ELIZABETHAN
AND
STUART PLAYS

ELIZABETHAN AND STUART PLAYS

EDITED BY

CHARLES READ BASKERVILL
LATE PROFESSOR OF ENGLISH
UNIVERSITY OF CHICAGO

VIRGIL B. HELTZEL
PROFESSOR OF ENGLISH
NORTHWESTERN UNIVERSITY

ARTHUR H. NETHERCOT
PROFESSOR OF ENGLISH
NORTHWESTERN UNIVERSITY

HOLT, RINEHART AND WINSTON
New York · Chicago · San Francisco
Toronto · London

PREFACE

This collection of Elizabethan and Stuart plays exclusive of Shakespeare has the advantage of a larger compass than similar anthologies for students. It opens with such plays as *Roister Doister*, *Gammer Gurton's Needle*, and *Gorboduc*, in which, through imitation of the classics, English drama broke with medieval tradition as represented in the hybrid moralities, and it extends to the closing of the theaters in 1642, when the tone of the drama was already foreshadowing the Restoration period. Enough plays are included, moreover, to show the richness and variety of the great dramatic art of the era without neglecting the various phases of its historical development. It has been possible, for example, to print five plays and a masque as representative of Jonson's work, and at the same time to give specimens of popular romantic drama like *Mucedorus* or of a hitherto neglected form like the jig. All the significant types of drama in the period are illustrated here.

The plays have been arranged in two groups as Elizabethan and Stuart for the purpose of emphasizing what is distinctive in each period. In this way the Elizabethan group may more readily be studied in connection with medieval drama or Shakespeare, and the Stuart group as a background for Restoration drama. The division is useful even when the two eras are studied together. In Shakespeare's immediate predecessors and contemporaries, the Elizabethan characteristics of boldness of conception and execution are obvious, resulting in an imaginative and emotional power which is frequently accompanied by a disregard for restraint, structure, and form. This distinctive quality survives in the final work of Shakespeare and in the two great tragedies of Webster, so that *The Duchess of Malfi*, in spite of its late date, is included with the Elizabethan plays. Already, however, Jonson had written his chief works that represent the Stuart reaction in drama, following classical ideals of restraint and unity in design; and a change of attitude, with a more searching study of manners, resulted. The centering of interest on form and technique, even in romantic plays, gives a sufficiently distinct character to the plays of the Stuart period as a whole.

The text used as a basis of the editing is indicated in the introduction to each play. For about half the plays, original early editions, photostatic copies of them, reproductions in the Farmer Facsimile Texts, or facsimile reprints of the Malone Society have been used. The rest are based on standard modern editions, in most cases recent critical editions. These have also been checked with other modern editions, or where possible with Farmer Facsimiles or the Malone Society reproductions. In whatever affects the actual content of the play, including stage directions, the principle followed has been one of strict fidelity to the original. Emendations have been avoided when any logical interpretation of the reading given seemed possible, and those adopted are duly recorded in the footnotes. Added material has been enclosed in square brackets. When no source of an emendation is stated, it has been made on the authority of the basic text, except that in stage directions the bracketed material has usually been added by the present editors. Plays with no act and scene division have been divided simply into scenes, with bracketed numbers. Likewise few liberties have been taken with the verse arrangement found in the sixteenth and seventeenth century originals, unless by a simple change in the division of lines a whole passage could be made to fall into pattern. Footnotes call attention to such revision in the plays in which it occurs. In *George a Greene* and the additions to *The Spanish Tragedy*, there are so many doubtful cases or cases in which no satisfactory arrangement of the lines is possible that no attempt has been made to change the original arrangement even in the passages where the dramatist's intention seems fairly clear.

In matters of less fundamental importance, the editing has been done with a view to

v

aiding the student who is interested primarily in the literary and dramatic qualities of the plays. Hence spelling, punctuation, and capitalization have been modernized. Where differences in spelling, however, suggest significant differences in pronunciation resulting from the survival in Elizabethan times of variant forms now obsolete (as in *hunderd, renowm, accompt*, for example), the original has been followed, at times even in doubtful cases. On the other hand, in certain very common words where the vowel varies so frequently as to suggest that perhaps to an Elizabethan there was little distinction in sound, the modern spelling has been adopted. Examples include the use of *than* for *then* (in the modern sense of *than*), *whither* and *hither* for *whether* and *hether* (except in dialect or consciously archaic passages or for rime), *devil* for *divel*, *show* for *shew*, *ambassador* for *embassador*, and many *in-* combinations for *en-* combinations (for instance, *increase* for *encrease*). In such original forms as *marchant* and *clark*, *-er-* has regularly been substituted for *-ar-*. The spellings *dost* and *doth*, rather than *doest* and *doeth*, are regularly used for the words as auxiliaries. *Wive's* as a possessive singular is printed *wife's*, but in general such voicings have been retained whenever any modern justification for them could be found. Again, obvious misprints have been silently corrected throughout. Numerals also are written out, and a compound form like *24* is expanded into the common Elizabethan form *four-and-twenty*. In many of the plays, speech heads vary so irrationally that they have been frankly reduced to some consistency. The prevalent or the most logical form of each speaker's name, usually an abbreviation, has been adopted throughout a play, except that, where there are two or three different names for the same speaker, they are retained, with explanation in the notes. As the original speech heads in *Cambises* are printed in full consistently, however, they have been left unchanged. It is perhaps unnecessary to mention the omission of imprints, colophons, titles repeated at the head of the text proper, and running heads, or the occasional disregard of certain unusual arrangements of the material on the page of the original.

As an aid in the matter of meter, an accent has been placed over *e* in the verbal suffix *-ed* when it is pronounced as an additional syllable contrary to ordinary usage, and an apostrophe marks the omission of a vowel when a shortening in pronunciation seems to be indicated by the spelling of the original (as in *wav'ring*, for example). For the rest, it is felt that with a little attention to Elizabethan practice, the reader will quickly fall into the rhythm of the various dramatists, representing various periods. Especially after playwrights learned to give verse some of the flexibility of speech, blank verse was handled very freely. Occasionally the line is as short as one foot, or as long as six. The foot may have an extra syllable, or a syllable may be omitted, usually at the beginning of a line or after a pause. Inverted stress is frequent in the first foot and occasionally occurs elsewhere, especially after a pause. It is to be noted also that some Elizabethan words differ from modern usage in the position of the accent, and a much larger number seems to have been very flexible as to accent, at least in verse. *Ácademy, revénue, infámous, envý, cómplete, canónize, obdúrate, pórtray, déprive*, and *aspéct* are a few examples taken from the plays printed here. Another large group of words, especially those with endings in *-ion, -ian, -ia, -ience, -ier*, etc., are often to be scanned as having a syllable more than is normal in modern pronunciation (as in *motion, ocean, Christian, Persia, Delia, soldier, marriage*). Not infrequently, too, an extra syllable is developed, especially in connection with *l* and *r* (as in *fair, fire, hour, mild, sure, sworn*).

Webster's *Collegiate Dictionary* has been taken as the standard of what the reader might properly be expected to know in the matter of current vocabulary. Old forms that are not obvious, and words and phrases that are obsolete, or have shifted meaning, or for any other reason might not be understood, have been explained in the notes for each play, but as a rule only in the first occurrence in a given play.

The editors wish to thank Professor J. C. Murley, Professor J. G. Fucilla, and Dr. N. A. Bennetton for help in translating a few difficult or corrupt passages from Latin, Italian, and Spanish, and Professor F. H. Heidbrink, Professor M. E. Prior, Dr. L. S. Wright, and Dr. Z. S. Fink for help in proof-reading the second part.

CONTENTS

PART ONE: ELIZABETHAN PLAYS

	PAGE
Roister Doister, *by Nicholas Udall*	1
Gammer Gurton's Needle, *by "Mr. [William] S [tevenson?]"*	47
Gorboduc, *by Thomas Norton and Thomas Sackville*	77
Supposes, *by George Gascoigne*	111
Cambises, *by Thomas Preston*	143
Endymion, *by John Lyly*	171
The Arraignment of Paris, *by George Peele*	205
The Old Wives' Tale, *by George Peele*	231
Friar Bacon and Friar Bungay, *by Robert Greene*	247
George a Greene, *by Robert Greene* (?)	285
Tamburlaine, Part I, *by Christopher Marlowe*	307
Doctor Faustus, *by Christopher Marlowe*	349
Edward II, *by Christopher Marlowe*	375
The Spanish Tragedy, *by Thomas Kyd*	421
Arden of Feversham	475
Attowell's Jig (Francis' New Jig)	519
Mucedorus	525
The Shoemakers' Holiday, *by Thomas Dekker*	553
The Honest Whore, Part I, *by Thomas Dekker*	593
A Woman Killed with Kindness, *by Thomas Heywood*	641
The Malcontent, *by John Marston and John Webster*	679
Bussy d'Ambois, *by George Chapman*	723
The Duchess of Malfi, *by John Webster*	771

PART TWO: STUART PLAYS

Every Man in His Humor, *by Ben Jonson*	827
Sejanus His Fall, *by Ben Jonson*	881
Volpone, or The Fox, *by Ben Jonson*	941
The Alchemist, *by Ben Jonson*	1003
The Hue and Cry after Cupid, *by Ben Jonson*	1067
The Sad Shepherd, *by Ben Jonson*	1075
The Knight of the Burning Pestle, *by Francis Beaumont and John Fletcher*	1090

PAGE

The Faithful Shepherdess, *by John Fletcher* 1147

Philaster, *by Francis Beaumont and John Fletcher* 1189

The Maid's Tragedy, *by Francis Beaumont and John Fletcher* 1233

A Trick to Catch the Old One, *by Thomas Middleton* 1279

The Changeling, *by Thomas Middleton and William Rowley* 1317

A New Way to Pay Old Debts, *by Philip Massinger* 1355

The Maid of Honor, *by Philip Massinger* 1401

The Witch of Edmonton, *by John Ford, Thomas Dekker, and William Rowley* 1443

The Broken Heart, *by John Ford* 1485

Perkin Warbeck, *by John Ford* 1531

The Lady of Pleasure, *by James Shirley* 1577

The Cardinal, *by James Shirley* 1625

ELIZABETHAN PLAYS

EDITED BY

CHARLES READ BASKERVILL
VIRGIL B. HELTZEL
ARTHUR H. NETHERCOT

NICHOLAS UDALL

Nicholas Udall, born about 1505 or 1506, was educated at Winchester College and at Corpus Christi College, Oxford, where he proceeded M.A. in 1534. In 1533 he prepared, with the help of John Leland, the great antiquary, a verse pageant for the coronation of Anne Boleyn, in which Paris bestowed the golden apple on the queen instead of on Venus, and about the same time he brought out *Flowers for Latin Speaking*, selections from Terence, with an English translation. Both enterprises illustrate the increasing influence of humanism, of which the most important early monument in the field of drama is his *Roister Doister*. Udall was Vicar of Braintree, Essex, from 1533 to 1537, and Master of Eton from 1534 to 1541, when charges against him and a confession of misconduct caused his dismissal. In the succeeding years he enjoyed the patronage of different noblemen, wrote or translated several works, and took some part in Protestant propaganda. Nevertheless he retained the favor of the Catholic Mary on her accession in 1553. He was appointed Master of Westminster School in 1555 and died in 1556.

Though Bishop Bale states in his *Catalogus* that Udall wrote several plays ("*Comœdias plures*"), it was not known that any had survived until the unique copy of *Roister Doister*, now at Eton, was discovered early in the nineteenth century. The copy lacks a title-page, and the authorship of the play was established by the fact that the ambiguous letter of III, iv, was quoted as Udall's in Thomas Wilson's *The Rule of Reason* in 1553. Though *Roister Doister* was clearly written for acting by boys, the school, the date, and the occasion are uncertain. The traditional view is that it was written for the boys of Eton, and it has been conjectured that this was the play performed when they played before Cromwell in 1538. Arguments have been advanced, however, for its composition shortly before Wilson's use of the letter. The extant copy is usually dated 1566/7 because the play was licensed by the Stationers' Company for printing in that year, and because the prayer for the queen at the end is obviously for Elizabeth. The edition is possibly a revised form, however.

Roister Doister seems to be the earliest of a small group of extant plays which represent a change in the style of English comedy through the imitation of the classics. The formal act and scene structure, the simple setting of a town street, and the observation of the unities of action, time, and place belong to a new technique, which the humanists developed through a study of classical comedy and criticism. The characters and the incidents are also modeled on Roman comedy. For the group of characters and their relations centering in the household of Dame Custance, parallels are found in the plays of both Plautus and Terence, but especially in Terence's *Eunuchus*. Roister Doister, the braggart, and Merrygreek, a combination of parasite and intriguer, are drawn from the stock figures of Roman comedy. Udall's use of the *Miles gloriosus* of Plautus, in which the portrayal of the braggart soldier is perfected, is especially obvious, though perhaps modified by Terence's portrait of Thraso. Udall, however, blends his classical material rather skillfully with details of English life to give an English atmosphere to the play. The whole is also handled in a spirit of burlesque and extravagance which harmonizes perfectly with the spirit of revelry and misrule that prevailed in the games and pastimes of the holiday seasons in English institutional life of all types. Particularly the boys in schools connected with cathedrals and chapels, led by a boy bishop, celebrated Christmas with parodies of the regular services of the church, a tradition which is preserved in the mock liturgical material woven into *Roister Doister*.

Of the several modern reprints of the play, the best is that of Flügel in Gayley's *Representative English Comedies*, and it has been followed here even to the extent of beginning a new line for each speech, though in the original the speeches, if short or irregular in length, are run along on the same line until a rime word is reached.

1

ROISTER DOISTER[1]

BY
NICHOLAS UDALL

[DRAMATIS PERSONÆ

RALPH ROISTER DOISTER, *a braggart.*
MATTHEW MERRYGREEK, *a parasite.*
GAWIN GOODLUCK, *betrothed to Dame Custance.*
TRISTRAM TRUSTY, *his friend.*
DOBINET DOUGHTY, *a boy* ⎫ *servants to*
HARPAX   ⎬ *Roister Dois-*
               ⎭ *ter.*
TOM TRUEPENNY, *a boy, servant to Dame Custance.*

SIM SURESBY, *servant to Goodluck.*
SCRIVENER.
MUSICIANS *and* OTHERS.

DAME CHRISTIAN CUSTANCE, *a widow.*
MARGERY, *or* MADGE, MUMBLECRUST, *her old nurse.*
TIBET TALKAPACE ⎫ *her maids.*
ANNOT ALYFACE [2] ⎬

SCENE: *A street, probably in London.*

TIME: *Contemporary.*]

THE PROLOGUE

What creature is in health, either young or
    old,
  But some mirth with modesty will be
    glad to use,
As[3] we in this interlude shall now unfold,
  Wherein all scurrility we utterly refuse,
  Avoiding such mirth wherein is abuse,
Knowing nothing more commendable for a
    man's recreation
Than mirth which is used in an honest
    fashion?

For mirth prolongeth life and causeth
    health;
  Mirth recreates our spirits and voideth
    pensiveness;
Mirth increaseth amity, not hind'ring our
    wealth;   10
  Mirth is to be used both of more and less,[4]
  Being mixed with virtue in decent come-
    liness,

As we trust no good nature can gainsay
    the same—
Which mirth we intend to use, avoiding
    all blame.

The wise poets long time heretofore,
  Under merry comedies secrets did declare,
Wherein was contained very virtuous lore,
  With mysteries and forewarnings very
    rare.
  Such to write neither Plautus nor Ter-
    ence did spare,
Which among the learned at this day bears
    the bell;   20
These with such other therein did excel.

Our comedy or interlude which we intend
    to play
Is naméd *Roister Doister* indeed,
Which against the vainglorious doth inveigh,
  Whose humor the roisting [5] sort contin-
    ually doth feed.
Thus by your patience we intend to
    proceed
In this our interlude by God's leave and
    grace,
And here I take my leave for a certain space.

---

[1] Since the title-page is missing from the only copy of the play in existence, this title has been supplied from the prologue.
[2] *I.e.,* beery face.
[3] Such as.   [4] By great and small.   [5] Blustering.

FINIS.

3

Actus I. Scena i.[1]

Matthew Merrygreek. He ent'reth singing.

[M. Merry.] As long liveth the merry man,
  they say,
  As doth the sorry man, and longer by a
    day.
  Yet the grasshopper, for all his summer
    piping,
  Starveth in winter with hungry griping;
  Therefore another sayd [2] saw doth men
    advise
  That they be together both merry and
    wise.
  This lesson must I practice, or else ere
    long,
  With me, Matthew Merrygreek, it will
    be wrong.
  Indeed men so call me, for by Him that
    us bought,
  Whatever chance betide, I can take no
    thought; 10
  Yet wisdom would that I did myself
    bethink
  Where to be provided this day of meat
    and drink;
  For know ye that, for all this merry
    note of mine,
  He might appose [3] me now that should
    ask where I dine.
  My living lieth here and there, of God's
    grace:
  Sometime with this good man, sometime
    in that place;
  Sometime Lewis Loit'rer biddeth me
    come near;
  Somewhiles Watkin Waster maketh us
    good cheer;
  Sometime Davy Diceplayer, when he
    hath well cast,
  Keepeth revel rout as long as it will
    last; 20
  Sometime Tom Titivile maketh us a
    feast;
  Sometime with Sir Hugh Pie I am a
    bidden guest;
  Sometime at Nichol Neverthrive's I get
    a sop;
  Sometime I am feasted with Bryan
    Blinkinsop;

Sometime I hang on Hankin Hoddy-
  doddy's sleeve,
  But this day on Ralph Roister Doister's
    by his leave.
  For truly of all men he is my chief
    banker
  Both for meat and money, and my chief
    shoot-anchor.[4]
  For, sooth [5] Roister Doister in that he
    doth say,
  And, require what ye will, ye shall have
    no nay. 30
  But now of Roister Doister somewhat to
    express,
  That ye may esteem him after his
    worthiness,
  In these twenty towns and seek them
    throughout,
  Is not the like stock, whereon to graff [6]
    a lout.
  All the day long is he facing and craking [7]
  Of his great acts in fighting and fray-
    making;
  But when Roister Doister is put to his
    proof,
  To keep the queen's peace is more for
    his behoof.
  If any woman smile or cast on him an
    eye,
  Up is he to the hard ears in love by-and-
    by,[8] 40
  And in all the hot haste must she be his
    wife,
  Else farewell his good days, and farewell
    his life.
  Master Rafe [9] Roister Doister is but
    dead and gone
  Except she on him take some compas-
    sion;
  Then chief of counsel must be Matthew
    Merrygreek.
  "What if I for marriage to such an one
    seek?"
  Then must I sooth it, whatever it is;
  For what he saith or doth cannot be
    amiss.
  Hold up his yea and nay, be his nown
    white son,[10]
  Praise and rouse him well, and ye have
    his heart won, 50

---

[1] The scene remains fixed throughout as a street, with the house of Custance on one side and that of Roister Doister on the other.
[2] Sad, serious.   [3] Nonplus.

[4] Sheet-anchor.   [8] Immediately.
[5] Soothe, support.   [9] Variant of *Ralph*.
[6] Graft.   [10] His own dear friend.
[7] Bullying and boasting.

For so well liketh he his own fond [1] fash-
ions
That he taketh pride of false commenda-
tions.
But such sport have I with him as I
would not leese, [2]
Though I should be bound to live with
bread and cheese.
For exalt him, and have him as ye lust [3]
indeed—
Yea, to hold his finger in a hole for a
need.
I can with a word make him fain or loath;
I can with as much make him pleased or
wroth;
I can when I will make him merry and
glad;
I can when me lust make him sorry and
sad;   60
I can set him in hope and eke in despair;
I can make him speak rough and make
him speak fair.
But I marvel I see him not all this same
day.
I will seek him out.—But lo, he cometh
this way!
I have yond espied him sadly coming,
And in love for twenty pound, by his
glomming. [4]

Actus I. Scena ii.

Rafe Roister Doister, Matthew Merrygreek.

R. Roister. Come, death, when thou wilt!
I am weary of my life!
M. Merry. [*Aside.*] I told you, I, we
should woo another wife.
R. Roister. Why did God make me such
a goodly person?
M. Merry. [*Aside.*] He is in by the
week; [5] we shall have sport anon. [6]
R. Roister. And where is my trusty
friend, Matthew Merrygreek?
M. Merry. [*Aside.*] I will make as I saw
him not; he doth me seek.
R. Roister. I have him espied, methink-
eth; yond is he.
Ho! Matthew Merrygreek, my friend,
a word with thee.
M. Merry. [*Aside.*] I will not hear him,
but make as I had haste.—

[*To the audience.*] Farewell, all my good
friends; the time away doth waste.   10
And the tide, they say, tarrieth for no
man.
R. Roister. Thou must with thy good
counsel help me if thou can.
M. Merry. God keep thee, worshipful
Master Roister Doister,
And fare well thee, lusty Master Roister
Doister.
R. Roister. I must needs speak with thee
a word or twain.
M. Merry. Within a month or two I will
be here again.
Negligence in great affairs, ye know, may
mar all.
R. Roister. Attend upon me now, and
well reward thee I shall.
M. Merry. I have take my leave, and the
tide is well spent.
R. Roister. I die except thou help; I pray
thee, be content.   20
Do thy part well now, and ask what thou
wilt,
For without thy aid my matter is all
spilt.
M. Merry. Then to serve your turn I will
some pains take,
And let all mine own affairs alone for your
sake.
R. Roister. My whole hope and trust
resteth only in thee.
M. Merry. Then can ye not do amiss,
whatever it be.
R. Roister. Gramercies, Merrygreek, most
bound to thee I am.
M. Merry. But up with that heart, and
speak out like a ram.
Ye speak like a capon that had the cough
now.
Be of good cheer; anon ye shall do well
enow.   30
R. Roister. Upon thy comfort, I will all
things well handle.
M. Merry. So, lo! that is a breast [7] to
blow out a candle!
But what is this great matter, I would
fain know?
We shall find remedy therefore, I trow.
Do ye lack money? Ye know mine old
offers;
Ye have always a key to my purse and
coffers.

---

[1] Foolish.
[2] Lose.
[3] Desire.
[4] Sullenness.
[5] Trapped.
[6] At once.
[7] Pair of lungs.

R. Roister. I thank thee. Had ever man
such a friend?

M. Merry. Ye give unto me; I must needs
to you lend.

R. Roister. Nay, I have money plenty
all things to discharge.

M. Merry. [*Aside.*] That knew I right
well when I made offer so large.   40

R. Roister. But it is no such matter.

M. Merry.   What is it then?
Are ye in danger of debt to any man?
If ye be, take no thought nor be not
afraid.
Let them hardly [1] take thought how they
shall be paid.

R. Roister. Tut, I owe naught.

M. Merry.   What
then? Fear ye imprisonment?

R. Roister. No.

M. Merry.   No, I wist [2] ye offend
not, so to be shent.[3]
But if ye had, the Tower could not you
so hold,
But to break out at all times ye would
be bold.
What is it? Hath any man threatened
you to beat?

R. Roister. What is he that durst have
put me in that heat?   50
He that beateth me, by His arms, shall
well find
That I will not be far from him nor run
behind.

M. Merry. That thing know all men ever
since ye overthrew
The fellow of the lion which Hercules
slew.
But what is it then?

R. Roister.   Of love I make my
moan.

M. Merry. Ah, this foolish a[h]-love, wilt
ne'er let us alone?
But, because ye were refused the last day,
Ye said ye would ne'er more be entangled
that way.
I would meddle no more, since I find all
so unkind.

R. Roister. Yea, but I cannot so put love
out of my mind.   60

M. Merry. But is your love, tell me first,
in any wise,
In the way of marriage, or of merchandise?

<hr>

[1] Assuredly.   [2] Knew.   [3] Shamed.

If it may otherwise than lawful be found,
Ye get none of my help for a hundred
pound.

R. Roister. No, by my troth, I would
have her to my wife.

M. Merry. Then are ye a good man, and
God save your life!
And what or who is she with whom ye
are in love?

R. Roister. A woman whom I know not
by what means to move.

M. Merry. Who is it?

R. Roister.   A woman yond.

M. Merry.   What is her name?

R. Roister. Her yonder.

M. Merry.   Whom?

R. Roister.   Mistress—ah—

M. Merry.   Fie, fie,
for shame!   70
Love ye, and know not whom but "her
yond," "a woman"?
We shall then get you a wife—I cannot
tell when.

R. Roister. The fair woman that supped
with us yesternight;
And I heard her name twice or thrice,
and had it right.

M. Merry. Yea, ye may see ye ne'er take
me to good cheer with you;
If ye had, I could have told you her name
now.

R. Roister. I was to blame indeed, but
the next time perchance—
And she dwelleth in this house.

M. Merry.   What,
Christian Custance?

R. Roister. Except I have her to my wife,
I shall run mad.

M. Merry. [*Aside.*] Nay, unwise perhaps,
but I warrant you for mad.   80

R. Roister. I am utterly dead unless I
have my desire.

M. Merry. Where be the bellows that
blew this sudden fire?

R. Roister. I hear she is worth a thousand pound and more.

M. Merry. Yea, but learn this one lesson
of me afore:
An hundred pound of marriage-money,
doubtless,
Is ever thirty pound sterling, or somewhat less,
So that her thousand pound, if she be
thrifty,

Is much near [1] about two hundred and
    fifty,
Howbeit wooers and widows are never
    poor.

R. ROISTER. Is she a widow? I love her
    better therefore.   90

M. MERRY. But I hear she hath made
    promise to another.

R. ROISTER. He shall go without her, and [2]
    he were my brother.

M. MERRY. I have heard say—I am right
    well advised—
    That she hath to Gawin Goodluck prom-
    ised.

R. ROISTER. What is that Gawin Good-
    luck?

M. MERRY.   A merchant man.

R. ROISTER. Shall he speed afore me?
    Nay, sir, by sweet Saint Anne.
Ah, sir, "'*Backare*,' [3] quod [4] Mortimer to
    his sow." [5]
I will have her mine own self, I make
    God avow.
For, I tell thee, she is worth a thousand
    pound.

M. MERRY. Yet a fitter wife for your
    ma'ship might be found: 100
Such a goodly man as you might get one
    with land,
Besides pounds of gold a thousand, and a
    thousand,
And a thousand, and a thousand, and a
    thousand,
And so to the sum of twenty hundred
    thousand.
Your most goodly personage is worthy of
    no less.

R. ROISTER. I am sorry God made me so
    comely, doubtless.
For that maketh me each where so highly
    favored,
And all women on me so enamored.

M. MERRY. "Enamored," quod you?
    Have ye spied out that?
Ah sir, marry, now I see you know what
    is what.   110
"Enamored," ka? [6] Marry, sir, say that
    again!
But I thought not ye had marked it so
    plain.

R. ROISTER. Yes, each where they gaze
    all upon me and stare.

M. MERRY. Yea, Malkin! [7] I warrant you
    as much as they dare!
And ye will not believe what they say
    in the street,
When your ma'ship passeth by, all such
    as I meet,
That sometimes I can scarce find what
    answer to make.
"Who is this?" saith one. "Sir Launcelot
    du Lake?"
"Who is this? Great Guy of Warwick?"
    saith another.
"No," say I, "it is the thirteenth
    Hercules, brother."   120
"Who is this? Noble Hector of Troy?"
    saith the third.
"No, but of the same nest," say I, "it is
    a bird."
"Who is this? Great Goliah, Sampson,
    or Colbrand?"
"No," say I, "but it is a Brute [8] of the
    Alie [9] land."
"Who is this? Great Alexander or
    Charles le Maigne?"
"No, it is the tenth Worthy," say I to
    them again.
I know not if I said well?

R. ROISTER.   Yes, for so I am.

M. MERRY. Yea, for there were but nine
    Worthies before ye came.
To some others, the third Cato I do you
    call.   129
And so, as well as I can, I answer them all.
"Sir, I pray you, what lord or great
    gentleman is this?"
"Master Ralph Roister Doister, dame,"
    say I, "iwis." [10]
"O Lord," saith she then, "what a
    goodly man it is!
Would Christ I had such a husband as
    he is!"
"O Lord," say some, "that the sight
    of his face we lack!"
"It is enough for you," say I, "to see
    his back.
His face is for ladies of high and noble
    parages, [11]
With whom he hardly scapeth great
    marriages."—
With much more than this, and much
    otherwise.

---

[1] Nearer.   [3] Keep back.   [5] An old proverb.
[2] An, if.   [4] Quoth, said.   [6] Quoth he.

[7] Probably *by Malkin.*
[8] A Brutus, an exemplary hero; with a pun on
brute.   [9] Holy(?).   [10] Certainly.   [11] Lineage

R. Roister. I can thee thank that thou
    canst such answers devise;   140
But I perceive thou dost me throughly
    know.
M. Merry. I mark your manners for mine
    own learning, I trow.
But such is your beauty, and such are
    your acts,
Such is your personage, and such are
    your facts,[1]
That all women fair and foul, more and
    less,
They eye you, they "lub you," they talk
    of you doubtless.
Your p[l]easant look maketh them all
    merry,
Ye pass not by, but they laugh till they
    be weary;
Yea, and money could I have, the truth
    to tell,
Of many, to bring you that way where
    they dwell.   150
R. Roister. Merrygreek, for this thy re-
    porting well of me—
M. Merry. What should I else, sir? It
    is my duty, pardee.[2]
R. Roister. I promise thou shalt not lack,
    while I have a groat.
M. Merry. Faith, sir, and I ne'er had
    more need of a new coat.
R. Roister. Thou shalt have one to-
    morrow, and gold for to spend.
M. Merry. Then I trust to bring the day
    to a good end.
For, as for mine own part having money
    enow,
I could live only with the remembrance
    of you.
But now to your widow whom you love
    so hot.
R. Roister. By Cock,[3] thou sayest truth.
    I had almost forgot.   160
M. Merry. What if Christian Custance
    will not have you, what?
R. Roister. Have me? Yes, I warrant
    you, never doubt of that;
I know she loveth me, but she dare not
    speak.
M. Merry. Indeed, meet it were some-
    body should it break.[4]

R. Roister. She looked on me twenty
    times yesternight,
And laughed so.
M. Merry.   That she could not sit
    upright.
R. Roister. No, faith, could she not.
M. Merry.   No, even
    such a thing I cast.[5]
R. Roister. But for wooing, thou know-
    est, women are shamefast.[6]
But, and she knew my mind, I know
    she would be glad,
And think it the best chance that ever
    she had.   170
M. Merry. To her then like a man, and
    be bold forth to start.
Wooers never speed well that have a
    false heart.
R. Roister. What may I best do?
M. Merry.   Sir, re-
    main ye awhile [here].[7]
Ere long one or other of her house will
    appear.
Ye know my mind.
R. Roister.   Yea, now hardly let
    me alone.
M. Merry. In the meantime, sir, if you
    please, I will home,
And call your musicians, for in this your
    case
It would set you forth, and all your
    wooing grace.
Ye may not lack your instruments to
    play and sing.
R. Roister. Thou knowest I can do that.
M. Merry.   As well as anything.   180
Shall I go call your folks, that ye may
    show a cast?[8]
R. Roister. Yea, run, I beseech thee, in
    all possible haste.
M. Merry. I go.   Exeat.[9]
R. Roister.   Yea, for I love singing
    out of measure,
It comforteth my spirits and doth me
    great pleasure.
But who cometh forth yond from my
    sweetheart Custance?
My matter frameth well; this is a lucky
    chance.

---

[1] Deeds.
[2] From *par Dieu* (by God), an oath that had
become innocuous.
[3] Corruption of *By God*.   [4] Reveal.

[5] Forecast, expected.
[6] Shamefaced, bashful.
[7] Added by Cooper.
[8] Specimen.
[9] Let him go out.

Actus I. Scena iii.

*Madge Mumblecrust, spinning on the distaff.
Tibet Talkapace, sewing. Annot Alyface,[1] knitting. R[alph] Roister.*

M. Mumbl. If this distaff were spun,
Margery Mumblecrust—

Tib. Talk. Where good stale ale is, will
drink no water, I trust.

M. Mumbl. Dame Custance hath promised us good ale and white bread.

Tib. Talk. If she keep not promise, I will
beshrew [2] her head!

But it will be stark night before I shall
have done.

R. Roister. [*Aside.*] I will stand here
awhile, and talk with them anon.

I hear them speak of Custance, which
doth my heart good.

To hear her name spoken doth even
comfort my blood.

M. Mumbl. Sit down to your work, Tibet,
like a good girl.

Tib. Talk. Nurse, meddle you with your
spindle and your whirl.[3]   10

No haste but good, Madge Mumblecrust;
for "Whip and whir," [4]

The old proverb doth say, "never made
good fur."

M. Mumbl. Well, ye will sit down to your
work anon, I trust.

Tib. Talk. "Soft fire maketh sweet malt,"
good Madge Mumblecrust.

M. Mumbl. And sweet malt maketh jolly
good ale for the nonce.

Tib. Talk. Which will slide down the lane
without any bones.   *Cantet.*[5]

Old brown bread crusts must have much
good mumbling,

But good ale down your throat hath
good easy tumbling.

R. Roister. [*Aside.*] The jolliest wench
that e'er I heard, little mouse!

May I not rejoice that she shall dwell in
my house?   20

Tib. Talk. So, sirrah, now this gear [6] beginneth for to frame.

M. Mumbl. Thanks to God, though your
work stand still, your tongue is not
lame.

Tib. Talk. And though your teeth be
gone, both so sharp and so fine,

Yet your tongue can renne on pattens [7]
as well as mine.

M. Mumbl. Ye were not for naught named
Tib Talkapace.

Tib. Talk. Doth my talk grieve you?
Alack, God save your grace.

M. Mumbl. I hold [8] a groat, ye will drink
anon for this gear.

Tib. Talk. And I will pray you the stripes
for me to bear.

M. Mumbl. I hold a penny, ye will drink
without a cup.

Tib. Talk. Whereinsoe'er ye drink, I wot [9]
ye drink all up.   30

[*Enter Annot.*]

An. Alyface. By Cock, and well sewed,
my good Tibet Talkapace.

Tib. Talk. And e'en as well knit, my
nown Annot Alyface.

R. Roister. [*Aside.*] See what a sort [10] she
keepeth that must be my wife!

Shall not I, when I have her, lead a merry
life?

Tib. Talk. Welcome, my good wench, and
sit here by me just.

An. Alyface. And how doth our old beldame here, Madge Mumblecrust?

Tib. Talk. Chide, and find faults, and
threaten to complain.

An. Alyface. To make us poor girls shent,
to her is small gain.

M. Mumbl. I did neither chide, nor complain, nor threaten.

R. Roister. [*Aside.*] It would grieve my
heart to see one of them beaten.   40

M. Mumbl. I did nothing but bid her
work and hold her peace.

Tib. Talk. So would I, if you could your
clattering cease;

But the devil cannot make old trot [11] hold
her tongue.

An. Alyface. Let all these matters pass,
and we three sing a song.

So shall we pleasantly both the time
beguile now,

And eke despatch all our works ere we
can tell how.

---

[1] Enters later.   [4] Sound of a whip.
[2] Curse.   [5] Let her sing.
[3] Small flywheel on the spindle.   [6] Affair.
[7] Run on wooden shoes, *i.e.*, clatter.
[8] Wager.   [9] Know.   [10] Company.   [11] Hag.

Tib. Talk. I shrew [1] them that say nay,
and that shall not be I.

M. Mumbl. And I am well content.

Tib. Talk.   Sing on then by-and-by.

R. Roister. [*Aside.*] And I will not away,
but listen to their song.

Yet Merrygreek and my folks tarry very
long.   50

Tib[et], An[not], and Margery do sing here.
    Pipe, merry Annot, etc.
Trilla, trilla, trillarie.
Work, Tibet; work, Annot; work, Margery.
Sew, Tibet; knit, Annot; spin, Margery.
Let us see who shall win the victory.

Tib. Talk. This sleeve is not willing to be
sewed, I trow.
A small thing might make me all in [2] the
ground to throw.

                Then they sing again.
    Pipe, merry Annot, etc.
Trilla, trilla, trillarie.
What, Tibet! what, Annot! what, Marg-
ery!   60
Ye sleep, but we do not; that shall we try.
Your fingers be numbed; our work will not
lie.

Tib. Talk. If ye do so again, well I would
advise you nay.
In good sooth, one stop [3] more, and I
make holiday.

                They sing the third time.
    Pipe, merry Annot, etc.
Trilla, trilla, trillarie.
Now, Tibet; now, Annot; now, Margery.
Now whippet [4] apace for the mast'ry;
But it will not be, our mouth is so dry.

Tib. Talk. Ah, each finger is a thumb
today, methink;   70
I care not to let all alone, choose it swim
or sink.

                They sing the fourth time.
    Pipe, merry Annot, etc.
Trilla, trilla, trillarie.
When, [5] Tibet! When, Annot! When, Mar-
gery!
I will not, I cannot, no more can I.
Then give we all over, and there let it lie.
    Let her cast down her work.

[1] Beshrew, curse.   [2] On.   [3] Hindrance.
[4] Whip it (?) *i.e.*, move briskly.
[5] An exclamation of impatience.

Tib. Talk. There it lieth! The worst is
but a curried coat. [6]
Tut, I am used thereto; I care not a
groat.

An. Alyface. Have we done singing since?
Then will I in again.
Here I found you, and here I leave both
twain.   *Exeat.* 80

M. Mumbl. And I will not be long after.
[*She sees Roister Doister.*] Tib Talkapace!

Tib. Talk. What is the matter?

M. Mumbl.   Yond
stood a man all this space
And hath heard all that ever we spake
togither.

Tib. Talk. Marry, the more lout he for
his coming hither.
And the less good he can to listen maidens
talk.
I care not and I go bid him hence for to
walk.
It were well done to know what he maketh hereaway.

R. Roister. [*Aside.*] Now might I speak
to them, if I wist what to say.

M. Mumbl. Nay, we will go both off, and
see what he is.

R. Roister. One that hath heard all your
talk and singing, iwis.   90

Tib. Talk. The more to blame you; a good
thrifty husband [7]
Would elsewhere have had some better
matters in hand.

R. Roister. I did it for no harm, but for
good love I bear
To your dame, Mistress Custance, I did
your talk hear.
And, mistress nurse, I will kiss you for
acquaintance.

M. Mumbl. I come anon, sir.

Tib. Talk.   Faith, I
would our Dame Custance
Saw this gear.

M. Mumbl.   I must first wipe all
clean, yea, I must.

Tib. Talk. Ill chieve it, [8] doting fool, but
it must be cust. [9]
        [*He kisses Madge Mumblecrust.*]

[6] A whipping.
[7] Manager of a household.
[8] Achieve, succeed.
[9] Kost, kissed.

M. Mumbl. God yeld [1] you, sir; chad not
　so much, ichotte not when,
Ne'er since chwas bore, chwine, of such
　a gay gentleman. [2]   100
R. Roister. I will kiss you too, maiden,
　for the good will I bear you.
Tib. Talk. No, forsooth, by your leave,
　ye shall not kiss me.
R. Roister. Yes, be not afeard; I do not
　disdain you a whit.
Tib. Talk. Why should I fear you? I have
　not so little wit.
Ye are but a man, I know very well.
R. Roister.   Why then?
Tib. Talk. Forsooth, for I will not; I use
　not to kiss men.
R. Roister. I would fain kiss you too,
　good maiden, if I might.
Tib. Talk. What should that need?
R. Roister.   But to honor you,
　by this light.
I use to kiss all them that I love, to God
　I vow.
Tib. Talk. Yea, sir? I pray you, when
　did ye last kiss your cow?   110
R. Roister. Ye might be proud to kiss
　me, if ye were wise.
Tib. Talk. What promotion were therein?
R. Roister.   Nurse is not so nice. [3]
Tib. Talk. Well, I have not been taught
　to kissing and licking.
R. Roister. Yet I thank you, mistress
　nurse; ye made no sticking.
M. Mumbl. I will not stick for a koss [4]
　with such a man as you.
Tib. Talk. They that lust. I will again to
　my sewing now.

[Enter Annot Alyface.]

An. Alyface. Tidings, ho! tidings! Dame
　Custance greeteth you well.
R. Roister. Whom? me?
An. Alyface.   You, sir? No,
　sir! I do no such tale tell.
R. Roister. But, and she knew me here—
An. Alyface.   Tibet Talkapace,
Your mistress, Custance, and mine must
　speak with your grace.   120

Tib. Talk. With me?
An. Alyface.   Ye must come in
　to her, out of all doubts.
Tib. Talk. And my work not half done?
　A mischief on all louts.
　　　　　　　　　　Ex[eant] am[bæ]. [5]
R. Roister. Ah, good sweet nurse!
M. Mumbl.   A
　good sweet gentleman.
R. Roister.   What?
M. Mumbl. Nay, I cannot tell, sir, but
　what thing would you?
R. Roister. How doth sweet Custance,
　my heart of gold, tell me how?
M. Mumbl. She doth very well, sir, and
　command me to you.
R. Roister. To me?
M. Mumbl.   Yea, to you, sir.
R. Roister.   To me? Nurse,
　tell me plain,
　To me?
M. Mumbl.   Ye.
R. Roister.   That word maketh
　me alive again.
M. Mumbl. She command me to one last
　day, [6] whoe'er it was.
R. Roister. That was e'en to me and
　none other, by the Mass.   130
M. Mumbl. I cannot tell you surely, but
　one it was.
R. Roister. It was I and none other; this
　cometh to good pass.
I promise thee, nurse, I favor her.
M. Mumbl.   E'en so, sir.
R. Roister. Bid her sue to me for mar-
　riage.
M. Mumbl.   E'en so, sir.
R. Roister. And surely for thy sake she
　shall speed.
M. Mumbl.   E'en so, sir.
R. Roister. I shall be contented to take
　her.
M. Mumbl.   E'en so, sir.
R. Roister. But at thy request and for
　thy sake.
M. Mumbl.   E'en so, sir.
R. Roister. And, come, hark in thine ear
　what to say.
M. Mumbl.   E'en so, sir.

*Here let him tell her a great long tale in
　　　　　　　　　　　　　　her ear.*

---

[1] Reward.
[2] Madge speaks an artificial Southern dialect,
regularly used by stage rustics. Chad = ich
had = I had; ichotte = ich wot = I know; chwas =
I was; chwine = I ween = I think; etc.
[3] Fastidious.   [4] Kiss.
[5] Let both go out.
[6] Yesterday.

Actus I. Scena iv.

Matthew Merrygreek, Dobinet Doughty, Harpax, [Musicians,] Ralph Roister, Margery Mumblecrust.

M. MERRY. Come on, sirs, apace, and quit
yourselves like men.
Your pains shall be rewarded.

D. DOUGH.   But I
wot not when.

M. MERRY. Do your master worship as ye
have done in time past.

D. DOUGH. Speak to them; of mine office
he shall have a cast.

M. MERRY. Harpax, look that thou do
well too, and thy fellow.

HARPAX. I warrant, if he will mine example follow.

M. MERRY. Curtsy, whoresons, duck you
and crouch at every word.

D. DOUGH. Yes, whether our master speak
earnest or bord.[1]

M. MERRY. For this lieth upon [2] his preferment, indeed.

D. DOUGH. Oft is he a wooer, but never
doth he speed.   10

M. MERRY. But with whom is he now so
sadly rounding [3] yond?

D. DOUGH. With *Nobs nicebecetur miserere* [4] fond.

[M.] MERRY. God be at your wedding! Be
ye sped already?
                    [*Approaches Roister Doister.*]
I did not suppose that your love was so
greedy.
I perceive now ye have chose of devotion,
And joy have ye, lady, of your promotion.

R. ROISTER. Tush, fool, thou art deceived; this is not she.

M. MERRY. Well, mock [5] much of her, and
keep her well, I vise [6] ye.
I will take no charge of such a fair piece
keeping.

M. MUMBL. What aileth this fellow? He
driveth me to weeping.   20

M. MERRY. What, weep on the wedding
day? Be merry, woman.
Though I say it, ye have chose a good
gentleman.

---

[1] Jest.   [2] Is necessary to.   [3] Whispering.
[4] The meaning of the burlesque Latin is uncertain.
[5] Hazlitt suggests *make*   [6] Advise.

R. ROISTER. Kock's nowns,[7] what meanest thou, man? Tut, a whistle!

[M. MERRY.] [8] Ah, sir, be good to her; she
is but a gristle.[9]
Ah, sweet lamb and cony! [10]

R. ROISTER.   Tut, thou
art deceived.

M. MERRY. Weep no more, lady; ye shall
be well received.—
[*To Musicians.*] Up with some merry
noise, sirs, to bring home the bride.

R. ROISTER. Gog's [11] arms, knave, art thou
mad? I tell thee thou art wide.

M. MERRY. Then ye intend by night to
have her home brought.

R. ROISTER. I tell thee no.

M. MERRY.   How then?

R. ROISTER.   'Tis neither
meant ne [12] thought.   30

M. MERRY. What shall we then do with
her?

R. ROISTER.   Ah, foolish harebrain,
This is not she.

M. MERRY.   No, is? Why then, unsaid
again!
And what young girl is this with your
ma'ship so bold?

R. ROISTER. A girl?

M. MERRY.   Yea. I dare say,
scarce yet three score year old.

R. ROISTER. This same is the fair widow's
nurse, of whom ye wot.

M. MERRY. Is she but a nurse of a house?
Hence home, old trot,
Hence at once!

R. ROISTER. No, no.

M. MERRY.   What, an please
your ma'ship,
A nurse talk so homely [13] with one of your
worship?

R. ROISTER. I will have it so; it is my
pleasure and will.

M. MERRY. Then I am content. Nurse,
come again; tarry still.   40

R. ROISTER. What! She will help forward
this my suit for her part.

M. MERRY. Then is't mine own pigsnie,[14]
and blessing on my heart.

---

[7] God's wounds.
[8] This speech is assigned to Roister Doister
in the original.
[9] A delicate person; with a pun on the meaning
tough.   [10] Rabbit, a term of endearment.   [11] God's.
[12] Nor.   [13] Familiarly.   [14] Pig's eye, darling.

R. ROISTER. This is our best friend, man.
M. MERRY. Then teach her what to say.
M. MUMBL. I am taught already.
M. MERRY. Then go; make no delay.
R. ROISTER. Yet hark, one word in thine ear.
M. MERRY. Back, sirs, from his tail.
R. ROISTER. Back, villains, will ye be privy of my counsel?
M. MERRY. Back, sirs, so. I told you afore ye would be shent.
R. ROISTER. She shall have the first day a whole peck of argent.[1]
M. MUMBL. A peck? *Nomine patris*,[2] have ye so much spare?
R. ROISTER. Yea, and a cart-load thereto, or else were it bare, 50
Besides other movables, household stuff, and land.
M. MUMBL. Have ye lands too?
R. ROISTER. An hundred marks.
M. MERRY. Yea, a thousand.
M. MUMBL. And have ye cattle too, and sheep too?
R. ROISTER. Yea, a few.
M. MERRY. He is ashamed the number of them to shew.
E'en round about him, as many thousand sheep goes,
As he and thou, and I too, have fingers and toes.
M. MUMBL. And how many years old be you?
R. ROISTER. Forty at least.
M. MERRY. Yea, and thrice forty to them.
R. ROISTER. Nay, now thou dost jest. I am not so old; thou misreckonest my years.
M. MERRY. I know that; but my mind was on bullocks and steers. 60
M. MUMBL. And what shall I show her your mastership's name is?
R. ROISTER. Nay, she shall make suit ere she know that, iwis.
M. MUMBL. Yet let me somewhat know.
M. MERRY. This is he, understand,
That killed the blue spider in Blanchepowder land.
M. MUMBL. Yea, Jesus! William! Zee, law! Did he zo? Law![3]

M. MERRY. Yea, and the last elephant that ever he saw,
As the beast passed by, he start out of a busk,[4]
And e'en with pure strength of arms plucked out his great tusk.
M. MUMBL. Jesus, *nomine patris*, what a thing was that?
R. ROISTER. Yea, but, Merrygreek, one thing thou hast forgot.
M. MERRY. What? 70
R. ROISTER. Of th' other elephant.
M. MERRY. O, him that fled away.
R. ROISTER. Yea.
M. MERRY. Yea, he knew that his match was in place that day.
Tut, he bet[5] the king of crickets on Christmas day,
That he crept in a hole, and not a word to say.
M. MUMBL. A sore[6] man, by zembletee.[7]
M. MERRY. Why, he wrong[8] a club
Once in a fray out of the hand of Belzebub.
R. ROISTER. And how when Mumfision—
M. MERRY. O, your coustreling[9]
Bore the lantern afield so before the gozeling[10]—
Nay, that is too long a matter now to be told.
Never ask his name, nurse; I warrant thee, be bold. 80
He conquered in one day from Rome to Naples,
And won towns, nurse, as fast as thou canst make apples.
M. MUMBL. O Lord, my heart quaketh for fear! He is too sore!
R. ROISTER. Thou makest her too much afeard, Merrygreek; no more.
This tale would fear my sweetheart Custance right evil.
M. MERRY. Nay, let her take him, nurse, and fear not the devil.
But thus is our song dashed. [*To Musicians.*] Sirs, ye may home again.
R. ROISTER. No, shall they not. I charge you all here to remain.
The villain slaves, a whole day ere they can be found!

---

[1] Silver, money.
[2] In the name of the Father.
[3] Madge relapses into dialect.
[4] Bush.   [5] Beat.   [6] Terrible.
[7] Semblety, semblance—a rustic oath.
[8] Wrung.   [9] Servant.
[10] Gosling, *i.e.*, a foolish person(?).

M. MERRY. Couch on your marybones,[1]
   whoresons, down to the ground!   90
Was it meet he should tarry so long in
   one place
Without harmony of music, or some
   solace?
Whoso hath such bees as your master in
   his head,
Had need to have his spirits with music
   to be fed.
By your mastership's license—
[*Picks something from Roister Doister's
                              coat.*]
R. ROISTER.   What is that? A mote?
M. MERRY. No, it was a fool's [2] feather
   had light on your coat.
R. ROISTER. I was nigh no feathers since
   I came from my bed.
M. MERRY. No, sir, it was a hair that was
   fall from your head.
R. ROISTER. My men come when it please
   them.
M. MERRY.   By your leave—
R. ROISTER.   What is
   that?
M. MERRY. Your gown was foul spotted
   with the foot of a gnat.   100
R. ROISTER. Their master to offend they
   are nothing afeard.
What now?
M. MERRY.   A lousy hair from your
   mastership's beard.
OMNES FAMULÆ.[3] And, sir, for nurse's sake,
   pardon this one offense.
We shall not after this show the like
   negligence.
R. ROISTER. I pardon you this once, and
   come, sing ne'er the worse.
M. MERRY. How like you the goodness of
   this gentleman, nurse?
M. MUMBL. God save his mastership that
   so can his men forgive!
And I will hear them sing ere I go, by his
   leave.
R. ROISTER. Marry and thou shalt, wench.
   Come, we two will dance.
M. MUMBL. Nay, I will by mine own self
   foot the song perchance.   110
R. ROISTER. Go to it, sirs, lustily.

M. MUMBL.   Pipe up a
   merry note.
Let me hear it played; I will foot it for a
   groat.   *Cantent.*[4]
R. ROISTER. Now, nurse, take this same
   letter here to thy mistress;
And, as my trust is in thee, ply my busi-
   ness.
M. MUMBL. It shall be done.
M. MERRY.   Who made it?
R. ROISTER.   I wrote it each
   whit.
M. MERRY. Then needs it no mending.
R. ROISTER.   No, no.
M. MERRY.   No, I know
   your wit.
I warrant it well.
M. MUMBL.   It shall be delivered.
But, if ye speed, shall I be con-
   sidered?
M. MERRY. Whough! Dost thou doubt of
   that?
MADGE [MUMBL.] What shall I have? 120
M. MERRY. An hundred times more than
   thou canst devise to crave.
M. MUMBL. Shall I have some new gear?
   For my old is all spent.
M. MERRY. The worst kitchen wench shall
   go in ladies' raiment.
M. MUMBL. Yea?
M. MERRY.   And the worst drudge
   in the house shall go better
Than your mistress doth now.
MAR. [MUMBL.]   Then I trudge
   with your letter.   [*Exeat.*]
R. ROISTER. Now may I repose me. Cus-
   tance is mine own.
Let us sing and play homeward that it
   may be known.
M. MERRY. But are you sure that your
   letter is well enough?
R. ROISTER. I wrote it myself.
M. MERRY.   Then sing
   we to dinner.
       Here they sing, and go out singing.

ACTUS I. SCENA v.

Christian Custance, Margery Mumblecrust.

C. CUSTANCE. Who took [5] thee this letter,
   Margery Mumblecrust?

---

[1] Marrowbones.
[2] With a pun on *fowl's.*
[3] All the servants.

[4] Let them sing (probably "The Second Song,"
printed at the end of the play).   [5] Gave.

M. MUMBL. A lusty gay bachelor took it me of trust,
  And, if ye seek to him, he will low [1] your doing.
C. CUSTANCE. Yea, but where learned he that manner of wooing?
M. MUMBL. If to sue to him you will any pains take,
  He will have you to his wife, he saith, for my sake.
C. CUSTANCE. Some wise gentleman, belike. I am bespoken; [2]
  And I thought verily this had been some token
  From my dear spouse Gawin Goodluck, whom, when him please,
  God luckily send home to both our hearts' ease.   10
M. MUMBL. A joyly [3] man it is, I wot well by report,
  And would have you to him for marriage resort.
  Best open the writing, and see what it doth speak.
C. CUSTANCE. At this time, nurse, I will neither read ne break. [4]
M. MUMBL. He promised to give you a whole peck of gold.
C. CUSTANCE. Perchance, lack of a pint when it shall be all told.
M. MUMBL. I would take a gay rich husband, and I were you.
C. CUSTANCE. In good sooth, Madge, e'en so would I, if I were thou.
  But no more of this fond talk now; let us go in,
  And see thou no more move me folly to begin,   20
  Nor bring me no mo [5] letters for no man's pleasure,
  But thou know from whom.
M. MUMBL.   I warrant ye shall be sure.

ACTUS II. SCENA i.

Dobinet Doughty.

D. DOUGH. Where is the house I go to, before or behind?
  I know not where nor when nor how I shall it find.

If I had ten men's bodies and legs and strength,
This trotting that I have must needs lame me at length.
And now that my master is new set on wooing,
I trust there shall none of us find lack of doing.
Two pair of shoes a day will now be too little
To serve me, I must trot to and fro so mickle. [6]
"Go bear me this token!" "Carry me this letter!"
Now, "This is the best way;" now, "That way is better!"   10
"Up before day, sirs, I charge you, an hour or twain!"
"Trudge! Do me this message, and bring word quick again!"
If one miss but a minute, then, "His arms and wounds,
I would not have slacked for ten thousand pounds.
Nay, see, I beseech you, if my most trusty page
Go not now about to hinder my marriage."
So fervent hot wooing, and so far from wiving,
I trow, never was any creature living.
With every woman is he in some love's pang,
Then up to our lute at midnight, twangledom twang;   20
Then twang with our sonnets, and twang with our dumps, [7]
And heigh-ho from our heart, as heavy as lead lumps;
Then to our recorder [8] with toodle-loodle poop,
As the howlet out of an ivy bush should hoop. [9]
Anon to our gittern, thrumpledum, thrumpledum thrum,
Thrumpledum, thrumpledum, thrumpledum, thrumpledum thrum.
Of songs and ballads also he is a maker,
And that can he as finely do as Jack Raker;
Yea, and extempore will he ditties compose—

---

[1] Allow, approve.
[2] Promised, betrothed.
[3] Pretty, elegant.
[4] Break the seal.
[5] More.

[6] Much.
[7] Melancholy music.
[8] Flute.
[9] Whoop.

Foolish Marsyas ne'er made the like, I
   suppose.   30
Yet must we sing them; as good stuff, I
   undertake,
As for such a penman is well fitting to
   make.
"Ah, for these long nights! Heigh-ho!
   When will it be day?
I fear ere I come she will be wooed
   away."
Then when answer is made that it may
   not be,
"O death, why comest thou not?" by-
   and-by saith he.
But then, from his heart to put away
   sorrow,
He is as far in with some new love next
   morrow.
But in the mean season we trudge and
   we trot;
From dayspring to midnight I sit not
   nor rest not.   40
And now am I sent to Dame Christian
   Custance,
But I fear it will end with a mock for
   pastance.[1]
I bring her a ring, with a token in a
   clout [2]—
And by all guess this same is her house
   out of doubt.
I know it now perfect; I am in my right
   way.
And lo! yond the old nurse that was with
   us last day.

ACTUS II. SCENA ii.

Madge Mumblecrust, Dobinet Doughty.

M. MUMBL. I was ne'er so shoke up [3] afore
   since I was born.
That our mistress could not have chid,
   I would have sworn;
And I pray God I die if I meant any
   harm,
But for my lifetime this shall be to me
   a charm.
D. DOUGH. God you save and see,[4] nurse,
   and how is it with you?
M. MUMBL. Marry, a great deal the worse
   it is for such as thou.
D. DOUGH. For me? Why so?

M. MUMBL.   Why, were not thou
   one of them, say,
That song and played here with the
   gentleman last day?
D. DOUGH. Yes, and he would know if
   you have for him spoken,
And prays you to deliver this ring and
   token.   10
M. MUMBL. Now by the token that God
   tokened, brother,
I will deliver no token, one nor other.
I have once been so shent for your mas-
   ter's pleasure,
As I will not be again for all his trea-
   sure.
D. DOUGH. He will thank you, woman.
M. MUMBL.   I will none of his
   thank.   *Ex[eat]*.
D. DOUGH. I ween I am a prophet! This
   gear will prove blank.[5]
But what! should I home again without
   answer go?
It were better go to Rome on my head
   than so.
I will tarry here this month, but some of
   the house
Shall take it of me, and then I care not
   a louse.   20
But yonder cometh forth a wench or a
   lad;
If he have not one Lombard's [6] touch,
   my luck is bad.

ACTUS II. SCENA iii.

*Truepenny, D[obinet] Dough[ty], Tibet T[alk-
   apace], Annot Al[yface].*[7]

TRUEPENNY. I am clean lost for lack of
   merry company;
We gree [8] not half well within, our wenches
   and I.
They will command like mistresses; they
   will forbid;
If they be not served, Truepenny must
   be chid.
Let them be as merry now as ye can
   desire,
With turning of a hand, our mirth lieth
   in the mire.

---

[1] Pastime.
[2] Cloth.
[3] Scolded.
[4] Watch over.
[5] Unsuccessful.
[6] The Lombard was proverbially a money changer. Here, one who likes to handle gold.
[7] Last two enter later.
[8] Agree.

I cannot skill of [1] such changeable
    mettle;
There is nothing with them but "in
    dock, out nettle." [2]

D. Dough. Whether is it better that I
    speak to him first,
Or he first to me? It is good to cast the
    worst.   10
If I begin first, he will smell all my pur-
    pose;
Otherwise I shall not need anything to
    disclose.

Truepenny. What boy have we yonder?
    I will see what he is.

D. Dough. He cometh to me.—It is here-
    about, iwis.

Truepenny. Wouldest thou aught, friend,
    that thou lookest so about?

D. Dough. Yea, but whether ye can help
    me or no, I doubt.
I seek to one Mistress Custance' house,
    here dwelling.

Truepenny. It is my mistress ye seek to,
    by your telling.

D. Dough. Is there any of that name here
    but she?

Truepenny. Not one in all the whole
    town that I know, pardee.   20

D. Dough. A widow she is, I trow.

Truepenny.   And what
    and she be?

D. Dough. But insured to an husband.

Truepenny.   Yea, so think we.

D. Dough. And I dwell with her husband
    that trusteth to be.

Truepenny. In faith, then must thou
    needs be welcome to me.
Let us for acquaintance shake hands
    togither,
And whate'er thou be, heartily welcome
    hither.

[Enter Tibet and Annot.]

Tib. Talk. Well, Truepenny, never but
    flinging? [3]

An. Alyface.   And frisking?

Truepenny. Well, Tibet and Annot, still
    swinging and whisking?

Tib. Talk. But ye roil [4] abroad.

An. Alyface.   In the street
    everywhere.

Truepenny. Where are ye twain, in
    chambers when ye meet me there?   30
But come hither, fools; I have one now
    by the hand,
Servant to him that must be our mistress'
    husband.
Bid him welcome.

An. Alyface.   To me truly is he
    welcome.

Tib. Talk. Forsooth, and as I may say,
    heartily welcome.

D. Dough. I thank you, mistress maids.

An. Alyface.   I hope we shall
    better know.

Tib. Talk. And when will our new master
    come?

D. Dough.   Shortly, I trow.

Tib. Talk. I would it were tomorrow; for
    till he resort,
Our mistress, being a widow, hath small
    comfort,
And I heard our nurse speak of an hus-
    band today
Ready for our mistress, a rich man and
    a gay.   40
And we shall go in our French hoods
    every day,
In our silk cassocks, I warrant you,
    fresh and gay,
In our trick ferdegews [5] and billiments [6]
    of gold;
Brave [7] in our suits of change, seven
    double fold.
Then shall ye see Tibet, sirs, tread the
    moss so trim—
Nay, why said I tread? Ye shall see her
    glide and swim,
Not lumperdee clumperdee like our span-
    iel Rig.

Truepenny. Marry, then, prick-me-dain-
    ty, [8] come toast me a fig!
Who shall then know our Tib Talkapace,
    trow ye?

An. Alyface. And why not Annot Aly-
    face as fine as she?   50

Truepenny. And what had Tom True-
    penny, a father or none?

An. Alyface. Then our pretty new-come
    man will look to be one.

---

[1] Understand.
[2] Proverbial phrase for inconstancy, referring
to the curing of nettle stings by dock leaves.
[3] Running about.   [4] Gad.
[5] Neat farthingales.
[6] Habiliments, perhaps headdresses.
[7] Gay.   [8] Finical person.

TRUEPENNY. We four, I trust, shall be a joyly merry knot.

Shall we sing a fit [1] to welcome our friend, Annot?

AN. ALYFACE. Perchance he cannot sing.

D. DOUGH.   I am at all essays. [2]

TIB. TALK. By Cock, and the better welcome to us always.

Here they sing.

A thing very fit
For them that have wit
And are fellows knit,
　　Servants in one house to be,   60
Is fast, fast for to sit,
And not oft to flit,
Nor vary a whit,
　　But lovingly to agree.

No man complaining,
No other disdaining,
For loss or for gaining,
　　But fellows or friends to be.
No grudge remaining,
No work refraining,   70
Nor help restraining,
　　But lovingly to agree.

No man for despite,
By word or by write
His fellow to twite, [3]
　　But further in honesty;
No good turns entwite, [3]
Nor old sores recite,
But let all go quite,
　　And lovingly to agree.   80

After drudgery,
When they be weary,
Then to be merry,
　　To laugh and sing they be free;
With chip and cherry, [4]
Heigh derry derry,
Trill on the bery, [5]
　　And lovingly to agree.
　　　　　　　FINIS.

TIB. TALK. Will you now in with us unto our mistress go?

D. DOUGH. I have first for my master an errand or two.   90

But I have here from him a token and a ring;

They shall have most thank of her that first doth it bring.

[1] Song.   [4] Chirp and coo.
[2] Ready for all contingencies.
[3] Twit, blame.   [5] Dance on the hill.

TIB. TALK. Marry, that will I.

TRUEPENNY.   See, and Tibet snatch not now!

TIB. TALK. And why may not I, sir, get thanks as well as you?   *Exeat.*

AN. ALYFACE. Yet get ye not all; we will go with you both

And have part of your thanks, be ye never so loath.

[Exeant all but Doughty.]

D. DOUGH. So my hands are rid of it; I care for no more.

I may now return home; so durst I not afore.   *Exeat.*

ACTUS II. SCENA iv.

C[hristian] Custance, Tibet, Annot Alyface,
Truepenny.

C. CUSTANCE. Nay, come forth all three; and come hither, pretty maid.

Will not so many forewarnings make you afraid?

TIB. TALK. Yes, forsooth.

C. CUSTANCE.   But still be a runner up and down,

Still be a bringer of tidings and tokens to town.

TIB. TALK. No, forsooth, mistress.

C. CUSTANCE.   Is all your delight and joy

In whisking and ramping abroad like a tomboy?

TIB. TALK. Forsooth, these were there too, Annot and Truepenny.

TRUEPENNY. Yea, but ye alone took it, ye cannot deny.

AN. ALYFACE. Yea, that ye did.

TIB. TALK.   But if I had not, ye twain would.

C. CUSTANCE. You great calf, ye should have more wit, so ye should.   10

But why should any of you take such things in hand?

TIB. TALK. Because it came from him that must be your husband.

C. CUSTANCE. How do ye know that?

TIB. TALK.   Forsooth, the boy did say so.

C. CUSTANCE. What was his name?

AN. ALYFACE.   We asked not.

C. CUSTANCE.   No, did? [6]

[6] This word might be omitted for the sake of the rime.

An. Alyface. He is not far gone, of likelihood.

Truepenny.　　　I will see.

C. Custance. If thou canst find him in
the street, bring him to me.

Truepenny. Yes.　　　　　　*Exeat.*

C. Custance.　　　Well, ye naughty girls,
if ever I perceive
That henceforth you do letters or tokens
receive,
To bring unto me from any person or
place,
Except ye first show me the party face
to face,　　　　　　　　　　　20
Either thou or thou, full truly aby [1] thou
shalt.

Tib. Talk. Pardon this, and the next time
powder me in salt.

C. Custance. I shall make all girls by
you twain to beware.

Tib. Talk. If ever I offend again, do not
me spare.
But if ever I see that false boy any more,
By your mistress-ship's license, I tell you
afore,
I will rather have my coat twenty times
swinged [2]
Than on the naughty wag not to be
avenged.

C. Custance. Good wenches would not so
ramp abroad idly,
But keep within doors, and ply their work
earnestly.　　　　　　　　　30
If one would speak with me that is a
man likely,
Ye shall have right good thank to bring
me word quickly.
But otherwise with messages to come in
post
From henceforth, I promise you, shall
be to your cost.
Get you in to your work.

Tib. [Talk.]　╲
　　　　　　　 〉　Yes, forsooth.
An. [Alyface.]　╱

C. Custance.　　　Hence, both twain.
And let me see you play me such a part
again!　　　　[*Exeant Tibet and Annot.*]

[*Enter Truepenny.*]

Truepenny. Mistress, I have run past the
far end of the street,
Yet can I not yonder crafty boy see nor
meet.

C. Custance. No?

Truepenny.　　　Yet I looked as far
beyond the people
As one may see out of the top of Paul's
steeple.　　　　　　　　　40

C. Custance. Hence, in at doors, and let
me no more be vexed.

Truepenny. Forgive me this one fault,
and lay on for the next.　　[*Exeat.*]

C. Custance. Now will I in too, for I
think, so God me mend,
This will prove some foolish matter in
the end.　　　　　　　　*Exeat.*

Actus II[I].　Scena i.

Matthew Merrygreek.

M. Merry. Now say this again: he hath
somewhat to doing
Which followeth the trace of one that is
wooing,
Specially that hath no more wit in his
head
Than my cousin Roister Doister withal
is led.
I am sent in all haste to espy and to mark
How our letters and tokens are likely to
wark. [3]
Master Roister Doister must have answer
in haste,
For he loveth not to spend much labor
in waste.
Now as for Christian Custance, by this
light,
Though she had not her troth to Gawin
Goodluck plight,　　　　　　10
Yet rather than with such a loutish dolt
to marry,
I dare say would live a poor life solitary.
But fain would I speak with Custance,
if I wist how,
To laugh at the matter.—Yond cometh
one forth now.

Actus III.　Scena ii.

*Tibet, M[atthew] Merrygreek, Christian Cus-
tance.* [4]

Tib. Talk. Ah, that I might but once in
my life have a sight
Of him that made us all so ill shent! By
this light,
He should never escape if I had him by
the ear,

---

[1] Pay the penalty.　　　[2] Beaten.　　　[3] Work.　　　[4] Enters later.

But even from his head I would it bite or
   tear!
Yea, and if one of them were not enow,
I would bite them both off, I make God
   avow.[1]
M. MERRY. [*Aside*.] What is he whom
   this little mouse doth so threaten?
TIB. TALK. I would teach him, I trow, to
   make girls shent or beaten.
M. MERRY. [*Aside*.] I will call her.—Maid,
   with whom are ye so hasty?
TIB. TALK. Not with you, sir, but with a
   little wagpasty,[2]   10
A deceiver of folks by subtle craft and
   guile.
M. MERRY. [*Aside*.] I know where she is:[3]
   Dobinet hath wrought some wile.
TIB. TALK. He brought a ring and token
   which he said was sent
From our dame's husband, but I wot
   well I was shent;
For it liked her as well, to tell you no lies,
As water in her ship, or salt cast in her
   eyes.
And yet whence it came neither we nor
   she can tell.
M. MERRY. [*Aside*.] We shall have sport
   anon; I like this very well.—
And dwell ye here with Mistress Cus-
   tance, fair maid?
TIB. TALK. Yea, marry, do I, sir. What
   would ye have said?   20
M. MERRY. A little message unto her by
   word of mouth.
TIB. TALK. No messages, by your leave,
   nor tokens forsooth.
M. MERRY. Then help me to speak with
   her.
TIB. TALK.   With a good will that.
Here she cometh forth. Now speak ye
   know best what.

[*Enter Custance.*]

C. CUSTANCE. None other life with you,
   maid, but abroad to skip?
TIB. TALK. Forsooth, here is one would
   speak with your mistress-ship.
C. CUSTANCE. Ah, have ye been learning
   of mo messages now?
TIB. TALK. I would not hear his mind, but
   bade him show it to you.

C. CUSTANCE. In at doors!
TIB. TALK.   I am gone.   *Ex[eat.]*
M. MERRY.   Dame Custance,
   God ye save.
C. CUSTANCE. Welcome, friend Merry-
   greek, and what thing would ye
   have?   30
M. MERRY. I am come to you a little
   matter to break.
C. CUSTANCE. But see it be honest; else
   better not to speak.
M. MERRY. How feel ye yourself affected
   here of late?
C. CUSTANCE. I feel no manner change but
   after the old rate.
But whereby do ye mean?
M. MERRY.   Concerning
   marriage.
Doth not love lade you?
C. CUSTANCE.   I feel no such
   carriage.[4]
M. MERRY. Do ye feel no pangs of dotage?
   Answer me right.
C. CUSTANCE. I dote so that I make but
   one sleep all the night.
But what need all these words?
M. MERRY.   O Jesus,
   will ye see
What dissembling creatures these same
   women be?   40
The gentleman ye wot of, whom ye do so
   love
That ye would fain marry him, if ye
   durst it move,
Among other rich widows, which are of
   him glad,
Lest ye for leesing of him perchance
   might run mad,
Is now contented that, upon your suit
   making,
Ye be as one in election of taking.
C. CUSTANCE. What a tale is this! That I
   wot of? Whom I love?
M. MERRY. Yea, and he is as loving a
   worm,[5] again, as a dove.
E'en of very pity he is willing you to take,
Because ye shall not destroy yourself for
   his sake.   50
C. CUSTANCE. Marry, God yeld his ma'-
   ship whatever he be.
It is gentmanly[6] spoken.

---

[1] An oath, a promise.   [2] Rogue.
[3] I know what's the matter with her.
[4] Burden.
[5] Little creature; a term of endearment.
[6] Colloquial for *gentlemanly*.

M. MERRY.   Is it not,
   trow ye?
  If ye have the grace now to offer your-
   self, ye speed.
C. CUSTANCE. As much as though I did,
   this time it shall not need.
  But what gentman is it, I pray you tell
   me plain,
  That wooeth so finely?
M. MERRY.   Lo, where ye be
   again,
  As though ye knew him not.
C. CUSTANCE.   Tush, ye
   speak in jest.
M. MERRY. Nay, sure, the party is in
   good knacking [1] earnest,
  And have you he will, he saith, and have
   you he must.
C. CUSTANCE. I am promised during my
   life; that is just.   60
M. MERRY. Marry, so thinketh he, unto
   him alone.
C. CUSTANCE. No creature hath my faith
   and troth but one—
  That is Gawin Goodluck; and, if it be
   not he,
  He hath no title this way whatever he be,
  Nor I know none to whom I have such
   word spoken.
M. MERRY. Yea, know him not you by his
   letter and token?
C. CUSTANCE. Indeed, true it is that a
   letter I have,
  But I never read it yet, as God me
   save.
M. MERRY. Ye a woman, and your letter
   so long unread?
C. CUSTANCE. Ye may thereby know what
   haste I have to wed.   70
  But now, who it is for my hand I know
   by guess.
M. MERRY. Ah, well I say.
C. CUSTANCE.   It is Roister
   Doister, doubtless.
M. MERRY. Will ye never leave this dis-
   simulation?
  Ye know him not?
C. CUSTANCE.   But by imagination,
  For no man there is but a very dolt and
   lout
  That to woo a widow would so go about.
  He shall never have me his wife while
   he do live.

[1] Downright.

M. MERRY. Then will he have you if he
   may, so mote [2] I thrive,
  And he biddeth you send him word by me,
  That ye humbly beseech him, ye may his
   wife be,   80
  And that there shall be no let [3] in you
   nor mistrust,
  But to be wedded on Sunday next if he
   lust,
  And biddeth you to look for him.
C. CUSTANCE.   Doth
   he bid so?
M. MERRY. When he cometh, ask him
   whether he did or no.
C. CUSTANCE. Go, say that I bid him keep
   him warm at home,
  For, if he come abroad, he shall cough
   me a mome.[4]
  My mind was vexed; I shrew his head,
   sottish dolt!
M. MERRY. He hath in his head—
C. CUSTANCE.   As much
   brain as a burbolt.[5]
M. MERRY. Well, Dame Custance, if he
   hear you thus play choploge [6]—
C. CUSTANCE. What will he?
M. MERRY.   Play the
   devil in the horologe.[7]   90
C. CUSTANCE. I defy him, lout!
M. MERRY.   Shall I
   tell him what ye say?
C. CUSTANCE. Yea, and add whatsoever
   thou canst, I thee pray,
  And I will avouch it, whatsoever it be.
M. MERRY. Then let me alone; we will
   laugh well, ye shall see.
  It will not be long ere he will hither resort.
C. CUSTANCE. Let him come when him
   lust; I wish no better sport.
  Fare ye well. I will in, and read my
   great letter.
  I shall to my wooer make answer the
   better.   *Exeat.*

ACTUS III. SCENA iii.

Matthew Merrygreek, Roister Doister.

M. MERRY. Now that the whole answer
   in my devise doth rest,
  I shall paint out our wooer in colors of
   the best.

[2] May.   [3] Hindrance.
[4] Show what a blockhead he is.
[5] Birdbolt, sometimes carried by jesters;
hence, a fool.   [6] Choplogic.   [7] Clock.

And all that I say shall be on Custance's
    mouth;
She is author of all that I shall speak
    forsooth.
But yond cometh Roister Doister now
    in a trance.
R. ROISTER. Juno send me this day good
    luck and good chance.
I cannot but come see how Merrygreek
    doth speed.
M. MERRY. [*Aside.*] I will not see him, but
    give him a jut [1] indeed.—
                [*Runs into him.*]
I cry your mastership mercy!
R. ROISTER.   And
    whither now?
M. MERRY. As fast as I could run, sir, in
    post against you.   10
But why speak ye so faintly, or why are
    ye so sad?
R. ROISTER. Thou knowest the proverb—
    "Because I cannot be had."
Hast thou spoken with this woman?
M. MERRY.   Yea, that I have.
R. ROISTER. And what will this gear be?
M. MERRY.   No, so God me save.
R. ROISTER. Hast thou a flat answer?
M. MERRY.   Nay, a sharp answer.
R. ROISTER.   What?
M. MERRY. Ye shall not, she saith, by her
    will, marry her cat.
Ye are such a calf, such an ass, such a
    block,
Such a lilburn,[2] such a hoball,[3] such a
    lobcock,[4]
And because ye should come to her at
    no season,
She despised your ma'ship out of all
    reason.   20
"Bawawe [5] what ye say," ko [6] I, "of such
    a gentman!"
"Nay, I fear him not," ko she, "do the
    best he can.
He vaunteth himself for a man of prowess
    great,
Whereas a good gander, I dare say, may
    him beat.
And where he is louted [7] and laughed to
    scorn,
For the veriest dolt that ever was born,
And veriest lover,[8] sloven, and beast,

Living in this world from the west to the
    east,
Yet of himself hath he such opinion,
That in all the world is not the like
    minion.[9]   30
He thinketh each woman to be brought
    in dotage
With the only sight of his goodly per-
    sonage;
Yet none that will have him. We do him
    lout and flock,[10]
And make him among us our common
    sporting stock,
And so would I now," ko she, "save only
    because—"
"Better nay," ko I; "I lust not meddle
    with daws.[11]
Ye are happy," ko I, "that ye are a
    woman;
This would cost you your life in case ye
    were a man."
R. ROISTER. Yea, an hundred thousand
    pound should not save her life.
M. MERRY. No, but that ye woo her to
    have her to your wife.   40
But I could not stop her mouth.
R. ROISTER.   Heigh-
    ho, alas!
M. MERRY. Be of good cheer, man, and
    let the world pass.
R. ROISTER. What shall I do or say now
    that it will not be?
M. MERRY. Ye shall have choice of a
    thousand as good as she,
And ye must pardon her; it is for lack of
    wit.
R. ROISTER. Yea, for were not I an hus-
    band for her fit?
Well, what should I now do?
M. MERRY.   In faith, I
    cannot tell.
R. ROISTER. I will go home and die.
M. MERRY.   Then shall
    I bid toll the bell?
R. ROISTER. No.
M. MERRY.   God have mercy on
    your soul! Ah, good gentleman,
That e'er ye should thus die for an un-
    kind woman!   50
Will ye drink once ere ye go?
R. ROISTER.   No, no,
    I will none.

---

[1] Jolt.   [4] Lubber.   [7] Ridiculed.
[2] Dolt.   [5] Beware(?).   [8] Lubber(?).
[3] Clodhopper.   [6] Quoth, said.
[9] Darling, favorite.   [11] Fools.
[10] Treat contemptuously.

M. MERRY. How feel your soul to God? [1]
R. ROISTER.   I am nigh gone.
M. MERRY. And shall we hence straight?
R. ROISTER.   Yea.
M. MERRY.   Placebo.[2] Dilexi.[3]
Master Roister Doister will straight go
   home and die.   Ut infra.[4]
R. ROISTER. Heigh-ho, alas, the pangs of
   death my heart do break!
M. MERRY. Hold your peace! For shame,
   sir, a dead man may not speak!
Nequando.[5] What mourners and what
   torches shall we have?
R. ROISTER. None.
M. MERRY.   Dirige.[6] He will go
   darkling to his grave—
Neque lux, neque crux, neque mourners,
   neque clink.[7]
He will steal to heaven, unknowing to
   God, I think.   60
A porta inferi.[8] Who shall your goods
   possess?
R. ROISTER. Thou shalt be my sector,[9]
   and have all, more and less.
M. MERRY. Requiem æternam.[10] Now, God
   reward your mastership.
And I will cry halfpenny-dole for your
   worship.
Come forth, sirs, hear the doleful news
   I shall you tell. Evocat servos militis.[11]

[Enter four Servants.]

Our good master here will no longer with
   us dwell.
But, in spite of Custance, which hath
   him wearied,
Let us see his ma'ship solemnly buried.
And while some piece of his soul is yet
   him within,   69
Some part of his funerals let us here begin.
Audivi vocem.[12] All men take heed by
   this one gentleman,

[1] From the service for the visitation of the sick.
[2] I shall be acceptable(?). This word begins
a parody on the Catholic service for the dead.
[3] I have loved(?).
[4] As below. (See "Psalmody" at end of play.)
[5] Never.
[6] Direct [my way].
[7] Neither light nor cross nor mourners nor bell.
[8] From the gate of hell.
[9] Executor.
[10] Eternal rest.
[11] He calls the soldier's [Roister Doister's]
servants.
[12] I have heard a voice.

How you set your love upon an unkind
   woman.
For these women be all such mad peevish
   elves,
They will not be won except it please
   themselves.
But in faith, Custance, if ever ye come
   in hell,
Master Roister Doister shall serve you
   as well.
And will ye needs go from us thus in
   very deed?
R. ROISTER. Yea, in good sadness.
M. MERRY.   Now,
   Jesus Christ be your speed.
Good night, Roger, old knave; farewell,
   Roger, old knave!
Good night, Roger, old knave; knave,
   knap! [13]   Ut infra. 80
Pray for the late Master Roister Dois-
   ter's soul,
And come forth, parish clerk, let the
   passing bell toll.   Ad servos militis.[14]

[Enter Parish Clerk.]

Pray for your master, sirs, and for him
   ring a peal.[15]
He was your right good master while he
   was in heal.[16]
Qui Lazarum.[17]
R. ROISTER.   Heigh-ho!
M. MERRY.   Dead men go
   not so fast
In paradisum.[18]
R. ROISTER. Heigh-ho!
M. MERRY.   Soft, hear what
   I have cast.
R. ROISTER. I will hear nothing; I am
   past.
M. MERRY.   Whough, wellaway!
Ye may tarry one hour, and hear what
   I shall say.
Ye were best, sir, for a while to revive
   again,
And quite [19] them ere ye go.
R. ROISTER.   Trowest thou so?

[13] This word may mean either knave or nap or
strike (the bell).
[14] To the servants of the soldier.
[15] See "Peal of Bells" at the end of play.
[16] Health.
[17] Thou who [didst raise] Lazarus.
[18] Into paradise.
[19] Requite, get even with.

M. MERRY.　　　　　Yea, plain.　90

R. ROISTER. How may I revive, being now
so far past?

M. MERRY. I will rub your temples, and
fet [1] you again at last.

R. ROISTER. It will not be possible.

M. MERRY.　　　　　Yes,
for twenty pound.

R. ROISTER. Arms! [2] what dost thou?

M. MERRY.　　　　　Fet
you again out of your sound. [3]

By this cross, ye were nigh gone indeed;
I might feel

Your soul departing within an inch of
your heel.

Now follow my counsel.

R. ROISTER.　　　What is it?

M. MERRY.　　　If I were you,
Custance should eft [4] seek to me, ere I
would bow.

R. ROISTER. Well, as thou wilt have me,
even so will I do.

M. MERRY. Then shall ye revive again for
an hour or two.　　　　　100

R. ROISTER. As thou wilt; I am content
for a little space.

M. MERRY. "Good hap is not hasty;"
yet "In space com[e]th grace."

To speak with Custance yourself should
be very well;

What good thereof may come, nor I
nor you can tell.

But now the matter standeth upon your
marriage,

Ye must now take unto you a lusty courage;

Ye may not speak with a faint heart to
Custance,

But with a lusty breast and countenance,

That she may know she hath to answer
to a man.

R. ROISTER. Yes, I can do that as well
as any can.　　　　　110

M. MERRY. Then because ye must Custance face to face woo,

Let us see how to behave yourself ye
can do.

Ye must have a portly brag after your
estate. [5]

R. ROISTER. Tush, I can handle that after
the best rate.

M. MERRY. Well done! so, lo! up, man,
with your head and chin,

Up with that snout, man! so, lo! now ye
begin!

So, that is somewhat like! But, pranky-
coat, [6] nay, whan? [7]

That is a lusty brute; hands under your
side, man.

So, lo! now is it even as it should be;

That is somewhat like, for a man of your
degree.　　　　　120

Then must ye stately go, jetting [8] up
and down.

Tut, can ye no better shake the tail of
your gown?

There, lo, such a lusty brag it is ye must
make.

R. ROISTER. To come behind, and make
curtsy, thou must some pains take.

M. MERRY. Else were I much to blame, I
thank your mastership.

The Lord one day all-to [9] begrime you
with worship.

"Back, sir sauce, let gentlefolks have
elbow room.

[Shoves imaginary persons out of the way.]

Void, [10] sirs, see ye not Master Roister
Doister come?

Make place, my masters."

　　　　　[Jostles Roister Doister.]

R. ROISTER.　　　　　Thou justlest
now too nigh.　　　　　129

M. MERRY. "Back, all rude louts!"

R. ROISTER.　　　　　Tush!

M. MERRY.　　I cry your ma'ship mercy!
Hoiday, if fair fine Mistress Custance
saw you now,

Ralph Roister Doister were her own, I
warrant you!

R. ROISTER. Ne'er an M [11] by your girdle? [12]

M. MERRY.　　Your good mastership's
Mastership were her own mistress-ship's
mistress-ship's! [13]

Ye were take up for hawks [14]— ye were
gone, ye were gone.

But now one other thing more yet I
think upon.

---

[1] Fetch.　　　　　　　　[3] Swoon.
[2] By God's arms.　　　　[4] Again.
[5] Pompous bearing befitting your rank.

[6] Frolicsome fellow.　　[9] Completely.
[7] When.　　　　　　　　[10] Make room.
[8] Strutting.
[11] Abbreviation for *master* or *mistress.*
[12] *I.e.,* Can't you speak respectfully—address
me as master?　　[13] Supply *property, husband.*
[14] Farmer suggests: "You would be snapped
up for a husband like hawks' meat."

R. ROISTER. Show what it is.

M. MERRY.   A wooer, be
   he never so poor,
Must play and sing before his best-
   belove's door;
How much more, then, you?

R. ROISTER.   Thou
   speakest well, out of doubt.

M. MERRY. And perchance that would
   make her the sooner come out.   140

R. ROISTER. Go, call my musicians; bid
   them hie apace.

M. MERRY. I will be here with them ere
   ye can say "trey ace."   *Exeat.*

R. ROISTER. This was well said of Merrygreek; I low his wit.
Before my sweetheart's door we will have
   a fit,
That if my love come forth, that I may
   with her talk,
I doubt not but this gear shall on my
   side walk.
But lo, how well Merrygreek is returned
   sence.[1]

[*Enter Merrygreek with Musicians.*]

M. MERRY. There hath grown no grass on
   my heel since I went hence;
Lo, here have I brought that shall make
   you pastance.

R. ROISTER. Come, sirs, let us sing to win
   my dear love Custance.   150
                     Cantent.[2]

M. MERRY. Lo, where she cometh! Some
   countenance to her make,
And ye shall hear me be plain with her
   for your sake.

ACTUS III. SCENA iv.

Custance, Merrygreek, Roister Doister.

C. CUSTANCE. What gauding[3] and fooling is this afore my door?

M. MERRY. May not folks be honest,
   pray you, though they be poor?

C. CUSTANCE. As that thing may be true,
   so rich folks may be fools.

R. ROISTER. Her talk is as fine as she
   had learned in schools.

M. MERRY. Look partly toward her, and
   draw a little near.

C. CUSTANCE. Get ye home, idle folks.

M. MERRY.   Why may not we be here?
Nay, and ye will ha's,[4] ha's; otherwise,
   I tell you plain,
And ye will not ha's, then give us our
   gear again.

C. CUSTANCE. Indeed, I have of yours
   much gay things, God save all.

R. ROISTER. Speak gently unto her, and
   let her take all.   10

M. MERRY. Ye are too tender-hearted.
   Shall she make us daws?
Nay, dame, I will be plain with you in
   my friend's cause.

R. ROISTER. Let all this pass, sweetheart,
   and accept my service.

C. CUSTANCE. I will not be served with a
   fool in no wise;
When I choose an husband, I hope to
   take a man.

M. MERRY. And where will ye find one
   which can do that he can?
Now this man toward you being so kind,
You not to make him an answer somewhat to his mind!

C. CUSTANCE. I sent him a full answer by
   you, did I not?

M. MERRY. And I reported it.

C. CUSTANCE.   Nay, I
   must speak it again.   20

R. ROISTER. No, no, he told it all.

M. MERRY.   Was
   I not metely[5] plain?

R. ROISTER. Yes.

M. MERRY.   But I would not tell
   all; for faith, if I had,
With you, Dame Custance, ere this hour
   it had been bad,
And not without cause; for this goodly
   personage
Meant no less than to join with you in
   marriage.

C. CUSTANCE. Let him waste no more labor nor suit about me.

M. MERRY. Ye know not where your preferment lieth, I see,
He sending you such a token, ring,
   and letter.

C. CUSTANCE. Marry, here it is; ye never
   saw a better.

M. MERRY. Let us see your letter.

---

[1] Since.
[2] Probably "The Fourth Song," printed at the end of the play.   [3] Jesting.
[4] Have us.   [5] Tolerably.

C. Custance.   Hold,
  read it if ye can.   30
And see what letter it is to win a woman.
M. Merry. "To mine own dear cony,
  bird, sweetheart, and pigsnie,
Good Mistress Custance, present these
  by-and-by."
Of this superscription do ye blame the
  style?
C. Custance. With the rest, as good stuff
  as ye read a great while.
M. Merry. "Sweet mistress, whereas I
  love you nothing at all,
Regarding your substance and richesse
  chief of all,
For your personage, beauty, demeanor,
  and wit,
I commend me unto you never a whit;
Sorry to hear report of your good wel-
  fare,   40
For, as I hear say, such your conditions
  are,
That ye be worthy favor of no living
  man;
To be abhorred of every honest man;
To be taken for a woman inclined to
  vice;
Nothing at all to virtue giving her due
  price.
Wherefore, concerning marriage, ye are
  thought
Such a fine paragon as ne'er honest
  man bought.
And now by these presents I do you
  advertise
That I am minded to marry you in no
  wise.
For your goods and substance, I could
  be content   50
To take you as ye are. If ye mind to be
  my wife,
Ye shall be assured for the time of my
  life,
I will keep ye right well from good raiment and fare;
Ye shall not be kept but in sorrow and
  care.
Ye shall in no wise live at your own
  liberty;
Do and say what ye lust, ye shall never
  please me;
But, when ye are merry, I will be all
  sad;
When ye are sorry, I will be very glad

When ye seek your heart's ease, I will
  be unkind.
At no time in me shall ye much gentleness find.   60
But all things contrary to your will and
  mind
Shall be done; otherwise I will not be
  behind
To speak. And, as for all them that
  would do you wrong,
I will so help and maintain, ye shall not
  live long.
Nor any foolish dolt shall cumber you
  but I.
I, whoe'er say nay, will stick by you
  till I die.
Thus, good Mistress Custance, the Lord
  you save and keep
From me, Roister Doister, whether I
  wake or sleep.
Who favoreth you no less (ye may be
  bold)
Than this letter purporteth, which ye
  have unfold."   70
C. Custance. How by this letter of love?
  Is it not fine?
R. Roister. By the arms of Calais, it is
  none of mine.
M. Merry. Fie, you are foul to blame;
  this is your own hand!
C. Custance. Might not a woman be
  proud of such an husband?
M. Merry. Ah, that ye would in a letter
  show such despite!
R. Roister. O, I would I had him here,
  the which did it indite.
M. Merry. Why, ye made it yourself, ye
  told me by this light.
R. Roister. Yea, I meant I wrote it mine
  own self yesternight.
C. Custance. Iwis, sir, I would not have
  sent you such a mock.
R. Roister. Ye may so take it, but I
  meant it not so, by Cock.   80
M. Merry. Who can blame this woman to
  fume and fret and rage?
Tut, tut! yourself now have marred your
  own marriage.
Well, yet, Mistress Custance, if ye can
  this remit,
This gentleman otherwise may your love
  requit.
C. Custance. No, God be with you both,
  and seek no more to me.   *Exeat.*

R. ROISTER. Wough! she is gone forever; I shall her no more see.

M. MERRY. What, weep? Fie, for shame! And blubber? For manhood's sake,

Never let your foe so much pleasure of you take.

Rather play the man's part, and do love refrain.[1]

If she despise you, e'en despise ye her again.   90

R. ROISTER. By Goss,[2] and for thy sake I defy her indeed.

M. MERRY. Yea, and perchance that way ye shall much sooner speed,

For one mad property these women have, in fay:[3]

When ye will, they will not; will not ye, then will they.

Ah, foolish woman! ah, most unlucky Custance!

Ah, unfortunate woman! ah, peevish Custance!

Art thou to thine harms so obstinately bent

That thou canst not see where lieth thine high preferment?

Canst thou not lub dis man, which could lub dee so well?

Art thou so much thine own foe?

R. ROISTER.   Thou dost the truth tell.   100

M. MERRY. Well, I lament.

R. ROISTER.   So do I.

M. MERRY.   Wherefore?

R. ROISTER.   For this thing:

Because she is gone.

M. MERRY.   I mourn for another thing.

R. ROISTER. What is it, Merrygreek, wherefore thou dost grief take?

M. MERRY. That I am not a woman myself for your sake;

I would have you myself—and a straw for yond Gill[4]—

And mock[5] much of you though it were against my will.

I would not, I warrant you, fall in such a rage[6]

As so to refuse such a goodly personage.

R. ROISTER. In faith, I heartily thank thee, Merrygreek.

M. MERRY. And I were a woman——

R. ROISTER.   Thou wouldest to me seek.   110

M. MERRY. For, though I say it, a goodly person ye be.

R. ROISTER. No, no.

M. MERRY.   Yes, a goodly man as e'er I did see.

R. ROISTER. No, I am a poor homely man, as God made me.

M. MERRY. By the faith that I owe to God, sir, but ye be.

Would I might, for your sake, spend a thousand pound land.

R. ROISTER. I dare say thou wouldest have me to thy husband.

M. MERRY. Yea; and I were the fairest lady in the shire,

And knew you as I know you, and see you now here—

Well, I say no more.

R. ROISTER.   Gramercies, with all my heart.

M. MERRY. But since that cannot be, will ye play a wise part?   120

R. ROISTER. How should I?

M. MERRY.   Refrain from Custance a while now,

And I warrant her soon right glad to seek to you.

Ye shall see her anon come on her knees creeping,

And pray you to be good to her, salt tears weeping.

R. ROISTER. But what and she come not?

M. MERRY.   In faith, then, farewell she.

Or else, if ye be wroth, ye may avengéd be.

R. ROISTER. By Cock's precious potstick,[7] and e'en so I shall.

I will utterly destroy her, and house and all!

But I would be avenged in the mean space

On that vile scribbler that did my wooing disgrace.   130

M. MERRY. "Scribbler," ko you? Indeed, he is worthy no less.

I will call him to you, and ye bid me doubtless.

---

[1] Desist from.
[2] By God (a mild oath).
[3] Faith.
[4] Wench.
[5] Make (?).
[6] Madness.

[7] Farmer suggests the stick used to extend the sponge to Christ on the cross.

R. ROISTER. Yes, for although he had as
  many lives
As a thousand widows, and a thousand
  wives,
As a thousand lions, and a thousand
  rats,
A thousand wolves, and a thousand
  cats,
A thousand bulls, and a thousand calves,
And a thousand legions divided in halves,
He shall never scape death on my sword's
  point,
Though I should be torn therefor joint
  by joint.   140
M. MERRY. Nay, if ye will kill him, I will
  not fet him;
I will not in so much extremity set
  him.
He may yet amend, sir, and be an honest
  man;
Therefore pardon him, good soul, as
  much as ye can.
R. ROISTER. Well, for thy sake, this once
  with his life he shall pass,
But I will hew him all to pieces, by the
  Mass.
M. MERRY. Nay, faith, ye shall promise
  that he shall no harm have,
Else I will not fet him.
R. ROISTER.   I shall, so God
  me save.
But I may chide him agood.[1]
M. MERRY.   Yea, that
  do hardly.[2]
R. ROISTER. Go, then.
M. MERRY.   I return, and bring
  him to you by-and-by.   Ex[eat]. 150

ACTUS III. SCENA v.

Roister Doister, Matthew Merrygreek, Scrivener.[3]

R. ROISTER. What is a gentleman but his
  word and his promise?
I must now save this villain's life in any
  wise,
And yet at him already my hands do
  tickle;
I shall uneath [4] hold them, they will be
  so fickle.
But lo, and Merrygreek have not brought
  him sence.

---

[1] In earnest.   [3] Last two enter later.
[2] Hardily, boldly.   [4] With difficulty.

[*Enter Merrygreek and Scrivener.*]

M. MERRY. Nay, I would I had of my
  purse paid forty pence.
SCRIVENER. So would I too; but it needed
  not that stound.[5]
M. MERRY. But the gentman had rather
  spent five thousand pound,
For it disgraced him at least five times
  so much.
SCRIVENER. He disgraced himself, his lout-
  ishness is such.   10
R. ROISTER. [*Aside.*] How long they stand
  prating!—Why com'st thou not away?
M. MERRY. Come now to himself, and
  hark what he will say.
SCRIVENER. I am not afraid in his presence
  to appear.
R. ROISTER. Art thou come, fellow?
SCRIVENER.   How
  think you? Am I not here?
R. ROISTER. What hindrance hast thou
  done me, and what villainy!
SCRIVENER. It hath come of thyself, if
  thou hast had any.
R. ROISTER. All the stock thou comest of,
  later or rather,[6]
From thy first father's grandfather's
  father's father,
Nor all that shall come of thee to the
  world's end,
Though to threescore generations they
  descend,   20
Can be able to make me a just recom-
  pense
For this trespass of thine and this one
  offense.
SCRIVENER. Wherein?
R. ROISTER.   Did not you make
  me a letter, brother?
SCRIVENER. Pay the like hire, I will make
  you such another.
R. ROISTER. Nay, see and these whoreson [7]
  Pharisees and Scribes
Do not get their living by polling and
  bribes! [8]
If it were not for shame——
SCRIVENER.   Nay, hold
  thy hands still!
M. MERRY. Why, did ye not promise that
  ye would not him spill? [9]

---

[5] Amazement; *i.e.*, the shock of the letter was
unnecessary (?).   [6] Sooner.   [7] Rascally.
[8] Swindling and robbery.   [9] Destroy.

SCRIVENER. Let him not spare me.

R. ROISTER.   Why,
   wilt thou strike me again?

SCRIVENER. Ye shall have as good as ye
   bring of me, that is plain.   30

M. MERRY. I cannot blame him, sir,
   though your blows would him grieve,
   For he knoweth present death to ensue
   of all ye give.

R. ROISTER. Well, this man for once hath
   purchased thy pardon.

SCRIVENER. And what say ye to me? Or
   else I will be gone.

R. ROISTER. I say the letter thou madest
   me was not good.

SCRIVENER. Then did ye wrong copy it,
   of likelihood.

R. ROISTER. Yes, out of thy copy word
   for word I wrote.

SCRIVENER. Then was it as ye prayed to
   have it, I wot,
   But in reading and pointing [1] there was
   made some fault.

R. ROISTER. I wot not, but it made all
   my matter to halt.   40

SCRIVENER. How say you, is this mine
   original or no?

R. ROISTER. The selfsame that I wrote
   out of, so mote I go. [2]

SCRIVENER. Look you on your own fist,
   and I will look on this,
   And let this man be judge whether I
   read amiss.
   "To mine own dear cony, bird, sweetheart, and pigsnie,
   Good Mistress Custance, present these
   by-and-by."
   How now? Doth not this superscription
   agree?

R. ROISTER. Read that is within, and
   there ye shall the fault see.

SCRIVENER. "Sweet mistress, whereas I
   love you—nothing at all
   Regarding your richesse and substance,
   chief of all   50
   For your personage, beauty, demeanor,
   and wit—
   I commend me unto you; never a whit
   Sorry to hear report of your good welfare.
   For, as I hear say, such your conditions
   are
   That ye be worthy favor; of no living
   man

[1] Punctuating.   [2] *I.e.*, so may I live.

To be abhorred; of every honest man
To be taken for a woman inclined to vice
Nothing at all; to virtue giving her due
   price.
Wherefore concerning marriage, ye are
   thought
Such a fine paragon as ne'er honest man
   bought.   60
And now by these presents I do you
   advertise
That I am minded to marry you—in no
   wise
For your goods and substance. I can be
   content
To take you as you are. If ye will be my
   wife,
Ye shall be assured for the time of my
   life,
I will keep you right well. From good
   raiment and fare
Ye shall not be kept; but in sorrow and
   care
Ye shall in no wise live; at your own
   liberty
Do and say what ye lust. Ye shall never
   please me
But when ye are merry; I will be all sad 70
When ye are sorry; I will be very glad
When ye seek your heart's ease; I will
   be unkind
At no time; in me shall ye much gentle-
   ness find.
But all things contrary to your will and
   mind
Shall be done otherwise. I will not be
   behind
To speak.   And as for all them that
   would do you wrong
(I will so help and maintain ye) shall
   not live long.
Nor any foolish dolt shall cumber you,
   but I,
I, whoe'er say nay, will stick by you till
   I die.
Thus, good Mistress Custance, the Lord
   you save and keep.   80
From me, Roister Doister, whether I
   wake or sleep,
Who favoreth you no less (ye may be
   bold)
Than this letter purporteth, which ye
   have unfold."
Now, sir, what default can ye find in this
   letter?

R. Roister. Of truth, in my mind there
   cannot be a better.
Scrivener. Then was the fault in reading,
   and not in writing;
   No, nor I dare say in the form of inditing.
   But who read this letter, that it sounded
   so naught?
M. Merry. I read it, indeed.
Scrivener.   Ye read it
   not as ye ought.
R. Roister. Why, thou wretched villain,
   was all this same fault in thee?   90
M. Merry. I knock your costard [1] if ye
   offer to strike me.
R. Roister. Strikest thou, indeed, and I
   offer but in jest?
M. Merry. Yea, and rap you again ex-
   cept ye can sit in rest.
   And I will no longer tarry here, me be-
   lieve.
R. Roister. What, wilt thou be angry,
   and I do thee forgive?
   Fare thou well, scribbler; I cry thee
   mercy indeed.
Scrivener. Fare ye well, bibbler, and
   worthily may ye speed.
R. Roister. If it were another but thou,
   it were a knave.
M. Merry. Ye are another yourself, sir,
   the Lord us both save,
   Albeit in this matter I must your pardon
   crave.   100
   Alas, would ye wish in me the wit that
   ye have?
   But as for my fault I can quickly amend;
   I will show Custance it was I that did
   offend.
R. Roister. By so doing her anger may
   be reformed.
M. Merry. But, if by no entreaty she will
   be turned,
   Then set light by her and be as testy as
   she,
   And do your force upon her with ex-
   tremity.
R. Roister. Come on, therefore, let us go
   home in sadness.
M. Merry. That if force shall need, all
   may be in a readiness.   109
   And, as for this letter, hardly let all go.
   We will know whe'er [2] she refuse you for
   that or no.   *Exeant am[bo]*.

---

[1] Apple, *i.e.*, head.   [2] Whether.

Actus IV. Scena i.

Sim Suresby.

Sim Sure. Is there any man but I, Sim
   Suresby alone,
That would have taken such an enter-
   prise him upon,
In such an outrageous tempest as this
   was,
Such a dangerous gulf of the sea to
   pass?
I think, verily, Neptune's mighty god-
   ship
Was angry with some that was in our
   ship,
And, but for the honesty which in me
   he found,
I think for the others' sake we had been
   drowned.
But fie on that servant which for his
   master's wealth [3]
Will stick for to hazard both his life and
   his health.   10
My master, Gawin Goodluck, after me
   a day,
Because of the weather, thought best his
   ship to stay;
And now that I have the rough surges so
   well passed,
God grant I may find all things safe here
   at last.
Then will I think all my travail well
   spent.
Now the first point wherefore my master
   hath me sent
Is to salute Dame Christian Custance,
   his wife
Espoused, whom he tend'reth no less
   than his life.
I must see how it is with her, well or
   wrong,
And whether for him she doth not now
   think long.   20
Then to other friends I have a message
   or tway, [4]
And then so to return and meet him on
   the way.
Now will I go knock that I may despatch
   with speed,
But lo, forth cometh herself happily, [5]
   indeed.

---

[3] Welfare.
[4] Two.
[5] Fortunately.

ACTUS IV. SCENA ii.

Christian Custance, Sim Suresby.

C. CUSTANCE. [*Aside.*] I come to see if any
　more stirring be here.
But what stranger is this which doth to
　me appear?
SIM SURE. [*Aside.*] I will speak to her.—
　Dame, the Lord you save and see.
C. CUSTANCE. What, friend Sim Suresby?
　Forsooth, right welcome ye be!
How doth mine own Gawin Goodluck?
　I pray thee tell.
SIM SURE. When he knoweth of your
　health, he will be perfect well.
C. CUSTANCE. If he have perfect health,
　I am as I would be.
SIM SURE. Such news will please him well;
　this is as it should be.
C. CUSTANCE. I think now long for him.
SIM SURE.　　　　　And he as long for you.
C. CUSTANCE. When will he be at home?
SIM SURE.　　　His heart is here e'en now;
　His body cometh after.
C. CUSTANCE.　　　　　I would see that
　fain.　　　　　　　　　　　　11
SIM SURE. As fast as wind and sail can
　carry it amain.
But what two men are yond coming
　hitherward?
C. CUSTANCE. Now I shrew their best
　Christmas cheeks,[1] both togetherward!

ACTUS IV. SCENA iii.

*Christian Custance, Sim Suresby, Ralph
Roister, Matthew Merrygreek, True-
　　　　　　　　　penny.*[2]

C. CUSTANCE. [*Aside.*] What mean these
　lewd fellows thus to trouble me still?
Sim Suresby here perchance shall thereof
　deem some ill,
And shall suspect in me some point of
　naughtiness,
And[3] they come hitherward.
SIM SURE.　　　　　　　　What is
　their business?
C. CUSTANCE. I have naught to them, nor
　they to me, in sadness.[4]
SIM SURE. Let us hearken them.—[*Aside.*]
　Somewhat there is, I fear it.

R. ROISTER. I will speak out aloud best,
　that she may hear it.
M. MERRY. Nay, alas, ye may so fear[5]
　her out of her wit.
R. ROISTER. By the cross of my sword, I
　will hurt her no whit.
M. MERRY. Will ye do no harm indeed?
　Shall I trust your word?　　　　10
R. ROISTER. By Roister Doister's faith, I
　will speak but in bord.
SIM SURE. Let us hearken them.—[*Aside.*]
　Somewhat there is, I fear it.
R. ROISTER. I will speak out aloud; I care
　not who hear it.
　　[*Pretends to call to his servants within.*]
Sirs, see that my harness, my target,
　and my shield
Be made as bright now as when I was
　last in field,
As white as I should to war again to-
　morrow;
For sick shall I be, but I work some folk
　sorrow.
Therefore see that all shine as bright as
　Saint George,
Or as doth a key newly come from the
　smith's forge.
I would have my sword and harness to
　shine so bright[6]　　　　　20
That I might therewith dim mine
　enemies' sight.
I would have it cast beams as fast, I tell
　you plain,
As doth the glittering grass after a shower
　of rain.
And see that, in case I should need to
　come to arming,
All things may be ready at a minute's
　warning.
For such chance may chance in an hour—
　do ye hear?
M. MERRY. As perchance shall not chance
　again in seven year.
R. ROISTER. Now draw we near to her,
　and hear what shall be said.
M. MERRY. But I would not have you
　make her too much afraid.
R. ROISTER. Well found, sweet wife (I
　trust), for all this your sour look.　30
C. CUSTANCE. Wife? Why call ye me
　wife?

---

[1] A defiant curse (*N.E.D.*); *i.e.*, I curse their
unrestrained effrontery.
[2] Enters later.　　　[3] If.　　　[4] Seriousness.

[5] Frighten.
[6] This passage is based on Plautus, *Miles
gloriosus*, I, i.

SIM SURE. [*Aside.*]   Wife? This gear
go'th acrook.

M. MERRY. Nay, Mistress Custance, I
warrant you, our letter

Is not as we read e'en now, but much
better,

And, where ye half stomached this gentleman afore,

For this same letter, ye will love him now
therefor;

Nor it is not this letter, though ye were a
queen,

That should break marriage between
you twain, I ween.[1]

C. CUSTANCE. I did not refuse him for the
letter's sake.

R. ROISTER. Then ye are content me for
your husband to take.

C. CUSTANCE. You for my husband to
take? Nothing less truly.   40

R. ROISTER. Yea, say so, sweet spouse,
afore strangers hardly.

M. MERRY. And, though I have here his
letter of love with me,

Yet his ring and tokens he sent, keep
safe with ye.

C. CUSTANCE. A mischief take his tokens,
and him and thee too.

But what prate I with fools? Have I
nought else to do?

Come in with me, Sim Suresby, to take
some repast.

SIM SURE. I must, ere I drink, by your
leave, go in all haste

To a place or two with earnest letters of
his.

C. CUSTANCE. Then come drink here with
me.

SIM SURE.   I thank you!

C. CUSTANCE.   Do not miss.
You shall have a token to your master
with you.   50

SIM SURE. No tokens this time, gramercies!
God be with you.   *Exeat.*

C. CUSTANCE. Surely this fellow misdeemeth some ill in me—

Which thing, but God help, will go near
to spill me.

R. ROISTER. Yea, farewell, fellow, and tell
thy master Goodluck

That he cometh too late of this blossom
to pluck.

Let him keep him there still, or at least-
wise make no haste,

As for his labor hither he shall spend in
waste.

His betters be in place now.

M. MERRY. [*Aside.*]   As long as it
will hold.

C. CUSTANCE. I will be even with thee,
thou beast, thou mayst be bold.[2]

R. ROISTER. Will ye have us then?

C. CUSTANCE.   I will
never have thee.   60

R. ROISTER. Then will I have you!

C. CUSTANCE.   No,
the devil shall have thee.

I have gotten this hour more shame and
harm by thee

Than all thy life-days thou canst do me
honesty.

M. MERRY. [*To Roister Doister.*] Why, now
may ye see what it com'th to, in the
end,

To make a deadly foe of your most loving friend.—

And iwis this letter, if ye would hear it
now——

C. CUSTANCE. I will hear none of it.

M. MERRY.   In
faith, would ravish you.

C. CUSTANCE. He hath stained my name
forever, this is clear.

R. ROISTER. I can make all as well in an
hour—

M. MERRY. [*Aside.*]   As ten year.—
How say ye, will ye have him?

C. CUSTANCE.   No.

M. MERRY.   Will ye take him? 70

C. CUSTANCE. I defy him.

M. MERRY.   At my word?

C. CUSTANCE.   A shame take him.
Waste no more wind, for it will never
be.

M. MERRY. This one fault with twain shall
be mended, ye shall see.

Gentle Mistress Custance now, good
Mistress Custance!

Honey Mistress Custance now, sweet
Mistress Custance!

Golden Mistress Custance now, white [3]
Mistress Custance!

Silken Mistress Custance now, fair Mistress Custance!

---

[1] Imagine.   [2] Certain.   [3] Dear.

C. Custance. Faith, rather than to marry with such a doltish lout
I would match myself with a beggar, out of doubt.

M. Merry. Then I can say no more; to speed we are not like,   80
Except ye rap out a rag of your rhetoric.[1]

C. Custance. Speak not of winning me, for it shall never be so.

R. Roister. Yes, dame, I will have you, whether ye will or no.
I command you to love me! Wherefore should ye not?
Is not my love to you chafing and burning hot?

M. Merry. To her! That is well said!

R. Roister.   Shall I so break my brain
To dote upon you, and ye not love us again?

M. Merry. Well said yet.

C. Custance.   Go to, you goose.

R. Roister.   I say, Kit Custance,
In case ye will not ha's—well, better yes, perchance.

C. Custance. Avaunt, losel;[2] pick thee hence![3]

M. Merry.   Well, sir, ye perceive,   90
For all your kind offer, she will not you receive.

R. Roister. Then a straw for her, and a straw for her again;
She shall not be my wife, would she never so fain;
No, and though she would be at ten thousand pound cost.

M. Merry. Lo, dame, ye may see what an husband ye have lost.

C. Custance. Yea, no force;[4] a jewel much better lost than found.

M. Merry. Ah, ye will not believe how this doth my heart wound.
How should a marriage between you be toward,
If both parties draw back, and become so froward?

R. Roister. Nay, dame, I will fire thee out of thy house,   100
And destroy thee and all thine, and that by-and-by.

M. Merry. Nay, for the passion of God, sir, do not so.

R. Roister. Yes, except she will say yea to that she said no.

C. Custance. And what! be there no officers, trow we, in town
To check idle loiterers, bragging up and down?
Where be they by whom vacabunds[5] should be repressed,
That poor silly[6] widows might live in peace and rest?
Shall I never rid thee out of my company?
I will call for help. What ho! come forth, Truepenny!

Truepenny. [Within.] Anon.[7]

[Enters.]
        What is your will, mistress?
Did ye call me?   110

C. Custance. Yea; go run apace, and, as fast as may be,
Pray Tristram Trusty, my most assured friend,
To be here by-and-by, that he may me defend.

Truepenny. That message so quickly shall be done, by God's grace,
That at my return ye shall say I went apace.   Exeat.

C. Custance. Then shall we see, I trow, whether ye shall do me harm.

R. Roister. Yes, in faith, Kit, I shall thee and thine so charm
That all women incarnate by thee may beware.

C. Custance. Nay, as for charming me, come hither if thou dare;
I shall clout thee till thou stink, both thee and thy train,   120
And coil thee[8] mine own hands, and send thee home again.

R. Roister. Yea, sayest thou me that, dame? Dost thou me threaten?
Go we; I still[9] see whether I shall be beaten.

M. Merry. Nay, for the pashe[10] of God, let me now treat peace,
For bloodshed will there be in case this strife increase.
Ah, good Dame Custance, take better way with you.

---

[1] I.e., unless you spout a bit of your rhetoric.
[2] Rascal.
[3] Away with you!   [4] No matter.

[5] Vagabonds.   [8] Beat thee [with].
[6] Simple.   [9] Cooper suggests *will*.
[7] The usual answer of servants.   [10] Passion.

C. Custance. Let him do his worst!

M. Merry.   Yield in time!

R. Roister.   Come hence,
thou!

Exeant Roister et Merry[greek].

Actus IV. Scena iv.

*Christian Custance, Annot Alyface, Tibet
T[alkapace], M[adge] Mumblecrust.*[1]

C. Custance. So, sirrah, if I should not
with him take this way,

I should not be rid of him, I think, till
doomsday.

I will call forth my folks, that, without
any mocks,[2]

If he come again, we may give him raps
and knocks.

Madge Mumblecrust, come forth, and
Tibet Talkapace.

Yea, and come forth too, Mistress Annot
Alyface.

[Enter the three Maids.]

An. Alyface. I come.

Tib. Talk.   And I am here.

M. Mumbl.   And I am here too,
at length.

C. Custance. Like warriors, if need be,
ye must show your strength.

The man that this day hath thus beguiled you,

Is Ralph Roister Doister, whom ye know
well inowe,[3]   10

The most lout and dastard that ever on
ground trod.

Tib. Talk. I see all folk mock him when
he go'th abroad.

C. Custance. What, pretty maid, will ye
talk when I speak?

Tib. Talk. No, forsooth, good mistress.

C. Custance.   Will ye my tale break?

He threat'neth to come hither with all
his force to fight.

I charge you, if he come, on him with all
your might!

M. Mumbl. I with my distaff will reach
him one rap!

Tib. Talk. And I with my new broom
will sweep him one swap,

And then with our great club I will reach
him one rap!

An. Alyface. And I with our skimmer
will fling him one flap!   20

Tib. Talk. Then Truepenny's firefork[4]
will him shrewdly fray,[5]

And you with the spit may drive him
quite away.

C. Custance. Go, make all ready, that
it may be e'en so.

Tib. Talk. For my part, I shrew them
that last about it go.   *Exeant.*

Actus IV. Scena v.

*Christian Custance, Truepenny, Tristram
Trusty.*[6]

C. Custance. Truepenny did promise me
to run a great pace,

My friend Tristram Trusty to fet into
this place.

Indeed he dwelleth hence a good start,[7]
I confess;

But yet a quick messenger might twice
since, as I guess,

Have gone and come again. Ah, yond
I spy him now.

*[Enter Truepenny, followed by Tristram
Trusty.]*

Truepenny. Ye are a slow goer, sir, I
make God avow.

My mistress Custance will in me put all
the blame.

Your legs be longer than mine; come
apace for shame.

C. Custance. I can thee thank, Truepenny; thou hast done right well.

Truepenny. Mistress, since I went, no
grass hath grown on my heel,   10

But Master Tristram Trusty here maketh no speed.

C. Custance. That he came at all, I
thank him in very deed,

For now have I need of the help of some
wise man.

T. Trusty. Then may I be gone again,
for none such I [a]m.

Truepenny. Ye may be, by your going,[8]
for no alderman

Can go, I dare say, a sadder[9] pace than
ye can.

---

[1] The last three enter later.   [2] Pretenses.
[3] *I.e.*, enow. Emendation suggested by Cooper,
original reads *mowe*.

[4] Poker.
[5] Frighten.
[6] Last two enter later.

[7] Distance.
[8] Gait.
[9] Soberer.

C. Custance. Truepenny, get thee in;
thou shalt among them know
How to use thyself like a proper man, I
trow.

Truepenny. I go.   [*Exeat.*]

C. Custance.   Now, Tristram Trusty,
I thank you right much,
For, at my first sending, to come ye
never grutch.[1]   20

T. Trusty. Dame Custance, God ye save,
and while my life shall last,
For my friend Goodluck's sake ye shall
not send in waste.

C. Custance. He shall give you thanks.

T. Trusty.   I will do much for his sake.

C. Custance. But, alack, I fear great displeasure shall be take.

T. Trusty. Wherefore?

C. Custance.   For a foolish matter.

T. Trusty.   What is your cause?

C. Custance. I am ill accumbered with a
couple of daws.

T. Trusty. Nay, weep not, woman, but
tell me what your cause is.
As concerning my friend, is anything
amiss?

C. Custance. No, not on my part. But
here was Sim Suresby—

T. Trusty. He was with me and told me so.

C. Custance.   And he stood by   30
While Ralph Roister Doister with help
of Merrygreek
For promise of marriage did unto me
seek.

T. Trusty. And had ye made any promise
before them twain?

C. Custance. No, I had rather be torn in
pieces and slain.
No man hath my faith and troth but
Gawin Goodluck,
And that before Suresby did I say, and
there stuck.
But of certain letters there were such
words spoken—

T. Trusty. He told me that too.

C. Custance.   And of
a ring and token,
That Suresby, I spied, did more than
half suspect
That I my faith to Gawin Goodluck did
reject.   40

T. Trusty. But there was no such matter,
Dame Custance, indeed?

C. Custance. If ever my head thought it,
God send me ill speed.
Wherefore, I beseech you, with me to be
a witness,
That in all my life I never intended thing
less;
And what a brainsick fool Ralph Roister
Doister is,
Yourself know well enough.

T. Trusty.   Ye say full
true, iwis.

C. Custance. Because to be his wife I ne
grant nor apply,[2]
Hither will he come, he sweareth, by-
and-by,
To kill both me and mine, and beat
down my house flat.
Therefore I pray your aid.

T. Trusty.   I warrant
you that.   50

C. Custance. Have I so many years lived
a sober life,
And showed myself honest, maid, widow,
and wife,
And now to be abused in such a vile sort?
Ye see how poor widows live all void of
comfort.

T. Trusty. I warrant him do you no harm
nor wrong at all.

C. Custance. No, but Matthew Merrygreek doth me most appall,
That he would join himself with such a
wretched lout.

T. Trusty. He doth it for a jest; I know
him out of doubt.—
And here cometh Merrygreek.

C. Custance.   Then
shall we hear his mind.

Actus IV. Scena vi.

Merrygreek, Christian Custance, Trist[ram]
                                Trusty.

M. Merry. Custance and Trusty both, I
do you here well find.

C. Custance. Ah, Matthew Merrygreek,
ye have used me well!

M. Merry. Now for altogether [3] ye must
your answer tell.
Will ye have this man, woman, or else
will ye not?
Else will he come never boar so brim
nor toast so hot.

---

[1] Grumble.   [2] Incline.   [3] Once for all.   [4] Fierce

Tris. AND Cus. But why join ye with him?

T. Trusty.   For mirth?

C. Custance.   Or else in
   sadness?

M. Merry. The more fond of you! Both?
   Hardly! The matter guess!

T. Trusty. Lo, how say ye, dame?

M. Merry.   Why,
   do ye think, Dame Custance,

That in this wooing I have meant aught
   but pastance?

C. Custance. Much things ye spake, I
   wot, to maintain his dotage.   10

M. Merry. But well might ye judge I
   spake it all in mockage.

For why? Is Roister Doister a fit husband for you?

T. Trusty. I dare say ye never thought it.

M. Merry.   No, to God I vow.

And did not I know afore of the insur-
   ance [1]

Between Gawin Goodluck and Christian
   Custance?

And did not I for the nonce, by my conveyance,[2]

Read his letter in a wrong sense for
   dalliance,

That, if you could have take it up at the
   first bound,

We should thereat such a sport and
   pastime have found,

That all the whole town should have been
   the merrier?   20

C. Custance. Ill ache your heads both!
   I was never wearier,

Nor never more vexed since the first day
   I was born.

T. Trusty. But very well I wist he here
   did all in scorn.

C. Custance. But I feared thereof to take
   dishonesty.[3]

M. Merry. This should both have made
   sport and showed your honesty,

And Goodluck, I dare swear, your wit
   therein would low.

T. Trusty. Yea, being no worse than we
   know it to be now.

M. Merry. And nothing yet too late; for
   when I come to him,

Hither will he repair with a sheep's look
   full grim,

By plain force and violence to drive you
   to yield.   30

[1] Betrothal, promise.   [2] Trickery.   [3] Dishonor.

C. Custance. If ye two bid me, we will
   with him pitch a field,[4]

I and my maids together.

M. Merry.   Let us see;
   be bold.

C. Custance. Ye shall see women's war.

T. Trusty.   That fight will I behold.

M. Merry. If occasion serve, taking his
   part full brim,

I will strike at you, but the rap shall
   light on him,

When we first appear.

C. Custance.   Then will I run
   away

As though I were afeard.

T. Trusty.   Do you that
   part well play

And I will sue for peace.

M. Merry.   And I will set
   him on.

Then will he look as fierce as a Cotswold
   lion.[5]

T. Trusty. But when goest thou for him?

M. Merry.   That do I very now.   40

C. Custance. Ye shall find us here.

M. Merry.   Well, God have
   mercy on you.   *Ex[eat].*

T. Trusty. There is no cause of fear; the
   least boy in the street——

C. Custance. Nay, the least girl I have
   will make him take his feet.

But hark! methink they make preparation.

T. Trusty. No force, it will be a good
   recreation.

C. Custance. I will stand within, and
   step forth speedily,

And so make as though I ran away
   dreadfully.[6]   [*Exeant.*]

Actus IV. Scena vii.

*R[alph] Roister, M[atthew] Merrygreek, C[hris-
tian] Custance,[7] D[obinet] Doughty,[7]
Harpax, Tristram Trusty.[7]*

R. Roister. Now, sirs, keep your ray,[8]
   and see your hearts be stout.

But where be these caitiffs? Methink
   they dare not rout.[9]

How sayest thou, Merrygreek? What
   doth Kit Custance say?

[4] Engage in a battle.   [7] Enters later.
[5] *I.e.*, a sheep.   [8] Array, due order.
[6] Full of fear.   [9] Assemble.

M. MERRY. I am loath to tell you.

R. ROISTER. Tush, speak, man: yea or nay?

M. MERRY. Forsooth, sir, I have spoken for you all that I can.

But if ye win her, ye must e'en play the man;

E'en to fight it out, ye must a man's heart take.

R. ROISTER. Yes, they shall know, and thou knowest I have a stomach.[1]

[M. MERRY.] "A stomach," quod you? Yea, as good as e'er man had.

R. ROISTER. I trow they shall find and feel that I am a lad. 10

M. MERRY. By this cross, I have seen you eat your meat as well

As any that e'er I have seen of or heard tell.

"A stomach," quod you? He that will that deny

I know was never at dinner in your company.

R. ROISTER. Nay, the stomach of a man it is that I mean.

M. MERRY. Nay, the stomach of a horse or a dog, I ween.

R. ROISTER. Nay, a man's stomach with a weapon, mean I.

M. MERRY. Ten men can scarce match you with a spoon in a pie.

R. ROISTER. Nay, the stomach of a man to try in strife.

M. MERRY. I never saw your stomach cloyed yet in my life. 20

R. ROISTER. Tush, I mean in strife or fighting to try.

M. MERRY. We shall see how ye will strike now, being angry.

R. ROISTER. Have at thy pate then, and save thy head if thou may.

 [They strike at each other.]

M. MERRY. Nay, then have at your pate again by this day.

R. ROISTER. Nay, thou mayst not strike at me again in no wise.

M. MERRY. I cannot in fight make to you such warrantize;[2]

But as for your foes, here let them the bargain by.[3]

R. ROISTER. Nay, as for they, shall every mother's child die.

And in this my fume a little thing might make me

To beat down house and all, and else the devil take me. 30

M. MERRY. If I were as ye be, by Gog's dear mother,

I would not leave one stone upon another,

Though she would redeem it with twenty thousand pounds.

R. ROISTER. It shall be even so, by his lily wounds.

M. MERRY. Be not at one with her, upon any amends.

R. ROISTER. No, though she make to me never so many friends,

Nor if all the world for her would undertake, [4]

No, not God himself neither shall not her peace make.

On, therefore, march forward—soft, stay a while yet!

M. MERRY. On!

R. ROISTER. Tarry!

M. MERRY. Forth!

R. ROISTER. Back!

M. MERRY. On!

R. ROISTER. Soft! Now forward set! 40

 [Enter Custance.]

C. CUSTANCE. What business have we here? Out! alas, alas! [Exeat.]

R. ROISTER. Ha, ha, ha, ha, ha!

Didst thou see that, Merrygreek, how afraid she was?

Didst thou see how she fled apace out of my sight?

Ah, good sweet Custance, I pity her, by this light.

M. MERRY. That tender heart of yours will mar altogether;

Thus will ye be turned with wagging of a feather.

R. ROISTER. On, sirs, keep your ray!

M. MERRY. On, forth, while this gear is hot!

R. ROISTER. Soft, the arms of Calais! I have one thing forgot.

M. MERRY. What lack we now?

R. ROISTER. Retire, or else we be all slain. 50

M. Merry. Back, for the pashe of God!
Back, sirs, back again!

What is the great matter?

R. Roister. This hasty
forthgoing

Had almost brought us all to utter undoing;

It made me forget a thing most necessary.

M. Merry. Well remembered of a captain, by Saint Mary.

R. Roister. It is a thing must be had.

M. Merry. Let us have it then.

R. Roister. But I wot not where nor how.

M. Merry. Then wot not I when.
But what is it?

R. Roister. Of a chief thing I am to
seek.

M. Merry. Tut, so will ye be, when ye
have studied a week.
But tell me what it is?

R. Roister. I lack yet an
headpiece. 60

M. Merry. The kitchen collocavit,[1] the
best hens to grease! [2]

Run, fet it, Dobinet, and come at once
withal,

And bring with thee my potgun,[3] hanging
by the wall. [*Exeat Dobinet.*]

I have seen your head with it full many
a time

Covered as safe as it had been with a
skrine; [4]

And I warrant it save your head from
any stroke,

Except perchance to be amazed [5] with
the smoke.

I warrant your head therewith, except
for the mist,

As safe as if it were fast locked up in a
chist.[6]

And lo, here our Dobinet cometh with it
now. 70

[Enter Dobinet.]

D. Dough. It will cover me to the shoulders well enow.

M. Merry. Let me see it on.

R. Roister. In faith,
it doth metely well.

M. Merry. There can be no fitter thing.
Now ye must us tell

What to do.

R. Roister. Now forth in ray, sirs,
and stop no more.

M. Merry. Now, Saint George to borrow,[7] drum dub-a-dub afore.

[Enter Trusty.]

T. Trusty. What mean you to do, sir,
commit manslaughter?

R. Roister. To kill forty such is a matter
of laughter.

T. Trusty. And who is it, sir, whom ye
intend thus to spill?

R. Roister. Foolish Custance here force-
eth me against my will.

T. Trusty. And is there no mean your
extreme wrath to slake? 80

She shall some amends unto your good
ma'ship make.

R. Roister. I will none amends.

T. Trusty. Is her
offense so sore?

M. Merry. And he were a lout, she could
have done no more.

She hath called him fool, and dressed [8]
him like a fool,

Mocked him like a fool, used him like a
fool.

T. Trusty. Well, yet the sheriff, the justice, or constable,

Her misdemeanor to punish might be able.

R. Roister. No, sir, I mine own self will,
in this present cause,

Be sheriff, and justice, and whole judge
of the laws;

This matter to amend, all officers be I
shall, 90

Constable, bailiff, sergeant—

M. Merry. And hang-
man and all.

T. Trusty. Yet a noble courage, and the
heart of a man,

Should more honor win by bearing with
a woman.

Therefore take the law, and let her
answer thereto.

R. Roister. Merrygreek, the best way
were even so to do.

What honor should it be with a woman to
fight?

---

[1] Humorous latinization of *collock*, a large
kitchen pail.
[2] Or, punning, "the best hence to Greece."
[3] Popgun. [5] Stupefied, bewildered.
[4] Box, chest. [6] Chest.
[7] Saint George for a pledge; Saint George help
us. [8] Addressed.

M. Merry. And what then? Will ye thus forgo and leese your right?

R. Roister. Nay, I will take the law on her withouten grace.

T. Trusty. Or if your ma'ship could pardon this one trespace,[1]
I pray you forgive her.

R. Roister.　　　　　　Hoh!

M. Merry.　　　　　　　Tush,
tush, sir, do not.　　　　　　　　100

[T. Trusty.] Be good, master, to her.

R. Roister.　　　Hoh!

M. Merry.　　　　　Tush, I say, do not.
And what! shall your people here return straight home?

T. Trusty.[2] Yea; levy the camp,[3] sirs, and hence again each one.

R. Roister.[2] But be still in readiness, if I hap to call;
I cannot tell what sudden chance may befall.

M. Merry. Do not off your harness, sirs, I you advise,
At the least for this fortnight in no manner wise.
Perchance in an hour when all ye think least,
Our master's appetite to fight will be best.
But soft, ere ye go, have once at Custance' house.　　　　　　　110

R. Roister. Soft, what wilt thou do?

M. Merry.　　Once discharge my harquebouse,　　[Shoots the harquebus.]
And, for my heart's ease, have once more with my potgun. [Shoots the popgun.]

R. Roister. Hold thy hands; else is all our purpose clean fordone!

M. Merry. And it cost me my life—

R. Roister.　　　　　　　I say,
thou shalt not.

M. Merry. By the Matte,[4] but I will.
Have once more with hail shot.
I will have some pennyworth! I will not leese all!

Actus IV. Scena viii.[5]

*M[atthew] Merrygreek, C[hristian] Custance,
R[alph] Roister, Tib[et] T[alkapace],[6]
An[not] Alyface,[6] M[adge] Mumblecrust,[6]*

*Truepenny, Dobinet Doughty, Harpax,
two Drums [7] with their ensigns.*

C. Custance. What caitiffs are those that so shake my house wall?

M. Merry. Ah, sirrah! now Custance, if ye had so much wit,
I would see you ask pardon, and yourselves submit.

C. Custance. Have I still this ado with a couple of fools?

M. Merry. Hear ye what she saith?

C. Custance.　　　Maidens, come forth with your tools.

[Enter Maids.]

R. Roister. In a ray!

M. Merry.　　　Dubbadub, sirrah.

R. Roister.　　　　　　In a ray!
They come suddenly on us.

M. Merry.　　　Dubbadub.

R. Roister.　　　　　　In a ray!
That ever I was born! We are taken tardy! [8]

M. Merry. Now, sirs, quit ourselves like tall men and hardy!

C. Custance. On afore, Truepenny! Hold thine own, Annot!　　　　10
On toward them, Tibet! for scape us they cannot.
Come forth, Madge Mumblecrust! So stand fast togither.

M. Merry. God send us a fair day!

R. Roister. See, they march on hither.

Tib. Talk. But, mistress——

C. Custance. What sayest you?

Tib. Talk.　　　Shall I go fet our goose?

C. Custance. What to do?

Tib. Talk.　　　　　To yonder captain I will turn her loose.
And she gape and hiss at him, as she doth at me,
I durst jeopard my hand she will make him flee.

C. Custance. On! Forward!

R. Roister.　　　They come!

M. Merry.　　　　　　Stand!

R. Roister.　　　　　　　Hold!

M. Merry.　　Keep! [9]

R. Roister.　　　There!

M. Merry.　　　　　Strike!

R. Roister.　　　　　　Take heed!

---

[1] Trespass.　　　[3] Raise the siege.
[2] Speakers are reversed in original.　[4] Mass.
[5] For this scene *cf.* Plautus, *Miles gloriosus*, V.
[6] Enters later.

[7] *I.e.*, drummers.　[8] Unprepared.　[9] Take care!

C. CUSTANCE. Well said, Truepenny!

TRUEPENNY.   Ah, whoresons!

C. CUSTANCE.   Well done,
  indeed!   20

M. MERRY. Hold thine own, Harpax;
  down with them, Dobinet!

C. CUSTANCE. Now, Madge! There, Annot! Now stick them, Tibet!

TIB. TALK. [To Dobinet.] All my chief
  quarrel is to this same little knave
  That beguiled me last day; nothing shall
  him save.

D. DOUGH. Down with this little quean [1]
  that hath at me such spite;
  Save you from her, master; it is a very
  sprite.

C. CUSTANCE. I myself will *mounsire
  graunde captaine* undertake.[2]

R. ROISTER. They win ground.

M. MERRY.   Save yourself, sir, for God's sake!

R. ROISTER. Out, alas! I am slain, help!

M. MERRY.   Save yourself!

R. ROISTER.   Alas!

M. MERRY. Nay, then, have at you, mistress!

R. ROISTER.   Thou hittest me, alas! 30

M. MERRY. I will strike at Custance
  here.

R. ROISTER.   Thou hittest me!

M. MERRY. [Aside.]   So I
  will. —
  Nay, Mistress Custance!

R. ROISTER.   Alas, thou
  hittest me still!
  Hold!

M. MERRY.   Save yourself, sir!

R. ROISTER.   Help!
  Out, alas! I am slain!

M. MERRY. Truce, hold your hands; truce
  for a pissing while or twain.
  Nay, how say you, Custance? For saving
  of your life,
  Will ye yield and grant to be this gentman's wife?

C. CUSTANCE. Ye told me he loved me.
  Call ye this love?

M. MERRY. He loved a while even like a
  turtledove.

C. CUSTANCE. Gay love, God save it!
  So soon hot, so soon cold!

M. MERRY. I am sorry for you. He could
  love you yet, so he could.   40

[1] Wench.   [2] Engage with.

R. ROISTER. Nay, by Cock's precious,[3]
  she shall be none of mine.

M. MERRY. Why so?

R. ROISTER.   Come away; by the
  Matte, she is mankine.[4]
  I durst adventure the loss of my right
  hand,
  If she did not slee [5] her other husband.
  And see if she prepare not again to fight!

M. MERRY. What then? Saint George to
  borrow, our Lady's knight!

R. ROISTER. Slee else whom she will, by
  Gog, she shall not slee me!

M. MERRY. How then?

R. ROISTER.   Rather than to be
  slain, I will flee.

C. CUSTANCE. To it again, my knightesses;
  down with them all!

R. ROISTER. Away, away, away! She will
  else kill us all.   50

M. MERRY. Nay, stick to it, like an hardy
  man and a tall.

R. ROISTER. O bones, thou hittest me!
  Away, or else die we shall!

M. MERRY. Away, for the pashe of our
  sweet Lord Jesus Christ!

C. CUSTANCE. Away, lout and lubber, or
  I shall be thy priest!

*Exeant om[nes; i.e., Roister Doister and
                    his Men].*
  So this field is ours; we have driven them
  all away.

TIB. TALK. Thanks to God, mistress, ye
  have had a fair day.

C. CUSTANCE. Weil, now go ye in, and
  make yourself some good cheer.

OMNES PARITER.[6] We go! [*Exeant Maids.*]

T. TRUSTY.   Ah, sir, what a
  field we have had here!

C. CUSTANCE. Friend Tristram, I pray
  you be a witness with me.

T. TRUSTY. Dame Custance, I shall depose for your honesty.   60
  And now fare ye well, except something
  else ye would.

C. CUSTANCE. Not now, but when I need
  to send I will be bold.
                    Exeat [Trusty].
  I thank you for these pains. And now I
  will get me in.
  Now Roister Doister will no more wooing
  begin.   *Ex[eat]*

[3] By God's precious (blood, bones, etc.).
[4] Fierce, Amazonian.   [5] Slay.   [6] All together

Actus V. Scena i.

Gawin Goodluck, Sim Suresby.

[G. Good.] Sim Suresby, my trusty man,
    now advise thee well,
And see that no false surmises thou me
    tell.
Was there such ado about Custance, of a
    truth?
Sim Sure. To report that I heard and saw,
    to me is ruth,
But both my duty and name and prop-
    erty [1]
Warneth me to you to show fidelity.
It may be well enough, and I wish it so
    to be;
She may herself discharge [2] and try her
    honesty.
Yet their claim to her methought was
    very large,
For with letters, rings, and tokens, they
    did her charge;   10
Which when I heard and saw I would
    none [3] to you bring.
G. Good. No, by Saint Mary, I allow [4]
    thee in that thing.
Ah, sirrah, now I see truth in the proverb
    old,
"All things that shineth is not by-and-by
    pure gold."
If any do live a woman of honesty,
I would have sworn Christian Custance
    had been she.
Sim Sure. Sir, though I to you be a serv-
    ant true and just,
Yet do not ye therefore your faithful
    spouse mistrust,
But examine the matter, and, if ye shall
    it find
To be all well, be not ye for my words
    unkind.   20
G. Good. I shall do that is right, and as
    I see cause why.
But here cometh Custance forth; we shall
    know by-and-by.

Actus V. Scena ii.

*C[hristian] Custance, Gawin Goodluck, Sim
Suresby.*

C. Custance. I come forth to see and
    hearken for news good,

For about this hour is the time of likeli-
    hood
That Gawin Goodluck by the sayings of
    Suresby
Would be at home, and lo, yond I see
    him, I.
What! Gawin Goodluck, the only hope
    of my life!
Welcome home, and kiss me, your true
    espoused wife.
G. Good. Nay, soft, Dame Custance! I
    must first, by your license,
See whether all things be clear in your
    conscience.
I hear of your doings to me very strange.
C. Custance. What, fear ye that my faith
    towards you should change?   10
G. Good. I must needs mistrust ye be
    elsewhere entangled;
For I hear that certain men with you
    have wrangled
About the promise of marriage by you
    to them made.
C. Custance. Could any man's report
    your mind therein persuade?
G. Good. Well, ye must therein declare
    yourself to stand clear;
Else I and you, Dame Custance, may
    not join this year.
C. Custance. Then would I were dead,
    and fair laid in my grave.
Ah, Suresby, is this the honesty that ye
    have,
To hurt me with your report, not know-
    ing the thing?
Sim Sure. If ye be honest, my words can
    hurt you nothing.   20
But what I heard and saw, I might not
    but report.
C. Custance. Ah, Lord, help poor widows,
    destitute of comfort!
Truly, most dear spouse, naught was
    done but for pastance.
G. Good. But such kind of sporting is
    homely [5] dalliance.
C. Custance. If ye knew the truth, ye
    would take all in good part.
G. Good. By your leave, I am not half
    well skilled in that art.
C. Custance. It was none but Roister
    Doister, that foolish mome.
G. Good. Yea, Custance, better, they say,
    a bad scuse than none.

---

[1] Character.   [3] *I.e.*, tokens. *Cf.* IV, iii, 50–51.
[2] Clear.   [4] Agree with.
[5] Rude.

C. Custance. Why, Tristram Trusty, sir,
　your true and faithful friend,
Was privy both to the beginning and the
　end.　　　　　　　　　　　　　　　30
Let him be the judge, and for me testify.
G. Good. I will the more credit that [1] he
　shall verify,
And because I will the truth know e'en
　as it is,
I will to him myself, and know all without
　miss.
Come on, Sim Suresby, that before my
　friend thou may
Avouch the same words which thou didst
　to me say.　　　　　　　　*Exeant.*

Actus V. Scena iii.

Christian Custance.

C. Custance. O Lord! how necessary it
　is now-of-days
That each body live uprightly all manner
　ways;
For let never so little a gap be open,
And be sure of this—the worst shall be
　spoken.
How innocent stand I in this for deed or
　thought,
And yet see what mistrust towards me
　it hath wrought.
But thou, Lord, knowest all folks'
　thoughts and eke intents,
And thou art the deliverer of all inno-
　cents.
Thou didst help the advoutress,[2] that
　she might be amended;
Much more then help, Lord, that [3] never
　ill intended.　　　　　　　　　10
Thou didst help Susanna, wrongfully
　accused,
And no less dost thou see, Lord, how I
　am now abused.
Thou didst help Hester, when she should
　have died;
Help also, good Lord, that my truth may
　be tried.
Yet if Gawin Goodluck with Tristram
　Trusty speak,
I trust of ill report the force shall be but
　weak.
And lo, yond they come, sadly talking
　togither.
I will abide, and not shrink for their
　coming hither.

---

[1] That which.　　[2] Adulteress.　　[3] One that.

Actus V. Scena iv.

*Gawin Goodluck, Tristram Trusty, C[hris-
tian] Custance, Sim Suresby.*

G. Good. And was it none other than ye
　to me report?
T. Trusty. No, and here were ye wished [4]
　to have seen the sport.
G. Good. Would I had, rather than half
　of that in my purse.
Sim Sure. And I do much rejoice the
　matter was no worse,
And like as to open it I was to you faith-
　ful,
So of Dame Custance' honest truth I am
　joyful.
For God forfend that I should hurt her
　by false report.
G. Good. Well, I will no longer hold her
　in discomfort.
C. Custance. Now come they hitherward;
　I trust all shall be well.
G. Good. Sweet Custance, neither heart
　can think nor tongue tell　　　10
How much I joy in your constant fidel-
　ity.
Come now, kiss me, the pearl of perfect
　honesty.
C. Custance. God let me no longer to
　continue in life
Than I shall towards you continue a true
　wife.
G. Good. Well, now to make you for this
　some part of amends,
I shall desire first you, and then such of
　our friends
As shall to you seem best, to sup at home
　with me,
Where at your fought field we shall
　laugh and merry be.
Sim Sure. And, mistress, I beseech you,
　take with me no grief.
I did a true man's part, not wishing you
　reprief.[5]　　　　　　　　　20
C. Custance. Though hasty reports
　through surmises growing
May of poor innocents be utter over-
　throwing,
Yet because to thy master thou hast a
　true heart,
And I know mine own truth, I forgive
　thee for my part.

---

[4] "By me" is understood.
[5] Reproof, reproach.

G. Good. Go we all to my house, and of this gear no more.

Go, prepare all things, Sim Suresby; hence, run afore.

Sim Sure. I go.   Ex[eat].

G. Good.   But who cometh yond, M[aster] Merrygreek?

C. Custance. Roister Doister's champion, I shrew his best cheek.

T. Trusty. Roister Doister self, your wooer, is with him too.

Surely something there is with us they have to do.   30

Actus V. Scena v.[1]

M[atthew] Merrygreek, Ralph Roister, Gawin Goodluck, Tristram Trusty, C[hristian] Custance.

M. Merry. Yond I see Gawin Goodluck, to whom lieth my message.

I will first salute him after his long voyage,

And then make all thing well concerning your behalf.

R. Roister. Yea, for the pashe of God!

M. Merry.   Hence, out of sight, ye calf, Till I have spoke with them, and then I will you fet.

R. Roister. In God's name.   [Exeat.]

M. Merry.   What, Master Gawin Goodluck, well met!

And from your long voyage I bid you right welcome home.

G. Good. I thank you.

M. Merry.   I come to you from an honest mome.

G. Good. Who is that?

M. Merry.   Roister Doister, that doughty kite.

C. Custance. Fie! I can scarce abide ye should his name recite.   10

M. Merry. Ye must take him to favor, and pardon all past.—

He heareth of your return, and is full ill aghast.

G. Good. I am right well content he have with us some cheer.

C. Custance. Fie upon him, beast! Then will not I be there.

G. Good. Why, Custance, do ye hate him more than ye love me?

C. Custance. But for your mind,[2] sir, where he were would I not be.

T. Trusty. He would make us all laugh.

M. Merry.   Ye ne'er had better sport.

G. Good. I pray you, sweet Custance, let him to us resort.

C. Custance. To your will I assent.

M. Merry.   Why, such a fool it is, As no man for good pastime would forgo or miss.   20

G. Good. Fet him to go with us.

M. Merry.   He will be a glad man.   Ex[eat].

T. Trusty. We must to make us mirth maintain him all we can.

And lo, yond he cometh, and Merrygreek with him.

C. Custance. At his first entrance ye shall see I will him trim.

But first let us hearken the gentleman's wise talk.

T. Trusty. I pray you, mark if ever ye saw crane so stalk.

Actus V. Scena vi.

R[alph] Roister, M[atthew] Merrygreek, C[hristian] Custance, G[awin] Goodluck, T[ristram] Trusty, D[obinet] Doughty, Harpax.[3]

R. Roister. May I then be bold?

M. Merry.   I warrant you on my word,

They say they shall be sick but ye be at their board.

R. Roister. They were not angry then?

M. Merry.   Yes, at first, and made strange;[4]

But, when I said your anger to favor should change,

And therewith had commended you accordingly,

They were all in love with your ma'ship by-and-by,

And cried you mercy that they had done you wrong.

R. Roister. Forwhy[5] no man, woman, nor child can hate me long.

M. Merry. "We fear," quod they, "he will be avenged one day;

Then for a penny give all our lives we may!"   10

R. Roister. Said they so indeed?

---

[1] Cf. final scene of Terence, *Eunuchus.*

[2] Except for your desire.   [4] Acted shocked.
[3] Last two enter later.   [5] Because.

M. Merry.   Did
   they? Yea, even with one voice.
"He will forgive all," quod I. O, how
   they did rejoice!
R. Roister. Ha, ha, ha!
M. Merry. "Go fet him," say they,
   "while he is in good mood,
For have his anger who lust, we will not,
   by the Rood."
R. Roister. I pray God that it be all
   true, that thou hast me told,
And that she fight no more.
M. Merry.   I warrant
   you, be bold.
To them, and salute them.
R. Roister. [*Advancing.*]   Sirs, I greet
   you all well.
Omnes. Your mastership is welcome.
C. Custance.   Saving my quarrel,
For sure I will put you up into the
   Exchequer.[1]   20
M. Merry. Why so? Better nay. Where-
   fore?
C. Custance.   For an usurer.
R. Roister. I am no usurer, good mis-
   tress, by His arms!
M. Merry. When took he gain of money
   to any man's harms?
C. Custance. Yes, a foul usurer he is;
   ye shall see; else [2]—
R. Roister. Didst not thou promise she
   would pick no mo quarrels?
C. Custance. He will lend no blows but
   he have in recompense
Fifteen for one, which is too much, of
   conscience.[3]
R. Roister. Ah, dame, by the ancient
   law of arms, a man
Hath no honor to foil [4] his hands on a
   woman.
C. Custance. And where other usurers
   take their gains yearly,   30
This man is angry but he have his by-
   and-by.
G. Good. Sir, do not for her sake bear me
   your displeasure.
M. Merry. Well, he shall with you talk
   thereof more at leisure.
Upon your good usage, he will now shake
   your hand.
R. Roister. And much heartily welcome
   from a strange land.

M. Merry. Be not afeard, Gawin, to let
   him shake your fist.
G. Good. O, the most honest gentleman
   that e'er I wist.
  I beseech your ma'ship to take pain to
   sup with us.
M. Merry. He shall not say you nay,
   and I too, by Jesus,
Because ye shall be friends, and let all
   quarrels pass.   40
R. Roister. I will be as good friends with
   them as ere I was.
M. Merry. Then let me fet your quire
   that we may have a song.
R. Roister. Go.

[*Merrygreek beckons to the Musicians, who
                                 enter.*]

G. Good.   I have heard no melody
   all this year long.
M. Merry. Come on, sirs, quickly.
R. Roister.   Sing on,
   sirs, for my friends' sake.
D. Dough. Call ye these your friends?
R. Roister.   Sing on,
   and no mo words make.
                    Here they sing.[5]
G. Good. The Lord preserve our most
   noble queen of renown,
And her virtues reward with the heavenly
   crown.
C. Custance. The Lord strengthen her
   most excellent majesty,
Long to reign over us in all prosperity.
T. Trusty. That her godly proceedings
   the faith to defend,   50
He may stablish and maintain through
   to the end.
M. Merry. God grant her, as she doth,
   the Gospel to protect,
Learning and virtue to advance, and
   vice to correct.
R. Roister. God grant her loving subjects
   both the mind and grace,
Her most godly proceedings worthily to
   embrace.
Harpax. Her highness' most worthy counselors God prosper,
With honor and love of all men to minister.

---

[1] Law court.   [3] A mild oath.
[2] Besides.   [4] Soil.

[5] Whether the lines following represent the
song sung here, or an epilogue in addition to
the song, is uncertain.

OMNES. God grant the nobility her to
serve and love,
With all the whole commonty,[1] as doth
them behove.

AMEN.

CERTAIN SONGS TO BE SONG BY THOSE
WHICH SHALL USE THIS COMEDY OR
INTERLUDE

THE SECOND SONG

Whoso to marry a minion wife
Hath had good chance and hap,
Must love her and cherish her all his life,
And dandle her in his lap.

If she will fare well, if she will go gay,
A good husband ever still,
Whatever she lust to do or to say,
Must let her have her own will.

About what affairs soever he go,
He must show her all his mind.   10
None of his counsel she may be kept fro;[2]
Else is he a man unkind.

THE FOURTH SONG

I mun[3] be married a[4] Sunday;
I mun be married a Sunday;
Whosoever shall come that way,
    I mun be married a Sunday.

Roister Doister is my name;
Roister Doister is my name;
A lusty brute I am the same;
    I mun be married a Sunday.

Christian Custance have I found;
Christian Custance have I found;   10
A widow worth a thousand pound;
    I mun be married a Sunday.

Custance is as sweet as honey;
Custance is as sweet as honey;
I her lamb and she my cony;
    I mun be married a Sunday.

When we shall make our wedding feast,
When we shall make our wedding feast,
There shall be cheer for man and beast;
I mun be married a Sunday.   20
    I mun be married a Sunday, etc.

THE PSALMODY

Placebo dilexi,
Master Roister Doister will straight go
home and die;
Our Lord Jesus Christ his soul have mercy
upon.
Thus you see today a man, tomorrow John.[5]
Yet saving for a woman's extreme cru-
elty,
He might have lived yet a month or two
or three,
But in spite of Custance, which hath him
wearied,
His ma'ship shall be worshipfully buried.
And while some piece of his soul is yet
him within,
Some part of his funerals let us here begin.
    Dirige. He will go darkling to his grave. 10
Neque lux, neque crux, nisi solum clink,[6]
Never gentman so went toward heaven, I
think.
Yet, sirs, as ye will the bliss of heaven win,
When he cometh to the grave, lay him
softly in,
And all men take heed by this one gentle-
man,
How you set your love upon an unkind
woman.
For these women be all such mad peevish
elves,
They will not be won except it please
themselves.
But in faith, Custance, if ever ye come in
hell,
Master Roister Doister shall serve you as
well.   20
Good night, Roger, old knave; farewell,
Roger, old knave!
Good night, Roger, old knave; knave, nap!
    *Nequando. Audivi vocem. Requiem
    æternam.*

THE PEAL OF BELLS RONG BY THE PARISH CLERK AND ROISTER DOISTER'S FOUR MEN

The first bell a triple. When died he? When
died he?
The second. We have him! We have him!
The third. Roister Doister! Roister Doister!
The fourth bell. He cometh! He cometh!
The great bell. Our own! Our own!

FINIS.

---

[1] Commons.   [2] From.   [3] Must.   [4] On.
[5] *I.e.*, anybody.   [6] Except only a bell.

GAMMER GURTON'S NEEDLE

In 1563, according to the Stationers' Register, Thomas Colwell was granted a license to print a play entitled *Dyccon of Bedlam*, probably a provisional title for *Gammer Gurton's Needle*, the earliest extant edition of which was issued by him in 1575. The authorship of the play, in spite of a great deal of discussion, still remains a matter of dispute. According to the title-page the play was "made by Mr. S., Mr. of Art," and had been performed "not long ago in Christ's College in Cambridge." As early as 1782 Isaac Reed attributed it to John Still, Bishop of Bath and Wells, but in 1838 Joseph Hunter set forth the claims of Dr. John Bridges. In 1903 Henry Bradley presented strong evidence in favor of William Stevenson, Fellow of Christ's College, Cambridge, whose claim is now generally favored. Stevenson was born at Hunwick, Durham, matriculated at Christ's College in November, 1546, and proceeded B.A. in 1550, M.A. in 1553, and B.D. in 1560. He may have been the William Stevenson who was Fellow of Christ's from 1551 to 1554, and he was certainly Fellow from 1559 to 1561. He was ordained deacon in London in 1552, and was appointed Prebendary of Durham in January, 1561. He died in 1575.

In *Gammer Gurton's Needle*, as in *Roister Doister*, the influence of classical Latin comedy is to be seen in the five-act division with subdivision into scenes, the simple stage setting, and the narrow limitation of the time and place of the action. The broadly farcical treatment, however, follows a tradition reaching back through John Heywood to *Secunda Pastorum* of the Towneley cycle and to medieval farce in general. As an intriguer and manipulator of the action, Diccon is a figure parallel to the tricky rascals of Roman comedy, but, both as a practical joker and as a rogue and vagabond, he is more clearly a successor of the vices of the morality play. Above all, the characters and the life portrayed are far more distinctly English than in *Roister Doister*. In the words of Bradley, "as the first known attempt to present a picture of contemporary rustic life in the form of a regular comedy, it [*Gammer Gurton's Needle*] may be admitted to represent a distinct advance in the development of English dramatic art."

The language of the play is an inaccurate representation of the dialect of the southwestern counties of England, the language which was to be established as the conventional speech of the stage rustic. In making the first attempt to modernize the play, the editors have sought to preserve all forms which may be regarded as dialectal variations from the normal speech of the period.

The text of the present edition is based upon the 1575 quarto as reprinted by H. F. Brett-Smith.

GAMMER GURTON'S NEEDLE[1]

BY
MR. S.

THE NAMES OF THE SPEAKERS IN THIS COMEDY

DICCON *the bedlam.*[2]
HODGE, *Gammer Gurton's servant.*
TIB, *Gammer Gurton's maid.*
GAMMER GURTON.
COCK,[3] *Gammer Gurton's boy.*
DAME CHAT.

DOCTOR RAT, *the curate.*
MASTER BAILY.[4]
DOLL, *Dame Chat's maid.*
SCAPETHRIFT, *Mast[er] Baily's servant.*
MUTES.

[SCENE: *A village in England.*

TIME: *Contemporary.*]

GOD SAVE THE QUEEN!

THE PROLOGUE

As Gammer Gurton with many a wide stitch
Sat piecing and patching of Hodge her
  man's breech,
By chance or misfortune as she her gear[5]
  tossed,
In Hodge' leather breeches her needle she
  lost.
When Diccon the bedlam had heard by
  report
That good Gammer Gurton was robbed in
  this sort,
He quietly persuaded with her in that
  stound[6]
Dame Chat, her dear gossip,[7] this needle
  had found.
Yet knew she no more of this matter, alas,
Than knoweth Tom, our clerk,[8] what the
  priest saith at Mass! 10
Hereof there ensued so fearful a fray

Mas' Doctor was sent for, these gossips to
  stay,
Because he was curate, and esteemed full
  wise,
Who found that[9] he sought not, by Diccon's device.
When all things were tumbled and clean
  out of fashion,
Whether it were by fortune or some other
  constellation,
Suddenly the neele[10] Hodge found by the
  pricking,
And drew it out of his buttock where he
  felt it sticking.
Their hearts then at rest with perfect
  security,
With a pot of good nale[11] they stroke[12] up
  their plaudity.[13] 20

THE I ACT. THE i SCENE.[14]

Diccon.

DICCON Many a mile have I walked, divers and sundry ways,
And many a good man's house have I
  been at in my days,

[1] The complete title runs: "A Right Pithy, Pleasant, and Merry Comedy Entitled Gammer Gurton's Needle, Played on Stage Not Long Ago in Christ's College in Cambridge. Made by Mr. S., Mr. of Art."
[2] A partially cured lunatic discharged from the Hospital of St. Mary of Bethlehem in London; he was licensed to make his living by begging. [3] Original reads *Docke.*
[4] Bailiff. [6] Occasion.
[5] *I.e.,* sewing materials. [7] Crony.
[8] The original spelling, *clarke,* indicates the pronunciation.

[9] That which. [11] Ale. [13] Applause.
[10] Needle. [12] Struck.
[14] The scene for the entire play is a village street with Gammer Gurton's house on one side and Dame Chat's alehouse on the other.

Many a gossip's cup in my time have I
  tasted,
And many a broach and spit have I both
  turned and basted,
Many a piece of bacon have I had out of
  their balks [1]
In running over the country with long
  and weary walks;
Yet came my foot never within those
  doorcheeks,[2]
To seek flesh, or fish, garlic, onions, or
  leeks,
That ever I saw a sort [3] in such a plight
As here within this house appeareth to
  my sight!   10
There is howling and scowling, all cast in
  a dump,
With whewling and puling, as though
  they had lost a trump; [4]
Sighing and sobbing they weep and they
  wail.
I marvel in my mind what the devil they
  ail.
The old trot [5] sits groaning, with "alas!"
  and "alas!"
And Tib wrings her hands, and takes on in
  worse case.
With poor Cock, their boy, they be driven
  in such fits
I fear me the folks be not well in their
  wits.
Ask them what they ail, or who brought
  them in this stay,[6]
They answer not at all but "slack!" and
  "welaway!"   20
When I saw it booted not, out at doors I
  hied me,
And caught a slip of bacon, when I saw
  that none spied me,
Which I intend not far hence, unless my
  purpose fail,
Shall serve for a shoeing-horn to draw on
  two pots of ale.

THE I ACT.   THE ii SCENE.

Hodge, Diccon.

HODGE. See! So cham [7] arrayed with
  dabbling in the dirt!

[1] Lofts.   [3] Company.   [5] Hag.
[2] Doorjambs. [4] A game of cards. [6] State.
[7] I am. For use and characteristics of this
conventional stage dialect for rustics, see *Roister
Doister* I, iii, 100, n.

She that set me to ditching, ich wold [8] she
  had the squirt! [9]
Was never poor soul that such a life had!
Gog's bones,[10] this vilthy glay [11] has
  dressed me too bad!
God's soul, see how this stuff tears!
Ich were better to be a bearward and set
  to keep bears!
By the Mass, here is a gash! A shameful
  hole indeed!
And [12] one stitch tear furder,[13] a man may
  thrust in his head.
DICCON. By my father's soul, Hodge, if I
  shuld now be sworn,
I cannot choose but say thy breech is
  foul be-torn!   10
But the next remedy in such a case and
  hap
Is to planch [14] on a piece as broad as thy
  cap.
HODGE. Gog's soul, man, 'tis not yet two
  days fully ended
Since my Dame Gurton, cham sure, these
  breeches amended!
But cham made such a drudge, to trudge
  at every need,
Chwold rend it, though it were stitched
  with sturdy packthread.
DICCON. Hodge, let thy breeches go, and
  speak and tell me soon
What devil aileth Gammer Gurton and
  Tib, her maid, to frown.
HODGE. Tush, man, th'art deceived! 'Tis
  their daily look;
They cower so over the coals, their eyes
  be bleared with smoke.   20
DICCON. Nay, by the Mass, I perfectly
  perceived, as I came hether,[15]

[8] Both *wold* and *would*, *cold* and *could*, *shold*
or *shuld* and *should*, and these words, especially
would, in combination with *ch* for *ich* (*I*)—*chold*
and *chould* with a few other variants—occur in
the play. In part the variations in this series of
words are probably unintentional, but the shorter
forms predominate so decidedly in the aggregate
that they cannot be disregarded as a feature of
dialect. Hence it has seemed best to retain the
spelling of the original with its inconsistencies,
except for dropping the meaningless final *e* wherever it occurs.
[9] Diarrhea.
[10] By God's bones.
[11] In the rustic dialect, initial *v* = *f*, *g* = *c*, *z* = *s*.
[12] If.   [13] Further.   [14] Plank, clap.
[15] A common form for *hither*, which has been
retained in this play because of the dialect and
rime.

That either Tib and her dame hath been
   by the ears together,
Or else as great a matter, as thou shalt
   shortly see.
HODGE. Now ich beseech our Lord they
   never better agree!
DICCON. By Gog's soul, there they sit as
   still as stones in the street,
As though they had been taken [1]
   with fairies, or else with some ill
   sprite.[2]
HODGE. Gog's heart, I durst have laid my
   cap to a crown
Chwould learn of some prancome [3] as
   soon as ich came to town!
DICCON. Why, Hodge, art thou inspired?
   Or didst thou thereof hear?
HODGE. Nay, but ich saw such a wonder
   as ich saw nat this seven year: 30
Tom Tankard's cow, by Gog's bones,
   she set me up her sail,
And flinging about his half-acre, fisking [4]
   with her tail,
As though there had been in her arse a
   swarm of bees,
And chad not cried, "Tphrowh, whore!"
   she'd leaped out of his leas. [5]
DICCON. Why, Hodge, lies the cunning [6]
   in Tom Tankard's cow's tail?
HODGE. Well, ich chave hard [7] some say
   such tokens do not fail.
But canst thou not tell,[8] in faith, Diccon,
   why she frowns, or whereat?
Hath no man stolen her ducks or hens,
   or gelded Gib, her cat?
DICCON. What devil can I tell, man?   I
   cold not have one word;
They gave no more heed to my talk than
   thou woldst to a lord.   40
HODGE. Ich cannot still but muse what
   marvelous thing it is!
Chill in and know myself what matters
   are amiss.
DICCON. Then farewell, Hodge, awhile,
   since thou dost inward haste,
For I will into the Goodwife Chat's, to
   feel how the ale doth taste.   [Exit.]

THE I ACT.   THE iii SCENE.

Hodge, Tib.

HODGE. [*To himself.*] Cham aghast, by the
   Mass! Ich wot [9] not what to do.
Chad need bless me well before ich go
   them to!
Perchance some felon sprite may haunt
   our house indeed,
And then chwere but a [10] noddy to ven-
   ter [11] where cha' [12] no need!
TIB. [*To herself.*] Cham worse than mad,
   by the Mass, to be at this stay!
Cham chid, cham blamed, and beaten all
   thours [13] on the day,
Lamed, and hunger-starved, pricked up
   all in jags,[14]
Having no patch to hide my back save a
   few rotten rags!
HODGE. I say, Tib—if thou be Tib, as
   I trow sure thou be—
What devil make-ado is this between our
   dame and thee?   10
TIB. Gog's bread, Hodge, thou had a good
   turn thou wert not here [this while!] [15]
It had been better for some of us to have
   been hence a mile!
My gammer is so out of course and fran-
   tic all at once
That Cock, our boy, and I, poor wench,
   have felt it on our bones.
HODGE. What is the matter—say on, Tib—
   whereat she taketh so on?
TIB. She is undone, she saith; alas, her
   joy and life is gone!
If she hear not of some comfort, she is,
   saith, but dead;
Shall never come within her lips one inch
   of meat ne [16] bread!
HODGE. By'r Lady, cham not very glad to
   see her in this dump.
Chold a noble [17] her stool hath fallen and
   she hath broke her rump!   20
TIB. Nay, and that were the worst, we
   wold not greatly care,

---

[1] Bewitched.
[2] Probably pronounced *spreet*.
[3] Unusual incident, freak.
[4] Frisking.
[5] Pastures.
[6] *I.e.*, prophetic power.
[7] Heard.
[8] Original reads *till*.

[9] Know.
[10] Original reads *at*.
[11] Venture.
[12] I have.
[13] The hours.
[14] Dressed in tatters.
[15] This line is partially cut away in copies of early edns., but is completed by Brett-Smith from 1661 quarto.
[16] Nor.
[17] I hold (*i.e.*, wager) a noble (*i.e.*, a piece of money). The form *ichold* also appears.

For bursting of her huckle bone,[1] or
 breaking of her chair;
But greater, greater, is her grief, as,
 Hodge, we shall all feel.
HODGE. Gog's wounds, Tib, my gammer
 has never lost her—neele?
TIB. Her neele!
HODGE.   Her neele?
TIB.   Her neele!
 By Him that made me, it is true, Hodge,
 I tell thee.
HODGE. Gog's sacrament, I would she had
 lost thart [2] out of her belly!
The devil, or else his dame, they ought [3]
 her, sure, a shame!
How a murrion [4] came this chance—say,
 Tib—unto our dame?
TIB. My gammer sat her down on
 her pess,[5] and bade me reach thy
 breeches;   30
And by-and-by [6]—a vengeance in it!—
 or [7] she had take two stitches
To clap a clout [8] upon thine arse, by
 chance aside she leers,
And Gib, our cat, in the milk pan she
 spied over head and ears.
"Ah, whore! Out, thief!" she cried aloud,
 and swapt [9] the breeches down.
Up went her staff, and out leaped Gib at
 doors into the town,[10]
And since that time was never wight
 cold set their eyes upon it.
Gog's malison chave Cock and I bid
 twenty times light on it.
HODGE. And is not then my breeches
 sewed up, tomorrow that I shuld
 wear?
TIB. No, in faith, Hodge, thy breeches lie,
 for all this, never the near.[11]
HODGE. Now a vengeance light on all the
 sort, that better shold have kept
 it—   40
The cat, the house, and Tib, our maid,
 that better shold have swept it!
See where she cometh crawling! Come
 on, in twenty devils' way!
Ye have made a fair day's work, have
 you not? Pray you, say!

THE I ACT. THE iv SCENE.

Gammer, Hodge, Tib, Cock. [12]

GAMMER. Alas, Hodge, alas, I may well
 curse and ban
This day, that ever I saw it, with Gib
 and the milk pan!
For these and ill luck together, as knoweth Cock, my boy,
Have stack [13] away my dear neele, and
 robbed me of my joy—
My fair, long, straight neele, that was
 mine only treasure!
The first day of my sorrow is, and last
 end of my pleasure!
HODGE. Might ha' kept it when ye had it,
 but fools will be fools still!
Lose that is vast in your hands? Ye
 need not, but ye will!
GAMMER. Go hie thee, Tib, and run, thou
 whore, to th'end here of the town!
Didst carry out dust in thy lap. Seek
 where thou pourest it down; 10
And, as thou sawest me roking [14] in the
 ashes where I mourned,
So see in all the heap of dust thou leave
 no straw unturned.
TIB. That chall, gammer, swith and
 tight, [15] and soon be here again!
GAMMER. Tib, stoop and look down to
 the ground to it, and take some
 pain!   [*Exit Tib.*]
HODGE. Here is a pretty matter, to see
 this gear [16] how it goes!
By Gog's soul, I think you wold lose
 your arse and it were loose!
Your neele lost? It is pity you shold
 lack care and endless sorrow.
Gog's death, how shall my breeches be
 sewed? Shall I go thus tomorrow?
GAMMER. Ah, Hodge, Hodge, if that ich
 cold find my neele, by the Reed,[17]
Chould sew thy breeches, ich promise
 thee, with full good double thread, 20
And set a patch on either knee, shuld
 last this moneths [18] twain.
Now God and good Saint Sith [19] I pray to
 send it home again!
HODGE. Whereto served your hands and
 eyes but this your neele to keep?

---

[1] Hip bone.
[2] The heart.
[3] Owed.
[4] Murrain, plague.
[5] Hassock.
[6] At once.
[7] Ere, before.
[8] Cloth, patch.
[9] Swept.
[10] Yard.
[11] Nearer.

[12] Enters later.
[13] Stuck.
[14] Raking, searching.
[15] Quickly and speedily.
[16] Business.
[17] Rood, Cross.
[18] Months.
[19] Bradley suggests St. Osyth.

What devil had you else to do? Ye kept,
  ich wot, no sheep!
Cham fain abroad to dig and delve, in
  water, mire, and clay,
Sossing [1] and possing [2] in the dirt still [3]
  from day to day;
A hundred things that be abroad, cham
  set to see them weal [4]—
And four of you sit idle at home, and
  cannot keep a neele!
GAMMER. My neele, alas! Ich lost it,
  Hodge, what time ich me uphasted
To save the milk set up for thee, which
  Gib, our cat, hath wasted.   30
HODGE. The devil he burst both Gib and
  Tib, with all the rest!
Cham always sure of the worst end,
  whoever have the best!
Where ha' you been fidging [5] abroad
  since you your neele lost?
GAMMER. Within the house, and at the
  door, sitting by this same post,
Where I was looking a long hour before
  these folks came here.
But, welaway! All was in vain; my neele
  is never the near!
HODGE. Set me a candle; let me seek and
  grope wherever it be.
Gog's heart, ye be so foolish, ich think
  you know it not when you it see!
GAMMER. Come hether, Cock! What,
  Cock, I say!

[Enter Cock.]

COCK.   How, gammer!
GAMMER.   Go hie thee soon,
And grope behind the old brass pan;
  which thing when thou hast done, [6]
There shalt thou find an old shoe, where-
  in, if thou look well,   41
Thou shalt find lying an inch of a white
  tallow candle.
Light it, and bring it tight away.
COCK.   That shall be done anon. [7]
          [Exit.]
GAMMER. Nay, tarry, Hodge, till thou
  hast light, and then we'll seek each
  one.

HODGE. Come away, ye whoreson [8] boy!
  Are ye asleep? Ye must have a crier! [9]
COCK. [*Within.*] Ich cannot get the candle
  light; here is almost no fire.
HODGE. Chill hold thee a penny chill
  make thee come if that ich may catch
  thine ears!
Art deaf, thou whoreson boy? Cock, I
  say, why canst not hear 's?
GAMMER. Beat him not, Hodge, but help
  the boy, and come you two together.
          [Exit Hodge.]

THE I ACT. THE V SCENE.

Gammer, Tib, Cock, Hodge. [10]

GAMMER. How now, Tib? Quick, let's hear
  what news thou hast brought hether!

[Enter Tib.]

TIB. Chave tossed and tumbled yender [11]
  heap over and over again,
And winnowed it through my fingers as
  men wold winnow grain;
Not so much as a hen's turd but in
  pieces I tare it,
Or whatsoever clod or clay I found, I
  did not spare it,
Looking within, and eke without, to
  find your neele, alas!
But all in vain, and without help—your
  neele is where it was!
GAMMER. Alas, my neele! We shall never
  meet! Adieu, adieu, for aye!
TIB. Not so, gammer; we might it find
  if we knew where it lay.

[Enter Cock.]

COCK. Gog's Cross, gammer, if ye will
  laugh, look in but at the door,   10
And see how Hodge lieth tumbling and
  tossing amids the floor.
Raking there some fire to find among
  the ashes dead,
Where there is not one spark so big as a
  pin's head,
At last in a dark corner two sparks he
  thought he sees,
Which were [12] indeed naught else but
  Gib our cat's two eyes.
"Puff!" quod [13] Hodge, thinking thereby
  to have fire without doubt;

---

[1] Sousing, making oneself muddy.
[2] Pushing, beating out.
[3] Continuously.   [4] Prosper.   [5] Fidgeting.
[6] Line division in this couplet made by Manly.
[7] At once.

[8] Rascally.   [10] Last three enter later.
[9] Town crier.   [11] Yonder.
[12] Original reads *where*.   [13] Quoth, **said.**

With that Gib shut her two eyes, and
    so the fire was out,
And by-and-by them opened, even as
    they were before;
With that the sparks appeared, even
    as they had done of yore.
And, even as Hodge blew the fire, as he
    did think,   20
Gib, as she felt the blast, straightway
    began to wink,[1]
Till Hodge fell of swearing, as came best
    to his turn,
The fire was sure bewitched, and there-
    fore wold not burn.
At last Gib up [2] the stairs among the
    old posts and pins;
And Hodge he hied him after till broke
    were both his shins—
Cursing and swearing oaths, were never
    of his making,
That Gib wold fire the house if that she
    were not taken.
GAMMER. See, here is all the thought that
    the foolish urchin taketh,
And Tib, methink, at his elbow almost
    as merry maketh!
This is all the wit ye have, when others
    make their moan.   30
Come down, Hodge! Where art thou?
    And let the cat alone!
HODGE. [*Within.*] Gog's heart, help and
    come up! Gib in her tail hath fire,
And is like to burn all if she get a little
    higher!
"Come down," quoth you? Nay, then
    you might count me a patch! [3]
The house cometh down on your heads
    if it take once the thatch.
GAMMER. It is the cat's eyes, fool, that
    shineth in the dark!
HODGE. [*Within.*] Hath the cat, do you
    think, in every eye a spark?
GAMMER. No, but they shine as like fire
    as ever man see.
HODGE. [*Within.*] By the Mass, and she
    burn all, you sh' bear the blame for
    me!
GAMMER. Come down, and help to seek
    here our neele, that it were found.   40
Down, Tib, on the knees, I say! Down,
    Cock, to the ground!

[1] Close the eyes; not merely to blink.
[2] *I.e.*, ran up.
[3] Fool.

To God I make avow,[4] and so to good
    Saint Anne,
A candle shall they have apiece, get it
    where I can,
If I may my neele find in one place or in
    other.

[*Enter Hodge.*]

HODGE. Now a vengeance on Gib light,
    on Gib and Gib's mother,
And all the generation of cats both far
    and near!
Look on the ground, whoreson? Thinks
    then the neele is here?
COCK. By my troth, gammer, methought
    your neele here I saw,
But, when my fingers touched it, I felt
    it was a straw.
TIB. See, Hodge, what's t[h]is? May it
    not be within it?   50
HODGE. Break it, fool, with thy hand,
    and see and thou canst find it.
TIB. Nay, break it you, Hodge, accord-
    ing to your word.
HODGE. Gog's sides, fie, it stinks! It
    is a cat's turd!
It were well done to make thee eat it,
    by the Mass!
GAMMER. This matter amendeth not; my
    neele is still where it was.
Our candle is at an end; let us all in
    quite,
And come another time, when we have
    more light.   [*Exeunt.*]

THE II ACT.

First a song.

Back and side, go bare, go bare;
  Both foot and hand, go cold;
But, belly, God send thee good ale enough,
  Whether it be new or old!

I cannot eat but little meat,
  My stomach is not good;
But sure I think that I can drink
  With him that wears a hood.[5]
Though I go bare, take ye no care,
  I am nothing acold,   10
I stuff my skin so full within
  Of jolly good ale and old.

Back and side, go bare, go bare;
  Both foot and hand, go cold;
But, belly, God send thee good ale enough,
  Whether it be new or old!

[4] Promise.   [5] *I.e.*, a friar.

I love no roast but a nut-brown toast [1]
  And a crab [2] laid in the fire;
A little bread shall do me stead,
  Much bread I not desire.   20
No frost nor snow, no wind, I trow,
  Can hurt me if I wold,
I am so wrapped and throughly lapped
  Of jolly good ale and old.

Back and side, go bare, etc.

And Tib, my wife, that as her life
  Loveth well good ale to seek,
Full oft drinks she till ye may see
  The tears run down her cheeks;
Then doth she troll [3] to me the bowl,
  Even as a maltworm [4] shuld,   30
And saith, "Sweetheart, I took my part
  Of this jolly good ale and old."

Back and side, go bare, etc.

Now let them drink till they nod and wink,
  Even as good fellows should do;
They shall not miss to have the bliss
  Good ale doth bring men to.
And all poor souls that have scoured [5] bowls
  Or have them lustily trolled,
God save the lives of them and their wives,
  Whether they be young or old!   40

Back and side, go bare, etc.[6]

The i Scene.

Diccon, Hodge. [7]

DICCON. Well done, by Gog's malt! Well
  sung, and well said!
Come on, Mother Chat, as thou art true
  maid;
One fresh pot of ale let's see, to make an
  end,
Against this cold weather my naked
  arms to defend!   [*Drinks.*]
This gear it warms the soul! Now, wind,
  blow on the worst,
And let us drink and swill till that our
  bellies burst!
Now were he a wise man, by cunning
  cold define

Which way my journey lieth, or where
  Diccon will dine.
But one good turn I have: be it by night
  or day,
South, east, north, or west, I am never
  out of my way!   10

[Enter Hodge.]

HODGE. Cham goodly rewarded, cham I
  not, do you think?
Chad a goodly dinner for all my sweat
  and swink! [8]
Neither butter, cheese, milk, onions,
  flesh, nor fish,
Save this poor piece of barley bread—
  'tis a pleasant, costly dish!
DICCON. Hail, fellow Hodge, and well [9] to
  fare with thy meat—if thou have
  any!
But by thy words, as I them smelled, thy
  daintrels [10] be not many.
HODGE. Daintrels, Diccon? Gog's soul,
  man, save this piece of dry horse-
  bread,
Cha' bit no bit this livelong day; no
  crumb come in my head;
My guts they yawl, [11] crawl, and all my
  belly rumbleth;
The puddings [12] cannot lie still; each one
  over other tumbleth.   20
By Gog's heart, cham so vexed and in my
  belly penned
Chould one piece were at the spittle-
  house,[13] another at the Castle's End!
DICCON. Why, Hodge, was there none at
  home thy dinner for to set?
HODGE. Gog's bread, Diccon, ich came too
  late; was nothing there to get,
Gib—a foul fiend might on her light—
  licked the milk pan so clean!
See, Diccon, 'twas not so well washed
  this seven year, as ich ween!
A pestilence light on all ill luck! Chad
  thought yet, for all this,
Of a morsel of bacon behind the door at
  worst shuld not miss;
But when ich sought a slip to cut, as ich
  was wont to do,

---

[1] Toast soaked in ale.   [3] Pass around.
[2] Crab apple.   [4] Tippler.
[5] Emptied by drinking healths.
[6] This is a shortened version of an earlier drinking song printed in Dyce's edn. of Skelton.
[7] Enters later.

[8] Labor.
[9] Emended by Dodsley. Original reads *will*.
[10] Delicacies.
[11] Howl.
[12] Entrails.
[13] Almshouse.

Gog's soul, Diccon, Gib, our cat, had eat
the bacon too! 30
Which bacon Diccon stole, as is declared before.
DICCON. Ill luck, quod he? Marry, swear
it, Hodge, this day, the truth to tell.
Thou rose not on thy right side, or else
blessed thee not well.
Thy milk slopped up, thy bacon filched—
that was too bad luck, Hodge!
HODGE. Nay, nay, there was a fouler fault:
my gammer ga' me the dodge! [1]
Seest not how cham rent and torn—my
heels, my knees, and my breech?
Chad thought as ich sat by the fire, help
here and there a stitch;
But there ich was pooped [2] indeed!
DICCON. Why, Hodge?
HODGE. Boots not, man, to tell.
Cham so dressed [3] amongst a sort of fools,
chad better be in hell!
My gammer, cham ashamed to say, by
God, served me not weel! [4]
DICCON. How so, Hodge?
HODGE. Has she not gone, trowest
now, and lost her neele? 40
DICCON. Her eel, Hodge? Who fished of
late? That was a dainty dish!
HODGE. Tush, tush, her neele! her neele!
her neele, man! 'Tis neither flesh nor
fish.
A little thing with an hole in the end, as
bright as any siller, [5]
Small, long, sharp at the point, and
straight as any pillar.
DICCON. I know not what a devil thou
meanest. Thou bring'st me more in
doubt.
HODGE. Knowest not with what Tom
Tailor's man sits broaching [6] through
a clout?
A neele! neele! a neele! My gammer's
neele is gone!
DICCON. Her neele, Hodge? Now I smell
thee! That was a chance alone! [7]
By the Mass, thou hadst a shameful
loss, and it were but for thy breeches!
HODGE. Gog's soul, man, could give a
crown chad it but three stitches! 50
DICCON. How sayest thou, Hodge? What
shuld he have, again thy neele got?

HODGE. Bem [8] vather's soul, and chad it,
chould give him a new groat!
DICCON. Canst thou keep counsel in this
case?
HODGE. Else chwold my tongue were
out.
DICCON. Do thou [9] but then by my advice,
and I will fetch it without doubt.
HODGE. Chill run, chill ride, chill dig,
chill delve, chill toil, chill trudge, shalt
see;
Chill hold, chill draw, chill pull, chill
pinch, chill kneel on my bare knee;
Chill scrape, chill scratch, chill sift, chill
seek, chill bow, chill bend, chill sweat,
Chill stoop, chill stir, chill cap, [10] chill
kneel, chill creep on hands and feet;
Chill be thy bondman, Diccon, ich swear
by sun and moon.
And channot somewhat to stop this gap,
cham utterly undone! 60
Pointing behind to his torn breeches.
DICCON. Why, is there any special cause
thou takest hereat such sorrow?
HODGE. Kirstian Clack, Tom Simson's
maid, by the Mass, comes hether to-
morrow!
Cham not able to say, between us what
may hap—
She smiled on me the last Sunday when
ich put off my cap.
DICCON. Well, Hodge, this is a matter of
weight, and must be kept close;
It might else turn to both our costs, as
the world now goes.
Shalt swear to be no blab, Hodge?
HODGE. Chill, Diccon!
DICCON. Then, go to!
Lay thine hand here; say after me as thou
shalt hear me do.
Hast no book?
HODGE. Cha' no book, I!
DICCON. Then needs must force
us both
Upon my breech to lay thine hand, and
there to take thine oath. 70
HODGE. [*Repeating after Diccon.*] I,
Hodge, breechless,
Swear to Diccon rechless, [11]
By the Cross that I shall kiss,

---

[1] Deceived me.
[2] Befooled.
[3] Mistreated.
[4] Well.
[5] Silver.
[6] Piercing.
[7] Unique mishap.
[8] By my.
[9] Emended by Dodsley. Original reads *than.*
[10] Doff the cap.
[11] Without reservation.

To keep his counsel close,
And always me to dispose
To work that his pleasure is.
   Here he kisseth Diccon's breech.
DICCON. Now, Hodge, see thou take heed
And do as I thee bid,
 For so I judge it meet.
This needle again to win   80
There is no shift therein
 But conjure up a sprite.

HODGE. What, the great devil, Diccon, I
 say?
DICCON. Yea, in good faith, that is the
 way—
 Fet ¹ with some pretty charm.
   [*Begins to draw a magic circle.*]
HODGE. Soft, Diccon! Be not too hasty
 yet,
 By the Mass, for ich begin to sweat!
 Cham afraid of some harm!

DICCON. Come hether then, and stir thee
 not
One inch out of this circle plot, 90
 But stand as I thee teach.
HODGE. And shall ich be here safe from
 their claws?
DICCON. The master devil with his long
 paws
 Here to thee cannot reach.

Now will I settle me to this gear.
HODGE. I say, Diccon, hear me, hear!
 Go softly to this matter!
DICCON. What devil, man, art afraid of
 naught?
HODGE. Canst not tarry a little thought
Till ich make a curtsy of water? 100

DICCON. Stand still to it! Why shuldest
 thou fear him?
HODGE. Gog's sides, Diccon, methink ich
 hear him!
 And tarry, chall mar all!
DICCON. The matter is no worse than I
 told it.
HODGE. By the Mass, cham able no longer
 to hold it!
 Too bad ich must bewray ² the hall!
DICCON. Stand to it, Hodge' Stir not,
 you whoreson!

What devil, be thine arse-strings brus-
 ten? ³
 Thyself awhile but stay;
The devil—I smell him—will be here
 anon. 110
HODGE. Hold him fast, Diccon! Cham
 gone! Cham gone!
 Chill not be at that fray!
   [*Exit, running.*]

THE II ACT. THE ii SCENE.

*Diccon, Chat.*⁴

DICCON. Fie, shitten knave, and out upon
 thee!
Above all other louts, fie on thee!
 Is not here a cleanly prank?
But ⁵ thy matter was no better,
Nor thy presence here no sweeter,
 To fly I can thee thank.

Here is a matter worthy glozing ⁶
Of Gammer Gurton's needle losing,
 And a foul piece of wark! ⁷
A man, I think, might make a play 10
And need no word to ⁸ this they say,
 Being but half a clerk.

Soft, let me alone! I will take the charge
This matter further to enlarge
 Within a time short.
If ye will mark my toys,⁹ and note,
I will give ye leave to cut my throat
 If I make not good sport.

Dame Chat, I say, where be ye? Within?

[*Enter Dame Chat with cards in her hand.*]

CHAT. Who have we there maketh such
 a din? 20
DICCON. Here is a good fellow, maketh
 no great danger.¹⁰
CHAT. What, Diccon? Come near; ye
 be no stranger!
We be fast set at trump, man, hard by
 the fire.
Thou shalt set on the king, if thou come
 a little nigher.

---

³ Burst, broken. ⁴ Enters later. ⁵ Because (?).
⁶ Worth glossing, *i.e.*, commenting on.
⁷ Work.   ⁹ Tricks, pranks.
⁸ In addition to.   ¹⁰ Trouble.

¹ Fetched.   ² Befoul.

DICCON. Nay, nay, there is no tarrying,
  I must be gone again.
  But, first, for you, in counsel I have a
  word or twain.
CHAT. Come hether, Doll!

[Enter Doll.]

  Doll, sit down and play this game,
And, as thou sawest me do, see thou do
  even the same.
There is five trumps beside the queen—
  the hindmost thou shalt find her.
Take heed of Sim Glover's wife; she hath
  an eye behind her!   [*Exit Doll.*] 30
Now, Diccon, say your will.
DICCON.   Nay, soft a little yet!
  I wold nct tell it my sister, the matter
  is so great.
There I will have you swear by our dear
  Lady of Bullain,[1]
S[aint] Dunstan, and S[aint] Donnick,[2]
  three Kings of Kullain,[3]
That ye shall keep it secret.
CHAT.   Gog's bread, that will I do!
  As secret as mine own thought, by God,
  and the devil too!
DICCON. Here is Gammer Gurton, your
  neighbor, a sad and heavy wight—
  Her goodly fair red cock at home was
  stole this last night.
CHAT. Gog's soul! Her cock with the
  yellow legs, that nightly crowed so
  just?[4]
DICCON. That cock is stolen.
CHAT.   What, was he fet out of
  the hens' rust?[5]   40
DICCON. I cannot tell where the devil he
  was kept, under key or lock;
  But Tib hath tickled[6] in gammer's
  ear that you should steal the cock.
CHAT. Have I? Strong whore! By bread
  and salt—
DICCON.   What, soft, I say! Be still!
  Say not one word for all this gear.
CHAT.   By the Mass, that I will!
  I will have the young whore by the head
  and the old trot by the throat!
DICCON. Not one word, Dame Chat, I
  say! Not one word, for my coat!
CHAT. Shall such a beggar's brawl[7] as
  that, thinkest thou, make me a thief?

The pox light on her whore's sides, a
  pestilence and a mischief!—
Come out, thou hungry, needy bitch!
  O, that my nails be short!   49
DICCON. Gog's bread, woman, hold your
  peace! This gear will else pass sport!
  I wold not for an hundred pound this
  matter shuld be known,
  That I am auctor[8] of this tale or have
  abroad it blown!
  Did ye not swear ye wold be ruled, be-
  fore the tale I told?
  I said ye must all secret keep, and ye
  said sure ye wold.
CHAT. Wold you suffer, yourself, Dic-
  con, such a sort to revile you,
  With slanderous words to blot your
  name, and so to defile you?
DICCON. No, Goodwife Chat; I wold be
  loath such drabs shuld blot my
  name;
  But yet ye must so order all that Diccon
  bear no blame.
CHAT. Go to, then! What is your rede?[9]
  Say on your mind; ye shall me rule
  herein.
DICCON. God-a-mercy[10] to Dame Chat!
  In faith, thou must the gear begin.   60
  It is twenty pound to a goose turd, my
  gammer will not tarry,
  But hetherward she comes as fast as her
  legs can her carry,
  To brawl with you about her cock. For
  well I heard Tib say
  The cock was roasted in your house to
  breakfast yesterday;
  And, when ye had the carcass eaten, the
  feathers ye out flung;
  And Doll, your maid, the legs she hid a
  foot deep in the dung.
CHAT. O gracious God, my heart it[11]
  bursts!
DICCON.   Well, rule yourself a space!
  And Gammer Gurton when she cometh
  anon into this place—
  Then to the quean! Let's see! Tell her
  your mind, and spare not,
  So[12] shall Diccon blameless be; and then
  go to, I care not!   70
CHAT. Then, whore, beware her throat!
  I can abide no longer!

---

[1] Boulogne.   [2] Dominic.   [3] Cologne.
[4] Regularly.   [5] Roost.   [6] Whispered.   [7] Brat.

[8] Author.   [9] Advice.   [10] Thanks.
[11] Emended by Dodsley. Original reads *is*.
[12] So long as.

In faith, old witch, it shall be seen which
of us two be stronger!
And, Diccon, but at your request, I
wold not stay one hour.
DICCON. Well, keep it in till she be here,
and then—out let it pour!
In the meanwhile get you in, and make
no words of this.
More of this matter within this hour
to hear you shall not miss.
Because I know you are my friend, hide
it I cold not, doubtless.
Ye know your harm; see ye be wise
about your own business!
So fare ye well! [1]
CHAT.   Nay, soft, Diccon, and drink!
What, Doll, I say!
Bring here a cup of the best ale; let's
see! Come quickly away! [*Exeunt.*] 80

THE II ACT. THE iii SCENE.

Hodge,[2] Diccon.

DICCON. Ye see, masters, the one end
tapped of this my short device!
Now must we broach tother [3] too, be-
fore the smoke arise.
And, by the time they have awhile run,
I trust ye need not crave it;
But look, what lieth in both their hearts,
ye are like, sure, to have it.

[*Enter Hodge, wearing his other breeches.*]

HODGE. Yea, Gog's soul, art alive yet?
What, Diccon, dare ich come?
DICCON. A man is well hied [4] to trust to
thee! I will say nothing but mum.
But, and ye come any nearer, I pray
you see all be sweet!
HODGE. Tush, man! Is gammer's neele
found? That chould gladly weet! [5]
DICCON. She may thank thee it is not found,
for, if thou had kept thy standing,
The devil he wold have fet it out, even,
Hodge, at thy commanding. 10
HODGE. Gog's heart! And cold he tell noth-
ing where the neele might be found?
DICCON. Ye foolish dolt, ye were to seek
ere we had got our ground;
Therefore his tale so doubtful was that
I cold not perceive it.

HODGE. Then ich see well something was
said. Chope [6] one day yet to have it.
But, Diccon, Diccon, did not the devil
cry "Ho, ho, ho"?
DICCON. If thou hadst tarried where thou
stood'st, thou woldest have said so.
HODGE. Durst swear of [7] a book, chard [8]
him roar, straight after ich was gone!
But tell me, Diccon, what said the
knave? Let me hear it anon.
DICCON. The whoreson talked to me, I
know not well of what:
One while his tongue it ran and paltered
of a cat;   20
Another while he stammered still upon
a rat;
Last of all, there was nothing but every
word "Chat! Chat!"
But this I well perceived, before I wold
him rid,
Between "Chat" and the "rat" and
the "cat," the needle is hid.
Now, whether Gib, our cat, have eat it in
her maw,
Or Doctor Rat, our curate, have found it
in the straw,
Or this Dame Chat, your neighbor, have
stolen it, God he knoweth!
But by the morrow at this time we shall
learn how the matter goeth.
HODGE. Canst not learn tonight, man?
Seest not what is here?
Pointing behind to his torn breeches.
DICCON. 'Tis not possible to make it
sooner appear.   30
HODGE. Alas, Diccon, then chave no shift
but, lest ich tarry too long,
Hie me to Sim Glover's shop, there to
seek for a thong,
Therewith this breech to tatch [9] and tie
as ich may.
DICCON. Tomorrow, Hodge, if we chance
to meet, shalt see what I will say.
[*Exit Hodge.*]

THE II ACT. THE iv SCENE.

Diccon, Gammer.[10]

DICCON. Now this gear must forward go,
for here my gammer cometh.
Be still awhile, and say nothing; make
here a little romth! [11]

---

[1] Dodsley's reading. Original reads *will.*
[2] Enters later.   [4] Sped.
[3] That other.   [5] Know.

[6] I hope.   [7] On.   [8] I heard.   [9] Attach, fasten.
[10] Enters later.   [11] Room.

[*Enter Gammer.*]

GAMMER. Good Lord, shall never be my
  luck my neele again to spy?
 Alas the while, 'tis past my help! Where
  'tis, still it must lie!
DICCON. Now Jesus, Gammer Gurton,
  what driveth you to this sadness?
 I fear me, by my conscience, you will sure
  fall to madness.
GAMMER. Who is that? What, Diccon?
  Cham lost, man. Fie! fie!
DICCON. Marry, fie on them that be
  worthy! But what shuld be your
  trouble?
GAMMER. Alas, the more ich think on it,
  my sorrow it waxeth double!
 My goodly tossing[1] spurrier's neele,
  chave lost, ich wot not where.   10
DICCON. Your neele! When?
GAMMER.   My neele! Alas, ich might
  full ill it spare!
 As God himself he knoweth, ne'er one
  beside chave.
DICCON. If this be all, good gammer, I
  warrant you all is save.
GAMMER. Why, know you any tidings
  which way my neele is gone?
DICCON. Yea, that I do, doubtless, as ye
  shall hear anon.
 A[2] see a thing this matter toucheth,
  within these twenty hours,
 Even at this gate,[3] before my face, by a
  neighbor of yours:
 She stooped me down, and up she took a
  needle or a pin.
 I durst be sworn it was even yours, by all
  my mother's kin.
GAMMER. It was my neele, Diccon, ich
  wot; for here, even by this post,   20
 Ich sat what time as ich upstart, and so
  my neele it lost.
 Who was it, lief[4] son? Speak, ich pray
  thee, and quickly tell me that!
DICCON. A subtle quean as any in this
  town, your neighbor here, Dame Chat.
GAMMER. Dame Chat, Diccon? Let me
  be gone! Chill thither in posthaste.
DICCON. Take my counsel yet or ye go,
  for fear ye walk in waste!
 It is a murrion crafty drab, and froward
  to be pleaséd;

And ye take not the better way, our
  needle yet ye lose[5] it.
For, when she took it up, even here before your doors,
 "What, soft, Dame Chat," quoth I,
  "that same is none of yours!"
 "Avaunt," quoth she, "sir knave! What
  pratest thou of that I find?   30
 I wold thou hadst kissed me I wot where"
  (she meant, I know, behind).
 And home she went as brag[6] as it had
  been a bodylouse,
 And I after as bold as it had been the
  goodman of the house.
 But there and ye had hard her how she
  began to scold—
 The tongue it went on pattens,[7] by Him
  that Judas sold!
 Each other word I was a knave, and you
  a whore of whores,
 Because I spake in your behalf and said
  the neele was yours.
GAMMER. Gog's bread! And thinks the
  callet[8] thus to keep my neele me
  fro?[9]
DICCON. Let her alone, and she minds none
  other but even to dress you so!
GAMMER. By the Mass, chill rather spend
  the coat that is on my back!   40
 Thinks the false quean by such a sleight[10]
  that chill my neele lack?
DICCON. Slepe[11] not you[r] gear, I counsel you, but of this take good heed:
 Let not be known I told you of it, how
  well soever ye speed.
GAMMER. Chill in, Diccon, a clean apern[12]
  to take and set before me;
 And ich may my neele once see, chill sure
  remember thee!   [*Exit.*]

THE II ACT. THE V SCENE.

Diccon.

DICCON. Here will the sport begin! If
  these two once may meet,
 Their cheer, durst lay money, will prove
  scarcely sweet!
 My gammer, sure, intends to be upon her
  bones

---

[1] Brett-Smith suggests the movement of the
needle in sewing with a long thread.
[2] I.   [3] Door.   [4] Dear.

[5] Rime would require *leese*.   [6] Briskly.
[7] On wooden shoes, *i.e.*, noisily.
[8] Strumpet.   [9] From.
[10] Dodsley's reading. Original reads *slygh*.
[11] Slip, neglect.   [12] Apron.

With staves or with clubs or else with
　cobblestones.
Dame Chat, on the other side, if she be
　far behind,
I am right far deceived; she is given to it
　of kind.[1]
He that may tarry by it awhile, and that
　but short,
I warrant him—trust to it—he shall see
　all the sport.
Into the town will I, my friends to visit
　there,
And hether straight again to see th'end of
　this gear.—[*Turns to musicians.*]　　10
In the meantime, fellows, pipe up your
　fiddles! I say, take them,
And let your friends hear such mirth as
　ye can make them!　　　　　[*Exit.*]

The III Act. The i Scene.

Hodge.

Hodge. Sim Glover, yet gramercy! Cham
　meetly well sped now.
Th'art even as good a fellow as ever
　kissed a cow!
Here is a thing [2] indeed; by the Mass,
　though ich speak it,
Tom Tankard's great bald curtal,[3] I
　think, could not break it!
And, when he spied my need to be so
　straight and hard,
Hais [4] lent me here his nawl [5] to set the
　jib forward.[6]
As for my gammer's neele, the flying
　fiend go weet! [7]
Chill not now go to the door again with it
　to meet.
Chould make shift good enough and chad
　a candle's end.
The chief hole in my breech with these
　two chill amend.　　　　　10

The III Act. The ii Scene.

Gammer, Hodge.

Gammer. How, Hodge! mayst now be
　glad! Cha' news to tell thee.
Ich know who hais my neele; ich trust
　soon shalt it see.

Hodge. The devil thou does! Hast hard,
　gammer, indeed, or dost but jest?
Gammer. 'Tis as true as steel, Hodge.
Hodge.　　　　　Why, knowest well where
　didst leese it?
Gammer. Ich know who found it, and
　took it up; shalt see, or it be long.
Hodge. God's Mother dear, if that be
　true, farewell both nawl an' thong!
　But who hais it, gammer? Say on!
　Chould fain hear it disclosed.
Gammer. That false fixen,[8] that same
　Dame Chat, that counts herself so
　honest!
Hodge. Who told you so?
Gammer.　　　　　That same did Diccon
　the bedlam, which saw it done.
Hodge. Diccon? It is a vengeable knave,
　gammer! 'Tis a bonable [9] whoreson!　10
Can do mo [10] things than that, else cham
　deceived evil.
By the Mass, ich saw him of late call up
　a great black devil!
O, the knave cried, "Ho! ho!" He roared,
　and he thundered.
And ye'd been here, cham sure you'ld
　murrainly ha' wondered!
Gammer. Was not thou afraid, Hodge,
　to see him in this place?
Hodge. No! And chad come to me,
　chould have laid him on the face,
Chould have promised him!
Gammer.　　　　　But, Hodge, had he no
　horns to push?
Hodge. As long as your two arms! Saw
　ye never Friar Rush [11]
Painted on a cloth, with a side [12] long
　cow's tail,
And crooked cloven feet, and many a
　hooked nail?　　　　　20
For all the world, if I shuld judge,
　chould reckon him his brother.
Look, even what face Friar Rush had,
　the devil had such another!
Gammer. Now [13] Jesus' mercy, Hodge, did
　Diccon in him bring?
Hodge. Nay, gammer, hear me speak!
　Chill tell you a greater thing:

---

[1] By nature.　　　　　[4] Has.
[2] *I.e.*, the thong he had gone for.　　[5] Awl.
[3] Horse with a docked tail.
[6] *I.e.*, help things on.　　[7] Wi' it, with it.

[8] Vixen.
[9] Powerful; Hodge's mispronunciation of *abominable.*　　　　　[10] More.
[11] A name assumed by the devil in a popular German folk tale.
[12] Great (literally, *long*).
[13] Dodsley's reading. Early edns. read *new.*

The devil, when Diccon had him—ich
  hard him wondrous weel—
Said plainly, here before us, that Dame
  Chat had your neele.

GAMMER. Then let us go and ask her
  wherefore she minds to keep it!
Seeing we know so much, 'twere a madness now to slepe it.

HODGE. Go to her, gammer.

[Enter Chat.]

See ye not where she stands in her doors?
Bid her give you the neele. 'Tis none
  of hers, but yours!   30

THE III ACT. THE iii SCENE.

Gammer, Chat, Hodge.

GAMMER. Dame Chat, chold pray thee
  fair, let me have that is mine!
Chill not this twenty years take one
  fart that is thine.
Therefore give me mine own, and let
  me live beside thee!

CHAT. Why art thou crept from home
  hether to mine own doors to chide me?
Hence, doting drab, avaunt, or I shall
  set thee further!
Intends thou and that knave me in my
  house to murther?

GAMMER. Tush, gape not so on[1] me,
  woman! Shalt not yet eat me!
Nor all the friends thou hast, in this
  shall not entreat me!
Mine own goods I will have, and ask
  thee on beleve.[2]
What, woman! Poor folks must have
  right, though the thing you aggrieve. 10

CHAT. Give thee thy right, and hang thee
  up, with all thy bagger's[3] brood!
What, wilt thou make me a thief, and
  say I stole thy good?

GAMMER. Chill say nothing, ich warrant
  thee, but that ich can prove it well.
Thou fet my good even from my door,
  cham able this to tell!

CHAT. Did I, old witch, steal oft[4] was
  thine? How should that thing be
  known?

GAMMER. Ich cannot tell; but up thou
  tookest it, as though it had been thine
  own.

CHAT. Marry, fie on thee, thou old gib,[5]
  with all my very heart!

GAMMER. Nay, fie on thee, thou ramp,[6]
  thou rig,[7] with all that take thy
  part!

CHAT. A vengeance on those lips that
  layeth such things to my charge!

GAMMER. A vengeance on those callet-
  ships whose conscience is so large![8] 20

CHAT. Come out, Hodge!

GAMMER.   Come out, Hodge, and
  let me have[9] right!

CHAT. Thou arrant witch!

GAMMER.   Thou bawdy bitch, chill
  make thee curse this night!

CHAT. A bag and a wallet![10]

GAMMER. A cart for a callet![11]

CHAT.   Why, weenest thou thus to
  prevail?
I hold thee a groat I shall patch thy
  coat!

GAMMER.   Thou wart[12] as good
  kiss my tail!
Thou slut, thou cut,[13] thou rakes,[14] thou
  jakes![15] Will not shame make thee
  hide thee?

CHAT. Thou scald,[16] thou bald, thou rotten, thou glutton! I will no longer
  chide thee!
But I will teach thee to keep home.

GAMMER.   Wilt thou, drunken beast?
                  [They fight.]

HODGE. Stick to her, gammer! Take her by
  the head! Chill warrant you this feast!
Smite, I say, gammer! Bite, I say, gammer! I trow ye will be keen!
Where be your nails? Claw her by the
  jaws! Pull me out both her eyen![17] 30
         [Chat throws Gammer down.]
Gog's bones, gammer, hold up your head!

CHAT. I trow, drab, I shall dress thee.—
[To Hodge.] Tarry, thou knave! I hold
  thee a groat I shall make these hands
  bless thee!—

                [Hodge retires.]

---

[1] Emended by Hazlitt. Original reads *no.*
[2] Belive, lively, at once.
[3] Beggar's (?).   [4] Aught.

[5] Cat.   [7] Wanton woman.
[6] Shameless woman.   [8] Liberal, easy.
[9] Manly's reading. Original reads *let have me.*
[10] Accouterments of a beggar.
[11] A drab was commonly punished by being
whipped at the tail of a cart as it was driven
through the streets.
[12] Wert.   [15] Privy.
[13] Docked horse or dog.   [16] Scabby person.
[14] Dissolute person.   [17] Old plural of *eye.*

Take thou this, old whore, for amends,
and learn thy tongue well to tame,
And say thou met at this bickering, not
thy fellow, but thy dame!

[*Hodge returns with a club.*]

HODGE. Where is the strong stewed
whore? Chill gear [1] a whore's mark!
Stand out one's way that ich kill none
in the dark!
Up, gammer, and ye be alive! Chill
fight now for us both.
Come no near me, thou scald callet! To
kill thee ich were loath.

CHAT. Art here again, thou hoddypeak! [2]
What, Doll, bring me out my spit!

HODGE. Chill broach thee with this!
Bim father soul, chill conjure that
foul sprite!—   40
Let door stand, Cock! Why comes indeed? Keep door, thou whoreson boy!

CHAT. Stand to it, thou dastard, for thine
ears! Ise [3] teach thee a sluttish toy!

HODGE. Gog's wounds, whore, chill make
thee avaunt! [*Flees into the house.*]
Take heed, Cock, pull in the latch!

CHAT. I' faith, sir loose-breech, had ye
tarried, ye shold have found your
match!

[*Gammer attacks Chat from behind.*]

GAMMER. Now ware thy throat, losel! [4]
Thouse [5] pay [6] for all!

[*Throws Chat down.*]

HODGE.   Well said, gammer,
by my soul!
Hoise [7] her! Souse her! Bounce her!
Trounce her! Pull out her throatboll! [8]

CHAT. Com'st behind me, thou withered
witch? And I get once on foot,
Thouse pay for all, thou old tarleather! [9]
I'll teach thee what longs [10] to it!
Take thee this to make up thy mouth till
time thou come by more!

[*Chat beats Gammer and goes out.*]

HODGE. Up, gammer! Stand on your
feet. Where is the old whore?   50
Faith, would chad her by the face!
Chould crack her callet crown!

GAMMER. Ah, Hodge, Hodge, where was
thy help, when fixen had me down?

HODGE. By the Mass, gammer, but for my
staff, Chat had gone nigh to spill you!
Ich think the harlot had not cared, and
chad not come, to kill you.
But shall we lose our neele thus?

GAMMER.   No, Hodge, chwar [11] loath
do so.
Thinkest thou chill take that at her
hand? No, Hodge, ich tell thee, no!

HODGE. Chold yet this fray were well take
up, and our own neele at home.
'Twill be my chance else some to kill,
wherever it be, or whom!

GAMMER. We have a parson, Hodge, thou
knows, a man esteeméd wise,
Mast' Doctor Rat; chill for him send,
and let me hear his advice.   60
He will her shrive for all this gear, and
give her penance straight;
Wese [12] have our neele, else Dame Chat
comes ne'er within heaven-gate!

HODGE. Yea, marry, gammer, that ich
think best. Will you now for him send?
The sooner Doctor Rat be here, the
sooner wese ha' an end.
And here, gammer! Diccon's devil, as
ich remember well,
Of cat, and Chat, and Doctor Rat a
felonious tale did tell.
Chold you forty pound that is the way
your neele to get again!

GAMMER. Chill ha' him straight! Call out
the boy; wese make him take the pain.

HODGE. What, Cock, I say! Come out!
What devil, canst not hear?

[*Enter Cock.*]

COCK. [13] How now, Hodge? How does
gammer? Is yet the weather clear?   70
What wold chave me to do?

GAMMER.   Come hether, Cock, anon!
Hence swith to Doctor Rat! Hie thee
that thou were gone!
And pray him come speak with me; cham
not well at ease.
Shalt have him at his chamber, or [14] else
at Mother Bee's;
Else seek him at Hob Filcher's shop, for,
as chard it reported,
There is the best ale in all the town, and
now is most resorted.

---

[1] Gi' her, give her.   [4] Worthless person.
[2] Simpleton.   [5] Thou shalt.
[3] I shall.
[6] Emended by Dodsley. Original reads *pray.*
[7] Lift.   [9] Strip of dried sheepskin.
[8] Adam's apple.   [10] Belongs.

[11] Ich were, I were. Bradley's emendation for
chwarde.   [12] We shall.
[13] Original assigns this speech to Gammer.
[14] Original reads *of.*

Cock. And shall ich bring him with me,
    gammer?
Gammer.   Yea, by-and-by, good Cock.
Cock. Shalt see that shall be here anon,
    else let me have on the dock! [1] [*Exit.*]
Hodge. Now, gammer, shall we two go in,
    and tarry for his coming?
    What devil, woman, pluck up your heart,
    and leave off all this glumming! [2]   80
    Though she were stronger at the first, as
    ich think ye did find her,
    Yet there ye dressed the drunken sow,
    what time ye came behind her.
Gammer. Nay, nay, cham sure she lost
    not all; for set th'end to the beginning,
    And ich doubt not but she will make
    small boast of her winning.
                  [*They start to go in.*]

The III Act. The iv Scene.

Tib [*with a cat*], *Hodge, Gammer, Cock.*[3]

Tib. See, gammer, gammer, Gib, our cat!
    Cham afraid what she aileth!
    She stands me gasping behind the door,
    as though her wind her faileth.
    Now let ich doubt what Gib shuld mean,
    that now she doth so dote.[4]
Hodge. Hold hether! [5] Ichold twenty
    pound your neele is in her throat!
    Grope [6] her, ich say! Methinks ich feel
    it. Does not prick your hand?
Gammer. Ich can feel nothing.
Hodge.   No? Ich know thar's not
    within this land
    A murrainer cat than Gib is, betwixt the
    Thames and Tyne;
    Sh'as as much wit in her head almost as
    chave in mine!
Tib. Faith, sh'as eaten something that
    will not easily down.
    Whether she gat it at home or abroad
    in the town   10
    Ich cannot tell.
Gammer.   Alas, ich fear it be some
    crooked pin!
    And then, farewell Gib! She is undone
    and lost—all save the skin.
Hodge. Tib, your neele, woman, I say!
    Gog's soul, give me a knife,
    And chill have it out of her maw, or else
    chall lose my life!

Gammer. What! Nay, Hodge, fie! Kill not
    our cat! 'Tis all the cats we ha' now!
Hodge. By the Mass, Dame Chat hais
    me so moved ich care not what I
    kill, ma' [7] God avow!
    Go to, then, Tib! To this gear! Hold up
    her tail, and take her!
    Chill see what devil is in her guts! Chill
    take the pains to rake [8] her!
Gammer. Rake a cat, Hodge? What
    woldst thou do?
Hodge.   What! Think'st that
    cham not able?
    Did not Tom Tankard rake his curtal
    t'or [9] day, standing in the stable?   20

[*Enter Cock.*]

Gammer. Soft, be content; let's hear what
    news Cock bringeth from Mast' Rat!
Cock. Gammer, chave been there as you
    bade, you wot well about what.
    'Twill not be long before he come, ich
    durst swear of a book.
    He bids you see ye be at home, and there
    for him to look.
Gammer. Where didst thou find him, boy?
    Was he not where I told thee?
Cock. Yes, yes, even at Hob Filcher's
    house, by him that bought and sold me;
    A cup of ale had in his hand, and a crab
    lay in the fire.
    Chad much ado to go and come, all was
    so full of mire.
    And, gammer, one thing I can tell: Hob
    Filcher's nawl was lost,
    And Doctor Rat found it again, hard be-
    side the doorpost.   30
    Ichold a penny, can say something your
    neele again to fet.
Gammer. Cham glad to hear so much,
    Cock; then trust he will not let [10]
    To help us herein best he can; therefore,
    till time he come,
    Let us go in. If there be aught to get,
    thou shalt have some.   [*Exeunt.*]

The IV Act. The i Scene [11]

Doctor Rat, Gammer Gurton.

D. Rat. [*To himself.*] A man were better
    twenty times be a bandog and bark,
    Than here, among such a sort, be parish
    priest or clerk,

[1] Tail, *i.e.*, a beating.   [4] Act foolishly.
[2] Sullenness.   [5] Give her to me!
[3] Enters later.   [6] Feel.
[7] I make.   [8] Clean.   [9] Tother.   [10] Forbear.
[11] Original reads *The II Act. The iv Scene.*

Where he shall never be at rest one
pissing-while a day,
But he must trudge about the town, this
way and that way,
Here to a drab, there to a thief, his shoes
to tear and rent,
And, that which is worst of all, at every
knave's commandment!
I had not sit the space to drink two pots
of ale
But Gammer Gurton's sorry boy was
straightway at my tail,
And she was sick, and I must come—to
do I wot not what!
If once her finger's end but ache,
"Trudge! Call for Doctor Rat!"   10
And, when I come not at their call, I only
thereby lose;
For I am sure to lack therefore a tithe-
pig or a goose.
I warrant you, when truth is known, and
told they have their tale,
The matter whereabout I come is not
worth a halfpennyworth of ale!
Yet must I talk so sage and smooth as
though I were a glozier,[1]
Else, or the year come at an end, I shall
be sure the loser.
      [*He spies Gammer Gurton working.*]
What work ye, Gammer Gurton! How,
here is your friend M[aster] Rat!
GAMMER. Ah, good M[aster] Doctor, cha'
troubled, cha' troubled you, chwot
well that!
D. RAT. How do ye, woman? Be ye lusty,
or be ye not well at ease?
GAMMER. By Gis,[2] master, cham not
sick,[3] but yet chave a disease.[4]   20
Chad a foul turn now of late; chill tell it
you, by Gigs!
D. RAT. Hath your brown cow cast her
calf, or your sandy sow her pigs?
GAMMER. No, but chad been as good they
had, as this, ich wot weel.
D. RAT. What is the matter?
GAMMER.   Alas! alas! cha' lost my good
neele!
My neele, I say! And, wot ye what? A
drab came by and spied it,
And, when I asked her for the same, the
filth flatly denied it.

D. RAT. What was she that—
GAMMER.   A dame, ich warrant you!
She began to scold and brawl—
Alas, alas! Come hether, Hodge! This
wr[e]tch can tell you all.

THE IV ACT. THE ii SCENE.[5]

Hodge, Doctor Rat, Gammer, Diccon, Chat.[6]

HODGE. Good morrow, Gaffer Vicar!
D. RAT.   Come on, fellow; let us hear.
Thy dame hath said to me, thou knowest
of all this gear;
Let's see what thou canst say.
HODGE.   Bym fay,[7] sir, that ye shall!
What matter soever here was done, ich
can tell your ma'ship all.
My Gammer Gurton here, see now, sat
her down at this door, see now;
And, as she began to stir her, see now, her
neele fell in the floor, see now;
And, while her staff she took, see now, at
Gib, her cat, to fling, see now,
Her neele was lost in the floor, see now.
Is not this a wondrous thing, see now?
Then came the quean, Dame Chat, see
now, to ask for her black cup, see
now;
And even here at this gate, see now,
she took that neele up, see now.   10
My gammer then she yeed,[8] see now,
her neele again to bring, see now,
And was caught by the head, see now.
Is not this a wondrous thing, see now?
She tare my gammer's coat, see now,
and scratched her by the face, see
now;
Chad thought sh'ad stopped her throat,
see now. Is not this a wondrous case,
see now?
When ich saw this, ich was wroth,[9] see
now, and start between them twain,
see now;
Else, ich durst take a book oath, see
now, my gammer had been slain, see
now.
GAMMER. This is even the whole matter,
as Hodge has plainly told.
And chould fain be quiet, for my part,
that chould.

---

[1] Flatterer.   [2] Jesus.
[3] Emended by Dodsley. Original reads *sich*.
[4] Dis-ease, anxiety.

[5] Hazlitt, Manly, and Adams begin a new
scene at l. 52 and again at l. 94.
[6] The last two enter later.
[7] By my faith.   [8] Went.
[9] Original misprints *worth*.

But help us, good master—beseech ye
   that ye do—
Else shall we both be beaten, and lose
   our neele too.   20
D. RAT. What wold ye have me to do?
   Tell me, that I were gone.
I will do the best that I can to set you
   both at one.
But be ye sure Dame Chat hath this
   your neele found?
GAMMER. Here comes the man that see
   her take it up of [1] the ground;
Ask him yourself, Master Rat, if ye be-
   lieve not me;
And help me to my neele, for God's sake
   and Saint Charity!

[*Enter Diccon.*]

D. RAT. Come near, Diccon, and let us
   hear what thou can express.
Wilt thou be sworn thou seest Dame
   Chat this woman's neele have?
DICCON. Nay, by S[aint] Benit,[2] will I not!
   Then might ye think me rave.[3]
GAMMER. Why, didst not thou tell me so
   even here?   Canst thou for shame
   deny it?   30
DICCON. Ay, marry, gammer; but I said
   I wold not abide by it.
D. RAT. Will you say a thing, and not
   stick to it to try it?
DICCON. "Stick to it," quoth you, Master
   Rat? Marry, sir, I defy it!
Nay, there is many an honest man,
   when he such blasts hath blown
In his friend's ears, he would be loath
   the same by him were known.
If such a toy be uséd oft among the
   honesty,[4]
It may beseem a simple man of [5] your
   and my degree.
D. RAT. Then we be never the nearer,
   for all that you can tell?
DICCON. Yes, marry, sir, if ye will do by
   mine advice and counsel.
If Mother Chat see all us here, she know-
   eth how the matter goes;   40
Therefore I rede [6] you three go hence,
   and within keep close;
And I will into Dame Chat's house, and
   so the matter use

That, or you cold go twice to church, I
   warrant you hear news.
She shall look well about her, but, I
   durst lay a pledge,
Ye shall of gammer's neele have shortly
   better knowledge.
GAMMER. Now, gentle Diccon. do so; and,
   good sir, let us trudge.
D. RAT. By the Mass, I may not tarry so
   long to be your judge.
DICCON. 'Tis but a little while, man.
   What, take so much pain!
If I hear no news of it, I will come sooner
   again.
HODGE. Tarry so much, good Master
   Doctor, of your gentleness!   50
D. RAT. Then let us hie us inward; and,
   Diccon, speed thy business!
DICCON. Now, sirs, do you no more but
   keep my counsel just,
And Doctor Rat shall thus catch some
   good, I trust.—
   [*Exeunt Hodge, Rat, and Gammer.*
To himself.]   But Mother Chat, my
   gossip, talk first withal I must,
For she must be chief captain to lay the
   Rat in the dust.

[*Enter Dame Chat.*]

God deven,[7] Dame Chat, in faith, and
   well met in this place!
CHAT. God deven, my friend Diccon.
   Whether [8] walk ye this pace?
DICCON. By my truth, even to you, to
   learn how the world goeth.
Hard ye no more of the other matter,
   say me now, by your troth?
CHAT. O, yes, Diccon. Here the old whore
   and Hodge, that great knave—   60
But, in faith, I would thou hadst seen!—
   O Lord, I dressed them brave! [9]
She bare me two or three souses [10] be-
   hind in the nape of the neck,
Till I made her old wesen [11] to answer
   again, "keck"! [12]
And Hodge, that dirty dastard that at
   her elbow stands.
If one pair of legs had not been worth
   two pair of hands,

---

[1] Off.
[2] Benedict.
[3] To be mad.
[4] Persons of quality.
[5] Original reads *if.*
[6] Advise.
[7] God give you good even.
[8] Whither.
[9] Finely.
[10] Thwacks.
[11] Weasand, throat.
[12] Sound of vomiting.

He had had his beard shaven if my nails
　　wold have served!
And not without a cause, for the knave
　　it well deserved!
DICCON. By the Mass, I can thee thank,
　　wench, thou didst so well acquit
　　thee!
CHAT. And th'adst seen him, Diccon, it
　　wold have made thee beshit thee
For laughter. The whoreson dolt at last
　　caught up a club　　　　　　　　70
As though he would have slain the
　　master devil, Belsabub;
But I set him soon inward.
DICCON.　　　O Lord, there is the thing
　That Hodge is so offended, that makes
　　him start and fling!
CHAT. Why, makes the knave any moil-
　　ing,[1] as ye have seen or hard?
DICCON. Even now I saw him last. Like
　　a madman he fared,
And sware by heaven and hell he would
　　awreak[2] his sorrow,
And leave you never a hen on-live by
　　eight of the clock tomorrow.
Therefore mark what I say, and my
　　words see that ye trust:
Your hens be as good as dead if ye leave
　　them on the rust!
CHAT. The knave dare as well go hang
　　himself as go upon my ground!　80
DICCON. Well, yet take heed, I say! I
　　must tell you my tale round.[3]
Have you not about your house, behind
　　your furnace or lead,[4]
A hole where a crafty knave may creep
　　in for need?
CHAT. Yes, by the Mass, a hole broke
　　down even within these two days.
DICCON. Hodge he intends this same
　　night to slip in thereaways.
CHAT. O Christ, that I were sure of it!
　　In faith, he shuld have his meed!
DICCON. Watch well, for the knave will
　　be there as sure as is your creed.
I wold spend myself a shilling to have
　　him swingéd well.
CHAT. I am as glad as a woman can be of
　　this thing to hear tell.
By Gog's bones, when he cometh, now
　　that I know the matter,　　　　90

He shall sure at the first skip to leap in
　　scalding water—
With a worse turn besides! When he will,
　　let him come!
DICCON. I tell you as my sister. You
　　know what meaneth "mum"!—
　　　　　　　　　　　　　　[Exit Chat.]
Now lack I but my doctor to play his
　　part again.
And lo, where he cometh towards—per-
　　adventure to his pain!

　　　　　　　　[Enter Rat.]

D. RAT. What good news, Diccon? Fel-
　　low, is Mother Chat at home?
DICCON. She is, sir, and she is not, but it
　　please her to whom.
Yet did I take her tardy,[5] as subtle as
　　she was!
D. RAT. The thing that thou went'st for,
　　hast thou brought it to pass?
DICCON. I have done that I have done,
　　be it worse, be it better!　　　100
And Dame Chat at her wit's end I have
　　almost set her.
D. RAT. Why, hast thou spied the neele?
　　Quickly, I pray thee, tell!
DICCON. I have spied it, in faith, sir, I
　　handled myself so well.
And yet the crafty quean had almost
　　take my trump.
But, or all came to an end, I set her in
　　a dump!
D. RAT. How so, I pray thee, Diccon?
DICCON.　　　　Marry, sir, will ye hear?
She was clapped down on the back side,[6]
　　by Cock's Mother dear,
And there she sat sewing a halter, or a band,
With no other thing save gammer's
　　needle in her hand.
As soon as any knock, if the filth be in
　　doubt,　　　　　　　　　　110
She needs but once puff, and her candle
　　is out.
Now I, sir, knowing of every door the pin,
Came nicely,[7] and said no word till
　　time I was within;
And there I saw the neele, even with
　　these two eyes.
Whoever say the contrary, I will swear
　　he lies!

[1] Worry, vexation.
[2] Avenge.
[3] Directly.
[4] Pot.
[5] Unaware.
[6] Seated in the back of the house.
[7] Stealthily.

D. Rat. O Diccon, that I was not there
   then in thy stead!
Diccon. Well, if ye will be ordered and
   do by my rede,
   I will bring you to a place, as the house
   stands,
   Where ye shall take the drab with the
   neele in her hands.
D. Rat. For God's sake, do so, Diccon,
   and I will gage [1] my gown   120
   To give thee a full pot of the best ale
   in the town!
Diccon. Follow me but a little, and mark
   what I will say.
   Lay down your gown beside you. [*Rat
   takes off his gown.*] Go to, come on
   your way!
   See ye not what is here? A hole wherein
   ye may creep
   Into the house, and suddenly unwares
   among them leap.
   There shall ye find the bitch fox and the
   neele together.
   Do as I bid you, man; come on your
   ways hether!
D. Rat. Art thou sure, Diccon, the swill-
   tub stands not hereabout?
Diccon. I was within myself, man, even
   now, there is no doubt.
   Go softly, make no noise. Give me your
   foot, Sir John! [2]   130
   Here will I wait upon you till you come
   out anon.
[*Rat climbs through the hole and is beaten.*]
D. Rat. Help, Diccon! Out, alas! I
   shall be slain among them!
Diccon. If they give you not the needle,
   tell them that ye will hang them.
   Ware that!—How, my wenches, have ye
   caught the fox
   That used to make revel among your
   hens and cocks?
   Save his life yet for his order, though he
   sustain some pain.—
   Gog's bread, I am afraid they will beat
   out his brain!   [*Exit Diccon.*

Enter Rat.]

D. Rat. Woe worth the hour that I came
   here!
   And woe worth him that wrought this
   gear!

[1] Pledge.   [2] Conventional name for a parson.

A sort of drabs and queans have me
   blessed! [3]   140
Was ever creature half so evil dressed?
Whoever it wrought and first did invent
   it,
He shall, I warrant him, ere long repent
   it!
I will spend all I have, without [4] my skin,
But he shall be brought to the plight I
   am in!
Master Baily, I trow, and he be worth his
   ears,
Will snaffle these murderers and all that
   them bears. [5]
I will surely neither bite nor sup
Till I fetch him hether, this matter to
   take up.   [*Exit.*]

The V Act. The i Scene.

*Master Bailey, [attended by Scapethrift,] Doc-
   tor Rat.*

Baily. I can perceive none other, I speak
   it from my heart,
   But either ye are in all the fault, or else
   in the greatest part.
D. Rat. If it be counted his fault, besides
   all his grieves, [6]
   When a poor man is spoiled and beaten
   among thieves,
   Then I confess my fault herein at this
   season;
   But I hope you will not judge so much
   against reason.
Baily. And methinks, by your own tale,
   of all that ye name,
   If any played the thief, you were the very
   same.
   The women they did nothing, as your
   words make probation,
   But stoutly withstood your forcible invasion.   10
   If that a thief at your window to enter
   should begin,
   Wold you hold forth your hand and help
   to pull him in?
   Or you wold keep him out? I pray you,
   answer me.
D. Rat. Marry, keep him out, and a good
   cause why!
   But I am no thief, sir, but an honest,
   learned clerk.

[3] Wounded.   [4] Except.
[5] Everybody that supports them.   [6] Griefs.

BAILY. Yea, but who knoweth that when
he meets you in the dark?
I am sure your learning shines not out at
your nose.
Was it any marvel though the poor
woman arose
And start up, being afraid of that was in
her purse?
Methink you may be glad that you[r]
luck was no worse. 20
D. RAT. Is not this evil enough, I pray
you, as you think?
Showing his broken head.
BAILY. Yea, but a man in the dark, if [1]
chances do wink,
As soon he smites his father as any other
man,
Because for lack of light discern him he
ne can.
Might it not have been your luck with a
spit to have been slain?
D. RAT. I think I am little better—my
scalp is cloven to the brain!
If there be all the remedy, I know who
bears the k[n]ocks.
BAILY. By my troth, and well worthy besides to kiss the stocks!
To come in on the back side, when ye
might go about!
I know none such, unless they long to
have their brains knocked out. 30
D. RAT. Well, will you be so good, sir, as
talk with Dame Chat,
And know what she intended? I ask no
more but that.
BAILY. [*To Scapethrift.*] Let her be
called, fellow, because of Master Doctor. [*Exit Scapethrift.*]
I warrant in this case she will be her own
proctor;
She will tell her own tale, in meter or in
prose,
And bid you seek your remedy, and so go
wipe your nose!

THE V ACT. THE ii SCENE.

*M[aster] Baily, Chat, [led in by Scapethrift,]
D[octor] Rat, Gammer, Hodge, Diccon.* [2]

BAILY. Dame Chat, Master Doctor upon
you here complained
That you and your maids shuld him
much misorder,

And taketh many an oath that no word
he feigned,
Laying to your charge how you thought
him to murder;
And, on his part again, that same man
saith furder
He never offended you in word nor in-
tent.
To hear you answer hereto, we have now
for you sent.
CHAT. That I wold have murdered him?
Fie on him, wretch!
And evil mought he thee [3] for it, our
Lord I beseech.
I will swear on all the books that opens
and shuts, 10
He feigneth this tale out of his own guts!
For this seven weeks with me, I am sure,
he sat not down.
Nay, ye have other minions, [4] in the other
end of the town,
Where ye were liker to catch such a blow
Than anywhere else, as far as I know!
BAILY. Belike then, Master Doctor, yon
stripe there ye got not?
D. RAT. Think you I am so mad that
where I was bet [5] I wot not?
Will ye believe this quean before she
hath tried [6] it?
It is not the first deed she hath done and
afterward denied it.
CHAT. What, man, will you say I broke
your head? 20
D. RAT. How canst thou prove the con-
trary?
CHAT. Nay, how provest thou that I did
the deed?
D. RAT. Too plainly, by S[aint] Mary!
This proof, I trow, may serve though I no
word spoke!
Showing his broken head.
CHAT. Because thy head is broken, was it
I that it broke?
I saw thee, Rat, I tell thee, not once
within this fortnight.
D. RAT. No, marry, thou sawest me not,
forwhy [7] thou hadst no light;
But I felt thee, for all the dark, beshrew
thy smooth cheeks!
And thou groped me—this will declare,
any day this six weeks.
Showing his head.

----

[1] Original reads *of*.　　[2] Last three enter later.
[3] Ill may he thrive.　　[5] Beaten.　　[7] Because.
[4] Darlings.　　[6] Proved.

BAILY. Answer me to this, M[aster] Rat:
when caught you this harm of yours? 30
D. RAT. A while ago, sir, God he know-
eth; within less than these two hours.
BAILY. Dame Chat, was there none with
you—confess, i'faith—about that season?
What, woman! Let it be what it will,
'tis neither felony nor treason.
CHAT. Yes, by my faith, Master Baily,
there was a knave not far
Who caught one good fillip on the brow
with a door bar,
And well was he worthy, as it seemed to
me.
But what is that to this man, since this
was not he?
BAILY. Who was it then? Let's hear!
D. RAT.   Alas, sir, ask you that?
Is it not made plain enough by the own
mouth of Dame Chat?
The time agreeth, my head is broken, her
tongue cannot lie;   40
Only upon a bare "nay" she saith it was
not I.
CHAT. No, marry, was it not, indeed. Ye
shall hear by this one thing:
This afternoon a friend of mine, for good
will, gave me warning,
And bade we [1] well look to my rust and
all my capons' pens,
For, if I took not better heed, a knave
wold have my hens.
Then I, to save my goods, took so much
pains as him to watch;
And, as good fortune served me, it was
my chance him for to catch.
What strokes he bare away, or other what
was his gains,
I wot not—but sure I am he had some-
thing for his pains!
BAILY. Yet tells thou not who it was.
CHAT.   Who it was? A false thief, 50
That came like a false fox my pullen [2] to
kill and mischief!
BAILY. But knowest thou not his name?
CHAT.   I know it. But what than? [3]
It was that crafty cullion,[4] Hodge, my
Gammer Gurton's man.

BAILY. Call me the knave hether.   He
shall sure kiss the stocks.
I shall teach him a lesson for filching hens
or cocks!   [Exit Scapethrift.]
D. RAT. I marvel, Master Baily, so
bleared be your eyes!
An egg is not so full of meat as she is full
of lies.
When she hath played this prank, to
excuse all this gear
She layeth the fault in such a one as I
know was not there.
CHAT. Was he not there?   Look on his
pate! That shall be his witness!   60
D. RAT. I wold my head were half so
whole, I wold seek no redress!

[Enter Gammer.]

BAILY. God bless you, Gammer Gurton!
GAMMER.   God dyld you,[5] master mine!
BAILY. Thou hast a knave within thy
house—Hodge, a servant of thine.
They tell me that busy knave is such a
filching one
That hen, pig, goose, or capon thy neigh-
bor can have none.
GAMMER. By God, cham much ameved [6]
to hear any such report!
Hodge was not wont, ich trow, to b'ave [7]
him in that sort.
CHAT. A thievisher knave is not on-live,
more filching nor more false!
Many a truer man than he has hanged up
by the hals.[8]
And thou, his dame, of all his theft thou
art the sole receiver.   70
For Hodge to catch and thou to keep, I
never knew none better.
GAMMER. Sir [9] reverence of your masterdom, and you were out-a-door,
Chold be so bold, for all her brags, to call
her arrant whore!
And ich knew Hodge so bad as tow,[10] ich
wish me endless sorrow
And chould not take the pains to hang
him up before tomorrow!
CHAT. What have I stolen from thee or
thine, thou ill-favored old trot?

---

[1] Me (?).
[2] Poultry.
[3] A common Elizabethan spelling of *then*, retained here for the rime.
[4] Rascal.

[5] God yield you; God reward you.
[6] Moved, disturbed.
[7] Behave.   [8] Neck.
[9] Probably a contraction of *save your*.
[10] Thou.

GAMMER. A great deal more, by God's
blessed,[1] than chever [2] by thee got!
That thou knowest well. I need not say it.

BAILY.   Stop there, I say!
And tell me here, I pray you, this matter
by the way:
How chance Hodge is not here? Him
wold [3] I fain have had.   80

GAMMER. Alas, sir, he'll be here anon; ha'
be handled too bad!

CHAT. Master Baily, sir, ye be not such a
fool, well I know,
But ye perceive by this lingering there
is a pad [4] in the straw.

*Thinking that Hodge his head was broke,
and that Gammer would not let him come
before them.*

GAMMER. Chill show you his face, ich warrant thee.—Lo now, where he is!

[*Enter Hodge, led in by Scapethrift.*]

BAILY. Come on, fellow! It is told me
thou art a shrew, iwis.[5]
Thy neighbors' hens thou takest, and
plays the two-legged fox;
Their chickens and their capons too, and
now and then their cocks.

HODGE. Ich defy them all that dare it say!
Cham as true as the best!

BAILY. Wart not thou take within this
hour in Dame Chat's hens' nest?

HODGE. Take there? No, master. Chold
not do't for a house full of gold! 90

CHAT. Thou, or the devil in thy coat!
Swear this, I dare be bold.

D. RAT. Swear me no swearing, quean!
The devil he give thee sorrow!
All is not worth a gnat thou canst swear
till tomorrow.
Where is the harm he hath? Show it, by
God's bread!
Ye beat him, with a witness, but the
stripes light on my head!

HODGE. Bet me? Gog's blessed body,
chold first, ich trow, have burst thee.
Ich think, and chad my hands loose, callet, should have crust [6] thee!

CHAT. Thou shitten knave, I trow thou
knowest the full weight of my fist!
I am foully deceived unless thy head and
my door bar kissed!

HODGE. Hold thy chat, whore! Thou
criest so loud, can no man else be
hard.   100

CHAT. Well, knave, and I had thee alone, I
wold surely rap thy costard! [7]

BAILY. Sir, answer me to this: is thy head
whole or broken?

CHAT. Yea, Master Baily, blessed be every
good token!

HODGE. Is my head whole? Ich warrant
you 'tis neither scurvy nor scald!
What, you foul beast, does think 'tis
either pilled [8] or bald?
Nay, ich thank God, chill not, for all that
thou mayst spend,
That chad one scab on my narse as
broad as thy finger's end.

BAILY. Come nearer here!

HODGE.   Yes, that ich dare.

BAILY. [*Examining Hodge's head.*] By our
Lady, here is no harm.
Hodge's head is whole enough, for all
Dame Chat's charm.[9]

CHAT. By Gog's blessed, however the
thing he clocks or smolders,[10]   110
I know the blows he bare away either
with head or shoulders.
Camest thou not, knave, within this
hour creeping into my pens,
And there was caught within my house
groping among my hens?

HODGE. A plague both on thy hens and
thee! A cart, whore, a cart!
Chould I were hanged as high as a tree
and chware as false as thou art!
Give my gammer again her washical [11]
thou stole away in thy lap!

GAMMER. Yea, Master Baily, there is a
thing you know not, mayhap:
This drab she keeps away my good—the
devil he might her snare!
Ich pray you that ich might have a right
action on her.

CHAT. Have I thy good, old filth, or any
such, old sows? [12]   120
I am as true, I wold thou knew, as skin
between thy brows!

GAMMER. Many a truer hath been hanged,
though you escape the danger!

CHAT. Thou shalt answer, by God's pity,
for this thy foul slander!

---

[1] *Cf.* l. 96.   [2] I ever.   [3] Original reads *wole.*
[4] Toad; a proverbial term for something hid-
den.   [5] Indeed.   [6] Crushed.

[7] Apple, head.   [10] Cloaks or smothers.
[8] Peeled, shorn.   [11] What-you-call-it.
[9] Chatter.   [12] Souse (?).

BAILY. Why, what can ye charge her
    withal? To say so, ye do not well.
GAMMER. Marry, a vengeance to her heart,
    that whore has stolen my neele!
CHAT. Thy needle, old witch? How so?
    It were alms thy skull to knock!
  So didst thou say the other day that I
    had stolen thy cock,
  And roasted him to my breakfast—which
    shall not be forgotten.
  The devil pull out thy lying tongue and
    teeth that be so rotten!
GAMMER. Give me my neele! As for my
    Cock, chould be very loath   130
  That chuld hear tell he shuld hang on
    thy false faith and troth.
BAILY. Your talk is such I can scarce
    learn who shuld be most in fault.
GAMMER. Yet shall ye find no other wight
    save she, by bread and salt!
BAILY. Keep ye content awhile; see that
    your tongues ye hold;
  Methinks you shuld remember this is
    no place to scold.
  How knowest thou, Gammer Gurton,
    Dame Chat thy needle had?
GAMMER. To name you, sir, the party,
    chould not be very glad.
BAILY. Yea, but we must needs hear it,
    and therefore say it boldly.
GAMMER. Such one as told the tale full
    soberly and coldly;
  Even he that looked on—will swear on
    a book—   140
  What time this drunken gossip my fair
    long neele up took:
  Diccon, master, the bedlam. Cham very
    sure ye know him.
BAILY. A false knave, by God's pity! Ye
    were but a fool to trow [1] him.
  I durst aventure well the price of my
    best cap
  That when the end is known all will
    turn to a jape.[2]
  Told he not you that, besides, she stole
    your cock that tide?[3]
GAMMER. No, master, no, indeed; for then
    he shuld have lied!
  My cock is, I thank Christ, safe and well,
    a-fine.[4]
CHAT. Yea, but that ragged colt, that
    whore, that Tib of thine,

Said plainly thy cock was stolen and in
    my house was eaten.   150
That lying cut is lost that she is not
    swinged and beaten,
And yet for all my good name it were a
    small amends!
I pick not this gear, hear'st thou, out of
    my fingers' ends;
But he that hard it told me, who thou
    of late didst name:
Diccon, whom all men knows; it was
    the very same.
BAILY. This is the case: you lost your
    needle about the doors,
  And she answers again she has no cock
    of yours;
  Thus, in your talk and action, from that
    you do intend
  She is whole five mile wide from that
    she doth defend.[5]
  Will you say she hath your cock?
GAMMER.   No, marry, sir, that chill
    not!   160
BAILY. Will you confess her neele?
CHAT.   Will I? No, sir, will I not![6]
BAILY. Then there lieth all the matter.
GAMMER.   Soft, master, by the way!
  Ye know she could do little and she cold
    not say nay.
BAILY. Yea, but he that made one lie
    about your cock-stealing,
  Will not stick to make another what
    time lies be in dealing.
  I ween the end will prove this brawl did
    first arise
  Upon no other ground but only Diccon's
    lies.
CHAT. Though some be lies, as you belike
    have espied them,
  Yet other some be true—by proof I
    have well tried them.
BAILY. What other thing beside this,
    Dame Chat?
CHAT.   Marry, sir, even this: 170
  The tale I told before, the selfsame
    tale it was his;
  He gave me, like a friend, warning
    against my loss,
  Else had my hens be stolen, each one,
    by God's Cross!
  He told me Hodge wold come, and in he
    came indeed;

---

[1] Believe, trust.
[2] Jest.
[3] Time.
[4] Finally.
[5] Deny.
[6] Rime would require "I will not."

But, as the matter chanced, with greater
  haste than speed.
This truth was said, and true was found,
  as truly I report.
BAILY. If Doctor Rat be not deceived, it
  was of another sort.
D. RAT. By God's Mother, thou and he
  be a couple of subtle foxes!
Between you and Hodge I bear away
  the boxes.[1]
Did not Diccon appoint the place where
  thou shuldst stand to meet him?   180
CHAT. Yes, by the Mass; and, if he came,
  bade me not stick to speet[2] him.
D. RAT. God's sacrament, the villain
  knave hath dressed us round about!
He is the cause of all this brawl, that
  dirty, shitten lout!
When Gammer Gurton here complained,
  and made a rueful moan,
I heard him swear that you had gotten
  her needle that was gone;
And this to try, he furder said, he was
  full loath; howbeit
He was content, with small ado, to
  bring me where to see it.
And where ye sat, he said full certain,
  if I wold follow his rede,
Into your house a privy way he wold me
  guide and lead,
And where ye had it in your hands,
  sewing about a clout;   190
And set me in the back hole, thereby to
  find you out.
And, whiles I sought a quietness, creep-
  ing upon my knees,
I found the weight of your door bar for
  my reward and fees.
Such is the luck that some men gets
  while they begin to mell[3]
In setting at one such as were out,
  minding to make all well.
HODGE. Was not well blessed, gammer, to
  scape that scour?[4] And chad been
  there,
Then chad been dressed, belike, as ill,
  by the Mass, as Gaffer Vicar.
BAILY. Marry, sir, here is a sport alone.
  I looked for such an end.
If Diccon had not played the knave,
  this had been soon amend.

My gammer here he made a fool, and
  dressed her as she was;   200
And Goodwife Chat he set to scole,[5]
  till both parts cried "alas";
And D[octor] Rat was not behind, whiles
  Chat his crown did pare;
I wold the knave had been stark blind,
  if Hodge had not his share!
HODGE. Cham meetly well sped already
  amongs; cham dressed like a colt!
And chad not had the better wit, chad
  been made a dolt.
BAILY. [To Scapethrift.] Sir knave, make
  haste Diccon were here; fetch him
  wherever he be!   [Exit Scapethrift.]
CHAT. Fie on the villain, fie, fie, that
  makes us thus agree!
GAMMER. Fie on him, knave, with all my
  heart! Now fie! and fie again!
D. RAT. "Now fie on him!" may I best
  say, whom he hath almost slain.

[Enter Diccon, led in by Scapethrift.]

BAILY. Lo, where he cometh at hand.
  Belike he was not far!   210
Diccon, here be two or three thy com-
  pany cannot spare.
DICCON. God bless you—and you may
  be blessed, so many all at once!
CHAT. Come, knave, it were a good deed
  to geld thee, by Cock's bones!
Seest not thy handiwark? Sir Rat, can
  ye forbear[6] him?
        [Doctor Rat strikes Diccon.]
DICCON. A vengeance on those hands
  light, for my hands came not near
  him!
The whoreson priest hath lift the pot[7]
  in some of these alewives' chairs
That his head wold not serve him, belike, to come down the stairs.
BAILY. Nay, soft! Thou mayst not play
  the knave and have this language
  too!
If thou thy tongue bridle awhile, the
  better mayst thou do.
Confess the truth, as I shall ask, and
  cease awhile to fable;   220
And for thy fault, I promise thee, thy
  handling shall be reasonable.
Hast thou not made a lie or two to set
  these two by the ears?

---

[1] Blows.
[2] Spit, *i.e.*, beat with a spit.
[3] Meddle.   [4] Scouring, beating.
[5] School.   [6] Tolerate, spare.   [7] Tankard.

Diccon. What if I have? Five hundred
  such have I seen within these seven
  years.
I am sorry for nothing else but that I
  see not the sport
Which was between them when they
  met, as they themselves report.
Baily. The greatest thing—Master Rat!
  Ye see how he is dressed!
Diccon. What devil need he be groping
  so deep in Goodwife Chat's hens'
  nest?
Baily. Yea, but it was thy drift to bring
  him into the briers.
Diccon. God's bread! hath not such an
  old fool wit to save his ears?
He showeth himself herein, ye see, so
  very a cox [1]   230
The cat was not so madly allured by the
  fox
To run into the snares was set for him,
  doubtless;
For he leaped in for mice, and this Sir
  John for madness.
D. Rat. Well, and ye shift no better, ye
  losel, lither [2] and lazy,
I will go near, for this, to make ye leap
  at a daisy. [3]
In the king's name, Master Baily, I
  charge you set him fast!
Diccon. What, fast at cards, or fast on
  sleep? It is the thing I did last.
D. Rat. Nay, fast in fetters, false varlet,
  according to thy deeds!
Baily. Master Doctor, there is no remedy;
  I must entreat you, needs,
Some other kind of punishment.
D. Rat.   Nay, by All Hallows,   240
His punishment, if I may judge, shall
  be naught else but the gallows.
Baily. That were too sore. A spiritual
  man to be so extreme!
D. Rat. Is he worthy any better, sir?
  How do ye judge and deem?
Baily. I grant him worthy punishment,
  but in no wise so great.
Gammer. It is a shame, ich tell you plain,
  for such false knaves entreat!
He has almost undone us all; that is as
  true as steel.
And yet for all this great ado cham
  never the near my neele!

Baily. Canst thou not say anything to
  that, Diccon, with least or most?
Diccon. Yea, marry, sir, thus much I
  can say well: the needle is lost!
Baily. Nay, canst not thou tell which
  way that needle may be found?   250
Diccon. No, by my fay, sir, though I
  might have an hundred pound.
Hodge. Thou liar, lickdish, [4] didst not say
  the neele wold be gitten? [5]
Diccon. No, Hodge, by the same token
  you were [6] that time beshitten
For fear of Hobgobling—you wot well
  what I mean;
As long as it is sence, [7] I fear me yet ye
  be scarce clean.
Baily. Well, Master Rat, you must both
  learn and teach us to forgeve. [8]
Since Diccon hath confession made and
  is so clean shreve, [9]
If ye to me consent, to amend this heavy
  chance
I will enjoin him here some open kind of
  penance,
Of this condition. Where ye know my
  fee is twenty pence   260
For the bloodshed, [10] I am agreed with
  you here to dispense.
Ye shall go quite, [11] so that ye grant the
  matter now to run
To end with mirth among us all, even
  as it was begun.
Chat. Say yea, Master Vicar, and he shall
  sure confess to be your debtor,
And all we that be here present will
  love you much the better.
D. Rat. My part is the worst; but, since
  you all hereon agree,
Go even to, [12] Master Baily—let it be so
  for me!
Baily. How sayest thou, Diccon? Art
  content this shall on me depend?
Diccon. Go to, M[aster] Baily, say on
  your mind. I know ye are my friend.
Baily. Then mark ye well to recompense this thy former action,   270
Because thou hast offended all, to make
  them satisfaction,

---

[1] Fool.   [2] Worthless, idle.   [3] *I.e.*, be hanged.

[4] Scullion.   [5] Gotten.
[6] Dodsley's reading. Original reads *where*.
[7] Since, past.
[8] Forgive; a common spelling retained here for
the rime.   [11] Quit, free.
[9] Shriven.   [12] Go ahead then.
[10] Case involving violence.

Before their faces here kneel down, and
as [1] I shall thee teach.

For thou shalt take an [2] oath of Hodge's
leather breech:

First, for Master Doctor, upon pain of
his curse,

Where he will pay for all, thou never
draw thy purse,

And when ye meet at one pot, he shall
have the first pull,

And thou shalt never offer him the cup
but it be full;

To Goodwife Chat thou shalt be sworn,
even on the same wise,

If she refuse thy money once, never to
offer it twice;

Thou shalt be bound by the same, here
as thou dost take it,   280

When thou mayst drink of free cost,
thou never forsake it;

For Gammer Gurton's sake, again sworn
shalt thou be,

To help her to her needle again, if it do
lie in thee;

And likewise be bound, by the virtue of
that,

To be of good abearing [3] to Gib, her
great cat;

Last of all, for Hodge, the oath to scan,

Thou shalt never take him for fine
gentleman.

HODGE. [*Stooping over.*] Come on, fellow
Diccon! Chall be even with thee now!

BAILY. Thou wilt not stick to do this,
Diccon, I trow?

DICCON. No, by my father's skin; my
hand down I lay it!   290

Look! As I have promised, I will not
denay [4] it.

But, Hodge, take good heed now thou
do not beshit me!

And gave him a good blow on the buttock.

HODGE. Gog's heart! Thou false villain,
dost thou bite me?

BAILY. What, Hodge, doth he hurt thee
or ever he begin?

HODGE. He thrust me into the buttock
with a bodkin or a pin!

           [*He draws out the needle.*]

I say, gammer! gammer!

GAMMER.   How now, Hodge? How
now?

HODGE. God's malt, Gammer Gurton!

GAMMER.   Thou art mad, ich trow!

HODGE. Will you see the devil, gammer?

GAMMER.   The devil, son? God
bless us!

HODGE. Chould ich were hanged, gammer!

GAMMER.   Marry, see, ye might
dress us—

HODGE. Chave it, by the Mass, gammer!

GAMMER.   What, not my neele,
Hodge?   300

HODGE. Your neele, gammer, your neele!

GAMMER.   No, fie, dost but dodge! [5]

HODGE. Cha' found your neele, gammer!
Here in my hand be it!

GAMMER. For all the loves on earth,
Hodge, let me see it!

HODGE. Soft, gammer!

GAMMER.   Good Hodge!

HODGE.   Soft, ich say; tarry awhile!

GAMMER. Nay, sweet Hodge, say truth,
and do not me beguile!

HODGE. Cham sure on it, ich warrant
you it goes no more astray.

GAMMER. Hodge, when I speak so fair,
wilt still say me nay?

HODGE. Go near the light, gammer.
This—well, in faith, good luck!—
Chwas almost undone, 'twas so far in
my buttock!

GAMMER. 'Tis mine own dear neele,
Hodge. sikerly [6] I wot!   310

HODGE. Cham I not a good son, gammer, cham I not?

GAMMER. Christ's blessing light on thee!
Hast made me forever!

HODGE. Ich knew that ich must find it,
else choud 'a' [7] had it never!

CHAT. By my troth, Gossip Gurton, I
am even as glad

As though I mine own self as good a
turn had!

BAILY. And I, by my conscience, to see
it so come forth,

Rejoice so much at it as three needles
be worth!

D. RAT. I am no whit sorry to see you
so rejoice!

---

[1] In the manner that.
[2] Dodsley's reading. Original reads *on.*
[3] Bearing, behavior.
[4] Deny.

[5] Trick me.   [7] I would have.
[6] Truly.

DICCON. Nor I much the gladder for all this noise!
Yet say, "Gramercy, Diccon," for springing of the game. 320
GAMMER. Gramercy, Diccon, twenty times! O, how glad cham!
If that chould do so much, your masterdom to come hether,
Master Rat, Goodwife Chat, and Diccon, together—
Cha' but one halfpenny, as far as ich know it,
And chill not rest this night till ich bestow it.
If ever ye love me, let us go in and drink!

BAILY. I am content, if the rest think as I think.
Master Rat, it shall be best for you if we so do;
Then shall you warm you and dress yourself too.
DICCON. Soft, sirs, take us with you; the company shall be the more! 330
As proud comes behind, they say, as any goes before!— [*Addresses the audience.*]
But now, my good masters, since we must be gone
And leave you behind us here, all alone—
Since at our last ending thus merry we be,
For Gammer Gurton's needle sake let us have a plaudity!

FINIS, GURTON. PERUSED AND ALLOWED, ETC.

THOMAS NORTON AND THOMAS SACKVILLE

The Tragedy of Gorboduc, historically significant as the first regular English tragedy and the first English play to be written in blank verse, was acted by the gentlemen of the Inner Temple during their Christmas festival in 1561/2 and again before Queen Elizabeth at Whitehall Palace, January 18, 1561/2. It was surreptitiously printed by William Griffith in 1565, but an authorized edition was issued by John Day in 1570. In 1590 Edward Allde published a reprint of the edition of 1565. The title-page of the edition of 1565 informs us that three acts were by Thomas Norton and the last two by Thomas Sackville.

Thomas Norton, born in 1532, probably attended Cambridge University, was admitted to the Inner Temple in 1555, became a successful lawyer, and served as a member of parliament in 1571, 1572, and 1580. Much of his time was devoted to literature, however. He wrote Latin and English poetry, including versions of twenty-eight Psalms printed in the Psalter of Sternhold and Hopkins. He produced a number of controversial pamphlets against the Catholics and a political tract on a Catholic rebellion under Elizabeth which has some interest in view of the theme of *Gorboduc*. He also translated various works, among them Calvin's *Institution of Christian Religion*. In spite of his share in *Gorboduc*, his Puritan connection led him in later years to open hostility toward the stage. He died in 1584.

Thomas Sackville, born in 1536, was a son of Sir Richard Sackville, a first cousin to Anne Boleyn, mother of Queen Elizabeth. Nothing is known of his academic career. In 1563 he contributed to *The Mirror for Magistrates* his well known "Induction" and "The Complaint of Henry Duke of Buckingham," which gave promise of a brilliant literary future. But he soon forsook literature for a political career. After an extensive tour of Europe he was called home in 1566 by his father's death to become heir to a vast estate. He became a special favorite of the queen and was rapidly advanced to a distinguished career of public service. He was knighted and raised to the peerage June 8, 1567, served later on various diplomatic missions, was elected in 1591 to the chancellorship of the University of Oxford, and in 1603 became a member of the privy council and was made lord treasurer for life. In 1604 he was created Earl of Dorset. He died at the council table at Whitehall, April 19, 1608.

For the main elements of the story the authors follow the account of King Gorboduc in Geoffrey of Monmouth's *Historia Regum Britanniæ*, although their immediate source may have been Grafton's *Chronicle* (1556), which follows Geoffrey's version closely. For their dramatic model they chose the Senecan tragedy, a fact which accounts for the division into five acts, the general rhetorical quality of the style with emphasis on balance of structure, the sententious moralizing, the use of the chorus at the end of each act, and the exclusion of violence from the stage by having it announced by a messenger (*Nuntius*). It is noteworthy, however, that the authors drew their story from English legendary history and that they departed from precedent in disregarding the unities of time and place. Italian adaptations of Seneca may have suggested the use of blank verse, and the *intermedii* (allegorical representations between the acts) in Italian tragedy may have furnished the idea of the dumb show, but blank verse had already appeared in Surrey's translation of the *Æneid*, published in 1557, and the dumb show may have been a native development.

Sackville and Norton, both of them prominent members of Queen Elizabeth's first parliament, were keenly interested in the problem of providing for her successor, and they made this tragic story from the apocryphal history of England the vehicle for a special warning to her of the dangers of civil war in its most terrible aspects if she died without definite provision for the succession (see particularly Act V).   The warning is set, however, in a general body of political discussion which reflects ideas common in classical and humanistic treatises.   Senecan tragedy, didactic in its nature, readily lent itself to this type of moralizing.

The text of the play is based on the second edition, that of 1570, as reprinted by J. W. Cunliffe in his *Early Classical Tragedies* (Oxford, 1912).

THE TRAGEDY OF [GORBODUC; OR OF][1] FERREX AND PORREX[2]

BY

THOMAS NORTON AND THOMAS SACKVILLE

THE P[RINTER] TO THE READER

Where this tragedy was for furniture of part of the grand Christmas in the Inner Temple first written about nine years ago by the Right Honorable Thomas, now Lord Buckhurst, and by T. Norton, and after showed before her majesty, and never intended by the authors thereof to be published; yet one W. G., getting a copy thereof at some young man's hand that lacked a little money and much discretion, in [10 the last great plague, an[no] 1565, about five years past, while the said lord was out of England, and T. Norton far out of London, and neither of them both made privy, put it forth exceedingly corrupted—even as if by means of a broker, for hire, he should have enticed into his house a fair maid and done her villainy, and after all-to[3] bescratched her face, torn her apparel, bewrayed and disfigured her, and then [20 thrust her out of doors dishonested. In such plight, after long wandering, she came at length home to the sight of her friends, who scant knew her but by a few tokens and marks remaining. They—the authors, I mean—though they were very much displeased that she so ran abroad without leave, whereby she caught her shame, as many wantons do, yet seeing the case, as it is, remediless, have for common hon- [30 esty and shamefastness new appareled, trimmed, and attired her in such form as she was before. In which better form since she hath come to me, I have harbored her for her friends' sake and her own; and I do not doubt her parents, the authors, will not now be discontent that she go abroad among you, good readers, so it be in honest company. For she is by my encouragement and others' somewhat less ashamed of [40 the dishonesty done to her, because it was by fraud and force. If she be welcome among you, and gently entertained, in favor of the house from whence she is descended and of her own nature courteously disposed to offend no man, her friends will thank you for it. If not, but that she shall be still reproached with her former mishap, or quarreled at by envious persons, she, poor gentlewoman, will surely play [50 Lucrece's part, and of herself die for shame; and I shall wish that she had tarried still at home with me, where she was welcome, for she did never put me to more charge but this one poor black gown lined with white that I have now given her to go abroad among you withal.

THE ARGUMENT OF THE TRAGEDY [4]

Gorboduc, King of Britain, divided his realm in his lifetime to his sons, Ferrex and Porrex. The sons fell to dissension. The younger killed the elder. The mother, that more dearly loved the elder, for revenge killed the younger. The people, moved with the cruelty of the fact,[5] rose

[1] Added by Adams. The title of the 1565 edn. runs: "The Tragedy of Gorboduc, Whereof Three Acts Were Written by Thomas Norton, and the Two Last by Thomas Sackville."
[2] The title continues: "Set Forth without Addition or Alteration but Altogether As the Same Was Showed on Stage before the Queen's Majesty, about Nine Years Past, viz., the xviii Day of January, 1561. By the Gentlemen of the Inner Temple. Seen and Allowed, etc."
[3] Thoroughly.
[4] In the original this argument, or synopsis of plot, is printed on the back of the title-page.
[5] Deed.

in rebellion and slew both father and mother. The nobility assembled and most terribly destroyed the rebels. And [10 afterwards, for want of issue of the prince, whereby the succession of the crown became uncertain, they fell to civil war, in which both they and many of their issues were slain, and the land for a long time almost desolate and miserably wasted.

THE NAMES OF THE SPEAKERS

GORBODUC, *King of Great Britain.*
VIDENA, *queen and wife to King Gorboduc.*
FERREX, *elder son to King Gorboduc.*
PORREX, *younger son to King Gorboduc.*
CLOTYN, *Duke of Cornwall.*
FERGUS, *Duke of Albany.*
MANDUD, *Duke of Logris.*
GWENARD, *Duke of Cumberland.*
EUBULUS, *secretary to the king.*
AROSTUS, *a counselor to the king.*
DORDAN, *a counselor assigned by the king to his eldest son, Ferrex.*

PHILANDER, *a counselor assigned by the king to his youngest son, Porrex. Both being of the old king's counsel before.*
HERMON, *a parasite remaining with Ferrex.*
TYNDAR, *a parasite remaining with Porrex.*
NUNTIUS, *a messenger of the elder brother's death.*
NUNTIUS, *a messenger of Duke Fergus' rising in arms.*
MARCELLA, *a lady of the queen's privy-chamber.*
CHORUS, *four ancient and sage men of Britain.*

[SCENE: *Britain.*

TIME: *Legendary.*]

THE ORDER OF THE DUMB SHOW BEFORE THE FIRST ACT, AND THE SIGNIFICATION THEREOF

First, the music of violins began to play, during which came in upon the stage six wild men, clothed in leaves. Of whom the first bare in his neck a fagot of small sticks, which they all, both severally and together, assayed with all their strength to break; but it could not be broken by them. At the length one of them pulled out one of the sticks and brake it, and the rest, plucking out all the other sticks one after another, did easily break them, the same being severed which, being conjoined, they had before attempted in vain. After they had this done, they departed the stage, and the music ceased. Hereby was signified that a state knit in unity doth continue strong against all force, but, being divided, is easily destroyed; as befell upon Duke Gorboduc dividing his land to his two sons, which he before held in monarchy, and upon the dissension of the brethren, to whom it was divided.

ACTUS PRIMUS. SCENA PRIMA.

[*A room in Gorboduc's palace.*]

Viden[a], Ferrex.

VID. The silent night, that brings the quiet pause
From painful travails of the weary day,
Prolongs my careful [1] thoughts, and makes me blame
The slow Aurore, that so for love or shame
Doth long delay to show her blushing face;
And now the day renews my griefful plaint.
FER. My gracious lady and my mother dear,
Pardon my grief for your so grievéd mind
To ask what cause tormenteth so your heart.
VID. So great a wrong and so unjust despite,   10
Without all cause against all course of kind! [2]

[1] Full of care.
[2] Nature.

FER. Such causeless wrong and so unjust despite
May have redress or, at the least, revenge.
VID. Neither, my son; such is the froward will,
The person such, such my mishap and thine.
FER. Mine know I none, but grief for your distress.
VID. Yes, mine for thine, my son.   A father? No.
In kind a father, not in kindliness.
FER. My father? Why, I know nothing at all
Wherein I have misdone unto his grace.   20
VID. Therefore, the more unkind to thee and me.
For, knowing well, my son, the tender love
That I have ever borne and bear to thee,
He, grieved thereat, is not content alone
To spoil thee of my sight, my chiefest joy;
But thee, of thy birthright and heritage,
Causeless, unkindly, and in wrongful wise,
Against all law and right, he will bereave:
Half of his kingdom he will give away.
FER. To whom?
VID.   Even to Porrex, his younger son; 30
Whose growing pride I do so sore suspect
That, being raised to equal rule with thee,
Methinks I see his envious heart to swell,
Filled with disdain and with ambitious hope.
The end the gods do know, whose altars I
Full oft have made in vain of cattle slain
To send the sacred smoke to heaven's throne,
For thee, my son, if things do so succeed,
As now my jealous mind misdeemeth sore.
FER. Madam, leave care and careful plaint for me.   40
Just hath my father been to every wight;
His first unjustice he will not extend
To me, I trust, that give no cause thereof;
My brother's pride shall hurt himself, not me.
VID. So grant the gods! But yet thy father so

Hath firmly fixéd his unmovéd mind
That plaints and prayers can no whit avail;
For those have I assayed, but even this day
He will endeavor to procure assent
Of all his council to his fond devise.[1] 50
FER. Their ancestors from race to race [2] have borne
True faith to my forefathers and their seed;
I trust they eke will bear the like to me.
VID. There resteth all. But if they fail thereof,
And if the end bring forth an ill success,
On them and theirs the mischief shall befall,
And so I pray the gods requite it them;
And so they will, for so is wont to be.
When lords and trusted rulers under kings,
To please the present fancy of the prince,   60
With wrong transpose the course of governance,
Murders, mischief, or civil sword at length,
Or mutual treason, or a just revenge,
When right succeeding line returns again,
By Jove's just judgment and deservéd wrath,
Brings them to cruel and reproachful death,
And roots their names and kindreds from the earth.
FER. Mother, content you, you shall see the end.
VID. The end? Thy end, I fear! Jove end me first!   [Exeunt.]

ACTUS PRIMUS. SCENA SECUNDA.

[The council chamber in Gorboduc's palace.]

Gorboduc, Arostus, Philander, Eubulus.

GORB. My lords, whose grave advice and faithful aid
Have long upheld my honor and my realm,
And brought me to this age from tender years,
Guiding so great estate with great renowm,

---

[1] Foolish design.
[2] From generation to generation.

Now more importeth me [1] than erst [2] to
   use
Your faith and wisdom, whereby yet I
   reign;
That, when by death my life and rule
   shall cease,
The kingdom yet may with unbroken
   course
Have certain prince, by whose undoubted
   right
Your wealth and peace may stand in
   quiet stay;   10
And eke that they whom nature hath
   prepared
In time to take my place in princely
   seat,
While in their father's time their pliant
   youth
Yields to the frame of skillful governance,
May so be taught and trained in noble
   arts
As what their fathers, which have
   reigned before,
Have with great fame derivéd down to
   them,
With honor they may leave unto their
   seed;
And not be thought, for their unworthy
   life,
And for their lawless swerving out of
   kind,   20
Worthy to lose what law and kind them
   gave;
But that they may preserve the common
   peace,
The cause that first began and still main-
   tains
The lineal course of kings' inheritance,
For me, for mine, for you, and for the
   state
Whereof both I and you have charge and
   care.
Thus do I mean to use your wonted faith
To me and mine and to your native land.
My lords, be plain without all wry [3] re-
   spect
Or poisonous craft to speak in pleasing
   wise,   30
Lest, as the blame of ill-succeeding things
Shall light on you, so light the harms
   also.

Aros. Your good acceptance so, most
   noble king,
Of such our faithfulness as heretofore
We have employed in duties to your
   grace
And to this realm, whose worthy head
   you are,
Well proves that neither you mistrust
   at all,
Nor we shall need in boasting wise to
   show
Our truth to you, nor yet our wakeful
   care
For you, for yours, and for our native
   land.   40
Wherefore, O king—I speak as one for all,
Sith [4] all as one do bear you egal [5] faith—
Doubt not to use our counsels and our
   aids,
Whose honors, goods, and lives are whole
   avowed
To serve, to aid, and to defend your
   grace.
Gorb. My lords, I thank you all. This is
   the case:
Ye know, the gods, who have the sov-
   ereign care
For kings, for kingdoms, and for com-
   monweals,
Gave me two sons in my more lusty age,
Who now in my decaying years are
   grown   50
Well towards riper state of mind and
   strength
To take in hand some greater princely
   charge.
As yet they live and spend [their] [6] hope-
   ful days
With me and with their mother here in
   court.
Their age now asketh other place and
   trade,
And mine also doth ask another change—
Theirs to more travail, mine to greater
   ease.
When fatal death shall end my mortal
   life,
My purpose is to leave unto them twain
The realm divided into two sundry
   parts: 60
The one, Ferrex, mine elder son, shall
   have;

[1] It is more important for me.
[2] Formerly.   [3] Twisted, dissembled.
[4] Since.   [5] Equal.   [6] From 1565 edn.

The other shall the younger, Porrex, rule.
That both my purpose may more firmly
  stand,
And eke that they may better rule their
  charge,
I mean forthwith to place them in the
  same,
That in my life they may both learn to
  rule,
And I may joy to see their ruling well.
This is, in sum, what I would have ye
  weigh:
First, whether ye allow my whole devise,
And think it good for me, for them, for
  you,   70
And for our country, mother of us all;
And if ye like it and allow it well,
Then for their guiding and their gov-
  ernance
Show forth such means of circumstance
As ye think meet to be both known and
  kept.
Lo, this is all. Now tell me your advice.
AROS. And this is much, and asketh great
  advice.
But for my part, my sovereign lord and
  king,
This do I think: your majesty doth know
How under you, in justice and in
  peace,   80
Great wealth and honor long we have
  enjoyed,
So as we cannot seem with greedy minds
To wish for change of prince or gov-
  ernance;
But, if we like your purpose and devise,
Our liking must be deeméd to proceed
Of rightful reason and of heedful care,
Not for ourselves, but for the common
  state,
Sith our own state doth need no better
  change.
I think in all as erst your grace hath
  said.
First, when you shall unload your aged
  mind   90
Of heavy care and troubles manifold,
And lay the same upon my lords, your
  sons,
Whose growing years may bear the bur-
  den long—
And long I pray the gods to grant it
  so!—
And in your life, while you shall so behold

Their rule, their virtues, and their noble
  deeds,
Such as their kind behighteth [1] to us all,
Great be the profits that shall grow
  thereof.
Your age in quiet shall the longer last;
Your lasting age shall be their longer
  stay;   100
For cares of kings that rule as you have
  ruled,
For public wealth and not for private joy,
Do waste man's life and hasten crooked
  age,
With furrowed face and with enfeebled
  limbs,
To draw on creeping death a swifter pace.
They two, yet young, shall bear the
  parted reign
With greater ease than one, now old,
  alone
Can wield the whole, for whom much
  harder is
With lessened strength the double weight
  to bear.
Your eye, your counsel, and the grave
  regard   110
Of father, yea, of such a father's name,
Now at beginning of their sundered reign,
When is the hazard of their whole success,
Shall bridle so their force of youthful
  heats
And so restrain the rage of insolence,
Which most assails the young and noble
  minds,
And so shall guide and train in tempered
  stay
Their yet green bending wits with rev-
  erend awe,
As—now inured with virtues at the
  first—
Custom, O king, shall bring delightful-
  ness.   120
By use of virtue, vice shall grow in hate.
But, if you so dispose it that the day
Which ends your life shall first begin
  their reign,
Great is the peril what will be the end,
When such beginning of such liberties,
Void of such stays as in your life do lie,
Shall leave them free to randon [2] of their
  will,
An open prey to traitorous flattery,
The greatest pestilence of noble youth;

[1] Promises.   [2] Random. rove.

Which peril shall be past if, in your
    life,   130
Their tempered youth with aged father's
    awe
Be brought in ure [1] of skillful stayédness;
And, in your life, their lives disposéd so
Shall length your noble life in joyfulness.
Thus think I that your grace hath wisely
    thought,
And that your tender care of common
    weal [2]
Hath bred this thought, so to divide
    your land,
And plant your sons to bear the present
    rule,
While you yet live to see their ruling well,
That you may longer live by joy
    therein.   140
What furder [3] means behooveful are and
    meet;
At greater leisure may your grace devise,
When all have said, and when we be
    agreed
If this be best, to part the realm in twain,
And place your sons in present govern-
    ment;
Whereof, as I have plainly said my mind,
So would I hear the rest of all my lords.
PHIL. In part I think as hath been said
    before;
In part, again, my mind is otherwise.
As for dividing of this realm in twain, 150
And lotting out the same in egal parts
To either of my lords, your grace's sons,
That think I best for this your realm's
    behoof,
For profit and advancement of your sons,
And for your comfort and your honor eke.
But so to place them while your life do
    last,
To yield to them your royal governance,
To be above them only in the name
Of father, not in kingly state also,
I think not good for you, for them, nor
    us.   160
This kingdom, since the bloody civil field
Where Morgan slain did yield his con-
    quered part
Unto his cousin's sword in Camberland,
Containeth all that whilom [4] did suffice
Three noble sons of your forefather
    Brute;

So your two sons it may suffice also.
The mo [5] the stronger, if they gree [6] in
    one.
The smaller compass that the realm doth
    hold,
The easier is the sway thereof to weld,[7]
The nearer justice to the wrongéd
    poor,   170
The smaller charge, and yet enough for
    one.
And when the region is divided so
That brethren be the lords of either part,
Such strength doth nature knit between
    them both,
In sundry bodies by conjoinéd love,
That, not as two, but one of doubled
    force,
Each is to other as a sure defense;
The nobleness and glory of the one
Doth sharp the courage of the other's
    mind,
With virtuous envy to contend for
    praise.   180
And such an egalness hath nature made
Between the brethren of one father's
    seed
As an unkindly wrong it seems to be
To throw the brother subject under feet
Of him whose peer he is by course of
    kind;
And nature, that did make this egalness,
Oft so repineth at so great a wrong
That oft she raiseth up a grudging grief
In younger brethren at the elder's state,
Whereby both towns and kingdoms have
    been razed,   190
And famous stocks of royal blood de-
    stroyed.
The brother, that should be the brother's
    aid,
And have a wakeful care for his defense,
Gapes for his death, and blames the
    lingering years
That draw not forth his end with faster
    course;
And, oft impatient of so long delays,
With hateful slaughter he prevents [8] the
    fates,
And heaps a just reward for brother's
    blood,
With endless vengeance, on his stock for
    aye.

[1] Use, practice.   [3] Further.
[2] Welfare.   [4] Formerly.
[5] More.   [7] Wield, govern.
[6] Agree.   [8] Anticipates.

Such mischiefs here are wisely met
withal,   200
If egal state may nourish egal love,
Where none hath cause to grudge at
other's good.
But now the head to stoop beneath them
both,
Ne [1] kind, ne reason, ne good order bears.
And oft it hath been seen, where nature's
course
Hath been perverted in disordered wise,
When fathers cease to know that they
should rule,
The children cease to know they should
obey;
And often over-kindly tenderness
Is mother of unkindly stubbornness. 210
I speak not this in envy or reproach,
As if I grudged the glory of your sons,
Whose honor I beseech the gods increase;
Nor yet as if I thought there did remain
So filthy cankers in their noble breasts,
Whom I esteem—which is their greatest
praise—
Undoubted children of so good a king.
Only I mean to show by certain rules,
Which kind hath graft within the mind
of man,
That nature hath her order and her
course,   220
Which, being broken, doth corrupt the
state
Of minds and things, even in the best of
all.
My lords, your sons, may learn to rule
of you;
Your own example in your noble court
Is fittest guider of their youthful years.
If you desire to see some present joy
By sight of their well ruling in your life,
See them obey—so shall you see them
rule.
Whoso obeyeth not with humbleness
Will rule with outrage and with inso-
lence.   230
Long may they rule, I do beseech the
gods,
But long may they learn, ere they begin
to rule.
If kind and fates would suffer,[2] I would
wish
Them aged princes and immortal kings.
Wherefore, most noble king, I well assent

Between your sons that you divide your
realm,
And, as in kind, so match them in degree.
But, while the gods prolong your royal
life,
Prolong your reign; for thereto [3] live you
here,
And therefore have the gods so long
forborne   240
To join you to themselves, that still you
might
Be prince and father of our commonweal.
They, when they see your children ripe
to rule,
Will make them room, and will remove
you hence,
That yours, in right ensuing of your life,
May rightly honor your immortal name.
EUB. Your wonted true regard of faithful
hearts
Makes me, O king, the bolder to presume
To speak what I conceive within my
breast,
Although the same do not agree at all 250
With that which other here my lords
have said,
Nor which yourself have seeméd best to
like.
Pardon I crave, and that my words be
deemed
To flow from hearty zeal unto your grace,
And to the safety of your commonweal.
To part your realm unto my lords, your
sons,
I think not good for you, ne yet for them,
But worst of all for this our native land.
Within one land one single rule is best:
Divided reigns do make divided
hearts,   260
But peace preserves the country and the
prince.
Such is in man the greedy mind to reign,
So great is his desire to climb aloft,
In worldly stage the stateliest parts to
bear,
That faith and justice and all kindly love
Do yield unto desire of sovereignty,
Where egal state doth raise an egal hope
To win the thing that either would attain.
Your grace rememb'reth how in passéd
years
The mighty Brute, first prince of all this
land.   270

[1] Not, nor.   [2] Allow.   [3] For this purpose.

Possessed the same and ruled it well in
one;
He, thinking that the compass did suf-
fice
For his three sons three kingdoms eke to
make,
Cut it in three, as you would now in
twain.
But how much British blood hath since
been spilt
To join again the sundered unity,
What princes slain before their timely
hour,
What waste of towns and people in the
land,
What treasons heaped on murders and
on spoils—
Whose just revenge even yet is scarcely
ceased—　　　　　　　　　　　　280
Ruthful remembrance is yet raw in mind.
The gods forbid the like to chance again!
And you, O king, give not the cause
thereof.
My Lord Ferrex, your elder son, per-
haps—
Whom kind and custom gives a rightful
hope
To be your heir and to succeed your
reign—
Shall think that he doth suffer greater
wrong
Than he perchance will bear, if power
serve.
Porrex, the younger, so upraised in state,
Perhaps in courage will be raised also. 290
If flattery then, which fails not to assail
The tender minds of yet unskillful youth,
In one shall kindle and increase disdain,
And envy in the other's heart inflame,
This fire shall waste their love, their lives,
their land,
And ruthful ruin shall destroy them both.
I wish not this, O king, so to befall,
But fear the thing that I do most abhor.
Give no beginning to so dreadful end;
Keep them in order and obedience,　300
And let them both, by now obeying you,
Learn such behavior as beseems their
state—
The elder, mildness in his governance;
The younger, a yielding contentedness.
And keep them near unto your presence
still,
That they, restrainéd by the awe of you,

May live in compass of well tempered
stay,
And pass the perils of their youthful
years.
Your aged life draws on to feebler time,
Wherein you shall less able be to bear
The travails that in youth you have sus-
tained,　　　　　　　　　　　　311
Both in your person's and your realm's
defense.
If planting now your sons in furder parts,
You send them furder from your present
reach,
Less shall you know how they them-
selves demean;
Traitorous corrupters of their pliant
youth
Shall have unspied a much more free
access;
And, if ambition and inflamed disdain
Shall arm the one, the other, or them
both,
To civil war or to usurping pride,　320
Late shall you rue that you ne recked [1]
before.
Good is, I grant, of all to hope the best,
But not to live still [2] dreadless of the
worst.
So trust the one that the other be fore-
seen.
Arm not unskillfulness with princely
power,
But you that long have wisely ruled the
reins
Of royalty within your noble realm,
So hold them, while the gods for our
avails [3]
Shall stretch the thread of your pro-
longéd days.
Too soon he clamb [4] into the flaming
car,　　　　　　　　　　　　　　330
Whose want of skill did set the earth on
fire.
Time and example of your noble grace
Shall teach your sons both to obey and
rule.
When time hath taught them, time shall
make them place,
The place that now is full; and so I pray
Long it remain to comfort of us all.
GORB.　I take your faithful hearts in thank-
ful part.

---

[1] Did not heed.　　　　[3] Profit.
[2] Always.　　　　　　　[4] Climbed.

But, sith I see no cause to draw my mind
To fear the nature of my loving sons,
Or to misdeem that envy or disdain   340
Can there work hate where nature plant-
    eth love,
In one self purpose do I still abide.
My love extendeth egally to both;
My land sufficeth for them both also.
Humber shall part the marches [1] of their
    realms:
The southern part the elder shall possess;
The northern shall Porrex, the younger,
    rule.
In quiet I will pass mine aged days,
Free from the travail and the painful
    cares   349
That hasten age upon the worthiest kings.
But, lest the fraud, that ye do seem to
    fear,
Of flattering tongues, corrupt their tender
    youth,
And writhe them to the ways of youthful
    lust,
To climbing pride, or to revenging hate,
Or to neglecting of their careful charge
Lewdly to live in wanton recklessness,
Or to oppressing of the rightful cause,
Or not to wreak the wrongs done to the
    poor,
To tread down truth, or favor false
    deceit,
I mean to join to either of my sons   360
Some one of those whose long approvéd
    faith
And wisdom tried may well assure my
    heart
That mining fraud shall find no way to
    creep
Into their fencéd ears with grave advice.
This is the end; and so I pray you all
To bear my sons the love and loyalty
That I have found within your faithful
    breasts.
AROS. You nor your sons, our sovereign
    lord, shall want
Our faith and service while our lives do
    last.   [*Exeunt.*]

CHORUS

When settled stay doth hold the royal
    throne   370
    In steadfast place, by known and
    doubtless [2] right,

And chiefly when descent on one alone
    Makes single and unparted reign to
    light,
Each change of course unjoints the whole
    estate,
And yields it thrall to ruin by debate. [3]

The strength that, knit by fast accord in
    one,
    Against all foreign power of mighty
    foes,
Could of itself defend itself alone,
    Disjoinéd once, the former force doth
    lose.
The sticks, that sundered brake so soon
    in twain,   380
In fagot bound attempted were in vain.

Oft tender mind that leads the partial eye
    Of erring parents in their children's
    love,
Destroys   the   wrongly   lovéd   child
    thereby.
    This doth the proud son of Apollo
    prove.
Who, rashly set in chariot of his sire,
Inflamed the parchéd earth with heav-
    en's fire.

And this great king, that doth divide
    his land
    And change the course of his descend-
    ing crown,
And yields the reign into his children's
    hand,   390
    From blissful state of joy and great
    renown,
A mirror shall become to princes all,
To learn to shun the cause of such a fall. [4]

THE ORDER AND SIGNIFICATION OF THE
    DUMB SHOW BEFORE THE SECOND ACT

First, the music of cornets began to play,
    during which came in upon the stage a
    king accompanied with a number of his
    nobility and gentlemen. And, after he
    had placed himself in a chair of estate
    prepared for him, there came and kneeled
    before him a grave and aged gentleman,
    and offered up a cup unto him of wine
    in a glass, which the king refused. After

[3] Strife.
[4] None of the choruses are divided into stanzas
in the original.

[1] Borders.   [2] Undoubted.

him comes a brave and lusty young gentle-
man, and presents the king with a cup
of gold filled with poison, which the king
accepted, and, drinking the same, imme-
diately fell down dead upon the stage,
and so was carried thence away by his
lords and gentlemen, and then the music
ceased. Hereby was signified that, as
glass by nature holdeth no poison, but is
clear and may easily be seen through ne
boweth [1] *by any art, so a faithful coun-*
selor holdeth no treason, but is plain and
open, ne yieldeth to any undiscreet affec-
tion, but giveth wholesome counsel, which
the ill-advised prince refuseth. The de-
lightful gold filled with poison betokeneth
flattery, which under fair seeming of
pleasant words beareth deadly poison,
which destroyeth [2] *the prince that re-*
ceiveth it. As befell in the two brethren,
Ferrex and Porrex, who, refusing the
wholesome advice of grave counselors,
credited these young parasites and
brought to themselves death and destruc-
tion thereby.

Actus Secundus. Scena Prima.

[*The court of Ferrex.*]

Ferrex, Hermon, Dordan.

Fer. I marvel much what reason led the
  king,
My father, thus, without all my desert,
To reave me [3] half the kingdom, which
  by course
Of law and nature should remain to me.
Her. If you with stubborn and untaméd
  pride
Had stood against him in rebelling wise,
Or if with grudging mind you had envied
So slow a sliding of his aged years,
Or sought before your time to haste the
  course
Of fatal death upon his royal head,   10
Or stained your stock with murder of
  your kin,
Some face of reason might perhaps have
  seemed
To yield some likely cause to spoil ye
  thus.

[1] Bendeth.
[2] From 1565 edn. Original reads *destroyea.*
[3] Bereave me of, rob me of.

Fer. The wreakful [4] gods pour on my
  curséd head
Eternal plagues and never-dying woes,
The hellish prince adjudge my damnéd
  ghost
To Tantale's thirst, or proud Ixion's
  wheel,
Or cruel gripe [5] to gnaw my growing
  heart,
To during [6] torments and unquenchéd
  flames,
If ever I conceived so foul a thought, 20
To wish his end of life or yet of reign.
Dor. Ne yet your father, O most noble
  prince,
Did ever think so foul a thing of you;
For he, with more than father's tender
  love,
While yet the fates do lend him life to
  rule—
Who long might live to see your ruling
  well—
To you, my lord, and to his other son,
Lo, he resigns his realm and royalty;
Which never would so wise a prince have
  done
If he had once misdeemed that in your
  heart   30
There ever lodgéd so unkind a thought.
But tender love, my lord, and settled
  trust
Of your good nature and your noble mind
Made him to place you thus in royal
  throne,
And now to give you half his realm to
  guide;
Yea, and that half which, in abounding
  store
Of things that serve to make a wealthy
  realm,
In stately cities, and in fruitful soil,
In temperate breathing of the milder
  heaven,
In things of needful use, which friendly
  sea   40
Transports by traffic from the foreign
  parts,
In flowing wealth, in honor, and in force,
Doth pass the double value of the part
That Porrex hath allotted to his reign.
Such is your case, such is your father's
  love.

[4] Vengeful.   [5] Griffin.   [6] Enduring.

FER. Ah! love, my friends? Love wrongs
not whom he loves!

DOR. Ne yet he wrongeth you that giveth
you

So large a reign ere that the course of time
Bring you to kingdom by descended
right,

Which time perhaps might end your
time before.   50

FER. Is this no wrong, say you, to reave
from me

My native right of half so great a realm,
And thus to match his younger son with
me

In egal power and in as great degree?
Yea, and what son?   The son whose
swelling pride

Would never yield one point of reverence,
When I, the elder and apparent heir,
Stood in the likelihood to possess the
whole;

Yea, and that son which from his childish
age

Envieth mine honor and doth hate my
life.   60

What will he now do, when his pride, his
rage,

The mindful malice of his grudging heart
Is armed with force, with wealth, and
kingly state?

HER. Was this not wrong—yea, ill-advisèd
wrong—

To give so mad a man so sharp a sword,
To so great peril of so great mishap,
Wide open thus to set so large a way?

DOR. Alas, my lord, what griefful thing is
this,

That of your brother you can think so ill?
I never saw him utter likely sign   70
Whereby a man might see or once mis-
deem

Such hate of you ne such unyielding
pride.

Ill is their counsel, shameful be their end,
That raising such mistrustful fear in you,
Sowing the seed of such unkindly hate,
Travail by treason to destroy you both.
Wise is your brother and of noble hope,
Worthy to wield a large and mighty
realm.

So much a stronger friend have you
thereby,

Whose strength is your strength if you
gree in one.   80

HER. If nature and the gods had pinchèd
so

Their flowing bounty and their noble
gifts

Of princely qualities, from you, my lord,
And poured them all at once in wasteful
wise

Upon your father's younger son alone,
Perhaps there be [1] that in your prejudice [2]

Would say that birth should yield to
worthiness.

But sith in each good gift and princely art
Ye are his match, and, in the chief of
all,

In mildness and in sober governance 90
Ye far surmount; and sith there is in you
Sufficing skill and hopeful towardness
To weld the whole and match your
elder's praise,

I see no cause why ye should lose the
half.

Ne would I wish you yield to such a loss,
Lest your mild sufferance of so great a
wrong

Be deemèd cowardish and simple dread,
Which shall give courage to the fiery
head

Of your young brother to invade the
whole.

While yet therefore sticks in the people's
mind   100

The loathèd wrong of your disheritance;
And ere your brother have, by settled
power,

By guileful cloak of an alluring show,
Got him some force and favor in the
realm;

And, while the noble queen, your mother,
lives,

To work and practice all for your avail,
Attempt redress by arms, and wreak
yourself

Upon his life that gaineth by your loss,
Who now to shame of you and grief of us
In your own kingdom triumphs over
you.   110

Show now your courage meet for kingly
state,

That they which have avowed to spend
their goods,

Their lands, their lives and honors in
your cause,

[1] Supply *those*.   [2] To your damage.

May be the bolder to maintain your part,
When they do see that coward fear in you
Shall not betray ne fail their faithful
    hearts.
If once the death of Porrex end the strife,
And pay the price of his usurpéd reign,
Your mother shall persuade [1] the angry
    king.
The lords, your friends, eke shall appease
    his rage;   120
For they be wise, and well they can
    foresee
That ere long time your aged father's
    death
Will bring a time when you shall well
    requite
Their friendly favor or their hateful spite,
Yea, or their slackness to advance your
    cause.
" Wise men do not so hang on passing
    state
Of present princes, chiefly in their age,
But they will further cast their reaching
    eye,
To view and weigh the times and reigns
    to come." [2]
Ne is it likely, though the king be
    wroth,   130
That he yet will or that the realm will
    bear
Extreme revenge upon his only son;
Or, if he would, what one is he that dare
Be minister to such an enterprise?
And here you be now placéd in your
    own,
Amid your friends, your vassals, and your
    strength.
We shall defend and keep your person
    safe,
Till either counsel turn his tender mind,
Or age or sorrow end his weary days.
But, if the fear of gods and secret
    grudge   140
Of nature's law, repining at the fact,
Withhold your courage from so great
    attempt,
Know ye that lust of kingdoms hath no
    law.
The gods do bear and well allow in kings
The thinges [3] they abhor in rascal routs.[4]

[1] Win over.
[2] Quotation marks were commonly used to
call attention to sententious sayings.
[3] Dissyllabic.   [4] The rabble.

"When kings on slender quarrels run to
    wars,
And then in cruel and unkindly wise
Command thefts, rapes, murders of in-
    nocents,
The spoil of towns, ruins of mighty
    realms,
Think you such princes do suppose them-
    selves   150
Subject to laws of kind and fear of gods?"
Murders and violent thefts in private
    men
Are heinous crimes and full of foul re-
    proach,
Yet none offense, but decked with glo-
    rious name
Of noble conquests in the hands of kings.
But, if you like not yet so hot devise,
Ne list to take such vantage of the time,
But, though with peril of your own estate,
You will not be the first that shall invade,
Assemble yet your force for your de-
    fense,   160
And for your safety stand upon your
    guard.
DOR. O heaven! was there ever heard or
    known
So wicked counsel to a noble prince?
Let me, my lord, disclose unto your
    grace
This heinous tale, what mischief it con-
    tains:
Your father's death, your brother's, and
    your own—
Your present murder and eternal shame.
Hear me, O king, and suffer not to sink
So high a treason in your princely breast.
FER. The mighty gods forbid that ever I
    Should once conceive such mischief in
    my heart.   171
Although my brother hath bereft my
    realm,
And bear perhaps to me an hateful mind,
Shall I revenge it with his death there-
    fore?
Or shall I so destroy my father's life
That gave me life? The gods forbid, I
    say.
Cease you to speak so any more to me;
Ne you, my friend, with answer once
    repeat
So foul a tale. In silence let it die.
What lord or subject shall have hope at
    all   180

That under me they safely shall enjoy
Their goods, their honors, lands, and
  liberties,
With whom neither one only brother
  dear
Ne father dearer could enjoy their lives?
But, sith I fear my younger brother's
  rage,
And sith perhaps some other man may
  give
Some like advice, to move his grudging
  head
At mine estate—which counsel may per-
  chance
Take greater force with him than this
  with me—
I will in secret so prepare myself   190
As, if his malice or his lust to reign
Break forth in arms or sudden violence,
I may withstand his rage and keep mine
  own.   [*Exeunt Ferrex and Hermon.*]
Dor. I fear the fatal time now draweth on
When civil hate shall end the noble line
Of famous Brute and of his royal seed.
Great Jove, defend [1] the mischiefs now
  at hand!
O, that the secretary's wise advice
Had erst been heard when he besought
  the king
Not to divide his land, nor send his
  sons   200
To further parts from presence of his
  court,
Ne yet to yield to them his governance!
Lo, such are they now in the royal throne
As was rash Phaëton in Phœbus' car;
Ne then the fiery steeds did draw the
  flame
With wilder randon [2] through the kindled
  skies
Than traitorous counsel now will whirl
  about
The youthful heads of these unskillful
  kings.
But I hereof their father will inform;
The reverence of him perhaps shall
  stay   210
The growing mischiefs while they yet are
  green.
If this help not, then woe unto them-
  selves,
The prince, the people, the divided land!
  [*Exit.*]

[1] Prevent.   [2] Impetuosity.

ACTUS SECUNDUS. SCENA SECUNDA.

[*The court of Porrex.*]

Porrex, Tyndar, Philander.

Por. And is it thus? And doth he so
  prepare
Against his brother as his mortal foe?
And now while yet his aged father lives?
Neither regards he him, nor fears he me?
War would he have? And he shall have
  it so!
Tyn. I saw, myself, the great preparéd
  store
Of horse, of armor, and of weapons there;
Ne bring I to my lord reported tales
Without the ground of seen and searchéd
  truth.
Lo, secret quarrels run about his court 10
To bring the name of you, my lord, in
  hate.
Each man, almost, can now debate the
  cause,
And ask a reason of so great a wrong—
Why he, so noble and so wise a prince,
Is, as unworthy, reft his heritage,
And why the king, misled by crafty
  means,
Divided thus his land from course of
  right.
The wiser sort hold down their griefful
  heads;
Each man withdraws from talk and
  company
Of those that have been known to favor
  you.   20
To hide the mischief of their meaning
  there,
Rumors are spread of your preparing
  here.
The rascal numbers of unskillful sort
Are filled with monstrous tales of you
  and yours.
In secret I was counseled by my friends
To haste me thence, and brought you,
  as you know,
Letters from those that both can truly
  tell
And would not write unless they knew it
  well.
Phil. My lord, yet ere you move unkindly
  war,
Send to your brother to demand the
  cause.   30

Perhaps some traitorous tales have filled his ears
With false reports against your noble grace;
Which, once disclosed, shall end the growing strife
That else, not stayed with wise foresight in time,
Shall hazard both your kingdoms and your lives.
Send to your father eke; he shall appease
Your kindled minds and rid you of this fear.

Por. Rid me of fear? I fear him not at all;
Ne will to him ne to my father send.
If danger were for one to tarry there, 40
Think ye it safety to return again?
In mischiefs such as Ferrex now intends,
The wonted courteous laws to messengers
Are not observed, which in just war they use.
Shall I so hazard any one of mine?
Shall I betray my trusty friends to him,
That have disclosed his treason unto me?
Let him entreat that fears; I fear him not.
Or shall I to the king, my father, send?
Yea, and send now, while such a mother lives, 50
That loves my brother and that hateth me?
Shall I give leisure, by my fond [1] delays,
To Ferrex to oppress me all unware?
I will not; but I will invade his realm
And seek the traitor prince within his court.
Mischief for mischief is a due reward.
His wretched head shall pay the worthy price
Of this his treason and his hate to me.
Shall I abide, and treat, and send, and pray,
And hold my yelden [2] throat to traitor's knife, 60
While I, with valiant mind and conquering force,
Might rid myself of foes and win a realm?
Yet rather, when I have the wretch's head,
Then to the king, my father, will I send.
The bootless case may yet appease his wrath;
If not, I will defend me as I may.
[*Exeunt Porrex and Tyndar.*]

¹ Foolish. ² Yielded, submissive.

Phil. Lo, here the end of these two youthful kings,
The father's death, the ruin of their realms!
"O most unhappy state of counselors,
That light on so unhappy lords and times
That neither can their good advice be heard, 71
Yet must they bear the blames of ill success."
But I will to the king, their father, haste,
Ere this mischief come to the likely end;
That, if the mindful wrath of wreakful gods—
Since mighty Ilion's fall not yet appeased
With these poor remnants of the Trojan name—
Have not determined by unmovéd fate
Out of this realm to raze the British line,
By good advice, by awe of father's name,
By force of wiser lords, this kindled hate 81
May yet be quenched ere it consume us all. [*Exit.*]

Chorus

When youth, not bridled with a guiding stay,
Is left to randon of their own delight,
And welds whole realms by force of sovereign sway,
Great is the danger of unmastered might,
Lest skilless rage throw down, with headlong fall,
Their lands, their states, their lives, themselves and all.

When growing pride doth fill the swelling breast,
And greedy lust [3] doth raise the climbing mind, 90
O, hardly may the peril be repressed.
Ne fear of angry gods, ne lawes' [4] kind,
Ne country's care can firéd hearts restrain,
When force hath arméd envy and disdain.

When kings of foresight [5] will neglect the rede [6]
Of best advice, and yield to pleasing tales

³ Desire. ⁵ Of set purpose
⁴ Dissyllabic. ⁶ Counsel.

That do their fancies' noisome humor
  feed,
Ne reason nor regard of right avails.
Succeeding heaps of plagues shall teach,
  too late,   99
To learn the mischiefs of misguided state.

Foul fall the traitor false that under-
  mines
The love of brethren to destroy them
  both.
Woe to the prince that pliant ear inclines
And yields his mind to poisonous tale
  that floweth
From flattering mouth!   And woe to
  wretched land
That wastes itself with civil sword in
  hand!

Lo, thus it is, poison in gold to take,
And wholesome drink in homely cup
  forsake.

THE ORDER AND SIGNIFICATION OF THE
DUMB SHOW BEFORE THE THIRD ACT

*First, the music of flutes began to play, dur-
  ing which came in upon the stage a
  company of mourners, all clad in black,
  betokening death and sorrow to ensue
  upon the ill-advised misgovernment and
  dissension of brethren, as befell upon the
  murder of Ferrex by his younger brother.
  After the mourners had passed thrice
  about the stage, they departed, and then
                         the music ceased.*

ACTUS TERTIUS. SCENA PRIMA.

[*The court of Gorboduc.*]

*Gorboduc, Eubulus, Arostus, Philander,
                           Nuntius.*[1]
GORB. O cruel fates, O mindful wrath of
  gods,
Whose vengeance neither Simois' stainéd
  streams
Flowing with blood of Trojan princes
  slain,
Nor Phrygian fields made rank with
  corpses dead
Of Asian kings and lords, can yet ap-
  pease;
Ne slaughter of unhappy Priam's race,
Nor Ilion's fall, made level with the soil,

[1] Last two enter later.

Can yet suffice; but still continued rage
Pursues our lives, and from the farthest
  seas
Doth chase the issues of destroyéd
  Troy.   10
"O, no man happy till his end be seen."
If any flowing wealth and seeming joy
In present years might make a happy
  wight,
Happy was Hecuba, the woefullest wretch
That ever lived to make a mirror of;
And happy Priam, with his noble sons;
And happy I, till now, alas, I see
And feel my most unhappy wretched-
  ness.
Behold, my lords, read ye this letter
  here.
Lo, it contains the ruin of our realm,   20
If timely speed provide not hasty help.
Yet, O ye gods, if ever woeful king
Might move ye, kings of kings, wreak it
  on me
And on my sons, not on this guiltless
  realm!
Send down your wasting flames from
  wrathful skies,
To reave me and my sons the hateful
  breath.
Read, read, my lords; this is the matter
  why
I called ye now to have your good advice.

*The letter from Dordan, the counselor of the
              elder prince.*

Eubulus readeth the letter.

"My sovereign lord, what I am loath to
  write,
But loathest am to see, that I am
  forced   30
By letters now to make you understand.
My Lord Ferrex, your eldest son, misled
By traitorous fraud of young untempered
  wits,
Assembleth force against your younger
  son,
Ne can my counsel yet withdraw the heat
And furious pangs of his inflaméd head.
Disdain, saith he, of his disheritance
Arms him to wreak the great pretended
  wrong
With civil sword upon his brother's life.
If present help do not restrain this
  rage,   40

This flame will waste your sons, your
 land, and you.
Your majesty's faithful and most humble
 subject,

DORDAN."

AROS. O king, appease your grief and stay
 your plaint;
 Great is the matter, and a woeful case,
 But timely knowledge may bring timely
  help.
 Send for them both unto your presence
  here.
 The reverence of your honor, age, and
  state,
 Your grave advice, the awe of father's
  name,
 Shall quickly knit again this broken
  peace.
 And, if in either of my lords, your sons, 50
 Be such untaméd and unyielding pride
 As will not bend unto your noble hests; [1]
 If Ferrex, the elder son, can bear no peer,
 Or Porrex, not content, aspires to more
 Than you him gave above his native
  right,
 Join with the juster side; so shall you
  force
 Them to agree, and hold the land in
  stay.
EUB. What meaneth this? Lo, yonder
 comes in haste
 Philander from my lord, your younger
 son.

[Enter Philander.]

GORB. The gods send joyful news!
PHIL.   The mighty Jove 60
 Preserve your majesty, O noble king.
GORB. Philander, welcome! But how doth
 my son?
PHIL. Your son, sir, lives, and healthy I
 him left.
 But yet, O king, the want of lustful
  health
 Could not be half so griefful to your
  grace
 As these most wretched tidings that I
  bring.
GORB. O heavens, yet more? Not end of
 woes to me?
PHIL. Tyndar, O king, came lately from
 the court

Of Ferrex to my lord, your younger son,
And made report of great preparéd
 store   70
For war, and saith that it is wholly meant
Against Porrex, for high disdain that he
Lives now a king, and egal in degree
With him that claimeth to succeed the
 whole,
As by due title of descending right.
Porrex is now so set on flaming fire,
Partly with kindled rage of cruel wrath,
Partly with hope to gain a realm thereby,
That he in haste prepareth to invade 79
His brother's land, and with unkindly war
Threatens the murder of your elder son;
Ne could I him persuade that first he
 should
Send to his brother to demand the cause,
Nor yet to you to stay this hateful strife.
Wherefore, sith there no more I can be
 heard,
I come myself now to inform your grace,
And to beseech you, as you love the life
And safety of your children and your
 realm,
Now to employ your wisdom and your
 force
To stay this mischief ere it be too late. 90
GORB. Are they in arms? Would he not
 send to me?
Is this the honor of a father's name?
In vain we travail to assuage their minds,
As if their hearts, whom neither brother's
 love,
Nor father's awe, nor kingdom's cares
 can move,
Our counsels could withdraw from raging
 heat.
Jove slay them both, and end the curséd
 line.
For, though perhaps fear of such mighty
 force
As I, my lords, joined with your noble
 aids,
May yet raise, shall repress their present
 heat,   100
The secret grudge and malice will remain;
The fire, not quenched, but kept in close
 restraint,
Fed still within, breaks forth with double
 flame.
Their death and mine must pease [2] the
 angry gods.

---

[1] Behests, commands.

[2] Appease.

PHIL. Yield not, O king, so much to weak
    despair;
Your sons yet live, and long, I trust,
    they shall.
If fates had taken you from earthly life
Before beginning of this civil strife,
Perhaps your sons in their unmastered
    youth,
Loose from regard of any living wight, 110
Would run on headlong, with unbridled
    race,
To their own death and ruin of this
    realm.
But, sith the gods, that have the care for
    kings,
Of things and times dispose the order so
That in your life this kindled flame
    breaks forth,
While yet your life, your wisdom, and
    your power
May stay the growing mischief, and
    repress
The fiery blaze of their enkindled heat,
It seems—and so ye ought to deem
    thereof—
That loving Jove hath tempered so the
    time   120
Of this debate to happen in your days,
That you yet living may the same ap-
    pease,
And add it to the glory of your latter
    age,
And they your sons may learn to live in
    peace.
Beware, O king, the greatest harm of all,
Lest by your wailful plaints your has-
    tened death
Yield larger room unto their growing
    rage.
Preserve your life, the only hope of stay.
And, if your highness herein list to use
Wisdom or force, counsel or knightly
    aid,   130
Lo, we, our persons, powers, and lives
    are yours.
Use us till death, O king; we are your
    own.
EUB. Lo, here the peril that was erst fore-
    seen,
When you, O king, did first divide your
    land,
And yield your present reign unto your
    sons.
But now, O noble prince, now is no time

To wail and plain,[1] and waste your woeful
    life;
Now is the time for present good advice.
Sorrow doth dark the judgment of the
    wit.
"The heart unbroken and the courage
    free   140
From feeble faintness of bootless despair
Doth either rise to safety or renowm
By noble valure [2] of unvanquished mind,
Or yet doth perish in more happy sort."
Your grace may send to either of your
    sons
Some one both wise and noble personage,
Which with good counsel and with
    weighty name
Of father shall present before their eyes
Your hest, your life, your safety, and
    their own,
The present mischief of their deadly
    strife.   150
And, in the while, assemble you the force
Which your commandment and the
    speedy haste
Of all my lords here present can prepare.
The terror of your mighty power shall
    stay
The rage of both, or yet of one at least.

[Enter Nuntius.]

NUN. O king, the greatest grief that ever
    prince did hear,
That ever woeful messenger did tell,
That ever wretched land hath seen be-
    fore,
I bring to you: Porrex, your younger son,
With sudden force invaded hath the
    land   160
That you to Ferrex did allot to rule,
And with his own most bloody hand he
    hath
His brother slain, and doth possess his
    realm.
GORB. O heavens, send down the flames of
    your revenge!
Destroy, I say, with flash of wreakful
    fire
The traitor son, and then the wretched
    sire!
But let us go, that yet perhaps I may
Die with revenge and pease the hateful
    gods.   *[Exeunt.]*

---

[1] Complain.   [2] Valor, worth.

CHORUS

The lust of kingdom knows no sacred
  faith,
  No rule of reason, no regard of
    right,   170
No kindly love, no fear of heaven's
  wrath,
  But, with contempt of gods and man's
    despite,
Through bloody slaughter doth prepare
  the ways
To fatal scepter and accursèd reign.
The son so loathes the father's lingering
  days,
  Ne dreads his hand in brother's blood
    to stain.
O wretched prince, ne dost thou yet
  record
  The yet fresh murthers done within
    the land
Of thy forefathers, when the cruel sword
  Bereft Morgan his life with cousin's
    hand?   180
Thus fatal plagues pursue the guilty race
  Whose murderous hand, imbrued with
    guiltless blood,
Asks vengeance still before the heaven's
  face,
  With endless mischiefs on the cursèd
    brood.
The wicked child thus brings to woeful
  sire
  The mournful plaints to waste his very
    life.
Thus do the cruel flames of civil fire
  Destroy the parted reign with hateful
    strife;
And hence doth spring the well from
  which doth flow
  The dead black streams of mourning,
    plaints, and woe.   190

THE ORDER AND SIGNIFICATION OF THE
  DUMB SHOW BEFORE THE FOURTH
  ACT

*First, the music of hautboys began to play,
  during which there came forth from under the stage, as though out of hell,
  three Furies, Alecto, Megæra, and Tisiphone, clad in black garments sprinkled
  with blood and flames, their bodies girt
  with snakes, their heads spread with
  serpents instead of hair, the one bear-*

*ing in her hand a snake, the other a
whip, and the third a burning firebrand,
each driving before them a king and a
queen, which, moved by Furies, unnaturally had slain their own children. The
names of the kings and queens were
these: Tantalus, Medea, Athamas, Ino,
Cambises, Althea. After that the Furies
and these had passed about the stage
thrice, they departed, and then the music
ceased.   Hereby was signified the unnatural murders to follow; that is to
say, Porrex slain by his own mother,
and of King Gorboduc and Queen
Viden[a], killed by their own subjects.*

ACTUS QUARTUS. SCENA PRIMA.

[*A room in Gorboduc's palace.*]

Viden[a] sola.

VID. Why should I live, and linger forth my
    time
In longer life to double my distress?
O me, most woeful wight, whom no mishap
Long ere this day could have bereavéd
    hence!
Mought [1] not these hands, by fortune or by
    fate,
Have pierced this breast, and life with iron
    reft?
Or in this palace here, where I so long
Have spent my days, could not that happy
    hour
Once, once have happed, in which these
    hugy frames
With death by fall might have oppressèd
    me?   10
Or should not this most hard and cruel soil,
So oft where I have pressed my wretched
    steps,
Sometime had ruth of mine accursèd life
To rend in twain, [and] [2] swallow me
    therein?
So had my bones possessèd now in peace
Their happy grave within the closèd
    ground,
And greedy worms had gnawn this pinéd
    heart
Without my feeling pain; so should not now
This living breast remain the ruthful tomb
Wherein my heart, yelden to death, is
    gravèd; [3]   20

[1] Might.
[2] Supplied from 1565 edn.   [3] Buried.

Nor dreary thoughts, with pangs of pining
   grief,
My doleful mind had not afflicted thus.
O my beloved son! O my sweet child!
My dear Ferrex, my joy, my life's delight!
Is my beloved son, is my sweet child,
My dear Ferrex, my joy, my life's delight,
Murdered with cruel death?   O hateful
   wretch!
O heinous traitor both to heaven and earth!
Thou, Porrex, thou this damnéd deed hast
   wrought;
Thou, Porrex, thou shalt dearly by [1] the
   same.   30
Traitor to kin and kind, to sire and me,
To thine own flesh, and traitor to thyself!
The gods on thee in hell shall wreak their
   wrath,
And here in earth this hand shall take
   revenge
On thee, Porrex, thou false and caitiff
   wight.
If after blood so eager were thy thirst,
And murderous mind had so possesséd thee,
If such hard heart of rock and stony flint
Lived in thy breast that nothing else could
   like [2]
Thy cruel tyrant's thought but death and
   blood,   40
Wild savage beasts, mought not their
   slaughter serve
To feed thy greedy will, and in the midst
Of their entrails to stain thy deadly hands
With blood deserved, and drink thereof
   thy fill?
Or if naught else but death and blood of
   man
Mought please thy lust, could none in
   Britain land—
Whose heart betorn out of his panting
   breast
With thine own hand, or work what death
   thou wouldest—
Suffice to make a sacrifice to pease
That deadly mind and murderous thought
   in thee,   50
But he who in the selfsame womb was
   wrapped,
Where thou in dismal hour receivédst life?
Or if needs, needs thy hand must slaughter
   make,
Moughtest thou not have reached a mortal
   wound,

And with thy sword have pierced this
   curséd womb
That the accurséd Porrex brought to light,
And given me a just reward therefor?
So Ferrex yet sweet life mought have en-
   joyed
And to his aged father comfort brought,
With some young son in whom they both
   might live.   60
But whereunto waste I this ruthful speech,
To thee that hast thy brother's blood thus
   shed?
Shall I still think that from this womb thou
   sprung,
That I thee bare, or take thee for my son?
No, traitor, no; I thee refuse for mine.
Murderer, I thee renounce; thou art not
   mine.
Never, O wretch, this womb conceivéd thee,
Nor never bode [3] I painful throes for thee.
Changeling to me thou art, and not my
   child,   69
Nor to no wight that spark of pity knew.
Ruthless, unkind, monster of nature's
   work,
Thou never sucked the milk of woman's
   breast,
But from thy birth the cruel tiger's teats
Have nurséd thee; nor yet of flesh and
   blood
Formed is thy heart, but of hard iron
   wrought;
And wild and desert woods bred thee to life.
But canst thou hope to scape my just re-
   venge,
Or that these hands will not be wroke [4]
   on thee?
Dost thou not know that Ferrex' mother
   lives,
That lovéd him more dearly than herself? 80
And doth she live, and is not venged on
   thee?   [*Exit.*]

ACTUS QUARTUS.   SCENA SECUNDA.

[*The court of Gorboduc.*]

*Gorboduc, Arostus, Eubulus, Porrex, Mar-
   cella.*[5]

GORB.   We marvel much whereto this lin-
   g'ring stay
 Falls out so long.   Porrex unto our court.
By order of our letters, is returned,

---

[1] Aby; pay the penalty for.   [2] Please.
[3] Suffered.   [5] Wreaked, avenged.
[4] Last three enter later.

And Eubulus received from us behest,[1]
At his arrival here, to give him charge
Before our presence straight to make re-
pair;
And yet we have no word whereof he
stays.
AROS. Lo, where he comes, and Eubulus
with him.

[*Enter Eubulus and Porrex.*]

EUB. According to your highness' hest to
me,
Here have I Porrex brought, even in such
sort   10
As from his wearied horse he did alight,
For that your grace did will such haste
therein.
GORB. We like and praise this speedy will
in you
To work the thing that to your charge
we gave.
Porrex, if we so far should swerve from
kind,
And from those bounds which law of
nature sets,
As thou hast done by vile and wretched
deed,
In cruel murder of thy brother's life,
Our present hand could stay no longer
time,
But straight should bathe this blade in
blood of thee   20
As just revenge of thy detested crime.
No, we should not offend the law of
kind,
If now this sword of ours did slay thee
here;
For thou hast murdered him whose
heinous death
Even nature's force doth move us to re-
venge
By blood again; and justice forceth us
To measure death for death, thy due
desert.
Yet sithens [2] thou art our child, and sith
as yet
In this hard case what word thou canst
allege
For thy defense by us hath not been
heard,   30
We are content to stay our will for that

Which justice bids us presently to work,
And give thee leave to use thy speech at
full,
If aught thou have to lay for thine excuse.
POR. Neither, O king, I can or will deny
But that this hand from Ferrex life hath
reft—
Which fact how much my doleful heart
doth wail,
O, would it mought as full appear to
sight
As inward grief doth pour it forth to me!
So yet perhaps, if ever ruthful heart,   40
Melting in tears within a manly breast,
Through deep repentance of his bloody
fact,
If ever grief, if ever woeful man
Might move regret with sorrow of his
fault,
I think the torment of my mournful case,
Known to your grace, as I do feel the
same,
Would force even Wrath herself to pity
me.
But as the water, troubled with the mud,
Shows not the face which else the eye
should see,
Even so your ireful mind with stirréd
thought   50
Cannot so perfectly discern my cause.
But this unhap, amongst so many heaps,[3]
I must content me with, most wretched
man,
That to myself I must reserve my woe
In pining thoughts of mine accurséd fact,
Since I may not show here my smallest
grief,
Such as it is, and as my breast endures,
Which I esteem the greatest misery
Of all mishaps that fortune now can send.
Not that I rest in hope with plaint and
tears   60
To purchase life; for to the gods I clepe [4]
For true record of this my faithful
speech:
Never this heart shall have the thought-
ful dread
To die the death that by your grace's
doom,
By just desert, shall be pronounced to me;
Nor never shall this tongue once spend
the speech

---

[1] Suggested by Thorndike; all preceding edns.
have *by hest.*
[2] Since (probably pronounced as one syllable).

[3] Among so many heaps (of unhaps). *Cf.* V,
ii, 109.   [4] Call.

Pardon to crave, or seek by suit to live.
I mean not this as though I were not
  touched
With care of dreadful death, or that I
  held
Life in contempt, but that I know the
  mind   70
Stoops to no dread, although the flesh be
  frail.
And for my guilt, I yield the same so
  great
As in myself I find a fear to sue
For grant of life.
GORB.   In vain, O wretch,
  thou showest
A woeful heart! Ferrex now lies in grave,
Slain by thy hand.
POR.   Yet this, O father,
  hear,
And then I end. Your majesty well
  knows
That when my brother Ferrex and my-
  self
By your own hest were joined in gov-
  ernance
Of this your grace's realm of Britain
  land,   80
I never sought nor travailed for the same;
Nor by myself nor by no friend I
  wrought,
But from your highness' will alone it
  sprung,
Of your most gracious goodness bent to
  me.
But how my brother's heart even then
  repined
With swollen disdain against mine egal
  rule,
Seeing that realm which by descent
  should grow
Wholly to him allotted half to me!
Even in your highness' court he now re-
  mains,
And with my brother then in nearest
  place,   90
Who can record what proof thereof was
  showed,
And how my brother's envious heart ap-
  peared.
Yet I that judgéd it my part to seek
His favor and good will, and loath to
  make
Your highness know the thing which
  should have brought

Grief to your grace and your offense to
  him,
Hoping my earnest suit should soon have
  won
A loving heart within a brother's breast,
Wrought in that sort that for a pledge
  of love
And faithful heart he gave to me his
  hand.   100
This made me think that he had ban-
  ished quite
All rancor from his thought, and bare to
  me
Such hearty love as I did owe to him.
But, after once we left your grace's court,
And from your highness' presence lived
  apart,
This egal rule still, still did grudge him so
That now those envious sparks, which
  erst lay raked
In living cinders of dissembling breast,
Kindled so far within his heart disdain
That longer could he not refrain from
  proof   110
Of secret practice to deprive me life
By poison's force, and had bereft me so,
If mine own servant, hired to this fact
And moved by truth with hate to work
  the same,
In time had not bewrayed [1] it unto me.
When thus I saw the knot of love unknit,
All honest league and faithful promise
  broke,
The law of kind and truth thus rent in
  twain,
His heart on mischief set, and in his
  breast
Black treason hid, then, then did I de-
  spair   120
That ever time could win him friend to
  me;
Then saw I how he smiled with slaying
  knife
Wrapped under cloak; then saw I deep
  deceit
Lurk in his face and death prepared for
  me.
Even nature moved me then to hold my
  life
More dear to me than his, and bade this
  hand—
Since by his life my death must needs
  ensue

[1] Betrayed, divulged.

And by his death my life to be pre-
    served—
To shed his blood and seek my safety so.
And wisdom willéd me without pro-
    tract [1]   130
In speedy wise to put the same in ure.
Thus have I told the cause that movéd
    me
To work my brother's death; and so I
    yield
My life, my death, to judgment of your
    grace.
GORB. O cruel wight, should any cause
    prevail
To make thee stain thy hands with
    brother's blood?
But what of thee we will resolve to do
Shall yet remain unknown. Thou in the
    mean
Shalt from our royal presence banished be,
Until our princely pleasure furder shall
To thee be showed. Depart therefore
    our sight,   141
Accurséd child! [Exit Porrex.] What
    cruel destiny,
What froward fate hath sorted us this
    chance,
That, even in those where we should
    comfort find,
Where our delight now in our aged days
S[h]ould rest and be, even there our only
    grief
And deepest sorrows to abridge our life,
Most pining cares, and deadly thoughts
    do grow?
AROS. Your grace should now, in these
    grave years of yours,
Have found ere this the price of mortal
    joys: 150
How short they be, how fading here in
    earth,
How full of change, how brittle our es-
    tate,
Of nothing sure, save only of the death
To whom both man and all the world
    doth owe
Their end at last. Neither should na-
    ture's power
In other sort against your heart prevail
Than as the naked hand whose stroke
    assays
The arméd breast where force doth light
    in vain.

[1] Delay.

GORB. Many can yield right sage and
    grave advice
Of patient sprite to others wrapped in
    woe,   160
And can in speech both rule and conquer
    kind,
Who, if by proof they might feel nature's
    force,
Would show themselves men as they are
    indeed,
Which now will needs be gods. But what
    doth mean
The sorry cheer of her that here doth
    come?

[Enter Marcella.]

MAR. O, where is ruth, or where is pity
    now?
Whither is gentle heart and mercy fled?
Are they exiled out of our stony breasts,
Never to make return? Is all the world
Drownéd in blood, and sunk in cru-
    elty?   170
If not in women mercy may be found,
If not, alas, within the mother's breast,
To her own child, to her own flesh and
    blood,
If ruth be banished thence, if pity there
May have no place, if there no gentle
    heart
Do live and dwell, where should we seek
    it then?
GORB. Madam, alas, what means your
    woeful tale?
MAR. O silly [2] woman I, why to this hour
Have kind and fortune thus deferred my
    breath,
That I should live to see this doleful
    day?   180
Will ever wight believe that such hard
    heart
Could rest within the cruel mother's
    breast,
With her own hand to slay her only son?
But out, alas! these eyes beheld the
    same—
They saw the dreary sight, and are be-
    come
Most ruthful records of the bloody fact.
Porrex, alas, is by his mother slain,
And with her hand—a woeful thing to
    tell—

[2] Helpless.

While slumb'ring on his careful bed he
  rests,
His heart stabbed in with knife, is reft of
  life.   190
GORB. O Eubulus, O, draw this sword of
  ours,
And pierce this heart with speed! O
  hateful light,
O loathsome life, O sweet and welcome
  death!
Dear Eubulus, work this, we thee be-
  seech!
EUB. Patient [1] your grace; perhaps he liv-
  eth yet,
With wound received, but not of certain
  death.
GORB. O, let us then repair unto the place,
And see if Porrex live or thus be slain.
      [*Exeunt Gorboduc and Eubulus.*]
MAR. Alas, he liveth not! It is too true
That, with these eyes, of him a peerless
  prince,   200
Son to a king, and in the flower of youth,
Even with a twink a senseless stock I
  saw.[2]
AROS. O damnéd deed!
MAR.   But hear his ruth-
  ful end:
The noble prince, pierced with the sud-
  den wound,
Out of his wretched slumber hastely
  start,[3]
Whose strength now failing, straight he
  overthrew,[4]
When in the fall his eyes, even new
  unclosed,
Beheld the queen, and cried to her for
  help.
We then, alas, the ladies which that time
Did there attend, seeing that heinous
  deed,   210
And hearing him oft call the wretched
  name
Of mother, and to cry to her for aid
Whose direful hand gave him the mortal
  wound,
Pitying, alas—for nought else could we
  do—
His ruthful end, ran to the woeful bed,

Despoiléd straight his breast, and, all we
  might,
Wipéd in vain with napkins next at hand
The sudden streams of blood that flushéd
  fast
Out of the gaping wound. O, what a look,
O, what a ruthful, steadfast eye me-
  thought   220
He fixed upon my face, which to my
  death
Will never part fro [5] me, when with a
  braid [6]
A deep-fet [7] sigh he gave, and there-
  withal,
Clasping his hands, to heaven he cast his
  sight;
And straight—pale death pressing within
  his face—
The flying ghost his mortal corpse for-
  sook.
AROS. Never did age bring forth so vile a
  fact.
MAR. O hard and cruel hap, that thus as-
  signed
Unto so worthy a wight so wretched end;
But most hard cruel heart, that could
  consent   230
To lend the hateful destinies that hand
By which, alas, so heinous crime was
  wrought!
O queen of adamant! O marble breast!
If not the favor of his comely face,
If not his princely cheer and countenance,
His valiant active arms, his manly breast,
If not his fair and seemly personage,
His noble limbs in such proportion cast
As would have rapt a silly woman's
  thought—
If this mought not have moved thy
  bloody heart   240
And that most cruel hand the wretched
  weapon
Even to let fall, and kissed him in the
  face,
With tears for ruth to reave such one by
  death,
Should nature yet consent to slay her
  son?
O mother, thou to murder thus thy child!
Even Jove with justice must with light-
  ning flames
From heaven send down some strange
  revenge on thee.

---

[1] Used as a reflexive verb.
[2] An awkward passage. The sense seems to be:
"It is too true that with these eyes even in an
instant I saw a senseless corpse made of him," etc.
[3] Hastily started.   [4] Fell over.
[5] From.   [6] A start.   [7] Deep-fetched.

Ah, noble prince, how oft have I beheld
Thee mounted on thy fierce and tram-
pling steed,
Shining in armor bright before the
tilt,   250
And with thy mistress' sleeve tied on
thy helm,
And charge thy staff [1]—to please thy
lady's eye—
That bowed the headpiece of thy friendly
foe;
How oft in arms on horse to bend the
mace,
How oft in arms on foot to break the
sword,
Which never now these eyes may see
again!
AROS. Madam, alas, in vain these plaints
are shed;
Rather with me depart, and help to
swage [2]
The thoughtful griefs that in the aged
king
Must needs by nature grow by death of
this   260
His only son, whom he did hold so
dear.
MAR. What wight is that which saw that
I did see,
And could refrain to wail with plaint
and tears?
Not I, alas! That heart is not in me.—
But let us go, for I am grieved anew
To call to mind the wretched father's
woe.   [_Exeunt._]

CHORUS

When greedy lust in royal seat to reign
Hath reft all care of gods and eke of
men,
And cruel heart, wrath, treason, and
disdain,
Within ambitious breast are lodgéd,
then   270
Behold how mischief wide herself displays,
And with the brother's hand the brother
slays.

When blood thus shed doth stain the
heaven's face,
Crying to Jove for vengeance of the
deed,

[1] Level thy lance.   [2] Assuage.

The mighty god even moveth from his
place
With wrath to wreak. Then sends he
forth with speed
The dreadful Furies, daughters of the
night,
With serpents girt, carrying the whip
of ire,
With hair of stinging snakes, and shining
bright
With flames and blood, and with a
brand of fire.   280
These, for revenge of wretched murder
done,
Do make the mother kill her only son.

Blood asketh blood, and death must
death requite;
Jove, by his just and everlasting doom,
Justly hath ever so requited it.
The times before record, and times to
come
Shall find it true, and so doth present
proof
Present before our eyes for our behoof.

O happy wight that suffers not the snare
Of murderous mind to tangle him in
blood;   290
And happy he that can in time beware
By other's harms and turn it to his
good.
But woe to him that, fearing not to
offend,
Doth serve his lust and will not see the
end.

THE ORDER AND SIGNIFICATION OF THE DUMB SHOW BEFORE THE FIFTH ACT

_First, the drums and flutes began to sound,
during which there came forth upon the
stage a company of harquebusiers and
of armed men, all in order of battle.
These, after their pieces discharged, and
that the armed men had three times
marched about the stage, departed, and
then the drums and flutes did cease.
Hereby was signified tumults, rebellions,
arms, and civil wars to follow, as fell
in the realm of Great Britain, which,
by the space of fifty years and more,
continued in civil war between the nobility after the death of King Gorboduc_

and of his issues, for want of certain
limitation in succession of the crown,
till the time of Dunwallo Molmutius,
who reduced the land to monarchy.

ACTUS QUINTUS. SCENA PRIMA.

[*The court of Gorboduc.*]

Clotyn, Mandud, Gwenard, Fergus, Eubulus.

CLOT. Did ever age bring forth such ty-
  rants' hearts?
The brother hath bereft the brother's life;
The mother, she hath dyed her cruel
  hands
In blood of her own son; and now at last
The people, lo, forgetting truth and love,
Contemning quite both law and loyal
  heart,
Even they have slain their sovereign lord
  and queen.
MAND. Shall this their traitorous crime
  unpunished rest?
Even yet they cease not, carried on with
  rage,
In their rebellious routs, to threaten
  still   10
A new bloodshed unto the prince's kin,
To slay them all, and to uproot the race
Both of the king and queen; so are they
  moved
With Porrex' death, wherein they falsely
  charge
The guiltless king without desert at all,
And traitorously have murdered him
  therefor,
And eke the queen.
GWEN.   Shall subjects dare
  with force
To work revenge upon their prince's fact?
Admit the worst that may—as sure in
  this
The deed was foul, the queen to slay
  her son—   20
Shall yet the subject seek to take the
  sword,
Arise against his lord, and slay his king?
O wretched state where those rebellious
  hearts
Are not rent out even from their living
  breasts,
And with the body thrown unto the
  fowls,
As carrion food, for terror of the rest!

FERG. There can no punishment be
  thought too great
For this so grievous crime. Let speed
  therefore
Be used therein, for it behooveth so.
EUB. Ye all, my lords, I see, consent in
  one,   30
And I as one consent with ye in all.
I hold it more than need, with sharpest
  law
To punish this tumultuous bloody rage.
For nothing more may shake the com-
  mon state
Than sufferance of uproars without re-
  dress,
Whereby how some kingdoms of mighty
  power,
After great conquests made, and flour-
  ishing
In fame and wealth, have been to ruin
  brought.
I pray to Jove that we may rather wail
Such hap in them than witness in our-
  selves.   40
Eke fully with the duke my mind agrees,
Though kings forget to govern as they
  ought,
Yet subjects must obey as they are
  bound.
But now, my lords, before ye farder
  wade,[1]
Or spend your speech, what sharp re-
  venge shall fall
By justice' plague on these rebellious
  wights,
Methinks ye rather should first search
  the way
By which in time the rage of this uproar
Mought be repressed, and these great
  tumults ceased.
Even yet the life of Britain land doth
  hang   50
In traitors' balance of unegal weight.
Think not, my lords, the death of Gor-
  boduc
Nor yet Videna's blood will cease their
  rage.
Even our own lives, our wives, and chil-
  dren dear,
Our country, dearest of all, in danger
  stands,
Now to be spoiled, now, now made des-
  olate,

[1] Proceed.

And by ourselves a conquest to ensue.
For, give once sway unto the people's
    lusts
To rush forth on, and stay them not in
    time,
And, as the stream that rolleth down
    the hill,   60
So will they headlong run with raging
    thoughts
From blood to blood, from mischief
    unto mo,
To ruin of the realm, themselves, and
    all—
So giddy are the common people's minds,
So glad of change, more wavering than
    the sea.
Ye see, my lords, what strength these
    rebels have,
What hugy number is assembled still;
For, though the traitorous fact for which
    they rose
Be wrought and done, yet lodge they
    still in field;
So that, how far their furies yet will
    stretch,   70
Great cause we have to dread. That we
    may seek
By present battle to repress their power,
Speed must we use to levy force there-
    for;
For either they forthwith will mischief
    work,
Or their rebellious roars forthwith will
    cease.
These violent things may have no last-
    ing long.
Let us, therefore, use this for present
    help:
Persuade by gentle speech, and offer
    grace
With gift of pardon, save unto the chief,
And that upon condition that forth-
    with   80
They yield the captains of their enter-
    prise,
To bear such guerdon of their traitorous
    fact
As may be both due vengeance to them-
    selves
And wholesome terror to posterity.
This shall, I think, scatter the greatest
    part,
That now are holden, with desire of
    home,

Wearied in field with cold of winter's
    nights,
And some, no doubt, stricken with dread
    of law.
When this is once proclaiméd, it shall
    make
The captains to mistrust the multi-
    tude,   90
Whose safety bids them to betray their
    heads;
And so much more, because the rascal
    routs
In things of great and perilous attempts
Are never trusty to the noble race.
And, while we treat and stand on terms
    of grace,
We shall both stay their fury's rage the
    while,
And eke gain time, whose only help
    sufficeth
Withouten war to vanquish rebels'
    power.
In the meanwhile, make you in readiness
Such band of horsemen as ye may pre-
    pare.   100
Horsemen, you know, are not the com-
    mons' strength,
But are the force and store of noblemen,
Whereby the unchosen and unarméd sort
Of skilless rebels, whom none other power
But number makes to be of dreadful
    force,
With sudden brunt may quickly be op-
    pressed.
And, if this gentle mean of proffered grace
With stubborn hearts cannot so far avail
As to assuage their desperate courages,
Then do I wish such slaughter to be
    made   110
As present age and eke posterity
May be adrad [1] with horror of revenge
That justly then shall on these rebels
    fall.
This is, my lords, the sum of mine advice.
CLOT. Neither this case admits debate at
    large,
And, though it did, this speech that hath
    been said
Hath well abridged the tale I would
    have told.
Fully with Eubulus do I consent
In all that he hath said; and, if the
    same

[1] Adread, afraid.

To you, my lords, may seem for best
   advice,   120
I wish that it should straight be put in
   ure.
MAND. My lords, then let us presently [1]
   depart,
And follow this that liketh us so well.
[*Exeunt Clotyn, Mandud, Gwenard, and
                Eubulus.*]
FERG. If ever time to gain a kingdom here
   Were offered man, now it is offered me.
The realm is reft both of their king and
   queen;
The offspring of the prince is slain and
   dead;
No issue now remains, the heir unknown;
The people are in arms and mutinies;
The nobles they are busied how to
   cease   130
These great rebellious tumults and up-
   roars;
And Britain land, now desert, left alone,
Amid these broils uncertain where to
   rest,
Offers herself unto that noble heart
That will or dare pursue to bear her
   crown.
Shall I, that am the Duke of Albany,
Descended from that line of noble blood
Which hath so long flourished in worthy
   fame
Of valiant hearts, such as in noble breasts
Of right should rest above the baser
   sort,   140
Refuse to venture life to win a crown?
Whom shall I find enemies that will
   withstand
My fact herein, if I attempt by arms
To seek the same now in these times of
   broil?
These dukes'[2] power can hardly well
   appease
The people that already are in arms.
But, if perhaps my force be once in
   field,
Is not my strength in power above the
   best
Of all these lords now left in Britain land?
And though they should match me with
   power of men,   150
Yet doubtful is the chance of battles
   joined.
If victors of the field we may depart,

Ours is the scepter then of Great Britain;
If slain amid the plain this body lie,
Mine enemies yet shall not deny me
   this,
But that I died giving the noble charge
To hazard life for conquest of a crown.
Forthwith, therefore, will I in post de-
   part
To Albany, and raise in armor there
All power I can; and here my secret
   friends   160
By secret practice shall solicit still
To seek to win to me the people's hearts.
                [*Exit.*]

ACTUS QUINTUS. SCENA SECUNDA.

[*The same.*]

Eubulus, Clotyn, Mandud, Gwenard, Arostus,
              Nuntius.[3]
EUB. O Jove, how are these people's hearts
   abused!
What blind fury thus headlong carries
   them,
That, though so many books, so many
   rolls
Of ancient time, record what grievous
   plagues
Light on these rebels aye, and though so
   oft
Their ears have heard their aged fathers
   tell
What just reward these traitors still re-
   ceive,
Yea, though themselves have seen deep
   death and blood,
By strangling cord and slaughter of the
   sword,
To such assigned, yet can they not be-
   ware,   10
Yet cannot stay their lewd rebellious
   hands,
But suffering, lo, foul treason to distain
Their wretched minds, forget their loyal
   heart,
Reject all truth, and rise against their
   prince?
A ruthful case, that those whom duty's
   bond,
Whom grafted law, by nature, truth, and
   faith,
Bound to preserve their country and
   their king,

---

[1] At once.   [2] Dissyllabic.

[3] The last five enter later.

Born to defend their commonwealth and
  prince,
Even they should give consent thus to
  subvert
Thee, Britain land, and from thy womb
  should spring,   20
O native soil, those that will needs de-
  stroy
And ruin thee and eke themselves in fine.
For lo, when once the dukes had offered
  grace
Of pardon sweet, the multitude misled
By traitorous fraud of their ungracious
  heads,
One sort that saw the dangerous success
Of stubborn standing in rebellious war,
And knew the difference of prince's power
From headless number of tumultuous
  routs,
Whom common country's care and pri-
  vate fear   30
Taught to repent the error of their rage,
Laid hands upon the captains of their
  band,
And brought them bound unto the
  mighty dukes.
And other sort, not trusting yet so well
The truth of pardon, or mistrusting more
Their own offense than that they could
  conceive
Such hope of pardon for so foul misdeed,
Or for that they their captains could not
  yield,
Who, fearing to be yielded, fled before,
Stale [1] home by silence of the secret
  night.   40
The third unhappy and enragéd sort
Of desperate hearts who, stained in
  princes' blood,
From traitorous furor could not be with-
  drawn
By love, by law, by grace, ne yet by fear,
By proffered life, ne yet by threatened
  death,
With minds hopeless of life, dreadless of
  death,
Careless of country, and aweless of God,
Stood bent to fight, as Furies did them
  move
With violent death to close their traitor-
  ous life.
These all by power of horsemen were op-
  pressed,   50

[1] Stole.

And with revenging sword slain in the
  field,
Or with the strangling cord hanged on
  the trees,
Where yet their carrion carcasses do
  preach
The fruits that rebels reap of their uproars,
And of the murder of their sacred prince.
But lo, where do approach the noble
  dukes
By whom these tumults have been thus
  appeased.

[*Enter Clotyn, Mandud, Gwenard, and
  Arostus.*]

CLOT. I think the world will now at length
  beware
And fear to put on arms against their
  prince.
MAND. If not, those traitorous hearts that
  dare rebel,   60
Let them behold the wide and hugy fields
With blood and bodies spread of rebels
  slain,
The lofty trees clothed with the corpses
  dead,
That, strangled with the cord, do hang
  thereon.
AROS. A just reward, such as all times
  before
Have ever lotted to those wretched folks.
GWEN. But what means he that cometh
  here so fast?

[*Enter Nuntius.*]

NUN. My lords, as duty and my troth doth
  move,
And of my country work a care in me,
That, if the spending of my breath
  availed   70
To do the service that my heart desires,
I would not shun to embrace a present
  death,
So have I now, in that wherein I thought
My travail mought perform some good
  effect,
Ventered [2] my life to bring these tidings
  here.
Fergus, the mighty Duke of Albany,
Is now in arms and lodgeth in the field
With twenty thousand men; hither he
  bends

[2] Ventured.

His speedy march, and minds to invade
  the crown.
Daily he gathereth strength, and spreads
  abroad   80
That to this realm no certain heir re-
  mains,
That Britain land is left without a guide,
That he the scepter seeks for nothing
  else
But to preserve the people and the land,
Which now remain as ship without a
  stern.
Lo, this is that which I have here to say.
CLOT. Is this his faith? And shall he falsely
  thus
Abuse the vantage of unhappy times?
O wretched land, if his outrageous pride,
His cruel and untempered willfulness, 90
His deep dissembling shows of false pre-
  tense,
Should once attain the crown of Britain
  land!
Let us, my lords, with timely force resist
The new attempt of this our common
  foe,
As we would quench the flames of com-
  mon fire.
MAND. Though we remain without a cer-
  tain prince
To weld the realm or guide the wand'ring
  rule,
Yet now the common mother of us all,
Our native land, our country, that con-
  tains
Our wives, children, kindred, ourselves,
  and all   100
That ever is or may be dear to man,
Cries unto us to help ourselves and her.
Let us advance our powers to repress
This growing foe of all our liberties.
GWEN. Yea, let us so, my lords, with hasty
  speed.
And ye, O gods, send us the welcome
  death
To shed our blood in field, and leave us
  not
In loathsome life to linger out our days,
To see the hugy heaps of these unhaps
That now roll down upon the wretched
  land,   110
Where empty place of princely govern-
  ance,
No certain stay now left of doubtless
  heir,

Thus leaves [1] this guideless realm an open
  prey
To endless storms and waste of civil war.
AROS. That ye, my lords, do so agree in
  one,
To save your country from the violent
  reign
And wrongfully usurpéd tyranny
Of him that threatens conquest of you all,
To save your realm, and in this realm
  yourselves,
From foreign thraldom of so proud a
  prince,   120
Much do I praise; and I beseech the gods
With happy honor to requite it you.
But, O my lords, sith now the heaven's
  wrath
Hath reft this land the issue of their
  prince;
Sith of the body of our late sovereign
  lord
Remains no mo since the young kings
  be slain,
And of the title of descended crown
Uncertainly the divers minds do think
Even of the learned sort, and more un-
  certainly
Will partial fancy and affection deem, 130
But most uncertainly will climbing pride
And hope of reign withdraw to sundry
  parts
The doubtful right and hopeful lust to
  reign;
When once this noble service is achieved
For Britain land, the mother of ye all;
When once ye have with arméd force
  repressed
The proud attempts of this Albanian
  prince
That threatens thraldom to your native
  land;
When ye shall vanquishers return from
  field
And find the princely state an open
  prey   140
To greedy lust and to usurping power,
Then, then, my lords, if ever kindly care
Of ancient honor of your ancestors,
Of present wealth and noblesse of your
  stocks,
Yea, of the lives and safety yet to come
Of your dear wives, your children, and
  yourselves,

[1] Original reads *leave.*

Might move your noble hearts with
gentle ruth,
Then, then, have pity on the torn estate;
Then help to salve the well-near hopeless
sore;
Which ye shall do if ye yourselves with-
hold   150
The slaying knife from your own mother's
throat.
Her shall you save, and you, and yours
in her,
If ye shall all with one assent forbear
Once to lay hand or take unto yourselves
The crown, by color of pretended right,
Or by what other means soever it be,
Till first by common counsel of you all
In parliament the regal diadem
Be set in certain place of governance—
In which your parliament, and in your
choice,   160
Prefer the right, my lords, without re-
spect
Of strength or friends or whatsoever
cause
That may set forward any other's part.
For right will last, and wrong cannot en-
dure.
Right mean I his or hers upon whose
name
The people rest by mean of native line,
Or by the virtue of some former law,
Already made their title to advance.
Such one, my lords, let be your chosen
king,
Such one so born within your native
land,   170
Such one prefer, and in no wise admit
The heavy yoke of foreign governance;
Let foreign titles yield to public wealth.
And with that heart wherewith ye now
prepare
Thus to withstand the proud invading
foe,
With that same heart, my lords, keep out
also
Unnatural thralldom of stranger's reign;
Ne suffer you, against the rules of kind,
Your mother land to serve a foreign
prince.
Eub. Lo, here the end of Brutus' royal
line,   180
And lo, the entry to the woeful wreck
And utter ruin of this noble realm!
The royal king and eke his sons are slain;

No ruler rests within the regal seat;
The heir to whom the scepter longs [1] un-
known,
That [2] to each force of foreign princes'
power,
Whom vantage of our wretched state may
move
By sudden arms to gain so rich a realm,
And to the proud and greedy mind at
home,
Whom blinded lust to reign leads to as-
pire,   190
Lo, Britain realm is left an open prey,
A present spoil by conquest to ensue.
Who seeth not now how many rising
minds
Do feed their thoughts with hope to
reach a realm?
And who will not by force attempt to
win
So great a gain, that hope persuades to
have?
A simple color [3] shall for title serve.
Who wins the royal crown will want no
right,
Nor such as shall display by long descent
A lineal race to prove him lawful
king.   200
In the meanwhile these civil arms shall
rage,
And thus a thousand mischiefs shall un-
fold,
And far and near spread [4] thee, O Britain
land.
All right and law shall cease, and he that
had
Nothing today, tomorrow shall enjoy
Great heaps of gold, and he that flowed
in wealth,
Lo, he shall be bereft of life and all;
And happiest he that then possesseth
least.
The wives shall suffer rape; the maids
deflowered
And children fatherless shall weep and
wail;   210
With fire and sword thy native folk shall
perish;
One kinsman shall bereave another's life;
The father shall unwitting slay the son;
The son shall slay the sire and know it
not;

---

[1] Belongs.   [3] Pretense.
[2] So that.   [4] Spread over.

Women and maids the cruel soldier's
  sword
Shall pierce to death; and silly children,
  lo,
That playing [1] in the streets and fields
  are found,
By violent hands shall close their latter
  day.
Whom shall the fierce and bloody soldier
Reserve to life?   Whom shall he spare
  from death?   220
Even thou, O wretched mother, half
  alive,
Thou shalt behold thy dear and only child
Slain with the sword while he yet sucks
  thy breast.
Lo, guiltless blood shall thus each where
  be shed.
Thus shall the wasted soil yield forth no
  fruit,
But dearth and famine shall possess the
  land.
The towns shall be consumed and burnt
  with fire,
The peopled cities shall wax desolate;
And thou, O Britain, whilom in renowm,
Whilom in wealth and fame, shalt thus
  be torn,   230
Dismembered thus, and thus be rent in
  twain,
Thus wasted and defaced, spoiled and
  destroyed.
These be the fruits your civil wars will
  bring.
Hereto it comes when kings will not
  consent
To grave advice, but follow willful will.
This is the end when in fond princes'
  hearts
Flattery prevails and sage rede hath no
  place.
These are the plagues when murder is the
  mean
To make new heirs unto the royal crown.
Thus wreak the gods when that the
  mother's wrath   240
Naught but the blood of her own child
  may swage.
These mischiefs spring when rebels will
  arise
To work revenge and judge their prince's
  fact.

[1] From 1565 edn. Original reads *play*.

This, this ensues, when noble men do fail
In loyal truth, and subjects will be kings.
And this doth grow, when lo, unto the
  prince
Whom death or sudden hap of life be-
  reaves,
No certain heir remains—such certain
  heir,
As not all-only [2] is the rightful heir,
But to the realm is so made known to be,
And troth thereby vested in subjects'
  hearts   251
To owe faith there where right is known
  to rest.
Alas, in parliament what hope can be,
When is of parliament no hope at all,
Which, though it be assembled by consent,
Yet is not likely with consent to end?
While each one for himself, or for his
  friend,
Against his foe shall travail what he may,
While now the state, left open to the man
That shall with greatest force invade the
  same,   260
Shall fill ambitious minds with gaping
  hope,
When will they once with yielding hearts
  agree?
Or in the while, how shall the realm be
  used?
No, no; then parliament should have
  been holden,
And certain heirs appointed to the crown,
To stay the title of established right,
And in the people plant obedience,
While yet the prince did live whose name
  and power
By lawful summons and authority   269
Might make a parliament to be of force,
And might have set the state in quiet stay.
But now, O happy man whom speedy
  death
Deprives of life, ne is enforced to see
These hugy mischiefs and these miseries,
These civil wars, these murders, and
  these wrongs
Of justice! Yet must God in fine restore
This noble crown unto the lawful heir:
For right will always live, and rise at
  length,
But wrong can never take deep root to
  last.   [*Exeunt.*]

[2] Alonely, solely.

THE END OF THE TRAGEDY OF KING GORBODUC.

GEORGE GASCOIGNE

George Gascoigne is an early Elizabethan example of the passionate striving for full-ness of achievement and for fame in the Renaissance. Apparently he was born about 1542 or earlier. His career includes stays at Trinity College, Cambridge, and at Gray's Inn, a wealthy marriage with the widowed mother of Nicholas Breton, elections to parliament and charges that prevented him from sitting in 1572, notorious escapades and disinheritance by his father, the patronage of nobles and bids for the favor of the queen herself, travels on the Continent, and service under William of Orange in the Netherlands in 1573–74. In his motto, "*Tam Marti quam Mercurio*," he claims equal devotion to arms and to wit. His literary activity was very varied. In addition to his dramatic work, which includes what has been called the first regular masque in English— devised for Leicester's entertainment of Elizabeth at Kenilworth in 1575—he wrote lyrics, satire, fiction, and criticism, and distinguished himself in each field. He died in his prime, apparently in 1577, although some evidence has been advanced for 1578.

Gascoigne wrote two plays besides *Supposes*. *Jocasta*, a blank verse tragedy presented at Gray's Inn in 1566, was written in collaboration with Francis Kinwelmarsh. The play is not, as its title-page implies, a direct translation of Euripides' *Phœnissæ*, but rather a fairly close translation of an Italian adaptation, made by Lodovico Dolce and printed in 1549 with the title *Giocasta*. *The Glass of Government*, printed in 1575, belongs to a group of English plays dealing with the Prodigal Son theme, which followed the models furnished by a large body of Continental school plays in Latin, chiefly the work of Dutch humanists. Gascoigne's play was written under the influence of several of these Dutch dramatists.

Like *Jocasta*, *Supposes* was performed at Gray's Inn in 1566 and shows the Italian in-fluence on English drama. It is a somewhat free translation of Ariosto's *I Suppositi*, which was acted in a prose form in 1509 and later put into verse. Gascoigne seems to have used both versions for his play. In addition to its literary interest, *Supposes* has great historical importance, first, because it seems to be the first English translation of Italian adaptations of Roman comedy; second, because it is the first extant English play to be written in prose throughout; and third, because it apparently furnished Shake-speare with his underplot in *The Taming of the Shrew*.

Italian adaptations of Roman comedy, like Italian *novelle*, contributed important ele-ments to English romantic comedy. Much more than the English adaptations, they de-veloped the plot interests of comedy, especially love intrigue, disguise, and mistaken identity. For his foundation Ariosto took the young master's exchange of rôles with his servant from the *Captivi* of Plautus, and his entering in disguise the house of a girl from the *Eunuchus* of Terence, adding various elements adapted from these and other Roman plays—the substitute for the father, the discovery of a long lost son, the parasite, and the rich old wooer who developed into the stock character of Italian comedy called the pantaloon. In his preface Ariosto speaks of his imitation as poetic creation, and his plot is superior to those from which he borrowed, in variety of incident and in the heightening of the love interest through the introduction of the rival wooer, comic though the treat-ment here is.

Supposes was first printed about 1572–73. An improved edition was included in *The Posies* of 1575, a miscellany of different types of work, at least in the main Gascoigne's. A reprint of the text of 1575 by R. W. Bond in his *Early Plays from the Italian* is the basis of the present text. J. W. Cunliffe's edition of the play in his *Works of Gascoigne* has been used for comparison.

SUPPOSES[1]

BY

GEORGE GASCOIGNE

THE NAMES OF THE ACTORS

BALIA, *the nurse.*
POLYNESTA, *the young woman.*
CLEANDER, *the doctor,*[2] *suitor to Polynesta.*
PASIPHILO, *the parasite.*
CARION, *the doctor's man.*
DULIPPO, *feigned servant, and lover of Polynesta.*
EROSTRATO, *feigned master, and suitor to Polynesta.*
DALIO *and* } *servants to feigned Erostrato.*
CRAPINO

SIENESE, *a gentleman stranger.*
PAQUETTO *and* } *his servants.*
PETRUCHIO
DAMON, *father to Polynesta.*
NEVOLA *and* TWO OTHER HIS SERVANTS.
PSITERIA, *an old hag in his house.*
PHILOGANO, *a Sicilian gentleman, father to Erostrato.*
LITIO, *his servant.*
FERRARESE, *an innkeeper of Ferrara.*

The comedy presented as it were in Ferrara.

[TIME: *About 1500.*]

THE PROLOGUE OR ARGUMENT

I suppose you are assembled here supposing to reap the fruit of my travails;[3] and, to be plain, I mean presently to present you with a comedy called *Supposes*,[4] the very name whereof may peradventure drive into every of your heads a sundry suppose, to suppose the meaning of our Supposes. Some, percase,[5] will suppose we mean to occupy your ears with sophistical handling of subtile suppositions; some other will [10 suppose we go about to decipher unto you some quaint conceits,[6] which hitherto have been only supposed, as it were, in shadows;[7] and some I see smiling as though they supposed we would trouble you with the vain suppose of some wanton suppose.[8] But, understand, this our Suppose is noth-ing else but a mistaking or imagination of one thing for another. For you shall see the master supposed for the servant, the [20 servant for the master; the freeman for a slave, and the bondslave for a freeman; the stranger for a well-known friend, and the familiar for a stranger. But what? I suppose that even already you suppose me very fond[9] that have so simply disclosed unto you the subtilties of these our Supposes; where otherwise, indeed, I suppose you should have heard almost the last of our Supposes before you could [30 have supposed any of them aright. Let this then suffice.

ACTUS I. SCENA i.[10]

Balia, the nurse, [followed by] Polynesta, the young woman.

[BAL.] Here is nobody. Come forth, Polynesta. Let us look about, to be sure lest any man hear our talk; for I think within the house the tables, the planks,

---

[1] The original title continues: "A Comedy Written in the Italian Tongue by Ariosto, Englished by George Gascoigne, of Gray's Inn, Esquire, and There Presented. 1566."
[2] Of law.   [3] Labors.
[4] Ariosto's title, *I Suppositi*, carried the meaning of "substitutions" rather than of "suppositions."
[5] Perchance.
[6] Ingeniously elaborated conceptions.
[7] Pictures.   [8] "Prostitute" (Adams).
[9] Foolish.
[10] The whole action, which occupies only a few hours, takes place in a street between the houses of Damon and Erostrato.

113

the beds, the portals,[1] yea, and the cupboards themselves have ears.

POLY. You might as well have said the windows and the doors. Do you not see how they hearken?

BAL. Well, you jest fair; but I would [10 advise you take heed! I have bidden you a thousand times beware. You will be spied one day talking with Dulippo.

POLY. And why should I not talk with Dulippo as well as with any other, I pray you?

BAL. I have given you a wherefore for this why many times. But go to! Follow your own advice till you overwhelm us all with sudden mishap.   20

POLY. A great mishap, I promise you! Marry, God's blessing on their heart that set such a brooch on my cap.[2]

BAL. Well, look well about you! A man would think it were enough for you secretly to rejoice that by my help you have passed so many pleasant nights together. And yet, by my troth, I do it more than half against my will, for I would rather you had settled your fancy in [30 some noble family. Yea, and it is no small grief unto me that, rejecting the suits of so many nobles and gentlemen, you have chosen for your darling a poor servant of your father's, by whom shame and infamy is the best dower you can look for to attain.

POLY. And, I pray you, whom may I thank but gentle nurse, that continually praising him, what for his personage,[3] [40 his courtesy, and, above all, the extreme passions[4] of his mind—in fine, you would never cease till I accepted him, delighted in him, and at length desired him with no less affection than he erst[5] desired me.

BAL. I cannot deny but at the beginning I did recommend him unto you (as, indeed, I may say that for myself I have a pitiful heart), seeing the depth of his unbridled affection, and that continually [50 he never ceased to fill mine ears with lamentable complaints.

POLY. Nay, rather that he filled your purse with bribes and rewards, nurse!

BAL. Well, you may judge of nurse as you list.[6] Indeed, I have thought it always a deed of charity to help the miserable young men whose tender youth consumeth with the furious flames of love. But, be you sure, if I had thought you [60 would have passed to the terms you now stand in, pity nor pension,[7] penny nor paternoster,[8] should ever have made nurse once to open her mouth in the cause.

POLY. No? Of honesty, I pray you, who first brought him into my chamber, who first taught him the way to my bed but you? Fie, nurse, fie! Never speak of it for shame! You will make me tell a wise tale anon.[9]   70

BAL. And have I these thanks for my good will? Why then, I see well I shall be counted the cause of all mishap.

POLY. Nay, rather the author of my good hap, gentle nurse. For I would thou knewest I love not Dulippo, nor any of so mean estate, but have bestowed my love more worthily than thou deemest. But I will say no more at this time.   79

BAL. Then I am glad you have changed your mind yet.

POLY. Nay, I neither have changed nor will change it.

BAL. Then I understand you not. How said you?

POLY. Marry, I say that I love not Dulippo, nor any such as he; and yet I neither have changed nor will change my mind.

BAL. I cannot tell. You love to lie [90 with Dulippo very well. This gear[10] is Greek to me. Either it hangs not well together or I am very dull of understanding. Speak plain, I pray you.

POLY. I can speak no plainer; I have sworn to the contrary.

BAL. How! Make you so dainty[11] to tell it nurse, lest she should reveal it? You have trusted me as far as may be (I may show to you) in things that touch your [100 honor if they were known, and make you strange to tell me this? I am sure it is but a trifle in comparison of those things whereof heretofore you have made me privy.

POLY. Well, it is of greater importance

---

[1] Passages.
[2] I.e., "put such a feather in my cap."
[3] Bodily form.
[4] Heroic sentiments.   [5] First.

[6] Please.   [7] Payment.   [8] Prayer.   [9] Soon.
[10] Affair.   [11] Are you so squeamish?

than you think, nurse; yet would I tell it you—under condition and promise that you shall not tell it again, nor give any sign or token to be suspected that you know it. [110

BAL. I promise you, of my honesty. Say on.

POLY. Well, hear you me then. This young man whom you have always taken for Dulippo is a noble-born Sicilian, his right name Erostrato, son to Philogano, one of the worthiest men in that country.

BAL. How, Erostrato? Is it not our neighbor, which ——

POLY. Hold thy talking, nurse, and [120 hearken to me that I may explain the whole case unto thee. The man whom to this day you have supposed to be *The first sup-* Dulippo is, as I say, Erostrato, *pose and* a gentleman that came from *ground of all* Sicilia to study in this city; *the supposes.* and even at his first arrival met me in the street, fell enamored of me, and of such vehement force were the passions he suffered that immediately he cast aside [130 both long gown and books, and determined on me only to apply his study. And to the end he might the more commodiously both see me and talk with me, he exchanged both name, habit, clothes, and credit with his servant Dulippo, whom only he brought with him out of Sicilia. And so, with the turning of a hand, of Erostrato, a gentleman, he became Dulippo, a serving-man, and soon after [140 sought service of my father and obtained it.

BAL. Are you sure of this?

POLY. Yea, out of doubt. On the other side, Dulippo took upon him the name of Erostrato, his master, the habit, the credit, books, and all things needful to a student, and in short space profited very much, and is now esteemed as you see.

BAL. Are there no other Sicilians here nor none that pass this way, which [150 may discover them?

POLY. Very few that pass this way, and few or none that tarry here any time.

BAL. This hath been a strange adventure! But, I pray you, how hang these things together—that the student, whom you say to be the servant and not the master, is become an earnest suitor to you and requireth you of your father in marriage? 160

POLY. That is a policy devised between them to put Doctor Dotipole [1] out of conceit [2]—the old dotard!—he that so instantly doth lie upon [3] my father for me. But look where he comes—as God help me, it is he. Out upon him! What a lusky yonker [4] is this! Yet I had rather be a nun a thousand times than be cumbered with such a coistrel. [5] 169

BAL. Daughter, you have reason. But let us go in before he come any nearer.

Polynesta goeth in, and Balia stayeth a little while after, speaking a word or two to the doctor, and then departeth.

SCENA ii.

Cleander, doctor; Pasiphilo, parasite; Balia, nurse.

[CLE.] Were these dames [6] here, or did mine eyes dazzle?

PASI. Nay, sir, here were Polynesta and her nurse.

CLE. Was my Polynesta here? Alas, I knew her not!

BAL. [*Aside.*] He must have better eyesight that should marry your Polynesta—or else he may chance to oversee the best point in his tables [7] sometimes. [*Exit.*] 10

PASI. Sir, it is no marvel; the air is very misty today. I myself knew her better by her apparel than by her face.

CLE. In good faith, and I thank God, I have mine eyesight good and perfit [8]—little worse than when I was but twenty years old.

PASI. How can it be otherwise? You are but young.

CLE. I am fifty years old. 20

PASI. [*Aside.*] He tells [9] ten less than he is.

CLE. What sayst thou of ten less?

PASI. I say I would have thought you ten less; you look like one of six-and-thirty, or seven-and-thirty at the most.

CLE. I am no less than I tell.

PASI. You are like enough to live fifty more. Show me your hand.

---

[1] A common name for a blockhead.
[2] *I.e.*, humble his pride.
[3] So insistently urges. [4] Lazy youngster.
[5] Rascal. [6] Great ladies.
[7] "*I.e.*, be made a cuckold; metaphor from backgammon" (Bond).
[8] Perfect. [9] Counts.

Cle. Why, is Pasiphilo a chiro- [30 mancer? [1]

Pasi. What is not Pasiphilo? I pray you, show me it a little.

Cle. Here it is.

Pasi. O, how straight and infract [2] is this line of life! You will live to the years of Melchisedec.

Cle. Thou wouldest say Methusalem.

Pasi. Why, is it not all one?

Cle. I perceive you are no very [40 good Bibler, Pasiphilo.

Pasi. Yes, sir, an excellent good bibler,[3] specially in a bottle. O, what a mount of Venus here is! But this light serveth not very well. I will behold it another day, when the air is clearer, and tell you somewhat, peradventure, to your contentation.[4]

Cle. You shall do me great pleasure. But tell me, I pray thee, Pasiphilo, [50 whom dost thou think Polynesta liketh better, Erostrato or me?

Pasi. Why, you, out of doubt! She is a gentlewoman of a noble mind, and maketh greater accompt of the reputation she shall have in marrying your worship, than that poor scholar, whose birth and parentage God knoweth, and very few else.

Cle. Yet he taketh it upon him bravely [5] in this country. 60

Pasi. Yea, where no man knoweth the contrary. But let him brave it, boast his birth, and do what he can, the virtue and knowledge that is within this body of yours is worth more than all the country he came from.

Cle. It becometh not a man to praise himself; but indeed I may say, and say truly, that my knowledge hath stood me in better stead at a pinch than could all [70 the goods in the world. I came out of Otranto when the Turks won it, and first I came to Padua, after [6] hither, where, by reading,[7] counseling, and pleading, within twenty years I have gathered and gained as good as ten thousand ducats.

Pasi. Yea, marry, this is the right knowledge! Philosophy, Poetry, Logic, and all the rest are but pickling [8] sciences in comparison to this. 80

Cle. But pickling indeed; whereof we have a verse:

The trade of law doth fill the boist'rous bags; [9]
They swim in silk, when others roist [10] in rags.

Pasi. O excellent verse! Who made it? Virgil?

Cle. Virgil? Tush, it is written in one of our glosses.[11]

Pasi. Sure, whosoever wrote it, the moral is excellent, and worthy to be [90 written in letters of gold. But to the purpose! I think you shall never recover the wealth that you lost at Otranto.

Cle. I think I have doubled it, or rather made it four times as much. *Another sup-* But, indeed, I lost mine only *pose.* son there, a child of five years old.

Pasi. O great pity!

Cle. Yea, I had rather have lost all the goods in the world. 100

Pasi. Alas! alas! by God! And grafts of such a stock are very gayson [12] in these days.

Cle. I know not whether he were slain, or the Turks took him and kept him as a bondslave.

Pasi. Alas, I could weep for compassion! But there is no remedy but patience. You shall get many by this young damsel, with the grace of God. 110

Cle. Yea, if I get her.

Pasi. Get her? Why doubt you of that?

Cle. Why? Her father holds me off with delays, so that I must needs doubt.

Pasi. Content yourself, sir. He is a wise man and desirous to place his daughter well. He will not be too rash in his determination; he will think well of the matter. And let him think, for the longer he thinketh, the more good of you shall he [120 think. Whose wealth, whose virtue, whose skill, or whose estimation can he compare to yours in this city?

Cle. And hast thou not told him that I would make his daughter a dower of two thousand ducats?

Pasi. Why, even now. I came but from thence since.[13]

[9] Large pouches to hold the back hair of the wigs worn by judges.   [12] Geason, rare.
[10] Bluster.   [13] Straightway.
[11] Commentaries on the law.

[1] Palmist.   [4] Satisfaction.   [7] Lecturing.
[2] Unbroken.   [5] Lives showily. [8] Trifling.
[3] Tippler.   [6] Afterward.

Cle. What said he?

Pasi. Nothing but that Erostrato [130 had proffered the like.

Cle. Erostrato? How can he make any dower, and his father yet alive?

Pasi. Think you I did not tell him so? Yes, I warrant you, I forgot nothing that may furder [1] your cause. And doubt you not, Erostrato shall never have her—unless it be in a dream.

Cle. Well, gentle Pasiphilo, go thy ways and tell Damon I require nothing but [140 his daughter; I will none of his goods; I shall enrich her of mine own; and, if this dower of two thousand ducats seem not sufficient, I will make it five hundreth more, yea, a thousand, or whatsoever he will demand, rather than fail. Go to, Pasiphilo! Show thyself friendly in working this feat for me; spare for no cost. Since I have gone thus far, I will be loath to be outbidden. Go!　　　　150

Pasi. Where shall I come to you again?

Cle. At my house.

Pasi. When?

Cle. When thou wilt.

Pasi. Shall I come at dinner time?

Cle. I would bid thee to dinner, but it is a saint's even, which I have ever fasted.

Pasi. [Aside.] Fast till thou famish!

Cle. Hark!

Pasi. [Aside.] He speaketh of a dead [160 man's fast.[2]

Cle. Thou hearest me not.

Pasi. [Aside.] Nor thou understandest me not.

Cle. I dare say thou art angry I bid thee not to dinner, but come if thou wilt; thou shalt take such as thou findest.

Pasi. What! think you I know not where to dine?

Cle. Yes, Pasiphilo, thou art not to [170 seek.[3]

Pasi. No, be you sure; there are enow will pray me.

Cle. That I know well enough, Pasiphilo. But thou canst not be better welcome in any place than to me. I will tarry for thee.

Pasi. Well, since you will needs, I will come.

Cle. Despatch then, and bring no [180 news but good.

Pasi. [Aside.] Better than my reward, by the Rood!

Cleander exit; Pasiphilo restat.[4]

Scena iii.

Pasiphilo, Dulippo.[5]

[Pasi.] O miserable, covetous wretch! He findeth an excuse by St. Nicholas' fast, because [6] I should not dine with him—as though I should dine at his own dish! He maketh goodly feasts, I promise you! It is no wonder though he think me bound unto him for my fare; for, over and besides that his provision is as scant as may be, yet there is great difference between his diet and mine. I never so much as [10 sip of the wine that he tasteth; I feed at the board's end with brown bread. Marry, I reach always to his own dish, for there are no more but that only on the table. Yet he thinks that for one such dinner I am bound to do him all the service that I can, and thinks me sufficiently rewarded for all my travail with one such festival promotion! And yet, peradventure, some men think I have great gains under him, [20 but I may say, and swear, that this dozen year I have not gained so much in value as the points at my hose,[7] which are but three, with codpiece-point and all. He thinks that I may feed upon his favor and fair words, but, if I could not otherwise provide for one, Pasiphilo were in a wise case.[8] Pasiphilo hath mo [9] pastures to pass in than one, I warrant you! I am of household with this scholar Eros- [30 trato, his rival, as well as with Domine [10] Cleander—now with the one, and then with the other, according as I see their caters [11] provide good cheer at the market—and I find the means so to handle the matter that I am welcome to both. If the one see me talk with the other, I make him believe it is to hearken news in the furtherance of his cause, and thus I become a broker on both sides. Well, [40 let them both apply the matter as well as

---

[1] Further.

[2] *I.e.*, one which, like Cleander's own, is never broken.　　　　[3] Not deficient in that respect.

[4] Remains.

[5] Enters later.

[6] By cause; why.

[7] Laces on my breeches.

[8] In a bad way.

[9] More.

[10] Master.

[11] Caterers.

they can, for indeed I will travail for none of them both, yet will I seem to work wonders on each hand. But is not this one of Damon's servants that cometh forth? It is. Of him I shall understand where his master is. Whither goeth this joyly[1] gallant?

[Enter Dulippo from Damon's house.]

DUL. I come to seek somebody that may accompany my master at dinner. [50 He is alone and would fain have good company.

PASI. Seek no further. You could never have found one better than me.

DUL. I have no commission to bring so many.

PASI. How,[2] many? I will come alone.

DUL. How canst thou come alone that hast continually a legion of ravening wolves within thee?   60

PASI. Thou dost, as servants commonly do, hate all that love to visit their masters.

DUL. And why?

PASI. Because they have too many teeth, as you think.

DUL. Nay, because they have too many tongues.

PASI. Tongues? I pray you, what did my tongue ever hurt you?

DUL. I speak but merrily with you, [70 Pasiphilo. Go in; my master is ready to dine.

PASI. What, dineth he so early?

DUL. He that riseth early, dineth early.

PASI. I would I were his man. Master Doctor never dineth till noon, and how delicately then, God knoweth! I will be bold to go in, for I count myself bidden.

DUL. You were best so.

Pasiphilo intrat;[3] *Dul[ippo] restat.*

Hard hap had I when I first be- [80 gan this unfortunate enterprise! For I supposed the readiest medicine to my miserable affects[4] had been to change name, clothes, and credit with my serv-ant, and to place myself in Damon's serv-ice; thinking that, as shivering cold by glowing fire, thirst by drink, hunger by pleasant repasts, and a thousand such like

passions find remedy by their contraries, so my restless desire might have found [90 quiet by continual contemplation. But, alas, I find that only love is unsatiable, for, as the fly playeth with the flame till at last she is cause of her own decay, so the lover that thinketh with kissing and coll-ing[5] to content his unbridled appetite, is commonly seen the only cause of his own consumption. Two years are now past since, under the color[6] of Damon's service, I have been a sworn servant to Cupid [100 —of whom I have received as much favor and grace as ever man found in his service. I have free liberty at all times to behold my desired, to talk with her, to embrace her, yea, be it spoken in secret, to lie with her. I reap the fruits of my desire; yet, as my joys abound, even so my pains in-crease. I fare like the covetous man that, having all the world at will, is never yet content. The more I have, the more I [110 desire. Alas! what wretched estate have I brought myself unto, if in the end of all my far fetches[7] she be given by her father to this old doting doctor, this buzzard, this bribing villain, that by so many means seeketh to obtain her at her father's hands! I know she loveth me best of all others. But what may that prevail when perforce she shall be constrained to marry another? Alas! the pleasant taste of my sugared [120 joys doth yet remain so perfect in my remembrance that the least sop of sorrow seemeth more sour than gall in my mouth. If I had never known delight, with better contentation might I have passed these dreadful dolors. And if this old *mump-simus*[8]—whom the pox consume!—should win her, then may I say, "Farewell the pleasant talk, the kind embracings, yea, farewell the sight of my Polynesta!" [130 For he, like a jealous wretch, will pen her up, that I think the birds of the air shall not win the sight of her. I hoped to have cast a block in his way by the means that my servant, who is supposed to be Eros-trato and with my habit and credit is well esteemed, should proffer himself a suitor—at the least to countervail the doctor's proffers. But my master, knowing the wealth of the one and doubting the [140

---

[1] Elegant, well-dressed.   [3] Goes in.
[2] In what way?   [4] Feelings.

[5] "Necking," embracing.   [7] Clever plots.
[6] Pretense.   [8] Obstinate dolt.

state [1] of the other, is determined to be fed no longer with fair words, but to accept the doctor, whom he right well knoweth, for his son-in-law. Well, my servant promised me yesterday to devise yet again some new conspiracy to drive Master Doctor out of conceit, and to lay a snare that the fox himself might be caught in! What it is, I know not, nor I saw him not since he went about it. I will go see if he be [150 within, that at least if he help me not, he may yet prolong my life for this once. But here cometh his lackey. Ho, Jackpack, where is Erostrato?

Here must Crapine be coming in with a basket and a stick in his hand.

Scena iv.

Crapino, the lackey; Dulippo.

[Cra.] Erostrato? Marry, he is in his skin!

Dul. Ah, whoreson [2] boy! I say, how shall I find Erostrato?

Cra. Find [3] him? How mean you—by the week or by the year?

Dul. You crackhalter! [4] If I catch you by the ears, I shall make you answer me directly.

Cra. Indeed?   10

Dul. Tarry me a little.

Cra. In faith, sir, I have no leisure.

Dul. Shall we try who can run fastest?

Cra. Your legs be longer than mine; you should have given me the advantage.

Dul. Go to! Tell me where is Erostrato?

Cra. I left him in the street, where he gave me this casket—this basket, I would have said—and bade me bear it to [20 Dalio, and return to him at the duke's palace.

Dul. If thou see him, tell him I must needs speak with him immediately; or abide awhile! I will go seek him myself rather than be suspected by going to his house.

Crapino departeth, and Dulippo also; after, Dulippo cometh in again seeking Erostrato.

Finis Actus i.

[1] Estate.   [4] Gallows bird.
[2] Rascally.
[3] Punning on *find*, to board, support.

Actus II. Scena i.

Dulippo, Erostrato. [5]

[Dul.] I think if I had as many eyes as Argus I could not have sought a man more narrowly in every street and every by-lane. There are not many gentlemen, scholars, nor merchants in the city of Ferrara but I have met with them, except him. Peradventure he is come home another way. But look where he cometh at the last!

[Enter Erostrato.]

Ero. In good time have I spied my good master!   10

Dul. For the love of God, call me "Dulippo," not "master." Maintain the credit that thou hast hitherto kept, and let me alone.

Ero. Yet, sir, let me sometimes do my duty unto you, especially where nobody heareth.

Dul. Yea, but so long the parrot useth to cry "knap" [6] in sport that at the last she calleth her master "knave" in [20 earnest; so long you will use to call me "master," that at the last we shall be heard. What news?

Ero. Good!

Dul. Indeed?

Ero. Yea, excellent. We have as good as won the wager.

Dul. O, how happy were I if this were true!

Ero. Hear you me. Yesternight in [30 the evening I walked out and found Pasiphilo, and with small entreating I had him home to supper; where, by such means as I used, he became my great friend, and told me the whole order of our adversary's determination, yea, and what Damon doth intend to do also; and hath promised me that from time to time, what he can espy he will bring me word of it.

Dul. I cannot tell whether you [40 know him or no. He is not to trust unto— a very flattering and a lying knave.

Ero. I know him very well; he cannot deceive me. And this that he hath told me I know must needs be true.

Dul. And what was it in effect?

Ero. That Damon had purposed to give

[5] Enters later.   [6] Knave, rascal.

his daughter in marriage to this *Another sup-*
doctor upon the dower that he *pose.*
hath proffered.   50

DUL. Are these your good news, your
excellent news?

ERO. Stay awhile; you will understand
me before you hear me.

DUL. Well, say on.

ERO. I answered to that, I was ready to
make her the like dower.

DUL. Well said.

ERO. Abide; you hear not the worst yet.

DUL. O God, is there any worse [60
behind?

ERO. Worse? Why, what assurance could
you suppose that I might make without
some special consent from Philogano, my
father?

DUL. Nay, you can tell; you are better
scholar than I.

ERO. Indeed, you have lost your time,
for the books that you toss [1] nowadays
treat of small science!   70

DUL. Leave thy jesting and proceed.

ERO. I said, further, that I received
letters lately from my father, whereby I
understood that he would be here very
shortly to perform all that I had proffered.
Therefore I required him to request Damon
on my behalf that he would stay his promise to the doctor for a fortnight or more.

DUL. This is somewhat yet, for by this
means I shall be sure to linger and live [80
in hope one fortnight longer. But, at the
fortnight's end when Philogano cometh not,
how shall I then do? Yea, and though he
came, how may I any way hope of his consent, when he shall see that to follow this
amorous enterprise I have set aside all
study, all remembrance of my duty, and
all dread of shame? Alas, alas, I may go
hang myself!

ERO. Comfort yourself, man, and [90
trust in me. There is a salve for every sore,
and doubt you not, to this mischief we
shall find a remedy.

DUL. O, friend, revive me, that hitherto,
since I first attempted this matter, have
been continually dying.

ERO. Well, hearken awhile then. This
morning I took my horse and rode into the
fields to solace myself; and, as I passed the
ford beyond St. Anthony's Gate, I met [100

[1] Turn the leaves of.

at the foot of the hill a gentleman riding
with two or three men; and, as methought
by his habit and his looks, he should be
none of the wisest. He saluted me, and I
him. I asked him from whence he came,
and whither he would. He answered that
he had come from Venice, then from Padua,
now was going to Ferrara, and so to his
country, which is Siena. As soon as I
knew him to be a Sienese, suddenly [110
lifting up mine eyes, as it were with an admiration,[2] I said unto him, "Are you a
Sienese, and come to Ferrara?" "Why
not?" said he. Quoth I, half and more
with a trembling voice, "Know you the
danger that should ensue if you be known
in Ferrara to be a Sienese?" He, more than
half amazed, desired me earnestly to tell
him what I meant.

DUL. I understand not whereto this [120
tendeth.

ERO. I believe you. But hearken to me.

DUL. Go to, then.

ERO. I answered him in this sort: "Gentleman, because I have heretofore found
very courteous entertainment in your
country, being a student there, I accompt
myself, as it were, bound to a Sienese, and
therefore if I knew of any mishap towards
any of that country, God forbid but I [130
should disclose it. And I marvel that you
knew not of the injury that your countrymen offered this other day to the ambassadors of County [3] Hercules."

DUL. What tales he telleth me! What
appertain these to me?

ERO. If you will hearken awhile, you
shall find them no tales, but that they appertain to you more than you think for.

DUL. Forth.   140

ERO. I told him further, these ambassadors of County Hercules had divers
mules, wagons, and charettes,[4] laden with
divers costly jewels, gorgeous furniture, and
other things, which they carried as presents,
passing that way, to the King of Naples;
the which were not only stayed in Siene
by the officers whom you call customers,[5]
but searched, ransacked, tossed, and
turned, and in the end exacted for trib- [150
ute, as if they had been the goods of a
mean merchant.

[2] Wondering look.   [4] Carts.
[3] Count.   [5] Customs officers.

DUL. Whither the devil will he? Is it possible that this gear appertain anything to my cause? I find neither head nor foot in it.

ERO. O, how impatient you are! I pray you, stay awhile.

DUL. Go to yet awhile, then.

ERO. I proceeded that upon these [160 causes the duke sent his chancellor to declare the case unto the senate there, of whom he had the most uncourteous answer that ever was heard; whereupon he was so enraged with all of that country that for revenge he had sworn to spoil as many of them as ever should come to Ferrara, and to send them home in their doublet and their hose.

DUL. And, I pray thee, how could- [170 est thou upon the sudden devise or imagine such a lie, and to what purpose?

ERO. You shall hear by-and-by [1] a thing as fit for our purpose as any could have happened.

DUL. I would fain hear you conclude.

ERO. You would fain leap over the stile before you come at the hedge. I would you had heard me, and seen the gestures that I enforced to make him believe this! [180

DUL. I believe you, for I know you can counterfeit well.

ERO. Further, I said, the duke had charged, upon great penalties, that the inn-holders and victualers should bring word daily of as many Sieneses as came to their houses. The gentleman, being, as I guessed at the first, a man of small *sapientia*,[2] when he heard these news, would have turned his horse another way.   190

DUL. By likelihood he was not very wise when he would believe that of his country which, if it had been true, every man must needs have known it.

ERO. Why not, when he had not been in his country for a month past, and I told him this had happened within these seven days?

DUL. Belike [3] he was of small experience.

ERO. I think, of as little as may be. [200 But best of all for our purpose, and good adventure it was, that I met with such an one. Now hearken, I pray you.

DUL. Make an end, I pray thee.

ERO. He, as I say, when he heard these

words, would have turned the bridle; and I, feigning a countenance as though I were somewhat pensive and careful for him, paused awhile, and after, with a great sigh, said to him: "Gentleman, for the cour- [210 tesy that, as I said, I have found in your country, and because your affair shall be the better despatched, I will find the means to lodge you in my house, and you shall say to every man that you are a Sicilian of Cathanea, your name Philogano, father to me—that am indeed of that country and city—called here Erostrato. And I, to pleasure you, will during your abode here do you reverence as you were my [220 father."

DUL. Out upon me! What a gross-headed fool am I! Now I perceive whereto this tale tendeth.

ERO. Well, and how like you of it?

DUL. Indifferently.[4] But one thing I doubt.

ERO. What is that?

DUL. Marry, that when he hath been here two or three days, he shall hear of [230 every man that there is no such thing between the duke and the town of Siene.

ERO. As for that, let me alone. I do entertain and will entertain him so well that within these two or three days I will disclose unto him all the whole matter, and doubt not but to bring him in for performance of as much as I have promised to Damon. For what hurt can it be to him, when he shall bind [5] a strange name and [240 not his own?

DUL. What! Think you he will be entreated to stand bound for a dower of two thousand ducats by the year?

ERO. Yea, why not, if it were ten thousand, as long as he is not indeed the man that is bound?

DUL. Well, if it be so, what shall we be the nearer to our purpose?

ERO. Why, when we have done as [250 much as we can, how can we do any more?

DUL. And where have you left him?

ERO. At the inn, because of his horses. He and his men shall lie in my house.

DUL. Why brought you him not with you?

ERO. I thought better to use your advice first.

Dul. Well, go take him home. Make him all the cheer you can; spare for no [260 cost. I will allow it.

Ero. Content. Look where he cometh.

Dul. Is this he? Go meet him. By my troth, he looks even like a good soul! He that fisheth for him might be sure to catch a cod's head![1] I will rest here awhile to decipher him.

Erostrato espieth the Sienese and goeth towards him; Dulippo standeth aside.

Scena ii.

The Sienese; Paquetto and Petruchio, his servants; Erostrato.

[Sien.] He that traveleth in this world passeth by many perils.

Paq. You say true, sir. If the boat had been a little more laden *Another sup-* this morning at the ferry, we *pose.* had been all drowned, for I think there are none of us that could have swum.

Sien. I speak not of that.

Paq. O, you mean the foul way that we had since we came from this Padua. I [10 promise you, I was afraid twice or thrice that your mule would have lien [2] fast in the mire.

Sien. Jesu, what a blockhead thou art! I speak of the peril we are in presently since we came into this city.

Paq. A great peril, I promise you, that we were no sooner arrived but you found a friend that brought you from the inn and lodged you in his own house! 20

Sien. Yea, marry, God reward the gentle young man that we met, for else we had been in a wise case by this time. But have done with these tales. *A doltish* And take you heed, and you *suppose.* also, sirrah, take heed that none of you say we be Sieneses; and remember that you call me Philogano of Cathanea.

Paq. Sure, I shall never remember these outlandish words! I could well re- [30 member Haccanea.[3]

Sien. I say, "Cathanea," and not "Haccanea," with a vengeance!

Paq. Let another name it, then, when need is, for I shall never remember it.

Sien. Then hold thy peace, and take heed thou name not Siene.

Paq. How say you if I feign myself dumb, as I did once in the house of Crisobolus? 40

Sien. Do as thou thinkest best. [*Erostrato advances.*] But look where cometh the gentleman whom we are so much bound unto.

Ero. Welcome, my dear father Philogano.

Sien. Gramercy, my good son Erostrato.

Ero. That is well said. Be mindful of your tongue, for these Ferrareses be [50 as crafty as the devil of hell.

Sien. No, no; be you sure we will do as you have bidden us!

Ero. For, if you should name Siene, they would spoil you immediately, and turn you out of the town with more shame than I would should befall you for a thousand crowns.

Sien. I warrant you, I was giving them warning as I came to you; and I doubt [60 not but they will take good heed.

Ero. Yea, and trust not the servants of my household too far, for they are Ferrareses all, and never knew my father, nor came never in Sicilia.—This is my house. Will it please you to go in? I will follow.

They go in. Dulippo tarrieth, and espieth the Doctor coming in with his Man.

Scena iii.

Dulippo alone.

[Dul.] This gear hath had no evil beginning. If it continue so and fall to happy end! But is not this the silly doctor with the side [4] bonnet—the doting fool that dare presume to become a suitor to such a peerless paragon? O, how covetousness doth blind the common sort of men! Damon, more desirous of the dower than mindful of his gentle and gallant daughter, hath determined to make him his [10 son-in-law, who for his age may be his father-in-law, and hath greater respect to the abundance of goods than to his own natural child. He beareth well in mind to fill his own purse, but he little rememb'reth

---

[1] Fool.   [2] Lain.
[3] "Possibly a pun on *hackney* . . . a prostitute" (Adams).

[4] Large.

that his daughter's purse shall be continually empty—unless Master Doctor fill it with double duck eggs.[1] Alas, I jest, and have no joy! I will stand here aside and laugh a little at this lobcock.[2]   20

Dulippo espieth the Doctor and his Man coming.

Scena iv.

Carion, the Doctor's Man; Cleander; Dulippo [, who stands aside].

[Car.] Master, what the devil mean you to go seek guests at this time of the day? The mayor's officers have dined ere this time, which are alway the last in the market.

Cle. I come to seek Pasiphilo, to the end he may dine with me.

Car. As though six mouths, and the cat for the seventh, be not sufficient to eat an harlotry shotterell,[3] a penny-[10 worth of cheese, and half a score spurlings![4] This is all the dainties you have dressed for you and your family.

Cle. Ah, greedy gut, art thou afeard thou shalt want?

Car. I am afeard indeed! It is not the first time I have found it so.

Dul. [*Aside.*] Shall I make some sport with this gallant? What shall I say to him?   20

Cle. Thou art afeard, belike, that he will eat thee and the rest.

Car. Nay, rather that he will eat your mule, both hair and hide.

Cle. Hair and hide? And why not flesh and all?

Car. Because she hath none! If she had any flesh, I think you had eaten her yourself by this time.

Cle. She may thank you, then, for [30 your good attendance.

Car. Nay, she may thank you for your small allowance.

Dul. [*Aside.*] In faith, now, let me alone.

Cle. Hold thy peace, drunken knave, and espy me Pasiphilo.

Dul. [*Aside.*] Since I can do no better,

I will set such a stance[5] between him and Pasiphilo that all this town shall not [40 make them friends.

Car. Could you not have sent to seek him, but you must come yourself? Surely you come for some other purpose, for, if you would have had Pasiphilo to dinner, I warrant you he would have tarried here an hour since.[6]

Cle. Hold thy peace! Here is one of Damon's servants. Of him I *Another sup-* shall understand where he is. *pose.* Good fellow, art not thou one of Damon's servants?   52

Dul. Yes, sir, at your knamandement.[7]

Cle. Gramercy. Tell me, then, hath Pasiphilo been there this day or no?

Dul. Yes, sir, and I think he be there still. Ah, ah, ah!

Cle. What[8] laughest thou?

Dul. At a thing that every man may not laugh at.   60

Cle. What?

Dul. Talk that Pasiphilo had with my master this day.

Cle. What talk, I pray thee?

Dul. I may not tell it.

Cle. Doth it concern me?

Dul. Nay, I will say nothing.

Cle. Tell me.

Dul. I can say no more.

Cle. I would but know if it concern [70 me. I pray thee tell me.

Dul. I would tell you if I were sure you would not tell it again.

Cle. Believe me, I will keep it close. Carion, give us leave a little; go aside.

                    [*Carion stands aside.*]

Dul. If my master should know that it came by me, I were better die a thousand deaths.

Cle. He shall never know it. Say on.

Dul. Yea, but what assurance shall [80 I have?

Cle. I lay thee my faith and honesty in pawn.

Dul. A pretty pawn! The fulkers[9] will not lend you a farthing on it.

Cle. Yea, but amongst honest men it is more worth than gold.

---

[1] "Pun on 'duckets,' and also with a further and coarse meaning" (Adams).
[2] Lubber.   [4] Sparlings, smelts.
[3] Scurvy pike.

[5] Distance, disagreement.
[6] He would have been waiting here an hour ago.
[7] Commandment. So all early edns.
[8] Why.   [9] Pawnbrokers.

Dul. Yea, marry, sir, but where be they? But will you needs have me tell it unto you?   90

Cle. Yea, I pray thee, if it anything appertain to me.

Dul. Yes, it is of you. And I would gladly tell it you, because I would not have such a man of worship so scorned by a villain ribald.[1]

Cle. I pray thee tell me then.

Dul. I will tell you, so that you will swear never to tell it to Pasiphilo, to my master, nor to any other body.   100

Car. [*Aside.*] Surely it is some toy[2] devised to get some money of him.

Cle. I think I have a book here.

Car. [*Aside.*] If he knew him as well as I, he would never go about it, for he may as soon get one of his teeth from his jaws with a pair of pinchers as a penny out of his purse with such a conceit.

Cle. Here is a letter will serve the turn. I swear to thee by the contents hereof [110 never to disclose it to any man.

Dul. I will tell you. I am sorry to see how Pasiphilo doth abuse you, persuading you that always he laboreth for you, where, indeed, he lieth on my master continually, as it were with tooth and nail, for a stranger, a scholar, born in Sicilia. They call him Roscus, or Arsekiss—he hath a mad name; I can never hit upon it.

Cle. And thou reckonest it as madly. Is it not Erostrato?   121

Dul. That same. I should never have remembered it. And the villain[3] speaketh all the evil of you that can be devised.

Cle. To whom?

Dul. To my master; yea, and to Polynesta herself sometimes.

Cle. Is it possible? Ah, slave! And what saith he?

Dul. More evil than I can imagine: [130 that you are the miserablest and most niggardly man that ever was.

Cle. Sayeth Pasiphilo so by me?

Dul. And that as often as he cometh to your house he is like to die for hunger, you fare so well.

Cle. That the devil take him else!

Dul. And that you are the testiest man,

and most divers[4] to please, in the whole world, so that he cannot please you un- [140 less he should even kill himself with continual pain.

Cle. O devilish tongue!

Dul. Furthermore, that you cough continually and spit, so that a dog cannot abide it.

Cle. I never spit nor cough more than thus—vho, vho; and that but since I caught this murre.[5] But who is free from it?

Dul. You say true, sir. Yet further, [150 he saith your armholes stink, your feet worse than they, and your breath worst of all.

Cle. If I quite[6] him not for this gear!

Dul. And that you are bursten in the cods.[7]

Cle. O villain! He lieth! And if I were not in the street thou shouldest see them.

Dul. And he saith that you desire [160 this young gentlewoman as much for other men's pleasure as for your own.

Cle. What meaneth he by that?

Dul. Peradventure that by her beauty you would entice many young men to your house.

Cle. Young men? To what purpose?

Dul. Nay, guess you that.

Cle. Is it possible that Pasiphilo speaketh thus of me?   170

Dul. Yea, and much more.

Cle. And doth Damon believe him?

Dul. Yea, more than you would think; in such sort that long ere this he would have given you a flat repulse, but Pasiphilo entreated him to continue you a suitor for his advantage.

Cle. How for his advantage?

Dul. Marry, that during your suit he might still have some reward for his [180 great pains.

Cle. He shall have a rope, and yet that is more than he deserveth. I had thought to have given him these hose when I had worn them a little nearer, but he shall have a &c.[8]

Dul. In good faith, sir, they were but lost on him. Will you anything else with me, sir?

---

[1] Lewd scoundrel.   [2] Trick.
[3] So other edns. than original, which has *villainy.*

[4] Diverse, perverse, difficult.
[5] Catarrh.   [7] Scrotum.
[6] Requite.   [8] To be filled out by the actor.

CLE. Nay, I have heard too much [190 of [1] thee already.

DUL. Then I will take my leave of you.

CLE. Farewell! But tell me, may I not know thy name?

DUL. Sir, they call me Foul-fall-you.

CLE. An ill-favored name, by my troth! Art thou this countryman? [2]

DUL. No, sir, I was born by a castle men call Scab-catch-you. Fare you well, sir!   [*Exit.*] 200

CLE. Farewell! O God, how have I been abused! What a spokesman! What a messenger had I provided!

CAR. Why, sir, will you tarry for Pasiphilo till we die for hunger?

CLE. Trouble me not. That the devil take you both!

CAR. [*Aside.*] These news, whatsoever they be, like him not.

CLE. Art thou so hungry yet? I pray [210 to God thou be never satisfied!

CAR. By the Mass, no more I shall, as long as I am your servant.

CLE. Go, with mischance!

CAR. Yea, and a mischief to you and to all such covetous wretches!   [*Exeunt.*]

FINIS ACTUS II.

ACTUS III. SCENA i.

Dalio, the cook; Crapine, the lackey; Erostrato; Dulippo. [3]

[DAL.] By that time we come to the house I trust that of these twenty eggs in the basket we shall find but very few whole. But it is a folly to talk to him. What the devil! Wilt thou never lay that stick out of thy hand? He fighteth with the dogs, beateth the bears; at everything in the street he findeth occasion to tarry. If he spy a slipstring [4] by the way—such another as himself, a page, a lackey, or a [10 dwarf—the devil of hell cannot hold him in chains but he will be doing with him. I cannot go two steps but I must look back for my yonker. Go to, haltersick! [5] If you break one egg, I may chance break &c.

CRA. What will you break? Your nose in mine, &c.?

DAL. Ah, beast!

CRA. If I be a beast, yet I am no horned [6] beast.   20

DAL. Is it even so? Is the wind in that door? If I were unloaden, I would tell you whether I be a horned beast or no.

CRA. You are alway laden either with wine or with ale.

DAL. Ah, spiteful boy! Shall I suffer him?   [*Strikes him.*]

CRA. Ah, cowardly beast, darest thou strike and say never a word?

DAL. Well, my master shall know of [30 this gear. Either he shall redress it or he shall lose one of us.

CRA. Tell him the worst thou canst by me.

Erostra[to] et Du[lippo] ex improviso. [7]

ERO. What noise, what a rule [8] is this?

CRA. Marry, sir, he striketh me because I tell him of his swearing.

DAL. The villain lieth deadly! He reviles me because I bid him make haste.

ERO. Holla! no more of this. Dalio, [40 do you make in a readiness those pigeons, stock doves, and also the breast of veal; and let your vessel be as clear as glass against I return, that I may tell you which I will have roasted and which boiled. [*Exit Dalio.*] Crapine, lay down that basket and follow me. O, that I could tell where to find Pasiphilo!—But look where he cometh that can tell me of him.

Dulippo is espied by Erostrato.

DUL. What have you done with [50 Philogano, your father?

ERO. I have left him within. I would fain speak with Pasiphilo. Can you tell me where he is?

DUL. He dined this day with my master, but whither he went from thence I know not. What would you with him?

ERO. I would have him go tell Damon that Philogano, my father, is come, and ready to make assurance of as much as [60 he will require. Now shall I teach Master Doctor a school point. He travaileth to none other end but to catch *cornua*,[9] and he shall have them, for, as old as he is, and

---

[1] From.   [2] A man of this country.

[3] Last two enter later.

[4] Eluder of the gallows.

[5] Haltersack, gallows bird.

[6] Alluding to the horns of a cuckold.

[7] Enter unexpectedly. (But Erostrato does not notice Dulippo immediately.)

[8] Conduct, unruliness.   [9] Horns.

as many subtilties as he hath learned in the law, he cannot go beyond me one ace.

Dul. O dear friend, go thy ways, seek Pasiphilo, find him out, and conclude somewhat to our contentation.

Ero. But where shall I find him? 70

Dul. At the feasts, if there be any, or else in the market with the poulters or the fishmongers.

Ero. What should he do with them?

Dul. Marry, he watcheth whose caters buy the best meat. If any buy a fat capon, a good breast of veal, fresh salmon, or any such good dish, he followeth to the house, and either with some news or some stale jest, he will be sure to make himself [80 a guest.

Ero. In faith, and I will seek there for him.

Dul. Then must you needs find him, and, when you have done, I will make you laugh.

Ero. Whereat?

Dul. At certain sport I made today with Master Doctor.

Ero. And why not now?

Dul. No, it asketh further leisure. [90 I pray thee despatch and find out Pasiphilo, that honest man.

Dulippo tarrieth. Erostrato goeth out [with Crapine].

Scena ii.

Dulippo alone.

[Dul.] This amorous cause that hangeth in controversy between Domine Doctor and me may be compared to them that play at primero:[1] of whom someone, peradventure, shall leese[2] a great sum of money before he win one stake, and at last, half in anger, shall set up his rest, win it, and after that another, another, and another, till at last he draw the most part of the money to his heap, the other by [10 little and little still diminishing his rest, till at last he be come as near the brink as erst the other was; yet again, peradventure, fortune smiling on him, he shall, as it were by piecemeal, pull out the guts of his fellow's bags, and bring him barer than he himself was tofore;[3] and so in play continue still, fortune favoring now this way, now that way, till at last the one of them

---

¹ Game of cards. ² Lose. ³ Before.

is left with as many crosses[4] as God [20 hath brethren.[5] O, how often have I thought myself sure of the upper hand herein!—but I triumphed before the victory. And then how oft again have I thought the field lost! Thus have I been tossed, now over, now under, even as fortune list to whirl the wheel, neither sure to win nor certain to lose the wager. And this practice that now my servant hath devised, although hitherto it hath not [30 succeeded amiss, yet can I not count myself assured of it; for I fear still that one mischance or other will come and turn it topsy-turvy. But look where my master cometh.

Damon, coming in, espieth Dulippo and calleth him.

Scena iii.

Damon, Dulippo, Nevola, and two mo Servants.[6]

[Dam.] Dulippo!

Dul. Here, sir.

Dam. Go in and bid Nevola and his fellows come hither, that I may tell them what they shall go about. And go you into my study; there upon the shelf you shall find a roll of writings which John of the Dean[7] made to my father when he sold him the Grange farm, endorsed with both their names. Bring it hither to me. 10

Dul. It shall be done, sir. [*Exit.*]

Dam. Go. I will prepare other manner of writings for you than you are aware of. O fools, that trust any man but themselves nowadays! O spiteful fortune! Thou dost me wrong, I think, that from the depth of hell-pit thou hast sent me this servant to be the subversion of me and all mine!— Come hither, sirs, and hear what I shall say unto you. (*The Servants come in.*) [20 Go into my study, where you shall find Dulippo. Step to him all at once, take him, and, with a cord that I have laid on the table for the nonce, bind him hand and foot, carry him into the dungeon under the stairs, make fast the door, and bring me the key—it hangeth by upon a pin on the wall. Despatch, and do this gear as privily as

---

⁴ Coins. ⁶ Last three enter later.
⁵ *I.e.*, none at all. ⁷ Valley.

you can. And thou, Nevola, come hither
to me again with speed.   30

NEV. Well, I shall. [*Exit with Servants.*]

DAM. Alas, how shall I be revenged of
this extreme despite? If I punish my servant according to his devilish deserts, I
shall heap further cares upon mine own
head. For to such detestable offenses no
punishment can seem sufficient but only
death, and in such cases it is not lawful for
a man to be his own carver. The laws are
ordained, and officers appointed to min- [40
ister justice for the redress of wrongs; and,
if to the potestates [1] I complain me, I shall
publish mine own reproach to the world.
Yea, what should it prevail [2] me to use all
the punishments that can be devised? The
thing, once done, cannot be undone. My
daughter is deflowered, and I utterly dishonested.[3] How can I then wipe that blot
off my brow? And on whom shall I seek
revenge? Alas, alas, I myself have been [50
the cause of all these cares, and have deserved to bear the punishment of all these
mishaps! Alas, I should not have committed my dearest darling in custody to so
careless a creature as this old nurse; for we
see by common proof that these old women
be either peevish [4] or pitiful, either easily
inclined to evil or quickly corrupted with
bribes and rewards. O wife, my good wife,
that now liest cold in the grave, now [60
may I well bewail the want of thee, and,
mourning, now may I bemoan that I miss
thee! If thou hadst lived, such was thy
government of the least things that thou
wouldest prudently have provided for the
preservation of this pearl. A costly jewel
may I well accompt her, that hath been
my chief comfort in youth, and is now become the corrosive of mine age! O Polynesta, full evil hast thou requited the [70
clemency of thy careful father! And yet
to excuse thee guiltless before God and to
condemn thee guilty before the world, I
can count none other but my wretched
self the caitiff [5] and causer of all my cares.
For of all the duties that are requisite in
human life, only obedience is by the parents to be required of the child, where, on
the other side, the parents are bound, first
to beget them, then to bring them forth, [80

after to nourish them, to preserve them
from bodily perils in the cradle, from danger
of soul by godly education, to match them
in consort [6] inclined to virtue, to banish
them all idle and wanton company, to
allow them sufficient for their sustentation,
to cut off excess (the open gate of sin),
seldom or never to smile on them unless it
be to their encouragement in virtue, and
finally to provide them marriages in [90
time convenient, lest, neglected of us, they
learn to set either too much or too little
by themselves. Five years are past since
I might have married her, when by continual excuses I have prolonged it to my
own perdition. Alas, I should have considered she is a collop [7] of my own flesh.
What should I think to make her a princess? Alas, alas, a poor kingdom have
I now caught to endow her with! It is [100
too true that of all sorrows this is the head
source and chief fountain of all furies: the
goods of the world are incertain, the gains
[little] [8] to be rejoiced at, and the loss not
greatly to be lamented; only the children,
cast away, cutteth the parents' throat with
the knife of inward care, which knife will
kill me surely—I make none other accompt.

Damon's Servants come to him again.

SCENA iv.

Nevola, Damon, Pasiphilo.[9]

[NEV.] Sir, we have done as you bade us,
and here is the key.

DAM. Well, go then, Nevola, and seek
Master Casteling, the jailor; he dwelleth by
St. Antony's Gate. Desire him to lend
me a pair of the fetters he useth for his
prisoners; and come again quickly.

NEV. Well, sir.

DAM. Hear you. If he ask what I
would do with them, say you cannot [10
tell. And tell neither him nor any other
what is become of Dulippo.

Damon goeth out.

[NEV.] I warrant you, sir.—Fie upon the
devil! It is a thing almost unpossible
for a man nowadays to handle money but
the metal will stick on his *Another sup-*
fingers. I marveled alway at *pose.*
this fellow of mine, Dulippo, that of the

---

[1] Chief magistrates.   [2] Avail.
[3] Dishonored.   [4] Silly, weak.   [5] Captive.

[6] Companionship.   [8] Suggested by Bond.
[7] Slice, chip.   [9] Enters later.

wages he received he could maintain himself so bravely appareled, but now [20 I perceive the cause. He had the disbursing and receipt of all my master's affairs, the keys of the graner; [1] Dulippo here, Dulippo there; [in] favor with my master, in favor with his daughter—what would you more? He was *magister factotum*.[2] He was as fine as the crusado,[3] and we silly wretches as coarse as canvas. Well, behold what it is come to in the end! He had been better to have done less.   30

Pasi[philo] subito et improviso venit.[4]

PASI. Thou sayst true, Nevola! He hath done too much, indeed.

NEV. From whence comest thou, in the devil's name?

PASI. Out of the same house thou camest from, but not out of the same door.

NEV. We had thought thou hadst been gone long since.

PASI. When I arose from the table, I felt a rumbling in my belly, which [40 made me run to the stable, and there I fell on sleep [5] upon the straw and have lien there ever since. And thou—whither goest thou?

NEV. My master hath sent me on an errand in great haste.

PASI. Whither, I pray thee?

NEV. Nay, I may not tell. Farewell.
                                        [*Exit.*]

PASI. As though I need any further instructions! O God, what news I heard [50 even now, as I lay in the stable! O good Erostrato, and poor Cleander, that have so earnestly stroven for this *Another sup-* damsel! Happy is he that can *pose.* get her, I promise you! He shall be sure of mo than one at a clap that catcheth her—either Adam or Eve within her belly. O God, how men may be deceived in a woman! Who would have believed the contrary but that she had [60 been a virgin? Ask the neighbors, and you shall hear very good report of her. Mark her behaviors, and you would have judged her very maidenly—seldom seen abroad but in place of prayer and there very devout, and no gazer at outward sights, no

blazer of her beauty above in the windows, no stale [6] at the door for the bypassers. You would have thought her a holy young woman. But much good do it Domine [70 Doctor! He shall be sure to lack no CORN [7] in a dear year, whatsoever he have with her else. I beshrew me if I let [8] the marriage any way. But is not this the old scabbed quean [9] that I heard disclosing all this gear to her master as I stood in the stable ere now? It is she. Whither goeth, Psiteria?

Pasiphilo espieth Psiteria coming.

SCENA V.

Psiteria, Pasiphilo.

[PSIT.] To a gossip [10] of mine hereby.

PASI. What, to tattle of the goodly stir that thou kept'st concerning Polynesta?

PSIT. No, no. But how knew you of that gear?

PASI. You told me.

PSIT. I? When did I tell you?

PASI. Even now when you told it to Damon. I both saw you and heard you, though you saw not me. A good part, [10 I promise you, to accuse the poor wench, kill the old man with care, over and besides the danger you have brought Dulippo and the nurse unto, and many mo! Fie! fie!

PSIT. Indeed, I was to blame, but not so much as you think.

PASI. And how not so much? Did I not hear you tell?

PSIT. Yes, but I will tell you how it [20 came to pass. I have known for a great while that this Dulippo and Polynesta have lien together, and all by the means of the nurse; yet I held my peace and never told it. Now this other day the nurse fell on scolding with me, and twice or thrice called me "drunken old whore" and such names that it was too bad; and I called her "bawd" and told her that I knew well enough how often she had brought [30 Dulippo to Polynesta's bed. Yet all this while I thought not that anybody had heard me; but it befell clean contrary, for my master was on the other side of

---

[1] Granary.   [2] Master Do-all.   [3] A coin.
[4] Pasiphilo enters suddenly and unexpectedly.
[5] Asleep.

[6] Decoy.
[7] Pun on the Latin word for *horn.*
[8] Hinder.   [9] Vile slut.   [10] Crony.

the wall and heard all our talk, whereupon he sent for me and forced me to confess all that you heard.

PASI. And why wouldest thou tell him? I would not for &c.

PSIT. Well, if I had thought my [40 master would have taken it so, he should rather have killed me.

PASI. Why, how could he take it?

PSIT. Alas, it pitieth me to see the poor young woman, how she weeps, wails, and tears her hair, not esteeming her own life half so dear as she doth poor Dulippo's; and her father, he weeps on the other side, that it would pierce an heart of stone with pity. But I must be gone.   50

PASI. Go! That the gunpowder consume thee, old trot! [1]   [Exeunt.]

FINIS ACTUS III.

ACTUS IV. SCENA i.

Erostrato, feigned [,accompanied by Crapine].

[ERO.] What shall I do? Alas! what remedy shall I find for my rueful estate? What escape or what excuse may I now devise to shift over [2] our subtile supposes? For, though to this day I have usurped the name of my master, and that without check or control of any man, now shall I be openly deciphered, and that in the sight of every man. Now shall it openly be known whether I be Erostrato the [10 gentleman, or Dulippo the servant. We have hitherto played our parts in abusing [3] others, but now cometh the man that will not be abused—the right Philogano, the right father of the right Erostrato. Going to seek Pasiphilo and hearing that he was at the water gate, behold I espied my fellow Litio, and by-and-by my old master Philogano setting forth his first step on land. I to fuge,[4] and away [20 hither as fast as I could to bring word to the right Erostrato of his right father Philogano, that to so sudden a mishap some subtile shift might be upon the sudden devised. But what can be imagined to serve the turn, although we had months' respite to beat our brains about it, since we are commonly known—at the least supposed—in this town, he for Dulippo,

[1] Hag.   [2] Conceal.   [3] Deceiving.   [4] Flight.

a slave and servant to Damon, and I [30 for Erostrato, a gentleman and a student? But behold, run, Crapine, to yonder old woman before she get within the doors, and desire her to call out Dulippo. But hear you—if she ask who would speak with him, say thyself and none other.

*Erostrato espieth Psiteria coming, and send-
eth his Lackey to her.*

SCENA ii.

Crapine, Psiteria, Erostrato, feigned.

[CRA.] Honest woman! you gossip! thou rotten whore! Hearest thou not, old witch?

PSIT. A rope stretch your young bones! Either you must live to be as old as I or be hanged while you are young.

CRA. I pray thee, look if Dulippo be within.

PSIT. Yes, that he is, I warrant him!

CRA. Desire him, then, to come hither and speak a word with me. He shall [10 not tarry.

PSIT. Content yourself; he is otherwise occupied.

CRA. Yet tell him so, gentle girl.

PSIT. I tell you, he is busy.

CRA. Why, is it such a matter to tell him so, thou crooked crone?

PSIT. A rope stretch you, marry!

CRA. A pox eat you, marry!

PSIT. Thou wilt be hanged, I war- [20 rant thee, if thou live to it.

CRA. And thou wilt be burnt, I warrant thee, if the canker consume thee not.

PSIT. If I come near you, hempstring,[5] I will teach you to sing sol fa! [6]

CRA. Come on! and if I get a stone I will scare crows with you.

PSIT. Go, with a mischief! I think thou be some devil that would tempt me. [Exit.]

ERO. Crapine! Hear you? Come [30 away. Let her go, with a vengeance! Why come you not? Alas, look where my master Philogano cometh! What shall I do? Where shall I hide me? He shall not see me in these clothes, nor before I have spoken with the right Erostrato.

*Erostrato espieth Philogano coming and
runneth about to hide him*

[5] Gallows bird.   [6] I.e., scream.

Scena iii.

Philogano; Ferrarese, the innkeeper; Litio, a servant.

[PHI.] Honest man, it is even so. Be you sure there is no love to be compared like the love of the parents towards their children. It is not long since I thought that a very weighty matter should not have made me come out of Sicilia; and yet now I have taken this tedious toil and travail upon me, only to see my son and to have him home with me.

FER. By my faith, sir, it hath been a [10 great travail indeed, and too much for one of your age.

PHI. Yea, be you sure. I came in company with certain gentlemen of my country, who had affairs to despatch as far as to Ancona, from thence by water to Ravenna, and from Ravenna hither, continually against the tide.

FER. Yea, and I think that you had but homely lodging by the way. 20

PHI. The worst that ever man had. But that was nothing to the stir that the searchers [1] kept with me when I came aboard the ship. Jesus, how often they untrussed my male [2] and ransacked a little capcase [3] that I had, tossed and turned all that was within it, searched my bosom, yea, my breeches, that I assure you I thought they would have flayed me to search between the fell [4] and the flesh [30 for fardings. [5]

FER. Sure, I have heard no less, and that the merchants bob [6] them sometimes; but they play the knaves still.

PHI. Yea, be you well assured; such an office is the inheritance of a knave, and an honest man will not meddle with it.

FER. Well, this passage shall seem pleasant unto you when you shall find your child in health and well. But, I pray you, [40 sir, why did you not rather send for him into Sicilia than to come yourself, specially since you had none other business? Peradventure you had rather endanger yourself by this noisome [7] journey than hazard to draw him from his study.

PHI. Nay, that was not the matter, for I had rather have him give over his study altogether and come home.

FER. Why, if you minded not to [50 make him learned, to what end did you send him hither at the first?

PHI. I will tell you. When he was at home, he did as most young men do—he played many mad pranks and did many things that liked me not very well; and I, thinking that by that time he had seen the world he would learn to know himself better, exhorted him to study and put in his election what place he would go to. [60 At the last he came hither, and I think he was scarce here so soon as I felt the want of him, in such sort as from that day to this I have passed few nights without tears. I have written to him very often that he should come home, but continually he refused, still beseeching me to continue his study, wherein he doubted not, as he said, but to profit greatly.

FER. Indeed, he is very much com- [70 mended of all men, and specially of the best reputed students.

PHI. I am glad he hath not lost his time, but I care not greatly for so much knowledge. I would not be without the sight of him again so long for all the learning in the world. I am old now, and, if God should call me in his absence, I promise you I think it would drive me into desperation. 80

FER. It is commendable in a man to love his children, but to be so tender over them is more womanlike.

PHI. Well, I confess it is my fault. And yet I will tell you another cause of my coming hither, more weighty than this. Divers of my country have been here since he came hither, by whom I have sent unto him, and some of them have been thrice, some four or five times at his house, [90 and yet could never speak with him. I fear he applies his study so that he will not leese the minute of an hour from his book. What, alas, he might yet talk with his countrymen for awhile! He is a young man, tenderly brought up, and, if he fare thus continually night and day at his book, it may be enough to drive him into a frenzy.

FER. Indeed, enough were as good [100

---

[1] Customs officers. [3] Bag.
[2] Opened my trunk. [4] Skin.
[5] Farthings, *i.e.*, taxable goods.
[6] Deceive, cheat. [7] Annoying.

as a feast. Lo you, sir, here is your son
Erostrato's house. I will knock.

PHI. Yea, I pray you knock.

[*Knocks on the door.*]

FER. They hear not.

PHI. Knock again.

FER. I think they be on sleep.

LIT. If this gate were your grandfather's soul, you could not knock more
softly. Let me come! [*Knocks violently.*]
Ho, ho! Is there anybody within? 110
Dalio cometh to the window, and there maketh
them answer.

SCENA iv.

Dalio, the cook; Ferrarese, the innholder;
Philogano; Litio, his man.

[DAL.] What devil of hell is there? I
think he will break the gates in pieces!

LIT. Marry, sir, we had thought you had
been on sleep within, and therefore we
thought best to wake you. What doth
Erostrato?

DAL. He is not within.

PHI. Open the door, good fellow, I pray
thee.

DAL. If you think to lodge here, [10
you are deceived, I tell you; for here are
guests enow already.

PHI. A good fellow, and much for thy
master['s] honesty, by our Lady! And
what guests, I pray thee?

DAL. Here is Philogano, my *Another sup-*
master's father, lately come *pose.*
out of Sicilia.

PHI. Thou speakest truer than thou art
aware of. He will be, by that time thou [20
hast opened the door. Open, I pray thee
heartily.

DAL. It is a small matter for me to open
the door, but here is no lodging for you. I
tell you plain, the house is full.

PHI. Of whom?

DAL. I told you. Here is Philogano, my
master's father, come from Cathanea.

PHI. And when came he?

DAL. He came three hours since, or [30
more. He alighted at the Angel and left
his horses there. Afterward my master
brought him hither.

PHI. Good fellow, I think thou hast
good sport to mock me.

DAL. Nay, I think you have good sport

to make me tarry here, as though I have
nothing else to do. I am matched with an
unruly mate in the kitchen. I will go look
to him another while. 40

PHI. I think he be drunken.

FER. Sure he seems so. See you not how
red he is about the gills?

PHI. Abide, fellow. What Philogano
is it whom thou talkest of?

DAL. An honest gentleman, father to
Erostrato, my master.

PHI. And where is he?

DAL. Here within.

PHI. May we see him? 50

DAL. I think you may if you be not
blind.

PHI. Go to! Go tell him here is one
would speak with him.

DAL. Marry, that I will willingly do.
Dalio draweth his head in at the window.[1]

PHI. I cannot tell what I should say to
this gear. Litio, what thinkest thou of it?

LIT. I cannot tell you what I should say,
sir. The world is large and long; there [59
may be mo Philoganos and mo *Another sup-*
Erostratos than one, yea, and *pose.*
mo Ferraras, mo Sicilias, and mo Ca-
thaneas. Peradventure this is not that
Ferrara which you sent your son unto.

PHI. Peradventure thou art a fool, and
he was another that answered us even
now.—But be you sure, honest man, that
you mistake not the house?

FER. Nay, then God help! Think you
I know not Erostrato's house? Yes, and [70
himself also. I saw him here no longer
since than yesterday. But here comes one
that will tell us tidings of him. I like his
countenance better than the other's that
answered at the window erewhile.

The Sienese cometh out.

SCENA v.

Sienese, Philogano, [Ferrarese, Litio,] Dalio.

[SIEN.] Would you speak with me, sir?

PHI. Yea, sir; I would fain know whence
you are.

SIEN. Sir, I am a Sicilian, at your commandment.

PHI. What part of Sicilia?

SIEN. Of Cathanea.

[1] This direction appears at the end of the scene
in all early edns.

Phi. What shall I call your name?

Sien. My name is Philogano.

Phi. What trade do you occupy?   10

Sien. Merchandise.

Phi. What merchandise brought you hither?

Sien. None. I came only to see a son that I have here whom I saw not these two years.

Phi. What call they your son?

Sien. Erostrato.

Phi. Is Erostrato your son?

Sien. Yea, verily.

Phi. And are you Philogano?   20

Sien. The same.

Phi. And a merchant of Cathanea?

Sien. What need I tell you so often? I will not tell you a lie.

Phi. Yes, you have told me a false lie, and thou art a villain, and no better!

Sien. Sir, you offer me great wrong with these injurious words.

Phi. Nay, I will do more than I have yet proffered to do, for I will prove thee a [30 liar and a knave to take upon thee that thou art not.

Sien. Sir, I am Philogano of Cathanea, out of all doubt. If I were not, *A stout sup-* I would be loath to tell you so. *pose.*

Phi. O, see the boldness of this brute beast! What a brazen face he setteth on it!

Sien. Well, you may believe me if you list. What wonder you?

Phi. I wonder at thy impudency; for [40 thou, nor nature that framed thee, can ever counterfeit thee to be me, ribald villain and lying wretch that thou art!

Dal. Shall I suffer a knave to abuse my master's father thus? [*Draws A pleasant his sword.*] Hence, villain! *suppose.* Hence, or I will sheathe this good fawchion [1] in your paunch! If my master Erostrato find you prating here on this fashion to his father, I would not be in [50 your coat for mo cony skins [2] than I gat these twelve months. Come you in again, sir, and let this cur bark here till he burst!

Dalio pulleth the Sienese in at the doors.

Scena vi.

Philogano, Litio, Ferrarese.

[Phi.] Litio, how likest thou this gear?

Lit. Sir, I like it as evil as may be. But have you not often heard tell of the false-

[1] Falchion.   [2] Rabbit skins.

hood of Ferrara? And now may you see, it falleth out accordingly.

Fer. Friend, you do not well to slander the city. These men are no Ferrareses, you may know by their tongue.

Lit. Well, there is never a barrel better herring between you both.[3] But indeed [10 your officers are most to blame, that suffer such faults to escape unpunished.

Fer. What know the officers of this? Think you they know of every fault?

Lit. Nay, I think they will know as little as may be, specially when they have no gains by it. But they ought to have their ears as open to hear of such offenses as the inn gates be to receive guests.

Phi. Hold thy peace, fool!   20

Lit. By the Mass, I am afeard that we shall be proved fools, both two.

Phi. Well, what shall we do?

Lit. I would think best we should go seek Erostrato himself.

Fer. I will wait upon you willingly, and, either at the schools or at the convocations, we shall find him.

Phi. By our Lady, I am weary. I will run no longer about to seek him. I am [30 sure hither he will come at the last.

Lit. Sure, my mind gives *A true sup-* me that we shall find a new *pose.* Erostrato ere it be long.

Fer. Look where he is! Whither runs he? Stay you awhile; I will go tell him that you are here. Erostrato! Erostrato! ho, Erostrato! I would speak with you!

Erostrato is espied upon the stage running about.

Scena vii.

Feigned Erostrato, Ferrarese, Philogano, Litio, Dalio.

[Ero. (*Aside.*)] Now can I hide me no longer. Alas! what shall I do? I will set a good face on, to bear out the matter.

Fer. O Erostrato, Philogano, your father, is come out of Sicilia.

Ero. Tell me that I know not. I have been with him, and seen him already.

Fer. Is it possible? And it seemeth by him that you know not of his coming.

[3] Proverb meaning, "There is no difference between you two."

Ero. Why, have you spoken with [10 him? When saw you him, I pray you?

Fer. Look you where he stands. Why go you not to him? Look you, Philogano; behold your dear son Erostrato.

Phi. Erostrato? This is not Erostrato. This seemeth rather to be Dulippo—and it is Dulippo indeed.

Lit. Why, doubt you of that?

Ero. What saith this honest man?

Phi. Marry, sir, indeed you are so [20 honorably clad it is no marvel if you look big.

Ero. To whom speaketh he?

Phi. What! God help! Do you not know me?

Ero. As far as I remember, sir, I never saw you before.

Phi. Hark, Litio, here is good gear! This honest man will not know me!

Ero. Gentleman, you take your [30 marks amiss.

Lit. Did I not tell you of the *A shameless* falsehood of Ferrara, master? *suppose.* Dulippo hath learned to play the knave in-differently well since he came hither.

Phi. Peace, I say.

Ero. Friend, my name is not Dulippo. Ask you thoroughout this town of great and small; they know me. Ask this honest man that is with you, if you will not [40 believe me.

Fer. Indeed, I never knew him other-wise called than Erostrato; and so they call him, as many as know him.

Lit. Master, now you may see the falsehood of these fellows. This *A needless* honest man, your host, is of *suppose.* counsel with him, and would face us down that it is Erostrato. Beware of these mates! [1]   50

Fer. Friend, thou doest me wrong to suspect me, for sure I never heard him otherwise called than Erostrato.

Ero. What name could you hear me called by but by my right name? But I am wise enough to stand prating here with this old man! I think he be mad.

[*Enter Dalio and other Servants, armed.*]

Phi. Ah, runagate! Ah, villain traitor! Dost thou use thy master thus? What hast thou done with my son, villain? [60

[1] Fellows.

Dal. Doth this dog bark here still? And will you suffer him, master, thus to revile you?

Ero. Come in, come in. What wilt thou do with this pestil? [2]

Dal. I will rap the old cackabed [3] on the costard. [4]

Ero. Away with it! And you, sirrah, lay down these stones! Come in at door, every one of you. Bear with him, for [70 his age. I pass not of [5] his evil words.

Erostrato taketh all his Servants in at the doors.

Scena viii.

Philogano, Ferrarese, Litio.

[Phi.] Alas, who shall relieve my miser-able estate? To whom shall I complain, since he whom I brought up of a child, yea, and cherished him as if he had been mine own, doth now utterly deny to know me? And you, whom I took for an honest man and he that should have brought me to the sight of my son, are compact [6] with this false wretch, and would face me down that he is Erostrato. Alas, you might have [10 some compassion of mine age, *Another sup-* to the misery I am now in, and *pose.* that I am a stranger desolate of all comfort in this country; or, at the least, you should have feared the vengeance of God, the supreme judge, which knoweth the secrets of all hearts, in bearing this false witness with him whom heaven and earth do know to be Dulippo and not Erostrato.

Lit. If there be many such witnesses [20 in this country, men may go about to prove what they will in controversies here.

Fer. Well, sir, you may judge of me as it pleaseth you; and how the matter cometh to pass I know not, but, truly, ever since he came first hither I have known him by the name of Erostrato, the son of Philogano, a Cathanese. Now, whether he be so indeed or whether he be Dulippo, as you allege, let that be proved by them that knew [30 him before he came hither. But I protest before God that which I have said is neither a matter compact with him nor any

[2] Pestle, pig's leg.
[3] Vulgar term of abuse.
[4] Apple, head.
[5] Care not for.
[6] In conspiracy.

other, but even as I have heard him called and reputed of all men.

PHI. Out and alas! He whom I sent hither with my son to be his servant and to give attendance on him, hath either cut his throat or by some evil means made [39 him away, and hath not only *A shrewd sup-* taken his garments, his books, *pose.* his money, and that which he brought out of Sicilia with him, but usurpeth his name also, and turneth to his own commodity the bills of exchange that I have always allowed for my son's expenses. O miserable Philogano, O unhappy old man! O eternal God, is there no judge, no officer, no higher powers whom I may complain unto for redress of these wrongs?   50

FER. Yes, sir, we have potestates, we have judges, and, above all, we have a most just prince. Doubt you not but you shall have justice, if your cause be just.

PHI. Bring me then to the judges, to the potestates, or to whom you think best; for I will disclose a pack of the greatest knavery, a fardel [1] of the foulest falsehood, that ever was heard of!

LIT. Sir, he that will go to the law [60 must be sure of four things: first, a right and a just cause; then, a righteous advocate to plead; next, favor *coram judice;* [2] and, above all, a good purse to procure it.

FER. I have not heard that the law hath any respect to favor; what you mean by it I cannot tell.

PHI. Have you no regard to his words; he is but a fool.

FER. I pray you, sir, let him tell me [70 what is favor.

LIT. Favor call I to have a friend near about the judge, who may so solicit thy cause as, if it be right, speedy sentence may ensue without any delays; if it be not good, then to prolong it, till at the last thine adversary, being weary, shall be glad to compound with thee.

FER. Of thus much (although I never heard thus much in this country before) [80 doubt you not, Philogano: I will bring you to an advocate that shall speed you accordingly.

PHI. Then shall I give myself, as it were, a prey to the lawyers, whose insatiable jaws I am not able to feed, although I had

here all the goods and lands which I possess in mine own country—much less, being a stranger in this misery. I know their cautels [3] of old. At the first time I come [90 they will so extol my cause as though it were already won; but within a sevennight or ten days, if I do not continually feed them, as the crow doth her brats, twenty times in an hour, they will begin to wax cold and to find cavils in my cause, saying that at the first I did not well instruct them; till, at the last, they will not only draw the stuffing out of my purse but the marrow out of my bones.   100

FER. Yea, sir; but this man that I tell you of is half a saint.

LIT. And the other half a devil, I hold [4] a penny!

PHI. Well said, Litio. Indeed, I have but small confidence in their smooth looks.

FER. Well, sir, I think this whom I mean is no such manner of man. But if he were, there is such hatred and evil- *Another sup-* will between him and this *pose.* gentleman (whether he be Erostrato or [111 Dulippo, whatsoever he be) that I warrant you he will do whatsoever he can do for you, were it but to spite him.

PHI. Why, what hatred is betwixt them?

FER. They are both in love and suitors to one gentlewoman, the daughter of a wealthy man in this city.

PHI. Why, is the villain become of such estimation that he dare presume to be [120 a suitor to any gentlewoman of a good family?

FER. Yea, sir, out of all doubt.

PHI. How call you his adversary?

FER. Cleander, one of the excellentest doctors in our city.

PHI. For God's love, let us go to him!

FER. Go we then.   [*Exeunt.*]

FINIS ACTUS IV.

ACTUS V. SCENA i.

Feigned Erostrato.

[ERO.] What a mishap was this, that before I could meet with Erostrato I have light even full in the lap of Philogano, where I was constrained to deny my name, to deny my master, and to feign that I knew him not, to contend with him, and to

---

[1] Bundle.   [2] Before the judge.   [3] Artifices.   [4] Wager.

revile him in such sort that, hap what hap can, I can never hap well in favor with him again! Therefore, if I could come to speak with the right Erostrato, I will renounce [10 unto him both habit and credit, and away as fast as I can trudge into some strange country where I may never see Philogano again—alas, he that of a little child hath brought me up unto this day and nourished me as if I had been his own, and, indeed, to confess the truth, I have no father to *Another suppose.* trust unto but him. But look where Pasiphilo cometh, the fittest man in the world [20 to go on my message to Erostrato.

Erostrato espieth Pasiphilo coming towards him.

Scena ii.

Pasiphilo, Erostrato.

[Pasi.] Two good news have I heard to-day already: one, that Erostrato prepared a great feast this night; the other, that he seeketh for me. And I, to ease him of his travail, lest he should run up and down seeking me, and because no man loveth better than I to have an errand where good cheer is, come in posthaste even home to his own house. And look where he is.

Ero. Pasiphilo, thou must do one [10 thing for me, if thou love me.

Pasi. If I love you not, who loves you? Command me.

Ero. Go then a little there, to Damon's house; ask for Dulippo, and tell him—

Pasi. Wot[1] you what? I cannot speak with him. He is in prison.

Ero. In prison! How cometh that to pass? Where is he in prison?

Pasi. In a vile dungeon, there, within [20 his master's house.

Ero. Canst thou tell wherefore?

Pasi. Be you content to know he is in prison. I have told you too much.

Ero. If ever you will do anything for me, tell me.

Pasi. I pray you, desire me not. What were you the better if you knew?

Ero. More than thou thinkest, Pasiphilo, by God.　　　　　　　　　30

Pasi. Well, and yet it stands me upon,[2] more than you think, to keep it secret.

[1] Know.　　　[2] It is incumbent upon me.

Ero. Why, Pasiphilo, is this the trust I have had in you? Are these the fair promises you have a[l]ways made me?

Pasi. By the Mass, I would I had fasted this night with Master Doctor rather than have come hither.

Ero. Well, Pasiphilo, either tell me, or, at few words, never think to be welcome [40 to this house from henceforth.

Pasi. Nay, yet I had rather leese all the gentlemen in this town. But, if I tell you anything that displease you, blame nobody but yourself now.

Ero. There is nothing can grieve me more than Dulippo's mishap—no, not mine own; and therefore I am sure thou canst tell me no worse tidings.

Pasi. Well, since you would needs [50 have it, I will tell you. He *Another* was taken abed with your *plain and* beloved Polynesta. *homely suppose.*

Ero. Alas, and doth Damon know it?

Pasi. An old trot in the house disclosed it to him; whereupon he took both Dulippo and the nurse, which hath been the broker of all this bargain, and clapped them both in a cage—where, I think, they shall [60 have sour[3] sops to[4] their sweetmeats.

Ero. Pasiphilo, go thy ways into the kitchen; command the cook to boil and roast what liketh thee best. I make thee supervisor of this supper.

Pasi. By the Mass, if you should have studied this sevennight you could not have appointed me an office to please me better! You shall see what dishes I will devise.

Pasiphilo goeth in; Erostrato tarrieth.

Scena iii.

Feigned Erostrato alone.

[Ero.] I was glad to rid him out of the way, lest he should see me burst out of these swelling tears, which hitherto with great pain I have prisoned in my breast, and lest he should hear the echo of my doubled sighs, which bounce from the bottom of my heavy heart. O cursed I! O cruel fortune, that so many dispersed griefs as were sufficient to subvert a legion of lovers hast suddenly assem- [10

[3] From 1573 edn. Original has *sorowe.*
[4] In addition to.

bled within my careful carcass to fret this fearful heart in sunder with desperation! Thou that hast kept my master all his youth within the realm of Sicilia, reserving the wind and waves in a temperate calm— as it were at his command—now to convey his aged limbs hither, neither sooner nor later, but even in the worst time that may be! If, at any time before, thou haddest conducted him, this enterprise [20 had been cut off without care in the beginning; and, if never so little longer thou hadst lingered [1] his journey, this happy day might then have fully finished our drifts [2] and devises. But, alas, thou hast brought him even in the very worst time, to plunge us all in the pit of perdition! Neither art thou content to entangle me alone in thy ruinous ropes, but thou must also catch the right Erostrato in thy [30 crooked claws, to reward us both with open shame and rebuke. Two years hast thou kept secret our subtile supposes, even this day to decipher them with a sorrowful success. What shall I do? Alas, what shift shall I make? It is too late now to imagine any further deceit, for every minute seemeth an hour till I find some succor for the miserable captive Erostrato. Well, since there is no other remedy, I [40 will go to my master Philogano, and to him will I tell the whole truth of the matter, that at the least he may provide in time before his son feel the smart of some sharp revenge and punishment. This is the best, and thus will I do. Yet I know that for mine own part I shall do bitter penance for my faults forepassed! But such is the good will and duty that I bear to Erostrato as even with the loss [50 of my life I must not stick to adventure anything which may turn to his commodity. But what shall I do? Shall I go seek my master about the town, or shall I tarry his return hither? If I meet him in the streets, he will cry out upon me, neither will he hearken to anything that I shall say till he have gathered all the people wondering about me as it were at an owl. Therefore I were better to abide here. And yet, [60 if he tarry long, I will go seek him rather than prolong the time to Erostrato's peril.

Pasiphilo returneth to Erostrato.

---

[1] Delayed.　　　　　[2] Plots.

Scena iv.

Pasiphilo, feigned Erostrato.

[Pasi. (*To Dalio within.*)] Yea, dress them, but lay them not to the fire till they will be ready to sit down.—This gear goeth in order, but if I had not gone in, there had fallen a foul fault.

Ero. And what fault, I pray thee?

Pasi. Marry, Dalio would have laid the shoulder of mutton and the capon both to the fire at once, like a fool! He did not consider that the one would have more [10 roasting than the other.

Ero. Alas, I would this were the greatest fault.

Pasi. Why? And either the one should have been burned before the other had been roasted, or else he must have drawn them off the spit, and they would have been served to the board either cold or raw.

Ero. Thou hast reason, Pasiphilo.

Pasi. Now, sir, if it please you, I will [20 go into the town and buy oranges, olives, and caphers; [3] for without such sauce the supper were more than half lost.

Ero. There are [4] within already, doubt you not; there shall lack nothing that is necessary.　　　　　*Erostrato exit.*

Pasi. Since I told him these news of Dulippo, he is clean beside himself. He hath so many hammers in his head that his brains are ready to burst. And let them [30 break. So I may sup with him tonight, what care I? But is not this *A knavish Dominus noster Cleandrus* [5] that *suppose.* cometh before? Well said. By my truth, we will teach Master Doctor to wear a cornered cap [6] of a new fashion. By God, Polynesta shall be his! He shall have her, out of doubt; for I have told Erostrato such news of her that he will none of her.

Cleander and Philogano come in, talking of the matter in controversy.

Scena v.

Cleander, Philogano, Litio, Pasiphilo.

[Cle.] Yea, but how will ye prove that he is not Erostrato, having such presumptions to the contrary? Or how shall it be thought that you are Philogano, when another taketh upon him this same name,

---

[3] Capers.　　　　　　[5] Our master, Cleander.
[4] Supply *some.*　　　[6] Horns of the cuckold.

and for proof bringeth him for a witness which hath been ever reputed here for Erostrato?

PHI. I will tell you, sir. Let me be kept here fast in prison, and at my [10 charges let there be some man sent into Sicilia that may bring hither with him two or three of the honestest men in Cathanea, and by them let it be proved if I or this other be Philogano, and whether he be Erostrato or Dulippo my servant; and, if you find me contrary,[1] let me suffer death for it.

PASI. I will go salute Master Doctor.

CLE. It will ask great labor and great [20 expenses to prove it this way, but it is the best remedy that I can see.

PASI. God save you, sir!

CLE. And reward you as you have deserved.

PASI. Then shall he give me your favor continually.

CLE. He shall give you a halter, knave and villain that thou art!

PASI. I know I am a knave, but no [30 villain. I am your servant.

CLE. I neither take thee for my servant nor for my friend.

PASI. Why, wherein have I offended you, sir?

CLE. Hence to the gallows, knave!

PASI. What! Soft and fair, sir, I pray you. *"I præ, sequar;"* [2] you are mine elder.

CLE. I will be even with you, be you sure, honest man.   40

PASI. Why, sir? I never offended you.

CLE. Well, I will teach you. Out of my sight, knave!

PASI. What! I am no dog, I would you wist.[3]

CLE. Pratest thou yet, villain? I will make thee—

PASI. What will you make me? I see well the more a man doth suffer you, the worse you are.   50

CLE. Ah, villain, if it were not for this gentleman, I would tell you what I—

PASI. Villain? Nay, I am as honest a man as you.

CLE. Thou liest in thy throat, knave!

PHI. O, sir, stay your wisdom.

[1] Wrong.
[2] Terence, *Andria*, I, i, 144: "Go ahead; I'll follow."
[3] Knew.

PASI. What! Will you fight? Marry, come on!

CLE. Well, knave, I will meet with you another time. Go your way.   60

PASI. Even when you list, sir, I will be your man.

CLE. And if I be not even with thee, call me cut! [4]

PASI. Nay, by the Mass, all is one. I care not, for I have nothing. If I had either lands or goods, peradventure you would pull me into the law.   [*Exit.*]

PHI. Sir, I perceive your patience is moved.   70

CLE. This villain! But let him go. I will see him punished as he hath deserved. Now to the matter. How said you?

PHI. This fellow hath disquieted you, sir. Peradventure you would *Lawyers* be loath to be troubled any *are never* further.   *weary to get*

CLE. Not a whit. Say on, *money.* and let him go—with a vengeance!

PHI. I say, let them send at my [80 charge to Cathanea.

CLE. Yea, I remember that well, and it is the surest way as this case requireth. But tell me, how is he your servant, and how come you by him? Inform me fully in the matter.

PHI. I will tell you, sir. When the Turks won Otranto—

CLE. O, you put me in remembrance of my mishaps!   90

PHI. How, sir?

CLE. For I was driven among the rest out of the town (it is my native country), and there I lost more than ever I shall recover again while I live.

PHI. Alas, a pitiful case, by St. Anne!

CLE. Well, proceed.

PHI. At that time, as I said, there were certain of our country that scoured those coasts upon the seas with a good bark, [100 well appointed for the purpose, and had espial of a Turkey vessel that came laden from thence with great abundance of riches.

CLE. And peradventure most *A gentle* of mine.   *suppose.*

PHI. So they boarded them, and in the end overcame them, and brought the goods to Palermo, from whence they came; and amongst other things that they

[4] Gelded horse.

had was this villain, my servant, a [110 boy at that time, I think not past five years old.

Cle. Alas, I lost one of that same age there!

Phi. And I, being there, and liking the child's favor well, proffered them four and twenty ducats for him, and had him.

Cle. What! was the child a Turk? Or had the Turks brought him from Otranto?

Phi. They said he was a child of [120 Otranto. But what is that to the matter? Once four and twenty ducats he cost me— that I wot well.

Cle. Alas, I speak it not for that, sir. I would it were he whom I mean.

Phi. Why, whom mean you, sir?

Lit. Beware, sir; be not too   *A crafty* lavish!   *suppose.*

Cle. Was his name Dulippo then or had he not another name?   130

Lit. Beware what you say, sir!

Phi. What the devil hast thou to do!— Dulippo? No, sir, his name was Carino.

Lit. Yea, well said! Tell all, and more too; do!

Cle. O Lord, if it be as I think, how happy were I! And why did you change his name then?

Phi. We called him Dulippo because when he cried, as children do some- [140 times, he would always cry on that name, Dulippo.

Cle. Well, then I see well it is my own only child, whom I lost when I lost my country! He was named Carino after his grandfather; and this Dulippo, whom he always remembered in his lamenting, was his foster-father that nourished him and brought him up.

Lit. Sir, have I not told you enough [150 of the falsehood of Ferrara? This gentleman will not only pick your purse, but beguile you of your servant also, and make you believe he is his son.

Cle. Well, good fellow, I have not used to lie.

Lit. Sir, no; but everything hath a beginning.

Cle. Fie! Philogano, have you not the least suspect [1] that may be of me.   160

Lit. No, marry; but it were good he had the most suspect that may be.

    [1] Suspicion.

Cle. Well, hold thou thy peace a little, good fellow. I pray you tell me, Philogano, had the child any remembrance of his father's name, his mother's name, or the name of his family?

Phi. He did remember them, and could name his mother also, but sure I have forgotten the name.   170

Lit. I remember it well enough!

Phi. Tell it then.

Lit. Nay, that I will not, marry! You have told him too much already.

Phi. Tell it, I say, if thou can.

Lit. Can? Yes, by the Mass, I can well enough! But I will have my tongue pulled out rather than tell it unless he tell it first. Do you not perceive, sir, what he goeth about?   180

Cle. Well, I will tell you then. My name you know already; my wife, his mother's, name was Sophronia; the house that I came of they call Spiagia.

Lit. I never heard him speak of Spiagia, but indeed I have heard him say his mother's name was Sophronia. But what of that? A great matter, I promise you! It is like enough that you two have compact together to deceive my master. [190

Cle. What needeth me more evident tokens? This is my son out of doubt, whom I lost eighteen years since, and a thousand thousand times have I lamented for him. He should have also a mold [2] on his left shoulder.

Lit. He hath a mold there indeed, and an hole in another place, too—I would your nose were in it!

Cle. Fair words, fellow Litio! O, [200 I pray you, let us go talk with him! O fortune, how much am I bound to thee if I find my son!

Phi. Yea, how little am I beholden to fortune, that know not where my son is become; and you, whom I chose to be mine advocate, will now, by the means of this Dulippo, become mine adversary!

Cle. Sir, let us first go find mine, [209 and, I warrant you, yours will *A right sup-* be found also ere it be long. *pose.*

Phi. God grant! Go we then.

Cle. Since the door is open, I will never knock nor call, but we will be bold to go in.

    [2] Mole.

LIT. [*To Philogano.*] Sir, take you heed lest he lead you to some mischief.

PHI. Alas, Litio, if my son be lost, what care I what become of me?

LIT. Well, I have told you my mind, sir. Do you as you please.   221

Exeunt. Damon and Psiteria come in.

SCENA vi.

Damon, Psiteria.

[DAM.] Come hither, you old callet,[1] you tattling huswife! That the devil cut out your tongue! Tell me, how could Pasiphilo know of this gear but by you?

PSIT. Sir, he never knew it of me; he was the first that told me of it.

DAM. Thou liest, old drab! But I would advise you tell me the truth, or I will make those old bones rattle in your skin.

PSIT. Sir, if you find me contrary, [10 kill me.

DAM. Why, where should he talk with thee?

PSIT. He talked with me of it here in the street.

DAM. What did you here?

PSIT. I was going to the weaver's for a web of cloth you have there.

DAM. And what cause could Pasiphilo have to talk of it, unless thou began the [20 matter first?

PSIT. Nay, he began with me, sir, reviling me because I had told you of it. I asked him how he knew of it, and he said he was in the stable when you examined me erewhile.

DAM. Alas, alas, what shall I do then? In at doors, old whore! I will pluck that tongue of thine out by the roots one day. [*Exit Psiteria.*] Alas, it grieveth me [30 more that Pasiphilo knoweth it than all the rest. He that will have a thing kept secret, let him tell it to Pasiphilo! The people shall know it, and as many as have ears, and no mo. By this time he hath told it in a hundreth places! Cleander was the first, Erostrato the second; and so from one to another throughout the city. Alas, what dower, what marriage shall I now prepare for my daughter? O poor [40 dolorous Damon, more miserable than misery itself! Would God it were true

that Polynesta told me erewhile—that he who hath deflowered her is of no servile estate, as hitherto he hath been supposed in my service, but that he is a gentleman, born of a good parentage in Sicilia. Alas, small riches should content me if he be but of an honest family! But [50 I fear that he hath devised these toys to allure my daughter's love. Well, I will go examine her again. My mind giveth me that I shall perceive by her tale whether it be true or not. But is not this Pasiphilo that cometh out of my neighbor's house? What the devil aileth him to leap and laugh so like a fool in the highway?

The first suppose brought to conclusion.

Pasiphilo cometh out of the house laughing.

SCENA vii.

Pasiphilo,[2] Damon.

[PASI. (*To himself.*)] O God, that I might find Damon at home!

DAM. What the devil would he with me?

PASI. [*To himself.*] That I may be the first that shall bring him these news!

DAM. What will he tell me, in the name of God?

PASI. [*To himself.*] O Lord, how happy am I!—Look where he is.

DAM. What news, Pasiphilo, that [10 thou art so merry?

PASI. Sir, I am merry to make you glad. I bring you joyful news!

DAM. And that I have need of, Pasiphilo.

PASI. I know, sir, that you are a sorrowful man for this mishap that hath chanced in your house. Peradventure you thought I had not known of it. But let it pass! Pluck up your sprites,[3] and rejoice! For [20 he that hath done you this injury is so well born and hath so rich parents that you may be glad to make him your son-in-law.

DAM. How knowest thou?

PASI. His father, Philogano, one of the worthiest men in all Cathanea, is now come to the city, and is here in your neighbor's house.

DAM. What, in Erostrato's house?

PASI. Nay, in Dulippo's house. For [30 where you have always supposed this gentleman to be Erostrato, it is not so; but

---

[1] Whore.   [2] Original prints *Philogano.*   [3] Spirits.

your servant, whom you have imprisoned, hitherto supposed to be Dulippo, he is indeed Erostrato, and that other is Dulippo. And thus they have always, even since their first arrival in this city, exchanged names, to the end that Erostrato, the master, under the name of Dulippo, a servant, might be entertained in your house [40 and so win the love of your daughter.

DAM. Well, then I perceive it is even as Polynesta told me.

PASI. Why, did she tell you so?

DAM. Yea, but I thought it but a tale.

PASI. Well, it is a true tale. And here they will be with you by-and-by—both Philogano, this worthy man, and Master Doctor Cleander.

DAM. Cleander? What to do?   50

PASI. Cleander? Why thereby lies another tale—the most fortunate adventure that ever you heard! Wot you what? This other Dulippo, whom all this while we supposed to be Erostrato, is found to be the son of Cleander, whom he lost at the loss of Otranto, and was after sold in Sicilia to this Philogano. The strangest case that ever you heard! A man might make a comedy of it. They will come even [60 straight and tell you the whole circumstance of it themselves.

DAM. Nay, I will first go hear the story of this Dulippo, be it Dulippo or Erostrato, that I have here within, before I speak with Philoganc.

PASI. So shall you do well, sir. I will go tell them that they may stay awhile.— But look where they come.

Damon goeth in; Sienese, Cleander, and Philogano come upon the stage.

SCENA viii.

Sienese, Cleander, [Carino,] [1] Philogano.

[SIEN.] Sir, you shall not need to excuse the matter any further. Since I have received no greater injury than by words, let them pass like wind. I take them well in worth and am rather well pleased than offended. For it shall both be a good warning to me another time how to trust every man at the first sight, yea, and I shall have good game hereafter to tell this pleasant story another day in mine own country. [10

[1] *I.e.,* the real Dulippo.

CLE. Gentleman, you have reason; and be you sure that as many as hear it will take great pleasure in it. And you, Philogano, may think that God in heaven above hath ordained your coming hither at this present to the end I might recover my lost son, whom by no other means I could ever have found out.

PHI. Surely, sir, I think no less; for I think that not so much as a leaf falleth [20 from the tree without the ordinance of God. But let us go seek Damon, for methinketh every day a year, every hour a day, and every minute too much, till I see my Erostrato.

CLE. I cannot blame you. Go we then. Carino, take you that gentleman home in the meantime. The fewer the better to be present at such affairs.

Pasiphilo stayeth their going in.

SCENA ix.

Pasiphilo,[2] Cleander.

[PASI.] Master Doctor, will you not show me this favor, to tell me the cause of your displeasure?

CLE. Gentle Pasiphilo, I must needs confess I have done thee wrong, and that I believed tales of thee, which indeed I find now contrary.

PASI. I am glad, then, that it proceeded rather of ignorance than of malice.

CLE. Yea, believe me, Pasiphilo.   10

PASI. O, sir, but yet you should not have given me such foul words.

CLE. Well, content thyself, Pasiphilo. I am thy friend, as I have always been; for proof whereof, come sup with me tonight, and from day to day this sevennight be thou my guest. But behold, here cometh Damon out of his house.

Here they come all together.

SCENA x.

Cleander, Philogano, Damon, Erostrato, Pasiphilo, Polynesta; Nevola and other Servants.[3]

[CLE. (*To Damon.*)] We are come unto you, sir, to turn your sorrow into joy and gladness—the sorrow, we mean, that of force you have sustained since this mishap

[2] Original has *Philogano.*   [3] Enter later.

of late fallen in your house. But be you of good comfort, sir, and assure yourself that this young man, which youthfully and not maliciously hath committed this amorous offense, is very well able, with consent of this worthy man, his father, to make [10 you sufficient amends, being born in Cathanea of Sicilia, of a noble house, no way inferior unto you, and of wealth, by the report of such as know it, far exceeding that of yours.

PHI. And I here, in proper person, do present unto you, sir, not only my assured friendship and brotherhood, but do earnestly desire you to accept my poor child, though unworthy, as your son-in-law. [20 And for recompense of the injury he hath done you, I proffer my whole lands in dower to your daughter; yea, and more would, if more I might.

CLE. And I, sir, who have hitherto so earnestly desired your daughter in marriage, do now willingly yield up and quit claim to this young man, who, both for his years and for the love he beareth her, is most meetest to be her husband. For [30 where I was desirous of a wife by whom I might have issue, to leave that little which God hath sent me, now have I little need, that, thanks be to God, have found my dearly beloved son, whom I lost of a child at the siege of Otranto.

DAM. Worthy gentleman, your friendship, your alliance, and the nobility of your birth are such as I have much more cause to desire them of you than you to re- [40 quest of me that which is already granted. Therefore I gladly and willingly receive the same, and think myself most happy now

of all my life past that I have gotten so toward [1] a son-in-law to myself and so worthy a father-in-law to my daughter. Yea, and much the greater is my contentation since this worthy gentleman, Master Cleander, doth hold himself satisfied. And now, behold your son!　　　50

ERO. O father!

PASI. Behold the natural love of the child to the father. For inward joy he cannot pronounce one word; instead whereof he sendeth sobs and tears to tell the effect of his inward intention.[2] But why do you abide here abroad? Will it please you to go into the house, sir?

DAM. Pasiphilo hath said well. Will it please you to go in, sir?　　　60

[Enter Nevola with fetters.]

NEV. Here I have brought you, sir, both fetters and bolts.

DAM. Away with them, now!

NEV. Yea, but what shall I do with them?

DAM. Marry, I will tell thee, Nevola. To make a right end of our supposes, lay one of those bolts in the fire, and make thee a suppository as long as mine arm— God save the sample!—[*Turns to the audience.*] Nobles and gentlemen, if you [71 suppose that our Supposes have given you sufficient cause of delight, show some token whereby we may suppose you are content.

Et plauserunt.[3]

---

[1] Promising.
[2] From 1573 edn. Original reads *invention.*
[3] And they applauded.

FINIS.

THOMAS PRESTON

The identity of the Thomas Preston named as author at the end of the hybrid morality-tragedy *Cambises* is uncertain. Early students of the stage were inclined to identify him with the Thomas Preston who was Fellow of King's College, Cambridge, took his B.A. and M.A. there—the latter in 1561—and became Master of Trinity Hall in 1584 and Vice-Chancellor in 1587. He won Elizabeth's favor and a pension as her "scholar" in 1564 by disputing before her in Latin and acting in the Latin play *Dido*. It is not probable, however, that a man admired for his Latinity would write a play of such an extremely miscellaneous and popular nature as *Cambises*, one clearly designed for the use of some professional or semi-professional troupe of actors, whose personnel of six men and two boys is indicated by "The Division of the Parts" on the title-page of the published version. A more likely conjecture, as Chambers points out, is that the author was the ballad-writer two of whose ballads have at the end a subscription, "Finis, Quod Thomas Preston," similar to that in *Cambises*. He was publishing ballads at the time *Cambises* appeared in print.

As a tragedy *Cambises* offers a sharp contrast to *Gorboduc* in technique, and especially, in the very nature of great tragedy, through the failure of the catastrophe to develop logically out of the preceding incidents. While the spread of humanism may have had its effect on Preston's choice of a story from ancient history and on his attempt at a tragic treatment of it, the play probably represents more definitely the continuance of medieval literary and dramatic motives in the popular drama of the era. The story of Cambises, derived from Herodotus, was often retold in the Middle Ages and the Renaissance. The form found in the play is akin in spirit to the medieval type of narrative "tragedy" in the emphasis on the fall of a great figure at the height of his arrogant pride. A continued interest in such themes is indicated in the reprint of Lydgate's *Fall of Princes* and the production of *The Mirror for Magistrates*. The brutal character of the hero and the presentation of scenes of horror may reflect also an influence of scenes like the torturing of Christ or of the martyrs in medieval drama. For the rest, the technique is clearly that of the late hybrid moralities, in a number of which historical and farcical material was freely mixed with allegory. The story is carried and explained largely by abstract or generic characters, and the action is manipulated largely by Ambidexter, a brilliant example of the morality vice. Tendencies of later Elizabethan tragedy are foreshadowed in *Cambises* in the loose structure, based on a series of historical incidents, in the mixture of tragic and comic scenes, and in the presentation of crude horror on the stage.

The play was entered in the Stationers' Register in 1569/70 by John Allde, but had probably been performed several years earlier. The first edition, undated, appeared simultaneously with the entry or soon afterward. A second edition, also undated, was issued not earlier than 1584, by Edward Allde, John Allde's son, who succeeded to his father's business in that year. This later text, reproduced photographically by Farmer in his Tudor Facsimile Texts in 1910, has been followed by the present editors. Of critical editions, that in Manly's *Specimens of the Pre-Shaksperean Drama* has been most helpful.

CAMBISES, KING OF PERSIA[1]

BY

THOMAS PRESTON

[DRAMATIS PERSONÆ

CAMBISES, *King of Persia.*
SMIRDIS, *his brother.*
SISAMNES, *the judge.*
OTIAN, *his son.*
PRAXASPES, *a courtier.*
YOUNG CHILD, *his son.*
FIRST LORD ⎫
SECOND LORD ⎬ *attendants of the king.*
THIRD LORD ⎭

A LADY, *kinswoman of the king and later*
QUEEN.
WAITING-MAID, *attending her.*
MOTHER *of Young Child and wife of Prax-*
aspes.

HUF ⎫
RUF ⎬ *ruffianly soldiers.*
SNUF ⎭
MERETRIX, *a courtesan.*
HOB ⎫
LOB ⎬ *clownish countrymen.*
MARIAN-MAY-BE-GOOD, *Hob's wife.*

LORD.[2]
KNIGHT.[2]
COUNSEL.[2]

SHAME.
ATTENDANCE.
DILIGENCE.
PREPARATION.
SMALL HABILITY.[3]
COMMONS' CRY.
COMMONS' COMPLAINT.
TRIAL.
PROOF.
EXECUTION.
CRUELTY.
MURDER.

AMBIDEXTER, *the Vice.*

VENUS.
CUPID.

SCENE: *Persia.*
TIME: *Sixth century B.C.*]

THE DIVISION OF THE PARTS

COUNSEL ⎫
HUF ⎪
PRAXASPES ⎪
MURDER ⎬ *for one man.*
LOB ⎪
THE THIRD LORD ⎭

LORD ⎫
RUF ⎪
COMMONS' CRY ⎬ *for one man.*
COMMONS' COMPLAINT ⎪
LORD SMIRDIS ⎪
VENUS ⎭

KNIGHT ⎫
SNUF ⎪
SMALL HABILITY ⎪
PROOF ⎬ *for one man.*
EXECUTION ⎪
ATTENDANCE ⎪
SECOND LORD ⎭

[1] The complete title reads as follows: "A Lamentable Tragedy, Mixed Full of Pleasant Mirth, Containing the Life of Cambises, King of Persia, from the Beginning of His Kingdom unto His Death, His One Good Deed of Execution, after That Many Wicked Deeds and Tyrannous Murders Committed by and through Him, and Last of All, His Odious Death by God's Justice Appointed. Done in Such Order as Followeth." The running-title, however, reads: "A Comedy of King Cambises."

[2] The character is generic, representing the entire class. [3] Ability.

145

CAMBISES ⎫ *for one man.*
EPILOGUS ⎭

PROLOGUE ⎫
SISAMNES ⎪
DILIGENCE ⎪
CRUELTY ⎬ *for one man.*
HOB ⎪
PREPARATION ⎪
THE FIRST LORD ⎭

AMBIDEXTER ⎫ *for one man.*
TRIAL ⎭

MERETRIX ⎫
SHAME ⎪
OTIAN ⎪
MOTHER ⎬ *for one man.*
LADY ⎪
QUEEN ⎭

YOUNG CHILD ⎫ *for one man.*
CUPID ⎭

The Prologue entereth.

Agathon, he whose counsel wise to princes'
   weal [1] extended,
By good advice unto a prince three things
   he hath commended:
First is, that he hath government and rul-
   eth over men;
Secondly, to rule with laws, eke justice,
   saith he, then;
Thirdly, that he must well conceive he may
   not always reign.
Lo, thus the rule unto a prince Agathon
   squaréd plain.
Tully the wise, whose sapience in volumes
   great doth tell,
Who in wisdom in that time did many men
   excel,
"A prince," saith he, "is of himself a plain
   and speaking law;
The law, a schoolmaster divine"—this by
   his rule I draw.   10
The sage and witty Seneca his words
   thereto did frame:
"The honest exercise of kings, men will
   ensue [2] the same;
But, contrariwise, if that a king abuse his
   kingly seat,
His ignomy and bitter shame in fine shall
   be more great."
In Persia there reigned a king, who Cyrus
   hight [3] by name,
Who did deserve, as I do read, the lasting
   blast of fame;
But he, when Sisters Three had wrought to
   shear his vital thread,
As heir due, to take the crown Cambises did
   proceed.

He in his youth was trainéd up by trace [4]
   of virtue's lore;
Yet, being king, did clean forget his perfect
   race before;   20
Then, cleaving more unto his will, such vice
   did imitate
As one of Icarus his kind; forewarning then
   did hate,
Thinking that none could him dismay, ne [5]
   none his fact [6] could see.
Yet at the last a fall he took, like Icarus to
   be;
Else,[7] as the fish, which oft had take the
   pleasant bait from hook,
In safe [8] did spring and pierce the streams
   when fisher fast [9] did look
To hoist up from the wat'ry waves unto
   the driéd land,
Then scaped, at last by subtle bait come to
   the fisher's hand:
Even so this King Cambises here, when he
   had wrought his will,
Taking delight the innocent his guiltless
   blood to spill,   30
Then mighty Jove would not permit to
   prosecute offense;
But, what measure the king did mete, the
   same did Jove commence,
To bring to end with shame his race—two
   years he did not reign.
His cruelty we will delate,[10] and make the
   matter plain.
Craving that this may suffice now your
   patience to win,
I take my way. Behold, I see the players
   coming in.   [*Exit.*]

FINIS.

---

[1] Welfare.
[2] Follow.
[3] Was called.
[4] Track, course.
[5] Nor.
[6] Deed.
[7] Or.
[8] Safety.
[9] Intently.
[10] Describe fully.

First enter [1] *Cambises the King, Knight,*
[*Lord,*] *and Counselor.* [2]

CAMBISES. My counsel grave and sapient,
with lords of legal train,
Attentive ears towards me bend, and
mark what shall be sain; [3]
So you likewise, my valiant knight, whose
manly acts doth fly
By bruit of Fame, that sounding trump
doth pierce the azure sky—
My sapient words, I say, perpend, [4] and
so your skill delate!
You know that Mors [5] vanquished hath
Cyrus, that king of state,
And I, by due inheritance, possess that
princely crown,
Ruling by sword of mighty force in place
of great renown.
You know, and often have heard tell, my
father's worthy facts—
A manly Mars's heart he bare, appearing
by his acts. 10
And what, shall I to ground let fall my
father's golden praise?
No, no! I mean for to attempt this same
more large to raise.
In that, that I, his son, succeed his
kingly seat, as due,
Extend your counsel unto me in that I
ask of you.
I am the King of Persia, a large and
fertile soil;
The Egyptians against us repugn [6] as
varlets slave and vile;
Therefore I mean with Mars's heart with
wars them to frequent,
Them to subdue as captives mine—this
is my heart's intent;
So shall I win honor's delight, and praise
of me shall go.
My counsel, speak, and, lordings, eke:
is it not best do so? 20
COUNSEL. O puissant king, your blissful
words deserves abundant praise,
That you in this do go about your father's fame to raise.

---

[1] "As this play is not divided into acts and
scenes, and as the events occur apparently in a
place which is now a council-chamber, now a
street, and now a garden, it seems improper to
subdivide the play or to indicate changes of
scene. When necessary for intelligibility, the
location is announced in the text" (Manly).
[2] *I.e.,* Counsel.   [3] Said.   [4] Consider.
[5] Death.   [6] Oppose.

O blissful day, that king so young such
profit should conceive,
His father's praise and his to win from
those that would deceive!
Sure, my true and sovereign king, I fall
before you prest, [7]
Answer to give, as duty mine, in that
your grace request.
If that your heart addicted be the Egyptians to convince, [8]
Through Mars's aid the conquest won,
then deed of happy prince
Shall pierce the skies unto the throne of
the supernal seat,
And merit there a just reward of Jupiter
the Great. 30
But then your grace must not turn back
from this pretenséd [9] will;
For to proceed in virtuous life employ
endeavor still;
Extinguish vice, and in that cup to drink
have no delight;
To martial feats and kingly sport fix all
your whole delight.
KING. My counsel grave, a thousand
thanks with heart I do you render,
That you my case so prosperous entirely
do tender.
I will not swerve from those your steps
whereto you would me train.
But now, my lord and valiant knight,
with words give answer plain:
Are you content with me to go the
Mars's games to try?
LORD. Yea, peerless prince! To aid your
grace myself will live and die! 40
KNIGHT. And I, for my hability, for fear
will not turn back,
But, as the ship against the rocks, sus-
tain and bide the wrack.
KING. O willing hearts! A thousand
thanks I render unto you!
Strike up your drums with courage great;
we will march forth even now!
COUNSEL. Permit, O king, few words to
hear—my duty serves no less.
Therefore give leave to counsel thine his
mind for to express.
KING. Speak on, my counsel; what it be,
you shall have favor mine.
COUNSEL. Then will I speak unto your
grace as duty doth me bind.

---

[7] Quickly.   [8] Overpower.   [9] Intended.

Your grace doth mean for to attempt of
    war the manly art;
Your grace therein may hap receive, with
    others, for your part,   50
The dent of death—in those affairs all
    persons are alike.
The heart courageous oftentimes his det-
    riment doth seek.
It's best therefore for to permit a ruler
    of your land
To sit and judge with equity when things
    of right are scanned.
KING. My grace doth yield to this your
    talk. To be thus now it shall.
My knight, therefore prepare yourself
    Sisamnes for to call.
A judge he is of prudent skill; even he
    shall bear the sway
In absence mine, when from the land I
    do depart my way.
KNIGHT. Your knight before your grace
    even here himself hath ready pressed
With willing heart for to fulfill as your
    grace made request.   *Exit.* 60
COUNSEL. Pleaseth your grace, I judge of
    him to be a man right fit;
For he is learned in the law, having the
    gift of wit.
In your grace's precinct I do not view for
    it a meeter man.
His learning is of good effect—bring
    proof thereof I can.
I do not know what is his life—his con-
    science hid from me;
I doubt not but the fear of God before
    his eyes to be.
LORD. Report declares he is a man that
    to himself is nigh,[1]
One that favoreth much the world and
    sets too much thereby.
But this I say of certainty: if he your
    grace succeed
In your absence but for awhile, he will be
    warned indeed   70
No injustice for to frequent, no partial
    judge to prove,
But rule all things with equity, to win
    your grace's love.
KING. Of that he shall a warning have my
    hests [2] for to obey;
Great punishment for his offense against
    him will I lay.

[1] *I.e.,* self-seeking.
[2] Behests, commands.

[*Enter Sisamnes.*]

COUNSEL. Behold, I see him now aggress [3]
    and enter into place.
SISAMNES. O puissant prince and mighty
    king, the gods preserve your grace!
Your grace's message came to me, your
    will purporting forth;
With grateful mind I it received accord-
    ing to mine oath,
Erecting then myself with speed before
    your grace's eyes,
The tenor of your princely will from you
    for to agnize.[4]   80
KING. Sisamnes, this the whole effect the
    which for you I sent:
Our mind it is to elevate you to great
    preferment.
My grace, and gracious counsel eke,
    hath chose you for this cause;
In judgment you do office bear, which
    have the skill in laws.
We think that you accordingly by jus-
    tice' rule will deal,
That for offense none shall have cause,
    of wrong you to appeal.[5]
SISAMNES. Abundant thanks unto your
    grace for this benignity!
To you, his counsel, in like case, with
    lords of clemency!
Whatso your grace to me permits, if I
    therein offend,
Such execution then commence (and use
    it to this end)   90
That all other, by that my deed, example
    so may take
To admonish them to flee the same by
    fear it may them make.
KING. Then, according to your words, if
    you therein offend,
I assure you, even from my breast cor-
    rection shall extend.
From Persia I mean to go into the Egypt
    land,
Them to convince by force of arms and
    win the upper hand.
While I therefor absent shall be, I do
    you full permit,
As governor in this my right, in that
    estate to sit,
For to detect and eke correct those that
    abuse my grace.
This is the total of my will. Give answer
    in this case!   100

[3] Approach.   [4] Learn.   [5] Accuse.

SISAMNES. Unworthy much, O prince, am
   I, and for this gift unfit;
But, sith [1] that it hath pleased your grace
   that I in it must sit,
I do avouch, unto my death, according to
   my skill,
With equity for to observe your grace's
   mind and will,
And naught from it to swarve,[2] indeed,
   but sincerely to stay;
Else let me taste the penalty, as I before
   did say.
KING. Well then, of this authority I give
   you full possession.
SISAMNES. And I will it fulfill also as I
   have made profession.
KING. My counsel, then let us depart a
   final stay to make;
To Egypt land now forth with speed my
   voyage I will take.   110
Strike up your drums, us to rejoice to
   hear the warlike sound.
Stay you here, Sisamnes, judge, and look
   well to your bound! [3]
    Exeunt King, Lord, and Counsel.
SISAMNES. Even now the king hath me
   extolled, and set me up aloft.
Now may I wear the bordered guard,[4]
   and lie in down-bed soft;
Now may I purchase house and land,
   and have all at my will;
Now may I build a princely place, my
   mind for to fulfill;
Now may I abrogate the law as I shall
   think it good;
If anyone me now offend, I may demand
   his blood.
According to the proverb old, my mouth
   I will up-make.[5]
Now it doth lie all in my hand to leave,
   or else to take,   120
To deal with justice to me bound, and
   so to live in hope.
But oftentimes the birds be gone while
   one for nest doth grope.
Do well or ill, I dare avouch some evil on
   me will speak.
No, truly—yet I do not mean the king's
   precepts to break;
To place I mean for to return my duty
   to fulfill.   *Exit.*

*Enter the Vice, with an old capcase [6] on his
   head, an old pail about his hips for
   harness,[7] a scummer [8] and a potlid by
   his side, and a rake on his shoulder.*

AMBIDEXTER. Stand away, stand away, for
   the passion of God!
Harnessed I am, prepared to the field!
I would have been content at home to
   have bode,
But I am sent forth with my spear and
   shield.
I am appointed to fight against a
   snail,   130
And Wilkin Wren the ancient [9] shall
   bear.
I doubt not but against him to prevail—
To be a man my deeds shall declare!
If I overcome him, then a butterfly
   takes his part.
His weapon must be a blue-specked
   hen;
But you shall see me overthrow him with
   a fart.
So, without conquest, he shall go home
   again.
If I overcome him, I must fight with a
   fly,
And a black-pudding the fly's weapon
   must be.
At the first blow on the ground he shall
   lie;   140
I will be sure to thrust him through
   the mouth to the knee.
To conquest these fellows the man I will
   play.
Ha, ha, ha! now ye will make me to
   smile.
.   .   .   .   [10]
To see if I can all men beguile.
Ha! my name? My name would ye so
   fain know?
Yea, iwis,[11] shall ye, and that with all
   speed!—
I have forgot it; therefore I cannot show.
Ah! ah! now I have it! I have it, in-
   deed!
My name is Ambidexter. I signify
   one   150
That with both hands finely can play;
Now with King Cambises, and by-and-
   by [12] gone.

---

[1] Since.   [4] Trimming.
[2] Swerve.   [5] Please my palate.
[3] Bond, contract.

[6] Bandbox.   [7] Armor.   [8] Skimmer.   [9] Ensign.
[10] The rime indicates that a line is missing here.
[11] Certainly.   [12] Immediately.

Thus do I run this way and that way.
For while I mean with a soldier to be;
Then give I a leap to Sisamnes the
    judge.
I dare avouch you shall his destruction
    see!
To all kind of estates I mean for to
    trudge.
Ambidexter? Nay, he is a fellow, if ye
    knew all!
Cease for a while; hereafter hear more ye
    shall.

Enter three ruffians, Huf, Ruf, and Snuf,
                                singing.

HUF. Gog's [1] flesh and His wounds, these
    wars rejoice my heart!   160
By His wounds, I hope to do well, for
    my part!
By Gog's heart, the world shall go hard
    if I do not shift;
At some old carl's budget [2] I mean for
    to lift.
RUF. By His flesh, nose, eyes, and ears,
    I will venter,[3] void of all cares!
He is not a soldier that doth fear any
    doubt,
If that he would bring his purpose about.
SNUF. Fear that fear list,[4] it shall not be I.
By Gog's wounds, I will make some neck
    stand awry!
If I lose my share—I swear by Gog's
    heart—   170
Then let another take up my part!
HUF. Yet I hope to come the richest sol-
    dier away.
RUF. If a man ask ye, ye may hap to say
    nay.
SNUF. Let all men get what they can;
    not to leese [5] I hope;
Wheresoever I go, in each corner I will
    grope.
AMBIDEXTER. What and [6] ye run in the
    corner of some pretty maid?
SNUF. To grope there, good fellow, I will
    not be afraid.
HUF. Gog's wounds, what art thou that
    with us dost mell? [7]
Thou seemest to be a soldier, the truth
    to tell;

Thou seemest to be harnessed—I cannot
    tell how;   180
I think he came lately from riding some
    cow.
Such a deformed slave did I never see!
Ruf, dost thou know him? I pray thee,
    tell me.
RUF. No, by my troth, fellow Huf, I never
    see him before.
SNUF. As for me, I care not if I never see
    him more.
Come, let us run his arse against the post!
AMBIDEXTER. Ah, ye slaves! I will be
    with you at ost! [8]
            Here let him swinge them about.
Ah, ye knaves! I will teach ye how ye
    shall me deride!
Out of my sight! I can ye not abide!
Now, goodman pouchmouth, I am a slave
    with you?   190
Now have at ye afresh—again—even
    now!
Mine arse against the post you will
    run?
But I will make you from that saying to
    turn!
HUF. I beseech ye heartily to be content.
RUF. I insure you, by mine honesty, no
    hurt we meant.
Beside that, again, we do not know what
    ye are.
Ye know that soldiers their stoutness will
    declare;
Therefore, if we have anything offended,
Pardon our rudeness, and it shall be
    amended.
AMBIDEXTER. Yea, God's pity, begin ye to
    entreat me?   200
Have at ye once again! By the Mass, I
    will beat ye!   *Fight again.*
HUF. Gog's heart, let us kill him! Suffer no
    longer!   *Draw their swords.*
SNUF. Thou slave, we will see if thou be
    the stronger!
RUF. Strike off his head at one blow!
That we be soldiers, Gog's heart, let him
    know!
AMBIDEXTER. O the passion of God, I
    have done, by mine honesty!
I will take your part hereafter, verily.
ALL. Then come, let us agree!
AMBIDEXTER. Shake hands with me—I
    shake hands with thee.

[1] God's.
[2] Countryman's wallet.
[3] Venture.
[4] Pleases.
[5] Lose.
[6] If.
[7] Meddle.
[8] Host; *i.e.*, be intimate with you.

Ye are full of courtesy; that is the best.
And you take great pain; ye are a man-
    nerly guest.   211
Why, masters, do you not know me?
    The truth to me tell.
ALL. No, trust us, not very well.
AMBIDEXTER. Why, I am Ambidexter,
    who [1] many soldiers do love.
HUF. Gog's heart, to have thy company
    needs we must prove!
We must play with both hands, with our
    hostess and host,
Play with both hands, and score on the
    post; [2]
Now and then, with our captain, for
    many a delay,
We will not stick with both hands to play.
AMBIDEXTER. The honester man, ye may
    me trust!   220

Enter Meretrix, with a staff on her shoulder.

MERETRIX. What! is there no lads here
    that hath a lust
To have a passing trull to help at their
    need?
HUF. Gog's heart, she is come, indeed!
What, Mistress Meretrix, by His wounds,
    welcome to me!
MERETRIX. What will ye give me? I pray
    you, let me see.
RUF. By His heart, she looks for gifts
    by-and-by!
MERETRIX. What? Master Ruf? I cry
    you mercy!
The last time I was with you I got a
    broken head,
And lay in the street all night for want
    of a bed.
SNUF. Gog's wounds, kiss me, my trull so
    white! [3]   230
In thee, I swear, is all my delight!
If thou shouldst have had a broken head
    for my sake,
I would have made his head to ache.
MERETRIX. What? Master Ambidexter?
    Who looked for you?
AMBIDEXTER. Mistress Meretrix, I thought
    not to see you here now.
There is no remedy—at meeting I must
    have a kiss!

MERETRIX. What, man, I will not stick
    for that, by Gis! [4]   *Kiss.*
AMBIDEXTER. So now, gramercy! I pray
    thee be gone!
MERETRIX. Nay, soft, my friend; I mean
    to have one!
Nay, soft! I swear, and if ye were my
    brother,   240
Before I let go, I will have another!
                              Kiss, kiss, kiss.
RUF. Gog's heart, the whore would not
    kiss me yet!
MERETRIX. If I be a whore, thou art a
    knave; then it is quit.
HUF. But hear'st thou, Meretrix? With
    who this night wilt thou lie?
MERETRIX. With him that giveth the most
    money.
HUF. Gog's heart, I have no money in
    purse, ne yet in clout! [5]
MERETRIX. Then get thee hence and pack,
    like a lout!
HUF. Adieu, like a whore!   *Exit Huf.*
MERETRIX.   Farewell, like
    a knave! [6]
RUF. Gog's nails, Mistress Meretrix, now
    he is gone,
    A match ye shall make straight with
    me: 250
I will give thee sixpence to lie one night
    with thee.
MERETRIX. Gog's heart, slave, dost think
    I am a sixpenny Jug? [7]
No, wis [8] ye, Jack, I look a little more
    smug!
SNUF. I will give her eighteenpence to
    serve me first.
MERETRIX. Gramercy, Snuf, thou art not
    the worst!
RUF. By Gog's heart, she were better be
    hanged, to forsake me and take thee!
SNUF. Were she so? That shall we see!
RUF. By Gog's heart, my dagger into her
    I will thrust!
SNUF. Ah, ye boy, ye would do it and ye
    durst!
AMBIDEXTER. Peace, my masters; ye shall
    not fight.   260
He that draws first, I will him smite.
RUF. Gog's wounds, Master Snuf, are ye
    so lusty?

---

[1] Whom(?).
[2] *I.e.*, mark the reckonings on the tavern
doorposts.   [3] Dear.

[4] Jesus.   [5] In my clothes.
[6] " The rhyme seems to demand some such word
as *whoreson*" (Manly).   [7] Joan, a whore.   [8] Know.

SNUF. Gog's sides, Master Ruf, are ye so crusty?

RUF. You may happen to see!

SNUF. Do what thou darest to me!

Here draw and fight. Here she must lay on and coil [1] *them both; the Vice must run his way for fear; Snuf fling down his sword and buckler and run his way.*

MERETRIX. Gog's sides, knaves! Seeing to fight ye be so rough,

Defend yourselves, for I will give ye both enough!

I will teach ye how ye shall fall out for me!

Yea, thou slave, Snuf, no more blows wilt thou bide?

To take thy heels a time hast thou spied?   270

Thou villain, seeing Snuf has gone away,

A little better I mean thee to pay!

He falleth down; she falleth upon him, and beats him, and taketh away his weapons.

RUF. Alas, good Mistress Meretrix, no more!

My legs, sides, and arms with beating be sore!

MERETRIX. Thou a soldier, and lose thy weapon!

Go hence, sir boy; say a woman hath thee beaten!

RUF. Good Mistress Meretrix, my weapon let me have;

Take pity on me, mine honesty [2] to save.

If it be known this repulse I sustain,

It will redound to my ignomy and shame.   280

MERETRIX. If thou wilt be my man and wait upon me,

This sword and buckler I will give thee.

RUF. I will do all at your commandment;

As servant to you I will be obedient.

MERETRIX. Then let me see how before me you can go.

When I speak to you, you shall do so:

Off with your cap at place [3] and at board [4]—

"Forsooth, Mistress Meretrix," at every word.

Tut! tut! in the camp such soldiers there be,

One good woman would beat away two or three!   290

[1] Beat.   [3] House.
[2] Honor.   [4] Table.

Well, I am sure customers tarry at home.

Mannerly before, and let us be gone!

Exeunt.

Enter Ambidexter.

[AMBIDEXTER.] O the passion of God! Be they here still or no?

I durst not abide to see her beat them so!

I may say to you, iwis, in such a flight, [5]

Body of me, I see the hair of my head stand upright!

When I saw her so hard upon them lay on,

"O the passion of God!" thought I, "she will be with me anon!"

I made no more [6] ado, but avoided the thrust,

And to my legs began for to trust,   300

And fell a-laughing to myself when I was once gone.

"It is wisdom," quoth I, "by the Mass, to save one!"

Then into this place I intended to trudge,

Thinking to meet Sisamnes the judge.

Behold where he cometh! I will him meet,

And like a gentleman I mean him to greet.

Enter Sisamnes.

SISAMNES. Since that the king's grace's majesty in office did me set,

What abundance of wealth to me might I get!

Now and then some vantage I achieve; much more yet may I take,

But that I fear unto the king that some complaint will make.   310

AMBIDEXTER. Jesu, Master Sisamnes, you are unwise!

SISAMNES. Why so? I pray thee, let me agnize.

What, Master Ambidexter, is it you?

Now welcome to me, I make God avow!

AMBIDEXTER. Jesu, Master Sisamnes, with me you are well acquainted.

By me rulers may be trimly painted. [7]

Ye are unwise if ye take not time while ye may;

If ye will not now, when ye would ye shall have nay.

[5] Possibly a misprint for *fright*.
[6] Original reads *mare*.   [7] Cheated.

What is he that of you dare make ex-
clamation,
Of your wrong-dealing to make explica-
tion? 320
Can you not play with both hands, and
turn with the wind?
SISAMNES. Believe me, your words draw
deep in my mind.
In color wise unto this day,[1] to bribes I
have inclinéd;
More the same for to frequent, of truth
I am now minded.
Behold, even now unto me suitors do
proceed.

[*Enter Small Hability.*]

SMALL HABILITY. I beseech you here, good
Master Judge, a poor man's cause to
tender![2]
Condemn me not in wrongful wise that
never was offender.
You know right well my right it is. I
have not for to give.
You take away from me my due, that
should my corpse[3] relieve.
The commons of you do complain from
them you devocate;[4] 330
With anguish great and grievous words
their hearts do penetrate;
The right you sell unto the wrong, your
private gain to win;
You violate the simple man, and count it
for no sin.
SISAMNES. Hold thy tongue, thou prattling knave, and give to me reward;
Else, in this wise, I tell thee truth, thy
tale will not be heard.
Ambidexter, let us go hence, and let the
knave alone.
AMBIDEXTER. Farewell, Small Hability, for
help now get you none;
Bribes hath corrupt him good laws to
pollute.
Exeunt [Sisamnes and Ambidexter].
SMALL HABILITY. A naughty man, that
will not obey the king's constitute![5]
With heavy heart I will return, till God
redress my pain. *Exit.* 340

[1] Taking color from the practices of the day (?)
[2] Regard favorably.
[3] Body.
[4] Call away, take away.
[5] Law.

Enter Shame, with a trump, black.

SHAME. From among the grisly ghosts I
come, from tyrants' testy train.
Unseemly Shame, of sooth, I am, pro-
curéd to make plain
The odious facts and shameless deeds
that Cambises king doth use.
All piety and virtuous life he doth it
clean refuse;
Lechery and drunkenness he doth it
much frequent.
The tiger's kind[6] to imitate he hath
given full consent.
He naught esteems his Counsel grave ne
virtuous bringing-up,
But daily still receives the drink of
damnéd Vice's cup.
He can bide no instruction, he takes so
great delight
In working of iniquity for to frequent his
spite. 350
As Fame doth sound the royal trump of
worthy men and trim,
So Shame doth blow with strainéd blast
the trump of shame on him. *Exit.*

*Enter the King, Lord, Praxaspes, and
Sisamnes.*

KING. My judge, since my departure
hence, have you used judgment right?
If faithful steward I ye find, the same I
will requite.
SISAMNES. No doubt your grace shall not
once hear that I have done amiss.
PRAXASPES. I much rejoice to hear so good
news as this.

*Enter Commons' Cry running in, speak this
verse, and go out again hastily.*

COMMONS' CRY. Alas, alas, how are the
commons oppressed
By that vile judge, Sisamnes by name!
I do not know how it should be redressed.
To amend his life no whit he doth
frame. 360
We are undone and thrown out of door;
His damnable dealing doth us so tor-
ment;
At his hand we can find no relief nor suc-
cor.
God grant him grace for to repent!
Run away crying.

[6] Nature.

KING. What doleful cries be these, my
l[ord], that sound do in mine ear?
Intelligence if you can give, unto your
king declare.
To me it seemeth my commons all they
do lament and cry
Out of [1] Sisamnes, judge most chief, even
now standing us by.
PRAXASPES. Even so, O king, it seemed to
me, as you rehearsal made.
I doubt [2] the judge culpable be in some
respect or trade.[3]   370
SISAMNES. Redoubted king, have no mistrust! No whit your mind dismay!
There is not one that can me charge, or
aught against me lay.

Enter Commons' Complaint, with Proof and
Trial.

COMMONS' COMPLAINT. Commons' Complaint I represent, with thrall of doleful state.
My urgent cause erected forth my grief
for to dilate.
Unto the king I will prepare my misery
to tell,
To have relief of this my grief and fettered feet so fell.[4]
Redoubted prince and mighty king, myself I prostrate here.
Vouchsafe, O king, with me to bear for
this that I appear.
With humble suit I pardon crave of your
most royal grace
To give me leave my mind to break before you in this place.   380
KING. Commons' Complaint, keep nothing
back! Fear not thy tale to tell.
Whate'er he be within this land that
hath not used thee well,
As prince's mouth shall sentence give, he
shall receive the same.
Unfold the secrets of thy breast, for I
extinguish blame.
COMMONS' COMPLAINT. God preserve your
royal grace, and send you blissful days,
That all your deeds might still accord to
give the God the praise!
My complaint is, O mighty king, against
that judge you by,
Whose careless deeds, gain to receive,
hath made the commons cry.

He, by taking bribes and gifts, the poor
he doth oppress,
Taking relief from infants young, widows,
and fatherless.   390
KING. Untrustful traitor and corrupt
judge, how likest thou this complaint?
Forewarning I to thee did give of this to
make restraint;
And hast thou done this devilish deed
mine ire for to augment?
I sentence give, thou Judas judge. Thou
shalt thy deed repent!
SISAMNES. O pusant [5] prince, it is not so.
His complaint I deny.
COMMONS' COMPLAINT. If it be not so,
most mighty king, in place then let me
die.
Behold that I have brought with me both
Proof and Trial true,
To stand even here, and sentence give
what by him did ensue.
PROOF. I, Proof, do him in this appeal: he
did the commons wrong;
Unjustly he with them hath dealt, his
greedy [6] was so strong.   400
His heart did covet in to get, he caréd
not which way;
The poor did leese their due and right,
because they want [7] to pay
Unto him for bribes. Indeed, this was
his wonted use.
Whereas your grace good laws did make,
he did the same abuse.
TRIAL. I, Trial, here to verify what Proof
doth now unfold,
To stand against him in his wrong, as
now I dare be bold.
KING. How likest thou this, thou caitiff
vile? Canst thou the same deny?
SISAMNES. O noble king, forgive my fact!
I yield to thy mercy.
KING. Complaints and Proof, redress will
I all this your misery.
Depart with speed from whence you
came, and straight command by
me   410
The execution man to come before my
grace with haste.
ALL. For to fulfill this your request no
time we mean to waste.
                    Exeunt they three.

---

[1] On.   [3] Course, practice.
[2] Suspect.   [4] Cruel, cruelly treated.
[5] Puissant.
[6] Greediness(?); greed it(?).
[7] *I.e.,* lacked the wherewithal.

KING. My lord, before my grace go call
    Otian, this judge's son,
And he shall hear and also see what his
    father hath done.
The father he shall suffer death, the son
    his room succeed;
And, if that he no better prove, so like-
    wise shall he speed.
PRAXASPES. As your grace hath command-
    ment given, I mean for to fulfill.
                Step aside and fetch him.
KING. Accursèd judge, couldst thou con-
    sent to do this cursèd ill?
According unto thy demand, thou shalt,
    for this thy guilt,
Receive thy death before mine eyes. Thy
    blood it shall be spilt.   420

            [*Enter Praxaspes with Otian.*]
PRAXASPES. Behold, O king, Sisamnes' son
    before you doth appear.
KING. Otian, this is my mind; therefore
    to me come near:
Thy father here for judgment wrong pro-
    curèd hath his death,
And thou, his son, shalt him succeed
    when he hath lost his breath;
And, if that thou dost once offend, as
    thou seest thy father have,
In like wise thou shalt suffer death. No
    mercy shall thee save!
OTIAN. O mighty king, vouchsafe your
    grace my father to remit.
Forgive his fault. His pardon I do ask
    of you as yet.
Alas, although my father hath your
    princely heart offended,
Amends for miss [1] he will now make, and
    faults shall be amended.   430
Instead of his requested life, pleaseth
    your grace take mine.
This offer I as tender child, so duty doth
    me bind.
KING. Do not entreat my grace no more,
    for he shall die the death!
Where is the execution man him to be-
    reave of breath?

            Enter Execution.
EXECUTION. At hand, and if it like your
    grace, my duty to despatch,
In hope that I, when deed is done, a good
    reward shall catch.
[1] Wrongdoing.

KING. Despatch with sword this judge's
    life; extinguish fear and cares.
So done, draw thou his cursèd skin
    straight over both his ears.
I will see the office done, and that before
    mine eyes.
EXECUTION. To do the thing my king com-
    mands I give the enterprise.[2]   440
SISAMNES. Otian, my son, the king to
    death by law hath me condemnèd,
And you in room and office mine his
    grace's will hath placèd;
Use justice, therefore, in this case, and
    yield unto no wrong,
[Lest thou do purchase the like death ere
    ever it be long.][3]
OTIAN. O father dear, these words to hear
    —that you must die by force—
Bedews my cheeks with stillèd tears.
    The king hath no remorse.
The grievous griefs and strainèd sighs
    my heart doth break in twain,
And I deplore, most woeful child, that I
    should see you slain.
O false and fickle frowning dame, that
    turneth as the wind,
Is this the joy in father's age thou me
    assignest to find?   450
O doleful day, unhappy hour, that loving
    child should see
His father dear before his face thus put
    to death should be!
Yet, father, give me blessing thine, and
    let me once embrace
Thy comely corpse in folded arms, and
    kiss thy ancient face!
SISAMNES. O child, thou makes my eyes to
    run, as rivers do, by stream.
My leave I take of thee, my son. Be-
    ware of this my Beam![4]
KING. Despatch even now, thou man of
    death; no longer seem to stay!
EXECUTION. Come, M[aster] Sisamnes,
    come on your way.
My office I must pay; forgive therefore
    my deed.
SISAMNES. I do forgive it thee, my friend;
    despatch therefore with speed!   460
Smite him in the neck with a sword to signify
                           his death.
[2] I readily undertake.
[3] Line supplied from first edn.
[4] Affliction, alluding to the Cross.

PRAXASPES. Behold, O king, how he doth bleed, being of life bereft!

KING. In this wise he shall not yet be left.
Pull his skin over his eyes to make his death more vile.
A wretch he was, a cruel thief, my commons to beguile!
Flay him with a false skin.

OTIAN. What child [1] is he of nature's mold could bide the same to see—
His father flayéd in this wise? O, how it grieveth me!

KING. Otian, thou seest thy father dead, and thou art in his room;
If thou beest proud, as he hath been, even thereto shalt thou come.

OTIAN. O king, to me this is a glass; with grief in it I view
Example that unto your grace I do not prove untrue.   470

PRAXASPES. Otian, convey your father hence to tomb where he shall lie.

OTIAN. And if it please your lordship, it shall be done by-and-by.
Good execution man, for need, help me with him away.

EXECUTION. I will fulfill, as you to me did say.   *They take him away.*

KING. My l[ord], now that my grace hath seen that finished is this deed,
To question mine give tentive [2] ear, and answer make with speed:
Have not I done a gracious deed, to redress my commons' woe?

PRAXASPES. Yea, truly, if it please your grace, you have indeed done so.
But now, O king, in friendly wise I counsel you in this:
Certain vices for to leave that in you placéd is—   480
The vice of drunkenness, O king, which doth you sore infect,
With other great abuses, which I wish you to detect.

KING. Peace, my lord! What needeth this? Of this I will not hear!
To palace now I will return, and thereto make good cheer.
God Bacchus he bestows his gifts—we have good store of wine—
And also that the ladies be both passing brave and fine.

[1] Suggested by Manly. Original reads *thilde.*
[2] Attentive.

But stay! I see a lord now come, and eke a valiant knight.
What news, my lord? To see you here my heart it doth delight.

Enter Lord and Knight to meet the King.

LORD. No news, O king; but of duty come to wait upon your grace.

KING. I thank you, my l[ord] and loving knight. I pray you with me trace. [3] 490
My lords and knight, I pray ye tell—I will not be offended—
Am I worthy of any crime once to be reprehended?

PRAXASPES. The Persians much do praise your grace, but one thing discommend,
In that to wine subject you be, wherein you do offend.
Sith that the might of wine's effect doth oft subdue your brain,
My counsel is, to please their hearts, from it you would refrain.

LORD. No, no, my lord, it is not so! For this of prince they tell,
For virtuous proof and princely facts Cyrus he doth excel.
By that his grace by conquest great the Egyptians did convince,
Of him report abroad doth pass to be a worthy prince.   500

KNIGHT. In person of Crœsus I answer make: we may not his grace compare
In whole respect for to be like Cyrus, the king's father,
Insomuch your grace hath yet no child as Cyrus left behind;
Even you I mean, Cambises King, in whom I favor find.

KING. Crœsus said well in saying so. But, Praxaspes, tell me why
That to my mouth in such a sort thou should avouch a lie,
Of drunkenness me thus to charge. But thou with speed shalt see
Whether that I a sober king or else a drunkard be.
I know thou hast a blissful babe, wherein thou dost delight;
Me to revenge of these thy words I will go wreak this spite.   510
When I the most have tasted wine, my bow it shall be bent.

[3] Walk.

At heart of him even then to shoot is
now my whole intent,
And, if that I his heart can hit, the king
no drunkard is;
If heart of his I do not kill, I yield to
thee in this.
Therefore, Praxaspes, fetch to me thy
youngest son with speed.
There is no way, I tell thee plain, but I
will do this deed.
PRAXASPES. Redoubted prince, spare my
sweet child. He is mine only joy!
I trust your grace to infant's heart no
such thing will employ.
If that his mother hear of this, she is so
nigh her flight,
In clay her corpse will soon be shrined
to pass from world's delight. 520
KING. No more ado! Go fetch me him.
It shall be as I say.
And if that I do speak the word, how
dare ye once say nay?
PRAXASPES. I will go fetch him to your
grace; but so, I trust, it shall not be!
KING. For fear of my displeasure great, go
fetch him unto me. [*Exit Praxaspes.*]
Is he gone? Now, by the gods, I will do
as I say!
My lord, therefore fill me some wine, I
heartily you pray;
For I must drink to make my brain
somewhat intoxicate.
When that the wine is in my head, O,
trimly I can prate!
LORD. Here is the cup, with filléd wine,
thereof to take repast.
KING. Give it me to drink it off, and see
no wine be waste. *Drink.* 530
Once again enlarge this cup, for I must
taste it still. *Drink.*
By the gods, I think of pleasant wine I
cannot take my fill!
Now drink is in, give me my bow and
arrows from Sir Knight.
At heart of child I mean to shoot, hoping
to cleave it right.
KNIGHT. Behold, O king, where he doth
come, his infant young in hand.

[*Enter Praxaspes with the Child.*]

PRAXASPES. O mighty king, your grace'
behest with sorrow I have scanned,
And brought my child fro mother's knee
before you to appear,

And she thereof no whit doth know that
he in place is here.
KING. Set him up, my mark to be. I
will shoot at his heart.
PRAXASPES. I beseech your grace not so
to do! Set this pretense apart!— 540
Farewell, my dear and loving babe!
Come, kiss thy father dear!
A grievous sight to me it is to see thee
slain even here.
Is this the gain now from the king for
giving counsel good—
Before my face with such despite to spill
my son's heart-blood?
O heavy day to me this is, and mother
in like case!
YOUNG CHILD. O father, father, wipe your
face;
I see the tears run from your eye.
My mother is at home sewing of a band.
Alas, dear father, why do you cry?
KING. Before me as a mark now let him
stand. 550
I will shoot at him my mind to fulfill.
YOUNG CHILD. Alas, alas, father, will you
me kill?
Good Master King, do not shoot at me;
my mother loves me best of all. *Shoot.*
KING. I have despatched him! Down he
doth fall!
As right as a line his heart I have hit.
Nay, thou shalt see, Praxaspes, stranger
news yet.
My knight, with speed his heart cut out
and give it unto me.
KNIGHT. It shall be done, O mighty king,
with all celerity.
LORD. My Lord Praxaspes, this had not
been but your tongue must be walking.
To the king of correction you must needs
be talking. 560
PRAXASPES. No correction, my lord, but
counsel for the best.
KNIGHT. Here is the heart, according to
your grace's behest.
KING. Behold, Praxaspes, thy son's own
heart! O, how well the same was hit!
After this wine to do this deed I thought
it very fit.
Esteem thou mayst right well thereby
no drunkard is the king
That in the midst of all his cups could
do this valiant thing.

My lord and knight, on me attend. To
    palace we will go,
And leave him here to take his son when
    we are gone him fro.
ALL. With all our hearts we give consent
    to wait upon your grace.
               [*Exeunt all but Praxaspes.*]
PRAXASPES. A woeful man, O Lord, am I,
    to see him in this case!   570
My days, I deem, desires their end. This
    deed will help me hence.
To have the blossoms of my field de-
    stroyed by violence!

Enter Mother.

[MOTHER.] Alas, alas, I do hear tell the
    king hath killed my son!
If it be so, woe worth the deed that ever
    it was done!
It is even so! My lord I see, how by him
    he doth weep.
What meant I that from hands of him
    this child I did not keep?
Alas, husband and lord, what did you
    mean to fetch this child away?
PRAXASPES. O lady wife, I little thought
    for to have seen this day.
MOTHER. O blissful babe! O joy of womb!
    Heart's comfort and delight!
For counsel given unto the king is this
    thy just requite?   580
O heavy day and doleful time, these
    mourning tunes to make!
With blubbered eyes, into mine arms
    from earth I will thee take,
And wrap thee in mine apron white.
    But, O my heavy heart!
The spiteful pangs that it sustains would
    make it in two to part,
The death of this my son to see!   O
    heavy mother now,
That from thy sweet and sugared joy to
    sorrow so shouldst bow!
What grief in womb did I retain before I
    did thee see!
Yet at the last, when smart was gone,
    what joy wert thou to me!
How tender was I of thy food, for to
    preserve thy state!
How stillèd I thy tender heart at times
    early and late!   590
With velvet paps I gave thee suck with
    issue from my breast,

And dancéd thee upon my knee to bring
    thee unto rest!
Is this the joy of thee I reap?   O king of
    tiger's brood!
O tiger's whelp, hadst thou the heart
    to see this child's heart-blood?
Nature enforceth me, alas, in this wise
    to deplore,
To wring my hands. O welaway, that I
    should see this hour!
Thy mother yet will kiss thy lips, silk-
    soft and pleasant white,
With wringing hands lamenting for to see
    thee in this plight!
My lording dear, let us go home our
    mourning to augment.
PRAXASPES. My lady dear, with heavy
    heart to it I do consent,   600
Between us both the child to bear unto
    our lordly place.   *Exeunt.*

Enter Ambidexter.

[AMBIDEXTER. (*To the audience.*)] Indeed, as
    ye say, I have been absent a long space.
But is not my cousin Cutpurse with you
    in the meantime?
To it, to it, cousin, and do your office
    fine!
How like you Sisamnes for using of me?
He played with both hands, but he sped
    ill-favoredly!
The king himself was godly uptrained;
He professed virtue—but I think it was
    feigned.
He plays with both hands, good deeds
    and ill;
But it was no good deed Praxaspes' son
    for to kill.   610
As he for the good deed on the judge was
    commended,
For all his deeds else he is reprehended.
The most evil-disposed person that ever
    was
All the state of his life he would not let
    pass,
Some [1] good deeds he will do, though they
    be but few.
The like things this tyrant Cambises
    doth shew.
No goodness from him to none is ex-
    hibited,
But still malediction abroad is distrib-
    uted;

[1] *I.e.,* but some.

And yet ye shall see in the rest of his race
What infamy he will work against his
  own grace.   620
Whist! No more words! Here comes
the king's brother.

Enter Lord Smirdis with Attendance and
                                  Diligence.

SMIRDIS. The king's brother by birth am
  I, issued from Cyrus' loins;
A grief to me it is to hear of this the
  king's repines.[1]
I like not well of those his deeds that he
  doth still frequent;
I wish to God that other ways his mind
  he could content.
Young I am, and next to him; no mo[2] of
  us there be.
I would be glad a quiet realm in this his
  reign to see.
ATTENDANCE. My lord, your good a[nd][3]
  willing heart the gods will recompense,
In that your mind so pensive is for those
  his great offense.
My lord, his grace shall have a time to
  pair[4] and to amend.   630
Happy is he that can escape and not his
  grace offend.
DILIGENCE. If that wicked vice he could
  refrain, from wasting wine forbear,
A moderate life he would frequent,
  amending this his square.[5]
AMBIDEXTER. My lord, and if your honor
  it shall please,
I can inform you what is best for your
  ease:
Let him alone; of his deeds do not talk;
Then by his side ye may quietly walk.
After his death you shall be king;
Then may you reform each kind of thing.
In the meantime live quietly; do not
  with him deal;   640
So shall it redound much to your weal.
SMIRDIS. Thou say'st true, my friend; that
  is the best.
I know not whether he love me or do me
  detest.
ATTENDANCE. Lean from his company all
  that you may.
I, faithful Attendance, will your honor
  obey;

_{1 Dissatisfactions.}   _{4 Repair.}
_{2 More.}   _{5 Regularity of conduct.}
_{3 Added by Manly.}

If against your honor he take any ire,
  His grace is as like to kindle his fire
To your honor's destruction as otherwise.
DILIGENCE. Therefore, my lord, take good
  advice,
And I, Diligence, your case will so
  tender   650
That to his grace your honor shall be
  none offender.
SMIRDIS. I thank you both, entire friends.
  With my honor still remain.
AMBIDEXTER. Behold where the king doth
  come with his train!

Enter King and a Lord.

KING. O lording dear and brother mine, I
  joy your state to see,
Surmising much what is the cause you
  absent thus from me.
SMIRDIS. Pleaseth your grace, no absence
  I, but ready to fulfill,
At all assays, my prince and king, in that
  your grace me will.
What I can do in true defense to you, my
  prince, aright,
In readiness I always am to offer forth
  my might.
KING. And I the like to you again do here
  avouch the same.   660
ALL. For this your good agreement here,
  now praiséd be God's name!
AMBIDEXTER. [*To Smirdis.*] But hear ye,
  noble prince; hark in your ear:
It is best to do as I did declare.
KING. My lord and brother Smirdis, now
  this is my mind and will:
That you to court of mine return, and
  there to tarry still
Till my return within short space your
  honor for to greet.
SMIRDIS. At your behest so will I do till
  time again we meet.
My leave I take from you, O king; even
  now I do depart.
Exeunt Smirdis, Attendance, and Diligence.
KING. Farewell, lord and brother mine!
  farewell with all my heart!
My lord, my brother Smirdis is of youth
  and manly might,   670
And in his sweet and pleasant face my
  heart doth take delight.
LORD. Yea, noble prince, if that your
  grace before his honor die,

He will succeed, a virtuous king, and rule
　with equity.

KING. As you have said, my lord, he is
　chief heir next my grace,
And, if I die tomorrow, next he shall
　succeed my place.

AMBIDEXTER. And, if it please your grace,
　O king, I heard him say,
For your death unto the God day and
　night he did pray;
He would live so virtuously and get him
　such a praise
That Fame by trump his due deserts in
　honor should upraise;
He said your grace deservéd had the
　cursing of all men,　　　　680
That ye should never after him get any
　praise again.

KING. Did he speak thus of my grace in
　such despiteful wise?
Or else dost thou presume to fill my
　princely ears with lies?

LORD. I cannot think it in my heart that
　he would report so.

KING. How sayst thou? Speak the truth:
　was it so or no?

AMBIDEXTER. I think so, if it please your
　grace, but I cannot tell.

KING. Thou play'st with both hands, now
　I perceive well!
But, for to put all doubts aside and to
　make him leese his hope,
He shall die by dint of sword or else by
　choking rope.
Shall he succeed when I am gone, to have
　more praise than I?　　　　690
Were he father, as brother mine, I swear
　that he shall die!
To palace mine I will therefore, his death
　for to pursue.
　　　　　　　Exit [King with the Lord].

AMBIDEXTER. Are ye gone? Straightway
　I will follow you.—
[To the audience.] How like ye now, my
　masters? Doth not this gear cotton? [1]
The proverb old is verified: "Soon ripe,
　and soon rotten!"
He will not be quiet till his brother be
　killed;
His delight is wholly to have his blood
　spilled.
Marry, sir, I told him a notable lie!
If it were to do again, I durst [not] do it, I!

[1] Affair succeed.

Marry, when I had done, to it I durst
　not stand;　　　　700
Thereby ye may perceive I use to play
　with each hand.
But how now, cousin Cutpurse, with
　whom play you?
Take heed, for his hand is groping even
　now!
Cousin, take heed, if you do secretly
　grope;
If ye be taken, cousin, ye must look
　through a rope.　　　　Exit.

Enter Lord Smirdis alone.

[SMIRDIS.] I am wandering alone, here and
　there to walk;
The court is so unquiet, in it I take
　no joy.
Solitary to myself now I may talk.
If I could rule, I wist what to say.

Enter Cruelty and Murder with bloody hands.

CRUELTY. My coequal partner, Murder,
　come away;　　　　710
From me long thou mayst not stay.

MURDER. Yes, from thee I may stay, but
　not thou from me;
Therefore I have a prerogative above
　thee.

CRUELTY. But in this case we must to-
　gether abide.
Come, come! Lord Smirdis I have spied.
Lay hands on him with all festination,[2]
That on him we may work our indigna-
　tion!　　　　[They seize him.]

SMIRDIS. How now, my friends? What
　have you to do with me?

MURDER. King Cambises hath sent us
　unto thee,
Commanding us straightly, without
　mercy or favor,　　　　720
Upon thee to bestow our behavior,
With cruelty to murder you and make
　you away.

SMIRDIS. Yet pardon me, I heartily you
　pray!
Consider, the king is a tyrant tyran-
　nious,
And all his doings be damnable and per-
　nicious.
Favor me therefore; I did him never
　offend.

[2] Speed

CRUELTY. No favor at all! Your life is at
an end!

Even now I strike, his body to wound.
Strike him in divers places.[1]

Behold, now his blood springs out on
the ground!
A little bladder of vinegar pricked.[2]

MURDER. Now he is dead, let us present
him to the king. 730

CRUELTY. Lay to your hand, away him to
bring. *Exeunt.*

Enter Ambidexter.

AMBIDEXTER. O the passion of God, yonder
is a heavy court!

Some weeps, some wails—and some make
great sport.

Lord Smirdis by Cruelty and Murder is
slain;

But Jesus! for want of him how some do
complain!

If I should have had a thousand pound I
could not forbear weeping.

Now Jesus have his blessed soul in keeping!

Ah, good lord, to think on him, how it
doth me grieve!

I cannot forbear weeping, ye may me
believe. *Weep.*

O my heart, how my pulses do beat! 740

With sorrowful lamentations I am in
such a heat!

Ah, my heart, how for him it doth sorrow!

Nay, I have done, in faith, now. And
God give ye good morrow!

Ha, ha! Weep? Nay, laugh, with both
hands to play!

The king through his cruelty hath made
him away;

But hath not he wrought a most wicked
deed,

Because king after him he should not
proceed,

His own natural brother, and having no
more,

To procure his death by violence sore?

In spite, because his brother should never
be king, 750

His heart, being wicked, consented to
this thing.

Now he hath no more brothers nor kinred [3] alive.

If the king use this gear still, he cannot
long thrive.

Enter Hob and Lob.

HOB. God's hat, neighbor, come away!
It's time to market to go!

LOB. God's vast,[4] neighbor, zay ye zo?

The clock hath stricken vive, ich [5] think,
by Lakin! [6]

Bum vay,[7] vrom sleep cham not very well
waken!

But, neighbor Hob, neighbor Hob, what
have ye to zell?

HOB. Bum troth, neighbor Lob, to you I
chill tell:

Chave two goslings and a chine of
pork— 760

There is no vatter between this and York.

Chave a pot of strawberries and a calve's
head;

A zennight zince, tomorrow, it hath been
dead.

LOB. Chave a score of eggs and of butter
a pound:

Yesterday a nest of goodly young rabbits
I vound;

Chave vorty things mo, of more and of
less—

My brain is not very good them to express.

But, God's hat, neighbor, wot'st [8] what?

HOB. No, not well, neighbor; what's that?

LOB. Bum vay, neighbor, master king is a
zhrode [9] lad! 770

Zo God help me, and halidom, I think the
vool be mad!

Zome zay he deal cruelly: his brother he
did kill,

And also a goodly young lad's heart-
blood he did spill.

HOB. Vorbod of God,[10] neighbor! Has he
played zuch a voolish deed?

AMBIDEXTER. Goodman Hob and Goodman Lob, God be your speed!

As you two towards market do walk,

---

[1] In the original this stage direction is printed
in the margin at line 723.

[2] In the original this stage direction is printed
in the margin at line 727.

[3] Kindred.

[4] Fast. In the following rustic dialect, initial
$z=s$ and initial $v=f$.

[5] I. See *Roister Doister*, I, iii, 100, n.

[6] Ladykin; *i.e.*, the Virgin.

[7] By my faith.   [9] Shrewd.

[8] Knowest.   [10] God forbid!

Of the king's cruelty I did hear you talk.
I insure you he is a king most vile and
  pernicious;
His doings and life are odious and vicious.
Lob. It were a good deed zomebody would
  break his head.   780
Hob. Bum vay, neighbor Lob, I chuld he
  were dead!
Ambidexter. So would I, Lob and Hob,
  with all my heart!—
[To audience.] Now with both hands will
  you see me play my part.—
Ah, ye whoreson [1] traitorly knaves,
Hob and Lob, out upon you, slaves!
Lob. And thou call'st me knave, thou art
  another!
My name is Lob, and Hob my next
  neighbor.
Ambidexter. Hob and Lob! Ah, ye coun-
  try patches, [2]
Ah, ye fools, ye have made wrong
  matches!
Ye have spoken treason against the
  king's grace!   790
For it I will accuse ye before his face;
Then for the same ye shall be martyred.
At the least ye shall be hanged, drawn,
  and quartered!
Hob. O gentleman, ye shall have two
  pear-pies, and tell not of me!
Lob. By God, a vat goose chill give thee.
I think no hurt, by my vather's soul I
  zwear!
Hob. Chave lived well all my lifetime, my
  neighbors among,
And now chould be loath to come to zuch
  wrong—
To be hanged and quartered, the grief
  would be great!
Lob. A foul evil on thee, Hob! Who bid
  thee on it treat?   800
Vor it was thou that first did him
  name.
Hob. Thou liest like a varlet and thou
  zayst the zame!
It was zuch a foolish Lob as thou.
Lob. Speak many words, and, by Cod's
  nails I vow,
Upon thy pate my staff I will lay!
Ambidexter. [Aside.] By the Mass, I will
  cause them to make a fray.—
Yea, Lob, thou sayst true: all came
  through him.

Lob. Bum vay, thou hod,[3] a little would
  make me ye trim!
Give thee a zwap on thy nose till thy
  heart ache!
Hob. If thou darest, do it! Else, man,
  cry "creak!" [4]   810
I trust, before thou hurt me,
With my staff chill make a Lob of
  thee!
*Here let them fight with their staves, not come
  near another by three or four yards; the
  Vice set them on as hard as he can; one
  of their wives come out, and all-to [5] beat
  the Vice; he run away.*

*Enter Marian-May-Be-Good, Hob's Wife,
running in with a broom, and part them.*

Marian. O the body of me! Husband
  Hob, what mean ye to fight?
For the passion of God, no more blows
  smite!
Neighbors and friends so long, and now
  to fall out?
What! in your age to seem so stout?
If I had not parted ye, one had killed
  another.
Lob. I had not cared, I swear by God's
  Mother!
Marian. Shake hands again at the re-
  quest of me;
As ye have been friends, so friends still
  be.   820
Hob. Bum troth, cham content and zayst
  word, neighbor Lob.
Lob. I am content; agreed, neighbor
  Hob!
*Shake hands and laugh heartily one at
  another.*
Marian. So, get you to market; no longer
  stay.
And with yonder knave let me make a
  fray.
Hob. Content, wife Marian; chill do as
  thou dost say.
But buss me, ich pray thee, at going
  away!   *Exeunt Hob, Lob.*
Marian. Thou whoreson knave and prick-
  eared boy, why didst thou let them
  fight?
If one had killed another here, couldst
  thou their deaths requite?

[1] Rascally.   [2] Clowns, bumpkins.
[3] Hob(?).   [4] I.e., confess yourself beaten
[5] Thoroughly.

It bears a sign by this thy deed a cow-
    ardly knave thou art,
Else wouldst thou draw that weapon
    thine, like a man,[1] them to part. 830
AMBIDEXTER. What, Marian-May-Be-
    Good, are you come prattling?
Ye may hap get a box on the ear with
    your talking!
If they had killed one another, I had not
    cared a pease.
*Here let her swinge him in her broom; she
    gets him down, and he her down; thus
    one on the top of another make pastime.*
MARIAN. Ah, villain, myself on thee I
    must ease!
Give me a box on the ear? That will I try.
Who shall be master, thou shalt see by-
    and-by!
AMBIDEXTER. O, no more, no more, I be-
    seech you heartily!
Even now I yield, and give you the
    mast'ry.
        Run his way out while she is down.
MARIAN. Ah, thou knave! dost thou throw
    me down and run thy [2] way?
If he were here again, O, how I would
    him pay! 840
I will after him, and, if I can him meet,
With these my nails his face I will greet.
            [Exit.]

*Enter Venus leading out her son Cupid,
    blind. He must have a bow and two
    shafts, one headed with gold and th'
            other with lead.*

VENUS. Come forth, my son. Unto my
    words attentive ears resign;
What I pretend,[3] see you frequent, to
    force this game of mine.
The king a kinswoman hath, adorned
    with beauty store; [4]
And I wish that Diana's gifts they twain
    shall keep no more,
But use my silver sugared game their
    joys for to augment.
When I do speak, to wound his heart,
    Cupid my son, consent,
And shoot at him the shaft of love that
    bears the head of gold,
To wound his heart in lover's wise, his
    grief for to unfold. 850

Though kin she be unto his grace, that
    nature me expel,
Against the course thereof he may in my
    game please me well.
Wherefore, my son, do not forget; forth-
    with pursue the deed!
CUPID. Mother, I mean for to obey as
    you have whole decreed;
But you must tell me, mother dear,
    when I shall arrow draw,
Else your request to be attained will not
    be worth a straw;
I am blind and cannot see, but still do
    shoot by guess.
The poets well, in places, store [5] of my
    might do express.
VENUS. Cupid my son, when time shall
    serve that thou shalt do this deed,
Then warning I to thee will give; but see
    thou shoot with speed. 860

Enter a Lord, a Lady, and a Waiting-maid.

[FIRST] LORD. Lady dear, to king akin,
    forthwith let us proceed
To trace abroad the beauty fields, as erst
    we had decreed.
The blowing buds whose savory scents
    our sense will much delight,
The sweet smell of musk white-rose to
    please the appetite,
The chirping birds whose pleasant tunes
    therein shall here record
That our great joy we shall it find in
    field to walk abroad,
On lute and cittern there to play a heav-
    enly harmony;
Our ears shall hear, heart to content, our
    sports to beautify.
LADY. Unto your words, most comely lord,
    myself submit do I;
To trace with you in field so green I mean
    not to deny. 870
        Here trace up and down, playing.
MAID. And I, your waiting-maid, at hand
    with diligence will be,
For to fulfill with heart and hand, when
    you shall command me.

Enter King, Lord, and Knight.

KING. Come on, my lord and knight,
    abroad; our mirth let us employ.
Since he is dead, this heart of mine in
    corpse I feel it joy.

[1] Suggested by Manly. Original reads *knave.*
[2] Emended by Manly; original has *the.*
[3] Intend.   [4] Store of beauty.
[5] Greatness, abundance.

Should brother mine have reignéd king
    when I had yielded breath?
A thousand brothers I rather had to put
    them all to death.
But, O behold, where I do see a lord and
    lady fair!
For beauty she most worthy is to sit in
    prince's chair.

VENUS. Shoot forth, my son! Now is
    the time that thou must wound his
    heart.

CUPID. Content you, mother; I will do
    my part.   880
Shoot there, and go out Venus and Cupid.

KING. Of truth, my lord, in eye of mine
    all ladies she doth excel.
Can none report what dame she is, and to
    my grace it tell?

LORD. Redoubted prince, pleaseth your
    grace, to you she is akin,
Cousin-german, nigh of birth, by moth-
    er's side come in.

KNIGHT. And that her waiting-maiden is,
    attending her upon.
He is a lord of prince's court, and will be
    there anon.
They sport themselves in pleasant field,
    to former uséd use.

KING. My lord and knight, of truth I
    speak. My heart it cannot choose
But with my lady I must speak and so
    express my mind.—
My lord and ladies, walking there, if you
    will favor find,   890
Present yourselves unto my grace, and
    by my side come stand.

FIRST LORD. We will fulfill, most mighty
    king, as your grace doth command.

KING. Lady dear, intelligence my grace
    hath got of late,
You issued out of mother's stock and kin
    unto my state.
According to rule of birth you are cousin-
    german mine;
Yet do I wish that farther off this kinred
    I could find;
For Cupid he, that eyeless boy, my heart
    hath so enflamed
With beauty, you me to content the like
    cannot be named;
For, since I entered in this place and on
    you fixed mine eyes,
Most burning fits about my heart in
    ample wise did rise.   900

The heat of them such force doth yield,
    my corpse they scorch, alas!
And burns the same with wasting heat,
    as Titan doth the grass.
And, sith this heat is kindled so and
    fresh in heart of me,
There is no way but of the same the
    quencher you must be.
My meaning is that beauty yours my
    heart with love doth wound;
To give me love mind [1] to content, my
    heart hath you out found;
And you are she must be my wife, else
    shall I end my days.
Consent to this, and be my queen, to
    wear the crown with praise!

LADY. If it please your grace, O mighty
    king, you shall not this request.
It is a thing that nature's course doth
    utterly detest,   910
And high it would the God displease; of
    all, that is the worst.
To grant your grace to marry so, it is
    not I that durst.
Yet humble thanks I render now unto
    you, mighty king,
That you vouchsafe to great estate so
    gladly would me bring.
Were it not it were offense, I would it
    not deny,
But such great honor to achieve my
    heart I would apply.
Therefore, O king, with humble heart in
    this I pardon crave;
My answer is: in this request your mind
    ye may not have.

KING. May I not? Nay, then, I will, by
    all the gods I vow!
And I will marry thee as wife. This is
    mine answer now!   920
Who dare say nay what I pretend, who
    dare the same withstand,
Shall lose his head, and have report as
    traitor through my land.
There is no nay. I will you have, and
    you my queen shall be!

LADY. Then, mighty king, I crave your
    grace to hear the words of me:
Your counsel take of lordings' wit; the
    laws aright peruse;
If I with safe may grant this deed, I will
    it not refuse.

[1] Desire.

KING. No, no! What I have said to you,
 I mean to have it so.
For counsel theirs I mean not, I, in this
 respect to go;
But to my palace let us go, the marriage
 to prepare;
For, to avoid [1] my will in this, I can it
 not forbear. 930
LADY. O God, forgive me, if I do amiss!
 The king by compulsion enforceth me
 this.
MAID. Unto the gods for your estate I
 will not cease to pray,
That you may be a happy queen, and see
 most joyful day.
KING. Come on, my lords; with gladsome
 hearts let us rejoice with glee!
Your music show to joy this deed at the
 request of me!
BOTH. For to obey your grace's words our
 honors do agree. *Exeunt.*

Enter Ambidexter.

AMBIDEXTER. O the passion of me! Marry,
 as ye say, yonder is a royal court!
There is triumphing and sport upon
 sport,
Such loyal lords, with such lordly exercise, 940
Frequenting such pastime as they can
 devise,
Running at tilt, jousting, with running
 at the ring,
Masking and mumming, with each kind
 of thing,
Such dancing, such singing, with musical
 harmony!
Believe me, I was loath to absent their
 company.
But will you believe? Jesu, what haste
 they made till they were married!
Not for a million of pounds one day
 longer they would have tar[ri]ed!
O, there was a banquet royal and super-
 excellent!
Thousands and thousands at that banquet was spent.
I muse of nothing but how they can be
 married so soon. 950
I care not if I be married before tomorrow at noon,
If marriage be a thing that so may be
 had.

[*To a girl in the audience.*] How say you,
 maid? To marry me will ye be glad?
Out of doubt, I believe it is some excellent
 treasure;
Else to the same belongs abundant pleas-
 ure.
Yet with mine ears I have heard some
 say,
"That ever I was married, now cursèd
 be the day!"
Those be they [that] [2] with curst [3] wives
 be matched.
That husband for hawk's meat [4] of [5]
 them is up-snatched,
Head broke with a bedstaff, face all-to
 bescratched— 960
"Knave!" "Slave!" and "Villain!"—a
 coiled coat [6] now and then.
When the wife hath given it, she will say,
 "Alas, good man!"
Such were better unmarried, my masters,
 I trow,
Than all their life after be matched with
 a shrow.[7]

Enter Preparation.

[PREPARATION.] With speed I am sent all
 things to prepare,
My message to do as the king did de-
 clare.
His grace doth mean a banquet to
 make,
Meaning in this place repast for to take.
Well, the cloth shall be laid, and all
 things in readiness,
To court to return when done is my
 business. 970
AMBIDEXTER. A proper man and also fit
For the king's estate to prepare a ban-
 quet!
PREPARATION. What, Ambidexter? Thou
 art not unknown!
A mischief on all good faces, so that I
 curse not mine own!
Now, in the knave's name, shake hands
 with me.
AMBIDEXTER. Well said, goodman pouch-
 mouth; your reverence I see.
I will teach ye, if your manners no better
 be.

---

[1] Make void, give up.
[2] Supplied from first edn.
[3] Shrewish.
[4] Something seized greedily.
[5] By.
[6] A beating.
[7] Shrew.

Ah, ye slave, the king doth me a gentle-
man allow;
Therefore I look that to me ye should
bow.   *Fight.*
PREPARATION. Good Master Ambidexter,
pardon my behavior;   980
For this your deeds you are a knave, for
your labor!
AMBIDEXTER. Why, ye stale counterly [1]
villain, nothing but "knave"? *Fight.*
PREPARATION. I am sorry your mastership
offended I have;
Shake hands, that between us agreement
may be.
I was overshot with myself, I do see.
Let me have your help this furniture to
provide.
The king from this place will not long
abide.   *Set the fruit on the board.*
AMBIDEXTER. Content; it is the thing that
I would wish.
I myself will go fetch one dish.
*Let the Vice fetch a dish of nuts, and let them
fall in the bringing of them in.*
PREPARATION. Cleanly, Master Ambidex-
ter, for fair on the ground they lie. 990
AMBIDEXTER. I will have them up again
by-and-by.
PREPARATION. To see all in readiness I
will put you in trust;
There is no nay, to the court needs I
must.   *Exit Preparation.*
AMBIDEXTER. Have ye no doubt but all
shall be well.—
Marry, sir, as you say, this gear doth
excel!
All things is in a readiness, when they
come hither,
The king's grace and the queen both togither.—
[*To the audience.*] I beseech ye, my masters, tell me, is it not best
That I be so bold as to bid a guest?
He is as honest a man as ever spurred
cow—   1000
My cousin Cutpurse, I mean; I beseech
ye, judge you.
Believe me, cousin, if to be the king's
guest ye could be taken,
I trust that offer will never be for-
saken.
But, cousin, because to that office ye are
not like to come,

[1] Fit for the Counter, a prison.

Frequent your exercises—a horn [2] on
your thumb,
A quick eye, a sharp knife, at hand a
receiver. [3]
But then take heed, cousin, ye be a
cleanly conveyor.
Content yourself, cousin; for this banquet
you are unfit,
When such as I at the same am unworthy
to sit.

Enter King, Queen, and his Train.

KING. My queen and lords, to take re-
past, let us attempt the same.   1010
Here is the place; delay no time, but to
our purpose frame.
QUEEN. With willing hearts your whole
behest we mind for to obey.
ALL. And we, the rest of prince's train, will
do as you do say.   *Sit at the banquet.*
KING. Methink mine ears doth wish the
sound of music's harmony;
Here, for to play before my grace, in place
I would them spy. *Play at the banquet.*
AMBIDEXTER. They be at hand, sir, with
stick and fiddle;
They can play a new dance, called " Hey-
diddle-diddle."
KING. My queen, perpend. What I pro-
nounce, I will not violate,
But one thing which my heart makes
glad I mind to explicate.
You know in court uptrainéd is a lion
very young;   1020
Of one litter two whelps [4] beside, as yet
not very strong.
I did request one whelp to see and this
young lion fight;
But lion did the whelp convince by
strength of force and might.
His brother whelp, perceiving that the
lion was too good,
And he by force was like to see the other
whelp his [5] blood,
With force to lion he did run, his brother
for to help.
A wonder great it was to see that friendship in a whelp!
So then the whelps between them both
the lion did convince.

[2] A thimble of horn, worn by cutpurses.
[3] A confederate to whom stolen goods were
handed.   [4] Dogs, in this case.
[5] *Whelp his* is an old form of the possessive.

Which thing to see before mine eyes did
glad the heart of prince.

At this tale told, let the Queen weep.

QUEEN. These words to hear makes stilling
tears issue from crystal eyes.   1030

KING. What dost thou mean, my spouse,
to weep for loss of any prize? [1]

QUEEN. No, no, O king, but, as you see,
friendship in brother's whelp;

When one was like to have repulse, the
other yielded help.

And was this favor showed in dogs, to
shame of royal king?

Alack, I wish these ears of mine had not
once heard this thing!

Even so should you, O mighty king, to
brother been a stay,

And not, without offense to you, in such
wise him to slay.

In all assays it was your part his cause
to have defended,

And whosoever had him misused to have
them reprehended.

But faithful love was more in dog than it
was in your grace.   1040

KING. O cursèd caitiff, vicious and vile,
I hate thee in this place!

This banquet is at an end; take all these
things away.

Before my face thou shalt repent the
words that thou dost say.

O wretch most vile, didst thou the cause
of brother mine so tender

The loss of him should grieve thy heart,
he being none offender?

It did me good his death to have—so will
it to have thine!

What friendship he had at my hands, the
same even thou shalt find.

I give consent, and make a vow, that
thou shalt die the death!

By Cruel's sword and Murder fell even
thou shalt lose thy breath.

Ambidexter, see with speed to Cruelty
ye go;   1050

Cause him hither to approach, Murder
with him also.

AMBIDEXTER. I ready am for to fulfill if
that it be your grace's will.

KING. Then naught oblite [2] my message
given; absent thyself away.

AMBIDEXTER. Then in this place I will no
longer stay.—

[*Aside to the Queen.*] If that I durst, I
would mourn your case;

But, alas! I dare not, for fear of his
grace.   *Exit Ambidex[ter].*

KING. Thou cursèd Jill! [3] by all the gods I
take an oath and swear

That flesh of thine these hands of mine
in pieces small could tear!

But thou shalt die by dent [4] of sword;
there is no friend ne fee

Shall find remorse at prince's hand to
save the life of thee!   1060

QUEEN. O mighty king and husband mine,
vouchsafe to hear me speak,

And license give to spouse of thine her
patient mind to break.

For tender love unto your grace my
words I did so frame;

For pure love doth heart of king me violate and blame.

And to your grace is this offense that I
should purchase death?

Then cursèd time that I was queen to
shorten this my breath!

Your grace doth know by marriage true
I am your wife and spouse,

And one to save another's health at
troth-plight made our vows.

Therefore, O king, let loving queen at
thy hand find remorse;

Let pity be a mean to quench that cruel
raging force,   1070

And pardon, plight [5] from prince's mouth,
yield grace unto your queen,

That amity with faithful zeal may ever
be us between.

KING. Ah, caitiff vile! to pity thee my
heart it is not bent;

Ne yet to pardon your offense it is not
mine intent.

FIRST LORD. Our mighty prince, with
humble suit of your grace this I crave,

That this request it may take place, your
favor for to have.

Let mercy yet abundantly the life of
queen preserve,

Sith she in most obedient wise your
grace's will doth serve.

As yet your grace but while with her hath
had cohabitation,

And sure this is no desert why to yield
her indignation. [6]   1080

---

[1] Contest.   [2] Forget.

[3] Wench.   [5] Plighted, pledged.
[4] Dint.   [6] Indignity.

Therefore, O king, her life prolong, to joy
   her days in bliss!
SECOND LORD. Your grace shall win immortal fame in granting unto this.
She is a queen whose goodly hue excels
   the royal rose,
For beauty bright Dame Nature she a
   large gift did dispose.
For comeliness who may compare? Of
   all she bears the bell.[1]
This should give cause to move your
   grace to love her very well.
Her silver breast in those your arms to
   sing the songs of love—
Fine qualities most excellent to be in her
   you prove;
A precious pearl of price to prince, a
   jewel passing all!
Therefore, O king, to beg remorse on both
   my knees I fall;   1090
To grant her grace to have her life, with
   heart I do desire.
KING. You villains twain, with raging
   force ye set my heart on fire!
If I consent that she shall die, how dare
   ye crave her life?
You two to ask this at my hand doth
   much enlarge my strife.
Were it not for shame, you two should
   die, that for her life do sue.
But favor mine from you is gone, my
   lords, I tell you true.
I sent for Cruelty of late; if he would
   come away,
I would commit her to his hands his
   cruel part to play.
Even now I see where he doth come; it
   doth my heart delight.

Enter Cruelty and Murder.

CRUELTY. Come, Murder, come; let us go
   forth with might;   1100
Once again the king's commandment we
   must fulfill.
MURDER. I am contented [2] to do it with a
   good will.
KING. Murder and Cruelty, for both of
   you I sent,
With all festination your offices to frequent.
Lay hold on the queen; take her to your
   power,
And make her away within this hour!

Spare for no fear; I do you full permit.
So I from this place do mean for to flit.
BOTH. With courageous hearts, O king, we
   will obey.
KING. Then come, my lords, let us depart
   away.   1110
BOTH THE LORDS. With heavy hearts we
   will do all your grace doth say.
        Exeunt King and Lord[s].
CRUELTY. Come, lady and queen, now are
   you in our handling;
In faith, with you we will use no dandling.
MURDER. With all expedition I, Murder,
   will take place;
Though thou be a queen, ye be under my
   grace.
QUEEN. With patience I will you both
   obey.[3]
CRUELTY. No more words, but go with us
   away!
QUEEN. Yet before I die, some psalm to
   God let me sing.
BOTH. We be content to permit you that
   thing.
QUEEN. Farewell, you ladies of the court,
   with all your masking hue!   1120
I do forsake these broidered guards, and
   all the fashions new,
The court and all the courtly train,
   wherein I had delight;
I banished am from happy sport, and all
   by spiteful spite;
Yet with a joyful heart to God a psalm
   I mean to sing,
Forgiving all [men] [4] and the king of
   each kind of thing. *Sing,[5] and exeunt.*

Enter Ambidexter weeping.

AMBIDEXTER. Ah, ah, ah, ah! I cannot
   choose but weep for the queen!
Nothing but mourning now at the court
   there is seen.
O, O, my heart, my heart! O, my bum
   will break!
Very grief so torments me that scarce I
   can speak.
Who could but weep for the loss of such
   a lady?   1130
That cannot I do, I swear by mine hon-
   esty.
But, Lord! so the ladies mourn, crying
   "Alack!"

---

[1] Wins the prize.   [2] Original reads *contended*.
[3] Original interchanges *obey* and *away* of next
line.   [4] Supplied by Manly.   [5] The song is lost.

Nothing is worn now but only black.
I believe all [the] [1] cloth in Watling
  Street to make gowns would not serve.
If I make a lie, the devil let ye sterve! [2]
All ladies mourn, both young and old;
There is not one that weareth a point's
  worth of gold.
There is a sort for fear for the king do
  pray
That would have him dead, by the Mass,
  I dare say. [3]
What a king was he that hath used such
  tyranny!   1140
He was akin to Bishop Bonner, [4] I think
  verily!
For both their delights was to shed blood,
But never intended to do any good.
Cambises put a judge to death—that was
  a good deed;
But to kill the young child was worse to
  proceed;
To murder his brother, and then his own
  wife—
So help me God and halidom, it is pity
  of his life!
Hear ye? I will lay twenty thousand
  pound
That the king himself doth die by some
  wound;
He hath shed so much blood that his will
  be shed.   1150
If it come to pass, in faith, then he is
  sped.

*Enter the King, without a gown, a sword
  thrust up into his side, bleeding.*

KING. Out, alas! What shall I do? My
  life is finishéd!
Wounded I am by sudden chance; my
  blood is minishéd.
Gog's heart, what means might I make
  my life to preserve?
Is there naught to be my help, nor is
  there naught to serve?
Out upon the court and lords that there
  remain!
To help my grief in this my case will
  none of them take pain?

Who but I, in such a wise, his death's
  wound could have got?
As I on horseback up did leap, my sword
  from scabbard shot,
And ran me thus into the side, as you
  right well may see.   1160
A marvel's chance unfortunate, that in
  this wise should be!
I feel myself a-dying now; of life bereft
  am I;
And Death hath caught me with his
  dart; for want of blood I spy. [5]
Thus, gasping, here on ground I lie; for
  nothing I do care.
A just reward for my misdeeds my death
  doth plain declare.
            Here let him quake and stir.
AMBIDEXTER. How now, noble king? Pluck
  up your heart!
What, will you die, and from us depart?
Speak to me and ye be alive!
He cannot speak. But behold, how with
  Death he doth strive.   [*King dies.*]
Alas, good king! Alas, he is gone! 1170
The devil take me if for him I make any
  moan.
I did prognosticate of his end, by the
  Mass!
Like as I did say, so is it come to pass.
I will be gone. If I should be found here,
That I should kill him it would appear.
For fear with his death they do me
  charge,
Farewell, my masters, I will go take
  barge.
I mean to be packing; now is the tide;
Farewell, my masters, I will no longer
  abide!   *Exit Ambidexter.*

Enter three Lords.

FIRST LORD. Behold, my lord, it is even
  so as he to us did tell.   1180
His grace is dead, upon the ground, by
  dint of sword most fell.
SECOND LORD. As he in saddle would have
  leaped, his sword from sheath did go,
Goring him up into the side. His life was
  ended so.
THIRD LORD. His blood so fast did issue
  out that naught could him prolong;
Yet, before he yielded up the ghost, his
  heart was very strong.

---

[1] Supplied by Hazlitt.   [2] Die.
[3] *I.e.*, there is a group who pray for the king
out of fear, but wish him dead.
[4] Bishop of London, who was hated because
of his persecution of the Protestants.

[5] Spyre, 'spire, expire(?).

FIRST LORD. A just reward for his misdeeds the God above hath wrought,
For certainly the life he led was to be
counted naught.
SECOND LORD. Yet a princely burial he
shall have, according to his estate;
And more of him here at this time we
have not to dilate.
THIRD LORD. My lords, let us take him
up and carry him away.   1190
BOTH. Content we are with one accord to
do as you do say.   *Exeunt all.*

EPILOGUE

Right gentle audience, here have you pe-
rused
The tragical history of this wicked king.
According to our duty, we have not refused,
But to our best intent expressed every-
thing.
We trust none is offended for this our
doing.
Our author craves likewise, if he have
squared [1] amiss,
By gentle admonition to know where
the fault is.
His good will shall not be neglected to
amend the same.

[1] Shaped, built.

Praying all to bear, therefore, with this
simple deed
Until the time serve a better he may
frame;   10
Thus yielding you thanks, to end we
decreed
That you so gently have suffered us to
proceed,
In such patient wise as to hear and see,
We can but thank ye therefor; we can do
no more, we!

As duty binds us, for our noble queen let
us pray,
And for her honorable council, the truth
that they may use,
To practice justice and defend her grace
each day;
To maintain God's word they may not
refuse,
To correct all those that would her grace
and grace's laws abuse;
Beseeching God over us she may reign
long,   20
To be guided by truth and defended from
wrong.

AMEN, QUOD [2] THOMAS PRESTON.

[2] Quoth, said.

JOHN LYLY

John Lyly was probably born in Canterbury in 1553 or 1554. He took his B.A. at Oxford in 1573 and his M.A. in 1575, and was made an M.A. by Cambridge University also in 1579. Late in 1578 his *Euphues: The Anatomy of Wit* was issued, a work intended to set a pattern for English prose, in which he wove into a thin thread of fiction dissertations on such subjects as education and contemporary manners. A second part, *Euphues and His England,* appeared in 1580. In spite of the vogue of *Euphues,* whose style was imitated in a series of romantic novels for many years to come, Lyly turned from fiction to devote himself to drama, possibly under the influence of the Earl of Oxford. Beginning about 1580 as his secretary, Lyly served the earl at least until about 1585. He was esquire of the body to Elizabeth in 1588, probably wrote a pamphlet and plays for the bishops' party in the Marprelate controversy of 1589–90, and secured election to parliament on four separate occasions. Disappointed of his chief hopes, however, he died in 1606, after a decade marked for us only by some petty records of his family life and some letters complaining of failure and neglect.

Lyly's dramatic work was part of his disappointing effort to advance his fortunes at court, especially in connection with the office of the revels, but it was also designed for the professional theater. The records of the activities and interrelations of the boy companies by whom his plays were acted are complicated and often obscure. *Campaspe* and *Sapho and Phao* were printed in 1584 as having been acted early in the year at court, by the Children of the Chapel and the Boys of St. Paul's Choir School, but official payment for the two performances was made to Oxford's "servants" under Lyly. Possibly the boy company under Oxford's patronage was combined with the other two companies in this year to perform at court plays written by Lyly and Oxford. According to the prologues, however, Lyly's two plays were also publicly acted at the "private" theater of Blackfriars, where the Children of the Chapel had given periodic performances for profit since 1576. Apparently Lyly and Oxford acquired an interest in this playhouse just as it was closed by a suit in 1584. Later Lyly wrote plays for Paul's boys, as the title-pages show, clearly for both court and public performances, until the public acting of the boys came to an end in 1591. These plays, with the dates of publication, are *Endymion* (1591), *Galathea* (1592), *Midas* (1592), *Mother Bombie* (1594), and *Love's Metamorphosis* (1601). *The Woman in the Moon* (1597) has no indication of the company, and may have been the result of some other connection.

It is in keeping with this effort to please the court and the public that Lyly's dramatic work marks the first stage in the development toward the Elizabethan popular drama of superb literary quality which was to follow. In the words of Bond, Lyly struck a "balance between classic precedent and romantic freedom." Titles of lost plays suggest that court taste had turned from the stricter classicism of academic circles to romance, sometimes disguised by the use of classical story. Lyly used as a basis of his plots love stories drawn from ancient history or mythology, most often from Ovid, adding at times pastoral or sylvan settings, and always reflecting the ideals of courtly circles. Indirect effects of classical influence, possibly in part derived from Italian influence, are seen in both structure and style. There is good motivation of action, variety and skillful complication of incidents, and suspense, especially in the love story. A simplified form of the famous euphuistic prose style, with new elements of conceit and wit appropriate to brisk dialogue, makes Lyly's dramatic prose significant for the future of Elizabethan drama. In his pages, with their quotations from the classics and their parody of the forms and devices of logic, Lyly developed rôles appropriate to his actors as school boys, and the amount of singing in the plays gives scope for them as choir boys. Probably his style and his reflection of court life and taste account for the early printing of his plays, which in turn probably led to the printing of other romantic plays written for the London stage, especially those of the University Wits.

In *Endymion* the main incidents of the long sleep and the kiss of Cynthia, drawn from Ovid and Lucian, furnished a basis for Lyly's best blend of classic story, love intrigue, courtly and sylvan setting, satire, and wit. A long tradition of interpreting classic myth freely as shadowing historical events or embodying allegory was responsible for popularizing in the Renaissance the use of myths for presentation of contemporary events or figures, either for flattery or for satire, in poetry generally but perhaps chiefly in pageants and plays. Lyly availed himself of the fashion to flatter Elizabeth boldly as Cynthia and possibly to glance at events in the court. Many attempts have been made to read the apparent allegory of the play. In 1843 Halpin argued that Endymion's story represents Leicester's love for Elizabeth and his relations to others at court. Other interpretations of the play as personal allegory have been advanced by various scholars. P. W. Long argues, however, perhaps correctly, that the allegory is primarily one of Platonic love, in which Endymion passes from love of Tellus (Earth), or earthly beauty, to adoration of Cynthia as a symbol of heavenly beauty.

Endymion, probably composed some time between 1585 and 1588, was entered in the Stationers' Register on October 4, 1591, and published anonymously later that year. The play was printed as Lyly's by Blount in *Six Court Comedies* of 1632. The style, however, would leave no doubt as to Lyly's authorship. The text of the present edition is based on Bond's reprint of the quarto of 1591 in his *Works of Lyly*.

ENDYMION, THE MAN IN THE MOON[1]

[BY

JOHN LYLY

DRAMATIS PERSONÆ

ENDYMION, *in love with Cynthia.*
EUMENIDES, *his friend, in love with Sem-ele.*
CORSITES, *a captain, in love with Tellus.*
PANELION ⎫
ZONTES ⎭ *lords of Cynthia's court.*
PYTHAGORAS, *a philosopher.*
GYPTES, *an Egyptian soothsayer.*
GERON, *an old man, husband to Dip-sas.*
SIR TOPHAS, *a braggart.*
DARES, *page to Endymion.*
SAMIAS, *page to Eumenides.*
EPITON, *page to Sir Tophas.*

MASTER CONSTABLE.
FIRST *and* SECOND WATCHMAN.

CYNTHIA, *the queen.*
TELLUS, *her rival, in love with Endymion.*
FLOSCULA, *her friend.*
SEMELE, *a lady at the court.*
SCINTILLA ⎫
FAVILLA ⎭ *maids at the court.*
DIPSAS, *an old enchantress.*
BAGOA, *her servant.*
FAIRIES.
THREE LADIES *and an* OLD MAN *in the dumb show.*

SCENE: *Cynthia's realm.*

TIME: *Mythical.*]

THE PROLOGUE

MOST high and happy princess, we must tell you a tale of the Man in the Moon, which, if it seem ridiculous for the method, or superfluous for the matter, or for the means incredible, for three faults we can make but one excuse: it is a tale of the Man in the Moon.

It was forbidden in old time to dispute of Chimera because it was a fiction. We hope in our times none will apply [10 pastimes,[2] because they are fancies; for there liveth none under the sun that knows what to make of the Man in the Moon. We present neither comedy, nor tragedy, nor story, nor anything but that whosoever heareth may say this: "Why, here is a tale of the Man in the Moon."

[1] The title continues: "Played before the Queen's Majesty at Greenwich on Candlemas Day at Night by the Children of Paul's."
[2] Read actual events into the play.

ACTUS PRIMUS. SCENA PRIMA.

[A grove near the cell of Endymion.]

Endymion, Eumenides.

END. I find, Eumenides, in all things both variety to content and satiety to glut, saving only in my affections, which are so staid, and withal so stately that I can neither satisfy my heart with love, nor mine eyes with wonder. My thoughts, Eumenides, are stitched to the stars, which, being as high as I can see, thou mayst imagine how much higher they are than I can reach. 10

EUM. If you be enamored of anything above the moon, your thoughts are ridiculous, for that[3] things immortal are not subject to affections; if allured or enchanted with these transitory things under the moon, you show yourself senseless to attribute such lofty titles to such low[4] trifles.

[3] Because.   [4] Suggested by Bond. Both early edns. read *loue.*

END. My love is placed neither under the moon nor above.

EUM. I hope you be not sotted[1] [20 upon the Man in the Moon.

END. No; but settled either to die or possess the moon herself.

EUM. Is Endymion mad, or do I mistake? Do you love the moon, Endymion?

END. Eumenides, the moon.

EUM. There was never any so peevish[2] to imagine the moon either capable of affection or shape of a mistress; for as impossible it is to make love fit to her hu- [30 mor, which no man knoweth, as a coat to her form, which continueth not in one bigness whilst she is measuring. Cease off, Endymion, to feed so much upon fancies. That melancholy blood must be purged which draweth you to a dotage no less miserable than monstrous.

END. My thoughts have no veins, and yet, unless they be let blood, I shall perish.   40

EUM. But they have vanities, which being reformed, you may be restored.

END. O fair Cynthia, why do others term thee unconstant whom I have ever found unmovable? Injurious time, corrupt manners, unkind men, who, finding a constancy not to be matched in my sweet mistress, have christened her with the name of wavering, waxing, and waning! Is she inconstant that keepeth a settled [50 course, which, since her first creation, altereth not one minute in her moving? There is nothing thought more admirable or commendable in the sea than the ebbing and flowing; and shall the moon, from whom the sea taketh this virtue, be accounted fickle for increasing and decreasing? Flowers in their buds are nothing worth till they be blown, nor blossoms accounted[3] till they be ripe fruit; [60 and shall we then say they be changeable for that they grow from seeds to leaves, from leaves to buds, from buds to their perfection? Then why not twigs that become trees, children that become men, and mornings that grow to evenings, termed wavering, for that they continue not at one stay?[4] Ay, but Cynthia, being in her fulness, decayeth, as not delighting

in her greatest beauty, or withering [70 when she should be most honored. When malice cannot object anything, folly will, making that a vice which is the greatest virtue. What thing (my mistress excepted) being in the pride of her beauty and latter minute of her age, that waxeth young again? Tell me, Eumenides, what is he that, having a mistress of ripe years and infinite virtues, great honors, and unspeakable beauty, but would wish that [80 she might grow tender again, getting youth by years, and never-decaying beauty by time; whose fair face neither the summer's blaze can scorch, nor winter's blast chap, nor the numbering of years breed altering of colors? Such is my sweet Cynthia, whom time cannot touch because she is divine, nor will offend because she is delicate. O Cynthia, if thou shouldest always continue at thy fulness, both gods and [90 men would conspire to ravish thee. But thou, to abate the pride of our affections, dost detract from thy perfections, thinking it sufficient if once in a month we enjoy a glimpse of thy majesty; and then, to increase our griefs, thou dost decrease thy gleams, coming out of thy royal robes, wherewith thou dazzlest our eyes, down into thy swathe clouts,[5] beguiling our eyes. And then—   100

EUM. Stay there, Endymion. Thou that committest idolatry wilt straight blaspheme if thou be suffered. Sleep would do thee more good than speech. The moon heareth thee not or, if she do, regardeth thee not.

END. Vain Eumenides, whose thoughts never grow higher than the crown of thy head! Why troublest thou me, having neither head to conceive the cause of [110 my love or a heart to receive the impressions? Follow thou thine own fortunes, which creep on the earth, and suffer me to fly to mine, whose fall, though it be desperate, yet shall it come by daring. Farewell!
                                        [Exit.]

EUM. Without doubt Endymion is bewitched; otherwise in a man of such rare virtues there could not harbor a mind of such extreme madness. I will follow him, lest in this fancy of the moon he de- [120 prive himself of the sight of the sun.   Exit.

---

[1] Besotted, infatuated.   [3] Computed.
[2] Silly.   [4] State.
                                 [5] Swaddling clothes.

SCENA SECUNDA.

[The gardens of Cynthia's palace.]

Tellus, Floscula.

TELLUS. Treacherous and most perjured Endymion, is Cynthia the sweetness of thy life and the bitterness of my death? What revenge may be devised so full of shame as my thoughts are replenished with malice? Tell me, Floscula, if falseness in love can possibly be punished with extremity of hate. As long as sword, fire, or poison may be hired, no traitor to my love shall live unrevenged. Were thy [10 oaths without number, thy kisses without measure, thy sighs without end, forged to deceive a poor credulous virgin, whose simplicity had been worth thy favor and better fortune? If the gods sit unequal[1] beholders of injuries, or laughers at lovers' deceits, then let mischief be as well forgiven in women as perjury winked at in men.

FLOSC. Madam, if you would com- [20 pare the state of Cynthia with your own, and the height of Endymion his [2] thoughts with the meanness of your fortune, you would rather yield than contend, being between you and her no comparison; and rather wonder than rage at the greatness of his mind, being affected with a thing more than mortal.

TELLUS. No comparison, Floscula? And why so? Is not my beauty divine, [30 whose body is decked with fair flowers, and veins are vines, yielding sweet liquor to the dullest spirits; whose ears are corn, to bring strength; and whose hairs are grass, to bring abundance? Doth not frankincense and myrrh breathe out of my nostrils, and all the sacrifice of the gods breed in my bowels? Infinite are my creatures, without which neither thou nor Endymion nor any could love or live.   40

FLOSC. But know you not, fair lady, that Cynthia governeth all things? Your grapes would be but dry husks, your corn but chaff, and all your virtues vain, were it not Cynthia that preserveth the one in the bud and nourisheth the other in the blade, and by her influence both comforteth all things, and by her authority com-

mandeth all creatures. Suffer, then, Endymion to follow his affections, though to [50 obtain her be impossible, and let him flatter himself in his own imaginations, because they are immortal.

TELLUS. Loath I am, Endymion, thou shouldest die, because I love thee well; and that thou shouldest live, it grieveth me, because thou lovest Cynthia too well. In these extremities what shall I do? Floscula, no more words; I am resolved. He shall neither live nor die!   60

FLOSC. A strange practice,[3] if it be possible.

TELLUS. Yes, I will entangle him in such a sweet net that he shall neither find the means to come out, nor desire it. All allurements of pleasure will I cast before his eyes, insomuch that he shall slake that love which he now voweth to Cynthia, and burn in mine, of which he seemeth careless. In this languishing, be- [70 tween my amorous devices and his own loose desires, there shall such dissolute thoughts take root in his head and over his heart grow so thick a skin that neither hope of preferment nor fear of punishment nor counsel of the wisest nor company of the worthiest shall alter his humor nor make him once to think of his honor.

FLOSC. A revenge incredible, and, if it may be, unnatural.   80

TELLUS. He shall know the malice of a woman to have neither mean nor end; and of a woman deluded in love to have neither rule nor reason. I can do it; I must; I will! All his virtues will I shadow with vices. His person—ah, sweet person!— shall he deck with such rich robes as he shall forget it is his own person; his sharp wit—ah, wit too sharp that hath cut off all my joys!—shall he use in flattering of [90 my face and devising sonnets in my favor. The prime of his youth and pride of his time shall be spent in melancholy passions, careless behavior, untamed thoughts, and unbridled affections.

FLOSC. When this is done, what then? Shall it continue till his death, or shall he dote forever in this delight?

TELLUS. Ah, Floscula, thou rendest my heart in sunder in putting me in [100 remembrance of the end.

---

[1] Prejudiced.   [2] *I.e.,* Endymion's.   [3] Stratagem.

FLOSC. Why, if this be not the end, all the rest is to no end.

TELLUS. Yet suffer me to imitate Juno, who would turn Jupiter's lovers to beasts on the earth, though she knew afterwards they should be stars in heaven.

FLOSC. Affection that is bred by enchantment is like a flower that is wrought in silk— in color and form most like, but [110 nothing at all in substance or savor.

TELLUS. It shall suffice me, if the world talk, that I am favored of Endymion.

FLOSC. Well, use your own will; but you shall find that love gotten with witchcraft is as unpleasant as fish taken with medicines [1] unwholesome.

TELLUS. Floscula, they that be so poor that they have neither net nor hook will rather poison dough than pine with [120 hunger; and she that is so oppressed with love that she is neither able with beauty nor wit to obtain her friend, will rather use unlawful means than try untolerable pains. I will do it. *Exit.*

FLOSC. Then about it! Poor Endymion, what traps are laid for thee because thou honorest one that all the world wond'reth at! And what plots are cast to make thee unfortunate that studiest of all men [130 to be the faithfulest! *Exit.*

SCENA TERTIA.

[*The same.*]

Dares, Samias, Sir Tophas, Epiton. [2]

DAR. Now our masters are in love up to the ears, what have we to do but to be in knavery up to the crowns?

SAM. O, that we had Sir Tophas, that brave squire, in the midst of our mirth—*et ecce autem,* [3] "Will you see the devil?"—

Enter Sir Tophas [and Epiton].

TOP. Epi!

EPI. Here, sir!

TOP. I brook not this idle humor of [10 love; it tickleth not my liver, from whence the lovemongers in former ages seemed to infer they should proceed.

[1] Caught with poisoned bait (here, dough balls).
[2] Last two enter later.
[3] And behold indeed!

EPI. Love, sir, may lie in your lungs— and I think it doth, and that is the cause you blow and are so pursy.

TOP. Tush, boy, I think it but some device of the poet to get money.

EPI. A poet? What's that?

TOP. Dost thou not know what a [20 poet is?

EPI. No.

TOP. Why, fool, a poet is as much as one should say—a poet.—But soft, yonder be two wrens; shall I shoot at them?

EPI. They are two lads!

TOP. Larks or wrens, I will kill them.

EPI. Larks! Are you blind? They are two little boys.

TOP. Birds or boys, they are both [30 but a pittance for my breakfast; therefore have at them, for their brains must as it were embroider my bolts. [4]

SAM. Stay your courage, valiant knight, for your widsom is so weary that it stayeth itself.

DAR. Why, Sir Tophas, have you forgotten your old friends?

TOP. Friends? *Nego argumentum.* [5]

SAM. And why not friends? 40

TOP. Because *amicitia* (as in old annuals [6] we find) is *inter pares.* [7] Now, my pretty companions, you shall see how unequal you be to me. But I will not cut you quite off—you shall be my half-friends for reaching to my middle; so far as from the ground to the waist I will be your friend.

DAR. Learnedly! But what shall become of the rest of your body, from the waist to the crown? 50

TOP. My children, *quod supra vos, nihil ad vos.* [8] You must think the rest immortal, because you cannot reach it.

EPI. Nay, I tell ye my master is more than a man.

DAR. And thou less than a mouse.

TOP. But what be you two?

SAM. I am Samias, page to Eumenides. [9]

DAR. And I Dares, page to Endymion.

TOP. Of what occupation are your [60 masters?

[4] Flat-headed arrows.
[5] I deny the proof.
[6] Annals (?).
[7] Friendship is among equals.
[8] What is above you is nothing to you.
[9] Bond correctly transposes the names of the masters, in this and the following line.

DAR. Occupation, you clown! Why, they are honorable, and warriors.

TOP. Then are they my prentices.

DAR. Thine? And why so?

TOP. I was the first that ever devised war, and therefore by Mars himself given me for my arms a whole armory; and thus I go, as you see, clothed with artillery. It is not silks—milksops!—nor [70 tissues, nor the fine wool of Seres,[1] but iron, steel, swords, flame, shot, terror, clamor, blood, and ruin, that rocks asleep my thoughts, which never had any other cradle but cruelty. Let me see, do you not bleed?

DAR. Why so?

TOP. Commonly my words wound.

SAM. What then do your blows?

TOP. Not only wound,[2] but also con- [80 found.

SAM. How dar'st thou come so near thy master, Epi? Sir Tophas, spare us!

TOP. You shall live: you, Samias, because you are little; you, Dares, because you are no bigger; and both of you, because you are but two, for commonly I kill by the dozen, and have for every particular adversary a peculiar weapon.

SAM. May we know the use, for our [90 better skill in war?

TOP. You shall. Here is a burbolt [3] for the ugly beast the blackbird.

DAR. A cruel sight!

TOP. Here is the musket for the untamed or, as the vulgar sort term it, the wild mallard.

SAM. O desperate attempt!

EPI. Nay, my master will match them.

DAR. Ay, if he catch them.   100

TOP. Here is a spear and shield, and both necessary, the one to conquer, the other to subdue or overcome the terrible trout, which, although he be under the water, yet tying a string to the top of my spear and an engine of iron to the end of my line, I overthrow him, and then herein I put him.

SAM. O wonderful war!—[Aside.] Dares, didst thou ever hear such a dolt?   110

DAR. [Aside.] All the better; we shall have good sport hereafter, if we can get leisure.

SAM. [Aside.] Leisure! I will rather lose my master's service than his company! Look how he struts!—But what is this? Call you it your sword?

TOP. No, it is my scimitar, which I, by construction often studying to be compendious, call my smiter.   120

DAR. What, are you also learned, sir?

TOP. Learned? I am all Mars and Ars.[4]

SAM. Nay, you are all mass and ass.

TOP. Mock you me? You shall both suffer, yet with such weapons as you shall make choice of the weapon wherewith you shall perish. Am I all a mass or lump? Is there no proportion in me? Am I all ass? Is there no wit in me? Epi, prepare them to the slaughter.   130

SAM. I pray, sir, hear us speak! We call you mass, which your learning doth well understand is all man, for *mas, maris* is a man. Then *as*, as you know, is a weight, and we for your virtues account you a weight.

TOP. The Latin hath saved your lives, the which a world of silver could not have ransomed. I understand you, and pardon you.   140

DAR. Well, Sir Tophas, we bid you farewell, and at our next meeting we will be ready to do you service.

TOP. Samias, I thank you; Dares, I thank you; but especially I thank you both.

SAM. [Aside.] Wisely! Come, next time we'll have some pretty gentlewomen with us to walk, for without doubt with them he will be very dainty.   150

DAR. Come, let us see what our masters do; it is high time.

Exeunt [*Samias and Dares*].

TOP. Now will I march into the field, where, if I cannot encounter with my foul enemies, I will withdraw myself to the river, and there fortify for fish, for there resteth no minute free from fight.

Exit [*Sir Tophas with Epiton*].

SCENA QUARTA.

[*Another part of the same.*]

Tellus, Floscula, Dipsas.

TELLUS. Behold, Floscula, we have met with the woman by chance that we

---

[1] Chinese silk. Original reads *Ceres;* changed by Bond.   [2] Early edns. read *confound.*   [3] Birdbolt.   [4] War and art.

sought for by travel.[1] I will break my mind to her without ceremony or circumstance, lest we lose that time in advice that should be spent in execution.

FLOSC. Use your discretion; I will in this case neither give counsel nor consent, for there cannot be a thing more monstrous than to force affection by sorcery, [10 neither do I imagine anything more impossible.

TELLUS. Tush, Floscula, in obtaining of love, what impossibilities will I not try? And for the winning of Endymion, what impieties will I not practice?—Dipsas, whom as many honor for age as wonder at for cunning, listen in few words to my tale, and answer in one word to the purpose, for that neither my burning desire [20 can afford long speech, nor the short time I have to stay many delays. Is it possible by herbs, stones, spells, incantation, enchantment, exorcisms, fire, metals, planets, or any practice, to plant affection where it is not, and to supplant it where it is?

DIPSAS. Fair lady, you may imagine that these hoary hairs are not void of experience, nor the great name that goeth of my cunning to be without cause. I [30 can darken the sun by my skill and remove the moon out of her course; I can restore youth to the aged and make hills without bottoms; there is nothing that I cannot do but that only which you would have me do; and therein I differ from the gods, that I am not able to rule hearts, for, were it in my power to place affection by appointment, I would make such evil appetites, such inordinate lusts, such [40 cursed desires, as all the world should be filled both with superstitious heats and extreme love.

TELLUS. Unhappy Tellus, whose desires are so desperate that they are neither to be conceived of any creature, nor to be cured by any art!

DIPSAS. This I can: breed slackness in love, though never root it out. What is he whom you love, and what she that [50 he honoreth?

TELLUS. Endymion, sweet Endymion, is he that hath my heart; and Cynthia, too-too fair Cynthia, the miracle of nature, of time, of fortune, is the lady that

he delights in, and dotes on every day, and dies for ten thousand times a day.

DIPSAS. Would you have his love either by absence or sickness aslaked?[2] Would you that Cynthia should mistrust him, [60 or be jealous of him without color?[3]

TELLUS. It is the only thing I crave that, seeing my love to Endymion, unspotted, cannot be accepted, his truth to Cynthia, though it be unspeakable, may be suspected.

DIPSAS. I will undertake it, and overtake[4] him, that all his love shall be doubted of, and therefore become desperate. But this will wear out with time, that [70 treadeth all things down but truth.

TELLUS. Let us go.

DIPSAS. I follow.   *Exeunt.*

ACTUS SECUNDUS. SCENA PRIMA

[*A grove near the cell of Endymion.*]

Endymion, Tellus.[5]

END. O fair Cynthia! O unfortunate Endymion! Why was not thy birth as high as thy thoughts, or her beauty less than heavenly; or why are not thine honors as rare as her beauty, or thy fortunes as great as thy deserts? Sweet Cynthia, how wouldst thou be pleased, how possessed? Will labors, patient of all extremities, obtain thy love? There is no mountain so steep that I will not climb, no monster [10 so cruel that I will not tame, no action so desperate that I will not attempt. Desirest thou the passions of love, the sad and melancholy moods of perplexed minds, the not-to-be-expressed torments of racked thoughts? Behold my sad tears, my deep sighs, my hollow eyes, my broken sleeps, my heavy countenance! Wouldst thou have me vowed only to thy beauty and consume every minute of time in [20 thy service? Remember my solitary life almost these seven years. Whom have I entertained but mine own thoughts and thy virtues? What company have I used but contemplation? Whom have I wondered at but thee? Nay, whom have I not contemned for thee? Have I not crept to those on whom I might have trodden,

---

[1] Travail (?).

[2] Slaked, abated.

[3] Reason, excuse.

[4] Overcome.

[5] Enters later.

only because thou didst shine upon them?
Have not injuries been sweet to me if [30
thou vouchsafest I should bear them?
Have I not spent my golden years in hopes,
waxing old with wishing, yet wishing
nothing but thy love? With Tellus, fair
Tellus, have I dissembled, using her but
as a cloak for mine affections, that others,
seeing my mangled and disordered mind,
might think it were for one that loveth
me, not for Cynthia, whose perfection
alloweth no companion nor comparison. [40
In the midst of these distempered
thoughts of mine thou art not only jealous
of my truth, but careless, suspicious, and
secure,[1] which strange humor maketh my
mind as desperate as thy conceits[2] are
doubtful. I am none of those wolves that
bark most when thou shinest brightest,
but that fish (thy fish, Cynthia, in the
flood Araris)[3] which at thy waxing is as
white as the driven snow, and at thy [50
waning as black as deepest darkness. I
am that Endymion, sweet Cynthia, that
have carried my thoughts in equal balance
with my actions, being always as free from
imagining ill as enterprising; that Endymion whose eyes never esteemed anything
fair but thy face, whose tongue termed
nothing rare but thy virtues, and whose
heart imagined nothing miraculous but
thy government; yea, that Endymion, [60
who, divorcing himself from the amiable-
ness of all ladies, the bravery[4] of all courts,
the company of all men, hath chosen in
a solitary cell to live, only by feeding on
thy favor, accounting in the world—but
thyself—nothing excellent, nothing immortal. Thus mayst thou see every vein,
sinew, muscle, and artery of my love, in
which there is no flattery, nor deceit, error,
nor art. But soft, here cometh Tellus. [70
I must turn my other face to her, like
Janus, lest she be as suspicious as Juno.

Enter Tellus [*, Floscula, and Dipsas*].

TELLUS. Yonder I espy Endymion. I
will seem to suspect nothing, but soothe
him, that, seeing I cannot obtain the depth
of his love, I may learn the height of his

[1] Overconfident.
[2] Fancies, imaginings, ideas.
[3] Emended by Baker. Original reads *Aranis.*
[4] Splendor.

dissembling. Floscula and Dipsas, withdraw yourselves out of our sight, yet be
within the hearing of our saluting.— 79
[*Exeunt Floscula and Dipsas.*]
How now, Endymion, always solitary?
No company but your own thoughts, no
friend but melancholy fancies?
END. You know, fair Tellus, that the
sweet remembrance of your love is the only
companion of my life, and thy presence,
my paradise, so that I am not alone when
nobody is with me, and in heaven itself
when thou art with me.
TELLUS. Then you love me, Endymion?
END. Or else I live not, Tellus. 90
TELLUS. Is it not possible for you, Endymion, to dissemble?
END. Not, Tellus, unless I could make
me a woman.
TELLUS. Why, is dissembling joined to
their sex inseparable, as heat to fire, heaviness to earth, moisture to water, thinness
to air?
END. No, but found in their sex as
common as spots upon doves, moles [100
upon faces, caterpillars upon sweet apples,
cobwebs upon fair windows.
TELLUS. Do they all dissemble?
END. All but one.
TELLUS. Who is that?
END. I dare not tell; for, if I should
say you, then would you imagine my
flattery to be extreme; if another, then
would you think my love to be but indifferent. 110
TELLUS. You will be sure I shall take
no vantage of your words. But, in sooth,
Endymion, without more ceremonies, is
it not Cynthia?
END. You know, Tellus, that of the
gods we are forbidden to dispute, because
their deities come not within the compass
of our reasons; and of Cynthia we are allowed not to talk but to wonder, because
her virtues are not within the reach [120
of our capacities.
TELLUS. Why, she is but a woman.
END. No more was Venus.
TELLUS. She is but a virgin.
END. No more was Vesta.
TELLUS. She shall have an end.
END. So shall the world.
TELLUS. Is not her beauty subject to
time?

END. No more than time is to [130
standing still.

TELLUS. Wilt thou make her immortal?

END. No, but incomparable.

TELLUS. Take heed, Endymion, lest
like the wrastler in Olympia, that, striving to lift an impossible weight, catched
an incurable strain, thou, by fixing thy
thoughts above thy reach, fall into a disease
without all recure.[1] But I see thou art now
in love with Cynthia.   140

END. No, Tellus; thou knowest that
the stately cedar, whose top reacheth unto
the clouds, never boweth his head to the
shrubs that grow in the valley; nor ivy,
that climbeth up by the elm, can ever get
hold of the beams of the sun. Cynthia I
honor in all humility, whom none ought
or dare adventure to love, whose affections
are immortal, and virtues infinite. Suffer
me, therefore, to gaze on the moon, [150
at whom, were it not for thyself, I would
die with wondering.   *Exeunt.*

SCENA SECUNDA.

[*The gardens of Cynthia's palace.*]

Dares, Samias, Scintilla, Favilla.

DAR. Come, Samias, diddest thou ever
hear such a sighing, the one for Cynthia,
the other for Semele, and both for moonshine in the water?

SAM. Let them sigh, and let us sing.
How say you, gentlewomen, are not our
masters too far in love?

SCINT. Their tongues, happily,[2] are
dipped to the root in amorous words and
sweet discourses, but I think their [10
hearts are scarce tipped on the side with
constant desires.

DAR. How say you, Favilla, is not love
a lurcher,[3] that taketh men's stomachs
away that they cannot eat, their spleen
that they cannot laugh, their hearts that
they cannot fight, their eyes that they cannot sleep, and leaveth nothing but livers
to make nothing but lovers?

FAVIL. Away, peevish boy! A rod [20
were better under thy girdle than love in
thy mouth. It will be a forward cock that
croweth in the shell.

DAR. Alas, good old gentlewoman, how
it becometh you to be grave!

SCINT. Favilla, though she be but a
spark,[4] yet is she fire.

FAVIL. And you, Scintilla, be not much
more than a spark, though you would be
esteemed a flame.   30

SAM. [*Aside to Dares.*] It were good
sport to see the fight between two sparks.

DAR. [*Aside to Samias.*] Let them to
it, and we will warm us by their words.

SCINT. You are not angry, Favilla?

FAVIL. That is, Scintilla, as you list
to take it.

SAM. That, that!

SCINT. This it is to be matched with
girls who, coming but yesterday from [40
making of babies,[5] would before tomorrow
be accounted matrons.

FAVIL. I cry your matronship mercy.
Because your pantables[6] be higher with
cork, therefore your feet must needs be
higher in the insteps. You will be mine
elder because you stand upon a stool and
I on the floor.

SAM. Good, good!

DAR. [*To Samias.*] Let them alone, [50
and see with what countenance they will
become friends.

SCINT. Nay, you think to be the wiser,
because you mean to have the last word.

SAM. [*To Dares.*] Step between them
lest they scratch.—In faith, gentlewomen,
seeing we came out to be merry, let not
your jarring mar our jests; be friends.
How say you?

SCINT. I am not angry, but it spited [60
me to see how short she was.

FAVIL. I meant nothing till she would
needs cross me.

DAR. Then, so let it rest.

SCINT. I am agreed.

FAVIL. And I. [*Weeping.*] Yet I never
took anything so unkindly in my life.

SCINT. [*Weeping.*] 'Tis I have the cause,
that never offered the occasion.

DAR. Excellent, and right like a [70
woman!

SAM. A strange sight to see water come
out of fire!

---

[1] Recovery.   [3] Lurker, thief.
[2] Haply, perhaps.

[4] Punning on *spark*, a person of gay disposition.
[5] Dolls.   [6] Pantofles, slippers.

DAR. It is their property to carry in their eyes fire and water, tears and torches, and in their mouths honey and gall.

SCINT. You will be a good one if you live. But what is yonder formal fellow?

Enter Sir Tophas [, followed by Epiton].

DAR. Sir Tophas, Sir Tophas, of whom we told you. If you be good wenches, [80 make as though you love him, and wonder at him.

FAVIL. We will do our parts.

DAR. But first let us stand aside, and let him use his garb,[1] for all consisteth in his gracing.[2]   [*The four retire.*]

TOP. Epi!

EPI. At hand, sir.

TOP. How likest thou this martial life, where nothing but blood besprinkleth [90 our bosoms? Let me see, be our enemies[3] fat?

EPI. Passing fat; and I would not change this life to be a lord; and yourself passeth all comparison, for other captains kill and beat, and there is nothing you kill but you also eat.

TOP. I will draw out their guts out of their bellies, and tear the flesh with my teeth, so mortal is my hate, and so [100 eager my unstaunched stomach.

EPI. [*Aside.*] My master thinks himself the valiantest man in the world if he kill a wren; so warlike a thing he accompteth to take away life, though it be from a lark.

TOP. Epi, I find my thoughts to swell and my spirit to take wings, insomuch that I cannot continue within the compass of so slender combats.   110

FAVIL. }   This passeth!
SCINT. } [*Aside.*] Why, is he not mad?
SAM. }   No, but a little vainglorious.

TOP. Epi!

EPI. Sir?

TOP. I will encounter that black and cruel enemy that beareth rough and untewed[4] locks upon his body, whose sire throweth down the strongest walls, [120

whose legs are as many as both ours, on whose head are placed most horrible horns by nature as a defense from all harms.

EPI. What mean you, master, to be so desperate?

TOP. Honor inciteth me, and very hunger compelleth me.

EPI. What is that monster?

TOP. The monster *Ovis*. I have said; let thy wits work.   130

EPI. I cannot imagine it. Yet let me see: a black enemy with rough locks—it may be a sheep, and *Ovis* is a sheep; his sire so strong—a ram is a sheep's sire, that being also an engine of war; horns he hath, and four legs—so hath a sheep. Without doubt, this monster is a black sheep. Is it not a sheep that you mean?

TOP. Thou hast hit it. That monster will I kill and sup with.   140

SAM. [*Aside.*] Come, let us take him off.—[*Samias, Dares, Favilla, and Scintilla advance.*] Sir Tophas, all hail!

TOP. Welcome, children. I seldom cast mine eyes so low as to the crowns of your heads, and therefore pardon me that I spake not all this while.

DAR. No harm done. Here be fair ladies come to wonder at your person, your valor, your wit, the report where- [150 of hath made them careless of their own honors, to glut their eyes and hearts upon yours.

TOP. Report cannot but injure me, for that, not knowing fully what I am, I fear she hath been a niggard in her praises.

SCINT. No, gentle knight, Report hath been prodigal; for she hath left you no equal, nor herself credit, so much hath she told—yet no more than we now see. [160

DAR. [*Aside.*] A good wench!

FAVIL. If there remain as much pity toward women as there is in you courage against your enemies, then shall we be happy, who, hearing of your person, came to see it, and, seeing it, are now in love with it.

TOP. Love me, ladies? I easily believe it, but my tough heart receiveth no impression with sweet words. Mars may [170 pierce it; Venus shall not paint on it.

FAVIL. A cruel saying.

SAM. [*Aside.*] There's a girl!

---

[1] Show his demeanor.
[2] All depends on honoring him.
[3] *I.e.,* the fish Epiton carries.
[4] Uncombed.

DAR. Will you cast these ladies away, and all for a little love? Do but speak kindly!

TOP. There cometh no soft syllable within my lips; custom hath made my words bloody and my heart barbarous. That pelting [1] word love, how wat'rish [180 it is in my mouth; it carrieth no sound. Hate, horror, death are speeches that nourish my spirits. I like honey, but I care not for the bees; I delight in music, but I love not to play on the bagpipes; I can vouchsafe to hear the voice of women, but to touch their bodies, I disdain it as a thing childish and fit for such men as can digest nothing but milk.

SCINT. A hard heart! Shall we die [190 for your love and find no remedy?

TOP. I have already taken a surfeit.

EPI. Good master, pity them.

TOP. Pity them, Epi? No, I do not think that this breast shall be pestered with such a foolish passion.—What is that the gentlewoman carrieth in [2] a chain?

EPI. Why, it is a squirrel.

TOP. A squirrel? O gods, what things are made for money!   200

DAR. [Aside.] Is not this gentleman overwise?

FAVIL. [Aside.] I could stay all day with him, if I feared not to be shent. [3]

SCINT. [Aside.] Is it not possible to meet again?

DAR. [Aside.] Yes, at any time.

FAVIL. [Aside.] Then let us hasten home.   209

SCINT. Sir Tophas, the god of war deal better with you than you do with the god of love.

FAVIL. Our love we may dissemble—digest [4] we cannot; but I doubt not but time will hamper you and help us.

TOP. I defy time, who hath no interest in my heart. Come, Epi, let me to the battle with that hideous beast. Love is pap, and hath no relish in my taste because it is not terrible.—   220

DAR. Indeed, a black sheep is a perilous beast. But let us in till another time.

FAVIL. I shall long for that time.
    Exeunt.

[1] Paltry, contemptible.
[2] On.
[3] Scolded.   [4] Digest, stomach, put up with.

SCENA TERTIA.

[*A grove near the cell of Endymion.*]

Endymion, Dipsas, Bagoa. [5]

END. No rest, Endymion? Still uncertain how to settle thy steps by day or thy thoughts by night? Thy truth is measured by thy fortune, and thou art judged unfaithful because thou art unhappy. I will see if I can beguile myself with sleep, and, if no slumber will take hold in my eyes, yet will I embrace the golden thoughts in my head, and wish to melt by musing; that, as ebony, which no fire [10 can scorch, is yet consumed with sweet savors, so my heart, which cannot be bent by the hardness of fortune, may be bruised by amorous desires. On yonder bank never grew anything but lunary, [6] and hereafter I will never have any bed but that bank. O Endymion, Tellus was fair, but what availeth beauty without wisdom? Nay, Endymion, she was wise, but what availeth wisdom without honor? She [20 was honorable, Endymion; belie her not. Ay, but how obscure is honor without fortune! Was she not fortunate whom so many followed? Yes, yes, but base is fortune without majesty. Thy majesty, Cynthia, all the world knoweth and wondereth at, but not one in the world that can imitate it or comprehend it. No more. Endymion! Sleep or die! Nay, die, for to sleep, it is impossible.—And yet I [30 know not how it cometh to pass, I feel such a heaviness both in mine eyes and heart that I am suddenly benumbed, yea, in every joint. It may be weariness, for when did I rest? It may be deep melancholy, for when did I not sigh? Cynthia! Ay, so—I say, Cynthia!   *He falls asleep.*

[*Enter Dipsas and Bagoa.*]

DIPSAS. Little dost thou know, Endymion, when thou shalt wake, for, hadst thou placed thy heart as low in love as [40 thy head lieth now in sleep, thou mightest have commanded Tellus, whom now, instead of a mistress, thou shalt find a tomb. These eyes must I seal up by art, not nature, which are to be opened neither by art nor nature. Thou that lay'st down with

[5] Last two enter later.   [6] Moonwort.

golden locks shalt not awake until they
be turned to silver hairs; and that chin on
which scarcely appeareth soft down shall
be filled with bristles as hard as   [50
broom. Thou shalt sleep out thy youth and
flowering time, and become dry hay before thou knewest thyself green grass; and
ready by age to step into the grave when
thou wakest, that was youthful in the
court when thou laid'st thee down to
sleep. The malice of Tellus hath brought
this to pass, which, if she could not have
entreated of me by fair means, she would
have commanded by menacing, for   [60
from her gather we all our simples to maintain our sorceries.—Fan with this hemlock
over his face, and sing the enchantment
for sleep, whilst I go in and finish those
ceremonies that are required in our art.
Take heed ye touch not his face, for the
fan is so seasoned that whoso it toucheth
with a leaf shall presently die, and over
whom the wind of it breatheth, he shall
sleep forever.   *Exit.*   [70
    BAGOA. Let me alone; I will be careful.
What hap hadst thou, Endymion, to come
under the hands of Dipsas! O fair Endymion, how it grieveth me that that fair
face must be turned to a withered skin
and taste the pains of death before it feel
the reward of love! I fear Tellus will repent that which the heavens themselves
seemed to rue. But I hear Dipsas coming!
I dare not repine, lest she make me   [80
pine, and rock me into such a deep sleep
that I shall not awake to my marriage.

Enter Dipsas.

    DIPSAS. How now, have you finished?
    BAGOA. Yea.
    DIPSAS. Well then, let us in. And see
that you do not so much as whisper that
I did this, for, if you do, I will turn
thy hairs to adders and all thy teeth in
thy head to tongues. Come away, come
away!   *Exeunt.*   [90

A DUMB SHOW[1]

*Music sounds. Three Ladies enter: one
with a knife and a looking-glass, who, by*

[1] This scene, representing the dream of Endymion, first appeared in Blount's edition of 1632.
Cf. Endymion's account of the incident, V, i,
109 ff.

the procurement [2] of one of the other two,
offers to stab Endymion as he sleeps; but
the third wrings her hands, lamenteth, offering still to prevent it, but dares not.*

*At last, the first Lady, looking in the
glass, casts down the knife.   Exeunt.*

*Enters an Ancient Man with books with
three leaves; offers the same twice. Endymion refuseth. He rendeth two, and offers
the third, where he stands awhile; and then
Endymion offers to take it.*

                    Exit [the Old Man].

ACTUS TERTIUS. SCENA PRIMA.
[The gardens of Cynthia's palace.]

*Cynthia, Three Lords [Eumenides, Zontes,
    and Panelion], Tellus [,Semele, Corsites].*

    CYNTH. Is the report true that En-
dymion is stricken into such a dead sleep
that nothing can either wake him or move
him?
    EUM. Too true, madam, and as much
to be pitied as wondered at.
    TELLUS. As good sleep and do no harm
as wake and do no good.
    CYNTH. What maketh you, Tellus, to
be so short? The time was, Endymion   [10
only was.
    EUM. It is an old saying, madam, that
a waking dog doth afar off bark at a sleeping lion.
    SEM. It were good, Eumenides, that
you took a nap with your friend, for your
speech beginneth to be heavy.
    EUM. Contrary to your nature, Semele,
which hath been always accounted light.
    CYNTH. What, have we here before   [20
my face these unseemly and malapert over-
thwarts! [3] I will tame your tongues and
your thoughts, and make your speeches
answerable to your duties, and your conceits fit for my dignity, else will I banish
you both my person and the world.
    EUM. Pardon I humbly ask; but such
is my unspotted faith to Endymion that
whatsoever seemeth a needle to prick his
finger is a dagger to wound my heart.   [30
    CYNTH. If you be so dear to him, how
happeneth it you neither go to see him,
nor search for remedy for him?

[2] Instigation, urging.
[3] Impertinent wranglings.

EUM. I have seen him to my grief, and sought recure with despair, for that I cannot imagine who should restore him that is the wonder to all men. Your highness, on whose hands the compass of the earth is at command, though not in possession, may show yourself both worthy [40 your sex, your nature, and your favor, if you redeem that honorable Endymion, whose ripe years foretell rare virtues, and whose unmellowed conceits promise ripe counsel.

CYNTH. I have had trial of Endymion, and conceive greater assurance of his age than I could hope of his youth.

TELLUS. But timely,[1] madam, crooks that tree that will be a cammock,[2] and [50 young it pricks that will be a thorn; and therefore he that began without care to settle his life, it is a sign without amendment he will end it.

CYNTH. Presumptuous girl, I will make thy tongue an example of unrecoverable displeasure. Corsites, carry her to the castle in the desert, there to remain and weave. 59

CORS. Shall she work stories or poetries?

CYNTH. It skilleth[3] not which. Go to! In both, for she shall find examples infinite in either what punishment long tongues have. Eumenides, if either the soothsayers in Egypt, or the enchanters in Thessaly, or the philosophers in Greece, or all the sages of the world can find remedy, I will procure it. Therefore, despatch with all speed: you, Eumenides, into [70 Thessaly; you, Zontes, into Greece, because you are acquainted in Athens; you, Panelion, to Egypt; saying that Cynthia sendeth, and, if you will, commandeth.

EUM. On bowed knee I give thanks, and with wings on my legs I fly for remedy.

ZON. We are ready at your highness' command, and hope to return to your full content.

CYNTH. It shall never be said that [80 Cynthia, whose mercy and goodness filleth the heavens with joys and the world with marvels, will suffer either Endymion or any to perish, if he may be protected.

[1] Early.
[2] Tree artificially bent.
[3] Matters.

EUM. Your majesty's words have been always deeds, and your deeds virtues.
Exeunt.

SCENA SECUNDA.

[Before the castle of Corsites in a desert.]

Corsites, Tellus.

CORS. Here is the castle, fair Tellus, in which you must weave, till either time end your days, or Cynthia her displeasure. I am sorry so fair a face should be subject to so hard a fortune, and that the flower of beauty, which is honored in courts, should here wither in prison.

TELLUS. Corsites, Cynthia may restrain the liberty of my body; of my thoughts she cannot, and therefore do I [10 esteem myself most free, though I am in greatest bondage.

CORS. Can you then feed on fancy, and subdue the malice of envy by the sweetness of imagination?

TELLUS. Corsites, there is no sweeter music to the miserable than despair; and therefore the more bitterness I feel, the more sweetness I find; for so vain were liberty, and so unwelcome the following [20 of higher fortune, that I choose rather to pine in this castle than to be a prince in any other court.

CORS. A humor contrary to your years and nothing agreeable to your sex—the one commonly allured with delights, the other always with sovereignty.

TELLUS. I marvel, Corsites, that you, being a captain, who should sound nothing but terror and suck nothing but blood, [30 can find in your heart to talk such smooth words, for that it agreeth not with your calling to use words so soft as that of love.

CORS. Lady, it were unfit of wars to discourse with women, into whose minds nothing can sink but smoothness; besides, you must not think that soldiers be so rough-hewn, or of such knotty mettle, that beauty cannot allure, and you, [40 being beyond perfection, enchant.

TELLUS. Good Corsites, talk not of love, but let me to my labor. The little beauty I have shall be bestowed on my loom, which I now mean to make my lover.

Cors. Let us in, and what favor Corsites can show, Tellus shall command.

Tellus. The only favor I desire is now
and then to walk.   *Exeunt.*

Scena Tertia.

[*The gardens of Cynthia's palace.*]

Sir Tophas and Epi[ton].

Top. Epi!

Epi. Here, sir.

Top. Unrig me. Heigh-ho!

Epi. What's that?

Top. An interjection, whereof some are
of mourning: as *eho, vah.*[1]

Epi. I understand you not.

Top. Thou seest me.

Epi. Ay.

Top. Thou hear'st me.   10

Epi. Ay.

Top. Thou feelest me.

Epi. Ay.

Top. And not understand'st me?

Epi. No.

Top. Then am I but three-quarters of
a noun substantive. But alas, Epi, to tell
thee the troth, I am a noun adjective.

Epi. Why?

Top. Because I cannot stand with-   [20
out another.

Epi. Who is that?

Top. Dipsas.

Epi. Are you in love?

Top. No; but love hath, as it were,
milked my thoughts and drained from my
heart the very substance of my accustomed
courage. It worketh in my head like new
wine, so as I must hoop my sconce with
iron, lest my head break, and so I be-   [30
wray[2] my brains. But, I pray thee, first
discover me in all parts, that I may be
like a lover, and then will I sigh and die.
Take my gun and give me a gown: "*Ce-
dant arma togæ.*"[3]

Epi. Here.

Top. Take my sword and shield and
give me beard-brush and scissors: "*Bella
gerant alii; tu, Pari, semper ama.*"[4]

Epi. Will you be trimmed, sir?   40

Top. Not yet; for I feel a contention
within me whether I shall frame the bodkin beard or the bush.[5] But take my pike
and give me pen: "*Dicere quæ puduit,
scribere jussit amor.*"[6]

Epi. I will furnish you, sir.

Top. Now, for my bow and bolts give
me ink and paper, for my smiter a penknife; for

*Scalpellum, calami, atramentum, charta, li-
    belli,*   50
Sint semper studiis arma parata meis.[7]

Epi. Sir, will you give over wars and play
with that bable[8] called love?

Top. Give over wars? No, Epi, "*Mili-
tat omnis amans, et habet sua castra Cupido.*"[9]

Epi. Love hath made you very eloquent, but your face is nothing fair.

Top. "*Non formosus erat, sed erat facun-
dus Ulysses.*"[10]

Epi. Nay, I must seek a new master   [60
if you can speak nothing but verses.

Top. "*Quicquid conabar dicere, versus
erat.*"[11] Epi, I feel all *Ovid de Arte Amandi*
lie as heavy at my heart as a load of logs.
O, what a fine, thin hair hath Dipsas!
What a pretty, low forehead! What a tall
and stately nose! What little, hollow eyes!
What great and goodly lips! How harmless she is, being toothless! Her fingers
fat and short, adorned with long nails   [70
like a bitter![12] In how sweet a proportion

---

[4] Combination of verses from Ovid, *Heroides*,
xiii, 84; xvii, 254: "Let others wage wars; thou,
O Paris, must always love."

[5] Shape the beard like a dagger or leave it
untrimmed.

[6] Ovid, *Heroides*, iv, 10: "Those things which
one has hesitated to say, Love has bidden to
write."

[7] Lines apparently invented by Lyly: A penknife, quills, ink, paper, booklets—let these
weapons [*i.e.*, implements] be always in readiness
for my studies.

[8] Bauble.

[9] Ovid, *Amores*, i, 9, 1: "Every lover goes to
war, and Cupid holds his camp."

[10] Ovid, *Ars amatoria*, ii, 123: "Ulysses was
not handsome, but he was eloquent."

[11] Ovid, *Tristia*, iv, 10, 26: "Whatever I was
trying to express was poetry."

[12] Bittern.

[1] The discussion of grammatical terms in this
and the following lines is modeled upon passages
in William Lilly's famous Latin grammar.

[2] Uncover.

[3] From Cicero, *De officiis*, i, 22, 76: "Let
arms give place to the toga."

her cheeks hang down to her breasts like dugs and her paps to her waist like bags! What a low stature she is, and yet what a great foot she carrieth! How thrifty must she be in whom there is no waist! How virtuous is she like to be over whom no man can be jealous!

Epi. Stay, master, you forget yourself.

Top. O Epi, even as a dish melteth [80 by the fire, so doth my wit increase by love.

Epi. Pithily, and to the purpose! But what, begin you to nod?

Top. Good Epi, let me take a nap; for, as some man may better steal a horse than another look over the hedge, so divers shall be sleepy when they would fainest take rest. *He sleeps.* [89

Epi. Who ever saw such a woodcock! [1] Love Dipsas! Without doubt all the world will now account him valiant, that ventureth on her whom none durst undertake. But here cometh two wags.

Enter Dares and Samias.

Sam. Thy master hath slept his share.

Dar. I think he doth it because he would not pay me my board wages.

Sam. It is a thing most strange, and I think mine will never return, so that we must both seek new masters, for we [100 shall never live by our manners.

Epi. If you want masters, join with me and serve Sir Tophas, who must needs keep more men because he is toward marriage.

Sam. What, Epi, where's thy master?

Epi. Yonder, sleeping in love.

Dar. Is it possible?

Epi. He hath taken his thoughts a hole lower, and saith, seeing it is the fashion of the world, he will vail [2] bonnet to beauty.

Sam. How is he attired? 111

Epi. Lovely.

Dar. Whom loveth this amorous knight?

Epi. Dipsas.

Sam. That ugly creature? Why, she is a fool, a scold, fat, without fashion, and quite without favor.

Epi. Tush, you be simple; my master hath a good marriage.

Dar. Good? As how? 120

Epi. Why, in marrying Dipsas he shall have every day twelve dishes of meat to his dinner, though there be none but Dipsas with him: four of flesh, four of fish, four of fruit.

Sam. As how, Epi?

Epi. For flesh these: woodcock, goose, bitter, and rail.

Dar. Indeed, he shall not miss if Dipsas be there. 130

Epi. For fish these: crab, carp, lump, and pouting.

Sam. Excellent, for of my word she is both crabbish, lumpish, and carping.

Epi. For fruit these: fretters, [3] medlars, hartichokes, [4] and lady-longings. Thus you see he shall fare like a king, though he be but a beggar.

Dar. Well, Epi, dine thou with him, for I had rather fast than see her face. [140 But, see, thy ma[ster] is asleep; let us have a song to wake this amorous knight.

Epi. Agreed.

Sam. Content.

THE FIRST SONG [5]

Epi. Here snores Tophas,
That amorous ass,
Who loves Dipsas,
With face so sweet,
Nose and chin meet.

All Three. { At sight of her each Fury skips 150
And flings into her lap their whips.

Dar. Holla, holla in his ear.

Sam. The witch, sure, thrust her fingers there.

Epi. Cramp him, or wring the fool by th' nose;

Dar. Or clap some burning flax to his toes.

Sam. What music's best to wake him?

Epi. Baw-wow, let bandogs shake him!

Dar. Let adders hiss in 's ear!

Sam. Else earwigs wriggle there!

Epi. No, let him batten! When his tongue 160
Once goes, a cat is not worse strung.

All Three. { But if he ope nor mouth nor eyes,
He may in time sleep himself wise.

---

[1] Fool.   [2] Doff.

[3] An unidentified fruit.   [4] Artichokes.

[5] All the songs in the play appeared first in Blount's edn.

Top. [*Waking.*] Sleep is a binding of the senses, love a loosing.

Epi. [*Aside.*] Let us hear him awhile.

Top. There appeared in my sleep a goodly owl, who, sitting upon my shoulder, cried, "Twit, twit," and before mine eyes presented herself the express image of [170 Dipsas. I marveled what the owl said, till at the last I perceived "Twit, twit"— "To it, to it," only by contraction—admonished by this vision to make account of my sweet Venus.

Sam. Sir Tophas, you have overslept yourself.

Top. No, youth, I have but slept over my love.   179

Dar. Love? Why, it is impossible that into so noble and unconquered a courage love should creep, having first a head as hard to pierce as steel, then to pass to a heart armed with a shirt of mail.

Epi. Ay, but my master yawning one day in the sun, Love crept into his mouth before he could close it, and there kept such a tumbling in his body that he was glad to untruss the points [1] of his heart and entertain Love as a stranger.   190

Top. If there remain any pity in you, plead for me to Dipsas.

Dar. Plead? Nay, we will press her to it.—[*Aside to Samias.*] Let us go with him to Dipsas, and there shall we have good sport.—But, Sir Tophas, when shall we go? For I find my tongue voluble, and my heart venturous, and all myself like myself.   199

Sam. [*Aside to Dares.*] Come, Dares, let us not lose him till we find our masters, for, as long as he liveth, we shall lack neither mirth nor meat.

Epi. We will travice.[2] Will you go, sir?

Top. "*I præ; sequar.*"[3]   *Exeunt.*

Scena Quarta.

[*Near a fountain in the desert.*]

Eumenides, Geron.

Eum. Father, your sad music, being tuned on the same key that my hard fortune is, hath so melted my mind that I

---

[1] Untie the laces.   [2] Traverse, proceed.
[3] Terence, *Andria*, I, i, 144: "Go ahead; I'll follow."

wish to hang at your mouth's end till my life end.

Ger. These tunes, gentleman, have I been accustomed with these fifty winters, having no other house to shroud myself but the broad heavens. And so familiar with me hath use made misery that I [10 esteem sorrow my chiefest solace, and welcomest is that guest to me that can rehearse the saddest tale or the bloodiest tragedy.

Eum. A strange humor. Might I inquire the cause?

Ger. You must pardon me if I deny to tell it, for, knowing that the revealing of griefs is, as it were, a renewing of sorrow, I have vowed therefore to conceal them, [20 that I might not only feel the depth of everlasting discontentment, but despair of remedy. But whence are you? What fortune hath thrust you to this distress?

Eum. I am going to Thessaly, to seek remedy for Endymion, my dearest friend, who hath been cast into a dead sleep almost these twenty years, waxing old and ready for the grave, being almost but newly come forth of the cradle.   30

Ger. You need not for recure travel far, for whoso can clearly see the bottom of this fountain shall have remedy for anything.

Eum. That, methinketh, is unpossible. Why, what virtue can there be in water?

Ger. Yes, whosoever can shed the tears of a faithful lover shall obtain anything he would. Read these words engraven about the brim.   40

Eum. Have you known this by experience, or is it placed here of purpose to delude men?

Ger. I only would have experience of it, and then should there be an end of my misery; and then would I tell the strangest discourse that ever yet was heard.

Eum. Ah, Eumenides!

Ger. What lack you, gentleman? Are you not well?   50

Eum. Yes, father, but a qualm that often cometh over my heart doth now take hold of me. But did never any lovers come hither?

Ger. Lusters, but not lovers; for often have I seen them weep, but never could I hear they saw the bottom.

Eum. Came there women also?

Ger. Some.

Eum. What did they see?   60

Ger. They all wept, that the fountain overflowed with tears, but so thick became the water with their tears that I could scarce discern the brim, much less behold the bottom.

Eum. Be faithful lovers so scant?

Ger. It seemeth so, for yet heard I never of any.

Eum. Ah, Eumenides, how art thou perplexed! Call to mind the beauty of [70 thy sweet mistress and the depth of thy never-dying affections. How oft hast thou honored her, not only without spot, but suspicion of falsehood! And how hardly hath she rewarded thee without cause or color of despite.[1] How secret hast thou been these seven years, that hast not, nor once darest not, to name her, for [2] discontenting her. How faithful, that hast offered to die for her, to please her! Un- [80 happy Eumenides!

Ger. Why, gentleman, did you once love?

Eum. Once? Ay, father, and ever shall.

Ger. Was she unkind and you faithful?

Eum. She of all women the most froward, and I of all creatures the most fond.

Ger. You doted then, not loved, for affection is grounded on virtue, and virtue is never peevish; or on beauty, and [90 beauty loveth to be praised.

Eum. Ay, but, if all virtuous ladies should yield to all that be loving, or all amiable gentlewomen entertain all that be amorous, their virtues would be accounted vices, and their beauties deformities; for that love can be but between two, and that not proceeding of [3] him that is most faithful but most fortunate.

Ger. I would you were so faithful [100 that your tears might make you fortunate.

Eum. Yea, father, if that my tears clear not this fountain, then may you swear it is but a mere mockery.

Ger. So saith every one yet that wept.

Eum. Ah, I faint, I die! Ah, sweet Semele, let me alone, and dissolve,[4] by weeping, into water.

[Gazes into the fountain.]

Ger. This affection [5] seemeth strange. If he see nothing, without doubt this [110 dissembling passeth,[6] for nothing shall draw me from the belief.

Eum. Father, I plainly see the bottom, and there in white marble engraven these words: *Ask one for all, and but one thing at all.*

Ger. O fortunate Eumenides (for so have I heard thee call thyself), let me see.— I cannot discern any such thing. I think thou dreamest.   120

Eum. Ah, father, thou art not a faithful lover, and therefore canst not behold it.

Ger. Then ask, that I may be satisfied by the event, and thyself blessed.

Eum. Ask? So I will. And what shall I do but ask, and whom should I ask but Semele, the possessing of whose person is a pleasure that cannot come within the compass of comparison; whose golden locks seem most curious [7] when they seem [130 most careless; whose sweet looks seem most alluring when they are most chaste; and whose words the more virtuous they are, the more amorous they be accounted? I pray thee, Fortune, when I shall first meet with fair Semele, dash my delight with some light disgrace, lest, embracing sweetness beyond measure, I take a surfeit without recure. Let her practice her accustomed coyness that I may diet myself upon [140 my desires; otherwise the fulness of my joys will diminish the sweetness, and I shall perish by them before I possess them.

Why do I trifle the time in words? The least minute being spent in the getting of Semele is more worth than the whole world; therefore let me ask. What now, Eumenides! Whither art thou drawn? Hast thou forgotten both friendship and duty, care of Endymion, and the com- [150 mandment of Cynthia? Shall he die in a leaden sleep because thou sleepest in a golden dream? Ay, let him sleep ever, so I slumber but one minute with Semele. Love knoweth neither friendship nor kindred.

Shall I not hazard the loss of a friend for the obtaining of her for whom I would often lose myself? Fond [8] Eumenides, shall the enticing beauty of a most disdainful lady be of more force than the [160

[1] With no occasion or reason for ill will.
[2] For fear of.   [3] Caused by.   [4] Let me dissolve.

[5] Passion.   [7] Artfully arranged.
[6] This hypocrisy is excessive.   [8] Foolish.

rare fidelity of a tried friend? The love of men to women is a thing common and of course; the friendship of man to man infinite and immortal.—Tush! Semele doth possess my love.—Ay, but Endymion hath deserved it. I will help Endymion. I found Endymion unspotted in his truth.— Ay, but I shall find Semele constant in her love. I will have Semele.—What shall I do? Father, thy gray hairs are ambas- [170 sadors of experience. Which shall I ask?

GER. Eumenides, release Endymion, for all things, friendship excepted, are subject to fortune. Love is but an eyeworm, which only tickleth the head with hopes and wishes; friendship the image of eternity, in which there is nothing movable, nothing mischievous. As much difference as there is between beauty and virtue, bodies and shadows, colors and life, so great [180 odds is there between love and friendship.

Love is a chameleon, which draweth nothing into the mouth but air, and nourisheth nothing in the body but lungs. Believe me, Eumenides, desire dies in the same moment that beauty sickens, and beauty fadeth in the same instant that it flourisheth. When adversities flow, then love ebbs; but friendship standeth stiffly in storms. Time draweth wrinkles in [190 a fair face, but addeth fresh colors to a fast friend, which neither heat, nor cold, nor misery, nor place, nor destiny can alter or diminish. O friendship, of all things the most rare, and therefore most rare because most excellent, whose comforts in misery is always sweet, and whose counsels in prosperity are ever fortunate! Vain love, that, only coming near to friendship in name, would seem to be the [200 same or better in nature!

EUM. Father, I allow your reasons, and will therefore conquer mine own. Virtue shall subdue affections, wisdom lust, friendship beauty. Mistresses are in every place, and as common as hares in Athos, bees in Hybla, fowls in the air; but friends to be found are like the phœnix in Arabia, but one; or the philadelphi [1] in Arays, never above two. I will have Endymion. [210 Sacred fountain, in whose bowels are hidden divine secrets, I have increased your waters with the tears of unspotted thoughts,

¹ Shrubs on which the flowers grow in pairs.

and therefore let me receive the reward you promise. Endymion, the truest friend to me, and faithfulest lover to Cynthia, is in such a dead sleep that nothing can wake or move him.

GER. Dost thou see anything?

EUM. I see in the same pillar these [220 words: *When she whose figure of all is the perfectest, and never to be measured—always one, yet never the same—still inconstant, yet never wavering—shall come and kiss Endymion in his sleep, he shall then rise; else never.* This is strange.

GER. What see you else?

EUM. There cometh over mine eyes either a dark mist, or upon the fountain a deep thickness, for I can perceive [230 nothing. But how am I deluded, or what difficult—nay, impossible—thing is this?

GER. Methinketh it easy.

EUM. Good father, and how?

GER. Is not a circle of all figures the perfectest?

EUM. Yes.

GER. And is not Cynthia of all circles the most absolute?

EUM. Yes.   240

GER. Is it not impossible to measure her, who still worketh by her influence, never standing at one stay?

EUM. Yes.

GER. Is she not always Cynthia, yet seldom in the same bigness; always wavering in her waxing or waning, that our bodies might the better be governed, our seasons the dailier give their increase; yet never to be removed from her course, [250 as long as the heavens continue theirs?

EUM. Yes.

GER. Then who can it be but Cynthia, whose virtues, being all divine, must needs bring things to pass that be miraculous? Go, humble thyself to Cynthia; tell her the success, of which myself shall be a witness. And this assure thyself, that she that sent to find means for his safety will now work her cunning.   260

EUM. How fortunate am I, if Cynthia be she that may do it!

GER. How fond art thou, if thou do not believe it!

EUM. I will hasten thither that I may entreat on my knees for succor, and embrace in mine arms my friend.

GER. I will go with thee, for unto Cynthia must I discover all my sorrows, who also must work in me a contentment.

EUM. May I now know the cause? [271

GER. That shall be as we walk, and I doubt not but the strangeness of my tale will take away the tediousness of our journey.

EUM. Let us go.

GER. I follow.   *Exeunt.*

ACTUS QUARTUS. SCENA PRIMA.

[*Before the castle of Corsites in a desert.*]

Tellus, Corsites.[1]

TELLUS. I marvel Corsites giveth me so much liberty—all the world knowing his charge [2] to be so high and his nature to be most strange—who hath so ill entreated ladies of great honor that he hath not suffered them to look out of windows, much less to walk abroad. It may be he is in love with me, for (Endymion, hardhearted Endymion, excepted) what is he that is not enamored of my beauty? [10 But what respectest thou the love of all the world? Endymion hates thee. Alas, poor Endymion, my malice hath exceeded my love, and thy faith to Cynthia quenched my affections. Quenched, Tellus? Nay, kindled them afresh; insomuch that I find scorching flames for dead embers, and cruel encounters of war in my thoughts instead of sweet parleys. Ah, that I might once again see Endymion! Accursed [20 girl, what hope hast thou to see Endymion, on whose head already are grown gray hairs, and whose life must yield to nature before Cynthia end her displeasure? Wicked Dipsas and most devilish Tellus, the one for cunning too exquisite, the other for hate too intolerable! Thou wast commanded to weave the stories and poetries wherein were showed both examples and punishments of tattling tongues, and [30 thou hast only embroidered [3] the sweet face of Endymion, devices of love, melancholy imaginations, and what not, out of thy work, that thou shouldst study to pick out of thy mind. But here cometh Corsites. I must seem yielding and stout;

full of mildness, yet tempered with a majesty, for, if I be too flexible, I shall give him more hope than I mean; if too froward, enjoy less liberty than I would. [40 Love him I cannot, and therefore will practice that which is most contrary [4] to our sex, to dissemble.

Enter Corsites.

COR. Fair Tellus, I perceive you rise with the lark, and to yourself sing with the nightingale.

TELLUS. My lord, I have no playfellow but fancy. Being barred of all company, I must question with myself, and make my thoughts my friends.   50

COR. I would you would account my thoughts also your friends, for they be such as are only busied in wondering at your beauty and wisdom; and some such as have esteemed your fortune too hard; and divers of that kind that offer to set you free, if you will set them free.

TELLUS. There are no colors so contrary as white and black, nor elements so disagreeing as fire and water, nor [60 anything so opposite as men's thoughts and their words.

COR. He that gave Cassandra the gift of prophesying, with the curse that, spake she never so true, she should never be believed, hath I think poisoned the fortune of men, that, uttering the extremities of their inward passions, are always suspected of outward perjuries.

TELLUS. Well, Corsites, I will flatter [70 myself and believe you. What would you do to enjoy my love?

COR. Set all the ladies of the castle free, and make you the pleasure of my life. More I cannot do; less I will not.

TELLUS. These be great words, and fit your calling, for captains must promise things impossible. But will you do one thing for all?

COR. Anything, sweet Tellus, that [80 am ready for all.

TELLUS. You know that on the lunary bank sleepeth Endymion.

COR. I know it.

TELLUS. If you will remove him from that place by force, and convey him into

---

[1] Enters later.
[2] Military position.   [3] Embroidered.

[4] Bond suggests *customary.*

some obscure cave by policy, I give you here the faith of an unspotted virgin that you only shall possess me as a lover, and in spite of malice have me for a wife. 90

COR. Remove him, Tellus? Yes, Tellus, he shall be removed, and that so soon as [1] thou shalt as much commend my diligence as my force. I go.

TELLUS. Stay, will yourself attempt it?

COR. Ay, Tellus; as I would have none partaker of my sweet love, so shall none be partners of my labors. But I pray thee go at your best leisure, for Cynthia beginneth to rise, and, if she discover our [100 love, we both perish, for nothing pleaseth her but the fairness of virginity. All things must be not only without lust but without suspicion of lightness.

TELLUS. I will depart, and go you to Endymion.

COR. I fly, Tellus, being of all men the most fortunate. *Exit.*

TELLUS. Simple Corsites, I have set thee about a task, being but a man, [110 that the gods themselves cannot perform, for little dost thou know how heavy his head lies, how hard his fortune. But such shifts must women have to deceive men, and, under color of things easy, entreat that which is impossible; otherwise we should be cumbered with importunities, oaths, sighs, letters, and all implements of love, which to one resolved to the contrary are most loathsome. I will in, and laugh [120 with the other ladies at Corsites' sweating. *Exit.*

SCENA SECUNDA.

[*The gardens of Cynthia's palace.*]

Samias and Dares; Epiton. [2]

SAM. Will thy master never awake?

DAR. No; I think he sleeps for a wager. But how shall we spend the time? Sir Tophas is so far in love that he pineth in his bed and cometh not abroad.

SAM. But here cometh Epi in a pelting chafe. [3]

[*Enter Epiton.*]

EPI. A pox of all false proverbs, and were a proverb a page, I would have him by the ears! 10

SAM. Why art thou angry?

EPI. Why? You know it is said, "The tide tarrieth no man."

SAM. True.

EPI. A monstrous lie; for I was tied two hours, and tarried for one to unloose me.

DAR. Alas, poor Epi!

EPI. Poor? No, no, you base, conceited slaves, I am a most complete [20 gentleman, although I be in disgrace with Sir Tophas.

DAR. Art thou out with him?

EPI. Ay, because I cannot get him a lodging with Endymion. He would fain take a nap for forty or fifty years.

DAR. A short sleep, considering our long life.

SAM. Is he still in love?

EPI. In love? Why, he doth noth- [30 ing but make sonnets!

SAM. Canst thou remember any one of his poems?

EPI. Ay, this is one:

The beggar Love, that knows not where
    to lodge,
  At last within my heart, when I slept,
        He crept.
  I waked, and so my fancies began to
    fodge. [4]

SAM. That's a very long verse.

EPI. Why, the other was short. The [40 first is called from the thumb to the little finger; the second from the little finger to the elbow; and some he hath made to reach to the crown of his head, and down again to the sole of his foot. It is set to the tune of the Black Saunce; [5] *ratio est*,[6] because Dipsas is a black saint.

DAR. Very wisely. But pray thee, Epi, how art thou complete, and, being from thy master, what occupation wilt thou [50 take?

EPI. Know,[7] my hearts, I am an absolute *microcosmus*, a petty world of myself: my library is my head, for I have no other books but my brains; my wardrope [8] on my back, for I have no more apparel

[1] That. [2] Enters later. [3] Petty rage.

[4] Move.
[5] The Black Sanctus was a hymn to Saint Satan in ridicule of the monks.
[6] The reason is.
[7] Emended by Baker. Early edns. read *No.*
[8] Wardrobe.

than is on my body; my armory at my
fingers' ends, for I use no other artillery
than my nails; my treasure in my purse.
" *Sic omnia mea mecum porto.*" [1]   60

DAR. Good!

EPI. Now, sirs, my palace is paved with
grass and tiled with stars, for " *Cælo tegitur
qui non habet urnam* " [2]—" he that hath no
house must lie in the yard."

SAM. A brave resolution! But how wilt
thou spend thy time?

EPI. Not in any melancholy sort; for
mine exercise I will walk horses.

DAR. Too bad!   70

EPI. Why, is it not said, "It is good
walking when one hath his horse in his
hand"?

SAM. Worse and worse! But how wilt
thou live?

EPI. By angling. O, 'tis a stately occupation to stand four hours in a cold morning, and to have his nose bitten with frost
before his bait be mumbled with a fish.

DAR. A rare attempt! But wilt thou   [80
never travel?

EPI. Yes, in a western barge,[3] when,
with a good wind and lusty pugs,[4] one may
go ten miles in two days.

SAM. Thou art excellent at thy choice.
But what pastime wilt thou use? None?

EPI. Yes, the quickest of all.

SAM. What, dice?

EPI. No, when I am in haste, one-and-
twenty games at chess, to pass a few   [90
minutes.

DAR. A life for a little lord, and full of
quickness.[5]

EPI. Tush, let me alone! But I must
needs see if I can find where Endymion
lieth, and then go to a certain fountain
hard by, where they say faithful lovers
shall have all things they will ask. If I
can find out any of these, *Ego et magister
meus erimus in tuto*—I and my master   [100
shall be friends. He is resolved to weep
some three or four pailfuls to avoid [6] the
rheum of love that wambleth [7] in his stomach.

---

[1] Quoted by Cicero in *Paradoxa Stoicorum,*
i, 1: "Thus all my possessions I carry with me."
[2] Lucan, vii, 819.
[3] *I.e.,* on the Thames.
[4] Bargemen.
[5] Liveliness.
[6] Empty.   [7] Rumbles.

Enter the Watch.

SAM. Shall we never see thy master,
Dares?

DAR. Yes; let us go now, for tomorrow
Cynthia will be there.

EPI. I will go with you. But how shall
we see for the watch?   110

SAM. Tush, let me alone! I'll begin to
them. Masters, God speed you.

1 WATCH. Sir boy, we are all sped already.

EPI. [*Aside.*]   So methinks, for they
smell all of drink, like a beggar's beard.

DAR. But I pray, sirs, may we see Endymion?

2 WATCH. No, we are commanded in
Cynthia's name that no man shall see   [120
him.

SAM. No man? Why, we are but boys.

1 WATCH. Mass, neighbors, he says
true, for, if I swear I will never drink my
liquor by the quart, and yet call for two
pints, I think with a safe conscience I may
carouse both.

DAR. Pithily, and to the purpose!

2 WATCH. Tush, tush, neighbors, take
me with you.[8]   130

SAM. [*Aside.*] This will grow hot.

DAR. [*Aside.*] Let them alone.

2 WATCH. If I say to my wife, "Wife,
I will have no raisins in my pudding,"
she puts in currants. Small raisins are
raisins, and boys are men; even as my
wife should have put no raisins in my pudding, so shall there no boys see Endymion.

DAR. Learnedly!

EPI. Let Master Constable speak;   [140
I think he is the wisest among you.

MA. CONST. You know, neighbors, 'tis
an old said [9] saw, "Children and fools speak
true."

ALL *say:* True.

MA. CONST. Well, there you see the
men be the fools, because it is provided
from the children.

DAR. Good!

MA. CONST. Then say I, neighbors,   [150
that children must not see Endymion, because children and fools speak true.

EPI. O wicked application!

SAM. Scurvily brought about!

---

[8] Let me understand you.
[9] Sad, serious.

1 WATCH. Nay, he says true, and therefore till Cynthia have been here, he shall not be uncovered. Therefore, away!

DAR. [*Aside to Samias and Epiton.*] A watch, quoth you! A man may watch seven years for a wise word, and yet [160 go without it. Their wits are all as rusty as their bills.[1] But come on, Ma[ster] Const[able], shall we have a song before we go?

MA. CONST. With all my heart.

THE SECOND SONG

WATCH. Stand! Who goes there?
We charge you, appear
Fore our constable here,
In the name of the Man in the Moon.
To us billmen relate
Why you stagger so late,   170
And how you come drunk so soon.
    PAGES. What are ye, scabs?[2]
    WATCH.   The watch;
This the constable.
    PAGES.   A patch![3]
MA. CONST. Knock 'em down unless
    they all stand!
If any run away,
'Tis the old watchman's play,
To reach him a bill of his hand.
    PAGES. O gentlemen, hold;
Your gowns freeze with cold,   179
And your rotten teeth dance in your head.
    EPI. Wine nothing shall cost ye;
    SAM. Nor huge fires to roast ye;
    DAR. Then soberly let us be led.
    MA. CONST. Come, my brown bills, we'll
        roar,[4]
Bounce loud at tavern door,
    OMNES. And i' th' morning steal all to
        bed!
                            Exeunt.

SCENA TERTIA.

[*A grove near Endymion's cell.*]

Corsites solus. [*Endymion sleeps on the bank
                    in the grove.*]

CORS. I am come in sight of the lunary bank. Without doubt Tellus doteth upon me, and cunningly, that I might not perceive her love, she hath set me to a task that is done before it is begun. Endymion, you must change your pillow, and if you be not weary of sleep, I will carry you

[1] Halberds.
[2] Rascals, sheriff's officers.
[3] Fool.   [4] Revel.

where at ease you shall sleep your fill. It were good that without more ceremonies I took him, lest, being espied, I be en- [10 trapped, and so incur the displeasure of Cynthia, who commonly setteth watch that Endymion have no wrong. (*He lifts.*) What now, is your mastership so heavy, or are you nailed to the ground? Not stir one whit? Then use all thy force, though he feel it and wake. What, stone-still? Turned, I think, to earth with lying so long on the earth. Didst not thou, Corsites, before Cynthia, pull up a tree that [20 forty years was fastened with roots and wreathed in knots to the ground? Didst not thou with main force pull open the iron gates which no ram or engine could move? Have my weak thoughts made brawn-fallen my strong arms? Or is it the nature of love or the quintessence of the mind to breed numbness or litherness,[5] or I know not what languishing in my joints and sinews, being but the base strings [30 of my body? Or doth the remembrance of Tellus so refine my spirits into a matter so subtle and divine that the other fleshy parts cannot work whilst they muse? Rest thyself, rest thyself; nay, rent[6] thyself in pieces, Corsites, and strive, in spite of love, fortune, and nature, to lift up this dulled body, heavier than dead and more senseless than death.

Enter Fairies.

But what are these so fair fiends that [40 cause my hairs to stand upright and spirits to fall down? Hags—out, alas, nymphs, I crave pardon! Ay me, out! What do I hear?
*The Fairies dance and with a song pinch
    him, and he falleth asleep. They kiss
                Endymion and depart.*

THE THIRD SONG BY FAIRIES

OMNES. Pinch him, pinch him, black and
    blue,
Saucy mortals must not view
What the Queen of Stars is doing,
Nor pry into our fairy wooing.
    1 FAIRY. Pinch him blue,
    2 FAIRY. And pinch him black;   50
    3 FAIRY. Let him not lack

[5] Flaccidity, sloth.   [6] Rend, **tear.**

Sharp nails to pinch him blue and red,
Till sleep has rocked his addle head.

    4 FAIRY. For the trespass he hath done,
Spots o'er all his flesh shall run.
Kiss Endymion, kiss his eyes,
Then to our midnight hay-de-guise.[1]

                            Exeunt.

Cynthia, Floscula, Semele, Panelion, Zontes,
                Pythagoras, Gyptes.

  CYNTH. You see, Pythagoras, what ridiculous opinions you hold, and I doubt not but you are now of another mind.   60

  PYTHAG. Madam, I plainly perceive that the perfection of your brightness hath pierced through the thickness that covered my mind; insomuch that I am no less glad to be reformed than ashamed to remember my grossness.

  GYPTES. They are thrice fortunate that live in your palace where truth is not in colors but life, virtues not in imagination but execution.   70

  CYNTH. I have always studied to have rather living virtues than painted gods, the body of truth than the tomb. But let us walk to Endymion; it may be it lieth in your arts to deliver him. As for Eumenides, I fear he is dead.

  PYTHAG. I have alleged all the natural reasons I can for such a long sleep.

  GYPTES. I can do nothing till I see him.

  CYNTH. Come, Floscula; I am sure [80 you are glad that you shall behold Endymion.

  FLOSC. I were blessed, if I might have him recovered.

  CYNTH. Are you in love with his person?

  FLOSC. No, but with his virtue.

  CYNTH. What say you, Semele?

  SEM. Madam, I dare say nothing for fear I offend.

  CYNTH. Belike you cannot speak [90 except you be spiteful; but as good be silent as saucy. Panelion, what punishment were fit for Semele, in whose speech and thoughts is only contempt and sourness?

  PANEL. I love not, madam, to give any judgment; yet, sith[2] your highness commandeth, I think to commit her tongue close prisoner to her mouth.

  CYNTH. Agreed. Semele, if thou speak this twelvemonth, thou shalt forfeit [100

thy tongue.—Behold Endymion! Alas, poor gentleman, hast thou spent thy youth in sleep, that once vowed all to my service? Hollow eyes, gray hairs, wrinkled cheeks, and decayed limbs! Is it destiny or deceit that hath brought this to pass? If the first, who could prevent thy wretched stars? If the latter, I would I might know thy cruel enemy. I favored thee, Endymion, for thy honor, thy virtues, thy af- [110 fections. But[3] to bring thy thoughts within the compass of thy fortunes, I have seemed strange, that I might have thee stayed;[4] and now are thy days ended before my favor begin! But whom have we here? Is it not Corsites?

  ZON. It is, but more like a leopard than a man.

  CYNTH. Awake him. [*Zontes wakens Corsites.*] How now, Corsites, what [120 make[5] you here? How came you deformed? Look on thy hands, and then thou seest the picture of thy face.

  CORS. Miserable wretch, and accursed! How am I deluded! Madam, I ask pardon for my offense, and you see my fortune deserveth pity.

  CYNTH. Speak on; thy offense cannot deserve greater punishment. But see thou rehearse the truth, else shalt thou not [130 find me as thou wishest me.

  CORS. Madam, as it is no offense to be in love, being a man mortal, so I hope can it be no shame to tell with whom, my lady being heavenly. Your majesty committed to my charge fair Tellus, whose beauty in the same moment took my heart captive that I undertook to carry her body prisoner. Since that time have I found such combats in my thoughts [140 between love and duty, reverence and affection, that I could neither endure the conflict nor hope for the conquest.

  CYNTH. In love? A thing far unfitting the name of a captain, and, as I thought, the tough and unsmoothed nature of Corsites. But forth!

  CORS. Feeling this continual war, I thought rather by parley to yield than by certain danger to perish. I unfolded [150 to Tellus the depth of my affections, and framed my tongue to utter a sweet tale of love, that was wont to sound nothing but

---

[1] Rustic dance.   [2] Since.

[3] Only.   [4] Checked (*i.e.*, in his ambitions).   [5] Do.

threats of war. She, too fair to be true and too false for one so fair, after a nice [1] denial, practiced a notable deceit, commanding me to remove Endymion from this cabin,[2] and carry him to some dark cave; which I, seeking to accomplish, found impossible, and so by fairies or fiends [160 have been thus handled.

CYNTH. How say you, my lords, is not Tellus always practicing of some deceits? In sooth, Corsites, thy face is now too foul for a lover, and thine heart too fond for a soldier. You may see when warriors become wantons how their manners alter with their faces. Is it not a shame, Corsites, that, having lived so long in Mars his camp, thou shouldest now be rocked [170 in Venus' cradle? Dost thou wear Cupid's quiver at thy girdle and make lances of looks? Well, Corsites, rouse thyself and be as thou hast been; and let Tellus, who is made all of love, melt herself in her own looseness.

CORS. Madam, I doubt not but to recover my former state, for Tellus' beauty never wrought such love in my mind as now her deceit hath despite; and yet to be [180 revenged of a woman were a thing than love itself more womanish.

GYPTES. These spots, gentleman, are to be worn out, if you rub them over with this lunary, so that in place where you received this main,[3] you shall find a medicine.

CORS. I thank you for that. The gods bless [4] me from love and these pretty ladies that haunt this green.   190

FLOSC. Corsites, I would Tellus saw your amiable face.

ZON. How spitefully Semele laugheth, that dare not speak!

CYNTH. Could you not stir Endymion with that doubled strength of yours?

CORS. Not so much as his finger with all my force.

CYNTH. Pythagoras and Gyptes, what think you of Endymion? What rea- [200 son is to be given, what remedy?

PYTHAG. Madam, it is impossible to yield reason for things that happen not in compass of nature. It is most certain that some strange enchantment hath bound all his senses.

CYNTH. What say you, Gyptes?

GYPTES. With Pythagoras, that it is enchantment, and that so strange that no art can undo it (for that heaviness [210 argueth a malice unremovable in the enchantress) and that no power can end it, till she die that did it, or the heavens show some means more than miraculous.

FLOSC. O Endymion, could spite itself devise a mischief so monstrous as to make thee dead with life, and living being altogether dead? Where others number their years, their hours, their minutes, and step to age by stairs, thou only hast [220 thy years and times in a cluster, being old before thou rememb'rest thou wast young.

CYNTH. No more, Floscula; pity doth him no good. I would anything else might, and I vow by the unspotted honor of a lady he should not miss it. But is this all, Gyptes, that is to be done?

GYPTES. All as yet. It may be that either the enchantress shall die or else be discovered. If either happen, I will [230 then practice the utmost of my art. In the mean season, about this grove would I have a watch, and the first living thing that toucheth Endymion to be taken.

CYNTH. Corsites, what say you? Will you undertake this?

CORS. Good madam, pardon me! I was overtaken [5] too late. I should rather break into the middest of a main battle than again fall into the hands of those [240 fair babies.[6]

CYNTH. Well, I will provide others. Pythagoras and Gyptes, you shall yet remain in my court, till I hear what may be done in this matter.

PYTHAG. We attend.

CYNTH. Let us go in.   *Exeunt.*

ACTUS QUINTUS. SCENA PRIMA.

[*The same.*]

Samias, Dares.

SAM. Eumenides hath told such strange tales as I may well wonder at them, but never believe them.

---

[1] Overscrupulous, fastidious.
[2] Shelter (represented by the overhanging inner stage?).   [3] Maim.   [4] Protect.
[5] Overpowered.   [6] *I.e.*, the fairies.

Dar. The other old man, what a sad speech used he, that caused us almost all to weep. Cynthia is so desirous to know the experiment of her own virtue,[1] and so willing to ease Endymion's hard fortune, that she no sooner heard the discourse but she made herself in a readiness to [10 try the event.

Sam. We will also see the event. But whist, here cometh Cynthia with all her train! Let us sneak in amongst them.

Enter Cynthia, Floscula, Semele, [Eumenides,] Panelion, etc.

Cynth. Eumenides, it cannot sink into my head that I should be signified by that sacred fountain, for many things are there in the world to which those words may be applied.

Eum. Good madam, vouchsafe but [20 to try; else shall I think myself most unhappy that I asked not my sweet mistress.

Cynth. Will you not yet tell me her name?

Eum. Pardon me, good madam, for if Endymion awake, he shall; myself have sworn never to reveal it.

Cynth. Well, let us to Endymion. I will not be so stately, good Endymion, not to stoop to do thee good; and, if thy [30 liberty consist in a kiss from me, thou shalt have it. And, although my mouth hath been heretofore as untouched as my thoughts, yet now to recover thy life, though to restore thy youth it be impossible, I will do that to Endymion which yet never mortal man could boast of heretofore, nor shall ever hope for hereafter. *She kisseth him.*

Eum. Madam, he beginneth to stir!

Cynth. Soft, Eumenides; stand still! [40

Eum. Ah, I see his eyes almost open!

Cynth. I command thee once again, stir not! I will stand behind him.

Panel. What do I see? Endymion almost awake?

Eum. Endymion! Endymion! Art thou deaf or dumb, or hath this long sleep taken away thy memory? Ah, my sweet Endymion, seest thou not Eumenides, thy faithful friend, thy faithful Eumenides, who [50 for thy safety hath been careless of his own content? Speak, Endymion! Endymion! Endymion!

[1] Make trial of her power.

End. Endymion? I call to mind such a name.

Eum. Hast thou forgotten thyself, Endymion? Then do I not marvel thou rememb'rest not thy friend. I tell thee thou art Endymion, and I Eumenides. Behold also Cynthia, by whose favor thou art [60 awaked, and by whose virtue thou shalt continue thy natural course.

Cynth. Endymion, speak, sweet Endymion! Knowest thou not Cynthia?

End. O heavens, whom do I behold? Fair Cynthia, divine Cynthia?

Cynth. I am Cynthia, and thou Endymion.   68

End. "Endymion"! What do I hear? What! a gray beard, hollow eyes, withered body, decayed limbs—and all in one night?

Eum. One night! Thou hast here slept forty years—by what enchantress as yet it is not known—and behold, the twig to which thou laid'st thy head is now become a tree. Callest thou not Eumenides to remembrance?

End. Thy name I do remember by the sound, but thy favor[2] I do not yet call to mind; only divine Cynthia, to whom [80 time, fortune, destiny, and death are subject, I see and remember, and in all humility I regard and reverence.

Cynth. You have good cause to remember Eumenides, who hath for thy safety forsaken his own solace.

End. Am I that Endymion who was wont in court to lead my life, and in jousts, tourneys, and arms, to exercise my youth? Am I that Endymion?   90

Eum. Thou art that Endymion, and I Eumenides. Wilt thou not yet call me to remembrance?

End. Ah, sweet Eumenides, I now perceive thou art he, and that myself have the name of Endymion; but that this should be my body I doubt, for how could my curled locks be turned to gray hairs and my strong body to a dying weakness, having waxed old, and not knowing it? [100

Cynth. Well, Endymion, arise. [*Endymion attempts to rise, but sinks back.*] A while sit down, for that thy limbs are stiff and not able to stay thee, and tell what hast thou seen in thy sleep all this while, what dreams, visions, thoughts, and for-

[2] Appearance, face.

tunes; for it is impossible but in so long time thou shouldest see things strange.

END. Fair Cynthia, I will rehearse what I have seen, humbly desiring that, [110 when I exceed in length, you give me warning, that I may end; for to utter all I have to speak would be troublesome, although happily the strangeness may somewhat abate the tediousness.

CYNTH. Well, Endymion, begin.

END. Methought I saw a lady passing fair, but very mischievous, who in the one hand carried a knife with which she offered to cut my throat, and in the other a [120 looking-glass, wherein seeing how ill anger became ladies, she refrained from intended violence. She was accompanied with other damsels, one of which, with a stern countenance, and as it were with a settled malice engraven in her eyes, provoked her to execute mischief; another, with visage sad, and constant only in sorrow, with her arms crossed and watery eyes, seemed to lament my fortune, but durst not offer to pre- [130 vent the force. I started in my sleep, feeling my very veins to swell and my sinews to stretch with fear, and such a cold sweat bedewed all my body that death itself could not be so terrible as the vision.

CYNTH. A strange sight! Gyptes, at our better leisure, shall expound it.

END. After long debating with herself, mercy overcame anger, and there appeared in her heavenly face such a divine maj- [140 esty mingled with a sweet mildness that I was ravished with the sight above measure, and wished that I might have enjoyed the sight without end. And so she departed with the other ladies, of which the one retained still an unmovable cruelty, the other a constant pity.

CYNTH. Poor Endymion, how wast thou affrighted! What else?   149

END. After her, immediately appeared an aged man with a beard as white as snow, carrying in his hand a book with three leaves, and speaking, as I remember, these words: "Endymion, receive this book with three leaves, in which are contained counsels, policies, and pictures," and with that he offered me the book, which I rejected; wherewith, moved with a disdainful pity, he rent the first leaf in a thousand shivers. The second time he [160

offered it, which I refused also; at which, bending his brows, and pitching his eyes fast to the ground, as though they were fixed to the earth and not again to be removed, then suddenly casting them up to the heavens, he tore in a rage the second leaf, and offered the book only with one leaf. I know not whether fear to offend or desire to know some strange thing moved me. I took the book, and so the old [170 man vanished.

CYNTH. What diddest thou imagine was in the last leaf?

END. There—ay, portrayed to life— with a cold quaking in every joint, I beheld many wolves barking at thee, Cynthia, who, having ground their teeth to bite, did with striving bleed themselves to death. There might I see Ingratitude with an hundred eyes gazing for benefits, [180 and with a thousand teeth gnawing on the bowels wherein she was bred. Treachery stood all clothed in white, with a smiling countenance, but both her hands bathed in blood. Envy with a pale and meager face (whose body was so lean that one might tell [1] all her bones, and whose garment was so tottered [2] that it was easy to number every thread) stood shooting at stars, whose darts fell down again on [190 her own face. There might I behold drones, or beetles—I know not how to term them— creeping under the wings of a princely eagle, who, being carried into her nest, sought there to suck that vein that would have killed the eagle. I mused that things so base should attempt a fact [3] so barbarous, or durst imagine a thing so bloody. And many other things, madam, the repetition whereof may at your better [200 leisure seem more pleasing, for bees surfeit sometimes with honey, and the gods are glutted with harmony, and your highness may be dulled with delight.

CYNTH. I am content to be dieted; therefore, let us in. Eumenides, see that Endymion be well tended, lest, either eating immoderately or sleeping again too long, he fall into a deadly surfeit or into his former sleep.   210

See this also be proclaimed: that whosoever will discover this practice shall

---

[1] Count.
[2] Tattered.

[3] Deed, act.

have of Cynthia infinite thanks and no small rewards.

Exit [*with all but Floscula, Eumenides, Semele, and Endymion*].

FLOSC. Ah, Endymion, none so joyful as Floscula of thy restoring.

EUM. Yes, Floscula, let Eumenides be somewhat gladder, and do not that wrong to the settled friendship of a man as to compare it with the light affection [220 of a woman. Ah, my dear friend Endymion, suffer me to die with gazing at thee!

END. Eumenides, thy friendship is immortal and not to be conceived; and thy good will, Floscula, better than I have deserved. But let us all wait on Cynthia. I marvel Semele speaketh not a word.

EUM. Because if she do, she loseth her tongue!

END. But how prospereth your love?

EUM. I never yet spake word since [231 your sleep.

END. I doubt not but your affection is old and your appetite cold.

EUM. No, Endymion, thine hath made it stronger, and now are my sparks grown to flames and my fancies almost to frenzies. But let us follow, and within we will debate all this matter at large.   *Exeunt.*

SCENA SECUNDA.

[*The gardens of Cynthia's palace.*]

Sir Tophas, Epiton.

TOP. Epi, Love hath justled my liberty from the wall, and taken the upper hand of my reason.

EPI. Let me then trip up the heels of your affection and thrust your good will into the gutter.

TOP. No, Epi, Love is a lord of misrule and keepeth Christmas in my corpse.[1]

EPI. No doubt there is good cheer. What dishes of delight doth his lord- [10 ship feast you withal?

TOP. First, with a great platter of plum porridge of pleasure, wherein is stewed the mutton of mistrust.

EPI. Excellent love lap.[2]

TOP. Then cometh a pie of patience, a hen of honey, a goose of gall, a capon of care, and many other viands, some sweet

and some sour, which proveth love to be, as it was said of in old years, *dulce* [20 *venenum.*[3]

EPI. A brave banquet!

TOP. But, Epi, I pray thee feel on my chin; something pricketh me. What dost thou feel or see?

EPI. There are three or four little hairs.

TOP. I pray thee call it my beard. How shall I be troubled when this young spring [4] shall grow to a great wood!

EPI. O, sir, your chin is but a quiller[5] [30 yet; you will be most majestical when it is full-fledge. But I marvel that you love Dipsas, that old crone.

TOP. "*Agnosco veteris vestigia flammæ*"[6]—"I love the smoke of an old fire."

EPI. Why, she is so cold that no fire can thaw her thoughts.

TOP. It is an old goose, Epi, that will eat no oats; old kine will kick, old rats gnaw cheese, and old sacks will have [40 much patching. I prefer an old cony before a rabbit-sucker,[7] and an ancient hen before a young chicken-peeper.

EPI. [*Aside.*] *Argumentum ab antiquitate;*[8] my master loveth antique work.

TOP. Give me a pippin that is withered like an old wife!

EPI. Good, sir.

TOP. Then—*a contrario sequitur argumentum*[9]—give me a wife that looks [50 like an old pippin.

EPI. [*Aside.*] Nothing hath made my master a fool but flat scholarship.

TOP. Knowest thou not that old wine is best?

EPI. Yes.

TOP. And thou knowest that like will be like?

EPI. Ay.

TOP. And thou knowest that Venus [60 loved the best wine?

EPI. So.

TOP. Then I conclude that Venus was an old woman in an old cup of wine, for "*Est Venus in vinis, ignis in igne fuit.*" [10]

---

[1] Body.   [2] Love broth.

[3] Sweet poison.   [5] An unfledged bird.

[4] Sprout.   [6] Virgil, *Æneid*, iv, 23.

[7] An old rabbit before a sucking one.

[8] Argument from antiquity.

[9] From the contrary follows the proof.

[10] Adapted from Ovid, *Ars amat.*, i, 244, meaning, "Love is in wines as surely as fire is [lit., *was*] in fire."

Epi. "*O lepidum caput,*"[1] O madcap master! You were worthy to win Dipsas, were she as old again, for in your love you have worn the nap of your wit quite off and made it threadbare. But soft, who [70 comes here?

[*Enter Samias and Dares.*]

Top. My solicitors.

Sam. All hail, Sir Tophas. How feel you yourself?

Top. Stately in every joint, which the common people term stiffness. Doth Dipsas stoop? Will she yield? Will she bend?

Dar. O, sir, as much as you would wish, for her chin almost toucheth her knees.   80

Epi. Master, she is bent, I warrant you.

Top. What conditions doth she ask?

Sam. She hath vowed she will never love any that hath not a tooth in his head less than she.

Top. How many hath she?

Dar. One.

Epi. That goeth hard, master, for then you must have none.   90

Top. A small request, and agreeable to the gravity of her years. What should a wise man do with his mouth full of bones like a charnel[2]-house? The turtle [3] true hath ne'er a tooth.

Sam. [*Aside to Epiton.*] Thy master is in a notable vein, that will lose his teeth to be like a turtle.

Epi. [*Aside to Samias.*] Let him lose his tongue, too; I care not!   100

Dar. Nay, you must also have no nails, for she long since hath cast hers.

Top. That I yield to. What a quiet life shall Dipsas and I lead when we can neither bite nor scratch! You may see, youths, how age provides for peace.

Sam. [*Aside to Epiton.*] How shall we do to make him leave his love, for we never spake to her?

Dar. [*Aside to Samias.*] Let me [110 alone.—[*To Sir Tophas.*] She is a notable witch, and hath turned her maid Bagoa to an aspen tree, for bewraying her secrets.

Top. I honor her for her cunning, for now when I am weary of walking on two legs, what a pleasure may she do me to turn me to some goodly ass, and help me to four.

Dar. Nay, then I must tell you the troth: her husband, Geron, is come [120 home, who this fifty years hath had her to wife.

Top. What do I hear? Hath she an husband? Go to the sexton and tell him Desire is dead, and will him to dig his grave. O heavens, an husband! What death is agreeable to my fortune?

Sam. Be not desperate, and we will help you to find a young lady.

Top. I love no grissels; [4] they are [130 so brittle they will crack like glass, or so dainty that if they be touched they are straight of the fashion of wax. "*Animus majoribus instat*" [5]—"I desire old matrons." What a sight would it be to embrace one whose hair were as orient as the pearl, whose teeth shall be so pure a watchet [6] that they shall stain the truest turkis,[7] whose nose shall throw more beams from it than the fiery carbuncle, whose eyes [140 shall be environed about with redness exceeding the deepest coral, and whose lips might compare with silver for the paleness! Such a one if you can help me to, I will by piecemeal curtal [8] my affections towards Dipsas, and walk my swelling thoughts till they be cold.

Epi. Wisely provided! How say you, my friends, will you angle for my master's cause?   150

Sam. Most willingly.

Dar. If we speed him not shortly, I will burn my cap. We will serve him of the spades, and dig an old wife out of the grave that shall be answerable to his gravity.

Top. Youths, adieu. He that bringeth me first news, shall possess mine inheritance.
                                          [*Exit.*]

Dar. What, is thy master landed?

Epi. Know you not that my master [160 is *liber tenens*?

Sam. What's that?

---

[1] Terence, *Adelphi,* v, ix, 9: "O fine head!"
[2] Original reads *channel.*
[3] Turtledove.

[4] Griseldas, young girls.
[5] Ovid, *Ars Amat.,* ii, 535.
[6] Pale blue.
[7] Turquoise.
[8] Curtail.

EPI. A freeholder. But I will after him.

SAM. And we to hear what news of Endymion for the conclusion.   *Exeunt.*

SCENA TERTIA.

[The same.]

Panelion, Zontes.

PANEL. Who would have thought that Tellus, being so fair by nature, so honorable by birth, so wise by education, would have entered into a mischief to the gods so odious, to men so detestable, and to her friend so malicious!

ZON. If Bagoa had not bewrayed it, how then should it have come to light? But we see that gold and fair words are of force to corrupt the strongest men, and [10 therefore able to work silly women like wax.

PANEL. I marvel what Cynthia will determine in this cause.

ZON. I fear, as in all causes: hear of it in justice, and then judge of it in mercy; for how can it be that she that is unwilling to punish her deadliest foes with disgrace will revenge injuries of her train with death?   20

PANEL. That old witch, Dipsas, in a rage, having understood her practice to be discovered, turned poor Bagoa to an aspen tree. But let us make haste and bring Tellus before Cynthia, for she was coming out after us.

ZON. Let us go.   *Exeunt.*

*Cynthia, Semele, Floscula, Dipsas, Endym-
ion, Eumenides [,Geron, Pythagoras,
Gyptes, Sir Tophas].*

CYNTH. Dipsas, thy years are not so many as thy vices, yet more in number than commonly nature doth afford or [30 justice should permit. Hast thou almost these fifty years practiced that detested wickedness of witchcraft? Wast thou so simple as for to know the nature of simples of all creatures to be most sinful?

Thou hast threatened to turn my course awry and alter by thy damnable art the government that I now possess by the eternal gods; but know thou, Dipsas, and let all the enchanters know, that Cyn- [40 thia, being placed for light on earth, is also

protected by the powers of heaven. Breathe out thou mayst words; gather thou mayst herbs; find out thou mayst stones agreeable to thine art; yet of no force to appall my heart, in which courage is so rooted, and constant persuasion of the mercy of the gods so grounded, that all thy witchcraft I esteem as weak as the world doth thy case wretched.   50

This noble gentleman, Geron, once thy husband but now thy mortal hate, didst thou procure to live in a desert, almost desperate; Endymion, the flower of my court and the hope of succeeding time, hast thou bewitched by art, before thou wouldest suffer him to flourish by nature.

DIPSAS. Madam, things past may be repented, not recalled. There is nothing so wicked that I have not done, nor [60 anything so wished for as death; yet among all the things that I committed, there is nothing so much tormenteth my rented and ransacked thoughts as that in the prime of my husband's youth I divorced him by my devilish art; for which if to die might be amends, I would not live till tomorrow; if to live and still be more miserable would better content him, I would wish of all creatures to be oldest and [70 ugliest.

GER. Dipsas, thou hast made this difference between me and Endymion, that being both young, thou hast caused me to wake in melancholy, losing the joys of my youth, and him to sleep, not remem'bring youth.

CYNTH. Stay, here cometh Tellus; we shall now know all.

*[Enter Panelion and Zontes, with Corsites
and Tellus.]*

CORS. I would to Cynthia thou [80 couldest make as good an excuse in truth as to me thou hast done by wit.

TELLUS. Truth shall be mine answer, and therefore I will not study for an excuse.

CYNTH. Is it possible, Tellus, that so few years should harbor so many mischiefs? Thy swelling pride have I borne, because it is a thing that beauty maketh blameless, which the more it exceedeth fairness in measure, the more it stretch- [90 eth itself in disdain. Thy devices against Corsites I smile at, for that wits, the sharper they are, the shrewder [1] they are; but this unacquainted [2] and most unnatural practice with a vile enchantress against so noble a gentleman as Endymion I abhor as a thing most malicious, and will revenge as a deed most monstrous.

And as for you, Dipsas, I will send you into the desert amongst wild beasts, [100 and try whether you can cast lions, tigers, boars, and bears into as dead a sleep as you did Endymion, or turn them to trees, as you have done Bagoa. But tell me, Tellus, what was the cause of this cruel part, far unfitting thy sex, in which nothing should be but simpleness, and much disagreeing from thy face, in which nothing seemed to be but softness?

TELLUS. Divine Cynthia, by whom [110 I receive my life and am content to end it, I can neither excuse my fault without lying, nor confess it without shame; yet were it possible that in so heavenly thoughts as yours there could fall such earthly motions as mine, I would then hope, if not to be pardoned without extreme punishment, yet to be heard without great marvel.

CYNTH. Say on, Tellus; I cannot [120 imagine anything that can color such a cruelty.

TELLUS. Endymion, that Endymion, in the prime of his youth, so ravished my heart with love that to obtain my desires I could not find means, nor to recite them, reason.

What was she that favored not Endymion, being young, wise, honorable, and virtuous? Besides, what metal was she [130 made of (be she mortal) that is not affected with the spice, nay, infected with the poison of that not-to-be-expressed, yet always-to-be-felt love, which breaketh the brains and never bruiseth the brow, consumeth the heart and never toucheth the skin, and maketh a deep scar to be seen before any wound at all be felt? My heart, too tender to withstand such a divine fury, yielded to love. Madam, I, [140 not without blushing, confess [I] yielded to love.

CYNTH. A strange effect of love, to work such an extreme hate. How say you, Endymion? All this was for love?

[1] More mischievous.   [2] Unheard of.

END. I say, madam, then the gods send me a woman's hate.

CYNTH. That were as bad, for then by contrary you should never sleep. But on, Tellus; let us hear the end.   150

TELLUS. Feeling a continual burning in all my bowels, and a bursting almost in every vein, I could not smother the inward fire, but it must needs be perceived by the outward smoke; and, by the flying abroad of divers sparks, divers judged of my scalding flames. Endymion, as full of art as wit, marking mine eyes (in which he might see almost his own), my sighs (by which he might ever hear his [160 name sounded), aimed at my heart, in which he was assured his person was imprinted, and by questions wrung out that which was ready to burst out. When he saw the depth of my affections, he sware that mine in respect of his were as fumes to Ætna, valleys to Alps, ants to eagles, and nothing could be compared to my beauty but his love and eternity. Thus drawing a smooth shoe upon a crooked foot, [170 he made me believe that (which all of our sex willingly acknowledge) I was beautiful, and to wonder (which indeed is a thing miraculous) that any of his sex should be faithful.

CYNTH. Endymion, how will you clear yourself?

END. Madam, by mine own accuser.

CYNTH. Well, Tellus, proceed; but [179 briefly, lest, taking delight in uttering thy love, thou offend us with the length of it.

TELLUS. I will, madam, quickly make an end of my love and my tale. Finding continual increase of my tormenting thoughts, and that the enjoying of my love made deeper wounds than the entering into it, I could find no means to ease my grief but to follow Endymion, and continually to have him in the ob- [190 ject of mine eyes who had me slave and subject to his love.

But in the moment that I feared his falsehood and fried myself most in mine affections, I found—ah, grief, even then I lost myself!—I found him in most melancholy and desperate terms, cursing his stars, his state, the earth, the heavens, the world, and all for the love of—

CYNTH. Of whom? Tellus, speak [200 boldly.

TELLUS. Madam, I dare not utter, for fear to offend.

CYNTH. Speak, I say; who dare take offense, if thou be commanded by Cynthia?

TELLUS. For the love of Cynthia.

CYNTH. For my love, Tellus? That were strange. Endymion, is it true?

END. In all things, madam, Tellus doth not speak false.   210

CYNTH. What will this breed to in the end? Well, Endymion, we shall hear all.

TELLUS. I, seeing my hopes turned to mishaps, and a settled dissembling towards me, and an unmovable desire to Cynthia, forgetting both myself and my sex, fell into this unnatural hate; for, knowing your virtues, Cynthia, to be immortal, I could not have an imagination to withdraw him; [1] and, finding mine [220 own affections unquenchable, I could not carry the mind that any else should possess what I had pursued. For, though in majesty, beauty, virtue, and dignity I always humbled and yielded myself to Cynthia, yet in affections I esteemed myself equal with the goddesses; and all other creatures, according to their states, with myself; for stars to their bigness have their lights, and the sun hath no more; [230 and little pitchers, when they can hold no more, are as full as great vessels that run over. Thus, madam, in all truth have I uttered the unhappiness of my love and the cause of my hate, yielding wholly to that divine judgment which never erred for want of wisdom or envied for too much partiality.

CYNTH. How say you, my lords, to this matter? But what say you, En- [240 dymion? Hath Tellus told troth?

END. Madam, in all things but in that she said I loved her and swore to honor her.

CYNTH. Was there such a time whenas for my love thou didst vow thyself to death, and in respect of it loathed thy life? Speak, Endymion; I will not revenge it with hate.

END. The time was, madam, and is, and ever shall be, that I honored [250 your highness above all the world, but to stretch it so far as to call it love I never

[1] Hope to draw him away.

durst. There hath none pleased mine eye but Cynthia, none delighted mine ears but Cynthia, none possessed my heart but Cynthia. I have forsaken all other fortunes to follow Cynthia, and here I stand ready to die, if it please Cynthia. Such a difference hath the gods set between our states that all must be duty, [260 loyalty, and reverence; nothing (without it vouchsafe your highness) be termed love. My unspotted thoughts, my languishing body, my discontented life, let them obtain by princely favor that which to challenge they must not presume, only wishing of impossibilities; with imagination of which I will spend my spirits, and to myself, that no creature may hear, softly call it love; and, if any urge to utter what I [270 whisper, then will I name it honor. From this sweet contemplation if I be not driven. I shall live of all men the most content, taking more pleasure in mine aged thoughts than ever I did in my youthful actions.

CYNTH. Endymion, this honorable respect of thine shall be christened love in thee, and my reward for it, favor. Persevere, Endymion, in loving me, and I account more strength in a true heart [280 than in a walled city. I have labored to win all, and study to keep such as I have won; but those that neither my favor can move to continue constant, nor my offered benefits get to be faithful, the gods shall either reduce to truth, or revenge their treacheries with justice. Endymion, continue as thou hast begun, and thou shalt find that Cynthia shineth not on thee in vain.   [Endymion regains his youth.] [290

END. Your highness hath blessed me, and your words have again restored my youth; methinks I feel my joints strong and these moldy hairs to molt, and all by your virtue, Cynthia, into whose hands the balance that weigheth time and fortune are committed.

CYNTH. What, young again! Then it is pity to punish Tellus.

TELLUS. Ah, Endymion, now I [300 know thee and ask pardon of thee; suffer me still to wish thee well.

END. Tellus, Cynthia must command what she will.

FLOSC. Endymion, I rejoice to see thee in thy former estate.

END. Good Floscula, to thee also am I in my former affections.

EUM. Endymion, the comfort of my life, how am I ravished with a joy match- [310 less, saving only the enjoying of my mistress!

CYNTH. Endymion, you must now tell who Eumenides shrineth for his saint.

END. Semele, madam.

CYNTH. Semele, Eumenides? Is it Semele, the very wasp of all women, whose tongue stingeth as much as an adder's tooth?

EUM. It is Semele, Cynthia, the [320 possessing of whose love must only prolong my life.

CYNTH. Nay, sith Endymion is restored, we will have all parties pleased. Semele, are you content after so long trial of his faith, such rare secrecy, such unspotted love, to take Eumenides? Why speak you not? Not a word?

END. Silence, madam, consents; that is most true.   330

CYNTH. It is true, Endymion. Eumenides, take Semele; take her, I say.

EUM. Humble thanks, madam; now only do I begin to live.

SEM. A hard choice, madam, either to be married if I say nothing, or to lose my tongue if I speak a word. Yet do I rather choose to have my tongue cut out than my heart distempered—I will not have him.

CYNTH. Speaks the parrot? She [340 shall nod hereafter with signs. Cut off her tongue, nay, her head, that, having a servant of honorable birth, honest manners, and true love, will not be persuaded!

SEM. He is no faithful lover, madam, for then would he have asked his mistress.

GER. Had he not been faithful, he had never seen into the fountain, and so lost his friend and mistress.

EUM. Thine own thoughts, sweet [350 Semele, witness against thy words, for what hast thou found in my life but love? And as yet what have I found in my love but bitterness? Madam, pardon Semele, and let my tongue ransom hers.

CYNTH. Thy tongue, Eumenides? What, shouldst thou live wanting a tongue to blaze the beauty of Semele? Well, Semele, I will not command love, for it cannot be enforced; let me entreat it.   360

SEM. I am content your highness shall command, for now only do I think Eumenides faithful, that is willing to lose his tongue for my sake; yet loath, because it should do me better service. Madam, I accept of Eumenides.

CYNTH. I thank you, Semele.

EUM. Ah, happy Eumenides, that hast a friend so faithful and a mistress so fair! With what sudden mischief will the [370 gods daunt this excess of joy? Sweet Semele, I live or die as thou wilt.

CYNTH. What shall become of Tellus? Tellus, you know Endymion is vowed to a service from which death cannot remove him. Corsites casteth still a lovely [1] look towards you. How say you, will you have your Corsites, and so receive pardon for all that is past?

TELLUS. Madam, most willingly.   380

CYNTH. But I cannot tell whether Corsites be agreed.

CORS. Ay, madam, more happy to enjoy Tellus than the monarchy of the world.

EUM. Why, she caused you to be pinched with fairies!

CORS. Ay, but her fairness hath pinched my heart more deeply.

CYNTH. Well, enjoy thy love. But what have you wrought in the castle, [390 Tellus?

TELLUS. Only the picture of Endymion.

CYNTH. Then so much of Endymion as his picture cometh to, possess and play withal.

CORS. Ah, my sweet Tellus, my love shall be as thy beauty is, matchless.

CYNTH. Now it resteth, Dipsas, that if thou wilt forswear that vile art of enchanting, Geron hath promised again to re- [400 ceive thee; otherwise, if thou be wedded to that wickedness, I must and will see it punished to the uttermost.

DIPSAS. Madam, I renounce both substance and shadow of that most horrible and hateful trade, vowing to the gods continual penance, and to your highness obedience.

CYNTH. How say you, Geron? Will you admit her to your wife?   410

GER. Ay, with more joy than I did the first day, for nothing could happen to make me happy but only her forsaking

[1] Loving.

that lewd [1] and detestable course. Dipsas, I embrace thee.

DIPSAS. And I thee, Geron, to whom I will hereafter recite the cause of these my first follies.

CYNTH. Well, Endymion, nothing resteth now but that we depart. Thou hast my favor; Tellus her friend; Eumenides [421 in paradise with his Semele; Geron contented with Dipsas.

TOP. Nay, soft; I cannot handsomely go to bed without Bagoa.

CYNTH. Well, Sir Tophas, it may be there are more virtues in me than myself knoweth of, for Endymion I awaked, and at my words he waxed young. I will try whether I can turn this tree again to [430 thy true love.

TOP. Turn her to a true love or false, so she be a wench I care not.

CYNTH. Bagoa, Cynthia putteth an end to thy hard fortunes; for, being turned to a tree for revealing a truth, I will recover thee again, if in my power be the effect of truth.　[Bagoa recovers human shape.]

TOP. Bagoa, a bots [2] upon thee!

CYNTH. Come, my lords, let us in. [440 You, Gyptes and Pythagoras, if you can content yourselves in our court, to fall from vain follies of philosophers to such virtues as are here practiced, you shall be entertained according to your deserts, for Cynthia is no stepmother to strangers.

¹ Base.　　　　　　　² Worms.

PYTHAG. I had rather in Cynthia's court spend ten years than in Greece one hour.

GYPTES. And I choose rather to [450 live by the sight of Cynthia than by the possessing of all Egypt.

CYNTH. Then follow.

EUM. We all attend.　　　　　　Exeunt.

FINIS.

THE EPILOGUE

A MAN walking abroad, the Wind and Sun strove for sovereignty, the one with his blast, the other with his beams. The Wind blew hard; the man wrapped his garment about him harder. It blustered more strongly; he then girt it fast to him. "I cannot prevail," said the Wind. The Sun, casting her crystal beams, began to warm the man; he unloosed his gown. Yet it shined brighter; he then put it [10 off. "I yield," said the Wind, "for, if thou continue shining, he will also put off his coat."

Dread sovereign, the malicious that seek to overthrow us with threats do but stiffen our thoughts and make them sturdier in storms; but, if your highness vouchsafe with your favorable beams to glance upon us, we shall not only stoop, but with all humility lay both our hands and [20 hearts at your majesty's feet.

GEORGE PEELE

George Peele was born about 1558, and was educated at the grammar school of Christ's Hospital, of which his father James Peele, a maker of pageants, was clerk, and at Oxford, where he proceeded B.A. in 1577 and M.A. in 1579. When he returned to Oxford on business in 1583, two years after his departure for London, he was called upon to manage the performance of two Latin plays by William Gager for the entertainment of Alasco, a Polish prince, and in two sets of Latin elegiacs Gager commended Peele as wit and poet. The rest of his life was apparently spent in literary work in London among such friends as Greene, Lodge, Nashe, and Watson. Like other convivial spirits among the literary men of the time, Peele seems to have been given to excesses. These probably hastened his end, and were no doubt responsible for the ascription to him of a series of escapades and sayings, chiefly fabulous in all likelihood, which furnished material for the *Jests of George Peele*, published about 1605. He was buried in the Parish of St. James, Clerkenwell, November 9, 1596.

Peele's extant work is predominantly dramatic. His first play, *The Arraignment of Paris*, was prepared for boys and acted before Elizabeth. Its poetic fancy, like the wit and conceit of Lyly's prose dialogue, made its appeal to courtly taste. Nashe in the preface to Greene's *Menaphon* (1589) declares that it reveals the "pregnant dexterity of wit and manifold variety of invention" of Peele, whom he calls the great maker of phrases (*"primum verborum artifex"*). Peele was soon writing for the companies of professional players, and had his share, with other University Wits, in transforming the crude popular drama of the London stage into literary drama. His great contribution lay in his poetic diction, but with his fellows he experimented in the various types of plays in vogue between 1585 and 1595. In addition to the two plays reprinted here, Peele wrote the crude chronicle play of *King Edward the First*, published in mutilated form in 1593 and 1599; *The Battle of Alcazar*, which, although it was published anonymously in 1594, is generally recognized as Peele's from internal evidence and from the fact that six lines from it were printed as his in *England's Parnassus* (1600); and *The Love of King David and Fair Bethsabe*, published in 1599, regarding the merit of whose ornate verse there is a wide range of opinion. He also wrote several plays now lost and verse for London pageants.

The masque-like pastoral, *The Arraignment of Paris*, often considered Peele's best play, was published anonymously, and apparently without entry in the Stationers' Register, by Henry Marsh in 1584. Its authorship is established by Nashe's allusion in the preface to *Menaphon* and by the attribution of two of its songs to Peele in *England's Parnassus*. From the Greek myth of Paris' award of the golden apple, used by Udall to flatter Anne Boleyn, Peele fashioned an elaborate compliment to her daughter Elizabeth. No specific source has been found for the play, but Peele followed pastoral traditions. He is indebted to Spenser's *Shepherd's Calendar* for the names of the shepherds, and, as Miss Jeffrey has shown, to Paulilli's *Il Giuditio di Paride* for many conventional devices. The present text is based on the Malone Society reprint prepared by Child.

The Old Wives' Tale was entered in the Stationers' Register, April 16, 1595, and printed by John Danter the same year. The identification of the initials "G. P." on the title-page as those of George Peele, which was made by Herbert in *Typographical Antiquities*, has never been challenged. The date of composition is usually thought to lie between 1590 and 1593, but recently Larsen has argued for a date between January, 1593, and May, 1594. The play is essentially a medley of motives and incidents drawn from folk tales. Thus the main incident of the pursuit of Delia and her rescue from the conjuror gives the earliest extant version of a tale found also in a section of Christopher Middleton's *Chinon of England* (1597) and in Milton's *Comus*. All three are modified forms of the folk tale *Childe Rowland*, in which the youngest of three brothers rescues his sister from the elf king after the other two have failed. In the play the successful brother is replaced by a suitor and his helper, who come from a tale of "The Lady and the Monster" type. Peele probably followed some form of it closely, for the main incidents and most of the details of the Eumenides plot appear in one version or another of a modern folk tale which is best known as one of the components of *Jack the Giant Killer*. A stock motive in the tale of this type is that of "The Grateful Dead," which Peele used in its most conventional form—the ghostly helper exacting a promise of half the hero's gains and as a test of loyalty demanding that the rescued lady be cut in two. In this form the motive is found, much earlier than the play, in *Oliver of Castile*, translated from French and printed in England in 1518. Still another folk tale introduced into the play is *The Three Heads of the Well*, with its contrasted sisters, which is linked to the main thread by the marriage of the sisters to two who have failed in the quest for Delia. While Peele possibly found many of these various incidents already combined in some folk tale which he followed, evidently he made modifications in details. For instance, the contrast between the husbands of the two sisters in *The Three Heads of the Well* has been subordinated in the play to the treatment of them as stock comic figures, one a clown and the other a braggart. Though the induction, as in *The Taming of the Shrew* and *The Knight of the Burning Pestle*, satirizes the taste of the audience, its primary purpose here is to indicate the source of the material in folk tale. The name Sacrapant and some of the lines in the play came from Greene's *Orlando Furioso*, derived from Ariosto. The present text is based on W. W. Greg's reprint for the Malone Society.

THE ARRAIGNMENT OF PARIS[1]

[BY

GEORGE PEELE

DRAMATIS PERSONÆ

SATURN	JUNO
JUPITER	PALLAS
NEPTUNE	VENUS
PLUTO	DIANA
APOLLO	POMONA
MARS	FLORA
BACCHUS	RHANIS
MERCURY	ATE
VULCAN	CLOTHO
PAN	LACHESIS
FAUNUS	ATROPOS
SILVANUS	THE MUSES
PARIS	A NYMPH OF DIANA
COLIN	ŒNONE
HOBBINOL	HELEN
DIGGON	THESTYLIS
THENOT	

CUPIDS, CYCLOPS, SHEPHERDS, KNIGHTS, A
CHURL, etc.

SCENE: *A vale in Ida.*

TIME: *Mythical.*]

Ate, Prologus.[2]

Condemnéd soul, Ate, from lowest hell
And deadly rivers of the infernal Jove,
Where bloodless ghosts in pains of endless
   date
Fill ruthless ears with never-ceasing cries,
Behold, I come in place, and bring beside
The bane of Troy! Behold, the fatal fruit,
Raught[3] from the golden tree of Proser-
   pine!
Proud Troy must fall, so bid the gods
   above,
And stately Ilium's lofty towers be razed
By conquering hands of the victorious
   foe;   10
King Priam's palace waste with flaming fire,
Whose thick and foggy smoke, piercing
   the sky,

Must serve for messenger of sacrifice,
T' appease the anger of the angry heav-
   ens;
And Priam's younger son, the shepherd
   swain,
Paris, th' unhappy organ[4] of the Greeks.
So loath and weary of her heavy load,
The Earth complains unto the hellish
   prince,
Surchargéd with the burden that she
   nill[5] sustain.
Th' unpartial daughters of Necessity   20
Bin aides[6] in her suit; and so the twine
That holds old Priam's house, the thread
   of Troy,
Dame Atropos with knife in sunder cuts.
Done be the pleasure of the powers above,

---

[1] The original title continues: "A Pastoral.
Presented before the Queen's Majesty by the
Children of Her Chapel."
[2] *I.e.*, speaking as Prologue.
[3] Reached, taken.

[4] Provocation (?).
[5] Will not.
[6] Are aids. Such archaisms as these plurals
(with the final -*es* here pronounced as a syllable)
are fairly common throughout the play to represent shepherds' speech.

Whose hests [1] men must obey; and I my
　part
Perform in Ida vales. Lordings, adieu;
Imposing silence for your task, I end,
Till just assembly of the goddesses
Make me begin the tragedy of Troy.
　　　　　　Exit Ate cum aureo pomo. [2]

Act[us] I. Scena i.

[A vale in Ida.] [3]

*Pan, Faunus, and Silvanus, with their At-
tendants, enter to give welcome to the
Goddesses. Pan's Shepherd hath a lamb,
Faunus' Hunter hath a fawn, Silvanus'
Woodman with an oaken bough laden
with acorns.*

Pan incipit. [4]

PAN. Silvanus, either Flora doth us
　wrong
Or Faunus made us tarry all too long,
For by this morning mirth it should
　appear
The Muses or the goddesses be near.
FAUN. My fawn was nimble, Pan, and
　whipped apace—
'Twas happy that we caught him up
　at last—
The fattest, fairest fawn in all the chase;
I wonder how the knave could skip so
　fast.
PAN. And I have brought a twagger for
　the nonce, [5]
A bunting [6] lamb; nay, pray, you feel
　no bones.　　　　　　　　　　　10
Believe me now, my cunning much I
　miss
If ever Pan felt fatter lamb than this.
SIL. Sirs, you may boast your flocks and
　herds that bin both fresh and fair,
Yet hath Silvanus walks, [7] iwis, [8] that
　stand in wholesome air;
And, lo, the honor of the woods, the
　gallant oaken bough,
Do I bestow, laden with acorns and with
　mast enow! [9]

PAN. Peace, man, for shame! Shalt have
　both lambs and dams and flocks and
　herds and all,
And all my pipes to make the[e] glee;
　we meet not now to brawl.
FAUN. There's no such matter, Pan! We
　are all friends assembled hether, [10]
To bid Queen Juno and her feres [11]
　most humbly welcome hether.　　20
Diana, mistress of our woods, her pres-
　ence will not want; [12]
Her courtesy to all her friends, we wot, [13]
　is nothing scant.

Act[us] I. Scena ii.

*Pomona entereth with her fruit. Manenti-
bus Pan cum reliquis.* [14]

POM. Yea, Pan, no farther yet, and had
　the start of me?
Why, then, Pomona with her fruit comes
　time enough, I see.
Come on awhile; with country store,
　like friends, we venter [15] forth.
Thinkest, Faunus, that these goddesses
　will take our gifts in worth? [16]
FAUN. Yea, doubtless, for shall tell thee,
　dame, 'twere better give a thing,
A sign of love, unto a mighty person or
　a king,
Than to a rude and barbarous swain,
　but bad and basely born;
For gently takes the gentleman that [17]
　oft the clown will scorn.
PAN. Say'st truly, Faunus. I myself
　have given good tidy [18] lambs
To Mercury—may say to thee—to Phœ-
　bus, and to Jove,　　　　　　　10
When to a country mops, [19] forsooth,
　chave [20] offered all their dams,
And piped and prayed for little worth,
　and ranged about the grove.
POM. God Pan, that makes your flock so
　thin, and makes you look so lean,
To kiss in corners.

---

[1] Behests, commands.
[2] Ate goes out with the golden apple.
[3] The setting is the same throughout the play.
[4] Pan begins.
[5] A male lamb for the occasion.
[6] With budding horns.　　　[8] Certainly.
[7] Tracts of forest.　　　　[9] Nuts enough.

[10] Hither.　　　　　　　　[12] Be lacking.
[11] Companions.　　　　　　[13] Know.
[14] Pan with the others remaining.
[15] Venture.
[16] "In good part" (Bullen).
[17] That which.
[18] Plump; fit for sacrifice.
[19] Wench, from Mopsa, a common name for a
shepherdess or a rustic girl.
[20] Dialect for *ich have*, I have.

PAN.   Well said, wench! Some other
thing you mean.
POM. Yea, jest it out till it go alone; but
marvel where we miss
Fair Flora all this merry morn.
FAUN.   Some news; see where she is.

ACT[US] I. SCENA iii.

Flora entereth to the country gods.

PAN. Flora, well met, and for thy taken
pain,
Poor country gods, thy debtors we re-
main.
FLO. Believe me, Pan, not all thy lambs
and yoes,[1]
Nor, Faunus, all thy lusty bucks and
does
(But that I am instructed well to know
What service to the hills and dales I
owe)
Could have enforced me to so strange a
toil,
Thus to enrich this gaudy, gallant [2] soil.
FAUN. But tell me, wench, hast done't
so trick [3] indeed
That heaven itself may wonder at the
deed?   10
FLO. Not Iris, in her pride and bravery,[4]
Adorns her arch [5] with such variety,
Nor doth the milk-white way in frosty
night
Appear so fair and beautiful in sight
As done [6] these fields and groves and
sweetest bowers,
Bestrewed and decked with parti-colored
flowers.
Along the bubbling brooks and silver
glide [7]
That at the bottom doth in silence
slide,
The watery flowers and lilies on the
banks,
Like blazing comets, burgeon all in
ranks;   20
Under the hawthorn and the poplar
tree,
Where sacred Phœbe may delight to be,
The primrose and the purple hyacinth,
The dainty violet and the wholesome
minth,[8]

The double daisy and the cowslip, queen
Of summer flowers, do overpeer the
green;
And round about the valley as ye pass,
Ye may ne [9] see for peeping flowers the
grass—
That [10] well the mighty Juno and the
rest   29
May boldly think to be a welcome guest
On Ida hills, when to approve the thing
The Queen of Flowers prepares a second
spring.
SIL. Thou gentle nymph, what thanks
shall we repay
To thee that makest our fields and
woods so gay?
FLO. Silvanus, when it is thy hap to see,
My workmanship in portraying all the
three—
First stately Juno with her port and
grace,
Her robes, her lawns, her crownet,[11] and
her mace—
Would make thee muse [12] this picture
to behold
Of yellow oxlips bright as burnished
gold.   40
POM. A rare device; and Flora well, perdy,[13]
Did paint her yellow for her jealousy.
FLO. Pallas in flowers of hue and colors
red,
Her plumes, her helm, her lance, her
Gorgon's head,
Her trailing tresses that hang flaring
round,
Of July flowers so grafféd [14] in the ground
That, trust me, sirs, who did the cun-
ning see,
Would at a blush [15] suppose it to be
she.
PAN. Good Flora, by my flock, 'twere
very good
To dight [16] her all in red resembling
blood.   50
FLO. Fair Venus of sweet violets in blue,
With other flowers infixed for change
of hue;
Her plumes, her pendants, bracelets,
and her rings,
Her dainty fan, and twenty other things,

---

[1] Ewes.   [3] Neatly.
[2] Excellent.   [4] Finery.
[5] Rainbow, personified in Iris.
[6] Do, an archaic plural. [7] Current. [8] Mint.

[9] Not.   [13] *Par Dieu.*
[10] So that.   [14] Grafted.
[11] Coronet.   [15] Glance.
[12] Marvel.   [16] Dress.

Her lusty mantle waving in the wind,
And every part in color and in kind;[1]
And for her wreath of roses, she nill
    dare
With Flora's cunning counterfeit com-
    pare;
So that what living wight shall chance
    to see
These goddesses, each placed in her
    degree,   60
Portrayed by Flora's workmanship alone,
Must say that art and nature met in
    one.

SIL. A dainty draught[2] to lay her down
    in blue,
The color commonly betokening "true."

FLO. This piece of work, compact with
    many a flower,
And well laid in at entrance of the
    bower,
Where Phœbe means to make this meet-
    ing royal,
Have I prepared to welcome them
    withal.

POM. And are they yet dismounted, Flora,
    say,
That we may wend to meet them on
    the way?   70

FLO. That shall not need. They are at
    hand by this,
And the conductor of the train hight[3]
    Rhanis.
Juno hath left her chariot long ago,
And hath returned her peacocks by her
    rainbow,
And bravely, as becomes the wife of
    Jove,
Doth honor by her presence to our
    grove.
Fair Venus she hath let her sparrows
    fly,
To tend on her and make her melody;
Her turtles[4] and her swans unyokéd
    be,
And flicker near her side for company. 80
Pallas hath set her tigers loose to
    feed,
Commanding them to wait when she
    hath need.
And hitherward with proud and stately
    pace,
To do us honor in the sylvan chase,

They march, like to the pomp of heaven
    above,
Juno, the wife and sister of King Jove,
The warlike Pallas, and the Queen of
    Love.

PAN. Pipe, Pan, for joy, and let thy shep-
    herds sing;
Shall never age forget this memorable
    thing.

FLO. Clio, the sagest of the Sisters Nine, 90
To do observance to this dame divine,
Lady of learning and of chivalry,
Is here arrived in fair assembly;[5]
And, wand'ring up and down th' un-
    beaten ways,
Ring through the wood sweet songs of
    Pallas' praise.

POM. Hark, Flora, Faunus! Here is mel-
    ody,
A charm[6] of birds, and more than ordi-
    nary.

An artificial charm of birds being heard
                    within, Pan speaks.

PAN. The silly[7] birds make mirth; then
    should we do them wrong,
Pomona, if we nill bestow an echo to
    their song.   *An echo to their song.*

THE SONG

(A choir within and without.)

GODS. O Ida, O Ida, O Ida, happy hill! 100
This honor done to Ida, may it continue
    still!

MUSES. [*Within.*] Ye country gods that in
    this Ida wone,[8]
Bring down your gifts of welcome,
For honor done to Ida.

GODS. Behold, in sign of joy we sing,
And signs of joyful welcome bring,
For honor done to Ida.

MUSES. [*Within.*] The Muses give you mel-
    ody to gratulate this chance,[9]
And Phœbe, chief of sylvan chase, com-
    mands you all to dance.

GODS. (*Dance.*) Then[10] round in a circle our
    sportance must be;   110
Hold hands in a hornpipe, all gallant in
    glee.

MUSES. [*Within.*] Reverence, reverence,
    most humble reverence!

GODS. Most humble reverence!

---

[1] *I.e.*, suitable and natural.   [3] Is called.
[2] Rare device in painting.   [4] Turtledoves.

[5] Last syllable pronounced as two.   [7] Simple.
[6] Chorus.   [8] Dwell.
[9] To greet this occasion.
[10] Original reads *the*.

Act[us] I. Scena iv.

Pallas, Juno, and Venus enter, Rhanis lead-
ing the way.   Pan alone sings.

THE SONG

The god of shepherds and his mates
With country cheer salutes your states,
Fair, wise, and worthy as you be,
And thank the gracious ladies three
    For honor done to Ida. *The birds sing.*

The song being done, Juno speaks.

JUNO. Venus, what shall I say?   For,
    though I be a dame divine,
This welcome and this melody exceeds
    these wits of mine.
VEN. Believe me, Juno, as I hight the
    Sovereign of Love,
These rare delights in pleasures pass the
    banquets of King Jove.
PAL. Then, Venus, I conclude, it easily
    may be seen   10
That in her chaste and pleasant walks
    fair Phœbe is a queen.
RHA. Divine Pallas, and you sacred
    dames,
Juno and Venus, honored by your
    names,
Juno, the wife and sister of King Jove,
Fair Venus, lady-president of love,
If any entertainment in this place
That can afford but homely, rude, and
    base,
It please your godheads to accept in
    gree,[1]
That gracious thought our happiness
    shall be.
My mistress Dian, this right well I
    know,   20
For love that to this presence she doth
    owe,
Accounts more honor done to her this
    day
Than ever whilom[2] in these woods of
    Ida.
And for our country gods, I dare be
    bold,
They make such cheer, your presence
    to behold,
Such jouissance,[3] such mirth, and merri-
    ment,

As nothing else their mind might more
    content.
And that you do believe it to be so,
Fair goddesses, your lovely looks do
    show.
It rests in fine, for to confirm my talk,   30
Ye deign to pass along to Dian's walk,
Where she among her troop of maids
    attends
The fair arrival of her welcome friends.
FLO. And we will wait with all observ-
    ance due,
And do just honor to this heavenly crew.
PAN. The god of shepherds, Juno, ere thou
    go,
Intends a lamb on thee for to bestow.
FAUN. Faunus, high ranger in Diana's
    chase,
Presents a fawn to Lady Venus' grace.
SIL. Silvanus gives to Pallas' deity   40
This gallant bough raught from the
    oaken tree.
POM. To them that doth this honor to
    our fields
Her mellow apples poor Pomona yields.
JUNO. And, gentle gods, these signs of
    your good will
We take in worth, and shall accept them
    still.
VEN. And, Flora, this to thee among the
    rest:
Thy workmanship comparing with the
    best,
Let it suffice thy cunning to have [pow-
    er][4]
To call King Jove from forth his heavenly
    bower.
Hadst thou a lover, Flora, credit me,   50
I think thou wouldst bedeck him gal-
    lantly.
But wend we on; and, Rhanis, lead the
    way,
That kens the painted paths of pleasant
    Ida.   *Exeunt omnes.*

Act[us] I. Scena v et Ultima.[5]

Paris and Œnone.

PAR. Œnone, while[6] we bin disposed to
    walk,
Tell me what shall be subject of our
    talk.

---

[1] With good will.   [2] Formerly.   [3] Jollity.   [4] Suggested by Dyce.   [5] And last.   [6] Until.

Thou hast a sort [1] of pretty tales in store;
Dare say no nymph in Ida woods hath more.
Again, beside thy sweet alluring face,
In telling them thou hast a special grace.
Then, prithee, sweet, afford some pretty thing,
Some toy that from thy pleasant wit doth spring.

ŒN. Paris, my heart's contentment and my choice,
Use thou thy pipe, and I will use my voice; 10
So shall thy just request not be denied,
And time well spent, and both be satisfied.

PAR. Well, gentle nymph, although thou do me wrong,
That can ne tune my pipe unto a song,
Me list [2] this once, Œnone, for thy sake,
This idle task on me to undertake.

They sit under a tree together.

ŒN. And whereon, then, shall be my roundelay?
For thou hast heard my store long since, dare say: [3]
How Saturn did divide his kingdom tho [4]
To Jove, to Neptune, and to Dis below; 20
How mighty men made foul successless war
Against the gods and state of Jupiter;
How Phorcys' imp, that was so trick and fair,
That tangled Neptune in her golden hair,
Became a Gorgon for her lewd misdeed—
A pretty fable, Paris, for to read,
A piece of cunning, trust me, for the nonce,
That wealth and beauty alter men to stones;
How Salmacis, resembling idleness,
Turns men to women all through wantonness; 30
How Pluto raught Queen Ceres' daughter thence

And what did follow of that love-offense;
Of Daphne turned into the laurel tree,
That shows a mirror of virginity;
Now fair Narcissus, tooting on his shade, [5]
Reproves disdain, and tells how form doth vade; [6]
How cunning Philomela's needle tells
What force in love, what wit in sorrow dwells;
What pains unhappy souls abide in hell,
They say, because on earth they lived not well— 40
Ixion's wheel, proud Tantal's pining woe,
Prometheus' torment, and a many mo; [7]
How Danaus' daughters ply their endless task;
What toil the toil of Sisyphus doth ask.
All these are old and known, I know; yet if thou wilt have any,
Choose some of these, for, trust me, else Œnone hath not many.

PAR. Nay, what thou wilt; but, sith [8] my cunning not compares with thine,
Begin some toy [9] that I can play upon this pipe of mine.

ŒN. There is a pretty sonnet, [10] then— we call it "Cupid's Curse:" 49
"They that do change old love for new, pray gods they change for worse!"
The note is fine and quick withal; the ditty will agree,
Paris, with that same vow of thine upon our poplar tree.

PAR. No better thing; begin it then. Œnone, thou shalt see
Our music figure of [11] the love that grows twixt thee and me.

They sing, and, while Œnone singeth, he pipeth. Incipit Œnone.

ŒN. Fair and fair, and twice so fair,
As fair as any may be,
The fairest shepherd on our green,
A love for any lady.

PAR. Fair and fair, and twice so far,
As fair as any may be, 60
Thy love is fair for thee alone,
And for no other lady.

---

[1] Collection.   [2] It pleases me.
[3] Original has *Fabula* in margin here, and the following thirteen stories are numbered.
[4] Then.

[5] Gazing on his reflection.   [7] More.
[6] Fade, vanish.   [8] Since.
[9] Trifle, here a light musical air.
[10] Song.   [11] Portray.

Œn. My love is fair, my love is gay,
　As fresh as bin the flowers in May,
　And of my love my roundelay,
　My merry, merry, merry roundelay,
　　Concludes with Cupid's curse:
　They that do change old love for new,
　Pray gods they change for worse!
Ambo simul.[1] They that do change, etc. 70
Œn. Fair and fair, etc.
Par. Fair and fair, etc. Thy love is fair,
　etc.

Œn. My love can pipe, my love can sing,
　My love can many a pretty thing,
　And of his lovely praises ring
　My merry, merry roundelays;
　　Amen to Cupid's curse:
　They that do change, etc.
Par. They that do change, etc.
Ambo. Fair and fair, etc. *Finis camenæ.*[2]

The song being ended, they rise, and Œnone
　　　　　　　　　　　　　　　speaks.
Œn. Sweet shepherd, for Œnone's sake
　be cunning[3] in this song,　　　　 81
And keep thy love, and love thy choice,
　or else thou dost her wrong.
Par. My vow is made and witnessèd;
　the poplar will not start,[4]
Nor shall the nymph Œnone's love from
　forth my breathing heart.
I will go bring thee on thy way, my
　flock are here behind,
And I will have a lover's fee; they say,
　"Unkissed, unkind."　　　 *Exeunt ambo.*

Act[us] II. Scena i.

Venus, Juno, Pallas.

Ven. (*Ex abrupto.*[5]) But pray you, tell
　me, Juno, was it so,
As Pallas told me here the tale of Echo?
Jun. She was a nymph indeed, as Pallas
　tells,
　A walker,[6] such as in these thickets
　　dwells;
And as she told what subtle, juggling
　pranks
She played with Juno, so she told her
　thanks:[7]

A tattling trull to come at every call,
And now, forsooth, nor tongue nor life
　at all.
And, though perhaps she was a help to
　Jove,
And held me chat[8] while he might court
　his love,　　　　　　　　　　　 10
Believe me, dames, I am of this opinion,
He took but little pleasure in the minion;
And whatsoe'er his scapes[9] have been
　beside,
Dare say for him, a[10] never strayed so
　wide.
A lovely nut-brown lass or lusty trull
Have power perhaps to make a god a
　bull.
Ven. Gramercy, gentle Juno, for that
　jest;
I'faith, that item was worth all the rest.
Pal. No matter, Venus, howsoe'er you
　scorn,
My father Jove at that time ware the
　horn.[11]　　　　　　　　　　　 20
Jun. Had every wanton god above, Venus,
　not better luck,
Then heaven would be a pleasant park,
　and Mars a lusty buck.
Ven. Tut, Mars hath horns to butt withal,
　although no bull a shows.
A never needs to mask in nets; a fears
　no jealous froes.[12]
Jun. Forsooth the better is his turn, for,
　if a speak too loud,
Must find some shift to shadow him, a
　net or else a cloud.
Pal. No more of this, fair goddesses; un-
　rip not so your shames,
To stand all naked to the world, that
　been such heavenly dames.
Jun. Nay, Pallas, that's a common trick
　with Venus, well we know;
And all the gods in heaven have seen her
　naked long ago.　　　　　　　 30
Ven. And then she was so fair and bright,
　and lovely and so trim,
As Mars is but for Venus' tooth,[13] and
　she will sport with him.
And, but me list not here to make com-
　parison with Jove,
Mars is no ranger, Juno, he, in every
　open grove.

[1] Both together.
[2] The end of the song.
[3] Skillful, expert.
[4] *I.e.*, tremble in token of a false vow.
[5] Abruptly.
[6] Forest-dweller.
[7] An ironical phrase for *dismissed her.*

[8] In conversation.　　[9] Escapades.　　[10] He.
[11] Wore the horn—the proverbial sign of the
cuckold.　　[12] Women.　　[13] Taste, pleasure.

PAL. Too much of this! We wander far;
   the skies begin to scowl.
Retire we to Diana's bower; the weather
   will be foul.
The storm being past of thunder and light-
   ning, and Ate having trundled the ball
   into place, crying, "Fatum Trojæ," [1]
   Juno taketh the ball up and speaketh.
JUN. Pallas, the storm is past and gone,
   and Phœbus clears the skies,
And, lo, behold a ball of gold, a fair and
   worthy prize!
VEN. [*Reading.*] This posy [2] wills the ap-
   ple to the fairest given be;
Then is it mine, for Venus hight the
   fairest of the three.   40
PAL. The fairest here, as fair is meant,
   am I; ye do me wrong;
And, if the fairest have it must, to me it
   doth belong.
JUN. Then Juno may it not enjoy, so
   everyone says no;
But I will prove myself the fairest, ere
   I lose it so.   *They read the posy.*
The brief [3] is this, *Detur pulcherrimæ*—
Let this unto the fairest given be,
The fairest of the three—and I am she.
PAL. (*Reads.*) *Detur pulcherrimæ*—
Let this unto the fairest given be,
The fairest of the three—and I am she. 50
VEN. (*Reads.*) *Detur pulcherrimæ*—
Let this unto the fairest given be,
The fairest of the three—and I am
   she.
JUN. My face is fair; but yet the majesty
That all the gods in heaven have seen
   in me
Have made them choose me of the
   planets seven
To be the wife of Jove and Queen of
   Heaven;
If then this prize be but bequeathed to
   beauty,
The only she that wins this prize am I.
VEN. That Venus is the fairest, this doth
   prove: 60
That Venus is the lovely Queen of Love.
The name of Venus is indeed but beauty,
And men me fairest call per excellency; [4]
If then this prize be but bequeathed to
   beauty,
The only she that wins this prize am I.

PAL. To stand on terms of beauty as you
   take it,
Believe me, ladies, is but to mistake it.
The beauty that this subtle prize must
   win,
No outward beauty hight, but dwells
   within;
And sift it as you please, and you shall
   find   70
This beauty is the beauty of the mind.
This fairness, Virtue hight in general,
That many branches hath in special;
This beauty Wisdom hight, whereof am I
By heaven appointed goddess worthily.
And look, how much the mind, the bet-
   ter part,
Doth overpass the body in desert, [5]
So much the mistress of those gifts di-
   vine
Excels thy beauty, and that state of
   thine.
Then, if this prize be thus bequeathed
   to beauty,   80
The only she that wins this prize am I.
VEN. Nay, Pallas, by your leave you
   wander clean.
We must not conster [6] hereof as you
   mean,
But take the sense as it is plainly meant;
And let the fairest ha't, I am content.
PAL. Our reasons will be infinite, I trow,
Unless unto some other point we grow.
But first here's none, methinks, dis-
   posed to yield,
And none but will with words maintain
   the field.
JUN. Then, if you will, to avoid a tedious
   grudge,   90
Refer it to the sentence of a judge;
Whoe'er he be that cometh next in place,
Let him bestow the ball and end the
   case.
VEN. So can it not go wrong with me at
   all. [7]
PAL. I am agreed, however it befall.
And yet by common doom, [8] so may it
   be,
I may be said the fairest of the three.
JUN. Then yonder, lo, that shepherd swain
   is he,
That must be umpire in this controversy!

---

[1] The fate of Troy.   [3] Writing.
[2] Inscription.   [4] Above all.

[5] Pronounced *desart*.   [6] Construe.
[7] Emended by Dyce. Original reads *not at all.*
[8] Judgment.

ACT[US] II. SCENA ii.

Paris alone. Manentibus Pal[lade], Junone,
Venere.

VEN. Juno, in happy time, I do accept
the man;
  It seemeth by his looks some skill of
love he can.[1]
PAR. [*Aside.*] The nymph is gone, and I,
all solitary,
  Must wend to tend my charge, oppressed
with melancholy.
  This day (or else me fails my shepherd's
skill)
  Will tide [2] me passing good or passing ill.
JUN. Shepherd, abash not, though at sud-
den thus
  Thou be arrived by ignorance among us,
  Not earthly but divine, and goddesses
all three;
  Juno, Pallas, Venus, these our titles be. 10
  Nor fear to speak for reverence of the
place,
  Chosen to end a hard and doubtful case.
  This apple, lo (nor ask thou whence it
came),
  Is to be given unto the fairest dame.
  And fairest is, nor she, nor she, but she
  Whom, shepherd, thou shalt fairest name
to be.
  This is thy charge; fulfill without of-
fense,
  And she that wins shall give thee recom-
pense.
PAL. Dread not to speak, for we have
chosen thee,
  Sith in this case we can no judges be. 20
VEN. And, shepherd, say that I the fair-
est am,
  And thou shalt win good guerdon for
the same.
JUN. Nay, shepherd, look upon my stately
grace,
  Because the pomp that longs [3] to Juno's
mace
  Thou mayst not see; and think Queen
Juno's name,
  To whom old shepherds title works of
fame,[4]
  Is mighty, and may easily suffice,
  At Phœbus' hand, to gain a golden prize.

And for thy meed, sith I am queen of
riches,
  Shepherd, I will reward thee with great
monarchies, 30
  Empires, and kingdoms, heaps of massy
gold,
  Scepters and diadems curious to behold,
  Rich robes, of sumptuous workman-
ship and cost,
  And thousand things whereof I make
no boast.
  The mold whereon thou treadest shall
be of Tagus' sands,
  And Xanthus shall run liquid gold for
thee to wash thy hands;
  And, if thou like to tend thy flock, and
not from them to fly,
  Their fleeces shall be curléd gold to
please their master's eye.
  And last, to set thy heart on fire, give
this one fruit to me,
  And, shepherd, lo, this tree of gold will
I bestow on thee! 40

JUNO'S SHOW

Hereupon did rise a tree of gold, laden
with diadems and crowns of gold.

The ground whereon it grows, the grass,
the root of gold,
  The body and the bark of gold, all
glist'ring to behold,
  The leaves of burnished gold, the fruits
that thereon grow
  Are diadems set with pearl in gold, in
gorgeous glist'ring show:
  And, if this tree of gold in lieu may not
suffice,
  Require a grove of golden trees, so Juno
bear the prize. *The tree sinketh.*
PAL. Me list not tempt thee with decaying
wealth,
  Which is embased by want of lusty
health;
  But, if thou have a mind to fly above,
  Ycrowned [5] with fame, near to the seat
of Jove, 50
  If thou aspire to wisdom's worthiness,
  Whereof thou mayst not see the bright-
ness,
  If thou desire honor of chivalry,
  To be renowned for happy victory,
  To fight it out, and in the champaign [6]
field

---

[1] Knows. [2] Betide, befall. [3] Belongs.
[4] *I.e.*, to whom old poets address famous
works.

[5] Old form of the past participle. [6] Open.

To shroud thee under Pallas' warlike
　shield,
To prance on barbéd steeds—this honor,
　lo,
Myself for guerdon shall on thee bestow!
And for encouragement, that thou mayst
　see
What famous knights Dame Pallas'
　warriors be,　　　　　　　　　60
Behold in Pallas' honor here they come,
Marching along with sound of thund'-
　ring drum.

Pallas' Show

Hereupon did enter nine Knights in armor,
*　treading a warlike almain,[1] by drum and*
*　fife, and then having marched forth again,*
*　　　　　　Venus speaketh.*

Ven. Come, shepherd, come, sweet shep-
　herd, look on me;
These been too hot alarums,[2] these, for
　thee.
But, if thou wilt give me the golden
　ball,
Cupid my boy shall ha't to play withal,
That, whensoe'er this apple he shall see,
The God of Love himself shall think
　on thee,
And bid thee look and choose, and he
　will wound
Whereso thy fancy's[3] object shall be
　found;　　　　　　　　　70
And lightly when he shoots he doth
　not miss.
And I will give thee many a lovely kiss,
And come and play with thee on Ida
　here;
And, if thou wilt a face that hath no peer,
A gallant girl, a lusty minion trull,
That can give sport to thee thy belly-
　ful,
To ravish all thy beating veins with
　joy,
Here is a lass of Venus' court, my boy,

Helen ent'reth with four Cupids.

Here, gentle shepherd, here's for thee
　a piece,
The fairest face, the flower of gallant
　Greece.　　　　　　　　　80

---

[1] Dance.　　　[2] Calls to arms.　　　[3] Love's.

Here Helen ent'reth in her bravery, with four
*　Cupids attending on her, each having his*
*　fan in his hand to fan fresh air in her*
*　　face. She singeth as followeth:*

Se Diana nel cielo è una stella,
Chiara e lucente, piena di splendore,
Che porge luc' all' affanato cuore;

Se Diana nel ferno è una dea,
Che da conforto all' anime dannate
Che per amor son morte desperate;

Se Diana, ch' in terra è delle ninfe
Reina imperativa di dolci fiori,
Tra bosch' e selve da morte a pastori;

Io son un Diana dolce e rara,　　　90
Che con li guardi io posso far guerra
A Dian' in fern', in cielo, e in terra.[4] *Exit.*

The song being ended, Helen departeth, and
*　　　　　　Paris speaketh.*

Par. Most heavenly dames, was never
　man as I,
Poor shepherd swain, so happy and un-
　happy;
The least of these delights that you de-
　vise,
Able to rap[5] and dazzle human eyes.
But, since my silence may not pardoned
　be,
And I appoint which is the fairest she,
Pardon, most sacred dames, sith one,
　not all,
By Paris' doom must have this golden
　ball.　　　　　　　　　100
Thy beauty, stately Juno, dame divine,
That like to Phœbus' golden beams doth
　shine,

[4] If Diana is a star in heaven,
bright and shining, full of splendor,
giving light to the grieving heart;

If Diana is a goddess in hell,
who gives comfort to the tormented souls
who on account of love have died in despair;

If Diana, who on earth is of the nymphs
the reigning queen of sweet flowers,
amid woods and groves gives death to shep-
　herds;

I am a Diana gentle and rare,
for with my glances I can make war
upon Diana in hell, in heaven, and on earth.

[5] Affect with rapture.

Approves itself to be most excellent;
But that fair face that doth me most
    content,
Sith fair, fair dames, is neither she nor she,
But she whom I shall fairest deem to be,
That face is hers that hight the Queen
    of Love,
Whose sweetness doth both gods and
    creatures move.

      He giveth the golden ball to Venus.

And, if the fairest face deserve the ball,
Fair Venus, ladies, bears it from ye all.
VEN. And in this ball doth Venus more
    delight   111
Than in her lovely boy fair Cupid's
    sight.
Come, shepherd, come; sweet Venus is
    thy friend,
No matter how thou other gods offend.
Venus taketh Paris with her. Exeunt [ambo].
JUN. But he shall rue and ban the dis-
    mal day
Wherein his Venus bare the ball away;
And heaven and earth just witnesses
    shall be
I will revenge it on his progeny.
PAL. Well, Juno, whether we be lief [1] or
    loath,   119
Venus hath got the apple from us both.
            Exeunt ambo.

Act[us] III. Scena i.

Colin, th' enamored shepherd, singeth his
                passion of love.

THE SONG

O gentle Love, ungentle for thy deed,
    Thou makest my heart
    A bloody mark
With piercing shot to bleed!
Shoot soft, sweet Love, for fear thou shoot
        amiss,
    For fear too keen
    Thy arrows been,
And hit the heart where my beloved is.
Too fair that fortune were, nor never I
    Shall be so blessed,   10
    Among the rest,
That Love shall seize on her by sympathy.
Then since with Love my prayers bear no
    boot,[2]
    This doth remain
    To cease my pain,
I take the wound, and die at Venus' foot.
            Exit Colin.

[1] Willing.   [2] Profit.

Act[us] III. Scena ii.

Hobbinol, Diggon, Thenot.

HOB. Poor Colin, woeful man, thy life
    forespoke [3] by love,
What uncouth [4] fit, what malady, is
    this that thou dost prove? [5]
DIG. Or [6] Love is void of physic clean,
    or Love's our common wrack,
That gives us bane [7] to bring us low,
    and let[s] us medicine lack.
HOB. That ever Love had reverence
    'mong silly shepherd swains!
Belike [8] that humor hurts them most
    that most might be their pains.
THE. Hobbin, it is some other god that
    cherisheth their [9] sheep,
For sure this Love doth nothing else
    but make our herdmen weep.
DIG. And what a hap is this, I pray, when
    all our woods rejoice,
For Colin thus to be denied his young
    and lovely choice!   10
THE. She hight indeed so fresh and fair
    that well it is for thee,
Colin—and kind [10] hath been thy friend—
    that Cupid could not see.
HOB. And whither wends yon thriveless [11]
    swain? Like to the stricken deer,
Seeks he dictamum [12] for his wound with-
    in our forest here?
DIG. He wends to greet the Queen of Love,
    that in these woods doth wone,
With mirthless lays to make complaint
    to Venus of her son.
THE. Ah, Colin, thou art all deceived!
    She dallies with the boy,
And winks at all his wanton pranks,
    and thinks thy love a toy.
HOB. Then leave him to his luckless love;
    let him abide his fate.
The sore is rankled all too far; our com-
    fort comes too late.   20
DIG. Though Thestylis the scorpion be
    that breaks his sweet assault,
Yet will Rhamnusia [13] vengeance take
    on her disdainful fault.

[3] Predetermined.   [6] Either.
[4] Strange.   [7] Poison.
[5] Experience.   [8] Perhaps.
[9] Emended by Dyce. Original reads *her.*
[10] Nature.   [11] Unfortunate.
[12] Dictamnum, a healing herb.
[13] Nemesis.

THE. Lo, yonder comes the lovely nymph, that in these Ida vales
Plays with Amyntas' lusty boy and coys [1] him in the dales!

HOB. Thenot, methinks her cheer is changed; her mirthful looks are laid;
She frolics not. Pray God the lad have not beguiled the maid!

ACT[US] III. SCENA iii.

Œnone ent'reth with a wreath of poplar on her head. Manent Pastores. [2]

ŒN. Beguiled, disdained, and out of love! Live long, thou poplar tree,
And let thy letters grow in length, to witness this with me.
Ah, Venus, but for reverence unto thy sacred name,
To steal a silly maiden's love, I might account it blame!
And, if the tales be true I hear, and blush for to recite,
Thou dost me wrong to leave the plains and dally out of sight.
False Paris, this was not thy vow, when thou and I were one,
To range and change old love for new; but now those days be gone.
But I will find the goddess out, that she thy vow may read,
And fill these woods with my laments for thy unhappy deed.   10

HOB. So fair a face, so foul a thought to harbor in his breast!
Thy hope consumed, poor nymph, thy hap is worse than all the rest.

ŒN. Ah, shepherds, you bin full of wiles, and whet your wits on books,
And rap poor maids with pipes and songs, and sweet alluring looks!

DIG. Misspeak [3] not all for his amiss; [4] there bin that keepen [5] flocks,
That never chose but once, nor yet beguiléd love with mocks.

ŒN. False Paris, he is none of those; his trothless double deed
Will hurt a many shepherds else that might go nigh to speed. [6]

[1] Caresses.
[2] The shepherds remain.
[3] Reproach.
[4] Fault.
[5] Those who keep.
[6] Prosper (in love).

THE. Poor Colin, that is ill for thee, that art as true in trust
To thy sweet smart as to his nymph Paris hath been unjust.   20

ŒN. Ah, well is she hath Colin won, that nill no other love!
And woe is me. My luck is loss, my pains no pity move.

HOB. Farewell, fair nymph, sith he must heal alone that gave the wound;
There grows no herb of such effect upon Dame Nature's ground.

Exeunt Pastores.

[ACTUS III. SCENA iv.]

Manet Œnone.   Mercu[ry] ent'r[eth] with Vulcan's Cyclops. [7]

MER. Here is a nymph that sadly sits, and she belike
Can tell some news, Pyracmon, of the jolly swain we seek.
Dare wage my wings, the lass doth love, she looks so bleak and thin;
And 'tis for anger or for grief—but I will talk begin.

ŒN. [*Aside.*] Break out, poor heart, and make complaint, the mountain flocks to move,
What proud repulse and thankless scorn thou hast received of love.

MER. She singeth; sirs, be hushed awhile.

Œnone singeth as she sits.

ŒNONE'S COMPLAINT

Melpomene, the Muse of tragic songs,
With mournful tunes, in stole of dismal hue,
Assist a silly nymph to wail her woe,   10
And leave thy lusty company behind.

Thou luckless wreath! Becomes not me to wear
The poplar tree for triumph of my love.
Then, as my joy, my pride of love, is left,
Be thou unclothéd of thy lovely green;

And in thy leaves my fortune written be,
And them some gentle wind let blow abroad,
That all the world may see how false of love
False Paris hath to his Œnone been.

The song ended, Œnone sitting still, Mercury speaketh.

MER. Good day, fair maid; weary belike with following of your game,   20
I wish thee cunning at thy will, to spare or strike the same.

[7] Used in this play for both singular and plural.

Œn. I thank you, sir; my game is quick,[1]
and rids [2] a length of ground,
And yet I am deceived, or else a had a
deadly wound.
Mer. Your hand perhaps did swarve [3]
awry.
Œn. Or else it was my heart.
Mer. Then sure a plied his footmanship.
Œn. A played a ranging part.
Mer. You should have given a deeper
wound.
Œn. I could not that for pity.
Mer. You should have eyed him better,
then.
Œn. Blind Love was not so witty.
Mer. Why, tell me, sweet, are you in love?
Œn. O,[4] would I were not so!
Mer. Ye mean because a does ye wrong?
Œn. Perdy, the more my woe.
Mer. Why, mean ye Love, or him ye
loved?
Œn. Well may I mean them both. 30
Mer. Is Love to blame?
Œn. The Queen of Love hath
made him false his troth.[5]
Mer. Mean ye, indeed, the Queen of
Love?
Œn. Even wanton Cupid's dame.
Mer. Why, was thy love so lovely then?
Œn. His beauty hight [6] his shame—
The fairest shepherd on our green.
Mer. Is he a shepherd, than? [7]
Œn. And sometime kept a bleating flock.
Mer. Enough, this is the man.
Where wones he, then?
Œn. About these woods, far
from the poplar tree.
Mer. What poplar mean ye?
Œn. Witness of the vows
betwixt him and me.
And come and wend a little way, and
you shall see his skill.
Mer. Sirs, tarry you.
Œn. Nay, let them go.
Mer. Nay, not unless you will.
Stay, nymph, and hark what I say of
him thou blamest so, 40
And, credit me, I have a sad discourse
to tell thee ere I go.

Know then, my pretty mops, that I
hight Mercury,
The messenger of heaven, and hether
fly,
To seize upon the man whom thou dost
love,
To summon him before my father Jove,
To answer matter of great consequence;
And Jove himself will not be long from
hence.
Œn. Sweet Mercury, and have poor
Œnon's cries
For Paris' fault ypierced th' unpartial
skies?
Mer. The same is he, that jolly shep-
herd's swain. 50
Œn. His flock do graze upon Aurora's
plain;
The color of his coat is lusty green;
That would these eyes of mine had never
seen
His ticing [8] curléd hair, his front of
ivory,
Then had not I, poor I, bin unhappy.
Mer. No marvel, wench, although we
cannot find him,
When all-too late [9] the Queen of Heaven
doth mind him.
But, if thou wilt have physic for thy
sore,
Mind him who list, remember thou him
no more;
And find some other game, and get thee
gone; 60
For here will lusty suitors come anon,
Too hot and lusty for thy dying vein,
Such as ne'er wont [10] to make their suits
in vain.
  Exit Mer[cury] cum Cyclop[e].
Œn. I will go sit and pine under the
poplar tree,
And write my answer to his vow, that
every eye may see. *Exit.*

Act[us] III. Scena v.

Venus, Paris, and a company of Shepherds.

Ven. Shepherds, I am content, for this
sweet shepherd's sake,
A strange revenge upon the maid and
her disdain to take.

---

[1] Alive. [2] Traverses. [3] Swerve.
[4] Suggested by Child. Original reads *or.*
[5] Break his promise. [6] Promised, assured.
[7] Then, a common Elizabethan spelling here
retained for the rime.

[8] Enticing.
[9] Very lately.
[10] Suggested by Dyce; original reads *were monte.*

Let Colin's corpse be brought in place,
   and buried [1] in the plain,
And let this be the verse, "The love
   whom Thestylis hath slain."
And, trust me, I will chide my son for
   partiality,
That gave the swain so deep a wound,
   and let her scape him by.
Pasto[r]. Alas, that ever Love was blind,
   to shoot so far amiss!
Ven. Cupid, my son, was more to blame;
   the fault not mine, but his.
Pastores exeunt. Manet Ven[us] cum Pa-
                        r[ide].
Par. O madam, if yourself would deign
   the handling of the bow,
  Albeit it be a task, yourself more skill,
   more justice know.   10
Ven. Sweet shepherd, didst thou ever
   love?
Par.   Lady, a little once.
Ven. And art thou changed?
Par.   Fair Queen of Love,
   I loved not all attonce. [2]
Ven. Well, wanton, wert thou wounded
   so deep as some have been,
  It were a cunning cure to heal, and rue-
   ful to be seen.
Par. But tell me, gracious goddess, for
   a start [3] and false offense
  Hath Venus or her son the power at
   pleasure to dispense? [4]
Ven. My boy, I will instruct thee in a
   piece of poetry
  That haply erst [5] thou hast not heard:
   in hell there is a tree
  Where once a day do sleep the souls of
   false forsworen lovers,
  With open hearts; and thereabout in
   swarms the number hovers   20
Of poor forsaken ghosts, whose wings
   from off this tree do beat
Round drops of fiery Phlegiton to scorch
   false hearts with heat.
This pain did Venus and her son en-
   treat the Prince of Hell
T' impose to such as faithless were to
   such as loved them well.
And therefore this, my lovely boy, fair
   Venus doth advise thee:

---

[1] Emended by Dyce. Original reads *burned.*
[2] At once.
[3] Deviation (from right).
[4] Give dispensation.   [5] Before.

Be true and steadfast in thy love; beware thou do disguise [6] thee,
For he that makes but love a jest, when
   pleaseth him to start,
Shall feel those fiery water drops consume his faithless heart.
Par. Is Venus and her son so full of
   justice and severity?
Ven. Pity it were that love should not
   be linkéd with indifferency.   30
However lovers can exclaim for hard
   success in love,
Trust me, some more than common
   cause that painful hap doth move;
And Cupid's bow is not alone his tri-
   umph, but his rod.
Nor is he only but a boy—he hight a
   mighty god;
And they that do him reverence have
   reason for the same;
His shafts keep heaven and earth in
   awe, and shape rewards for shame.
Par. And hath he reason to maintain why
   Colin died for love?
Ven. Yea, reason good, I warrant thee;
   in right it might behove. [7]
Par. Then be the name of Love adored;
   his bow is full of might,
His wounds are all but for desert, his
   laws are all but right.   40
[Ven.] Well, for this once me list [8] apply
   my speeches to thy sense, [9]
And Thestylis shall feel the pain for
   Love's supposed offense.
The Shepherds bring in Colin's hearse, sing-
                          ing:

Welladay, welladay, poor Colin, thou art
   going to the ground,
  The love whom Thestylis hath slain—
  Hard heart, fair face, fraught with dis-
   dain,
Disdain in love a deadly wound.
  Wound her, sweet Love, so deep again,
  That she may feel the dying pain
  Of this unhappy shepherd's swain,   49
And die for love as Colin died, as Colin died.
                  Finis camenæ.

Ven. Shepherds, abide; let Colin's corpse
   be witness of the pain
  That Thestylis endures in love, a plague
   for her disdain.

---

[6] Alter.   [7] It was needful.   [8] It pleases me.
[9] *I.e.*, adapt my commands to thy judgment.

Behold the organ of our wrath, this
   rusty churl is he;
She dotes on his ill-favored face, so
   much accursed is she.
She singeth an old song called "The Wooing
                of Colman."

A foul, crooked Churl enters, and Thestylis,
   a fair lass, wooeth him. He crabbedly
   refuseth her, and goeth out of place. She
              tarrieth behind.

PAR. Ah, poor unhappy Thestylis, unpitied is thy pain!
VEN. Her fortune not unlike to hers [1]
   whom cruel thou hast slain.
Thestylis singeth, and the Shepherds reply.

THE SONG

[THEST.] The strange affects [2] of my tor-
   mented heart,
   Whom cruel love hath woeful prisoner
      caught,
   Whom cruel hate hath into bondage
      brought,
   Whom wit no way of safe escape hath
      taught,   60
   Enforce me say, in witness of my smart,
   There is no pain to [3] foul disdain in
      hardy suits of love.
SHEP. There is no pain, etc.
THEST. Cruel, farewell.
SHEP. Cruel, farewell.
THEST. Most cruel thou, of all that nature
   framed.
SHEP. Most cruel, etc.
THEST. To kill thy love with thy disdain.
SHEP. To kill thy love with thy disdain.
THEST. Cruel Disdain, so live thou named.
SHEP. Cruel Disdain, etc.   71
THEST. And let me die of Iphis' pain.
SHEP. A life too good for thy disdain.
THEST. Sith this my stars to me allot,
   And thou thy love hast all forgot.
               Exit Thest[ylis].
SHEP. And thou, etc.

The grace of this song is in the Shepherds'
            echo to her verse.
VEN. Now, shepherds, bury Colin's
   corpse, perfume his hearse with flowers,
   And write what justice Venus did amid
   these woods of yours.
     The Shepherds carry out Colin. [4]

How now, how cheers my lovely boy
   after this dump [5] of love?
PAR. Such dumps, sweet lady, as bin
   these are deadly dumps to prove.   80
VEN. Cease, shepherd; there [6] are other
   news after this melancholy.
My mind presumes some tempest toward [7] upon the speech of Mercury.

ACT[US] III. SCENA vi.

Mercury with Vulcan's Cyclops enter. Ma-
   nentibus Ven[ere] cum Par[ide].

MER. Fair Lady Venus, let me pardoned
   be,
That have of long been well-beloved of
   thee,
If, as my office bids, myself first brings
To my sweet madam these unwelcome
   tidings.
VEN. What news, what tidings, gentle
   Mercury,
In middest of my delights to trouble
   me?
MER. At Juno's suit, Pallas assisting her,
Sith both did join in suit to Jupiter,
Action is entered in the court of heaven;
And me, the swiftest of the planets
   seven,   10
With warrant they have thence des-
   patched away
To apprehend and find the man, they
   say,
That gave from them that selfsame ball
   of gold,
Which, I presume, I do in place behold;
Which man, unless my marks be taken
   wide, [8]
Is he that sits so near thy gracious side.
This being so, it rests he go from hence,
Before the gods to answer his offense.
VEN. What tale is this? Doth Juno and
   her mate
Pursue this shepherd with such deadly
   hate,   20
As what was then our general agree-
   ment
To stand unto, they nill be now content?
Let Juno jet, [9] and Pallas play her part;
What here I have, I won it by desert;

---

[1] Emended by Dyce. Original reads *his.*
[2] Feelings; original has *effects.*
[3] Comparable to.
[4] In the original this direction appears immediately after the song.

[5] Mournful song.
[6] Original reads *these.*
[7] Near at hand.
[8] Unless I am wide of the mark.
[9] Strut.

And heaven and earth shall both con-
    founded be,
Ere wrong in this be done to him or me.
MER. This little fruit, if Mercury can
    spell,[1]
Will send, I fear, a world of souls to
    hell.
VEN. What mean these Cyclops, Mercury?
    Is Vulcan waxed so fine,
To send his chimney-sweepers forth to
    fetter any friend of mine?—   30
Abash not, shepherd, at the thing; my-
    self thy bail will be.—
He shall be present at the court of
    Jove, I warrant thee.
MER. Venus, give me your pledge.
VEN.   My ceston,[2] or my fan, or both?
MER. (*Taketh her fan.*) Nay, this shall
    serve, your word to me as sure as is
    your oath,
At Diana's bower! And, lady, if my wit
    or policy
May profit him, for Venus' sake let him
    make bold with Mercury.
                Exit [with the Cyclops].
VEN. Sweet Paris, whereon dost thou
    muse?
PAR. The angry heavens, for this fatal jar,
Name me the instrument of dire and
    deadly war.
Explicit Actus Tertius. Exeunt Venus et
                        Paris.

ACT[US] IV. SCENA i.

Vulcan, following one of Diana's Nymphs.

VUL. Why, nymph, what need ye run so
    fast? What though but black I be?
I have more pretty knacks to please
    than every eye doth see;
And though I go not so upright, and
    though I am a smith,
To make me gracious you may have
    some other thing therewith.

ACT[US] IV. SCENA ii.

Bacchus, Vulcan, Nymph.

BAC. Yea, Vulcan, will ye so indeed?—
    Nay, turn and tell him, trull,
He hath a mistress of his own to take
    his bellyful.

VUL. Why, sir, if Phœbe's dainty nymph
    please lusty Vulcan's tooth,
Why may not Vulcan tread awry as well
    as Venus doth?
NYM. Ye shall not taint your troth for
    me. You wot it very well,
All that be Dian's maids are vowed to
    halter apes [3] in hell.[4]
BAC. I' faith, i' faith, my gentle mops, but
    I do know a cast[5]—
Lead apes who list—that we would help
    t'unhalter them as fast.
NYM. Fie, fie, your skill is wondrous great!
    Had thought the God of Wine
Had tended but his tubs and grapes,
    and not been half so fine.   10
VUL. Gramercy for that quirk, my girl.
BAC.   That's one of dainty's frumps.[6]
NYM. I pray, sir, take't with all amiss;
    our cunning comes by lumps.
VUL. Sh'ath capped his answer in the Q.[7]
NYM.   How says a, has she so?
As well as she that capped your head
    to keep you warm below.
VUL. Yea, then you will be curst,[8] I see.
BAC.   Best let her even alone.
NYM. Yea, gentle gods, and find some
    other string to harp upon.
BAC. Some other string! Agreed, i'faith,
    some other pretty thing;
'Twere shame fair maids should idle
    be. How say you, will ye sing?
NYM. Some rounds or merry roundelays;
    we sing no other songs.
Your melancholic notes not to our
    country mirth belongs.   20
VUL. Here comes a crew will help us
    trim.[9]

ACTUS IV. SCENA iii.

Mercury with the Cyclops.

MER. Yea, now our task is done.
BAC. Then, merry Mercury, more than
    time this round were well begun.
They sing "Hey down, down, down," etc.

The song done, she windeth a horn in Vul-
    can's ear, and runneth out. Manent
    Vulc[an], Bac[chus], Mer[cury], Cyclops.

---

[1] Foretell.   [2] Cestus, girdle.

[3] Emended by Dyce. Original reads *apples.*
[4] Proverbial reward of spinsterhood.
[5] Trick.   [7] Question.
[6] Mocks, sneers.   [8] Shrewish.
[9] Balance the parts (of the song).

Vul. A harlotry,[1] I warrant her!

Bac.   A peevish, elvish shroe![2]

Mer. Have seen as far to come as near,
   for all her ranging so.
But, Bacchus, time well-spent; I wot
   our sacred father Jove
With Phœbus and the God of War are
   met in Dian's grove.

Vul. Then we are here before them yet;
   but stay—the earth doth swell!
God Neptune, too (this hap is good),
   doth meet the Prince of Hell.

Pluto ascendeth from below in his chair;
   Neptune ent'reth at another way.

Plu. What jars are these that call the
   gods of heaven and hell below?

Nep. It is a work of wit and toil to rule
   a lusty shroe.   10

Act[us] IV. Scena iv.

Enter Jupiter, Saturn, Apollo, Mars, Pluto,
Neptune, Bacchus, Vulcan, Mer[cury],
Juno, Pallas, Diana, Cyclops. Jupiter
speaketh.

Jup. Bring forth the man of Troy, that
   he may hear
Whereof he is to be arraignéd here.

Nep. Lo, where a comes, prepared to plead
   his case,
Under conduct of lovely Venus' grace!

[*Enter Venus with Paris.*]

Mer. I have not seen a more alluring boy.

Apol. So beauty hight the wrack of
   Priam's Troy.

The Gods being set in Diana's bower, Juno,
Pallas, Diana, Venus, and Paris stand
on sides before them.

Ven. Lo, sacred Jove, at Juno's proud
   complaint,
As erst I gave my pledge to Mercury,
I bring the man whom he did late at-
   taint,[3]
To answer his indictment orderly;   10
And crave this grace of this immortal
   senate,
That ye allow the man his advocate.

Pal. That may not be; the laws of heaven
   deny
A man to plead or answer by attorney.

Ven. Pallas, thy doom is all too peremptory.

Apol. Venus, that favor is denied him
   flatly:
He is a man, and therefore by our laws,
Himself, without his aid, must plead
   his cause.

Ven. Then bash not,[4] shepherd, in so
   good a case;
And friends thou hast, as well as foes,
   in place.   20

Jun. Why, Mercury, why do ye not in-
   dict him?

Ven. Soft, gentle Juno, I pray you, do
   not bite him.

Jun. Nay, gods, I trow you are like to
   have great silence
Unless this parrot be commanded hence.

Jup.[5] Venus, forbear, be still.—Speak,
   Mercury.

Ven. If Juno jangle, Venus will reply.

Mer. Paris, King Priam's son, thou art
   arraigned of partiality,
Of sentence partial and unjust, for that
   without indifferency,[6]
Beyond desert or merit fair, as thine
   accusers say,
From them to Lady Venus here thou
   gavest the prize away.   30
What is thine answer?

Paris' Oration to the Council of the Gods

[Par.] Sacred and just, thou great and
   dreadful Jove,
And you thrice-reverend powers, whom
   love nor hate
May wrest awry, if this to me, a man,
This fortune fatal[7] be, that I must plead
For safe excusal of my guiltless thought,
The honor more makes my mishap the less
That I, a man, must plead before the
   gods—
Gracious forbearers[8] of the world's
   amiss—
For her, whose beauty how it hath en-
   ticed,   40
This heavenly senate may with me aver.
But sith nor that nor this may do me boot,
And for myself myself must speaker be,
A mortal man amidst this heavenly
   presence,

---

1 "Baggage."   2 Shrew.   3 Accuse, arrest.

4 Be not abashed.   7 Decreed.
5 Original reads *Jov.*   8 Tolerators.
6 Impartiality.

Let me not shape a long defense to them
That been beholders of my guiltless
  thoughts.
Then for the deed that I may not deny,
Wherein consists the full of mine of-
  fense,
I did upon command; if then I erred,
I did no more than to a man belonged. 50
And if, in verdit [1] of their forms divine,
My dazzled eye did swarve or surfeit
  more
On Venus' face than any face of theirs,
It was no partial fault, but fault of his,
Belike, whose eyesight not so perfect
  was
As might discern the brightness of the
  rest.
And, if it were permitted unto men,
Ye gods, to parley with your secret
  thoughts,
There been that sit upon that sacred
  seat
That would with Paris err in Venus'
  praise.   60
But let me cease to speak of error here,
Sith what my hand, the organ of my
  heart,
Did give with good agreement of mine
  eye,
My tongue is void with process to main-
  tain. [2]
PLU. A jolly shepherd, wise and eloquent!
PAR. First, then, arraigned of partiality,
Paris replies, "Unguilty of the fact;" [3]
His reason is, because he knew no more
Fair Venus' ceston than Dame Juno's
  mace,
Nor never saw wise Pallas' crystal
  shield.   70
Then, as I looked, I loved and liked
  attonce,
And, as it was referred from them to
  me,
To give the prize to her whose beauty
  best
My fancy did commend, so did I praise
And judge as might my dazzled eye
  discern.
NEP. A piece of art, that cunningly,
  perdy,
Refers the blame to weakness of his eye.

PAR. Now—for I must add reason for
  my deed—
Why Venus rather pleased me of the
  three: 79
First, in the entrails [4] of my mortal ears,
The question standing upon beauty's
  blaze, [5]
The name of her that hight the Queen
  of Love,
Methought [6] in beauty should not be
  excelled.
Had it been destinéd to majesty—
Yet will I not rob Venus of her grace—
Then stately Juno might have borne
  the ball.
Had it to wisdom been intituléd,
My human wit had given it Pallas then.
But, sith unto the fairest of the three
That power that threw it for my far-
  ther ill   90
Did dedicate this ball, and safest durst
My shepherd's skill adventure, as I
  thought,
To judge of form and beauty rather
  than
Of Juno's state or Pallas' worthiness,
That learned to ken the fairest of the
  flock,
And praiséd beauty but by nature's
  aim,
Behold, to Venus Paris gave this fruit,
A daysman [7] chosen there by full consent;
And heavenly powers should not repent
  their deeds.
Where it is said beyond desert of hers 100
I honored Venus with this golden prize,
Ye gods, alas, what can a mortal man
Discern betwixt the sacred gifts of
  heaven?
Or, if I may with reverence reason thus,
Suppose I gave—and judged corruptly
  then,
For hope of that that best did please
  my thought—
This apple, not for beauty's praise alone,
I might offend, sith I was pardonéd, [8]
And tempted more than ever creature
  was
With wealth, with beauty, and with
  chivalry,   110

---

[4] Turnings.   [5] Blazon, proclamation.
[6] Emended by Dyce.   Original reads *my·
thought*.   [7] Judge.
[8] Released from liability to punishment.

[1] Verdict.
[2] Unable to explain in a detailed story.
[3] Deed.

And so preferred beauty before them all,
The thing that hath enchanted heaven
 itself.
And for the one, contentment is my
 wealth;
A shell of salt will serve a shepherd swain,
A slender banquet in a homely scrip,[1]
And water running from the silver
 spring.
For arms, they dread no foes that sit so
 low;
A thorn [2] can keep the wind from off
 my back;
A sheepcote thatched, a shepherd's
 palace hight.
Of tragic muses shepherds con [3] no
 skill;   120
Enough is them, if Cupid been dis-
 pleased,
To sing his praise on slender oaten pipe.
And thus, thrice-reverend, have I told
 my tale,
And crave the torment of my guiltless
 soul
To be measured by my faultless thought.
If warlike Pallas or the Queen of Heaven
Sue to reverse my sentence by appeal,
Be it as please your majesties divine;
The wrong, the hurt, not mine, if any
 be,
But hers whose beauty claimed the prize
 of me.   130
    Paris having ended, Jupiter speaketh.
JUP. Venus, withdraw your shepherd for
 a space,
Till he again be called for into place.
                    Exeunt Venus et Paris.
Juno, what will ye after this reply,
But doom with sentence of indifferency?
And, if you will but justice in the cause,
The man must quited [4] be by heaven's
 laws.
JUN. Yea, gentle Jove, when Juno's suits
 are moved,
Then heaven may see how well she is
 beloved!
APOL. But, madam, fits it majesty divine
In any sort from justice to decline?   140
PAL. Whether the man be guilty, yea or
 no,
That doth not hinder our appeal, I
 trow.

JUN. Phœbus, I wot, amid this heavenly
 crew,
There be that have to say as well as you.
APOL. And, Juno, I with them, and they
 with me,
In law and right must needfully agree.
PAL. I grant ye may agree, but be content
To doubt upon regard of [5] your agree-
 ment.
PLU. And, if ye marked, the man in his
 defense
Said thereof as a might with rever-
 ence.   150
VUL. And did ye very well, I promise ye.
JUN. No doubt, sir, you could note it
 cunningly.
SAT. Well, Juno, if ye will appeal, ye may;
But first despatch the shepherd hence
 away.
MARS. Then Vulcan's dame is like to have
 the wrong.
JUN. And that in passion [6] doth to Mars
 belong!
JUP. Call Venus and the shepherd in
 again.   [*Exit Mercury.*]
BAC. And rid [7] the man that he may
 know his pain.[8]
APOL. His pain, his pain, his never-dying
 pain,   159
A cause to make a many mo complain.

    Mercury bringeth in Venus and Paris.

JUP. Shepherd, thou hast been heard with
 equity and law,
And, for [9] thy stars do thee to other call-
 ing draw,
We here dismiss thee hence, by order
 of our senate;
Go take thy way to Troy, and there
 abide thy fate.
VEN. Sweet shepherd, with such luck in
 love, while thou dost live,
As may the Queen of Love to any lover
 give!
PAR. My luck is loss, howe'er my love do
 speed.
I fear me Paris shall but rue his deed.
                              Paris exit.
APOL. From Ida woods now wends the
 shepherd's boy,
That in his bosom carries fire to Troy. 170

---

[1] Wallet.   [3] Know, have.
[2] Thorn tree.   [4] Freed.
[5] Hesitate in respect to.   [8] Sentence, fate.
[6] Sorrow.   [9] Because.
[7] Free.

Jup. Venus, these ladies do appeal, you
　　see,
And that they may appeal the gods
　　agree.
It resteth, then, that you be well content
To stand in this unto our final judg-
　　ment;
And, if King Priam's son did well in
　　this,
The law of heaven will not lead amiss.
Ven. But, sacred Jupiter, might thy
　　daughter choose,
She might with reason this appeal re-
　　fuse;
Yet, if they be unmovéd in their shames,
Be it a stain and blemish to their
　　names,　　　　　　　　　　　　　180
A deed too far unworthy of the place,
Unworthy Pallas' lance or Juno's mace;
And, if to beauty it bequeathéd be,
I doubt not but it will return to me.
　　　　　　　　She layeth down the ball.
Pal. Venus, there is no more ado than
　　so;
It resteth where the gods do it bestow.
Nep. But, ladies—under favor of your
　　rage—
Howe'er it be, you play upon the van-
　　tage.[1]
Jup. Then, dames, that we more freely
　　may debate,
And hear th' indifferent sentence of
　　this senate,　　　　　　　　　　190
Withdraw you from this presence for
　　a space,
Till we have throughly questioned of
　　the case.
Dian shall be your guide; nor shall you
　　need
Yourselves t' inquire how things do
　　here succeed;
We will, as we resolve, give you to know,
By general doom how everything doth go.
Dian. Thy will, my wish.—Fair ladies,
　　will ye wend?
Jun. Beshrew her whom this sentence
　　doth offend.
Ven. Now, Jove, be just; and, gods, you
　　that be Venus' friends,
If you have ever done her wrong, then
　　may you make amends.　　　　　200
Manent dii.[2] *Exeunt Diana, Pallas, Juno,*
　　　　　　　　　　　　　　　Venus.

Jup. Venus is fair; Pallas and Juno too.
Vul. But tell me now, without some
　　more ado,
Who is the fairest she, and do not
　　flatter.
Plu. Vulcan, upon comparison hangs all
　　the matter;
That done, the quarrel and the strife
　　were ended.
Mars. Because 'tis known the quarrel
　　is pretended.
Vul. Mars, you have reason for your
　　speech, perdy;
My dame, I trow, is fairest in your
　　eye.
Mars. Or, Vulcan, I should do her double
　　wrong.
Sat. About a toy we tarry here so long. 210
Give it by voices; voices give the
　　odds;
A trifle so to trouble all the gods!
Nep. Believe me, Saturn, be it so for me.
Bac. For me.
Plu. 　　　　　For me.
Mars. 　　　　　　　　For me, if Jove agree.
Mer. And, gentle gods, I am indifferent;
But then I know who's likely to be
　　shent.[3]
Apol. Thrice-reverend gods, and thou,
　　immortal Jove,
If Phœbus may, as him doth much be-
　　hove,
Be licpenséd, according to our laws,
To speak uprightly in this doubted [4]
　　cause　　　　　　　　　　　　220
(Sith women's wits work men's unceas-
　　ing woes)
To make them friends, that now bin
　　friendless foes,
And peace to keep with them, with us,
　　and all,
That make their title to this golden
　　ball—
Nor think, ye gods, my speech doth de-
　　rogate
From sacred power of this immortal
　　senate—
Refer this sentence where it doth be-
　　long.
In this, say I, fair Phœbe hath the
　　wrong;
Not that I mean her beauty bears the
　　prize,　　　　　　　　　　　　229

---

[1] Have the advantage.　　[2] The gods remain.

[3] Reproved.　　　　　　[4] Dreaded.

But that the holy law of heaven denies
One god to meddle in another's power;
And this befell so near Diana's bower
As, for th' appeasing this unpleasant
    grudge,
In my conceit [1] she hight the fittest
    judge.
If Jove comptrol [2] not Pluto's hell with
    charms,
If Mars have sovereign power to man-
    age arms,
If Bacchus bear no rule in Neptune['s]
    sea,
Nor Vulcan's fire doth Saturn's scythe
    obey,
Suppress not then, gainst law and equity,
Diana's power in her own territory,   240
Whose regiment,[3] amid her sacred bow-
    ers,
As proper hight as any rule of yours.
Well may we so wipe all the speech away
That Pallas, Juno, Venus hath to say,
And answer that, by justice of our laws,
We were not suffered to conclude the
    cause.
And this to me most egal [4] doom ap-
    pears—
A woman to be judge among her feres.
MER. Apollo hath found out the only
    mean
To rid the blame from us and trouble
    clean.   250
VUL. We are beholding [5] to his sacred wit.
JUP. I can commend and well allow of it;
And so derive [6] the matter from us all,
That Dian have the giving of the ball.
VUL. So Jove may clearly excuse him in
    the case,
Where Juno else would chide and brawl
    apace.   *All they rise to [7] go forth.*
MER. And now it were some cunning to
    divine
To whom Diana will this prize resign.
VUL. Sufficeth me, it shall be none of
    mine!
BAC. Vulcan, though thou be black,
    th'art nothing fine.   260
VUL. Go bathe thee, Bacchus, in a tub
    of wine;
The ball's as likely to be mine as thine!
Exeunt omnes. Explicit Act[us] Quartus.

[1] Opinion.   [3] Rule.   [5] Beholden, indebted.
[2] Control.   [4] Equal.   [6] Divert.
[7] Emended by Bullen. Original reads *and*

ACT[US] V ET ULTIMI SCENA i.[8]

Diana, Pallas, Juno, Venus.

DIAN. Lo, ladies, far beyond my hope
    and will, you see,
This thankless office is imposed to me;
Wherein, if you will rest as well content
As Dian will be judge indifferent,
My egal doom shall none of you offend,
And of this quarrel make a final end.
And therefore, whether you be lief or
    loath,
Confirm your promise with some sacred
    oath.
PAL. Phœbe, chief mistress of this sylvan
    chase,
Whom gods have chosen to conclude
    the case   10
That yet in balance undecided lies,
Touching bestowing of this golden prize,
I give my promise and mine oath withal,
By Styx, by heaven's power imperial,
By all that longs to Pallas' deity,
Her shield, her lance, ensigns of chivalry,
Her sacred wreath of olive and of bay,
Her crested helm, and else what Pallas
    may,
That wheresoe'er this ball of purest gold,
That chaste Diana here in hand doth
    hold,   20
Unpartially her wisdom shall bestow,
Without mislike or quarrel any mo
Pallas shall rest content and satisfied,
And say the best desert doth there abide.
JUN. And here I promise and protest
    withal,
By Styx, by heaven's power imperial,
By all that longs to Juno's deity,
Her crown, her mace, ensigns of maj-
    esty,
Her spotless marriage rites, her league
    divine,
And by that holy name of Proserpine,   30
That wheresoe'er this ball of purest gold,
That chaste Diana here in hand doth
    hold,
Unpartially her wisdom shall bestow,
Without mislike or quarrel any mo
Juno shall rest content and satisfied,
And say the best desert doth there
    abide.
VEN. And, lovely Phœbe, for I know thy
    doom

[8] The first scene of the fifth and last act.

Will be no other than shall thee become,
Behold, I take thy dainty hand to kiss,
And with my solemn oath confirm my
    promise,   40
By Styx, by Jove's immortal empery,
By Cupid's bow, by Venus' myrtle tree,
By Vulcan's gift, my ceston and my
    fan,
By this red rose, whose color first began
When erst my wanton boy (the more
    his blame)
Did draw his bow awry and hurt his
    dame,
By all the honor and the sacrifice
That from Cithæron and from Paphos
    rise,

The con-	That wheresoe'er,	
clusion	etc.	*ut supra.*[1]
above	Venus shall rest,	
	etc.	

Diana, having taken their oaths, speaketh.
    Diana describeth the nymph Eliza, a
        figure of the queen.[2]
DIAN. It is enough, and, goddesses, at-
    tend: 51
There wones within these pleasant
    shady woods,
Where neither storm nor sun's dis-
    temperature
Have power to hurt by cruel heat or
    cold,
Under the climate of the milder heaven,
Where seldom lights Jove's angry thun-
    derbolt,
For favor of that sovereign earthly
    peer,
Where whistling winds make music
    'mong the trees,
Far from disturbance of our country
    gods,
Amids the cypress-springs, a gracious
    nymph,   60
That honor[s] Dian for her chastity,
And likes the labors well of Phœbe's
    groves.
The place Elysium hight, and of the
    place
Her name that governs there Eliza is—
A kingdom that may well compare with
    mine,
An ancient seat of kings, a second Troy,

Ycompassed round with a commodious
    sea;
Her people are yclepéd [3] *Angeli*,
Or, if I miss, a letter is the most.   69
She giveth laws of justice and of peace;
And on her head, as fits her fortune best,
She wears a wreath of laurel, gold, and
    palm;
Her robes of purple and of scarlet dye;
Her veil of white, as best befits a maid.
Her ancestors live in the House of Fame.
She giveth arms of happy victory,
And flowers to deck her lions crowned
    with gold.
This peerless nymph, whom heaven and
    earth beloves,
This paragon, this only, this is she,   79
In whom do meet so many gifts in one,
On whom our country gods so often
    gaze,
In honor of whose name the Muses
    sing—
In state Queen Juno's peer, for power
    in arms
And virtues of the mind Minerva's mate,
As fair and lovely as the Queen of Love,
As chaste as Dian in her chaste desires.
The same is she, if Phœbe do no wrong,
To whom this ball in merit doth belong.
PAL. If this be she whom some Zabeta
    call,
To whom thy wisdom well bequeaths
    the ball,   90
I can remember, at her day of birth,
How Flora with her flowers strewed the
    earth,
How every power with heavenly maj-
    esty
In person honored that solemnity.
JUN. The lovely Graces were not far
    away;
They threw their balm for triumph [4]
    of the day.
VEN. The Fates, against their kind, be-
    gan a cheerful song,
And vowed her life with favor to prolong.
Then first gan [5] Cupid's eyesight wexen [6]
    dim;
Belike Eliza's beauty blinded him.   100
To this fair nymph, not earthly, but
    divine,
Contents it me my honor to resign.

[1] As above.
[2] Symbol of Queen Elizabeth, who was present at the performance.

[3] Called.
[4] Joy.

[5] Did.
[6] Wax, grow.

PAL. To this fair queen, so beautiful and wise,
Pallas bequeaths her title in the prize.
JUN. To her whom Juno's looks so well become,
The Queen of Heaven yields at Phœbe's [1] doom;
And glad I am Diana found the art,
Without offense so well to please desert.
DIAN. Then mark my tale: the usual time is nigh,
When wont [2] the dames of life and destiny,   110
In robes of cheerful colors, to repair
To this renownéd queen so wise and fair,
With pleasant songs this peerless nymph to greet.
Clotho lays down her distaff at her feet;
And Lachesis doth pull the thread at length;
The third with favor gives it stuff and strength,
And, for [3] contrary kind, affords her leave,
As her best likes, her web of life to weave.
This time we will attend, and in the mean while
With some sweet song the tediousness beguile.   120

The music sound, and the Nymphs within sing or solfa with voices and instruments awhile. Then enter Clotho, Lachesis, and Atropos, singing as follows, the state [4] being in place:

THE SONG

CLOTH. *Humanæ vitæ filum sic volvere Parcæ.*
LACH. *Humanæ vitæ filum sic tendere Parcæ.*
ATRO. *Humanæ vitæ filum sic scindere Parcæ.*
CLOTH. *Clotho colum bajulat.*
LACH.   *Lachesis trahit.*
ATRO.   *Atropos occat.*

---

[1] Emended by Dyce. Original reads *Phœbus.*
[2] Are wont, accustomed.
[3] Probably a misprint for *far. Cf.* l. 152 for the phrase *far indeed contrary kind* (*i.e.*, nature) and also l. 144 for the Latin equivalent.
[4] Chair of state.

TRES SIMUL. *Vive diu, felix votis hominumque deumque,*
Corpore, mente, libro, doctissima, candida, casta. [5]

They lay down their properties at the Queen's feet.

CLOTH. *Clotho colum pedibus,*
LACH. *Lachesis tibi pendula fila,*
ATRO. *Et fatale tuis manibus ferrum Atropos offert.*
[TRES SIMUL.] *Vive diu, felix, etc.* [6]   130

The song being ended, Clotho speaks to the Queen.

CLOTH. Gracious and wise, fair queen of rare renown,
Whom heaven and earth beloves, amid thy train—
Noble and lovely peers—to honor thee
And do thee favor more than may belong
By nature's law to any earthly wight, [7]
Behold continuance of our yearly due.
Th' unpartial dames of destiny, we meet,
As have the gods and we agreed in one,
In reverence of Eliza's noble name;
And humbly, lo, her distaff Clotho yields!   140
LACH. Her spindle Lachesis, and her fatal reel,
Lays down in reverence at Eliza's feet.
Te tamen in terris unam tria numina Divam
Invita statuunt naturæ lege sorores,
Et tibi, non aliis, didicerunt parcere Parcæ. [8]

[5] CLOTH. Thus the Fates spin the thread of human life.
LACH. Thus the Fates measure the thread of human life.
ATRO. Thus the Fates cut the thread of human life.
CLOTH. Clotho bears the distaff.
LACH.   Lachesis measures.
ATRO.   Atropos cuts.
THE THREE TOGETHER. Live long, happy in the prayers of men and gods,
Chaste in body, pure in mind, most skilled in learning.
[6] CLOTH. Clotho [places] the distaff at thy feet,
LACH. Lachesis [gives] thee the pendent threads,
ATRO. And Atropos puts into your hands the fateful shears.
[THE THREE TOGETHER.] Live long, happy, etc.
[7] Person.
[8] The three divine sisters, despite the law of nature, appoint thee a goddess unique, though on earth; and thee and no others have the Fates learned to spare.

Atro. Dame Atropos, according as her
　feres,
　To thee, fair queen, resigns her fatal
　knife.
　Live long the noble phœnix of our age,
　Our fair Eliza, our Zabeta fair!　　149
Dian. And lo, beside this rare solemnity
　And sacrifice these dames are wont to
　do,
　A favor, far indeed contrary kind,
　Bequeathéd is unto thy worthiness—
*She delivereth the ball of gold to the Queen's
own hands.*
　This prize from heaven and heavenly
　goddesses!
　Accept it, then, thy due by Dian's doom,
　Praise of the wisdom, beauty, and the
　state,

　That best becomes thy peerless excel-
　lency.
Ven. So, fair Eliza, Venus doth resign
　The honor of this honor to be thine.
Jun. So is the Queen of Heaven content
　likewise　　160
　To yield to thee her title in the prize.
Pal. So Pallas yields the praise hereof
　to thee,
　For wisdom, princely state, and peerless
　beauty.

Epilogus

Omnes simul. *Vive diu felix, votis homi-
　numque deumque,*
　Corpore, mente, libro, doctissima, candida,
　casta.　　　　　　　*Exeunt omnes.*
　　　　Finis.

THE OLD WIVES' TALE[1]

BY

GEORGE PEELE

[*DRAMATIS PERSONÆ*

SACRAPANT, *the conjurer.*
FIRST BROTHER, *named* CALYPHA.
SECOND BROTHER, *named* THELEA.
EUMENIDES, *the Wandering Knight.*
OLD MAN, *named* ERESTUS.
LAMPRISCUS.
HUANEBANGO.
COREBUS, *or* BOOBY, *the clown.*
WIGGEN.
CHURCHWARDEN, *named* STEVEN LOACH.
SEXTON.
GHOST OF JACK.
FRIAR, HARVESTMEN, *and* HARVESTWOMEN,
   TWO FURIES, *and* FIDDLERS.

DELIA, *sister to Calypha and Thelea.*
VENELIA, *betrothed to Erestus.*
ZANTIPPA, *the Curst* [2] *Daughter of Lampriscus.*
CELANTA, *the Foul Wench, another daughter.*
HOSTESS.
ANTIC
FROLIC
FANTASTIC
A SMITH, *named* CLUNCH   } *Characters of induction and interscenes.*
OLD WOMAN, *his wife, named* MADGE

SCENE: *England.*

TIME: *Mythical.*]

Enter Antic, Frolic, and Fantastic.[3]

ANT. How now, fellow Frolic![4] What, all amort?[5] Doth this sadness become thy madness? What though we have lost our way in the woods, yet never hang the head as though thou hadst no hope to live till tomorrow; for Fantastic and I will warrant thy life tonight for twenty in the hundred.

FROL. Antic and Fantastic, as I am frolic franion,[6] never in all my life was I so dead slain. What, to lose our way in [10 the wood, without either fire or candle, so uncomfortable! *O cælum! O terra!*[7] *O Maria! O Neptune!*

FANT. Why makes thou it so strange, seeing Cupid hath led our young master to the fair lady, and she is the only saint that he hath sworn to serve?

FROL. What resteth[8] then but we commit him to his wench, and each of us take his stand up in a tree, and sing out our [20 ill fortune to the tune of "O man in desperation"?

ANT. Desperately spoken, fellow Frolic, in the dark; but, seeing it falls out thus, let us rehearse the old proverb:

"Three merry men, and three merry men,
  And three merry men be we;
I in the wood, and thou on the ground,
  And Jack sleeps in the tree."

FANT. Hush! A dog in the wood, or [30 a wooden[9] dog! O comfortable hearing! I had even as lief the chamberlain of the White Horse had called me up to bed.

[1] The traditional title of the play is retained, although *wives* was a common possessive singular, and although the original entry in the Stationers' Register for April 16, 1595, reads: "A booke or interlude, intituled a pleasant Conceipte called the owlde wifes tale." The title continues: "A Pleasant Conceited Comedy, Played by the Queen's Majesty's Players. Written by G. P."
[2] Peevish.
[3] In the original there is no scene division or indication of setting. The action represents what Madge and her group visualize.
[4] Original has *Franticke.*
[5] Dejected.   [6] An idle, carefree fellow.
[7] O heaven! O earth!
[8] Remaineth.   [9] Punning on *wood*, mad.

231

FROL. Either hath this trotting cur gone out of his circuit, or else are we near some

Enter a Smith, with a lantern and candle.

village, which should not be far off, for I perceive the glimmering of a glowworm, a candle, or a cat's eye, my life for a half-penny! In the name of my own father, be thou ox or ass that appearest, tell us [40 what thou art.

SMITH. What am I? Why, I am Clunch the smith. What are you? What make [1] you in my territories at this time of the night?

ANT. What do we make, dost thou ask? Why, we make faces for fear, such as, if thy mortal eyes could behold, would make thee water the long seams of thy side slops,[2] smith. 50

FROL. And, in faith, sir, unless your hospitality do relieve us, we are like to wander, with a sorrowful heigh-ho, among the owlets and hobgoblins of the forest. Good Vulcan, for Cupid's sake that hath cozened us all, befriend us as thou mayst; and command us howsoever, wheresoever, whensoever, in whatsoever, for ever and ever.

SMITH. Well, masters, it seems to [60 me you have lost your way in the wood; in consideration whereof, if you will go with Clunch to his cottage, you shall have house-room and a good fire to sit by, although we have no bedding to put you in.

ALL. O blessed smith, O bountiful Clunch!

SMITH. For your further entertainment, it shall be as it may be, so and so.

Hear a dog bark.

Hark! [3] This is Ball, my dog, that [70 bids you all welcome in his own language. Come, take heed for stumbling on the threshold.—Open door, Madge; take in guests.

Enter Old Woman.

OLD WOM. Welcome, Clunch, and good fellows all, that come with my goodman. For my goodman's sake, come on, sit down. Here is a piece of cheese and a pudding of my own making.

ANT. Thanks, gammer; a good ex- [80 ample for the wives of our town.

FROL. Gammer, thou and thy goodman sit lovingly together. We come to chat, and not to eat.

SMITH. Well, masters, if you will eat nothing, take away. Come, what do we to pass away the time? Lay a crab in the fire to roast for lamb's wool.[4] What, shall we have a game at trump or ruff [5] to drive away the time? How say you? 90

FANT. This smith leads a life as merry as a king with Madge his wife. Sirrah Frolic, I am sure thou art not without some round [6] or other; no doubt but Clunch can bear his part.

FROL. Else think you me ill brought up; so set to it when you will. *They sing.*

SONG

Whenas the rye reach to the chin,
And chopcherry, chopcherry ripe [7] within,
Strawberries swimming in the cream, 100
And schoolboys playing in the stream;
Then O, then O, then O, my true love said,
Till that time come again,
She could not live a maid.

ANT. This sport does well, but methinks, gammer, a merry winter's tale would drive away the time trimly. Come, I am sure you are not without a score.

FANT. I' faith, gammer, a tale of an hour long were as good as an hour's sleep. 110

FROL. Look you, gammer, of the giant and the king's daughter, and I know not what. I have seen the day, when I was a little one, you might have drawn me a mile after you with such a discourse.

OLD WOM. Well, since you be so im-portunate, my goodman shall fill the pot and get him to bed. They that ply their work must keep good hours. One of you go lie with him; he is a clean-skinned [120 man, I tell you, without either spavin or windgall. So I am content to drive away the time with an old wives' winter's tale.

FANT. No better hay in Devonshire. O' my word, gammer, I'll be one of your audience.

[4] Ale mixed with the pulp of roasted crab-apples.
[5] Card games. [6] Song.
[7] A game of catching a suspended cherry with the teeth.

[1] Do. [2] Loose breeches.
[3] The scene is now at the cottage.

FROL. And I another, that's flat.

ANT. Then must I to bed with the good-man.—*Bona nox*,[1] gammer. Good night, Frolic. 130

SMITH. Come on, my lad, thou shalt take thy unnatural rest with me.

Exeunt Antic and the Smith.

FROL. Yet this vantage shall we have of them in the morning, to be ready at the sight thereof extempore.

OLD WOM. Now this bargain, my masters, must I make with you, that you will say hum and ha to my tale. So shall I know you are awake.

BOTH. Content, gammer; that will [140 we do.

OLD WOM. Once upon a time, there was a king, or a lord, or a duke, that had a fair daughter, the fairest that ever was, as white as snow and as red as blood; and once upon a time his daughter was stolen away, and he sent all his men to seek out his daughter, and he sent so long that he sent all his men out of his land.

FROL. Who dressed his dinner, then? [150

OLD WOM. Nay, either hear my tale, or kiss my tail.

FANT. Well said! On with your tale, gammer.

OLD WOM. O Lord, I quite forgot! There was a conjurer, and this conjurer could do anything, and he turned himself into a great dragon, and carried the king's daughter away in his mouth to a castle that he made of stone, and there he [160 kept her I know not how long, till at last all the king's men went out so long that her two brothers went to seek her. O, I forget! She—he, I would say—turned a proper young man to a bear in the night, and a man in the day, and keeps [2] by a cross that parts three several ways, and he made his lady run mad.—God's me bones, who comes here?

Enter the Two Brothers.

FROL. Soft, gammer, here some [170 come to tell your tale for you.

FANT. Let them alone; let us hear what they will say.

1 BRO. Upon these chalky cliffs of Albion
We are arrivéd now with tedious toil,

[1] Good night.

[2] Dwells (referring to the young man).

And compassing the wide world round about,
To seek our sister, to seek fair Delia forth,
Yet cannot we so much as hear of her.

2 BRO. O fortune cruel, cruel and unkind!
Unkind in that we cannot find our sister, 180
Our sister, hapless in her cruel chance!
Soft! Who have we here?

Enter Senex [Old Man] at the Cross, stooping to gather.

1 BRO. Now, father, God be your speed! What do you gather there?

OLD MAN. Hips and haws, and sticks and straws, and things that I gather on the ground, my son.

1 BRO. Hips and haws, and sticks and straws! Why, is that all your food, father?

OLD MAN. Yea, son. 190

2 BRO. Father, here is an alms penny for me; and, if I speed in that I go for, I will give thee as good a gown of gray as ever thou diddest wear.

1 BRO. And, father, here is another alms penny for me; and, if I speed in my journey, I will give thee a palmer's staff of ivory and a scallop shell of beaten gold.

OLD MAN. Was she fair?

2 BRO. Ay, the fairest for white, [200
and the purest for red, as the blood of the deer or the driven snow.

OLD MAN. Then hark well, and mark well, my old spell:
Be not afraid of every stranger;
Start not aside at every danger;
Things that seem are not the same;
Blow a blast at every flame;
For, when one flame of fire goes out,
Then comes your wishes well about.
If any ask who told you this good, 210
Say the white bear of England's wood.

1 BRO. Brother, heard you not what the old man said?
"Be not afraid of every stranger;
Start not aside for every danger;
Things that seem are not the same;
Blow a blast at every flame;
[For, when one flame of fire goes out,
Then comes your wishes well about.]
If any ask who told you this good,
Say the white bear of England's wood." 220

2 BRO. Well, if this do us any good,

Well fare the white bear of England's
    wood!   *Ex[eunt the Two Brothers]*.
OLD MAN. Now sit thee here, and tell a
    heavy tale.
Sad in thy mood, and sober in thy cheer,
Here sit thee now, and to thyself relate
The hard mishap of thy most wretched
    state.
In Thessaly I lived in sweet content,
Until that fortune wrought my over-
    throw;
For there I wedded was unto a dame
That lived in honor, virtue, love, and
    fame.   230
But Sacrapant, that cursèd sorcerer,
Being besotted with my beauteous love,
My dearest love, my true betrothèd wife,
Did seek the means to rid me of my life.
But, worse than this, he with his chant-
    ing spells
Did turn me straight unto an ugly bear;
And, when the sun doth settle in the west,
Then I begin to don my ugly hide.
And all the day I sit, as now you see,
And speak in riddles, all inspired with
    rage,   240
Seeming an old and miserable man;
And yet I am in April of my age.

Enter Venelia his lady, mad, and goes in
                             again.

See where Venelia, my betrothèd love,
Runs madding, all enraged, about the
    woods,
All by his cursèd and enchanting spells.—

Enter Lampriscus with a pot of honey.

But here comes Lampriscus, my discontented neighbor. How now, neighbor! You
look toward the ground as well as I; you
muse on something.
LAMP. Neighbor, on nothing but on [250
the matter I so often moved to you. If you
do anything for charity, help me; if for
neighborhood or brotherhood, help me.
Never was one so cumbered as is poor
Lampriscus. And, to begin, I pray receive
this pot of honey to mend your fare.
OLD MAN. Thanks, neighbor, set it
down. Honey is always welcome to the
bear. And now, neighbor, let me hear the
cause of your coming.   260
LAMP. I am, as you know, neighbor, a

man unmarried, and lived so unquietly
with my two wives that I keep every year
holy the day wherein I buried them both.
The first was on Saint Andrew's day,[1] the
other on Saint Luke's.[2]
OLD MAN. And now, neighbor, you of
this country say your custom is out. But
on with your tale, neighbor.
LAMP. By my first wife, whose [270
tongue wearied me alive, and sounded in
my ears like the clapper of a great bell,
whose talk was a continual torment to all
that dwelt by her or lived nigh her, you
have heard me say I had a handsome
daughter.
OLD MAN. True, neighbor.
LAMP. She it is that afflicts me with her
continual clamors, and hangs on me like a
bur. Poor she is, and proud she is; as [280
poor as a sheep new-shorn, and as proud
of her hopes as a peacock of her tail well
grown.
OLD MAN. Well said, Lampriscus! You
speak it like an Englishman.
LAMP. As curst as a wasp and as froward as a child new-taken from the
mother's teat; she is to my age as smoke
to the eyes or as vinegar to the teeth.
OLD MAN. Holily praised, neighbor. [290
As much for the next.
LAMP. By my other wife I had a daughter so hard-favored, so foul and ill-faced,
that I think a grove full of golden trees,
and the leaves of rubies and diamonds,
would not be a dowry answerable to her
deformity.
OLD MAN. Well, neighbor, now you
have spoke, hear me speak. Send them to
the well for the water of life; there shall [300
they find their fortunes unlooked for.
Neighbor, farewell.   *Exit.*
LAMP. Farewell, and a thousand! And
now goeth poor Lampriscus to put in execution this excellent counsel.   *Exit.*[3]

FROL. Why, this goes round without a
fiddling stick. But, do you hear, gammer,
was this the man that was a bear in the
night and a man in the day?
OLD WOM. Ay, this is he; and this [310

[1] Lovers' lucky day.
[2] "St. Luke was jocularly regarded as the
patron saint of cuckolds" (Bullen).
[3] Original reads *Exeunt*.

man that came to him was a beggar, and
dwelt upon a green. But soft! Who comes
here? O, these are the harvestmen. Ten
to one they sing a song of mowing.

*Enter the Harvestmen a-singing, with this
song double repeated.*

All ye that lovely lovers be,
Pray you for me.
Lo, here we come a-sowing, a-sowing,
And sow sweet fruits of love;
In your sweet hearts well may it prove!
Exeunt.

*Enter Huanebango with his two-hand sword,
and Booby, the clown.*

FANT. Gammer, what is he? 320
OLD WOM. O, this is one that is going to
the conjurer. Let him alone; hear what he
says.

HUAN. Now, by Mars and Mercury,
Jupiter and Janus, Sol and Saturnus,
Venus and Vesta, Pallas and Proserpina,
and by the honor of my house, Polimacker-
oeplacidus, it is a wonder to see what this
love will make silly fellows adventure, even
in the wane of their wits and infancy of [330
their discretion. Alas, my friend, what fortune calls thee forth to seek thy fortune
among brazen gates, enchanted towers, fire
and brimstone, thunder and lightning?
Beauty, I tell thee, is peerless, and she
precious whom thou affectest. Do off these
desires, good countryman; good friend, run
away from thyself; and, so soon as thou
canst, forget her, whom none must inherit
but he that can monsters tame, labors [340
achieve, riddles absolve, loose enchantments, murther magic, and kill conjuring—
and that is the great and mighty Huanebango.
BOOBY. Hark you, sir, hark you. First
know I have here the flirting [1] feather, and
have given the parish the start for the long
stock.[2] Now, sir, if it be no more but running
through a little lightning and thunder, and
"riddle me, riddle me what's this?" [350
I'll have the wench from the conjurer, if he
were ten conjurers.

[1] Swaying.
[2] Either *startled the parish with my long stockings* or *started the style for long stockings in the
parish.*

HUAN. I have abandoned the court and
honorable company, to do my devoir
against this sore sorcerer and mighty
magician. If this lady be so fair as she is
said to be, she is mine, she is mine; *meus,
mea, meum, in contemptum omnium gram-
maticorum.*[3]
BOOBY. *O falsum Latinum!* The fair [360
maid is *minum, cum apurtinantibus gib-
letes* [4] and all.
HUAN. If she be mine, as I assure myself the heavens will do somewhat to reward
my worthiness, she shall be allied to none
of the meanest gods, but be invested in the
most famous stock of Huanebango—Poli-
mackeroeplacidus, my grandfather; my
father, Pergopolineo; my mother, Dionora
de Sardinia, famously descended. 370
BOOBY. Do you hear, sir? Had not you
a cousin that was called Gusteceridis?
HUAN. Indeed, I had a cousin that sometime followed the court infortunately, and
his name Bustegusteceridis.
BOOBY. O Lord, I know him well! He
is the knight of the neat's feet.
HUAN. O, he loved no capon better! He
hath oftentimes deceived his boy of his dinner. That was his fault, good Buste- [380
gusteceridis.
BOOBY. Come, shall we go along?

[Enter Old Man.]

Soft! Here is an old man at the cross; let us
ask him the way thither.—Ho, you gaffer!
I pray you tell where the wise man, the
conjurer, dwells.
HUAN. Where that earthly goddess
keepeth her abode, the commander of
my thoughts and fair mistress of my heart.
OLD MAN. Fair enough, and far [390
enough from thy fingering, son.
HUAN. I will follow my fortune after
mine own fancy, and do according to mine
own discretion.
OLD MAN. Yet give something to an old
man before you go.
HUAN. Father, methinks a piece of this
cake might serve your turn.
OLD MAN. Yea, son.
HUAN. Huanebango giveth no [400
cakes for alms; ask of them that give gifts

[3] Mine, mine, mine, in contempt of all gram-
marians. [4] Mine, with her appurtenant parts.

for poor beggars.—Fair lady, if thou wert once shrined in this bosom, I would buckler [1] thee haratantara. *Exit.*

BOOBY. Father, do you see this man? You little think he'll run a mile or two for such a cake, or pass [2] for a pudding. I tell you, father, he has kept such a begging of me for a piece of this cake! Whoo! He comes upon me with "a superfantial [410 substance, and the foison [3] of the earth," that I know not what he means. If he came to me thus, and said, "My friend Booby," or so, why, I could spare him a piece with all my heart; but, when he tells me how God hath enriched me above other fellows with a cake, why, he makes me blind and deaf at once. Yet, father, here is a piece of cake for you, as hard as the world goes. [4]   420

OLD MAN. Thanks, son, but list to me:
He shall be deaf when thou shalt not see.
Farewell, my son. Things may so hit,
Thou mayst have wealth to mend thy wit.

BOOBY. Farewell, father, farewell; for I must make haste after my two-hand sword that is gone before. *Exeunt omnes.*

Enter Sacrapant in his study.

SACR. The day is clear, the welkin bright and gray,
The lark is merry and records her notes;
Each thing rejoiceth underneath the sky   430
But only I, whom heaven hath in hate,
Wretched and miserable Sacrapant.
In Thessaly was I born and brought up;
My mother Meroe hight, [5] a famous witch,
And by her cunning I of her did learn
To change and alter shapes of mortal men.
There did I turn myself into a dragon,
And stole away the daughter to the king,
Fair Delia, the mistress of my heart,
And brought her hither to revive the man   440
That seemeth young and pleasant to behold,
And yet is aged, crooked, weak, and numb.
Thus by enchanting spells I do deceive

[1] Protect.   [2] Care.
[3] Plentiful harvest. Booby imitates the stilted language of Huanebango.
[4] Though times are hard.   [5] Was called.

Those that behold and look upon my face;
But well may I bid youthful years adieu.

Enter Delia with a pot in her hand.

See where she comes from whence my sorrows grow!
How now, fair Delia, where have you been?

DEL. At the foot of the rock for running water, and gathering roots for your dinner, sir.   450

SACR. Ah, Delia, fairer art thou than the running water, yet harder far than steel or adamant!

DEL. Will it please you to sit down, sir?

SACR. Ay, Delia, sit and ask me what thou wilt,
Thou shalt have it brought into thy lap.

DEL. Then, I pray you, sir, let me have the best meat from the King of England's table, and the best wine in all France, brought in by the veriest knave in all [460 Spain.

SACR. Delia, I am glad to see you so pleasant. Well, sit thee down.—
Spread, table, spread
Meat, drink, and bread!
Ever may I have
What I ever crave,
When I am spread,
For meat for my black cock,
And meat for my red.   470

Enter a Friar with a chine of beef and a pot of wine.

Here, Delia, will ye fall to?

DEL. Is this the best meat in England?

SACR. Yea.

DEL. What is it?

SACR. A chine of English beef, meat for a king and a king's followers.

DEL. Is this the best wine in France?

SACR. Yea.

DEL. What wine is it?

SACR. A cup of neat wine of Or- [480 leans, that never came near the brewers in England.

DEL. Is this the veriest knave in all Spain?

SACR. Yea.

DEL. What is he, a friar?

SACR. Yea, a friar indefinite, and a knave infinite.

DEL. Then, I pray ye, Sir Friar, tell me before you go which is the most greed- [490 iest Englishman?

FRIAR. The miserable and most covetous usurer.

SACR. Hold thee there, friar. *Exit Friar.* But soft! Who have we here? Delia, away, be gone!

Enter the Two Brothers.

Delia, away, for beset are we!—
But heaven [n]or hell shall rescue her for [1] me.

[*Exeunt Delia and Sacrapant.*]

1 BRO. Brother, was not that Delia did appear?
Or was it but her shadow that was here?

2 BRO. Sister, where art thou? Delia, come again! 500
He calls, that of thy absence doth complain.—
Call out, Calypha, that she may hear,
And cry aloud, for Delia is near.

ECHO. Near.

1 BRO. Near! O, where? Hast thou any tidings?

ECHO. Tidings.

2 BRO. Which way is Delia, then—or that, or this?

ECHO. This.

1 BRO. And may we safely come where Delia is?

ECHO. Yes. 510

2 BRO. Brother, remember you the white bear of England's wood?
"Start not aside for every danger;
Be not afeard of every stranger;
Things that seem are not the same."

1 BRO. Brother, why do we not then courageously enter?

2 BRO. Then, brother, draw thy sword and follow me.

Enter the Conjurer; it lightens and thunders; the 2 Brother falls down.

1 BRO. What, brother, dost thou fall?

SACR. Ay, and thou too, Calypha. 520

Fall 1 Brother. Enter two Furies.

Adeste, dæmones! [2] Away with them!
Go carry them straight to Sacrapanto's cell,
There in despair and torture for to dwell.

[1] Because of. [2] Come, spirits!

These are Thenores' sons of Thessaly,
That come to seek Delia, their sister, forth;
But, with a potion I to her have given,
My arts hath made her to forget herself.

He removes a turf and shows a light in a glass.[3]

See here the thing which doth prolong my life.
With this enchantment I do anything;
And, till this fade, my skill shall still endure, 530
And never none shall break this little glass,
But she that's neither wife, widow, nor maid.
Then cheer thyself; this is thy destiny,
Never to die but by a dead man's hand.

Exeunt.

Enter Eumenides, the Wandering Knight, and the Old Man at the Cross.

EUM. Tell me, Time, tell me, just Time,
When shall I Delia see?
When shall I see the lodestar of my life?
When shall my wand'ring course end with her sight,
Or I but view my hope, my heart's delight?—
Father, God speed! If you tell fortunes, [540
I pray, good father, tell me mine.

OLD MAN. Son, I do see in thy face
Thy blessed fortune work apace.
I do perceive that thou hast wit;
Beg of thy fate to govern it,
For wisdom governed by advice
Makes many fortunate and wise.
Bestow thy alms, give more than all,
Till dead men's bones come at thy call.
Farewell, my son! Dream of no rest [550
Till thou repent that thou didst best.

Exit Old M[an].

EUM. This man hath left me in a labyrinth:
He biddeth me give more than all,
"Till dead men's bones come at thy call;"
He biddeth me dream of no rest,
Till I repent that I do best.

[*He lies down and sleeps.*]

[3] "The 'Life-Index,' so called, of popular tales, connected with the equally popular *motif* of the 'Thankful Dead'" (Gummere).

Enter Wiggen, Corebus,[1] Churchwarden, and Sexton.

WIG. You may be ashamed, you whoreson [2] scald [3] sexton and churchwarden, if you had any shame in those shameless faces of yours, to let a poor man lie so [560 long above ground unburied. A rot on you all, that have no more compassion of a good fellow when he is gone!

CHURCH.[4] What, would you have us to bury him, and to answer it ourselves to the parish?

SEX. Parish me no parishes! Pay me my fees, and let the rest run on in the quarter's accounts, and put it down for one of your good deeds, o' God's name, for I [570 am not one that curiously [5] stands upon merits.

COR. You whoreson, sodden-headed sheep's-face, shall a good fellow do less service and more honesty to the parish, and will you not, when he is dead, let him have Christmas [6] burial?

WIG. Peace, Corebus! As sure as Jack was Jack, the frolic'st franion amongst you, and I, Wiggen, his sweet sworn [580 brother, Jack shall have his funerals, or some of them shall lie on God's dear earth for it, that's once.[7]

CHURCH. Wiggen, I hope thou wilt do no more than thou dar'st answer.

WIG. Sir, sir, dare or dare not, more or less, answer or not answer, do this, or have this.

Wiggen sets upon the parish [8] with a pikestaff.

SEX. Help, help, help!

Eumenides awakes and comes to them.

EUM. Hold thy hands, good fellow. [590

COR. Can you blame him, sir, if he take Jack's part against this shake-rotten parish that will not bury Jack?

EUM. Why, what was that Jack?

COR. Who, Jack, sir? Who, our Jack, sir? As good a fellow as ever trod upon neat's-leather.

WIG. Look you, sir, he gave fourscore and nineteen mourning gowns to the parish

when he died, and, because he would [600 not make them up a full hundred, they would not bury him. Was not this good dealing?

CHURCH. O Lord, sir, how he lies! He was not worth a halfpenny, and drunk out every penny; and now his fellows, his drunken companions, would have us to bury him at the charge of the parish. And [9] we make many such matches, we may pull down the steeple, sell the bells, and [610 thatch the chancel. He shall lie above ground till he dance a galliard about the churchyard, for Steven Loach.

WIG. *Sic argumentaris, Domine* Loach:[10] "and we make many such matches, we may pull down the steeple, sell the bells, and thatch the chancel!"—In good time, sir, and hang yourselves in the bell ropes when you have done. *Domine, opponens præpono tibi hanc quæstionem,*[11] whether [620 will you have the ground broken or your pates broken first? For one of them shall be done presently, and, to begin mine, I'll seal it upon your coxcomb.

EUM. Hold thy hands, I pray thee, good fellow; be not too hasty.

COR. You capon's face, we shall have you turned out of the parish one of these days, with never a tatter to your arse. Then you are in worse taking than [630 Jack.

EUM. Faith, and he is bad enough. This fellow does but the part of a friend, to seek to bury his friend. How much will bury him?

WIG. Faith, about some fifteen or sixteen shillings will bestow him honestly.

SEX. Ay, even thereabouts, sir.

EUM. Here, hold it then. [*Starts to give money; then speaks to himself.*] And [640 I have left me but one poor three halfpence. Now do I remember the words the old man spake at the cross, "Bestow all thou hast," and this is all, "till dead men's bones come at thy call."—Here, hold it. [*Gives money.*] And so farewell.

WIG. God and all good be with you, sir! Nay, you cormorants, I'll bestow one peal of [12] Jack at mine own proper costs and charges. 650

---

[1] Previously, Booby, the clown.
[2] Rascally.
[3] Scabby.
[4] Original has *Simon.*
[5] Carefully.
[6] Corebus' blunder for *Christian.*
[7] "That's settled once for all" (Bullen).
[8] Sexton.
[9] If.
[10] Thus you argue, Master Loach.
[11] Master, responding, I put before you this question.
[12] Peal of bells on.

Cor. You may thank God the long staff and the bilbo-blade crossed not your coxcomb. Well, we'll to the church-stile [1] and have a pot, and so trill-lill.

Both [Churchwarden and Sexton]. Come, let's go.   *Exeunt.*

Fant. But, hark you, gammer, methinks this Jack bore a great sway in the parish.   658
Old Wom. O, this Jack was a marvelous fellow! He was but a poor man, but very well beloved. You shall see anon what this Jack will come to.

Enter the Harvestmen singing, with Women in their hands.

Frol. Soft! Who have we here? Our amorous harvesters. [2]
Fant. Ay, ay, let us sit still, and let them alone.
Here they begin to sing, the song doubled.

Lo, here we come a-reaping, a-reaping,
To reap our harvest fruit,
And thus we pass the year so long,
And never be we mute.   670
                Exit the Harvestmen.

Enter Huanebango and Corebus, the clown.

Frol. Soft! Who have we here?
Old Wom. O, this is a choleric gentleman! All you that love your lives, keep out of the smell of his two-hand sword. Now goes he to the conjurer.
Fant. Methinks the conjurer should put the fool into a juggling-box.

Huan. Fee, fa, fum, here is the English-
                man—
Conquer him that can—
Came for his lady bright,   680
To prove himself a knight,
And win her love in fight.
Cor. Who-haw, Master Bango, are you here? Hear you, you had best sit down here and beg an alms with me.
Huan. Hence, base cullion! Here is he that commandeth ingress and egress with

[1] Gummere quotes Overbury's *Characters:* "For at every church stile commonly ther's an ale-house."
[2] Original has *harvest starres.*

his weapon, and will enter at his voluntary, whosoever saith no.
A voice and flame of fire; Huanebango falleth down.
Voice. No!   690

Old Wom. So with that they kissed, and spoiled the edge of as good a two-hand sword as ever God put life in. Now goes Corebus in, spite of the conjurer.

Enter the Conjurer [with two Furies] and strike Corebus blind.

Sacr. Away with him into the open fields,
To be a ravening prey to crows and kites.
        [*The Furies carry Huanebango out.*]
And, for this villain, let him wander up and down
In naught but darkness and eternal night.
Cor. Here hast thou slain Huan, a slashing knight,
And robbéd poor Corebus of his sight.
                                Exit.
Sacr. Hence, villain, hence!—   701
Now I have unto Delia given a potion of forgetfulness,
That, when she comes, she shall not know her brothers.
Lo, where they labor, like to country slaves
With spade and mattock on this enchanted ground!
Now will I call her by another name;
For never shall she know herself again,
Until that Sacrapant hath breathed his last.
See where she comes.

Enter Delia.

Come hither, Delia, take this goad.   710
Here hard at hand two slaves do work and dig for gold;
Gore them with this, and thou shalt have enough.   *He gives her a goad.*
Del. Good sir, I know not what you mean.
Sacr. [*Aside.*] She hath forgotten to be Delia,
But not forgot the same she should forget;
But I will change her name.—
Fair Berecynthia, so this country calls you,
Go ply these strangers, wench; they dig for gold.   *Exit Sacrapant.*
Del. O heavens, how am I beholding [3] to this fair young man!
[3] Beholden, indebted.

But I must ply these strangers to their
work.   720
See where they come.

*Enter the Two Brothers in their shirts, with
spades, digging.*

1 Bro. O brother, see where Delia is!

2 Bro. O Delia, happy are we to see thee
here!

Del. What tell you me of Delia, prating
swains?
I know no Delia, nor know I what you
mean.
Ply you your work, or else you're like to
smart.

1 Bro. Why, Delia, know'st thou not thy
brothers here?
We come from Thessaly to seek thee
forth;
And thou deceivest thyself, for thou art
Delia.   729

Del. Yet more of Delia? Then take this,
and smart.   [*Pricks them with the goad.*]
What, feign you shifts for to defer your
labor?
Work, villains, work; it is for gold you dig.

2 Bro. Peace, brother, peace! This vild [1]
enchanter
Hath ravished Delia of her senses clean,
And she forgets that she is Delia.

1 Bro. Leave, cruel thou, to hurt the
miserable.—
Dig, brother, dig, for she is hard as steel.

*Here they dig, and descry the light under a
little hill.*

2 Bro. Stay, brother; what hast thou
descried?

Del. Away, and touch it not; it is something that my lord hath hidden there.
She covers it again.

Enter Sacrapant.

Sacr. Well said!   Thou plyest these
pioners [2] well.—Go, get you in, you
laboring slaves.—   740
Come, Berecynthia, let us in likewise,
And hear the nightingale record her
notes.   *Exeunt omnes.*

*Enter Zantippa, the Curst Daughter, to the
well, with a pot in her hand.* [3]

Zant. Now for a husband, house, and
home. God send a good one or none, I pray

[1] Vile.   [2] Diggers.
[3] This scene is a reworking of *The Three Heads
of the Well.*

God! My father hath sent me to the well
for the water of life, and tells me, if I give
fair words, I shall have a husband.

*Enter [Celanta,] the Foul Wench, to the well
for water with a pot in her hand.*

But here comes Celanta, my sweet sister.
I'll stand by and hear what she says.   [749

Cel. My father hath sent me to the
well for water, and he tells me, if I speak
fair, I shall have a husband and none of the
worst. Well, though I am black, [4] I am sure
all the world will not forsake me; and, as
the old proverb is, though I am black, I am
not the devil.

Zant. Marry-gup with a murrain, [5] I
know wherefore thou speakest that. But
go thy ways home as wise as thou   [759
cam'st, or I'll set thee home with a wanion. [6]

*Here she strikes her pitcher against her sis-
ter's, and breaks them both, and goes
her way.*

Cel. I think this be the curstest quean
in the world. You see what she is, a little
fair but as proud as the devil, and the
veriest vixen that lives upon God's earth.
Well, I'll let her alone, and go home and
get another pitcher, and for all this get me
to the well for water.   *Exit*

*Enter two Furies out of the Conjurer's cell
and lays Huanebango by the Well of
Life [and then exeunt]. Enter Zantippa
with a pitcher to the well.*

Zant. Once again for a husband; and
in faith, Celanta, I have got the start   [769
of you. Belike husbands grow by the well-
side. Now my father says I must rule my
tongue. Why, alas, what am I then?   A
woman without a tongue is as a soldier without his weapon. But I'll have my water
and be gone.

*Here she offers to dip her pitcher in, and a
Head speaks in the well.*

Head. Gently dip, but not too deep;
For fear you make the golden beard [7] to
weep,
Fair maiden, white and red,
Stroke me smooth, and comb my head;
And thou shalt have some cockle-bread. [8]

[4] Ugly.
[5] Plague take you!   [6] Vengeance.
[7] Original has *birde*, but see l. 959.
[8] Bread kneaded in a peculiar fashion and used
as a love charm.

Zant. What is this: "Fair maiden, white
and red, 781
Comb me smooth, and stroke my head,
And thou shalt have some cockle-bread"?
"Cockle," callest thou it, boy? Faith,
I'll give you cockle-bread!
*She breaks her pitcher upon his head; then it
thunders and lightens, and Huanebango
rises up. Huanebango is deaf and can-
not hear.*
Huan. Philida phileridos, Pamphilida flo-
rida flortos,
Dub dub-a-dub, bounce, quoth the guns,
with a sulphurous huff-snuff; [1]
Waked with a wench, pretty peat, [2] pretty
love, and my sweet pretty pigsnie, [3]
Just by thy side shall sit surnamed great
Huanebango;
Safe in my arms will I keep thee, threat
Mars or thunder Olympus. 790
Zant. [*Aside.*] Foh, what greasy groom
have we here? He looks as though he crept
out of the backside of the well, and speaks
like a drum perished at the west end. [4]
Huan. O, that I might—but I may not,
woe to my destiny therefore! [5]—
Kiss that I clasp, but I cannot. Tell me,
my destiny, wherefore?
Zant. [*Aside.*] Whoop! Now I have my
dream. Did you never hear so great a wonder as this? Three blue beans in a blue
bladder—rattle, bladder, rattle. 800
Huan. [*Aside.*] I'll now set my countenance, and to her in prose. It may be this
rim-ram-ruff [6] is too rude an encounter.—
Let me, fair lady, if you be at leisure, revel
with your sweetness, and rail upon that
cowardly conjurer that hath cast me, or
congealed me rather, into an unkind sleep,
and polluted my carcass.
Zant. [*Aside.*] Laugh, laugh, Zantippa;
thou hast thy fortune, a fool and a hus- [810
band under one.
Huan. Truly, sweetheart, as I seem,
about some twenty years, the very April of
mine age.
Zant. [*Aside.*] Why, what a prating ass
is this!
Huan. Her coral lips, her crimson chin,
Her silver teeth so white within,

Her golden locks, her rolling eye,
Her pretty parts, let them go by, 820
Heigh-ho, hath wounded me,
That I must die this day to see!
Zant. By Gog's [7] bones, thou art a
flouting knave. "Her coral lips, her crimson chin"! ka, wilshaw! [8]
Huan. True, my own, and my own
because mine, and mine because mine, ha,
ha! Above a thousand pounds in possibility, and things fitting thy desire in possession. 830
Zant. [*Aside.*] The sot thinks I ask of
his lands. Lob be your comfort, [9] and cuckold be your destiny!—Hear you, sir; and,
if you will have us, you had best say so
betime.
Huan. True, sweetheart, and will royalize thy progeny with my pedigree.
Exeunt omnes.

Enter Eumenides, the Wandering Knight.

Eum. Wretched Eumenides, still unfortu-
nate,
Envied by fortune and forlorn by
fate, 839
Here pine and die, wretched Eumenides!
Die in the spring, the April of my age?
Here sit thee down, repent what thou
hast done.
I would to God that it were ne'er begun.

Enter [the Ghost of] Jack.

Jack. You are well overtaken, sir.
Eum. Who's that?
Jack. You are heartily well met, sir.
Eum. Forbear, I say. Who is that which
pincheth me?
Jack. Trusting in God, good Master
Eumenides, that you are in so good [850
health as all your friends were at the making hereof, God give you good morrow, sir!
Lack you not a neat, handsome, and cleanly
young lad, about the age of fifteen or sixteen years, that can run by your horse,
and, for a need, make your mastership's
shoes as black as ink? How say you, sir?
Eum. Alas, pretty lad, I know not how
to keep myself, and much less a serv-

[1] Apparently a parody of Stanyhurst's hexam-
eters.
[2] Pet.
[3] Pig's eye, darling.
[4] *I.e.*, brokenly.
[5] A quotation from Harvey's *Encomium Lauri.*
[6] Chaucer's phrase for alliteration.
[7] God's.
[8] Quotha wilta-shalta, *i.e.*, quoth he willy-
nilly.
[9] "May you be brought into 'Lob's pound,'
the thralldom of the hen-pecked married man"
(Bullen).

ant, my pretty boy, my state is so [860
bad.

JACK. Content yourself, you shall not
be so ill a master but I'll be as bad a servant. Tut, sir, I know you, though you
know not me. Are not you the man, sir,
deny it if you can, sir, that came from a
strange place in the land of Catita, where
Jackanapes flies with his tail in his mouth,
to seek out a lady as white as snow and
as red as blood? Ha, ha! Have I [870
touched you now?

EUM. [Aside.] I think this boy be a
spirit.—How know'st thou all this?

JACK. Tut, are not you the man, sir,
deny it if you can, sir, that gave all the
money you had to the burying of a poor
man, and but one three halfpence left in
your purse? Content you, sir, I'll serve you,
that is flat.   879

EUM. Well, my lad, since thou art so
impor[tu]nate, I am content to entertain
thee, not as a servant, but a copartner in
my journey. But whither shall we go, for
I have not any money more than one bare
three halfpence?

JACK. Well, master, content yourself,
for, if my divination be not out, that shall be
spent at the next inn or alehouse we come
to, for, master, I know you are passing
hungry; therefore I'll go before and [890
provide dinner until that you come. No
doubt but you'll come fair and softly after.

EUM. Ay, go before; I'll follow thee.

JACK. But do you hear, master? Do
you know my name?

EUM. No, I promise thee, not yet.

JACK. Why, I am Jack.   Exit[1] Jack.

EUM. Jack! Why, be it so then.

Enter the Hostess and Jack, setting meat on
the table; and Fiddlers come[2] to play.
Eumenides walketh up and down, and
will eat no meat.

HOST. How say you, sir? Do you please
to sit down?   900

EUM. Hostess, I thank you, I have no
great stomach.

HOST. Pray, sir, what is the reason your
master is so strange? Doth not this meat
please him?

JACK. Yes, hostess, but it is my mas-

[1] Original reads Exeunt.
[2] Original reads came.

ter's fashion to pay before he eats; therefore, a reckoning, good hostess.

HOST. Marry, shall you, sir, presently.
                                              Exit.

EUM. Why, Jack, what dost thou [910
mean? Thou knowest I have not any money;
therefore, sweet Jack, tell me, what shall I
do?

JACK. Well, master, look in your purse.

EUM. Why, faith, it is a folly, for I have
no money.

JACK. Why, look you, master; do so
much for me.

EUM. [Looking into his purse.] Alas,
Jack, my purse is full of money!   920

JACK. "Alas," master! Does that word
belong to this accident? Why, methinks I
should have seen you cast away your cloak,
and in a bravado danced a galliard round
about the chamber. Why, master, your
man can teach you more wit than this.

[Enter Hostess.]

Come, hostess, cheer up my master.

HOST. You are heartily welcome; and,
if it please you to eat of a fat capon, a
fairer bird, a finer bird, a sweeter bird, [930
a crisper bird, a neater bird, your worship
never eat of.

EUM. Thanks, my fine, eloquent hostess.

JACK. But hear you, master, one word
by the way. Are you content I shall be
halves in all you get in your journey?

EUM. I am, Jack; here is my hand.

JACK. Enough, master, I ask no more.

EUM. Come, hostess, receive your [939
money; and I thank you for my good entertainment.   [Gives money.]

HOST. You are heartily welcome, sir.

EUM. Come, Jack, whither go we now?

JACK. Marry, master, to the conjurer's
presently.[3]

EUM. Content, Jack.—Hostess, fare-
well.   Exe[unt] om[nes].

Enter Corebus and Celanta, the Foul Wench,
to the well for water.

COR. Come, my duck, come. I have
now got a wife. Thou art fair, art thou
not?   950

CEL. My Corebus, the fairest alive;
make no doubt of that.

COR. Come, wench, are we almost at
the well?   [3] At once.

CEL. Ay, Corebus, we are almost at the well now. I'll go fetch some water. Sit down while I dip my pitcher in.

VOICE. Gently dip, but not too deep,
For fear you make the golden beard to weep.

A Head comes up with ears of corn, and she combs them in her lap.

Fair maiden, white and red,   960
Comb me smooth, and stroke my head,
And thou shalt have some cockle-bread.

A Head comes up full of gold; she combs it into her lap.[1]

Gently dip, but not too deep,
For fear thou make the golden beard to weep.
Fair maid, white and red,
Comb me smooth, and stroke my head,
And every hair a sheaf shall be,
And every sheaf a golden tree.

CEL. O, see, Corebus, I have combed a great deal of gold into my lap, [970 and a great deal of corn!

COR. Well said, wench! Now we shall have just enough. God send us coiners to coin our gold. But, come, shall we go home, sweetheart?

CEL. Nay, come, Corebus, I will lead you.

COR. So, Corebus, things have well hit;
Thou hast gotten wealth to mend thy wit.
Exit [Corebus with Celanta].

Enter Jack and the Wandering Knight.

JACK. Come away, master, come. [980

EUM. Go along, Jack; I'll follow thee. Jack, they say it is good to go cross-legged, and say his prayers backward. How sayest thou?

JACK. Tut, never fear, master; let me alone. Here sit you still; speak not a word. And, because you shall not be enticed with his enchanting speeches, with this same wool I'll stop your ears. And so, master, sit still, for I must to the conjurer. [990
Exit Jack.

Enter the Conjurer to the Wandering Knight.

SACR. How now! What man art thou that sits so sad?
Why dost thou gaze upon these stately trees

[1] This stage direction occurs in original after l. 968.

Without the leave and will of Sacrapant?
What, not a word but mum?
Then, Sacrapant, thou art betrayed.

Enter Jack, invisible, and taketh off Sacrapant's wreath from his head and his sword out of his hand.

What hand invades the head of Sacrapant?
What hateful Fury doth envy my happy state?
Then, Sacrapant, these are thy latest days.
Alas, my veins are numbed, my sinews shrink,
My blood is pierced, my breath fleeting away,   1000
And now my timeless date is come to end!
He in whose life his actions hath been so foul,
Now in his death to hell descends his soul.   *He dieth.*

JACK. O, sir, are you gone? Now I hope we shall have some other coil.[2]—Now, master, how like you this? The conjurer he is dead, and vows never to trouble us more. Now get you to your fair lady, and see what you can do with her.—Alas, he heareth me not all this while; but [1010 I will help that.
He pulls the wool out of his ears.

EUM. How now, Jack! What news?

JACK. Here, master, take this sword, and dig with it at the foot of this hill.
He digs and spies a light.

EUM. How now, Jack! What is this?

JACK. Master, without this the conjurer could do nothing; and so long as this light lasts, so long doth his art endure, and, this being out, then doth his art decay.   1020

EUM. Why, then, Jack, I will soon put out this light.

JACK. Ay, master, how?

EUM. Why, with a stone I'll break the glass, and then blow it out.

JACK. No, master, you may as soon break the smith's anvil as this little vial; nor the biggest blast that ever Boreas blew cannot blow out this little light but she that is neither maid, wife, nor widow. [1030 Master, wind this horn, and see what will happen.

[2] Trouble.

He winds the horn. Here enters Venelia, and breaks the glass, and blows out the light, and goeth in again.

So, master, how like you this? This is she that ran madding in the woods, his betrothed love that keeps the cross. And now, this light being out, all are restored to their former liberty. And now, master, to the lady that you have so long looked for. *He draweth a curtain, and there Delia sitteth asleep.*

EUM. God speed, fair maid, sitting alone—
there is once; 1039
God speed, fair maid—there is twice;
God speed, fair maid—that is thrice.
DEL. Not so, good sir, for you are by.
JACK. Enough, master, she hath spoke;
now I will leave her with you. [*Exit.*]
EUM. Thou fairest flower of these western parts,
Whose beauty so reflecteth in my sight
As doth a crystal mirror in the sun,
For thy sweet sake I have crossed the frozen Rhine; [1]
Leaving fair Po, I sailed up Danuby
As far as Saba, whose enhancing streams
Cuts twixt the Tartars and the Russians; 1051
These have I crossed for thee, fair Delia.
Then grant me that which I have sued for long.
DEL. Thou gentle knight, whose fortune is so good
To find me out and set my brothers free,
My faith, my heart, my hand I give to thee.
EUM. Thanks, gentle madam. But here comes Jack. Thank him, for he is the best friend that we have. 1059

Enter Jack, with a head in his hand.

How now, Jack! What hast thou there?
JACK. Marry, master, the head of the conjurer.
EUM. Why, Jack, that is impossible; he was a young man.
JACK. Ah, master, so he deceived them that beheld him! But he was a miserable, old, and crooked man, though to each man's eye h[e see]med young and fresh; for, master, this conjurer took the shape

[1] "This and the next three lines are found, with slight variations, in Greene's *Orlando Furioso*" (Dyce)

of the old man that kept the cross, [1070 and that old man was in the likeness of the conjurer. But now, master, wind your horn.

He winds his horn. Enter Venelia, the Two Brothers, and [Erestus,] he that was at the cross.

EUM. Welcome, Erestus! Welcome, fair Venelia!
Welcome, Thelea and Calypha both!
Now have I her that I so long have sought;
So saith fair Delia, if we have your consent.
1 BRO. Valiant Eumenides, thou well deservest
To have our favors; so let us rejoice
That by thy means we are at liberty.
Here may we joy each in other's sight,
And this fair lady have her Wand'ring Knight. 1081
JACK. So, master, now ye think you have done, but I must have a saying to you. You know you and I were partners, I to have half in all you got.
EUM. Why, so thou shalt, Jack.
JACK. Why, then, master, draw your sword, part your lady, let me have half of her presently.
EUM. Why, I hope, Jack, thou dost [1090 but jest. I promised thee half I got, but not half my lady.
JACK. But what else, master? Have you not gotten her? Therefore divide her straight, for I will have half; there is no remedy.
EUM. Well, ere I will falsify my word unto my friend, take her all. Here, Jack, I'll give her thee.
JACK. Nay, neither more nor less, [1100 master, but even just half.
EUM. Before I will falsify my faith unto my friend, I will divide her. Jack, thou shalt have half.
1 BRO. Be not so cruel unto our sister, gentle knight.
2 BRO. O, spare fair Delia! She deserves no death.
EUM. Content yourselves; my word is passed to him.—Therefore prepare [1110 thyself, Delia, for thou must die.
DEL. Then farewell, world! Adieu, Eumenides!

He offers to strike, and Jack stays him.

JACK. Stay, master; it is sufficient I have tried your constancy. Do you now remember since you paid for the burying of a poor fellow?

EUM. Ay, very well, Jack.

JACK. Then, master, thank that good deed for this good turn; and so God be with you all!   *Jack leaps down in the ground.*

EUM. Jack, what, art thou gone? Then
        farewell, Jack!—   1121
Come, brothers, and my beauteous
        Delia,
Erestus, and thy dear Venelia,
We will to Thessaly with joyful hearts.

ALL. Agreed! We follow thee and Delia.
                        Exeunt omnes.

FANT. What, gammer, asleep?

OLD WOM. By the Mass, son, 'tis almost day, and my windows shuts at the cock's crow.   1129

FROL. Do you hear, gammer, methinks this Jack bore a great sway amongst them.

OLD WOM. O, man, this was the ghost of the poor man that they kept such a coil to bury; and that makes him to help the Wand'ring Knight so much. But come, let us in; we will have a cup of ale and a toast this morning, and so depart.[1]

FANT. Then you have made an end of your tale, gammer?   [1140

OLD WOM. Yes, faith. When this was done, I took a piece of bread and cheese, and came my way; and so shall you have, too, before you go, to your breakfast.
                                    [*Exeunt.*]

[1] Separate.

ROBERT GREENE

Robert Greene, certainly the most picturesque and one of the most important of the University Wits, was born at Norwich in 1558. He took his B.A. in 1578 and his M.A in 1583 at Cambridge, and became an M.A. of Oxford in 1588. By 1583 he had begun his literary career with the publication of a long euphuistic romance, *Mamillia*, licensed in 1580, and he continued to produce romances written in a highly wrought style under such different influences as *Euphues, novella* collections, and pastoral and Greek romance, reaching his highest level in *Pandosto* (1588) and *Menaphon* (1589). Short poems and songs incorporated in some of the romances gave him high rank as a lyric poet also. By rapid production of such works Greene became one of the first authors in England to support himself, however precariously, with his pen. He soon began to capitalize on the bohemian existence which he had led from youth, writing his "repentance" pamphlets from 1590 to 1592, with many facts of his own life thinly veiled as fiction. He pictures his early riotous living, his marriage and desertion of his wife and child for the sister of a notorious character of the London underworld, a meeting with players, and his success in the production of plays for them. During this same period he was writing other journalistic and realistic prose, particularly a series of cony-catching pamphlets portraying the life of London rogues. He died September 3, 1592, from what Nashe called a "banquet of Rhenish wine and pickled herring," having written on his deathbed his famous *Groatsworth of Wit Bought with a Million of Repentance* and having despatched a letter to his wife asking her to forgive him and to settle his debts.

The earliest of Greene's plays is perhaps *The Comical History of Alphonsus, King of Aragon*, printed in 1599, which mentions "mighty Tamburlaine," and seems clearly modeled on Marlowe's conqueror play. Besides *The Honorable History of Friar Bacon and Friar Bungay* Greene's other known plays are *The History of Orlando Furioso*, drawn from Ariosto; *The Scottish History of James the Fourth*, with a plot of a *novella* type; and *A Looking-Glass for London and England*, written with Thomas Lodge, which pictures the wickedness of Nineveh as a warning to London. All of these plays were printed in 1594 or later, apparently from playhouse manuscripts, and give evidence of more or less corruption or even mutilation. It is probable that Greene wrote other plays. Of the several ascribed to him by different scholars, *George a Greene* perhaps has the best claim to be considered.

Nashe, in *Have with You to Saffron Walden*, calls Greene the master of his craft in the plotting of plays. His best work shows also effective characterization, especially in his romantic heroines, and a genuinely poetic style. His limitation is indicated by the charge, which he resents in the preface to *Perimedes the Blacksmith*, that he could not make his verses "jet upon the stage in tragical buskins." Greene defended his style by appeal to his prose romances and by bitter denunciation of players and playwrights for their "bumbast." While the type of sentimental and romantic comedy which represents his best work had to yield around 1590 to the turgid and passionate tragedy in vogue, by the end of the century it was carried to its zenith by Shakespeare, who had been the apparent object of Greene's bitterest attack on actors and dramatists in the *Groatsworth of Wit*.

The first record of *Friar Bacon and Friar Bungay* is Henslowe's note of a performance of it as an old play in 1592. Like *Alphonsus*, the play is supposed to have been written in emulation of Marlowe, and it is usually assigned to about 1589 as a rival to *Doctor Faustus*. If, however, as some scholars suggest, the proper date of Marlowe's play is 1592, then the relationship between the two must be reversed. Except for similar treat-

ment of the marvelous powers of magicians, common in such stories, there is little kinship between the two plays. Greene drew his plot from *The Famous History of Friar
Bacon*, a tale first known in the form of a chapbook, himself adding the romantic story
of Margaret from a very slight hint in the romance. The text is apparently corrupt in
several passages, and one or more whole scenes may have been omitted as a result of
stage adaptation. In 1594 Henslowe has a second record of performance of the play, and
it was entered in the Stationers' Register and printed in that year. The Malone Society
reprint of this quarto of 1594, prepared by W. W. Greg, is the basis of the present text.

A *Pleasant Conceited Comedy of George a Greene* was acted for Henslowe as an old play
in 1593. It was entered in the Stationers' Register in 1595, but the earliest extant edition
is dated 1599. There is no indication of the authorship, but a copy of this edition, formerly
in the Chatsworth Collection, has on the title-page the following two notes in an early
seventeenth century script: "Written by .... a minister, who ac[ted] the
pinners part in it himself. Teste W. Shakespea[re]," and "Ed. Juby saith that the play
was made by Ro. Gree[ne]." Opinion, long divided, is represented at the present by Tan-
nenbaum's claim that the entries are forgeries of Collier, and by Greg's that they are in
the hand of Sir George Buc, Master of the Revels from 1608 to 1622. If they are Buc's, the
second, perhaps correcting the first or perhaps adding to it, furnishes reliable contemporary
evidence, since Juby, as an actor prominent from 1594 to 1618, would have known playhouse traditions. On the internal evidence of verse and style, the play is generally ascribed to Greene. He is supposed to have written it before 1590, basing it on an early
version, now lost, of the prose tale *The Famous History of George a Greene*. The superiority
of the stalwart hero of some trade to the old woodland outlaw and folk hero, Robin Hood,
is a fairly frequent theme of ballad and tale, and *George a Greene* has many suggestions
of the style and the conventions of the popular ballad. In its extant form the play has
clearly been cut and corrupted in the course of use by a traveling company. The present
text is based on the Malone Society reprint of the edition of 1599, prepared by F. W.
Clarke.

THE HONORABLE HISTORY OF FRIAR BACON AND FRIAR BUNGAY[1]

BY

ROBERT GREENE

[DRAMATIS PERSONÆ

KING HENRY THE THIRD.
EDWARD, *Prince of Wales, his son.*
EMPEROR OF GERMANY.
KING OF CASTILE.
LACY, *Earl of Lincoln* ⎫
WARREN, *Earl of Sussex* ⎬ *Edward's friends.*
ERMSBY, *a gentleman* ⎭
RALPH SIMNELL, *the king's fool.*
FRIAR BACON.
MILES, *his poor scholar.*
FRIAR BUNGAY.
JAQUES VANDERMAST, *a German magician.*
BURDEN ⎫
MASON ⎬ *doctors of Oxford.*
CLEMENT ⎭
LAMBERT ⎫
SERLSBY ⎬ *gentlemen.*

TWO SCHOLARS, *their sons.*
THE KEEPER OF FRESSINGFIELD.
HIS FRIEND.
THOMAS ⎫
RICHARD ⎬ *rustics.*
CONSTABLE.
A POST BOY.
LORDS, COUNTRY CLOWNS, *etc.*

ELINOR, *daughter to the King of Castile.*
MARGARET,[2] *the keeper's daughter.*
JOAN, *a country wench.*
HOSTESS OF THE BELL AT HENLEY.

A DEVIL.
A SPEAKER FOR THE BRAZEN HEAD.
A SPIRIT IN THE SHAPE OF HERCULES.

SCENE: *England.*

TIME: *Thirteenth Century.*]

[SCENE i.

Framlingham.]

Enter Edward the First,[3] malcontented, with Lacy, Earl of Lincoln, John Warren, Earl of Sussex, and Ermsby, gentleman; Rafe[4] Simnell, the king's fool.

LACY. Why looks my lord like to a troubled sky
When heaven's bright shine is shadowed with a fog?
Alate[5] we ran the deer, and through the lawns[6]

Stripped[7] with our nags the lofty frolic bucks
That scudded fore the teasers[8] like the wind.
Ne'er was the deer of merry Fressingfield
So lustily pulled down by jolly mates,
Nor shared the farmers such fat venison,
So frankly dealt,[9] this hundred years before;
Nor have I seen my lord more frolic in the chase,   10
And now—changed to a melancholy dump.[10]

WARREN. After the prince got to the keeper's lodge,

---

[1] The original title continues: "As It Was Played by Her Majesty's Servants."
[2] In the original usually spelled *Margret.*
[3] Should be Prince Edward, since Henry III is still king at the end of the play.
[4] Variant of *Ralph.*   [5] Of late, lately.   [6] Glades.

[7] Outstripped.   [9] Generously divided.
[8] Hunting dogs.   [10] Fit of abstraction.

249

And had been jocund in the house
   awhile,
Tossing off ale and milk in country
   cans,
Whether it was the country's sweet
   content,
Or else the bonny damsel filled us drink,
That seemed so stately in her stammel [1]
   red,
Or that a qualm did cross his stomach
   then,
But straight he fell into his passions.
ERMSBY. Sirrah Rafe, what say you to
   your master? 20
Shall he thus all amort [2] live mal-
   content?
RAFE. Hearest thou, Ned?—Nay, look if
he will speak to me!
EDWARD. What say'st thou to me, fool?
RAFE. I prithee, tell me, Ned, art thou
in love with the keeper's daughter?
EDWARD. How if I be, what then?
RAFE. Why, then, sirrah, I'll teach thee
how to deceive Love.
EDWARD. How, Rafe? 30
RAFE. Marry, sirrah Ned, thou shalt
put on my cap and my coat and my dagger,
and I will put on thy clothes and thy
sword; and so thou shalt be my fool.
EDWARD. And what of this?
RAFE. Why, so thou shalt beguile Love,
for Love is such a proud scab that he will
never meddle with fools nor children. Is
not Rafe's counsel good, Ned?
EDWARD. Tell me, Ned Lacy, didst thou
   mark the maid, 40
How lively in her country weeds she
   looked?
A bonnier wench all Suffolk cannot yield.
All Suffolk! Nay, all England holds
   none such!
RAFE. Sirrah Will Ermsby, Ned is deceived.
ERMSBY. Why, Rafe?
RAFE. He says all England hath no
such, and I say, and I'll stand to it, there
is one better in Warwickshire.
WARREN. How provest thou that, Rafe?
RAFE. Why, is not the abbot a [51
learned man, and hath read many books,
and thinkest thou he hath not more learning than thou to choose a bonny wench?

[1] Woolen cloth.
[2] *A la mort*, spiritless.

Yes, I warrant thee, by his whole gram-
mar. [3]
ERMSBY. A good reason, Rafe.
EDWARD. I tell thee, Lacy, that her spar-
   kling eyes
Do lighten forth sweet love's alluring
   fire;
And in her tresses she doth fold the looks
Of such as gaze upon her golden hair; 61
Her bashful white, mixed with the morn-
   ing's red,
Luna doth boast upon her lovely cheeks;
Her front is Beauty's table, where she
   paints
The glories of her gorgeous excellence;
Her teeth are shelves of precious mar-
   garites, [4]
Richly enclosed with ruddy coral
   cleeves. [5]
Tush, Lacy, she is Beauty's overmatch,
If thou survey'st her curious imagery. [6]
LACY. I grant, my lord, the damsel is as
   fair 70
As simple Suffolk's homely towns can
   yield;
But in the court be quainter [7] dames
   than she,
Whose faces are enriched with honor's
   taint, [8]
Whose beauties stand upon the stage
   of fame,
And vaunt their trophies in the courts
   of love.
EDWARD. Ah, Ned, but hadst thou watched
   her as myself,
And seen the secret beauties of the
   maid,
Their courtly coyness were but foolery.
ERMSBY. Why, how watched you her,
   my lord?
EDWARD. Whenas she swept like Venus
   through the house, 80
And in her shape fast folded up my
   thoughts,
Into the milk house went I with the
   maid,
And there amongst the cream bowls
   she did shine
As Pallas 'mongst her princely hus-
   wifery. [9]

[3] Learning.
[4] Pearls.
[5] Cliffs.
[6] Rare appearance.
[7] Daintier, more fastidious.
[8] Tint.
[9] Housekeeping.

She turned her smock over her lily arms,
And dived them into milk to run her
  cheese;
But, whiter than the milk, her crystal
  skin,
Checked with lines of azure, made her [1]
  blush
That art or nature durst bring for com-
  pare.
Ermsby, if thou hadst seen, as I did
  note it well,   90
How Beauty played the huswife, how
  this girl,
Like Lucrece, laid her fingers to the work,
Thou wouldest with Tarquin hazard
  Rome and all
To win the lovely maid of Fressingfield.
RAFE. Sirrah Ned, wouldst fain have
her?
EDWARD. Ay, Rafe.
RAFE. Why, Ned, I have laid the plot
in my head; thou shalt have her already.
EDWARD. I'll give thee a new coat, and
learn me that.[2]   101
RAFE. Why, sirrah Ned, we'll ride to
Oxford to Friar Bacon. O, he is a brave
scholar, sirrah; they say he is a brave
nigromancer,[3] that he can make women of
devils, and he can juggle cats into costermongers.
EDWARD. And how then, Rafe?
RAFE. Marry, sirrah, thou shalt go to
him, and because [4] thy father Harry [110
shall not miss thee, he shall turn me into
thee; and I'll to the court, and I'll prince it
out; and he shall make thee either a silken
purse full of gold or else a fine-wrought
smock.
EDWARD. But how shall I have the
maid?
RAFE. Marry, sirrah, if thou be'st a
silken purse full of gold, then on Sundays
she'll hang thee by her side, and you [120
must not say a word. Now, sir, when
she comes into a great press of people, for
fear of the cutpurse, on a sudden she'll
swap thee into her plackerd;[5] then, sirrah,
being there, you may plead for yourself.
ERMSBY. Excellent policy!
EDWARD. But how if I be a wrought
smock?

RAFE. Then she'll put thee into her
chest and lay thee into lavender, and [130
upon some good day she'll put thee on;
and at night when you go to bed, then being
turned from a smock to a man, you may
make up the match.
LACY. Wonderfully wisely counseled,
Rafe.
EDWARD. Rafe shall have a new coat.
RAFE. God thank you—when I have
it on my back, Ned.
EDWARD. Lacy, the fool hath laid a per-
  fect plot,   140
Forwhy [6] our country Margaret is so
  coy
And stands so much upon her honest
  points
That marriage or no market with the
  maid.
Ermsby, it must be nigroma[n]tic spells
And charms of art that must enchain
  her love,
Or else shall Edward never win the girl.
Therefore, my wags, we'll horse us in
  the morn,
And post to Oxford to this jolly friar.
Bacon shall by his magic do this deed.
WARREN. Content, my lord; and that's
  a speedy way   150
To wean these headstrong puppies from
  the teat.
EDWARD. I am unknown, not taken for
  the prince;
They only deem us frolic courtiers,
That revel thus among our liege's game;
Therefore I have devised a policy.
Lacy, thou know'st next Friday is
  S[aint] James',[7]
And then the country flocks to Harles-
  ton Fair;
Then will the keeper's daughter frolic
  there,
And overshine the troop of all the maids
That come to see and to be seen that
  day.   160
Haunt thee disguised among the coun-
  try swains;
Feign th'art a farmer's son, not far
  from thence;
Espy her loves, and who she liketh best;
Cote [8] him, and court her, to control
  the clown;[9]

---

[1] *I.e.*, any other woman.   [4] In order that.
[2] If you teach me that.   [5] Placket.
[3] Necromancer.

[6] Because.   [8] Outstrip.
[7] July 25.   [9] Overmaster the rustic.

Say that the courtier tired [1] all in green,
That helped her handsomely to run her
  cheese,
And filled her father's lodge with venison,
Commends him, and sends fairings,[2]
  to herself.
Buy something worthy of her parentage,
Not worth her beauty, for, Lacy, then
  the fair   170
Affords no jewel fitting for the maid.
And, when thou talkest of me, note if
  she blush.
O, then she loves! But, if her cheeks
  wax pale,
Disdain it is. Lacy, send [3] how she fares,
And spare no time nor cost to win her loves.
LACY. I will, my lord, so execute this charge
As if that Lacy were in love with her.
EDWARD. Send letters speedily to Ox-
  ford of the news.
RAFE. And, sirrah Lacy, buy me a
thousand thousand million of fine bells.
LACY. What wilt thou do with them,
Rafe?   182
RAFE. Marry, every time that Ned sighs
for the keeper's daughter, I'll tie a bell
about him; and so within three or four
days I will send word to his father Harry
that his son and my master Ned is be-
come Love's morris dance.
EDWARD. Well, Lacy, look with care unto
  thy charge,   189
And I will haste to Oxford to the friar,
That he by art and thou by secret gifts
Mayst make me lord of merry Fressingfield.
LACY. God send your honor your heart's
  desire.   *Exeunt.*

[SCENE ii.

*Friar Bacon's study at Brazenose College,
                              Oxford.*]

*Enter Friar Bacon, with Miles, his poor
    scholar, with books under his arm; with
    them Burden, Mason, Clement, three
                              doctors.*

BACON. Miles, where are you?
MILES. *Hic sum, dostissime et reveren-
dissime doctor.*[4]

[1] Attired.   [2] Gifts bought at the fair.
[3] Send news of.
[4] Here I am, most learned and venerable doctor. (The Latin throughout the play is corrupt.
Translations are approximate.)

BACON. *Attulisti nos libros meos de
necromantia?*[5]
MILES. *Ecce quam bonum et quam
jocundum, habitares libros in unum!*[6]
BACON. Now, masters of our academic
  state,
That rule in Oxford, viceroys in your
  place,
Whose heads contain maps of the liberal
  arts,   10
Spending your time in depth of learned
  skill,
Why flock you thus to Bacon's secret
  cell,
A friar newly stalled [7] in Brazen-nose?
Say what's your mind, that I may make
  reply.
BURDEN. Bacon, we hear that long we
  have suspect,
That thou art read in magic's mystery—
In pyromancy, to divine by flames;
To tell, by hydroma[n]tic, ebbs and tides;
By aeromancy to discover doubts,
To plain out [8] questions, as Apollo did. 20
BACON. Well, Master Burden, what of
all this?
MILES. Marry, sir, he doth but fulfill,
by rehearsing of these names, the fable of
the Fox and the Grapes; that which is
above us pertains nothing to us.
BURDEN. I tell thee, Bacon, Oxford makes
  report—
Nay, England and the court of Henry
  says—
Th'art making of a brazen head by art,
Which shall unfold strange doubts and
  aphorisms,[9]   30
And read a lecture in philosophy;
And, by the help of devils and ghastly
  fiends,
Thou mean'st, ere many years or days
  be past,
To compass England with a wall of
  brass.
BACON. And what of this?
MILES. What of this, master? Why,
he doth speak mystically, for he knows,
if your skill fail to make a brazen head, yet
Mother Waters' strong ale will fit his turn
to make him have a copper nose.   40

[5] Have you brought us my books on magic?
[6] How good and how pleasant it is to live
together among books!   [7] Installed.   [8] Explain.
[9] Statement of scientific principles.

CLEMENT. Bacon, we come not grieving
at thy skill,
But joying that our academy yields
A man supposed the wonder of the
world;
For, if thy cunning work these miracles,
England and Europe shall admire thy
fame,
And Oxford shall in characters of brass
And statues such as were built up in
Rome
Eternize Friar Bacon for his art.
MASON. Then, gentle friar, tell us thy
intent.
BACON. Seeing you come as friends unto
the friar,   50
Resolve you,[1] doctors, Bacon can by
books
Make storming Boreas thunder from
his cave,
And dim fair Luna to a dark eclipse.
The great archruler, potentate of hell,
Trembles when Bacon bids him or his
fiends
Bow to the force of his pentagoron.[2]
What art can work, the frolic friar
knows;
And therefore will I turn my magic
books,
And strain out nigromancy to the deep.[3]
I have contrived and framed a head of
brass   60
(I made Belcephon hammer out the
stuff),
And that by art shall read philosophy.
And I will strengthen England by my
skill,
That, if ten Cæsars lived and reigned
in Rome,
With all the legions Europe doth con-
tain,
They should not touch a grass of English
ground.
The work that Ninus reared at Babylon,
The brazen walls framed by Semiramis,
Carved out like to the portal of the sun,
Shall not be such as rings the English
strand   70
From Dover to the market place of Rye.
BURDEN. Is this possible?

MILES. I'll bring ye two or three wit-
nesses.
BURDEN. What be those?
MILES. Marry, sir, three or four as
honest devils and good companions as
any be in hell.
MASON. No doubt but magic may do
much in this;   79
For he that reads but mathematic rules
Shall find conclusions that avail to
work
Wonders that pass the common sense
of men.
BURDEN. But Bacon roves a bow beyond
his reach,[4]
And tells of more than magic can per-
form,
Thinking to get a fame by fooleries.
Have I not passed as far in state of
schools,
And read of many secrets? Yet to
think
That heads of brass can utter any voice,
Or more, to tell of deep philosophy—
This is a fable Æsop had forgot.   90
BACON. Burden, thou wrong'st me in
detracting thus;
Bacon loves not to stuff himself with
lies.
But tell me fore these doctors, if thou
dare,
Of certain questions I shall move to
thee.
BURDEN. I will; ask what thou can.
MILES. Marry, sir, he'll straight be
on your pickpack,[5] to know whether the
feminine or the masculine gender be most
worthy.   99
BACON. Were you not yesterday, Mas-
ter Burden, at Henley upon the Thames?
BURDEN. I was. What then?
BACON. What book studied you thereon
all night?
BURDEN. I? None at all; I read not
there a line.
BACON. Then, doctors, Friar Bacon's art
knows naught.
CLEMENT. What say you to this, Master
Burden? Doth he not touch you?
BURDEN. I pass not of[6] his frivolous
speeches.   111

---

[1] Understand.
[2] Pentagonon, a five-pointed emblem with magical powers.
[3] Exert my magic to the utmost.

[4] Shoots at a target beyond his range.
[5] Pickaback.
[6] Care not for.

MILES. Nay, Master Burden, my master, ere he hath done with you, will turn you from a doctor to a dunce, and shake you so small that he will leave no more learning in you than is in Balaam's ass.

BACON. Masters, for that learned Burden's skill is deep,
And sore he doubts of Bacon's cabalism,
I'll show you why he haunts to Henley oft:
Not, doctors, for to taste the fragrant air,   120
But there to spend the night in alchemy,
To multiply with secret spells of art.
Thus private steals he learning from us all.
To prove my sayings true, I'll show you straight
The book he keeps at Henley for himself.

MILES. Nay, now my master goes to conjuration, take heed!

BACON. Masters, stand still; fear not, I'll show you but his book. (*Here he conjures.*)
Per omnes deos infernales, Belcephon! [1]   130

Enter a Woman with a shoulder of mutton on a spit, and a Devil.

MILES. O master, cease your conjuration, or you spoil all, for here's a she-devil come with a shoulder of mutton on a spit. You have marred the devil's supper; but no doubt he thinks our college fare is slender, and so hath sent you his cook with a shoulder of mutton, to make it exceed. [2]

HOSTESS. O, where am I, or what's become of me?

BACON. What art thou?   140

HOSTESS. Hostess at Henley, mistress of the Bell.

BACON. How camest thou here?

HOSTESS. As I was in the kitchen 'mongst the maids,
Spitting the meat against supper for my guess, [3]
A motion [4] moved me to look forth of door.
No sooner had I pried into the yard,
But straight a whirlwind hoisted me from thence,

[1] By all the infernal gods, Belcephon!
[2] Become better.   [3] Guests.   [4] Impulse.

And mounted me aloft unto the clouds.
As in a trance, I thought nor fearéd naught,
Nor know I where or whither I was ta'en,   150
Nor where I am nor what these persons be.

BACON. No?   Know you not Master Burden?

HOSTESS. O, yes, good sir, he is my daily guest.—
What, Master Burden, 't was but yesternight
That you and I at Henley played at cards.

BURDEN. I know not what we did!—
A pox of all conjuring friars!

CLEMENT. Now, jolly friar, tell us, is this the book
That Burden is so careful to look on?

BACON. It is.—But, Burden, tell me now,
Thinkest thou that Bacon's nigromantic skill   161
Cannot perform his head and wall of brass,
When he can fetch thine hostess in such post?

MILES. I'll warrant you, master, if Master Burden could conjure as well as you, he would have his book every night from Henley to study on at Oxford.

MASON. Burden, what, are you mated [5] by this frolic friar?—
Look how he droops; his guilty conscience
Drives him to bash, [6] and makes his hostess blush.   170

BACON. Well, mistress, for I will not have you missed,
You shall to Henley to cheer up your guests
Fore supper gin. [7]—Burden, bid her adieu;
Say farewell to your hostess fore she goes.—
Sirrah, away, and set her safe at home.

HOSTESS. Master Burden, when shall we see you at Henley?
                          Exeunt Hostess and the Devil.

BURDEN. The devil take thee and Henley too!   179

MILES. Master, shall I make a good motion?

[5] Confounded.   [6] Be abashed.   [7] Begin.

BACON. What's that?

MILES. Marry, sir, now that my hostess is gone to provide supper, conjure up another spirit, and send Doctor Burden flying after.

BACON. Thus, rulers of our academic state,
You have seen the friar frame his art by proof;
And as the college calléd Brazen-nose
Is under him, and he the master there,
So surely shall this head of brass be framed, 191
And yield forth strange and uncouth [1] aphorisms,
And hell and Hecate shall fail the friar,
But I will circle England round with brass.

MILES. So be it *et nunc et semper*,[2] amen. *Exeunt omnes.*

[SCENE iii.

Harleston Fair.]

Enter Margaret, the Fair Maid of Fressingfield, with Thomas, [Richard,] and Joan, and other clowns; Lacy disguised in country apparel.

THOMAS. By my troth, Margaret, here's a weather is able to make a man call his father whoreson. If this weather hold, we shall have hay good cheap,[3] and butter and cheese at Harleston will bear no price.

MARGARET. Thomas, maids, when they come to see the fair,
Count not to make a cope [4] for dearth of hay.
When we have turned our butter to the salt,
And set our cheese safely upon the racks,
Then let our fathers price it as they please. 10
We country sluts of merry Fressingfield
Come to buy needless naughts to make us fine,
And look that young men should be frank this day,
And court us with such fairings as they can.
Phœbus is blithe, and frolic looks from heaven,

As when he courted lovely Semele,
Swearing the peddlers shall have empty packs,
If that fair weather may make chapmen buy.

LACY. But, lovely Peggy, Semele is dead,
And therefore Phœbus from his palace pries, 20
And, seeing such a sweet and seemly saint,
Shows all his glories for to court yourself.

MARGARET. This is a fairing, gentle sir, indeed,
To soothe me up with such smooth flattery;
But, learn of me, your scoff's too broad before.[5]—
Well, Joan, our beauties must abide their jests;
We serve the turn in jolly Fressingfield.

JOAN. Margaret, a farmer's daughter for a farmer's son!
I warrant you, the meanest of us both
Shall have a mate to lead us from the church. 30
But, Thomas, what's the news? What, in a dump?
Give me your hand; we are near a peddler's shop.
Out with your purse; we must have fairings now.

THOMAS. Faith, Joan, and shall. I'll bestow a fairing on you, and then we will to the tavern, and snap off a pint of wine or two.

All this while Lacy whispers Margaret in the ear.

MARGARET. Whence are you, sir? Of Suffolk? For your terms
Are finer than the common sort of men.

LACY. Faith, lovely girl, I am of Beccles by,[6] 40
Your neighbor, not above six miles from hence,
A farmer's son, that never was so quaint
But that he could do courtesy to such dames.
But trust me, Margaret, I am sent in charge
From him that reveled in your father's house,

---

[1] Unusual.
[2] Now and forever.
[3] At a good price.
[4] Bargain.
[5] *I.e.*, obvious.
[6] From near Beccles.

And filled his lodge with cheer and
   venison,
Tired in green. He sent you this rich
   purse,
His token that he helped you run your
   cheese,
And in the milk house chatted with
   yourself.
MARGARET. To me?   You forget your-
   self.[1]   50
LACY. Women are often weak in mem-
   ory.
MARGARET. O, pardon, sir, I call to mind
   the man.
'Twere little manners to refuse his gift,
And yet I hope he sends it not for love;
For we have little leisure to debate of
   that.
JOAN. What, Margaret, blush not; maids
   must have their loves!
THOMAS. Nay, by the Mass, she looks
pale as if she were angry.
RICHARD. Sirrah, are you of Beccles?
I pray, how doth Goodman Cob? My [60
father bought a horse of him.—I'll tell
you, Margaret, a[2] were good to be a
gentleman's jade, for of all things the
foul hilding[3] could not abide a dung cart.
MARGARET. [Aside.] How different is this
   farmer from the rest
That erst as yet[4] have pleased my
   wand'ring sight!
His words are witty, quickened with
   a smile,
His courtesy gentle, smelling of the
   court;
Facile and debonair in all his deeds,
Proportioned as was Paris, when, in
   gray,[5]   70
He courted Œnon in the vale by Troy.
Great lords have come and pleaded for
   my love—
Who but the keeper's lass of Fressing-
   field?
And yet methinks this farmer's jolly
   son
Passeth the proudest that hath pleased
   mine eye.
But, Peg, disclose not that thou art in
   love,
And show as yet no sign of love to him,

Although thou well wouldst wish him
   for thy love.
Keep that to thee till time doth serve
   thy turn,
To show the grief wherein thy heart
   doth burn.—   80
Come, Joan and Thomas, shall we to
   the fair?
You, Beccles man, will not forsake us
   now?
LACY. Not whilst I may have such quaint
   girls as you.
MARGARET. Well, if you chance to come
   by Fressingfield,
Make but a step into the keeper's lodge,
And such poor fare as woodmen can
   afford,
Butter and cheese, cream and fat venison,
You shall have store, and welcome
   therewithal.
LACY. Gramercies, Peggy; look for me
   ere long.   *Exeunt omnes.*

[SCENE iv.

Hampton Court.]

Enter Henry the Third, the Emperor, the
   King of Castile, Elinor, his daughter,
   Jaques Vandermast, a German.

HENRY. Great men of Europe, monarchs
   of the West,
Ringed with the walls of old Oceanus,
Whose lofty surge is[6] like the battle-
   ments
That compassed high-built Babel in
   with towers,
Welcome, my lords, welcome, brave
   western kings,
To England's shore, whose promontory
   cleeves
Shows Albion is another little world.
Welcome says English Henry to you
   all;
Chiefly unto the lovely Elinor,
Who dared for Edward's sake cut
   through the seas,   10
And venture as Agenor's damsel through
   the deep,
To get the love of Henry's wanton son.
CASTILE. England's rich monarch, brave
   Plantagenet,

---

[1] Surely you mistake.   [3] Good-for-nothing.
[2] He.   [4] Until now.
[5] Traditional garb of shepherds.

[6] Original has *surges.*

The Pyren Mounts swelling above the
  clouds
That ward the wealthy Castile in with
  walls
Could not detain the beauteous Elinor;
But, hearing of the fame of Edward's
  youth,
She dared to brook Neptunus' haughty
  pride,
And bide the brunt of froward Æolus.
Then may fair England welcome her
  the more.   20
ELINOR. After that English Henry by
  his lords
Had sent Prince Edward's lovely coun-
  terfeit,[1]
A present to the Castile Elinor,
The comely portrait of so brave a man,
The virtuous fame discoursèd of his
  deeds,
Edward's courageous resolution,
Done at the Holy Land fore Damas'
  walls,
Led both mine eye and thoughts in
  equal links
To like so of the English monarch's
  son
That I attempted perils for his sake.   30
EMPEROR. Where is the prince, my lord?
HENRY. He posted down, not long since,
  from the court
To Suffolk side, to merry Framlingham,
To sport himself amongst my fallow
  deer;
From thence, by packets sent to Hamp-
  ton House,
We hear the prince is ridden with his
  lords
To Oxford, in the academy there
To hear dispute amongst the learned
  men.
But we will send forth letters for my son,
To will him come from Oxford to the
  court.   40
EMPEROR. Nay, rather, Henry, let us,
  as we be,
Ride for to visit Oxford with our train.
Fain would I see your universities,
And what learned men your academy
  yields.
From Hapsburg have I brought a
  learned clerk
To hold dispute with English orators.

This doctor, surnamed Jaques Vander-
  mast,
A German born, passed into Padua,
To Florence and to fair Bolonia,
To Paris, Rheims, and stately Orleans, 50
And, talking there with men of art,
  put down
The chiefest of them all in aphorisms,
In magic, and the mathematic rules.
Now let us, Henry, try him in your
  schools.
HENRY. He shall, my lord; this motion
  likes me well.
We'll progress straight to Oxford with
  our trains,
And see what men our academy brings.—
And, wonder Vandermast, welcome to
  me.
In Oxford shalt thou find a jolly friar
Called Friar Bacon, England's only
  flower.   60
Set him but nonplus in his magic spells,
And make him yield in mathematic
  rules,
And for thy glory I will bind thy brows,
Not with a poet's garland made of bays,
But with a coronet of choicest gold.
Whilst then [2] we f[l]it to Oxford with
  our troops,
Let's in and banquet in our English
  court.   *Exit [with his Train].*

[SCENE V.

An Oxford street.]

*Enter Rafe Simnell in Edward's apparel;
Edward, Warren, Ermsby, disguised.*

RAFE. Where be these vagabond knaves,
that they attend no better on their master?
EDWARD. If it please your honor, we
are all ready at an inch.[3]
RAFE. Sirrah Ned, I'll have no more
post horse to ride on. I'll have another
fetch.[4]
ERMSBY. I pray you, how is that, my
lord?   10
RAFE. Marry, sir, I'll send to the Isle
of Ely for four or five dozen of geese, and
I'll have them tied six and six together
with whipcord. Now upon their backs
will I have a fair field bed [5] with a canopy;

[1] Picture.
[2] Until the time that.   [3] At any instant.   [4] Trick.
[5] Portable bed used in campaigns.

and so, when it is my pleasure, I'll flee into what place I please. This will be easy.
WARREN. Your honor hath said well.
But shall we to Brazen-nose College before we pull off our boots?   20
ERMSBY. Warren, well motioned; we will
    to the friar
Before we revel it within the town.—
Rafe, see you keep your countenance
    like a prince.
RAFE. Wherefore have I such a company of cutting [1] knaves to wait upon me,
but to keep and defend my countenance
against all mine enemies? Have you not
good swords and bucklers?

Enter Bacon and Miles.

ERMSBY. Stay, who comes here?
WARREN. Some scholar; and we'll [30
ask him where Friar Bacon is.
BACON. Why, thou arrant dunce, shall
I never make thee good scholar? Doth
not all the town cry out and say, "Friar
Bacon's subsizer [2] is the greatest block-
head in all Oxford"? Why, thou canst not
speak one word of true Latin.
MILES. No, sir? Yes, what is this else?
Ego sum tuus homo—"I am your man."
I warrant you, sir, as good Tully's [40
phrase as any is in Oxford.
BACON. Come on, sirrah! What part
of speech is *Ego?*
MILES. *Ego*, that is "I"; marry, *nomen
substantivo.*
BACON. How prove you that?
MILES. Why, sir, let him prove him-
self, and a will; "I" can be heard, felt,
and understood.   49
BACON. O gross dunce!   *Here beat him.*
EDWARD. Come, let us break off this
dispute between these two.—Sirrah, where
is Brazen-nose College?
MILES. Not far from Coppersmiths'
Hall.
EDWARD. What, dost thou mock me?
MILES. Not I, sir. But what would
you at Brazen-nose?
ERMSBY. Marry, we would speak with
Friar Bacon.   60
MILES. Whose men be you?

ERMSBY. Marry, scholar, here's our
master.
RAFE. Sirrah, I am the master of these
good fellows. Mayst thou not know me to
be a lord by my reparel?
MILES. Then here's good game for the
hawk; for here's the master fool and a
covey of coxcombs. One wise man, I
think, would spring [3] you all.   70
EDWARD. Gog's [4] wounds!   Warren,
kill him!
WARREN. Why, Ned, I think the
devil be in my sheath; I cannot get out
my dagger.
ERMSBY. Nor I mine. 'Swones,[5] Ned,
I think I am bewitched.
MILES. A company of scabs! The
proudest of you all draw your weapon, if he
can.—[*Aside.*] See how boldly I speak, [80
now my master is by.
EDWARD. I strive in vain; but, if my sword
    be shut
And conjured fast by magic in my sheath,
Villain, here is my fist!
                Strike him a box on the ear.
MILES. O, I beseech you, conjure his
hands too, that he may not lift his arms
to his head, for he is light-fingered!
RAFE. Ned, strike him; I'll warrant [6]
thee, by mine honor.
BACON. What means the English prince
    to wrong my man?   90
EDWARD. To whom speakest thou?
BACON. To thee.
EDWARD. Who art thou?
BACON. Could you not judge when all
    your swords grew fast
That Friar Bacon was not far from
    hence?
Edward, King Henry's son and Prince
    of Wales,
Thy fool disguised cannot conceal thy-
    self.
I know both Ermsby and the Sussex
    earl,
Else Friar Bacon had but little skill.
Thou comest in post from merry Fres-
    singfield,   100
Fast-fancied [7] to the keeper's bonny
    lass,
To crave some succor of the jolly friar;

---

[1] Swaggering.
[2] Student who worked for his board and tui-
tion.
[3] Springe, ensnare.
[4] God's.
[5] Swounds, God's wounds.
[6] Back, support.
[7] Bound by love.

And Lacy, Earl of Lincoln, hast thou left
To treat [1] fair Margaret to allow thy
  loves.
But friends are men, and love can baffle
  lords;
The earl both woos and courts her for
  himself.
WARREN. Ned, this is strange; the friar
  knoweth all.
ERMSBY. Apollo could not utter more than
  this.
EDWARD. I stand amazed to hear this
  jolly friar
Tell even the very secrets of my
  thoughts.—   110
But, learned Bacon, since thou knowest
  the cause
Why I did post so fast from Fressingfield,
Help, friar, at a pinch, that I may have
The love of lovely Margaret to myself,
And, as I am true Prince of Wales, I'll give
Living and lands to strength thy college state.
WARREN. Good friar, help the prince in
  this.
RAFE. Why, servant Ned, will not the
friar do it? Were not my sword glued to
my scabbard by conjuration, I would [120
cut off his head, and make him do it by
force.
MILES. In faith, my lord, your man-
hood and your sword is all alike; they are
so fast conjured that we shall never see
them.
ERMSBY. What, doctor, in a dump?
  Tush, help the prince,
And thou shalt see how liberal he will
  prove.
BACON. Crave not such actions greater
  dumps than these?
I will, my lord, strain out my magic
  spells;   130
For this day comes the earl to Fressing-
  field,
And fore that night shuts in the day
  with dark,
They'll be betrothéd each to other fast.
But come with me; we'll to my study
  straight,
And in a glass prospective [2] I will show
What's done this day in merry Fres-
  singfield.

EDWARD. Gramercies, Bacon; I will
  quite [3] thy pain.
BACON. But send your train, my lord,
  into the town.
My scholar shall go bring them to their
  inn.
Meanwhile we'll see the knavery of
  the earl.   140
EDWARD. Warren, leave me, and, Erms-
  by, take the fool;
Let him be master, and go revel it
Till I and Friar Bacon talk awhile.
WARREN. We will, my lord.
RAFE. Faith, Ned, and I'll lord it out
till thou comest. I'll be Prince of Wales
over all the blackpots [4] in Oxford.   *Exeunt.*

[SCENE vi.

Bacon's study.]

Bacon and Edward goes into the study.

BACON. Now, frolic Edward, welcome
  to my cell.
Here tempers Friar Bacon many toys,
And holds this place his consistory
  court,
Wherein the devils plead homage to
  his words.
Within this glass prospective thou shalt
  see
This day what's done in merry Fressingfield
Twixt lovely Peggy and the Lincoln
  earl.
EDWARD. Friar, thou glad'st me. Now
  shall Edward try
How Lacy meaneth to his sovereign
  lord.
BACON. Stand there and look directly
  in the glass.   10

Enter Margaret and Friar Bungay. [5]

What sees my lord?
EDWARD. I see the keeper's lovely lass
  appear,
As bright-sun [6] as the paramour of
  Mars,
Only attended by a jolly friar.

---

[1] Entreat.   [2] Magic mirror.

[3] Requite, reward.
[4] Leather wine jugs.
[5] The persons in the magic glass are seen but
not heard by Edward.
[6] Brightsome (?).

BACON. Sit still, and keep the crystal in
  your eye.

MARGARET. But tell me, Friar Bungay,
  is it true
That this fair courteous country swain,
Who says his father is a farmer nigh,
Can be Lord Lacy, Earl of Lincolnshire?
BUNGAY. Peggy, 'tis true; 'tis Lacy for
  my life,   20
Or else mine art and cunning both doth
  fail,
Left by Prince Edward to procure his
  loves;
For he in green, that holp you run your
  cheese,
Is son to Henry, and the Prince of Wales.
MARGARET. Be what he will, his lure is
  but for lust.
But did Lord Lacy like poor Margaret,
Or would he deign to wed a country
  lass,
Friar, I would his humble handmaid be,
And for great wealth quite him with
  courtesy.
BUNGAY. Why, Margaret, dost thou love
  him?   30
MARGARET. His personage, like the pride
  of vaunting Troy,
Might well avouch to shadow [1] Helen's
  scape. [2]
His wit is quick and ready in conceit,
As Greece afforded in her chiefest prime,
Courteous, ah, friar, full of pleasing
  smiles!
Trust me, I love too much to tell thee
  more;
Suffice, to me he's England's paramour. [3]
BUNGAY. Hath not each eye that viewed
  thy pleasing face
Surnaméd thee Fair Maid of Fressing-
  field?
MARGARET. Yes, Bungay; and would
  God the lovely earl   40
Had that *in esse* [4] that so many sought.
BUNGAY. Fear not, the friar will not be
  behind
To show his cunning to entangle love.

EDWARD. I think the friar courts the
  bonny wench;
Bacon, methinks he is a lusty churl.
BACON. Now look, my lord.

Enter Lacy [disguised as before].

EDWARD. Gog's wounds, Bacon, here
  comes Lacy!
BACON. Sit still, my lord, and mark the
  comedy.

BUNGAY. Here's Lacy; Margaret, step
  aside awhile.   [*They withdraw.*]
LACY. Daphne, the damsel that caught
  Phœbus fast,   50
And locked him in the brightness of
  her looks,
Was not so beauteous in Apollo's eyes
As is fair Margaret to the Lincoln earl.
Recant thee, Lacy.   Thou art put in
  trust.
Edward, thy sovereign's son, hath
  chosen thee,
A secret friend, to court her for himself,
And darest thou wrong thy prince with
  treachery?
Lacy, love makes no exception of a
  friend,
Nor deems it of a prince but as a man.
Honor bids thee control him in his lust.
His wooing is not for to wed the girl,   61
But to entrap her and beguile the lass.
Lacy, thou lovest; then brook not such
  abuse,
But wed her, and abide thy prince's
  frown,
For better die than see her live disgraced.
MARGARET. Come, friar, I will shake him
  from his dumps.—   [*Comes forward.*]
How cheer you, sir?   A penny for your
  thought!
You're early up, pray God it be the
  near. [5]
What, come from Beccles in a morn
  so soon?
LACY. Thus watchful are such men as
  live in love,   70
Whose eyes brook broken slumbers for
  their sleep.
I tell thee, Peggy, since last Harleston
  fair
My mind hath felt a heap of passions.
MARGARET. A trusty man, that court it
  for your friend!
Woo you still for the courtier all in
  green?
I marvel that he sues not for himself.

---

[1] Excuse.   [3] Darling.
[2] Original reads *cape*.   [4] In actuality.
[5] A common expression meaning *the nearer
to your purpose.*

LACY. Peggy, I pleaded first to get your
    grace for him;
But, when mine eyes surveyed your
    beauteous looks,
Love, like a wag,[1] straight dived into
    my heart,
And there did shrine the idea [2] of your-
    self.   80
Pity me, though I be a farmer's son;
And measure not my riches, but my
    love.
MARGARET. You are very hasty; for to
    garden well,
Seeds must have time to sprout before
    they spring.
Love ought to creep as doth the dial's
    shade,
For timely [3] ripe is rotten too-too soon.
BUNGAY. [*Coming forward.*]   *Deus hic.*[4]
    Room for a merry friar!
What, youth of Beccles, with the keeper's
    lass?
'Tis well.   But, tell me, hear you any
    news?
MARGARET. No, friar.   What news?   90
BUNGAY. Hear you not how the pursui-
    vants do post
With proclamations through each coun-
    try town?
LACY. For what, gentle friar?   Tell the
    news.
BUNGAY. Dwell'st thou in Beccles, and
    hear'st not of these news?
Lacy, the Earl of Lincoln, is late fled
From Windsor court, disguiséd like a
    swain,
And lurks about the country here un-
    known.
Henry suspects him of some treachery,
And therefore doth proclaim in every
    way
That who can take the Lincoln earl
    shall have,   100
Paid in the Exchequer, twenty thousand
    crowns.
LACY. The Earl of Lincoln!   Friar, thou
    art mad!
It was some other; thou mistakest the
    man.
The Earl of Lincoln!   Why, it cannot be!
MARGARET. Yes, very well, my lord, for
    you are he.

The keeper's daughter took you prisoner.
Lord Lacy, yield; I'll be your jailer
    once.

EDWARD. How familiar they be, Bacon!
BACON. Sit still, and mark the sequel of
    their loves.
LACY. Then am I double prisoner to thy-
    self.   110
Peggy, I yield!   But are these news in
    jest?
MARGARET. In jest with you, but earnest
    unto me,
Forwhy these wrongs do wring me at
    the heart.
Ah, how these earls and noble men of
    birth
Flatter and feign, to forge poor women's
    ill!
LACY. Believe me, lass, I am the Lincoln
    earl;
I not deny but, tired thus in rags,
I lived disguised to win fair Peggy's
    love.
MARGARET. What love is there where wed-
    ding ends not love?
LACY. I meant, fair girl, to make thee
    Lacy's wife.   120
MARGARET. I little think that earls will
    stoop so low.
LACY. Say, shall I make thee countess
    ere I sleep?
MARGARET. Handmaid   unto   the   earl,
    so please himself;
A wife in name, but servant in obedi-
    ence.
LACY. The Lincoln countess, for it shall
    be so!
I'll plight the bands, and seal it with a
    kiss.

EDWARD. Gog's wounds, Bacon, they kiss!
    I'll stab them!
BACON. O, hold your hands, my lord!
    It is the glass!
EDWARD. Choler to see the traitors gree [5]
    so well   129
Made me think the shadows substances.
BACON. 'Twere a long poinard,[6] my lord,
    to reach between
Oxford and Fressingfield.   But sit still
    and see more.

---

[1] Mischievous boy.   [3] Prematurely.
[2] Image.   [4] God here.
[5] Agree.   [6] Poniard.

Bungay. Well, Lord of Lincoln, if your
    loves be knit,
And that your tongues and thoughts do
    both agree,
To avoid ensuing jars, I'll hamper up [1]
    the match.
I'll take my portace [2] forth and wed you
    here;
Then go to bed and seal up your desires.
Lacy. Friar, content.—Peggy, how like
    you this?
Margaret. What likes my lord is pleas-
    ing unto me.
Bungay. Then handfast [3] hand, and I
    will to my book.   140

Bacon. What sees my lord now?
Edward. Bacon, I see the lovers hand
    in hand,
The friar ready with his portace there
To wed them both.   Then am I quite
    undone!
Bacon, help now, if e'er thy magic served;
Help, Bacon! Stop the marriage now,
If devils or nigromancy may suffice,
And I will give thee forty thousand
    crowns.
Bacon. Fear not, my lord, I'll stop the
    jolly friar   149
For [4] mumbling up his orisons this day.

Lacy. Why speak'st not, Bungay? Friar,
    to thy book!
    Bungay is mute, crying, "Hud, hud."
Margaret. How lookest thou, friar, as
    a man distraught!
Reft of thy senses. Bungay? Show by
    signs,
If thou be dumb, what passions holdeth
    thee.
Lacy. He's dumb indeed. Bacon hath
    with his devils
Enchanted him, or else some strange
    disease
Or apoplexy hath possessed his lungs.
But, Peggy, what he cannot with his
    book,
We'll twixt us both unite it up in heart.
Margaret. Else let me die, my lord, a
    miscreant.   160

Edward. Why stands Friar Bungay [5] so
    amazed?
Bacon. I have struck him dumb, my
    lord; and, if your honor please,
I'll fetch this Bungay straightway from
    Fressingfield
And he shall dine with us in Oxford here.
Edward. Bacon, do that, and thou con-
    tentest me.

Lacy. Of courtesy, Margaret, let us lead
    the friar
Unto thy father's lodge, to comfort him
With broths, to bring him from this
    hapless trance.
Margaret. Or else, my lord, we were
    passing unkind   169
To leave the friar so in his distress.

Enter a Devil, and carry Bungay on his
back.

O, help, my lord! A devil, a devil, my
    lord!
Look how he carries Bungay on his back!
Let's hence, for Bacon's spirits be
    abroad.
    Exeunt [Margaret and Lacy].

Edward. Bacon, I laugh to see the jolly
    friar
Mounted upon the devil, and how the
    earl
Flees with his bonny lass for fear.
As soon as Bungay is at Brazen-nose,
And I have chatted with the merry
    friar,
I will in post hie me to Fressingfield,
And quite these wrongs on Lacy ere it
    be long.   180
Bacon. So be it, my lord. But let us to
    our dinner,
For, ere we have taken our repast awhile,
We shall have Bungay brought to
    Brazen-nose.   *Exeunt.*

[Scene vii.
The Regent House at Oxford.]
Enter three doctors, Burden, Mason,
Clement.

Mason. Now that we are gathered in
    the Regent House,
It fits us talk about the king's repair,[6]

---

[1] Make fast.   [2] Breviary for outdoor use.
[3] Join; used of marriage contracts.   [4] From.
[5] Original reads *Bacon.*   [6] Visit.

For he, troopéd with [1] all the western
  kings
That lie alongst the Danzig seas by
  east,
North by the clime of frosty Germany,
The Almain [2] monarch, and the Saxon
  duke,[3]
Castile and lovely Elinor with him,
Have in their jests resolved for Oxford
  town.
BURDEN. We must lay plots of stately
  tragedies,
Strange comic shows such as proud
  Roscius   10
Vaunted before the Roman emperors—
CLEMENT. To welcome all the western
  potentates.
But more: the king by letters hath fore-
  told
That Frederick, the Almain emperor,
Hath brought with him a German of
  esteem,
Whose surname is Don Jaques Vander-
  mast,
Skillful in magic and those secret arts.
MASON. Then must we all make suit
  unto the friar,
To Friar Bacon, that he vouch [4] this
  task,
And undertake to countervail in skill   20
The German; else there's none in Ox-
  ford can
Match and dispute with learned Vander-
  mast.
BURDEN. Bacon, if he will hold the Ger-
  man play,
We'll teach him what an English friar
  can do.
The devil, I think, dare not dispute
  with him.
CLEMENT. Indeed, Mas' Doctor, he pleas-
  ured you,
In that he brought your hostess with
  her spit
From Henley, posting unto Brazen-nose!
BURDEN. A vengeance on the friar for his
  pains!
But, leaving that, let's hie to Bacon
  straight,   30
To see if he will take this task in hand.

CLEMENT. Stay, what rumor is this?
The town is up in a mutiny. What hurly-
burly is this?

Enter a Constable, with Rafe, Warren,
Ermsby, and Miles.

CONSTABLE. Nay, masters, if you were
ne'er so good, you shall before the doctors
to answer your misdemeanor.
BURDEN. What's the matter, fellow?
CONSTABLE. Marry, sir, here's a company of rufflers, that, drinking in   [40
the tavern, have made a great brawl,
and almost killed the vintner.
MILES. *Salve,*[5] Doctor Burden!   This
  lubberly lurden,[6]
Ill-shaped and ill-faced, disdained and
  disgraced,
What he tells unto *vobis mentitur de*
  nobis.[7]
BURDEN. Who is the master and chief
of this crew?
MILES. *Ecce asinum mundi fugura ro-*
  tundi,[8]
Neat, sheat,[9] and fine, as brisk as a cup
  of wine.
BURDEN. What are you?   50
RAFE. I am, father doctor, as a man
would say, the bellwether of this company; these are my lords, and I the Prince
of Wales.
CLEMENT. Are you Edward, the king's
son?
RAFE. Sirrah Miles, bring hither the
tapster that drew the wine, and, I warrant, when they see how soundly I have
broke his head, they'll say 'twas done [60
by no less man than a prince.
MASON. I cannot believe that this is
the Prince of Wales.
WARREN. And why so, sir?
MASON. For they say the prince is a
brave and a wise gentleman.
WARREN. Why, and thinkest thou, doctor, that he is not so?
Dar'st thou detract and derogate from
  him,
Being so lovely and so brave a youth?
ERMSBY. Whose face, shining with many
  a sugared smile,   70

---

[1] Accompanied by.   [2] German.
[3] Original reads *Scocon duke.* This character
does not actually appear, although again referred
to.   [4] Avouch, make good.
[5] Hail!   [6] Blockhead.
[7] Whatever he tells you, he is lying about us.
[8] Behold the jackass of the round-shaped world.
[9] Trim (?); lively (?).

Bewrays[1] that he is bred of princely
race.
MILES. And yet, Master Doctor, to speak
like a proctor,
And tell unto you what is veriment[2]
and true;
To cease of this quarrel, look but on
his apparel;
Then mark but my talis, he is great
Prince of Walis,
The chief of our *grepis*, and *filius regis;*[3]
Then ware what is done, for he is
Henry's white[4] son.
RAFE. Doctors, whose doting nightcaps
are not capable of my ingenious dignity,
know that I am Edward Plantage-   [80
net, whom if you displease will make a
ship that shall hold all your colleges, and
so carry away the Niniversity with a
fair wind to the Bankside in Southwark.
—How say'st thou, Ned Warren? Shall I
not do it?
WARREN. Yes, my good lord; and, if
it please your lordship, I will gather up
all your old pantofles,[5] and with the cork
make you a pinnace of five hundred   [90
ton, that shall serve the turn marvelous
well, my lord.
ERMSBY. And I, my lord, will have
pioners[6] to undermine the town, that the
very gardens and orchards be carried
away for your summer walks.
MILES. And I, with *scientia* and great
diligentia,
Will conjure and charm, to keep you
from harm;
That, *utrum horum mavis,*[7] your very
great *navis,*[8]
Like Bartlet's[9] ship, from Oxford do
skip   100
With colleges and schools, full-loaden
with fools.
Quid dices ad hoc,[10] worshipful *Domine
Dawcock?*[11]
CLEMENT. Why, hare-brained courtiers,
are you drunk or mad,
To taunt us up with such scurrility?

Deem you us men of base and light
esteem,
To bring us such a fop for Henry's
son?—
Call out the beadles and convey them
hence
Straight to Bocardo;[12] let the roisters
lie
Close clapped in bolts, until their wits
be tame.
ERMSBY. Why, shall we to prison,   [110
my lord?
RAFE. What sayst, Miles, shall I
honor the prison with my presence?
MILES. No, no! Out with your blades,
and hamper these jades;
Have a flirt[13] and a crash, now play
revel-dash,[14]
And teach these *sacerdos*[15] that the
Bocardos,
Like peasants and elves, are meet for
themselves.
MASON. To the prison with them, con-
stable!
WARREN. Well, doctors, seeing I have
sported me
With laughing at these mad and merry
wags,   120
Know that Prince Edward is at Brazen-
nose,
And this, attiréd like the Prince of
Wales,
Is Rafe, King Henry's only lovéd fool,
I, Earl of Sussex,[16] and this Ermsby,
One of the privy chamber to the king,
Who, while the prince with Friar Bacon
stays,
Have reveled it in Oxford as you see.
MASON. My lord, pardon us, we knew
not what you were.
But courtiers may make greater scapes[17]
than these.
Will 't please your honor dine with me
today?   130
WARREN. I will, Master Doctor, and
satisfy the vintner for his hurt; only I must
desire you to imagine him all this fore-
noon the Prince of Wales.
MASON. I will, sir.
RAFE. And upon that I will lead the
way; only I will have Miles go before me,

[1] Betrays.   [2] Truth.
[3] The chief of our company and son of the
king.   [4] Dear.   [5] Slippers.   [6] Diggers.
[7] Whichever of these you prefer.   [8] Ship.
[9] Miles's mistake for Barclay, the translator of
Brandt's *Ship of Fools.*
[10] What do you say to this?
[11] Jackdaw, dolt.

[12] A prison at Oxford.   [15] Priests.
[13] Quick blow.   [16] Original reads *Essex.*
[14] Rowdy game.   [17] Escapades.

because I have heard Henry say that wisdom must go before majesty.

Exeunt omnes.

[SCENE viii.

Fressingfield.]

Enter Prince Edward with his poinard in his hand, Lacy, and Margaret.

EDWARD. Lacy, thou canst not shroud thy trait'rous thoughts,
Nor cover, as did Cassius, all his wiles;
For Edward hath an eye that looks as far
As Lynceus from the shores of Grecia.
Did not I sit in Oxford by the friar,
And see thee court the maid of Fressingfield,
Sealing thy flattering fancies with a kiss?
Did not proud Bungay draw his portace forth,
And, joining hand in hand, had married you,
If Friar Bacon had not stroke [1] him dumb,   10
And mounted him upon a spirit's back,
That we might chat at Oxford with the friar?
Traitor, what answer'st?   Is not all this true?
LACY. Truth all, my lord; and thus I make reply:
At Harleston Fair, there courting for your grace,
Whenas mine eye surveyed her curious shape,
And drew the beauteous glory of her looks
To dive into the center of my heart,
Love taught me that your honor did but jest,   19
That princes were in fancy [2] but as men;
How that the lovely maid of Fressingfield
Was fitter to be Lacy's wedded wife
Than concubine unto the Prince of Wales.
EDWARD. Injurious Lacy, did I love thee more
Than Alexander his Hephestion?
Did I unfold the passion[s] of my love,

And lock them in the closet of thy thoughts?
Wert thou to Edward second to himself,
Sole friend, and partner of his secret loves?
And could a glance of fading beauty break   30
The enchainéd fetters of such private friends?
Base coward, false, and too effeminate
To be corrival [3] with a prince in thoughts!
From Oxford have I posted since I dined,
To quite a traitor fore that Edward sleep.
MARGARET. 'Twas I, my lord, not Lacy stepped awry;
For oft he sued and courted for yourself,
And still wooed for the courtier all in green.   38
But I, whom fancy made but overfond,
Pleaded myself with looks as if I loved;
I fed mine eye with gazing on his face,
And still bewitched loved Lacy with my looks.
My heart with sighs, mine eyes pleaded with tears,
My face held pity and content at once,
And more I could not cipher out [4] by signs
But that I loved Lord Lacy with my heart.
Then, worthy Edward, measure with thy mind
If women's favors will not force men fall,
If beauty and if darts of piercing love
Are not of force to bury thoughts of friends.   50
EDWARD. I tell thee, Peggy, I will have thy loves;
Edward or none shall conquer Margaret.
In frigates bottomed with rich Sethin [5] planks,
Topped with the lofty firs of Lebanon,
Stemmed and incased with burnished ivory,
And overlaid with plates of Persian wealth,
Like Thetis shalt thou wanton on the waves,
And draw the dolphins to thy lovely eyes,

---

[1] Struck.   [2] Love.   [3] Partner.   [4] Express.   [5] Shittim.

To dance lavoltas [1] in the purple streams.
Sirens, with harps and silver psalteries, 60
Shall wait with music at thy frigate's
  stem,
And entertain fair Margaret with their [2]
  lays.
England and England's wealth shall
  wait on thee;
Britain shall bend unto her prince's
  love,
And do due homage to thine excellence,
If thou wilt be but Edward's Margaret.
MARGARET. Pardon, my lord; if Jove's
  great royalty
Sent me such presents as to Danaë,
If Phœbus, tired [3] in Latona's webs,
Come courting from the beauty of his
  lodge,   70
The dulcet tunes of frolic Mercury
Nor [4] all the wealth heaven's treasury
  affords
Should make me leave Lord Lacy or
  his love.
EDWARD. I have learned at Oxford, then,
  this point of schools: [5]
Ablata causa, tollitur effectus.[6]
Lacy, the cause that Margaret cannot
  love
Nor fix her liking on the English prince,
Take him away, and then the effects
  will fail.
Villain, prepare thyself; for I will bathe
My poinard in the bosom of an earl.   80
LACY. Rather than live, and miss fair
  Margaret's love,
Prince Edward, stop not at the fatal
  doom,
But stab it home. End both my loves
  and life.
MARGARET. Brave Prince of Wales, hon-
  ored for royal deeds,
'Twere sin to stain fair Venus' courts
  with blood;
Love's conquests ends, my lord, in
  courtesy.
Spare Lacy, gentle Edward; let me die,
For so both you and he do cease your
  loves.

[1] Lively dances.
[2] Original reads *her.*
[3] Attired. Original has *tied.*
[4] Emended by Dyce. Original reads *not.*
[5] Principle of scholastic argument.
[6] The cause being removed, the effect is
taken away.

EDWARD. Lacy shall die as traitor to his
  lord.
LACY. I have deserved it, Edward; act
  it well.   90
MARGARET. What hopes the prince to
  gain by Lacy's death?
EDWARD. To end the loves twixt him
  and Margaret.
MARGARET. Why, thinks King Henry's
  son that Margaret's love
Hangs in the uncertain balance of
  proud time?
That death shall make a discord of our
  thoughts?
No, stab the earl, and, fore the morn-
  ing sun
Shall vaunt him thrice over the lofty
  east,
Margaret will meet her Lacy in the
  heavens.
LACY. If aught betides to lovely Margaret
That wrongs or wrings her honor from
  content,   100
Europe's rich wealth nor England's
  monarchy
Should not allure Lacy to overlive.[7]
Then, Edward, short my life, and end
  her loves.
MARGARET. Rid [8] me, and keep a friend
  worth many loves.
LACY. Nay, Edward, keep a love worth
  many friends.
MARGARET. And, if thy mind be such as
  fame hath blazed,
Then, princely Edward, let us both
  abide
The fatal resolution of thy rage.
Banish thou fancy and embrace re-
  venge,
And in one tomb knit both our car-
  casses,   110
Whose hearts were linkéd in one perfect
  love.
EDWARD. [*Aside.*]   Edward, art thou
  that famous Prince of Wales
Who at Damasco beat the Saracens,
And brought'st home triumph on thy
  lance's point,
And shall thy plumes be pulled by Venus
  down?
Is it princely to dissever lovers' leagues,
To part such friends as glory in their
  loves?

[7] Outlive, survive.   [8] Get rid of.

Leave, Ned, and make a virtue of this
fault,
And further Peg and Lacy in their loves.
So in subduing fancy's passion,   120
Conquering thyself, thou gett'st the
richest spoil.—
Lacy, rise up! Fair Peggy, here's my
hand!
The Prince of Wales hath conquered
all his thoughts,
And all his loves he yields unto the earl.
Lacy, enjoy the maid of Fressingfield;
Make her thy Lincoln countess at the
church,
And Ned, as he is true Plantagenet,
Will give her to thee frankly for thy
wife.
LACY. Humbly I take her of my sover-
eign,
As if that Edward gave me England's
right,   130
And riched me with the Albion diadem.
MARGARET. And doth the English prince
mean true?
Will he vouchsafe to cease his former
loves,
And yield the title of a country maid
Unto Lord Lacy?
EDWARD. I will, fair Peggy, as I am true
lord.
MARGARET. Then, lordly sir, whose con-
quest is as great
In conquering love as Cæsar's victories,
Margaret, as mild and humble in her
thoughts
As was Aspasia unto Cyrus' self,   140
Yields thanks, and, next Lord Lacy,
doth enshrine
Edward the second secret in her heart.[1]
EDWARD. Gramercy, Peggy. Now that
vows are passed,
And that your loves are not [to] be
revolt,[2]
Once, Lacy, friends again, come, we will
post
To Oxford; for this day the king is
there,
And brings for Edward Castile Elinor.
Peggy, I must go see and view my wife;
I pray God I like her as I loved thee.
Beside, Lord Lincoln, we shall hear
dispute   150

[1] *I.e.*, the second (next to Lacy) in her affection.   [2] Withdrawn, overturned.

Twixt Friar Bacon and learned Vander-
mast.
Peggy, we'll leave you for a week or two.
MARGARET. As it please Lord Lacy; but
love's foolish looks
Think footsteps miles and minutes to
be hours.
LACY. I'll hasten, Peggy, to make short
return.—
But, please your honor, go unto the
lodge.
We shall have butter, cheese, and veni-
son;
And yesterday I brought for Margaret
A lusty bottle of neat claret wine.
Thus can we feast and entertain your
grace.   160
EDWARD. 'Tis cheer, Lord Lacy, for an
emperor,
If he respect the person and the place.
Come, let us in; for I will all this night
Ride post until I come to Bacon's cell.
Exeunt.

[SCENE ix.

Oxford.]

Enter Henry, Emperor, Castile, Elinor,
Vandermast, Bungay.

EMPEROR. Trust me, Plantagenet, these
Oxford schools
Are richly seated near the riverside,
The mountains full of fat and fallow
deer,
The battling [3] pastures lade [4] with kine
and flocks,
The town gorgeous with high-built
colleges,
And scholars seemly in their grave at-
tire,
Learned in searching principles of art.—
What is thy judgment, Jaques Vander-
mast?
VANDER. That lordly are the buildings of
the town,
Spacious the rooms, and full of pleasant
walks;   10
But for the doctors, how that they be
learned,
It may be meanly, for aught I can hear.
BUNGAY. I tell thee, German, Hapsburg
holds none such,
None read so deep as Oxenford contains.

[3] Nourishing.   [4] Laden.

There are within our academic state
Men that may lecture it in Germany
To all the doctors of your Belgic schools.
HENRY. Stand to him, Bungay; charm
   this Vandermast,
And I will use thee as a royal king.
VANDER. Wherein darest thou dispute with
   me?   20
BUNGAY. In what a doctor and a friar
   can.
VANDER. Before rich Europe's worthies
   put thou forth
The doubtful question unto Vander-
   mast.
BUNGAY. Let it be this: Whether the
spirits of pyromancy or geomancy be most
predominant in magic?
   VANDER. I say, of pyromancy.
   BUNGAY. And I, of geomancy.
VANDER. The cabalists that write of
   magic spells,
As Hermes, Melchie, and Pythagoras, 30
Affirm that, 'mongst the quadruplicity
Of elemental essence, *terra* is but thought
To be a *punctum* squaréd to [1] the rest;
And that the compass of ascending
   elements
Exceed in bigness as they do in height;
Judging the concave circle of the sun
To hold the rest in his circumference.
If, then, as Hermes says, the fire be
   great'st,
Purest, and only giveth shapes to
   spirits,
Then must these *dæmones* [2] that haunt
   that place   40
Be every way superior to the rest.
BUNGAY. I reason not of elemental shapes,
Nor tell I of the concave latitudes,
Noting their essence nor their quality,
But of the spirits that pyromancy calls,
And of the vigor of the geomantic
   fiends.
I tell thee, German, magic haunts the
   grounds,
And those strange necromantic spells,
That work such shows and wondering
   in the world,
Are acted by those geomantic spirits   50
That Hermes calleth *terræ filii*.[3]
The fiery spirits are but transparent
   shades,

That lightly pass as heralds to bear
   news;
But earthly fiends, closed in the lowest
   deep,
Dissever mountains, if they be but
   charged,
Being more gross and massy in their
   power.
VANDER. Rather these earthly geomantic
   spirits
Are dull and like the place where they
   remain;
For, when proud Lucifer fell from the
   heavens,
The spirits and angels that did sin with
   him   60
Retained their local essence as their
   faults,
All subject under Luna's continent.
They which offended less hang in the
   fire,
And second faults did rest within the
   air;
But Lucifer and his proud-hearted
   fiends
Were thrown into the center of the
   earth,
Having less understanding than the
   rest,
As having greater sin and lesser grace.
Therefore such gross and earthly spirits
   do serve
For jugglers, witches, and vild [4] sor-
   cerers;   70
Whereas the pyromantic genii
Are mighty, swift, and of far-reaching
   power.
But, grant that geomancy hath most
   force,
Bungay, to please these mighty poten-
   tates,
Prove by some instance what thy art
   can do.
BUNGAY. I will.
EMPEROR. Now, English Harry, here be-
   gins the game;
We shall see sport between these learned
   men.
VANDER. What wilt thou do?
BUNGAY. Show thee the tree, leaved with
   refinéd gold,   80
Whereon the fearful dragon held his
   seat,

[1] An atom compared with.
[2] Spirits.   [3] Sons of the earth.
[4] Vile, low in rank.

That watched the garden called Hes-
  perides,
Subdued and won by conquering Her·
  cules.
VANDER. Well done!

Here Bungay conjures, and the tree appears
      with the Dragon shooting fire.

HENRY. What say you, royal lordings,
  to my friar?
  Hath he not done a point of cunning
    skill?
VANDER. Each scholar in the nigromantic
  spells
Can do as much as Bungay hath per-
  formed.
But as Alcmena's bastard razed this
  tree,
So will I raise him up as when he lived, 90
And cause him pull the dragon from
  his seat,
And tear the branches piecemeal from
  the root.—
Hercules! *Prodi, prodi,*[1] Hercules!

Hercules appears in his lion's skin.

HERCULES. *Quis me vult?* [2]
VANDER. Jove's bastard son, thou Lib-
  yan Hercules,
Pull off the sprigs from off the Hespe-
  rian tree,
As once thou didst to win the golden
  fruit.
HERCULES. *Fiat.*[3]
  Here he begins to break the branches.
VANDER. Now, Bungay, if thou canst
  by magic charm   99
The fiend appearing like great Hercules
From pulling down the branches of the
  tree,
Then art thou worthy to be counted
  learned.
BUNGAY. I cannot.
VANDER. Cease, Hercules, until I give
  thee charge.—
Mighty commander of this English isle,
Henry, come from the stout Plantag-
  enets,
Bungay is learned enough to be a friar;
But, to compare with Jaques Vander-
  mast,

Oxford and Cambridge must go seek
  their cells
To find a man to match him in his art. 110
I have given nonplus to the Paduans,
To them of Sien, Florence, and Bologna,
Rheims, Louvain, and fair Rotherdam,
Frankfort, Lutrech,[4] and Orleans.
And now must Henry, if he do me right,
Crown me with laurel, as they all have
  done.

Enter Bacon.

BACON. All hail to this royal company,
That sit to hear and see this strange
  dispute!—
Bungay, how stand'st thou as a man
  amazed!
What, hath the German acted more
  than thou?   120
VANDER. What art thou that questions
  thus?
BACON. Men call me Bacon.
VANDER. Lordly thou look'st, as if that
  thou wert learned;
Thy countenance as if science held her
  seat
Between the circled arches of thy brows.
HENRY. Now, monarchs, hath the German
  found his match.
EMPEROR. Bestir thee, Jaques; take not
  now the foil,[5]
Lest thou dost lose what foretime thou
  didst gain.
VANDER. Bacon, wilt thou dispute?
BACON. No, unless he were more learned
  than Vandermast;   130
For yet, tell me, what hast thou done?
VANDER. Raised Hercules to ruinate that
  tree
That Bungay mounted by his magic
  spells.
BACON. Set Hercules to work.
VANDER. Now, Hercules, I charge thee
  to thy task;
Pull off the golden branches from the
  root.
HERCULES. I dare not. Seest thou not
  great Bacon here,
Whose frown doth act more than thy
  magic can?
VANDER. By all the thrones and domina-
  tions,   139

---

[1] Come forth.   [2] Who wishes me?
[3] Let it be done.

[4] Utrecht, or Lutetia (Paris) (?).
[5] Fall, a wrestling term.

Virtues, powers, and mighty hierarchies,
I charge thee to obey to Vandermast.

HERCULES. Bacon, that bridles headstrong Belcephon,
And rules Asmenoth, guider of the north,
Binds me from yielding unto Vandermast.

HENRY. How now, Vandermast! Have
you met with your match?

VANDER. Never before was't known to
Vandermast
That men held devils in such obedient
awe.
Bacon doth more than art, or else I
fail.

EMPEROR. Why, Vandermast, art thou
overcome?—
Bacon, dispute with him, and try his
skill.   150

BACON. I come not, monarchs, for to
hold dispute
With such a novice as is Vandermast;
I come to have your royalties to dine
With Friar Bacon here in Brazen-nose.
And, for this German troubles but the
place,
And holds this audience with a long
suspense,
I'll send him to his academy hence.—
Thou Hercules, whom Vandermast did
raise,
Transport the German unto Hapsburg
straight,
That he may learn by travail, gainst
the spring,[1]   160
More secret dooms and aphorisms of art.
Vanish the tree, and thou away with
him!

Exit the Spirit with Vandermast and the tree.

EMPEROR. Why, Bacon, whither dost
thou send him?

BACON. To Hapsburg; there your highness at return
Shall find the German in his study safe.

HENRY. Bacon, thou hast honored England with thy skill,
And made fair Oxford famous by thine
art;
I will be English Henry to thyself.
But tell me, shall we dine with thee
today?

BACON. With me, my lord. And, while I
fit my cheer,   170

[1] Original reads *springs*.

See where Prince Edward comes to welcome you,
Gracious as the morning star of heaven.
                                                   Exit.

Enter Edward, Lacy, Warren, Ermsby.

EMPEROR. Is this Prince Edward, Henry's
royal son?
How martial is the figure of his face,
Yet lovely and beset with amorets![2]

HENRY. Ned, where hast thou been?

EDWARD. At Framlingham, my lord, to
try your bucks
If they could scape the teasers or the
toil.
But, hearing of these lordly potentates
Landed and progressed up to Oxford
town,   180
I posted to give entertain [3] to them—
Chief, to the Almain monarch; next to
him,
And joint with him, Castile and Saxony
Are welcome as they may be to the
English court.
Thus for the men. But see, Venus ap-
pears,
Or one that overmatcheth Venus in
her shape!—
Sweet Elinor, beauty's high-swelling
pride,
Rich nature's glory and her wealth at
once,
Fair of all fairs, welcome to Albion;
Welcome to me, and welcome to thine
own,   190
If that thou deign'st the welcome from
myself.

ELINOR. Martial Plantagenet, Henry's
high-minded son,
The mark that Elinor did count her aim,
I liked thee fore I saw thee. Now I
love,
And so as in so short a time I may;
Yet so as time shall never break that
so,
And therefore so accept of Elinor.

CASTILE. Fear not, my lord, this couple
will agree,
If love may creep into their wanton
eyes.
And therefore, Edward, I accept thee
here,   200
Without suspense, as my adopted son.

[2] Loving looks.   [3] Reception.

HENRY. Let me that joy in these consort-
ing greets,
And glory in these honors done to Ned,
Yield thanks for all these favors to my
son,
And rest a true Plantagenet to all.

*Enter Miles with a cloth and trenchers and
salt.*

MILES.[1] *Salvete, omnes reges,*[2] that govern
your *greges* [3]
In Saxony and Spain, in England and
in Almain!
For all this frolic rable [4] must I cover
thee, table,[5]
With trenchers, salt, and cloth; and
then look for your broth.   209
EMPEROR. What pleasant fellow is this?
HENRY. 'Tis, my lord, Doctor Bacon's
poor scholar.
MILES. [*Aside.*] My master hath made
me sewer [6] of these great lords; and, God
knows, I am as serviceable at a table as
a sow is under an apple tree. 'Tis no matter; their cheer shall not be great, and
therefore what skills [7] where the salt stand,[8]
before or behind?   [*Exit.*]
CASTILE. These scholars knows more skill
in axioms,   220
How to use quips and sleights of soph-
istry,
Than for to cover [9] courtly for a king.

*Enter Miles with a mess of pottage and
broth; and, after him, Bacon.*

MILES. [10] Spill, sir? Why, do you think
I never carried twopenny chop [11] before
in my life?—
By your leave, *nobile decus,*[12] for here
comes Doctor Bacon's *pecus,*[13]
Being in his full age, to carry a mess of
pottage.

[1] The following speech appears as prose in the
original.
[2] Hail, all you kings. [5] The table (?).
[3] Peoples.   [6] Butler.
[4] Rabble.   [7] What does it matter?
[8] A large saltcellar usually marked the dividing line between superior and inferior guests.
[9] Set a table.
[10] All of the following speech is printed as prose
in the original.
[11] Chopped meat in broth (?).
[12] Your worshipful honor.
[13] Beast of burden.

BACON. Lordings, admire [14] not if your
cheer be this,
For we must keep our academic fare;
No riot where philosophy doth reign.
And therefore, Henry, place these po-
tentates,   231
And bid them fall unto their frugal
cates.
EMPEROR. Presumptuous friar! What,
scoff'st thou at a king?
What, dost thou taunt us with thy
peasants' fare,
And give us cates fit for country
swains?—
Henry, proceeds this jest of thy consent,
To twit us with such a pittance of such
price?
Tell me, and Frederick will not grieve
thee long.
HENRY. By Henry's honor, and the royal
faith
The English monarch beareth to his
friend,   240
I knew not of the friar's feeble fare,
Nor am I pleased he entertains you
thus.
BACON. Content thee, Frederick, for I
showed the cates
To let thee see how scholars use to feed,
How little meat refines our English
wits.—
Miles, take away, and let it be thy din-
ner.
MILES. Marry, sir, I will. This day shall
be a festival day with me,
For I shall exceed in the highest degree.
    Exit Miles.
BACON. I tell thee, monarch, all the Ger-
man peers
Could not afford thy entertainment
such,   250
So royal and so full of majesty,
As Bacon will present to Frederick.
The basest waiter that attends thy cups
Shall be in honors greater than thyself;
And for thy cates, rich Alexandria
drugs,[15]
Fetched by carvels from Egypt's rich-
est straits,
Found in the wealthy strond of Africa,
Shall royalize the table of my king.
Wines richer than the 'Gyptian courte-
san

[14] Wonder.   [15] Spices.

Quaffed to Augustus' kingly counter-
  match,[1]   260
Shall be caroused in English Henry's
  feast;
Kandy shall yield the richest of her
  canes;
Persia, down her Volga by canoes,
Send down the secrets of her spicery;
The Afric dates, mirabiles [2] of Spain,
Conserves and suckets [3] from Tiberias,
Cates from Judea, choicer than the
  lamp [4]
That fired Rome with sparks of glut-
  tony,
Shall beautify the board for Frederick.
And therefore grudge not at a friar's
  feast.   [*Exeunt.*]

[SCENE x.

Fressingfield.]

Enter two gentlemen, Lambert and Serlsby,
                          with the Keeper.

LAMBERT. Come, frolic keeper of our
  liege's game,
Whose table spread hath ever venison
And jacks [5] of wine to welcome passen-
  gers,
Know I am in love with jolly Margaret,
That overshines our damsels as the moon
Dark'neth the brightest sparkles of
  the night.
In Laxfield here my land and living
  lies.
I'll make thy daughter jointer [6] of it
  all,
So thou consent to give her to [7] my wife;
And I can spend five hundreth marks
  a year.   10
SERLSBY. I am the lands-lord, keeper, of
  thy holds;
By copy [8] all thy living lies in me;
Laxfield did never see me raise my due.
I will enfeoff fair Margaret in all
So she will take her to a lusty squire.
KEEPER. Now, courteous gentles, if the
  keeper's girl
Hath pleased the liking fancy of you
  both,

And with her beauty hath subdued your
  thoughts,
'Tis doubtful to decide the question.
It joys me that such men of great esteem
Should lay their liking on this base
  estate,   21
And that her state should grow so for-
  tunate
To be a wife to meaner men than you.
But sith [9] such squires will stoop to
  keeper's fee,
I will, to avoid displeasure of you both,
Call Margaret forth, and she shall make
  her choice.   *Exit.*
LAMBERT. Content, keeper; send her un-
  to us.
Why, Serlsby, is thy wife so lately dead,
Are all thy loves so lightly passéd over,
As thou canst wed before the year be
  out?   30
SERLSBY. I live not, Lambert, to content
  the dead,
Nor was I wedded but for life to her.
The grave [10] ends and begins a married
  state.

Enter Margaret.

LAMBERT. Peggy, the lovely flower of
  all towns,
Suffolk's fair Helen, and rich England's
  star,
Whose beauty, tempered with her hus-
  wifery,
Makes England talk of merry Fressing-
  field!
SERLSBY. I cannot trick it up with poesies,
Nor paint my passions with compari-
  sons,   39
Nor tell a tale of Phœbus and his loves;
But this believe me: Laxfield here is
  mine,
Of ancient rent seven hundred pounds
  a year,
And, if thou canst but love a country
  squire,
I will enfeoff thee, Margaret, in all.
I cannot flatter; try me, if thou please.
MARGARET. Brave neighboring squires,
  the stay of Suffolk's clime,
A keeper's daughter is too base in gree [11]
To match with men accompted [12] of
  such worth.

---

[1] Rival.
[2] Myrobalans, dried plums.
[3] Sweetmeats.
[4] Ward suggests *lamprey.*

[5] Pitchers.
[6] Joint-possessor.
[7] For.
[8] Copyhold.

[9] Since.
[10] Original reads *graves.*

[11] Degree.
[12] Accounted.

But might I not displease, I would reply.

LAMBERT. Say, Peggy; naught shall make us discontent.   50

MARGARET. Then, gentles, note that love hath little stay,
Nor can the flames that Venus sets on fire
Be kindled but by fancy's motion.
Then pardon, gentles, if a maid's reply
Be doubtful, while [1] I have debated with myself,
Who, or of whom, love shall constrain me like.

SERLSBY. Let it be me; and trust me, Margaret,
The meads environed with the silver streams,
Whose battling pastures fatt'neth all my flocks,
Yielding forth fleeces stapled [2] with such wool   60
As Leominster [3] cannot yield more finer stuff,
And forty kine with fair and burnished heads,
With strouting [4] dugs that paggle [5] to the ground,
Shall serve thy dairy, if thou wed with me.

LAMBERT. Let pass the country wealth, as flocks and kine,
And lands that wave with Ceres' golden sheaves,
Filling my barns with plenty of the fields.
But, Peggy, if thou wed thyself to me,
Thou shalt have garments of embrodered [6] silk,
Lawns, and rich networks for thy head-attire.   70
Costly shall be thy fair abiliments,[7]
If thou wilt be but Lambert's loving wife.

MARGARET. Content you, gentles; you have proffered fair,
And more than fits a country maid's degree;
But give me leave to counsel me a time,
For fancy blooms not at the first assault.

Give me but ten days' respite, and I will reply,
Which or to whom myself affectionates.

SERLSBY. Lambert, I tell thee, thou art importunate;   79
Such beauty fits not such a base esquire.
It is for Serlsby to have Margaret.

LAMBERT. Think'st thou with wealth to overreach me?
Serlsby, I scorn to brook thy country braves.[8]
I dare thee, coward, to maintain this wrong,
At dint of rapier, single in the field.

SERLSBY. I'll answer, Lambert, what I have avouched!—
Margaret, farewell; another time shall serve.   *Exit Serlsby.*

LAMBERT. I'll follow! — Peggy, farewell to thyself;
Listen how well I'll answer for thy love.
     Exit Lambert.

MARGARET. How Fortune tempers lucky haps with frowns,   90
And wrongs me with the sweets of my delight!
Love is my bliss, and love is now my bale.
Shall I be Helen in my forward [9] fates,
As I am Helen in my matchless hue,
And set rich Suffolk with my face afire?
If lovely Lacy were but with his Peggy,
The cloudy darkness of his bitter frown
Would check the pride of these aspiring squires.
Before the term of ten days be expired,
Whenas they look for answer of their loves,   100
My lord will come to merry Fressing-field,
And end their fancies and their follies both.
Till when, Peggy, be blithe and of good cheer.

Enter a Post with a letter and a bag of gold.

POST. Fair lovely damsel, which way leads this path?
How might I post me unto Fressingfield?
Which footpath leadeth to the keeper's lodge?

MARGARET. Your way is ready, and this path is right.

---

[1] Until.   [2] Fibered.
[3] The original spelling, *Lempster*, indicates the pronunciation.
[4] Swelling.   [6] Embroidered.
[5] Hang loosely down.   [7] Habiliments.
[8] Boasts, insults.   [9] Froward.

Myself do dwell hereby in Fressingfield,
And, if the keeper be the man you seek,
I am his daughter. May I know the
  cause? 110
POST. Lovely, and once beloved of my
  lord—
No marvel if his eye was lodged so
  low,
When brighter beauty is not in the
  heavens—
The Lincoln earl hath sent you letters
  here,
And, with them, just an hundred pounds
  in gold.
Sweet, bonny wench, read them and
  make reply.
MARGARET. The scrolls that Jove sent
  Danaë,
Wrapped in rich closures [1] of fine bur-
  nished gold,
Were not more welcome than these
  lines to me.
Tell me, whilst that I do unrip the
  seals, 120
Lives Lacy well? How fares my lovely
  lord?
POST. Well, if that wealth may make men
  to live well.

The letter, and Margaret reads it.

" The blooms of the almond tree grow in
a night, and vanish in a morn; the flies
hœmeræ,[2] fair Peggy, take life with the
sun, and die with the dew; fancy, that
slippeth in with a gaze, goeth out with
a wink; and too timely loves have ever
the shortest length. I write this as thy
grief, and my folly, who at Fressing- [130
field loved that which time hath taught
me to be but mean dainties. Eyes are
dissemblers, and fancy is but queasy.
Therefore know, Margaret, I have chosen
a Spanish lady to be my wife, chief waiting-
woman to the Princess Elinor—a lady
fair, and no less fair than thyself, honorable and wealthy. In that I forsake thee,
I leave thee to thine own liking; and for
thy dowry I have sent thee an hundred [140
pounds, and ever assure thee of my favor,
which shall avail thee and thine much.
  Farewell. Not thine, nor his own,
           EDWARD LACY."

[1] Coverings.
[2] Ephemeræ.

Fond Ate, doomer of bad-boding fates,
That wraps proud Fortune in thy snaky
  locks,
Didst thou enchant my birthday with
  such stars
As lightened mischief from their in-
  fancy?
If heavens had vowed, if stars had made
  decree, 149
To show on me their froward influ-
  ence,
If Lacy had but loved, heavens, hell,
  and all
Could not have wronged the patience
  of my mind.
POST. It grieves me, damsel; but the earl
  is forced
To love the lady by the king's command.
MARGARET. The wealth combined within
  the English shelves,
Europe's commander, nor the English
  king
Should not have moved the love of
  Peggy from her lord.
POST. What answer shall I return to
  my lord?
MARGARET. First, for thou cam'st from
  Lacy whom I loved—
Ah, give me leave to sigh at every
  thought!— 160
Take thou, my friend, the hundred
  pound he sent,
For Margaret's resolution craves no
  dower.
The world shall be to her as vanity;
Wealth, trash; love, hate; pleasure,
  despair.
For I will straight to stately Framling-
  ham,
And in the abbey there be shorn a nun,
And yield my loves and liberty to God.
Fellow, I give thee this, not for the
  news,
For those be hateful unto Margaret,
But for th'art Lacy's man, once Mar-
  garet's love. 170
POST. What I have heard, what passions
  I have seen,
I'll make report of them unto the earl.
                  Exit Post.
MARGARET. Say that she joys his fancies
  be at rest,
And prays that his misfortune may be
  hers. *Exit.*

[Scene xi.

Bacon's study.]

Enter Friar Bacon, drawing the curtains
with a white stick, a book in his hand,
and a lamp lighted by him; and the
Brazen Head, and Miles with weapons
by him.

BACON. Miles, where are you?

MILES. Here, sir.

BACON. How chance you tarry so long?

MILES. Think you that the watching
of the Brazen Head craves no furniture?
I warrant you, sir, I have so armed myself that, if all your devils come, I will not
fear them an inch.

BACON. Miles, thou knowest that I have
dived into hell,

And sought the darkest palaces of
fiends; 10

That with my magic spells great Belcephon

Hath left his lodge and kneeléd at my
cell;

The rafters of the earth rent from the
poles,

And three-formed Luna hid her silver
looks,

Trembling upon her concave continent,

When Bacon read upon his magic book.

With seven years' tossing nigromantic
charms,

Poring upon dark Hecat's principles,

I have framed out a monstrous head
of brass,

That, by the enchanting forces of the
devil, 20

Shall tell out strange and uncouth aphorisms,

And girt fair England with a wall of
brass.

Bungay and I have watched these threescore days,

And now our vital spirits crave some
rest.

If Argus lived, and had his hundred
eyes,

They could not overwatch Phobetor's
night.

Now, Miles, in thee rests Friar Bacon's
weal;

The honor and renown of all his life

Hangs in the watching of this Brazen
Head.

Therefore I charge thee by the immortal
God, 30

That holds the souls of men within his
fist,

This night thou watch, for, ere the
morning star

Sends out his glorious glister on the
north,

The head will speak. Then, Miles,
upon thy life,

Wake me; for then by magic art I'll
work

To end my seven years' task with excellence.

If that a wink but shut thy watchful
eye,

Then farewell Bacon's glory and his
fame!

Draw close the curtains, Miles. Now,
for thy life,

Be watchful, and— 40

Here he falleth asleep.

MILES. So! I thought you would talk
yourself asleep anon; and 'tis no marvel,
for Bungay on the days, and he on the
nights, have watched just these ten-and-
fifty days. Now this is the night, and
'tis my task, and no more. Now, Jesus
bless me, what a goodly head it is! And
a nose! You talk of *nos autem glorificare*,[1]
but here's a nose that I warrant may be
called *nos autem popelare* for the people [50
of the parish. Well, I am furnished with
weapons. Now, sir, I will set me down by
a post, and make it as good as a watchman
to wake me if I chance to slumber. I
thought, Goodman Head, I would call
you out of your *memento.*

Sit down and knock your head.

Passion o' God, I have almost broke my
pate! Up, Miles, to your task; take your
brown bill [2] in your hand. Here's some of
your master's hobgoblins abroad. 60

With this a great noise. The Head speaks.

HEAD. Time is!

MILES. Time is! Why, Master Brazen
Head, have you such a capital nose, and
answer you with syllables, "Time is"?
Is this all my master's cunning, to spend
seven years' study about "Time is"?
Well, sir, it may be we shall have some
better orations of it anon. Well, I'll watch

[1] Miles's impossible Latin pun on a liturgical
phrase.   [2] Halbert.

you as narrowly as ever you were watched, and I'll play with you as the nightingale [70 with the slowworm:[1] I'll set a prick against my breast. [*Places the halbert against his breast.*] Now rest there, Miles. [*He falls over.*] Lord, have mercy upon me! I have almost killed myself! [*A great noise.*] Up, Miles; list how they rumble.

HEAD. Time was!

MILES. Well, Friar Bacon, you spent your seven years' study well, that can make your head speak but two words [80 at once. "Time was"! Yea, marry, time was when my master was a wise man, but that was before he began to make the Brazen Head. You shall lie while your arse ache, and your head speak no better. Well, I will watch, and walk up and down, and be a peripatetian and a philosopher of Aristotle's stamp. [*A great noise.*] What, a fresh noise? Take thy pistols in hand, Miles!   90

Here the Head speaks, and a lightning flasheth forth, and a hand appears that breaketh down the Head with a hammer.

HEAD. Time is past!

MILES. Master, master, up! Hell's broken loose! Your head speaks; and there's such a thunder and lightning that I warrant all Oxford is up in arms. Out of your bed, and take a brown bill in your hand. The latter day is come!

BACON. Miles, I come. O, passing warily watched!

Bacon will make thee next himself in love.

When spake the head?   100

MILES. When spake the head! Did not you say that he should tell strange principles of philosophy? Why, sir, it speaks but two words at a time.

BACON. Why, villain, hath it spoken oft?

MILES. Oft! Ay, marry, hath it, thrice; but in all those three times it hath uttered but seven words.

BACON. As how?   110

MILES. Marry, sir, the first time he said, "Time is," as if Fabius Cumentator[2] should have pronounced a sentence; he said, "Time was;" and the third time,

with thunder and lightning, as in great choler, he said, "Time is past."

BACON. 'Tis past indeed! A villain! Time is past!

My life, my fame, my glory, all are past.—

Bacon, the turrets of thy hope are ruined down;   119

Thy seven years' study lieth in the dust!

Thy Brazen Head lies broken through a slave

That watched, and would not when the head did will.—

What said the head first?

MILES. Even, sir, "Time is."

BACON. Villain, if thou hadst called to Bacon then,

If thou hadst watched, and waked the sleepy friar,

The Brazen Head had uttered aphorisms,

And England had been circled round with brass.

But proud Astmeroth,[3] ruler of the North,   129

And Demogorgon, master of the fates,

Grudge that a mortal man should work so much.

Hell trembled at my deep, commanding spells;

Fiends frowned to see a man their overmatch;

Bacon might boast more than a man might boast.

But now the braves of Bacon hath an end;

Europe's conceit[4] of Bacon hath an end;

His seven years' practice sorteth[5] to ill end;

And, villain, sith my glory hath an end,

I will appoint thee fatal to some end.[6]

Villain, avoid! Get thee from Bacon's sight!   140

Vagrant, go roam and range about the world,

And perish as a vagabond on earth!

MILES. Why, then, sir, you forbid me your service?

BACON. My service, villain, with a fatal curse

That direful plagues and mischief fall on thee!

---

[1] Small snake.
[2] Grosart suggests that Miles confuses *commentator* and *cunctator*.

[3] Same as *Asmenoth*.
[4] Conception, opinion.
[5] Tends.   [6] To some fatal end (?).

MILES. 'Tis no matter; I am against you with the old proverb, "The more the fox is cursed, the better he fares."[1] God be with you, sir. I'll take but a book in my hand, a wide-sleeved gown on my [150 back, and a crowned cap on my head, and see if I can want promotion.   [*Exit.*]

BACON. Some fiend or ghost haunt on thy weary steps
Until they do transport thee quick to hell;
For Bacon shall have never merry day,
To lose the fame and honor of his Head.
         Exit.

[SCENE xii.

At court.]

Enter Emperor, Castile, Henry, Elinor,
        Edward, Lacy, Rafe.

EMPEROR. Now, lovely prince, the prince of Albion's wealth,
How fares the Lady Elinor and you?
What, have you courted and found Castile fit
To answer England in equivalence?
Will 't be a match twixt bonny Nell and thee?

EDWARD. Should Paris enter in the courts of Greece,
And not lie fettered in fair Helen's looks,
Or Phœbus scape those piercing amorets
That Daphne glancéd at his deity?
Can Edward then sit by a flame and freeze,   10
Whose heat puts Helen and fair Daphne down?
Now, monarchs, ask the lady if we gree.

HENRY. What, madam, hath my son found grace or no?

ELINOR. Seeing, my lord, his lovely counterfeit,
And hearing how his mind and shape agreed,
I come not, trooped with all this warlike train,
Doubting of love, but so affectionate
As [2] Edward hath in England what he won in Spain.

CASTILE. A match, my lord; these wantons needs must love.
Men must have wives, and women will be wed.   20
Let's haste the day to honor up the rites.

RAFE. Sirrah Harry, shall Ned marry Nell?

HENRY. Ay, Rafe; how then?

RAFE. Marry, Harry, follow my counsel: send for Friar Bacon to marry them, for he'll so conjure him and her with his nigromancy that they shall love together like pig and lamb whilst they live.

CASTILE. But hear'st thou, Rafe? [30 Art thou content to have Elinor to thy lady?

RAFE. Ay, so she will promise me two things.

CASTILE. What's that, Rafe?

RAFE. That she will never scold with Ned, nor fight with me.—Sirrah Harry, I have put her down with a thing unpossible.

HENRY. What's that, Rafe?   40

RAFE. Why, Harry, didst thou ever see that a woman could both hold her tongue and her hands? No! But when egg pies grows on apple trees, then will thy gray mare prove a bagpiper.

EMPEROR. What says the Lord of Castile and the Earl of Lincoln, that they are in such earnest and secret talk?

CASTILE. I stand, my lord, amazéd at his talk,
How he discourseth of the constancy
Of one surnamed, for beauty's excellence,   51
The Fair Maid of merry Fressingfield.

HENRY. 'Tis true, my lord, 'tis wondrous for to hear;
Her beauty passing Mars's paramour,
Her virgin's right as rich as Vesta's was.
Lacy and Ned hath told me miracles.

CASTILE. What says Lord Lacy? Shall she be his wife?

LACY. Or else Lord Lacy is unfit to live.—
May it please your highness give me leave to post
To Fressingfield, I'll fetch the bonny girl,   60

---

[1] With puns on *coursed* (pursued) and *fares* (*goes*).   [2] That.

And prove, in true appearance at the
     court,
What I have vouchéd often with my
     tongue.
HENRY. Lacy, go to the querry [1] of my
     stable,
And take such coursers as shall fit thy
     turn.
Hie thee to Fressingfield, and bring
     home the lass;
And, for her fame flies through the
     English coast,
If it may please the Lady Elinor,
One day shall match your excellence
     and her.
ELINOR. We Castile ladies are not very
     coy.[2]
Your highness may command a greater
     boon;   70
And glad were I to grace the Lincoln
     earl
With being partner of his marriage
     day.
EDWARD. Gramercy, Nell, for I do love
     the lord,
As he that's second to myself in love.
RAFE. You love her?—Madam Nell,
never believe him you, though he swears
he loves you.
ELINOR. Why, Rafe?
RAFE. Why, his love is like unto a tap-
ster's glass that is broken with every [80
touch; for he loved the Fair Maid of Fres-
singfield once out of all ho.[3]— Nay,
Ned, never wink upon me; I care not, I.
HENRY. Rafe tells all; you shall have
a good secretary of him.—
But, Lacy, haste thee post to Fressing-
     field;
For, ere thou hast fitted all things for
     her state,
The solemn marriage day will be at
     hand.
LACY. I go, my lord.   *Exit Lacy.*
EMPEROR. How shall we pass this day,
     my lord?   90
HENRY. To horse, my lord. The day is
     passing fair;
We'll fly the partridge or go rouse the
     deer.
Follow, my lords; you shall not want
     for sport.   *Exeunt.*

[1] Equerry.
[2] Distant, disdainful.
[3] Out of all bounds.

     Bacon's study.]
*Enter Friar Bacon with Friar Bungay to
     his cell.*

BUNGAY. What means the friar that
     frolicked it of late,
To sit as melancholy in his cell
As if he had neither lost nor won today?
BACON. Ah, Bungay, my Brazen Head
     is spoiled,
My glory gone, my seven years' study
     lost!
The fame of Bacon, bruited through
     the world,
Shall end and perish with this deep dis-
     grace.
BUNGAY. Bacon hath built foundation
     of [4] his fame
So surely on the wings of true report,
With acting strange and uncouth mir-
     acles,   10
As this cannot infringe what he de-
     serves.
BACON. Bungay, sit down, for by pro-
     spective skill
I find this day shall fall out ominous:
Some deadly act shall tide [5] me ere I
     sleep;
But what and wherein little can I
     guess.
BUNGAY. My mind is heavy, whatsoe'er
     shall hap.

*Enter two Scholars, sons to Lambert and
     Serlsby. Knock.*

BACON. Who's that knocks?
BUNGAY. Two scholars that desires to
     speak with you.
BACON. Bid them come in.—   19
Now, my youths, what would you have?
1 SCHOLAR. Sir, we are Suffolk men and
     neighboring friends;
Our fathers in their countries lusty
     squires;
Their lands adjoin. In Crackfield [6] mine
     doth dwell,
And his in Laxfield. We are college
     mates,
Sworn brothers, as our fathers lives as
     friends.

[4] Original reads *on.*
[5] Betide.
[6] Now Cratfield.

BACON. To what end is all this?

2 SCHOLAR. Hearing your worship kept
within your cell
A glass prospective, wherein men might
see
Whatso their thoughts or hearts' desire could wish,
We come to know how that our fathers
fare.   30

BACON. My glass is free for every honest
man.
Sit down, and you shall see ere long
how
Or in what state your friendly father
lives.
Meanwhile, tell me your names.

1 SCHOLAR.[1] Mine Lambert.

2 SCHOLAR. And mine Serlsby.

BACON. Bungay, I smell there will be a
tragedy.

*Enter [in the glass] Lambert and Serlsby
with rapiers and daggers.*

LAMBERT. Serlsby, thou hast kept thine
hour like a man.
Th'art worthy of the title of a squire,
That durst, for proof of thy affection   40
And for thy mistress' favor, prize[2]
thy blood.
Thou know'st what words did pass at
Fressingfield,
Such shameless braves as manhood can-
not brook.
Ay, for I scorn to bear such piercing
taunts,
Prepare thee, Serlsby; one of us will die.

SERLSBY. Thou see'st I single [meet] thee
[in] the field,[3]
And what I spake, I'll maintain with
my sword.
Stand on thy guard; I cannot scold it
out.
And, if thou kill me, think I have a son
That lives in Oxford in the Broadgates
Hall,   50
Who will revenge his father's blood with
blood.

LAMBERT. And, Serlsby, I have there a
lusty boy
That dares at weapon buckle with thy
son,

And lives in Broadgates too, as well as
thine.
But draw thy rapier, for we'll have a
bout.

BACON. Now, lusty younkers, look within
the glass,
And tell me if you can discern your
sires.

1 SCHOLAR. Serlsby, 'tis hard; thy father
offers wrong,
To combat with my father in the field.

2 SCHOLAR. Lambert, thou liest; my father's is the abuse,[4]   60
And thou shalt find it, if my father
harm.[5]

BUNGAY. How goes it, sirs?

1 SCHOLAR. Our fathers are in combat,
hard by Fressingfield.

BACON. Sit still, my friends, and see the
event.

LAMBERT. Why stand'st thou, Serlsby?
Doubt'st thou of thy life?
A veney,[6] man! Fair Margaret craves
so much.

SERLSBY. Then this for her!

1 SCHOLAR. Ah, well thrust!

2 SCHOLAR. But mark the ward.[7]

They fight and kill each other.

LAMBERT. O, I am slain!   70

SERLSBY. And I.—Lord, have mercy on
me!

1 SCHOLAR. My father slain!—Serlsby,
ward that!

2 SCHOLAR. And so is mine!—Lambert,
I'll quite thee well.

The two Scholars stab one another.[8]

BUNGAY. O, strange stratagem![9]

BACON. See, friar, where the fathers[10] both
lie dead!—
Bacon, thy magic doth effect this massacre.
This glass prospective worketh many
woes;

---

[1] Original reads *Lambert.*
[2] Risk.   [3] Insertions by Dyce.
[4] *I.e.*, my father is the offended one.   [6] Bout.
[5] Come to harm.   [7] Guard.
[8] Stage direction appears before the 2 Scholar's speech in original.
[9] Violent deed.   [10] Scholars (?)

And therefore, seeing these brave lusty
  Brutes,[1]
These friendly youths, did perish by
  thine art,
End all thy magic and thine art at
  once.   80
The poniard that did end the fatal [2]
  lives
Shall break the cause efficiat of [3] their
  woes.
So fade the glass, and end with it the
  shows
That nigromancy did infuse the crystal
  with.   *He breaks the glass.*
BUNGAY. What means learned Bacon
  thus to break his glass?
BACON. I tell thee, Bungay, it repents
  me sore
That ever Bacon meddled in this art.
The hours I have spent in pyromantic
  spells,
The fearful tossing in the latest night
Of papers full of nigromantic charms,   90
Conjuring and adjuring devils and
  fiends,
With stole and alb and strange pentag-
  onon;
The wresting [4] of the holy name of God,
As Sother, Eloim, and Adonai,
Alpha, Manoth, and Tetragrammaton,
With praying to the fivefold powers
  of heaven,
Are instances that Bacon must be
  damned
For using devils to countervail his God.—
Yet, Bacon, cheer thee; drown not in
  despair.
Sins have their salves; repentance can
  do much.   100
Think Mercy sits where Justice holds
  her seat,
And from those wounds those bloody
  Jews did pierce,
Which by thy magic oft did bleed afresh,
From thence for thee the dew of mercy
  drops
To wash the wrath of high Jehovah's
  ire,
And make thee as a new-born babe from
  sin.—
Bungay, I'll spend the remnant of my
  life

In pure devotion, praying to my God
That he would save what Bacon vainly
  lost.   *Exit [with Bungay].*

[SCENE xiv.

Fressingfield.]

*Enter Margaret in nun's apparel; Keeper,
  her father; and their Friend.*

KEEPER. Margaret, be not so headstrong
  in these vows!
O, bury not such beauty in a cell,
That England hath held famous for
  the hue!
Thy father's hair, like to the silver
  blooms
That beautify the shrubs of Africa,
Shall fall before the dated time of death,
Thus to forgo his lovely Margaret.
MARGARET. Ah, father, when the harmony
  of heaven
Soundeth the measures of a lively faith,
The vain illusions of this flattering
  world   10
Seems odious to the thoughts of Mar-
  garet.
I lovéd once—Lord Lacy was my love;
And now I hate myself for that I loved,
And doted more on him than on my God.
For this I scourge myself with sharp
  repents.
But now the touch of such aspiring sins
Tells me all love is lust but love of
  heavens;
That beauty used for love is vanity.
The world contains naught but alluring
  baits,   19
Pride, flattery, and inconstant thoughts.
To shun the pricks of death, I leave the
  world,
And vow to meditate on heavenly bliss,
To live in Framlingham a holy nun,
Holy and pure in conscience and in
  deed;
And for to wish all maids to learn of me
To seek heaven's joy before earth's
  vanity.
FRIEND. And will you then, Margaret,
be shorn a nun, and so leave us all?
MARGARET. Now farewell, world, the
  engine of all woe!
Farewell to friends and father! Wel-
  come, Christ!   30

---

[1] Britons (or heroes?).   [3] Effecting.
[2] Fated.   [4] Misusing.

Adieu to dainty robes! This base attire
Better befits an humble mind to God
Than all the show of rich abiliments.
Love, O love, and, with fond love, fare-
   well,
Sweet Lacy, whom I lovéd once so dear.
Ever be well, but never in my thoughts,
Lest I offend to think on Lacy's love.
But even to that, as to the rest, farewell!

Enter Lacy, Warren, Ermsby, booted and
                   spurred.

LACY. Come on, my wags, we're near
   the keeper's lodge.
Here have I oft walked in the wat'ry
   meads,   40
And chatted with my lovely Margaret.
WARREN. Sirrah Ned, is not this the
   keeper?
LACY. 'Tis the same.
ERMSBY. The old lecher hath gotten holy
mutton [1] to him—a nun, my lord!
LACY. Keeper, how farest thou? Holla,
   man, what cheer?
How doth Peggy, thy daughter and my
   love?
KEEPER. Ah, good my lord! O, woe is me
   for Peg!
See where she stands clad in her nun's
   attire,
Ready for to be shorn in Framling-
   ham.   50
She leaves the world because she left
   your love.
O, good my lord, persuade her if you
   can!
LACY. Why, how now, Margaret! What,
   a malcontent?
A nun? What holy father taught you
   this,
To task yourself to such a tedious life
As die a maid? 'Twere injury to me
To smother up such beauty in a cell.
MARGARET. Lord Lacy, thinking of thy
   former miss,[2]
How fond [3] the prime of wanton years
   were spent
In love—O, fie upon that fond con-
   ceit,   60
Whose hap and essence hangeth in the
   eye!—

---

[1] Loose woman.   [2] Error.   [3] Foolishly.

I leave both love and love's content
   at once,
Betaking me to Him that is true love,
And leaving all the world for love of
   Him.
LACY. Whence, Peggy, comes this meta-
   morphosis?
What, shorn a nun, and I have from the
   court
Posted with coursers to convey thee
   hence
To Windsor, where our marriage shall
   be kept?
Thy wedding robes are in the tailor's
   hands.
Come, Peggy, leave these peremptory
   vows.   70
MARGARET. Did not my lord resign his
   interest,
And make divorce twixt Margaret and
   him?
LACY. 'Twas but to try sweet Peggy's
   constancy.
But will fair Margaret leave her love and
   lord?
MARGARET. Is not heaven's joy before
   earth's fading bliss,
And life above sweeter than life in love?
LACY. Why, then, Margaret will be shorn
   a nun?
MARGARET. Margaret hath made a vow
   which may not be revoked.
WARREN. We cannot stay, my lord; and,
   if she be so strict,   79
Our leisure grants us not to woo afresh.
ERMSBY. Choose you, fair damsel; yet
   the choice is yours,
Either a solemn nunnery or the court,
God or Lord Lacy. Which contents you
   best,
To be a nun or else Lord Lacy's wife?
LACY. A good motion.—Peggy, your an-
   swer must be short.
MARGARET. The flesh is frail. My lord
   doth know it well,
That when he comes with his enchanting
   face,
Whatsoe'er betide, I cannot say him
   nay.
Off goes the habit of a maiden's heart,
And, seeing fortune will, fair Framling-
   ham,   90
And all the show of holy nuns, farewell!
Lacy for me, if he will be my lord.

LACY. Peggy, thy lord, thy love, thy husband!

Trust me, by truth of knighthood, that the king

Stays for to marry matchless Elinor,

Until I bring thee richly to the court,

That one day may both marry her and thee.—

How sayst thou, keeper? Art thou glad of this?

KEEPER. As if the English king had given

The park and deer of Fressingfield to me.   100

ERMSBY. I pray thee, my Lord of Sussex, why art thou in a brown study?

WARREN. To see the nature of women— that be they never so near God, yet they love to die in a man's arms.

LACY. What have you fit for breakfast? We have hied

And posted all this night to Fressingfield.

MARGARET. Butter and cheese, and umbles [1] of a deer,

Such as poor keepers have within their lodge.

LACY. And not a bottle of wine?   110

MARGARET. We'll find one for my lord.

LACY. Come, Sussex, let's in; we shall have more,

For she speaks least, to hold her promise sure.   *Exeunt.*

[SCENE XV.

Bacon's study.]

Enter a Devil to seek Miles.

DEVIL. How restless are the ghosts of hellish spirits,

When every charmer with his magic spells

Calls us from ninefold-trenchéd Phlegeton, [2]

To scud and overscour the earth in post

Upon the speedy wings of swiftest winds!

Now Bacon hath raised me from the darkest deep,

To search about the world for Miles his man,

For Miles, and to torment his lazy bones

For careless watching of his Brazen Head.

See where he comes. O, he is mine!   10

---

[1] Numbles; heart, liver, etc.

[2] Emended by Dyce. Original reads *Blegiton.*

Enter Miles with a gown and a cornercap.

MILES. A scholar, quoth you! Marry, sir, I would I had been made a bottle maker when I was made a scholar; for I can get neither to be a deacon, reader, nor schoolmaster, no, not the clerk of a parish. Some call me dunce; another saith my head is as full of Latin as an egg's full of oatmeal. Thus I am tormented, that the devil and Friar Bacon haunts me.— Good Lord, here's one of my master's [20] devils! I'll go speak to him.—What, Master Plutus, how cheer you?

DEVIL. Dost thou know me?

MILES. Know you, sir! Why, are not you one of my master's devils that were wont to come to my master, Doctor Bacon, at Brazen-nose?

DEVIL. Yes, marry, am I.

MILES. Good Lord, M[aster] Plutus, I have seen you a thousand times at my [30] master's, and yet I had never the manners to make you drink. But, sir, I am glad to see how conformable you are to the statute.—[*To audience.*] I warrant you, he's as yeomanly a man as you shall see. Mark you, masters, here's a plain, honest man, without welt or guard. [3]—But I pray you, sir, do you come lately from hell?

DEVIL. Ay, marry; how then?

MILES. Faith, 'tis a place I have de- [40] sired long to see. Have you not good tippling houses there? May not a man have a lusty fire there, a pot of good ale, a pair [4] of cards, a swingeing [5] piece of chalk, [6] and a brown toast that will clap a white waistcoat [7] on a cup of good drink?

DEVIL. All this you may have there.

MILES. You are for me, friend, and I am for you. But I pray you, may I not have an office there?   50

DEVIL. Yes, a thousand! What wouldst thou be?

MILES. By my troth, sir, in a place where I may profit myself. I know hell is a hot place, and men are marvelous dry, and much drink is spent there. I would be a tapster.

DEVIL. Thou shalt.

MILES. There's nothing lets [8] me from

---

[3] Facing or trimming.   [4] Pack.

[5] Striking, huge.

[6] Used in marking up alehouse accounts.

[7] *I.e.*, foam.   [8] Hinders.

going with you, but that 'tis a long [60
journey, and I have never a horse.

DEVIL. Thou shalt ride on my back.

MILES. Now surely here's a courteous
devil, that, for to pleasure his friend, will
not stick to make a jade of himself.—
But I pray you, goodman friend, let me
move a question to you.

DEVIL. What's that?

MILES. I pray you, whether is your pace
a trot or an amble?   70

DEVIL. An amble.

MILES. 'Tis well; but take heed it be
not a trot. But 'tis no matter, I'll prevent
it.   [*Puts on spurs.*]

DEVIL. What dost?

MILES. Marry, friend, I put on my
spurs; for, if I find your pace either a trot
or else uneasy, I'll put you to a false gallop;
I'll make you feel the benefit of my
spurs.   80

DEVIL. Get up upon my back.

MILES. O Lord, here's even a goodly
marvel, when a man rides to hell on the
devil's back!   *Exeunt, roaring.*

[SCENE xvi.

At court.]

*Enter the Emperor with a pointless sword;
next, the King of Castile, carrying a
sword with a point; Lacy, carrying the
globe; Ed[ward]; Warr[en], carrying a rod
of gold with a dove on it; Ermsby with
a crown and scepter; the Queen [i.e.,
Princess Elinor] with the Fair Maid of
Fressingfield on her left hand; Henry;
Bacon; with other Lords attending.*

EDWARD. Great potentates, earth's miracles for state,
Think that Prince Edward humbles at
your feet,
And, for these favors, on his martial
sword
He vows perpetual homage to yourselves,
Yielding these honors unto Elinor.

HENRY. Gramercies, lordings. Old Plan-
tagenet,
That rules and sways the Albion diadem,
With tears discovers these conceivéd
joys,
And vows requital, if his men-at-arms,

The wealth of England, or due honors
done   10
To Elinor, may quite his favorites.
But all this while what say you to the
dames
That shine like to the crystal lamps of
heaven?

EMPEROR. If but a third were added to
these two,
They did surpass those gorgeous images
That gloried Ida with rich beauty's
wealth.

MARGARET. 'Tis I, my lords, who humbly
on my knee
Must yield her orisons to mighty Jove
For lifting up his handmaid to this state,
Brought from her homely cottage to
the court,   20
And graced with kings, princes, and
emperors;
To whom (next to the noble Lincoln
earl)
I vow obedience, and such humble love
As may a handmaid to such mighty
men.

ELINOR. Thou martial man that wears
the Almain crown,
And you the western potentates of
might,
The Albion princess, English Edward's
wife,
Proud that the lovely star of Fressingfield,
Fair Margaret, countess to the Lincoln earl,
Attends on Elinor—gramercies, lord,
for her—   30
'Tis I give thanks for Margaret to you
all,
And rest,[1] for her, due bounden to yourselves.

HENRY. Seeing the marriage is solemnizéd,
Let's march in triumph to the royal
feast.—
But why stands Friar Bacon here so
mute?

BACON. Repentant for the follies of my
youth,
That magic's secret mysteries misled,
And joyful that this royal marriage
Portends such bliss unto this matchless
realm.

[1] Remain.

HENRY. Why, Bacon, what strange event
    shall happen to this land?   40
Or what shall grow from Edward and
    his queen?
BACON. I find by deep prescience of mine
    art,
Which once I tempered in my secret cell,
That here where Brute did build his
    Troynovant,[1]
From forth the royal garden of a king
Shall flourish out so rich and fair a bud [2]
Whose brightness shall deface proud
    Phœbus' flower,
And overshadow Albion with her leaves.
Till then Mars shall be master of the
    field,
But then the stormy threats of wars
    shall cease.   50
The horse shall stamp as careless of the
    pike;
Drums shall be turned to timbrels of
    delight;
With wealthy favors plenty shall enrich
The strond that gladded wand'ring
    Brute to see,
And peace from heaven shall harbor in
    these leaves
That gorgeous beautifies this matchless
    flower.
Apollo's hellitropian [3] then shall stoop,
And Venus' hyacinth shall vail [4] her top;

[1] London, which according to legend was
founded by Brutus, friend of Æneas.
[2] Referring to Queen Elizabeth.
[3] Heliotrope.   [4] Lower.

Juno shall shut her gilliflowers up,
And Pallas' bay shall bash her bright-
    est green;   60
Ceres' carnation, in consort with those,
Shall stoop and wonder at Diana's rose.
HENRY. This prophecy is mystical.—
But, glorious commanders of Europa's
    love,
That makes fair England like that
    wealthy isle
Circled with Gihon and swift [5] Euphrates,
In royalizing Henry's Albion
With presence of your princely mighti-
    ness,
Let's march. The tables all are spread,
And viands such as England's wealth
    affords   70
Are ready set to furnish out the boards.
You shall have welcome, mighty po-
    tentates.
It rests to furnish up this royal feast.
Only your hearts be frolic, for the time
Craves that we taste of naught but
    jouissance.[6]
Thus glories England over all the West.
    Exeunt omnes.

FINIS FRIAR BACON, MADE BY ROBERT
    GREENE, MASTER OF ARTS.

"Omne tulit punctum qui miscuit utile dulci."[7]

[5] Dyce's emendation. Original reads *first*.
[6] Pleasure.
[7] "He has everybody's approval who mingles
the useful with the agreeable" (Horace).

GEORGE A GREENE, THE PINNER OF WAKEFIELD[1]

[DRAMATIS PERSONÆ

EDWARD, *King of England.*[2]
EARL OF WARWICK.
JAMES, *King of Scotland.*[2]
LORD HUMES.
EARL OF KENDAL ⎫
LORD BONFIELD ⎪
SIR NICHOLAS MANNERING ⎬ *rebels.*
SIR GILBERT ARMSTRONG ⎭
MUSGROVE, *keeper of Sandown Castle.*
CUDDY, *his son.*
GEORGE A GREENE, *the pinner*[3] *of Wake-field.*
JENKIN, *a clown* ⎫ *servants to*
WILY, *a boy* ⎭ *George a Greene.*

GRIME.
WOODROFFE, *the justice of Wakefield.*
ROBIN HOOD.
SCARLET ⎫ *Robin Hood's men.*
MUCH ⎭
JOHN TAYLOR, *post of King James.*
NED A BARLEY, *a small boy.*
A SHOEMAKER.

JANE A BARLEY, *mother of Ned.*
BETTRIS, *daughter to Grime.*
MAID MARIAN.
TOWNSMEN, SHOEMAKERS, SOLDIERS, MESSENGER, *etc.*

SCENE: *England.*

TIME: *Indefinite.*]

[SCENE i.

Near Bradford.]

Enter the Earl of Kendal; with him the Lord Bonfield, Sir Gilbert Armstrong, [Sir Nicholas Mannering,] and John [Taylor].

KEND. Welcome to Bradford, martial gentlemen,
L[ord] Bonfield and Sir Gilbert Armstrong both;
And all my troops, even to my basest groom,
Courage and welcome, for the day is ours!
Our cause is good—it is for the land's avail.
Then let us fight and die for England's good!
OMNES. We will, my lord!

KEND. As I am Henry Momford, Kendal's earl,
You honor me with this assent of yours;
And here upon my sword I make protest
For to relieve the poor or die myself. 11
And know, my lords, that James, the King of Scots,
Wars hard upon the borders of this land.—
Here is his post.—Say, John Taylor,
What news with King James?
JOHN. War, my lord! Tall[4] and good news, I trow;
For King Jamie vows to meet you the twenty-sixth of this month,
God willing; marry, doth he, sir.
KEND. My friends, you see what we have to win.—
Well, John, commend me to King James, 20
And tell him I will meet him the twenty-sixth of this month
And all the rest; and so, farewell.
Exit John.

---

[1] The complete title reads: "A Pleasant Conceited Comedy of George a Greene, the Pinner of Wakefield. As It Was Sundry Times Acted by the Servants of the Right Honorable the Earl of Sussex."
[2] Identity not clear.
[3] An officer who impounds stray animals.

[4] Excellent. Suggested by Adams; original reads *tell*.

Bonfield, why stand'st thou as a man in
    dumps?
Courage! For, if I win, I'll make thee
    duke.
I, Henry Momford, will be king myself;
And I will make thee Duke of Lancaster,
And Gilbert Armstrong Lord of Don-
    caster.
Bon. Nothing, my lord, makes me
    amazed [1] at all
But that our soldiers finds our victuals
    scant.
We must make havoc of those country
    swains;   30
For so will the rest tremble and be afraid,
And humbly send provision to your
    camp.
Gilb. My Lord Bonfield gives good ad-
    vice.
They make a scorn,[2] and stand upon [3]
    the king;
So what is brought is sent from them per-
    force.
Ask Mannering else.
Kend. What sayest thou, Mannering?
Man. Whenas [4] I showed your high com-
    mission,
They made this answer,
Only to send provision for your horses. 40
Kend. Well, hie thee to Wakefield, bid the
    town
To send me all provision that I want,
Lest I, like martial Tamburlaine, lay
    waste
Their bordering countries,
And leaving none alive that contradicts
    my commission.
Man. Let me alone, my lord; I'll make
    them
Vail [5] their plumes; for whatsoe'er he be,
The proudest knight, justice, or other,
    that gainsayeth
Your word, I'll clap him fast,[6] to make
    the rest to fear.
Kend. Do so, Nick. Hie thee thither pres-
    ently,[7]   50
And let us hear of thee again tomorrow.
Man. Will you not remove, my lord?
Kend. No, I will lie at Bradford all this
    night

And all the next.—Come, Bonfield, let
    us go,
And listen out [8] some bonny lasses here.
                        Exeunt omnes.

[Scene ii.

Wakefield.]

*Enter the Justice, a Townsman, George a
    Greene, and Sir Nicholas Mannering
              with his commission.*

Just. M[aster] Mannering, stand aside,
    whilst we confer
What is best to do.—
Townsmen of Wakefield, the Earl of
    Kendal
Here hath sent for victuals;
And in aiding him we show ourselves
No less than traitors to the king;
Therefore let me hear, townsmen,
What is your consents.[9]
Towns. Even as you please, we are all
    content.
Just. Then, M[aster] Mannering, we are
    resolved.   10
Man. As how?
Just. Marry, sir, thus.
We will send the Earl of Kendal no
    victuals,
Because he is a traitor to the king,
And in aiding him we show ourselves no
    less.
Man. Why, men of Wakefield, are you
    waxen mad,
That present danger cannot whet your
    wits
Wisely to make provision of yourselves?
The earl is thirty thousand men strong
    in power,
And what town soever him resist,   20
He lays it flat and level with the
    ground.
Ye silly men, you seek your own decay;
Therefore send my lord such provision as
    he wants,
So he will spare your town, and come no
    nearer
Wakefield than he is.
Just. Master Mannering, you have your
    answer;
You may be gone.
Man. Well, Woodroffe, for so I guess is
    thy name,

---

[1] Perplexed.
[2] *I.e.,* they scorn us.
[3] With.
[4] When.
[5] Lower.
[6] Imprison.
[7] At once.
[8] Get news of.
[9] Opinion.

I'll make thee curse thy overthwart [1]
  denial;
And all that sit upon the bench this day
Shall rue the hour they have withstood
  my lord's   31
Commission.
JUST.   Do thy worst; we fear thee not.
MAN.   See you these seals?   Before you
  pass the town,
I will have all things my lord doth want,
In spite of you.
GEORGE.   Proud dapper Jack,[2] vail bonnet
  to
The bench
That represents the person of the king,
Or, sirrah, I'll lay thy head before thy
  feet!   40
MAN.   Why, who art thou?
GEORGE.   Why, I am George a Greene,
  True liegeman to my king,
Who scorns that men of such esteem as
  these
Should brook the braves [3] of any traitor-
  ous squire.
You of the bench, and you, my fellow-
  friends,
Neighbors, we subjects all unto the
  king,
We are English born, and therefore Ed-
  ward's friends,
Vowed unto him even in our mothers'
  womb,
Our minds to God, our hearts unto our
  king.   50
Our wealth, our homage, and our car-
  casses
Be all King Edward's.   Then, sirrah,
  we have
Nothing left for traitors but our swords,
Whetted to bathe them in your bloods,
And die against you, before we send you
  any victuals.
JUST.   Well spoken, George a Greene!
TOWNS.   Pray let George a Greene speak
  for us.
GEORGE.   Sirrah, you get no victuals here,
Not if a hoof of beef would save your
  lives.
MAN.   Fellow, I stand amazed at thy pre-
  sumption.   60
Why, what art thou that darest gainsay
  my lord,

Knowing his mighty puissance and his
  stroke?
Why, my friend, I come not barely of
  myself,
For, see, I have a large commission.
GEORGE.   Let me see it, sirrah.
                   [*Takes the commission.*]
Whose seals be these?
MAN.   This is the Earl of Kendal's seal-
  at-arms,
This Lord Charnel Bonfield's,
And this Sir Gilbert Armstrong's.
GEORGE.   I tell thee, sirrah, did good King
  Edward's son   70
Seal a commission against the king his
  father,
Thus would I tear it in despite of him,
              He tears the commission.
Being traitor to my sovereign.
MAN.   What, hast thou torn my lord's
  commission?
Thou shalt rue it, and so shall all Wake-
  field.
GEORGE.   What, are you in choler?   I will
  give you pills
To cool your stomach.[4]
Seest thou these seals?
Now, by my father's soul, which was a
  yeoman
When he was alive, eat them,   80
Or eat my dagger's point, proud squire.
MAN.   But thou dost but jest, I hope.
GEORGE.   Sure, that shall you see before
  we two part.
MAN.   Well, and [5] there be no remedy, so,
  George—
              [*Swallows one of the seals.*]
One is gone; I pray thee, no more now.
GEORGE.   O, sir, if one be good, the others
  cannot hurt!
         [*Mannering swallows the other seals.*]
So, sir; now you may go tell the Earl of
  Kendal,
Although I have rent his large com-
  mission,
Yet of courtesy I have sent all his seals
Back again by you.   90
MAN.   Well, sir, I will do your arrant.[6]
                           Exit.
GEORGE.   Now let him tell his lord that he
  hath
Spoke with George a Greene,
Right [7] pinner of merry Wakefield town,

[1] Perverse.   [3] Endure the threats.
[2] Knave.
[4] Angry temper.   [5] If.   [6] Errand.   [7] True.

That hath physic for a fool,
Pills for a traitor that doth wrong his
　sovereign.
Are you content with this that I have
　done?

Just. Aye, content, George;
　For highly hast thou honored Wakefield
　town　　　　　　　　　　　　　　　　99
　In cutting of proud Mannering so short.
　Come, thou shalt be my welcome guest
　today,
　For well thou hast deserved reward and
　favor.　　　　　　　　　　　　*Exeunt omnes.*

[SCENE iii.

Before Musgrove's castle.]

*Enter Old Musgrove and Young Cuddy, his
　　　　　　　　　　　　　　　　　　son.*

CUDDY. Now, gentle father, list unto thy
　son,
And for my mother's love,
That erst[1] was blithe and bonny in
　thine eye,
Grant one petition that I shall demand.

Mus. What is that, my Cuddy?

CUDDY. Father, you know the ancient en-
　mity of late
Between the Musgroves and the wily
　Scots,
Whereof they have oath
Not to leave one alive that strides a
　lance.[2]
O father, you are old and, waning, age
　unto the grave.　　　　　　　　　　　10
Old William Musgrove, which whilom[3]
　was thought
The bravest horseman in all Westmore-
　land,
Is weak, and forced to stay his arm upon
　a staff,
That erst could wield a lance.
Then, gentle father, resign the hold[4]
　to me;
Give arms to youth, and honor unto age.

Mus. Avaunt, false-hearted boy!　My
　joints do quake
Even with anguish of thy very words.
Hath William Musgrove seen an hundred
　years,
Have I been feared and dreaded of the
　Scots,　　　　　　　　　　　　　　　20

That, when they heard my name in any
　road,[5]
They fled away, and posted thence
　amain,[6]
And shall I die with shame now in mine
　age?
No, Cuddy, no.　Thus resolve I:
Here have I lived, and here will Mus-
　grove die.　　　　　　　　　　*Exeunt omnes.*

[SCENE iv.

Before Grime's house at Bradford.]

*Enter Lord Bonfield, Sir Gilbert Armstrong,
　M[aster] Grime, and Bettris, his daughter.*

Bon. Now, gentle Grime, God-a-mercy[7]
　for our good cheer;
Our fare was royal, and our welcome
　great;
And, sith[8] so kindly thou hast enter-
　tained us,
If we return with happy victory,
We will deal as friendly with thee in
　recompense.

Grime. Your welcome was but duty,
　gentle lord;
For wherefore have we given us our
　wealth
But to make our betters welcome when
　they come?
[*Aside.*]　O, this goes hard when traitors
　must be flattered!
But life is sweet, and I cannot with-
　stand it.　　　　　　　　　　　　　10
God, I hope, will revenge the quarrel
　of my king.—

Gilb. What said you, Grime?

Grime. I say, Sir Gilbert, looking on my
　daughter,
I curse the hour that e'er I got[9] the girl:
For, sir, she may have many wealthy
　suitors,
And yet she disdains them all to have
Poor George a Greene unto her hus-
　band.

Bon. On that, good Grime, I am talking
　with thy
　Daughter;
But she, in quirks and quiddities of
　love,　　　　　　　　　　　　　　20
Sets me to school, she is so overwise.—

---

[1] Formerly.
[2] *I.e.*, even the children.
[3] Formerly.
[4] Fort, castle.
[5] Raid.
[6] At full speed.
[7] God reward you; thank you.
[8] Since.
[9] Begot.

But, gentle girl, if thou wilt forsake
The pinner and be my love, I will ad-
vance thee high.
To dignify those hairs of amber hue,
I'll grace them with a chaplet made of
pearl,
Set with choice rubies, sparks,[1] and dia-
monds,
Planted upon a velvet hood, to hide
that head
Wherein two sapphires burn like spar-
kling fire.
This will I do, fair Bettris, and far more,
If thou wilt love the Lord of Doncaster.
BETTRIS. Heigh-ho! My heart is in a
higher place,   31
Perhaps on the earl, if that be he.
See where he comes, or[2] angry or in
love,
Forwhy[3] his color[4] looketh discontent.
KEND. [Entering.] Come, Nick, follow me.

*Enter the Earl of Kendal and Nicholas
Mannering.*

BON. How now, my lord? What news?
KEND. Such news, Bonfield, as will make
thee laugh,
And fret thy fill, to hear how Nick was
used.
Why, the justices stand on their terms.
Nick, as you know, is haughty in his
words;   40
He laid the law unto the justices
With threat'ning braves, that one looked
on another,
Ready to stoop; but that a churl came
in,
One George a Greene, the pinner of the
town,
And with his dagger drawn laid hands
on Nick,
And by no beggars[5] swore that we were
traitors,
Rent our commission, and upon a brave
Made Nick to eat the seals or brook the
stab.
Poor Mannering, afraid, came posting
hither straight.
BETTRIS. O lovely George, fortune be
still[6] thy friend!   50

And as thy thoughts be high, so be thy
mind
In all accords, even to thy heart's de-
sire!
BON. What says fair Bettris?
GRIME. My lord, she is praying for George
a Greene.
He is the man, and she will none but him.
BON. But him? Why, look on me, my
girl!
Thou knowest that yesternight I courted
thee,
And swore at my return to wed with
thee.
Then tell me, love, shall I have all thy
fair?[7]
BETTRIS. I care not for earl, nor yet for
knight,   60
Nor baron that is so bold;
For George a Greene, the merry pinner,
He hath my heart in hold.
BON. Bootless, my lord, are many vain
replies.
Let us hie us to Wakefield, and send her
the pinner's head.
KEND. It shall be so.—Grime, gramercy.
Shut up thy daughter; bridle her af-
fects.[8]
Let me not miss her when I make return;
Therefore look to her, as to thy life, good
Grime.
GRIME. I warrant you, my lord.   70
Ex[eunt] Grime and Bettris.
KEND. And, Bettris, leave a base pinner
for to love an earl.
Fain would I see this pinner, George a
Greene.
It shall be thus:
Nick Mannering shall lead on the battle,[9]
And we three will go to Wakefield in
some disguise.
But howsoever, I'll have his head today.
Ex[eunt] omnes.

[SCENE V.

Before Sir John a Barley's castle.]

*Enter the King of Scots, Lord Humes, with
Soldiers, and Johnny [Taylor].*

JAMES.[10] Why, Johnny, then the Earl of
Kendal is blithe,

---

[1] Precious stones.   [4] Appearance.
[2] Either.   [5] By no small oath.
[3] Because.   [6] Always.

[7] Beauty.   [8] Affections.   [9] Army.
[10] In the original *King* is used here and at line
6 to designate the speaker.

And hath brave men that troop along
with him?

JOHNNY. Ay, marry, my liege, and hath
good men
That come along with him,
And vows to meet you at Scrasblesea,
God willing.

JAMES. If good S[aint] Andrew lend King
Jamie leave,
I will be with him at the pointed ¹ day.
But, soft!—Whose pretty boy art thou?

Enter Jane a Barley's Son.

NED. Sir, I am son unto Sir John a Barley,
Eldest, and all that e'er my mother
had;   10
Edward my name.

JAMES. And whither art thou going,
pretty Ned?

NED. To seek some birds, and kill them,
if I can.
And now my schoolmaster is also gone,
So have I liberty to ply my bow;
For, when he comes, I stir not from my
book.

JAMES. Lord Humes, but mark the visage
of this child.
By him I guess the beauty of his mother;
None but Leda could breed Helena.
Tell me, Ned, who is within with thy
mother?   20

NED. Not ² but herself and household
servants, sir.
If you would speak with her, knock at
this gate.

JAMES. Johnny, knock at that gate.
[*John knocks.*]

Enter Jane a Barley upon the walls.

JANE. O, I am betrayed! What multitudes
be these?

JAMES. Fear not, fair Jane, for all these
men are mine,
And all thy friends, if thou be friend to
me.
I am thy lover, James the King of Scots,
That oft have sued and wooed with
many letters,
Painting my outward passions with my
pen,
Whenas my inward soul did bleed for
woe.   30

Little regard was given to my suit,
But haply thy husband's presence
wrought it.
Therefore, sweet Jane, I fitted me to
time,
And, hearing that thy husband was from
home,
Am come to crave what long I have desired.

NED. Nay, soft you, sir! You get no en-
trance here,
That seek to wrong Sir John a Barley so,
And offer such dishonor to my mother.

JAMES. Why, what dishonor, Ned?

NED. Though young, yet often have I
heard   40
My father say
No greater wrong than to be made
cuckold.
Were I of age, or were my body strong,
Were he ten kings, I would shoot him
to the heart
That should attempt to give Sir John
the horn.³
Mother, let him not come in.
I will go lie at Jockie Miller's house.

JAMES. Stay him!

JANE. Ay, well said; Ned, thou hast given
the king
His answer,   50
For, were the ghost of Cæsar on the
earth,
Wrapped in the wonted glory of his
honor,
He should not make me wrong my hus-
band so.
But good King James is pleasant,⁴ as I
guess,
And means to try what humor I am in;
Else would he never have brought an
host of men
To have them witness of his Scottish lust.

JAMES. Jane, in faith, Jane!

JANE. Never reply, for I protest by the
highest
Holy God,   60
That doometh just revenge for things
amiss,
King James, of all men, shall not have
my love.

JAMES. Then list to me: Saint Andrew
be my boot,⁵

---

¹Appointed.   ² Naught (?)

³ Proverbial sign of the cuckold.
⁴ Jocular.   ⁵ Aid.

But I'll raze thy castle to the very ground
Unless thou open the gate, and let me in.
JANE. I fear thee not, King Jamie; do thy
   worst.
This castle is too strong for thee to scale;
Besides, tomorrow will Sir John come
   home.
JAMES. Well, Jane, since thou disdain'st
   King James' love,
I'll draw thee on with sharp and deep
   extremes;   70
For, by my father's soul, this brat of
   thine
Shall perish here before thine eyes,
Unless thou open the gate, and let me in.
JANE. O deep extremes! My heart begins
   to break!
My little Ned looks pale for fear!
Cheer thee, my boy; I will do much for
   thee.
NED. But not so much as to dishonor me.
JANE. And if thou diest, I cannot live,
   sweet Ned.
NED. Then die with honor, mother, dy-
   ing chaste.
JANE. I am armed: 80
My husband's love, his honor, and his
   fame
Joins [1] victory by virtue.
Now, King James, if mother's tears can-
   not allay thine ire,
Then butcher him, for I will never yield.
The son shall die before I wrong the
   father.
JAMES. Why, then, he dies.

Alarum within. Enter a Messenger.

MESSENGER. My lord, Musgrove is at
   hand.
JAMES. Who, Musgrove? The devil he
   is! Come,
My horse!   *Exeunt omnes.*

[SCENE vi.

The same.]

*Enter Old Musgrove with King James
               prisoner.*

MUS. Now, King James, thou art my
   prisoner.
JAMES. Not thine, but fortune's prisoner!

[1] Enjoins.

Enter Cuddy.

CUDDY. Father, the field is ours. Their
   colors we
Have seized,
And Humes is slain—I slew him hand
   to hand.
MUS. God and Saint George!
CUDDY. O father, I am sore athirst!
JANE. Come in, young Cuddy, come and
   drink thy fill.
Bring in King Jamie with you as a guest;
For all this broil was cause [2] he could
   not enter.   10
             Exeunt omnes.

[SCENE vii.

Wakefield.]

Enter George a Greene alone.

GEORGE. The sweet content of men that
   live in love
Breeds fretting humors in a restless mind;
And fancy,[3] being checked by fortune's
   spite,
Grows too impatient in her sweet de-
   sires—
Sweet to those men whom love leads on
   to bliss,
But sour to me whose hap is still amiss.

Enter [Jenkin,] the clown.

JEN. Marry, amen, sir.
GEORGE. Sir, what do you cry "amen" at?
JEN. Why, did not you talk of love?
GEORGE. How do you know that?   10
JEN. Well, though I say it that should not
   say it,
There are few fellows in our parish
So nettled with love as I have been of
   late.
GEORGE. Sirrah, I thought no less when
   the other morning
You rose so early to go to your wenches.
Sir, I had thought you had gone about
   my honest business.
JEN. Trow, you have hit it; for, master,
   be it known
To you,
There is some good will betwixt Madge
   the sousewife [4]

[2] Because.   [4] Seller of souse, or pickled pork.
[3] Love.

And I;   20
Marry, she hath another lover.
GEORGE. Canst thou brook any rivals
   in thy love?
JEN. A rider? No, he is a sow-gelder and
   goes afoot.
But Madge pointed to meet me in your
   wheat close.[1]
GEORGE. Well, did she meet you there?
JEN. Never make question of that.
And first I saluted her with a green
   gown,[2]
And after fell as hard a-wooing
As if the priest had been at our backs
   to have married us.
GEORGE. What, did she grant?   30
JEN. Did she grant? Never make question
   of that.
And she gave me a shirt collar
Wrought over with no counterfeit stuff.
GEORGE. What, was it gold?
JEN. Nay, 'twas better than gold.
GEORGE. What was it?
JEN. Right Coventry blue.[3]
We[4] had no sooner come there but wot
   you who came by?
GEORGE. No, who?
JEN. Clim, the sow-gelder.   40
GEORGE. Came he by?
JEN. He spied Madge and I sit together.
He leapt from his horse, laid his hand
   on his dagger, and
Began to swear.
Now I seeing he had a dagger,
And I nothing but this twig in my
   hand,
I gave him fair words and said nothing.
He comes to me, and takes me by the
   bosom.
"You whoreson[5] slave," said he, "hold
   my horse.
And look he take no cold in his feet." 50
"No, marry, shall he, sir," quoth I;
"I'll lay my cloak underneath him."
I took my cloak, spread it all along,
And his horse on the midst of it.
GEORGE. Thou clown, didst thou set his
   horse upon
Thy cloak?
JEN. Ay, but mark how I served him:

Madge and he was no sooner gone down
   into the ditch
But I plucked out my knife,
Cut four holes in my cloak, and made
   his horse stand   60
On the bare ground.
GEORGE. 'Twas well done. Now, sir, go
   and survey my fields.
If you find any cattle in the corn, to
   pound[6] with them!
JEN. And, if I find any in the pound,
I shall turn them out.
                          Exit Jenkin.

Enter the Earl of Kendal, Lord Bonfield,
   Sir Gilbert, all disguised, with a Train
                                of Men.

KEND. Now we have put the horses in
   the corn,
Let us stand in some corner for to hear
What braving terms the pinner will
   breathe
When he spies our horses in the corn.
                 [*They conceal themselves.*]

Enter Jenkin[7] blowing of his horn.

JEN. O master, where are you? We have
a prize.   71
   GEORGE. A prize! What is it?
   JEN. Three goodly horses in our wheat
close.
   GEORGE. Three horses in our wheat
close? Whose be they?
   JEN. Marry, that's a riddle to me, but
they are there, velvet horses, and I never
saw such horses before. As my duty was,
I put off my cap, and said as followeth: [80
"My masters, what do you make[8] in
our close?" One of them, hearing me ask
what he made there, held up his head and
neighed, and after his manner laughed as
heartily as if a mare had been tied to his
girdle. "My masters," said I, "it is no
laughing matter; for, if my master take you
here, you go as round as a top to the
pound." Another untoward jade, hearing
me threaten him to the pound and to [90
tell you of them, cast up both his heels, and
let such a monstrous great fart that was
as much as in his language to say, "A fart

---

[1] Field.   [2] Tumbled her in the grass.
[3] Superior blue embroidery thread made at
Coventry, with a pun on *black and blue.*
[4] Original reads *who.*   [5] Rascally.

[6] Public enclosure for stray cattle.
[7] Original reads *Jack,* possibly the name of the
actor of the part.   [8] Do.

for the pound, and a fart for George a
Greene!" Now I, hearing this, put on my
cap, blew my horn, called them all jades,
and came to tell you.

GEORGE. Now, sir, go and drive me those
   three horses
   To the pound.

JEN. Do you hear? I were best take a
   constable   100
   With me.

GEORGE. Why so?

[JEN.] Why, they, being gentlemen's
   horses, may stand on their
   Reputation, and will not obey me.

GEORGE. Go, do as I bid you, sir.

JEN. Well, I may go.

*The Earl of Kendal, the Lord Bonfield, and
   Sir Gilbert Armstrong meet them.*

KEND. Whither away, sir?

JEN. Whither away? I am going to put
   the horses
   In the pound.

KEND. Sirrah, those three horses belong
   to us, and we put   110
   Them in, and they must tarry there and
   eat their fill.

JEN. Stay, I will go tell my master.—
   Hear you, master? We have another
   prize:
   Those three horses be in your wheat close
   still,
   And here be three geldings more.

GEORGE. What be these?

JEN. These are the masters of the horses.

GEORGE. Now, gentlemen—I know not
   your degrees,
   But more you cannot be, unless you be
   kings—
   Why wrong you us of Wakefield with
   your horses?   120
   I am the pinner, and, before you pass,
   You shall make good the trespass they
   have done.

KEND. Peace, saucy mate, prate not to us!
   I tell thee, pinner, we are gentlemen.

GEORGE. Why, sir, so may I, sir, although
   I give no arms.[1]

KEND. Thou? How art thou a gentleman?

JEN. And such is my master, and he may
   give as good

---

[1] Bear no coat of arms.

Arms as ever your great-grandfather
   could give.

KEND. Pray thee, let me hear how.

JEN. Marry, my master may give for his
   arms   130
   The picture of April in a green jerkin,
   With a rook on one fist and an horn on
   the other;
   But my master gives his arms the wrong
   way,
   For he gives the horn on his fist,
   And your grandfather, because he would
   not lose his
   Arms,
   Wears the horn on his own head.

KEND. Well, pinner, sith our horses be in,
   In spite of thee they now shall feed their
   fill,
   And eat until our leisures serve to go. 140

GEORGE. Now, by my father's soul,
   Were good King Edward's horses in the
   corn,
   They shall amend the scath or kiss [2] the
   pound;
   Much more yours, sir, whatsoe'er you be.

KEND. Why, man, thou knowest not us.
   We do belong to Henry Momford, Earl of
   Kendal,
   Men that, before a month be full expired,
   Will be King Edward's betters in the
   land.

GEORGE. King Edward's better! Rebel,
   thou liest!   *George strikes him.*

BON. Villain, what hast thou done? Thou
   hast stroke [3]   150
   An earl.

GEORGE. Why, what care I? A poor man
   that is true
   Is better than an earl, if he be false.
   Traitors reap no better favors at my
   hands.

KEND. Ay, so methinks; but thou shalt
   dear aby [4] this blow.—
   Now or never lay hold on the pinner!

Enter all the Ambush.

GEORGE. Stay, my lords, let us parley on
   these broils.—
   [*Aside.*] Not Hercules against two, the
   proverb is,
   Nor I against so great a multitude.

---

[2] Be imprisoned in (slang).   [4] Dearly pay for.
[3] Struck.

Had not your troops come marching as
　　they did,　　　　　　　　　　160
I would have stopped your passage unto
　　London.
But now I'll fly to secret policy.

KEND. What dost thou murmur, George?

GEORGE. Marry, this, my lord; I muse,[1]
　　If thou be Henry Momford, Kendal's
　　　　earl,
　　That thou wilt do poor G[eorge] a Greene
　　　　this wrong,
　　Ever to match me with a troop of men.

KEND. Why dost thou strike me then?

GEORGE. Why, my lord, measure me but
　　by yourself:
　　Had you a man had served you long,
　　And heard your foe misuse you behind
　　　　your back,　　　　　　　　171
　　And would not draw his sword in your
　　　　defense,
　　You would cashier him.
　　Much more, King Edward is my king;
　　And before I'll hear him so wronged,
　　I'll die within this place,
　　And maintain good whatsoever I have
　　　　said.
　　And, if I speak not reason in this case,
　　What I have said I'll maintain in this
　　　　place.

BON. A pardon, my lord, for this pinner,
　　For, trust me, he speaketh like a man of
　　　　worth.　　　　　　　　　181

KEND. Well, George, wilt thou leave
　　Wakefield and
　　Wend with me,
　　I'll freely put up all and pardon thee.

GEORGE. Ay, my lord, considering[2] me one
　　thing:
　　You will leave these arms, and follow
　　　　your good king.

KEND. Why, George, I rise not against
　　King Edward,
　　But for the poor that is oppressed by
　　　　wrong;
　　And, if King Edward will redress the
　　　　same,
　　I will not offer him disparagement,　190
　　But otherwise; and so let this suffice.
　　Thou hear'st the reason why I rise in
　　　　arms.
　　Now, wilt thou leave Wakefield and
　　　　wend with me,
　　I'll make thee captain of a hardy band,

And, when I have my will, dub thee a
　　knight.

GEORGE. Why, my lord, have you any
　　hope to win?

KEND. Why, there is a prophecy doth say
　　That King James and I shall meet at
　　　　London,
　　And make the king vail bonnet to us both.

GEORGE. If this were true, my lord, this
　　were a mighty reason.　　　　200

KEND. Why, it is a miraculous prophecy,
　　and cannot fail.

GEORGE. Well, my lord, you have almost
　　turned me.—
　　Jenkin, come hither.

JEN. Sir?

GEORGE. Go your ways home, sir,
　　And drive me those three horses home
　　　　unto my house,
　　And pour them down a bushel of good
　　　　oats.

JEN. Well, I will.—[Aside]. Must I give
　　these scurvy horses
　　Oats?　　　　　　　　Exit Jenkin.

GEORGE. Will it please you to command
　　your train aside?　　　　　210

KEND. Stand aside.　　　Exit the Train.

GEORGE. Now list to me:
　　Here in a wood not far from hence,
　　There dwells an old man in a cave alone,
　　That can foretell what fortunes shall
　　　　befall you,
　　For he is greatly skillful in magic art.
　　Go you three to him early in the morning,
　　And question him. If he says good,
　　Why, then, my lord, I am the foremost
　　　　man!
　　We will march up with your camp to
　　　　London.　　　　　　　　220

KEND. George, thou honorest me in this.
　　But where shall we find him out?

GEORGE. My man shall conduct you to the
　　place.
　　But, good my lords, tell me true what the
　　　　wise man saith.

KEND. That will I, as I am Earl of Kendal.

GEORGE. Why, then, to honor G[eorge] a
　　Greene the more,
　　Vouchsafe a piece of beef at my poor
　　　　house.
　　You shall have wafer cakes your fill,
　　A piece of beef hung up since Martle-
　　　　mas.[3]

---

[1] Marvel.　　　　　　[2] Granting, noting.

[3] Martinmas, November 11.

If that like you not, take what you bring,
for me! [1]   230
KEND. Gramercies, George.
                              Exeunt omnes.

[SCENE viii.

Before Grime's house at Bradford.]

*Enter George a Greene's boy, Wily, disguised
like a woman, to M[aster] Grime's.*

WILY. O, what is love? It is some mighty
    power,
Else could it never conquer G[eorge] a
    Greene.
Here dwells a churl that keeps away his
    love.
I know the worst, and, if I be espied,
'Tis but a beating; and, if I by this
    means
Can get fair Bettris forth her father's
    door,
It is enough. Venus for me, and all gods
    above [2]
Be aiding to my wily enterprise!
                    He knocks at the door.

Enter Grime.

GRIME. How now! Who knocks there?
    What would you have?
From whence came you? Where do you
    dwell?   10
WILY. I am, forsooth, a sempster's [3] maid
    hard by,
That hath brought work home to your
    daughter.
GRIME. Nay, are you not some crafty
    quean
That comes from George a Greene, that
    rascal,
With some letters to my daughter?
I will have you searched.
WILY. Alas, sir, it is Hebrew unto me
To tell me of George a Greene or any
    other!
Search me, good sir,
And, if you find a letter about me,   20
Let me have the punishment that is
    due.
GRIME. Why are you muffled? I like you
    the worse
For that.

WILY. I am not, sir, ashamed to show my
    face;
Yet loath I am my cheeks should take the
    air—
Not that I am chary of my beauty's
    hue,
But that I am troubled with the tooth-
    ache sore.   [*Uncovers his face.*]
GRIME. [*Aside.*] A pretty wench, of smil-
    ing countenance!
Old men can like, although they cannot
    love;
Ay, and love, though not so brief [4] as
    young men can.—   30
Well, go in, my wench, and speak with
    my daughter.   *Exit* [*Wily*].
I wonder much at the Earl of Kendal,
Being a mighty man, as still he is;
Yet for to be a traitor to his king
Is more than God or man will well
    allow.
But what a fool am I to talk of him!
My mind is more here of the pretty
    lass.
Had she brought some forty pounds to
    town,
I could be content to make her my
    wife.
Yet I have heard it in a proverb said,   40
He that is old and marries with a lass,
Lies but at home, and proves himself an
    ass.

Enter Bettris in Wily's apparel, to Grime.

How now, my wench! How is't? What,
    not a word?
Alas, poor soul, the toothache plagues
    her sore!
Well, my wench, here is an angel [5] for to
    buy thee pins,
And I pray thee use mine house,
The oft'ner, the more welcome. Farewell.
                                Exit.
BETTRIS. O blessed love, and blessed for-
    tune both!
But, Bettris, stand not here to talk of
    love,
But hie thee straight unto thy George a
    Greene.   50
Never went roebuck swifter on the downs
Than I will trip it till I see my George.
                                Exit.

---

[1] For all I care.   [3] Seamstress'.
[2] Original reads *all goes alone.*

[4] Readily.   [5] Gold coin.

[SCENE ix.

Before a cave near Wakefield.]

*Enter the Earl of Kendal, L[ord] Bonfield,
Sir Gilbert, and Jenkin, the clown.*

KEND. Come away, Jenkin.

JEN. Come, here is his house.—Where be
you, ho?

GEORGE. [*Within.*] Who knocks there?

KEND. Here are two or three poor men,
father,
Would speak with you.

GEORGE. [*Within.*] Pray, give your man
leave to lead me forth.

KEND. Go, Jenkin, fetch him forth.

JEN. Come, old man.

Enter George a Greene, disguised.

KEND. Father, here is three poor men come
to question
Thee a word in secret that concerns their
lives.   10

GEORGE. Say on, my sons.

KEND. Father, I am sure you hear the
news,
How that the Earl of Kendal wars
against the king.
Now, father, we three are gentlemen by
birth,
But younger brethren that want reven-
ues,
And for the hope we have to be preferred,
If that we knew that we shall win,
We will march with him;
If not, we will not march a foot to
London more.
Therefore, good father, tell us what shall
happen,   20
Whether the king or the Earl of Kendal
shall win.

GEORGE. The king, my son.

KEND. Art thou sure of that?

GEORGE. Ay, as sure as thou art Henry
Momford,
The one L[ord] Bonfield, the other Sir
Gilbert.

KEND. Why, this is wondrous, being blind
of sight,
His deep perseverance [1] should be such to
know us.

GILB. Magic is mighty and foretelleth
great matters.

¹ Perceiverance, perception.

Indeed, father, here is the earl come to
see thee,
And therefore, good father, fable not
with him.   30

GEORGE. Welcome is the earl to my poor
cell,
And so are you, my lords; but let me
counsel you
To leave these wars against your king,
And live in quiet.

KEND. Father, we come not for advice in
war,
But to know whether we shall win or
leese. [2]

GEORGE. Lose, gentle lords, but not by
good King Edward;
A baser man shall give you all the foil. [3]

KEND. Ay, marry, father, what man is
that?

GEORGE. Poor George a Greene, the pinner.   40

KEND. What shall he?

GEORGE. Pull all your plumes, and sore
dishonor you.

KEND. He! As how?

GEORGE. Nay, the end tries all; but so
it will fall out.

KEND. But so it shall not, by my honor!
Christ!
I'll raise my camp, and fire Wakefield
town,
And take that servile pinner, George a
Greene,
And butcher him before King Edward's
face.

GEORGE. Good my lord, be not offended,
For I speak no more than art reveals
to me.   50
And for greater proof
Give your man leave to fetch me my staff.

KEND. Jenkin, fetch him his walking staff.

JEN. Here is your walking staff.

GEORGE. I'll prove it good upon your
carcasses;
A wiser wizard never met you yet,
Nor one that better could foredoom
your fall.
Now I have singled you here alone, [4]
I care not, though you be three to one.
[*Throws off his disguise.*]

KEND. Villain, hast thou betrayed us? 60

² Lose.   ³ Defeat.
⁴ *I.e.*, as an animal is selected from a herd for
hunting.

GEORGE. Momford, thou liest! Never was
　I traitor yet;
　Only devised this guile to draw you on
　For to be combatants.
　Now conquer me, and then march on
　　to London!
　But shall go hard but I will hold you
　　task.[1]
GILB. Come, my lord, cheerly; I'll kill
　him hand to hand.
KEND. A thousand pound to him that
　strikes that stroke!
GEORGE. Then give it me, for I will have
　the first.
Here they fight; George kills Sir Gilbert and
　　takes the other two prisoners.
BON. Stay, George; we do appeal.
GEORGE. To whom?　　　　　　　70
BON. Why, to the king!
　For rather had we bide what he appoints,
　Than here be murthered by a servile
　　groom.
KEND. What wilt thou do with us?
GEORGE. Even as Lord Bonfield wished,[2]
　You shall unto the king;
　And, for that purpose, see where the
　　justice is placed.

Enter Justice.

JUST. Now, my Lord of Kendal, where be
　all your threats?
　Even as the cause, so is the combat
　　fallen;
　Else one could never have conquered
　　three.　　　　　　　　　　　　80
KEND. I pray thee, Woodroffe, do not
　twit me;
　If I have faulted, I must make amends.
GEORGE. Master Woodroffe, here is not a
　place for many
　Words;
　I beseech ye, sir, discharge all his sol-
　　diers,
　That every man may go home unto his
　　own house.
JUST. It shall be so. What wilt thou do,
　George?
GEORGE. Master Woodroffe, look to your
　charge;
　Leave me to myself.
JUST. Come, my lords.　　　　　90
　　　　　　　Exit all but George.

[1] If I do not keep you busy.
[2] Original reads *wist.*

GEORGE. Here sit thou, George, wearing
　a willow wreath,
　As one despairing of thy beauteous
　　love.
　Fie, George, no more!
　Pine not away for that which cannot be.
　I cannot joy in any earthly bliss
　So long as I do want my Bettris.

Enter Jenkin.

JEN. Who see a master of mine?
GEORGE. How now, sirrah! Whither away?
JEN. Whither away? Why, who do you
　take me to be?
GEORGE. Why, Jenkin, my man.　　100
JEN. I was so once indeed, but now the
　case is altered.
GEORGE. I pray thee, as how?
JEN. Were not you a fortune teller today?
GEORGE. Well, what of that?
JEN. So sure am I become a juggler.
　What will you say if I juggle your sweet-
　　heart?
GEORGE. Peace, prating losel![3] Her jeal-
　ous father
　Doth wait over her with such suspicious
　　eyes
　That, if a man but dally by her feet,
　He thinks it straight a witch[4] to charm
　　his daughter.　　　　　　　116
JEN. Well, what will you give me if I
　bring her hither?
GEORGE. A suit of green and twenty
　crowns besides.
JEN. Well, by your leave, give me room.
　You must give me something that you
　have lately worn.
GEORGE. Here is a gown. Will that serve
　you?　　　　　　　　*[Gives his gown.]*
JEN. Ay, this will serve me. Keep out of
　my circle,
　Lest you be torn in pieces with she-
　　devils.—
　Mistress Bettris—once, twice, thrice!

He throws the gown [5] in, and she comes out.

　O, is this no cunning?
GEORGE. Is this my love, or is it but her
　shadow?　　　　　　　　　120
JEN. Ay, this is the shadow, but here is
　the substance.

[3] Worthless fellow.
[4] Spell.
[5] Original reads *ground.*

GEORGE. Tell me, sweet love, what good
fortune
  Brought thee hither?
  For one it was that favored George a
  Greene.
BETTRIS. Both love and fortune brought
me to my George,
  In whose sweet sight is all my heart's
content.
GEORGE. Tell me, sweet love, how cam'st
thou from thy
Father's?
BETTRIS. A willing mind hath many slips
in love.   129
  It was not I, but Wily, thy sweet boy.
GEORGE. And where is Wily now?
BETTRIS. In my apparel, in my chamber
still.
GEORGE. Jenkin, come hither.   Go to
Bradford,
  And listen out your fellow Wily.—
  Come, Bettris, let us in,
  And in my cottage we will sit and talk.
                          Exeunt omnes.

[SCENE X.

Edward's court at London.]

*Enter King Edward, the King of Scots,
  Lord Warwick, Young Cuddy, and their
                                    Train.*

EDWARD. Brother of Scotland, I do hold
it hard,
  Seeing a league of truce was late confirmed
  Twixt you and me, without displeasure
  offered
  You should make such invasion in my
  land.
  The vows of kings should be as oracles,
  Not blemished with the stain of any
  breach,
  Chiefly [1] where fealty and homage will-
  eth it.
JAMES. Brother of England, rub not the
sore afresh;
  My conscience grieves me for my deep
  misdeed.
  I have the worst; of thirty thousand
  men,   10
  There scaped not full five thousand from
  the field.

EDWARD. [*To Cuddy.*] Gramercy, Mus-
grove, else it had gone hard.
  Cuddy, I'll quite [2] thee well ere we two
  part.
JAMES. But had not his old father, Wil-
liam Musgrove,
  Played twice the man, I had not now
  been here.
  A stronger man I seldom felt before;
  But one of more resolute valiance
  Treads not, I think, upon the English
  ground.
EDWARD. I wot well. Musgrove shall not
lose his hire.
CUDDY. And it please your grace, my
father was   20
  Fivescore and three at midsummer last
  past;
  Yet had King Jamie been as good as
  George a Greene,
  Yet Billy Musgrove would have fought
  with him.
EDWARD. As George a Greene? I pray
thee, Cuddy,
  Let me question thee.
  Much have I heard, since I came to my
  crown;
  Many in manner of a proverb say,
  "Were he as good as G[eorge] a Greene,
  I would strike him sure."
  I pray thee, tell me, Cuddy, canst thou
  inform me,
  What is that George a Greene?   30
CUDDY. Know, my lord, I never saw the
man,
  But mickle [3] talk is of him in the coun-
  try.
  They say he is the pinner of Wakefield
  town,
  But for his other qualities, I let alone.
WAR. May it please your grace, I know
the man too well.
EDWARD. Too well? Why so, Warwick?
WAR. For once he swinged me till my
bones did ache.
EDWARD. Why, dares he strike an earl?
WAR. An earl, my lord? Nay, he will
strike a king,
  Be it not King Edward.   40
  For stature he is framed
  Like to the picture of stout Hercules,
  And for his carriage passeth Robin
  Hood.

---

[1] Especially.

[2] Requite, reward.   [3] Much.

The boldest earl or baron of your land
That offereth scath unto the town of
Wakefield,
George will arrest his pledge unto the
pound;[1]
And whoso resisteth bears away the
blows,
For he himself is good enough for three.

EDWARD. Why, this is wondrous, my
L[ord] of Warwick!
Sore do I long to see this George a
Greene.   50
But leaving him, what shall we do, my
lord,
For to subdue the rebels in the north?
They are now marching up to Don-
caster.—

Enter one with the Earl of Kendal prisoner.

Soft! Who have we there?
CUDDY. Here is a traitor, the Earl of
Kendal.
EDWARD. Aspiring traitor, how dar'st
thou once
Cast thine eyes upon thy sovereign
That honored thee with kindness and
with favor?
But I will make thee bye[2] this treason
dear.
KEND. Good my lord—   60
EDWARD. Reply not, traitor![3]—
Tell me, Cuddy, whose deed of honor
Won the victory against this rebel?
CUDDY. George a Greene, the pinner of
Wakefield.
EDWARD. George a Greene! Now shall I
hear news
Certain, what this pinner is.
Discourse it briefly, Cuddy, how it be-
fell.
CUDDY. Kendal and Bonfield, with Sir
Gilbert Armstrong,
Came to Wakefield town disguised,
And there spoke ill of your grace;   70
Which George but hearing, felled them
at his feet,
And, had not rescue come into the place,
George had slain them[4] in his close of
wheat.

EDWARD. But, Cuddy, canst thou not
tell
Where I might give and grant some-
thing
That might please and highly gratify
the pinner's thoughts?
CUDDY. This at their parting George did
say to me:[5]
"If the king vouchsafe of this my serv-
ice,
Then, gentle Cuddy, kneel upon thy
knee,
And humbly crave a boon of him for
me."   80
EDWARD. Cuddy, what is it?
CUDDY. It is his will your grace would
pardon them,
And let them live, although they have
offended.
EDWARD. I think the man striveth to be
glorious.[6]
Well, George hath craved it, and it shall
be granted,
Which none but he in England should
have gotten.—
Live, Kendal, but as prisoner;
So shalt thou end thy days within the
Tower.
KEND. Gracious is Edward to offending
subjects.
JAMES. My Lord of Kend[al], you are
welcome to the court.   90
EDWARD. Nay, but "ill-come" as it falls
out now;
Ay, "ill-come" indeed, were it not for
George a Greene.
But, "gentle king," for so you would
aver,
And, "Edward's betters," I salute you
both,
[*He mockingly vails bonnet to them.[7]*]
And here I vow by good Saint George,
You will gain but little when your sums
are counted!
I sore do long to see this George a
Greene.
And, for because I never saw the north,
I will forthwith go see it;
And, for that to none I will be known, 100

---

[1] *I.e.*, keep him in the pound as a hostage.
[2] Aby, pay for.
[3] In the original this line and the preceding are
printed on one line.
[4] Original reads *him*.
[5] The contradiction between this statement
and l. 31 may be due to the careless rewriting
of the play for use by a touring company.
[6] Vainglorious.
[7] Suggested by Adams as a fulfillment of the
prophecy in sc. vii, ll. 197–99.

We will disguise ourselves and steal down
  secretly,
Thou and I, King James, Cuddy, and
  two or three,
And make a merry journey for a
  month.—
Away, then, conduct him to the Tower.—
Come on, King James, my heart must
  needs be merry,
If fortune makes such havoc of our foes.
                  Ex[eunt] omnes.

[SCENE xi.

Sherwood Forest.]

*Enter Robin Hood, Maid Marian, Scarlet,
  and Much, the miller's son.*

ROBIN. Why is not lovely Marian blithe
  of cheer?
What ails my leman,[1] that she gins[2]
  to lour?
Say, good Marian, why art thou so sad?
MARIAN. Nothing, my Robin, grieves me
  to the heart
But, whensoever I do walk abroad,
I hear no songs but all of George a
  Greene;
Bettris, his fair leman, passeth me,
And this, my Robin, galls my very soul.
ROBIN. Content [thee].[3] What wreaks[4]
  it us though George a
Greene be stout,   10
So long as he does proffer us no scath?
Envy doth seldom hurt but to itself;
And therefore, Marian, smile upon thy
  Robin.
MARIAN. Never will Marian smile upon
  her Robin,
Nor lie with him under the greenwood
  shade,
Till that thou go to Wakefield on a green,
And beat the pinner for the love of me.
ROBIN. Content thee, Marian; I will ease
  thy grief.
My merry men and I will thither stray;
And here I vow that, for the love of thee,
I will beat George a Greene, or he shall
  beat me.   21
SCARLET. As I am Scarlet, next to Little
  John,
One of the boldest yeomen of the crew,

So will I wend with Robin all along,
And try this pinner what he dares do.
MUCH. As I am Much, the miller's son,
That left my mill to go with thee
(And nill[5] repent that I have done;
This pleasant life contenteth me),
In aught I may, to do thee good,   30
I'll live and die with Robin Hood.
MARIAN. And, Robin, Marian she will go
  with thee
To see fair Bettris how bright she is of
  blee.[6]
ROBIN. Marian, thou shalt go with thy
  Robin.—
Bend up your bows, and see your strings
  be tight,
The arrows keen, and everything be ready,
And each of you a good bat[7] on his neck,
Able to lay a good man on the ground.
SCARLET. I will have Friar Tuck's.
MUCH. I will have Little John's.   40
ROBIN. I will have one made of an ashen
  plank,[8]
Able to bear a bout or two.—
Then come on, Marian, let us go,
For, before the sun doth show the morn-
  ing day,
I will be at Wakefield to see this pinner,
George a Greene.   *Exeunt omnes.*

[SCENE xii.

Bradford.]

*Enter a Shoemaker sitting upon the stage at
  work; Jenkin to him [,carrying a staff].*

JEN. My masters, he that hath neither
  meat nor money,
And hath lost his credit with the ale-wife,
For anything I know, may go supper-
  less to bed.—
But soft! Who is here? Here is a shoe-
  maker;
He knows where is the best ale.
Shoemaker, I pray thee tell me,
Where is the best ale in the town?
SHOE. Afore, afore, follow thy nose!
At the sign of the Eggshell.
JEN. Come, shoemaker, if thou wilt,   10
And take thy part of a pot.
SHOE. [*Rising.*] Sirrah, down with your
  staff!
Down with your staff!

---

[1] Sweetheart.   [3] Supplied by Dyce.
[2] Begins.   [4] Recks, matters.
[5] Will not.   [6] Complexion.   [7] Staff.
[8] Emended by Mitford. Original reads *plunk.*

JEN. Why, how now! Is the fellow mad?
I pray thee tell me, why should I hold
down my staff?

SHOE. You will down with him, will you
not, sir?

JEN. Why, tell me wherefore?

SHOE. My friend, this is the town of
merry Bradford,[1]
And here is a custom held
That none shall pass with his staff on
his shoulders 20
But he must have a bout with me;
And so shall you, sir.

JEN. And so will not I, sir!

SHOE. That will I try. Barking dogs bite
not the sorest.

JEN. [Aside.] I would to God I were once
well rid of him.

SHOE. Now, what, will you down with
your staff?

JEN. Why, you are not in earnest, are
you?

SHOE. If I am not, take that!
[Strikes him.]

JEN. You whoreson, cowardly scab,
It is but the part of a clapperdudgeon[2]
To strike a man in the street. 31
But darest thou walk to the town's
end with me?

SHOE. Ay, that I dare do; but stay till I
lay in my
Tools, and I will go with thee to the
town's end
Presently.[3]

JEN. [Aside.] I would I knew how to be
rid of this fellow.

SHOE. Come, sir, will you go to the
town's end now, sir?

JEN. Ay, sir, come.—
[They cross the stage.]
Now we are at the town's end. What
say you now?

SHOE. Marry, come, let us even have a
bout. 40

JEN. Ha, stay a little; hold thy hands,
I pray thee!

SHOE. Why, what's the matter?

JEN. Faith, I am underpinner of a town,
And there is an order, which if I do not
keep,
I shall be turned out of mine office.

SHOE. What is that, sir?

JEN. Whensoever I go fight with anybody,
I use to flourish my staff thrice about
my head
Before I strike, and then show no
favor.

SHOE. Well, sir, and till then I will not
strike thee. 50

JEN. Well, sir, here is once, twice—
Here is my hand; I will never do it the
third time.

SHOE. Why, then, I see we shall not fight.

JEN. Faith, no! Come, I will give thee
two pots
Of the best ale, and be friends.

SHOE. [Aside.] Faith, I see it is as hard
to get water out of a flint
As to get him to have a bout with me;
Therefore I will enter into him for some
good cheer.—
My friend, I see thou art a faint-hearted
fellow;
Thou hast no stomach[4] to fight; 60
Therefore let us go to the alehouse and
drink.

JEN. Well, content! Go thy ways, and
say thy prayers;
Thou scap'st my hands today.
Exeunt omnes.

[SCENE xiii.

Wakefield.]

Enter George a Greene and Bettris.

GEORGE. Tell me, sweet love, how is thy
mind content?
What, canst thou brook to live with
George a Greene?

BETTRIS. O, George, how little pleasing
are these words!
Came I from Bradford for the love of
thee,
And left my father for so sweet a friend!
Here will I live until my life do end.

Enter Robin Hood, and Marian, and his
Train.

GEORGE. Happy am I to have so sweet
a love.—
But what are these come tracing[5] here
along?

---

[1] Original reads Wakefield.
[2] Beggar.   [3] Immediately
[4] Courage.   [5] Walking.

BETTRIS. Three men come striking
through the corn,
My love.   10
GEORGE. Back again, you foolish travelers,
For you are wrong, and may not wend
this way.
ROBIN. That were great shame.
Now, by my soul, proud sir,
We be three tall yeomen, and thou art
but one.—
Come, we will forward in despite of him.
GEORGE. Leap the ditch, or I will make
you skip.
What, cannot the highway serve your
turn,
But you must make a path over the
corn?
ROBIN. Why, art thou mad? Dar'st thou
encounter three?   20
We are no babes, man; look upon our
limbs.
GEORGE. Sirrah, the biggest limbs have
not the stoutest hearts.
Were ye as good as Robin Hood and
his three merry men,
I'll drive you back the same way that
ye came.
Be ye men, ye scorn to encounter me
all at once;
But be ye cowards, set upon me all
three,
And try the pinner what he dares per-
form.
SCARLET. Were thou as high in deeds
As thou art haughty in words,
Thou well mightest be a champion for
a king.   30
But empty vessels have the loudest
sounds,
And cowards prattle more than men of
worth.
GEORGE. Sirrah, darest thou try me?
SCARLET. Ay, sirrah, that I dare.
They fight, and George a Greene beats him.
MUCH. How now! What, art thou down?—
Come, sir, I am next.
They fight, and George a Greene beats him.
ROBIN. Come, sirrah, now to me! Spare
me not,
For I'll not spare thee.
GEORGE. Make no doubt I will be as
liberal to thee.
        They fight. Robin Hood stays.[1]

[1] Desists, rests.

ROBIN. Stay, George, for here I do pro-
test   40
Thou art the stoutest champion that
ever I laid
Hands upon.
GEORGE. Soft you, sir! By your leave,
you lie;
You never yet laid hands on me.
ROBIN. George, wilt thou forsake Wake-
field,
And go with me?
Two liveries will I give thee every year,
And forty crowns shall be thy fee.
GEORGE. Why, who art thou?
ROBIN. Why, Robin Hood!   50
I am come hither with my Marian
And these my yeomen for to visit thee.
GEORGE. Robin Hood! Next to King
Edward
Art thou lief [2] to me.
Welcome, sweet Robin; welcome, Maid
Marian;
And welcome, you, my friends.
Will you to my poor house?
You shall have wafer cakes your fill,
A piece of beef hung up since Martlemas,
Mutton and veal. If this like you not, 60
Take that you find, or that you bring,
for me.
ROBIN. God-a-mercies, good George,
I'll be thy guest today.
GEORGE. Robin, therein thou honorest me.
I'll lead the way.   *Exeunt omnes.*

[SCENE xiv.

Bradford.]

*Enter King Edward and King James dis-
guised, with two staves.*

EDWARD. Come on, King James; now we
are
Thus disguised,
There is none, I know, will take us to
be kings.
I think we are now in Bradford,
Where all the merry shoemakers dwell.

Enter a Shoemaker [with his Comrades].

SHOE. Down with your staves, my friends,
Down with them!
EDWARD. Down with our staves? I pray
thee, why so?

[2] Dear.

SHOE. My friend, I see thou art a stranger here,
Else wouldest thou not have questioned
of the thing.   10
This is the town of merry Bradford,
And here hath been a custom kept of
old,
That none may bear his staff upon his
neck,
But trail it all along throughout the
town,
Unless they mean to have a bout with
me.

EDWARD. But hear you, sir, hath the king
Granted you this custom?

SHOE. King or kaiser, none shall pass
this way,
Except King Edward;
No, not the stoutest groom that haunts
his court.   20
Therefore down with your staves!

EDWARD. [Aside.] What were we best to
do?

JAMES. [Aside.] Faith, my lord, they are
stout fellows;
And, because we will see some sport,
We will trail our staves.

EDWARD. Hear'st thou, my friend?
Because we are men of peace and travel-
ers,
We are content to trail our staves.

SHOE. The way lies before you; go along.

Enter Robin Hood and George a Greene,
disguised.

ROBIN. See, George, two men are passing
Through the town,   31
Two lusty men, and yet they trail their
staves.

GEORGE. Robin, they are some peasants
Tricked in yeoman's weeds.—Hollo,
you two travelers!

EDWARD. Call you us, sir?

GEORGE. Ay, you. Are ye not big enough
to bear
Your bats upon your necks,
But you must trail them along the
streets?

EDWARD. Yes, sir, we are big enough;
but here is a custom
Kept, that none may pass, his staff
upon his neck,   40
Unless he trail it at the weapon's point.

Sir, we are men of peace, and love to
sleep
In our whole skins, and therefore quietness is best.

GEORGE. Base-minded peasants, worthless to be men!
What, have you bones and limbs to
strike a blow,
And be your hearts so faint you cannot
fight?
Were't not for shame, I would shrub [1]
your shoulders well,
And teach you manhood against [2] another time.

SHOE. Well preached, Sir Jack! Down
with your staff!

EDWARD. Do you hear, my friends? And
you be wise,   50
Keep down your staves,
For all the town will rise upon you.

GEORGE. Thou speakest like an honest,
quiet fellow.
But hear you me. In spite of all the
swains
Of Bradford town, bear me your staves
upon your necks,
Or, to begin withal, I'll baste you both
so well,
You were never better basted in your
lives.

EDWARD. We will hold up our staves.

George a Greene fights with the Shoemakers,
and beats them all down.

GEORGE. What, have you any more?
Call all your town forth, cut and long-
tail. [3]   60

The Shoemakers spy [4] George a Greene.

SHOE. What, George a Greene, is it you?
A plague found [5] you!
I think you longed to swinge me well.
Come, George, we will crush [6] a pot
before we part.

GEORGE. A pot, you slave! We will have
an hundred.—
Here, Will Perkins, take my purse;
Fetch me a stand [7] of ale, and set in the
market place,
That all may drink that are athirst this
day;

---

[1] Scrub, beat.   [2] In preparation for.
[3] Docked and undocked (said of dogs and
horses); hence, all classes of people.
[4] Recognize.   [6] Drink.
[5] Confound.   [7] Cask.

For this is for a fee to welcome Robin
Hood
To Bradford town.　　　　　　　　　　70
*They bring out the stand of ale and fall
a-drinking.*
Here, Robin, sit thou here; for thou art
the best man
At the board this day.
You that are strangers, place yourselves
where you will.
Robin, here's a carouse to good King
Edward's self;
And they that love him not, I would
we had
The basting of them a little.

*Enter the Earl of Warwick with other Noble-
men, bringing out the King's garments;
then George a Greene and the rest kneel
down to the King.*

EDWARD. Come, masters, all fellows!—
Nay, Robin, you are the best man at
the board today.—
Rise up, George.
GEORGE. Nay, good my liege, ill-nurtured
we were, then.　　　　　　　　　　80
Though we Yorkshire men be blunt of
speech,
And little skilled in court or such quaint
fashions,
Yet nature teacheth us duty to our king;
Therefore I humbly beseech you pardon
George a Greene.
ROBIN. And, good my lord, a pardon for
poor Robin;
And for us all a pardon, good King Ed-
ward.
SHOE. I pray you, a pardon for the shoe-
makers.
EDWARD. I frankly grant a pardon to you
all.　　　　　　　　　　　　[*They rise.*]
And, George a Greene, give me thy hand;
There's none in England that shall do
thee wrong.　　　　　　　　　　　90
Even from my court I came to see thy-
self;
And now I see that fame speaks naught
but truth.
GEORGE. I humbly thank your royal
majesty.
That which I did against the Earl of
Kendal,
It was but a subject's duty to his sov-
ereign,

And therefore little merit such good
words.
EDWARD. But, ere I go, I'll grace thee with
good deeds.
Say what King Edward may perform,
And thou shalt have it, being in Eng-
land's bounds.
GEORGE. I have a lovely leman,　　　100
As bright of blee as is the silver moon,
And old Grime her father will not let
her match
With me, because I am a pinner,
Although I love her, and she me, dearly.
EDWARD. Where is she?
GEORGE. At home at my poor house,
And vows never to marry unless her
father
Give consent; which is my great grief,
my lord.
EDWARD. If this be all, I will despatch it
straight;
I'll send for Grime and force him give
his grant;　　　　　　　　　　　110
He will not deny King Edward such a
suit.

Enter Jenkin and speaks.

[JEN.] Ho, who saw a master of mine?
O, he is gotten into company, and a body
should rake
Hell for company!
GEORGE. Peace, ye slave!　See where
King Edward is.
EDWARD. George, what is he?
GEORGE. I beseech your grace pardon
him; he is my man.
SHOE. Sirrah, the king hath been drink-
ing with us,
And did pledge us too.
JEN. Hath he so?　Kneel!　I dub you
"gentlemen."　　　　　　　　　　120
SHOE. Beg it of the king, Jenkin.
JEN. I will.—I beseech your worship grant
me one thing.
EDWARD. What is that?
JEN. Hark in your ear.
　　　　He whispers the King in the ear.
EDWARD. Go your ways, and do it.
JEN. Come, down on your knees; I have
got it.
SHOE. Let us hear what it is first.
JEN. Marry, because you have drunk
with the king,

And the king hath so graciously pledged
   you,
You shall be no more called shoe-
   makers,   130
But you and yours, to the world's end,
Shall be called "the trade of the gentle [1]
   craft."
SHOE. I beseech your majesty reform
   this
Which he hath spoken.
JEN. I beseech your worship consume
   this
Which he hath spoken.
EDWARD. Confirm it, you would say.—
   Well, he hath done it for you; it is suf-
   ficient.
Come, George, we will go to Grime,
And have thy love.   140
JEN. I am sure your worship will
   abide;
For yonder is coming old Musgrove
And mad Cuddy, his son.—
Master, my fellow Wily comes dressed
   like a woman,
And Master Grime will marry Wily.
   Here they come.

*Enter Musgrove and Cuddy; and Master
Grime, Wily, Maid Marian, and Bettris.*

EDWARD. Which is thy old father, Cuddy?
CUDDY. This, if it please your majesty.
            [*Musgrove kneels.*]
EDWARD. Ah, old Musgrove, stand[2] up;
   It fits not such gray hairs to kneel.
MUS. [*Rising.*] Long live my sovereign!
   Long and happy be his days!   151
Vouchsafe, my gracious lord, a simple
   gift
At Billy Musgrove's hand.
King James at Middleham [3] Castle
   gave me this;
This won the honor, and this give I
   thee.   [*Gives sword to Edward.*]
EDWARD. God-a-mercy, Musgrove, for
   this friendly gift;
And, for thou felledst a king with this
   same weapon,
This blade shall here dub valiant Mus-
   grove knight.

[1] Genteel, elegant.
[2] Original reads *kneel*.
[3] The original form *Meddellom* shows the pronunciation.

MUS. Alas, what hath your highness
   done? I am poor.
EDWARD. To mend thy living take thou
   Middleham Castle,   160
The hold of both. And if thou want
   living, complain;
Thou shalt have more to maintain thy
   estate.—
George, which is thy love?
GEORGE. This, if please your majesty.
EDWARD. Art thou her aged father?
GRIME. I am, and it like your majesty.
EDWARD. And wilt not give thy daughter
   unto George?
GRIME. Yes, my lord, if he will let me
   marry
With this lovely lass.
EDWARD. What sayst thou, George? 170
GEORGE. With all my heart, my lord, I
   give consent.
GRIME. Then do I give my daughter unto
   George.
WILY. Then shall the marriage soon be
   at an end.
Witness, my lord, if that I be a woman;
        [*Throws off his disguise.*]
For I am Wily, boy to George a Greene,
Who for my master wrought this subtle
   shift.
EDWARD. What, is it a boy?—What sayst
   thou to this, Grime?
GRIME. Marry, my lord, I think this boy
   hath
More knavery than all the world be-
   sides.
Yet am I content that George shall
   both have   180
My daughter and my lands.
EDWARD. Now, George, it rests I gratify
   thy worth;
And therefore here I do bequeath to
   thee,
In full possession, half that Kendal
   hath;
And whatas [4] Bradford holds of me in
   chief,
I give it frankly unto thee forever.
Kneel down, George.
GEORGE. What will your majesty do?
EDWARD. Dub thee a knight, George.
GEORGE. I beseech your grace, grant me
   one thing.   190
EDWARD. What is that?

[4] Whatsoever.

GEORGE. Then let me live and die a yeo-
　man still.
So was my father, so must live his son.
For 'tis more credit to men of base de-
　gree
To do great deeds than men of dignity.
EDWARD. Well, be it so, George.
JAMES. I beseech your grace, despatch
　with me,
And set down my ransom.
EDWARD. George a Greene, set down the
　King of Scots
His ransom.　　　　　　　　　　200
GEORGE. I beseech your grace, pardon
　me;
It passeth my skill.
EDWARD. Do it; the honor's thine.
GEORGE. Then let King James make good
　Those towns which he hath burnt upon
　　the borders;
　Give a small pension to the fatherless,
　Whose fathers he caused murthered in
　　those wars;

Put in pledge for these things to your
　grace,
And so return.
[EDWARD.] King James, are you content? [1]
JAMES. I am content, and like [2] your
　majesty,　　　　　　　　　　211
And will leave good castles in security.
EDWARD. I crave no more.—Now, George
　a Greene,
I'll to thy house; and when I have
　supped, I'll go to ask
And see if Jane a Barley be so fair
As good King James reports her for to
　be.
And for the ancient custom of *Vail staff*,
　keep it still;
Claim privilege from me.
If any ask a reason why or how,
Say English Edward vailed his staff to
　you.

[1] In the original this sentence is given to
George a Greene, completing the last line of his
speech.　　　　　　[2] If it please.

FINIS.

CHRISTOPHER MARLOWE

Christopher Marlowe—the name is also spelled Marly and Marlin in the records—was born in 1564, the son of a well-to-do shoemaker and a clergyman's daughter. He was educated at King's School in his native Canterbury and at Corpus Christi College, Cambridge, where he proceeded B.A. in 1584 and M.A. in 1587. The privy council intervened to see that his employment on some confidential mission for the government, in which he had proved "orderly and discreet," should not put him at a disadvantage in the matter of his M.A. degree. For the remaining six years of his life there is evidence of exceptional activity. Apparently he continued to serve as a confidential agent for the government; he engaged in the philosophical or theological speculation of a circle centering around Raleigh; he achieved distinction by his non-dramatic verse, of which the unfinished *Hero and Leander* is the most important example; and he became the outstanding dramatist of London, in association chiefly with the Admiral's Company of players. Many details of his life were a source of scandal to some of his contemporaries, and for us are still shrouded in mystery. In May, 1593, a manuscript was discovered in Kyd's possession which he declared to be Marlowe's, left with Kyd in 1591 when he was in the service of a noble lord for whose players Marlowe was writing. The document—merely a copy of part of a theological treatise already published—though unitarian in nature, was atheistic in the eyes of the orthodox. Testimony as to blasphemous conversations on Marlowe's part was also produced. Before the privy council took definite action about the charges, Marlowe was killed. Puritan disapproval of his connection with the stage and of his free-thinking perhaps influenced Meres' statement that he was stabbed "by a bawdy serving-man, a rival of his in his lewd love." Records discovered by Hotson merely show that he was stabbed in a tavern in Deptford by Friser, one of three companions who also were, or had been, in the service of the government. The procedure of the coroner's inquest by which Friser was exonerated is regarded by some modern students as regular, by others as an attempt to cover official secrets or even a political assassination. Marlowe was buried on June 1, 1593.

Tamburlaine, unanimously accepted as Marlowe's first play, was attracting attention by 1588, when Greene in the preface to *Perimedes the Blacksmith* speaks of "atheist Tamburlaine" in what is pretty clearly an attack on Marlowe. Evidence of his authorship is chiefly to be found in the character of the play, however. The two parts were published together anonymously in 1590, with some omissions, as the printer's preface indicates. Perhaps the success of the first part led Marlowe to write the inferior second part—not printed in this anthology—in which Tamburlaine is followed to his boasting and unrepentant end. A Renaissance interest in the oriental conqueror and his barbaric passions and display, surviving no doubt in part from medieval story and drama, and stimulated by new contacts with the East, is reflected by the popularity of the type on the London stage. The story of Tamburlaine apparently held an especial fascination for writers, and had become mythical before Marlowe created his conqueror. Marlowe seems to have consulted a number of historical or pseudo-historical accounts of the East for his material, and even contemporary geographical works for some of his sonorous references to distant places. In this first play Marlowe developed his "mighty line," as Jonson calls it, and made it a fit instrument for the intense and passionate characters created by him. While at times, especially in *Tamburlaine*, his style approaches bombast, his swelling periods and bold figures contributed greatly to the effectiveness of tragic style in his successors.

Doctor Faustus has usually been assigned to the winter of 1588–89, but recent scholars like Tucker Brooke and Boas (in his edition of the play for *The Works and Life of Marlowe*

307

under the general editorship of Case) argue for the date 1592. The German *Faustbuch*, translated into English, seems to have been the source, and there is evidence that this was not published before 1592. The first certain record of the play is of its being acted for Henslowe in 1594. The problem of the text is a difficult one. The earliest known edition was not published until 1604, and it contains some material which bears evidence of composition after Marlowe's death. Some scholars trace Dekker's hand in this version, possibly through revision for acting in 1594. Apparently the serious parts of the play have been cut, with an enlargement of the spectacular and comic scenes of conjuring and dancing, the sort of thing always loved by the London populace. In 1602 Henslowe paid William Bird and Samuel Rowley for "additions" to the play. Presumably these were included in the enlarged edition which came out in 1616. The new material in this version, though added to the poetic scenes, is still primarily of a spectacular nature, and does not often suggest Marlowe. Boas argues that Rowley collaborated with Marlowe from the beginning, contributing most of the original comic prose as well as many of the later verse additions. Accordingly he constructs a composite text for the play, but one based primarily on the edition of 1616. It is, however, in the tragic portrayal of the scholar who, irked by the limitations of academic studies, purchased supreme knowledge and power with his soul, that the play represents Marlowe at his best, in spite of the imperfections of the surviving texts. Hence the present editors have preferred to follow the shorter version of 1604, with sparing use of later editions for corrupt passages.

Edward II was entered in the Stationers' Register on July 6, 1593. The first complete edition known was printed in 1594 with the statement that the play had been acted by the Earl of Pembroke's players. The winter of 1592–93 is suggested as the date of composition by indications of maturity in the play and by the fact that Pembroke's Company was prominent in London only at that time. The source is Holinshed's *Chronicles*. *Edward II* represents a great advance over the known plays on English history that preceded, and is the best of Marlowe's work in construction, in characterization, and in sustained tone. Against a background of the fierce feudal barons, Marlowe has drawn a very effective picture of the sentimental and weak but stubborn king.

Of the three extant plays by Marlowe in addition to those printed here, the most important is *The Jew of Malta*, written possibly around 1590. It was being played for Henslowe early in 1592, and was entered in the Stationers' Register early in 1594. The earliest form to survive, however, is an edition by Thomas Heywood in 1633, which has clearly been revamped. *The Massacre at Paris* was printed without date about 1593. *Dido, Queen of Carthage*, printed in 1594, was written in collaboration with Thomas Nashe. It has been claimed that Marlowe had a hand in several other extant plays, particularly in the two parts of *The Contention of York and Lancaster*, which are versions of Shakespeare's Second and Third Parts of *Henry VI*.

Tucker Brooke's variorum *Works of Marlowe* has furnished the basis for the texts of the three plays printed here, which in each case go back to the earliest edition. *Doctor Faustus* has been checked with the edition of 1604 in Farmer's Tudor Facsimile Texts, and *Edward II* with the Malone Society reprint of the edition of 1594 prepared under the direction of W. W. Greg.

TAMBURLAINE THE GREAT

[BY

CHRISTOPHER MARLOWE

THE FIRST PART

DRAMATIS PERSONÆ

MYCETES, *King of Persia.*
COSROE, *his brother.*
ORTYGIUS ⎫
CENEUS   ⎪
MEANDER ⎬ *Persian lords and leaders.*
MENAPHON ⎪
THERIDAMAS ⎭
TAMBURLAINE, *a Scythian shepherd.*
TECHELLES ⎫ *his followers.*
USUMCASANE ⎭
BAJAZETH, *Emperor of the Turks.*
KING OF ARABIA.
KING OF FEZ.
KING OF MOROCCO.
KING OF ARGIER.[2]

SOLDAN of EGYPT.
GOVERNOR of DAMASCUS.
AGYDAS   ⎫ *Median lords.*
MAGNETES ⎭
CAPOLIN, *an Egyptian captain.*
PHILEMUS, *a messenger.*
BASSOES,[3] LORDS, CITIZENS, MOORS, SOLDIERS, *and* ATTENDANTS.

ZENOCRATE, *daughter of the Soldan of Egypt.*
ANIPPE, *her maid.*
ZABINA, *wife of Bajazeth.*
EBEA, *her maid.*
VIRGINS OF DAMASCUS.

SCENE: *Western Asia.*

TIME: *Fourteenth Century.*]

To THE GENTLEMEN READERS, AND OTHERS THAT TAKE PLEASURE IN READING HISTORIES.

Gentlemen, and courteous readers whosoever: I have here published in print for your sakes the two tragical discourses of the Scythian shepherd, Tamburlaine, that became so great a conqueror and so mighty a monarch. My hope is that they will be now no less acceptable unto you to read after your serious affairs and studies than they have been, lately, delightful for many of you to see, when the same were [10 showed in London upon stages. I have, purposely, omitted and left out some fond[4] and frivolous gestures, digressing and, in my poor opinion, far unmeet for the matter, which I thought might seem more tedious unto the wise than any way else to be regarded, though haply they have been of some vain, conceited fondlings[5] greatly gaped at, what times they were showed upon the stage in their graced deformities; [20 nevertheless, now, to be mixtured in print with such matter of worth, it would prove a great disgrace to so honorable and stately a history. Great folly were it in me to commend unto your wisdoms either the eloquence of the author that writ them, or the worthiness of the matter itself; I therefore leave unto your learned censures[6] both the one and the other, and myself, the poor

---

[1] The title continues: "Who, from a Scythian Shepherd, by His Rare and Wonderful Conquests Became a Most Puissant and Mighty Monarch, and (for His Tyranny and Terror in War) Was Termed the Scourge of God. Divided into Two Tragical Discourses, as They Were Sundry Times Showed upon Stages in the City of London, by the Right Honorable the Lord Admiral His Servants. Now First and Newly Published."

[2] Algiers.   [3] Bashaws.

[4] Foolish.   [5] Fools.   [6] Judgments.

printer of them, unto your most cour- [30
teous and favorable protection, which if you
vouchsafe to accept, you shall evermore
bind me to employ what travail and service
I can to the advancing and pleasuring of
your excellent degree.

Yours, most humble at commandment,
R[ichard] J[ones], Printer.

The Prologue

From jigging veins of riming mother wits
And such conceits as clownage keeps in pay,
We'll lead you to the stately tent of war,
Where you shall hear the Scythian Tam-
burlaine
Threat'ning the world with high astound-
ing terms,
And scourging kingdoms with his conquer-
ing sword.
View but his picture in this tragic glass,
And then applaud his fortunes as you
please.

Actus I. Scena i.

[*The Persian court.*]

*Mycetes, Cosroe, Meander, Theridamas,
Ortygius, Ceneus, [Menaphon,] with
Others.*

Myc. Brother Cosroe, I find myself ag-
grieved,
  Yet insufficient to express the same,
  For it requires a great and thund'ring
speech.
  Good brother, tell the cause unto my
lords;
  I know you have a better wit than I.
Cos. Unhappy Persia, that in former age
  Hast been the seat of mighty conquerors
  That, in their prowess and their policies,
  Have triumphed over Afric and the
bounds
  Of Europe, where the sun dares scarce
appear   10
  For freezing meteors and congealéd cold,
  Now to be ruled and governed by a man
  At whose birthday Cynthia with Saturn
joined,
  And Jove, the Sun, and Mercury denied
  To shed their[1] influence in his fickle
brain!

[1] Suggested by Dyce. Original has *his*.

Now Turks and Tartars shake their
swords at thee,
  Meaning to mangle all thy provinces.
Myc. Brother, I see your meaning well
enough,
  And thorough[2] your planets I perceive
you think
  I am not wise enough to be a king;   20
  But I refer me to my noblemen
  That know my wit, and can be witnesses.
  I might command you to be slain for this.
  Meander, might I not?
Mean. Not for so small a fault, my sov-
ereign lord.
Myc. I mean it not, but yet I know I
might.
  Yet live; yea, live. Mycetes wills it so.
  Meander, thou, my faithful counselor,
  Declare the cause of my conceivéd grief,
  Which is, God knows, about that Tam-
burlaine,   30
  That, like a fox in midst of harvest
time,
  Doth prey upon my flocks of passengers,[3]
  And, as I hear, doth mean to pull my
plumes;
  Therefore 'tis good and meet for to be
wise.
Mean. Oft have I heard your majesty
complain
  Of Tamburlaine, that sturdy Scythian
thief,
  That robs your merchants of Persepolis,
  Treading by land unto the Western Isles,
  And in your confines with his lawless
train
  Daily commits incivil[4] outrages,   40
  Hoping (misled by dreaming prophecies)
  To reign in Asia, and with barbarous
arms
  To make himself the monarch of the
East.
  But, ere he march in Asia, or display
  His vagrant ensign in the Persian fields,
  Your grace hath taken order by Theri-
damas,
  Charged with a thousand horse, to appre-
hend
  And bring him captive to your highness'
throne.
Myc. Full true thou speak'st, and like
thyself, my lord,

[2] Through.   [4] Barbarous.
[3] Travelers, traders.

Whom I may term a Damon for thy
    love.   50
Therefore 'tis best, if so it like you all,
To send my thousand horse incontinent [1]
To apprehend that paltry Scythian.
How like you this, my honorable lords?
Is it not a kingly resolution?
Cos. It cannot choose, because it comes
    from you.
Myc. Then hear thy charge, valiant Theri-
    damas,
The chiefest captain of Mycetes' host,
The hope of Persia, and the very legs
Whereon our state doth lean, as on a
    staff   60
That holds us up, and foils our neighbor
    foes.
Thou shalt be leader of this thousand
    horse,
Whose foaming gall with rage and high
    disdain
Have sworn the death of wicked Tam-
    burlaine.
Go frowning forth; but come thou smiling
    home,
As did Sir Paris with the Grecian dame.
Return with speed—time passeth swift
    away;
Our life is frail, and we may die today.
Ther. Before the moon renew her bor-
    rowed light,
Doubt not, my lord and gracious sov-
    ereign,   70
But Tamburlaine and that Tartarian
    rout
Shall either perish by our warlike hands
Or plead for mercy at your highness'
    feet.
Myc. Go, stout Theridamas; thy words
    are swords,
And with thy looks thou conquerest all
    thy foes.
I long to see thee back return from
    thence,
That I may view these milk-white steeds
    of mine,
All loaden with the heads of killéd men,
And from their knees even to their hoofs
    below,
Besmeared with blood that makes a
    dainty [2] show.   80
Ther. Then now, my lord, I humbly take
    my leave.

Myc. Therid[amas], farewell ten thousand
    times!   *Exit* [*Theridamas*].
Ah, Menaphon, why stayest thou thus
    behind,
When other men press forward for re-
    nown?
Go, Menaphon, go into Scythia,
And foot by foot follow Theridamas.
Cos. Nay, pray you let him stay; a greater
    [task] [3]
Fits Menaphon than warring with a
    thief.
Create him prorex [4] of [all] [5] Africa,
That he may win the Babylonians'
    hearts,   90
Which will revolt from Persian govern-
    ment,
Unless they have a wiser king than you.
Myc. "Unless they have a wiser king than
    you"!
These are his words. Meander, set them
    down.
Cos. And add this to them—that all
    Asia
Lament to see the folly of their king.
Myc. Well, here I swear by this my royal
    seat—
Cos. You may do well to kiss it then!
Myc. Embossed with silk as best beseems
    my state,
To be revenged for these contemptuous
    words.   100
O, where is duty and allegiance now?
Fled to the Caspian or the Ocean main?
What, shall I call thee brother? No, a foe,
Monster of nature, shame unto thy
    stock,
That dar'st presume thy sovereign for to
    mock!
Meander, come! I am abused, Meander.
Exit [*with his Train*]. *Manent* [6] *Cosroe*
                et Menaphon.
Mena. How now, my lord? What, mated [7]
    and amazed
To hear the king thus threaten like him-
    self?
Cos. Ah, Menaphon, I pass [8] not for his
    threats.
The plot is laid by Persian noblemen 110
And captains of the Median garrisons
To crown me Emperor of Asia.

[1] Immediately.   [2] Fine, rare.

[3] Added by Robinson.   [5] From 1605 edn.
[4] Viceroy.   [6] Remain.
[7] Checkmated, confounded.   [8] Care.

But this it is that doth excruciate
The very substance of my vexéd soul—
To see our neighbors, that were wont to
quake
And tremble at the Persian monarch's
name,
Now sits and laughs our regiment [1] to
scorn;
And, that which might resolve [2] me into
tears,
Men from the farthest equinoctial line
Have swarmed in troops into the Eastern
India,   120
Lading their ships with gold and precious
stones,
And made their spoils from all our prov-
inces.
MENA. This should entreat your highness
to rejoice,
Since fortune gives you opportunity
To gain the title of a conqueror
By curing of this maiméd empery.
Afric and Europe bordering on your land,
And continent [3] to your dominions,
How easily may you, with a mighty host,
Pass into Grecia, as did Cyrus once,   130
And cause them to withdraw their forces
home,
Lest you subdue the pride of Christen-
dom!   [*Trumpet within.*]
COS. But, Menaph[on], what means this
trumpet's sound?
MENA. Behold, my lord, Ortygius and the
rest
Bringing the crown to make you em-
peror!

*Enter Ortygius and Ceneus [4] bearing a
crown, with Others.*

ORTY. Magnificent and mighty Prince Cos-
roe,
We, in the name of other Persian states [5]
And commons of this mighty monarchy,
Present thee with th' imperial diadem.
CEN. The warlike soldiers and the gentle-
men,   140
That heretofore have filled Persepolis
With Afric captains taken in the field,
Whose ransom made them march in coats
of gold,

With costly jewels hanging at their ears,
And shining stones upon their lofty
crests,
Now living idle in the walléd towns,
Wanting both pay and martial discipline,
Begin in troops to threaten civil war,
And openly exclaim against the king.
Therefore, to stay all sudden muti-
nies,   150
We will invest your highness emperor,
Whereat the soldiers will conceive more
joy
Than did the Macedonians at the spoil
Of great Darius and his wealthy host.
COS. Well, since I see the state of Persia
droop
And languish in my brother's govern-
ment,
I willingly receive th' imperial crown,
And vow to wear it for my country's
good,
In spite of them [6] shall malice [7] my es-
tate.
ORTY. And, in assurance of desired suc-
cess,   160
We here do crown thee Monarch of the
East,
Emperor of Asia and of Persia,
Great Lord of Media and Armenia,
Duke of Africa and Albania,
Mesopotamia and of Parthia,
East India and the late-discovered isles,
Chief Lord of all the wide, vast Euxine
sea,
And of the ever-raging Caspian lake!
Long live Cosroe, mighty emperor!
COS. And Jove may [8] never let me longer
live   170
Than I may seek to gratify your love,
And cause the soldiers that thus honor
me
To triumph over many provinces!
By whose desires of discipline in arms
I doubt not shortly but to reign sole
king,
And with the army of Theridamas,
Whither we presently will fly, my lords,
To rest secure against my brother's force.
ORTY. We knew, my lord, before we
brought the crown,
Intending your investion [9] so near   180

---

[1] Rule, government.   [3] Contiguous.
[2] Dissolve.
[4] Emended by Dyce. Original reads *Cornerus.*
[5] Persons of state.
[6] Them who.
[7] Bear malice to, seek to injure.
[8] May Jove.   [9] Investiture.

The residence of your despiséd brother,
The lord[s] would not be too exasperate [1]
To injure or suppress your worthy title;
Or, if they would, there are in readiness
Ten thousand horse to carry you from
    hence,
In spite of all suspected enemies.

Cos. I know it well, my lord, and thank
    you all.

Orty. Sound up the trumpets then. God
    save the king!   *Exeunt.*

ACTUS I. SCENA ii.

[*Tamburlaine's camp in Scythia.*]

*Tamburlaine leading Zenocrate; Techelles,
    Usumcasane, [Agydas, Magnetes;]
    other Lords and Soldiers loaden with
                            treasure.*

Tam. Come, lady, let not this appall your
    thoughts.
The jewels and the treasure we have ta'en
Shall be reserved, and you in better state
Than if you were arrived in Syria,
Even in the circle of your father's arms,
The mighty Soldan of Egyptia.

Zen. Ah, shepherd, pity my distresséd
    plight
(If, as thou seemst, thou art so mean a
    man)
And seek not to enrich thy followers
By lawless rapine from a silly [2] maid   10
Who, traveling with these Median lords
To Memphis, from my uncle's country
    of Media,
Where all my youth I have been gov-
    ernéd,
Have passed the army of the mighty
    Turk,
Bearing his privy signet and his hand
To safe conduct us thorough Africa.

Mag. And, since we have arrived in
    Scythia,
Besides rich presents from the puissant
    Cham,
We have his highness' letters to com-
    mand
Aid and assistance, if we stand in
    need.   20

Tam. But now you see these letters and
    commands
Are countermanded by a greater man;

And through my provinces you must
    expect
Letters of conduct from my mightiness,
If you intend to keep your treasure safe.
But, since I love to live at liberty,
As easily may you get the soldan's crown
As any prizes out of my precinct,
For they are friends that help to wean my
    state
Till men and kingdoms help to strengthen
    it,   30
And must maintain my life exempt from
    servitude.—
But, tell me, madam, is your grace be-
    trothed?

Zen. I am, my lord—for so you do import. [3]

Tam. I am a lord, for so my deeds shall
    prove,
And yet a shepherd by my parentage.
But, lady, this fair face and heavenly hue
Must grace his bed that conquers Asia,
And means to be a terror to the world,
Measuring the limits of his empery
By east and west, as Phœbus doth his
    course.   40
Lie here, ye weeds that I disdain to
    wear!
This complete armor and this curtle-ax [4]
Are adjuncts more beseeming Tambur-
    laine.
And, madam, whatsoever you esteem
Of this success [5] and loss unvaluéd, [6]
Both may invest you Empress of the
    East;
And these that seem but silly country
    swains
May have the leading of so great an host
As with their weight shall make the
    mountains quake,
Even as when windy exhalations,   50
Fighting for passage, tilt within the
    earth.

Tech. As princely lions, when they rouse
    themselves,
Stretching their paws, and threat'ning
    herds of beasts,
So in his armor looketh Tamburlaine.
Methinks I see kings kneeling at his feet,
And he, with frowning brows and fiery
    looks,
Spurning their crowns from off their
    captive heads.

[1] Old form of past participle.
[2] Simple, innocent.

[3] Bear yourself.
[4] Cutlass.
[5] Event.
[6] Invaluable.

Usum. And making thee and me, Techelles, kings,
 That even to death will follow Tamburlaine.
Tam. Nobly resolved, sweet friends and followers!   60
 These lords, perhaps, do scorn our estimates,
 And think we prattle with distempered spirits;
 But, since they measure our deserts so mean,
 That in conceit [1] bear empires on our spears,
 Affecting thoughts coequal with the clouds,
 They shall be kept our forcéd followers,
 Till with their eyes they view us emperors.
Zen. The gods, defenders of the innocent,
 Will never prosper your intended drifts,[2]
 That thus oppress poor friendless passengers.   70
 Therefore at least admit us liberty,
 Even as thou hop'st to be eternizéd [3]
 By living Asia's mighty emperor.
Agyd. I hope our lady's treasure and our own
 May serve for ransom to our liberties.
 Return our mules and empty camels back,
 That we may travel into Syria,
 Where her betrothéd lord, Alcidamus,
 Expects th' arrival of her highness' person.
Mag. And, wheresoever we repose ourselves,   80
 We will report but well of Tamburlaine.
Tam. Disdains Zenocrate to live with me?
 Or you, my lords, to be my followers?
 Think you I weigh this treasure more than you?
 Not all the gold in India's wealthy arms
 Shall buy the meanest soldier in my train.
 Zenocrate, lovelier than the love of Jove,
 Brighter than is the silver Rhodope,[4]
 Fairer than whitest snow on Scythian hills,
 Thy person is more worth to Tamburlaine   90

Than the possession of the Persian crown,
 Which gracious stars have promised at my birth.
 A hundreth Tartars shall attend on thee,
 Mounted on steeds swifter than Pegasus.
 Thy garments shall be made of Median silk,
 Enchased with precious jewels of mine own,
 More rich and valurous [5] than Zenocrate's.
 With milk-white harts upon an ivory sled
 Thou shalt be drawn amidst the frozen pools,
 And scale the icy mountains' lofty tops,   100
 Which with thy beauty will be soon resolved.
 My martial prizes with five hundred men,
 Won on the fifty-headed Volga's waves,
 Shall all we offer to Zenocrate—
 And then myself to fair Zenocrate.
Tech. What now!—In love?
Tam. Techelles, women must be flatteréd,
 But this is she with whom I am in love.

Enter a Soldier.

Sold. News! News!
Tam. How now, what's the matter?   110
Sold. A thousand Persian horsemen are at hand,
 Sent from the king to overcome us all.
Tam. How now, my lords of Egypt, and Zenocrate!
 Now must your jewels be restored again,
 And I that triumphed so be overcome?
 How say you, lordings? Is not this your hope?
Agyd. We hope yourself will willingly restore them.
Tam. Such hope, such fortune, have the thousand horse.
 Soft ye, my lords and sweet Zenocrate!
 You must be forcéd from me ere you go.   120
 A thousand horsemen? We five hundred foot?
 An odds too great for us to stand against!
 But are they rich? And is their armor good?

---

[1] Idea, fancy, imagination.   [3] Made immortal.
[2] Plans, schemes.
[4] Suggested by Dyce; original has *Rhodolfe*.

[5] Valuable.

Sold. Their pluméd helms are wrought
    with beaten gold,
  Their swords enameled, and about their
    necks
  Hangs massy chains of gold down to the
    waist,
  In every part exceeding brave [1] and rich.
Tam. Then shall we fight courageously
    with them,
  Or look [2] you I should play the orator?
Tech. No; cowards and faint-hearted run-
    aways   130
  Look for orations when the foe is near.
  Our swords shall play the orators for us.
Usum. Come! Let us meet them at the
    mountain foot,
  And with a sudden and an hot alarum
  Drive all their horses headlong down the
    hill.
Tech. Come, let us march!
Tam. Stay, Techelles! Ask a parley first.

The Soldiers enter.

  Open the mails,[3] yet guard the treasure
    sure;
  Lay out our golden wedges to the
    view
  That their reflections may amaze the
    Persians;   140
  And look we friendly on them when they
    come.
  But, if they offer word or violence,
  We'll fight five hundred men-at-arms to
    one
  Before we part with our possession.
  And gainst the general we will lift our
    swords,
  And either lanch [4] his greedy, thirsting
    throat,
  Or take him prisoner, and his chain shall
    serve
  For manacles till he be ransomed home.
Tech. I hear them come. Shall we en-
    counter them?
Tam. Keep all your standings and not stir
    a foot;   150
  Myself will bide the danger of the brunt.

Enter Theridamas with Others.

Ther. Where is this Scythian Tambur-
    laine?
Tam. Whom seek'st thou, Persian?—I am
    Tamburlaine.

Ther. Tamburlaine?—
  [*Aside.*] A Scythian shepherd so em-
    bellishéd
  With nature's pride and richest furni-
    ture!
  His looks do menace heaven and dare the
    gods;
  His fiery eyes are fixed upon the earth,
  As if he now devised some stratagem,
  Or meant to pierce Avernus' darksome
    vaults   160
  To pull the triple-headed dog from hell.
Tam. [*Aside.*] Noble and mild this Persian
    seems to be,
  If outward habit judge [5] the inward man.
Tech. [*Aside.*] His deep affections [6] make
    him passionate.
Tam. [*Aside.*] With what a majesty he
    rears his looks!—
  In thee, thou valiant man of Persia,
  I see the folly of thy emperor.
  Art thou but captain of a thousand horse,
  That, by characters graven in thy brows
  And by thy martial face and stout as-
    pect,   170
  Deserv'st to have the leading of an host?
  Forsake thy king, and do but join with
    me,
  And we will triumph over all the world.
  I hold the Fates bound fast in iron chains,
  And with my hand turn Fortune's
    wheel about;
  And sooner shall the sun fall from his
    sphere
  Than Tamburlaine be slain or overcome.
  Draw forth thy sword, thou mighty
    man-at-arms,
  Intending but to race [7] my charméd skin,
  And Jove himself will stretch his hand
    from heaven   180
  To ward the blow and shield me safe
    from harm.
  See how he rains down heaps of gold in
    showers,
  As if he meant to give my soldiers pay!
  And, as a sure and grounded argument
  That I shall be the monarch of the East,
  He sends this soldan's daughter, rich
    and brave,
  To be my queen and portly [8] emperess.
  If thou wilt stay with me, renowméd
    man,

---

[1] Fine. [2] Expect, wish. [3] Baggage. [4] Lance, cut.

[5] Indicate.   [7] Rase, scratch.
[6] Feelings.   [8] Stately.

And lead thy thousand horse with my
   conduct,
Besides thy share of this Egyptian
   prize,   190
Those thousand horse shall sweat with
   martial spoil
Of conquered kingdoms and of cities
   sacked.
Both we will walk upon the lofty clifts;[1]
And Christian merchants[2] that with
   Russian stems
Plow up huge furrows in the Caspian sea
Shall vail[3] to us as lords of all the lake.
Both we will reign as consuls of the earth,
And mighty kings shall be our senators.
Jove sometime maskéd in a shepherd's
   weed;
And by those steps that he hath scaled
   the heavens   200
May we become immortal like the gods!
Join with me now in this my mean
   estate
(I call it mean because, being yet ob-
   scure,
The nations far removed admire[4] me
   not),
And, when my name and honor shall be
   spread
As far as Boreas claps his brazen wings,
Or fair Boötes sends his cheerful light,
Then shalt thou be competitor[5] with
   me,
And sit with Tamburlaine in all his maj-
   esty.
THER. Not Hermes, prolocutor to the
   gods,   210
Could use persuasions more pathetical.[6]
TAM. Nor are Apollo's oracles more true
   Than thou shalt find my vaunts sub-
   stantial.
TECH. We are his friends, and, if the Per-
   sian king
Should offer present dukedoms to our
   state,
We think it loss to make exchange for
   that
We are assured of by our friend's suc-
   cess.
USUM. And kingdoms at the least we all
   expect,
Besides the honor in assured conquests,

Where kings shall crouch unto our con-
   quering swords,   220
And hosts of soldiers stand amazed at
   us,
When with their fearful tongues they
   shall confess
These are the men that all the world
   admires.
THER. What strong enchantments tice[7]
   my yielding soul!
Are these resolvéd noble Scythians?
But shall I prove a traitor to my king?
TAM. No, but the trusty friend of Tam-
   burlaine.
THER. Won with thy words, and con-
   quered with thy looks,
I yield myself, my men, and horse to
   thee,
To be partaker of thy good or ill   230
As long as life maintains Theridamas.
TAM. Theridamas, my friend, take here
   my hand,
Which is as much as if I swore by heaven
And called the gods to witness of my
   vow!
Thus shall my heart be still combined
   with thine
Until our bodies turn to elements,
And both our souls aspire[8] celestial
   thrones.
Techelles and Casane, welcome him!
TECH. Welcome, renowméd Persian, to us
   all!
USUM. Long may Theridamas remain
   with us!   240
TAM. These are my friends, in whom I
   more rejoice
Than doth the King of Persia in his
   crown,
And by the love of Pylades and Orestes,
Whose statues[9] we adore in Scythia,
Thyself and them shall never part from
   me
Before I crown you kings in Asia.
Make much of them, gentle Theridamas,
And they will never leave thee till the
   death.
THER. Nor thee nor them, thrice noble
   Tamburlaine,
Shall want my heart to be with glad-
   ness pierced   250
To do you honor and security.

---

[1] Cliffs.
[2] Merchantmen.
[3] Lower their topsails in salute.
[4] Wonder at.
[5] Partner.
[6] Moving.
[7] Entice.
[8] Aspire to.
[9] Probably *statues*

TAM. A thousand thanks, worthy Ther-
  idamas.—
And now, fair madam and my noble
  lords,
If you will willingly remain with me,
You shall have honors as your merits
  be;
Or else you shall be forced with slavery.
AGYD. We yield unto thee, happy Tambur-
  laine.
TAM. For you then, madam, I am out
  of doubt.
ZEN. I must be pleased perforce. Wretched
  Zenocrate!   *Exeunt.*

ACTUS II. SCENA i.

[*Cosroe's camp.*]

*Cosroe, Menaphon, Ortygius, Ceneus, with
              other Soldiers.*

COS. Thus far are we towards Theridamas
And valiant Tamburlaine, the man of
  fame,
The man that in the forehead of his
  fortune
Bears figures of renown and miracle.
But tell me, that hast seen him, Mena-
  phon,
What stature wields [1] he, and what
  personage?
MENA. Of stature tall, and straightly fash-
  ionéd,
Like his desire, lift [2] upwards and di-
  vine;
So large of limbs, his joints so strongly
  knit,
Such breadth of shoulders as might
  mainly bear   10
Old Atlas' burthen. Twixt his manly
  pitch,[3]
A pearl [4] more worth than all the world
  is placed,
Wherein by curious sovereignty of art
Are fixed his piercing instruments of
  sight,
Whose fiery circles bear encompasséd
A heaven of heavenly bodies in their
  spheres,
That guides his steps and actions to
  the throne,

Where honor sits invested royally.
Pale of complexion, wrought in him with
  passion,
Thirsting with sovereignty, with love of
  arms,   20
His lofty brows, in folds, do figure [5]
  death
And, in their smoothness, amity and
  life.
About them hangs a knot of amber hair,
Wrappéd in curls, as fierce Achilles' was,
On which the breath of heaven delights
  to play,
Making it dance with wanton majesty.
His arms and fingers, long and sinewy,[6]
Betokening valor and excess of strength—
In every part proportioned like the
  man—
Should make the world subdued to Tam-
  burlaine.   30
COS. Well hast thou portrayed in thy
  terms of life
The face and personage of a wondrous
  man.
Nature doth strive with fortune and
  his stars
To make him famous in accomplished
  worth;
And well his merits show him to be
  made
His fortune's master and the king of
  men,
That could persuade at such a sudden
  pinch,
With reasons of his valor and his life.
A thousand sworn and overmatching
  foes.
Then, when our powers in points of
  swords are joined   40
And closed in compass of the killing
  bullet,
Though strait the passage and the port [7]
  be made
That leads to palace of my brother's life,
Proud is his fortune if we pierce it not.
And, when the princely Persian diadem
Shall overweigh his weary, witless head,
And fall like mellowed fruit with shakes
  of death,
In fair Persia, noble Tamburlaine
Shall be my regent and remain as king.

[1] Possesses.   [2] Lifted.
[3] Height (falconry); here, shoulders.
[4] *I.e.*, the head.
[5] Foreshadow.
[6] Suggested by Dyce; original has *snowy.*
[7] Portal, gate.

ORTY. In happy hour we have set the crown 50
Upon your kingly head, that seeks our honor
In joining with the man ordained by heaven
To further every action to the best.
CEN. He that with shepherds and a little spoil
Durst, in disdain of wrong and tyranny,
Defend his freedom gainst a monarchy,
What will he do supported by a king,
Leading a troop of gentlemen and lords,
And stuffed with treasure for his highest thoughts!
Cos. And such shall wait on worthy Tamburlaine. 60
Our army will be forty thousand strong,
When Tamburlaine and brave Theridamas
Have met us by the river Araris,
And all conjoined to meet the witless king
That now is marching near to Parthia.
And with unwilling soldiers faintly armed,
To seek revenge on me and Tamburlaine—
To whom, sweet Menaphon, direct me straight.
MEN. I will, my lord. *Exeunt.*

ACTUS II. SCENA ii.

[*Mycetes' camp in the Caucasus.*]

Mycetes, Meander, with other Lords and Soldiers.

MYC. Come, my Meander, let us to this gear.[1]
I tell you true, my heart is swoln with wrath
On this same thievish villain, Tamburlaine,
And of [2] that false Cosroe, my traitorous brother.
Would it not grieve a king to be so abused
And have a thousand horsemen ta'en away,

And, which is worst, to have his diadem
Sought for by such scald [3] knaves as love him not?
I think it would. Well then, by heavens I swear,
Aurora shall not peep out of her doors, 10
But I will have Cosroe by the head,
And kill proud Tamburlaine with point of sword.
Tell you the rest, Meander; I have said.
MEAN. Then having passed Armenian deserts now,
And pitched [4] our tents under the Georgian hills,
Whose tops are covered with Tartarian thieves,
That lie in ambush, waiting for a prey,
What should we do but bid them battle straight,
And rid the world of those detested troops,
Lest, if we let them linger here awhile, 20
They gather strength by power of fresh supplies?
This country swarms with vile, outrageous men
That live by rapine and by lawless spoil,
Fit soldiers for the wicked Tamburlaine;
And he that could with gifts and promises
Inveigle him that led a thousand horse,
And make him false [5] his faith unto his king,
Will quickly win such as are like himself.
Therefore cheer up your minds; prepare to fight.
He that can take or slaughter Tamburlaine 30
Shall rule the province of Albania.
Who brings that traitor's head, Theridamas',
Shall have a government in Media,
Beside the spoil of him and all his train.
But, if Cosroe—as our spials [6] say,
And as we know—remains with Tamburlaine,
His highness' pleasure is that he should live,
And be reclaimed with princely lenity.

---

[1] Business.　　　　　　　　　　[2] On.

[3] Scabby, base.　　　　　　　[5] Betray.
[4] Original has *pitch*.　　　[6] Spies.

[Enter a Spy.]

A SPY. An hundred horsemen of my company,
　　Scouting abroad upon these champion [1]
　　　plains,   40
　　Have viewed the army of the Scythians,
　　Which make reports it far exceeds the
　　　king's.
MEAN. Suppose they be in number infinite,
　　Yet, being void of martial discipline,
　　All running headlong after greedy spoils,
　　And more regarding gain than victory,
　　Like to the cruel brothers of the earth,
　　Sprung of the teeth of dragons venomous,
　　Their careless swords shall lanch their
　　　fellows' throats,
　　And make us triumph in their overthrow.   50
MYC. Was there such brethren, sweet
　　　Meander, say,
　　That sprung of teeth of dragons venomous?
MEAN. So poets say, my lord.
MYC. And 'tis a pretty toy to be a poet.
　　Well, well, Meander, thou art deeply
　　　read,
　　And, having thee, I have a jewel sure.
　　Go on, my lord, and give your charge,
　　　I say;
　　Thy wit will make us conquerors today.
MEAN. Then, noble soldiers, to entrap
　　　these thieves,
　　That live confounded in disordered
　　　troops,   60
　　If wealth or riches may prevail with
　　　them,
　　We have our camels laden all with gold,
　　Which you that be but common soldiers
　　Shall fling in every corner of the field;
　　And, while the baseborn Tartars take
　　　it up,
　　You, fighting more for honor than for
　　　gold,
　　Shall massacre those greedy-minded
　　　slaves,
　　And, when their scattered army is subdued,
　　And you march on their slaughtered
　　　carcasses,
　　Share equally the gold that bought their
　　　lives,   70

[1] Champaign, level.

And live like gentlemen in Persia.
　　Strike up the drum and march courageously!
　　Fortune herself doth sit upon our crests.
MYC. He tells you true, my masters; so
　　he does.
　　Drums, why sound ye not, when Me-
　　　and[er] speaks?   *Exeunt.*

ACTUS II. SCENA iii.

[Tamburlaine's camp.]

*Cosroe, Tamburlaine, Theridamas, Techelles,
　　Usumcasane, Ortygius, with Others.*

COS. Now, worthy Tamburlaine, have I
　　reposed
　　In thy approvéd fortunes all my hope.
　　What think'st thou, man, shall come of
　　　our attempts?
　　For, even as from assuréd oracle,
　　I take thy doom [2] for satisfaction.
TAM. And so mistake you not a whit, my
　　lord;
　　For fates and oracles [of] heaven have
　　　sworn
　　To royalize the deeds of Tamburlaine,
　　And make them blessed that share in
　　　his attempts.
　　And doubt you not but, if you favor
　　　me,   10
　　And let my fortunes and my valor sway
　　To some direction in your martial deeds,
　　The world will strive with hosts of men-
　　　at-arms,
　　To swarm unto the ensign I support.
　　The host of Xerxes, which by fame is
　　　said
　　To drink the mighty Parthian Araris,
　　Was but a handful to that we will have.
　　Our quivering lances, shaking in the
　　　air,
　　And bullets, like Jove's dreadful thunderbolts,
　　Enrolled in flames and fiery smoldering
　　　mists,   20
　　Shall threat the gods more than Cyclopian wars;
　　And, with our sun-bright armor as we
　　　march,
　　We'll chase the stars from heaven and
　　　dim their eyes
　　That stand and muse at our admiréd
　　　arms.

[2] Opinion.

THER. You see, my lord, what working
  words he hath;
But, when you see his actions stop his
  speech,
Your speech will stay [1] or so extol his
  worth
As I shall be commended and excused
For turning my poor charge to his di-
  rection.
And these his two renowmèd friends,
  my lord,   30
Would make one thrust and strive to be
  retained
In such a great degree of amity.
TECH. With duty and with amity we
  yield
Our utmost service to the fair Cosroe.
Cos. Which I esteem as portion of my
  crown.
  Usumcasane and Techelles both,
When she [2] that rules in Rhamnis'
  golden gates,
And makes a passage for all prosperous
  arms,
Shall make me solely Emperor of Asia,
Then shall your meeds and valors be
  advanced   40
To rooms of honor and nobility.
TAM. Then haste, Cosroe, to be king
  alone,
That I with these, my friends, and all
  my men
May triumph in our long-expected
  fate.
The king, your brother, is now hard
  at hand;
Meet with the fool, and rid your royal
  shoulders
Of such a burthen as outweighs the
  sands
And all the craggy rocks of Caspia.

[*Enter a Messenger.*]

MESS. My lord, we have discovered the
  enemy
Ready to charge you with a mighty
  army.   50
Cos. Come, Tamburlaine! Now whet thy
  wingèd sword,
And lift thy lofty arm into the clouds

That it may reach the King of Persia's
  crown,
And set it safe on my victorious head.
TAM. See where it is, the keenest cuttle-
  ax [3]
That e'er made passage thorough Per-
  sian arms.
These are the wings shall make it fly
  as swift
As doth the lightning or the breath of
  heaven,
And kill as sure as it swiftly flies.   59
Cos. Thy words assure me of kind success.
Go, valiant soldier, go before and charge
The fainting army of that foolish king.
TAM. Usumcasane and Techelles, come!
We are enough to scare the enemy,
And more than needs to make an em-
  peror.   [*Exeunt.*]

[ACTUS II. SCENA iv.

Part of the battlefield.]

*To the battle, and Mycetes comes out alone
  with his crown in his hand, offering
                                      to hide it.*

MYC. Accursed be he that first invented
  war.
They knew not, ah, they knew not,
  simple men,
How those [4] were hit by pelting cannon
  shot
Stand staggering like a quivering aspen
  leaf
Fearing the force of Boreas' boist'rous
  blasts.
In what a lamentable case were I
If nature had not given me wisdom's
  lore!
For kings are clouts [5] that every man
  shoots at,
Our crown the pin [6] that thousands seek
  to cleave.
Therefore in policy I think it good   10
To hide it close—a goodly stratagem,
And far from any man that is a fool.
So shall I not be known; or, if I be,
They cannot take away my crown from
  me.
Here will I hide it in this simple hole.

---

[1] *I.e.*, you will be speechless.
[2] "Nemesis, who had a temple at Rhamnus"
(Bullen).

[3] Curtle-ax, cutlass.
[4] Those who.
[5] Center of an archer's target.
[6] Peg fastening the clout.

Enter Tamburlaine.

TAM. What, fearful coward, straggling
    from the camp
  When kings themselves are present in
    the field?
MYC. Thou liest!
TAM.   Base villain, dar'st thou
    give the lie?
MYC. Away; I am the king! Go; touch me
    not!
  Thou break'st the law of arms, unless
    thou kneel   20
  And cry me, "Mercy, noble king!"
TAM. Are you the witty King of Persia?
  MYC. Ay, marry am I. Have you any
suit to me?
  TAM. I would entreat you to speak but
three wise words.
  MYC. So I can when I see my time.
  TAM. Is this your crown?
  MYC. Ay, didst thou ever see a fairer?
  TAM. You will not sell it, will ye?   30
  MYC. Such another word and I will
have thee executed. Come, give it me!
  TAM. No; I took it prisoner.
  MYC. You lie; I gave it you.
  TAM. Then 'tis mine.
  MYC. No; I mean I let you keep it.
  TAM. Well, I mean you shall have it again.
  Here, take it for awhile. I lend it thee
  Till I may see thee hemmed with arméd
    men.
  Then shalt thou see me pull it from thy
    head.   40
  Thou art no match for mighty Tambur-
    laine.   [*Exit.*]
MYC. O gods! Is this Tamburlaine the
    thief?
  I marvel much he stole it not away.
Sound trumpets to the battle, and he runs in.

[ACTUS II. SCENA V.

Tamburlaine's camp.]

Cosroe, Tamburlaine, Theridamas, Mena-
    phon, Meander, Ortygius, Techelles,
        Usumcasane, with Others.

TAM. Hold thee, Cosroe! Wear two im-
    perial crowns!
  Think thee invested now as royally,
  Even by the mighty hand of Tambur-
    laine,

As if as many kings as could encompass
    thee
  With greatest pomp had crowned thee
    emperor.
COS. So do I, thrice renowméd man-at-
    arms,
  And none shall keep the crown but Tam-
    burlaine.
  Thee do I make my regent of Persia,
  And general lieftenant [1] of my armies.
  Meander, you that were our brother's
    guide   10
  And chiefest counselor in all his acts,
  Since he is yielded to the stroke of war,
  On your submission we with thanks
    excuse,
  And give you equal place in our affairs.
MEAN. Most happy emperor, in humblest
    terms
  I vow my service to your majesty,
  With utmost virtue of my faith and duty.
COS. Thanks, good Meander. Then, Cos-
    roe, reign
  And govern Persia in her former pomp!
  Now send ambassage to thy neighbor
    kings,   20
  And let them know the Persian king is
    changed
  From one that knew not what a king
    should do,
  To one that can command what longs [2]
    thereto.
  And now we will to fair Persepolis,
  With twenty thousand expert soldiers.
  The lords and captains of my brother's
    camp
  With little slaughter take Meander's
    course,
  And gladly yield them to my gracious
    rule.
  Ortygius and Menaphon, my trusty
    friends,
  Now will I gratify your former good,   30
  And grace your calling with a greater
    sway.
ORTY. And, as we ever aimed [3] at your
    behoof,[4]
  And sought your state all honor it de-
    served,
  So will we with our powers and our lives
  Endeavor to preserve and prosper it.

[1] Lieutenant.   [2] Belongs.
[3] From 1605 edn. Original reads *and*.
[4] Advantage.

Cos. I will not thank thee, sweet Ortygius;
   Better replies shall prove my purposes.
   And now, Lord Tamburlaine, my broth-
      er's camp
   I leave to thee and to Theridamas,
   To follow me to fair Persepolis.   40
   Then will we march to all those Indian
      mines
   My witless brother to the Christians lost,
   And ransom [1] them with fame and
      usury.[2]
   And, till thou overtake me, Tamburlaine,
   Staying to order all the scattered troops,
   Farewell, lord regent and his happy
      friends!
   I long to sit upon my brother's throne.
Mena. Your majesty shall shortly have
      your wish,
   And ride in triumph through Persepolis.
Exeunt. Manent Tamb[urlaine], Tech[elles],
         Ther[idamas], Usum[casane].
Tam. "And ride in triumph through Per-
      sepolis"!   50
   Is it not brave to be a king, Techelles?
   Usumcasane and Theridamas,
   Is it not passing brave to be a king,
   "And ride in triumph through Persep-
      olis"?
Tech. O, my lord, 'tis sweet and full of
      pomp.
Usum. To be a king is half to be a god.
Ther. A god is not so glorious as a king.
   I think the pleasure they enjoy in heaven
   Cannot compare with kingly joys in
      earth.
   To wear a crown enchased with pearl and
      gold,   60
   Whose virtues carry with it life and
      death;
   To ask and have, command and be
      obeyed;
   When looks breed love, with looks to gain
      the prize—
   Such power attractive shines in princes'
      eyes!
Tam. Why, say, Theridamas, wilt thou be
      a king?
Ther. Nay, though I praise it, I can live
      without it.
Tam. What says my other friends? Will
      you be kings?
Tech. Ay, if I could, with all my heart,
      my lord.

Tam. Why, that's well said, Techelles.
      So would I,
   And so would you, my masters, would
      you not?   70
Usum. What then, my lord?
Tam. Why then, Casane, shall we wish for
      aught
   The world affords in greatest novelty,
   And rest attemptless, faint, and desti-
      tute?
   Methinks we should not. I am strongly
      moved
   That, if I should desire the Persian
      crown,
   I could attain it with a wondrous ease.
   And would not all our soldiers soon con-
      sent,
   If we should aim at such a dignity?
Ther. I know they would with our per-
      suasions.   80
Tam. Why then, Theridamas, I'll first
      assay
   To get the Persian kingdom to myself;
   Then thou for Parthia; they for Scythia
      and Media;
   And, if I prosper, all shall be as sure
   As if the Turk, the pope, Afric, and
      Greece,
   Came creeping to us with their crowns
      apace.
Tech. Then shall we send to this triumph-
      ing king,
   And bid him battle for his novel crown?
Usum. Nay, quickly then, before his room
      be hot.
Tam. 'Twill prove a pretty jest, in faith,
      my friends.   90
Ther. A jest to charge on twenty thou-
      sand men?
   I judge the purchase [3] more important
      far.
Tam. Judge by thyself, Theridamas, not
      me,
   For presently Techelles here shall haste
   To bid him battle ere he pass too far,
   And lose more labor than the gain will
      quite.[4]
   Then shalt thou see the Scythian Tam-
      burlaine
   Make but a jest to win the Persian
      crown.
   Techelles, take a thousand horse with
      thee,

---

[1] Deliver.   [2] Profit.   [3] Undertaking.   [4] Requite.

And bid him turn his back [1] to war with
  us,   100
That only made him king to make us
  sport.
We will not steal upon him cowardly,
But give him warning and more warriors.
Haste thee, Techelles; we will follow
  thee.—
What saith Theridamas?
THER.   Go on for me.   *Exeunt.*

ACTUS II. SCENA vi.

[Cosroe's camp.]

Cosroe, Meander, Ortygius, Menaphon, with
other Soldiers.

COS. What means this devilish shepherd to
  aspire
With such a giantly presumption
To cast up hills against the face of
  heaven,
And dare the force of angry Jupiter?
But, as he thrust them underneath the
  hills,
And pressed out fire from their burning
  jaws,
So will I send this monstrous slave to hell,
Where flames shall ever feed upon his
  soul.
MEAN. Some powers divine, or else in-
  fernal, mixed
Their angry seeds at his conception,   10
For he was never sprung of human race,
Since with the spirit of his fearful pride
He dare so doubtlessly [2] resolve of [3] rule,
And by profession [4] be ambitious.
ORTY. What god, or fiend, or spirit of the
  earth,
Or monster turnéd to a manly shape,
Or of what mold or mettle he be made,
What star or state soever govern him,
Let us put on our meet, encount'ring [5]
  minds
And, in detesting such a devilish thief,   20
In love of honor and defense of right,
Be armed against the hate of such a foe,
Whether from earth, or hell, or heaven he
  grow.
COS. Nobly resolved, my good Ortygius!
And, since we all have sucked one whole-
  some air,

And with the same proportion of ele-
  ments
Resolve, I hope we are resembled,[6]
Vowing our loves to equal death and life.
Let's cheer our soldiers to encounter him,
That grievous image of ingratitude,   30
That fiery thirster after sovereignty,
And burn him in the fury of that flame
That none can quench [7] but blood and
  empery.
Resolve, my lords and loving soldiers,
  now
To save your king and country from
  decay.
Then strike up, drum; and all the stars
  that make
The loathsome circle of my dated life,
Direct my weapon to his barbarous heart,
That thus opposeth him against the gods,
And scorns the powers that govern
  Persia!   *[Exeunt.]*   40

[ACTUS II. SCENA vii.

A plain.]

Enter to the battle, and after the battle enter
Cosroe, wounded, Theridamas, Tam-
burlaine, Techelles, Usumcasane, with
Others.

COS. Barbarous and bloody Tamburlaine,
Thus to deprive me of my crown and life!
Treacherous and false Theridamas,
Even at the morning of my happy state,
Scarce being seated in my royal throne,
To work my downfall and untimely end!
An uncouth [8] pain torments my grievéd
  soul,
And death arrests the organ of my voice,
Who, ent'ring at the breach thy sword
  hath made,
Sacks every vein and artier [9] of my
  heart.   10
Bloody and insatiate Tamburlaine!
TAM. The thirst of reign and sweetness of a
  crown
That caused the eldest son of heavenly
  Ops
To thrust his doting father from his
  chair,
And place himself in the emperial [10]
  heaven,

---

[1] *I.e.*, turn himself, return.   [4] Open avowal.
[2] Fearlessly.   [5] Warlike.
[3] Upon.

[6] Alike.   [8] Strange.
[7] Quench.   [9] Artery.
[10] Imperial or empyreal?

Moved me to manage arms against thy
  state.
What better president [1] than mighty
  Jove?
Nature, that framed us of four elements,
Warring within our breasts for regiment,
Doth teach us all to have aspiring
  minds.   20
Our souls, whose faculties can compre-
  hend
The wondrous architecture of the world,
And measure every wand'ring planet's
  course,
Still climbing after knowledge infinite,
And always moving as the restless
  spheres,
Wills us to wear ourselves and never rest
Until we reach the ripest fruit of all,
That perfect bliss and sole felicity,
The sweet fruition of an earthly crown.
THER. And that made me to join with
  Tamburlaine,   30
For he is gross and like the massy earth,
That moves not upwards, nor by princely
  deeds
Doth mean to soar above the highest sort.
TECH. And that made us the friends of
  Tamburlaine,
To lift our swords against the Persian
  king.
USUM. For, as when Jove did thrust old
  Saturn down,
Neptune and Dis gained each of them a
  crown,
So do we hope to reign in Asia,
If Tamburlaine be placed in Persia.
COS. The strangest men that ever nature
  made!   40
I know not how to take their tyrannies.
My bloodless body waxeth chill and cold,
And with my blood my life slides through
  my wound.
My soul begins to take her flight to hell,
And summons all my senses to depart.
The heat and moisture, which did feed
  each other,
For want of nourishment to feed them
  both,
Is dry and cold; and now doth ghastly
  Death,
With greedy talents [2] gripe my bleeding
  heart,
And like a harpy tires [3] on my life. 50

Theridamas and Tamburlaine, I die!
And fearful vengeance light upon you
  both!
[Dies.] He [4] takes the crown and puts it on.
TAM. Not all the curses which the Furies
  breathe
Shall make me leave so rich a prize as
  this.
Theridamas, Techelles, and the rest,
Who think you now is King of Persia?
ALL. Tamburlaine! Tamburlaine
TAM. Though Mars himself, the angry god
  of arms,
And all the earthly potentates conspire
To dispossess me of this diadem,   60
Yet will I wear it in despite of them,
As great commander of this eastern
  world,
If you but say that Tamburlaine shall
  reign.
ALL. Long live Tamburlaine and reign in
  Asia!
TAM. So now it is more surer on my head
Than if the gods had held a parliament,
And all pronounced me King of Persia.
                  [Exeunt.]

FINIS ACTUS SECUNDI.

ACTUS III. SCENA i.

[Before Constantinople.]

Bajazeth, the Kings of Fez, Morocco, and
  Argier, with Others, in great pomp.

BAJ. Great kings of Barbary and my
  portly bassoes,
We hear the Tartars and the eastern
  thieves,
Under the conduct of one Tamburlaine,
Presume a bickering [5] with your emperor,
And thinks to rouse us from our dreadful
  siege
Of the famous Grecian Constantinople.
You know our army is invincible;
As many circumciséd Turks we have,
And warlike bands of Christians renied,[6]
As hath the ocean or the Terrene sea [7] [10
Small drops of water when the moon be-
  gins
To join in one her semicircled horns.
Yet would we not be braved with foreign
  power,

[1] Precedent.   [2] Talons.   [3] Preys.

[4] I.e., Tamburlaine.   [6] Apostates.
[5] Battle.   [7] The Mediterranean.

Nor raise our siege before the Grecians
   yield,
Or breathless lie before the city walls.
Fez. Renowmèd emperor and mighty
   general,
What if you sent the bassoes of your
   guard
To charge him to remain in Asia,
Or else to threaten death and deadly arms
As from the mouth of mighty Baja-
   zeth?   20
Baj. Hie thee, my basso, fast to Persia.
Tell him thy lord, the Turkish emperor,
Dread lord of Afric, Europe, and Asia,
Great king and conqueror of Grecia,
The ocean, Terrene, and the coal-black
   sea,[1]
The high and highest monarch of the
   world,
Wills and commands—for say not I
   entreat—
Not once to set his foot in Africa,
Or spread his colors in Grecia,
Lest he incur the fury of my wrath.   30
Tell him I am content to take a truce,
Because I hear he bears a valiant mind.
But if, presuming on his silly power,
He be so mad to manage arms with me,
Then stay thou with him. Say I bid thee
   so.
And if, before the sun have measured
   heaven
With triple circuit, thou regreet us not,
We mean to take his morning's next arise
For messenger he will not be reclaimed,
And mean to fetch thee in despite of
   him.   40
Basso. Most great and puissant monarch
   of the earth,
Your basso will accomplish your behest,
And show your pleasure to the Persian,
As fits the legate of the stately Turk.
                  Exit Bass[o].
Arg. They say he is the King of Persia;
But, if he dare attempt to stir your siege,
'Twere requisite he should be ten times
   more,
For all flesh quakes at your magnificence.
Baj. True, Argier, and tremble at my
   looks.
Mor. The spring is hindered by your
   smothering host,   50
For neither rain can fall upon the earth,

Nor sun reflex[2] his virtuous beams
   thereon,
The ground is mantled with such multi-
   tudes.
Baj. All this is true as holy Mahomet;
And all the trees are blasted with our
   breaths.
Fez. What thinks your greatness best to
   be achieved
In pursuit of the city's overthrow?
Baj. I will the captive pioners[3] of Argier
Cut off the water that by leaden pipes
Runs to the city from the mountain
   Carnon.   60
Two thousand horse shall forage up and
   down,
That no relief or succor come by land;
And all the sea my galleys countermand.[4]
Then shall our footmen lie within the
   trench,
And with their cannons, mouthed like
   Orcus' gulf,
Batter the walls, and we will enter in.
And thus the Grecians shall be con-
   querèd.   *Exeunt.*

Actus III. Scena ii.

[*Tamburlaine's camp.*]

Agydas, Zenocrate, Anippe, with Others.

[Agyd.] Madam Zenocrate, may I presume
To know the cause of these unquiet fits,
That work such trouble to your wonted
   rest?
'Tis more than pity such a heavenly face
Should by heart's sorrow wax so wan and
   pale,
When your offensive rape[5] by Tambur-
   laine—
Which of your whole displeasures should
   be most—
Hath seemed to be digested long ago.
Zen. Although it be digested long ago,
As his exceeding favors have deserved, 10
And might content the Queen of Heaven,
   as well
As it hath changed my first conceived
   disdain,
Yet, since, a farther passion feeds my
   thoughts
With ceaseless and disconsolate conceits,

[1] The Black Sea.
[2] Throw.
[3] Miners.
[4] Control.
[5] Capture.

Which dyes my looks so lifeless as they
  are,
And might, if my extremes had full
  events,[1]
Make me the ghastly counterfeit of
  death.
AGYD. Eternal heaven sooner be dissolved,
And all that pierceth Phœbe's silver eye,
Before such hap fall to Zenocrate!   20
ZEN. Ah, life and soul, still hover in his
  breast
And leave my body senseless as the earth,
Or else unite you to his life and soul,
That I may live and die with Tambur-
  laine!

Enter [, unseen,] Tamburlaine with Techelles
and Others.

AGYD. With Tamburlaine? Ah, fair Zeno-
  crate,
Let not a man so vile and barbarous,
That holds you from your father in
  despite,
And keeps you from the honors of a
  queen,
Being supposed his worthless concubine,
Be honored with your love but for neces-
  sity.   30
So, now [2] the mighty soldan hears of you,
Your highness needs not doubt but in
  short time
He will with Tamburlaine's destruction
Redeem you from this deadly servitude.
ZEN. Leave to wound me with these words,
And speak of Tamburlaine as he deserves.
The entertainment we have had of him
Is far from villainy [3] or servitude,
And might in noble minds be counted
  princely.
AGYD. How can you fancy one that looks
  so fierce,   40
Only disposed to martial stratagems,
Who, when he shall embrace you in his
  arms,
Will tell how many thousand men he
  slew,
And, when you look for amorous dis-
  course,
Will rattle forth his facts [4] of war and
  blood,
Too harsh a subject for your dainty
  ears?

ZEN. As looks the Sun through Nilus' flow-
  ing stream,
Or when the Morning holds him in her
  arms,
So looks my lordly love, fair Tambur-
  laine;
His talk much sweeter than the Muses'
  song   50
They sung for honor gainst Pierides,
Or when Minerva did with Neptune
  strive.
And higher would I rear my estimate
Than Juno, sister to the highest god,
If I were matched with mighty Tambur-
  laine.
AGYD. Yet be not so inconstant in your
  love,
But let the young Arabian live in hope
After your rescue to enjoy his choice.
You see, though first the King of Persia,
Being a shepherd, seemed to love you
  much,   60
Now in his majesty he leaves those
  looks,
Those words of favor, and those com-
  fortings,
And gives no more than common cour-
  tesies.
ZEN. Thence rise the tears that so distain [5]
  my cheeks,
Fearing his love through my unworthi-
  ness.—

Tamburlaine goes to her and takes her away
lovingly by the hand, looking wrathfully
on Agydas, and says nothing. [Exeunt
all but Agydas.]

AGYD. Betrayed by fortune and suspicious
  love,
Threatened with frowning wrath and
  jealousy,
Surprised with fear of hideous revenge,
I stand aghast; but most astoniéd [6]   69
To see his choler shut in secret thoughts,
And wrapped in silence of his angry soul.
Upon his brows was portrayed ugly
  death,
And in his eyes the fury of his heart,
That shine as comets, menacing revenge,
And casts a pale complexion on his
  cheeks.
As, when the seaman sees the Hyades
Gather an army of Cimmerian clouds
(Auster and Aquilon with wingéd steeds,

---

[1] If my extremities were carried to their outcome.   [2] Now that.   [3] Serfdom.   [4] Deeds.
[5] Stain.   [6] Astonished.

All sweating, tilt about the watery heav-
ens,
With shivering spears enforcing thunder-
claps,   80
And from their shields strike flames of
lightening),
All fearful folds his sails and sounds the
main,
Lifting his prayers to the heavens for aid
Against the terror of the winds and
waves,
So fares Agydas for the late-felt frowns
That sent a tempest to my daunted
thoughts,
And makes my soul divine her over-
throw.

*Enter [Usumcasane and] Techelles with a
naked dagger.*

TECH. See you, Agydas, how the king
salutes you.
He bids you prophesy what it imports.
Exit.[1]
AGYD. I prophesied before, and now I
prove   90
The killing frowns of jealousy and love.
He needed not with words confirm my
fear,
For words are vain where working tools
present
The naked action of my threatened end.
It says, Agydas, thou shalt surely die,
And of extremities elect the least;
More honor and less pain it may procure
To die by this resolvéd hand of thine
Than stay the torments he and heaven
have sworn.
Then haste, Agydas, and prevent the
plagues   100
Which thy prolongéd fates may draw
on thee.
Go, wander free from fear of tyrant's
rage,
Removéd from the torments and the
hell
Wherewith he may excruciate thy soul;
And let Agydas by Agydas die,
And with this stab slumber eternally.
[Stabs himself.][2]
TECH. Usumcasane, see how right the man
Hath hit the meaning of my lord the
king.

[1] He and Usumcasane stand aside.
[2] Supplied from 1605 edn.

USUM. Faith, and, Techelles, it was manly
done.
And, since he was so wise and honor-
able,   110
Let us afford him now the bearing
hence,
And crave his triple-worthy burial.
TECH. Agreed, Casane; we will honor him.
[Exeunt, bearing out the body.]

ACTUS III. SCENA iii.

[The same.]

*Tamburlaine, Techelles, Usumcasane, Theri-
damas, Basso, Zenocrate, [Anippe,] with
Others.*

TAM. Basso, by this thy lord and master
knows
I mean to meet him in Bithynia.
See how he comes! Tush, Turks are full
of brags,
And menace more than they can well
perform.
He meet me in the field, and fetch thee
hence?
Alas, poor Turk! His fortune is too weak
T' encounter with the strength of Tam-
burlaine.
View well my camp, and speak indiffer-
ently.[3]
Do not my captains and my soldiers
look
As if they meant to conquer Africa?   10
BASSO. Your men are valiant, but their
number few,
And cannot terrify his mighty host.
My lord, the great commander of the
world,
Besides fifteen contributory kings,
Hath now in arms ten thousand Janis-
saries,
Mounted on lusty Mauritanian steeds,
Brought to the war by men of Tripoli;
Two hundred thousand footmen that
have served
In two set battles fought in Grecia;
And for the expedition of this war,   20
If he think good, can from his garri-
sons
Withdraw as many more to follow him.
TECH. The more he brings, the greater is
the spoil,

[3] Impartially.

For, when they perish by our warlike
  hands,
We mean to seat our footmen on their
  steeds,
And rifle all those stately Janisars.
TAM. But will those kings accompany
  your lord?
BASSO. Such as his highness please; but
  some must stay
To rule the provinces he late subdued.
TAM. [*To his Captains.*] Then fight coura-
  geously; their crowns are yours!   30
This hand shall set them on your con-
  quering heads,
That made me Emperor of Asia.
USUM. Let him bring millions infinite
  of men,
Unpeopling Western Africa and Greece,
Yet we assure us of the victory.
THER. Even he that in a trice vanquished
  two kings
More mighty than the Turkish emperor,
Shall rouse him out of Europe and pur-
  sue
His scattered army till they yield or die.
TAM. Well said, Theridamas. Speak in
  that mood;   40
For *will* and *shall* best fitteth Tambur-
  laine,
Whose smiling stars gives him assuréd
  hope
Of martial triumph ere he meet his foes.
I that am termed the scourge and wrath
  of God,
The only fear and terror of the world,
Will first subdue the Turk, and then
  enlarge
Those Christian captives, which you
  keep as slaves,
Burdening their bodies with your heavy
  chains,
And feeding them with thin and slender
  fare,
That naked row about the Terrene sea, 50
And, when they chance to breathe and
  rest a space,
Are punished with bastones [1] so griev-
  ously
That they lie panting on the galley's
  side,
And strive for life at every stroke they
  give.
These are the cruel pirates of Argier,

[1] Cudgels.

That damnéd train, the scum of Africa,
Inhabited with straggling runagates,
That make quick havoc of the Christian
  blood.
But, as I live, that town shall curse the
  time
That Tamburlaine set foot in Africa.   60

*Enter Bajazeth with his Bassoes and con-
  tributory Kings [; Zabina and Ebea].*

BAJ. Bassoes and Janissaries of my guard,
Attend upon the person of your lord,
The greatest potentate of Africa.
TAM. Techelles and the rest, prepare your
  swords;
I mean t' encounter with that Bajazeth.
BAJ. Kings of Fez, Moroccus, and Argier,
He calls me Bajazeth, whom you call
  lord!
Note the presumption of this Scythian
  slave!
I tell thee, villain, those that lead my
  horse
Have to their names titles of dignity,   70
And dar'st thou bluntly call me Baja-
  zeth?
TAM. And know thou, Turk, that those
  which lead my horse
Shall lead thee captive thorough Africa.
And dar'st thou bluntly call me Tam-
  burlaine?
BAJ. By Mahomet my kinsman's sep-
  ulcher
And by the holy Alcoran,[2] I swear
He shall be made a chaste and lustless
  eunuch,
And in my sarell [3] tend my concubines;
And all his captains that thus stoutly
  stand
Shall draw the chariot of my emperess, 80
Whom I have brought to see their over-
  throw.
TAM. By this my sword that conquered
  Persia,
Thy fall shall make me famous through
  the world.
I will not tell thee how I'll handle thee,
But every common soldier of my camp
Shall smile to see thy miserable state.
FEZ. What means the mighty Turkish
  emperor,
To talk with one so base as Tambur-
  laine?

[2] The Koran.   [3] Seraglio.

Mor. Ye Moors and valiant men of Bar-
    bary,
How can ye suffer these indignities? 90
Arg. Leave words, and let them feel your
    lances' points
Which glided through the bowels of
    the Greeks.
Baj. Well said, my stout contributory
    kings!
Your threefold army and my hugy host
Shall swallow up these baseborn Persians.
Tech. Puissant, renowmed, and mighty
    Tamburlaine,
Why stay we thus prolonging all their
    lives?
Ther. I long to see those crowns won by
    our swords,
That we may reign as kings of Africa.
Usum. What coward would not fight for
    such a prize?   100
Tam. Fight all courageously, and be you
    kings;
I speak it, and my words are oracles.
Baj. Zabina, mother of three braver boys
Than Hercules, that in his infancy
Did pash [1] the jaws of serpents ven-
    omous;
Whose hands are made to gripe a war-
    like lance,
Their shoulders broad for complete
    armor fit,
Their limbs more large and of a bigger
    size
Than all the brats ysprung [2] from Ty-
    phon's loins;
Who, when they come unto their fa-
    ther's age,   110
Will batter turrets with their manly
    fists—
Sit here upon this royal chair of state,
And on thy head wear my imperial
    crown
Until I bring this sturdy Tamburlaine
And all his captains bound in captive
    chains.
Zab. Such good success happen to Ba-
    jazeth!
Tam. Zenocrate, the loveliest maid alive,
Fairer than rocks of pearl and precious
    stone,
The only paragon of Tamburlaine,
Whose eyes are brighter than the lamps
    of heaven   120

[1] Dash to pieces.   [2] Old past participle.

And speech more pleasant than sweet
    harmony;
That with thy looks canst clear the
    darkened sky,
And calm the rage of thund'ring Jupi-
    ter,
Sit down by her, adornéd with my
    crown,
As if thou wert the empress of the world.
Stir not, Zenocrate, until thou see
Me march victoriously with all my men,
Triumphing over him and these his
    kings,
Which I will bring as vassals to thy feet;
Till then take thou my crown, vaunt
    of my worth,   130
And manage words with her, as we will
    arms.
Zen. And may my love, the King of
    Persia,
Return with victory and free from
    wound!
Baj. Now shalt thou feel the force of
    Turkish arms,
Which lately made all Europe quake
    for fear.
I have of Turks, Arabians, Moors, and
    Jews
Enough to cover all Bithynia.
Let thousands die; their slaughtered
    carcasses
Shall serve for walls and bulwarks to
    the rest;
And, as the heads of Hydra, so my
    power,   140
Subdued, shall stand as mighty as be-
    fore.
If they should yield their necks unto
    the sword,
Thy soldiers' arms could not endure to
    strike
So many blows as I have heads for
    thee.
Thou knowest not, foolish-hardy Tam-
    burlaine,
What 'tis to meet me in the open field,
That leave no ground for thee to march
    upon.
Tam. Our conquering swords shall mar-
    shal us the way
We used to march upon the slaughtered
    foe,
Trampling their bowels with our horses'
    hoofs —   150

Brave horses bred on the white Tar-
  tarian hills.
My camp is like to Julius Cæsar's host,
That never fought but had the victory;
Nor in Pharsalia was there such hot
  war
As these my followers willingly would
  have.
Legions of spirits fleeting [1] in the air
Direct our bullets and our weapons'
  points,
And make our strokes to wound the
  senseless lure,[2]
And, when she sees our bloody colors
  spread,　　　　　　　　　　159
Then Victory begins to take her flight,
Resting herself upon my milk-white
  tent.—
But come, my lords, to weapons let us
  fall;
The field is ours, the Turk, his wife, and
  all.　　　　*Exit with his Followers.*
BAJ. Come, kings and bassoes, let us glut
  our swords,
That thirst to drink the feeble Persians'
  blood.　　　　*Exit with his Followers.*
ZAB. Base concubine, must thou be placed
  by me,
That am the empress of the mighty
  Turk?
ZEN. Disdainful Turkess and unreverend
  boss,[3]
Call'st thou me concubine, that am be-
  trothed
Unto the great and mighty Tambur-
  laine?　　　　　　　　　　170
ZAB. To Tamburlaine, the great Tarta-
  rian thief!
ZEN. Thou wilt repent these lavish words
  of thine,
When thy great basso-master and thy-
  self
Must plead for mercy at his kingly feet,
And sue to me to be your advocates.[4]
ZAB. And sue to thee? I tell thee, shame-
  less girl,
Thou shalt be laundress to my waiting
  maid!—
How lik'st thou her, Ebea? Will she
  serve?

EBEA. Madam, she thinks perhaps she
  is too fine,
But I shall turn her into other weeds, 180
And make her dainty fingers fall to work.
ZEN. Hear'st thou, Anippe, how thy
  drudge doth talk?
And how my slave, her mistress, men-
  aceth?
Both for their sauciness shall be em-
  ployed
To dress the common soldiers' meat
  and drink,
For we will scorn they should come
  near ourselves.
ANIP. Yet sometimes let your highness
  send for them
To do the work my chambermaid dis-
  dains.
  They sound the battle within and stay.[5]
ZEN. Ye gods and powers that govern
  Persia,
And made my lordly love her worthy
  king,　　　　　　　　　　190
Now strengthen him against the Turk-
  ish Bajazeth,
And let his foes, like flocks of fearful
  roes
Pursued by hunters, fly his angry looks,
That I may see him issue conqueror!
ZAB. Now, Mahomet, solicit God him-
  self,
And make him rain down murthering
  shot from heaven
To dash the Scythians' brains, and strike
  them dead,
That dare to manage arms with him
That offered jewels to thy sacred shrine,
When first he warred against the Chris-
  tians!　　　　　　　　　　200
  　　　　　To the battle again.
ZEN. By this the Turks lie welt'ring in
  their blood,
And Tamburlaine is Lord of Africa.
ZAB. Thou art deceived. I heard the trum-
  pets sound
As when my emperor overthrew the
  Greeks,
And led them captive into Africa.
Straight will I use thee as thy pride de-
  serves.
Prepare thyself to live and die my slave!
ZEN. If Mahomet should come from
  heaven and swear

---

[1] Floating.
[2] Dyce suggests: "And make *your* strokes to
wound the senseless *air.*"
[3] Fat woman.　　[4] Wagner suggests *advocatess.*
[5] Cease, pause.

My royal lord is slain or conqueréd,
Yet should he not persuade me otherwise   210
But that he lives and will be conqueror.
Bajazeth flies and he [1] *pursues him. The*
battle short, and they enter. Bajazeth is
overcome.
Tam. Now, king of bassoes, who is conqueror?
Baj. Thou, by the fortune of this damnéd
soil.
Tam. Where are your stout contributory
kings?

Enter Techelles, Theridamas, Usumcasane.

Tech. We have their crowns; their bodies
strow the field.
Tam. Each man a crown? Why, kingly
fought, i' faith!
Deliver them into my treasury.
Zen. Now let me offer to my gracious
lord
His royal crown again, so highly won.
Tam. Nay, take the Turkish crown from
her, Zenocrate,   220
And crown me Emperor of Africa.
Zab. No, Tamburlaine; though now thou
gat the best,
Thou shalt not yet be lord of Africa.
Ther. Give her the crown, Turkess; you
were best.
He takes it from her and gives it Zenocrate.
Zab. Injurious villains, thieves, runa-
gates,
How dare you thus abuse my majesty?
Ther. Here, madam, you are empress;
she is none.
Tam. Not now, Theridamas; her time is
past.
The pillars that have bolstered up those
terms
Are fallen in clusters at my conquering
feet.   230
Zab. Though he be prisoner, he may be
ransomed.
Tam. Not all the world shall ransom Ba-
jazeth.
Baj. Ah, fair Zabina, we have lost the
field!
And never had the Turkish emperor
So great a foil by any foreign foe.
Now will the Christian miscreants be glad,

Ringing with joy their superstitious
bells,
And making bonfires for my overthrow.
But, ere I die, those foul idolaters
Shall make me bonfires with their
filthy bones,   240
For, though the glory of this day be
lost,
Afric and Greece have garrisons enough
To make me sovereign of the earth
again.
Tam. Those walléd garrisons will I sub-
due,
And write myself great Lord of Africa.
So from the East unto the furthest
West
Shall Tamburlaine extend his puissant
arm.
The galleys and those pilling [2] brigan-
dines
That yearly sail to the Venetian gulf
And hover in the Straits for Christians'
wrack   250
Shall lie at anchor in the isle Asant,
Until the Persian fleet and men of war,
Sailing along the oriental sea,
Have fetched [3] about the Indian conti-
nent,
Even from Persepolis to Mexico,
And thence unto the straits of Jubal-
ter, [4]
Where they shall meet and join their
force in one,
Keeping in awe the Bay of Portingale, [5]
And all the ocean by the British shore;
And by this means I'll win the world
at last.   260
Baj. Yet set a ransom on me, Tambur-
laine.
Tam. What, think'st thou Tamburlaine
esteems thy gold?
I'll make the kings of India, ere I die,
Offer their mines to sue for peace to me,
And dig for treasure to appease my
wrath.
Come, bind them both, and one lead
in the Turk;
The Turkess let my love's maid lead
away.   *They bind them.*
Baj. Ah, villains, dare ye touch my sacred
arms?
O Mahomet!—O sleepy Mahomet!

[1] *I.e.,* Tamburlaine.

[2] Pillaging.   [3] Sailed.   [4] Gibraltar.
[5] Bay of Portugal, *i.e.,* Bay of Biscay.

ZAB. O cursèd Mahomet, that makest us
    thus 270
The slaves to Scythians rude and bar-
    barous!
TAM. Come, bring them in, and for this
    happy conquest
Triumph and solemnize a martial feast.
                         Exeunt.

FINIS ACTUS TERTII.

ACTUS IV. SCENA i.

[*The Egyptian court.*]

Soldan of Egypt, with three or four Lords,
    Capolin [,and a Messenger].

SOLD. Awake, ye men of Memphis! Hear
    the clang
Of Scythian trumpets! Hear the basi-
    lisks [1]
That, roaring, shake Damascus' turrets
    down!
The rogue of Volga holds Zenocrate,
The soldan's daughter, for his concubine,
And with a troop of thieves and vaga-
    bonds
Hath spread his colors to our high dis-
    grace,
While you, faint-hearted, base Egyp-
    tians,
Lie slumbering on the flowery banks of
    Nile,
As crocodiles that unaffrighted rest, 10
While thund'ring cannons rattle on their
    skins.
MESS. Nay, mighty soldan, did your great-
    ness see
The frowning looks of fiery Tamburlaine,
That with his terror and imperious eyes
Commands the hearts of his associates,
It might amaze your royal majesty.
SOLD. Villain, I tell thee, were that Tam-
    burlaine
As monstrous as Gorgon, prince of hell,
The soldan would not start a foot from
    him.
But speak, what power hath he?
MESS.   Mighty lord, 20
Three hundred thousand men in armor
    clad,
Upon their prancing steeds disdainfully
With wanton paces trampling on the
    ground;

Five hundred thousand footmen threat'-
    ning shot,
Shaking their swords, their spears, and
    iron bills,
Environing their standard round, that
    stood
As bristle-pointed as a thorny wood.
Their warlike engines and munition
Exceed the forces of their martial men.
SOLD. Nay, could their numbers counter-
    vail [2] the stars, 30
Or ever-drizzling drops of April showers,
Or withered leaves that autumn shaketh
    down,
Yet would the soldan by his conquering
    power
So scatter and consume them in his rage
That not a man should live to rue their
    fall.
CAP. So might your highness, had you
    time to sort [3]
Your fighting men, and raise your royal
    host;
But Tamburlaine, by expedition,
Advantage takes of your unreadiness.
SOLD. Let him take all th' advantages he
    can. 40
Were all the world conspired to fight for
    him,
Nay, were he devil, as he is no man,
Yet in revenge of fair Zenocrate,
Whom he detaineth in despite of us,
This arm should send him down to Ere-
    bus
To shroud his shame in darkness of the
    night.
MESS. Pleaseth your mightiness to under-
    stand,
His resolution far exceedeth all.
The first day when he pitcheth down his
    tents,
White is their hue, and on his silver
    crest 50
A snowy feather spangled white he
    bears,
To signify the mildness of his mind,
That, satiate with spoil, refuseth blood.
But, when Aurora mounts the second
    time,
As red as scarlet is his furniture.
Then must his kindled wrath be
    quenched with blood,
Not sparing any that can manage arms

---

[1] Cannon.   [2] Equal.   [3] Select.

But, if these threats move not submis-
    sion,
Black are his colors, black pavilion;
His spear, his shield, his horse, his
    armor, plumes,   60
And jetty feathers menace death and
    hell.
Without respect of sex, degree, or age,
He razeth all his foes with fire and sword.
COLD. Merciless villain, peasant, ignorant
    Of lawful arms or martial discipline!
Pillage and murder are his usual trades;
The slave usurps the glorious name of
    war.
See, Capolin, the fair Arabian king,
That hath been disappointed by this
    slave
Of my fair daughter and his princely
    love,   70
May have fresh warning to go war with
    us,
And be revenged for her disparagement.
                                      [Exeunt.]

ACTUS IV. SCENA ii.

[*Tamburlaine's camp outside Damascus.*]

Tamburlaine, Techelles, Theridamas, Usum-
    casane, Zenocrate, Anippe, two Moors
    drawing Bajazeth in his cage, and his
    Wife following him.

TAM. Bring out my footstool!
        They take him out of the cage.
BAJ. Ye holy priests of heavenly Ma-
    homet,
That, sacrificing, slice and cut your flesh,
Staining his altars with your purple
    blood,
Make heaven to frown and every fixéd
    star
To suck up poison from the moorish fens,
And pour it in this glorious [1] tyrant's
    throat!
TAM. The chiefest God, first mover of that
    sphere,
Enchased with thousands ever-shining
    lamps,
Will sooner burn the glorious frame of
    heaven   10
Than it should so conspire my over-
    throw.
But, villain, thou that wishest this to me,

[1] Vainglorious.

Fall prostrate on the low disdainful
    earth,
And be the footstool of great Tambur-
    laine,
That I may rise into my royal throne.
BAJ. First shalt thou rip my bowels with
    thy sword,
And sacrifice my heart to death and hell,
Before I yield to such a slavery.
TAM. Base villain, vassal, slave to Tam-
    burlaine,
Unworthy to embrace or touch the
    ground   20
That bears the honor of my royal
    weight,
Stoop, villain, stoop! Stoop! For so he
    bids
That may command thee piecemeal to be
    torn,
Or scattered like the lofty cedar trees
Struck with the voice of thund'ring
    Jupiter.
BAJ. Then, as I look down to the damnéd
    fiends,
Fiends, look on me! And thou, dread
    god of hell,
With ebon scepter strike this hateful
    earth,
And make it swallow both of us at once!
        He gets up upon him to his chair.
TAM. Now clear the triple region of the
    air,   30
And let the majesty of heaven behold
Their scourge and terror tread on em-
    perors.
Smile, stars, that reigned at my nativity,
And dim the brightness of their neighbor
    lamps!
Disdain to borrow light of Cynthia!
For I, the chiefest lamp of all the earth,
First rising in the east with mild aspect,
But fixéd now in the meridian line,
Will send up fire to your turning spheres,
And cause the sun to borrow light of
    you.   40
My sword stroke [2] fire from his coat of
    steel,
Even in Bithynia, when I took this Turk,
As when a fiery exhalation,
Wrapped in the bowels of a freezing
    cloud,
Fighting for passage, make[s] the welkin
    crack,

[2] Struck.

And casts a flash of lightning to the
earth.
But, ere I march to wealthy Persia,
Or leave Damascus and th' Egyptian
fields,
As was the fame of Clymene's brainsick
son,[1]
That almost brent [2] the axletree of
heaven,   50
So shall our swords, our lances, and our
shot
Fill all the air with fiery meteors.
Then, when the sky shall wax as red as
blood,
It shall be said I made it red myself,
To make me think of naught but blood
and war.
ZAB. Unworthy king, that by thy cruelty
Unlawfully usurpest the Persian seat,
Dar'st thou, that never saw an emperor
Before thou met my husband in the
field,
Being thy captive, thus abuse his
state,   60
Keeping his kingly body in a cage,
That roofs of gold and sun-bright palaces
Should have prepared to entertain his
grace,
And treading him beneath thy loathsome
feet,
Whose feet the kings of Africa have
kissed?
TECH. You must devise some torment
worse, my lord,
To make these captives rein their lavish
tongues.
TAM. Zenocrate, look better to your slave!
ZEN. She is my handmaid's slave, and she
shall look
That these abuses flow not from her
tongue.   70
Chide her, Anippe!
ANIP. Let these be warnings for you then,
my slave,
How you abuse the person of the king;
Or else I swear to have you whipped,
stark-naked.
BAJ. Great Tamburlaine, great in my over-
throw,
Ambitious pride shall make thee fall as
low
For treading on the back of Bajazeth,

[1] *I.e.*, Phaëton. Original reads *Clymeus*.
[2] Burnt.

That should be horséd on four mighty
kings.
TAM. Thy names and titles and thy digni-
ties
Are fled from Bajazeth and remain with
me,   80
That will maintain it against a world of
kings.
Put him in again!
          [*They put him back into the cage.*]
BAJ. Is this a place for mighty Bajazeth?
Confusion light on him that helps thee
thus!
TAM. There, whiles he lives, shall Bajazeth
be kept,
And, where I go, be thus in triumph
drawn;
And thou, his wife, shalt feed him with
the scraps
My servitures [3] shall bring thee from my
board,
For he that gives him other food than this
Shall sit by him and starve to death
himself.   90
This is my mind and I will have it so.
Not all the kings and emperors of the
earth,
If they would lay their crowns before my
feet,
Shall ransom him or take him from his
cage.
The ages that shall talk of Tamburlaine,
Even from this day to Plato's wondrous
year,
Shall talk how I have handled Bajazeth.
These Moors, that drew him from Bithy-
nia
To fair Damascus, where we now remain,
Shall lead him with us wheresoe'er we
go.   100
Techelles and my loving followers,
Now may we see Damascus' lofty towers,
Like to the shadows of pyramides,[4]
That with their beauties graced the
Memphian fields.
The golden stature [5] of their feathered
bird
That spreads her wings upon the city
walls
Shall not defend it from our battering
shot.
The townsmen mask in silk and cloth of
gold,

[3] Servitors.   [4] Quadrisyllabic.   [5] Statue.

And every house is as a treasury.
The men, the treasure, and the town is
   ours.   110
THER. Your tents of white now pitched
   before the gates,
And gentle flags of amity displayed,
I doubt not but the governor will yield,
Offering Damascus to your majesty.
TAM. So shall he have his life, and all the
   rest.
But, if he stay until the bloody flag
Be once advanced on my vermilion tent,
He dies, and those that kept us out so
   long.
And, when they see me march in black
   array,
With mournful streamers hanging down
   their heads,   120
Were in that city all the world contained,
Not one should scape, but perish by our
   swords.
ZEN. Yet would you have some pity for
   my sake,
Because it is my country's, and my
   father's!
TAM. Not for the world, Zenocrate, if I
   have sworn.
Come; bring in the Turk!   *Exeunt.*

ACTUS IV. SCENA iii.

[*The Egyptian court.*]

Soldan, Arabia, Capolin, with steeming [1]
   colors and Soldiers.

SOLD. Methinks we march as Meleager did,
   Environéd with brave Argolian knights,
To chase the savage Cal[y]donian boar,
Or Cephalus with lusty Theban youths
Against the wolf that angry Themis sent
To waste and spoil the sweet Aonian
   fields,
A monster of five hundred thousand
   heads,
Compact of rapine, piracy, and spoil.
The scum of men, the hate and scourge of
   God,
Raves in Egyptia and annoyeth us.   10
My lord, it is the bloody Tamburlaine,
A sturdy felon and a base-bred thief,
By murder raiséd to the Persian crown,
That dares control us in our territories.
To tame the pride of this presumptuous
   beast,

[1] Bright, gleaming.

Join your Arabians with the soldan's
   power;
Let us unite our royal bands in one,
And hasten to remove Damascus' siege.
It is a blemish to the majesty
And high estate of mighty emperors   20
That such a base, usurping vagabond
Should brave a king, or wear a princely
   crown.
ARAB. Renowméd soldan, have ye lately
   heard
The overthrow of mighty Bajazeth
About the confines of Bithynia,
The slavery wherewith he persecutes
The noble Turk and his great emperess?
SOLD. I have, and sorrow for his bad
   success.
But, noble lord of great Arabia,
Be so persuaded that the soldan is   30
No more dismayed with tidings of his fall
Than in the haven when the pilot stands
And views a stranger's ship rent in the
   winds,
And shiveréd against a craggy rock.
Yet, in compassion of his wretched state,
A sacred vow to heaven and him I make,
Confirming it with Ibis' holy name,
That Tamburlaine shall rue the day, the
   hour,
Wherein he wrought such ignominious
   wrong
Unto the hallowed person of a prince,   40
Or kept the fair Zenocrate so long
As concubine, I fear, to feed his lust.
ARAB. Let grief and fury hasten on re-
   venge;
Let Tamburlaine for his offenses feel
Such plagues as heaven and we can pour
   on him.
I long to break my spear upon his crest,
And prove the weight of his victorious
   arm,
For fame, I fear, hath been too prodigal
In sounding through the world his partial
   praise.
SOLD. Capolin, hast thou surveyed our
   powers?   50
CAP. Great Emperors of Egypt and
   Arabia,
The number of your hosts united is
A hundred and fifty thousand horse,
Two hundred thousand foot, brave men-
   at-arms,
Courageous, and full of hardiness,

As frolic as the hunters in the chase
Of savage beasts amid the desert woods.
ARAB. My mind presageth fortunate suc-
cess;
And, Tamburlaine, my spirit doth fore-
see
The utter ruin of thy men and thee. 60
SOLD. Then rear your standards; let your
sounding drums
Direct our soldiers to Damascus' walls.
Now, Tamburlaine, the mighty soldan
comes,
And leads with him the great Arabian
king
To dim thy baseness and obscurity,
Famous for nothing but for theft and
spoil;
To raze and scatter thy inglorious crew
Of Scythians and slavish Persians.
Exeunt.

ACTUS IV. SCENA iv.[1]

[*Tamburlaine's camp outside Damascus.*]

*The banquet; and to it cometh Tamburlaine,
all in scarlet, [Zenocrate,] Theridamas,
Techelles, Usumcasane, the Turk [Ba-
jazeth in his cage, Zabina], with Others.*

TAM. Now hang our bloody colors by Da-
mascus,
Reflexing hues of blood upon their heads,
While they walk quivering on their city
walls,
Half dead for fear before they feel my
wrath;
Then let us freely banquet and carouse [2]
Full bowls of wine unto the God of War,
That means to fill your helmets full of
gold,
And make Damascus' spoils as rich to
you
As was to Jason Colchos' golden fleece.—
And now, Bajazeth, hast thou any
stomach? 10
BAJ. Ay, such a stomach, cruel Tamburlaine, as I could willingly feed upon thy
blood-raw heart.
TAM. Nay, thine own is easier to come
by; pluck out that, and 'twill serve thee
and thy wife. Well, Zenocrate, Techelles,
and the rest, fall to your victuals.
BAJ. Fall to, and never may your meat
digest!

Ye Furies, that can mask invisible,
Dive to the bottom of Avernus' pool, 20
And in your hands bring hellish poison
up
And squeeze it in the cup of Tambur-
laine!
Or, wingéd snakes of Lerna, cast your
stings,
And leave your venoms in this tyrant's
dish!
ZAB. And may this banquet prove as
ominous
As Progne's to th' adulterous Thracian
king,
That fed upon the substance of his child!
ZEN. My lord, how can you suffer these
Outrageous curses by these slaves of
yours?
TAM. To let them see, divine Zenocrate, 30
I glory in the curses of my foes,
Having the power from the emperial
heaven
To turn them all upon their proper heads.
TECH. I pray you give them leave,
madam; this speech is a goodly refreshing
to them.
THER. But, if his highness would let
them be fed, it would do them more good.
TAM. Sirrah, why fall you not to? Are
you so daintily brought up you cannot [40
eat your own flesh?
BAJ. First, legions of devils shall tear
thee in pieces!
USUM. Villain, knowest thou to whom
thou speakest?
TAM. O, let him alone. Here, eat, sir.
Take it from my sword's point, or I'll thrust
it to thy heart.

He [3] takes it and stamps upon it.

THER. He stamps it under his feet, my
lord. 50
TAM. Take it up, villain, and eat it, or I
will make thee slice the brawns of thy arms
into carbonadoes [4] and eat them.
USUM. Nay, 'twere better he killed his
wife, and then she shall be sure not to be
starved, and he be provided for a month's
victual beforehand.
TAM. Here is my dagger. Despatch her
while she is fat, for, if she live but awhile
longer, she will fall into a consumption [60
with fretting, and then she will not be
worth the eating.

---

[1] Original has *5*. [2] Drink. [3] *I.e.*, Bajazeth. [4] Steaks.

THER. Dost thou think that Mahomet will suffer this?

TECH. 'Tis like he will, when he cannot let [1] it.

TAM. Go to; fall to your meat!—What, not a bit? Belike he hath not been watered today; give him some drink.

They give him water to drink, and he flings it on the ground.

Fast, and welcome, sir, while [2] hunger [70 make you eat. How now, Zenocrate, doth not the Turk and his wife make a goodly show at a banquet?

ZEN. Yes, my lord.

THER. Methinks 'tis a great deal better than a consort [3] of music.

TAM. Yet music would do well to cheer up Zenocrate. Pray thee, tell why art thou so sad? If thou wilt have a song, the Turk shall strain his voice. But why is it?   80

ZEN. My lord, to see my father's town besieged,
The country wasted where myself was born,
How can it but afflict my very soul?
If any love remain in you, my lord,
Or if my love unto your majesty
May merit favor at your highness' hands,
Then raise your siege from fair Damascus' walls,
And with my father take a friendly truce.

TAM. Zenocrate, were Egypt Jove's own land,
Yet would I with my sword make Jove to stoop.   90
I will confute those blind geographers
That make a triple region in the world,
Excluding regions which I mean to trace, [4]
And with this pen [5] reduce them to a map,
Calling the provinces, cities, and towns,
After my name and thine, Zenocrate.
Here at Damascus will I make the point
That shall begin the perpendicular;
And wouldst thou have me buy thy father's love
With such a loss? Tell me, Zenocrate. 100

ZEN. Honor still wait on happy Tamburlaine!

Yet give me leave to plead for him, my lord.

TAM. Content thyself. His person shall be safe
And all the friends of fair Zenocrate,
If with their lives they will be pleased to yield
Or may be forced to make me emperor;
For Egypt and Arabia must be mine.—
Feed, you slave! Thou mayst think thyself happy to be fed from my trencher.

BAJ. My empty stomach, full of idle heat,   110
Draws bloody humors from my feeble parts,
Preserving life by hasting cruel death.
My veins are pale, my sinews hard and dry,
My joints benumbed; unless I eat, I die.

ZAB. Eat, Bajazeth. Let us live in spite of them, looking [6] some happy power will pity and enlarge [7] us.

TAM. Here, Turk, wilt thou have a clean trencher?

BAJ. Ay, tyrant, and more meat.   120

TAM. Soft, sir; you must be dieted; too much eating will make you surfeit.

THER. So it would, my lord, specially having so small a walk and so little exercise.

Enter a second course of crowns.

TAM. Theridamas, Techelles, and Casane, here are the cates [8] you desire to finger, are they not?

THER. Ay, my lord, but none save kings must feed with these.

TECH. 'Tis enough for us to see [130 them, and for Tamburlaine only to enjoy them.

TAM. Well, here is now to the Soldan of Egypt, the King of Arabia, and the Governor of Damascus. Now take these three crowns, and pledge me, my contributory kings. I crown you here, Theridamas, King of Argier; Techelles, King of Fez; and Usumcasane, King of Moroccus. How say you to this, Turk? These are not your [140 contributory kings.

BAJ. Nor shall they long be thine, I warrant them.

TAM. Kings of Argier, Moroccus, and of Fez,

---

[1] Prevent.
[2] Until.
[3] Concert.
[4] Travel over.
[5] *I.e.*, sword.
[6] Expecting.   [7] Free.   [8] Delicacies

You that have marched with happy Tam-
　burlaine
As far as from the frozen place of heaven
Unto the wat'ry morning's ruddy hour,[1]
And thence by land unto the torrid zone,
Deserve these titles I endow you with
By value [2] and by magnanimity.[3]
Your births shall be no blemish to your
　fame,　　　　　　　　　　　　　150
For virtue is the fount whence honor
　springs,
And they are worthy she investeth kings.
Ther. And, since your highness hath so
　well vouchsafed,
If we deserve them not with higher
　meeds [4]
Than erst our states and actions have
　retained,
Take them away again and make us
　slaves.
Tam. Well said, Theridamas; when holy
　fates
Shall stablish me in strong Egyptia,
We mean to travel to th' antartic [5] pole,
Conquering the people underneath our
　feet,　　　　　　　　　　　　　160
And be renowmed as never emperors
　were.
Zenocrate, I will not crown thee yet,
Until with greater honors I be graced.
　　　　　　　　　　　　　[Exeunt.]

　　　　Finis Actus Quarti.

　　　　Actus V. Scena i.

[Outside the walls of Damascus.]

*The Governor of Damasco, with three or four
Citizens, and four Virgins with branches
　　　　of laurel in their hands.*

Gov. Still doth this man, or rather god, of
　war,
Batter our walls and beat our turrets
　down,
And to resist with longer stubbornness
Or hope of rescue from the soldan's
　power
Were but to bring our willful overthrow,
And make us desperate of our threatened
　lives.
We see his tents have now been altered

[1] *I.e.*, dawn, the east.　　　[3] Courage.
[2] Worth, goodness.　　　[4] Merits.
[5] Antarctic. From 1592 edn. Original reads
antatique.

With terrors to the last and cruelest
　hue.
His coal-black colors everywhere ad-
　vanced
Threaten our city with a general spoil. 10
And, if we should with common rites of
　arms
Offer our safeties to his clemency,
I fear the custom, proper to his sword,
Which he observes as parcel of his fame,
Intending so to terrify the world,
By any innovation or remorse
Will never be dispensed with till our
　deaths.
Therefore, for these our harmless vir-
　gins' sakes,
Whose honors and whose lives rely on
　him,
Let us have hope that their unspotted
　prayers,　　　　　　　　　　　20
Their blubbered cheeks, and hearty,
　humble moans,
Will melt his fury into some remorse,[6]
And use us like a loving conqueror.
[1] Virg. If humble suits or imprecations,[7]
Uttered with tears of wretchedness and
　blood
Shed from the heads and hearts of all
　our sex
(Some made your wives, and some your
　children),
Might have entreated your obdurate
　breasts
To entertain some care of our securities
Whiles [8] only danger beat upon our
　walls,　　　　　　　　　　　30
These more than dangerous warrants
　of our death
Had never been erected as they be,
Nor you depend on such weak helps as
　we.
Gov. Well, lovely virgins, think our
　country's care,
Our love of honor, loath to be enthralled
To foreign powers and rough imperious
　yokes,
Would not with too much cowardice
　or fear,
Before all hope of rescue were denied,
Submit yourselves and us to servitude.
Therefore, in that your safeties and our
　own,　　　　　　　　　　　40

[6] Pity.　　　　　　[8] During the time that.
[7] Prayers.

Your honors, liberties, and lives were
    weighed
In equal care and balance with our own,
Endure as we the malice of our stars,
The wrath of Tamburlaine, and power
    of wars;
Or be the means the overweighing [1]
    heavens
Have kept to qualify [2] these hot ex-
    tremes,
And bring us pardon in your cheerful
    looks.
2 VIRG. Then here before the majesty of
    heaven
And holy patrons of Egyptia,
With knees and hearts submissive we
    entreat   50
Grace to our words and pity to our looks
That this device may prove propitious,
And through the eyes and ears of Tam-
    burlaine
Convey events [3] of mercy to his heart.
Grant that these signs of victory we
    yield
May bind the temples of his conquering
    head,
To hide the folded furrows of his brows,
And shadow his displeaséd countenance
With happy looks of ruth and lenity.
Leave us, my lord and loving country-
    men;   60
What simple virgins may persuade, we
    will.
Gov. Farewell, sweet virgins, on whose
    safe return
Depends our city, liberty, and lives.
        Exeunt [all but the Virgins].

ACTUS V. SCENA ii.

[*The same.*]

[*The Virgins are approached by*] *Tambur-
    laine, Techelles, Theridamas, Usumca-
    san[e], with Others; Tamburlaine all in
    black and very melancholy.*

TAM. What, are the turtles [4] frayed [5] out
    of their nests?
Alas, poor fools! Must you be first
    shall feel
The sworn destruction of Damascus?

[1] Overruling.   [4] Turtledoves.
[2] Mollify.   [5] Frightened.
[3] Effects.

They know my custom. Could they
    not as well
Have sent ye out when first my milk-
    white flags,
Through which sweet Mercy threw her
    gentle beams,
Reflexing them on your disdainful eyes,
As now, when fury and incenséd hate
Flings slaughtering terror from my coal-
    black tents,
And tells for truth submissions comes
    too late?   10
1 VIRG. Most happy king and emperor
    of the earth,
Image of honor and nobility,
For whom the powers divine have made
    the world,
And on whose throne the holy Graces
    sit,
In whose sweet person is comprised the
    sum
Of nature's skill and heavenly majesty,
Pity our plights! O, pity poor Damascus!
Pity old age, within whose silver hairs
Honor and reverence evermore have
    reigned!
Pity the marriage bed, where many a
    lord,   20
In prime and glory of his loving joy,
Embraceth now with tears of ruth and
    blood
The jealous body of his fearful wife,
Whose cheeks and hearts, so punished
    with conceit
To think thy puissant, never-stayéd
    arm
Will part their bodies, and prevent their
    souls
From heavens of comfort yet their age
    might bear,
Now wax all pale and withered to the
    death,
As well for grief our ruthless governor
Hath thus refused the mercy of thy
    hand   30
(Whose scepter angels kiss and furies
    dread)
As for their liberties, their loves, or
    lives!
O, then for these, and such as we our-
    selves,
For us, for infants, and for all our bloods,
That never nourished thought against
    thy rule,

Pity, O, pity, sacred emperor,
The prostrate service of this wretched town,
And take in sign thereof this gilded wreath,
Whereto each man of rule hath given his hand,
And wished, as worthy subjects, happy means   40
To be investers of thy royal brows
Even with the true Egyptian diadem!
TAM. Virgins, in vain ye labor to prevent
That which mine honor swears shall be performed.
Behold my sword! What see you at the point?
[1] VIRG. Nothing but fear and fatal steel, my lord.
TAM. Your fearful minds are thick and misty then;
For there sits Death, there sits imperious Death,
Keeping his circuit [1] by the slicing edge.
But I am pleased you shall not see him there;   50
He now is seated on my horsemen's spears,
And on their points his fleshless body feeds.
Techelles, straight go charge a few of them
To charge these dames, and show my servant, Death,
Sitting in scarlet on their arméd spears.
OMNES. O, pity us!
TAM. Away with them, I say, and show them Death!   *They take them away.*
I will not spare these proud Egyptians,
Nor change my martial observations
For all the wealth of Gihon's golden waves,   60
Or for the love of Venus, would she leave
The angry god of arms and lie with me.
They have refused the offer of their lives,
And know my customs are as peremptory
As wrathful planets, death, or destiny.

[1] Law court.

Enter Techelles.

What, have your horsemen shown the virgins Death?
TECH. They have, my lord, and on Damascus' walls
Have hoisted up their slaughtered carcasses.
TAM. A sight as baneful to their souls, I think,
As are Thessalian drugs or mithridate.[2]—   70
But go, my lords, put the rest to the sword.
    Exeunt [all except Tamburlaine].
Ah, fair Zenocrate, divine Zenocrate,
Fair is too foul an epithet for thee,
That in thy passion [3] for thy country's love,
And fear to see thy kingly father's harm,
With hair disheveled wip'st thy watery cheeks,
And, like to Flora in her morning's pride,
Shaking her silver tresses [4] in the air,
Rain'st on the earth resolvéd pearl in showers,
And sprinklest sapphires on thy shining face,   80
Where Beauty, mother to the Muses, sits
And comments [5] volumes with her ivory pen,
Taking instructions from thy flowing eyes,
Eyes, when that Ebena steps to heaven,
In silence of thy solemn evening's walk,
Making the mantle of the richest night,
The moon, the planets, and the meteors, light!
There angels in their crystal armors fight
A doubtful battle with my tempted thoughts
For Egypt's freedom, and the soldan's life—   90
His life that so consumes Zenocrate,
Whose sorrows lay more siege unto my soul
Than all my army to Damascus' walls;
And neither Persians' sovereign nor the Turk

[2] Usually an antidote against poison; here, a poison.
[3] Suffering.
[4] Tresses.
[5] Writes.

Troubled my senses with conceit of
  foil [1]
So much by much as doth Zenocrate.
What is beauty, saith my sufferings,
  then?
If all the pens that ever poets held
Had fed the feeling of their masters'
  thoughts,
And every sweetness that inspired their
  hearts,   100
Their minds, and muses on admired
  themes;
If all the heavenly quintessence they
  still [2]
From their immortal flowers of poesy,
Wherein, as in a mirror, we perceive
The highest reaches of a human wit;
If these had made one poem's period, [3]
And all combined in beauty's worthi-
  ness,
Yet should there hover in their restless
  heads
One thought, one grace, one wonder, at
  the least,   109
Which into words no virtue can digest.
But how unseemly is it for my sex,
My discipline of arms and chivalry,
My nature, and the terror of my name,
To harbor thoughts effeminate and
  faint!
Save only that in beauty's just applause,
With whose instinct the soul of man is
  touched
(And every warrior that is rapt with
  love
Of fame, of valor, and of victory
Must needs have beauty beat on his
  conceits),
I, thus conceiving and subduing both   120
That which hath stopped the tempest
  of the gods,
Even from the fiery-spangled veil of
  heaven,
To feel the lovely warmth of shepherds'
  flames,
And march [4] in cottages of strowéd
  weeds,
Shall give the world to note, for all my
  birth,
That virtue solely is the sum of glory,
And fashions men with true nobility.—
Who's within there?

Enter two or three [Attendants].

Hath Bajazeth been fed today?
A[TTE]N. Ay, my lord.   130
TAM. Bring him forth; and let us know
the town be ransacked.

                       [Exeunt Attendants.]

Enter Techelles, Theridamas, Usumcasan[e],
                           and Others.

TECH. The town is ours, my lord, and
  fresh supply
Of conquest and of spoil is offered us.
TAM. That's well, Techelles. What's the
  news?
TECH. The soldan and the Arabian king
  together
March on us with such eager violence
As if there were no way but one with
  us.
TAM. No more there is not, I warrant
  thee, Techelles.

      They bring in the Turk [and Zabina].

THER. We know the victory is ours, my
  lord;   140
But let us save the reverend soldan's
  life
For fair Zenocrate, that so laments his
  state.
TAM. That will we chiefly see unto, Theri-
  damas,
For sweet Zenocrate, whose worthiness
Deserves a conquest over every heart.—
And now, my footstool, if I lose the
  field,
You hope of liberty and restitution.
Here let him stay, my masters, from the
  tents,
Till we have made us ready for the
  field.
Pray for us, Bajazeth; we are going.   150
Exeunt [all except Bajazeth and Zabina].
BAJ. Go, never to return with victory!
Millions of men encompass thee about,
And gore thy body with as many wounds!
Sharp, forkéd arrows light upon thy
  horse!
Furies from the black Cocytus lake
Break up the earth, and with their fire-
  brands
Enforce thee run upon the baneful
  pikes!
Volleys of shot pierce through thy
  charméd skin,

---

[1] Thought of defeat.   [3] Climax.
[2] Distil.   [4] Move about.

And every bullet dipped in poisoned
drugs, 159
Or roaring cannons sever all thy joints,
Making thee mount as high as eagles
soar!

ZAB. Let all the swords and lances in the
field
Stick in his breast as in their proper
rooms!
At every pore let blood come dropping
forth,
That ling'ring pains may massacre his
heart,
And madness send his damnéd soul to
hell!

BAJ. Ah, fair Zabina, we may curse his
power,
The heavens may frown, the earth for
anger quake,
But such a star hath influence in his
sword
As rules the skies and countermands
the gods 170
More than Cimmerian Styx or destiny;
And then shall we in this detested
guise,
With shame, with hunger, and with
horror lie,[1]
Griping our bowels with retorquéd[2]
thoughts,
And have no hope to end our ecstasies.[3]

ZAB. Then is there left no Mahomet, no
God,
No fiend, no fortune, nor no hope of
end
To our infamous, monstrous slaveries?
Gape, earth, and let the fiends infernal
view
A hell as hopeless and as full of fear 180
As are the blasted banks of Erebus,
Where shaking ghosts with ever-howling
groans
Hover about the ugly ferryman,
To get a passage to Elysian!
Why should we live? O, wretches, beg-
gars, slaves!
Why live we, Bajazeth, and build up
nests
So high within the region of the air
By living long in this oppression
That all the world will see and laugh to
scorn

The former triumphs of our mightiness 190
In this obscure, infernal servitude?

BAJ. O life, more loathsome to my vexéd
thoughts
Than noisome parbreak[4] of the Stygian
snakes,
Which fills the nooks of hell with stand-
ing air,
Infecting all the ghosts with cureless
griefs!
O dreary engines[5] of my loathéd sight,
That sees my crown, my honor, and my
name
Thrust under yoke and thralldom of a
thief,
Why feed ye still on day's accurséd beams
And sink not quite into my tortured
soul? 200
You see my wife, my queen and em-
peress,
Brought up and proppéd by the hand of
Fame,
Queen of fifteen contributory queens,
Now thrown to rooms[6] of black abjec-
tion,
Smeared with blots of basest drudgery,
And villainess[7] to shame, disdain, and
misery.
Accurséd Bajazeth, whose words of
ruth,
That would with pity cheer Zabina's
heart,
And make our souls resolve in ceaseless
tears,
Sharp hunger bites upon, and gripes
the root 210
From whence the issues of my thoughts
do break!
O poor Zabina, O my queen, my queen,
Fetch me some water for my burning
breast,
To cool and comfort me with longer date
That in the shortened sequel of my life
I may pour forth my soul into thine arms
With words of love, whose moaning
intercourse
Hath hitherto been stayed with wrath
and hate
Of our expressless banned[8] inflic-
tions.

---

[1] Original has *aie.*   [3] Frenzies.
[2] Twisted inward.

[4] Vomit.   [7] Slave.
[5] Instruments, *i.e.*, eyes.   [8] Cursed.
[6] Positions.

ZAB. Sweet Bajazeth, I will prolong thy
     life   220
    As long as any blood or spark of breath
    Can quench or cool the torments of
      my grief.   *She goes out.*
BAJ. Now, Bajazeth, abridge thy bane-
     ful days,
    And beat thy brains out of thy conquered
     head,
    Since other means are all forbidden me
    That may be ministers of my decay.
    O highest lamp of ever-living Jove,
    Accursèd day, infected with my griefs,
    Hide now thy stainèd face in endless
     night,
    And shut the windows of the lightsome
     heavens!   230
    Let ugly Darkness with her rusty coach,
    Engirt with tempests, wrapped in pitchy
     clouds,
    Smother the earth with never-fading
     mists,
    And let her horses from their nostrils
     breathe
    Rebellious winds and dreadful thunder-
     claps,
    That in this terror Tamburlaine may
     live,
    And my pined soul, resolved in liquid
     air,[1]
    May still excruciate his tormented
     thoughts!
    Then let the stony dart of senseless
     cold
    Pierce through the center of my withered
     heart,   240
    And make a passage for my loathèd
     life!
       He brains himself against the cage.

Enter Zabina.

ZAB. What do mine eyes behold? My
     husband dead!
    His skull all riven in twain! His brains
     dashed out,
    The brains of Bajazeth, my lord and
     sovereign!
    O Bajazeth, my husband and my lord!
    O Bajazeth, O Turk, O emperor!
    Give him his liquor? Not I. Bring milk
   and fire, and my blood I bring him again!—
   Tear me in pieces! Give me the sword

with a ball of wildfire upon it!—Down   [250
   with him, down with him!—Go to my child!
   Away, away, away! Ah, save that infant,
   save him, save him!—I, even I, speak to
   her.—The sun was down; streamers white,
   red, black, here, here, here!—Fling the
   meat in his face!—Tamburlaine, Tamburlaine!—Let the soldiers be buried.—Hell!
   Death! Tamburlaine! Hell!—Make ready
   my coach, my chair, my jewels. I come,
   I come, I come!   260
   She runs against the cage and brains herself.

       [Enter] Zenocrate with Anippe.

[ZEN.] Wretched Zenocrate, that livest
     to see
    Damascus' walls dyed with Egyptian
     blood,
    Thy father's subjects and thy country-
     men;
    Thy streets strowed with dissevered
     joints of men
    And wounded bodies gasping yet for
     life!
    But most accursed, to see the sun-bright
     troop
    Of heavenly virgins and unspotted
     maids,
    Whose looks might make the angry god
     of arms
    To break his sword and mildly treat
     of love,   269
    On horsemen's lances to be hoisted up
    And guiltlessly endure a cruel death!
    For every fell and stout Tartarian steed,
    That stamped on others with their thun-
     d'ring hoofs,
    When all their riders charged their
     quivering spears,
    Began to check [2] the ground and rein
     themselves,
    Gazing upon the beauty of their looks.
    Ah, Tamburlaine, wert thou the cause
     of this
    That term'st Zenocrate thy dearest
     love,
    Whose lives were dearer to Zenocrate
    Than her own life, or aught save thine
     own love?—   280
    But see another bloody spectacle!
    Ah, wretched eyes, the enemies of my
     heart,

---

[1] Original has *ay.*

[2] Push against.

How are ye glutted with these grievous
  objects,
And tell my soul more tales of bleeding
  ruth!
See, see, Anippe, if they breathe or no.

ANIP. No breath, nor sense, nor motion
  in them both.
Ah, madam, this their slavery hath enforced,
And ruthless cruelty of Tamburlaine.

ZEN. Earth, cast up fountains from thy
  entrails,
And wet thy cheeks for their untimely
  deaths!   290
Shake with their weight in sign of fear
  and grief!
Blush, Heaven, that gave them honor
  at their birth
And let them die a death so barbarous!
Those that are proud of fickle empery
And place their chiefest good in earthly
  pomp,
Behold the Turk and his great emperess!
Ah, Tamburlaine, my love, sweet Tam-
  burlaine,
That fights for scepters and for slippery
  crowns,
Behold the Turk and his great emper-
  ess!
Thou, that in conduct of thy happy
  stars   300
Sleep'st every night with conquests on
  thy brows,
And yet wouldst shun the wavering
  turns of war,
In fear and feeling of the like distress
Behold the Turk and his great emperess!
Ah, mighty Jove and holy Mahomet,
Pardon my love!—O, pardon his con-
  tempt
Of earthly fortune and respect of pity,
And let not conquest, ruthlessly pur-
  sued,
Be equally against his life incensed   309
In this great Turk and hapless emper-
  ess!
And pardon me that was not moved
  with ruth
To see them live so long in misery!
Ah, what may chance to thee, Zenocrate?

ANIP. Madam, content yourself, and be
  resolved;
Your love hath Fortune so at his command

That she shall stay and turn her wheel
  no more,
As long as life maintains his mighty
  arm
That fights for honor to adorn your
  head.

Enter [Philemus,] a Messenger.

ZEN. What other heavy news now brings
  Philemus?

PHIL. Madam, your father, and the Ara-
  bian king,   320
The first affecter [1] of your excellence,
Comes now, as Turnus gainst Æneas
  did,
Arméd with lance into the Egyptian
  fields,
Ready for battle gainst my lord, the king

ZEN. Now shame and duty, love and fear
  presents
A thousand sorrows to my martyred soul.
Whom should I wish the fatal victory
When my poor pleasures are divided
  thus
And racked by duty from my curséd
  heart?   329
My father and my first-betrothéd love
Must fight against my life and present
  love,
Wherein the change I use condemns my
  faith,
And makes my deeds infamous through
  the world.
But as the gods, to end the Troyans'
  toil,
Prevented [2] Turnus of Lavinia
And fatally enriched Æneas' love,
So, for a final issue to my griefs,
To pacify my country and my love
Must Tamburlaine by their resistless
  powers
With virtue of a gentle victory   340
Conclude a league of honor to my hope;
Then, as the powers divine have pre-
  ordained,
With happy safety of my father's life
Send like defense of fair Arabia.

They sound to the battle [within], and Tam-
* burlaine enjoys the victory. After,*
*   Arabia enters wounded.*

ARAB. What curséd power guides the
  murthering hands

[1] Lover.   [2] Deprived.

Of this infamous tyrant's soldiers
That no escape may save their enemies,
Nor fortune keep themselves from vic-
tory?
Lie down, Arabia, wounded to the death,
And let Zenocrate's fair eyes behold
That, as for her thou bear'st these
wretched arms,   351
Even so for her thou diest in these arms,
Leaving thy blood for witness of thy
love.
ZEN. Too dear a witness for such love, my
lord!
Behold Zenocrate, the curséd object,
Whose fortunes never masteréd her
griefs;
Behold her wounded, in conceit, for
thee,
As much as thy fair body is for me,
ARAB. Then shall I die with full, con-
tented heart,
Having beheld divine Zenocrate,   360
Whose sight with joy would take away
my life
As now it bringeth sweetness to my
wound,
If I had not been wounded as I am.
Ah, that the deadly pangs I suffer now
Would lend an hour's license to my
tongue,
To make discourse of some sweet acci-
dents
Have chanced [1] thy merits in this worth-
less [2] bondage,
And that I might be privy to the state
Of thy deserved contentment, and thy
love.   369
But, making now a virtue of thy sight
To drive all sorrow from my fainting
soul,
Since death denies me further cause of
joy,
Deprived of care, my heart with com-
fort dies,
Since thy desiréd hand shall close mine
eyes.   [Dies.]

*Enter Tamburlaine, leading the Soldan,
Techelles, Theridamas, Usumcasane,
with Others.*

TAM. Come, happy father of Zenocrate,
A title higher than thy soldan's name.

[1] Befallen.   [2] Unworthy.

Though my right hand have thus en-
thralléd thee,
Thy princely daughter here shall set
thee free,
She that hath calmed the fury of my
sword,
Which had ere this been bathed in
streams of blood   380
As vast and deep as Euphrates or Nile.
ZEN. O sight thrice welcome to my joy-
ful soul,
To see the king, my father, issue safe
From dangerous battle of my conquer-
ing love!
SOLD. Well met, my only dear Zenocrate,
Though with the loss of Egypt and my
crown.
TAM. 'Twas I, my lord, that gat the vic-
tory,
And therefore grieve not at your over-
throw,
Since I shall render all into your hands,
And add more strength to your domin-
ions   390
Than ever yet confirmed th' Egyptian
crown.
The God of War resigns his room to me,
Meaning to make me general of the
world.
Jove, viewing me in arms, looks pale
and wan,
Fearing my power should pull him from
his throne.
Where'er I come, the Fatal Sisters
sweat
And grisly Death, by running to and
fro,
To do their ceaseless homage to my
sword.
And here in Afric, where it seldom
rains,
Since I arrived with my triumphant
host,   400
Have swelling clouds, drawn from wide-
gasping wounds,
Been oft resolved in bloody, purple
showers,
A meteor that might terrify the earth,
And make it quake at every drop it
drinks.
Millions of souls sit on the banks of
Styx,
Waiting the back return of Charon's
boat;

Hell and Elysian swarm with ghosts
of men
That I have sent from sundry foughten
fields,
To spread my fame through hell and up
to heaven.
And see, my lord, a sight of strange im-
port: 410
Emperors and kings lie breathless at
my feet.
The Turk and his great empress, as it
seems,
Left to themselves while we were at
the fight,
Have desperately despatched their
slavish lives;
With them Arabia, too, hath left his
life—
All sights of power to grace my victory.
And such are objects fit for Tambur-
laine,
Wherein, as in a mirror, may be seen
His honor, that consists in shedding
blood,
When men presume to manage arms
with him.   420
SOLD. Mighty hath God and Mahomet
made thy hand,
Renowmèd Tamburlaine, to whom all
kings
Of force [1] must yield their crowns and
emperies;
And I am pleased with this my over-
throw,
If, as beseems a person of thy state,
Thou hast with honor used Zenocrate.
TAM. Her state and person wants no
pomp, you see;
And for all blot of foul inchastity
I record [2] heaven her heavenly self is
clear.
Then let me find no further time to
grace   430
Her princely temples with the Persian
crown,
But here these kings that on my for-
tunes wait,
And have been crowned for provèd
worthiness,
Even by this hand that shall establish
them,
Shall now, adjoining all their hands
with mine,

[1] Of necessity.   [2] Take to witness.

Invest her here my Queen of Persia.
What saith the noble soldan and Zeno-
crate?
SOLD. I yield with thanks and protesta-
tions
Of endless honor to thee for her love.
TAM. Then doubt I not but fair Zeno-
crate   440
Will soon consent to satisfy us both.
ZEN. Else should I much forget myself,
my lord.
THER. Then let us set the crown upon
her head,
That long hath lingered for so high a
seat.
TECH. My hand is ready to perform the
deed,
For now her marriage time shall work
us rest.
USUM. And here's the crown, my lord,
help set it on.
TAM. Then sit thou down, divine Zeno-
crate;
And here we crown thee Queen of
Persia   449
And all the kingdoms and dominions
That late the power of Tamburlaine
subdued.
As Juno, when the giants were sup-
pressed,
That darted mountains at her brother
Jove,
So looks my love, shadowing in her
brows
Triumphs and trophies for my victories;
Or as Latona's daughter, bent to arms,
Adding more courage to my conquering
mind.
To gratify the sweet Zenocrate,
Egyptians, Moors, and men of Asia,
From Barbary unto the western Indie,
Shall pay a yearly tribute to thy sire; 461
And from the bounds of Afric to the
banks
Of Ganges shall his mighty arm extend.
And now, my lords and loving followers
That purchased kingdoms by your mar-
tial deeds,
Cast off your armor, put on scarlet
robes,
Mount up your royal places of estate,
Environèd with troops of noblemen,
And there make laws to rule your prov-
inces.

Hang up your weapons on Alcides'
  post,[1]   470
For Tamburlaine takes truce with all
  the world.
Thy first-betrothéd love, Arabia,
Shall we with honor, as beseems, entomb
With this great Turk and his fair em-
  peress.

[1] Doorpost of the temple.

Then, after all these solemn exequies,
We will our celebrated rites of marriage solemnize.   *[Exeunt.]*

FINIS ACTUS QUINTI ET ULTIMI HUJUS
        PRIMÆ PARTIS.[2]

[2] The end of the fifth and last act of this first
part.

THE TRAGICAL HISTORY OF D[OCTOR] FAUSTUS[1]

BY
CHRISTOPHER MARLOWE

[DRAMATIS PERSONÆ

THE POPE.
CARDINAL OF LORRAIN.
EMPEROR OF GERMANY.
DUKE OF VANHOLT.
FAUSTUS.
VALDES } friends to Faustus.
CORNELIUS AGRIPPA }
WAGNER, servant to Faustus.
CLOWN.
ROBIN.
RAFE.[2]
VINTNER.
HORSE-CORSER.[3]
KNIGHT.
OLD MAN.

SCHOLARS, FRIARS, and ATTENDANTS.

DUCHESS OF VANHOLT.

LUCIFER.
BELZEBUB.
MEPHISTOPHILIS.
GOOD ANGEL.
EVIL ANGEL.
THE SEVEN DEADLY SINS.
DEVILS.
SPIRITS in the shapes of ALEXANDER THE
GREAT, of his PARAMOUR, and of HELEN
OF TROY.

CHORUS.

PLACE: Germany and Rome.
TIME: Early sixteenth century.]

Enter Chorus.

Not marching now in fields of Thrasi-
mene,
Where Mars did mate [4] the Carthagin-
ians,
Nor sporting in the dalliance of love,
In courts of kings where state is over-
turned,
Nor in the pomp of proud audacious
deeds,
Intends our Muse to daunt [5] his heavenly
verse.
Only this, gentlemen: we must perform
The form [6] of Faustus' fortunes, good or
bad.

To patient judgments we appeal our
plaud,[7]
And speak for Faustus in his infancy. 10
Now is he born, his parents base of stock,
In Germany, within a town called
Rhodes;
Of riper years to Wertenberg [8] he went,
Whereas [9] his kinsmen chiefly brought
him up.
So soon he profits in divinity,
The fruitful plot of scholarism graced,
That shortly he was graced with doctor's
name,
Excelling all whose sweet delight disputes
In heavenly matters of theology;
Till swollen with cunning,[10] of a self-
conceit,   20
His waxen wings did mount above his
reach,

[1] The title continues: "As It Hath Been Acted
by the Right Honorable the Earl of Nottingham
His Servants. Written by Ch. Marl."
[2] Variant of Ralph.   [4] Join with (?).
[3] Dealer in horses.
[5] Wear out, exhaust. The 1616 edn. has vaunt.
[6] Course.

[7] For our applause.   [9] Where.
[8] Wittenberg.   [10] Learning.

349

And, melting, heavens conspired his over-
throw,
For, falling to a devilish exercise,
And glutted more with learning's golden
gifts,
He surfeits upon cursèd negromancy.[1]
Nothing so sweet as magic is to him,
Which he prefers before his chiefest
bliss.
And this the man that in his study sits!
                   Exit.

[SCENE i.]

Enter Faustus in his study.

FAUST. Settle thy studies, Faustus, and
begin
To sound the depth of that thou wilt
profess.
Having commenced,[2] be a divine in
show;
Yet level at the end of [3] every art,
And live and die in Aristotle's works.
Sweet analytics,[4] 'tis thou hast ravished
me!
[*Reads.*] *"Bene disserere est finis logices."*
Is to dispute well logic's chiefest end?
Affords this art no greater miracle?
Then read no more; thou hast attained
the end.   10
A greater subject fitteth Faustus' wit.
Bid *Oncaymæon* [5] farewell. [*Puts down
Aristotle and takes up Galen.*] Galen,
come,
Seeing *"Ubi desinit Philosophus, ibi
incipit Medicus."* [6]
Be a physician, Faustus, heap up gold,
And be eternized [7] for some wondrous
cure.
[*Reads.*] *"Summum bonum medicinæ sa-
nitas."*
"The end of physic is our body's health."
Why, Faustus, hast thou not attained
that end?
Is not thy common talk sound apho-
risms? [8]

Are not thy bills [9] hung up as monu-
ments   20
Whereby whole cities have escaped the
plague,
And thousand desperate maladies been
eased?
Yet art thou still but Faustus, and a man.
Wouldst thou make man to live eternally,
Or, being dead, raise them to life again,
Then this profession were to be esteemed.
Physic, farewell.—Where is Justinian?
[*Puts down Galen, takes up Justinian, and
reads.*]
*"Si una eademque res legatur duobus, alter
rem, alter valorem rei,"* [10] *etc.*
A pretty case of paltry legacies!
[*Reads.*] *"Exhæreditare filium non potest
pater nisi—"* [11]   30
Such is the subject of the Institute [12]
And universal Body of the Law.[13]
His [14] study fits a mercenary drudge,
Who aims at nothing but external trash,
Too servile [15] and illiberal for me.
When all is done, divinity is best.
Jerome's Bible,[16] Faustus, view it well.
[*Puts down Justinian, takes up the Vulgate,
and reads.*]
"Stipendium peccati mors est." Ha!
"Stipendium," *etc.:*
"The reward of sin is death." That's
hard.
[*Reads.*] *"Si peccasse negamus, fallimur,
et nulla est in nobis veritas:"*   40
"If we say that we have no sin,
We deceive ourselves, and there's no
truth in us."
Why then, belike,
We must sin and so consequently die.
Ay, we must die an everlasting death.
What doctrine call you this? *Che sera,
sera:*
"What will be, shall be." Divinity,
adieu!
[*Puts down the Vulgate and takes up his
book of magic.*]

---

[1] Necromancy.   [3] Aim at perfection in.
[2] Proceeded to a degree.   [4] Logic.
[5] Bullen points out that this is a corruption
of Aristotle's phrase for "being and not being."
[6] "Where the philosopher stops, there the
physician begins." This and the following quotation are from Aristotle.
[7] Immortalized.
[8] Maxims of medicine.

[9] Doctor's prescriptions.
[10] "If one and the same thing is willed to two
persons, one gets the thing and the other the
value of the thing."
[11] "A father cannot disinherit the son unless—"
[12] Of Justinian.
[13] From 1616 edn. Original has *church.*
[14] Its.
[15] From 1616 edn. Original reads *The devil.*
[16] The Vulgate.

These metaphysics of magicians
And negromantic books are heavenly;
Lines, circles, scenes, letters, and char-
　acters,　　　　　　　　　　　　　50
Ay, these are those that Faustus most
　desires.
O, what a world of profit and delight,
Of power, of honor, of omnipotence
Is promised to the studious artisan! [1]
All things that move between the quiet
　poles
Shall be at my command.　Emperors and
　kings
Are but obeyed in their several provinces,
Nor can they raise the wind or rend the
　clouds;
But his dominion that exceeds [2] in this
Stretcheth as far as doth the mind of
　man.　　　　　　　　　　　　　60
A sound magician is a mighty god.
Here, Faustus, try thy brains to gain a
　deity.—

Enter Wagner.

Wagner!　Commend me to my dearest
　friends,
The German Valdes and Cornelius;
Request them earnestly to visit me.
WAG.　I will, sir.　　　　　　*Exit.*
FAUST.　Their conference will be a greater
　help to me
Than all my labors, plod I ne'er so fast.

Enter the Good Angel and the Evil Angel.

GOOD A.　O Faustus, lay that damnéd book
　aside,　　　　　　　　　　　　　69
And gaze not on it lest it tempt thy soul,
And heap God's heavy wrath upon thy
　head!
Read, read the Scriptures.　That is blas-
　phemy.
EVIL A.　Go forward, Faustus, in that fa-
　mous art
Wherein all Nature's treasury [3] is con-
　tained.
Be thou on earth, as Jove is in the sky,
Lord and commander of these elements.
　　　　　　　　　Exeunt [Angels].
FAUST.　How am I glutted with conceit [4]
　of this!

---

[1] Student of a liberal art.　　[3] Treasure.
[2] Excels.　　　　　　　　　[4] Thought.

Shall I make spirits fetch me what I
　please,
Resolve me of all ambiguities, [5]
Perform what desperate enterprise I
　will?　　　　　　　　　　　　　80
I'll have them fly to India [6] for gold,
Ransack the ocean for orient pearl,
And search all corners of the new-found
　world
For pleasant fruits and princely delicates;
I'll have them read me strange philos-
　ophy
And tell the secrets of all foreign kings;
I'll have them wall all Germany with
　brass,
And make swift Rhine circle fair Werten-
　berg;
I'll have them fill the public schools [7]
　with silk, [8]
Wherewith the students shall be bravely
　clad;　　　　　　　　　　　　　90
I'll levy soldiers with the coin they
　bring,
And chase the Prince of Parma from our
　land,
And reign sole king of all our provinces;
Yea, stranger engines [9] for the brunt of
　war
Than was the fiery keel at Antwerp's
　bridge,
I'll make my servile spirits to invent.
Come, German Valdes and Cornelius,
And make me blessed with your sage con-
　ference.

Enter Valdes and Cornelius.

Valdes, sweet Valdes, and Cornelius,
Know that your words have won me at
　the last　　　　　　　　　　　100
To practice magic and concealéd
　arts—
Yet not your words only, but mine own
　fantasy,
That will receive no object, [10] for my
　head
But ruminates on negromantic skill.
Philosophy is odious and obscure;

---

[5] Free me from all uncertainties.
[6] The American Indies.
[7] University lecture rooms.
[8] Emended by Dyce.　Original reads *skill.*
[9] Machines.
[10] "Will not be impressed by solid realities"
(Boas).

Both law and physic are for petty wits;
Divinity is basest of the three,
Unpleasant, harsh, contemptible, and
vild.[1]
'Tis magic, magic, that hath ravished
me!
Then, gentle friends, aid me in this
attempt;   110
And I that have with concise syllo-
gisms
Graveled the pastors of the German
church,
And made the flow'ring pride of Werten-
berg
Swarm to my problems,[2] as the infernal
spirits
On sweet Musæus when he came to hell,
Will be as cunning as Agrippa was,
Whose shadows[3] made all Europe honor
him.
VALD. Faustus,
These books, thy wit, and our experi-
ence
Shall make all nations to canonize us.
As Indian Moors[4] obey their Spanish
lords,   121
So shall the subjects[5] of every element
Be always serviceable to us three.
Like lions shall they guard us when we
please;
Like Almain rutters[6] with their horse-
men's staves,
Or Lapland giants, trotting by our
sides;
Sometimes like women or unwedded
maids,
Shadowing more beauty in their airy[7]
brows
Than has the[8] white breasts of the Queen
of Love;
From Venice shall they drag[9] huge
argosies,   130
And from America the golden fleece
That yearly stuffs old Philip's treasury,
If learned Faustus will be resolute.
FAUST. Valdes, as resolute am I in this
As thou to live; therefore object it
not.

[1] Vile.   [5] Servants, *i.e.*, spirits.
[2] Lectures.   [6] German cavalry.
[3] Spirits, here shown in a mirror. [7] Ethereal.
[4] American Indians.
[8] From 1616 edn. Original has *Then in their.*
[9] From 1609 edn. Original has *For Venice
shall they dregge* (dredge?).

CORN. The miracles that magic will per-
form
Will make thee vow to study nothing
else.
He that is grounded in astrology,
Enriched with tongues, well seen[10] [in][11]
minerals,
Hath all the principles magic doth re-
quire.   140
Then doubt not, Faustus, but to be
renowmed,
And more frequented for this mystery
Than heretofore the Delphian oracle.
The spirits tell me they can dry the
sea,
And fetch the treasure of all foreign
wracks,
Ay, all the wealth that our forefathers
hid
Within the massy entrails of the earth.
Then tell me, Faustus, what shall we
three want?
FAUST. Nothing, Cornelius! O, this cheers
my soul!
Come, show me some demonstrations
magical,   150
That I may conjure in some lusty
grove,
And have these joys in full posses-
sion.
VALD. Then haste thee to some solitary
grove,
And bear wise Bacon's and Albanus'
works,
The Hebrew Psalter and New Testa-
ment;
And whatsoever else is requisite
We will inform thee ere our conference
cease.
CORN. Valdes, first let him know the words
of art,
And then, all other ceremonies learned,
Faustus may try his cunning by him-
self.
VALD. First I'll instruct thee in the rudi-
ments,   161
And then wilt thou be perfecter than I.
FAUST. Then come and dine with me, and
after meat
We'll canvass every quiddity thereof;
For ere I sleep I'll try what I can do.
This night I'll conjure though I die
therefor.   *Exeunt.*
[10] Versed.   [11] From 1616 edn.

[SCENE ii.

Before Faustus' house.]

Enter two Scholars.

1 SCH. I wonder what's become of Faustus that was wont to make our schools ring with *sic probo?* [1]

2 SCH. That shall we know, for see here comes his boy.

Enter Wagner.

1 SCH. How now, sirrah! Where's thy master?

WAG. God in heaven knows!

2 SCH. Why, dost not thou know?

WAG. Yes, I know. But that fol- [10 lows not.

1 SCH. Go to, sirrah! Leave your jesting, and tell us where he is.

WAG. That follows not necessary by force of argument, that you, being licentiate, should stand upon 't; therefore, acknowledge your error and be attentive.

2 SCH. Why, didst thou not say thou knew'st?

WAG. Have you any witness on 't? [20

1 SCH. Yes, sirrah, I heard you.

WAG. Ask my fellow if I be a thief.

2 SCH. Well, you will not tell us?

WAG. Yes, sir, I will tell you; yet if you were not dunces, you would never ask me such a question, for is not he *corpus naturale*,[2] and is not that *mobile?*[2] Then wherefore should you ask me such a question? But that I am by nature phlegmatic, slow to wrath, and prone to lechery (to [30 love, I would say), it were not for you to come within forty foot of the place of execution,[3] although I do not doubt to see you both hanged the next sessions. Thus having triumphed over you, I will set my countenance like a precisian,[4] and begin to speak thus: "Truly, my dear brethren, my master is within at dinner with Valdes and Cornelius, as this wine, if it could speak, would inform your worships; and so [40 the Lord bless you, preserve you, and keep you, my dear brethren, my dear brethren." *Exit.*

[1] Thus I prove.
[2] Terms used in the physics of the day.
[3] The room within, where Faustus is dining.
[4] Puritan.

1 SCH. Nay, then, I fear he has fallen into that damned art for which they two are infamous through the world.

2 SCH. Were he a stranger, and not allied to me, yet should I grieve for him. But come, let us go and inform the rector, and see if he by his grave counsel can reclaim him. 51

1 SCH. O, but I fear me nothing can reclaim him.

2 SCH. Yet let us try what we can do.
Exeunt.

[SCENE iii.

A grove.]

Enter Faustus to conjure.

FAUST. Now that the gloomy shadow of the earth,
Longing to view Orion's drizzling look,
Leaps from th' antartic world unto the sky,
And dims the welkin with her pitchy breath,
Faustus, begin thine incantations,
And try if devils will obey thy hest,[5]
Seeing thou hast prayed and sacrificed to them.
Within this circle is Jehovah's name,
Forward and backward anagrammatized,[6]
The breviated names of holy saints, 10
Figures of every adjunct[7] to the heavens,
And characters of signs and erring stars,[8]
By which the spirits are enforced to rise.
Then fear not, Faustus, but be resolute,
And try the uttermost magic can perform.

Sint mihi Dei Acherontis propitii! Valeat numen triplex Jehovæ! Ignei, aerii, aquatani spiritus, salvete! Orientis Princeps, Belzebub, inferni ardentis monarcha, et Demogorgon, propitiamus vos, ut appareat [20 *et surgat Mephistophilis.*[9] *Quid tu moraris?*[10]

[5] Behest, command.
[6] From 1616 edn. Original has *and Agramithist.*
[7] *I.e.,* star.
[8] Moving stars, *i.e.,* planets.
[9] The spelling of this name varies in the original.
[10] Suggested by Schröer; original has *Quod tumeraris.*

Per Jehovam, Gehennam, et consecratam
aquam quam nunc spargo, signumque crucis
quod nunc facio, et per vota nostra, ipse
nunc surgat nobis dicatus Mephistophilis! [1]

Enter [Mephistophilis,] a Devil.

I charge thee to return and change thy
    shape;
Thou art too ugly to attend on me.
Go, and return an old Franciscan friar;
That holy shape becomes a devil best.
                         Exit Devil.
I see there's virtue in my heavenly
    words.   30
Who would not be proficient in this art?
How pliant is this Mephistophilis,
Full of obedience and humility!
Such is the force of magic and my spells.
No, Faustus, thou art conjuror laureate,
That canst command great Mephis-
    tophilis;
Quin regis, Mephistophilis, fratris ima-
    gine. [2]

Enter Mephistophilis [as a Franciscan
                        friar].

MEPH. Now, Faustus, what wouldst thou
    have me do?
FAUST. I charge thee wait upon me whilst
    I live,
To do whatever Faustus shall com-
    mand,   40
Be it to make the moon drop from her
    sphere,
Or the ocean to overwhelm the world.
MEPH. I am a servant to great Lucifer,
And may not follow thee without his
    leave;
No more than he commands must we
    perform.
FAUST. Did he not charge thee to appear to
    me?

[1] May the gods of Acheron be propitious
to me! Away with the threefold godhead of
Jehovah! Spirits of fire, air, water, hail! Belzebub, Prince of the East, monarch of burning
hell, and Demogorgon, we propitiate you, that
Mephistophilis may appear and rise. Why dost
thou delay? By Jehovah, Gehenna, and the
holy water which I now sprinkle, and the sign
of the cross which I now make, and by our
prayers, may Mephistophilis himself, invoked
by us, now rise!

[2] Verily thou rulest in the image of a brother
(*i.e.*, a friar), Mephistophilis.

MEPH. No, I came now hither of mine own
    accord.
FAUST. Did not my conjuring speeches
    raise thee? Speak!
MEPH. That was the cause, but yet per
    accident;
For, when we hear one rack the name of
    God,   56
Abjure the Scriptures and his Savior
    Christ,
We fly in hope to get his glorious soul;
Nor will we come, unless he use such
    means
Whereby he is in danger to be damned.
Therefore the shortest cut for conjur-
    ing
Is stoutly to abjure the Trinity,
And pray devoutly to the Prince of Hell.
FAUST. So Faustus hath
Already done, and holds this principle:
There is no chief but only Belzebub,   60
To whom Faustus doth dedicate him-
    self.
This word "damnation" terrifies not
    him,
For he confounds hell in Elysium. [3]
His ghost be with the old philosophers!
But, leaving these vain trifles of men's
    souls,
Tell me what is that Lucifer, thy lord?
MEPH. Arch-regent and commander of all
    spirits.
FAUST. Was not that Lucifer an angel
    once?
MEPH. Yes, Faustus, and most dearly
    loved of God.
FAUST. How comes it then that he is
    prince of devils?   70
MEPH. O, by aspiring pride and insolence,
For which God threw him from the face
    of heaven.
FAUST. And what are you that live with
    Lucifer?
MEPH. Unhappy spirits that fell with
    Lucifer,
Conspired against our God with Lucifer,
And are forever damned with Lucifer.
FAUST. Where are you damned?
MEPH. In hell.
FAUST. How comes it then that thou **art**
    out of hell?
MEPH. Why, this is hell, nor am I out of
    it.   80

[3] *I.e.*, makes no distinction between them.

Think'st thou that I who saw the face of
God,
And tasted the eternal joys of heaven,
Am not tormented with ten thousand
hells,
In being deprived of everlasting bliss?
O Faustus, leave these frivolous de-
mands,
Which strike a terror to my fainting soul!

FAUST. What, is great Mephistophilis so
passionate [1]
For being deprived of the joys of heaven?
Learn thou of Faustus manly fortitude,
And scorn those joys thou never shalt
possess.   90
Go bear those tidings to great Lucifer:
Seeing Faustus hath incurred eternal
death
By desp'rate thoughts against Jove's
deity,
Say he surrenders up to him his soul,
So he will spare him four-and-twenty
years,
Letting him live in all voluptuousness,
Having thee ever to attend on me,
To give me whatsoever I shall ask,
To tell me whatsoever I demand,
To slay mine enemies, and aid my
friends,   100
And always be obedient to my will.
Go and return to mighty Lucifer,
And meet me in my study at midnight,
And then resolve [2] me of thy master's
mind.

MEPH. I will, Faustus.   Exit.

FAUST. Had I as many souls as there be
stars,
I'd give them all for Mephistophilis.
By him I'll be great emp'ror of the
world,
And make a bridge through the moving
air,
To pass the ocean with a band of men. 110
I'll join the hills that bind the Afric
shore,
And make that land continent [3] to
Spain,
And both contributory to my crown.
The emp'ror shall not live but by my
leave,
Nor any potentate of Germany.
Now that I have obtained what I de-
sire,

I'll live in speculation [4] of this art
Till Mephistophilis return again.   Exit.

[SCENE iv.

A street.]

Enter Wagner and the Clown.

WAG. Sirrah boy, come hither.

CLO. How, "boy"? Swowns,[5] "boy"! I
hope you have seen many boys with such
pickadevaunts [6] as I have. "Boy," quotha!

WAG. Tell me, sirrah, hast thou any
comings-in?

CLO. Ay, and goings-out too. You
may see else.

WAG. Alas, poor slave! See how poverty
jesteth in his nakedness! The villain is [10
bare and out of service, and so hungry
that I know he would give his soul to the
devil for a shoulder of mutton, though it
were blood-raw.

CLO. How? My soul to the devil for
a shoulder of mutton, though 'twere
blood-raw! Not so, good friend. Bur [7]
Lady, I had need have it well roasted and
good sauce to it, if I pay so dear.

WAG. Well, wilt thou serve me, and [20
I'll make thee go like "*Qui mihi discipu-
lus?*" [8]

CLO. How, in verse?

WAG. No, sirrah; in beaten [9] silk and
stavesacre.[10]

CLO. How, how, Knave's Acre! [11] Ay,
I thought that was all the land his father
left him. Do you hear? I would be sorry
to rob you of your living.

WAG. Sirrah, I say in stavesacre.   30

CLO. Oho! Oho! Stavesacre! Why, then,
belike if I were your man I should be full
of vermin.

WAG. So thou shalt, whether thou beest
with me or no. But, sirrah, leave your
jesting, and bind yourself presently [12] unto
me for seven years, or I'll turn all the lice
about thee into familiars,[13] and they shall
tear thee in pieces.

---

[1] Moved.   [2] Inform.   [3] Contiguous.

[4] Contemplation, study.   [6] Pointed beards.
[5] God's wounds.   [7] By'r, by our.
[8] "You who are my pupil" (Dyce notes that the
source of this phrase is William Lilly's *Ad dis-
cipulos carmen de moribus*).
[9] Stamped with metal and embroidered.
[10] Larkspur, used as lice-killer.
[11] A low street in London.
[12] Immediately.   [13] Familiar spirits.

CLO. Do you hear, sir? You may [40 save that labor; they are too familiar with me already. Swowns! They are as bold with my flesh as if they had paid for my meat and drink.

WAG. Well, do you hear, sirrah? Hold, take these guilders.   [Gives money.]

CLO. Gridirons! What be they?

WAG. Why, French crowns.

CLO. Mass, but for the name of French crowns, a man were as good have as [50 many English counters. And what should I do with these?

WAG. Why, now, sirrah, thou art at an hour's warning, whensoever and wheresoever the devil shall fetch thee.

CLO. No, no. Here, take your gridirons again.

WAG. Truly, I'll none of them.

CLO. Truly, but you shall.

WAG. Bear witness I gave them him.

CLO. Bear witness I give them you [61 again.

WAG. Well, I will cause two devils presently to fetch thee away—Baliol and Belcher.

CLO. Let your Balio and your Belcher come here, and I'll knock them, they were never so knocked since they were devils. Say I should kill one of them, what would folks say? "Do you see [70 yonder tall [1] fellow in the round slop? [2]— He has killed the devil." So I should be called Kill-devil all the parish over.

Enter two Devils, and the Clown runs up and down crying.

WAG. Baliol and Belcher!   Spirits, away!   *Exeunt [Devils].*

CLO. What, are they gone? A vengeance on them, they have vild long nails! There was a he-devil and a she-devil! I'll tell you how you shall know them: all he-devils has horns, and all she-devils has clifts [3] and cloven feet.   81

WAG. Well, sirrah, follow me.

CLO. But, do you hear—if I should serve you, would you teach me to raise up Banios and Belcheos?

WAG. I will teach thee to turn thyself to anything—to a dog, or a cat, or a mouse, or a rat, or anything.

CLO. How? A Christian fellow to a

[1] Brave.   [2] Wide breeches.   [3] Clefts.

dog or a cat, a mouse or a rat? No, [90 no, sir. If you turn me into anything, let it be in the likeness of a little pretty frisking flea, that I may be here and there and everywhere. O, I'll tickle the pretty wenches' plackets; I'll be amongst them, i' faith.

WAG. Well, sirrah, come.

CLO. But, do you hear, Wagner?

WAG. How!—Baliol and Belcher!

CLO. O Lord! I pray, sir, let Banio and Belcher go sleep.   101

WAG. Villain, call me Master Wagner, and let thy left eye be diametarily [4] fixed upon my right heel, with *quasi vestigias nostras insistere.* [5]   *Exit.*

CLO. God forgive me, he speaks Dutch fustian. Well, I'll follow him; I'll serve him; that's flat.   *Exit.*

[SCENE v.]

Enter Faustus in his study.

FAUST. Now, Faustus, must thou needs be damned,
And canst thou not be saved.
What boots it then to think of God or heaven?
Away with such vain fancies, and despair.[6]
Despair in God, and trust in Belzebub.
Now go not backward; no, Faustus, be resolute.
Why waverest thou?   O, something soundeth in mine ears:
"Abjure this magic; turn to God again!"
Ay, and Faustus will turn to God again
To God?—He loves thee not.   10
The God thou servest is thine own appetite,
Wherein is fixed the love of Belzebub.
To him I'll build an altar and a church,
And offer lukewarm blood of newborn babes.

Enter Good Angel and Evil.

GOOD A. Sweet Faustus, leave that execrable art!

FAUST. Contrition, prayer, repentance! What of them?

GOOD A. O, they are means to bring thee unto heaven.

[4] Wagner's blunder for *diametrically.*
[5] As if to walk in my footsteps.
[6] Be without hope.

EVIL A. Rather illusions, fruits of lunacy,
That makes men foolish that do trust
    them most.
GOOD A. Sweet Faustus, think of heaven
    and heavenly things.   20
EVIL A. No, Faustus, think of honor
    and [of] wealth!   *Exeunt [Angels].*
FAUST. Of wealth!
    Why, the signiory of Emden shall be
    mine.
    When Mephistophilis shall stand by me,
    What God can hurt thee, Faustus?
    Thou art safe;
    Cast no more doubts. Come, Mephis-
    tophilis,
    And bring glad tidings from great Luci-
    fer.
    Is't not midnight? Come, Mephistoph-
    ilis;
    Veni,[1] *veni, Mephistophile!*

Enter Meph[istophilis].

    Now tell [me],[2] what says Lucifer, thy
    lord?   30
MEPH. That I shall wait on Faustus
    whilst he lives,[3]
    So he will buy my service with his soul.
FAUST. Already Faustus hath hazarded
    that for thee.
MEPH. But, Faustus, thou must bequeath
    it solemnly,
    And write a deed of gift with thine own
    blood,
    For that security craves great Lucifer.
    If thou deny it, I will back to hell.
FAUST. Stay, Mephistophilis, and tell me
    what good
    Will my soul do thy lord.
MEPH.   Enlarge his kingdom.
FAUST. Is that the reason he tempts us
    thus?   40
MEPH. *Solamen miseris socios habuisse
    doloris.*[4]
FAUST. Have you any pain that tortures
    others?
MEPH. As great as have the human souls
    of men.
    But tell me, Faustus, shall I have thy
    soul?

[1] Come.   [2] From 1616 edn.
[3] From 1616 edn. Original has *I live.*
[4] It is a solace to the wretched to have had
companions in sorrow.

And I will be thy slave, and wait on
    thee,
    And give thee more than thou hast wit
    to ask.
FAUST. Ay, Mephistophilis, I give it
    thee.
MEPH. Then stab thine arm courageously,
    And bind thy soul that at some certain
    day
    Great Lucifer may claim it as his own; 50
    And then be thou as great as Lucifer.
FAUST. [*Stabbing his arm.*] Lo, Mephis-
    tophilis, for love of thee
    I cut mine arm, and with my proper [5]
    blood
    Assure my soul to be great Lucifer's,
    Chief lord and regent of perpetual
    night!
    View here the blood that trickles from
    mine arm,
    And let it be propitious for my wish.
MEPH. But, Faustus, thou must
    Write it in manner of a deed of gift.
FAUST. Ay, so I will.   [*Writes.*]   But,
    Mephistophilis,   60
    My blood congeals, and I can write no
    more.
MEPH. I'll fetch thee fire to dissolve it
    straight.   *Exit.*
FAUST. What might the staying of my
    blood portend?
    Is it unwilling I should write this bill?
    Why streams it not that I may write
    afresh?
    "Faustus gives to thee his soul." Ah,
    there it stayed.
    Why shouldst thou not? Is not thy
    soul thine own?
    Then write again, "Faustus gives to
    thee his soul."

Enter Mephistophilis with a chafer[6] *of
    coals.*

MEPH. Here's fire. Come, Faustus, set
    it on.
FAUST. So now the blood begins to clear
    again;   70
    Now will I make an end immediately.
            [*Writes.*]
MEPH. [*Aside.*] O, what will not I do to
    obtain his soul?
FAUST. *Consummatum est:*[7] this bill is
    ended,

[5] Own.   [6] Portable grate.   [7] It is finished.

And Faustus hath bequeathed his soul
to Lucifer.
But what is this inscription on mine arm?
"*Homo, fuge!*" [1] Whither should I fly?
If unto God, he'll throw me down to
hell.
My senses are deceived; here's nothing
writ.
I see it plain; here in this place is writ,
"*Homo, fuge!*" Yet shall not Faustus
fly.   80
MEPH. I'll fetch him somewhat to de-
light his mind.   *Exit.*

*Enter with Devils, giving crowns and rich
    apparel to Faustus, and dance, and
                            then depart.*

FAUST. Speak, Mephistophilis, what means
this show?
MEPH. Nothing, Faustus, but to delight
thy mind withal,
And to show thee what magic can per-
form.
FAUST. But may I raise up spirits when I
please?
MEPH. Ay, Faustus, and do greater
things than these.
FAUST. Then there's enough for a thou-
sand souls.
Here, Mephistophilis, receive this scroll,
A deed of gift of body and of soul—
But yet conditionally that thou perform   90
All articles prescribed between us both.
MEPH. Faustus, I swear by hell and Lucifer
To effect all promises between us made.
FAUST. Then hear me read them: "On
these conditions following:—First, that
Faustus may be a spirit in form and substance; secondly, that Mephistophilis
shall be his servant, and at his command;
thirdly, that Mephistophilis shall do for
him and bring him whatsoever; [2] [100
fourthly, that he shall be in his chamber or
house invisible; lastly, that he shall appear
to the said John Faustus, at all times, in
what form or shape soever he please—I,
John Faustus, of Wertenberg, Doctor, by
these presents do give both body and soul
to Lucifer, Prince of the East, and his
minister, Mephistophilis; and further-

more grant unto them that, four-and-
twenty years being expired, the articles [110
above written inviolate, full power to fetch
or carry the said John Faustus, body and
soul, flesh, blood, or goods, into their
habitation wheresoever.   By me, John
Faustus."
MEPH. Speak, Faustus, do you deliver
this as your deed?
FAUST. Ay, take it, and the devil give
thee good on 't.
MEPH. Now, Faustus, ask what thou
wilt.
FAUST. First will I question with thee
about hell.
Tell me, where is the place that men call
hell?   120
MEPH. Under the heavens.
FAUST.   Ay, but whereabout?
MEPH. Within the bowels of these ele-
ments,
Where we are tortured and remain for-
ever.
Hell hath no limits, nor is circumscribed
In one self [3] place, for where we are is
hell,
And where hell is [there] [4] must we ever
be;
And, to conclude, when all the world
dissolves,
And every creature shall be purified,
All places shall be hell that is not heaven.
FAUST. Come, I think hell's a fable.   130
MEPH. Ay, think so still, till experience
change thy mind.
FAUST. Why, think'st thou then that
Faustus shall be damned?
MEPH. Ay, of necessity, for here's the
scroll
Wherein thou hast given thy soul to
Lucifer.
FAUST. Ay, and body too; but what of
that?
Think'st thou that Faustus is so fond [5]
to imagine
That, after this life, there is any pain?
Tush, these are trifles, and mere old
wives' tales.
MEPH. But, Faustus, I am an instance
to prove the contrary,   139
For I am damnéd, and am now in hell.
FAUST. How? Now in hell? Nay, and [6]

[1] "Man, fly!"   [2] Ellipsis for *whatsoever it be.*

[3] One and the same.   [5] Foolish.
[4] Added from 1616 edn.   [6] If

this be hell, I'll willingly be damned here. What? Walking, disputing, etc.? But, leaving off this, let me have a wife, the fairest maid in Germany, for I am wanton and lascivious, and cannot live without a wife.

MEPH. How? A wife? I prithee, Faustus, talk not of a wife.

FAUST. Nay, sweet Mephistophilis, fetch me one, for I will have one.   151

MEPH. Well—thou wilt have one. Sit there till I come. I'll fetch thee a wife in the devil's name.   [*Exit.*]

Enter with a Devil dressed like a woman,
with fireworks.

MEPH. Tell, Faustus, how dost thou like thy wife?

FAUST. A plague on her for a hot whore!

MEPH.   Tut, Faustus,
Marriage is but a ceremonial toy;
If thou lovest me, think [no] [1] more of it.
I'll cull thee out the fairest courte-
sans,
And bring them every morning to thy
bed.   160
She whom thine eye shall like, thy heart
shall have,
Be she as chaste as was Penelope,
As wise as Saba,[2] or as beautiful
As was bright Lucifer before his fall.
Hold, take this book; peruse it thor-
oughly.   [*Gives a book.*]
The iterating of these lines brings gold;
The framing of this circle on the ground
Brings whirlwinds, tempests, thunder,
and lightning;
Pronounce this thrice devoutly to thy-
self,   169
And men in armor shall appear to thee,
Ready to execute what thou desir'st.

FAUST. Thanks, Mephistophilis; yet fain would I have a book wherein I might be-hold all spells and incantations, that I might raise up spirits when I please.

MEPH. Here they are, in this book.
        There turn to them.

FAUST. Now would I have a book where I might see all characters and planets of the heavens, that I might know their mo-tions and dispositions.[3]   180

MEPH. Here they are too.
        Turn to them.

FAUST. Nay, let me have one book more—and then I have done—wherein I might see all plants, herbs, and trees that grow upon the earth.

MEPH. Here they be.

FAUST. O, thou art deceived.

MEPH. Tut, I warrant thee.
        Turn to them.
        [*Exeunt.*]

[SCENE vi.

The same.

Enter Faustus in his study and Mephis-
tophilis.] [4]

FAUST. When I behold the heavens, then
I repent,
And curse thee, wicked Mephistophilis,
Because thou hast deprived me of those
joys.

MEPH. Why, Faustus,
Think'st thou heaven is such a glorious
thing?
I tell thee 'tis not half so fair as thou,
Or any man that breathes on earth.

FAUST. How provest thou that?

MEPH. It was made for man; therefore
is man more excellent.

FAUST. If it were made for man, 'twas
made for me;   10
I will renounce this magic and repent.

Enter Good Angel and Evil Angel.

GOOD A. Faustus, repent; yet God will
pity thee.

EVIL A. Thou art a spirit; God cannot
pity thee.

FAUST. Who buzzeth in mine ears I am a
spirit?
Be I a devil, yet God may pity me;
Ay, God will pity me if I repent.

EVIL A. Ay, but Faustus never shall repent.   *Exeunt* [*Angels*].

FAUST. My heart's so hardened I cannot
repent.
Scarce can I name salvation, faith, or
heaven,
But fearful echoes thunders in mine
ears,   20

_____
[1] Added from 1609 edn.   [2] Sheba.
[3] Situations in relation to their influence upon men.

[4] Stage direction from 1616 edn.

"Faustus, thou art damned!" Then
  swords and knives,
Poison, guns, halters, and envenomed
  steel
Are laid before me to despatch myself,
And long ere this I should have slain
  myself,
Had not sweet pleasure conquered deep
  despair.
Have not I made blind Homer sing to
  me
Of Alexander's love and Œnon's death?
And hath not he that built the walls of
  Thebes
With ravishing sound of his melodious
  harp
Made music with my Mephistophilis? 30
Why should I die then, or basely despair?
I am resolved: Faustus shall ne'er re-
  pent.
Come, Mephistophilis, let us dispute
  again,
And argue of divine astrology.
Tell me, are there many heavens above
  the moon?
Are all celestial bodies but one globe,
As is the substance of this centric earth?
Meph. As are the elements, such are the
  spheres
Mutually folded in each other's orb,
And, Faustus,   40
All jointly move upon one axletree
Whose terminine [1] is termed the world's
  wide pole;
Nor are the names of Saturn, Mars, or
  Jupiter
Feigned, but are erring stars.
Faust. But tell me, have they all one
motion, both *situ et tempore?* [2]
Meph. All jointly move from east to
west in four-and-twenty hours upon the
poles of the world, but differ in their motion
upon the poles of the zodiac.   50
Faust. Tush, these slender trifles Wagner
  can decide.
Hath Mephistophilis no greater skill?
Who knows not the double motion of the
  planets?
The first is finished in a natural day;
the second thus: as Saturn in thirty years;
Jupiter in twelve; Mars in four; the sun,
Venus, and Mercury in a year; the moon
in eight-and-twenty days. Tush, these are

[1] Limit.   [2] In space and in time.

freshmen's suppositions. But tell me, hath
every sphere a dominion or *intelligentia?* [3] [60
Meph. Ay.
Faust. How many heavens, or spheres,
are there?
Meph. Nine: the seven planets, the
firmament, and the imperial [4] heaven.
Faust. Well, resolve me in this question: Why have we not conjunctions, oppo-
sitions, aspects, eclipses, all at one time, but
in some years we have more, in some less?
Meph. *Per inæqualem motum respectu*
  totius. [5]   70
Faust. Well, I am answered. Tell me who
  made the world.
Meph. I will not.
Faust. Sweet Mephistophilis, tell me.
Meph. Move me not, for I will not tell
  thee.
Faust. Villain, have I not bound thee to
  tell me anything?
Meph. Ay, that is not against our king-
  dom; but this is.
Think thou on hell, Faustus, for thou art
  damned.
Faust. Think, Faustus, upon God that
  made the world.
Meph. Remember this.   *Exit.*
Faust. Ay, go, accursèd spirit, to ugly hell.
'Tis thou hast damned distressèd Faus-
  tus' soul.   80
Is't not too late?

Enter Good Angel, and Evil.

Evil A. Too late.
Good A. Never too late, if Faustus can
  repent.
Evil A. If thou repent, devils shall tear
  thee in pieces.
Good A. Repent, and they shall never
  rase [6] thy skin.   *Exeunt [Angels].*
Faust. Ah, Christ, my Savior,
  Seek to save distressèd Faustus' soul!

*Enter Lucifer, Belzebub, and Mephis-
               tophilis.*

Luc. Christ cannot save thy soul, for he is
  just;
  There's none but I have int'rest in the
  same.

[3] Intelligence, spirit. From 1616 edn.; original
has *intelligentii.*   [4] Empyreal.
[5] Because of their uneven motion in regard to
the whole.   [6] Scratch.

FAUST. O, who art thou that look'st so terrible? 90

LUC. I am Lucifer,

And this is my companion prince in hell.

FAUST. O Faustus, they are come to fetch away thy soul!

LUC. We come to tell thee thou dost injure us.

Thou talk'st of Christ, contrary to thy promise;

Thou shouldst not think of God. Think of the devil,

And of his dame, too.

FAUST. Nor will I henceforth. Pardon me in this,

And Faustus vows never to look to heaven, 99

Never to name God, or to pray to him;

To burn his Scriptures, slay his ministers,

And make my spirits pull his churches down.

LUC. Do so, and we will highly gratify [1] thee. Faustus, we are come from hell to show thee some pastime. Sit down, and thou shalt see all the Seven Deadly Sins appear in their proper shapes.

FAUST. That sight will be as pleasing unto me

As paradise was to Adam the first day Of his creation. 110

LUC. Talk not of paradise nor creation, but mark this show. Talk of the devil, and nothing else.—Come away!

Enter the Seven Deadly Sins.

Now, Faustus, examine them of their several names and dispositions.

FAUST. What art thou, the first?

PRIDE. I am Pride. I disdain to have any parents. I am like to Ovid's flea: I can creep into every corner of a wench. [119 Sometimes, like a periwig, I sit upon her brow; or, like a fan of feathers, I kiss her lips; indeed I do—what do I not? But, fie, what a scent is here! I'll not speak another word except the ground were perfumed, and covered with cloth of arras.

FAUST. What art thou, the second?

COVET. I am Covetousness, begotten of an old churl in an old leathern bag; and, might I have my wish, I would desire that this house and all the people in it [130

were turned to gold, that I might lock you up in my good chest. O, my sweet gold!

FAUST. What art thou, the third?

WRATH. I am Wrath. I had neither father nor mother. I leaped out of a lion's mouth when I was scarce half an hour old and, ever since, I have run up and down the world with this case [2] of rapiers, wounding myself when I had nobody to fight withal. I was born in hell; and look to it, [140 for some of you shall be my father.

FAUST. What art thou, the fourth?

ENVY. I am Envy, begotten of a chimney sweeper and an oyster wife. I cannot read, and therefore wish all books were burnt. I am lean with seeing others eat. O, that there would come a famine through all the world, that all might die, and I live alone! Then thou shouldst see how fat I would be. But must thou sit and I [150 stand? Come down with a vengeance!

FAUST. Away, envious rascal!—What art thou, the fifth?

GLUT. Who, I, sir? I am Gluttony. My parents are all dead, and the devil a penny they have left me but a bare pension, and that is thirty meals a day and ten bevers [3]— a small trifle to suffice nature. O, I come of a royal parentage! My grandfather was a Gammon of Bacon, my grandmother [160 a Hogshead of Claret Wine. My godfathers were these—Peter Pickleherring and Martin Martlemas-beef. O, but my godmother she was a jolly gentlewoman, and well beloved in every good town and city. Her name was Mistress Margery Marchbeer. Now,[4] Faustus, thou hast heard all my progeny,[5] wilt thou bid me to supper?

FAUST. No, I'll see thee hanged; thou wilt eat up all my victuals. 170

GLUT. Then the devil choke thee!

FAUST. Choke thyself, glutton!—What art thou, the sixth?

SLOTH. I am Sloth. I was begotten on a sunny bank, where I have lain ever since; and you have done me great injury to bring me from thence. Let me be carried thither again by Gluttony and Lechery. I'll not speak another word for a king's ransom.

FAUST. What are you, Mistress Minx, the seventh and last? 180

LECH. Who, I, sir? I am one that loves

---

[1] Reward.

[2] Pair. [4] Now that.

[3] Refreshments between meals. [5] Lineage.

an inch of raw mutton better than an ell of fried stockfish; and the first letter of my name begins with Lechery.

Luc.[1] Away to hell, to hell! (*Exeunt the Sins.*)—Now, Faustus, how dost thou like this?

Faust. O, this feeds my soul!

Luc. Tut, Faustus, in hell is all manner of delight.　　　　　　　　　　　190

Faust. O, might I see hell, and return again,

How happy were I then!

Luc. Thou shalt; I will send for thee at midnight.

In meantime take this book; peruse it throughly,

And thou shalt turn thyself into what shape thou wilt.

Faust. Great thanks, mighty Lucifer!

This will I keep as chary as my life.

Luc. Farewell, Faustus, and think on the devil.

Faust. Farewell, great Lucifer! Come, Mephistophilis.　　　　　*Exeunt omnes.*

[Chorus]
Enter Wagner solus.[2]

Wag. Learned Faustus,　　　　　　200

To know the secrets of astronomy

Graven in the book of Jove's high firmament,

Did mount himself to scale Olympus' top,

Being seated in a chariot burning bright,

Drawn by the strength of yoky dragons' necks.

He now is gone to prove cosmography,

And, as I guess, will first arrive at Rome,

To see the pope and manner of his court,

And take some part of holy Peter's feast,　　　　　　　　　　　209

That to this day is highly solemnized.

Exit Wagner.

[Scene vii.
The Pope's privy chamber.]

Enter Faustus and Mephistophilis.

Faust. Having now, my good Mephistophilis,

Passed with delight the stately town of Trier,

Environed round with airy mountain tops,

With walls of flint, and deep entrenchéd lakes,[3]

Not to be won by any conquering prince,

From Paris next, coasting [4] the realm of France,

We saw the river Maine fall into Rhine,

Whose banks are set with groves of fruitful vines;

Then up to Naples, rich Campania,

Whose buildings fair and gorgeous to the eye,　　　　　　　　　　　　10

The streets straight forth, and paved with finest brick,

Quarters the town in four equivalents.

There saw we learned Maro's golden tomb,

The way he cut, an English mile in length,

Thorough a rock of stone in one night's space;[5]

From thence to Venice, Padua, and the rest,

In midst of which a sumptuous temple stands,

That threats the stars with her aspiring top.

Thus hitherto hath Faustus spent his time.

But tell me, now, what resting place is this?　　　　　　　　　　　20

Hast thou, as erst I did command,

Conducted me within the walls of Rome?

Meph. Faustus, I have; and, because we will not be unprovided, I have taken up his holiness' privy chamber for our use.

Faust. I hope his holiness will bid us welcome.

Meph. Tut, 'tis no matter, man; we'll be bold with his good cheer.

And now, my Faustus, that thou mayst perceive

What Rome containeth to delight thee with,　　　　　　　　　　　　30

Know that this city stands upon seven hills

That underprops the groundwork of the same.

[Just through the midst runs flowing Tiber's stream,

With winding banks that cut it in two parts,][6]

---

[1] Placed before *Now, Faustus* in the original.
[2] 1616 edn. reads *Enter the Chorus.*
[3] Moats.　　　　　　　　　　[4] Skirting.
[5] Virgil was regarded as a magician in the Middle Ages.　　　[6] From 1616 edn.

Over the which four stately bridges lean,
That makes safe passage to each part of
Rome.
Upon the bridge called Ponto Angelo,
Erected is a castle passing strong,
Within whose walls such store of ordo-
nance are,
And double cannons, framed of carvéd
brass,   40
As match the days within one complete
year,
Besides the gates and high pyramides,
Which Julius Cæsar brought from Africa.
FAUST. Now by the kingdoms of infernal
rule,
Of Styx, Acheron, and the fiery lake
Of ever-burning Phlegeton, I swear
That I do long to see the monuments
And situation of bright, splendent Rome.
Come therefore; let's away.
MEPH. Nay, Faustus, stay; I know you'd
fain see the pope,   50
And take some part of holy Peter's
feast,
Where thou shalt see a troop of baldpate
friars,
Whose *summum bonum* [1] is in belly-cheer.
FAUST. Well, I am content to compass then
some sport,
And by their folly make us merriment.
Then charm me, that I may be invisible,
to do what I please,
Unseen of any whilst I stay in Rome.
MEPH. [*Charming him.*] So, Faustus, now
Do what thou wilt; thou shalt not be
discerned.

Sound a sennet. [2] *Enter the Pope and the
Cardinal of Lorrain to the banket,* [3] *with
Friars attending.*

POPE. My Lord of Lorrain, wilt please you
draw near?   60
FAUST. Fall to, and the devil choke you,
and [4] you spare!
POPE. How now! Who's that which spake?
—Friars, look about.
FRIAR. Here's nobody, if it like your holi-
ness.
POPE. My lord, here is a dainty dish
was sent me from the Bishop of Milan.
FAUST. I thank you, sir.   *Snatch it.*

POPE. How now! Who's that which
snatched the meat from me? Will no man
look? My lord, this dish was sent me from
the Cardinal of Florence.   70
FAUST. You say true; I'll ha't.
                              [*Snatch it.*]
POPE. What, again? My lord, I'll drink
to your grace.
FAUST. I'll pledge your grace.
                          [*Snatch the cup.*]
LOR. My lord, it may be some ghost
newly crept out of purgatory, come to beg a
pardon of your holiness.
POPE. It may be so. Friars, prepare a
dirge to lay the fury of this ghost. Once
again, my lord, fall to.   80
                The Pope crosseth himself.
FAUST. What, are you crossing of your-
self?
Well, use that trick no more, I would
advise you.   *Cross again.*
Well, there's the second time. Aware the
third,
I give you fair warning.
*Cross again, and Faustus hits him a box of
the ear; and they all run away.*
FAUST. Come on, Mephistophilis, what
shall we do?
MEPH. Nay, I know not. We shall be
cursed with bell, book, and candle.
FAUST. How? Bell, book, and candle;
candle, book, and bell—
Forward and backward to curse Faustus
to hell!
Anon you shall hear a hog grunt, a calf
bleat, and an ass bray, because it is
S[aint] Peter's holiday.

Enter all the Friars to sing the dirge.

FRIAR. Come, brethren, let's about our
business with good devotion.   90
                              Sing this:
Cursed be he that stole away his holi-
ness' meat from the table! *Maledicat
Dominus!* [5]
Cursed be he that struck his holiness a
blow on the face! *Maledicat Dominus!*
Cursed be he that took Friar Sandelo a
blow on the pate! *Male., etc.*
Cursed be he that disturbeth our holy
dirge! *Male., etc.*
Cursed be he that took away his holi-

[1] Highest good.   [3] Banquet.
[2] Trumpet call. Original has *sonnet.* [4] If.

[5] The Lord curse him!

ness' wine! *Maledicat Dominus! Et omnes sancti!* [1] *Amen.*

[*Mephistophilis and Faustus*] *beat the Friars, and fling fireworks among them, and so exeunt.*

Enter Chorus.

When Faustus had with pleasure ta'en
    the view
Of rarest things and royal courts of kings,
He stayed his course, and so returnéd
    home,
Where such as bear his absence but with
    grief—   100
I mean his friends and nearest compan-
    ions—
Did gratulate his safety with kind words,
And in their conference of what befell,
Touching his journey through the world
    and air,
They put forth questions of astrology,
Which Faustus answered with such
    learned skill,
As they admired and wondered at his wit.
Now is his fame spread forth in every land.
Amongst the rest the emperor is one, 109
Carolus the Fifth, at whose palace now
Faustus is feasted 'mongst his noblemen.
What there he did in trial of his art,
I leave untold—your eyes shall see per-
    formed.   *Exit.*

[Scene viii.

An innyard.]

*Enter Robin the Ostler with a book in his
    hand.*

Robin. O, this is admirable! Here I ha'
stolen one of Doctor Faustus' conjuring
books, and i' faith I mean to search some
circles for my own use. [*Draws circles on
the ground.*] Now will I make all the
maidens in our parish dance at my pleasure, stark naked before me; and so by that
means I shall see more than e'er I felt or
saw yet.

Enter Rafe, calling Robin.

Rafe. Robin, prithee come away. [10
There's a gentleman tarries to have his
horse, and he would have his things rubbed
and made clean. He keeps such a chafing
with my mistress about it, and she has

sent me to look thee out. Prithee come
away.

Robin. Keep out, keep out, or else you
are blown up; you are dismembered, Rafe!
Keep out, for I am about a roaring piece
of work.   20

Rafe. Come, what doest thou with
that same book thou canst not read?

Robin. Yes, my master and mistress
shall find that I can read, he for his forehead, she for her private study. She's born
to bear with me, or else my art fails.

Rafe. Why, Robin, what book is that?

Robin. What book? Why, the most
intolerable book for conjuring that e'er was
invented by any brimstone devil.   30

Rafe. Canst thou conjure with it?

Robin. I can do all these things easily
with it: first, I can make thee drunk with
ippocras [2] at any tabern [3] in Europe for
nothing; that's one of my conjuring works.

Rafe. Our Master Parson says that's
nothing.

Robin. True, Rafe. And more, Rafe,
if thou hast any mind to Nan Spit, our
kitchenmaid, then turn her and wind [40
her to thy own use as often as thou wilt,
and at midnight.

Rafe. O brave Robin, shall I have Nan
Spit, and to mine own use? On that condition I'll feed thy devil with horse bread
as long as he lives, of free cost.

Robin. No more, sweet Rafe. Let's go
and make clean our boots, which lie foul
upon our hands, and then to our conjuring
in the devil's name.   *Exeunt.* 50

[Scene ix.

The same.]

Enter Robin and Rafe with a silver goblet.

Robin. Come, Rafe, did not I tell thee
we were forever made by this Doctor
Faustus' book? *Ecce signum.* [4] Here's a
simple purchase [5] for horse keepers; our
horses shall eat no hay as long as this lasts.

Enter the Vintner.

Rafe. But, Robin, here comes the
vintner.

Robin. Hush! I'll gull him supernatu-

---

[1] And all the saints.

[2] A sweetened, spiced wine.　　[4] Behold the sign.
[3] Tavern.　　　　　　　　　　　[5] Spoil, plunder.

rally. Drawer, I hope all is paid. God be
with you! Come, Rafe.   10

Vint. Soft, sir; a word with you. I must
yet have a goblet paid from you ere you go.

Robin. I a goblet? Rafe, I a goblet? I
scorn you, and you are but a &c. [1] I a
goblet? Search me!

Vint. I mean so, sir, with your favor.
                        [Searches him.]

Robin. How say you now?

Vint. I must say somewhat to your
fellow. You, sir!

Rafe. Me, sir? Me, sir? Search your [20
fill. [Vintner searches him.] Now, sir, you
may be ashamed to burden honest men
with a matter of truth.[2]

Vint. Well, t'one of you hath this
goblet about you.

Robin. [Aside.] You lie, drawer, 'tis
afore me.—Sirrah you, I'll teach ye to
impeach honest men! Stand by! I'll
scour you for a goblet! Stand aside you
had best, I charge you in the name   [30
of Belzebub.—[Aside to Rafe.] Look to the
goblet, Rafe.

Vint. What mean you, sirrah?

Robin. I'll tell you what I mean. (He
reads.) Sanctobulorum Periphrasticon!—
Nay, I'll tickle you, vintner.—[Aside.]
Look to the goblet, Rafe.—Polypragmos
Belseborams framanto pacostiphos tostu,
Mephistophilis, etc.[3]

Enter Mephistophilis, sets squibs at their
    backs [, and then exit]. They run about.

Vint. O, nomine Domine! [4] What   [40
mean'st thou, Robin, thou hast no goblet?

Rafe. Peccatum peccatorum! [5] Here's
thy goblet, good vintner.
   [Gives goblet to Vintner. Exit Vintner.]

Robin. Misericordia pro nobis! [6] What
shall I do? Good devil, forgive me now,
and I'll never rob thy library more.

      Enter to them Meph[istophilis].

Meph.[7] Monarch of hell, under whose
    black survey

  [1] Here the actor extemporizes.
  [2] Question of their honesty.
  [3] Latin and Greek gibberish used as an incantation.
  [4] Ungrammatical phrase for "O, in the name
of the Lord."   [5] Sin of sins!   [6] Mercy on us!
  [7] Here the original inserts two lines of prose
roughly approximating ll. 57–59.

Great potentates do kneel with awful
    fear,
Upon whose altars thousand souls do lie,
How am I vexéd with these villains'
    charms!   50
From Constantinople am I hither come
Only for pleasure of these damnéd slaves.

Robin. How, from Constantinople? You
have had a great journey. Will you take
sixpence in your purse to pay for your
supper, and be gone?

Meph. Well, villains, for your presumption I transform thee into an ape, and thee
into a dog. And so be gone.   Exit.

Robin. How, into an ape? That's [60
brave! I'll have fine sport with the boys.
I'll get nuts and apples enow.

Rafe. And I must be a dog.

Robin. I' faith, thy head will never be
out of the pottage pot.   Exeunt.

             [Scene x.

        The German Court.]

Enter Emperor, Faustus, [Mephistophilis,]
     and a Knight, with Attendants.

Emp. Master Doctor Faustus, I have
heard strange report of thy knowledge in
the black art, how that none in my empire
nor in the whole world can compare with
thee for the rare effects of magic. They say
thou hast a familiar spirit, by whom thou
canst accomplish what thou list.[8] This,
therefore, is my request, that thou let me
see some proof of thy skill, that mine eyes
may be witnesses to confirm what mine [10
ears have heard reported; and here I swear
to thee by the honor of mine imperial
crown that, whatever thou doest, thou
shalt be no ways prejudiced or endamaged.

Knight. (Aside.) I' faith, he looks much
like a conjuror.

Faust. My gracious sovereign, though
I must confess myself far inferior to the
report men have published, and nothing
answerable [9] to the honor of your im- [20
perial majesty, yet for that [10] love and duty
binds me thereunto, I am content to do
whatsoever your majesty shall command
me.

Emp. Then, Doctor Faustus, mark what I
    shall say.

  [8] Desirest.   [10] Because.
  [9] Not at all corresponding.

As I was sometime solitary set
Within my closet, sundry thoughts arose
About the honor of mine ancestors,
How they had won by prowess such ex-
    ploits,
Got such riches, subdued so many king-
    doms,   30
As we that do succeed, or they that shall
Hereafter possess our throne, shall,
I fear me, never attain to that degree
Of high renown and great authority;
Amongest which kings is Alexander the
    Great,
Chief spectacle of the world's preemi-
    nence,
The bright shining of whose glorious acts
Lightens the world with his reflecting
    beams,
As,[1] when I heard but motion[2] made of
    him,   39
It grieves my soul I never saw the man.
If, therefore, thou by cunning of thine
    art
Canst raise this man from hollow vaults
    below,
Where lies entombed this famous con-
    queror,
And bring with him his beauteous par-
    amour,
Both in their right shapes, gesture, and
    attire
They used to wear during their time of
    life,
Thou shalt both satisfy my just desire,
And give me cause to praise thee whilst
    I live.
FAUST. My gracious lord, I am ready to
accomplish your request so far forth as [50
by art and power of my spirit I am able to
perform.
KNIGHT. (*Aside.*) I' faith, that's just
nothing at all.
FAUST. But, if it like your grace, it is
not in my ability to present before your
eyes the true substantial bodies of those
two deceased princes, which long since are
consumed to dust.
KNIGHT. (*Aside.*) Ay, marry, Master [60
Doctor, now there's a sign of grace in you,
when you will confess the truth.
FAUST. But such spirits as can lively[3]
resemble Alexander and his paramour shall

appear before your grace in that manner
that they best lived in, in their most flourishing estate, which I doubt not shall sufficiently content your imperial majesty.
EMP. Go to, Master Doctor, let me see
them presently.   70
KNIGHT. Do you hear, Master Doctor?
You bring Alexander and his paramour
before the emperor!
FAUST. How then, sir?
KNIGHT. I' faith, that's as true as Diana
turned me to a stag!
FAUST. No, sir, but when Actæon died,
he left the horns for you. Mephistophilis,
begone!   *Exit Meph[istophilis].*
KNIGHT. Nay, and you go to con- [80
juring, I'll be gone.   *Exit Kn[ight].*
FAUST. I'll meet with you[4] anon for interrupting me so. Here they are, my gracious lord.

*Enter Meph[istophilis] with Alexander and
                    his Paramour.*

EMP. Master Doctor, I heard this lady
while she lived had a wart or mole in her
neck. How shall I know whether it be so
or no?
FAUST. Your highness may boldly go
and see.   90

*[Emperor examines her.]   Exit Alex[ander
                    with his Paramour].*

EMP. Sure, these are no spirits, but the
true substantial bodies of those two deceased princes.
FAUST. Will 't please your highness now
to send for the knight that was so pleasant
with me here of late?
EMP. One of you call him forth.
                        [Attendant calls.]

*Enter the Knight with a pair of horns on his
                    head.*

EMP. How now, Sir Knight! Why, I had
thought thou hadst been a bachelor, but
now I see thou hast a wife, that not [100
only gives thee horns, but makes thee wear
them. Feel on thy head!
KNIGHT. Thou damnéd wretch and ex-
    ecrable dog,
Bred in the concave[5] of some monstrous
    rock,

---

[1] So that.   [3] In a lifelike way.
[2] *I.e.,* mention.
[4] Get even with you.   [5] Hollow.

How dar'st thou thus abuse a gentleman?
Villain, I say, undo what thou hast done!

FAUST. O, not so fast, sir; there's no haste. But, good,[1] are you remembered how you crossed me in my conference with the emperor? I think I have met with [110 you for it.

EMP. Good Master Doctor, at my entreaty release him; he hath done penance sufficient.

FAUST. My gracious lord, not so much for the injury he offered me here in your presence, as to delight you with some mirth, hath Faustus worthily requited this injurious knight, which being all I desire, I am content to release him of his horns. [120 And, Sir Knight, hereafter speak well of scholars. Mephistophilis, transform him straight. [*Mephistophilis removes the horns.*] Now, my good lord, having done my duty, I humbly take my leave.

EMP. Farewell, Master Doctor; yet, ere you go,
Expect from me a bounteous reward.
         Exit Emperor [*with the Others*].

[SCENE xi.

A common.

Enter Faustus and Mephistophilis.]

FAUST. Now, Mephistophilis, the restless course
  That Time doth run with calm and silent foot,
  Short'ning my days and thread of vital life,
  Calls for the payment of my latest years;
  Therefore, sweet Mephistophilis, let us
  Make haste to Wertenberg.

MEPH. What, will you go on horseback or on foot?

FAUST. Nay, till I am past this fair and pleasant green, I'll walk on foot.

Enter a Horse-Corser.[2]

HORSE-C. I have been all this day seeking one Master Fustian. Mass, see [10 where he is! God save you, Master Doctor!

FAUST. What, horse-corser! You are well met.

HORSE-C. Do you hear, sir? I have brought you forty dollars for your horse.

[1] *I.e.*, good man.   [2] Horse dealer.

FAUST. I cannot sell him so. If thou lik'st him for fifty, take him.

HORSE-C. Alas, sir, I have no more.—I pray you speak for me.

MEPH. I pray you let him have him. [20 He is an honest fellow, and he has a great charge, neither wife nor child.

FAUST. Well, come, give me your money.
  [*Horse-Corser gives Faustus the money.*]
My boy will deliver him to you. But I must tell you one thing before you have him: ride him not into the water at any hand.[3]

HORSE-C. Why, sir, will he not drink of all waters?

FAUST. O, yes, he will drink of all waters, but ride him not into the water. [30 Ride him over hedge or ditch, or where thou wilt, but not into the water.

HORSE-C. Well, sir.—[*Aside.*] Now am I made man forever. I'll not leave my horse for forty. If he had but the quality of hey-ding-ding, hey-ding-ding, I'd make a brave living on him. He has a buttock as slick as an eel.—Well, God buy,[4] sir. Your boy will deliver him me. But hark ye, sir; if my horse be sick or ill at ease, if [40 I bring his water to you, you'll tell me what it is?   *Exit Horse-Corser.*

FAUST. Away, you villain! What, dost think I am a horse doctor?
        [*Retires into his study.*]

[SCENE xii.

Faustus' study.]

FAUST. What art thou, Faustus, but a man condemned to die?
  Thy fatal time doth draw to final end;
  Despair doth drive distrust into my thoughts;
  Confound these passions with a quiet sleep.
  Tush, Christ did call the thief upon the Cross;
  Then rest thee, Faustus, quiet in conceit.
        Sleep in his chair.

Enter Horse-Corser, all wet, crying.

HORSE-C. Alas, alas! Doctor Fustian, quotha? Mass, Doctor Lopus[5] was never

[3] In any case.   [4] God be with you (good bye).
[5] Dr. Lopez, Queen Elizabeth's physician, who was hanged in 1594 for a supposed attempt to poison her. This passage, therefore, could not have been written by Marlowe.

such a doctor. Has given me a purgation, has purged me of forty dollars; I shall [10 never see them more. But yet, like an ass as I was, I would not be ruled by him, for he bade me I should ride him into no water. Now I, thinking my horse had had some rare quality that he would not have had me known of, I, like a vent'rous youth, rid him into the deep pond at the town's end. I was no sooner in the middle of the pond, but my horse vanished away, and I sat upon a bottle [1] of hay, never so near [20 drowning in my life. But I'll seek out my doctor, and have my forty dollars again, or I'll make it the dearest horse!—

[Enter Mephistophilis.]

O, yonder is his snipper-snapper.—Do you hear? You hey-pass,[2] where's your master?

MEPH. Why, sir, what would you? You cannot speak with him.

HORSE-C. But I will speak with him.

MEPH. Why, he's fast asleep. Come some other time.   30

HORSE-C. I'll speak with him now, or I'll break his glass windows [3] about his ears.

MEPH. I tell thee he has not slept this eight nights.

HORSE-C. And he have not slept this eight weeks, I'll speak with him.

MEPH. See where he is, fast asleep.

HORSE-C. Ay, this is he. God save ye, Master Doctor! Master Doctor, Master Doctor Fustian!—Forty dollars, forty [40 dollars for a bottle of hay!

MEPH. Why, thou seest he hears thee not.

HORSE-C. So ho, ho!—So ho, ho! (*Hallo in his ear.*) No, will you not wake? I'll make you wake ere I go! (*Pull him by the leg, and pull it away.*) Alas, I am undone! What shall I do?   48

FAUST. O, my leg, my leg! Help, Mephistophilis! Call the officers. My leg, my leg!

MEPH. Come, villain, to the constable.

HORSE-C. O Lord, sir, let me go, and I'll give you forty dollars more.

MEPH. Where be they?

HORSE-C. I have none about me. Come to my ostry [4] and I'll give them you.

MEPH. Be gone quickly!

Horse-Corser runs away.

FAUST. What, is he gone? Farewell he Faustus has his leg again, and the horse corser, I take it, a bottle of hay for [60 his labor. Well, this trick shall cost him forty dollars more.

Enter Wagner.

How now, Wagner, what's the news with thee?

WAG. Sir, the Duke of Vanholt doth earnestly entreat your company.

FAUST. The Duke of Vanholt! An honorable gentleman, to whom I must be no niggard of my cunning. Come, [69 Mephistophilis, let's away to him. *Exeunt.*

[SCENE xiii.

The court of the Duke of Vanholt.]

Enter the Duke of Vanholt, the Duchess, Faustus, and Mephistophilis.[5]

DUKE. Believe me, Master Doctor, this merriment hath much pleased me.

FAUST. My gracious lord, I am glad it contents you so well.—But it may be, madam, you take no delight in this. I have heard that great-bellied women do long for some dainties or other. What is it, madam? Tell me, and you shall have it.

DUCH. Thanks, good Master Doctor; [10 and, for I see your courteous intent to pleasure me, I will not hide from you the thing my heart desires. And were it now summer, as it is January and the dead time of the winter, I would desire no better meat than a dish of ripe grapes.

FAUST. Alas, madam, that's nothing! Mephistophilis, begone. (*Exit Meph[istophilis].*) Were it a greater thing than this, so it would content you, you should [20 have it.

Enter Mephisto[philis] with the grapes.

Here they be, madam. Wilt please you taste on them?

DUKE. Believe me, Master Doctor, this makes me wonder above the rest, that being in the dead time of winter, and in the month of January, how you should come by these grapes.

FAUST. If it like your grace, the year

---

[1] Load, bundle.   [3] Spectacles (?).
[2] Juggler.   [4] Ostlery, inn.

[5] Original reads: "Enter to them the Duke and the Duchess. The Duke speaks."

is divided into two circles over the whole [30 world, that, when it is here winter with us, in the contrary circle it is summer with them, as in India, Saba, and farther countries in the East; and by means of a swift spirit that I have, I had them brought hither, as ye see.—How do you like them, madam; be they good?

DUCH. Believe me, Master Doctor, they be the best grapes that e'er I tasted in my life before. 40

FAUST. I am glad they content you so, madam.

DUKE. Come, madam, let us in, where you must well reward this learned man for the great kindness he hath showed to you.

DUCH. And so I will, my lord; and, whilst I live,
Rest beholding [1] for this courtesy.

FAUST. I humbly thank your grace.

DUKE. Come, Master Doctor, follow us and receive your reward. *Exeunt.* 50

[SCENE xiv.

Faustus' study.]

Enter Wagner solus.

WAG. I think my master means to die shortly,
For he hath given to me all his goods;
And yet methinks, if that death were near,
He would not banquet and carouse and swill
Amongst the students, as even now he doth,
Who are at supper with such belly-cheer
As Wagner ne'er beheld in all his life.
See where they come! Belike the feast is ended.

Enter Faustus, with two or three Scholars [and Mephistophilis].

1 SCH. Master Doctor Faustus, since our conference about fair ladies, which [10 was the beautifull'st in all the world, we have determined with ourselves that Helen of Greece was the admirablest lady that ever lived. Therefore, Master Doctor, if you will do us that favor, as to let us see that peerless dame of Greece, whom all

[1] Beholden, indebted.

the world admires for majesty, we should think ourselves much beholding unto you.

FAUST.[2] Gentlemen,
For that I know your friendship is unfeigned, 20
And Faustus' custom is not to deny
The just requests of those that wish him well,
You shall behold that peerless dame of Greece,
No otherways for pomp and majesty
Than when Sir Paris crossed the seas with her,
And brought the spoils to rich Dardania.
Be silent, then, for danger is in words.

Music sounds, and Helen passeth over the stage.

2 SCH. Too simple is my wit to tell her praise,
Whom all the world admires for majesty.

3 SCH. No marvel though the angry Greeks pursued 30
With ten years' war the rape [3] of such a queen,
Whose heavenly beauty passeth all compare.

1 SCH. Since we have seen the pride of Nature's works
And only paragon of excellence,

Enter an Old Man.

Let us depart; and for this glorious deed
Happy and blessed be Faustus evermore.

FAUSTUS. Gentlemen, farewell—the same I wish to you. *Exeunt Scholars.*

OLD MAN. Ah, Doctor Faustus, that I might prevail
To guide thy steps unto the way of life,
By which sweet path thou mayst attain the goal 40
That shall conduct thee to celestial rest!
Break heart, drop blood, and mingle it with tears,
Tears falling from repentant heaviness
Of thy most vild and loathsome filthiness,
The stench whereof corrupts the inward soul
With such flagitious crimes of heinous sins
As no commiseration may expel,

[2] The following speech is printed as prose in the original, but as verse in the 1616 ewn.
[3] Capture.

But mercy, Faustus, of thy Savior sweet,
Whose blood alone must wash away
thy guilt.
FAUST. Where art thou, Faustus? Wretch,
what hast thou done? 50
Damned art thou, Faustus, damned;
despair and die!
Hell calls for right, and with a roaring
voice
Says, "Faustus, come! Thine hour is
come!"
And Faustus will come to do thee right.
   Mephi[stophilis] gives him a dagger.
OLD MAN. Ah, stay, good Faustus, stay
thy desperate steps!
I see an angel hovers o'er thy head,
And, with a vial full of precious grace,
Offers to pour the same into thy soul.
Then call for mercy, and avoid despair.
FAUST. Ah, my sweet friend, I feel 60
Thy words to comfort my distressèd
soul.
Leave me a while to ponder on my sins.
OLD MAN. I go, sweet Faustus, but with
heavy cheer,
Fearing the ruin of thy hopeless soul.
        [Exit.]
FAUST. Accursèd Faustus, where is mercy
now?
I do repent, and yet I do despair;
Hell strives with grace for conquest in
my breast.
What shall I do to shun the snares of
death?
MEPH. Thou traitor Faustus, I arrest
thy soul
For disobedience to my sovereign lord; 70
Revolt, or I'll in piecemeal tear thy flesh.
FAUST. Sweet Mephistophilis, entreat thy
lord
To pardon my unjust presumption,
And with my blood again I will confirm
My former vow I made to Lucifer.
MEPH. Do it then quickly, with unfeignèd
heart,
Lest greater danger do attend thy drift.
[Faustus pricks his arm and signs a paper
            with his blood.]
FAUST. Torment, sweet friend, that base
and crooked age,[1]
That durst dissuade me from thy Lucifer,
With greatest torments that our hell
affords. 80
[1] Old Man.

MEPH. His faith is great; I cannot touch
his soul.
But what I may afflict his body with
I will attempt, which is but little worth.
FAUST. One thing, good servant, let me
crave of thee,
To glut the longing of my heart's desire:
That I might have unto my paramour
That heavenly Helen, which I saw of
late,
Whose sweet embraces may extinguish
clean
These thoughts that do dissuade me
from my vow,
And keep mine oath I made to Lucifer. 90
MEPH. Faustus, this or what else thou
shalt desire
Shall be performed in twinkling of an
eye.

       Enter Helen.

FAUST. Was this the face that launched
a thousand ships,
And burnt the topless towers of Ilium?
Sweet Helen, make me immortal with
a kiss.   *[Kisses her.]*
Her lips sucks forth my soul; see where
it flies!—
Come, Helen, come, give me my soul
again.
Here will I dwell, for heaven be in these
lips,
And all is dross that is not Helena.

      Enter Old Man.

I will be Paris, and for love of thee, 100
Instead of Troy, shall Wertenberg be
sacked;
And I will combat with weak Menelaus,
And wear thy colors on my plumèd
crest;
Yea, I will wound Achilles in the heel,
And then return to Helen for a kiss.
O, thou art fairer than the evening air
Clad in the beauty of a thousand stars;
Brighter art thou than flaming Jupiter
When he appeared to hapless Semele;
More lovely than the monarch of the
sky 110
In wanton Arethusa's azured arms;
And none but thou shalt be my para-
mour.   *Exeunt [all except Old Man].*
OLD MAN. Accursèd Faustus, miserable
man,

That from thy soul exclud'st the grace
  of heaven,
And fliest the throne of his tribunal
  seat!

Enter the Devils.

Sathan begins to sift me with his pride.
As in this furnace God shall try my
  faith,
My faith, vile hell, shall triumph over
  thee.
Ambitious fiends, see how the heavens
  smiles
At your repulse, and laughs your state
  to scorn!   120
Hence, hell; for hence I fly unto my
  God!   *Exeunt.*

[SCENE xv.

The same.]

Enter Faustus with the Scholars.

FAUST. Ah, gentlemen!
  1 SCH. What ails Faustus?
  FAUST. Ah, my sweet chamber-fellow,
had I lived with thee, then had I lived
still, but now I die eternally. Look, comes
he not, comes he not?
  2 SCH. What means Faustus?
  3 SCH. Belike he is grown into some
sickness by being oversolitary.
  1 SCH. If it be so, we'll have physi- [10
cians to cure him. 'Tis but a surfeit.
Never fear, man.
  FAUST. A surfeit of deadly sin that
hath damned both body and soul.
  2 SCH. Yet, Faustus, look up to
heaven; remember God's mercies are infinite.
  FAUST. But Faustus' offense can ne'er
be pardoned. The serpent that tempted
Eve may be saved, but not Faustus. [20
Ah, gentlemen, hear me with patience,
and tremble not at my speeches! Though
my heart pants and quivers to remember
that I have been a student here these
thirty years, O, would I had never seen
Wertenberg, never read book! And what
wonders I have done, all Germany can
witness, yea, all the world; for which
Faustus hath lost both Germany and the
world, yea, heaven itself, heaven, the [30
seat of God, the throne of the blessed, the

kingdom of joy, and must remain in hell
forever, hell, ah, hell, forever! Sweet
friends, what shall become of Faustus,
being in hell forever?
  3 SCH. Yet, Faustus, call on God.
  FAUST. On God, whom Faustus hath
abjured! On God, whom Faustus hath
blasphemed! Ah, my God, I would weep,
but the devil draws in my tears. Gush [40
forth blood instead of tears! Yea, life
and soul! O, he stays my tongue! I would
lift up my hands, but see, they hold them,
they hold them!
  ALL. Who, Faustus?
  FAUST. Lucifer and Mephistophilis. Ah,
gentlemen, I gave them my soul for my
cunning!
  ALL. God forbid!
  FAUST. God forbade it indeed, but [50
Faustus hath done it. For vain pleasure
of four-and-twenty years hath Faustus
lost eternal joy and felicity. I writ them
a bill with mine own blood. The date is
expired; the time will come, and he will
fetch me.
  1 SCH. Why did not Faustus tell us of
this before, that divines might have prayed
for thee?
  FAUST. Oft have I thought to have [60
done so; but the devil threatened to tear
me in pieces if I named God; to fetch both
body and soul if I once gave ear to divinity. And now 'tis too late. Gentlemen,
away, lest you perish with me!
  2 SCH. O, what shall we do to [save][1]
Faustus?
  FAUST. Talk not of me, but save yourselves, and depart.
  3 SCH. God will strengthen me. I [70
will stay with Faustus.
  1 SCH. Tempt not God, sweet friend;
but let us into the next room, and there
pray for him.
  FAUST. Ay, pray for me, pray for me,
and what noise soever ye hear, come not
unto me, for nothing can rescue me.
  2 SCH. Pray thou, and we will pray
that God may have mercy upon thee.
  FAUST. Gentlemen, farewell! If I [80
live till morning, I'll visit you. If not—
Faustus is gone to hell.
  ALL. Faustus, farewell!
Exeunt Sch[olars]. The clock strikes eleven.

[1] Added from 1616 edn.

FAUST. Ah, Faustus,
Now hast thou but one bare hour to
    live,
And then thou must be damned per-
    petually!
Stand still, you ever-moving spheres of
    heaven,
That time may cease, and midnight
    never come!
Fair Nature's eye, rise, rise again and
    make
Perpetual day; or let this hour be but   90
A year, a month, a week, a natural day,
That Faustus may repent and save his
    soul!
O lente, lente, currite, noctis equi! [1]
The stars move still,[2] time runs, the
    clock will strike,
The devil will come, and Faustus must
    be damned.
O, I'll leap up to my God! Who pulls
    me down?
See, see where Christ's blood streams
    in the firmament!
One drop would save my soul—half a
    drop. Ah, my Christ!
Ah, rend not my heart for naming of
    my Christ!
Yet will I call on him! O, spare me,
    Lucifer!—   100
Where is it now? 'Tis gone; and see
    where God
Stretcheth out his arm, and bends his
    ireful brows!
Mountains and hills, come, come and
    fall on me,
And hide me from the heavy wrath of
    God!
No! No!
Then will I headlong run into the earth.
Earth gape! O, no, it will not harbor
    me!
You stars that reigned at my nativity,
Whose influence hath allotted death
    and hell,
Now draw up Faustus like a foggy
    mist   110
Into the entrails of yon lab'ring clouds,
That, when you vomit forth into the
    air,
My limbs may issue from your smoky
    mouths,

[1] Run slowly, slowly, horses of night.
[2] Continuously.

So that my soul may but ascend to
    heaven.   *The watch strikes.*
Ah, half the hour is past!
'Twill all be past anon!
O God!
If thou wilt not have mercy on my soul,
Yet, for Christ's sake whose blood hath
    ransomed me,
Impose some end to my incessant
    pain.   120
Let Faustus live in hell a thousand years,
A hundred thousand, and at last be
    saved!
O, no end is limited to damnèd souls!
Why wert thou not a creature wanting
    soul?
Or why is this immortal that thou hast?
Ah, Pythagoras' metempsychosis! Were
    that true,
This soul should fly from me, and I
    be changed
Unto some brutish beast! All beasts
    are happy,
For, when they die,
Their souls are soon dissolved in ele-
    ments.   130
But mine must live, still to be plagued
    in hell.
Cursed be the parents that engendered me!
No, Faustus, curse thyself; curse Lucifer
That hath deprived thee of the joys of
    heaven.   *The clock striketh twelve.*
O, it strikes, it strikes! Now, body,
    turn to air,
Or Lucifer will bear thee quick [3] to hell.
    Thunder and lightning.
O soul, be changed into little water-
    drops,
And fall into the ocean—ne'er be found.
My God, my God, look not so fierce on
    me!

Enter Devils.

Adders and serpents, let me breathe
    awhile!   140
Ugly hell, gape not! Come not, Lucifer!
I'll burn my books!—Ah, Mephistoph-
    ilis!   *Exeunt with him.*

Enter Chorus.

Cut is the branch that might have grown
    full straight,
And burnèd is Apollo's laurel bough

[3] Alive.

That sometime [1] grew within this
     learned man.
Faustus is gone; regard his hellish
     fall,
Whose fiendful fortune may exhort the
     wise
Only to wonder at unlawful things,

[1] Once.

Whose deepness doth entice such for-
     ward wits
To practice more than heavenly power
     permits.   [*Exit.*] 150

TERMINAT HORA DIEM; TERMINAT
          AUTHOR OPUS. [2]

[2] The hour (midnight) ends the day; the
author ends his work.

THE TROUBLESOME REIGN AND LAMENTABLE DEATH OF EDWARD THE SECOND[1]

BY
CHRISTOPHER MARLOWE

[DRAMATIS PERSONÆ

KING EDWARD THE SECOND.
PRINCE EDWARD, *his son, afterwards King Edward the Third.*
EDMUND, *Earl of Kent, brother to King Edward the Second.*
PIERS GAVESTON.
ARCHBISHOP OF CANTERBURY.
BISHOP OF COVENTRY.
BERKELEY, *Bishop of Winchester.*
EARL OF WARWICK.
EARL OF LANCASTER.
EARL OF PEMBROKE.[2]
EARL OF ARUNDEL.
EARL OF LEICESTER.
BEAUMONT.
SIR THOMAS BERKELEY.[3]
MORTIMER, SENIOR.
MORTIMER, JUNIOR, *his nephew.*
SPENCER, THE ELDER.
SPENCER, THE YOUNGER, *his son.*

BALDOCK, *a clerk.*
SIR WILLIAM TRUSSEL,[4] *Proctor of Parliament.*
GURNEY } *creatures of young*
MATREVIS[5] } *Mortimer.*
LIGHTBORN, *a murderer.*
SIR JOHN OF HAINAULT.
LEVUNE, *a Frenchman.*
RICE AP HOWELL.
JAMES, *servant to Pembroke.*
AN ABBOT, MONKS, A HERALD, LORDS, POOR MEN, A MOWER, THE KING'S CHAMPION, MESSENGERS, SOLDIERS, *and* ATTENDANTS.

QUEEN ISABELLA, *wife to King Edward the Second.*
A LADY, *niece to King Edward the Second and daughter to the Duke of Gloucester.*
OTHER LADIES.

SCENE: *England and Paris.*

TIME: *Early fourteenth century.*]

[SCENE i.

Near the court in London.]

Enter Gaveston, reading on a letter that was brought him from the King.

[GAV.] "My father is deceased! Come, Gaveston,
And share the kingdom with thy dearest friend."

Ah, words that make me surfeit with delight!
What greater bliss can hap to Gaveston
Than live and be the favorite of a king?
Sweet prince, I come. These, these thy amorous lines
Might have enforced me to have swum from France,

---

[1] The title continues: "King of England, with the Tragical Fall of Proud Mortimer, As It Was Sundry Times Publicly Acted in the Honorable City of London by the Right Honorable the Earl of Pembroke His Servants. Written by Chri. Marlowe, Gent."

[2] This name regularly appears as *Penbrook* in original.

[3] Consistent spelling of this name as *Bartley* indicates the pronunciation in this play.

[4] Dyce suggests that this character is represented in the speech head *Tru.* in Scene xviii.

[5] Dyce suggests Sir John Maltravers.

375

And, like Leander, gasped upon the sand,
So thou wouldst smile, and take me in
    thy arms.
The sight of London to my exiled eyes 10
Is as Elysium to a newcome soul;
Not that I love the city, or the men,
But that it harbors him I hold so dear—
The king, upon whose bosom let me die,
And with the world be still at enmity.
What need the artic people love starlight,
To whom the sun shines both by day
    and night?
Farewell, base stooping to the lordly
    peers!
My knee shall bow to none but to the
    king.
As for the multitude, that are but
    sparks   20
Raked up in embers of their poverty,
Tanti! [1] I'll fawn [2] first on the wind
That glanceth at my lips, and flyeth
    away.
But how now, what are these?

Enter three Poor Men.

POOR MEN. Such as desire your worship's
    service.
GAV. What canst thou do?
1 POOR. I can ride.
GAV. But I have no horses.—What art
    thou?
2 POOR. A traveler.
GAV.   Let me see. Thou wouldst do well
    To wait at my trencher and tell me lies
    at dinner time;   30
    And, as I like your discoursing, I'll have
    you.—
    And what art thou?
3 POOR. A soldier that hath served
    against the Scot.
GAV. Why, there are hospitals for such as
    you.
    I have no war, and therefore, sir, begone.
SOLDIER. [3] Farewell, and perish by a sol-
    dier's hand,
    That wouldst reward them with an hos-
    pital.
GAV. [*Aside.*] Ay, ay, these words of his
    move me as much
    As if a goose should play the porpen-
    tine, [4]

And dart her plumes, thinking to pierce
    my breast.   40
But yet it is no pain to speak men fair;
I'll flatter these, and make them live in
    hope.—
You know that I came lately out of
    France,
And yet I have not viewed my lord the
    king;
If I speed well, I'll entertain you all.
OMNES. We thank your worship.
GAV. I have some business; leave me to
    myself.
OMNES. We will wait here about the court.
    Exeunt.
GAV. Do.—These are not men for me.   49
I must have wanton poets, pleasant wits,
Musicians that with touching of a string
May draw the pliant king which way I
    please.
Music and poetry is his delight;
Therefore I'll have Italian masques by
    night,
Sweet speeches, comedies, and pleasing
    shows;
And in the day, when he shall walk
    abroad,
Like sylvan nymphs my pages shall be
    clad;
My men, like satyrs grazing on the lawns,
Shall with their goat feet dance an antic
    hay. [5]   59
Sometime a lovely boy in Dian's shape
With hair that gilds the water as it glides,
Crownets [6] of pearl about his naked arms,
And in his sportful hands an olive tree,
To hide those parts which men delight
    to see,
Shall bathe him in a spring; and there
    hard by,
One like Acteon peeping through the
    grove
Shall by the angry goddess be trans-
    formed,
And running in the likeness of an hart
By yelping hounds pulled down, and
    seem to die.
Such things as these best please his
    majesty,   70
My lord.—Here comes the king and the
    nobles
From the parliament. I'll stand aside.
    [*Retires.*]

---

[1] So much for them.   [3] *I.e., 3 Poor.*
[2] Original reads *fanne.*   [4] Porcupine.
[5] Country dance.   [6] Coronets, garlands.

Enter the King; Lancaster; Mortimer, Senior; Mortimer, Junior; Edmund, Earl of Kent; Guy, Earl of Warwick; etc.

EDW. Lancaster!

LAN. My lord.

GAV. [*Aside.*] That Earl of Lancaster do I abhor!

EDW. Will you not grant me this?—[*Aside.*] In spite of them
I'll have my will; and these two Morti-
mers,
That cross me thus, shall know I am displeased.

MOR. SEN. If you love us, my lord, hate Gaveston.

GAV. [*Aside.*] That villain Mortimer! I'll be his death. 80

MOR. JUN. Mine uncle here, this earl, and I myself
Were sworn to your father at his death
That he should ne'er return into the realm;
And know, my lord, ere I will break my oath,
This sword of mine, that should offend your foes,
Shall sleep within the scabbard at thy need,
And underneath thy banners march who will,
For Mortimer will hang his armor up.

GAV. [*Aside.*] *Mort Dieu!* [1]

EDW. Well, Mortimer, I'll make thee rue these words. 90
Beseems it thee to contradict thy king?
Frown'st thou thereat, aspiring Lan-
caster?
The sword shall plane the furrows of thy brows,
And hew these knees that now are grown so stiff.
I will have Gaveston; and you shall know
What danger 'tis to stand against your king.

GAV. [*Aside.*] Well done, Ned!

LAN. My lord, why do you thus incense your peers,
That naturally would love and honor you 99
But for that base and obscure Gaveston?
Four earldoms have I, besides Lancas-
ter—

Derby, Salisbury, Lincoln, Leicester;
These will I sell, to give my soldiers pay,
Ere Gaveston shall stay within the realm.
Therefore, if he be come, expel him straight.

EDM.[2] Barons and earls, your pride hath made me mute;
But now I'll speak, and to the proof, I hope.
I do remember, in my father's days,
Lord Percy of the north, being highly moved,
Braved Mowbery [3] in presence of the king, 110
For which, had not his highness loved him well,
He should have lost his head; but with his look
The undaunted spirit of Percy was ap-
peased,
And Mowbery and he were reconciled.
Yet dare you brave the king unto his face!—
Brother, revenge it, and let these their heads
Preach upon poles, for trespass of their tongues.

WAR. O, our heads!

EDW. Ay, yours; and therefore I would wish you grant— 119

WAR. Bridle thy anger, gentle Mortimer.

MOR. JUN. I cannot, nor I will not; I must speak.—
Cousin, our hands I hope shall fence our heads,
And strike off his that makes you threaten us.
Come, uncle, let us leave the brainsick king,
And henceforth parley with our naked swords.

MOR. SEN. Wiltshire hath men enough to save our heads.

WAR. [*Ironically.*] All Warwickshire will love him for my sake!

LAN. [*Ironically.*] And northward Gaves-
ton hath many friends!—
Adieu, my lord; and either change your mind,
Or look to see the throne, where you should sit, 130

[1] God's death!

[2] The name of this character appears inter-changeably as *Edmund* or *Kent* in speech heads throughout the play. [3] Mowbray.

To float in blood, and at thy wanton head
The glozing [1] head of thy base minion thrown.

Exeunt Nobles [except Kent].

EDW. I cannot brook these haughty menaces.
Am I a king, and must be overruled?—
Brother, display my ensigns in the field;
I'll bandy [2] with the barons and the earls,
And either die or live with Gaveston.

GAV. I can no longer keep me from my lord. *[Comes forward.]*

EDW. What, Gaveston! Welcome! Kiss not my hand; 139
Embrace me, Gaveston, as I do thee.
Why shouldst thou kneel? Knowest thou not who I am? [3]
Thy friend, thyself, another Gaveston!
Not Hylas was more mourned of Hercules
Than thou hast been of me since thy exile.

GAV. And, since I went from hence, no soul in hell
Hath felt more torment than poor Gaveston.

EDW. I know it.—Brother, welcome home my friend.
Now let the treacherous Mortimers conspire,
And that high-minded [4] Earl of Lancaster. 149
I have my wish, in that I joy [5] thy sight;
And sooner shall the sea o'erwhelm my land
Than bear the ship that shall transport thee hence.
I here create thee lord high chamberlain,
Chief secretary to the state and me,
Earl of Cornwall, King and Lord of Man.[6]

GAV. My lord, these titles far exceed my worth.

KENT. Brother, the least of these may well suffice
For one of greater birth than Gaveston.

EDW. Cease, brother, for I cannot brook these words.

Thy worth, sweet friend, is far above my gifts. 160
Therefore, to equal it, receive my heart.
If for these dignities thou be envied,
I'll give thee more, for, but to honor thee,
Is Edward pleased with kingly regiment.[7]
Fear'st thou [8] thy person? Thou shalt have a guard!
Wants thou gold? Go to my treasury!
Wouldst thou be loved and feared? Receive my seal;
Save or condemn, and in our name command
Whatso thy mind affects,[9] or fancy likes.

GAV. It shall suffice me to enjoy your love, 170
Which, whiles I have, I think myself as great
As Cæsar riding in the Roman street,
With captive kings at his triumphant ear.

Enter the Bishop of Coventry.

EDW. Whither goes my Lord of Coventry so fast?

BISH. To celebrate your father's exequies.
But is that wicked Gaveston returned?

EDW. Ay, priest, and lives to be revenged on thee,
That wert the only cause of his exile.

GAV. 'Tis true, and, but for reverence of these robes,
Thou shouldst not plod one foot beyond this place. 180

BISH. I did no more than I was bound to do;
And, Gaveston, unless thou be reclaimed,
As then I did incense the parliament,
So will I now, and thou shalt back to France.

GAV. Saving your reverence, you must pardon me.

EDW. Throw off his golden miter, rend his stole,
And in the channel [10] christen him anew.

KENT. Ah, brother, lay not violent hands on him,
For he'll complain unto the see of Rome!

GAV. Let him complain unto the see of hell; 190
I'll be revenged on him for my exile.

---

[1] Flattering. [2] Fight.
[3] Here and in a few other passages the line division has been regularized. [5] Enjoy.
[4] Arrogant. [6] Isle of Man.
[7] Rule. [9] Desires.
[8] Fear'st thou for. [10] Gutter.

EDW. No, spare his life, but seize upon
   his goods.
Be thou lord bishop and receive his rents,
And make him serve thee as thy chaplain.
I give him thee—here, use him as thou
   wilt.
GAV. He shall to prison, and there die in
   bolts.
EDW. Ay, to the Tower, the Fleet, or
   where thou wilt.
BISH. For this offense, be thou accursed of
   God!
EDW. Who's there? Convey this priest to
   the Tower.
BISH. True, true.[1]   200
EDW. But in the meantime, Gaveston,
   away,
And take possession of his house and
   goods.
Come, follow me, and thou shalt have
   my guard
To see it done, and bring thee safe again.
GAV. What should a priest do with so fair
   a house?
A prison may best beseem his holiness.
                      [*Exeunt.*]

[SCENE ii.

Westminster.]

*Enter [on one side] both the Mortimers; [on
the other,] Warwick and Lancaster.*

WAR. 'Tis true, the bishop is in the Tower,
And goods and body given to Gaveston.
LAN. What, will they tyrannize upon the
   church?
Ah, wicked king! Accursèd Gaveston!
This ground, which is corrupted with
   their steps,
Shall be their timeless[2] sepulcher or
   mine.
MOR. JUN. Well, let that peevish French-
   man guard him sure;
Unless his breast be swordproof, he shall
   die.
MOR. SEN. How now! Why droops the
   Earl of Lancaster?
MOR. JUN. Wherefore is Guy of Warwick
   discontent?   10
LAN. That villain Gaveston is made an
   earl.

MOR. SEN. An earl!
WAR. Ay, and besides, lord chamberlain
   of the realm,
And secretary too, and Lord of Man.
MOR. SEN. We may not nor we will not
   suffer this.
MOR. JUN. Why post we not from hence
   to levy men?
LAN. "My Lord of Cornwall" now at ev-
   ery word!
And happy is the man whom he vouch-
   safes
For vailing[3] of his bonnet one good look.
Thus, arm in arm, the king and he doth
   march.   20
Nay, more, the guard upon his lordship
   waits,
And all the court begins to flatter him.
WAR. Thus leaning on the shoulder of the
   king,
He nods and scorns and smiles at those
   that pass.
MOR. SEN. Doth no man take exceptions
   at the slave?
LAN. All stomach[4] him, but none dare
   speak a word.
MOR. JUN. Ah, that bewrays[5] their base-
   ness, Lancaster!
Were all the earls and barons of my
   mind,
We'll hale him from the bosom of the
   king,
And at the court gate hang the peasant
   up,   30
Who, swoln with venom of ambitious
   pride,
Will be the ruin of the realm and us.

*Enter the [Arch]bishop of Canterbury [and
an Attendant].*

WAR. Here comes my Lord of Canterbury's grace.
LAN. His countenance bewrays he is displeased.
[ARCH]BISH. First were his sacred garments
   rent and torn;
Then laid they violent hands upon him;
   next,
Himself imprisoned, and his goods as-
   seized.[6]
This certify the pope.—Away, take
   horse!   [*Exit Attendant.*]

---

[1] Alluding to euphemistic use of *convey*, taking the word in the sense of *steal, carry away
feloniously.*
[2] Untimely.
[3] Lowering, doffing.
[4] Resent.
[5] Reveals.
[6] Seized upon.

LAN. My lord, will you take arms against the king?

[ARCH]BISH. What need I? God himself is up in arms,   40
When violence is offered to the church.

MOR. JUN. Then will you join with us that be his peers,
To banish or behead that Gaveston?

[ARCH]BISH. What else, my lords? For it concerns me near;
The bishopric of Coventry is his.

Enter the Queen.

MOR. JUN. Madam, whither walks your majesty so fast?

QUEEN. Unto the forest, gentle Mortimer,
To live in grief and baleful discontent;
For now my lord the king regards me not,
But dotes upon the love of Gaveston. 50
He claps his cheeks, and hangs about his neck,
Smiles in his face, and whispers in his ears;
And, when I come, he frowns, as who should say,
"Go whither thou wilt, seeing I have Gaveston."

MOR. SEN. Is it not strange that he is thus bewitched?

MOR. JUN. Madam, return unto the court again.
That sly, inveigling Frenchman we'll exile
Or lose our lives; and yet, ere that day come,
The king shall lose his crown, for we have power,   59
And courage too, to be revenged at full.

[ARCH]BISH. But yet lift not your swords against the king.

LAN. No, but we'll lift Gaveston from hence.

WAR. And war must be the means, or he'll stay still.

QUEEN. Then let him stay; for rather than my lord
Shall be oppressed by civil mutinies,
I will endure a melancholy life,
And let him frolic with his minion.

[ARCH]BISH. My lords, to ease all this, but hear me speak:
We and the rest, that are his counselors,
Will meet and with a general consent 70
Confirm his banishment with our hands and seals.

LAN. What we confirm the king will frustrate.

MOR. JUN. Then may we lawfully revolt from him.

WAR. But say, my lord, where shall this meeting be?

[ARCH]BISH. At the New Temple.

MOR. JUN. Content.

[ARCH]BISH. And, in the meantime, I'll entreat you all
To cross to Lambeth, and there stay with me.

LAN. Come then, let's away.

MOR. JUN. Madam, farewell!   80

QUEEN. Farewell, sweet Mortimer, and for my sake
Forbear to levy arms against the king.

MOR. JUN. Ay, if words will serve; if not, I must.   [*Exeunt.*]

[SCENE iii.

A street in London.]

Enter Gaveston and the Earl of Kent.

GAV. Edmund, the mighty Prince of Lancaster,
That hath more earldoms than an ass can bear,
And both the Mortimers, two goodly men,
With Guy of Warwick, that redoubted knight,
Are gone towards Lambeth—there let them remain!   *Exeunt.*

[SCENE iv.

The New Temple.]

Enter Nobles.

LAN. Here is the form of Gaveston's exile.
May it please your lordship to subscribe your name.

[ARCH]BISH. Give me the paper!
                    [*He signs, followed by the others.*]

LAN. Quick, quick, my lord! I long to write my name.

WAR. But I long more to see him banished hence.

MOR. JUN. The name of Mortimer shall fright the king,
Unless he be declined [1] from that base peasant.

[1] Turned aside, parted.

Enter the King [, Kent,] and Gaveston.

EDW. What, are you moved that Gaveston
  sits here?
It is our pleasure; we will have it so.
LAN. Your grace doth well to place him by
  your side,   10
For nowhere else the new earl is so safe.
MOR. SEN. What man of noble birth can
  brook this sight?
Quam male conveniunt! [1]
See what a scornful look the peasant
  casts!
PEM. Can kingly lions fawn on creeping
  ants?
WAR. Ignoble vassal, that like Phaëton
Aspir'st unto the guidance of the sun!
MOR. JUN. Their downfall is at hand, their
  forces down;
We will not thus be faced and over-
  peered. [2]   19
EDW. Lay hands on that traitor Mortimer!
MOR. SEN. Lay hands on that traitor Gav-
  eston!
KENT. Is this the duty that you owe your
  king?
WAR. We know our duties—let him know
  his peers.
EDW. Whither will you bear him? Stay,
  or ye shall die.
MOR. SEN. We are no traitors; therefore
  threaten not.
GAV. No, threaten not, my lord, but pay
  them home!
Were I a king—
MOR. JUN. Thou villain, wherefore talks
  thou of a king,
That hardly art a gentleman by birth?
EDW. Were he a peasant, being my min-
  ion,   30
I'll make the proudest of you stoop to
  him.
LAN. My lord, you may not thus disparage
  us.—
Away, I say, with hateful Gaveston!
MOR. SEN. And with the Earl of Kent that
  favors him!
[*Attendants remove Kent and Gaveston.*]
EDW. Nay, then, lay violent hands upon
  your king.
Here, Mortimer, sit thou in Edward's
  throne;

Warwick and Lancaster, wear you my
  crown.
Was ever king thus overruled as I?
LAN. Learn then to rule us better, and the
  realm.
MOR. JUN. What we have done, our heart
  blood shall maintain.   40
WAR. Think you that we can brook this
  upstart pride?
EDW. Anger and wrathful fury stops my
  speech.
[ARCH]BISH. Why are you moved? Be pa-
  tient, my lord,
And see what we your counselors have
  done.
MOR. JUN. My lords, now let us all be
  resolute,
And either have our wills or lose our
  lives.
EDW. Meet you for this, proud, overdaring
  peers?
Ere my sweet Gaveston shall part from
  me,
This isle shall fleet [3] upon the ocean,
And wander to the unfrequented Inde. 50
[ARCH]BISH. You know that I am legate to
  the pope!
On your allegiance to the see of Rome
Subscribe, as we have done, to his exile.
MOR. JUN. Curse him, if he refuse; and
  then may we
Depose him and elect another king.
EDW. Ay, there it goes! But yet I will
  not yield.
Curse me, depose me, do the worst you
  can.
LAN. Then linger not, my lord, but do it
  straight.
[ARCH]BISH. Remember how the bishop
  was abused!
Either banish him that was the cause
  thereof,   60
Or I will presently [4] discharge these lords
Of duty and allegiance due to thee.
EDW. [*Aside.*] It boots me not to threat; I
  must speak fair.—
The legate of the pope will be obeyed.
My lord, you shall be chancellor of the
  realm;
Thou, Lancaster, high admiral of our
  fleet;
Young Mortimer and his uncle shall be
  earls;

[1] How ill they agree!
[2] Looked down upon, scorned.
[3] Float.   [4] Immediately.

And you, Lord Warwick, President of the
  North;
And thou, of Wales. If this content you
  not,   69
Make several kingdoms of this monarchy,
And share it equally amongst you all,
So I may have some nook or corner left
To frolic with my dearest Gaveston.
[Arch]bish. Nothing shall alter us; we are
  resolved.
Lan. Come, come, subscribe.
Mor. Jun. Why should you love him
  whom the world hates so?
Edw. Because he loves me more than all
  the world.
  Ah, none but rude and savage-minded men
  Would seek the ruin of my Gaveston. 79
  You that be noble born should pity him.
War. You that are princely born should
  shake him off.
  For shame, subscribe, and let the lown [1]
  depart.
Mor. Sen. Urge him, my lord.
[Arch]bish. Are you content to banish him
  the realm?
Edw. I see I must, and therefore am con-
  tent.
  Instead of ink, I'll write it with my tears.
                               [Signs.]
Mor. Jun. The king is lovesick for his
  minion.
Edw. 'Tis done; and now, accursèd hand,
  fall off!
Lan. Give it me; I'll have it published in
  the streets.
Mor. Jun. I'll see him presently des-
  patched away.   90
[Arch]bish. Now is my heart at ease.
War.   And so is mine.
Pem. This will be good news to the com-
  mon sort.
Mor. Sen. Be it or no, he shall not linger
  here.   Exeunt Nobles.
Edw. How fast they run to banish him I
  love!
  They would not stir, were it to do me
  good.
  Why should a king be subject to a priest?
  Proud Rome, that hatchest such im-
  perial grooms,
  For these thy superstitious taper lights,
  Wherewith thy antichristian churches
  blaze,   99

[1] Worthless fellow.

I'll fire thy crazèd buildings, and enforce
The papal towers to kiss the lowly
  ground!
With slaughtered priests may Tiber's
  channel swell,
And banks raised higher with their sep-
  ulchers!
As for the peers that back the clergy thus,
If I be king, not one of them shall live.

              Enter Gaveston.

Gav. My lord, I hear it whispered every-
  where
  That I am banished, and must fly the
  land.
Edw. 'Tis true, sweet Gaveston—O, were
  it false!
  The legate of the pope will have it so,
  And thou must hence, or I shall be de-
  posed.   110
  But I will reign to be revenged of them,
  And therefore, sweet friend, take it pa-
  tiently.
  Live where thou wilt, I'll send thee gold
  enough;
  And long thou shalt not stay, or, if thou
  dost,
  I'll come to thee. My love shall ne'er
  decline.
Gav. Is all my hope turned to this hell of
  grief?
Edw. Rend not my heart with thy too
  piercing words.
  Thou from this land, I from myself am
  banished.
Gav. To go from hence grieves not poor
  Gaveston,
  But to forsake you, in whose gracious
  looks   120
  The blessedness of Gaveston remains;
  For nowhere else seeks he felicity.
Edw. And only this torments my wretched
  soul
  That, whether I will or no, thou must
  depart.
  Be governor of Ireland in my stead,
  And there abide till fortune call thee
  home.
  Here take my picture, and let me wear
  thine;   [They exchange pictures.]
  O, might I keep thee here as I do this,
  Happy were I, but now most miser-
  able!
Gav. 'Tis something to be pitied of a king.

EDW. Thou shalt not hence—I'll hide thee,
Gaveston.   131
GAV. I shall be found, and then 'twill
grieve me more.
EDW. Kind words and mutual talk makes
our grief greater;
Therefore, with dumb embracement, let
us part.—
Stay, Gaveston, I cannot leave thee thus!
GAV. For every look, my lord drops down
a tear.
Seeing I must go, do not renew my sor-
row.
EDW. The time is little that thou hast to
stay,
And, therefore, give me leave to look
my fill.
But come, sweet friend, I'll bear thee on
thy way.   140
GAV. The peers will frown.
EDW. I pass [1] not for their anger.—Come,
let's go;
O, that we might as well return as go.

Enter Edmund and Queen Isabel.

QUEEN. Whither goes my lord?
EDW. Fawn not on me, French strumpet!
Get thee gone!
QUEEN. On whom but on my husband
should I fawn?
GAV. On Mortimer, with whom, ungentle
queen—
I say no more. Judge you the rest, my
lord.
QUEEN. In saying this, thou wrong'st
me, Gaveston.
Is't not enough that thou corrupts my
lord,   150
And art a bawd to his affections,
But thou must call mine honor thus in
question?
GAV. I mean not so; your grace must
pardon me.
EDW. Thou art too familiar with that
Mortimer,
And by thy means is Gaveston exiled.
But I would wish thee reconcile the lords,
Or thou shalt ne'er be reconciled to me.
QUEEN. Your highness knows it lies not in
my power.
EDW. Away then! Touch me not.—Come,
Gaveston.

[1] Care

QUEEN. Villain, 'tis thou that robb'st me
of my lord!   160
GAV. Madam, 'tis you that rob me of my
lord.
EDW. Speak not unto her; let her droop
and pine.
QUEEN. Wherein, my lord, have I deserved
these words?
Witness the tears that Isabella sheds,
Witness this heart, that, sighing for thee,
breaks,
How dear my lord is to poor Isabel!
EDW. And witness heaven how dear thou
art to me!
There weep, for till my Gaveston be re-
pealed,[2]
Assure thyself thou com'st not in my
sight.   *Exeunt Edward and Gaveston.*
QUEEN. O miserable and distresséd queen!
Would, when I left sweet France and
was embarked,   171
That charming Circes,[3] walking on the
waves,
Had changed my shape, or at the mar-
riage day
The cup of Hymen had been full of
poison,
Or with those arms that twined about
my neck
I had been stifled, and not lived to see
The king my lord thus to abandon me!
Like frantic Juno will I fill the earth
With ghastly murmur of my sighs and
cries;
For never doted Jove on Ganymede 180
So much as he on curséd Gaveston.
But that will more exasperate his wrath.
I must entreat him, I must speak him
fair,
And be a means to call home Gaveston.
And yet he'll ever dote on Gaveston,
And so am I forever miserable.

Enter the Nobles to the Queen.

LAN. Look where the sister of the King of
France
Sits wringing of her hands, and beats
her breast!
WAR. The king, I fear, hath ill entreated [4]
her.
PEM. Hard is the heart that injures such
a saint.   190

[2] Recalled from exile.   [4] Treated, used.
[3] Circe.

MOR. JUN. I know 'tis long [1] of Gaveston
    she weeps.

MOR. SEN. Why? He is gone.

MOR. JUN.   Madam, how fares
    your grace?

QUEEN. Ah, Mortimer, now breaks the
    king's hate forth,
    And he confesseth that he loves me
    not.

MOR. JUN. Cry quittance, madam, then,
    and love not him.

QUEEN. No, rather will I die a thousand
    deaths!
    And yet I love in vain. He'll ne'er love
    me.

LAN. Fear ye not, madam; now his min-
    ion's gone,
    His wanton humor will be quickly left.

QUEEN. O never, Lancaster! I am en-
    joined   200
    To sue unto you all for his repeal.
    This wills my lord, and this must I per-
    form,
    Or else be banished from his highness'
    presence.

LAN. For his repeal? Madam, he comes
    not back,
    Unless the sea cast up his shipwrack [2]
    body.

WAR. And to behold so sweet a sight as
    that,
    There's none here but would run his
    horse to death.

MOR. JUN. But, madam, would you have
    us call him home?

QUEEN. Ay, Mortimer, for till he be re-
    stored,
    The angry king hath banished me the
    court;   210
    And, therefore, as thou lovest and ten-
    d'rest [3] me,
    Be thou my advocate unto these peers.

MOR. JUN. What! Would you have me
    plead for Gaveston?

MOR. SEN. Plead for him he that will, I
    am resolved.

LAN. And so am I, my lord. Dissuade the
    queen.

QUEEN. O Lancaster, let him dissuade the
    king,
    For 'tis against my will he should return.

WAR. Then speak not for him; let the
    peasant go.

---
[1] Because.   [2] Shipwrecked.   [3] Carest for.

QUEEN. 'Tis for myself I speak, and not
    for him.

PEM. No speaking will prevail, and there-
    fore cease.   220

MOR. JUN. Fair queen, forbear to angle
    for the fish
    Which, being caught, strikes him that
    takes it dead;
    I mean that vile torpedo, Gaveston,
    That now, I hope, floats on the Irish
    seas. [4]

QUEEN. Sweet Mortimer, sit down by me
    awhile,
    And I will tell thee reasons of such weight
    As thou wilt soon subscribe to his repeal.

MOR. JUN. It is impossible; but speak your
    mind.

QUEEN. Then thus—but none shall hear
    it but ourselves.   [They stand aside.]

LAN. My lords, albeit the queen win Mor-
    timer,   230
    Will you be resolute, and hold with me?

MOR. SEN. Not I, against my nephew.

PEM. Fear not; the queen's words cannot
    alter him.

WAR. No? Do but mark how earnestly she
    pleads!

LAN. And see how coldly his looks make
    denial!

WAR. She smiles. Now for my life his
    mind is changed!

LAN. I'll rather lose his friendship, I, than
    grant.

MOR. JUN. Well, of necessity it must be so.
    My lords, that I abhor base Gaveston,
    I hope your honors make no question, 240
    And therefore, though I plead for his
    repeal,
    'Tis not for his sake, but for our avail;
    Nay, for the realm's behoof, and for the
    king's.

LAN. Fie, Mortimer, dishonor not thyself!
    Can this be true, 'twas good to banish
    him?
    And is this true, to call him home again?
    Such reasons make white black, and dark
    night day.

MOR. JUN. My Lord of Lancaster, mark
    the respect. [5]

LAN. In no respect can contraries be true.

QUEEN. Yet, good my lord, hear what he
    can allege.   250

---
[4] A sample of Marlowe's telescoping of time.
[5] Reason.

WAR. All that he speaks is nothing; we are resolved.

MOR. JUN. Do you not wish that Gaveston were dead?

PEM. I would he were!

MOR. JUN. Why, then, my lord, give me but leave to speak.

MOR. SEN. But, nephew, do not play the sophister.

MOR. JUN. This which I urge is of a burning zeal
To mend the king, and do our country good.
Know you not Gaveston hath store of gold,
Which may in Ireland purchase him such friends   259
As he will front the mightiest of us all?
And whereas [1] he shall live and be beloved,
'Tis hard for us to work his overthrow.

WAR. Mark you but that, my Lord of Lancaster.

MOR. JUN. But were he here, detested as he is,
How easily might some base slave be suborned
To greet his lordship with a poniard,
And none so much as blame the murtherer,
But rather praise him for that brave attempt, [2]
And in the chronicle enroll his name
For purging of the realm of such a plague!   270

PEM. He saith true.

LAN. Ay, but how chance this was not done before?

MOR. JUN. Because, my lords, it was not thought upon.
Nay, more, when he shall know it lies in us
To banish him, and then to call him home,
'Twill make him vail the top flag of his pride,
And fear to offend the meanest nobleman.

MOR. SEN. But how if he do not, nephew?

MOR. JUN. Then may we with some color [3] rise in arms;
For, howsoever we have borne it out,   280
'Tis treason to be up against the king.

So shall we have the people of [4] our side,
Which for his father's sake lean to the king,
But cannot brook a night-grown mushrump, [5]
Such a one as my Lord of Cornwall is,
Should bear us down of the nobility.
And when the commons and the nobles join,
'Tis not the king can buckler Gaveston;
We'll pull him from the strongest hold he hath.
My lords, if to perform this I be slack, 290
Think me as base a groom as Gaveston.

LAN. On that condition, Lancaster will grant.

WAR. And so will Pembroke and I.

MOR. SEN. And I.

MOR. JUN. In this I count me highly gratified,
And Mortimer will rest at your command.

QUEEN. And when this favor Isabel forgets,
Then let her live abandoned and forlorn.—
But see, in happy time, [6] my lord the king,
Having brought the Earl of Cornwall on his way,   300
Is new returned. This news will glad him much,
Yet not so much as me. I love him more
Than he can Gaveston. Would he loved me
But half so much, then were I treble-blessed.

Enter King Edward, mourning.

EDW. He's gone, and for his absence thus I mourn.
Did never sorrow go so near my heart
As doth the want of my sweet Gaveston;
And could my crown's revenue bring him back,
I would freely give it to his enemies,
And think I gained, having bought so dear a friend.   310

QUEEN. [*Aside.*] Hark, how he harps upon his minion!

[1] Where.   [2] Enterprise.   [3] Excuse.
[4] On.   [6] At an appropriate moment.
[5] Mushroom.

EDW. My heart is as an anvil unto sorrow,
Which beats upon it like the Cyclops'
  hammers,
And with the noise turns up my giddy
  brain,
And makes me frantic for my Gaveston.
Ah, had some bloodless Fury rose from
  hell,
And with my kingly scepter stroke [1] me
  dead,
When I was forced to leave my Gaveston!
LAN. *Diablo!* [2] What passions call you
  these?
QUEEN. My gracious lord, I come to
  bring you news.   320
EDW. That you have parleyed with your
  Mortimer!
QUEEN. That Gaveston, my lord, shall be
  repealed.
EDW. Repealed! The news is too sweet to
  be true.
QUEEN. But will you love me, if you find
  it so?
EDW. If it be so, what will not Edward do?
QUEEN. For Gaveston, but not for Isabel.
EDW. For thee, fair queen, if thou lovest
  Gaveston.
I'll hang a golden tongue about thy neck,
Seeing thou hast pleaded with so good
  success.
QUEEN. No other jewels hang about my
  neck   330
Than these, my lord; nor let me have
  more wealth
Than I may fetch from this rich treasury.
O, how a kiss revives poor Isabel!
EDW. Once more receive my hand; and
  let this be
A second marriage twixt thyself and me.
QUEEN. And may it prove more happy
  than the first!
My gentle lord, bespeak these nobles
  fair,
That wait attendance for a gracious look,
And on their knees salute your majesty.
EDW. Courageous Lancaster, embrace thy
  king!   340
And, as gross vapors perish by the sun,
Even so let hatred with thy sovereign's [3]
  smile.
Live thou with me as my companion.
LAN. This salutation overjoys my heart.

[1] Struck.   [2] The devil.
[3] From 1612 edn. Original reads *sovereign.*

EDW. Warwick shall be my chiefest coun-
  selor.
These silver hairs will more adorn my
  court
Than gaudy silks, or rich imbrothery. [4]
Chide me, sweet Warwick, if I go astray.
WAR. Slay me, my lord, when I offend
  your grace.
EDW. In solemn triumphs and in public
  shows,   350
Pembroke shall bear the sword before
  the king.
PEM. And with this sword Pembroke will
  fight for you.
EDW. But wherefore walks young Morti-
  mer aside?
Be thou commander of our royal fleet;
Or, if that lofty office like thee not,
I make thee here lord marshal of the
  realm.
MOR. JUN. My lord, I'll marshal so your
  enemies
As England shall be quiet, and you safe.
EDW. And as for you, Lord Mortimer of
  Chirke,
Whose great achievements in our foreign
  war   360
Deserves no common place nor mean
  reward,
Be you the general of the levied troops
That now are ready to assail the Scots.
MOR. SEN. In this your grace hath highly
  honored me,
For with my nature war doth best agree.
QUEEN. Now is the King of England rich
  and strong,
Having the love of his renownéd peers.
EDW. Ay, Isabel, ne'er was my heart so
  light.
Clerk of the crown, direct our warrant
  forth
For Gaveston to Ireland.—Beaumont,
  fly   370
As fast as Iris or Jove's Mercury.
BEAU. It shall be done, my gracious lord.
EDW. Lord Mortimer, we leave you to
  your charge.
Now let us in, and feast it royally.
Against our friend the Earl of Corn-
  wall comes,
We'll have a general tilt and tournament; [5]

[4] Embroidery.
[5] *I.e.,* in anticipation of his coming, we'll prepare for a general tilt, etc.

And then his marriage shall be solemnized.

For wot you not that I have made him
sure [1]

Unto our cousin, [2] the Earl of Gloucester's
heir?

LAN. Such news we hear, my lord.   380

EDW. That day, if not for him, yet for
my sake,

Who [3] in the triumph [4] will be challenger,

Spare for no cost. We will requite your
love.

WAR. In this, or aught, your highness
shall command us.

EDW. Thanks, gentle Warwick. Come,
let's in and revel.

Exeunt. Manent [5] *Mortimers.*

MOR. SEN. Nephew, I must to Scotland;
thou stayest here.

Leave now to oppose thyself against the
king.

Thou seest by nature he is mild and
calm,

And, seeing his mind so dotes on Gaveston,

Let him without controlment have his
will.   390

The mightiest kings have had their
minions:

Great Alexander loved Ephestion;

The conquering Hercules [6] for Hylas
wept;

And for Patroclus stern Achilles drooped;

And not kings only, but the wisest
men:

The Roman Tully loved Octavius;

Grave Socrates, wild Alcibiades.

Then let his grace, whose youth is
flexible,

And promiseth as much as we can wish,

Freely enjoy that vain, light-headed earl;

For riper years will wean him from such
toys.   401

MOR. JUN. Uncle, his wanton humor
grieves not me;

But this I scorn, that one so basely born

Should by his sovereign's favor grow so
pert,

And riot it with the treasure of the realm.

While soldiers mutiny for want of pay,

He wears a lord's revenue on his back,

And Midas-like he jets [7] it in the court,

With base, outlandish cullions [8] at his
heels,

Whose proud, fantastic liveries make
such show   410

As if that Proteus, god of shapes,
appeared.

I have not seen a dapper Jack [9] so brisk.

He wears a short Italian-hooded cloak

Larded with pearl, and in his Tuscan
cap

A jewel of more value than the crown.

Whiles other walk below, the king and he

From out a window laugh at such as we,

And flout our train, and jest at our attire.

Uncle, 'tis this that makes me impatient.

MOR. SEN. But, nephew, now you see the
king is changed.   420

MOR. JUN. Then so am I, and live to do
him service.

But, whiles I have a sword, a hand, a heart,

I will not yield to any such upstart.

You know my mind; come, uncle, let's
away.   *Exeunt.*

[SCENE V.

A room in Gloucester's castle.]

Enter Spencer [10] *and Baldock.*

BALD. Spencer, seeing that our lord th'
Earl of Gloucester's dead,

Which of the nobles dost thou mean to
serve?

SPEN. Not Mortimer, nor any of his side,

Because the king and he are enemies.

Baldock, learn this of me, a factious lord

Shall hardly do himself good, much less
us;

But he that hath the favor of a king

May with one word advance us while we
live.

The liberal Earl of Cornwall is the man

On whose good fortune Spencer's hope
depends.   10

BALD. What, mean you then to be his
follower?

SPEN. No, his companion, for he loves me
well,

And would have once preferred [11] me to
the king.

---

[1] Betrothed him.   [4] Tournament.
[2] Relative; here, niece.   [5] Remain.
[3] Whoever.   [6] Original reads *Hector.*

[7] Struts.   [10] *I.e.*, young Spencer.
[8] Rascals.   [11] Recommended.
[9] Knave.

BALD. But he is banished; there's small
   hope of him.
SPEN. Ay, for a while, but, Baldock, mark
   the end.
  A friend of mine told me in secrecy
  That he's repealed, and sent for back
    again;
  And even now a post came from the
    court
  With letters to our lady from the king,
  And as she read she smiled, which makes
    me think   20
  It is about her lover Gaveston.
BALD. 'Tis like enough, for, since he was
   exiled,
  She neither walks abroad, nor comes in
    sight.
  But I had thought the match had been
    broke off.
  And that his banishment had changed
    her mind.
SPEN. Our lady's first love is not waver-
   ing;
  My life for thine, she will have Gaveston.
BALD. Then hope I by her means to be pre-
   ferred,
  Having read unto her since she was a
    child.
SPEN. Then, Baldock, you must cast the
   scholar off,   30
  And learn to court it like a gentleman.
  'Tis not a black coat and a little band,
  A velvet-caped coat, faced before with
    serge,
  And smelling to a nosegay all the day,
  Or holding of a napkin in your hand,
  Or saying a long grace at a table's end,
  Or making low legs [1] to a nobleman,
  Or looking downward with your eyelids
    close,
  And saying, "Truly, an't [2] may please
    your honor,"
  Can get you any favor with great
    men.   40
  You must be proud, bold, pleasant,
    resolute,
  And now and then stab, as occasion
    serves.
BALD. Spencer, thou knowest I hate such
   formal toys,
  And use them but of mere hypocrisy.
  Mine old lord whiles he lived was so
    precise

  That he would take exceptions at my
    buttons,
  And, being like pin's heads, blame me for
    the bigness,
  Which made me curatelike in mine
    attire,
  Though inwardly licentious enough
  And apt for any kind of villainy.   50
  I am none of these common pedants, [3] I,
  That cannot speak without *propterea
    quod.* [4]
SPEN. But one of those that saith *quando-
   quidem,* [5]
  And hath a special gift to form a verb.
BALD. Leave off this jesting; here my lady
   comes.

Enter the Lady [*, Gloucester's daughter*].

LADY. The grief for his exile was not so
   much
  As is the joy of his returning home.
  This letter came from my sweet Gaves-
    ton.
  What need'st thou, love, thus to excuse
    thyself?
  I know thou couldst not come and visit
    me.   60
  [*Reads.*] "I will not long be from thee,
    though I die."
  This argues the entire love of my lord.
  [*Reads.*] "When I forsake thee, death
    seize on my heart."
  But rest thee here where Gaveston shall
    sleep.   [*Puts the letter into her bosom.*]
  Now to the letter of my lord the king.—
  He wills me to repair unto the court,
  And meet my Gaveston. Why do I stay,
  Seeing that he talks thus of my marriage
    day?—
  Who's there? Baldock!
  See that my coach be ready; I must
    hence.   70
BALD. It shall be done, madam.   *Exit.*
LADY. And meet me at the park-pale pres-
   ently.—
  Spencer, stay you and bear me company,
  For I have joyful news to tell thee of.
  My Lord of Cornwall is a-coming over,
  And will be at the court as soon as we.
SPEN. I knew the king would have him
   home again.

[1] Bows.   [2] If it.

[3] From 1598 edn. Original reads *pendants*.
[4] On account of which.
[5] Seeing that.

LADY. If all things sort out [1] as I hope they will,
  Thy service, Spencer, shall be thought upon.
SPEN. I humbly thank your ladyship. 80
LADY. Come, lead the way; I long till I am there.   [*Exeunt.*]

[SCENE vi.

Before Tynemouth Castle.]

Enter Edward, the Queen, Lancaster, Mortimer [, Junior], Warwick, Pembroke, Kent, Attendants.

EDW. The wind is good—I wonder why he stays;
  I fear me he is wracked upon the sea.
QUEEN. Look, Lancaster, how passionate [2] he is,
  And still [3] his mind runs on his minion!
LAN. My lord—
EDW. How now! What news? Is Gaveston arrived?
MOR. JUN. Nothing but Gaveston! What means your grace?
  You have matters of more weight to think upon;
  The King of France sets foot in Normandy.
EDW. A trifle! We'll expel him when we please. 10
  But tell me, Mortimer, what's thy device
  Against the stately triumph we decreed?
MOR. JUN. A homely one, my lord, not worth the telling.
EDW. Prithee, let me know it.
MOR. JUN. But, seeing you are so desirous, thus it is:
  A lofty cedar tree, fair flourishing,
  On whose top branches kingly eagles perch,
  And by the bark a canker creeps me up,
  And gets unto the highest bough of all.
  The motto: *Æque tandem.* [4]   20
EDW. And what is yours, my Lord of Lancaster?
LAN. My lord, mine's more obscure than Mortimer's.
  Pliny reports there is a flying fish
  Which all the other fishes deadly hate,
  And therefore, being pursued, it takes the air;

No sooner is it up, but there's a fowl
That seizeth it. This fish, my lord, I bear.
The motto this: *Undique mors est.* [5]
EDW. Proud Mortimer, ungentle Lancaster,
Is this the love you bear your sovereign? 30
Is this the fruit your reconcilement bears?
Can you in words make show of amity,
And in your shields display your rancorous minds?
What call you this but private libeling
Against the Earl of Cornwall and my brother?
QUEEN. Sweet husband, be content; they all love you.
EDW. They love me not that hate my Gaveston.
I am that cedar; shake me not too much.
And you, the eagles, soar ye ne'er so high,
I have the jesses [6] that will pull you down; 40
And *Æque tandem* shall that canker cry
Unto the proudest peer of Britainy.
Though thou compar'st him to a flying fish,
And threatenest death whether he rise or fall,
'Tis not the hugest monster of the sea
Nor foulest harpy that shall swallow him.
MOR. JUN. [*Aside.*] If in his absence thus he favors him,
What will he do whenas [7] he shall be present?
LAN. [*Aside.*]   That shall we see; look where his lordship comes.

Enter Gaveston.

EDW. My Gaveston! Welcome to Tynemouth! Welcome to thy friend! 50
Thy absence made me droop and pine away;
For, as the lovers of fair Danaë,
When she was locked up in a brazen tower,
Desired her more, and waxed outrageous,
So did it sure with me; and now thy sight
Is sweeter far than was thy parting hence
Bitter and irksome to my sobbing heart.

---

[1] Chance, turn out.   [3] Always.
[2] Sorrowful.   [4] Justly at last.
[5] Death is everywhere.
[6] Legstraps fastening a hawk to his leash.
Original reads *gresses.*   [7] When.

GAV. Sweet lord and king, your speech
     preventeth [1] mine,
Yet have I words left to express my joy.
The shepherd, nipped with biting win-
     ter's rage,   60
Frolics not more to see the painted
     spring
Than I do to behold your majesty.

EDW. Will none of you salute my Gaves-
     ton?

LAN. Salute him? Yes. Welcome, lord
     chamberlain!

MOR. JUN. Welcome is the good Earl of
     Cornwall!

WAR. Welcome, Lord Governor of the Isle
     of Man!

PEM. Welcome, Master Secretary!

EDM. Brother, do you hear them?

EDW. Still will these earls and barons
     use me thus?

GAV. My lord, I cannot brook these in-
     juries.   70

QUEEN. [*Aside.*] Ay me, poor soul, when
     these begin to jar.

EDW. Return it to their throats; I'll be
     thy warrant.

GAV. Base, leaden earls, that glory in
     your birth,
Go sit at home and eat your tenants'
     beef;
And come not here to scoff at Gaveston,
Whose mounting thoughts did never
     creep so low
As to bestow a look on such as you.

LAN. Yet I disdain not to do this for you!
               [*Offers to stab Gaveston.*]

EDW. Treason! Treason! Where's the
     traitor?

PEM.   Here! Here!

[EDW.] [2] Convey hence Gaveston; they'll
     murder him!   80

GAV. The life of thee shall salve this foul
     disgrace.

MOR. JUN. Villain, thy life, unless I miss
     mine aim.   [*Wounds Gaveston.*]

QUEEN. Ah, furious Mortimer, what hast
     thou done?

MOR. JUN. No more than I would answer,
     were he slain.

EDW. Yes, more than thou canst answer,
     though he live.

[1] Anticipateth.
[2] Original has *King* printed as part of preceding
speech.

Dear shall you both aby [3] this riotous
     deed.
Out of my presence! Come not near
     the court!

MOR. JUN. I'll not be barred the court
     for Gaveston.

LAN. We'll hale him by the ears unto the
     block.

EDW. Look to your own heads; his is
     sure enough.   90

WAR. Look to your own crown, if you
     back him thus.

EDM. Warwick, these words do ill be-
     seem thy years.

EDW. Nay, all of them conspire to cross
     me thus;
But, if I live, I'll tread upon their
     heads
That think with high looks thus to
     tread me down.
Come, Edmund, let's away and levy
     men;
'Tis war that must abate these barons'
     pride.
            Exit the King [*with his Train*].

WAR. Let's to our castles, for the king
     is moved.

MOR. JUN. Moved may he be, and perish
     in his wrath!   99

LAN. Cousin, it is no dealing with him now.
He means to make us stoop by force
     of arms,
And therefore let us jointly here protest
To prosecute that Gaveston to the
     death.

MOR. JUN. By heaven, the abject villain
     shall not live!

WAR. I'll have his blood, or die in seeking
     it.

PEM. The like oath Pembroke takes.

LAN.   And so doth Lancaster.
Now send our heralds to defy the
     king;
And make the people swear to put him
     down.

            Enter a Post.

MOR. JUN. Letters! From whence?

MESS. From Scotland, my lord.   110
           [*Gives letters to Mortimer.*]

LAN. Why, how now, cousin, how fares
     all our friends?

[3] Pay for.

Mor. Jun. My uncle's taken prisoner by the Scots.

Lan. We'll have him ransomed, man; be of good cheer.

Mor. Jun. They rate his ransom at five thousand pound.
Who should defray the money but the king,
Seeing he is taken prisoner in his wars?
I'll to the king.

Lan. Do, cousin, and I'll bear thee company.

War. Meantime, my Lord of Pembroke and myself
Will to Newcastle here, and gather head.[1]   120

Mor. Jun. About it then, and we will follow you.

Lan. Be resolute and full of secrecy.

War. I warrant you.
                              [Exit with Pembroke.]

Mor. Jun. Cousin, and if[2] he will not ransom him,
I'll thunder such a peal into his ears
As never subject did unto his king.

Lan. Content, I'll bear my part.—Holla! Who's there?

[Enter Guard.]

Mor. Jun. Ay, marry, such a guard as this doth well.

Lan. Lead on the way.

Guard. Whither will your lordships?   129

Mor. Jun. Whither else but to the king?

Guard. His highness is disposed to be alone.

Lan. Why, so he may, but we will speak to him.

Guard. You may not in, my lord.

Mor. Jun. May we not?

[Enter Edward and Kent.]

Edw. How now! What noise is this?
Who have we there? Is't you?

Mor. Jun. Nay, stay, my lord; I come to bring you news;
Mine uncle's taken prisoner by the Scots.

Edw. Then ransom him.

Lan. 'Twas in your wars; you should ransom him.   140

Mor. Jun. And you shall ransom him, or else——

Edm. What, Mortimer, you will not threaten him?

Edw. Quiet yourself; you shall have the broad seal
To gather for him thoroughout the realm.

Lan. Your minion Gaveston hath taught you this.

Mor. Jun. My lord, the family of the Mortimers
Are not so poor but, would they sell their land,
Would levy men enough to anger you.
We never beg, but use such prayers as these.

Edw. Shall I still be haunted thus?   150

Mor. Jun. Nay, now you're here alone, I'll speak my mind.

Lan. And so will I, and then, my lord, farewell.

Mor. Jun. The idle triumphs, masques, lascivious shows,
And prodigal gifts bestowed on Gaveston
Have drawn thy treasury dry, and made thee weak,
The murmuring commons overstretchéd hath.[3]

Lan. Look for rebellion; look to be deposed.
Thy garrisons are beaten out of France,
And, lame and poor, lie groaning at the gates.
The wild O'Neill, with swarms of Irish kerns,[4]   160
Lives uncontrolled within the English pale.
Unto the walls of York the Scots made road,
And unresisted drave away rich spoils.

Mor. Jun. The haughty Dane commands the narrow seas,
While in the harbor ride thy ships unrigged.

Lan. What foreign prince sends thee ambassadors?

Mor. Jun. Who loves thee but a sort[5] of flatterers?

Lan. Thy gentle queen, sole sister to Valois,
Complains that thou hast left her all forlorn.

---

[3] I.e., the idle triumphs, etc., have overstretched the murmuring commons.

[4] Foot soldiers.   [5] Company.

[1] Troops.   [2] Emphatic form of if.

Mor. Jun. Thy court is naked, being
  bereft of those   170
That makes a king seem glorious to the
  world—
I mean the peers, whom thou shouldst
  dearly love.
Libels are cast again [1] thee in the street;
Ballads and rimes made of thy over-
  throw.
Lan. The northern borderers, seeing the
  houses burnt,
Their wives and children slain, run up
  and down,
Cursing the name of thee and Gaveston.
Mor. Jun. When wert thou in the field
  with banner spread,
But once? And then thy soldiers marched
  like players,
With garish robes, not armor; and thy-
  self,   180
Bedaubed with gold, rode laughing at
  the rest,
Nodding and shaking of thy spangled
  crest,
Where women's favors hung like labels
  down.
Lan. And therefore came it that the
  fleering Scots,
To England's high disgrace, have made
  this jig: [2]

  Maids of England, sore may you mourn
  For your lemans [3] you have lost at Ban-
    nocksbourn.[4]
    With a heave and a ho!
  What, weeneth [5] the King of England
  So soon to have won Scotland?   190
    With a rombelow!

Mor. Jun. Wigmore shall fly [6] to set my
  uncle free.
Lan. And, when 'tis gone, our swords
  shall purchase more.
If ye be moved, revenge it as you can;
Look next to see us with our ensigns
  spread.   Exeunt Nobles.
Edw. My swelling heart for very anger
  breaks!
How oft have I been baited by these
  peers,
And dare not be revenged, for their
  power is great!

[1] Against.   [2] Carol.   [3] Lovers.
[4] Bannockburn was not actually fought until
1314.   [5] Imagineth.
[6] I.e., Mortimer will sell his estate.

Yet shall the crowing of these cocker-
  els
Affright a lion? Edward, unfold thy
  paws,   200
And let their lives' blood slake thy
  fury's hunger.
If I be cruel and grow tyrannous,
Now let them thank themselves, and
  rue too late.
Kent. My lord, I see your love to Gaveston
Will be the ruin of the realm and you,
For now the wrathful nobles threaten
  wars,
And therefore, brother, banish him for-
  ever.
Edw. Art thou an enemy to my Gaves-
  ton?
Kent. Ay, and it grieves me that I fa-
  vored him.
Edw. Traitor, begone! Whine thou with
  Mortimer.   210
Kent. So will I, rather than with Gaves-
  ton.
Edw. Out of my sight, and trouble me
  no more!
Kent. No marvel though thou scorn thy
  noble peers,
When I thy brother am rejected thus.
                             Exit.
Edw. Away!—Poor Gaveston, that hast
  no friend but me,
Do what they can, we'll live in Tyne-
  mouth here,
And, so I walk with him about the walls,
What care I though the earls begirt
  us round?—
Here comes she that's cause of all these
  jars.

Enter the Queen, Ladies three, [Gaveston,]
              Baldock, and Spencer.

Queen. My lord, 'tis thought the earls
  are up in arms.   220
Edw. Ay, and 'tis likewise thought you
  favor him.[7]
Queen. Thus do you still suspect me
  without cause.
Lady.[8] Sweet uncle, speak more kindly
  to the queen.
Gav. [Aside.] My lord, dissemble with
  her; speak her fair.
Edw. Pardon me, sweet, I forgot myself

[7] I.e., Mortimer.   [8] Gloucester's daughter.

QUEEN. Your pardon is quickly got of
Isabel.
EDW. The younger Mortimer is grown
so brave
That to my face he threatens civil wars.
GAV. Why do you not commit him to the
Tower?
EDW. I dare not, for the people love him
well.   230
GAV. Why, then we'll have him privily
made away.
EDW. Would Lancaster and he had both
caroused [1]
A bowl of poison to each other's health!
But let them go, and tell me what are
these.
LADY. Two of my father's servants whilst
he lived.
May't please your grace to entertain
them now.
EDW. Tell me, where wast thou born?
What is thine arms?
BALD. My name is Baldock, and my
gentry
I fetched from Oxford, not from heraldry.
EDW. The fitter art thou, Baldock, for
my turn.   240
Wait on me, and I'll see thou shalt not
want.
BALD. I humbly thank your majesty.
EDW. Knowest thou him, Gaveston?
GAV.   Ay, my lord;
His name is Spencer; he is well allied.
For my sake, let him wait upon your
grace;
Scarce shall you find a man of more
desert.
EDW. Then, Spencer, wait upon me; for
his sake
I'll grace thee with a higher style ere long.
SPEN. No greater titles happen unto me
Than to be favored of your majesty.
EDW. Cousin, this day shall be your mar-
riage feast.   251
And, Gaveston, think that I love thee
well
To wed thee to our niece, the only heir
Unto the Earl of Gloucester late de-
ceased.
GAV. I know, my lord, many will stomach
me,
But I respect neither their love nor
hate.

[1] Drunk.

EDW. The headstrong barons shall not
limit me;
He that I list to favor shall be great.
Come, let's away; and, when the mar-
riage ends,   259
Have at the rebels, and their complices! [2]
                            Exeunt omnes.

[SCENE vii.

The rebels' camp near Tynemouth Castle.]

*Enter Lancaster, Mortimer, Jun[ior,] War-
wick, Pembroke, Kent.*

KENT. My lords, of love to this our na-
tive land
I come to join with you and leave the
king,
And in your quarrel and the realm's
behoof
Will be the first that shall adventure
life.
LAN. I fear me, you are sent of policy,[3]
To undermine us with a show of love.
WAR. He is your brother; therefore have
we cause
To cast [4] the worst, and doubt of your
revolt.
EDM. Mine honor shall be hostage of my
truth;
If that will not suffice, farewell, my
lords!   10
MOR. JUN. Stay, Edmund; never was
Plantagenet
False to his word, and therefore trust
we thee.
PEM. But what's the reason you should
leave him now?
KENT. I have informed the Earl of Lan-
caster.
LAN. And it sufficeth. Now, my lords,
know this,
That Gaveston is secretly arrived,
And here in Tynemouth frolics with
the king.
Let us with these our followers scale
the walls,
And suddenly surprise them unawares. 19
MOR. JUN. I'll give the onset.
WAR.   And I'll follow thee.
MOR. JUN. This tottered [5] ensign of my
ancestors,

[2] Accomplices.   [4] Forecast, suspect
[3] In trickery.   [5] Tattered.

Which swept the desert shore of that
    dead sea
Whereof we got the name of Mortimer,
Will I advance upon this castle walls.
Drums, strike alarum, raise them from
    their sport,
And ring aloud the knell of Gaveston!
LAN. None be so hardy as to touch the
    king;
But neither spare you Gaveston nor
    his friends.   *Exeunt.*

[SCENE viii.

In Tynemouth Castle.]

Enter the King and Spencer; to them
                    Gaveston, etc.

EDW. O, tell me, Spencer, where is Gaves-
    ton?
SPEN. I fear me he is slain, my gracious
    lord.
EDW. No, here he comes; now let them
    spoil and kill.—
    Fly, fly, my lords; the earls have got
    the hold!
    Take shipping and away to Scarborough!
    Spencer and I will post away by land.
GAV. O, stay, my lord; they will not in-
    jure you.
EDW. I will not trust them; Gaveston,
    away!
GAV. Farewell, my lord.
EDW. Lady, farewell.   10
LADY. Farewell, sweet uncle, till we meet
    again.
EDW. Farewell, sweet Gaveston, and fare-
    well, niece.
QUEEN. No farewell to poor Isabel, thy
    queen?
EDW. Yes, yes, for Mortimer, your lover's
    sake.   *Exeunt omnes; manet Isabella.*
QUEEN. Heavens can witness I love none
    but you!
    From my embracements thus he breaks
    away.
    O, that mine arms could close this isle
    about,
    That I might pull him to me where I
    would,
    Or that these tears that drizzle from mine
    eyes
Had power to mollify his stony heart, 20
That when I had him we might never
    part!

Enter the Barons. Alarums.

LAN. I wonder how he scaped!
MOR. JUN.   Who's this? The queen!
QUEEN. Ay, Mortimer, the miserable
    queen,
    Whose pining heart her inward sighs have
    blasted,
    And body with continual mourning
    wasted.
    These hands are tired with haling of my
    lord
    From Gaveston, from wicked Gaveston;
    And all in vain, for, when I speak him fair,
    He turns away, and smiles upon his
    minion.
MOR. JUN. Cease to lament, and tell us
    where's the king.   30
QUEEN. What would you with the king?
    Is't him you seek?
LAN. No, madam, but that cursèd Gaves-
    ton.
    Far be it from the thought of Lancaster
    To offer violence to his sovereign.
    We would but rid the realm of Gaveston.
    Tell us where he remains, and he shall die.
QUEEN. He's gone by water unto Scar-
    borough;
    Pursue him quickly, and he cannot scape.
    The king hath left him, and his train is
    small.
WAR. Foreslow [1] no time, sweet Lancaster;
    let's march.   40
MOR. JUN. How comes it that the king and
    he is parted?
QUEEN. That this your army, going several
    ways,
    Might be of lesser force, and, with the
    power
    That he intendeth presently to raise,
    Be easily suppressed. And therefore be-
    gone!
MOR. JUN. Here in the river rides a Flem-
    ish hoy; [2]
    Let's all aboard, and follow him amain.
LAN. The wind that bears him hence will
    fill our sails.
    Come, come aboard; 'tis but an hour's
    sailing.
MOR. JUN. Madam, stay you within this
    castle here.   50
QUEEN. No, Mortimer, I'll to my lord the
    king.

---

[1] Delay, lose.   [2] Small ship.

Mor. Jun. Nay, rather sail with us to Scarborough.

Queen. You know the king is so suspicious As, if he hear I have but talked with you, Mine honor will be called in question; And therefore, gentle Mortimer, begone.

Mor. Jun. Madam, I cannot stay to answer you, But think of Mortimer as he deserves.

Queen. [*Aside.*] So well hast thou deserved, sweet Mortimer, As Isabel could live with thee forever! 60 In vain I look for love at Edward's hand, Whose eyes are fixed on none but Gaveston; Yet once more I'll importune him with prayers. If he be strange and not regard my words, My son and I will over into France, And to the king my brother there complain How Gaveston hath robbed me of his love. But yet I hope my sorrows will have end, And Gaveston this blessed day be slain.

Exeunt.

[Scene ix.

A field near Pembroke's castle.]

Enter Gaveston, pursued.

Gav. Yet, lusty lords, I have escaped your hands, Your threats, your larums, and your hot pursuits; And, though divorcéd from King Edward's eyes, Yet liveth Pierce of Gaveston unsurprised,[1] Breathing, in hope (*malgrado*[2] all your beards, That muster rebels thus against your king) To see his royal sovereign once again.

Enter the Nobles [with Attendants].

War. Upon him, soldiers; take away his weapons!

Mor. Jun. Thou proud disturber of thy country's peace, Corrupter of thy king, cause of these broils,   10

Base flatterer, yield! And were it not for shame, Shame and dishonor to a soldier's name, Upon my weapon's point here shouldst thou fall, And welter in thy gore.

Lan.   Monster of men, That, like the Greekish strumpet,[3] trained[4] to arms And bloody wars so many valiant knights, Look for no other fortune, wretch, than death! King Edward is not here to buckler thee.

War. Lancaster, why talk'st thou to the slave? Go, soldiers, take him hence, for, by my sword,   20 His head shall off. Gaveston, short warning Shall serve thy turn; it is our country's cause That here severely we will execute Upon thy person. Hang him at a bough.

Gav. My lord—!

War.   Soldiers, have him away!— But, for[5] thou wert the favorite of a king, Thou shalt have so much honor at our hands—[6]

Gav. I thank you all, my lords. Then I perceive That heading is one, and hanging is the other, And death is all.

Enter Earl of Arundel.

Lan.   How now, my Lord of Arundel?

Arun. My lords, King Edward greets you all by me.   31

War. Arundel, say your message.

Arun.   His majesty, Hearing that you had taken Gaveston, Entreateth you by me, yet but he may See him before he dies; forwhy,[7] he says, And sends you word, he knows that die he shall; And, if you gratify his grace so far, He will be mindful of the courtesy.

War. How now?

[3] Helen of Troy   [6] *I.e.,* as to be beheaded.
[4] Lured.   [7] Because.
[1] Uncaptured.   [2] In spite of.
[5] Since.

GAV.   Renowmèd Edward, how
    thy name   39
Revives poor Gaveston!
WAR.   No, it needeth not;
    Arundel, we will gratify the king
In other matters; he must pardon us in
    this.
Soldiers, away with him!
GAV.   Why, my Lord of Warwick,
Will not these delays beget my hopes?
I know it, lords, it is this life you aim at;
Yet grant King Edward this.
MOR. JUN.   Shalt thou appoint
What we shall grant? Soldiers, away
    with him!
Thus we'll gratify the king:
We'll send his head by thee. Let him be-
    stow   49
His tears on that, for that is all he gets
Of Gaveston, or else his senseless trunk.
LAN. Not so, my lord, lest he bestow more
    cost
In burying him than he hath ever earned.
ARUN. My lords, it is his majesty's request,
And in the honor of a king he swears,
He will but talk with him, and send him
    back.
WAR. When? Can you tell? Arundel, no!
    We wot
He that the care of realm remits,
And drives his nobles to these exigents [1]
For Gaveston, will, if he sees him once,
Violate any promise to possess him.   61
ARUN. Then if you will not trust his grace
    in keep, [2]
My lords, I will be pledge for his return.
MOR. JUN. It is honorable in thee to offer
    this;
But, for we know thou art a noble gentle-
    man,
We will not wrong thee so,
To make away a true man for a thief.
GAV. How mean'st thou, Mortimer? That
    is overbase.
MOR. JUN. Away, base groom, robber of
    king's renowm!
Question with thy companions and thy
    mates.   70
PEM. My Lord Mortimer, and you, my
    lords, each one,
To gratify the king's request therein,
Touching the sending of this Gaveston,
Because his majesty so earnestly

Desires to see the man before his death,
I will upon mine honor undertake
To carry him, and bring him back again;
Provided this, that you, my Lord of
    Arundel,
Will join with me.
WAR.   Pembroke, what wilt thou do?
    Cause yet more bloodshed? Is it not
    enough   80
That we have taken him, but must we
    now
Leave him on "had I wist," [3] and let
    him go?
PEM. My lords, I will not overwoo your
    honors,
But, if you dare trust Pembroke with the
    prisoner,
Upon mine oath, I will return him back.
ARUN. My Lord of Lancaster, what say
    you in this?
LAN. Why, I say, let him go on Pem-
    broke's word.
PEM. And you, Lord Mortimer?
MOR. JUN. How say you, my Lord of War-
    wick?
WAR. Nay, do your pleasures; I know how
    'twill prove.   90
PEM. Then give him me.
GAV.   Sweet sovereign, yet I come
To see thee ere I die.
WAR. [Aside.]   Yet not perhaps,
If Warwick's wit and policy prevail.
MOR. JUN. My Lord of Pembroke, we de-
    liver him you;
Return him on your honor. Sound away!
Exeunt.   Manent Pembroke, Arundel, [4]
    Gavest[on], and Pembroke's Men for
                                          soldiers.
PEM. My lord, you shall go with me.
My house is not far hence, out of the way
A little; but our men shall go along.
We that have pretty wenches to our
    wives,
Sir, must not come so near and balk
    their lips.   100
ARUN. [4] 'Tis very kindly spoke, my Lord
    of Pembroke;
Your honor hath an adamant [5] of power
To draw a prince.

---

[1] Straits.   [2] Custody.

[3] "Had I known—the exclamation of those
who repent of what they have rashly done"
(Dyce).
[4] Original reads Mat[revis], probably, as Dyce
suggests, because the parts of Arundel and Matrevis were taken by the same actor.   [5] Magnet.

Pem.   So, my lord. Come
hither, James.
I do commit this Gaveston to thee;
Be thou this night his keeper; in the
    morning
We will discharge thee of thy charge.
    Begone!
Gav. Unhappy Gaveston, whither goest
    thou now?   *Exit cum servis Pem.*[1]
Horse Boy. My lord, we'll quickly be at
    Cobham.   *Exeunt ambo.*

[Scene x.

A road to Boroughbridge, Yorkshire.]

*Enter Gaveston, mourning, and the Earl of
                        Pembroke's Men.*

Gav. O treacherous Warwick, thus to
    wrong thy friend!
James. I see it is your life these arms pur-
    sue.
Gav. Weaponless must I fall, and die in
    bands?
O, must this day be period of my life?
Center of all my bliss! And ye be men,
Speed to the king!

Enter Warwick and his Company.

War.   My Lord of Pembroke's men,
Strive you no longer—I will have that
    Gaveston.
James. Your lordship doth dishonor to
    yourself,
And wrong our lord, your honorable
    friend.
War. No, James, it is my country's cause
    I follow.   10
Go, take the villain; soldiers, come away.
We'll make quick work. Commend me
    to your master,
My friend, and tell him that I watched
    it well.
Come, let thy shadow [2] parley with King
    Edward.
Gav. Treacherous earl, shall I not see the
    king?
War. The King of Heaven, perhaps; no
    other king.
Away!
*Exeunt Warwick and his Men with Gavest[on].
            Manet James cum cæteris.*[3]

[1] With Pembroke's servants.   [3] With the rest.
[2] Ghost.

[James.] Come, fellows, it booted not for
    us to strive.
We will in haste go certify our lord.
                                    Exeunt.

[Scene xi.

Near Boroughbridge.]

*Enter King Edward, [Baldock,] and Spencer,
                with drums and fifes.*

Edw. I long to hear an answer from the
    barons
Touching my friend, my dearest Gaves-
    ton.
Ah, Spencer, not the riches of my realm
Can ransom him! Ah, he is marked to
    die!
I know the malice of the younger Mor-
    timer;
Warwick, I know, is rough; and Lan-
    caster
Inexorable; and I shall never see
My lovely Pierce, my Gaveston again!
The barons overbear me with their pride.
Spen. Were I King Edward, England's
    sovereign,   10
Son to the lovely Eleanor of Spain,
Great Edward Longshanks' issue, would
    I bear
These braves, this rage, and suffer un-
    controlled
These barons thus to beard me in my
    land,
In mine own realm? My lord, pardon my
    speech:
Did you retain your father's magnanim-
    ity,
Did you regard the honor of your name,
You would not suffer thus your majesty
Be counterbuffed of [4] your nobility.
Strike off their heads, and let them
    preach on poles!   20
No doubt, such lessons they will teach
    the rest
As by their preachments they will profit
    much,
And learn obedience to their lawful king.
Edw. Yea, gentle Spencer, we have been
    too mild,
Too kind to them, but now have drawn
    our sword.
And, if they send me not my Gaveston,

[4] Curbed by.

We'll steel it [1] on their crest, and poll [2]
　their tops.
BALD. This haught [3] resolve becomes your
　majesty,
Not to be tied to their affection,
As though your highness were a school-
　boy still,　　　　　　　　　　　　　30
And must be awed and governed like a
　child.

*Enter Hugh Spencer, an old man, father to
　the young Spencer, with his truncheon,
　　　　　　　　　　　and Soldiers.*

SPEN. FA[THER.] Long live my sovereign,
　the noble Edward,
In peace triumphant, fortunate in
　wars!
EDW. Welcome, old man; com'st thou in
　Edward's aid?
Then tell thy prince of whence, and what
　thou art.
SPEN. FA. Lo, with a band of bowmen and
　of pikes,
Brown bills and targeteers, four hundred
　strong,
Sworn to defend King Edward's royal
　right,
I come in person to your majesty,
Spencer, the father of Hugh Spencer
　there,　　　　　　　　　　　　　40
Bound to your highness everlastingly,
For favors done, in him, unto us all.
EDW. Thy father, Spencer?
SPEN.　　　　　True, and it like your grace,
That pours, in lieu of all your goodness
　shown,
His life, my lord, before your princely
　feet.
EDW. Welcome ten thousand times, old
　man, again.
Spencer, this love, this kindness to thy
　king,
Argues thy noble mind and disposition.
Spencer, I here create thee Earl of Wilt-
　shire,
And daily will enrich thee with our fa-
　vor,　　　　　　　　　　　　　50
That, as the sunshine, shall reflect o'er
　thee.
Beside, the more to manifest our love,
Because we hear Lord Bruce doth sell
　his land,

And that the Mortimers are in hand [4]
　withal,
Thou shalt have crowns of us t' outbid
　the barons.
And, Spencer, spare them not, but lay
　it on.
Soldiers, a largess, and thrice welcome
　all!
SPEN. My lord, here comes the queen.

*Enter the Queen and her Son, and Levune,
　　　　　　　　　　　a Frenchman.*

EDW.　　　　　　　　Madam, what news?
QUEEN. News of dishonor, lord, and dis-
　content.
Our friend Levune, faithful and full of
　trust,　　　　　　　　　　　　　60
Informeth us, by letters and by words,
That Lord Valois, our brother, King of
　France,
Because your highness hath been slack
　in homage,
Hath seizéd Normandy into his hands.
These be the letters, this the messenger.
EDW. Welcome, Levune. Tush, Sib, [5] if
　this be all,
Valois and I will soon be friends again.—
But to my Gaveston! Shall I never see,
Never behold thee now?—Madam, in
　this matter　　　　　　　　　　69
We will employ you and your little son;
You shall go parley with the King of
　France.—
Boy, see you bear you bravely to the
　king,
And do your message with a majesty.
PRINCE. Commit not to my youth things
　of more weight
Than fits a prince so young as I to bear,
And fear not, lord and father, heaven's
　great beams
On Atlas' shoulder shall not lie more safe
Than shall your charge committed to
　my trust.
QUEEN. Ah, boy, this towardness [6] makes
　thy mother fear
Thou art not marked to many days on
　earth.　　　　　　　　　　　　80
EDW. Madam, we will that you with speed
　be shipped,
And this our son. Levune shall follow you

[1] Use steel(?).　　[2] Crop.　　[3] Haughty, bold.
[4] In negotiation (to sell their lands).
[5] Either *gossip, dear*, or an abbreviation for
Isabella.　　　　　　　　　　　　[6] Aptness.

With all the haste we can despatch him
  hence.
Choose of our lords to bear you company,
And go in peace; leave us in wars at
  home.
QUEEN. Unnatural wars, where subjects
  brave their king.
God end them once! My lord, I take
  my leave,
To make my preparation for France.
         [Exit with Prince Edward.]

Enter Lord Arundel.[1]

EDW. What, Lord Arundel, dost thou
  come alone?
ARUN. Yea, my good lord, for Gaveston is
  dead.   90
EDW. Ah, traitors! Have they put my
  friend to death?
Tell me, Arundel, died he ere thou
  cam'st,
Or didst thou see my friend to take his
  death?
ARUN. Neither, my lord; for, as he was
  surprised,
Begirt with weapons and with enemies
  round,
I did your highness' message to them all,
Demanding him of them, entreating
  rather,
And said, upon the honor of my name,
That I would undertake to carry him
Unto your highness, and to bring him
  back.   100
EDW. And tell me, would the rebels deny
  me that?
SPEN. Proud recreants!
EDW.   Yea, Spencer, traitors all.
ARUN. I found them at the first inexorable.
The Earl of Warwick would not bide the
  hearing;
Mortimer hardly; Pembroke and Lan-
  caster
Spake least. And, when they flatly had
  denied,
Refusing to receive me pledge for him,
The Earl of Pembroke mildly thus be-
  spake:
"My lords, because our sovereign sends
  for him,   109
And promiseth he shall be safe returned,

I will this undertake, to have him hence,
And see him redelivered to your hands."
EDW. Well, and how fortunes that he came
  not?
SPEN. Some treason, or some villainy, was
  cause.
ARUN. The Earl of Warwick seized him on
  his way,
For, being delivered unto Pembroke's
  men,
Their lord rode home, thinking his pris-
  oner safe.
But, ere he came, Warwick in ambush
  lay,
And bare him to his death, and in a
  trench
Strake[2] off his head, and marched unto
  the camp.   120
SPEN. A bloody part, flatly against law of
  arms!
EDW. O, shall I speak, or shall I sigh and
  die?
SPEN. My lord, refer your vengeance to
  the sword
Upon these barons; hearten up your men;
Let them not unrevenged murther your
  friends!
Advance your standard, Edward, in the
  field,
And march to fire them from their start-
  ing holes.[3]
EDWARD (*Kneels and saith:*)
By earth, the common mother of us all,
By heaven and all the moving orbs
  thereof,
By this right hand, and by my father's
  sword,   130
And all the honors longing[4] to my
  crown,
I will have heads and lives for him, as
  many
As I have manors, castles, towns, and
  towers!—   *[Rises.]*
Treacherous Warwick! Traitorous Mor-
  timer!
If I be England's king, in lakes of gore
Your headless trunks, your bodies will I
  trail,
That you may drink your fill, and quaff
  in blood,
And stain my royal standard with the
  same,

---

[1] Original gives Arundel's part to Matrevis
throughout the scene.

[2] Struck.   [4] Belonging.
[3] Refuges taken by hunted animals.

That so my bloody colors may suggest 139
Remembrance of revenge immortally
On your accursèd traitorous progeny,
You villains, that have slain my Gaves-
ton!
And in this place of honor and of trust,
Spencer, sweet Spencer, I adopt thee
here;
And merely [1] of our love we do create
thee
Earl of Gloucester and lord chamber-
lain,
Despite of times, despite of enemies.
SPEN. My lord, here is a messenger from
the barons,
Desires access unto your majesty.
EDW. Admit him near.   150

Enter the Herald from the Barons with his
coat-of-arms.

MESS. Long live King Edward, England's
lawful lord!
EDW. So wish not they, iwis,[2] that sent
thee hither.
Thou com'st from Mortimer and his
complices;
A ranker rout of rebels never was.
Well, say thy message.
MESS. The barons, up in arms, by me
salute
Your highness with long life and happi-
ness,
And bid me say, as plainer[3] to your
grace,
That, if without effusion of blood
You will this grief have ease and rem-
edy,   160
That from your princely person you re-
move
This Spencer, as a putrefying branch,
That deads the royal vine, whose golden
leaves
Empale your princely head, your diadem,
Whose brightness such pernicious up-
starts dim,
Say they, and lovingly advise your
grace
To cherish virtue and nobility,
And have old servitors in high esteem,
And shake off smooth dissembling flat-
terers.

---

[1] Purely.   [3] Complainer, petitioner.
[2] Certainly.

This granted, they, their honors, and
their lives   170
Are to your highness vowed and conse-
crate.
SPEN. Ah, traitors, will they still display
their pride?
EDW. Away, tarry no answer, but begone!
Rebels, will they appoint their sover-
eign
His sports, his pleasures, and his com-
pany?
Yet, ere thou go, see how I do divorce
                    Embrace Spencer.
Spencer from me.—Now get thee to thy
lords,
And tell them I will come to chastise
them
For murthering Gaveston. Hie thee, get
thee gone!
Edward with fire and sword follows at
thy heels.   180
My lords, perceive you how these rebels
swell?
Soldiers, good hearts, defend your sov-
ereign's right,
For now, even now, we march to make
them stoop.
Away!   *Exeunt.*
Alarums, excursions, a great fight, and a
                    retreat.

Enter the King, Spencer the Father, Spencer
the Son, and the Noblemen of the King's
                    side.

EDW. Why do we sound retreat? Upon
them, lords!
This day I shall pour vengeance with my
sword
On those proud rebels that are up in
arms
And do confront and countermand[4] their
king.
SPEN. I doubt it not, my lord, right will
prevail.
SPEN. FA. 'Tis not amiss, my liege, for
either part   190
To breathe awhile. Our men, with sweat
and dust
All choked well near, begin to faint for
heat;
And this retire refresheth horse and man.
SPEN. Here come the rebels.

---

[4] Oppose.

Enter the Barons, Mortimer, [Junior,] Lancaster, Warwick, Pembroke, cum cæteris.

MOR. JUN. Look, Lancaster; yonder is
Edward among his flatterers.

LAN. And there let him be
Till he pay dearly for their company.

WAR. And shall, or Warwick's sword shall
smite in vain.

EDW. What, rebels, do you shrink and
sound retreat?

MOR. JUN. No, Edward, no; thy flatterers
faint and fly.   200

LAN. Th'ad[1] best betimes forsake them[2]
and their trains,[3]
For they'll betray thee, traitors as they
are.

SPEN. Traitor on thy face, rebellious Lancaster!

PEM. Away, base upstart! Brav'st thou
nobles thus?

SPEN. FA. A noble attempt and honorable
deed
Is it not, trow ye, to assemble aid
And levy arms against your lawful king!

EDW. For which ere long their heads shall
satisfy,
T' appease the wrath of their offended
king.

MOR. JUN. Then, Edward, thou wilt fight
it to the last,   210
And rather bathe thy sword in subjects'
blood
Than banish that pernicious company?

EDW. Ay, traitors all, rather than thus be
braved,
Make England's civil towns huge heaps
of stones,
And plows to go about our palace gates.

WAR. A desperate and unnatural resolution!
Alarum! To the fight!
St. George for England, and the barons'
right!

EDW. Saint George for England, and King
Edward's right! *[Alarums. Exeunt.]*

*Enter Edward [and his Followers,] with the
Barons captives.*

EDW. Now, lusty lords, now, not by chance
of war,   220
But justice of the quarrel and the cause,

Vailed is your pride. Methinks you hang
the heads;
But we'll advance[4] them, traitors.
Now 'tis time
To be avenged on you for all your
braves,[5]
And for the murther of my dearest friend,
To whom right well you knew our soul
was knit,
Good Pierce of Gaveston, my sweet
favorite.
Ah, rebels, recreants, you made him
away!

EDM. Brother, in regard of thee and of thy
land
Did they remove that flatterer from thy
throne.   230

EDW. So, sir, you have spoke; away, avoid
our presence!—   *[Exit Kent.]*
Accursèd wretches, was't in regard of us,
When we had sent our messenger to request
He might be spared to come to speak
with us,
And Pembroke undertook for his return,
That thou, proud Warwick, watched the
prisoner,
Poor Pierce, and headed[6] him against law
of arms?
For which thy head shall overlook the
rest,
As much as thou in rage outwent'st the
rest.

WAR. Tyrant, I scorn thy threats and
menaces;   240
'Tis but temporal[7] that thou canst inflict.

LAN. The worst is death, and better die to
live
Than live in infamy under such a king.

EDW. Away with them, my Lord of Winchester!
These lusty leaders, Warwick and Lancaster,
I charge you roundly, off with both their
heads!
Away!

WAR. Farewell, vain world!

LAN.   Sweet Mortimer, farewell.

MOR. JUN. England, unkind to thy nobility,
Groan for this grief; behold how thou art
maimed!   250

---

[1] Thou had.   [3] Plots.
[2] Original reads *thee*.

[4] Raise.   [6] Beheaded.
[5] Boasts.   [7] Supply *punishment*.

EDW. Go take that haughty Mortimer to
the Tower;
There see him safe bestowed. And, for
the rest,
Do speedy execution on them all.
Begone!
MOR. JUN. What, Mortimer, can ragged,
stony walls
Immure thy virtue that aspires to
heaven?
No, Edward, England's scourge, it may
not be;
Mortimer's hope surmounts his fortune
far. [*The Barons are led away.*]
EDW. Sound drums and trumpets! March
with me, my friends.
Edward this day hath crowned him king
anew.　　　　　　　　　　260
Exit [*with his Train*]. *Manent Spencer
filius,*[1] *Levune, and Baldock.*
SPEN. Levune, the trust that we repose in
thee
Begets the quiet of King Edward's
land.
Therefore begone in haste, and with
advice
Bestow that treasure on the lords of
France,
That, therewith all enchanted, like the
guard
That suffered Jove to pass in showers of
gold
To Danaë, all aid may be denied
To Isabel, the queen, that now in France
Makes friends, to cross the seas with her
young son,
And step into his father's regiment. 270
LEVUNE. That's it these barons and the
subtle queen
Long levied[2] at.
BAL.　　　　　Yea, but, Levune, thou seest
These barons lay their heads on blocks
together.
What they intend, the hangman frus-
trates clean.
LEVUNE. Have you no doubts, my lords,
I'll clap s' close[3]
Among the lords of France with Eng-
land's gold
That Isabel shall make her plaints in
vain,

And France shall be obdurate with her
tears.
SPEN. Then make for France amain;
Levune, away!
Proclaim King Edward's wars and vic-
tories.　　　　　*Exeunt omnes.* 280

[SCENE xii.

Near the Tower of London.]

Enter Edmund.

EDM. Fair blows the wind for France.
Blow, gentle gale,
Till Edmund be arrived for England's
good!
Nature, yield to my country's cause in
this.
A brother? No, a butcher of thy friends!
Proud Edward, dost thou banish me thy
presence?
But I'll to France, and cheer the wrongéd
queen,
And certify what Edward's looseness is.
Unnatural king, to slaughter noble men
And cherish flatterers! Mortimer, I
stay[4]
Thy sweet escape; stand gracious, gloomy
night,　　　　　　　　　　10
To his device.

Enter Mortimer, [*Junior,*] *disguised.*

MOR. JUN.　　　Holla! Who walketh there?
Is't you, my lord?
EDM.　　　　　　Mortimer, 'tis I.
But hath thy potion wrought so happily?
MOR. JUN. It hath, my lord; the warders
all asleep,
I thank them, gave me leave to pass in
peace.
But hath your grace got shipping unto
France?
EDM. Fear it not.　　　　　*Exeunt.*

[SCENE xiii.

Paris.]

Enter the Queen and her Son.

QUEEN. Ah, boy, our friends do fail us all
in France.
The lords are cruel, and the king unkind.
What shall we do?

---

[1] Son.
[2] Frequently misused for *leveled* in this period.
[3] Contrive so secretly.

[4] Await.

PRINCE. Madam, return to England,
And please my father well, and then a fig
For all my uncle's friendship here in
France.
I warrant you, I'll win his highness
quickly;
A [1] loves me better than a thousand
Spencers.
QUEEN. Ah, boy, thou art deceived, at
least in this,
To think that we can yet be tuned to-
gether.
No, no, we jar too far. Unkind Valois! 10
Unhappy Isabel, when France rejects,
Whither, O, whither dost thou bend thy
steps?

Enter Sir John of Hainault.

SIR J. Madam, what cheer?
QUEEN. Ah, good Sir John of Hainault,
Never so cheerless, nor so far distressed.
SIR J. I hear, sweet lady, of the king's un-
kindness.
But droop not, madam; noble minds
contemn
Despair. Will your grace with me to
Hainault,
And there stay time's advantage with
your son?
How say you, my lord, will you go with
your friends, 19
And shake off all our fortunes equally?
PRINCE. So pleaseth the queen, my mother,
me it likes.
The King of England nor the court of
France
Shall have me from my gracious mother's
side,
Till I be strong enough to break a staff;
And then have at the proudest Spencer's
head.
SIR J. Well said, my lord!
QUEEN. O, my sweet heart, how do I moan
thy wrongs,
Yet triumph in the hope of thee, my joy!
Ah, sweet Sir John, even to the utmost
verge
Of Europe, or the shore of Tanais, 30
Will we with thee to Hainault—so we will.
The marquis is a noble gentleman;
His grace, I dare presume, will welcome
me.
But who are these?
[1] He.

Enter Edmund and Mortimer [, Junior].

EDM. Madam, long may you live,
Much happier than your friends in
England do!
QUEEN. Lord Edmund and Lord Morti-
mer alive!
Welcome to France! The news was here,
my lord,
That you were dead, or very near your
death.
MOR. JUN. Lady, the last was truest of the
twain;
But Mortimer, reserved for better hap, 40
Hath shaken off the thralldom of the
Tower,
And lives t' advance your standard, good
my lord.
PRINCE. How mean you, and [2] the king,
my father, lives?
No, my Lord Mortimer, not I, I trow.
QUEEN. Not, son? Why not? I would it
were no worse.
But, gentle lords, friendless we are in
France.
MOR. JUN. Monsieur le Grand, a noble
friend of yours,
Told us at our arrival all the news:
How hard the nobles, how unkind the
king
Hath showed himself. But, madam, right
makes room 50
Where weapons want; and, though a
many friends
Are made away, as Warwick, Lancaster,
And others of our party and faction,
Yet have we friends—assure your grace—
in England
Would cast up caps and clap their hands
for joy
To see us there, appointed [3] for our foes.
EDM. Would all were well, and Edward
well reclaimed,
For England's honor, peace, and quiet-
ness.
MOR. JUN. But by the sword, my lord, it
must be deserved; [4]
The king will ne'er forsake his flat-
terers. 60
SIR J. My lords of England, sith [5] the
ungentle king
Of France refuseth to give aid of arms
To this distresséd queen his sister here,

[2] If.   [4] Earned.
[3] Equipped.   [5] Since.

Go you with her to Hainault. Doubt ye
　not,
We will find comfort, money, men, and
　friends
Ere long, to bid the English king a base.[1]
How say, young prince? What think you
　of the match?
PRINCE. I think King Edward will outrun
　us all.
QUEEN. Nay, son, not so; and you must
　not discourage
Your friends, that are so forward in your
　aid.　　　　　　　　　　　　　70
EDM. Sir John of Hainault, pardon us, I
　pray ;
These comforts that you give our woeful
　queen
Bind us in kindness all at your command.
QUEEN. Yea, gentle brother; and the God
　of heaven
Prosper your happy motion,[2] good Sir
　John.
MOR. JUN. This noble gentleman, forward
　in arms,
Was born, I see, to be our anchor-hold.
Sir John of Hainault, be it thy renown,
That England's queen and nobles in
　distress
Have been by thee restored and com-
　forted.　　　　　　　　　　　　80
SIR J. Madam, along, and you, my lord,
　with me,
That England's peers may Hainault's
　welcome see.　　　　　　[Exeunt.]

[SCENE xiv.

The King's palace in London.]

Enter the King, Arundel,[3] *the two Spencers,
　　　　　　　　　　　　with Others.*

EDW. Thus, after many threats of wrathful
　war,
Triumpheth England's Edward with his
　friends.
And triumph, Edward, with his friends
　uncontrolled!
My Lord of Gloucester, do you hear the
　news?
SPEN. What news, my lord?
EDW. Why, man, they say there is great
　execution

[1] To challenge, as in the game of prisoner's
base.　　　　　　　　　　　　　[2] Proposal.
[3] As before, original reads *Matr[evis]*.

Done through the realm. My Lord of
　Arundel,
You have the note, have you not?
ARUN.[3] From the lieutenant of the Tower,
　my lord.
EDW. I pray let us see it. What have we
　there?　　　　　　　　　　　　10
Read it, Spencer.
　　　　　　Spencer reads their names.
Why, so; they barked apace a month
　ago.
Now, on my life, they'll neither bark nor
　bite.
Now, sirs, the news from France. Glou-
　cester, I trow
The lords of France love England's gold
　so well
As Isabel gets no aid from thence.
What now remains? Have you pro-
　claimed, my lord,
Reward for them can bring in Morti-
　mer?
SPEN. My lord, we have, and, if he be in
　England,
A will be had ere long, I doubt it not.　20
EDW. "If," dost thou say? Spencer, as
　true as death,
He is in England's ground. Our port
　masters
Are not so careless of their king's com-
　mand.

　　　　　　Enter a Post.

How now, what news with thee? From
　whence come these?
POST. Letters, my lord, and tidings forth
　of France—
To you, my Lord of Gloucester, from
　Levune.　　[*Gives letters to Spencer.*]
EDW. Read.
SPEN. (*Reads the letter.*)
"My duty to your honor premised,[4] etc.
I have, according to instructions in that
behalf, dealt with the King of France　[30
his lords, and effected that the queen, all
discontented and discomforted, is gone.
Whither, if you ask: with Sir John of
Hainault, brother to the marquis, into
Flanders. With them are gone Lord Ed-
mund and the Lord Mortimer, having in
their company divers of your nation, and
others; and, as constant report goeth, they
intend to give King Edward battle in

[4] From 1598 edn. Original reads *promised.*

England sooner than he can look for [40
them. This is all the news of import.
   Your honor's in all service,
                    LEVUNE."
EDW. Ah, villains, hath that Mortimer
   escaped?
   With him is Edmund gone associate?
   And will Sir John of Hainault lead the
   round? [1]
   Welcome, a God's name, madam, and
   your son;
   England shall welcome you and all your
   rout.
   Gallop apace, bright Phœbus, through
   the sky,
   And dusky Night, in rusty iron car; 50
   Between you both shorten the time, I
   pray,
   That I may see that most desiréd day
   When we may meet these traitors in the
   field.
   Ah, nothing grieves me but my little boy
   Is thus misled to countenance their ills.
   Come, friends, to Bristow,[2] there to make
   us strong;
   And, winds, as equal be to bring them in
   As you injurious were to bear them
   forth!   [*Exeunt.*]

[SCENE XV.

Near Harwich.]

*Enter the Queen, her Son, Edmund, Morti-
mer, [Junior,] and Sir John.*

QUEEN. Now, lords, our loving friends and
   countrymen,
   Welcome to England all, with prosperous
   winds!
   Our kindest friends in Belgia have we
   left,
   To cope with friends at home; a heavy
   case
   When force to force is knit, and sword
   and glaive
   In civil broils makes kin and countrymen
   Slaughter themselves in others, and their
   sides
   With their own weapons gored! But
   what's the help?
   Misgoverned kings are cause of all this
   wrack;
   And, Edward, thou art one among them
   all,   10

[1] Dance.   [2] Bristol.

   Whose looseness hath betrayed thy land
   to spoil,
   And made the channels overflow with
   blood.
   Of thine own people patron shouldst
   thou be,
   But thou—
MOR. JUN.   Nay, madam, if you be a
   warrior,
   Ye must not grow so passionate in
   speeches.
   Lords,
   Sith that we are by sufferance of heaven
   Arrived and arméd in this prince's right,
   Here for our country's cause swear we to
   him
   All homage, fealty, and forwardness. 20
   And, for the open wrongs and injuries
   Edward hath done to us, his queen, and
   land,
   We come in arms to wreak it with the
   swords,
   That England's queen in peace may re-
   possess
   Her dignities and honors, and withal
   We may remove these flatterers from
   the king,
   That havocs England's wealth and
   treasury.
SIR J. Sound trumpets, my lord, and for-
   ward let us march.
   Edward will think we come to flatter
   him.
EDM. I would he never had been flattered
   more.   [*Exeunt.*] 30

[SCENE XVI.

Near Bristol.]

*Enter the King, Baldock, and Spencer the
Son, flying about the stage.*

SPEN. Fly, fly, my lord! The queen is
   overstrong;
   Her friends do multiply, and yours do
   fail.
   Shape we our course to Ireland, there to
   breathe.
EDW. What! Was I born to fly and run
   away,
   And leave the Mortimers conquerors
   behind?
   Give me my horse, and let's r'enforce our
   troops,
   And in this bed of honors die with fame.

Bald. O, no, my lord, this princely resolution
Fits not the time. Away! We are pursued.   [*Exeunt.*]

[*Enter*] *Edmund alone with a sword and target.*[1]

Edm. This way he fled, but I am come too late.   10
Edward, alas, my heart relents for thee!
Proud traitor, Mortimer, why dost thou chase
Thy lawful king, thy sovereign, with thy sword?
Vild[2] wretch, and why hast thou, of all unkind,[3]
Borne arms against thy brother and thy king?
Rain showers of vengeance on my cursèd head,
Thou God, to whom in justice it belongs
To punish this unnatural revolt!
Edward, this Mortimer aims at thy life!
O, fly him, then! But, Edmund, calm this rage;   20
Dissemble, or thou diest, for Mortimer
And Isabel do kiss while they conspire,
And yet she bears a face of love forsooth.
Fie on that love that hatcheth death and hate!
Edmund, away! Bristow to Longshanks' blood
Is false. Be not found single for suspect.[4]
Proud Mortimer pries near into thy walks.

Enter the Queen, Mortimer, [Junior,] the young Prince, and Sir John of Hainault.

Queen. Successful battles gives the God of kings
To them that fight in right and fear his wrath.
Since then successfully we have prevailed,   30
Thanks be heaven's great Architect, and you.
Ere farther we proceed, my noble lords,

We here create our well-belovèd son,
Of love and care unto his royal person,
Lord warden of the realm, and, sith the fates
Have made his father so infortunate,
Deal you, my lords, in this, my loving lords,
As to your wisdoms fittest seems in all.
Edm. Madam, without offense, if I may ask,
How will you deal with Edward in his fall?   40
Prince. Tell me, good uncle, what Edward do you mean?
Edm. Nephew, your father; I dare not call him king.
Mor. Jun. My Lord of Kent, what needs these questions?
'Tis not in her controlment, nor in ours,
But as the realm and parliament shall please,
So shall your brother be disposèd of.—
[*Aside to the Queen.*] I like not this relenting mood in Edmund.
Madam, 'tis good to look to him betimes.
Queen. My lord, the Mayor of Bristow knows our mind.
Mor. Jun. Yea, madam, and they scape not easily   50
That fled the field.
Queen.   Baldock is with the king.
A goodly chancellor, is he not, my lord?
Sir J. So are the Spencers, the father and the son.
Edm. This, Edward, is the ruin of the realm.

Enter Rice ap Howell and the Mayor of Bristow, with Spencer the Father [, and Attendants].

Rice. God save Queen Isabel and her princely son!
Madam, the mayor and citizens of Bristow,
In sign of love and duty to this presence,
Present by me this traitor to the state,
Spencer, the father to that wanton Spencer,   59
That, like the lawless Catiline of Rome,
Reveled in England's wealth and treasary.

[1] Shield.   [2] Vile.   [3] Most unnatural of all.
[4] Alone for fear of suspicion.

QUEEN. We thank you all.

MOR. JUN. Your loving care in this
Deserveth princely favors and rewards.
But where's the king and the other
Spencer fled?

RICE. Spencer the son, created Earl of
Gloucester,
Is with that smooth-tongued scholar
Baldock gone
And shipped but late for Ireland with
the king.

MOR. JUN. Some whirlwind fetch them
back or sink them all!
They shall be started [1] thence, I doubt it
not.

PRINCE. Shall I not see the king my father
yet? 70

EDM. [Aside.] Unhappy's Edward, chased
from England's bounds!

SIR J. Madam, what resteth? Why stand
ye in a muse?

QUEEN. I rue my lord's ill fortune. But,
alas,
Care of my country called me to this
war!

MOR. JUN. Madam, have done with care
and sad complaint;
Your king hath wronged your country
and himself,
And we must seek to right it as we
may.—
Meanwhile, have hence this rebel to the
block.—
Your lordship cannot privilege [2] your
head.

SPEN. FA. Rebel is he that fights against
his prince; 80
So fought not they that fought in Edward's right.

MOR. JUN. Take him away; he prates.
[Exeunt Attendants with the Elder
Spencer.]—You, Rice ap Howell,
Shall do good service to her majesty,
Being of countenance [3] in your country
here,
To follow these rebellious runagates.
We in meanwhile, madam, must take
advice
How Baldock, Spencer, and their com-
plices
May in their fall be followed to their end.
Exeunt omnes.

[1] Routed out.
[2] Exempt, free.
[3] In authority, favor.

[SCENE xvii.

The Abbey of Neath.]

*Enter the Abbot, Monks, Edward, Spencer,
and Baldock [, the last three disguised].*

ABBOT. Have you no doubt, my lord; have
you no fear.
As silent and as careful will we be
To keep your royal person safe with us,
Free from suspect and fell invasion
Of such as have your majesty in chase,
Yourself, and those your chosen company,
As danger of this stormy time requires.

EDW. Father, thy face should harbor no
deceit.
O, hadst thou ever been a king, thy heart,
Piercéd deeply with sense of my dis-
tress, 10
Could not but take compassion of my
state.
Stately and proud, in riches and in train,
Whilom [4] I was powerful and full of
pomp.
But what is he whom rule and empery
Have not in life or death made miserable?
Come, Spencer; come, Baldock, come, sit
down by me.
Make trial now of that philosophy
That in our famous nurseries of arts
Thou suckedst from Plato and from
Aristotle. 19
Father, this life contemplative is heaven.
O, that I might this life in quiet lead!
But we, alas, are chased; and you, my
friends,
Your lives, and my dishonor they pursue.
Yet, gentle monks, for treasure, gold,
nor fee,
Do you betray us and our company.

MONKS. Your grace may sit secure, if none
but we
Do wot of your abode.

SPEN. Not one alive; but shrewdly I sus-
pect
A gloomy fellow in a mead below.
A gave a long look after us, my lord, 30
And all the land, I know, is up in arms,
Arms that pursue our lives with deadly
hate.

BALD. We were embarked for Ireland,
wretched we!
With awkward winds and sore tempests
driven

[4] Formerly.

To fall on shore, and here to pine in fear
Of Mortimer and his confederates.

Edw. Mortimer! Who talks of Mortimer?
Who wounds me with the name of
   Mortimer,
That bloody man? Good father, on thy
   lap   39
Lay I this head, laden with mickle care.
O, might I never open these eyes again,
Never again lift up this drooping head,
O, never more lift up this dying heart!

Spen. Look up, my lord.—Baldock, this
   drowsiness
Betides no good; here, even, we are
   betrayed!

Enter, with Welsh hooks,[1] *Rice ap Howell, a*
   Mower, and the Earl of Leicester.

Mow. Upon my life, those be the men ye
   seek!

Rice. Fellow, enough!—My lord, I pray
   be short;
A fair commission warrants what we do.

Leices. [*Aside.*] The queen's commission,
   urged by Mortimer.
What cannot gallant Mortimer with the
   queen?   50
Alas, see where he sits, and hopes unseen
T' escape their hands that seek to reave[2]
   his life.
Too true it is: *"Quem dies vidit veniens*
   superbum,
Hunc dies vidit fugiens jacentem."[3]
But, Leicester, leave to grow so passion-
   ate.—
Spencer and Baldock, by no other names,
I arrest you of high treason here.
Stand not on titles, but obey th' arrest;
'Tis in the name of Isabel the queen.—
My lord, why droop you thus?   60

Edw. O day, the last of all my bliss on
   earth!
Center of all misfortune! O my stars,
Why do you lour unkindly on a king?
Comes Leicester, then, in Isabella's name
To take my life, my company, from me?
Here, man, rip up this panting breast of
   mine,
And take my heart in rescue of my
   friends!

---

[1] A kind of weapon.   [2] Rob, take away.
[3] "Whom the dawning day sees proud, departing day sees prostrate" (Seneca, *Thyestes,*
l. 613).

Rice. Away with them!

Spen.   It may become thee yet
To let us take our farewell of his grace.

Abbot. [*Aside.*] My heart with pity earns[4]
   to see this sight—   70
A king to bear these words and proud
   commands!

Edw. Spencer, ah, sweet Spencer, thus
   then must we part?

Spen. We must, my lord; so will the angry
   heavens.

Edw. Nay, so will hell and cruel Mortimer;
The gentle heavens have not to do in
   this.

Bald. My lord, it is in vain to grieve or
   storm.
Here humbly of your grace we take our
   leaves;
Our lots are cast; I fear me, so is thine.

Edw. In heaven we may, in earth never
   shall we meet—
And, Leicester, say, what shall become of
   us?   80

Leices. Your majesty must go to Killingworth.[5]

Edw. "Must!" 'Tis somewhat hard when
   kings "must" go.

Leices. Here is a litter ready for your
   grace,
That waits your pleasure; and the day
   grows old.

Rice. As good be gone as stay and be benighted.

Edw. A litter hast thou? Lay me in a
   hearse,
And to the gates of hell convey me
   hence.
Let Pluto's bells ring out my fatal knell,
And hags howl for my death at Charon's
   shore,
For friends hath Edward none but these
   and these,   90
And these must die under a tyrant's
   sword.

Rice. My lord, be going; care not for
   these,
For we shall see them shorter by the
   heads.

Edw. Well, that shall be, shall be! Part
   we must!
Sweet Spencer, gentle Baldock, part we
   must!

---

[4] Yearns, sorrows.   [5] Kenilworth.

Hence, feignéd weeds! [*Throws off his
   disguise.*] Unfeignéd are my woes!
Father, farewell! Leicester, thou stay'st
   for me,
And go I must. Life, farewell, with my
   friends.
          Exeunt Edward and Leicester.
SPEN. O, is he gone? Is noble Edward
   gone?
Parted from hence, never to see us
   more?   100
Rent,[1] sphere of heaven, and, fire, forsake
   thy orb!
Earth, melt to air! Gone is my sovereign,
Gone, gone, alas, never to make return!
BALD. Spencer, I see our souls are fleeted
   hence;
We are deprived the sunshine of our life.
Make for a new life, man; throw up thy
   eyes,
And heart, and hand to heaven's im-
   mortal throne;
Pay nature's debt with cheerful coun-
   tenance.
Reduce we all our lessons unto this:
To die, sweet Spencer, therefor live we
   all;   110
Spencer, all live to die, and rise to fall.
RICE. Come, come, keep these preach-
ments till you come to the place appointed.
You, and such as you are, have made wise
work in England. Will your lordships
away?
MOW. Your lordship, I trust, will remem-
   ber me?
RICE. Remember thee, fellow! What else?
   Follow me to the town.   [*Exeunt.*]

[SCENE xviii.

A room in Killingworth Castle.]

Enter the King, Leicester, with a Bishop [2] *for
the crown* [, *and Trussel*].

LEICES. Be patient, good my lord; cease
   to lament.
Imagine Killingworth Castle were your
   court,
   And that you lay for pleasure here a
      space,
Not of compulsion or necessity.
EDW. Leicester, if gentle words might com-
   fort me,

[1] Rend, split.
[2] Berkeley, Bishop of Winchester.

Thy speeches long ago had eased my
   sorrows,
For kind and loving hast thou always
   been.
The griefs of private men are soon al-
   layed,
But not of kings. The forest deer, being
   struck,
Runs to an herb that closeth up the
   wounds;   10
But, when the imperial lion's flesh is
   gored,
He rends and tears it with his wrathful
   paw,
[And,][3] highly scorning that the lowly
   earth
Should drink his blood, mounts up into
   the air.
And so it fares with me, whose dauntless
   mind
The ambitious Mortimer would seek to
   curb,
And that unnatural queen, false Isabel,
That thus hath pent and mewed me in a
   prison;
For such outrageous passions cloy my
   soul,
As with the wings of rancor and dis-
   dain   20
Full often am I soaring up to heaven,
To plain me [4] to the gods against them
   both.
But, when I call to mind I am a king,
Methinks I should revenge me of the
   wrongs
That Mortimer and Isabel have done.
But what are kings, when regiment is
   gone,
But perfect shadows in a sunshine day?
My nobles rule; I bear the name of
   king.
I wear the crown, but am controlled by
   them,   29
By Mortimer, and my unconstant queen,
Who spots my nuptial bed with infamy,
Whilst I am lodged within this cave of
   care,
Where sorrow at my elbow still attends,
To company my heart with sad laments,
That bleeds within me for this strange
   exchange.
But tell me, must I now resign my crown,
To make usurping Mortimer a king?

[3] Supplied by Dodsley.   [4] Complain.

BISH. Your grace mistakes; it is for England's good

And princely Edward's right we crave the crown.

EDW. No, 'tis for Mortimer, not Edward's head; 40

For he's a lamb, encompasséd by wolves,

Which in a moment will abridge his life.

But, if proud Mortimer do wear this crown,

Heavens turn it to a blaze of quenchless fire,

Or, like the snaky wreath of Tisiphon,

Engirt the temples of his hateful head!

So shall not England's vines be perishéd,

But Edward's name survives, though Edward dies.

LEICES. My lord, why waste you thus the time away?

They stay your answer. Will you yield your crown? 50

EDW. Ah, Leicester, weigh how hardly I can brook

To lose my crown and kingdom without cause;

To give ambitious Mortimer my right—

That like a mountain overwhelms my bliss,

In which extreme my mind here murthered is.

But what the heavens appoint, I must obey!

Here, take my crown—the life of Edward too; [Takes off the crown.]

Two kings in England cannot reign at once.

But stay awhile; let me be king till night,

That I may gaze upon this glittering crown. 60

So shall my eyes receive their last content,

My head, the latest honor due to it,

And jointly both yield up their wishéd right.

Continue ever, thou celestial sun;

Let never silent night possess this clime.

Stand still, you watches of the element; [1]

All times and seasons, rest you at a stay,

That Edward may be still fair England's king!

But day's bright beams doth vanish fast away,

And needs I must resign my wishéd crown. 70

Inhuman creatures, nursed with tiger's milk,

Why gape you for your sovereign's overthrow—

My diadem, I mean, and guiltless life?

See, monsters, see, I'll wear my crown again! [Puts on the crown.]

What, fear you not the fury of your king?

But, hapless Edward, thou art fondly [2] led;

They pass [3] not for thy frowns as late they did,

But seeks to make a new-elected king;

Which fills my mind with strange, despairing thoughts,

Which thoughts are martyréd with endless torments, 80

And, in this torment, comfort find I none,

But that I feel the crown upon my head;

And therefore let me wear it yet awhile.

TRU. My lord, the parliament must have present news,

And therefore say, will you resign or no? *The King rageth.*

EDW. I'll not resign, but whilst I live—

Traitors, be gone and join you with Mortimer!

Elect, conspire, install, do what you will—

Their blood and yours shall seal these treacheries!

BISH. This answer we'll return, and so farewell. 90

LEICES. Call them again, my lord, and speak them fair;

For, if they go, the prince shall lose his right.

EDW. Call thou them back; I have no power to speak.

LEICES. My lord, the king is willing to resign.

BISH. If he be not, let him choose.

EDW. O, would I might, but heavens and earth conspire

To make me miserable! Here receive my crown;

Receive it? No, these innocent hands of mine

Shall not be guilty of so foul a crime.

He of you all that most desires my blood,

---

[1] *I.e.*, celestial bodies.

[2] Foolishly.

[3] Care.

And will be called the murtherer of a
  king,   101
Take it. What, are you moved? Pity
  you me?
Then send for unrelenting Mortimer,
And Isabel, whose eyes, being [1] turned
  to steel,
Will sooner sparkle fire than shed a tear.
Yet stay, for rather than I will look on
  them—
Here, here! [*Gives the crown.*] Now,
  sweet God of heaven,
Make me despise this transitory pomp,
And sit for aye enthronizéd in heaven!
Come, death, and with thy fingers close
  my eyes,   110
Or, if I live, let me forget myself.

Enter [Sir Thomas] Berkeley.

BISH. [2] My lord—
EDW. Call me not lord. Away—out of my
  sight!
Ah, pardon me. Grief makes me lunatic!
Let not that Mortimer protect my son;
More safety is there in a tiger's jaws
Than [3] his embracements. Bear this to
  the queen,
Wet with my tears, and dried again with
  sighs;   [*Gives a handkerchief.*]
If with the sight thereof she be not
  moved,   119
Return it back and dip it in my blood.
Commend me to my son, and bid him
  rule
Better than I. Yet how have I trans-
  gressed,
Unless it be with too much clemency?
TRU. And thus most humbly do we take
  our leave.
EDW. Farewell. [*Exeunt the Bishop of
  Winchester and Trussel.*] I know the
  next news that they bring
Will be my death, and welcome shall it
  be;
To wretched men, death is felicity.
LEICES. [*Noticing Berkeley.*] Another post!
  What news brings he?
EDW. Such news as I expect.—Come,
  Berkeley, come,   129
And tell thy message to my naked breast.

[1] From 1598 edn. Original reads *been.*
[2] Original assigns this speech to Sir Thomas
Berkeley.
[3] From 1598 edn. Original reads *this.*

BERK. My lord, think not a thought so
  villainous
Can harbor in a man of noble birth.
To do your highness service and devoir,
And save you from your foes, Berkeley
  would die.
LEICES. My lord, the council of the queen
  commands
That I resign my charge.
EDW. And who must keep me now? Must
  you, my lord?
BERK. Ay, my most gracious lord; so 'tis
  decreed.
EDW. [*Taking the paper.*] By Mortimer,
  whose name is written here!
Well may I rent his name that rends my
  heart!   [*Tears it.*]   140
This poor revenge hath something eased
  my mind.
So may his limbs be torn, as is this paper!
Hear me, immortal Jove, and grant it
  too!
BERK. Your grace must hence with me to
  Berkeley straight.
EDW. Whither you will; all places are
  alike,
And every earth is fit for burial.
LEICES. Favor him, my lord, as much as
  lieth in you.
BERK. Even so betide my soul as I use
  him.
EDW. Mine enemy hath pitied my estate,
And that's the cause that I am now
  removed.   150
BERK. And thinks your grace that Berk-
  eley will be cruel?
EDW. I know not, but of this am I as-
  sured,
That death ends all, and I can die but
  once.
Leicester, farewell!
LEICES. Not yet, my lord; I'll bear you on
  your way.   *Exeunt omnes.*

[SCENE xix.

The King's palace in London.]

Enter Mortimer [, Junior,] and Queen Isabel.

MOR. JUN. Fair Isabel, now have we our
  desire;
The proud corrupters of the light-brained
  king
Have done their homage to the lofty
  gallows,

And he himself lies in captivity.
Be ruled by me, and we will rule the realm.
In any case take heed of childish fear,
For now we hold an old wolf by the ears,
That, if he slip, will seize upon us both,
And gripe the sorer, being gripped himself.
Think therefore, madam, that imports us [1] much   10
To erect [2] your son with all the speed we may,
And that I be protector over him;
For our behoof will bear the greater sway
Whenas a king's name shall be underwrit.

QUEEN. Sweet Mortimer, the life of Isabel,
Be thou persuaded that I love thee well,
And therefore, so the prince my son be safe,
Whom I esteem as dear as these mine eyes,
Conclude against his father what thou wilt,
And I myself will willingly subscribe.   20

MOR. JUN. First would I hear news that he were deposed,
And then let me alone to handle him.

Enter Messenger.

MOR. JUN. Letters! From whence?
MESS.   From Killingworth, my lord.
QUEEN. How fares my lord the king?
MESS. In health, madam, but full of pensiveness.
QUEEN. Alas, poor soul, would I could ease his grief!

[*Enter the Bishop of Winchester with the crown.*]

Thanks, gentle Winchester.—[*To the Messenger.*] Sirrah, begone.
                    [*Exit Messenger.*]
WIN. [3] The king hath willingly resigned his crown.
QUEEN. O happy news! Send for the prince my son.
BISH. Further, or [4] this letter was sealed,
Lord Berkeley came,   30

So that he now is gone from Killingworth;
And we have heard that Edmund laid a plot
To set his brother free; no more but so.
The Lord of Berkeley is so [5] pitiful
As Leicester, that had charge of him before.
QUEEN. Then let some other be his guardian.
MOR. JUN. Let me alone. Here is the privy seal.—
          [*Exit the Bishop of Winchester.*]
[*To Attendants within.*] Who's there?—
Call hither Gurney and Matrevis.
To dash the heavy-headed Edmund's drift, [6]
Berkeley shall be discharged, the king removed,   40
And none but we shall know where he lieth.
QUEEN. But, Mortimer, as long as he survives,
What safety rests for us or for my son?
MOR. JUN. Speak, shall he presently be despatched and die?
QUEEN. I would he were, so 'twere not by my means.

Enter Matrevis and Gurney.

MOR. JUN. Enough.—Matrevis, write a letter presently
Unto the Lord of Berkeley from ourself
That he resign the king to thee and Gurney;
And, when 'tis done, we will subscribe our name.
MAT. It shall be done, my lord.
MOR. JUN.   Gurney!
GUR.   My lord. 50
MOR. JUN. As thou intendest to rise by Mortimer,
Who now makes Fortune's wheel turn as he please,
Seek all the means thou canst to make him droop,
And neither give him kind word nor good look.
GUR. I warrant you, my lord.
MOR. JUN. And this above the rest: because we hear
That Edmund casts [7] to work his liberty,
Remove him still from place to place by night,

---

[1] From 1612 edn. Original reads *as*.   [4] Ere.
[2] Crown.
[3] Regularly *Bish.* in speech heads.

[5] As.   [6] Plot.   [7] Plots.

Till at the last he come to Killingworth,
And then from thence to Berkeley back
   again.   60
And by the way, to make him fret the
   more,
Speak curstly [1] to him, and in any case
Let no man comfort him; if he chance
   to weep,
But amplify his grief with bitter words.

MAT. Fear not, my lord, we'll do as you
   command.

MOR. JUN. So now away; post thither-
   wards amain.

QUEEN. Whither goes this letter? To my
   lord the king?
Commend me humbly to his majesty,
And tell him that I labor all in vain
To ease his grief, and work his lib-
   erty;   70
And bear him this as witness of my love.
                     [Gives a ring.]

MAT. I will, madam.

Exeunt Matrevis and Gurney.   Manent
                Isabel and Mortimer.

Enter the young Prince, and the Earl of
             Kent talking with him.

MOR. JUN. [*Aside.*] Finely dissembled!
   Do so still, sweet queen.
Here comes the young prince with the
   Earl of Kent.

QUEEN. [*Aside.*] Something he whispers
   in his childish ears.

MOR. JUN. [*Aside.*] If he have such access
   unto the prince,
Our plots and stratagems will soon be
   dashed.

QUEEN. [*Aside.*] Use Edmund friendly, as
   if all were well.—

MOR. JUN. How fares my honorable
   Lord of Kent?

EDM. In health, sweet Mortimer.—How
   fares your grace?   80

QUEEN. Well, if my lord your brother were
   enlarged.[2]

EDM. I hear of late he hath deposed himself.

QUEEN. The more my grief.

MOR. JUN.   And mine.

EDM. [*Aside.*]   Ah, they do dissemble!

QUEEN. Sweet son, come hither; I must
   talk with thee.

MOR. JUN. Thou, being his uncle, and
   the next of blood,
Do look to be protector over the prince.

EDM. Not I, my lord. Who should protect
   the son
But she that gave him life? I mean the
   queen.

PRINCE. Mother, persuade me not to wear
   the crown.
Let him be king—I am too young to
   reign.   90

QUEEN. But be content, seeing it his
   highness' pleasure.

PRINCE. Let me but see him first, and then
   I will.

EDM. Ay, do, sweet nephew.

QUEEN. Brother, you know it is impossible.

PRINCE. Why, is he dead?

QUEEN. No, God forbid!

EDM. I would those words proceeded from
   your heart.

MOR. JUN. Inconstant Edmund, dost thou
   favor him,
That wast the cause of his imprisonment?

EDM. The more cause have I now to make
   amends.   100

MOR. JUN. [*Aside to queen.*] I tell thee,
   'tis not meet that one so false
Should come about the person of a
   prince.—
My lord, he hath betrayed the king his
   brother,
And therefore trust him not.

PRINCE. But he repents, and sorrows for
   it now.

QUEEN. Come, son, and go with this gentle
   lord and me.

PRINCE. With you I will, but not with
   Mortimer.

MOR. JUN. Why, youngling, 'sdain'st thou
   so of Mortimer?
Then I will carry thee by force away.

PRINCE. Help, uncle Kent! Mortimer will
   wrong me.   110

QUEEN. Brother Edmund, strive not; we
   are his friends;
Isabel is nearer than the Earl of Kent.

EDM. Sister, Edward is my charge; redeem him.

QUEEN. Edward is my son, and I will keep
   him.

EDM. Mortimer shall know that he hath
   wronged me!—

---

[1] Ill-temperedly.   [2] Freed.

[*Aside.*] Hence will I haste to Killing-
worth Castle,
And rescue aged Edward from his foes,
To be revenged on Mortimer and thee.
Exeunt omnes.

[SCENE xx.

An outbuilding at Killingworth Castle.]

*Enter Matrevis and Gurney [and Soldiers,]
with the King.*

MAT. My lord, be not pensive; we are your
friends.
Men are ordained to live in misery;
Therefore come—dalliance dangereth
our lives.
EDW. Friends, whither must unhappy Ed-
ward go?
Will hateful Mortimer appoint no rest?
Must I be vexéd like the nightly bird,
Whose sight is loathsome to all wingéd
fowls?
When will the fury of his mind assuage?
When will his heart be satisfied with
blood?
If mine will serve, unbowel straight this
breast,   10
And give my heart to Isabel and him.
It is the chiefest mark they level at.
GUR. Not so, my liege; the queen hath
given this charge
To keep your grace in safety.
Your passions make your dolors to in-
crease.
EDW. This usage makes my misery in-
crease.
But can my air of life continue long
When all my senses are annoyed with
stench?
Within a dungeon England's king is kept,
Where I am starved for want of suste-
nance.   20
My daily diet is heart-breaking sobs,
That almost rents the closet of my heart.
Thus lives old Edward, not relieved by
any,
And so must die, though pitiéd by many.
O, water, gentle friends, to cool my thirst,
And clear my body from foul excre-
ments!
MAT. Here's channel water, as our charge
is given.
Sit down, for we'll be barbers to your
grace.

EDW. Traitors, away! What, will you
murther me,
Or choke your sovereign with puddle
water?   30
GUR. No, but wash your face, and shave
away your beard,
Lest you be known and so be rescuéd.
MAT. Why strive you thus? Your labor
is in vain!
EDW. The wren may strive against the
lion's strength,
But all in vain; so vainly do I strive
To seek for mercy at a tyrant's hand.
*They wash him with puddle water, and shave
his beard away.*
Immortal powers, that knows the pain-
ful cares
That waits upon my poor distresséd
soul,
O, level all your looks upon these daring
men
That wrongs their liege and sovereign,
England's king!   40
O Gaveston, it is for thee that I am
wronged!
For me, both thou and both the Spencers
died,
And for your sakes a thousand wrongs
I'll take.
The Spencers' ghosts, wherever they
remain,
Wish well to mine; then tush—for them
I'll die!
MAT. Twixt theirs and yours shall be no
enmity.
Come, come away; now put the torches
out;
We'll enter in by darkness to Killing-
worth.

Enter Edmund.

GUR. How now, who comes there?
MAT. Guard the king sure; it is the Earl
of Kent.   50
EDW. O, gentle brother, help to rescue
me!
MAT. Keep them asunder; thrust in the
king.
EDM. Soldiers, let me but talk to him one
word.
GUR. Lay hands upon the earl for this
assault.
EDM. Lay down your weapons, traitors!
Yield the king!

MAT. Edmund, yield thou thyself, or thou
　shalt die!
EDM. Base villains, wherefore do you gripe
　me thus?
GUR. Bind him and so convey him to the
　court.
EDM. Where is the court but here? Here is
　the king.
　And I will visit him; why stay you me? 60
MAT. The court is where Lord Mortimer
　remains.
　Thither shall your honor go; and so fare-
　well.
Exeunt Matr[evis] and Gurney, with the
　King.　Manent Edmund and the
　Soldiers.
EDM. O, miserable is that commonweal
　Where lords keep courts, and kings are
　locked in prison!
SOL. Wherefore stay we? On, sirs, to the
　court!
EDM. Ay, lead me whither you will, even
　to my death,
　Seeing that my brother cannot be re-
　leased.　　　　　　　　　*Exeunt omnes.*

[SCENE xxi.

The King's palace in London.]

Enter Mortimer alone.

MOR. JUN. The king must die or Mor-
　timer goes down;
　The commons now begin to pity him.
　Yet he that is the cause of Edward's
　death
　Is sure to pay for it when his son is of
　age,
　And therefore will I do it cunningly.
　This letter, written by a friend of ours,
　Contains his death, yet bids them save
　his life.　　　　　　　　　[*Reads.*]
　"*Edwardum occidere nolite timere bonum
　est:*"
　"Fear not to kill the king; 'tis good he
　die."
　But read it thus, and that's another
　sense:　　　　　　　　　　　　10
　"*Edwardum occidere nolite timere bonum
　est:*"
　"Kill not the king; 'tis good to fear the
　worst."
　Unpointed as it is, thus shall it go,
　That, being dead, if it chance to be
　found,

Matrevis and the rest may bear the
　blame,
　And we be quit that caused it to be
　done.
　Within this room is locked the mes-
　senger
　That shall convey it, and perform the
　rest;
　And, by a secret token that he bears,
　Shall he be murdered when the deed is
　done.—　　　　　　　　　　20
　Lightborn,
　Come forth!

[*Enter Lightborn.*]

　Art thou as resolute as thou wast?
LIGHT. What else, my lord? And far
　more resolute!
MOR. JUN. And hast thou cast how to
　accomplish it?
LIGHT. Ay, ay, and none shall know
　which way he died.
MOR. JUN. But at his looks, Lightborn,
　thou wilt relent.
LIGHT. Relent! Ha, ha! I use much to
　relent!
MOR. JUN. Well, do it bravely, and be
　secret.
LIGHT. You shall not need to give in-
　structions;　　　　　　　　29
　'Tis not the first time I have killed a man.
　I learned in Naples how to poison
　flowers;
　To strangle with a lawn [1] thrust through [2]
　the throat;
　To pierce the windpipe with a needle's
　point;
　Or, whilst one is asleep, to take a quill
　And blow a little powder in his ears;
　Or open his mouth and pour quick-
　silver down.
　But yet I have a braver way than these.
MOR. JUN. What's that?
LIGHT. Nay, you shall pardon me; none
　shall know my tricks.
MOR. JUN. I care not how it is, so it be
　not spied.　　　　　　　　　40
　Deliver this to Gurney and Matrevis.
　　　　　　　　　　　　[*Gives letter.*]
　At every ten miles' end thou hast a
　horse.
　Take this. [*Gives money.*] Away, and
　never see me more!

---

[1] Handkerchief.　　　　　　[2] Down.

Light. No?

Mor. Jun. No;
Unless you bring me news of Edward's
death.

Light. That will I quickly do. Farewell,
my lord. [*Exit.*]

Mor. Jun. The prince I rule, the queen
do I command,
And with a lowly congé to the ground   49
The proudest lords salute me as I pass.
I seal, I cancel, I do what I will.
Feared am I more than loved; let me
be feared,
And, when I frown, make all the court
look pale.
I view the prince with Aristarchus' eyes,
Whose looks were as a breeching [1] to a
boy.
They thrust upon me the protectorship,
And sue to me for that that I desire.
While at the council table, grave enough,
And not unlike a bashful Puritan,
First I complain of imbecility,   60
Saying it is *onus quam gravissimum*,[2]
Till, being interrupted by my friends,
Suscepi that *provinciam*,[3] as they term
it;
And, to conclude, I am protector now.
Now is all sure. The queen and Morti-
mer
Shall rule the realm, the king, and none
rule us.
Mine enemies will I plague, my friends
advance;
And what I list command who dare
control?
" *Major sum quam cui possit fortuna no-
cere*." [4]   69
And that this be the coronation day,
It pleaseth me and Isabel the queen.
[*Trumpets within.*]
The trumpets sound; I must go take my
place.

*Enter the young King, [Arch]bishop, Cham-
pion, Nobles, Queen.*

[Arch]bish. Long live King Edward, by
the grace of God
King of England and Lord of Ireland!

[1] Flogging.
[2] A very heavy burden.
[3] I have undertaken that office.
[4] "I am too great for fortune to harm me"
(Ovid, *Metamorphoses*, vi, 195).

Cham. If any Christian, heathen, Turk,
or Jew
Dares but affirm that Edward's not
true king,
And will avouch his saying with the
sword,
I am the champion that will combat him!

Mor. Jun. None comes; sound trumpets.
[*Trumpets sound.*]

King.[5]   Champion, here's to thee!
[*Gives a purse.*]

Queen. Lord Mortimer, now take him
to your charge.   80

*Enter Soldiers, with the Earl of Kent
prisoner.*

Mor. Jun. What traitor have we there
with blades and bills?

Sol. Edmund, the Earl of Kent.

King.   What hath he done?

Sol. A would have taken the king away
perforce,
As we were bringing him to Killingworth.

Mor. Jun. Did you attempt his rescue,
Edmund? Speak.

Edm. Mortimer, I did; he is our king,
And thou compell'st this prince to wear
the crown.

Mor. Jun. Strike off his head! He shall
have martial law.

Edm. Strike off my head? Base traitor,
I defy thee!

King. My lord, he is my uncle, and shall
live.   90

Mor. Jun. My lord, he is your enemy,
and shall die.

Edm. Stay, villains!

King. Sweet mother, if I cannot pardon
him,
Entreat my lord protector for his life.

Queen. Son, be content; I dare not speak
a word.

King. Nor I, and yet methinks I should
command;
But, seeing I cannot, I'll entreat for
him.—
My lord, if you will let my uncle live,
I will requite it when I come to age.

Mor. Jun. 'Tis for your highness' good,
and for the realm's.—   100
How often shall I bid you bear him
hence?

[5] Formerly the prince, now Edward the Third.

EDM. Art thou king? Must I die at thy
command?

MOR. JUN. At our command.—Once more
away with him!

EDM. Let me but stay and speak; I will
not go.

Either my brother or his son is king,
And none of both [1] then thirst for Edmund's blood.

And, therefore, soldiers, whither will
you hale me?

They hale Edmund away, and carry him to
be beheaded.

KING. What safety may I look for at his
hands,

If that my uncle shall be murthered
thus?

QUEEN. Fear not, sweet boy; I'll guard
thee from thy foes;   110

Had Edmund lived, he would have
sought thy death.

Come, son, we'll ride a-hunting in the
park.

KING. And shall my uncle Edmund ride
with us?

QUEEN. He is a traitor; think not on him.

Come.   *Exeunt omnes.*

[SCENE xxii.

A subterranean room in Berkeley Castle.]

Enter Matr[evis] and Gurney.

MAT. Gurney, I wonder the king dies not,
Being in a vault up to the knees in
water,

To which the channels of the castle run,
From whence a damp continually ariseth,
That were enough to poison any man,
Much more a king brought up so ten-
derly.

GUR. And so do I, Matrevis. Yesternight

I opened but the door to throw him
meat,

And I was almost stifled with the savor.

MAT. He hath a body able to endure   10
More than we can inflict; and therefore now

Let us assail his mind another while.

GUR. Send for him out thence, and I
will anger him.

MAT. But stay, who's this?

[1] Neither.

Enter Lightborn,

LIGHT.   My lord protector greets you.
                    [*Gives letter.*]

GUR. [*Reads.*] What's here? I know not
how to conster [2] it.

MAT. Gurney, it was left unpointed for
the nonce; [3]

"*Edwardum occidere nolite timere*"—
That's his meaning.

LIGHT. Know ye this token? I must have
the king.   [*Gives token.*]

MAT. Ay, stay awhile; thou shalt have
answer straight.—   20

[*Aside.*] This villain's sent to make away
the king.

GUR. [*Aside.*] I thought as much.

MAT. [*Aside.*]   And, when the murder's
done,

See how he must be handled for his
labor.

Pereat iste! [4] Let him have the king.—
What else? Here is the keys; this is the
lake. [5]

Do as you are commanded by my lord.

LIGHT. I know what I must do. Get
you away.

Yet be not far off; I shall need your
help.

See that in the next room I have a fire.
And get me a spit, and let it be red-
hot.   30

MAT. Very well.

GUR.   Need you anything besides?

LIGHT. What else? A table and a feather
bed.

GUR. That's all?

LIGHT. Ay, ay; so, when I call you, bring
it in.

MAT. Fear not you that.

GUR. Here's a light, to go into the dungeon.

[*Gives a light, and then exit with Matrevis.*]

LIGHT. So now must I about this gear; [6]
ne'er was there any

So finely handled as this king shall be.
                    [*Opens the door.*]

Foh! Here's a place indeed, with all
my heart!

EDW. Who's there? What light is that?
Wherefore comes thou?   40

[2] Construe.   [5] Vault, dungeon.
[3] For the occasion, on purpose.   [6] Affair.
[4] Let this man die.

Light. To comfort you, and bring you
joyful news.

Edw. Small comfort finds poor Edward
in thy looks.
Villain, I know thou com'st to murther
me.

Light. To murther you, my most gracious
lord?
Far is it from my heart to do you harm.
The queen sent me to see how you were
used,
For she relents at this your misery.
And what eyes can refrain from shedding
tears,
To see a king in this most piteous state?

Edw. Weep'st thou already? List awhile
to me   50
And then thy heart, were it as Gurney's
is,
Or as Matrevis', hewn from the Cauca-
sus,
Yet will it melt, ere I have done my tale.
This dungeon where they keep me is
the sink
Wherein the filth of all the castle falls.

Light. O villains!

Edw. And there in mire and puddle have
I stood
This ten days' space; and, lest that I
should sleep,
One plays continually upon a drum.
They give me bread and water, being
a king;   60
So that, for want of sleep and suste-
nance,
My mind's distempered, and my body's
numbed,
And whether I have limbs or no I know
not.
O, would my blood dropped out from
every vein
As doth this water from my tattered
robes.
Tell Isabel, the queen, I looked not
thus
When for her sake I ran at tilt in France,
And there unhorsed the Duke of Clere-
mont.

Light. O, speak no more, my lord! This
breaks my heart.
Lie on this bed,[1] and rest yourself
awhile.   70

[1] Dyce suggests that the feather bed has been
thrust in from the wing.

Edw. These looks of thine can harbor
naught but death.
I see my tragedy written in thy brows.
Yet stay awhile; forbear thy bloody
hand,
And let me see the stroke before it
comes,
That—and even then when I shall lose
my life—
My mind may be more steadfast on
my God.

Light. What means your highness to
mistrust me thus?

Edw. What means thou to dissemble
with me thus?

Light. These hands were never stained
with innocent blood,
Nor shall they now be tainted with a
king's.   80

Edw. Forgive my thought for having
such a thought.
One jewel have I left; receive thou this.
                              [Gives jewel.]
Still fear I, and I know not what's the
cause,
But every joint shakes as I give it thee.
O, if thou harbor'st murther in thy
heart,
Let this gift change thy mind, and save
thy soul!
Know that I am a king! O, at that
name
I feel a hell of grief! Where is my crown?
Gone, gone! And do I remain alive?

Light. You're overwatched, my lord;
lie down and rest.   90

Edw. But that grief keeps me waking, I
should sleep,
For not these ten days have these eyelids closed.
Now as I speak, they fall, and yet with
fear
Open again. O, wherefore sits thou
here?

Light. If you mistrust me, I'll be gone,
my lord.

Edw. No, no, for if thou mean'st to murther me,
Thou wilt return again; and therefore
stay.   [Dozes.]

Light. He sleeps.

Edw. O, let me not die yet! Stay, O,
stay a while!

Light. How now, my lord?   100

EDW. [*Waking.*] Something still buzzeth
in mine ears,
And tells me if I sleep I never wake;
This fear is that which makes me tremble
thus.
And therefore tell me, wherefore art
thou come?
LIGHT. To rid thee of thy life.—Matrevis, come!

[*Enter Matrevis and Gurney.*]

EDW. I am too weak and feeble to resist.—
Assist me, sweet God, and receive my
soul!
LIGHT. Run for the table.
EDW. O, spare me, or despatch me in a
trice.   [*Matrevis brings in a table.*]
LIGHT. So, lay the table down, and stamp
on it,   110
But not too hard, lest that you bruise
his body.   [*They murder the King.*]
MAT. I fear me that this cry will raise
the town,
And therefore let us take horse and away.
LIGHT. Tell me, sirs, was it not bravely
done?
GUR. Excellent well; take this for thy
reward!
    Then Gurney stabs Lightborn.
Come, let us cast the body in the moat,
And bear the king's to Mortimer our
lord.
Away!   *Exeunt omnes.*

[SCENE xxiii.

The royal palace in London.]

Enter Mortimer and Matrevis.

MOR. JUN. Is't done, Matrevis, and the
murtherer dead?
MAT. Ay, my good lord; I would it were
undone!
MOR. JUN. Matrevis, if thou now growest
penitent
I'll be thy ghostly father; [1] therefore
choose
Whether thou wilt be secret in this,
Or else die by the hand of Mortimer.
MAT. Gurney, my lord, is fled, and will, I
fear,
Betray us both; therefore let me fly.
MOR. JUN. Fly to the savages!   9
MAT. I humbly thank your honor. [*Exit.*]

[1] Father confessor.

MOR. JUN. As for myself, I stand as
Jove's huge tree,
And others are but shrubs compared to me.
All tremble at my name, and I fear none.
Let's see who dare impeach me for his
death!

Enter the Queen.

QUEEN. Ah, Mortimer, the king my son
hath news
His father's dead, and we have murdered
him!
MOR. JUN. What if he have? The king is
yet a child.
QUEEN. Ay, ay, but he tears his hair, and
wrings his hands,
And vows to be revenged upon us both.
Into the council chamber he is gone,   20
To crave the aid and succor of his peers.
Ay me! See where he comes, and they
with him.
Now, Mortimer, begins our tragedy.

Enter the King with the Lords.

LORDS. Fear not, my lord; know that you
are a king.—
KING. Villain!
MOR. JUN. How now, my lord?
KING. Think not that I am frighted with
thy words!
My father's murdered through thy
treachery;
And thou shalt die, and on his mournful
hearse   29
Thy hateful and accurséd head shall lie,
To witness to the world that by thy means
His kingly body was too soon interred.
QUEEN. Weep not, sweet son!
KING. Forbid not me to weep; he was my
father.
And, had you loved him half so well as I,
You could not bear his death thus
patiently.
But you, I fear, conspired with Mortimer.
LORDS. Why speak you not unto my lord
the king?
MOR. JUN. Because I think scorn to be
accused.
Who is the man dares say I murdered
him?   40
KING. Traitor, in me my loving father
speaks,
And plainly saith 'twas thou that mur-
d'redst him

MOR. JUN. But hath your grace no other proof than this?

KING. Yes, if this be the hand of Mortimer. [*Shows letter.*]

MOR. JUN. [*Aside.*] False Gurney hath betrayed me and himself.

QUEEN. [*Aside.*] I feared as much; murther cannot be hid.

MOR. JUN. 'Tis my hand. What gather you by this?

KING. That thither thou didst send a murtherer.

MOR. JUN. What murtherer? Bring forth the man I sent!

KING. Ah, Mortimer, thou knowest that he is slain,   50
And so shalt thou be too.—Why stays he here?
Bring him unto a hurdle; drag him forth;
Hang him, I say, and set his quarters up;
But bring his head back presently to me.

QUEEN. For my sake, sweet son, pity Mortimer!

MOR. JUN. Madam, entreat not; I will rather die
Than sue for life unto a paltry boy.

KING. Hence with the traitor, with the murderer!

MOR. JUN. Base Fortune, now I see that in thy wheel
There is a point to which when men aspire,   60
They tumble headlong down. That point I touched,
And, seeing there was no place to mount up higher,
Why should I grieve at my declining fall?—
Farewell, fair queen. Weep not for Mortimer,
That scorns the world, and, as a traveler,
Goes to discover countries yet unknown.

KING. What, suffer you the traitor to delay? [*Mortimer is led away.*]

QUEEN. As thou receivedst thy life from me,
Spill not the blood of gentle Mortimer!

KING. This argues that you spilt my father's blood,   70
Else would you not entreat for Mortimer.

QUEEN. I spill his blood? No!

KING. Ay, madam, you, for so the rumor runs.

QUEEN. That rumor is untrue; for loving thee
Is this report raised on poor Isabel.

KING. I do not think her so unnatural.

LORDS. My Lord, I fear me it will prove too true.

KING. Mother, you are suspected for his death,
And therefore we commit you to the Tower
Till further trial may be made thereof.   80
If you be guilty, though I be your son,
Think not to find me slack or pitiful.

QUEEN. Nay, to my death, for too long have I lived
Whenas my son thinks to abridge my days.

KING. Away with her! Her words enforce these tears,
And I shall pity her if she speak again.

QUEEN. Shall I not mourn for my beloved lord,
And with the rest accompany him to his grave?

LORDS. Thus, madam, 'tis the king's will you shall hence.

QUEEN. He hath forgotten me. Stay, I am his mother.   90

LORDS. That boots not; therefore, gentle madam, go.

QUEEN. Then come, sweet death, and rid me of this grief.   [*Exit.*]

[*Enter Lords with the head of Mortimer.*]

LORDS. My lord, here is the head of Mortimer.

KING. Go fetch my father's hearse where it shall lie,
And bring my funeral robes. [*Exeunt Attendants.*]—Accurséd head,
Could I have ruled thee then, as I do now,
Thou hadst not hatched this monstrous treachery!—
Here comes the hearse; help me to mourn, my lords.

[*Enter Attendants with the hearse and funeral robes.*]

Sweet father, here unto thy murdered ghost
I offer up this wicked traitor's head;   100
And let these tears, distilling from mine eyes,
Be witness of my grief and innocency.
    [*Exeunt.*]

FINIS.

THOMAS KYD

Thomas Kyd was born in London in 1558, the son of Francis Kyd, a scrivener. He was educated at the Merchant Tailors' School, of which Richard Mulcaster was head master. Probably he followed his father's calling for a while, but little or nothing more is known of him until he reached his thirties. He seems to have had some acquaintance with French, Italian, Spanish, and Latin, and to have done hack work in translating and in pamphleteering. Certainly with his *Spanish Tragedy* at least, he had a part in the outburst of popular tragedy around 1590. It has been supposed that he afterward capitalized on the popularity of this play by writing what might be called a first part, though the extant *First Part of Jeronimo* (printed in 1605) is probably by another hand. *Soliman and Perseda* is usually assigned to him on the basis of style and of the fact that it has the same plot as the play produced by Hieronimo in *The Spanish Tragedy*. The claim that he wrote *Arden of Feversham* is discussed in connection with that play. Kyd is also credited with an early version of *Hamlet*, now lost, especially by those who regard as aimed at him an allusion to one who "will afford you whole *Hamlets*, I should say handfuls of tragical speeches," in Nashe's preface to Greene's *Menaphon*. Nashe's satire in the same connection on the scrivener born who leaves his trade to write tragedies plundered from Seneca is usually accepted as inspired by the success of Kyd's plays. At any rate Nashe here and Greene in his *Groatsworth of Wit* show resentment at the rise of dramatists without classical training who were proving more effective than the University Wits. Kyd was connected with the coterie around the Countess of Pembroke who were interested in developing a literary tragedy, and he translated from Robert Garnier, called the "French Seneca," the tragedy of *Cornelia*, printed in 1594—the only extant play to bear Kyd's name on the title-page. Arrested in 1593 on suspicion of having posted libels on foreigners, he was found in possession of papers considered heretical or atheistic. He was released on his testimony that the papers had been left among his effects by Marlowe in 1591, when the two of them, in the service of an unidentified lord, had used the same room. Kyd died in 1594.

The authorship of *The Spanish Tragedy* is known only from a chance reference in Thomas Heywood's *Apology for Actors* in 1612. The date assigned to the play varies from 1582 to 1589, with the evidence in favor of the latter date, when the vogue of revenge tragedies—most of them now lost—seems to have begun. The known history of the tragedy opens with Henslowe's record of frequent performances in 1592. License to print was granted in October of that year. What is apparently the earliest extant edition is undated; the earliest with date is that of 1594. Both, however, refer to a "first impression," now lost. In 1597 Henslowe records a number of performances of the play as new, perhaps on account of revision. In September, 1601, and June, 1602, he paid Jonson for additions to "*Jeronimo*," possibly in competition with the closely related *Hamlet*, which Shakespeare was reviving for the Chamberlain's players at the same time, and with several new revenge plays of other companies modeled on these two. In 1602 an edition appeared with "new additions," which develop certain impassioned parts, and which have been assigned to Jonson on the basis of Henslowe's payments. The amounts paid would suggest a more thorough revision, however, and the style of the additions is regarded as against Jonson's authorship, though no real evidence has been adduced in favor of anyone else. The play had an extraordinary popularity. It ran into many editions, at least one of them pirated, was freely imitated, was the subject of numerous allusions, especially by way of stage parody and satire, and finally made its way to Germany. The romantic plot, for which no source has been traced, is strongly colored by the influence of Senecan tragedy—in the chorus, the ghost, the sententious and balanced speeches, the declamation, and the melodramatic treatment of character. The style differs from Marlowe's, with its "high astounding terms," in the emphasis on conceit and on elaborate rhetorical devices of repetition and balance.

The present text is based on the recension of the undated quarto in the British Museum (printed for Allde by White) made by Schick in his variorum edition of *The Spanish Tragedy*, except that the additions have been taken from the Malone Society reprint of the edition of 1602 prepared by Greg. Boas' standard edition of *The Works of Thomas Kyd* has been consulted.

THE SPANISH TRAGEDY[1]

[BY

THOMAS KYD

DRAMATIS PERSONÆ

GHOST OF ANDREA, *a Span-* | *induction*
  ish courtier | *and chorus.*
REVENGE |

KING OF SPAIN.
DON CYPRIAN, *Duke of Castile, his brother.*
LORENZO, *Don Cyprian's son.*
PAGE OF LORENZO.
HIERONIMO, *Marshal of Spain.*
HORATIO, *his son.*
SPANISH GENERAL.
DEPUTY.
VICEROY OF PORTUGAL.
BALTHAZAR, *his son.*
SERBERINE, *Balthazar's servant.*
DON PEDRO, *the viceroy's brother.*
ALEXANDRO | *Portuguese noblemen.*
VILLUPPO |
PORTUGUESE AMBASSADOR.
TWO PORTUGUESE.
DON BAZULTO, *an old man.*

PEDRINGANO, *Bel-imperia's servant.*
CHRISTOPHIL, *Bel-imperia's custodian.*
THREE CITIZENS.
MESSENGER.
HANGMAN.
ARMY, ROYAL SUITES, NOBLEMEN, OF-
FICERS, HALBERDIERS, SERVANTS, THREE
WATCHMEN, ETC.

BEL-IMPERIA, *Don Cyprian's daughter.*
ISABELLA, *Hieronimo's wife.*
MAID OF ISABELLA.

Three KINGS *and three* KNIGHTS, *in the first
dumb show;* HYMEN *and two* TORCH-
BEARERS *in the second.*

BAZARDO, *a painter* | *in the addi-*
PEDRO *and* JAQUES, | *tions to the*
  Hieronimo's servants | *play.*

SCENE: *Spain and Portugal.*

TIME: *Contemporary.*]

ACTUS PRIMUS.

[INDUCTION, *or* CHORUS]

*Enter the Ghost of Andrea, and with him
Revenge.*

GHOST. When this eternal substance of my
  soul
Did live imprisoned in my wanton flesh,
Each in their function serving other's
  need,
I was a courtier in the Spanish court.
My name was Don Andrea, my descent,
Though not ignoble, yet inferior far
To gracious fortunes of my tender youth.

For there in prime and pride of all my
  years,
By duteous service and deserving love,
In secret I possessed a worthy dame, 10
Which hight [2] sweet Bel-imperia by
  name.
But in the harvest of my summer joys
Death's winter nipped the blossoms of
  my bliss,
Forcing divorce betwixt my love and me.
For in the late conflict with Portingale
My valor drew me into danger's mouth
Till life to death made passage through
  my wounds.
When I was slain, my soul descended
  straight
To pass the flowing stream of Acheron;

[1] The title continues: "Containing the Lamentable End of Don Horatio and Bel-imperia,
with the Pitiful Death of Old Hieronimo." In
the 1615 edn. a sub-title is substituted: "Or
Hieronimo Is Mad Again."

[2] Who was called.

423

But churlish Charon, only boatman
there, 20
Said that, my rites of burial not per-
formed,
I might not sit amongst his passengers.
Ere Sol had slept three nights in Thetis'
lap,
And slaked his smoking chariot in her
flood,
By Don Horatio, our knight marshal's
son,
My funerals and obsequies were done.
Then was the ferryman of hell content
To pass me over to the slimy strand
That leads to fell Avernus' ugly waves.
There, pleasing Cerberus with honeyed
speech, 30
I passed the perils of the foremost porch.
Not far from hence, amidst ten thousand
souls,
Sat Minos, Æacus, and Rhadamanth,
To whom no sooner gan [1] I make ap-
proach
To crave a passport for my wand'ring
ghost,
But Minos, in graven leaves of lottery,
Drew forth the manner of my life and
death.
"This knight," quoth he, "both lived
and died in love,
And for his love tried fortune of the wars,
And by war's fortune lost both love and
life." 40
"Why then," said Æacus, "convey him
hence,
To walk with lovers in our fields of love,
And spend the course of everlasting time
Under green myrtle trees and cypress
shades."
"No, no," said Rhadamanth, "it were
not well
With loving souls to place a martialist.
He died in war, and must to martial
fields,
Where wounded Hector lives in lasting
pain,
And Achilles' Myrmidons do scour the
plain." 49
Then Minos, mildest censor [2] of the three,
Made this device to end the difference:
"Send him," quoth he, "to our infernal
king,
To doom him as best seems his majesty."

To this effect my passport straight was
drawn.
In keeping on my way to Pluto's court,
Through dreadful shades of ever-
glooming night,
I saw more sights than thousand tongues
can tell,
Or pens can write, or mortal hearts can
think.
Three ways there were. That on the
right-hand side 59
Was ready way unto the foresaid fields,
Where lovers live and bloody martialists,
But either sort contained within his
bounds.
The left-hand path, declining fearfully,
Was ready downfall to the deepest hell,
Where bloody Furies shakes their whips
of steel,
And poor Ixion turns an endless wheel;
Where usurers are choked with melting
gold,
And wantons are embraced with ugly
snakes,
And murderers groan with never-killing
wounds,
And perjured wights scalded in boiling
lead, 70
And all foul sins with torments over-
whelmed.
Twixt these two ways I trod the middle
path,
Which brought me to the fair Elysian
green,
In midst whereof there stands a stately
tower,
The walls of brass, the gates of adamant.
Here finding Pluto with his Proserpine,
I showed my passport, humbled on my
knee,
Whereat fair Proserpine began to smile,
And begged that only she might give
my doom.
Pluto was pleased, and sealed it with a
kiss. 80
Forthwith, Revenge, she rounded [3] thee
in th' ear,
And bade thee lead me through the gates
of horn,
Where dreams have passage in the silent
night.
No sooner had she spoke, but we were
here—

[1] Did.   [2] Judge.   [3] Whispered.

I wot [1] not how—in twinkling of an eye.

REVENGE. Then know, Andrea, that thou
art arrived

Where thou shalt see the author of thy
death,

Don Balthazar, the prince of Portingale,

Deprived of life by Bel-imperia.

Here sit we down to see the mystery,[2] 90

And serve for Chorus in this tragedy.

[SCENA PRIMA.

The Spanish court.]

*Enter Spanish King, General, Castile, and
Hieronimo.*

KING. Now say, l[ord] general, how fares
our camp?

GEN. All well, my sovereign liege, except
some few

That are deceased by fortune of the war.

KING. But what portends thy cheerful
countenance,

And posting to our presence thus in
haste?

Speak, man, hath fortune given us victory?

GEN. Victory, my liege, and that with little
loss.

KING. Our Portingales will pay us tribute
then?

GEN. Tribute and wonted homage therewithal.

KING. Then blessed be heaven and guider
of the heavens,   10

From whose fair influence such justice
flows.

CAS. "*O multum dilecte Deo, tibi militat
æther,*

Et conjuratæ curvato poplite gentes

*Succumbunt: recti soror est victoria
juris.*" [3]

KING. Thanks to my loving brother of
Castile.—

But, general, unfold in brief discourse

Your form of battle and your war's success,

That, adding all the pleasure of thy news

Unto the height of former happiness,

With deeper wage and greater dignity 20

We may reward thy blissful chivalry.

GEN. Where Spain and Portingale do
jointly knit

Their frontiers, leaning on each other's
bound,

There met our armies in their proud
array,

Both furnished well, both full of hope
and fear,

Both menacing alike with daring shows,

Both vaunting sundry colors of device,

Both cheerly sounding trumpets, drums,
and fifes,

Both raising dreadful clamors to the sky

That valleys, hills, and rivers made re-
bound,   30

And heaven itself was frighted with the
sound.

Our battles both were pitched in squadron form,

Each corner strongly fenced with wings
of shot,

But, ere we joined and came to push of
pike,

I brought a squadron of our readiest shot

From out our rearward [4] to begin the
fight;

They brought another wing t' encounter
us.

Meanwhile, our ordinance played on
either side,

And captains strove to have their valors
tried.

Don Pedro, their chief horsemen's colonel,   40

Did with his cornet [5] bravely make attempt

To break the order of our battle ranks;

But Don Rogero, worthy man of war,

Marched forth against him with our
musketeers,

And stopped the malice of his fell approach.

While they maintain hot skirmish to and
fro,

Both battles join, and fall to handy-
blows,[6]

Their violent shot resembling th' ocean's
rage,

When, roaring loud and with a swelling
tide,

---

[1] Know.   [2] Play.

[3] "O thou much loved of God, for thee heaven
wars, and the peoples of earth, united, submit on bended knee. The triumph of justice
is the sister of righteousness" (adapted from
Claudian's *De Tertio Consulatu Honorii*, ll. 96–
98).

[4] Rear division.   [6] Hand-to-hand fighting.
[5] Troop of horse.

It beats upon the rampiers [1] of huge
  rocks,   50
And gapes to swallow neighbor-bounding
  lands.
Now, while Bellona rageth here and
  there,
Thick storms of bullets ran like winter's
  hail,
And shivered lances dark the troubled
  air.
             Pede pes et cuspide cuspis;
Arma sonant armis, vir petiturque viro. [2]
On every side drop captains to the
  ground,
And soldiers, some ill maimed, some slain
  outright.
Here falls a body sindered [3] from his
  head;
There legs and arms lie bleeding on the
  grass,   60
Mingled with weapons and unboweled
  steeds,
That scattering overspread the purple
  plain.
In all this turmoil, three long hours and
  more,
The victory to neither part inclined,
Till Don Andrea, with his brave lan-
  ciers,
In their main battle made so great a
  breach
That, half dismayed, the multitude re-
  tired.
But Balthazar, the Portingales' young
  prince,
Brought rescue, and encouraged them
  to stay.
Herehence [4] the fight was eagerly re-
  newed,   70
And in that conflict was Andrea slain—
Brave man at arms, but weak to Baltha-
  zar.
Yet while the prince, insulting [5] over
  him,
Breathed out proud vaunts, sounding to
  our reproach,
Friendship and hardy valor joined in one
Pricked forth Horatio, our knight mar-
  shal's son,

[1] Rampires, ramparts, embankments.
[2] Foot against foot and spear against spear,
arms clash on arms, hero is assailed by hero
(a combination of phrases from Statius, Virgil,
and Curtius).   [4] From this point.
[3] Sundered.   [5] Triumphing scornfully.

To challenge forth that prince in single
  fight.
Not long between these twain the fight
  endured,
But straight the prince was beaten from
  his horse,
And forced to yield him prisoner to his
  foe.   80
When he was taken, all the rest they fled,
And our carbines pursued them to the
  death,
Till, Phœbus waving [6] to the western
  deep,
Our trumpeters were charged to sound
  retreat.
KING. Thanks, good l[ord] general, for
  these good news;
And, for some argument of more to come,
Take this and wear it for thy sovereign's
  sake.   *Give him his chain.*
But tell me now, hast thou confirmed a
  peace?
GEN. No peace, my liege, but peace con-
  ditional,
That, if with homage tribute be well
  paid,   90
The fury of your forces will be stayed;
And to this peace their viceroy hath
  subscribed,   *Give the K[ing] a paper.*
And made a solemn vow that, during
  life,
His tribute shall be truly paid to Spain.
KING. These words, these deeds, become
  thy person well.
But now, knight marshal, frolic with
  thy king,
For 'tis thy son that wins this battle's
  prize.
HIER. Long may he live to serve my sov-
  ereign liege,
And soon decay, unless he serve my
  liege.
KING. Nor thou nor he shall die without
  reward.   *A tucket [7] afar off.* 100
What means this warning of this trump-
  et's sound?
GEN. This tells me that your grace's men
  of war,
Such as war's fortune hath reserved
  from death,
Come marching on towards your royal
  seat,
To show themselves before your majesty,

[6] 1603 edn. has *waning.*   [7] Flourish of trumpets.

For so I gave in charge at my depart,
Whereby by demonstration shall appear
That all, except three hundred or few
    more,
Are safe returned, and by their foes en-
    riched.

*The Army enters, Balthazar, between Lorenzo
                    and Horatio, captive.*

KING. A gladsome sight! I long to see
    them here. *They enter and pass by.* 110
Was that the warlike prince of Portin-
    gale
That by our nephew was in triumph
    led?
GEN. It was, my liege, the prince of Portin-
    gale.
KING. But what was he that on the other
    side
Held him by th' arm as partner of the
    prize?
HIER. That was my son, my gracious sov-
    ereign,
Of whom though from his tender infancy
My loving thoughts did never hope but
    well,
He never pleased his father's eyes till
    now,
Nor filled my heart with overcloying
    joys.   120
KING. Go, let them march once more about
    these walls,
That, staying them, we may confer and
    talk
With our brave prisoner and his double
    guard.   [*Exit a Messenger.*]
Hieronimo, it greatly pleaseth us
That in our victory thou have a share,
By virtue of thy worthy son's exploit.

Enter again.

Bring hither the young prince of Portin-
    gale.
The rest march on; but, ere they be dis-
    missed,
We will bestow on every soldier
Two ducats and on every leader ten,   130
That they may know our largess wel-
    comes them.
*Exeunt all but [the King,] Bal[thazar],
            Lor[enzo], Hor[atio].*
Welcome, Don Balthazar! Welcome,
    nephew!

And thou, Horatio, thou art welcome
    too.
Young prince, although thy father's hard
    misdeeds,
In keeping back the tribute that he owes,
Deserve but evil measure at our hands,
Yet shalt thou know that Spain is hon-
    orable.
BAL. The trespass that my father made in
    peace
Is now controlled [1] by fortune of the
    wars,
And, cards once dealt, it boots not ask
    why so.   140
His men are slain—a weakening to his
    realm;
His colors seized—a blot unto his name;
His son distressed—a corsive [2] to his
    heart.
These punishments may clear his late
    offense.
KING. Ay, Balthazar, if he observe this
    truce,
Our peace will grow the stronger for
    these wars.
Meanwhile live thou, though not in lib-
    erty,
Yet free from bearing any servile yoke,
For in our hearing thy deserts were great,
And in our sight thyself art gracious. 150
BAL. And I shall study to deserve this
    grace.
KING. But tell me—for their holding
    makes me doubt—
To which of these twain art thou pris-
    oner?
LOR. To me, my liege.
HOR.   To me, my sovereign.
LOR. This hand first took his courser by
    the reins.
HOR. But first my lance did put him from
    his horse.
LOR. I seized his weapon, and enjoyed it
    first.
HOR. But first I forced him lay his weap-
    ons down.
KING. Let go his arm, upon our privilege.
                            Let him go.
Say, worthy prince, to whether [3] didst
    thou yield?   160
BAL. To him in courtesy; to this perforce.
He spake me fair; this other gave me
    strokes.

[1] Checked.   [2] Corrosive.   [3] Which one.

He promised life; this other threatened
  death.
He won my love; this other conquered
  me—
And, truth to say, I yield myself to both.
HIER. But that I know your grace for
  just and wise,
And might seem partial in this difference,
Enforced by nature and by law of arms,
My tongue should plead for young
  Horatio's right.   169
He hunted well that was a lion's death,
Not he that in a garment wore his skin;
So hares may pull dead lions by the
  beard.
KING. Content thee, marshal, thou shalt
  have no wrong;
And, for thy sake, thy son shall want no
  right.
Will both abide the censure [1] of my
  doom?
LOR. I crave no better than your grace
  awards.
HOR. Nor I, although I sit beside my
  right.
KING. Then by my judgment thus your
  strife shall end:
You both deserve, and both shall have
  reward.
Nephew, thou took'st his weapon and
  his horse;   180
His weapons and his horse are thy re-
  ward.
Horatio, thou didst force him first to
  yield;
His ransom therefore is thy valor's fee.
Appoint the sum, as you shall both agree.
But, nephew, thou shalt have the prince
  in guard,
For thine estate best fitteth such a guest.
Horatio's house were small for all his
  train.
Yet, in regard thy substance passeth his,
And that just guerdon may befall desert,
To him we yield the armor of the
  prince.   190
How likes Don Balthazar of this device?
BAL. Right well, my liege, if this proviso
  were
That Don Horatio bear us company,
Whom I admire and love for chivalry.
KING. Horatio, leave him not that loves
  thee so.—

[1] Judgment.

Now let us hence to see our soldiers paid,
And feast our prisoner as our friendly
  guest.   *Exeunt.*

[SCENA SECUNDA.
The Portuguese court.]

Enter Viceroy, Alexandro, Villuppo.

VIC. Is our ambassador despatched for
  Spain?
ALEX. Two days, my liege, are past since
  his depart.
VIC. And tribute payment gone along with
  him?
ALEX. Ay, my good lord.
VIC. Then rest we here awhile in our un-
  rest,
And feed our sorrows with some inward
  sighs,
For deepest cares break never into tears.
But wherefore sit I in a regal throne?
This better fits a wretch's endless moan.
          Falls to the ground.
Yet this is higher than my fortunes
  reach,   10
And therefore better than my state de-
  serves.
Ay, ay, this earth, image of melancholy,
Seeks him whom fates adjudge to misery.
Here let me lie; now am I at the lowest.
Qui jacet in terra, non habet unde cadat.
In me consumpsit vires Fortuna nocendo;
Nil superest ut jam possit obesse magis. [2]
Yes, Fortune may bereave me of my
  crown—
Here, take it now. Let Fortune do her
  worst,
She will not rob me of this sable weed. 20
O, no, she envies none but pleasant
  things.
Such is the folly of despiteful chance!
Fortune is blind, and sees not my deserts;
So is she deaf, and hears not my laments;
And could she hear, yet is she willful-mad,
And therefore will not pity my distress.
Suppose that she could pity me, what
  then?
What help can be expected at her hands
Whose foot [is] [3] standing on a rolling
  stone,

[2] He who lies upon the ground hath not
whence he may fall. On me hath Fortune exhausted her powers of injury. There remains
no further damage that she can inflict (source
unknown).   [3] Added by Dodsley.

And mind more mutable than fickle
winds?   30
Why wail I, then, where's hope of no
redress?
O, yes, complaining makes my grief seem
less.
My late ambition hath distained [1] my
faith;
My breach of faith occasioned bloody
wars;
Those bloody wars have spent my treas-
ure;
And with my treasure my people's blood;
And with their blood, my joy and best
beloved,
My best beloved, my sweet and only son.
O, wherefore went I not to war myself?
The cause was mine; I might have died
for both.   40
My years were mellow; his but young
and green.
My death were natural, but his was
forced.
ALEX. No doubt, my liege, but still the
prince survives.
VIC. Survives! Ay, where?
ALEX. In Spain, a prisoner by mischance
of war.
VIC. Then they have slain him for his
father's fault.
ALEX. That were a breach to common
law of arms.
VIC. They reck no laws that meditate re-
venge.
ALEX. His ransom's worth will stay from
foul revenge.
VIC. No; if he lived, the news would soon
be here.   50
ALEX. Nay, evil news fly faster still than
good.
VIC. Tell me no more of news, for he is
dead.
VIL. My sovereign, pardon the author of
ill news,
And I'll bewray [2] the fortune of thy son.
VIC. Speak on, I'll guerdon thee, whate'er
it be.
Mine ear is ready to receive ill news,
My heart grown hard gainst mischief's
battery.
Stand up, I say, and tell thy tale at large.
VIL. Then hear that truth which these
mine eyes have seen.

When both the armies were in battle
joined,   60
Don Balthazar, amidst the thickest
troops,
To win renown did wondrous feats of
arms.
Amongst the rest, I saw him, hand to
hand,
In single fight with their lord general,
Till Alexandro, that here counterfeits
Under the color of a duteous friend,
Discharged his pistol at the prince's back
As though he would have slain their
general—
But therewithal Don Balthazar fell down,
And, when he fell, then we began to
fly;   70
But, had he lived, the day had sure been
ours.
ALEX. O wicked forgery! O traitorous mis-
creant!
VIC. Hold thou thy peace! But now, Vil-
luppo, say,
Where then became [3] the carcass of my
son?
VIL. I saw them drag it to the Spanish
tents.
VIC. Ay, ay, my nightly dreams have told
me this.—
Thou false, unkind, unthankful, traitor-
ous beast,
Wherein had Balthazar offended thee
That thou shouldst thus betray him to
our foes?
Was't Spanish gold that bleared so
thine eyes   80
That thou couldst see no part of our
deserts?
Perchance, because thou art Terceira's
lord,
Thou hadst some hope to wear this
diadem,
If first my son and then myself were
slain.
But thy ambitious thought shall break
thy neck.
Ay, this was it that made thee spill his
blood,
    Take the crown and put it on again.
But I'll now wear it till thy blood be
spilt.
ALEX. Vouchsafe, dread sovereign, to hear
me speak.

[1] Stained, defiled.   [2] Disclose.   [3] What became of.

VIC. Away with him! His sight is second
 hell.
Keep him till we determine of his
 death.   [*They take him out.*]   90
If Balthazar be dead, he shall not live.
Villuppo, follow us for thy reward.
                    Exit Vice[*roy*].
VIL. Thus have I with an envious, forgéd
 tale
Deceived the king, betrayed mine enemy,
And hope for guerdon of my villainy.
                    Exit.

[SCENA TERTIA.

Hieronimo's garden.[1]]

Enter Horatio and Bel-imperia.

BEL. Signior Horatio, this is the place and
 hour,
Wherein I must entreat thee to relate
The circumstance of Don Andrea's death,
Who, living, was my garland's sweetest
 flower,
And in his death hath buried my de-
 lights.
HOR. For love of him and service to your-
 self,
I nill[2] refuse this heavy, doleful charge;
Yet tears and sighs, I fear, will hinder
 me.
When both our armies were enjoined in
 fight,
Your worthy chevalier amidst the
 thick'st,   10
For glorious cause still aiming at the
 fairest,
Was at the last by young Don Balthazar
Encountered hand to hand. Their fight
 was long,
Their hearts were great, their clamors
 menacing,
Their strength alike, their strokes both
 dangerous.
But wrathful Nemesis, that wicked
 power,
Envying at Andrea's praise and worth,

Cut short his life to end his praise and
 worth.
She, she herself, disguised in armor's
 mask—
As Pallas was before proud Perga-
 mus—   20
Brought in a fresh supply of halberdiers,
Which paunched[3] his horse, and dinged[4]
 him to the ground.
Then young Don Balthazar with ruthless
 rage,
Taking advantage of his foe's distress,
Did finish what his halberdiers begun,
And left not till Andrea's life was done.
Then, though too late, incensed with just
 remorse,[5]
I with my band set forth against the
 prince
And brought him prisoner from his
 halberdiers.
BEL. Would thou hadst slain him that so
 slew my love!   30
But then was Don Andrea's carcass lost?
HOR. No, that was it for which I chiefly
 strove,
Nor stepped I back till I recovered him.
I took him up, and wound him in mine
 arms;
And, welding[6] him unto my private tent,
There laid him down, and dewed him
 with my tears,
And sighed and sorrowed as became a
 friend.
But neither friendly sorrow, sighs, nor
 tears
Could win pale Death from his usurpéd
 right.
Yet this I did, and less I could not do: 40
I saw him honored with due funeral.
This scarf I plucked from off his lifeless
 arm,
And wear it in remembrance of my
 friend.
BEL. I know the scarf. Would he had kept
 it still!
For, had he lived, he would have kept it
 still,
And worn it for his Bel-imperia's sake,
For 'twas my favor at his last depart.
But now wear thou it both for him and
 me,
For after him thou hast deserved it best.

---

[1] If II, ii, 42–43, refers to I, iii, 48–54, the
scene here is Hieronimo's garden, and, according to ll. 110–15, close to the place of the banquet in I, iv. Possibly, however, I, iii and iv, are
to be regarded as one scene, beginning in some
indefinite locality and shifting to a banqueting
hall.
[2] Ne will; will not.

[3] Stabbed in the belly.   [5] Sorrow.
[4] Knocked down.   [6] Wielding, carrying.

But, for thy kindness in his life and
    death,   50
Be sure, while Bel-imperia's life endures,
She will be Don Horatio's thankful
    friend.

Hor. And, madam, Don Horatio will not
    slack
Humbly to serve fair Bel-imperia.
But now, if your good liking stand
    thereto,
I'll crave your pardon to go seek the
    prince,
For so the duke, your father, gave me
    charge.   *Exit.*

Bel. Ay, go, Horatio, leave me here
    alone,
For solitude best fits my cheerless mood.
Yet what avails to wail Andrea's
    death,   60
From whence Horatio proves my second
    love?
Had he not loved Andrea as he did,
He could not sit in Bel-imperia's
    thoughts.
But how can love find harbor in my
    breast
Till I revenge the death of my beloved?
Yes, second love shall further my re-
    venge!
I'll love Horatio, my Andrea's friend,
The more to spite the prince that
    wrought his end;
And, where Don Balthazar, that slew
    my love,
Himself now pleads for favor at my
    hands,   70
He shall, in rigor of my just disdain,
Reap long repentance for his murderous
    deed.
For what was't else but murderous
    cowardice,
So many to oppress one valiant knight,
Without respect of honor in the fight?
And here he comes that murdered my
    delight.

Enter Lorenzo and Balthazar.

Lor. Sister, what means this melancholy
    walk?
Bel. That for a while I wish no company.
Lor. But here the prince is come to visit
    you.
Bel. That argues that he lives in lib-
    erty.   80

Bal. No, madam, but in pleasing servi-
    tude.
Bel. Your prison then, belike, is your
    conceit.[1]
Bal. Ay, by conceit my freedom is en-
    thralled.
Bel. Then with conceit enlarge [2] yourself
    again.
Bal. What if conceit have laid my heart
    to gage? [3]
Bel. Pay that you borrowed, and recover
    it.
Bal. I die, if it return from whence it lies.
Bel. A heartless man, and live? A mir-
    acle!
Bal. Ay, lady, love can work such mir-
    acles.
Lor. Tush, tush, my lord! Let go these
    ambages,[4]   90
And in plain terms acquaint her with
    your love.
Bel. What boots complaint, when there's
    no remedy?
Bal. Yes, to your gracious self must I com-
    plain,
In whose fair answer lies my remedy;
On whose perfection all my thoughts
    attend;
On whose aspect mine eyes find beauty's
    bower;
In whose translucent breast my heart is
    lodged.
Bel. Alas, my lord, these are but words of
    course,[5]
And but devise[d] to drive me from this
    place.

*She in going in lets fall her glove, which
    Horatio, coming out, takes up.*

Hor. Madam, your glove.   100
Bel. Thanks, good Horatio; take it for thy
    pains.
Bal. Signior Horatio stooped in happy
    time!
Hor. I reaped more grace than I deserved
    or hoped.
Lor. My lord, be not dismayed for what
    is past;
You know that women oft are humor-
    ous.[6]
These clouds will overblow with little
    wind;

---

[1] Thought, imagination.   [4] Roundabout phrases.
[2] Free.   [5] Formal phrases.
[3] As security.   [6] Variable, capricious.

Let me alone, I'll scatter them myself.
Meanwhile, let us devise to spend the
time
In some delightful sports and reveling.
Hor. The king, my lords, is coming hither
straight   110
To feast the Portingale ambassador;
Things were in readiness before I came.
Bal. Then here it fits us to attend the king,
To welcome hither our ambassador,
And learn my father and my country's
health.

[Scena Quarta.

The banqueting hall in the Spanish court.]

*Enter the banquet, Trumpets, the King, and
Ambassador.*

King. See, lord ambassador, how Spain
entreats [1]
Their prisoner Balthazar, thy viceroy's
son.
We pleasure more in kindness than in
wars.
Amb. Sad is our king, and Portingale la-
ments,
Supposing that Don Balthazar is slain.
Bal. So am I—slain by beauty's tyranny!
You see, my lord, how Balthazar is slain:
I frolic with the Duke of Castile's son,
Wrapped every hour in pleasures of the
court,
And graced with favors of his majesty. 10
King. Put off your greetings till our feast
be done;
Now come and sit with us, and taste our
cheer.   *Sit to the banquet.*
Sit down, young prince; you are our
second guest.
Brother, sit down; and, nephew, take
your place.
Signior Horatio, wait thou upon our cup,
For well thou hast deserved to be hon-
ored.
Now, lordings, fall to. Spain is Portugal,
And Portugal is Spain; we both are
friends;
Tribute is paid, and we enjoy our right.
But where is old Hieronimo, our mar-
shal?   20
He promised us, in honor of our guest,
To grace our banquet with some pom-
pous jest. [2]

[1] Treats.   [2] Stately entertainment.

*Enter Hieronimo, with a drum, three
Knights, each [with] his scutcheon; then
he fetches three Kings; they take their
crowns and them captive.*

Hieronimo, this masque contents mine
eye,
Although I sound not well the mystery.
Hier. The first armed knight that hung
his scutcheon up
*He takes the scutcheon and gives it to the
King.*
Was English Robert, Earl of Gloucester,
Who, when King Stephen bore sway in
Albion,
Arrived with five-and-twenty thousand
men
In Portingale, and by success of war
Enforced the king, then but a Saracen, 30
To bear the yoke of the English mon-
archy.
King. My lord of Portingale, by this you
see
That which may comfort both your king
and you,
And make your late discomfort seem the
less.
But say, Hieronimo, what was the next?
Hier. The second knight that hung his
scutcheon up   *He doth as he did before.*
Was Edmund, Earl of Kent in Albion,
When English Richard wore the diadem.
He came likewise, and razéd Lisbon
walls,
And took the King of Portingale in
fight,   40
For which and other suchlike service
done
He after was created Duke of York.
King. This is another special argument
That Portingale may deign to bear our
yoke,
When it by little England hath been
yoked.
But now, Hieronimo, what were the last?
Hier. The third and last, not least, in our
account,   *Doing as before.*
Was, as the rest, a valiant Englishman,
Brave John of Gaunt, the Duke of Lan-
caster,
As by his scutcheon plainly may ap-
pear.   50
He with a puissant army came to Spain
And took our King of Castile prisoner.

Amb. This is an argument for our viceroy
　That Spain may not insult for her suc-
　　cess,
　Since English warriors likewise conquered
　　Spain,
　And made them bow their knees to
　　Albion.
King. Hieronimo, I drink to thee for this
　device,
　Which hath pleased both the ambassador
　　and me.
　Pledge me, Hieronimo, if thou love the
　　king.　　　*Takes the cup of Horatio.*
　My lord, I fear we sit but overlong,　60
　Unless our dainties were more delicate,
　But welcome are you to the best we have.
　Now let us in, that you may be des-
　　patched.
　I think our council is already set.
　　　　　　　　　　　Exeunt omnes.

[Chorus]

Andrea. Come we for this from depth of
　underground,
　To see him feast that gave me my
　　death's wound?
　These pleasant sights are sorrow to my
　　soul—
　Nothing but league,[1] and love, and ban-
　　queting!
Revenge. Be still, Andrea; ere we go from
　hence,
　I'll turn their friendship into fell de-
　　spite,　　　　　　　　　　　70
　Their love to mortal hate, their day to
　　night,
　Their hope into despair, their peace to
　　war,
　Their joys to pain, their bliss to misery.

Actus Secundus. [Scena Prima.

A room in Don Cyprian's palace.]

Enter Lorenzo and Balthazar.

Lor. My lord, though Bel-imperia seem
　thus coy,
　Let reason hold you in your wonted joy.
　In time the savage bull sustains the
　　yoke,[2]

---

[1] Friendship.
[2] Lines 3–6, 9–10, are modeled on Sonnet 47
of Watson's *Hecatompathia.*

In time all haggard [3] hawks will stoop to
　lure,
　In time small wedges cleave the hardest
　　oak,
　In time the flint is pierced with softest
　　shower,
　And she in time will fall from her dis-
　　dain,
　And rue the sufferance of your friendly
　　pain.
Bal. No, she is wilder and more hard
　withal
　Than beast or bird or tree or stony
　　wall.　　　　　　　　　　　10
　But wherefore blot I Bel-imperia's name?
　It is my fault, not she, that merits blame.
　My feature is not to content her sight,
　My words are rude and work her no
　　delight.
　The lines I send her are but harsh and ill,
　Such as do drop from Pan and Marsyas'
　　quill.
　My presents are not of sufficient cost,
　And, being worthless, all my labor's lost.
　Yet might she love me for my valiancy—
　Ay, but that's slandered by captivity. 20
　Yet might she love me to content her
　　sire—
　Ay, but her reason masters his desire.
　Yet might she love me as her brother's
　　friend—
　Ay, but her hopes aim at some other end.
　Yet might she love me to uprear her
　　state—
　Ay, but perhaps she hopes some nobler
　　mate.
　Yet might she love me as her beauty's
　　thrall—
　Ay, but I fear she cannot love at all.
Lor. My lord, for my sake leave this
　ecstasy,[4]
　And doubt not but we'll find some
　　remedy.　　　　　　　　　　30
　Some cause there is that lets you not be
　　loved;
　First that must needs be known, and
　　then removed.
　What if my sister love some other knight?
Bal. My summer's day will turn to win-
　ter's night.
Lor. I have already found a stratagem
　To sound the bottom of this doubtful
　　theme.

---

[3] Wild.　　　　　　　　　　　[4] Frenzy.

My lord, for once you shall be ruled by
me;
Hinder me not, whate'er you hear or see.
By force or fair means will I cast about
To find the truth of all this question
out.   40
Ho, Pedringano!

PED.   Signior!

LOR.   Vien qui presto.[1]

Enter Pedringano.

PED. Hath your lordship any service to
command me?

LOR. Ay, Pedringano, service of import,
And—not to spend the time in trifling
words—
Thus stands the case: it is not long, thou
know'st,
Since I did shield thee from my father's
wrath,
For thy conveyance[2] in Andrea's love,
For which thou wert adjudged to punish-
ment.
I stood betwixt thee and thy punishment,
And, since, thou knowest how I have
favored thee.   50
Now to these favors will I add reward,
Not with fair words, but store of golden
coin,
And lands and living joined with dig-
nities,
If thou but satisfy my just demand.
Tell truth, and have me for thy lasting
friend.

PED. Whate'er it be your lordship shall de-
mand,
My bounden duty bids me tell the truth,
If case[3] it lie in me to tell the truth.

LOR. Then, Pedringano, this is my de-
mand:
Whom loves my sister Bel-imperia?   60
For she reposeth all her trust in thee.
Speak, man, and gain both friendship and
reward.
I mean, whom loves she in Andrea's
place?

PED. Alas, my lord, since Don Andrea's
death
I have no credit with her as before,
And therefore know not if she love or no.

LOR. Nay, if thou dally, then I am thy foe,
[*Draw his sword.*][4]

And fear shall force what friendship
cannot win.
Thy death shall bury what thy life con-
ceals;
Thou diest for more esteeming her than
me.   70

PED. O, stay, my lord!

LOR. Yet speak the truth, and I will
guerdon thee,
And shield thee from whatever can
ensue,
And will conceal whate'er proceeds from
thee.
But, if thou dally once again, thou diest.

PED. If Madam Bel-imperia be in love—

LOR. What, villain! If's and and's?
[*Offer to kill him.*][4]

PED. O, stay, my lord! She loves Horatio.
Balthazar starts back.

LOR. What, Don Horatio, our knight
marshal's son?

PED. Even him, my lord.   80

LOR. Now say but how know'st thou he
is her love,
And thou shalt find me kind and liberal.
Stand up, I say, and fearless tell the
truth.

PED. She sent him letters, which myself
perused,
Full fraught with lines and arguments of
love,
Preferring him before Prince Balthazar.

LOR. Swear on this cross[5] that what thou
sayst is true,
And that thou wilt conceal what thou
hast told.

PED. I swear to both, by Him that made
us all.

LOR. In hope thine oath is true, here's thy
reward;   90
But, if I prove thee perjured and unjust,
This very sword whereon thou took'st
thine oath
Shall be the worker of thy tragedy.

PED. What I have said is true, and shall—
for me—
Be still concealed from Bel-imperia.
Besides, your honor's liberality
Deserves my duteous service, even till
death.

LOR. Let this be all that thou shalt do for
me:

---

[1] Come here quickly.   [3] In case.
[2] Trickery.   [4] From 1602 edn.

[5] *I.e.*, sword hilt.

Be watchful when and where these lovers
    meet,
And give me notice in some secret
    sort.   100
PED. I will, my lord.
LOR. Then shalt thou find that I am
    liberal.
Thou know'st that I can more advance
    thy state
Than she. Be therefore wise, and fail me
    not.
Go and attend her, as thy custom is,
Lest absence make her think thou dost
    amiss.   *Exit Pedringano.*
Why, so: *tam armis quam ingenio.*[1]
Where words prevail not, violence pre-
    vails;
But gold doth more than either of them
    both.
How likes Prince Balthazar this strata-
    gem?   110
BAL. Both well and ill. It makes me glad
    and sad:
Glad that I know the hinderer of my
    love—
Sad that I fear she hates me whom I
    love;
Glad that I know on whom to be re-
    venged—
Sad that she'll fly me if I take revenge.
Yet must I take revenge or die myself,
For love resisted grows impatient.
I think Horatio be my destined plague.
First, in his hand he brandishéd a sword,
And with that sword he fiercely wagéd
    war,   120
And in that war he gave me dangerous
    wounds,
And by those wounds he forcéd me to
    yield,
And by my yielding I became his slave.
Now in his mouth he carries pleasing
    words,
Which pleasing words do harbor sweet
    conceits,
Which sweet conceits are limed with sly
    deceits,
Which sly deceits smooth Bel-imperia's
    ears,
And through her ears dive down into her
    heart,
And in her heart set him where I should
    stand.

[1] As much by force as by wisdom.

Thus hath he ta'en my body by his
    force,   130
And now by sleight would captivate my
    soul.
But in his fall I'll tempt the destinies,
And either lose my life or win my love.
LOR. Let's go, my lord; your staying stays
    revenge.
Do you but follow me, and gain your love.
Her favor must be won by his remove.
                                    Exeunt.

                    [SCENA SECUNDA.

                    The same.]

        Enter Horatio and Bel-imperia.

HOR. Now, madam, since by favor of your
    love
Our hidden smoke is turned to open flame,
And that with looks and words we feed
    our thought
(Two chief contents, where more cannot
    be had),
Thus, in the midst of love's fair blandish-
    ments,
Why show you sign of inward languish-
    ments?
Pedringano showeth all to the Prince and
            Lorenzo, placing them in secret.
BEL. My heart, sweet friend, is like a ship
    at sea.
She wisheth port, where, riding all at ease,
She may repair what stormy times have
    worn,
And, leaning on the shore, may sing with
    joy   10
That pleasure follows pain, and bliss
    annoy.
Possession of thy love is th' only port
Wherein my heart, with fears and hopes
    long tossed,
Each hour doth wish and long to make
    resort,
There to repair the joys that it hath lost,
And, sitting safe, to sing in Cupid's choir
That sweetest bliss is crown of love's
    desire.

        Balthazar [and Lorenzo] above.
BAL. O, sleep, mine eyes; see not my love
    profaned.
Be deaf, my ears; hear not my discontent.
Die, heart; another joys what thou de-
    servest.   20

LOR. Watch still, mine eyes, to see this
    love disjoined;
  Hear still, mine ears, to hear them both
    lament;
  Live, heart, to joy at fond Horatio's fall.

BEL. Why stands Horatio speechless all
    this while?
HOR. The less I speak, the more I medi-
    tate.
BEL. But whereon dost thou chiefly medi-
    tate?
HOR. On dangers past, and pleasures to
    ensue.

BAL. On pleasures past, and dangers to
    ensue.

BEL. What dangers and what pleasures
    dost thou mean?
HOR. Dangers of war, and pleasures of our
    love.   30

LOR. Dangers of death, but pleasures none
    at all.

BEL. Let dangers go; thy war shall be
    with me,
  But such a war as breaks no bond of
    peace.
  Speak thou fair words, I'll cross them
    with fair words;
  Send thou sweet looks, I'll meet them
    with sweet looks;
  Write loving lines, I'll answer loving lines;
  Give me a kiss, I'll countercheck thy kiss.
  Be this our warring peace, or peaceful
    war.
HOR. But, gracious madam, then appoint
    the field,
  Where trial of this war shall first be
    made.   40

BAL. Ambitious villain, how his boldness
    grows!

BEL. Then be thy father's pleasant bower
    the field,
  Where first we vowed a mutual amity.
  The court were dangerous; that place is
    safe.
  Our hour shall be when Vesper gins to
    rise,
  That summons home distressful trav-
    elers.[1]

[1] The meaning *travailers, workers,* is also possible.

There none shall hear us but the harmless
    birds;
Happily [2] the gentle nightingale
Shall carol us asleep, ere we be ware,
And, singing with the prickle at her
    breast,   50
Tell our delight and mirthful dalliance.
Till then each hour will seem a year and
    more.
HOR. But, honeysweet and honorable love,
  Return we now into your father's sight;
  Dangerous suspicion waits on our de-
    light.

LOR. Ay, danger mixed with jealous de-
    spite
  Shall send thy soul into eternal night.
                    Exeunt.

[SCENA TERTIA.

The Spanish court.]

Enter King of Spain, Portingale Ambassa-
    dor, Don Cyprian, etc.

KING. Brother of Castile, to the prince's
    love
  What says your daughter Bel-imperia?
CYP. Although she coy it,[3] as becomes her
    kind,
  And yet dissemble that she loves the
    prince,
  I doubt not, I, but she will stoop in time.
  And, were she froward, which she will
    not be,
  Yet herein shall she follow my advice,
  Which is to love him, or forgo my love.
KING. Then, lord ambassador of Portin-
    gale,
  Advise thy king to make this marriage
    up   10
  For strengthening of our late-confirméd
    league.
  I know no better means to make us
    friends.
  Her dowry shall be large and liberal.
  Besides that she is daughter and half-
    heir
  Unto our brother here, Don Cyprian,
  And shall enjoy the moiety of his land,
  I'll grace her marriage with an uncle's
    gift,
  And this it is: in case the match go for-
    ward,

[2] Haply, perhaps.   [3] Pretend to be shy.

The tribute which you pay shall be re-
leased;
And, if by Balthazar she have a son,   20
He shall enjoy the kingdom after us.

AMB. I'll make the motion to my sovereign
liege,
And work it, if my counsel may prevail.

KING. Do so, my lord, and, if he give
consent,
I hope his presence here will honor us
In celebration of the nuptial day;
And let himself determine of the time.

AMB. Will 't please your grace command
me aught beside?

KING. Commend me to the king, and so
farewell.
But where's Prince Balthazar to take his
leave?   30

AMB. That is performed already, my good
lord.

KING. Amongst the rest of what you have
in charge,
The prince's ransom must not be forgot.
That's none of mine, but his that took
him prisoner,
And well his forwardness deserves re-
ward.
It was Horatio, our knight marshal's son.

AMB. Between us there's a price already
pitched,
And shall be sent with all convenient
speed.

KING. Then once again farewell, my lord.

AMB. Farewell, my Lord of Castile, and the
rest.   *Exit.* 40

KING. Now, brother, you must take some
little pains
To win fair Bel-imperia from her will.
Young virgins must be rulèd by their
friends.
The prince is amiable and loves her well.
If she neglect him and forgo his love,
She both will wrong her own estate and
ours.
Therefore, whiles I do entertain the
prince
With greatest pleasure that our court
affords,
Endeavor you to win your daughter's
thought.
If she give back,[1] all this will come to
naught.   50
                                      Exeunt.

[1] Decline.

[SCENA QUARTA.

Hieronimo's garden.]

Enter Horatio, Bel-imperia, and Pedringano.

HOR. Now that the night begins with
sable wings
To overcloud the brightness of the sun,
And that in darkness pleasures may be
done,
Come, Bel-imperia, let us to the bower,
And there in safety pass a pleasant hour.

BEL. I follow thee, my love, and will not
back,
Although my fainting heart controls my
soul.

HOR. Why, make you doubt of Pedringano's faith?

BEL. No, he is as trusty as my second
self.—
Go, Pedringano, watch without the
gate,   10
And let us know if any make approach.

PED. [*Aside.*] Instead of watching, I'll deserve more gold
By fetching Don Lorenzo to this match.
                              Exit Ped[ringano].

HOR. What means my love?

BEL.   I know not what myself,
And yet my heart foretells me some mischance.

HOR. Sweet, say not so; fair fortune is our
friend,
And heavens have shut up day to pleasure us.
The stars, thou seest, hold back their
twinkling shine,
And Luna hides herself to pleasure us.

BEL. Thou hast prevailed; I'll conquer my
misdoubt,   20
And in thy love and counsel drown my
fear.
I fear no more; love now is all my
thoughts.
Why sit we not, for pleasure asketh ease?

HOR. The more thou sitt'st within these
leafy bowers,
The more will Flora deck it with her
flowers.

BEL. Ay, but, if Flora spy Horatio here,
Her jealous eye will think I sit too near.

HOR. Hark, madam, how the birds record[2]
by night,
For joy that Bel-imperia sits in sight.

[2] Sing.

BEL. No, Cupid counterfeits the nightin-
gale,   30
  To frame sweet music to Horatio's tale.
HOR. If Cupid sing, then Venus is not far.
  Ay, thou art Venus, or some fairer star.
BEL. If I be Venus, thou must needs be
Mars;
  And, where Mars reigneth, there must
needs be wars.
HOR. Then thus begin our wars. Put forth
thy hand,
  That it may combat with my ruder hand.
BEL. Set forth thy foot to try the push of
mine.
HOR. But first my looks shall combat
against thine.
BEL. Then ward thyself: I dart this kiss
at thee.   40
HOR. Thus I retort the dart thou threw'st
at me.
BEL. Nay, then, to gain the glory of the
field
  My twining arms shall yoke and make
thee yield.
HOR. Nay, then, my arms are large and
strong withal.
  Thus elms by vines are compassed, till
they fall.
BEL. O, let me go, for in my troubled eyes
  Now mayst thou read that life in passion
dies.
HOR. O, stay awhile, and I will die with
thee;
  So shalt thou yield, and yet have conquered me.
BEL. Who's there? Pedringano?—We are
betrayed!   50

*Enter Lorenzo, Balthazar, Serberine, Pedrin-
gano, disguised.*

LOR. My lord, away with her; take her
aside.—
  O, sir, forbear! Your valor is already
tried.—
  Quickly despatch, my masters.
          They hang him in the arbor.
HOR.   What, will you murder me?
LOR. Ay, thus, and thus! These are the
fruits of love.   *They stab him.*
BEL. O, save his life, and let me die for
him!
  O, save him, brother! Save him, Baltha-
zar!
  I loved Horatio, but he loved not me.

BAL. But Balthazar loves Bel-imperia.
LOR. Although his life were still ambitious,
proud,
  Yet is he at the highest now he is dead. 60
BEL. Murder! Murder! Help, Hieronimo,
help!
LOR. Come, stop her mouth; away with
her.   *Exeunt.*

Enter Hieronimo in his shirt, etc.

HIER. What outcries pluck me from my
naked bed,
  And chill my throbbing heart with
trembling fear,
  Which never danger yet could daunt
before?
  Who calls Hieronimo? Speak, here I am.
  I did not slumber; therefore 'twas no
dream.
  No, no, it was some woman cried for help,
  And here within this garden did she cry,
  And in this garden must I rescue her.— 70
  But stay, what murd'rous spectacle is
this?
  A man hanged up and all the murderers
gone!
  And in my bower, to lay the guilt on me!
  This place was made for pleasure, not
for death.   *He cuts him down.*
  Those garments that he wears I oft have
seen—
  Alas, it is Horatio, my sweet son!
  O, no, but he that whilom [1] was my son!
  O, was it thou that calledst me from my
bed?
  O, speak, if any spark of life remain.
  I am thy father. Who hath slain my
son?   80
  What savage monster, not of human
kind,
  Hath here been glutted with thy harm-
less blood,
  And left thy bloody corpse dishonored
here,
  For me, amidst these dark and deathful
shades,
  To drown thee with an ocean of my tears?
  O heavens, why made you night to cover
sin?
  By day this deed of darkness had not
been.
  O earth, why didst thou not in time
devour

[1] Formerly.

The vild [1] profaner of this sacred bower?
O poor Horatio, what hadst thou mis-
   done,   90
To leese [2] thy life ere life was new begun?
O wicked butcher, whatsoe'er thou wert,
How could thou strangle virtue and
   desert?
Ay me most wretched, that have lost my
   joy,
In leesing my Horatio, my sweet boy!

Enter Isabel[la].

ISAB. My husband's absence makes my
   heart to throb.—
Hieronimo!
HIER. Here, Isabella, help me to lament,
For sighs are stopped, and all my tears
   are spent.
ISAB. What world of grief!   My son
   Horatio!   100
O, where's the author of this endless
   woe?
HIER. To know the author were some ease
   of grief,
For in revenge my heart would find relief.
ISAB. Then is he gone? And is my son gone
   too?
O, gush out, tears, fountains and floods
   of tears;
Blow, sighs, and raise an everlasting
   storm,
For outrage fits our cursèd wretchedness! [3]
Ay me, Hieronimo, sweet husband, speak!
HIER. He supped with us tonight, frolic
   and merry,
And said he would go visit Balthazar 110
At the duke's palace—there the prince
   doth lodge.
He had no custom to stay out so late;
He may be in his chamber. Some go see.
Roderigo, ho!

Enter Pedro and Jaques.

ISAB. Ay me, he raves!—Sweet Hier-
   onimo!
HIER. True, all Spain takes note of it.
Besides, he is so generally beloved;
His majesty the other day did grace him

With waiting on his cup. These be favors
Which do assure me [he] [4] cannot be
   short-lived.
ISAB. Sweet Hieronimo!   120
HIER. I wonder how this fellow got his
   clothes!—
Sirrah, sirrah, I'll know the truth of all.
Jaques, run to the Duke of Castile's
   presently,
And bid my son Horatio to come home.
I and his mother have had strange
   dreams tonight.
Do ye hear me, sir?
JAQUES. Ay, sir.
HIER. Well, sir, be gone.   Pedro, come
   hither. Know'st thou who this is?
PED. Too well, sir.
HIER. Too well! Who, who is it? Peace,
   Isabella! Nay, blush not, man.   130
PED. It is my lord Horatio.
HIER. Ha, ha! St. James, but this doth
   make me laugh,
That there are more deluded than my-
   self.
PED. Deluded?
HIER. Ay, I would have sworn myself,
   within this hour,
That this had been my son Horatio,
His garments are so like. Ha! Are they
   not great persuasions?
ISAB. O, would to God it were not so!
HIER. Were not, Isabella?   Dost thou
   dream it is?   139
Can thy soft bosom entertain a thought
That such a black deed of mischief should
   be done
On one so pure and spotless as our son?
Away, I am ashamed.
ISAB. Dear Hieronimo, cast a more serious
   eye upon thy grief;
Weak apprehension gives but weak
   belief.
HIER. It was a man, sure, that was hanged
   up here;
A youth, as I remember. I cut him down.
If it should prove my son now after all—
Say you? Say you?—Light! Lend me
   a taper;
Let me look again.—   150
O God! Confusion, mischief, torment,
   death, and hell,
Drop all your stings at once in my cold
   bosom,

---

[1] Vile.   [2] Lose.
[3] The first of the additions begins here and extends through l. 160. Some modern editors have attempted without success to improve the form of the verse in these additions by changing the division of lines. Here the line division of the original has been kept in all the additions.

[4] From 1603 edn.

That now is stiff with horror. Kill me
quickly!
Be gracious to me, thou infective [1] night,
And drop this deed of murder down on
me.
Gird in my waste of grief with thy large
darkness,
And let me not survive to see the light
May put me in the mind I had a son.

ISAB. O sweet Horatio! O my dearest
son!

HIER. How strangely had I lost my way
to grief! 160
Sweet, lovely rose, ill-plucked before thy
time,
Fair, worthy son, not conquered, but
betrayed,
I'll kiss thee now, for words with tears
are stayed.

ISAB. And I'll close up the glasses of his
sight,
For once these eyes were only my delight.

HIER. Seest thou this handkercher be-
smeared with blood?
It shall not from me, till I take revenge.
Seest thou those wounds that yet are
bleeding fresh?
I'll not entomb them, till I have revenged.
Then will I joy amidst my discontent; 170
Till then my sorrow never shall be spent.

ISAB. The heavens are just; murder cannot be hid.
Time is the author both of truth and
right,
And time will bring this treachery to
light.

HIER. Meanwhile, good Isabella, cease thy
plaints,
Or, at the least, dissemble them awhile.
So shall we sooner find the practice [2] out,
And learn by whom all this was brought
about.
Come, Isabel, now let us take him up,
They take him up.
And bear him in from out this cursèd
place. 180
I'll say his dirge; singing fits not this case.

*O aliquis mihi quas pulchrum ver educat
herbas,*   Hiero[nimo] *sets his
breast unto his sword.*
Misceat, et nostro detur medicina dolori;

[1] Infectious.   [2] Plot.

*Aut, si qui faciunt annorum oblivia,
succos
Præbeat; ipse metam magnum quæcunque
per orbem
Gramina Sol pulchras effert in luminis oras,
Ipse bibam quicquid meditatur saga veneni,
Quicquid et herbarum vi cæca nenia nectit:
Omnia perpetiar, lethum quoque, dum
semel omnis
Noster in extincto moriatur pectore sen-
sus.* 190
*Ergo tuos oculos nunquam, mea vita,
videbo?
Et tua perpetuus sepelivit lumina somnus?
Emoriar tecum: sic, sic, juvat ire sub
umbras.
At tamen absistam properato cedere letho,
Ne mortem vindicta tuam tam nulla
sequatur.* [3]

     Here he throws it from him
     and bears the body away.

[CHORUS]

ANDREA. Brought'st thou me hither to in-
crease my pain?
I looked that Balthazar should have
been slain,
But 'tis my friend Horatio that is slain,
And they abuse fair Bel-imperia,
On whom I doted more than all the
world, 200
Because she loved me more than all the
world.

REVENGE. Thou talk'st of harvest when
the corn is green.
The end is crown of every work well
done;

[3] O, let some one mingle for me herbs which
beautiful spring brings forth, and let a medicine
be given for my pain. Or let one furnish whatever juices provide forgetfulness of the years.
Myself shall reap whatever grasses throughout
the great world the sun brings forth to the fair
shores of light. Myself shall drink whatever
poison a witch devises and whatever of herbs
the incantation weaves by secret power. All
things shall I suffer patiently, even death, provided once for all all feeling die in my extinguished breast. And so shall I never see your
eyes, my life? And hath perpetual sleep buried
your orbs? I shall die with you: so, so it pleases
me to go down to the shades. But yet I shall
abstain from going in hastened death [i.e., by
suicide], lest by so doing no vengeance should
follow your death (a patchwork of verses from
Virgil, Lucretius, Horace, Tibullus, Catullus,
etc.).

The sickle comes not till the corn be ripe.
Be still, and, ere I lead thee from this place,
I'll show thee Balthazar in heavy case.

ACTUS TERTIUS. [SCENA PRIMA.

The Portuguese court.]

Enter Viceroy of Portingale, Nobles, Alexandro, Villuppo.

VIC. Infortunate condition of kings,
Seated amidst so many helpless doubts!
First we are placed upon extremest height,
And oft supplanted with exceeding hate,
But ever subject to the wheel of chance.
And at our highest never joy we so
As we both doubt and dread our overthrow.
So striveth not the waves with sundry winds
As Fortune toileth in the affairs of kings,
That would be feared, yet fear to be beloved, 　　　　10
Sith [1] fear or love to kings is flattery.[2]
For instance, lordings, look upon your king,
By hate deprivéd of his dearest son,
The only hope of our successive line.
[1] NOB. I had not thought that Alexandro's heart
Had been envenomed with such extreme hate;
But now I see that words have several works,
And there's no credit in the countenance.
VIL. No; for, my lord, had you beheld the train [3]
That feignéd love had colored in his looks, 　　　　20
When he in camp consorted [4] Balthazar,
Far more inconstant had you thought the sun,
That hourly coasts [5] the center of the earth,
Than Alexandro's purpose to the prince.
VIC. No more, Villuppo, thou hast said enough,
And with thy words thou slayest our wounded thoughts.

[1] Since.
[2] The preceding passage is based on Seneca's *Agamemnon*, ll. 57–73.　　[4] Accompanied.
[3] Deception.　　　　[5] Moves round.

Nor shall I longer dally with the world,
Procrastinating Alexandro's death.
Go, some of you, and fetch the traitor forth
That, as he is condemnéd, he may die. 30

Enter Alexandro with a Nobleman and Halberts.

NOB. In such extremes will naught but patience serve.
ALEX. But in extremes what patience shall I use?
Nor discontents it me to leave the world,
With whom there nothing can prevail but wrong.
NOB. Yet hope the best.
ALEX. 　　　　'Tis heaven is my hope.
As for the earth, it is too much infect
To yield me hope of any of her mold.
VIC. Why linger ye? Bring forth that daring fiend,
And let him die for his accurséd deed.
ALEX. Not that I fear the extremity of death 　　　　40
(For nobles cannot stoop to servile fear)
Do I, O king, thus discontented live.
But this, O, this, torments my laboring soul,
That thus I die suspected of a sin
Whereof, as heavens have known my secret thoughts,
So am I free from this suggestion.
VIC. No more, I say! To the tortures! When? [6]
Bind him, and burn his body in those flames, 　　*They bind him to the stake.*
That shall prefigure those unquenchéd fires
Of Phlegeton, preparéd for his soul. 　　50
ALEX. My guiltless death will be avenged on thee,
On thee, Villuppo, that hath maliced [7] thus,
Or for thy meed hast falsely me accused.
VIL. Nay, Alexandro, if thou menace me,
I'll lend a hand to send thee to the lake [8]
Where those thy words shall perish with thy works,
Injurious traitor! Monstrous homicide!

[6] An expression of impatience.
[7] Entertained malice.
[8] *I.e.*, Avernus.

Enter Ambassador.

[Amb.] Stay, hold awhile;
And here—with pardon of his maj-
    esty—
Lay hands upon Villuppo.
Vic.   Ambassador, 60
    What news hath urged this sudden
    entrance?
Amb. Know, sovereign l[ord], that Baltha-
    zar doth live.
Vic. What sayest thou? Liveth Balthazar
    our son?
Amb. Your highness' son, L[ord] Baltha-
    zar, doth live,
And, well entreated in the court of Spain,
Humbly commends him to your majesty.
These eyes beheld, and these my fol-
    lowers';
With these, the letters of the king's
    commends   *Gives him letters.*
Are happy witnesses of his highness'
    health.
The King looks on the letters, and proceeds.
Vic. "Thy son doth live; your tribute is
    received.   70
Thy peace is made, and we are satis-
    fied.
The rest resolve upon as things proposed
For both our honors and thy benefit."
Amb. These are his highness' farther
    articles. *He gives him more letters.*
Vic. Accurséd wretch, to intimate these
    ills
Against the life and reputation
Of noble Alexandro! Come, my lord,
    unbind him.—
Let him unbind thee, that is bound to
    death,
To make a quital ¹ for thy discontent.
                      They unbind him.
Alex. Dread lord, in kindness ² you could
    do no less   80
Upon report of such a damnéd fact.
But thus we see our innocence hath saved
The hopeless life which thou, Villuppo,
    sought
By thy suggestions to have massacred.
Vic. Say, false Villuppo, wherefore didst
    thou thus
Falsely betray Lord Alexandro's life—
Him whom thou knowest that no un-
    kindness else

But even the slaughter of our dearest
    son
Could once have moved us to have mis-
    conceived?
Alex. Say, treacherous Villuppo, tell the
    king: 90
Wherein ³ hath Alexandro used thee ill?
Vil. Rent with remembrance of so foul a
    deed,
My guilty soul submits me to thy doom;
For not for Alexandro's injuries,
But for reward and hope to be preferred,
Thus have I shamelessly hazarded his
    life.
Vic. Which, villain, shall be ransomed
    with thy death,
And not so mean ⁴ a torment as we here
Devised for him who, thou said'st, slew
    our son,
But with the bitterest torments and ex-
    tremes   100
That may be yet invented for thine end.
                Alex[andro] seems to entreat.
Entreat me not.—Go, take the traitor
    hence.—   *Exit Vil[luppo].*
And, Alexandro, let us honor thee
With public notice of thy loyalty.—
To end those things articulated here
By our great lord, the mighty King of
    Spain,
We with our council will deliberate.
Come, Alexandro, keep us company.
                              Exeunt.

[Scena Secunda.

Near the place of Bel-imperia's confinement.]

Enter Hieronimo.

Hier. O eyes! No eyes, but fountains
    fraught with tears!
O life! No life, but lively form of death!
O world! No world, but mass of public
    wrongs,
Confused and filled with murder and
    misdeeds!
O sacred heavens, if this unhallowed
    deed,
If this inhuman and barbarous attempt,
If this incomparable murder thus
Of mine, but now no more my son,
Shall unrevealed and unrevengéd pass,

¹ Requital.   ² Nature.

³ Emended by Hazlitt. Early edns. read *Or
wherein.*   ⁴ Moderate.

How should we term your dealings to be
　just,　　　　　　　　　　　　　　10
If you unjustly deal with those that in
　your justice trust?
The night, sad secretary to my moans,
With direful visions wake my vexéd soul,
And with the wounds of my distressful
　son
Solicit me for notice of his death.
The ugly fiends do sally forth of hell,
And frame my steps to unfrequented
　paths,
And fear my heart with fierce inflaméd
　thoughts.
The cloudy day my discontents records
Early begins to register my dreams,　20
And drive me forth to seek the murderer.
Eyes, life, world, heavens, hell, night,
　and day,
See, search, show, send some man, some
　mean, that may—　　*A letter falleth.*
What's here? A letter? Tush! It is not
　so!—
A letter written to Hieronimo!　*Red ink.*
"For want of ink, receive this bloody
　writ.
Me hath my hapless brother hid from
　thee.
Revenge thyself on Balthazar and him,
For these were they that murderéd thy
　son.
Hieronimo, revenge Horatio's death,　30
And better fare than Bel-imperia doth."
What means this unexpected miracle?
My son slain by Lorenzo and the prince!
What cause had they Horatio to malign?
Or what might move thee, Bel-imperia,
To accuse thy brother, had he been the
　mean?
Hieronimo, beware!　　Thou art be-
　trayed,
And to entrap thy life this train is laid.
Advise thee therefore; be not credulous.
This is deviséd to endanger thee,　　40
That thou, by this, Lorenzo shouldst
　accuse;
And he, for thy dishonor done, should
　draw
Thy life in question and thy name in
　hate.
Dear was the life of my beloved son,
And of his death behoves me be revenged;
Then hazard not thine own, Hieronimo,
But live t' effect thy resolution.

I therefore will by circumstances [1] try
What I can gather to confirm this writ;
And, hearkening near the Duke of Cas-
　tile's house,　　　　　　　　　50
Close, if I can, with Bel-imperia,
To listen more, but nothing to bewray.

　　　　　Enter Pedringano.

　Now, Pedringano!
PED.　　　　　　　　Now, Hieronimo!
HIER.　Where's thy lady?
PED.　　　　　I know not. Here's my lord.

　　　　　Enter Lorenzo.

LOR.　How now, who's this? Hieronimo?
HIER.　　　　　　　　　　My lord!
PED.　He asketh for my lady Bel-imperia.
LOR.　What to do, Hieronimo? The duke,
　my father, hath
Upon some disgrace awhile removed her
　hence;
But, if it be aught I may inform her of,
Tell me, Hieronimo, and I'll let her know
　it.　　　　　　　　　　　　　60
HIER.　Nay, nay, my lord, I thank you; it
　shall not need.
I had a suit unto her, but too late,
And her disgrace makes me unfortunate.
LOR.　Why so, Hieronimo? Use me.[2]
HIER.　Who? You, my lord?
I reserve your favor for a greater honor;
This is a very toy,[3] my lord, a toy.
LOR.　All's one, Hieronimo; acquaint me
　with it.
HIER.　I' faith, my lord, 'tis an idle thing,
　I must confess;
I ha' been too slack, too tardy, too re-
　miss unto your honor.　　　　70
LOR.　How now, Hieronimo?
HIER.　In troth, my lord, it is a thing of
　nothing,
The murder of a son, or so—
A thing of nothing, my lord!
LOR.　　　　　　　Why then, farewell.
HIER.　My grief no heart, my thoughts no
　tongue can tell.　　　　　　*Exit.*

[1] Roundabout methods.
[2] The passage from this point through "nothing, my lord!" in l. 74 is substituted in the
1602 edn. for the following speech of Hieronimo
in the original:
　　O, no, my lord, I dare not; it must not be.
　　I humbly thank your lordship.
[3] Trifle.

Lor. Come hither, Pedringano, seest thou
   this?
Ped. My lord, I see it, and suspect it too.
Lor. This is that damnéd villain Serberine
   That hath, I fear, revealed Horatio's
   death.
Ped. My lord, he could not, 'twas so
   lately done;   80
And, since, he hath not left my company.
Lor. Admit he have not, his condition's
   such
As fear or flattering words may make
   him false.
I know his humor, and therewith re-
   pent
That e'er I used him in this enterprise.
But, Pedringano, to prevent the worst,
And cause I know thee secret as my
   soul,
Here, for thy further satisfaction, take
   thou this,   *Gives him more gold.*
And hearken to me. Thus it is devised:
This night thou must (and, prithee, so
   resolve)   90
Meet Serberine at S[aint] Luigi's Park—
Thou know'st 'tis here hard by behind
   the house.
There take thy stand, and see thou
   strike him sure,
For die he must, if we do mean to live.
Ped. But how shall Serberine be there,
   my lord?
Lor. Let me alone; I'll send to him to
   meet
The prince and me, where thou must
   do this deed.
Ped. It shall be done, my l[ord], it shall
   be done;
And I'll go arm myself to meet him
   there.
Lor. When things shall alter, as I hope
   they will,   100
Then shalt thou mount for this; thou
   knowest my mind.
               Exit Ped[ringano].
Che le Ieron![1]

Enter Page.

Page.   **My lord?**
Lor.   Go, sirrah,
To Serberine, and bid him forthwith
   meet

[1] Unintelligible. Probably a call to the page.

The prince and me at S[aint] Luigi's
   Park,
Behind the house, this evening, boy.
Page.   I go, my lord.
Lor. But, sirrah, let the hour be eight
   a-clock.
Bid him not fail.
Page.   I fly, my lord. *Exit.*
Lor. Now to confirm the complot thou
   hast cast
Of all these practices, I'll spread the
   watch,
Upon precise commandment from the
   king,   110
Strongly to guard the place where Ped-
   ringano
This night shall murder hapless Serber-
   ine.
Thus must we work that will avoid dis-
   trust;
Thus must we practice to prevent mis-
   hap;
And thus one ill another must expulse.
This sly inquiry of Hieronimo
For Bel-imperia breeds suspicion,
And this suspicion bodes a further ill.
As for myself, I know my secret fault,
And so do they. But I have dealt for
   them.   120
They that for coin their souls endangeréd,
To save my life, for coin shall venture
   theirs;
And better it's that base companions
   die
Than by their life to hazard our good
   haps.
Nor shall they live, for me to fear their
   faith.
I'll trust myself, myself shall be my
   friend;
For die they shall; slaves are ordained
   to no other end.   *Exit.*

[Scena Tertia.

Saint Luigi's Park.]

Enter Pedringano, with a pistol.

[Ped.] Now, Pedringano, bid thy pistol
   hold;
And hold on, Fortune; once more favor
   me.
Give but success to mine attempting
   spirit,
And let me shift for taking of mine aim.

Here is the gold. This is the gold proposed.
It is no dream that I adventure for,
But Pedringano is possessed thereof.
And he that would not strain his conscience
For him that thus his liberal purse hath stretched,
Unworthy such a favor, may he fail,   10
And, wishing, want when such as I prevail.
As for the fear of apprehension,
I know, if need should be, my noble lord
Will stand between me and ensuing harms.
Besides, this place is free from all suspect.
Here therefore will I stay and take my stand.

Enter the Watch.

1 [WATCH.] I wonder much to what intent it is
That we are thus expressly charged to watch.
2 [WATCH.] 'Tis by commandment in the king's own name.
3 [WATCH.] But we were never wont to watch and ward   20
So near the duke his brother's house before.
2 [WATCH.] Content yourself. Stand close; there's somewhat in 't.

Enter Serberine.

SER. Here, Serberine, attend and stay thy pace,
For here did Don Lorenzo's page appoint
That thou by his command shouldst meet with him.
How fit a place—if one were so disposed—
Methinks this corner is to close with one.
PED. Here comes the bird that I must seize upon.
Now, Pedringano, or never, play the man!
SER. I wonder that his lordship stays so long,   30
Or wherefore should he send for me so late?

PED. For this, Serberine!—and thou shalt ha't.   *Shoots the dag.*[1]
So, there he lies; my promise is performed.

The Watch.

1 [WATCH.] Hark, gentlemen, this is a pistol shot.
2 [WATCH.] And here's one slain! Stay the murderer.
PED. Now by the sorrows of the souls in hell,   *He strives with the Watch.*
Who first lays hand on me, I'll be his priest.
3 [WATCH.] Sirrah, confess, and therein play the priest.
Why hast thou thus unkindly[2] killed the man?
PED. Why? Because he walked abroad so late.   40
3 [WATCH.] Come, sir, you had been better kept your bed
Than have committed this misdeed so late.
2 [WATCH.] Come, to the marshal's with the murderer!
1 [WATCH.] On to Hieronimo's! Help me here
To bring the murdered body with us too.
PED. Hieronimo? Carry me before whom you will.
Whate'er he be, I'll answer him and you;
And do your worst, for I defy you all.   *Exeunt.*

[SCENA QUARTA.

A room in Don Cyprian's palace.]

Enter Lorenzo and Balthazar.

BAL. How now, my lord, what makes you rise so soon?
LOR. Fear of preventing our mishaps too late.
BAL. What mischief is it that we not mistrust?[3]
LOR. Our greatest ills we least mistrust, my lord,
And inexpected harms do hurt us most.

<hr>

[1] Pistol.   [3] Suspect.
[2] Unnaturally.

BAL. Why, tell me, Don Lorenzo, tell me, man,
If aught concerns our honor and your own.
LOR. Nor you, nor me, my lord, but both in one;
For I suspect—and the presumption's great—
That by those base confederates in our fault   10
Touching the death of Don Horatio,
We are betrayed to old Hieronimo.
BAL. Betrayed, Lorenzo? Tush! It cannot be.
LOR. A guilty conscience, urgéd with the thought
Of former evils, easily cannot err.
I am persuaded—and dissuade me not—
That all's revealéd to Hieronimo.
And therefore know that I have cast it thus—

[Enter Page.] [1]

But here's the page. How now? What news with thee?
PAGE. My lord, Serberine is slain.
BAL.   Who? Serberine, my man?   20
PAGE. Your highness' man, my lord.
LOR.   Speak, page, who murdered him?
PAGE. He that is apprehended for the fact. [2]
LOR. Who?
PAGE.   Pedringano.
BAL. Is Serberine slain, that loved his lord so well?
Injurious villain, murderer of his friend!
LOR. Hath Pedringano murdered Serberine?
My lord, let me entreat you to take the pains
To exasperate and hasten his revenge
With your complaints unto my l[ord] the king.   30
This their dissension breeds a greater doubt.
BAL. Assure thee, Don Lorenzo, he shall die,
Or else his highness hardly shall deny. [3]
Meanwhile I'll haste the marshal-sessions,
For die he shall for this his damnéd deed.
          Exit Balt[hazar].

LOR. Why so, this fits our former policy,
And thus experience bids the wise to deal.
I lay the plot; he prosecutes the point.
I set the trap; he breaks the worthless twigs,
And sees not that wherewith the bird was limed.   40
Thus hopeful men, that mean to hold their own,
Must look like fowlers to their dearest friends.
He runs to kill whom I have holp [4] to catch,
And no man knows it was my reaching fatch. [5]
'Tis hard to trust unto a multitude,
Or anyone, in mine opinion,
When men themselves their secrets will reveal.

Enter a Messenger with a letter.

Boy!
PAGE. My lord.
LOR. What's he?
MES.   I have a letter to your lordship.
LOR. From whence?
MES.   From Pedringano that's imprisoned.   51
LOR. So he is in prison then?
MES.   Ay, my good lord.
LOR. What would he with us?—He writes us here
To stand good lord, and help him in distress.—
Tell him I have his letters, know his mind,
And what we may, let him assure him of.
Fellow, begone; my boy shall follow thee.   *Exit Mes[senger].*
This works like wax; yet once more try thy wits.
Boy, go, convey this purse to Pedringano.
Thou know'st the prison. Closely [6] give it him,   60
And be advised that none be there about.
Bid him be merry still, but secret;
And, though the marshal-sessions be today,

---

[1] From 1615 edn.   [2] Deed.
[3] *I.e.*, shall with difficulty deny my demand.

[4] Helped.   [5] Deep-reaching trick.   [6] Secretly.

Bid him not doubt of his delivery.
Tell him his pardon is already signed,
And thereon bid him boldly be re-
　solved;
For, were he ready to be turnéd off[1]—
As 'tis my will the uttermost be tried—
Thou with his pardon shalt attend him
　still.
Show him this box; tell him his pardon's
　in't;　　　　　　　　　　　　　　　70
But open't not, an if[2] thou lov'st thy
　life,
But let him wisely keep his hopes un-
　known.
He shall not want while Don Lorenzo
　lives.
Away!
PAGE.　I go, my lord, I run.
LOR.　But, sirrah, see that this be cleanly[3]
　done.　　　　　　　　　　　Exit Page.
Now stands our fortune on a tickle
　point,
And now or never ends Lorenzo's doubts.
One only thing is uneffected yet,
And that's to see the executioner.　　80
But to what end?　I list not trust the
　air
With utterance of our pretense[4] therein,
For fear the privy whisp'ring of the
　wind
Convey our words amongst unfriendly
　ears,
That lie too open to advantages.[5]
E quel che voglio io, nessun lo sa;
Intendo io; quel mi basterà.[6]　　Exit.

[SCENA QUINTA.

A street.]

Enter Boy with the box.

[BOY.]　My master hath forbidden me to
look in this box, and, by my troth, 'tis
likely, if he had not warned me, I should
not have had so much idle time; for we
men's-kind in our minority are like women
in their uncertainty—that they are most
forbidden, they will soonest attempt.　So
I now.—By my bare honesty, here's nothing but the bare empty box!　Were it not
sin against secrecy, I would say it　[10
were a piece of gentlemanlike knavery.
I must go to Pedringano, and tell him his
pardon is in this box; nay, I would have
sworn it, had I not seen the contrary.　I
cannot choose but smile to think how the
villain will flout the gallows, scorn the
audience, and descant on the hangman,
and all presuming of his pardon from
hence.　Will 't not be an odd jest for me
to stand and grace every jest he makes,　[20
pointing my finger at this box, as who
would say, "Mock on, here's thy warrant"?　Is 't not a scurvy jest that a man
should jest himself to death?　Alas, poor
Pedringano, I am in a sort sorry for thee;
but, if I should be hanged with thee, I
cannot weep.　　　　　　　　　　　Exit.

[SCENA SEXTA.

The Court of Justice.]

Enter Hieronimo and the Deputy.

HIER.　Thus must we toil in other men's
　extremes,
That know not how to remedy our
　own,
And do them justice, when unjustly
　we,
For all our wrongs, can compass no
　redress.
But shall I never live to see the day
That I may come, by justice of the
　heavens,
To know the cause that may my cares
　allay?
This toils[7] my body, this consumeth
　age,
That only I to all men just must be,
And neither gods nor men be just to
　me.　　　　　　　　　　　　　10
DEP.　Worthy Hieronimo, your office asks
A care to punish such as do transgress.
HIER.　So is 't my duty to regard his death
Who, when he lived, deserved my
　dearest blood.
But come, for that we came for!　Let's
　begin,
For here lies that which bids me to be
　gone.

---

[1] Hanged.　　　　　　[4] Intention.
[2] An emphatic form of *if*.　[5] Opportunities.
[3] Adroitly.
[6] And what I wish, that no one knows.　I
intend it; that will be enough for me (source
unknown).

[7] Taxes.

Enter Officers, [Hangman,] Boy, and Ped-
ringano, with a letter in his hand, bound.

DEP. Bring forth the prisoner, for the
court is set.

PED. Gramercy, boy, but it was time to
come,

For I had written to my lord anew

A nearer matter that concerneth him,   20

For fear his lordship had forgotten me.

But sith he hath remembered me so
well—

Come, come, come on, when shall we
to this gear? ¹

HIER. Stand forth, thou monster, murderer of men,

And here, for satisfaction of the world,

Confess thy folly, and repent thy fault;

For there's thy place of execution.

PED. This is short work. Well, to your
marshalship

First I confess—nor fear I death therefor—

I am the man; 'twas I slew Serberine.   30

But, sir, then you think this shall be
the place

Where we shall satisfy you for this gear?

DEP. Ay, Pedringano.

PED.   Now I think not so.

HIER. Peace, impudent, for thou shalt
find it so;

For blood with blood shall, while I sit
as judge,

Be satisfiéd, and the law discharged.

And, though myself cannot receive the
like,

Yet will I see that others have their
right.

Despatch! The fault's approvéd ² and
confessed,

And by our law he is condemned to die. 40

HANG. Come on, sir, are you ready?

PED. To do what, my fine, officious
knave?

HANG. To go to this gear.

PED. O, sir, you are too forward. Thou
wouldst fain furnish me with a halter, to
disfurnish me of my habit.³ So I should
go out of this gear, my raiment, into that
gear, the rope. But, hangman, now I spy
your knavery, I'll not change without
boot; that's flat.   50

¹ Business.   ² Proved.
³ The hangman received the criminal's garments.

HANG. Come, sir.

PED. So, then, I must up?

HANG. No remedy.

PED. Yes, but there shall be for my
coming down.

HANG. Indeed, here's a remedy for that.

PED. How? Be turned off?

HANG. Ay, truly. Come, are you ready?
I pray, sir, despatch; the day goes away.

PED. What, do you hang by the hour?
If you do, I may chance to break your
old custom.   62

HANG. Faith, you have reason, for I
am like to break your young neck.

PED. Dost thou mock me, hangman?
Pray God, I be not preserved to break
your knave's pate for this.

HANG. Alas, sir, you are a foot too low
to reach it, and I hope you will never
grow so high while I am in the office.   70

PED. Sirrah, dost see yonder boy with
the box in his hand?

HANG. What, he that points to it with
his finger?

PED. Ay, that companion.

HANG. I know him not. But what of
him?

PED. Dost thou think to live till his
old doublet will make thee a new truss? ⁴

HANG. Ay, and many a fair year after, [80
to truss up many an honester man than
either thou or he.

PED. What hath he in his box, as thou
think'st?

HANG. Faith, I cannot tell, nor I care
not greatly. Methinks you should rather
hearken to your soul's health.

PED. Why, sirrah hangman, I take it
that that is good for the body is likewise
good for the soul; and, it may be, in [90
that box is balm for both.

HANG. Well, thou art even the merriest piece of man's flesh that e'er groaned
at my office door!

PED. Is your roguery become an office
with a knave's name?

HANG. Ay, and that shall all they witness that see you seal it with a thief's
name.

PED. I prithee, request this good [100
company to pray with me.

⁴ The term was used both for a close-fitting
body garment and for tight, short breeches or
drawers.

HANG. Ay, marry, sir, this is a good motion.—My masters, you see here's a good fellow.

PED. Nay, nay, now I remember me, let them alone till some other time, for now I have no great need.

HIER. I have not seen a wretch so impudent.

    O monstrous times, where murder's set so light,
And where the soul, that should be shrinèd in heaven,   110
Solely delights in interdicted things,
Still wand'ring in the thorny passages,
That intercepts itself of [1] happiness.
Murder! O bloody monster! God forbid
A fault so foul should scape unpunishèd.
Despatch, and see this execution done!—
This makes me to remember thee, my son.   *Exit Hiero[nimo].*

PED. Nay, soft, no haste.

DEP. Why, wherefore stay you? Have you hope of life?

PED. Why, ay!   120

HANG. As how?

PED. Why, rascal, by my pardon from the king.

HANG. Stand you on that? Then you shall off with this.   *He turns him off.*

DEP. So, executioner!—Convey him hence, But let his body be unburièd.
Let not the earth be chokèd or infect
With that which heaven contemns, and men neglect.   *Exeunt.*

[SCENA SEPTIMA.

A room in Hieronimo's house.]

Enter Hieronimo.

[HIER.] Where shall I run to breathe abroad my woes,
My woes, whose weight hath weariéd the earth,
Or mine exclaims, [2] that have surcharged the air
With ceaseless plaints for my deceasèd son?
The blust'ring winds, conspiring with my words,
At my lament have moved the leafless trees,
Disrobed the meadows of their flowered green,

Made mountains marsh with spring tides of my tears,
And broken through the brazen gates of hell.
Yet still tormented is my tortured soul 10
With broken sighs and restless passions,
That, wingèd, mount, and hovering in the air,
Beat at the windows of the brightest heavens,
Soliciting for justice and revenge.
But they are placed in those imperial heights,
Where, countermured [3] with walls of diamond,
I find the place impregnable; and they
Resist my woes, and give my words no way.

Enter Hangman with a letter.

HANG. O Lord, sir! God bless you, sir! The man, sir, Petergade, sir, he that [20 was so full of merry conceits—

HIER. Well, what of him?

HANG. O Lord, sir, he went the wrong way; the fellow had a fair commission to the contrary. Sir, here is his passport. I pray you, sir, we have done him wrong.

HIER. I warrant thee; give it me.

HANG. You will stand between the gallows and me?

HIER. Ay, ay.   30

HANG. I thank your l[ord] worship.   *Exit Hangman.*

HIER. And yet, though somewhat nearer me concerns,
I will, to ease the grief that I sustain,
Take truce with sorrow while I read on this.
"My lord, I write, [4] as mine extremes required,
That you would labor my delivery.
If you neglect, my life is desperate,
And in my death I shall reveal the troth.
You know, my lord, I slew him for your sake,
And was confederate with the prince and you;   40
Won by rewards and hopeful promises,
I holp to murder Don Horatio too."—
Holp he to murder mine Horatio?
And actors in th' accursèd tragedy
Wast thou, Lorenzo, Balthazar and thou,

---

[1] Bars itself from.   [2] Exclamations.

[3] Doubly walled.   [4] Manly emends to *writ.*

Of whom my son, my son, deserved so
   well?
What have I heard? What have mine
   eyes beheld?
O sacred heavens, may it come to pass
That such a monstrous and detested
   deed,
So closely smothered, and so long con-
   cealed,   50
Shall thus by this be vengéd or revealed?
Now see I what I durst not then sus-
   pect,
That Bel-imperia's letter was not feigned.
Nor feignéd she, though falsely they have
   wronged
Both her, myself, Horatio, and them-
   selves.
Now may I make compare twixt hers
   and this,
Of every accident I ne'er could find
Till now, and now I feelingly perceive
They did what heaven unpunished would
   not leave.
O false Lorenzo! Are these thy flattering
   looks?   60
Is this the honor that thou didst my
   son?
And Balthazar—bane to thy soul and
   me!—
Was this the ransom he reserved thee
   for?
Woe to the cause of these constrainéd
   wars!
Woe to thy baseness and captivity!
Woe to thy birth, thy body, and thy
   soul,
Thy curséd father, and thy conquered
   self!
And banned with bitter execrations be
The day and place where he did pity
   thee!
But wherefore waste I mine unfruitful
   words,   70
When naught but blood will satisfy my
   woes?
I will go plain me [1] to my lord the king,
And cry aloud for justice through the
   court,
Wearing the flints with these my with-
   ered feet;
And either purchase justice by entreats,
Or tire them all with my revenging
   threats.   *Exit.*

[1] Complain.

[SCENA OCTAVA.

The same.]

Enter Isabell[a] and her Maid.

ISAB. So that you say this herb will purge
   the eye,
And this, the head?
Ah, but none of them will purge the
   heart!
No, there's no medicine left for my dis-
   ease,
Nor any physic to recure the dead.
             She runs lunatic.
Horatio! O, where's Horatio?
MAID. Good madam, affright not thus
   yourself
With outrage [2] for your son Horatio.
He sleeps in quiet in the Elysian fields.
ISAB. Why, did I not give you gowns and
   goodly things,   10
Bought you a whistle and a whipstalk [3]
   too,
To be revengéd on their villainies?
MAID. Madam, these humors do torment
   my soul.
ISAB. My soul—poor soul, thou talks of
   things
Thou know'st not what—my soul hath
   silver wings,
That mounts me up unto the highest
   heavens.
To heaven? Ay, there sits my Horatio,
Backed with a troop of fiery cherubins,
Dancing about his newly healéd wounds,
Singing sweet hymns and chanting heav-
   enly notes,   20
Rare harmony to greet his innocence,
That died, ay, died, a mirror in our days.
But say, where shall I find the men, the
   murderers,
That slew Horatio? Whither shall I run
To find them out that murderéd my son?
             Exeunt.

[SCENA NONA.

*Outside the place of Bel-imperia's con-
finement.*]

Bel-imperia at a window.

BEL. What means this outrage that is offered me?
Why am I thus sequestered from the
   court?

[2] Outcry.   [3] Whipstock.

No notice! Shall I not know the cause
Of these my secret and suspicious ills?
Acccurséd brother, unkind murderer,
Why bends thou thus thy mind to martyr
    me?
Hieronimo, why writ I of thy wrongs,
Or why art thou so slack in thy revenge?
Andrea, O Andrea! That thou saw'st
Me for thy friend Horatio handled thus,
And him for me thus causeless mur-
    deréd!—   11
Well, force perforce, I must constrain
    myself
To patience, and apply me [1] to the time,
Till heaven, as I have hoped, shall set
    me free.

Enter Christophil.

CHRIS. Come, Madam Bel-imperia, this
    may not be.   *Exeunt.*

Enter Lorenzo, Balthazar, and the Page.[2]

LOR. Boy, talk no further. Thus far things
    go well.
Thou art assuréd that thou sawest him
    dead?
PAGE. Or else, my lord, I live not.
LOR.   That's enough.
As for his resolution in his end,
Leave that to him with whom he so-
    journs now.   20
Here, take my ring and give it Christo-
    phil,
And bid him let my sister be enlarged,
And bring her hither straight.—
                                  Exit Page.
This that I did was for a policy,
To smooth and keep the murder secret,
Which, as a nine-days' wonder, being
    o'erblown,
My gentle sister will I now enlarge.
BAL. And time, Lorenzo, for my lord the
    duke,
You heard, inquired for her yesternight.
LOR. Why, and, my lord, I hope you heard
    me say   30
Sufficient reason why she kept away.
But that's all one. My lord, you love her?
BAL.   Ay.

LOR. Then in your love beware. Deal
    cunningly;
Salve all suspicions; only soothe me up, [3]
And, if she hap to stand on terms [4] with
    us—
As for her sweetheart and concealment
    so—
Jest with her gently. Under feignéd jest
Are things concealed that else would
    breed unrest.
But here she comes.

Enter Bel-imperia.

                         Now, sister—
BEL.   Sister? No!
Thou art no brother, but an enemy;   40
Else wouldst thou not have used thy
    sister so:
First, to affright me with thy weapons
    drawn,
And with extremes abuse my company; [5]
And then to hurry me, like whirlwind's
    rage,
Amidst a crew of thy confederates,
And clap me up where none might come
    at me,
Nor I at any to reveal my wrongs.
What madding [6] fury did possess thy
    wits?
Or wherein is 't that I offended thee?
LOR. Advise you better, Bel-imperia,   50
For I have done you no disparagement—
Unless, by more discretion than deserved,
I sought to save your honor and mine own.
BEL. Mine honor? Why, Lorenzo, wherein
    is 't
That I neglect my reputation so
As you, or any, need to rescue it?
LOR. His highness and my father were
    resolved
To come confer with old Hieronimo
Concerning certain matters of estate
That by the viceroy was determinéd.   60
BEL. And wherein was mine honor touched
    in that?
BAL. Have patience, Bel-imperia; hear the
    rest.
LOR. Me, next in sight, as messenger they
    sent
To give him notice that they were so
    nigh.

[1] Conform myself.
[2] It is conventional to make a new scene here.
Lorenzo and Balthazar probably enter on the
lower stage, however, as Bel-imperia leaves the
upper.

[3] Support me.
[4] Insist on her rights.
[5] Do violence to my companion.
[6] Raving.

Now when I came, consorted with the prince,
And unexpected in an arbor there
Found Bel-imperia with Horatio—
BEL.   How then?
LOR. Why then, remembering that old disgrace,
Which you for Don Andrea had endured,
And now were likely longer to sustain   70
By being found so meanly accompanied,
Thought rather—for I knew no readier mean—
To thrust Horatio forth my father's way.
BAL. And carry you obscurely somewhere else,
Lest that his highness should have found you there.
BEL. Even so, my lord?   And you are witness
That this is true which he entreateth of?
You, gentle brother, forged this for my sake,
And you, my lord, were made his instrument?
A work of worth, worthy the noting too!   80
But what's the cause that you concealed me since?
LOR. Your melancholy, sister, since the news
Of your first favorite Don Andrea's death
My father's old wrath hath exasperate.
BAL. And better was 't for you, being in disgrace,
To absent yourself, and give his fury place.
BEL. But why had I no notice of his ire?
LOR. That were to add more fuel to your fire,
Who burnt like Ætna for Andrea's loss.
BEL. Hath not my father then inquired for me?   90
LOR. Sister, he hath, and thus excused I thee.   *He whispereth in her ear.*
But, Bel-imperia, see the gentle prince;
Look on thy love, behold young Balthazar,
Whose passions by thy presence are increased,
And in whose melancholy thou mayst see
Thy hate, his love; thy flight, his following thee.

BEL. Brother, you are become an orator—
I know not, I, by what experience—
Too politic for me, past all compare,
Since last I saw you. But content yourself;   100
The prince is meditating higher things.
BAL. 'Tis of thy beauty, then, that conquers kings;
Of those thy tresses, Ariadne's twines,
Wherewith my liberty thou hast surprised;
Of that thine ivory front, my sorrow's map,
Wherein I see no haven to rest my hope.
BEL. To love and fear, and both at once, my lord,
In my conceit, are things of more import
Than women's wits are to be busied with.
BAL. 'Tis I that love.
BEL.   Whom?
BAL.   Bel-imperia. 110
BEL. But I that fear.
BAL.   Whom?
BEL.   Bel-imperia.
LOR. Fear yourself?
BEL.   Ay, brother.
LOR.   How?
BEL.   As those
That what they love are loath and fear to lose.
BAL. Then, fair, let Balthazar your keeper be.
BEL. No, Balthazar doth fear as well as we:
Et [1] *tremulo metui pavidum junxere timorem—*
Et vanum stolidæ proditionis opus. [2] *Exit.*
LOR. Nay, and you argue things so cunningly,
We'll go continue this discourse at court.
BAL. Led by the lodestar of her heavenly looks,   120
Wends poor oppressèd Balthazar,
As o'er the mountains walks the wanderer,
Incertain to effect his pilgrimage.
                                        Exeunt.

[1] Emended by Hazlitt. Early edns. read *Est.*
[2] And to quivering fear they added trembling terror—and the vain task of stupid betrayal (source unknown).

[SCENA DECIMA.

A street.]

*Enter two Portingales, and Hieronimo
meets them.*

1 [PORT.] By your leave, sir.

HIER.[1] 'Tis neither as you think, nor as
you think,
Nor as you think. You're wide all.
These slippers are not mine; they were
my son Horatio's.
My son? And what's a son?
A thing begot within a pair of minutes—
thereabout;
A lump bred up in darkness, and doth
serve
To ballace[2] these light creatures we call
women;
And, at nine months' end, creeps forth
to light.
What is there yet in a son   10
To make a father dote, rave, or run mad?
Being born, it pouts, cries, and breeds
teeth.
What is there yet in a son? He must be
fed,
Be taught to go, and speak. Ay, or yet
Why might not a man love a calf as well,
Or melt in passion o'er a frisking kid,
As for a son? Methinks a young bacon
Or a fine little smooth horse colt
Should move a man as much as doth a
son,
For one of these, in very little time,   20
Will grow to some good use, whereas a
son,
The more he grows in stature and in
years,
The more unsquared, unbeveled,[3] he
appears,
Reckons his parents among the rank of
fools,
Strikes care upon their heads with his
mad riots,
Makes them look old before they meet
with age.
This is a son! And what a loss were this,
considered truly?—
O, but my Horatio grew out of reach of
these
Insatiate humors. He loved his loving
parents;

He was my comfort and his mother's
joy,   30
The very arm that did hold up our house;
Our hopes were storéd up in him.
None but a damnéd murderer could hate
him.
He had not seen the back of nineteen
year,
When his strong arm unhorsed the proud
Prince Balthazar,
And his great mind, too full of honor,
Took him unto [4] mercy, that valiant but
ignoble Portingale!
Well, heaven is heaven still,
And there is Nemesis, and Furies,
And things called whips,   40
And they sometimes do meet with mur-
derers.
They do not always scape, that is some
comfort.
Ay, ay, ay; and then time steals on, and
steals, and steals,
Till violence leaps forth like thunder
Wrapped in a ball of fire,
And so doth bring confusion to them all.—
Good leave have you; nay, I pray you go,
For I'll leave you, if you can leave me so.

2 [PORT.] Pray you, which is the next way
to my lord the duke's?

HIER. The next way from me.

1 [PORT.]   To his house, we mean. 50

HIER. O, hard by; 'tis yon house that you
see.

2 [PORT.] You could not tell us if his son
were there?

HIER. Who, my Lord Lorenzo?

1 [PORT.]   Ay, sir.

*He goeth in at one door and comes out at
another.*

HIER.   O, forbear!
For other talk for us far fitter were.
But, if you be importunate to know
The way to him, and where to find him
out,
Then list to me, and I'll resolve your
doubt.
There is a path upon your left-hand side
That leadeth from a guilty conscience
Unto a forest of distrust and fear,   60
A darksome place, and dangerous to pass.
There shall you meet with melancholy
thoughts,
Whose baleful humors if you but uphold,

---

[1] The following speech except the last two
lines is an addition.   [2] Ballast.   [3] Unpolished.
[4] Early edns. read *us to.*

It will conduct you to despair and
  death—
Whose rocky cliffs when you have once
  beheld,
Within a hugy dale of lasting night,
That, kindled with the world's iniquities,
Doth cast up filthy and detested fumes—
Not far from thence, where murderers
  have built
A habitation for their curséd souls,   70
There, in a brazen caldron, fixed by Jove
In his fell wrath, upon a sulphur flame,
Yourselves shall find Lorenzo bathing
  him
In boiling lead and blood of innocents.
1 [PORT.] Ha, ha, ha!
HIER. Ha, ha, ha! Why, ha, ha, ha! Fare-
  well, good ha, ha, ha!   *Exit.*
2 [PORT.] Doubtless this man is passing lu-
  natic,
Or imperfection of his age doth make him
  dote.
Come, let's away to seek my lord the
  duke.   [*Exeunt.*] [1]

[SCENA UNDECIMA.

The Spanish court.]

*Enter Hieronimo, with a poniard in one
  hand and a rope in the other.*

HIER. Now, sir, perhaps I come and see the
  king;
The king sees me, and fain would hear
  my suit.
Why, is not this a strange and seld-seen [2]
  thing,
That standers-by with toys should
  strike me mute?
Go to, I see their shifts, and say no more.
Hieronimo, 'tis time for thee to trudge.
Down by the dale that flows with purple
  gore
Standeth a fiery tower. There sits a judge
Upon a seat of steel and molten brass,
And twixt his teeth he holds a fire-
  brand,   10
That leads unto the lake where hell doth
  stand.
Away, Hieronimo! To him be gone;
He'll do thee justice for Horatio's death.
Turn down this path, [3] thou shalt be with
  him straight;

[1] From 1602 edn.   [3] *I.e.*, the poniard.
[2] Seldom seen.

Or this [4] and then thou need'st not take
  thy breath.
This way, or that way?—Soft and fair!
  Not so!
For, if I hang or kill myself, let's know
Who will revenge Horatio's murder then?
No, no! Fie, no! Pardon me, I'll none
  of that.
    He flings away the dagger and halter.
This way I'll take; and this way comes
  the king, *He takes them up again.* 20
And here I'll have a fling at him, that's
  flat;
And, Balthazar, I'll be with thee to
  bring, [5]
And thee, Lorenzo! Here's the king—
  nay, stay;
And here, ay, here—there goes the hare
  away.

*Enter King, Ambassador, Castile, and
                  Lorenzo.*

KING. Now show, ambassador, what our
  viceroy saith.
Hath he received the articles we sent?
HIER. Justice, O, justice to Hieronimo!
LOR. Back! Seest thou not the king is
  busy?
HIER.   O, is he so?
KING. Who is he that interrupts our
  business?
HIER. Not I. [*Aside.*] Hieronimo, beware!
  Go by, go by! [6]   30
AMB. Renowméd king, he hath received
  and read
Thy kingly proffers and thy promised
  league;
And, as a man extremely overjoyed
To hear his son so princely entertained,
Whose death he had so solemnly be-
  wailed,
This for thy further satisfaction
And kingly love he kindly lets thee
  know.
First, for the marriage of his princely son
With Bel-imperia, thy beloved niece,
The news are more delightful to his
  soul   40
Than myrrh or incense to the offended
  heavens.

[4] *I.e.*, the rope.   [5] Get the upper hand of thee.
[6] A phrase which was widely quoted in Elizabethan literature; probably used to denote impatience.

In person, therefore, will he come himself,
To see the marriage rites solemnizéd,
And, in the presence of the court of Spain.
To knit a sure inextricable [1] band
Of kingly love and everlasting league
Betwixt the crowns of Spain and Portin-
gale.
There will he give his crown to Balthazar,
And make a queen of Bel-imperia.
KING. Brother, how like you this our vice-
roy's love? 50
CAS. No doubt, my lord, it is an argu-
ment
Of honorable care to keep his friend,
And wondrous zeal to Balthazar his son;
Nor am I least indebted to his grace
That bends his liking to my daughter
thus.
AMB. Now last, dread lord, here hath his
highness sent
(Although he send not that his son re-
turn)
His ransom due to Don Horatio.
HIER. Horatio! Who calls Horatio?
KING. And well remembered, thank his
majesty! 60
Here, see it given to Horatio.
HIER. Justice, O, justice, justice, gentle
king!
KING. Who is that? Hieronimo?
HIER. Justice, O, justice! O my son, my
son!
My son, whom naught can ransom or
redeem!
LOR. Hieronimo, you are not well-advised.
HIER. Away, Lorenzo, hinder me no more,
For thou hast made me bankrupt of my
bliss.
Give me my son! You shall not ransom
him!
Away! I'll rip the bowels of the earth, 70
He diggeth with his dagger.
And ferry over to th' Elysian plains,
And bring my son to show his deadly
wounds.
Stand from about me!
I'll make a pickax of my poniard,
And here surrender up my marshalship,
For I'll go marshal up the fiends in hell
To be avengéd on you all for this.
KING. What means this outrage?
Will none of you restrain his fury?

HIER. Nay, soft and fair! You shall not
need to strive. 80
Needs must he go that the devils drive.
Exit.
KING. What accident hath happed Hier-
onimo?
I have not seen him to demean him so.
LOR. My gracious lord, he is with extreme
pride,
Conceived of young Horatio his son,
And covetous of having to himself
The ransom of the young prince Balthazar,
Distract, and in a manner lunatic.
KING. Believe me, nephew, we are sorry
for 't.
This is the love that fathers bear their
sons. 90
But, gentle brother, go give to him this
gold,
The prince's ransom; let him have his due.
For what he hath, Horatio shall not want.
Happily Hieronimo hath need thereof.
LOR. But, if he be thus helplessly distract,
'Tis requisite his office be resigned,
And given to one of more discretion.
KING. We shall increase his melancholy so.
'Tis best that we see further in it first,
Till when, ourself will exempt [him] [2] the
place. 100
And, brother, now bring in the ambassa-
dor,
That he may be a witness of the match
Twixt Balthazar and Bel-imperia,
And that we may prefix a certain time
Wherein the marriage shall be solemnized,
That we may have thy lord, the viceroy,
here.
AMB. Therein your highness highly shall
content
His majesty, that longs to hear from
hence.
KING. On, then, and hear you, lord am-
bassador— *Exeunt.*

[SCENA DUODECIMA.
Hieronimo's garden.]

[3] *Enter Jaques and Pedro.*

JAQ. I wonder, Pedro, why our master thus
At midnight sends us with our torches
light,

[1] Emended by Hawkins. Original reads *in-
execrable.*

[2] Added by Boas; meaning to excuse him from
his duties.
[3] The following scene through l. 156 is an
addition.

When man and bird and beast are all at
  rest,
Save those that watch for rape and
  bloody murder.
PED. O Jaques, know thou that our mas-
  ter's mind
Is much distraught since his Horatio died,
And—now his aged years should sleep in
  rest,
His heart in quiet—like a desperate man,
Grows lunatic and childish for his son.
Sometimes, as he doth at his table sit, 10
He speaks as if Horatio stood by him;
Then starting in a rage, falls on the
  earth,
Cries out, "Horatio, where is my Hora-
  tio?"
So that with extreme grief and cutting
  sorrow
There is not left in him one inch of
  man.—
See, where he comes.

Enter Hieronimo.

HIER. I pry through every crevice of each
  wall,
Look on each tree, and search through
  every brake,
Beat at the bushes, stamp our grandam
  earth,
Dive in the water, and stare up to
  heaven,   20
Yet cannot I behold my son Horatio.—
How now, who's there? Sprites, sprites?
PED. We are your servants that attend
  you, sir.
HIER. What make you with your torches
  in the dark?
PED. You bid us light them, and attend
  you here.
HIER. No, no, you are deceived! Not I;
  you are deceived!
Was I so mad to bid you light your
  torches now?
Light me your torches at the mid of noon,
Whenas the sun-god rides in all his glory;
Light me your torches then.
PED.　　　Then we burn daylight. 30
HIER. Let it be burnt! Night is a murder-
  ous slut,
That would not have her treasons to be
  seen;
And yonder pale-faced Hecate there, the
  moon,

Doth give consent to that is done in
  darkness;
And all those stars that gaze upon her
  face
Are aglots [1] on her sleeve, pins on her
  train;
And those that should be powerful and
  divine
Do sleep in darkness when they most
  should shine.
PED. Provoke them not, fair sir, with
  tempting words.
The heavens are gracious, and your mis-
  eries and sorrow   40
Makes you speak you know not what.
HIER. Villain, thou liest! And thou doest
  naught
But tell me I am mad. Thou liest! I am
  not mad!
I know thee to be Pedro, and he Jaques.
I'll prove it to thee; and, were I mad, how
  could I?
Where was she that same night when my
  Hor[atio] was murdered?
She should have shone—search thou the
  book.
Had the moon shone, in my boy's face
  there was a kind of grace,
That I know—nay, I do know—had the
  murderer seen him,
His weapon would have fall'n and cut
  the earth,   50
Had he been framed of naught but blood
  and death.
Alack, when mischief doth it knows not
  what,
What shall we say to mischief?

Enter Isabella.

ISAB. Dear Hieronimo, come in a-doors;
O, seek not means so to increase thy
  sorrow.
HIER. Indeed, Isabella, we do nothing here.
I do not cry—ask Pedro, and ask Jaques.
Not I indeed; we are very merry, very
  merry.
ISAB. How? Be merry here, be merry
  here?
Is not this the place, and this the very
  tree,   60
Where my Horatio died, where he was
  murdered?

---

[1] Metal ornaments. From 1610 edn. Original
reads *aggots.*

HIER. Was—do not say what. Let her
  weep it out.
This was the tree. I set it of a kernel;
And, when our hot Spain could not let
  it grow,
But that the infant and the human sap
Began to wither, duly twice a morning
Would I be sprinkling it with fountain
  water.
At last it grew and grew, and bore and
  bore,
Till at the length it grew a gallows, and
  did bear our son.
It bore thy fruit and mine—O wicked,
  wicked plant!   70
      One knocks within at the door.
See who knocks there.
PED.   It is a painter, sir.
HIER. Bid him come in, and paint some
  comfort,
For surely there's none lives but painted
  comfort.
Let him come in!—One knows not what
  may chance.
God's will that I should set this tree!
But even so, masters ungrateful servants
  rear from naught,
And then they hate them that did bring
  them up.

Enter the Painter.

PAIN. God bless you, sir.
HIER. Wherefore? Why, thou scornful
  villain?
How, where, or by what means should I
  be blessed?   80
ISAB. What wouldst thou have, good fel-
  low?
PAIN.   Justice, madam.
HIER. O ambitious beggar! Wouldst thou
  have that
That lives not in the world?
Why, all the undelved mines cannot buy
An ounce of justice, 'tis a jewel so in-
  estimable.
I tell thee, God hath engrossed all jus-
  tice in his hands,
And there is none but what comes from
  him.
PAIN. O, then I see that God must right
  me for my murdered son.
HIER. How, was thy son murdered?
PAIN. Ay, sir. No man did hold a son so
  dear.   90

HIER. What, not as thine? That's a lie
As massy as the earth. I had a son
Whose least unvalued hair did weigh
A thousand of thy sons; and he was
  murdered.
PAIN. Alas, sir, I had no more but he.
HIER. Nor I, nor I! But this same one of
  mine
Was worth a legion. But all is one.
Pedro, Jaques, go in a-doors; Isabella, go!
And this good fellow here and I
Will range this hideous orchard up and
  down   100
Like to two lions reavéd of their young.
Go in a-doors, I say.
    Exeunt. The Painter and he sits down.
        Come, let's talk wisely now.
Was thy son murdered?
PAIN.   Ay, sir.
HIER.   So was mine.
How dost take it? Art thou not some-
  times mad?
Is there no tricks[1] that comes before
  thine eyes?
PAIN. O Lord, yes, sir.[2]
HIER. Art a painter? Canst paint me a
  tear, or a wound,
A groan, or a sigh? Canst paint me such
  a tree as this?
PAIN. Sir, I am sure you have heard of
  my painting; my name's Bazardo.
HIER. Bazardo! Afore God, an excellent
  fellow. Look you, sir,   110
Do you see, I'd have you paint me [for]
  my gallery
In your oil colors matted,[3] and draw me
  five
Years younger than I am—do ye see, sir,
  let five
Years go; let them go—like the marshal
  of Spain,
My wife Isabella standing by me,
With a speaking look to my son Horatio,
Which should intend to this or some
  suchlike purpose:
"God bless thee, my sweet son;" and
  my hand leaning upon his head, thus,
  sir, do you see? May it be done?

[1] Illusions.
[2] The remainder of the added passage is so
chaotic in form that it has been printed as
prose by some editors.
[3] Meaning doubtful; probably either *set in a
mat* or *a mount*, or *lacking in luster.*

PAIN. Very well, sir.

HIER. Nay, I pray mark me, sir. Then, sir, would I have you paint me this tree, this very tree.   120

Canst paint a doleful cry?

PAIN. Seemingly, sir.

HIER. Nay, it should cry; but all is one. Well, sir, paint me a youth, run thorough and thorough with villains' swords, hanging upon this tree.

Canst draw a murderer?

PAIN. I'll warrant you, sir; I have the pattern of the most notorious villains that ever lived in all Spain.

HIER. O, let them be worse, worse. Stretch thine art,

And let their beards be of Judas his own color,[1]

And let their eyebrows jutty over—in any case observe that.   130

Then, sir, after some violent noise, Bring me forth in my shirt, and my gown under mine arm, with my torch in my hand, and my sword reared up thus, and with these words:

"What noise is this? Who calls Hieronimo?"

May it be done?

PAIN. Yea, sir.

[HIER.] Well, sir, then bring me forth, bring me thorough alley and alley, still with a distracted countenance going along, and let my hair heave up my nightcap.

Let the clouds scowl, make the moon dark, the stars extinct, the winds blowing, the bells tolling, the owl shrieking, the toads croaking, the minutes jerring,[2] and the clock striking twelve.

And then at last, sir, starting, behold a man hanging, and tottering, and tottering as you know the wind will weave a man, and I, with a trice[3] to cut him down,

And, looking upon him by the advantage of my torch, find it to be my son Horatio.

There you may [show][4] a passion, there you may show a passion!   140

Draw me like old Priam of Troy,

---

[1] I.e., red, according to medieval tradition.
[2] Jarring, ticking.
[3] Moment.   [4] Added by Dodsley.

Crying, "The house is afire! The house is afire!"

As the torch over my head. Make me curse,

Make me rave, make me cry, make me mad,

Make me well again, make me curse hell, Invocate heaven, and, in the end, leave me In a trance, and so forth.

PAIN. And is this the end?

HIER. O no, there is no end! The end is death and madness,

As I am never better than when I am mad.   150

Then methinks I am a brave fellow;

Then I do wonders. But reason abuseth me,

And there's the torment, there's the hell.

At the last, sir, bring me to one of the murderers.

Were he as strong as Hector, thus would I Tear and drag him up and down.

He beats the Painter in, then comes out again with a book in his hand.[5]

"*Vindicta mihi!*"[6]

Ay, heaven will be revenged of every ill, Nor will they suffer murder unrepaid.

Then stay, Hieronimo; attend their will,   160

For mortal men may not appoint their time!—

"*Per scelus semper tutum est sceleribus iter.*"[7]

Strike, and strike home, where wrong is offered thee,

For evils unto ills conductors be,

And death's the worst of resolution.

For he that thinks with patience to contend

To quiet life, his life shall easily end.—

"*Fata si miseros juvant, habes salutem;*
Fata si vitam negant, habes sepulchrum:"[8]

If destiny thy miseries do ease,   170

Then hast thou health, and happy shalt thou be;

---

[5] This stage direction is a substitute for "Enter Hieronimo, with a book in his hand" in the earlier editions.
[6] "Vengeance for me" (from Seneca's *Octavia*).
[7] "The path to crimes is always made safe by crime" (from Seneca's *Agamemnon*, l. 115).
[8] "If the Fates aid the unfortunate, you have safety; if the Fates deny you life, you have a tomb" (from Seneca's *Troades*, ll. 511–512). Paraphrased in the following four lines.

If destiny deny thee life, Hieronimo,
Yet shalt thou be assuréd of a tomb;
If neither, yet let this thy comfort be:
Heaven covereth him that hath no burial.
And, to conclude, I will revenge his death!
But how? Not, as the vulgar wits of men,
With open, but inevitable ills,[1]
As by a secret, yet a certain mean,
Which under kindship [2] will be cloakéd
    best.   180
Wise men will take their opportunity,
Closely and safely fitting things to time.
But in extremes advantage hath no time,
And therefore all times fit not for revenge.
Thus therefore will I rest me in unrest,
Dissembling quiet in unquietness,
Not seeming that I know their villainies,
That my simplicity may make them
    think
That ignorantly I will let all slip,
For ignorance, I wot, and well they
    know,   190
"Remedium malorum iners est." [3]
Nor aught avails it me to menace them
Who, as a wintry storm upon a plain,
Will bear me down with their nobility.
No, no, Hieronimo, thou must enjoin
Thine eyes to observation, and thy
    tongue
To milder speeches than thy spirit
    affords,
Thy heart to patience, and thy hands to
    rest,
Thy cap to courtesy, and thy knee to
    bow,
Till to revenge thou know when, where,
    and how.   A noise within. 200
How now, what noise? What coil [4] is that
you keep?

Enter a Servant.

SER. Here are a sort [5] of poor petitioners
    That are importunate, and [6] it shall
    please you, sir,
    That you should plead their cases to the
    king.
HIER. That I should plead their several
    actions?
    Why, let them enter, and let me see
    them.

[1] Injuries, attacks.   [2] Kindness.
[3] "Ignorance is a cowardly remedy for misfortunes" (from Seneca's Œdipus, l. 515).
[4] Disturbance.   [5] Company.   [6] If.

Enter three Citizens and an Old Man.

1 [CIT.] So, I tell you this: for learning and
    for law
    There is not any advocate in Spain
    That can prevail, or will take half the
    pain
    That he will, in pursuit of equity.   210
HIER. Come near, you men, that thus
    importune me.—
[Aside.] Now must I bear a face of gravity;
    For thus I used, before my marshalship,
    To plead in causes as corregidor.[7]—
    Come on, sirs, what's the matter?
2 [CIT.]   Sir, an action.
HIER. Of battery?
1 [CIT.]   Mine of debt.
HIER.   Give place.
2 [CIT.] No, sir, mine is an action of the
    case.[8]
3 [CIT.] Mine an *ejectione firmæ* [9] by a
    lease.
HIER. Content you, sirs. Are you
    determinéd   219
    That I should plead your several actions?
1 [CIT.] Ay, sir, and here's my declaration.
2 [CIT.] And here's my band.[10]
3 [CIT.]   And here's my lease.
                    They give him papers.
HIER. But wherefore stands yon silly man
    so mute,
    With mournful eyes and hands to heaven
    upreared?
    Come hither, father, let me know thy
    cause.
SENEX.[11] O worthy sir, my cause, but
    slightly known,
    May move the hearts of warlike Myrmi-
    dons,
    And melt the Corsic rocks with ruthful
    tears.
HIER. Say, father, tell me what's thy suit.
SENEX. No, sir, could my woes   230
    Give way unto my most distressful words,
    Then should I not in paper, as you see,
    With ink bewray what blood began in me.
HIER. What's here? "The humble sup-
    plication
    Of Don Bazulto for his murdered son."

[7] Advocate; properly, magistrate.
[8] "A universal remedy given for all personal
wrongs . . . so called because the plaintiff's
whole case . . . is set forth at length in the
original writ" (Blackstone).
[9] A writ to eject a tenant.   [10] Bond.
[11] *I.e.*, Old Man; also *Baz.* in speech heads.

SENEX. Ay, sir.
HIER.   No, sir, it was my murdered
          son.
O, my son, my son; O, my son Horatio!
But mine, or thine, Bazulto, be content.
Here, take my handkercher and wipe
          thine eyes,
Whiles wretched I in thy mishaps may
          see   240
The lively portrait of my dying self.
          He draweth out a bloody napkin.
O, no, not this! Horatio, this was thine,
And, when I dyed it in thy dearest blood,
This was a token twixt thy soul and me
That of thy death revengéd I should be.
But here, take this, and this—what,
          my purse?—
Ay, this, and that, and all of them are
          thine,
For all as one are our extremities.
1 [CIT.] O, see the kindness of Hieronimo!
2 [CIT.] This gentleness shows him a gen-
          tleman.   250
HIER. See, see, O, see thy shame,
          Hieronimo!
See here a loving father to his son!
Behold the sorrows and the sad laments
That he delivereth for his son's decease!
If love's effects so strives in lesser things,
If love enforce such moods in meaner
          wits,
If love express such power in poor estates,
Hieronimo, whenas a raging sea,
Tossed with the wind and tide, o'er-
          turnest then
The upper billows, course of waves to
          keep,   260
Whilst lesser waters labor in the deep,
Then shamest thou not, Hieronimo, to
          neglect
The sweet revenge of thy Horatio?
Though on this earth justice will not be
          found,
I'll down to hell, and in this passion
Knock at the dismal gates of Pluto's
          court,
Getting by force, as once Alcides did,
A troop of furies and tormenting hags
To torture Don Lorenzo and the rest.
Yet lest the triple-headed porter should
Deny my passage to the slimy strand, 271
The Thracian poet thou shalt counter-
          feit.
Come on, old father, be my Orpheus,

And, if thou canst [1] no notes upon the
          harp,
Then sound the burden [2] of thy sore
          heart's grief,
Till we do gain that Proserpine may
          grant
Revenge on them that murderéd my son.
Then will I rent and tear them, thus and
          thus,
Shivering their limbs in pieces with my
          teeth.   *Tear the papers.*
1 [CIT.] O sir, my declaration!
          Exit Hieronimo, and they after.
2 [CIT.]   Save my bond! 280

          Enter Hieronimo.

2 [CIT.] Save my bond!
3 [CIT.] Alas, my lease! It cost me ten
          pound,
And you, my lord, have torn the same.
HIER. That cannot be; I gave it never a
          wound.
Show me one drop of blood fall from the
          same!
How is it possible I should slay it then?
Tush, no; run after, catch me if you can.
Exeunt all but the Old Man. Bazulto re-
mains till Hieronimo enters again, who,
          staring him in the face, speaks.
HIER. And art thou come, Horatio, from
          the depth,
To ask for justice in this upper earth,
To tell thy father thou art unrevenged,
To wring more tears from Isabella's
          eyes,   291
Whose lights are dimmed with overlong
          laments?
Go back, my son; complain to Æacus,
For here's no justice. Gentle boy, begone,
For justice is exiléd from the earth.
Hieronimo will bear thee company.
Thy mother cries on righteous Rhada-
          manth
For just revenge against the murderers.
SENEX. Alas, my lord, whence springs this
          troubled speech?
HIER. But let me look on my Horatio. 300
Sweet boy, how art thou changed in
          death's black shade!
Had Proserpine no pity on thy youth,
But suffered thy fair crimson-colored
          spring
With withered winter to be blasted thus?
[1] Knowest.   [2] Bass accompaniment.

Horatio, thou art older than thy father.
Ah, ruthless fate,[1] that favor[2] thus
　transforms!
Baz. Ah, my good lord, I am not your
　young son.
Hier. What, not my son? Thou then a
　Fury art,
Sent from the empty kingdom of black
　night
To summon me to make appearance　310
Before grim Minos and just Rhada-
　manth,
To plague Hieronimo that is remiss,
And seeks not vengeance for Horatio's
　death.
Baz. I am a grievéd man, and not a ghost,
That came for justice for my murdered
　son.
Hier. Ay, now I know thee, now thou
　namest my son.
Thou art the lively image of my grief;
Within thy face my sorrows I may see.
Thy eyes are gummed with tears, thy
　cheeks are wan,
Thy forehead troubled, and thy mut-
　t'ring lips　　　　　　　　　　320
Murmur sad words abruptly broken off
By force of windy sighs thy spirit
　breathes.
And all this sorrow riseth for thy son,
And selfsame sorrow feel I for my son.
Come in, old man, thou shalt to Isabel.
Lean on my arm; I thee, thou me, shalt
　stay,
And thou, and I, and she will sing a song,
Three parts in one, but all of discords
　framed.—
Talk not of chords, but let us now be
　gone,
For with a cord Horatio was slain.　330
　　　　　　　　　　　　　Exeunt.

[Scena Tertia Decima.

The Spanish court.]

*Enter King of Spain, the Duke, Viceroy, and
　Lorenzo, Balthazar, Don Pedro, and
　　　　　　　　　　　　Bel-imperia.*

King. Go, brother, it is the Duke of
　Castile's cause;
Salute the viceroy in our name.
Cas.　　　　　　　　　　　I go.

---

[1] Emended by Dodsley. Original reads *Father.*
[2] Appearance.

Vic. Go forth, Don Pedro, for thy
　nephew's sake,
And greet the Duke of Castile.
Ped.　　　　　　　　It shall be so.
King. And now to meet these Portuguese,
For as we now are, so sometimes were
　these,
Kings and commanders of the western
　Indies.—
Welcome, brave viceroy, to the court of
　Spain,
And welcome all his honorable train!
'Tis not unknown to us for why you
　come,　　　　　　　　　　　10
Or have so kingly crossed the seas.
Sufficeth it, in this we note the troth
And more than common love you lend
　to us.
So is it that mine honorable niece
(For it beseems us now that it be known)
Already is betrothed to Balthazar;
And by appointment and our condescent[3]
Tomorrow are they to be married.
To this intent we entertain thyself,
Thy followers, their pleasure, and our
　peace.　　　　　　　　　　　20
Speak, men of Portingale, shall it be so?
If ay, say so; if not, say flatly no.
Vic. Renowméd king, I come not, as thou
　think'st,
With doubtful followers, unresolvéd men,
But such as have upon thine articles
Confirmed thy motion, and contented me.
Know, sovereign, I come to solemnize
The marriage of thy beloved niece,
Fair Bel-imperia, with my Balthazar—
With thee, my son, whom sith I live to
　see,　　　　　　　　　　　30
Here take my crown, I give it her and
　thee,
And let me live a solitary life,
In ceaseless prayers,
To think how strangely heaven hath thee
　preserved.
King. See, brother, see, how nature strives
　in him!
Come, worthy viceroy, and accompany
Thy friend with thine extremities.[4]
A place more private fits this princely
　mood.
Vic. Or here, or where your highness
　thinks it good.
　　　Exeunt all but Cas[tile] and Lor[enzo].

---

[3] Consent.　[4] Unrestrained expression of feelings.

CAS. Nay, stay, Lorenzo, let me talk with
　you.　　　　　　　　　　　　　　　　40
Seest thou this entertainment of these
　kings?
LOR. I do, my lord, and joy to see the
　same.
CAS. And knowest thou why this meeting
　is?
LOR. For her, my lord, whom Balthazar
　doth love,
And to confirm their promised marriage.
CAS. She is thy sister?
LOR.　　　　　　　Who, Bel-imperia? Ay,
My gracious lord, and this is the day
That I have longed so happily to see.
CAS. Thou wouldst be loath that any
　fault of thine　　　　　　　　　　　49
Should intercept her in her happiness?
LOR. Heavens will not let Lorenzo err so
　much.
CAS. Why then, Lorenzo, listen to my
　words.
It is suspected, and reported too,
That thou, Lorenzo, wrong'st Hieronimo,
And in his suits towards his majesty
Still keep'st him back, and seeks to cross
　his suit.
LOR. That I, my lord—?
CAS. I tell thee, son, myself have heard
　it said,
When, to my sorrow, I have been
　ashamed
To answer for thee, though thou art
　my son.　　　　　　　　　　　　　60
Lorenzo, knowest thou not the common
　love
And kindness that Hieronimo hath won
By his deserts within the court of Spain?
Or seest thou not the k[ing] my brother's
　care
In his behalf, and to procure his health?
Lorenzo, shouldst thou thwart his
　passions,
And he exclaim against thee to the king,
What honor were 't in this assembly,
Or what a scandal were't among the
　kings
To hear Hieronimo exclaim on thee!　70
Tell me—and look thou tell me truly
　too—
Whence grows the ground of this report
　in court?
LOR. My l[ord], it lies not in Lorenzo's
　power

To stop the vulgar,[1] liberal of their
　tongues.
A small advantage makes a water-breach,
And no man lives that long contenteth
　all.
CAS. Myself have seen thee busy to keep
　back
Him and his supplications from the king.
LOR. Yourself, my l[ord], hath seen his
　passions　　　　　　　　　　　　　79
That ill beseemed the presence of a king;
And, for I pitied him in his distress,
I held him thence with kind and cour-
　teous words
As free from malice to Hieronimo
As to my soul, my lord.
CAS. Hieronimo, my son, mistakes thee
　then.
LOR. My gracious father, believe me, so he
　doth.
But what's a silly man, distract in mind,
To think upon the murder of his son?
Alas, how easy is it for him to err!　89
But for his satisfaction and the world's,
'Twere good, my l[ord], that Hieronimo
　and I
Were reconciled, if he misconster [2] me.
CAS. Lorenzo, thou hast said; it shall be so.
Go one of you, and call Hieronimo.

Enter Balthazar and Bel-imperia.

BAL. Come, Bel-imperia, Balthazar's con-
　tent,
My sorrow's ease and sovereign of my
　bliss,
Sith heaven hath ordained thee to be
　mine,
Disperse those clouds and melancholy
　looks,
And clear them up with those thy sun-
　bright eyes,
Wherein my hope and heaven's fair
　beauty lies.　　　　　　　　　　100
BEL. My looks, my lord, are fitting for my
　love,
Which, new-begun, can show [no] [3]
　brighter yet.
BAL. New-kindled flames should burn as
　morning sun.
BEL. But not too fast, lest heat and all be
　done.
I see my lord my father.

1 Common people.　　　3 From 1602 edn.
2 Misconstrue.

BAL. Truce, my love;
I will go salute him.
CAS. Welcome, Balthazar.
Welcome, brave prince, the pledge of
Castile's peace!
And welcome, Bel-imperia!—How now,
girl?
Why comest thou sadly to salute us thus?
Content thyself, for I am satisfied. 110
It is not now as when Andrea lived;
We have forgotten and forgiven that,
And thou art gracéd with a happier
love.—
But, Balthazar, here comes Hieronimo;
I'll have a word with him.

Enter Hieronimo and a Servant.

HIER. And where's the duke?
SER. Yonder.
HIER. Even so.—
[*Aside.*] What new device have they
deviséd, trow? [1]
Pocas palabras! [2] Mild as the lamb!
Is 't I will be revenged? No, I am not
the man.—
CAS. Welcome, Hieronimo. 120
LOR. Welcome, Hieronimo.
BAL. Welcome, Hieronimo.
HIER. My lords, I thank you for Horatio.
CAS. Hieronimo, the reason that I sent
To speak with you, is this—
HIER. What, so short?
Then I'll be gone; I thank you for 't.
CAS. Nay, stay, Hieronimo!—Go call him,
son.
[LOR.] Hieronimo, my father craves a word
with you.
HIER. With me, sir? Why, my l[ord], I
thought you had done. 129
LOR. [*Aside.*] No. Would he had!
CAS. Hieronimo, I hear
You find yourself aggrievéd at my son,
Because you have not access unto the
king,
And say 'tis he that intercepts your suits.
HIER. Why, is not this a miserable thing,
my lord?
CAS. Hieronimo, I hope you have no cause,
And would be loath that one of your
deserts
Should once have reason to suspect my
son,
Considering how I think of you myself.

HIER. Your son Lorenzo? Whom, my
noble lord?
The hope of Spain, mine honorable
friend? 140
Grant me the combat of them, if they
dare. *Draws out his sword.*
I'll meet him face to face, to tell me so!
These be the scandalous reports of such
As love not me, and hate my lord too
much.
Should I suspect Lorenzo would prevent
Or cross my suit, that loved my son so
well?
My lord, I am ashamed it should be
said.
LOR. Hieronimo, I never gave you cause.
HIER. My good lord, I know you did
not.
CAS. There then pause;
And for the satisfaction of the world, 150
Hieronimo, frequent my homely house,
The Duke of Castile, Cyprian's ancient
seat,
And, when thou wilt, use me, my son,
and it.
But here, before Prince Balthazar and
me,
Embrace each other, and be perfect
friends.
HIER. Ay, marry, my lord, and shall.
Friends, quoth he? See, I'll be friends
with you all—
Specially with you, my lovely lord;
For divers causes it is fit for us
That we be friends. The world's sus-
picious, 160
And men may think what we imagine
not.
BAL. Why, this is friendly done, Hiero-
nimo.
LOR. And that I hope. Old grudges are
forgot?
HIER. What else? It were a shame it
should not be so.
CAS. Come on, Hieronimo, at my re-
quest;
Let us entreat your company today.
Exeunt.
HIER. Your lordship's to command.—Pha!
keep your way.
*Mi. Chi mi fa? Piu Correzza Che no sule
Tradito viha otrade vule.* [3] *Exit.* 169

---

[1] Think you? [2] Few words.

[3] A corrupt version of a proverb from Piovanc
Arlotto.

[CHORUS]

Enter Ghost and Revenge.

GHOST. Awake, Erichtho! Cerberus, awake!
  Solicit Pluto, gentle Proserpine!
  To combat, Acheron and Erebus!
  For ne'er, by Styx and Phlegeton in hell,
  O'er-ferried Charon to the fiery lakes
  Such fearful sights as poor Andrea sees.[1]
  Revenge, awake!
REVENGE.   Awake? For why?
GHOST. Awake, Revenge, for thou art ill-
    advised
  To sleep away what thou art warned to
    watch!
REVENGE. Content thyself, and do not
    trouble me.
GHOST. Awake, Revenge, if love—as love
    hath had—   180
  Have yet the power or prevalence in hell!
  Hieronimo with Lorenzo is joined in
    league,
  And intercepts our passage to revenge.
  Awake, Revenge, or we are woebegone!
REVENGE. Thus worldlings ground [2] what
    they have dreamed upon.
  Content thyself, Andrea.   Though I
    sleep,
  Yet is my mood soliciting their souls.
  Sufficeth thee that poor Hieronimo
  Cannot forget his son Horatio.
  Nor dies Revenge, although he sleep
    awhile;   190
  For, in unquiet, quietness is feigned,
  And slumb'ring is a common worldly
    wile.
  Behold, Andrea, for an instance, how
  Revenge hath slept, and then imagine
    thou
  What 'tis to be subject to destiny.

Enter a Dumb Show.

GHOST. Awake, Revenge; reveal this mys-
    tery.
REVENGE. The two first the nuptial
    torches bore
  As brightly burning as the midday's sun;
  But after them doth Hymen hie as fast,
  Clothéd in sable and a saffron robe, 200
  And blows them out, and quencheth
    them with blood,
  As discontent that things continue so.

[1] Lines 171–74, corrupt in the original, have
been emended by Schick.   [2] Rely on.

GHOST. Sufficeth me; thy meaning's under-
    stood,
  And thanks to thee and those infernal
    powers
  That will not tolerate a lover's woe.
  Rest thee, for I will sit to see the rest.
REVENGE. Then argue not, for thou hast
    thy request.   *Exeunt.*

ACTUS QUARTUS. [SCENA PRIMA.

A room in Don Cyprian's palace.]

Enter Bel-imperia and Hieronimo.

BEL. Is this the love thou bear'st Horatio?
  Is this the kindness that thou counter-
    feits?
  Are these the fruits of thine incessant
    tears?
  Hieronimo, are these thy passions,
  Thy protestations and thy deep laments,
  That thou wert wont to weary men
    withal?
  O unkind father! O deceitful world!
  With what excuses canst thou show thy-
    self—
  With what dishonor and the hate of
    men—
  From this dishonor and the hate of
    men,   10
  Thus to neglect the loss and life of him
  Whom both my letters and thine own
    belief
  Assures thee to be causeless slaughteréd?
  Hieronimo, for shame, Hieronimo,
  Be not a history to aftertimes
  Of such ingratitude unto thy son.
  Unhappy mothers of such children then!
  But monstrous fathers to forget so soon
  The death of those whom they with care
    and cost
  Have tendered so, thus careless should
    be lost.   20
  Myself, a stranger in respect of thee,
  So loved his life as still I wish their
    deaths.
  Nor shall his death be unrevenged by
    me,
  Although I bear it out for fashion's sake,
  For here I swear, in sight of heaven and
    earth,
  Shouldst thou neglect the love thou
    shouldst retain,
  And give it over and devise no more,

Myself should send their hateful souls
  to hell
That wrought his downfall with extrem-
  est death.
HIER. But may it be that Bel-imperia 30
  Vows such revenge as she hath deigned
    to say?
  Why, then I see that heaven applies our
    drift,[1]
  And all the saints do sit soliciting
  For vengeance on those cursèd murder-
    ers.
  Madam, 'tis true, and now I find it so,
  I found a letter, written in your name,
  And, in that letter, how Horatio died.
  Pardon, O, pardon, Bel-imperia,
  My fear and care in not believing it;
  Nor think I thoughtless think upon a
    mean   40
  To let his death be unrevenged at full.
  And here I vow—so you but give consent,
  And will conceal my resolution—
  I will ere long determine of their deaths
  That causeless thus have murder[è]d my
    son.
BEL. Hieronimo, I will consent, conceal,
  And aught that may effect for thine
    avail,
  Join with thee to revenge Horatio's
    death.
HIER. On, then; [and] whatsoever I devise,
  Let me entreat you, grace my practices,
  Forwhy [2] the plot's already in mine
    head.   51
  Here they are.

Enter Balthazar and Lorenzo.

BAL.   How now, Hieronimo?
  What, courting Bel-imperia?
HIER.   Ay, my lord;
  Such courting as, I promise you,
  She hath my heart, but you, my lord,
    have hers.
LOR. But now, Hieronimo, or never,
  We are to entreat your help.
HIER.   My help?
  Why, my good lords, assure yourselves
    of me,
  For you have given me cause—ay, by
    my faith, have you!
BAL. It pleased you, at the entertainment
  of the ambassador,   60

To grace the king so much as with a
  show.
Now, were your study so well furnishèd,
As, for the passing of the first night's
  sport,
To entertain my father with the like,
Or any suchlike pleasing motion,
Assure yourself, it would content them
  well.
HIER. Is this all?
BAL.   Ay, this is all.
HIER. Why then, I'll fit you; say no more.
  When I was young, I gave my mind
  And plied myself to fruitless poetry,   70
  Which, though it profit the professor
    naught,
  Yet is it passing pleasing to the world.
LOR. And how for that?
HIER.   Marry, my good lord, thus
  (And yet methinks, you are too quick
    with us):
  When in Toledo there I studièd,
  It was my chance to write a tragedy—
  See here, my lords—
           He shows them a book.
  Which, long forgot, I found this other day.
  Now would your lordships favor me so
    much
  As but to grace me with your acting
    it—   80
  I mean each one of you to play a part—
  Assure you it will prove most passing
    strange,
  And wondrous plausible [3] to that as-
    sembly.
BAL. What, would you have us play a
  tragedy?
HIER. Why, Nero thought it no dispar-
  agement,
  And kings and emperors have ta'en de-
  light
  To make experience of their wits in
    plays.[4]
LOR. Nay, be not angry, good Hieronimo;
  The prince but asked a question.
BAL. In faith, Hieronimo, an you be in
    earnest,   90
  I'll make one.
LOR.   And I another.
HIER. Now, my good lord, could you en-
  treat

---

[1] Approves our plan.   [2] Because.
[3] Acceptable.
[4] These lines, which are quoted by Heywood,
give the clue to Kyd's authorship.

Your sister Bel-imperia to make one?
For what's a play without a woman in it?
BEL. Little entreaty shall serve me, Hiero-
nimo,
For I must needs be employed in your
play.
HIER. Why, this is well. I tell you, lord-
ings,
It was determinéd to have been acted
By gentlemen and scholars too,
Such as could tell what to speak.
BAL. And now 100
It shall be played by princes and court-
iers,
Such as can tell how to speak,
If, as it is our country manner,
You will but let us know the argument.
HIER. That shall I roundly. The chron-
icles of Spain
Record this written of a knight of
Rhodes:
He was betrothed, and wedded at the
length,
To one Perseda, an Italian dame,
Whose beauty ravished all that her be-
held,
Especially the soul of Soliman, 110
Who at the marriage was the chiefest
guest.[1]
By sundry means sought Soliman to
win
Perseda's love, and could not gain the
same.
Then gan he break his passions to a
friend,
One of his bashaws, whom he held full
dear.
Her had this bashaw long solicited,
And saw she was not otherwise to be
won
But by her husband's death, this knight
of Rhodes,
Whom presently by treachery he slew.
She, stirred with an exceeding hate
therefor, 120
As cause of this, slew Soliman
And, to escape the bashaw's tyranny,
Did stab herself. And this the tragedy.
LOR. O excellent!
BEL. But say, Hieronimo,
What then became of him that was the
bashaw?

[1] Cf. the play Soliman and Perseda, attributed
to Kyd.

HIER. Marry, thus: moved with remorse
of his misdeeds,
Ran to a mountain top, and hung him-
self.
BAL. But which of us is to perform that
part?
HIER. O, that will I, my lords; make no
doubt of it.
I'll play the murderer, I warrant you, 130
For I already have conceited that.
BAL. And what shall I?
HIER. Great Soliman, the Turkish em-
peror.
LOR. And I?
HIER. Erastus, the knight of Rhodes.
BEL. And I?
HIER. Perseda, chaste and resolute.
And here, my lords, are several abstracts
drawn,
For each of you to note your parts,
And act it, as occasion's offered you.
You must provide a Turkish cap,
A black mustachio and a falchion; 140
    Gives a paper to Bal[thazar].
You with a cross, like to a knight of
Rhodes;
    Gives another to Lor[enzo].
And, madam, you must attire yourself
    He giveth Bel[-imperia] another.
Like Phœbe, Flora, or the huntress,[2]
Which to your discretion shall seem
best.
And, as for me, my lords, I'll look to
one,
And, with the ransom that the viceroy
sent,
So furnish and perform this tragedy
As all the world shall say Hieronimo
Was liberal in gracing of it so.
BAL. Hieronimo, methinks a comedy were
better. 150
HIER. A comedy?
Fie! Comedies are fit for common wits;
But to present a kingly troop withal,
Give me a stately-written tragedy,
Tragedia cothurnata,[3] fitting kings,
Containing matter, and not common
things.
My lords, all this must be performed,
As fitting for the first night's reveling.
The Italian tragedians were so sharp
of wit

[2] *I.e.*, Diana.
[3] Wearing the buskin of the tragic actor.

That in one hour's meditation 160
They would perform anything in action.

LOR. And well it may, for I have seen
the like

In Paris 'mongst the French tragedians.

HIER. In Paris? Mass! And well remembered!

There's one thing more that rests for us
to do.

BAL. What's that, Hieronimo? Forget
not anything.

HIER. Each one of us
Must act his part in unknown lan-
guages,
That it may breed the more variety:
As you, my lord, in Latin, I in Greek, 170
You in Italian; and, for because I know
That Bel-imperia hath practicéd the
French,
In courtly French shall all her phrases
be.

BEL. You mean to try my cunning then,
Hieronimo?

BAL. But this will be a mere confusion
And hardly shall we all be understood.

HIER. It must be so, for the conclusion
Shall prove the invention and all was
good.
And I myself in an oration,
And with a strange and wondrous show
besides, 180
That I will have there behind a cur-
tain,
Assure yourself, shall make the matter
known.
And all shall be concluded in one scene,
For there's no pleasure ta'en in tedious-
ness.

BAL. [Aside.] How like you this?

LOR. [Aside.] Why, thus, my lord:
We must resolve to soothe his humors
up.

BAL. On then, Hieronimo. Farewell till
soon.

HIER. You'll ply this gear?

LOR. I warrant you.
  Exeunt all but Hiero[nimo].

HIER. Why, so!
Now shall I see the fall of Babylon,
Wrought by the heavens in this con-
fusion. 190
And, if the world like not this tragedy,
Hard is the hap of old Hieronimo. *Exit.*

[SCENA SECUNDA.

Hieronimo's garden.]

Enter Isabella with a weapon.

[ISAB.] Tell me no more!—O monstrous
homicides!
Since neither piety or pity moves
The king to justice or compassion,
I will revenge myself upon this place,
Where thus they murdered my beloved
son. *She cuts down the arbor.*
Down with these branches and these
loathsome boughs
Of this unfortunate and fatal pine!
Down with them, Isabella; rent them
up,
And burn the roots from whence the
rest is sprung!
I will not leave a root, a stalk, a tree, 10
A bough, a branch, a blossom, nor a
leaf,
No, not an herb within this garden
plot—
Acccurséd complot of my misery!
Fruitless forever may this garden be,
Barren the earth, and blissless whosoever
Imagines not to keep it unmanured![1]
An eastern wind, commixed with noi-
some airs,
Shall blast the plants and the young
saplings;
The earth with serpents shall be pesteréd,
And passengers, for fear to be infect, 20
Shall stand aloof, and, looking at it,
tell,
"There, murdered, died the son of Isa-
bel."
Ay, here he died, and here I him em-
brace.
See, where his ghost solicits with his
wounds
Revenge on her that should revenge his
death.
Hieronimo, make haste to see thy son,
For sorrow and despair hath cited me
To hear Horatio plead with Rhada-
manth.
Make haste, Hieronimo, to hold ex-
cused[2]
Thy negligence in pursuit of their
deaths 30
Whose hateful wrath bereaved him of
his breath.

[1] Uncultivated.   [2] Make excuses for.

Ah, nay, thou dost delay their deaths,
Forgives the murderers of thy noble
   son,
And none but I bestir me—to no end!
And, as I curse this tree from further
   fruit,
So shall my womb be cursèd for his
   sake,
And with this weapon will I wound the
   breast,
The hapless breast, that gave Horatio
   suck.   *She stabs herself.*

[SCENA TERTIA.

A room in Don Cyprian's palace.]

Enter Hieronimo; he knocks up the curtain.
   Enter the Duke of Castile.

CAS. How now, Hieronimo, where's your
   fellows,
   That you take all this pain?
HIER. O, sir, it is for the author's credit
   To look that all things may go well.
   But, good my lord, let me entreat your
     grace
   To give the king the copy of the play.
   This is the argument of what we show.
CAS. I will, Hieronimo.
HIER. One thing more, my good lord.
CAS. What's that?
HIER.   Let me entreat your grace   10
   That, when the train are passed into the
     gallery,
   You would vouchsafe to throw me down
     the key.
CAS. I will, Hieronimo.   *Exit Cas[tile].*
HIER. What, are you ready, Balthazar?
   Bring a chair and a cushion for the king.

   Enter Balthazar, with a chair.

Well done, Balthazar! Hang up the title:
"Our scene is Rhodes." What, is your
   beard on?
BAL. Half on; the other is in my hand.
HIER. Despatch, for shame. Are you so
   long?   *Exit Balthazar.*
Bethink thyself, Hieronimo,   20
Recall thy wits, recount thy former
   wrongs
Thou hast received by murder of thy
   son,
And lastly, not least, how Isabel,
Once his mother and thy dearest wife,
All woebegone for him, hath slain herself.

Behoves thee then, Hieronimo, to be
   revenged!
The plot is laid of dire revenge.
On then, Hieronimo, pursue revenge,
For nothing wants but acting of revenge!
               Exit Hieronimo.

Enter Spanish King, Viceroy, the Duke of
   Castile, and their Train [*to the gallery*].[1]

KING. Now, viceroy, shall we see the
   tragedy   30
   Of Soliman, the Turkish emperor,
   Performed of pleasure by your son the
     prince,
   My nephew Don Lorenzo, and my niece.
VIC. Who? Bel-imperia?
KING. Ay, and Hieronimo, our marshal,
   At whose request they deign to do't
     themselves.
   These be our pastimes in the court of
     Spain.
   Here, brother, you shall be the book-
     keeper.
   This is the argument of that they show.
              He giveth him a book.
   (*Gentlemen, this play of Hieronimo, in* [40
   sundry languages, was thought good to be set
   down in English, more largely, for the easier
   understanding to every public reader.)

Enter Balthazar, Bel-imperia, and Hiero-
                      nimo.

BAL. Bashaw, that Rhodes is ours, yield
   heavens the honor,
   And holy Mahomet, our sacred prophet!
   And be thou graced with every excellence
   That Soliman can give, or thou desire.
   But thy desert in conquering Rhodes is
     less
   Than in reserving this fair Christian
     nymph,
   Perseda, blissful lamp of excellence,   50
   Whose eyes compel, like powerful ada-
     mant,
   The warlike heart of Soliman to wait.

KING. See, viceroy, that is Balthazar, your
   son,
   That represents the emperor Soliman.
   How well he acts his amorous passion!
VIC. Ay, Bel-imperia hath taught him
   that.

[1] Added by Manly.

Cas. That's because his mind runs all on
 Bel-imperia.

Hier. Whatever joy earth yields, betide
 your majesty.
Bal. Earth yields no joy without Perseda's
 love.
Hier. Let then Perseda on your grace
 attend.   60
Bal. She shall not wait on me, but I on
 her.
 Drawn by the influence of her lights, I
 yield.
 But let my friend, the Rhodian knight,
 come forth,
 Erasto, dearer than my life to me,
 That he may see Perseda, my beloved.

Enter Erasto.

King. Here comes Lorenzo. Look upon
 the plot
 And tell me, brother, what part plays he?

Bel. Ah, my Erasto, welcome to Perseda.
Lor. Thrice happy is Erasto that thou
 livest;
 Rhodes' loss is nothing to Erasto's joy. 70
 Sith his Perseda lives, his life survives.
Bal. Ah, bashaw, here is love between
 Erasto
 And fair Perseda, sovereign of my soul.
Hier. Remove Erasto, mighty Soliman,
 And then Perseda will be quickly won.
Bal. Erasto is my friend, and, while he
 lives,
 Perseda never will remove her love.
Hier. Let not Erasto live to grieve great
 Soliman.
Bal. Dear is Erasto in our princely eye.
Hier. But, if he be your rival, let him
 die.   80
Bal. Why, let him die!—So love com-
 mandeth me;
 Yet grieve I that Erasto should so die.
Hier. Erasto, Soliman saluteth thee,
 And lets thee wit by me his highness' will,
 Which is, thou shouldst be thus em-
 ployed.   *Stab him.*
Bel.   Ay me!
 Erasto! See, Soliman, Erasto's slain!
Bal. Yet liveth Soliman to comfort thee.
 Fair queen of beauty, let not favor die,
 But with a gracious eye behold his
 grief   89

That with Perseda's beauty is increased,
If by Perseda [hi]s grief be not released.
Bel. Tyrant, desist soliciting vain suits.
 Relentless are mine ears to thy laments
 As thy butcher is pitiless and base,
 Which seized on my Erasto, harmless
 knight.
 Yet by thy power thou thinkest to
 command,
 And to thy power Perseda doth obey;
 But, were she able, thus she would
 revenge
 Thy treacheries on thee, ignoble prince;
          Stab him.
 And on herself she would be thus re-
 venged.   *Stab herself.*

King. Well said!—Old marshal, this was
 bravely done!   101
Hier. But Bel-imperia plays Perseda
 well!
Vic. Were this in earnest, Bel-imperia,
 You would be better to my son than so.
King. But now what follows for Hiero-
 nimo?
Hier. Marry, this follows for Hieronimo.
 Here break we off our sundry languages,
 And thus conclude I in our vulgar tongue.
 Happily you think—but bootless are
 your thoughts—
 That this is fabulously counterfeit, 110
 And that we do as all tragedians do—
 To die today (for fashioning our scene,
 The death of Ajax or some Roman peer),
 And, in a minute starting up again,
 Revive to please tomorrow's audience.
 No, princes; know I am Hieronimo,
 The hopeless father of a hapless son,
 Whose tongue is tuned to tell his latest
 tale,
 Not to excuse gross errors in the play.
 I see, your looks urge instance of these
 words;   120
 Behold the reason urging me to this!
        Shows his dead son.
 See here my show; look on this spectacle!
 Here lay my hope, and here my hope
 hath end;
 Here lay my heart, and here my heart
 was slain;
 Here lay my treasure, here my treasure
 lost;
 Here lay my bliss, and here my bliss
 bereft.

But hope, heart, treasure, joy, and bliss,
All fled, failed, died, yea, all decayed
  with this.
From forth these wounds came breath
  that gave me life;
They murdered me that made these fatal
  marks.   130
The cause was love, whence grew this
  mortal hate;
The hate—Lorenzo and young Baltha-
  zar;
The love—my son to Bel-imperia.
But night, the coverer of accurséd
  crimes,
With pitchy silence hushed these trai-
  tors' harms,
And lent them leave, for they had sorted [1]
  leisure
To take advantage in my garden plot
Upon my son, my dear Horatio.
There merciless they butchered up my
  boy,
In black, dark night, to pale, dim, cruel
  death.   140
He shrieks. I heard—and yet, methinks,
  I hear—
His dismal outcry echo in the air.
With soonest speed I hasted to the noise,
Where hanging on a tree I found my son,
Through-girt [2] with wounds, and slaugh-
  tered as you see.
And grieved I, think you, at this spec-
  tacle?
Speak, Portuguese, whose loss resembles
  mine.
If thou canst weep upon thy Balthazar,
'Tis like I wailed for my Horatio.   149
And you, my l[ord], whose reconciléd son
Marched in a net, and thought himself
  unseen,
And rated me for brainsick lunacy,
With "God amend that mad Hiero-
  nimo!"—
How can you brook our play's catastro-
  phe?
And here behold this bloody handker-
  cher,
Which at Horatio's death I weeping
  dipped
Within the river of his bleeding wounds.
It as propitious, see, I have reserved,
And never hath it left my bloody
  heart,

Soliciting remembrance of my vow   160
With these, O, these accurséd murderers,
Which now performed, my heart is
  satisfied.
And to this end the bashaw I became
That might revenge me on Lorenzo's life,
Who therefore was appointed to the part,
And was to represent the knight of
  Rhodes
That I might kill him more conveniently.
So, viceroy, was this Balthazar, thy son,
That Soliman which Bel-imperia,
In person of Perseda, murderéd,   170
So[le]ly appointed to that tragic part
That she might slay him that offended
  her.
Poor Bel-imperia missed her part in this:
For, though the story saith she should
  have died,
Yet I of kindness, and of care to her,
Did otherwise determine of her end;
But love of him whom they did hate too
  much
Did urge her resolution to be such.
And, princes, now behold Hieronimo,
Author and actor in this tragedy,   180
Bearing his latest fortune in his fist,
And will as resolute conclude his part
As any of the actors gone before.
And, gentles, thus I end my play.
Urge no more words; I have no more to
  say.   *He runs to hang himself.*
KING. O, hearken, viceroy! Hold, Hiero-
  nimo!
Brother, my nephew and thy son are
  slain!
VIC. We are betrayed; my Balthazar is
  slain!
Break ope the doors; run, save Hiero-
  nimo.
      [*They break in and hold Hieronimo.*][3]
Hieronimo, do but inform the king of
  these events;   190
Upon mine honor, thou shalt have no
  harm.
HIER. Viceroy, I will not trust thee with
  my life,
Which I this day have offered to my son.
Accurséd wretch!
Why stay'st thou him that was resolved
  to die?
KING. Speak, traitor! Damnéd, bloody
  murderer, speak!

[1] Selected.   [2] Pierced.

[3] From 1602 edn.

For now I have thee, I will make thee
 speak.
Why hast thou done this undeserving
 deed?
VIC. Why hast thou murderéd my Baltha-
 zar?
CAS. Why hast thou butchered both my
 children thus? [1]   200
HIER. But are you sure they are dead?
CAS.   Ay, slave, too sure.
HIER. What, and yours too?
VIC. Ay, all are dead; not one of them
 survive.
HIER. Nay, then I care not. Come, and we
 shall be friends.
 Let us lay our heads together;
 See, here's a goodly noose will hold them
 all.
VIC. O damnéd devil, how secure [2] he is!
HIER. Secure? Why, dost thou wonder
 at it?
 I tell thee, viceroy, this day I have seen
 revenged,
 And in that sight am grown a prouder
 monarch   210
 Than ever sat under the crown of Spain.
 Had I as many lives as there be stars,
 As many heavens to go to as those lives,

[1] Lines 201–249 are substituted in the 1602
edn. for the following passage in the original:
HIER. O, good words!
 As dear to me was my Horatio
 As yours, or yours, or yours, my l[ord], to you.
 My guiltless son was by Lorenzo slain,
 And by Lorenzo and that Balthazar
 Am I at last revengéd thoroughly,
 Upon whose souls may heavens be yet avenged
 With greater far than these afflictions.
CAS. But who were thy confederates in this?
VIC. That was thy daughter Bel-imperia,
 For by her hand my Balthazar was slain.
 I saw her stab him.
KING.   Why speakest thou not?
HIER. What lesser liberty can kings afford
 Than harmless silence? Then afford it me.
 Sufficeth, I may not, nor I will not tell thee.
KING. Fetch forth the tortures. Traitor as
 thou art,
 I'll make thee tell.
HIER. Indeed? Thou mayest torment me as
 his wretched son
 Hath done in murd'ring my Horatio,
 But never shalt thou force me to reveal
 The thing which I have vowed inviolate.
 And therefore, in despite of all thy threats,
 Pleased with their deaths, and eased with their
 revenge,
 First take my tongue, and afterwards my
 heart.
[2] Assured.

I'd give them all, ay, and my soul to boot,
But I would see thee ride in this red pool.
CAS. Speak, who were thy confederates in
 this?
VIC. That was thy daughter Bel-imperia,
 For by her hand my Balthazar was
 slain.
 I saw her stab him.
HIER. O, good words! As dear to me was
 my Horatio,   220
 As yours, or yours, or yours, my lord, to
 you.
 My guiltless son was by Lorenzo slain,
 And by Lorenzo and that Balthazar
 Am I at last revengéd thoroughly,
 Upon whose souls may heavens be yet
 revenged
 With greater far than these afflictions.
 Methinks, since I grew inward with
 revenge,
 I cannot look with scorn enough on
 death.
KING. What, dost thou mock us, slave?—
 Bring tortures forth.
HIER. Do, do, do; and meantime I'll tor-
 ture you.   230
 You had a son, as I take it, and your son
 Should ha' been married to your
 daughter. Ha, was't not so?—
 You had a son too; he was my liege's
 nephew.
 He was proud and politic. Had he lived,
 He might ha' come to wear the crown of
 Spain.
 I think 'twas so; 'twas I that killed him.
 Look you, this same hand, 'twas it that
 stabbed
 His heart—do you see, this hand?—
 For one Horatio, if you ever knew him, a
 youth,
 One that they hanged up in his father's
 garden;   240
 One that did force your valiant son to
 yield,
 While your more valiant son did take him
 prisoner.
VIC. Be deaf, my senses; I can hear no
 more.
KING. Fall, heaven, and cover us with thy
 sad ruins.
CAS. Roll all the world within thy pitchy
 cloud.
HIER. Now do I applaud what I have
 acted.

Nunc mers cadæ manus.[1]
Now to express the rupture of my
part—
First take my tongue, and afterward my
heart.   *He bites out his tongue.* 249
KING. O, monstrous resolution of a wretch!
See, viceroy, he hath bitten forth his
tongue
Rather than to reveal what we required.
CAS. Yet can he write.
KING. And, if in this he satisfy us not,
We will devise th' extremest kind of
death
That ever was invented for a wretch.
Then he makes signs for a knife to mend
his pen.
CAS. O, he would have a knife to mend his
pen.
VIC. Here, and advise thee that thou write
the troth.—
Look to my brother! Save Hieronimo!
He with a knife stabs the Duke and himself.
KING. What age hath ever heard such
monstrous deeds? 260
My brother, and the whole succeeding
hope
That Spain expected after my decease!
Go, bear his body hence, that we may
mourn
The loss of our beloved brother's death,
That he may be entombed whate'er be-
fall.
I am the next, the nearest, last of all.
VIC. And thou, Don Pedro, do the like for
us.
Take up our hapless son, untimely
slain;
Set me with him, and he with woeful
me, 269
Upon the mainmast of a ship unmanned,
And let the wind and tide haul me
along
To Scylla's barking and untaméd gulf,
Or to the loathsome pool of Acheron,
To weep my want for my sweet Baltha-
zar.
Spain hath no refuge for a Portingale.
The trumpets sound a dead march, the King
of Spain mourning after his brother's
body, and the King of Portingale bearing
the body of his son.

[CHORUS]

Enter Ghost and Revenge.

GHOST. Ay, now my hopes have end in
their effects,
When blood and sorrow finish my desires:
Horatio murdered in his father's bower;
Vild Serberine by Pedringano slain;
False Pedringano hanged by quaint de-
vice;
Fair Isabella by herself misdone;
Prince Balthazar by Bel-imperia stabbed;
The Duke of Castile and his wicked son
Both done to death by old Hieronimo;
My Bel-imperia fall'n as Dido fell; 10
And good Hieronimo slain by himself.
Ay, these were spectacles to please my
soul!
Now will I beg at lovely Proserpine
That, by the virtue of her princely doom,[2]
I may consort my friends in pleasing sort,
And on my foes work just and sharp re-
venge.
I'll lead my friend Horatio through those
fields
Where never-dying wars are still inured;[3]
I'll lead fair Isabella to that train[4] 19
Where pity weeps, but never feeleth pain;
I'll lead my Bel-imperia to those joys
That vestal virgins and fair queens pos-
sess;
I'll lead Hieronimo where Orpheus plays,
Adding sweet pleasure to eternal days.
But say, Revenge (for thou must help,
or none),
Against the rest how shall my hate be
shown?
REVENGE. This hand shall hale them down
to deepest hell,
Where none but furies, bugs,[5] and tor-
tures dwell.
GHOST. Then, sweet Revenge, do this at
my request:
Let me be judge, and doom them to un-
rest. 30
Let loose poor Tityus from the vulture's
gripe,
And let Don Cyprian supply his room;
Place Don Lorenzo on Ixion's wheel,
And let the lover's endless pains surcease
(Juno forgets old wrath, and grants
him ease);

---

[1] Reading *iners cadat* for *mers cadæ*, the meaning seems to be, "Now let my hand fall lifeless"
(source unknown).

[2] Decree.   [4] Company.
[3] Carried on.   [5] Bugbears, terrors.

Hang Balthazar about Chimera's neck,
And let him there bewail his bloody love,
Repining at our joys that are above;
Let Serberine go roll the fatal stone,
And take from Sisyphus his endless
   moan;   40
False Pedringano, for his treachery,
Let him be dragged through boiling
   Acheron,
And there live, dying still in endless
   flames,

Blaspheming gods and all their holy
   names.
REVENGE. Then haste we down to meet
   thy friends and foes,
To place thy friends in ease, the rest in
   woes,
For here, though death hath [1] end their
   misery,
I'll there begin their endless tragedy.
                 Exeunt.

[1] 1623 edn. has *doth.*

ARDEN OF FEVERSHAM

The authorship of *Arden of Feversham* has been a source of much conjecture. In 1770 Edward Jacob reprinted the play with a brief preface in which, without advancing any evidence of value, he attributed it to Shakespeare. In spite of much able criticism written in support of Shakespearean authorship in the last century, this view is now discredited. Boas, as editor of Kyd's works, holds that the author was an imitator of Kyd, rather than Kyd himself, as Fleay had argued many years earlier. Kyd's claim is supported, however, by Charles Crawford in his *Collectanea* and by H. Dugdale Sykes in his *Sidelights on Shakespeare*. Sykes gives the following recapitulation of his evidence: "The play echoes the phrasing not only of Kyd's earlier dramas, but of his later work as well. It uses his vocabulary and exhibits the characteristic features of his diction even to the least conspicuous of his mannerisms. It was written by a dramatist, who like Kyd, had a technical knowledge of legal documents and legal procedure. It deals with just such a crime as he had chosen for the subject of a prose tract [*The Murder of John Brewen*]. Like *Soliman and Perseda* it borrows from Marlowe's *Edward II*. Like *The Spanish Tragedy* and *Soliman and Perseda* it shows the influence of Seneca and of Garnier. Like them it was published anonymously by Edward White. It is with some confidence that I submit that there is here conclusive proof that it is Kyd's play." Though able scholars have accepted this argument, the case for Kyd is very doubtful. Sykes's impressionistic method of determining authorship has been shown to be fallacious in similar cases. Here the argument from diction is especially questionable, first, because he does not confine himself to Kyd's one authentic original play, *The Spanish Tragedy*, for comparison, but speaks of *Arden of Feversham* as echoing Kyd's "earlier dramas" and "later work"; and, second, because there was extensive borrowing of effective phrases and devices in plays around 1590.

The play is founded on an actual murder committed in 1551, a murder so notorious that Holinshed almost a generation later gave a lengthy account of it in his *Chronicles*. The dramatist apparently used the chronicle, but he may have been acquainted with other accounts or even with local legends. Significant variations from Holinshed are the addition of the confidant Franklin, the omission of Arden's winking at his wife's infidelity, and the use of a fog to frustrate the plans of Shakebag and Will. The free use of chronicle material around 1592, especially for tragedy, may have influenced the selection of this story for dramatization. The author handles it realistically, presenting, as he claims in the epilogue, "a naked tragedy" without embellishments of style. Perhaps the fact that the story deals with characters of the middle and lower classes, rather than with kings and nobles common in tragedy drawn from romance and history, led the author to avoid the pomp and rhetoric prevailing in the tragedy of the period. *Arden of Feversham* is the first extant example of the domestic tragedy, and one of the best. The success of the play, with its dramatic force and its vivid impressions of moods and places, probably had much to do with the vogue of the type.

The play was entered in the Stationers' Register on April 3, 1592, and was printed anonymously for Edward White later in the same year. Other editions appeared in 1599 and 1633. The present text is based on Farmer's reproduction of the quarto of 1592 in *Tudor Facsimile Texts* and on Tucker Brooke's reprint in his *Shakespeare Apocrypha*.

THE LAMENTABLE AND TRUE TRAGEDY OF M[ASTER] ARDEN OF FEVERSHAM IN KENT[1]

[DRAMATIS PERSONÆ

LORD CHEINY.
THOMAS ARDEN, *a gentleman of Feversham.*
FRANKLIN, *his friend.*
MICHAEL, *Arden's servant.*
MOSBIE, *lover of Arden's wife.*
MAYOR OF FEVERSHAM.
ADAM FOWLE, *landlord of the Flower-de-Luce.*
CLARKE, *a painter.*
GREENE, *a tenant.*

BRADSHAW, *a goldsmith.*
DICK REEDE, *a sailor.*
BLACK WILL } *murderers.*
SHAKEBAG }

ALICE, *Arden's wife.*
SUSAN, *Mosbie's sister.*

ATTENDANTS OF LORD CHEINY, THE WATCH, A SAILOR, A PRENTICE, A FERRYMAN.

SCENE: *Feversham, London, and the surrounding country.*

TIME: *1551.*]

[SCENE i.

Before and in Arden's house.]

Enter Arden and Franklin.

FRANK. Arden, cheer up thy spirits, and droop no more!
My gracious lord, the Duke of Somerset,
Hath freely given to thee and to thy heirs,
By letters patents from his majesty,
All the lands of the Abbey of Feversham.
Here are the deeds, sealed and subscribed with his name and the king's.
[*Gives the papers.*]
Read them, and leave this melancholy mood.
ARD. Franklin, thy love prolongs my weary life;
And but for thee how odious were this life,
That shows me nothing, but torments my soul,   10
And those foul objects that offend mine eyes,
Which makes me wish that for this veil of heaven
The earth hung over my head and covered me!
Love letters passed twixt Mosbie and my wife,
And they have privy meetings in the town.
Nay, on his finger did I spy the ring
Which at our marriage day the priest put on.
Can any grief be half so great as this?
FRANK. Comfort thyself, sweet friend. It is not strange   19
That women will be false and wavering.
ARD. Ay, but to dote on such a one as he
Is monstrous, Franklin, and intolerable.
FRANK. Why, what is he?
ARD. A botcher,[2] and no better at the first

---

[1] The title continues: "Who Was Most Wickedly Murdered by the Means of His Disloyal and Wanton Wife, Who for the Love She Bare to One Mosbie Hired Two Desperate Ruffians, Black Will and Shakebag, to Kill Him. Wherein Is Showed the Great Malice and Dissimulation of a Wicked Woman, the Unsatiable Desire of Filthy Lust, and the Shameful End of All Murderers."

[2] A patcher of old clothes, a tailor.

477

Who, by base brokage getting some small
　stock,
Crept into service of a nobleman,
And by his servile flattery and fawning
Is now become the steward of his house,
And bravely jets it [1] in his silken gown.

FRANK. No nobleman will count'nance
　such a peasant.　　　　　　　　　30

ARD. Yes, the Lord Clifford, he that loves
　not me.
But through his favor let him not grow
　proud;
For, were he by the lord protector
　backed,
He should not make me to be pointed at.
I am by birth a gentleman of blood,
And that injurious ribald that attempts
To violate my dear wife's chastity
(For dear I hold her love, as dear as
　heaven)
Shall on the bed which he thinks to defile
See his dissevered joints and sinews torn,
Whilst on the planchers [2] pants his weary
　body,　　　　　　　　　　　　41
Smeared in the channels of his lustful
　blood.

FRANK. Be patient, gentle friend, and
　learn of me
To ease thy grief and save her chastity.
Entreat her fair; sweet words are fittest
　engines
To race [3] the flint walls of a woman's
　breast.
In any case be not too jealous, [4]
Nor make no question of her love to thee;
But, as securely, [5] presently [6] take horse,
And lie with me at London all this term;
For women, when they may, will not, 51
But, being kept back, straight grow out-
　rageous.

ARD. Though this abhors from [7] reason, yet
　I'll try it,
And call her forth and presently take
　leave.—How! Alice!

Here enters Alice.

ALICE. Husband, what mean you to get
　up so early?
Summer nights are short, and yet you
　rise ere day.

Had I been wake, you had not rise [8] so
　soon.

ARD. Sweet love, thou know'st that we
　two, Ovid-like,
Have often chid the morning when it gan
　to peep,
And often wished that dark Night's pur-
　blind steeds　　　　　　　　　60
Would pull her by the purple mantle
　back,
And cast her in the ocean to her love.
But this night, sweet Alice, thou hast
　killed my heart:
I heard thee call on Mosbie in thy sleep.

ALICE. 'Tis like I was asleep when I named
　him,
For, being awake, he comes not in my
　thoughts.

ARD. Ay, but you started up and suddenly,
Instead of him, caught me about the
　neck.

ALICE. Instead of him? Why, who was
　there but you?　　　　　　　　69
And where but one is, how can I mistake?

FRANK. Arden, leave [9] to urge her overfar.

ARD. Nay, love, there is no credit in a
　dream;
Let it suffice I know thou lovest me well.

ALICE. Now I remember whereupon it
　came:
Had we no talk of Mosbie yesternight?

FRANK. Mistress Alice, I heard you name
　him once or twice.

ALICE. And thereof came it, and therefore
　blame not me.

ARD. I know it did, and therefore let it
　pass.
I must to London, sweet Alice, presently.

ALICE. But, tell me, do you mean to stay
　there long?　　　　　　　　　80

ARD. No longer there till my affairs be
　done.

FRANK. He will not stay above a month at
　most.

ALICE. A month? Ay me! Sweet Arden,
　come again
Within a day or two, or else I die.

ARD. I cannot long be from thee, gentle
　Alice.
Whilst Michael fetch our horses from the
　field,
Franklin and I will down unto the quay,

---

[1] Struts.
[2] Planks, wooden floor.
[3] Raze.
[4] Common form for *jealous*
[5] As if unsuspicious.
[6] Immediately.
[7] Is at variance with.

[8] An old form of the past participle.
[9] Cease.

For I have certain goods there to unload.
Meanwhile prepare our breakfast, gentle
  Alice,
For yet ere noon we'll take horse and
  away. 90
     Exeunt Arden and Franklin.
ALICE. Ere noon he means to take horse
  and away!
Sweet news is this. O, that some airy
  spirit
Would in the shape and likeness of a
  horse
Gallop with Arden cross the ocean,
And throw him from his back into the
  waves!
Sweet Mosbie is the man that hath my
  heart,
And he usurps it, having naught but this,
That I am tied to him by marriage.
Love is a god, and marriage is but words;
And therefore Mosbie's title is the best.
Tush! whether it be or no, he shall be
  mine, 101
In spite of him, of Hymen, and of rites.

Here enters Adam of the Flower-de-Luce.

And here comes Adam of the Flower-de-
  Luce.
I hope he brings me tidings of my love.—
How now, Adam, what is the news with
  you?
Be not afraid; my husband is now from
  home.
ADAM. He whom you wot [1] of, Mosbie,
  Mistress Alice,
Is come to town, and sends you word by
  me
In any case you may not visit him.
ALICE. Not visit him? 110
ADAM. No, nor take no knowledge of his
  being here.
ALICE. But, tell me, is he angry or dis-
  pleased?
ADAM. Should seem so, for he is wondrous
  sad.
ALICE. Were he as mad as raving Hercules,
  I'll see him, I; and, were thy house of
  force, [2]
These hands of mine should race it to
  the ground,
Unless that thou wouldst bring me to
  my love.

ADAM. Nay, and [3] you be so impatient, I'll
  be gone.
ALICE. Stay, Adam, stay; thou wert wont
  to be my friend.
Ask Mosbie how I have incurred his
  wrath; 120
Bear him from me these pair of silver
  dice,
With which we played for kisses many a
  time,
And, when I lost, I won, and so did he
(Such winning and such losing Jove send
  me!);
And bid him, if his love do not decline,
[To] [4] come this morning but along my
  door,
And as a stranger but salute me there.
This may he do without suspect [5] or fear.
ADAM. I'll tell him what you say, and so
  farewell. *Exit Adam.*
ALICE. Do, and one day I'll make amends
  for all.— 130
I know he loves me well, but dares not
  come,
Because my husband is so jealous,
And these my marrow [6]-prying neigh-
  bors' blab
Hinder our meetings, when we would
  confer.
But, if I live, that block shall be removed,
And, Mosbie, thou that comes to me by
  stealth
Shalt neither fear the biting speech of
  men
Nor Arden's looks. As surely shall he die
As I abhor him and love only thee.

Here enters Michael.

How now, Michael, whither are you go-
  ing? 140
MICH. To fetch my master's nag.
I hope you'll think on me.
ALICE. Ay; but, Michael, see you keep
  your oath,
And be as secret as you are resolute.
MICH. I'll see he shall not live above a
  week.
ALICE. On that condition, Michael, here is
  my hand;
None shall have Mosbie's sister but thy-
  self.

[1] Know.   [2] Fortified.
[3] If.   [4] Added in 1633 edn.
[5] Suspicion.   [6] Later quartos have *narrow*.

MICH. I understand the painter here hard
    by
Hath made report that he and Sue is
    sure.[1]
ALICE. There's no such matter, Michael;
    believe it not.   150
MICH. But he hath sent a dagger sticking
    in a heart,
With a verse or two stolen from a painted
    cloth,[2]
The which I hear the wench keeps in her
    chest.
Well, let her keep it! I shall find a fellow
That can both write and read and make
    rime too.
And if I do—well, I say no more.
I'll send from London such a taunting
    letter
As [3] [she] [4] shall eat the heart he sent
    with salt
And fling the dagger at the painter's
    head.
ALICE. What needs all this? I say that
    Susan's thine.   160
MICH. Why, then I say that I will kill
    my master,
Or anything that you will have me do.
ALICE. But, Michael, see you do it cun-
    ningly.
MICH. Why, say I should be took, I'll
    ne'er confess
That you know anything; and Susan,
    being a maid,
May beg me from the gallows of the
    shrieve.[5]
ALICE. Trust not to that, Michael.
MICH. You cannot tell me; I have seen
    it, I.
But, mistress, tell her, whether I live or
    die,
I'll make her more worth than twenty
    painters can,   170
For I will rid mine elder brother away,
And then the farm of Bolton is mine
    own.
Who would not venture upon house and
    land,
When he may have it for a right-down [6]
    blow?

[1] Betrothed.   [3] That.
[2] Hangings for a room.   [4] Supplied by Delius.
[5] Sheriff. "It was a popular belief that an
offer of marriage from a virgin might save a
criminal from the gallows" (Oliphant).
[6] Downright.

Here enters Mosbie.

ALICE. Yonder comes Mosbie! Michael,
    get thee gone,
And let not him nor any know thy drifts.[7]
             Exit Michael.
Mosbie, my love!
MOS. Away, I say, and talk not to me
    now!
ALICE. A word or two, sweetheart, and
    then I will.
'Tis yet but early days; [8] thou needest
    not fear.   180
MOS. Where is your husband?
ALICE. 'Tis now high water, and he is at
    the quay.
MOS. There let him be; henceforward
    know me not.
ALICE. Is this the end of all thy solemn
    oaths?
Is this the fruit thy reconcilement buds?
Have I for this given thee so many favors,
Incurred my husband's hate, and, out
    alas,
Made shipwrack of mine honor for thy
    sake?
And dost thou say, "Henceforward know
    me not"?
Remember, when I locked thee in my
    closet,[9]   190
What were thy words and mine. Did
    we not both
Decree to murder Arden in the night?
The heavens can witness, and the world
    can tell,
Before I saw that falsehood look of thine,
Fore I was tangled with thy ticing [10]
    speech,
Arden to me was dearer than my soul—
And shall be still. Base peasant, get thee
    gone,
And boast not of thy conquest over me,
Gotten by witchcraft and mere [11] sorcery!
For what hast thou to countenance [12] my
    love,   200
Being descended of a noble house,
And matched already with a gentleman
Whose servant thou mayst be? And so
    farewell.
MOS. Ungentle and unkind Alice, now I see
That which I ever feared, and find too
    true:

[7] Plots.   [10] Enticing.
[8] Early in the day.   [11] Absolute.
[9] Private chamber.   [12] Be in keeping with.

A woman's love is as the lightning-
flame,
Which even in bursting forth consumes
itself.
To try thy constancy have I been
strange.
Would I had never tried, but lived in
hope!
ALICE. What needs thou try me whom
thou never found false?   210
Mos. Yet pardon me, for love is jealous.
ALICE. So list [1] the sailor to the mermaid's
song;
So looks the traveler to the basilisk.
I am content for to be reconciled,
And that, I know, will be mine over-
throw.
Mos. Thine overthrow? First let the world
dissolve.
ALICE. Nay, Mosbie, let me still enjoy
thy love,
And, happen what will, I am resolute.
My saving husband hoards up bags of
gold   219
To make our children rich, and now is he
Gone to unload the goods that shall be
thine,
And he and Franklin will to London
straight.
Mos. To London, Alice? If thou'lt be
ruled by me,
We'll make him sure enough for coming
there.
ALICE. Ah, would we could!
Mos. I happened on a painter yesternight,
The only cunning man of Christendom,
For he can temper poison with his oil,
That whoso looks upon the work he
draws
Shall, with the beams that issue from
his [2] sight,   230
Suck venom to his breast and slay him-
self.
Sweet Alice, he shall draw thy counter-
feit,
That Arden may, by gazing on it, perish.
ALICE. Ay, but, Mosbie, that is dangerous,
For thou, or I, or any other else,
Coming into the chamber where it hangs,
may die.
Mos. Ay, but we'll have it covered with a
cloth
And hung up in the study for himself.

[1] Listens.   [2] Its.

ALICE. It may not be, for, when the pic-
ture's drawn,   239
Arden, I know, will come and show it me.
Mos. Fear not; we'll have that shall serve
the turn.   [*They cross the stage.*]
This is the painter's house; I'll call him
forth.
ALICE. But, Mosbie, I'll have no such pic-
ture, I.
Mos. I pray thee leave it to my discretion.
How, Clarke!

Here enters Clarke.

O, you are an honest man of your word;
you served me well.
CLARKE. Why, sir, I'll do it for you at
any time,
Provided, as you have given your word,
I may have Susan Mosbie to my wife.
For, as sharp-witted poets, whose sweet
verse
Make heavenly gods break off their nec-
tar draughts   250
And lay their ears down to the lowly
earth,
Use humble promise to their sacred muse,
So we that are the poets' favorites
Must have a love. Ay, Love is the
painter's muse,
That makes him frame a speaking coun-
tenance,
A weeping eye that witnesses heart's
grief.
Then tell me, Master Mosbie, shall I
have her?
ALICE. 'Tis pity but he should; he'll use
her well.
Mos. Clarke, here's my hand; my sister
shall be thine.
CLARKE. Then, brother, to requite this
courtesy,   260
You shall command my life, my skill,
and all.
ALICE. Ah, that thou couldst be secret!
Mos. Fear him not. Leave; I have talked
sufficient.
CLARKE. You know not me that ask such
questions.
Let it suffice I know you love him well,
And fain would have your husband made
away;
Wherein, trust me, you show a noble
mind.

That rather than you'll live with him
you hate,
You'll venture life, and die with him
you love.
The like will I do for my Susan's sake. 270
ALICE. Yet nothing could enforce me to
the deed
But Mosbie's love. Might I without
control
Enjoy thee still, then Arden should not
die;
But, seeing I cannot, therefore let him
die.
Mos. Enough, sweet Alice; thy kind words
makes me melt.
Your trick of poisoned pictures we dis-
like;
Some other poison would do better far.
ALICE. Ay, such as might be put into his
broth,
And yet in taste not to be found at all.
CLARKE. I know your mind, and here I
have it for you. 280
Put but a dram of this into his drink,
Or any kind of broth that he shall eat,
And he shall die within an hour after.
ALICE. As I am a gentlewoman, Clarke,
next day
Thou and Susan shall be marriéd.
Mos. And I'll make her dowry more than
I'll talk of, Clarke.
CLARKE. Yonder's your husband. Mosbie,
I'll be gone.

Here enters Arden and Franklin.

ALICE. In good time [1] see where my hus-
band comes.
Master Mosbie, ask him the question
yourself. *Exit Clarke.*
Mos. Master Arden, being at London yes-
ternight, 290
The Abbey lands, whereof you are now
possessed,
Were offered me on some occasion
By Greene, one of Sir Antony Ager's men.
I pray you, sir, tell me, are not the lands
yours?
Hath any other interest herein?
ARD. Mosbie, that question we'll decide
anon.
Alice, make ready my breakfast; I must
hence. *Exit Alice.*

[1] At the right moment.

As for the lands, Mosbie, they are mine
By letters patents from his majesty. 299
But I must have a mandate for my wife;
They say you seek to rob me of her love.
Villain, what makes thou in her com-
pany?
She's no companion for so base a groom.
Mos. Arden, I thought not on her; I came
to thee;
But rather than I pocket up this wrong—
FRANK. [*Interposing.*] What will you do,
sir?
Mos. Revenge it on the proudest of you
both.
Then Arden draws forth Mosbie's sword.
ARD. So, sirrah. You may not wear a
sword—
The statute makes against artificers. [2]
I warrand that I do. [3] Now use your bod-
kin, 310
Your Spanish needle, and your pressing
iron,
For this shall go with me. And mark my
words—
You goodman botcher, 'tis to you I
speak—
The next time that I take thee near my
house,
Instead of legs I'll make thee crawl on
stumps.
Mos. Ah, Master Arden, you have injured
me;
I do appeal to God and to the world.
FRANK. Why, canst thou deny thou wert
a botcher once?
Mos. Measure me what I am, not what I
was.
ARD. Why, what art thou now but a velvet
drudge, 320
A cheating steward, and base-minded
peasant?
Mos. Arden, now thou hast belched and
vomited
The rancorous venom of thy misswoln
heart,
Hear me but speak. As I intend to live
With God and his elected saints in
heaven,
I never meant more to solicit her;
And that she knows, and all the world
shall see.

[2] Provides against the wearing of swords by
handicraftsmen.
[3] I have warrant for what I do.

I loved her once—sweet Arden, pardon
    me.
I could not choose; her beauty fired my
    heart!
But time hath quenched these over-
    raging coals;   330
And, Arden, though I now frequent thy
    house,
'Tis for my sister's sake, her waiting-
    maid,
And not for hers. Mayest thou enjoy
    her long!
Hell-fire and wrathful vengeance light
    on me,
If I dishonor her or injure thee.
ARD. Mosbie, with these thy protestations
    The deadly hatred of my heart is ap-
    peased,
    And thou and I'll be friends, if this prove
    true.
    As for the base terms I gave thee late,
    Forget them, Mosbie; I had cause to
    speak,   340
    When all the knights and gentlemen of
    Kent
    Make common table talk of her and thee.
MOS. Who lives that is not touched with
    slanderous tongues?
FRANK. Then, Mosbie, to eschew the
    speech of men,
    Upon whose general bruit [1] all honor
    hangs,
    Forbear his house.
ARD. Forbear it! Nay, rather frequent it
    more.
    The world shall see that I distrust her
    not.
    To warn him on the sudden from my
    house
    Were to confirm the rumor that is
    grown.   350
MOS. By my faith, sir,[2] you say true,
    And therefore will I sojourn here awhile,
    Until our enemies have talked their fill;
    And then, I hope, they'll cease, and at
    last confess
    How causeless they have injured her and
    me.
    [*They pass to a room on the inner stage.*]
ARD. And I will lie at London all this term
    To let them see how light I weigh their
    words.

[1] Report.
[2] All early edns. read *By faith, my sir.*

Here enters Alice.

ALICE. Husband, sit down; your breakfast
    will be cold.
ARD. Come, M[aster] Mosbie, will you sit
    with us?
MOS. I cannot eat, but I'll sit for com-
    pany.   360
ARD. Sirrah Michael, see our horse be
    ready.
ALICE. Husband, why pause ye? Why eat
    you not?
ARD. I am not well. There's something
    in this broth
    That is not wholesome. Didst thou make
    it, Alice?
ALICE. I did, and that's the cause it likes
    not you.
Then she throws down the broth on the ground.
    There's nothing that I do can please your
    taste.
    You were best to say I would have poi-
    soned you.
    I cannot speak or cast aside my eye,
    But he imagines I have stepped awry.
    Here's he that you cast in my teeth so
    oft;   370
    Now will I be convinced or purge myself.
    I charge thee speak to this mistrustful
    man,
    Thou that wouldst see me hang, thou,
    Mosbie, thou.
    What favor hast thou had more than a
    kiss
    At coming or departing from the town?
MOS. You wrong yourself and me to cast
    these doubts;
    Your loving husband is not jealous.
ARD. Why, gentle Mistress Alice, cannot
    I be ill
    But you'll accuse yourself?—
    Franklin, thou hast a box of mithri-
    date;   380
    I'll take a little to prevent the worst.
FRANK. Do so, and let us presently take
    horse;
    My life for yours, ye shall do well enough.
ALICE. Give me a spoon; I'll eat of it my-
    self.
    Would it were full of poison to the brim,
    Then should my cares and troubles have
    an end!
    Was ever silly [3] woman so tormented?

[3] Simple.

ARD. Be patient, sweet love; I mistrust
    not thee.
ALICE. God will revenge it, Arden, if thou
    dost;
    For never woman loved her husband
    better than I do thee.   390
ARD. I know it, sweet Alice. Cease to
    complain,
    Lest that in tears I answer thee again.
FRANK. Come, leave this dallying, and let
    us away.
ALICE. Forbear to wound me with that
    bitter word;
    Arden shall go to London in my arms.
ARD. Loath am I to depart, yet I must go.
ALICE. Wilt thou to London, then, and
    leave me here?
    Ah, if thou love me, gentle Arden, stay.
    Yet, if thy business be of great im-
    port,   399
    Go, if thou wilt; I'll bear it as I may.
    But write from London to me every week,
    Nay, every day, and stay no longer there
    Than thou must needs, lest that I die for
    sorrow.
ARD. I'll write unto thee every other tide.
    And so farewell, sweet Alice, till we meet
    next.
ALICE. Farewell, husband, seeing you'll
    have it so;
    And, M[aster] Franklin, seeing you take
    him hence,
    In hope you'll hasten him home, I'll give
    you this.   *And then she kisseth him.*
FRANK. And if he stay, the fault shall not
    be mine.
    Mosbie, farewell, and see you keep your
    oath.   410
MOS. I hope he is not jealous of me now.
ARD. No, Mosbie, no; hereafter think of
    me
    As of your dearest friend, and so farewell.
    Exeunt Arden, Franklin, and Michael.
ALICE. I am glad he is gone; he was about
    to stay,
    But did you mark me then how I brake
    off?
MOS. Ay, Alice, and it was cunningly per-
    formed.
    But what a villain is that painter Clarke!
ALICE. Was it not a goodly poison that he
    gave?
    Why, he's as well now as he was be-
    fore.   419

It should have been some fine confection
That might have given the broth some
    dainty taste.
This powder was too gross and populous.[1]
MOS. But, had he eaten but three spoon-
    fuls more,
    Then had he died and our love continued.
ALICE. Why, so it shall, Mosbie, albeit he
    live.
MOS. It is unpossible, for I have sworn
    Never hereafter to solicit thee,
    Or, whilst he lives, once more importune
    thee.
ALICE. Thou shalt not need; I will impor-
    tune thee.
    What? Shall an oath make thee forsake
    my love?   430
    As if I have not sworn as much myself
    And given my hand unto him in the
    church!
    Tush, Mosbie; oaths are words, and
    words is wind,
    And wind is mutable. Then, I conclude,
    'Tis childishness to stand upon an oath.
MOS. Well proved, Mistress Alice; yet by
    your leave
    I'll keep mine unbroken whilst he lives.
ALICE. Ay, do, and spare not; his time is
    but short;
    For, if thou beest as resolute as I,
    We'll have him murdered as he walks the
    streets.   440
    In London, many alehouse ruffians keep,[2]
    Which, as I hear, will murther men for
    gold.
    They shall be soundly feed to pay him
    home.

Here enters Greene.

MOS. Alice, what's he that comes yonder?
    Knowest thou him?
ALICE. Mosbie, begone! I hope 'tis one
    that comes
    To put in practice our intended drifts.
                            Exit Mosbie.
GREENE. Mistress Arden, you are well
    met.
    I am sorry that your husband is from
    home,
    Whenas[3] my purposed journey was to
    him;   449
    Yet all my labor is not spent in vain,

[1] Thick.   [2] Lodge.   [3] Since.

For I suppose that you can full dis-
    course
And flat resolve [1] me of the thing I
    seek.
ALICE. What is it, Master Greene? If that
    I may
Or can with safety, I will answer you.
GREENE. I heard your husband had the
    grant of late,
Confirmed by letters patents from the
    king,
Of all the lands of the Abbey of Fever-
    sham,
Generally intitled, [2] so that all former
    grants
Are cut off, whereof I myself had one;
But now my interest by that is void. 460
This is all, Mistress Arden. Is it true
    or no? [3]
ALICE. True, Master Greene; the lands
    are his in state, [4]
And whatsoever leases were before
Are void for term of Master Arden's life.
He hath the grant under the chancery
    seal.
GREENE. Pardon me, Mistress Arden, I
    must speak,
For I am touched. Your husband doth
    me wrong
To wring me from the little land I have.
My living is my life; only that
Resteth remainder of my portion. 470
Desire of wealth is endless in his mind,
And he is greedy-gaping still [5] for gain;
Nor cares he though young gentlemen do
    beg,
So he may scrape and hoard up in his
    pouch.
But, seeing he hath taken my lands, I'll
    value life
As careless as he is careful for to get;
And tell him this from me, I'll be re-
    venged,
And so as he shall wish the Abbey lands
Had rested still within their former
    state. 479
ALICE. Alas, poor gentleman, I pity you,
And woe is me that any man should
    want!
God knows 'tis not my fault. But wonder
    not

Though he be hard to others, when to
    me—
Ah, Master Greene, God knows how I
    am used!
GREENE. Why, Mistress Arden, can the
    crabbéd churl
Use you unkindly? Respects he not your
    birth,
Your honorable friends, nor what you
    brought?
Why, all Kent knows your parentage and
    what you are.
ALICE. Ah, M[aster] Greene, be it spoken
    in secret here, 489
I never live good day with him alone.
When he is at home, then have I froward
    looks,
Hard words, and blows to mend the
    match withal;
And, though I might content as good a
    man,
Yet doth he keep in every corner trulls;
And, weary with his trugs [6] at home,
Then rides he straight to London; there,
    forsooth,
He revels it among such filthy ones
As counsels him to make away his wife.
Thus live I daily in continual fear,
In sorrow, so despairing of redress 500
As every day I wish with hearty prayer
That he or I were taken forth the world.
GREENE. Now trust me, Mistress Alice, it
    grieveth me
So fair a creature should be so abused.
Why, who would have thought the civil
    sir so sullen?
He looks so smoothly. Now, fie upon
    him, churl!
And, if he live a day, he lives too long.
But frolic, woman! I shall be the man
Shall set you free from all this discon-
    tent;
And, if the churl deny my interest 510
And will not yield my lease into my hand,
I'll pay him home, whatever hap to
    me.
ALICE. But speak you as you think?
GREENE. Ay, God's my witness, I mean
    plain dealing,
For I had rather die than lose my land.
ALICE. Then, Master Greene, be coun-
    seléd by me.
Endanger not yourself for such a churl,

---

[1] Completely satisfy.   [2] Deeded.
[3] From 1599 edn. Original has *nor*.
[4] By law.   [5] Always.
[6] Wenches.

But hire some cutter [1] for to cut him
    short,
And here's ten pound to wager them
    withal.
When he is dead, you shall have twenty
    more,   520
And the lands whereof my husband is
    possessed
Shall be intitled as they were before.
GREENE. Will you keep promise with me?
ALICE. Or count me false and perjured
    whilst I live.
GREENE. Then here's my hand; I'll have
    him so despatched.
I'll up to London straight; I'll thither
    post,
And never rest till I have compassed it.
Till then farewell.
ALICE. Good fortune follow all your for-
    ward thoughts,   529
                    Exit Greene.
And whosoever doth attempt the deed,
A happy hand I wish, and so farewell.—
All this goes well. Mosbie, I long for
    thee
To let thee know all that I have con-
    trived.

      Here enters Mosbie and Clarke.

MOS. How now, Alice, what's the news?
ALICE. Such as will content thee well,
    sweetheart.
MOS. Well, let them pass awhile, and tell
    me, Alice,
How have you dealt and tempered with [2]
    my sister?
What, will she have my neighbor, Clarke,
    or no?
ALICE. What, M[aster] Mosbie! Let him
    woo himself!
Think you that maids look not for fair
    words?   540
Go to her, Clarke; she's all alone within.
Michael, my man, is clean out of her
    books.
CLARKE. I thank you, Mistress Arden. I
    will in;
And, if fair Susan and I can make a
    gree,[3]
You shall command me to the uttermost,
As far as either goods or life may stretch.
                    Exit Clarke.

MOS. Now, Alice, let's hear thy news.
ALICE. They be so good that I must laugh
    for joy
Before I can begin to tell my tale.
MOS. Let's hear them, that I may laugh
    for company.   550
ALICE. This morning, M[aster] Greene—
    Dick Greene, I mean,
From whom my husband had the Abbey
    land—
Came hither, railing, for to know the
    truth
Whether my husband had the lands by
    grant.
I told him all, whereat he stormed amain
And swore he would cry quittance with [4]
    the churl,
And, if he did deny his interest,
Stab him, whatsoever did befall himself.
Whenas [5] I saw his choler thus to rise,
I whetted on the gentleman with words;
And, to conclude, Mosbie, at last we
    grew   561
To composition [6] for my husband's death.
I gave him ten pound to hire knaves,
By some device to make away the churl;
When he is dead, he should have twenty
    more
And repossess his former lands again.
On this we greed, and he is ridden
    straight
To London to bring his death about.
MOS. But call you this good news?
ALICE. Ay, sweetheart, be they not?   570
MOS. 'Twere cheerful news to hear the
    churl were dead;
But trust me, Alice, I take it passing ill
You would be so forgetful of our state
To make recount of it to every groom.
What! to acquaint each stranger with our
    drifts,
Chiefly in case of murther, why, 'tis the
    way
To make it open unto Arden's self
And bring thyself and me to ruin both.
Forewarned, forearmed; who threats his
    enemy,
Lends him a sword to guard himself
    withal.   580
ALICE. I did it for the best.
MOS. Well, seeing 'tis done, cheerly [7] let
    it pass.

---

[1] Cutthroat.   [3] Reach an agreement.
[2] Worked upon.

[4] Be even with.   [5] When.
[6] Agreement.   [7] Cheerfully.

You know this Greene; is he not re-
  ligious? [1]
A man, I guess, of great devotion?
ALICE. He is.
Mos. Then, sweet Alice, let it pass; I
  have a drift
Will quiet all, whatever is amiss.

Here enters Clarke and Susan.

ALICE. How now, Clarke?   Have you
  found me false?
Did I not plead the matter hard for you?
CLARKE. You did.   590
Mos. And what? Wilt be a match?
CLARKE. A match, i' faith, sir; ay, the
  day is mine.
  The painter lays his colors to the life;
  His pencil draws no shadows in his love.
  Susan is mine.
ALICE. You make her blush.
Mos. What, sister, is it Clarke must be
  the man?
Sus. It resteth in your grant. Some words
  are passed,
  And happily [2] we be grown unto a match,
  If you be willing that it shall be so. 600
Mos. Ah, Master Clarke, it resteth at my
  grant;
  You see my sister's yet at my dispose.
  But, so you'll grant me one thing I shall
  ask,
  I am content my sister shall be yours.
CLARKE. What is it, M[aster] Mosbie?
Mos. I do remember once in secret talk
  You told me how you could compound
  by art
  A crucifix impoisoned,
  That whoso look upon it should wax
  blind
  And with the scent be stifled, that ere
  long   610
  He should die poisoned that did view it
  well.
  I would have you make me such a
  crucifix,
  And then I'll grant my sister shall be
  yours.
CLARKE. Though I am loath, because it
  toucheth life,
  Yet, rather or I'll leave sweet Susan's
  love,
  I'll do it, and with all the haste I may.
  But for whom is it?

[1] Conscientious.   [2] Haply, perchance.

ALICE. Leave that to us. Why, Clarke, is
  it possible
  That you should paint and draw it out
  yourself,   619
  The colors being baleful and impoisoned,
  And no ways prejudice [3] yourself withal?
Mos. Well   questioned,   Alice.—Clarke,
  how answer you that? [4]
CLARKE. Very easily: I'll tell you straight
  How I do work of these impoisoned drugs.
  I fasten on my spectacles so close
  As nothing can any way offend my sight;
  Then, as I put a leaf within my nose,
  So put I rhubarb to avoid the smell,
  And softly as another work I paint.
Mos. 'Tis very well. But against when
  shall I have it?   630
CLARKE. Within this ten days.
Mos.   'Twill serve the turn.
  Now, Alice, let's in and see what cheer
  you keep.
  I hope, now M[aster] Arden is from home,
  You'll give me leave to play your hus-
  band's part.
ALICE. Mosbie, you know, who's master
  of my heart,
  He well may be the master of the house.
                                  E[x]eunt.

[SCENE ii.

The road between Feversham and London.]

Here enters Greene and Bradshaw.

BRAD. See you them that comes yonder,
  M[aster] Greene?
GREENE. Ay, very well. Do you know
  them?

Here enters Black Will and Shakebag.

BRAD. The one I know not, but he seems a
  knave,
  Chiefly for bearing the other company;
  For such a slave, so vile a rogue as he,
  Lives not again upon the earth.
  Black Will is his name. I tell you,
  M[aster] Greene,
  At Boulogne he and I were fellow soldiers,
  Where he played such pranks
  As all the camp feared him for his
  villainy.   10
  I warrant you he bears so bad a mind
  That for a crown he'll murther any man.

[3] Endanger.
[4] Here and in a few later passages the line
divisions have been regularized.

GREENE. The fitter is he for my purpose, marry!

WILL. How now, fellow Bradshaw? Whither away so early?

BRAD. O Will, times are changed. No fellows now,
Though we were once together in the field;
Yet thy friend to do thee any good I can.

WILL.[1] Why, Bradshaw, was not thou and I fellow soldiers at Boulogne, [20 where I was a corporal, and thou but a base mercenary groom? No fellows now, because you are a goldsmith and have a little plate in your shop! You were glad to call me "fellow Will," and with a cursy[2] to the earth, "One snatch, good corporal," when I stole the half ox from John the victualer, and domineered[3] with it amongst good fellows in one night. 29

BRAD. Ay, Will, those days are past with me.

WILL. Ay, but they be not past with me, for I keep that same honorable mind still. Good neighbor Bradshaw, you are too proud to be my fellow, but, were it not that I see more company coming down the hill, I would be fellows with you once more, and share crowns with you too. But let that pass, and tell me whither you go. 40

BRAD. To London, Will, about a piece of service
Wherein happily thou mayst pleasure me.

WILL. What is it?

BRAD. Of late Lord Cheiny lost some plate,
Which one did bring and sold it at my shop,
Saying he served Sir Antony Cooke.
A search was made, the plate was found with me,
And I am bound to answer at the size.[4]
Now, Lord Cheiny solemnly vows,
If law will serve him, he'll hang me for his plate. 50
Now I am going to London upon hope
To find the fellow. Now, Will, I know
Thou art acquainted with such companions.

WILL. What manner of man was he?

BRAD. A lean-faced, writhen[5] knave,
Hawk-nosed and very hollow-eyed,
With mighty furrows in his stormy brows;
Long hair down his shoulders curled;
His chin was bare, but on his upper lip
A mutchado,[6] which he wound about his ear. 60

WILL. What apparel had he?

BRAD. A watchet[7] satin doublet all-to[8] torn
(The inner side did bear the greater show),
A pair of threadbare velvet hose, seam-rent,
A worsted stocking rent above the shoe,
A livery cloak, but all the lace was off;
'Twas bad, but yet it served to hide the plate.

WILL. Sirrah Shakebag, canst thou remember since we trolled the bowl[9] at Sittingburgh, where I broke the tap- [70 ster's head of the Lion with a cudgel-stick?

SHAKE. Ay, very well, Will.

WILL. Why, it was with the money that the plate was sold for. Sirrah Bradshaw, what wilt thou give him that can tell thee who sold thy plate?

BRAD. Who, I pray thee, good Will?

WILL. Why, 'twas one Jack Fitten. He's now in Newgate for stealing a horse, and shall be arraigned the next size. 80

BRAD. Why, then let Lord Cheiny seek Jack Fitten forth,
For I'll back and tell him who robbed him of his plate.
This cheers my heart. M[aster] Greene, I'll leave you,
For I must to the Isle of Sheppy with speed.

GREENE. Before you go, let me entreat you
To carry this letter to Mistress Arden of Feversham
And humbly recommend me to herself.

BRAD. That will I, M[aster] Greene, and so farewell.—
Here, Will, there's a crown for thy good news.   Exit Bradshaw.

WILL. Farewell, Bradshaw; I'll [90

---

[1] The passages printed as prose throughout the play are printed as rough verse in the original (with the exception of the letters).

[2] Curtsey.
[3] Lived like a lord, feasted.
[4] Assizes.

[5] Twisted.
[6] Mustache.
[7] Pale blue.
[8] Completely
[9] Passed the drinking cup.

drink no water for thy sake whilst this lasts.
—Now, gentleman, shall we have your company to London?

GREENE. Nay, stay, sirs.

A little more I needs must use your help,
And in a matter of great consequence,
Wherein if you'll be secret and profound,
I'll give you twenty angels for your pains.

WILL. How? Twenty angels? Give my fellow George Shakebag and me twenty [100 angels, and, if thou'lt have thy own father slain, that thou mayst inherit his land, we'll kill him.

SHAKE. Ay, thy mother, thy sister, thy brother, or all thy kin.

GREENE. Well, this it is: Arden of Feversham
Hath highly wronged me about the Abbey land,
That no revenge but death will serve the turn.
Will you two kill him? Here's the angels down,
And I will lay the platform [1] of his death.   110

WILL. Plat me no platforms. Give me the money, and I'll stab him as he stands pissing against a wall, but I'll kill him.

SHAKE. Where is he?

GREENE. He is now at London, in Aldersgate Street.

SHAKE. He's dead as if he had been condemned by an act of parliament, if once Black Will and I swear his death.

GREENE. Here is ten pound, and, [120 when he is dead, ye shall have twenty more.

WILL. My fingers itches to be at the peasant. Ah, that I might be set awork thus through the year, and that murther would grow to an occupation, that a man might, without danger of law—Zounds, I warrant I should be warden of the company! Come, let us be going, and we'll bait [2] at Rochester, where I'll give thee a gallon of sack to hansel [3] the match withal.   *Exeunt.* 131

[SCENE iii.

A street near St. Paul's, London.]

Here enters Michael.

MICH. I have gotten such a letter as will touch the painter; and thus it is:

[1] Plan.   [2] Stop to feed.   [3] Confirm.

Here enters Arden and Franklin and hears
Michael read this letter.

"My duty remembered, Mistress Susan, hoping in God you be in good health, as I Michael was at the making hereof. This is to certify you that as the turtle [4] true, when she hath lost her mate, sitteth alone, so I, mourning for your absence, do walk up and down Paul's till one day I fell asleep and lost my master's pantofles. [5] [10 Ah, Mistress Susan, abolish that paltry painter, cut him off by the shins with a frowning look of your crabbed countenance, and think upon Michael, who, drunk with the dregs of your favor, will cleave as fast to your love as a plaster of pitch to a galled horseback. Thus hoping you will let my passions penetrate, or rather impetrate [6] mercy of your meek hands, I end.   20
    Yours,
        MICHAEL, or else not MICHAEL."

ARD. Why, you paltry knave,
Stand you here loitering, knowing my affairs,
What haste my business craves to send to Kent?

FRANK. Faith, friend Michael, this is very ill,
Knowing your master hath no more but you,
And do ye slack his business for your own?

ARD. Where is the letter, sirrah? Let me see it.   *Then he gives him the letter.*
See, Master Franklin, here's proper stuff: 30
Susan my maid, the painter, and my man,
A crew of harlots, [7] all in love, forsooth.
Sirrah, let me hear no more of this.
Now for thy life once write to her a word!

Here enters Greene, Will, and Shakebag.

Wilt thou be married to so base a trull?
'Tis Mosbie's sister. Come I once at home,
I'll rouse her from remaining in my house.

[4] Turtledove.   [6] Obtain by entreaty.
[5] Slippers.   [7] Worthless persons of either sex.

Now, M[aster] Franklin, let us go walk in Paul's;
Come but a turn or two, and then away.
Exeunt [Arden, Franklin, and Michael].
GREENE. The first is Arden, and that's his man;   40
The other is Franklin, Arden's dearest friend.
WILL. Zounds, I'll kill them all three.
GREENE. Nay, sirs, touch not his man in any case;
But stand close, and take you fittest standing,
And, at his coming forth, speed [1] him.
To the Nag's Head; there is this coward's haunt.
But now I'll leave you till the deed be done.   *Exit Greene.*
SHAKE. If he be not paid his own, ne'er trust Shakebag.
WILL. Sirrah Shakebag, at his coming forth
I'll run him through, and then to the Blackfriars,   50
And there take water and away.
SHAKE. Why, that's the best; but see thou miss him not.
WILL. How can I miss him, when I think on the forty angels I must have more?

Here enters a Prentice.

PREN. [*Aside.*] 'Tis very late; I were best shut up my stall,
For here will be old filching, [2] when the press
Comes forth of Paul's.
Then lets he down his window, and it breaks Black Will's head.
WILL. Zounds, draw, Shakebag, draw! I am almost killed.   60
PREN. We'll tame you, I warrant.
WILL. Zounds, I am tame enough already.

Here enters Arden, Fran[klin], and Michael.

ARD. What troublesome fray or mutiny is this?
FRANK. 'Tis nothing but some brabbling paltry fray,
Devised to pick men's pockets in the throng.

[1] Despatch.   [2] Abundant stealing.

ARD. Is't nothing else? Come, Franklin, let us away.   *Exeunt.*
WILL. What mends [3] shall I have for my broken head?
PREN. Marry, this mends: that, if you get you not away all the sooner, you [70 shall be well beaten and sent to the Counter. [4]   *Exit Prentice.*
WILL. Well, I'll be gone, but look to your signs, for I'll pull them down all. Shakebag, my broken head grieves me not so much as by this means Arden hath escaped.

Here enters Greene.

I had a glimpse of him and his companion.   79
GREENE. Why, sirs, Arden's as well as I. I met him and Franklin going merrily to the ordinary. What, dare you not do it?
WILL. Yes, sir, we dare do it; but, were my consent to give again, we would not do it under ten pound more. I value every drop of my blood at a French crown. I have had ten pound to steal a dog, and we have no more here to kill a man. But [89 that a bargain is a bargain, and so forth, you should do it yourself.
GREENE. I pray thee, how came thy head broke?
WILL. Why, thou seest it is broke, dost thou not?
SHAKE. Standing against a stall, watching Arden's coming, a boy let down his shop window and broke his head, whereupon arose a brawl, and in the tumult Arden escaped us and passed by un- [100 thought on. But forbearance is no acquittance; another time we'll do it, I warrant thee.
GREENE. I pray thee, Will, make clean thy bloody brow,
And let us bethink us on some other place
Where Arden may be met with handsomely.
Remember how devoutly thou hast sworn
To kill the villain; think upon thine oath.
WILL. Tush, I have broken five hundred oaths!

[3] Amends.   [4] A London prison.

But wouldst thou charm me to effect
  this deed, 110
Tell me of gold, my resolution's fee;
Say thou seest Mosbie kneeling at my
  knees,
Off'ring me service for my high attempt,
And sweet Alice Arden, with a lap of
  crowns,
Comes with a lowly cursy to the earth,
Saying, "Take this but for thy quarter-
  age;[1]
Such yearly tribute will I answer [2] thee."
Why, this would steel soft-mettled cow-
  ardice,
With which Black Will was never tainted
  with.
I tell thee, Greene, the forlorn trav-
  eler 120
Whose lips are glued with summer's
  parching heat
Ne'er longed so much to see a running
  brook
As I to finish Arden's tragedy.
Seest thou this gore that cleaveth to
  my face?
From hence ne'er will I wash this bloody
  stain,
Till Arden's heart be panting in my hand.
GREENE. Why, that's well said; but what
  saith Shakebag?
SHAKE. I cannot paint my valor out with
  words;
But, give me place and opportunity,
Such mercy as the starven lioness, 130
When she is dry-sucked of her eager
  young,
Shows to the prey that next encounters
  her,
On Arden so much pity would I take.
GREENE. So should it fare with men of
  firm resolve.
And now, sirs, seeing this accident
Of meeting him in Paul's hath no suc-
  cess,
Let us bethink us on some other place
Whose earth may swallow up this Ar-
  den's blood.

     Here enters Michael.

See, yonder comes his man. And wot
  you what?
The foolish knave is in love with Mosbie's sister, 140

[1] Quarterly payment.   [2] Render.

And for her sake, whose love he cannot
  get
Unless Mosbie solicit his suit,
The villain hath sworn the slaughter
  of his master.
We'll question him, for he may stead [3]
  us much.—
How now, Michael, whither are you
  going?
MICH. My master hath new supped,
And I am going to prepare his chamber.
GREENE. Where supped M[aster] Arden?
MICH. At the Nag's Head, at the
eighteenpence ordinary. How now, [150
M[aster] Shakebag? What, Black Will!
God's dear Lady, how chance your face is
so bloody?
WILL. Go to, sirrah, there is a chance
in it; this sauciness in you will make you
be knocked.
MICH. Nay, and you be offended, I'll be
  gone.
GREENE. Stay, Michael; you may not
  scape us so.
Michael, I know you love your m[aster]
  well.
MICH. Why, so I do; but wherefore urge
  you that? 160
GREENE. Because I think you love your
  mistress better.
[MICH.] So think not I; but say, i' faith,
  what if I should?
SHAKE. Come to the purpose, Michael;
  we hear
You have a pretty love in Feversham.
MICH. Why, have I two or three, what's
  that to thee?
WILL. You deal too mildly with the
  peasant. Thus it is:
'Tis known to us you love Mosbie's
  sister;
We know besides that you have ta'en
  your oath
To further Mosbie to your mistress'
  bed,
And kill your m[aster] for his sister's
  sake. 170
Now, sir, a poorer coward than yourself
Was never fostered in the coast of Kent.
How comes it then that such a knave as
  you
Dare swear a matter of such conse-
  quence?

[3] Help.

GREENE. Ah, Will—

WILL. Tush, give me leave; there's no more but this:

Sith [1] thou hast sworn, we dare discover all;

And, hadst thou or shouldst thou utter it,

We have devised a complat [2] under hand,

Whatever shall betide to any of us, 180

To send thee roundly to the devil of hell.

And therefore thus: I am the very man,

Marked in my birth hour by the destinies,

To give an end to Arden's life on earth;

Thou but a member [3] but to whet the knife

Whose edge must search the closet of his breast.

Thy office is but to appoint the place,

And train thy m[aster] to his tragedy;

Mine to perform it when occasion serves. 189

Then be not nice,[4] but here devise with us

How and what way we may conclude his death.

SHAKE. So shalt thou purchase Mosbie for thy friend,

And by his friendship gain his sister's love.

GREENE. So shall thy mistress be thy favorer,

And thou disburdened of the oath thou made.

MICH. Well, gentlemen, I cannot but confess,

Sith you have urged me so apparently,

That I have vowed my M[aster] Arden's death;

And he whose kindly love and liberal hand

Doth challenge naught but good deserts of me, 200

I will deliver over to your hands.

This night come to his house at Aldersgate;

The doors I'll leave unlocked against [5] you come.

No sooner shall ye enter through the latch,

Over the threshold to the inner court,

But on your left hand shall you see the stairs

That leads directly to my m[aster's] chamber.

There take him and dispose him as ye please.

Now it were good we parted company. 209

What I have promiséd, I will perform.

WILL. Should you deceive us, 'twould go wrong with you.

MICH. I will accomplish all I have revealed.

WILL. Come, let's go drink; choler makes me as dry as a dog.

Exeunt Will, Gre[ene], and Shak[ebag].
    Manet [6] Michael.

MICH. Thus feeds the lamb securely on the down,

Whilst through the thicket of an arbor brake

The hunger-bitten wolf o'erpries [7] his haunt

And takes advantage to eat him up.

Ah, harmless Arden, how, how hast thou misdone,

That thus thy gentle life is leveled at?

The many good turns that thou hast done to me, 220

Now must I quittance [8] with betraying thee.

I, that should take the weapon in my hand

And buckler thee from ill-intending foes,

Do lead thee with a wicked, fraudful smile,

As unsuspected, to the slaughterhouse.

So have I sworn to Mosbie and my mistress;

So have I promised to the slaughtermen;

And, should I not deal currently [9] with them,

Their lawless rage would take revenge on me.

Tush, I will spurn at mercy for this once. 230

Let pity lodge where feeble women lie;

I am resolved, and Arden needs must die. *Exit Michael.*

---

[1] Since.   [3] Helper.
[2] Complot, plan. [4] Squeamish.
[5] In expectation of the time when.

[6] Remains.   [8] Requite.
[7] Looks over.   [9] Genuinely, honestly.

[Scene iv.

A room in Franklin's house at Aldersgate.]

Here enters Arden and Fran[klin].

Ard. No, Franklin, no. If fear or stormy
      threats,
  If love of me or care of womanhood,
  If fear of God or common speech of men,
  Who mangle credit with their wounding
      words,
  And couch dishonor as dishonor buds,
  Might join repentance in her wanton
      thoughts,
  No question then but she would turn the
      leaf
  And sorrow for her dissolution.[1]
  But she is rooted in her wickedness,
  Perverse and stubborn, not to be re-
      claimed;   10
  Good counsel is to her as rain to weeds,
  And reprehension makes her vice to grow
  As Hydra's head that flourished[2] by
      decay.
  Her faults, methink, are painted in my
      face,
  For every searching eye to overread;
  And Mosbie's name, a scandal unto mine,
  Is deeply trenchéd in my blushing brow.
  Ah, Franklin, Franklin, when I think on
      this,
  My heart's grief rends my other powers
  Worse than the conflict at the hour of
      death.   20
Frank. Gentle Arden, leave this sad la-
      ment.
  She will amend, and so your griefs will
      cease;
  Or else she'll die, and so your sorrows
      end.
  If neither of these two do happily fall,
  Yet let your comfort be that others bear
  Your woes, twice doubled all, with pa-
      tience.
Ard. My house is irksome; there I cannot
      rest.
Frank. Then stay with me in London; go
      not home.
Ard. Then that base Mosbie doth usurp
      my room
  And makes his triumph of my being
      thence.   30

[1] Degeneration.
[2] Suggested by Delius; early edns. read *perished.*

At home or not at home, where'er I be,
Here, here it lies [*Points to his heart.*], ah,
    Franklin, here it lies
That will not out till wretched Arden
    dies.

Here enters Michael.

Frank. Forget your griefs awhile. Here
      comes your man.
Ard. What a-clock is 't, sirrah?
Mich. Almost ten.
Ard. See, see, how runs away the weary
      time!
  Come, M[aster] Franklin, shall we go to
      bed?
Exeunt Arden and Michael. Manet Franklin.
Frank. I pray you, go before; I'll follow
      you.—
  Ah, what a hell is fretful jealousy!   40
  What pity-moaning[3] words, what deep-
      fetched sighs,
  What grievous groans and overlading
      woes
  Accompanies this gentle gentleman!
  Now will he shake his care-oppresséd
      head,
  Then fix his sad eyes on the sullen
      earth,
  Ashamed to gaze upon the open world.
  Now will he cast his eyes up towards the
      heavens,
  Looking that ways for redress of wrong;
  Sometimes he seeketh to beguile his grief
  And tells a story with his careful[4]
      tongue;   50
  Then comes his wife's dishonor in his
      thoughts
  And in the middle cutteth off his tale,
  Pouring fresh sorrow on his weary limbs.
  So woebegone, so inly charged with woe,
  Was never any lived and bare it so.

Here enters Michael.

Mich. My m[aster] would desire you come
      to bed.
Frank. Is he himself already in his bed?
      Exit Fran[klin]. Manet Mic[hael].
Mich. He is, and fain would have the light
      away.—
  Conflicting thoughts, encampéd in my
      breast,

[3] In the original *moning*, possibly a misprint
for *mouing* (*i.e., moving*).   [4] Full of care.

Awake me with the echo of their
  strokes,   60
And I, a judge to censure either side,
Can give to neither wishéd victory.
My master's kindness pleads to me for life
With just demand, and I must grant it
  him;
My mistress she hath forced me with an
  oath,
For Susan's sake, the which I may not
  break,
For that is nearer than a master's love.
That grim-faced fellow, pitiless Black
  Will,
And Shakebag, stern in bloody strata-
  gem—
Two rougher ruffians never lived in
  Kent—   70
Have sworn my death, if I infringe my
  vow,
A dreadful thing to be considered of.
Methinks I see them with their bol-
  stered [1] hair,
Staring and grinning in thy gentle face,
And in their ruthless hands their daggers
  drawn,
Insulting o'er thee [2] with a peck of oaths,
Whilst thou, submissive, pleading for
  relief,
Art mangled by their ireful instruments.
Methinks I hear them ask where Michael
  is,
And pitiless Black Will cries, "Stab the
  slave!   80
The peasant will detect the tragedy!"
The wrinkles in his foul death-threat'ning
  face
Gapes open wide, like graves to swallow
  men.
My death to him is but a merriment,
And he will murther me to make him
  sport.
He comes, he comes!   Ah, M[aster]
  Franklin, help!
Call up the neighbors, or we are but dead!

Here enters Fran[klin] and Arden.

FRANK. What dismal outcry calls me from
  my rest?
ARD. What hath occasioned such a fearful
  cry?   89
Speak, Michael! Hath any injured thee?

[1] Disheveled.
[2] From 1633 edn. Original reads *there*.

MICH. Nothing, sir; but, as I fell asleep,
Upon the threshold leaning to the stairs,
I had a fearful dream that troubled me,
And in my slumber thought I was beset
With murtherer thieves that came to
  rifle me.
My trembling joints witness my inward
  fear.
I crave your pardons for disturbing you.
ARD. So great a cry for nothing I ne'er
  heard.
What? Are the doors fast locked and all
  things safe?
MICH. I cannot tell; I think I locked the
  doors.   100
ARD. I like not this, but I'll go see my-
  self.—   [*He tries the doors.*]
Ne'er trust me but the doors were all un-
  locked.
This negligence not half contenteth me.
Get you to bed, and, if you love my favor,
Let me have no more such pranks as
  these.
Come, M[aster] Franklin, let us go to bed.
FRANK. Ay, by my faith; the air is very
  cold.—
Michael, farewell; I pray thee dream no
  more.   *Exeunt.*

[SCENE v.

Before Franklin's house.]

Here enters Will, Gre[ene], and Shak[ebag]. [3]

SHAKE. Black night hath hid the pleasures
  of the day,
And sheeting darkness overhangs the
  earth,
And with the black fold of her cloudy
  robe
Obscures [4] us from the eyesight of the
  world,
In which sweet silence such as we tri-
  umph.
The lazy minutes linger on their time,
Loath to give due audit to the hour,
Till in the watch [5] our purpose be com-
  plete
And Arden sent to everlasting night.
Greene, get you gone, and linger here
  about,   10

[3] The stage direction follows l. 1 in the
original.
[4] From 1633 edn. Earlier edns. read *obscure*.
[5] Time division of the night.

And at some hour hence come to us
  again,
Where we will give you instance [1] of his
  death.
GREENE. Speed to my wish, whose will so-
  e'er says no; [2]
And so I'll leave you for an hour or two.
                  Exit Gre[ene].
WILL. I tell thee, Shakebag, would this
  thing were done.
I am so heavy that I can scarce go;
This drowsiness in me bodes little good.
SHAKE. How now, Will? Become a Preci-
  sian? [3]
Nay, then let's go sleep, when bugs [4] and
  fears
Shall kill our courages with their fancy's
  work.   20
WILL. Why, Shakebag, thou mistakes me
  much,
And wrongs me too in telling me of fear.
Were 't not a serious thing we go about,
It should be slipped [5] till I had fought
  with thee,
To let thee know I am no coward, I.
I tell thee, Shakebag, thou abusest me.
SHAKE. Why, thy speech bewrayed an
  inly kind of fear,
And savored of a weak, relenting spirit.
Go forward now in that we have begun,
And afterwards attempt [6] me when thou
  darest.   30
WILL. And, if I do not, heaven cut me
  off!
But let that pass, and show me to this
  house,
Where thou shalt see I'll do as much as
  Shakebag.
SHAKE. This is the door; but, soft, me-
  thinks 'tis shut.
The villain Michael hath deceivéd us.
WILL. Soft, let me see, Shakebag; 'tis shut
  indeed.
Knock with thy sword; perhaps the slave
  will hear.
SHAKE. It will not be. The white-livered
  peasant is gone to bed,
And laughs us both to scorn.
WILL. And he shall buy his merriment as
  dear   40

As ever coistrel [7] bought so little sport.
Ne'er let this sword assist me when I
  need,
But rust and canker after I have sworn,
If I, the next time that I meet the hind,
Lop not away his leg, his arm, or both.
SHAKE. And let me never draw a sword
  again,
Nor prosper in the twilight, cockshut
  light, [8]
When I would fleece the wealthy pas-
  senger, [9]
But lie and languish in a loathsome den.
Hated and spit at by the goers-by,   50
And in that death may die unpitiéd,
If I, the next time that I meet the slave,
Cut not the nose from off the coward's
  face
And trample on it for this villainy.
WILL. Come, let's go seek out Greene. I
  know he'll swear.
SHAKE. He were a villain, and [10] he would
  not swear.
'Twould make a peasant swear amongst
  his boys,
That ne'er durst say before but "yea"
  and "no,"
To be thus flouted of a coisterel.
WILL. Shakebag, let's seek out Greene, and
  in the morning   60
At the alehouse butting [11] Arden's house
Watch the outcoming of that prick-
  eared cur,
And then let me alone to handle him.
                      Exeunt.

[SCENE vi.

A room in Franklin's house.]

Here enters Ard[en], Fra[nklin], and Michael.

ARD. Sirrah, get you back to Billens-
  gate [12]
And learn what time the tide will serve
  our turn;
Come to us in Paul's. First go make the
  bed,
And afterwards go hearken for the flood. [13]
                  Exit Michael.
Come, M[aster] Franklin, you shall go
  with me.

---

[1] Evidence.
[2] *I.e.*, no matter who wills the contrary.
[3] Puritan.   [5] Let go, put aside.
[4] Bugaboos.   [6] Make trial of, attack.

[7] Varlet.
[8] Time when woodcocks (*i.e.*, gulls) are caught.
[9] Passer-by. [11] Abutting on. [12] Billingsgate.
[10] If.   [13] Flood tide.

This night I dreamed that, being in a park,
A toil [1] was pitched to overthrow the deer,
And I upon a little rising hill
Stood whistly [2] watching for the herd's approach.
Even there, methoughts, a gentle slumber took me, 10
And summoned all my parts to sweet repose;
But in the pleasure of this golden rest
An ill-thewed foster [3] had removed the toil
And rounded me with that beguiling home [4]
Which late, methought, was pitched to cast [5] the deer.
With that he blew an evil-sounding horn,
And at the noise another herdman came,
With fauchon [6] drawn, and bent it at my breast,
Crying aloud, "Thou art the game we seek!"
With this I waked and trembled every joint, 20
Like one obscuréd in a little bush,
That sees a lion foraging about,
And, when the dreadful forest-king is gone,
He pries about with timorous suspect
Throughout the thorny casements of the brake,
And will not think his person dangerless,
But quakes and shewers,[7] though the cause be gone.
So, trust me, Franklin, when I did awake,
I stood in doubt whether I waked or no—
Such great impression took [8] this fond [9] surprise. 30
God grant this vision bedeem [10] me any good.
FRANK. This fantasy doth rise from Michael's fear,
Who being awakéd with the noise he made,
His troubled senses yet could take no rest;
And this, I warrant you, procured your dream.

[1] Net.
[2] Silently.　　　　[3] Unmannerly forester.
[4] Surrounded me completely with that snare.
[5] Throw.　　　　[8] Gave.
[6] Falchion, sword.　[9] Foolishly credulous.
[7] Shivers.　　　　[10] Forebode (').

ARD. It may be so; God frame it to the best.
But oftentimes my dreams presage too true.
FRANK. To such as note their nightly fantasies,
Some one in twenty may incur belief.
But use it not: [11] 'tis but a mockery. 40
ARD. Come, M[aster] Franklin, we'll now walk in Paul's
And dine together at the ordinary,
And by my man's direction draw to the quay,
And with the tide go down to Feversham.
Say, M[aster] Franklin, shall it not be so?
FRANK. At your good pleasure, sir;
I'll bear you company.　　　　Exeunt.

[SCENE vii.

A street in Aldersgate.]

Here enters Michael at one door. Here enters Greene, Will, and Shakebag at another door.

WILL. Draw, Shakebag, for here's that villain Michael.
GREENE. First, Will, let's hear what he can say.
WILL. Speak, milksop slave, and never after speak!
MICH. For God's sake, sirs, let me excuse myself!
For here I swear, by heaven and earth and all,
I did perform the outmost [12] of my task,
And left the doors unbolted and unlocked.
But see the chance: Franklin and my master
Were very late conferring in the porch,
And Franklin left his napkin [13] where he sat 10
With certain gold knit in it, as he said.
Being in bed, he did bethink himself,
And coming down he found the doors unshut.
He locked the gates, and brought away the keys,
For which offense my master rated me.
But now I am going to see what flood it is,

[11] Do not make a practice of it.
[12] Utmost.　　　　[13] Handkerchief.

For with the tide my m[aster] will away,
Where you may front [1] him well on
  Rainham Down,
A place well fitting such a stratagem.

WILL. Your excuse hath somewhat molli-
  fied my choler.   20
  Why now, Greene, 'tis better now nor [2]
  e'er it was.

GREENE. But, Michael, is this true?

MICH. As true as I report it to be true.

SHAKE. Then, Michael, this shall be your
  penance:
To feast us all at the Salutation,
Where we will plat [3] our purpose
  throughly.

GREENE. And, Michael, you shall bear no
  news of this tide,
Because [4] they two may be in Rainham
  Down
Before your m[aster].

MICH. Why, I'll agree to anything you'll
  have me,   30
So you will except of my company. [5]
                                    Exeunt.

[SCENE viii.

A room in Arden's house at Feversham.]

Here enters Mosbie.

MOS. Disturbéd thoughts drives me from
  company
And dries my marrow with their watch-
  fulness;
Continual trouble of my moody brain
Feebles my body by excess of drink,
And nips me as the bitter northeast
  wind
Doth check the tender blossoms in the
  spring.
Well fares the man, howe'er his cates [6] do
  taste,
That tables not with foul suspicion;
And he but pines amongst his delicates,
Whose troubled mind is stuffed with dis-
  content.   10
My golden time was when I had no
  gold.
Though [7] then I wanted, yet I slept
  secure;
My daily toil begat me night's repose,

My night's repose made daylight fresh
  to me.
But, since I climbed the top bough of the
  tree
And sought to build my nest among the
  clouds,
Each gentle, stary [8] gale doth shake my
  bed,
And makes me dread my downfall to the
  earth.
But whither doth contemplation carry
  me?
The way I seek to find, where pleasure
  dwells,   20
Is hedged behind me that I cannot
  back,
But needs must on, although to danger's
  gate.
Then, Arden, perish thou by that decree;
For Greene doth ear [9] the land and weed
  thee up
To make my harvest nothing but pure
  corn.
And for his pains I'll heave him up
  awhile,
And after smother him to have his
  wax—
Such bees as Greene must never live to
  sting.
Then is there Michael and the painter
  too,
Chief actors to Arden's overthrow,   30
Who, when they shall see me sit in
  Arden's seat,
They will insult upon me for my meed, [10]
Or fright me by detecting [11] of his end.
I'll none of that, for I can cast a bone
To make these curs pluck out each
  other's throat,
And then am I sole ruler of mine own.
Yet Mistress Arden lives; but she's my-
  self,
And holy church rites makes us two but
  one.
But what for that? I may not trust you,
  Alice.
You have supplanted Arden for my
  sake,   40
And will extirpen [12] me to plant another.
'Tis fearful sleeping in a serpent's bed,
And I will cleanly rid my hands of her.

---

[1] From 1633 edn.; original reads *frons.*
[2] Than.   [3] Plot.   [4] In order that.
[5] Excuse me from accompanying you.
[6] Dainties.   [7] Original reads *thought.*

[8] Stirry (?); stirring (?).   [11] Betraying.
[9] Plow.   [12] Extirpate.
[10] Assail me for my bribe (?).

Here enters Alice.

But here she comes, and I must flatter
her.—
How now, Alice? What, sad and pas-
sionate? [1]
Make me partaker of thy pensiveness;
Fire divided burns with lesser force.
ALICE. But I will dam that fire in my
breast
Till by the force thereof my part con-
sume. Ah, Mosbie!
Mos. Such deep pathaires,[2] like to a can-
non's burst   50
Discharged against a ruinated wall,
Breaks my relenting heart in thousand
pieces.
Ungentle Alice, thy sorrow is my sore;
Thou know'st it well, and 'tis thy policy
To forge distressful looks to wound a
breast
Where lies a heart that dies where thou
art sad.
It is not love that loves to anger love.
ALICE. It is not love that loves to murther
love.
Mos. How mean you that?
ALICE. Thou knowest how dearly Arden
lovéd me.   60
Mos. And then?
ALICE. And then—conceal the rest, for
'tis too bad,
Lest that my words be carried with the
wind,
And published in the world to both our
shames.
I pray thee, Mosbie, let our springtime
wither;
Our harvest else will yield but loathsome
weeds.
Forget, I pray thee, what hath passed
betwix us,
For now I blush and tremble at the
thoughts!
Mos. What, are you changed?
ALICE. Ay, to my former happy life
again,   70
From title of an odious strumpet's name
To honest Arden's wife, not Arden's
honest [3] wife.
Ha, Mosbie, 'tis thou hast rifled me of
that
And made me sland[e]rous to all my kin;

[1] Full of emotion.   [2] Sighs (?).   [3] Chaste

Even in my forehead is thy name en-
graven,
A mean artificer, that low-born name.
I was bewitched; woe worth the hapless
hour
And all the causes that enchanted me!
Mos. Nay, if thou ban,[4] let me breathe
curses forth,
And, if you stand so nicely [5] at your
fame,   80
Let me repent the credit I have lost.
I have neglected matters of import
That would have stated [6] me above thy
state,
Forslowed [7] advantages, and spurned at
time;
Ay, Fortune's right hand Mosbie hath
forsook
To take a wanton giglot [8] by the left.
I left the marriage of an honest maid,
Whose dowry would have weighed down
all thy wealth,
Whose beauty and demeanor far ex-
ceeded thee—
This certain good I lost for changing
bad,   90
And wrapped my credit in thy company.
I was bewitched—that is no theme of
thine!—
And thou unhallowed hast enchanted me.
But I will break thy spells and exorcisms,
And put another sight upon these eyes
That showed my heart a raven for a
dow.[9]
Thou art not fair—I viewed thee not till
now;
Thou art not kind—till now I knew thee
not.
And now the rain hath beaten off thy
gilt,
Thy worthless copper shows thee coun-
terfeit.   100
It grieves me not to see how foul thou
art,
But mads me that ever I thought thee
fair.
Go, get thee gone, a copesmate [10] for thy
hinds;
I am too good to be thy favorite.
ALICE. Ay, now I see, and too soon find it
true,

[4] Curse.   [7] Delayed.   [10] Companion.
[5] Fastidiously.   [8] Wench.
[6] Placed.   [9] Dove.

Which often hath been told me by my
    friends,
That Mosbie loves me not but for my
    wealth,
Which, too incredulous, I ne'er believed.
Nay, hear me speak, Mosbie, a word or
    two;   109
I'll bite my tongue if it speak bitterly.
Look on me, Mosbie, or I'll kill myself;
Nothing shall hide me from thy stormy
    look.
If thou cry war, there is no peace for me.
I will do penance for offending thee,
And burn this prayer book, where I here
    use
The holy word that had converted me.
See, Mosbie, I will tear away the leaves,
And all the leaves, and in this golden
    cover
Shall thy sweet phrases and thy letters
    dwell;
And thereon will I chiefly meditate, 120
And hold no other sect but such devotion.
Wilt thou not look? Is all thy love over-
    whelmed?
Wilt thou not hear? What malice stops
    thine ears?
Why speaks thou not? What silence ties
    thy tongue?
Thou hast been sighted [1] as the eagle is,
And heard [2] as quickly as the fearful hare,
And spoke [3] as smoothly as an orator,
When I have bid thee hear or see or
    speak,
And art thou sensible in none of these?
Weigh all thy good turns with this little
    fault,   130
And I deserve not Mosbie's muddy looks.
A fence of trouble is not thickened still. [4]
Be clear again; I'll ne'er more trouble
    thee.
Mos. O, no, I am a base artificer;
My wings are feathered for a lowly flight.
Mosbie? Fie! No, not for a thousand
    pound.
Make love to you? Why, 'tis unpardon-
    able;
We beggars must not breathe where
    gentles are.

[1] Endowed with sight.
[2] Endowed with hearing.
[3] Endowed with speech.
[4] Meaning not certain. The sense seems to be:
"A troubled pool is not always turbid."

ALICE. Sweet Mosbie is as gentle as a king,
And I too blind to judge him otherwise.
Flowers do sometimes spring in fallow
    lands,   141
Weeds in gardens, roses grow on thorns;
So, whatsoe'er my Mosbie's father was,
Himself [is] [5] valued gentle by his worth.
Mos. Ah, how you women can insinuate,
And clear a trespass with your sweet-set
    tongue!
I will forget this quarrel, gentle Alice,
Provided I'll be tempted so no more.

Here enters Bradshaw.

ALICE. Then with thy lips seal up this
    new-made match.   149
Mos. Soft, Alice, for here comes somebody.
ALICE. How now, Bradshaw, what's the
    news with you?
BRAD. I have little news, but here's a letter
That M[aster] Greene importuned me to
    give you.
ALICE. Go in, Bradshaw; call for a cup of
    beer.   *Exit [Bradshaw].*
'Tis almost supper time; thou shalt stay
    with us.
              Then she reads the letter.
"We have missed of our purpose at Lon-
don, but shall perform it by the way. We
thank our neighbor Bradshaw.
        Yours,
           RICHARD GREENE." 160
How likes my love the tenor of this letter?
Mos. Well, were his date complete and
    expired!
ALICE. Ah, would it were! Then comes
    my happy hour;
Till then my bliss is mixed with bitter
    gall.
Come, let us in to shun suspicion.
Mos. [6] Ay, to the gates of death to follow
    thee.   *Exeunt.*

[SCENE ix.

The country near Rochester.]

Here enters Greene, Will, and Shakebag.

SHAKE. Come, Will, see thy tools be in a
    readiness!
Is not thy powder dank, or will thy flint
    strike fire?

[5] Supplied by Jacob.
[6] From 1633 edn. Original has *Alice.*

WILL. Then ask me if my nose be on my
  face,
Or whether my tongue be frozen in my
  mouth.
Zounds, here's a coil! [1]
You were best swear me on the interga-
  tories [2]
How many pistols I have took in hand,
Or whether I love the smell of gun-
  powder,
Or dare abide the noise the dag [3] will
  make,
Or will not wink at flashing of the fire. 10
I pray thee, Shakebag, let this answer
  thee,
That I have took more purses in this
  down
Than e'er thou handledst pistols in thy
  life.
SHAKE. Ay, happily thou hast picked more
  in a throng;
But, should I brag what booties I have
  took,
I think the overplus that's more than
  thine
Would mount to a greater sum of money
Than either thou or all thy kin are worth.
Zounds, I hate them (as I hate a toad)
That carry a muscado [4] in their tongue,
And scarce a hurting weapon in their
  hand. 21
WILL. O Greene, intolerable!
It is not for mine honor to bear this.
Why, Shakebag, I did serve the king at
  Boulogne,
And thou canst brag of nothing that
  thou hast done.
SHAKE. Why, so can Jack of Feversham,
That sounded [5] for a fillip on the nose,
When he that gave it him holloed in his
  ear,
And he supposed a cannon-bullet hit him.
  Then they fight.
GREENE. I pray you, sirs, list to Æsop's
  talk: 30
Whilst two stout dogs were striving for a
  bone,
There comes a cur and stole it from
  them both;
So, while you stand striving on these
  terms of manhood,
Arden escapes us, and deceive[s] us all.

SHAKE. Why, he begun.
WILL.   And thou shalt find I'll end;
I do but slip it until better time.
But, if I do forget—
Then he kneels down and holds up his hands
                                to heaven.
GREENE. Well, take your fittest standings,
  and once more
Lime your twigs to catch this weary [6]
  bird.   39
I'll leave you, and at your dags' discharge
Make towards, like the longing water dog
That coucheth till the fowling piece be
  off,
Then seizeth on the prey with eager
  mood.
Ah, might I see him stretching forth his
  limbs,
As I have seen them beat their wings ere
  now!
SHAKE. Why, that thou shalt see, if he
  come this way.
GREENE. Yes, that he doth, Shakebag, I'll
  warrant thee.
But brawl not when I am gone in any
  case.
But, sirs, be sure to speed him when he
  comes,
And in that hope I'll leave you for an
  hour.   *Exit Gre[ene].* 50

Here enters Arden, Fran[klin], and Mic[hael].

MICH. 'Twere best that I went back to
  Rochester.
The horse halts downright; it were not
  good
He traveled in such pain to Feversham.
Removing of a shoe may happily help it.
ARD. Well, get you back to Rochester;
  but, sirrah, see
Ye overtake us ere we come to Rainham
  Down,
For it will be very late ere we get home.
MICH. [*Aside.*] Ay, God he knows, and so
  doth Will and Shakebag,
That thou shalt never go further than
  that down;
And therefore have I pricked the horse
  on purpose,   60
Because I would not view the massacre.
                              Exit Michael.

---

[1] Bother.   [3] Pistol.   [5] Swooned.
[2] Interrogatories. [4] Musket.

[5] Troublesome, vexatious. Jacob suggests
wary.

ARD. Come, M[aster] Franklin, onwards
  with your tale.
FRANK. I assure you, sir, you task me
  much.
  A heavy blood is gathered at my heart,
  And on the sudden is my wind so short
  As hindereth the passage of my speech;
  So fierce a qualm yet ne'er assailéd me.
ARD. Come, M[aster] Franklin, let us go
  on softly.
  The annoyance of the dust or else some
  meat
  You eat [1] at dinner cannot brook [2] [with] [3]
  you.   70
  I have been often so, and soon amended.
FRANK. Do you remember where my tale
  did leave?
ARD. Ay, where the gentleman did check [4]
  his wife.
FRANK. She being reprehended for the
  fact, [5]
  Witness produced that took her with the
  deed,
  Her glove brought in which there she left
  behind,
  And many other assured arguments,
  Her husband asked her whether it were
  not so.
ARD. Her answer then? I wonder how she
  looked,
  Having forsworn it with such vehement
  oaths,   80
  And at the instant so approved [6] upon her.
FRANK. First did she cast her eyes down
  to the earth,
  Watching the drops that fell amain from
  thence;
  Then softly draws she forth her handker-
  cher,
  And modestly she wipes her tear-stained
  face;
  Then hemmed she out, to clear her voice
  should seem,
  And with a majesty addressed herself
  To encounter all their accusations.—
  Pardon me, M[aster] Arden, I can no
  more;
  This fighting at my heart makes short
  my wind.   90
ARD. Come, we are almost now at Rain-
  ham Down.

Your pretty tale beguiles the weary way;
  I would you were in state to tell it out.
SHAKE. [Aside.] Stand close, Will; I hear
  them coming.

Here enters Lord Cheiny with his Men.

WILL. [Aside.] Stand to it, Shakebag, and
  be resolute.
LORD C. Is it so near night as it seems,
  Or will this black-faced evening have a
  shower?—
  What, M[aster] Arden? You are well
  met;
  I have longed this fortnight's day to
  speak with you.
  You are a stranger, man, in the Isle of
  Sheppy.   100
ARD. Your honor's always! Bound to do
  you service!
LORD C. Come you from London, and
  ne'er a man with you?
ARD. My man's coming after, but here's
  My honest friend that came along with
  me.
LORD C. My lord protector's man I take
  you to be.
FRANK. Ay, my good lord, and highly
  bound to you.
LORD C. You and your friend come home
  and sup with me.
ARD. I beseech your honor, pardon me;
  I have made a promise to a gentleman,
  My honest friend, to meet him at my
  house.   110
  The occasion is great, or else would I
  wait on you.
LORD C. Will you come tomorrow and dine
  with me,
  And bring your honest friend along with
  you?
  I have divers matters to talk with you
  about.
ARD. Tomorrow we'll wait upon your
  honor.
LORD C. One of you stay my horse at the
  top of the hill.—
  What! Black Will? For whose purse
  wait you?
  Thou wilt be hanged in Kent, when all
  is done.
WILL. Not hanged, God save your honor;
  I am your bedesman, [7] bound to pray for
  you.   120

----

[1] Preterit.   [4] Reprove.
[2] Agree.   [5] Deed.
[3] Added in 1633 edn.   [6] Proved.

[7] One who says prayers for charity received.

LORD C. I think thou ne'er saidest prayer
in all thy life.—
One of you give him a crown.—
And, sirrah, leave this kind of life;
If thou beest tainted [1] for a penny mat-
ter,
And come in question, surely thou wilt
truss.[2]—
Come, M[aster] Arden, let us be going;
Your way and mine lies four mile to-
gether.
Exeunt. Manet Black Will and Shakebag.
WILL. The devil break all your necks at
four miles' end!
Zounds, I could kill myself for very
anger!
His lordship chops me in,[3]   130
Even when my dag was leveled at his
heart.
I would his crown were molten down his
throat.
SHAKE. Arden, thou hast wondrous holy
luck.
Did ever man escape as thou hast done?
Well, I'll discharge my pistol at the
sky,
For by this bullet Arden might not die.

Here enters Greene.

GREENE. What, is he down? Is he des-
patched?
SHAKE. Ay, in health towards Feversham,
to shame us all.
GREENE. The devil he is! Why, sirs, how
escaped he?
SHAKE. When we were ready to shoot, 140
Comes my Lord Cheiny to prevent his
death.
GREENE. The Lord of Heaven hath pre-
served him.
WILL. Preserved a fig! The L[ord] Cheiny
hath preserved him,
And bids him to a feast to his house at
Shorlow.
But by the way once more I'll meet with
him,
And, if all the Cheinies in the world say
no,
I'll have a bullet in his breast tomorrow.
Therefore come, Greene, and let us to
Feversham.

[1] Accused.   [3] Thrusts in, interrupts.
[2] Hang.

GREENE. Ay, and excuse ourselves to Mistress Arden.
O, how she'll chafe when she hears of
this!   150
SHAKE. Why, I'll warrant you she'll think
we dare not do it.
WILL. Why, then let us go, and tell her
all the matter,
And plat the news [4] to cut him off tomorrow.   *Exeunt.*

[SCENE X.

Arden's house at Feversham.]

*Here enters Arden and his Wife, Franklin,
and Michael.*

ARD. See how the hours, the guardant [5]
of heaven's gate,
Have by their toil removed the darksome
clouds,
That Sol may well discern the trampled
pace [6]
Wherein he wont to guide his golden car.
The season fits; come, Franklin, let's
away.
ALICE. I thought you did pretend some
special hunt
That made you thus cut short the time
of rest.
ARD. It was no chase that made me rise
so early,
But, as I told thee yesternight, to go
To the Isle of Sheppy,   10
There to dine with my Lord Cheiny;
For so his honor late commanded me.
ALICE. Ay, such kind husbands seldom
want excuses;
Home is a wild cat to a wandering wit.
The time hath been—would God it were
not past!—
That honor's title nor a lord's command
Could once have drawn you from these
arms of mine.
But my deserts or your desires [7] decay,
Or both; yet if true love may seem desert,
I merit still to have thy company.   20
FRANK. Why, I pray you, sir, let her go
along with us.
I am sure his honor will welcome her
And us the more for bringing her along.

[4] Plot a new means.   [6] Course, path.
[5] Guardian.
[7] Suggested by Warnke. Original reads *deserves.*

ARD. Content; sirrah, saddle your mistress' nag.

ALICE. No, begged favor merits little thanks.

If I should go, our house would run away,
Or else be stolen; therefore I'll stay behind.

ARD. Nay, see how mistaking you are!
I pray thee, go.

ALICE. No, no, not now.

ARD. Then let me leave thee satisfied in this,   30
That time nor place nor persons alter me,
But that I hold thee dearer than my life.

ALICE. That will be seen by your quick return.

ARD. And that shall be ere night, and if I live.
Farewell, sweet Alice; we mind to sup with thee.   *Exit Al[ice]*.

FRANK. Come, Michael, are our horses ready?

MICH. Ay, your horse are ready, but I am not ready, for I have lost my purse, with six-and-thirty shillings in it, with taking up of [1] my m[aster's] nag.   40

FRANK. Why, I pray you, let us go before,
Whilst he stays behind to seek his purse.

ARD. Go to, sirrah; see you follow us to the Isle of Sheppy
To my Lord Cheiny's, where we mean to dine.

Exeunt Arden and Franklin. Manet Michael.

MICH. So, fair weather after you, for before you lies Black Will and Shakebag in the broom close,[2] too close for you. They'll be your ferrymen to long home.[3]

Here enters the Painter.

But who is this? The painter, my corrival, that would needs win M[istress] [50 Susan.

CLARKE. How now, Michael? How doth my mistress and all at home?

MICH. Who? Susan Mosbie? She is your mistress too?

CLARKE. Ay, how doth she and all the rest?

MICH. All's well but Susan; she is sick.

CLARKE. Sick? Of what disease?

MICH. Of a great fear.   60

CLARKE. A fear of what?

MICH. A great fever.

CLARKE. A fever? God forbid!

MICH. Yes, faith, and of a lordaine,[4] too, as big as yourself.

CLARKE. O, Michael, the spleen prickles you. Go to; you carry an eye over Mistress Susan.

MICH. Ay, faith, to keep her from the painter.   70

CLARKE. Why more from a painter than from a serving creature like yourself?

MICH. Because you painters make but a painting-table of a pretty wench, and spoil her beauty with blotting.

CLARKE. What mean you by that?

MICH. Why, that you painters paint lambs in the lining of wenches' petticoats, and we serving-men put horns to them to make them become sheep.   80

CLARKE. Such another word will cost you a cuff or a knock.

MICH. What, with a dagger made of a pencil? Faith, 'tis too weak, and therefore thou too weak to win Susan.

CLARKE. Would Susan's love lay upon this stroke! *Then he breaks Michael's head.*

Here enters Mosbie, Greene, and Alice.

ALICE. I'll lay my life, this is for Susan's love.
Stayed you behind your m[aster] to this end?   89
Have you no other time to brabble in
But now when serious matters are in hand?—
Say, Clarke, hast thou done the thing thou promised?

CLARKE. Ay, here it is. The very touch is death!

ALICE. Then this, I hope, if all the rest do fail,
Will catch M[aster] Arden,
And make him wise in death that lived a fool.
Why should he thrust his sickle in our corn,
Or what hath he to do with thee, my love,
Or govern me that am to rule myself?

---

[1] Making gambol.
[2] Field.
[3] *I.e.*, the grave.
[4] Clown, with a play on *lurdan*, meaning "fever of idleness."

Forsooth, for credit sake, I must leave
thee!   100
Nay, he must leave to live that we may
love,
May live, may love; for what is life but
love?
And love shall last as long as life remains,
And life shall end before my love depart.
Mos. Why, what's love without true
constancy?
Like to a pillar built of many stones,
Yet neither with good mortar well com-
pact
Nor cement [1] to fasten it in the joints,
But that it shakes with every blast of
wind,
And, being touched, straight falls unto
the earth,   110
And buries all his [2] haughty pride in dust.
No, let our love be rocks of adamant,
Which time nor place nor tempest can
asunder.[3]
Greene. Mosbie, leave protestations now,
And let us bethink us what we have to do.
Black Will and Shakebag I have placed
In the broom close, watching Arden's
coming.
Let's to them and see what they have
done.   *Exeunt.*

[SCENE xi.

*The Kentish coast opposite the Isle of
Sheppy.*]

Here enters Ard[en] and Fra[nklin].

Ard. O ferryman, where art thou?

Here enters the Ferryman.

Fer. Here, here! Go before to the boat,
and I will follow you.
Arden. We have great haste; I pray
thee, come away.
Fer. Fie, what a mist is here!
Ard. This mist, my friend, is mystical,
Like to a good companion's smoky brain
That was half drowned with new ale
overnight.
Fer. 'Twere pity but his skull were [10
opened to make more chimney room.
Frank. Friend, what's thy opinion of
this mist?
Fer. I think 'tis like to a curst[4] wife in a

little house, that never leaves her husband
till she have driven him out at doors with
a wet pair of eyes. Then looks he as if his
house were afire, or some of his friends
dead.
Ard. Speaks thou this of thine own [20
experience?
Fer. Perhaps, ay; perhaps, no; for my
wife is as other women are, that is to say,
governed by the moon.
Frank. By the moon? How, I pray
thee?
Fer. Nay, thereby lies a bargain, and
you shall not have it fresh and fasting.[5]
Ard. Yes, I pray thee, good ferryman.
Fer. Then for this once. Let it be [30
midsummer moon, but yet my wife has
another moon.
Frank. Another moon?
Fer. Ay, and it hath influences and
eclipses.
Ard. Why, then, by this reckoning you
sometimes play the man in the moon?
Fer. Ay, but you had not best to meddle with that moon, lest I scratch you by
the face with my bramble bush.   40
Ard. I am almost stifled with this fog.
Come, let's away.
Frank. And, sirrah, as we go, let us have
some more of your bold yeomandry.[6]
Fer. Nay, by my troth, sir, but flat
knavery.   *Exeunt.*

[SCENE xii.

Another part of the coast.]

*Here enters Will at one door, and Shakebag
at another.*

Shake. O, Will, where art thou?
Will. Here, Shakebag, almost in hell's
mouth, where I cannot see my way for
smoke.
Shake. I pray thee, speak still that we
may meet by the sound, for I shall fall
into some ditch or other, unless my feet
see better than my eyes.
Will. Didst thou ever see better
weather to run away with another man's [10
wife, or play with a wench at potfinger?
Shake. No; this were a fine world for
chandlers if this weather would last, for

---

[1] From 1633 edn. Original reads *semell.*
[2] Its.   [3] Part.   [4] Cross, shrewish.

[5] Before eating; in your eagerness; for nothing (?).   [6] Yeoman's talk.

then a man should never dine nor sup without candlelight. But, sirrah Will, what horses are those that passed?

WILL. Why, didst thou hear any?

SHAKE. Ay, that I did.

WILL. My life for thine, 'twas Arden and his companion, and then all our [20 labor's lost.

SHAKE. Nay, say not so, for, if it be they, they may happily lose their way as we have done, and then we may chance meet with them.

WILL. Come, let us go on like a couple of blind pilgrims.

Then Shakebag falls into a ditch.

SHAKE. Help, Will, help! I am almost drowned!

Here enters the Ferryman.

FER. Who's that that calls for help? 30

WILL. 'Twas none here; 'twas thou thyself.

FER. I came to help him that called for help. Why, how now? Who is this that's in the ditch? You are well enough served to go without a guide such weather as this.

WILL. Sirrah, what companies hath passed your ferry this morning?

FER. None but a couple of gentle- [40 men, that went to dine at my Lord Cheiny's.

WILL. Shakebag, did not I tell thee as much?

FER. Why, sir, will you have any letters carried to them?

WILL. No, sir; get you gone.

FER. Did you ever see such a mist as this?

WILL. No, nor such a fool as will [50 rather be hought [1] than get his way.

FER. Why, sir, this is no Hough-Monday; [2] you are deceived.—What's his name, I pray you, sir?

SHAKE. His name is Black Will.

FER. I hope to see him one day hanged upon a hill. *Exit Ferryman.*

SHAKE. See how the sun hath cleared the foggy mist,

Now we have missed the mark of our intent.

[1] Hamstrung.
[2] Hock Monday, a festival shortly after Easter.

Here enters Greene, Mosbie, and Alice.

MOS. Black Will and Shakebag, what make [3] you here? 60

What, is the deed done? Is Arden dead?

WILL. What could a blinded man perform in arms?

Saw you not how till now the sky was dark,

That neither horse nor man could be discerned?

Yet did we hear their horses as they passed.

GREENE. Have they escaped you, then, and passed the ferry?

SHAKE. Ay, for awhile; but here we two will stay,

And at their coming back meet with them once more.

Zounds, I was ne'er so toiled [4] in all my life

In following so slight a task as this. 70

MOS. How cam'st thou so berayed? [5]

WILL. With making false footing in the dark.

He needs would follow them without a guide.

ALICE. Here's to pay for a fire and good cheer.

Get you to Feversham to the Flower-de-Luce,

And rest yourselves until some other time.

GREENE. Let me alone; it most concerns my state.

WILL. Ay, Mistress Arden, this will serve the turn,

In case we fall into a second fog.

Exeunt Greene, Will, and Shake[bag].

MOS. These knaves will never do it; let us give it over. 80

ALICE. First tell me how you like my new device:

Soon, when my husband is returning back,

You and I both marching arm in arm,

Like loving friends, we'll meet him on the way,

And boldly beard and brave him to his teeth.

When words grow hot and blows begin to rise,

[3] Do.   [4] Entangled or fatigued.
[5] Befouled with mud.

I'll call those cutters forth your tene-
    ment,
Who, in a manner to take up the fray,
Shall wound my husband Hornsby [1] to
    the death.
Mos. Ah, fine device! Why, this deserves
    a kiss.   *Exeunt.*   90

[SCENE xiii.

Near the Flower-de-Luce in Feversham.]

Here enters Dick Reede and a Sailor.

SAIL. Faith, Dick Reede, it is to little end.
    His conscience is too liberal, and he too
        niggardly
    To part from anything may do thee good.
REEDE. He is coming from Shorlow, as I
        understand.
    Here I'll intercept him, for at his house
    He never will vouchsafe to speak with
        me.
    If prayers and fair entreaties will not
        serve,
    Or make no batt'ry in his flinty breast,

Here enters Fra[nklin], Ard[en], and Michael.

    I'll curse the carl, and see what that will
        do.
    See where he comes to further my in-
        tent!—   10
    M[aster] Arden, I am now bound to the
        sea.
    My coming to you was about the plat of
        ground
    Which wrongfully you detain from me.
    Although the rent of it be very small,
    Yet will it help my wife and children,
    Which here I leave in Feversham, God
        knows,
    Needy and bare. For Christ's sake, let
        them have it!
ARD. Franklin, hearest thou this fellow
        speak?
    That which he craves I dearly bought of
        him,
    Although the rent of it was ever
        mine.—   20
    Sirrah, you that ask these questions,
    If with thy clamorous impeaching [2]
        tongue
    Thou rail on me, as I have heard thou
        dost,

I'll lay thee up so close a twelvemonth's
    day,
As thou shalt neither see the sun nor
    moon.
Look to it, for, as surely as I live,
I'll banish pity if thou use me thus.
REEDE. What, wilt thou do me wrong and
        threat me too?
    Nay, then, I'll tempt thee, Arden; do thy
        worst.
    God, I beseech thee, show some mir-
        acle   30
    On thee or thine, in plaguing thee for this.
    That plot of ground which thou detains
        from me—
    I speak it in an agony of spirit—
    Be ruinous and fatal unto thee!
    Either there be butchered by thy dearest
        friends,
    Or else be brought for men to wonder at,
    Or thou or thine miscarry in that place,
    Or there run mad and end thy cursèd
        days!
FRANK. Fie, bitter knave, bridle thine
        envious [3] tongue;
    For curses are like arrows shot up-
        right,   40
    Which, falling down, light on the shoot-
        er's [4] head.
REEDE. Light where they will! Were I
        upon the sea,
    As oft I have in many a bitter storm,
    And saw a dreadful southern flaw at
        hand,
    The pilot quaking at the doubtful [5]
        storm,
    And all the sailors praying on their knees,
    Even in that fearful time would I fall
        down,
    And ask of God, whate'er betide of me,
    Vengeance on Arden or some misevent [6]
    To show the world what wrong the carl
        hath done.   50
    This charge I'll leave with my distressful
        wife;
    My children shall be taught such prayers
        as these;
    And thus I go, but leave my curse with
        thee.   *Exeunt Reede and Sailor.*
ARD. It is the railingest knave in Chris-
        tendom,

[3] Spiteful.
[4] From 1633 edn. Original reads *sutors.*
[5] Fearful.   [6] Mischance.

[1] Cuckold.   [2] Accusing.

And oftentimes the villain will be mad.
It greatly matters not what he says,
But I assure you I ne'er did him
    wrong.

FRANK. I think so, M[aster] Arden.

ARD. Now that our horses are gone home
    before,
My wife may happily meet me on the
    way.   60
For God knows she is grown passing kind
    of late,
And greatly changéd from the old humor
Of her wonted frowardness,
And seeks by fair means to redeem old
    faults.

FRANK. Happy the change that alters for
    the best!
But see in any case you make no speech
Of the cheer we had at my Lord
    Cheiny's,
Although most bounteous and liberal,
For that will make her think herself more
    wronged,
In that we did not carry her along;   70
For sure she grieved that she was left
    behind.

ARD. Come, Franklin, let us strain to
    mend our pace,
And take her unawares playing the cook;

Here enters Alice and Mosbie.

For I believe she'll strive to mend our
    cheer.

FRANK. Why, there's no better creatures
    in the world
Than women are when they are in good
    humors.

ARD. Who is that? Mosbie? What, so
    familiar?
Injurious strumpet, and thou ribald
    knave,
Untwine those arms.

ALICE. Ay, with a sugared kiss let them
    untwine.   80

ARD. Ah, Mosbie, perjured beast! Bear
    this and all!

MOS. And yet no hornéd beast; the horns
    are thine.

FRANK. O monstrous! Nay, then 'tis time
    to draw.
    [*Arden, Franklin, and Mosbie draw.*]

ALICE. Help, help! They murther my hus-
    band.

Here enters Will and Shak[ebag].

SHAKE. Zounds, who injures M[aster]
Mosbie?   [*He and Mosbie are wounded.*]
—Help, Will! I am hurt.

MOS. I may thank you, Mistress Arden,
    for this wound.
    Exeunt Mosbie, Will, and Shakebag.

ALICE. Ah, Arden, what folly blinded
    thee?
Ah, jealous harebrain man, what hast
    thou done!   90
When we, to welcome thee,[1] intended
    sport,
Came lovingly to meet thee on thy way,
Thou drew'st thy sword, enraged with
    jealousy,
And hurt thy friend whose thoughts were
    free from harm—
All for a worthless kiss and joining arms,
Both done but merrily to try thy pa-
    tience.
And me unhappy that devised the jest,
Which, though begun in sport, yet ends
    in blood!

FRANK. Marry, God defend me from such
    a jest!

ALICE. Couldst thou not see us friendly
    smile on thee,   100
When we joined arms and when I kissed
    his cheek?
Hast thou not lately found me overkind?
Didst thou not hear me cry, they murther
    thee?
Called I not help to set my husband free?
No, ears and all were witched. Ah, me ac-
    cursed,
To link in liking with a frantic man!
Henceforth I'll be thy slave, no more thy
    wife,
For with that name I never shall content
    thee.
If I be merry, thou straightways thinks
    me light;
If sad, thou sayest the sullens[2] trouble
    me;   110
If well attired, thou thinks I will be gad-
    ding;
If homely, I seem sluttish in thine eye.
Thus am I still, and shall be while[3] I die.
Poor wench, abused by thy misgovern-
    ment!

---

[1] Original reads *thy.*   [3] Until.
[2] Dumps.

ARD. But is it for truth that neither thou
   nor he
Intendedst malice in your misdemeanor?
ALICE. The heavens can witness of our
   harmless thoughts.
ARD. Then pardon me, sweet Alice,
   And forgive this fault!   119
Forget but this and never see the like.
Impose me penance, and I will perform it,
For in thy discontent I find a death,
A death tormenting more than death it-
   self.
ALICE. Nay, hadst thou loved me as thou
   dost pretend,
Thou wouldst have marked the speeches
   of thy friend,
Who going wounded from the place, he
   said
His skin was pierced only through my de-
   vice.
And, if sad sorrow taint thee for this
   fault,
Thou wouldst have followed him, and
   seen him dressed,
And cried him mercy whom thou hast
   misdone.   130
Ne'er shall my heart be eased till this
   be done.
ARD. Content thee, sweet Alice, thou shalt
   have thy will,
Whate'er it be. For that I injured thee
And wronged my friend, shame scourgeth
   my offense.
Come thou thyself, and go along with me,
And be a mediator twixt us two.
FRANK. Why, M[aster] Arden, know you
   what you do?
Will you follow him that hath dishonored
   you?
ALICE. Why, canst thou prove I have been
   disloyal?
FRANK. Why, Mosbie taunts your [1] hus-
   band with the horn.   140
ALICE. Ay, after he had reviled him
By the injurious name of perjured beast!
He knew no wrong could spite a jealous
   man
More than the hateful naming of the horn.
FRANK. Suppose 'tis true; yet is it dan-
   gerous
To follow him whom he hath lately hurt.
ALICE. A fault confessed is more than half
   amends;

[1] From 1633 edn. Original reads *traunt you*.

But men of such ill spirit as yourself
Work crosses and debates twixt man and
   wife.
ARD. I pray thee, gentle Franklin, hold
   thy peace.   150
I know my wife counsels me for the best.
I'll seek out Mosbie where his wound is
   dressed,
And salve his hapless quarrel if I may.
          Exeunt Arden and Alice.
FRANK. He whom the devil drives must go
   perforce.
Poor gentleman, how soon he is be-
   witched!
And yet, because his wife is the instru-
   ment,
His friends must not be lavish in their
   speech.   *Exit Fran[klin].*

[SCENE xiv.

A room in Arden's house.]

Here enters Will, Shakebag, and Greene.

WILL. Sirrah Greene, when was I so
long in killing a man?
GREENE. I think we shall never do it.
Let us give it over.
SHAKE. Nay, zounds! We'll kill him,
though we be hanged at his door for our
labor.
WILL. Thou knowest, Greene, that I have
lived in London this twelve years, where
I have made some go upon wooden [10
legs for taking the wall on me;[2] divers
with silver noses for saying, "There goes
Black Will!" I have cracked as many
blades as thou hast done nuts.
GREENE. O monstrous lie!
WILL. Faith, in a manner I have. The
bawdyhouses have paid me tribute; there
durst not a whore set up unless she have
agreed with me first for opening her shop
windows. For a cross word of a tapster [20
I have pierced one barrel after another
with my dagger, and held him be [3] the ears
till all his beer hath run out. In Thames
Street a brewer's cart was like to have
run over me. I made no more ado, but
went to the clerk and cut all the natches
off his tails [4] and beat them about his head.
I and my company have taken the constable from his watch, and carried him

[2] For pushing me into the street.   [3] By.
[4] Notches off his tallies (sticks on which his
accounts were kept).

about the fields on a coltstaff.[1] I have [30
broken a sergeant's head with his own
mace, and bailed whom I list with my
sword and buckler. All the tenpenny
alehouses would stand every morning with
a quart pot in his hand, saying, "Will it
please your worship drink?" He that had
not done so, had been sure to have had his
sign pulled down and his lattice borne away
the next night. To conclude, what have I
not done? Yet cannot do this. Doubt-   [40
less he is preserved by miracle.

Here enters Alice and Michael.

GREENE. Hence, Will!   Here comes
M[istress] Arden.
ALICE. Ah, gentle Michael, art thou sure
they're friends?
MICH. Why, I saw them when they both
shook hands.
When Mosbie bled, he even wept for
sorrow,
And railed on Franklin that was cause
of all.
No sooner came the surgeon in at doors,
But my m[aster] took to his purse and
gave him money,
And, to conclude, sent me to bring you
word   50
That Mosbie, Franklin, Bradshaw, Adam
Fowle,
With divers of his neighbors and his
friends,
Will come and sup with you at our house
this night.
ALICE. Ah, gentle Michael, run thou
back again,
And, when my husband walks into the
fair,
Bid Mosbie steal from him and come
to me;
And this night shall thou and Susan be
made sure.
MICH. I'll go tell him.
ALICE. And, as thou goest, tell John cook
of our guests,
And bid him lay it on—spare for no
cost.   *Exit Michael.*   60
WILL. Nay, and there be such cheer, we
will bid ourselves.—
Mistress Arden, Dick Greene and I do
mean to sup with you.

[1] Staff used for carrying tubs.

ALICE. And welcome shall you be.   Ah,
gentlemen,
How missed you of your purpose yesternight?
GREENE. 'Twas long of [2] Shakebag, that
unlucky villain.
SHAKE. Thou dost me wrong; I did as
much as any.
WILL. Nay then, M[istress] Alice, I'll
tell you how it was.
When he should have locked with both
his hilts,[3]
He in a bravery [4] flourished over his head;
With that comes Franklin at him lustily,   70
And hurts the slave; with that he slinks
away.
Now his way had been to have come
hand and feet, one and two round, at his
costard;[5] he like a fool bears his sword-
point half a yard out of danger. I lie here
for my life. [*Takes a position of defense.*]
If the devil come, and he have no more
strength than fence,[6] he shall never beat
me from this ward.[7]
I'll stand to it, a buckler in a skillful
hand   80
Is as good as a castle; nay,
'Tis better than a sconce,[8] for I have
tried it.
Mosbie, perceiving this, began to faint.
With that comes Arden with his arming sword,[9]
And thrust him through the shoulder in
a trice.
ALICE. Ay, but I wonder why you both
stood still.
WILL. Faith, I was so amazed, I could
not strike.
ALICE. Ah, sirs, had he yesternight been
slain,
For every drop of his detested blood
I would have crammed [10] in angels [11] in
thy fist,   90
And kissed thee, too, and hugged thee
in my arms.
WILL. Patient yourself; we cannot help
it now.

[2] Because of.
[3] Sword. *Hilts* was often used for singular.
[4] Bravado.   [7] Guard.
[5] Apple, head.   [8] Fort.
[6] Fencing skill.   [9] A two-handed sword.
[10] From 1633 edn.; original reads *would
cramme.*   [11] Coins.

Greene and we two will dog him through
the fair,
And stab him in the crowd, and steal
away.

Here enters Mosbie.

ALICE. It is unpossible; but here comes
he
That will, I hope, invent some surer
means.
Sweet Mosbie, hide thy arm; it kills my
heart.
Mos. Ay, Mistress Arden, this is your
favor.
ALICE. Ah, say not so, for, when I saw
thee hurt,
I could have took the weapon thou
lett'st fall,   100
And run at Arden, for I have sworn
That these mine eyes, offended with
his sight,
Shall never close till Arden's be shut up.
This night I rose and walked about the
chamber,
And twice or thrice I thought to have
murthered him.
Mos. What, in the night? Then had we
been undone.
ALICE. Why, how long shall he live?
Mos. Faith, Alice, no longer than this
night.—
Black Will and Shakebag, will you two
Perform the complot that I have laid? 110
WILL. Ay, or else think me as a villain.
GREENE. And rather than you shall
want,[1] I'll help, myself.
Mos. You, M[aster] Greene, shall single
Franklin forth,
And hold him with a long tale of strange
news,
That he may not come home till supper
time.
I'll fetch M[aster] Arden home, and we,
like friends,
Will play a game or two at tables [2] here.
ALICE. But what of all this? How shall he
be slain?
Mos. Why, Black Will and Shakebag,
locked within the countinghouse,
Shall, at a certain watchword given,
rush forth.   120
WILL. What shall the watchword be?

Mos. "Now I take you"—that shall be
the word.
But come not forth before in any case.
WILL. I warrant you. But who shall
lock me in?
ALICE. That will I do; thou'st keep the
key thyself.
Mos. Come, M[aster] Greene; go you
along with me.
See all things ready, Alice, against we
come.
ALICE. Take no care for that; send you
him home,
Exeunt Mosbie and Greene.
And, if he e'er go forth again, blame me.
Come, Black Will, that in mine eyes
art fair;   130
Next unto Mosbie do I honor thee.
Instead of fair words and large promises
My hands shall play you golden har-
mony.[3]
How like you this? Say, will you do it,
sirs?
WILL. Ay, and that bravely, too. Mark
my device:
Place Mosbie, being a stranger, in a
chair,
And let your husband sit upon a stool,
That I may come behind him cun-
ningly,   138
And with a towel pull him to the ground,
Then stab him till his flesh be as a sine;[4]
That done, bear him behind the Abbey,
That those that find him murthered
may suppose
Some slave or other killed him for his
gold.
ALICE. A fine device! You shall have
twenty pound,
And, when he is dead, you shall have
forty more,
And, lest you might be suspected stay-
ing here,
Michael shall saddle you two lusty geld-
ings;
Ride whither you will, to Scotland, or
to Wales,
I'll see you shall not lack, where'er you be.
WILL. Such words would make one kill
a thousand [5] men!   150
Give me the key! Which is the count-
inghouse?

[1] Fail.   [2] Backgammon.
[3] *I.e.*, give you money.   [4] Seine, sieve.
[5] Original reads *1000* without the article.

ALICE. Here would I stay and still encourage you,
But that I know how resolute you are.
SHAKE. Tush, you are too faint-hearted; we must do it.
ALICE. But Mosbie will be there, whose very looks
Will add unwonted courage to my thought,
And make me the first that shall adventure on him.
WILL. Tush, get you gone; 'tis we must do the deed.
When this door opens next, look for his death.
            [*Exeunt Will and Shakebag.*]
ALICE. Ah, would he now were here that it might open!   160
I shall no more be closed in Arden's arms,
That like the snakes of black Tisiphone
Sting me with their embracings. Mosbie's arms
Shall compass me, and, were I made a star,
I would have none other spheres but those.
There is no nectar but in Mosbie's lips!
Had chaste Diana kissed him, she like me
Would grow lovesick, and from her wat'ry bower
Fling down Endymion and snatch[1] him up.
Then blame not me that slay a silly man   170
Not half so lovely as Endymion.

Here enters Michael.

MICH. Mistress, my master is coming hard by.
ALICE. Who comes with him?
MICH. Nobody but Mosbie.
ALICE. That's well, Michael. Fetch in the tables, and, when thou hast done, stand before the countinghouse door.
MICH. Why so?   179
ALICE. Black Will is locked within to do the deed.
MICH. What? Shall he die tonight?
ALICE. Ay, Michael.
MICH. But shall not Susan know it?

ALICE. Yes, for she'll be as secret as ourselves.
MICH. That's brave.[2] I'll go fetch the tables.
ALICE. But, Michael, hark to me a word or two.
When my husband is come in, lock the street door;   190
He shall be murthered or[3] the guests come in.   *Exit Mic[hael].*

Here enters Arden and Mosbie.

Husband, what mean you to bring Mosbie home?
Although I wished you to be reconciled,
'Twas more for fear of you than love of him.
Black Will and Greene are his companions,
And they are cutters, and may cut you short;
Therefore I thought it good to make you friends.
But wherefore do you bring him hither now?
You have given me my supper with his sight.[4]
Mos. M[aster] Arden, methinks your wife would have me gone.   200
ARD. No, good M[aster] Mosbie; women will be prating.
Alice, bid him welcome; he and I are friends.
ALICE. You may enforce me to it if you will;
But I had rather die than bid him welcome.
His company hath purchased me ill friends,
And therefore will I ne'er frequent it more.
Mos. [*Aside.*] O, how cunningly she can dissemble!
ARD. Now he is here, you will not serve me so.
ALICE. I pray you be not angry or displeased;
I'll bid him welcome, seeing you'll have it so.   210
You are welcome, M[aster] Mosbie; will you sit down?

---

[1] Snatch.
[2] Splendid.   [4] *I.e.*, taken my appetite away.
[3] Before.

Mos. I know I am welcome to your loving
　husband;
　But for yourself you speak not from your
　heart.
Alice. And, if I do not, sir, think I have
　cause.
Mos. Pardon me, M[aster] Arden; I'll
　away.
Ard. No, good M[aster] Mosbie.
Alice. We shall have guests enough, though
　you go hence.
Mos. I pray you, M[aster] Arden, let me
　go.
Ard. I pray thee, Mosbie, let her prate
　her fill.
Alice. The doors are open, sir; you may
　be gone.　　　　　　　　　　　　　220
Mich. [Aside.] Nay, that's a lie, for I have
　locked the doors.
Ard. Sirrah, fetch me a cup of wine;
　I'll make them friends.
　And, gentle M[istress] Alice, seeing you
　are so stout,[1]
　You shall begin. Frown not; I'll have it
　so.
Alice. I pray you meddle with that you
　have to do.
Ard. Why, Alice, how can I do too much
　for him
　Whose life I have endangered without
　cause?
Alice. 'Tis true; and, seeing 'twas partly
　through my means,
　I am content to drink to him for this
　once.
　Here, M[aster] Mosbie—and, I pray you,
　henceforth　　　　　　　　　　　　230
　Be you as strange to me as I to you.
　Your company hath purchased me ill
　friends,
　And I for you, God knows, have un-
　deserved
　Been ill spoken of in every place;
　Therefore henceforth frequent my house
　no more.
Mos. I'll see your husband in despite of
　you.
　Yet, Arden, I protest to thee by heaven,
　Thou ne'er shalt see me more after this
　night.
　I'll go to Rome rather than be forsworn.
Ard. Tush, I'll have no such vows made
　in my house.　　　　　　　　　　240

[1] Stubborn, proud.

Alice. Yes, I pray you, husband, let him
　swear;
　And, on that condition, Mosbie, pledge
　me here.
Mos. Ay, as willingly as I mean to live.
Ard. Come, Alice, is our supper ready
　yet?
Alice. It will by then you have played a
　game at tables.
Ard. Come, M[aster] Mosbie, what shall
　we play for?
Mos. Three games for a French crown,
　sir, and [2] please you.
Ard. Content.

Then they play at the tables.

[*Enter Will and Shakebag.*]

Will. [*Aside.*] Can he not take him yet?
　What a spite is that!
Alice. [*Aside.*] Not yet, Will. Take heed
　he see thee not.　　　　　　　　250
Will. [*Aside.*] I fear he will spy me as I
　am coming.
Mich. [*Aside.*] To prevent that, creep
　betwixt my legs.
Mos. One ace, or else I lose the game.
Ard. Marry, sir, there's two for failing.[3]
Mos. Ah, M[aster] Arden, "now I can take
　you."
Then Will pulls him down with a towel.
Ard. Mosbie! Michael! Alice! What
　will you do?
Will. Nothing but take you up, sir,
　nothing else.
Mos. There's for the pressing iron you
　told me of.　　　　　[*Stabs him.*]
Shake. And there's for the ten pound in
　my sleeve.　　　　　[*Stabs him.*]
Alice. What! Groans thou? Nay, then
　give me the weapon!　　　　　260
　Take this for hind'ring Mosbie's love
　and mine!　　　　　[*She stabs him.*]
Mich. O, mistress!
Will. Ah, that villain will betray us all.
Mos. Tush, fear him not; he will be
　secret.
Mich. Why, dost thou think I will betray
　myself?
Shake. In Southwark dwells a bonny
　northern lass,
　The widow Chambley; I'll to her house
　now,

[2] An't, if it.　　　[3] If one is not sufficient.

And, if she will not give me harborough,[1]
I'll make booty of the quean even to her
     smock.
WILL. Shift for yourselves; we two will
     leave you now.   270
ALICE. First lay the body in the counting-
     house.
Then they lay the body in the countinghouse.
WILL. We have our gold; Mistress Alice,
     adieu;
     Mosbie, farewell, and, Michael, farewell
     too.   *Exeunt.*

Enter Susan.

SUS. Mistress, the guests are at the doors.
     Hearken, they knock. What, shall I let
     them in?
ALICE. Mosbie, go thou, and bear them
     company.   *Exit M[osbie].*
     And, Susan, fetch water and wash away
     this blood.
SUS. The blood cleaveth to the ground
     and will not out.
ALICE. But with my nails I'll scrape away
     the blood.—
     The more I strive, the more the blood
     appears!   280
SUS. What's the reason, m[istress], can you
     tell?
ALICE. Because I blush not at my hus-
     band's death.

Here enters Mosbie.

MOS. How now? What's the matter? Is
     all well?
ALICE. Ay, well, if Arden were alive again.
     In vain we strive, for here his blood re-
     mains.
MOS. Why, strew rushes on it, can you
     not?
     This wench doth nothing. Fall unto the
     work.
ALICE. 'Twas thou that made me murther
     him.
MOS.   What of that?
ALICE. Nay, nothing, Mosbie, so it be not
     known.
MOS. Keep thou it close, and 'tis unpos-
     sible.   290
ALICE. Ah, but I cannot! Was he not slain
     by me?
     My husband's death torments me at the
     heart.

[1] Harbor.

MOS. It shall not long torment thee, gentle
     Alice.
     I am thy husband; think no more of him.

Here enters Adam Fowle and Brad[shaw].

BRAD. How now, M[istress] Arden? What
     ail you weep?[2]
MOS. Because her husband is abroad so
     late.
     A couple of ruffians threatened him yes-
     ternight,
     And she, poor soul, is afraid he should be
     hurt.
ADAM. Is 't nothing else? Tush, he'll be
     here anon.

Here enters Greene.

GREENE. Now, M[istress] Arden, lack you
     any guests?   300
ALICE. Ah, M[aster] Greene, did you see
     my husband lately?
GREENE. I saw him walking behind the
     Abbey even now.

Here enters Franklin.

ALICE. I do not like this being out so
     late.—
     M[aster] Franklin, where did you leave
     my husband?
FRANK. Believe me, I saw him not since
     morning.
     Fear you not; he'll come anon. Mean-
     time
     You may do well to bid his guests sit
     down.
ALICE. Ay, so they shall. M[aster] Brad-
     shaw, sit you there;
     I pray you, be content; I'll have my will.
     M[aster] Mosbie, sit you in my husband's
     seat.   310
MICH. [*Aside.*] Susan, shall thou and I
     wait on them?
     Or, and thou sayst the word, let us sit
     down too.
SUS. [*Aside.*] Peace, we have other mat-
     ters now in hand.
     I fear me, Michael, all will be bewrayed.
MICH. [*Aside.*] Tush, so it be known
that I shall marry thee in the morning,
I care not though I be hanged ere night.
But to prevent the worst I'll buy some
ratsbane.   319

[2] *I.e.*, what ails you that you weep?

Sus. [*Aside.*] Why, Michael, wilt thou poison thyself?

Mich. [*Aside.*] No, but my mistress, for I fear she'll tell.

Sus. [*Aside.*] Tush, Michael, fear not her; she's wise enough.

Mos. Sirrah Michael, give's a cup of beer.—

M[istress] Arden, here's to your husband.

Alice.   My husband!

Frank. What ails you, woman, to cry so suddenly?

Alice. Ah, neighbors, a sudden qualm came over my heart;

My husband's being forth torments my mind.   330

I know something's amiss; he is not well Or else I should have heard of him ere now.

Mos. [*Aside.*] She will undo us through her foolishness.

Greene. Fear not, M[istress] Arden; he's well enough.

Alice. Tell not me; I know he is not well. He was not wont for to stay thus late.

Good M[aster] Franklin, go and seek him forth,

And, if you find him, send him home to me,

And tell him what a fear he hath put me in.

Frank. [*Aside.*] I like not this; I pray God all be well.—   340

Exeunt Fra[nklin], Mos[bie], and Gre[ene].

I'll seek him out, and find him if I can.

Alice. [*Aside.*] Michael, how shall I do to rid the rest away?

Mich. [*Aside.*] Leave that to my charge; let me alone.—

'Tis very late, M[aster] Bradshaw,

And there are many false knaves abroad,

And you have many narrow lanes to pass.

Brad. Faith, friend Michael, and thou sayest true.

Therefore I pray thee light's forth and lend's a link.[1]

Exeunt Brad[shaw], Adam, and Michael.

Alice. Michael, bring them to the doors, but do not stay;   349

You know I do not love to be alone.—

Go, Susan, and bid thy brother come.

But wherefore should he come? Here is naught but fear;

Stay, Susan, stay, and help to counsel me.

[1] Torch.

Sus. Alas, I counsel! Fear frights away my wits.

Then they open the countinghouse door, and look upon Arden.

Alice. See, Susan, where thy quondam master lies,

Sweet Arden, smeared in blood and filthy gore.

Sus. My brother, you, and I shall rue this deed.

Alice. Come, Susan, help to lift his body forth,

And let our salt tears be his obsequies.

Here enters Mosbie and Greene.

Mos. How now, Alice, whither will you bear him?   360

Alice. Sweet Mosbie, art thou come? Then weep that will;

I have my wish in that I joy thy sight.

Greene. Well, it hoves[2] us to be circumspect.

Mos. Ay, for Franklin thinks that we have murthered him.

Alice. Ay, but he cannot prove it for his life.

We'll spend this night in dalliance and in sport.

Here enters Michael.

Mich. O mistress, the mayor and all the watch

Are coming towards our house with glaives and bills![3]

Alice. Make the door fast; let them not come in.

Mos. Tell me, sweet Alice, how shall I escape?   370

Alice. Out at the back door, over the pile of wood,

And for one night lie at the Flower-de-Luce.

Mos. That is the next way to betray myself.

Greene. Alas, M[istress] Arden, the watch will take me here,

And cause suspicion where else would be none.

Alice. Why, take that way that M[aster] Mosbie doth;

But first convey the body to the fields.

Then they bear the body into the fields.

[2] Behooves.   [3] Swords and halberts.

Mos. Until tomorrow, sweet Alice, now
farewell.
And see you confess nothing in any case.
Greene. Be resolute, M[istress] Alice; be-
tray us not,   380
But cleave to us as we will stick to you.
                        Exeunt Mosbie and Greene.
Alice. Now, let the judge and juries do
their worst.
My house is clear, and now I fear them
not.
Sus. As we went, it snowéd all the way,
Which makes me fear our footsteps will
be spied.
Alice. Peace, fool, the snow will cover
them again.
Sus. But it had done before we came back
again.
Alice. Hark, hark, they knock!   Go,
Michael, let them in.

Here enters the Mayor and the Watch.

How now, M[aster] Mayor, have you
brought my husband home?
Mayor. I saw him come into your house
an hour ago.   390
Alice. You are deceived; it was a Lon-
doner.
Mayor. Mistress Arden, know you not
one that is called Black Will?
Alice. I know none such.   What mean
these questions?
Mayor. I have the council's warrand to
apprehend him.
Alice. [*Aside.*] I am glad it is no worse.—
Why, M[aster] Mayor, think you I har-
bor any such?
Mayor. We are informed that here he is;
And therefore pardon us, for we must
search.
Alice. Ay, search, and spare you not,
through every room.
Were my husband at home, you would
not offer this.   400

Here enters Franklin.

M[aster] Franklin, what mean you come
so sad?
Frank. Arden, thy husband and my
friend, is slain!
Alice. Ah, by whom? M[aster] Franklin,
can you tell?

Frank. I know not; but behind the Ab-
bey
There he lies murthered in most piteous
case.
Mayor. But, M[aster] Franklin, are you
sure 'tis he?
Frank. I am too sure; would God I were
deceived.
Alice. Find out the murtherers; let them
be known.
Frank. Ay, so they shall. Come you along
with us.
Alice. Wherefore?
Frank.   Know you this hand towel
and this knife?   410
Sus. [*Aside.*] Ah, Michael, through this
thy negligence
Thou hast betrayéd and undone us all.
Mich. [*Aside.*] I was so afraid I knew not
what I did;
I thought I had thrown them both into
the well.
Alice. It is the pig's blood we had to
supper.
But wherefore stay you? Find out the
murtherers.
Mayor. I fear me you'll prove one of
them yourself.
Alice. I one of them? What mean such
questions?
Frank. I fear me he was murthered in
this house
And carried to the fields, for from that
place   420
Backwards and forwards may you see
The print of many feet within the
snow.
And look about this chamber where we
are,
And you shall find part of his guiltless
blood,
For in his slipshoe [1] did I find some
rushes,
Which argueth he was murthered in this
room.
Mayor. Look in the place where he was
wont to sit.
See, see! His blood! It is too manifest.
Alice. It is a cup of wine that Michael
shed.
Mich. Ay, truly.   430
Frank. It is his blood, which, strumpet,
thou hast shed!
_____
[1] Slipper.

But, if I live, thou and thy complices
Which have conspired and wrought his
　death shall rue it.
ALICE. Ah, M[aster] Franklin, God and
　heaven can tell
I loved him more than all the world be-
　side.
But bring me to him; let me see his body.
FRANK. Bring that villain and Mosbie's
　sister too;
And one of you go to the Flower-de-Luce,
And seek for Mosbie, and apprehend him
　too.　　　　　　　　　　　*Exeunt.*

[SCENE xv.

An obscure street in Southwark.]

Here enters Shakebag solus.

SHAKE. The widow Chambley in her hus-
　band's days I kept;
And, now he's dead, she is grown so stout
She will not know her old companions.
I came thither, thinking to have had
Harbor as I was wont,
And she was ready to thrust me out at
　doors.
But, whether she would or no, I got me up,
And, as she followed me, I spurned her
　down the stairs,
And broke her neck, and cut her tapster's
　throat,
And now I am going to fling them in the
　Thames.　　　　　　　　　　　10
I have the gold; what care I though it be
　known!
I'll cross the water and take sanctuary.
　　　　　　　　　　　Exit Shakebag.

[SCENE xvi.

A room in Arden's house.]

Here enters the Mayor, Mosbie, Alice, Frank-
lin, Michael, and Susan.

MAYOR. See, M[istress] Arden, where your
　husband lies.
Confess this foul fault and be penitent.
ALICE. Arden, sweet husband, what shall
　I say?
The more I sound his name, the more he
　bleeds;
This blood condemns me, and in gushing
　forth
Speaks as it falls, and asks me why I did it.

Forgive me, Arden; I repent me now,
And, would my death save thine, thou
　shouldst not die.
Rise up, sweet Arden, and enjoy thy love,
And frown not on me when we meet in
　heaven;　　　　　　　　　　　10
In heaven I love thee, though on earth
　I did not.
MAYOR. Say, Mosbie, what made thee
　murther him?
FRANK. Study not for an answer; look not
　down.
His purse and girdle found at thy bed's
　head
Witness sufficiently thou didst the deed.
It bootless is to swear thou didst it not.
MOS. I hired Black Will and Shakebag,
　ruffians both,
And they and I have done this mur-
　therous deed.
But wherefore stay we? Come and bear
　me hence.
FRANK. Those ruffians shall not escape; I
　will up to London,　　　　　　　　20
And get the council's warrand to appre-
　hend them.　　　　　　　　　　*Exeunt.*

[SCENE xvii.

The Kentish coast.]

Here enters Will.

WILL. Shakebag, I hear, hath taken sanc-
　tuary,
But I am so pursued with hues and cries
For petty robberies that I have done
That I can come unto no sanctuary.
Therefore must I in some oyster boat
At last be fain to go aboard some hoy,[1]
And so to Flushing. There is no staying
　here.
At Sittinburgh the watch was like to take
　me,
And, had not I with my buckler covered
　my head,
And run full blank at all adventures,[2] 10
I am sure I had ne'er gone further than
　that place,
For the constable had twenty warrands
　to apprehend me;
Besides that, I robbed him and his man
　once at Gadshill.
Farewell, England; I'll to Flushing now.
　　　　　　　　　　　Exit Will.

[1] Small boat.　　　　[2] *I.e.*, taken all risks.

[SCENE xviii.

A courtroom at Feversham.]

Here enters the Mayor, Mosbie, Alice, Michael, Susan, and Bradshaw.

MAYOR. Come, make haste and bring away the prisoners.

BRAD. M[istress] Arden, you are now going to God,
And I am by the law condemned to die
About a letter I brought from M[aster] Greene.
I pray you, M[istress] Arden, speak the truth.
Was I ever privy to your intent or no?

ALICE. What should I say? You brought me such a letter,
But I dare swear thou knewest not the contents.
Leave now to trouble me with worldly things,
And let me meditate upon my Savior Christ,   10
Whose blood must save me for the blood I shed.

MOS. How long shall I live in this hell of grief?
Convey me from the presence of that strumpet.

ALICE. Ah, but for thee I had never been strumpet.
What cannot oaths and protestations do,
When men have opportunity to woo?
I was too young to sound thy villainies,
But now I find it and repent too late.

SUS. Ah, gentle brother, wherefore should I die?   19
I knew not of it till the deed was done.

MOS. For thee I mourn more than for myself;
But let it suffice, I cannot save thee now.

MICH. And, if your brother and my mistress
Had not promised me you in marriage,
I had ne'er given consent to this foul deed.

MAYOR. Leave to accuse each other now,
And listen to the sentence I shall give.
Bear Mosbie and his sister to London straight,
Where they in Smithfield must be executed;   29
Bear M[istress] Arden unto Canterbury,
Where her sentence is she must be burnt,
Michael and Bradshaw in Feversham must suffer death.

ALICE. Let my death make amends for all my sins.

MOS. Fie upon women!—this shall be my song.
But bear me hence, for I have lived too long.

SUS. Seeing no hope on earth, in heaven is my hope.

MICH. Faith, I care not, seeing I die with Susan.

BRAD. My blood be on his head that gave the sentence.

MAYOR. To speedy execution with them all!   *Exeunt.*

[EPILOGUE]

Here enters Franklin.

FRANK. Thus have you seen the truth of Arden's death.
As for the ruffians, Shakebag and Black Will,
The one took sanctuary, and, being sent for out,
Was murthered in Southwark as he passed
To Greenwich, where the lord protector lay.
Black Will was burnt in Flushing on a stage;
Greene was hangéd at Osbridge in Kent;
The painter fled and how he died we know not.
But this above the rest is to be noted:
Arden lay murthered in that plot of ground   10
Which he by force and violence held from Reede,
And in the grass his body's print was seen
Two years and more after the deed was done.
Gentlemen, we hope you'll pardon this naked tragedy,
Wherein no filéd [1] points are foisted in
To make it gracious to the ear or eye;
For simple truth is gracious enough,
And needs no other points of glozing stuff.   [*Exit.*]

FINIS.

[1] Polished.

ATTOWELL'S JIG

Attowell's Jig is one of the most interesting specimens—though perhaps not the most typical—of a dramatic form that achieved a remarkable popularity with London audiences by the end of the sixteenth century. Many satiric allusions go to show that the masses were not satisfied without a jig at the end of every play. About the middle of the century the term jig begins to appear in literary allusions as applied to simple song or dance or to the two combined. During the Elizabethan period, song and dance entertainments under the name jig developed in complexity and were popularized on the stage among the various song and dance specialties of the players. These stage jigs apparently showed considerable variety, but the typical form was that of the ballad, which lent itself to the presentation of jest, tale, and satiric skit, with clowns, fools, vagabonds, and other figures traditional in farce and popular drama. The more formal stage jig was usually a brief ballad farce, sung and accompanied by dance. The chief rôles in the jigs, emphasizing the drollery or rascality of the clown, were taken by outstanding comedians of the various companies. Richard Tarlton, the great clown of the Queen's Company, who died in 1588, was the first to win fame for his jigs, both as author and as performer. In the last decade of the century the most famous exponent of the jig was William Kemp, the leading comedian of Shakespeare's company. In spite of the vogue of the jig until well into the seventeenth century, only six farce jigs are known to have survived in English. A larger number are extant in German, however, for English actors carried the formal jig to the Continent, where it remained popular for nearly a century, especially in Germany. *Rowland*, the most famous of the jigs, is lost in English, but preserved in several German texts. Another favorite was *Singing Simpkin*, almost certainly one of Kemp's successes, which survives in several languages.

Attowell's Jig was entered in the Stationers' Register on October 14, 1595, as "A Pretty New Jig between Francis the Gentleman, Richard the Farmer, and Their Wives." It was published as a broadside ballad in two parts, with the name George Attowell at the end. A manuscript form, published in *Shirburn Ballads*, has the title "Mr. Attowell's Jig between Francis," etc. There is also an early seventeenth century version in German, somewhat freely translated. Probably the name of Attowell is connected with the jig because he popularized it by his performances, not because he wrote it. Little is known of him beyond his connection with the jig. He was associated with Strange's men in 1590–91, and is mentioned, without reference to any company, in a business transaction of Henslowe's in 1595. One interesting feature of the jig is its early use of several scenes with different airs. Of the four tunes, "Walsingham" and "Go from My Window" had an extraordinary vogue. No exact source for the plot is known. Similar intrigue plots with a substitution motive are found in a German jest and in the story from the *Decameron* used by Shakespeare in *All's Well*, but the husband of the faithful wife does not appear. The coarse and farcical handling of characters usual in the dramatic jig is lacking. Instead of the droll, stupid, or crafty country clown and the light, tricky wife common in the jig, the farmer and his wife are presented with sympathy and a measure of dignity. The style is characteristic of the ballad, and, while not distinguished, it is also not without occasional quaintness and charm. The text here is based on that of the only extant copy of the broadside, from the Pepys Collection, as printed by Baskervill in *The Elizabethan Jig*.

ATTOWELL'S JIG[1]

[*DRAMATIS PERSONÆ*

MASTER FRANCIS, *a gentleman.*   MISTRESS FRANCIS.
RICHARD, *a farmer.*   BESS, *Richard's wife.*

SCENE: *The farmer's home.*

TIME: *Contemporary.*]

BESS. [*Singing.*]

> As I went to Walsingham,
>   To the shrine with speed,
> Met I with a jolly palmer
>   In a pilgrim's weed.

[*Enter Francis.*]

Now God you save, you jolly palmer!

FRAN. Welcome, lady gay!
Oft have I sued to thee for love.
BESS.[2] Oft have I said you nay.

FRAN. My love is fixed. BESS. And so
  is mine,
But not on you;   10
For to my husband whilst I live
  I will ever be true.
FRAN. I'll give thee gold and rich array—
BESS. Which I shall buy too dear.
FRAN. Naught shalt thou want; then say
  not nay.
  BESS. "Naught" would you make me,
  I fear!

What though you be a gentleman,
  And have lands great store?
I will be chaste, do what you can,
  Though I live ne'er so poor.   20
FRAN. Thy beauty rare hath wounded
  me,
  And pierced my heart.

[1] This is the conventional title. The first part of the broadside on which the present text is based has the title "Francis' New Jig, between Francis, a Gentleman, and Richard, a Farmer. To the Tune of 'Walsingham'."

[2] Except for an initial *Bess, Fran.,* and *Rich.,* the speech heads are *B., F.,* and *R.* in the original, with *W.,* that is, *Wife,* for Mistress Francis.

BESS. Your foolish love doth trouble me.
  Pray you, sir, depart.

FRAN. Then tell me, sweet, wilt thou con-
  sent
  Unto my desire?
BESS. And, if I should, then tell me, sir,
  What is it you require?
FRAN. For to enjoy thee as my love.
  BESS. Sir, you have a wife;   30
Therefore let your suit have an end.
  FRAN. First will I lose my life!

All that I have thou shalt command.
  BESS. Then my love you have.
FRAN. Your meaning I well understand.
  BESS. I yield to what you crave.
FRAN. But tell me, sweet, when shall I
  enjoy
  My heart's delight?
I prithee, sweetheart, be not coy.
  BESS. Even soon, at night.   40

My husband is rid ten miles from home,
  Money to receive.
In the evening see you come.
  FRAN. Till then, I take my leave.   *Exit.*
BESS. Thus have I rid my hands full well
  Of my amorous love,
And my sweet husband will I tell
  How he doth me move.

*Enter Richard, Bess's husband. To the tune
of the "Jewish Dance."*

RICH. [*Not observing Bess.*] Hey, down a
  down,
Hey, down a down, a down!   50
There is never a lusty farmer
  In all our town

That hath more cause
  To lead a merry life
Than I that am married
  To an honest,[1] faithful wife.
BESS. [*Coming forward.*] I thank you,
  gentle husband;
  You praise me to my face.
RICH. I cry thee mercy, Bessie;
  I knew thee not in place.   60

BESS. Believe me, gentle husband,
  If you knew as much as I,
The words that you have spoken
  You quickly would deny;
For, since you went from home,
  A suitor I have had,
Who is so far in love with me
  That he is almost mad.
He'll give me gold and silver store,
  And money for to spend,   70
And I have promised him therefore
  To be his loving friend.

RICH. Believe me, gentle wife,
  But this makes me to frown!
There is no gentleman nor knight
  Nor lord of high renown
That shall enjoy thy love, girl,
  Though he were ne'er so good!
Before he wrong my Bessie so,
  I'll spend on him my blood!   80
And therefore tell me who it is
  That doth desire thy love.
BESS. Our neighbor, Master Francis,
  That often did me move;

To whom I gave consent,
  His mind for to fulfill,
And promised him this night
  That he should have his will.
Nay, do not frown, good Dickie,
  But hear me speak my mind;   90
For thou shalt see, I'll warrant thee,
  I'll use him in his kind.
For unto thee I will be true
  So long as I do live;
I'll never change thee for a new,
  Nor once my mind so give.

Go you to Mistress Francis,
  And this to her declare,
And will her with all speed
  To my house to repair,   100
[1] Chaste.

Where she and I'll devise
  Some pretty knavish wile;
For I have laid the plot,
  Her husband to beguile.
Make haste, I pray, and tarry not,
  For long he will not stay.
RICH. Fear not; I'll tell her such a tale
  Shall make her come away!   [*Exit.*]

BESS. Now, Bess, bethink thee
  What thou hast to do.   110
Thy lover will come presently,
  And hardly will he woo.
I will teach my gentleman
  A trick that he may know
I am too crafty and too wise
  To be o'erreachéd so.
But here he comes now! Not a word,
  But fall to work again.
        She sews [*as Francis enters*].
FRAN. How now, sweetheart, at work so
  hard?
BESS. Ay, sir, I must take pains.   120

FRAN. But say, my lovely sweeting,
  Thy promise wilt thou keep?
Shall I enjoy thy love,
  This night with me to sleep?
BESS. My husband rid [2] from home;
  Here safely may you stay.
FRAN. And I have made my wife believe
  I rid another way.
BESS. Go in, good sir, whate'er betide,
  This night and lodge with me.   130
FRAN. The happiest night that ever I
  had!
  Thy friend still will I be.   [*Exit.*]

Enter Mistress Francis with Richard. To
    the tune of "Bugle Bow." [3]

WIFE. I thank you, neighbor Richard,
  For bringing me this news.
RICH. Nay, thank my wife that loves me
  so,
  And will not you abuse.

WIFE. But see whereas [4] she stands
  And waiteth our return.

[2] Rode.
[3] The first sheet ends here with a separate
colophon. The second is headed: "The Second
Part of Attowell's New Jig. To the Tune of 'As
I Went to Walsingham'." There is no division
into stanzas marked in the section sung to the
tune of "Bugle Bow."
[4] Where.

Rich. You must go cool your husband's
  heat,
  That so in love doth burn.   140

Bess. Now, Dickie, welcome home,
  And, mistress, welcome hither.
Grieve not, although you find
  Your husband and I together.

For you shall have your right,
  Nor will I wrong you so.
Then change apparel with me straight,
  And unto him do go.
                [*They exchange clothes.*]

Wife. For this your kind good will
  A thousand thanks I give;   150
And make account I will requite
  This kindness, if I live.

Bess. I hope it shall not need;
  Dick will not serve me so.
I know he loves me not so ill
  A-ranging for to go.

Rich. No, faith, my lovely Bess;
  First will I lose my life
Before I'll break my wedlock bonds
  Or seek to wrong my wife.   160
                [*Exit Mistress Francis.*]

Now thinks good Master Francis
  He hath thee in his bed,
And makes account he is grafting
  Of horns upon my head.

But softly! Stand aside!
  Now shall we know his mind,
And how he would have uséd thee,
  If thou hadst been so kind.
                [*They stand aside.*]

Enter Master Francis with his own Wife,
having a mask before her face, supposing
her to be Bess. To the tune of "Go from
                My Window."

Fran. Farewell, my joy and heart's de-
  light,
  Till next we meet again.   170
Thy kindness to requite
For lodging me all night,
  Here's ten pound for thy pain;

And more to show my love to thee
  Wear this ring for my sake.

Wife. Without your gold or fee
You shall have more of me.
Fran. No doubt of that I make.

Wife. Then let your love continue still.
  Fran. It shall, till life doth end.   180
Wife. Your wife I greatly fear.
Fran. For her thou need'st not care
  So I remain thy friend.

Wife. But you'll suspect me, without
  cause,
  That I am false to you;
And then you'll cast me off
And make me but a scoff,
  Since that I prove untrue.

Fran. Then never trust man for my sake,
  If I prove so unkind!   190
[Wife.] So often have you sworn,
Sir, since that you were born,
  And soon have changed your mind.

[Fran.] Nor wife nor life, nor goods nor
  lands,
  Shall make me leave my love,
Nor any worldly treasure
Make me forgo my pleasure,
  Nor once my mind remove.

                [*Richard and Bess come forward.*]

Wife. But soft awhile! Who is yonder?
  Do you see
My husband? Out, alas!   200
Fran. And yonder is my wife!
Now shall we have a life!
  How cometh this to pass?

Rich. Come hither, gentle Bess! I charge
  thee, do confess
What makes Master Francis here?
Wife.[1] Good husband, pardon me!
I'll tell the troth to thee.
  Rich. Then speak, and do not fear.

Fran. Nay, neighbor Richard, hark to
  me!
  I'll tell the troth to you.   210
Bess. Nay, tell it unto me,
Good sir, that I may see
  What you have here to do.

[1] In this stanza and the next, the names of
the women are reversed in the original, probably
because of the disguise.

But you can make no scuse ¹ to color this
   abuse;
  This wrong is too-too great!
RICH. Good sir, I take great scorn
You should proffer me the horn.
  WIFE. Now must I cool this heat.²

Nay, neighbor Richard, be content;
  Thou hast no wrong at all.   220
             [*Discloses herself.*]
Thy wife hath done thee right,
And pleasured me this night!
  FRAN. This frets me to the gall!

Good wife, forgive me this offense;
  I do repent mine ill.
WIFE. I thank you with mine heart
For playing this kind part,
  Though sore against your will.

Nay, gentle husband, frown not so,
  For you have made amends;   230
I think it is good gain
To have ten pound for my pain!
  Then let us both be friends.

FRAN. Ashamed I am, and know not what
  to say.
  Good wife, forgive this crime!
Alas, I do repent!
WIFE. Tut, I could be content
  To be served so many a time!

FRAN. Good neighbor Richard, be content;
  I'll woo thy wife no more—   240

¹ Excuse.
² In the original, the rest of this speech is assigned to Francis.

I have enough of this.
  WIFE. Then all forgiven is.—
  I thank thee, Dick, therefore,

And to thy wife I'll give this gold,
  I hope you'll not say no.
Since I have had the pleasure,
Let her enjoy the treasure!
  FRAN. Good wife, let it be so.

BESS. I thank you, gentle mistress,
  RICH. Faith, and so do I,
  Sir, learn your own wife to know,   250
And shoot not in the dark
For fear you miss the mark.
  BESS. He hath paid for this, I trow.

All women learn of me. FRAN. All men
  by me take heed
  How you a woman trust.
WIFE. Nay, women, trust no men.
FRAN. And, if they do, how then?
  WIFE. There's few of them prove just.

Farewell, neighbor Richard!   Farewell,
  honest Bess!
  I hope we are all friends.   260
[*To Francis.*] ³ And, if you stay at home,
And use not thus to roam,
  Here all our quarrel ends.

              FINIS.

         GEORGE ATTOWELL.

³ In the original, the speech head for "Wife"
is repeated here.

MUCEDORUS

If the evidence of editions may be accepted, *Mucedorus* was the most popular play in all pre-Restoration drama, for after its initial publication in 1598 it went through at least sixteen new editions by 1668. The distribution of the parts suggests, however, that the unusual number of editions may have been called forth by a ready sale to small troupes of actors. The Citizen's Wife in *The Knight of the Burning Pestle* remarks of Ralph, the apprentice with histrionic ambitions, "Nay, gentlemen, he hath played before, my husband says—*Mucedorus* before the wardens of our company." In Cowley's *Guardian* and in his Restoration revision of that play as *The Cutter of Coleman Street*, Jolly's servant Will disclaims having acted the clown, but modestly admits to the bear. *Mucedorus* was surreptitiously presented by strolling players while the theaters were closed during the Commonwealth, and was performed by village actors in the north of England as late as 1666. The reduction of the play to a ballad also emphasizes its popular character. The form printed here shows revision for acting before James I.

The bare outline of the play was derived from Sidney's *Arcadia:* the hero's name, his disguise as a shepherd, his rescue of the heroine from the bear, and the elopement, capture, and happy union of the two. With the action set in the forest, the author of the play has added the wild man, whose offer of rustic gifts to Amadine is an ancient convention of pastoral poetry. The wild man represents, however, the ogre of folk tale rather than the savage of pastoral or of Spenser's *Fairy Queen*. The constantly appearing clown is of the droll and stupid type that popular taste seems to have demanded not only in farces and jigs but in the romantic plays of the University Wits and Shakespeare, and even in chronicle plays and tragedies. Thus the author of *Mucedorus* has shifted the treatment from Sidney's courtly mixture of pastoral and chivalric romance to make a play of the type that Sidney condemns in his *Apology for Poetry*, with its romantic absurdities and its inappropriate clown crowding to the very throne of the king. The induction and the epilogue, which like those of several other sixteenth century plays show the continued interest in debates, or flytings, are here used to emphasize the mixed nature of the play as a "tragi-comedy."

The fact that in spite of its vogue the author of *Mucedorus* is unknown reveals a characteristic attitude of the sixteenth century. The cultured looked upon a play as mere entertainment rather than as literature, and printers were inclined to disregard the playwright unless he had achieved popularity with some class of readers. The author of *Mucedorus* was, however, a man of some literary as well as dramatic gifts, and from the characteristics of the play many attempts have been made to identify him as one of the better known dramatists. The older attribution in part or in whole to Shakespeare is now discarded by virtually all scholars. Claims have been made for Peele, Greene, and more especially Lodge. More likely, Tucker Brooke, who edited the play in his *Shakespeare Apocrypha*, is right in his suggestion that it was written by "an obscure and only moderately gifted disciple" of the University Wits.

The present text is based on the edition of 1610, with its added scenes showing the bear and the court of Mucedorus' father. The editors are indebted to the authorities of the Huntington Library for permission to use photostats of the copy of this quarto in the Library.

MUCEDORUS[1]

Most sacred majesty, whose great deserts
Thy subject England, nay, the world admires—
Which heaven grant still increase—O, may your praise,
Multiplying with your hours, your fame still raise;
Embrace your council; love, with faith, them guide,
That both, as one, bench by each other's side.
So may your life pass on and run so even
That your firm zeal plant you a throne in heaven,
Where smiling angels shall your guardians be
From blemished traitors, stained with perjury.   10
And, as the night's inferior to the day,
So be all earthly regions to your sway.
Be as the sun to day, the day to night;
For, from your beams, Europe shall borrow light.
Mirth drown your bosom, fair delight your mind,
And may our pastime your contentment find.   *Exit.*

[DRAMATIS PERSONÆ]

Ten persons may easily play it.[3]

THE KING *and* RUMBELO } *for one.*

KING VALENCIA } *for one.*

MUCEDORUS, *the Prince of Valencia* } *for one.*

ANSELMO } *for one.*

AMADINE, *the king's daughter of Aragon* } *for one.*

SEGASTO, *a nobleman* } *for one.*

ENVY; TREMELIO, *a captain;* BREMO, *a wild man* } *for one.*

COMEDY; A BOY; AN OLD WOMAN; ARIENA, *Amadine's maid* } *for one.*

COLLEN, *a councilor;* A MESSENGER } *for one.*

MOUSE, *the clown* } *for one.*

[SCENE: *Valencia and Aragon.*

TIME: *Uncertain.*]

[INDUCTION]

Enter Comedy, joyfully, with a garland of bays on her head.

[COM.] Why, so! Thus do I hope to please.
Music revives, and mirth is tolerable.
Comedy, play thy part and please;
Make merry them that comes to joy with thee.
Joy, then, good gentles;[4] I hope to make you laugh.
Sound forth Bellona's silver-tunéd strings.
Time fits us well; the day and place is ours.

Enter Envy, his arms naked, besmeared with blood.

ENV. Nay, stay, minion; there lies a block.
What, all on mirth? I'll interrupt your tale
And mix your music with a tragic end.   10
COM. What monstrous, ugly hag is this,
That dares control the pleasures of our will?

---

[1] The complete title of 1610 reads: "A Most Pleasant Comedy of Mucedorus, the King's Son of Valencia, and Amadine, the King's Daughter of Aragon, with the Merry Conceits of Mouse. Amplified with New Additions, As It Was Acted before the King's Majesty at Whitehall on Shrove Sunday Night. By His Highness' Servants, Usually Playing at the Globe. Very Delectable and Full of Conceited Mirth."

[2] The prologue first appeared in the 1610 edn.

[3] In the following list no provision is made for Roderigo, Borachius, and the Bear.

[4] Gentlefolk.

Vaunt,[1] churlish cur, besmeared with
    gory blood,
That seem'st to check the blossom of
    delight,
And stifle [2] the sound of sweet Bellona's
    breath.
Blush, monster, blush, and post away
    with shame,
That seekest disturbance of a goddess'
    deeds.
Env. Post hence thyself, thou counter-
    checking trull!
I will possess this habit,[3] spite of thee,
And gain the glory of thy wishéd port.[4] 20
I'll thunder music shall appall the
    nymphs,
And make them shiver their clattering
    strings,
Flying for succor to their dankish [5]
    caves.
Sound drums within and cry, "Stab! Stab!"
Hearken, thou shalt hear a noise
Shall fill the air with a shrilling sound,
And thunder music to [the] [6] gods above;
Mars shall himself breathe down
A peerless crown upon brave Envy's
    head,
And raise his chivall [7] with a lasting
    fame. 29
In this brave music Envy takes delight,
Where I may see them wallow in their
    blood,
To spurn at arms and legs quite shivered
    off,
And hear the cries of many thousand
    slain.
How lik'st thou this, my trull? This
    sport alone for me!
Com. Vaunt, bloody cur, nursed up with
    tiger's sap,
That so dost [seek to] [8] quail a woman's
    mind.
Comedy is mild, gentle, willing for to
    please,
And seeks to gain the love of all estates,
Delighting in mirth, mixed all with
    lovely tales,

And bringeth things with treble joy
    to pass. 40
Thou, bloody, envious disdainer of men's
    joys,
Whose name is fraught with bloody
    stratagems,
Delights in nothing but in spoil and
    death,
Where thou mayst trample in their
    lukewarm blood,
And grasp their hearts within thy curséd
    paws.
Yet vail thy mind;[9] revenge thou not
    on me—
A silly woman begs it at thy hands.
Give me the leave to utter out my play.
Forbear this place, I humbly crave thee;
    hence,
And mix not death 'mongst pleasing
    comedies, 50
That treats naught else but pleasure
    and delight!
If any spark of human rests in thee,
Forbear, begone, tender [10] the suit of
    me.
Env. Why, so I will; forbearance [11] shall
    be such
As treble death shall cross thee with
    despite,
And make thee mourn where most thou
    joyest,
Turning thy mirth into a deadly dole,
Whirling thy pleasures with a peal of
    death,
And drench thy methods [12] in a sea of
    blood.
This will I do; thus shall I bear with
    thee; 60
And, more to vex thee with a deeper
    spite,
I will with threats of blood begin thy
    play,
Favoring thee with envy and with hate.
Com. Then, ugly monster, do thy worst;
I will defend them in despite of thee.
And, though thou think'st with tragic
    fumes [13]
To prave [14] my play unto my deep dis-
    grace,

---

[1] Avaunt, be off.
[2] From 1598 edn. Original reads *stiffe*.
[3] Costume.
[4] Station.
[5] Emended by Collier. Original reads *Danish*.
[6] Supplied from 1598 edn.
[7] 'Chieval, achieval, achievement (?).
[8] From 1598 edn.

[9] Modify thy intention.
[10] Regard favorably.
[11] From 1598 edn. Original reads *forbear*.
[12] Designs, *i.e.*, the plot of her play.
[13] Fits of anger.
[14] Deprave, ruin.

I force it not;[1] I scorn what thou canst
    do;
I'll grace it so thyself shall it confess
From tragic stuff to be a pleasant
    comedy.   70
ENV. Why then, Comedy, send thy actors
    forth
And I will cross the first steps of their
    trade,
Making them fear the very dart of
    death.
COM. And I'll defend them mauger all
    thy spite.
So, ugly fiend, farewell, till time shall
    serve
That we may meet to parley for the best.
ENV. Content, Comedy; I'll go spread
    my branch,
And scattered blossoms from mine en-
    vious tree
Shall prove to [2] monsters, spoiling of
    their joys.   *Exit [with Comedy].*

[SCENE i.[3]

The court of Valencia.]

Sound. Enter Mucedorus and Anselmo, his
                                  friend.
MU. Anselmo!
ANS. My lord and friend!
MU. True, my Anselmo, both thy lord
    and friend
Whose dear affections bosom with my
    heart,
And keep their domination in one orb.
ANS. Whence ne'er disloyalty shall root
    it forth,
But faith plant firmer in your choice
    respect.
MU. Much blame were mine if I should
    other deem,
Nor can coy Fortune contrary allow.
But, my Anselmo, loath I am to say
I must estrange that friendship.   11
Misconster [4] not—'tis from the realm,
    not thee;
Though lands part bodies, hearts keep
    company.
Thou know'st that I imparted often
    have
Private relations with my royal sire,

Had as concerning beauteous Amadine,
Rich Aragon's bright jewel, whose face
    some say
That blooming lilies never shone so gay,
Excelling, not excelled. Yet, lest re-
    port
Does mangle verity, boasting of what is
    not,   20
Winged with desire, thither I'll straight
    repair,
And be my fortunes, as my thoughts
    are, fair.
ANS. Will you forsake Valencia, leave
    the court,
Absent you from the eye of sovereignty?
Do not, sweet prince, adventure on that
    task,
Since danger lurks each where. Be won
    from it.
MU. Desist dissuasion;
My resolution brooks no battery;
Therefore, if thou retain thy wonted
    form,
Assist what I intend.   30
ANS. Your miss will breed a blemish in
    the court,
And throw a frosty dew upon that
    beard
Whose front Valencia stoops to.
MU. If thou my welfare tender, then no
    more;
Let love's strong magic charm thy
    trivial phrase,
Wasted as vainly as to gripe [5] the sun.
Augment not then more answers; lock
    thy lips,
Unless thy wisdom suit [6] me with dis-
    guise
According to my purpose.
ANS. That action craves no counsel,   40
Since what you rightly are will more
    command
Than best usurpéd shape.
MU. Thou still art opposite in disposi-
    tion.
A more obscure, servile habiliment
Beseems this enterprise.
ANS. Then like a Florentine or mounte-
    bank?
MU. 'Tis much too tedious; I dislike thy
    judgment.
My mind is grafted on an humbler
    stock.

[1] I care not for it.   [2] Become.
[3] This scene appears first in the 1610 edn.
[4] Misconstrue.

[5] Seize.   [6] Clothe.

Ans. Within my closet does there hang
  a cassock;
Though base the weed is, 't was a shep-
  herd's   50
Which J presented in Lord Julio's
  masque.
Mu. That, my Anselmo, and none else
  but that,
Mask Mucedorus from the vulgar view!
That habit suits my mind; fetch me
  that weed.   *Exit Anselmo.*
Better than kings have not disdained
  that state,
And much inferior, to obtain their mate!

Enter Anselmo with a shepherd's coat.

So let our respect command thy secrecy.
At once a brief farewell!
Delay to lovers is a second hell!
                              Exit Mucedorus.
Ans. Prosperity forerun thee; awkward
  chance   60
Never be neighbor to thy wish's ven-
  ture;
Content and fame advance thee; ever
  thrive,
And glory thy mortality survive.   *Exit.*

[Scene ii.[1]

A forest in Aragon.]

Enter Mouse with a bottle [2] of hay.

Mouse. O, horrible, terrible! Was ever
poor gentleman so scared out of his seven
senses? A bear? Nay, sure it cannot be
a bear, but some devil in a bear's doublet,
for a bear could never have had that agility
to have frighted me. Well, I'll see my
father hanged before I'll serve his horse
any more. Well, I'll carry home my bottle
of hay, and for once make my father's
horse turn Puritan and observe fasting [10
days, for he gets not a bit. But soft! This
way she followed me; therefore I'll take
the other path; and, because I'll be sure
to have an eye on him, I will take hands
with some foolish creditor, and make
every step backward.
*As he goes backwards the bear comes in,
and he tumbles over her, and runs away and
      leaves his bottle of hay behind him.*

[1] This scene appeared first in the 1610 edn.
[2] Bundle.

*Enter Segasto running and Amadine after
      him, being pursued with a bear.*

Seg. O, fly, madam, fly or else we are
  but dead!
Am. Help, Segasto, help! Help, sweet
  Segasto, or else I die!
Seg. Alas, madam, there is no way but
  flight;
Then haste and save yourself!
                      Segasto runs away.[3]
Am. Why, then I die; ah, help me in dis-
  tress!

*Enter Mucedorus like a shepherd, with a
      sword drawn and a bear's head in his
                                          hand.*

Mu. Stay, lady, stay, and be no more
  dismayed.
That cruel beast most merciless and fell,
Which hath bereavéd thousands of their
  lives,
Affrighted many with his hard pursues,
Prying from place to place to find his
  prey,   10
Prolonging thus his life by others'
  death,
His carcass now lies headless, void of
  breath.
Am. That foul, deforméd monster, is he
  dead?
Mu. Assure yourself thereof; behold his
  head,
Which, if it please you, lady, to accept,
With willing heart I yield it to your
  majesty.
Am. Thanks, worthy shepherd, thanks
  a thousand times.
This gift, assure thyself, contents me more
Than greatest bounty of a mighty prince,
Although he were the monarch of the
  world.   20
Mu. Most gracious goddess, more than
  mortal wight—
Your heavenly hue of right imports
  no less—
Most glad am I in that it was my chance
To undertake this enterprise in hand,
Which doth so greatly glad your princely
  mind.

[3] All early edns. place this direction after l. 2.

Am. No goddess, shepherd, but a mortal
   wight,
A mortal wight distresséd as thou seest.
My father here is king of Aragon.
I, Amadine, his only daughter am,   25
And after him sole heir unto the crown.
Now, whereas it is my father's will
To marry me unto Segasto, one [1]
Whose wealth through father's former
   usury
Is known to be no less than wonderful,
We both of custom oftentimes did use,
Leaving the court, to walk within the
   fields
For recreation, especially [in][2] the spring,
In that it yields great store of rare de-
   lights,
And, passing further than our wonted
   walks,
Scarce entered were within these luck-
   less woods,   40
But right before us down a steep-fall
   hill
A monstrous, ugly bear did hie him fast
To meet us both. I faint to tell the rest,
Good shepherd, but suppose the ghastly
   looks,
The hideous fears, the thousand hun-
   dred woes,
Which at this instant Amadine sustained.
Mu. Yet, worthy princess, let thy sorrow
   cease,
And let this sight your former joys re-
   vive.
Am. Believe me, shepherd, so it doth no
   less.
Mu. Long may they last unto your heart's
   content.   50
But tell me, lady, what is become of
   him,
Segasto called, what is become of him?
Am. I know not, I; that know the powers
   divine;
But God grant this, that sweet Segasto
   live.
Mu. Yet hard-hearted he in such a case,
So cowardly to save himself by flight,
And leave so brave a princess to the
   spoil.
Am. Well, shepherd, for thy worthy valor
   tried,

[1] Here and in a few other cases line divisions
have been regularized.
[2] Supplied by Hazlitt.

Endangering thyself to set me free,
Unrecompenséd sure thou shalt not be. 60
In court thy courage shall be plainly
   known;
Throughout the kingdom will I spread
   thy name,
To thy renown and never-dying fame.
And, that thy courage may be better
   known,
Bear thou the head of this most mon-
   strous beast
In open sight to every courtier's view.
So will the king my father thee reward.
Come, let's away, and guard me to
   the court.
Mu. With all my heart.   *Exeunt.*

[SCENE iv.

The outskirts of the forest.]

Enter Segasto solus.

Seg. When heaps of harms do hover over-
   head,
'Tis time as then, some say, to look
   about,
And of [3] ensuing harms to choose the
   least.
But hard, yea, hapless, is that wretch's
   chance,
Luckless his lot and caitiff-like accursed,
At whose proceedings fortune ever
   frowns—
Myself I mean, most subject unto
   thrall,
For I, the more I seek to shun the
   worst,
The more by proof I find myself accursed.
Erewhiles assaulted with an ugly bear, 10
Fair Amadine in company all alone,
Forthwith by flight I thought to save
   myself,
Leaving my Amadine unto her shifts;
For death it was for to resist the bear,
And death no less of Amadine's harms to
   hear.
Acccurséd I in ling'ring life thus long!
In living thus, each minute of an hour
Doth pierce my heart with darts of
   thousand deaths.
If she by flight her fury do escape,
What will she think?   20
Will she not say—yea, flatly to my face,

[3] From 1613 edn. Original reads *so.*

Accusing me of mere [1] disloyalty—
A trusty friend is tried in time of need?
But I, when she in danger was of death
And needed me, and cried, "Segasto,
  help!"
I turned my back and quickly ran away.
Unworthy I to bear this vital breath!
But what! What needs these plaints?
If Amadine do live, then happy I;
She will in time forgive and so forget.   30
Amadine is merciful, not Juno-like,
In harmful heart to harbor hatred long.

Enter Mouse, the clown, running, crying,
                          "Clubs!"

MOUSE. Clubs, prongs, pitchforks, bills! [2]
O, help! A bear, a bear, a bear! [3]
SEG. Still bears, and nothing else but
bears! Tell me, sirrah, where she is.
CLO. [4] O, sir, she is run down the woods!
I saw her white head and her white
belly.
SEG. Thou talkest of wonders, to tell me
  of white bears.   40
But, sirrah, didst thou ever see any
  such?
CLO. No, faith, I never saw any such,
but I remember my father's words: he
bade me take heed I was not caught with
a white bear.
SEG. A lamentable tale, no doubt.
CLO. I tell you what, sir, as I was going
afield to serve my father's great horse, and
carried a bottle of hay upon my head—now
do you see, sir—I, fast hoodwinked [5] [50
that I could see nothing, I perceiving the
bear coming, I threw my hay into the hedge
and ran away.
SEG. What, from nothing?
CLO. I warrant you, yes, I saw something, for there was two load of thorns
besides my bottle of hay, and that made
three.
SEG. But tell me, sirrah, the bear that
  thou didst see,   59
Did she not bear a bucket on her arm?
CLO. Ha, ha, ha! I never saw bear go
a-milking in all my life. But hark you,

sir, I did not look so high as her arm; I
saw nothing but her white head and her
white belly.
SEG. But tell me, sirrah, where dost
thou dwell?
CLO. Why, do you not know me?
SEG. Why, no, how should I know thee?
CLO. Why, then, you know nobody, [70
and [6] you know not me. I tell you, sir,
I am the Goodman Rat's son of the next
parish over the hill.
SEG. Goodman Rat's son?   Why,
what's thy name?
CLO. Why, I am very near kin unto
him.
SEG. I think so, but what's thy name?
CLO. My name? I have a very pretty
name. I'll tell you what my name is; my
name is Mouse.   81
SEG. What, plain Mouse?
CLO. Ay, plain Mouse without either
welt or guard. [7] But do you hear, sir, I am
but a very young mouse, for my tail is
scarce grown out yet; look you here else.
SEG. But, I pray thee, who gave thee
that name?
CLO. Faith, sir, I know not that, but,
if you would fain know, ask my father's [90
great horse, for he hath been half a year
longer with my father than I have.
SEG. [*Aside.*] This seems to be a merry
  fellow;
I care not if I take him home with me.
Mirth is a comfort to a troubled mind;
A merry man a merry master makes.—
How sayst thou, sirrah, wilt thou dwell
  with me?
CLO. Nay, soft, sir, two words to a bar-
gain! Pray you, what occupation are
you?   100
SEG. No occupation; I live upon my
lands.
CLO. Your lands! Away, you are no
master for me! Why, do you think that
I am so mad, to go seek my living in the
lands amongst the stones, briers, and
bushes, and tear my holiday apparel? Not
I, by your leave.
SEG. Why, I do not mean thou shalt.
CLO. How then?   110
SEG. Why, thou shalt be my man, and
wait upon me at the court.

---

[1] Absolute.   [2] Pruning hooks.
[3] Ll. 33–45 and a number of other passages
printed as rough verse in the original are here
printed as prose.
[4] Clown, *i.e.*, Mouse.
[5] Completely blindfolded.

[6] If. The whole expression is proverbial.
[7] *I.e.*, undecorated.

CLO. What's that?

SEG. Where the king lies.

CLO. What's that same king, a man or a woman?

SEG. A man as thou art.

CLO. As I am? Hark you, sir; pray you, what kin is he to Goodman King of our parish, the churchwarden? 120

SEG. No kin to him; he is the king of the whole land.

CLO. King of the land! I never see him.

SEG. If thou wilt dwell with me, thou shalt see him every day.

CLO. Shall I go home again to be torn in pieces with bears? No, not I. I will go home and put on a clean shirt, and then go drown myself. 129

SEG. Thou shalt not need; if thou wilt dwell with me, thou shalt want nothing.

CLO. Shall I not? Then here's my hand; I'll dwell with you. And hark you, sir; now you have entertained me, I will tell you what I can do. I can keep my tongue from picking and stealing, and my hands from lying and slandering, I warrant you, as well as ever you had man in all your life. 140

SEG. Now will I to court with sorrowful heart, rounded [1] with doubts. If Amadine do live, then happy I; yea, happy I, if Amadine do live. [*Exeunt.*]

[SCENE V.

The camp of the King of Aragon.]

Enter the King with a young Prince prisoner, Amadine, Tremelio, [2] *with Collen and Councilors.*

KING. Now, brave lords, our wars are brought to end,

Our foes, the foil, [3] and we in safety rest.

It us behooves to use such clemency in peace

As valor in the wars.

It is as great honor to be bountiful at home

As to be conquerors in the field.

Therefore, my lords, the more to my content,

Your liking, and your country's safeguard,

We are disposed in marriage for to give

Our daughter to Lord Segasto here, 10

Who shall succeed the diadem after me,

And reign hereafter as I tofore [4] have done,

Your sole and lawful King of Aragon.

What say you, lordings? Like you of my advice?

COL. An't [5] please your majesty, we do not only allow of your highness' pleasure, but also vow faithfully in what we may to further it.

KING. Thanks, good my lords; if long Adrostus live,

He will at full requite your courtesies. 20

Tremelio, in recompense of thy late valor done,

Take unto thee the Catalone, [6] a prince,

Lately our prisoner taken in the wars.

Be thou his keeper; his ransom shall be thine;

We'll think of it when leisure shall afford.

Meanwhile, do use him well; his father is a king.

TRE. Thanks to your majesty! His usage shall be such

As he thereat shall think no cause to grutch. [7]

Exeunt [*Tremelio and Prince*].

KING. Then march we on to court, and rest our wearied limbs.

But, Collen, I have a tale in secret kept for thee: 30

When thou shalt hear a watchword from thy king,

Think then some weighty matter is at hand

That highly shall concern our state;

Then, Collen, look thou be not far from me.

And, for the service thou tofore hast done,

Thy truth and valor proved in every point,

I shall with bounties thee enlarge therefor.

So guard us to the court.

COL. Whatso my sovereign doth command me do, 39

With willing mind I gladly yield consent.

Exeunt.

---

[1] Surrounded.   [3] *I.e.*, to defeat.

[2] Appears first in 1610 edn.

[4] Before.   [6] Man from Catalonia.

[5] If it.   [7] Grudge, murmur.

[SCENE vi.

The same.]

Enter Segasto and the Clown, with weapons about him.

SEG. Tell me, sirrah, how do you like your weapons?

CLO. O, very well, very well; they keep my sides warm.

SEG. They keep the dogs from your shins very well, do they not?

CLO. How, keep the dogs from my shins? I would scorn but my shins could keep the dogs from them.

SEG. Well, sirrah, leaving idle talk, [10 tell me dost thou know Captain Tremelio's chamber?

CLO. Ay, very well; it hath a door.

SEG. I think so, for so hath every chamber. But dost thou know the man?

CLO. Ay, forsooth; he hath a nose on his face.

SEG. Why, so hath everyone.

CLO. That's more than I know.

SEG. But dost thou remember the [20 captain that was here with the king even now, that brought the young prince prisoner?

CLO. O, very well.

SEG. Go unto him and bid him come unto me. Tell him I have a matter in secret to impart to him.

CLO. I will, Master.—Master, what's his name?

SEG. Why, Captain Tremelio. 30

CLO. O, the mealman! I know him very well. He brings meal every Saturday. But hark you, master, must I bid him come to you or must you come to him?

SEG. No, sirrah, he must come to me.

CLO. Hark you, master, how if he be not at home? What shall I do then?

SEG. Why, then leave word with some of his folks.

CLO. O, master, if there be nobody [40 within, I will leave word with his dog.

SEG. Why, can his dog speak?

CLO. I cannot tell; wherefore doth he keep his chamber else?

SEG. To keep out such knaves as thou art.

CLO. Nay, by Lady; then go yourself.

SEG. You will go, sir, will you not?

CLO. Yes, marry, will I. O, 'tis come to my head; and a [1] be not within, I'll [50 bring his chamber to you.

SEG. What, wilt thou pluck down the king's house?

CLO. Nay, by Lady, I'll know the price of it first. Master, it is such a hard name I have forgotten it again. I pray you, tell me his name.

SEG. I tell thee, Captain Tremelio.

CLO. O, Captain Treble-knave, Captain Treble-knave. 60

Enter Tremelio.

TRE. How now, sirrah, dost thou call me?

CLO. You must come to my master, Captain Treble-knave.

TRE. My Lord Segasto, did you send for me?

SEG. I did, Tremelio.—Sirrah, about your business.

CLO. Ay, marry, what's that? Can you tell? 70

SEG. No, not well.

CLO. Marry, then, I can; straight to the kitchen-dresser, to John the cook, and get me a good piece of beef and brewis,[2] and then to the buttery hatch to Thomas the butler for a jack [3] of beer, and there for an hour I'll so belabor myself! And therefore, I pray you, call me not till you think I have done, I pray you, good master.

Exit.

SEG. Well, sir, away.—Tremelio, this [80 it is: thou knowest the valor of Segasto spread through all the kingdom of Aragon, and such as have found triumph and favors, never daunted at any time; but now a shepherd [is][4] admired at in court for worthiness, and Segasto's honor laid aside. My will, therefore, is this: that thou dost find some means to work the shepherd's death. I know thy strength sufficient to perform my desire, and thy [90 love no otherwise than to revenge my injuries.

TRE. It is not the frowns of a shepherd that Tremelio fears. Therefore, account it accomplished, what I take in hand.

[1] He.
[2] Thickened broth.
[3] Leather pitcher.
[4] Added by Hazlitt.

SEG. Thanks, good Tremelio, and assure
    thyself
What I promise that will I perform.
TRE. Thanks, my good lord, and in good
    time see where
He cometh. Stand by awhile, and you
    shall see
Me put in practice your intended
    drift.[1]   100

Enter Mucedorus.[2]

Have at thee, swain, if that I hit thee
    right!
MU. Vild [3] coward, so without cause to
    strike a man!
Turn, coward, turn; now strike and do
    thy worst!   *Mucedorus killeth him.*
SEG. Hold, shepherd, hold; spare him,
    kill him not!
Accursed villain, tell me, what hast
    thou done?
Ah, Tremelio, trusty Tremelio!
I sorrow for thy death, and, since that thou,
Living, didst prove faithful to Segasto,
So Segasto now, living, will honor
The dead corpse of Tremelio with re-
    venge.   110
Bloodthirsty villain, born and bred in
    merciless murther,
Tell me, how durst thou be so bold as
    once
To lay thy hands upon the least of
    mine?
Assure thyself, thou shalt be used ac-
    cording to the law.
MU. Segasto, cease; these threats are
    needless.
Accuse not me of murther, that have
    done nothing
But in mine own defense.
SEG. Nay, shepherd, reason not with me.
I'll manifest thy fact [4] unto the king,
Whose doom [5] will be thy death, as thou
    deserv'st.   120
What ho, Mouse, come away!

Enter Mouse.

CLO. Why, how now, what's the matter? I thought you would be calling before
I had done.

SEG. Come, help; away with my friend!
CLO. Why, is he drunk? Cannot he
stand on his feet?
SEG. No, he is not drunk; he is slain.
CLO. Flain?[6] No, by Lady; he is not
flain.   130
SEG. He's killed, I tell thee.
CLO. What, do you use to kill your
friends? I will serve you no longer.
SEG. I tell thee, the shepherd killed
him.
CLO. O, did a so? But, master, I will
have all his apparel if I carry him away?
SEG. Why, so thou shalt.
CLO. Come, then, I will help. Mass,[7]
master, I think his mother sung [140
"looby"[8] to him, he is so heavy.
        Exeunt [Segasto and Mouse].
MU. Behold the fickle state of man, al-
    ways mutable,
Never at one. Sometimes we feed on
    fancies
With the sweet of our desires; some-
    times again
We feel the heat of extreme miseries.
Now am I in favor about the court and
    country;
Tomorrow those favors will turn to
    frowns.
Today I live revengéd on my foe;
Tomorrow I die, my foe revenged on me.
                Exit.

[SCENE vii.

The forest.]

Enter Bremo, a wild man.

BRE. No passenger [9] this morning? What,
    not one?
A chance that seldom doth befall.
What, not one? Then lie thou there,
And rest thyself till I have further need.
             [Puts down his club.]
Now, Bremo, sith [10] thy leisure so af-
    fords—
An endless thing. Who knows not
    Bremo's strength,
Who like a king commands [11] within
    these woods?
The bear, the boar, dares not abide my
    sight,

---

[1] Scheme.
[2] All early edns. have stage direction after next
line.   [4] Deed, crime.
   [3] Vile.   [5] Judgment. sentence.

[6] Flayed.   [9] Traveler.
[7] By the Mass.   [10] Since.
[8] Lubber.   [11] Original reads *commander.*

But haste away to save themselves by
  flight.
The crystal waters in the bubbling
  brooks,   10
When I come by, doth swiftly slide away,
And claps themselves in closets under
  banks,
Afraid to look bold Bremo in the face.
The aged oaks at Bremo's breath doth
  bow,
And all things else are still at my com-
  mand.
Else, what would I?
Rend them in pieces and pluck them
  from the earth,
And each way else I would revenge my-
  self.
Why, who comes here with whom I
  dare not fight?
Who fights with me and doth not die the
  death? Not one.   20
What favor shows this sturdy stick to
  those
That here within these woods are com-
  batants with me?
Why, death, and nothing else but pres-
  ent death.
With restless rage I wander through
  these woods;
No creature here but feareth Bremo's
  force;
Man, woman, child, beast, and bird,
And everything that doth approach
  my sight,
Are forced to fall if Bremo once do frown.
Come, cudgel, come, my partner in my
  spoils,
For here I see this day it will not be;   30
But, when it falls that I encounter any,
One pat sufficeth for to work my will.
What, comes not one? Then let's begone;
A time will serve when we shall better
  speed.   *Exit.*

[SCENE viii.

A room of state at the court of Aragon.]

*Enter the King, Segasto, the Shepherd, and
                        the Clown, with Others.*

KING. Shepherd, thou hast heard thine
  accusers;
Murther is laid to thy charge.
What canst thou say? Thou hast deservéd death.

MU. Dread sovereign, I must needs con-
  fess
I slew this captain in mine own defense,
Not of any malice, but by chance;
But mine accuser hath a further mean-
  ing.

SEG. Words will not here prevail;
I seek for justice, and justice craves
  his death.

KING. Shepherd, thine own confession
  hath condemned thee.   10
Sirrah, take him away, and do him to
  execution straight.

CLO. So he shall, I warrant him. But
do you hear, master king, he is kin to a
monkey; his neck is bigger than his head.

SEG. Come, sirrah, away with him, and
hang him about the middle.

CLO. Yes, forsooth, I warrant you.
Come on, sir. Ah, so like a sheepbiter a
looks! [1]

*Enter Amadine and a Boy with a bear's
                        head.*

AM. Dread sovereign and well-belovéd
  sire,   20
On bended knee I crave the life of this
Condemnéd shepherd, which heretofore preserved
The life of thy sometime distresséd
  daughter.

KING. Preserved the life of my sometime
  distresséd daughter?
How can that be? I never knew the time
Wherein thou wast distressed; I never
  knew the day
But that I have maintainéd thy estate
As best beseemed the daughter of a
  king.
I never saw the shepherd until now.
How comes it, then, that he preserved
  thy life?   30

AM. Once walking with Segasto in the
  woods,
Further than our accustomed manner
  was,
Right before us, down a steep-fall hill,
A monstrous, ugly bear did hie him fast
To meet us both. Now whether this be
  true,
I refer it to the credit of Segasto.

SEG. Most true, an't like your majesty.

KING.   How then?

_____
[1] *I.e.*, he has a hangdog look.

Am. The bear, being eager to obtain his
    prey,
Made forward to us with an open mouth,
As if he meant to swallow us both at
    once,   40
The sight whereof did make us both to
    dread,
But specially your daughter Amadine,
Who, for I saw no succor incident
But in Segasto's valor, I grew desperate,
And he most cowardlike began to fly—
Left me distressed to be devoured of him.
How say you, Segasto, is it not true?
King. His silence verifies it to be true.
    What then?   48
Am. Then I amazed, distresséd, all alone,
Did hie me fast to scape that ugly bear;
But all in vain, forwhy[1] he reachéd
    after me,
And hardly I did oft escape his paws,
Till at the length this shepherd came,
And brought to me his head. Come
    hither, boy.
Lo, here it is, which I present unto
    your majesty.
King. The slaughter of this bear deserves
    great fame.
Seg. The slaughter of a man deserves
    great blame.
King. Indeed, occasion oftentimes so falls
    out.
Seg. Tremelio in the wars, O king, pre-
    servéd thee.
Am. The shepherd in the woods, O king,
    preservéd me.   60
Seg. Tremelio fought when many men
    did yield.
Am. So would the shepherd, had he been
    in field.
Clo. [Aside.] So would my master, had
    he not run away.
Seg. Tremelio's force saved thousands
    from the foe.
Am. The shepherd's force hath[2] savéd
    thousands mo.[3]
Clo. [Aside.] Ay, shipsticks,[4] nothing
    else.
King. Segasto, cease to accuse the shep-
    herd;
His worthiness deserves a recompense;
All we are bound to do the shepherd
    good.

[1] Because.   [2] Brooke suggests *would have.*
[3] More.   [4] Sheep's ticks (?).

Shepherd, whereas it was my sentence
    thou shouldst die,   70
So shall my sentence stand, for thou
    shalt die.
Seg. Thanks to your majesty.
King. But soft, Segasto, not for this
    offense!—
Long mayst thou live, and, when the
    Sisters shall decree
To cut in twain the twisted thread of
    life,
Then let him die. For this I set him
    free.—
And for thy valor I will honor thee.
Mu. Thanks to your majesty!
King. Come, daughter, let us now de-
part, to honor the worthy valor of the [80
shepherd with our rewards.
        Exeunt [all but Clown and Segasto].
Clo. O master, hear you. You have
made a fresh hand now. You would be
slow, you! What will you do now? You
have lost me a good occupation by the
means. Faith, master, now I cannot hang
the shepherd, I pray you, let me take the
pains to hang you—it is but half an hour's
exercise.   89
Seg. You are still in your knavery, but,
sith I cannot have his life, I will procure
his banishment forever. Come on, sirrah.
Clo. Yes, forsooth, I come.—[*To audience.*] Laugh at him, I pray you.   *Exeunt.*

[Scene ix.

A grove near the court.]

Enter Mucedorus solus.

Mu. From Amadine and from her father's
    court,
With gold and silver and with rich re-
    wards,
Flowing from the banks of golden
    treasures [5]—
More may I boast and say; but I
Was never shepherd in such dignity.

Enter the Messenger and the Clown.

Mess. All hail, worthy shepherd!
Clo. All rain, lousy shepherd!
Mu. Welcome, my friends.   From
whence come you?   9
Mess. The king and Amadine greet

[5] Treasuries.

thee well, and, after greeting done, bids thee depart the court. Shepherd, begone!

CLO. Shepherd!   Take law,[1] legs; fly away, shepherd!

MU. Whose words are these?   Came these from Amadine?

MESS. Ay, from Amadine.

CLO. Ay, from Amladine.

MU. Ah, luckless fortune, worse than
     Phaëton's tale,   19
My former bliss is now become my bale.

CLO. What, wilt thou poison thyself?

MU. My former heaven is now become
     my hell.

CLO. The worst alehouse that ever I came in, in all my life.

MU. What shall I do?

CLO. Even go hang thyself half an hour.

MU. Can Amadine so churlishly command
     To banish the shepherd from her father's
     court?

MESS. What should shepherds do in   [30
the court?

CLO. What should shepherds do amongst us? Have we not lords enough on us in the court?

MU. Why, shepherds are men, and kings are no more.

MESS. Shepherds are men, and masters over their flock.

CLO. That's a lie.   Who pays them
     their wages then?   40

MESS. Well, you are always interrupting of me, but you were best to look to him, lest you hang for him when he is gone.   *Exit.*

The Clown sings.

CLO. And you shall hang for company,
     For leaving me alone.

Shepherd, stand forth and hear my sentence: Shepherd, begone within three days in pain of my displeasure. Shepherd, begone; shepherd, begone; begone, begone, be-   [50 gone, shepherd, shepherd, shepherd.
                           Exit.

MU. And must I go, and must I needs
     depart?
Ye goodly groves, partakers of my
     songs
In time tofore when fortune did not
     frown,

[1] Take a good lead (a hunting term).

Pour forth your plaints and wail
     awhile with me!
And thou, bright sun, my comfort in
     the cold,
Hide, hide thy face and leave me comfortless!
Ye wholesome herbs and sweet-smelling savors,
Yea, each thing else prolonging life of
     man,
Change, change your wonted course,
     that I,   60
Wanting your aid, in woeful sort may
     die.

Enter Amadine and Ariena, her maid.

AM. Ariena, if anybody ask for me,
Make some excuse till I return.

ARI. What and Segasto call?

AM. Do thou the like to him; I mean not to stay long.   *Exit [Ariena].*[2]

MU. This voice so sweet my pining spirits
     revives.

AM. Shepherd, well met; tell me how
     thou doest.

MU. I linger life, yet wish for speedy
     death.

AM. Shepherd, although thy banishment
     already   70
Be decreed, and all against my will,
Yet Amadine—

MU. Ah, Amadine, to hear of banishment
Is death, ay, double death to me;
But, since I must depart, one thing I
     crave.

AM. Say on with all my heart.

MU. That in absence, either far or near,
You honor me, as servant, with your
     name.

AM. Not so.

MU. And why?   80

AM. I honor thee as sovereign of my
     heart.

MU. A shepherd and a sovereign? Nothing
     like.

AM. Yet like enough where there is no
     dislike.

MU. Yet great dislike, or else no banishment.

AM. Shepherd, it is only
     Segasto that procures thy banishment.

[2] Stage direction appears after l. 63 in 1610 and later edns.

Mu. Unworthy wights are more in jealousy.

Am. Would God they would free thee from banishment,
Or likewise banish me.

Mu. Amen, say I, to have your company. 90

Am. Well, shepherd, sith thou suff'rest this for my sake,
With thee in exile also let me live—
On this condition, shepherd, thou canst love.

Mu. No longer love, no longer let me live!

Am. Of late I lovéd one indeed; now love
I none but only thee.

Mu. Thanks, worthy princess.
I burn likewise, yet smother up the blast;
I dare not promise what I may perform.

Am. Well, shepherd, hark what I shall say:
I will return unto my father's court, 100
There for to provide me of such necessaries
As for my journey I shall think most fit;
This being done, I will return to thee.
Do thou, therefore, appoint the place
Where we may meet.

Mu. Down in the valley where I slew the bear.
And there doth grow a fair, broad-branchéd beech
That overshades a well; so who comes first
Let them abide the happy meeting of us both.
How like you this?

Am. I like it very well. 110

Mu. Now, if you please, you may appoint the time.

Am. Full three hours hence, God willing, I will return.

Mu. The thanks that Paris gave the Grecian queen
The like doth Mucedorus yield.

Am. Then, Mucedorus, for three hours farewell. *Exit.*

Mu. Your departure, lady, breeds a privy pain. *Exit.*

[SCENE x.

The court of Aragon.]

Enter Segasto solus.

Seg. 'Tis well, Segasto, that thou hast thy will.
Should such a shepherd, such a simple swain
As he, eclipse thy credit famous through
The court? No, ply,[1] Segasto, ply!
Let it not in Aragon be said,
A shepherd hath Segasto's honor won.

Enter Mouse, the clown, calling his master.

Clo. What ho, master, will you come away?

Seg. Will you come hither? I pray you, what's the matter? 10

Clo. Why, is it not past eleven a-clock?

Seg. How then, sir?

Clo. I pray you, come away to dinner.

Seg. I pray you, come hither.

Clo. Here's such ado with you! Will you never come?

Seg. I pray you, sir, what news of the message I sent you about?

Clo. I tell you all the messes be on the table already. There wants not so [20 much as a mess of mustard half an hour ago.

Seg. Come, sir, your mind is all upon your belly;
You have forgotten what I bid you do.

Clo. Faith, I know nothing, but you bade me go to breakfast.

Seg. Was that all?

Clo. Faith, I have forgotten it; the very scent of the meat hath made me forget[2] it quite. 30

Seg. You have forgotten the errand I bid you do?

Clo. What arrant? An arrant knave, or an arrant whore?

Seg. Why, thou knave, did I not bid thee banish the shepherd?

Clo. O, the shepherd's bastard.

Seg. I tell thee, the shepherd's banishment.

Clo. I tell you, the shepherd's bas- [40 tard shall be well kept. I'll look to it myself. But, I pray you, come away to dinner.

[1] Apply, work.
[2] Original reads *made me hath forgot.*

SEG. Then you will not tell me whether you have banished him or no?

CLO. Why, I cannot say "banishment," and you would give me a thousand pounds to say so.

SEG. Why, you whoreson [1] slave, have you forgotten that I sent you and another to drive away the shepherd? 50

CLO. What an ass are you! Here's a stir indeed! Here's "message," "arrant," "banishment," and I cannot tell what.

SEG. I pray you, sir, shall I know whether you have drove him away?

CLO. Faith, I think I have; and you will not believe me, ask my staff.

SEG. Why, can thy staff tell?

CLO. Why, he was with me too.

SEG. Then happy I, that have [60 obtained my will.

CLO. And happier I, if you would go to dinner.

SEG. Come, sirrah, follow me.

CLO. I warrant you, I will not lose an inch of you, now you are going to dinner.— [*To audience.*] I promise you, I thought seven year before I could get him away.

Exeunt.

[SCENE xi.

The forest.]

Enter Amadine sola. [2]

AM. God grant my long delay procures no harm

Nor this my tarrying frustrate my pretense. [3]

My Mucedorus surely stays for me,

And thinks me overlong. At length I come,

My present promise to perform.

Ah, what a thing is firm, unfeignéd love!

What is it which true love dares not attempt?

My father he may make, but I must match;

Segasto loves, but Amadine must like

Where Segasto likes her best; compulsion is a thrall. 10

No, no, the hearty choice is all in all;

The shepherd's virtue Amadine esteems.

But what! Methinks my shepherd is not come.

I muse at that; the hour is at hand.

Well, here I'll rest till Mucedorus come.

She sits down.

Enter Bremo, looking about; hastily takes hold of her.

BRE. A happy prey! Now, Bremo, feed on flesh!

Dainties, Bremo, dainties, thy hungry panch [4] to fill!

Now glut thy greedy guts with lukewarm blood!

Come, fight with me; I long to see thee dead.

AM. How can she fight that weapons cannot wield? 20

BRE. What, canst not fight? Then lie thee down and die.

AM. What, must I die?

BRE. What need these words? I thirst to suck thy blood!

AM. Yet pity me and let me live awhile.

BRE. No pity I; I'll feed upon thy flesh; I'll tear thy body piecemeal joint from joint.

AM. Ah, how I want my shepherd's company.

BRE. I'll crush thy bones betwixt two oaken trees.

AM. Haste, shepherd, haste, or else thou com'st too late!

BRE. I'll suck the sweetness from thy marrowbones. 30

AM. Ah, spare, ah, spare to shed my guiltless blood!

BRE. With this my bat will I beat out thy brains!

Down, down, I say; prostrate thyself upon the ground.

AM. Then, Mucedorus, farewell; my hopéd joys, farewell.

Yea, farewell, life, and welcome, present death! *She kneels.*

To thee, O God, I yield my dying ghost.

BRE. Now, Bremo, play thy part.—

How now, what sudden chance is this?

My limbs do tremble and my sinews shake;

My unweakened arms hath lost their former force. 40

Ah, Bremo, Bremo, what a foil [5] hast thou

[1] Rascally.

[2] Original reads *solus.*

[3] Intention.

[4] Paunch.

[5] Disgrace.

That yet at no time [ever][1] wast afraid
To dare the greatest gods to fight with
thee,   *He strikes.*
And now wants strength for one down-
driving blow!
Ah, how my courage fails when I should
strike!
Some newcome spirit, abiding in my
breast,
Saith, "Spare her," which never spared
any.
Shall I spare her, Bremo? Spare her;
do not kill.[2]
To it, Bremo, to it! Say [3] again.—
I cannot wield my weapons in my hand;
Methinks I should not strike so fair a
one.   51
I think her beauty hath bewitched my
force
Or else within me altered nature's course.
Ay, woman, wilt thou live in woods with
me?
Am. Fain would I live, yet loath to live in
woods.
Bre. Thou shalt not choose; it shall be
as I say,
And, therefore, follow me.   *Exeunt.*

[Scene xii.
The same.]

Enter Mucedorus solus.

Mu. It was my will an hour ago and more,
As was my promise, for to make return,
But other business hindered my pre-
tense.
It is a world [4] to see, when man appoints
And purposely one certain thing de-
crees,
How many things may hinder his intent.
What one would wish, the same is
farthest off.
But yet th'appointed time cannot be
past,
Nor hath her presence yet prevented [5]
me.
Well, here I'll stay, and expect [6] her com-
ing.   10
They cry within, "Hold him, hold him!"
Mu. Someone or other is pursued, no
doubt;

[1] From 1598 edn.
[2] Ll. 47 and 48 are interchanged in the original.
[3] Essay.   [5] Preceded.
[4] It is wonderful.   [6] Await.

Perhaps some search for me. 'Tis good
to doubt the worst;
Therefore I'll be gone.   *Exit.*

*Cry within, "Hold him, hold him!" Enter
Mouse, the clown, with a pot.*

Clo. Hold him, hold him, hold him!
Here's a stir indeed. Here came hue after
the crier; and I was set close at Mother
Nip's house, and there I called for three
pots of ale, as 'tis the manner of us courtiers. Now, sirrah, I had taken the maidenhead of two of them. Now, as I was [20
lifting up the third to my mouth, there
came, "Hold him, hold him!" Now I could
not tell whom to catch hold on, but I am
sure I caught one—perchance a may be in
this pot. Well, I'll see! Mass, I cannot
see him yet. Well, I'll look a little further.
Mass, he is a little slave, if a be here. Why,
here's nobody. All this goes well yet; but
if the old trot should come for her pot—
ay, marry, there's the matter. But I [30
care not; I'll face her out, and call her old
rusty, dusty, musty, fusty, crusty firebrand, and worse than all that, and so
face her out of her pot. But soft, here
she comes!

Enter the Old Woman.

Old W. Come, you knave! Where's
my pot, you knave?
Clo. Go, look your pot; come not to
me for your pot, 'twere good for you.
Old W. Thou liest, thou knave; [40
thou hast my pot.
Clo. You lie, and you say it. I your
pot? I know what I'll say.
[Old W.] [7] Why, what wilt thou say?
Clo. But say I have him, and thou
dar'st.
Old W. Why, thou knave, thou hast
not only my pot but my drink unpaid for.
Clo. You lie like an old—I will not
say whore.   50
Old W. Dost thou call me whore? I'll
cap [8] thee for my pot.
Clo. Cap me and thou darest! Search
me whether I have it or no.
*She searcheth him, and he drinketh over
her head and casteth down the pot; she
stumbleth at it; then they fall together by
the ears; she takes up her pot and goes out.*

[7] From 1598 edn.   [8] Arrest.

Enter Segasto.

SEG. How now, sirrah, what's the matter?

CLO. O, flies, master, flies.

SEG. Flies? Where are they?

CLO. O, here, master, all about your face.   60

SEG. Why, thou liest; I think thou art mad.

CLO. Why, master, I have killed a dungcartful at the least.

SEG. Go to, sirrah! Leaving this idle talk, give ear to me.

CLO. How? Give you one of my ears? Not and you were ten masters.

SEG. Why, sir, I bid you give ear to my words.   70

CLO. I tell you I will not be made a curtal [1] for no man's pleasure.

SEG. I tell thee, attend what I say. Go thy ways straight and rear the whole town.

CLO. How? Rear the whole town? Even go yourself; it is more than I can do. Why, do you think I can rear a town, that can scarce rear a pot of ale to my head? I should rear a town, should I not! [80

SEG. Go to the constable and make a privy search, for the shepherd is run away with the king's daughter.

CLO. How? Is the shepherd run away with the king's daughter, or is the king's daughter run away with the shepherd?

SEG. I cannot tell, but they are both gone together.

CLO. What a fool is she to run away with the shepherd! Why, I think I am [90 a little handsomer man than the shepherd myself. But tell me, master, must I make a privy search, or search in the privy?

SEG. Why, dost thou think they will be there?

CLO. I cannot tell.

SEG. Well, then, search everywhere; leave no place unsearched for them.   *Exit.*

CLO. O, now am I in office; now will I to that old firebrand's house and [100 will not leave one place unsearched; nay, I'll to the alestand [2] and drink as long as I can stand, and, when I have done, I'll let out all the rest, to see if he be not hid in the barrel. And, if I find him not there, I'll to the cupboard; I'll not leave one

[1] Docked animal.   [2] Barrel.

corner of her house unsearched. I' faith, ye old crust, I will be with you now.   *Exit.*

[SCENE xiii. [3]

The court of Valencia.]

Sound music.

Enter the King of Valencia, Anselmo, Roderigo, Lord Borachius, with Others.

KING [OF] VAL. Enough of music; it but adds to torment;

Delights to vexéd spirits are as dates
Set to a sickly man, which rather cloy than comfort.

Let me entreat you to entreat no more.

ROD. Let your strings sleep; have done there.   *Let the music cease.*

KING [OF] VAL. Mirth to a soul disturbed are embers turned,

Which sudden gleam with molestation,
But sooner lose their sight for't;
'Tis gold bestowed upon a rioter,
Which not relieves, but murders him.   10
'Tis a drug given to the healthful,
Which infects, not cures.

How can a father that hath lost his son,

A prince both wise, virtuous, and valiant,
Take pleasure in the idle acts of time?
No, no; till Mucedorus I shall see again,
All joy is comfortless, all pleasure pain.

ANS. Your son, my lord, is well.

KING [OF] VAL. I prithee, speak that thrice.

ANS. The prince, your son, is safe.   20

KING [OF] VAL. O, where, Anselmo? Surfeit me with that.

ANS. In Aragon, my liege; and at his parture

Bound my secrecy
By his affectious love, not to disclose it.
But care of him and pity of your age
Makes my tongue blab what my breast vowed concealment.

KING [OF] VAL. Thou not deceiv'st me?

I ever thought thee what I find thee now,
An upright, loyal man. But what desire,

Or young-fed humor nursed within the brain,   30

Drew him so privately to Aragon?

[3] This scene appeared first in the 1610 edn.

Ans. A forcing adamant: [1]

Love, mixed with fear and doubtful
　jealousy,
Whether report gilded a worthless trunk,
Or Amadine deserved her high extol-
　ment.

King [of] Val. See our provision be in
　readiness;
Collect us followers of the comeliest
　hue
For our chief guardians; we will thither
　wend.
The crystal eye of heaven shall not
　thrice wink,
Nor the green flood six times his shoul-
　ders turn,　　　　　　　　　　40
Till we salute the Aragonian king.
Music, speak loudly now; the season's
　apt,
For former dolors are in pleasure
　wrapped.　　　　　*Exeunt omnes.*

[Scene xiv.

The forest.]

Enter Mucedorus to disguise himself.

Mu. Now, Mucedorus, whither wilt thou
　go?
Home to thy father to thy native soil,
Or try some long abode within these
　woods?
Well, I will hence depart and hie me
　home.
What, hie me home, said I? That may
　not be;
In Amadine rests my felicity.
Then, Mucedorus, do as thou didst
　decree:
Attire thee hermit-like within these
　groves,
Walk often to the beech and view the
　well,
Make settles there and seat thyself
　thereon,　　　　　　　　　　10
And, when thou feelest thyself to be
　athirst,
Then drink a hearty draught to Ama-
　dine.
No doubt she thinks on thee,
And will one day come pledge thee at
　this well.
Come, habit, thou art fit for me.
　　　　　　　He disguiseth himself.

[1] Compelling magnet.

No shepherd now, a hermit must I be.
Methinks this fits me very well;
Now must I learn to bear a walking
　staff,
And exercise some gravity withal.

Enter the Clown.

Clo. Here's through the woods, and　[20
through the woods, to look out a shepherd
and a stray king's daughter.—But soft,
who have we here? What art thou?

Mu. I am an hermit.

Clo. An emmet? I never saw such a
big emmet in all my life before.

Mu. I tell you, sir, I am an hermit,
one that leads a solitary life within these
woods.

Clo. O, I know thee now; thou art　[30
her that eats up all the hips and haws;
we could not have one piece of fat bacon
for thee all this year.

Mu. Thou dost mistake me. But, I
pray thee, tell me who dost thou seek in
these woods.

Clo. What do I seek? For a stray
king's daughter run away with a shepherd.

Mu. A stray king's daughter run away
with a shepherd! Wherefore, canst　[40
thou tell?

Clo. Yes, that I can; 'tis this: my
master and Amadine, walking one day
abroad, nearer to these woods than they
were used—about what I cannot tell—but
towards them comes running a great
bear. Now my master, he played the man
and ran away, and Amadine crying after
him. Now, sir, comes me a shepherd and
he strikes off the bear's head. Now　[50
whether the bear were dead before or no I
cannot tell, for bring twenty bears before
me and bind their hands and feet, and
I'll kill them all. Now, ever since, Amadine
hath been in love with the shepherd, and
for good will she's even run away with the
shepherd.

Mu. What manner of man was he?
Canst describe him unto me?

Clo. 'Scribe him? Ay, I warrant　[60
you that I can. A was a little, low, broad,
tall, narrow, big, well-favored fellow—a
jerkin of white cloth, and buttons of the
same cloth.

Mu. Thou describest him well, but, if

I chance to see any such, pray you, where
shall I find you, or what's your name?

Clo. My name is called Master Mouse.

Mu. O, Master Mouse, I pray you,
what office might you bear in the [70
court?

Clo. Marry, sir, I am a rusher of the
stable.

Mu. O, usher of the table!

Clo. Nay, I say "rusher," and I'll
prove mine office good; for look, sir, when
any comes from under the sea or so, and
a dog chance to blow his nose backward,
then with a whip I give him the good time
of the day, and strow rushes presently.[1] [80
Therefore, I am a rusher, a high office,
I promise ye.

Mu. But where shall I find you in the
court?

Clo. Why, where it is best being, either
in the kitching a-eating or in the buttery
drinking. But, if you come, I will provide
for thee a piece of beef and brewis knuckle-
deep in fat. Pray you, take pains; remember Master Mouse.   *Exit.* [90

Mu. Ay, sir, I warrant I will not forget
you.—
Ah, Amadine, what should become of
thee?
Whither shouldst thou go so long unknown?
With watch and ward each passage is
beset,
So that she cannot long escape unknown.
Doubtless she hath lost herself within
these woods
And, wand'ring to and fro, she seeks the
well,
Which yet she cannot find; therefore
will I seek her out.   *Exit.*

[Scene xv.

The same.]

Enter Bremo and Amadine.

Bre. Amadine, how like you Bremo and
his woods?

Am. As like the woods of Bremo's cruelty!
Though I were dumb and could not
answer him,
The beasts themselves would with re-
lenting tears
Bewail thy savage and unhuman deeds.

[1] Strew rushes immediately.

Bre. My love, why dost thou murmur to
thyself?
Speak louder, for thy Bremo hears thee
not.

Am. My Bremo? No, the shepherd is my
love.

Bre. Have I not savéd thee from sudden
death,
Giving thee leave to live that thou
mightst love?   10
And dost thou whet me on to cruelty?
Come, kiss me, sweet, for all my favors
past.

Am. I may not, Bremo, and therefore
pardon me.

Bre. [*Aside.*] See how she flings away
from me; I will follow
And give attend to her.—Deny my
love!
Ah, worm of beauty, I will chastise thee!
Come, come, prepare thy head upon
the block.

Am. O, spare me, Bremo! Love should
limit life,
Not to be made a murderer of himself.
If thou wilt glut thy loving heart with
blood,   20
Encounter with the lion or the bear,
And like a wolf prey not upon a lamb.

Bre. Why then dost thou repine at me?
If thou wilt love me, thou shalt be my
queen;
I will crown thee with a chaplet [2] made
of ivory,
And make the rose and lily wait on thee.
I'll rend the burly branches from the
oak,[3]
To shadow thee from burning sun.
The trees shall spread themselves where
thou dost go,
And, as they spread, I'll trace [4] along
with thee.   30

Am. [*Aside.*] You may, for who but you?

Bre. Thou shalt be fed with quails and
partridges,
With blackbirds, larks, thrushes, and
nightingales.
Thy drink shall be goat's milk and crystal
water,
Distilled from the fountains and the
clearest springs.

[2] Original reads *complet.*
[3] From 1598 edn. Original reads *oxe.*
[4] Walk.

And all the dainties that the woods afford
I'll freely give thee to obtain thy love.
Am. [*Aside.*] You may, for who but you?
Bre. The day I'll spend to recreate my love   39
With all the pleasures that I can devise,
And in the night I'll be thy bedfellow,
And lovingly embrace thee in mine arms.
Am. [*Aside.*] One may; so may not you.
Bre. The satyrs and the wood-nymphs shall attend on thee
And lull thee asleep with music's sound,
And in the morning when thou dost awake,
The lark shall sing good morrow to my queen,
And, whilst he sings, I'll kiss my Amadine.
Am. [*Aside.*] You may, for who but you?
Bre. When thou art up, the wood lanes shall be strowed   50
With violets, cowslips, and sweet marigolds
For thee to trample and to trace upon,
And I will teach thee how to kill the deer,
To chase the hart and how to rouse the roe,
If thou wilt live to love and honor me.
Am. [*Aside.*] You may, for who but you?

Enter Mucedorus.

Bre. Welcome, sir;
An hour ago I looked for such a guest.
Be merry, wench, we'll have a frolic feast.
Here's flesh enough for to suffice us both.   60
Say, sirrah, wilt thou fight or dost thou mean to die?
Mu. I want a weapon; how can I fight?
Bre. Thou wants a weapon? Why then, thou yield'st to die.
Mu. I say not so; I do not yield to die.
Bre. Thou shalt not choose. I long to see thee dead!
Am. Yet spare him, Bremo, spare him!
Bre. Away, I say; I will not spare him.
Mu. Yet give me leave to speak.
Bre.   Thou shalt not speak.
Am. Yet give him leave to speak for my sake.

Bre. Speak on, but be not overlong.   70
Mu. In time of yore, when men like brutish beasts
Did lead their lives in loathsome cells and woods
And wholly gave themselves to witless will,
A rude, unruly rout, then man to man
Became a present prey; then might prevailed;
The weakest went to walls.
Right was unknown, for wrong was all in all.
As men thus livéd in their great outrage,[1]
Behold, one Orpheus came, as poets tell,
And them from rudeness unto reason brought,   80
Who, led by reason, some forsook the woods.
Instead of caves they built them castles strong;
Cities and towns were founded by them then.
Glad were they, they found such ease, and in
The end they grew to perfect amity.
Weighing their former wickedness,
They termed the time wherein they livéd then
A golden age, a goodly golden age.
Now, Bremo, for so I hear thee called,
If men which lived tofore, as thou dost now,   90
Wild in wood, addicted all to spoil,
Returnéd were by worthy Orpheus' means,
Let me like Orpheus cause thee to return
From murther, bloodshed, and like cruelty.
What, should we fight before we have a cause?
No, let's live and love together faithfully.
I'll fight for thee.
Bre.   Fight for me or die!
Or fight, or else thou diest!
Am.   Hold, Bremo, hold!
Bre. Away, I say; thou troublest me.
Am. You promised me to make me your queen.   100
Bre. I did; I mean no less.
Am. You promised that I should have my will.
Bre. I did; I mean no less.

---

[1] Violent conduct.

Am. Then save this hermit's life, for he may save us both.

Bre. At thy request I'll spare him, but never any after him. Say, hermit, what canst thou do?

Mu. I'll wait on thee; sometime upon thy queen. Such service shalt thou shortly have as Bremo never had.　　*Exeunt.* [110

[Scene xvi.

The court of Aragon.]

Enter Segasto, the Clown, and Rumbelo.

Seg. Come, sirs; what, shall I never have you find out Amadine and the shepherd?

Clo. And I have been through the woods, and through the woods, and could see nothing but an emmet.

Ru. Why, I see a thousand emmets. Thou mean'st a little one?

Clo. Nay, that emmet that I saw was bigger than thou art.　　　　　　10

Ru. Bigger than I?—What a fool have you to your man; I pray you, master, turn him away.

Seg. But dost thou hear? Was he not a man?

Clo. Think he was, for he said he did lead a saltseller's life about the woods.

Seg. Thou wouldest say a solitary life about the woods.

Clo. I think it was so, indeed.　　20

Ru. I thought what a fool thou art.

Clo. Thou art a wise man! Why, he did nothing but sleep since he went.

Seg. But tell me, Mouse, how did he go?

Clo. In a white gown, and a white hat on his head, and a staff in his hand.

Seg. I thought so; it was an hermit that walked a solitary life in the woods. Well, get you to dinner, and after, never leave seeking till you bring some news of [30 them, or I'll hang you both.　　*Exit.*

Clo. How now, Rumbelo? What shall we do now?

Ru. Faith, I'll home to dinner, and afterward to sleep.

Clo. Why, then, thou wilt be hanged.

Ru. Faith, I care not, for I know I shall never find them. Well, I'll once more abroad, and, if I cannot find them, I'll never come home again.　　　　　40

Clo. I tell thee what, Rumbelo, thou shalt go in at one end of the wood and I at the other, and we will meet both together in the midst.

Ru. Content! Let's away to dinner.
　　　　　　　　　　　　　　Exeunt.

[Scene xvii.

The forest.]

Enter Mucedorus solus.

Mu. Unknown to any here within these woods,
With bloody Bremo do I lead my life.
The monster, he doth murder all he meets;
He spareth none, and none doth him escape.
Who would continue—who but only I—
In such a cruel cutthroat's company?
Yet Amadine is there. How can I choose?
Ah, silly soul, how oftentimes she sits
And sighs, and calls, "Come, shepherd, come;
Sweet Mucedorus, come and set me free,"　　　　　　　　　　10
When Mucedorus present [1] stands her by!—
But here she comes!

Enter Amadine. [2]

What news, fair lady, as you walk these woods?

Am. Ah, hermit, none but bad and such as thou knowest.

Mu. How do you like your Bremo and his woods?

Am. Not my Bremo nor Bremo his [3] woods.

Mu. And why not yours? Methinks he loves you well.

Am. I like not him; his love to me is nothing worth.

Mu. Lady, in this methinks you offer wrong,
To hate the man that ever loves you best.　　　　　　　　　　20

Am. Ah, hermit, I take no pleasure in his love;
Neither doth Bremo like me best.

[1] Suggested by Hazlitt. Original reads *peasant.*
[2] In the original this stage direction follows the next line.
[3] Original reads *his Bremo.*

MU. Pardon my boldness, fair lady; sith
we both
May safely talk now out of Bremo's
sight,
Unfold to me, if so you please, the full
discourse
How, when, and why you came into
these woods,
And fell into this bloody butcher's
hands.
AM. Hermit, I will.
Of late a worthy shepherd I did love—
MU. A shepherd, lady? Sure, a man un-
fit　　　　　　　　　　　　　　30
To match with you.
AM. Hermit, this is true; and, when we
had—
MU. Stay there; the wild man comes!
Refer [1] the rest until another time.

Enter Bremo.

BRE. What secret tale is this? What
whisp'ring have we here?
Villain, I charge thee tell thy tale again.
MU. If needs I must, lo, here it is again:
Whenas we both had lost the sight of
thee,
It grieved us both, but specially thy
queen,　　　　　　　　　　39
Who in thy absence ever fears the worst,
Lest some mischance befall your royal
grace.
"Shall my sweet Bremo wander through
the woods?
Toil to and fro for to redress my want,
Hazard his life, and all to cherish me?
I like not this," quoth she,
And thereupon cravéd to know of me
If I could teach her handle weapons
well.
My answer was I had small skill therein,
But gladsome, mighty king, to learn of
thee.
And this was all.　　　　　　50
BRE. Was't so? None can dislike of this.
I'll teach
You both to fight; but first, my queen,
begin.
Here, take this weapon; see how thou
canst use it.
AM. This is too big; I cannot wield it in
my arm.

[1] Postpone.

BRE. Is't so? We'll have a knotty crab-
tree staff
For thee.—But, sirrah, tell me, what
sayest thou?
MU. With all my heart I willing am to
learn.
BRE. Then take my staff and see how
thou canst wield it.
MU. First teach me how to hold it in my
hand.
BRE. Thou hold'st it well.　　　　60
Look how he doth; thou mayst the
sooner learn.
MU. Next tell me how and when 'tis best
to strike.
BRE. 'Tis best to strike when time doth
serve;
'Tis best to lose no time.
MU. [*Aside.*] Then now or never is my
time to strike.
BRE. And, when thou strikest, be sure to
hit the head.
MU. The head?
BRE.　　　　The very head.
MU.　　　　　　Then have at thine!
He strikes him down dead.
So, lie there and die,
A death no doubt according to desert,
Or else a worse as thou deserv'st a
worse.　　　　　　70
AM. It glads my heart this tyrant's death
to see.
MU. Now, lady, it remains in you
To end the tale you lately had begun,
Being interrupted by this wicked wight.
You said you loved a shepherd?
AM. Ay, so I do, and none but only him,
And will do still as long as life shall
last.
MU. But tell me, lady, sith I set you free,
What course of life do you intend to
take?
AM. I will disguiséd wander through the
world,　　　　　　80
Till I have found him out.
MU. How if you find your shepherd in
these woods?
AM. Ah, none so happy then as Amadine.
He discloseth [2] himself.
MU. In tract of time a man may alter
much.
Say, lady, do you know your shepherd
well?

[2] Early edns. read *disguiseth.*

Am. My Mucedorus! Hath he set me free?

Mu. He hath set thee free.

Am. And lived so long unknown to Amadine?

Mu. Ay, that's a question whereof you may not be resolved.
You know that I am banished from the court?   90
I know likewise each passage is beset
So that we cannot long escape unknown;
Therefore my will is this: that we return
Right through the thickets to the wild man's cave,
And there awhile live on his provision,
Until the search and narrow watch be past.
This is my counsel, and I think it best.

Am. I think the very same.

Mu.   Come, let's begone.

The Clown [enters and] searcheth, and falls over the Wild Man, and so carries him away.

Clo. Nay, soft, sir; are you here? A bots [1] on you! I was like to be hanged [100 for not finding you. We would borrow a certain stray king's daughter of you—a wench, a wench, sir, we would have.

Mu. A wench of me? I'll make thee eat my sword!

Clo. O Lord! Nay, and you are so lusty, I'll call a cooling card [2] for you. Ho, master, master, ay, come away quickly!

Enter Seg[asto].

Seg. What's the matter?   109

Clo. Look, master, Amadine and the shepherd! O, brave!

Seg. What, minion, have I found you out?

Clo. Nay, that's a lie; I found her out myself.

Seg. Thou gadding huswife, what cause hadst thou to gad abroad,
Whenas thou knowest our wedding day so nigh?

Am. Not so, Segasto; no such thing in hand.
Show your assurance; [3] then I'll answer you.

---

[1] *I.e.*, plague.
[2] A card that dashes the hopes of the adversary.   [3] Pledge of betrothal.

Seg. Thy father's promise my assurance is.   120

Am. But what he promised he hath not performed.

Seg. It rests in thee for to perform the same.

Am. Not I.

Seg. And why?

Am. So is my will, and therefore even so.

Clo. Master, with a nonny, nonny, no! [4]

Seg. Ah, wicked villain, art thou here?

Mu. What needs these words? We weigh them not.

Seg. We weigh them not? Proud shepherd, I scorn thy company.

Clo. We'll not have a corner of thy company.   130

Mu. I scorn not thee, nor yet the least of thine.

Clo. That's a lie; a would have killed me with his pugsnando.

Seg. This stoutness, Amadine, contents me not.

Am. Then seek another that may you better please.

Mu. Well, Amadine, it only rests in thee
Without delay to make thy choice of three:
There stands Segasto; here a shepherd stands;
There stands the third. Now make thy choice.

Clo. A lord at the least I am.   140

Am. My choice is made, for I will none but thee.

Seg. A worthy mate, no doubt, for such a wife.

Mu. And, Amadine, why wilt thou none but me?
I cannot keep thee as thy father did;
I have no lands for to maintain thy state.
Moreover, if thou mean to be my wife,
Commonly this must be thy use:
To bed at midnight, up at four,
Drudge all day and trudge from place to place,   149
Whereby our daily victual for to win;
And last of all, which is the worst of all,
No princess then, but plain a shepherd's wife.

Clo. Then, God gi' you good morrow, goody shepherd!

---

[4] Refrain in popular songs.

Am. It shall not need; if Amadine do
    live,
Thou shalt be crownéd King of Aragon.
Clo. O, master, laugh! When he's
king, then I'll be a queen!
Mu. Then know that which ne'er to-
    fore was known:
I am no shepherd, no Aragonian I,
But born of royal blood—my father's
    of   160
Valencia king, my mother, queen—
    who for
Thy sacred sake took this hard task in
    hand.
Am. Ah, how I joy my fortune is so good!
Seg. Well, now I see Segasto shall not
    speed;
But, Mucedorus, I as much do joy
To see thee here within our court of
    Aragon,
As if a kingdom had befall'n me this
    time.
I with my heart surrender her to thee,
    He gives her to him.
And loose [1] what right to Amadine I
    have!   169
Clo. What barn's door, and born
where my father was constable! A bots
on thee! How dost thee?
Mu. Thanks, Segasto; but yet you leveled
    at the crown.
Clo. Master, bear this and bear all.
Seg. Why so, sir?
Clo. He sees you take a goose by the
    crown.
Seg. Go to, sir! Away, post you to the
    king,
Whose heart is fraught with careful
    doubts,[2]
Glad him up and tell him these good
    news,   179
And we will follow as fast as we may.
Clo. I go, master; I run, master!
    Exeunt.

[Scene xviii.

An open place near the court of Aragon.]

Enter the King and Collen.

King. Break, heart, and end my pallid
    woes!
My Amadine, the comfort of my life,

[1] Emended by Hazlitt. Original reads *looke.*
[2] Anxious fears.

How can I joy except she were in sight?
Her absence breeds sorrow to my soul
And with a thunder breaks my heart in
    twain.
Col. Forbear those passions, gentle king,
And you shall see 'twill turn unto the
    best,
And bring your soul to quiet and to joy.
King. Such joy as death, I do assure me
    that,
And naught but death, unless of her
    I hear,   10
And that with speed; I cannot sigh thus
    long—
But what a tumult do I hear within?
They cry within, "Joy and happiness!"
Col. I hear a noise of overpassing joy
Within the court; my lord, be of good
    comfort.—
And here comes one in haste.

Enter the Clown running.

Clo. A king! a king! a king!
Col. Why, how now, sirrah? What's
the matter?
Clo. O, 'tis news for a king; 'tis worth
money.   20
King. Why, sirrah, thou shalt have sil-
ver and gold if it be good.
Clo. O, 'tis good, 'tis good! Amadine—
King. O, what of her? Tell me, and I
will make thee a knight.
Clo. How, a sprite? No, by Lady, I
will not be a sprite. Masters, get you
away; if I be a sprite, I shall be so lean I
shall make you all afraid.
Col. Thou sot, the king means to [30
make thee a gentleman.
Clo. Why, I shall want parel.[3]
King. Thou shalt want for nothing.
Clo. Then stand away; strike up thy-
self. Here they come.

Enter Segasto, Mucedorus, and Amadine.

Am. My gracious father, pardon thy dis-
    loyal daughter.
King. What, do mine eyes behold my
    daughter Amadine?
Rise up, dear daughter, and let these
    my embracing arms
Show some token of thy father's joy,
Which ever since thy departure hath
    languished in sorrow.   40

[3] Apparel.

Am. Dear father, never were your sorrows
Greater than my griefs,
Never you so desolate as I comfortless;
Yet, nevertheless, acknowledging myself
To be the cause of both, on bended knees
I humbly crave your pardon.

King. I'll pardon thee, dear daughter;
but, as for him—

Am. Ah, father, what of him?

King. As sure as I am king and wear the
crown,   49
I will revenge on that accurséd wretch.

Mu. Yet, worthy prince, work not thy
will in wrath;
Show favor.

King.   Ay, such favor as thou
deservest.

Mu. I do deserve the daughter of a king.

King. O, impudent! A shepherd and so
insolent?

Mu. No shepherd I, but a worthy prince.

King. In fair conceit,[1] not princely born.

Mu. Yes, princely born: my father is a
king,
My mother a queen, and of Valencia
both.

King. What, Mucedorus? Welcome to
our court!
What cause hadst thou to come to me
disguised?   60

Mu. No cause to fear; I causéd no of-
fense
But this: desiring thy daughter's virtues
for to see,
Disguised myself from out my father's
court,
Unknown to any. In secret I did rest,
And passéd many troubles near to death;
So hath your daughter my partaker been,
As you shall know hereafter more at
large,
Desiring you, you will give her to me,
Even as mine own and sovereign of
my life;
Then shall I think my travails are well
spent.   70

King. With all my heart, but this—
Segasto claims my promise made tofore,
That he should have her as his only
wife,
Before my council when we came from
war.

[1] Imagination.

Segasto, may I crave thee let it pass,
And give Amadine as wife to Mucedorus?

Seg. With all my heart, were it a far
greater thing;
And what I may to furnish up their rites
With pleasing sports and pastimes you
shall see.

King. Thanks, good Segasto, I will think
of this.   80

Mu. Thanks, good my lord, and, while I
live,
Account of me in what I can or may.

Am. And, good Segasto, these great courtesies
Shall not be forgot.

Clo. Why, hark you, master! Bones,[2]
what have you done? What, given away
the wench you made me take such pains
for? You are wise indeed! Mass, and I
had known of that, I would have had her
myself! Faith, master, now we may go   [90
to breakfast with a woodcock pie!

Seg. Go, sir; you were best leave this
knavery.

King. Come on, my lords, let's now to
court,
Where we may finish up the joyfulest day
That ever happed to a distresséd king.[3]
Were but thy father, the Valencia lord,
Present in view of this combining knot!

A shout within. Enter a Messenger.

What shout was that?   98

Mess. My lord, the great Valencia king,
Newly arrived, entreats your presence.

Mu. My father?

King. Preparéd welcomes give him enter-
tainment.
A happier planet never reigned than that
Which governs at this hour.   *Sound.*

*Enter the King of Valencia, Anselmo,
Roderigo, Borachius, with Others; the
King runs and embraces his Son.*

King [of] Val. Rise, honor of my age,
food to my rest!
Condemn not, mighty King of Aragon,
My rude behavior, so compelled by
nature,
That manners stood unknowledged.

[2] By God's bones.
[3] The rest of the scene is different in the 1598
edn., in which the King of Valencia does not
appear.

King. What we have to recite would
    tedious prove   109
By declaration; therefore, in and feast.
Tomorrow the performance shall ex-
    plain
What words conceal; till then, drums,
    speak; bells, ring.
Give plausive [1] welcomes to our brother
    king.
Sound drums and trumpets. Exeunt omnes.

[Epilogue]

Enter Comedy and Envy.

Com. How now, Envy? What, blushest
    thou already?
Peep forth; hide not thy head with
    shame,
But with a courage praise a woman's
    deeds.
Thy threats were vain; thou couldst
    do me no hurt.
Although thou seemest to cross me with
    despite,
I overwhelmed, and turnéd upside down
    thy blocks
And made thyself to stumble at the
    same.
Env. Though stumbled, yet not over-
    thrown!
Thou canst not draw my heart to mild-
    ness;
Yet must I needs confess thou hast done
    well,   10
And played thy part with mirth and
    pleasant glee.
Say all this, yet canst thou not conquer
    me;
Although this time thou hast got—yet
    not the conquest neither.
A double revenge another time I'll have.[2]
Com. Envy, spit thy gall;
Plot, work, contrive; create new fal-
    lacies;
Teem from thy womb each minute a
    black traitor,
Whose blood and thoughts have twins'
    conception;
Study to act deeds yet unchronicled;
Cast native monsters in the molds of
    men;   20

Case vicious devils under sancted roch-
    ets; [3]
Unhasp the wicket [4] where all perjureds
    roost,
And swarm this ball with treasons. Do
    thy worst,
Thou canst not, hellhound, cross my
    steer [5] tonight,
Nor blind that glory where I wish de-
    light.
Env. I can, I will.
Com.   Nefarious hag, begin,
And let us tug till one the mast'ry win.
Env. Comedy, thou art a shallow goose;
I'll overthrow thee in thine own intent, 29
And make thy fall my comic merriment.
Com. Thy policy wants gravity; thou art
Too weak. Speak, fiend! As how?
Env. Why, thus:
From my foul study will I hoist a wretch,
A lean and hungry neger [6] cannibal,
Whose jaws swell to his eyes with chaw-
    ing malice;
And him I'll make a poet!
Com.   What's that to th' purpose?
Env. This scrambling raven, with his
    needy beard,
Will I whet on to write a comedy,
Wherein shall be composed dark sen-
    tences,   40
Pleasing to factious brains;
And every other where place me a jest,
Whose high abuse shall more torment
    than blows.
Then I myself, quicker than lightning,
Will fly me to a puissant magistrate,
And, waiting with a trencher at his
    back,
In midst of jollity, rehearse those galls,
With some additions,
So lately vented in your theater.
He, upon this, cannot but make com-
    plaint,   50
To your great danger, or at least re-
    straint.
Com. Ha, ha, ha! I laugh to hear thy
    folly;
This is a trap for boys, not men, nor
    such,
Especially desertful in their doings,
Whose staid discretion rules their pur-
    poses.

---

[1] Applauding.
[2] In the 1598 edn. the remainder of the epilogue
consists of nineteen lines in honor of Elizabeth.

[3] Holy surplices.   [5] Interfere with my rudder.
[4] Gate (in hell).   [6] Negro.

I and my faction do eschew those vices.
But see, O, see! The weary sun for rest
Hath lain his golden compass to the
  west,
Where he perpetual bide and ever shine,
As David's offspring, in his happy
  clime.   60
Stoop, Envy, stoop; bow to the earth
  with me;
Let's beg our pardons on our bended
  knee.   *They kneel.*[1]
Env. My power has lost her might;
  Envy's date's expired.
Yon splendent majesty hath felled my
  sting,
And I amazéd am. *Fall down and quake.*
Com. Glorious and wise Arch-Cæsar on
  this earth,

[1] To King James, before whom one performance was given.

At whose appearance Envy's stroken
  dumb,
And all bad things cease operation,
Vouchsafe to pardon our unwilling
  error,   69
So late presented to your gracious view,
And we'll endeavor with excess of pain
To please your senses in a choicer strain.
Thus we commit you to the arms of
  Night,
Whose spangled carcass would, for your
  delight,
Strive to excel the Day; be blessed,
  then.
Who other wishes, let him never speak.
Env.   Amen!
To Fame and Honor we commend your
  rest;
Live still more happy, every hour more
  blessed.

FINIS.

THOMAS DEKKER

Thomas Dekker the dramatist—there are records of several contemporaries with this name—was born in London about 1572, but no details of his family relations or of his education are known. The first record of his work is a payment to him in January, 1598, as a member of Henslowe's group of dramatists. For the next six years he was actively engaged in playwriting, chiefly under Henslowe, first for the Admiral's men and later for Worcester's, and he continued to write plays sporadically during the remainder of a comparatively long life. From early in the seventeenth century, however, he devoted most of his time to the composition of prose pamphlets, which are among the best records of London life in his day. The most important are *The Bellman of London* (1608) and *The Gull's Hornbook* (1609). In spite of his prolific literary output, Dekker lived a life of hardship as a result of debt. He borrowed money of Henslowe in 1598 to secure his release from prison, and in 1619 he had been in prison some years. He may have been the Thomas Dekker who was buried in 1632; he was certainly dead by 1640 or 1641.

In his connection with Henslowe, Dekker had a hand in over forty plays, only a few of which survive. *The Shoemakers' Holiday* and *Old Fortunatus* he wrote alone, but most of his work was done in collaboration with Henslowe's writers, chiefly with Drayton, Chettle, and Wilson, but not infrequently with Jonson, Day, Haughton, Munday, Heywood, Middleton, and Webster. The group exploited many fields—the classics, romance of many periods, history, especially English chronicles, and, to a considerable extent, contemporary life. Thus the French civil wars of the period were stretched to four plays, at least two plays were domestic tragedies, and several apparently dealt with the lower levels of English life. Of the individual plays extant, *Old Fortunatus*, printed in 1600, is Dekker's best romance. *Patient Grissel*, written with Chettle and Haughton in 1598 in the spirit of the domestic play, inaugurated a vogue of the patient wife. In 1601 Dekker was drawn into the stage quarrel and acquitted himself well in *Satiromastix*, a reply to Jonson's *Poetaster*. *The Honest Whore* of 1604 is the first of a series of dramatic studies in which contact of London gallants with the rising merchant classes is depicted. The more realistic *Westward Ho* and *Northward Ho*, written with Webster, followed soon after, and *The Roaring Girl*, in which he collaborated with Middleton, about 1610. Among the later plays, *The Virgin Martyr*, written with Massinger about 1620, and *The Witch of Edmonton*, with Ford and Rowley about 1621, are masterly tragedies. Appropriately Dekker also made his contributions to the great civic pageants of London.

Dekker is the first of a group of writers included in this anthology who represent the culmination of Elizabethan drama proper. The literary decade extending from the first known publication of work by Lyly and Peele in 1584 to the death of Kyd shows the dramatists utilizing a wide range of story and history and developing not only a variety of characters from both the real and the supernatural world, but also a variety of structural devices and styles. For a period of a little over a decade from the middle of the nineties, the early literary drama continued with even greater imaginative fervor and range of style, as illustrated in the work of Shakespeare. Significant new forces, however, were producing a more searching and realistic interpretation of character and a more critical attitude to structure and style. In these respects the drama of this decade prepares for the early Stuart drama or indeed merges with it, for the later work of most of the men represented here is at times more Jacobean than Elizabethan. In Dekker the reaction is indicated not so much by the loss of the romantic or idealizing tendency of the age as by the centering of it on contemporary life, as a result no doubt of the growing wealth and splendor of courts and cities and of man's new adventures in travel.

exploration, and war. With old elements of romance Dekker blends new ones of commerce in the portrayal of the merchant class. Primarily, however, he reflects the infinite Elizabethan zest of life, even in realistic scenes.

The Shoemakers' Holiday is first mentioned by Henslowe under date of July 15, 1599, evidently having been written during the preceding six weeks. A court performance was secured for it on the night of January 1, 1600, and it was printed in the same year by Valentine Sims. Other quartos appeared in 1610, 1618, 1624, 1631, and 1657, each one being a reprint of its immediate predecessor. The plot of *The Shoemakers' Holiday* is derived from the three shoemaker stories that make up the first part of Thomas Deloney's *Gentle Craft* (1598). The last story, "Simon Eyre," which furnished Dekker with most of his material for the play, is Deloney's romanticized account of a historical figure, who rose from the position of upholsterer and draper (in Deloney, shoemaker) to become a wealthy lord mayor of London (1445–46). To the other two stories Dekker is indebted for suggestions for characters. He may also have made use of popular ballads for the incident of Ralph, Jane, and Hammon. The play shows the patriotism and many of the romantic conventions of *George a Greene*, transferred to London tradesmen of 1599. The present text is based on Lange's reprint of the quarto of 1600 in Gayley's *Representative English Comedies*.

The first part of *The Honest Whore* was printed by Valentine Sims in 1604 (other editions appeared in 1605, 1615, 1616, and 1635), and the second part (not reprinted here) by Elizabeth Allde in 1630, with the original subtitle considerably expanded: "With the humors of the patient man, the impatient wife; the honest whore, persuaded by strong arguments to turn courtesan again; her brave refuting those arguments; and lastly, the comical passages of an Italian Bridewell, where the scene ends." Although the title-pages of both plays give Dekker alone as the author, from a passage in Henslowe's Diary it appears that Middleton collaborated with him in the first part. Middleton's exact part in the play cannot be determined, but modern scholars are inclined to agree with Dyce that his "share is comparatively small." The source of the plots and characters has never been discovered. It is probable that the plays are compounded of characters whom Dekker had known in the London streets and of stuff of his own imagination, with the use, however, of some conventional motives, especially in the story of Hippolito. The present text is based on the Pearson reprint of the quarto of 1605.

THE SHOEMAKERS' HOLIDAY[1]

BY

THOMAS DEKKER

[DRAMATIS PERSONÆ

THE KING.

THE EARL OF CORNWALL.

SIR HUGH LACY, Earl of Lincoln.

ROWLAND LACY,
  otherwise HANS } his nephews.
ASKEW

SIR ROGER OTELEY, Lord Mayor of London.

MASTER HAMMON[2]
MASTER WARNER } citizens of London.
MASTER SCOTT

SIMON EYRE, a shoemaker.

ROGER, commonly
  called HODGE
FIRK } Eyre's journeymen.
RAFE[3] DAMPORT

LOVELL, a courtier.

DODGER, a servant to the Earl of Lincoln.

A DUTCH SKIPPER.

A BOY.

COURTIERS, ATTENDANTS, OFFICERS, SOLDIERS, HUNTERS, SHOEMAKERS, APPRENTICES, SERVANTS.

ROSE, daughter of Sir Roger.

SYBIL, her maid.

MARGERY, wife of Simon Eyre.

JANE, wife of Rafe.

SCENE: *London and Old Ford.*

TIME: *Middle of the fifteenth century.*]

TO ALL GOOD FELLOWS, PROFESSORS[4] OF THE GENTLE CRAFT,[5] OF WHAT DEGREE SOEVER.

Kind gentlemen and honest boon companions, I present you here with a merry-conceited[6] comedy, called *The Shoemakers' Holiday*, acted by my Lord Admiral's players this present Christmas before the queen's most excellent majesty, for the mirth and pleasant matter by her highness graciously accepted, being indeed no way offensive. The argument of the play I will set down in this epistle: Sir Hugh [10 Lacy, Earl of Lincoln, had a young gentleman of his own name, his near kinsman, that loved the lord mayor's daughter of London; to prevent and cross which love, the earl caused his kinsman to be sent coronel[7] of a company into France; who resigned his place to another gentleman, his friend, and came disguised like a Dutch shoemaker to the house of Simon Eyre in Tower Street, who served the mayor [20 and his household with shoes; the merriments that passed in Eyre's house, his coming to be mayor of London, Lacy's getting his love, and other accidents,[8] with two merry three-men's songs.[9] Take all in good worth that is well intended, for nothing is purposed but mirth; mirth length'neth long life, which, with all other blessings, I heartily wish you.

FAREWELL!

THE PROLOGUE

As it was pronounced before the queen's majesty

As wretches in a storm, expecting day,
With trembling hands and eyes cast up to heaven,
Make prayers the anchor of their conquered hopes,
So we, dear goddess, wonder of all eyes,
Your meanest vassals, through mistrust and fear
To sink into the bottom of disgrace
By our imperfit pastimes, prostrate thus
On bended knees, our sails of hope do strike,
Dreading the bitter storms of your dislike.
Since then, unhappy men, our hap is such
That to ourselves ourselves no help can bring,   11
But needs must perish, if your saintlike ears,
Locking the temple where all mercy sits,
Refuse the tribute of our begging tongues,
O, grant, bright mirror of true chastity,
From those life-breathing stars, your sun-like eyes,
One gracious smile, for your celestial breath
Must send us life, or sentence us to death.

[SCENE i.

A street in London.]

Enter Lord Mayor, Lincoln.

LINC. My lord mayor, you have sundry times
Feasted myself and many courtiers more;
Seldom or never can we be so kind
To make requital of your courtesy.
But, leaving this, I hear my cousin [1] Lacy
Is much affected to [2] your daughter Rose.
L. MAYOR. True, my good lord, and she loves him so well
That I mislike her boldness in the chase.
LINC. Why, my lord mayor, think you it then a shame
To join a Lacy with an Oteley's name? 10

[1] Applied to any collateral relative more distant than brother or sister.   [2] In love with.

L. MAYOR. Too mean is my poor girl for his high birth;
Poor citizens must not with courtiers wed,
Who will in silks and gay apparel spend
More in one year than I am worth, by far.
Therefore your honor need not doubt [3] my girl.
LINC. Take heed, my lord; advise you what you do!
A verier unthrift lives not in the world
Than is my cousin; for I'll tell you what:
'Tis now almost a year since he requested
To travel countries for experience;   20
I furnished him with coin, bills of exchange,
Letters of credit, men to wait on him,
Solicited my friends in Italy
Well to respect him. But, to see the end,
Scant had he journeyed through half Germany,
But all his coin was spent, his men cast off,
His bills embezzled,[4] and my jolly coz,[5]
Ashamed to show his bankrupt presence here,
Became a shoemaker in Wittenberg,
A goodly science for a gentleman   30
Of such descent!   Now judge the rest by this:
Suppose your daughter have a thousand pound,
He did consume me more in one half year;
And, make him heir to all the wealth you have,
One twelvemonth's rioting will waste it all.
Then seek, my lord, some honest citizen
To wed your daughter to.
L. MAYOR.   I thank your lordship.
[*Aside.*] Well, fox, I understand your subtilty.—
As for your nephew, let your lordship's eye
But watch his actions, and you need not fear,   40
For I have [sent][6] my daughter far enough.

[3] Fear.   [5] Cousin.
[4] Wasted.   [6] Supplied from 1610 edn.

And yet your cousin Rowland might
do well,
Now he hath learned an occupation;
And yet I scorn to call him son-in-law.
LINC. Ay, but I have a better trade for
him.
I thank his grace, he hath appointed
him
Chief colonel of all those companies
Mustered in London and the shires
about,
To serve his highness in those wars of
France.
See where he comes!—Lovell, what news
with you? 50

Enter Lovell, Lacy, and Askew.

Lov. My Lord of Lincoln, 'tis his high-
ness' will
That presently [1] your cousin ship for
France
With all his powers; he would not for a
million
But they should land at Dieppe within
four days.
LINC. Go certify his grace it shall be done.
Exit Lovell.
Now, cousin Lacy, in what forwardness
Are all your companies?
LACY. All well prepared.
The men of Hertfordshire lie at Mile
End;
Suffolk and Essex train in Tothill [2]
Fields;
The Londoners and those of Middle-
sex, 60
All gallantly prepared in Finsbury,
With frolic spirits long for their parting
hour.
L. MAYOR. They have their imprest,[3]
coats, and furniture; [4]
And, if it please your cousin Lacy come
To the Guildhall, he shall receive his
pay;
And twenty pounds besides my brethren
Will freely give him, to approve [5] our
loves
We bear unto my lord, your uncle here.
LACY. I thank your honor.
LINC. Thanks, my good lord mayor.

L. MAYOR. At the Guildhall we will
expect [6] your coming. *Exit.* 70
LINC. To approve your loves to me? No
subtilty!
Nephew, that twenty pound he doth
bestow
For joy to rid you from his daughter
Rose.
But, cousins both, now here are none
but friends,
I would not have you cast an amorous
eye
Upon so mean a project as the love
Of a gay, wanton, painted citizen.
I know this churl even in the height of
scorn
Doth hate the mixture of his blood with
thine.
I pray thee, do thou so! Remember,
coz, 80
What honorable fortunes wait on thee.
Increase the king's love, which so
brightly shines,
And gilds thy hopes. I have no heir but
thee—
And yet not thee if with a wayward
spirit
Thou start [7] from the true bias of my
love.
LACY. My lord, I will for honor, not de-
sire
Of land or livings, or to be your heir,
So guide my actions in pursuit of
France
As shall add glory to the Lacys' name.
LINC. Coz, for those words here's thirty
Portuguese,[8] 90
And, nephew Askew, there's a few for
you.
Fair Honor, in her loftiest eminence,
Stays in France for you, till you fetch
her thence.
Then, nephews, clap swift wings on
your designs.
Begone, begone, make haste to the
Guildhall;
There presently I'll meet you. Do not
stay.
Where Honor beckons,[9] Shame at-
tends delay. *Exit.*
ASKEW. How gladly would your uncle
have you gone!

[1] At once.
[2] The spelling *Tuttle* in the original indicates
the pronunciation.
[3] Advance pay.
[4] Equipment.
[5] Prove.
[6] Await.
[7] Turn aside.
[8] Gold coins.
[9] Malone's emendation of *becomes.*

LACY. True, coz, but I'll o'erreach his policies.[1]

I have some serious business for three days, 100
Which nothing but my presence can despatch.
You, therefore, cousin, with the companies
Shall haste to Dover; there I'll meet with you.
Or, if I stay past my prefixéd time,
Away for France; we'll meet in Normandy.
The twenty pounds my lord mayor gives to me
You shall receive, and these ten Portuguese,
Part of mine uncle's thirty. Gentle coz,
Have care to our great charge; I know your wisdom 109
Hath tried itself in higher consequence.

ASKEW. Coz, all myself am yours; yet have this care,
To lodge in London with all secrecy.
Our uncle Lincoln hath, besides his own,
Many a jealous eye, that in your face
Stares only to watch means for your disgrace.

LACY. Stay, cousin. Who be these?

Enter Simon Eyre, his Wife, Hodge, Firk, Jane, and Rafe with a piece.[2]

EYRE. Leave whining, leave whining! Away with this whimp'ring, this puling, these blubbering tears, and these wet eyes! I'll get thy husband discharged, [120 I warrant thee, sweet Jane; go to!

HODGE. Master, here be the captains.

EYRE. Peace, Hodge; husht, ye knave, husht!

FIRK. Here be the cavaliers and the coronels, master.

EYRE. Peace, Firk; peace, my fine Firk! Stand by with your pishery-pashery.[3] Away! I am a man of the best presence; I'll speak to them, and[4] they were [130 popes.—Gentlemen, captains, colonels, commanders! Brave men, brave leaders, may it please you to give me audience. I am Simon Eyre, the mad shoemaker of Tower Street; this wench with the mealy

mouth that will never tire, is my wife, I can tell you; here's Hodge, my man and my foreman; here's Firk, my fine firking [5] journeyman; and this is blubbered Jane. All we come to be suitors for this hon- [140 est Rafe. Keep him at home, and, as I am a true shoemaker and a gentleman of the gentle craft, buy spurs yourself, and I'll find[6] ye boots these seven years.

WIFE. Seven years, husband?

EYRE. Peace, midriff, peace! I know what I do. Peace!

FIRK. Truly, master cormorant,[7] you shall do God good service to let Rafe and his wife stay together. She's a young [150 new-married woman; if you take her husband away from her a-night, you undo her; she may beg in the daytime; for he's as good a workman at a prick and an awl as any is in our trade.

JANE. O, let him stay; else I shall be undone!

FIRK. Ay, truly, she shall be laid at one side like a pair of old shoes else, and be occupied for no use. 160

LACY. Truly, my friends, it lies not in my power.
The Londoners are pressed,[8] paid, and set forth
By the lord mayor; I cannot change a man.

HODGE. Why, then you were as good be a corporal as a colonel, if you cannot discharge one good fellow; and, I tell you true, I think you do more than you can answer, to press a man within a year and a day of his marriage.

EYRE. Well said, melancholy [170 Hodge; gramercy, my fine foreman.

WIFE. Truly, gentlemen, it were ill done for such as you to stand so stiffly against a poor young wife, considering her case, she is new-married; but let that pass. I pray, deal not roughly with her; her husband is a young man, and but newly entered; but let that pass.

EYRE. Away with your pishery-pashery, your pols and your edipols![9] Peace, [180 midriff;[10] silence, Cisly Bumtrinket! Let your head speak.

---

[5] Frisking. [6] Provide.
[7] His corruption of *coronel.*
[8] Impressed, drafted.
[9] Forms of *By Pollux.* [10] Original has *midaffe.*

[1] Tricks. [3] Trifling talk.
[2] *I.e.,* of leather. [4] An, if.

FIRK. Yea, and the horns too, master.

EYRE. Too soon, my fine Firk, too soon! Peace, scoundrels! See you this man? Captains, you will not release him? Well, let him go. He's a proper shot; let him vanish! Peace, Jane, dry up thy tears; they'll make his powder dankish. Take him, brave men. Hector of Troy was [190 an hackney to him; Hercules and Termagant, scoundrels; Prince Arthur's Round Table—by the Lord of Ludgate—ne'er fed such a tall,[1] such a dapper swordman; by the life of Pharaoh, a brave, resolute swordman! Peace, Jane! I say no more, mad knaves.

FIRK. See, see, Hodge, how my master raves in commendation of Rafe!

HODGE. Rafe, th'art a gull,[2] by this [200 hand, and thou goest.[3]

ASKEW. I am glad, good Master Eyre, it is my hap
To meet so resolute a soldier.
Trust me, for your report and love to him,
A common slight regard shall not respect him.

LACY. Is thy name Rafe?

RAFE. Yes, sir.

LACY. Give me thy hand.
Thou shalt not want, as I am a gentleman.
Woman, be patient. God, no doubt, will send
Thy husband safe again; but he must go— 209
His country's quarrel says it shall be so.

HODGE. Th'art a gull, by my stirrup,[4] if thou dost not go. I will not have thee strike thy gimlet into these weak vessels; prick thine enemies, Rafe.

Enter Dodger.

DOLGER. My lord, your uncle on the Tower Hill
Stays with the lord mayor and the aldermen,
And doth request you, with all speed you may,
To hasten thither.

ASKEW. Cousin, let's go.

LACY. Dodger, run you before; tell them we come.— *Exit Dodger.*[5] 219
This Dodger is mine uncle's parasite,
The arrant'st varlet that e'er breathed on earth;
He sets more discord in a noble house
By one day's broaching of his pickthank[6] tales
Than can be salved again in twenty years,
And he, I fear, shall go with us to France
To pry into our actions.

ASKEW. Therefore, coz,
It shall behoove you to be circumspect.

LACY. Fear not, good cousin.—Rafe, hie to your colors.
[*Exeunt Lacy and Askew.*]

RAFE. I must, because there's no remedy; 229
But, gentle master and my loving dame,
As you have always been a friend to me,
So in mine absence think upon my wife.

JANE. Alas, my Rafe!

WIFE. She cannot speak for weeping.

EYRE. Peace, you cracked groats, you mustard tokens;[7] disquiet not the brave soldier. Go thy ways, Rafe!

JANE. Ay, ay, you bid him go. What shall I do when he is gone?

FIRK. Why, be doing with me or my fellow Hodge; be not idle. 240

EYRE. Let me see thy hand, Jane. This fine hand, this white hand, these pretty fingers must spin, must card, must work; work, you bombast cotton-candle[8] quean; work for your living, with a pox to you![9]— Hold thee, Rafe, here's five sixpences for thee. Fight for the honor of the gentle craft, for the gentlemen shoemakers, the courageous cordwainers, the flower of S[aint] Martin's, the mad knaves of Bedlam, [250 Fleet Street, Tower Street, and Whitechapel; crack me the crowns of the French knaves; a pox on them, crack them; fight, by the Lord of Ludgate; fight, my fine boy!

FIRK. Here, Rafe, here's three twopences. Two carry into France; the third

[1] Brave. [2] Fool.
[3] Lange and other editors add *not*.
[4] A strap for steadying the shoemaker's last on his knee.
[5] This direction follows Dodger's speech in original. [6] Talebearer's.
[7] Yellow spots from the plague.
[8] "Bombast: cotton-wool; cotton-candle: a candle with a cotton wick. Jane's hands are as white as the wax of a candle, as soft as bombast" (Sutherland). [9] A plague to you!

shall wash our souls at parting, for sorrow is dry. For my sake, firk the *Basa mon cues.*[1] 259

HODGE. Rafe, I am heavy at parting; but here's a shilling for thee. God send thee to cram thy slops [2] with French crowns, and thy enemies' bellies with bullets.

RAFE. I thank you, master, and I thank you all.
  Now, gentle wife, my loving, lovely Jane,
  Rich men, at parting, give their wives rich gifts,
  Jewels and rings, to grace their lily hands.
  Thou know'st our trade makes rings for women's heels.
  Here take this pair of shoes, cut out by Hodge,
  Stitched by my fellow Firk, seamed by myself, 270
  Made up and pinked [3] with letters for thy name.
  Wear them, my dear Jane, for thy husband's sake,
  And every morning when thou pull'st them on,
  Remember me, and pray for my return.
  Make much of them, for I have made them so
  That I can know them from a thousand mo.[4]

Sound drum. Enter Lord Mayor, Lincoln, Lacy, Askew, Dodger, and Soldiers. They pass over the stage; Rafe falls in amongst them; Firk and the rest cry "Farewell," etc., and so exeunt.

[SCENE ii.

A garden at Old Ford.]

Enter Rose, alone, making a garland.

[ROSE.] Here sit thou down upon this flow'ry bank
  And make a garland for thy Lacy's head.
  These pinks, these roses, and these violets,
  These blushing gilliflowers, these marigolds,
  The fair embroidery [5] of his coronet,

Carry not half such beauty in their cheeks
As the sweet count'nance of my Lacy doth.
O my most unkind father! O my stars,
Why lowered you so at my nativity,
To make me love, yet live robbed of my love? 10
Here as a thief am I imprisonéd
For my dear Lacy's sake within those walls
Which by my father's cost were builded up
For better purposes. Here must I languish
For him that doth as much lament, I know,
Mine absence as for him I pine in woe.

Enter Sybil.

SYB. Good morrow, young mistress. I am sure you make that garland for me, against [6] I shall be Lady of the Harvest.

ROSE. Sybil, what news at London? [20

SYB. None but good. My lord mayor, your father, and Master Philpot, your uncle, and Master Scot, your cousin, and Mistress Frigbottom by Doctors' Commons do all, by my troth, send you most hearty commendations.

ROSE. Did Lacy send kind greetings to his love?

SYB. O, yes, out of cry,[7] by my troth. I scant knew him. Here a [8] wore [a] [9] [30 scarf, and here a scarf; here a bunch of feathers, and here precious stones and jewels, and a pair of garters—O, monstrous! —like one of our yellow silk curtains at home here in Old Ford House, here in Master Bellymount's chamber. I stood at our door in Cornhill, looked at him, he at me indeed, spake to him, but he not to me, not a word. "Marry gup," [10] thought I, "with a wanion!" [11] He passed by me as proud— [40 "Marry foh! Are you grown humorous?" [12] thought I, and so shut the door, and in I came.

ROSE. O Sybil, how dost thou my Lacy wrong!

---

[1] *I.e.*, the Frenchmen. *Cf.* vulgar French, *baisez mon queue.*
[2] Breeches.
[3] Perforated.
[5] Embroidery.
[6] For the time when.
[7] Beyond all description.
[8] He.
[9] From 1618 edn.
[10] Exclamation of impatience.
[11] With a vengeance.
[12] Capricious.

My Rowland is as gentle as a lamb;
No dove was ever half so mild as he.

SYB. Mild? Yea, as a bushel of stamped crabs.[1] He looked upon me as sour as verjuice. "Go thy ways," thought I; "thou mayst be much in my gaskins,[2] [50 but nothing in my netherstocks."[3] This is your fault, mistress, to love him that loves not you; he thinks scorn to do as he's done to; but, if I were as you, I'd cry, "Go by, Jeronimo, go by!"[4]

I'd set mine old debts against my new driblets,
And the hare's foot against the goose giblets,
For, if ever I sigh, when sleep I should take,
Pray God I may lose my maidenhead when I wake.[5]   60

ROSE. Will my love leave me then, and go to France?

SYB. I know not that, but I am sure I see him stalk before the soldiers. By my troth, he is a proper[6] man; but he is proper that proper doth. Let him go snick-up,[7] young mistress.

ROSE. Get thee to London, and learn perfectly
Whether my Lacy go to France, or no.
Do this, and I will give thee for thy pains
My cambric apron and my Romish gloves,   70
My purple stockings and a stomacher.
Say, wilt thou do this, Sybil, for my sake?

SYB. Will I, quotha? At whose suit? By my troth, yes, I'll go. A cambric apron, gloves, a pair of purple stockings, and a stomacher! I'll sweat in purple, mistress, for you; I'll take anything that comes a God's name. O, rich! A cambric apron! Faith, then have at "Up tails all."[8] I'll go jiggy-joggy to [80

London, and be here in a trice, young mistress.   *Exit.*

ROSE. Do so, good Sybil.—Meantime wretched I
Will sit and sigh for his lost company.
                                          Exit.

[SCENE iii.

Tower Street, London.]

*Enter Rowland Lacy, like a Dutch shoe-
maker.*

LACY. How many shapes have gods and kings devised
Thereby to compass their desired loves!
It is no shame for Rowland Lacy, then,
To clothe his cunning with the gentle craft,
That, thus disguised, I may unknown possess
The only happy presence of my Rose.
For her have I forsook my charge in France,
Incurred the king's displeasure, and stirred up
Rough hatred in mine uncle Lincoln's breast.
O love, how powerful art thou, that canst change   10
High birth to bareness,[9] and a noble mind
To the mean semblance of a shoemaker!
But thus it must be, for her cruel father,
Hating the single union of our souls,
Has secretly conveyed my Rose from London
To bar me of her presence; but I trust
Fortune and this disguise will furder me
Once more to view her beauty, gain her sight.
Here in Tower Street with Eyre the shoemaker
Mean I a while to work; I know the trade;   20
I learnt it when I was in Wittenberg.
Then cheer thy hoping sprites; be not dismayed;
Thou canst not want. Do Fortune what she can,
The gentle craft is living for a man. *Exit.*

---

[1] Crushed crab apples.   [2] Wide trousers.
[3] Stockings. "The meaning seems to be that, though we may be acquainted, we are not intimate friends" (Neilson).
[4] This tag from Kyd's *Spanish Tragedy* was a popular slang phrase.
[5] Lange suggests that these verses mean, "Off with the old love, on with the new." In these couplets and a few other passages the line division has been regularized.
[6] Handsome.   [7] Go and be hanged!
[8] *I.e.*, make speed; the name of a dance tune.
[9] 1631 edn. reads *baseness.*

[SCENE iv.

...a open yard before Eyre's house in Tower Street.]

Enter Eyre, making himself ready.

EYRE. Where be these boys, these girls, these drabs, these scoundrels? They wallow in the fat brewis [1] of my bounty, and lick up the crumbs of my table, yet will not rise to see my walks cleansed. Come out, you powder-beef [2] queans! What, Nan! What, Madge Mumblecrust! Come out, you fat midriff-swag-belly-whores, and sweep me these kennels [3] that the noisome stench offend not the nose of my neighbors. [10 What, Firk, I say! What, Hodge! Open my shop windows! What, Firk, I say!

Enter Firk.

FIRK. O master, is 't you that speak bandog and bedlam [4] this morning? I was in a dream, and mused what madman was got into the street so early. Have you drunk this morning that your throat is so clear?

EYRE. Ah, well said, Firk; well said, Firk. To work, my fine knave, to [20 work! Wash thy face, and thou't be more blessed.

FIRK. Let them wash my face that will eat it. Good master, send for a souse-wife, [5] if you'll have my face cleaner.

Enter Hodge.

EYRE. Away, sloven! Avaunt, scoundrel! —Good morrow, Hodge; good morrow, my fine foreman.

HODGE. O master, good morrow; y'are an early stirrer. Here's a fair morning.— [30 Good morrow, Firk; I could have slept this hour. Here's a brave day towards.

EYRE. O, haste to work, my fine foreman, haste to work.

FIRK. Master, I am dry as dust to hear my fellow Roger talk of fair weather. Let us pray for good leather, and let clowns and plowboys and those that work in the fields pray for brave days. We work in a dry shop; what care I if it rain? 40

[1] Thickened broth.
[2] Salted beef.
[3] Channels, gutters.
[4] *I.e.*, like a watchdog and a madman.
[5] Pig-pickler.

Enter Eyre's Wife.

EYRE. How now, Dame Margery, can you see to rise? Trip and go; call up the drabs, your maids.

WIFE. See to rise? I hope 'tis time enough; 'tis early enough for any woman to be seen abroad. I marvel how many wives in Tower Street are up so soon. God's me, [6] 'tis not noon! Here's a yawling!

EYRE. Peace, Margery, peace! Where's Cisly Bumtrinket, your maid? She has a [50 privy fault—she farts in her sleep. Call the quean up; if my men want shoe thread, I'll swinge her in a stirrup.

FIRK. Yet that's but a dry beating; here's still a sign of drought.

Enter Lacy singing.

LACY. *Der was een bore van Gelderland*
　　(Frolick si byen!);
　　He was als dronck he cold nyet stand
　　Upsolce se byen.
　　Tap eens de canneken;　　　　　　60
　　Drincke, schone mannekin. [7]

FIRK. Master, for my life, yonder's a brother of the gentle craft; if he bear not Saint Hugh's bones, [8] I'll forfeit my bones; he's some uplandish [9] workman. Hire him, good master, that I may learn some gibble-gabble; 'twill make us work the faster.

EYRE. Peace, Firk! A hard world! Let him pass, let him vanish; we have journeymen enow. Peace, my fine Firk! 70

WIFE. Nay, nay, y'are best follow your man's counsel; you shall see what will come on 't. We have not men enow, but we must entertain every butterbox; [10] but let that pass.

HODGE. Dame, fore God, if my master follow your counsel, he'll consume little beef. He shall be glad of men and he can catch them.

[6] An exclamation of impatience.
[7] Adopting Baugh's emendation, "Op zulke zeebeenen," in line 4, we may translate the song thus:
　There was a boor from Gelderland
　　(Jolly they be!);
　He was so drunk he could not stand
　　On such sea legs.
　Tap once the cannikin;
　Drink, pretty mannikin.
[8] St. Hugh's bones were believed to have been made into shoemakers' tools.
[9] Up-country; perhaps an error for *outlandish,* foreign.　　[10] Dutchman.

FIRK. Ay, that he shall.   80
HODGE. Fore God, a proper man and, I warrant, a fine workman. Master, farewell; dame, adieu. If such a man as he cannot find work, Hodge is not for you.

Offers to go.

EYRE. Stay, my fine Hodge.
FIRK. Faith, and your foreman go, dame, you must take a journey to seek a new journeyman; if Roger remove, Firk follows. If St. Hugh's bones shall not be set awork, I may prick mine awl in the walls, [90 and go play. Fare ye well, master; good-by, dame.
EYRE. Tarry, my fine Hodge, my brisk foreman! Stay, Firk! Peace, pudding-broth! By the Lord of Ludgate, I love my men as my life. Peace, you gallimaufry![1] Hodge, if he want work, I'll hire him. One of you to him. Stay—he comes to us.
LACY. *Goeden dach, meester, ende u, vro, oak.*[2]   100
FIRK. Nails,[3] if I should speak after him without drinking, I should choke. And you, friend Oak, are you of the gentle craft?
LACY. *Yaw, yaw, ik bin den skomawker.*[4]
FIRK. "*Den skomaker,*" quotha! And hark you, *skomaker,* have you all your tools, a good rubbing pin, a good stopper, a good dresser, your four sorts of awls, and your two balls of wax, your paring knife, your hand-and-thumb-leathers, and [110 good St. Hugh's bones to smooth up your work?
LACY. *Yaw, yaw; be niet vorveard. Ik hab all de dingen voour mack skoes groot and cleane.*[5]
FIRK. Ha, ha! Good master, hire him; he'll make me laugh so that I shall work more in mirth than I can in earnest.
EYRE. Hear ye, friend, have ye any skill in the mystery[6] of cordwainers?   120
LACY. *Ik weet niet wat yow seg; ich verstaw you niet.*[7]
FIRK. Why, thus, man: [*Imitating a shoemaker at work.*] "*Ich verste u niet,*"[8] quotha.

---

[1] Ragout of hashed meats.
[2] Good day, master, and you, wife, too.
[3] By God's nails.
[4] Yes, yes, I am the shoemaker.
[5] Yes, yes; be not afraid. I have everything to make shoes big and little.   [6] Trade.
[7] I don't know what you say; I don't understand you.   [8] "I don't understand you."

LACY. *Yaw, yaw, yaw; ick can dat wel doen.*[9]
FIRK. "*Yaw, yaw!*" He speaks yawing like a jackdaw that gapes to be fed with cheese curds. O, he'll give a villainous [130 pull at a can of double beer; but Hodge and I have the vantage—we must drink first because we are the eldest journeymen.
EYRE. What is thy name?
LACY. Hans—Hans Meulter.
EYRE. Give me thy hand; th'art welcome.—Hodge, entertain him; Firk, bid him welcome; come, Hans. Run, wife, bid your maids, your trullibubs,[10] make ready my fine men's breakfasts. To him, Hodge! [140
HODGE. Hans, th'art welcome. Use thyself friendly, for we are good fellows; if not, thou shalt be fought with, wert thou bigger than a giant.
FIRK. Yea, and drunk with, wert thou Gargantua. My master keeps no cowards, I tell thee.—Ho, boy, bring him an heel block;[11] here's a new journeyman.

Enter Boy.

LACY. *O, ich wersto you; ich moet een halve dossen cans betaelen. Here, boy,* [150 *nempt dis skilling; tap eens freelicke.*[12]

Exit Boy.

EYRE. Quick, snippersnapper, away! Firk, scour thy throat; thou shalt wash it with Castilian liquor.

Enter Boy.

Come, my last of the fives,[13] give me a can. Have to thee, Hans; here, Hodge; here, Firk; drink, you mad Greeks, and work like true Trojans, and pray for Simon Eyre, the shoemaker.—Here, Hans, and th'art welcome.   160
FIRK. Lo, dame, you would have lost a good fellow that will teach us to laugh. This beer came hopping in well.
WIFE. Simon, it is almost seven.
EYRE. Is't so, Dame Clapperdudgeon?[14]

---

[9] Yes, yes, yes, I can do that well.
[10] Tripes, sluts.
[11] A last for making heels.
[12] O, I understand you; I must pay for a half dozen cans. Here, boy, take this shilling; tap once freely.
[13] My smallest last; my little one.
[14] Because her mouth rattles like a beggar's clapdish.

Is't seven a-clock, and my men's breakfast not ready? Trip and go, you soused cunger,[1] away! Come, you mad hyperboreans. Follow me, Hodge; follow me, Hans; come after, my fine Firk; to work, to work [170 awhile, and then to breakfast!   *Exit.*

FIRK. Soft! *Yaw, yaw,* good Hans, though my master have no more wit but to call you afore me, I am not so foolish to go behind you, I being the elder journeyman.   *Exeunt.*

[SCENE V.

A field near Old Ford.]

Halloaing within.   Enter Warner and Hammon, like hunters.

HAM. Cousin, beat every brake; the game's not far.
This way with wingéd feet he fled from death,
Whilst the pursuing hounds, scenting his steps,
Find out his highway to destruction.
Besides, the miller's boy told me even now,
He saw him take soil,[2] and he halloaed him,
Affirming him so embossed [3]
That long he could not hold.
WARN.   If it be so,
'Tis best we trace these meadows by Old Ford.

A noise of Hunters within.   Enter a Boy.

HAM. How now, boy? Where's the deer?
Speak! Saw'st thou him?   10
BOY. O, yea; I saw him leap through a hedge, and then over a ditch; then, at my lord mayor's pale, over he skipped me, and in he went me, and "Holla" the hunters cried, and "There, boy; there, boy!" But there he is, a mine honesty.
HAM. Boy, God-a-mercy.[4] Cousin, let's away;
I hope we shall find better sport today.   *Exeunt.*

---

[1] Pickled cucumber, or perhaps a misspelling for *conger*, eel.
[2] Take to water. From 1610 edn. Original reads *saile*.
[3] Foaming at the mouth from exhaustion.
[4] Thanks.

Hunting within.   Enter Rose and Sybil.

ROSE. Why, Sybil, wilt thou prove a forester?   20
SYB. Upon some,[5] no. Forester? Go by; no, faith, mistress. The deer came running into the barn through the orchard and over the pale. I wot [6] well I looked as pale as a new cheese to see him. But whip, says Goodman Pinclose, up with his flail, and our Nick with a prong, and down he fell, and they upon him, and I upon them. By my troth, we had such sport; and in the end we ended him; his throat we cut, flayed [30 him, unhorned him, and my lord mayor shall eat of him anon, when he comes.
     Horns sound within.
ROSE. Hark, hark, the hunters come.
     Y'are best take heed;
They'll have a saying to you for this deed.

Enter Hammon, Warner, Huntsmen, and Boy.

HAM. God save you, fair ladies.
SYB.   Ladies! O, gross! [7]
WARN. Came not a buck this way?
ROSE.   No, but two does.
HAM. And which way went they? Faith, we'll hunt at those.
SYB. At those? Upon some, no. When, can you tell?
WARN. Upon some, ay!
SYB.   Good Lord!
WARN.   Wounds! [8] Then farewell!
HAM. Boy, which way went he?
BOY.   This way, sir, he ran.   40
HAM. This way he ran indeed, fair Mistress Rose;
Our game was lately in your orchard seen.
WARN. Can you advise which way he took his flight?
SYB. Follow your nose; his horns will guide you right.
WARN. Th' art a mad wench.
SYB.   O, rich!
ROSE.   Trust me, not I.
It is not like [that] [9] the wild forest deer
Would come so near to places of resort.
You are deceived; he fled some other way.

---

[5] An intensive cant phrase of uncertain origin.
[6] Know.
[7] Stupid.
[8] God's wounds!
[9] Supplied from 1610 edn.

WARN. Which way, my sugar candy, can you show? [*Puts his arm about Sybil.*]

SYB. Come up, good honeysops; upon some, no! 50

ROSE. Why do you stay, and not pursue your game?

SYB. I'll hold[1] my life, their hunting nags be lame.

HAM. A deer more dear is found within this place.

ROSE. But not the deer, sir, which you had in chase.

HAM. I chased the deer, but this dear chaseth me.

ROSE. The strangest hunting that ever I see.

But where's your park?
She offers to go away.

HAM. 'Tis here. O, stay!

ROSE. Impale me, and then I will not stray.

WARN. They wrangle, wench; we are more kind than they.

SYB. What kind of hart is that dear heart you seek? 60

WARN. A hart, dear heart!

SYB. Who ever saw the like?

ROSE. To lose your heart, is 't possible you can?

HAM. My heart is lost.

ROSE. Alack, good gentleman!

HAM. This poor lost heart would I wish you might find.

ROSE. You, by such luck, might prove your hart a hind.

HAM. Why, Luck had horns, so have I heard some say.

ROSE. Now, God, and 't be his will, send Luck into your way.

Enter L[ord] Mayor and Servants.

L. MAYOR. What, M[aster] Hammon? Welcome to Old Ford!

SYB. God's pitikins, hands off, sir! Here's my lord.

L. MAYOR. I hear you had ill luck, and lost your game. 70

HAM. 'Tis true, my lord.

L. MAYOR. I am sorry for the same. What gentleman is this?

HAM. My brother-in-law.

L. MAYOR. Y'are welcome both. Sith[2] Fortune offers you

Into my hands, you shall not part from hence

Until you have refreshed your wearied limbs.

Go, Sybil, cover the board! You shall be guest

To no good cheer, but even a hunter's feast.

HAM. I thank your lordship.—Cousin, on my life,

For our lost venison I shall find a wife.
Exeunt [all but Mayor].

L. MAYOR. In, gentlemen; I'll not be absent long.— 80

This Hammon is a proper gentleman,

A citizen by birth, fairly allied;

How fit an husband were he for my girl!

Well, I will in, and do the best I can

To match my daughter to this gentleman.
Exit.

[SCENE vi.

A room in Eyre's house.]

Enter Lacy, Skipper, Hodge, and Firk.

SKIP. *Ick sal yow wat seggen, Hans; dis skip dat comen from Candy, is al vol,[3] by Got's sacrament, van sugar, civet, almonds, cambrick, end alle dingen—towsand towsand ding. Nempt it, Hans, nempt it vor u meester. Daer be de bils van laden. Your meester Simon Eyre sal hae good copen. Wat seggen yow, Hans?*[4]

FIRK. *Wat seggen de reggen de copen, slopen*—Laugh, Hodge, laugh! 10

LACY. *Mine liever broder Firk, bringt Meester Eyre tot[5] det signe un Swannekin; daer sal yow finde dis skipper end me. Wat seggen yow, broder Firk? Doot it, Hodge.[6] Come, skipper.* *Exeunt.*

---

[1] Wager.

[2] Since.

[3] From 1610 edn. Original reads *wel.*

[4] I'll tell you what, Hans; this ship that is come from Candia is all full, by God's sacrament, of sugar, civet, almonds, cambric, and all things—a thousand thousand things. Take it, Hans, take it for your master. There are the bills of lading. Your master, Simon Eyre, shall have a good bargain. What say you, Hans?

[5] In early edns. *lot.*

[6] My dear brother Firk, bring Master Eyre to the sign of the Swan; there shall you find this skipper and me. What say you, brother Firk? Do it, Hodge.

FIRK. Bring him, quod you? Here's no knavery, to bring my master to buy a ship worth the lading of two or three hundred thousand pounds. Alas, that's nothing; a trifle, a bable,[1] Hodge.   20

HODGE. The truth is, Firk, that the merchant owner of the ship dares not show his head, and therefore this skipper that deals for him, for the love he bears to Hans, offers my master Eyre a bargain in the commodities. He shall have a reasonable day of payment; he may sell the wares by that time, and be an huge gainer himself.

FIRK. Yea, but can my fellow Hans lend my master twenty porpentines as an [30 earnest penny?

HODGE. Portuguese, thou wouldst say. Here they be, Firk; hark, they jingle in my pocket like St. Mary Overy's bells.

Enter Eyre and his Wife.

FIRK. Mum, here comes my dame and my master. She'll scold, on my life, for loitering this Monday; but all's one—let them all say what they can, Monday's our holiday.

WIFE. You sing, Sir Sauce, but I beshrew[2]
        your heart.   40
    I fear for this your singing we shall
        smart.

FIRK. Smart for me, dame? Why, dame, why?

HODGE. Master, I hope you'll not suffer my dame to take down your journeymen.

FIRK. If she take me down, I'll take her up; yea, and take her down too, a button-hole lower.

EYRE. Peace, Firk; not I, Hodge; by the life of Pharaoh, by the Lord of Ludgate, [50 by this beard, every hair whereof I value at a king's ransom, she shall not meddle with you.—Peace, you bombast cotton-candle quean; away, queen of clubs! Quarrel not with me and my men, with me and my fine Firk; I'll firk you if you do!

WIFE. Yea, yea, man, you may use me as you please; but let that pass.

EYRE. Let it pass, let it vanish away! Peace! Am I not Simon Eyre? Are not [60 these my brave men, brave shoemakers, all gentlemen of the gentle craft? Prince am I none, yet am I nobly born, as being the sole son of a shoemaker. Away, rubbish! Vanish; melt, melt like kitchen stuff.

WIFE. Yea, yea, 'tis well; I must be called rubbish, kitchen stuff, for a sort[3] of knaves.

FIRK. Nay, dame, you shall not weep and wail in woe for me. Master, I'll stay [70 no longer; here's a venentory[4] of my shop tools. Adieu, master; Hodge, farewell.

HODGE. Nay, stay, Firk; thou shalt not go alone.

WIFE. I pray, let them go; there be mo maids than Mawkin, more men than Hodge, and more fools than Firk.

FIRK. Fools? Nails! If I tarry now, I would my guts might be turned to shoe thread.   80

HODGE. And, if I stay, I pray God I may be turned to a Turk, and set in Finsbury for boys to shoot at.—Come, Firk.

EYRE. Stay, my fine knaves, you arms of my trade, you pillars of my profession. What, shall a tittle-tattle's words make you forsake Simon Eyre?—Avaunt, kitchen stuff! Rip, you brown bread Tannikin;[5] out of my sight! Move me not! Have not I ta'en you from selling tripes in East- [90 cheap, and set you in my shop, and made you hail-fellow with Simon Eyre, the shoemaker? And now do you deal thus with my journeymen? Look, you powder-beef quean, on the face of Hodge; here's a face for a lord.

FIRK. And here's a face for any lady in Christendom.

EYRE. Rip, you chitterling, avaunt! Boy, bid the tapster of the Boar's Head [100 fill me a dozen cans of beer for my journeymen.

FIRK. A dozen cans? O, brave! Hodge, now I'll stay.

EYRE. [*Aside to the Boy.*] And the knave fills any more than two, he pays for them.—[*Exit Boy.—Aloud.*] A dozen cans of beer for my journeymen. [*Enter Boy.*] Heave,[6] you mad Mesopotamians; wash your livers with this liquor. Where be [110 the odd ten?—[*Aside.*] No more, Madge, no more.—Well said.[7] Drink and to work! —What work dost thou, Hodge? What work?

---

[1] Bauble.   [2] Curse.

[3] Pack.   [4] Firk's corruption of *inventory*.
[5] Dutch nickname for Anne.
[6] *I.e.*, lift your tankards.   [7] Well done.

Hodge. I am a-making a pair of shoes for my lord mayor's daughter, Mistress Rose.

Firk. And I a pair of shoes for Sybil, my lord's maid. I deal with her.

Eyre. Sybil? Fie, defile not thy [120 fine workmanly fingers with the feet of kitchen stuff and basting ladles. Ladies of the court, fine ladies, my lads, commit their feet to our appareling; put gross work to Hans. Yark [1] and seam, yark and seam!

Firk. For yarking and seaming let me alone, and I come to 't.

Hodge. Well, master, all this is from the bias. Do you remember the ship my fellow Hans told you of? The skipper and [130 he are both drinking at the Swan. Here be the Portuguese to give earnest. If you go through with it, you cannot choose but be a lord at least.

Firk. Nay, dame, if my master prove not a lord, and you a lady, hang me.

Wife. Yea, like enough, if you may loiter and tipple thus.

Firk. Tipple, dame? No, we have been bargaining with Skellum Skanderbag [2] [140 Can-You-Dutch-Spreaken for a ship of silk Cyprus,[3] laden with sugar candy.

Enter the Boy with a velvet coat and an alder-man's gown. Eyre puts it on.

Eyre. Peace, Firk; silence, Tittle-tattle! Hodge, I'll go through with it. Here's a seal ring, and I have sent for a garded [4] gown and a damask cassock. See where it comes. Look here, Maggy; help me, Firk; apparel me, Hodge; silk and satin, you mad Philistines, silk and satin!

Firk. Ha, ha, my master will be as [150 proud as a dog in a doublet, all in beaten [5] damask and velvet.

Eyre. Softly, Firk, for rearing of the nap, and wearing threadbare my garments. How dost thou like me, Firk? How do I look, my fine Hodge?

Hodge. Why, now you look like yourself, master. I warrant you, there's few in the city but will give you the wall,[6] and

[1] Pull stitches tight.
[2] Equivalent to *Rascal*.   [3] Black lawn.
[4] Edged with an ornamental band.
[5] Stamped.
[6] *I.e.*, yield him the favored position in walking the streets.

come upon you with the "right wor- [160 shipful."

Firk. Nails, my master looks like a threadbare cloak new turned and dressed! Lord, Lord, to see what good raiment doth! Dame, dame, are you not enamored?

Eyre. How sayst thou, Maggy, am I not brisk? Am I not fine?

Wife. Fine? By my troth, sweetheart, very fine! By my troth, I never liked thee so well in my life, sweetheart; but let [170 that pass. I warrant there be many women in the city have not such handsome husbands, but only for their apparel; but let that pass too.

Enter Hans and Skipper.

Hans. *Godden day, mester. Dis be de skipper dat heb de skip van marchandice. De commodity ben good; nempt it, master, nempt it.*[7]

Eyre. God-a-mercy, Hans; welcome, skipper. Where lies this ship of merchandise?

Skip. *De skip ben in rouere; dor be* [181 *van sugar, cyvet, almonds, cambrick, and a towsand towsand tings. Gotz sacrament, nempt it, mester; yo sal heb good copen.*[8]

Firk. To him, master! O sweet master! O sweet wares! Prunes, almonds, sugar candy, carrot roots, turnips! O brave, fatting meat![9] Let not a man buy a nutmeg but yourself.

Eyre. Peace, Firk! Come, skipper, [190 I'll go aboard [10] with you.—Hans, have you made him drink?

Skip. *Yaw, yaw, ic heb veale gedrunck.*[11]

Eyre. Come, Hans, follow me. Skipper, thou shalt have my countenance in the city.

Exeunt.

Firk. "*Yaw, heb veale gedrunck,*" quotha. They may well be called butterboxes, when they drink fat veal and thick beer too. But come, dame, I hope you'll chide us no more.   200

Wife. No, faith, Firk; no, perdy,[12]

[7] Good day, master. This is the skipper that has the ship of merchandise. The commodity is good; take it, master, take it.
[8] The ship is in the river; there are sugar, civet, almonds, cambric, and a thousand thousand things. By God's sacrament, take it, master; you shall have a good bargain.
[9] Fattening food.
[10] First two edns. read *abroade*.
[11] Yes, yes, I have drunk much.
[12] *Par Die*i, truly.

Hodge. I do feel honor creep upon me,
and, which is more, a certain rising in my
flesh; but let that pass.

FIRK. Rising in your flesh do you feel,
say you? Ay, you may be with child, but
why should not my master feel a rising in
his flesh, having a gown and a gold ring on?
But you are such a shrew, you'll soon pull
him down.   210

WIFE. Ha, ha! Prithee, peace! Thou
mak'st my worship laugh; but let that
pass. Come, I'll go in. Hodge, prithee, go
before me; Firk, follow me.

FIRK. Firk doth follow; Hodge, pass out
in state.   *Exeunt.*

[SCENE vii.

A room in Lincoln's house at London.]

Enter Lincoln and Dodger.

LINC. How now, good Dodger, what's the
    news in France?

DODGER. My lord, upon the eighteen day
    of May
The French and English were prepared
    to fight;
Each side with eager fury gave the sign
Of a most hot encounter. Five long hours
Both armies fought together; at the
    length
The lot of victory fell on our sides.
Twelve thousand of the Frenchmen that
    day died,
Four thousand English, and no man of
    name
But Captain Hyam and young Arding-
    ton,   10
Two gallant gentlemen—I knew them
    well.

LINC. But, Dodger, prithee, tell me, in this
    fight
How did my cousin Lacy bear himself?

DODGER. My lord, your cousin Lacy was
    not there.

LINC. Not there?

DODGER.   No, my good lord.

LINC.   Sure, thou mistakest.
I saw him shipped, and a thousand eyes
    beside
Were witnesses of the farewells which he
    gave,
When I, with weeping eyes, bid him
    adieu.
Dodger, take heed.

DODGER.   My lord, I am advised
That what I spake is true. To prove it
    so,   20
His cousin Askew, that supplied his place,
Sent me for him from France, that se-
    cretly
He might convey himself hither.

LINC.   Is 't even so?
Dares he so carelessly venture his life
Upon the indignation of a king?
Hath he despised my love, and spurned
    those favors
Which I with prodigal hand poured on
    his head?
He shall repent his rashness with his soul;
Since of my love he makes no estimate,
I'll make him wish he had not known my
    hate.   30
Thou hast no other news?

DODGER.   None else, my lord.

LINC. None worse I know thou hast.—
    Procure the king
To crown his giddy brows with ample
    honors,
Send him chief colonel—and all my hope
Thus to be dashed! But 'tis in vain to
    grieve;
One evil cannot a worse relieve.
Upon my life, I have found out his plot;
That old dog, Love, that fawned upon
    him so,
Love to that puling girl, his fair-cheeked
    Rose,
The lord mayor's daughter, hath dis-
    tracted him,   40
And in the fire of that love's lunacy
Hath he burnt up himself, consumed his
    credit,
Lost the king's love, yea, and, I fear, his
    life,
Only to get a wanton to his wife.
Dodger, it is so.

DODGER.   I fear so, my good lord.

LINC. It is so—nay, sure it cannot be!
I am at my wits' end. Dodger!

DODGER.   Yea, my lord.

LINC. Thou art acquainted with my neph-
    ew's haunts;
Spend this gold for thy pains; go seek him
    out.
Watch at my lord mayor's—there if he
    live,   50
Dodger, thou shalt be sure to meet with
    him.

Prithee, be diligent.—Lacy, thy name
Lived once in honor, now dead in
   shame!—
Be circumspect.   *Exit.*
DODGER.   I warrant you, my lord.   *Exit.*

[SCENE viii.

*A room in the Lord Mayor's house at
London.]*

Enter Lord Mayor and Master Scott.

L. MAYOR. Good Master Scott, I have
   been bold with you
To be a witness to a wedding knot
Betwixt young Master Hammon and my
   daughter.
O, stand aside; see where the lovers come.

Enter Hammon and Rose.

ROSE. Can it be possible you love me so?
No, no, within those eyeballs I espy
Apparent likelihoods of flattery.
Pray now, let go my hand.
HAM.   Sweet Mistress Rose,
Misconstrue not my words, nor miscon-
   ceive
Of my affection, whose devoted soul   10
Swears that I love thee dearer than my
   heart.
ROSE. As dear as your own heart? I judge
   it right,
Men love their hearts best when th' are
   out of sight.
HAM. I love you, by this hand.
ROSE.   Yet hands off now!
If flesh be frail, how weak and frail's
   your vow!
HAM. Then by my life I swear.
ROSE.   Then do not brawl;
One quarrel loseth wife and life and all.
Is not your meaning thus?
HAM.   In faith, you jest.
ROSE. Love loves to sport; therefore leave
   love, y'are best.
L. MAYOR. What? Square [1] they, Master
   Scott?
SCOTT.   Sir, never doubt,   20
Lovers are quickly in, and quickly out.
HAM. Sweet Rose, be not so strange in
   fancying me.
Nay, never turn aside, shun not my
   sight.

[1] Quarrel.

I am not grown so fond,[2] to fond [3] my
   love
On any that shall quit [4] it with disdain;
If you will love me, so—if not, farewell.
L. MAYOR. Why, how now, lovers, are you
   both agreed?
HAM. Yes, faith, my lord.
L. MAYOR.   'Tis well; give me your hand.
Give me yours, daughter.—How now,
   both pull back!
What means this, girl?
ROSE.   I mean to live a maid.   30
HAM. (*Aside.*) But not to die one; pause
   ere that be said.
L. MAYOR. Will you still cross me, still be
   obstinate?
HAM. Nay, chide her not, my lord, for
   doing well;
If she can live an happy virgin's life,
'Tis far more blessed than to be a wife.
ROSE. Say, sir, I cannot. I have made a
   vow.
Whoever be my husband, 'tis not you.
L. MAYOR. Your tongue is quick; but,
   Master Hammon, know,
I bade you welcome to another end.
HAM. What, would you have me pule and
   pine and pray,   40
With "lovely lady," "mistress of my
   heart,"
"Pardon your servant," and the rimer
   play,
Railing on Cupid and his tyrant's dart?
Or shall I undertake some martial spoil,
Wearing your glove at tourney and at
   tilt,
And tell how many gallants I unhorsed?
Sweet, will this pleasure you?
ROSE.   Yea, when wilt begin?
What, love rimes, man? Fie on that
   deadly sin!
L. MAYOR. If you will have her, I'll make
   her agree.
HAM. Enforcéd love is worse than hate
   to me.—   50
[*Aside.*] There is a wench keeps shop in
   the Old Change;
To her will I. It is not wealth I seek;
I have enough, and will prefer her love
Before the world.—My good lord mayor,
   adieu.
Old love for me; I have no luck with new.
                    Exit.

[2] Foolish.   [3] Found, set.   [4] Requite, return.

L. MAYOR. Now, mammet,[1] you have well
behaved yourself,
But you shall curse your coyness if I
live.—
Who's within there? See you convey
your mistress
Straight to th' Old Ford! I'll keep you
straight enough.
Fore God, I would have sworn the puling
girl   60
Would willingly accepted Hammon's
love;
But banish him, my thoughts!—Go,
minion, in!   *Exit Rose.*
Now tell me, Master Scott, would you
have thought
That Master Simon Eyre, the shoe-
maker,
Had been of wealth to buy such mer-
chandise?
SCOTT. 'Twas well, my lord, your honor
and myself
Grew partners with him, for your bills of
lading
Show that Eyre's gains in one commodity
Rise at the least to full three thousand
pound
Besides like gain in other merchandise. 70
L. MAYOR. Well, he shall spend some of
his thousands now,
For I have sent for him to the Guildhall.

Enter Eyre.

See, where he comes.—Good morrow,
Master Eyre.
EYRE. Poor Simon Eyre, my lord, your
shoemaker.
L. MAYOR. Well, well, it likes [2] yourself to
term you so.

Enter Dodger.[3]

Now, M[aster] Dodger, what's the news
with you?
DODGER. I'd gladly speak in private to
your honor.
L. MAYOR. You shall, you shall.—Master
Eyre and M[aster] Scott,
I have some business with this gentle-
man;
I pray, let me entreat you to walk
before   80

To the Guildhall; I'll follow presently.
Master Eyre, I hope ere noon to call you
sheriff.
EYRE. I would not care, my lord, if you
might call me King of Spain.—Come, Mas-
ter Scott.   [*Exeunt Eyre and Scott.*]
L. MAYOR. Now, Master Dodger, what's
the news you bring?
DODGER. The Earl of Lincoln by me greets
your lordship,
And earnestly requests you, if you can,
Inform him where his nephew Lacy keeps.
L. MAYOR. Is not his nephew Lacy now in
France?   90
DODGER. No, I assure your lordship, but
disguised
Lurks here in London.
L. MAYOR.   London? Is 't even so?
It may be; but, upon my faith and soul,
I know not where he lives, or whether
he lives;
So tell my Lord of Lincoln.—Lurk in
London?
Well, Master Dodger, you perhaps may
start him;
Be but the means to rid him into France,
I'll give you a dozen angels [4] for your
pains,
So much I love his honor, hate his
nephew.   99
And, prithee, so inform thy lord from me.
DODGER. I take my leave.   *Exit Dodger.*
L. MAYOR.   Farewell, good Master
Dodger.—
Lacy in London? I dare pawn my life
My daughter knows thereof, and for that
cause
Denied young M[aster] Hammon in his
love.
Well, I am glad I sent her to Old Ford.
God's Lord, 'tis late! To Guildhall I must
hie;
I know my brethren stay [5] my company.
Exit.

[SCENE ix.

A room in Eyre's house.]

Enter Firk, Eyre's Wife, Hans, and Roger.

WIFE. Thou goest too fast for me,
Roger. [O, Firk!] [6]
FIRK. Ay, forsooth.

---

[1] Puppet, doll.   [2] Pleases.
[3] Early edns. print this direction after the
following line.

[4] Gold coins.   [5] Await.
[6] Supplied from 1618 edn.

WIFE. I pray thee, run—do you hear?—run to Guildhall, and learn if my husband, Master Eyre, will take that worshipful vocation of m[aster] sheriff upon him. Hie thee, good Firk.

FIRK. Take it? Well, I go; and he should not take it, Firk swears to for- [10 swear him. Yes, forsooth, I go to Guildhall.

WIFE. Nay, when? Thou art too compendious and tedious.

FIRK. O, rare! Your excellence is full of eloquence; how like a new cart wheel my dame speaks, and she looks like an old musty ale bottle [1] going to scalding.

WIFE. Nay, when? Thou wilt make me melancholy.

FIRK. God forbid your worship [20 should fall into that humor. I run. *Exit.*

WIFE. Let me see now, Roger and Hans.

HODGE. Ay, forsooth, dame—mistress, I should say, but the old term so sticks to the roof of my mouth I can hardly lick it off.

WIFE. Even what thou wilt, good Roger; dame is a fair name for any honest Christian; but let that pass. How dost thou, Hans?

HANS. *Mee tanck you, vro.*　　　　30

WIFE. Well, Hans and Roger, you see God hath blessed your master, and, perdy, if ever he comes to be m[aster] sheriff of London—as we are all mortal—you shall see, I will have some odd thing or other in a corner for you; I will not be your back-friend; [2] but let that pass. Hans, pray thee, tie my shoe.

HANS. *Yaw, ic sal, vro.*

WIFE. Roger, thou know'st the [40 length of my foot; as it is none of the biggest, so, I thank God, it is handsome enough. Prithee, let me have a pair of shoes made—cork, [3] good Roger, wooden heel too.

HODGE. You shall.

WIFE. Art thou acquainted with never a fardingale-maker nor a French hood-maker? I must enlarge my bum—ha, ha! How shall I look in a hood, I wonder! [50 Perdy, oddly, I think.

HODGE. [4] [*Aside.*] As a cat out of a

pillory.—Very well, I warrant you, mistress.

WIFE. Indeed, all flesh is grass; and, Roger, canst thou tell where I may buy a good hair?

HODGE. Yes, forsooth, at the poulterer's in Gracious Street.

WIFE. Thou art an ungracious wag; [60 perdy, I mean a false hair for my periwig.

HODGE. Why, mistress, the next time I cut my beard, you shall have the shavings of it; but they are all true hairs.

WIFE. It is very hot; I must get me a fan or else a mask.

HODGE. [*Aside.*] So you had need, to hide your wicked face.

WIFE. Fie upon it, how costly this world's calling is; perdy, but that it is [70 one of the wonderful works of God, I would not deal with it.—Is not Firk come yet? Hans, be not so sad; let it pass and vanish, as my husband's worship says.

HANS. *Ick bin vrolicke; lot see yow soo.* [5]

HODGE. Mistress, will you drink [6] a pipe of tobacco?

WIFE. O, fie upon it, Roger, perdy! These filthy tobacco pipes are the most idle, slavering bables that ever I felt. [80 Out upon it! God bless us, men look not like men that use them.

Enter Rafe, being lame.

HODGE. What, fellow Rafe? Mistress, look here, Jane's husband! Why, how [now], [7] lame? Hans, make much of him; he's a brother of our trade, a good workman, and a tall soldier.

HANS. *You be welcome, broder.*

WIFE. Perdy, I knew him not. How dost thou, good Rafe? I am glad [to] see [90 thee well.

RAFE. I would to God you saw me, dame, as well

As when I went from London into France.

WIFE. Trust me, I am sorry, Rafe, to see thee impotent. Lord, how the wars have made him sunburnt! The left leg is not well; 'twas a fair gift of God the infirmity took not hold a little higher, considering thou camest from France; but let that pass.　　　　　　　　100

---

[1] Bottles made of leather.
[2] Reluctant friend.
[3] *I.e.*, with an inner pad of cork.
[4] The name now appears as Roger to the end of this scene.
[5] I am merry; let's see you so.
[6] Smoke.　　　　　　　[7] From 1610 edn.

Rafe. I am glad to see you well, and I rejoice
To hear that God hath blessed my master so
Since my departure.

Wife. Yea, truly, Rafe, I thank my Maker; but let that pass.

Hodge. And, sirrah Rafe, what news, what news in France?

Rafe. Tell me, good Roger, first, what news in England?
How does my Jane? When didst thou see my wife?
Where lives my poor heart? She'll be poor indeed, 110
Now I want limbs to get whereon to feed.

Hodge. Limbs? Hast thou not hands, man? Thou shalt never see a shoemaker want bread, though he have but three fingers on a hand.

Rafe. Yet all this while I hear not of my Jane.

Wife. O Rafe, your wife—perdy, we know not what's become of her. She was here awhile, and, because she was married, grew more stately than became her; I [120 checked [1] her, and so forth; away she flung, never returned, nor said bye nor bah; and, Rafe, you know, "ka me, ka thee." [2] And, so as I tell ye—Roger, is not Firk come yet?

Hodge. No, forsooth.

Wife. And so, indeed, we heard not of her, but I hear she lives in London; but let that pass. If she had wanted, she might have opened her case to me or my hus- [130 band, or to any of my men; I am sure, there's not any of them, perdy, but would have done her good to his power. Hans, look if Firk be come.

Hans. Yaw, ik sal, vro.   Exit Hans.

Wife. And so, as I said—but, Rafe, why dost thou weep? Thou knowest that naked we came out of our mother's womb, and naked we must return; and, therefore, thank God for all things. 140

Hodge. No, faith, Jane is a stranger here; but, Rafe, pull up a good heart— I know thou hast one. Thy wife, man, is in London; one told me he saw her a while ago very brave and neat; we'll ferret her out, and [3] London hold her.

[1] Scolded.
[2] "Scratch me and I'll scratch thee."   [3] If.

Wife. Alas, poor soul, he's overcome with sorrow; he does but as I do—weep for the loss of any good thing. But, Rafe, get thee in, call for some meat and drink; [150 thou shalt find me worshipful towards thee.

Rafe. I thank you, dame; since I want limbs and lands,
I'll trust to God, my good friends, and to my hands. [4]   Exit.

Enter Hans and Firk running.

Firk. Run, good Hans! O Hodge, O mistress! Hodge, heave up thine ears; mistress, smug up [5] your looks; on with your best apparel! My master is chosen, my master is called, nay, condemned by the cry of the country to be sheriff of the city for this famous year now to come. And, [160 time now being, a great many men in black gowns were asked for their voices and their hands, and my master had all their fists about his ears presently, and they cried, "Ay, ay, ay, ay,"—and so I came away.
Wherefore, without all other grieve, [6]
I do salute you, Mistress Shrieve. [7]

Hans. *Yaw, my mester is de groot man, de shrieve.*

Hodge. Did not I tell you, mistress? [170 Now I may boldly say, "Good morrow to your worship."

Wife. Good morrow, good Roger. I thank you, my good people all.—Firk, hold up thy hand; here's a threepenny piece for thy tidings.

Firk. 'Tis but three halfpence, I think. Yes, 'tis threepence; I smell the rose. [8]

Hodge. But, mistress, be ruled by me, and do not speak so pulingly. 180

Firk. 'Tis her worship speaks so, and not she. No, faith, mistress, speak me in the old key: "To it, Firk;" "There, good Firk;" "Ply your business, Hodge;" "Hodge, with a full mouth;" "I'll fill your bellies with good cheer, till they cry twang."

Enter Simon Eyre, wearing a gold chain.

Hans. *See, myn liever broder, heer compt my meester.* [9]

[4] From 1618 edn. Original reads *I'll to God, my good friends, and to these my hands.*
[5] Smarten up.   [6] Beyond every other sherif..
[7] Sheriff.   [8] This coin had a rose on it.
[9] See, my dear brothers, here comes my master.

WIFE. Welcome home, Master [190 Shrieve; I pray God continue you in health and wealth.

EYRE. See here, my Maggy, a chain, a gold chain for Simon Eyre! I shall make thee a lady; here's a French hood for thee; on with it, on with it! Dress thy brows with this flap of a shoulder of mutton,[1] to make thee look lovely. Where be my fine men? Roger, I'll make over my shop and tools to thee; Firk, thou shalt be the [200 foreman; Hans, thou shalt have an hundred for twenty.[2] Be as mad knaves as your master Sim Eyre hath been, and you shall live to be sheriffs of London.—How dost thou like me, Margery? Prince am I none, yet am I princely born. Firk, Hodge, and Hans!

ALL THREE. Ay, forsooth, what says your worship, Master[3] Sheriff?

EYRE. Worship and honor, you [210 Babylonian knaves, for the gentle craft. But I forgot myself; I am bidden by my lord mayor to dinner to Old Ford. He's gone before; I must after. Come, Madge, on with your trinkets! Now, my true Trojans, my fine Firk, my dapper Hodge, my honest Hans, some device, some odd crochets, some morris, or suchlike, for the honor of the gentle shoemakers. Meet me at Old Ford; you know my mind. [220 Come, Madge, away. Shut up the shop, knaves, and make holiday. *Exeunt.*

FIRK. O, rare! O, brave! Come, Hodge; follow me, Hans;
We'll be with them for a morris dance.
Exeunt.

[SCENE X.

A room at Old Ford.]

Enter Lord Mayor, Eyre his Wife in a French hood,[4] [Rose,] Sybil, and other Servants.

L. MAYOR. Trust me, you are as welcome to Old Ford
As I myself.

WIFE.   Truly, I thank your lordship.

L. MAYOR. Would our bad cheer were worth the thanks you give.

EYRE. Good cheer, my lord mayor,

fine cheer! A fine house, fine walls, all fine and neat.

L. MAYOR. Now, by my troth, I'll tell thee, Master Eyre,
It does me good, and all my brethren,
That such a madcap fellow as thyself
Is entered into our society.   10

WIFE. Ay, but, my lord, he must learn now to put on gravity.

EYRE. Peace, Maggy, a fig for gravity! When I go to Guildhall in my scarlet gown, I'll look as demurely as a saint, and speak as gravely as a justice of peace; but, now I am here at Old Ford, at my good lord mayor's house, let it go by, vanish, Maggy; I'll be merry. Away with flip-flap, these fooleries, these guller- [20 ies! What, honey? Prince am I none, yet am I princely born. What says my lord mayor?

L. MAYOR. Ha, ha, ha! I had rather than a thousand pound I had an heart but half so light as yours.

EYRE. Why, what should I do, my lord? A pound of care pays not a dram of debt. Hum, let's be merry whiles we are young; old age, sack, and sugar will steal upon us, ere we be aware.   31

THE FIRST THREE-MAN'S SONG[5]

O, the month of May, the merry month of May,
So frolic, so gay, and so green, so green, so green!
O, and then did I unto my true love say:
"Sweet Peg, thou shalt be my summer's queen!

"Now the nightingale, the pretty nightingale,
The sweetest singer in all the forest's choir,
Entreats thee, sweet Peggy, to hear thy true love's tale;
Lo, yonder she sitteth, her breast against a brier.

"But, O, I spy the cuckoo, the cuckoo, the cuckoo;   40
See where she sitteth. Come away, my joy;
Come away, I prithee. I do not like the cuckoo
Should sing where my Peggy and I kiss and toy."

---

[1] "The flap of a hood trimmed with fur or sheep's wool" (Rhys).

[2] *I.e.*, the twenty Portuguese already lent.

[3] From 1657 edn. Earlier edns. read *Mistress.*

[4] First two edns. give Sybil the French hood.

[5] This seems the most appropriate place to insert this song.

O, the month of May, the merry month of
   May,
So frolic, so gay, and so green, so green,
   so green!
And then did I unto my true love say:
   "Sweet Peg, thou shalt be my summer's
   queen!"

L. MAYOR. It's well done. Mistress
Eyre, pray give good counsel to my
daughter. 50
WIFE. I hope Mistress Rose will have
the grace to take nothing that's bad.
L. MAYOR. Pray God she do; for, i' faith,
   Mistress Eyre,
I would bestow upon that peevish
   girl
A thousand marks more than I mean
   to give her
Upon condition she'd be ruled by me.
The ape [1] still crosseth me. There came
   of late
A proper gentleman of fair revenues,
Whom gladly I would call son-in-
   law;
But my fine cockney [1] would have none
   of him. 60
You'll prove a coxcomb [2] for it, ere you
   die;
A courtier, or no man, must please
   your eye.
EYRE. Be ruled, sweet Rose; th' art
ripe for a man. Marry not with a boy
that has no more hair on his face than thou
hast on thy cheeks. A courtier! Wash, go
by, stand not upon pishery-pashery.
Those silken fellows are but painted images, outsides, outsides, Rose; their inner
linings are torn. No, my fine mouse, [70
marry me with a gentleman grocer like my
lord mayor, your father. A grocer is a
sweet trade—plums, plums! Had I a son or
daughter should marry out of the generation and blood of the shoemakers, he should
pack. What! The gentle trade is a living
for a man through Europe, through the
world.
A noise within of a tabor and a pipe.
MAYOR. What noise is this?
EYRE. O my lord mayor, a crew of [80
good fellows that for love to your honor are
come hither with a morris dance. Come
in, my Mesopotamians, cheerily.

*Enter Hodge, Hans, Rafe, Firk, and other
   Shoemakers in a morris; after a little
   dancing, the Lord Mayor speaks.*

MAYOR. Master Eyre, are all these shoe-
makers?
EYRE. All cordwainers, my good lord
mayor.
ROSE. [*Aside.*] How like my Lacy looks
   yond shoemaker!
HANS. [*Aside.*] O, that I durst but speak
   unto my love! 89
MAYOR. Sybil, go fetch some wine to
make these drink. You are all welcome.
ALL. We thank your lordship.
Rose takes a cup of wine and goes to Hans.
ROSE. For his sake whose fair shape thou
   represent'st,
Good friend, I drink to thee.
HANS. *Ic bedancke, good frister.* [3]
EYRE'S WIFE. I see, Mistress Rose,
you do not want judgment; you have drunk
to the properest man I keep.
FIRK. Here be some have done their
parts to be as proper as he. 100
MAYOR. Well, urgent business calls me
   back to London.
Good fellows, first go in and taste our
   cheer,
And, to make merry as you homeward go,
Spend these two angels in beer at Strat-
   ford Bow.
EYRE. To these two, my mad lads,
Sim Eyre adds another; then cheerily,
Firk; tickle it, Hans, and all for the honor
of shoemakers. *All go dancing out.*
MAYOR. Come, Master Eyre, let's have
   your company. *Exeunt.*
ROSE. Sybil, what shall I do?
SYB.   Why, what's the matter? 110
ROSE. That Hans the shoemaker is my
   love Lacy,
Disguised in that attire to find me out.
How should I find the means to speak
   with him?
SYB. What, mistress, never fear; I
dare venter [4] my maidenhead to nothing,
and that's great odds, that Hans the Dutchman, when we come to London, shall
not only see and speak with you, but in
spite of all your father's policies steal you
away and marry you. Will not this [120
please you?

---

[1] Pet.   [2] Fool.

[3] I thank you, good maid.   [4] Venture.

Rose. Do this, and ever be assured of my love.

Syb. Away, then, and follow your father to London, lest your absence cause him to suspect something.

Tomorrow, if my counsel be obeyed, I'll bind you prentice to the gentle trade.   *Exeunt.*

[Scene xi.

A street in London.]

Enter Jane in a semster's [1] *shop, working; and Hammon, muffled, at another door. He stands aloof.*

Ham. Yonder's the shop, and there my fair love sits.

She's fair and lovely, but she is not mine.

O, would she were! Thrice have I courted her;

Thrice hath my hand been moistened with her hand,

Whilst my poor famished eyes do feed on that

Which made them famish. I am infortunate:

I still love one, yet nobody loves me.

I muse [2] in other men what women see

That I so want! Fine Mistress Rose was coy,

And this too curious! [3] O, no, she is chaste,   10

And, for she thinks me wanton, she denies

To cheer my cold heart with her sunny eyes.

How prettily she works! O pretty hand!

O happy work! It doth me good to stand

Unseen to see her. Thus I oft have stood

In frosty evenings, a light burning by her,

Enduring biting cold, only to eye her.

One only look hath seemed as rich to me

As a king's crown; such is love's lunacy.

Muffled I'll pass along, and by that try   20

Whether she know me.—

Jane.   Sir, what is 't you buy?

What is 't you lack, sir, calico, or lawn,

Fine cambric shirts, or bands? What will you buy?

Ham. [*Aside.*] That which thou wilt not sell. Faith, yet I'll try.—

How do you sell this handkercher?

Jane.   Good cheap. [4]

Ham. And how these ruffs?

Jane.   Cheap too.

Ham.   And how this band?

Jane. Cheap too.

Ham.   All cheap! How sell you then this hand?

Jane. My hands are not to be sold.

Ham.   To be given then!

Nay, faith, I come to buy.

Jane.   But none knows when.

Ham. Good sweet, leave work a little while; let's play.   30

Jane. I cannot live by keeping holiday.

Ham. I'll pay you for the time which shall be lost.

Jane. With me you shall not be at so much cost.

Ham. Look, how you wound this cloth, so you wound me.

Jane. It may be so.

Ham.   'Tis so.

Jane.   What remedy?

Ham. Nay, faith, you are too coy.

Jane.   Let go my hand.

Ham. I will do any task at your command;

I would let go this beauty, were I not

In mind to disobey you by a power

That controls kings. I love you!

Jane.   So, now part. 40

Ham. With hands I may, but never with my heart.

In faith, I love you.

Jane.   I believe you do.

Ham. Shall a true love in me breed hate in you?

Jane. I hate you not.

Ham.   Then you must love?

Jane.   I do.

What, are you better now? I love not you.

Ham. All this, I hope, is but a woman's fray,

That means, "Come to me," when she cries, "Away!"

In earnest, mistress, I do not jest;

---

[1] Seamstress'.   [2] Wonder.   [3] Scrupulous.

[4] At a bargain.

A true, chaste love hath entered in my
  breast.
I love you dearly, as I love my life;   50
I love you as a husband loves a wife;
That, and no other love, my love re-
  quires.
Thy wealth, I know, is little; my de-
  sires
Thirst not for gold. Sweet, beauteous
  Jane, what's mine
Shall, if thou make myself thine, all be
  thine.
Say, judge, what is thy sentence, life
  or death?
Mercy or cruelty lies in thy breath.
JANE. Good sir, I do believe you love me
  well;
For 'tis a silly conquest, silly pride,
For one like you—I mean a gentle-
  man—   60
To boast that by his love tricks he hath
  brought
Such and such women to his amorous
  lure.
I think you do not so, yet many do,
And make it even a very trade to woo.
I could be coy, as many women be,
Feed you with sunshine smiles and
  wanton looks,
But I detest witchcraft; say that I
Do constantly believe you, constant [1]
  have—
HAM. Why dost thou not believe me?
JANE.   I believe you;
But yet, good sir, because I will not
  grieve you   70
With hopes to taste fruit which will
  never fall,
In simple truth this is the sum of all:
My husband lives—at least, I hope he
  lives.
Pressed was he to these bitter wars in
  France;
Bitter they are to me by wanting him.
I have but one heart, and that heart's
  his due.
How can I then bestow the same on you?
Whilst he lives, his I live, be it ne'er
  so poor,
And rather be his wife than a king's
  whore.
HAM. Chaste and dear woman, I will not
  abuse thee,   80

[1] Constantly.

Although it cost my life, if thou refuse
  me.
Thy husband, pressed for France, what
  was his name?
JANE. Rafe Damport.
HAM.   Damport?—Here's a letter sent
From France to me, from a dear friend
  of mine,
A gentleman of place; here he doth
  write
Their names that have been slain in
  every fight.
JANE. I hope death's scroll contains not
  my love's name.
HAM. Cannot you read?
JANE.   I can.
HAM.   Peruse the same.
To my remembrance such a name I read
Amongst the rest. See here!
JANE.   Ay me, he's dead! 90
He's dead! If this be true, my dear
  heart's slain!
HAM. Have patience, dear love.
JANE.   Hence, hence!
HAM.   Nay, sweet Jane,
Make not poor sorrow proud with these
  rich tears.
I mourn thy husband's death because
  thou mourn'st.
JANE. That bill is forged; 'tis signed by
  forgery.
HAM. I'll bring thee letters sent besides
  to many,
Carrying the like report. Jane, 'tis too
  true.
Come, weep not; mourning, though it
  rise from love,
Helps not the mournéd, yet hurts them
  that mourn.
JANE. For God's sake, leave me.
HAM.   Whither dost thou turn? 100
Forget the dead; love them that are
  alive.
His love is faded; try how mine will
  thrive.
JANE. 'Tis now no time for me to think
  on love.
HAM. 'Tis now best time for you to think
  on love,
Because your love lives not.
JANE.   Though he be dead,
My love to him shall not be buried.
For God's sake, leave me to myself
  alone.

HAM. 'Twould kill my soul to leave thee
    drowned in moan.
  Answer me to my suit, and I am gone;
  Say to me yea or no.
JANE.   No.
HAM.   Then farewell!— 110
  One farewell will not serve; I come
    again.
  Come, dry these wet cheeks; tell me,
    faith, sweet Jane,
  Yea or no, once more.
JANE.   Once more I say no;
  Once more be gone, I pray; else will I
    go.
HAM. Nay, then I will grow rude, by this
    white hand,
  Until you change that cold "no"; here
    I'll stand
  Till by your hard heart—
JANE.   Nay, for God's love, peace!
  My sorrows by your presence more in-
    crease.
  Not that you thus are present, but all
    grief
  Desires to be alone; therefore in brief 120
  Thus much I say, and saying bid adieu:
  If ever I wed man, it shall be you.
HAM. O blessed voice! Dear Jane, I'll
    urge no more;
  Thy breath hath made me rich.
JANE.   Death makes me poor.
                                    Exeunt.

[SCENE xii.

The shop in Tower Street.]

*Enter Hodge, at his shopboard, Rafe, Firk,
    Hans, and a Boy at work [, singing].*

ALL. Hey, down a down, down derry!

HODGE. Well said, my hearts. Ply your
work today; we loitered yesterday; to it
pell-mell, that we may live to be lord
mayors, or aldermen at least.

FIRK. Hey, down a down, derry!

HODGE. Well said, i' faith! How sayst
thou, Hans, doth not Firk tickle it? [1]

HANS. *Yaw, mester.*

FIRK. Not so neither; my organ pipe [10
squeaks this morning for want of liquoring.

Hey, down a down, derry!

HANS. *Forward, Firk; tow best un jolly*
* "Go it."*

*yongster. Hort, I, mester, ic bid yo, cut me un
pair vampres vor Mester Jeffre's bootes.* [2]

HODGE. Thou shalt, Hans.

FIRK. Master!

HODGE. How now, boy?

FIRK. Pray, now you are in the cutting
vein, cut me out a pair of counterfeits, [3] [20
or else my work will not pass current.

  Hey, down a down!

HODGE. Tell me, sirs, are my cousin
M[istress] Priscilla's shoes done?

FIRK. Your cousin? No, master; one of
your aunts, [4] hang her; let them alone.

RAFE. I am in hand with them; she
gave charge that none but I should do them
for her.

FIRK. Thou do for her? Then 'twill [30
be a lame doing, and that she loves not.
Rafe, thou mightst have sent her to me
in faith; I would have yerked and firked
your Priscilla.

  Hey, down a down, derry.

This gear [5] will not hold.

HODGE. How sayst thou, Firk, were we
not merry at Old Ford?

FIRK. How, merry? Why, our buttocks
went jiggy-joggy like a quagmire. Well, [40
Sir Roger Oatmeal, [6] if I thought all
meal of that nature, I would eat nothing
but bagpuddings.

RAFE. Of all good fortunes my fellow
Hans had the best.

FIRK. 'Tis true, because Mistress Rose
drank to him.

HODGE. Well, well, work apace. They
say seven of the aldermen be dead, or very
sick.   50

FIRK. I care not; I'll be none.

RAFE. No, nor I; but then my M[as-
ter] Eyre will come quickly to be l[ord]
mayor.

Enter Sybil.

FIRK. Whoop, yonder comes Sybil.

HODGE. Sybil, welcome, i' faith; and
how dost thou, mad wench?

FIRK. Sib [7]-whore, welcome to London.

[2] Go on, Firk, thou art a jolly youngster.
Hark, ay, master, I pray you cut me a pair of
vamps for Master Jeffrey's boots.
[3] With a pun on the sense of *anything made
after a pattern.*
[4] Women.   [5] Matter.
[6] Punning reference to Sir Roger Oteley.
[7] Punning on the sense of *friend.*

Syb. God-a-mercy, sweet Firk. Good Lord, Hodge, what a delicious shop you [60 have got! You tickle it, i' faith.

Rafe. God-a-mercy, Sybil, for our good cheer at Old Ford.

Syb. That you shall have, Rafe.

Firk. Nay, by the Mass, we had tickling cheer, Sybil. And how the plague dost thou and Mistress Rose and my l[ord] mayor? I put the women in first.

Syb. Well, God-a-mercy. But, God's me, I forget myself; where's Hans the Fleming?

Firk. Hark, butterbox, now you must yelp out some *spreken*. 72

Hans. *Vat begaie gou? Vat vod gou, frister?* [1]

Syb. Marry, you must come to my young mistress, to pull on her shoes you made last.

Hans. *Vare ben your egle fro?* [2] *Vare ben your mistris?*

Syb. Marry, here at our London [80 house in Cornhill. [3]

Firk. Will nobody serve her turn but Hans?

Syb. No, sir. Come, Hans, I stand upon needles.

Hodge. Why then, Sybil, take heed of pricking.

Syb. For that let me alone. I have a trick in my budget. Come, Hans. 89

Hans. *Yaw, yaw, ic sall meete yo gane.* [4]
Exit Hans and Sybil.

Hodge. Go, Hans, make haste again. Come, who lacks work?

Firk. I, master, for I lack my breakfast; 'tis munching time, and past.

Hodge. Is't so? Why, then leave work, Rafe. To breakfast! Boy, look to the tools. Come, Rafe; come, Firk. *Exeunt.*

[Scene xiii.
The same.]

Enter a Serving-man.

Serv. Let me see now, the sign of the Last in Tower Street. Mass, yonder's the house. What, haw! Who's within?

Enter Rafe.

Rafe. Who calls there? What want you, sir?

---

[1] What do you want? What would you, girl?
[2] Where is your noble lady?
[2] First three edns. read *Cornwall*.
[4] I shall with you go.

Serv. Marry, I would have a pair of shoes made for a gentlewoman against tomorrow morning. What, can you do them?

Rafe. Yes, sir, you shall have them. But what length's her foot? 10

Serv. [*Presenting a shoe.*] Why, you must make them in all parts like this shoe; but, at any hand, fail not to do them, for the gentlewoman is to be married very early in the morning.

Rafe. How? By this shoe must it be made? By this? Are you sure, sir, by this?

Serv. How, by this? Am I sure, by this? Art thou in thy wits? I tell thee, I must have a pair of shoes, dost thou [20 mark me? A pair of shoes, two shoes, made by this very shoe, this same shoe, against tomorrow morning by four a-clock. Dost understand me? Canst thou do 't?

Rafe. Yes, sir, yes—I—I—I can do 't. By this shoe, you say? I should know this shoe. Yes, sir, yes, by this shoe, I can do 't. Four a-clock, well. Whither shall I bring them?

Serv. To the sign of the Golden Ball [30 in Watling Street; inquire for one Master Hammon, a gentleman, my master.

Rafe. Yea, sir; by this shoe, you say?

Serv. I say, Master Hammon at the Golden Ball; he's the bridegroom, and those shoes are for his bride.

Rafe. They shall be done by this shoe. Well, well, Master Hammon at the Golden Shoe—I would say, the Golden Ball; very well, very well. But I pray you, sir, [40 where must Master Hammon be married?

Serv. At Saint Faith's Church, under Paul's. But what's that to thee? Prithee, despatch those shoes, and so farewell. *Exit.*

Rafe. "By this shoe," said he. How am I amazed
At this strange accident! Upon my life,
This was the very shoe I gave my wife,
When I was pressed for France—since when, alas!
I never could hear of her. It is the same,
And Hammon's bride no other but my Jane. 50

Enter Firk.

Firk. 'Snails, Rafe, thou hast lost thy part of three pots a countryman of mine gave me to breakfast.

RAFE. I care not; I have found a better thing.

FIRK. A thing? Away! Is it a man's thing, or a woman's thing?

RAFE. Firk, dost thou know this shoe?

FIRK. No, by my troth; neither doth that know me! I have no acquaintance [60 with it; 'tis a mere stranger to me.

RAFE. Why, then I do; this shoe, I durst be sworn,
Once covéred the instep of my Jane.
This is her size, her breadth; thus trod my love;
These truelove knots I pricked. I hold my life,
By this old shoe I shall find out my wife.

FIRK. Ha, ha! Old shoe, that wert new! How a murrain [1] came this ague fit of foolishness upon thee?

RAFE. Thus, Firk: even now here came a serving-man;   70
By this shoe would he have a new pair made
Against tomorrow morning for his mistress,
That's to be married to a gentleman.
And why may not this be my sweet Jane?

FIRK. And why mayst not thou be my sweet ass? Ha, ha!

RAFE. Well, laugh and spare not! But the truth is this:
Against tomorrow morning I'll provide
A lusty crew of honest shoemakers   78
To watch the going of the bride to church.
If she prove Jane, I'll take her in despite
From Hammon and the devil, were he by.
If it be not my Jane, what remedy?
Hereof am I sure, I shall live till I die,
Although I never with a woman lie. *Exit.*

FIRK. Thou lie with a woman to build nothing but Cripplegates! Well, God sends fools fortune, and it may be he may light upon his matrimony by such a device, for wedding and hanging goes by destiny. *Exit.*

[SCENE xiv.

A room in the Lord Mayor's house at London.]

Enter Hans and Rose, arm in arm.

HANS. How happy am I by embracing thee!
O, I did fear such cross mishaps did reign
That I should never see my Rose again.

[1] Plague.

ROSE. Sweet Lacy, since fair opportunity
Offers herself to furder our escape,
Let not too overfond esteem of me
Hinder that happy hour. Invent the means,
And Rose will follow thee through all the world.

HANS. O, how I surfeit with excess of joy,
Made happy by thy rich perfection! 10
But since thou pay'st sweet int'rest to my hopes,
Redoubling love on love, let me once more
Like to a bold-faced debtor crave of thee
This night to steal abroad, and at Eyre's house,
Who now by death of certain aldermen
Is mayor of London,[2] and my master once,
Meet thou thy Lacy, where in spite of change,
Your father's anger, and mine uncle's hate,
Our happy nuptials will we consummate.

Enter Sybil.

SYB. O God, what will you do, mis- [20 tress? Shift for yourself; your father is at hand! He's coming, he's coming! Master Lacy, hide yourself in my mistress! For God's sake, shift for yourselves!

HANS. Your father come! Sweet Rose, what shall I do?
Where shall I hide me? How shall I escape?

ROSE. A man, and want wit in extremity?
Come, come, be Hans still; play the shoemaker;
Pull on my shoe.

Enter Lord Mayor.

HANS.   Mass, and that's well remembered.

SYB. Here comes your father.   30

HANS. *Forware, metresse, 'tis un good skow; it sal vel dute, or ye sal neit betallen.*[3]

ROSE. O God, it pincheth me. What will you do?

HANS. [*Aside.*] Your father's presence pincheth, not the shoe.

[2] Sir Roger Oteley, however, is called lord mayor in stage directions and speech heads throughout the play.

[3] Indeed, mistress, 'tis a good shoe; it shall well do it, or you shall not pay.

L. Mayor. Well done; fit my daughter well, and she shall please thee well.

Hans. *Yaw, yaw, ick weit dat well; for ware, 'tis un good skoo; 'tis gimait van neits leither. Se ever, mine here.*[1]

Enter a Prentice.

L. Mayor. I do believe it.—What's the
    news with you?   40

Pren. Please you, the Earl of Lincoln at
    the gate
Is newly lighted, and would speak with
    you.

L. Mayor. The Earl of Lincoln come
    speak with me?
Well, well, I know his errand.—Daughter
    Rose,
Send hence your shoemaker, despatch,
    have done!—
Syb, make things handsome.—Sir boy,
    follow me.   *Exit [with Prentice].*

Hans. Mine uncle come! O, what may
    this portend?
Sweet Rose, this of our love threatens
    an end.

Rose. Be not dismayed at this; whate'er
    befall,
Rose is thine own. To witness I speak
    truth,   50
Where thou appoints the place, I'll meet
    with thee.
I will not fix a day to follow thee,
But presently steal hence. Do not reply.
Love which gave strength to bear my
    father's hate
Shall now add wings to further our
    escape.   *Exeunt.*

Enter L[ord] Mayor and Lincoln.

L. Mayor. Believe me, on my credit, I
    speak truth;
Since first your nephew Lacy went to
    France,
I have not seen him. It seemed strange
    to me,
When Dodger told me that he stayed
    behind,
Neglecting the high charge the king
    imposed.   60

Linc. Trust me, Sir Roger Oteley, I did
    think

[1] Yes, yes, I know that well; indeed, 'tis a good shoe; 'tis made of neat's leather. See here, good sir!

Your counsel had given head to this
    attempt,
Drawn to it by the love he bears your
    child.
Here I did hope to find him in your
    house;
But now I see mine error, and confess
My judgment wronged you by conceiving
    so.

L. Mayor. Lodge in my house, say you?
    Trust me, my lord,
I love your nephew Lacy too-too dearly,
So much to wrong his honor; and he hath
    done so,
That first gave him advice to stay from
    France.   70
To witness I speak truth, I let you know
How careful I have been to keep my
    daughter
Free from all conference or speech of
    him—
Not that I scorn your nephew, but in
    love
I bear your honor, lest your noble
    blood
Should by my mean worth be dishonoréd.

Linc. [*Aside.*] How far the churl's tongue
    wanders from his heart!—
Well, well, Sir Roger Oteley, I believe
    you,
With more than many thanks for the
    kind love
So much you seem to bear me. But, my
    lord,   80
Let me request your help to seek my
    nephew,
Whom if I find, I'll straight embark for
    France.
So shall your Rose be free, my thoughts
    at rest,[2]
And much care die which now lies [3] in
    my breast.

Enter Sybil.

Syb. O Lord! Help, for God's sake!
My mistress; O, my young mistress!

L. Mayor. Where is thy mistress? What's
    become of her?

Syb. She's gone, she's fled!

L. Mayor.   Gone! Whither is she fled?

Syb. I know not, forsooth. She's fled

[2] First two edns. have *my Rose . . . your thoughts.*

[3] From 1610 edn. Original reads *dies.*

out of doors with Hans the shoemaker; I saw them scud, scud, scud, apace, apace!

L. MAYOR. Which way? What, John! Where be my men? Which way?   92

SYB. I know not, and it please your worship.

L. MAYOR. Fled with a shoemaker? Can this be true?

SYB. O Lord, sir, as true as God's in heaven.

LINC. [Aside.] Her love turned shoemaker? I am glad of this.

L. MAYOR. A Fleming butterbox, a shoemaker!
Will she forget her birth, requite my care   100
With such ingratitude?   Scorned she young Hammon
To love a honnikin,[1] a needy knave?
Well, let her fly; I'll not fly after her.
Let her starve, if she will; she's none of mine.

LINC. Be not so cruel, sir.

Enter Firk with shoes.

SYB.   I am glad she's scaped.

L. MAYOR. I'll not account of her as of my child.
Was there no better object for her eyes
But a foul drunken lubber, swill-belly,
A shoemaker?   That's brave!   109

FIRK. Yea, forsooth; 'tis a very brave shoe, and as fit as a pudding.

L. MAYOR. How now, what knave is this? From whence comest thou?

FIRK. No knave, sir. I am Firk the shoemaker, lusty Roger's chief lusty journeyman, and I come hither to take up the pretty leg of sweet Mistress Rose, and thus hoping your worship is in as good health as I was at the making hereof, I bid you farewell, yours—Firk.

L. MAYOR. Stay, stay, Sir Knave!   120

LINC. Come hither, shoemaker!

FIRK. 'Tis happy the knave is put before the shoemaker, or else I would not have vouchsafed to come back to you. I am moved, for I stir.

L. MAYOR. My lord, this villain calls us knaves by craft.

FIRK. Then 'tis by the gentle craft, and to call one knave gently, is no harm.   [129

Sit your worship merry!   Syb, your young mistress—I'll so bob[2] them,[3] now my master, M[aster] Eyre, is lord mayor of London.

L. MAYOR. Tell me, sirrah, whose man are you?

FIRK. I am glad to see your worship so merry.   I have no maw[4] to this gear, no stomach as yet to a red petticoat.
Pointing to Sybil.

LINC. He means not, sir, to woo you to his maid,
But only doth demand whose man you are.   140

FIRK. I sing now to the tune of "Rogero."   Roger, my fellow, is now my master.

LINC. Sirrah, know'st thou one Hans, a shoemaker?

FIRK. Hans, shoemaker?   O, yes; stay, yes, I have him. I tell you what (I speak it in secret): Mistress Rose and he are by this time—no, not so, but shortly are to come over one another with "Can [149 you dance the shaking of the sheets?"[5] It is that Hans—[Aside.] I'll so gull these diggers![6]

L. MAYOR. Know'st thou, then, where he is?

FIRK. Yes, forsooth; yea, marry!

LINC. Canst thou, in sadness[7]—

FIRK. No, forsooth; no, marry!

L. MAYOR. Tell me, good honest fellow, where he is,
And thou shalt see what I'll bestow of thee.

FIRK. Honest fellow? No, sir; not so, sir; my profession is the gentle craft.   I [160 care not for seeing; I love feeling. Let me feel it here; *aurium tenus*, ten pieces of gold; *genuum tenus*,[8] ten pieces of silver; and then Firk is your man—[Aside.] in a new pair of stretchers.[9]

L. MAYOR. Here is an angel, part of thy reward,
Which I will give thee; tell me where he is.   167

FIRK. No point![10]   Shall I betray my brother? No! Shall I prove Judas to Hans?

[2] Fool.   [3] From 1610 edn.   Original reads *then*.
[4] Appetite.   [6] *I.e.*, for information.
[5] An old dance song.   [7] Seriousness.
[8] Firk's Latin phrases actually mean *up to the ears, up to the knees.*
[9] Shoe stretchers; also lies.
[10] Not at all.

[1] Low fellow.

No! Shall I cry treason to my corporation?
No, I shall be firked and yerked then. But
give me your angel; your angel shall tell you.

LINC. Do so, good fellow; 'tis no hurt to
thee.

FIRK. Send simpering Syb away.

L. MAYOR. Huswife, get you in.

Exit Syb[il].

FIRK. Pitchers have ears, and maids
have wide mouths; but for Hans Prans,
upon my word, tomorrow morning he and
young Mistress Rose go to this gear; they
shall be married together, by this rush, [180
or else turn Firk to a firkin of butter, to tan
leather withal.

L. MAYOR. But art thou sure of this?

FIRK. Am I sure that Paul's steeple is a
handful higher than London Stone, or that
the Pissing Conduit leaks nothing but
pure Mother Bunch? [1] Am I sure I am
lusty Firk? God's nails, do you think I
am so base to gull you?

LINC. Where are they married? Dost
thou know the church?   191

FIRK. I never go to church, but I know
the name of it; it is a swearing church—
stay awhile! 'Tis—ay, by the Mass! No,
no! 'Tis—ay, by my troth! No, nor that.
'Tis—ay, by my faith! That, that, 'tis,
ay, by my Faith's Church under Paul's
Cross. There they shall be knit like a pair
of stockings in matrimony; there they'll be
incony. [2]   200

LINC. Upon my life, my nephew Lacy
walks

In the disguise of this Dutch shoemaker.

FIRK. Yes, forsooth.

LINC.   Doth he not, honest fellow?

FIRK. No, forsooth; I think Hans is
nobody but Hans, no spirit.

L. MAYOR. My mind misgives me now,
'tis so, indeed.

LINC. My cousin speaks the language,
knows the trade.

L. MAYOR. Let me request your company,
my lord;

Your honorable presence may, no doubt,
Refrain their headstrong rashness, when
myself,   210
Going alone, perchance may be o'erborne.
Shall I request this favor?

LINC.   This, or what else.

FIRK. Then you must rise betimes, for

they mean to fall to their hey-pass and re-
pass, [3] pindy-pandy, [4] which hand will you
have, very early.

L. MAYOR. My care shall every way equal
their haste.
This night accept your lodging in my
house;
The earlier shall we stir, and at Saint
Faith's   219
Prevent this giddy hare-brained nuptial.
This traffic of hot love shall yield cold
gains;
They ban [5] our loves, and we'll forbid
their banes. [6]   *Exit.* [7]

LINC. At Saint Faith's Church, thou
say'st?

FIRK.   Yes, by their troth.

LINC. Be secret, on thy life.   *Exit.*

FIRK. Yes, when I kiss your wife! Ha,
ha, here's no craft in the gentle craft. I
came hither of purpose with shoes to Sir
Roger's worship, whilst Rose, his daughter,
be cony-catched [8] by Hans. Soft now; these
two gulls will be at Saint Faith's [230
Church tomorrow morning, to take Master
Bridegroom and Mistress Bride napping,
and they, in the meantime, shall chop up [9]
the matter at the Savoy. But the best
sport is, Sir Roger Oteley will find my fellow, lame Rafe's, wife going to marry a
gentleman, and then he'll stop her instead
of his daughter. O, brave! There will be fine
tickling sport. Soft now, what have I to
do? O, I know; now a mess of shoe- [240
makers meet at the Woolsack in Ivy Lane,
to cozen my gentleman of lame Rafe's
wife; that's true.

Alack, alack!
Girls, hold out tack! [10]
For now smocks for this jumbling
Shall go to wrack.

Exit.

[SCENE XV.

A room in Eyre's house.]

Enter Eyre, his Wife, Hans, and Rose.

EYRE. This is the morning, then; stay,
my bully, my honest Hans, is it not?

HANS. This is the morning that must

---

[1] A well-known alewife.   [2] Fine.

[3] Conjuring terms.   [5] Curse.
[4] Game of handy-dandy.   [6] Banns.
[7] From 1618 edn. First two edns. have *Exeunt.*
[8] Tricked.   [10] *I.e.*, hold out against attack (?).
[9] Conclude.

make us two happy or miserable; therefore, if you—

EYRE. Away with these if's and and's, Hans, and these *et cetera's!* By mine honor, Rowland Lacy, none but the king shall wrong thee. Come, fear nothing. Am not I Sim Eyre? Is not Sim Eyre lord [10 mayor of London? Fear nothing, Rose. Let them all say what they can, "Dainty, come thou to me." [1]—Laughest thou?

WIFE. Good my lord, stand her friend in what thing you may.

EYRE. Why, my sweet Lady Madgy, think you Simon Eyre can forget his fine Dutch journeyman? No, vah! Fie, I scorn it; it shall never be cast in my teeth that I was unthankful. Lady Madgy, thou [20 hadst never covered thy Saracen's head with this French flap, nor loaden thy bum with this farthingale ('tis trash, trumpery, vanity); Simon Eyre had never walked in a red petticoat, nor wore a chain of gold, but for my fine journeyman's Portuguese. —And shall I leave him? No! Prince am I none, yet near a princely mind.

HANS. My lord, 'tis time for us to part from hence. 30

EYRE. Lady Madgy, Lady Madgy, take two or three of my piecrust eaters, my buff jerkin varlets, that do walk in black gowns at Simon Eyre's heels; take them, good Lady Madgy; trip and go, my brown queen of periwigs, with my delicate Rose and my jolly Rowland to the Savoy; see them linked; countenance the marriage; and, when it is done, cling, cling together, you Hamborough turtledoves. I'll bear [40 you out; come to Simon Eyre. Come, dwell with me, Hans; thou shalt eat minced pies and marchpane.[2] Rose, away, cricket; trip and go, my Lady Madgy, to the Savoy; Hans, wed, and to bed; kiss, and away! Go, vanish!

WIFE. Farewell, my lord.

ROSE. Make haste, sweet love.

WIFE. She'd fain the deed were done.

HANS. Come, my sweet Rose; faster than deer we'll run. *They go out.*

EYRE. Go, vanish, vanish! Avaunt, [50 I say! By the Lord of Ludgate, it's a mad life to be a lord mayor; it's a stirring life, a fine life, a velvet life, a careful life. Well,

---

[1] The opening of a popular song.
[2] A sweetmeat.

Simon Eyre, yet set a good face on it, in the honor of Saint Hugh. Soft, the king this day comes to dine with me, to see my new buildings; his majesty is welcome; he shall have good cheer, delicate cheer, princely cheer. This day my fellow prentices of London come to dine with me too; [60 they shall have fine cheer, gentlemanlike cheer. I promised the mad Cappadocians, when we all served at the Conduit together, that, if ever I came to be mayor of London, I would feast them all, and I'll do 't, I'll do 't, by the life of Pharaoh; by this beard, Sim Eyre will be no flincher. Besides, I have procured that upon every Shrove Tuesday, at the sound of the pancake bell, my fine dapper Assyrian lads [70 shall clap up their shop windows, and away. This is the day, and this day they shall do 't, they shall do 't.

Boys, that day are you free, let masters care,
And prentices shall pray for Simon Eyre. *Exit.*

[SCENE xvi.

A street near St. Faith's church.]

Enter Hodge, Firk, Rafe, and five or six Shoemakers, all with cudgels or such weapons.

HODGE. Come, Rafe; stand to it, Firk. My masters, as we are the brave bloods of the shoemakers, heirs apparent to Saint Hugh, and perpetual benefactors to all good fellows, thou shalt have no wrong. Were Hammon a king of spades, he should not delve in thy close [3] without thy sufferance. But tell me, Rafe, art thou sure 'tis thy wife?

RAFE. Am I sure this is Firk? This [10 morning, when I stroked on her shoes, I looked upon her, and she upon me, and sighed—asked me if ever I knew one Rafe. "Yes," said I. "For his sake," said she, tears standing in her eyes, "and for thou art somewhat like him, spend this piece of gold." I took it; my lame leg and my travel beyond sea made me unknown. All is one for that; I know she's mine.

FIRK. Did she give thee this gold? O [20 glorious, glittering gold! She's thine own,

[3] Field.

'tis thy wife, and she loves thee; for I'll
stand to 't there's no woman will give gold
to any man, but she thinks better of him
than she thinks of them she gives silver to.
And for Hammon, neither Hammon nor
hangman shall wrong thee in London! Is
not our old master Eyre lord mayor?
Speak, my hearts.

ALL. Yes, and Hammon shall know it to
his cost.   31

Enter Hammon, his Man, Jane, and Others.

HODGE. Peace, my bullies; yonder they
come.

RAFE. Stand to 't, my hearts. Firk, let
me speak first.

HODGE. No, Rafe, let me.—Hammon,
whither away so early?

HAM. Unmannerly, rude slave, what's that
    to thee?

FIRK. To him, sir? Yes, sir, and to me,
and others. Good morrow, Jane, how [40
dost thou? Good Lord, how the world is
changed with you! God be thanked!

HAM. Villains, hands off! How dare you
    touch my love?

ALL. Villains? Down with them! Cry
clubs [1] for prentices!

HODGE. Hold, my hearts! Touch her,
Hammon? Yea, and, more than that,
we'll carry her away with us. My masters
and gentlemen, never draw your bird-
spits; shoemakers are steel to the back,
men every inch of them, all spirit.   51

ALL OF HAMMON'S SIDE. Well, and what
of all this?

HODGE. I'll show you.—Jane, dost thou
know this man? 'Tis Rafe, I can tell thee;
nay, 'tis he in faith, though he be lamed
by the wars. Yet look not strange, but run
to him, fold him about the neck, and kiss
him.

JANE. Lives then my husband? O God,
    let me go;   60
Let me embrace my Rafe.

HAM.   What means my Jane?

JANE. Nay what meant you, to tell me he
    was slain?

HAM. Pardon me, dear love, for being
    misled.—
[*To Rafe.*] 'Twas rumored here in London thou wert dead.

FIRK. Thou seest he lives. Lass, go, pack
    home with him.
Now, M[aster] Hammon, where's your
    mistress, your wife?

SERV. 'Swounds,[2] m[aster], fight for her!
Will you thus lose her?

ALL. Down with that creature! Clubs!
Down with him!   70

HODGE. Hold, hold!

HAM.   Hold, fool! Sirs, he shall
    do no wrong.
Will my Jane leave me thus, and break
    her faith?

FIRK. Yea, sir! She must, sir! She shall,
sir! What then? Mend it!

HODGE. Hark, fellow Rafe, follow my
counsel: set the wench in the midst, and
let her choose her man, and let her be his
woman.

JANE. Whom should I choose? Whom
    should my thoughts affect
But him whom heaven hath made to be
    my love?   80
Thou art my husband, and these humble
    weeds
Makes thee more beautiful than all his
    wealth.
Therefore, I will but put off his attire,
Returning it into the owner's hand,
And after ever be thy constant wife.

HODGE. Not a rag, Jane! The law's
on our side; he that sows in another
man's ground, forfeits his harvest. Get thee
home, Rafe; follow him, Jane; he shall not
have so much as a busk point[3] from thee. [90

FIRK. Stand to that, Rafe; the appurte-
nances are thine own. Hammon, look not
at her!

SERV. O, 'swounds, no!

FIRK. Blue coat, be quiet. We'll give
you a new livery else; we'll make Shrove
Tuesday Saint George's Day [4] for you.
Look not, Hammon; leer not! I'll firk
you! For thy head now, one glance, one
sheep's eye, anything, at her! Touch [100
not a rag, lest I and my brethren beat you
to clouts.

SERV. Come, Master Hammon, there's no
    striving here.

HAM. Good fellows, hear me speak; and,
    honest Rafe,

---

[1] The rallying cry of the London apprentices.

[2] God's wounds.   [3] Corset lace.
[4] The day on which blue coats were worn.
Firk means, "We'll beat you black and blue."

Whom I have injured most by loving
  Jane,
Mark what I offer thee. Here in fair gold
Is twenty pound; I'll give it for thy Jane;
If this content thee not, thou shalt have
  more.

HODGE. Sell not thy wife, Rafe; make her
  not a whore.

HAM. Say, wilt thou freely cease thy claim
  in her,   110
And let her be my wife?

ALL.   No, do not, Rafe.

RAFE. Sirrah Hammon, Hammon, dost
thou think a shoemaker is so base to be a
bawd to his own wife for commodity?
Take thy gold; choke with it! Were I
not lame, I would make thee eat thy words.

FIRK. A shoemaker sell his flesh and
blood? O indignity!

HODGE. Sirrah, take up your pelf, and
be packing.   120

HAM. I will not touch one penny, but in
  lieu
Of that great wrong I offeréd thy Jane,
To Jane and thee I give that twenty
  pound.
Since I have failed of her, during my
  life
I vow no woman else shall be my wife.
Farewell, good fellows of the gentle trade.
Your morning's mirth my mourning day
  hath made.   *Exit.*

FIRK. [*To Serving-man.*] Touch the gold,
creature, if you dare! Y'are best be trudg-
ing. Here, Jane, take thou it. Now [130
let's home, my hearts.

HODGE. Stay! Who comes here? Jane,
on again with thy mask!

Enter Lincoln, L[ord] Mayor, and Servants.

LINC. Yonder's the lying varlet mocked
  us so.

L. MAYOR. Come hither, sirrah!

FIRK. I, sir? I am "sirrah"? You mean
me, do you not?

LINC. Where is my nephew married?

FIRK. Is he married? God give him joy,
I am glad of it. They have a fair [140
day, and the sign is in a good planet,
Mars in Venus.

L. MAYOR. Villain, thou told'st me that
  my daughter Rose
  This morning should be married at Saint
    Faith's;

We have watched there these three hours
  at the least,
Yet see we no such thing.

FIRK. Truly, I am sorry for 't; a bride's
a pretty thing.

HODGE. Come to the purpose. Yonder's
the bride and bridegroom you look for, [150
I hope. Though you be lords, you are not
to bar by your authority men from women,
are you?

L. MAYOR. See, see, my daughter's masked.

LINC.   True, and my nephew,
To hide his guilt, counterfeits him lame.

FIRK. Yea, truly; God help the poor
couple, they are lame and blind.

L. MAYOR. I'll ease her blindness.

LINC.   I'll his lameness cure.

FIRK. [*Aside to his friends.*] Lie down,
sirs, and laugh! My fellow Rafe is [160
taken for Rowland Lacy, and Jane for Mistress Damask Rose. This is all my knavery.

L. MAYOR. What, have I found you,
minion?

LINC.   O base wretch!
Nay, hide thy face; the horror of thy
  guilt
Can hardly be washed off. Where are
  thy powers?
What battles have you made? O, yes,
  I see,
Thou fought'st with Shame, and Shame
  hath conquered thee.
This lameness will not serve.

L. MAYOR.   Unmask yourself.

LINC. Lead home your daughter.

L. MAYOR.   Take your nephew hence.

RAFE. Hence! 'Swounds, what mean [170
you? Are you mad? I hope you cannot enforce my wife from me. Where's Hammon?

L. MAYOR. Your wife?

LINC. What, Hammon?

RAFE. Yea, my wife; and, therefore, the
proudest of you that lays hands on her
first, I'll lay my crutch cross his pate.

FIRK. To him, lame Rafe! Here's brave
sport!

RAFE. Rose call you her? Why, [180
her name is Jane. Look here else; do you
know her now?   [*Unmasks Jane.*]

LINC. Is this your daughter?

L. MAYOR.   No, nor this your nephew.
My Lord of Lincoln, we are both abused
By this base, crafty varlet.

FIRK. Yea, forsooth, no varlet; forsooth,

no base; forsooth, I am but mean;[1] no
crafty neither, but of the gentle craft.

L. MAYOR. Where is my daughter Rose?
  Where is my child?   189

LINC. Where is my nephew Lacy marriéd?

  FIRK. Why, here is good laced mutton,[2]
as I promised you.

LINC. Villain, I'll have thee punished for
  this wrong.

  FIRK. Punish the journeyman villain,
but not the journeyman shoemaker.

Enter Dodger.

DODGER. My lord, I come to bring unwel-
  come news.
  Your nephew Lacy and your daughter
    Rose
  Early this morning wedded at the Savoy,
  None being present but the lady
    mayoress.   199
  Besides, I learned among the officers
  The lord mayor vows to stand in their
    defense
  Gainst any that shall seek to cross the
    match.

LINC. Dares Eyre the shoemaker uphold
  the deed?

  FIRK. Yes, sir, shoemakers dare stand in
a woman's quarrel, I warrant you, as deep
as another, and deeper too.

DODGER. Besides, his grace today dines
  with the mayor,
  Who on his knees humbly intends to fall
  And beg a pardon for your nephew's
    fault.

LINC. But I'll prevent him! Come, Sir
  Roger Oteley;   210
  The king will do us justice in this cause.
  Howe'er their hands have made them
    man and wife,
  I will disjoin the match, or lose my life.
Exeunt [*Lincoln, Mayor, Dodger, and
                                Servants*].

  FIRK. Adieu, Monsieur Dodger! Farewell, fools! Ha, ha! O, if they had stayed, I
would have so lammed them with flouts!
O heart, my codpiece point is ready to fly
in pieces every time I think upon Mistress
Rose. But let that pass, as my lady
mayoress says.   220

HODGE. This matter is answered. Come,
Rafe; home with thy wife. Come, my fine

shoemakers, let's to our master's, the new
lord mayor, and there swagger this Shrove
Tuesday. I'll promise you wine enough,
for Madge keeps the cellar.

ALL. O, rare! Madge is a good wench.

  FIRK. And I'll promise you meat enough,
for simp'ring Susan keeps the larder. I'll
lead you to victuals, my brave sol-   [230
diers; follow your captain. O, brave! Hark,
hark!   *Bell rings.*

ALL. The pancake bell rings, the pancake bell! Trilill, my hearts!

  FIRK. O, brave! O sweet bell! O delicate pancakes! Open the doors, my hearts,
and shut up the windows! Keep in the
house; let out the pancakes! O, rare, my
hearts! Let's march together for the honor
of Saint Hugh to the great new hall   [240
in Gracious Street corner, which our
master, the new lord mayor, hath built.

  RAFE. O, the crew of good fellows that
will dine at my lord mayor's cost today!

HODGE. By the Lord, my lord mayor is
a most brave man. How shall prentices be
bound to pray for him and the honor of
the gentlemen shoemakers! Let's feed and
be fat with my lord's bounty.   249

  FIRK. O musical bell, still! O Hodge, O
my brethren! There's cheer for the heavens.[3]
Ven'son pasties[4] walk up and down piping
hot, like serjeants; beef and brewis comes
marching in dryfats;[5] fritters and pancakes
comes trolling in in wheelbarrows; hens and
oranges hopping in porters' baskets, collops
and eggs in scuttles; and tarts and custards
comes quavering in in malt shovels.

Enter more Prentices.

ALL. Whoop, look here, look here!   259

HODGE. How now, mad lads, whither
away so fast?

  1 PREN. Whither? Why, to the great new
hall, know you not why? The lord mayor
hath bidden all the prentices in London to
breakfast this morning.

ALL. O brave shoemaker, O brave lord of
incomprehensible good-fellowship! Whoo!
Hark you! The pancake bell rings.
                          Cast up caps.

  FIRK. Nay, more, my hearts! Every
Shrove Tuesday is our year of jubilee; [270

---

[1] *I.e.*, with a tenor, not "bass" voice.
[2] Loose woman, with a pun on *Lacy*.
[3] Food for the gods.
[4] From 1610 edn. Original has *pastimes.*
[5] Large containers.

and, when the pancake bell rings, we are as free as my lord mayor; we may shut up our shops, and make holiday. I'll have it called Saint Hugh's Holiday.

ALL. Agreed, agreed! Saint Hugh's Holiday!

HODGE. And this shall continue forever!

ALL. O, brave! Come, come, my hearts. Away, away!

FIRK. O, eternal credit to us of the gentle craft! March fair, my hearts! O rare! [281

Exeunt.

[SCENE xvii.

A street in London.]

Enter King and his Train over the stage.

KING. Is our lord mayor of London such a gallant?

NOBLEMAN. One of the merriest madcaps in your land.
Your grace will think, when you behold the man,
He's rather a wild ruffian than a mayor.
Yet thus much I'll ensure your majesty,
In all his actions that concern his state
He is as serious, provident, and wise,
As full of gravity amongst the grave,
As any mayor hath been these many years.

KING. I am with child [1] till I behold this huffcap.[2]   10
But all my doubt is, when we come in presence,
His madness will be dashed clean out of countenance.

NOBLEMAN. It may be so, my liege.

KING.   Which to prevent,
Let someone give him notice, 'tis our pleasure
That he put on his wonted merriment.
Set forward!

ALL.   On afore!   *Exeunt.*

[SCENE xviii.

A great hall.]

Enter Eyre, Hodge, Firk, Rafe, and other Shoemakers, all with napkins on their shoulders.

EYRE. Come, my fine Hodge, my jolly gentlemen shoemakers! Soft, where be these cannibals, these varlets, my officers?

Let them all walk and wait upon my brethren; for my meaning is that none but shoemakers, none but the livery of my company, shall in their satin hoods wait upon the trencher of my sovereign.

FIRK. O my lord, it will be rare!

EYRE. No more, Firk; come, lively! [10 Let your fellow prentices want no cheer; let wine be plentiful as beer, and beer as water. Hang these penny-pinching fathers, that cram wealth in innocent lambskins.[3] Rip, knaves, avaunt! Look to my guests!

HODGE. My lord, we are at our wits' end for room; those hundred tables will not feast the fourth part of them.

EYRE. Then cover me those hundred tables again, and again, till all my jolly [20 prentices be feasted. Avoid, Hodge! Run, Rafe! Frisk about, my nimble Firk! Carouse me fadom healths [4] to the honor of the shoemakers. Do they drink lively, Hodge? Do they tickle it, Firk?

FIRK. Tickle it? Some of them have taken their liquor standing so long that they can stand no longer; but, for meat, they would eat it and they had it.

EYRE. Want they meat? Where's [30 this swagbelly, this greasy kitchen stuff cook? Call the varlet to me! Want meat? Firk, Hodge, lame Rafe, run, my tall men, beleaguer the shambles, beggar all Eastcheap, serve me whole oxen in chargers,[5] and let sheep whine upon the tables like pigs for want of good fellows to eat them. Want meat? Vanish, Firk! Avaunt, Hodge!

HODGE. Your lordship mistakes my man Firk; he means their bellies want meat, [40 not the boards, for they have drunk so much, they can eat nothing.

THE SECOND THREE-MAN'S SONG [6]

Cold's the wind, and wet's the rain—
    Saint Hugh be our good speed.
Ill is the weather that bringeth no gain,
    Nor helps good hearts in need.

Troll [7] the bowl, the jolly nut-brown bowl,
    And here, kind mate, to thee.
Let's sing a dirge for Saint Hugh's soul,
    And down it merrily.   50

[1] Impatient.   [2] Swaggerer.

[3] Purses.   [5] Large platters.
[4] Fathom-deep healths.
[6] A direction, "This is to be sung at the latter end," suggests the insertion of this song here.
[7] Pass.

Down a down, hey down a down,
    (*Close with the tenor boy*)
Hey derry derry, down a down!
Ho, well done; to me let come!
Ring compass,[1] gentle joy.

Troll the bowl, the nut-brown bowl,
  And here, kind, etc.
    As often as there be men to drink.

At last, when all have drunk, this verse:

Cold's the wind, and wet's the rain—
  Saint Hugh be our good speed.
Ill is the weather that bringeth no gain,
  Nor helps good hearts in need.   60

Enter Hans, Rose, and Wife.

WIFE. Where is my lord?

EYRE. How now, Lady Madgy?

WIFE. The king's most excellent majesty is new come; he sends me for thy honor. One of his most worshipful peers bade me tell thou must be merry, and so forth; but let that pass.

EYRE. Is my sovereign come? Vanish, my tall shoemakers, my nimble brethren; look to my guests, the prentices. Yet [70 stay a little! How now, Hans? How looks my little Rose?

HANS. Let me request you to remember me.

I know your honor easily may obtain
Free pardon of the king for me and Rose,
And reconcile me to my uncle's grace.

EYRE. Have done, my good Hans, my honest journeyman; look cheerily! I'll fall upon both my knees, till they be as hard as horn, but I'll get thy pardon.   80

WIFE. Good my lord, have a care what you speak to his grace.

EYRE. Away, you Islington whitepot![2] Hence, you hopper[3]-arse! Hence, you barley pudding, full of maggots! You broiled carbonado![4] Avaunt, avaunt, avoid, Mephostophilus! Shall Sim Eyre learn to speak of you, Lady Madgy? Vanish, Mother Miniver-cap;[5] vanish, go, trip and go; meddle with your partlets[6] and [90 your pishery-pashery, your flews[7] and your whirligigs; go, rub,[8] out of mine alley!

[1] The fullest range of tones possible.
[2] Custard.
[3] Shaped like a hopper.
[4] Steak.
[5] Fur cap.
[6] Ruffs for the neck.
[7] Flaps.
[8] An obstruction in bowling.

Sim Eyre knows how to speak to a pope, to Sultan Soliman, to Tamburlaine, and he were here; and shall I melt, shall I droop before my sovereign? No, come, my Lady Madgy! Follow me, Hans! About your business, my frolic freebooters! Firk, frisk about, and about, and about, for the honor of mad Simon Eyre, lord mayor [100 of London.

FIRK. Hey, for the honor of the shoemakers!   *Exeunt.*

[SCENE xix.

An open yard before the hall.]

A long flourish or two. Enter King, Nobles,
    Eyre, his Wife, Lacy, Rose. Lacy and
            Rose kneel.

KING. Well, Lacy, though the fact was very foul
Of your revolting from our kingly love
And your own duty, yet we pardon you.
Rise both, and, Mistress Lacy, thank my lord mayor
For your young bridgroom here.

EYRE. So, my dear liege, Sim Eyre and my brethren, the gentlemen shoemakers, shall set your sweet majesty's image cheek by jowl by Saint Hugh for this honor you have done poor Simon Eyre. I beseech [10 your grace, pardon my rude behavior; I am a handicraftsman, yet my heart is without craft; I would be sorry at my soul that my boldness should offend my king.

KING. Nay, I pray thee, good lord mayor, be even as merry
As if thou wert among thy shoemakers;
It does me good to see thee in this humor.

EYRE. Sayst thou me so, my sweet Dioclesian? Then, hump! Prince am I none, yet am I princely born. By the [20 Lord of Ludgate, my liege, I'll be as merry as a pie.[9]

KING. Tell me, in faith, mad Eyre, how old thou art.

EYRE. My liege, a very boy, a stripling, a younker; you see not a white hair on my head, not a gray in this beard. Every hair, I assure thy majesty, that sticks in this beard, Sim Eyre values at the King of Babylon's ransom; Tamar Cham's beard was a rubbing brush to 't. Yet I'll [30

[9] Magpie

shave it off, and stuff tennis balls with it, to please my bully king.

KING. But all this while I do not know your age.

EYRE. My liege, I am six-and-fifty year old, yet I can cry "hump!" with a sound heart for the honor of Saint Hugh. Mark this old wench, my king; I danced the shaking of the sheets with her six-and-thirty years ago, and yet I hope to get two or three young lord mayors ere I die. [40 I am lusty still, Sim Eyre still. Care and cold lodging brings white hairs. My sweet majesty, let care vanish, cast it upon thy nobles; it will make thee look always young like Apollo, and cry "hump!" Prince am I none, yet am I princely born.

KING. Ha, ha!
Say, Cornwall, didst thou ever see his like?

NOBLEMAN. Not I, my lord.

Enter Lincoln and Lord Mayor.

KING. Lincoln, what news with you?

LINC. My gracious lord, have care unto yourself, 50
For there are traitors here.

ALL. Traitors? Where? Who?

EYRE. Traitors in my house? God forbid! Where be my officers? I'll spend my soul, ere my king feel harm.

KING. Where is the traitor, Lincoln?

LINC. [*Pointing to Lacy.*] Here he stands.

KING. Cornwall, lay hold on Lacy!—Lincoln, speak;
What canst thou lay unto thy nephew's charge?

LINC. This, my dear liege: your grace, to do me honor,
Heaped on the head of this degenerous [1] boy 59
Desertless favors; you made choice of him
To be commander over powers in France.
But he—

KING. Good Lincoln, prithee, pause awhile!
Even in thine eyes I read what thou wouldst speak.
I know how Lacy did neglect our love,
Ran himself deeply, in the highest degree,
Into vile treason—

LINC. Is he not a traitor?

---
[1] Degenerate.

KING. Lincoln, he was; now have we pardoned him.
'Twas not a base want of true valor's fire
That held him out of France, but love's desire.

LINC. I will not bear his shame upon my back. 70

KING. Nor shalt thou, Lincoln; I forgive you both.

LINC. Then, good my liege, forbid the boy to wed
One whose mean birth will much disgrace his bed.

KING. Are they not married?

LINC. No, my liege.

BOTH. We are.

KING. Shall I divorce them then? O, be it far
That any hand on earth should dare untie
The sacred knot, knit by God's majesty;
I would not for my crown disjoin their hands
That are conjoined in holy nuptial bands.
How say'st thou, Lacy, wouldst thou lose thy Rose? 80

HANS. Not for all Indians' wealth, my sovereign.

KING. But Rose, I am sure, her Lacy would forgo?

ROSE. If Rose were asked that question, she'd say no!

KING. You hear them, Lincoln?

LINC. Yea, my liege, I do.

KING. Yet canst thou find i' th' heart to part these two?
Who seeks, besides you, to divorce these lovers?

L. MAYOR. I do, my gracious lord; I am her father.

KING. Sir Roger Oteley, our last mayor, I think?

NOBLEMAN. The same, my liege.

KING. Would you offend Love's laws?
Well, you shall have your wills; you sue to me 90
To prohibit the match. Soft, let me see—
You both are married, Lacy, art thou not?

HANS. I am, dread sovereign.

KING. Then, upon thy life,
I charge thee not to call this woman wife.

L. MAYOR. I thank your grace.

Rose.   O my most gracious lord!
                                          Kneel.
King. Nay, Rose, never woo me; I tell you
    true,
    Although as yet I am a bachelor,
    Yet I believe I shall not marry you.
Rose. Can you divide the body from the
    soul,   99
    Yet make the body live?
King.   Yea, so profound?
    I cannot, Rose, but you I must divide.
    Fair maid, this bridegroom cannot be
        your bride.[1]—
    Are you pleased, Lincoln? Oteley, are
        you pleased?
Both. Yes, my lord.
King.   Then must my heart be eased;
    For, credit me, my conscience lives in
        pain,
    Till these whom I divorced be joined
        again.
    Lacy, give me thy hand; Rose, lend me
        thine!
    Be what you would be! Kiss now! So,
        that's fine.   108
    At night, lovers, to bed!—Now let me see
    Which of you all mislikes this harmony.
L. Mayor. Will you then take from me
    my child perforce?
King. Why, tell me, Oteley, shines not
    Lacy's name
    As bright in the world's eye as the gay
        beams
    Of any citizen?
Linc.   Yea, but, my gracious lord,
    I do mislike the match far more than he;
    Her blood is too-too base.
King.   Lincoln, no more.
    Dost thou not know that love respects
        no blood,
    Cares not for difference of birth or state?
    The maid is young, well born, fair, virtu-
        ous,
    A worthy bride for any gentleman. 120
    Besides, your nephew for her sake did
        stoop
    To bear necessity, and, as I hear,
    Forgetting honors and all courtly pleas-
        ures,
    To gain her love became a shoemaker.
    As for the honor which he lost in France,
    Thus I redeem it: Lacy, kneel thee
        down!—

[1] Used of both sexes.

    Arise, Sir Rowland Lacy! Tell me now,
    Tell me in earnest, Oteley, canst thou
        chide,
    Seeing thy Rose a lady and a bride?
L. Mayor. I am content with what your
    grace hath done.   130
Linc. And I, my liege, since there's no
    remedy.
King. Come on, then, all shake hands.
    I'll have you friends;
    Where there is much love, all discord
        ends.
    What says my mad lord mayor to all
        this love?
Eyre. O my liege, this honor you have
done to my fine journeyman here, Rowland
Lacy, and all these favors which you have
shown to me this day in my poor house
will make Simon Eyre live longer by one
dozen of warm summers more than he
should.   141
King. Nay, my mad lord mayor, that shall
    be thy name;
    If any grace of mine can length thy life,
    One honor more I'll do thee: that new
        building,
    Which at thy cost in Cornhill is erected,
    Shall take a name from us; we'll have it
        called
    The Leadenhall, because in digging it
    You found the lead that covereth the
        same.
Eyre. I thank your majesty.
Wife.   God bless your grace!
King. Lincoln, a word with you!   150

Enter Hodge, Firk, Rafe, and more Shoe-
                                      makers.

Eyre. How now, my mad knaves?
Peace, speak softly; yonder is the king.
King. With the old troop which there we
    keep in pay,
    We will incorporate a new supply.
    Before one summer more pass o'er my
        head,
    France shall repent England was injuréd.
    What are all those?
Hans.   All shoemakers, my liege,
    Sometimes my fellows; in their com-
        panies
    I lived as merry as an emperor.
King. My mad lord mayor, are all these
    shoemakers?   160
    Eyre. All shoemakers, my liege; all

gentlemen of the gentle craft, true Trojans, courageous cordwainers; they all kneel to the shrine of holy Saint Hugh.

ALL. God save your majesty, all shoe-maker[s]!

KING. Mad Simon, would they anything with us?

EYRE. Mum, mad knaves! Not a word! I'll do 't; I warrant you. They are all beggars, my liege; all for themselves, [170 and I for them all, on both my knees do entreat that, for the honor of poor Simon Eyre and the good of his brethren, these mad knaves, your grace would vouchsafe some privilege to my new Leadenhall, that it may be lawful for us to buy and sell leather there two days a week.

KING. Mad Sim, I grant your suit; you shall have patent

To hold two market days in Leadenhall, Mondays and Fridays—those shall be the times.   180

Will this content you?

ALL.   Jesus bless your grace!

EYRE. In the name of these my poor brethren shoemakers, I most humbly thank your grace. But, before I rise, seeing you are in the giving vein and we in the beg-ging, grant Sim Eyre one boon more.

KING. What is it, my lord mayor?

EYRE. Vouchsafe to taste of a poor banquet that stands sweetly waiting for your sweet presence.   190

KING. I shall undo thee, Eyre, only with feasts;

Already have I been too troublesome. Say, have I not?

EYRE. O my dear king, Sim Eyre was taken unawares upon a day of shroving [1] which I promised long ago to the prentices of London.

For, and 't please your highness, in time past,   198
I bare the water tankard,[2] and my coat Sits not a whit the worse upon my back; And then, upon a morning, some mad boys
(It was Shrove Tuesday, even as 'tis now) gave me my breakfast, and I swore then by the stopple of my tankard, if ever I came to be lord mayor of London, I would feast all the prentices. This day, my liege, I did it, and the slaves had an hundred tables five times covered. They are gone home and vanished.   209
Yet add more honor to the gentle trade; Taste of Eyre's banquet, Simon's happy made.

KING. Eyre, I will taste of thy banquet, and will say

I have not met more pleasure on a day. Friends of the gentle craft, thanks to you all;

Thanks, my kind lady mayoress, for our cheer.—

Come, lords, awhile let's revel it at home! When all our sports and banquetings are done,

Wars must right wrongs which French-men have begun.   *Exeunt.*

FINIS.

[1] Merrymaking.   [2] As an apprentice.

THE HONEST¹ WHORE²

[PART I]

BY

THOMAS DEKKER

SCENA i.³

[*A street in Milan.*]

Enter at one door a funeral (a coronet lying on the hearse, scutcheons and garlands hanging on the sides), attended by Gasparo Trebazzi, Duke of Milan, Castruchio, Sinezi, Pioratto, Fluello, and Others. At another door enter Hippolito, in discontented appearance, Matheo, a gentleman, his friend, laboring to hold him back.

DUKE. Behold, yon comet shows his head again!
Twice hath he thus at cross turns⁴ thrown on us

Prodigious⁵ looks; twice hath he troubled
The waters of our eyes. See, he's turned wild!
Go on, in God's name.

ALL.   On afore there, ho!

DUKE. Kinsmen and friends, take from your manly sides
Your weapons to keep back the desperate boy
From doing violence to the innocent dead.

HIP. I prithee, dear Matheo—

MAT.   Come, y'are mad!

HIP. I do arrest thee, murderer! Set down,
Villains, set down that sorrow; 'tis all mine.   11

DUKE. I do beseech you all, for my blood's sake
Send hence your milder spirits, and let wrath
Join in confederacy with your weapons' points;

---

¹ Chaste.
² The title of the first edn. continues: "With the Humors of the Patient Man and the Longing Wife."
³ Original reads *Actus Primus, Scena Prima,* but from this point on, the play is not divided into acts, although some scene divisions are indicated.
⁴ Street crossings.
⁵ Portentous.

593

If he proceed to vex us, let your swords
Seek out his bowels. Funeral grief loathes
   words.

ALL. Set on!

HIP.   Set down the body!

MAT.   O my lord!
Y'are wrong! I' th' open street? You see
   she's dead.

HIP. I know she is not dead.

DUKE.   Frantic young man,
Wilt thou believe these gentlemen? Pray
   speak.   20
Thou dost abuse my child, and mock'st
   the tears
That here are shed for her. If to behold
Those roses withered that set out her
   cheeks;
That pair of stars that gave her body light,
Darkened and dim forever; all those
   rivers
That fed her veins with warm and crim-
   son streams
Frozen and dried up—if these be signs of
   death,
Then is she dead.   Thou unreligious
   youth,
Art not ashamed to empty all these eyes
Of funeral tears, a debt due to the
   dead,   30
As mirth is to the living? Sham'st thou
   not
To have them stare on thee? Hark, thou
   art cursed
Even to thy face, by those that scarce
   can speak.

HIP. My lord—

DUKE.   What wouldst thou have?
   Is she not dead?

HIP. O, you ha' killed her by your cruelty!

DUKE. Admit I had, thou kill'st her now
   again,
And art more savage than a barbarous
   Moor.

HIP. Let me but kiss her pale and bloodless
   lip.

DUKE. O fie, fie, fie!

HIP. Or, if not touch her, let me look on
   her.   40

MAT. As you regard your honor—

HIP.   Honor? Smoke!

MAT. Or, if you loved her living, spare her
   now.

DUKE. Ay, well done, sir; you play the
   gentleman.—

Steal hence.—'Tis nobly done.—Away!
   —I'll join
My force to yours to stop this violent
   torment.—
Pass on.

Exeunt with funeral [all except the Duke,
             Hippolito, and Matheo].

HIP.   Matheo, thou dost wound me
   more.

MAT. I give you physic, noble friend, not
   wounds.

DUKE. O, well said, well done, a true
   gentleman!
Alack, I know the sea of lovers' rage
Comes rushing with so strong a tide, it
   beats   50
And bears down all respects of life, of
   honor,
Of friends, of foes. Forget her, gallant
   youth.

HIP. Forget her?

DUKE.   Nay, nay, be but patient,
Forwhy [1] death's hand hath sued a strict
   divorce
Twixt her and thee. What's beauty but a
   corse?
What but fair sand-dust are earth's purest forms?
Queen's bodies are but trunks to put in
   worms.

MAT. Speak no more sentences,[2] my
good lord, but slip hence; you see they are
but fits. I'll rule him, I warrant ye.   [60
Ay, so, tread gingerly; your grace is here
somewhat too long already. [*Exit Duke.
Aside.*] 'Sblood,[3] the jest were now, if
having ta'en some knocks o' th' pate already, he should get loose again, and, like
a mad ox, toss my new black cloaks into
the kennel.[4] I must humor his lordship.—
My Lord Hippolito, is it in your stomach
to go to dinner?

HIP. Where is the body?   70

MAT. The body, as the duke spake very
wisely, is gone to be wormed.

HIP. I cannot rest; I'll meet it at next
turn. I'll see how my love looks.

      Matheo holds him in 's arms.

MAT. How your love looks? Worse than

---

[1] Because.   [2] Sententious sayings.
[3] God's blood. *Cf.* other mild oaths in this
play, such as *'Sfoot, 'Swounds, 'Snails, Ud's life,
Godso.*
[4] Channel, gutter.

a scarecrow. Wrastle not with me; the great fellow gives the fall for a ducat.

HIP. I shall forget myself.

MAT. Pray, do so; leave yourself behind yourself, and go whither you will. [80 'Sfoot, do you long to have base rogues that maintain a Saint Anthony's fire in their noses by nothing but twopenny ale, make ballads of you? If the duke had but so much mettle in him as is in a cobbler's awl, he would ha' been a vexed thing. He and his train had blown you up but that their powder has taken the wet of cowards. You'll bleed three pottles of Alicant,[1] by this light, if you follow 'em, and then [90 we shall have a hole made in a wrong place, to have surgeons roll thee up like a baby in swaddling clouts.

HIP. What day is today, Matheo?

MAT. Yea, marry, this is an easy question. Why, today is—let me see—Thursday.

HIP. O, Thursday!

MAT. Here's a coil [2] for a dead commodity. 'Sfoot, women when they are [100 alive are but dead commodities, for you shall have one woman lie upon many men's hands.

HIP. She died on Monday then.

MAT. And that's the most villainous day of all the week to die in. And she was well, and eat a mess of water gruel on Monday morning.

HIP. Ay? It cannot be
Such a bright taper should burn out so
    soon.   110

MAT. O yes, my lord. So soon? Why, I ha' known them that at dinner have been as well, and had so much health that they were glad to pledge it, yet before three a-clock have been found dead—drunk.

HIP. On Thursday buried! And on Monday died!
Quick haste, by'r Lady. Sure her winding
    sheet
Was laid out fore her body, and the
    worms
That now must feast with her were even
    bespoke,
And solemnly invited like strange
    guests.   120

MAT. Strange feeders they are indeed,

my lord, and, like your jester or young courtier, will enter upon any man's trencher without bidding.

HIP. Cursed be that day forever that
    robbed her
Of breath, and me of bliss! Henceforth
    let it stand
Within the wizard's book (the calendar)
Marked with a marginal finger, to be
    chosen
By thieves, by villains, and black mur-
    derers,
As the best day for them to labor in. 130
If henceforth this adulterous, bawdy
    world
Be got with child with treason, sacrilege,
Atheism, rapes, treacherous friendship,
    perjury,
Slander (the beggar's sin), lies (sin of
    fools),
Or any other damned impieties,
On Monday let 'em be deliveréd.
I swear to thee, Matheo, by my soul,
Hereafter weekly on that day I'll glue
Mine eyelids down, because they shall
    not gaze
On any female cheek. And, being locked
    up   140
In my close [3] chamber, there I'll meditate
On nothing but my Infelice's end,
Or on a dead man's skull draw out mine
    own.

MAT. You'll do all these good works now every Monday, because it is so bad; but I hope upon Tuesday morning I shall take you with a wench.

HIP. If ever, whilst frail blood through
    my veins run,
On woman's beams I throw affection,
Save her that's dead, or that I loosely
    fly   150
To th' shore of any other wafting eye,
Let me not prosper, Heaven! I will be
    true
Even to her dust and ashes. Could her
    tomb
Stand whilst I lived, so long that it
    might rot,
That should fall down, but she be ne'er
    forgot.

MAT. If you have this strange monster, honesty,[4] in your belly, why, so jig-[5] makers and chroniclers shall pick something

<hr>

[1] Six quarts of Spanish wine.
[2] Disturbance.
[3] Private.   [4] Chastity.   [5] Ballad.

out of you; but, and [1] I smell not you and a bawdyhouse out within these ten [160 days, let my nose be as big as an English bag pudding. I'll follow your lordship, though it be to the place aforenamed.

Exeunt.

[SCENA ii.

Another street.]

Enter Fustigo in some fantastic sea suit at one door; a Porter meets him at another.

FUS. How now, porter, will she come?

POR. If I may trust a woman, sir, she will come.

FUS. There's for thy pains. [*Gives money.*] God-a-mercy,[2] if I ever stand in need of a wench that will come with a wet finger,[3] porter, thou shalt earn my money before any clarissimo[4] in Milan; yet, so God sa' me, she's mine own sister, body and soul, as I am a Christian gentleman. Farewell; I'll ponder till she come. Thou [11 hast been no bawd in fetching this woman, I assure thee.

POR. No matter if I had, sir; better men than porters are bawds.

FUS. O God, sir, many that have borne offices. But, porter, art sure thou went'st into a true [5] house?

POR. I think so, for I met with no thieves.   20

FUS. Nay, but art sure it was my sister Viola?

POR. I am sure, by all superscriptions, it was the party you ciphered.[6]

FUS. Not very tall?

POR. Nor very low; a middling woman.

FUS. 'Twas she, faith, 'twas she. A pretty plump cheek, like mine?

POR. At a blush,[7] a little very much like you.   30

FUS. Godso, I would not for a ducat she had kicked up her heels, for I ha' spent an abomination this voyage; marry, I did it amongst sailors and gentlemen. There's a little modicum more, porter, for making thee stay. [*Gives money.*] Farewell, honest porter.

POR. I am in your debt, sir; God preserve you.   *Exit.*

Enter Viola.

FUS. Not so neither, good porter. God's lid, yonder she comes.—Sister Viola, I [41 am glad to see you stirring. It's news to have me here, is't not, sister?

VIO. Yes, trust me. I wondered who should be so bold to send for me. You're welcome to Milan, brother.

FUS. Troth, sister, I heard you were married to a very rich chuff,[8] and I was very sorry for it that I had no better clothes, and that made me send; for you know we Milaners love to strut upon Span- [51 ish leather. And how does all our friends?

VIO. Very well. You ha' traveled enough now, I trow, to sow your wild oats.

FUS. A pox on 'em! Wild oats? I ha' not an oat to throw at a horse. Troth, sister, I ha' sowed my oats, and reaped two hundred ducats—if I had 'em here. Marry, I must entreat you to lend me some thirty or forty till the ship come. By this hand, I'll discharge at my day, by [61 this hand.

VIO. These are your old oaths.

FUS. Why, sister, do you think I'll forswear my hand?

VIO. Well, well, you shall have them. Put yourself into better fashion, because I must employ you in a serious matter.

FUS. I'll sweat like a horse if I like the matter.   [70

VIO. You ha' cast off all your old swaggering humors?

FUS. I had not sailed a league in that great fishpond, the sea, but I cast up my very gall.

VIO. I am the more sorry, for I must employ a true swaggerer.

FUS. Nay, by this iron, sister, they shall find I am powder and touch-box,[9] if they put fire once into me.   80

VIO. Then lend me your ears.

FUS. Mine ears are yours, dear sister.

VIO. I am married to a man that has wealth enough, and wit enough.

FUS. A linen draper, I was told, sister.

VIO. Very true, a grave citizen; I want nothing that a wife can wish from a husband. But here's the spite [10]—he has not all things belonging to a man.

---

[1] If.
[2] Thank you.
[3] Promptly.
[4] Grandee.

[5] Respectable.
[6] Described.
[7] Glance.

[8] Old miser.
[9] A box containing powder for priming a firearm.   [10] Vexation.

Fus. God's my life, he's a very mandrake,[1] or else, God bless us, one a [2] [91 these whiblins,[3] and that's worse, and then all the children that he gets lawfully of your body, sister, are bastards by a statute.

Vio. O, you run over me too fast, brother. I have heard it often said that he who cannot be angry is no man. I am sure my husband is a man in print,[4] for all things else save only in this: no tempest can move him.   100

Fus. 'Slid, would he had been at sea with us! He should ha' been moved, and moved again, for I'll be sworn, la, our drunken ship reeled like a Dutchman.

Vio. No loss of goods can increase in him a wrinkle; no crabbed language make his countenance sour; the stubbornness of no servant shake him. He has no more gall in him than a dove, no more sting than an ant. Musician will he never be, yet I find much music in him; but he loves no [111 frets,[5] and is so free from anger that many times I am ready to bite off my tongue, because it wants that virtue which all women's tongues have, to anger their husbands. Brother, mine can by no thunder turn him into a sharpness.

Fus. Belike his blood, sister, is well brewed then.

Vio. I protest to thee, Fustigo, I love him most affectionately; but I know not— [121 I ha' such a tickling within me—such a strange longing; nay, verily I do long.

Fus. Then y'are with child, sister, by all signs and tokens; nay, I am partly a physician, and partly something else. I ha' read Albertus Magnus and Aristotle's Emblems.

Vio. Y'are wide a th' bow hand [6] still, brother; my longings are not wanton, but wayward. I long to have my patient [131 husband eat up a whole porcupine, to the intent the bristling quills may stick about his lips like a Flemish mustacho, and be shot at me. I shall be leaner than the new moon unless I can make him horn-mad.[7]

Fus. 'Sfoot, half a quarter of an hour does that: make him a cuckold.

Vio. Pooh, he would count such a cut no unkindness.

Fus. The honester citizen he. Then [141 make him drunk and cut off his beard.

Vio. Fie, fie, idle,[8] idle! He's no Frenchman, to fret at the loss of a little scald [9] hair. No, brother, thus it shall be—you must be secret.

Fus. As your midwife, I protest, sister, or a barber-surgeon.

Vio. Repair to the Tortoise here in St. Christopher's Street. I will send you money; turn yourself into a brave [10] [151 man. Instead of the arms of your mistress, let your sword and your military scarf hang about your neck.

Fus. I must have a great horseman's French feather too, sister.

Vio. O, by any means, to show your light head, else your hat will sit like a coxcomb. To be brief, you must be in all points a most terrible wide-mouthed swaggerer.   161

Fus. Nay, for swaggering points let me alone.

Vio. Resort then to our shop, and, in my husband's presence, kiss me, snatch rings, jewels, or anything, so you give it back again, brother, in secret.

Fus. By this hand, sister.

Vio. Swear as if you came but new from knighting.   170

Fus. Nay, I'll swear after [11] four hundred a year.

Vio. Swagger worse than a lievetenant [12] among freshwater soldiers; [13] call me your love, your ingle,[14] your cousin, or so—but sister at no hand.

Fus. No, no, it shall be cousin, or rather coz; that's the gulling word between the citizens' wives and their madcaps that man [15] 'em to the Garden.[16] To call you one a mine "aunts," sister, were as good [181 as call you arrant whore; no, no, let me alone to "cousin" you rarely.

Vio. H'as heard I have a brother, but

---

[1] The root of this plant was supposed to resemble the human figure.
[2] Of.   [3] Weak, impotent creatures.
[4] To the letter, exactly; with a pun.
[5] A common pun with reference to the frets of a stringed instrument.   [6] Wide of the mark.
[7] Stark mad; with a pun on the "horns" of a cuckold.

[8] Foolish.   [11] According to an income of.
[9] Scurfy.   [12] Lieutenant.
[10] Richly dressed.
[13] Soldiers who had never crossed the sea.
[14] Darling.   [16] Presumably Paris Garden
[15] Accompany.

never saw him; therefore put on a good face.

Fus. The best in Milan, I warrant.

Vio. Take up wares, but pay nothing; rifle my bosom, my pocket, my purse, the boxes for money to dice withal; but, brother, you must give all back again [191 in secret.

Fus. By this welkin that here roars I will, or else let me never know what a secret is. Why, sister, do you think I'll cunny-catch [1] you, when you are my cousin? God's my life, then I were a stark ass. If I fret not his guts, beg me for a fool. [2]

Vio. Be circumspect, and do so then. Fare-well. 200

Fus. The Tortoise, sister? I'll stay there. Forty ducats! *Exit.*

Vio. Thither I'll send.—This law can none deny:
Women must have their longings, or they die. *Exit.*

[Scena iii.

A room in the Duke's palace.]

Gasparo the Duke, Doctor Benedict, two Servants.

Duke. Give charge that none do enter; lock the doors.
And, fellows, what your eyes and ears receive,
Upon your lives trust not the gadding air
To carry the least part of it. The glass,
The hourglass!

Doc. Here, my lord.

Duke. Ah, 'tis near [3] spent! [4]
But, Doctor Benedict, does your art speak truth?
Art sure the soporiferous stream will ebb,
And leave the crystal banks of her white body
Pure as they were at first, just at the hour?

---

¹ Cheat.
² Beg the king for the custody of me as an idiot.
³ Emended by Dyce. Original reads *meere.*
⁴ The line division here and in a few later passages has been regularized. A few passages printed as prose in the original have also been changed to verse.

Doc. Just at the hour, my lord.

Duke. Uncurtain her! 10
[*A curtain is drawn back, revealing Infelice lying on a couch.*]
Softly!—See, doctor, what a coldish heat
Spreads over all her body!

Doc. Now it works.
The vital spirits that by a sleepy charm
Were bound up fast, and threw an icy rust [5]
On her exterior parts, now gin [6] to break.
Trouble her not, my lord.

Duke. Some stools! You called
For music, did you not? O ho, it speaks!
[*Music.*]
It speaks! Watch, sirs, her waking; note those sands.
Doctor, sit down. A dukedom that should weigh
Mine own down twice, being put into one scale, 20
And that fond [7] desperate boy, Hippo-lito,
Making the weight up, should not at my hands
Buy her i' th' tother [8] were her state more light
Than hers who makes a dowry up with alms.
Doctor, I'll starve her on the Apennine
Ere he shall marry her. I must confess
Hippolito is nobly born, a man—
Did not mine enemies' blood boil in his veins—
Whom I would court to be my son-in-law;
But princes, whose high spleens for empery [9] swell, 30
Are not with easy art made parallel.

2 Ser. She wakes, my lord.

Duke. Look, Doctor Benedict.—
I charge you, on your lives, maintain for truth
Whate'er the doctor or myself aver,
For you shall bear her hence to Ber-gamo.

Inf. [*Waking.*] O God, what fearful dreams!

Doc. Lady.

---

⁵ Coating.
⁶ Begin.
⁷ Foolish.
⁸ Other.
⁹ Sovereignty.

INF.　　　　　　Ha!

DUKE.　　　　　　Girl.

Why, Infelice, how is't now, ha? Speak.

INF. I'm well. What makes[1] this doctor
here? I'm well.

DUKE. Thou wert not so even now; sickness' pale hand

Laid hold on thee even in the midst of
feasting;　　　　　　40

And, when a cup crowned with thy
lover's health

Had touched thy lips, a sensible, cold
dew

Stood on thy cheeks, as if that death
had wept

To see such beauty alter.

INF.　　　　　　I remember

I sate at banquet, but felt no such
change.

DUKE. Thou hast forgotten, then, how
a messenger

Came wildly in, with this unsavory
news,

That he was dead?

INF.　　What messenger? Who's dead?

DUKE. Hippolito. Alack, wring not thy
hands.

INF. I saw no messenger, heard no such
news.　　　　　　50

Doc. Trust me, you did, sweet lady.

DUKE.　　　　　　La you now!

2 SER. Yes, indeed, madam.

DUKE.　　　La you now!—[Aside.]
'Tis well, good knaves!

INF. You ha' slain him, and now you'll
murder me.

DUKE. Good Infelice, vex not thus thyself.

Of this the bad report before did strike

So coldly to thy heart that the swift
currents

Of life were all frozen up.

INF.　　　　　　It is untrue,

'Tis most untrue, O most unnatural
father!

DUKE. And we had much to do by art's
best cunning

To fetch life back again.

Doc.　　　　Most certain, lady. 60

DUKE. Why, la you now, you'll not believe me. Friends,

Sweat we not all? Had we not much to
do?

[1] Does.

2 SER. Yes, indeed, my lord, much.

DUKE. Death drew such fearful pictures
in thy face

That, were Hippolito alive again,

I'd kneel and woo the noble gentleman

To be thy husband. Now I sore repent

My sharpness to him and his family.

Nay, do not weep for him; we all must
die.—

Doctor, this place where she so oft hath
seen　　　　　　70

His lively presence, hurts her, does it
not?

Doc. Doubtless, my lord, it does.

DUKE.　　　　　　It does, it does!

Therefore, sweet girl, thou shalt to Bergamo.

INF. Even where you will; in any place
there's woe.

DUKE. A coach is ready. Bergamo doth
stand

In a most wholesome air—sweet walks—
there's deer.

Ay, thou shalt hunt and send us venison,

Which, like some goddess in the Cyprian groves,

Thine own fair hand shall strike.—Sirs,
you shall teach her

To stand, and how to shoot; ay, she
shall hunt.　　　　　　80

Cast off this sorrow. In, girl, and prepare

This night to ride away to Bergamo.

INF. O, most unhappy maid!　　Exit.

DUKE.　　　　　　Follow her close.

No words that she was buried, on your
lives,

Or that her ghost walks now after she's
dead.

I'll hang you if you name a funeral.

1 SER. I'll speak Greek, my lord, ere
I speak that deadly word.

2 SER. And I'll speak Welsh, which [88
is harder than Greek.　Exeunt [Servants].

DUKE. Away, look to her.—Doctor Benedict,

Did you observe how her complexion
altered

Upon his name and death? O, would
'twere true.

Doc. It may, my lord.

DUKE.　May! How? I wish his death.

Doc. And you may have your wish: say
but the word,

And 'tis a strong spell to rip up his
grave.
I have good knowledge with Hippolito;
He calls me friend. I'll creep into his
bosom,
And sting him there to death; poison
can do 't.
Duke. Perform it; I'll create thee half
mine heir. 100
Doc. It shall be done, although the fact [1]
be foul.
Duke. Greatness hides sin; the guilt upon
my soul! *Exeunt.*

[Scena iv.

A street.]

Enter Castruchio, Pioratto, and Fluello.

Cas. Signior Pioratto, Signior Fluello,
shall 's be merry? Shall 's play the wags
now?
Flu. Ay, anything that may beget the
child of laughter.
Cas. Truth, I have a pretty sportive
conceit [2] new crept into my brain, will
move excellent mirth.
Pio. Let's ha't, let's ha't. And where
shall the scene of mirth lie? 10
Cas. At Signior Candido's house, the
patient man, nay, the monstrous patient
man. They say his blood is immovable,
that he has taken all patience from a man,
and all constancy from a woman.
Flu. That makes so many whores nowadays.
Cas. Ay, and so many knaves too.
Pio. Well, sir.
Cas. To conclude, the report goes, [20
he's so mild, so affable, so suffering, that
nothing indeed can move him. Now do
but think what sport it will be to make
this fellow, the mirror of patience, as angry,
as vexed, and as mad as an English cuckold.
Flu. O, 'twere admirable mirth, that.
But how will 't be done, signior?
Cas. Let me alone; I have a trick, a
conceit, a thing, a device will sting [30
him, i' faith, if he have but a thimbleful of
blood in 's belly, or a spleen not so big as
a tavern token.[3]

Pio. Thou stir him? Thou move him?
Thou anger him? Alas, I know his approved [4] temper. Thou vex him? Why,
he has a patience above man's injuries.
Thou mayst sooner raise a spleen in an
angel than rough humor in him. Why,
I'll give you instance for it. This won- [40
derfully tempered Signior Candido upon a
time invited home to his house certain
Neapolitan lords, of curious [5] taste and
no mean palates, conjuring his wife, of all
loves,[6] to prepare cheer fitting for such
honorable trenchermen. She—just of a
woman's nature, covetous to try the uttermost of vexation, and thinking at last to
get the start of his humor—willingly neglected the preparation, and became [50
unfurnished not only of dainty but of ordinary dishes. He, according to the mildness of his breast, entertained the lords,
and with courtly discourse beguiled the
time, as much as a citizen might do. To
conclude, they were hungry lords, for
there came no meat in; their stomachs
were plainly gulled, and their teeth deluded, and, if anger could have seized a
man, there was matter enough, i' faith, [60
to vex any citizen in the world, if he were
not too much made a fool by his wife.
Flu. Ay, I'll swear for 't. 'Sfoot, had
it been my case, I should ha' played mad
tricks with my wife and family. First, I
would ha' spitted the men, stewed the
maids, and baked the mistress, and so
served them in.
Pio. Why, 't would ha' tempted any
blood but his.
And thou to vex him? Thou to anger
him 70
With some poor, shallow jest?
Cas. 'Sblood, Signior Pioratto, you that
disparage my conceit, I'll wage a hundred
ducats upon the head on 't that it moves
him, frets him, and galls him.
Pio. Done! 'Tis a lay;[7] join golls [8] on 't.
Witness, Signior Fluello.
Cas. Witness; 'tis done.
Come, follow me. The house is not far off.
I'll thrust him from his humor, vex his
breast, 80
And win a hundred ducats by one
jest. *Exeunt.*

---

[1] Deed.
[2] Idea.
[3] Small metal check.
[4] Proved.
[5] Fastidious.
[6] For love's sake.
[7] Bet.
[8] Hands.

[SCENA v.

Candido's shop.]

Enter Candido's Wife, George, and two Prentices in the shop.

WIFE.[1] Come, you put up your wares in good order here, do you not, think you? One piece cast this way, another that way! You had need have a patient master indeed.

GEO. [*Aside.*] Ay, I'll be sworn, for we have a curst [2] mistress.

WIFE. You mumble, do you? Mumble? I would your master or I could be a note more angry, for two patient folks in a [10 house spoil all the servants that ever shall come under them.

1 PREN. [*Aside.*] You patient! Ay, so is the devil when he is horn-mad.

Enter Castruchio, Fluello, and Pioratto.

ALL THREE.[3] Gentlemen, what do you lack? What is 't you buy? See, fine hollands, fine cambrics, fine lawns.

GEO. What is 't you lack?

2 PREN. What is 't you buy?

CAS. Where's Signior Candido, thy master? 20

GEO. Faith, signior, he's a little negotiated; he'll appear presently.

CAS. Fellow, let's see a lawn, a choice one, sirrah.

GEO. The best in all Milan, gentlemen, and this is the piece. I can fit you gentlemen with fine calicoes too for doublets, the only sweet fashion now, most delicate and courtly, a meek gentle calico, cut upon two double affable taffetas—ah, most neat, [30 feat, and unmatchable!

FLU. A notable, voluble-tongued villain!

PIO. I warrant this fellow was never begot without much prating.

CAS. What, and is this she, say'st thou?

GEO. Ay, and the purest she that ever you fingered since you were a gentleman. Look how even she is, look how clean she is! Ha, as even as the brow of Cynthia, and as clean as your sons and heirs [40 when they ha' spent all!

CAS. Pooh, thou talk'st! Pox on 't, 'tis rough.

GEO. How? Is she rough? But, if you bid pox on 't, sir, 'twill take away the roughness presently.

FLU. Ha, signior! Has he fitted your French curse?

GEO. Look you, gentleman, here's another. Compare them, I pray. *Compara* [50 *Virgilium cum Homero:* compare virgins with harlots.

CAS. Pooh, I ha' seen better, and, as you term them, evener and cleaner.

GEO. You may see further for your mind, but, trust me, you shall not find better for your body.

Enter Candido.

CAS. [*Aside.*] O, here he comes; let's make as though we pass.—
Come, come, we'll try in some other shop.

CAND. How now? What's the matter? 60

GEO. The gentlemen find fault with this lawn, fall out with it, and without a cause too.

CAND. Without a cause?
And that makes you to let 'em pass away.
Ah, may I crave a word with you, gentlemen?

FLU. He calls us.

CAS. Makes the better for the jest.

CAND. I pray come near; y'are very welcome, gallants.
Pray pardon my man's rudeness, for I fear me
H'as talked above a prentice with you.
Lawns? [*Shows lawns.*] 70
Look you, kind gentlemen, this—no—ay—this.
Take this upon my honest-dealing faith
To be a true weave, not too hard nor slack,
But e'en as far from falsehood as from black.

CAS. Well, how do you rate it?

CAND. Very conscionably—eighteen shillings a yard.

CAS. That's too dear. How many yards does the whole piece contain, think you?

CAND. Why, some seventeen yards, I think, or thereabouts. 80

[1] From this point Viola appears as *Wife* in speech heads.
[2] Ill-tempered.
[3] *I.e.*, George and the two prentices.

How much would serve your turn, I
  pray?

Cas. Why, let me see—would it were
  better too!

Cand. Truth, 'tis the best in Milan, at
  few words.

Cas. Well, let me have then—a whole
  pennyworth.

Cand. Ha, ha! Y'are a merry gentleman.

  Cas. A penn'orth, I say.

  Cand. Of lawn!

Cas. Of lawn? Ay, of lawn, a penn'orth.
'Sblood, dost not hear? A whole penn'orth!
Are you deaf?   90

Cand. Deaf? No, sir; but I must tell
  you,
  Our wares do seldom meet such customers.

Cas. Nay, and you and your lawns be
so squeamish, fare you well.

Cand. Pray stay; a word, pray, signior.
For what purpose is it, I beseech you?

Cas. 'Sblood, what's that to you? I'll
have a pennyworth.

Cand. A pennyworth! Why, you shall.
I'll serve you presently.[1]   100

2 Pren. 'Sfoot, a pennyworth, mistress!

Wife.[2] A pennyworth! Call you these
  gentlemen?

Cas. [To Candido.] No, no. Not there.

Cand.   What then, kind
  gentleman?
  What, at this corner here?

Cas.   No, nor there neither;
  I'll have it just in the middle, or else
  not.

Cand. Just in the middle? Ha, you shall
  too. What?
  Have you a single penny?

Cas.   Yes, here's one.

  Cand. Lend it me, I pray.

Flu. An excellent-followed jest!   109

Wife. What, will he spoil the lawn
now?

Cand. Patience, good wife.

Wife. Ay, that patience makes a fool
of you.—Gentlemen, you might ha' found
some other citizen to have made a kind
gull on besides my husband.

Cand. Pray, gentlemen, take her to be a
  woman;
  Do not regard her language.—O kind
  soul,

Such words will drive away my customers.

Wife. Customers with a murrain![3]
Call you these customers?   121

  Cand. Patience, good wife.

  Wife. Pox a your patience.

Geo. 'Sfoot, mistress, I warrant these
are some cheating companions.[4]

Cand. Look you, gentleman, there's
your ware. I thank you; I have your
money here. Pray know my shop; pray
let me have your custom.

  Wife. Custom, quotha!   130

  Cand. Let me take more of your money.

  Wife. You had need so.

Pio. Hark in thine ear; th'ast lost an
  hundred ducats.

Cas. Well, well, I know 't. Is 't possible
  that homo
  Should be nor man nor woman--not
  once moved—
  No, not at such an injury, not at all!
  Sure he's a pigeon, for he has no gall.

Flu. Come, come, y'are angry though you
  smother it.
  Y'are vexed, i' faith; confess.

Cand.   Why, gentlemen,
  Should you conceit[5] me to be vexed or
  moved?   140
  He has my ware; I have his money
  for 't,
  And that's no argument I'm angry. No,
  The best logician cannot prove me so.

Flu. O, but the hateful name of a pennyworth of lawn,
  And then cut out i' th' middle of the
  piece—
  Pah, I guess it by myself—would move
  a lamb
  Were he a linen draper; 'twould, i'
  faith.

Cand. Well, give me leave to answer you
  for that.
  We're set here to please all customers,
  Their humors and their fancies—offend
  none;   150
  We get by many, if we leese[6] by one.
  May be his mind stood to no more than
  that;
  A pennyworth serves him, and, 'mongst
  trades 'tis found,
  Deny a penn'orth, it may cross a pound.

---

[1] At once.   [2] Original has Mist[ress].
[3] Plague.   [5] Imagine.
[4] Fellows.   [6] Lose.

O, he that means to thrive, with patient
eye
Must please the devil if he come to
buy!

FLU. O wondrous man, patient 'bove
wrong or woe,
How blessed were men, if women could be
so!

CAND. And to express how well my breast
is pleased,
And satisfied in all—George, fill a beaker.
Exit George.
I'll drink unto that gentleman who
lately 161
Bestowed his money with me.

WIFE. God's my life,
We shall have all our gains drunk out in
beakers
To make amends for pennyworths of
lawn!

Enter Geor[ge with beaker].

CAND. Here, wife, begin you to the gentleman.

WIFE. I begin to him! [*Spills the wine.*]

CAND. George, fill 't up again.
'Twas my fault; my hand shook.
Exit George.

PIO. How strangely this doth show!
A patient man linked with a waspish
shrow.[1]

FLU. [*Aside.*] A silver and gilt beaker! I
have a trick
To work upon that beaker. Sure 'twill
fret him; 170
It cannot choose but vex him. Signior
Castruchio,
In pity to thee I have a conceit
Will save thy hundred ducats yet. 'Twill
do 't,
And work him to impatience.

CAS. [*Aside.*] Sweet Fluello, I should be
bountiful to that conceit.

FLU. [*Aside.*] Well, 'tis enough.

Enter George [with beaker].

CAND. Here, gentlemen, to you!
I wish your custom; y'are exceeding
welcome. [*Drinks.*]

CAS. I pledge you, Signior Candido! [*Drinks.*]

[1] Shrew.

Here, you that must receive a hundred
ducats!

PIO. I'll pledge them deep, i' faith, Castruchio.— 180
Signior Fluello. [*Drinks.*]

FLU. Come; play 't off to me;
I am your last man.

CAND. George, supply the cup

FLU. So, so, good honest George.
Here, Signior Candido, all this to you.

CAND. O, you must pardon me; I use it
not.

FLU. Will you not pledge me then?

CAND. Yes, but not that;
Great love is shown in little.

FLU. Blurt on [2] your sentences!
'Sfoot, you shall pledge me all.

CAND. Indeed, I shall not.

FLU. Not pledge me? 'Sblood, I'll carry
away the beaker then.

CAND. The beaker? O, that at your
pleasure, sir. 190

FLU. Now by this drink I will. [*Drinks.*]

CAS. Pledge him; he'll do 't else.

FLU. So; I ha' done you right on my thumb
nail.[3]
What, will you pledge me now?

CAND. You know me, sir!
I am not of that sin.

FLU. Why, then, farewell!
I'll bear away the beaker, by this light.

CAND. That's as you please; 'tis very good.

FLU. Nay, it doth please me, and, as you
say, 'tis a very good one.
Farewell, Signior Candido.

PIO. Farewell, Candido.

CAND. Y'are welcome, gentlemen.

CAS. Heart, not moved yet?
I think his patience is above our wit.

*Exeunt [Castruchio, Fluello with the beaker,
and Pioratto].*

GEO. I told you before, mistress, [201
they were all cheaters.

WIFE. Why, fool! Why, husband! Why,
madman! I hope you will not let 'em
sneak away so with a silver and gilt beaker,
the best in the house too.—Go, fellows,
make hue and cry after them.

CAND. Pray let your tongue lie still; all
will be well.—
Come hither, George; hie to the constable,

[2] A fig for.
[3] So that only enough to stand on a thumb
nail is left.

And in calm order wish him to attach
  them. 210
Make no great stir, because they're
  gentlemen,
And a thing partly done in merri-
  ment.
'Tis but a size above a jest, thou
  know'st;
Therefore pursue it mildly. Go, begone;
The constable's hard by; bring him
  along.
Make haste again.

WIFE. O, y'are a goodly, patient woodcock,[1] are you not now? (*Exit George.*)
See what your patience comes to: everyone
saddles you, and rides you; you'll be shortly
the common stone-horse [2] of Milan. [221
A woman's well holped [3] up with such a
meacock.[4] I had rather have a husband
that would swaddle [5] me thrice a day than
such a one that will be gulled twice in half
an hour. O, I could burn all the wares in
my shop for anger.

CAND. Pray wear a peaceful temper; be
  my wife,
That is, be patient; for a wife and
  husband
Share but one soul between them. This
  being known, 230
Why should not one soul then agree in
  one? *Exit.*

WIFE. Hang your agreements! But if
my beaker be gone!

*Enter Castruchio, Fluello, Pioratto, and
                George.*

CAND. O, here they come.

GEO. The constable, sir, let 'em come
along with me, because [6] there should be
no wond'ring. He stays at door.

CAS. Constable, Goodman Abram! [7]

FLU. Now, Signior Candido, 'sblood,
why do you attach us? 240

CAS. 'Sheart! Attach us!

CAND. Nay, swear not, gallants;
Your oaths may move your souls, but
  not move me;
You have a silver beaker of my wife's.

FLU. You say not true. 'Tis gilt.

---

[1] Simpleton.
[2] Stallion.
[3] Helped.
[7] A man who shams madness to gain his ends.

[4] Milksop.
[5] Beat.
[6] In order that.

CAND. Then you say true;
And, being gilt, the guilt lies more on you.

CAS. I hope y'are not angry, sir.

CAND. Then you hope right; for I am
  not angry.

FLU. No, but a little moved.

CAND. I moved! 'Twas you were moved—
you were brought hither.

CAS. But you, out of your anger and impatience, 250
Caused us to be attached.

CAND. Nay, you misplace it.
Out of my quiet sufferance I did that,
And not of any wrath. Had I shown
  anger,
I should have then pursued you with the
  law,
And hunted you to shame, as many
  worldlings
Do build their anger upon feebler
  grounds,
The more's the pity. Many lose their lives
For scarce so much coin as will hide their
  palm—
Which is most cruel. Those have vexéd
  spirits
That pursue lives. In this opinion rest:
The loss of millions could not move my
  breast. 261

FLU. Thou art a blessed man, and with
  peace dost deal;
Such a meek spirit can bless a commonweal.

CAND. Gentlemen, now 'tis upon eating
  time.
Pray, part not hence, but dine with me
  today.

CAS. I never heard a carter yet say nay
To such a motion. I'll not be the first.

PIO. Nor I.

FLU. Nor I.

CAND. The constable shall bear you
  company. 270
George, call him in. Let the world say
  what it can,
Nothing can drive me from a patient
  man. *Exeunt.*

[SCENA vi.

A room in Bellafront's house.]

*Enter Roger with a stool, cushion, looking-
glass, and chafing dish;[8] those being
set down, he pulls out of his pocket a*

---

[8] Used for heating the poker mentioned below.

*vial with white color in it, and two boxes,
one with white, another red painting.
He places all things in order, and a
candle by them, singing with the ends of
old ballads as he does it. At last Bellafront, as he rubs his cheek with the
colors, whistles within.*

Rog. Anon, forsooth.

Bell. [*Within.*] What are you playing
the rogue about?

Rog. About you, forsooth; I'm drawing
up a hole in your white silk stocking.

Bell. Is my glass there and my boxes
of complexion?

Rog. Yes, forsooth. Your boxes of
complexion are here, I think; yes, 'tis here.
Here's your two complexions—[*Aside.*] 10
and, if I had all the four complexions,[1]
I should ne'er set a good face upon 't.
Some men, I see, are born under hard-
favored planets as well as women. Zounds,
I look worse now than I did before, and it
makes her face glister most damnably.
There's knavery in daubing, I hold my
life; or else this is only female pomatum.

*Enter Bellafront not full ready,[2] without a
gown; she sits down; with her bodkin[3]
curls her hair; colors her lips.*

Bell. Where's my ruff and poker,[4]
you blockhead?　　　　　　　　　　20

Rog. Your ruff, your poker, are engend'ring together upon the cupboard of
the court, or the court-cupboard.[5]

Bell. Fetch 'em. Is the pox in your
hams, you can go no faster? [*Strikes him.*]

Rog. Would the pox were in your
fingers, unless you could leave flinging![6]
Catch—　　　　　　　　　　*Exit.*

Bell. I'll catch you, you dog, by-and-
by. Do you grumble?　*She sings.* 30

Cupid is a God, as naked as my nail;
I'll whip him with a rod, if he my true love
fail.

[*Enter Roger with ruff and poker.*]

Rog. There's your ruff. Shall I poke
it?

Bell. Yes, honest Ro[ger]—no, stay;
prithee, good boy, hold here.

[*Sings. Roger holds the glass and candle.*]

Down, down, down, down, I fall down and
arise—down—
I never shall arise.

Rog. Troth, m[istress], then leave the
trade if you shall never rise.　　　40

Bell. What trade, Goodman Abram?

Rog. Why, that of down and arise, or
the falling trade.

Bell. I'll fall with you by-and-by.

Rog. If you do, I know who shall
smart for 't. Troth, mistress, what do I look
like now?

Bell. Like as you are, a panderly
sixpenny rascal.

Rog. I may thank you for that; in [50
faith, I look like an old proverb, "Hold
the candle before the devil."

Bell. Ud's life, I'll stick my knife in
your guts and you prate to me so!—
What?　　　　　　　　　　*She sings.*

"Well met, pug,[7] the pearl of beauty—
umh, umh."
"How now, Sir Knave? You forget your
duty—umh, umh.
Marry muff,[8] sir!" "Are you grown so
dainty? Fa, la, la, etc."
"Is it you, sir?" "The worst of twenty!
Fa, la, la, leera, la."

Pox on you, how dost thou hold my [60
glass?

Rog. Why, as I hold your door—with
my fingers.

Bell. Nay, pray thee, sweet honey
Ro[ger], hold up handsomely.　[*Sings.*]

Sing, pretty wantons, warble, etc.

We shall ha' guests today, I lay my little
maidenhead; my nose itches so.

Rog. I said so too last night, when our
fleas twinged me.　　　　　　70

Bell. So, poke my ruff now. My
gown, my gown! Have I my fall?[9] Where's
my fall, Roger?　　　*One knocks.*

Rog. Your fall, forsooth, is behind.

Bell. God's my pitikins! Some fool
or other knocks.

Rog. Shall I open to the fool, mistress?

Bell. And all these bables[10] lying
thus? Away with it quickly.—Ay, ay,

---

[1] Temperaments constituted by the four
humors.　　　　[4] Rod for pleating ruffs.
[2] Dressed.　　　　[5] Movable sideboard.
[3] Long hairpin.　　[6] Smiting, striking.
[7] Darling; also harlot.　　[9] A flat collar.
[8] An expression of contempt.　[10] Baubles.

knock, and be damned, whosoever you [80 be!—So; give the fresh salmon line now; let him come ashore. He shall serve for my breakfast, though he go against my stomach.

Roger fetch in Fluello, Castruchio, and Pioratto.

FLU. Morrow, coz.

CAS. How does my sweet acquaintance?

PIO. Save thee, little marmoset! How dost thou, good, pretty rogue?

BELL. Well, God-a-mercy, good, pretty rascal. 90

FLU. Roger, some light, I pray thee.

ROG. You shall, signior, for we that live here in this vale of misery are as dark as hell. *Exit for a candle.*

CAS. Good tobacco, Fluello?

FLU. Smell.

Enter Roger.

PIO. It may be tickling gear, for it plays with my nose already.

ROG. Here's another light angel,[1] signior. 100

BELL. What, you pied curtal,[2] what's that you are neighing?

ROG. I say God send us the light of heaven, or some more angels.

BELL. Go fetch some wine, and drink half of it.

ROG. I must fetch some wine, gentlemen, and drink half of it.

FLU. Here, Roger.

CAS. No, let me send, prithee. 110

FLU. Hold, you cankerworm.

ROG. You shall send both, if you please, signiors.

PIO. Stay, what's best to drink a-mornings?

ROG. Hippocras, sir, for my mistress, if I fetch it, is most dear to her.

FLU. Hippocras? There then, here's a teston[3] for you, you snake.

ROG. Right, sir, here's three shil- [120 lings sixpence for a pottle and a manchet.[4] *Ex[it].*

CAS. Here's most Herculanean tobacco; ha' some, acquaintance?

---

[1] Also a gold coin.
[2] A docked horse.
[3] Sixpence.
[4] Loaf of fine bread.

BELL. Faugh, not I—makes your breath stink like the piss of a fox. Acquaintance, where supped you last night?

CAS. At a place, sweet acquaintance, where your health danced the canaries,[5] i' faith. You should ha' been there.

BELL. I there among your punks![6] [130 Marry, faugh, hang 'em; I scorn 't! Will you never leave sucking of eggs in other folks' hens' nests?

CAS. Why, in good troth, if you'll trust me, acquaintance, there was not one hen at the board. Ask Fluello.

FLU. No, faith, coz, none but cocks. Signior Malavella drunk to thee.

BELL. O, a pure beagle; that horse-leech there? 140

FLU. And the knight, Sir Oliver Lollio, swore he would bestow a taffeta petticoat on thee, but to break his fast with thee.

BELL. With me? I'll choke him then, hang him, molecatcher! It's the dreaming'st snottynose.

PIO. Well, many took that Lollio for a fool, but he's a subtle fool.

BELL. Ay, and he has fellows. Of all filthy, dry-fisted knights, I cannot [150 abide that he should touch me.

CAS. Why, wench, is he scabbed?

BELL. Hang him, he'll not live to be so honest, nor to the credit to have scabs about him; his betters have 'em. But I hate to wear out any of his coarse knighthood, because he's made like an alderman's nightgown, faced all with cony[7] before, and within nothing but fox. This sweet Oliver will eat mutton[8] till he be ready [160 to burst, but the lean-jawed slave will not pay for the scraping of his trencher.

PIO. Plague him! Set him beneath the salt, and let him not touch a bit till everyone has had his full cut.

FLU. Lord Ello, the gentleman usher, came in to us too. Marry, 'twas in our cheese,[9] for he had been to borrow money for his lord, of a citizen.

CAS. What an ass is that lord to [170 borrow money of a citizen!

BELL. Nay, God's my pity, what an ass is that citizen to lend money to a lord!

---

[5] A lively dance.
[6] Prostitutes.
[7] Rabbit skin.
[8] Strumpet.
[9] During the cheese course (?).

*Enter Matheo and Hippolito, who, saluting
the company as a stranger, walks off.
Roger comes in sadly behind them, with
a pottle pot, and stands aloof off.*

MAT. Save you, gallants. Signior Fluello, exceedingly well met, as I may say.

FLU. Signior Matheo, exceedingly well
met too, as I may say.

MAT. And how fares my little pretty
mistress?   180

BELL. E'en as my little pretty servant—sees three court dishes before her,
and not one good bit in them.—How now?
Why the devil stand'st thou so? Art in
a trance?

ROG. Yes, forsooth.

BELL. Why dost not fill out their wine?

ROG. Forsooth, 'tis filled out already.
All the wine that the signior has bestowed
upon you is cast away; a porter ran [190
a little at me, and so faced me down that
I had not a drop.

BELL. I'm accursed to let such a withered, artichoke-faced rascal grow under
my nose. Now you look like an old hecat, going to the gallows. I'll be hanged if
he ha' not put up the money to cony-
catch us all.

ROG. No, truly, forsooth, 'tis not put
up yet.   200

BELL. How many gentlemen hast thou
served thus?

ROG. None but five hundred, besides
prentices and serving-men.

BELL. Dost think I'll pocket it up at
thy hands?

ROG. Yes, forsooth, I fear you will
pocket it up.

BELL. Fie, fie, cut my lace, good servant; I shall ha' the mother [1] presently, [210
I'm so vexed at this horse-plum.[2]

FLU. Plague, not for a scald [3] pottle
of wine!

MAT. Nay, sweet Bellafront, for a little
pig's wash!

CAS. Here, Roger, fetch more. [*Gives
money.*] A mischance, i' faith, acquaintance.

BELL. Out of my sight, thou ungodly,
puritanical creature.   220

ROG. For the tother pottle?   Yes,
forsooth.   *Exit.*

BELL. Spill that too!—What gentleman
is that, servant? Your friend?

MAT. Godso; a stool, a stool! If you
love me, mistress, entertain this gentleman respectively,[4] and bid him welcome.

BELL. He's very welcome.   Pray, sir,
sit.

HIP. Thanks, lady.   230
[*Matheo and Bellafront stand aside conversing.*]

FLU. Count Hippolito, is 't not? Cry
you mercy, signior; you walk here all this
while, and we not heard you? Let me
bestow a stool upon you, beseech you.
You are a stranger here; we know the
fashions a th' house.

CAS. Please you, be here, my lord.
[*Offers*] *tobacco.*

HIP. No, good Castruchio.

FLU. You have abandoned the court, I
see, my lord, since the death of your [240
mistress. Well, she was a delicate piece.—
Beseech you, sweet, come let us serve
under the colors of your acquaintance still
for all that.—Please you to meet here at
my lodging of my coz, I shall bestow a banquet upon you.

HIP. I never can deserve this kindness,
sir. What may this lady be, whom you call
coz?   249

FLU. Faith, sir, a poor gentlewoman,
of passing good carriage; one that has
some suits in law, and lies here in an attorney's house.

HIP. Is she married?

FLU. Ha, as all your punks are, a captain's wife, or so. Never saw her before,
my lord?

HIP. Never, trust me! A goodly creature!

FLU. By gad, when you know her [260
as we do, you'll swear she is the prettiest,
kindest, sweetest, most bewitching, honest
ape under the pole. A skin, your satin is
not more soft, nor lawn whiter.

HIP. Belike, then, she's some sale
courtesan.

FLU. Troth, as all your best faces are.
A good wench!

HIP. Great pity that she's a good
wench.   270

MAT. [*To Bellafront.*]   Thou shalt
ha', i' faith, mistress.—How now, signiors?

---

[1] Hysteria.   [2] Wild plum.   [3] Paltry.

[4] Respectfully.

What, whispering? Did not I lay a wager I should take you within seven days in a house of vanity?

HIP. You did; and, I beshrew your heart, you have won.

MAT. How do you like my mistress?

HIP. Well, for such a mistress; better, if your mistress be not your mas- [280 ter.—I must break manners, gentlemen; fare you well.

MAT. 'Sfoot, you shall not leave us.

BELL. The gentleman likes not the taste of our company.

OMNES. Beseech you, stay.

HIP. Trust me, my affairs beckon for me; pardon me.

MAT. Will you call for me half an hour hence here? 290

HIP. Perhaps I shall.

MAT. Perhaps? Faugh! I know you can swear to me you will.

HIP. Since you will press me, on my word, I will. *Exit.*

BELL. What sullen picture is this, servant?

MAT. It's Count Hippolito, the brave count.

PIO. As gallant a spirit as any in [300 Milan, you sweet Jew.[1]

FLU. O, he's a most essential gentleman, coz!

CAS. Did you never hear of Count Hippolito, acquaintance?

BELL. Marry muff a your counts, and be no more life in 'em!

MAT. He's so malcontent, sirrah Bellafronta.—And you be honest gallants, let's sup together and have the count [310 with us.—Thou shalt sit at the upper end, punk.

BELL. Punk, you soused gurnet?[2]

MAT. King's truce! Come, I'll bestow the supper to have him but laugh.

CAS. He betrays his youth too grossly to that tyrant melancholy.

MAT. All this is for a woman.

BELL. A woman? Some whore! What sweet jewel is 't? 320

PIO. Would she heard you!

FLU. Troth, so would I.

CAS. And I, by heaven.

BELL. Nay, good servant, what woman?

MAT. Pah!

BELL. Prithee, tell me; a buss,[3] and tell me. I warrant he's an honest fellow, if he take on thus for a wench. Good rogue, who?

MAT. By th' Lord, I will not, must not, faith, mistress. Is 't a match, sirs? [330 This night, at th' Antelope. Ay, for there's best wine, and good boys.

OMNES. It's done; at th' Antelope.

BELL. I cannot be there tonight.

MAT. Cannot? By th' Lord, you shall.

BELL. By the Lady, I will not. Shall!

FLU. Why, then, put it off till Friday; woot[4] come then, coz?

BELL. Well.

Enter Roger.

MAT. Y'are the waspishest ape. [340 Roger, put your mistress in mind to sup with us on Friday next. Y'are best come like a madwoman, without a band, in your waistcoat,[5] and the linings of your kirtle outward, like every common hackney[6] that steals out at the back gate of her sweet knight's lodging.

BELL. Go, go, hang yourself!

CAS. It's dinner time, Matheo. Shall 's hence? 350

OMNES. Yes, yes.—Farewell, wench.

Exeunt [all but Bellafront and Roger].

BELL. Farewell, boys.—Roger, what wine sent they for?

ROG. Bastard wine,[7] for, if it had been truly begotten, it would not ha' been ashamed to come in. Here's six shillings to pay for nursing the bastard.

BELL. A company of rooks![8] O good sweet Roger, run to the poulter's, and buy me some fine larks! 360

ROG. No woodcocks?

BELL. Yes, faith, a couple, if they be not dear.

ROG. I'll buy but one; there's one[9] already here. *Exit.*

Enter Hippolito.

HIP. Is the gentleman, my friend, departed, mistress?

BELL. His back is but new turned, sir.

HIP. Fare you well.

BELL. I can direct you to him.

[3] Kiss.   [4] Wilt thou.
[5] *I.e.*, without your upper dress.   [6] Harlot.
[7] Sweet Spanish wine.   [8] Simpletons.
[9] *I.e.*, Hippolito, with a play on *woodcock* as simpleton.

[1] Term of endearment.   [2] Pickled fish.

Hip.   Can you, pray?
Bell. If you please stay, he'll not be absent long.
Hip. I care not much.
Bell.   Pray sit, forsooth.
Hip.   I'm hot.
  If I may use your room, I'll rather
    walk.
Bell. At your best pleasure.—Whew!
    Some rubbers [1] there!   370
Hip. Indeed, I'll none—indeed I will not;
    thanks.
  Pretty fine lodging.   I perceive my
    friend
  Is old in your acquaintance.
Bell.   Troth, sir, he comes,
  As other gentlemen, to spend spare
    hours.
  If yourself like our roof, such as it is,
  Your own acquaintance may be as old
    as his.
Hip. Say I did like, what welcome should
    I find?
Bell. Such as my present fortunes can
    afford.
Hip. But would you let me play Matheo's
    part?
Bell. What part?
Hip.   Why, embrace you,
    dally with you, kiss.   380
  Faith, tell me, will you leave him and
    love me?
Bell. I am in bonds to no man, sir.
Hip.   Why then,
  Y'are free for any man; if any, me.
  But I must tell you, lady, were you
    mine,
  You should be all mine. I could brook
    no sharers;
  I should be covetous, and sweep up all.
  I should be pleasure's usurer; faith, I
    should.
Bell. O fate!
Hip.   Why sigh you, lady? May
    I know?
Bell. 'T has never been my fortune yet
    to single
  Out that one man whose love could fellow mine,   390
  As I have ever wished it. O my stars!
  Had I but met with one kind gentleman,
  That would have purchased sin alone
    to himself,

[1] Towels.

For his own private use, although scarce
    proper[2]—
Indifferent handsome, meetly legged
    and thighed—
And my allowance reasonable, i' faith,
According to my body, by my troth,
I would have been as true unto his
    pleasures,
Yea, and as loyal to his afternoons,   399
As ever a poor gentlewoman could be.
Hip. This were well now to one but newly
    fledged,
  And scarce a day old in this subtle
    world;
  'Twere pretty art, good birdlime, cunning net.
  But come, come, faith, confess. How
    many men
  Have drunk this selfsame protestation,
  From that red ticing [3] lip?
Bell.   Indeed, not any.
Hip. "Indeed," and blush not!
Bell.   No, in truth, not any.
Hip. "Indeed!" "In truth!"—how warily you swear!
  'Tis well, if ill it be not; yet had I
  The ruffian in me, and were drawn before you   410
  But in light colors, I do know indeed
  You could not swear "Indeed," but
    thunder oaths
  That should shake heaven, drown the
    harmonious spheres,
  And pierce a soul that loved her Maker's
    honor
  With horror and amazement.
Bell.   Shall I swear?
  Will you believe me then?
Hip.   Worst then of all;
  Our sins by custom seem at last but
    small.
  Were I but o'er your threshold, a next
    man,
  And after him a next, and then a fourth,
  Should have this golden hook and lascivious bait   420
  Thrown out to the full length. Why,
    let me tell you,
  I ha' seen letters sent from that white
    hand,
  Tuning such music to Matheo's ear.
Bell. Matheo! That's true, but, believe
    it, I

[2] Fine-looking.   [3] Enticing.

No sooner had laid hold upon your pres-
   ence,
But straight mine eye conveyed you to
   my heart.
HIP. O, you cannot feign with me! Why,
   I know, lady,
This is the common passion of you all,
   To hook in a kind gentleman, and then
Abuse his coin, conveying it to your
   lover,   430
And in the end you show him a French
   trick,
And so you leave him, that a coach may
   run
Between his legs for breadth.
BELL.   O, by my soul,
   Not I! Therein I'll prove an honest
   whore,
In being true to one, and to no more.
HIP. If any be disposed to trust your oath,
   Let him; I'll not be he. I know you
   feign
All that you speak; ay, for a mingled
   harlot
Is true in nothing but in being false.
What! shall I teach you how to loathe
   yourself?   440
And mildly too, not without sense or
   reason?
BELL. I am content; I would feign loathe
   myself
If you not love me.
HIP.   Then, if your gracious blood
   Be not all wasted, I shall assay to do 't.
Lend me your silence and attention.
   You have no soul;
That makes you weigh so light. Heaven's
   treasure bought it,
And half a crown hath sold it. For your
   body
Is like the common shore, that still re-
   ceives
All the town's filth. The sin of many
   men
Is within you; and thus much I sup-
   pose   450
That, if all your committers stood in
   rank,
They'd make a lane in which your
   shame might dwell,
And with their spaces reach from hence
   to hell.
Nay, shall I urge it more? There has
   been known

As many by one harlot maimed and
   dismembered
As would ha' stuffed an hospital. This
   I might
Apply to you, and perhaps do you right.
O, y'are as base as any beast that bears;
Your body is e'en hired, and so are
   theirs.
For gold and sparkling jewels, if he
   can,   460
You'll let a Jew get you with Christian—
Be he a Moor, a Tartar, though his
   face
Look uglier than a dead man's skull.
Could the devil put on a human shape,
If his purse shake out crowns, up then
   he gets;
Whores will be rid to hell with golden
   bits.
So that y'are crueler than Turks, for
   they
Sell Christians only; you sell yourselves
   away.
Why, those that love you, hate you, and
   will term you
Lickerish [1] damnation; wish themselves
   half-sunk   470
After the sin is laid out, and e'en curse
Their fruitless riot (for what one begets
Another poisons); lust and murder hit.
A tree being often shook, what fruit
   can knit?
BELL. O me unhappy!
HIP.   I can vex you more.
A harlot is like Dunkirk, true to none,
Swallows both English, Spanish, ful-
   some Dutch,
Back-doored [2] Italian, last of all, the
   French,
And he sticks to you, faith, gives you
   your diet,
Brings you acquainted, first, with Mon-
   sieur Doctor,   480
And then you know what follows.
BELL.   Misery!
Rank, stinking, and most loathsome
   misery!
HIP. Methinks a toad is happier than a
   whore.
That, with one poison, swells; with
   thousands more
The other stocks her veins. Harlot?
   Fie, fie!

[1] Lascivious.   [2] Sneaking.

You are the miserablest creatures breathing,

The very slaves of nature. Mark me else.

You put on rich attires—others' eyes wear them;

You eat, but to supply your blood with sin.

And this strange curse e'en haunts you to your graves. 490

From fools you get, and spend it upon slaves.

Like bears and apes, y'are baited and show tricks

For money; but your bawd the sweetness licks.

Indeed, you are their journeywomen, and do

All base and damned works they list set you to,

So that you ne'er are rich; for do but show me,

In present memory or in ages past,

The fairest and most famous courtesan,

Whose flesh was dear'st; that raised the price of sin,

And held it up; to whose intemperate bosom, 500

Princes, earls, lords, the worst has been a knight,

The mean'st a gentleman, have offered up

Whole hecatombs of sighs, and rained in showers

Handfuls of gold; yet, for all this, at last

Diseases sucked her marrow, then grew so poor

That she has begged e'en at a beggar's door.

And (wherein heaven has a finger) when this idol,

From coast to coast, has leaped on foreign shores,

And had more worship than the outlandish whores;

When several nations have gone over her; 510

When, for each several city she has seen,

Her maidenhead has been new, and been sold dear;

Did live well there, and might have died unknown

And undefamed—back comes she to her own,

And there both miserably lives and dies,

Scorned even of those that once adored her eyes,

As if her fatal, circled life thus ran:

Her pride should end there where it first began.

What, do you weep to hear your story read?

Nay, if you spoil your cheeks, I'll read no more. 520

BELL. O yes, I pray, proceed.

Indeed, 'twill do me good to weep, indeed.

HIP. To give those tears a relish, this I add—

Y'are like the Jews, scattered, in no place certain;

Your days are tedious, your hours burdensome;

And, were 't not for full suppers, midnight revels,

Dancing, wine, riotous meetings, which do drown

And bury quite in you all virtuous thoughts,

And on your eyelids hang so heavily

They have no power to look so high as heaven, 530

You'd sit and muse on nothing but despair,

Curse that devil Lust, that so burns up your blood,

And in ten thousand shivers break your glass

For his temptation. Say you taste delight,

To have a golden gull from rise to set,

To mete [1] you in his hot, luxurious [2] arms,

Yet your nights pay for all. I know you dream

Of warrants, whips, and beadles, and then start

At a door's windy creak; think every weasel

To be a constable, and every rat 540

A long-tailed officer. Are you now not slaves?

O, you have damnation without pleasure for it!

[1] Measure, embrace.   [2] Lecherous.

Such is the state of harlots. To conclude:
When you are old and can well paint
  no more,
You turn bawd, and are then worse
  than before.
Make use of this. Farewell.
BELL.   O, I pray, stay.
HIP. I see Matheo comes not; time hath
  barred me.
Would all the harlots in the town had
  heard me.   *Exit.*
BELL. Stay yet a little longer!   No?
  Quite gone!
Cursed be that minute—for it was no
  more,   550
So soon a maid is changed into a whore—
Wherein I first fell! Be it forever black!
Yet why should sweet Hippolito shun
  mine eyes,
For whose true love I would become
  pure-honest,
Hate the world's mixtures, and the
  smiles of gold?
Am I not fair? Why should he fly me
  then?
Fair creatures are desired, not scorned
  of men.
How many gallants have drunk healths
  to me,
Out of their daggered arms, and thought
  them blessed,
Enjoying but mine eyes at prodigal
  feasts!   560
And does Hippolito detest my love?
O, sure their heedless lusts but flattered
  me;
I am not pleasing, beautiful, nor young.
Hippolito hath spied some ugly blemish,
Eclipsing all my beauties. I am foul.
Harlot! Ay, that's the spot that taints
  my soul.
His weapon left here? O fit instrument
To let forth all the poison of my flesh!
Thy master hates me, cause my blood
  hath ranged;
But, when 'tis forth, then he'll believe
  I'm changed.   570

[*As she prepares to stab herself,*] *enter*
                                Hipp[olito].

HIP. Mad woman, what art doing?
BELL.   Either love me,
  Or cleave my bosom on thy rapier's
  point.

Yet do not neither; for thou then de-
  stroy'st
That which I love thee for—thy virtues.
  Here, here;
                [*Gives sword to Hippolito.*]
Th' art crueler, and kill'st me with dis-
  dain.
To die so, sheds no blood, yet 'tis worse
  pain.   *Exit Hipp[olito].*
Not speak to me? Not look? Not bid
  farewell?
Hated! This must not be; some means
  I'll try.
Would all whores were as honest now as
  I!   *Exit.*[1]

SCENA vii.

*Enter Candido, his Wife, George, and two
    Prentices in the shop. Fustigo enters,
                              walking by.*

GEO. See, gentlemen, what you lack—
a fine holland, a fine cambric! See what you
buy.
  1 PREN. Holland for shirts, cambric for
bands! What is 't you lack?
  FUS. [*Aside.*] 'Sfoot, I lack 'em all; nay,
more, I lack money to buy 'em. Let me
see, let me look again. Mass, this is the
shop.—What, coz! Sweet coz! How dost,
i' faith, since last night after candle- [10
light? We had good sport, i' faith, had we
not? And when shall 's laugh again?
  WIFE. When you will, cousin.
  FUS. Spoke like a kind Lacedemonian.
I see yonder's thy husband.
  WIFE. Ay, there's the sweet youth, God
bless him!
  FUS. And how is 't, cousin? And how,
how is 't, thou squall?[2]
  WIFE. Well, cousin. How fare you? [20
  FUS. How fare I? Troth, for sixpence a
meal, wench, as well as heart can wish, with
calves' chaldrons[3] and chitterlings;[4] be-
sides, I have a punk after supper, as good
as a roasted apple.
  CAND. Are you my wife's cousin?
  FUS. I am, sir. What hast thou to do
with that?
  CAND. O, nothing, but y'are welcome.
  FUS. The devil's dung in thy teeth! [30

---

[1] Original reads *Exeunt.*   [3] Edible entrails.
[2] Minx.   [4] Tripe.

I'll be welcome whether thou wilt or no,
I.—What ring's this, coz? Very pretty and
fantastical, i' faith! Let's see it.

WIFE. Pooh! Nay, you wrench my
finger.

FUS. I ha' sworn I'll ha't, and I hope you
will not let my oaths be cracked in the
ring,[1] will you? [*Seizes the ring.*] I hope, sir,
you are not malicolly [2] at this, for all your
great looks. Are you angry? 40

CAND. Angry? Not I, sir; nay, if she
 can part
So easily with her ring, 'tis with my
 heart.

GEO. Suffer this, sir, and suffer all. A
whoreson [3] gull, to—

CAND. Peace, George! When she has
 reaped what I have sown,
She'll say one grain tastes better of her
 own
Than whole sheaves gathered from another's land.
Wit's never good till bought at a dear
 hand.[4]

GEO. But in the meantime she makes an
ass of somebody. 50

2 PREN. See, see, see, sir; as you turn
your back, they do nothing but kiss.

CAND. No matter; let 'em. When I touch
 her lip,
I shall not feel his kisses, no, nor miss
Any of her lip; no harm in kissing is.
Look to your business, pray; make up
 your wares.

FUS. Troth, coz, and well remembered.
I would thou wouldst give me five yards of
lawn, to make my punk some falling bands
a the fashion—three falling one upon [60
another, for that's the new edition [5] now.
She's out of linen horribly, too; troth,
sh'as never a good smock to her back
neither, but one that has a great many
patches in 't, and that I'm fain to wear
myself for want of shift, too. Prithee, put
me into wholesome napery, and bestow
some clean commodities upon us.

WIFE. Reach me those cambrics, and the
lawns hither. 70

CAND. What to do, wife? To lavish out
my goods upon a fool?

FUS. Fool? 'Snails, eat the "fool," or

I'll so batter your crown that it shall
scarce go for five shillings.

2 PREN. Do you hear, sir? Y'are best
be quiet, and say a fool tells you so.

FUS. Nails, I think so, for thou tell'st
me.

CAND. Are you angry, sir, because I
 named thee fool? 80
Trust me, you are not wise in my own
 house
And to my face to play the antic [6] thus.
If you'll needs play the madman, choose
 a stage
Of lesser compass, where few eyes may
 note
Your action's error; but, if still you miss,
As here you do, for one clap, ten will
 hiss.

FUS. 'Swounds, cousin, he talks to me
as if I were a scurvy tragedian.

2 PREN. [*Aside.*] Sirrah George, I ha'
thought upon a device how to break [90
his pate, beat him soundly, and ship him
away.

GEO. [*Aside.*] Do 't.

2 PREN. [*Aside.*] I'll go in, pass through
the house, give some of our fellow prentices
the watchword when they shall enter, then
come and fetch my master in by a wile, and
place one in the hall to hold him in conference, whilst we cudgel the gull out of his
coxcomb. 100

GEO. [*Aside.*] Do 't; away, do 't.
       [*Exit 2 Prentice.*]

WIFE. Must I call twice for these cambrics and lawns?

CAND. Nay, see, you anger her, George;
prithee despatch.

1 PREN. Two of the choicest pieces are
in the warehouse, sir.

CAND. Go fetch them presently.
        Exit 1 Prentice.

FUS. Ay, do, make haste, sirrah.

CAND. Why were you such a stran- [110
ger all this while, being my wife's cousin?

FUS. Stranger? No, sir, I'm a natural
Milaner born.

CAND. I perceive still it is your natural
guise to mistake me, but you are welcome,
sir; I much wish your acquaintance.

FUS. My acquaintance? I scorn that,
i' faith; I hope my acquaintance goes in
chains of gold three-and-fifty times double.

---

[1] Invalid, like a damaged coin.
[2] Corruption of *melancholy*. [4] High price.
[3] Rascally. [5] Kind, fashion.
[6] Buffoon.

You know who I mean, coz; the posts of his gate are a-painting too.[1]　　　121

Enter the 2 Prentice.

2 PREN. Signior Pandulfo, the merchant, desires conference with you.

CAND. Signior Pandulfo? I'll be with him straight.

Attend your mistress and the gentleman.
　　　　　　　　　　　　　　　　Exit.

WIFE. When do you show those pieces?

FUS. Ay, when do you show those pieces?

OMNES. [*Within.*] Presently, sir, presently; we are but charging them.　　　130

FUS. Come, sirrah. You flatcap,[2] where be these whites?

[*Enter 1 Prentice with cloth.*]

GEO. [*Whispering.*] Flatcap? Hark in your ear, sir; y'are a flat fool, an ass, a gull, and I'll thrum[3] you.—Do you see this cambric, sir?

FUS. 'Sfoot, coz, a good jest! Did you hear him? He told me in my ear, I was a "flat fool, an ass, a gull, and I'll thrum you.—Do you see this cambric, sir?"　　140

WIFE. What, not my men, I hope?

FUS. No, not your men, but one of your men, i' faith.

1 PREN. I pray, sir, come hither. What say you to this? Here's an excellent good one.

FUS. Ay, marry, this likes[4] me well. Cut me off some half-score yards.

2 PREN. [*Whispering.*] Let your whores cut. Y'are an impudent coxcomb. [150 You get none, and yet I'll thrum you.—A very good cambric, sir.

FUS. Again, again, as God judge me! 'Sfoot, coz, they stand thrumming here with me all day, and yet I get nothing.

2 PREN. [*Whispering.*] A word, I pray, sir; you must not be angry. Prentices have hot bloods, young fellows.—What say you to this piece? Look you, 'tis so delicate, so soft, so even, so fine a thread, that [160 a lady may wear it.

FUS. 'Sfoot, I think so. If a knight

marry my punk, a lady shall wear it. Cut me off twenty yards. Th'art an honest lad.

1 PREN. Not without money, gull, and I'll thrum you too.

OMNES. Gull, we'll thrum you!

FUS. O Lord, sister, did you not hear something cry "thump"? Zounds, your men here make a plain ass of me.　　170

WIFE. What, to my face so impudent?

GEO. Ay, in a cause so honest, we'll not suffer
Our master's goods to vanish moneyless.

WIFE. You will not suffer them?

2 PREN.　　　　　No, and you may blush
In going about to vex so mild a breast
As is our master's.

WIFE.　　　　　Take away those pieces!
Cousin, I give them freely.

FUS. Mass, and I'll take 'em as freely.
　　　　　　　[*Other Prentices rush in.*]

OMNES. We'll make you lay 'em down again more freely.
　　　　　[*They attack Fustigo with their clubs.*]

WIFE. Help, help! My brother will be murderéd.　　180

Enter Can[dido].

CAND. How now, what coil is here? Forbear, I say.

[*Exeunt all the Prentices except the 1 and 2.*]

GEO. He calls us flatcaps, and abuses us.

CAND. Why, sirs, do such examples flow from me?

WIFE. They are of your keeping, sir. Alas, poor brother!

FUS. I' faith, they ha' peppered me, sister. Look, dost not spin? Call you these prentices? I'll ne'er play at cards more when clubs is trump. I have a goodly coxcomb, sister, have I not?

CAND. Sister and brother? Brother [190 to my wife?

FUS. If you have any skill in heraldry, you may soon know that; break but her pate, and you shall see her blood and mine is all one.

CAND. A surgeon! Run, a surgeon! [*Exit 1 Prentice.*] Why then wore you that forged name of cousin?

FUS. Because it's a common thing to call coz and ningle[5] nowadays all the [200 world over.

---

[1] In reference to the painting of the sheriff's gateposts for displaying proclamations.

[2] Derisive name for apprentice.

[3] Beat.

[4] Pleases.

[5] Mine ingle, my intimate.

CAND. Cousin! A name of much deceit, folly, and sin,
For under that common abuséd word
Many an honest-tempered citizen
Is made a monster, and his wife trained out
To foul adulterous action, full of fraud.
I may well call that word a city's bawd.

FUS. Troth, brother, my sister would needs ha' me take upon me to gull your patience a little; but it has made [210 double gules [1] on my coxcomb.

WIFE. What, playing the woman? Blabbing now, you fool?

CAND. O, my wife did but exercise a jest upon your wit.

FUS. 'Sfoot, my wit bleeds for 't, methinks.

CAND. Then let this warning more of sense afford;
The name of cousin is a bloody word.

FUS. I'll ne'er call coz again whilst [220 I live, to have such a coil about it. This should be a coronation day, for my head runs claret lustily.   *Exit.*

Enter an Officer.

CAND. Go, wish the surgeon to have great respect—   *Exit 2 Prentice.*
How now, my friend? What, do they sit today?

OFF. Yes, sir, they expect you at the senate house.

CAND. I thank your pains; I'll not be last man there.—   *Exit Offi[cer].*
My gown, George, go, my gown.—A happy land,
Where grave men meet each cause to understand;
Whose consciences are not cut out in bribes   230
To gull the poor man's right; but in even scales,
Peise [2] rich and poor, without corruption's vails. [3]
Come, where's the gown?

GEO.   I cannot find the key, sir.

CAND. Request it of your mistress.

WIFE. Come not to me for any key;
I'll not be troubled to deliver it.

CAND. Good wife, kind wife, it is a needful trouble,
But for my gown!

WIFE.   Moths swallow down your gown!
You set my teeth on edge with talking on 't.

CAND. Nay, prithee, sweet, I cannot meet without it.   240
I should have a great fine set on my head.

WIFE. Set on your coxcomb; tush, fine me no fines.

CAND. Believe me, sweet, none greets the senate house
Without his robe of reverence—that's his gown.

WIFE. Well, then, y'are like to cross that custom once;
You get nor key nor gown. And so depart.—
[*Aside.*] This trick will vex him sure, and fret his heart.   *Exit.*

CAND. Stay, let me see; I must have some device.
My cloak's too short; fie, fie, no cloak will do 't.
It must be something fashioned like a gown,   250
With my arms out. O, George, come hither, George!
I prithee, lend me thine advice.

GEO. Troth, sir, were it any but you, they would break open chest.

CAND. O, no! Break open chest! That's a thieves' office.
Therein you counsel me against my blood;
'Twould show impatience, that. Any meek means
I would be glad to embrace. Mass, I have got it.
Go, step up, fetch me down one of the carpets, [4]
The saddest [5]-colored carpet, honest George;   260
Cut thou a hole i' th' middle for my neck,
Two for mine arms. Nay, prithee, look not strange.

GEO. I hope you do not think, sir, as you mean.

CAND. Prithee, about it quickly; the hour chides me.
Warily, George, softly, take heed of eyes.
     Exit George.
Out of two evils he's accounted wise

---

[1] Heraldic term for red.   [2] Weigh.   [3] Bribes, tips.
[4] Table covers.   [5] Quietest.

That can pick out the least. The fine
  imposed
For an ungownéd senator is about
Forty crusadoes,[1] the carpet not 'bove
  four.
Thus have I chosen the lesser evil yet,
Preserved my patience, foiled her desper-
  ate wit.   271

Enter George.

GEO. Here, sir, here's the carpet.
CAND. O, well done, George; we'll cut it
  just i' th' midst. [*They cut the carpet.*]
'Tis very well; I thank thee. Help it on.
GEO. It must come over your head, sir,
like a wench's petticoat.
CAND. Th'art in the right, good George; it
  must indeed.
Fetch me a nightcap, for I'll gird it close,
As if my health were queasy. 'Twill show
  well
For a rude, careless nightgown,[2] will 't
  not, think'st?   280
GEO. Indifferent well, sir, for a night-
gown, being girt and pleated.
CAND. Ay, and a nightcap on my head.
GEO. That's true, sir; I'll run and fetch
one, and a staff.   *Ex[it] Ge[orge].*
CAND. For thus they cannot choose but
  conster [3] it:
One that is out of health takes no delight,
Wears his apparel without appetite,
And puts on heedless raiment without
  form.—

Enter Geo[rge with nightcap and staff].

So, so, kind George. [*Puts on nightcap.*]
Be secret now; and, prithee,   290
Do not laugh at me till I'm out of
  sight.
GEO. I laugh? Not I, sir.
CAND.   Now to the senate house.
  Methinks I'd rather wear, without a
  frown,
A patient carpet than an angry gown.
                                   Exit.
GEO. Now looks my m[aster] just like
one of our carpet knights,[4] only he's some-
what the honester of the two.

[1] Portuguese coins.
[2] Dressing gown.   [3] Construe.
[4] A contemptuous term for a knight whose
achievements belong rather to the carpet (the
lady's boudoir) than to the field of battle.

Enter Candido's Wife.

WIFE. What, is your master gone?
GEO. Yes, forsooth, his back is but new
  turned.
WIFE. And in his cloak? Did he not vex
  and swear?   300
GEO. [*Aside.*] No, but he'll make you
swear anon.—No, indeed, he went away
like a lamb.
WIFE. Key, sink to hell! Still patient,
  patient still?
I am with child [5] to vex him. Prithee,
  George,
If e'er thou look'st for favor at my
  hands,
Uphold one jest for me.
GEO.   Against my master?
WIFE. 'Tis a mere jest, in faith. Say, wilt
  thou do 't?
GEO. Well, what is 't?
WIFE. Here, take this key; thou know'st
  where all things lie.   310
Put on thy master's best apparel—gown,
Chain, cap, ruff, everything. Be like
  himself,
And, gainst his coming home, walk in the
  shop;
Feign the same carriage and his patient
  look.
'Twill breed but a jest, thou know'st.
  Speak, wilt thou?
GEO. 'Twill wrong my master's patience.
WIFE.   Prithee, George.
GEO. Well, if you'll save me harmless,
and put me under covert-barn,[6] I am con-
tent to please you, provided it may breed
no wrong against him.   320
WIFE. No wrong at all. Here, take the
  key; begone.
If any vex him, this; if not this, none.
                                  Exeunt.

SCENA viii.

[*A room in Bellafront's house.*]

Enter a Bawd and Roger.

BAWD. O Roger, Roger, where's your
mistress, where's your mistress? There's
the finest, neatest gentleman at my house,
but newly come over. O, where is she,
where is she, where is she?

[5] Filled with longing.
[6] Covert-baron, *i.e.*, under protection.

Rog. My mistress is abroad, but not amongst 'em. My mistress is not the whore now that you take her for.

Bawd. How? Is she not a whore? Do you go about to take away her good [10 name, Roger? You are a fine pander indeed.

Rog. I tell you, Madonna Fingerlock, I am not sad for nothing; I ha' not eaten one good meal this three-and-thirty days. I had wont to get sixteenpence by fetching a pottle of hippocras, but now those days are past. We had as good doings, Madonna Fingerlock, she within doors, and I without, as any poor young couple [20 in Milan.

Bawd. God's my life, and is she changed now?

Rog. I ha' lost by her squeamishness more than would have builded twelve bawdyhouses.

Bawd. And had she no time to turn honest but now? What a vile woman is this! Twenty pound a night, I'll be sworn, Roger, in good gold and no silver. Why, [30 here was a time! If she should ha' picked out a time, it could not be better—gold enough stirring, choice of men, choice of hair, choice of beards, choice of legs, and choice of every, every, everything. It cannot sink into my head that she should be such an ass. Roger, I never believe it.

Rog. Here she comes now.

Enter Bellafront.

Bawd. O sweet madonna, on with your loose gown, your felt,[1] and your feather. [40 There's the sweetest, prop'rest, gallantest gentleman at my house; he smells all of musk and ambergris, his pocket full of crowns, flame-colored doublet, red satin hose, carnation silk stockings, and a leg, and a body—O!

Bell. Hence, thou, our sex's monster, poisonous bawd,
Lust's factor,[2] and damnation's orator!
Gossip of hell! Were all the harlots' sins
Which the whole world contains, numbered together,　　　　　50
Thine far exceeds them all!; of all the creatures
That ever were created, thou art basest.

What serpent would beguile thee of thy office?
It is destestable, for thou liv'st
Upon the dregs of harlots, guard'st the door
Whilst couples go to dancing. O coarse devil!
Thou art the bastard's curse—thou brand'st his birth;
The lecher's French disease, for thou drysuck'st him;
The harlot's poison, and thine own confusion.

Bawd. Marry come up, with a pox! [60 Have you nobody to rail against but your bawd now?

Bell. And you, knave pander, kinsman to a bawd!

Rog. You and I, madonna, are cousins.

Bell. Of the same blood and making, near allied.
Thou, that slave to sixpence, basemetaled villain!

Rog. Sixpence? Nay, that's not so. I never took under two shillings fourpence; I hope I know my fee.

Bell. I know not against which most to inveigh,　　　　　70
For both of you are damned so equally.
Thou never spar'st for oaths, swear'st anything,
As if thy soul were made of shoe leather:
"God damn me, gentlemen, if she be within!"—
When in the next room she's found dallying.

Rog. If it be my vocation to swear, every man in his vocation. I hope my betters swear and damn themselves, and why should not I?

Bell. Roger, you cheat kind gentle- [80 men.

Rog. The more gulls they.

Bell. Slave, I cashier thee.

Bawd. And you do cashier him, he shall be entertained.

Rog. Shall I? Then blurt a[3] your service!

Bell. As hell would have it, entertained by you! I dare the devil himself to match those two.　　　　　*Exit.*　90

Bawd. Marry gup,[4] are you grown so holy, so pure, so honest, with a pox?

---

[1] Hat.　　　　　[2] Agent.

[3] On.　　　　　[4] Go up, get along!

Rog. Scurvy, honest punk! But stay, madonna, how must our agreement be now? For you know I am to have all the comings-in at the hall door, and you at the chamber door.

Bawd. True, Roger, except my vails.

Rog. Vails? What vails?

Bawd. Why, as thus: if a couple [100 come in a coach, and light to lie down a little, then, Roger, that's my fee, and you may walk abroad, for the coachman himself is their pander.

Rog. Is a [1] so? In truth, I have almost forgot for want of exercise. But how if I fetch this citizen's wife to that gull, and that madonna to that gallant, how then?

Bawd. Why then, Roger, you are [110 to have sixpence a lain; [2] so many lains, so many sixpences.

Rog. Is 't so? Then I see we two shall agree, and live together.

Bawd. Ay, Roger, so long as there be any taverns and bawdyhouses in Milan.
Exeunt.

SCENA ix.

[*Another room in Bellafront's house.*]

Enter Bellafront with lute, pen, ink, and paper being placed before her.

SONG

[Bell.] The courtier's flattering jewels,
    Temptation's only fuels;
    The lawyer's ill-got moneys,
    That suck up poor bees' honeys;
    The citizen's son's riot,
    The gallant, costly diet;
    Silks and velvets, pearls and ambers—
    Shall not draw me to their chambers.
        Silks and velvets, etc.

She writes.
O, 'tis in vain to write! It will not please.   10
Ink on this paper would ha' but presented
The foul black spots that stick upon my soul,
And rather make me loathsomer than wrought
My love's impression in Hippolito's thought.

[1] He.   [2] Lying down (?).

No, I must turn the chaste leaves of my breast,
And pick out some sweet means to breed my rest.
Hippolito, believe me, I will be
As true unto thy heart as thy heart to thee,
And hate all men, their gifts and company!

Enter Matheo, Castruchio, Fluello, Pioratto.

Mat. You, goody punk—*subaudi,* [3] [20 cockatrice—O, y'are a sweet whore or your promise, are you not, think you? How well you came to supper to us last night! Mew, a whore, and break her word! Nay, you may blush, and hold down your head at it well enough. 'Sfoot, ask these gallants if we stayed not till we were as hungry as serjeants. [4]

Flu. Ay, and their yeomen [5] too.

Cas. Nay, faith, acquaintance, let [30 me tell you, you forgat yourself too much. We had excellent cheer, rare vintage, and were drunk after supper.

Pio. And, when we were in, our woodcocks, sweet rogue, a brace of gulls, dwelling here in the city, came in, and paid all the shot. [6]

Mat. Pox on her! Let her alone.

Bell. O, I pray do, if you be gentlemen;
I pray, depart the house. Beshrew the door [7]   40
For being so easily entreated! Faith,
I lent but little ear unto your talk;
My mind was busied otherwise, in troth,
And so your words did unregarded pass.
Let this suffice—I am not as I was.

Flu. I am not what I was? No, I'll be sworn thou art not, for thou wert honest at five, and now th'art a punk at fifteen. Thou wert yesterday a simple whore, and now th'art a cunning, cony-catching baggage today.   51

Bell. I'll say I'm worse; I pray, forsake me then.
I do desire you leave me, gentlemen,
And leave yourselves. O, be not what you are,
Spendthrifts of soul and body!

[3] Understand.   [6] Reckoning, bill.
[4] Sheriff's officers.   [7] Doorkeeper.
[5] Assistants.

Let me persuade you to forsake all
   harlots,
Worse than the deadliest poisons—they
   are worse,
For o'er their souls hangs an eternal
   curse.
In being slaves to slaves, their labors
   perish;
Th'are seldom blessed with fruit, for,
   ere it blossoms,   60
Many a worm confounds it.
They have no issue but foul, ugly ones,
That run along with them, e'en to their
   graves;
For, stead of children, they breed rank
   diseases,
And all you gallants can bestow on them
Is that French infant, which ne'er acts,
   but speaks.
What shallow son and heir then, foolish
   gallants,
Would waste all his inheritance to pur-
   chase
A filthy, loathed disease, and pawn his
   body
To a dry evil? That usury's worst of all,
When th' int'rest will eat out the princi-
   pal.   71
MAT. [Aside.] 'Sfoot, she gulls 'em the
best! This is always her fashion, when
she would be rid of any company that she
cares not for, to enjoy mine alone.
FLU. What's here? Instructions, ad-
monitions, and caveats? Come out, you
scabbard of vengeance.
MAT. Fluello, spurn your hounds when
they foist[1]— you shall not spurn my punk,
I can tell you; my blood is vexed.   81
FLU. Pox a your blood! Make it a
quarrel.
MAT. Y'are a slave! Will that serve
turn?
OMNES. 'Sblood, hold, hold!
CAS. Matheo, Fluello, for shame, put up!
BELL. O, how many, thus
Moved with a little folly, have let out
Their souls in brothel houses, fell down
   and died   90
Just at their harlot's foot, as 'twere in
   pride!
FLU. Matheo, we shall meet.
MAT. Ay, ay; anywhere saving at church;
pray take heed we meet not there.

[1] Break wind silently.

FLU. Adieu, damnation!
CAS.   Cockatrice, farewell!
PIO. There's more deceit in women than in
   hell.
Exeunt [Castruchio, Fluello, and Pioratto].
   MAT. Ha, ha, thou dost gull 'em so
rarely, so naturally! If I did not think
thou hadst been in earnest! Thou art a
sweet rogue for 't, i' faith.   100
BELL. Why are not you gone too, Signior
   Matheo?
I pray depart my house; you may be-
   lieve me,
In troth, I have no part of harlot in
   me.
MAT. How is this?
BELL. Indeed, I love you not, but hate
   you worse
Than any man, because you were the first
Gave money for my soul. You brake the
   ice,
Which after turned a puddle; I was led
By your temptation to be miserable.
I pray, seek out some other that will
   fall,   110
Or rather, I pray, seek out none at all.
MAT. Is 't possible to be impossible! An
honest whore! I have heard many honest
wenches turn strumpets with a wet finger,
but for a harlot to turn honest is one of
Hercules' labors. It was more easy for
him in one night to make fifty queans[2]
than to make one of them honest again in
fifty years. Come, I hope thou dost but
jest.   120
BELL. 'Tis time to leave off jesting; I
   had almost
Jested away salvation. I shall love you
If you will soon forsake me.
MAT.   God be with thee!
BELL. O, tempt no more women! Shun
   their weighty curse!
Women at best are bad; make them not
   worse.
You gladly seek our sex's overthrow,
But not to raise our states. For all your
   wrongs,
Will you vouchsafe me but due recom-
   pense,
To marry with me?
   MAT. How! Marry with a punk, a [130
cockatrice, a harlot? Marry, foh, I'll be
burnt thorough the nose first.

[2] Whores.

BELL. Why, la, these are your oaths!
You love to undo us,
To put heaven from us, whilst our best
hours waste;
You love to make us lewd, but never
chaste.
MAT. I'll hear no more of this, this ground
upon.
Th'art damned for alt'ring thy religion.
Exit.
BELL. Thy lust and sin speak so much.
Go thou, my ruin,
The first fall my soul took! By my ex-
ample,
I hope few maidens now will put their
heads   140
Under men's girdles; who least trusts is
most wise.
Men's oaths do cast a mist before our
eyes.
My best of wit, be ready! Now I go
By some device to greet Hippolito.

SCENA x.

[*An apartment in Hippolito's house.*]

*Enter a Servant, setting out a table, on which
he places a skull, a picture [of Infelice],
a book, and a taper.*

SER. So, this is Monday morning, and
now must I to my huswif'ry. Would I
had been created a shoemaker, for all the
gentle craft are gentlemen every Monday
by their copy,[1] and scorn then to work one
true stitch. My master means sure to turn
me into a student, for here's my book,
here my desk, here my light, this my close
chamber, and here my punk—so that this
dull, drowsy first day of the week [10
makes me half a priest, half a chandler, half a
painter, half a sexton, ay, and half a bawd;
for all this day my office is to do nothing but
keep the door. To prove it, look you, this
good face and yonder gentleman, so soon as
ever my back is turned, will be naught together.

Enter Hippolito.

HIP. Are all the windows shut?
SER. Close, sir, as the fist of a courtier
that hath stood [2] in three reigns.   20

[1] Membership certificate.
[2] Waited without advancement (?).

HIP. Thou art a faithful servant, and ob-
serv'st
The calendar both of my solemn vows
And ceremonious sorrow. Get thee gone;
I charge thee on thy life, let not the
sound
Of any woman's voice pierce through
that door.
SER. If they do, my lord, I'll pierce some
of them.
What will your lordship have to break-
fast?
HIP. Sighs.
SER. What to dinner?
HIP. Tears.   30
SER. The one of them, my lord, will fill
you too full of wind, the other wet you too
much. What to supper?
HIP. That which now thou canst not
get me, the constancy of a woman.
SER. Indeed, that's harder to come by
than ever was Ostend.[3]
HIP. Prithee, away!
SER. I'll make away myself presently,
which few servants will do for their [40
lords, but rather help to make them away.
Now to my doorkeeping; I hope to pick
something out of it.   *Exit.*
HIP. [*Taking up the picture.*]   My In-
felice's face, her brow, her eye,
The dimple on her cheek! And such
sweet skill
Hath from the cunning workman's
pencil flown,
These lips look fresh and lively as her
own,
Seeming to move and speak. 'Las, now
I see
The reason why fond women love to buy
Adulterate complexion! Here 'tis
read: 50
False colors last after the true be dead.
Of all the roses grafted on her cheeks,
Of all the graces dancing in her eyes,
Of all the music set upon her tongue,
Of all that was past woman's excellence,
In her white bosom—look!—a painted
board
Circumscribes all. Earth can no bliss
afford.
Nothing of her but this? This cannot
speak,

[3] Taken Sept. 8, 1604, after holding out for
more than three years.

It has no lap for me to rest upon,
No lip worth tasting; here the worms
will feed,   60
As in her coffin. Hence, then, idle art!
True love's best pictured in a truelove's
heart.
Here art thou drawn, sweet maid, till
this be dead,
So that thou liv'st twice, twice art buriéd.
Thou figure of my friend, lie there.
What's here?   [*Takes up the skull.*]
Perhaps this shrewd [1] pate was mine
enemy's.
'Las, say it were! I need not fear him
now!
For all his braves,[2] his contumelious
breath,
His frowns, though dagger-pointed, all
his plot,
Though ne'er so mischievous, his Italian
pills,   70
His quarrels, and that common fence,
his law,
See, see, they're all eaten out! Here's
not left one!
How clean they're picked away to the
bare bone!
How mad are mortals, then, to rear
great names
On tops of swelling houses, or to wear out
Their fingers' ends in dirt, to scrape up
gold,
Not caring, so that sumpter horse, the
back,
Be hung with gaudy trappings! With
what coarse,
Yea, rags most beggarly, they clothe the
soul!
Yet, after all, their gayness looks thus
foul.   80
What fools are men to build a garish
tomb,
Only to save the carcass whilst it rots,
To maintain 't long in stinking, make
good carrion,
But leave no good deeds to preserve
them sound!
For good deeds keep men sweet, long
above ground.
And must all come to this? Fools, wise,
all hither?
Must all heads thus at last be laid together?

Draw me my picture then, thou grave
neat workman,
After this fashion, not like this. These
colors   89
In time, kissing but air, will be kissed off;
But here's a fellow—that which he lays
on
Till doomsday alters not complexion.
Death's the best painter then; they that
draw shapes
And live by wicked faces are but God's
apes.
They come but near the life, and there
they stay.
This fellow draws life too; his art is
fuller—
The pictures which he makes are with-
out color.

Enter his Servant.

SER. Here's a person would speak with
you, sir.
HIP. Hah!   100
SER. A parson,[3] sir, would speak with
you.
HIP. Vicar?
SER. Vicar? No, sir; h'as too good a
face to be a vicar yet; a youth, a very
youth.
HIP. What youth? Of man or woman?
Lock the doors.
SER. If it be a woman, maribones and
potato pies [4] keep me from meddling with
her, for the thing has got the breeches! [110
'Tis a male-varlet sure, my lord, for a
woman's tailor ne'er measured him.
HIP. Let him give thee his message and be
gone.
SER. He says he's Signior Matheo's
man, but I know he lies.
HIP. How dost thou know it?
SER. Cause h'as ne'er a beard. 'Tis
his boy, I think, sir, whosoe'er paid for his
nursing.
HIP. Send him and keep the door.   120
[*Exit Servant.*]
(*Reads.*) "*Fata si liceat mihi,*
Fingere arbitrio meo,
Temperem zephyro levi vela." [5]

---

[1] Accursed.   [2] Boasts.

[3] Common pronunciation of *person.*
[4] Marrow bones and potato pies were regarded
as aphrodisiacs.
[5] "If I were permitted to determine my fate
according to my wish, I should regulate my sails
by a light breeze" (Seneca, *Œdipus,* l. 882).

I'd sail, were I to choose, not in the
  ocean;
Cedars are shaken when shrubs do feel no
  bruise.

Enter Bellafront, like a Page [, giving a letter].

How? From Matheo?
BELL.   Yes, my lord.
HIP.   Art sick?
BELL. Not all in health, my lord.
HIP.   Keep off!
BELL.   I do.—
  [*Aside.*] Hard fate when women are com-
    pelled to woo.
HIP. This paper does speak nothing.
BELL.   Yes, my lord,
  Matter of life it speaks, and therefore
    writ   130
  In hidden character; to me instruction
  My master gives, and, less you please to
    stay
  Till you both meet, I can the text dis-
    play.
HIP. Do so; read out.
BELL.   I am already out.[1]
                          [*Discloses herself.*]
  Look on my face, and read the strangest
    story!
HIP. What, villain, ho!

Enter his Servant.

SER. Call you, my lord?
HIP. Thou slave, thou hast let in the
  devil!
SER. Lord bless us, where? He's [140
not cloven, my lord, that I can see; besides, the devil goes more like a gentleman
than a page. Good my lord, *buon coraggio.*[2]
HIP. Thou hast let in a woman in man's
shape. And thou art damned for 't.
SER. Not damned, I hope, for putting
in a woman to a lord.
HIP. Fetch me my rapier!—Do not—I
  shall kill thee!
  Purge this infected chamber of that
    plague
  That runs upon me thus. Slave, thrust
    her hence!   150
SER. Alas, my lord, I shall never be able
to thrust her hence without help. Come,
mermaid, you must to sea again.

---

[1] *I.e.*, out of words.   [2] Good courage.

BELL. Hear me but speak; my words shall
  be all music;
  Hear me but speak.   [*Knocking within.*]
HIP.   Another beats the door;
  Tother she-devil! Look!
SER. Why, then, hell's broke loose. *Exit.*
HIP. Hence; guard the chamber! Let no
  more come on!
  One woman serves for man's damnation.
  Beshrew thee, thou dost make me violate
  The chastest and most sanctimonious
    vow   160
  That e'er was entered in the court of
    heaven!
  I was, on meditation's spotless wings,
  Upon my journey thither; like a storm
  Thou beat'st my ripened cogitations
  Flat to the ground, and like a thief dost
    stand
  To steal devotion from the holy land.
BELL. If woman were thy mother, if thy
    heart
  Be not all marble, or, if 't marble be,
  Let my tears soften it, to pity me.
  I do beseech thee, do not thus with
    scorn   170
  Destroy a woman!
HIP.   Woman, I beseech thee,
  Get thee some other suit; this fits thee
    not.
  I would not grant it to a kneeling queen;
  I cannot love thee, nor I must not. See
                  [*Points to Infelice's picture.*]
  The copy of that obligation,
  Where my soul's bound in heavy pen-
    alties.
BELL. She's dead, you told me; she'll let
  fall her suit.
HIP. My vows to her fled after her to
  heaven.
  Were thine eyes clear as mine, thou
    mightst behold her,   179
  Watching upon yon battlements of stars.
  How I observe them! Should I break
    my bond,
  This board would rive in twain, these
    wooden lips
  Call me most perjured villain. Let it
    suffice,
  I ha' set thee in the path; is't not a sign
  I love thee, when with one so most most
    dear
  I'll have thee fellows? All are fellows
    there.

BELL. Be greater than a king; save not a body,
But from eternal shipwreck keep a soul.
If not, and that again sin's path I tread,
The grief be mine, the guilt fall on thy head! 190
HIP. Stay, and take physic for it. Read this book;
Ask counsel of this head what's to be done.
He'll strike it dead [1] that 'tis damnation
If you turn Turk again. O, do it not!
Though heaven cannot allure you to do well,
From doing ill let hell fright you; and learn this:
The soul whose bosom lust did never touch
Is God's fair bride, and maidens' souls are such;
The soul that, leaving chastity's white shore,
Swims in hot sensual streams, is the devil's whore.— 200
How now, who comes?

Enter his Servant [with a letter].

SER. No more knaves, my lord, that wear smocks! Here's a letter from Doctor Benedict. I would not enter his man, though he had hairs at his mouth, for fear he should be a woman, for some women have beards; marry, they are half witches. 'Slid, you are a sweet youth to wear a codpiece, and have no pins to stick upon 't.
HIP. I'll meet the doctor, tell him; yet tonight 210
I cannot; but at morrow rising sun
I will not fail.—Go, woman; fare thee well.
Exeunt [Hippolito and Servant].
BELL. The lowest fall can be but into hell.
It does not move him. I must therefore fly
From this undoing city, and with tears
Wash off all anger from my father's brow.
He cannot sure but joy, seeing me new born.
A woman honest first, and then turn whore,

[1] *I.e.*, state flatly.

Is, as with me, common to thousands more;
But from a strumpet to turn chaste, that sound 220
Has oft been heard, that woman hardly found. *Exit.*

SCENA xi.[2]

[A street near Candido's shop.]

Enter Fustigo, Crambo, and Poli.

FUS. Hold up your hands, gentlemen. Here's one, two, three. [*Gives money.*] Nay, I warrant they are sound pistoles, and without flaws; I had them of my sister and I know she uses to put [up] nothing that's cracked—four, five, six, seven, eight, and nine. By this hand, bring me but a piece of his blood, and you shall have nine more. I'll lurk in a tavern not far off, and provide supper to close up the end of the [10 tragedy. The linen draper's, remember. Stand to 't, I beseech you, and play your parts perfectly.
CRAM. Look you, signior, 'tis not your gold that we weigh.
FUS. Nay, nay, weigh it and spare not; if it lack one grain of corn, I'll give you a bushel of wheat to make it up.
CRAM. But by your favor, signior, which of the servants is it? Because we'll [20 punish justly.
FUS. Marry, 'tis the head man; you shall taste him by his tongue; a pretty, tall, prating fellow, with a Tuscalonian beard.
POLI. Tuscalonian? Very good.
FUS. God's life, I was ne'er so thrummed since I was a gentleman. My coxcomb was dry-beaten, as if my hair had been hemp.
CRAM. We'll dry-beat some of them.
FUS. Nay, it grew so high that my [30 sister cried out murder, very manfully. I have her consent, in a manner, to have him peppered; else I'll not do 't, to win more than ten cheaters do at a rifling.[3] Break but his pate, or so, only his mazer,[4] because I'll have his head in a cloth as well as mine. He's a linen draper, and may take enough. I could enter mine action of battery against him, but we may perhaps be both dead and rotten before the lawyers would end it. [40
CRAM. No more to do, but ensconce

[2] Original reads *11. SCE.* [4] Mazzard, head
[3] A game with dice.

yourself i' th' tavern. Provide no great cheer—a couple of capons, some pheasants, plovers, an orangeado [1] pie, or so. But how bloody soe'er the day be, sally you not forth.

Fus. No, no; nay, if I stir, somebody shall stink. I'll not budge; I'll lie like a dog in a manger.

Cram. Well, well, to the tavern; let [50 not our supper be raw, for you shall have blood enough, your belly full.

Fus. That's all (so God sa' me) I thirst after: blood for blood, bump for bump, nose for nose, head for head, plaster for plaster. And so farewell. What shall I call your names? Because I'll leave word, if any such come to the bar.

Cram. My name is Corporal Crambo.

Poh. And mine, Lieutenant Poh.   60
                                        Exit.[2]

Cram. Poli is as tall [3] a man as ever opened oyster; I would not be the devil to meet Poh. Farewell.

Fus. Nor I, by this light, if Poh be such a Poli.   *Exeunt.*

[Scena xii.]

Enter Candido's Wife in her shop, and the two Prentices.

Wife. What's a-clock now?

2 Pren.   'Tis almost twelve.

Wife.   That's well.
The Senate will leave wording [4] presently.
But is George ready?

2 Pren.   Yes, forsooth, he's furbished.[5]

Wife. Now, as you ever hope to win my favor,
Throw both your duties and respects on him
With the like awe as if he were your master.
Let not your looks betray it with a smile
Or jeering glance to any customer;
Keep a true settled countenance, and beware
You laugh not, whatsoe'er you hear or see.   10

2 Pren. I warrant you, mistress, let us alone for keeping our countenance; for, if I list, there's never a fool in all Milan shall

make me laugh, let him play the fool never so like an ass, whether it be the fat court fool or the lean city fool.

Wife. Enough then; call down George.

2 Pren.   I hear him coming.

Enter George [in Candido's dress].

Wife. Be ready with your legs [6] then; let me see
How court'sy would become him.—Gallantly!
Beshrew my blood, a proper, seemly man,   20
Of a choice carriage, walks with a good port!

Geo. I thank you, mistress, my back's broad enough, now my master's gown's on.

Wife. Sure, I should think 'twere the least of sin
To mistake the master, and to let him in.

Geo. 'Twere a good *Comedy of Errors* that, i' faith.

2 Pren. Whist, whist! My master!

Enter Candido, and exit presently.

Wife. You all know your tasks.—God's my life,
What's that he has got on 's back? Who can tell?   30

Geo. [*Aside.*] That can I, but I will not.

Wife. Girt about him like a madman! What, has he lost his cloak too? This is the maddest fashion that e'er I saw. What said he, George, when he passed by thee?

Geo. Troth, mistress, nothing! Not so much as a bee, he did not hum; not so much as a bawd, he did not hem; not so much as a cuckold, he did not ha; neither hum, [40 hem, nor ha; only stared me in the face, passed along, and made haste in, as if my looks had wrought with him to give him a stool.

Wife. Sure he's vexed now; this trick has moved his spleen.
He's angered now, because he uttered nothing;
And wordless wrath breaks out more violent.
May be he'll strive for place when he comes down,
But, if thou lov'st me, George, afford him none.

___
[1] Candied orange peel.
[2] Original reads *Exeunt.*
[3] Bold.
[4] Disputing.
[5] Furbished.
[6] Bows.

GEO. Nay, let me alone to play [50 my master's prize,[1] as long as my mistress warrants me. I'm sure I have his best clothes on, and I scorn to give place to any that is inferior in apparel to me; that's an axiom, a principle, and is observed as much as the fashion. Let that persuade you, then, that I'll shoulder with him for the upper hand in the shop as long as this chain [2] will maintain it.

WIFE. Spoke with the spirit of a [60 master, though with the tongue of a prentice.

Enter Candido like a prentice.

Why, how now, madman? What, in your tricksy coats?

CAND. O, peace, good mistress.—

Enter Crambo and Poli.

See, what you lack? What is 't you buy? Pure calicoes, fine hollands, choice cambrics, neat lawns! See what you buy! Pray come near; my master will use you well; he can afford you a pennyworth.

WIFE. Ay, that he can, out of a whole piece of lawn, i' faith. 70

CAND. Pray see your choice here, gentlemen.

WIFE. O fine fool! What a madman, a patient madman! Who ever heard of the like? Well, sir, I'll fit you and your humor presently. What, cross-points? [3] I'll untie 'em all in a trice; I'll vex you, i' faith. Boy, take your cloak; quick, come.
                    Exit [with 1 Prentice].
CAND. Be covered, George! This chain and welted gown
Bare to this coat? Then the world's upside down! 80

GEO. Umh, umh, hum.

CRAM. That's the shop, and there's the fellow.

POH. Ay, but the master is walking in there.

CRAM. No matter, we'll in.

POH. 'Sblood, dost long to lie in limbo?

CRAM. And limbo be in hell, I care not.

CAND. Look you, gentlemen, your choice. Cambrics? 90

[1] A public contest for a master's degree in fencing.
[2] Symbol of office.
[3] Crossed laces by which garments were fastened.

CRAM. No, sir, some shirting.

CAND. You shall.

CRAM. Have you none of this striped canvas for doublets?

CAND. None striped, sir, but plain.

2 PREN. I think there be one piece striped within.

GEO. Step, sirrah, and fetch it.—Hum, hum, hum. 99
[*Exit 2 Prentice and returns with the canvas.*]

CAND. Look you, gentlemen, I'll make but one spreading; here's a piece of cloth, fine yet shall wear like iron. 'Tis without fault; take this upon my word, 'tis without fault.

CRAM. Then 'tis better than you, sirrah.

CAND. Ay, and a number more. O, that each soul
Were but as spotless as this innocent white,
And had as few breaks in it!

CRAM.   'Twould have some then.
There was a fray here last day in this shop.

CAND. There was, indeed, a little flea-biting. 110

POLI. A gentleman had his pate broke; call you that but a flea-biting?

CAND. He had so.

CRAM. Zounds, do you stand to it?
                    He strikes him.

GEO. 'Sfoot, clubs, clubs! Prentices, down with 'em!

[*Enter Prentices, who disarm Crambo and Poli.*]

Ay, you rogues, strike a citizen in 's shop?

CAND. None of you stir, I pray. Forbear, good George.

CRAM. I beseech you, sir, we mistook our marks; deliver us our weapons. 120

GEO. Your head bleeds, sir; cry clubs!

CAND. I say you shall not; pray be patient;
Give them their weapons. Sirs, y'are best be gone;
I tell you here are boys more tough than bears.
Hence, lest more fists do walk about your ears.

BOTH. We thank you, sir.   *Exeunt.*

CAND.   You shall not follow them;
Let them alone, pray. This did me no harm;

Troth, I was cold, and the blow made
  me warm;
I thank 'em for 't.   Besides, I had
  decreed [1]
To have a vein pricked—I did mean to
  bleed,   130
So that there's money saved. They are
  honest men;
Pray use 'em well when they appear
  again.
GEO. Yes, sir, we'll use 'em like honest
men.
CAND. Ay, well said, George, like honest
men, though they be arrant knaves, for
that's the phrase of the city. Help to lay
up these wares.

[*He and the Prentices retire to the back of the
    shop.*] *Enter his Wife with Officers.*

WIFE. Yonder he stands.
[1] OFF.   What, in a prentice's coat?
WIFE. Ay, ay; mad, mad. Pray, take heed.
CAND.   How now,   140
  What news with them? What make they
    with my wife?—
  Officers, is she attached?—Look to your
    wares.
WIFE. He talks to himself. O, he's much
  gone indeed.
[1] OFF. Pray, pluck up a good heart; be
  not so fearful.
  Sirs, hark, we'll gather to him by de-
    grees.
WIFE. Ay, ay, by degrees, I pray. O me!
  What makes he with the lawn in his
    hand?
  He'll tear all the ware in my shop.
[1] OFF. Fear not, we'll catch him on a
  sudden.
WIFE. You had need do so; pray take
  heed of your warrant.   150
[1] OFF. I warrant, mistress. Now, Signior
  Candido.
CAND. Now, sir, what news with you, sir?
WIFE. [*Aside to 1 Officer.*] "What news
  with you?" he says. O, he's far gone!
[1] OFF. [*Aside to Wife.*] I pray, fear
  nothing; let's alone with him.—
  Signior, you look not like yourself, me-
    thinks.—
  Steal you a tother side.—Y'are changed,
    y'are altered.

---

[1] Decided.

CAND. Changed, sir? Why, true, sir. Is
  "changed" strange? 'Tis not
The fashion unless it alter. Monarchs
  turn
To beggars, beggars creep into the
  nests
Of princes, masters serve their prentices,
Ladies their serving-men, men turn to
  women.   161
[1] OFF. And women turn to men.
CAND. Ay, and women turn to men, you
say true. Ha, ha, a mad world, a mad
world.   [*Officers seize him.*]
[1] OFF. Have we caught you, sir?
CAND. Caught me? Well, well, you have
caught me.
WIFE. He laughs in your faces.
GEO. A rescue, prentices! My master's
  catchpolled. [2]   170
[1] OFF. I charge you, keep the peace, or
  have your legs
  Gartered with irons! We have from the
    duke
  A warrant strong enough for what we do.
CAND. I pray, rest quiet; I desire no rescue.
WIFE. La, he desires no rescue! 'Las, poor
  heart,
  He talks against himself.
CAND.   Well, what's the matter?
[1] OFF. [*Binding Candido.*] Look to that
  arm.
  Pray, make sure work; double the cord.
CAND.   Why, why?
WIFE. Look how his head goes. Should he
  get but loose,
  O, 'twere as much as all our lives were
    worth!   180
[1] OFF. Fear not; we'll make all sure for
  our own safety.
CAND. Are you at leisure now?   Well,
  what's the matter?
  Why do I enter into bonds thus, ha?
[1] OFF. Because y'are mad, put fear upon
  your wife.
WIFE. O, ay, I went in danger of my life
every minute.
CAND. What, am I mad, say you, and I
  not know it?
[1] OFF. That proves you mad, because
  you know it not.
WIFE. Pray talk to him as little as you
  can;
  You see he's too far spent.

---

[2] Caught by a bumbailiff.

CAND.   Bound with strong cord!
A sister's [1] thread, i' faith, had been
   enough   191
To lead me anywhere.—Wife, do you
   long?
You are mad too, or else you do me
   wrong.
GEO. But are you mad indeed, master?
CAND.   My wife says so,
And what she says, George, is all truth,
   you know.—
And whither now, to Bethlem Mon-
   astery?
Ha! whither?
[1] OFF.   Faith, e'en to the madmen's pound.
CAND. A God's name! Still I feel my
   patience sound.   Exit [with Officers].
GEO. Come, we'll see whither he goes.
If the master be mad, we are his [200
servants, and must follow his steps; we'll
be madcaps too.   Farewell, mistress; you
shall have us all in Bedlam.
               Exeunt [George and Prentices].
WIFE. I think I have fitted you now, you
   and your clothes.
If this move not his patience, nothing
   can;
I'll swear then I have a saint, and not a
   man.   [Exit.]

SCENA xiii.

[A street near an abbey.]

Enter Duke, Doctor, Fluello, Castruchio,
                            Pioratto.

DUKE. Give us a little leave.
[Exeunt Fluello, Castruchio, and Pioratto.]
                   Doctor, your news.
DOC. I sent for him, my lord. At last he
   came,
And did receive all speech that went
   from me
As gilded pills made to prolong his health.
My credit with him wrought it, for some
   men
Swallow even empty hooks, like fools
   that fear
No drowning where 'tis deepest, cause
   'tis clear.
In th' end we sat and eat; [2] a health I
   drank
To Infelice's sweet, departed soul.

This train [3] I knew would take.
DUKE.   'Twas excellent. 10
Doc. He fell with such devotion on his
   knees
To pledge the same—
DUKE.   Fond, superstitious fool!
Doc. That had he been inflamed with zeal
   of prayer,
He could not pour 't out with more
   reverence.
About my neck he hung, wept on my
   cheek,
Kissed it, and swore he would adore my
   lips,
Because they brought forth Infelice's
   name.
DUKE. Ha, ha! Alack, alack!
Doc. The cup he lifts up high, and thus he
   said,
"Here, noble maid!"—drinks, and was
   poisonéd.   20
DUKE. And died?
DOC.   And died, my lord.
DUKE.   Thou in that word
Hast pieced mine aged hours out with
   more years
Than thou hast taken from Hippolito.
A noble youth he was, but lesser
   branches
Hind'ring the greater's growth must be
   lopped off,
And feed the fire. Doctor, we're now all
   thine,
And use us so; be bold.
DOC.   Thanks, gracious lord.
My honored lord—
DUKE. Hum.
Doc. I do beseech your grace to bury deep
This bloody act of mine.
DUKE.   Nay, nay, for that, 31
Doctor, look you to 't; me it shall not
   move.
They're cursed that ill do, not that ill do
   love.
Doc. You throw an angry forehead on my
   face;
But, be you pleased backward thus far
   to look,
That, for your good, this evil I under-
   took—
DUKE. Ay, ay, we conster so.
Doc. And only for your love.
DUKE.   Confessed; 'tis true.

---

[1] Sewster's, seamstress'.   [2] Preterit.   [3] Device.

Doc. Nor let it stand against me as a bar
To thrust me from your presence; nor
believe, 40
As princes have quick thoughts, that
now, my finger
Being dipped in blood, I will not spare
the hand,
But that for gold—as what can gold not
do?—
I may be hired to work the like on you.
DUKE. Which to prevent—
Doc. 'Tis from my heart as far—
DUKE. No matter, doctor; cause I'll
fearless sleep,
And that you shall stand clear of that
suspicion,
I banish thee forever from my court.
This principle is old, but true as fate:
Kings may love treason, but the traitor
hate. *Exit.*
Doc. Is 't so? Nay then, duke, your stale
principle, 51
With one as stale, the doctor thus shall
quit: [1]
He falls himself that digs another's
pit.—
How now! Where is he? Will he not
meet me?

Enter the Doctor's Man.

Do. MAN. Meet you, sir? He might
have met with three fencers in this time,
and have received less hurt than by meeting one doctor of physic. Why, sir, he has
walked under the old abbey wall yonder
this hour, till he's more cold than a [60
citizen's country house in Janivere. You
may smell him behind, sir. La you, yonder he comes.
Doc. Leave me.

Enter Hippolito.

Do. MAN. Ich lurch,[2] if you will. *Exit.*
Doc. O my most noble friend!
HIP. Few but yourself
Could have enticed me thus to trust
the air
With my close sighs. You sent for me.
What news?
Doc. Come, you must doff this black,
dye that pale cheek

[1] Repay.
[2] Perhaps dialect for *I lurk* (*i.e.*, wait); or
perhaps a misprint for *i' th' lurch.*

Into his own color, go, attire yourself
Fresh as a bridegroom when he meets
his bride. 71
The duke has done much treason to
thy love,
'Tis now revealed; 'tis now to be re-
venged.
Be merry, honored friend. Thy lady
lives.
HIP. What lady?
Doc. Infelice; she's revived.
Revived? Alack, Death never had the
heart
To take breath from her.
HIP. Umh! I thank you, sir;
Physic prolongs life when it cannot
save.
This helps not my hopes; mine are in
their grave.
You do some wrong to mock me.
Doc. By that love
Which I have ever borne you, what I
speak 81
Is truth. The maiden lives; that fun-
eral,
Duke's tears, the mourning, was all
counterfeit.
A sleepy draught cozened the world and
you;
I was his minister, and then chambered
up
To stop discovery.
HIP. O treacherous duke!
Doc. He cannot hope so certainly for
bliss
As he believes that I have poisoned you.
He wooed me to 't; I yielded, and con-
firmed him
In his most bloody thoughts.
HIP. A very devil!
Doc. Her did he closely coach to Ber-
gamo, 91
And thither—
HIP. Will I ride. Stood Bergamo
In the Low Countries of black hell, I'll
to her.
Doc. You shall to her, but not to Bergamo.
How passion makes you fly beyond
yourself!
Much of that weary journey I ha' cut
off,
For she by letters hath intelligence
Of your supposéd death, her own inter-
ment,

And all those plots which that false
duke, her father,
Has wrought against you; and she'll
meet you—
Hip.　　　　　　　　　　O, when? 100
Doc. Nay, see how covetous are your
desires.
Early tomorrow morn.
Hip.　　　　　　O where, good father?
Doc. At Bethlem Monastery. Are you
pleased now?
Hip. At Bethlem Monastery! The place
well fits;
It is the school where those that lose
their wits
Practice again to get them. I am sick
Of that disease; all love is lunatic.
Doc. We'll steal away this night in some
disguise.
Father Anselmo, a most reverend friar,
Expects our coming, before whom we'll
lay　　　　　　　　　　　　　110
Reasons so strong that he shall yield
in bands
Of holy wedlock to tie both your hands.
Hip. This is such happiness
That, to believe it, 'tis impossible.
Doc. Let all your joys then die in mis-
belief;
I will reveal no more.
Hip.　　　　　　　O, yes, good father,
I am so well acquainted with despair
I know not how to hope; I believe all.
Doc. We'll hence this night. Much must
be done, much said;
But, if the doctor fail not in his
charms,　　　　　　　　　　　120
Your lady shall ere morning fill these
arms.
Hip. Heavenly physician! Far thy fame
shall spread,
That mak'st two lovers speak when
they be dead.　　　　　　　Exeunt.

[Scena xiv.

A hall in the Duke's palace.]

Candido's Wife and George; Pioratto meets
them.

Wife. O, watch, good George, watch
which way the duke comes.
Geo. Here comes one of the butterflies; ask him.

Wife. Pray, sir, comes the duke this
way?
Pio. He's upon coming, mistress. Exit.
Wife. I thank you, sir. George, are
there many mad folks where thy master
lies?　　　　　　　　　　　　　10
Geo. O, yes, of all countries some, but
especially mad Greeks—they swarm. Troth,
mistress, the world is altered with you;
you had not wont to stand thus with
a paper "humbly complaining."[1] But
you're well enough served; provender
pricked[2] you, as it does many of our city
wives besides.
Wife. Dost think, George, we shall
get him forth?　　　　　　　　　20
Geo. Truly, mistress, I cannot tell;
I think you'll hardly[3] get him forth. Why,
'tis strange! 'Sfoot, I have known many
women that have had mad rascals to their
husbands, whom they would belabor by
all means possible to keep 'em in their
right wits; but of a woman to long to turn
a tame man into a madman, why, the
devil himself was never used so by his
dam.　　　　　　　　　　　　　30
Wife. How does he talk, George?
Ha! Good George, tell me.
Geo. Why, you're best go see.
Wife. Alas, I am afraid!
Geo. Afraid! You had more need be
ashamed. He may rather be afraid of you.
Wife. But, George, he's not stark mad,
is he? He does not rave; he is not horn-
mad, George, is he?
Geo. Nay, I know not that, but he　[40
talks like a justice of peace, of a thousand
matters, and to no purpose.
Wife. I'll to the monastery. I shall be
mad till I enjoy him; I shall be sick until
I see him; yet, when I do see him, I shall
weep out mine eyes.
Geo. Ay, I'd fain see a woman weep
out her eyes! That's as true as to say a
man's cloak burns, when it hangs in the
water. I know you'll weep, mistress, but　[50
what says the painted cloth?[4]

Trust not a woman when she cries,
For she'll pump water from her eyes
With a wet finger, and in faster showers
Than April when he rains down flowers.

[1] The opening phrase of a petition.　　[2] Urged.
[3] With difficulty.　[4] Hanging with mottoes on it.

WIFE. Ay, but, George, that painted cloth is worthy to be hanged up for lying. All women have not tears at will, unless they have good cause.

GEO. Ay, but, mistress, how easily [60 will they find a cause, and, as one of our cheese trenchers [1] says very learnedly:

As out of wormwood bees suck honey,
As from poor clients lawyers firk [2] money,
As parsley from a roasted cunny [3]—
So, though the day be ne'er so sunny,
If wives will have it rain, down then it drives;
The calmest husbands make the storm[i]est wives.

WIFE. Tame, George; but I ha' done storming now.   70

GEO. Why, that's well done. Good mistress, throw aside this fashion of your humor; be not so fantastical in wearing it; storm no more, long no more. This longing has made you come short of many a good thing that you might have had from my master. Here comes the duke.

Enter Duke, Fluello, Pioratto, Sinezi.

WIFE. O, I beseech you, pardon my offense,
In that I durst abuse your grace's warrant;
Deliver forth my husband, good my lord.   80

DUKE. Who is her husband?

FLU.   Candido, my lord.

DUKE. Where is he?

WIFE.   He's among the lunatics.
He was a man made up without a gall;
Nothing could move him, nothing could convert
His meek blood into fury; yet, like a monster,
I often beat at the most constant rock
Of his unshaken patience, and did long
To vex him.

DUKE.   Did you so?

WIFE.   And for that purpose
Had warrant from your grace to carry him
To Bethlem Monastery, whence they will not free him   90
Without your grace's hand that sent him in.

[1] *I.e.,* inscriptions on cheese trenchers.
[2] Trick.   [3] Cony, rabbit.

DUKE. You have longed fair; 'tis you are mad, I fear.
It's fit to fetch him thence, and keep you there.
If he be mad, why would you have him forth?

GEO. And please your grace, he's not stark mad, but only talks like a young gentleman, somewhat fantastically, that's all. There's a thousand about your court, city, and country madder than he.

DUKE. Provide a warrant; you shall have our hand.   100

GEO. Here's a warrant ready drawn, my lord.

DUKE. Get pen and ink, get pen and ink.   [*Exit George.*]

Enter Castruchio.

CAS. Where is my lord the duke?

DUKE.   How now! More madmen?

CAS. I have strange news, my lord.

DUKE.   Of what? Of whom?

CAS. Of Infelice, and a marriage.

DUKE. Ha! Where? With whom?

CAS.   Hippolito.

[*Enter George, with pen and ink.*]

GEO.   Here, my lord.

DUKE. Hence with that woman! Void the room!

FLU.   Away!
The duke's vexed.

GEO.   Whoop, come, mistress, the duke's mad too.
                     Exeunt [*Wife and George*].

DUKE. Who told me that Hippolito was dead?   109

CAS. He that can make any man dead, the doctor. But, my lord, he's as full of life as wildfire, and as quick. Hippolito, the doctor, and one more rid hence this evening; the inn at which they light is Bethlem Monastery; Infelice comes from Bergamo and meets them there. Hippolito is mad, for he means this day to be married. The afternoon is the hour, and Friar Anselmo is the knitter.

DUKE. From Bergamo? Is 't possible?
It cannot be.   120
It cannot be!

CAS.   I will not swear, my lord,
But this intelligence I took from one
Whose brains work in the plot.

DUKE.   What's he?

CAS.   Matheo.

FLU. Matheo knows all.

PIO.   He's Hippolito's bosom.[1]

DUKE. How far stands Bethlem hence?

OMNES.   Six or seven miles.

DUKE. Is 't so? Not married till the afternoon?

Stay, stay, let's work out some prevention. How?

This is most strange. Can none but
madmen serve

To dress their wedding dinner? All of
you

Get presently to horse, disguise yourselves   130

Like country gentlemen,

Or riding citizens, or so; and take

Each man a several path, but let us
meet

At Bethlem Monastery, some space of
time

Being spent between the arrival each
of other,

As if we came to see the lunatics.

To horse, away! Be secret, on your
lives.

Love must be punished that unjustly
thrives.

                  Exeunt [all but Fluello].

FLU. Be secret, on your lives! Castruchio,

Y'are but a scurvy spaniel. Honest
lord,   140

Good lady! Zounds, their love is just,
'tis good,

And I'll prevent you, though I swim in
blood.   *Exit.*

[SCENA XV.

A room in Bethlem Monastery.]

*Enter Friar Anselmo, Hippolito, Matheo,
Infelice.*

HIP. Nay, nay, resolve,[2] good father, or
deny.

ANS. You press me to an act both full of
danger

And full of happiness; for I behold

Your father's frowns, his threats, nay,
perhaps death

To him that dare do this. Yet, noble
lord,

Such comfortable beams break through
these clouds

By this blessed marriage, that, your honored word

Being pawned in my defense, I will
tie fast

The holy wedding knot.

HIP.   Tush, fear not the duke.

ANS. O son, wisely to fear is to be free
from fear.   10

HIP. You have our words, and you shall
have our lives,

To guard you safe from all ensuing
danger.

MAT. Ay, ay, chop 'em up, and away.

ANS. Stay! When is 't fit for me, and
safest for you,

To entertain this business?

HIP.   Not till the evening.

ANS. Be it so. There is a chapel stands
hard by,

Upon the west end of the abbey wall;

Thither convey yourselves, and, when
the sun

Hath turned his back upon this upper
world,

I'll marry you; that done, no thund'ring
voice   20

Can break the sacred bond. Yet, lady,
here

You are most safe.

INF.   Father, your love's most dear.

MAT. Ay, well said; lock us into some
little room by ourselves, that we may be
mad for an hour or two.

HIP. O, good Matheo, no; let's make no
noise.

MAT. How! No noise! Do you know
where you are? 'Sfoot, amongst all the
madcaps in Milan; so that to throw the
house out at window will be the better, [30
and no man will suspect that we lurk here
to steal mutton.[3] The more sober we are,
the more scurvy 'tis. And, though the
friar tell us that here we are safest, I am
not of his mind; for, if those lay here that
had lost their money, none would ever look
after them; but here are none but those
that have lost their wits, so that if hue
and cry be made, hither they'll come. And
my reason is, because none goes to be [40
married till he be stark mad.

HIP. Muffle yourselves; yonder's Fluello.

---

[1] Bosom friend.   [2] Agree.   [3] *I.e.*, a wench.

Enter Fluello.

MAT.   Zounds!

FLU. O my lord, these cloaks are not
for this rain. The tempest is too great. I
come sweating to tell you of it, that you
may get out of it.

MAT. Why, what's the matter?

FLU. What's the matter? You have mat-
tered it fair; the duke's at hand.   49

OMNES. The duke?

FLU.   The very duke.

HIP.   Then all our plots
Are turned upon our heads and we're
    blown up
With our own underminings. 'Sfoot,
    how comes he?
What villain durst betray our being
    here?

FLU. Castruchio told the duke, and
Matheo here told Castruchio.

HIP. Would you betray me to Castruchio?

MAT. 'Sfoot, he damned himself to the
pit of hell, if he spake on 't again.

HIP. So did you swear to me; so were you
    damned.   59

MAT. Pox on 'em, and there be no
faith in men, if a man shall not believe
oaths. He took bread and salt,[1] by this
light, that he would never open his lips.

HIP. O God, O God!

ANS.   Son, be not desperate;
Have patience. You shall trip your
    enemy
Down by his own sleights. How far is
    the duke hence?

FLU. He's but new set out. Castruchio,
Pioratto, and Sinezi come along with him.
You have time enough yet to prevent[2]
them, if you have but courage.   70

ANS. Ye shall steal secretly into the
    chapel,
And presently be married. If the duke
Abide here still, spite of ten thousand
    eyes,
You shall scape hence like friars.

HIP. O blessed disguise! O happy man!

ANS. Talk not of Happiness till your
    closed hand
Have her by th' forehead, like the lock
    of Time.
Be nor too slow, nor hasty, now you
    climb

Up to the tower of bliss; only be wary
And patient, that's all. If you like my
    plot,   80
Build and despatch; if not, farewell;
    then not.

HIP. O, yes, we do applaud it! We'll dis-
    pute
No longer, but will hence and execute.
Fluello, you'll stay here; let us be gone.
The ground that frighted lovers tread
    upon
Is stuck with thorns.

ANS.   Come, then away, 'tis meet,
Exeunt [Anselmo, Hippolito, and Infelice.]
To escape those thorns, to put on wingéd
    feet.

MAT. No words, I pray, Fluello, for
it stands us upon.[3]

FLU. O, sir, let that be your lesson!   90
                                [*Exit Matheo.*]
Alas, poor lovers! On what hopes and
    fears
Men toss themselves for women! When
    she's got,
The best has in her that which pleaseth
    not.

*Enter to Fluello, the Duke, Castruchio,
    Pioratto, and Sinezi from several doors,
                                    muffled.*

DUKE. Who's there?

CAS.   My lord—

DUKE.   Peace;
    send that "lord" away.
A lordship will spoil all; let's be all
    fellows.
What's he?

CAS. Fluello, or else Sinezi, by his little
legs.

OMNES. All friends, all friends.

DUKE. What? Met upon the very point
    of time?   100
Is this the place?

PIO.   This is the place, my lord.

DUKE. Dream you on lordships? Come
    no more "lords," I pray.
You have not seen these lovers yet?

OMNES.   Not yet.

DUKE. Castruchio, art thou sure this
    wedding feat
Is not till afternoon?

CAS.   So it is given out, my lord.

---

[1] To seal the oath.   [2] Anticipate.

DUKE. Nay, nay, 'tis like. Thieves must observe their hours;

Lovers watch minutes like astronomers.

How shall the interim hours by us be spent?

FLU. Let's all go see the madmen.

OMNES.   Mass, content.   109

Enter Towne [1] *like a sweeper.*

DUKE. O, here comes one.   Question him, question him.

FLU. Now, honest fellow, dost thou belong to the house?

TOWNE. Yes, forsooth, I am one of the implements; I sweep the madmen's rooms, and fetch straw for 'em, and buy chains to tie 'em, and rods to whip 'em. I was a mad wag myself here once, but, I thank Father Anselmo, he lashed me into my right mind again.   120

DUKE. Anselmo is the friar must marry them;

Question him where he is.

CAS. And where is Father Anselmo now?

TOWNE. Marry, he's gone but e'en now.

DUKE. Ay, well done. Tell me, whither is he gone?

TOWNE. Why, to God A'mighty.

FLU. Ha, ha! This fellow's a fool, talks idly.

PIO. Sirrah, are all the mad folks in Milan brought hither?   130

TOWNE. How, all? There's a question indeed! Why, if all the mad folks in Milan should come hither, there would not be left ten men in the city.

DUKE. Few gentlemen or courtiers here, ha?

TOWNE. O, yes, abundance, abundance. Lands no sooner fall into their hands, but straight they run out a their wits. Citizens' sons and heirs are free of the [140 house by their fathers' copy. Farmers' sons come hither like geese, in flocks, and, when they ha' sold all their cornfields, here they sit and pick the straws.

SIN. Methinks you should have women here as well as men.

TOWNE. O, ay, a plague on 'em, there's no "ho!"[2] with 'em; they're madder than March hares.   149

FLU. Are there no lawyers amongst you?

TOWNE. O, no, not one; never any lawyer. We dare not let a lawyer come in, for he'll make 'em mad faster than we can recover 'em.

DUKE. And how long is 't ere you recover any of these?

TOWNE. Why, according to the quantity of the moon [3] that's got into 'em. An alderman's son will be mad a great [160 while, a very great while, especially if his friends left him well. A whore will hardly come to her wits again. A Puritan, there's no hope of him, unless he may pull down the steeple, and hang himself i' th' bell ropes.

FLU. I perceive all sorts of fish come to your net.

TOWNE. Yes, in truth, we have blocks for all heads. We have good store of wild oats here; for the courtier is mad [170 at the citizen, the citizen is mad at the countryman; the shoemaker is mad at the cobbler, the cobbler at the carman; [4] the punk is mad that the merchant's wife is no whore, the merchant's wife is mad that the punk is so common a whore. Godso, here's Father Anselmo; pray, say nothing that I tell tales out of the school.   *Exit.*

Enter Anselmo [5] [*and Servants*].

OMNES. God bless you, father.

ANS.   I thank you, gentlemen.

CAS. Pray, may we see some of those wretched souls   180

That here are in your keeping?

ANS.   Yes, you shall;

But, gentlemen, I must disarm you then.

There are of mad men, as there are of tame,

All humored not alike. We have here some

So apish and fantastic, play with a feather,

And, though 'twould grieve a soul to see God's image

So blemished and defaced, yet do they act

Such antic and such pretty lunacies,

<hr>

[1] Thomas Towne, the name of the actor who took the part.   [2] A cry commanding to stop.

[3] Alluding to the superstition that the moon's rays made lunatics.

[4] Carter.

[5] This direction appears after line 180 in the original.

That spite of sorrow they will make
you smile; 189
Others again we have like hungry lions,
Fierce as wild bulls, untamable as flies,
And these have oftentimes from stran-
gers' sides
Snatched rapiers suddenly, and done
much harm,
Whom if you'll see, you must be weapon-
less.

OMNES. With all our hearts.

[*They give Anselmo their weapons.*]

ANS.   Here, take these weapons in.—

[*Exit Servant with weapons.*]

Stand off a little, pray; so, so, 'tis well.
I'll show you here a man that was some-
times
A very grave and wealthy citizen,
Has served a prenticeship to this mis-
fortune,
Been here seven years, and dwelt in
Bergamo. 200

DUKE. How fell he from his wits?

ANS.   By loss at sea.
I'll stand aside; question him you alone,
For, if he spy me, he'll not speak a word,
Unless he's throughly vexed.

Discovers an Old Man, wrapped in a net.

FLU.   Alas, poor soul!

CAS. A very old man.

DUKE. God speed, father!

1 MAD. God speed the plow; thou
shalt not speed me.

PIO. We see you, old man, for all you
dance in a net. 210

1 MAD. True, but thou wilt dance in
a halter, and I shall not see thee.

ANS. O, do not vex him, pray.

CAS. Are you a fisherman, father?

1 MAD. No, I am neither fish nor flesh.

FLU. What do you with that net then?

1 MAD. Dost not see, fool? There's a
fresh salmon in 't. If you step one foot
furder, you'll be over shoes, for you see I'm
over head and ears in the salt water; [220
and, if you fall into this whirlpool where
I am, y'are drowned—y'are a drowned
rat. I am fishing here for five ships, but
I cannot have a good draught, for my net
breaks still,[1] and breaks; but I'll break
some of your necks and I catch you in my
clutches. Stay, stay, stay, stay, stay,
where's the wind? Where's the wind?

[1] Always.

Where's the wind? Where's the wind? Out,
you gulls, you goosecaps,[2] you gud- [230
geon-eaters![3] Do you look for the wind in
the heavens? Ha, ha, ha, ha! No, no!
Look there, look there, look there! The
wind is always at that door; hark how it
blows, puff, puff, puff!

OMNES. Ha, ha, ha!

1 MAD. Do you laugh at God's creatures? Do you mock old age, you rogues?
Is this gray beard and head counterfeit
that you cry, "Ha, ha, ha"? Sirrah, [240
art not thou my eldest son?

PIO. Yes, indeed, father.

1 MAD. Then th'art a fool, for my eldest son had a polt foot,[4] crooked legs, a
verjuice face, and a pear-colored beard.
I made him a scholar, and he made himself a fool.—Sirrah, thou there, hold out
thy hand!

DUKE. My hand? Well, here 'tis. 249

1 MAD. Look, look, look, look! Has
he not long nails and short hair?

FLU. Yes, monstrous short hair, and
abominable long nails.

1 MAD. Tenpenny nails, are they not?

FLU. Yes, tenpenny nails.

1 MAD. Such nails had my second boy.
Kneel down, thou varlet, and ask thy father
blessing. Such nails had my middlemost
son, and I made him a promoter;[5] and
he scraped, and scraped, and scraped, [260
till he got the devil and all; but he scraped
thus, and thus, and thus, and it went
under his legs, till at length a company
of kites, taking him for carrion, swept up
all, all, all, all, all, all, all. If you love
your lives, look to yourselves! See, see, see,
see, the Turks' galleys are fighting with
my ships! "Bounce," goes the guns.
"Oooh!" cry the men. "Rumble, rumble,"
go the waters. Alas, there, 'tis sunk, [270
'tis sunk! I am undone, I am undone! You
are the damned pirates have undone me.
You are, by the Lord, you are, you are!
Stop 'em! You are!

ANS. Why, how now, sirrah! Must I fall
to tame you?

1 MAD. Tame me! No, I'll be madder
than a roasted cat. See, see, I am burnt
with gunpowder. These are our close
fights! 280

[2] Boobies.   [4] Club foot.
[3] Simpletons.   [5] Informer.

Ans. I'll whip you if you grow unruly thus.

1 Mad. Whip me? Out, you toad! Whip me? What justice is this, to whip me because I am a beggar? Alas, I am a poor man, a very poor man! I am starved, and have had no meat, by this light, ever since the great flood; I am a poor man.

Ans. Well, well, be quiet, and you shall have meat.   290

1 Mad. Ay, ay, pray do; for, look you, here be my guts. These are my ribs—you may look through my ribs—see how my guts come out! These are my red guts, my very guts, O, O!

Ans. Take him in there.
                    [Servants take 1 Madman in.]
Omnes. A very piteous sight.

Cas. Father, I see you have a busy charge.

Ans. They must be used like children, pleased with toys,   300
And anon whipped for their unruliness.
I'll show you now a pair quite different
From him that's gone. He was all words;
        and these,
Unless you urge 'em, seldom spend their speech,
But save their tongues. [Discovers 2 and
        3 Madmen.] La you, this hithermost
Fell from the happy quietness of mind
About a maiden that he loved, and died.
He followed her to church, being full
        of tears,
And, as her body went into the ground,
He fell stark mad. This is a married
        man   310
Was jealous of a fair, but, as some say,
A very virtuous wife; and that spoiled him.

2 Mad. All these are whoremongers, and lay with my wife! Whore, whore, whore, whore, whore!

Flu. Observe him.

2 Mad. Gaffer shoemaker, you pulled on my wife's pumps, and then crept into her pantofles.[1] Lie there, lie there!—This was her tailor. You cut out her loose- [320 bodied gown, and put in a yard more than I allowed her. Lie there by the shoe-maker.—O Master Doctor, are you here? You gave me a purgation, and then crept

into my wife's chamber to feel her pulses, and you said, and she said, and her maid said, that they went pit-a-pat, pit-a-pat, pit-a-pat. Doctor, I'll put you anon [328 into my wife's urinal.—Heigh, come aloft, Jack![2] This was her schoolmaster, and taught her to play upon the virginals,[3] and still his jacks[4] leapt up, up. You pricked[5] her out nothing but bawdy les-sons, but I'll prick you all, fiddler—doc-tor—tailor—shoemaker—shoemaker—fid-dler—doctor—tailor! So, lie with my wife again, now!

Cas. See how he notes the other, now[6] he feeds.

2 Mad. Give me some porridge.   340
3 Mad. I'll give thee none.
2 Mad. Give me some porridge.
3 Mad. I'll not give thee a bit.
2 Mad. Give me that flapdragon.[7]
3 Mad. I'll not give thee a spoonful. Thou liest; it's no dragon—'tis a par-rot that I bought for my sweetheart, and I'll keep it.
2 Mad. Here's an almond for parrot.[8]
3 Mad. Hang thyself!   350
2 Mad. Here's a rope for parrot.[8]
3 Mad. Eat it, for I'll eat this.
2 Mad. I'll shoot at thee, and thou 't give me none.
3 Mad. Woot thou?
2 Mad. I'll run a tilt at thee, and thou 't give me none.
3 Mad. Woot thou? Do, and thou dar'st.
2 Mad. Bounce!   [Strikes him.]   360
3 Mad. O, O! I am slain! Murder, murder, murder! I am slain; my brains are beaten out.
Ans. How now, you villains! Bring me whips; I'll whip you.
3 Mad. I am dead! I am slain! Ring out the bell, for I am dead.
Duke. How will you do now, sirrah? You ha' killed him.   368
2 Mad. I'll answer 't at sessions. He was eating of almond butter, and I longed

[1] Slippers.

[2] Command to a performing monkey.
[3] Musical instrument with keys.
[4] Devices which plucked the strings of the virginals.
[5] Wrote in musical notes.
[6] Now that.
[7] A tidbit in a flaming cup of liquor.
[8] Proverbial phrase of uncertain meaning.

for 't.   The child had never been delivered out of my belly, if I had not killed
him. I'll answer 't at sessions, so my wife
may be burnt i' th' hand,[1] too.

ANS. Take 'em in both. Bury him, for
he's dead.

3 MAD. Indeed, I am dead; put me,
I pray, into a good pit-hole.

2 MAD. I'll answer 't at sessions.   379

Exeunt [Servants with 2 and 3 Madmen].

Enter Bellafront mad.

ANS. How now, huswife, whither gad
you?

BELL. A-nutting, forsooth.   How do
you, gaffer? How do you, gaffer? There's
a French curtsy for you, too.

FLU. 'Tis Bellafront!

PIO. 'Tis the punk, by th' Lord!

DUKE. Father, what's she, I pray?

ANS.   As yet I know not.
She came in but this day, talks little
    idly,
And therefore has the freedom of the
    house.   389

BELL. Do not you know me?—nor
you?—nor you?—nor you?

OMNES. No, indeed.

BELL. Then you are an ass—and you
an ass—and you are an ass—for I know
you.

ANS. Why, what are they?   Come,
tell me, what are they?

BELL. They're fishwives. Will you buy
any gudgeons? God's santy![2] Yonder
come friars; I know them too.—How   [400
do you, friar?

*Enter Hippolito, Matheo, and Infelice dis-
        guised in the habits of friars.*

ANS. Nay, nay, away, you must not
    trouble friars.—
[*Aside to Hippolito, etc.*] The duke is
here; speak nothing.

BELL. Nay, indeed, you shall not go.
We'll run at barleybreak first, and you
shall be in hell.[3]

MAT. [*Aside.*] My punk turned mad
whore, as all her fellows are?

HIP. [*Aside.*] Say nothing, but steal hence,
    when you spy time.   410

ANS. I'll lock you up, if y'are unruly. Fie!

BELL. Fie! Marry, so! They shall not
go indeed, till I ha' told 'em their fortunes.

DUKE. Good father, give her leave.

BELL. Ay, pray, good father, and I'll
give you my blessing.

ANS. Well then, be brief, but, if you are
    thus unruly,
I'll have you locked up fast.

PIO.   Come, to their fortunes.   419

BELL. Let me see: one, two, three, and
four. I'll begin with the little friar [4] first.
Here's a fine hand, indeed! I never saw
friar have such a dainty hand. Here's a
hand for a lady! Here's your fortune:—
    You love a friar better than a nun;
    Yet long you'll love no friar, nor no
        friar's son.
    Bow a little; the line of life is out; yet
        I am afraid,
    For all y'are holy, you'll not die a maid.
    God give you joy!—Now to you, Friar
        Tuck.

MAT. God send me good luck!   430

BELL. You love one, and one loves you;
    You are a false knave, and she's a Jew.
    Here is a dial that false ever goes—

MAT. O, your wit drops!

BELL.   Troth, so does your nose.—
[*To Hippolito.*] Nay, let's shake hands
with you too. Pray open. Here's a fine
hand!
    Ho, friar, ho! God be here!   438
    So he had need. You'll keep good cheer,
    Here's a free table,[5] but a frozen breast,
    For you'll starve those that love you
        best;
    Yet you have good fortune, for, if I am
        no liar,
    Then you are no friar, nor you, nor you
        no friar!
    Ha, ha, ha, ha!   *Discovers them.*

DUKE. Are holy habits cloaks for villainy?
Draw all your weapons!

HIP.   Do; draw all your weapons.

DUKE. Where are your weapons? Draw!

OMNES. The friar has gulled us of 'em.

---

[1] Punishment for adultery.
[2] Sanctity.
[3] Name of the middle compartment in the
game of barleybreak.

[4] *I.e.*, Infelice.
[5] A quibble on a term in palmistry for a section of the hand.

MAT.   O rare trick!
You ha' learned one mad point of arith-
metic.
HIP. Why swells your spleen so high?
Against what bosom   450
Would you your weapons draw? Hers?
'Tis your daughter's.
Mine? 'Tis your son's.
DUKE.   Son?
MAT.   Son, by yonder sun.
HIP. You cannot shed blood here but 'tis
your own;
To spill your own blood were damnation.
Lay smooth that wrinkled brow, and
I will throw
Myself beneath your feet.
Let it be rugged still and flinted ore,
What can come forth but sparkles, that
will burn
Yourself and us? She's mine; my claim's
most good;
She's mine by marriage, though she's
yours by blood.   460
[ANS. (Kneeling.)] I have a hand, dear
lord, deep in this act,
For I foresaw this storm, yet willingly
Put forth to meet it. Oft have I seen a
father
Washing the wounds of his dear son in
tears,
A son to curse the sword that struck his
father,
Both slain i' th' quarrel of your fami-
lies.
Those scars are now ta'en off, and I
beseech you
To seal our pardon! All was to this end,
To turn the ancient hates of your two
houses
To fresh green friendship, that your
loves might look   470
Like the Spring's forehead, comfortably
sweet,
And your vexed souls in peaceful union
meet.
Their blood will now be yours, yours
will be theirs,
And happiness shall crown your silver
hairs.
FLU. You see, my lord, there's now no
remedy.
OMNES. Beseech your lordship!
DUKE. You beseech fair; you have me in
place fit

To bridle me.—Rise, friar. You may be
glad
You can make madmen tame, and tame
men mad.
Since Fate hath conquered, I must rest
content;   480
To strive now would but add new pun-
ishment.
I yield unto your happiness; be blessed.
Our families shall henceforth breathe in
rest.
OMNES. O, happy change!
DUKE.   Yours now is my content;
I throw upon your joys my full consent.
BELL. Am not I a good girl, for find-
ing "the friar in the well"?[1] Godso, you
are a brave man! Will not you buy me some
sugarplums, because I am so good a fortune
teller?   490
DUKE. Would thou hadst wit, thou pretty
soul, to ask,
As I have will to give.
BELL. Pretty soul? A pretty soul is
better than a pretty body. Do not you
know my pretty soul? I know you. Is not
your name Matheo?
MAT. Yes, lamb.   497
BELL. Baa, lamb! There you lie, for
I am mutton.—Look, fine man! He was
mad for me once, and I was mad for him
once, and he was mad for her once, and
were you never mad? Yes, I warrant. I had
a fine jewel once, a very fine jewel, and
that naughty man stole it away from me—
a very fine and a rich jewel.
DUKE. What jewel, pretty maid?
BELL. Maid? Nay, that's a lie. O,
'twas a very rich jewel, called a maiden-
head, and had not you it, leerer?   509
MAT. Out, you mad ass! Away!
DUKE.   Had he thy maidenhead?
He shall make thee amends, and marry
thee.
BELL. Shall he? O brave Arthur of
Bradley [2] then!
DUKE. And, if he bear the mind of a
gentleman, I know he will.
MAT. I think I rifled her of some such
paltry jewel.
DUKE. Did you? Then marry her; you
see the wrong
Has led her spirits into a lunacy.   519

[1] The name of a popular ballad.
[2] The opening of a well-known ballad.

MAT. How? Marry her, my lord?
'Sfoot, marry a madwoman? Let a man
get the tamest wife he can come by, she'll
be mad enough afterward, do what he
can.

DUKE. Nay, then, Father Anselmo here
　shall do his best
To bring her to her wits. And will you
　then?

MAT. I cannot tell; I may choose.

DUKE. Nay, then, law shall compel. I
　tell you, sir,
So much her hard fate moves me, you
　should not breathe　　　　　529
Under this air unless you married her.

MAT. Well, then, when her wits stand
　in their right place,
I'll marry her.

BELL. I thank your grace.—Matheo, thou
　art mine.—
[To Hippolito.] I am not mad, but put
　on this disguise,
Only for you, my lord; for you can tell
Much wonder of me; but you are gone.
　Farewell.—
Matheo, thou didst first turn my soul
　black;
Now make it white again. I do pro-
　test,
I'm pure as fire now, chaste as Cynthia's
　breast.

HIP. I durst be sworn, Matheo, she's in-
　deed.　　　　　540

MAT. Cony-catched, gulled! Must I sail
　in your flyboat
Because I helped to rear your main-
　mast first?
Plague found [1] you for 't, 'tis well.
The cuckold's stamp goes current in
　all nations.
Some men ha' horns giv'n them at their
　creations;
If I be one of those, why so. 'Tis better
To take a common wench, and make
　her good,
Than one that simpers, and at first will
　scarce
Be tempted forth over the threshold
　door,
Yet in one sennight, zounds, turns ar-
　rant whore.　　　　　550
Come, wench, thou shalt be mine. Give
　me thy golls;

[1] Confound.

We'll talk of legs hereafter.—See, my
　lord,
God give us joy!

OMNES. God give you joy!

Enter Candido's Wife and George.

GEO. Come, mistress, we are in Bedlam
now. Mass, and see, we come in pudding
time,[2] for here's the duke.

WIFE. My husband, good my lord!

DUKE. Have I thy husband?　　　　　559

CAS. It's Candido, my lord; he's here
among the lunatics. Father Anselmo, pray
fetch him forth. [*Exit Anselmo.*] This mad
woman is his wife, and, though she were
not with child, yet did she long most spitefully to have her husband mad; and, because she would be sure he should turn
Jew, she placed him here in Bethlem.
Yonder he comes.

Enter Candido with Anselmo.

DUKE. Come hither, signior. Are you
mad?　　　　　570

CAND. You are not mad.

DUKE. Why, I know that.

CAND. Then may you know I am not mad,
　that know
You are not mad, and that you are the
　duke.
None is mad here but one.—How do
　you, wife?
What do you long for now?—Pardon,
　my lord.
She had lost her child's nose else. I did
　cut out
Pennyworths of lawn; the lawn was yet
　mine own.
A carpet was my gown, yet 'twas mine
　own.
I wore my man's coat, yet the cloth
　mine own;　　　　　580
Had a cracked crown, the crown was
　yet mine own.
She says for this I'm mad. Were her
　words true,
I should be mad indeed. O foolish skill![3]
Is patience madness? I'll be a madman
　still.

WIFE. [*Kneeling.*] Forgive me, and I'll
　vex your spirit no more.

[2] In good time.
[3] Reason.

DUKE. Come, come, we'll have you
    friends; join hearts, join hands.
CAND. See, my lord, we are even.—
    Nay, rise, for ill deeds kneel unto none
    but heaven.
DUKE. Signior, methinks patience has
    laid on you
    Such heavy weight that you should
    loathe it—
CAND.   Loathe it?   590
DUKE. For he whose breast is tender,
    blood so cool,
    That no wrongs heat it, is a patient fool.
    What comfort do you find in being so
    calm?
CAND. That which green wounds receive
    from sovereign balm.
    Patience, my lord? Why, 'tis the soul
    of peace;
    Of all the virtues, 'tis near'st kin to
    heaven;
    It makes men look like gods. The best
    of men
    That e'er wore earth about him was a
    sufferer,
    A soft, meek, patient, humble, tranquil
    spirit,
    The first true gentleman that ever
    breathed.   600
    The stock of patience then cannot be
    poor;
    All it desires, it has; what monarch
    more?
    It is the greatest enemy to law
    That can be, for it doth embrace all
    wrongs,

And so chains up lawyers' and women's
    tongues.
'Tis the perpetual prisoner's liberty,
His walks and orchards. 'Tis the bond-
    slave's freedom,
And makes him seem proud of each iron
    chain,
As though he wore it more for state
    than pain.   609
It is the beggars' music, and thus sings,
Although their bodies beg, their souls
    are kings.
O my dread liege, It is the sap of bliss
Rears us aloft, makes men and angels
    kiss.
And last of all, to end a household
    strife,
It is the honey gainst a waspish wife.
DUKE. Thou giv'st it lively colors. Who
    dare say
    He's mad, whose words march in so good
    array?
    'Twere sin all women should such hus-
    bands have,
    For every man must then be his wife's
    slave.
    Come, therefore, you shall teach our
    court to shine;   620
    So calm a spirit is worth a golden
    mine.
    Wives with meek husbands that to vex
    them long,
    In Bedlam must they dwell, else dwell
    they wrong.   *Exeunt.*

FINIS.

THOMAS HEYWOOD

Thomas Heywood, who, though not a genius, at times achieved dramatic work of the finest quality, was for more than forty years an industrious literary journeyman, willing for profit to turn his hand to any respectable job. Born in Lincolnshire about 1573 or 1574 into the family of a country parson who in descent and education seems to have been considerably above his station, Heywood had some pretensions to gentility. He studied at Cambridge and took an active interest in the many dramatic productions there. About 1594 he went to London, and soon afterward his name began to appear in Henslowe's Diary as playwright and actor. By 1598 he had won sufficient distinction to be listed by Meres in *Palladis Tamia* as among the "best for comedy" in England. He wrote and acted at first chiefly for the Admiral's Company and afterwards for Worcester's, which continued as Queen Anne's from 1603 until her death in 1619. In some of his work he collaborated with Wentworth Smith, Chettle, Dekker, Webster, or others. The average pay for an original play was about six pounds—a sum, however, which had in the Elizabethan period several times its present value—and this was sometimes shared with collaborators. Yet Heywood's productivity enabled him to support a wife and several children apparently in some comfort. In 1633 he stated that he had had "either an entire hand or at the least a main finger" in some two hundred and twenty plays. Of these probably not thirty survive. The dramatic work of his later years seems to have been confined to a series of lord mayors' pageants from 1631 to 1639 and the printing of plays that had been written by himself and others, usually long before. Besides *An Apology for Actors* (1612), his non-dramatic works include an epic on London, a history of Elizabeth's early life, and, in his later years, various semi-learned compilations. He died in 1641.

Heywood's university training may have led him to write plays drawn from classical sources, chiefly mythological, as in his series *The Four Ages*, in *The Rape of Lucrece*, and in *Love's Mistress*. The largest part of his extant work, however, and the best, depicts phases of English life, all classes being presented with unusual insight and sympathy. Even his stories from foreign sources, as in the Plautine plot of *The Captives*, are used for the portrayal of English characters. The outburst of national self-glorification that followed the defeat of the Armada is fully reflected in his plays. In one or the other of the double plots common in them, place is frequently found for one or more characters who illustrate the sterling qualities of the yeoman or the citizen—his patriotism, sturdy independence, thrift, generosity. The extreme example is the glorification of the apprentice in *The Four Prentices of London* (an adaptation of the story of Godfrey of Boulogne), which was satirized in *The Knight of the Burning Pestle*. There is the same emphasis, however, in the two chronicle plays, each in two parts—*Edward IV* (printed in 1599) and *If You Know Not Me, You Know Nobody* (printed in 1605 and 1606), which deals with the life of Queen Elizabeth, especially the early part. Romantic tales of English adventure on sea or in far lands are found in *Fortune by Land and Sea*, written with William Rowley, *A Challenge for Beauty*, and *The Fair Maid of the West*, in two parts. *The Fair Maid of the Exchange* and *The Wise Woman of Hogsdon* are more realistic studies of London life. Heywood's most sympathetic vein, however, is found in plays portraying the gentry, as in his *Royal King and Loyal Subject*. Two of these dealing with rural England are *A Woman Killed with Kindness* and *The English Traveler*, both domestic plays written in the restrained style considered appropriate for the type.

A Woman Killed with Kindness, Heywood's undoubted masterpiece, was begun, and probably acted, in 1603 for Henslowe, who squandered thirty-five shillings more on

Mistress Frankford's black velvet gown than he paid for the play. Printed in 1607, it was the first of Heywood's extant plays to carry his name on the title-page. A third edition is dated 1617, but no copy of the second is known. Heywood may have taken from life the basis of his main plot, with its thoroughly English tone, but it has been suggested that he reworked a story one form of which was translated from the *Heptameron* in Painter's *Palace of Pleasure*. The subplot comes from a novella of Illicini, which was translated into English by Fenton in his *Tragical Discourses* as well as by Painter, but the characters are as typically English as is the rest of the play. The basis of the present edition is the reproduction of the text of 1617 by Katherine Lee Bates in the Belles-Lettres Series.

A WOMAN KILLED WITH KINDNESS [1]

BY

THOMAS HEYWOOD

[*DRAMATIS PERSONÆ*

SIR FRANCIS ACTON, *brother to Mistress
Frankford.*
SIR CHARLES MOUNTFORD.
MASTER JOHN FRANKFORD.
MASTER MALBY, *friend to Sir Francis.*
MASTER WENDOLL, *friend to Frankford.*
MASTER CRANWELL.
MASTER SHAFTON, *false friend to Sir
Charles.*
OLD MOUNTFORD, *uncle to Sir Charles.*
MASTER SANDY, *former friend to Sir Charles.*
MASTER RODER, *former tenant to Sir
Charles.*
MASTER TIDY, *cousin to Sir Charles.*
NICHOLAS ⎱ *household servants to*
JENKIN ⎰ *Frankford.*
SPIGOT

ROGER BRICKBAT ⎱ *country fellows.*
JACK SLIME ⎰
SHERIFF.
KEEPER OF PRISON.
SHERIFF'S OFFICERS, SERJEANT, HUNTS-
MEN, FALCONERS, COACHMEN, CARTERS,
SERVANTS, MUSICIANS.
FRANKFORD'S CHILDREN.

MISTRESS ANNE FRANKFORD.
SUSAN, *sister to Sir Charles Mountford.*
SISLY,[2] *maid to Mistress Frankford.*
WOMEN SERVANTS *in Master Frankford's
household.*
JOAN MINIVER ⎱
JANE TRUBKIN ⎰ *country wenches.*
ISBEL MOTLEY

SCENE: *Yorkshire.*

TIME: *Contemporary.*]

PROLOGUE

I COME but as a harbinger, being sent
To tell you what these preparations mean.
Look for no glorious state; our Muse is bent
Upon a barren subject, a bare scene.
We could afford this twig a timber tree,
Whose strength might boldly on your favors
build;
Our russet, tissue;[3] drone, a honeybee;
Our barren plot, a large and spacious field;
Our coarse fare, banquets; our thin water,
wine;
Our brook, a sea; our bat's eyes, eagle's
sight; 10
Our poet's dull and earthy Muse, divine;
Our ravens, doves; our crow's black feath-
ers, white.

But gentle thoughts, when they may give
the foil,[4]
Save them that yield, and spare where
they may spoil.

[SCENE i.

A room in Frankford's house.]

*Enter M[aster] John Frankford, Mistress
Anne, Sir Francis Acton, Sir Charles
Mountford, Master Malby, Master
Wendoll, and M[aster] Cranwell.*

FRAN. Some music there! None lead the
bride a dance?
CHAR. Yes, would she dance "The Shaking
of the Sheets";[5]
But that's the dance her husband means
to lead her.

---

[1] The title continues: "As It Hath Been Oftentimes Acted by the Queen's Majest. Servants."
[2] Cicely.
[3] Fine cloth interwoven with gold or silver
threads.

[4] Repulse, disapproval.
[5] A popular ballad and dance tune, also known
as "The Dance of Death."

WEN. That's not the dance that every man must dance,
According to the ballet.[1]

FRAN. Music, ho!
By your leave, sister—by your husband's leave,
I should have said—the hand that but this day
Was given you in the church I'll borrow.—Sound!
This marriage music hoists me from the ground.

FRANK. Ay, you may caper; you are light and free! 10
Marriage hath yoked my heels; pray, pardon me.

FRAN. I'll have you dance too, brother!

CHAR. Master Frankford,
Y'are a happy man, sir, and much joy
Succeed your marriage mirth, you have a wife
So qualified, and with such ornaments
Both of the mind and body. First, her birth
Is noble, and her education such
As might become the daughter of a prince;
Her own tongue speaks all tongues, and her own hand
Can teach all strings to speak in their best grace, 20
From the shrill'st treble to the hoarsest bass.
To end her many praises in one word,
She's Beauty and Perfection's eldest daughter,
Only found by yours, though many a heart hath sought her.

FRANK. But that I know your virtues and chaste thoughts,
I should be jealous of your praise, Sir Charles.

CRAN. He speaks no more than you approve.

MAL. Nor flatters he that gives to her her due.

ANNE. I would your praise could find a fitter theme
Than my imperfect beauty to speak on. 30
Such as they be, if they my husband please,
They suffice me now I am marriéd.

His sweet content is like a flatt'ring glass,
To make my face seem fairer to mine eye;
But the least wrinkle from his stormy brow
Will blast the roses in my cheeks that grow.

FRAN. A perfect wife already, meek and patient!
How strangely the word husband fits your mouth,
Not married three hours since! Sister, 'tis good;
You that begin betimes thus, must needs prove 40
Pliant and duteous in your husband's love.—
Gramercies,[2] brother! Wrought her to 't already:
"Sweet husband," and a curtsy the first day!
Mark this, mark this, you that are bachelors,
And never took the grace of honest man,[3]
Mark this, against you marry,[4] this one phrase:
"In a good time that man both wins and woos
That takes his wife down in her wedding shoes."[5]

FRANK. Your sister takes not after you, Sir Francis.
All his wild blood your father spent on you; 50
He got her in his age, when he grew civil.
All his mad tricks were to his land entailed,
And you are heir to all; your sister, she
Hath to her dower her mother's modesty.

CHAR. Lord, sir, in what a happy state live you!
This morning, which to many seems a burthen
Too heavy to bear, is unto you a pleasure.
This lady is no clog, as many are;
She doth become you like a well-made suit,

[1] Ballad.
[2] Many thanks.
[3] "Assumed the honorable estate of husband" (Bates).
[4] In preparation for your marriage.
[5] *I.e.*, tames her at once.

In which the tailor hath used all his
　art,　　　　　　　　　　　　　　60
Not like a thick coat of unseasoned
　frieze,
Forced on your back in summer. She's
　no chain
To tie your neck, and curb ye to the yoke;
But she's a chain of gold to adorn your
　neck.
You both adorn each other, and your
　hands,
Methinks, are matches. There's equality
In this fair combination; y'are both
Scholars, both young, both being de-
　scended nobly.
There's music in this sympathy; it
　carries
Consort [1] and expectation of much
　joy,　　　　　　　　　　　　　70
Which God bestow on you from this
　first day
Until your dissolution—that's for aye!
FRAN. We keep you here too long, good
　brother Frankford.
Into the hall; away! Go cheer your
　guests.
What! Bride and bridegroom both with-
　drawn at once?
If you be missed, the guests will doubt
　their welcome,
And charge you with unkindness.
FRANK.　　　　　　　To prevent it,
I'll leave you here, to see the dance
　within.
ANNE. And so will I.
　　　　　Exeunt [Frankford and Anne].
FRAN.　　　　　To part you it were sin.—
Now, gallants, while the town musi-
　cians　　　　　　　　　　　　80
Finger their frets within, and the mad
　lads
And country lasses, every mother's child,
With nosegays and bride-laces [2] in their
　hats,
Dance all their country measures,
　rounds, and jigs,
What shall we do? Hark! They're all
　on the hoigh; [3]
They toil like mill horses, and turn as
　round;

[1] Harmony as well as companionship.
[2] Ribbons used for tying up the rosemary
sprigs carried by wedding guests.
[3] In a state of excitement.

Marry, not on the toe! Ay, and they
　caper,
Not without cutting; [4] you shall see to-
　morrow
The hall floor pecked and dinted like a
　millstone,
Made with their high shoes. Though
　their skill be small,　　　　　90
Yet they tread heavy where their hob-
　nails fall.
CHAR. Well, leave them to their sports!—
　Sir Francis Acton,
I'll make a match with you. Meet to-
　morrow
At Chevy Chase; I'll fly my hawk with
　yours.
FRAN. For what? For what?
CHAR.　　　　　Why, for a hundred pound.
FRAN. Pawn [5] me some gold of that!
CHAR.　　　　　　　Here are ten angels;
I'll make them good a hundred pound
　tomorrow
Upon my hawk's wing.
FRAN.　　　　　'Tis a match; 'tis done.
Another hundred pound upon your dogs,
Dare ye, Sir Charles?
CHAR.　　I dare. Were I sure to lose,　100
I durst do more than that; here's my
　hand,
The first course for a hundred pound!
FRAN.　　　　　　　　　　A match!
WEN. Ten angels on Sir Francis Acton's
　hawk;
As much upon his dogs!
CRAN. I'm for Sir Charles Mountford; I
　have seen
His hawk and dog both tried. What,
　clap [6] ye hands,
Or is 't no bargain?
WEN.　　　　Yes, and stake them down.
Were they five hundred, they were all
　my own.
FRAN. Be stirring early with the lark to-
　morrow;
I'll rise into my saddle ere the sun　110
Rise from his bed.
CHAR.　　　　　If there you miss me, say
I am no gentleman! I'll hold my day.
FRAN. It holds on all sides.—Come, to-
　night let's dance;
Early tomorrow let's prepare to ride.
We had need be three hours up before
　the bride.　　　　　　　　*[Exeunt.]*

[4] Curveting.　　[5] Pledge, "put up."　　[6] Shake.

[SCENE ii.

The yard of Frankford's house.]

Enter Nick and Jenkin, Jack Slime, Roger Brickbat, with Country Wenches, and two or three Musicians.

JENK. Come, Nick, take you Joan Miniver, to trace[1] withal; Jack Slime, traverse[1] you with Sisly Milkpail; I will take Jane Trubkin, and Roger Brickbat shall have Isbel Motley. And now that they are busy in the parlor, come, strike up; we'll have a crash[2] here in the yard.

NICK. My humor is not compendious. Dancing I possess not, though I can foot it; yet, since I am fallen into the hands [10 of Sisly Milkpail, I consent.

SLIME.[3] Truly, Nick, though we were never brought up like serving courtiers, yet we have been brought up with serving creatures, ay, and God's creatures, too, for we have been brought up to serve sheep, oxen, horses, hogs, and suchlike; and, though we be but country fellows, it may be in the way of dancing we can do the horse-trick[4] as well as the serv- [20 ing-men.

ROGER. Ay, and the crosspoint[4] too.

JENK. O Slime! O Brickbat! Do not you know that comparisons are odious? Now we are odious ourselves, too; therefore there are no comparisons to be made betwixt us.

NICK. I am sudden, and not superfluous;
I am quarrelsome, and not seditious;
I am peaceable, and not contentious; 30
I am brief, and not compendious.

SLIME. Foot it quickly! If the music overcome not my melancholy, I shall quarrel; and, if they suddenly do not strike up, I shall presently strike thee down.

JENK. No quarreling, for God's sake! Truly, if you do, I shall set a knave between ye.

SLIME. I come to dance, not to quarrel. Come, what shall it be? "Rogero"? [40

JENK. "Rogero"? No; we will dance "The Beginning of the World."

SISLY. I love no dance so well as "John, come kiss me now."

NICK. I, that have ere now deserved a cushion, call for the "Cushion Dance."

ROGER. For my part, I like nothing so well as "Tom Tyler."

JENK. No; we'll have "The Hunting of the Fox." 50

SLIME. The hay,[5] the hay! There's nothing like the hay.

NICK. I have said, do say, and will say again—

JENK. Every man agree to have it as Nick says!

ALL. Content.

NICK. It hath been, it now is, and it shall be— 59

SISLY. What, Master Nich'las? What?

NICK. "Put on your Smock a Monday."

JENK. So the dance will come cleanly off! Come, for God's sake, agree of something; if you like not that, put it to the musicians; or let me speak for all, and we'll have "Sellenger's Round."

ALL. That, that, that!

NICK. No, I am resolved thus it shall be;
First take hands, then take ye to your heels.

JENK. Why, would ye have us run [70 away?

NICK. No; but I would have you shake your heels.—Music, strike up!

They dance; Nick, dancing, speaks stately and scurvily, the rest after the country fashion.

JENK. Hey! Lively, my lasses! Here's a turn for thee! [*Exeunt.*]

[SCENE iii.

The open country.]

Wind horns. Enter Sir Charles, Sir Francis, Malby, Cranwell, Wendoll, Falconer, and Huntsmen.

CHAR. So; well cast off! Aloft, aloft! Well flown!
O, now she takes her at the souse,[6] and strikes her
Down to th' earth, like a swift thunderclap.[7]

WEN. She hath stroke ten angels out of my way.

FRAN. A hundred pound from me.

CHAR. What, falc'ner!

FALC. At hand, sir!

---

[1] Dance. [3] Original reads *Jack*.
[2] Revel. [4] Vigorous movement of the dance.
[5] A winding country dance. [6] Swoop.
[7] Here and in a few other passages the line divisions have been regularized.

CHAR. Now she hath seized the fowl and
  gins to plume [1] her;
  Rebeck her not; [2] rather stand still and
    check her! 10
  So, seize her gets, [3] her jesses, [4] and her
    bells!
  Away!
FRAN. My hawk killed, too.
CHAR.   Ay, but 'twas at the querre, [5]
  Not at the mount like mine.
FRAN.   Judgment, my masters!
CRAN. Yours missed her at the ferre. [6]
WEN. Ay, but our merlin first had plumed
    the fowl,
  And twice renewed [7] her from the river
    too.
  Her bells, Sir Francis, had not both one
    weight,
  Nor was one semitune above the other.
  Methinks these Milan bells do sound
    too full, 20
  And spoil the mounting of your hawk.
CHAR.   'Tis lost.
FRAN. I grant it not. Mine likewise
    seized a fowl
  Within her talents, [8] and you saw her
    paws
  Full of the feathers; both her petty
    singles [9]
  And her long singles griped her more
    than other;
  The terrials [10] of her [11] legs were stained
    with blood,
  Not of the fowl only; she did discomfit
  Some of her feathers, but she [12] brake
    away.
  Come, come; your hawk is but a rifler. [13]
CHAR.   How!
FRAN. Ay, and your dogs are trindle-
    tails [14] and curs. 30
CHAR. You stir my blood!
  You keep not one good hound in all
    your kennel,
  Nor one good hawk upon your perch.
FRAN.   How, knight!

CHAR. So, knight! You will not swagger,
    sir?
FRAN. Why, say I did?
CHAR.   Why, sir,
  I say you would gain as much by swag-
    g'ring
  As you have got by wagers on your
    dogs.
  You will come short in all things.
FRAN.   Not in this!
  Now I'll strike home.
    [Strikes Sir Charles.]
CHAR.   Thou shalt to thy long home,
  Or I will want my will. 40
FRAN. All they that love Sir Francis,
    follow me!
CHAR. All that affect Sir Charles, draw on
    my part!
CRAN. On this side heaves my hand.
WEN.   Here goes my heart.
*They divide themselves. Sir Charles, Cran-
  well, Falconer, and Huntsman fight
  against Sir Francis, Wendoll, his Fal-
  coner, and Huntsman; and Sir Charles
  hath the better, and beats them away,
  killing both of Sir Francis his men.*
    [Exeunt all but Sir Charles.]
CHAR. My God, what have I done! What
    have I done!
  My rage hath plunged into a sea of
    blood,
  In which my soul lies drowned. Poor
    innocents,
  For whom we are to answer! Well, 'tis
    done,
  And I remain the victor. A great con-
    quest,
  When I would give this right hand, nay,
    this head,
  To breathe in them new life whom I
    have slain! 50
  Forgive me, God! 'Twas in the heat of
    blood,
  And anger quite removes me from my-
    self.
  It was not I, but rage, did this vile
    murther;
  Yet I, and not my rage, must answer it.
  Sir Francis Acton, he is fled the field;
  With him all those that did partake his
    quarrel;
  And I am left alone with sorrow dumb,
  And in my heighth of conquest over-
    come.

---

[1] Begins to pluck.   [2] Do not call her off.
[3] Part of the hawk's harness.   [4] Leg straps.
[5] At the quarry, *i.e.*, before the prey rose
from the ground.
[6] At the far, *i.e.*, at a higher point.   [8] Talons.
[7] Driven again.   [9] Claws.
[10] Perhaps a misprint for *terrets*, a part of the
jesses.
[11] Mountford's hawk's.   [13] Bungler.
[12] The fowl.   [14] Curly-tailed dogs.

Enter Susan.

SUS. O God! My brother wounded 'mong
　　the dead!
　Unhappy jests, that in such earnest
　　ends!　　　　　　　　　　　　　　　60
　The rumor of this fear stretched to my
　　ears,
　And I am come to know if you be wound-
　　ed.
CHAR. O, sister, sister, wounded at the
　　heart!
SUS. My God forbid!
CHAR. In doing that thing which he for-
　　bade,
　I am wounded, sister.
SUS.　　　　　I hope, not at the heart.
CHAR. Yes, at the heart.
SUS.　　　　　O God! A surgeon, there!
CHAR. Call me a surgeon, sister, for my
　　soul!
　The sin of murther, it hath pierced my
　　heart
　And made a wide wound there; but for
　　these scratches,　　　　　　　　　70
　They are nothing, nothing.
SUS.　　Charles, what have you done?
　Sir Francis hath great friends, and will
　　pursue you
　Unto the utmost danger [1] of the law.
CHAR. My conscience is become mine
　　enemy,
　And will pursue me more than Acton
　　can.
SUS. O, fly, sweet brother!
CHAR.　　　　Shall I fly from thee?
　Why, Sue, art weary of my company?
SUS. Fly from your foe!
CHAR.　　　You, sister, are my friend,
　And, flying you, I shall pursue my end.
SUS. Your company is as my eyeball dear;
　Being far from you, no comfort can be
　　near.　　　　　　　　　　　　　81
　Yet fly to save your life! What would I
　　care
　To spend my future age in black de-
　　spair,
　So you were safe? And yet to live one
　　week
　Without my brother Charles, through
　　every cheek
　My streaming tears would downwards
　　run so rank,

Till they could set on either side a bank,
And in the midst a channel; so my face
For two saltwater brooks shall still
　find place.
CHAR. Thou shall not weep so much, for
　I will stay,　　　　　　　　　　90
In spite of danger's teeth. I'll live with
　thee,
Or I'll not live at all. I will not sell
My country and my father's patrimony,
Nor [2] thy sweet sight, for a vain hope
　of life.

Enter Sheriff with Officers.

SHER. Sir Charles, I am made the un-
　willing instrument
Of your attach [3] and apprehension.
I'm sorry that the blood of innocent
　men
Should be of you exacted. [4] It was told me
That you were guarded with a troop of
　friends,
And therefore [I] came thus armed.
CHAR.　　　　O, Master Sheriff,　100
I came into the field with many friends,
But see, they all have left me; only one
Clings to my sad misfortune, my dear
　sister.
I know you for an honest gentleman;
I yield my weapons, and submit to you.
Convey me where you please!
SHER.　　　　　　To prison, then,
To answer for the lives of these dead
　men.
SUS. O God! O God!
CHAR.　　　Sweet sister, every strain
Of sorrow from your heart augments
　my pain;
Your grief abounds, and hits against
　my breast.　　　　　　　　　　110
SHER. Sir, will you go?
CHAR.　Even where it likes you best.
　　　　　　　　　　　　[*Exeunt.*]

[SCENE iv.

A room in Frankford's house.]

Enter Master Frankford in a study. [5]

FRANK. How happy am I amongst other
　men,
That in my mean estate embrace content!

[2] Original has *no.*　　　　　[3] Arrest
[4] From 1607 edn. Original reads *enacted.*
[5] Reverie.

I am a gentleman, and by my birth
Companion with a king; a king's no more.
I am possessed of many fair revenues,
Sufficient to maintain a gentleman;
Touching my mind, I am studied in all
arts,
The riches of my thoughts; and of my
time
Have been a good proficient;[1] but, the
chief
Of all the sweet felicities on earth,   10
I have a fair, a chaste, and loving wife—
Perfection all, all truth, all ornament.
If man on earth may truly happy be,
Of these at once possessed, sure I am he.

Enter Nicholas.

NICK. Sir, there's a gentleman attends
without
To speak with you.
FRANK.   On horseback?
NICK.   Yes, on horseback.
FRANK. Entreat him to alight, and I'll
attend him.
Know'st thou him, Nick?
NICK.   Know him? Yes; his name's
Wendoll.
It seems he comes in haste. His horse is
booted[2]
Up to the flank in mire, himself all
spotted   20
And stained with plashing. Sure, he rid
in fear,
Or for a wager. Horse and man both
sweat;
I ne'er saw two in such a smoking heat.
FRANK. Entreat him in. About it in-
stantly!   [*Exit Nick.*]
This Wendoll I have noted, and his car-
riage
Hath pleased me much; by observation
I have noted many good deserts in
him.
He's affable, and seen[3] in many things;
Discourses well, a good companion,
And, though of small means, yet a gentle-
man   30
Of a good house, somewhat pressed by
want.
I have preferred him to a second place
In my opinion and my best regard.

[1] Have made good use.
[2] Covered.
[3] Skilled, accomplished.

Enter Wendoll, Mistress Frankford, and
Nick.

ANNE. O, M[aster] Frankford, Master
Wendoll here
Brings you the strangest news that e'er
you heard.
FRANK. What news, sweet wife? What
news, good M[aster] Wendoll?
WEN. You knew the match made twixt
Sir Francis Acton
And Sir Charles Mountford?
FRANK.   True; with their hounds
and hawks.
WEN. The matches were both played.
FRANK.   Ha? And which won?
WEN. Sir Francis, your wife's brother, had
the worst,   40
And lost the wager.
FRANK.   Why, the worse his chance;
Perhaps the fortune of some other day
Will change his luck.
WEN.[4]   O, but you hear not all.
Sir Francis lost, and yet was loath to
yield.
At length the two knights grew to dif-
ference,
From words to blows, and so to banding
sides,
Where valorous Sir Charles slew, in his
spleen,
Two of your brother's men—his falc'ner
And his good huntsman whom he loved
so well.
More men were wounded, no more slain
outright.   50
FRANK. Now, trust me, I am sorry for the
knight.
But is my brother safe?
WEN.   All whole and sound,
His body not being blemished with one
wound.
But poor Sir Charles is to the prison led,
To answer at th' assize for them that's
dead.
FRANK. I thank your pains, sir. Had the
news been better,
Your will was to have brought it, M[as-
ter] Wendoll.
Sir Charles will find hard friends; his case
is heinous
And will be most severely censured on.[5]
I'm sorry for him. Sir, a word with you!

[4] Original reads *Anne.*   [5] Judged.

I know you, sir, to be a gentleman   61
In all things; your possibility [1] but mean.
Please you to use my table and my purse;
They are yours.

WEN.   O Lord, sir, I shall ne'er
  deserve it!

FRANK. O, sir, disparage not your worth
  too much;
You are full of quality and fair desert.
Choose of my men which shall attend
  you, sir,
And he is yours. I will allow you, sir,
Your man, your gelding, and your
  table,
All at my own charge. Be my compan-
  ion!   70

WEN. M[aster] Frankford, I have oft been
  bound to you
By many favors; this exceeds them all,
That I shall never merit your least favor;
But, when your last remembrance I for-
  get,
Heaven at my soul exact that weighty
  debt!

FRANK. There needs no protestation, for
  I know you
Virtuous, and therefore grateful.—
  Prithee, Nan,
Use him with all thy loving'st courtesy!

ANNE. As far as modesty may well extend,
It is my duty to receive your friend. 80

FRANK. To dinner! Come, sir, from this
  present day,
Welcome to me forever! Come, away!
  [Exeunt Frankford, Anne, and Wendoll.]

NICK. I do not like this fellow by no
  means.
I never see him but my heart still earns.[2]
Zounds! I could fight with him, yet
  know not why;
The devil and he are all one, in mine eye.

Enter Jenkin.

JENK. O Nick, what gentleman is that
that comes to lie at our house? My master
allows him one to wait on him, and I believe it will fall to thy lot.   90

NICK. I love my master; by these hilts, I
  do;
But rather than I'll ever come to serve
  him,
I'll turn away my master.

[1] Possessions.   [2] Yearns, grieves.

Enter Sisly.

SISLY. Nich'las, where are you, Nich'-
las? You must come in, Nich'las, and
help the gentleman off with his boots.

NICK. If I pluck off his boots, I'll eat the
  spurs,
And they shall stick fast in my throat
  like burrs.

SISLY. Then, Jenkin, come you!   99

JENK. Nay, 'tis no boot [3] for me to
deny it. My master hath given me a coat
here, but he takes pains himself to brush it
once or twice a day with a holly wand.

SISLY. Come, come, make haste, that
you may wash your hands again, and help
to serve in dinner!

JENK. You may see, my masters, though
it be afternoon with you, 'tis but early days [4]
with us, for we have not dined yet. Stay
but a little; I'll but go in and help   [110
to bear up the first course, and come to you
again presently.   *Exeunt.*

[SCENE v.

The jail.]

Enter Malby and Cranwell.

MAL. This is the sessions day. Pray, can
  you tell me
How young Sir Charles hath sped? Is he
  acquit,
Or must he try the law's strict penalty?

CRAN. He's cleared of all, spite of his
  enemies,
Whose earnest labor was to take his life.
But in this suit of pardon he hath spent
All the revenues that his father left him;
And he is now turned a plain country
  man,
Reformed [5] in all things. See, sir, here he
  comes.

Enter Sir Charles and his Keeper.

KEEP. Discharge your fees, and you are
  then at freedom.   10

CHAR. Here, M[aster] Keeper, take the
  poor remainder
Of all the wealth I have! My heavy foes

[3] Use.
[4] Jenkin addresses the audience, for whom the
time is afternoon, although on the stage it is
early morning.
[5] Transformed.

Have made my purse light, but, alas, to me
'Tis wealth enough that you have set me free.

MAL. God give you joy of your delivery!
I am glad to see you abroad, Sir Charles.

CHAR. The poorest knight in England, M[aster] Malby.
My life hath cost me all my patrimony
My father left his son. Well, God forgive them
That are the authors of my penury!   20

Enter Shafton.

SHAFT. Sir Charles! A hand, a hand! At liberty?
Now, by the faith I owe, I am glad to see it.
What want you? Wherein may I pleasure you?

CHAR. O me, O, most unhappy gentleman!
I am not worthy to have friends stirred up,
Whose hands may help me in this plunge of want.
I would I were in heaven, to inherit there
Th' immortal birthright which my Savior keeps,
And by no unthrift [1] can be bought and sold;
For here on earth what pleasures should we trust?   30

SHAFT. To rid you from these contemplations,
Three hundred pounds you shall receive of me;
Nay, five for fail.[2] Come, sir, the sight of gold
Is the most sweet receipt for melancholy,
And will revive your spirits. You shall hold law
With your proud adversaries. Tush! Let Frank Acton
Wage [3] his knighthood like expense [4] with me,
And a [5] will sink, he will. Nay, good Sir Charles,
Applaud your fortune and your fair escape
From all these perils.

CHAR.   O, sir, they have undone me!   40
Two thousand and five hundred pound a year
My father at his death possessed me of,
All which the envious [6] Acton made me spend;
And, notwithstanding all this large expense,
I had much ado to gain my liberty;
And I have only now a house of pleasure,
With some five hundred pounds, reserved
Both to maintain me and my loving sister.

SHAFT. [*Aside.*] That must I have; it lies convenient for me.
If I can fasten but one finger on him,   50
With my full hand I'll gripe him to the heart.
'Tis not for love I proffered him this coin,
But for my gain and pleasure.—Come, Sir Charles,
I know you have need of money; take my offer.

CHAR. Sir, I accept it, and remain indebted
Even to the best of my unable power.
Come, gentlemen, and see it tendered down!   [*Exeunt.*]

[SCENE vi.

A room in Frankford's house.]

Enter Wendoll, melancholy.

WEN. I am a villain, if I apprehend
But such a thought! Then, to attempt the deed—
Slave, thou art damned without redemption!
I'll drive away this passion with a song.
A song! Ha, ha! A song! As if, fond [7] man,
Thy eyes could swim in laughter when thy soul
Lies drenched and drownéd in red tears of blood!
I'll pray, and see if God within my heart
Plant better thoughts. Why, prayers are meditations,
And when I meditate (O, God forgive me!)   10

---

[1] Spendthrift or unthriftiness.
[2] For fear of failure to give enough.
[3] Hazard.   [4] Expenditure.   [5] He.
[6] Malicious.   [7] Foolish.

It is on her divine perfections.
I will forget her; I will arm myself
Not t' entertain a thought of love to her;
And, when I come by chance into her
    presence,
I'll hale [1] these balls until my eyestrings
    crack
From being pulled and drawn to look
    that way.

Enter, over the stage, Frankford, his Wife,
                    and Nick [, and exeunt].

O God, O God! With what a violence
I'm hurried to mine own destruction!
There goest thou, the most perfect's[t]
    man
That ever England bred a gentleman, 20
And shall I wrong his bed?—Thou God
    of Thunder,
Stay, in thy thoughts of vengeance and
    of wrath,
Thy great, almighty, and all-judging
    hand
From speedy execution on a villain,
A villain and a traitor to his friend!

Enter Jenkin.

JENK. Did your worship call?
WEN. [*Not noticing Jenkin.*] He doth
    maintain me; he allows me largely
Money to spend—
    JENK. By my faith, so do not you me;
I cannot get a cross [2] of you.   30
WEN. My gelding, and my man—
    JENK. That's Sorrel and I.
WEN. This kindness grows of no alliance [3]
    twixt us—
    JENK. Nor is my service of any great ac-
quaintance. [4]
WEN. I never bound him to me by desert.
Of a mere stranger, a poor gentleman,
A man by whom in no kind he could
    gain,
He hath placed me in the height of all
    his thoughts, [5]
Made me companion with the best and
    chiefest   40
In Yorkshire. He cannot eat without
    me,

[1] Draw away, turn away.   [3] Kinship.
[2] Coin.   [4] Close relationship.
[5] From 1607 edn. Original reads, *And he
hath placed me in his highest thoughts.*

Nor laugh without me; I am to his body
As necessary as his digestion,
And equally do make him whole or sick.
And shall I wrong this man? Base man!
    Ingrate!
Hast thou the power, straight with thy
    gory hands,
To rip thy image from his bleeding heart,
To scratch thy name from out the holy
    book
Of his remembrance, and to wound his
    name
That holds thy name so dear, or rend his
    heart   50
To whom thy heart was knit and joined
    together?
And yet I must. Then, Wendoll, be con-
    tent!
Thus villains, when they would, cannot
    repent.
    JENK. What a strange humor is my new
master in! Pray God he be not mad; if he
should be so, I should never have any mind
to serve him in Bedlam. It may be he's
mad for missing of me.
    WEN. [*Seeing Jenkin.*] What, Jenkin!
Where's your mistress?   60
    JENK. Is your worship married?
    WEN. Why dost thou ask?
    JENK. Because you are my master; and,
if I have a mistress, I would be glad, like a
good servant, to do my duty to her.
    WEN. I mean Mistress Frankford.
    JENK. Marry, sir, her husband is riding
out of town, and she went very lovingly to
bring him on his way to horse. Do you
see, sir? Here she comes, and here I go.
    WEN. Vanish!   [*Exit Jenkin.*] 71

Enter Mistress Frankford.

ANNE. Y'are well met, sir. Now, in troth,
    my husband,
Before he took horse, had a great desire
To speak with you; we sought about the
    house,
Hallooed into the fields, sent every way,
But could not meet you. Therefore he
    enjoined me
To do unto you his most kind commends.
Nay, more; he wills you, as you prize his
    love,
Or hold in estimation his kind friendship,
To make bold in his absence, and com-
    mand   80

Even as himself were present in the house;
For you must keep his table, use his servants,
And be a present Frankford in his absence.

WEN. I thank him for his love.—
[*Aside.*] Give me a name, you whose infectious tongues
Are tipped with gall and poison. As you would
Think on a man that had your father slain,
Murdered your children, made your wives base strumpets,
So call me, call me so; print in my face
The most stigmatic title of a villain,   90
For hatching treason to so true a friend!

ANNE. Sir, you are much beholding to my husband;
You are a man most dear in his regard.

WEN. I am bound unto your husband, and you too.—
[*Aside.*] I will not speak to wrong a gentleman
Of that good estimation, my kind friend.
I will not, zounds! I will not. I may choose,
And I will choose. Shall I be so misled?
Or shall I purchase [1] to my father's crest
The motto of a villain? If I say   100
I will not do it, what thing can enforce me?
What can compel me? What sad destiny
Hath such command upon my yielding thoughts?
I will not. Ha! Some fury pricks me on;
The swift Fates drag me at their chariot wheel,
And hurry me to mischief. Speak I must;
Injure myself, wrong her, deceive his trust!—

ANNE. Are you not well, sir, that ye seem thus troubled?
There is sedition in your countenance.

WEN. And in my heart, fair angel, chaste and wise.   110
I love you! Start not, speak not, answer not.
I love you—nay, let me speak the rest.
Bid me to swear, and I will call to record
The host of heaven.

[1] Acquire, add.

ANNE.   The host of heaven forbid
Wendoll should hatch such a disloyal thought!

WEN. Such is my fate; to this suit I was born,
To wear rich pleasure's crown, or fortune's scorn.

ANNE. My husband loves you.
WEN.   I know it.
ANNE.   He esteems you
Even as his brain, his eyeball, or his heart.

WEN. I have tried it.   120
ANNE. His purse is your exchequer, and his table
Doth freely serve you.

WEN.   So I have found it.
ANNE. O, with what face of brass, what brow of steel,
Can you, unblushing, speak this to the face
Of the espoused wife of so dear a friend?
It is my husband that maintains your state.
Will you dishonor him—I am his wife—
That in your power hath left his whole affairs?
It is to me you speak?

WEN.   O, speak no more,
For more than this I know, and have recorded   130
Within the red-leaved table [2] of my heart.
Fair, and of all beloved, I was not fearful
Bluntly to give my life into your hand,
And at one,[3] hazard all my earthly means.
Go, tell your husband; he will turn me off,
And I am then undone. I care not, I;
'Twas for your sake. Perchance in rage he'll kill me;
I care not, 'twas for you. Say I incur
The general name of villain through the world,
Of traitor to my friend; I care not, I.
Beggary, shame, death, scandal, and reproach—   141
For you I'll hazard all. Why, what care I?
For you I'll love, and in your love I'll die.

ANNE. You move me, sir, to passion and to pity.

[2] Tablet, notebook.   [3] At one throw.

The love I bear my husband is as precious
As my soul's health.

WEN.   I love your husband too,
And for his love I will engage my life.
Mistake me not; the augmentation
Of my sincere affection borne to you
Doth no whit lessen my regard of him.
I will be secret, lady, close as night; 151
And not the light of one small glorious
star
Shall shine here in my forehead, to be-
wray
That act of night.

ANNE.   What shall I say?
My soul is wand'ring, and hath lost her
way.
O, Master Wendoll! O!

WEN.   Sigh not, sweet saint,
For every sigh you breathe draws from
my heart
A drop of blood.

ANNE.   I ne'er offended yet.
My fault, I fear, will in my brow be writ.
Women that fall, not quite bereft of
grace,   160
Have their offenses noted in their
face.
I blush, and am ashamed. O, Master
Wendoll,
Pray God I be not born to curse your
tongue
That hath enchanted me! This maze I
am in
I fear will prove the labyrinth of sin.

Enter Nick [behind].

WEN. The path of pleasure and the gate
to bliss,
Which on your lips I knock at with a kiss!

NICK. [*Aside.*] I'll kill the rogue.

WEN. Your husband is from home; your
bed's no blab.
Nay, look not down and blush!
           [*Exeunt Wendoll and Anne.*]

NICK.   Zounds! I'll stab!
Ay, Nick, was it thy chance to come just
in the nick?   171
I love my master, and I hate that slave;
I love my mistress, but these tricks I like
not.
My master shall not pocket up this
wrong;

I'll eat my fingers first. What sayst thou,
metal?
Does not that rascal Wendoll go on legs
That thou must cut off? Hath he not
hamstrings
That thou must hock? [1] Nay, metal,
thou shalt stand
To all I say. I'll henceforth turn a spy,
And watch them in their close convey-
ances. [2]   180
I never looked for better of that ras-
cal,
Since he came miching [3] first into our
house.
It is that Sathan hath corrupted her,
For she was fair and chaste. I'll have an
eye
In all their gestures. Thus I think of
them,
If they proceed as they have done before:
Wendoll's a knave, my mistress is a ——.
           Exit.

[SCENE vii.

Near Mountford's house.]

Enter Charles and Susan.

CHAR. Sister, you see we are driven to hard
shift
To keep this poor house we have left
unsold.
I am now enforced to follow husbandry,
And you to milk. And do we not live
well?
Well, I thank God.

SUS.   O brother, here's a change
Since old Sir Charles died in our father's
house.

CHAR. All things on earth thus change,
some up, some down;
Content's a kingdom, and I wear that
crown.

Enter Shafton, with a Serjeant.

SHAFT. Good morrow, morrow, Sir Charles!
What, with your sister,
Plying your husbandry?—Serjeant, stand
off!—   10
You have a pretty house here, and a
garden,
And goodly ground about it. Since it lies
So near a lordship that I lately bought,

---

[1] Hack, cut.   [2] Secret trickery.   [3] Skulking.

I would fain buy it of you. I will give
you—

CHAR. O, pardon me; this house successively

Hath longed[1] to me and my progenitors

Three hundred years. My great-great-
grandfather,

He in whom first our gentle style[2] began,

Dwelt here, and in this ground increased
this molehill

Unto that mountain which my father
left me.   20

Where he, the first of all our house, begun,

I now, the last, will end, and keep this
house,

This virgin title never yet deflowered

By any unthrift of the Mountfords' line.

In brief, I will not sell it for more gold

Than you could hide or pave the ground
withal.

SHAFT. Ha, ha! A proud mind and a
beggar's purse!

Where's my three hundred pounds, besides the use?[3]

I have brought it to execution

By course of law. What, is my monies
ready?   30

CHAR. An execution, sir, and never tell me

You put my bond in suit? You deal extremely.

SHAFT. Sell me the land, and I'll acquit
you straight.

CHAR. Alas, alas! 'Tis all trouble hath
left me

To cherish me and my poor sister's life.

If this were sold, our names[4] should then
be quite

Raced[5] from the beadroll of gentility.

You see what hard shift we have made
to keep it

Allied still to our own name. This palm
you see,

Labor hath glowed within; her silver
brow,   40

That never tasted a rough winter's blast

Without a mask or fan, doth with a grace

Defy cold winter, and his storms outface.

SUS. Sir, we feed sparing, and we labor
hard;

We lie uneasy, to reserve to us

And our succession this small spot of
ground.

CHAR. I have so bent my thoughts to husbandry

That I protest I scarcely can remember

What a new fashion is, how silk or satin

Feels in my hand. Why, pride is grown
to us   50

A mere, mere stranger. I have quite
forgot

The names of all that ever waited on me.

I cannot name ye any of my hounds,

Once from whose echoing mouths I
heard all music

That e'er my heart desired. What should
I say?

To keep this place, I have changed myself away.

SHAFT. [To the Serjeant.] Arrest him at my
suit!—Actions and actions

Shall keep thee in continual bondage fast;

Nay, more, I'll sue thee by a late appeal,

And call thy former life in question.   60

The keeper is my friend; thou shalt have
irons,

And usage such as I'll deny to dogs.—

Away with him!

CHAR. Ye are too timorous.[6] But trouble
is my master,

And I will serve him truly.—My kind
sister,

Thy tears are of no force to mollify

This flinty man. Go to my father's
brother,

My kinsmen, and allies; entreat them for
me,

To ransom me from this injurious man

That seeks my ruin.

SHAFT.   Come, irons, irons! Come away!

I'll see thee lodged far from the sight of
day.   [Exeunt all except Susan.]   70

SUS. My heart's so hardened with the
frost of grief,

Death cannot pierce it through.—Tyrant
too fell!

So lead the fiends condemnéd souls to
hell.

Enter Acton and Malby.

FRAN. Again to prison! Malby, hast thou
seen

A poor slave better tortured? Shall we
hear

---

[1] Belonged.   [4] Old edns. read *means.*
[2] Title of gentleman.   [5] Erased, scraped.
[3] Interest.

[6] Terrible.

The music of his voice cry from the
grate,[1]
"Meat, for the Lord's sake"? No, no;
yet I am not
Throughly revenged. They say he hath
a pretty wench
To his sister. Shall I, in my mercy
sake   79
To him and to his kindred, bribe the fool
To shame herself by lewd, dishonest lust?
I'll proffer largely; but, the deed being
done,
I'll smile to see her base confusion.

MAL. Methinks, Sir Francis, you are full
revenged
For greater wrongs than he can proffer
you.
See where the poor sad gentlewoman
stands!

FRAN. Ha, ha! Now will I flout her
poverty,
Deride her fortunes, scoff her base
estate.
My very soul the name of Mountford
hate.
But stay, my heart! O,[2] what a look
did fly   90
To strike my soul through with thy
piercing eye!
I am enchanted, all my spirits are fled,
And with one glance my envious spleen
strook dead.

SUS. Acton, that seeks our blood!
                 Runs away.

FRAN.   O chaste and fair!

MAL. Sir Francis, why, Sir Francis, in a
trance?
Sir Francis, what cheer, man? Come,
come, how is 't?

FRAN. Was she not fair? Or else this judging eye
Cannot distinguish beauty.

MAL.   She was fair.

FRAN. She was an angel in a mortal's
shape,
And ne'er descended from old Mountford's line.   100
But soft, soft, let me call my wits together!
A poor, poor wench, to my great adversary
Sister, whose very souls denounce stern
war

[1] Grating of prison.   [2] Original reads *Or.*

Each against other! How now, Frank?
Turned fool
Or madman, whether?[3] But no! Master
of
My perfect senses and directest wits.
Then why should I be in this violent
humor
Of passion and of love? And with a per-
son
So different every way, and so opposed
In all contractions[4] and still-warring
actions?   110
Fie, fie! How I dispute against my soul!
Come, come; I'll gain her, or in her fair
quest
Purchase my soul free and immortal rest.
                 [*Exeunt.*]

[SCENE viii.

A room in Frankford's house.]

*Enter three or four Serving-men, one with a
voider[5] and a wooden knife, to take
away; another the salt and bread; another
the tablecloth and napkins; another the
carpet;[6] Jenkin with two lights after
them.*

JENK. So; march in order, and retire in
battle array! My master and the guests
have supped already; all's taken away.
Here, now spread for the serving-men in the
hall!—Butler, it belongs to your office.

BUT. I know it, Jenkin. What d' ye call
the gentleman that supped there tonight?

JENK. Who? My master?

BUT. No, no; Master Wendoll, he's a
daily guest. I mean the gentleman that   [10
came but this afternoon.

JENK. His name's M[aster] Cranwell.
God's light! Hark, within there; my master
calls to lay more billets upon the fire.
Come, come! Lord, how we that are in
office here in the house are troubled! One
spread the carpet in the parlor, and stand
ready to snuff the lights; the rest be ready
to prepare their stomachs! More lights in
the hall there! Come, Nich'las.   20
            [*Exeunt all but Nick.*]

NICK. I cannot eat, but, had I Wendoll's
heart,

[3] Which one?
[4] Lawsuits.
[5] Tray for clearing the remains of the meal.
[6] Heavy covering for a table.

I would eat that. The rogue grows impudent!

O, I have seen such vild,[1] notorious
tricks,

Ready to make my eyes dart from my
head!

I'll tell my master; by this air, I will.

Fall what may fall, I'll tell him. Here
he comes.

*Enter Master Frankford, as it were brushing
the crumbs from his clothes with a
napkin, as newly risen from supper.*

FRANK. Nich'las, what make [2] you here?
Why are not you

At supper in the hall, among your
fellows?

NICK. Master, I stayed [3] your rising from
the board,   29
To speak with you.

FRANK.   Be brief then, gentle Nich'las;
My wife and guests attend [4] me in the
parlor.

Why dost thou pause? Now, Nich'las,
you want money,

And, unthriftlike, would eat into your
wages

Ere you have earned it. Here, sir, 's
half a crown;

Play the good husband.[5] And away to
supper!

NICK. [*Aside.*] By this hand, an honorable gentleman! I will not see him
wronged.—Sir, I have served you long;
you entertained me seven years before
your beard; you knew me, sir, before [40
you knew my mistress.

FRANK. What of this, good Nich'las?

NICK. I never was a makebate [6] or a
knave;

I have no fault but one—I'm given to
quarrel,

But not with women. I will tell you,
master,

That which will make your heart leap
from your breast,

Your hair to startle from your head,
your ears to tingle.

FRANK. What preparation's this to dismal
news?

NICK. 'Sblood![7] Sir, I love you better
than your wife.
I'll make it good.   50

FRANK. Y'are a knave, and I have much
ado

With wonted patience to contain my
rage,

And not to break thy pate. Th' art a
knave.

I'll turn you, with your base comparisons,
Out of my doors.

NICK.   Do, do!
There is not room for Wendoll and me
too,

Both in one house. O master, master,
That Wendoll is a villain!

FRANK. [*Striking him.*]   Ay, saucy!

NICK. Strike, strike, do strike; yet hear
me! I am no fool;

I know a villain, when I see him act 60
Deeds of a villain. Master, master,
that base slave

Enjoys my mistress, and dishonors you.

FRANK. Thou hast killed me with a weapon
whose sharp point

Hath pricked quite through and through
my shiv'ring heart.

Drops of cold sweat sit dangling on my
hairs,

Like morning's dew upon the golden
flowers,

And I am plunged into strange agonies.
What didst thou say? If any word that
touched

His credit or her reputation,
It is as hard to enter my belief   70
As Dives into heaven.

NICK.   I can gain nothing.
They are two that never wronged me. I
knew before

'Twas but a thankless office, and perhaps
As much as is my service, or my life is
worth.

All this I know; but this, and more,
More by a thousand dangers, could not
hire me

To smother such a heinous wrong from
you.

I saw, and I have said.

FRANK. [*Aside.*] 'Tis probable. Though
blunt, yet he is honest.

Though I durst pawn my life, and on
their faith   80

---

[1] Vile.   [4] Await.
[2] Do.   [5] *I.e.*, be thrifty.
[3] Awaited.   [6] Maker of debates, quarrels.
[7] God's blood.

Hazard the dear salvation of my soul,
Yet in my trust I may be too secure.
May this be true? O, may it? Can it be?
Is it by any wonder possible?
Man, woman, what thing mortal can we
    trust,
When friends and bosom wives prove so
    unjust?—
What instance [1] hast thou of this strange
    report?

NICK. Eyes, master, eyes.

FRANK. Thy eyes may be deceived, I tell
    thee;
For, should an angel from the heavens
    drop down,   90
And preach this to me that thyself hast
    told,
He should have much ado to win belief,
In both their loves I am so confident.

NICK. Shall I discourse the same by cir-
    cumstance?

FRANK. No more! To supper, and com-
    mand your fellows
To attend us and the strangers. Not a
    word,
I charge thee, on thy life! Be secret then,
For I know nothing.

NICK. I am dumb; and, now that I have
    eased my stomach,[2]
I will go fill my stomach.   *Exit.*

FRANK.   Away! Begone!— 100
She is well born, descended nobly;
Virtuous her education; her repute
Is in the general voice of all the country
Honest and fair; her carriage, her de-
    meanor,
In all her actions that concern the love
To me her husband, modest, chaste, and
    godly.
Is all this seeming gold plain copper?
But he, that Judas that hath borne my
    purse,
And sold me for a sin! O God! O God!
Shall I put up these wrongs? No! Shall
    I trust   110
The bare report of this suspicious groom
Before the double gilt,[3] the well-hatch[4]
    ore
Of their two hearts? No, I will loose [5]
    these thoughts;

---

[1] Evidence.   [2] Anger.
[3] Gold; with a pun on the meaning *guilt*.
[4] Well-hatched, nobly wrought.
[5] Possibly a spelling of *lose*.

Distraction I will banish from my brow,
And from my looks exile sad discontent.
Their wonted favors in my tongue shall
    flow;
Till I know all, I'll nothing seem to
    know.—
Lights and a table there! Wife, M[aster]
    Wendoll,
And gentle Master Cranwell!

*Enter Mistress Frankford, Master Wendoll,
    Master Cranwell, Nick, and Jenkin
    with cards, carpets, stools, and other
                              necessaries.*

FRANK. O, Master Cranwell, you are a
    stranger here,   120
And often balk [6] my house; faith, y'are a
    churl!
Now we have supped, a table and to
    cards!

JENK. A pair [7] of cards, Nich'las, and a
carpet to cover the table! Where's Sisly,
with her counters and her box? Candles
and candlesticks there! Fie! We have
such a household of serving-creatures! Unless it be Nick and I, there's not one
amongst them all can say "bo" to a
goose!—Well said,[8] Nick!   130

*They spread a carpet, set down lights and
                                      cards.*

ANNE. Come, M[aster] Frankford, who
shall take my part? [9]

FRANK. Marry, that will I, sweet wife.

WEN. No, by my faith, when you are together, I sit out. It must be Mistress
Frankford and I, or else it is no match.

FRANK. I do not like that match.

NICK. [*Aside.*] You have no reason,
marry, knowing all.   139

FRANK. 'Tis no great matter, neither.—
Come, Master Cranwell, shall you and I
take them up?

CRAN. At your pleasure, sir.

FRANK. I must look to you, Master
Wendoll, for you'll be playing false. Nay,
so will my wife, too.

NICK. [*Aside.*] I will be sworn she will.

ANNE. Let them that are taken false,
forfeit the set!

FRANK. Content; it shall go hard but I'll
    take you.   150

---

[6] Avoid.   [8] Well done.
[7] Pack.   [9] Be my partner.

CRAN. Gentlemen, what shall our game be?

WEN. Master Frankford, you play best at noddy.[1]

FRANK. You shall not find it so; indeed, you shall not.

ANNE. I can play at nothing so well as double-ruff.[2]

FRANK. If Master Wendoll and my wife be together, there's no playing against them at double-hand.[3]

NICK. I can tell you, sir, the game that Master Wendoll is best at.

WEN. What game is that, Nick? 160

NICK. Marry, sir, knave-out-of-doors.

WEN. She and I will take you at loadum.

ANNE. Husband, shall we play at saint?

FRANK. [Aside.] My saint's turned devil.—No, we'll none of saint.

You are best at new-cut, wife; you'll play at that.

WEN. If you play at new-cut, I'm soonest[4] hitter of any here, for a wager.

FRANK. [Aside.] 'Tis me they play on.—

Well, you may draw out;

For all your cunning, 'twill be to your shame;

I'll teach you, at your new-cut, a new game. 170

Come, come!

CRAN. If you cannot agree upon the game, To post and pair!

WEN. We shall be soonest pairs, and my good host,

When he comes late home, he must kiss the post.[5]

FRANK. Whoever wins, it shall be to thy cost.

CRAN. Faith, let it be vide-ruff, and let's make honors!

FRANK. If you make honors, one thing let me crave:

Honor the king and queen; except[6] the knave.

WEN. Well, as you please for that.—Lift![7] Who shall deal? 180

ANNE. The least in sight. What are you, Master Wendoll?

WEN. I am a knave.

NICK. [Aside.] I'll swear it.

ANNE.   I am queen.

FRANK. [Aside.] A quean, thou shouldst say.—Well, the cards are mine;

They are the grossest pair that e'er I felt.

ANNE. Shuffle; I'll cut. Would I had never dealt!

FRANK. [Misdealing]. I have lost my dealing.

WEN.   Sir, the fault's in me;

This queen I have more than mine own, you see.

Give me the stock![8]

FRANK.   My mind's not on my game.

Many a deal I've lost; the more's your shame.

You have served me a bad trick, Master Wendoll. 190

WEN. Sir, you must take your lot. To end this strife,

I know I have dealt better with your wife.

FRANK. Thou hast dealt falsely, then.

ANNE. What's trumps?

WEN. Hearts. Partner, I rub.

FRANK. [Aside.] Thou robb'st me of my soul, of her chaste love;

In thy false dealing thou hast robbed my heart.—

Booty you play;[9] I, like a loser, stand,

Having no heart, or[10] here or in my hand.

I will give o'er the set; I am not well.

Come, who will hold my cards? 201

ANNE. Not well, sweet M[aster] Frankford?

Alas, what ail you? 'Tis some sudden qualm.

WEN. How long have you been so, Master Frankford?

FRANK. Sir, I was lusty, and I had my health,

But I grew ill when you began to deal.—

Take hence this table!—Gentle Master Cranwell,

Y'are welcome; see your chamber at your pleasure!

I am sorry that this megrim takes me so;

I cannot sit and bear you company.—

Jenkin, some lights, and show him to his chamber! 211

[Exeunt Cranwell and Jenkin.]

[1] A game like cribbage; also, a simpleton.

[2] Forerunner of whist; with a double meaning.

[3] The names of this and the following games, the nature of which is not known, are of course used with double meanings.

[4] Quickest, speediest.

[5] I.e., be shut out.

[6] Exclude.

[7] Cut.

[8] Remainder of the pack.

[9] Lose, by arrangement with a confederate, in order to draw the opponent on.

[10] Either.

ANNE. A nightgown [1] for my husband;
　quickly there!
It is some rheum or cold.
WEN.　　　　　Now, in good faith,
　This illness you have got by sitting late
　Without your gown.
FRANK.　　I know it, M[aster] Wendoll.
　Go, go to bed, lest you complain like
　　me!—
　Wife, prithee, wife, into my bedcham-
　　ber!
　The night is raw and cold and rheumatic.
　Leave me my gown and light; I'll walk
　　away my fit.
WEN. Sweet sir, good night!　　　220
FRANK. Myself, good night!
　　　　　　　　　　[Exit Wendoll.]
ANNE.　　Shall I attend you, husband?
FRANK. No, gentle wife, thou't catch cold
　in thy head.
　Prithee, begone, sweet; I'll make haste to
　　bed.
ANNE. No sleep will fasten on mine eyes,
　you know,
　Until you come.　　　　　　Exit.
FRANK.　Sweet Nan, I prithee, go!—
　I have bethought me. Get me by degrees
　The keys of all my doors, which I will
　　mold
　In wax, and take their fair impression,
　To have by them new keys. This being
　　compassed,　　　　　　229
　At a set hour a letter shall be brought me,
　And, when they think they may securely
　　play,
　They nearest are to danger. Nick, I must
　　rely
　Upon thy trust and faithful secrecy.
NICK. Build on my faith!
FRANK.　　　To bed, then, not to rest!
　Care lodges in my brain, grief in my
　　breast.　　　　　　[Exeunt.]

[SCENE ix.

Near the home of Old Mountford.]

Enter Sir Charles his [2] *Sister, Old Mountford,*
　　　Sandy, Roder, and Tidy.

MOUNT. You say my nephew is in great
　distress.
　Who brought it to him but his own
　　lewd life?

---

[1] Dressing gown.　　　　[2] *I.e.*, Charles's.

I cannot spare a cross. I must confess
　He was my brother's son; why, niece,
　　what then?
This is no world in which to pity men.
SUS. I was not born a beggar, though his
　extremes
　Enforce this language from me. I pro-
　　test
　No fortune of mine own could lead my
　　tongue
　To this base key. I do beseech you,
　　uncle,
　For the name's sake, for Christianity, 10
　Nay, for God's sake, to pity his dis-
　　tress.
　He is denied the freedom of the prison,
　And in the hole is laid with men con-
　　demned.
　Plenty he hath of nothing but of irons,
　And it remains in you to free him thence.
MOUNT. Money I cannot spare; men
　should take heed.
　He lost my kindred when he fell to need.
　　　　　　　　　　　[Exit.]
SUS. Gold is but earth; thou earth enough
　shalt have,
　When thou hast once took measure of
　　thy grave.
　You know me, Master Sandy, and my
　　suit.　　　　　　　　　20
SANDY. I knew you, lady, when the old
　man lived;
　I knew you ere your brother sold his
　　land.
　Then you were Mistress Sue, tricked up
　　in jewels;
　Then you sung well, played sweetly on
　　the lute.
　But now I neither know you nor your
　　suit.　　　　　　　[Exit.]
SUS. You, Master Roder, was my brother's
　tenant;
　Rent-free he placed you in that wealthy
　　farm
　Of which you are possessed.
RODER.　　　　　　True, he did;
　And have I not there dwelt still for his
　　sake?
　I have some business now; but without
　　doubt　　　　　　　30
　They that have hurled him in will help
　　him out.　　　　　　Exit.
SUS. Cold comfort still. What say you,
　cousin Tidy?

TIDY. I say this comes of roisting,[1] swag-
g'ring.
  Call me not cousin. Each man for him-
    self!
  Some men are born to mirth, and some
    to sorrow;
  I am no cousin unto them that borrow.
                                    Exit.
SUS. O Charity, why art thou fled to
    heaven,
  And left all things on this earth uneven?
  Their scoffing answers I will ne'er re-
    turn,   39
  But to myself his grief in silence mourn.

              Enter Sir Francis and Malby.

FRAN. She is poor; I'll therefore tempt
    her with this gold.
  Go, Malby, in my name deliver it,
  And I will stay thy answer.
MAL. Fair mistress, as I understand your
    grief
  Doth grow from want, so I have here
    in store
  A means to furnish you, a bag of gold,
  Which to your hands I freely tender you.
SUS. I thank you, heavens! I thank you,
    gentle sir;
  God make me able to requite this favor!
MAL. This gold Sir Francis Acton sends
    by me,   50
  And prays you—
SUS. Acton? O God! That name I'm
    born to curse.
  Hence, bawd; hence, broker![2] See, I
    spurn his gold.
  My honor never shall for gain be sold.
FRAN. Stay, lady, stay!
SUS.   From you I'll posting hie,
  Even as the doves from feathered eagles
    fly.   *Exit.*
FRAN. She hates my name, my face. How
    should I woo?
  I am disgraced in everything I do.
  The more she hates me, and disdains my
    love,
  The more I am rapt in admiration   60
  Of her divine and chaste perfections.
  Woo her with gifts I cannot, for all gifts
  Sent in my name she spurns; with looks
    I cannot,
  For she abhors my sight; nor yet with
    letters,

For none she will receive. How then?
    How then?
  Well, I will fasten such a kindness on
    her
  As shall o'ercome her hate and conquer it.
  Sir Charles, her brother, lies in execu-
    tion
  For a great sum of money; and, besides,
  The appeal is sued still for my hunts-
    men's death,   70
  Which only I have power to reverse.
  In her I'll bury all my hate of him.—
  Go seek the keeper, Malby; bring him
    to me!
  To save his body, I his debts will pay;
  To save his life, I his appeal will stay.
                                 [*Exeunt.*]

                  [SCENE X.

            A dungeon in York Castle.]

*Enter Sir Charles in prison, with irons, his
feet bare, his garments all ragged and
                                      torn.*

CHAR. Of all on the earth's face most
    miserable,
  Breathe in this hellish dungeon thy la-
    ments,
  Thus like a slave ragg'd, like a felon
    gyved!
  That hurls thee headlong to this base
    estate!
  O unkind uncle! O my friends ingrate,
  Unthankful kinsmen, Mountfords all-
    too[3] base,
  To let thy name be fettered in disgrace!
  A thousand deaths here in this grave I
    die!
  Fear, hunger, sorrow, cold, all threat
    my death,   9
  And join together to deprive my breath.
  But, that which most torments me, my
    dear sister
  Hath left[4] to visit me, and from my
    friends
  Hath brought no hopeful answer; there-
    fore, I
  Divine they will not help my misery.
  If it be so, shame, scandal, and contempt
  Attend their covetous thoughts; need
    make their graves!
  Usurers they live, and may they die
    like slaves!

---

[1] Roistering. rioting.   [2] Go-between.

[3] Entirely.   [4] Ceased.

Enter Keeper.

KEEP. Knight, be of comfort, for I bring
    thee freedom
From all thy troubles.
CHAR.   Then I am doomed to die:
Death is the end of all calamity.   20
KEEP. Live! Your appeal is stayed; the
    execution
Of all your debts discharged; your
    creditors
Even to the utmost penny satisfied;
In sign whereof your shackles I knock
    off.
You are not left so much indebted to us
As for your fees; all is discharged, all
    paid.
Go freely to your house, or where you
    please;
After long miseries, embrace your ease.
CHAR. Thou grumblest out the sweetest
    music to me
That ever organ played.—Is this a
    dream?   30
Or do my waking senses apprehend
The pleasing taste of these applausive [1]
    news?
Slave that I was, to wrong such honest
    friends,
My loving kinsmen, and my near allies!
Tongue, I will bite thee for the scandal
    breath [2]
Against such faithful kinsmen; they are
    all
Composed of pity and compassion,
Of melting charity and of moving ruth.
That which I spake before was in my
    rage;
They are my friends, the mirrors [3] of
    this age,   40
Bounteous and free. The noble Mount-
    fords' race
Ne'er bred a covetous thought, or humor
    base.

Enter Susan.

SUS. [*Aside.*] I can no longer stay from
    visiting
My woeful brother. While I could, I
    kept
My hapless tidings from his hopeful
    ear.

CHAR. Sister, how much am I indebted
    to thee
And to thy travail!
SUS.   What, at liberty?
CHAR. Thou seest I am, thanks to thy
    industry.
O, unto which of all my courteous friends
Am I thus bound? My uncle Mount-
    ford, he   50
Even of an infant loved me. Was it he?
So did my cousin Tidy. Was it he?
So Master Roder, Master Sandy, too.
Which of all these did this high kind-
    ness do?
SUS. Charles, can you mock me in your
    poverty,
Knowing your friends deride your
    misery?
Now, I protest I stand so much amazed,
To see your bonds free, and your irons
    knocked off,
That I am rapt into a maze of wonder;
The rather for I know not by what
    means   60
This happiness hath chanced.
CHAR.   Why, by my uncle,
My cousins, and my friends. Who else,
    I pray,
Would take upon them all my debts to
    pay?
SUS. O brother, they are men all of flint,
Pictures of marble, and as void of pity
As chaséd bears. I begged, I sued, I
    kneeled,
Laid open all your griefs and miseries,
Which they derided; more than that,
    denied us
A part in their alliance, but, in pride,
Said that our kindred with our plenty
    died.   70
CHAR. Drudges too much [4]—what did
    they? O, known evil!
Rich fly the poor as good men shun the
    devil.
Whence should my freedom come? Of
    whom alive,
Saving of those, have I deserved so well?
Guess, sister, call to mind, remember me!
These I have raised,[5] they follow the
    world's guise,
Whom, rich in honor, they in woe despise.[6]

[1] Worthy of applause, joyful.   [3] Paragons.
[2] Scandalous talk.
[4] Menials too base.   [5] Recalled, named.
[6] *I.e.*, those who are honorable but unfortunate they despise.

Sus. My wits have lost themselves; let's
   ask the keeper!

Char. Jailer!

Keep. At hand, sir. 80

Char. Of courtesy resolve me one demand![1]

   What was he took the burthen of my
     debts

   From off my back, stayed my appeal to
     death,

   Discharged my fees, and brought me
     liberty?

Keep. A courteous knight, and called
   Sir Francis Acton.

Char. Ha! Acton! O me, more distressed in this

   Than all my troubles! Hale me back,

   Double my irons, and my sparing meals

   Put into halves, and lodge me in a
     dungeon

   More deep, more dark, more cold, more
     comfortless! 90

   By Acton freed! Not all thy manacles

   Could fetter so my heels as this one
     word

   Hath thralled my heart, and it must now
     lie bound

   In more strict prison than thy stony
     jail.

   I am not free; I go but under bail.

Keep. My charge is done, sir, now I have
   my fees.

   As we get little, we will nothing leese.[2]
                     Exit.

Char. By Acton freed, my dangerous opposite!

   Why, to what end? Or what occasion?
     Ha!

   Let me forget the name of enemy, 100

   And with indifference balance[3] this
     high favor! Ha!

Sus. [*Aside.*] His love to me! Upon my
   soul, 'tis so!

   That is the root from whence these
     strange things grow.

Char. Had this proceeded from my father, he

   That by the law of nature is most bound

   In offices of love, it had deserved

   My best employment to requite that
     grace.

   Had it proceeded from my friends, or him,

[1] Answer me one question.
[2] Lose.   [3] Weigh with impartiality.

From them this action had deserved my
   life,

And from a stranger more, because
   from such 110

There is less execution of good deeds.

But he, nor father, nor ally, nor friend,

More than a stranger, both remote in
   blood,

And in his heart opposed my enemy,

That this high bounty should proceed
   from him—

O, there I lose myself! What should I say,

What think, what do, his bounty to repay?

Sus. You wonder, I am sure, whence this
   strange kindness

Proceeds in Acton; I will tell you,
   brother.

He dotes on me, and oft hath sent me
   gifts, 120

Letters, and tokens; I refused them all.

Char. I have enough, though poor; my
   heart is set

   In one rich gift to pay back all my debt.
                     Exeunt.

[Scene xi.

A room in Frankford's house.]

Enter Frankford and Nick, with keys and
         a letter in his hand.

Frank. This is the night that I must play
   my part,

   To try two seeming angels.—Where's
     my keys?

Nick. They are made according to your
   mold in wax.

   I bade the smith be secret, gave him
     money,

   And here they are. The letter, sir!

Frank. [*Giving letter.*] True, take it; there
   it is;

   And, when thou seest me in my pleas-
     ant's[t] vein,

   Ready to sit to supper, bring it me!

Nick. I'll do 't; make no more question
   but I'll do 't.   *Exit.*

Enter Mistress Frankford, Cranwell, Wen-
        doll, and Jenkin.

Anne. Sirrah, 'tis six a-clock already
   stroke; 10

   Go bid them spread the cloth, and serve
     in supper.

JENK. It shall be done, forsooth, mistress. Where's Spigot, the butler, to give us our salt and trenchers?   [*Exit.*]

WEN. We that have been a-hunting all the day
Come with prepared stomachs.—Master Frankford,
We wished you at our sport.

FRANK. My heart was with you, and my mind was on you.—
Fie, Master Cranwell! You are still thus sad?—
A stool, a stool! Where's Jenkin, and where's Nick?   20
'Tis supper time at least an hour ago.
What's the best news abroad?

WEN. I know none good.

FRANK. [*Aside.*]   But I know too much bad.

Enter Butler and Jenkin, with a tablecloth, bread, trenchers, and salt.

CRAN. Methinks, sir, you might have that interest
In [1] your wife's brother, to be more remiss [2]
In his hard dealing against poor Sir Charles,
Who, as I hear, lies in York Castle,
Needy and in great want.
        [Exeunt Jenkin and Butler.]

FRANK. Did not more weighty business of mine own
Hold me away, I would have labored peace   30
Betwixt them with all care; indeed I would, sir.

ANNE. I'll write unto my brother earnestly
In that behalf.

WEN.   A charitable deed,
And will beget the good opinion
Of all your friends that love you, Mistress Frankford.

FRANK. That's you, for one; I know you love Sir Charles,
And my wife too, well.

WEN.   He deserves the love
Of all true gentlemen; be yourselves judge!

FRANK. But supper, ho!—Now, as thou lov'st me, Wendoll,
Which I am sure thou dost, be merry, pleasant,   40

And frolic it tonight! Sweet Master Cranwell,
Do you the like! Wife, I protest, my heart
Was ne'er more bent on sweet alacrity.
Where be those lazy knaves to serve in supper?

Enter Nick.

NICK. Here's a letter, sir.

FRANK. Whence comes it, and who brought it?

NICK. A stripling that below attends your answer,
And, as he tells me, it is sent from York.

FRANK. Have him into the cellar; let him taste
A cup of our March beer; go, make him drink!   *[Reads the letter.]*   50

NICK. I'll make him drunk, if he be a Trojan. [3]

FRANK. My boots and spurs! Where's Jenkin? God forgive me,
How I neglect my business! Wife, look here!
I have a matter to be tried tomorrow
By eight a-clock, and my attorney writes me
I must be there betimes with evidence,
Or it will go against me. Where's my boots?

Enter Jenkin, with boots and spurs.

ANNE. I hope your business craves no such despatch
That you must ride tonight?

WEN. [*Aside.*]   I hope it doth.

FRANK. God's me! No such despatch!   60
Jenkin, my boots! Where's Nick? Saddle my roan,
And the gray dapple for himself!—Content ye,
It much concerns me.—Gentle Master Cranwell,
And Master Wendoll, in my absence use
The very ripest pleasures of my house!

WEN. Lord, Master Frankford, will you ride tonight?
The ways are dangerous.

FRANK.   Therefore will I ride
Appointed [4] well; and so shall Nick, my man.

---

[1] Influence with.   [2] Lenient.

[3] Good fellow.   [4] Equipped, armed.

ANNE. I'll call you up by five a-clock to-morrow.

FRANK. No, by my faith, wife, I'll not trust to that. 70
'Tis not such easy rising in a morning
From one I love so dearly. No, by my faith,
I shall not leave so sweet a bedfellow
But with much pain. You have made me a sluggard
Since I first knew you.

ANNE. Then, if you needs will go
This dangerous evening, Master Wendoll,
Let me entreat you bear him company.

WEN. With all my heart, sweet mistress.—
My boots there!

FRANK. Fie, fie, that for my private business 79
I should disease [1] a friend, and be a trouble
To the whole house!—Nick!

NICK. Anon, sir!

FRANK. Bring forth my gelding! [Exit Nick.]—As you love me, sir,
Use no more words. A hand, good Master Cranwell!

CRAN. Sir, God be your good speed!

FRANK. Good night, sweet Nan; nay, nay, a kiss, and part!—
[Aside.] Dissembling lips, you suit not with my heart. Exit.

WEN. [Aside.] How business, time, and hours all gracious prove,
And are the furtherers to my new-born love!
I am husband now in Master Frankford's place,
And must command the house.—My pleasure is 90
We will not sup abroad so publicly,
But in your private chamber, Mistress Frankford.

ANNE. [Aside to Wendoll.] O, sir, you are too public in your love,
And Master Frankford's wife—

CRAN. Might I crave favor,
I would entreat you I might see my chamber.
I am on the sudden grown exceeding ill,
And would be spared from supper.

WEN. Light there, ho!—
See you want nothing, sir, for, if you do,
You injure that good man, and wrong me too. 99

[1] Dis-ease, inconvenience.

CRAN. I will make bold. Good night!
Exit.

WEN. How all conspire
To make our bosom [2] sweet, and full entire! [3]
Come, Nan, I prithee let us sup within!

ANNE. O, what a clog unto the soul is sin!
We pale offenders are still full of fear;
Every suspicious eye brings danger near,
When they whose clear heart from offense are free
Despise report, base scandals do outface,
And stand at mere [4] defiance with disgrace.

WEN. Fie, fie! You talk too like a Puritan.

ANNE. You have tempted me to mischief, M[aster] Wendoll; 110
I have done I know not what. Well, you plead custom;
That which for want of wit I granted erst, [5]
I now must yield through fear. Come, come, let's in;
Once o'er shoes, we are straight o'er head in sin.

WEN. My jocund soul is joyful above measure;
I'll be profuse in Frankford's richest treasure. Exeunt.

[SCENE xii.

Another room in the house.]

Enter Sisly, Jenkin, Butler.

JENK. My mistress and Master Wendoll, my master, sup in her chamber tonight. Sisly, you are preferred [6] from being the cook to be chambermaid. Of all the loves betwixt thee and me, tell me what thou think'st of this.

SISLY. Mum; there's an old proverb, "When the cat's away, the mouse may play."

JENK. Now you talk of a cat, Sisly, I [10 smell a rat.

SISLY. Good words, Jenkin, lest you be called to answer them!

JENK. Why, God make my mistress an honest woman! Are not these good words? Pray God my new master play not the knave with my old master! Is there any

[2] Intimacy.
[3] Very complete.
[4] Absolute.
[5] Formerly.
[6] Promoted.

hurt in this? God send no villainy intended; and, if they do sup together, pray God they do not lie together! God make my mis- [20 tress chaste, and make us all His servants! What harm is there in all this? Nay, more; here is my hand; thou shalt never have my heart unless thou say amen.

SISLY. Amen, I pray God, I say.

Enter Serving-men.

SERVING-MAN. My mistress sends that you should make less noise, to lock up the doors, and see the household all got to bed. You, Jenkin, for this night are made the porter, to see the gates shut in. 30

JENK. Thus by little and little I creep into office. Come, to kennel, my masters, to kennel; 'tis eleven a-clock already.

SERV. When you have locked the gates in, you must send up the keys to my mistress.

SISLY. Quickly, for God's sake, Jenkin, for I must carry them. I am neither pillow nor bolster, but I know more than both.

JENK. To bed, good Spigot; to bed, [40 good honest serving-creatures; and let us sleep as snug as pigs in pea straw! *Exeunt.*

[SCENE xiii.

Outside Frankford's house.[1]]

Enter Frankford and Nick.

FRANK. Soft, soft! We have tied our [2] geldings to a tree,
Two flight-shot [3] off, lest by their thun-
  dering hoofs
They blab our coming. Hear'st thou no
  noise?

NICK. I hear nothing but the owl and you.

FRANK. So; now my watch's hand points upon twelve,
And it is just midnight. Where are my keys?

NICK. Here, sir.

FRANK. This is the key that opes my outward gate;
This, the hall door; this, the withdraw-
  ing-chamber; 10

---

[1] This scene shifts gradually to the hall of the house.
[2] From 1607 edn. Original reads *your.*
[3] Early edns. read *flight shoot;* long bow-shot.

But this, that door that's bawd unto my shame,
Fountain and spring of all my bleeding thoughts,
Where the most hallowed order and true knot
Of nuptial sanctity hath been profaned.
It leads to my polluted bedchamber,
Once my terrestrial heaven, now my earth's hell,
The place where sins in all their ripeness dwell.—
But I forget myself; now to my gate!

NICK. It must ope with far less noise than Cripplegate, or your plot's dashed. [20

FRANK. So, reach me my dark lanthorn to the rest! [4]
Tread softly, softly!

NICK. I will walk on eggs this pace.
[*They enter the house.*]

FRANK. A general silence hath surprised the house,
And this is the last door. Astonishment,
Fear, and amazement beat upon my heart,
Even as a madman beats upon a drum.
O, keep my eyes, you heavens, before I enter,
From any sight that may transfix my soul;
Or, if there be so black a spectacle,
O, strike mine eyes stark blind; or, if not so, 30
Lend me such patience to digest my grief,
That I may keep this white and virgin hand
From any violent outrage or red murther!
And with that prayer I enter.
[*Peers into the bedchamber.*]

NICK. [*Aside.*] Here's a circumstance, indeed! A man may be made cuckold in the time that he's about it. And [5] the case were mine, as 'tis my master's—'sblood, that he makes me swear!—I would have placed his action,[6] entered there; [40 I would, I would!

FRANK. [*Turning away.*] O! O!

NICK. Master! 'Sblood! Master, master!

FRANK. O me unhappy! I have found them lying

---

[4] *I.e.,* in addition to the other equipment.
[5] If.
[6] Established his case (Ward).

Close in each other arms, and fast asleep.
But that I would not damn two precious
　souls,
Bought with my Savior's blood, and send
　them laden
With all their scarlet sins upon their
　backs
Unto a fearful judgment, their two lives
Had met upon my rapier.　　　　　50
NICK. Master, what, have you left them
　sleeping still?
Let me go wake 'em!
FRANK.　　　　Stay, let me pause awhile!—
O God! O God! That it were possible
To undo things done, to call back yester-
　day;
That Time could turn up his swift sandy
　glass,
To untell the days, and to redeem these
　hours;
Or that the sun
Could, rising from the west, draw his
　coach backward,
Take from th' account of time so many
　minutes,　　　　　59
Till he had all these seasons called again,
Those minutes, and those actions done
　in them,
Even from her first offense that I might
　take her
As spotless as an angel in my arms!
But, O, I talk of things impossible,
And cast beyond the moon.[1] God give
　me patience,
For I will in, and wake them.　　*Exit.*
NICK.　　　　Here's patience perforce!
He needs must trot afoot that tires his
　horse.

*Enter Wendoll, running over the stage in a
　nightgown, he [Frankford] after him
　with his sword drawn; the Maid in her
　smock stays his hand, and clasps hold
　on him. He pauses for a while.*

FRANK. I thank thee, maid; thou, like an
　angel's hand,
Hast stayed me from a bloody sacrifice.—
Go, villain, and my wrongs sit on thy
　soul　　　　　70
As heavy as this grief doth upon mine!
When thou record'st my many courtesies,
And shall compare them with thy treach-
　erous heart,

[1] *I.e.*, speak wildly.

Lay them together, weigh them equally,
'Twill be revenge enough. Go, to thy
　friend
A Judas; pray, pray, lest I live to see
Thee, Judas-like, hanged on an eldertree!

*Enter Mistress Frankford in her smock,
　nightgown, and night attire.*

ANNE. O, by what word, what title, or
　what name,
Shall I entreat your pardon? Pardon! O,
I am as far from hoping such sweet grace
As Lucifer from heaven. To call you
　husband—　　　　　81
O me, most wretched! I have lost that
　name;
I am no more your wife.
NICK.　　　　'Sblood, sir, she sounds.[2]
FRANK. Spare thou thy tears, for I will
　weep for thee;
And keep thy count'nance, for I'll blush
　for thee.
Now, I protest, I think 'tis I am tainted,
For I am most ashamed; and 'tis more
　hard
For me to look upon thy guilty face
Than on the sun's clear brow. What
　wouldst thou speak?
ANNE. I would I had no tongue, no ears,
　no eyes,　　　　　90
No apprehension, no capacity.
When do you spurn me like a dog? When
　tread me
Under feet? When drag me by the hair?
Though I deserve a thousand thousand
　fold
More than you can inflict, yet, once my
　husband,
For womanhood—to which I am a
　shame,[3]
Though once an ornament—even for His
　sake
That hath redeemed our souls, mark not
　my face,
Nor hack me with your sword, but let
　me go　　　　　99
Perfect and undeforméd to my tomb!
I am not worthy that I should prevail
In the least suit; no, not to speak to you,
Nor look on you, nor to be in your
　presence;
Yet, as an abject, this one suit I crave.
This granted, I am ready for my grave.

[2] Swoons.　　　[3] Early edns. read *ashamed*.

FRANK. My God, with patience arm me!—
　　Rise, nay, rise,
And I'll debate with thee. Was it for
　　want
Thou playedst the strumpet? Wast thou
　　not supplied
With every pleasure, fashion, and new
　　toy,
Nay, even beyond my calling? [1]
ANNE.　　　　　　　　I was.　　110
FRANK. Was it, then, disability in me?
Or in thine eye seemed he a properer [2]
　　man?
ANNE. O, no!
FRANK.　　　　　Did not I lodge thee in
　　my bosom?
Wear thee in my heart?
ANNE.　　　　　　　You did.
FRANK. I did, indeed; witness my tears, I
　　did.—
Go, bring my infants hither!—
[*Exit Maid and returns with two Children.*]
　　　　　　　　　O Nan! O Nan!
If neither fear of shame, regard of honor,
The blemish of my house, nor my dear love
Could have withheld thee from so lewd
　　a fact,[3]
Yet for these infants, these young, harm-
　　less souls,　　120
On whose white brows thy shame is
　　charactered,
And grows in greatness as they wax in
　　years—
Look but on them, and melt away in
　　tears!—
Away with them, lest, as her spotted
　　body
Hath stained their names with stripe of
　　bastardy,
So her adulterous breath may blast their
　　spirits
With her infectious thoughts! Away with
　　them!　　[*Exeunt Maid and Children.*]
ANNE. In this one life, I die ten thousand
　　deaths.
FRANK. Stand up, stand up! I will do
　　nothing rashly.
I will retire awhile into my study,　　130
And thou shalt hear thy sentence pres-
　　ently.[4]　　　　　　　　　*Exit.*
ANNE. 'Tis welcome, be it death. O me,
　　base strumpet,

That, having such a husband, such sweet
　　children,
Must enjoy neither! O, to redeem mine
　　honor,
I would have this hand cut off, these my
　　breasts seared;
Be racked, strappadoed, put to any
　　torment;
Nay, to whip but this scandal out, I
　　would hazard
The rich and dear redemption of my soul!
He cannot be so base as to forgive me,
Nor I so shameless to accept his par-
　　don.　　　　　　　　　　140
O women, women, you that yet have
　　kept
Your holy matrimonial vow unstained,
Make me your instance; when you tread
　　awry,
Your sins, like mine, will on your con-
　　science lie.

*Enter Sisly, Spigot, all the Serving-men, and
　　　　Jenkin, as newly come out of bed.*

ALL. O mistress, mistress! What have you
　　done, mistress?
NICK. What a caterwauling keep you here!
JENK. O Lord, mistress, how comes this
　　to pass? My master is run away in his
　　shirt, and never so much as called me to
　　bring his clothes after him.　　150
ANNE. See what guilt is! Here stand I in
　　this place,
Ashamed to look my servants in the
　　face.

*Enter M[aster] Frankford and Cranwell,
　　whom seeing, she falls on her knees.*

FRANK. My words are registered in heaven
　　already.
With patience hear me. I'll not martyr
　　thee,
Nor mark thee for a strumpet, but with
　　usage
Of more humility torment thy soul,
And kill thee even with kindness.
CRAN.　　　　　M[aster] Frankford—
FRANK. Good M[aster] Cranwell!—Wo-
　　man, hear thy judgment!
Go make thee ready in thy best attire,
Take with thee all thy gowns, all thy
　　apparel,　　160
Leave nothing that did ever call thee
　　mistress,

---

[1] Estate, station.
[2] Handsomer.
[3] Act.
[4] Immediately.

Or by whose sight, being left here in the house,
I may remember such a woman by.
Choose thee a bed and hangings for thy chamber,
Take with thee everything which hath thy mark,
And get thee to my manor seven mile off,
Where live. 'Tis thine; I freely give it thee.
My tenants by [1] shall furnish thee with wains
To carry all thy stuff within two hours;
No longer will I limit [2] thee my sight. 170
Choose which of all my servants thou lik'st best,
And they are thine to attend thee.

ANNE.   A mild sentence.

FRANK. But, as thou hop'st for heaven, as thou believ'st
Thy name's recorded in the Book of Life,
I charge thee never after this sad day
To see me, or to meet me, or to send,
By word or writing, gift or otherwise,
To move me, by thyself or by thy friends,
Nor challenge any part in my two children.
So farewell, Nan; for we will henceforth be   180
As we had never seen, ne'er more shall see.

ANNE. How full my heart is, in mine eyes appears;
What wants in words, I will supply in tears.

FRANK. Come, take your coach, your stuff; all must along.
Servants and all make ready; all begone!
It was thy hand cut two hearts out of one.   *Exeunt.*

[SCENE xiv.

Before Sir Francis Acton's house.]

Enter Sir Charles, gentlemanlike, and his Sister, gentlewomanlike.

SUS. Brother, why have you tricked [3] me like a bride,
Bought me this gay attire, these ornaments?
Forget you our estate, our poverty?

CHAR. Call me not brother, but imagine me
Some barbarous outlaw, or uncivil kern; [4]
For, if thou shutt'st thy eye, and only hear'st
The words that I shall utter, thou shalt judge me
Some staring ruffian, not thy brother Charles.
O sister!—

SUS. O brother, what doth this strange language mean?   10

CHAR. Dost love me, sister? Wouldst thou see me live
A bankrout [5] beggar in the world's disgrace,
And die indebted to mine enemies?
Wouldst thou behold me stand like a huge beam
In the world's eye, a byword and a scorn?
It lies in thee of these to acquit me free,
And all my debt I may outstrip by thee.

SUS. By me? Why, I have nothing, nothing left;
I owe even for the clothes upon my back;
I am not worth—

CHAR.   O sister, say not so!   20
It lies in you my downcast state to raise,
To make me stand on even points with the world.
Come, sister, you are rich; indeed you are,
And in your power you have, without delay,
Acton's five hundred pound back to repay.

SUS. Till now I had thought y' had loved me. By my honor,
Which I have kept as spotless as the moon,
I ne'er was mistress of that single doit [6]
Which I reserved not to supply your wants;
And d' ye think that I would hoard from you?   30
Now, by my hopes in heaven, knew I the means
To buy you from the slavery of your debts
(Especially from Acton, whom I hate),
I would redeem it with my life or blood!

CHAR. I challenge it, and, kindred set apart,

[1] Near by.   [3] Tricked out, dressed.
[2] Allot, permit.

[4] Peasant.   [5] Bankrupt.   [6] Half a farthing.

Thus, ruffianlike, I lay siege to thy heart.
What do I owe to Acton?

Sus. Why, some five hundred pounds,
towards which, I swear,
In all the world I have not one denier.[1]

Char. It will not prove so. Sister, now
resolve me: 40
What do you think (and speak your conscience)
Would Acton give, might he enjoy your
bed?

Sus. He would not shrink to spend a thousand pound
To give the Mountfords' name so deep a
wound.

Char. A thousand pound! I but five hundred owe;
Grant him your bed; he's paid with
int'rest so.

Sus. O brother!

Char.   O sister! Only this one way,
With that rich jewel you my debts may
pay.
In speaking this my cold heart shakes
with shame;
Nor do I woo you in a brother's name, 50
But in a stranger's. Shall I die in debt
To Acton, my grand foe, and you still wear
The precious jewel that he holds so dear?

Sus. My honor I esteem as dear and precious
As my redemption.

Char.   I esteem you, sister,
As dear, for so dear prizing it.

Sus.   Will Charles
Have me cut off my hands, and send
them Acton?
Rip up my breast, and with my bleeding
heart
Present him as a token?

Char.   Neither, sister;
But hear me in my strange assertion! 60
Thy honor and my soul are equal in my
regard;
Nor will thy brother Charles survive thy
shame.
His kindness, like a burthen, hath sur-
charged me,
And under his good deeds I stooping go,
Not with an upright soul. Had I re-
mained
In prison still, there doubtless I had died.
Then, unto him that freed me from that
prison,

[1] Penny.

Still do I owe this life. What moved my
foe
To enfranchise [2] me? 'Twas, sister, for
your love.
With full five hundred pounds he bought
your love,   70
And shall he not enjoy it? Shall the
weight
Of all this heavy burthen lean on me,
And will not you bear part? You did
partake
The joy of my release; will you not stand
In joint bond bound to satisfy the debt?
Shall I be only charged?

Sus.   But that I know
These arguments come from an honored
mind,
As in your most extremity of need
Scorning to stand in debt to one you
hate—
Nay, rather would engage your unstained
honor   80
Than to be held ingrate—I should con-
demn you.
I see your resolution, and assent.
So Charles will have me, and I am content.

Char. For this I tricked you up.

Sus.   But here's a knife,
To save mine honor, shall slice out my life.

Char. I know thou pleasest me a thousand
times
More in thy resolution than thy grant.—
[Aside.] Observe her love; to soothe it to
my suit,
Her honor she will hazard, though not
lose;
To bring me out of debt, her rigorous
hand   90
Will pierce her heart. O wonder, that
will choose,
Rather than stain her blood, her life to
lose.—
Come, you sad sister to a woeful brother,
This is the gate. I'll bear him such a
present,
Such an acquittance for the knight to seal,
As will amaze his senses, and surprise
With admiration [3] all his fantasies.

Enter Acton and Malby.

Sus. Before his unchaste thoughts shall
seize on me,
'Tis here shall my imprisoned soul set free.

[2] Set free.   [3] Wonder.

FRAN. How! Mountford with his sister,
hand in hand! 100
What miracle's afoot?

MAL. It is a sight
Begets in me much admiration.

CHAR. Stand not amazed to see me thus
attended!
Acton, I owe thee money, and, being
unable
To bring thee the full sum in ready coin,
Lo, for thy more assurance, here's a
pawn—
My sister, my dear sister, whose chaste
honor
I prize above a million. Here! Nay, take
her;
She's worth your money, man; do not
forsake her.

FRAN. I would he were in earnest! 110

SUS. Impute it not to my immodesty.
My brother, being rich in nothing else
But in his interest that he hath in me,
According to his poverty hath brought
you
Me, all his store, whom, howsoe'er you
prize,
As forfeit to your hand, he values highly,
And would not sell, but to acquit your
debt,
For any emperor's ransom.

FRAN. [Aside.] Stern heart, relent;
Thy former cruelty at length repent!
Was ever known, in any former age, 120
Such honorable, wrested [1] courtesy?
Lands, honors, life, and all the world forgo
Rather than stand engaged to such a foe!

CHAR. Acton, she is too poor to be thy
bride,
And I too much opposed to be thy
brother.
There, take her to thee. If thou hast the
heart
To seize her as a rape or lustful prey,
To blur our house, that never yet was
stained,
To murther her that never meant thee
harm,
To kill me now, whom once thou savedst
from death, 130
Do them at once; on her all these rely,
And perish with her spotted chastity.

FRAN. You overcome me in your love, Sir
Charles.

¹ Distorted.

I cannot be so cruel to a lady
I love so dearly. Since you have not
spared
To engage your reputation to the world,
Your sister's honor, which you prize so
dear,
Nay, all the comfort which you hold on
earth,
To grow out of my debt, being your foe,
Your honored thoughts, lo! thus I recom-
pense. 140
Your metamorphosed foe receives your
gift
In satisfaction of all former wrongs.
This jewel I will wear here in my heart;
And, where before I thought her, for her
wants,
Too base to be my bride, to end all strife
I seal you my dear brother, her my wife.

SUS. You still exceed us. I will yield to
fate,
And learn to love, where I till now did
hate.

CHAR. With that enchantment you have
charmed my soul
And made me rich even in those very
words! 150
I pay no debt, but am indebted more;
Rich in your love, I never can be poor.

FRAN. All's mine is yours; we are alike in
state;
Let's knit in love what was opposed in
hate!
Come, for our nuptials we will straight
provide,
Blessed only in our brother and fair bride.
Exeunt.

[SCENE XV.

A room in Frankford's house.]

Enter Cranwell, Frankford, and Nick.

CRAN. Why do you search each room
about your house,
Now that you have despatched your
wife away?

FRANK. O, sir, to see that nothing may be
left
That ever was my wife's. I loved her
dearly,
And, when I do but think of her unkindness,
My thoughts are all in hell; to avoid
which torment,

I would not have a bodkin or a cuff,
A bracelet, necklace, or rabato wire,[1]
Nor anything that ever was called hers
Left me, by which I might remember her.
Seek round about. 11
NICK. 'Sblood! Master, here's her lute
   flung in a corner.
FRANK. Her lute! O God! Upon this in-
   strument
Her fingers have rung quick division,[2]
Sweeter than that which now divides our
   hearts.
These frets have made me pleasant, that
   have now
Frets of my heartstrings made. O, Mas-
   ter Cranwell,
Oft hath she made this melancholy wood
(Now mute and dumb for her disastrous
   chance)[3]
Speak sweetly many a note, sound many
   a strain 20
To her own ravishing voice, which being
   well strung,
What pleasant strange airs have they
   jointly rung!—
Post with it after her!—Now nothing's left;
Of her and hers I am at once bereft.
NICK. I'll ride and overtake her, do my
   message,
And come back again. [Exit.]
CRAN. Meantime, sir, if you please,
I'll to Sir Francis Acton, and inform him
Of what hath passed betwixt you and
   his sister.
FRANK. Do as you please.—How ill am I
   bestead, 29
To be a widower ere my wife be dead!
   [Exeunt.]

[SCENE xvi.

On the road to Frankford's manor.]

*Enter Mistress Frankford, with Jenkin, her
maid Sisly, her Coachmen, and three
Carters.*
ANNE. Bid my coach stay! Why should I
   ride in state,
Being hurled so low down by the hand
   of fate?
A seat like to my fortunes let me have—
Earth for my chair, and for my bed a
   grave!

[1] Wire to support a ruff.
[2] Variations. [3] Because of her misfortune.

JEN. Comfort, good mistress; you have
watered your coach with tears already.
You have but two mile now to go to
your manor. A man cannot say by my
old master Frankford as he may say by
me, that he wants manors; for he hath [10
three or four, of which this is one that we
are going to now.
SISLY. Good mistress, be of good cheer!
Sorrow, you see, hurts you, but helps you
not; we all mourn to see you so sad.
CARTER. Mistress, I see some of my landlord's men
Come riding post;[4] 'tis like he brings
   some news.
ANNE. Comes he from M[aster] Frankford,
   he is welcome;
So is his news, because they come from
   him.

Enter Nick.

NICK. [*Presents lute.*] There! 20
ANNE. I know the lute. Oft have I sung
   to thee;
We both are out of tune, both out of
   time.
NICK. Would that had been the worst
instrument that e'er you played on! My
master commends him unto ye. There's
all he can find that was ever yours; he
hath nothing left that ever you could lay
claim to but his own heart—and he could
afford you that! All that I have to deliver you is this: he prays you to [30
forget him, and so he bids you farewell.
ANNE. I thank him; he is kind, and ever
   was.
All you that have true feeling of my grief,
That know my loss, and have relenting
   hearts,
Gird me about, and help me with your
   tears
To wash my spotted sins! My lute shall
   groan;
It cannot weep, but shall lament my
   moan. [*She plays.*]

Enter Wendoll [behind].

WEN. Pursued with horror of a guilty soul,
And with the sharp scourge of repentance
   lashed, 39
I fly from mine own shadow. O my stars!
[4] Posthaste.

What have my parents in their lives
　deserved,
That you should lay this penance on
　their son?
When I but think of Master Frankford's
　love,
And lay it to my treason, or compare
My murthering him for his relieving
　me,
It strikes a terror like a lightning's flash,
To scorch my blood up. Thus I, like
　the owl,
Ashamed of day, live in these shadowy
　woods,
Afraid of every leaf or murmuring blast.
Yet longing to receive some perfect
　knowledge　　　　　　　　　　　50
How he hath dealt with her.　[Sees
　Anne.] O my sad fate!
Here, and so far from home, and thus
　attended!
O God! I have divorced the truest
　turtles [1]
That ever lived together, and, being
　divided,
In several places make their several
　moan;
She in the fields laments, and he at home.
So poets write that Orpheus made the
　trees
And stones to dance to his melodious
　harp,
Meaning the rustic and the barbarous
　hinds,　　　　　　　　　　　　　59
That had no understanding part in them;
So she from these rude carters tears
　extracts,
Making their flinty hearts with grief to
　rise,
And draw down rivers from their rocky
　eyes.
ANNE. [To Nick.] If you return unto my
　master, say
(Though not from me, for I am all
　unworthy
To blast his name so with a strumpet's
　tongue)
That you have seen me weep, wish my-
　self dead!
Nay, you may say, too (for my vow is
　passed),
Last night you saw me eat and drink
　my last.

[1] Turtledoves.

This to your master you may say and
　swear,　　　　　　　　　　　　70
For it is writ in heaven, and decreed here.
NICK. I'll say you wept; I'll swear you
　made me sad.
Why, how now, eyes? What now?
　What's here to do?
I'm gone, or I shall straight turn baby too.
WEN. [Aside.] I cannot weep; my heart is
　all on fire.
Cursed be the fruits of my unchaste
　desire!
ANNE. Go, break this lute upon my coach's
　wheel,
As the last music that I e'er shall make—
Not as my husband's gift, but my
　farewell
To all earth's joy; and so your master
　tell!　　　　　　　　　　　　　80
NICK. If I can for crying.
WEN. [Aside.]　　　　　Grief, have done,
Or, like a madman, I shall frantic run.
ANNE. You have beheld the woefull'st
　wretch on earth,
A woman made of tears. Would you
　had words
To express but what you see! My inward
　grief
No tongue can utter, yet unto your power
You may describe my sorrow, and disclose
To thy sad master my abundant woes.
NICK. I'll do your commendations.
ANNE.　　　　　　　　　　O, no!
I dare not so presume; nor to my
　children!　　　　　　　　　　　90
I am disclaimed in both; alas, I am!
O, never teach them, when they come to
　speak,
To name the name of mother. Chide
　their tongue,
If they by chance light on that hated
　word;
Tell them 'tis naught, for, when that
　word they name,
Poor, pretty souls, they harp on their
　own shame.
WEN. [Aside.] To recompense her wrongs,
　what canst thou do?
Thou hast made her husbandless and
　childless too.
ANNE. I have no more to say.—Speak not
　for me;
Yet you may tell your master what you
　see.　　　　　　　　　　　　100

NICK. I'll do 't.   *Exit.*
WEN. [*Aside.*] I'll speak to her, and com-
    fort her in grief.
O, but her wound cannot be cured with
    words!
No matter, though; I'll do my best good
    will
To work a cure on her whom I did kill.
ANNE. So, now unto my coach, then to
    my home,
So to my deathbed, for from this sad
    hour
I never will nor eat, nor drink, nor taste
Of any cates [1] that may preserve my life.
I never will nor smile, nor sleep, nor rest;
But, when my tears have washed my
    black soul white,   111
Sweet Savior, to Thy hands I yield my
    sprite.
WEN. [*Coming forward.*] O, Mistress
    Frankford!
ANNE.   O, for God's sake, fly!
The devil doth come to tempt me, ere
    I die.
My coach!—This sin, that with an
    angel's face
Conjured [2] mine honor, till he sought my
    wrack,
In my repentant eye seems ugly black.
*Exeunt all [except Wendoll and Jenkin], the
                        Carters whistling.*
JENK. What, my young master, that fled
in his shirt! How come you by your
clothes again? You have made our [120
house in a sweet pickle, ha' ye not, think
you? What, shall I serve you still, or
cleave to the old house?
WEN. Hence, slave! Away with thy un-
    seasoned mirth!
Unless thou canst shed tears, and sigh,
    and howl,
Curse thy sad fortunes, and exclaim on
    fate,
Thou art not for my turn.
JENK. Marry, and you will not, another
will; farewell, and be hanged! Would you
had never come to have kept this [130
quoil [3] within our doors! We shall ha'
you run away like a sprite again. [*Exit.*]
WEN. She's gone to death; I live to want
    and woe,
Her life, her sins, and all upon my head.

And I must now go wander, like a Cain,
In foreign countries and remoted climes,
Where the report of my ingratitude
Cannot be heard. I'll over first to
    France,
And so to Germany and Italy,
Where, when I have recovered, and by
    travel   140
Gotten those perfect tongues, [4] and that
    these rumors
May in their height abate, I will return;
And I divine (however now dejected),
My worth and parts being by some great
    man praised,
At my return I may in court be raised.
                                        Exit.

[SCENE xvii.

Before the manor house.[5]]

*Enter Sir Francis, Sir Charles, Cranwell,
                    [Malby,] and Susan.*

FRAN. Brother, and now my wife, I think
    these troubles
Fall on my head by justice of the heav-
    ens,
For being so strict to you in your ex-
    tremities;
But we are now atoned.[6] I would my
    sister
Could with like happiness o'ercome her
    griefs
As we have ours.
SUS. You tell us, Master Cranwell, won-
    drous things
Touching the patience of that gentle-
    man,
With what strange virtue he demeans [7]
    his grief.
CRAN. I told you what I was witness of; 10
It was my fortune to lodge there that
    night.
FRAN. O, that same villain, Wendoll!
    'Twas his tongue
That did corrupt her; she was of her-
    self
Chaste and devoted well.[8] Is this the
    house?

---

[1] Food.   [3] Coil, disturbance.
[2] Enchanted, seduced.

[4] Learned those languages perfectly.
[5] The scene shifts to the interior of the house
during the action.
[6] Reconciled.
[7] Manages.
[8] *I.e.,* true to her marriage vow.

CRAN. Yes, sir; I take it, here your sister lies.

FRAN. My brother Frankford showed too mild a spirit

In the revenge of such a loathéd crime.

Less than he did, no man of spirit could do.

I am so far from blaming his revenge,

That I commend it. Had it been my case,   20

Their souls at once had from their breasts been freed;

Death to such deeds of shame is the due meed.

Enter Jenkin [and Sisly].

JEN. O my mistress, mistress! My poor mistress!

SISLY. Alas, that ever I was born! What shall I do for my poor mistress?

CHAR. Why, what of her?

JENK. O Lord, sir, she no sooner heard that her brother and her friends were come to see how she did, but she, for [30 very shame of her guilty conscience, fell into such a swound that we had much ado to get life in her.

SUS. Alas, that she should bear so hard a fate!

Pity it is repentance comes too late.

FRAN. Is she so weak in body?

JENK. O, sir, I can assure you there's no hope of life in her, for she will take no sust'nance. She hath plainly starved herself, and now she's as lean as a lath. She [40 ever looks for the good hour. Many gentlemen and gentlewomen of the country are come to comfort her.

Enter Mistress Frankford in her bed.[1]

MAL. How fare you, Mistress Frankford?

ANNE. Sick, sick, O, sick! Give me some air, I pray!

Tell me, O, tell me, where's Master Frankford?

Will not [he] deign to see me ere I die?

MAL. Yes, Mistress Frankford; divers gentlemen,

Your loving neighbors, with that just request

---

[1] Either the bed was pushed onto the stage or the curtains of the inner stage were drawn to disclose her.

Have moved and told him of your weak estate,   50

Who, though with much ado to get belief,

Examining of the general circumstance,

Seeing your sorrow and your penitence,

And hearing therewithal the great desire

You have to see him, ere you left the world,

He gave to us his faith to follow us,

And sure he will be here immediately.

ANNE. You have half revived me with the pleasing news.

Raise me a little higher in my bed.

Blush I not, brother Acton? Blush I not, Sir Charles?   60

Can you not read my fault writ in my cheek?

Is not my crime there? Tell me, gentlemen.

CHAR. Alas, good mistress, sickness hath not left you

Blood in your face enough to make you blush.

ANNE. Then sickness, like a friend, my fault would hide.

Is my husband come? My soul but tarries

His arrive; then I am fit for heaven.

FRAN. I came to chide you, but my words of hate

Are turned to pity and compassionate grief.

I came to rate you, but my brawls, you see,   70

Melt into tears, and I must weep by thee.—

Here's M[aster] Frankford now.

Enter Frankford.

FRANK. Good morrow, brother; morrow, gentlemen!

God, that hath laid this cross upon our heads,

Might, had He pleased, have made our cause of meeting

On a more fair and more contented ground;

But He that made us, made us to this woe.

ANNE. And is he come? Methinks that voice I know.

FRANK. How do you, woman?

ANNE. Well, M[aster] Frankford, well;
  but shall be better,   80
  I hope, within this hour. Will you vouch-
    safe,
  Out of your grace and your humanity,
  To take a spotted strumpet by the
    hand?

FRANK. This hand once held my heart
    in faster bonds
  Than now 'tis griped by me. God pardon
    them
  That made us first break hold!

ANNE.   Amen, amen!
  Out of my zeal to heaven, whither I'm
    now bound,
  I was so impudent to wish you here,
  And once more beg your pardon. O,
    good man,   89
  And father to my children, pardon me.
  Pardon, O, pardon me! My fault so
    heinous is
  That, if you in this world forgive it not,
  Heaven will not clear it in the world to
    come.
  Faintness hath so usurped upon my
    knees,
  That kneel I cannot; but on my heart's
    knees
  My prostrate soul lies thrown down at
    your feet,
  To beg your gracious pardon. Pardon,
    O, pardon me!

FRANK. As freely, from the low depth of
    my soul,
  As my Redeemer hath forgiven His
    death,
  I pardon thee. I will shed tears for thee,
    pray with thee,   100
  And, in mere pity of thy weak estate,
  I'll wish to die with thee.

ALL.   So do we all.

NICK.   So will not I;
  I'll sigh and sob, but, by my faith, not die.

FRAN. O, Master Frankford, all the near
    alliance
  I lose by her shall be supplied in thee.
  You are my brother by the nearest way;
  Her kindred hath fallen off, but yours
    doth stay.

FRANK. Even as I hope for pardon at
    that day
  When the great Judge of Heaven in
    scarlet sits,

So be thou pardoned! Though thy rash
    offense   110
  Divorced our bodies, thy repentant
    tears
  Unite our souls.

CHAR.   Then comfort, Mistress
    Frankford!
  You see your husband hath forgiven
    your fall;
  Then rouse your spirits, and cheer your
    fainting soul!

SUS. How is it with you?

FRAN.   How d' ye feel yourself?

ANNE. Not of this world.

FRANK. I see you are not, and I weep
    to see it.
  My wife, the mother to my pretty
    babes!
  Both those lost names I do restore thee
    back,   119
  And with this kiss I wed thee once again.
  Though thou art wounded in thy honored
    name,
  And with that grief upon thy deathbed
    liest,
  Honest in heart, upon my soul, thou
    diest.

ANNE. Pardoned on earth, soul, thou in
    heaven art free;
  Once more thy wife dies, thus embrac-
    ing thee.   [Dies.]

FRANK. New-married, and new-widowed!—
    O! she's dead,
  And a cold grave must be her nuptial
    bed.

CHAR. Sir, be of good comfort, and your
    heavy sorrow
  Part equally amongst us. Storms di-
    vided
  Abate their force, and with less rage
    are guided.   130

CRAN. Do, Master Frankford; he that
    hath least part
  Will find enough to drown one troubled
    heart.

FRAN. Peace with thee, Nan!—Brothers
    and gentlemen,
  All we that can plead interest in her
    grief,
  Bestow upon her body funeral tears!
  Brother, had you with threats and usage
    bad
  Punished her sin, the grief of her of-
    fense

Had not with such true sorrow touched
  her heart.
FRANK. I see it had not; therefore, on her
  grave
Will I bestow this funeral epitaph,   140
Which on her marble tomb shall be en-
  graved.
In golden letters shall these words be
  filled:
Here lies she whom her husband's kind-
* ness killed.*
          FINIS.

THE EPILOGUE

AN honest crew, disposéd to be merry,
  Came to a tavern by, and called for
  wine.
The drawer brought it, smiling like a
  cherry,
  And told them it was pleasant, neat,[1]
  and fine.
"Taste it," quoth one. He did so. "Fie!"
  quoth he,
[1] Pure.

"This wine was good; now 't runs too near
  the lee."[2]

Another sipped, to give the wine his due,
  And said unto the rest it drunk too
  flat;
The third said it was old; the fourth,
  too new;
  "Nay," quoth the fift, "the sharpness
  likes me not."   10
Thus, gentlemen, you see how, in one hour,
The wine was new, old, flat, sharp, sweet,
  and sour.

Unto this wine we do allude [3] our play,
  Which some will judge too trivial, some
  too grave.
You as our guests we entertain this day,
  And bid you welcome to the best we
  have.
Excuse us, then; good wine may be disgraced
When every several mouth hath sundry
  taste.
[2] Lees.   [3] Compare.

JOHN MARSTON

John Marston was born about 1576, seemingly at Coventry. His father was a lawyer, his mother the daughter of an Italian physician resident in England. Marston took his B.A. at Oxford in 1594 and entered the Middle Temple to study law. Turning to literature, he won a reputation by his satiric verse published in 1598, especially by *The Scourge of Villainy*. The first record of his dramatic work is Henslowe's payment to him in 1599 toward an unnamed play. His chief work, however, was done for the boy companies, for the Children of Paul's apparently from 1599 until 1604, when he acquired an interest in the Children of the Queen's Revels. He was a prominent figure in the stage quarrel, or war of the theaters as it was called because of the several companies at different theaters involved. According to Jonson, it arose from Marston's representing him on the stage, but in spite of much study the early history of the affair remains obscure. It lasted from about 1599 until 1601. In 1601 Marston apparently satirized Jonson in *What You Will*, and possibly aided Dekker in preparing the attack in *Satiromastix*. Marston's eulogistic dedication of *The Malcontent* to Jonson indicates a renewal of friendly relations by 1604, and in the same year the two joined Chapman in writing *Eastward Ho*. Marston escaped the imprisonment which his collaborators suffered for *Eastward Ho*, but he was committed to Newgate by the privy council in 1608—it has been conjectured for satire on King James in a play now lost. After this he apparently abandoned the theater and sold his interest in the Children of the Revels. He took orders before 1616, held a living in Hampshire until the end of 1631, and died in 1634. His misanthropy—or his pose—was carried to the grave, for the inscription on his tombstone read, *Oblivioni sacrum*.

Marston's plays follow many of the romantic conventions of Elizabethan drama, but with a fundamental change in spirit. By the end of the sixteenth century, the growth of conservatism and nationalism in the middle classes had brought a sharp reaction against the Italianate elements in English life and literature. Marston and others, taking as their model the rugged style of the Roman satirists, made bitter attacks on the affected gallants of the day and on the artifices of romance and poetry. But their satire reflects also a reaction of Europe as a whole against the idealism of the earlier Renaissance, for many forces were tending to weaken man's faith in the glory of the world and in his own perfectibility. The mood of disillusion is reflected in the misanthropy and melancholy of many writers, who picture the follies of the age as inordinate, its crimes as monstrous. Marston's satire impressed even his contemporaries by its extravagance, its bitterness, and cynicism. As a vehicle for it, he developed—with an affectation equal to that he satirized—a style both blunt and tumid, which is the chief point of Jonson's ridicule in *The Poetaster*. Both mood and manner were carried over into Marston's plays, with a malcontent character used as a critic or an intriguer to set the tone. In keeping with the current conception of the evil of Italian life, he drew the material for his plots and his characters largely from Italy. Here libertinism and Machiavellian intrigue had indeed produced many sinister figures, which were vividly portrayed by Italian writers in both history and story, and which had already been utilized to some extent in Elizabethan novels and plays. But, where direct sources seem to be lacking, dramatists like Marston and Tourneur were able to outdo their models in creating characters and situations of morbid lust and villainy.

Marston's first acknowledged play was *Antonio and Mellida*, an extravagant tragicomedy with disguises and other conventions of romance. The characters were quickly used as a basis for *Antonio's Revenge*, a form of revenge tragedy in which a malcontent revenger carried the type to new depths of gloom and terror. The double play was printed in 1602. *What You Will* (printed in 1607) and *The Malcontent* in its first form were also probably early. In *The Dutch Courtesan* (printed in 1605), with an English setting instead of the usual Italian scene, Marston has used a modification of the plot found in Bandello's famous story of the Countess of Celant, translated by Painter in *The Palace of Pleasure* and by Fenton in *Tragical Discourses*. The comic plot is drawn from a story of Masuccio translated by Painter. *Parasitaster, or the Fawn* (printed in 1606) is based on a story from Boccaccio's *Decameron*. Incidents from Roman history furnished the plot for *The Wonder of Women, or The Tragedy of Sophonisba* (printed in 1606). In *The Insatiate Countess* (published in 1613), which was apparently completed by William Barksted, Marston has used the story of the Countess of Celant for the main plot and another *novella* of Bandello for the subplot.

The Malcontent, for which no source has been discovered, is a tragi-comedy with the dominating atmosphere of tragedy. It was published in 1604, but an allusion (I, vii) to a "horn . . . growing in the woman's forehead, twelve years since" would seem to carry at least part of the play back to 1600 or 1601. A second edition, which quickly followed in the same year, was provided with "additions" by Webster (apparently consisting of little more than an inferior though topically interesting induction) and "augmented" by many passages, primarily comic, presumably from Marston's own pen. The reference to the woman's horn first occurred in one of these "augmentations." *The Works of Mr. John Marston* published in a single volume in 1633 failed to include *The Malcontent*, as well as *Eastward Ho* and *The Insatiate Countess*, in which others had had a hand. The present text is based directly on a photostatic copy of the second edition (1604) in the possession of the Huntington Library, with the permission of the authorities of the Library. The editions of Bullen in *The Works of Marston* and of Neilson in *The Chief Elizabethan Dramatists* have also been consulted.

THE MALCONTENT[1]

BY

JOHN MARSTON

BENJAMINO [2] JONSONIO, POETÆ ELEGANTISSIMO, GRAVISSIMO, AMICO SUO, CANDIDO ET CORDATO, JOHANNES MARSTON, MUSARUM ALUMNUS, ASPERAM HANC SUAM THALIAM D.D.[3]

To the Reader

I am an ill orator, and, in truth, use to indite more honestly than eloquently, for it is my custom to speak as I think, and write as I speak.

In plainness, therefore, understand that in some things I have willingly erred, as in supposing a Duke of Genoa, and in taking names different from that city's families, for which some may wittily accuse me; but my defense shall be as honest as many [10 reproofs unto me have been most malicious, since, I heartily protest, it was my care to write so far from reasonable offense that even strangers in whose state I laid my scene should not from thence draw any disgrace to any, dead or living. Yet, in despite of my endeavors, I understand some have been most unadvisedly overcunning in misinterpreting me, and with subtility as deep as hell have maliciously spread [20 ill rumors, which, springing from themselves, might to themselves have heavily returned. Surely I desire to satisfy every firm spirit, who, in all his actions, proposeth to himself no more ends than God and vir-

tue do, whose intentions are always simple. To such I protest that, with my free understanding, I have not glanced at disgrace of any, but of those whose unquiet studies labor [4] innovation, contempt of holy [30 policy, reverent, comely superiority, and established unity. For the rest of my supposed tartness, I fear not but unto every worthy mind it will be approved so general and honest as may modestly pass with the freedom of a satire. I would fain leave the paper; only one thing afflicts me, to think that scenes invented merely to be spoken should be enforcively [5] published to be read, and that the least hurt I [40 can receive is to do myself the wrong. But, since others otherwise would do me more, the least inconvenience is to be accepted. I have myself, therefore, set forth this comedy, but so [6] that my enforced absence must much rely upon the printer's discretion; but I shall entreat slight errors in orthography may be as slightly overpassed, and that the unhandsome shape which this trifle in reading presents, may be par- [50 doned for the pleasure it once afforded you when it was presented with the soul of lively action.

Sine aliqua dementia nullus Phœbus.[7]

---

[1] The title continues: "Augmented by Marston. With the Additions Played by the King's Majesty's Servants. Written by John Webster."

[2] Original reads *Beniamini.*

[3] "To Benjamin Jonson, poet most accomplished and most eminent, his frank and judicious friend—John Marston, follower of the Muses—dedicates this his unpolished comedy."

[4] Work for.

[5] Compulsorily.

[6] In such a manner.

[7] No poet is without some madness.

DRAMATIS PERSONÆ

GIOVANNI ALTOFRONTO,[1] *disguised Male-*
vole, sometime Duke of Genoa.
PIETRO JACOMO, *Duke of Genoa.*
MENDOZA, *a minion*[2] *to the duchess of Pietro*
Jacomo.
CELSO, *a friend to Altofront.*
BILIOSO, *an old choleric marshal.*
PREPASSO, *a gentleman usher.*
FERNEZE, *a young courtier, and enamored*
on the duchess.

FERRARDO, *a minion to Duke Pietro Jacomo.*
EQUATO ⎫ *two courtiers.*
GUERRINO ⎭
AURELIA, *duchess to Duke Pietro Jacomo.*
MARIA, *duchess to Duke Altofront.*
EMILIA ⎫ *two ladies attending the*
BIANCHA ⎭ *duchess [, Aurelia].*
MAQUERELLE, *an old panderess.*
PASSARELLO, *fool to Bilioso.*
[CAPTAIN *of the citadel.*

SCENE: *Genoa.*

TIME: *Contemporary.*]

THE INDUCTION [3]

TO

THE MALCONTENT, AND THE ADDITIONS[4] ACTED BY THE KING'S MAJESTY'S
SERVANTS

WRITTEN BY JOHN WEBSTER

Enter W[illiam] Sly,[5] *a Tireman*[6] *following*
him with a stool.

TIRE. Sir, the gentlemen will be angry
if you sit here.

SLY. Why? We may sit upon the stage
at the private house.[7] Thou dost not take
me for a country gentleman, dost? Dost
think I fear hissing? I'll hold my life thou
took'st me for one of the players.

TIRE. No, sir.

SLY. By God's slid,[8] if you had, I would
have given you but sixpence for your [10
stool. Let them that have stale suits sit in
the galleries. Hiss at me! He that will be
laughed out of a tavern or an ordinary
shall seldom feed well, or be drunk in good
company.—Where's Harry Condell, D[ick]

Burbadge, and W[illiam] Sly? Let me speak
with some of them.

TIRE. An't [9] please you to go in, sir, you
may.

SLY. I tell you, no. I am one that [20
hath seen this play often, and can give them
intelligence for their action. I have most
of the jests here in my table-book.[10]

Enter Sinklo.

SINK. Save you, coz! [11]

SLY. O, cousin, come, you shall sit between my legs here.

SINK. No, indeed, cousin; the audience
then will take me for a viol-de-gambo, and
think that you play upon me.

SLY. Nay, rather that I work upon [30
you, coz.

SINK. We stayed for you at supper last
night at my cousin Honeymoon's, the
woolen draper. After supper we drew cuts
for a score of apricocks,[12] the longest cut
still to draw an apricock. By this light,
'twas Mistress Frank Honeymoon's fortune
still to have the longest cut; I did measure
for the women.—What be these, coz?

---

[1] The significance of many of these names as
indicating "humors" or offices is obvious.
[2] Favorite, lover.
[3] The induction does not appear in the first
edn.
[4] The significant additions are indicated in
footnotes.
[5] William Sly, John Sinklo, Richard Burbadge,
etc., were prominent members of the King's
Company.
[6] Property man.
[7] The Blackfriars Theater.
[8] Eyelid.

[9] If it.
[10] Notebook.

[11] Cousin, friend.
[12] Apricots.

Enter D[ick] Burbadge, H[arry] Condell, J[ohn] Lowin.

SLY. The players.—God save you! 40
BUR. You are very welcome.
SLY. I pray you, know this gentleman, my cousin; 'tis Master Doomsday's son, the usurer.
CON. I beseech you, sir, be covered.[1]
SLY. No, in good faith, for mine ease. Look you, my hat's the handle to this fan. God's so,[2] what a beast was I, I did not leave my feather at home! Well, but I'll take an order with you. 50
Puts his feather in his pocket.
BUR. Why do you conceal your feather, sir?
SLY. Why? Do you think I'll have jests broken upon me in the play, to be laughed at? This play hath beaten all your gallants out of the feathers. Blackfriars hath almost spoiled Blackfriars for feathers.[3]
SINK. God's so, I thought 'twas for somewhat our gentlewomen at home counseled me to wear my feather to the [60 play; yet I am loath to spoil it.
SLY. Why, coz?
SINK. Because I got it in the tiltyard; there was a herald broke my pate for taking it up. But I have worn it up and down the Strand, and met him forty times since, and yet he dares not challenge it.
SLY. Do you hear, sir? This play is a bitter play.
CON. Why, sir, 'tis neither satire nor [70 moral, but the mean[4] passage of a history; yet there are a sort of discontented creatures that bear a stingless envy to great ones, and these will wrest the doings of any man to their base, malicious applyment; but, should their interpretation come to the test, like your marmoset they presently turn their teeth to their tail and eat it.
SLY. I will not go so far with you; but I say any man that hath wit may cen- [80 sure,[5] if he sit in the twelvepenny room;[6] and I say again the play is bitter.
BUR. Sir, you are like a patron that, presenting a poor scholar to a benefice, enjoins him not to rail against anything

that stands within compass of his patron's folly. Why should not we enjoy the ancient freedom of poesy? Shall we protest to the ladies that their painting makes them angels, or to my young gallant [90 that his expense in the brothel shall gain him reputation? No, sir, such vices as stand not accountable to law should be cured as men heal tetters, by casting ink upon them. Would you be satisfied[7] in anything else, sir?
SLY. Ay, marry, would I: I would know how you came by this play.
CON. Faith, sir, the book was lost; and, because 'twas pity so good a play [100 should be lost, we found it, and play it.
SLY. I wonder you would play it, another company having interest in it.
CON. Why not Malevole in folio with us, as Jeronimo in decimo-sexto with them?[8] They taught us a name for our play; we call it *One for Another.*
SLY. What are your additions?
BUR. Sooth, not greatly needful; only as your sallet[9] to your great feast, to [110 entertain a little more time, and to abridge the not-received custom of music in our theater.[10] I must leave you, sir.
Exit Burbadge.
SINK. Doth he play the Malcontent?
CON. Yes, sir.
SINK. I durst lay four of mine ears the play is not so well acted as it hath been.
CON. O, no, sir, nothing *ad Parmenonis suem.*[11]

---

[1] Put your hat on. [2] A mild oath.
[3] This presumably refers to V, ii, 47–48, and perhaps means that gallants wearing feathers were so ridiculed that they quit the district.
[4] Common. [5] Judge, criticize. [6] Box.

[7] Answered.
[8] "*I.e.* Why should not the King's Company of grown up (folio) actors play *The Malcontent* (which was the property of the children's company playing at Blackfriars), since the children (16mo actors) have appropriated *The Spanish Tragedy*, in which the King's Company had rights?" (Neilson).
[9] Salad.
[10] *I.e.*, fill in the interval ordinarily taken by music in other theaters.
[11] "'Tis reported that Parmeno, being very famous for imitating the grunting of a pig, some endeavoured to rival and outdo him. And when the hearers, being prejudiced, cried out, 'Very well, indeed, but nothing comparable to Parmeno's sow,' one took a pig under his arm and came upon the stage; and when, tho' they heard the very pig, they still continued, 'This is nothing comparable to Parmeno's sow,' he threw the pig among them to show that they judged according to opinion and not truth" (Plutarch's *Symposium*, V, i, cited by "L. S." and Bullen).

Low. Have you lost your ears, sir, [120 that you are so prodigal of laying them?

Sink. Why did you ask that, friend?

Low. Marry, sir, because I have heard of a fellow would offer to lay a hundred pound wager, that was not worth five baubees;[1] and in this kind you might venter[2] four of your elbows; yet God defend[3] your coat should have so many!

Sink. Nay, truly, I am no great censurer; and yet I might have been one of [130 the College of Critics once. My cousin here hath an excellent memory, indeed, sir.

Sly. Who, I? I'll tell you a strange thing of myself; and I can tell you, for one that never studied the art of memory, 'tis very strange too.

Con. What's that, sir?

Sly. Why, I'll lay a hundred pound I'll walk but once down by the Goldsmiths' Row in Cheap, take notice of the signs, [140 and tell you them with a breath instantly.

Low. 'Tis very strange.

Sly. They begin as the world did, with Adam and Eve. There's in all just five-and-fifty. I do use to meditate much when I come to plays too. What do you think might come into a man's head now, seeing all this company?

Con. I know not, sir.

Sly. I have an excellent thought. [150 If some fifty of the Grecians that were crammed in the horse-belly had eaten garlic, do you not think the Trojans might have smelt out their knavery?

Con. Very likely.

Sly. By God, I would he had, for I love Hector horribly.

Sink. O, but, coz, coz!—
"Great Alexander, when he came to the tomb of Achilles,
Spake with a big loud voice, 'O thou thrice blessed and happy!'"[4]   [160

Sly. Alexander was an ass to speak so well of a filthy cullion.[5]

Low. Good sir, will you leave the stage? I'll help you to a private room.[6]

Sly. Come, coz, let's take some tobacco.—Have you never a prologue?

Low. Not any, sir.

---

[1] Halfpennies.   [2] Venture.   [3] Forbid.
[4] From John Harvey's translation of Petrarch's 153rd sonnet.
[5] Knave.   [6] Box.

Sly. Let me see, I will make one extempore.

*Come to them, and fencing of a congee[7] with
    arms and legs, be round[8] with them.[9]*
Gentlemen, I could wish for the [170 women's sakes you had all soft cushions; and, gentlewomen, I could wish that for the men's sakes you had all more easy standings.—What would they wish more but the play now? And that they shall have instantly.   *[Exeunt.]*

Actus Primus.[10]   Scena Prima.

[The palace of the Duke of Genoa.]

*The vilest out-of-tune music being heard,
            enter Bilioso and Prepasso.*

Bil. Why, how now! Are ye mad, or drunk, or both, or what?

Pre. Are ye building Babylon there?

Bil. Here's a noise in court! You think you are in a tavern, do you not?

Pre. You think you are in a brothel house, do you not?—This room is ill-scented.

Enter One with a perfume.

So, perfume, perfume; some upon me, I
    pray thee.—
The duke is upon instant entrance; so,
    make place there!   10

Scena Secunda.

[The same.]

*Enter the Duke Pietro, Ferrardo, Count
    Equato, Count Celso before, and
                  Guerrino.[11]*

Piet. Where breathes that music?

Bil. The discord rather than the music is heard from the malcontent Malevole's chamber.

Fer. *[Calling.]* Malevole!

---

[7] Making a bow.
[8] Plain-spoken.
[9] This stage direction is printed as part of Sly's speech in the original.
[10] The title is repeated before this line, and in the margin appears Juvenal's phrase, *Vexat censura columbas*, "Censorship disturbs the doves" (*i.e.*, the peace).
[11] The characters from the preceding scene remain, as in general they do throughout the play.

MAL. (*Out of his chamber.*) Yaugh, God
a [1] man, what dost thou there? Duke's
Ganymede, Juno's jealous of thy long
stockings. Shadow of a woman, what
wouldst, weasel? Thou lamb a court, [10
what dost thou bleat for? Ah, you smooth-
chinned catamite! [2]

PIET. Come down, thou ragged cur, and
snarl here. I give thy dogged sullenness
free liberty; trot about and bespurtle [3]
whom thou pleasest.

MAL. I'll come among you, you goatish-
blooded toderers,[4] as gum into taffeta, to
fret, to fret.[5] I'll fall like a sponge into
water, to suck up, to suck up. Howl [20
again! I'll go to church and come to you.
　　　　　　　　　　　　　[*Exit above.*]

PIET. This Malevole is one of the most
prodigious affections [6] that ever conversed
with nature; a man, or rather a monster,
more discontent than Lucifer when he was
thrust out of the presence. His appetite
is unsatiable as the grave, as far from any
content as from heaven. His highest delight is to procure others vexation, and
therein he thinks he truly serves heaven; [30
for 'tis his position, whosoever in this earth
can be contented is a slave and damned;
therefore does he afflict all in that to which
they are most affected.[7] Th' elements
struggle within him; his own soul is at
variance within herself; his speech is halter-
worthy at all hours. I like him; faith, he
gives good intelligence to my spirit, makes
me understand those weaknesses which
others' flattery palliates.—Hark! They [40
sing.[8]

SCENA TERTIA.

[*The same.*]

Enter Malevole after the song.

[PIET.] See, he comes. Now shall you
hear the extremity of a malcontent. He
is as free as air; he blows over every man.—
And, sir, whence come you now?

MAL. From the public place of much
dissimulation, the church.[9]

PIET. What didst there?

---

[1] Of.　　　　　[2] Male prostitute.　[3] Besprinkle.
[4] Perhaps dealers in sheep or mutton, *i.e.*, in
prostitutes.　[5] *I.e.*, to wear you out quickly.
[6] Passions.　[7] Inclined.　[8] The song is not given.
[9] *The church* does not appear in the first
edn. and is erased in some copies of the second.

MAL. Talk with a usurer; take up at
interest.

PIET. I wonder what religion thou [10
art of.

MAL. Of a soldier's religion.

PIET. And what dost think makes most
infidels now?

MAL. Sects, sects. I have seen seeming
Piety change her robe so oft that sure
none but some arch-devil can shape her
a petticoat.

PIET. O, a religious policy.

MAL. But damnation on a politic re- [20
ligion! I am weary. Would I were one
of the duke's hounds now!

PIET. But what's the common news
abroad, Malevole? Thou dogg'st rumor
still.

MAL. Common news? Why, common
words are, "God save ye," "Fare ye well;"
common actions, flattery and cozenage;
common things, women and cuckolds.—
And how does my little Ferrard? Ah, ye [30
lecherous animal! My little ferret, he goes
sucking up and down the palace into every
hen's nest, like a weasel. And to what
dost thou addict thy time to now more
than to those antique painted drabs that
are still affected of [10] young courtiers,
Flattery, Pride, and Venery?

FER. I study languages. Who dost
think to be the best linguist of our age?

MAL. Phew, the devil! Let him pos- [40
sess thee; he'll teach thee to speak all
languages most readily and strangely; and
great reason, marry, he's traveled greatly
in the world, and is everywhere.

FER. Save i' th' court.

MAL. Ay, save i' th' court.—(*To Bilioso.*) And how does my old muckhill, overspread with fresh snow? Thou half a man,
half a goat, all a beast! How does thy
young wife, old huddle? [11]　　　　　50

BIL. Out, you improvident rascal!

MAL. Do, kick, thou hugely-horned old
duke's ox, good Master Make-pleas.

PIET. How dost thou live nowadays,
Malevole?

MAL. Why, like the knight, Sir Pat-
rick Penlolians, with killing a spiders
for my lady's monkey.

PIET. How dost spend the night? I
hear thou never sleep'st.　　　　　60

---

[10] Liked by.　　　　[11] Decrepit old man.

MAL. O, no, but dream the most fantastical! O heaven! O fubbery, fubbery![1]

PIET. Dream! What dream'st?

MAL. Why, methinks I see that signior pawn his footcloth,[2] that *metreza*[3] her plate; this madam takes physic that tother[4] *monsieur* may minister to her. Here is a pander jeweled; there's a fellow in shift of satin this day, that could not shift a shirt tother night. Here a Paris [70 supports that Helen; there's a Lady Guinevere bears up that Sir Lancelot. Dreams, dreams, visions, fantasies, chimeras, imaginations, tricks, conceits![5] —(*To Prepasso.*) Sir Tristram Trimtram, come aloft, Jackanapes,[6] with a whim-wham. Here's a knight of the land of Catito shall play at trap[7] with any page in Europe, do the sword dance with any morris dancer in Christendom, ride at the [80 ring[8] till the fin[9] of his eyes look as blue as the welkin, and run the wild goose chase even with Pompey the Huge.

PIET. You run!

MAL. To the devil. Now, Signior Guerrino, that thou from a most pitied prisoner shouldst grow a most loathed flatterer!— Alas, poor Celso, thy star's oppressed: thou art an honest lord. 'Tis pity.

EQU. Is 't pity? 90

MAL. Ay, marry is 't, philosophical Equato; and 'tis pity that thou, being so excellent a scholar by art, shouldst be so ridiculous a fool by nature.—I have a thing to tell you, duke; bid um avaunt, bid um avaunt.

PIET. Leave us, leave us.—Now, sir, what is 't?

Exeunt all saving Pietro and Malevole.

MAL. Duke, thou art a *becco*,[10] a *cornuto*.[11]

PIET. How? 100

MAL. Thou art a cuckold.

PIET. Speak; unshale[12] him quick.

MAL. With most tumblerlike nimbleness.

PIET. Who? By whom? I burst with desire.

MAL. Mendoza is the man makes thee a horned beast; duke, 'tis Mendoza cornutes thee.

PIET. What conformance?[13] Relate; [110 short, short!

MAL. As a lawyer's beard.
There is an old crone in the court— her name is Maquerelle;
She is my mistress, sooth to say, and she doth ever tell me.
Blurt a rime,[14] blurt a rime! Maquerelle is a cunning bawd; I am an honest villain; thy wife is a close drab;[15] and thou art a notorious cuckold. Farewell, duke.

PIET. Stay, stay.

MAL. Dull, dull duke, can lazy pa- [120 tience make lame revenge? O God, for a woman to make a man that which God never created, never made!

PIET. What did God never make?

MAL. A cuckold! To be made a thing that's hoodwinked with kindness, whilst every rascal fillips his brows; to have a coxcomb with egregious horns pinned to a lord's back, every page sporting himself with delightful laughter, whilst he [130 must be the last must know it! Pistols and poniards! Pistols and poniards!

PIET. Death and damnation!

MAL. Lightning and thunder!

PIET. Vengeance and torture!

MAL. *Catso!*[16]

PIET. O, revenge![17]

MAL. Nay, to select among ten thousand fairs
A lady far inferior to the most,
In fair proportion both of limb and soul; 140
To take her from austerer check of parents,
To make her his by most devoutful rites,
Make her commandress of a better essence
Than is the gorgeous world, even of a man;
To hug her with as raised an appetite
As usurers do their delved-up treasury[18]

---

[1] Deceit.
[2] The housings of a horse.
[3] Mistress.
[4] That other.
[5] Fancies.
[6] The ape-trainer's call to his monkey.
[7] A game played with a bat, a ball, and a trap.
[8] Tilt at a ring.
[9] Lid.
[10] Cuckold.
[11] A horned one.
[12] Unshell.
[13] Confirmance (?), proof.
[14] A fig for rime.
[15] Secret harlot.
[16] A provocative exclamation.
[17] Lines 138–85 are the first significant addition.
[18] Treasure.

(Thinking none tells [1] it but his private
   self);
To meet her spirit in a nimble kiss,
Distilling panting ardor to her heart;
True to her sheets, nay, diets strong his
   blood,   150
To give her height of hymeneal sweets—
PIET. O God!
MAL. Whilst she lisps, and gives him some
   court *quelquechose*,[2]
Made only to provoke, not satiate;
And yet, even then, the thaw of her de-
   light
Flows from lewd heat of apprehension,
Only from strange imagination's rank-
   ness,
That forms the adulterer's presence in
   her soul,
And makes her think she clips [3] the
   foul knave's loins.
PIET. Affliction to my blood's root! [160
MAL. Nay, think, but think what may
proceed of this; adultery is often the
mother of incest.
PIET. Incest?
MAL. Yes, incest. Mark! Mendoza of
his wife begets perchance a daughter;
Mendoza dies; his son marries this daughter. Say you? Nay, 'tis frequent, not
only probable, but no question often acted,
whilst ignorance, fearless ignorance, [170
clasps his own seed.
PIET. Hideous imagination!
MAL. Adultery! Why, next to the sin
of simony, 'tis the most horrid transgres-
sion under the cope of salvation.[4]
PIET. Next to simony?
MAL. Ay, next to simony, in which our
men in next age shall not sin.
PIET. Not sin? Why?
MAL. Because (thanks to some [180
churchmen) our age will leave them nothing to sin with. But adultery, O dullness, should show [5] exemplary punishment, that intemperate bloods may freeze
but to think it. I would dam [6] him and
all his generation; my own hands should
do it; ha, I would not trust heaven with
my vengeance anything.
PIET. Anything, anything, Malevole!
Thou shalt see instantly what temper [190

my spirit holds. Farewell; remember I
forget thee not; farewell.   *Exit Pietro.*
MAL.[7] Farewell.
Lean thoughtfulness, a sallow meditation,
Suck thy veins dry! Distemperance rob
   thy sleep!
The heart's disquiet is revenge most deep;
He that gets blood, the life of flesh but
   spills,[8]
But he that breaks heart's peace, the dear
   soul kills.[9]—
Well, this disguise doth yet afford me
   that
Which kings do seldom hear, or great
   men use,   200
Free speech; and, though my state's
   usurped,
Yet this affected strain gives me a
   tongue
As fetterless as is an emperor's.
I may speak foolishly, ay, knavishly,
Always carelessly, yet no one thinks it
   fashion
To poise [10] my breath, "for he that laughs
   and strikes
Is lightly felt, or seldom struck again."
Duke, I'll torment thee; now my just
   revenge
From thee than crown a richer gem
   shall part.
Beneath God, naught's so dear as a calm
   heart.   210

SCENA QUARTA.

[*The same.*]

Enter Celso.

CEL. My honored lord—
MAL. Peace, speak low; peace! O Celso,
   constant lord,
Thou to whose faith I only rest dis-
   covered,
Thou, one of full ten millions of men,
That lovest virtue only for itself,
Thou in whose hands old Ops [11] may put
   her soul,
Behold forever-banished Altofront,

---

[1] Counts.   [2] Kickshaws, delicacies.   [3] Embraces.
[4] Under the expanse of heaven.
[5] Original reads *show should*.   [6] Stop up, choke.

[7] This speech is an addition.
[8] Destroys.
[9] Italics or quotation marks were often used
to mark sententious passages.
[10] Weigh seriously.
[11] The goddess of plenty.

This Genoa's last year's duke. O truly
　　noble!
I wanted [1] those old instruments of
　　state—
Dissemblance and suspect.[2] I could not
　　time it, [3] Celso;　　　　　　　　　10
My throne stood like a point in middest
　　of a circle,
To all of equal nearness; bore with none;
Reined all alike; so slept in fearless virtue,
Suspectless, too suspectless; till the
　　crowd,
Still lickerous of [4] untried novelties,
Impatient with severer government,
Made strong with Florence, banished
　　Altofront.
CEL. Strong with Florence! Ay, thence
　　your mischief rose;
For, when the daughter of the Florentine
Was matched once with this [5] Pietro,
　　now duke,　　　　　　　　　　20
No stratagem of state untried was left,
Till you of all— [6]
MAL.　　　　Of all was quite bereft.
Alas, Maria too, close prisonéd,
My true-faithed duchess, i' the citadel!
CEL. I'll still adhere; let's mutiny and die.
MAL. O, no, climb not a falling tower,
　　Celso;
'Tis well held desperation, no zeal,
Hopeless to strive with fate. Peace!
　　Temporize!
Hope, hope, that never forsak'st the
　　wretched'st man,
Yet bidd'st me live, and lurk in this
　　disguise!　　　　　　　　　　30
What, play I well the free-breathed
　　discontent?
Why, man, we are all philosophical
　　monarchs
Or natural fools. Celso, the court's afire;
The duchess' sheets will smoke for 't ere
　　it be long.
Impure Mendoza, that sharp-nosed lord,
　　that made
The curséd match linked Genoa with
　　Florence,

Now broad-horns the duke, which he now
　　knows.
Discord to malcontents is very manna;
When the ranks are burst, then scuffle,
　　Altofront.
CEL. Ay, but durst—　　　　　　40
MAL. 'Tis gone; 'tis swallowed like a min-
　　eral. [7]
Some way 'twill work. Pheut, I'll not
　　shrink!
"He's resolute who can no lower sink."

[8] *Bilioso entering, Malevole shifteth his
　　　　　　　　　　　　　speech.*

MAL. O, the father of Maypoles! Did
you never see a fellow whose strength con-
sisted in his breath, respect in his office,
religion in [9] his lord, and love in himself?
Why, then, behold!
BIL. Signior—
MAL. My right worshipful lord, [50
your court nightcap makes you have a
passing high forehead.
BIL. I can tell you strange news, but I
am sure you know them already: the duke
speaks much good of you.
MAL. Go to, then; and shall you and I
now enter into a strict friendship?
BIL. Second one another?
MAL. Yes.
BIL. Do one another good offices?　　60
MAL. Just. What though I called thee
old ox, egregious wittol, [10] broken-bellied
coward, rotten mummy? Yet, since I am
in favor—
BIL. Words, of course, terms of disport.
His grace presents you by me a chain, as
his grateful remembrance for—I am ignorant for what; marry, ye may impart. Yet
howsoever—come, dear friend. Dost know
my son?　　　　　　　　　　70
MAL. Your son?
BIL. He shall eat woodcocks, dance jigs,
make possets, and play at shuttlecock with
any young lord about the court. He has
as sweet a lady, too. Dost know her little
bitch?
MAL. 'Tis a dog, man.
BIL. Believe me, a she-bitch. O, 'tis a

[1] Lacked.　　　　　　　　[2] Suspicion.
[3] *I.e.*, could not force myself into time with
conditions.
[4] Craving.　　　　　[5] Original reads *his*.
[6] Here and in a few other passages the line
division has been regularized. Some later
passages printed in the original as prose have
been set as verse.

[7] Medicine.
[8] The passage from this point through the
stage direction in l. 103 is an addition.
[9] Original reads *on*.
[10] A man who winks at his own cuckoldry.

good creature! Thou shalt be her servant.
I'll make thee acquainted with my [80
young wife too. What, I keep her not at
court for nothing! 'Tis grown to supper
time; come to my table; that—anything I
have—stands open to thee.

MAL. ([*Aside*] *to Cel*[*so*].) How smooth
  to him that is in state of grace,
How servile is the rugged'st courtier's
  face!
What profit, nay, what nature would keep
  down,
Are heaved [1] *to them are minions to a crown.*
Envious ambition never sates his thirst,
Till, sucking all, he swells and swells,
  and bursts.   90

BIL. I shall now leave you with my
always-best wishes; only let's hold betwixt us a firm correspondence, a mutual
friendly-reciprocal kind of steady-unani-
mous-heartily-leagued—

MAL. Did your signiorship ne'er see
a pigeonhouse that was smooth, round,
and white without, and full of holes and
stink within? Ha' ye not, old courtier?

BIL. O, yes, 'tis the form, the fashion
of them all.   101

MAL. Adieu, my true court friend; farewell, my dear Castilio.[2]   *Exit Bilioso.*

CEL. Yonder's Mendoza.

MAL.   True, the privy-key.
                    Descries Mendoza.

CEL. I take my leave, sweet lord.
                       Exit Celso.

MAL.   'Tis fit; away!

SCENA QUINTA.

[*The same.*]

Enter Mendoza with three or four Suitors.

MEN. Leave your suits with me; I
can and will. Attend my secretary; leave
me.   [*Exeunt Suitors.*]

MAL. Mendoza, hark ye, hark ye. You
are a treacherous villain, God b' wi' ye!

MEN. Out, you baseborn rascal!

MAL. We are all the sons of heaven,
though a tripe-wife were our mother. Ah,
you whoreson,[3] hot-reined[4] he-marmoset!
Ægistus—didst ever hear of one Ægistus?

MEN. Gistus?   11

---

[1] Lifted.
[2] Alluding to Castiglione, author of *Il Corte-*
giano (*The Courtier*).
[3] Rascally.   [4] Lecherous.

MAL. Ay, Ægistus; he was a filthy, incontinent fleshmonger, such a one as thou
art.

MEN. Out, grumbling rogue!

MAL. Orestes, beware Orestes!

MEN. Out, beggar!

MAL. I once shall rise!

MEN. Thou rise?

MAL. Ay, at the resurrection.   20
"No vulgar seed but once may rise and
  shall;
No king so huge but fore he die may
  fall."   *Exit.*

MEN. Now, good Elysium! What a
delicious heaven is it for a man to be in a
prince's favor! O sweet God! O pleasure!
O fortune! O all thou best of life! What
should I think, what say, what do, to be a
favorite, a minion? To have a general
timorous respect, observe [5] a man, a [29
stateful silence in his presence, solitariness in his absence, a confused hum and
busy murmur of obsequious suitors training [6] him, the cloth held up, and way
proclaimed before him, petitionary vassals
licking the pavement with their slavish
knees, whilst some odd palace-lampreels [7]
that engender with snakes, and are full
of eyes on both sides, with a kind of
insinuated humbleness, fix all their delights upon his brow! O blessed state! [40
What a ravishing prospect doth the Olympus of favor yield! Death, I cornute
the duke! Sweet women, most sweet
ladies, nay, angels! By heaven, he is more
accursed than a devil that hates you, or
is hated by you, and happier than a god
that loves you, or is beloved by you. You
preservers of mankind, lifeblood of society,
who would live, nay, who can live without you? O paradise, how majes- [50
tical is your austerer presence! How
imperiously chaste is your more modest
face! But, O, how full of ravishing attraction is your pretty, petulant, languishing, lasciviously-composed countenance!
These amorous smiles, those soul-warming
sparkling glances, ardent as those flames
that singed the world by heedless Phaëton! In body how delicate, in soul how [59
witty, in discourse how pregnant, in life
how wary, in favors how judicious, in day
how sociable, and in night how—! O

---

[5] Be obsequious to.   [6] Following.   [7] Lampreys.

pleasure unutterable! Indeed, it is most certain, one man cannot deserve only to enjoy a beauteous woman. But a duchess! In despite of Phœbus, I'll write a sonnet instantly in praise of her.　　　　　*Exit.*

Scena Sexta.

[*The same.*]

Enter Ferneze ushering Aurelia, Emilia and
*　　Maquerelle bearing up her train,*
*　　Biancha attending; all go out but*
*　　Aurelia, Maquerelle, and Ferneze.*

Aur. And is 't possible? Mendoza slight me! Possible?

Fer. Possible! What can be strange in
　　him that's drunk with favor,
　　Grows insolent with grace?—Speak,
　　Maquerelle, speak.

Maq. To speak feelingly, more, more richly in solid sense than worthless words, give me those jewels of your ears to receive my enforced duty. As for my part, 'tis well known.　　(*Ferneze privately feeds Ma-*　[10
querelle's hands with jewels during
this speech.)　I can put [1] anything, can bear patiently with any man. But, when I heard he wronged your precious sweetness, I was enforced to take deep offense. 'Tis most certain he loves Emilia with high appetite; and, as she told me (as you know we women impart our secrets one to an-other), when she repulsed his suit, in that he was possessed with your endeared grace, Mendoza most ingratefully renounced　[20
all faith to you.

Fer. Nay, called you—speak, Ma-querelle, speak.

Maq. By heaven, witch, dried bisque, [2] and contested blushlessly he loved you but for a spurt or so.

Fer. For maintenance.

Maq. Advancement and regard.

Aur. O villain! O impudent Mendoza!

Maq. Nay, he is the rustiest jade,　[30
the foulest-mouthed knave in railing against our sex! He will rail against women—

Aur. How? How?

Maq. I am ashamed to speak 't, I.

Aur. I love to hate him. Speak.

Maq. Why, when Emilia scorned his base unsteadiness, the black-throated rascal scolded, and said—

Aur. What?

Maq. Troth, 'tis too shameless.　　40

Aur. What said he?

Maq. Why, that, at four, women were fools; at fourteen, drabs, at forty, bawds; at fourscore, witches; and [at] [3] a hundred, cats.

Aur. O unlimitable impudency!

Fer. But, as for poor Ferneze's fixéd
　　heart,
　　Was never shadeless meadow drier
　　parched
　　Under the scorching heat of heaven's Dog
　　Than is my heart with your enforcing [4]
　　eyes.　　　　　　　　　　　50

Maq. A hot simile!

Fer. Your smiles have been my heaven,
　　your frowns my hell.
　　O, pity, then! Grace should with beauty
　　dwell.

Maq. Reasonable perfect, by 'r Lady.

Aur. I will love thee, be it but in despite
　　Of that Mendoza. "Witch," Ferneze,
　　"witch"!
　　Ferneze, thou art the duchess' favorite;
　　Be faithful, private; but 'tis dangerous.

Fer. "His love is liveless that for love
　　fears breath;
　　The worst that's due to sin, O, would
　　'twere death!"　　　　　　　60

Aur. Enjoy my favor. I will be sick instantly and take physic; therefore in depth of night visit—

Maq. Visit her chamber, but condition-ally: you shall not offend her bed, by this diamond!

Fer. By this diamond.
　　　　　　　Gives it to Maquerelle.

Maq. Nor tarry longer than you please, by this ruby!

Fer. By this ruby.　　*Gives again.*　70

Maq. And that the door shall not creak.

Fer. And that the door shall not creak.

Maq. Nay, but swear.

Fer. By this purse.　*Gives her his purse.*

Maq. Go to, I'll keep your oaths for you. Remember, visit.

Enter Mendoza, reading a sonnet.

Aur. "Dried biscuit"!—Look where the base wretch comes.

Men. "Beauty's life, heaven's model, love's queen—"　　　　　　80

---

[1] Endure.　　　　　　[2] Biscuit.　　　　　[3] Supplied by Bullen.　　　[4] Ravishing.

Maq. [*Aside.*] That's his Emilia.

Men. "Nature's triumph, best on earth—"

Maq. [*Aside.*] Meaning Emilia.

Men. "Thou only wonder that the world hath seen—"

Maq. [*Aside.*] That's Emilia.

Aur. [*Aside.*] Must I then hear her praised?—Mendoza!

Men. Madam, your excellency is [90 graciously encountered; I have been writing passionate flashes in honor of—

Exit Fer[neze].

Aur. Out, villain, villain! O judgment, where have been my eyes? What bewitched election made me dote on thee? What sorcery made me love thee? But be gone; bury thy head. O, that I could do more than loathe thee! Hence, worst of ill! No reason ask; our reason is our will.

Exit with Maquerelle.

Men. Women! Nay, furies; nay, [100 worse, for they torment only the bad, but women good and bad. Damnation of mankind! Breath, hast thou praised them for this? And is't you, Ferneze, are wriggled into smock-grace? Sit sure. O, that I could rail against these monsters in nature, models of hell, curse of the earth, women that dare attempt anything, and what they attempt they care not how they accomplish; without all premeditation or prevention; [110 rash in asking, desperate in working, impatient in suffering, extreme in desiring, slaves unto appetite, mistresses in dissembling, only constant in unconstancy, only perfect in counterfeiting. Their words are feigned, their eyes forged, their sights [1] dissembled, their looks counterfeit, their hair false, their given hopes deceitful, their very breath artificial. *Their blood is their only god; bad clothes and old age are* [120 *only the devils they tremble at.* That I could rail now!

Scena Septa.

[*The same.*]

Enter Pietro, his sword drawn.

Piet. A mischief fill thy throat, thou foul-jawed slave!

Say thy prayers.

Men. I ha' forgot um.

¹ Sighs.

Piet. Thou shalt die!

Men. So shalt thou. I am heart-mad.

Piet. I am horn-mad.²

Men. Extreme mad.

Piet. Monstrously mad.

Men. Why?

Piet. Why? Thou, thou hast dishonoréd my bed.

Men. I? Come, come, sit; here's my bare heart to thee,

As steady as is this center to the glorious world.

And yet, hark, thou art a cornuto—but by me?

Piet. Yes, slave, by thee.

Men. Do not, do not with tart and spleenful breath 10

Lose him can lose thee. I offend my duke?

Bear record, O ye dumb and raw-aired nights,

How vigilant my sleepless eyes have been

To watch the traitor! Record, thou spirit of truth,

With what debasement I ha' thrown myself

To under offices, only to learn

The truth, the party, time, the means, the place,

By whom, and when, and where thou wert disgraced!

And am I paid with "slave"? Hath my intrusion

To places private and prohibited, 20

Only to observe the closer passages

(Heaven knows with vows of revelation),

Made me suspected, made me deemed a villain?

What rogue hath wronged us?

Piet. Mendoza, I may err.

Men. Err? 'Tis too mild a name; but err and err,

Run giddy with suspect fore through me thou know

That which most creatures, save thyself, do know.

Nay, since my service hath so loathed reject,³

Fore I'll reveal, shalt find them clipped together.

Piet. Mendoza, thou know'st I am [30 a most plain-breasted ⁴ man.

² Intensive, with a double meaning.

³ Rejection. ⁴ Plain-spoken.

MEN. The fitter to make a cuckold!
Would your brows were most plain too!
PIET. Tell me; indeed, I heard thee rail.
MEN. At women, true. Why, what cold
fleam [1] could choose,
Knowing a lord so honest, virtuous,
So boundless-loving, bounteous, fair-
shaped, sweet,
To be contemned, abused, defamed,
made cuckold?
Heart! I hate all women for 't—sweet
sheets, wax lights, antique bedposts, [40
cambric smocks, villainous curtains, arras
pictures, oiled hinges, and all the tongue-
tied lascivious witnesses of great creatures'
wantonness! What salvation can you
expect?
PIET. Wilt thou tell me?
MEN. Why, you may find it yourself;
observe, observe.
PIET. I ha' not the patience. Wilt thou
deserve [2] me? Tell, give it.   50
MEN. Take 't! Why, Ferneze is the
man, Ferneze. I'll prove 't; this night you
shall take him in your sheets. Will 't serve?
PIET. It will; my bosom's in some peace.
Till night!
MEN. What?
PIET. Farewell.
MEN.   God! How weak a lord are you!
Why, do you think there is no more but
so?
PIET. Why?
MEN.   Nay, then will I presume to
counsel you.
It should be thus. You with some guard
upon the sudden
Break into the princess' chamber; I stay
behind,
Without the door through which he needs
must pass.   60
Ferneze flies—let him. To me he comes.
He's killed
By me—observe—by me. You follow; [3]
I rail,
And seem to save the body. Duchess
comes,
On whom (respecting her advancéd birth
And your fair nature) I know, nay, I do
know,
No violence must be used. She comes; I
storm;

[1] Phlegm.
[2] Be serviceable to.
[3] Original reads *fellow*.

I praise, excuse Ferneze, and still maintain
The duchess' honor; she for this loves me.
I honor you, shall know her soul, you
mine.
Then naught shall she contrive in
vengeance   70
(As women are most thoughtful in revenge)
Of her Ferneze, but you shall sooner
know' t
Than she can think 't. Thus shall his
death come sure;
Your duchess brain-caught, so your life
secure.
PIET. It is too well, my bosom and my
heart!
"When nothing helps, cut off the rotten
part."   *Exit.*
MEN. "Who cannot feign friendship can
ne'er produce the effects of hatred." Honest fool duke, subtile lascivious duchess, silly
novice Ferneze, I do laugh at ye. My [80
brain is in labor till it produce mischief,
and I feel sudden throes, proofs sensible the
issue is at hand.
"As bears shape young, so I'll form my
device,
Which grown proves horrid. Vengeance
makes men wise."   [*Exit.*] [4]

Enter Malevole and Passarello.

MAL. Fool, most happily encountered!
Canst sing, fool?
PASS. Yes, I can sing, fool, if you'll bear
the burden; [5] and I can play upon instruments, scurvily, as gentlemen do. O, [90
that I had been gelded! I should then have
been a fat fool for a chamber, a squeaking
fool for a tavern, and a private fool for all
the ladies.
MAL. You are in good case since you
came to court, fool. What, garded, [6]
garded!
PASS. Yes, faith, even as footmen and
bawds wear velvet, not for an ornament
of honor, but for a badge of drudgery; [100
for, now the duke is discontented, I am
fain to fool him asleep every night.
MAL. What are his griefs?
PASS. He hath sore eyes.
MAL. I never observed so much.

[4] The remainder of the scene is an addition.
[5] Sing the bass.   [6] Trimmed up.

PASS. Horrible sore eyes; and so hath every cuckold, for the roots of the horns spring in the eyeballs, and that's the reason the horn of a cuckold is as tender as his eye, or as that growing in the woman's [110 forehead, twelve years since, that could not endure to be touched.[1] The duke hangs down his head like a columbine.

MAL. Passarello, why do great men beg fools? [2]

PASS. As the Welshman stole rushes when there was nothing else to filch—only to keep begging in fashion.

MAL. Pooh, thou givest no good reason; thou speakest like a fool.   120

PASS. Faith, I utter small fragments, as your knight courts your city widow with something of his gilt,[3] some advancing his high-colored [4] beard, and taking tobacco. This is all the mirror of their knightly complements.[5] Nay, I shall talk when my tongue is a-going once; 'tis like a citizen on horseback, evermore in a false gallop.

MAL. And how doth Maquerelle fare nowadays?   130

PASS. Faith, I was wont to salute her as our English women are at their first landing in Flushing—I would call her whore. But now that antiquity leaves her as an old piece of plastic [6] t' work by, I only ask her how her rotten teeth fare every morning, and so leave her. She was the first that ever invented perfumed smocks for the gentlewomen, and woolen shoes for fear of creaking for the visitant. She were [140 an excellent lady but that her face peeleth like Muscovy glass.[7]

MAL. And how doth thy old lord, that hath wit enough to be a flatterer, and conscience enough to be a knave?

PASS. O, excellent; he keeps beside me fifteen jesters to instruct him in the art of fooling, and utters their jests in private to the duke and duchess. He'll lie like to your Switzer or lawyer; he'll be of any side [150 for most money.

MAL. I am in haste; be brief.

PASS. As your fiddler when he is paid. He'll thrive, I warrant you, while your

[1] A pamphlet describing this monstrosity was printed in 1588.
[2] Seek the custody of idiots to enjoy their estates.
[3] Money (?).
[4] Deeply dyed.
[5] Accomplishments.
[6] Sculpture.
[7] Talc.

young courtier stands like Good Friday in Lent; men long to see it, because more fatting days come after it; else he's the leanest and pitifull'st actor in the whole pageant. Adieu, Malevole.

MAL. [Aside.] O world most vild,[8] when thy loose vanities,   160
Taught by this fool, do make the fool seem wise!

PASS. You'll know me again, Malevole.

MAL. O, ay, by that velvet.

PASS. Ay, as a pettifogger by his buckram bag. I am as common in the court as an hostess's lips in the country; knights, and clowns, and knaves, and all share me; the court cannot possibly be without me. Adieu, Malevole.   [Exeunt.]

ACTUS SECUNDUS. SCENA PRIMA.

[A hall outside the Duchess' chamber.]

Enter Mendoza, with a sconce,[9] to observe Ferneze's entrance, who, whilst the act is playing, enter [10] unbraced,[11] two Pages before him with lights; is met by Maquerelle and conveyed in; the Pages are sent away.

MEN. He's caught; the woodcock's head is i' th' noose.
Now treads Ferneze in dangerous path of lust,
Swearing his sense is merely [12] deified.
The fool grasps clouds, and shall beget centaurs;
And now, in strength of panting, faint delight,
The goat bids heaven envy him.—Good goose,
I can afford thee nothing but the poor comfort of calamity, pity.
"Lust's like the plummets hanging on clock lines,
Will ne'er ha' done till all is quite undone."
Such is the course salt [13] sallow lust doth run,   10
Which thou shalt try. I'll be revenged. Duke, thy suspect,
Duchess, thy disgrace, Ferneze, thy rivalship

[8] Vile.
[9] Lantern.
[10] I.e., should enter.
[11] With garments unfastened.
[12] Absolutely.
[13] Salacious.

Shall have swift vengeance. Nothing so
　　holy,
No band of nature so strong,
No law of friendship so sacred,
But I'll profane, burst, violate,
Fore I'll endure disgrace, contempt, and
　　poverty.
Shall I, whose very "Hum" strook all
　　heads bare,
Whose face made silence, creaking of
　　whose shoe
Forced the most private passages fly
　　ope,　　　　　　　　　　　　　　20
Scrape like a servile dog at some latched
　　door;
Learn now to make a leg[1] and cry,
　　"Beseech ye,
Pray ye, is such a lord within?"; be
　　awed
At some odd usher's scoffed formality?
First sear[2] my brains! "*Unde cadis non
　　quo, refert.*"[3]
My heart cries, "Perish all!" How!
　　How! "What fate
Can once avoid revenge, that's desper-
　　ate?"
I'll to the duke. If all should ope—If?
　　Tush!
"Fortune still dotes on those who cannot
　　blush."　　　　　　　　　　　　[*Exit.*]

SCENA SECUNDA.

[*The same.*]

*Enter Malevole at one door; Biancha,
　　Emilia, and Maquerelle at the other
　　　　　　　　　　　　　　　　door.*

MAL. Bless ye, cast[4] a ladies!—Ha,
dip-sauce![5] How dost thou, old coal?
MAQ. Old coal?
MAL. Ay, old coal; methinks thou liest
like a brand under billets of green wood.
He that will inflame a young wench's
heart, let him lay close to her an old coal
that hath first been fired, a panderess, my
half-burnt lint, who, though thou canst
[not] flame thyself, yet art able to set a　[10

[1] Bow.
[2] Emended by Bullen. Original reads *seate.*
[3] "No matter whither, but from whence you
fall" (Seneca, *Thyestes,* 1. 929. *Cf. Antonio and
Mellida,* Part I, III, ii, 115).
[4] Pair.
[5] With an allusion to *dipsas,* a fabulous snake,
and perhaps to Lyly's Dipsas.

thousand virgins' tapers afire.—[*Turns
to Biancha.*] And how doth Janivere thy
husband, my little periwinkle? Is he
troubled with the cough of th' lungs still?
Does he hawk a-nights still? He will not
bite.
BIAN. No, by my troth, I took him with
his mouth empty of old teeth.
MAL. And he took thee with thy belly
full of young bones. Marry, he took　[20
his maim by the stroke of his enemy.
BIAN. And I mine by the stroke of my
friend.
MAL. The close stock![6] O mortal
wench! Lady, ha' ye now no restoratives[7]
for your decayed Jasons? Look ye: crabs'
guts baked, distilled ox-pith, the pul-
verized hairs of a lion's upper lip, jelly of
cock sparrows, he-monkeys' marrow, or
pouldre[8] of fox-stones? And whither　[30
are you ambling now?
BIAN. To bed, to bed.
MAL. Do your husbands lie with ye?
BIAN. That were country fashion, i' faith.
MAL. Ha' ye no foregoers[9] about you?
Come, whither in good deed, la now?
BIAN. In good indeed, la now, to eat
the most miraculously, admirably, astonish-
able-composed posset with three curds,　[39
without any drink. Will ye help me with
a he-fox?—Here's the duke.
　　　　　　　　　　　The Ladies go out.
MAL.[10] (*To Bian[cha].*) Fried frogs are
very good, and Frenchlike too!

SCENA TERTIA.

[*The same.*]

*Enter Duke Pietro, Count Celso, Count
　　Equato, Bilioso, Ferrard, and Mendoza.*

PIET. The night grows deep and foul.
What hour is 't?
CEL. Upon the stroke of twelve.
MAL. Save ye, duke!
PIET. From thee! Begone, I do not love
thee! Let me see thee no more; we are
displeased.
MAL. Why, God be with thee! Heaven
hear my curse—may thy wife and thee
live long together!　　　　　　　　10
PIET. Begone, sirrah!

[6] A thrust in fencing.　　　　　[9] Ushers.
[7] Aphrodisiacs.　　[10] This speech is an addition.
[8] Powder.

MAL. "When Arthur first in court began"—Agamemnon—Menelaus—was ever
any duke a cornuto?

PIET. Begone hence!

MAL. What religion wilt thou be of
next?

MEN. Out with him!

MAL. With most servile patience time
    will come
When wonder of thy error will strike
    dumb   20
Thy bezzled [1] sense.—Slaves! Ay, favor!
    Ay, marry, shall he rise?
"Good God! How subtile hell doth
    flatter vice,
Mounts him aloft, and makes him seem
    to fly,
As fowl the tortoise mocked, who to the
    sky
Th' ambitious shellfish raised! Th' end
    of all
Is only that from height he might dead
    fall." [2]

BIL. Why, when? Out, ye rogue! Begone,
ye rascal!

MAL. I shall now leave ye with all my
best wishes.   30

BIL. Out, ye cur!

MAL. Only let's hold together a firm
correspondence.

BIL. Out!

MAL. A mutual-friendly-reciprocal-per-
petual kind of steady-unanimous-heartily-
leagued—

BIL. Hence, ye gross-jawed, peasantly
—out, go!

MAL. Adieu, pigeon house; thou burr,
that only stickest to nappy fortunes. [41
The sarpego,[3] the strangury,[4] an eternal,
uneffectual priapism seize thee!

BIL. Out, rogue!

MAL. Mayest thou be a notorious wit-
tolly pander to thine own wife, and yet
get no office, but live to be the utmost
misery of mankind, a beggarly cuckold!
                       Exit.

PIET. It shall be so.

MEN. It must be so, for, where great states
    revenge,   50
"'Tis requisite the parts with piety [5]

(And loft [6] respect forbears) be closely
    dogged.
Lay one into his breast shall sleep with
    him,
Feed in the same dish, run in self-
    faction,
Who may discover any shape of danger;
For once disgraced, displayéd in offense,
It makes man blushless, and man is
    (all confess)
More prone to vengeance than to grate-
    fulness.
Favors are writ in dust; but stripes we feel
Depravéd nature stamps in lasting steel."

PIET. You shall be leagued with the   [61
duchess.

EQU. The plot is very good.

MEN. You shall both kill, and seem the
    corse to save.

FER. A most fine brain-trick.

CEL. (*Tacite.*) [7]   Of a most cunning
    knave.

PIET. My lords, the heavy action we in-
    tend
Is death and shame, two of the ugliest
    shapes
That can confound a soul. Think, think
    of it.
I strike, but yet, like him that gainst
    stone walls
Directs his shafts, rebounds in his own
    face;   70
My lady's shame is mine, O God,
    'tis mine!
Therefore I do conjure all secrecy.
Let it be as very little as may be, pray
    ye, as may be.
Make frightless entrance, salute her with
    soft eyes,
Strain [8] naught with blood.   Only
    Ferneze dies,
But not before her brows. O gentle-
    men,
God knows I love her! Nothing else
    but this.
I am not well. If grief, that sucks veins
    dry,
Rivels [9] the skin, casts ashes in men's
    faces,
Bedulls the eye, unstrengthens all the
    blood,   80

---

[1] Drunken.
[2] Lines 27–48 are an addition.
[3] Serpigo, a skin eruption.
[4] Disease of the bladder.
[5] Devotion.
[6] Proud.
[7] Silently, aside.
[8] Do violence to; or perhaps a misprint for
stain.
[9] Wrinkles

Chance to remove me to another
world,
As sure I once must die, let him succeed.
I have no child; all that my youth begot
Hath been your loves, which shall in-
herit [1] me;
Which as it ever shall, I do conjure it,
Mendoza may succeed; he's noble born,
With me of much desert.

CEL. (*Tacite.*) Much!

PIET. Your silence answers, "Ay."
I thank you. Come on now. O, that I
might die   90
Before her shame's displayed! Would
I were forced
To burn my father's tomb, unheal [2]
his bones,
And dash them in the dirt, rather than
this!
This both the living and the dead of-
fends:
"Sharp surgery where naught but death
amends."   *Exit with the others.*

SCENA QUARTA.

[*The same.*]

*Enter Maquerelle, Emilia, and Biancha
with the posset.*

MAQ. Even here it is, three curds in
three regions individually distinct, most
methodical according to art composed,
without any drink.

BIAN. Without any drink?

MAQ. Upon my honor. Will you sit
and eat?   [*They eat.*]

EM. Good! The composure, the receipt,
how is 't?

MAQ. 'Tis a pretty pearl; by this [10
pearl (how does it with me?) [3] thus it is:
Seven-and-thirty yelks of Barbary hens'
eggs; eighteen spoonfuls and a half of
the juice of cock sparrow bones; one ounce,
three drams, four scruples, and one quarter
of the syrup of Ethiopian dates; sweetened
with three-quarters of a pound of pure
candied Indian eryngoes; [4] strewed over
with the powder of pearl of America, amber of Cataia, and lamb-stones of [20
Muscovia.

BIAN. Trust me, the ingredients are
very cordial, and, no question, good, and
most powerful in restoration.

MAQ. I know not what you mean by restoration, but this it doth—it purifieth the
blood, smootheth the skin, enliveneth the
eye, strengtheneth the veins, mundi-
fieth [5] the teeth, comforteth the stomach,
fortifieth the back, and quickeneth the [30
wit; that's all.

EM. By my troth, I have eaten but two
spoonfuls, and methinks I could discourse
most swiftly and wittily already.

MAQ. Have you the art to seem honest? [6]

BIAN. I thank advice and practice.

MAQ. Why, then, eat me of this posset,
quicken your blood, and preserve your
beauty. Do you know Doctor Plaster- [40
face? By this curd, he is the most exquisite
in forging of veins, sprightening [7] of eyes,
dyeing of hair, sleeking of skins, blushing
of cheeks, surphling [8] of breasts, blanch-
ing and bleaching of teeth, that ever
made an old lady gracious by torchlight;
by this curd, la!

BIAN. We, we are resolved; what God
has given us we'll cherish.

MAQ. Cherish anything saving your [50
husband; keep him not too high, lest he
leap the pale. But, for your beauty, let
it be your saint; bequeath two hours to
it every morning in your closet. I ha'
been young, and yet, in my conscience,
I am not above five-and-twenty; but,
believe me, preserve and use your beauty;
for youth and beauty once gone, we are
like beehives without honey, out-a-fashion,
apparel that no man will wear; there- [60
fore use me your beauty.

EM. Ay, but men say—

MAQ. Men say! Let men say what they
will. Life a woman! They are ignorant
of your wants. The more in years, the
more in perfection they grow; if they lose
youth and beauty, they gain wisdom and
discretion. But when our beauty fades,
good night with us. There cannot be an
uglier thing to see than an old woman, [70
from which—O pruning, pinching, and
painting!—deliver all sweet beauties!
                              [*Music within.*]

BIAN. Hark! Music!

---

[1] Be heir to.   [3] How does it become me?
[2] Uncover.   [4] Candied sea-holly.

[5] Cleanseth.   [7] Brightening.
[6] Virtuous.   [8] Tinting

MAQ. Peace, 'tis in the duchess' bedchamber. Good rest, most prosperously-
graced ladies.

EM. Good night, sentinel.

BIAN. Night, dear Maquerelle.

Exeunt all but Maq[uerelle].

MAQ. May my posset's operation send
you my wit and honesty; and me, your　[80
youth and beauty. The pleasing'st rest!

Exit Maq[uerelle].

SCENA QUINTA.

[*The same.*]

A song [within].

*Whilst the song is singing, enter Mendoza
with his sword drawn, standing ready to
murder Ferneze as he flies from the
Duchess' chamber.*

ALL. [*Within.*] Strike, strike!

AUR. [*Within.*] Save my Ferneze! O, save
my Ferneze!

*Enter Ferneze in his shirt, and is received
upon Mendoza's sword.*

ALL. [*Within.*] Follow, pursue!

AUR. [*Within.*] O, save Ferneze!

MEN. Pierce, pierce!—Thou shallow fool,
drop there!
"He that attempts a princess' lawless
love
Must have broad hands, close heart, with
Argus' eyes,
And back of Hercules, or else he dies."

Thrusts his rapier in Fer[neze].

*Enter Aurelia, Duke Pietro, Ferrard, Bilioso,
Celso, and Equato.*

ALL. Follow, follow!

MEN. Stand off, forbear, ye most uncivil
lords!　　　　　　　　　　　　　10

PIET. Strike!

MEN. Do not; tempt not a man resolved.
Would you, inhuman murtherers, more
than death?

AUR. O poor Ferneze!

MEN. Alas, now all defense too late!

AUR. He's dead.

PIET. I am sorry for our shame.—Go to
your bed;

Weep not too much, but leave some tears
to shed
When I am dead.

AUR. What, weep for thee? My soul no
tears shall find.

PIET. Alas, alas, that women's souls are
blind!

MEN. Betray such beauty! Murther such
youth! Contemn civility!　　　　20
He loves him not that rails not at him.

PIET. Thou canst not move us; we have
blood enough.—
And please you, lady, we have quite forgot
All your defects; if not, why, then—

AUR. Not.

PIET. Not. The best of rest; good night.

Exit Pietro with other Courtiers.

AUR. Despite go with thee!

MEN. Madam, you ha' done me foul
disgrace; you have wronged him much,
loves[1] you too much. Go to, your soul　[30
knows you have.

AUR. I think I have.

MEN. Do you but think so?

AUR. Nay, sure, I have; my eyes have
witnessed thy love. Thou hast stood too
firm for me.

MEN. Why, tell me, fair-cheeked lady, who
even in tears
Art powerfully beauteous, what unad-
vised passion
Strook ye into such a violent heat against
me?
Speak, what mischief wronged us? What
devil injured us?　　　　　　　　40
Speak.

AUR. That thing ne'er worthy of the name
of man, Ferneze;
Ferneze swore thou lov'st Emilia;
Which to advance, with most reproachful breath,
Thou both didst blemish and denounce
my love.

MEN. Ignoble villain! Did I for this be-
stride
Thy wounded limbs? For this? O God!
For this
Sunk all my hopes, and with my hopes
my life?
Ripped bare my throat unto the hang-
man's ax?—　　　　　　　　　　49
Thou most dishonored trunk!—Emilia!

[1] *I.e.*, who loves.

By life, I know her not—Emilia—!
Did you believe him?

Aur.   Pardon me, I did.

Men. Did you? And thereupon you graced
him?

Aur. I did.

Men. Took him to favor, nay, even
clasped with him?

Aur. Alas, I did!

Men.   This night?

Aur.   This night.

Men. And in your lustful twines the duke
took you?

Aur. A most sad truth.

Men. O God, O God! How we dull honest
souls,
Heavy-brained men, are swallowed in the
bogs   60
Of a deceitful ground, whilst nimble
bloods,
Light-jointed spirits, spent,[1] cut good
men's throats,
And scape! Alas, I am too honest for
this age,
Too full of fleam and heavy steadiness;
Stood still whilst this slave cast a noose
about me;
Nay, then to stand in honor of him and
her
Who had even sliced my heart!

Aur.   Come, I did err,
And am most sorry I did err.

Men. Why, we are both but dead; the
duke hates us.
"And those whom princes do once
groundly [2] hate,   70
Let them provide to die, as sure as fate.
Prevention is the heart of policy."

Aur. Shall we murder him?

Men. Instantly?

Aur. Instantly! Before he casts a plot,
Or further blaze my honor's much-known
blot,
Let's murther him!

Men. I would do much for you; will ye
marry me?

Aur. I'll make thee duke. We are of Med-
icis;   79
Florence our friend; in court my faction
Not meanly strengthful; the duke then
dead;
We well prepared for change; the multitude

Irresolutely reeling; we in force;
Our party seconded; the kingdom
mazed—
No doubt of swift success; all shall be
graced.

Men. You do confirm me; we are resolute.
Tomorrow look for change; rest confi-
dent.
'Tis now about the immodest waist of
night;
The mother of moist dew with pallid
light
Spreads gloomy shades about the numbéd
earth.   90
Sleep, sleep, whilst we contrive our mis-
chief's birth.
This man I'll get inhumed.   Farewell;
to bed.
Ay, kiss the pillow; dream the duke is
dead.   *Exit Aurelia.*
So, so, good night. How fortune dotes on
impudence!
I am in private the adopted son of yon
good prince.
I must be duke. Why, if I must, I must!
Most seely [3] lord, name me! O heaven!
I see God made honest fools to maintain
crafty knaves.
The duchess is wholly mine too; must
kill her husband
To quit her shame. Much! [4] Then marry
her! Ay.   100
O, I grow proud in prosperous treachery!
As wrastlers clip, so I'll embrace you all,
Not to support, but to procure your fall.

Enter Malevole.

Mal. God arrest thee!

Men. At whose suit?

Mal. At the devil's. Ah, you treacherous,
damnable monster!
How dost? How dost, thou treacherous
rogue?
Ah, ye rascal! I am banished the court,
sirrah.

Men. Prithee, let's be acquainted; I do
love thee, faith.   110

Mal. At your service, by the Lord, la!
Shall's go to supper? Let's be once drunk
together, and so unite a most virtuously
strengthened friendship. Shall's, Hugue-
not? Shall 's?

[1] Exhausted, dissolute.   [2] Completely.

[3] Silly, simple.
[4] Great! Excellent!

MEN. Wilt fall upon my chamber to-morrow morn?

MAL. As a raven to a dunghill. They say there's one dead here—pricked for the pride of the flesh. 120

MEN. Ferneze. There he is; prithee, bury him.

MAL. O, most willingly; I mean to turn pure Rochelle [1] churchman, I.

MEN. Thou churchman! Why, why?

MAL. Because I'll live lazily, rail upon authority, deny kings' supremacy in things indifferent, and be a pope in mine own parish. 129

MEN. Wherefore dost thou think churches were made?

MAL. To scour plowshares; I have seen oxen plow up altars; "*et nunc seges ubi Sion fuit.*" [2]

MEN. Strange!

MAL. Nay, monstrous! I ha' seen a sumptuous steeple turned to a stinking privy; more beastly, the sacred'st place made a dogs' kennel; nay, most inhuman, the stoned coffins of long-dead Chris- [140 tians burst up, and made hogs' troughs: *Hic finis Priami.* [3] Shall I ha' some sack and cheese at thy chamber? Good night, good mischievous incarnate devil; good night, Mendoza; ah, you inhuman villain, good night! Night, fub. [4]

MEN. Good night; tomorrow morn.
Exit Mendoza.

MAL. Ay, I will come, friendly damnation, I will come. I do descry crosspoints: [5] honesty and courtship straddle as far [150 asunder as a true Frenchman's legs.

FER. O!

MAL. Proclamations! More proclamations!

FER. O! A surgeon!

MAL. Hark! Lust cries for a surgeon. What news from Limbo? How doth the grand cuckold, Lucifer?

FER. O, help, help! Conceal and save me. 160

Ferneze stirs, and Malevole helps him up and conveys him away.

MAL. Thy shame more than thy wounds do grieve me far;

"Thy wounds but leave upon thy flesh some scar;
But fame ne'er heals, still rankles worse and worse;
Such is of uncontrolléd lust the curse.
Think what it is in lawless sheets to lie;
But, O, Ferneze, what in lust to die!
Then thou that shame respect's[t], O, fly converse
With women's eyes and lisping wantonness!
Stick candles gainst a virgin wall's white back;
If they not burn, yet at the least they'll black." 170
Come, I'll convey thee to a private port,
Where thou shalt live (O happy man!) from court.
The beauty of the day begins to rise,
From whose bright form night's heavy shadow flies.
Now gins [6] close plots to work; the scene grows full,
And craves his eyes who hath a solid skull. [7]   *Exeunt.*

ACTUS TERTIUS. SCENA PRIMA.

[*A room in the Duke's palace.*]

Enter Pietro the Duke, Mendoza, Count Equato, and Bilioso.

PIET. 'Tis grown to youth of day; how shall we waste this light?
My heart's more heavy than a tyrant's crown.
Shall we go hunt? Prepare for field.
Exit Equato.

MEN. Would ye could be merry!

PIET. Would God I could! Mendoza, bid um haste. *Exit Mendoza.*
I would fain shift place; O vain relief!
"Sad souls may well change place, but not change grief."
As deer, being struck, fly thorough many soils, [8]
Yet still the shaft sticks fast, so—

BIL. A good old simile, my honest lord. 10

PIET. I am not much unlike to some sick man
That long desired hurtful drink; at last

---

[1] Where persecuted Huguenots took refuge.
[2] Paraphrased from Ovid: "Now the corn grows where Sion stood."
[3] Here the end of Priam.
[4] Impostor. [5] A step in dancing.
[6] Begins. [7] Sound head. [8] Streams.

Swills in and drinks his last, ending at
  once
Both life and thirst. O, would I ne'er
  had known
My own dishonor! Good God, that men
  should
Desire to search out that which, being
  found, kills all
Their joy of life! To taste the tree of
  knowledge,
And then be driven from out paradise!
Canst give me some comfort?

BIL. My lord, I have some books [20
which have been dedicated to my honor,
and I ne'er read um, and yet they had
very fine names—*Physic for Fortune,
Lozenges of Sanctified Sincerity*, very pretty
works of curates, scriveners, and school-
masters. Marry, I remember one Seneca,
Lucius Annæus Seneca—

PIET. Out upon him! He writ of temperance and fortitude, yet lived like a
voluptuous epicure, and died like an [30
effeminate coward.—
Haste thee to Florence.
Here, take our letters; see um sealed;
  away!
Report in private to the honored duke
His daughter's forced disgrace; tell him
  at length
We know too much; due compliments
  advance.
"There's naught that's safe and sweet
  but ignorance."   *Exit Duke.*[1]

Enter Bilioso[2] *and Bianc[h]a.*

BIL. Madam, I am going ambassador
for Florence; 'twill be great charges to me.

BIAN. No matter, my lord, you [40
have the lease of two manors come out next
Christmas; you may lay your tenants on
the greater rack for it; and, when you come
home again, I'll teach you how you shall
get two hundred pounds a year by your
teeth.

BILL. How, madam?

BIAN. Cut off so much from housekeeping; that which is saved by the teeth,
you know, is got by the teeth.   50

BIL. Fore God, and so I may; I am in
wondrous credit, lady.

BIAN. See the use of flattery; I did
ever counsel you to flatter greatness, and
you have profited well. Any man that will
do so shall be sure to be like your Scotch
barnacle,[3] now a block, instantly a worm,
and presently a great goose. This it is to
rot and putrefy in the bosom of greatness.

BIL. Thou art ever my politician. [60
O, how happy is that old lord that hath a
politician to his young lady! I'll have
fifty gentlemen shall attend upon me.
Marry, the most of them shall be farmer's
sons, because they shall bear their own
charges; and they shall go appareled thus—
in sea-water-green suits, ash-color cloaks,
watchet[4] stockings, and popinjay-green
feathers. Will not the colors do excellent?

BIAN. Out upon 't! They'll look like [70
citizens riding to their friends at Whitsuntide, their apparel just so many several
parishes.[5]

BIL. I'll have it so; and Passarello, my
fool, shall go along with me; marry, he
shall be in velvet.

BIAN. A fool in velvet?

BIL. Ay, 'tis common for your fool to
wear satin; I'll have mine in velvet.   79

BIAN. What will you wear, then, my
lord?

BIL. Velvet too; marry, it shall be embroidered, because I'll differ from the fool
somewhat. I am horribly troubled with
the gout; nothing grieves me but that my
doctor hath forbidden me wine, and you
know your ambassador must drink. Didst
thou ask thy doctor what was good for
the gout?   89

BIAN. Yes; he said ease, wine, and
women were good for it.

BIL. Nay, thou hast such a wit! What
was good to cure it, said he?

BIAN. Why, the rack. All your em-
pirics could never do the like cure upon
the gout the rack did in England, or your
Scotch boot.[6] The French harlequin will
instruct you.

BIL. Surely, I do wonder how thou,
having for the most part of thy life- [100

---

[1] The rest of this scene is an addition.
[2] Apparently, however, he has really remained
on the stage.

[3] "It was formerly thought that this species of
shell-fish, which is found on timber exposed to
the action of the sea, became, when broken off,
a kind of geese " (Halliwell).
[4] Pale blue.
[5] *I.e.*, mismatched.
[6] Instrument of torture.

time been a country body, shouldst have so good a wit.

BIAN. Who, I? Why, I have been a courtier thrice two months.

BIL. So have I this twenty year, and yet there was a gentleman usher called me coxcomb tother day, and to my face too. Was 't not a backbiting rascal? I would I were better traveled, that I might have been better acquainted [110 with the fashions of several countrymen; but my secretary, I think, he hath sufficiently instructed me.

BIAN. How, my lord?

BIL. "Marry, my good lord," quoth he, "your lordship shall ever find amongst a hundred Frenchmen forty hotshots;[1] amongst a hundred Spaniards, threescore braggarts; amongst a hundred Dutchmen, fourscore drunkards; [120 amongst an hundred Englishmen, fourscore and ten madmen; and amongst an hundred Welshmen"—

BIAN. What, my lord?

BIL. "Fourscore and nineteen gentlemen."

BIAN. But, since you go about a sad embassy, I would have you go in black, my lord.　　　　　　　　　　　129

BIL. Why, dost think I cannot mourn, unless I wear my hat in cypress,[2] like an alderman's heir? That's vile, very old, in faith.

BIAN. I'll learn of you shortly. O, we should have a fine gallant of you, should not I instruct you! How will you bear yourself when you come into the Duke of Florence' court?

BIL. Proud enough, and 'twill do well enough. As I walk up and down the [140 chamber, I'll spit frowns about me, have a strong perfume in my jerkin, let my beard grow to make me look terrible, salute no man beneath[3] the fourth button; and 'twill do excellent.

BIAN. But there is a very beautiful lady there; how will you entertain her?

BIL. I'll tell you that when the lady hath entertained me. But to satisfy thee, here comes the fool.—Fool, thou shalt [150 stand for the fair lady.

Enter Passarello.

PASS. Your fool will stand for your lady most willingly and most uprightly.

BIL. I'll salute her in Latin.

PASS. O, your fool can understand no Latin.

BIL. Ay, but your lady can.

PASS. Why, then, if your lady take down your fool, your fool will stand no longer for your lady.　　　　　　160

BIL. A pestilent fool! Fore God, I think the world be turned upside down too.

PASS. O, no, sir; for then your lady and all the ladies in the palace should go with their heels upward, and that were a strange sight, you know.

BIL. There be many will repine at my preferment.

PASS. O, ay, like the envy of an [170 elder sister, that hath her younger made a lady before her.

BIL. The duke is wondrous discontented.

PASS. Ay, and more melancholic than a usurer having all his money out at the death of a prince.

BIL. Didst thou see Madam Floria today?

PASS. Yes, I found her repairing her face today. The red upon the white [180 showed as if her cheeks should have been served in for two dishes of barberries in stewed broth, and the flesh to them a woodcock.

BIL. A bitter fowl![4] Come, madam, this night thou shalt enjoy me freely, and tomorrow for Florence.

　　　　　　[*Exeunt Bilioso and Biancha.*]

PASS. What a natural fool is he that would be a pair of bodies[5] to a woman's petticoat, to be trussed and pointed to them! Well, I'll dog my lord; and the [191 word is proper, for, when I fawn upon him, he feeds me; when I snap him by the fingers, he spits in my mouth. If a dog's death were not strangling, I had rather be one than a serving-man; for the corruption of coin is either the generation of a usurer or a lousy beggar.　　　　　　　*Exit.*[6]

---

[1] Reckless persons.
[2] Crape.
[3] Bow no lower than.

[4] With a pun on *fool.*
[5] Bodice, pair of stays.
[6] In the original, this direction appears at the end of Passarello's preceding speech.

Scena Secunda.

[Another room in the Duke's palace.]

Enter Malevole in some frieze gown, whilst Bilioso reads his patent.[1]

MAL. I cannot sleep; my eyes' ill-neigh-
boring lids
Will hold no fellowship. O thou pale,
sober night,
Thou that in sluggish fumes all sense
dost steep;
Thou that gives all the world full leave
to play,
Unbend'st the feebled veins of sweaty
labor!
The galley slave, that all the toilsome
day
Tugs at his oar against the stubborn
wave,
Straining his rugged veins, snores fast;
The stooping scythe-man, that doth
barb [2] the field,
Thou makest wink [3] sure. In night all
creatures sleep;   10
Only the malcontent, that gainst his
fate
Repines and quarrels, alas, he's goodman tell-clock! [4]
His sallow jawbones sink with wasting
moan;
Whilst others' beds are down, his pillow's stone.
BIL. Malevole!
MAL. *(To Bilioso.)* Elder of Israel,
thou honest defect of wicked nature and
obstinate ignorance, when did thy wife let
thee lie with her?   19
BIL. I am going ambassador to Florence.
MAL. Ambassador? Now, for thy
country's honor, prithee, do not put up
mutton and porridge in thy cloak bag.
Thy young lady wife goes to Florence with
thee too, does she not?
BIL. No, I leave her at the palace.
MAL. At the palace? Now, discretion
shield, man! For God's love, let's ha' no
more cuckolds! Hymen begins to put   [30
off his saffron robe; keep thy wife i' the
state of grace. Heart a truth, I would
sooner leave my lady singled in a bordello [5]
than in the Genoa palace.

Sin, there appearing in her sluttish shape,
Would soon grow loathsome, even to
blushes' sense;
Surfeit would cloak [6] intemperate appe-
tite,
Make the soul scent the rotten breath of
lust.
When in an Italian lascivious palace, a
lady guardianless,
Left to the push of all allurement,   40
The strongest incitements to immodesty,
To have her bound, incensed with wan-
ton sweets,
Her veins filled high with heating deli-
cates,
Soft rest, sweet music, amorous mas-
querers,
Lascivious banquets, sin itself gilt o'er,
Strong fantasy tricking up strange de-
lights,
Presenting it dressed pleasingly to
sense,
Sense leading it unto the soul, con-
firmed
With potent example, impudent custom,
Enticed by that great bawd, Oppor-
tunity—   50
Thus being prepared, clap to her easy ear
Youth in good clothes, well-shaped, rich,
Fair-spoken, promising-noble, ardent,
blood-full,
Witty, flattering—Ulysses absent,
O Ithaca, can [7] chastest Penelope hold
out?
BIL. Mass, I'll think on't. Farewell.
                                  Exit Bilioso.
MAL. Farewell. Take thy wife with thee.
Farewell.—
To Florence; umh! It may prove good,
it may!
And we may once unmask our brows.

Scena Tertia.

[The same.]

Enter Count Celso.

CEL. My honored lord—
MAL. Celso, peace! How is 't? Speak
low. Pale fears suspect that hedges, walls,
and trees have ears. Speak, how runs all?
CEL. I' faith, my lord, that beast with
many heads,

----

[1] Commission.   [2] Mow.   [3] Sleep.
[4] Counter of the clock; idler.   [5] Brothel.

[6] Bullen emends to *choke*.
[7] From first edn. Original has *Ithacan chastest*.

The staggering multitude, recoils apace.
Though thorough great men's envy, most
　men's malice,
Their much-intemperate heat hath ban-
　ished you,
Yet now they find envy and malice ne'er
Produce faint reformation.　　　　　　10
The duke, the too soft duke, lies as a
　block,
For which two tugging factions seem to
　saw;
But still the iron through the ribs they
　draw.
MAL. I tell thee, Celso, I have ever found
Thy breast most far from shifting cow-
　ardice
And fearful baseness; therefore I'll tell
　thee, Celso,
I find the wind begins to come about;
I'll shift my suit of fortune.
I know the Florentine, whose only force,[1]
By marrying his proud daughter to this
　prince,　　　　　　　　　　　　　20
Both banished me and made this weak
　lord duke,
Will now forsake them all; be sure he
　will.
I'll lie in ambush for conveniency,
Upon their severance to confirm myself.
CEL. Is Ferneze interred?
MAL. Of that at leisure; he lives.
CEL. But how stands Mendoza? How
is 't with him?
MAL. Faith, like a pair of snuffers—
snibs [2] filth in other men, and retains　[30
it in itself.
CEL. He does fly from public notice,
methinks, as a hare does from hounds; the
feet whereon he flies betrays him.
MAL. I can track him, Celso.
O, my disguise fools him most power-
　fully!
For that I seem a desperate malcontent,
He fain would clasp with me; he is the
　true slave
That will put on the most affected grace
For some vild second cause.

　　　　　　Enter Mendoza.

CEL.　　　　　　　　He's here.
MAL.　　　　　　　　　　Give place.—　40
Illo, ho, ho, ho! Art there, old truepenny?
　　　　　　　　　　　　Exit Celso.

[1] Whose force alone.　　　　[2] Snips off.

Where hast thou spent thyself this morn-
ing? I see flattery in thine eyes, and
damnation in thy soul. Ha, thou huge
rascal!
MEN. Thou art very merry.
MAL. As a scholar, *futuens gratis.*[3] How
doth the devil go with thee now?
MEN. Malevole, thou art an arrant
knave.　　　　　　　　　　　　　50
MAL. Who, I? I have been a sergeant,
man.
MEN. Thou art very poor.
MAL. As Job, an alcumist,[4] or a poet.
MEN. The duke hates thee.
MAL. As Irishmen do bum-cracks.
MEN. Thou hast lost his amity.
MAL. As pleasing as maids lose their
virginity.
MEN. Would thou wert of a lusty　[60
spirit! Would thou wert noble!
MAL. Why, sure my blood gives me I
am noble, sure I am of noble kind; for I
find myself possessed with all their qualities: love dogs, dice, and drabs; scorn
wit in stuff-clothes;[5] have beat my shoemaker, knocked my semsters,[6] cuckold[ed] my potecary, and undone my
tailor. Noble, why not? Since the stoic
said, "*Neminem servum non ex regibus,*　[70
*neminem regem non ex servis esse oriun-
dum,*"[7] only busy Fortune touses,[8] and
the provident Chances blends them together. I'll give you a simile. Did you
e'er see a well with two buckets—whilst
one comes up full to be emptied, another
goes down empty to be filled? Such is the
state of all humanity. Why, look you, I
may be the son of some duke; for, believe
me, intemperate lascivious bastardy　[80
makes nobility doubtful. I have a lusty,
daring heart, Mendoza.
MEN. Let's grasp; I do like thee infinitely. Wilt enact one thing for me?
MAL. Shall I get by it?　　([*Mendoza*]
gives him his purse.) Command me; I am
thy slave, beyond death and hell.
MEN. Murther the duke.
MAL. My heart's wish, my soul's desire, my fantasy's dream, my blood's　[90

[3] Loving freely.　　　[5] Persons coarsely dressed.
[4] Alchemist.　　　　[6] Seamstresses.
[7] "There is no slave who has not sprung
from kings, and no king who has not sprung
from slaves" (Seneca, *Epist.*, xliv).
[8] Tears apart.

longing, the only height of my hopes! How,
O God, how? O, how my united spirits
throng together! So strengthen my resolve!

MEN. The duke is now a-hunting.

MAL. Excellent, admirable, as the devil
would have it! Lend me, lend me rapier,
pistol, crossbow. So, so, I'll do it.

MEN. Then we agree.

MAL. As Lent and fishmongers. Come,
à cap-a-pie. How? Inform.   100

MEN. Know that this weak-brained duke,
      who only stands
On Florence' stilts, hath out of witless
      zeal
Made me his heir, and secretly confirmed
The wreath to me after his life's full
      point.

MAL. Upon what merit?

MEN.   Merit! By heaven, I horn him.
Only Ferneze's death gave me state's
      life.
Tut, we are politic; he must not live now.

MAL. No reason, marry. But how must
      he die now?   108

MEN. My utmost project is to murder
the duke, that I might have his state, because he makes me his heir; to banish the
duchess, that I might be rid of a cunning
Lacedæmonian, because I know Florence
will forsake her; and then to marry Maria,
the banished Duke Altofront's wife, that
her friends might strengthen me and my
faction. This is all, la.

MAL. Do you love Maria?   118

MEN. Faith, no great affection, but as
wise men do love great women, to ennoble
their blood and augment their revenue. To
accomplish this now, thus now: the duke
is in the forest, next the sea; single him,
kill him, hurl him in the main, and proclaim thou sawest wolves eat him.

MAL. Umh! Not so good. Methinks when
      he is slain,
To get some hypocrite, some dangerous
      wretch
That's muffled[1] or with[2] feigned holiness,
To swear he heard the duke on some
      steep cliff
Lament his wife's dishonor, and, in an
      agony   130
Of his heart's torture, hurled his groan-
      ing sides
Into the swoln sea. This circumstance,

Well made, sounds probable; and here-
      upon
The duchess—

MEN. May well be banished.
O unpeerable[3] invention! Rare!
Thou god of policy, it honeys me.

MAL. Then fear not for the wife of Alto-
      front;
I'll close to her.

MEN. Thou shalt, thou shalt. Our ex-
      cellency is pleased.   140
Why wert not thou an emperor? When
      we
Are duke, I'll make thee some great man,
      sure.

MAL. Nay, make me some rich knave, and
      I'll make myself
Some great man.

MEN.   In thee be all my spirit.
Retain ten souls; unite thy virtual
      powers.
Resolve; ha, remember greatness! Heart,
      farewell.

Enter Celso.

"The fate of all my hopes in thee doth
      dwell."   [*Exit.*]

MAL. Celso, didst hear? O heaven, didst
      hear
Such devilish mischief? Sufferest thou
      the world
Carouse damnation even with greedy
      swallow,   150
And still dost wink, still does thy ven-
      geance slumber?
"If now thy brows are clear, when will
      they thunder?"   *Exit* [*with Celso*].

SCENA QUARTA.

[*A forest near the sea.*]

Enter Pietro, Ferrard, Prepasso, and three
                                    Pages.

FER. The dogs are at a fault.
                        Cornets like horns.

PIET. Would God nothing but the dogs
were at it! Let the deer pursue safety,[4]
the dogs follow the game, and do you follow
the dogs. As for me, 'tis unfit one beast
should hunt another. I ha' one chaseth

---

[1] Disguised.   [2] *I.e.*, one with.

[3] Peerless.

[4] Emended by Bullen. Original reads *safely.*

me; and 't [1] please you, I would be rid of you a little.

FER. Would your grief would as soon leave you, as we, to quietness. 10

Exeunt [Ferrardo and Prepasso].

PIET. I thank you.—Boy, what dost thou dream of now?

[1] PAGE. Of a dry summer, my lord; for here's a hot world towards.[2] But, my lord, I had a strange dream last night.

PIET. What strange dream?

[1] PAGE. Why, methought I pleased you with singing, and then I dreamt you gave me that short sword.

PIET. Prettily begged. Hold thee, [20 I'll prove thy dream true; take 't.

[Gives sword.]

[1] PAGE. My duty! But still I dreamt on, my lord; and methought, and 't shall please your excellency, you would needs out of your royal bounty give me that jewel in your hat.

PIET. O, thou didst but dream, boy; do not believe it. Dreams prove not always true; they may hold in a short sword, but not in a jewel. But now, sir, you dreamt [30 you had pleased me with singing; make that true, as I have made the other.

[1] PAGE. Faith, my lord, I did but dream, and dreams, you say, prove not always true; they may hold in a good sword, but not in a good song. The truth is, I ha' lost my voice.

PIET. Lost thy voice! How?

[1] PAGE. With dreaming, faith. But here's a couple of sirenical [3] rascals shall [40 enchant ye. What shall they sing, my good lord?

PIET. Sing of the nature of women, and then the song shall be surely full of variety, old crotchets,[4] and most sweet closes; it shall be humorous, grave, fantastic, amorous, melancholy, sprightly, one in all, and all in one.

[1] PAGE. All in one?

PIET. By 'r Lady, too many. Sing! [50 My speech grows culpable of unthrifty idleness.[5] Sing!

Song [by 2 and 3 Pages].

[1] If it.
[2] Approaching.
[3] Sirenlike.
[4] Quarter notes, with a pun.
[5] Triviality, folly.

SCENA QUINTA.

[The same.]

Enter Malevole, with crossbow and pistol.

[PIET.] Ah, so, so, sing. I am heavy. Walk off; I shall talk in my sleep. Walk off.

Exeunt Pages.

MAL. [*Aside.*] Brief,[6] brief, who? The duke? Good heaven, that fools
Should stumble upon greatness!—Do not sleep, duke;
Give ye good morrow. You must be brief, duke;
I am feed to murther thee. Start not! Mendoza,
Mendoza hired me; here's his gold, his pistol,
Crossbow, and sword. 'Tis all as firm as earth.
O fool, fool, choked with the common maze
Of easy idiots, credulity! 10
Make him thine heir! What, thy sworn murtherer!

PIET. O, can it be?

MAL. Can?

PIET. Discovered he not Ferneze?

MAL. Yes, but why? But why? For love to thee?
Much, much! To be revenged upon his rival,
Who had thrust his jaws awry;
Who being slain, supposed by thine own hands,
Defended by his sword, made thee most loathsome,
Him most gracious with thy loose princess;
Thou, closely [7] yielding egress and regress to her, 19
Madest him heir; whose hot unquiet lust
Straight toused [8] thy sheets, and now would seize thy state.
Politician! Wise man! Death! To be
Led to the stake like a bull by the horns;
To make even kindness cut a gentle throat!
Life, why art thou numbed? Thou foggy dullness, speak!
Lives not more faith in a home-thrusting tongue
Than in these fencing tip-tap [9] courtiers?

[6] In short.
[7] Privately.
[8] Disturbed.
[9] Light-thrusting.

Enter Celso, with a hermit's gown and beard.

Piet.[1] Lord Malevole, if this be true—
Mal. If? Come, shade thee with this
disguise. If? Thou shalt handle it; he　[30
shall thank thee for killing thyself. Come,
follow my directions, and thou shalt see
strange sleights.
Piet. World, whither wilt thou?
Mal. Why, to the devil. Come, the morn
　grows late.
　A steady quickness is the soul of state.
　　　　　　　　　　　　　　Exeunt.

Actus Quartus. Scena Prima.

[*A hall outside the chamber of Biancha and
　　　　　　　　　　　　　Emilia.*]

*Enter Maquerelle, knocking at the Ladies'
　　　　　　　　　　　　　door.*

Maq. Medam, medam, are you stirring,
medam? If you be stirring, medam—if I
thought I should disturb ye—

[*Enter Page.*]

Page. My lady is up, forsooth.
Maq. A pretty boy, faith. How old art
thou?
Page. I think fourteen.
Maq. Nay, and ye be in the teens—Are
ye a gentleman born? Do you know me?
My name is Medam Maquerelle; I lie in　[10
the old cunnycourt.[2]—See, here the ladies.

Enter Biancha and Emilia.

Bian. A fair day to ye, Maquerelle.
Em. Is the duchess up yet, sentinel?
Maq. O ladies, the most abominable
mischance! O dear ladies, the most piteous
disaster! Ferneze was taken last night in
the duchess' chamber. Alas, the duke
catched him and killed him!
Bian. Was he found in bed?
Maq. O, no; but the villainous cer-　[20
tainty is, the door was not bolted; the
tongue-tied hatch[3] held his peace. So the
naked troth is, he was found in his shirt,
whilst I, like an arrand beast, lay in the
outward chamber, heard nothing; and yet
they came by me in the dark, and yet I felt
them not, like a senseless creature as I was.
O beauties, look to your busk-points,[4] if

not chastely, yet charily; be sure the door
be bolted.—Is your lord gone to Flor-　[30
ence?
Bian. Yes, Maquerelle.
Maq. I hope you'll find the discretion
to purchase a fresh gown for his return.—
Now, by my troth, beauties, I would ha'
ye once wise. He loves ye; pish! He is
witty; bubble! Fair-proportioned; meaw!
Nobly-born; wind! Let this be still your
fixed position: esteem me every man according to his good gifts, and so ye shall　[40
ever remain most dear and most worthy
to be most dear—ladies.
Em. Is the duke returned from hunting
　yet?
Maq. They say not yet.
Bian. 'Tis now in midst of day.
Em. How bears the duchess with this
　blemish now?
Maq. Faith, boldly; strongly defies defame, as one that has a duke to her father.
And there's a note to you: be sure of a stout
friend in a corner, that may always awe
your husband. Mark the havior of the　[50
duchess now. She dares defame; cries,
"Duke, do what thou canst, I'll quite[5]
mine honor." Nay, as one confirmed in her
own virtue against ten thousand mouths
that mutter her disgrace, she's presently for
dances.

Enter Ferrard.

Bian. For dances?
Maq. Most true.
Em. Most strange. [*Aside to Maque-*　[59
relle.] See, here's my servant,[6] young Ferrard. How many servants think'st thou I
have, Maquerelle?[7]
Maq. [*Aside to Emilia.*] The more, the
merrier. 'Twas well said, use your servants
as you do your smocks; have many, use
one, and change often, for that's most sweet
and courtlike.
Fer. Save ye, fair ladies! Is the duke returned?
Bian. Sweet sir, no voice of him as yet in
　court.
Fer. 'Tis very strange.　　　　　　　70
Bian. [*Aside to Maquerelle.*] And how like
　you my servant, Maquerelle?
Maq. [*Aside to Biancha.*] I think he

[1] Original reads *Cel.*　　　[3] Half-door.
[2] Quarters for women.　　　[4] Stay-laces.
[5] Quit, acquit.　　　　　　[6] Lover.
[7] Neilson suggests that this speech should
probably be given to Biancha.

could hardly draw Ulysses' bow; but, by my
fidelity, were his nose narrower, his eyes
broader, his hands thinner, his lips thicker,
his legs bigger, his feet lesser, his hair
blacker, and his teeth whiter, he were a
tolerable sweet youth, i' faith. And he will
come to my chamber, I will read him the
fortune of his beard. *Cornets sound.* [80

FER. Not yet returned! I fear—But the
duchess approacheth.

SCENA SECUNDA.[1]

[*The same.*]

*Enter Mendoza supporting the Duchess;
Guerrino. The Ladies that are on the
stage rise. Ferrard ushers in the
Duchess, and then takes a Lady to tread
a measure.*[2]

AUR. We will dance; music! We will
dance.

GUER. "*Les quanto,*" lady, "*Pensez
bien,*" "*Passa regis,*" or Biancha's brawl?[3]

AUR. We have forgot the brawl.

FER. So soon? 'Tis wonder.

GUER. Why, 'tis but two singles on the
left, two on the right, three doubles
forward, a traverse of six round; do this
twice, three singles side, galliard trick-　[10
of-twenty, coranto-pace; a figure of eight,
three singles broken down, come up, meet,
two doubles, fall back, and then honor.

AUR. O Dædalus, thy maze! I have
quite forgot it.

MAQ. Trust me, so have I, saving the
falling-back, and then honor.

Enter Prepasso.

AUR. Music, music!

PREP. Who saw the duke? The duke?

Enter Equato.

AUR. Music!　　　　　　　　　　　20

EQU.[4] The duke? Is the duke returned?

AUR. Music!

Enter Celso.

CEL. The duke is either quite invisible
or else is not.

---

[1] Follows stage direction in the original.
[2] A grave or stately dance.
[3] Names of old dances.
[4] Original reads *Pre.*

AUR. We are not pleased with your
intrusion upon our private retirement;
we are not pleased. You have forgot
yourselves.

Enter a Page.

CEL. Boy, thy master? Where's the　[30
duke?

PAGE. Alas, I left him burying the
earth with his spread, joyless limbs. He
told me he was heavy, would sleep; bid
me walk off, for that the strength of fantasy oft made him talk in his dreams. I
straight obeyed, nor ever saw him since;
but, wheresoe'er he is, he's sad.

AUR. Music, sound high, as is our
heart! Sound high!　　　　　　　40

SCENA TERTIA.

[*The same.*]

*Enter Malevole, and Pietro disguised like
　　　　　　　　　　an hermit.*

MAL. The duke—peace!—the duke is
dead.

AUR. Music!

MAL. Is 't music?

MEN. Give proof.

FER. How?

CEL. Where?

PRE. When?

MAL. Rest in peace, as the duke does;
quietly sit! For my own part, I beheld　[10
him but dead; that's all. Marry, here's
one can give you a more particular account of him.

MEN. Speak, holy father, nor let any
　　brow
Within this presence fright thee from
　　the truth;
Speak confidently and freely.

AUR.　　　　　　　　　　We attend.

PIET. Now had the mounting sun's all-
　　ripening wings
Swept the cold sweat of night from
　　earth's dank breast,
When I, whom men call Hermit of the
　　Rock,
Forsook my cell, and clambered up a
　　cliff,　　　　　　　　　　　20
Against whose base the heady Neptune
　　dashed
His high-curled brows; there 'twas I
　　eased my limbs,

When, lo, my entrails melted with the moan
Someone, who far 'bove me was climbed, did make—
I shall offend.
MEN. Not.
AUR. On.
PIET. Methinks I hear him yet: "O female faith!
Go sow the ingrateful sand, and love a woman!
And do I live to be the scoff of men?
To be the wittol-cuckold, even to hug my poison?   31
Thou knowest, O truth,
Sooner hard steel will melt with southern wind,
A seaman's whistle calm the ocean,
A town on fire be extinct with tears,
Than women, vowed to blushless impudence,
With sweet behavior and soft minioning
Will turn from that where appetite is fixed.
O powerful blood, how thou dost slave their soul!
I washed an Ethiope, who, for recompense,   40
Sullied my name. And must I, then, be forced
To walk, to live thus black? Must! Must! Fie!
He that can bear with 'must,' he cannot die."
With that he sighed so [1] passionately deep
That the dull air even groaned. At last he cries,
"Sink shame in seas, sink deep enough!" so dies,
For then I viewed his body fall and souse
Into the foamy main. O, then I saw
That which methinks I see: it was the duke
Whom straight the nicer-stomached sea
Belched up, but then—   51
MAL. Then came I in; but, 'las, all was too late,
For even straight he sunk!
PIET.   Such was the duke's sad fate.
CEL. A better fortune to our Duke Mendoza!
OMNES. Mendoza!

[1] From first edn. Original has *too.*

Cornets flourish. Enter a Guard.

MEN. A guard, a guard! We, full of hearty tears,
For our good father's loss—
For so we well may call him
Who did beseech your loves for our succession—   59
Cannot so lightly overjump his death
As leave his woes revengeless.—(*To Aurelia.*) Woman of shame,
We banish thee forever to the place
From whence this good man comes;
Nor permit, on death, unto the body any ornament;
But, base as was thy life, depart away!
AUR. Ungrateful!
MEN.   Away!
AUR.   Villain, hear me!
Prepasso and Guerrino lead away the Duchess.
MEN. Begone! My lords, address to [2] public council;
'Tis most fit
The train of Fortune is borne up by wit.
Away! Our presence shall be sudden; haste.   70
All depart saving Mendoza, Malevole, and Pietro.
MAL. Now, you egregious devil! Ha, ye murthering politician! [3] How dost, duke? How dost look now? Brave duke, i' faith!
MEN. How did you kill him?
MAL. Slatted his brains out, then soused him in the briny sea.
MEN. Brained him, and drowned him too?
MAL. O, 'twas best, sure work; *for* [80 *he that strikes a great man, let him strike home, or else ware he'll prove no man. Shoulder not a huge fellow, unless you may be sure to lay him in the kennel.* [4]
MEN. A most sound brainpan!
I'll make you both emperors.
MAL. Make us Christians, make us Christians!
MEN. I'll hoist ye; ye shall mount.   89
MAL. To the gallows, say ye? Come!
"Præmium incertum petit certum scelus." [5]
How stands the progress? [6]

[2] Prepare for.   [3] Intriguer.   [4] Channel, gutter.
[5] "Uncertain is the reward sought, but certain the crime" (adapted from Seneca's *Phœnissæ*, l. 632).   [6] Plan of action.

MEN. [*Gives ring.*] Here, take my ring
　unto the citadel;
Have entrance to Maria, the grave
　duchess
Of banished Altofront. Tell her we love
　her;
Omit no circumstance to grace our per-
　son. Do 't.
MAL. I'll make an excellent pander.
Duke, farewell; 'dieu, adieu, duke.
　　　　　　　　　　　Exit Malevole.
MEN. Take Maquerelle with thee, for
　'tis found　　　　　　　　　　99
None cuts a diamond but a diamond.
Hermit, thou art a man for me, my con-
　fessor.
O thou selected spirit, born for my good,
Sure thou wouldst make
An excellent elder in a deformed church.
Come, we must be inward,[1] thou and I
　all one.
PIET. I am glad I was ordained for ye.
MEN. Go to, then; thou must know
that Malevole is a strange villain; danger-
ous, very dangerous. You see how broad a[2]
speaks; a gross-jawed rogue. I would [110
have thee poison him; he's like a corn upon
my great toe, I cannot go for him; he
must be cored out, he must. Wilt do 't, ha?
PIET. Anything, anything.
MEN. Heart of my life! Thus, then, to
　the citadel.
Thou shalt consort with this Malevole;
There being at supper, poison him.
It shall be laid upon Maria, who yields
　love or dies.
Scud quick like lightning.
PIET. "Good deeds crawl, but mischief
　flies."　　　　　　　　　　　120

Enter Malevole. Exit Pietro.

MAL. Your devilship's ring has no
virtue. The buff-captain, the sallow
Westphalian gammon-faced zaza, cries,
"Stand out! Must have a stiffer warrant,
or no pass into the Castle of Comfort."
MEN. Command our sudden letter.—
Not enter! Sh'a't![3] What place is there
in Genoa but thou shalt? Into my heart,
into my very heart! Come, let's love; we
must love, we two, soul and body.　　130
MAL. How didst like the hermit? A
strange hermit, sirrah.

MEN. A dangerous fellow, very peril-
ous. He must die.
MAL. Ay, he must die.
MEN. Thou'st[4] kill him. We are wise;
we must be wise.
MAL. And provident.
MEN. Yea, provident. Beware an hypo-
　crite;　　　　　　　　　　　139
A churchman once corrupted, O, avoid!
A fellow that makes religion his stalking-
　horse,[5]
He breeds a plague. Thou shalt poison
　him.
MAL. Ho, 'tis wondrous necessary! How?
MEN. You both go jointly to the citadel;
There sup, there poison him; and Maria,
Because she is our opposite,[6] shall
　bear
The sad suspect—on which she dies or
　loves us.
MAL. I run.　　　　　　*Exit Malevole.*
MEN. *We that are great, our sole self-good*
　still moves us.
They shall die both, for their deserts
　craves more　　　　　　　　　150
Than we can recompense; their pres-
　ence still
Imbraids[7] our fortunes with beholding-
　ness,
Which we abhor; like deed, not doer.
　Then conclude,
They live not to cry out, "Ingratitude!"
One stick burns tother; steel cuts steel
　alone.
'Tis good trust few; but, O, 'tis best trust
　none!
　　　　　　　　　　Exit Mendoza.

SCENA QUARTA.

[*The same.*]

Enter Malevole and Pietro still disguised, at
　　　　　　　　　　several doors.

MAL. How do you? How dost, duke?
PIET. O, let the last day fall! Drop, drop
　on our cursed heads!

---

[1] Intimate.　　[2] He.　　[3] Shall have it.

[4] Thou must.
[5] A marginal note for the reader, *Shoots under
his belly*, appears here, meaning, according to
Collier, that "a corrupted churchman makes
religion his *stalking-horse*, viz. by shooting at his
object under its belly."
[6] Opponent.
[7] Upbraids.

Let heaven unclasp itself, vomit forth
flames.

MAL. O, do not rand,[1] do not turn
player. There's more of them than can
well live one by another already. What,
art an infidel still?

PIET. I am amazed, struck in a swown
with wonder. I am commanded to poison
thee.   10

MAL. I am commanded to poison thee
at supper.

PIET. At supper?

MAL. In the citadel.

PIET. In the citadel?

MAL. Cross-capers! Tricks! Truth a
heaven! He would discharge us as boys
do eldern guns,[2] one pellet to strick[3] out
another. Of what faith art now?

PIET. All is damnation, wickedness extreme.   20
There is no faith in man.

MAL. In none but usurers and brokers;
they deceive no man. Men take um for
bloodsuckers, and so they are. Now, God
deliver me from my friends!

PIET. Thy friends?

MAL. Yes, from my friends, for from
mine enemies I'll deliver myself. O, cutthroat friendship is the rankest villainy!
Mark this Mendoza; mark him for a   [30
villain; but heaven will send a plague upon
him for a rogue.

PIET. O world!

MAL. World! 'Tis the only region of
death, the greatest shop of the devil, the
cruelest prison of men, out of the which
none pass without paying their dearest
breath for a fee. There's nothing perfect
in it but extreme, extreme calamity, such as
comes yonder.   40

SCENA QUINTA.

[The same.]

Enter Aurelia, two Halberts before and two
after, supported by Celso and Ferrard;
Aurelia in base mourning attire.

AUR. To banishment! Led on to banishment!

PIET. Lady, the blessedness of repentance
to you!

[1] Rant, storm.   [3] Strike.
[2] Elderwood guns, i.e., popguns.

AUR. Why? Why? I can desire nothing
but death,
Nor deserve anything but hell.
If heaven should give sufficiency of grace
To clear my soul, it would make heaven
graceless;
My sins would make the stock of mercy
poor.
O, they would tire heaven's goodness to
reclaim them!
Judgment is just, yet from that vast
villain—
But, sure, he shall not miss sad punish-
ment   10
Fore he shall rule.—On to my cell of
shame!

PIET. My cell 'tis, lady, where, instead of
masques,
Music, tilts, tourneys, and such court-
like shows,
The hollow murmur of the checkless
winds
Shall groan again, whilst the unquiet sea
Shakes the whole rock with foamy bat-
tery.
There usherless the air comes in and out;
The rheumy vault will force your eyes
to weep,
Whilst you behold true desolation.   19
A rocky barrenness shall pain your eyes,
Where all at once one reaches where he
stands,
With brows the roof, both walls with
both his hands.

AUR. It is too good.—Blessed spirit of my
lord,
O, in what orb soe'er thy soul is throned,
Behold me worthily most miserable!
O, let the anguish of my contrite spirit
Entreat some reconciliation!
If not, O, joy, triumph in my just grief!
Death is the end of woes, and tears' re-
lief.

PIET. Belike your lord not loved you, was
unkind.   30

AUR. O heaven!
As the soul loved the body, so loved he.
'Twas death to him to part my presence,
heaven
To see me pleased.
Yet I, like to a wretch given o'er to hell,
Brake all the sacred rites of marriage
To clip a base, ungentle, faithless villain.
O God, a very pagan reprobate—

What should I say?—ungrateful, throws
me out,
For whom I lost soul, body, fame, and
honor.   40
But 'tis most fit. Why should a better fate
Attend on any who forsake chaste sheets,
Fly the embrace of a devoted heart,
Joined by a solemn vow fore God and
man,
To taste the brackish blood of beastly
lust
In an adulterous touch? O ravenous
immodesty!
Insatiate impudence of appetite!
*Look, here's your end; for mark, what sap
in dust,*
What sin in good, even so much love in lust.
Joy to thy ghost, sweet lord! Pardon to
me!   50
CEL. 'Tis the duke's pleasure this night
you rest in court.
AUR. Soul, lurk in shades; run, shame,
from brightsome skies;
*In night the blind man misseth not his
eyes.*
Exit [with Celso, Ferrardo, and Halberts].
MAL. Do not weep, kind cuckold; take
comfort, man; thy betters have been bec-
cos. Agamemnon, emperor of all the merry
Greeks, that tickled all the true Troyans,
was a cornuto; Prince Arthur, that cut off
twelve kings' beards, was a cornuto; Hercules, whose back bore up heaven, and   [60
got forty wenches with child in one night—
PIET. Nay, 't was fifty.
MAL. Faith, forty's enow, a conscience
—yet was a cornuto. Patience; mischief
grows proud; be wise.
PIET. Thou pinchest too deep, art too
keen upon me.
MAL. Tut, a pitiful surgeon makes a
dangerous sore; I'll tent [1] thee to the
ground. Thinkest I'll sustain myself by [70
flattering thee, because thou art a prince?
I had rather follow a drunkard, and live by
licking up his vomit, than by servile
flattery.
PIET. Yet great men ha' done 't.
MAL. Great slaves fear better than love,
born naturally for a coal basket, though the
common usher of princes' presence, Fortune, hath blindly given them better place.
I am vowed to be thy affliction.   80

¹ Probe.

PIET. Prithee, be. I love much misery,
and be thou son to me.

Enter Bilioso.

MAL. Because you are an usurping
duke.—(*To Bilioso.*) Your lordship's well
returned from Florence.
BIL. Well returned, I praise my horse.
MAL. What news from the Floren-
tines?   88
BIL. I will conceal the great duke's
pleasure; only this was his charge. His
pleasure is that his daughter die; Duke
Pietro be banished for banishing his blood's
dishonor; and that Duke Altofront be re-
accepted. This is all. But I hear Duke
Pietro is dead.
MAL. Ay, and Mendoza is duke. What
will you do?
BIL. Is Mendoza strongest?
MAL. Yet he is.
BIL. Then yet I'll hold with him.   100
MAL. But if that Altofront should turn
straight again? [2]
BIL. Why, then, I would turn straight
again.
'Tis good run still with him that has most
might;
I had rather stand with wrong than fall
with right.
MAL. What religion will you be of
now?
BIL. Of the duke's religion, when I know
what it is.   110
MAL. O Hercules!
BIL. Hercules? Hercules was the son of
Jupiter and Alcmena.
MAL. Your lordship is a very wittol.
BIL. Wittol?
MAL. Ay, all-wit.
BIL. Amphitryo was a cuckold.   117
MAL. Your lordship sweats; your young
lady will get you a cloth for your old worship's brows. (*Exit Bilioso.*) Here's a
fellow to be damned! This is his inviolable
maxim—flatter the greatest and oppress
the least. A whoreson flesh-fly, that still
gnaws upon the lean, galled backs!
PIET. Why dost, then, salute him?
MAL. I' faith, as bawds go to church, for
fashion sake. Come, be not confounded;
thou art but in danger to lose a dukedom. Think this: this earth is the only grave

² Return straightway.

and Golgotha wherein all things that   [130
live must rot; 'tis but the draught wherein
the heavenly bodies discharge their corruption; the very muck hill on which the
sublunary orbs cast their excrements.
Man is the slime of this dung pit, and
princes are the governors of these men, for,
for our souls, they are as free as emperors,
all of one piece. There goes but a pair of
shears betwixt an emperor and the son of a
bagpiper;[1] only the dyeing, dressing,   [140
pressing, glossing, makes the difference.

Now, what art thou like to lose?
A jailer's office to keep men in bonds,
Whilst toil and treason all life's good con-
    founds.

PIET. I here renounce forever regency.
O Altofront, I wrong thee to supplant
    thy right,
To trip thy heels up with a devilish
    sleight,
For which I now from throne am thrown,
    world-tricks abjure;
For vengeance, though 't comes slow, yet it
    comes sure.
O, I am changed! For here, fore the
    dread power,   150
In true contrition, I do dedicate
My breath to solitary holiness,
My lips to prayer, and my breast's care
    shall be
Restoring Altofront to regency.

MAL. Thy vows are heard, and we accept
    thy faith.   *Undisguiseth himself.*

Enter Ferneze and Celso.[2]

Banish amazement; come, we four must
    stand
Full shock of fortune. Be not so wonder-
    stricken.
PIET. Doth Ferneze live?
FER.   For your pardon.
PIET. Pardon and love. Give leave to
    recollect
My thoughts dispersed in wild astonish-
    ment.   160
My vows stand fixed in heaven, and from
    hence
I crave all love and pardon.
MAL.   Who doubts of providence,

That sees this change? A hearty faith to
    all!
He needs must rise [who] [3] *can no lower*
    fall;
For still impetuous vicissitude
Touseth the world; then let no maze
    intrude
Upon your spirits. Wonder not I rise,
For who can sink that close can temporize?
The time grows ripe for action. I'll
    detect [4]
My privat'st plot, lest ignorance fear
    suspect.   170
Let's close to counsel, leave the rest to
    fate;
Mature discretion is the life of state.
                            Exeunt.

ACTUS QUINTUS. SCENA PRIMA.

[*Outside the citadel.*]

[5] *Enter Bilioso and Passarello.*

BIL. Fool, how dost thou like my calf in
a long stocking?
PASS. An excellent calf, my lord.
BIL. This calf hath been a reveler this
twenty year. When Monsieur Gundi lay
here ambassador, I could have carried a
lady up and down at arm's end in a platter;
and I can tell you, there were those at
that time who, to try the strength of a
man's back and his arm, would be   [10
coistered.[6] I have measured calves with
most of the palace, and they come nothing
near me; besides, I think there be not
many armors in the arsenal will fit me,
especially for the headpiece. I'll tell thee—
PASS. What, my lord?
BIL. I can eat stewed broth as it comes
seething off the fire, or a custard as it
comes reeking out of the oven, and I think
there are not many lords can do it. [20
[*Displaying his pomander.*] A good pomander—a little decayed in the scent, but six
grains of musk, ground with rosewater and
tempered with a little civet, shall fetch her
again presently!
PASS. O, ay, as a bawd with aqua vitæ.
BIL. And, what, dost thou rail upon the
ladies as thou wert wont?

---

[1] *I.e.*, they are cut out of the same cloth.
[2] Here original adds, *Altofront, Ferneze,
Celso, Pietro.*
[3] Supplied from first edn.
[4] Expose.
[5] The following lines to Bilioso's exit are an
addition.   [6] Coiled up (?).

Pass. I were better roast a live cat, and might do it with more safety. I am [30 as secret to [the] [1] thieves as their painting. There's Maquerelle, oldest bawd and a perpetual beggar. Did you never hear of her trick to be known in the city?

Bil. Never.

Pass. Why, she gets all the picter-[2] makers to draw her picture; when they have done, she most courtly finds fault with them one after another, and never fetcheth them. They, in revenge of this, [40 execute her in pictures as they do in Germany, and hang her in their shops. By this means is she better known to the stinkards [3] than if she had been five times carted.[4]

Bil. Fore God, an excellent policy.

Pass. Are there any revels tonight, my lord?

Bil. Yes.

Pass. Good my lord, give me leave to break a fellow's pate that hath abused [50 me.

Bil. Whose pate?

Pass. Young Ferrard, my lord.

Bil. Take heed, he's very valiant; I have known him fight eight quarrels in five days, believe it.

Pass. O, is he so great a quarreler? Why, then, he's an arrant coward.

Bil. How prove you that?

Pass. Why, thus: he that quarrels [60 seeks to fight; and he that seeks to fight seeks to die; and he that seeks to die seeks never to fight more; and he that will quarrel, and seeks means never to answer a man more, I think he's a coward.

Bil. Thou canst prove anything.

Pass. Anything but a rich knave, for I can flatter no man.

Bil. Well, be not drunk, good fool. I shall see you anon[5] in the presence. [70

Exit [with Passarello].

Enter Malevole and Maquerelle, at several doors opposite, singing.

Mal. The Dutchman for a drunkard—
Maq. The Dane for golden locks—
Mal. The Irishman for usquebath [6]—
Maq. The Frenchman for the ( ).[7]

Mal. O, thou art a blessed creature! Had I a modest woman to conceal, I would put her to thy custody, for no reasonable creature would ever suspect her to be in thy company. Ha, thou art a melodious Maquerelle, thou picture of a woman, [80 and substance of a beast!

[8] *Enter Passarello.*

Maq. O fool, will ye be ready anon to go with me to the revels? The hall will be so pestered [9] anon.

Pass. Ay, as the country is with attorneys.

Mal. What hast thou there, fool?

Pass. Wine; I have learned to drink since I went with my lord ambassador. I'll drink to the health of Madam [90 Maquerelle.

Mal. Why, thou wast wont to rail upon her.

Pass. Ay; but since I borrowed money of her, I'll drink to her health now, as gentlemen visit brokers, or as knights send venison to the city, either to take up more money, or to procure longer forbearance.

Mal. Give me the bowl. I drink a health to Altofront, our deposed duke. [100
[*Drinks.*]

Pass. I'll take it. [*Drinks.*] So? Now I'll begin a health to Madam Maquerelle.
[*Drinks.*]

Mal. Pugh! I will not pledge her.

Pass. Why, I pledged your lord.

Mal. I care not.

Pass. Not pledge Madam Maquerelle! Why, then will I spew up your lord again with this fool's finger.

Mal. Hold; I'll take it. [*Drinks.*]

Maq. Now thou hast drunk my health, fool, I am friends with thee. 111

Pass. Art? Art?

When Griffon saw the reconciléd quean
Offering about his neck her arms to cast,
He threw off sword and heart's malignant stream,
And lovely her below the loins embraced.—

Adieu, Madam Maquerelle.

Exit Passarello.

Mal. And how dost thou think a this transformation of state now? 119

---

[1] Supplied by Bullen. [2] Picture. [3] The mob.
[4] Bawds were punished by being carted through the streets. [5] Immediately.
[6] Usquebaugh, whiskey. [7] Pox.
[8] The passage from this point to the exit of Passarello is an addition.
[9] Crowded.

Maq. Verily, very well; for we women always note, the falling of the one is the rising of the other. Some must be fat, some must be lean; some must be fools, and some must be lords; some must be knaves, and some must be officers; some must be beggars, some must be knights; some must be cuckolds, and some must be citizens. As for example, I have two court dogs, the most fawning curs, the one called Watch, th' other Catch. [130 Now I, like Lady Fortune, sometimes love this dog, sometimes raise that dog, some-times favor Watch, most commonly fancy Catch. Now, that dog which I favor I feed; and he's so ravenous that what I give he never chaws it, gulps it down whole, with-out any relish of what he has, but with a greedy expectation of what he shall have. The other dog now—   139

Mal. No more dog, sweet Maquerelle, no more dog. And what hope hast thou of the Duchess Maria? Will she stoop to the duke's lure? Will she cow, [1] think'st?

Maq. Let me see, where's the sign now? Ha' ye e'er a calendar? Where's the sign, trow you?

Mal. Sign! Why, is there any moment in that?   148

Maq. O, believe me, a most secret power. Look ye, a Chaldean or an As-syrian, I am sure 'twas a most sweet Jew, told me, court any woman in the right sign, you shall not miss. But you must take her in the right vein then, as, when the sign is in Pisces, a fishmonger's wife is very sociable; in Cancer, a Precisian's [2] wife is very flexible; in Capricorn, a mer-chant's wife hardly holds out; in Libra, a lawyer's wife is very tractable, especially if her husband be at the term; [3] only in [160 Scorpio 'tis very dangerous meddling. Has the duke sent any jewel, any rich stones?

Enter Captain.

Mal. Ay, I think those are the best signs to take a lady in.—By your favor, signior, I must discourse with the Lady Maria, Altofront's duchess; I must enter for the duke.

Cap. She here shall give you interview. I received the guardship of this citadel

[1] Submit.
[2] Puritan's.

from the good Altofront, and for his [170 use I'll keep 't till I am of no use.

Mal. Wilt thou? O heavens, that a Christian should be found in a buff jerkin! Captain Conscience, I love thee, captain. (*Exit Captain.*) We attend. And what hope hast thou of this duchess' easiness?

Maq. 'Twill go hard. She was a cold creature ever; she hated monkeys, fools, jesters, and gentlemen ushers ex- [179 tremely; she had the vile trick on 't, not only to be truly modestly honorable in her own conscience, but she would avoid the least wanton carriage that might incur suspect, as, God bless me, she had almost brought bed-pressing out of fashion. I could scarce get a fine [4] for the lease of a lady's favor once in a fortnight.

Mal. Now, in the name of immodesty, how many maidenheads hast thou brought to the block?   190

Maq. Let me see. Heaven forgive us our misdeeds!—Here's the duchess.

Scena Secunda.

[*The same.*]

Enter Maria and Captain.

Mal. God bless thee, lady!

Mar. Out of thy company!

Mal. We have brought thee tender of a husband.

Mar. I hope I have one already.

Maq. Nay, by mine honor, madam, as good ha' ne'er a husband as a banished husband; he's in another world now. I'll tell ye, lady, I have heard of a sect that maintained, when the husband was [10 asleep, the wife might lawfully entertain another man, for then her husband was as dead. Much more when he is banished!

Mar. Unhonest creature!

Maq. Pish, honesty is but an art to seem so.

Pray ye, what's honesty, what's con-stancy,

But fables feigned, odd old fools' chat, devised

By jealous fools to wrong our liberty?

Mal. Mully,[5] he that loves thee is a duke, Mendoza. He will maintain thee [20 royally, love thee ardently, defend thee

[3] Court.

[4] Fee.
[5] Molly.

powerfully, marry thee sumptuously, and
keep thee in despite of Rosicleer or Donzel
del Phebo.[1] There's jewels. [*Gives jewels.*]
If thou wilt, so; if not, so.

MAR. Captain, for God's sake, save poor
    wretchedness
From tyranny of lustful insolence!
Enforce me in the deepest dungeon dwell,
Rather than here; here round about is
    hell.—
O my dear'st Altofront, where'er thou
    breathe,   30
Let my soul sink into the shades beneath
Before I stain thine honor! This thou
    hast,
And, long as I can die, I will live chaste.

MAL. Gainst him that can enforce, how
    vain is strife!

MAR. She that can be enforced has ne'er a
    knife;
She that through force her limbs with lust
    enrolls,
Wants Cleopatra's asps and Portia's coals.
God amend you!   *Exit with Captain.*

MAL. Now, the fear of the devil forever
go with thee!—Maquerelle, I tell thee, [40
I have found an honest woman. Faith, I
perceive, when all is done, there is of
women, as of all other things, some good,
most bad; some saints, some sinners. For
as nowadays no courtier but has his mistress, no captain but has his cockatrice,[2]
no cuckold but has his horns, and no fool
but has his feather, even so, no woman but
has her weakness and feather too, no sex
but has his—I can hunt the letter no [50
farder.—[*Aside.*] O God, how loathsome
this toying is to me! That a duke should
be forced to fool it! Well, "*Stultorum plena
sunt omnia.*"[3]   Better play the fool lord
than be the fool lord.—Now, where's your
sleights, Madam Maquerelle?

MAQ. Why, are ye ignorant that 'tis said
a squeamish, affected niceness is natural to
women, and that the excuse of their yielding
is only, forsooth, the difficult obtaining? [60
You must put her to 't. Women are flax,
and will fire in a moment.

MAL. Why, was the flax put into thy
mouth, and yet thou—thou set fire, thou
inflame her?

MAQ. Marry, but I'll tell ye now, you
were too hot.

MAL. The fitter to have inflamed the
flax-woman.

MAQ. You were too boisterous, [70
spleeny, for, indeed—

MAL. Go, go, thou art a weak pandress;
    now I see,
Sooner earth's fire heaven itself shall waste
    Than all with heat can melt a mind that's
    chaste.
Go thou, the duke's lime-twig![4] I'll make
the duke turn thee out of thine office.
What, not get one touch of hope, and had
her at such advantage!

MAQ. Now, a my conscience, now I
think in my discretion, we did not take [80
her in the right sign; the blood was not in
the true vein, sure.   *Exit.*

[5] *Enter Bilioso.*

BIL. Make way there! The duke returns
from the enthronement.—Malevole—

MAL. Out, rogue!

BIL. Malevole—

MAL. "Hence, ye gross-jawed, peasantly—out, go!"

BIL. Nay, sweet Malevole, since my
return I hear you are become the thing [90
I always prophesied would be—an advanced virtue, a worthily-employed faithfulness, a man a grace, dear friend.
Come, what! *Si quoties peccant homines*—
if as often as courtiers play the knaves,
honest men should be angry—why, look
ye, we must collogue[6] sometimes, forswear
sometimes.

MAL. Be damned sometimes.

BIL. Right.   *Nemo omnibus horis* [100
sapit: No man can be honest at all hours.
Necessity often depraves virtue.

MAL. I will commend thee to the duke.

BIL. Do let us be friends, man.

MAL. And knaves, man.

BIL. Right. Let us prosper and purchase;[7] our lordships shall live, and our
knavery be forgotten.

MAL. He that by any ways gets riches,
his means never shames him.   110

---

[1] Heroes of the Spanish romance translated as
The Mirror of Knighthood.   [2] Courtesan.
[3] "All things are full of fools" (Cicero).
[4] Snare, trap.
[5] The remainder of the scene is another addition.
[6] Confer secretly.
[7] Acquire wealth (by illegitimate means).

BIL. True.

MAL. For impudency and faithlessness are the main stays to greatness.

BIL. By the Lord, thou art a profound lad.

MAL. By the Lord, thou art a perfect knave. Out, ye ancient damnation!

BIL. Peace, peace! And thou wilt not be a friend to me as I am a knave, be not a knave to me as I am thy friend, and [120 disclose me. Peace! Cornets!

SCENA TERTIA.

[*The same.*]

Enter Prepasso and Ferrard, two Pages with lights, Celso and Equato, Mendoza in duke's robes, and Guerrino.[1] *Exeunt all saving Malevole [and Mendoza].*

MEN. On, on; leave us, leave us.— Stay, where is the hermit?

MAL. With Duke Pietro, with Duke Pietro.

MEN. Is he dead? Is he poisoned?

MAL. Dead as the duke is.

MEN. Good, excellent. He will not blab; secureness lives in secrecy. Come hither, come hither.

MAL. Thou hast a certain strong [10 villainous scent about thee my nature cannot endure.

MEN. Scent, man? What returns Maria—what answer to our suit?

MAL. Cold-frosty; she is obstinate.

MEN. Then she's but dead; 'tis resolute she dies.

Black deed only through black deed safely flees.

MAL. Pugh! "*Per scelera semper sceleribus tutum est iter.*"[2]   19

MEN. What, art a scholar? Art a politician? Sure, thou art an arrand knave.

MAL. Who, I? I have been twice an undersheriff, man.[3]

Well, I will go rail upon some great man, that I may purchase the bastinado, or else go marry some rich Genoan lady, and instantly go travel.

MEN. Travel, when thou art married?

MAL. Ay, 'tis your young lord's fashion to do so, though he was so lazy, being a [30 bachelor, that he would never travel so far as the university; yet, when he married her, tales of—and, catso, for England!

MEN. And why for England?

MAL. Because there is no brothel houses there.

MEN. Nor courtesans?

MAL. Neither; your whore went down with the stews, and your punk came up with your Puritan.   40

MEN. Canst thou empoison? Canst thou empoison?

MAL. Excellently; no Jew, potecary, or politician better. Look ye, here's a box. Whom wouldst thou empoison? Here's a box (*Giving it.*) which, opened and the fume taken up in conduits thorough which the brain purges itself, doth instantly for twelve hours' space bind up all show of life in a deep senseless sleep. Here's an- [50 other (*Giving it.*) which, being opened under the sleeper's nose, chokes all the power of life, kills him suddenly.

MEN. I'll try experiments; 'tis good not to be deceived.—So, so; catso!

Seems to poison Malevole [, who falls].

Who would fear that may destroy?
    Death hath no teeth or tongue;
And he that's great, to him are slaves
    Shame, murder, fame, and wrong.—

Celso!   60

Enter Celso.[4]

CEL. My honored lord?

MEN. The good Malevole, that plain-tongued man, alas, is dead on sudden, wondrous strangely! He held in our esteem good place. Celso, see him buried, see him buried.

CEL. I shall observe ye.

MEN. And, Celso, prithee, let it be thy care tonight

because with its repetition of the earlier part of the scene it was apparently an alternate reading for all or part of the first twenty-three lines.

[4] In the original this direction follows l. 53.

---

[1] Direction reads *Bilioso and Guerrino.*

[2] "The way to wickedness is always made safe by wickedness" (Seneca, *Agamemnon,* l. 115).

[3] Ll. 24–40 are an addition. In the original they are preceded by the passage:

"*Enter Malevole and Mendoza.*

MEN. Hast been with Maria?

MAL. As your scrivener to your usurer, I have dealt about taking of this commodity; but she's cold-frosty,"

The passage just quoted has been omitted here

To have some pretty show, to solem-
　nize
Our high installment; some music,
　masquery.　　　　　　　　　　70
We'll give fair entertain unto Maria,
The duchess to the banished Altofront.
Thou shalt conduct her from the citadel
Unto the palace.　　Think on some
　masquery.
CEL. Of what shape, sweet lord?
MEN. Why, shape? Why, any quick-done
　fiction,
As some brave spirits of the Genoan
　dukes
To come out of Elysium, forsooth,
Led in by Mercury, to gratulate　　　79
Our happy fortune; some such anything,
Some far-fet [1] trick good for ladies, some
　stale toy
Or other, no matter, so 't be of our de-
　vising.
Do thou prepare 't; 'tis but for a fashion
　sake.
Fear not; it shall be graced, man; it shall
　take.
CEL. All service.
MEN. All thanks; our hand shall not be
　close to thee; farewell.—
[*Aside.*] Now is my teachery secure, nor
　can we fall.
Mischief that prospers, men do virtue call.
I'll trust no man; he that by tricks gets
　wreaths
Keeps them with steel; no man securely
　breathes　　　　　　　　　　　90
Out of deservéd ranks; the crowd will
　mutter, "Fool!"
Who cannot bear with spite, he cannot rule.
The chiefest secret for a man of state
Is to live senseless of a strengthless hate.
　　　　　　　　　　　　　　[*Exit.*]
MAL. (*Starts up and speaks.*) Death of
the damned thief! I'll make one i' the
masque; thou shalt ha' some brave spirits
of the antique dukes.　　　　　　98
CEL. My lord, what strange delusion?
MAL. Most happy, dear Celso! Poisoned
with an empty box! I'll give thee all anon.
My lady comes to court; there is a whirl
of fate comes tumbling on; the castle's
captain stands for me, the people pray for
me, and the great leader of the just stands
for me. Then courage, Celso.

[1] Far-fetched.

For no disastrous chance can ever move him
That leaveth nothing but a God above him.
　　　　　　　　　　　　　　[*Exeunt.*]

SCENA QUARTA. [2]

[*The presence chamber.*]

Enter Prepasso and Bilioso, two Pages before
　them; Maquer[elle], Biancha, and
　　　　　　　　Emilia.

BIL. Make room there, room for the
ladies! Why, gentlemen, will not ye suffer
the ladies to be entered in the great chamber? Why, gallants! And you, sir, to drop
your torch where the beauties must sit too!
PRE. And there's a great fellow plays
the knave. Why dost not strike him?
BIL. Let him play the knave, a God's
name; think'st thou I have no more wit
than to strike a great fellow?—The　[10
music! More lights! Reveling-scaffolds! Do
you hear? Let there be oaths enow ready
at the door; swear out the devil himself.
Let's leave the ladies, and go see if the
lords be ready for them.
　　　　　　All save the Ladies depart.
MAQ. And, by my troth, beauties, why
do you not put you into the fashion? This
is a stale cut; you must come in fashion.
Look ye, you must be all felt, felt and
feather, a felt upon your bare hair. [20
Look ye, these tiring things [3] are justly out of
request now. And, do ye hear, you must
wear falling bands, [4] you must come into
the falling fashion; there is such a deal a
pinning these ruffs, when the fine clean fall
is worth all; and again, if you should chance
to take a nap in the afternoon, your falling
band requires no poting stick [5] to recover
his form. Believe me, no fashion to the
falling, I say.　　　　　　　　　30
BIAN. And is not Signior St. Andrew a
gallant fellow now?
MAQ. By my maidenhead, la, honor and
he agrees as well together as a satin suit
and woolen stockings.
EM. But is not Marshal Make-room,
my servant in reversion, [6] a proper gentleman?

[2] In the original the new scene begins at the
entry of the duke's procession.
[3] Headdresses.
[4] Flat collars.　　　　[5] Stick for plaiting ruffs.
[6] Upon the death or withdrawal of the present
owner.

MAQ. Yes, in reversion, as he had his office; as, in truth, he hath all things in [40 reversion. He has his mistress in reversion, his clothes in reversion, his wit in reversion, and, indeed, is a suitor to me for my dog in reversion. But, in good verity, la, he is as proper a gentleman in reversion as—and, indeed, as fine a man as may be, having a red beard and a pair of wrapped [1] legs.

BIAN. But, i' faith, I am most monstrously in love with Count Quidlibet-in-quodlibet. Is he not a pretty, dapper, [50 unidle gallant?

MAQ. He is even one of the most busy-fingered lords; he will put the beauties to the squeak most hideously.

Enter Bilioso.

BIL. Room! Make a lane there! The duke is entering. Stand handsomely, for beauty's sake; take up the ladies there! So, cornets, cornets!

Enter Prepasso; joins to Bilioso. Two Pages and lights; Ferrard; Mendoza. At the other door, two Pages with lights, and the Captain leading in Maria. The Duke meets Maria, and closeth with her. The rest fall back.

MEN. Madam, with gentle ear receive my suit;
A kingdom's safety should o'erpeise [2] slight rites;   60
Marriage is merely nature's policy.
Then since, unless our royal beds be joined,
Danger and civil tumult frights the state,
Be wise as you are fair, give way to fate.
MAR. What wouldst thou, thou affliction to our house?
Thou ever-devil, 'twas thou that banishedst
My truly noble lord!
MEN. I?
MAR. Ay, by thy plots, by thy black stratagems.
Twelve moons have suffered change since I beheld   70
The lovéd presence of my dearest lord.
O thou, far worse than Death! He parts but soul

From a weak body; but thou soul from soul
Disseverest, that which God's own hand did knit;
Thou, scant of honor, full of devilish wit!
MEN. We'll check your too-intemperate lavishness.
I can and will.
MAR. What canst?
MEN. Go to; in banishment thy husband dies.   79
MAR. *He ever is at home that's ever wise.*
MEN. You'st [3] never meet more; reason should love control.
MAR. Not meet?
She that dear loves, her love's still in her soul.
MEN. You are but a woman, lady; you must yield.
MAR. O, save me, thou innated [4] bashfulness,
Thou only ornament of woman's modesty!
MEN. Modesty? Death, I'll torment thee.
MAR. Do, urge all torments, all afflictions try;
I'll die my lord's as long as I can die.
MEN. Thou obstinate, thou shalt die.—Captain, that lady's   90
Life is forfeited [5] to justice. We have examined her,
And we do find she hath empoisonéd
The reverend hermit; therefore we command
Severest custody.—Nay, if you'll do 's no good,
You 'st do 's no harm. A tyrant's peace is blood.
MAR. O, thou art merciful! O gracious devil,
Rather by much let me condemnéd be
For seeming murder than be damned for thee!
I'll mourn no more; come, girt my brows with flowers;
Revel and dance. Soul, now thy wish thou hast;   100
Die like a bride; poor heart, thou shalt die chaste.

Enter Aurelia in mourning habit.

AUR. *Life is a frost of cold felicity,*
And death the thaw of all our vanity.
Was't not an honest priest [6] that wrote so?

---

[1] Padded. Perhaps a misprint for *warped.*
[2] Outweigh.
[3] You must.   [4] Innate.
[5] From first edn. Original reads *forteified.*
[6] Thomas Bastard.

MEN. Who let her in?

BIL. 　　　　　　　Forbear!

PRE. 　　　　　　　Forbear!

AUR. *Alas, calamity is everywhere.*
Sad misery, despite your double doors,
Will enter even in court.

BIL. Peace!

AUR. 　　　　　I ha' done. One word—take
heed! I ha' done.

Enter Mercury with loud music.

MER. Cyllenian Mercury, the god of
ghosts, 　　　　　　　　　110
From gloomy shades that spread the
lower coasts,
Calls four high-famed Genoan dukes to
come,
And make this presence their Elysium,
To pass away this high triumphal night
With song and dances, court's more soft
delight.

AUR. Are you god of ghosts? I have a
suit depending in hell betwixt me and my
conscience. I would fain have thee help
me to an advocate. 　　　　　　119

BIL. Mercury shall be your lawyer, lady.

AUR. Nay, faith, Mercury has too good
a face to be a right lawyer.

PRE. Peace, forbear! Mercury presents
the masque.

Cornets. The song to the cornets, which play-
ing, the masque enters; Malevole,
Pietro, Ferneze, and Celso, in white
robes, with duke's crowns upon laurel
wreaths, pistolets and short swords under
their robes.

MEN. Celso, Celso, court [1] Maria for our
love.—Lady, be gracious, yet grace—
Malevole takes his Wife to dance.

MAR. With me, sir?

MAL. 　　　　　Yes, more lovéd
than my breath;
With you I'll dance.

MAR. 　　　　　　Why, then, you
dance with death.
But, come, sir, I was ne'er more apt to
mirth. 　　　　　　　　129
Death gives eternity a glorious breath;
O, to die honored, who would fear to die?

MAL. *They die in fear who live in vil-*
lainy.

MEN. Yes, believe him, lady, and be ruled
by him.
Pietro takes his wife Aurelia to dance.

PIET. Madam, with me?

AUR. 　　　　Wouldst then be miserable?

PIET. I need not wish.

AUR. O, yet forbear my hand! Away, fly,
fly!
O, seek not her that only seeks to die!

PIET. Poor lovéd soul!

AUR. 　　　　What, wouldst court misery?

PIET. Yes.

AUR. 　　　　She'll come too soon. O my
grieved heart!

PIET. Lady, ha' done, ha' done. 　　140
Come, let's dance; be once from sorrow
free.

AUR. Art a sad man?

PIET. 　　　　　Yes, sweet.

AUR. 　　　　　　　Then we'll agree.
Ferneze takes Maquerelle, and Celso, Bi-
ancha; then the cornets sound the
measure, one change and rest.

FER. (*To Biancha.*) 　Believe it, lady;
shall I swear? Let me enjoy you in private,
and I'll marry you, by my soul.

BIAN. I had rather you would swear by
your body; I think that would prove the
more regarded oath with you.

FER. I'll swear by them both, to please
you. 　　　　　　　　　150

BIAN. O, damn them not both to please
me, for God's sake!

FER. Faith, sweet creature, let me enjoy
you tonight, and I'll marry you tomorrow
fortnight, by my troth, la.

MAQ. On his troth, la! Believe him not;
that kind of cunny-catching [2] is as stale as
Sir Oliver Anchovy's perfumed jerkin.
Promise of matrimony by a young gallant,
to bring a virgin lady into a fool's paradise;
make her a great woman, and then 　[161]
cast her off—'tis as common, as natural, to a
courtier, as jealousy to a citizen, gluttony
to a Puritan, wisdom to an alderman, pride
to a tailor, or an empty hand basket to one
of these sixpenny damnations.[3] Of his
troth, la, believe him not; traps to catch
polecats!

MAL. (*To Maria.*) Keep your face constant; let no sudden passion
Speak in your eyes. 　[*Reveals himself.*]

MAR. 　　　　　　O my Altofront!

[1] From first edn. Original reads *count.*

[2] Cony-catching, deceiving. 　　[3] Prostitutes.

PIET. [*To Aurelia.*] A tyrant's jealous-
   ies   171
Are very nimble; you receive it all.
AUR.[1] My heart, though not my knees, doth
   humbly fall
Low as the earth, to thee.
PIET. Peace! Next change; no words.
MAR. Speech to such, ay, O, what will
   affords!
Cornets sound the measure over again; which
                    danced, they unmask.
MEN. Malevole!
They environ Mendoza, bending their pistols
                         on him.
MAL. No!
MEN. Altofront! Duke Pietro! Ferneze!
   Ha!
ALL. Duke Altofront! Duke Altofront! 180
Cornets, a flourish.—They seize upon
                         Mendoza.
MEN. Are we surprised? What strange de-
   lusions mock
Our senses? Do I dream? Or have I
   dreamt
This two days' space? Where am I?
MAL. Where an archvillain is.
MEN. O, lend me breath till I am fit to die!
For peace with heaven, for your own
   souls' sake,
Vouchsafe me life!
PIET. Ignoble villain, whom neither heaven
   nor hell,
Goodness of God or man, could once
   make good!
MAL. Base, treacherous wretch, what
   grace canst thou expect,   190
That hast grown impudent in graceless-
   ness?
MEN. O, life!
MAL. Slave, take thy life.
Wert thou defenséd,[2] through blood and
   wounds,
The sternest horror of a civil fight
Would I achieve thee; but, prostrate at
   my feet,
I scorn to hurt thee. *'Tis the heart of slaves*
That deigns to triumph over peasants'
   graves;
For such thou art, since birth doth ne'er enroll
A man 'mong monarchs, but a glorious soul.[3]
O, I have seen strange accidents of
   state—   201

The flatterer, like the ivy, clip the oak,
And waste it to the heart; lust so con-
   firmed
That the black act of sin itself not
   shamed
To be termed courtship.
O, they that are as great as be their sins,
Let them remember that th' inconstant
   people
Love many princes merely for their faces
And outward shows; and they do covet
   more
To have a sight of these than of their
   virtues.   210
Yet thus much let the great ones still
   conceal.[4]
When they observe not heaven's imposed
   conditions,
They are no kings, but forfeit their commissions.
MAQ. O good my lord, I have lived in
the court this twenty year; they that have
been old courtiers, and come to live in the
city, they are spited at, and thrust to the
walls like apricocks, good my lord.   218
BIL. My lord, I did know your lordship
in this disguise; you heard me ever say, if
Altofront did return, I would stand for
him. Besides, 'twas your lordship's pleasure
to call me wittol and cuckold; you must not
think, but that I knew you, I would have
put it up so patiently.
[MAL.] (*To Pietro and Aurelia.*) You
o'erjoyed spirits, wipe your long-wet
   eyes.—
Hence with this man! (*Kicks out*
   Mendoza.) An eagle takes not flies.—
(*To Pietro and Aurelia.*) You to your
   vows—(*To Maquerelle.*) and thou
   unto the suburbs.[5]
You to my worst friend I would hardly
   give.—
(*To Bilioso.*) Thou art a perfect old
   knave.—(*To Celso and the Captain.*)
   All-pleased, live   230
You two unto my breast—(*To Maria.*)
   thou to my heart.
The rest of idle actors idly part;
And as for me, I here assume my right,
To which I hope all's pleased. To all,
   good night.
        Cornets, a flourish. Exeunt omnes.
             FINIS.

---

[1] Marginal note: *Aurelia to Pietro.*
[2] Defended.   [3] Lines 201–25 are an addition.

[4] Conceive (?).   [5] The disreputable district.

An Imperfect Ode, Being But One
Staff, Spoken by the Prologue

To wrest each hurtless thought to private
    sense
Is the foul use of ill-bred impudence.
    Immodest censure [1] now grows wild,
      All overrunning.
    Let Innocence be ne'er so chaste,
      Yet at the last
      She is defiled
    With too nice-brainéd cunning.
    O you of fairer soul,
      Control   10
    With an Herculean arm
      This harm;
And once teach all old freedom of a pen,
Which still must write of fools, whilst
    writes of men!

Epilogus

Your modest silence, full of heedy [2]
    stillness,
Makes me thus speak: a voluntary illness [3]

Is merely [4] senseless; but unwilling error,
Such as proceeds from too rash youthful
    fervor,
May well be called a fault, but not a sin.
*Rivers take names from founts where they
    begin.*
Then let not too severe an eye peruse
The slighter brakes [5] of our reforméd Muse,
Who could herself herself of faults detect,
But that she knows 'tis easy to correct,
Though [6] some men's labor. Troth, to err
    is fit,   11
As long as wisdom's not professed, but wit.
Then till another's [7] happier Muse appears,
Till his Thalia feast your learned ears,
To whose desertful lamps [8] pleased Fates
    impart
Art above Nature, Judgment above Art,
    Receive this piece, which hope nor fear
    yet daunteth:
*He that knows most, knows most how
    much he wanteth.*

Finis.

[1] Immoderate criticism.
[2] Heedful.
[3] Defect.
[4] Wholly.
[5] Flaws.
[6] Supply 'tis.
[7] Ben Jonson's.
[8] Nocturnal studies.

GEORGE CHAPMAN

George Chapman was born near Hitchin about 1559, and, according to Wood, "spent some time in Oxon, where he was observed to be most excellent in the Latin and Greek tongues, but not in logic or philosophy." He is first heard of upon the publication of his poem *The Shadow of Night* in 1594. He is first mentioned as a dramatist in Henslowe's record of the performance of his *Blind Beggar of Alexandria* by the Admiral's Men in February, 1596. In 1598 Meres placed him among the best for both comedy and tragedy. Not long after 1600 he seems to have been writing for the Children of the Chapel—called after 1604 the Children of the Queen's Revels—at Blackfriars Theater. His share in *Eastward Ho*, written for the children in collaboration with Jonson and Marston, caused his imprisonment for a short while because James I was offended by its satire on the Scots. In *Byron*, also written for the boy actors, Chapman offended again by his representation of French royalty on the stage. His major activity as a dramatist probably ceased by 1613. In the meanwhile he had published in 1598 *Seven Books of the Iliads* and a continuation of Marlowe's *Hero and Leander*. Minor poetic works and parts of the famous Homeric translation were published at intervals, the complete edition of the two epics appearing in 1616 and a volume of other Homeric poems about 1624. From Prince Henry, his chief patron, whom he had served as sewer, he received promise of a large reward and a pension for his Homer, but after the death of the prince in 1612 the promise was not fulfilled. Chapman wrote a poem on his death and prepared a court masque the next year, but he did not continue in favor at court. His later life was one of poverty. He died in 1634, and was honored with a monument designed by his friend, the great architect Inigo Jones.

In Chapman's plays the Elizabethan poetic and romantic treatment of life is united with the humanist's interest in classical learning. Early in his career he experimented with elements of the comedy of humors, or manners, which Jonson, the dominant figure of the Stuart era, established in 1598 with his *Every Man in His Humor*, using a classical technique to satirize the follies of contemporary society. After depicting characters warped by humors in *An Humorous Day's Mirth*, apparently written for Henslowe in 1597, Chapman made a still more searching study of follies in *All Fools* of 1599, based on two plays of Terence. But in his comic plots, drawn from various sources including the classics, he seems to be interested primarily in devices of romantic comedy—love story, intrigue, disguise, mistakes of identity, and other features of the complicated action developed under the influence chiefly of Italian comedy and novel. His later comedies with date of publication are *The Gentleman Usher* (1606), *Monsieur D'Olive* (1606), *May Day* (1611), and *The Widow's Tears* (1612). *Sir Giles Goosecap*, printed in 1606, is usually ascribed to Chapman. In tragedy also Chapman showed a kinship to Jonson in his combination of history, philosophic discourse drawn from classic writers, and Senecan technique, but he did not achieve the clarity and sustained tone that made Jonson a model for later writers. Chapman is distinctly Elizabethan in his style, which frequently rises to passionate intensity, with passages lighted by felicitous figures as vivid and elaborate as his Homeric similes, but at times becomes bombastic, strained, or "metaphysical." One of his tragedies, *Cæsar and Pompey*, published in 1631 as written long before, deals with a theme of ancient history popular in drama. With the omission of some tragedies doubtfully ascribed to him, the rest are drawn from contemporary or recent French history: *Bussy D'Ambois* (printed in 1607), the two parts of *The Conspiracy and the Tragedy of Charles, Duke of Byron* (printed in 1608), *The Revenge of Bussy D'Ambois* (printed in 1613), and *The Tragedy of Chabot* (printed in 1639 as written by Chapman and Shirley). The main incidents of *Byron* and *The Revenge of Bussy D'Ambois* Chapman apparently drew from Grimestone's *General Inventory of the History of France*, a translation of Jean de Serres, brought nearer to the date of publication in 1607 by the use of other French works. He modified or supplemented his material, however, to emphasize certain aspects of character or to secure tragic effects. The influence of Seneca on his tragedies is clear in such devices as the ghost and in his fondness for the declamatory and sententious. Ethical or metaphysical discourses are adapted from classical treatises, as F. L. Schoell has shown, often through Renaissance translations or through compilations like Erasmus' *Adagia*. Plutarch's moral treatises furnished Chapman with numerous passages, and the stoic philosophy of Cleremont in *The Revenge of Bussy D'Ambois* is built up from passages in a Latin translation of Epictetus.

Bussy D'Ambois, Chapman's best tragedy, may have been written as early as 1598, to judge from the names of the characters in an inventory of garments to be found in Henslowe's Diary for that year. If so, it was revised before publication in 1607. Possibly the play was inspired by Marlowe's *Massacre at Paris*, for several of the same historical figures appear in the two, and there is a not dissimilar portrayal of bold, arrogant characters. As in other cases, Chapman must have had contemporary accounts for his historical details, but the extant French works of importance covering the field seem to have been printed after the play was written—De Thou's *Historiæ sui temporis*, formerly regarded as a possible source, the memoirs of Brantôme and Marguerite de Valois, and Rosset's *Histoires tragiques*. Whatever his source, he has varied from historical fact, not only in a convention like the introduction of the ghost, but in giving a logical connection to the incidents chosen for plot, and in making Bussy a man of lower social status and more truculent nature than seems warranted. Bussy thus becomes an example of the aspiring spirits produced by the Renaissance, who dared much to win recognition, as other historical characters in the play have taken form as Renaissance types.

After its publication by Aspley in 1607, *Bussy D'Ambois* was reissued in 1608. Robert Lunne brought out another edition in 1641, which according to the title-page had been "much corrected and amended by the Author before his death." The present text is based on Parrott's reprint of this quarto of 1641 in *The Plays and Poems of George Chapman*. The edition of Boas in the Belles-Lettres Series has also been consulted.

BUSSY D'AMBOIS [1]

BY

GEORGE CHAPMAN

[DRAMATIS PERSONÆ

HENRY III, *King of France.*
MONSIEUR, *his brother.*
MAFFÉ, *steward to Monsieur.*
THE DUKE OF GUISE.
MONTSURRY, *a count.*
BUSSY D'AMBOIS.
BARRISOR ⎫ *courtiers; enemies*
L'ANOU ⎬ *of D'Ambois.*
PYRRHOT ⎭
BRISAC ⎫ *courtiers; friends*
MELYNELL ⎬ *of D'Ambois.*
FRIAR COMOLET.
NUNTIUS, *a messenger.*

MURDERERS.
BEHEMOTH ⎫ *spirits.*
CARTOPHYLAX ⎬
UMBRA of FRIAR.

ELENOR, *Duchess of Guise.*
ANNABELLE, *maid to Elenor.*
BEAUPRÉ, *niece to Elenor.*
CHARLOTTE, *maid to Beaupré.*
TAMYRA, *Countess of Montsurry.*
PERO, *maid to Tamyra.*
PYRA, *a court lady.*
LORDS, LADIES, PAGES, *etc.*

SCENE: *Paris.*

TIME: *Later sixteenth century.*]

PROLOGUE

NOT out of confidence that none but we [2]
Are able to present this tragedy,
Nor out of envy at the grace of late
It did receive, nor yet to derogate
From their deserts who [3] give out boldly
    that
They move with equal feet on the same
    flat; [4]
Neither for all nor any of such ends
We offer it, gracious and noble friends,
To your review. We, far from emulation
And (charitably judge) from imitation, 10
With this work entertain you, a piece
    known
And still believed in court to be our own.
To quit our claim, doubting our right or
    merit,

Would argue in us poverty of spirit
Which we must not subscribe to. Field [5]
    is gone,
Whose action first did give it name, and
    one
Who came the nearest to him, [6] is denied
By his gray beard to show the height and
    pride
Of D'Ambois' youth and bravery. Yet,
    to hold
Our title still afoot, and not grow cold 20
By giving it o'er, a third man [7] with his
    best
Of care and pains defends our interest;
As Richard he was liked, nor do we
    fear
In personating D'Ambois he'll appear
To faint, or go less, so [8] your free con-
    sent,
As heretofore, give him encouragement.

[1] The title continues: "A Tragedy, As It Hath Been Often Acted with Great Applause, Being Much Corrected and Amended by the Author before his Death."
[2] *I.e.*, the King's Men.
[3] A rival company which had given the play.
[4] Over the same ground.

[5] Nathan Field, one of the company when the play was acted about 1616.
[6] Unidentified.
[7] Probably Elliard Swanston.
[8] If.

725

Actus Primi Scena Prima.[1]

[A forest near Paris.]

Enter Bussy D'Ambois, poor.

[Bus.] Fortune, not Reason, rules the
state of things;
Reward goes backwards, Honor on his
head; [2]
Who is not poor, is monstrous; only
Need
Gives form and worth to every human
seed.
As cedars beaten with continual storms,
So great men flourish, and do imitate
Unskillful statuaries, who suppose,
In forming a colossus, if they make him
Straddle enough, strut, and look big,
and gape,
Their work is goodly. So men merely
great   10
In their affected gravity of voice,
Sourness of countenance, manners' cru-
elty,
Authority, wealth, and all the spawn of
fortune,
Think they bear all the kingdom's
worth before them,
Yet differ not from those colossic statues,
Which, with heroic forms without o'er-
spread,
Within are naught but mortar, flint,
and lead.
Man is a torch borne in the wind; a
dream
But of a shadow, summed [3] with all
his substance;
And, as great seamen, using all their
wealth   20
And skills in Neptune's deep invisible
paths,
In tall ships richly built and ribbed with
brass,
To put a girdle round about the world,
When they have done it, coming near
their haven,
Are fain to give a warning-piece,[4] and
call
A poor, staid fisherman, that never
passed
His country's sight, to waft and guide
them in;

So, when we wander furthest through
the waves
Of glassy glory, and the gulfs of state,
Topped with all titles, spreading all our
reaches,   30
As if each private arm would sphere the
earth,
We must to Virtue for her guide resort,
Or we shall shipwrack in our safest port.
                    Procumbit.[5]

[Enter] Monsieur, with two Pages.

[Mon.] There is no second place in nu-
merous state
That holds more than a cipher; in a
king
All places are contained. His words and
looks
Are like the flashes and the bolts of
Jove;
His deeds inimitable, like the sea
That shuts still as it opes, and leaves
no tracts
Nor prints of precedent for mean men's
facts.[6]   40
There's but a thread betwixt me and a
crown;
I would not wish it cut, unless by na-
ture;
Yet to prepare me for that possible
fortune,
'Tis good to get resolvéd spirits about
me.
I followed D'Ambois to this green re-
treat,
A man of spirit beyond the reach of
fear,
Who, discontent with his neglected
worth,
Neglects the light, and loves obscure
abodes;
But he is young and haughty, apt to
take
Fire at advancement, to bear state, and
flourish;   50
In his rise therefore shall my bounties
shine.
None loathes the world so much, nor
loves to scoff it,
But gold and grace will make him sur-
feit of it.—
What, D'Ambois?
Bus.   He, sir.

---

[1] The first scene of the first act. [3] Clothed.
[2] *I.e.*, upside down.   [4] Signal shot.   [5] He falls forward.   [6] Deeds.

Mon. Turned to earth, alive?
Up, man; the sun shines on thee.
Bus. Let it shine.
I am no mote to play in 't, as great men
are.
Mon. Callest thou men great in state,
motes in the sun?
They say so that would have thee
freeze in shades,
That, like the gross Sicilian gourmandist,
Empty their noses in the cates they
love, 60
That none may eat but they. Do thou
but bring
Light to the banquet Fortune sets be-
fore thee,
And thou wilt loathe lean darkness like
thy death.
Who would believe thy mettle could
let sloth
Rust and consume it? If Themistocles
Had lived obscured thus in th' Athe-
nian state,
Xerxes had made both him and it his
slaves.
If brave Camillus had lurked so in
Rome,
He had not five times been dictator
there,
Nor four times triumphed. If Epami-
nondas, 70
Who lived twice twenty years obscured
in Thebes,
Had lived so still, he had been still un-
named,
And paid his country nor himself their
right;
But, putting forth his strength, he res-
cued both
From imminent ruin, and, like bur-
nished steel,
After long use he shined; for, as the
light
Not only serves to show, but renders us
Mutually profitable, so our lives
In acts exemplary not only win
Ourselves good names, but do to others
give 80
Matter for virtuous deeds, by which we
live.
Bus. What would you wish me?
Mon. Leave the troubled streams,
And live, where thrivers do, at the well-
head.

Bus. At the wellhead? Alas, what should
I do
With that enchanted glass? See devils
there;
Or, like a strumpet, learn to set my
looks
In an eternal brake [1] or practice jug-
gling,
To keep my face still fast, my heart
still loose;
Or bear, like dame's schoolmistresses
their riddles,
Two tongues, and be good only for a
shift; [2] 90
Flatter great lords, to put them still in
mind
Why they were made lords; or please
humorous [3] ladies
With a good carriage, tell them idle
tales
To make their physic work; spend a
man's life
In sights and visitations that will make
His eyes as hollow as his mistress'
heart;
To do none good but those that have no
need;
To gain being forward, though you
break for haste
All the commandments ere you break
your fast;
But believe backwards, make your
period 100
And creed's last article, "I believe in
God;"
And, hearing villainies preached, t'un-
fold their art,
Learn to commit them? 'Tis a great
man's part.
Shall I learn this there?
Mon. No, thou need'st not learn;
Thou hast the theory; now go there and
practice.
Bus. Ay, in a thridbare suit. When men
come there,
They must have high naps, [4] and go
from thence bare.
A man may drown the parts [5] of ten
rich men
In one poor suit. Brave barks [6] and out-
ward gloss

[1] Vise.
[2] Deception.
[3] Capricious.

[4] Rich clothes.
[5] Abilities.
[6] Fine coverings.

Attract court loves, be in-parts ne'er
  so gross.   110
Mon. Thou shalt have gloss enough, and
  all things fit
T'enchase in all show thy long-smothered
  spirit.
Be ruled by me then. The old Scythians
Painted blind Fortune's powerful hands
  with wings,
To show her gifts come swift and sud-
  denly,
Which, if her favorite be not swift to
  take,
He loses them forever. Then be wise;
Stay but awhile here, and I'll send to
  thee.
Exit Mon[sieur with Pages].   Manet [1]
                                   Buss[y].
Bus. What will he send? Some crowns?
  It is to sow them
Upon my spirit, and make them spring
  a crown   120
Worth millions of the seed-crowns he
  will send.
Like to disparking [2] noble husbandmen,
He'll put his plow into me, plow me up.
But his unsweating thrift is policy,
And learning-hating policy is ignorant
To fit his seed-land soil; a smooth plain
  ground
Will never nourish any politic seed.
I am for honest actions, not for great.
If I may bring up a new fashion,
And rise in court for virtue, speed his
  plow!   130
The king hath known me long as well
  as he,
Yet could my fortune never fit the
  length
Of both their understandings till this
  hour.
There is a deep nick in Time's restless
  wheel
For each man's good; when which nick
  comes, it strikes;
As rhetoric yet works not persuasion,
But only is a mean to make it work,
So no man riseth by his real merit,
But when it cries "Clink" [3] in his rais-
  er's spirit.
Many will say, that cannot rise at all, 140

Man's first hour's rise is first step to his
  fall.
I'll venture that; men that fall low must
  die,
As well as men cast headlong from the sky.

                Ent[er] Maffé.

[Maf. (*Aside.*)] Humor of princes! Is this
  wretch indued
With any merit worth a thousand
  crowns?
Will my lord have me be so ill a steward
Of his revenue, to dispose a sum
So great with so small cause as shows in
  him?
I must examine this.—Is your name
  D'Ambois?
Bus. Sir?
Maf.   Is your name D'Ambois?
Bus.   Who have we here? 150
Serve you the Monsieur?
Maf.   How?
Bus.   Serve you the Monsieur?
Maf. Sir, y'are very hot. I do serve the
  Monsieur,
But in such place as gives me the com-
  mand [4]
Of all his other servants. And, because
His grace's pleasure is to give your good
His pass [5] through my command, me-
  thinks you might
Use me with more respect.
Bus.   Cry you mercy! [6]
Now you have opened my dull eyes, I
  see you,
And would be glad to see the good you
  speak of.
What might I call your name?
Maf.   Monsieur Maffé. 160
Bus. Monsieur Maffé? Then, good Mon-
  sieur Maffé,
Pray let me know you better.
Maf.   Pray do so,
That you may use me better. For your-
  self,
By your no better outside, I would judge
  you
To be some poet. Have you given my
  lord
Some pamphlet?

[4] At this point the original has the stage direction, "*Table, chessboard, and tapers behind the
arras,*" in preparation for the following scene.
[5] Passage.   [6] I beg your pardon!

[1] Remains.
[2] Changing parks into open fields.
[3] "Now is the hour."

Bus.   Pamphlet?

Maf.   Pamphlet, sir, I say.

Bus. Did your great master's goodness
leave the good
That is to pass your charge to my poor
use,
To your discretion?

Maf.   Though he did not, sir,
I hope 'tis no rude office to ask reason 170
How that [1] his grace gives me in charge,
goes from me?

Bus. That's very perfect, sir.

Maf.   Why, very good, sir.
I pray then give me leave; if for no
pamphlet,
May I not know what other merit in you
Makes his compunction willing to re-
lieve you?

Bus. No merit in the world, sir.

Maf.   That is strange.
Y'are a poor soldier, are you?

Bus.   That I am, sir.

Maf. And have commanded?

Bus.   Ay, and gone without, sir.

Maf. [Aside.] I see the man; a hundred
crowns will make him
Swagger and drink healths to his grace's
bounty,   180
And swear he could not be more bounti-
ful;
So there's nine hundred crowns saved.—
Here, tall [2] soldier,
His grace hath sent you a whole hundred
crowns.

Bus. A hundred, sir? Nay, do his high-
ness right;
I know his hand is larger, and perhaps
I may deserve more than my outside shows.
I am a poet, as I am a soldier,
And I can poetize; and, being well en-
couraged,
May sing his fame for giving, yours for
delivering—
Like a most faithful steward—what he
gives.   190

Maf. What shall your subject be?

Bus.   I care not much,
If to his bounteous grace I sing the
praise
Of fair great noses, and to you of long
ones. [3]

What qualities have you, sir, beside
your chain
And velvet jacket? [4] Can your worship
dance?

Maf. [Aside.] A pleasant fellow, faith.
It seems my lord
Will have him for his jester, and, by'r
Lady,
Such men are now no fools; 'tis a knight's
place.
If I, to save his grace some crowns,
should urge him
T'abate his bounty, I should not be
heard;   200
I would to heaven I were an arrant
ass,
For then I should be sure to have the
ears
Of these great men, where now their
jesters have them.
'Tis good to please him, yet I'll take no
notice
Of his preferment, but in policy
Will still be grave and serious, lest he
think
I fear his wooden dagger.[5]—Here, Sir
Ambo!

Bus. How, Ambo, sir?

Maf.   Ay, is not your name Ambo?

Bus. You called me lately D'Ambois.
Has your worship
So short a head?

Maf.   I cry thee mercy, D'Ambois. 210
A thousand crowns I bring you from
my lord.
If you be thrifty and [6] play the good
husband,[7] you may make
This a good standing living. 'Tis a
bounty
His highness might perhaps have bestowed better.

Bus. Go, y'are a rascal; hence, away, you
rogue!

Maf. What mean you, sir?

Bus.   Hence! Prate no more,

---

[4] Emblems of a steward's office.
[5] Emblem of the jester.
[6] As Parrott points out, If you be thrifty and
has been substituted for the better reading Serve
God of the 1607 edn. "to avoid the penalty fixed
by the law of 1606 for the abuse of the name of
God in stage-plays." Cf. II, i, 207, for the
omission of Mort Dieu, and V, i, 41, 61, where
Heaven replaces God of the 1607 edn.
[7] I.e., be economical.

---

[1] That which.   [2] Brave.
[3] Monsieur's large nose was the object of much
satire.

Or, by thy villain's blood, thou prat'st
    thy last!
A barbarous groom grudge at his mas-
    ter's bounty!
But, since I know he would as much ab-
    hor
His hind should argue what he gives his
    friend,   220
Take that, sir, [*Strikes him.*] for your
    aptness to dispute.   *Exit.*
MAF. These crowns are set in blood; blood
    be their fruit!   *Exit.*

[SCENA SECUNDA.

A room in the court.]

Henry, Guise, Montsurry, Elenor, Tamyra,
    Beaupré, Pero, Charlotte, Pyra, Anna-
    belle. [Henry and Guise are playing
                                        chess.]

HEN. Duchess of Guise, your grace is much
    enriched
In the attendance of that English virgin,
That will initiate her prime of youth
(Disposed to court conditions) under the
    hand
Of your preferred instructions and com-
    mand,
Rather than any in the English court,
Whose ladies are not matched in Chris-
    tendom
For graceful and confirmed behaviors,
More than the court, where they are
    bred, is equaled.
GUISE. I like not their court fashion; it is
    too crestfallen   10
In all observance, making demigods
Of their great nobles, and of their old
    queen
An ever young and most immortal god-
    dess.
MONT. No question she's the rarest queen
    in Europe.
GUISE. But what's that to her immortal-
    ity?
HEN. Assure you, cousin Guise, so great a
    courtier,
So full of majesty and royal parts,
No queen in Christendom may vaunt
    herself.
Her court approves it, that's a court
    indeed,
Not mixed with clowneries used in com-
    mon houses,   20

But, as courts should be th' abstracts of
    their kingdoms
In all the beauty, state, and worth they
    hold,
So is hers, amply, and by her informed.[1]
The world is not contracted in a man
With more proportion and expression
Than in her court, her kingdom. Our
    French court
Is a mere mirror of confusion to it.
The king and subject, lord and every
    slave,
Dance a continual hay;[2] our rooms of
    state
Kept like our stables; no place more ob-
    served[3]   30
Than a rude market place; and, though
    our custom
Keep this assured confusion from our eyes,
'Tis ne'er the less essentially unsightly,
Which they would soon see, would they
    change their form
To this of ours, and then compare them
    both,
Which we must not affect, because in
    kingdoms
Where the king's change doth breed the
    subject's terror,
Pure innovation is more gross than error.
MONT. No question we shall see them im-
    itate,
Though afar off, the fashions of our
    courts,   40
As they have ever aped us in attire,
Never were men so weary of their skins,
And apt to leap out of themselves as
    they,
Who, when they travel[4] to bring forth
    rare men,
Come home, delivered of a fine French
    suit.
Their brains lie with their tailors, and
    get babies
For their most complete issue; he's sole
    heir
To all the moral virtues that first greets
The light with a new fashion, which be-
    comes them
Like apes, disfigured with the attires of
    men.   50
HEN. No question they much wrong their
    real worth

[1] Molded, fashioned.   [3] Respected.
[2] Country dance.   [4] With a pun on *travail.*

In affectation of outlandish scum;
But they have faults, and we more; they
　foolish-proud
To jet [1] in others' plumes so haughtily;
We proud that they are proud of foolery,
Holding our worths more complete for
　their vaunts.

Enter Monsieur, D'Ambois.

MON.　Come, mine own sweetheart,[2] I will
　enter [3] thee.—
Sir, I have brought a gentleman to court,
And pray you would vouchsafe to do him
　grace.
HEN.　D'Ambois, I think?
BUS.　　That's still my name, my lord,　60
Though I be something altered in attire.
HEN.　We like your alteration, and must
　tell you
We have expected th' offer of your serv-
　ice;
For we, in fear to make mild virtue
　proud,
Use not to seek her out in any man.
BUS.　Nor doth she use to seek out any
　man.
They that will win must woo her [; she's
　not shameless].[4]
MON.[5]　I urged her modesty in him, my
　lord,
And gave her those rites that he says
　she merits.
HEN.　If you have wooed and won, then,
　brother, wear him.　　　　　　　70
MON.　Th' art mine, sweetheart. See, here's
　the Guise's duchess,
The Countess of Montsurreau, Beaupré.
Come, I'll enseam [6] thee.—Ladies, y'are
　too many
To be in council; I have here a friend
That I would gladly enter in your graces.
BUS.　Save you,[7] ladies.
DUCH.　If you enter him in our graces,
my lord, methinks by his blunt behavior he
should come out of himself.
TAM.　Has he never been courtier, [80
my lord?

MON.　Never, my lady.
BEAU.　And why did the toy [8] take him
in th' head now?
BUS.　'Tis leap year, lady, and therefore
very good to enter a courtier.
HEN.　Mark, Duchess of Guise, there is
one is not bashful.
DUCH.　No, my lord, he is much guilty of
the bold extremity.　　　　　　　　90
TAM.　The man's a courtier at first sight.
BUS.　I can sing pricksong,[9] lady, at
first sight; and why not be a courtier as
suddenly?
BEAU.　Here's a courtier rotten before
he be ripe.
BUS.　Think me not impudent, lady. I
am yet no courtier; I desire to be one, and
would gladly take entrance, [*To the Duchess.*] madam, under your princely colors.

Enter Barrisor, L'Anou, Pyrrhot.

DUCH.　Soft, sir, you must rise by [101
degrees, first being the servant [10] of some
common lady or knight's wife; then a little
higher to a lord's wife; next a little higher
to a countess; yet a little higher to a duchess, and then turn the ladder.[11]
BUS.　Do you allow a man, then, four
mistresses when the greatest mistress is
allowed but three servants?　　　　109
DUCH.　Where find you that statute, sir?
BUS.　Why, be judged by the groom
porters.[12]
DUCH.　The groom porters?
BUS.　Ay, madam; must not they judge
of all gamings i' th' court?
DUCH.　You talk like a gamester.
GUISE.　[*Rising from the chess table.*] Sir,
know you me?
BUS.　My lord?
GUISE.　I know not you. Whom do [120
you serve?
BUS.　Serve, my lord!
GUISE.　Go to, companion,[13] your court-
ship's too saucy.
BUS.　[*Aside.*] Saucy! Companion! 'Tis
the Guise, but yet those terms might have

---

[1] Strut.
[2] Merely a term of affectionate address.
[3] Introduce, be sponsor for.
[4] From 1607 edn.
[5] The following eight lines are printed as prose
in the original.
[6] Introduce.　　　　　　　[7] God save you.

[8] Whim.
[9] Music pricked or noted down as distinguished from extemporaneous music.
[10] Lover.
[11] *I.e.*, be hanged.
[12] Minor court officials in charge of gaming.
[13] Fellow.

been spared of the Guisard.[1] Companion!
He's jealous, by this light. Are you blind
of that side, duke? I'll to her again for
that.—Forth, princely mistress, for [130
the honor of courtship. Another riddle!

GUISE. Cease your courtship, or by
heaven I'll cut your throat.

BUS. Cut my throat? Cut a whetstone,
young Accius Nævius! Do as much with
your tongue as he did with a razor. Cut
my throat!

BAR. [Aside.] What newcome gallant
have we here, that dares mate [2] the Guise
thus?   140

L'AN. [Aside.] 'Sfoot,[3] 'tis D'Ambois.
The duke mistakes him, on my life, for
some knight of the new edition.[4]

BUS. Cut my throat! I would the king
feared thy cutting of his throat no more
than I fear thy cutting of mine.

GUISE. I'll do 't, by this hand.

BUS.[5] That hand dares not do 't. Y'ave
cut too many throats already, Guise, and
robbed the realm of many thousand [150
souls, more precious than thine own.—
Come, madam, talk on. 'Sfoot, can you not
talk? Talk on, I say. Another riddle!

PYR. Here's some strange distemper.

BAR. Here's a sudden transmigration
with D'Ambois—out of the Knight's
Ward [6] into the duchess' bed.

L'AN. See what a metamorphosis a
brave suit can work.

PYR. 'Slight, step to the Guise and [160
discover him.

BAR. By no means! Let the new suit
work; we'll see the issue.

GUISE. Leave your courting!

BUS. I will not.—I say, mistress, and I
will stand unto it, that, if a woman may
have three servants, a man may have three
score mistresses.

GUISE. Sirrah, I'll have you whipped
out of the court for this insolence.   170

BUS. Whipped? Such another syllable

out o' th' presence,[7] if thou dar'st, for thy
dukedom!

GUISE. Remember, poltroon!
                     [He returns to his game.]

MON. Pray thee, forbear.

BUS. Passion of death! Were not the
king here, he should strow the chamber
like a rush.

MON. But leave courting his wife, then.

BUS. I will not. I'll court her in [180
despite of him. Not court her!—Come,
madam, talk on, fear me nothing.—[To
Guise.] Well mayst thou drive thy master
from the court, but never D'Ambois.

MON. [Aside.] His great heart will not
down. 'Tis like the sea,
That, partly by his own internal heat,
Partly the stars' daily and nightly mo-
tion,
Their heat and light, and partly of the
place,
The divers frames,[8] but chiefly by the
moon,
Bristled with surges, never will be won
(No, not when th' hearts of all those
powers are burst)   191
To make retreat into his settled home,
Till he be crowned with his own quiet
foam.

HEN. You have the mate. Another?

GUISE. No more.   Flourish short.[9]
Exit Guise, after him the King, Mons[ieur]
                         whispering.

BAR. Why, here's the lion, scared with
the throat of a dunghill cock, a fellow that
has newly shaked off his shackles; now
does he crow for that victory.

L'AN. 'Tis one of the best jigs that [200
ever was acted.

PYR. Whom does the Guise suppose him
to be, trow? [10]

L'AN. Out of doubt, some new deni-
zened [11] lord, and thinks that suit newly
drawn out a [12] th' mercer's books.

BAR. I have heard of a fellow that, by
a fixed imagination looking upon a bull-
baiting, had a visible pair of horns grew
out of his forehead; and I believe [210
this gallant, overjoyed with the conceit of

---

[1] Follower of the Guise, with a probable pun
on *gizzard*, the throat.
[2] Checkmate, defy.
[3] God's foot.
[4] A reference to the recent creation of a number of knights by James I.
[5] Lines 148–53 and 241–44 are set as verse in
the original.
[6] Part of the Counter, a London prison for
debtors.

[7] Out of the king's presence.   [9] Trumpet call.
[8] Perhaps the bed of the sea.   [10] Think you.
[11] Naturalized, referring to James's new Scottish nobility.
[12] Of.

Monsieur's cast suit, imagines himself to be the Monsieur.

L'An. And why not, as well as the ass, stalking in the lion's case,[1] bare himself like a lion, braying all the huger beasts out of the forest?

Pyr. Peace, he looks this way.

Bar. Marry, let him look, sir. What will you say now if the Guise be gone to [220 fetch a blanket [2] for him?

L'An. Faith, I believe it for his honor sake.

Pyr. But, if D'Ambois carry it clean? [3]

Exeunt Ladies.

Bar. True, when he curvets in the blanket.

Pyr. Ay, marry, sir.

L'An. 'Sfoot, see how he stares on 's.

Bar. Lord bless us, let's away.

Bus. Now, sir, take your full view. [230 How does the object please ye?

Bar. If you ask my opinion, sir, I think your suit sits as well as if 't had been made for you.

Bus. So, sir, and was that the subject of your ridiculous jollity?

L'An. What's that to you, sir?

Bus. Sir, I have observed all your fleerings, and resolve yourselves ye shall give a strict account for 't.   240

Enter Brisac, Melynell.

Bar. O, miraculous jealousy![4] Do you think yourself such a singular subject for laughter that none can fall into the matter of our merriment but you?

L'An. This jealousy of yours, sir, confesses some close defect in yourself that we never dreamed of.

Pyr. We held discourse of a perfumed ass that, being disguised in a lion's case, imagined himself a lion. I hope that [250 touched not you.

Bus. So, sir; your descants do marvelous well fit this ground.[5]   We shall meet where your buffoonly laughters will cost ye the best blood in your bodies.

Bar. For life's sake let's be gone; he'll kill 's outright else.

Bus. Go, at your pleasures. I'll be your

ghost to haunt you; and ye sleep an 't,[6] hang me.   260

L'An. Go, go, sir; court your mistress.

Pyr. And, be advised, we shall have odds against you.

Bus. Tush! Valor stands not in number; I'll maintain it that one man may beat three boys.

Bris. Nay, you shall have no odds of him in number, sir; he's a gentleman as good as the proudest of you, and ye shall not wrong him.   270

Bar. Not, sir?

Mel. Not, sir. Though he be not so rich, he's a better man than the best of you, and I will not endure it.

L'An. Not you, sir?

Bris. No, sir, nor I.

Bus. I should thank you for this kindness, if I thought these perfumed musk cats, being out of this privilege, durst but once mew at us.   280

Bar. Does your confident spirit doubt that, sir? Follow us and try.

L'An. Come, sir, we'll lead you a dance.

Exeunt.

FINIS ACTUS PRIMI.

ACTUS SECUND[I]   SCENA PRIMA.

[A room in the court.]

Henry, Guise, Montsurry, [Beaumond,] and Attendants.

Hen. This desperate quarrel sprung out of their envies
   To D'Ambois' sudden bravery [7] and great spirit.

Guise. Neither is worth their envy.

Hen.   Less than either
   Will make the gall of Envy overflow.
   She feeds on outcast entrails like a kite,
   In which foul heap, if any ill lies hid,
   She sticks her beak into it, shakes it up,
   And hurls it all abroad, that all may view it.
   Corruption is her nutriment; but touch her
   With any precious ointment, and you kill her.   10
   Where she finds any filth in men, she feasts,

---

[1] Skin.   [3] *I.e.*, get the better of him.
[2] To toss him.   [4] Suspicion.
[5] With an additional reference to music, meaning variations on a theme.

[6] If you sleep on it.
[7] Presumably here in the common sense of *finery.*

And with her black throat bruits it
   through the world,
Being sound and healthful; but, if she
   but taste
The slenderest pittance of commended
   virtue,
She surfeits of it, and is like a fly
That passes all the body's soundest parts,
And dwells upon the sores; or, if her
   squint eye
Have power to find none there, she forges
   some.
She makes that crooked ever which is
   straight;
Calls valor giddiness, justice tyranny. 20
A wise man may shun her, she not her-
   self;
Whithersoever she flies from her harms,
She bears her foes still clasped in her own
   arms.
And therefore, cousin Guise, let us avoid
   her.

Enter Nuntius.

NUN. What Atlas or Olympus lifts his
   head
So far past covert that with air enough
My words may be informed, and from
   their height
I may be seen and heard through all the
   world?
A tale so worthy and so fraught with
   wonder   29
Sticks in my jaws, and labors with event.
HEN. Com'st thou from D'Ambois?
NUN.   From him, and the rest,
   His friends and enemies, whose stern
      fight I saw,
   And heard their words before and in the
      fray.
HEN. Relate at large what thou hast seen
   and heard.
NUN. I saw fierce D'Ambois and his two
   brave friends
Enter the field, and at their heels their
   foes,
Which were the famous soldiers, Bar-
   risor,
L'Anou, and Pyrrhot, great in deeds of
   arms;
All which arrived at the evenest piece of
   earth
The field afforded, the three challeng-
   ers   40

Turned head, drew all their rapiers, and
   stood ranked,
When face to face the three defendants
   met them,
Alike prepared, and resolute alike.
Like bonfires of contributory wood
Every man's look showed, fed with
   either's spirit,
As one had been a mirror to another,
Like forms of life and death, each took
   from other;
And so were life and death mixed at
   their heights
That you could see no fear of death, for
   life,
Nor love of life, for death; but in their
   brows   50
Pyrrho's opinion in great letters shone:
That life and death in all respects are one.
HEN. Passed there no sort of words at
   their encounter?
NUN. As Hector, twixt the hosts of Greece
   and Troy,
When Paris and the Spartan king should
   end
The nine years' war, held up his brazen
   lance
For signal that both hosts should cease
   from arms,
And hear him speak, so Barrisor, ad-
   vised,[1]
Advanced his naked rapier twixt both
   sides,
Ripped up [2] the quarrel, and compared
   six lives   60
Then laid in balance with six idle words;
Offered remission and contrition too;
Or else that he and D'Ambois might
   conclude
The others' dangers. D'Ambois liked the
   last;
But Barrisor's friends, being equally
   engaged
In the main quarrel, never would expose
His life alone to that they all deserved.
And, for the other offer of remission,
D'Ambois, that like a laurel put in fire
Sparkled and spit, did much, much more
   than scorn   70
That his wrong should incense him so like
   chaff
To go so soon out, and like lighted paper

[1] Cautious.
[2] Recalled the causes of.

Approve [1] his spirit at once both fire and
ashes.
So drew they lots and in them Fates
appointed
That Barrisor should fight with fiery
D'Ambois,
Pyrrhot with Melynell, with Brisac,
L'Anou.
And then like flame and powder they
commixed
So spritely that I wished they had been
spirits,
That the ne'er-shutting wounds they
needs must open
Might, as they opened, shut and never
kill.   80
But D'Ambois' sword, that lightened as
it flew,
Shot like a pointed comet at the face
Of manly Barrisor; and there it stuck.
Thrice plucked he at it, and thrice drew
on thrusts
From him that of himself was free as fire;
Who thrust still as he plucked, yet, past
belief,
He with his subtle eye, hand, body,
scaped.
At last, the deadly-bitten point tugged
off,
On fell his yet undaunted foe so fiercely
That, only made more horrid with his
wound,   90
Great D'Ambois shrunk, and gave a little
ground;
But soon returned, redoubled in [2] his
danger,
And at the heart of Barrisor sealed his
anger.
Then, as in Arden I have seen an oak
Long shook with tempests, and his lofty
top
Bent to his root, which being at length
made loose,
Even groaning with his weight, he gan to
nod
This way and that, as loath his curléd
brows,
Which he had oft wrapped in the sky with
storms,
Should stoop; and yet, his radical fibers
burst,   100
Stormlike he fell, and hid the fear-cold
earth,

So fell stout Barrisor, that had stood the
shocks
Of ten set battles in your highness' war
Gainst the sole soldier of the world,
Navarre.
GUISE. O, piteous and horrid murther!
BEAUM.   Such a life
Methinks had metal in it to survive
An age of men.
HEN.   Such often soonest end.—
Thy felt report calls on; [3] we long to
know
On what events the other have arrived.
NUN. Sorrow and fury, like two opposite
fumes   110
Met in the upper region of a cloud,
At the report made by this worthy's fall,
Brake from the earth, and with them rose
Revenge,
Ent'ring with fresh powers his two noble
friends;
And under that odds fell surcharged [4]
Brisac,
The friend of D'Ambois, before fierce
L'Anou;
Which D'Ambois seeing, as I once did
see
In my young travels through Armenia
An angry unicorn in his full career
Charge with too swift a foot a jew-
eler   120
That watched him for the treasure of his
brow, [5]
And, ere he could get shelter of a tree,
Nail him with his rich antler to the earth,
So D'Ambois ran upon revenged L'Anou,
Who, eying th' eager point borne in his
face,
And giving back, fell back, and in his
fall
His foe's uncurbéd sword stopped in his
heart;
By which time all the lifestrings of the
tw' other
Were cut, and both fell as their spirit[s]
flew
Upwards, and still hunt honor at the
view. [6]   130
And now, of all the six, sole D'Ambois
stood

---

[1] Prove.   [2] Coming a second time into.

[3] Thy affecting report calls for more.
[4] Overpowered.
[5] *I.e.,* his horn.
[6] Like dogs that have sighted the quarry.

Untouched, save only with the others'
    blood.

HEN. All slain outright but he?

NUN.   All slain outright but he,
Who, kneeling in the warm life of his
    friends,
All freckled with the blood his rapier
    rained,
He kissed their pale lips, and bade both
    farewell—
And see the bravest man the French
    earth bears!

Enter Monsieur, D'Amb[ois] bare.

BUS. Now is the time. Y'are princely
    vowed my friend;
Perform it princely, and obtain my
    pardon.

MON. Else heaven forgive not me! Come
    on, brave friend!—   [*They kneel.*]   140
If ever nature held herself her own,
When the great trial of a king and sub-
    ject
Met in one blood, both from one belly
    springing,
Now prove her virtue and her greatness
    one,
Or make the t' one the greater with the
    tother,
As true kings should, and for your
    brother's love,
Which is a special species of true virtue,
Do that you could not do, not being a
    king.

HEN. Brother, I know your suit; these
    willful murthers
Are ever past our pardon.

MON.   Manly slaughter   150
Should never bear th' account of willful
    murther,
It being a spice [1] of justice, where with life
Offending past law, equal life is laid
In equal balance, to scourge that offense
By law of reputation, which to men
Exceeds all positive law; and what that
    leaves
To true men's valors, not prefixing rights
Of satisfaction, suited to their wrongs,
A free man's eminence may supply and
    take.

HEN. This would make every man that
    thinks him wronged   160
Or is offended, or in wrong or right,

[1] Sort.

Lay on this violence, and all vaunt them-
    selves
Law-menders and suppliers, though mere
    butchers.
Should this fact, though of justice, be
    forgiven?

MON. O, no, my lord; it would make
    cowards fear
To touch the reputations of true men
When only they are left to imp [2] the law.
Justice will soon distinguish murtherous
    minds
From just revengers. Had my friend
    been slain,
His enemy surviving, he should die,   170
Since he had added to a murthered
    fame,
Which was in his intent, a murthered
    man,
And this had worthily been willful mur-
    ther.
But my friend only saved his fame's dear
    life,
Which is above life, taking th' under
    value,
Which, in the wrong it did, was forfeit
    to him;
And in this fact only preserves a man
In his uprightness, worthy to survive
Millions of such as murther men alive.

HEN. Well, brother, rise, and raise your
    friend withal   180
From death to life. And, D'Ambois, let
    your life,
Refined by passing through this merited
    death,
Be purged from more such foul pollution,
Nor on your scape nor valor more pre-
    suming
To be again so daring.

BUS.   My lord,
I loathe as much a deed of unjust death
As law itself doth, and to tyrannize,
Because I have a little spirit to dare
And power to do, as to be tyrannized.
This is a grace that, on my knees re-
    doubled, [3]   190
I crave to double this, my short life's gift,
And shall your royal bounty centuple,
That I may so make good what law and
    nature
Have given me for my good; since I am
    free,

[2] Piece out.   [3] Rekneeling.

Offending no just law, let no law make,
By any wrong it does, my life her slave.
When I am wronged, and that law fails
   to right me,
Let me be king myself, as man was made,
And do a justice that exceeds the law;
If my wrong pass the power of single
   valor   200
To right and expiate, then be you my
   king,
And do a right, exceeding law and nature.
Who to himself is law, no law doth need,
Offends no law, and is a king indeed.
HEN. Enjoy what thou entreat'st; we give
   but ours.
Bus. What you have given, my lord, is
   ever yours.
Exit Rex[1] *cum Beau[mond, Attendants,*
        Nuntius, and Montsurry].
GUISE. [*Mort Dieu!*][2] Who would have
   pardoned such a murther?   *Exit.*
MON. Now vanish horrors into court at-
   tractions,
For which let this balm make thee fresh
   and fair.
And now forth with thy service to the
   duchess,   210
As my long love will to Montsurry's
   countess.   *Exit.*
Bus. To whom my love hath long been
   vowed in heart,
Although in hand for show I held the
   duchess.
And now through blood and vengeance,
   deeds of height
And hard to be achieved, 'tis fit I make
Attempt of her perfection. I need fear
No check in his rivalry,[3] since her virtues
Are so renowned, and he of all dames
   hated.   *Exit.*

[SCENA SECUNDA.

A room in Montsurry's house.]

Enter Monsieur, Tamyra, and Pero with a
                book.

MON. Pray thee regard thine own good, if
   not mine,
And cheer my love for that. You do not
   know

[1] King.
[2] God's death! From 1607 edn.; omitted in
the original.
[3] Rivalry.

What you may be by me, nor what with-
   out me;
I may have power t' advance and pull
   down any.
TAM. That's not my study. One way I am
   sure
You shall not pull down me; my hus-
   band's height
Is crown to all my hopes, and his retiring
To any mean state shall be my aspiring.
Mine honor's in mine own hands, spite
   of kings.
MON. Honor, what's that? Your second
   maidenhead!   10
And what is that? A word. The word is
   gone;
The thing remains. The rose is plucked;
   the stalk
Abides. An easy loss where no lack's
   found!
Believe it, there's as small lack in the loss
As there is pain i' th' losing. Archers ever
Have two strings to a bow, and shall
   great Cupid,
Archer of archers both in men and
   women,
Be worse provided than a common
   archer?
A husband and a friend all wise wives
   have.
TAM. Wise wives they are that on such
   strings depend,   20
With a firm husband joining a loose
   friend!
MON. Still you stand on your husband; so
   do all
The common sex of you, when y'are
   encountered
With one ye cannot fancy. All men know
You live in court here by your own
   election,
Frequenting all our common sports and
   triumphs,
All the most youthful company of men.
And wherefore do you this? To please
   your husband?
'Tis gross and fulsome. If your husband's
   pleasure
Be all your object, and you aim at
   honor   30
In living close to him, get you from
   court;
You may have him at home. These
   common put-offs

For common women serve: "My honor!
　　Husband!"
Dames maritorious [1] ne'er were meri-
　　torious.
Speak plain and say, "I do not like you,
　　sir;
Y'are an ill-favored fellow in my eye,"
And I am answered.
TAM.　　　　　Then, I pray, be answered;
For in good faith, my lord, I do not like
　　you
In that sort you like.
MON.　　　　　Then have at you, here!
Take, with a politic hand, this rope
　　of pearl,　　　　　　　　　　　40
And, though you be not amorous, yet be
　　wise.
Take me for wisdom; he that you can love
Is ne'er the further from you.
TAM.　　　　　　　　　Now it comes
So ill prepared that I may take a poison
Under a medicine as good cheap [2] as it;
I will not have it were it worth the world.
MON. Horror of death! Could I but please
　　your eye,
You would give me the like ere you
　　would lose [3] me.
"Honor and husband!"
TAM.　　　　　By this light, my lord,
Y'are a vile fellow, and I'll tell the
　　king　　　　　　　　　　　　　50
Your occupation of dishonoring ladies
And of his court. A lady cannot live
As she was born, and with that sort of
　　pleasure
That fits her state, but she must be
　　defamed
With an infamous lord's detraction.
Who would endure the court if these
　　attempts
Of open and professed lust must be
　　borne?—
Who's there? Come on, dame; you are
　　at your book
When men are at your mistress. Have I
　　taught you
Any such waiting-woman's quality?　60
MON. Farewell, good "husband."
　　　　　　　　　　　　Exit Mons[ieur].
TAM.　　　　　Farewell, wicked lord.

[1] Excessively fond of their husbands.
[2] Cheaply, readily.
[3] The original spelling *loose* carries a possible
meaning.

Enter Mont[surry].
MONT. Was not the Monsieur here?
TAM.　　　　　　Yes, to good purpose;
And your cause is as good to seek him too,
And haunt his company.
MONT.　　　　　Why, what's the matter?
TAM. Matter of death, were I some hus-
　　bands' wife.
I cannot live at quiet in my chamber
For opportunities [4] almost to rapes
Offered me by him.
MONT.　　　　　Pray thee bear with him.
Thou know'st he is a bachelor and a
　　courtier,
Ay, and a prince; and their preroga-
　　tives　　　　　　　　　　　　70
Are to their laws as to their pardons are
Their reservations, after parliaments—
One quits another; form gives all their
　　essence.
That prince doth high in virtue's reck-
　　oning stand
That will entreat a vice, and not com-
　　mand.
So far bear with him; should another man
Trust to his privilege, he should trust
　　to death.
Take comfort, then, my comfort; nay,
　　triumph
And crown thyself; thou part'st [5] with
　　victory.
My presence is so only dear to thee　80
That other men's appear worse than
　　they be.
For this night yet, bear with my forcéd
　　absence;
Thou know'st my business, and with
　　how much weight
My vow hath charged it.
TAM.　　　　　True, my lord, and never
My fruitless love shall let [6] your serious
　　honor;
Yet, sweet lord, do not stay; you know
　　my soul
Is so long time without me, and I dead,
As you are absent.
MONT.　　　　　By this kiss, receive
My soul for hostage till I see my love.
TAM. The morn shall let me see you?
MONT.　　　　　　　With the sun　90
I'll visit thy more comfortable beauties.

[4] Importunities.　　　　　　[6] Hinder.
[5] Depart'st, com'st off.

Tam. This is my comfort, that the sun
    hath left
The whole world's beauty ere my sun
    leaves me.
Mont. 'Tis late night now indeed; fare-
    well, my light!   *Exit.*
Tam. Farewell, my light and life!—[*Aside.*]
    But not in him,
  In mine own dark love and light bent to
    another.
  Alas, that in the wave [1] of our affections
  We should supply it with a full dis-
    sembling,
  In which each youngest maid is grown a
    mother.
  Frailty is fruitful; one sin gets an-
    other.   100
  Our loves like sparkles are that bright-
    est shine
  When they go out; most vice shows most
    divine.—
  Go, maid, to bed; lend me your book, I
    pray—
  Not, like yourself, for form; I'll this night
    trouble
  None of your services. Make sure the
    doors,
  And call your other fellows to their rest.
Per. I will.—[*Aside.*] Yet I will watch to
    know why you watch.   *Exit.*
Tam. Now all ye peaceful regents of the
    night,
  Silently gliding exhalations,
  Languishing winds and murmuring falls
    of waters,   110
  Sadness of heart and ominous secure-
    ness,
  Enchantments, dead sleeps, all the
    friends of rest,
  That ever wrought upon the life of man,
  Extend your utmost strengths, and this
    charmed hour
  Fix like the center.[2] Make the violent
    wheels
  Of Time and Fortune stand, and great
    Existence,
  The Maker's treasury, now not seem to
    be,
  To all but my approaching friends and
    me!
  They come, alas, they come! Fear,
    fear and hope

Of one thing, at one instant fight in
    me;   120
I love what most I loathe, and cannot
    live
Unless I compass that which holds my
    death;
For life's mere death, loving one that
    loathes me,
And he I love will loathe me, when he
    sees
I fly my sex, my virtue, my renown,
To run so madly on a man unknown.
                The vault opens.[3]
See, see, a vault is opening that was
    never
Known to my lord and husband, nor to
    any
But him that brings the man I love,
    and me.
How shall I look on him? How shall I
    live,   130
And not consume in blushes? I will
    in,
And cast myself off, as I ne'er had been.[4]
                         Exit.

       Ascendit Friar and D'Ambois.

Fri. Come, worthiest son, I am past
    measure glad
That you, whose worth I have approved
    so long,
Should be the object of her fearful love,
Since both your wit and spirit can adapt
Their full force to supply her utmost
    weakness.
You know her worths and virtues, for
    report
Of all that know is to a man a knowl-
    edge;
You know, besides, that our affections'
    storm,   140
Raised in our blood, no reason can re-
    form.
Though she seek then their satisfaction,
Which she must needs, or rest unsat-
    isfied,
Your judgment will esteem her peace
    thus wrought,
Nothing less dear than if yourself had
    sought;

---

[1] Wavering. Dilke suggests *wane.*
[2] Center of the earth.
[3] This direction follows l. 123 in the original.
[4] Undress as if I had never been here (?); completely cast off my old self (?).

And with another color,[1] which my art
Shall teach you to lay on, yourself must
   seem
The only agent, and the first orb [2] move
In this our set and cunning world of
   love.
Bus. Give me the color, my most hon-
   ored father,   150
And trust my cunning then to lay it on.
Fri. 'Tis this, good son. Lord Barrisor,
   whom you slew,
Did love her dearly, and with all fit
   means
Hath urged his acceptation, of all which
She keeps one letter written in his blood.
You must say thus, then, that you
   heard from me
How much herself was touched in con-
   science
With a report, which is in truth dis-
   persed,
That your main quarrel grew about her
   love,   159
Lord Barrisor imagining your courtship
Of the great Guise's duchess in the pres-
   ence
Was by you made to his elected mistress;
And so made me your mean now to re-
   solve her,[3]
Choosing, by my direction, this night's
   depth
For the more clear avoiding of all note
Of your presuméd presence; and with
   this,
To clear her hands of such a lover's blood,
She will so kindly thank and entertain
   you—
Methinks I see how—ay, and ten to one,
Show you the confirmation in his blood,
Lest you should think report and she
   did feign,   171
That you shall so have circumstantial
   means
To come to the direct, which must be
   used;
For the direct is crooked; love comes
   flying;
The height of love is still won with deny-
   ing.
Bus. Thanks, honored father.

[1] Pretense.
[2] *Primum mobile*, the sphere which, according
to the Ptolemaic system, set the other spheres
in motion.   [3] Explain to her.

Fri.   She must never know
That you know anything of any love
Sustained on her part; for, learn this of
   me,
In anything a woman does alone,
If she dissemble, she thinks 'tis not
   done;   180
If not dissemble, nor a little chide,
Give her her wish, she is not satisfied.
To have a man think that she never
   seeks,
Does her more good than to have all she
   likes.
This frailty sticks in them beyond their
   sex,
Which to reform, reason is too perplex.[4]
Urge reason to them, it will do no good;
Humor, that is the chariot of our food
In everybody, must in them be fed,
To carry their affections by it bred.   190
Stand close.   *[They withdraw.]*

Enter Tamyra with a book.

Tam. Alas, I fear my strangeness will re-
   tire him.
If he go back, I die; I must prevent it,
And cheer his onset with my sight at
   least,
And that's the most. Though every step
   he takes
Goes to my heart, I'll rather die than
   seem
Not to be strange to that I most esteem.
Fri. [*Advancing.*] Madam!
Tam.   Ah!
Fri.   You will
   pardon me, I hope,
That so beyond your expectation,
And at a time for visitants so unfit,   200
I, with my noble friend here, visit you.
You know that my access at any time
Hath ever been admitted; and that friend
That my care will presume to bring with
   me
Shall have all circumstance of worth in
   him
To merit as free welcome as myself.
Tam. O father! But at this suspicious
   hour
You know how apt best men are to sus-
   pect us
In any cause that makes suspicious
   shadow

[4] Intricate.

No greater than the shadow of a hair; 210
And y'are to blame. What though my
  lord and husband
Lie forth tonight, and, since I cannot
  sleep
When he is absent, I sit up tonight;
Though all the doors are sure, and all
  our servants
As sure bound with their sleeps, yet
  there is One
That wakes above, whose eye no sleep
  can bind.
He sees through doors, and darkness, and
  our thoughts;
And therefore, as we should avoid with
  fear
To think amiss ourselves before his
  search,
So should we be as curious [1] to shun   220
All cause that other think not ill of us.
Bus. Madam, 'tis far from that; I only
  heard
By this my honored father that your
  conscience
Made some deep scruple with a false
  report
That Barrisor's blood should something
  touch your honor,
Since he imagined I was courting you
When I was bold to change words with
  the duchess,
And therefore made his quarrel, his long
  love
And service, as I hear, being deeply
  vowed
To your perfections, which my ready
  presence,   230
Presumed on with my father at this
  season
For the more care of your so curious
  honor,
Can well resolve [2] your conscience is most
  false.
Tam. And is it therefore that you come,
  good sir?
Then crave I now your pardon and my
  father's,
And swear your presence does me so
  much good
That all I have it binds to your requital.
Indeed, sir, 'tis most true that a report
Is spread, alleging that his love to me
Was reason of your quarrel, and, because

You shall not think I feign it for my
  glory   241
That he importuned me for his court
  service,[3]
I'll show you his own hand, set down in
  blood
To that vain purpose. Good sir, then
  come in.
Father, I thank you now a thousandfold.
              Exit Tamyra and D'Amb[ois].
Fri. May it be worth it to you, honored
  daughter.   *Descendit Friar.*

           Finis Actus Secundi.

           Actus Tertii   Scena Prima.

        [*A room in Montsurry's house.*]

*Enter D'Ambois, Tamyra, with a chain of
                              pearl.*

Bus. Sweet mistress, cease! Your con-
  science is too nice,[4]
And bites too hotly of the Puritan spice.
Tam. O, my dear servant, in thy close
  embraces
I have set open all the doors of danger
To my encompassed honor and my life.
Before, I was secure against death and
  hell,
But now am subject to the heartless fear
Of every shadow and of every breath,
And would change firmness with an as-
  pen leaf;
So confident a spotless conscience is,   10
So weak a guilty. O, the dangerous siege
Sin lays about us, and the tyranny
He exercises when he hath expunged! [5]
Like to the horror of a winter's thunder,
Mixed with a gushing storm, that suffer
  nothing
To stir abroad on earth but their own
  rages,
Is Sin, when it hath gathered head above
  us.
No roof, no shelter can secure us so,
But he will drown our cheeks in fear or
  woe.   19
Bus. Sin is a coward, madam, and insults
But on [6] our weakness, in his truest valor;

[1] Careful.   [2] Assure.
[3] *I.e.*, to accept him as courtly lover.
[4] Scrupulous, squeamish.
[5] Attacked successfully, been victorious.
[6] Merely exults scornfully over.

And so our ignorance tames us, that we
  let
His shadows fright us; and like empty
  clouds,
In which our faulty apprehensions forge
The forms of dragons, lions, elephants,
When they hold no proportion,[1] the sly
  charms
Of the witch, Policy, makes him like a
  monster
Kept only to show men for servile money.
That false hag often paints him in her
  cloth
Ten times more monstrous than he is in
  troth.   30
In three of us, the secret of our meeting
Is only guarded, and three friends as one
Have ever been esteemed, as our three
  powers
That in one soul are as one united.
Why should we fear then? For myself I
  swear
Sooner shall torture be the sire to pleas-
  ure,
And health be grievous to one long-time
  sick,
Than the dear jewel of your fame in me
Be made an outcast to your infamy;
Nor shall my value (sacred to your vir-
  tues)   40
Only give free course to it, from myself,
But make it fly out of the mouths of kings
In golden vapors and with awful wings.
Tam. It rests as all kings' seals were set in
  thee.[2]
Now let us call my father, whom I swear
I could extremely chide, but that I fear
To make him so suspicious of my love,
Of which, sweet servant, do not let him
  know
For all the world.
Bus.   Alas, he will not think it!
Tam. Come, then.—Ho, father, ope, and
  take your friend.   50

Ascendit Friar.

Fri. Now, honored daughter, is your doubt
  resolved?
Tam. Ay, father, but you went away too
  soon.
Fri. Too soon?

[1] Resemblance.
[2] *I.e.*, it remains inviolable.

Tam.   Indeed you did; you should
  have stayed.
Had not your worthy friend been of your
  bringing—
And that contains all laws to temper
  me—
Not all the fearful danger that besieged
  us
Had awed my throat from exclamation.
Fri. I know your serious disposition well.
Come, son, the morn comes on.
Bus.   Now, honored mistress,
Till farther service call, all bliss supply
  you!   60
Tam. And you this chain of pearl, and my
  love only!
       Descendit Friar and D'Amb[ois].
It is not I, but urgent destiny,
That (as great statesmen for their gen-
  eral end,
In politic justice, make poor men offend)
Enforceth my offense to make it just.
What shall weak dames do, when th'
  whole work of nature
Hath a strong finger in each one of us?
Needs must that sweep away the silly
  cobweb
Of our still undone labors, that lays still
Our powers to it; as to the line, the
  stone,   70
Not to the stone, the line should be op-
  posed.
We cannot keep our constant course in
  virtue.
What is alike at all parts? Every day
Differs from other—every hour and min-
  ute,
Ay, every thought in our false clock of
  life
Ofttimes inverts the whole circumference.
We must be sometimes one, sometimes
  another.
Our bodies are but thick clouds to our
  souls,
Through which they cannot shine when
  they desire.
When all the stars, and even the sun
  himself,   80
Must stay the vapors' times that he ex-
  hales
Before he can make good his beams to us,
O, how can we, that are but motes to
  him,
Wand'ring at random in his ordered rays,

Disperse our passions' fumes, with our
  weak labors,
That are more thick and black than all
  earth's vapors?

Enter Mont[surry].

MONT. Good day, my love! What, up and
  ready [1] too?
TAM. Both, my dear lord; not all this
  night made I
Myself unready, or could sleep a wink.
MONT. Alas, what troubled my true love,
  my peace,   90
From being at peace within her better
  self?
Or how could sleep forbear to seize thine
  eyes
When he might challenge them as his just
  prize?
TAM. I am in no power earthly, but in
  yours.
To what end should I go to bed, my lord,
That wholly missed the comfort of my
  bed?
Or how should sleep possess my faculties,
Wanting the proper closer of mine eyes?
MONT. Then will I never more sleep night
  from thee.
All mine own business, all the king's
  affairs,   100
Shall take the day to serve them; every
  night
I'll ever dedicate to thy delight.
TAM. Nay, good my lord, esteem not my
  desires
Such doters on their humors that my
  judgment
Cannot subdue them to your worthier
  pleasure;
A wife's pleased husband must her object
  be
In all her acts, not her soothed fantasy.
MONT. Then come, my love, now pay
  those rites to sleep
Thy fair eyes owe him. Shall we now to
  bed?   109
TAM. O, no, my lord; your holy friar says
All couplings in the day that touch the
  bed
Adulterous are, even in the married;
Whose grave and worthy doctrine, well
  I know,
Your faith in him will liberally allow.

MONT. He's a most learned and religious
  man.
Come to the presence then, and see great
  D'Ambois
(Fortune's proud mushroom shot up in
  a night)
Stand like an Atlas under our king's arm;
Which greatness with him Monsieur
  now envies
As bitterly and deadly as the Guise. 120
TAM. What, he that was but yesterday
  his maker,
His raiser and preserver?
MONT.   Even the same.
Each natural agent works but to this end,
To render that it works on like itself;
Which, since the Monsieur in his act
  on D'Ambois
Cannot to his ambitious end effect,
But that, quite opposite, the king hath
  power,
In his love borne to D'Ambois, to convert
The point of Monsieur's aim on his own
  breast,
He turns his outward love to inward
  hate.   130
A prince's love is like the lightning's
  fume,
Which no man can embrace, but must
  consume.   *Exeunt.*

[SCENA SECUNDA.

A room in the court.]

*Henry, D'Ambois, Monsieur, Guise, Duchess,
  Annabelle, Charlotte, Attendants.*

HEN. Speak home, Bussy! Thy impartial
  words
Are like brave falcons that dare truss [2]
  a fowl
Much greater than themselves. Flatterers are kites
That check at [3] sparrows; thou shalt be
  my eagle,
And bear my thunder underneath thy
  wings.
Truth's words like jewels hang in th'
  ears of kings.
BUS. Would I might live to see no Jews
  hang there
Instead of jewels—sycophants, I mean,
Who use Truth like the devil, his true
  foe,

[1] Dressed.   [2] Seize.   [3] Pursue.

Cast by the angel to the pit of fears,　10
And bound in chains; Truth seldom decks
　　kings' ears.
Slave Flattery (like a rippier's [1] legs
　　rolled up
In boots of hay ropes) with kings' soothéd
　　guts
Swaddled and strappled,[2] now lives only
　　free.
O, 'tis a subtle knave; how like the
　　plague
Unfelt he strikes into the brain of man,
And rageth in his entrails, when he can,
Worse than the poison of a red-haired
　　man! [3]
Hen. Fly at him and his brood! I cast
　　thee off,[4]
And once more give thee surname of
　　mine eagle.　　　　　　　　　　　20
Bus. I'll make you sport enough, then;
　　let me have
My lucerns [5] too, or dogs inured to hunt
Beasts of most rapine, but to put them
　　up,[6]
And, if I truss not, let me not be trusted.
Show me a great man (by the people's
　　voice,
Which is the voice of God) that by his
　　greatness
Bombasts [7] his private roofs with public
　　riches;
That affects royalty, rising from a clap-
　　dish; [8]
That rules so much more by his suffering
　　king [9]
That he makes kings of his subordinate
　　slaves;　　　　　　　　　　　　30
Himself and them graduate [10] (like wood-
　　mongers,
Piling a stack of billets) from the earth,
Raising each other into steeples' heights;
Let him convey this on the turning
　　props
Of Protean law, and, his own counsel
　　keeping,[11]

Keep all upright—let me but hawk at
　　him,
I'll play the vulture, and so thump his
　　liver
That, like a huge, unlading argosy,
He shall confess all, and you then may
　　hang him.
Show me a clergyman that is in voice　40
A lark of heaven, in heart a mole of
　　earth;
That hath good living, and a wicked life;
A temperate look, and a luxurious gut;
Turning the rents of his superfluous
　　cures [12]
Into your pheasants and your partridges;
Venting their quintessence as men read
　　Hebrew[13]—
Let me but hawk at him, and, like the
　　other,
He shall confess all, and you then may
　　hang him.
Show me a lawyer that turns sacred law
(The equal rend'rer of each man his
　　own,　　　　　　　　　　　　50
The scourge of rapine and extortion,
The sanctuary and impregnable defense
Of retired learning and besiegéd virtue)
Into a harpy, that eats all but 's own,
Into the damnéd sins it punisheth,
Into the synagogue of thieves and athe-
　　ists,
Blood into gold, and justice into lust—
Let me but hawk at him as at the rest,
He shall confess all, and you then may
　　hang him.

Enter Montsurry, Tamyra, and Pero.

Guise. Where will you find such game as
　　you would hawk at?　　　　　　60
Bus. I'll hawk about your house for one
　　of them.
Guise. Come, y'are a glorious [14] ruffian,
　　and run proud
Of [15] the king's headlong graces. Hold
　　your breath,
Or, by that poisoned vapor, not the king
Shall back your murtherous valor against
　　me.
Bus. I would the king would make his
　　presence free

---

[1] Fishmonger's.
[2] Strapped.
[3] Judas was supposed to have had red hair;
hence, a traitor.
[4] Release thee for flight.
[5] Properly lynxes; here, hunting dogs.
[6] Start them from cover.
[7] Stuffs out.　　　　[9] By his king's sufferance.
[8] Beggar's dish.　　[10] Rise by steps.
[11] Perhaps referring to the keeping of a private
lawyer.

[12] Income of his supplementary parishes.
[13] *I.e.*, backwards.
[14] Boastful.
[15] On account of.

But for one bout betwixt us; by the
　reverence
Due to the sacred space twixt kings
　and subjects,
Here would I make thee cast that
　popular purple,
In which thy proud soul sits and braves
　thy sovereign.　　　　　　　　70
Mon. Peace, peace, I pray thee, peace!
Bus. 　　　　　Let him peace first
　That made the first war.
Mon. 　　　　　He's the better man.
Bus. And therefore may do worst?
Mon. 　　　　　He has more titles.
Bus. So Hydra had more heads.
Mon. 　　　　　He's greater known.
Bus. His greatness is the people's; mine's
　mine own.
Mon. He's nobly [1] born.
Bus. 　　　　He is not; I am noble.
　And noblesse in his [2] blood hath no
　　gradation
　But in his merit.
Guise. 　　　Th' art not nobly born,
　But bastard to the Cardinal of Ambois.
Bus. Thou liest, proud Guisard. Let me
　fly, my lord!　　　　　　　　80
Hen. Not in my face, my eagle; violence
　flies
　The sanctuaries of a prince's eyes.
Bus. Still shall we chide and foam upon
　this bit?
　Is the Guise only great in faction?
　Stands he not by himself? Proves he
　th' opinion
　That men's souls are without them? Be
　a duke,
　And lead me to the field.
Guise. 　　　　Come, follow me
Hen. Stay them! Stay, D'Ambois! Cousin
　Guise, I wonder
　Your honored disposition brooks so ill
　A man so good, that only would uphold
　Man in his native noblesse, from whose
　　fall　　　　　　　　　　　91
　All our dissensions rise; that in himself
　(Without the outward patches of our
　　frailty,
　Riches and honor) knows he compre-
　　hends
　Worth with the greatest. Kings had
　　never borne
　Such boundless empire over other men,

Had all maintained the spirit and state
　of D'Ambois;
Nor had the full impartial hand of
　Nature,
That all things gave in her original [3]
Without these definite terms of "mine"
　and "thine,"　　　　　　　100
Been turned unjustly to the hand of
　Fortune,
Had all preserved her in her prime, like
　D'Ambois.
No envy, no disjunction had dissolved,
Or plucked one stick out of the golden
　faggot
In which the world of Saturn [4] bound
　our lives,
Had all been held together with the
　nerves,
The genius, and th' ingenious soul of
　D'Ambois.
Let my hand therefore be the Hermean
　rod [5]
To part and reconcile, and so conserve
　you,
As my combined embracers and sup-
　porters.　　　　　　　　110
Bus. 'Tis our king's motion,[6] and we shall
　not seem
　To worst eyes womanish, though we
　change thus soon
　Never so great grudge for his greater
　pleasure.
Guise. I seal to that; and, so the manly
　freedom
　That you so much profess, hereafter
　prove not
　A bold and glorious license to deprave,[7]
　To me his hand shall hold the Hermean
　virtue
　His grace affects, in which submissive
　sign
　On this his sacred right hand I lay mine.
Bus. 'Tis well, my lord, and, so your
　worthy greatness　　　　　120
　Decline not to the greater insolence,
　Nor make you think it a prerogative
　To rack men's freedoms with the ruder
　wrongs,
　My hand (stuck full of laurel, in true
　sign
　'Tis wholly dedicate to righteous peace)

[1] Boas emends to *noblier.*　　　[2] Its.

[3] In the beginning.　　　[6] Desire, proposal.
[4] The fabled Golden Age.　　[7] Vilify.
[5] Caduceus.

In all submission kisseth th' other side.

HEN. Thanks to ye both; and kindly I
　invite ye
Both to a banquet, where we'll sacrifice
Full cups to confirmation of your loves—
At which, fair ladies, I entreat your
　presence,　　　　　　　　　　　130
And hope you, madam, will take one
　carouse
For reconcilement of your lord and
　servant.

DUCH. If I should fail, my lord, some
　other lady
Would be found there to do that for
　my servant.

MON. Any of these here?

DUCH.　　　　　Nay, I know not that.

BUS. [*To Tamyra.*] Think your thoughts
　like my mistress', honored lady?

TAM. I think not on you, sir; y'are one I
　know not.

BUS. Cry you mercy, madam!

MONT.　　　　O, sir, has she met you?
　　Exeunt Henry, D'Amb[ois], Ladies.

MON. What had my bounty drunk when
　it raised him?

GUISE. Y'ave stuck us up a very worthy
　flag,　　　　　　　　　　　　　140
That takes more wind than we with all
　our sails.

MON. O, so he spreads and flourishes.

GUISE.　　　　　　　　He must down;
Upstarts should never perch too near
　a crown.

MON. 'Tis true, my lord; and as this dot-
　ing hand,
Even out of earth, like Juno, struck
　this giant,
So Jove's great ordinance [1] shall be here
　implied
To strike him under th' Etna of his pride,
To which work lend your hands, and
　let us cast
Where we may set snares for his ranging
　greatness.
I think it best amongst our greatest
　women;　　　　　　　　　　　150
For there is no such trap to catch an up-
　start
As a loose downfall, for you know their
　falls
Are th' ends of all men's rising.　If
　great men

[1] Ordnance, thunderbolt.

And wise make scapes to please ad-
　vantage,[2]
'Tis with a woman.　Women, that worst
　may,
Still hold men's candles:[3] they direct
　and know
All things amiss in all men; and their
　women,[4]
All things amiss in them, through whose
　charmed mouths
We may see all the close [5] scapes of the
　court.
When the most royal beast of chase,
　the hart,　　　　　　　　　　　160
Being old and cunning in his lairs and
　haunts,
Can never be discovered to the bow,
The piece,[6] or hound, yet where, behind
　some queach,[7]
He breaks his gall, and rutteth with his
　hind,
The place is marked, and by his venery
He still is taken.　Shall we then attempt
The chiefest mean to that discovery
　here,
And court our greatest ladies' chiefest
　women
With shows of love and liberal promises?
'Tis but our breath.　If something given
　in hand　　　　　　　　　　　170
Sharpen their hopes of more, 'twill be
　well ventured.

GUISE. No doubt of that; and 'tis the
　cunning'st point
Of your devised investigation.

MON.　　　　　　　I have broken
The ice to it already with the woman
Of your chaste lady, and conceive good
　hope
I shall wade thorough to some wishéd
　shore
At our next meeting.

MONT.　　Nay, there's small hope there.

GUISE. Take say of [8] her, my lord; she
　comes most fitly.

[2] "Commit escapades, and thereby give points
against themselves" (Boas).
[3] This passage is based on an old proverb.
"Women, who hold the candles because of their
inferiority to men, none the less know well how
the game is going" (Parrott).
[4] Waiting-women.
[5] Secret.
[6] Gun.
[7] Thicket.
[8] Assay, make trial of.

Enter Charlotte, Annabelle, Pero.

MON. Starting back?

GUISE. Y'are engaged, indeed.   180

ANN. Nay, pray, my lord, forbear.

MONT. What, skittish, servant?

ANN. No, my lord, I am not so fit for your service.

CHAR. Pray pardon me now, my lord; my lady expects me.

GUISE. I'll satisfy her expectation, as far as an uncle may.

MON. Well said; a spirit of courtship of all hands.   [*Takes Pero aside.*]

Now, mine own Pero, hast thou remembered me   190

For the discovery I entreated thee to make of thy mistress?

Speak boldly, and be sure of all things I have sworn to thee.

PER. Building on that assurance, my lord, I may speak, and much the rather because my lady hath not trusted me with that I can tell you, for now I cannot be said to betray her.

MON. That's all one, so we reach our objects. Forth, I beseech thee.

PER. To tell you truth, my lord, I   [200 have made a strange discovery.

MON. Excellent, Pero, thou reviv'st me. May I sink quick to perdition if my tongue discover it.

PER. 'Tis thus, then: this last night my lord lay forth, and I, watching my lady's sitting up, stole up at midnight from my pallet, and, having before made a hole both through the wall and arras to her inmost chamber, I saw D'Ambois and   [210 herself reading a letter.

MON. D'Ambois?

PER. Even he, my lord.

MON. Dost thou not dream, wench?

PER. I swear he is the man.

MON. The devil he is, and thy lady his dam! Why, this was the happiest shot that ever flew! The just plague of hypocrisy leveled it. O, the infinite regions betwixt a woman's tongue and her   [220 heart! Is this our goddess of chastity? I thought I could not be so slighted if she had not her fraught [1] besides, and therefore plotted this with her woman, never dreaming of D'Ambois. Dear Pero, I will advance thee forever. But tell me

now—God's precious, it transforms me with admiration [2]—sweet Pero, whom should she trust with this conveyance? [3] Or, all the doors being made sure, how   [230 should his conveyance be made?

PER. Nay, my lord, that amazes me; I cannot by any study so much as guess at it.

MON. Well, let's favor our apprehensions with forbearing that a little; for, if my heart were not hooped with adamant, the conceit [4] of this would have burst it. But hark thee!—   *Whispers.*

MONT. [*Aside to Annabelle.*] I pray   [240 thee, resolve me; the duke will never imagine that I am busy about 's wife. Hath D'Ambois any privy access to her?

ANN. No, my lord, D'Ambois neglects her, as she takes it, and is therefore suspicious that either your lady or the Lady Beaupré hath closely entertained him.

MONT. By'r Lady, a likely suspi-   [250 cion, and very near the life, especially of my wife.—

MON. [*Aside to Pero.*] Come, we'll disguise all with seeming only to have courted.—Away, dry palm! [5] Sh'as a liver as hard as a biscuit; a man may go a whole voyage with her, and get nothing but tempests from her windpipe.

GUISE. Here's one, I think, has swallowed a porcupine, she casts pricks   [260 from her tongue so.

MONT. And here's a peacock seems to have devoured one of the Alps, she has so swelling a spirit, and is so cold of her kindness.

CHAR. We are no windfalls, my lord; ye must gather us with the ladder of matrimony, or we'll hang till we be rotten.

MON. Indeed, that's the way to make ye right openarses. [6] But, alas, ye have   [270 no portions fit for such husbands as we wish you.

PER. Portions, my lord? Yes, and such portions as your principality cannot purchase.

MON. What, woman! What are those portions?

[1] Freight.

[2] Wonder.   [5] Sign of chastity.
[3] *I.e.*, of Bussy to her room.   [6] Medlars.
[4] Thought.

PER. Riddle my riddle, my lord.

MON. Ay, marry, wench, I think thy portion is a right riddle; a man shall [280 never find it out. But let's hear it.

PER. You shall, my lord.

What's that, that being most rare's most
*   cheap?*
That when you sow, you never reap?
That when it grows most, most you in [1] *it?*
And still you lose it when you win it;
That, when 'tis commonest, 'tis dearest,
And, when 'tis farthest off, 'tis nearest?

MON. Is this your great portion?

PER. Even this, my lord.   290

MON. Believe me, I cannot riddle it.

PER. No, my lord; 'tis my chastity, which you shall neither riddle nor fiddle.

MON. Your chastity? Let me begin with the end of it; how is a woman's chastity nearest a man when 'tis furthest off?

PER. Why, my lord, when you cannot get it, it goes to th' heart on you; and that, I think, comes most near [300 you; and I am sure it shall be far enough off. And so we leave you to our mercies.

                      Exeunt Women.

MON. Farewell, riddle!

GUISE. Farewell, medlar!

MONT. Farewell, winter plum!

MON. Now, my lords, what fruit of our inquisition? Feel you nothing budding yet? Speak, good my Lord Montsurry.

MONT. Nothing but this: D'Ambois is thought negligent in observing the [310 duchess, and therefore she is suspicious that your niece or my wife closely entertains him.

MON. Your wife, my lord? Think you that possible?

MONT. Alas, I know she flies him like her last hour.

MON. Her last hour? Why, that comes upon her the more she flies it. Does D'Ambois so, think you?   320

MONT. That's not worth the answering. 'Tis miraculous to think with what monsters women's imaginations engross them when they are once enamored, and what wonders they will work for their satisfaction. They will make a sheep valiant, a lion fearful.

MON. [*Aside.*] And an ass confident.—

---

[1] Boas suggests *thin*.

Well, my lord, more will come forth shortly; get you to the banquet.   330

GUISE. Come, my lord; I have the blind side of one of them.

           Exit Guise cum Mont[surry].

MON. O, the unsounded sea of women's bloods,

That, when 'tis calmest, is most dangerous;

Not any wrinkle creaming in their faces

When in their hearts are Scylla and Charybdis,

Which still are hid in dark and standing fogs,

Where never day shines, nothing never grows

But weeds and poisons that no statesman knows;

Not Cerberus ever saw the damnéd nooks   340

Hid with the veils of women's virtuous looks!

But what a cloud of sulphur have I drawn

Up to my bosom in this dangerous secret!

Which if my haste with any spark should light,

Ere D'Ambois were engaged in some sure plot,

I were blown up; he would be sure my death.

Would I had never known it, for before

I shall persuade th' importance to Montsurry,

And make him with some studied stratagem

Train D'Ambois to his wreak,[2] his maid may tell it,   350

Or I (out of my fiery thirst to play

With the fell tiger, up in darkness tied,

And give it some light) make it quite break loose.

I fear it, afore heaven, and will not see

D'Ambois again till I have told Montsurry

And set a snare with him to free my fears.

Who's there?

               Enter Maffé.[3]

MAF.   My lord?

MON.   Go call the Count Montsurry,

---

[2] *I.e.*, to Montsurry's vengeance.

[3] The scene apparently shifts to Monsieur's chamber.

And make the doors fast; I will speak
with none
Till he come to me.
MAF.   Well, my lord.   *Exiturus.*[1]
MON.   Or else
Send you some other, and see all the
doors   360
Made safe yourself, I pray; haste, fly
about it.
MAF. You'll speak with none but with
the Count Montsurry?
MON. With none but he, except it be the
Guise.
MAF. See even by this, there's one excep-
tion more!
Your grace must be more firm in the
command,
Or else shall I as weakly execute.
The Guise shall speak with you?
MON.   He shall, I say.
MAF. And Count Montsurry?
MON.   Ay, and Count Montsurry.
MAF. Your grace must pardon me, that I
am bold
To urge the clear and full sense of your
pleasure;   370
Which whensoever I have known, I hope
Your grace will say, I hit it to a hair.
MON. You have.
MAF.   I hope so, or I would be glad—
MON. I pray thee get thee gone; thou art
so tedious
In the strict form of all thy services
That I had better have one negligent.
You hit my pleasure well when D'Ambois
hit you;
Did you not, think you?
MAF.   D'Ambois? Why, my lord—
MON. I pray thee talk no more, but shut
the doors.
Do what I charge thee.
MAF.   I will, my lord, and yet   380
I would be glad the wrong I had of
D'Ambois—
MON. Precious! Then it is a fate that
plagues me
In this man's foolery! I may be mur-
thered
While he stands on protection of his folly.
Avaunt about thy charge!
MAF.   I go, my lord.—
[*Aside.*] I had my head broke in his
faithful service;

[1] About to go out.

I had no suit the more, nor any thanks,
And yet my teeth must still be hit with
D'Ambois.—
D'Ambois, my lord, shall know—
MON.   The devil and D'Ambois!
                                        Exit Maffé.
How am I tortured with this trusty fool!
Never was any curious [2] in his place 391
To do things justly, but he was an ass;
We cannot find one trusty that is witty,[3]
And therefore bear their disproportion.
Grant thou, great star and angel of my
life,[4]
A sure lease of it but for some few days,
That I may clear my bosom of the snake
I cherished there, and I will then defy
All check to it but Nature's, and her
altars
Shall crack with vessels crowned with
every liquor   400
Drawn from her highest and most bloody
humors.
I fear him strangely; his advancéd valor
Is like a spirit raised without a circle,
Endangering him that ignorantly raised
him,
And for whose fury he hath learnt no
limit.

Enter Maffé hastily.

MAF. I cannot help it; what should I do
more?
As I was gathering a fit guard to make
My passage to the doors, and the doors
sure,
The man of blood is entered.
MON.   Rage of death! 409
If I had told the secret, and he knew it,
Thus had I been endangered.

Enter D'Ambois.[5]

                              My sweetheart!
How now, what leap'st thou at?
BUS.   O royal object!
MON. Thou dream'st, awake; object in
th' empty air?
BUS. Worthy the brows of Titan, worth
his chair.
MON. Pray thee, what mean'st thou?
BUS.   See you not a crown

[2] Careful.   [3] Sensible.   [4] Guardian angel.
[5] In the original this direction comes at the
end of the speech.

Impale the forehead of the great King
    Monsieur?
Mon. O, fie upon thee!
Bus.   Prince, that is the subject
    Of all these your retired and sole dis-
    courses.
Mon. Wilt thou not leave that wrongful
    supposition?
Bus. Why wrongful, to suppose the doubt-
    less right   420
    To the succession worth the thinking
    on?
Mon. Well, leave these jests. How I am
    overjoyed
    With thy wished presence, and how fit
    thou com'st,
    For, of mine honor, I was sending for thee.
Bus. To what end?
Mon.   Only for thy company,
    Which I have still in thought; but that's
    no payment
    On thy part made with personal ap-
    pearance.
    Thy absence, so long suffered, often-
    times
    Put me in some little doubt thou dost
    not love me.
    Wilt thou do one thing therefore now
    sincerely?   430
Bus. Ay, anything but killing of the king.
Mon. Still in that discord and ill-taken
    note?
    How most unseasonable thou playest
    the cuckoo,
    In this thy fall of friendship! [1]
Bus.   Then do not doubt
    That there is any act within my nerves [2]
    But killing of the king, that is not yours.
Mon. I will not, then; to prove which
    by my love
    Shown to thy virtues, and by all fruits
    else
    Already sprung from that still flourish-
    ing tree,
    With whatsoever may hereafter spring,
    I charge thee utter (even with all the
    freedom   441
    Both of thy noble nature and thy friend-
    ship)
    The full and plain state of me in thy
    thoughts.

Bus. What, utter plainly what I think of
    you?
Mon. Plain as truth!
Bus. Why, this swims quite against the
    stream of greatness;
    Great men would rather hear their flat-
    teries,
    And, if they be not made fools, are not
    wise.
Mon. I am no such great fool, and there-
    fore charge thee,
    Even from the root of thy free heart,
    display me.   450
Bus. Since you affect [3] it in such serious
    terms,
    If yourself first will tell me what you think
    As freely and as heartily of me,
    I'll be as open in my thoughts of you.
Mon. A bargain, of mine honor! And
    make this,
    That, prove we in our full dissection
    Never so foul, live still the sounder
    friends.
Bus. What else, sir? Come, pay me home;
    I'll bide it bravely.
Mon. I will, I swear. I think thee then
    a man
    That dares as much as a wild horse or
    tiger;   460
    As headstrong and as bloody; and to
    feed
    The ravenous wolf of thy most cannibal
    valor,
    Rather than not employ it, thou wouldst
    turn
    Hackster to any whore,[4] slave to a Jew
    Or English usurer, to force possessions
    (And cut men's throats) of mortgagéd
    estates;
    Or thou wouldst tire [5] thee like a tinker's
    strumpet,
    And murther market folks, quarrel with
    sheep,
    And run as mad as Ajax, serve a
    butcher—
    Do anything but killing of the king; 470
    That in thy valor th' art like other
    naturals [6]
    That have strange gifts in nature, but
    no soul
    Diffused quite through, to make them
    of a piece,

---

[1] The cuckoo, known for its monotonous song, sings in spring rather than in autumn.
[2] Strength, power.

[3] Desire.   [4] Ruffian serving her as bodyguard.
[5] Attire, dress.   [6] Idiots.

But stop at humors that are more ab-
 surd,
Childish, and villainous than that hack-
 ster, whore,
Slave, cutthroat, tinker's bitch, com-
 pared before;
And in those humors wouldst envy, be-
 tray,
Slander, blaspheme, change each hour
 a religion—
Do anything but killing of the king;
That in thy valor (which is still the
 dunghill,   480
To which hath reference all filth in thy
 house)
Th' art more ridiculous and vainglori-
 ous
Than any mountebank, and impudent
Than any painted bawd; which, not to
 soothe
And glorify thee like a Jupiter Hammon,
Thou eat'st thy heart in vinegar; and
 thy gall
Turns all thy blood to poison, which is
 cause
Of that toad pool that stands in thy
 complexion,
And makes thee (with a cold and earthy
 moisture,
Which is the dam of putrefaction, 490
As plague to thy damned pride) rot as
 thou liv'st;
To study calumnies and treacheries;
To thy friends' slaughters like a screech
 owl sing,
And to all mischiefs—but to kill the
 king.
Bus. So! Have you said?
Mon.   How think'st thou? Do I
 flatter?
Speak I not like a trusty friend to thee?
Bus. That ever any man was blessed
 withal!
So here's for me! I think you are, at
 worst,
No devil, since y'are like to be no king;
Of which, with any friend of yours, I'll
 lay   500
This poor stillado [1] here gainst all the
 stars,
Ay, and gainst all your treacheries, which
 are more,
That you did never good, but to do ill;

[1] Stiletto.

But ill of all sorts, free and for itself,
That (like a murthering piece, making
 lanes in armies,
The first man of a rank, the whole rank
 falling),
If you have wronged one man, you are
 so far
From making him amends that all his
 race,
Friends, and associates fall into your
 chase;   508
That y'are for perjuries the very prince
Of all intelligencers; [2] and your voice
Is like an eastern wind, that where it
 flies
Knits nets of caterpillars, with which
 you catch
The prime of all the fruits the kingdom
 yields;
That your political head is the cursed
 fount
Of all the violence, rapine, cruelty,
Tyranny, and atheism flowing through
 the realm;
That y'ave a tongue so scandalous, 'twill
 cut
The purest crystal, and a breath that
 will
Kill to [3] that wall a spider; you will
 jest   520
With God, and your soul to the devil
 tender
For lust; kiss horror, and with death
 engender;
That your foul body is a Lernean fen
Of all the maladies breeding in all men;
That you are utterly without a soul;
And, for your life, the thread of that
 was spun
When Clotho slept, and let her breath-
 ing rock [4]
Fall in the dirt; and Lachesis still draws
 it,
Dipping her twisting fingers in a bowl
Defiled, and crowned with virtue's
 forcéd soul;   530
And lastly, which I must for gratitude
Ever remember, that of all my height
And dearest life, you are the only spring,
Only in royal hope to kill the king.

[2] Spies.
[3] At the distance of.
[4] "The distaff from whence she draws the
breath of life" (Dilke).

Mon. Why, now I see thou lovest me.
Come to the banquet. *Exeunt.*

Finis Actus Tertii.

Actus Quarti Scena Prima.

[*A room in the court.*]

Henry, Monsieur with a letter, Guise,
Montsurry, Bussy, Elenor, Tamyra,
Beaupré, Pero, Charlotte, Annabelle,
Pyra, with four Pages.

Hen. Ladies, ye have not done our ban-
quet right,
Nor looked upon it with those cheerful
rays
That lately turned your breaths to
floods of gold.
Your looks, methinks, are not drawn
out with thoughts
So clear and free as heretofore, but foul,
As if the thick complexions [1] of men
Governed within them.
Bus.   'Tis not like, my lord,
That men in women rule, but contrary;
For, as the moon, of all things God
created,
Not only is the most appropriate im-
age   10
Or glass to show them how they wax
and wane,
But in her height and motion likewise
bears
Imperial influences that command
In all their powers, and make them wax
and wane;
So women, that, of all things made of
nothing,
Are the most perfect idols of the moon,
Or still-unweaned, sweet mooncalves [2]
with white faces,
Not only are patterns of change to men,
But, as the tender moonshine of their
beauties
Clears or is cloudy, make men glad or
sad;   20
So then they rule in men, not men in
them.
Mon. But here the moons are changed,
as the king notes,
And either men rule in them, or some
power

[1] Humors, bodily fluids.
[2] Deformed creatures, monstrosities.

Beyond their voluntary faculty,
For nothing can recover their lost faces.
Mont. None can be always one. Our
griefs and joys
Hold several scepters in us, and have
times
For their divided empires; which grief
now in them
Doth prove as proper to his diadem.
Bus. And grief's a natural sickness of
the blood,   30
That time to part asks, as his coming
had;
Only slight fools, grieved, suddenly are
glad.
A man may say t' a dead man, "Be re-
vived,"
As well as to one sorrowful, "Be not
grieved."
[*To the Duchess.*] And therefore, princely
mistress, in all wars
Against these base foes that insult on
weakness,
And still fight housed behind the shield
of nature,
Of privilege, law, treachery, or beastly
need,
Your servant cannot help; authority
here
Goes with corruption, something like
some states,   40
That back worst men. Valor to them
must creep
That, to themselves left, would fear him
asleep.
Duch. Ye all take that for granted that
doth rest
Yet to be proved; we all are as we were,
As merry and as free in thought as ever.
Guise. And why then can ye not disclose
your thoughts?
Tam. Methinks the man hath answered
for us well.
Mon. The man? Why, madam, d' ye
not know his name?
Tam. Man is a name of honor for a king;
Additions [3] take away from each chief
thing.   50
The school of modesty not to learn
learns dames;
They sit in high forms [4] there, that know
men's names.

[3] Titles.
[4] "On the stools of disgrace" (Boas).

MON. [*To Bussy.*] Hark, sweetheart, here's
    a bar set to your valor!
It cannot enter here; no, not to notice
Of what your name is. Your great eagle's
    beak,
Should you fly at her, had as good en-
    counter
An Albion cliff as her more craggy liver.[1]
BUS. I'll not attempt her, sir; her sight
    and name,
    By which I only know her, doth deter me.
HEN. So they do all men else.
MON.   You would say so 60
    If you knew all.
TAM.   Knew all, my lord? What
    mean you?
MON. All that I know, madam.
TAM.   That you know? Speak it.
MON. No, 'tis enough I feel it.
HEN.   But, methinks
Her courtship is more pure than here-
    tofore;
True courtiers should be modest, and
    not nice;
Bold, but not impudent; pleasure love,
    not vice.
MON. Sweetheart, come hither! What if
    one should make
Horns at Montsurry? Would it not
    strike him jealous
Through all the proofs of his chaste
    lady's virtues?
BUS. If he be wise, not.   70
MON. What? Not if I should name the
    gardener
That I would have him think hath
    grafted him?
BUS. So the large license that your great-
    ness uses
To jest that all men may be taught in-
    deed
To make a difference of the grounds you
    play on,
Both in the men you scandal, and the
    matter.
MON. As how? As how?
BUS.   Perhaps led with a train,[2]
Where you may have your nose made
    less and slit,
Your eyes thrust out.
MON.   Peace, peace, I pray thee peace!
Who dares do that? The brother of his
    king?   80

[1] Supposed to be the seat of love.   [2] Trick.

BUS. Were your king brother in you; all
    your powers,
Stretched in the arms of great men and
    their bawds,
Set close down by you; all your stormy
    laws
Spouted with lawyers' mouths and gush-
    ing blood
Like to so many torrents; all your glo-
    ries
(Making you terrible, like enchanted
    flames)
Fed with bare coxcombs and with crooked
    hams; [3]
All your prerogatives, your shames, and
    tortures;
All daring heaven, and opening hell
    about you—
Were I the man ye wronged so and pro-
    voked,   90
Though ne'er so much beneath you, like
    a box tree
I would, out of the roughness of my root,
Ram hardness in my lowness, and, like
    Death
Mounted on earthquakes, I would trot
    through all
Honors and horrors, thorough foul and
    fair,
And from your whole strength toss you
    into the air.
MON. Go, th' art a devil! Such another
    spirit
Could not be stilled [4] from all th' Arme-
    nian dragons.
O my love's glory, heir to all I have
(That's all I can say, and that all I
    swear)   100
If thou outlive me, as I know thou must,
Or else hath Nature no proportioned
    end
To her great labors, she hath breathed
    a mind
Into thy entrails, of desert to swell
Into another great Augustus Cæsar,
Organs and faculties fitted to her great-
    ness;
And, should that perish like a common
    spirit,
Nature's a courtier and regards no merit.
HEN. Here's naught but whispering with
    us, like a calm

[3] The bare heads and bent knees of sycophants.
[4] Distilled.

Before a tempest, when the silent air   110
Lays her soft ear close to the earth to
     hearken
For that she fears steals on to ravish
     her,
Some fate doth join [1] our ears to hear
     it coming.
Come, my brave eagle, let's to covert
     fly;
I see almighty Æther in the smoke
Of all his clouds descending, and the
     sky
Hid in the dim ostents [2] of tragedy.

Exit Henr[y] with D'Amb[ois] and Ladies.

GUISE. [*Aside to Monsieur.*]   Now stir
     the humor, and begin the brawl.
MONT. The king and D'Ambois now are
     grown all one.
MON. [*Making horns at Montsurry.*] Nay,
     they are two, my lord.
MONT.   How's that?
MON.   No more. 120
MONT. I must have more, my lord.
MON.   What, more than two?
MONT. How monstrous is this!
MON.   Why?
MONT.   You make me horns!
MON. Not I; it is a work without my
     power.
Married men's ensigns are not made
     with fingers;
Of divine fabric they are, not men's
     hands.
Your wife, you know, is a mere [3] Cyn-
     thia,
And she must fashion horns out of her
     nature.
MONT. But doth she—dare you charge
     her? Speak, false prince!
MON. I must not speak, my lord; but, if
     you'll use
The learning of a nobleman and read, 130
Here's something to those points. Soft,
     you must pawn [4]
Your honor, having read it, to return
     it.

Enter Tamyra, Pero.

MONT. Not I! I pawn my honor for a
     paper?
MON. You must not buy it under.

Exeunt Guise and Monsieur.

[1] Enjoin.   [3] Absolute.
[2] Manifestations, omens.   [4] Pledge.

MONT.   Keep it then,
And keep fire in your bosom.
TAM.   What says he?
MONT. You must make good the rest.
TAM.   How fares my lord?
Takes my love anything to heart he
     says?
MONT. Come, y'are a—
TAM.   What, my lord?
MONT.   The plague of Herod
Feast in his rotten entrails.
TAM.   Will you wreak
Your anger's just cause given by him,
     on me?   140
MONT. By him?
TAM.   By him, my lord. I have
     admired [5]
You could all this time be at concord
     with him,
That still hath played such discords on
     your honor.
MONT. Perhaps 'tis with some proud
     string of my wife's.
TAM. How's that, my lord?
MONT.   Your tongue will still admire,
Till my head be the miracle of the world.
TAM. O, woe is me! *She seems to sound.* [6]
PER.   What does your lordship
     mean?—
Madam, be comforted; my lord but
     tries you.
Madam!—Help, good my lord, are you
     not moved?
Do your set looks print in your words
     your thoughts?   150
Sweet lord, clear up those eyes, unbend
     that masking forehead.
Whence is it you rush upon her with
     these Irish wars,
More full of sound than hurt? But it
     is enough.
You have shot home; your words are
     in her heart.
She has not lived to bear a trial now.
MONT. Look up, my love, and by this
     kiss receive
My soul amongst thy spirits for supply
To thine, chased with my fury.
TAM.   O, my lord,
I have too long lived to hear this from
     you.
MONT. 'Twas from my troubled blood,
     and not from me.—   160

[5] Wondered.   [6] Swound, swoon.

[*Aside.*] I know not how I fare; a sud-
  den night
Flows through my entrails, and a head-
  long chaos
Murmurs within me, which I must di-
  gest,
And not drown her in my confusions,
That was my life's joy, being best in-
  formed.—
Sweet, you must needs forgive me, that
  my love,
Like to a fire disdaining his suppression,
Raged, being discouraged; my whole
  heart is wounded
When any least thought in you is but
  touched,
And shall be till I know your former
  merits;   170
Your name and memory altogether
  crave
In just oblivion their eternal grave;
And then, you must hear from me,
  there's no mean
In any passion I shall feel for you.
Love is a razor, cleansing, being well
  used,
But fetcheth blood still, being the least
  abused.
To tell you briefly all, the man that
  left me
When you appeared, did turn me worse
  than woman,
And stabbed me to the heart thus, with
  his fingers.
TAM. O, happy woman! Comes my stain
  from him?   180
It is my beauty, and that innocence
  proves
That slew Chimera, rescued Peleus
From all the savage beasts in Pelion,
And raised the chaste Athenian prince
  from hell;
All suffering with me, they for women's
  lusts,
I for a man's, that the Augean stable
Of his foul sin would empty in my lap.
How his guilt shunned me! Sacred In-
  nocence
That where thou fear'st, art dreadful,
  and his face
Turned in flight from thee, that had
  thee in chase!   190
Come, bring me to him; I will tell the
  serpent

Even to his venomed teeth, from whose
  cursed seed
A pitched field [1] starts up twixt my lord
  and me,
That his throat lies, and he shall curse
  his fingers
For being so governed by his filthy soul.
MONT. I know not if himself will vaunt
  t' have been
The princely author of the slavish sin,
Or any other; he would have resolved me,
Had you not come, not by his word,
  but writing,
Would I have sworn to give it him
  again,   200
And pawned mine honor to him for a
  paper.
TAM. See how he flies me still; 'tis a foul
  heart
That fears his own hand. Good my lord,
  make haste
To see the dangerous paper; papers hold
Ofttimes the forms and copies of our
  souls,
And, though the world despise them,
  are the prizes
Of all our honors.   Make your honor
  then
A hostage for it, and with it confer [2]
My nearest woman here, in all she
  knows,
Who, if the sun or Cerberus could have
  seen   210
Any stain in me, might as well as they.
And, Pero, here I charge thee by my
  love,
And all proofs of it, which I might call
  bounties,
By all that thou hast seen seem good
  in me,
And all the ill which thou shouldst spit
  from thee,
By pity of the wound this touch hath
  given me,
Not as thy mistress now, but a poor
  woman,
To death given over, rid me of my pains;
Pour on thy powder; clear thy breast
  of me.
My lord is only here. Here speak thy
  worst;   220
Thy best will do me mischief. If thou
  spar'st me,

[1] Battle.   [2] Consult.

Never shine good thought on thy mem-
ory!
Resolve my lord, and leave me desper-
ate.
PER. My lord! My lord hath played a
prodigal's part,
To break his stock for nothing; and an
insolent,
To cut a Gordian [1] when he could not
loose it.
What violence is this, to put true fire
To a false train, to blow up long-crowned
peace
With sudden outrage, and believe a
man
Sworn to the shame of women, gainst
a woman, 230
Born to their honors? But I will to him.
TAM. No, I will write (for I shall never
more
Meet with the fugitive) where I will
defy him,
Were he ten times the brother of my
king.
To him, my lord, and I'll to cursing
him. *Exeunt.*

[SCENA SECUNDA.

A room in Montsurry's house.]

Enter D'Ambois and Friar.

BUS. I am suspicious, my most honored
father,
By some of Monsieur's cunning passages,
That his still ranging and contentious
nostrils,
To scent the haunts of Mischief, have
so used
The vicious virtue of his busy sense
That he trails hotly of him, and will
rouse him,
Driving him all enraged and foaming on
us,
And therefore have entreated your deep
skill
In the command of good aërial spirits,
To assume these magic rites, and call
up one 10
To know if any have revealed unto him
Anything touching my dear love and me.
FRI. Good son, you have amazed me but
to make

[1] Gordian knot.

The least doubt of it, it concerns so
nearly
The faith and reverence of my name and
order.
Yet will I justify, upon my soul,
All I have done; if any spirit i' th' earth
or air
Can give you the resolve, do not despair.

*Music; and Tamyra enters with Pero, her
maid,[2] bearing a letter.*

TAM. Away, deliver it! (*Exit Pero.*) O,
may my lines
Filled with the poison of a woman's
hate, 20
When he shall open them, shrink up
his cursed eyes
With torturous darkness, such as stands
in hell,
Stuck full of inward horrors, never
lighted,
With which are all things to be feared,
affrighted.
BUS. [*Advancing.*] How is it with my
honored mistress?
TAM. O servant, help, and save me from
the gripes
Of shame and infamy. Our love is known;
Your Monsieur hath a paper where is writ
Some secret tokens that decipher it.
BUS. What cold dull northern brain, what
fool but he 30
Durst take into his Epimethean breast
A box of such plagues as the danger
yields
Incurred in this discovery? He had
better
Ventured his breast in the consuming
reach
Of the hot surfeits cast out of the clouds,
Or stood the bullets that, to wreak the
sky,
The Cyclops ram in Jove's artillery.
FRI. We soon will take the darkness from
his face
That did that deed of darkness; we will
know
What now the Monsieur and your hus-
band do, 40
What is contained within the secret
paper
Offered by Monsieur, and your love's
events;

[2] Original reads *and her maid.*

To which ends, honored daughter, at
  your motion,
I have put on these exorcising rites,
And, by my power of learned holiness
Vouchsafed me from above, I will com-
  mand
Our resolution of [1] a raiséd spirit.

TAM. Good father, raise him in some
  beauteous form
That with least terror I may brook
  his sight.

FRI. Stand sure together, then, whate'er
  you see,   50
And stir not, as ye tender all our lives.
                     He puts on his robes.

Occidentalium legionum spiritualium im-
perator, magnus ille Behemoth, veni, veni,
comitatus cum Astaroth locotenente invicto!
Adjuro te per Stygis inscrutabilia arcana,
per ipsos irremeabiles anfractus Averni:
Adesto, O Behemoth, tu cui pervia sunt
Magnatum scrinia; veni, per Noctis et tene-
brarum abdita profundissima; per labentia
sidera; per ipsos motus horarum furtivos, [60
Hecatesque altum silentium! Appare in
forma spirituali, lucente, splendida, et ama-
bili! [2]

Thunder. Ascendit [Behemoth with Carto-
         phylax and other Spirits].

BEH. What would the holy friar?

FRI.   I would see
What now the Monsieur and Montsurry
  do,
And see the secret paper that the Mon-
  sieur
Offered to Count Montsurry, longing
  much
To know on what events the secret loves
Of these two honored persons shall
  arrive.

BEH. Why calledst thou me to this accursed light,   70

[1] From.

[2] O ruler of the legions of western spirits, that
mighty Behemoth, come, come, accompanied by
Astaroth, unconquered lieutenant! I command
thee by the hidden mysteries of the Styx, by the
unretraceable labyrinths of Avernus themselves:
Appear, O Behemoth, thou to whom the cabinets of the Mighty are accessible; come, by the
deepest caves of Night and the shades; by the
wandering stars; by the stealthy motions of the
hours themselves, and the deep silence of Hecate!
Appear in spirit form, shining, brilliant, and
lovely!

To these light purposes? I am emperor
Of that inscrutable darkness where are
  hid
All deepest truths and secrets never seen,
All which I know, and command legions
Of knowing spirits that can do more than
  these.
Any of this my guard that circle me
In these blue fires, and out of whose
  dim fumes
Vast murmurs use to break, and from
  their sounds
Articulate voices, can do ten parts
  more
Than open such slight truths as you
  require.   80

FRI. From the last night's black depth I
  called up one
Of the inferior ablest ministers,
And he could not resolve me. Send one
  then
Out of thine own command, to fetch the
  paper
That Monsieur hath to show to Count
  Montsurry.

BEH. I will. Cartophylax, thou that properly
Hast in thy power all papers so inscribed,
Glide through all bars to it and fetch
  that paper.

CART. I will.   *A torch* [3] *removes.*

FRI. Till he returns, great Prince of Darkness,   90
Tell me if Monsieur and the Count Montsurry
Are yet encountered?

BEH.   Both them and the Guise
Are now together.

FRI.   Show us all their persons,
And represent the place, with all their
  actions.

BEH. The spirit will straight return, and
  then I'll show thee.

[Enter Cartophylax.]

See, he is come; why brought'st thou
  not the paper?

CART. He hath prevented me, and got a
  spirit
Raised by another, great in our command,
To take the guard of it before I came.

[3] *I.e.,* a torchbearer (Cartophylax).

BEH. This is your slackness, not t' invoke
  our powers   100
  When first your acts set forth to their
    effects;
  Yet shall you see it and themselves.
    Behold,
  They come here, and the earl now holds
    the paper.

Ent[er] Mons[ieur], Gui[se], Mont[surry]
                            with a paper.

BUS. May we not hear them?
[FRI.][1]   No, be still and see.
BUS. I will go fetch the paper.
FRI.   Do not stir;
  There's too much distance and too many
    locks
  Twixt you and them, how near soe'er
    they seem,
  For any man to interrupt their secrets.
TAM. O honored spirit, fly into the fancy
  Of my offended lord, and do not let him
  Believe what there the wicked man
    hath written.   111
BEH.[2] Persuasion hath already entered
    him
  Beyond reflection.[3] Peace till their de-
    parture!—

MON. There is a glass of ink[4] where you
    may see
  How to make ready black-faced tragedy.
  You now discern, I hope, through all
    her paintings,
  Her gasping wrinkles and fame's sepul-
    chers.
GUISE. Think you he feigns, my lord?
    What hold you now?
  Do we malign your wife, or honor you?
MON. What, stricken dumb! Nay, fie,
    lord, be not daunted;   120
  Your case is common; were it ne'er so
    rare,
  Bear it as rarely. Now to laugh were
    manly.
  A worthy man should imitate the
    weather
  That sings in tempests, and, being clear,
    is silent.

[1] Original reads *Mon.*
[2] Original reads *Pre.*
[3] Turning back, return.
[4] *I.e.*, the letter is a mirror.

GUISE. Go home, my lord, and force your
    wife to write
  Such loving lines to D'Ambois as she
    used
  When she desired his presence.
MON.   Do, my lord,
  And make her name her concealed mes-
    senger,
  That close and most inennerable[5]
    pander,   129
  That passeth all our studies to exquire;[6]
  By whom convey the letter to her love;
  And so you shall be sure to have him
    come
  Within the thirsty reach of your revenge;
  Before which, lodge an ambush in her
    chamber
  Behind the arras, of your stoutest men
  All close and soundly armed, and let
    them share
  A spirit amongst them that would serve
    a thousand.

              Enter Pero with a letter.

GUISE. Yet stay a little; see, she sends
    for you.
MON. Poor, loving lady; she'll make all
    good yet.
  Think you not so, my lord?
      Exit Mont[surry] and stabs Pero.[7]
GUISE.   Alas, poor soul!   140
MON. This was cruelly done, i' faith.
PER.   'Twas nobly done.
  And I forgive his lordship from my soul.
MON. Then much good do 't thee, Pero!
  Hast a letter?
PER. I hope it rather be a bitter volume
  Of worthy curses for your perjury.
GUISE. To you, my lord.
MON.   To me? Now, out upon her.
GUISE. Let me see, my lord.
MON. You shall presently. How fares
    my Pero?
  Who's there?

              Enter Servant.

              Take in this maid—sh' as
    caught a clap—
  And fetch my surgeon to her. Come,
    my lord,   150

[5] Inenarrable, indescribable, unknown.
[6] Discover.
[7] Boas emends: *Mont[surry] stabs Pero, and exit.*

We'll now peruse our letter.
Exeunt Mons[ieur], Guise. Lead her out.
PER.   Furies rise
 Out of the black lines, and torment his
  soul!—

TAM. Hath my lord slain my woman?
BEH.   No, she lives.
FRI. What shall become of us?
BEH.   All I can say,
 Being called thus late, is brief, and darkly
  this:
 If D'Ambois' mistress dye not her [1]
  white hand
 In her forced blood, he shall remain un-
  touched;
 So, father, shall yourself, but by your-
  self.
 To make this augury plainer, when the
  voice
 Of D'Ambois shall invoke me, I will
  rise,   160
 Shining in greater light, and show him
  all
 That will betide ye all. Meantime be
  wise,
 And curb his valor with your policies.
        Descendit cum suis. [2]
BUS. Will he appear to me when I invoke
  him?
FRI. He will, be sure.
BUS.   It must be shortly then;
 For his dark words have tied my
  thoughts on knots,
 Till he dissolve and free them.
TAM.   In meantime,
 Dear servant, till your powerful voice
  revoke him,
 Be sure to use the policy he advised;
 Lest fury in your too quick knowledge
  taken   170
 Of our abuse, and your defense of me,
 Accuse me more than any enemy.
 And, father, you must on my lord im-
  pose
 Your holiest charges and the church's
  power
 To temper his hot spirit and disperse
 The cruelty and the blood I know his
  hand
 Will shower upon our heads, if you put
  not

[1] Original has *his.*
[2] He descends with his attendants.

Your finger to the storm, and hold it up,
As my dear servant here must do with
 Monsieur.
BUS. I'll soothe his plots, and strow my
  hate with smiles,   180
Till all at once the close mines of my
  heart
Rise at full date, and rush into his
  blood.
I'll bind his arm in silk, and rub his
  flesh,
To make the vein swell, that his soul
  may gush
Into some kennel, [3] where it longs to lie,
And policy shall be flanked [4] with policy.
Yet shall the feeling center [5] where we
  meet
Groan with the weight of my approach-
  ing feet;
I'll make th' inspired [6] thresholds of his
  court
Sweat with the weather of my horrid
  steps,[7]   190
Before I enter; yet will I appear
Like calm security before a ruin.
A politician must, like lightning, melt
The very marrow, and not taint the
  skin;
His ways must not be seen; the super-
  ficies
Of the green center must not taste his
  feet,
When hell is plowed up with his wound-
  ing tracts,[8]
And all his harvest reaped by hellish
  facts.   *Exeunt.*

FINIS ACTUS QUARTI.

ACTUS QUINTI SCENA PRIMA.

[*A room in Montsurry's house.*]

Montsurry, bare, unbraced,[9] *pulling Ta-*
 myra in by the hair; Friar; One bearing
 light, a standish,[10] *and paper, which* [11]
     sets a table [*and exit*].

TAM. O, help me, father!
FRI.   Impious earl, forbear!

[3] Channel, gutter.   [4] Outflanked.
[5] The conscious earth, considered the center
of the universe.
[6] Blown upon. [7] Storm of my terrifying steps.
[8] Tracks. [9] With his garments unfastened.
[10] Receptacle for pen and ink. [11] Who

Take violent hand from her, or by mine
  order
The king shall force thee.
Mont.   'Tis not violent.—
  Come you not willingly?
Tam.   Yes, good my lord.
Fri. My lord, remember that your soul
  must seek
Her peace, as well as your revengeful
  blood.
You ever to this hour have proved your-
  self
A noble, zealous, and obedient son
T' our Holy Mother; be not an apostate.
Your wife's offense serves not, were it the
  worst   10
You can imagine, without greater proofs,
To sever your eternal bonds and hearts,
Much less to touch her with a bloody
  hand;
Nor is it manly, much less husbandly,
To expiate any frailty in your wife
With churlish strokes or beastly odds of
  strength.
The stony birth of clouds [1] will touch no
  laurel,
Nor any sleeper; your wife is your laurel,
And sweetest sleeper. Do not touch her
  then;
Be not more rude than the wild seed of
  vapor,   20
To her that is more gentle than that rude,
In whom kind nature suffered one offense
But to set off her other excellence.
Mont. Good father, leave us; interrupt no
  more
The course I must run for mine honor
  sake.
Rely on my love to her, which her fault
Cannot extinguish. Will she but disclose
Who was the secret minister of her love,
And through what maze he served it, we
  are friends.
Fri. It is a damned work to pursue those
  secrets   30
That would ope more sin, and prove
  springs of slaughter;
Nor is't a path for Christian feet to tread,
But out of all way to the health of souls,
A sin impossible to be forgiven;
Which he that dares commit—
Mont. Good father, cease your terrors;
Tempt not a man distracted; I am apt

To outrages that I shall ever rue!
I will not pass the verge that bounds a
  Christian,
Nor break the limits of a man nor hus-
  band.   40
Fri. Then Heaven inspire you both with
  thoughts and deeds
Worthy His high respect and your own
  souls.
Tam. Father!
Fri.   I warrant thee, my dearest
  daughter,
He will not touch thee. Think'st thou
  him a pagan?
His honor and his soul lies for thy safety.
                        Exit.
Mont. Who shall remove the mountain
  from my breast,
Stand the opening furnace of my
  thoughts,
And set fit outcries for a soul in hell?
         Mont[surry] turns a key.
For now it nothing fits my woes to speak
But thunder, or to take into my throat 50
The trump of heaven, with whose deter-
  minate [2] blasts
The winds shall burst, and the devouring
  seas
Be drunk up in his sounds; that my hot
  woes,
Vented enough, I might convert to vapor,
Ascending from my infamy unseen,
Shorten the world, preventing [3] the last
  breath
That kills the living and regenerates
  death.
Tam. My lord, my fault (as you may cen-
  sure it
With too strong arguments) is past your
  pardon.
But how the circumstances may excuse
  me   60
Heaven knows, and your more temperate
  mind hereafter
May let my penitent miseries make you
  know.
Mont. Hereafter? 'Tis a supposed infinite,
That from this point will rise eternally.
Fame grows in going; in the scapes of
  virtue
Excuses damn her: they be fires in cities
Enraged with those winds that less lights
  extinguish.

---

[1] I.e., the thunderbolt.

[2] Final.   [3] Anticipating.

Come, siren, sing, and dash against my
　　rocks
Thy ruffian galley, rigged with quench
　　for lust; [1]
Sing, and put all the nets into thy
　　voice　　　　　　　　　　　　　70
With which thou drew'st into thy strum-
　　pet's lap
The spawn of Venus, and in which ye
　　danced,
That, in thy lap's stead, I may dig his
　　tomb,
And quit [2] his manhood with a woman's
　　sleight,
Who never is deceived in her deceit.
Sing (that is, write), and then take from
　　mine eyes
The mists that hide the most inscrutable
　　pander
That ever lapped up an adulterous
　　vomit,
That I may see the devil, and survive
To be a devil, and then learn to wive;　80
That I may hang him, and then cut him
　　down,
Then cut him up, and with my soul's
　　beams search
The cranks [3] and caverns of his brain, and
　　study
The errant wilderness of a woman's face,
Where men cannot get out, for all the
　　comets
That have been lighted at it.　Though
　　they know
That adders lie a-sunning in their smiles,
That basilisks drink their poison from
　　their eyes,
And no way there to coast out to their
　　hearts,
Yet still they wander there, and are not
　　stayed　　　　　　　　　　　　90
Till they be fettered, nor secure before
All cares devour them, nor in human
　　consort
Till they embrace within their wife's two
　　breasts
All Pelion and Cytheron with their
　　beasts.
Why write you not?
TAM.　　　　　　O, good my lord, forbear
In wreak of great faults to engender
　　greater,

And make my love's corruption generate
　　murther.
MONT. It follows needfully as child and
　　parent;
The chain shot of thy lust is yet aloft,
And it must murther; 'tis thine own dear
　　twin.　　　　　　　　　　　　100
No man can add height to a woman's sin.
Vice never doth her just hate so provoke
As when she rageth under virtue's cloak.
Write! For it must be—by this ruthless
　　steel,
By this impartial torture, and the death
Thy tyrannies have invented in my en-
　　trails,
To quicken life in dying, and hold up
The spirits in fainting, teaching to pre-
　　serve
Torments in ashes, that will ever last.
Speak! Will you write?
TAM.　　　　　　Sweet lord, enjoin my sin
Some other penance than what makes it
　　worse.　　　　　　　　　　　111
Hide in some gloomy dungeon my
　　loathed face,
And let condemnéd murtherers let me
　　down
(Stopping their noses) my abhorréd food.
Hang me in chains, and let me eat these
　　arms
That have offended; bind me face to face
To some dead woman, taken from the
　　cart
Of execution, till death and time
In grains of dust dissolve me; I'll endure;
Or any torture that your wrath's in-
　　vention　　　　　　　　　　　120
Can fright all pity from the world withal;
But to betray a friend with show of
　　friendship,
That is too common for the rare revenge
Your rage affecteth.　Here then are my
　　breasts,
Last night your pillows; here my
　　wretched arms,
As late the wishéd confines of your life;
Now break them as you please, and all
　　the bounds
Of manhood, noblesse, and religion.
MONT. Where all these have been broken,
　　they are kept,　　　　　　　　129
In doing their justice there with any show
Of the like cruel cruelty; thine arms have
　　lost

[1] *I.e.*, D'Ambois is to be lured with the desire to
quench his lust.　　[2] Requite.　　[3] Winding paths.

Their privilege in lust, and in their
  torture
Thus they must pay it.   *Stabs her.*
TAM.   O Lord!
MONT.   Till thou writ'st,
  I'll write in wounds (my wrong's fit
    characters)
Thy right of sufferance. Write!
TAM.   O, kill me, kill me!
  Dear husband, be not crueler than death.
  You have beheld some Gorgon; feel, O,
    feel
  How you are turned to stone. With my
    heartblood
  Dissolve yourself again, or you will grow
  Into the image of all tyranny.   140
MONT. As thou art of adultery; I will ever
  Prove thee my parallel, being most a
    monster;
  Thus I express thee yet.[1] *Stabs her again.*
TAM.   And yet I live.
MONT. Ay, for thy monstrous idol is not
    done yet;
  This tool hath wrought enough; now,
    torture, use

Ent[er] Servants.

This other engine[2] on th' habituate
    powers
Of her thrice-damned and whorish forti-
    tude.
Use the most madding pains in her that
    ever
Thy venoms soaked through, making
    most of death,
That she may weigh her wrongs with
    them, and then   150
Stand Vengeance on thy steepest rock, a
    victor.
TAM. O, who is turned into my lord and
    husband?
  Husband! My lord! None but my lord
    and husband!
  Heaven, I ask thee remission of my sins,
  Not of my pains. Husband, O, help me,
    husband!

Ascendit Friar with a sword drawn.

FRI. What rape of honor and religion—
  O, wrack of nature!   *Falls and dies.*
TAM.   Poor man! O, my father!

¹ "Thus I give a further stroke to my delinea-
tion of thee" (Boas).   ² Rack.

Father, look up; O, let me down, my lord,
  And I will write.
MONT.   Author of prodigies!
  What new flame breaks out of the fir-
    mament,   160
  That turns up counsels never known
    before?
  Now is it true earth moves, and heaven
    stands still;
  Even heaven itself must see and suffer
    ill.
  The too huge bias[3] of the world hath
    swayed
  Her backpart upwards, and with that
    she braves
  This hemisphere, that long her mouth
    hath mocked.
  The gravity of her religious face,
  Now grown too weighty with her sacri-
    lege,
  And here discerned sophisticate enough,
  Turns to th' antipodes; and all the
    forms   170
  That her illusions have impressed in her
  Have eaten through her back; and now
    all see
  How she is riveted with hypocrisy.
  Was this the way? Was he the mean be-
    twixt you?
TAM. He was, he was; kind worthy man,
    he was!
MONT. Write, write a word or two.
TAM.   I will, I will.
  I'll write, but with my blood, that he may
    see
  These lines come from my wounds, and
    not from me.   *Writes.*
MONT. Well might he die for thought;
    methinks the frame
  And shaken joints of the whole world
    should crack   180
  To see her parts so disproportionate,
  And that his general beauty cannot
    stand
  Without these stains in the particular
    man.
  Why wander I so far? Here, here was she
  That was a whole world without spot to
    me,
  Though now a world of spots. O, what a
    lightning
  Is man's delight in women! What a
    bubble

³ Slant.

He builds his state, fame, life on, when
    he marries!
Since all earth's pleasures are so short
    and small,
The way t' enjoy it, is t' abjure it all. 190
Enough! I must be messenger myself,
Disguised like this strange creature. In!
    I'll after,
To see what guilty light gives this cave
    eyes,
And to the world sing new impieties.

*Exeunt [Servants]. He puts the Friar in the
vault and follows. She wraps herself in
the arras.*

[SCENA SECUNDA.

Another room in Montsurry's house.]

Enter Monsieur and Guise.

MON. Now shall we see that Nature hath
    no end
In her great works responsive to their
    worths,
That she, that makes so many eyes and
    souls
To see and foresee, is stark blind herself;
And, as illiterate men say Latin prayers
By rote of heart and daily iteration,
Not knowing what they say, so Nature
    lays
A deal of stuff together, and by use,
Or by the mere necessity of matter,
Ends such a work, fills it, or leaves it
    empty 10
Of strength or virtue, error or clear
    truth,
Not knowing what she does; but usually
Gives that which she calls merit to a man,
And belief must arrive [1] him on huge
    riches,
Honor, and happiness, that effects his
    ruin,
Even as in ships of war, whole lasts [2] of
    powder
Are laid, methinks, to make them last
    and guard, [3]
When a disordered spark, that powder
    taking,

[1] Bring.
[2] Measures, in this case of twenty-four barrels.
[3] In ll. 13–17 the 1607 edition reads *wee call*
for *she calls*, *believe* for *beliefe*, *should* for *must*,
Right for *Even*, *men thinke* for *me thinks*, *gard
them* for *guard*. Parrott accepts all the readings
of 1607 as preferable.

Blows up with sudden violence and horror
Ships that, kept empty, had sailed long
    with terror. [4]   20
GUISE. He that observes but like a worldly
    man
That which doth oft succeed, and by th'
    events
Values the worth of things, will think it
    true
That Nature works at random, just with
    you;
But with as much proportion she may
    make
A thing that from the feet up to the
    throat
Hath all the wondrous fabric man should
    have,
And leave it headless, for a perfect man,
As give a full man valor, virtue, learning,
Without an end more excellent than
    those   30
On whom she no such worthy part be-
    stows.
MON. Yet shall you see it here; here will
    be one
Young, learned, valiant, virtuous, and
    full manned—
One on whom Nature spent so rich a
    hand
That with an ominous eye she wept to see
So much consumed her virtuous treas-
    ury. [5]
Yet, as the winds sing through a hollow
    tree
And (since it lets them pass through) lets
    it stand,
But a tree solid (since it gives no way
To their wild rage) they rend up by the
    root,   40
So this whole man
(That will not wind with every crooked
    way,
Trod by the servile world) shall reel and
    fall
Before the frantic puffs of blind-born
    chance,
That pipes through empty men, and
    makes them dance. [6]
Not so the sea raves on the Lybian
    sands,

[4] "Inspiring terror in their enemies" (Boas).
[5] Store of virtues.
[6] Lines 46–53 are adapted from Seneca's
Agamemnon.

Tumbling her billows in each other's
neck;
Not so the surges of the Euxine sea
(Near to the frosty pole, where free
Boötes
From those dark deep waves turns his
radiant team) 50
Swell, being enraged, even from their
inmost drop,
As Fortune swings about the restless
state
Of virtue, now thrown into all men's
hate.

*Enter Montsurry disguised [as the Friar,]
with the Murtherers.*

Away, my lord; you are perfectly dis-
guised;
Leave us to lodge your ambush.
MONT. Speed me, vengeance! *Exit.*
MON. Resolve, my masters, you shall meet
with one
Will try what proofs your privy coats [1]
are made on.
When he is entered, and you hear us
stamp,
Approach, and make all sure. 59
MURTHERERS. We will, my lord. *Exeunt.*

[SCENA TERTIA.

A room in Bussy's house.]

D'Ambois with two Pages with tapers.

BUS. Sit up tonight, and watch; I'll speak
with none
But the old friar, who bring to me.
PAGES. We will, sir. *Exeunt.*
BUS. What violent heat is this? Methinks
the fire
Of twenty lives doth on a sudden flash
Through all my faculties; the air goes
high
In this close chamber, and the frighted
earth *Thunder.*
Trembles, and shrinks beneath me; the
whole house
Nods with his shaken burthen.

Enter Umb[ra] [2] Friar.

Bless me, heaven!
UMB. [FRI.] Note what I want, [3] dear son,
and be forewarned;

O, there are bloody deeds past and to
come. 10
I cannot stay; a fate doth ravish me;
I'll meet thee in the chamber of thy
love. *Exit.*
BUS. What dismal change is here; the good
old friar
Is murthered, being made known to serve
my love;
And now his restless spirit would fore-
warn me
Of some plot dangerous and imminent.
Note what he wants? He wants his upper
weed;
He wants his life and body. Which of
these
Should be the want he means, and may
supply me
With any fit forewarning? This strange
vision 20
(Together with the dark prediction
Used by the Prince of Darkness that was
raised
By this embodied shadow) stir my
thoughts
With reminiscion [4] of the spirit's promise,
Who told me that by any invocation
I should have power to raise him, though
it wanted
The powerful words and decent rites of
art.
Never had my set brain such need of
spirit
T' instruct and cheer it; now, then, I will
claim 29
Performance of his free and gentle vow
T' appear in greater light, and make
more plain
His rugged [5] oracle. I long to know
How my dear mistress fares, and be
informed
What hand she now holds on the troubled
blood
Of her incenséd lord. Methought the
spirit,
When he had uttered his perplexed
presage,
Threw his changed countenance headlong
into clouds;
His forehead bent, as it would hide his
face,
He knocked his chin against his dark-
ened breast,

[1] Secret coats of mail. [2] Shade, ghost. [3] Lack. [4] Remembrance. [5] Unpolished, unfinished.

And struck a churlish silence through his
  powers.   40
Terror of Darkness! O thou King of
  Flames,
That with thy music-footed horse dost
  strike
The clear light out of crystal on dark
  earth,
And hurl'st instructive fire [1] about the
  world,
Wake, wake the drowsy and enchanted
  Night
That sleeps with dead eyes in this heavy
  riddle!
Or, thou great Prince of Shades, where
  never sun
Sticks his far-darted beams, whose eyes
  are made
To shine in darkness, and see ever best
Where men are blindest, open now the
  heart   50
Of thy abashéd oracle, that, for fear
Of some ill it includes, would fain lie hid,
And rise thou with it in thy greater light.

Thunders. *Surgit spiritus cum suis.* [2]

BEH. [3] Thus to observe my vow of appari-
  tion
In greater light, and explicate thy fate,
I come, and tell thee that, if thou obey
The summons that thy mistress next will
  send thee,
Her hand shall be thy death.
BUS.   When will she send?
BEH. Soon as I set again, where late I rose.
BUS. Is the old friar slain?
BEH.   No, and yet lives not. 60
BUS. Died he a natural death?
BEH.   He did.
BUS.   Who then
Will my dear mistress send?
BEH.   I must not tell thee.
BUS. Who lets [4] thee?
BEH.   Fate.
BUS.   Who are Fate's ministers?
BEH. The Guise and Monsieur.
BUS.   A fit pair of shears
To cut the threads of kings and kingly
  spirits,

[1] *I.e.*, the sun's rays.
[2] The spirit rises with his attendants.
[3] In the original this speaker is *Sp.* (for
Spirit), clearly Behemoth, come to fulfill his
promise of IV, ii, 159–62.
[4] Prevents.

And consorts [5] fit to sound forth har-
  mony,
Set to the falls of kingdoms! Shall the
  hand
Of my kind mistress kill me?
BEH.   If thou yield
To her next summons.   Y'are fair-
  warned. Farewell!   *Thunders. Exit.*
BUS. I must fare well, however, though I
  die,   70
My death consenting [6] with his augury.
Should not my powers obey when she
  commands,
My motion must be rebel to my will,
My will to life. If, when I have obeyed,
Her hand should so reward me, they must
  arm it,
Bind me, or force it; or, I lay my life,
She rather would convert it many times
On her own bosom, even to many deaths.
But, were there danger of such violence,
I know 'tis far from her intent to
  send,   80
And who she should send is as far from
  thought,
Since he is dead whose only mean she
  used.   *Knocks.*
Who's there? Look to the door, and let
  him in,
Though politic Monsieur or the violent
  Guise.

*Enter Montsurry, like the Friar, with a
           letter written in blood.*

MONT. Hail to my worthy son!
BUS.   O lying spirit,
To say the friar was dead! I'll now
  believe
Nothing of all his forged predictions.
My kind and honored father, well re-
  vived!
I have been frighted with your death and
  mine,
And told my mistress' hand should be my
  death   90
If I obeyed this summons.
MONT.   I believed
Your love had been much clearer than
  to give
Any such doubt a thought, for she is
  clear,
And, having freed her husband's jealousy

[5] Companions, with a pun on the meaning
concerts.   [6] Agreeing.

(Of which her much abused hand here is
witness),
She prays, for urgent cause, your instant
presence.
Bus. Why, then your Prince of Spirits may
be called
The prince of liars.
Mont. 　　　　　　　Holy Writ so calls him.
Bus. [*Opening the letter.*] What, writ in
blood?
Mont. 　　　　　　Ay, 'tis the ink of lovers.
Bus. O, 'tis a sacred witness of her
love. 　　　　　　　　　　　　　　100
So much elixir of her blood as this,
Dropped in the lightest dame, would
make her firm
As heat to fire, and, like to all the signs,[1]
Commands the life confined in all my
veins.
O, how it multiplies my blood with spirit,
And makes me apt t' encounter death
and hell.
But come, kind father, you fetch me to
heaven,
And to that end your holy weed was
given. 　　　　　　　　　　*Exeunt.*

[Scena Quarta.

Same as Scena Prima.]

Thunder. Intrat[2] *Umbra Friar, and discovers*[3] *Tamyra.*

[Umb.] Fri. Up with these stupid thoughts,
still lovéd daughter,
And strike away this heartless trance of
anguish.
Be like the sun, and labor in eclipses;[4]
Look to the end of woes! O, can you sit
Mustering the horrors of your servant's
slaughter
Before your contemplation, and not
study
How to prevent it? Watch when he shall
rise,
And, with a sudden outcry of his mur-
ther,
Blow[5] his retreat before he be revenged.[6]

[1] Signs of the heavens, the stars.
[2] Enters.
[3] Reveals, unwraps from the arras.
[4] *I.e.*, to throw them off.
[5] Give a signal for.
[6] *I.e.*, before your husband's vengeance overtake him.

Tam. O father, have my dumb woes
waked your death? 　　　　　　10
When will our human griefs be at their
height?
Man is a tree that hath no top in cares,
No root in comforts; all his power to live
Is given to no end, but t' have power to
grieve.
Umb. Fri. It is the misery of our creation.
Your true friend,
Led by your husband, shadowed in my
weed,
Now enters the dark vault.
Tam. 　　　　　　　But, my dearest father,
Why will not you appear to him yourself,
And see that none of these deceits annoy
him? 　　　　　　　　　　　　20
Umb. Fri. My power is limited; alas! I
cannot.
All that I can do—See, the cave opens!
　　　　　　Exit. D'Ambois at the gulf.[7]
Tam. Away, my love, away! Thou wilt be
murthered!

Enter Monsieur and Guise above.

Bus. Murthered? I know not what that
Hebrew means.
That word had ne'er been named had all
been D'Ambois.
Murthered? By heaven, he is my mur-
therer
That shows me not a murtherer; what
such bug[8]
Abhorreth not the very sleep of D'Am-
bois?
Murthered? Who dares give all the room
I see
To D'Ambois' reach, or look with any
odds 　　　　　　　　　　　　30
His fight i' th' face, upon whose hand sits
death,
Whose sword hath wings, and every
feather pierceth?
If I scape Monsieur's pothecary shops,
Foutre[9] for Guise's shambles! 'Twas ill
plotted;
They should have mauled me here
When I was rising. I am up and ready.
Let in my politic visitants; let them in,
Though ent'ring like so many moving
armors.

[7] Cave, vault.
[8] Object of terror, bogey.
[9] A fig (an expression of contempt).

Fate is more strong than arms and sly
  than treason,   39
And I at all parts buckled [1] in my fate.
Mon. ⎫ Why enter not the coward vil-
Guise. ⎭ lains?
Bus. Dare they not come?

Enter Murtherers with [Umbra] Friar at the
other door.

Tam.   They come!
First Mur.   Come all at once!
[Umb.] Fri. Back, coward murtherers,
  back!
Omnes.   Defend us, heaven!
  Exeunt all but the First [Murtherer].
First Mur. Come ye not on?
Bus.   No, slave, nor goest thou off!
  Stand you so firm? [*Strikes at him.*] Will
  it not enter here?
  You have a face yet. [*Kills him.*] So!
  In thy life's flame
  I burn the first rites to my mistress' fame.
Umb. Fri. Breathe thee, brave son, against
  the other charge.
Bus. O, is it true then that my sense first
  told me?
  Is my kind father dead?
Tam.   He is, my love.   50
  'Twas the earl, my husband, in his weed,
  that brought thee.
Bus. That was a speeding sleight,[2] and
  well resembled.
  Where is that angry earl? My lord, come
  forth
  And show your own face in your own
  affair;
  Take not into your noble veins the blood
  Of these base villains, nor the light re-
  ports
  Of blistered tongues for clear and weighty
  truth,
  But me against the world, in pure defense
  Of your rare lady, to whose spotless name
  I stand here as a bulwark, and project 60
  A life to her renown, that ever yet
  Hath been untainted, even in Envy's eye.
  And, where it would protect, a sanctuary,
  Brave earl, come forth, and keep your
  scandal in;
  'Tis not our fault if you enforce the spot,[3]
  Nor the wreak [4] yours, if you perform it
  not.

Enter Mont[surry], with all the Murtherers.

Mont. Cowards, a fiend or spirit beat ye
  off?
  They are your own faint spirits that have
  forged
  The fearful shadows that your eyes
  deluded.
  The fiend was in you; cast him out then,
  thus.   70
[*They fight.*]   *D'Ambois hath Montsurry*
down.
Tam. Favor my lord, my love, O, favor
  him!
Bus. I will not touch him; take your life,
  my lord,
  And be appeased.
Pistols shot within.[5]   [*Bussy is wounded.*]
                  O, then the coward Fates
  Have maimed themselves, and ever lost
  their honor.
Umb. Fri. What have ye done, slaves?
  Irreligious lord!
Bus. Forbear them, father; 'tis enough for
  me
  That Guise and Monsieur, death and
  destiny,
  Come behind D'Ambois. Is my body,
  then,
  But penetrable flesh? And must my
  mind   79
  Follow my blood? Can my divine part
  add
  No aid to th' earthly in extremity?
  Then these divines are but for form, not
  fact.
  Man is of two sweet courtly friends com-
  pact,
  A mistress and a servant; let my death
  Define life nothing but a courtier's
  breath.
  Nothing is made of naught, of all things
  made,
  Their abstract being a dream but of a
  shade.
  I'll not complain to earth yet, but to
  heaven,
  And, like a man, look upwards even in
  death.
  And, if Vespasian thought in majesty   90
  An emperor might die standing, why not
  I?   *She offers to help him.*[6]

----

[1] Armored.   [3] Emphasize the dishonor.
[2] Successful trick.   [4] Vengeance.

[5] In the original this direction follows l. 71.
[6] In the original this direction follows l. 93.

Nay, without help, in which I will exceed
  him;
For he died splinted with [1] his chamber
  grooms.
Prop me, true sword, as thou hast ever
  done!
The equal thought I bear of life and death
Shall make me faint on no side; I am up.
Here like a Roman statue I will stand
Till death hath made me marble. O my
  fame,
Live in despite of murther! Take thy
  wings
And haste thee where the gray-eyed
  Morn perfumes　　　　　　　　　　100
Her rosy chariot with Sabean spices;
Fly where the Evening from th' Iberian
  vales
Takes on her swarthy shoulders Hecate,
Crowned with a grove of oaks; fly where
  men feel
The burning axletree, and those that
  suffer
Beneath the chariot of the snowy Bear; [2]
And tell them all that D'Ambois now is
  hasting
To the eternal dwellers; that a thunder
Of all their sighs together (for their
  frailties
Beheld in me) may quit my worthless [3]
  fall　　　　　　　　　　　　　　110
With a fit volley for my funeral.
UMB. FRI. Forgive thy murtherers.
BUS.　　　　　　　　 I forgive them all,
And you, my lord, their fautor; [4] for true
  sign
Of which unfeigned remission, take my
  sword;
Take it, and only give it motion,
And it shall find the way to victory
By his own brightness, and th' inherent
  valor
My fight hath stilled [5] into 't, with
  charms of spirit.
Now let me pray you that my weighty
  blood,
Laid in one scale of your impartial
  spleen,　　　　　　　　　　　　120
May sway the forfeit of my worthy love
Weighed in the other; and be reconciled

With all forgiveness to your matchless
  wife.
TAM. Forgive thou me, dear servant, and
  this hand
That led thy life to this unworthy end;
Forgive it, for the blood with which 'tis
  stained,
In which I writ the summons of thy
  death
(The forcéd summons) by this bleeding
  wound,
By this here in my bosom, and by this
That makes me hold up both my hands
  imbrued　　　　　　　　　　　130
For thy dear pardon.
BUS.　　　　　　　 O, my heart is broken!
Fate nor these murtherers, Monsieur nor
  the Guise,
Have any glory in my death, but this,
This killing spectacle, this prodigy.
My sun is turned to blood, in whose red
  beams
Pindus and Ossa, hid in drifts of snow
Laid on my heart and liver, from their
  veins
Melt like two hungry torrents, eating
  rocks,
Into the ocean of all human life,
And make it bitter, only with my
  blood.　　　　　　　　　　　　140
O frail condition of strength, valor, vir-
  tue,
In me (like warning fire upon the top
Of some steep beacon on a steeper hill)
Made to express it, like a falling star
Silently glanced [6] that like a thunderbolt
Looked to have stuck [7] and shook the
  firmament.　　　　　　　　 Moritur.[8]
UMB. FRI. Farewell, brave relics of a com-
  plete man!
Look up and see thy spirit made a star;
Join flames with Hercules,[9] and, when
  thou sett'st
Thy radiant forehead in the firma-
  ment,　　　　　　　　　　　　150
Make the vast crystal [10] crack with thy
  receipt;
Spread to a world of fire, and the aged sky
Cheer with new sparks of old humanity.

[1] Supported by.
[2] *I.e.*, equatorial and arctic regions. This
passage is adapted from Seneca, *Hercules Œtæus*.
[3] Unworthy.　　　　[4] Patron.　　　　[5] Instilled.
[6] Glimpsed.
[7] Pierced. Boas conjectures *struck*.
[8] He dies.
[9] From 1607 edn. 1641 edn. has *Jove flames
with her rules.*　　　　[10] Crystalline sphere.

[*To Montsurry.*] Son of the earth, whom my
    unrested soul
  Rues t' have begotten in the faith of
    heaven,
  Assay to gratulate [1] and pacify
  The soul fled from this worthy by per-
    forming
  The Christian reconcilement he besought
  Betwixt thee and thy lady. Let her
    wounds
  Manlessly [2] digged in her, be eased and
    cured   160
  With balm of thine own tears, or be
    assured
  Never to rest free from my haunt and
    horror.
Mon. See how she merits this, still kneel-
    ing by,
  And mourning his fall more than her own
    fault.
Umb. Fri. Remove, dear daughter, and
    content thy husband;
  So piety wills thee, and thy servant's
    peace.
Tam. O wretched piety, that art so distract
  In thine own constancy, and in thy right
  Must be unrighteous! If I right my
    friend,
  I wrong my husband; if his wrong I
    shun,   170
  The duty of my friend I leave undone.
  Ill plays on both sides; here and there it
    riseth;
  No place, no good, so good but ill com-
    priseth.
  O, had I never married but for form,
  Never vowed faith but purposed to de-
    ceive,
  Never made conscience of any sin,
  But cloaked it privately and made it
    common,
  Nor never honored been in blood or
    mind,
  Happy had I been then, as others are
  Of the like license. I had then been
    honored;   180
  Lived without envy; custom had be-
    numbed
  All sense of scruple, and all note of
    frailty;
  My fame had been untouched, my heart
    unbroken;
  But, shunning all, I strike on all offense.

[1] Repay, please.   [2] In an unmanly fashion.

  O husband! Dear friend! O my con-
    science!
Mon. Come, let's away; my senses are not
    proof
  Against those plaints.
Exeunt Guise, Mon[sieur].   D'Ambois is
                                     borne off.
Mont. I must not yield to pity, nor to
    love
  So servile and so traitorous. Cease, my
    blood,
  To wrastle with my honor, fame, and
    judgment.—   190
  Away! Forsake my house; forbear com-
    plaints
  Where thou hast bred them. Here all
    things [are] [3] full
  Of their own shame and sorrow; leave my
    house.
Tam. Sweet lord, forgive me, and I will be
    gone,
  And till these wounds—that never balm
    shall close
  Till death hath entered at them, so I love
    them,
  Being opened by your hands—by death
    be cured,
  I never more will grieve you with my
    sight,
  Never endure that any roof shall part
  Mine eyes and heaven; but to the open
    deserts,   200
  Like to a hunted tigress, I will fly,
  Eating my heart, shunning the steps of
    men,
  And look on no side till I be arrived.
Mont. I do forgive thee, and upon my
    knees,
  With hands held up to heaven, wish that
    mine honor
  Would suffer reconcilement to my love;
  But, since it will not, honor never serve
  My love with flourishing object till it
    sterve! [4]
  And, as this taper, though it upwards
    look,
  Downwards must needs consume, so let
    our love!   210
  As having lost his honey, the sweet taste
  Runs into savor, and will needs retain
  A spice of his first parents, till, like life,
  It sees and dies, so let our love! And
    lastly,

[3] Added by Dilke.   [4] Perish.

As, when the flame is suffered to look up,
It keeps his luster, but, being thus turned
　　down,
His natural course of useful light in-
　　verted,
His own stuff puts it out, so let our
　　love!
Now turn from me, as here I turn from
　　thee,
And may both points of heaven's straight
　　axletree　　　　　　　　　　　　220
Conjoin in one, before thyself and me.

　　　　　　　　　　　Exeunt severally.

FINIS ACTUS QUINTI ET ULTIMI.

WITH many hands you have seen D'Ambois
　　slain,
Yet by your grace he may revive again,
And every day grow stronger in his skill
To please, as we presume he is in will.
The best deserving actors of the time
Had their ascents, and by degrees did climb
To their full height, a place to study due.
To make him tread in their path lies in you;
He'll not forget his makers, but still prove
His thankfulness as you increase your
　　love.

　　　　　　　　　　FINIS.

JOHN WEBSTER

No one has discovered when John Webster was born or when he died. He tells us himself that he was born "free" of the Merchant Tailors' Company, but there is no evidence that he ever followed in his father's footsteps or even attended the Merchant Tailors' School. In fact, his education is as obscure as his birth. Chambers has pointed out that a John Webster acted with an English company in Germany in 1596, and Lucas has tried to identify the dramatist with the John Webster who entered the Middle Temple in 1598 to study law. No certain record of him appears before 1602, however, when Henslowe's Diary shows that he had a part that year in several plays, now lost under the titles given, in which he collaborated in different combinations with Dekker, Drayton, Middleton, Heywood, and others. *Sir Thomas Wyatt*, published in 1607 as by Webster and Dekker, was probably a revised form of one of these plays. It is possible that Webster had only a secondary part in the later plays *Westward Ho* and *Northward Ho*, written with Dekker and probably acted in 1604 and 1605. He merely made slight "additions" to *The Malcontent*. The tragedy *Appius and Virginia*, about the date of which there is a wide difference of opinion, was published in 1654 as Webster's, but critics are now inclined to give Heywood a share in it. There is in all this work nothing to prepare one for the two great tragedies, *The White Devil*, printed in 1612, and *The Duchess of Malfi*, probably produced in 1613–14. After them Webster wrote *The Devil's Law Case*, a tragicomedy in the Fletcherian manner; he mentions a play of *Guise*, now lost; a share in *A Cure for a Cuckold* is doubtfully assigned to him; and in 1624 there is record of a new play by Ford and Webster, which from its title must have been a domestic tragedy. Besides some minor verse, he composed the lord mayor's pageant for 1624. Nothing specific is heard of him after that date. He may have been the John Webster who was buried in 1638.

Critics prefer *The White Devil* or *The Duchess of Malfi* according as they are impressed by the greater plausibility and dramatic effectiveness of the first or the greater poetry and pathos of the second. Both plays are concerned with actual events that occurred in Italy. *The White Devil*, which dramatizes a murder committed in 1585, may have been based on oral reports or on some lost news sheet. At least no printed source is known. *The Duchess of Malfi* came ultimately from a story of Bandello, translated into French by Belleforest in *Histoires tragiques*, and from the French version into English in Painter's *Palace of Pleasure*, which was Webster's direct source. Bandello claimed to have known intimately those involved in the tragedy, and he may even have been the original of the character Delio. To some extent, facts have been altered in both plays to meet the needs of drama, and have been overlaid with conventions of the Elizabethan tragedy of blood. In the treatment of revenge for honor, features of the older revenge plays have been used, but the tool-villain in each case is of the malcontent type, and the Italian characters breathe a spirit only less fraught with deadly passions than those of Marston and Tourneur. *The Duchess of Malfi* has a loosely constructed plot, whose dragging action leads to a climax at the end of the fourth act, only to be prolonged through a fifth. It is chiefly on the characters and the appropriateness and poetic power of their speech that Webster fixed his attention. His interest in humanizing his characters is suggested in a note printed at the end of *The White Devil* praising the actors for their "true imitation of life, without striving to make nature a monster." No doubt some of his power to give appropriate utterances to his characters and to illuminate them with an imaginative flash results from a study of sententious and pictorial language, indicated by his admiration for Seneca and, among his contemporaries, for Chapman, with his "full and heightened style." Occasionally one of his sententious passages can be traced to a classical writer or to a contemporary like Montaigne. Many of the vivid phrases in the scene in which the Duchess of Malfi is tortured and slain are borrowed from Sidney's *Arcadia*. The attention to effective lines is also suggested by the frequency with which Webster repeats the more vivid ones in different plays. In the poetic quality of his style, in his moving reflection on the mysteries of life, and in his understanding of character, Webster is most often compared to Shakespeare. Certainly the full imaginative and creative sweep of Elizabethan drama ends with *The Duchess of Malfi*.

The play was first published in 1623. Other editions followed in 1640, 1678, 1708. The present text is based on the critical edition of the quarto of 1623 printed by Sampson in the Belles-Lettres Series. The edition of the play published by Lucas in *The Complete Works of John Webster* has also been consulted.

THE DUCHESS OF MALFI[1]

BY

JOHN WEBSTER

THE ACTORS' NAMES

[DANIEL DE] BOSOLA [, *gentleman of the horse to the Duchess*]: *J. Lowin.*
FERDINAND [, *Duke of Calabria*]: 1. *R. Burbadge;* 2. *J. Taylor.*
CARDINAL [, *his brother*]: 1. *H. Condell;* 2. *R. Robinson.*
ANTONIO [BOLOGNA, *the Duchess' steward*]: 1. *W. Ostler;* 2. *R. Benfield.*
DELIO [, *his friend*]: *J. Underwood.*
FOROBOSCO[2] [, *an attendant*]: *N. Tooley.*
MALATESTE [, *a count*].
THE MARQUIS OF PESCARA: *J. Rice.*
SILVIO [, *a lord*]: *T. Pollard.*
[CASTRUCHIO, *an old lord*.]

[RODERIGO, *a lord.*]
[GRISOLAN, *a lord.*]
THE SEVERAL MADMEN: *N. Tooley, J. Underwood, etc.*
THE DUCHESS: *R. Sharp.*
[JULIA, *Castruchio's wife and*] the Cardinal's mis[tress]: *J. Thompson.*
DOCTOR ⎫
CARIOLA ⎬ : *R. Pallant.*
COURT OFFICERS ⎭
[OLD LADY.]
THREE YOUNG CHILDREN.
TWO PILGRIMS.
[LADIES, EXECUTIONERS, *and* ATTENDANTS.]

[SCENE: *Italy.*

TIME: *Early sixteenth century.*][3]

ACTUS I. SCENA i.

[*The presence chamber of the Duchess' palace at Amalfi.*]

Antonio and Delio; Bosola, Cardinal.[4]

DEL. You are welcome to your country, dear Antonio;
You have been long in France, and you return

A very formal Frenchman in your habit.
How do you like the French court?
ANT.   I admire it.
In seeking to reduce both state and people
To a fixed order, their judicious king
Begins at home, quits[5] first his royal palace
Of flatt'ring sycophants, of dissolute
And infamous persons, which he sweetly terms
His master's masterpiece, the work of heaven,   10
Consid'ring duly that a prince's court
Is like a common fountain, whence should flow
Pure silver drops in general,[6] but, if 't chance
Some cursed example poison 't near the head,

[1] The complete title reads: "The Tragedy of the Duchess of Malfi. As It Was Presented Privately at the Blackfriars, and Publicly at the Globe, by the King's Majesty's Servants. The Perfect and Exact Copy, with Divers Things Printed That the Length of the Play Would not Bear in the Presentment. Written by John Webster."
[2] In the printed version of the play this character does not speak.
[3] A dedication to George Harding, Baron Berkeley, and commendatory verses by Thomas Middleton, William Rowley, and John Ford are omitted in the present edition.
[4] Last two enter later.
[5] Clears.   [6] Without exception.

773

"Death and diseases through the whole
   land spread." [1]
And what is 't makes this blessed govern-
   ment
But a most provident council, who dare
   freely
Inform him the corruption of the times?
Though some o' th' court hold it pre-
   sumption
To instruct princes what they ought to
   do,   20
It is a noble duty to inform them
What they ought to foresee.—Here
   comes Bosola,
The only court-gall.

[Enter Bosola.]

         Yet I observe his railing
Is not for simple love of piety.
Indeed, he rails at those things which he
   wants,
Would be as lecherous, covetous, or
   proud,
Bloody, or envious as any man,
If he had means to be so.—Here's the
   cardinal.

[Enter Cardinal.]

Bos. I do haunt you still.
Card. So.   30
Bos.[2] I have done you better service
than to be slighted thus. Miserable age,
where only the reward of doing well is the
doing of it!
Card. You enforce your merit too much.
Bos. I fell into the galleys in your service, where, for two years together, I wore
two towels instead of a shirt, with a knot on
the shoulder, after the fashion of a Roman
mantle. Slighted thus! I will thrive [40
some way. Blackbirds fatten best in
hard weather; why not I in these dog
days?
Card. Would you could become honest!
Bos. With all your divinity, do but
direct me the way to it. I have known many
travel far for it, and yet return as arrant
knaves as they went forth, because they

carried themselves always along with them.
[Exit Cardinal.] Are you gone? Some [50
fellows, they say, are possessed with the
devil, but this great fellow were able to
possess the greatest devil, and make him
worse.
Ant. He hath denied thee some suit?
Bos. He and his brother are like plum
trees that grow crooked over standing
pools; they are rich and o'erladen with
fruit, but none but crows, pies, and caterpillars feed on them. Could I be one [60
of their flatt'ring panders, I would hang
on their ears like a horseleech, till I were
full, and then drop off. I pray, leave me.
Who would rely upon these miserable
dependences, in expectation to be advanced tomorrow? What creature ever
fed worse than hoping Tantalus? Nor
ever died [3] any man more fearfully than
he that hoped for a pardon.[3] There are
rewards for hawks and dogs when [4] [70
they have done us service; but, for a soldier
that hazards his limbs in a battle, nothing
but a kind of geometry is his last supporta-
tion.
Del. Geometry?
Bos. Ay, to hang in a fair pair of slings,
take his latter swing in the world upon
an honorable pair of crutches, from hospital to hospital. Fare ye well, sir. And
yet do not you scorn us, for places in [80
the court are but like beds in the hospital,
where this man's head lies at that man's
foot, and so lower and lower. *[Exit.]*
Del. I knew this fellow seven years in
   the galleys
For a notorious murther; and 'twas
   thought
The cardinal suborned it. He was released
By the French general, Gaston de Foix,[5]
When he recovered Naples.
Ant.   'Tis great pity
He should be thus neglected. I have
   heard
He's very valiant. This foul melancholy   90
Will poison all his goodness; for, I'll
   tell you,

---

[1] Sententious passages set off in the original
with quotation marks or italics are here indicated throughout by quotation marks.

[2] All prose passages in the play were originally
printed as irregular verse.

[3] Readings from 1640 edn. Original reads *did*
and *pleadon*.

[4] From 1640 edn. Earlier edns. read *and when*.

[5] Original reads *Foux*.

If too immoderate sleep be truly said
To be an inward rust unto the soul,
It then doth follow want of action
Breeds all black malcontents; and their
　close rearing,
Like moths in cloth, do hurt for want of
　wearing.[1]

Scena ii.
[*The same.*]

*Antonio, Delio, Ferdinand,[2] Cardinal,[2]
Duchess,[2] Castruchio, Silvio, Roderigo,
Grisolan, Bosola, Julia,[2] Cariola.[2]*

Del. The presence gins [3] to fill. You prom-
　ised me
To make me the partaker of the natures
Of some of your great courtiers.
Ant.　　　　　The lord cardinal's
And other strangers' that are now in
　court?
I shall.—Here comes the great Calabrian
　duke.

[*Enter Ferdinand and Attendants.*]

Ferd. Who took the ring oft'nest? [4]
Sil. Antonio Bologna, my lord.
Ferd. Our sister duchess' great master
of her household? Give him the jewel.—
When shall we leave this sportive ac-　[10
tion, and fall to action indeed?
Cast. Methinks, my lord, you should
not desire to go to war in person.
Ferd. [*Aside.*] Now for some gravity.—
Why, my lord?
Cast. It is fitting a soldier arise to be a
prince, but not necessary a prince descend
to be a captain.
Ferd. No?
Cast. No, my lord; he were far bet-　[20
ter do it by a deputy.
Ferd. Why should he not as well sleep
or eat by a deputy? This might take idle,
offensive, and base office from him, whereas
the other deprives him of honor.
Cast. Believe my experience: that realm
is never long in quiet where the ruler is a
soldier.
Ferd. Thou told'st me thy wife could
not endure fighting—　　　　　　30

[1] The scene division throughout appears to be
purely artificial, since the action continues without pause.　　　[3] Begins.
[2] Enters later.　[4] *I.e.*, in the tilting at the ring.

Cast. True, my lord.
Ferd. And of a jest she broke [5] of a captain she met full of wounds—I have forgot
it.
Cast. She told him, my lord, he was a
pitiful fellow, to lie, like the children of
Ismael, all in tents.[6]
Ferd. Why, there's a wit were able to
undo all the chirurgeons [7] o' the city, for,
although gallants should quarrel, and　[40
had drawn their weapons, and were ready
to go to it, yet her persuasions would make
them put up.
Cast. That she would, my lord.—How
do you like my Spanish jennet?
Rod. He is all fire.
Ferd. I am of Pliny's opinion; I think
he was begot by the wind; he runs as if he
were ballast with quicksilver.
Sil. True, my lord, he reels from　[50
the tilt often.
Rod.　⎫
Gris.　⎬ Ha, ha, ha!
　　　⎭
Ferd. Why do you laugh? Methinks you
that are courtiers should be my touchwood—
take fire when I give fire; that is, laugh when
I laugh, were the subject never so witty.
Cast. True, my lord; I myself have
heard a very good jest, and have scorned to
seem to have so silly a wit as to understand
it.　　　　　　　　　　　　　　　60
Ferd. But I can laugh at your fool, my
lord.
Cast. He cannot speak, you know, but
he makes faces. My lady cannot abide him.
Ferd. No?
Cast. Nor endure to be in merry company; for she says too much laughing and
too much company fills her too full of the
wrinkle.
Ferd. I would, then, have a mathe-　[70
matical instrument made for her face, that
she might not laugh out of compass.—I
shall shortly visit you at Milan, Lord
Silvio.
Sil. Your grace shall arrive most welcome.
Ferd. You are a good horseman, Antonio; you have excellent riders in France.
What do you think of good horsemanship?
Ant. Nobly, my lord. As out of　[80

[5] Told.
[6] With a pun on the meaning *lint*, for dressing
wounds.　　　　　　　[7] Surgeons.

the Grecian horse issued many famous princes, so out of brave horsemanship arise the first sparks of growing resolution, that raise the mind to noble action.

FERD. You have bespoke it worthily.

SIL. Your brother, the lord cardinal, and sister duchess.

[Enter Cardinal, Duchess, Cariola, and Julia.]

CARD. Are the galleys come about?

GRIS.   They are, my lord.

FERD. Here's the Lord Silvio, is come to take his leave.

DEL. [*Aside to Antonio.*] Now, sir, your promise. What's that cardinal?   90 I mean his temper. They say he's a brave fellow, Will play his five thousand crowns at tennis, dance, Court ladies, and one that hath fought single combats.

ANT. Some such flashes superficially hang on him for form, but, observe his inward character, he is a melancholy churchman. The spring in his face is nothing but the engend'ring of toads; where he is jealous of any man, he lays worse plots for them than ever was imposed [100 on Hercules, for he strews in his way flatter[er]s, panders, intelligencers,[1] atheists, and a thousand such political monsters. He should have been pope; but, instead of coming to it by the primitive decency of the church, he did bestow bribes so largely and so impudently as if he would have carried it away without heaven's knowledge. Some good he hath done—

DEL. You have given too much of him. What's his brother?   110

ANT. The duke there? A most perverse and turbulent nature. What appears in him mirth is merely outside; If he laugh heartily, it is to laugh All honesty out of fashion.

DEL.   Twins?

ANT.   In quality. He speaks with others' tongues, and hears men's suits With others' ears; will seem to sleep o' th' bench Only to entrap offenders in their answers;

Dooms men to death by information;[2] Rewards by hearsay.

DEL.   Then the law to him Is like a foul, black cobweb to a spider—   120 He makes it his dwelling and a prison To entangle those shall feed him.

ANT.   Most true. He never pays debts unless they be shrewd[3] turns, And those he will confess that he doth owe. Last, for his brother there, the cardinal, They that do flatter him most say oracles Hang at his lips; and verily I believe them, For the devil speaks in them. But for their sister, the right noble duchess, You never fixed your eye on three fair medals   130 Cast in one figure,[4] of so different temper. For her discourse, it is so full of rapture, You only will begin then to be sorry When she doth end her speech, and wish, in wonder, She held it less vainglory to talk much Than your penance to hear her. Whilst she speaks, She throws upon a man so sweet a look That it were able raise one to a galliard That lay in a dead palsy, and to dote On that sweet countenance; but in that look   140 There speaketh so divine a continence As cuts off all lascivious and vain hope. Her days are practiced in such noble virtue That sure her nights, nay, more, her very sleeps, Are more in heaven than other ladies' shrifts. Let all sweet ladies break their flatt'ring glasses, And dress themselves in her.

DEL.   Fie, Antonio, You play the wire-drawer with her commendations.[5]

ANT. I'll case the picture up only thus much—

---

[2] Informer's evidence.
[3] From 1640 edn. Original has *shewed*.
[4] Mold.
[5] You draw her praises out at great length.

[1] Spies.

All her particular worth grows to this
　　sum:　　　　　　　　　　　　　150
She stains [1] the time past, lights the time
　　to come.
Cari. You must attend my lady in the gal-
　　lery
Some half an hour hence.
Ant. I shall.
　　　　　　　　[*Exeunt Antonio and Delio.*]
Ferd. Sister, I have a suit to you.
Duch.　　　　　　　　　　To me, sir?
Ferd. A gentlemen here, Daniel de
　　Bosola,
One that was in the galleys—
Duch.　　　　　　　Yes, I know him.
Ferd. A worthy fellow h' is; pray, let me
　　entreat for
The provisorship [2] of your horse.
Duch.　　　　　Your knowledge of him
Commends him and prefers him.
Ferd.　　　　　　　　Call him hither.
　　　　　　　　　　[*Exeunt Attendants.*]
We now upon [3] parting, good Lord
　　Silvio,　　　　　　　　　　　161
Do us commend to all our noble friends
At the leaguer.[4]
Sil.　　　　　　Sir, I shall.
Ferd.[5]　　　　　　You are for Milan?
Sil. I am.
Duch. Bring the caroches.[6]—We'll bring
　　you down to the haven.

[*Exeunt all except Cardinal and Ferdinand.*]

Card. Be sure you entertain that Bosola
For your intelligence.[7] I would not be
　　seen in 't;
And therefore many times I have slighted
　　him
When he did court our furtherance, as
　　this morning.
Ferd. Antonio, the great master of her
　　household,　　　　　　　　　　170
Had been far fitter.
Card.　　　You are deceived in him.
His nature is too honest for such busi-
　　ness.—
He comes; I'll leave you.　　　[*Exit.*]

[1] "Deprives of luster" (Lucas).
[2] Office of purveyor.
[3] At the point of.
[4] Camp. From 1640 edn.; original reads
leagues.
[5] Sampson assigns this speech to the Duchess.
[6] Coaches.
[7] Information from spies.

[*Enter Bosola.*]

Bos.　　　　　　　　I was lured [8] to you.
Ferd. My brother here, the cardinal,
　　could never
Abide you.
Bos.　　　Never since he was in my debt.
Ferd. May be some oblique character in
　　your face
Made him suspect you.
Bos.　　　Doth he study physiognomy?
There's no more credit to be given to th'
　　face
Than to a sick man's urine, which some
　　call
The physician's whore, because she
　　cozens him.　　　　　　　　　180
He did suspect me wrongfully.
Ferd.　　　　　　　　　For that
You must give great men leave to take
　　their times.
Distrust doth cause us seldom be de-
　　ceived.
You see, the oft shaking of the cedar tree
Fastens it more at root.
Bos.　　　　　　　　Yet take heed,
For to suspect a friend unworthily
Instructs him the next way to suspect
　　you,
And prompts him to deceive you.
Ferd.　　　　　　　　There's gold.
Bos.　　　　　　　　　　　　So!
What follows? Never rained such
　　showers as these
Without thunderbolts i' th' tail of
　　them. Whose throat must I cut?
Ferd. Your inclination to shed blood rides
　　post [9]　　　　　　　　　　　191
Before my occasion to use you. I give
　　you that
To live i' th' court here, and observe the
　　duchess;
To note all the particulars of her havior,
What suitors do solicit her for marriage,
And whom she best affects.[10] She's a
　　young widow;
I would not have her marry again.
Bos.　　　　　　　　　　No, sir?
Ferd. Do not you ask the reason, but be
　　satisfied.
I say I would not.
Bos.　　　It seems you would create me
One of your familiars.

[8] Called.　　　[9] At full speed.　　　[10] **Likes.**

FERD.   Familiar! What's that?

Bos. Why, a very quaint invisible devil in
   flesh—   201
   An intelligencer.

FERD.   Such a kind of thriving thing
   I would wish thee; and ere long thou
   mayst arrive
   At a higher place by 't.

Bos.   Take your devils,
   Which hell calls angels![1] These cursed
   gifts would make
   You a corrupter, me an impudent traitor;
   And, should I take these, they'ld take
   me [to][2] hell.

FERD. Sir, I'll take nothing from you that
   I have given.
   There is a place that I procured for you
   This morning, the provisorship o' th'
   horse.   210
   Have you heard on 't?

Bos.   No.

FERD.   'Tis yours. Is 't not
   worth thanks?

Bos. I would have you curse yourself now,
   that your bounty
   (Which makes men truly noble) e'er
   should make me
   A villain. O, that to avoid ingratitude
   For the good deed you have done me, I
   must do
   All the ill man can invent! Thus the
   devil
   Candies all sins o'er;[3] and what heaven
   terms vild,[4]
   That names he complimental.

FERD.   Be yourself;
   Keep your old garb of melancholy. 'Twill
   express
   You envy those that stand above your
   reach,   220
   Yet strive not to come near 'em. This
   will gain
   Access to private lodgings, where yourself
   May, like a politic dormouse—

Bos.   As I have seen some
   Feed in a lord's dish, half asleep, not
   seeming
   To listen to any talk; and yet these
   rogues
   Have cut his throat in a dream. What's
   my place?

[1] Gold coins.   [2] From 1708 edn.
[3] From 1640 edn. Original reads are.
[4] Vile.

The provisorship o' th' horse? Say, then,
   my corruption
   Grew out of horse dung. I am your
   creature.

FERD.   Away!

Bos. [Aside.] Let good men, for good
   deeds, covet good fame,
   Since place and riches oft are bribes of
   shame.   230
   Sometimes the devil doth preach.
                         Exit Bosola.[5]

[Enter Duchess, Cardinal, and Cariola.]

CARD. We are to part from you, and your
   own discretion
   Must now be your director.

FERD.   You are a widow:
   You know already what man is; and
   therefore
   Let not youth, high promotion, eloquence—

CARD. No, nor anything without the addition,[6] Honor,
   Sway your high blood.

FERD.   Marry! They
   are most luxurious[7]
   Will wed twice.

CARD.   O, fie!

FERD.   Their livers[8] are
   more spotted
   Than Laban's sheep.

DUCH.   Diamonds are of most value,
   They say, that have passed through most
   jewelers' hands.   240

FERD. Whores by that rule are precious.

DUCH.   Will you hear me?
   I'll never marry.

CARD.   So most widows say;
   But commonly that motion[9] lasts no
   longer
   Than the turning of an hourglass—the
   funeral sermon
   And it end both together.

FERD.   Now hear me:
   You live in a rank pasture, here, i' th'
   court.
   There is a kind of honeydew that's
   deadly;

[5] With no indication of scene division the
scene apparently shifts slowly to the gallery of
the palace.
[6] Title.   [8] Seat of love.
[7] Lecherous.   [9] Intention.

'Twill poison your fame; look to 't. Be
　not cunning,
For they whose faces do belie their
　hearts
Are witches ere they arrive at twenty
　years—　　　　　　　　　　　　250
Ay, and give the devil suck.

Duch. This is terrible good counsel.

Ferd. Hypocrisy is woven of a fine, small
　thread,
Subtler than Vulcan's engine; [1] yet, be-
　lieve 't,
Your darkest actions, nay, your privat'st
　thoughts,
Will come to light.

Card.　　　　You may flatter yourself,
And take your own choice; privately be
　married
Under the eaves of night—

Ferd.　　　　Think 't the best voyage
That e'er you made, like the irregular
　crab,
Which, though 't goes backward, thinks
　that it goes right　　　　　　　260
Because it goes its own way. But ob-
　serve,
Such weddings may more properly be
　said
To be executed than celebrated.

Card.　　　　The marriage night
Is the entrance into some prison.

Ferd.　　　　And those joys,
Those lustful pleasures, are like heavy
　sleeps
Which do forerun man's mischief.

Card.　　　　Fare you well.
Wisdom begins at the end; remember it.
　　　　　　　　　　　　[Exit.]

Duch. I think this speech between you
　both was studied,
It came so roundly off.

Ferd.　　　　You are my sister.
This was my father's poniard, do you
　see?　　　　　　　　　　　　270
I'ld be loath to see 't look rusty, cause
　'twas his.
I would have you to give o'er these
　chargeable [2] revels;
A visor and a mask are whispering-
　rooms [3]
That were never built for goodness—
　fare ye well—

And women like that part which, like the
　lamprey,
Hath never a bone in 't.

Duch.　　　　　　　　Fie, sir!

Ferd.　　　　　　　　　　Nay,
I mean the tongue—variety of courtship.
What cannot a neat knave with a smooth
　tale
Make a woman believe? Farewell, lusty
　widow.　　　　　　　　　[Exit.]

Duch. Shall this move me? If all my royal
　kindred　　　　　　　　　　280
Lay in my way unto this marriage,
I'ld make them my low footsteps. [4] And
　even now,
Even in this hate, as men in some great
　battles,
By apprehending [5] danger, have achieved
Almost impossible actions (I have heard
　soldiers say so),
So I through frights and threat'nings will
　assay
This dangerous venture. Let old wives
　report
I winked [6] and chose a husband.—
　Cariola,
To thy known secrecy I have given up
More than my life—my fame.

Cari.　　　　Both shall be safe,　290
For I'll conceal this secret from the world
As warily as those that trade in poison
Keep poison from their children.

Duch.　　　　　　　Thy protestation
Is ingenious and hearty; [7] I believe it.
Is Antonio come?

Cari.　　　　He attends [8] you.

Duch.　　　　　　　Good dear soul,
Leave me, but place thyself behind the
　arras,
Where thou mayst overhear us. Wish
　me good speed,
　　　[Cariola hides behind the arras.]
For I am going into a wilderness
Where I shall find nor path nor friendly
　clew　　　　　　　　　　　299
To be my guide.—

　　　　　[Enter Antonio.]

　　　　　I sent for you; sit down.
Take pen and ink, and write. Are you
　ready?

[1] Device; here, a net.　　　　　[2] Costly.
[3] Private chambers.
[4] Rungs of a ladder.
[5] Grasping.　　　　　　　　　[6] Shut my eyes.
[7] Ingenuous and from the heart　[8] Awaits.

Ant.   Yes.

Duch. What did I say?

Ant. That I should write somewhat.

Duch.   O, I remember.
After these triumphs [1] and this large ex-
    pense
It's fit, like thrifty husbands,[2] we inquire
What's laid up for tomorrow.

Ant. So please your beauteous excellence.

Duch. Beauteous? Indeed, I thank you.
I look young for your sake;
You have ta'en my cares upon you.

Ant.   I'll fetch your grace [3]
The particulars of your revenue and
    expense.   310

Duch. O, you are an upright treasurer,
    but you mistook;
For, when I said I meant to make inquiry
What's laid up for tomorrow, I did mean
What's laid up yonder for me.

Ant.   Where?

Duch.   In heaven.
I am making my will (as 'tis fit princes
    should,
In perfect memory), and, I pray, sir, tell
    me,
Were not one better make it smiling,
    thus,
Than in deep groans and terrible ghastly
    looks,
As if the gifts we parted with procured [4]
That violent destruction? [5]

Ant.   O, much better.

Duch. If I had a husband now, this care
    were quit.   321
But I intend to make you overseer.[6]
What good deed shall we first remember?
    Say.

Ant. Begin with that first good deed began
    i' th' world
After man's creation, the sacrament of
    marriage.
I'ld have you first provide for a good
    husband;
Give him all.

Duch.   All?

Ant.   Yes, your excellent self.

[1] Festivities. Original misprints *this triumphs*.
[2] Housekeepers.
[3] Here and in a few other passages the line
division has been regularized.
[4] Produced.
[5] 1708 edn. prints *distraction*.
[6] *I.e.*, of the will. Double meanings run
throughout this passage.

Duch. In a winding sheet?

Ant.   In a couple.

Duch. Saint Winfrid, that were a strange
    will!

Ant.   'Twere strange
If there were no will in you to marry
    again.   330

Duch. What do you think of mar-
    riage?

Ant. I take 't, as those that deny purga-
    tory,
It locally contains or heaven or hell;
There's no third place in 't.

Duch.   How do you affect it?

Ant. My banishment, feeding my melan-
    choly,
Would often reason thus:—

Duch.   Pray, let's hear it.

Ant. Say a man never marry nor have
    children,
What takes that from him? Only the
    bare name
Of being a father, or the weak delight
To see the little wanton ride a cockhorse
Upon a painted stick, or hear him
    chatter   341
Like a taught starling.

Duch.   Fie, fie, what's all this?
One of your eyes is bloodshot. Use my
    ring to 't;
They say 'tis very sovereign. 'Twas my
    wedding ring,
And I did vow never to part with it
But to my second husband.

Ant. You have parted with it now.

Duch. Yes, to help your eyesight.

Ant. You have made me stark blind.

Duch. How?   350

Ant. There is a saucy and ambitious
    devil
Is dancing in this circle.

Duch.   Remove him.

Ant.   How?

Duch. There needs small conjuration
    when your finger
May do it: thus. [*She puts the ring upon
    his finger.*] Is it fit?

Ant.   What said you? *He kneels.*

Duch.   Sir,
This goodly roof of yours is too low built;
I cannot stand upright in 't nor discourse,
Without I raise it higher. Raise yourself;
Or, if you please, my hand to help you—so.
                        [*Raises him.*]

Ant. Ambition, madam, is a great man's madness,
That is not kept in chains and close-pent rooms, 360
But in fair, lightsome lodgings, and is girt
With the wild noise of prattling visitants,
Which makes it lunatic beyond all cure.
Conceive not I am so stupid but I aim [1]
Whereto your favors tend; but he's a fool
That, being acold, would thrust his hands i' th' fire
To warm them.
Duch. So, now the ground's broke,
You may discover what a wealthy mine
I make you lord of.
Ant. O, my unworthiness!
Duch. You were ill to sell yourself. 370
This dark'ning of your worth is not like that
Which tradesmen use i' th' city; their false lights
Are to rid bad wares off; and I must tell you,
If you will know where breathes a complete man
(I speak it without flattery), turn your eyes,
And progress through yourself.
Ant. Were there nor heaven nor hell,
I should be honest. I have long served virtue,
And never ta'en wages of her.
Duch. Now she pays it.
The misery of us that are born great!
We are forced to woo,[2] because none dare woo [2] us; 381
And, as a tyrant doubles with his words
And fearfully equivocates, so we
Are forced to express our violent passions
In riddles and in dreams, and leave the path
Of simple virtue, which was never made
To seem the thing it is not. Go, go brag
You have left me heartless; mine is in your bosom.
I hope 'twill multiply love there. You do tremble.
Make not your heart so dead a piece of flesh, 390

[1] Guess.
[2] Original spelling is *woe* with double meaning.

To fear more than to love me. Sir, be confident.
What is 't distracts you? This is flesh and blood, sir;
'Tis not the figure cut in alablaster [3]
Kneels at my husband's tomb. Awake, awake, man!
I do here put off all vain ceremony,
And only do appear to you a young widow
That claims you for her husband, and, like a widow,
I use but half a blush in 't.
Ant. Truth speak for me;
I will remain the constant sanctuary
Of your good name.
Duch. I thank you, gentle love, 400
And, cause you shall not come to me in debt,
Being now my steward, here upon your lips
I sign your *Quietus est.*[4] This you should have begged now.
I have seen children oft eat sweetmeats thus,
As fearful to devour them too soon.
Ant. But for your brothers?
Duch. Do not think of them.
All discord without this circumference
[*Puts her arms about him.*]
Is only to be pitied, and not feared.
Yet, should they know it, time will easily
Scatter the tempest.
Ant. These words should be mine,
And all the parts you have spoke, if some part of it 411
Would not have savored flattery.
Duch. Kneel!
[*Cariola discloses herself.*]
Ant. Ha!
Duch. Be not amazed. This woman's of my counsel.
I have heard lawyers say a contract in a chamber
Per verba [*de*] *presenti* [5] is absolute marriage. [*She and Antonio kneel.*]
Bless, heaven, this sacred Gordian,[6] which let violence
Never untwine. [*They rise.*]

[3] Common corrupt pronunciation of *alabaster*.
[4] He is acquitted of his obligations (an accountant's term).
[5] Using words (*i.e.*, vows) in the present tense: I take thee. etc.
[6] Knot.

ANT. And may our sweet affections, like
  the spheres,
  Be still [1] in motion!
DUCH.   Quick'ning, and make
  The like soft music!   420
ANT. That we may imitate the loving palms,
  Best emblem of a peaceful marriage,
  That never bore fruit, divided!
DUCH. What can the church force more?
ANT. That fortune may not know an acci-
  dent,
  Either of joy or sorrow, to divide
  Our fixéd wishes!
DUCH.   How can the church build faster?[2]
  We now are man and wife, and 'tis the
  church
  That must but echo this.[3]—Maid, stand
  apart.—
  I now am blind.
ANT.   What's your conceit [4] in this?
DUCH. I would have you lead your fortune
  by the hand   431
  Unto your marriage bed.
  (You speak in me this, for we now are one.)
  We'll only lie and talk together, and plot
  T' appease my humorous [5] kindred; and,
  if you please,
  Like the old tale in *Alexander and Lodo-
  wick*,
  Lay a naked sword between us, keep us
  chaste.
  O, let me shroud my blushes in your
  bosom,
  Since 'tis the treasury of all my secrets!
CARI. [*Aside.*] Whether the spirit of great-
  ness or of woman   440
  Reign most in her, I know not; but it
  shows
  A fearful madness. I owe her much of
  pity.   *Exeunt.*

ACTUS II. SCENA i.

[*An apartment in the Duchess' palace.*]

*Bosola, Castruchio, an Old Lady, Antonio,
  Delio, Duchess, Roderigo, Grisolan.*[6]

BOS. You say you would fain be taken
for an eminent courtier? [7]

CAST. 'Tis the very main [8] of my ambition.
  BOS. Let me see. You have a reasonable good face for 't already, and your
nightcap [9] expresses your ears sufficient
largely. I would have you learn to twirl
the strings of your band with a good grace,
and in a set speech, at th' end of every
sentence, to hum three or four times, [11
or blow your nose till it smart again, to
recover your memory. When you come
to be a president in criminal causes, if
you smile upon a prisoner, hang him; but,
if you frown upon him and threaten
him, let him be sure to scape the gallows.
  CAST. I would be a very merry president.   20
  BOS. Do not sup a-nights; 'twill beget
you an admirable wit.
  CAST. Rather it would make me have
a good stomach to quarrel; for they say
your roaring boys [10] eat meat seldom, and
that makes them so valiant. But how shall
I know whether the people take me for an
eminent fellow?   28
  BOS. I will teach a trick to know it.
Give out you lie a-dying, and, if you hear
the common people curse you, be sure you
are taken for one of the prime nightcaps.—

[*Enter an Old Lady.*]

You come from painting now?
  OLD LADY. From what?
  BOS. Why, from your scurvy face-
physic. To behold thee not painted inclines somewhat near a miracle. These in
thy face here were deep ruts and foul
sloughs the last progress.[11] There was
a lady in France that, having had the [40
small-pox, flayed the skin off her face to
make it more level; and, whereas before
she looked like a nutmeg-grater, after
she resembled an abortive hedgehog.
  OLD LADY. Do you call this painting?
  BOS. No, no, but you call [it] [12] carcen-
ing [13] of an old morphewed [14] lady, to make
her disembogue [15] again. There's rough-cast
phrase to your plastic.[16]

---

[1] Always.   [2] More firmly.
[3] Ordinarily it was expected that the church
ceremony should follow such a marriage.
[4] Idea.   [5] Temperamental.
[6] All but the first two enter later.
[7] Member of a law court.

[8] Goal.
[9] Lawyer's coif.   [11] Royal journey.
[10] Rowdies.   [12] Supplied from 1678 edn.
[13] Turning a boat on its side for repairs.
[14] Scabbed.   [15] Put to sea.   [16] Modeling.

OLD LADY. It seems you are well ac- [50
quainted with my closet.

BOS. One would suspect it for a shop of
witchcraft, to find in it the fat of serpents, spawn of snakes, Jews' spittle,
and their young children['s] ordures; and
all these for the face. I would sooner eat
a dead pigeon taken from the soles of the
feet of one sick of the plague than kiss one
of you fasting. Here are two of you whose
sin of your youth is the very patrimony [60
of the physician; makes him renew his footcloth with the spring, and change his high-
priced courtesan with the fall of the leaf.
I do wonder you do not loathe yourselves.
Observe my meditation now.

What thing is in this outward form of
　　man
To be beloved? We account it ominous
If nature do produce a colt, or lamb,
A fawn, or goat, in any limb resembling
A man, and fly from 't as a prodigy.
Man stands amazed to see his deformity
In any other creature but himself. 72
But in our own flesh, though we bear
　　diseases
Which have their true names only ta'en
　　from beasts,
As the most ulcerous wolf [1] and swinish
　　measle;
Though we are eaten up of lice and
　　worms;
And though continually we bear about
　　us
A rotten and dead body, we delight
To hide it in rich tissue. All our fear,
Nay, all our terror, is lest our physician
Should put us in the ground to be made
　　sweet.—　　　　　　　　　　　81
Your wife's gone to Rome; you two
　　couple; and get you
To the wells at Lucca to recover your
　　aches.
I have other work on foot.

　　　[Exeunt Castruchio and Old Lady.]
I observe our duchess
Is sick a-days. She pukes, her stomach
　　seethes,
The fins [2] of her eyelids look most teem-
　　ing blue,[3]

---

[1] Lupus (Lat. for *wolf*) is a medical term for
ulcer.
[2] Rims.
[3] Blue like those of a pregnant woman.

She wanes i' th' cheek, and waxes fat i'
　　th' flank,
And, contrary to our Italian fashion,
Wears a loose-bodied gown. There's
　　somewhat in 't.　　　　　　　90
I have a trick may chance discover it,
A pretty one; I have bought some ap-
　　ricocks,
The first our spring yields.

　　　　[Enter Antonio and Delio.]

DEL. [Aside to Antonio.]　　And so long
　　since married?
You amaze me.
ANT. [Aside to Delio.]　　　Let me seal
　　your lips forever,
For, did I think that anything but th' air
Could carry these words from you, I
　　should wish
You had no breath at all.—[To Bosola.]
　　Now, sir, in your contemplation?
You are studying to become a great
　　wise fellow?
BOS. O, sir, the opinion of wisdom is a
foul tetter that runs all over a man's [100
body. If simplicity direct us to have no
evil, it directs us to a happy being, for the
subtlest folly proceeds from the subtlest
wisdom. Let me be simply honest.
ANT. I do understand your inside.
BOS.　　　　　　　　Do you so?
ANT. Because you would not seem to ap-
　　pear to th' world
Puffed up with your preferment, you
　　continue
This out-of-fashion melancholy. Leave
　　it, leave it!
BOS. Give me leave to be honest in any
phrase, in any compliment whatsoever. [110
Shall I confess myself to you? I look no
higher than I can reach. They are the
gods that must ride on winged horses;
a lawyer's mule of a slow pace will both suit
my disposition and business; for, mark me,
when a man's mind rides faster than his
horse can gallop, they quickly both tire.
ANT. You would look up to heaven, but I
　　think
The devil, that rules i' th' air, stands
　　in your light.　　　　　　　119
BOS. O, sir, you are lord of the ascendant,[4] chief man with the duchess; a duke was

---

[4] Person of the highest influence (an astrological term).

your cousin-german removed. Say you
were lineally descended from King Pepin,
or he himself, what of this? Search the
heads of the greatest rivers in the world,
you shall find them but bubbles of water.
Some would think the souls of princes
were brought forth by some more weighty
cause than those of meaner persons. They
are deceived; there's the same hand to   [130
them. The like passions sway them; the
same reason that makes a vicar go to law
for a tithe-pig and undo his neighbors,
makes them spoil a whole province, and
batter down goodly cities with the cannon.

[Enter Duchess and Ladies.]

Duch. Your arm, Antonio. Do I not grow
  fat?
I am exceeding short-winded.—Bosola,
I would have you, sir, provide for me a
  litter,
Such a one as the Duchess of Florence
  rode in.
Bos. The duchess used one when she was
  great with child.   140
Duch. I think she did.—Come hither;
  mend my ruff.
Here, when? Thou art such a tedious
  lady, and
Thy breath smells of lemon pills.[1]
Would thou hadst done!
Shall I sound [2] under thy fingers? I am
So troubled with the mother! [3]
Bos. [*Aside.*]   I fear, too much.
Duch. I have heard you say that the
  French courtiers
Wear their hats on fore the king.
Ant. I have seen it.
Duch.   In the presence?
Ant.   Yes.
[Duch.] Why should not we bring up that
  fashion?
'Tis ceremony more than duty that con-
  sists   150
In the removing of a piece of felt.
Be you the example to the rest o' th'
  court;
Put on your hat first.
Ant.   You must pardon me.
I have seen, in colder countries than in
  France,

[1] Lemon peels.   [2] Swoon.
[3] Hysteria, with a double meaning.

Nobles stand bare to th' prince; and the
  distinction
Methought showed reverently.
Bos. I have a present for your grace.
Duch.   For me, sir?
Bos. Apricocks, madam.
Duch.   O, sir, where are they?
I have heard of none to-year.[4]
Bos. [*Aside.*]   Good; her color rises!
Duch. Indeed, I thank you; they are won-
  drous fair ones.   160
What an unskillful fellow is our gardener!
We shall have none this month.
Bos. Will not your grace pare them?
Duch. No. They taste of musk, methinks;
  indeed they do.
Bos. I know not; yet I wish your grace
  had pared 'em.
Duch. Why?
Bos.   I forgot to tell you, the
  knave gard'ner,
Only to raise his profit by them the sooner,
Did ripen them in horse dung.
Duch.   O, you jest!—
You shall judge. Pray, taste one.
Ant.   Indeed, madam,
I do not love the fruit.
Duch.   Sir, you are loath
To rob us of our dainties. 'Tis a delicate
  fruit;   171
They say they are restorative.
Bos.   'Tis a pretty
Art, this grafting.
Duch.   'Tis so; a bett'ring of nature.
Bos. To make a pippin grow upon a crab,
A damson on a blackthorn.—[*Aside.*]
  How greedily she eats them!
A whirlwind strike off these bawd-
  farthingales!
For, but for that and the loose-bodied
  gown,
I should have discovered apparently [5]
The young springal [6] cutting a caper in
  her belly.
Duch. I thank you, Bosola. They were
  right good ones,   180
If they do not make me sick.
Ant.   How now, madam?
Duch. This green fruit and my stomach
  are not friends.
How they swell me!
Bos. [*Aside.*] Nay, you are too much
  swelled already.

[4] This year.   [5] Clearly.   [6] Youngster.

Duch. O, I am in an extreme cold sweat!

Bos. I am very sorry.　　　　　　[*Exit.*]

Duch. Lights to my chamber!—O good
　　Antonio,
　I fear I am undone!
　　　　　Exit Duchess [with Ladies].

Del.　　　　　　Lights there, lights!

Ant. O my most trusty Delio, we are lost!
　I fear she's fall'n in labor; and there's left
　No time for her remove.

Del.　　　　　Have you prepared　191
　Those ladies to attend her, and procured
　That politic safe conveyance for the
　　midwife
　Your duchess plotted?

Ant. I have.

Del. Make use, then, of this forced occa-
　　sion.
　Give out that Bosola hath poisoned her
　With these apricocks; that will give some
　　color
　For her keeping close.

Ant.　　　　　Fie, fie, the physicians
　Will then flock to her.

Del.　　　For that you may pretend　200
　She'll use some prepared antidote of her
　　own,
　Lest the physicians should repoison her.

Ant. I am lost in amazement. I know not
　what to think on 't.　　　*Ex[eunt].*

Scena ii.

[*A hall in the palace.*]

*Bosola,　Old Lady,　Antonio,　Roderigo,
　Grisolan, Servants, Delio, Cariola.*[1]

Bos. So, so, there's no question but her
techiness and most vulturous eating of the
apricocks are apparent signs of breeding.—

[*Enter Old Lady.*]

Now?

Old Lady. I am in haste, sir.

Bos. There was a young waiting-woman
had a monstrous desire to see the Glass
House [2]—

Old Lady. Nay, pray, let me go.

Bos. And it was only to know what　[10
strange instrument it was should swell up
a glass to the fashion of a woman's belly.

Old Lady. I will hear no more of the
Glass House. You are still abusing women!

Bos. Who? I? No, only, by the way
now and then, mention your frailties. The
orange tree bear[s] ripe and green fruit
and blossoms all together; and some of
you give entertainment for pure love, but
more for more precious reward. The　[20
lusty spring smells well, but drooping autumn tastes well. If we have the same
golden showers that rained in the time of
Jupiter the thunderer, you have the same
Dan[ä]es [3] still, to hold up their laps to
receive them. Didst thou never study the
mathematics?

Old Lady. What's that, sir?

Bos. Why, to know the trick how to
make a many lines meet in one center. [30
Go, go, give your foster daughters good
counsel. Tell them that the devil takes delight to hang at a woman's girdle, like a
false, rusty watch, that she cannot discern how the time passes. [*Exit Old Lady.*

*Enter　Antonio,　Delio,　Roderigo,　and
　　　　　　　　　　　　　　　　Grisolan.*]

Ant. Shut up the court gates!

Rod.　　　Why, sir? What's the danger?

Ant. Shut up the posterns presently,[4] and
　call
　All the officers o' th' court.

Gris.　　　　　I shall instantly. [*Exit.*]

Ant. Who keeps the key o' th' park gate?

Rod.　　　　　　Forobosco.

Ant. Let him bring 't presently.　　40

[*Enter Grisolan with Servants.*]

[1] Ser. O, gentleman o' th' court, the
　　foulest treason!

Bos. [*Aside.*] If that these apricocks should
　be poisoned now,
　Without my knowledge!

[1] Ser. There was taken even now a
　　Switzer
　In the duchess' bedchamber—

2 Ser.　　　　　　　A Switzer?

[1] Ser. With a pistol in his great codpiece.

Bos. Ha, ha, ha!

[1] Ser. The codpiece was the case for 't.

2 Ser. There was a cunning traitor. [50
Who would have searched his codpiece?

[1] Ser. True, if he had kept out of the
ladies' chambers. And all the molds of his
buttons were leaden bullets.

---

[1] All except the first enter later.

[2] A London glass factory.

[3] Correction from 1708 edn.　　[4] At once.

2 SER. O wicked cannibal! A firelock
in 's codpiece?

[1] SER. 'Twas a French plot, upon my
life.

2 SER. To see what the devil can do!

ANT. All the officers [1] here?	60

[1] SER. We are.

ANT. Gentlemen,

We have lost much plate, you know;
and but this evening

Jewels, to the value of four thousand
ducats,

Are missing in the duchess' cabinet.

Are the gates shut?

[1] SER.	Yes.

ANT.	'Tis the duchess' pleasure

Each officer be locked into his chamber

Till the sun-rising, and to send the keys

Of all their chests and of their outward
doors	69

Into her bedchamber. She is very sick.

ROD. At her pleasure.

ANT. She entreats you take 't not ill. The
innocent

Shall be the more approved [2] by it.

Bos. Gentlemen o' th' woodyard,
where's your Switzer now?

[1] SER. By this hand, 'twas credibly reported by one o' th' black guard. [3]

[Exeunt all except Antonio and Delio.]

DEL. How fares it with the duchess?

ANT.	She's exposed

Unto the worst of torture—pain and
fear.

DEL. Speak to her all happy comfort.	80

ANT. How I do play the fool with mine
own danger!

You are this night, dear friend, to post
to Rome.

My life lies in your service.

DEL.	Do not doubt me.

ANT. O, 'tis far from me; and yet fear
presents me

Somewhat that look[s] like danger.

DEL.	Believe it,

'Tis but the shadow of your fear, no
more.

How superstitiously we mind our evils!

The throwing down salt, or crossing of a
hare,

Bleeding at nose, the stumbling of a
horse,

Or singing of a cricket are of power	90

To daunt whole man in us. Sir, fare you
well.

I wish you all the joys of a blessed
father;

And, for my faith, lay this unto your
breast:

Old friends, like old swords, still are
trusted best.	[Exit.]

[Enter Cariola with a Child.] [4]

CARI. Sir, you are the happy father of a
son.

Your wife commends him to you.

ANT.	Blessed comfort!—

For heaven sake, tend her well. I'll
presently

Go set a figure for 's nativity. [5]	Exeunt.

SCENA iii.

[The courtyard of the palace.]

Bosola, Antonio. [6]

Bos. Sure I did hear a woman shriek.
List, ha!

And the sound came, if I received it
right,

From the duchess' lodgings. There's
some stratagem

In the confining all our courtiers

To their several wards. I must have
part of it;

My intelligence will freeze else. List,
again!

It may be 'twas the melancholy bird,

Best friend of silence and of solitariness,

The owl, that screamed so.—Ha! Antonio?

[Enter Antonio with a candle, his sword
drawn.] [7]

ANT. I heard some noise.—Who's there?
What art thou? Speak.	10

Bos. Antonio, put not your face nor body

To such a forced expression of fear;

I am Bosola, your friend.

ANT.	Bosola!—

[Aside.] This mole does undermine me.—
Heard you not

A noise even now?

---

[1] From 1640 edn. Original reads *offices*.
[2] Proved.	[3] Scullions.
[4] From 1708 edn.	[5] Cast his horoscope.
[6] Antonio enters later. 1708 edn. reads *Enter
Bosola with a dark lanthorn*.
[7] From 1708 edn.

Bos.   From whence?

ANT.   From the duchess' lodging.

Bos. Not I. Did you?

ANT.   I did, or else I dreamed.

Bos. Let's walk towards it.

ANT.   No; it may be 'twas
But the rising of the wind.

Bos.   Very likely.
Methinks 'tis very cold, and yet you
    sweat.
You look wildly.

ANT.   I have been setting a figure 20
For the duchess' jewels.

Bos.   Ah, and how falls your question?
Do you find it radical? [1]

ANT.   What's that to you?
'Tis rather to be questioned what design,
When all men were commanded to their
    lodgings,
Makes you a night-walker.

Bos.   In sooth, I'll tell you.
Now all the court's asleep, I thought the
    devil
Had least to do here; I came to say my
    prayers;
And, if it do offend you I do so,
You are a fine courtier.

ANT. [Aside.]   This fellow will undo
    me.—
You gave the duchess apricocks to-
    day.   30
Pray heaven they were not poisoned!

Bos.   Poisoned? A Spanish fig
For the imputation!

ANT.   Traitors are ever confident
Till they are discovered. There were
    jewels stol'n too—
In my conceit, none are to be suspected
More than yourself.

Bos.   You are a false steward!

ANT. Saucy slave, I'll pull thee up by the
    roots!

Bos. May be the ruin will crush you to
    pieces.

ANT. You are an impudent snake indeed,
    sir.
Are you scarce warm, and do you show
    your sting?

[Bos.] [2]   40

ANT. You libel [3] well, sir?

Bos.   No, sir; copy it out,
And I will set my hand to 't.

ANT.   My nose bleeds.—
[Aside, taking out his handkerchief and care-
    lessly dropping a paper.] One that were
    superstitious would count
This ominous, when it merely comes by
    chance.
Two letters, that are wrought here for
    my name,
Are drowned in blood!
Mere accident!—For you, sir, I'll take
    order;
I' th' morn you shall be safe.—[Aside.]
    'Tis that must color
Her lying-in.—Sir, this door you pass not.
I do not hold it fit that you come near
The duchess' lodgings till you have
    quite [4] yourself.—   51
[Aside.] "The great are like the base,
    nay, they are the same,
When they seek shameful ways to avoid
    shame."   Ex[it].

Bos. Antonio hereabout did drop a paper.
Some of your help, false friend. [5]—O,
    here it is.
What's here? A child's nativity cal-
    culated!   [Reads.]
"The duchess was delivered of a son,
'tween the hours twelve and one in the
night, Anno Dom. 1504"—that's this
year—"decimo nono Decembris" [6]—that's
this night—"taken according to the [61
meridian of Malfi"—that's our duchess.
Happy discovery!—"The lord of the first
house being combust in the ascendant
signifies short life; and Mars being in a
human sign, joined to the tail of the
Dragon, in the eight house, doth threaten a
violent death. Cætera non scrutantur." [7]
Why, now 'tis most apparent; this pre-
    cise fellow
Is the duchess' bawd. I have it to my
    wish!   70
This is a parcel of intelligency [8]
Our courtiers were cased up for! It needs
    must follow
That I must be committed on pretense
Of poisoning her, which I'll endure, and
    laugh at.

[1] Fit to be decided (astrological term).
[2] The passage is obscure. Lucas suggests that
a speech by Bosola seems to have been omitted.
[3] Draw up a document, with a double meaning.
[4] Acquitted.
[5] I.e., his dark lantern.
[6] December 19.
[7] Other things are not investigated.
[8] News.

If one could find the father now! But
  that
Time will discover. Old Castruchio
I' th' morning posts to Rome; by him
  I'll send
A letter that shall make her brothers'
  galls
O'erflow their livers. This was a thrifty
  way!
"Though Lust do mask in ne'er so
  strange disguise.   80
She's oft found witty, but is never
  wise."   [Exit.]

Scena iv.

[An apartment in the Cardinal's palace at
            Rome.]

Cardinal and Julia; Servant and Delio.[1]

CARD. Sit; thou art my best of wishes.
  Prithee, tell me
What trick didst thou invent to come
  to Rome
Without thy husband?
JUL.   Why, my lord, I told him
I came to visit an old anchorite
Here, for devotion.
CARD.   Thou art a witty false one—
I mean, to him.
JUL.   You have prevailed with me
Beyond my strongest thoughts; I would
  not now
Find you inconstant.
CARD.   Do not put thyself
To such a voluntary torture, which pro-
  ceeds
Out of your own guilt.
JUL.   How, my lord!
CARD.   You fear   10
My constancy, because you have ap-
  proved[2]
Those giddy and wild turning[s] in
  yourself.
JUL. Did you e'er find them?
CARD.   Sooth, generally for women;
A man might strive to make glass mal-
  leable
Ere he should make them fixéd.
JUL.   So, my lord!
CARD. We had need go borrow that fan-
  tastic glass
Invented by Galileo the Florentine

To view another spacious world i' th'
  moon,
And look to find a constant woman
  there.
JUL. [Weeping.] This is very well, my lord.
CARD.   Why do you weep?   20
Are tears your justification? The self-
  same tears
Will fall into your husband's bosom,
  lady,
With a loud protestation that you love
  him
Above the world. Come, I'll love you
  wisely—
That's jealously, since I am very cer-
  tain
You cannot me make cuckold.
JUL.   I'll go home
To my husband.
CARD.   You may thank me, lady,
I have taken you off your melancholy
  perch,
Bore you upon my fist, and showed you
  game,
And let you fly at it. I pray thee, kiss
  me.   30
When thou wast with thy husband, thou
  wast watched
Like a tame elephant. (Still you are to
  thank me.)
Thou hadst only kisses from him, and
  high feeding;
But what delight was that? 'Twas just
  like one
That hath a little fing'ring on the lute,
Yet cannot tune it. (Still you are to
  thank me.)
JUL. You told me of a piteous wound i'
  th' heart
And a sick liver when you wooed me
  first,
And spake like one in physic.[3]
CARD.   Who's that?—

[Enter Servant.]

Rest firm; for my affection to thee,   40
Lightning moves slow to 't.
SER.   Madam, a gentleman
That's comes post from Malfi desires
  to see you.
CARD. Let him enter; I'll withdraw.   Exit.
SER.   He says

---

[1] Last two enter later.   [2] Experienced.

[3] I.e., sick.

Your husband, old Castruchio, is come
to Rome,
Most pitifully tired with riding post.
　　　　　　　　　　　　　[*Exit.*

Enter Delio.]

Jul. Signior Delio?—[*Aside.*] 'Tis one of
my old suitors.
Del. I was bold to come and see you.
Jul. 　　　　　Sir, you are welcome.
Del. Do you lie here?
Jul. 　　　　Sure, your own experience
Will satisfy you no—our Roman prel-
ates
Do not keep lodging for ladies.
Del. 　　　　　　　　Very well. 50
I have brought you no commendations
from your husband,
For I know none by him.
Jul. 　　　　　I hear he's come to Rome.
Del. I never knew man and beast, of a
horse and a knight,
So weary of each other. If he had had
a good back,
He would have undertook to have borne
his horse,
His breech was so pitifully sore.
Jul. 　　　　　　　Your laughter
Is my pity.
Del. 　　　　Lady, I know not whether
You want money, but I have brought
you some.
Jul. From my husband?
Del. 　No, from mine own allowance.
Jul. I must hear the condition, ere I
be bound to take it. 　　　　60
Del. Look on 't; 'tis gold. Hath it not a
fine color?
Jul. I have a bird more beautiful.
Del. 　　　　　Try the sound on 't.
Jul. A lutestring far exceeds it.
It hath no smell, like cassia or civet;
Nor is it physical,[1] though some fond [2]
doctors
Persuade us seethe 't [3] in cullises.[4] I'll
tell you,
This is a creature bred by—

[*Enter Servant.*]

Ser. 　　　　Your husband's come,
Hath delivered a letter to the Duke of
Calabria

[1] Medicinal. 　　　　　[2] Foolish.
[3] Boil it. Dyce's emendation. Original reads
seeth's. 　　　　[4] Strong broths.

That, to my thinking, hath put him out
of his wits. 　　　　　　　[*Exit.*]
Jul. Sir, you hear. 　　　　　　70
Pray, let me know your business and
your suit
As briefly as can be.
Del. 　　　　　With good speed.
I would wish you
(At such time as you are non-resident
With your husband) my mistress.
Jul. Sir, I'll go ask my husband if I shall,
And straight return your answer. 　*Exit.*
Del. 　　　　　　　　Very fine!
Is this her wit, or honesty, that speaks
thus?
I heard one say the duke was highly
moved
With a letter sent from Malfi. I do fear
Antonio is betrayed. How fearfully 　80
Shows his ambition now! Unfortunate
fortune!
"They pass through whirlpools, and
deep woes do shun,
Who the event weigh ere the action's
done." 　　　　　　　　*Exit.*

Scena v.

[*The same.*]

Cardinal and Ferdinand, with a letter.

Ferd. I have this night digged up a man-
drake.[5]
Card. 　　　　Say you?
Ferd. And I am grown mad with 't.
Card. 　　　　　　What's the prodigy?
Ferd. Read there—a sister damned! She's
loose i' th' hilts,
Grown a notorious strumpet.
Card. 　　　　　　Speak lower.
Ferd. 　　　　　　　　Lower?
Rogues do not whisper 't now, but seek
to publish 't
(As servants do the bounty of their
lords)
Aloud, and with a covetous, searching
eye,
To mark who note them. O, confusion
seize her!
She hath had most cunning bawds to
serve her turn, 　　　　　9
And more secure conveyances for lust
Than towns of garrison for service.

[5] The mandrake, when dug up, supposedly
gave forth shrieks which drove the hearer mad.

CARD. 　　　　　　Is 't possible?
Can this be certain?

FERD. 　　　　Rhubarb, O, for rhubarb
To purge this choler! [*Points to the
horoscope.*] Here's the cursed day
To prompt my memory; and here 't
shall stick
Till of her bleeding heart I make a
sponge
To wipe it out.

CARD. 　　　Why do you make yourself
So wild a tempest?

FERD. 　　　　　Would I could be one,
That I might toss her palace 'bout her ears,
Root up her goodly forests, blast her
meads,
And lay her general territory as waste 20
As she hath done her honors.

CARD. 　　　　　　Shall our blood,
The royal blood of Aragon and Castile,
Be thus attainted?

FERD. 　　　　Apply desperate physic.
We must not now use balsamum, but
fire—
The smarting cupping glass, for that's
the mean
To purge infected blood, such blood as
hers.
There is a kind of pity in mine eye;
I'll give it to my handkercher, and, now
'tis here,
I'll bequeath this to her bastard.

CARD. 　　　　　　What to do?

FERD. Why, to make soft lint for his
　　　mother's [1] wounds, 　　　　30
When I have hewed her to pieces.

CARD. 　　　　　　Cursed creature!
Unequal nature, to place women's
hearts
So far upon the left side! [2]

FERD. 　　　　　　Foolish men,
That e'er will trust their honor in a bark
Made of so slight, weak bulrush as is
woman,
Apt every minute to sink it!

CARD. 　　　　　　Thus
Ignorance, when it hath purchased
honor,
It cannot wield it.

FERD. 　　　Methinks I see her laughing—
Excellent hyena! Talk to me somewhat, quickly,

Or my imagination will carry me 　40
To see her in the shameful act of sin.

CARD. With whom?

FERD. 　　　　　Happily [3] with some
strong-thighed bargeman,
Or one [o'] [4] th' woodyard that can quoit
the sledge [5]
Or toss the bar, or else some lovely
squire
That carries coals up to her privy lodgings.

CARD. You fly beyond your reason.

FERD. 　　　　　Go to, mistress!
'Tis not your whore's milk that shall
quench my wildfire,
But your whore's blood.

CARD. How idly [6] shows this rage, which
carries you,
As men conveyed by witches through
the air, 　　　　　　　　50
On violent whirlwinds! This intemperate noise
Fitly resembles deaf men's shrill discourse,
Who talk aloud, thinking all other
men
To have their imperfection.

FERD. 　　　　　　Have not you
My palsy?

CARD. 　　Yes. I can be angry
Without this rupture. There is not in
nature
A thing that makes man so deformed,
so beastly,
As doth intemperate anger. Chide your-
self.
You have divers men who never yet
expressed
Their strong desire of rest but by un-
rest, 　　　　　　　　　　60
By vexing of themselves. Come, put
yourself
In tune.

FERD. 　　So! I will only study to seem
The thing I am not. I could kill her
now,
In you, or in myself; for I do think
It is some sin in us heaven doth re-
venge
By her.

CARD. 　　Are you stark mad?

FERD. 　　　　　I would have their bodies

---

[1] From 1640 edn. Original reads *mother*.
[2] *I.e.*, to make women so perverse.

[3] Haply, perhaps.　　　[5] Throw the hammer.
[4] From 1678 edn.　　　[6] Madly.

Burnt in a coalpit with the ventage stopped,
That their cursed smoke might not ascend to heaven;
Or dip the sheets they lie in in pitch or sulphur,
Wrap them in 't, and then light them like a match;　　　　　70
Or else to boil their bastard to a cullis,
And give 't his lecherous father to renew
The sin of his back.

CARD.　　　　　I'll leave you.
FERD.　　　　　Nay, I have done.
I am confident, had I been damned in hell,
And should have heard of this, it would have put me
Into a cold sweat. In, in! I'll go sleep.
Till I know who leaps my sister, I'll not stir.
That known, I'll find scorpions to string my whips,
And fix her in a general eclipse.　*Exeunt.*

ACTUS III. SCENA i.

[*An apartment in the Duchess' palace.*]

Antonio and Delio; Duchess, Ferdinand, Bosola.[1]

ANT. Our noble friend, my most beloved Delio!
O, you have been a stranger long at court.
Came you along with the Lord Ferdinand?
DEL. I did, sir. And how fares your noble duchess?
ANT. Right fortunately well. She's an excellent
Feeder of pedigrees; since you last saw her,
She hath had two children more, a son and daughter.
DEL. Methinks 'twas yesterday. Let me but wink,
And not behold your face, which to mine eye
Is somewhat leaner, verily I should dream　　　　　10
It were within this half hour.
ANT. You have not been in law, friend Delio,

---

[1] Last three enter later.

Nor in prison, nor a suitor at the court,
Nor begged the reversion of some great man's place,
Nor troubled with an old wife, which doth make
Your time so insensibly hasten.
DEL.　　　　　Pray, sir, tell me,
Hath not this news arrived yet to the ear
Of the lord cardinal?
ANT.　　　　　I fear it hath.
The Lord Ferdinand, that's newly come to court,
Doth bear himself right dangerously.
DEL.　　　　　Pray, why?　20
ANT. He is so quiet that he seems to sleep
The tempest out, as dormice do in winter.
Those houses that are haunted are most still
Till the devil be up.
DEL.　　　　　What say the common people?
ANT. The common rabble do directly say
She is a strumpet.
DEL.　　　　　And your graver heads
Which would be politic, what censure[2] they?
ANT. They do observe I grow to infinite purchase[3]
The left-hand way; and all suppose the duchess
Would amend it, if she could; for, say they,　　　　　30
Great princes, though they grudge their officers
Should have such large and unconfinéd means
To get wealth under them, will not complain,
Lest thereby they should make them odious
Unto the people. For other obligation
Of love or marriage between her and me,
They never dream of.

[*Enter Duchess, Ferdinand, Bosola, and Attendants.*]

DEL. [*Aside.*]　　　　　The Lord Ferdinand
Is going to bed.
FERD.　　　　　I'll instantly to bed,
For I am weary.—I am to bespeak
A husband for you.
DUCH. For me, sir? Pray, who is 't?　40
FERD. The great Count Malateste.
DUCH.　　　　　Fie upon him!

---

[2] Judge.　　　　　[3] Wealth.

A count? He's a mere stick of sugar
candy;
You may look quite thorough him.
When I choose
A husband, I will marry for your honor.
FERD. You shall do well in 't.—How is 't,
worthy Antonio?
DUCH. But, sir, I am to have private con-
ference with you
About a scandalous report is spread
Touching mine honor.
FERD.   Let me be ever deaf to 't—
One of Pasquil's paper bullets,[1] court
calumny,
A pestilent air which princes' palaces 50
Are seldom purged of. Yet, say that it
were true,
I pour it in your bosom, my fixed love
Would strongly excuse, extenuate, nay,
deny
Faults, were they apparent in you. Go,
be safe
In your own innocency.
DUCH. [Aside.]   O blessed comfort!
This deadly air is purged.
Exeunt [all except Ferdinand and Bosola].
FERD.   Her guilt treads on
Hot, burning cultures.[2] Now, Bosola,
How thrives our intelligence?
BOS.   Sir, uncertainly.
'Tis rumored she hath had three bas-
tards, but
By whom we may go read i' th' stars.
FERD.   Why, some 60
Hold opinion all things are written there.
BOS. Yes, if we could find spectacles to
read them.
I do suspect there hath been some sorcery
Used on the duchess.
FERD.   Sorcery! To what purpose?
BOS. To make her dote on some desertless
fellow
She shames to acknowledge.
FERD.   Can your faith give way
To think there's power in potions or in
charms,
To make us love whether we will or no?
BOS. Most certainly.
FERD. Away! These are mere gulleries,[3]
horrid things,   70
Invented by some cheating mountebanks
To abuse us. Do you think that herbs or
charms

Can force the will? Some trials have
been made
In this foolish practice, but the ingredi-
ents
Were lenitive poisons, such as are of
force
To make the patient mad; and straight
the witch
Swears by equivocation they are in
love.
The witchcraft lies in her rank blood.
This night
I will force confession from her. You told
me
You had got, within these two days, a
false key   80
Into her bedchamber.
BOS.   I have.
FERD.   As I would wish.
BOS. What do you intend to do?
FERD.   Can you guess?
BOS.   No.
FERD. Do not ask, then.
He that can compass me, and know my
drifts,
May say he hath put a girdle 'bout the
world,
And sounded all her quicksands.
BOS.   I do not
Think so.
FERD.   What do you think, then, pray?
BOS.   That you are
Your own chronicle too much, and grossly
Flatter yourself.
FERD.   Give me thy hand; I thank thee.
I never gave pension but to flatterers 90
Till I entertainéd thee. Farewell.
"That friend a great man's ruin strongly
checks,
Who rails into his belief all his defects."
          Exeunt.

SCENA ii.

[The Duchess' bedchamber.]

Duchess, Antonio, Cariola, Ferdinand,
          Bosola, Officers.[4]

DUCH. Bring me the casket hither, and the
glass.—
You get no lodging here tonight, my lord.
ANT. Indeed, I must persuade one.
DUCH.   Very good!
I hope in time 'twill grow into a custom

1 Lampoons.   2 Plowshares.   3 Deceptions.   4 Ferdinand, Bosola, and Officers enter later.

That noblemen shall come with cap and
knee
To purchase a night's lodging of their
wives.
ANT. I must lie here.
DUCH. Must? You are a lord of misrule.
ANT. Indeed, my rule is only in the night.
DUCH. To what use will you put me?
ANT.   We'll sleep together.
DUCH. Alas, what pleasure can two lovers
find in sleep?   10
CARI. My lord, I lie with her often, and I
know
She'll much disquiet you.
ANT.   See, you are complained of.
CARI. For she's the sprawling'st bedfellow.
ANT. I shall like her the better for that.
CARI. Sir, shall I ask you a question?
ANT. I pray thee, Cariola.
CARI. Wherefore still when you lie with my
lady
Do you rise so early?
ANT.   Laboring men
Count the clock oft'nest, Cariola,
Are glad when their task's ended.
DUCH.   I'll stop your mouth.   20
                                   [Kisses him.]
ANT. Nay, that's but one; Venus had two
soft doves
To draw her chariot; I must have
another.—   [Another kiss.]
When wilt thou marry, Cariola?
CARI.   Never, my lord.
ANT. O, fie upon this single life! Forgo it.
We read how Daphne, for her peevish
slight,[1]
Became a fruitless bay tree, Syrinx
turned
To the pale, empty reed, Anaxarete
Was frozen into marble; whereas those
Which married or proved kind unto their
friends
Were by a gracious influence trans-
shaped   30
Into the olive, pomegranate, mulberry,
Became flowers, precious stones, or
eminent stars.
CARI. This is a vain poetry   But I pray
you, tell me,
If there were proposed me wisdom,
riches, and beauty,
In three several young men, which should
I choose?

[1] I.e., of Apollo. Mod. edns. print flight.

ANT. 'Tis a hard question. This was Paris'
case,
And he was blind in 't, and there was a
great cause.
For how was 't possible he could judge
right,
Having three amorous goddesses in view,
And they stark naked? 'Twas a motion [2]
Were able to benight the apprehension
Of the severest counselor of Europe.   42
Now I look on both your faces so well
formed,
It puts me in mind of a question I would
ask.
CARI. What is 't?
ANT.   I do wonder why hard-
favored ladies
For the most part keep worse-favored
waiting-women
To attend them, and cannot endure fair
ones.
DUCH. O, that's soon answered.
Did you ever in your life know an ill
painter
Desire to have his dwelling next door to
the shop   50
Of an excellent picture maker? 'Twould
disgrace
His face-making, and undo him. I prithee,
When were we so merry?—My hair
tangles.
ANT. [Aside.]   Pray thee, Cariola, let's
steal forth the room,
And let her talk to herself. I have divers
times
Served her the like, when she hath
chafed extremely.
I love to see her angry. Softly, Cariola.
                 Exeunt [Antonio and Cariola].
DUCH. Doth not the color of my hair gin
to change?
When I wax gray, I shall have all the
court
Powder their hair with arras,[3] to be like
me.   60
You have cause to love me; I entered you
into my heart

[Enter Ferdinand unseen.][4]

Before you would vouchsafe to call for
the keys.

[2] Spectacle, show.   [3] Powder of orris-root.
[4] Stage direction from 1708 edn.

We shall one day have my brothers take
  you napping.
Methinks his presence, being now in court,
Should make you keep your own bed;
  but you'll say
Love mixed with fear is sweetest. I'll
  assure you,
You shall get no more children till my
  brothers
Consent to be your gossips.[1] Have you
  lost your tongue?—[*Sees Ferdinand
  with a poniard.*] 'Tis welcome;
For know, whether I am doomed to live
  or die,
I can do both like a prince.
        Ferdinand gives her a poniard.
FERD.   Die, then, quickly. 70
  Virtue, where art thou hid? What hid-
    eous thing
  Is it that doth eclipse [2] thee?
DUCH.   Pray, sir, hear me!
FERD. Or is it true thou art but a bare
    name,
  And no essential thing?
DUCH.   Sir—
FERD.   Do not speak.
DUCH. No, sir!
  I will plant my soul in mine ears, to hear
    you.
FERD. O most imperfect light of human
    reason,
  That mak'st [us] [3] so unhappy to foresee
  What we can least prevent! Pursue thy
    wishes,
  And glory in them; there's in shame no
    comfort   80
  But to be past all bounds and sense of
    shame.
DUCH. I pray, sir, hear me. I am married!
FERD.   So!
DUCH. Happily, not to your liking. But
    for that,
  Alas, your shears do come untimely now
  To clip the bird's wings that's already
    flown!
  Will you see my husband?
FERD.   Yes, if I
  Could change eyes with a basilisk.
DUCH.   Sure, you came hither
  By his confideracy.[4]

  [1] Godparents to your children.
  [2] Perhaps with a pun on *clip*, to embrace.
  [3] From 1708 edn.
  [4] Confederacy. It is not clear in the original
whether the word is *consideracy* or *confideracy*.

FERD.   The howling of a wolf
  Is music to thee, screech owl! Prithee,
    peace!—
  Whate'er thou art that hast enjoyed my
    sister,   90
  For I am sure thou hear'st me, for thine
    own sake
  Let me not know thee. I came hither
    prepared
  To work thy discovery, yet am now per-
    suaded
  It would beget such violent effects
  As would damn us both. I would not for
    ten millions
  I had beheld thee; therefore use all
    means
  I never may have knowledge of thy
    name;
  Enjoy thy lust still, and a wretched life,
  On that condition.—And for thee, vild
    woman,
  If thou do wish thy lecher may grow
    old   100
  In thy embracements, I would have thee
    build
  Such a room for him as our anchorites
  To holier use inhabit. Let not the sun
  Shine on him till he's dead; let dogs and
    monkeys
  Only converse with him, and such dumb
    things
  To whom nature denies use to sound his
    name;
  Do not keep a paraquito, lest she learn it;
  If thou do love him, cut out thine own
    tongue,
  Lest it bewray him.
DUCH.   Why might not I marry? 109
  I have not gone about in this to create
  Any new world or custom.
FERD.   Thou art undone;
  And thou hast ta'en that massy sheet of
    lead
  That hid thy husband's bones, and folded
    it
  About my heart.
DUCH.   Mine bleeds for 't.
FERD.   Thine? Thy heart?
  What should I name 't, unless a hollow
    bullet
  Filled with unquenchable wildfire?
DUCH.   You are in this
  Too strict, and, were you not my princely
    brother.

I would say, too willful. My reputation
Is safe.

FERD.　　　Dost thou know what reputa-
tion is?
I'll tell thee—to small purpose, since th'
instruction　　　　　　　　　　120
Comes now too late.
Upon a time Reputation, Love, and
Death
Would travel o'er the world; and it was
concluded
That they should part, and take three
several ways.
Death told them they should find him in
great battles,
Or cities plagued with plagues. Love
gives them counsel
To inquire for him 'mongst unambitious
shepherds,
Where dowries were not talked of and
sometimes
'Mongst quiet kindred that had nothing
left
By their dead parents. "Stay," quoth
Reputation,　　　　　　　　　130
"Do not forsake me; for it is my nature,
If once I part from any man I meet,
I am never found again." And so, for
you,
You have shook hands with Reputation,
And made him invisible. So, fare you
well;
I will never see you more.

DUCH.　　　Why should only I,
Of all the other princes of the world,
Be cased up, like a holy relic? I have
youth
And a little beauty.

FERD.　　　So you have some virgins
That are witches. I will never see thee
more.　　　　　　　　　　　　　Exit. 140

Enter Antonio with a pistol [, and Cariola].[1]

DUCH. You saw this apparition?

ANT.　　　　　　　Yes; we are
Betrayed. How came he hither? [*Points
the pistol at Cariola.*] I should turn
This to thee, for that.

CARI.　　　Pray, sir, do; and, when
That you have cleft my heart, you shall
read there
Mine innocence.

DUCH.　　That gallery gave him entrance.

[1] Direction in original follows next speech.

ANT. I would this terrible thing would
come again
That, standing on my guard, I might
relate
My warrantable love.—Ha! what means
this?　　　　　　*She shows the poniard.*

DUCH. He left this with me.

ANT.　　　　　And it seems did wish
You would use it on yourself?

DUCH.　　　　　His action seemed　150
To intend so much.

ANT.　　　　　This hath a handle to 't,
As well as a point—turn it towards him,
and
So fasten the keen edge in his rank gall.
　　　　　　　　　　　　[*Knocking within.*]
How now! Who knocks? More earth-
quakes?

DUCH.　　　I stand
As if a mine beneath my feet were ready
To be blown up.

CARI.　　　　　'Tis Bosola.

DUCH.　　　　　　　　Away!
O misery! Methinks unjust actions
Should wear these masks and curtains,
and not we.
You must instantly part hence; I have
fashioned it already. *Ex[it] Ant[onio].*

　　　　　　　[*Enter Bosola.*]

Bos. The duke your brother is ta'en up
in a whirlwind,　　　　　　　160
Hath took horse, and 's rid post to
Rome.

DUCH.　　　　　　　So late?

Bos. He told me, as he mounted into th'
saddle,
You were undone.

DUCH.　　　Indeed I am very near it.

Bos. What's the matter?

DUCH. Antonio, the master of our house-
hold,
Hath dealt so falsely with me in 's
accounts.
My brother stood engaged with me for
money
Ta'en up of certain Neapolitan Jews,
And Antonio lets the bonds be forfeit.

Bos. Strange!—[*Aside.*] This is cunning.

DUCH.　　　　　And hereupon　170
My brother's bills at Naples are pro-
tested
Against.—Call up our officers.

Bos.　　　　　　　I shall. *Exit.*

[*Enter Antonio.*]

DUCH. The place that you must fly to is Ancona.
Hire a house there; I'll send after you
My treasure and my jewels. Our weak safety
Runs upon enginous [1] wheels; short syllables
Must stand for periods. I must now accuse you
Of such a feignéd crime as Tasso calls
Magnanima menzogna, "a noble lie,"
Cause it must shield our honors.—Hark! they are coming.   180

[*Enter Bosola and Officers.*]

ANT. Will your grace hear me?
DUCH. I have got well by you; you have yielded me
A million of loss. I am like to inherit
The people's curses for your stewardship.
You had the trick in audit-time to be sick,
Till I had signed your *Quietus;* and that cured you
Without help of a doctor.—Gentlemen,
I would have this man be an example to you all;
So shall you hold my favor. I pray, let him, [2]
For h'as done that, alas, you would not think of,   190
And, because I intend to be rid of him,
I mean not to publish.—Use your fortune elsewhere.
ANT. I am strongly armed to brook my overthrow,
As commonly men bear with a hard year.
I will not blame the cause on 't; but do think
The necessity of my malevolent star
Procures this, not her humor. O, the inconstant
And rotten ground of service! You may see,
'Tis even like him that in a winter night
Takes a long slumber o'er a dying fire,   200
As loath [3] to part from 't, yet parts thence as cold
As when he first sat down.

[1] Ingenious, intricate.   [2] Let him go.
[3] Some apparently uncorrected copies of 1623 edn. read *a-loth.*

DUCH.   We do confiscate,
Towards the satisfying of your accounts,
All that you have.
ANT.   I am all yours; and 'tis very fit
All mine should be so.
DUCH.   So, sir, you have your pass.
ANT. You may see, gentlemen, what 'tis to serve
A prince with body and soul.   *Exit.*
Bos. Here's an example for extortion; what moisture is drawn out of the sea, when foul weather comes, pours down, and [210 runs into the sea again.
DUCH. I would know what are your opinions of this Antonio.
2 OFF. He could not abide to see a pig's head gaping; [4] I thought your grace would find him a Jew.
3 OFF. I would you had been his officer, for your own sake.
4 OFF. You would have had more money.   220
1 OFF. He stopped his ears with black wool, and to those came to him for money said he was thick of hearing.
2 OFF. Some said he was an hermaphrodite, for he could not abide a woman.
4 OFF. How scurvy proud he would look when the treasury was full! Well, let him go.
1 OFF. Yes, and the chippings of the butt'ry fly after him, to scour his gold [230 chain. [5]
DUCH. Leave us.—   (*Exeunt* [*Officers*].)
What do you think of these?
Bos. That these are rogues that, in 's prosperity,
But to have waited on his fortune could have wished
His dirty stirrup riveted through their noses,
And followed after 's mule, like a bear in a ring;
Would have prostituted their daughters to his lust;
Made their first-born intelligencers; thought none happy
But such as were born under his blessed planet,   240
And wore his livery—and do these lice drop off now?
Well, never look to have the like again.

[4] A roasted pig with an apple in its mouth.
[5] Symbol of a steward's office.

He hath left a sort [1] of flatt'ring rogues
　behind him;
Their doom must follow.　Princes pay
　flatterers
In their own money; flatterers dissemble
　their vices,
And they dissemble their lies.　That's
　justice.
Alas, poor gentleman!
Duch. Poor?　He hath amply filled his
　coffers.
Bos. Sure, he was too honest.　Pluto, the
　god of riches,
When he's sent by Jupiter to any
　man,　　　　　　　　　　　　　　　250
He goes limping, to signify that wealth
That comes on God's name comes slowly;
　but, when he's sent
On the devil's errand, he rides post and
　comes in by scuttles.[2]
Let me show you what a most unvalued
　jewel
You have in a wanton humor thrown
　away,
To bless the man shall find him.　He was
　an excellent
Courtier and most faithful; a soldier that
　thought it
As beastly to know his own value too
　little
As devilish to acknowledge it too much.
Both his virtue and form deserved a far
　better fortune;　　　　　　　　　260
His discourse rather delighted to judge
　itself than show itself;
His breast was filled with all perfec-
　tion,
And yet it seemed a private whisp'ring-
　room,
It made so little noise of 't.
Duch. But he was basely descended.
Bos. Will you make yourself a mercenary
　herald,
Rather to examine men's pedigrees than
　virtues?
You shall want him;
For know an honest statesman to a
　prince
Is like a cedar planted by a spring;　270
The spring bathes the tree's root; the
　grateful tree
Rewards it with his shadow.　You have
　not done so.

I would sooner swim to the Bermoothes [3]
　on two politicians'[4]
Rotten bladders, tied together with an
　intelligencer's heartstring,
Than depend on so changeable a prince's
　favor.
Fare thee well, Antonio! Since the malice
　of the world
Would needs down with thee, it cannot
　be said yet
That any ill happened unto thee, con-
　sidering thy fall
Was accompanied with virtue.
Duch. O, you render me excellent music!
Bos.　　　　　　　　　　　Say you?　280
Duch. This good one that you speak of is
　my husband.
Bos. Do I not dream?　Can this ambitious
　age
Have so much goodness in 't as to prefer
A man merely for worth, without these
　shadows
Of wealth and painted honors? Possible?
Duch. I have had three children by him.
Bos.　　　　　　　　　　　Fortunate lady!
For you have made your private nuptial
　bed
The humble and fair seminary of peace—
No question but.　Many an unbeneficed
　scholar
Shall pray for you for this deed, and
　rejoice　　　　　　　　　　　　290
That some preferment in the world can
　yet
Arise from merit.　The virgins of your
　land
That have no dowries shall hope your
　example
Will raise them to rich husbands.　Should
　you want
Soldiers, 'twould make the very Turks
　and Moors
Turn Christians, and serve you for this
　act.
Last, the neglected poets of your time,
In honor of this trophy of a man,
Raised by that curious engine, your white
　hand,
Shall thank you in your grave for 't, and
　make that　　　　　　　　　　　300
More reverend than all the cabinets [5]
Of living princes.　For Antonio,

[1] Crowd.　　　　　　[2] Quick steps.
[3] Bermudas.　　　　　　[5] Museums.
[4] Intriguers'.

His fame shall likewise flow from many a
   pen,
When heralds shall want coats to sell to
   men.
Duch. As I taste comfort in this friendly
   speech,
So would I find concealment.
Bos.   O, the secret of my prince,
   Which I will wear on th' inside of my
   heart!
Duch. You shall take charge of all my
   coin and jewels,
And follow him, for he retires himself 310
   To Ancona.
Bos.   So!
Duch.   Whither, within few days,
   I mean to follow thee.
Bos.   Let me think.
   I would wish your grace to feign a pil-
   grimage
   To our Lady of Loretto, scarce seven
   leagues
   From fair Ancona; so may you depart
   Your country with more honor, and your
   flight
   Will seem a princely progress, retaining
   Your usual train about you.
Duch.   Sir, your direction
   Shall lead me by the hand.
Cari.   In my opinion,
   She were better progress to the baths 320
   At Lucca, or go visit the Spa
   In Germany, for, if you will believe me,
   I do not like this jesting with religion,
   This feignéd pilgrimage.
Duch. Thou art a superstitious fool!
   Prepare us instantly for our departure.
   Past sorrows, let us moderately lament
   them,
   For those to come, seek wisely to prevent
   them.
           Exit [*Duchess with Cariola*].
Bos. A politician is the devil's quilted
   anvil;
   He fashions all sins on him, and the
   blows   330
   Are never heard. He may work in a
   lady's chamber,
   As here for proof. What rests [1] but I
   reveal
   All to my lord? O, this base quality [2]
   Of intelligencer! Why, every quality i'
   th' world

[1] Remains.   [2] Profession.

Prefers but gain or commendation.
Now, for this act I am certain to be
   raised,
"And men that paint weeds to the life
   are praised."   *Exit.*

Scena iii.

[*An apartment in the Cardinal's palace at
             Rome.*]

*Cardinal, Ferdinand, Malateste, Pescara,
        Silvio, Delio, Bosola.*[3]

Card. Must we turn soldier, then?
Mal.   The emperor,
   Hearing your worth that way ere you
   attained
   This reverend garment, joins you in
   commission
   With the right fortunate soldier, the
   Marquis of Pescara,
   And the famous Lannoy.
Card.   He that had the honor
   Of taking the French king prisoner?
Mal.   The same.
   Here's a plot drawn for a new fortifica-
   tion
   At Naples.

[*Cardinal and Malateste stand aside con-
             versing.*]

Ferd.   This great Count Mala-
   [teste], I perceive,
   Hath got employment?
Del.   No employment, my lord;
   A marginal note in the muster book that
   he is   10
   A voluntary [4] lord.
Ferd.   He's no soldier?
Del. He has worn gunpowder in 's hollow
   tooth for the toothache.
Sil. He comes to the leaguer with a full
   intent
   To eat fresh beef and garlic, means to
   stay
   Till the scent be gone, and straight re-
   turn to court.
Del. He hath read all the late service
   As the city chronicle relates it;
   And keep[s] two painters [5] going, only to
   express
   Battles in model.

[3] Enters later.   [4] *I.e.*, a volunteer.
[5] Some apparently uncorrected copies of 1623
edn. read *pewterers.*

Sil.   Then he'll fight by the book.
Del. By the almanac, I think,   20
To choose good days and shun the
critical.
That's his mistress' scarf.
Sil.   Yes, he protests
He would do much for that taffeta.
Del. I think he would run away from a
battle
To save it from taking prisoner.
Sil.   He is horribly afraid
Gunpowder will spoil the perfume on 't.
Del. I saw a Dutchman break his pate
once
For calling him potgun;[1] he made his
head
Have a bore in 't like a musket.
Sil. I would he had made a touchhole
to 't.   30
He is indeed a garded sumpter cloth,[2]
Only for the remove of the court.[3]

[Enter Bosola.]

Pes. Bosola arrived? What should be the
business?
Some falling out amongst the cardinals.
These factions amongst great men, they
are like
Foxes; when their heads are divided,
They carry fire in their tails, and all
the country
About them goes to wrack for 't.
Sil.   What's that Bosola?
Del. I knew him in Padua—a fantastical scholar, like such who study to [40
know how many knots was in Hercules'
club, of what color Achilles' beard was, or
whether Hector were not troubled with the
toothache. He hath studied himself half
blear-eyed to know the true symmetry of
Cæsar's nose by a shoeinghorn; and this
he did to gain the name of a speculative
man.
Pes. Mark Prince Ferdinand.
A very salamander lives in 's eye,   50
To mock the eager violence of fire.
Sil. That cardinal hath made more bad
faces with his oppression than ever Michael
Angelo made good ones. He lifts up 's nose
like a foul porpoise before a storm.
Pes. The Lord Ferdinand laughs.

Del.   Like a deadly cannon
That lightens ere it smokes.
Pes. These are your true pangs of death,
The pangs of life, that struggle with
great statesmen.
Del. In such a deformed silence, witches
whisper their charms.   60
[*Silvio, Pescara, and Delio stand aside.*]
Card. Doth she make religion her riding
hood
To keep her from the sun and tempest?
Ferd. That, that damns her. Methinks
her fault and beauty,
Blended together, show like leprosy—
The whiter the fouler. I make it a ques-
tion
Whether her beggarly brats were ever
christened.
Card. I will instantly solicit the state of
Ancona
To have them banished.
Ferd.   You are for Loretto?
I shall not be at your ceremony. Fare
you well.—
Write to the Duke of Malfi, my young
nephew   70
She had by her first husband, and ac-
quaint him
With 's mother's honesty.[4]
Bos.   I will.
Ferd.   Antonio!
A slave that only smelled of ink and
compters,[5]
And never in 's life looked like a gentle-
man
But in the audit-time.—Go, go pres-
ently;
Draw me out an hundreth and fifty of
our horse,
And meet me at the fort-bridge.
          Exeunt.

Scena iv.

Two Pilgrims to the Shrine of Our Lady of
Loretto.

1 Pil. I have not seen a goodlier shrine
than this;
Yet I have visited many.
2 Pil.   The Cardinal of Aragon
Is this day to resign his cardinal's hat;
His sister duchess likewise is arrived

---

[1] Popgun.
[2] Ornamented horse cloth.
[3] When the court moves from place to place.

[4] Chastity.   [5] Counters.

To pay her vow of pilgrimage. I expect
A noble ceremony.

1 PIL.   No question.—They come.

*Here the ceremony of the Cardinal's in-
stallment in the habit [of]* [1] *a soldier,
performed in delivering up his cross, hat,
robes, and ring at the shrine, and in-
vesting him with sword, helmet, shield,
and spurs. Then Antonio, the Duchess, and their Children, having presented
themselves at the shrine, are, by a form
of banishment in dumb show, expressed
towards them by the Cardinal and the
state of Ancona, banished. During all
which ceremony, this ditty is sung, to
very solemn music, by divers Churchmen; and then exeunt.*

Arms and honors deck thy story
To thy fame's eternal glory!
Adverse fortune ever fly thee;
No disastrous fate come nigh
   thee!
I alone will sing thy praises, ⎡ *The author*
Whom to honor virtue raises, ⎢ *disclaims this*
                              ⎣ *ditty to be his.*
And thy study, that divine is,
Bent to martial discipline is,
Lay aside all those robes lie by thee.
Crown thy arts with arms; they'll beautify
   thee.

O worthy of worthiest name, adorned in
   this manner,
Lead bravely thy forces on under war's
   warlike banner!
O, mayst thou prove fortunate in all martial courses!   19
Guide thou still by skill in arts and forces!
Victory attend thee nigh, whilst fame sings
   loud thy powers;
Triumphant conquest crown thy head, and
   blessings pour down showers!

1 PIL. Here's a strange turn of state! Who
   would have thought
So great a lady would have matched
   herself
Unto so mean a person? Yet the cardinal
Bears himself much too cruel.

2 PIL.   They are banished.

1 PIL. But I would ask what power hath
   this state
Of Ancona to determine of a free prince?

2 PIL. They are a free state, sir, and her
   brother showed

---

[1] Supplied from 1640 edn.

How that the pope, forehearing of her
   looseness,   30
Hath seized into th' protection of the
   church
The dukedom which she held as dowager.

1 PIL. But by what justice?

2 PIL.   Sure, I think by none,
Only her brother's instigation.

1 PIL. What was it with such violence he
   took
Off from her finger?

2 PIL.   'Twas her wedding ring,
Which he vowed shortly he would
   sacrifice
To his revenge.

1 PIL.   Alas, Antonio!
If that a man be thrust into a well,
No matter who sets hand to 't, his own
   weight   40
Will bring him sooner to th' bottom.
Come, let's hence.
Fortune makes this conclusion general,
"All things do help th' unhappy man to
   fall."   *Exeunt.*

SCENA V.

[*A road near Loretto.*]

*Antonio, Duchess, Children, Cariola, Serv-
   ants; Bosola, Soldiers with vizards.* [2]

DUCH. Banished Ancona!

ANT.   Yes, you see what power
Lightens in great men's breath.

DUCH.   Is all our train
Shrunk to this poor remainder?

ANT.   These poor men,
Which have got little in your service,
   vow
To take your fortune. But your wiser
   buntings,
Now they are fledged, are gone.

DUCH.   They have done wisely.
This puts me in mind of death; physi-
   cians thus,
With their hands full of money, use to
   give o'er
Their patients.

ANT.   Right the fashion of the world—
From decayed fortunes every flatterer
   shrinks;   10
Men cease to build where the foundation sinks.

---

[2] Bosola and Soldiers enter later.

Duch. I had a very strange dream tonight.
Ant.   What was 't?
Duch. Methought I wore my coronet of
    state,
And on a sudden all the diamonds
Were changed to pearls.
Ant.   My interpretation
Is, you'll weep shortly, for to me the
    pearls
Do signify your tears.
Duch.   The birds, that live i' th' field
On the wild benefit of nature, live
Happier than we, for they may choose
    their mates,
And carol their sweet pleasures to the
    spring.   20

    [*Enter Bosola with a letter.*]

Bos. You are happily o'erta'en.
Duch.   From my brother?
Bos. Yes, from the Lord Ferdinand your
    brother
All love and safety.
Duch.   Thou dost blanch mischief,
Wouldst make it white. See, see, like to
    calm weather
At sea before a tempest, false hearts
    speak fair
To those they intend most mischief.
        A Letter:
"Send Antonio to me; I want his head in
    a business."
A politic equivocation!
He doth not want your counsel, but your
    head;
That is, he cannot sleep till you be
    dead.   30
And here's another pitfall that's strewed
    o'er
With roses. Mark it; 'tis a cunning one:
"I stand engaged for your husband
for several debts at Naples. Let not
that trouble him; I had rather have his
heart than his money."
    And I believe so too.
Bos.   What do you believe?
Duch. That he so much distrusts my
    husband's love,
He will by no means believe his heart
    is with him
Until he see it. The devil is not cunning
    enough   40
To circumvent us in riddles.

Bos. Will you reject that noble and free
    league
Of amity and love which I present you?
Duch. Their league is like that of some
    politic kings,
Only to make themselves of strength and
    power
To be our after-ruin. Tell them so.
Bos. And what from you?
Ant.   Thus tell him: I will not come.
Bos. And what of this?
Ant.   My brothers have dispersed
Bloodhounds abroad, which till I hear
    are muzzled,
No truce, though hatched with ne'er
    such politic skill,   50
Is safe, that hangs upon our enemies'
    will.
I'll not come at them.
Bos.   This proclaims your breeding.
Every small thing draws a base mind to
    fear
As the adamant [1] draws iron. Fare you
    well, sir;
You shall shortly hear from 's. *Exit.*
Duch.   I suspect some ambush;
Therefore by all my love I do conjure
    you
To take your eldest son, and fly to-
    wards Milan.
Let us not venture all this poor re-
    mainder
In one unlucky bottom.
Ant.   You counsel safely.
Best of my life, farewell. Since we must
    part,   60
Heaven hath a hand in 't; but no other-
    wise
Than as some curious artist takes in
    sunder
A clock or watch, when it is out of
    frame,
To bring 't in better order.
Duch. I know not which is best,
To see you dead or part with you.
    Farewell, boy.
Thou art happy that thou hast not
    understanding
To know thy misery, for all our wit
And reading brings us to a truer sense
Of sorrow.—In the eternal church, sir,
I do hope we shall not part thus.
Ant.   O, be of comfort! 71

_____
[1] Magnet.

Make patience a noble fortitude,
And think not how unkindly we are
  used.
"Man, like to cassia, is proved best,
  being bruised."
Duch. Must I, like to a slave-born
  Russian,
Account it praise to suffer tyranny?
And yet, O heaven, thy heavy hand is
  in 't!
I have seen my little boy oft scourge [1]
  his top,
And compared myself to 't. Naught
  made me e'er
Go right but heaven's scourge-stick.
Ant.   Do not weep. 80
Heaven fashioned us of nothing, and
  we strive
To bring ourselves to nothing.—Fare-
  well, Cariola,
And thy sweet armful.—If I do never see
  thee more,
Be a good mother to your little ones,
And save them from the tiger. Fare
  you well.
Duch. Let me look upon you once more,
  for that speech
Came from a dying father. Your kiss is
  colder
Than that I have seen an holy anchorite
Give to a dead man's skull.
Ant. My heart is turned to a heavy lump
  of lead,   90
With which I sound my danger. Fare
  you well.   *Exit [with his Son].*
Duch. My laurel is all withered.
Cari. Look, madam, what a troop of
  arméd men
Make toward us!

Enter Bosola with a Guard.

Duch.   O, they are very welcome.
When Fortune's wheel is overcharged
  with princes,
The weight makes it move swift. I
  would have my ruin
Be sudden.—I am your adventure,[2] am
  I not?
Bos. You are. You must see your hus-
  band no more.
Duch. What devil art thou that counter-
  feits heaven's thunder?

---

[1] Whip, to keep in motion.
[2] Object of your quest.

Bos. Is that terrible? I would have you
  tell me whether   100
Is that note worse that frights the silly
  birds
Out of the corn, or that which doth al-
  lure them
To the nets? You have hearkened to
  the last too much.
Duch. O misery! Like to a rusty o'er-
  charged [3] cannon,
Shall I never fly in pieces? Come, to
  what prison?
Bos. To none.
Duch.   Whither, then?
Bos.   To your palace.
Duch.   I have heard
That Charon's boat serves to convey
  all o'er
The dismal lake, but brings none back
  again.
Bos. Your brothers mean you safety and
  pity.
Duch. Pity! With such a pity men pre-
  serve alive   110
Pheasants and quails, when they are
  not fat enough
To be eaten.
Bos.   These are your children?
Duch.   Yes.
Bos.   Can they prattle?
Duch. No.
But I intend, since they were born ac-
  cursed,
Curses shall be their first language.
Bos.   Fie, madam!
Forget this base, low fellow!
Duch.   Were I a man,
I'ld beat that counterfeit face [4] into thy
  other.
Bos. One of no birth.
Duch.   Say that he was born mean,
Man is most happy when 's own actions
Be arguments and examples of his vir-
  tue.   120
Bos. A barren, beggarly virtue!
Duch. I prithee, who is greatest? Can
  you tell?
Sad tales befit my woe; I'll tell you one.
A salmon, as she swam unto the sea,
Met with a dogfish, who encounters her
With this rough language, "Why art
  thou so bold

---

[3] From 1640 edn. Original reads *o'erchar'd.*
[4] His vizard.

To mix thyself with our high state of
    floods,
Being no eminent courtier, but one
That for the calmest and fresh time o' th'
    year
Dost live in shallow rivers, rank'st thy-
    self   130
With silly smelts and shrimps?   And
    darest thou
Pass by our dogship without reverence?"
"O," quoth the salmon, "sister, be at
    peace.
Thank Jupiter we both have passed the
    net!
Our value never can be truly known
Till in the fisher's basket we be shown;
I' th' market then my price may be the
    higher,
Even when I am nearest to the cook and
    fire."
So to great men the moral may be
    stretched,
"Men oft are valued high, when they're
    most wretch'd."   140
But come, whither you please.   I am
    armed gainst misery,
Bent to all sways of the oppressor's will.
"There's no deep valley but near some
    great hill."   Ex[eunt].

Actus IV. Scena i.

[The place of the Duchess' imprisonment.]

Ferdinand,   Bosola,   Duchess,   Cariola,
                            Servants.[1]

Ferd. How doth our sister duchess bear
    herself
In her imprisonment?
Bos.   Nobly. I'll describe her.
She's sad, as one long used to 't, and
    she seems
Rather to welcome the end of misery
Than shun it, a behavior so noble
As gives a majesty to adversity;
You may discern the shape of loveli-
    ness
More perfect in her tears than in her
    smiles.
She will muse four hours together, and
    her silence,
Methinks, expresseth more than if she
    spake.   10

[1] All but first two enter later.

Ferd. Her melancholy seems to be forti-
    fied
With a strange disdain.
Bos.   'Tis so; and this restraint,
Like English mastiffs that grow fierce
    with tying,
Makes her too passionately apprehend
Those pleasures she's kept from.
Ferd.   Curse upon her!
I will no longer study in the book
Of another's heart.   Inform her what I
    told you.   *Exit.*

[Enter Duchess and Attendants.]

Bos. All comfort to your grace!
Duch.   I will have none.
Pray thee, why dost thou wrap thy
    poisoned pills
In gold and sugar?   20
Bos. Your elder brother, the Lord Ferdi-
    nand,
Is come to visit you, and sends you
    word,
Cause once he rashly made a solemn
    vow
Never to see you more, he comes i' th'
    night;
And prays you gently neither torch nor
    taper
Shine in your chamber.   He will kiss
    your hand,
And reconcile himself; but for his vow
He dares not see you.
Duch.   At his pleasure.—
Take hence the lights.—He's come.
            [Exeunt Attendants with lights.

Enter Ferdinand.]

Ferd.   Where are you?
Duch.   Here, sir.
Ferd. This darkness suits you well.
Duch.   I would ask you pardon.   30
Ferd. You have it;
For I account it the honorabl'st revenge,
Where I may kill, to pardon.—Where
    are your cubs?
Duch. Whom?
Ferd. Call them your children;
For, though our national law distinguish
    bastards
From true legitimate issue, compassion-
    ate nature
Makes them all equal.

DUCH.   Do you visit me for this?
You violate a sacrament o' th' church
Shall make you howl in hell for 't.
FERD.   It had been well
Could you have lived thus always; for
  indeed   41
You were too much i' th' light. But
  no more;
I come to seal my peace with you. Here's
  a hand   *Gives her a dead man's hand.*
To which you have vowed much love;
  the ring upon 't
You gave.
DUCH.   I affectionately kiss it.
FERD. Pray do, and bury the print of it
  in your heart.
I will leave this ring with you for a love
  token;
And the hand as sure as the ring; and
  do not doubt
But you shall have the heart too. When
  you need a friend,
Send it to him that owed [1] it; you shall
  see   50
Whether he can aid you.
DUCH.   You are very cold.
I fear you are not well after your
  travel.—
Ha! Lights!—O, horrible!
FERD.   Let her have lights enough.
                                        Exit.
DUCH. What witchcraft doth he practice,
  that he hath left
A dead man's hand here?

[*By Servants who enter,*] *here is discovered,
  behind a traverse,*[2] *the artificial figures
  of Antonio and his Children, appearing as if they were dead.*

BOS. Look you, here's the piece from
  which 'twas ta'en.
He doth present you this sad spectacle,
That, now you know directly they are
  dead,
Hereafter you may wisely cease to
  grieve
For that which cannot be recoveréd.
DUCH. There is not between heaven and
  earth one wish   61
I stay for after this. It wastes me more
Than were 't my picture, fashioned out
  of wax,

Stuck with a magical needle, and then
  buried
In some foul dunghill; and yon's an ex-
  cellent property
For a tyrant, which I would account
  mercy.
BOS.   What's that?
DUCH. If they would bind me to that
  lifeless trunk,
And let me freeze to death.
BOS.   Come, you must live.
DUCH. That's the greatest torture souls
  feel in hell—
In hell, that they must live, and cannot
  die.   70
Portia, I'll new kindle thy coals again,
And revive the rare and almost dead
  example
Of a loving wife.
BOS.   O, fie! Despair? Remember
You are a Christian.
DUCH.   The church enjoins fasting.
I'll starve myself to death.
BOS.   Leave this vain sorrow.
Things being at the worst begin to mend.
The bee, when he hath shot his sting
  into your hand,
May then play with your eyelid.
DUCH.   Good comfortable fellow,
Persuade a wretch that's broke upon
  the wheel
To have all his bones new set; entreat
  him live   80
To be executed again! Who must des-
  patch me?
I account this world a tedious theater,
For I do play a part in 't gainst my
  will.
BOS. Come, be of comfort; I will save
  your life.
DUCH. Indeed, I have not leisure to tend
  so small a business.
BOS. Now, by my life, I pity you.
DUCH.   Thou art a fool, then,
To waste thy pity on a thing so wretched
As cannot pity it.[3] I am full of daggers.
Puff, let me blow these vipers from me.—
[*To a Servant.*] What are you?
SER.   One that wishes you long life.
DUCH. I would thou wert hanged for the
  horrible curse   91
Thou hast given me. I shall shortly
  grow one

---

[1] Owned.   [2] Curtain.   [3] *I.e.*, itself.

Of the miracles of pity. I'll go pray.—
  No,
I'll go curse.
Bos.   O, fie!
Duch.   I could curse the stars—
Bos.   O, fearful!
Duch. And those three smiling seasons
  of the year
Into a Russian winter; nay, the world
To its first chaos.
Bos.   Look you, the stars shine still.
Duch. O, but you must remember my
  curse hath a great way to go.—
Plagues, that make lanes through larg-
  est families,
Consume them!
Bos.   Fie, lady!
Duch.   Let them, like tyrants, 100
Never be remembered but for the ill
  they have done;
Let all the zealous prayers of mortified
Churchmen forget them!
Bos.   O, uncharitable!
Duch. Let heaven a little while cease
  crowning martyrs, to punish them!
Go, howl them this, and say I long to
  bleed:
"It is some mercy when men kill with
  speed."   Exit [with Servants.

Enter Ferdinand.]

Ferd. Excellent, as I would wish; she's
  plagued in art.
These presentations are but framed in
  wax
By the curious master in that quality,
Vincentio Lauriola, and she takes
  them   110
For true substantial bodies.
Bos.   Why do you do this?
Ferd. To bring her to despair.
Bos.   Faith, end here,
And go no farther in your cruelty.
Send her a penitential garment to put on
Next to her delicate skin, and furnish
  her
With beads and prayer books.
Ferd.   Damn her! That body of hers,
While that my blood ran pure in 't, was
  more worth
Than that which thou wouldst comfort,
  called a soul.
I will send her masques of common
  courtesans,

Have her meat served up by bawds and
  ruffians,   120
And, cause she'll needs be mad, I am
  resolved
To remove forth [1] the common hospital
All the mad folk, and place them near
  her lodging;
There let them practice together, sing
  and dance,
And act their gambols to the full o' th'
  moon.
If she can sleep the better for it, let her.
Your work is almost ended.
Bos.   Must I see her again?
Ferd. Yes.
Bos.   Never.
Ferd.   You must.
Bos.   Never in mine own shape;
That's forfeited by my intelligence
And this last cruel lie. When you send
  me next,   130
The business shall be comfort.
Ferd.   Very likely!
Thy pity is nothing of kin to thee. An-
  tonio
Lurks about Milan; thou shalt shortly
  thither
To feed a fire as great as my revenge,
Which never will slack till it hath
  spent his fuel.
"Intemperate agues make physicians
  cruel."   *Exeunt*

Scena ii.
[*The same.*]

*Duchess, Cariola, Servant, Madmen, Bosola,
          Executioners, Ferdinand.* [2]

Duch. What hideous noise was that?
Cari.   'Tis the wild consort [3]
Of madmen, lady, which your tyrant
  brother
Hath placed about your lodging. This
  tyranny,
I think, was never practiced till this hour.
Duch. Indeed, I thank him.   Nothing
  but noise and folly
Can keep me in my right wits, whereas
  reason
And silence make me stark mad.   Sit
  down;
Discourse to me some dismal tragedy.

[1] From.   [2] All but the first two enter later.
[3] Company, especially of musicians.

CARI. O, 'twill increase your melancholy!
DUCH.   Thou art deceived;
  To hear of greater grief would lessen
    mine.   10
  This is a prison?
CARI.   Yes, but you shall live
  To shake this durance off.
DUCH.   Thou art a fool.
  The robin redbreast and the nightin-
    gale
  Never live long in cages.
CARI.   Pray, dry your eyes.—
  What think you of, madam?
DUCH.   Of nothing;
  When I muse thus, I sleep.
CARI. Like a madman, with your eyes
  open?
DUCH. Dost thou think we shall know
  one another
  In th' other world?
CARI.   Yes, out of question.   19
DUCH. O, that it were possible we might
  But hold some two days' conference with
    the dead!
  From them I should learn somewhat, I
    am sure,
  I never shall know here. I'll tell thee a
    miracle:
  I am not mad yet, to my cause of sorrow.
  Th' heaven o'er my head seems made of
    molten brass,
  The earth of flaming sulphur, yet I am
    not mad.
  I am acquainted with sad misery
  As the tanned galley slave is with his
    oar.
  Necessity makes me suffer constantly,
  And custom makes it easy. Who do I
    look like now?   30
CARI. Like to your picture in the gallery,
  A deal of life in show, but none in prac-
    tice;
  Or rather like some reverend monument
  Whose ruins are even pitied.
DUCH.   Very proper;
  And Fortune seems only to have her
    eyesight
  To behold my tragedy.—How now!
  What noise is that?

[Enter Servant.]

SER.   I am come to tell you
  Your brother hath intended you some
    sport.

A great physician, when the pope was
    sick
Of a deep melancholy, presented him   40
With several sorts of madmen, which
    wild object,
Being full of change and sport, forced
    him to laugh,
And so th' imposthume [1] broke.   The
    selfsame cure
The duke intends on you.
DUCH.   Let them come in.
SER. There's a mad lawyer and a secular
    priest;
A doctor that hath forfeited his wits
By jealousy; an astrologian
That in his works said such a day o' th'
    month
Should be the day of doom, and, failing
    of 't,
Ran mad; an English tailor crazed i' th'
    brain   50
With the study of new fashion; a gentle-
    man usher
Quite beside himself with care to keep
    in mind
The number of his lady's salutations
(Or "How do you") she employed him
    in each morning;
A farmer, too, an excellent knave in
    grain, [2]
Mad cause he was hindered transporta-
    tion. [3]
And let one broker [4] that's mad loose to
    these,
You'ld think the devil were among them.
DUCH. Sit, Cariola.—Let them loose when
    you please,
For I am chained to endure all your tyr-
    anny.   60

[Enter Madmen.]

Here by a Madman this song is sung to a
                    dismal kind of music.

O, let us howl some heavy note,
  Some deadly dogged howl,
Sounding as from the threat'ning throat
  Of beasts and fatal fowl!
As ravens, scritch owls, bulls, and bears,
  We'll bill [5] and bawl our parts,

[1] Abscess.
[2] A pun on (1) in dye, *i.e.*, incorrigible, and
(2) in the grain trade.
[3] *I.e.*, forbidden to export his produce.
[4] Pawnbroker.
[5] Bell, bellow.

Till yerksome [1] noise have cloyed your ears
And corrasived [2] your hearts.
At last, whenas our choir wants breath,
Our bodies being blessed,   70
We'll sing, like swans, to welcome death,
And die in love and rest.

1 MAD. Doomsday not come yet? I'll draw it nearer by a perspective,[3] or make a glass that shall set all the world on fire upon an instant. I cannot sleep; my pillow is stuffed with a litter of porcupines.

2 MAD. Hell is a mere glass house, where the devils are continually blowing up women's souls on hollow irons, and [80 the fire never goes out.

3 MAD. I will lie with every woman in my parish the tenth night. I will tithe them over like haycocks.

4 MAD. Shall my pothecary outgo me, because I am a cuckold? I have found out his roguery: he makes alum of his wife's urine, and sells it to Puritans that have sore throats with overstraining.

1 [MAD.] I have skill in heraldry.   90

2 [MAD.] Hast?

1 [MAD.] You do give for your crest a woodcock's head with the brains picked out on 't; you are a very ancient gentleman.

3 [MAD.] Greek is turned Turk; we are only to be saved by the Helvetian translation.[4]

1 [MAD.] Come on, sir, I will lay [5] the law to you.

2 [MAD.] O, rather lay a corrasive; [100 the law will eat to the bone.

3 [MAD.] He that drinks but to satisfy nature is damned.

4 [MAD.] If I had my glass here, I would show a sight should make all the women here call me mad doctor.

1 [MAD. (Pointing at 3 Madman.)] What's he? A rope maker?

2 [MAD.] No, no, no; a snuffling knave that, while he shows the tombs, will [110 have his hand in a wench's placket.[6]

3 [MAD.] Woe to the caroche that brought home my wife from the masque at three a-clock in the morning! It had a large feather bed in it.

4 [MAD.] I have pared the devil's nails

forty times, roasted them in raven's eggs, and cured agues with them.

3 [MAD.] Get me three hundred milch-bats, to make possets to procure sleep. [120

4 [MAD.] All the college may throw their caps at me—I have made a soap boiler costive; it was my masterpiece.

Here the dance, consisting of eight Madmen,
    with music answerable thereunto, after
    which Bosola, like an old man, enters.

DUCH. Is he mad too?

SER. Pray, question him. I'll leave you.
                    [*Exeunt Servant and Madmen.*]

BOS. I am come to make thy tomb.

DUCH.   Ha! My tomb?
Thou speak'st as if I lay upon my death-bed,
Gasping for breath. Dost thou perceive me sick?

BOS. Yes, and the more dangerously since thy sickness is insensible.   130

DUCH. Thou art not mad, sure. Dost know me?

BOS.   Yes.

DUCH.   Who am I?

BOS. Thou art a box of worm-seed, at best but a salvatory of green mummy.[7] What's this flesh? A little crudded [8] milk, fantastical puff paste. Our bodies are weaker than those paper prisons boys use to keep flies in; more contemptible, since ours is to preserve earthworms. Didst thou ever see a lark in a cage? Such is the soul in the body; this world is like [140 her little turf of grass, and the heaven o'er our heads, like her looking-glass, only gives us a miserable knowledge of the small compass of our prison.

DUCH. Am not I thy duchess?

BOS. Thou art some great woman, sure, for riot begins to sit on thy forehead (clad in gray hairs) twenty years sooner than on a merry milkmaid's. Thou sleep'st worse than if a mouse should be forced to [150 take up her lodging in a cat's ear; a little infant that breeds its teeth, should it lie with thee, would cry out, as if thou wert the more unquiet bedfellow.

DUCH. I am Duchess of Malfi still!

BOS. That makes thy sleep so broken,

---

[1] Irksome.   [2] Corroded.   [3] Telescope.
[4] The Geneva Bible, prohibited in England because of its Puritan tone.
[5] Expound.   [6] Opening in petticoat.
[7] Ointment box filled with dried flesh, widely used as a medicine.
[8] Curdled.

Glories, like glowworms, afar off shine
　　bright,
But, looked to near, have neither heat
　　nor light.
Duch. Thou art very plain.　　　　159
Bos. My trade is to flatter the dead,
not the living; I am a tomb-maker.
Duch. And thou com'st to make my
tomb?
Bos. Yes.
Duch. Let me be a little merry.　Of
what stuff wilt thou make it?
Bos. Nay, resolve [1] me first, of what
fashion?
Duch. Why, do we grow fantastical in
　　our deathbed?
Do we affect fashion in the grave?　170
Bos. Most ambitiously.　Princes' images
　　on their tombs
　　Do not lie, as they were wont, seeming
　　　to pray
　　Up to heaven, but with their hands under
　　　their cheeks,
　　As if they died of the toothache.　They
　　　are not carved
　　With their eyes fixed upon the stars,
　　　but, as their
　　Minds were wholly bent upon the world,
　　The selfsame way they seem to turn
　　　their faces.
Duch. Let me know fully therefore the
　　effect
　　Of this thy dismal preparation,
　　This talk fit for a charnel.
Bos.　　　　　　　　　Now I shall.—

[*Enter Executioners, with*] *a coffin, cords,
　　　　　　　　　and a bell.*

　　Here is a present from your princely
　　　brothers;　　　　　　　　　181
　　And may it arrive welcome, for it brings
　　Last benefit, last sorrow.
Duch.　　　　　　　　Let me see it.
　　I have so much obedience in my blood,
　　I wish it in their veins to do them good.
Bos. This is your last presence chamber.
Cari. O, my sweet lady!
Duch.　　　　Peace; it affrights not me.
Bos. I am the common bellman
　　That usually is sent to condemned per-
　　　sons
　　The night before they suffer.

[1] Satisfy.

Duch.　　　　Even now thou said'st　190
　　Thou wast a tomb-maker.
Bos.　　　　　　　　'Twas to bring you
　　By degrees to mortification.　Listen.
　　　　　　　　　　　　[*Rings his bell.*][2]

　　Hark, now everything is still;
　　The scritch owl and the whistler shrill
　　Call upon our dame aloud,
　　And bid her quickly don her shroud!
　　Much you had of land and rent;
　　Your length in clay's now competent.
　　A long war disturbed your mind;
　　Here your perfect peace is signed.　　200
　　Of what is 't fools make such vain keeping?
　　Sin their conception, their birth weeping,
　　Their life a general mist of error,
　　Their death a hideous storm of terror.
　　Strew your hair with powders sweet,
　　Don clean linen, bathe your feet,
　　And (the foul fiend more to check)
　　A crucifix let bless your neck.
　　'Tis now full tide tween night and day;
　　End your groan, and come away.　　210

Cari. Hence, villains, tyrants, murderers!
　　Alas!
　　What will you do with my lady?—Call
　　　for help!
Duch. To whom?　To our next neighbors?
　　They are madfolks.
Bos. Remove that noise!
Duch.　　　　　　　Farewell, Cariola.
　　In my last will I have not much to give—
　　A many hungry guests have fed upon
　　　me;
　　Thine will be a poor reversion.[3]
Cari.　　　　　　I will die with her.
Duch. I pray thee, look thou giv'st my
　　little boy
　　Some syrup for his cold, and let the girl
　　Say her prayers ere she sleep.
　　　　　　　　　[*Cariola is forced off.*][4]
　　　　　　　　Now what you please—
　　What death?
Bos.　　　　　Strangling; here are your
　　executioners.　　　　　　　　221
Duch. I forgive them.
　　The apoplexy, cathar,[5] or cough o' th'
　　　lungs
　　Would do as much as they do.
Bos. Doth not death fright you?

[2] From 1708 edn.
[3] Right of future possession.
[4] From 1708 edn.
[5] Catarrh; here, cerebral hemorrhage.

Duch.　　　　Who would be afraid on 't,
　Knowing to meet such excellent company
　In th' other world?
Bos. Yet, methinks,
　The manner of your death should much afflict you—
　This cord should terrify you!
Duch.　　　　　　　　　　Not a whit.
　What would it pleasure me to have my
　　throat cut　　　　　　　　　　231
　With diamonds? Or to be smotheréd
　With cassia? Or to be shot to death
　　with pearls?
　I know death hath ten thousand several
　　doors
　For men to take their exits; and 'tis found
　They go on such strange geometrical
　　hinges,
　You may open them both ways. Any
　　way, for heaven sake,
　So I were out of your whispering. Tell
　　my brothers
　That I perceive death, now I am well
　　awake,
　Best gift is they can give or I can
　　take.　　　　　　　　　　　240
　I would fain put off my last woman's
　　fault:
　I'ld not be tedious to you.
[1] Exec.　　　　　　　　We are ready.
Duch. Dispose my breath how please
　you; but my body
　Bestow upon my women, will you?
[1] Exec.　　　　　　　　　　Yes.
Duch. Pull, and pull strongly, for your
　able strength
　Must pull down heaven upon me.—
　Yet stay. Heaven-gates are not so
　　highly arched
　As princes' palaces; they that enter
　　there
　Must go upon their knees.—[Kneels.]
　Come, violent death;
　Serve for mandragora to make me
　　sleep!—　　　　　　　　　　250
　Go tell my brothers, when I am laid
　　out,
　They then may feed in quiet.
　　　　　　　　　They strangle her.
Bos. Where's the waiting-woman?
　Fetch her. [Exeunt Executioners.] Some
　other strangle the children.

[Enter Cariola.]

　Look you, there sleeps your mistress.
Cari.　　　　　　　O, you are damned
　Perpetually for this! My turn is next.
　Is 't not so ordered?
Bos.　　　　　　Yes, and I am glad
　You are so well prepared for 't.
Cari.　　　　　　You are deceived, sir;
　I am not prepared for 't. I will not die;
　I will first come to my answer,[1] and
　　know　　　　　　　　　　260
　How I have offended.
　　　Bos.　　　　Come, despatch her.—
　You kept her counsel; now you shall
　　keep ours.
Cari. I will not die; I must not! I am
　contracted
　To a young gentleman.
[1] Exec.　　　　Here's your wedding ring.
Cari. Let me but speak with the duke.
　I'll discover
　Treason to his person.
Bos.　　　　　　Delays!—Throttle her!
[1] Exec. She bites and scratches.
Cari.　　　　　　If you kill me now,
　I am damned; I have not been at confession
　This two years.
Bos. [To Executioners.]　　　When![2]
Cari.　　　　I am quick with child.
Bos.　　　　　　　　Why, then,
　Your credit's saved. [Executioners
　　strangle Cariola.] Bear her into th'
　next room;　　　　　　　　270
　Let this lie still.
[Exeunt Executioners with body of Cariola.

Enter Ferdinand.]

Ferd.　　　　　　Is she dead?
Bos.　　　　　　　She is what
　You'ld have her. But here begin your
　　pity! Shows the Children strangled.
　Alas, how have these offended?
Ferd.　　　　　　　The death
　Of young wolves is never to be pitied.
Bos. Fix your eye here.
Ferd.　　　　Constantly.
Bos.　　　　　　Do you not weep?
　Other sins only speak; murther shrieks
　　out.
　The element of water moistens the earth,

[1] Opportunity for defense.
[2] Exclamation of impatience.

But blood flies upwards and bedews the
heavens.

FERD. Cover her face! Mine eyes dazzle;
she died young.

Bos. I think not so; her infelicity   280
Seemed to have years too many.

FERD. She and I were twins;
And, should I die this instant, I had
lived
Her time to a minute.

Bos.   It seems she was born first.
You have bloodily approved the ancient
truth
That kindred commonly do worse agree
Than remote strangers.

FERD.   Let me see her face
Again. Why didst thou not pity her?
What
An excellent, honest man mightst thou
have been,
If thou hadst borne her to some sanc-
tuary,   290
Or, bold in a good cause, opposed thy-
self
With thy advancéd sword above thy
head
Between her innocence and my revenge!
I bade thee, when I was distracted of my
wits,
Go kill my dearest friend, and thou hast
done 't.
For let me but examine well the cause.
What was the meanness of her match
to me?
Only I must confess I had a hope,
Had she continued widow, to have
gained
An infinite mass of treasure by her
death,   300
And that was the main cause. Her mar-
riage—
That drew a stream of gall quite through
my heart.
For thee (as we observe in tragedies
That a good actor many times is cursed
For playing a villain's part), I hate thee
for 't.
And, for my sake, say thou hast done
much ill well.

Bos. Let me quicken your memory, for
I perceive
You are falling into ingratitude. I chal-
lenge
The reward due to my service.

FERD.   I'll tell thee
What I'll give thee.

Bos.   Do.

FERD.   I'll give thee a pardon   310
For this murther.

Bos.   Ha!

FERD.   Yes, and 'tis
The largest bounty I can study to do
thee.
By what authority didst thou execute
This bloody sentence?

Bos. By yours.

FERD. Mine? Was I her judge?
Did any ceremonial form of law
Doom her to not-being? Did a complete
jury
Deliver her conviction up i' th' court?
Where shalt thou find this judgment
registered,   320
Unless in hell? See, like a bloody fool,
Th' hast forfeited thy life, and thou shalt
die for 't.

Bos. The office of justice is perverted quite
When one thief hangs another. Who
shall dare
To reveal this?

FERD.   O, I'll tell thee;
The wolf shall find her grave, and scrape
it up,
Not to devour the corpse, but to dis-
cover
The horrid murther.

Bos.   You, not I, shall quake for 't.

FERD. Leave me.

Bos.   I will first receive my pension.

FERD. You are a villain!

Bos.   When your ingratitude 330
Is judge, I am so.

FERD. O horror,
That not the fear of him which binds
the devils
Can prescribe man obedience!—
Never look upon me more.

Bos.   Why, fare thee well.
Your brother and yourself are worthy
men!
You have a pair of hearts are hollow
graves,
Rotten, and rotting others; and your
vengeance,
Like two chained-bullets, still goes arm
in arm.
You may be brothers, for treason, like
the plague,   340

Doth take much in a blood. I stand like one
That long hath ta'en a sweet and golden dream.
I am angry with myself, now that I wake.

FERD. Get thee into some unknown part o' th' world,
That I may never see thee.

BOS.　　　　　Let me know
Wherefore I should be thus neglected. Sir,
I served your tyranny, and rather strove
To satisfy yourself than all the world;
And, though I loathed the evil, yet I loved
You that did counsel it, and rather sought　　　350
To appear a true servant than an honest man.

FERD. I'll go hunt the badger by owl-light;
'Tis a deed of darkness.　　　　　*Exit.*

Bos. He's much distracted.　Off, my painted honor!
While with vain hopes our faculties we tire,
We seem to sweat in ice and freeze in fire.
What would I do, were this to do again?
I would not change my peace of conscience
For all the wealth of Europe. She stirs; here's life!
Return, fair soul, from darkness, and lead mine　　　360
Out of this sensible hell! She's warm; she breathes!
Upon thy pale lips I will melt my heart,
To store them with fresh color.—Who's there?
Some cordial drink!—Alas! I dare not call.
So pity would destroy pity. Her eye opes,
And heaven in it seems to ope, that late was shut,
To take me up to mercy.

DUCH. Antonio!

BOS.　　　　　Yes, madam, he is living;
The dead bodies you saw were but feigned statues.
He's reconciled to your brothers; the pope hath wrought　　　370

The atonement.[1]

DUCH. Mercy!　　　　　*She dies.*

Bos. O, she's gone again! There the cords of life broke.
O sacred Innocence, that sweetly sleeps
On turtles'[2] feathers, whilst a guilty conscience
Is a black register wherein is writ
All our good deeds and bad, a perspective
That shows us hell! That we cannot be suffered
To do good when we have a mind to it!
This is manly sorrow;　　　　　380
These tears, I am very certain, never grew
In my mother's milk. My estate is sunk
Below the degree of fear. Where were
These penitent fountains while she was living?
O, they were frozen up! Here is a sight
As direful to my soul as is the sword
Unto a wretch hath slain his father.
Come, I'll bear thee hence,
And execute thy last will—that's deliver
Thy body to the reverend dispose
Of some good women. That the cruel tyrant　　　390
Shall not deny me. Then I'll post to Milan,
Where somewhat I will speedily enact
Worth my dejection.
　　　　　Exit [with the body].[3]

ACTUS V. SCENA i.

[*A public place in Milan.*]

Antonio, Delio, Pescara, Julia.[4]

ANT. What think you of my hope of reconcilement
To the Aragonian brethren?

DELIO.　　　　　I misdoubt it;
For, though they have sent their letters of safe-conduct
For your repair to Milan, they appear
But nets to entrap you. The Marquis of Pescara,
Under whom you hold certain land in cheat,[5]

---

[1] Reconciliation.　　　[4] Last two enter later.
[2] Turtledoves'.　　　　[5] Escheat.
[3] From 1708 edn.

Much gainst his noble nature hath been
    moved
To seize those lands; and some of his
    dependants
Are at this instant making it their suit
To be invested in your revenues.   10
I cannot think they mean well to your
    life
That do deprive you of your means of
    life,
Your living.
ANT.   You are still an heretic
To any safety I can shape myself.
DEL. Here comes the marquis. I will make
    myself
Petitioner for some part of your land,
To know whither it is flying.
ANT.   I pray, do. [*Withdraws.*

Enter Pescara.]

DEL. Sir, I have a suit to you.
PES.   To me?
DEL.   An easy one.
There is the Citadel of Saint Bennet,
With some demesnes, of late in the
    possession   20
Of Antonio Bologna—please you bestow
    them on me.
PES. You are my friend; but this is such a
    suit
Nor fit for me to give nor you to take.
DEL. No, sir?
PES.   I will give you ample reason for 't
Soon in private.—Here's the cardinal's
    mistress.

[*Enter Julia.*]

JUL. My lord, I am grown your poor peti-
    tioner,
And should be an ill beggar, had I not
A great man's letter here, the cardinal's,
To court you in my favor. [*Gives a letter.*]
PES. [*After reading.*]   He entreats
    for you
The Citadel of Saint Bennet, that be-
    longed   30
To the banishéd Bologna.
JUL.   Yes.
PES. I could not have thought of a friend I
    could
Rather pleasure with it. 'Tis yours.
JUL.   Sir, I thank you;
And he shall know how doubly I am
    engaged

Both in your gift and speediness of
    giving,
Which makes your grant the greater.
                              Exit.
ANT. [*Aside.*]   How they fortify
Themselves with my ruin!
DEL.   Sir, I am
Little bound to you.
PES. Why?
DEL. Because you denied this suit to me,
    and gave 't   40
To such a creature.
PES.   Do you know what it was?
It was Antonio's land, not forfeited
By course of law, but ravished from his
    throat
By the cardinal's entreaty. It were not
    fit
I should bestow so main a piece of wrong
Upon my friend; 'tis a gratification
Only due to a strumpet, for it is injustice.
Shall I sprinkle the pure blood of in-
    nocents
To make those followers I call my friends
Look ruddier [1] upon me? I am glad   50
This land, ta'en from the owner by such
    wrong,
Returns again unto so foul an use
As salary for his lust. Learn, good Delio,
To ask noble things of me, and you shall
    find
I'll be a noble giver.
DEL.   You instruct me well.
ANT. [*Aside.*] Why, here's a man now
    would fright impudence
From sauciest beggars.
PES.   Prince Ferdi-
    nand's come to Milan,
Sick, as they give out, of an apoplexy;
But some say 'tis a frenzy. I am going
To visit him.   *Exit.*
ANT.   'Tis a noble old fellow!
DEL. What course do you mean to take,
    Antonio?   61
ANT. This night I mean to venture all my
    fortune,
Which is no more than a poor ling'ring
    life,
To the cardinal's worst of malice. I have
    got
Private access to his chamber, and in-
    tend
To visit him about the mid of night,
—————
[1] More favorably.

As once his brother did our noble
  duchess.
It may be that the sudden apprehension
Of danger (for I'll go in mine own shape),
When he shall see it fraight [1] with love
  and duty,   70
May draw the poison out of him, and
  work
A friendly reconcilement. If it fail,
Yet it shall rid me of this infamous
  calling;
For better fall once than be ever falling.
DEL. I'll second you in all danger; and,
  howe'er,
My life keeps rank with yours.
ANT. You are still my lovéd and best
  friend.   *Exeunt.*

SCENA ii.

[*A gallery in the palace of the Cardinal and
  Ferdinand at Milan.*]

*Pescara, a Doctor, Ferdinand, Cardinal,
  Malateste, Bosola, Julia.* [2]

PES. Now, doctor, may I visit your pa-
  tient?
DOC. If 't please your lordship; but he's
  instantly
To take the air here in the gallery
By my direction.
PES.   Pray thee, what's his disease?
DOC. A very pestilent disease, my lord,
They call lycanthropia.
PES.   What's that?
I need a dictionary to 't.
DOC.   I'll tell you.
In those that are possessed with 't there
  o'erflows
Such melancholy humor they imagine
Themselves to be transforméd into
  wolves,   10
Steal forth to churchyards in the dead
  of night,
And dig dead bodies up; as two nights
  since
One met the duke 'bout midnight in a
  lane
Behind Saint Mark's Church, with the
  leg of a man
Upon his shoulder; and he howled fear-
  fully;
Said he was a wolf, only the difference

[1] Fraught.   [2] Last five enter later.

Was, a wolf's skin was hairy on the out-
  side,
His on the inside; bade them take their
  swords,
Rip up his flesh, and try. Straight I was
  sent for,
And, having ministered to him, found his
  grace   20
Very well recovered.
PES. I am glad on 't.
DOC.   Yet not without some fear
Of a relapse. If he grow to his fit again,
I'll go a nearer way to work with him
Than ever Paracelsus dreamed of. If
They'll give me leave, I'll buffet his
  madness out of him.
Stand aside; he comes.

[*Enter Ferdinand, Cardinal, Malateste,
  and Bosola.*]

FERD. Leave me.
MAL. Why doth your lordship love this
solitariness?   30
FERD. Eagles commonly fly alone; they
are crows, daws, and starlings that flock
together.   Look, what's that follows
me?
MAL. Nothing, my lord.
FERD. Yes.
MAL. 'Tis your shadow.
FERD. Stay it; let it not haunt me.
MAL. Impossible, if you move, and the
sun shine.   40
FERD. I will throttle it.
[*Throws himself down on his shadow.*]
MAL. O, my lord, you are angry with
nothing.
FERD. You are a fool. How is 't possible
I should catch my shadow unless I fall
upon 't? When I go to hell, I mean to carry
a bribe, for, look you, good gifts evermore
make way for the worst persons.
PES. Rise, good my lord.   49
FERD. I am studying the art of patience.
PES. 'Tis a noble virtue.
FERD. To drive six snails before me
from this town to Moscow; neither use
goad nor whip to them, but let them take
their own time (the patient'st man i' th'
world match me for an experiment!), and
I'll crawl after like a sheepbiter.
CARD. Force him up. [*They raise him.*]
FERD. Use me well, you were best.

What I have done, I have done; I'll [60
confess nothing.

Doc. Now let me come to him.—Are you
mad, my lord?

Are you out of your princely wits?

FERD. What's he?

PES. Your doctor.

FERD. Let me have his beard sawed off,
and his eyebrows filed more civil.

Doc. I must do mad tricks with him, for
that's the only way on 't.—I have brought
your grace a salamander's skin to keep you
from sunburning.

FERD. I have cruel sore eyes. 70

Doc. The white of a cockatrix's egg is
present remedy.

FERD. Let it be a new-laid one, you were
best.

Hide me from him! Physicians are like
kings—

They brook no contradiction.

Doc. Now he begins to fear me; now let
me alone with him.

[Puts off his four cloaks one after another.][1]

CARD. How now! Put off your gown?

Doc. Let me have some forty urinals
filled with rose water. He and I'll go [80
pelt one another with them.—Now he begins
to fear me.—Can you fetch a frisk,[2] sir?—
Let him go, let him go, upon my peril!
I find by his eye he stands in awe of me;
I'll make him as tame as a dormouse.

FERD. Can you fetch your frisks, sir?—
I will stamp him into a cullis, flay off his
skin to cover one of the anatomies [3] this
rogue hath set i' th' cold yonder in Barber-
Chirurgeons'[4] Hall.—Hence, hence! [90
You are all of you like beasts for sacrifice.
[Throws the Doctor down and beats him.][5]
There's nothing left of you but tongue
and belly, flattery and lechery. [Exit.]

PES. Doctor, he did not fear you
throughly!

Doc. True; I was somewhat too forward.

BOS. Mercy upon me, what a fatal judgment
Hath fall'n upon this Ferdinand!

PES. Knows your grace
What accident hath brought unto the
prince

This strange distraction? 100

CARD. [Aside.] I must feign somewhat.—
Thus they say it grew:
You have heard it rumored, for these
many years,
None of our family dies but there is seen
The shape of an old woman, which is
given
By tradition to us to have been mur-
thered
By her nephews for her riches. Such a
figure
One night, as the prince sat up late at 's
book,
Appeared to him, when, crying out for
help,
The gentleman of 's chamber found his
grace 109
All on a cold sweat, altered much in face
And language; since which apparition,
He hath grown worse and worse, and I
much fear
He cannot live.

BOS. Sir, I would speak with you.

PES. We'll leave your grace,
Wishing to the sick prince, our noble
lord,
All health of mind and body.

CARD. You are most welcome.
[Exeunt. Manent[6] Cardinal and Bosola.][7]
Are you come? So.—[Aside.] This fellow
must not know
By any means I had intelligence
In our duchess' death; for, though I
counseled it,
The full of all th' engagement seemed to
grow 120
From Ferdinand.—Now, sir, how fares
our sister?
I do not think but sorrow makes her
look
Like to an oft-dyed garment. She shall
now
Taste comfort from me. Why do you
look so wildly?
O, the fortune of your master here, the
prince,
Dejects you; but be you of happy com-
fort.
If you'll do one thing for me I'll entreat,
Though he had a cold tombstone o'er his
bones,
I'ld make you what you would be.

---

[1] From 1708 edn.   [2] Cut a caper.   [3] Skeletons.
[4] Barber-Surgeons'.   Barbers often performed
some of the duties of the physician.
[5] From 1708 edn.

[6] Remain.   [7] From 1708 edn.

Bos.　　　　　　　　　　　Anything;
　Give it me in a breath, and let me fly
　　to 't.　　　　　　　　　　　　130
They that think long, small expedition
　win,
For musing much o' th' end, cannot
　begin.

[*Enter Julia.*]

Jul.　Sir, will you come in to supper?
Card.　I am busy; leave me.
Jul.　[*Aside.*]　What an excellent shape
　hath that fellow!　　　　　*Exit.*
Card.　'Tis thus.　Antonio lurks here in
　Milan;
Inquire him out, and kill him.　While he
　lives,
Our sister cannot marry; and I have
　thought
Of an excellent match for her.　Do this,
　and style me
Thy advancement.　　　　　　140
Bos.　But by what means shall I find him
　out?
Card.　There is a gentleman called Delio
Here in the camp, that hath been long
　approved
His loyal friend.　Set eye upon that
　fellow;
Follow him to mass; may be Antonio,
Although he do account religion
But a school-name, for fashion of the
　world
May accompany him; or else go inquire
　out
Delio's confessor, and see if you can bribe
Him to reveal it.　There are a thousand
　ways　　　　　　　　　　　　150
A man might find to trace him—as to
　know
What fellows haunt the Jews for taking up
Great sums of money, for sure he's in
　want;
Or else to go to th' picture makers, and
　learn
Who bought [1] her picture lately.　Some
　of these
Happily may take.
Bos.　Well, I'll not freeze i' th' business;
I would see that wretched thing, An-
　tonio,
Above all sights i' th' world.
Card.　　　　　Do, and be happy.　*Exit.*

[1] Dyce's emendation for *brought.*

Bos.　This fellow doth breed basilisks in 's
　eyes;
He's nothing else but murder; yet he
　seems　　　　　　　　　　　160
Not to have notice of the duchess' death.
'Tis his cunning; I must follow his
　example.
There cannot be a surer way to trace
Than that of an old fox.

[*Enter Julia, with a pistol.*]

Jul.　So, sir, you are well met.
Bos.　How now!
Jul.　Nay, the doors are fast enough.
Now, sir, I will make you confess your
treachery.
Bos.　Treachery?　　　　　　170
Jul.　Yes, confess to me
Which of my women 'twas you hired to
　put
Love powder into my drink.
Bos.　Love powder!
Jul.　　　　　Yes, when I was at Malfi.
Why should I fall in love with such a
　face else?
I have already suffered for thee so much
　pain,
The only remedy to do me good
Is to kill my longing.
Bos.　　　　　Sure, your pistol holds
Nothing but perfumes or kissing-comfits.[2]
Excellent lady,　　　　　　179
You have a pretty way on 't to discover
Your longing.　Come, come, I'll disarm
　you,
And arm [3] you thus.　Yet this is wondrous
　strange.
Jul.　Compare thy form and my eyes to-
　gether,
You'll find my love no such great miracle.
　Now you'll say
I am wanton.　This nice modesty in ladies
Is but a troublesome familiar [4]
That haunts them.
Bos.　Know you me; I am a blunt soldier.
Jul.　　　　　　　The better.
Sure, there wants fire where there are no
　lively sparks
Of roughness.　　　　　　190
Bos.　And I want compliment.
Jul.　　　　　　Why, ignorance

[2] Sweetmeats for the breath.
[3] Embrace.　　　　　　[4] Spirit.

In courtship cannot make you do amiss,
If you have a heart to do well.

Bos.   You are very fair.

Jul. Nay, if you lay beauty to my charge,
I must plead unguilty.

Bos.   Your bright eyes
Carry a quiver of darts in them, sharper
Than sunbeams.

Jul.   You will mar me with
commendation;
Put yourself to the charge of courting me,
Whereas now I woo you.

Bos. [*Aside.*] I have it; I will work upon
this creature.—   200
Let us grow most amorously familiar.
If the great cardinal now should see me
thus,
Would he not count me a villain?

Jul. No; he might count me a wanton,
Not lay a scruple of offense on you;
For, if I see and steal a diamond,
The fault is not i' th' stone, but in me,
the thief
That purloins it. I am sudden with you.
We that are great women of pleasure use
to cut off
These uncertain wishes and unquiet long-
ings,   210
And in an instant join the sweet delight
And the pretty excuse together. Had you
been i' th' street,
Under my chamber window, even
there
I should have courted you.

Bos. O, you are an excellent lady!

Jul. Bid me do somewhat for you presently
To express I love you.

Bos. I will; and, if you love me, fail not to
effect it.
The cardinal is grown wondrous melancholy;
Demand the cause; let him not put you
off   220
With feigned excuse; discover the main
ground on 't.

Jul. Why would you know this?

Bos.   I have depended on him,
And I hear that he is fall'n in some dis-
grace
With the emperor. If he be, like the
mice
That forsake falling houses, I would shift
To other dependence.

Jul.   You shall not need follow the
wars—
I'll be your maintenance.

Bos.   And I your loyal servant;
But I cannot leave my calling.

Jul.   Not leave an
Ungrateful general for the love of a sweet
lady!
You are like some cannot sleep in feather
beds,   230
But must have blocks for their pillows.

Bos.   Will you do this?

Jul. Cunningly.

Bos. Tomorrow I'll expect th' intelligence.

Jul. Tomorrow! Get you into my cabinet;
You shall have it with you. Do not delay
me,
No more than I do you. I am like one
That is condemned; I have my pardon
promised,
But I would see it sealed. Go, get you in;
You shall see me wind my tongue about
his heart
Like a skein of silk.   [*Exit Bosola.*

Enter Cardinal.]

Card.   Where are you?

[*Enter Servants.*]

Servants.   Here.

Card. Let none, upon your lives,   241
Have conference with the Prince Fer-
dinand,
Unless I know it. [*Exeunt Servants.*]—
[*Aside.*] In this distraction
He may reveal the murther.
Yond's my lingering consumption.
I am weary of her, and by any means
Would be quit of.

Jul. How now, my lord! What ails you?

Card. Nothing.

Jul.   O, you are much alteréd.
Come, I must be your secretary,[1] and
remove
This lead from off your bosom. What's
the matter?   250

Card. I may not tell you.

Jul. Are you so far in love with sorrow
You cannot part with part of it? Or
think you

_____
[1] Sharer of secrets.

I cannot love your grace when you are
　　sad
As well as merry? Or do you suspect
I, that have been a secret to your heart
These many winters, cannot be the same
Unto your tongue?
CARD.　　　　　　Satisfy thy longing—
　The only way to make thee keep my
　　counsel　　　　　　　　　　259
　Is not to tell thee.
JUL.　　　　　　Tell your echo this,
　Or flatterers, that like echoes still re-
　　port
　What they hear, though most imperfect,
　　and not me;
　For, if that you be true unto yourself,
　I'll know.
CARD.　　　Will you rack me?
JUL.　　　　　　No, judgment shall
　Draw it from you. It is an equal fault
　To tell one's secrets unto all or none.
CARD. The first argues folly.
JUL. But the last tyranny.
CARD. Very well; why, imagine I have
　　committed
　Some secret deed which I desire the
　　world　　　　　　　　　　270
　May never hear of.
JUL.　　　Therefore may not I know it?
　You have concealed for me as great a sin
　As adultery. Sir, never was occasion
　For perfect trial of my constancy
　Till now. Sir, I beseech you—
CARD.　　　　　　You'll repent it.
JUL. Never.
CARD. It hurries thee to ruin. I'll not tell
　　thee.
　Be well advised, and think what danger
　　'tis
　To receive a prince's secrets. They that
　　do,
　Had need have their breasts hooped with
　　adamant　　　　　　　　　280
　To contain them. I pray thee, yet be
　　satisfied;
　Examine thine own frailty; 'tis more easy
　To tie knots than unloose them. 'Tis a
　　secret
　That, like a ling'ring poison, may chance
　　lie
　Spread in thy veins, and kill thee seven
　　year hence.
JUL. Now you dally with me.
CARD. No more; thou shalt know it.

By my appointment, the great Duchess
　　of Malfi
And two of her young children, four
　　nights since,
Were strangled.
JUL.　　　　　　O heaven! Sir, what
　have you done?　　　　　　　290
CARD. How now? How settles this? Think
　you your
　Bosom will be a grave, dark and obscure
　　enough
　For such a secret?
JUL.　　　You have undone yourself, sir.
CARD. Why?
JUL.　　　It lies not in me to conceal it.
CARD. No? Come, I will swear you to 't
　upon this book.
JUL. Most religiously.
CARD. Kiss it.　　　　[She kisses the book.]
　Now you shall never utter it; thy curios-
　　ity
　Hath undone thee; thou'rt poisoned with
　　that book.
　Because I knew thou couldst not keep
　　my counsel,　　　　　　　300
　I have bound thee to 't by death.

　　　　　　[Enter Bosola.]

BOS. For pity sake, hold!
CARD.　　　　　　Ha, Bosola?
JUL.　　　　　　I forgive you
　This equal piece of justice you have done;
　For I betrayed your counsel to that
　　fellow.
　He overheard it; that was the cause I
　　said
　It lay not in me to conceal it.
BOS. O foolish woman,
　Couldst not thou have poisoned him?
JUL.　　　　　　'Tis weakness
　Too much to think what should have
　　been done.　　　　　　　309
　I go, I know not whither.　　　[Dies.]
CARD. Wherefore com'st thou hither?
BOS. That I might find a great man like
　　yourself,
　Not out of his wits, as the Lord Ferdi-
　　nand,
　To remember my service.
CARD.　　　I'll have thee hewed in pieces.
BOS. Make not yourself such a promise of
　　that life
　Which is not yours to dispose of.
CARD.　　　　　Who placed thee here?

Bos. Her lust, as she intended.

Card.   Very well;
  Now you know me for your fellow-
    murderer.

Bos. And wherefore should you lay fair
    marble colors
  Upon your rotten purposes to me,   320
  Unless you imitate some that do plot
    great treasons,
  And, when they have done, go hide them-
    selves i' th' graves
  Of those were actors in 't?

Card.   No more; there is
  A fortune attends thee.

Bos. Shall I go sue to Fortune any longer?
  'Tis the fool's pilgrimage.

Card. I have honors in store for thee.

Bos. There are a many ways that conduct
    to seeming
  Honor, and some of them very dirty ones.

Card. Throw to the devil   330
  Thy melancholy. The fire burns well;
  What need we keep a-stirring of 't, and
    make
  A greater smoother? [1] Thou wilt kill
    Antonio?

Bos. Yes.

Card.   Take up that body.

Bos.   I think I shall
  Shortly grow the common bier for
    churchyards!

Card. I will allow thee some dozen of
    attendants
  To aid thee in the murther.

  Bos. O, by no means. Physicians that
apply horseleeches to any rank swelling use
to cut off their tails, that the blood [340
may run through them the faster. Let
me have no train when I go to shed blood,
lest it make me have a greater when I
ride to the gallows.

Card. Come to me after midnight, to help
    to remove
  That body to her own lodging. I'll give out
  She died o' th' plague;
  'Twill breed the less inquiry after her
    death.

Bos. Where's Castruchio her husband?

Card. He's rode to Naples, to take pos-
    session   350
  Of Antonio's citadel.

Bos. Believe me, you have done a very
    happy turn.

  [1] Smother, smoke.

Card. Fail not to come. There is the
    master key
  Of our lodgings; and by that you may
    conceive
  What trust I plant in you.   Exit.

Bos.   You shall find me ready.—
  O poor Antonio, though nothing be so
    needful
  To thy estate as pity, yet I find
  Nothing so dangerous! I must look to my
    footing;
  In such slippery ice-pavements men had
    need
  To be frost-nailed well—they may break
    their necks else.   360
  The precedent's here afore me. How this
    man
  Bears up in blood, seems fearless! Why,
    'tis well.
  Security some men call the suburbs of
    hell,
  Only a dead wall between. Well, good
    Antonio,
  I'll seek thee out; and all my care shall be
  To put thee into safety from the reach
  Of these most cruel biters that have got
  Some of thy blood already. It may be,
  I'll join with thee in a most just revenge.
  The weakest arm is strong enough that
    strikes   370
  With the sword of justice. Still methinks
    the duchess
  Haunts me. There, there!—'Tis nothing
    but my melancholy.
  O Penitence, let me truly taste thy cup,
  That throws men down only to raise
    them up!   Exit.

SCENA iii.

[A fortification in Milan.]

Antonio, Delio. Echo (from the Duchess'
                                    grave).

Del. Yond's the cardinal's window. This
    fortification
  Grew from the ruins of an ancient abbey;
  And to yond side o' th' river lies a wall,
  Piece of a cloister, which in my opinion
  Gives the best echo that you ever heard,
  So hollow and so dismal, and withal
  So plain in the distinction of our words
  That many have supposed it is a spirit
  That answers.

ANT.   I do love these ancient ruins.
We never tread upon them but we set   10
Our foot upon some reverend history;
And, questionless, here in this open
    court,
Which now lies naked to the injuries
Of stormy weather, some men lie interred
Loved the church so well, and gave so
    largely to 't,
They thought it should have canopied
    their bones
Till doomsday. But all things have their
    end;
Churches and cities, which have diseases
    like to men,
Must have like death that we have.
ECHO.   Like death that we have.
DEL. Now the echo hath caught you.   20
ANT. It groaned, methought, and gave
A very deadly accent.
ECHO.   Deadly accent.
DEL. I told you 'twas a pretty one. You
    may make it
A huntsman, or a falconer, a musician,
Or a thing of sorrow.
ECHO.   A thing of sorrow.
ANT. Ay, sure, that suits it best.
ECHO.   That suits it best.
ANT. 'Tis very like my wife's voice.
ECHO.   Ay, wife's voice.
DEL. Come, let's us walk farther from 't.
I would not have you go to th' cardinal's
    tonight.
Do not.   30
ECHO. Do not.
DEL. Wisdom doth not more moderate
    wasting sorrow
Than time. Take time for 't; be mindful
    of thy safety.
ECHO. Be mindful of thy safety.
ANT. Necessity compels me.
Make scrutiny throughout the passes
Of your own life, you'll find it impossible
To fly your fate.
[ECHO.] O, fly your fate!
DEL. Hark! The dead stones seem to
    have pity on you,   40
And give you good counsel.
ANT. Echo, I will not talk with thee,
For thou art a dead thing.
ECHO. Thou art a dead thing.
ANT. My duchess is asleep now,
And her little ones, I hope sweetly. O
    heaven,

Shall I never see her more?
ECHO. Never see her more.
ANT. I marked not one repetition of the
    echo
But that; and on the sudden a clear
    light   50
Presented me a face folded in sorrow.
DEL. Your fancy merely.
ANT.   Come, I'll be out of this ague.
For to live thus is not indeed to live;
It is a mockery and abuse of life.
I will not henceforth save myself by
    halves;
Lose all, or nothing.
DEL.   Your own virtue save you!
I'll fetch your eldest son, and second you.
It may be that the sight of his own blood
Spread in so sweet a figure may beget
The more compassion. However, fare
    you well.   60
Though in our miseries Fortune have a
    part,
Yet in our noble suff'rings she hath none
Contempt of pain, that we may call our
    own.   Exe[unt].

SCENA iv.

[An apartment in the palace of the Cardinal
                    and Ferdinand at Milan.]

Cardinal, Pescara, Malateste, Roderigo,
    Grisolan, Bosola, Ferdinand, Antonio,
                              Servant.[1]

CARD. You shall not watch tonight by the
    sick prince;
His grace is very well recovered.
MAL. Good my lord, suffer us.
CARD.   O, by no means;
The noise, and change of object in his
    eye,
Doth more distract him. I pray, all to
    bed;
And, though you hear him in his violent
    fit,
Do not rise, I entreat you.
PES. So, sir; we shall not.
CARD.   Nay, I must have you promise
Upon your honors, for I was enjoined
to 't
By himself; and he seemed to urge it
    sensibly.   10
PES. Let our honors bind this trifle.
CARD. Nor any of your followers.

[1] Last four enter later.

MAL. Neither.

CARD. It may be, to make trial of your promise,
When he's asleep, myself will rise and feign
Some of his mad tricks, and cry out for help,
And feign myself in danger.

MAL.   If your throat were cutting,
I'ld not come at you, now I have protested against it.

CARD. Why, I thank you.

GRIS.   'Twas a foul storm tonight.   20

ROD. The Lord Ferdinand's chamber shook like an osier.

MAL. [Aside.] 'Twas nothing but pure kindness in the devil
To rock his own child.

              Exeunt [all except the Cardinal].

CARD. The reason why I would not suffer these
About my brother is because at midnight
I may with better privacy convey
Julia's body to her own lodging. O, my conscience!
I would pray now, but the devil takes away my heart
For having any confidence in prayer.
About this hour I appointed Bosola   30
To fetch the body. When he hath served my turn,
He dies.   Exit.

              [Enter Bosola.]

Bos. Ha! 'Twas the cardinal's voice; I heard him name
Bosola and my death. Listen; I hear one's footing.

              [Enter Ferdinand.]

FERD. Strangling is a very quiet death.

Bos. [Aside.] Nay, then, I see I must stand upon my guard.

FERD. What say to that? Whisper softly. Do you agree to 't? So; it must be done i' th' dark; the cardinal would not for a thousand pounds the doctor should   [40
see it.   Exit.

Bos. My death is plotted; here's the consequence of murther.
"We value not desert nor Christian breath,
When we know black deeds must be cured with death."

              [Enter Antonio and Servant.]

SER. Here stay, sir, and be confident, I pray;
I'll fetch you a dark lanthorn.   Exit.

ANT.   Could I take
Him at his prayers, there were hope of pardon.

Bos. Fall right, my sword! [Stabs him.]—
I'll not give thee so much leisure as to pray.

ANT. O, I am gone! Thou hast ended a long suit   50
In a minute.

Bos.   What art thou?

ANT.   A most wretched thing,
That only have thy benefit[1] in death,
To appear myself.

              [Enter Servant with a lantern.]

SER. Where are you, sir?

ANT. Very near my home!—Bosola!

SER.   O, misfortune!

Bos. [To Servant.] Smother thy pity; thou art dead else.—Antonio!
The man I would have saved 'bove mine own life!
We are merely the stars' tennis balls, strook[2] and banded[3]
Which way please them.—O good Antonio,
I'll whisper one thing in thy dying ear   60
Shall make thy heart break quickly!
Thy fair duchess
And two sweet children—

ANT.   Their very names
Kindle a little life in me.

Bos.   Are murdered!

ANT. Some men have wished to die
At the hearing of sad tidings; I am glad
That I shall do 't in sadness.[4] I would not now
Wish my wounds balmed nor healed, for I have no use
To put my life to. In all our quest of greatness,
Like wanton boys whose pastime is their care,
We follow after bubbles blown in th' air.   70
Pleasure of life, what is 't? Only the good hours

---

[1] Assistance.   [3] Bandied.
[2] Struck.   [4] Seriousness, reality.

Of an ague; merely a preparative to rest,
To endure vexation. I do not ask
The process ¹ of my death; only com-
     mend me
To Delio.
Bos. Break, heart!
ANT. And let my son fly the courts of
     princes.   [*Dies.*]
Bos. Thou seem'st to have loved An-
     tonio?
SER. I brought him hither,   79
To have reconciled him to the cardinal.
Bos. I do not ask thee that.
Take him up, if thou tender thine own
     life,
And bear him where the lady Julia
Was wont to lodge.—O, my fate moves
     swift!
I have this cardinal in the forge al-
     ready;
Now I'll bring him to th' hammer. O
     direful misprision! ²
I will not imitate things glorious,
No more than base; I'll be mine own
     example.—
On, on, and look thou represent, for
     silence,
The thing thou bear'st.   *Exeunt.* 90

SCENA V.

[*A hall and gallery of the same.*]

*Cardinal, with a book. Bosola, Pescara,
     Malateste, Roderigo, Ferdinand, Delio,
     Servant with Antonio's body.* ³

CARD. I am puzzled in a question about
     hell.
He says in hell there's one material fire,
And yet it shall not burn all men alike.
Lay him by. How tedious is a guilty
     conscience!
When I look into the fish ponds in my
     garden,
Methinks I see a thing armed with a
     rake,
That seems to strike at me.

[*Enter Bosola, and Servant bearing Antonio's
     body.*]

Now, art thou come?   Thou look'st
     ghastly;

¹ Account, story.   ² Mistake.
³ All but the first enter later.

There sits in thy face some great deter-
     mination,
Mixed with some fear.
Bos.   Thus it lightens into action; 10
I am come to kill thee.
CARD.   Ha!—Help! Our guard!
Bos. Thou art deceived; they are out of
     thy howling.
CARD. Hold, and I will faithfully divide
Revenues with thee.
Bos.   Thy prayers and proffers
Are both unseasonable.
CARD.   Raise the watch!
We are betrayed!
Bos.   I have confined your flight.
I'll suffer your retreat to Julia's chamber,
But no further.
CARD.   Help! We are betrayed!

[*Enter, above, Pescara, Malateste, Roderigo,
                    and Grisolan.*]

MAL. Listen!
CARD. My dukedom for rescue!   20
ROD. Fie upon his counterfeiting!
MAL. Why, 'tis not the cardinal.
ROD. Yes, yes, 'tis he.
But I'll see him hanged ere I'll go down
     to him.
CARD. Here's a plot upon me. I am as-
     saulted! I am lost,
Unless some rescue!
GRIS.   He doth this pretty well;
But it will not serve to laugh me out of
     mine honor.
CARD. The sword's at my throat!
ROD.   You would not bawl so loud then.
MAL. Come, come, lets 's go to bed. He
told us this much aforehand.   30
PES. He wished you should not come at
     him; but, believe 't,
The accent of the voice sounds not in
     jest.
I'll down to him, howsoever, and with
     engines
Force ope the doors.   [*Exit above.*]
ROD.   Let's follow him aloof,
And note how the cardinal will laugh
     at him.
[*Exeunt, above, Malateste, Roderigo, and
                    Grisolan.*]
Bos. There's for you first, cause you shall
     not unbarricade the door
To let in rescue.   *He kills the Servant.*

CARD. What cause hast thou to pursue my life?

Bos.   Look there.

CARD. Antonio?

Bos.   Slain by my hand unwittingly.
Pray, and be sudden. When thou killedst thy sister,   40
Thou took'st from Justice her most equal balance,
And left her naught but her sword.

CARD.   O, mercy!

Bos. Now it seems thy greatness was only outward;
For thou fall'st faster of thyself than calamity
Can drive thee. I'll not waste longer time. There!   [*Wounds him.*]

CARD. Thou hast hurt me!

Bos.   Again!

CARD.   Shall I die like a leveret,
Without any resistance?—Help, help, help!
I am slain!

[*Enter Ferdinand.*]

FERD.   Th' alarum! Give me a fresh horse;
Rally the vaunt-guard,[1] or the day is lost.
Yield, yield! I give you the honor of arms,   50
Shake my sword over you. Will you yield?

CARD. Help me; I am your brother!

FERD. The devil!
My brother fight upon the adverse party?

He wounds the Cardinal, and, in the scuffle,
gives Bosola his death wound.

There flies your ransom.

CARD. O justice!
I suffer now for what hath former been.
"Sorrow is held the eldest child of sin."

FERD. Now you're brave fellows. Cæsar's fortune was harder than Pompey's; [60
Cæsar died in the arms of prosperity,
Pompey at the feet of disgrace. You both died in the field. The pain's nothing;
pain many times is taken away with the apprehension of greater, as the toothache with the sight of a barber that comes to pull it out. There's philosophy for you.

[1] Vanguard.

Bos. Now my revenge is perfect.—Sink, thou main cause
Of my undoing!—The last part of my life
Hath done me best service.   70
               He kills Ferdinand.

FERD. Give me some wet hay; I am broken-winded.
I do account this world but a dog kennel.
I will vault credit[2] and affect[3] high pleasures
Beyond death.

Bos. He seems to come to himself, now he's so near the bottom.

FERD. My sister, O my sister! There's the cause on 't.
"Whether we fall by ambition, blood, or lust,
Like diamonds, we are cut with our own dust."   [*Dies.*]

CARD. Thou hast thy payment too.

Bos. Yes, I hold my weary soul in my teeth;   80
'Tis ready to part from me. I do glory
That thou, which stood'st like a huge pyramid
Begun upon a large and ample base,
Shalt end in a little point, a kind of nothing.

[*Enter, below, Pescara, Malateste, Roderigo,*
and Grisolan.]

PES. How now, my lord!

MAL.   O sad disaster!

ROD.   How comes this?

Bos. Revenge for the Duchess of Malfi, murderéd
By th' Aragonian brethren; for Antonio
Slain by this[4] hand; for lustful Julia
Poisoned by this man; and lastly for myself,
That was an actor in the main of all 90
Much gainst mine own good nature, yet i' th' end
Neglected.

PES.   How now, my lord!

CARD.   Look to my brother.
He gave us these large wounds, as we were struggling

[2] "Overleap rational expectation" (Lucas).
[3] Aspire to.
[4] From 1708 edn. Original has *his*.

Here i' th' rushes. And now, I pray, let
   me
Be laid by and never thought of. [*Dies.*]
PES. How fatally, it seems, he did with-
   stand
His own rescue!
MAL.   Thou wretched thing of blood,
How came Antonio by his death?
BOS. In a mist; I know not how;
Such a mistake as I have often seen   100
In a play. O, I am gone!
We are only like dead walls or vaulted
   graves,
That, ruined, yields no echo. Fare you
   well!
It may be pain, but no harm, to me to
   die
In so good a quarrel. O, this gloomy
   world!
In what a shadow, or deep pit of dark-
   ness,
Doth womanish and fearful mankind
   live!
Let worthy minds ne'er stagger in dis-
   trust
To suffer death or shame for what is
   just.
Mine is another voyage.   [*Dies.*] 110
PES. The noble Delio, as I came to th'
   palace.

Told me of Antonio's being here, and
   showed me
A pretty gentleman, his son and heir.

[*Enter Delio, and Antonio's Son.*]

MAL. O, sir, you come too late!
DEL.   I heard so, and
Was armed for 't, ere I came. Let us
   make noble use
Of this great ruin, and join all our force
To establish this young hopeful gentle-
   man
In 's mother's right. These wretched
   eminent things
Leave no more fame behind 'em than
   should one
Fall in a frost, and leave his print in
   snow.   120
As soon as the sun shines, it ever melts,
Both form and matter. I have ever
   thought
Nature doth nothing so great for great
   men
As when she's pleased to make them
   lords of truth.
"Integrity of life is fame's best friend,
Which nobly, beyond death, shall crown
   the end."   *Exeunt.*

FINIS.

STUART PLAYS

EDITED BY

VIRGIL B. HELTZEL
ARTHUR H. NETHERCOT

BEN JONSON

Intimately acquainted with the Greek and Roman classics, critically observant of life about him, and endowed beyond any other writer of his day with the satirist's gifts, Ben Jonson with his originality, his clearly defined principles of art, and his impatience with anything but the best, brought to the business of play-writing an equipment which enabled him to infuse into his work elements which profoundly influenced English drama for generations after his time. He was born in London or its environs in the year 1572, the posthumous son of a clergyman, and, according to Fuller, was sent to a private school in St. Martin's Church, and later to Westminster, where his tutor, the eminent antiquary, William Camden, probably instilled into him that taste for the classics which was to influence strongly the subsequent work of the dramatist. About 1589, probably because of his poverty, instead of pursuing a university education he left Westminster to follow his stepfather's trade of bricklaying. Except that he saw service as a soldier in the Netherlands, was married to one whom he later characterized as "a shrew, yet honest," was a member of a strolling company of actors in which he may have played the hero of Kyd's *Spanish Tragedy*, very little is known of his career until July 28, 1597, when Henslowe's Diary records a loan of £4 made to him as an actor at Paris Garden. On the same day the privy council ordered all London theaters suppressed as a result of the performance of a play now lost, *The Isle of Dogs*. Probably for his share with Nashe in the writing of this play, Jonson was imprisoned in the Marshalsea until an order was signed on October 3 for his release. In the same year he is thought to have composed *The Case Is Altered*, a comedy in the manner of Chapman. By September, 1598, he had acquired sufficient reputation to be accounted by Francis Meres one of the best for tragedy, but Meres' basis for such a pronouncement can now be but a subject of conjecture. About the middle of September, however, Jonson's reputation as a writer of comedy was definitely established when *Every Man in His Humor* was played by the Lord Chamberlain's Company at the Curtain, a performance in which Shakespeare acted a part, possibly that of the elder Knowell. On September 22, 1598, Jonson killed his fellow-actor, Gabriel Spencer, in a duel. When brought to trial, he confessed and claimed right of clergy; his property was confiscated and his thumb branded. The following year he collaborated with Dekker in two plays now lost, *The Page of Plymouth* and *Robert the Second, King of Scots*, and wrote *Every Man out of His Humor*, performed and published in 1600. By caricaturing Marston in this play he definitely committed himself to a part in the stage quarrel, in which his next two plays, *Cynthia's Revels* and *The Poetaster*, were to figure prominently. With the performance of *Sejanus* in 1603 Jonson appeared as a writer of a tragedy which not only was unpopular on the boards but which, because of political attacks made upon it, caused him to be questioned by the privy council. Late in 1604 he collaborated with Chapman and Marston in writing *Eastward Ho!* and, when they were sent to prison "for writing something against the Scots," Jonson voluntarily accompanied them. On January 6, 1605, he began his great career of masque-writing with the production of *The Masque of Blackness* at Whitehall, and during the reign of James he furnished twenty of the thirty-seven masques presented at court. Early in 1606 he composed *Volpone;* toward the close of 1609, *Epicoene;* in 1610, *The Alchemist;* and in 1611, another tragedy, *Catiline His Conspiracy*, which was as little of a success as *Sejanus* had been. During the first years of the century Jonson formed friendships with some of the greatest wits of the day and with such eminent patrons as the Countess of Bedford, the Countess of Rutland, Lady Wroth, and the Earl of Pembroke. About 1612 he had the first of several quarrels with Inigo Jones, the noted architect who designed costumes and scenery for masques at

827

court, and in the autumn he accompanied Raleigh's son to France in the capacity of tutor, returning before the end of June the following year. About this time he began the task of preparing his works for publication in the folio of 1616. Following the performance of *Bartholomew Fair* in October, 1614, and the rather unsuccessful, loosely constructed play, *The Devil Is an Ass*, in 1616, Jonson produced no plays for about nine years, although he wrote a few masques. In the summer of 1618 he set out for Scotland, where he visited William Drummond of Hawthornden, whose notes on Ben's conversations are invaluable for biographical details and for their criticisms upon contemporaries. On July 19, 1619, Jonson was made M.A. of Oxford. He now stood at the head of English men of letters, a past master about whom the wits of London gathered in tavern meetings, especially at the Devil's Head, where the upper chamber, known as the Apollo, was set aside for meetings of "The Tribe of Ben." The performance of *The Staple of News* in 1626 marks the dramatist's return to the stage, and by 1634 he had produced *The New Inn, The Magnetic Lady*, and *A Tale of a Tub*, probably, though not certainly, an old play revised. *The Sad Shepherd* he left unfinished at his death. Although in 1628 a paralytic stroke confined him to his chamber, he succeeded Thomas Middleton as city chronologer, and in the following year he was granted a pension of £100 by King Charles. From November, 1635, when his son died, until his own death, no biographical information is available. He died on August 6, 1637, and was buried three days later in Westminster Abbey. The following year saw the appearance of *Jonsonus Virbius*, a collection of thirty-three pieces of verse contributed to his memory by his admirers. In 1640 appeared a reprint of the 1616 folio, and a second volume of Jonson's works, printed 1631–41, was issued 1640–41 under the supervision of Sir Kenelm Digby.

Every Man in His Humor, not Jonson's greatest but probably his most influential play, first acted by the Lord Chamberlain's Men in 1598, was entered in the Stationers' Register August 4, 1600, and was printed the following year. This version, with its scene laid in Florence and its chief characters bearing Italian names, was later carefully revised by Jonson for publication in the 1616 folio. The scene was shifted to London, the characters were given English names and were more individualized, and the expression in general was much altered, the most notable change being the excision of Lorenzo's (Knowell's) defense of poetry at the end of the play, a passage which delayed the action and to Jonson's mind probably violated the principle of decorum because it was unsuited to such a gathering. The plot is of Jonson's own invention, but from Chapman's *An Humorous Day's Mirth* (1599) he drew hints for the gull, and from Plautine comedy he derived the suggestion of a pair of elderly persons deceived and outwitted by a pair of clever young men, as well as the shrewd serving-man and the braggart soldier. In its preservation of unity of tone, its observance of the unities of time, place, and action, and its truth to what is typical or normal in action and character, the play shows a definite adherence to the requirements of classical comedy as formulated by Renaissance criticism, notably by Sidney in his *Defense of Poesy*, published in 1595. The prologue to the later version of the play presents Jonson's essential dramatic theory for all his comedies. He here expresses condemnation of the wildly romantic tendencies in the drama and declares his purpose to "show the image of the times" by employing "deeds and language such as men do use," and to make follies, not crimes, his chief consideration. During the last twenty years of the sixteenth century, Lyly, Greene, Nashe, and Lodge in their didactic writings and, at the end of the century, Chapman in his *Blind Beggar of Alexandria* (1598) and *An Humorous Day's Mirth* (1599) had created characters dominated by humors. To exhibit the follies of men Jonson created the comedy of humors which, though illustrated by the present play, is fully developed in *Every Man out of His Humor* and *Cynthia's Revels*. The present text is based on Herford and Simpson's reprint of the 1616 folio checked by the original in the Newberry Library.

Perhaps prompted by the success of Shakespeare's *Julius Cæsar* and by the popularity of the tragedy of political adventure about the time of the conspiracy and trial of Essex, Jonson turned from the Comic Muse, who, as he says, had proved "so ominous" to him, and tried his hand at Roman tragedy. *Sejanus*, performed before the end of 1603 by the King's Men at the Globe, with Shakespeare among the actors, was entered in the Stationers' Register November 2, 1604, and published in 1605. In his address to the reader Jonson says "a second pen" had a good share in the original version of the play, but, since Jonson rewrote the parts of his collaborator, neither these passages nor their original author can be identified, though Chapman has been suggested with some probability. For the story of *Sejanus*, Jonson relied mainly upon Tacitus' *Annals* and Dion's *Roman History*, but he drew details from Suetonius' life of Tiberius, Juvenal's tenth satire, and Seneca's *De Tranquillitate*. Although he departs but little from his sources, the play is far more than a mosaic of translated passages, for he has thoroughly re-created and quickened his materials by the imaginative treatment required of the dramatist. He does not adhere nearly so closely to classical technique as in his earlier plays, but he achieves greater coherence and displays more constructive skill. In stressing the arrogance and fall of Sejanus, Jonson was influenced by the medieval conception of tragedy still surviving in the popular *Mirror for Magistrates*. The play was not and never can be popular. The characters are too numerous, too little individualized, and too imperfectly grouped. Moreover, the play is lacking in pity. As Herford says, "Jonsonian tragedy suffers from an inner poverty in the humanities of the heart." The present text is based on Herford and Simpson's reprint of the 1616 folio checked by the original in the Newberry Library.

Volpone, "fully penned" in five weeks early in 1606, was presented shortly after by the King's Men at the Globe and in the summer and autumn of the same year at both universities, and was published in 1607/8. The play is not confined merely to follies, as were the earlier comedies, but includes crimes, so that, as Coleridge remarks, "there is no goodness of heart in any of the prominent characters." Nevertheless, the production of *Volpone* restored Jonson's popularity, which had been temporarily dimmed by the poor reception accorded *Sejanus*. The latter play had taught him the necessity of a closely knit plot and the value of Roman history as a source. Legacy-hunting, so frequent in Roman literature, had impressed him as fertile soil for imposture and fraud, and for the materials of the play he drew suggestions from numerous classical sources, among which may be mentioned Lucian's dialogues, Horace's satires, and Libanius. Professor J. D. Rea in his edition of the play has stressed Jonson's debt to Erasmus' *Praise of Folly*. The scene of the action is quite appropriately laid in Italy, to the Elizabethan mind the land of villainy, and only in the sub-plot (which, although it affords some effective comic episodes, does not advance the action) does Jonson introduce a bit of his own England in the persons of Sir Politic and his lady. The play observes the unities carefully, and the arrangement of scenes is according to classical precedent. The present text is based on the Newberry Library copy of the 1616 folio.

Jonson's most popular and, in the light of his theory, most perfect play, *The Alchemist*, entered in the Stationers' Register October 3, 1610, and published in 1612, was written during the plague season of 1610 for performance before Londoners who, like Lovewit, would return to their homes after all danger of infection had passed. The practice of alchemy was as common to the life of the time as it had been in the Middle Ages, and exposures of impostures such as Jonson portrays were so frequent in life as well as in literature that it has been impossible to discover any source for this aspect of the play. From Plautus' *Mostellaria* he may have derived the quarrel scene at the opening of the play and the idea of the unexpected return of the owner of a house in which rogues are carrying on their practices; and he may have taken certain minor suggestions from Plautus' *Pœnulus* and Erasmus' colloquy on the alchemist. Professor Child's suggestion of Giordano Bruno's *Il Candelaio* (1582) as a source has not won general acceptance. The construction of the play reveals the hand of the master. All the unities are rigidly observed. The action takes place in a single day at a house in the Blackfriars district of London, and, while the three intrigues remain distinct, each being a unit in itself, they are actuated by similar motives, are pervaded by one comic tone, and are related to the general plan. Suspense as to the outcome of the action constantly increases to the very end of the play. The present text is based on Hathaway's reprint of the 1616 folio checked with the original in the Newberry Library. Occasional reference has also been made to Noel Douglas' replica of the 1612 quarto in the British Museum.

Lord Haddington's Masque or, as it is appropriately named by Gifford, *The Hue and Cry after Cupid,* was printed, probably in 1608, in an undated quarto, and in the folio of 1616. The classical legend upon which it was founded is as old at least as Moschus, and had been often retold in Italy and in France. None of these versions, however, can be designated as a source for Jonson's masque. The piece occupies an important place in the evolution of the masque, not only because in the rôles of Cupid and his twelve boys "most anticly attired" it offers a good example of the antimasque or foil, intended by its grotesqueness and drollery to set off the beauty of the main masque, but because in its brevity, simplicity, and high poetical quality it avoids the excesses which often characterized its successors. The present text is based on the 1616 folio in the Newberry Library.

Jonson's one extant attempt at pastoral drama, *The Sad Shepherd,* was found as a fragment among his papers after his death, and was published by Sir Kenelm Digby in the second folio with the date 1641 on its title-page. The circumstances and exact date of its composition are still to be ascertained, but there is some reason for regarding it as the work of the author's last years. Jonson here turns aside from examples set by his predecessors in the type, and boldly strikes out to produce a truly English pastoral play. He suppresses satire and symbolism, and for Arcadia with its shadowy shepherds as main characters he substitutes Sherwood Forest with Maid Marian and Robin Hood and his merry men; instead of the satyr of conventional pastoral tradition he introduces Maudlin the Witch and Puck-Hairy. In thus subordinating or ignoring many of the time-worn conventions of the pastoral and introducing freshness and real life, Jonson was reverting to the practice of the first pastoral poet, Theocritus. The present text is based on the second folio in the Newberry Library.

EVERY MAN IN HIS HUMOR [1]

BY

BEN JONSON

To the Most Learned, and My Honored Friend, Mr.[2] Camden, Clarencieux [3]

Sir:

There are, no doubt, a supercilious race in the world who will esteem all office done you in this kind an injury, so solemn a vice it is with them to use the authority of their ignorance to the crying down of poetry or the professors.[4] But my gratitude must not leave [5] to correct their error, since I am none of those that can suffer the benefits conferred upon my youth to perish with my age. It is a frail memory that remembers [10 but present things, and had the favor of the times so conspired with my disposition, as it could have brought forth other or better, you had had the same proportion and number of the fruits, the first. Now I pray you to accept this, such wherein neither the confession of my manners shall make you blush, nor of my studies repent you [6] to have been the instructor; and for the profession of my thankfulness, I am sure [20 it will, with good men, find either praise or excuse.

Your true lover,

Ben. Jonson.

THE PERSONS OF THE PLAY

Knowell,[7] *an old gentleman.*
Ed[ward] Knowell, *his son.*
Brainworm, *the father's man.*
Mr. Stephen, *a country gull.*
[George] Downright, *a plain squire.*
Wellbred, *his half-brother.*
Just[ice] Clement, *an old, merry magistrate.*
Roger Formal, *his clerk.*

Kitely, *a merchant.*
Dame Kitely, *his wife.*
Mrs.[8] Bridget, *his sister.*
Mr. Matthew, *the town gull.*
[Thomas] Cash, *Kitely's man.*
[Oliver] Cob, *a water bearer.*
Tib, *his wife.*
Cap[tain] Bobadill, *a Paul's man.*[9]
[Servants, *etc.*]

The scene: *London.*

[Time: *Contemporary.*]

PROLOGUE

Though need make many poets, and some such
As art and nature have not bettered much,
Yet ours for want hath not so loved the stage
As he dare serve th' ill customs of the age,
Or purchase your delight at such a rate,
As, for it, he himself must justly hate:
To make a child, now swaddled, to proceed
Man, and then shoot up, in one beard and weed,
Past threescore years; or, with three rusty swords,
And help of some few foot-and-half-foot words,   10
Fight over York and Lancaster's long jars,

[1] The title continues: "A Comedy. Acted in the Year 1598 by the Then Lord Chamberlain His Servants. The Author B. J."
[2] Master.
[3] One of the kings-at-arms in the Heralds' College.   [5] Omit.
[4] Supporters of poetry.   [6] Make you repent.
[7] Printed *Kno'well* throughout.
[8] Mistress.
[9] A lounger in the middle aisle of St. Paul's Cathedral, a social and business center.

And in the tiring-house [1] bring wounds to
   scars.
He rather prays you will be pleased to see
One such today, as other plays should be,
Where neither chorus wafts you o'er the
   seas,
Nor creaking throne comes down, the boys
   to please,
Nor nimble squib is seen, to make afeard
The gentlewomen, nor rolled bullet heard,
To say it thunders, nor tempestuous drum
Rumbles, to tell you when the storm doth
   come,   20
But deeds and language such as men do use,
And persons such as comedy would choose,
When she would show an image of the
   times,
And sport with human follies, not with
   crimes—
Except we make hem [2] such, by loving still
Our popular errors, when we know th' are
   ill.
I mean such errors as you'll all confess,
By laughing at them, they deserve no less—
Which when you heartily do, there's hope
   left then,
You, that have so graced [3] monsters, may
   like men.   30

Act I. Scene i.

[A street.]

Knowell, Brainworm, Mr. Stephen. [4]

[Know.] A goodly day toward, and a fresh
morning!—Brainworm,

[Enter Brainworm.]

Call up your young master; bid him rise,
   sir.
Tell him I have some business to employ
   him.
Bra. I will, sir, presently. [5]
Know.   But hear you, sirrah,
  If he be at [6] his book, disturb him not.
Bra. Well, sir.   [Exit.]
Know. How happy yet should I esteem
   myself,

---

[1] Dressing room.
[2] Them.   [4] Enters later.
[3] Approved.   [5] At once.
[6] Original reads *be 'at.* Jonson and other poets
often use the apostrophe thus to indicate elision,
but in deference to modern practice it has been
omitted in this anthology.

Could I, by any practice, [7] wean the boy
From one vain course of study he affects.
He is a scholar, if a man may trust   10
The liberal voice of fame, in her report
Of good accompt in both our universities,
Either of which hath favored him with
   graces.
But their indulgence must not spring in
   me
A fond [8] opinion that he cannot err.
Myself was once a student, and, indeed,
Fed with the selfsame humor [9] he is now,
Dreaming on naught but idle poetry,
That fruitless and unprofitable art,
Good unto none, but least to the pro-
   fessors,   20
Which then I thought the mistress of all
   knowledge;
But, since, time and the truth have
   waked my judgment,
And reason taught me better to distin-
   guish
The vain from th' useful learnings.—

[Enter Stephen.]

                Cousin [10] Stephen,
What news with you, that you are here
   so early?
Ste. Nothing, but e'en come to see how
you do, uncle.
Know. That's kindly done; you are
welcome, coz.
Ste. Ay, I know that, sir; I would not ha'
   come else.   30
How do my cousin Edward, uncle?
Know. O, well, coz; go in and see; I
doubt he be scarce stirring yet.
Ste. Uncle, afore I go in, can you tell
me, an [11] he have e'er a book of the sciences
of hawking and hunting? I would fain
borrow it.
Know. Why, I hope you will not a-hawk-
ing now, will you?
Ste. No, wusse; [12] but I'll practice   [40
against [13] next year, uncle. I have bought
me a hawk, and a hood, and bells, and all;
I lack nothing but a book to keep it by.
Know. O, most ridiculous!

---

[7] Artifice.   [8] Foolish.
[9] A dominating quality or caprice in a person's
temperament.
[10] A general term of relationship or intimacy.
[11] If.
[12] I wis, certainly.   [13] In preparation for.

STE. Nay, look you now, you are angry, uncle. Why, you know, an a man have not skill in the hawking and hunting languages nowadays, I'll not give a rush for him. They are more studied than the Greek or the Latin. He is for no gallant's company [50 without hem; and, by Gad's lid,[1] I scorn it, I, so I do, to be a consort for every humdrum;[2] hang hem, scroyles![3] There's nothing in hem i' the world. What[4] do you talk on it? Because I dwell at Hogsden, I shall keep company with none but the archers of Finsbury or the citizens that come a-ducking to Islington ponds? A fine jest, i' faith! 'Slid,[1] a gentleman mun[5] show himself like a gentleman. Uncle, [60 I pray you be not angry; I know what I have to do, I trow; I am no novice.

KNOW. You are a prodigal, absurd coxcomb; go to!
Nay, never look at me. It's I that speak.
Take 't as you will, sir, I'll not flatter you.
Ha' you not yet found means enow to waste
That which your friends have left you, but you must
Go cast away your money on a kite,
And know not how to keep it, when you ha' done?
O, it's comely! This will make you a gentleman!   70
Well, cousin, well, I see you are e'en past hope
Of all reclaim.—Ay, so, now you are told on it,
You look another way.

STE.   What would you ha' me do?
KNOW. What would I have you do? I'll tell you, kinsman;
Learn to be wise, and practice how to thrive.
That would I have you do, and not to spend
Your coin on every bable[6] that you fancy,
Or every foolish brain that humors you.
I would not have you to invade each place,
Nor thrust yourself on all societies, 80
Till men's affections, or your own desert,
Should worthily invite you to your rank.

He that is so respectless[7] in his courses
Oft sells his reputation at cheap market.
Nor would I you should melt away yourself
In flashing bravery,[8] lest, while you affect
To make a blaze of gentry to the world,
A little puff of scorn extinguish it,
And you be left like an unsavory snuff,
Whose property is only to offend.   90
I'ld ha' you sober, and contain yourself,
Not that your sail be bigger than your boat;
But moderate your expenses now, at first,
As[9] you may keep the same proportion still;[10]
Nor stand so much on your gentility,
Which is an airy and mere borrowed thing
From dead men's dust and bones, and none of yours
Except you make or hold it. Who comes here?

ACT I. SCENE ii.

[The same.]

Servant, Mr. Stephen, Knowell, Brainworm.[11]

[SERV.] Save you, gentlemen!
STE. Nay, we do not stand much on our gentility, friend; yet you are welcome; and I assure you mine uncle here is a man of a thousand a year, Middlesex land. He has but one son in all the world; I am his next heir, at the common law, Master Stephen, as simple as I stand here, if my cousin die, as there's hope he will. I have a pretty living o' mine own too, beside, hard [10 by here.
SERV. In good time,[12] sir.
STE. In good time, sir? Why, and in very good time, sir! You do not flout, friend, do you?
SERV. Not I, sir.
STE. Not you, sir? You were not best, sir; an you should, here be them can perceive it, and that quickly too. Go to! And they can give it again soundly too, [20 and[13] need be.

[7] Lacking in self-respect.
[8] Finery.
[9] So that.
[10] Always.
[11] Enters later.
[12] Certainly.
[13] If.

[1] God's eyelid.
[2] Commonplace person.
[3] Mangy fellows.
[4] Why.
[5] Must.
[6] Bauble.

SERV. Why, sir, let this satisfy you; good faith, I had no such intent.

STE. Sir, an I thought you had, I would talk with you, and that presently.

SERV. Good Master Stephen, so you may, sir, at your pleasure.

STE. And so I would, sir, good my saucy companion! An you were out o' mine uncle's ground, I can tell you, [30 though I do not stand upon my gentility neither in 't.

KNOW. Cousin, cousin, will this ne'er be left?

STE. Whoreson,[1] base fellow! A mechan- ical[2] serving-man! By this cudgel, and 'twere not for shame, I would—

KNOW. What would you do, you peremp-
 tory gull?[3]
If you cannot be quiet, get you hence.
You see the honest man demeans him-
 self 40
Modestly towards you, giving no re-
 ply
To your unseasoned, quarreling, rude
 fashion;
And still you huff it,[4] with a kind of
 carriage
As void of wit as of humanity.
Go, get you in; fore[5] heaven, I am
 ashamed
Thou hast a kinsman's interest in me.
 [Exit Stephen.]

SERV. I pray you, sir, is this Master Knowell's house?

KNOW. Yes, marry, is it, sir.

SERV. I should inquire for a gentle- [50 man here, one Master Edward Knowell. Do you know any such, sir, I pray you?

KNOW. I should forget myself else, sir.

SERV. Are you the gentleman? Cry you mercy,[6] sir! I was required by a gentleman i' the city, as I rode out at this end o' the town, to deliver you this letter, sir.

KNOW. To me, sir! What do you mean? Pray you, remember your court'sy.[7] [Reads.] "To his most selected friend, [60 Master Edward Knowell." What might the gentleman's name be, sir, that sent it? Nay, pray you be covered.

SERV. One Master Wellbred, sir.

KNOW. Master Wellbred! A young gentleman, is he not?

SERV. The same, sir. Master Kitely married his sister; the rich merchant i' the Old Jewry. 69

KNOW. You say very true.—Brainworm!

[Enter Brainworm.]

BRA. Sir?

KNOW. Make this honest friend drink here.
 Pray you, go in.—
 [Exeunt Brainworm and Servant.]
This letter is directed to my son;
Yet I am Edward Knowell too, and may,
With the safe conscience of good man-
 ners, use
The fellow's error to my satisfaction.
Well, I will break it ope (old men are
 curious),
Be it but for the style's sake and the
 phrase,
To see if both do answer my son's
 praises,
Who is almost grown the idolater 80
Of this young Wellbred. What have we
 here? What's this?

THE LETTER

" Why, Ned, I beseech thee, hast thou forsworn all thy friends i' the Old Jewry? Or dost thou think us all Jews that inhabit there yet? If thou dost, come over, and but see our frippery;[8] change an old shirt for a whole smock[9] with us. Do not con- ceive that antipathy between us and Hogsden, as was between Jews and [89 hog's flesh. Leave thy vigilant father alone, to number over his green apricots, eve- ning and morning, o' the northwest wall. An I had been his son, I had saved him the labor long since, if taking in all the young wenches that pass by at the backdoor, and coddling[10] every kernel of the fruit for hem, would ha' served. But, prithee, come over to me quickly this morning; I have such a present for thee! Our Turkey com- pany never sent the like to the Grand [100 Signior. One is a rimer, sir, o' your own batch, your own leaven, but doth think himself poet-major o' the town, willing to be shown, and worthy to be seen. The

---

[1] Rascally.   [2] Menial.
[3] Absolute, complete fool.
[4] Swagger.   [6] I beg your pardon.
[5] Before.   [7] I.e., put on your hat.

[8] Old clothes shop.
[9] I.e., wench.   [10] Stewing.

other—I will not venter [1] his description
with you till you come, because I would ha'
you make hither with an appetite. If the
worst of hem be not worth your journey, draw your bill of charges, as unconscionable as any Guildhall verdict [110
will give it you, and you shall be allowed
your viaticum. [2]

> From the Windmill." [3]

From the Burdello [4] it might come as
   well,
The Spittle, [5] or Pict-hatch. [6] Is this the
   man
My son hath sung so, for the happiest
   wit,
The choicest brain the times hath sent
   us forth?
I know not what he may be in the arts,
Nor what in schools; [7] but, surely, for
   his manners
I judge him a profane and dissolute
   wretch,
Worse by possession of such great good
   gifts,   120
Being the master of so loose a spirit.
Why, what unhallowed ruffian would
   have writ
In such a scurrilous manner to a friend!
Why should he think I tell [8] my apricots,
Or play th' Hesperian dragon with my
   fruit,
To watch it? Well, my son, I had thought
Y' had had more judgment t' have made
   election
Of your companions than t' have ta'en
   on trust
Such petulant, jeering gamesters, that
   can spare   129
No argument or subject from their jest.
But I perceive affection makes a fool
Of any man too much the father.—
   Brainworm!

[Enter Brainworm.]

Bra. Sir?
Know.   Is the fellow gone that brought
   this letter?
Bra. Yes, sir, a pretty while since.
Know. And where's your young master?

Bra. In his chamber, sir.
Know. He spake not with the fellow, did
he?
Bra. No, sir, he saw him not.   139
Know.[9] Take you this letter, and deliver
it my son, but with no notice that I have
opened it, on your life.
Bra. O Lord, sir, that were a jest indeed!
                                  [Exit.]
Know. I am resolved I will not stop his
   journey,
Nor practice any violent mean to stay
The unbridled course of youth in him,
   for that,
Restrained, grows more impatient, and
   in kind [10]
Like to the eager, but the generous, [11]
   grayhound,
Who, ne'er so little from his game with-
   held,
Turns head, and leaps up at his holder's
   throat.   150
There is a way of winning more by
   love
And urging of the modesty than fear;
Force works on servile natures, not the
   free.
He that's compelled to goodness may be
   good,
But 'tis but for that fit; [12] where others,
   drawn
By softness and example, get a habit.
Then, if they stray, but warn hem, and
   the same
They should for virtue have done, they'll
   do for shame.   [Exit.]

Act I. Scene ii[i].

[A room in Knowell's house.]

Edw[ard]   Knowell,   Brainworm,   Mr.
                                  Stephen. [13]

[E. Know. (With a letter in his hand.)]
Did he open it, sayest thou?
Bra. Yes, o' my word, sir, and read
the contents.
E. Know. That scarce contents me.
What countenance, prithee, made he i'
the reading of it? Was he angry or pleased?

[1] Venture.   [2] Traveling expenses.
[3] A tavern, formerly a synagogue.
[4] Bordello, a brothel.   [7] Lecture rooms.
[5] Hospital.   [8] Count.
[6] A low district of London.

[9] Here and in two or three other passages the
original verse has been changed to prose.
[10] Nature.   [12] Moment.
[11] Well-bred.   [13] Enters later.

BRA. Nay, sir, I saw him not read it, nor open it, I assure your worship.

E. KNOW. No! How know'st thou [10 then that he did either?

BRA. Marry, sir, because he charged me, on my life, to tell nobody that he opened it, which unless he had done, he would never fear to have it revealed.

E. KNOW. That's true; well, I thank thee, Brainworm.

[*Enter Stephen.*]

STE. O, Brainworm, didst thou not see a fellow here in a what-sha'-call-him doublet? He brought mine uncle a letter [20 e'en now.

BRA. Yes, Master Stephen. What of him?

STE. O, I ha' such a mind to beat him— where is he, canst thou tell?

BRA. Faith, he is not of that mind; he is gone, Master Stephen.

STE. Gone! Which way? When went he? How long since?

BRA. He is rid hence; he took horse [30 at the street door.

STE. And I stayed i' the fields! Whoreson Scanderbag[1] rogue! O, that I had but a horse to fetch him back again!

BRA. Why, you may ha' my m[aste]r's gelding, to save your longing, sir.

STE. But I ha' no boots—that's the spite on 't.

BRA. Why, a fine wisp of hay, rolled hard, Master Stephen.   40

STE. No, faith, it's no boot[2] to follow him now; let him e'en go and hang. Pray thee, help to truss me[3] a little. He does so vex me—

BRA. You'll be worse vexed when you are trussed,[4] Master Stephen. Best keep unbraced,[5] and walk yourself till you be cold; your choler may founder you else.

STE. By my faith, and so I will, now thou tell'st me on 't. How dost thou [50 like my leg, Brainworm?

BRA. A very good leg, Master Stephen; but the woolen stocking does not commend it so well.

STE. Foh!   The stockings be good

enough, now summer is coming on, for the dust; I'll have a pair of silk again' winter, that[6] I go to dwell i' the town. I think my leg would show in a silk hose—

BRA. Believe me, Master Stephen, [60 rarely well.

STE. In sadness,[7] I think it would; I have a reasonable good leg.

BRA. You have an excellent good leg, Master Stephen; but I cannot stay to praise it longer now, and I am very sorry for 't.

STE. Another time will serve, Brainworm; gramercy for this.

[*Exit Brainworm.*]

E. KNOW. Ha, ha, ha!   70

Knowell laughs, having read the letter.

STE. [*Aside.*] 'Slid, I hope he laughs not at me; and he do—

E. KNOW. Here was a letter indeed, to be intercepted by a man's father, and do him good with him! He cannot but think most virtuously both of me and the sender, sure, that make the careful costermonger of him in our familiar epistles. Well, if he read this with patience I'll be gelt,[8] and troll ballads for Mr. John Trundle[9] [80 yonder the rest of my mortality.[10] It is true, and likely, my father may have as much patience as another man, for he takes much physic; and oft taking physic makes a man very patient. But would your packet, Master Wellbred, had arrived at him in such a minute of his patience! Then we had known the end of it, which now is doubtful, and threatens—[*Notices Stephen. Aside.*] What, my wise [90 cousin! Nay, then I'll furnish our feast with one gull more toward the mess.[11] He writes to me of a brace, and here's one— that's three. O, for a fourth! Fortune, if ever thou'lt use thine eyes, I entreat thee—

STE. [*Aside.*] O, now I see who he laughed at. He laughed at somebody in that letter. By this good light, and he had laughed at me—   100

E. KNOW. How now, cousin Stephen, melancholy?

STE. Yes, a little. I thought you had laughed at me, cousin.

---

[1] *I.e.*, mighty, in reference to Iskender-beg, fifteenth century Albanian leader against the Turks.

[2] Use.
[3] Lace me up.

[4] Beaten.
[5] Unlaced.

[6] When.
[7] Seriously.
[8] Gelded.

[9] An actual publisher.
[10] Life.
[11] A group of four.

E. Know. Why, what an I had, coz? What would you ha' done?

Ste. By this light, I would ha' told mine uncle.

E. Know. Nay, if you would ha' told your uncle, I did laugh at you, coz. 110

Ste. Did you, indeed?

E. Know. Yes, indeed.

Ste. Why then—

E. Know. What then?

Ste. I am satisfied; it is sufficient.

E. Know. Why, be so, gentle coz. And, I pray you, let me entreat a courtesy of you. I am sent for this morning by a friend i' the Old Jewry to come to him; it's but crossing over the fields to Moor- [120 gate. Will you bear me company? I protest it is not to draw you into bond or any plot against the state, coz.

Ste. Sir, that's all one and 'twere; you shall command me twice so far as Moorgate, to do you good in such a matter. Do you think I would leave you? I protest—

E. Know. No, no, you shall not protest, coz.

Ste. By my fackins,[1] but I will, [130 by your leave; I'll protest more to my friend than I'll speak of at this time.

E. Know. You speak very well, coz.

Ste. Nay, not so neither; you shall pardon me. But I speak to serve my turn.

E. Know. Your turn, coz? Do you know what you say? A gentleman of your sort,[2] parts, carriage, and estimation, to talk o' your "turn"[3] i' this company, and to me alone, like a tankard bearer at [140 a conduit! Fie! A wight that, hitherto, his every step hath left the stamp of a great foot behind him, as every word the savor of a strong spirit, and he, this man, so graced, gilded, or, to use a more fit metaphor, so tin-foiled by nature, as not ten housewives' pewter again' a good time shows more bright to the world than he! And he (as I said last, so I say again, and still shall say it), this man, to conceal [150 such real ornaments as these, and shadow their glory, as a milliner's wife does her wrought stomacher, with a smoky lawn or a black cyprus![4] O, coz, it cannot be answered; go not about it! Drake's old

ship at Detford[5] may sooner circle the world again. Come, wrong not the quality of your desert, with looking downward, coz; but hold up your head, so; and let the idea of what you are be portrayed i' [160 your face, that men may read i' your physnomy,[6] "Here within this place is to be seen the true, rare, and accomplished monster, or miracle of nature," which is all one. What think you of this, coz?

Ste. Why, I do think of it; and I will be more proud, and melancholy, and gentlemanlike than I have been, I'll insure you.

E. Know. Why, that's resolute,[7] [170 Master Stephen!—[Aside.] Now, if I can but hold him up to his height, as it is happily begun, it will do well for a suburb[8] humor: we may hap have a match with the city, and play him for forty pound.— Come, coz.

Ste. I'll follow you.

E. Know. Follow me! You must go before.[9]

Ste. Nay, an I must, I will. Pray [180 you, show me, good cousin. [Exeunt.]

Act I. Scene iv.

[The lane before Cob's house.]

Mr. Matthew, Cob.[10]

[Mat.] I think this be the house. What, ho!

[Enter Cob.]

Cob. Who's there? O, Master Matthew! Gi' your worship good morrow.

Mat. What, Cob! How dost thou, good Cob? Dost thou inhabit here, Cob?

Cob. Ay, sir, I and my linage[11] ha' kept a poor house here in our days.

Mat. Thy linage, Monsieur Cob! What linage? What linage? 10

Cob. Why, sir, an ancient linage, and a princely. Mine ance'try came from a king's belly, no worse man; and yet no man neither (by your worship's leave, I did lie in that), but herring,[12] the king of

[1] Faith. [2] Station.
[3] A trip, according to which water-carriers were paid. [4] Transparent cloth.
[5] Deptford, where the *Golden Hind* was laid up.
[6] Physiognomy. [10] Enters later.
[7] Decided. [11] Lineage, family.
[8] Rustic. [12] A cob is a young herring.
[9] *I.e.*, like a servant.

fish (from his belly I proceed), one o' the monarchs o' the world, I assure you. The first red herring that was broiled in Adam and Eve's kitchen do I fetch my pedigree from, by the harrot's [1] books. His cob [20 was my great-great-mighty-great grandfather.

MAT. Why mighty, why mighty, I pray thee?

COB. O, it was a mighty while ago, sir, and a mighty great cob.

MAT. How know'st thou that?

COB. How know I? Why, I smell his ghost ever and anon.

MAT. Smell a ghost? O unsavory [30 jest! And the ghost of a herring cob? [2]

COB. Ay, sir. With favor of your worship's nose, Mr. Matthew, why not the ghost of a herring cob as well as the ghost of Rasher Bacon?

MAT. Roger Bacon, thou wouldst say?

COB. I say Rasher Bacon. They were both broiled o' the coals; and a man may smell broiled meat, I hope? You are a scholar; upsolve me that now.   40

MAT. O raw ignorance!—Cob, canst thou show me of a gentleman, one Captain Bobadill, where his lodging is?

COB. O, my guest, sir, you mean.

MAT. Thy guest! Alas! Ha, ha!

COB. Why do you laugh, sir? Do you not mean Captain Bobadill?

MAT. Cob, pray thee, advise thyself well; do not wrong the gentleman, and thyself too. I dare be sworn he scorns [50 thy house. He! He lodge in such a base, obscure place as thy house! Tut, I know his disposition so well he would not lie in thy bed if thou'ldst gi' it him.

COB. I will not give it him though, sir. Mass, I thought somewhat was in 't—we could not get him to bed all night! Well, sir, though he lie not o' my bed, he lies o' my bench; an 't please you to go up, sir, you shall find him with two cushions [60 under his head, and his cloak wrapped about him, as though he had neither won nor lost, and yet, I warrant, he ne'er cast [3] better in his life than he has done tonight.[4]

MAT. Why, was he drunk?

COB. Drunk, sir? You hear not me say

so. Perhaps he swallowed a tavern token,[5] or some such device, sir; I have nothing to do withal. I deal with water and not with wine.—Gi' me my tankard there, ho!— [70 God b' w' you, sir. It's six a-clock; I should ha' carried two turns by this. What ho! My stopple! [6] Come.

MAT. Lie in a water bearer's house! A gentleman of his havings! [7] Well, I'll tell him my mind.

[Enter Tib with a water tankard.]

COB. What, Tib; show this gentleman up to the captain.—*[Exit Tib with Master Matthew.]* O, an my house were the Brazen Head now, faith, it would e'en speak, [80 "Mo [8] fools yet." [9] You should ha' some now would take this Mr. Matthew to be a gentleman, at the least. His father's an honest man, a worshipful fishmonger, and so forth; and now does he creep and wriggle into acquaintance with all the brave gallants about the town, such as my guest is (O, my guest is a fine man!), and they flout him invincibly.[10] He useth [11] every day to a merchant's house where I serve [90 water, one Master Kitely's, i' the Old Jewry; and here's the jest: he is in love with my master's sister, Mistress Bridget, and calls her "Mistress"; and there he will sit you a whole afternoon sometimes, reading o' these same abominable, vile (a pox on hem, I cannot abide them), rascally verses, "poyetry," "poyetry," and speaking of "interludes"; 'twill make a man burst to hear him. And the [100 wenches, they do so jeer, and tee-hee at him. Well, should they do so much to me, I'ld forswear them all, by the foot of Pharaoh! There's an oath! How many water bearers shall you hear swear such an oath? O, I have a guest—he teaches me—he does swear the legiblest of any man christened: "By St. George! The foot of Pharaoh! The body of me! As I am [a] [109 gentleman and a soldier!" Such dainty oaths! And withal he does take this same filthy, roguish tabacco,[12] the finest and cleanliest! It would do a man good to see

---

[1] Herald's.   [2] Here, herring's head.
[3] Pun on *cast*, to throw dice, and to vomit.
[4] *I.e.*, last night.

[5] Slang term for *got drunk*.   [7] Possessions.
[6] Stopper.   [8] More.
[9] *Cf.* Greene's *Friar Bacon and Friar Bungay*.
[10] Exceedingly.   [11] Is accustomed to go.
[12] Tobacco.

the fume come forth at 's tonnels.[1] Well, he owes me forty shillings my wife lent him out of her purse, by sixpence a time, besides his lodging; I would I had it! I shall ha' it, he says, the next action.[2] Helter-skelter, hang sorrow, care 'll kill a cat, up-tails all, and a louse for the [120 hangman! [*Exit.*]

ACT I. SCENE V.

[*A room in Cob's house.*]

Bobadill, Tib, Matthew.[3] *Bobad*[*ill*] *is discovered lying on his bench.*

[BOB.] Hostess, hostess!

[*Enter Tib.*]

TIB. What say you, sir?

BOB. A cup o' thy small beer, sweet hostess.

TIB. Sir, there's a gentleman below would speak with you.

BOB. A gentleman! 'Odso,[4] I am not within.

TIB. My husband told him you were, sir. 10

BOB. What a plague—what meant he?

MAT. [*Below.*] Captain Bobadill?

BOB. Who's there?—(Take away the basin, good hostess!) Come up, sir.

TIB. He would desire you to come up, sir.

[*Enter Matthew.*]

You come into a cleanly house, here!

MAT. Save you, sir; save you, captain!

BOB. Gentle Master Matthew! Is it you, sir? Please you, sit down. 20

MAT. Thank you, good captain; you may see I am somewhat audacious.

BOB. Not so, sir. I was requested to supper last night by a sort[5] of gallants, where you were wished for and drunk to, I assure you.

MAT. Vouchsafe me, by whom, good captain?

BOB. Marry, by young Wellbred and others.—Why, hostess, a stool here [30 for this gentleman!

MAT. No haste, sir; 'tis very well.

BOB. Body of me! It was so late ere we parted last night I can scarce open my eyes yet; I was but new risen, as you came. How passes the day abroad, sir? You can tell.

MAT. Faith, some half hour to seven. Now, trust me, you have an exceeding fine lodging here, very neat and pri- [40 vate.

BOB. Ay, sir; sit down, I pray you. Master Matthew, in any case possess no gentlemen of our acquaintance with notice of my lodging.

MAT. Who? I, sir? No.

BOB. Not that I need to care who know it, for the cabin[6] is convenient; but in regard I would not be too popular, and generally visited, as some are. 50

MAT. True, captain, I conceive you.

BOB. For, do you see, sir, by the heart of valor in me, except it be to some peculiar and choice spirits, to whom I am extraordinarily engaged, as yourself or so, I could not extend thus far.

MAT. O Lord, sir! I resolve so.[7]

BOB. I confess I love a cleanly and quiet privacy, above all the tumult and roar of fortune. What new book [60 ha' you there? What! "Go by, Hieronymo"?[8]

MAT. Ay; did you ever see it acted? Is 't not well penned?

BOB. Well penned? I would fain see all the poets of these times pen such another play as that was! They'll prate and swagger, and keep a stir of art and devices, when, as I am a gentleman, read hem, they are the most shallow, pitiful, bar- [70 ren fellows that live upon the face of the earth again.

MAT. Indeed, here are a number of fine speeches in this book. "O eyes, no eyes, but fountains fraught with tears!" There's a conceit! "Fountains fraught with tears!"—"O life, no life, but lively form of death!" Another—"O world, no world, but mass of public wrongs!" A third—"Confused and filled with mur- [80 der and misdeeds!" A fourth—O, the muses! Is 't not excellent? Is 't not simply the best that ever you heard, captain? Ha! How do you like it?

---

[1] Tunnels, nostrils.
[2] *I.e.,* court action.
[3] Last two enter later.
[4] A mild oath.
[5] Company.
[6] Room.
[7] I am sure of it.
[8] *I.e.,* Kyd's *Spanish Tragedy.*

Bob. 'Tis good.

Mat. "To thee, the purest object to my
  sense,
The most refinéd essence heaven covers,
Send I these lines, wherein I do com-
  mence
The happy state of turtle-billing lovers.
 If they prove rough, unpolished, harsh,
  and rude,   90
 Haste made the waste: thus mildly I
  conclude." [1]

Bob. Nay, proceed, proceed. Where's
this?

Bobadill is making him ready all this while.

Mat. This, sir? A toy o' mine own, in
my nonage, the infancy of my muses. But
when will you come and see my study?
Good faith, I can show you some very good
things I have done of late.—That boot
becomes your leg passing well, captain,
methinks.   100

Bob. So, so; it's the fashion gentlemen
now use.

Mat. Troth, captain, and now you
speak o' the fashion, Master Wellbred's
elder brother and I are fall'n out exceedingly. This other day I happened to enter
into some discourse of a hanger,[2] which,
I assure you, both for fashion and workmanship, was most peremptory[3]-beauti-
ful and gentlemanlike! Yet he con- [110
demned and cried it down for the most
pied [4] and ridiculous that ever he saw.

Bob. Squire Downright, the half brother,
was 't not?

Mat. Ay, sir, he.

Bob. Hang him, rook! [5] He! Why, he has
no more judgment than a malt horse.[6]
By S[t]. George, I wonder you'ld loose a
thought upon such an animal; the most
peremptory-absurd clown of Chris- [120
tendom this day he is holden. I protest
to you, as I am a gentleman and a soldier,
I ne'er changed words with his like. By
his discourse, he should eat nothing but
hay; he was born for the manger, pannier,
or pack-saddle. He has not so much as a
good phrase in his belly, but all old iron

and rusty proverbs! A good commodity
for some smith to make hobnails of!

Mat. Ay, and he thinks to carry [130
it away with his manhood still, where he
comes. He brags he will gi' me the *bastinado*, as I hear.

Bob. How! He the *bastinado!* How
came he by that word, trow?

Mat. Nay, indeed, he said "cudgel
me"; I termed it so, for my more grace.

Bob. That may be, for I was sure it
was none of his word. But when? When
said he so?   140

Mat. Faith, yesterday, they say; a
young gallant, a friend of mine, told me so.

Bob. By the foot of Pharaoh, and
'twere my case now, I should send him a
chartel [7] presently. The *bastinado!* A most
proper and sufficient *dependence*,[8] warranted by the great Caranza.[9] Come
hither; you shall *chartel* him; I'll show you
a trick or two you shall kill him with at
pleasure; the first *stoccata*,[10] if you [150
will, by this air.

Mat. Indeed, you have absolute knowledge i' the mystery,[11] I have heard, sir.

Bob. Of whom? Of whom? Ha' you
heard it, I beseech you?

Mat. Troth, I have heard it spoken
of divers[12] that you have very rare and
un-in-one-breath-utterable skill, sir.

Bob. By heaven, no, not I; no skill
i' the earth; some small rudiments i' [160
the science, as to know my time, distance,
or so. I have professed it more for noblemen and gentlemen's use than mine own
practice, I assure you.—Hostess, accom-
modate us with another bedstaff [13] here
quickly. Lend us another bedstaff.—The
woman does not understand the words
of action.—[*Takes the position of a fencer.*]
Look you, sir; exalt not your point above
this state, at any hand, and let your [170
poinard [14] maintain your defense, thus.
(Give it the gentleman, and leave us.)—
[*Exit Tib.*] So, sir. Come on. O, twine
your body more about, that you may fall
to a more sweet, comely, gentlemanlike
guard; so, indifferent![15] Hollow your

---

[1] The source of these lines is unknown, although Matthew usually pilfers other poets.
 [2] A belt by which a weapon was hung from the
girdle.
 [3] Exceedingly.   [5] Simpleton.
 [4] Variegated.   [6] Drunkard.

[7] Challenge.   [8] Ground for a duel.
[9] Author of a Spanish book on fencing.
[10] Thrust. [11] Art, profession. [12] By many.
[13] For preparing a feather bed. [14] Poniard.
[15] Fairly well.

body more, sir, thus. Now, stand fast o'
your left leg, note your distance, keep
your due proportion of time. O, you disorder your point most irregularly!   180

MAT. How is the bearing of it now, sir?

BOB. O, out of measure ill. A well-
experienced hand would pass upon you
at pleasure.

MAT. How mean you, sir, pass upon
me?

BOB. Why, thus, sir: make a thrust at
me, come in upon the answer, control
your point, and make a full career [1] at the
body. The best-practiced gallants [190
of the time name it the *passada*. A most
desperate thrust, believe it!

MAT. Well, come, sir.

BOB. Why, you do not manage your
weapon with any facility or grace to invite
me. I have no spirit to play with you;
your dearth of judgment renders you
tedious.

MAT. But one *venue*,[2] sir.

BOB. "*Venue*"! Fie! Most gross [200
denomination as ever I heard. O, the
"*stoccata*," while you live, sir; note that.—
Come, put on your cloak, and we'll go
to some private place where you are acquainted—some tavern or so—and have
a bit. I'll send for one of these fencers,
and he shall breathe [3] you, by my direction; and then I will teach you your trick.
You shall kill him with it at the first, if
you please. Why, I will learn you, by [210
the true judgment of the eye, hand, and
foot, to control any enemy's point i' the
world. Should your adversary confront
you with a pistol, 'twere nothing, by this
hand! You should, by the same rule, control his bullet, in a line, except it were hail
shot, and spread. What money ha' you
about you, Mr. Matthew?

MAT. Faith, I ha' not past a two shillings or so.   220

BOB. 'Tis somewhat with the least.
But come; we will have a bunch of reddish [4] and salt to taste our wine, and a
pipe of tabacco to close the orifice of the
stomach; and then we'll call upon young
Wellbred. Perhaps we shall meet the
Corydon [5] his brother there, and put him
to the question.   [*Exeunt.*]

---

[1] Lunge.   [2] Thrust.   [3] Exercise.
[4] Radish.   [5] Rustic.

ACT II. SCENE i.

[A room in Kitely's house in the Old Jewry.]

Kitely, Cash, Downright.

[KITE.] Thomas, come hither.
There lies a note within upon my desk.
Here, take my key. It is no matter
neither.
Where is the boy?

CASH.   Within, sir, i' the warehouse.

KITE. Let him tell over straight that
Spanish gold,
And weigh it, with th' pieces of eight.
Do you
See the delivery of those silver stuffs
To Mr. Lucre; tell him, if he will,
He shall ha' the grograns [6] at the rate
I told him,
And I will meet him on the Exchange
anon.   10

CASH. Good, sir.   [*Exit.*]

KITE. Do you see that fellow, brother
Downright?

DOW. Ay, what of him?

KITE.   He is a jewel, brother.
I took him of [7] a child up at my door,
And christened him, gave him mine own
name, Thomas;
Since, bred him at the Hospital,[8] where
proving
A toward imp,[9] I called him home, and
taught him
So much as I have made him my cashier,
And given him who had none, a surname,
Cash,
And find him in his place so full of
faith   20
That I durst trust my life into his hands.

DOW. So would not I in any bastard's,
brother,
As it is like he is, although I knew
Myself his father. But you said yo' had
somewhat
To tell me, gentle brother. What is 't?
What is 't?

KITE. Faith, I am very loath to utter it,
As fearing it may hurt your patience;
But that I know your judgment is of
strength,
Against the nearness of affection—

---

[6] Coarse silk cloth.   [7] As.
[8] Christ's Hospital, where foundlings and
others were educated.   [9] Apt lad.

Dow. What need this circumstance? [1]
Pray you, be direct.   30

Kite. I will not say how much I do ascribe
Unto your friendship, nor in what regard
I hold your love; but let my past be-
havior
And usage of your sister but confirm
How well I've been affected to your—

Dow. You are too tedious; come to the
matter, the matter.

Kite. Then, without further ceremony,
thus.

My brother Wellbred, sir, I know not how,
Of late is much declined in what he was,
And greatly altered in his disposi-
tion.   40
When he came first to lodge here in my
house,
Ne'er trust me if I were not proud of him;
Methought he bare himself in such a
fashion,
So full of man [2] and sweetness in his car-
riage,
And, what was chief, it showed not bor-
rowed in him,
But all he did became him as his own,
And seemed as perfect, proper, and pos-
sessed
As breath with life, or color with the
blood.
But now, his course is so irregular,   49
So loose, affected, and deprived of grace,
And he himself withal so far fall'n off
From that first place as scarce no note
remains
To tell men's judgments where he lately
stood.
He's grown a stranger to all due respect,
Forgetful of his friends; and, not content
To stale himself in all societies,
He makes my house here common as a
mart,
A theater, a public receptacle
For giddy humor and diseasèd riot;
And here, as in a tavern or a stews,   60
He and his wild associates spend their
hours
In repetition of lascivious jests,
Swear, leap, drink, dance, and revel
night by night,
Control my servants, and, indeed, what
not?

Dow. 'Sdeynes,[3] I know not what I
should say to him, i' the whole world! He
values me at a cracked three farthings, for
aught I see. It will never out o' the flesh
that's bred i' the bone. I have told him
enough, one would think, if that would [70
serve; but counsel to him is as good as a
shoulder of mutton to a sick horse. Well,
he knows what to trust to, for George.[4]
Let him spend and spend and domineer,
till his heart ache; an he think to be relieved by me, when he is got into one o'
your city pounds, the counters,[5] he has
the wrong sow by the ear, i' faith, and claps
his dish [6] at the wrong man's door. I'll
lay my hand o' my halfpenny, ere I [80
part with 't to fetch him out, I'll assure
him.

Kite. Nay, good brother, let it not trouble
you thus.

Dow. 'Sdeath, he mads me! I could eat
my very spur-leathers for anger! But why
are you so tame? Why do you not speak
to him, and tell him how he disquiets your
house?

Kite. O, there are divers reasons to dis-
suade, brother.
But, would yourself vouchsafe to travail
in it   90
(Though but with plain and easy circum-
stance),
It would both come much better to his
sense,
And savor less of stomach [7] or of passion.
You are his elder brother, and that title
Both gives and warrants you authority,
Which, by your presence seconded, must
breed
A kind of duty in him, and regard;
Whereas, if I should intimate the least,
It would but add contempt to his neglect,
Heap worse on ill, make up a pile of
hatred,   100
That in the rearing would come tott'ring
down,
And in the ruin bury all our love.
Nay, more than this, brother; if I should
speak,
He would be ready, from his heat of
humor [8]

---

[1] Circuitous narration.   [2] Manliness.

[3] By God's dignesse, i.e., dignity(?).
[4] I.e., for all I care.   [6] I.e., like a beggar.
[5] Debtors' prisons.   [7] Anger.
[8] From his temper.

And overflowing of the vapor in him,
To blow the ears of his familiars
With the false breath of telling what dis-
　　graces
And low disparagements I had put upon
　　him,
Whilst they, sir, to relieve him in the
　　fable,[1]
Make their loose comments upon every
　　word,　　　　　　　　　　　　110
Gesture, or look I use; mock me all over,
From my flat cap[2] unto my shining
　　shoes;[2]
And, out of their impetuous, rioting
　　fant'sies,
Beget some slander that shall dwell with
　　me.
And what would that be, think you?
　　Marry, this:
They would give out, because my wife is
　　fair,
Myself but lately married, and my sister
Here sojourning a virgin in my house,
That I were jealous—nay, as sure as
　　death,
That they would say—and how that I
　　had quarreled[3]　　　　　　　120
My brother purposely, thereby to find
An apt pretext to banish them my
　　house.
Dow. Mass, perhaps so; they are like
　　enough to do it.
Kite. Brother, they would, believe it; so
　　should I,
Like one of these penurious quack-
　　salvers,
But set the bills[4] up to mine own dis-
　　grace,
And try experiments upon myself;
Lend scorn and envy opportunity
To stab my reputation and good
　　name—

Act II. Scene ii.

[The same.]

Matthew, Bobadill, Downright, Kitely.

[Mat. (*Enters, struggling with Bobadill.*)]
I will speak to him.
Bob. Speak to him? Away! By the foot
of Pharaoh, you shall not! You shall not
do him that grace.—The time of day to

you, gentleman o' the house. Is Mr. Well-
bred stirring?
Dow. How then? What should he do?
Bob. Gentleman of the house, it[5] is to
you. Is he within, sir?　　　　　　10
Kite. He came not to his lodging to-
night, sir, I assure you.
Dow. Why, do you hear? You!
Bob. The gentleman-citizen hath satis-
fied me; I'll talk to no scavenger.
　　　[*Exeunt Bobadill and Matthew.*]
Dow. How! Scavenger? Stay, sir, stay!
Kite. Nay, brother Downright—
Dow. Heart! Stand you away, and you
love me.
Kite. You shall not follow him now, [20
I pray you, brother; good faith, you shall
not. I will overrule you.
Dow. Ha! Scavenger? Well, go to, I say
little; but, by this good day (God forgive
me I should swear), if I put it up[6] so, say
I am the rankest cow that ever pissed.
'Sdeynes, and I swallow this, I'll ne'er draw
my sword in the sight of Fleet Street again
while I live; I'll sit in a barn with madge-
howlet,[7] and catch mice first. Scaven- [30
ger, heart!—and I'll go near to fill that
huge tumbrel-slop[8] of yours with somewhat, and I have good luck; your Gara-
gantua breech cannot carry it away so.
Kite. O, do not fret yourself thus; never
　　think on 't.
Dow. These are my brother's consorts,
these! These are his cam'rades, his walking
mates! He's a gallant, a *cavaliero* too, right
hangman cut![9] Let me not live, and I
could not find in my heart to swinge [40
the whole ging[10] of hem, one after another,
and begin with him first. I am grieved it
should be said he is my brother, and take
these courses. Well, as he brews, so shall
he drink, for George, again. Yet he shall
hear on 't, and that tightly[11] too, and I
live, i' faith.
Kite. But, brother, let your reprehension,
　　then,
Run in an easy current, not o'erhigh
Carried with rashness or devouring
　　choler;　　　　　　　　　　　50
But rather use the soft, persuading way,

---

[1] Narrating.　　　　　　[3] Quarreled with.
[2] Marks of the citizen.　[4] Advertisements.
[5] *I.e.*, my question.　　[7] The barn owl.
[6] Endure it.　　　　　　[8] Loose breeches.
[9] In the exact form of a hangman.
[10] Gang, crowd.　　　　　[11] Quickly.

Whose powers will work more gently,
and compose
Th' imperfect thoughts you labor to re-
claim,
More winning than enforcing the consent.
Dow. Ay, ay, let me alone for that, I war-
rant you. *Bell rings.*
Kite. How now! O, the bell rings to
breakfast.
Brother, I pray you go in, and bear my
wife
Company till I come; I'll but give order
For some despatch of business to my
servants— [*Exit Downright.*]

Act II. Scene iii.

[*The same.*]

¹ *Kitely, Cob, Dame Kitely.*²

[Kite.] What, Cob! Our maids will have
you by the back, i' faith,
For coming so late this morning.
Cob. Perhaps so, sir; take heed some-
body have not them by the belly for walk-
ing so late in the evening.
He passes by with his tankard.
Kite. Well, yet my troubled spirit's some-
what eased,
Though not reposed in that security
As I could wish; but I must be content,
Howe'er I set a face on 't to the world.
Would I had lost this finger at a venter,
So Wellbred had ne'er lodged within my
house. 11
Why, 't cannot be, where there is such
resort
Of wanton gallants and young revelers,
That any woman should be honest ³
long.
Is 't like that factious beauty will pre-
serve
The public weal of chastity unshaken,
When such strong motives muster and
make head ⁴
Against her single peace? No, no. Be-
ware.
When mutual appetite doth meet to
treat,
And spirits of one kind and quality 20
Come once to parley in the pride of blood,
It is no slow conspiracy that follows.

Well, to be plain, if I but thought the
time
Had answered their affections,⁵ all the
world
Should not persuade me but I were a
cuckold.
Marry, I hope they ha' not got that
start,
For opportunity hath balked hem yet,
And shall do still, while I have eyes and
ears
To attend the impositions ⁶ of my heart.
My presence shall be as an iron bar 30
Twixt the conspiring motions of desire;
Yea, every look or glance mine eye ejects
Shall check occasion, as one doth his
slave,
When he forgets the limits of prescrip-
tion.

[*Enter Dame Kitely.*]

Dame. [*Calling.*] Sister Bridget, pray
you, fetch down the rose water above in the
closet.—Sweetheart, will you come in to
breakfast?
Kite. An she have overheard me
now—! 40
Dame. I pray thee, good muss,⁷ we stay
for you.
Kite. By heaven, I would not for a
thousand angels.⁸
Dame. What ail you, sweetheart? Are
you not well? Speak, good muss.
Kite. Troth, my head aches extremely
on a sudden.
Dame. [*Putting her hand to his forehead.*]
O, the Lord! 50
Kite. How now! What?
Dame. Alas, how it burns! Muss, keep
you warm; good truth, it is this new
disease;⁹ there's a number are troubled
withal. For love's sake, sweetheart, come
in out of the air.
Kite. [*Aside.*] How simple and how subtle
are her answers!
A new disease, and many troubled with
it?
Why, true; she heard me, all ¹⁰ the world
to nothing.
Dame. I pray thee, good sweet- [60

¹ The marginal direction "*To them*" is erroneously printed here. ³ Virtuous.
² Enters later. ⁴ Gather their forces.

⁵ Suited their inclinations. ⁷ Mouse.
⁶ Promptings. ⁸ Gold coins.
⁹ A form of fever, probably typhoid.
¹⁰ *I.e.*, I wager all.

heart, come in; the air will do you harm, in
　troth.
KITE. [*Aside.*] The air! She has me i' the
　　wind.[1]—Sweetheart,
　I'll come to you presently; 'twill away,
　　I hope.
DAME. Pray heaven it do.　　　　　[*Exit.*]
KITE. A new disease? I know not, new or
　　old,
　But it may well be called poor mortals'
　　plague,
　For, like a pestilence, it doth infect
　The houses of the brain. First it begins
　Solely to work upon the fantasy,　　70
　Filling her seat with such pestiferous air
　As soon corrupts the judgment; and from
　　thence
　Sends like contagion to the memory,
　Still each to other giving the infection,
　Which as a subtle vapor spreads itself
　Confusedly through every sensive [2] part,
　Till not a thought or motion in the mind
　Be free from the black poison of suspect.[3]
　Ah, but what misery is it to know this!
　Or, knowing it, to want the mind's erec-
　　tion [4]　　　　　　　　　　　80
　In such extremes? Well, I will once more
　　strive,
　In spite of this black cloud, myself to be,
　And shake the fever off that thus shakes
　　me.　　　　　　　　　　[*Exit.*]

ACT II. SCENE iv.

[*Moorfields.*]

*Brainworm, Ed[ward] Knowell, Mr. Ste-
phen.*[5]

　BRA. [*Disguised like a maimed soldier.*]
'Slid, I cannot choose but laugh to see myself translated thus from a poor creature to
a creator; for now must I create an intolerable sort of lies, or my present profession
loses the grace. And yet the lie, to a man
of my coat, is as ominous a fruit as the
fico.[6] O, sir, it holds for good polity ever,
to have that outwardly in vilest estimation,
that inwardly is most dear to us. So　[10
much for my borrowed shape. Well, the
troth is, my old master intends to follow

my young, dry-foot,[7] over Moorfields to
London this morning; now I, knowing of
this hunting match, or rather conspiracy,
and to insinuate with my young master
(for so must we that are blue waiters [8] and
men of hope and service do, or perhaps we
may wear motley at the year's end, and
who wears motley,[9] you know—),　[20
have got me afore in this disguise, determining here to lie in *ambuscado*, and intercept him in the midway. If I can but get
his cloak, his purse, his hat, nay, any thing
to cut him off, that is, to stay his journey,
"*Veni, vidi, vici,*" [10] I may say, with Captain
Cæsar, I am made forever, i' faith. Well,
now must I practice to get the true garb
of one of these lance-knights,[11] my　arm
here, and my—young master, and his　[30
cousin, Mr. Stephen, as I am true counterfeit man of war, and no soldier!　[*Retires.*]

[*Enter Edward Knowell and Stephen.*]

E. KNOW. So, sir! And how then, coz?
STE. 'Sfoot, I have lost my purse, I
think.
E. KNOW. How?　Lost your purse?
Where? When had you it?
STE. I cannot tell. Stay.
BRA. 'Slid, I am afeard they will know
me. Would I could get by them!　　40
E. KNOW. What, ha' you it?
STE. No; I think I was bewitched, I—
　　　　　　　　　　　　　　[*Weeps.*]
E. KNOW. Nay, do not weep the loss;
hang it, let it go.
STE. [*Finding his purse.*] O, it's here.
No, and it had been lost, I had not cared,
but for a jet ring Mistress Mary sent me.
E. KNOW. A jet ring? O, the poesy,[12]
the poesy?
STE. Fine, i' faith.—　　　　　　50
　　"Though Fancy [13] sleep,
　　　My love is deep—"
meaning that, though I did not fancy her,
yet she loved me dearly.
E. KNOW. Most excellent!
STE. And then I sent her another, and
my poesy was,

---

[1] She's on my scent.
[2] Sensitive.　　[4] To lack elevation of mind.
[3] Suspicion.　　[5] The last two enter later.
[6] Fig, an insulting gesture.

[7] By the scent.　　[8] Blue-liveried servants.
[9] The fool's coat.
[10] "I came, I saw, I conquered."
[11] Mercenary footsoldiers.
[12] Posy, motto.　　　　　[13] Affection.

"The deeper, the sweeter,
I'll be judged by St. Peter."

E. Know. How, by St. Peter? I do [60 not conceive that.

Ste. Marry, St. Peter, to make up the meter.

E. Know. Well, there the saint was your good patron; he helped you at your need. Thank him, thank him.

Bra. (*He is come back.*)[1] [*Aside.*] I cannot take leave on hem so; I will venture, come what will.—Gentlemen, please you change a few crowns for a very excel- [70 lent good blade here? I am a poor gentleman, a soldier, one that, in the better state of my fortunes, scorned so mean a refuge; but now it is the humor of necessity to have it so. You seem to be gentlemen well affected to martial men, else I should rather die with silence than live with shame. However, vouchsafe to remember it is my want speaks, not myself; this condition agrees not with my spirit—   80

E. Know. Where hast thou served?

Bra. May it please you, sir, in all the late wars of Bohemia, Hungaria, Dalmatia, Poland—where not, sir? I have been a poor servitor by sea and land any time this fourteen years, and followed the fortunes of the best commanders in Christendom. I was twice shot at the taking of Aleppo, once at the relief of Vienna; I have been at Marseilles, Naples, and the Adriatic [90 gulf, a gentleman slave in the galleys thrice, where I was most dangerously shot in the head, through both the thighs; and yet, being thus maimed, I am void of maintenance, nothing left me but my scars, the noted marks of my resolution.

Ste. How will you sell this rapier, friend?

Bra. Generous sir, I refer it to your own judgment. You are a gentle- [100 man; give me what you please.

Ste. True, I am a gentleman, I know that, friend; but what though? I pray you say, what would you ask?

Bra. I assure you, the blade may become the side or thigh of the best prince in Europe.

E. Know. Ay, with a velvet scabbard, I think.

Ste. Nay, and 't be mine, it shall [110 have a velvet scabbard, coz, that's flat; I'd not wear it as 'tis, and you would give me an angel.

Bra. At your worship's pleasure, sir. [*Stephen examines the blade.*] Nay, 'tis a most pure Toledo.

Ste. I had rather it were a Spaniard. But tell me, what shall I give you for it? An it had a silver hilt—

E. Know. Come, come, you shall [120 not buy it. Hold, there's a shilling, fellow; take thy rapier.

Ste. Why, but I will buy it now, because you say so; and there's another shilling, fellow; I scorn to be outbidden. What, shall I walk with a cudgel, like Higginbottom,[2] and may have a rapier for money?

E. Know. You may buy one in the city.

Ste. Tut! I'll buy this i' the field, so I will; I have a mind to 't, because 'tis [130 a field rapier. Tell me your lowest price.

E. Know. You shall not buy it, I say.

Ste. By this money, but I will, though I give more than 'tis worth.

E. Know. Come away; you are a fool.

Ste. Friend, I am a fool, that's granted; but I'll have it, for that word's sake. Follow me for your money.

Bra. At your service, sir.   [*Exeunt.*]

Act II. Scene v.

[*Another part of Moorfields.*]

Knowell, Brainworm.[3]

[Know.] I cannot lose the thought yet of this letter

Sent to my son; nor leave t' admire [4] the change

Of manners and the breeding of our youth

Within the kingdom, since myself was one.

When I was young, he lived not in the stews

Durst have conceived a scorn and uttered it

On a gray head; age was authority

Against a buffon,[5] and a man had then

A certain reverence paid unto his years,

That had none due unto his life. So much

---

[1] This direction appears opposite the preceding line in the original.

[2] Unidentified; probably any rustic.

[3] Enters later.

[4] Wonder at.   [5] Buffoon.

The sanctity of some prevailed for others.
But now we all are fall'n, youth from
  their fear,   12
And age from that which bred it, good
  example.[1]
Nay, would ourselves were not the first
  even parents
That did destroy the hopes in our own
  children,
Or they not learned our vices in their
  cradles,
And sucked in our ill customs with their
  milk!
Ere all their teeth be born, or they can
  speak,
We make their palates cunning; the first
  words
We form their tongues with are licentious
  jests!   20
Can it call "whore"? Cry "bastard"?
O, then, kiss it!
A witty child! Can't swear? The father's
  dearling![2]
Give it two plums. Nay, rather than 't
  shall learn
No bawdy song, the mother herself will
  teach it!
But this is in the infancy, the days
Of the long coat; when it puts on the
  breeches,
It will put off all this. Ay, it is like,
When it is gone into the bone already!
No, no; this dye goes deeper than the
  coat,   29
Or shirt, or skin; it stains unto the liver[3]
And heart[4] in some. And, rather than it
  should not,
Note what we fathers do! Look how we
  live,
What mistresses we keep, at what ex-
  pense!
In our sons' eyes, where they may handle
  our gifts,
Hear our lascivious courtships, see our
  dalliance,
Taste of the same provoking meats with
  us,
To ruin of our states! Nay, when our own
Portion[5] is fled, to prey on their re-
  mainder,[5]

We call them into fellowship of vice;
Bait hem with the young chambermaid,
  to seal,[6]   40
And teach hem all bad ways to buy af-
  fiction.[7]
This is one path; but there are millions
  more,
In which we spoil our own with leading
  them.
Well, I thank heaven, I never yet was he
That traveled with my son, before six-
  teen,
To show him the Venetian courtesans;
Nor read the grammar of cheating I had
  made,
To my sharp boy, at twelve, repeating
  still
The rule,[8] "Get money;" still, "Get
  money, boy,   49
No matter by what means; money will do
More, boy, than my lord's letter." Nei-
  ther have I
Dressed snails or mushrooms curiously
  before him,
Perfumed my sauces, and taught him to
  make hem;
Preceding still, with my gray gluttony,
At all the ordinaries, and only feared
His palate should degenerate, not his
  manners.
These are the trade of fathers now; how-
  ever,
My son, I hope, hath met within my
  threshold
None of these household precedents,
  which are strong
And swift to rape youth to their preci-
  pice.[9]   60
But let the house at home be ne'er so
  clean-
Swept, or kept sweet from filth, nay,
  dust and cobwebs,
If he will live abroad with his compan-
  ions
In dung and leystalls,[10] it is worth a fear;
Nor is the danger of conversing less
Than all that I have mentioned of ex-
  ample.

---

[1] The following twenty lines are taken from
Quintilian.
[2] Darling.   [4] Seat of knowledge.
[3] Seat of the passions. [5] Inheritance.

[6] "Probably, to agree to the sale of family
estates" (Neilson).
[7] Affliction, from Lat. afficio.
[8] The following lines are based on passages
from Horace and Juvenal.
[9] Carry youth off to their downfall.
[10] Laystalls, rubbish heaps.

[*Enter Brainworm.*]

BRA. [*Aside.*] My master! Nay, faith, have at you; I am fleshed [1] now, I have sped so well.—Worshipful sir, I beseech you, respect the estate of a poor sol- [70 dier; I am ashamed of this base course of life—God's my comfort [2]—but extremity provokes me to 't. What remedy?

KNOW. I have not for you now.

BRA. By the faith I bear unto truth, gentleman, it is no ordinary custom in me, but only to preserve manhood. I protest to you, a man I have been; a man I may be, by your sweet bounty.

KNOW. Pray thee, good friend, be [80 satisfied.

BRA. Good sir, by that hand, you may do the part of a kind gentleman in lending a poor soldier the price of two cans of beer, a matter of small value; the king of heaven shall pay you, and I shall rest thankful. Sweet worship—

KNOW. Nay, and you be so importunate—

BRA. O, tender sir, need will have [90 his course; I was not made to this vile use! Well, the edge of the enemy could not have abated me so much. It's hard when a man hath served in his prince's cause, and be thus—(*He weeps.*) Honorable worship, let me derive a small piece of silver from you; it shall not be given in the course of time.[3] By this good ground, I was fain to pawn my rapier last night for a poor supper; I had sucked the hilts long before, I [100 am a pagan else. Sweet honor—

KNOW. Believe me, I am taken with some wonder
To think a fellow of thy outward presence
Should, in the frame and fashion of his mind,
Be so degenerate and sordid-base.
Art thou a man, and sham'st thou not to beg?
To practice such a servile kind of life?
Why, were thy education ne'er so mean,
Having thy limbs, a thousand fairer courses
Offer themselves to thy election. 110

Either the wars might still supply thy wants,
Or service of some virtuous gentleman,
Or honest labor; nay, what can I name
But would become thee better than to beg?
But men of thy condition feed on sloth,
As doth the beetle on the dung she breeds in,
Not caring how the metal of your minds
Is eaten with the rust of idleness.
Now, afore me, whate'er he be that should
Relieve a person of thy quality, 120
While thou insists in this loose, desperate course,
I would esteem the sin not thine, but his.

BRA. Faith, sir, I would gladly find some other course, if so—

KNOW. Ay, you'ld gladly find it, but you will not seek it.

BRA. Alas, sir, where should a man seek? In the wars there's no ascent by desert in these days; but—and, for service, would it were as soon purchased [4] as wished [130 for! The air's my comfort, I know. What I would say—

KNOW. What's thy name?

BRA. Please you, Fitzsword, sir.

KNOW. Fitzsword?
Say that a man should entertain thee now,
Wouldst thou be honest, humble, just, and true?

BRA. Sir, by the place and honor of a soldier—

KNOW. Nay, nay, I like not those affected oaths.
Speak plainly, man, what think'st thou of my words?

BRA. Nothing, sir, but wish my fortunes were as happy as my service [140 should be honest.

KNOW. Well, follow me; I'll prove [5] thee, if thy deeds
Will carry a proportion to thy words.

BRA. Yes, sir, straight; I'll but garter my hose.—[*Exit Knowell.*] O, that my belly were hooped now, for I am ready to burst with laughing! Never was bottle or bagpipe fuller. 'Slid, was there ever seen a fox in years to betray himself thus? Now shall

---

[1] Encouraged by success.
[2] Confirmation, witness.
[3] Not forever; *i.e.*, it will be repaid.
[4] Acquired.   [5] Test.

I be possessed of all his counsels, and, [150
by that conduit, my young master. Well,
he is resolved to prove my honesty; faith,
and I'm resolved to prove his patience. O,
I shall abuse [1] him intolerably. This small
piece of service will bring him clean out of
love with the soldier forever. He will never
come within the sign of it, the sight of a
cassock,[2] or a musket rest again. He will
hate the musters at Mile End for it, to his
dying day. It's no matter; let the [160
world think me a bad counterfeit, if I cannot give him the slip [3] at an instant. Why,
this is better than to have stayed [4] his
journey. Well, I'll follow him. O, how I
long to be employed!   [*Exit.*]

Act III. Scene i.

[*A room in the Windmill Tavern.*]

*Matthew, Wellbred, Bobadill, Ed[ward]
Knowell, Stephen.*[5]

[Mat.] Yes, faith, sir, we were at your
lodging to seek you too.

Well. O, I came not there tonight.

Bob. Your brother delivered us as much.

Well. Who, my brother Downright?

Bob. He. Mr. Wellbred, I know not
in what kind [6] you hold me, but let me say
to you this: as sure as honor, I esteem it
so much out of the sunshine of reputation
to throw the least beam of regard upon [10
such a——

Well. Sir, I must hear no ill words of
my brother.

Bob. I protest to you, as [7] I have a
thing to be saved about me, I never saw
any gentlemanlike part—

Well. Good captain, "faces about" [8]
to some other discourse.

Bob. With your leave, sir, and there
were no more men living upon the face [20
of the earth, I should not fancy him, by
St. George!

Mat. Troth, nor I; he is of a rustical
cut, I know not how, he doth not carry
himself like a gentleman of fashion.

Well. O, Mr. Matthew, that's a grace
peculiar but to a few, "*quos æquus amavit
Jupiter.*" [9]

Mat. I understand you, sir.

Well. No question, you do—[*Aside.*] [30
or you do not, sir.—

Young Knowell enters [with Stephen].

Ned Knowell! By my soul, welcome! How
doest thou, sweet spirit, my genius? 'Slid,
I shall love Apollo and the mad Thespian
girls [10] the better, while I live, for this, my
dear Fury; now I see there's some love in
thee! Sirrah, these be the two I writ to
thee of. Nay, what a drowsy humor is this
now! Why dost thou not speak?

E. Know. O, you are a fine gallant; [40
you sent me a rare letter!

Well. Why, was 't not rare?

E. Know. Yes, I'll be sworn, I was ne'er
guilty of reading the like; match it in all
Pliny, or Symmachus' epistles, and I'll
have my judgment burned in the ear for
a rogue.[11] Make much of thy vein, for it
is inimitable. But I mar'l [12] what camel it
was that had the carriage of it, for, doubtless, he was no ordinary beast that [50
brought it.

Well. Why?

E. Know. "Why?" say'st thou! Why,
dost thou think that any reasonable
creature, especially in the morning, the
sober time of the day too, could have
mista'en my father for me?

Well. 'Slid, you jest, I hope.

E. Know. Indeed, the best use we can
turn it to is to make a jest on't now; [60
but, I'll assure you, my father had the
full view o' your flourishing style some
hour before I saw it.

Well. What a dull slave was this!
But, sirrah, what said he to it, i' faith?

E. Know. Nay, I know not what he
said; but I have a shrewd guess what he
thought.

Well. What? What?

E. Know. Marry, that thou art [70
some strange, dissolute young fellow, and

---

[1] Deceive.   [2] A soldier's cloak.
[3] With a pun on *counterfeit coin.*
[4] Prevented. [5] The last two enter later.
[6] Fashion, relationship.
[7] As surely as.   [8] About face.

[9] "Whom friendly Jupiter has loved" (Virgil,
Æneid, VI, 129).
[10] The Muses.
[11] Common method of punishing criminals.
[12] Marvel.

I—a grain or two better for keeping thee company.

WELL. Tut! That thought is like the moon in her last quarter—'twill change shortly. But, sirrah, I pray thee be acquainted with my two hang-bys here; thou wilt take exceeding pleasure in hem if thou hear'st hem once go: my wind instruments. I'll wind hem up— [80 But what strange piece of silence is this? The Sign of the Dumb Man?

E. KNOW. O, sir, a kinsman of mine, one that may make your music the fuller, and he please; he has his humor, sir.

WELL. O, what is 't? What is 't?

E. KNOW. Nay, I'll neither do your judgment nor his folly that wrong as to prepare your apprehension; I'll leave him to the mercy o' your search. If you [90 can take him, so!

WELL. Well, Captain Bobadill, Mr. Matthew, pray you, know this gentleman here; he is a friend of mine, and one that will deserve your affection.—(To Master Stephen.) I know not your name, sir, but I shall be glad of any occasion to render me more familiar to you.

STE. My name is Mr. Stephen, sir; I am this gentleman's own cousin, sir; [100 his father is mine uncle, sir. I am somewhat melancholy, but you shall command me, sir, in whatsoever is incident to a gentleman.

BOB. (To [E.] Knowell.) Sir, I must tell you this, I am no general[1] man; but, for Mr. Wellbred's sake (you may embrace it at what height of favor you please), I do communicate with you, and conceive you to be a gentleman of some parts; I love [110 few words.

E. KNOW. And I fewer, sir; I have scarce enow to thank you.

MAT. (To Master Stephen.) But are you, indeed, sir, so given to it?

STE. Ay, truly, sir, I am mightily given to melancholy.

MAT. O, it's your only fine humor, sir; your true melancholy breeds your perfect, fine wit, sir. I am melancholy [120 myself, diver times, sir, and then do I no more but take pen and paper presently, and overflow you half a score or a dozen of sonnets at a sitting.

[1] Open to general acquaintance.

(2 E. KNOW. Sure he utters[3] them then by the gross.)

STE. Truly, sir, and I love such things out of measure.

E. KNOW. I' faith, better than in measure, I'll undertake.   130

MAT. Why, I pray you, sir, make use of my study; it's at your service.

STE. I thank you, sir; I shall be bold, I warrant you. Have you a stool there to be melancholy upon?

MAT. That I have, sir, and some papers there of mine own doing, at idle hours, that you'll say there's some sparks of wit in hem, when you see them.

WELL. [Aside.] Would the sparks [140 would kindle once, and become a fire amongst hem! I might see self-love burnt for her heresy.

STE. Cousin, is it well? Am I melancholy enough?

E. KNOW. O, ay, excellent.

WELL. Captain Bobadill, why muse you so?

E. KNOW. He is melancholy too. [149

BOB. Faith, sir, I was thinking of a most honorable piece of service, was performed tomorrow, being St. Mark's Day, shall be some ten years now.

E. KNOW. In what place, captain?

BOB. Why, at the beleag'ring of Strigonium, where, in less than two hours, seven hundred resolute gentlemen as any were in Europe lost their lives upon the breach. I'll tell you, gentlemen, it was the first, but the best leaguer that [160 ever I beheld with these eyes, except the taking-in of—what do you call it?—last year, by the Genoways;[4] but that, of all other, was the most fatal and dangerous exploit that ever I was ranged in, since I first bore arms before the face of the enemy, as I am a gentleman and soldier.

STE. So! I had as lief as an angel I could swear as well as that gentleman. [169

E. KNOW. Then you were a servitor at both, it seems; at Strigonium, and what do you call 't?

BOB. O Lord, sir! By S[t]. George, I was the first man that entered the breach;

[2] Jonson frequently encloses speeches in parenthesis to indicate an aside or a passage incidental to the main action.

[3] Puts into circulation.   [4] Genoese.

and, had I not effected it with resolution, I had been slain if I had had a million of lives.

E. Know. 'Twas pity you had not ten— a cat's and your own, i' faith. But—was it possible? 180

(Mat. Pray you, mark this discourse, sir!

Ste. So I do.)

Bob. I assure you, upon my reputation, 'tis true, and yourself shall confess.

E. Know. [*Aside.*] You must bring me to the rack first.

Bob. Observe me judicially, sweet sir: they had planted me three demi-culverings[1] just in the mouth of the breach; [190 now, sir, as we were to give on,[2] their master gunner (a man of no mean skill and mark, you must think) confronts me with his linstock,[3] ready to give fire; I, spying his intendment, discharged my petronel[4] in his bosom, and with these single arms, my poor rapier, ran violently upon the Moors that guarded the ordinance, and put hem pellmell to the sword. 199

Well. To the sword? To the rapier, captain?

E. Know. O, it was a good figure observed, sir. But did you all this, captain, without hurting your blade?

Bob. Without any impeach[5] o' the earth. You shall perceive, sir. [*Shows his rapier.*] It is the most fortunate weapon that ever rid on poor gentleman's thigh. Shall I tell you, sir? You talk of Morglay, Excalibur, Durindana, or so. Tut! [210 I lend no credit to that is fabled of hem. I know the virtue of mine own, and therefore I dare the boldlier maintain it.

Ste. I mar'l whether it be a Toledo or no?

Bob. A most perfect Toledo, I assure you, sir.

Ste. I have a countryman of his here.

Mat. Pray you, let's see, sir; yes, faith, it is! 220

Bob. This a Toledo? Pish!

Ste. Why do you pish, captain?

Bob. A Fleming, by heaven! I'll buy them for a guilder[6] apiece, an I would have a thousand of them.

E. Know. How say you, cousin? I told you thus much!

Well. Where bought you it, Mr. Stephen? 229

Ste. Of a scurvy rogue soldier. A hundred of lice go with him! He swore it was a Toledo.

Bob. A poor provant[7] rapier, no better.

Mat. Mass, I think it be indeed, now I look on 't better.

E. Know. Nay, the longer you look on 't, the worse. Put it up, put it up.

Ste. Well, I will put it up; but by— I ha' forgot the captain's oath; I [239 thought to ha' sworn by it—an e'er I meet/ him—

Well. O, it is past help now, sir; you must have patience.

Ste. Whoreson, cony-catching[8] rascal! I could eat the very hilts for anger.

E. Know. A sign of good digestion; you have an ostrich stomach, cousin!

Ste. A stomach? Would I had him here, you should see an I had a stomach.[9] 250

Well. It's better as 'tis.—Come, gentlemen, shall we go?

Act III. Scene ii.

[*The same.*]

E[dward] Knowell, Brainworm, Stephen, Wellbred, Bobadill, Matthew.

[*Enter Brainworm.*]

[E. Know.] A miracle, cousin; look here, look here!

Ste. O!—God's lid! By your leave, do you know me, sir?

Bra. Ay, sir, I know you by sight.

Ste. You sold me a rapier, did you not?

Bra. Yes, marry, did I, sir.

Ste. You said it was a Toledo, ha?

Bra. True, I did so.

Ste. But it is none? 10

Bra. No, sir, I confess it; it is none.

Ste. Do you confess it? Gentlemen, bear witness, he has confessed it.—By God's will, and you had not confessed it—

E. Know. O, cousin, forbear, forbear!

Ste. Nay, I have done, cousin.

---

[1] Small cannon. [4] Petronel, a large pistol.
[2] Charge. [5] Question.
[3] A lighted match. [6] A Dutch coin.

[7] Supplied by the government.
[8] Swindling. [9] Courage.

WELL. Why, you have done like a gentleman; he has confessed it; what would
you more?   20

STE. Yet, by his leave, he is a rascal,
under his favor, do you see?

E. KNOW. [*Aside.*] Ay, by his leave,
he is, and under favor—a pretty piece of
civility! Sirrah, how dost thou like him?

WELL. [*Aside.*] O, it's a most precious
fool; make much on him. I can compare
him to nothing more happily than a
drum, for everyone may play upon him.

E. KNOW. [*Aside.*] No, no, a child's
whistle were far the fitter.   31

BRA. Sir, shall I entreat a word with
you?

E. KNOW. With me, sir? You have
not another Toledo to sell, ha' you?

BRA. You are conceited,[1] sir. Your
name is Mr. Knowell, as I take it?

E. KNOW. You are i' the right; you
mean not to proceed in the catechism,
do you?   40

BRA. No, sir; I am none of that coat.[2]

E. KNOW. Of as bare a coat, though.
Well, say, sir.

BRA. [*Taking Edward Knowell aside.*]
Faith, sir, I am but servant to the drum
extraordinary, and, indeed, this smoky
varnish being washed off, and three or
four patches removed, I appear your
worship's in reversion, after the decease
of your good father.—Brainworm!   50

E. KNOW. Brainworm! 'Slight, what
breath of a conjurer hath blown thee
hither in this shape?

BRA. The breath o' your letter, sir,
this morning, the same that blew you to
the Windmill, and your father after you.

E. KNOW. My father?

BRA. Nay, never start; 'tis true. He
has followed you over the fields by the
foot, as you would do a hare i' the   [60
snow.

E. KNOW. Sirrah, Wellbred, what shall
we do, sirrah? My father is come over
after me.

WELL. Thy father? Where is he?

BRA. At Justice Clement's house here,
in Coleman Street, where he but stays my
return; and then—

WELL. Who's this? Brainworm?

BRA. The same, sir.   70

---

[1] Witty.   [2] *I.e.*, not a clergyman.

WELL. Why, how, i' the name of wit,
com'st thou transmuted thus?

BRA. Faith, a device, a device; nay,
for the love of reason, gentlemen, and
avoiding the danger, stand not here; withdraw, and I'll tell you all.

WELL. But art thou sure he will stay
thy return?

BRA. Do I live, sir? What a question
is that!   80

WELL. We'll prorogue his expectation,
then, a little. Brainworm, thou shalt go
with us.—Come on, gentlemen. Nay,
I pray thee, sweet Ned, droop not; heart,
and our wits be so wretchedly dull that
one old plodding brain can outstrip us all,
would we were e'en pressed[3] to make porters of us, and serve out the remnant of our
days in Thames Street, or at Custom-
house quay, in a civil war against [90
the carmen![4]

BRA. Amen, amen, amen, say I.
                                    [*Exeunt.*]

ACT III. SCENE iii.

[*Kitely's shop.*]

Kitely, Cash.

[KITE.] What says he, Thomas? Did you
    speak with him?

CASH. He will expect you, sir, within this
    half hour.

KITE. Has he the money ready, can you
    tell?

CASH. Yes, sir, the money was brought in
    last night.

KITE. O, that's well; fetch me my cloak,
    my cloak!—   [*Exit Cash.*]
Stay, let me see. An hour to go and come—
Ay, that will be the least; and then
    'twill be
An hour before I can despatch with him,
Or very near; well, I will say two hours.
Two hours? Ha! Things never dreamt
    of yet   10
May be contrived, ay, and effected too,
In two hours' absence; well, I will not go.
Two hours! No, fleering Opportunity,
I will not give your subtilty that scope.
Who will not judge him worthy to be
    robbed
That sets his doors wide open to a thief,

---

[3] Impressed.   [4] Carters.

And shows the felon where his treasure
　lies?
Again, what earthy spirit but will
　attempt
To taste the fruit of Beauty's golden
　tree,
When leaden sleep seals up the dragon's
　eyes?　　　　　　　　　　　　　20
I will not go. Business, go by for once.
No, beauty, no; you are of too good
　caract [1]
To be left so, without a guard, or open.
Your luster, too, 'll inflame at any dis-
　tance,
Draw courtship to you, as a jet doth
　straws,
Put motion in a stone, strike fire from
　ice,
Nay, make a porter leap you with his
　burden.
You must be then kept up, close, and
　well watched,
For, give you opportunity, no quicksand
Devours or swallows swifter! He that
　lends　　　　　　　　　　　　　30
His wife, if she be fair, or [2] time or place,
Compels her to be false. I will not go!
The dangers are too many—and then the
　dressing
Is a most main attractive! [3] Our great
　heads
Within the city never were in safety
Since our wives wore these little caps.
　I'll change hem;
I'll change hem straight in mine. Mine
　shall no more
Wear three-piled acorns [4] to make my
　horns ache.
Nor will I go; I am resolved for that.—

[Enter Cash with a cloak.]

Carry in my cloak again. Yet stay. Yet
　do, too.　　　　　　　　　　　40
I will defer going, on all occasions.
CASH. Sir, Snare, your scrivener, will be
　there with th' bonds.
KITE. That's true! "Fool" on me! I had
　clean forgot it;
I must go. What's a-clock?
CASH.　　　　　　Exchange time,[5] sir.

[1] Carat, worth.　　　　　　[2] Either.
[3] Mighty attraction.
[4] Fine velvet tags for hat cords.
[5] Time for opening the Exchange, i.e., about
ten.

KITE. Heart, then will Wellbred presently
　be here too,
With one or other of his loose consorts.
I am a knave if I know what to say,
What course to take, or which way to
　resolve.
My brain, methinks, is like an hour-
　glass,
Wherein my imaginations run like sands,
Filling up time, but then are turned and
　turned,　　　　　　　　　　　51
So that I know not what to stay upon,
And less, to put in act. It shall be so.
Nay, I dare build upon his secrecy;
He knows not to deceive me.—Thomas!
CASH.　　　　　　　　　　　　Sir.
KITE. Yet now I have bethought me, too,
　I will not.—
Thomas, is Cob within?
CASH.　　　　　　I think he be, sir.
KITE. [Aside.] But he'll prate too; there's
　no speech of him.
No, there were no man o' the earth to [6]
　Thomas,
If I durst trust him; there is all the
　doubt.　　　　　　　　　　　60
But should he have a chink in him, I were
　gone,
Lost i' my fame forever, talk for th'
　Exchange!
The manner he hath stood with, till this
　present,
Doth promise no such change. What
　should I fear then?
Well, come what will, I'll tempt my
　fortune once.—
Thomas—you may deceive me, but, I
　hope—
Your love to me is more—
CASH.　　　　　　Sir, if a servant's
Duty, with faith, may be called love,
　you are
More than in hope—you are possessed
　of it.
KITE. I thank you heartily, Thomas; gi'
　me your hand.　　　　　　　70
With all my heart, good Thomas. I have,
　Thomas,
A secret to impart unto you—but,
When once you have it, I must seal your
　lips up;
So far I tell you, Thomas.
CASH.　　　　　　Sir, for that—

[6] Compared to.

KITE. Nay, hear me out. Think I esteem you, Thomas,
When I will let you in thus to my private.[1]
It is a thing sits nearer to my crest
Than thou art ware of, Thomas; if thou shouldst
Reveal it, but—
CASH.   How? I reveal it?
KITE.   Nay,
I do not think thou wouldst; but, if thou shouldst,   80
'Twere a great weakness.
CASH.   A great treachery:
Give it no other name.
KITE.   Thou wilt not do 't, then?
CASH. Sir, if I do, mankind disclaim me ever!
KITE. [Aside.] He will not swear; he has some reservation,
Some concealed purpose, and close meaning, sure;
Else, being urged so much, how should he choose
But lend an oath to all this protestation?
H'is no Precisian [2] that I am certain of—
Nor rigid Roman Catholic. He'll play
At fayles and ticktack; [3] I have heard him swear.   90
What should I think of it? Urge him again,
And by some other way? I will do so.—
Well, Thomas, thou hast sworn not to disclose.
Yes, you did swear?
CASH.   Not yet, sir, but I will, Please you—
KITE. No, Thomas, I dare take thy word.
But, if thou wilt swear, do as thou think'st good;
I am resolved [4] without it; at thy pleasure.
CASH. By my soul's safety then, sir, I protest,
My tongue shall ne'er take knowledge of a word   99
Delivered me in nature of your trust.
KITE. It's too much; these ceremonies need not;
I know thy faith to be as firm as rock.
Thomas, come hither, near; [5] we cannot be

Too private in this business. So it is—
[Aside.] Now he has sworn, I dare the safelier venter.—
I have of late, by divers observations—
[Aside.] But whether his oath can bind him, yea, or no,
Being not taken lawfully? [6] Ha! Say you?
I will ask counsel ere I do proceed.—
Thomas, it will be now too long to stay;   110
I'll spy some fitter time soon, or tomorrow.
CASH. Sir, at your pleasure.
KITE.   I will think—and, Thomas,
I pray you, search the books gainst my return
For the receipts twixt me and Traps.
CASH.   I will, sir.
KITE. And hear you, if your mistress' brother, Wellbred,
Chance to bring hither any gentlemen
Ere I come back, let one straight bring me word.
CASH. Very well, sir.
KITE.   To the Exchange, do you hear?
Or here in Coleman Street, to Justice Clement's.
Forget it not, nor be not out of the way.   120
CASH. I will not, sir.
KITE.   I pray you have a care on 't.
Or, whether he come or no, if any other,
Stranger or else, fail not to send me word.
CASH. I shall not, sir.
KITE.   Be 't your special business
Now to remember it.
CASH.   Sir, I warrant you.
KITE. But, Thomas, this is not the secret, Thomas,
I told you of.
CASH.   No, sir; I do suppose it.
KITE. Believe me, it is not.
CASH.   Sir, I do believe you.
KITE. By heaven, it is not; that's enough.
But, Thomas,
I would not you should utter it, do you see,   130
To any creature living; yet I care not.
Well, I must hence. Thomas, conceive thus much;
It was a trial of you, when I meant
So deep a secret to you; I mean not this,

---

[1] Privacy.
[2] Puritan.
[3] Varieties of backgammon.
[4] Convinced.
[5] Nearer.
[6] I.e., before an officer.

But that [1] I have to tell you; this is
  nothing, this.
But, Thomas, keep this from my wife,
  I charge you—
Locked up in silence, midnight, buried
  here.—
[*Aside.*] No greater hell than to be slave
  to fear.   [*Exit.*]
CASH. "Locked up in silence, midnight,
  buried here!"
Whence should this flood of passion,
  trow, take head? Ha!   140
Best dream no longer of this running
  humor,
For fear I sink; the violence of the stream
Already hath transported me so far
That I can feel no ground at all. But
  soft—
O, 'tis our water bearer; somewhat has
  crossed him now.

ACT III. SCENE iv.

[*The same.*]

Cob, Cash.

[COB. (*To himself.*)] Fasting days! What
tell you me of fasting days? 'Slid, would
they were all on a light fire [2] for me! They
say the whole world shall be consumed
with fire one day, but would I had these
ember weeks and villainous Fridays burnt
in the meantime, and then—
CASH. Why, how now, Cob? What
moves thee to this choler, ha?
COB. Collar, Master Thomas? I [10
scorn your collar, I, sir; I am none o' your
cart horse, though I carry and draw water.
An you offer to ride me with your collar,
or halter either, I may hap show you a
jade's trick, sir.
CASH. O, you'll slip your head out of the
collar? Why, Goodman Cob, you mistake
me.
COB. Nay, I have my rheum, and I can
be angry as well as another, sir.   20
CASH. Thy rheum, Cob! Thy humor,
thy humor—thou mistak'st.[3]
COB. Humor? Mack,[4] I think it be so indeed. What is that humor? Some rare
thing, I warrant.
CASH. Marry, I'll tell thee, Cob: it is a

gentlemanlike monster, bred in the special
gallantry of our time, by affectation, and
fed by folly.
COB. How? Must it be fed?   30
CASH. O, ay, humor is nothing if it be
not fed; didst thou never hear that? It's a
common phrase, "Feed my humor."
COB. I'll none on it. Humor, avaunt!
I know you not; begone! Let who will,
make hungry meals for your monstership,
it shall not be I. Feed you, quoth he?
'Slid, I ha' much ado to feed myself, especially on these lean rascally days too;
and 't had been any other day but a [40
fasting day—a plague on them all for me—
by this light, one might have done the
commonwealth good service, and have
drowned them all i' the flood, two or three
hundred thousand years ago. O, I do
stomach [5] them hugely. I have a maw [6]
now, and 'twere for S[i]r Bevis his horse,
against hem.
CASH. I pray thee, good Cob, what
makes thee so out of love with fasting [50
days?
COB. Marry, that which will make any
man out of love with hem, I think—their
bad conditions, and you will needs know.
First, they are of a Flemish breed, I am
sure on 't, for they raven up [7] more butter
than all the days of the week beside; next,
they stink of fish and leek porridge miserably; thirdly, they'll keep a man devoutly
hungry all day, and at night send him [60
supperless to bed.
CASH. Indeed, these are faults, Cob.
COB. Nay, and this were all, 'twere
something; but they are the only known
enemies to my generation. A fasting day
no sooner comes but my lineage goes to
wrack. Poor cobs, they smoke for it, they
are made martyrs o' the gridiron, they melt
in passion; and your maids too know this,
and yet would have me turn Han- [70
nibal,[8] and eat my own fish and blood.
(*He pulls out a red herring.*) My princely
coz, fear nothing; I have not the heart to
devour you, and I might be made as rich
as King Cophetua. O, that I had room for
my tears! I could weep salt water enough
now to preserve the lives of ten thousand
of my kin! But I may curse none but these

---

[1] That which.   [2] Ablaze.
[3] *Humor* had superseded *rheum* as a fashionable term.   [4] Corruption of *Mass.*

[5] Resent.   [7] Devour.
[6] Stomach, appetite.   [8] *I.e.*, cannibal.

filthy almanacs; for, an 'twere not for them, these days of persecution would ne'er [80 be known. I'll be hanged an some fish-monger's son do not make of [1] hem, and puts in more fasting days than he should do, because he would utter [2] his father's dried stockfish and stinking conger.[3]

Cash. 'Slight, peace! Thou'lt be beaten like a stockfish else. Here is Mr. Matthew. Now must I look out for a messenger to my master. [*Exeunt.*]

Act III. Scene v.

[*The same.*]

Wellbred, Ed[ward] Knowell, Brainworm, Bobadill, Matthew, Stephen, Thomas,[4] *Cob.*[5]

[Well.] Beshrew me, but it was an absolute good jest, and exceedingly well carried!

E. Know. Ay, and our ignorance maintained it as well, did it not?

Well. Yes, faith; but was 't possible thou shouldst not know him? I forgive Mr. Stephen, for he is stupidity itself.

E. Know. Fore God, not I, and I might have been joined patten [6] with one of [10 the seven wise masters for knowing him. He had so writhen [7] himself into the habit of one of your poor *infanterie*,[8] your decayed, ruinous, worm-eaten gentlemen of the round,[9] such as have vowed to sit on the skirts of the city—let your provost and his half dozen of halberdiers do what they can—and have translated begging out of the old hackney pace to a fine easy amble, and made it run as smooth off [20 the tongue as a shovegroat shilling.[10] Into the likeness of one of these *reformados* [11] had he molded himself so perfectly, observing every trick of their action, as varying the accent, swearing with an emphasis, indeed, all with so special and exquisite a grace, that, hadst thou seen

him, thou wouldst have sworn he might have been sergeant major,[12] if not lieutenant coronel,[13] to the regiment. 30

Well. Why, Brainworm, who would have thought thou hadst been such an artificer?

E. Know. An artificer! An architect! Except a man had studied begging all his lifetime, and been a weaver of language from his infancy for the clothing of it, I never saw his rival.

Well. Where got'st thou this coat, I mar'l? 40

Bra. Of a Houndsditch man, sir, one of the devil's near kinsmen, a broker.[14]

Well. That cannot be, if the proverb hold; for "A crafty knave needs no broker."

Bra. True, sir; but I did need a broker; ergo—

Well. Well put off—no "crafty knave," you'll say.

E. Know. Tut, he has more of these shifts. 50

Bra. And yet, where I have one, the broker has ten,[15] sir.

[*Enter Cash.*]

Cash. Francis! Martin! Ne'er a one to be found now? What a spite's this?

Well. How now, Thomas? Is my brother Kitely within?

Cash. No, sir, my master went forth e'en now; but Master Downright is within.—Cob! What, Cob! Is he gone too?

Well. Whither went your master? [60 Thomas, canst thou tell?

Cash. I know not. To Justice Clement's, I think, sir.—Cob!

E. Know. Justice Clement! What's he?

Well. Why, dost thou not know him? He is a city magistrate, a justice here, an excellent good lawyer, and a great scholar, but the only mad, merry old fellow in Europe. I showed him you the other day. 70

E. Know. O, is that he? I remember him now. Good faith, and he has a very strange presence, methinks; it shows as if he stood out of the rank from other men. I have heard many of his jests i' univer-

---

[1] Make.   [2] Vend.
[3] "Wednesday and Friday were fast days legally enforced for the benefit of the fisheries" (Smithson).
[4] *I.e.*, Cash.   [7] Twisted.
[5] Last two enter later.   [8] Infantry.
[6] By letters patent.   [9] Military patrol.
[10] A smooth shilling used in the game of shovel-board.
[11] "Officers of a re-formed or disbanded company" (Simpson).

[12] A rank corresponding to the modern major.
[13] Colonel.   [14] Pawnbroker.
[15] Punning on the meaning of *changes of clothing*.

sity. They say he will commit a man for taking the wall [1] of his horse.

WELL. Ay, or wearing his cloak of [2] one shoulder, or serving of God; anything, indeed, if it come in the way of his humor.

Cash goes in and out calling.

CASH. Gasper! Martin! Cob! Heart, where should they be, trow?   82

BOB. Master Kitely's man, pray thee vouchsafe us the lighting of this match.

CASH. Fire on your match! No time but now to vouchsafe?—Francis! Cob! *[Exit.]*

BOB. Body of me! Here's the remainder of seven pound since yesterday was sevennight. 'Tis your right *Trinidado!* [3] Did you never take any, Master Stephen? [90

STE. No, truly, sir; but I'll learn to take it now, since you commend it so.

BOB. Sir, believe me upon my relation, for what I tell you the world shall not reprove.[4] I have been in the Indies, where this herb grows, where neither myself nor a dozen gentlemen more, of my knowledge, have received the taste of any other nutriment in the world for the space of one-and-twenty weeks but the fume of this simple [5] only; therefore it cannot be but 'tis [101 most divine. Further, take it in the nature, in the true kind; so, it makes an antidote, that, had you taken the most deadly poisonous plant in all Italy, it should expel it, and clarify you, with as much ease as I speak. And for your green wound, your balsamum and your St. John's wort are all mere gulleries and trash to it, especially your *Trinidado;* [110 your *Nicotian* [6] is good too. I could say what I know of the virtue of it, for the expulsion of rheums, raw humors, crudities, obstructions, with a thousand of this kind; but I profess myself no quacksalver. Only thus much: by Hercules, I do hold it, and will affirm it before any prince in Europe, to be the most sovereign and precious weed that ever the earth tendered to the use of man.   120

E. KNOW. This speech would ha' done decently in a tabacco trader's mouth.

[Enter Cash with Cob.]

CASH. At Justice Clement's he is, in the middle of Coleman Street.

COB. O! O!

BOB. Where's the match I gave thee, Master Kitely's man?

CASH. Would his match and he, and pipe and all, were at Sancto Domingo! I had forgot it.   *[Exit.]*

COB. By God's me,[7] I mar'l [131 what pleasure or felicity they have in taking this roguish tabacco! It's good for nothing but to choke a man, and fill him full of smoke and embers. There were four died out of one house last week with taking of it, and two more the bell [8] went for yesternight; one of them, they say, will ne'er scape it; he voided a bushel of soot yesterday, upward and downward. [140 By the stocks, an there were no wiser men than I, I'ld have it present whipping, man or woman, that should but deal with a tabacco pipe. Why, it will stifle them all in the end, as many as use it; it's little better than ratsbane or rosaker.[9]

Bobadill beats him with a cudgel.

ALL. O, good captain, hold, hold!

BOB. You base cullion, you!

[Enter Cash.]

CASH. Sir, here's your match.—Come, thou must needs be talking too; thou'rt [150 well enough served.

COB. Nay, he will not meddle with his match, I warrant you. Well, it shall be a dear beating, and I live.

BOB. Do you prate? Do you murmur?

E. KNOW. Nay, good captain, will you regard the humor of a fool? Away, knave!

WELL. Thomas, get him away.

[Exeunt Cash and Cob.]

BOB. A whoreson filthy slave, a dung worm, an excrement! Body o' Cæsar, [160 but that I scorn to let forth so mean a spirit, I'ld ha' stabbed him to the earth.

WELL. Marry, the law forbid, sir!

BOB. By Pharaoh's foot, I would have done it.

STE. *[Aside.]* O, he swears admirably! "By Pharaoh's foot!" "Body of Cæsar!"

---

[1] The cleanest part of the street was nearest the wall.

[2] On.   [4] Disprove.

[3] The best tobacco.   [5] Herb.

[6] A tobacco named from Jacques Nicot.

[7] A mild oath.

[8] Rung for one in mortal extremity.

[9] Poisons.

—I shall never do it, sure. Upon mine
honor, and by Saint George! No, I ha' not
the right grace.   170

MAT. Master Stephen, will you any?
By this air, the most divine tabacco that
ever I drunk.[1]

STE. None, I thank you, sir. O, this
gentleman does it rarely too; but nothing
like the other. "By this air!" "As I am
a gentleman!" "By—"
Master Stephen is practicing to the post.
     [*Exeunt Bobadill and Matthew.*]

BRA. Master, glance, glance! Master
Wellbred!

STE. As I have somewhat to be saved, I
protest—   181

WELL. You are a fool; it needs no
affidavit.

E. KNOW. Cousin, will you any tabacco?

STE. I, sir! Upon my reputation—

E. KNOW. How now, cousin!

STE. I protest, as I am a gentleman, but
no soldier, indeed—

WELL. No, Master Stephen! As [190
I remember, your name is entered in the
artillery garden.[2]

STE. Ay, sir, that's true. Cousin, may
I swear "as I am a soldier" by that?

E. KNOW. O, yes, that you may; it's all
you have for your money.

STE. Then, as I am a gentleman and a
soldier, it is "divine tabacco"!

WELL. But soft, where's Mr. Matthew?
Gone?   200

BRA. No, sir; they went in here.

WELL. O, let's follow them. Master Matthew is gone to salute his mistress in verse; we shall ha' the happiness
to hear some of his poetry now; he never
comes unfurnished.—Brainworm?

STE. Brainworm? Where? Is this
Brainworm?

E. KNOW. Ay, cousin; no words of it,
upon your gentility.   210

STE. Not I, "body of me"! "By this
air"! "S[t]. George"! And "the foot of
Pharaoh"!

WELL. Rare! Your cousin's discourse
is simply drawn out with oaths.

E. KNOW. 'Tis larded with hem—a kind
of French dressing, if you love it. [*Exeunt.*]

[1] Smoked.
[2] Practice grounds.

ACT III. SCENE vi.

*[A room in Justice Clement's house in
Coleman Street.]*

Kitely, Cob.

[KITE.] Ha! How many are there, sayest thou?

COB. Marry, sir, your brother, Master
Wellbred—

KITE. Tut, beside him? What strangers
are there, man?

COB. Strangers? Let me see, one, two;
Mass,
I know not well, there are so many.

KITE. How? So many?

COB. Ay, there's some five or six of them
at the most.

KITE. [*Aside.*] A swarm, a swarm!
Spite of the devil, how they sting my
head
With forkéd stings, thus wide and
large!—But, Cob,   10
How long hast thou been coming hither,
Cob?

COB. A little while, sir.

KITE. Didst thou come running?

COB. No, sir.

KITE. [*Aside.*] Nay, then I am familiar
with thy haste.
Bane to my fortunes! What meant I
to marry?
I, that before was ranked in such content,
My mind at rest too, in so soft a peace,
Being free master of mine own free
thoughts,
And now become a slave? What? Never
sigh;   20
Be of good cheer, man, for thou art a
cuckold.
'Tis done, 'tis done! Nay, when such
flowing store,
Plenty itself, falls in my wife's lap,
The *cornu-copiæ* [3] will be mine, I
know.—But, Cob,
What entertainment had they? I am
sure
My sister and my wife would bid them
welcome! Ha?

COB. Like enough, sir; yet I heard not a
word of it.

KITE. [*Aside.*] No; their lips were sealed
with kisses, and the voice,
Drowned in a flood of joy at their arrival,

[3] Horns of plenty, with an allusion to cuckoldry.

Had lost her motion, state, and faculty.—
Cob, which of them was 't that first
   kissed my wife,   31
My sister, I should say? My wife, alas,
I fear not her. Ha! Who was it, say'st
   thou?
Cob. By my troth, sir, will you have the
   truth of it?
Kite. O, ay, good Cob, I pray thee heartily.
Cob. Then I am a vagabond, and fitter
for Bridewell than your worship's company,
if I saw anybody to be kissed, unless they
would have kissed the post in the middle
of the warehouse,[1] for there I left them   [40
all at their tabacco, with a pox!
   Kite. How? Were they not gone in
then ere thou cam'st?
   Cob. O, no, sir.
   Kite. Spite of the devil! What do I
stay here then? Cob, follow me.   [Exit.]
   Cob. Nay, soft and fair, I have eggs
on the spit; I cannot go yet, sir. Now am
I, for some five-and-fifty reasons, hammering, hammering revenge. O, for three   [50
or four gallons of vinegar to sharpen my
wits! Revenge, vinegar revenge, vinegar
and mustard revenge! Nay, and he had
not lyen[2] in my house, 'twould never have
grieved me; but being my guest, one that,
I'll be sworn, my wife has lent him her
smock off her back, while his one shirt
has been at washing; pawned her necker-
chers[3] for clean bands for him; sold almost all my platters to buy him ta-   [60
bacco; and he to turn monster of ingratitude, and strike his lawful host! Well, I
hope to raise up an host of fury for 't! Here
comes Justice Clement.

Act III. Scene vii.

[The same.]

Clement, Knowell, Formal, Cob.

[Clem.] What, 's Master Kitely gone,
Roger?
   For. Ay, sir.
   Clem. Heart of me! What made him
leave us so abruptly?—How now, sirrah!
What make[4] you here? What would you
have, ha?

   Cob. And 't please your worship, I am
a poor neighbor of your worship's—
   Clem. A poor neighbor of mine?   [10
Why, speak, poor neighbor.
   Cob. I dwell, sir, at the sign of the
Water Tankard, hard by the Green Lattice;[5] I have paid scot and lot[6] there any
time this eighteen years.
   Clem. To the Green Lattice?
   Cob. No, sir, to the parish. Marry, I
have seldom scaped scot-free[7] at the Lattice.
   Clem. O, well; what business has   [20
my poor neighbor with me?
   Cob. And 't like your worship, I am
come to crave the peace of your worship.
   Clem. Of me, knave? Peace of me,
knave? Did I e'er hurt thee? Or threaten
thee? Or wrong thee, ha?
   Cob. No, sir; but your worship's warrant for one that has wronged me, sir. His
arms are at too much liberty; I would fain
have them bound to a treaty of peace,   [30
an my credit could compass it with your
worship.
   Clem. Thou goest far enough about
for 't, I am sure.
   Know. Why, dost thou go in danger of
thy life for him, friend?
   Cob. No, sir; but I go in danger of my
death every hour, by his means; an I die
within a twelvemonth and a day,[8] I may
swear by the law of the land that he   [40
killed me.
   Clem. How? How, knave? Swear he
killed thee? And by the law? What pretense? What color[9] hast thou for that?
   Cob. Marry, and 't please your worship, both black and blue; color enough,
I warrant you. I have it here to show your
worship.   [Shows his bruises.]
   Clem. What is he that gave you this,
sirrah?   50
   Cob. A gentleman and a soldier, he
says he is, o' the city here.
   Clem. A soldier o' the city? What call
you him?
   Cob. Captain Bobadill.
   Clem. Bobadill? And why did he bob[10]

---

[1] Shop.
[2] Lain.
[3] Neckerchiefs.
[4] Do.
[5] A tavern.   [7] Without paying a tavern bill.
[6] Parish taxes.
[8] A twelvemonth and a day was the legal time
for determining the cause of death from bodily
injury.
[9] Reason.   [10] Strike.

and beat you, sirrah? How began the quarrel betwixt you, ha? Speak truly, knave, I advise you.

Cob. Marry, indeed, and please [60 your worship, only because I spake against their vagrant tabacco, as I came by hem when they were taking on 't; for nothing else.

Clem. Ha! You speak against tabacco?— Formal, his name.

For. What's your name, sirrah?

Cob. Oliver, sir; Oliver Cob, sir.

Clem. Tell Oliver Cob he shall go to the jail, Formal.   70

For. Oliver Cob, my master, Justice Clement, says you shall go to the jail.

Cob. O, I beseech your worship, for God's sake, dear master justice!

Clem. Nay, God's precious![1] And such drunkards and tankards as you are come to dispute of tabacco once, I have done. Away with him!

Cob. O, good master justice!—[To Knowell.] Sweet old gentleman!   80

Know. Sweet Oliver, would I could do thee any good!—Justice Clement, let me entreat you, sir.

Clem. What? A threadbare rascal, a beggar, a slave that never drunk out of better than pisspot metal[2] in his life! And he to deprave[3] and abuse the virtue of an herb so generally received in the courts of princes, the chambers of nobles, the bowers of sweet ladies, the cabins[4] [90 of soldiers!—Roger, away with him! By God's precious—I say, go to.

Cob. Dear master justice, let me be beaten again; I have deserved it; but not the prison, I beseech you.

Know. Alas, poor Oliver!

Clem. Roger, make him a warrant.— [Aside.] He shall not go; I but fear[5] the knave.

For. [Aside.] Do not stink, sweet [100 Oliver; you shall not go.—My master will give you a warrant.

Cob. O, the Lord maintain his worship, his worthy worship!

Clem. Away, despatch him.—[Exeunt Formal and Cob.] How now, Master Knowell, in dumps? In dumps? Come, this becomes not.

Know. Sir, would I could not feel my cares.   110

Clem. Your cares are nothing; they are like my cap, soon put on, and as soon put off. What? Your son is old enough to govern himself. Let him run his course; it's the only way to make him a staid man. If he were an unthrift,[6] a ruffian, a drunkard, or a licentious liver, then you had reason; you had reason to take care; but, being none of these, mirth's my witness, an I had twice so [120 many cares as you have, I'd drown them all in a cup of sack. Come, come, let's try it. I muse[7] your parcel[8] of a soldier returns not all this while.   [Exeunt].

Act IV. Scene i.

[A room in Kitely's house.]

Downright, Dame Kitely.

[Dow.] Well, sister, I tell you true; and you'll find it so in the end.

Dame. Alas, brother, what would you have me to do? I cannot help it; you see my brother brings hem in here; they are his friends.

Dow. His friends? His fiends! 'Slud,[9] they do nothing but haunt him up and down like a sort of unlucky sprites, and tempt him to all manner of villainy [10 that can be thought of. Well, by this light, a little thing would make me play the devil with some of hem; and 'twere not more for your husband's sake than anything else, I'ld make the house too hot for the best on hem; they should say, and swear, hell were broken loose, ere they went hence. But, by God's will, 'tis nobody's fault but yours; for, an you had done as you might have done, they should have been [20 purboiled[10] and baked too, every mother's son, ere they should ha' come in, e'er a one of them.

Dame. God's my life! Did you ever hear the like? What a strange man is this! Could I keep out all them, think you? I should put myself against half a dozen men, should I? Good faith, you'ld mad the patient'st body in the world, to hear you talk so, without any sense [30 or reason.

---

[1] God's precious body.   [2] Pewter.
[3] Disparage.   [4] Tents.   [5] Frighten.
[6] Prodigal.   [8] Portion.
[7] Wonder.   [9] God's Lord.
[10] Parboiled, boiled thoroughly.

Act IV. Scene ii.

[*The same.*]

Mrs. Bridget, Mr. Matthew, [observed by] Dame Kitely, Downright, Wellbred, Stephen, Ed[ward] Knowell, Bobadill, Brainworm, Cash.[1]

[BRID.] Servant,[2] in troth you are too prodigal
Of your wit's treasure, thus to pour it forth
Upon so mean a subject as my worth.

MAT. You say well, mistress, and I mean as well.

Dow. Hoyday,[3] here is stuff!

WELL. O, now stand close;[4] pray heaven, she can get him to read! He should do it of his own natural impudency.

BRID. Servant, what is this same, I pray you?   10

MAT. Marry, an elegy, an elegy, an odd toy—

Dow. To mock an ape withal![5] O, I could sew up his mouth now.

DAME. Sister, I pray you let's hear it.

Dow. Are you rime-given too?

MAT. Mistress, I'll read it, if you please.

BRID. Pray you do, servant.

Dow. O, here's no foppery![6] Death, I can endure the stocks better. [*Exit.*] 20

E. KNOW. What ails thy brother? Can he not hold his water at reading of a ballad?

WELL. O, no; a rime to him is worse than cheese or a bagpipe. But mark, you lose the protestation.

MAT. Faith, I did it in an humor; I know not how it is. But please you come near, sir. This gentleman has judgment; he knows how to censure of a—pray you, sir, you can judge?   30

STE. Not I, sir; upon my reputation, and by the foot of Pharaoh!

WELL. O, chide your cousin for swearing.

E. KNOW. Not I, so long as he does not forswear himself.

BOB. Master Matthew, you abuse the expectation of your dear mistress and her fair sister. Fie! While you live, avoid this prolixity.   40

MAT. I shall, sir; well, *incipere dulce.*[7]

E. KNOW. How, *insipere dulce!* "A sweet thing to be a fool," indeed!

WELL. What, do you take *incipere* in that sense?

E. KNOW. You do not, you? This was your villainy, to gull him with a motte.[8]

WELL. O, the benchers'[9] phrase! *Pauca verba, pauca verba!*[10]

MAT. [*Reading.*] "Rare creature, let me speak without offense;   50
Would God my rude words had the influence
To rule thy thoughts, as thy fair looks do mine;
Then shouldst thou be his prisoner, who is thine."

E. KNOW. [*Aside.*] This is in *Hero and Leander!*

WELL. [*Aside.*] O, ay! Peace, we shall have more of this.

MAT. "Be not unkind and fair; misshapen stuff
Is of behavior boisterous and rough."

WELL. [*Aside.*] How like you that, sir? *Master Stephen answers with shaking his head.*

E. KNOW. [*Aside.*] 'Slight, he shakes [61 his head like a bottle, to feel and there be any brain in it!

MAT. But observe the catastrophe now:
"And I in duty will exceed all other,
As you in beauty do excel Love's mother."

E. KNOW. [*Aside.*] Well, I'll have him free of[11] the wit brokers, for he utters nothing but stol'n remnants.

WELL. [*Aside.*] O, forgive it him.   70

E. KNOW. A filching rogue, hang him! And from the dead? It's worse than sacrilege.

WELL. [*Coming forward.*] Sister, what ha' you here? Verses? Pray you, let's see. Who made these verses? They are excellent good.

MAT. O, Master Wellbred, 'tis your disposition to say so, sir. They were good i' the morning; I made hem *ex tem-* [80 *pore* this morning.

WELL. How? *Ex tempore?*

MAT. Ay, would I might be hanged

---

[1] Enters later.   [3] Exclamation of surprise.
[2] Lover.   [4] Aside.
[5] To dupe a simpleton with.   [6] Deceit.

[7] It is sweet to begin.   [8] *Mot*, word.
[9] Justices', or alehouse loafers'.
[10] Few words.   [11] Made a member of.

else. Ask Captain Bobadill; he saw me
write them, at the—pox on it!—the Star
yonder.

BRA. [*Aside.*] Can he find in his heart
to curse the stars so?

E. KNOW. [*Aside.*] Faith, his are even
with him; they ha' cursed him enough　[90
already.

STE. Cousin, how do you like this
gentleman's verses?

E. KNOW. O, admirable! The best
that ever I heard, coz.

STE. Body o' Cæsar, they are admirable!
The best that ever I heard, as I am a
soldier!

[Enter Downright.]

DOW. [*Aside.*] I am vexed; I can hold
ne'er a bone of me still! Heart, I think they
mean to build and breed here.　　　　100

WELL. Sister, you have a simple servant here, that crowns your beauty with
such *encomions* [1] and devices; you may see
what it is to be the mistress of a wit that
can make your perfections so transparent
that every blear eye may look through
them, and see him drowned over head and
ears in the deep well of desire. Sister Kitely,
I marvel you get you not a servant that
can rime, and do tricks too.　　　　110

DOW. [*Aside.*] O monster! Impudence
itself! Tricks? [2]

DAME. Tricks, brother? What tricks?

BRID. Nay, speak, I pray you, what
tricks?

DAME. Ay, never spare anybody here;
but say, what tricks?

BRID. Passion of my heart, do tricks?

WELL. 'Slight, here's a trick vied and
revied! [3] Why, you monkeys, you,　[120
what a caterwauling do you keep! Has he
not given you rimes and verses and tricks?

DOW. [*Aside.*] O, the fiend!

WELL. Nay, you lamp of virginity, that
take it in snuff [4] so, come, and cherish this
tame poetical fury in your servant; you'll
be begged else shortly for a concealment. [5]

[1] Encomiums.

[2] Punning on the sense of *wantonness*.

[3] A bet made and raised. [4] Take offense at.

[5] "This is a reference to the unauthorized holding of sequestered lands, such as those which
had belonged to the monasteries. Elizabeth had
appointed commissions to search such holdings
or 'concealments,' which her courtiers often
'begged'" (Neilson).

Go to, reward his muse. You cannot give
him less than a shilling, in conscience, for
the book he had it out of cost him a　[130
teston [6] at least. How now, gallants? Mr.
Matthew? Captain? What, all sons of
silence? No spirit?

DOW. Come, you might practice your
ruffian tricks somewhere else, and not here,
I wusse; this is no tavern nor drinking
school to vent your exploits in.

WELL. How now! Whose cow has
calved? [7]

DOW. Marry, that has mine, sir.　[140
Nay, boy, never look askance at me for
the matter; I'll tell you of it, I, sir. You
and your companions mend yourselves
when I ha' done.

WELL. My companions!

DOW. Yes, sir, your companions, so I
say; I am not afraid of you, nor them
neither; your hang-bys here. You must
have your poets and your potlings, [8] your
soldados and *foolados* to follow you up　[150
and down the city; and here they must
come to domineer and swagger.—Sirrah,
you ballad singer, and slops, [9] your fellow
there, get you out; get you home; or, by
this steel, I'll cut off your ears, and that
presently.

WELL. 'Slight, stay, let's see what he
dare do! Cut off his ears? Cut a whetstone! You are an ass, do you see? Touch
any man here, and, by this hand, I'll　[160
run my rapier to the hilts in you.

DOW. Yea, that would I fain see, boy.
*They all draw, and they of the house make
out to part them.*

DAME. O Jesu! Murder! Thomas!
Gasper!

BRID. Help, help! Thomas!

[Enter Cash and Servants.]

E. KNOW. Gentlemen, forbear, I pray
you.

BOB. Well, sirrah, you Holofernes; by
my hand, I will pink your flesh full of holes
with my rapier for this; I will, by this　[170
good heaven!—

They offer to fight again and are parted.
Nay, let him come, let him come, gentle-

[6] Sixpence.

[7] *I.e.,* what's the matter?

[8] Tipplers.　　　　　　[9] *I.e.,* Bobadill.

men; by the body of Saint George, I'll
not kill him.

CASH. Hold, hold, good gentlemen.

Dow. You whoreson, bragging cois-
tril! [1]

ACT IV. SCENE iii.

[The same.]

To them, Kitely.

[KITE.] Why, how now? What's the matter? What's the stir here?

Whence springs the quarrel? Thomas!
Where is he?

Put up your weapons, and put off this
rage.

My wife and sister, they are the cause of
this.

What, Thomas! Where is this knave?

CASH. Here, sir.

WELL. Come, let's go; this is one of my
brother's ancient humors, this.

STE. I am glad nobody was hurt by his
ancient humor.   10

[Exeunt Wellbred, Stephen, Edward Knowell, Bobadill, Brainworm, and Servants.]

KITE. Why, how now, brother, who enforced this brawl?

Dow. A sort of lewd rakehells that
care neither for God nor the devil. And
they must come here to read ballads, and
roguery, and trash! I'll mar the knot of
hem ere I sleep, perhaps—especially Bob
there, he that's all manner of shapes—and
Songs and Sonnets, his fellow.

BRID. Brother, indeed you are too violent,
Too sudden in your humor; and you
know   20
My brother Wellbred's temper will not
bear
Any reproof, chiefly in such a presence,
Where every slight disgrace he should
receive
Might wound him in opinion and respect.

Dow. Respect? What talk you of
respect 'mong such as ha' nor spark of
manhood nor good manners? 'Sdeynes,
I am ashamed to hear you! Respect! [Exit.]

BRID. Yes, there was one, a civil gentleman,
And very worthily demeaned himself.   30

KITE. O, that was some love of yours,
sister.

BRID. A love of mine? I would it were no
worse, brother;
You'ld pay my portion sooner than you
think for.

DAME. Indeed he seemed to be a gentleman of an exceeding fair disposition, and
of very excellent good parts.

[Exeunt Dame Kitely and Bridget.]

KITE. [Aside.] Her love, by heaven! My
wife's minion!
"Fair disposition"? "Excellent good
parts"?
Death, these phrases are intolerable!
Good parts? How should she know his
parts?   40
His parts? Well, well, well, well, well, well!
It is too plain, too clear.—Thomas, come
hither.
What, are they gone?

CASH.   Ay, sir, they went in.
My mistress and your sister—

KITE. Are any of the gallants within?

CASH. No, sir, they are all gone.

KITE.   Art thou sure of it?

CASH. I can assure you, sir.

KITE. What gentleman was that they
praised so, Thomas?

CASH. One, they call him Master [50
Knowell, a handsome young gentleman, sir.

KITE. Ay, I thought so; my mind gave me
as much.
I'll die, but they have hid him i' the house
Somewhere; I'll go and search; go with
me, Thomas.
Be true to me, and thou shalt find me a
master.   [Exeunt.]

ACT IV. SCENE iv.

[The lane before Cob's house.]

Cob, Tib. [2]

COB. [Knocking.] What, Tib! Tib, I
say!

TIB. [Within.] How now, what cuckold
is that knocks so hard? [Enters.] O husband, is 't you? What's the news?

COB. Nay, you have stonned [3] me, i'
faith; you ha' giv'n me a knock o' the
forehead will stick by me. Cuckold? 'Slid,
cuckold?

TIB. Away, you fool! Did I know it [10
was you that knocked? Come, come, you
may call me as bad when you list. [4]

----
[1] Knave.

[2] Enters later.   [3] Stunned.   [4] Please.

Cob. May I? Tib, you are a whore.

Tib. You lie in your throat, husband.

Cob. How, the lie? And in my throat too? Do you long to be stabbed, ha?

Tib. Why, you are no soldier, I hope?

Cob. O, must you be stabbed by a soldier? Mass, that's true! When was Bobadill here, your captain? That [20 rogue, that foist,[1] that fencing Burgullion?[2] I'll tickle him, i' faith.

Tib. Why, what's the matter, trow?

Cob. O, he has basted me rarely, sumptiously! But I have it here in black and white. [*Pulls out the warrant.*] For his black and blue, shall[3] pay him. O, the justice, the honestest old brave Trojan in London; I do honor the very flea of his dog. A plague on him, though, [30 he put me once in a villainous filthy fear; marry, it vanished away like the smoke of tabacco; but I was smoked[4] soundly first. I thank the devil and his good angel, my guest. Well, wife, or Tib, which you will, get you in and lock the door; I charge you let nobody in to you, wife; nobody in to you; those are my words. Not Captain Bob himself, nor the fiend in his likeness. You are a woman; you have [40 flesh and blood enough in you to be tempted; therefore keep the door shut upon all comers.

Tib. I warrant you, there shall nobody enter here without my consent.

Cob. Nor with your consent, sweet Tib; and so I leave you.

Tib. It's more than you know, whether you leave me so.

Cob. How?   50

Tib. Why, "sweet."

Cob. Tut, sweet or sour, thou art a flower. Keep close thy door; I ask no more.
                                    [*Exeunt.*]

Act IV. Scene v.

[*A room in the Windmill.*]

Ed[ward] Knowell, Wellbred, Stephen, Brainworm.

[E. Know.] Well, Brainworm, perform this business happily, and thou makest a purchase of my love forever.

Well. I' faith, now let thy spirits use their best faculties. But, at any hand,[5]

remember the message to my brother, for there's no other means to start him.

Bra. I warrant you, sir; fear nothing; I have a nimble soul has waked all forces of my fant'sy by this time, and put [10 hem in true motion. What you have possessed me withal,[6] I'll discharge it amply, sir; make it no question.

Well. Forth, and prosper, Brainworm.— [*Exit Brainworm.*] Faith, Ned, how dost thou approve of my abilities in this device?

E. Know. Troth, well, howsoever; but it will come excellent if it take.

Well. Take, man? Why, it cannot [20 choose but take, if the circumstances miscarry not. But tell me ingenuously, dost thou affect my sister Bridget as thou pretend'st?

E. Know. Friend, am I worth belief?

Well. Come, do not protest. In faith, she is a maid of good ornament and much modesty; and, except I conceived very worthily of her, thou shouldest not have her.   30

E. Know. Nay, that, I am afraid, will be a question yet, whether I shall have her or no.

Well. 'Slid, thou shalt have her; by this light, thou shalt.

E. Know. Nay, do not swear.

Well. By this hand, thou shalt have her; I'll go fetch her presently. Point[7] but where to meet, and as I am an honest man I'll bring her.   40

E. Know. Hold, hold, be temperate.

Well. Why, by—what shall I swear by? Thou shalt have her, as I am—

E. Know. Pray thee, be at peace; I am satisfied, and do believe thou wilt omit no offered occasion to make my desires complete.

Well. Thou shalt see and know I will not.   [*Exeunt.*]

Act IV. Scene vi.

[*A street in the Old Jewry.*]

Formal, Knowell, Brainworm.[8]

[For.] Was your man a soldier, sir?

Know. Ay, a knave; I took him begging o' the way,
 This morning as I came over Moorfields.

---

[1] Pickpocket.   [3] *I.e.,* I shall.
[2] Bully.   [4] Beaten.   [5] Rate.

[6] Informed me of.   [7] Appoint.   [8] Enters later.

[*Enter Brainworm.*]

O, here he is!—Yo' have made fair speed,
 believe me.
Where, i' the name of sloth, could you
 be thus—
Bra. Marry, peace be my comfort,
where I thought I should have had little
comfort of your worship's service.
Know. How so?
Bra. O, sir, your coming to the [10
city, your entertainment of me, and your
sending me to watch—indeed all the circumstances either of your charge or my
employment are as open to your son as to
yourself.
Know. How should that be, unless that
 villain, Brainworm,
Have told him of the letter, and discovered [1]
All that I strictly charged him to conceal? 'Tis so.
Bra. I am partly o' the faith, 'tis so,
indeed.
Know. But how should he know thee
to be my man? 21
Bra. Nay, sir, I cannot tell, unless it
be by the black art. Is not your son a
scholar, sir?
Know. Yes, but I hope his soul is not
 allied
Unto such hellish practice; if it were,
I had just cause to weep my part in him,
And curse the time of his creation.
But where didst thou find them, Fitzsword?
Bra. You should rather ask where [30
they found me, sir, for, I'll be sworn, I
was going along in the street, thinking
nothing, when, of a sudden, a voice calls,
"Mr. Knowell's man!" another cries,
"Soldier!" and thus half a dozen of hem,
till they had called me within a house,
where I no sooner came but they seemed
men, and out flew all their rapiers at my
bosom, with some three or four score
oaths to accompany hem; and all to [40
tell me I was but a dead man if I did not
confess where you were, and how I was
employed, and about what; which when
they could not get out of me (as, I protest,
they must ha' dissected and made an
anatomy [2] o' me first, and so I told hem),

they locked me up into a room i' the top
of a high house, whence by great miracle
(having a light heart) I slid down by a
bottom [3] of packthread into the [50
street, and so scaped. But, sir, thus much
I can assure you, for I heard it while I
was locked up: there were a great many
rich merchants and brave [4] citizens' wives
with hem at a feast; and your son, Mr. Edward, withdrew with one of hem, and has
pointed to meet her anon at one Cob's
house, a water bearer that dwells by the
Wall. Now there your worship shall be sure
to take him, for there he preys, and fail
he will not. 61
Know. Nor will I fail to break his match,
 I doubt not.
Go thou along with Justice Clement's
 man,
And stay there for me. At one Cob's
 house, say'st thou?
Bra. Ay, sir, there you shall have him.—
[*Exit Knowell.—Aside.*] Yes—invisible!
Much wench, or much son! 'Slight, when he
has stayed there three or four hours, travail-
ing with the expectation of wonders, and
at length be delivered of air, O, the [70
sport that I should then take to look on him,
if I durst! But now I mean to appear no
more afore him in this shape. I have another trick to act yet. O, that I were so
happy as to light on a nupson [5] now of [6]
this justice's novice!—Sir, I make you
stay somewhat long.
For. Not a whit, sir. Pray you, what
do you mean, sir?
Bra. I was putting up some papers—
For. You ha' been lately in the [81
wars, sir, it seems.
Bra. Marry, have I, sir, to my loss, and
expense of all, almost—
For. Troth, sir, I would be glad to bestow a pottle [7] of wine o' you, if it please
you to accept it—
Bra. O, sir—
For. But to hear the manner of your
services, and your devices in the wars, [90
they say they be very strange, and not like
those a man reads in the Roman histories,
or sees at Mile End.
Bra. No, I assure you, sir; why, at any

[1] Revealed.   [2] Skeleton.

[3] Ball.
[4] Finely dressed.   [6] In.
[5] Simpleton.   [7] Bottle.

time when it please you, I shall be ready to discourse to you all I know.—[*Aside.*] And more too somewhat.

For. No better time than now, sir. We'll go to the Windmill; there we shall have a cup of neat grist,[1] we call it. [100 I pray you, sir, let me request you to the Windmill.

Bra. I'll follow you, sir.—[*Aside.*] And make grist o' you, if I have good luck.

[*Exeunt.*]

Act IV. Scene vii.

[*The same.*]

[2] *Matthew, Ed[ward] Knowell, Bobadill, Stephen, Downright.*[3]

[Mat.] Sir, did your eyes ever taste the like clown of him where we were to-day, Mr. Wellbred's half brother? I think the whole earth cannot show his parallel, by this daylight.

E. Know. We were now speaking of him; Captain Bobadill tells me he is fall'n foul o' you too.

Mat. O, ay, sir, he threatened me with the *bastinado*.   10

Bob. Ay, but I think I taught you prevention this morning for that. You shall kill him beyond question, if you be so generously [4] minded.

Mat. Indeed, it is a most excellent trick.   [*Fences.*]

Bob. O, you do not give spirit enough to your motion; you are too tardy, too heavy! O, it must be done like lightning. Hay! [5]

    He practices at a post.

Mat. Rare, captain!   20

Bob. Tut! 'Tis nothing, and 't be not done in a—*punto*.[6]

E. Know. Captain, did you ever prove yourself upon any of our masters of defense here?

Mat. O good sir! Yes, I hope he has.

Bob. I will tell you, sir. Upon my first coming to the city, after my long travel [7]

for knowledge in that mystery only, there came three or four of hem to me, at [30 a gentleman's house where it was my chance to be resident at that time, to entreat my presence at their schools, and withal so much importuned me that, I protest to you as I am a gentleman, I was ashamed of their rude demeanor out of all measure. Well, I told hem that to come to a public school, they should pardon me, it was opposite, in diameter,[8] to my humor; but, if so they would [40 give their attendance at my lodging, I protested to do them what right or favor I could, as I was a gentleman, and so forth.

E. Know. So, sir, then you tried their skill?

Bob. Alas, soon tried! You shall hear, sir. Within two or three days after, they came; and, by honesty, fair sir, believe me, I graced them exceedingly, showed them some two or three tricks of pre- [50 vention have purchased hem, since, a credit—to admiration. They cannot deny this; and yet now they hate me; and why? Because I am excellent; and for no other vile reason on the earth.

E. Know. This is strange and barbarous, as ever I heard.

Bob. Nay, for a more instance of their preposterous natures, but note, sir. They have assaulted me some three, four, [60 five, six of them together, as I have walked alone in divers skirts i' the town, as Turnbull, Whitechapel, Shoreditch,[9] which were then my quarters, and since, upon the Exchange, at my lodging, and at my ordinary, where I have driven them afore me the whole length of a street, in the open view of all our gallants, pitying to hurt them, believe me. Yet all this lenity will not o'ercome their spleen; they [70 will be doing with the pismire,[10] raising a hill a man may spurn abroad with his foot at pleasure. By myself, I could have slain them all, but I delight not in murder. I am loath to bear any other than this *bastinado* for hem; yet I hold it good polity not to go disarmed, for, though I be skillful, I may be oppressed with multitudes.

E. Know. Ay, believe me, may you, sir; and, in my conceit,[11] our whole [80

---

[1] Liquor sold at the Windmill.
[2] The marginal direction *To them* is erroneously printed here.
[3] Enters later.   [4] Gentlemanly.
[5] A fencer's cry, meaning "a hit!"—"you have it!"
[6] Instant, with a pun on *thrust with a point.*
[7] With a pun on *travail.*

[8] *I.e.*, diametrically.   [10] Ant.
[9] Disreputable districts of London.   [11] Opinion.

nation should sustain the loss by it, if it were so.

Bob. Alas, no! What's a peculiar [1] man to a nation? Not seen.

E. Know. O, but your skill, sir!

Bob. Indeed, that might be some loss; but who respects it? I will tell you, sir, by the way of private, and under seal; I am a gentleman, and live here obscure, and to myself; but were I known to her [90 majesty and the lords, observe me, I would undertake, upon this poor head and life, for the public benefit of the state, not only to spare the entire lives of her subjects in general, but to save the one half, nay, three parts of her yearly charge in holding war, and against what enemy soever. And how would I do it, think you?

E. Know. Nay, I know not, nor [100 can I conceive.

Bob. Why thus, sir. I would select nineteen more to [2] myself throughout the land; gentlemen they should be of good spirit, strong and able constitution; I would choose them by an instinct, a character, that I have; and I would teach these nineteen the special rules, as your *punto*, your *reverso*, your *stoccata*, your *imbroccata*, your *passada*, your *mon- [110 tanto* [3]—till they could all play very near, or altogether, as well as myself. This done, say the enemy were forty thousand strong, we twenty would come into the field the tenth of March, or thereabouts; and we would challenge twenty of the enemy; they could not in their honor refuse us. Well, we would kill them; challenge twenty more, kill them; twenty more, kill them; twenty more, kill them too; and thus [120 would we kill every man his twenty a day—that's twenty score; twenty score, that's two hundreth; two hundreth a day, five days a thousand; forty thousand; forty times five, five times forty, two hundreth days kills them all up, by com- putation. And this will I venture my poor gentlemanlike carcass to perform, pro- vided there be no treason practiced upon us, by fair and discreet manhood; [130 that is, civilly by the sword.

E. Know. Why, are you so sure of your hand, captain, at all times?

Bob. Tut! Never miss [4] thrust, upon my reputation with you.

E. Know. I would not stand in Down- right's state then, an you meet him, for the wealth of any one street in London.

Bob. Why, sir, you mistake me. If he were here now, by this welkin, I would [140 not draw my weapon on him. Let this gentleman do his mind; but I will *bastinado* him, by the bright sun, wherever I meet him.

Mat. Faith, and I'll have a fling at him, at my distance.

Downright walks over the stage.

E. Know. God's so, look where he is! Yonder he goes.

Dow. What peevish luck have I, I cannot meet with these bragging [150 rascals?

Bob. It's not he, is it?

E. Know. Yes, faith, it is he.

Mat. I'll be hanged, then, if that were he.

E. Know. Sir, keep your hanging good for some greater matter, for I assure you that was he.

Ste. Upon my reputation, it was he.

Bob. Had I thought it had been [160 he, he must not have gone so; but I can hardly be induced to believe it was he yet.

E. Know. That I think, sir.

[*Enter Downright.*]

But see, he is come again!

Dow. O, Pharaoh's foot, have I found you? Come, draw, to your tools; draw, gipsy, or I'll thresh you.

Bob. Gentleman of valor, I do believe in thee; hear me—   170

Dow. Draw your weapon then.

Bob. Tall [5] man, I never thought on it till now: body of me, I had a warrant of the peace served on me, even now as I came along, by a water bearer; this gentle- man saw it, Mr. Matthew.

Dow. 'Sdeath, you will not draw then?

He beats him and disarms him; Matthew runs away.

Bob. Hold, hold! Under thy favor, forbear!

---

[1] Individual.

[2] In addition to.

[3] Italian fencing terms.

[4] *I.e.*, I never miss.   [5] Bold.

Dow. Prate again, as you like [180 this, you whoreson foist, you! You'll "control [1] the point," you! Your consort is gone; had he stayed, he had shared with you, sir. [*Exit.*]

Bob. Well, gentlemen, bear witness I was bound to the peace, by this good day.

E. Know. No, faith, it's an ill day, captain—never reckon it other; but, say you were bound to the peace, the law allows you to defend yourself. That'll prove [190 but a poor excuse.

Bob. I cannot tell, sir; I desire good construction in fair sort. I never sustained the like disgrace, by heaven! Sure I was strook [2] with a planet thence, for I had no power to touch my weapon.

E. Know. Ay, like enough; I have heard of many that have been beaten under a planet; go, get you to a surgeon. 'Slid, an these be your tricks, your *pas-* [200 *sadas* and your *montantos*, I'll none of them.—[*Exit Bobadill.*] O, manners! That this age should bring forth such creatures! That nature should be at leisure to make hem! Come, coz.

Ste. Mass, I'll ha' this cloak.

E. Know. God's will, 'tis Downright's.

Ste. Nay, it's mine now. Another might have ta'en up as well as I. I'll wear it, so I will. 210

E. Know. How an he see it? He'll challenge it, assure yourself.

Ste. Ay, but he shall not ha' it; I'll say I bought it.

E. Know. Take heed you buy it not too dear, coz. [*Exeunt.*]

Act IV. Scene viii.

[*A room in Kitely's house.*]

Kitely, Wellbred, Dame Kit[ely], Bridget, Brainworm, Cash. [3]

[Kite.] Now, trust me, brother, you were much to blame,

T' incense his anger, and disturb the peace

Of my poor house, where there are sentinels

That every minute watch to give alarms

Of civil war, without adjection [4]

Of your assistance or occasion.

Well. No harm done, brother, I warrant you. Since there is no harm done, anger costs a man nothing; and a tall man is never his own man till he be angry. [10 To keep his valure [5] in obscurity is to keep himself as it were in a cloak bag. What's a musician, unless he play? What's a tall man, unless he fight? For, indeed, all this my wise brother stands upon absolutely; and that made me fall in with him so resolutely.

Dame. Ay, but what harm might have come of it, brother?

Well. "Might," sister? So might [20 the good warm clothes your husband wears be poisoned, for anything he knows; or the wholesome wine he drunk, even now at the table—

Kite. [*Aside.*] Now, God forbid! O me! Now I remember

My wife drunk to me last, and changed the cup,

And bade me wear this curséd suit today.

See, if heaven suffer murder undiscovered!—

I feel me ill; give me some mithridate; [6]

Some mithridate and oil, good sister, fetch me. 30

O, I am sick at heart; I burn, I burn.

If you will save my life, go fetch it me.

Well. O strange humor! My very breath has poisoned him.

Brid. Good brother, be content. What do you mean?

The strength of these extreme conceits [7] will kill you.

Dame. Beshrew your heart-blood, brother Wellbred, now, for putting such a toy [8] into his head!

Well. Is a fit simile a "toy"? Will [40 he be poisoned with a simile? Brother Kitely, what a strange and idle [9] imagination is this! For shame, be wiser. O' my soul, there's no such matter.

Kite. Am I not sick? How am I then not poisoned?

Am I not poisoned? How am I then so sick?

Dame. If you be sick, your own thoughts make you sick.

---

[1] Beat down.
[2] Struck, bewitched.
[3] Last two enter later.
[4] Addition.
[5] Worth; 1640 edn. has *valor*.
[6] Antidote to poisons.
[7] Fancies.
[8] Whim.
[9] Foolish.

WELL. [*Aside*.] His jealousy is the poison he has taken.

BRA. (*He comes disguised like Justice Clement's man*.) Mr. Kitely, my master, [50 Justice Clement, salutes you, and desires to speak with you with all possible speed.

KITE. No time but now? When I think I am sick? Very sick! Well, I will wait upon his worship. Thomas! Cob! I must seek them out, and set hem sentinels till I return. Thomas! Cob! Thomas! [*Exit*.]

WELL. This is perfectly rare, Brainworm. [*Takes him aside*.] But how got'st thou this apparel of the justice's man?   60

BRA. [*Aside*.] Marry, sir, my proper fine penman would needs bestow the grist o' me at the Windmill, to hear some martial discourse, where so I marshaled him that I made him drunk—with admiration—and, because too much heat was the cause of his distemper, I stripped him stark naked as he lay along asleep, and borrowed his suit to deliver this counterfeit message in, leaving a rusty armor and [70 an old brown bill [1] to watch him till my return—which shall be when I ha' pawned his apparel, and spent the better part o' the money, perhaps.

WELL. [*Aside*.] Well, thou art a successful, merry knave, Brainworm; his absence will be a good subject for more mirth. I pray thee, return to thy young master, and will him to meet me and my sister Bridget at the Tower [2] instantly, for here, tell [80 him, the house is so stored with jealousy there is no room for love to stand upright in. We must get our fortunes committed to some larger prison, say, and than the Tower I know no better air, nor where the liberty of the house may do us more present service. Away!

[*Exit Brainworm.   Enter Kitely, talking aside to Cash.*]

KITE. Come hither, Thomas. Now my secret's ripe,
And thou shalt have it; lay to both thine ears.
Hark what I say to thee. I must go forth, Thomas;   90
Be careful of thy promise, keep good watch,

---
[1] Pike.
[2] Since the Tower was in no parish, a marriage might be performed there immediately.

Note every gallant, and observe him well,
That enters in my absence to thy mistress.
If she would show him rooms—the jest is stale[3]—
Follow hem, Thomas, or else hang on him,
And let him not go after. Mark their looks;
Note if she offer but to see his band,
Or any other amorous toy about him;
But praise his leg, or foot; or if she say
The day is hot, and bid him feel her hand,
How hot it is—O, that's a monstrous thing!   101
Note me all this, good Thomas; mark their sighs,
And, if they do but whisper, break hem off.
I'll bear thee out in it. Wilt thou do this?
Wilt thou be true, my Thomas?

CASH.   As truth's self, sir.

KITE. Why, I believe thee. Where is Cob, now? Cob!   [*Exit*.]

DAME. He's ever calling for Cob! I wonder how he employs Cob so.

WELL. Indeed, sister, to ask how he employs Cob is a necessary question for [110 you that are his wife, and a thing not very easy for you to be satisfied in; but this I'll assure you, Cob's wife is an excellent bawd, sister, and oftentimes your husband haunts her house—marry, to what end I cannot altogether accuse him; imagine you what you think convenient. But I have known fair hides have foul hearts ere now, sister.

DAME. Never said you truer than [120 that, brother; so much I can tell you for your learning. Thomas, fetch your cloak and go with me. I'll after him presently; I would to fortune I could take him there, i' faith. I'ld return him his own, I warrant him!   [*Exeunt Dame and Cash.*]

WELL. So, let hem go; this may make sport anon. Now, my fair sister-in-law, that you knew but how happy a thing it were to be fair and beautiful!   130

BRID. That touches not me, brother.

WELL. That's true; that's even the fault of it; for, indeed, beauty stands a woman in no stead, unless it procure her

---
[3] With a pun on the meaning *harlot*.

touching. But, sister, whether it touch you or no, it touches your beauties; and I am sure they will abide the touch. An they do not, a plague of all ceruse,[1] say I! And it touches me too in part, though not in the—Well, there's a dear and re- [140 spected friend of mine, sister, stands very strongly and worthily affected toward you, and hath vowed to inflame whole bonefires [2] of zeal at his heart, in honor of your perfections. I have already engaged my promise to bring you where you shall hear him confirm much more. Ned Knowell is the man, sister; there's no exception against the party. You are ripe for a husband; and a minute's loss to such an [150 occasion is a great trespass in a wise beauty. What say you, sister? On my soul, he loves you. Will you give him the meeting?

BRID. Faith, I had very little confidence in mine own constancy, brother, if I durst not meet a man; but this motion of yours savors of an old knight-adventurer's servant a little too much, methinks.

WELL. What's that, sister?

BRID. Marry, of the squire.[3]   160

WELL. No matter if it did, I would be such an one for my friend. But see who is returned to hinder us.

[Enter Kitely.]

KITE. What villainy is this? Called out on a false message?
This was some plot; I was not sent for.—
Bridget,
Where's your sister?

BRID.   I think she be gone forth, sir.

KITE. How! Is my wife gone forth? Whither, for God's sake?

BRID. She's gone abroad with Thomas.

KITE. Abroad with Thomas? O, that villain dors [4] me.   169
He hath discovered all unto my wife.
Beast that I was, to trust him! Whither,
I pray you,
Went she?

BRID.   I know not, sir.

WELL.   I'll tell you, brother,
Whither I suspect she's gone.

KITE.   Whither, good brother?

WELL. To Cob's house, I believe; but keep my counsel.

KITE. I will, I will. To Cob's house? Doth she haunt Cob's?
She's gone a purpose now to cuckold me
With that lewd rascal, who, to win her favor,
Hath told her all.   *[Exit.]*

WELL.   Come, he's once more gone;
Sister, let's lose no time; th' affair is worth it.   *[Exeunt.]*

ACT IV. SCENE ix.

[Another street in the Old Jewry.]

[5] *Matthew, Bobadill, Brainworm.*

[MAT.] I wonder, captain, what they will say of my going away, ha?

BOB. Why, what should they say, but as of a discreet gentleman, quick, wary, respectful of nature's fair lineaments? And that's all.

MAT. Why, so! But what can they say of your beating?

BOB. A rude part, a touch with soft wood, a kind of gross battery used, [10 laid on strongly, borne most patiently; and that's all.

MAT. Ay, but would any man have offered it in Venice, as you say?

BOB. Tut! I assure you, no; you shall have there your *nobilis*,[6] your *gentilezza*,[7] come in bravely upon your *reverse*, stand you close, stand you firm, stand you fair, save your *retricato* with his left leg, come to the *assalto* with the right, thrust [20 with brave steel, defy your base wood! But wherefore do I awake this remembrance? I was fascinated,[8] by Jupiter— fascinated. But I will be unwitched and revenged by law.

MAT. Do you hear? Is 't not best to get a warrant, and have him arrested and brought before Justice Clement?

BOB. It were not amiss. Would we had it!   30

[Enter Brainworm, disguised as Formal.]

MAT. Why, here comes his man; let's speak to him.

BOB. Agreed, do you speak.

MAT. Save you, sir.

---

[1] Cosmetic of white lead.   [2] Bonfires.
[3] Implying the meaning *pander*.   [4] Cheats.
[5] The marginal direction *To them* is erroneously printed here. The name of Downright also appears by mistake in the list of characters.
[6] Nobility.   [7] Gentility.   [8] Bewitched.

Bra. With all my heart, sir.

Mat. Sir, there is one Downright hath abused this gentleman and myself, and we determine to make our amends by law. Now, if you would do us the favor to procure a warrant to bring him afore your [40 master, you shall be well considered, I assure you, sir.

Bra. Sir, you know my service is my living; such favors as these, gotten of my master, is his only preferment,[1] and therefore you must consider me as I may make benefit of my place.

Mat. How is that, sir?

Bra. Faith, sir, the thing is extraordinary, and the gentleman may be of [50 great accompt; yet, be what he will, if you will lay me down a brace of angels in my hand, you shall have it; otherwise not.

Mat. How shall we do, captain? He asks a brace of angels; you have no money?

Bob. Not a cross,[2] by Fortune.

Mat. Nor I, as I am a gentleman, but twopence left of my two shillings in the morning for wine and reddish. Let's find him some pawn.   60

Bob. Pawn? We have none to the value of his demand.

Mat. O, yes. I'll pawn this jewel in my ear, and you may pawn your silk stockings, and pull up your boots; they will ne'er be missed. It must be done now.

Bob. Well, an there be no remedy, I'll step aside and pull hem off. [Withdraws.]

Mat. Do you hear, sir? We have no store of money at this time, but you [70 shall have good pawns. Look you, sir, this jewel, and that gentleman's silk stockings, because we would have it despatched ere we went to our chambers.

Bra. I am content, sir; I will get you the warrant presently. What's his name, say you? Downright?

Mat. Ay, ay, George Downright.

Bra. What manner of man is he?

Mat. A tall, big man, sir; he goes in [80 a cloak most commonly of silk russet, laid about with russet lace.

Bra. 'Tis very good, sir.

Mat. Here, sir, here's my jewel.

Bob. [Returning.] And here are stockings.

[1] I.e., the only reward he gives me.
[2] A small coin.

Bra. Well, gentlemen, I'll procure you this warrant presently. But who will you have to serve it?

Mat. That's true, captain; that [90 must be considered.

Bob. Body o' me, I know not; 'tis service of danger.

Bra. Why, you were best get one o' the varlets o' the city,[3] a serjeant. I'll appoint you one, if you please.

Mat. Will you, sir? Why, we can wish no better.

Bob. We'll leave it to you, sir.

      [Exeunt Bobadill and Matthew.]

Bra. This is rare! Now will I go [100 pawn this cloak of the justice's man's at the broker's for a varlet's suit, and be the varlet myself, and get either more pawns, or more money of Downright, for the arrest.   [Exit.]

Act IV. Scene x.

[The lane before Cob's house.]

Knowell, Tib, Cash, Dame Kitely, Kitely, Cob.[4]

[Know.] O, here it is; I am glad. I have
    found it now.
Ho! Who is within here?
Tib. [Within.] I am within, sir. What's
    your pleasure?
Know. To know who is within besides
    yourself.
Tib. Why, sir, you are no constable, I
    hope?
Know. O, fear you the constable? Then I
    doubt not
You have some guests within deserve
    that fear.
I'll fetch him straight.

[Enter Tib.]

Tib.   O' God's name, sir!
Know. Go to; come tell me, is not young
    Knowell here?
Tib. Young Knowell? I know none such,
    sir, o' mine honesty.   10
Know. Your honesty? Dame, it flies too
    lightly from you.
There is no way but fetch the constable.
Tib. The constable? The man is mad, I
    think.   [Exit.]

[3] Bailiffs.   [4] The last five enter later.

[*Enter Dame Kitely and Cash.*]

CASH. Ho! Who keeps house here?
KNOW. O, this is the female copesmate [1]
     of my son?
     Now shall I meet him straight.
DAME.   Knock, Thomas, hard.
CASH. Ho, goodwife!

[*Enter Tib.*]

TIB.   Why, what's the matter with you?
DAME. Why, woman, grieves it you to ope
     your door?
     Belike you get something to keep it shut.
TIB. What mean these questions, pray
     ye?   20
DAME. So strange you make it? Is not my
     husband here?
KNOW. Her husband!
DAME.   My tried husband, Master
     Kitely.
TIB. I hope he needs not to be triéd here.
DAME. No, dame, he does it not for need,
     but pleasure.
TIB. Neither for need nor pleasure is he
     here.
KNOW. This is but a device to balk me
     withal—

[*Enter Kitely with his face covered.*]

     Soft, who is this? 'Tis not my son dis-
     guised?
DAME. (*She spies her husband come, and
     runs to him.*) O, sir, have I forestalled
     your honest market?
     Found your close [2] walks? You stand
     amazed now, do you?
     I' faith, I am glad I have smoked [3] you
     yet at last.   30
     What is your jewel, trow? In, come, let's
     see her.
     Fetch forth your huswife, dame; if she
     be fairer,
     In any honest judgment, than myself,
     I'll be content with it; but she is change,
     She feeds you fat, she soothes your ap-
     petite,
     And you are well? Your wife, an honest
     woman,
     Is meat twice sod [4] to you, sir? O, you
     treachor! [5]

KNOW. [*Aside.*] She cannot counterfeit
     thus palpably.
KITE. Out on thy more than strumpet's
     impudence!
     Steal'st thou thus to thy haunts? And
     have I taken   40
     Thy bawd and thee, and thy companion,
               (*Pointing to old Knowell.*)
     This hoary-headed lecher, this old goat,
     Close at your villainy, and wouldst thou
     scuse [6] it
     With this stale harlot's jest, accusing
     me?—
     (*To him.*) O, old incontinent, dost not
     thou shame,
     When all thy powers in chastity is spent,
     To have a mind so hot, and to entice,
     And feed th' enticements of a lustful
     woman?
DAME. Out, I defy thee, I, dissembling
     wretch!
KITE. Defy me, strumpet? (*By [7] Thomas.*)
     Ask thy pander here,   50
     Can he deny it? Or that wicked elder?
KNOW. Why, hear you, sir—
KITE.   Tut, tut, tut; never speak.
     Thy guilty conscience will discover thee.
KNOW. What lunacy is this that haunts
     this man?
KITE. Well, good wife Bad,[8] Cob's wife,
     and you,
     That make your husband such a hoddy-
     doddy; [9]
     And you, young apple-squire; [10] and old
     cuckold-maker—
     I'll ha' you every one before a justice.
     Nay, you shall answer it; I charge you
     go.
KNOW. Marry, with all my heart, sir, I go
     willingly,   60
     Though I do taste this as a trick put on
     me,
     To punish my impertinent search, and
     justly,
     And half forgive my son for the device.
KITE. Come, will you go?
DAME.   Go? To thy shame, believe it.

[*Enter Cob.*]

COB. Why, what's the matter here?
What's here to do?

---

[1] Companion.
[2] Secret.
[3] Found.
[4] Boiled.
[5] Traitor.
[6] Excuse.
[7] *I. e.*, referring to.
[8] With a pun on *bawd*.
[9] Dupe, cuckold.
[10] Pimp.

KITE. O, Cob, art thou come? I have been abused,
And i' thy house; never was man so wronged!
COB. 'Slid, in my house? My master, Kitely? Who wrongs you in my house? [70
KITE. Marry, young lust in old, and old in young here;
Thy wife's their bawd; here have I taken hem.
COB. How? Bawd? (*He falls upon his Wife and beats her.*) Is my house come to that? Am I preferred thither? Did I charge you to keep your doors shut, Isbel? And do you let hem lie open for all comers?
KNOW. Friend, know some cause before thou beat'st thy wife.
This's madness in thee.
COB.   Why, is there no cause?
KITE. Yes, I'll show cause before the justice, Cob.   80
Come, let her go with me.
COB.   Nay, she shall go.
TIB. Nay, I will go. I'll see an you may be allowed to make a bundle o' hemp o' [1] your right and lawful wife thus at every cuckoldly knave's pleasure. Why do you not go?
KITE A bitter quean! Come, we'll ha' you tamed.   [*Exeunt.*]

ACT IV. SCENE xi.

[*A street near Justice Clement's house.*]

Brainworm, Matthew, Bobadill, Stephen, Downright.[2]

[BRA.] Well, of all my disguises yet, now am I most like myself, being in this serjeant's gown. A man of my present profession never counterfeits, till he lays hold upon a debtor and says he rests[3] him; for then he brings him to all manner of unrest. A kind of little kings we are, bearing the diminutive of a mace, made like a young artichock,[4] that always carries pepper and salt in itself.[5] Well, I know not [10 what danger I undergo by this exploit; pray heaven I come well off!

[*Enter Matthew and Bobadill.*]

MAT. See, I think, yonder is the varlet, by his gown.

BOB. Let's go in quest of him.
MAT. Save you, friend! Are not you here by appointment of Justice Clement's man?
BRA. Yes, an 't please you, sir; he told me two gentlemen had willed him to [20 procure a warrant from his master, which I have about me, to be served on one Downright.
MAT. It is honestly done of you both; and see where the party comes you must arrest. Serve it upon him quickly, afore he be aware.
BOB. Bear back, Master Matthew.

[*Enter Stephen, in Downright's cloak.*]

BRA. Master Downright, I arrest you i' the queen's name, and must carry [30 you afore a justice by virtue of this warrant.
STE. Me, friend? I am no Downright, I; I am Master Stephen. You do not well to arrest me, I tell you truly; I am in nobody's bonds nor books, I would you should know it. A plague on you heartily, for making me thus afraid afore my time!
BRA. Why, now are you deceived, gentlemen?
BOB. He wears such a cloak, and [40 that deceived us. But see, here a[6] comes indeed; this is he, officer.

[*Enter Downright.*]

DOW. Why, how now, signior gull! Are you turned filcher of late? Come, deliver my cloak.
STE. Your cloak, sir? I bought it even now in open market.
BRA. Master Downright, I have a warrant I must serve upon you, procured by these two gentlemen.   50
DOW. These gentlemen? These rascals?   [*Offers to beat them.*]
BRA. Keep the peace, I charge you in her majesty's name.
DOW. I obey thee. What must I do, officer?
BRA. Go before Master Justice Clement, to answer what they can object against you, sir. I will use you kindly, sir.   59
MAT. Come, let's before, and make[7] the justice, captain.

---

[1] *I. e.*, beat.   [2] Last four enter later.   [3] Arrests.
[4] Artichoke.   [5] Punning on *mace*, the spice.   [6] He.   [7] Prepare.

Bob. The varlet's a tall man, afore heaven! [*Exeunt Bobadill and Matthew.*]

Dow. Gull, you'll gi' me my cloak?

Ste. Sir, I bought it, and I'll keep it.

Dow. You will?

Ste. Ay, that I will.

Dow. Officer, there's thy fee; arrest him.

Bra. Master Stephen, I must arrest you.

Ste. Arrest me? I scorn it. There, take your cloak; I'll none on 't. 71

Dow. Nay, that shall not serve your turn now, sir. Officer, I'll go with thee to the justice's; bring him along.

Ste. Why, is not here your cloak? What would you have?

Dow. I'll ha' you answer it, sir.

Bra. Sir, I'll take your word, and this gentleman's too, for his appearance. 79

Dow. I'll ha' no words taken. Bring him along.

Bra. Sir, I may choose to do that; I may take bail.

Dow. 'Tis true, you may take bail, and choose at another time; but you shall not now, varlet. Bring him along, or I'll swinge you.

Bra. Sir, I pity the gentleman's case; here's your money again. 89

Dow. 'Sdeynes, tell not me of my money; bring him away, I say.

Bra. I warrant you he will go with you of himself, sir.

Dow. Yet more ado?

Bra. [*Aside.*] I have made a fair mash on 't.

Ste. Must I go?

Bra. I know no remedy, Master Stephen. 99

Dow. Come along afore me here; I do not love your hanging look behind.

Ste. Why, sir, I hope you cannot hang me for it. Can he, fellow?

Bra. I think not, sir; it is but a whipping matter, sure!

Ste. Why, then let him do his worst; I am resolute. [*Exeunt.*]

Act V. Scene i.

[*A hall in Justice Clement's house.*]

Clement, Knowell, Kitely, Dame Kitely, Tib, Cash, Cob, Servants.

[Clem.] Nay, but stay, stay, give me leave. My chair, sirrah.—You, Master Knowell, say you went thither to meet your son?

Know. Ay, sir.

Clem. But who directed you thither?

Know. That did mine own man, sir.

Clem. Where is he?

Know. Nay, I know not now; I left him with your clerk and appointed [10 him to stay here for me.

Clem. My clerk? About what time was this?

Know. Marry, between one and two, as I take it.

Clem. And what time came my man with the false message to you, Master Kitely?

Kite. After two, sir.

Clem. Very good; but, Mistress [20 Kitely, how that you were at Cob's, ha?

Dame. An please you, sir, I'll tell you: my brother Wellbred told me that Cob's house was a suspected place—

Clem. So it appears, methinks; but on.

Dame. And that my husband used thither daily.

Clem. No matter, so he used himself well, mistress. 30

Dame. True, sir, but you know what grows by such haunts oftentimes.

Clem. I see rank fruits of a jealous brain, Mistress Kitely; but did you find your husband there in that case as you suspected?

Kite. I found her there, sir.

Clem. Did you so? That alters the case. Who gave you knowledge of your wife's being there? 40

Kite. Marry, that did my brother Wellbred.

Clem. How? Wellbred first tell her? Then tell you after? Where is Wellbred?

Kite. Gone with my sister, sir, I know not whither.

Clem. Why, this is a mere trick, a device; you are gulled in this most grossly, all. Alas, poor wench, wert thou beaten for this? 50

Tib. Yes, most pitifully, and 't please you.

Cob. And worthily, I hope, if it shall prove so.

Clem. Ay, that's like, and a piece of a sentence.—

[*Enter a Servant.*]

How now, sir? What's the matter?

SER. Sir, there's a gentleman i' the court without, desires to speak with your worship.   60

CLEM. A gentleman? What's he?

SER. A soldier, sir, he says.

CLEM. A soldier? Take down my armor, my sword, quickly. A soldier speak with me! Why, when, knaves? Come on, come on. (*He arms himself.*) Hold my cap there, so; give me my gorget, my sword. Stand by. I will end your matters anon. Let the soldier enter. [*Exit Servant.*]— Now, sir,[1] what ha' you to say to me?

ACT V. SCENE ii.

[*The same.*]

[*To them,*] *Bobadill, Matthew.*

[BOB.] By your worship's favor—

CLEM. Nay, keep out, sir; I know not your pretense.[2] You send me word, sir, you are a soldier. Why, sir, you shall be answered here; here be them have been amongst soldiers. Sir, your pleasure.

BOB. Faith, sir, so it is, this gentleman and myself have been most uncivilly wronged and beaten by one Downright, a coarse fellow about the town here; [10 and, for mine own part, I protest, being a man in no sort given to this filthy humor of quarreling, he hath assaulted me in the way of my peace, despoiled me of mine honor, disarmed me of my weapons, and rudely laid me along in the open streets, when I not so much as once offered to resist him.

CLEM. O, God's precious! Is this the soldier? Here, take my armor off [20 quickly. 'Twill make him swoon, I fear; he is not fit to look on 't, that will put up[3] a blow.

MAT. An 't please your worship, he was bound to the peace.

CLEM. Why, and he were, sir, his hands were not bound, were they?

[*Enter Servant.*]

SER. There's one of the varlets of the city, sir, has brought two gentlemen here, one, upon your worship's warrant. 30

CLEM. My warrant!

SER. Yes, sir; the officer says, procured by these two.

CLEM. Bid him come in. [*Exit Servant.*] Set by this picture.[4]—What, Mr. Downright! Are you brought at Mr. Freshwater's[5] suit here?

ACT V. SCENE iii.

[*The same.*]

[*To them,*] *Downright, Stephen, Brainworm.*

[Dow.] I' faith, sir, and here's another brought at my suit.

CLEM. What are you, sir?

STE. A gentleman, sir—O, uncle!

CLEM. Uncle? Who? Master Knowell?

KNOW. Ay, sir; this is a wise kinsman of mine.

STE. God's my witness, uncle, I am wronged here monstrously; he charges me with stealing of his cloak, and would [10 I might never stir, if I did not find it in the street by chance.

DOW. O, did you find it now? You said you bought it erewhile.

STE. And you said I stole it. Nay, now my uncle is here, I'll do well enough with you.

CLEM. Well, let this breathe awhile. You that have cause to complain there, stand forth. Had you my warrant for [20 this gentleman's apprehension?

BOB. Ay, an 't please your worship.

CLEM. Nay, do not speak in passion[6] so. Where had you it?

BOB. Of your clerk, sir.

CLEM. That's well! An my clerk can make warrants, and my hand not at hem! Where is the warrant—officer, have you it?

BRA. No, sir. Your worship's man, Master Formal, bid me do it for these [30 gentlemen, and he would be my discharge.[7]

CLEM. Why, Master Downright, are you such a novice, to be served and never see the warrant?

DOW. Sir, he did not serve it on me.

CLEM. No? How then?

DOW. Marry, sir, he came to me, and said he must serve it, and he would use me kindly, and so—

---

[1] Notice that here and in the rest of the act Jonson does not indicate a formal scene division until the new characters actually speak.

[2] Intention.   [3] Put up with.

[4] Put aside this imitation of a soldier.

[5] A soldier who had seen no service abroad.

[6] Feeling.   [7] Guarantee.

CLEM. O, God's pity, was it so, sir? [40 "He must serve it"? Give me my long sword there, and help me off. So, come on, Sir Varlet. (*He flourishes over him with his long sword.*) I "*must*" cut off your legs, sirrah. [*Brainworm kneels.*] Nay, stand up! I'll "use you kindly"; I *must* cut off your legs, I say.

BRA. O, good sir, I beseech you; nay, good Master Justice!

CLEM. I "*must*" do it; there is no [50 remedy. I "*must*" cut off your legs, sirrah; I "*must*" cut off your ears, you rascal; I "*must*" do it. I "*must*" cut off your nose; I "*must*" cut off your head.

BRA. O, good your worship!

CLEM. Well, rise; how dost thou do now? Dost thou feel thyself well? Hast thou no harm?

BRA. No, I thank your good worship, sir.   60

CLEM. Why, so! I said I must cut off thy legs, and I must cut off thy arms, and I must cut off thy head; but I did not do it. So you said you must serve this gentleman with my warrant, but you did not serve him. You knave, you slave, you rogue, do you say you "must," sirrah! Away with him to the jail; I'll teach you a trick for your "must," sir.

BRA. Good sir, I beseech you, be [70 good to me.

CLEM. Tell him he shall to the jail; away with him, I say.

BRA. Nay, sir, if you will commit me, it shall be for committing more than this; I will not lose, by my travail, any grain of my fame, certain.   [*Reveals himself.*]

CLEM. How is this?

KNOW. My man Brainworm!

STE. O, yes, uncle; Brainworm has [80 been with my cousin Edward and I all this day.

CLEM. I told you all there was some device.

BRA. Nay, excellent justice, since I have laid myself thus open to you, now stand strong for me—both with your sword and your balance.

CLEM. Body o' me, a merry knave! Give me a bowl of sack. If he belong [90 to you, Master Knowell, I bespeak your patience.

BRA. That is it I have most need of.

Sir, if you'll pardon me only, I'll glory in all the rest of my exploits.

KNOW. Sir, you know I love not to have my favors come hard from me. You have your pardon, though I suspect you shrewdly for being of counsel with my son against me.   100

BRA. Yes, faith, I have, sir, though you retained me doubly this morning for yourself: first, as Brainworm; after, as Fitzsword. I was your reformed soldier, sir. 'Twas I sent you to Cob's upon the errand without end.

KNOW. Is it possible? Or that thou shouldst disguise thy language so as I should not know thee?

BRA. O, sir, this has been the day [110 of my metamorphosis. It is not that shape alone that I have run through today. I brought this gentleman, Master Kitely, a message too, in the form of Master Justice's man here, to draw him out o' the way, as well as your worship, while Master Wellbred might make a conveyance of Mistress Bridget to my young master.

KITE. How! My sister stol'n away?

KNOW. My son is not married, I [120 hope.

BRA. Faith, sir, they are both as sure as love, a priest, and three thousand pound, which is her portion, can make hem, and by this time are ready to bespeak their wedding supper at the Windmill, except some friend here prevent [1] hem, and invite hem home.

CLEM. Marry, that will I; I thank thee for putting me in mind on 't.—Sirrah, [130 go you and fetch hem hither upon my warrant.—[*Exit Servant.*] Neither's friends have cause to be sorry, if I know the young couple aright. Here, I drink to thee for thy good news. But, I pray thee, what hast thou done with my man Formal?

BRA. Faith, sir, after some ceremony past, as making him drunk, first with story, and then with wine (but all in kindness), and stripping him to his shirt, I left [140 him in that cool vein, departed, sold your worship's warrant to these two, pawned his livery for that varlet's gown to serve it in, and thus have brought myself by my activity to your worship's consideration.

[1] Forestall.

CLEM. And I will consider thee in another cup of sack. Here's to thee, which having drunk off, this is my sentence: Pledge me. Thou hast done, or assisted to, nothing, in my judgment, but de- [151 serves to be pardoned for the wit o' the offense. If thy master, or any man here, be angry with thee, I shall suspect his ingine,[1] while I know him, for 't. How now, what noise is that?

[Enter Servant.]

SER. Sir, it is Roger is come home.

CLEM. Bring him in, bring him in.— What! Drunk in arms against me? Your reason, your reason for this?　　　160

ACT V. SCENE iv.

[The same.]

To them, Formal [in armor].

[FOR.] I beseech your worship to pardon me; I happened into ill company by chance, that cast me into a sleep, and stripped me of all my clothes.

CLEM. Well, tell him I am Justice Clement, and do pardon him. But what is this to your armor? What may that signify?

FOR. And 't please you, sir, it hung up i' the room where I was stripped, and I borrowed it of one o' the drawers to [10 come home in, because I was loath to do penance through the street i' my shirt.

CLEM. Well, stand by a while.—Who be these? O, the young company; welcome, welcome! Gi' you joy. Nay, Mistress Bridget, blush not, you are not so fresh a bride, but the news of it is come hither afore you. Master Bridegroom, I ha' made your peace, give me your hand. So will I for all the rest ere you forsake [20 my roof.

ACT V. SCENE v.

[The same.]

To them Ed[ward] Knowell, Wellbred, Bridget.

[E. KNOW.] We are the more bound to your humanity, sir.

CLEM. Only these two have so little
_____
[1] Ingenuity, wit.

of man in hem, they are no part of my care.

WELL. Yes, sir, let me pray you for this gentleman; he belongs to my sister, the bride.

CLEM. In what place, sir?　　　9

WELL. Of her delight, sir, below the stairs, and in public: her poet, sir.

CLEM. A poet? I will challenge him myself presently at extempore.

Mount up thy Phlegon,[2] Muse, and testify
　　How Saturn, sitting in an ebon cloud,
Disrobed his podex,[3] white as ivory,
　　And through the welkin thundered all
　　　　aloud.[4]

WELL. He is not for extempore, sir; he is all for the pocket muse. Please you command a sight of it.　　　20

CLEM. Yes, yes, search him for a taste of his vein.　　　*[They search Matthew.]*

WELL. You must not deny the queen's justice, sir, under a writ o' rebellion.

CLEM. What! All this verse? Body o' me, he carries a whole realm,[5] a commonwealth of paper, in 's hose. Let's see some of his subjects.　　　*[Reads.]*

Unto the boundless ocean of thy face,
Runs this poor river, charged with streams
　　of eyes.　　　30

How? This is stol'n!

E. KNOW. A parody![6] A parody! With a kind of miraculous gift to make it absurder than it was!

CLEM. Is all the rest of this batch? Bring me a torch, lay it together, and give fire. Cleanse the air. *[Sets the papers on fire]* Here was enough to have infected the whole city, if it had not been taken in time. See, see how our poet's glory shines! Brighter and brighter! Still it increases! [41 O, now it's at the highest; and now it declines as fast. You may see, *sic transit gloria mundi!*[7]

KNOW. There's an emblem[8] for you, son, and your studies.
_____
[2] One of the Sun's horses.　　　[3] Fundament.
[4] These verses parody Marston.
[5] Pronounced *ream.*
[6] Of the opening lines of Daniel's *Delia.*
[7] Thus passes the glory of the world.
[8] Motto.

CLEM. Nay, no speech or act of mine be drawn against such as profess it worthily. They are not born every year, as an alderman. There goes more to the making of a good poet than a sheriff, Master [51 Kitely. You look upon me! Though I live i' the city here amongst you, I will do more reverence to him, when I meet him, than I will to the mayor out of his year.[1] But these paper-peddlers! These ink-dabblers! They cannot expect reprehension or reproach; they have it with the fact.[2]   59

E. KNOW. Sir, you have saved me the labor of a defense.[3]

CLEM. It shall be discourse for supper between your father and me, if he dare undertake me. But to despatch away these: you sign o' the soldier, and picture o' the poet (but both so false I will not ha' you hanged out at my door till midnight), while we are at supper, you two shall penitently fast it out in my court

[1] When his term is expired.   [2] Deed, crime.

[3] At approximately this point in the Italian version the following passage, based on Sidney's *Defense of Poesy*, occurs:

If it may stand with your most wished content,
I can refel [a] opinion and approve
The state of poesy, such as it is,
Blessed, eternal, and most true divine.
Indeed, if you will look on poesy
As she appears in many, poor and lame,
Patched up in remnants and old worn rags,
Half starved for want of her peculiar food,
Sacred invention, then I must confirm
Both your conceit and censure of her merit.
But view her in her glorious ornaments,
Attired in the majesty of art,
Set high in spirit with the precious taste
Of sweet philosophy, and, which is most,
Crowned with the rich traditions of a soul
That hates to have her dignity profaned
With any relish of an earthly thought—
O, then how proud a presence doth she bear!
Then is she like herself, fit to be seen
Of none but grave and consecrated eyes.
Nor is it any blemish to her fame
That such lean, ignorant, and blasted wits,
Such brainless gulls, should utter their stol'n wares
With such applauses in our vulgar ears,
Or that their slubbered lines have current pass
From the fat judgments of the multitude.
But that this barren and infected age
Should set no difference twixt these empty spirits
And a true poet, than which reverend name
Nothing can more adorn humanity!

[a] Refute.

without; and, if you will, you may [70 pray there that we may be so merry within as to forgive or forget you when we come out. Here's a third,[4] because we tender your safety, shall watch you; he is provided for the purpose.—Look to your charge, sir.

STE. And what shall I do?

CLEM. O! I had lost a sheep an he had not bleated. Why, sir, you shall give Mr. Downright his cloak; and I will entreat him to take it. A trencher and a nap- [81 kin you shall have i' the butt'ry, and keep Cob and his wife company here, whom I will entreat first to be reconciled, and you to endeavor with your wit to keep hem so.

STE. I'll do my best.

COB. Why, now I see thou art honest, Tib, I receive thee as my dear and mortal wife again.   90

TIB. And I you, as my loving and obedient husband.

CLEM. Good complement! It will be their bridal night too. They are married anew. Come, I conjure the rest to put off all discontent. You, Mr. Downright, your anger; you, Master Knowell, your cares; Master Kitely and his wife, their jealousy.

For, I must tell you both, while that is fed,
Horns i' the mind are worse than o' the head.   100

KITE. Sir, thus they go from me; kiss me, sweetheart.

See what a drove of horns fly in the air,
Winged with my cleansèd and my credulous breath!
Watch hem, suspicious eyes, watch where they fall.
See, see! On heads that think th' have none at all!
O, what a plenteous world of this will come!
When air rains horns, all may be sure of some.[5]

I ha' learned so much verse out of a jealous man's part in a play.   110

CLEM. 'Tis well, 'tis well! This night we'll dedicate to friendship, love, and laughter. Master Bridegroom, take your bride and lead, everyone, a fellow. Here

[4] I.e., Formal in his armor.
[5] From 1601 edn. Original has *fame*.

is my mistress, Brainworm, to whom all my addresses of courtship shall have their reference—whose adventures this day, when our grandchildren shall hear to be made a fable, I doubt not but it shall find both spectators and applause.   [*Exeunt.*]

THE END.

This comedy was first acted in the year 1598 by the then L[ord] Chamberlain his Servants. The principal comedians were:

Will. Shakespeare	*Ric. Burbadge*
Aug. Philips	*Joh. Hemings*
Hen. Condell	*Tho. Pope*
Will. Sly	*Chr. Beeston*
Will. Kemp	*Joh. Duke*

With the allowance of the Master of Revels.

SEJANUS HIS FALL[1]

BY

BEN JONSON

To the No Less Noble by Virtue Than
Blood, Esme, L[ord] Aubigny

My Lord:

If ever any ruin were so great as to survive, I think this be one I send you, *The Fall of Sejanus*. It is a poem, that, if I well remember, in your lo[rdship's] sight, suffered no less violence from our people here than the subject of it did from the rage of the people of Rome—but with a different fate as, I hope, merit; for this hath outlived their malice, and begot [10 itself a greater favor than he lost, the love of good men. Amongst whom, if I make your lo[rdship] the first it thanks, it is not without a just confession of the bond your benefits have, and ever shall hold, upon me.

Your lo[rdship's] most faithful honorer,
Ben. Jonson.

[2] To the Readers

The following and voluntary labors[3] of my friends, prefixed to my book, have relieved me in much whereat, without them, I should necessarily have touched. Now I will only use three or four short and needful notes, and so rest.

First, if it be objected that what I publish is no true poem, in the strict laws of time, I confess it, as also in the want of a proper chorus, whose habit and moods [10 are such and so difficult as not any whom I have seen since the ancients—no, not they who have most presently affected laws[4] —have yet come in the way of. Nor is it needful, or almost possible in these our times, and to such auditors as commonly things are presented, to observe the old state and splendor of dramatic poems, with preservation of any popular delight. But of this I shall take more seasonable [20 cause to speak, in my observations upon Horace his *Art of Poetry*, which, with the text translated, I intend shortly to publish.[5] In the meantime, if in truth of argument, dignity of persons, gravity and height of elocution, fullness and frequency of sentence,[6] I have discharged the other offices of a tragic writer, let not the absence of these forms be imputed to[7] me, wherein I shall give you occasion here- [30 after, and without my boast, to think I could better prescribe than omit the due use for want of a convenient knowledge.

The next is, lest in some nice nostril the quotations might savor affected, I do let you know that I abhor nothing more, and have only done it to show my integrity in the story, and save myself in those common torturers that bring all wit to the rack, whose noses are ever like swine [40 spoiling and rooting up the Muses' gardens, and their whole bodies like moles, as blindly working under earth to cast any, the least, hills upon virtue.

Whereas they are in Latin, and the work in English, it was presupposed none but the learned would take the pains to confer[8] them, the authors themselves being all in the learned tongues, save one,[9] with whose

---

[1] The title continues: "A Tragedy, Acted in the Year 1603 by the K. Majesty's Servants. The Author, B. J. Mart[ial]. *Non hic centauros, non Gorgonas, Harpyiasque invenies; hominem pagina nostra sapit.*" ("You will not find centaurs, nor Gorgons, nor Harpies here; our page deals with man.")

[2] This address occurs only in the 1605 edn.

[3] Commendatory verses by George Chapman, Hugh Holland, John Marston, etc., printed in the 1605 edn.

[4] Most recently favored the rules of dramatic composition.

[5] This commentary, but not the translation, was destroyed in the burning of his library.

[6] Sententious statement.

[7] Charged against.

[8] Compare.

[9] Tacitus, translated by Richard Greenwey in 1598.

English side I have had little to do. [50
To which it may be required, since I have
quoted the page, to name what edition
I followed: *Tacit. Lips. in 4.º, Antverp. edit.*
[1]600. *Dio. folio Hen. Step.* [15]92. For
the rest, as *Sueton., Seneca, etc.,* the chap-
ter doth sufficiently direct, or the edition
is not varied.[1]

Lastly, I would inform you that this
book, in all numbers,[2] is not the same with
that which was acted on the public [60
stage, wherein a second pen[3] had good share,
in place of which I have rather chosen to
put weaker, and, no doubt, less pleasing,
of mine own than to defraud so happy a
genius of his right by my loathed usurpa-
tion.

Fare you well. And if you read farder[4]
of me, and like, I shall not be afraid of it,
though you praise me out.　　　　　　　69

Neque enim mihi cornea fibra est.[5]

But that I should plant my felicity in
your general saying, "good," or "well," etc.,
were a weakness which the better sort of
you might worthily contemn, if not absolutely hate me for.

　　　　　　　BEN. JONSON, and no such,

　　　　　　　　　　　　　　　Quem
*Palma negata macrum, donata reducit
opimum.*[6]

THE ARGUMENT

Ælius Sejanus, son to Sejus Strabo, a
gentleman of Rome, and born at Vul-
sinium, after his long service in court—
first under Augustus, afterward, Tiberius—
grew into that favor with the latter, and
won him by those arts, as there wanted
nothing but the name to make him a copartner of the empire. Which greatness
of his, Drusus, the emperor's son, not brook-
ing, after many smothered dislikes, [10
it one day breaking out, the prince strook[7]

---

[1] The hundreds of marginal notes referring to
Jonson's sources appeared only in the 1605 edn.
[2] Verses.
[3] The identity of this writer is unknown.
[4] Farther.
[5] "For my fiber is not of cornel wood"
(Persius' *Satires*, I, 47); *i.e.*, I am not hardened
to praise.
[6] "Whom denied applause makes lean, but
bestowed applause makes happy" (Horace,
Epist., II, i, 181).
[7] Struck.

---

him publicly on the face. To revenge
which disgrace, Livia, the wife of Drusus
(being before corrupted by him to her dishonor, and the discovery of her husband's
counsels), Sejanus practiceth[8] with, together with her physician, called Eudemus,
and one Lygdus, an eunuch, to poison
Drusus. This their inhuman act having
successful and unsuspected passage,[9] [20
it emboldeneth Sejanus to farther and more
insolent projects, even the ambition of
the empire; where finding the lets[10] he
must encounter to be many and hard, in respect of the issue of Germanicus, who
were next in hope for the succession, he
deviseth to make Tiberius' self his means,
and instills into his ears many doubts and
suspicions, both against the princes, and
their mother Agrippina, which Cæsar [30
jealously heark'ning to, as covetously
consenteth to their ruin, and their friends'.
In this time, the better to mature and
strengthen his design, Sejanus labors to
marry Livia, and worketh with all his
ingine[11] to remove Tiberius from the
knowledge of public business, with allurements of a quiet and retired life; the
latter of which, Tiberius, out of a proneness to lust, and a desire to hide those [40
unnatural pleasures which he could not
so publicly practice, embraceth; the former
enkindleth his fears, and there gives him
first cause of doubt or suspect towards
Sejanus. Against whom he raiseth in
private a new instrument, one Sertorius
Macro, and by him underworketh, discovers the other's counsels, his means, his
ends, sounds the affections of the senators,
divides, distracts them; at last, when [50
Sejanus least looketh, and is most secure,
with pretext of doing him an unwonted
honor in the senate, he trains[12] him from
his guards, and with a long doubtful letter
in one day hath him suspected, accused,
condemned, and torn in pieces by the rage
of the people.[13]

---

[8] Conspires.　　　　　　[11] Ingenuity.
[9] Outcome.　　　　　　　[12] Tricks.
[10] Obstacles.
[13] The following passage, apparently alluding
to the Gunpowder Plot, occurs only in the 1605
edn.: "This do we advance as a mark of terror
to all traitors and treasons, to show how just
the heavens are in pouring and thund'ring down
a weighty vengeance on their unnatural intents,

THE PERSONS OF THE PLAY

TIBERIUS [, *the emperor*].
DRUSUS SE[NIOR, *his son*].
NERO ⎱ [, *sons of Germanicus*
DRUSUS JU[NIOR] ⎰ *and grandnephews*
CALIGULA ⎰ *of Tiberius*].
[LUCIUS] ARRUNTIUS ⎱
[CAIUS] SILIUS ⎰ [, *gentlemen*
[TITIUS] SABINUS ⎰ *opposed*
[MARCUS] LEPIDUS ⎰ *to*
[CREMUTIUS] CORDUS ⎰ *Sejanus*].
[ASINIUS] GALLUS ⎰
REGULUS [, *consul*].
TERENTIUS.
[GRACINUS] LACO.
EUDEMUS [, *a physician*].
RUFUS.
SEJANUS.
LATIARIS.
VARRO [, *consul*].
[SERTORIUS] MACRO.
COTTA.
[DOMITIUS] AFER.

HATERIUS.
SANQUINIUS.
POMPONIUS.
[JULIUS] POSTHUMUS.
[FULCINUS] TRIO, *consul*.
MINUTIUS.
SATRIUS [SECUNDUS].
[PINNARIUS] NATTA.
OPSIUS.

AGRIPPINA [, *widow of Germanicus*].
LIVIA [, *wife of Drusus Senior*].
SOSIA [, *wife of Caius Silius*].

TRIBUNI.
PRÆCONES.
FLAMEN.
TUBICINES.
NUNTIUS.
LICTORES.
MINISTRI.
TIBICINES.
SERVUS [, *etc.*]

THE SCENE: *Rome.*

[TIME: *23–31 A.D.*]

ACT I. [SCENE i.

A room of state in the palace.]

*Sabinus, Silius, Natta, Latiaris, Cordus,
Satrius, Arruntius, Eudemus, Haterius, etc.*

[SAB.] Hail, Caius Silius!
SIL.   Titius Sabinus, hail!
    Yo' are rarely met in court!
SAB.   Therefore, well met.
SIL. 'Tis true; indeed, this place is not our
        sphere.
SAB. No, Silius, we are no good inginers.[1]
    We want the fine arts, and their thriving
        use
    Should make us graced or favored of the
        times;
    We have no shift of faces, no cleft
        tongues,
    No soft and glutinous bodies that can
        stick

Like snails on painted walls, or on our
    breasts
Creep up, to fall from that proud height
    to which   10
We did by slavery, not by service, climb.
We are no guilty men, and then no great;
We have nor place in court, office in state,
That we can say we owe unto our crimes;
We burn with no black secrets, which
    can make
Us dear to the [pale][2] authors; or live
    feared
Of their still waking jealousies, to raise
Ourselves a fortune by subverting theirs.
We stand not in the lines that do advance
To that so courted point.
SIL. [*Pointing to Satrius and Natta*.]   But
        yonder lean   20
    A pair that do.
([3]SAB.   Good cousin Latiaris.)

even to the worst princes—much more to those,
for guard of whose piety and virtue the angels
are in continual watch, and God himself miraculously working."
[1] Plotters.

[2] Supplied from the Newberry Library copy
of the 1616 folio.
[3] Jonson frequently encloses speeches in parenthesis to indicate an aside or a passage incidental to the main action.

Sil. Satrius Secundus and Pinnarius
    Natta,
The great Sejanus' clients.[1] There be
    two
Know more than honest counsels, whose
    close [2] breasts,
Were they ripped up to light, it would
    be found
A poor and idle [3] sin to which their
    trunks
Had not been made fit organs. These
    can lie,
Flatter, and swear, forswear, deprave,
    inform,
Smile, and betray; make guilty men;
    then beg
The forfeit lives, to get the livings;
    cut   30
Men's throats with whisp'rings; sell to
    gaping suitors
The empty smoke that flies about the
    palace;
Laugh when their patron laughs; sweat
    when he sweats;
Be hot and cold with him; change every
    mood,
Habit, and garb as often as he varies;
Observe him, as his watch observes [4] his
    clock;
And, true as turkis [5] in the dear lord's
    ring,
Look well or ill with him; [6] ready to
    praise
His lordship, if he spit, or but piss
    fair,
Have an indifferent stool, or break wind
    well;   40
Nothing can scape their catch.
Sab.   Alas! These things
Deserve no note, conferred with other
    vile
And filthier flatteries that corrupt the
    times,
When, not alone our gentries chief are
    fain
To make their safety from such sordid
    acts,
But all our consuls, and no little part
Of such as have been prætors, yea, the
    most

Of senators, that else not use their
    voices,[7]
Start up in public senate, and there
    strive
Who shall propound most abject things
    and base,   50
So much as oft Tiberius hath been heard,
Leaving the court, to cry, "O race of men,
Prepared for servitude!"—which showed
    that he,
Who least the public liberty could like,
As loathly brooked their flat servility.
Sil. Well, all is worthy of us, were it more,
Who with our riots, pride, and civil hate
Have so provoked the justice of the
    gods—
We, that within these fourscore years
    were born
Free, equal lords of the triumphéd
    world,   60
And knew no masters but affections,
To which, betraying first our liberties,
We since became the slaves to one man's
    lusts,
And now to many; every minist'ring
    spy
That will accuse and swear is lord of you,
Of me, of all, our fortunes and our lives.
Our looks are called to question, and our
    words,
How innocent soever, are made crimes;
We shall not shortly dare to tell our
    dreams,
Or think, but 'twill be treason.
Sab.   "Tyrans' [8] arts   70
Are to give flatterers grace, accusers
    power,
That those may seem to kill whom they
    devour." [9]—
    [Turns to Cordus.] Now, good Cremutius
    Cordus.
Cor.   Hail to your lordship!
Nat. [To Latiaris.] Who's that salutes
    your cousin?
        They whisper. [Exeunt Satrius and
                                  Eudemus.]
Lat.   'Tis one Cordus,
A gentleman of Rome, one that has writ
Annals of late, they say, and very well.

[1] Dependents of a patrician family.
[2] Secret.   [4] Is set by.
[3] Empty.   [5] Turquoise.
[6] A common superstition.

[7] Jonson's marginal note reads Pedarii (i.e.,
senators who could speak only when called upon
by the presiding officer).
[8] Tyrants'.
[9] Sententious passages were commonly set in
quotation marks.

NAT. Annals? Of what times?

LAT.   I think of Pompey's
And Caius Cæsar's; and so down to
these.

NAT. How stands h' affected to the pres-
ent state?
Is he or [1] Drusian or Germanican?   80
Or ours or neutral?

LAT.   I know him not so far.

NAT. Those times are somewhat queasy to
be touched.
Have you or seen or heard part of his
work?

LAT. Not I; he means they shall be public shortly.

NAT. O, Cordus do you call him?

LAT.   Ay.

SAB.   But these our times
Are not the same, Arruntius.

ARR.   Times? The men,
The men are not the same! 'Tis we are
base,
Poor, and degenerate from th' exalted
strain
Of our great fathers. Where is now the
soul
Of godlike Cato—he that durst be
good   90
When Cæsar durst be evil, and had
power,
As not to live his slave, to die his master?
Or where the constant Brutus, that,
being proof
Against all charm of benefits, did strike
So brave a blow into the monster's heart
That sought unkindly to captive [2] his
country?
O, they are fled the light! Those mighty
spirits
Lie raked up with their ashes in their
urns,
And not a spark of their eternal fire
Glows in a present bosom. All's but
blaze,   100
Flashes, and smoke, wherewith we
labor so;
There's nothing Roman in us, nothing
good,
Gallant, or great. 'Tis true that Cordus
says,
"Brave Cassius was the last of all that
race."

[1] Either.
[2] Unnaturally to capture.

Drusus [Senior] passeth by.

SAB. Stand by! Lord Drusus!

HAT.   Th' emp'ror's son! Give place.

SIL. I like the prince well.

ARR.   A riotous youth;
There's little hope of him.

SAB.   That fault his age
Will, as it grows, correct. Methinks he
bears
Himself each day more nobly than other,
And wins no less on men's affections   110
Than doth his father lose. Believe me, I
love him,
And chiefly for opposing to Sejanus.

SIL. And I, for gracing his young kinsmen
so,
The sons of Prince Germanicus; it shows
A gallant clearness in him, a straight
mind
That envies not, in them, their father's
name.

ARR. His name was, while he lived, above
all envy,
And, being dead, without it. O, that man!
If there were seeds of the old virtue left,
They lived in him.

SIL.   He had the fruits, Arruntius,   120
More than the seeds; Sabinus and my-
self
Had means to know him within, and
can report him.
We were his followers (he would call us
friends).
He was a man most like to virtue; in all,
And every action, nearer to the gods
Than men, in nature; of a body as fair
As was his mind; and no less reverend
In face than fame. He could so use his
state,
Temp'ring his greatness with his gravity,
As it avoided all self-love in him   130
And spite in others. What his funerals
lacked
In images and pomp, they had supplied
With honorable sorrow, soldiers' sad-
ness,
A kind of silent mourning, such as men,
Who know no tears but from their cap-
tives, use
To show in so great losses.

COR.   I thought once,
Considering their forms, age, manner of
deaths,

The nearness of the places where they
  fell,
T' have paralleled him with great Alex-
  ander;
For both were of best feature, of high
  race,   140
Yeared [1] but to thirty, and, in foreign
  lands,
By their own people alike made away.
SAB. I know not, for his death, how you
  might wrest [2] it;
But, for his life, it did as much disdain
Comparison with that voluptuous, rash,
Giddy, and drunken Macedon's as mine
Doth with my bondman's. All the good
  in him,
His valor, and his fortune, he made his;
But he had other touches of late Romans,
That more did speak [3] him: Pompey's
  dignity,   150
The innocence of Cato, Cæsar's spirit,
Wise Brutus' temperance, and every
  virtue,
Which, parted unto others, gave them
  name,
Flowed mixed in him. He was the soul
  of goodness;
And all our praises of him are like
  streams
Drawn from a spring, that still rise
  full, and leave
The part remaining greatest.
ARR.   I am sure
He was too great for us, and that they
  knew
Who did remove him hence.
SAB.   When men grow fast [4]
Honored and loved, there is a trick in
  state   160
(Which jealous princes never fail to use)
How to decline [5] that growth, with fair
  pretext,
And honorable colors [6] of employment,
Either by embassy, the war, or such,
To shift them forth into another air
Where they may purge and lessen. So
  was he,
And had his seconds there, sent by
  Tiberius
And his more subtile dam, to discontent
  him,

To breed and cherish mutinies, detract
His greatest actions, give audacious
  check   170
To his commands, and work to put him
  out
In open act of treason. All which
  snares
When his wise cares prevented, a fine
  poison
Was thought on to mature their prac-
  tices.
COR. Here comes Sejanus.
SIL.   Now observe the stoops,
The bendings, and the falls.
ARR.   Most creeping base!

[*Enter*] *Sejanus, Satrius, Terentius, etc.*
          They pass over the stage.

[SEJ.] I note hem [7] well; no more. Say
  you?
SAT.   My lord,
There is a gentleman of Rome would
  buy—
SEJ. How call you him you talked with?
SAT.   Please your lordship,
It is Eudemus, the physician   180
To Livia, Drusus' wife.
SEJ.   On with your suit.
Would buy, you said—
SAT.   A tribune's place, my lord.
SEJ. What will he give?
SAT.   Fifty sestertia.
SEJ. Livia's physician, say you, is that
  fellow?
SAT. It is, my lord.   Your lordship's
  answer?
SEJ.   To what?
SAT. The place, my lord. 'Tis for a gen-
  tleman
Your lordship will well like of, when
  you see him,
And one you may make yours by the
  grant.
SEJ. Well, let him bring his money, and his
  name.
SAT. Thank your lordship. He shall, my
  lord.
SEJ.   Come hither.   190
Know you this same Eudemus? Is he
  learned?
SAT. Reputed so, my lord, and of deep
  practice.
SEJ. Bring him in to me in the gallery,

---

[1] Aged.
[2] Interpret.
[3] Celebrate.
[4] Greatly.
[5] Lower.
[6] Pretenses.
[7] Them.

And take you cause to leave us there
together;
I would confer with him, about a
grief.—On!

[*Exit Sejanus with Satrius, Terentius, and
Attendants.*]

Arr. So, yet! Another? Yet? O desperate
state
Of grov'ling honor! Seest thou this, O
sun,
And do we see thee after? Methinks,
day
Should lose his light when men do lose
their shames,
And for the empty circumstance of
life   200
Betray their cause of living.

Sil.   Nothing so.
Sejanus can repair, if Jove should ruin.
He is the now court-god; and, well ap-
plied
With sacrifice of knees, of crooks, and
cringe,
He will do more than all the house of
heav'n
Can for a thousand hecatombs. 'Tis
he
Makes us our day or night; hell and
Elysium
Are in his look. We talk of Radamanth,
Furies, and firebrands; but 'tis his frown
That is all these, where, on the adverse
part,   210
His smile is more than e'er yet poets
feigned
Of bliss, and shades, nectar—

Arr.   A serving boy!
I knew him at Caius' trencher, when for
hire
He prostituted his abuséd body
To that great gourmand, fat Apicius,
And was the noted pathic [1] of the time.

Sab. And, now, the second face of the
whole world,
The partner of the empire—hath his
image
Reared equal with Tiberius, borne in
ensigns;
Commands, disposes every dignity. 220
Centurions, tribunes, heads of provinces,
Prætors, and consuls, all that heretofore

Rome's general suffrage gave, is now his
sale. [2]
The gain, or rather spoil of all the earth.
One, and his house, receives.

Sil.   He hath of late
Made him a strength too, strangely, by
reducing
All the prætorian bands into one camp,
Which he commands, pretending that
the soldier,
By living loose and scattered, fell to riot;
And that, if any sudden enterprise 230
Should be attempted, their united
strength
Would be far more than severed; and
their life
More strict, if from the city more re-
moved—

Sab. Where now he builds what kind of
forts he please,
Is heard to court the soldier by his name,
Woos, feasts the chiefest men of action,
Whose wants, not loves, compel them
to be his.
And, though he ne'er were liberal by
kind, [3]
Yet, to his own dark ends, he's most
profuse,
Lavish, and letting fly he cares not
what   240
To his ambition.

Arr.   Yet hath he ambition?
Is there that step in state can make
him higher,
Or more, or anything he is, but less?

Sil. Nothing but emp'ror.

Arr.   The name Tiberius,
I hope, will keep, howe'er he hath for-
gone
The dignity and power.

Sil.   Sure, while he lives.

Arr. And dead, it comes to Drusus. [4]
Should he fail,
To the brave issue of Germanicus;
And they are three: too many—ha?—for
him
To have a plot upon?

Sab.   I do not know 250
The heart of his designs, but sure their
face
Looks farther than the present.

[2] At his disposal for sale.
[3] Nature.
[4] *I.e.*, Drusus Senior.

ARR.   By the gods,
If I could guess he had but such a
    thought,
My sword should cleave him down from
    head to heart
But I would find it out; and with my
    hand
I'ld hurl his panting brain about the
    air
In mites as small as *atomi* [1] to undo
The knotted bed—
SAB.   You are observed, Arruntius!
ARR. (*He turns to Sejanus' Clients.*) Death!
    I dare tell him so, and all his spies.
You, sir, I would—do you look?—and
    you.
SAB.   Forbear!   260

[*Enter*] *Satrius, Eudemus, Sejanus* [2] [*in the
                        gallery above*].

SAT. Here he will instant be; let's walk a
    turn;
Yo' are in a muse, Eudemus?
EUD.   Not I, sir.—
[*Aside.*] I wonder he should mark me
    out so. Well,
Jove and Apollo form it for the best!
SAT. Your fortune's made unto you now,
    Eudemus,
If you can but lay hold upon the means;
Do but observe his humor, and—believe
    it—
He's the noblest Roman, where he
    takes—
Here comes his lordship.

[*Enter Sejanus.*]

SEJ.   Now, good Satrius.
SAT. This is the gentleman, my lord.
SEJ.   Is this?   270
Give me your hand; we must be more ac-
    quainted.
Report, sir, hath spoke out your art and
    learning,
And I am glad I have so needful cause,
However in itself painful and hard,
To make me known to so great virtue.
    Look,
Who's that? Satrius—[*He motions and
    Satrius leaves.*] I have a grief, sir,
That will desire your help. Your name's
    Eudemus?

EUD. Yes.
SEJ.   Sir?
EUD.   It is, my lord.
SEJ.   I hear you are
Physician to Livia, the princess.   279
EUD. I minister unto her, my good lord.
SEJ. You minister to a royal lady, then.
EUD. She is, my lord, and fair.
SEJ.   That's understood
Of all their sex, who are or would be so;
And those that would be, physic soon
    can make hem;
For those that are, their beauties fear
    no colors. [3]
EUD. Your lordship is conceited. [4]
SEJ.   Sir, you know it,
And can, if need be, read a learned lec-
    ture
On this, and other secrets. Pray you,
    tell me,
What more of ladies, besides Livia,
Have you your patients?
EUD.   Many, my good lord: 290
The great Augusta, Urgulania,
Mutilia Prisca, and Plancina; divers—
SEJ. And all these tell you the particulars
Of every several grief: how first it grew,
And then increased; what action caused
    that;
What passion that; and answer to each
    point
That you will put hem?
EUD.   Else, my lord, we know not
How to prescribe the remedies.
SEJ.   Go to,
Yo' are a subtile nation, you physicians,
And grown the only cabinets in court 300
To ladies' privacies! Faith, which of
    these
Is the most pleasant lady in her physic?
Come, you are modest now.
EUD.   'Tis fit, my lord.
SEJ. Why, sir, I do not ask you of their
    urines,
Whose smell's most violet, or whose
    siege [5] is best,
Or who makes hardest faces on her
    stool,
Which lady sleeps with her own face
    a-nights,
Which puts her teeth off, with her
    clothes, in court,

---

[1] Atoms.   [2] Actually enters later.

[3] With a punning reference to *fear no enemy*.
[4] Witty.   [5] Defecation.

Or which her hair, which her complexion,
And in which box she puts it. These
  were questions   310
That might, perhaps, have put your
  gravity
To some defense of blush. But I inquired
Which was the wittiest, merriest, wantonest?
Harmless intergatories,[1] but conceits.[2]
Methinks Augusta should be most perverse,
And froward in her fit?
Eud.   She's so, my lord.
Sej. I knew it; and Mutilia the most
  jocund?
Eud. 'Tis very true, my lord.
Sej.   And why would you
  Conceal this from me, now? Come,
  what's Livia?
I know she's quick and quaintly spirited,   320
And will have strange thoughts, when
  she's at leisure.
She tells hem all to you?
Eud.   My noblest lord,
He breathes not in the empire, or on
  earth,
Whom I would be ambitious to serve
(In any act that may preserve mine
  honor)
Before your lordship.
Sej.   Sir, you can lose no honor
By trusting aught to me. The coarsest
  act
Done to my service I can so requite
As all the world shall style it honorable.
"Your idle, virtuous definitions   330
Keep honor poor, and are as scorned as
  vain;
Those deeds breathe honor that do suck
  in gain." [3]
Eud. But, good my lord, if I should thus
  betray
The counsels of my patient, and a lady's
Of her high place and worth, what might
  your lordship
(Who presently are to trust me with
  your own)
Judge of my faith?

Sej.   Only the best, I swear.
Say now that I should utter you my
  grief—
And with it the true cause—that it were
  love,
And love to Livia—you should tell her
  this?   340
Should she suspect your faith? I would
  you could
Tell me as much from her; see if my
  brain
Could be turned jealous.[4]
Eud.   Happily,[5] my lord,
I could in time tell you as much and
  more,
So I might safely promise but the first
To her from you.
Sej.   As safely, my Eudemus
(I now dare call thee so), as I have put
The secret into thee.
Eud.   My lord—
Sej.   Protest not;
Thy looks are vows to me; use only
  speed;   349
And but affect her with Sejanus' love,
Thou art a man made to make consuls.
  Go!
Eud. My lord, I'll promise you a private
  meeting
This day together.
Sej.   Canst thou?
Eud.   Yes.
Sej.   The place?
Eud. My gardens, whither I shall fetch
  your lordship.
Sej. Let me adore my Æsculapius![6]
Why, this indeed is physic, and outspeaks
The knowledge of cheap drugs, or any
  use
Can be made out of it! More comforting
Than all your opiates, *julebes*,[7] *apozems*,[8]
Magistral[9] syrups, or—begone, my
  friend,   360
Not barely styléd, but created so;
Expect things greater than thy largest
  hopes
To overtake thee. Fortune shall be
  taught

---

[1] Interrogatories.   [2] Merely fancies.
[3] As usual, quotation marks indicate sententious passages.
[4] Suspicious.   [5] Haply, perhaps.
[6] God of medicine, used here in reference to Venus.   [8] Decoctions.
[7] Juleps.   [9] Sovereign.

To know how ill she hath deserved thus
  long,
To come behind thy wishes.   Go, and
  speed.   [*Exit Eudemus.*]
"Ambition makes more trusty slaves
  than need."
These fellows, by the favor of their art,
Have still the means to tempt, ofttimes
  the power.
If Livia will be now corrupted, then
Thou hast the way, Sejanus, to work
  out   370
His secrets, who, thou knowest, endures
  thee not,
Her husband, Drusus; and to work
  against them.
Prosper it, Pallas, thou that better'st
  wit;
For Venus hath the smallest share in it.

[*Enter*] *Tiberius; Sejanus* [*from the gallery*];
                     Drusus [*Senior*].

[Tɪʙ.] (*One kneels to him.*) We not endure
  these flatteries; let him stand.
Our empire, ensigns, axes, rods, and state
Take not away our human nature from
  us.
Look up on us, and fall before the gods.
Sᴇᴊ. How like a god speaks Cæsar!
Aʀʀ. [*Aside to Cordus.*]   There,
  observe!
He can endure that second [1]—that's no
  flattery.   380
O, what is it proud slime will not believe
Of his own worth, to hear it equal
  praised
Thus with the gods?
Cᴏʀ. [*Aside.*]   He did not hear it, sir.
Aʀʀ. [*Aside.*] He did not? Tut, he must
  not; we think meanly.
'Tis your most courtly known confed-
  eracy,
To have your private parasite redeem
What he, in public subtilty, will lose
To making him a name.
Hᴀᴛ.   Right mighty lord—
                  [*Gives him letters.*]
Tɪʙ. We must make up our ears gainst
  these assaults
Of charming tongues. We pray you use
  no more   390
These contumelies to us; style not us

[1] Support.

Or "lord" or "mighty," who profess
  ourself
The servant of the senate, and are proud
T' enjoy them our good, just, and favor-
  ing lords.
Cᴏʀ. [*Aside.*] Rarely dissembled!
Aʀʀ. [*Aside.*]   Princelike to the life.
Sᴀʙ. "When power that may command,
  so much descends,
Their bondage, whom it stoops to, it
  intends."
Tɪʙ. Whence are these letters?
Hᴀᴛ.   From the senate.
Tɪʙ.   So.
          [*Latiaris gives him letters.*]
Whence these?
Lᴀᴛ.   From thence too.
         [*Tiberius reads the letters.*]
Tɪʙ.   Are they sitting now?
Lᴀᴛ. They stay [2] thy answer, Cæsar.
Sɪʟ. [*Aside.*]   If this man   400
Had but a mind allied unto his words,
How blessed a fate were it to us, and
  Rome!
We could not think [3] that state for
  which to change,[4]
Although the aim were our old liberty;
The ghosts of those that fell for that
  would grieve
Their bodies lived not now, again to
  serve.
"Men are deceived, who think there can
  be thrall
Beneath a virtuous prince. Wished
  liberty
Ne'er lovelier looks than under such a
  crown."
But, when his grace is merely but lip-
  good,   410
And that no longer than he airs himself
Abroad in public, there to seem to shun
The strokes and stripes of flatterers,
  which within
Are lechery unto him, and so feed
His brutish sense with their afflicting
  sound,
As, dead to virtue, he permits himself
Be carried like a pitcher by the ears,
To every act of vice—this is a case
Deserves our fear, and doth presage the
  nigh
And close approach of blood and tyr-
  anny.   420

[2] Await.   [3] Imagine.   [4] Exchange.

"Flattery is midwife unto prince's rage;
And nothing sooner doth help forth a
　tyran
Than that and whisperers' grace, who
　have the time,
The place, the power to make all men
　offenders."
ARR. [*Aside*.] He should be told this; and
　be bid dissemble
With fools and blind men. We that know
　the evil
Should hunt the palace rats, or give them
　bane;
Fright hence these worse than ravens,
　that devour
The quick, where they but prey upon
　the dead.
He shall be told it.
SAB. [*Aside*.]　　　　Stay, Arruntius,　430
We must abide our opportunity,
And practice what is fit, as what is
　needful.
"It is not safe t' enforce a sovereign's
　ear;
Princes hear well, if they at all will
　hear."
ARR. [*Aside*.] Ha, say you so? Well!
　In the meantime, Jove
(Say not but I do call upon thee now),
Of all wild beasts preserve me from a
　tyran;
And of all tame, a flatterer.
SIL. [*Aside*.]　　　　'Tis well prayed.
TIB. Return the lords this voice: We are
　their creature,
And it is fit a good and honest prince, 440
Whom they, out of their bounty, have
　instructed
With so dilate[1] and absolute a power,
Should owe the office of it to their service
And good of all and every citizen.
Nor shall it e'er repent us to have
　wished
The senate just and fav'ring lords unto
　us,
"Since their free loves do yield no less
　defense
T' a prince's state than his own inno-
　cence."
Say then, there can be nothing in their
　thought
Shall want to please us, that hath
　pleaséd them;　　　　　　450

[1] Extended.

Our suffrage rather shall prevent[2] than
　stay
Behind their wills; 'tis empire to obey,
Where such, so great, so grave, so good,
　determine.
Yet, for the suit of Spain t' erect a
　temple
In honor of our mother and ourself,
We must, with pardon of the senate, not
Assent thereto. Their lordships may ob-
　ject
Our not denying the same late request
Unto the Asian cities. We desire
That our defense for suffering that be
　known　　　　　　　　　　　　　460
In these brief reasons, with our after-
　purpose.
Since deified Augustus hindered not
A temple to be built at Pergamum,
In honor of himself and sacred Rome,
We, that have all his deeds and words
　observed
Ever, in place of laws, the rather followed
That pleasing precedent, because with
　ours
The senate's reverence, also, there was
　joined.
But as,[3] t' have once received it, may
　deserve
The gain of pardon, so to be adored　470
With the continued style and note[4]
　of gods,
Through all the provinces, were wild am-
　bition,
And no less pride. Yea, ev'n Augustus'
　name
Would early vanish, should it be pro-
　faned
With such promiscuous flatteries. For
　our part,
We here protest it, and are covetous
Posterity should know it: we are mortal,
And can[5] but deeds of men. 'Twere
　glory enough,
Could we be truly a prince. And they
　shall add
Abounding grace unto our memory,　480
That shall report us worthy our fore-
　fathers,
Careful of your affairs, constant in
　dangers,
And not afraid of any private frown

[2] Anticipate.　　　　[4] Manner of address.
[3] *I.e.*, as one.　　　[5] Can do.

For public good. These things shall be to
  us
Temples and statues, reared in your
  minds,
The fairest and most during imag'ry;
For those of stone or brass, if they be-
  come
Odious in judgment of posterity,
Are more contemned as dying sepulchers
Than ta'en for living monuments. We
  then   490
Make here our suit alike to gods and men:
The one, until the period of our race,
T' inspire us with a free and quiet mind,
Discerning both divine and human laws;
The other, to vouchsafe us after death
An honorable mention and fair praise
T' accompany our actions and our name.
The rest of greatness princes may com-
  mand,
And, therefore, may neglect; only, a long,
A lasting, high, and happy memory 500
They should, without being satisfied,
  pursue.
Contempt of fame begets contempt of
  virtue.
NAT. Rare!
SAT.   Most divine!
SEJ.   The oracles are ceased
That only Cæsar, with their tongue,
  might speak.
ARR. [Aside.] Let me be gone! Most
  felt and open this!
COR. [Aside.] Stay.
ARR. [Aside.]   What? To hear more
  cunning and fine words,
With their sound flattered, ere their
  sense be meant?
TIB. Their choice of Antium, there to
  place the gift,[1]
Vowed to the goddess for our mother's
  health,
We will the senate know we fairly
  like,   510
As also of their grant [2] to Lepidus
For his repairing the Æmilian place
And restoration of those monuments.
Their grace, too, in confining of Silanus
To th' other isle Cithera, at the suit
Of his religious sister, much commends
Their policy, so tempered with their
  mercy.

But for the honors which they have
  decreed
To our Sejanus, to advance [3] his statue
In Pompey's theater (whose ruining
  fire   520
His vigilance and labor kept restrained
In that one loss), they have therein
  outgone
Their own great wisdoms, by their
  skillful choice
And placing of their bounties on a man
Whose merit more adorns the dignity
Than that can him, and gives a benefit
In taking greater than it can receive.
Blush not, Sejanus, thou great aid of
  Rome,
Associate of our labors, our chief helper;
Let us not force thy simple modesty 530
With off'ring at [4] thy praise, for more
  we cannot,
Since there's no voice can take [5] it. No
  man here
Receive our speeches as hyperboles,
For we are far from flattering our
  friend,
Let envy know, as from the need to
  flatter.
Nor let them ask the causes of our
  praise;
Princes have still their grounds reared
  with themselves,
Above the poor low flats of common men;
And who will search the reasons of their
  acts,
Must stand on equal bases.   Lead,
  away.   540
Our loves unto the senate.
ARR.   Cæsar!—
SAB.   Peace!—
[Exeunt Tiberius, Sejanus, and Attendants.]
COR. Great Pompey's theater was never
  ruined
Till now that proud Sejanus hath a
  statue
Reared on his ashes.
ARR.   Place the shame of soldiers
Above the best of generals? Crack the
  world,
And bruise the name of Romans into
  dust,
Ere we behold it!
SIL.   Check your passion;
Lord Drusus tarries.

---

[1] Jonson's marginal note reads: "Fortuna
equestris."   [2] Permission.

[3] Set up.   [4] Attempting.   [5] Accomplish.

DRU.   Is my father mad,
    Weary of life and rule, lords, thus to
       heave
    An idol up with praise? Make him his
       mate,   550
    His rival in the empire?
ARR.   O, good prince!
DRU. Allow him statues, titles, honors,
     such
    As he himself refuseth?
ARR.   Brave, brave Drusus!
DRU. The first ascents to sovereignty are
     hard;
    But, entered once, there never wants or
       means
    Or ministers to help th' aspirer on.
ARR. True, gallant Drusus.
DRU.   We must shortly pray
    To Modesty, that he will rest con-
       tented—
ARR. Ay, where he is, and not write em-
       p'ror.

Sejanus,[1] *etc.; he enters, followed with Clients.*
[SEJ.] There is your bill, and yours.—[*To*
    Satrius.] Bring you your man.   560
    I have moved for you, too, Latiaris.
DRU.   What?
    Is your vast greatness grown so blindly
       bold
    That you will over us?
SEJ.   Why, then give way!
DRU. Give way, Colossus? Do you lift?
     Advance you?
    Take that!   *Drusus strikes him.*
ARR.   Good! Brave! Excellent
     brave prince!
DRU. Nay, come, approach. [*Draws his*
     sword.] What, stand you off? At
     gaze?
    It looks too full of death for thy cold
       spirits.
    Avoid mine eye, dull camel, or my sword
    Shall make thy brav'ry fitter for a grave
    Than for a triumph. I'll advance a
     statue   570
    O' your own bulk; but 't shall be on the
       cross,
    Where I will nail your pride at breadth
       and length,

[1] The fact that the names, *Drusus, Arruntius,*
are repeated at this point in the original would
perhaps indicate that Jonson conceived of his
act as being divided into scenes in classical fashion.

And crack those sinews, which are yet
     but stretched
    With your swol'n fortune's rage.
ARR.   A noble prince!
ALL. A Castor, a Castor, a Castor, a
    Castor!   [*Exeunt All but Sejanus.*]
SEJ. He that, with such wrong moved,
     can bear it through
    With patience and an even mind, knows
       how
    To turn it back. Wrath, covered, carries
       fate;
    Revenge is lost if I profess my hate.
    What was my practice [2] late, I'll now
       pursue   580
    As my fell justice. This hath styled it
       new.   [*Exit.*]

CHORUS—*of Musicians.*

ACT II. [SCENE i.

The garden of Eudemus.]

Sejanus, Livia, Eudemus.

[SEJ.] Physician, thou art worthy of a
    province
    For the great favors done unto our loves,
    And, but that greatest Livia bears a
       part
    In the requital of thy services,
    I should alone despair of aught like
       means
    To give them worthy satisfaction.
LIV. Eudemus, I will see it, shall receive
    A fit and full reward for his large merit.
    But for this potion we intend to Drusus
    (No more our husband now), whom
       shall we choose   10
    As the most apt and abled instrument
    To minister it to him?
EUD.   I say, Lygdus.
SEJ. Lygdus? What's he?
LIV.   An eunuch Drusus loves.
EUD. Ay, and his cupbearer.
SEJ.   Name not a second.
    If Drusus love him, and he have that
       place,
    We cannot think a fitter.
EUD.   True, my lord;
    For free access and trust are two main
       aids.
SEJ. Skillful physician!
LIV.   But he must be wrought
    To th' undertaking with some labored art.

[2] Trickery.

SEJ. Is he ambitious?
LIV.   No.
SEJ.   Or covetous?   20
LIV. Neither.
EUD.   Yet gold is a good general charm.
SEJ. What is he, then?
LIV.   Faith, only wanton, light.
SEJ. How! Is he young and fair?
EUD.   A delicate youth.
SEJ. Send him to me; I'll work him.—
    Royal lady,
    Though I have loved you long, and with
        that height
    Of zeal and duty, like the fire, which
        more
    It mounts it trembles, thinking naught
        could add
    Unto the fervor which your eye had
        kindled,
    Yet, now I see your wisdom, judgment,
        strength,
    Quickness, and will to apprehend the
        means   30
    To your own good and greatness, I
        protest
    Myself through rarefied, and turned all
        flame
    In your affection. Such a spirit as yours
    Was not created for the idle second
    To a poor flash, as Drusus, but to shine
    Bright as the moon among the lesser
        lights,
    And share the sov'reignty of all the
        world.
    Then Livia triumphs in her proper
        sphere,
    When she and her Sejanus shall divide
    The name of Cæsar, and Augusta's star
    Be dimmed with glory of a brighter
        beam,   41
    When Agrippina's fires are quite ex-
        tinct,
    And the scarce-seen Tiberius borrows
        all
    As little light from us, whose folded
        arms
    Shall make one perfect orb! [Knocking
        within.] Who's that? Eudemus,
    Look 'tis not Drusus.—[Exit Eudemus.]
    Lady, do not fear.
LIV. Not I, my lord. My fear and love
    of him
    Left me at once.[1]

¹ Simultaneously.

SEJ.   Illustr'ous lady, stay—
EUD. [Within.] I'll tell his lordship.

[Enter Eudemus.]

SEJ.   Who is 't, Eudemus?
EUD. One of your lordship's servants
    brings you word   50
    The emp'ror hath sent for you.
SEJ.   O! Where is he?—
    With your fair leave, dear princess, I'll
        but ask
    A question, and return.   He goes out.
EUD.   Fortunate princess!
    How are you blessed in the fruition
    Of this unequaled man, this soul of
        Rome,
    The empire's life, and voice of Cæsar's
        world!
LIV. So blessed, my Eudemus, as to know
    The bliss I have, with what I ought to
        owe
    The means that wrought it. How do I
        look today?
EUD. Excellent clear, believe it. This
    same fucus ²   60
    Was well laid on.
LIV.   Methinks 'tis here not white.
EUD. Lend me your scarlet, lady. 'Tis
    the sun
    Hath giv'n some little taint unto the
        ceruse; ³
    You should have used of the white oil
    I gave you.
    Sejanus for your love! His very name
    Commandeth above Cupid or his shafts—
                [Paints her cheek.]
(LIV. Nay, now yo' have made it worse.
EUD.   I'll help it straight.)
    —And, but pronounced, is a sufficient
        charm
    Against all rumor, and of absolute power
    To satisfy for any lady's honor.   70
(LIV. What do you now, Eudemus?
EUD.   Make a light fucus,
    To touch you o'er withal.) Honored
        Sejanus!
    What act, though ne'er so strange and
        insolent,
    But that addition ⁴ will at least bear out,
    If 't do not expiate?
LIV.   Here, good physician.

² Cosmetic.
³ Cosmetic containing white lead.
⁴ Title.

Eud. I like this study to preserve the love
  Of such a man, that comes not every
    hour
  To greet the world. ('Tis now well, lady;
    you should
  Use of the dentifrice I prescribed you,
    too,
  To clear your teeth, and the prepared
    pomatum,   80
  To smooth the skin.) A lady cannot be
  Too curious [1] of her form, that still
    would hold
  The heart of such a person, made her
    captive,
  As you have his; who, to endear him
    more
  In your clear eye, hath put away his
    wife,
  The trouble of his bed and your delights,
  Fair Apicata, and made spacious room
  To your new pleasures.

Liv.   Have not we returned
  That with our hate of Drusus, and dis-
    covery
  Of all his counsels?

Eud.   Yes, and wisely, lady.   90
  The ages that succeed, and stand far off
  To gaze at your high prudence, shall
    admire,
  And reckon it an act without [2] your sex;
  It hath that rare appearance. Some will
    think
  Your fortune could not yield a deeper
    sound
  Than mixed with Drusus'; but, when
    they shall hear
  That and the thunder of Sejanus meet,
  Sejanus, whose high name doth strike
    the stars,
  And rings about the concave—great
    Sejanus,
  Whose glories, style, and titles are him-
    self,   100
  The often iterating of Sejanus—
  They then will lose their thoughts, and
    be ashamed
  To take acquaintance of them.

[Enter Sejanus.]

Sej.   I must make
  A rude departure, lady; Cæsar sends
  With all his haste both of command and
    prayer.

Be resolute in our plot; you have my
    soul,
  As certain yours as it is my body's.
  And, wise physician, so prepare the
    poison
  As you may lay the subtile operation
  Upon some natural disease of his.   110
  Your eunuch send to me. I kiss your
    hands,
  Glory of ladies, and commend my love
  To your best faith and memory.

Liv.   My lord,
  I shall but change [3] your words. Fare-
    well. Yet, this
  Remember for your heed, he loves you
    not;
  You know what I have told you. His
    designs
  Are full of grudge and danger; we must
    use
  More than a common speed.

Sej.   Excellent lady,
  How you do fire my blood!

Liv.   Well, you must go?
  The thoughts be best, are least set forth
    to show.   *[Exit Sejanus.]*   120

Eud. When will you take some physic,
    lady?

Liv.   When
  I shall, Eudemus; but let Drusus' drug
  Be first prepared.

Eud.   Were Lygdus made,[4] that's done;
  I have it ready. And tomorrow morning
  I'll send you a perfume, first to resolve
  And procure sweat, and then prepare
    a bath
  To cleanse and clear the cutis; against
    when
  I'll have an excellent new fucus made,
  Resistive gainst the sun, the rain, or
    wind,
  Which you shall lay on with a breath,
    or oil,   130
  As you best like, and last some fourteen
    hours.
  This change came timely, lady, for your
    health,
  And the restoring your complexion,
  Which Drusus' choler had almost burnt
    up,
  Wherein your fortune hath prescribed
    you better
  Than art could do.

---

[1] Careful.   [2] Beyond.   [3] Reciprocate.   [4] Won to our purpose.

Liv.   Thanks, good physician;
I'll use my fortune, you shall see, with
    reverence.
Is my coach ready?
Eud.   It attends your highness.
                              [*Exeunt.*]

[Scene ii.

A room in the palace.]

Sejanus.

[Sej.] If this be not revenge, when I have
    done
And made it perfect, let Egyptian slaves,
Parthians, and barefoot Hebrews brand
    my face,
And print my body full of injuries.
Thou lost thyself, childe [1] Drusus, when
    thou thought'st
Thou couldst outskip my vengeance,
    or outstand [2]
The power I had to crush thee into air.
Thy follies now shall taste what kind
    of man
They have provoked, and this thy
    father's house   9
Crack in the flame of my incenséd rage,
Whose fury shall admit no shame or
    mean.
Adultery? It is the lightest ill
I will commit. A race of wicked acts
Shall flow out of my anger, and o'er-
    spread
The world's wide face, which no pos-
    terity
Shall e'er approve, nor yet keep silent—
    things
That, for their cunning, close, and cruel
    mark,
Thy father would wish his, and shall,
    perhaps,
Carry the empty name, but we the prize.
On, then, my soul, and start not in thy
    course;   20
Though heav'n drop sulphur, and hell
    belch out fire,
Laugh at the idle terrors. Tell proud
    Jove,
Between his power and thine there is
    no odds.
'Twas only fear first in the world made
    gods.

[*Enter*] *Tiberius* [*with Attendants*].[3]
[Tib.] Is yet Sejanus come?
Sej.   He's here, dread Cæsar.
Tib. Let all depart that chamber, and the
    next.—   [*Exeunt Attendants.*]
Sit down, my comfort. When the master-
    prince
Of all the world, Sejanus, saith he fears,
Is it not fatal?
Sej.   Yes, to those are feared.
Tib. And not to him?
Sej.   Not if he wisely turn   30
That part of fate he holdeth, first on
    them.
Tib. That nature, blood, and laws of
    kind forbid.
Sej. Do policy and state forbid it?
Tib.   No.
Sej. The rest of poor respects, then, let
    go by;
State [4] is enough to make th' act just,
    them guilty.
Tib. Long hate pursues such acts.
Sej.   Whom hatred frights,
Let him not dream on sov'reignty.
Tib.   Are rites
Of faith, love, piety, to be trod down,
Forgotten, and made vain?
Sej.   All for a crown.
The prince who shames a tyran's name
    to bear   40
Shall never dare do anything but fear;
All the command of scepters quite doth
    perish,
If it begin religious thoughts to cherish;
Whole empires fall, swayed by those
    nice respects;
It is the license of dark deeds protects
Ev'n states most hated, when no laws
    resist
The sword, but that it acteth what it
    list.
Tib. Yet so, we may do all things cruelly,
Not safely.
Sej.   Yes, and do them thoroughly.
Tib. Knows yet Sejanus whom we point
    at?
Sej.   Ay,   50
Or else my thought, my sense, or both
    do err:
'Tis Agrippina?
Tib.   She, and her proud race.

[1] A youth of noble birth.   [2] Withstand.
[3] The name *Sejanus* is repeated here.
[4] Reasons of state.

SEJ. Proud? Dangerous, Cæsar; for in
    them apace
The father's spirit shoots up. Germani-
    cus
Lives in their looks, their gait, their
    form, t' upbraid us
With his close death, if not revenge the
    same.
TIB. The act's not known.
SEJ.   Not proved; but whisp'ring Fame [1]
Knowledge and proof doth to the jeal-
    ous give,
Who, than to fail, would their own
    thought believe.
It is not safe the children draw long
    breath,   60
That are provokéd by a parent's death.
TIB. It is as dangerous to make them
    hence,
If nothing but their birth be their of-
    fense.
SEJ. Stay till they strike at Cæsar; then
    their crime
Will be enough; but late and out of time
For him to punish.
TIB.   Do they purpose it?
SEJ. You know, sir, thunder speaks not
    till it hit.
Be not secure; [2] none swiftlier are op-
    pressed
Than they whom confidence betrays to
    rest.
Let not your daring make your danger
    such;   70
All power's to be feared, where 'tis too
    much.
The youths are of themselves hot, vi-
    olent,
Full of great thought; and that male-
    spirited dame,
Their mother, slacks no means to put
    them on,
By large allowance, popular presentings,
Increase of train and state, suing for
    titles;
Hath them commended with like prayers,
    like vows,
To the same gods, with Caesar; days
    and nights
She spends in banquets and ambitious
    feasts
For the nobility, where Caius Silius,   80
Titius Sabinus, old Arruntius,

Asinius Gallus, Furnius, Regulus,
And others of that discontented list
Are the prime guests. There, and to
    these, she tells
Whose niece she was, whose daughter,
    and whose wife.
And then must they compare her with
    Augusta,
Ay, and prefer her too, commend her
    form,
Extol her fruitfulness, at which a
    shower
Falls for the memory of Germanicus,
Which they blow over straight with
    windy praise   90
And puffing hopes of her aspiring sons,
Who, with these hourly ticklings, grow
    so pleased
And wantonly conceited of themselves
As now they stick not to believe they're
    such
As these do give hem out, and would
    be thought
More than competitors,[3] immediate
    heirs,
Whilest to their thirst of rule they win
    the rout
(That's still the friend of novelty) with
    hope
Of future freedom, which on every
    change   99
That greedily, though emptily, expects.[4]
Cæsar, 'tis age in all things breeds neg-
    lects,
And princes that will keep old dignity
Must not admit too youthful heirs
    stand by—
Not their own issue—but so darkly set
As shadows are in picture, to give
    height
And luster to themselves.
TIB.   We will command
Their rank thoughts down, and with a
    stricter hand
Than we have yet put forth; their trains
    must bate,
Their titles, feasts, and factions.
SEJ.   Or your state.
But how, sir, will you work?
TIB.   Confine hem.
SEJ.   No.   110
They are too great, and that too faint
    a blow

---

[1] Rumor.   [2] Overconfident.   [3] Partners.   [4] Awaits.

To give them now; it would have served
　　at first,
When with the weakest touch their
　　knot had burst.
But now your care must be, not to de-
　　tect
The smallest cord or line of your suspect,
For such, who know the weight of
　　princes' fear,
Will, when they find themselves dis-
　　covered, rear
Their forces, like seen snakes, that else
　　would lie
Rolled in their circles, close. Naught is
　　more high,
Daring, or desperate than offenders
　　found;　　　　　　　　　　　　120
Where guilt is, rage and courage doth
　　abound.
The course must be, to let hem still
　　swell up,
Riot, and surfeit on blind Fortune's cup;
Give hem more place, more dignities,
　　more style,
Call hem to court, to senate; in the while,
Take from their strength some one or
　　twain or more
Of the main fautors [1] (it will fright the
　　store [2]),
And by some by-occasion. Thus, with
　　sleight
You shall disarm first, and they, in
　　night　　　　　　　　　　　　129
Of their ambition, not perceive the train,
Till in the ingine [3] they are caught and
　　slain.
TIB. We would not kill, if we knew how
　　to save;
Yet, than a throne, 'tis cheaper give a
　　grave.
Is there no way to bind them by deserts?
SEJ. Sir, wolves do change their hair, but
　　not their hearts.
While thus your thought unto a mean
　　is tied,
You neither dare enough, nor do provide.
All modesty is fond, [4] and chiefly where
The subject is no less compelled to bear,
Than praise, his sov'reign's acts.
TIB.　　　　　　We can no longer　140
Keep on our mask to thee, our dear
　　Sejanus;

[1] Adherents.　　　[2] Many.　　　[3] Trap.
[4] All moderation is foolish.

Thy thoughts are ours, in all, and we
　　but proved
Their voice, in our designs, which by as-
　　senting
Hath more confirmed us than if heart'n-
　　ing Jove
Had, from his hundred statues, bid us
　　strike,
And at the stroke clicked all his marble
　　thumbs.
But who shall first be strook?
SEJ.　　　　　　　　First, Caius Silius;
He is the most of mark, and most of
　　danger—
In power and reputation equal strong,
Having commanded an imperial army
Seven years together, vanquished Sa-
　　crovir　　　　　　　　　　　　151
In Germany, and thence obtained to
　　wear
The ornaments triumphal.　His steep
　　fall,
By how much it doth give the weightier
　　crack,
Will send more wounding terror to the
　　rest,
Command them stand aloof, and give
　　more way
To our surprising of the principal.
TIB. But what, Sabinus?
SEJ.　　　　　　Let him grow awhile;
His fate is not yet ripe.　We must not
　　pluck　　　　　　　　　　　　159
At all together, lest we catch ourselves.
And there's Arruntius too; he only talks.
But Sosia, Silius' wife, would be wound
　　in
Now, for she hath a fury in her breast
More than hell ever knew, and would
　　be sent
Thither in time.　Then is there one Cre-
　　mutius
Cordus, a writing fellow, they have got
To gather notes of the precedent times,
And make them into annals—a most
　　tart
And bitter spirit, I hear, who, under
　　color
Of praising those, doth tax [5] the present
　　state,　　　　　　　　　　　　170
Censures [6] the men, the actions, leaves
　　no trick,
No practice unexamined, parallels

[5] Accuse.　　　　　　　　[6] Judges.

The times, the governments—a professed champion
For the old liberty—

TIB. A perishing wretch!
As if there were that chaos bred in things,
That laws and liberty would not rather choose
To be quite broken and ta'en hence by us
Than have the stain to be preserved by such.
Have we the means to make these guilty first?

SEJ. Trust that to me. Let Cæsar, by his power, 180
But cause a formal meeting of the senate,
I will have matter and accusers ready.

TIB. But how? Let us consult.

SEJ. We shall misspend
The time of action. Counsels are unfit
In business where all rest is more pernicious
Than rashness can be. Acts of this close kind
Thrive more by execution than advice.
There is no ling'ring in that work begun,
Which cannot praiséd be, until through done.

TIB. Our edict shall forthwith command a court. 190
While I can live, I will prevent earth's fury:
'Εμοῦ θανόντος γαῖα μιχθήτω πυρί.[1]

[Exit.]

[Enter] Posthumus.[2]

[Pos.] My Lord Sejanus—

SEJ. Julius Posthumus,
Come with my wish! What news from Agrippina's?

Pos. Faith, none. They all lock up themselves alate,
Or talk in character;[3] I have not seen
A company so changed. Except they had
Intelligence by augury of our practice—

SEJ. When were you there?

Pos. Last night.

SEJ. And what guests found you?

Pos. Sabinus, Silius (the old list), Arruntius, 200
Furnius, and Gallus.

SEJ. Would not these talk?

Pos. Little.
And yet we offered choice of argument.[4]
Satrius was with me.

SEJ. Well. 'Tis guilt enough,
Their often meeting. You forgot t' extol
The hospitable lady?

Pos. No; that trick
Was well put home, and had succeeded too,
But that Sabinus coughed a caution out;
For she began to swell—

SEJ. And may she burst!
Julius, I would have you go instantly
Unto the palace of the great Augusta, 210
And, by your kindest friend,[5] get swift access;
Acquaint her with these meetings. Tell the words
You brought me, th' other day, of Silius;
Add somewhat to hem. Make her understand
The danger of Sabinus, and the times,
Out of his closeness. Give Arruntius' words
Of malice against Cæsar; so, to Gallus;
But, above all, to Agrippina. Say,
As you may truly, that her infinite pride,
Propped with the hopes of her too fruitful womb, 220
With popular studies[6] gapes for sovereignty,
And threatens Cæsar. Pray Augusta then
That for her own, great Cæsar's, and the public safety, she be pleased to urge these dangers.
Cæsar is too secure; he must be told,
And best he'll take it from a mother's tongue.
Alas! What is 't for us to sound, t' explore,

---

[1] When I am dead, let the earth be overwhelmed with fire.

[2] The name *Sejanus* is repeated here.

[3] Cipher.

[4] Subject.

[5] Marginal note reads "Mutilia Prisca."

[6] Jonson's questionable rendering of *popularibus studiis, i.e.*, "The zeal and devotion of the people" (Briggs).

To watch, oppose, plot, practice, or pre-
vent,
If he, for whom it is so strongly labored,
Shall, out of greatness and free spirit,
be   230
Supinely negligent? Our city's now
Divided as in time o' th' civil war,
And men forbear not to declare them-
selves
Of Agrippina's party. Every day
The faction multiplies, and will do more
If not resisted; you can best enlarge it,
As you find audience. Noble Posthumus,
Commend me to your Prisca, and pray
her
She will solicit this great business
To earnest and most present execu-
tion,   240
With all her utmost credit with Augusta.
Pos. I shall not fail in my instructions.
                        [*Exit.*]
SEJ. This second, from his mother, will
well urge
Our late design, and spur on Cæsar's
rage,
Which else might grow remiss. The way
to put
A prince in blood [1] is to present the
shapes
Of dangers greater than they are, like
late
Or early shadows, and, sometimes, to
feign
Where there are none, only to make him
fear.
His fear will make him cruel, and, once
entered,   250
He doth not easily learn to stop, or
spare
Where he may doubt. This have I
made my rule
To thrust Tiberius into tyranny,
And make him toil to turn aside those
blocks
Which I alone could not remove with
safety.
Drusus once gone, Germanicus' three
sons
Would clog my way, whose guards have
too much faith
To be corrupted, and their mother known
Of too-too unreproved [2] a chastity

[1] *I.e.*, make him angry.
[2] Too completely blameless.

To be attempted as light Livia was.   260
Work then, my art, on Cæsar's fears,
as they
On those they fear, till all my lets [3] be
cleared,
And he in ruins of his house, and hate
Of all his subjects, bury his own state,
When with my peace and safety I will
rise
By making him the public sacrifice.
                        [*Exit.*]

[SCENE iii.

A room in Agrippina's house.]

Satrius, Natta.

[SAT.] They are grown exceeding circum-
spect and wary.
NAT. They have us in the wind; [4] and yet
Arruntius
Cannot contain himself.
SAT.   Tut, he's not yet
Looked after; there are others more
desired
That are more silent.
NAT.   Here he comes. Away! [*Exeunt.*]

[*Enter*] *Sabinus, Arruntius, Cordus.*

[SAB.] How is it that these beagles haunt
the house
Of Agrippina?
ARR.   O, they hunt, they hunt!
There is some game here lodged, which
they must rouse,
To make the great ones sport.
COR.   Did you observe
How they inveighed gainst Cæsar?
ARR.   Ay, baits, baits
For us to bite at; would I have my
flesh   11
Torn by the public hook, these qualified
hangmen
Should be my company.
COR.   Here comes another.

[*Afer passes by.*]

ARR. Ay, there's a man, Afer the orator!
One that hath phrases, figures, and fine
flowers
To strew his rethoric [5] with, and doth
make haste

[3] From 1605 edn.; original reads *betts.*
[4] They are on our scent.
[5] Rhetoric.

To get him note or name by any offer
Where blood or gain be objects; steeps
  his words,
When he would kill, in artificial tears—
The crocodile of Tiber! Him I love, 20
That man is mine. He hath my heart
  and voice
When I would curse—he, he.
SAB.   Contemn the slaves;
Their present lives will be their future
  graves.   [*Exeunt.*]

[*Enter*] *Silius, Agrippina, Nero, Sosia.*

[SIL.] May 't please your highness not
  forget yourself;
  I dare not, with my manners, to attempt
  Your trouble farder.
AGR.   Farewell, noble Silius!
SIL. Most royal princess!
AGR.   Sosia stays with us?
SIL. She is your servant, and doth owe
  your grace
  An honest, but unprofitable love.
AGR. How can that be, when there's no
  gain but virtue's?   30
SIL. You take the moral, not the politic
  sense.
  I meant, as she is bold, and free of
  speech,
  Earnest to utter what her zealous
  thought
  Travails withal, in honor of your house—
  Which act, as it is simply borne in her,
  Partakes of love and honesty, but may,
  By th' over-often and unseasoned use,
  Turn to your loss and danger; for your
  state
  Is waited on by envies, as by eyes;
  And every second guest your tables take
  Is a fee'd spy, t' observe who goes, who
  comes,   41
  What conference you have, with whom,
  where, when,
  What the discourse is, what the looks,
  the thoughts
  Of ev'ry person there, they do extract
  And make into a substance.
AGR.   Hear me, Silius.
  Were all Tiberius' body stuck with
  eyes,
  And ev'ry wall and hanging in my house
  Transparent, as this lawn I wear, or air,
  Yea, had Sejanus both his ears as long
  As to my inmost closet, I would hate 50

To whisper any thought, or change an
  act,
To be made Juno's rival. Virtue's forces
Show ever noblest in conspicuous
  courses.
SIL. 'Tis great, and bravely spoken, like
  the spirit
  Of Agrippina; yet, your highness knows,
  There is nor loss nor shame in provi-
  dence;[1]
  Few can, what all should do, beware
  enough.
  You may perceive with what officious
  face
  Satrius and Natta, Afer and the rest
  Visit your house of late, t' inquire the
  secrets,   60
  And with what bold and privileged art
  they rail
  Against Augusta, yea, and at Tiberius;
  Tell tricks of Livia, and Sejanus—all
  T' excite, and call your indignation on,
  That they might hear it at more liberty.
AGR. Yo' are too suspicious, Silius.
SIL.   Pray the gods
  I be so, Agrippina; but I fear
  Some subtile practice. They that durst
  to strike
  At so exampless[2] and unblamed a life
  As that of the renowned Germanicus, 70
  Will not sit down with that exploit alone.
  "He threatens many that hath injured
  one."
NERO. 'Twere best rip forth their tongues,
  sear out their eyes,
  When next they come.
SOS.   A fit reward for spies.

[*Enter*] *Drusus Ju[nior].*[3]

DRU. Hear you the rumor?
AGR.   What?
DRU.   Drusus is dying.
AGR. Dying?
NERO.   That's strange!
AGR.   Yo' were with him yesternight.
DRU. One met Eudemus the physician,
  Sent for but now, who thinks he can-
  not live.
SIL. Thinks? If 't be arrived at that, he
  knows,
  Or none.

[1] Prudence.   [2] Example-less, unexampled.
[3] The names *Agrippina, Nero,* and *Silius* are
here repeated.

AGR.　　This 's quick! What should
be his disease?　　　　　　　　　80
SIL. Poison, poison—
AGR.　　　　　How, Silius!
NERO.　　　　　　　What's that?
SIL. Nay, nothing.　There was late a
certain blow
Giv'n o' the face.
NERO.　　　　　Ay, to Sejanus?
SIL.　　　　　　　　　　　True.
DRU. And what of that?
SIL.　　　　　I am glad I gave it not.
NERO. But there is somewhat else?
SIL.　　　　　Yes, private meetings,
With a great lady at a physician's,
And a wife turned away—
NERO.　　　Ha!
SIL.　　　　　　　　Toys, mere toys!
What wisdom's now i' th' streets? I'
th' common mouth?
DRU. Fears, whisp'rings, tumults, noise,
I know not what;
They say the senate sit.
SIL.　　　　　I'll thither straight,　90
And see what's in the forge.
AGR.　　　　　　　Good Silius, do;
Sosia and I will in.
SIL.　　　　　　Haste you, my lords,
To visit the sick prince; tender your
loves
And sorrows to the people. This Sejanus,
Trust my divining soul, hath plots on
all;
No tree that stops his prospect but must
fall.　　　　　　　　[Exeunt.]
　　　CHORUS—of Musicians.

ACT III. [SCENE i.]

The Senate.

Sejanus, Varro, Latiaris. Cotta, Afer.
[*Sabinus,*] *Gallus, Lepidus, Arruntius.*
　　　　　　Præcones,[1] *Lictores.*
[SEJ.] 'Tis only you must urge against him,
Varro;
Nor I nor Cæsar may appear therein,
Except in your defense, who are the
consul,
And, under color of late enmity
Between your father and his, may better
do it,
As free from all suspicion of a practice.

[1] Public criers.

Here be your notes, what points to touch
at. Read;
Be cunning in them. Afer has them too.
VAR. But is he summoned?
SEJ.　　　　　　No. It was debated
By Cæsar, and concluded as most fit　10
To take him unprepared.
AFER.　　　　　　And prosecute
All under name of treason.
VAR.　　　　　　I conceive.
SAB. Drusus being dead, Cæsar will not be
here.
GAL. What should the business of this
senate be?
ARR. That can my subtile whisperers tell
you: we
That are the good-dull-noble lookers-on
Are only called to keep the marble
warm.
What should we do with those deep
mysteries,
Proper to these fine heads? Let them
alone.
Our ignorance may, perchance, help us
be saved　　　　　　　　　20
From whips and Furies.
GAL.　　　　See, see, see their action!
ARR. Ay, now their heads do travail, now
they work;
Their faces run like shittles;[2] they are
weaving
Some curious cobweb to catch flies.
SAB.　　　　　　　　　Observe,
They take their places.
ARR.　　　　　What, so low?
GAL.　　　　　　　　O, yes,
They must be seen to flatter Cæsar's
grief,
Though but in sitting.
VAR.　　　　　Bid us silence.
PRÆ.　　　　　　　　Silence!
VAR. "Fathers conscript, may this our
present meeting
Turn fair and fortunate to the common-
wealth!"

　　　　　[*Enter*] *Silius.*[3]

SEJ. See, Silius enters.
SIL.　　　　　Hail, grave fathers!
LIC.　　　　　　　　Stand.　30
Silius, forbear thy place!
SEN[ATE].　　　　　　How!

[2] Shuttles.
[3] The word *Senate* is repeated here.

Præ.   Silius, stand forth;
The consul hath to charge thee.
Lic.   Room for Cæsar!
Arr. Is he come too? Nay, then, expect a
trick.
Sab. Silius accused? Sure he will answer
nobly.

[*Enter*] *Tiberius* [1] [*with Attendants*].

[Tib.] We stand amazéd, fathers, to be-
hold
This general dejection. Wherefore sit
Rome's consuls thus dissolved,[2] as they
had lost
All the remembrance both of style and
place?
It not becomes. No woes are of fit weight
To make the honor of the empire stoop,
Though I, in my peculiar self, may
meet   41
Just reprehension, that so suddenly,
And in so fresh a grief, would greet the
senate,
When private tongues of kinsmen and
allies,
Inspired with comforts, loathly are en-
dured,
The face of men not seen, and scarce the
day,
To thousands that communicate[3] our
loss.
Nor can I argue these of weakness, since
They take but natural ways; yet I must
seek
For stronger aids, and those fair helps
draw out   50
From warm embraces of the common-
wealth.
Our mother, great Augusta, is strook
with time,
Our self impressed with aged characters,
Drusus is gone, his children young and
babes.
Our aims must now reflect on those that
may
Give timely succor to these present ills,
And are our only glad-surviving hopes,
The noble issue of Germanicus,
Nero and Drusus. Might it please the
consul
Honor them in; they both attend with-
out.   60

I would present them to the senate's
care,
And raise those suns of joy that should
drink up
These floods of sorrow in your drownéd
eyes.
Arr. By Jove, I am not Œdipus enough
To understand this Sphinx.
Sab.   The princes come.

[*Enter*] [4] *Nero, Drusus Junior.*

[Tib.] Approach you, noble Nero, noble
Drusus.
These princes, fathers, when their parent
died,
I gave unto their uncle, with this prayer,
That though h' had proper issue of his
own,
He would no less bring up and foster
these   70
Than that self-blood, and by that act
confirm
Their worths to him and to posterity.
Drusus ta'en hence, I turn my prayers to
you,
And, fore [5] our country and our gods, be-
seech
You take and rule Augustus' nephew's
sons,
Sprung of the noblest ancestors, and so
Accomplish both my duty and your own.
Nero and Drusus, these shall be to you
In place of parents, these your fathers,
these;
And not unfitly, for you are so born   80
As all your good or ill's the common-
wealth's.
Receive them, you strong guardians, and,
blessed gods,
Make all their actions answer to their
bloods;
Let their great titles find increase by
them,
Not they by titles. Set them, as in place,
So in example, above all the Romans;
And may they know no rivals but them-
selves.
Let Fortune give them nothing, but
attend
Upon their virtue, and that still come
forth

Greater than hope, and better than their
    fame.   90
Relieve me, fathers, with your general
    voice.
SEN. "May all the gods consent to Cæsar's
    wish,
And add to any honors that may crown
The hopeful issue of Germanicus!" [1]
TIB. We thank you, reverend fathers, in
    their right.
ARR. [*Aside.*] If this were true now! But
    the space, the space
Between the breast and lips! Tiberius'
    heart
Lies a thought farder than another
    man's.
TIB. My comforts are so flowing in my
    joys,
As, in them, all my streams of grief are
    lost,   100
No less than are land-waters in the sea,
Or showers in rivers, though their cause
    was such
As might have sprinkled ev'n the gods
    with tears;
Yet, since the greater doth embrace the
    less,
We covetously obey.
(ARR.   Well acted, Cæsar.)
TIB. And, now I am the happy witness
    made
Of your so much desired affections
To this great issue, I could wish the
    Fates
Would here set peaceful period to my
    days;
However, to my labors I entreat—   110
And beg it of this senate—some fit ease.
(ARR. Laugh, fathers, laugh! Ha' you no
    spleens [2] about you?)
TIB. The burden is too heavy I sustain
On my unwilling shoulders; and I pray
It may be taken off, and reconferred
Upon the consuls, or some other Roman,
More able and more worthy.
(ARR.   Laugh on still!
SAB. Why, this doth render all the rest
    suspected!
GAL. It poisons all.
ARR.   O, do you taste it then?

SAB. It takes away my faith to anything
He shall hereafter speak.
ARR.   Ay, to pray that,   121
Which would be to his head as hot as
    thunder,
Gainst which he wears that charm,[3]
    should but the court
Receive him at his word.
GAL.   Hear!)
TIB.   For myself
I know my weakness, and so little covet,
Like some gone past, the weight that will
    oppress me,
As my ambition is the counterpoint.[4]
(ARR. Finely maintained; good still!)
SEJ.   But Rome, whose blood,
Whose nerves, whose life, whose very
    frame relies
On Cæsar's strength, no less than heaven
    on Atlas,   130
Cannot admit it but with general ruin.
(ARR. Ah, are you there to bring him off?)
SEJ.   Let Cæsar
No more then urge a point so contrary
To Cæsar's greatness, the grieved sen-
    ate's vows,
Or Rome's necessity.
(GAL.   He comes about.
ARR. More nimbly than Vertumnus.)
TIB.   For the public,
I may be drawn to show I can neglect
All private aims, though I affect my
    rest;
But, if the senate still command me
    serve,
I must be glad to practice my obedience.
(ARR. You must and will, sir. We do
    know it.)
SEN.   "Cæsar,   141
Live long and happy, great and royal
    Cæsar;
The gods preserve thee and thy modesty,
Thy wisdom and thy innocence!" [5]
(ARR.   Where is 't?
The prayer is made before the subject.)
SEN.   "Guard
His meekness, Jove, his piety, his care,
His bounty—"
ARR. [*Aside.*]   And his subtilty, I'll put
    in;

---

[1] Jonson's marginal note reads, "A form of
speaking they had."
[2] Supposed seat of the emotions such as
laughter.

[3] Jonson's marginal note reads, "A wreath
of laurel."   [4] Opposite.
[5] Jonson's marginal note reads, "Another
form."

Yet he'll keep that himself, without the
  gods.
All prayers are vain for him.
TIB.   We will not hold
Your patience, fathers, with long answer,
  but   150
Shall still contend [1] to be what you de-
  sire,
And work to satisfy so great a hope.
Proceed to your affairs.
ARR. [Aside.]   Now, Silius, guard thee;
The curtain's drawing. Afer advanceth.
PRÆ.   Silence!
AFER. Cite Caius Silius.
PRÆ.   Caius Silius!
SIL.   Here.
AFER. The triumph that thou hadst in
  Germany
For thy late victory on Sacrovir,
Thou hast enjoyed so freely, Caius Silius,
As no man it envied thee; nor would
  Cæsar
Or Rome admit that thou wert then de-
  frauded   160
Of any honors thy deserts could claim
In the fair service of the commonwealth;
But now, if after all their loves and
  graces
(Thy actions and their courses being dis-
  covered)
It shall appear to Cæsar and this senate,
Thou hast defiled those glories with thy
  crimes—
SIL. Crimes?
AFER.   Patience, Silius.
SIL.   Tell thy moil [2] of patience;
I am a Roman. What are my crimes?
  Proclaim them.
Am I too rich, too honest for the times?
Have I or treasure, jewels, land, or
  houses   170
That some informer gapes for? Is my
  strength
Too much to be admitted, or my knowl-
  edge?
These now are crimes.
AFER.   Nay, Silius, if the name
Of crime so touch thee, with what im-
  potence
Wilt thou endure the matter to be
  searched?
SIL. I tell thee, Afer, with more scorn than
  fear:

[1] Strive.   [2] Mule.

Employ your mercenary tongue and art.
Where's my accuser?
VAR.   Here.
ARR. [Aside.]   Varro? The consul?
Is he thrust in?
VAR.   'Tis I accuse thee, Silius.
Against the majesty of Rome and
  Cæsar,   180
I do pronounce thee here a guilty cause,
First, of beginning and occasioning,
Next, drawing out the war in Gallia,
For which thou late triumph'st; dissem-
  bling long
That Sacrovir to be an enemy,
Only to make thy entertainment [3] more,
Whilst thou and thy wife Sosia polled [4]
  the province—
Wherein, with sordid-base desire of gain,
Thou hast discredited thy actions' worth,
And been a traitor to the state.
SIL.   Thou liest! 190
ARR. [Aside.] I thank thee, Silius; speak
  so still and often.
VAR. If I not prove it, Cæsar, but injustly
Have called him into trial, here I bind
Myself to suffer what I claim gainst him,
And yield to have what I have spoke,
  confirmed
By judgment of the court and all good
  men.
SIL. Cæsar, I crave to have my cause
  deferred,
Till this man's consulship be out.
TIB.   We cannot,
  Nor may we grant it.
SIL.   Why? Shall he design [5]
My day of trial? Is he my accuser? 200
And must he be my judge?
TIB.   It hath been usual,
And is a right that custom hath allowed
The magistrate, to call forth private men
And to appoint their day, which privilege
We may not in the consul see infringed,
By whose deep watches and industrious
  care
It is so labored, as the commonwealth
Receive no loss, by any oblique course.
SIL. Cæsar, thy fraud is worse than vio-
  lence.
TIB. Silius, mistake us not; we dare not
  use   210

[3] Reward, proceeds.
[4] Plundered by extortion.
[5] Designate.

The credit of the consul to thy wrong,
But only do preserve his place and power
So far as it concerns the dignity
And honor of the state.

ARR.   Believe him, Silius.

COT. Why, so he may, Arruntius.

ARR.   I say so;
And he may choose too.

TIB.   By the Capitol
And all our gods, but that the dear
    republic,
Our sacred laws, and just authority
Are interested [1] therein, I should be
    silent.

AFER. Please Cæsar to give way unto his
    trial.   220
He shall have justice.

SIL.   Nay, I shall have law;
Shall I not, Afer? Speak!

AFER.   Would you have mo[re?] [2]

SIL. No, my well-spoken man, I would no
    more;
Nor less, might I enjoy it natural,
Not taught to speak unto your present
    ends,
Free from thine, his, and all your unkind
    handling,
Furious enforcing, most unjust pre-
    suming,
Malicious and manifold applying,
Foul wresting, and impossible construc-
    tion.

AFER. He raves, he raves!

SIL.   Thou durst not tell me so,   230
Hadst thou not Cæsar's warrant. I can
    see
Whose power condemns me.

VAR.   This betrays his spirit;
This doth enough declare him what he is.

SIL. What am I? Speak.

VAR.   An enemy to the state.

SIL. Because I am an enemy to thee,
And such corrupted ministers o' the
    state,
That here art made a present instru-
    ment
To gratify it with thine own disgrace.

SEJ. This, to the consul, is most insolent,
And impious!

SIL.   Ay, take part. Reveal yourselves.
Alas! I scent not your confed'racies,   241

---

[1] Concerned.

[2] Remainder of the word is dropped out in the
original.

Your plots, and combinations? I not
    know
Minion Sejanus hates me, and that all
This boast of law and law is but a form,
A net of Vulcan's filing, a mere ingine
To take that life by a pretext of justice,
Which you pursue in malice? I want
    brain
Or nostril to persuade me that your ends
And purposes are made to what they are,
Before my answer? O, you equal gods,
Whose justice not a world of wolf-turned
    men   251
Shall make me to accuse (howe'er pro-
    voke[d]),
Have I for this so oft engaged myself?
Stood in the heat and fervor of a fight,
When Phœbus sooner hath forsook the
    day
Than I the field, against the blue-eyed
    Gauls,
And crispéd [3] Germans, when our Roman
    eagles
Have fanned the fire with their laboring
    wings,
And no blow dealt that left not death
    behind it;
When I have charged, alone, into the
    troops   260
Of curled Sicambrians, routed them, and
    came
Not off with backward ensigns of a slave,
But forward marks, wounds on my breast
    and face,
Were meant to thee, O Cæsar, and thy
    Rome?
And have I this return? Did I, for this,
Perform so noble and so brave defeat
On Sacrovir? O Jove, let it become me
To boast my deeds, when he whom they
    concern
Shall thus forget them.

AFER.   Silius, Silius,
These are the common customs of thy
    blood   270
When it is high with wine, as now with
    rage.
This well agrees with that intemperate
    vaunt
Thou lately mad'st at Agrippina's table
That, when all other of the troops were
    prone
To fall into rebellion, only yours

---

[3] Curled-haired.

Remained in their obedience. You were
he
That saved the empire, which had then
been lost
Had but your legions there rebelled or
mutined; [1]
Your virtue met and fronted every peril.
You gave to Cæsar and to Rome their
surety.   280
Their name, their strength, their spirit,
and their state,
Their being was a donative from you.
ARR. [*Aside.*] Well worded, and most like
an orator.
TIB. Is this true, Silius?
SIL.   Save thy question, Cæsar;
Thy spy of famous credit hath affirmed
it.
ARR. [*Aside.*] Excellent Roman!
SAB. [*Aside.*]   He doth answer stoutly.
SEJ. If this be so, there needs no farder
cause
Of crime against him.
VAR.   What can more impeach
The royal dignity and state of Cæsar
Than to be urgéd with a benefit   290
He cannot pay.
COT.   In this, all Cæsar's fortune
Is made unequal to the courtesy.
LAT. His means are clean destroyed that
should requite.
GAL. [*Ironically.*] Nothing is great enough
for Silius' merit.
ARR. [*Aside.*] Gallus on that side too?
SIL.   Come, do not hunt
And labor so about for circumstance
To make him guilty whom you have
foredoomed.
Take shorter ways; I'll meet your pur-
poses.
The words were mine, and more I now
will say:
Since I have done thee that great service,
Cæsar,   300
Thou still hast feared me; and, in place
of grace,
Returned me hatred; so soon all best
turns,
With doubtful [2] princes, turn deep in-
juries
In estimation, when they greater rise
Than can be answered. Benefits, with
you,

Are of no longer pleasure than you can
With ease restore them; that transcended
once,
Your studies are not how to thank, but
kill.
It is your nature to have all men slaves
To you, but you acknowledging to none.
The means that makes your greatness
must not come   311
In mention of it; if it do, it takes
So much away, you think; and that
which helped
Shall soonest perish, if it stand in eye,
Where it may front [3] or but upbraid the
high.
COT. Suffer him speak no more.
VAR.   Note but his spirit.
AFER. This shows him in the rest.
LAT.   Let him be censured.[4]
SEJ. He hath spoke enough to prove him
Cæsar's foe.
COT. His thoughts look through his words.
SEJ.   A censure!
SIL.   Stay,
Stay, most officious senate, I shall
straight   320
Delude thy fury. Silius hath not placed
His guards within him, against Fortune's
spite,
So weakly but he can escape your gripe
That are but hands of Fortune. She
herself,
When Virtue doth oppose, must lose her
threats.
All that can happen in humanity,
The frown of Cæsar, proud Sejanus'
hatred,
Base Varro's spleen, and Afer's bloodying
tongue,
The senate's servile flattery, and these
Mustered to kill, I am fortified against,
And can look down upon; they are be-
neath me.   331
It is not life whereof I stand enamored,
Nor shall my end make me accuse my
fate.
The coward and the valiant man must
fall;
Only the cause, and manner how, dis-
cerns them[5]—
Which then are gladdest, when they cost
us dearest.

[1] Mutinied.   [2] Suspicious.
[3] Affront.   [4] Judged.
[5] Distinguishes them from each other.

Romans, if any here be in this senate,
Would know to mock Tiberius' tyranny,
Look upon Silius, and so learn to die.
                                    [*Stabs himself.*] [1]
VAR. O desperate act!
ARR. [*Aside.*]   An honorable hand! 340
TIB. Look, is he dead?
SAB. [*Aside.*]   'Twas nobly strook, and
    home.
ARR. [*Aside.*] My thought did prompt him
    to it. Farewell, Silius!
Be famous ever for thy great example.
TIB. We are not pleased in this sad acci-
    dent,
That thus hath stalléd,[2] and abused our
    mercy,
Intended to preserve thee, noble Roman,
And to prevent thy hopes.
ARR. [*Aside.*]   Excellent wolf!
Now he is full, he howls.
SEJ.   Cæsar doth wrong
His dignity and safety thus to mourn
The deserved end of so professed a
    traitor,   350
And doth, by this his lenity, instruct
Others as factious to the like offense.
TIB. The confiscation merely of his state
Had been enough.
ARR. [*Aside.*]   O, that was gaped for
    then?
VAR. Remove the body.
SEJ.   Let citation
Go out for Sosia.
GAL.   Let her be proscribed;
And for the goods, I think it fit that half
Go to the treasure,[3] half unto the chil-
    dren.
LEP. With leave of Cæsar, I would think
    that fourth
Part, which the law doth cast on the
    informers,   360
Should be enough; the rest go to the
    children—
Wherein the prince shall show humanity
And bounty, not to force them by their
    want,
Which in their parent's trespass they
    deserved,
To take ill courses.
TIB.   It shall please us.
ARR. [*Aside.*]   Ay,
Out of necessity. This Lepidus

---

[1] From 1692 edn.   [3] Treasury.
[2] Forestalled.

Is grave and honest, and I have observed
A moderation still in all his censures.
SAB. [*Aside.*] And bending to the better.—
    Stay, who's this?
Cremutius Cordus? What? Is he brought
    in?   370
ARR. [*Aside.*] More blood unto the ban-
    quet? Noble Cordus,
I wish thee good; be as thy writings, free
And honest.
TIB.   What is he?
SEJ.   For th' annals, Cæsar.

[*Enter*] *Præco*[*nes*], *Cordus* [*with Guards*],
                              Satrius, Natta.

[PRÆ.] Cremutius Cordus!
COR.   Here.
PRÆ.   Satrius Secundus,
Pinnarius Natta, you are his accusers.
ARR. [*Aside.*]   Two of Sejanus' blood-
    hounds, whom he breeds
With human flesh, to bay at citizens.
AFER. Stand forth before the senate, and
    confront him.
SAT. I do accuse thee here, Cremutius
    Cordus,
To be a man factious and dangerous, 380
A sower of sedition in the state,
A turbulent and discontented spirit,
Which I will prove from thine own writ-
    ings here,
The annals thou hast published, where
    thou bit'st
The present age, and with a viper's
    tooth,
Being a member of it, dar'st that ill
Which never yet degenerous [4] bastard
    did
Upon his parent.
NAT.   To this I subscribe,
And, forth [5] a world of more particu-
    lars,
Instance in only one: comparing men
And times, thou praisest Brutus, and
    affirm'st   391
That Cassius was the last of all the
    Romans.
COT. How! What are we then?
VAR.   What is Cæsar? Nothing?
AFER. My lords, this strikes at every
    Roman's private,[6]

---

[4] Degenerate.   [6] Private interest.
[5] From.

In whom reigns gentry and estate of
   spirit,[1]
To have a Brutus brought in parallel,
A parricide, an enemy of his country,
Ranked, and preferred to any real worth
That Rome now holds. This is most
   strangely invective,
Most full of spite, and insolent up-
   braiding.   400
Nor is 't the time alone is here disprized,[2]
But the whole man of time, yea, Cæsar's
   self,
Brought in disvalue; and he aimed at
   most
By oblique glance of his licentious pen.
Cæsar, if Cassius were the last of Ro-
   mans,
Thou hast no name.
TIB.   Let's hear him answer. Silence!
COR. So innocent I am of fact,[3] my lords,
As but my words are argued, yet those
   words
Not reaching either prince or prince's
   parent—
The which your law of treason compre-
   hends.   410
Brutus and Cassius I am charged t' have
   praised,
Whose deeds, when many more besides
   myself
Have writ, not one hath mentioned with-
   out honor.
Great Titus Livius, great for eloquence
And faith amongst us, in his history
With so great praises Pompey did extol,
As oft Augustus called him a Pompeian:
Yet this not hurt their friendship. In his
   book
He often names Scipio, Afranius,
Yea, the same Cassius, and this Brutus
   too,   420
As worthi'st men—not thieves and par-
   ricides,
Which notes upon their fames are now
   imposed.
Asinius Pollio's writings quite throughout
Give them a noble memory; so Messala
Renowned his general, Cassius; yet both
   these
Lived with Augustus, full of wealth and
   honors.

To Cicero's book, where Cato was heaved
   up
Equal with heaven, what else did Cæsar
   answer,
Being then dictator, but with a penned
   oration,
As if before the judges? Do but see   430
Antonius' letters; read but Brutus'
   pleadings—
What vile reproach they hold against
   Augustus,
False, I confess, but with much bitter-
   ness.
The epigrams of Bibaculus and Catullus
Are read, full stuffed with spite of both
   the Cæsars;
Yet deified Julius, and no less Augustus,
Both bore them, and contemned them.
   I not know,
Promptly to speak it, whether done with
   more
Temper, or wisdom; for such obloquies
If they despiséd be, they die suppressed;
But, if with rage acknowledged, they are
   confessed.   441
The Greeks I slip,[4] whose license not
   alone
But also lust did scape unpunishéd,
Or where someone, by chance, exception
   took,
He words with words revenged. But in
   my work
What could be aimed more free,[5] or
   farder off
From the time's scandal, than to write of
   those
Whom death from grace or hatred had
   exempted?
Did I, with Brutus and with Cassius,
Armed and possessed of the Philippi
   fields,   450
Incense the people in the civil cause,
With dangerous speeches? Or do they,
   being slain
Seventy years since, as by their images,
Which not the conqueror hath defaced,
   appears,
Retain that guilty memory with writers?
Posterity pays every man his honor.
Nor shall there want, though I con-
   demnéd am,
That [6] will not only Cassius well approve,

---

[1] Gentle blood and spirit befitting one of rank.
[2] Contemptuously depreciated.
[3] Deed.
[4] Pass over.   [6] Those who.
[5] Innocently.

And of great Brutus' honor mindful be,
But that will also mention make of
   me.   460
ARR. [*Aside.*] Freely and nobly spoken!
SAB. [*Aside.*]   With good temper;
I like him, that he is not moved with
   passion.
ARR. [*Aside.*] He puts hem to their whis-
   per.
TIB.   Take him hence;
We shall determine of him at next sit-
   ting.
        [*Exeunt Guards with Cordus.*]
COT. Meantime, give order that his books
   be burnt,
   To the ædiles.
SEJ.   You have well advised.
AFER. It fits not such licentious things
   should live
   T' upbraid the age.
ARR.   If th' age were good, they might.
LAT. Let hem be burnt.
GAL.   All sought and burnt today.
PRÆ. The court is up; lictors, resume the
   fasces.   470
[*Exeunt All but*] *Arruntius, Sabinus, Lepidus.*
[ARR.] Let hem be burnt! O, how ridic-
   ulous
   Appears the senate's brainless diligence,
   Who think they can, with present power,
      extinguish
   The memory of all succeeding times!
SAB. 'Tis true, when, contrary, the punish-
   ment
   Of wit doth make th' authority in-
      crease.
   Nor do they aught, that use this cruelty
   Of interdiction, and this rage of burn-
      ing,
   But purchase to themselves rebuke and
      shame,
   And to the writers an eternal name. 480
LEP. It is an argument the times are
   sore,
   When virtue cannot safely be advanced,
   Nor vice reproved.
ARR.   Ay, noble Lepidus;
   Augustus well foresaw what we should
      suffer
   Under Tiberius, when he did pronounce
   The Roman race most wretched, that
      should live
   Between so slow jaws, and so long
      a-bruising.   [*Exeunt.*]

[SCENE ii.

A room in the palace.]

Tiberius, Sejanus.

[TIB.] This business hath succeeded well,
   Sejanus,
   And quite removed all jealousy of prac-
      tice
   Gainst Agrippina and our nephews. Now
   We must bethink us how to plant our in-
      gines
   For th' other pair, Sabinus and Arrun-
      tius,
   And Gallus too; howe'er he flatter us,
   His heart we know.
SEJ.   Give it some respite, Cæsar.
   Time shall mature and bring to perfect
      crown
   What we, with so good vultures,[1] have
      begun;
   Sabinus shall be next.
TIB.   Rather Arruntius. 10
SEJ. By any means, preserve him. His
   frank tongue,
   Being lent the reins, will take away all
      thought
   Of malice, in your course against the
      rest.
   We must keep him to stalk with.
TIB.   Dearest head,
   To thy most fortunate design I yield it.
SEJ. Sir, I have been so long trained up
   in grace,
   First with your father, great Augustus,
      since
   With your most happy bounties so
      familiar,
   As I not sooner would commit my
      hopes
   Or wishes to the gods than to your
      ears.   20
   Nor have I ever yet been covetous
   Of overbright and dazzling honors—
      rather
   To watch and travail in great Cæsar's
      safety,
   With the most common soldier.
TIB.   'Tis confessed.
SEJ. The only gain, and which I count
   most fair
   Of all my fortunes, is that mighty Cæsar

   [1] *I.e.,* auspiciously, with reference to augury
by means of birds.

Hath thought me worthy his alliance.[1]
Hence
Begin my hopes.

Tib. H'mh?

Sej. I have heard Augustus,
In the bestowing of his daughter, thought
But even [2] of gentlemen of Rome; if
  so— 30
I know not how to hope so great a favor—
But, if a husband should be sought for
  Livia,
And I be had in mind, as Cæsar's friend,
I would but use the glory of the kindred.
It should not make me slothful, or less
  caring
For Cæsar's state; it were enough to me
It did confirm and strengthen my weak
  house
Against the now-unequal opposition
Of Agrippina; and for dear regard
Unto my children, this I wish. Myself 40
Have no ambition farder than to end
My days in service of so dear a master.

Tib. We cannot but commend thy piety,
Most loved Sejanus, in acknowledging
Those bounties, which we, faintly, such
  remember.
But to thy suit. The rest of mortal men,
In all their drifts and counsels, pursue
  profit;
Princes alone are of a different sort,
Directing their main actions still to
  fame.
We therefore will take time to think and
  answer. 50
For Livia she can best, herself, resolve
If she will marry, after Drusus, or
Continue in the family; besides,
She hath a mother, and a grandame yet,
Whose nearer counsels she may guide
  her by;
But I will simply deal. That enmity
Thou fear'st in Agrippina would burn
  more,
If Livia's marriage should, as 'twere in
  parts,
Divide th' imperial house; an emulation
Between the women might break forth,
  and discord 60
Ruin the sons and nephews on both
  hands.

[1] Jonson's marginal note reads, "His daughter was betrothed to Claudius his son."
[2] Without impartiality.

What if it cause some present difference?
Thou art not safe, Sejanus, if thou
  prove [3] it.
Canst thou believe that Livia, first the
  wife
To Caius Cæsar, then my Drusus, now
Will be contented to grow old with thee,
Born but a private gentleman of Rome,
And raise thee with her loss, if not her
  shame?
Or, say that I should wish it, cans't
  thou think
The senate or the people (who have
  seen 70
Her brother, father, and our ancestors
In highest place of empire) will endure it?
The state thou hold'st already, is in
  talk;
Men murmur at thy greatness; and the
  nobles
Stick not, in public, to upbraid thy
  climbing
Above our father's favors, or thy scale,
And dare accuse me, from their hate to
  thee.
Be wise, dear friend. We would not hide
  these things,
For friendship's dear respect. Nor will
  we stand
Adverse to thine or Livia's design-
  ments. 80
What we have purposed to thee, in our
  thought,
And with what near degrees of love to
  bind thee,
And make thee equal to us, for the pres-
  ent
We will forbear to speak. Only, thus
  much
Believe, our loved Sejanus, we not know
That height in blood or honor, which
  thy virtue
And mind to us may not aspire [4] with
  merit.
And this we'll publish on all watched
  occasion
The senate or the people shall present.

Sej. I am restored, and to my sense
  again, 90
Which I had lost in this so blinding suit.
Cæsar hath taught me better to refuse
Than I knew how to ask. How pleaseth
  Cæsar

[3] Try, attempt. [4] Aspire to.

T' embrace my late advice for leaving
   Rome?
Tib. We are resolved.
Sej.   Here are some motives more,
          [*Gives him a paper.*]
Which I have thought on since, may
   more confirm.
Tib. Careful Sejanus! We will straight
   peruse them.
   Go forward in our main design, and
      prosper.   [*Exit.*]
Sej. If those but take, I shall. Dull, heavy
   Cæsar!
Wouldst thou tell me thy favors were
   made crimes,   100
And that my fortunes were esteemed thy
   faults,
That thou for me wert hated, and not
   think
I would with wingéd haste prevent that
   change,
When thou might'st win all to thyself
   again
By forfeiture of me?   Did those fond
   words
Fly swifter from thy lips than this my
   brain,
This sparkling forge, created me an
   armor
T' encounter chance and thee?   Well,
   read my charms,
And may they lay that hold upon thy
   senses,
As thou hadst snuffed up hemlock, or
   ta'en down   110
The juice of poppy and of mandrakes.
   Sleep,
Voluptuous Cæsar, and security
Seize on thy stupid powers, and leave
   them dead
To public cares; awake but to thy
   lusts,
The strength of which makes thy li-
   bidinous soul
Itch to leave Rome—and I have thrust
   it on,
With blaming of the city business,
The multitude of suits, the confluence
Of suitors, then their importunacies,
The manifold distractions he must
   suffer,   120
Besides ill-rumors, envies, and re-
   proaches,
All which a quiet and retiréd life,

Larded with ease and pleasure, did
   avoid,
And yet for any weighty and great
   affair,
The fittest place to give the soundest
   counsels.
By this shall I remove him both from
   thought
And knowledge of his own most dear
   affairs;
Draw all despatches through my private
   hands;
Know his designments, and pursue mine
   own;
Make mine own strengths by giving suits
   and places,   130
Conferring dignities and offices;
And these that hate me now, wanting
   access
To him, will make their envy none, or
   less;
For, when they see me arbiter of all,
They must observe, or else with Cæsar
   fall.   [*Exit.*]

[Scene iii.

Another room in the palace.]

Tiberius, Servus.[1]

[Tib.] To marry Livia? Will no less,
   Sejanus,
Content thy aims? No lower object?
   Well!
Thou know'st how thou art wrought into
   our trust,
Woven in our design, and think'st we
   must
Now use thee, whatso'er thy projects
   are.
'Tis true—but yet with caution and fit
   care.
And, now we better think—who's there
   within?

[*Enter Servus.*]

Ser. Cæsar?
Tib. [*Aside.*]   To leave our journey off
   were sin
Gainst our decreed delights, and would
   appear
Doubt, or, what less becomes a prince,
   low fear.   20

----
[1] *I.e.*, a servant, who enters later.

Yet doubt hath law, and fears have their
    excuse,
Where princes' states plead necessary
    use,
As ours doth now more in Sejanus'
    pride,
Than all fell [1] Agrippina's hates beside.
Those are the dreadful enemies we raise
With favors and make dangerous with
    praise;
The injured by us may have will alike,
But 'tis the favorite hath the power to
    strike;
And fury ever boils more high and
    strong,
Heat' [2] with ambition, than revenge of
    wrong.   20
'Tis then a part of supreme skill, to
    grace
No man too much, but hold a certain
    space
Between th' ascender's rise and thine
    own flat,[3]
Lest, when all rounds [4] be reached, his
    aim be that.
'Tis thought—[To Servus.] Is Macro in
    the palace? See.
If not, go seek him, to come to us.—[Exit
    Servus.] He
Must be the organ we must work by
    now,
Though none less apt for trust; need
    doth allow
What choice would not. I have heard
    that aconite,
Being timely taken, hath a healing
    might   30
Against the scorpion's stroke; the proof
    we'll give,
That, while two poisons wrastle, we may
    live.
He hath a spirit too working [5] to be
    used
But to th' encounter of his like; ex-
    cused
Are wiser sov'reigns then, that raise
    one ill
Against another, and both safely kill.
The prince that feeds great natures,
    they will sway him;
Who nourisheth a lion, must obey him.—

[Enter Servus with] Macro.[6]

Macro, we sent for you.
MAC.   I heard so, Cæsar.   39
TIB. Leave us awhile.—   [Exit Servus.]
    When you shall know, good Macro,
The causes of our sending and the ends,
You will then hearken nearer, and be
    pleased
You stand so high both in our choice and
    trust.
MAC. The humblest place in Cæsar's
    choice or trust
May make glad Macro proud, with-
    out ambition
Save to do Cæsar service.
TIB.   Leave our courtings.
We are in purpose, Macro, to depart
The city for a time, and see Campania,
Not for our pleasures, but to dedicate
A pair of temples, one to Jupiter   50
At Capua, th' other at Nola to Augustus,
In which great work, perhaps, our stay
    will be
Beyond our will produced.[7] Now, since
    we are
Not ignorant what danger may be born
Out of our shortest absence, in a state
So subject unto envy, and embroiled
With hate and faction, we have thought
    on thee,
Amongst a field of Romans, worthiest
    Macro,
To be our eye and ear, to keep strict
    watch
On Agrippina, Nero, Drusus, ay,   60
And on Sejanus—not that we distrust
His loyalty, or do repent one grace
Of all that heap we have conferred on
    him
(For that were to disparage our elec-
    tion,[8]
And call that judgment now in doubt,
    which then
Seemed as unquestioned as an oracle);
But greatness hath his cankers. Worms
    and moths
Breed out of too fit matter, in the things
Which after they consume, transferring
    quite
The substance of their makers int'
    themselves.   70

---

[1] Fierce.   [4] *I.e.*, of the ladder.
[2] Heated.   [5] Active.
[3] Level.

[6] The name *Tiberius* is repeated here.
[7] Prolonged.   [8] Selection.

Macro is sharp, and apprehends. Besides,
I know him subtile, close, wise, and well-read
In man, and his large nature; he hath studied
Affections, passions, knows their springs, their ends,
Which way and whether they will work; 'tis proof
Enough of his great merit that we trust him.
Then to a point (because our conference
Cannot be long without suspicion):
Here, Macro, we assign thee both to spy,
Inform, and chastise; think, and use thy means,   80
Thy ministers, what, where, on whom thou wilt;
Explore, plot, practice. All thou dost in this
Shall be, as if the senate or the laws
Had giv'n it privilege, and thou thence styled
The savior both of Cæsar and of Rome,
We will not take thy answer but in act,
Whereto, as thou proceed'st, we hope to hear
By trusted messengers. If 't be inquired
Wherefore we called you, say you have in charge
To see our chariots ready, and our horse.   90
Be still our loved and, shortly, honored Macro.   [Exit.]
MAC. I will not ask why Cæsar bids do this,
But joy that he bids me. It is the bliss
Of courts to be employed, no matter how;
A prince's power makes all his actions virtue.
We whom he works by are dumb instruments,
To do, but not inquire; his great intents
Are to be served, not searched. Yet, as that bow
Is most in hand whose owner best doth know
T' affect [1] his aims, so let that statesman hope   100
Most use, most price, can hit his prince's scope.[2]

Nor must he look at what or whom to strike,
But loose [3] at all; each mark must be alike.
Were it to plot against the fame, the life
Of one with whom I twinned; remove a wife
From my warm side, as loved as is the air;
Practice away each parent; draw mine heir
In compass,[4] though but one; work all my kin
To swift perdition; leave no untrained engine [5]
For friendship, or for innocence; nay, make   110
The gods all guilty; I would undertake
This, being imposed me, both with gain and ease.
The way to rise is to obey and please.
He that will thrive in state, he must neglect
The trodden paths that truth and right respect,
And prove new, wilder ways; for virtue there
Is not that narrow thing she is elsewhere.
Men's fortune there is virtue; reason, their will;
Their license, law; and their observance, skill.
Occasion is their foil; conscience, their stain;   120
Profit, their luster; and what else is, vain.
If then it be the lust of Cæsar's power
T' have raised Sejanus up, and in an hour
O'erturn him, tumbling, down from height of all,
We are his ready engine, and his fall
May be our rise. It is no uncouth [6] thing
To see fresh buildings from old ruins spring.   [Exit.]

CHORUS—of Musicians.

[1] Know how to effect.   [2] Mark.
[3] Shoot.
[4] Into a trap.
[5] Instrument.
[6] Unknown.

Act IV. [Scene i.

A room in Agrippina's house.]

Gallus, Agrippina, Nero, Drusus, Caligula.[1]

[Gal.] You must have patience, royal Agrippina.

Agr. I must have vengeance first; and that were nectar
Unto my famished spirits. O, my fortune,
Let it be sudden thou prepar'st against me;
Strike all my powers of understanding blind,
And ignorant of destiny to come!
Let me not fear, that cannot hope.

Gal.   Dear princess,
These tyrannies[2] on yourself are worse than Cæsar's.

Agr. Is this the happiness of being born great?
Still to be aimed at? Still to be suspected?   10
To live the subject of all jealousies?
At least the color[3] made, if not the ground,
To every painted danger? Who would not
Choose once to fall than thus to hang forever?

Gal. You might be safe if you would—

Agr.   What, my Gallus?
Be lewd Sejanus' strumpet? Or the bawd
To Cæsar's lusts he now is gone to practice?
Not these are safe, where nothing is. Yourself,
While thus you stand but by me, are not safe.
Was Silius safe? Or the good Sosia safe?   20
Or was my niece, dear Claudia Pulchra, safe?
Or innocent Furnius? They that latest have
(By being made guilty) added reputation
To Afer's eloquence? O, foolish friends,
Could not so fresh example warn your loves,
But you must buy my favors with that loss

Unto yourselves, and when you might perceive
That Cæsar's cause of raging must forsake him
Before his will? Away, good Gallus, leave me.
Here to be seen is danger; to speak, treason;   30
To do me least observance is called faction.
You are unhappy in me, and I in all.
Where are my sons, Nero and Drusus? We
Are they be shot at; let us fall apart,
Not in our ruins sepulcher our friends.
Or shall we do some action, like offense,[4]
To mock their studies that would make us faulty,
And frustrate practice by preventing[5] it?
The danger's like; for what they can contrive
They will make good. No innocence is safe   40
When power contests; nor can they trespass more,
Whose only being was all crime before.

[*Enter Nero, Drusus, and Caligula.*]

Nero. You hear Sejanus is come back from Cæsar?

Gal. No. How? Disgraced?

Dru.   More gracéd now than ever.

Gal. By what mischance?

Cal.   A fortune like enough
Once to be bad.

Dru.   But turned too good to both.

Gal. What was 't?

Nero.   Tiberius sitting at his meat,
In a farmhouse they call Spelunca, sited
By the seaside, among the Fundane hills,
Within a natural cave, part of the grot   50
About the entry fell and overwhelmed
Some of the waiters; others ran away;
Only Sejanus with his knees, hands, face,
O'erhanging Cæsar, did oppose himself
To the remaining ruins, and was found
In that so laboring posture by the soldiers
That came to succor him. With which adventure

---

[1] Last three enter later.   [2] Cruelties.
[3] Pretext, although double meanings run through the sentence.
[4] Like what we are charged with.
[5] Anticipating.

He hath so fixed himself in Cæsar's trust
As thunder cannot move him, and is
    come
With all the height of Cæsar's praise to
    Rome.   60
AGR. And power to turn those ruins all
    on us,
And bury whole posterities beneath
    them.
Nero and Drusus and Caligula,
Your places are the next, and therefore
    most
In their offense. Think on your birth
    and blood,
Awake your spirits, meet their violence;
'Tis princely when a tyran doth oppose,
And is a fortune sent to exercise
Your virtue, as the wind doth try strong
    trees,
Who by vexation [1] grow more sound and
    firm.   70
After your father's fall, and uncle's fate,
What can you hope, but all the change
    of stroke
That force or sleight can give? Then
    stand upright;
And, though you do not act, yet suffer
    nobly.
Be worthy of my womb, and take strong
    cheer;
What we do know will come, we should
    not fear.   [*Exeunt.*]

[SCENE ii.

A room in the palace.]

Macro.

[MAC.] Returned so soon? Renewed in
    trust and grace?
Is Cæsar then so weak, or hath the
    place
But wrought this alteration with the
    air,
And he, on next remove, will all repair?
Macro, thou art engaged,[2] and what
    before
Was public, now must be thy private
    more.
The weal of Cæsar, fitness did imply;
But thine own fate confers necessity
On thy employment; and the thoughts
    borne nearest

[1] Shaking.   [2] Entangled.

Unto ourselves, move swiftest still and
    dearest.   10
If he recover, thou art lost; yea, all
The weight of preparation to his fall
Will turn on thee, and crush thee. There-
    fore strike
Before he settle, to prevent the like
Upon thyself. He doth his vantage
    know,
That makes [3] it home, and gives the
    foremost blow.   [*Exit.*]

[SCENE iii.

An upper room in Agrippina's house.]

Latiaris, Rufus, Opsius.

[LAT.] It is a service great Sejanus will
See well requited, and accept of nobly.
Here place yourselves between the roof
    and ceiling,
And, when I bring him to his words of
    danger,
Reveal yourselves, and take him.
RUF.   Is he come?
LAT. I'll now go fetch him.   [*Exit.*]
OPS.   With good speed.—I long
To merit from the state in such an action.
RUF. I hope it will obtain the consulship
    For one of us.
OPS.   We cannot think of less,
To bring in one so dangerous as Sa-
    binus.   10
RUF. He was a follower of Germanicus,
And still is an observer of [4] his wife
And children, though they be declined
    in grace—
A daily visitant, keeps them company
In private and in public, and is noted
To be the only client of the house.
Pray Jove, he will be free [5] to Latiaris.
OPS. H' is allied to him, and doth trust
    him well.
RUF. And he'll requite his trust?
OPS.   To do an office 19
So grateful to the state, I know no man
But would strain nearer bands than
    kindred—
RUF.   List!
I hear them come.
OPS.   Shift to our holes with silence.
                    [*They retire.*]

[3] Strikes.
[4] One who shows respectful attentions to.
[5] Outspoken.

[*Enter*] *Latiaris, Sabinus.*

[LAT.] It is a noble constancy you show
To this afflicted house, that not like
others,
The friends of season, you do follow
fortune,
And, in the winter of their fate, forsake
The place whose glories warmed you.
You are just,
And worthy such a princely patron's
love,
As was the world's-renowned Germani-
cus,
Whose ample merit when I call to
thought,   30
And see his wife and issue objects made
To so much envy, jealousy, and hate,
It makes me ready to accuse the gods
Of negligence, as men of tyranny.
SAB. They must be patient; so must we.
LAT.   O Jove,
What will become of us or of the times,
When to be high or noble are made
crimes,
When land and treasure are most dan-
gerous faults?
SAB. Nay, when our table, yea, our bed
assaults
Our peace and safety? When our writ-
ings are,   40
By any envious instruments that dare
Apply them to the guilty, made to speak
What they will have to fit their tyran-
nous wreak? [1]
When ignorance is scarcely innocence,
And knowledge made a capital offense?
When not so much but the bare empty
shade
Of liberty is reft us, and we made
The prey to greedy vultures and vile
spies,
That first transfix us with their murder-
ing eyes?
LAT. Methinks the genius of the Roman
race   50
Should not be so extinct, but that bright
flame
Of liberty might be revived again
(Which no good man but with his life
should lose)
And we not sit like spent and patient
fools,

Still puffing in the dark at one poor coal,
Held on by hope, till the last spark is
out.
The cause is public, and the honor,
name,
The immortality of every soul
That is not bastard or a slave in Rome
Therein concerned; whereto, if men
would change   60
The wearied arm, and for the weighty
shield
So long sustained employ the ready
sword,
We might have some assurance of our
vows.
This ass's fortitude doth tire us all;
It must be active valor must redeem
Our loss, or none. The rock and our hard
steel
Should meet t' enforce those glorious
fires again,
Whose splendor cheered the world, and
heat gave life
No less than doth the sun's.
SAB.   'Twere better stay
In lasting darkness and despair of day. 70
No ill should force the subject undertake
Against the sovereign, more than hell
should make
The gods do wrong. A good man should
and must
Sit rather down with loss than rise un-
just,
Though, when the Romans first did yield
themselves
To one man's power, they did not mean
their lives,
Their fortunes, and their liberties should
be
His absolute spoil, as purchased by the
sword.
LAT. Why, we are worse, if to be slaves,
and bond
To Cæsar's slave, be such, the proud
Sejanus!   80
He that is all, does all, gives Cæsar leave
To hide his ulcerous and anointed face,
With his bald crown at Rhodes, while
he here stalks
Upon the heads of Romans and their
princes,
Familiarly to empire. [2]

---

[1] Vengeance.

[2] *I.e.*, as if accustomed to the state of an
emperor.

Sab. Now you touch
A point indeed, wherein he shows his art
As well as power.
Lat. And villainy in both.
Do you observe where Livia lodges?
How
Drusus came dead? What men have
been cut off?
Sab. Yes, those are things removed. I
nearer looked 90
Into his later practice, where he stands
Declared a master in his mystery.[1]
First, ere Tiberius went, he wrought
his fear
To think that Agrippina sought his
death;
Then put those doubts in her; sent her
oft word,
Under the show of friendship, to beware
Of Cæsar, for he laid to poison her;
Drave them to frowns, to mutual jeal-
ousies,
Which now in visible hatred are burst
out.
Since, he hath had his hired instru-
ments 100
To work on Nero, and to heave him up;
To tell him Cæsar's old, that all the
people,
Yea, all the army have their eyes on him;
That both do long to have him under-
take
Something of worth, to give the world
a hope;
Bids him to court their grace. The easy
youth
Perhaps gives ear, which straight he
writes to Cæsar,
And with this comment: "See yon
dangerous boy;
Note but the practice of the mother
there;
She's tying him for purposes at hand, 110
With men of sword." Here's Cæsar put
in fright
Gainst son and mother. Yet he leaves
not thus.
The second brother, Drusus, a fierce
nature
And fitter for his snares, because am-
bitious
And full of envy, him he clasps and
hugs,

[1] Profession. art.

Poisons with praise, tells him what
hearts he wears,
How bright he stands in popular ex-
pectance,
That Rome doth suffer with him in the
wrong
His mother does him, by preferring
Nero.
Thus sets he them asunder, each gainst
other, 120
Projects the course that serves him to
condemn,
Keeps in opinion of a friend to all,
And all drives on to ruin.
Lat. Cæsar sleeps,
And nods at this?
Sab. Would he might ever sleep,
Bogged in his filthy lusts!
[Opsius and Rufus rush in.]
Ops. Treason to Cæsar!
Ruf. Lay hands upon the traitor, Latiaris,
Or take the name thyself.
Lat. I am for Cæsar.
Sab. Am I then catched?
Ruf. How think you, sir? You are.
Sab. Spies of this head, so white, so full
of years!
Well, my most reverend monsters, you
may live 130
To see yourselves thus snared.
Ops. Away with him!
Lat. Hale him away!
Ruf. To be a spy for traitors
Is honorable vigilance.
Sab. You do well,
My most officious instruments of state,
Men of all uses. Drag me hence, away.
The year is well begun, and I fall fit
To be an off'ring to Sejanus. Go!
Ops. Cover him with his garments; hide
his face.
Sab. It shall not need. Forbear your rude
assault.
The fault's not shameful, villainy makes
a fault. [Exeunt.] 140

[Scene iv.

A street before Agrippina's house.]

Macro, Caligula.

[Mac.] Sir, but observe how thick your
dangers meet
In his clear drifts! Your mother and
your brothers,

Now cited to the senate; their friend
Gallus,
Feasted today by Cæsar, since com-
mitted!
Sabinus here we met, hurried to fetters!
The senators all strook with fear and
silence,
Save those whose hopes depend not on
good means,
But force their private prey from public
spoil.
And you must know, if here you stay,
your state
Is sure to be the subject of his hate,   10
As now the object.
CAL.   What would you advise me?
MAC. To go for Capreæ presently,[1] and
there
Give up yourself entirely to your uncle.
Tell Cæsar (since your mother is accused
To fly for succors[2] to Augustus' statue,
And to the army, with your brethren)
you
Have rather chose to place your aids in
him
Than live suspected, or in hourly fear
To be thrust out by bold Sejanus' plots—
Which you shall confidently urge to be   20
Most full of peril to the state and Cæsar,
As being laid to his peculiar ends,
And not to be let run with common
safety.
All which, upon the second, I'll make
plain,
So both shall love and trust with Cæsar
gain.
CAL. Away then; let's prepare us for our
journey.   [Exeunt.]

[SCENE V.

Another street.]

Arruntius.

[ARR.] Still dost thou suffer, heaven?
Will no flame,
No heat of sin, make thy just wrath to
boil
In thy distempered bosom, and o'er-
flow
The pitchy blazes of impiety,
Kindled beneath thy throne? Still canst
thou sleep,

Patient, while vice doth make an antic
face
At thy drad[3] power, and blow dust and
smoke
Into thy nostrils?   Jove, will nothing
wake thee?
Must vile Sejanus pull thee by the beard
Ere thou wilt open thy black-lidded
eye   10
And look him dead? Well! Snore on,
dreaming gods,
And let this last of that proud giant race
Heave mountain upon mountain gainst
your state.
Be good unto me, Fortune, and you
powers
Whom I, expostulating, have profaned;
I see (what's equal with a prodigy)
A great, a noble Roman, and an honest,
Live an old man!—O Marcus Lepidus,
When is our turn to bleed? Thyself
and I,
Without our boast, are a'most all the
few   20
Left to be honest in these impious times.

[Enter] Lepidus.[4]

[LEP.] What we are left to be, we will be,
Lucius,
Though tyranny did stare as wide as
death
To fright us from it.
ARR.   'T hath so on Sabinus.
LEP. I saw him now drawn from the Gem-
onies,[5]
And, what increased the direness of
the fact,
His faithful dog, upbraiding all us Ro-
mans,
Never forsook the corpse, but, seeing it
thrown
Into the stream, leaped in, and drowned
with it.   29
ARR. O act, to be envied him of[6] us men!
We are the next the hook lays hold on,
Marcus.
What are thy arts (good patriot, teach
them me)

[3] Dread.
[4] The name Arruntius is repeated here.
[5] Steps on the Aventine, down which corpses
of criminals were dragged by the executioner's
hook and thrown into the river.
[6] By.

[1] At once.
[2] Accused of flying for the right of asylum.

That have preserved thy hairs to this
　　white dye,
And kept so reverend and so dear a head
Safe on his comely shoulders?
LEP.　　　　　　　　　Arts, Arruntius?
None but the plain and passive fortitude
To suffer and be silent, never stretch
These arms against the torrent, live at
　　home
With my own thoughts and innocence
　　about me,
Not tempting the wolves' jaws—these
　　are my arts.　　　　　　　　　　40
ARR. I would begin to study hem, if I
　　thought
They would secure me. May I pray to
　　Jove
In secret and be safe? Ay, or aloud?
With open wishes? So I do not mention
Tiberius or Sejanus? Yes, I must,
If I speak out. 'Tis hard, that. May I
　　think,
And not be racked? What danger is 't
　　to dream?
Talk in one's sleep, or cough? Who
　　knows the law?
May I shake my head without a com-
　　ment? Say
It rains, or it holds up, and not be
　　thrown　　　　　　　　　　　　50
Upon the Gemonies? These now are
　　things
Whereon men's fortune, yea, their fate
　　depends.
Nothing hath privilege gainst the violent
　　ear.
No place, no day, no hour, we see, is
　　free
(Not our religious and most sacred
　　times)
From some one kind of cruelty; all
　　matter,
Nay, all occasion pleaseth. Madmen's
　　rage,
The idleness of drunkards, women's
　　nothing,
Jester's simplicity, all, all is good
That can be catched at. Nor is now th'
　　event [1]　　　　　　　　　　　60
Of any person, or for any crime,
To be expected,[2] for 'tis always one:
Death, with some little difference of
　　place,

Or time—what's this? Prince Nero?
　　Guarded?

[*Enter*] *Laco, Nero* [, *with Guards*].[3]

[LAC.] On, lictors, keep your way. My
　　lords, forbear.
On pain of Cæsar's wrath, no man at-
　　tempt
Speech with the prisoner.
NERO.　　　　　　Noble friends, be safe;
To lose yourselves for words were as
　　vain hazard
As unto me small comfort. Fare you
　　well!
Would all Rome's suff'rings in my fate
　　did dwell!　　　　　　　　　　　70
LAC. Lictors, away!
LEP.　　　　　　Where goes he, Laco?
LAC.　　　　　　　　　　　　　Sir,
H' is banished into Pontia by the
　　senate.
ARR. Do I see, and hear, and feel? May
　　I trust sense?
Or doth my phant'sy form it?
LEP.　　　　　　　Where's his brother?
LAC. Drusus is prisoner in the palace.
ARR.　　　　　　　　　　　　Ha!
I smell it now; 'tis rank. Where's Agrip-
　　pina?
LAC. The princess is confined to Panda-
　　taria.
ARR. Bolts, Vulcan, bolts for Jove! Phœ-
　　bus, thy bow;
Stern Mars, thy sword; and, blue-eyed
　　Maid, thy spear;
Thy club, Alcides—all the armory　　80
Of heaven is too little!—Ha! To guard
The gods, I meant. Fine, rare despatch!
　　This same
Was swiftly borne! Confined? Im-
　　prisoned? Banished?
Most tripartite! The cause, sir?
LAC.　　　　　　　　　Treason.
ARR.　　　　　　　　　　　　　O!
The complement of all accusings? That
Will hit, when all else fails.
LEP.　　　　　　This turn is strange!
But yesterday the people would not
　　hear,
Far less objected, but cried Cæsar's
　　letters

---

[1] Fate.　　　　　　　[2] Dreaded.

[3] The names *Lepidus* and *Arruntius* are repeated here.

Were false and forged, that all these
plots were malice,
And that the ruin of the prince's house 90
Was practiced gainst his knowledge.
Where are now
Their voices, now that they behold his
heirs
Locked up, disgraced, led into exile?

ARR.   Hushed.
Drowned in their bellies. Wild Sejanus'
breath
Hath, like a whirlwind, scattered that
poor dust
With this rude blast.—(*He turns to Laco
and the Rest.*) We'll talk no treason, sir,
If that be it you stand for. Fare you well.
We have no need of horse-leeches. Good
spy,
Now you are spied, begone.
           [*Exeunt Laco, Nero, and Guards.*]

LEP.   I fear you wrong him.
He has the voice to be an honest Roman.   100

ARR. And trusted to this office? Lepidus,
I'ld sooner trust Greek Sinon than a
man
Our state employs. He's gone; and be-
ing gone,
I dare tell you, whom I dare better
trust,
That our night-eyed Tiberius doth not
see
His minion's drifts; or, if he do, h' is not
So arrant subtile as we fools do take
him.
To breed a mungrel [1] up in his own house,
With his own blood, and, if the good
gods please,
At his own throat flesh [2] him to take a
leap!   110
I do not beg it, heav'n; but, if the fates
Grant it these eyes, they must not wink.

LEP.   They must
Not see it, Lucius.

ARR.   Who should let [3] hem?

LEP.   Zeal
And duty; with the thought he is our
prince.

ARR. He is our monster, forfeited to vice
So far as no racked virtue can redeem
him;
His loathéd person fouler than all crimes;
An emp'ror only in his lusts. Retired,

From all regard of his own fame or
Rome's,
Into an obscure island, where he lives, 120
Acting his tragedies with a comic face,
Amidst his rout of Chaldees,[4] spending
hours,
Days, weeks, and months in the unkind [5]
abuse
Of grave astrology, to the bane of men,
Casting the scope of men's nativities,
And, having found aught worthy in
their fortune,
Kill, or precipitate them in the sea,
And boast he can mock fate. Nay,
muse not; these
Are far from ends of evil, scarce de-
grees.
He hath his slaughterhouse at Capreæ,
Where he doth study murder as an art;
And they are dearest in his grace that
can   132
Devise the deepest tortures. Thither,
too,
He hath his boys and beauteous girls
ta'en up
Out of our noblest houses, the best
formed,
Best nurtured, and most modest; what's
their good
Serves to provoke his bad. Some are
allured,
Some threatened; others, by their friends
detained,
Are ravished hence like captives, and,
in sight
Of their most grievéd parents, dealt
away   140
Unto his spintries,[6] sellaries,[7] and slaves,
Masters of strange and new-com-
mented [8] lusts,
For which wise nature hath not left a
name.
To this (what most strikes us and bleed-
ing Rome)
He is, with all his craft, become the
ward
To his own vassal, a stale catamite [9]
Whom he, upon our low and suffering
necks,

[1] Mongrel.   [2] Incite.   [3] Hinder.

[4] Chaldeans, astrologers.
[5] Unnatural.
[6] Male prostitutes.
[7] Lewd persons.
[8] New-invented.
[9] Male prostitute.

Hath raised from excrement to side [1]
the gods
And have his proper sacrifice in Rome,
Which Jove beholds, and yet will sooner
rive　　　　　　　　　　　　　　150
A senseless oak with thunder than his
trunk!

*Laco, Pomponius, Minutius, Terentius, to
them.*

[LAC.] These letters make men doubtful
what t' expect,
Whether his coming or his death.
POM.　　　　　　　　　Troth, both;
And which comes soonest, thank the
gods for.
(ARR.　　　　　　　　　　　　List!
Their talk is Cæsar; I would hear all
voices.)
　　[*Arruntius and Lepidus withdraw.*]
MIN. One day he's well and will return
to Rome;
The next day, sick, and knows not when
to hope it.
LAC. True; and today one of Sejanus'
friends
Honored by special writ, and on the
morrow
Another punished—
POM.　　　　　By more special writ.　160
MIN. This man receives his praises of
Sejanus;
A second, but slight mention; a third,
none;
A fourth, rebukes. And thus he leaves
the senate
Divided and suspended, all uncertain.
LAC. These forkéd tricks, I understand
hem not;
Would he would tell us whom he loves
or hates,
That we might follow, without fear or
doubt.
(ARR. Good Heliotrope! [2]　Is this your
honest man?
Let him be yours so still; he is my knave.)
POM. I cannot tell; Sejanus still goes
on,　　　　　　　　　　　　　170
And mounts, we see; new statues are
advanced,
Fresh leaves of titles, large inscriptions
read,

[1] Match.
[2] Because he keeps turning toward the sun.

His fortune sworn by, himself new gone
out
Cæsar's colleague in the fifth consulship;
More altars smoke to him than all the
gods.
What would we more?
(ARR.　　　　That the dear smoke would
choke him,
That would I more!
LEP.　　　　　　Peace, good Arruntius.)
LAC. But there are letters come, they
say, ev'n now,
Which do forbid that last.
MIN.　　　　　　　Do you hear so?
LAC.　　　　　　　　　　　　　Yes.
POM. By Pollux, that's the worst.
(ARR.　　　　　　　　By Hercules, best.)
MIN. I did not like the sign, when Regu-
lus,　　　　　　　　　　　　　181
Whom all we know no friend unto Se-
janus,
Did, by Tiberius' so precise command,
Succeed a fellow in the consulship;
It boded somewhat.
POM.　　　　　Not a mote. His partner,
Fulcinius Trio, is his own, and sure.—
Here comes Terentius. He can give us
more.

[*Enter Terentius.*]　　*They whisper with
　　　　　　　　　　　　　　Terentius.*

LEP. I'll ne'er believe but Cæsar hath
some scent
Of bold Sejanus' footing. These cross-
points
Of varying letters and opposing con-
suls,　　　　　　　　　　　　　190
Mingling his honors and his punish-
ments,
Feigning now ill, now well, raising Se-
janus,
And then depressing him, as now of late
In all reports we have it, cannot be
Empty of practice; 'tis Tiberius' art,
For (having found his favorite grown
too great,
And with his greatness strong, that all
the soldiers
Are, with their leaders, made at his de-
votion,
That almost all the senate are his crea-
tures,
Or hold on him their main dependen-
cies,　　　　　　　　　　　　　200

Either for benefit, or hope, or fear,
And that himself hath lost much of his
    own,
By parting unto him, and, by th' in-
    crease
Of his rank lusts and rages, quite dis-
    armed
Himself of love or other public means
To dare an open contestation)
His subtilty hath chose this doubling
    line,
To hold him even in, not so to fear him,
As wholly put him out, and yet give
    check   209
Unto his farder boldness; in meantime,
By his employments, makes him odious
Unto the staggering rout, whose aid,
    in fine,
He hopes to use, as sure, who, when
    they sway,
Bear down, o'erturn all objects in their
    way.
Arr. You may be a Lynceus, Lepidus;
    yet I
See no such cause but that a politic
    tyran,
Who can so well disguise it, should
    have ta'en
A nearer way: feigned honest, and come
    home
To cut his throat, by law.
Lep.   Ay, but his fear
Would ne'er be masked, allbe [1] his vices
    were.   220
Pom. His lordship then is still in grace?
Ter.   Assure you,
    Never in more, either of grace or power.
Pom. The gods are wise and just.
(Arr.   The fiends they are,
To suffer thee belie hem!)
Ter.   I have here
His last and present letters, where he
    writes him,
The "partner of his cares," and "his
    Sejanus"—
Lac. But is that true, it is [2] prohibited
To sacrifice unto him?
Ter.   Some such thing
Cæsar makes scruple of, but forbids it
    not,
No more than to himself; says he could
    wish   230

It were forborne to all.
Lac.   Is it no other?
Ter. No other, on my trust. For your
    more surety,
Here is that letter too.
(Arr.   How easily
Do wretched men believe what they
    would have!
Looks this like plot?
Lep.   Noble Arruntius, stay.)
Lac. He names him here without his
    titles.
(Lep.   Note!
Arr. Yes, and come off [3] your notable
    fool. I will.)
Lac. No other than Sejanus.
Pom.   That's but haste
In him that writes. Here he gives large
    amends.   239
Min. And with his own hand written?
Pom.   Yes.
Lac.   Indeed?
Ter. Believe it, gentlemen, Sejanus'
    breast
Never received more full contentments
    in
Than at this present.
Pom.   Takes he well th' escape
Of young Caligula with Macro?
Ter.   Faith,
At the first air it somewhat troubled
    him.
(Lep. Observe you?
Arr.   Nothing; riddles. Till I see
Sejanus strook, no sound thereof strikes
    me.)
Pom. I like it not. I muse h' would not
    attempt
Somewhat against him in the consul-
    ship,
Seeing the people gin [4] to favor him. 250
Ter. He doth repent it now; but h' has
    employed
Pagonianus after him; and he holds
That correspondence there, with all
    that are
Near about Cæsar,[5] as no thought can
    pass
Without his knowledge thence, in act
    to front [6] him.
Pom. I gratulate [7] the news.

[1] Although.
[2] From 1640 edn. Original reads 'tis.
[3] Turn out to be.   [6] Oppose.
[4] Begin.   [7] Welcome.
[5] I.e., Caligula.

LAC. But how comes Macro
So in trust and favor with Caligula?
POM. O, sir, he has a wife, and the young
  prince
An appetite. He can look up and spy
Flies in the roof, when there are fleas
  i' bed, 260
And hath a learned nose to assure his
  sleeps.
Who, to be favored of the rising sun,
Would not lend little of his waning moon?
'Tis the saf'st ambition. Noble Teren-
  tius!
TER. The night grows fast upon us. At
  your service. [*Exeunt.*]

CHORUS—*of Musicians.*

ACT V. [SCENE i.

An apartment in Sejanus' house.]

Sejanus.

[SEJ.] Swell, swell, my joys, and faint not
  to declare
Yourselves as ample as your causes are.
I did not live till now—this my first
  hour,
Wherein I see my thoughts reached by
  my power.
But this, and gripe my wishes.[1] Great
  and high,
The world knows only two, that's Rome
  and I.
My roof receives me not; 'tis air I
  tread;
And at each step I feel my advancéd
  head
Knock out a star in heaven! Reared to
  this height,
All my desires seem modest, poor, and
  slight, 10
That did before sound impudent; 'tis
  place,
Not blood, discerns the noble and the
  base.
Is there not something more than to
  be Cæsar?
Must we rest there? It irks t' have come
  so far,
To be so near a stay. Caligula,
Would thou stood'st stiff and many in
  our way!

---

[1] Only this obstacle (Caligula), and I shall
obtain my wishes.

Winds lose their strength, when they
  do empty fly,
Unmet of woods or buildings; great
  fires die,
That want their matter to withstand
  them; so,
It is our grief, and will be our loss, to
  know 20
Our power shall want opposites, unless
The gods, by mixing in the cause, would
  bless
Our fortune with their conquest. That
  were worth
Sejanus' strife, durst fates but bring it
  forth.

[*Enter*] *Terentius.*[2]

[TER.] Safety to great Sejanus!
SEJ. Now, Terentius?
TER. Hears not my lord the wonder?
SEJ. Speak it; no.
TER. I meet it violent in the people's
  mouths,
Who run in routs to Pompey's theater
To view your statue, which, they say,
  sends forth
A smoke, as from a fornace,[3] black and
  dreadful. 30
SEJ. Some traitor hath put fire in; you
  go see,
And let the head be taken off, to look
What 'tis. Some slave hath practiced
  an imposture
To stir the people.—[*Terentius starts to
  go.*] How now! Why return you?

Satrius, Natta, to them.

SAT. The head, my lord, already is ta'en
  off;
I saw it; and, at op'ning, there leaped
  out
A great and monstrous serpent.
SEJ. Monstrous! Why?
Had it a beard and horns, no heart, a
  tongue
Forkéd as flattery? Looked it of the
  hue
To such as live in great men's bosoms?
  Was 40
The spirit of it Macro's?
NAT. May it please

---

[2] The name *Sejanus* is repeated here.
[3] Furnace.

The most divine Sejanus, in my days
(And by his sacred fortune I affirm it)
I have not seen a more extended, grown,
Foul, spotted, venomous, ugly—
SEJ.   O, the Fates!
What a wild muster's here of attributes
T' express a worm, a snake?
TER.   But how that should
Come there, my lord?
SEJ.   What, and you too, Terentius?
I think you mean to make 't a prodigy
In your reporting!
TER.   Can the wise Sejanus   50
Think heav'n hath meant it less?
SEJ.   O, superstition!
Why, then the falling of our bed, that
   brake
This morning, burdened with the popu-
   lous weight
Of our expecting clients, to salute us,
Or running of the cat bewixt our legs,
As we set forth unto the Capitol,
Were prodigies.
TER.   I think them ominous,
And would they had not happened—
   as, today,
The fate of some your servants, who,
   declining
Their way, not able, for the throng, to
   follow,   60
Slipped down the Gemonies, and brake
   their necks!
Besides, in taking your last augury,
No prosperous bird appeared, but croak-
   ing ravens
Flagged up and down, and from the
   sacrifice
Flew to the prison, where they sat all
   night,
Beating the air with their obstreperous
   beaks!
I dare not counsel, but I could entreat
That great Sejanus would attempt the
   gods
Once more with sacrifice.
SEJ.   What excellent fools
Religion makes of men!   Believes
   Terentius,   70
If these were dangers, as I shame to
   think them,
The gods could change the certain
   course of fate?
Or, if they could, they would, now in a
   moment,

For a beeve's fat, or less, be bribed t'
   invert
Those long decrees?   Then think the
   gods, like flies,
Are to be taken with the steam of flesh,
Or blood, diffused about their altars:
   think
Their power as cheap as I esteem it
   small.
Of all the throng that fill th' Olympian
   hall,
And, without pity, lade poor Atlas'
   back,   80
I know not that one deity, but Fortune,
To whom I would throw up, in begging
   smoke,
One grain of incense, or whose ear I'ld
   buy
With thus much oil. Her I indeed adore,
And keep her grateful image in my
   house,
Sometimes belonging to a Roman king,
But now called mine, as by the better
   style;
To her I care not, if, for satisfying
Your scrupulous phant'sies, I go offer.
   Bid
Our priest prepare us honey, milk, and
   poppy,   90
His masculine odors and night vest-
   ments; say
Our rites are instant, which performed,
   you'll see
How vain, and worthy laughter, your
   fears be.   [*Exeunt.*]

[SCENE ii.

A street.]

Cotta, Pomponius.

[COT.] Pomponius, whither in such speed?
POM.   I go
To give my lord Sejanus notice—
COT.   What?
POM. Of Macro.
COT.   Is he come?
POM.   Entered but now
The house of Regulus.
COT.   The opposite consul?
POM. Some half hour since.
COT.   And by night too! Stay, sir;
I'll bear you company.
POM.   Along then. [*Exeunt.*]

[SCENE iii.

A room in Regulus' house.]

Macro, Regulus, Laco[1] [, *and Attendant*].

[MAC.] 'Tis Cæsar's will to have a fre-
      quent [2] senate;
And therefore must your edict lay deep
      mulct
On such as shall be absent.
REG.   So it doth.
   Bear it my fellow consul to adscribe.[3]
MAC. And tell him it must early be pro-
      claimed;
   The place Apollo's temple.
                           [*Exit Attendant.*]
REG.   That's remembered.
MAC. And at what hour?
REG.   Yes.
MAC.   You do forget
   To send one for the provost of the
      watch?
REG. I have not; here he comes.

                [Enter Laco.]

MAC.   Gracinus Laco,
   You are a friend most welcome; by-and-
      by   10
   I'll speak with you.—[*Aside.*] You must
      procure this list
   Of the prætorian cohorts, with the
      names
   Of the centurions and the tribunes.
REG. [*Aside.*]   Ay.
MAC. I bring you letters, and a health
   from Cæsar.
LAC. Sir, both come well.
(MAC.   And, hear you, with your note,
   Which are the eminent men, and most
      of action.
REG. That shall be done you too.)
               The Consul goes out.
MAC.   Most worthy Laco,
   Cæsar salutes you.—[*Aside.*] Consul!
      Death and furies!
   Gone now?—The argument will please
      you, sir.—
   [*Aside.*] Ho! Regulus? The anger of
      the gods   20
   Follow his diligent legs, and overtake
      hem,
   In likeness of the gout!—

[1] Enters later.   [2] Full.   [3] Sign.

[Regulus] returns.

                         O, good my lord,
   We lacked you present; I would pray
      you send
   Another to Fulcinius Trio straight,
   To tell him you will come and speak
      with him;
   The matter we'll devise, to stay him
      there,
   While I with Laco do survey the watch.—
                  [*Regulus*] *goes out again.*
   What are your strengths, Gracinus?
LAC.   Seven cohorts.
MAC. You see what Cæsar writes; and
   —[*Aside.*] Gone again?
   H' has sure a vein of mercury in his
      feet.—   30
   Knew you what store of the prætorian
      soldiers
   Sejanus holds about him for his
      guard?
LAC. I cannot the just number, but I
      think
   Three centuries.
MAC.   Three? Good.
LAC.   At most not four.
MAC. And who be those centurions?
LAC.   That the consul
   Can best deliver you.
(MAC.   When h' is away?
   Spite on his nimble industry!)—Graci-
      nus,
   You find what place you hold, there, in
      the trust
   Of royal Cæsar?
LAC.   Ay, and I am—
MAC.   Sir,
   The honors there proposed are but
      beginnings   40
   Of his great favors.
LAC.   They are more—
MAC.   I heard him
   When he did study what to add.
LAC.   My life,
   And all I hold—
MAC.   You were his own first choice,
   Which doth confirm as much as you can
      speak,
   And will, if we succeed, make more—
      Your guards
   Are seven cohorts, you say?
LAC.   Yes.
MAC.   Those we must

Hold still in readiness and undischarged.

LAC. I understand so much. But how it can—

MAC. Be done without suspicion, you'll object?

[Regulus] returns.

REG. What's that?

LAC.   The keeping of the watch in arms,   50
When morning comes.

MAC.   The senate shall be met, and set
So early in the temple, as all mark
Of that will be avoided.

REG.   If we need,
We have commission to possess the palace,
Enlarge [1] Prince Drusus, and make him our chief.

(MAC. That secret would have burnt his reverend mouth,
Had he not spit it out now.)—By the gods,
You carry things too. Let me borrow a man
Or two to bear these. That of freeing Drusus,
Cæsar projected as the last and utmost—   60
Not else to be remembered.

REG. *[Beckoning to Servants.]*   Here are servants.

MAC. These to Arruntius, these to Lepidus.
This bear to Cotta, this to Latiaris.
If they demand you of me, say I have ta'en
Fresh horse and am departed.—*[Exeunt Servants.]* You, my lord,
To your colleague, and be you sure to hold him
With long narration of the new fresh favors,
Meant to Sejanus, his great patron; I,
With trusted Laco here, are for the guards;
Then, to divide. For night hath many eyes,   70
Whereof, though most do sleep, yet some are spies.   *[Exeunt.]*

[1] Free.

[SCENE iv.

A chapel in Sejanus' house.]

Præcones, Flamen,[2] Ministri,[3] Sejanus, Terentius, Satrius, [Natta,] etc.

[PRÆ.] *Be all profane far hence; fly, fly far off.*
Be absent far; far hence be all profane!
Tub[icines], Tib[icines] [4] sound while the Flamen washeth.

FLA. *We have been faulty, but repent us now,*
And bring pure hands, pure vestments, and pure minds.

[1] MIN. *Pure vessels.*

[2] MIN.   *And pure off'rings.*

[3] MIN.   *Garlands pure.*

FLA. *Bestow your garlands; and, with reverence, place*
The vervine [5] on the altar.

PRÆ.   *Favor [6] your tongues.*
While they sound again, the Flamen takes of the honey with his finger, and tastes, then ministers to all the rest; so of the milk, in an earthen vessel, he deals about; which done, he sprinkleth upon the altar, milk; then imposeth the honey, and kindleth his gums, and after censing about the altar, placeth his censer thereon, into which they put several branches of poppy, and, the music ceasing, proceed.

FLA. *Great mother Fortune, queen of human state,*
Rectress [7] of action, arbitress of fate,
To whom all sway, all power, all empire bows,   10
Be present, and propitious to our vows!

PRÆ. *Favor it with your tongues.[8]*

MIN. *Be present, and propitious to our vows!*
Accept our off'ring, and be pleased, great goddess.

TER. See, see, the image stirs!

SAT.   And turns away!

NAT. Fortune averts her face!

FLA.   Avert, you gods,
The prodigy! Still! Still! Some pious rite
We have neglected. Yet, heav'n, be appeased,

[2] Priest.   [3] Servitors.
[4] Trumpeters, flute-players.
[5] Vervain, verbena.   [7] Governess.
[6] Silence.   [8] Speak the good words.

And be all tokens false or void that speak
Thy present wrath!
SEJ.   Be thou dumb, scrupulous [1] priest,
And gather up thyself, with these thy
    wares,   21
Which I, in spite of thy blind mistress, or
Thy juggling mystery, religion, throw
Thus scornéd on the earth.
        [*Overturns the statue and the altar.*]
                Nay, hold thy look
Averted till I woo thee turn again;
And thou shalt stand, to all posterity,
Th' eternal game and laughter, with thy
    neck
Writhed to thy tail, like a ridiculous cat.
Avoid [2] these fumes, these superstitious
    lights,   29
And all these coz'ning ceremonies—you,
Your pure and spicéd [3] conscience!
        [*Exit Flamen with his Attendants.*]
                I, the slave
And mock of fools (scorn on my worthy
    head!),
That have been titled and adored a god,
Yea, sacrificed unto, myself, in Rome,
No less than Jove—and I be brought
    to do
A peevish giglot rites! [4] Perhaps the
    thought
And shame of that made Fortune turn
    her face,
Knowing herself the lesser deity,
And but my servant.—Bashful queen,
    if so,
Sejanus thanks thy modesty.—Who's
    that?   40

[*Enter*] *Pomponius,* [5] *Minutius, etc.*

[POM.] His fortune suffers till he hears my
    news;
I have waited here too long. Macro, my
    lord—
SEJ. Speak lower and withdraw.
                [*Draws him aside.*]
TER.   Are these things true?
MIN. Thousands are gazing at it in the
    streets.
SEJ. What's that?
TER.   Minutius tells us here, my lord,

[1] Doubtful, untrustworthy.
[2] Remove.
[3] Overscrupulous.
[4] Do rites to a crazy wanton (*i.e.*, to Fortune).
[5] The name *Sejanus* is repeated here.

That, a new head being set upon your
    statue,
A rope is since found wreathed about it,
    and
But now a fiery meteor in the form
Of a great ball was seen to roll along
The troubled air, where yet it hangs un-
    perfect,   50
The amazing wonder of the multitude!
SEJ. No more. That Macro's come, is more
    than all!
TER. Is Macro come?
POM.   I saw him.
TER.   Where? With whom?
POM. With Regulus.
SEJ.   Terentius!
TER.   My lord?
SEJ. Send for the tribunes; we will straight
    have up
More of the soldiers for our guard.—[*Exit
    Terentius.*] Minutius,
We pray you go for Cotta, Latiaris,
Trio the consul, or what senators
You know are sure, and ours.—[*Exit
    Minutius.*] You, my good Natta,
For Laco, provost of the watch.—[*Exit
    Natta.*] Now, Satrius,   60
The time of proof comes on; arm all our
    servants,
And without tumult.—[*Exit Satrius.*]
    You, Pomponius,
Hold some good correspondence with the
    consul;
Attempt him, noble friend.—[*Exit Pom-
    ponius.*] These things begin
To look like dangers, now, worthy my
    fates.
Fortune, I see thy worst. Let doubtful
    states
And things uncertain hang upon thy will;
Me surest death shall render certain still.
Yet why is now my thought turned
    toward death,
Whom fates have let go on so far in
    breath,   70
Unchecked or unreproved? I, that did
    help
To fell the lofty cedar of the world,
Germanicus; that at one stroke cut down
Drusus, that upright elm; withered his
    vine;
Laid Silius and Sabinus, two strong oaks,
Flat on the earth; besides those other
    shrubs,

Cordus and Sosia, Claudia Pulchra,
Furnius and Gallus, which I have
  grubbed up;
And since, have set my ax so strong
  and deep
Into the root of spreading Agrippine; 80
Lopped off and scattered her proud
  branches, Nero,
Drusus, and Caius too, although re-
  planted;
If you will, Destinies, that, after all,
I faint now ere I touch my period,
You are but cruel; and I already have
  done
Things great enough. All Rome hath
  been my slave;
The senate sate an idle looker-on
And witness of my power, when I have
  blushed
More to command than it to suffer; [1] all
The fathers have sat ready and pre-
  pared   90
To give me empire, temples, or their
  throats,
When I would ask hem; and, what crowns
  the top,
Rome, senate, people, all the world have
  seen
Jove but my equal, Cæsar but my second.
'Tis then your malice, Fates, who, but
  your own,
Envy and fear t' have any power long
  known.   [*Exit.*]

[SCENE V.

A room in the same.]

Terentius, Tribunes.

[TER.] Stay here; I'll give [2] his lordship you
  are come.

[*Enter*] *Minutius, Cotta, Latiaris.*

[MIN.] Marcus Terentius, pray you, tell
  my lord
Here's Cotta and Latiaris.
TER.   Sir, I shall.
          [*Exit.*] *They confer their letters.*
COT. My letter is the very same with
  yours,
Only requires me to be present there,
And give my voice to strengthen his
  design.

---

[1] *I.e.*, than it has blushed to permit me to
command.   [2] *I.e.*, tell.

LAT. Names he not what it is?
COT.   No, nor to you.
LAT. 'Tis strange and singular doubtful!
COT.   So it is.
  It may be all is left to Lord Sejanus.

Natta, Laco, to them.

[NAT.] Gentlemen, where's my lord?
TRI.   We wait him here.   10
COT. The provost Laco? What's the
  news?
LAT.   My lord—

Sejanus, to them.

[SEJ.] Now, my right dear, noble, and
  trusted friends,
  How much I am a captive to your kind-
    ness!
  Most worthy Cotta, Latiaris, Laco,
  Your valiant hand; and, gentlemen, your
    loves.
I wish I could divide myself unto you,
Or that it lay within our narrow powers
To satisfy for so enlargéd bounty.
Gracinus, we must pray you, hold your
  guards
Unquit when morning comes. Saw you
  the consul?   20
MIN. Trio will presently be here, my lord.
COT. They are but giving order for the
  edict,
  To warn the senate?
SEJ.   How! The senate?
LAT.   Yes.
  This morning in Apollo's temple—
COT.   We
  Are charged by letter to be there, my
    lord.
SEJ. By letter? Pray you, let's see.
LAT.   Knows not his lordship?
COT. It seems so!
SEJ.   A senate warned? Without
  my knowledge?
And on this sudden? Senators by letters
Required to be there! Who brought
  these?
COT.   Macro.
SEJ. Mine enemy! And when?
COT.   This midnight.
SEJ.   Time, 30
  With ev'ry other circumstance, doth give
  It hath some strain of ingine in 't!—How
    now?

[Enter] Satrius.[1]

[SAT.] My lord, Sertorius Macro is without,

Alone, and prays t' have private conference

In business of high nature with your lordship,

He says to me, and which regards you much.

SEJ. Let him come here.

SAT.   Better, my lord, withdraw;

You will betray what store and strength of friends

Are now about you, which he comes to spy.

SEJ. Is he not armed?

SAT.   We'll search him.

SEJ.   No; but take   40

And lead him to some room, where you concealed

May keep a guard upon us.—*[Exit Satrius.]* Noble Laco,

You are our trust; and, till our own cohorts

Can be brought up, your strengths must be our guard.

Now, good Minutius, honored Latiaris.

He salutes them humbly.

Most worthy and my most unwearied friends,

I return instantly.   *[Exit.]*

LAT.   Most worthy lord!

COT. His lordship is turned instant kind, methinks;

I have not observed it in him heretofore.

TRI. 1. 'Tis true, and it becomes him nobly.

MIN.   I   50

Am rapt withal.

TRI. 2.   By Mars, he has my lives,

Were they a million, for this only grace.

LAC. Ay, and to name a man!

LAT.   As he did me!

MIN. And me!

LAT.   Who would not spend his life and fortunes

To purchase but the look of such a lord?

LAC. *[Aside.]* He that would nor be lord's fool nor the world's.   *[Exeunt.]*

[1] The words *Sejanus, etc.*, are repeated here.

[SCENE vi.

Another room in the same.]

Sejanus, Macro [, Satrius].

[SEJ.] Macro, most welcome as most coveted friend!

Let me enjoy my longings. When arrived you?

MAC. About the noon of night.

SEJ.   Satrius, give leave. *[Exit Satrius.]*

MAC. I have been, since I came, with both the consuls,

On a particular design from Cæsar.

SEJ. How fares it with our great and royal master?

MAC. Right plentifully well, as with a prince

That still holds out the great proportion

Of his large favors, where his judgment hath   9

Made once divine election, like the god

That wants not, nor is wearied to bestow

Where merit meets his bounty, as it doth

In you, already the most happy, and, ere

The sun shall climb the south, most high Sejanus.

Let not my lord be amused.[2] For to this end

Was I by Cæsar sent for to the isle,

With special caution to conceal my journey,

And thence had my despatch as privately

Again to Rome, charged to come here by night,   19

And only to the consuls make narration

Of his great purpose, that the benefit

Might come more full and striking, by how much

It was less looked for, or aspired by you,

Or least informéd to the common thought.

SEJ. What may this be? Part of myself, dear Macro,

If good, speak out, and share with your Sejanus.

MAC. If bad, I should forever loathe myself

To be the messenger to so good a lord.

I do exceed m' instructions to acquaint

Your lordship with thus much; but 'tis my venture   30

[2] Amazed.

On your retentive wisdom, and because
I would no jealous scruple should molest
Or rack your peace of thought. For I
　　assure
My noble lord, no senator yet knows
The business meant, though all by sev-
　　eral letters
Are warnéd to be there, and give their
　　voices,
Only to add unto the state and grace
Of what is purposed.
SEJ.　　　　　You take pleasure, Macro,
Like a coy wench, in torturing your
　　lover.
What can be worth this suffering?
MAC.　　　　　That which follows, 40
The tribunitial dignity and power—
Both which Sejanus is to have this day
Conferred upon him, and by public
　　senate.
SEJ. [*Aside.*] Fortune, be mine again! Thou
　　hast satisfied
For thy suspected loyalty.
MAC.　　　　　　　　My lord,
I have no longer time; the day approach-
　　eth,
And I must back to Cæsar.
SEJ.　　　　　　　Where's Caligula?
MAC. That I forgot to tell your lordship.
　　Why,
He lingers yonder about Capreæ,
Disgraced; Tiberius hath not seen him
　　yet.　　　　　　　　　　　　　50
He needs would thrust himself to go with
　　me,
Against my wish or will; but I have
　　quitted
His forward trouble,[1] with as tardy note
As my neglect or silence could afford
　　him.
Your lordship cannot now command me
　　aught,
Because I take no knowledge that I saw
　　you;
But I shall boast to live to serve your
　　lordship;
And so take leave.
SEJ.　　　　　Honest and worthy Macro,
Your love and friendship.—[*Exit Macro.*]
Who's there? Satrius,　　　　　　59
Attend my honorable friend forth.—O!
How vain and vile a passion is this
　　fear!

[1] Troublesome forwardness.

What base uncomely things it makes
　　men do:
Suspect their noblest friends, as I did
　　this,
Flatter poor enemies, entreat their ser-
　　vants,
Stoop, court, and catch at the benevo-
　　lence
Of creatures unto whom, within this hour,
I would not have vouchsafed a quarter-
　　look,
Or piece of face! By you that fools call
　　gods,
Hang all the sky with your prodigious
　　signs,
Fill earth with monsters, drop the scor-
　　pion down　　　　　　　　　　70
Out of the zodiac, or the fiercer lion,
Shake off the loosened globe from her
　　long henge, [2]
Roll all the world in darkness, and let
　　loose
Th' enragéd winds to turn up groves and
　　towns!
When I do fear again, let me be strook
With forked fire, and unpitied die;
Who fears, is worthy of calamity. [*Exit.*]

[SCENE vii.

Another room in the same.]

Pomponius, Regulus, Trio, to the Rest.[3]

P[OM.] Is not my lord here?
TER.　　　　　Sir, he will be straight.
COT. What news, Fulcinius Trio?
TRIO.　　　　　Good, good tidings;
But keep it to yourself. My lord Sejanus
Is to receive this day in open senate
The tribunitial dignity.
COT.　　　　　　Is 't true?
TRIO. No words, not to your thought; but,
　　sir, believe it.
LAT. What says the consul?
COT. [*Aside.*]　　　Speak it not again.—
He tells me that today my lord Seja-
　　nus—
(TRIO. I must entreat you, Cotta, on your
　　honor
Not to reveal it.
COT.　　　　　On my life, sir.)
LAT.　　　　　　　　Say. 10

[2] Hinge, axis.
[3] *I.e.*, Terentius, Minutius, Laco, Cotta,
Latiaris, and Tribunes.

Cot. Is to receive the tribunitial power.
But, as you are an honorable man,
　Let me conjure you not to utter it;
For it is trusted to me with that bond.
Lat. I am Harpocrates.
Ter.   Can you assure it?
Pom. The consul told it me; but keep it
　close.
Min. Lord Latiaris, what's the news?
Lat.   I'll tell you;
But you must swear to keep it secret.

To them, Sejanus.

[Sej.] I knew the Fates had on their distaff
　left
More of our thread than so.
Reg.   Hail, great Sejanus! 20
Trio. Hail, the most honored—!
Cot.   Happy—!
Lat.   High Sejanus!
Sej. Do you bring prodigies too?
Trio.   May all presage
Turn to those fair effects whereof we
　bring
Your lordship news.
Reg.   May 't please my lord withdraw.
Sej. Yes.—(*To Some that stand by*.) I
　will speak with you anon.
Ter.   My lord,
What is your pleasure for the tribunes?
Sej.   Why,
Let hem be thanked and sent away.
Min.   My lord—
Lac. Will 't please your lordship to
　command me—
Sej.   No.
You are troublesome.
Min.   The mood is changed.
Tri.[1.]   Not speak?
Tri.[2.] Nor look?
Lac.   Ay, he is wise, will
　make him friends   30
Of such who never love but for their
　ends.   [*Exeunt.*]

[Scene viii.

Before the Temple of Apollo.]

*Arruntius, Lepidus, divers other Senators
passing by them.*

[Arr.] Ay, go, make haste; take heed you
　be not last
To tender your "All hail" in the wide
　hall

Of huge Sejanus; run a lictor's pace;
Stay not to put your robes on, but
　away
With the pale troubled ensigns of great
　friendship
Stamped i' your face! Now, Marcus
　Lepidus,
You still believe your former augury?
Sejanus must go downward? You per-
　ceive
His wane approaching fast?
Lep.   Believe me, Lucius,
I wonder at this rising.
Arr.   Ay, and that we 10
Must give our suffrage to it? You will
　say,
It is to make his fall more steep and
　grievous?
It may be so. But think it, they that
　can
With idle wishes 'ssay to bring back
　time;
In cases desperate, all hope is crime.
See, see! What troops of his officious
　friends
Flock to salute my lord, and start before
My great proud lord, to get a lordlike
　nod!
Attend my lord unto the Senate House!
Bring back my lord! Like servile
　huishers,[1] make   20
Way for my lord! Proclaim his idol
　lordship,
More than ten criers, or six noise of
　trumpets![2]
Make legs,[3] kiss hands, and take a scat-
　tered hair
From my lord's eminent shoulder! See,
　Sanquinius,
With his slow belly, and his dropsy!
　Look,
What toiling haste he makes! Yet here's
　another
Retarded with the gout, will be afore
　him.
Get thee Liburnian porters, thou gross
　fool,
To bear thy obsequious fatness, like
　thy peers.
They are met! The gout returns, and
　his great carriage.   30

[1] Ushers.
[2] Companies of trumpeters.
[3] *I.e.,* bow.

Lictors, Consuls, Sejanus, etc., pass over
　　　　　　　　　　　　　the stage.

Lic. Give way, make place, room for the
　　consul!
San.　　　　Hail,
　　Hail, great Sejanus!
Hat.　　　　　　Hail, my honored lord!
Arr. [*Aside.*] We shall be marked anon
　　for our not "Hail."
Lep. [*Aside.*] That is already done.
Arr. [*Aside.*]　　　　　　It is a note
　　Of upstart greatness to observe and
　　　watch
　　For these poor trifles, which the noble
　　　mind
　　Neglects and scorns.
Lep. [*Aside.*]　Ay, and they think them-
　　　selves
　　Deeply dishonored where they are
　　　omitted,
　　As if they were necessities that helped
　　To the perfection of their dignities,　40
　　And hate the men that but refrain hem.
Arr. [*Aside.*]　　　　　　　　　O!
　　There is a farder cause of hate. Their
　　　breasts
　　Are guilty that we know their obscure
　　　springs
　　And base beginnings; thence the anger
　　　grows.　On! Follow!　　[*Exeunt.*]

　　　　　　[Scene ix.

　　　　　The same.]

　　　　　Macro, Laco.

[Mac.] When all are entered, shut the
　　temple doors,
　　And bring your guards up to the gate.
Lac.　　　　　　　　　　I will.
Mac. If you shall hear commotion in the
　　senate,
　　Present yourself, and charge on any man
　　Shall offer to come forth.
Lac.　　　　I am instructed. [*Exeunt.*]

　　　　　[Scene x.

The Temple of Apollo.]　*The Senate.*

Haterius, Trio, Sanquinius, Cotta, Regulus,
　　Sejanus, Pomponius, Latiaris, Lepidus,
　　Arruntius, Præcones, Lictores, [*etc.*]

[Hat.] How well his lordship looks today!
Trio.　　　　　　　　　　As if
　　He had been born or made for this
　　hour's state.

Cot. Your fellow consul's come about,
　　methinks?
Trio. Ay, he is wise.
San.　　　　Sejanus trusts him well.
Trio. Sejanus is a noble, bounteous lord.
Hat. He is so, and most valiant.
Lat.　　　　　　And most wise.
[1] Sen. He's everything.
Lat.　　　　Worthy of all, and more
　　Than bounty can bestow.
Trio.　　　　　　This dignity
　　Will make him worthy.
Pom.　　　　　Above Cæsar.
San.　　　　　　　　Tut,
　　Cæsar is but the rector of an isle,　10
　　He of the empire.
Trio.　　　　Now he will have power
　　More to reward than ever.
Cot.　　　　　　　Let us look
　　We be not slack in giving him our
　　　voices.
Lat. Not I.
San.　　　Nor I.
Cot.　　　　　The readier we seem
　　To propagate his honors, will more bind
　　His thought to ours.
Hat.　　I think right with your lordship;
　　It is the way to have us hold our places.
San. Ay, and get more.
Lat.　　　　More office and more titles.
Pom. I will not lose the part I hope to
　　share
　　In these his fortunes, for my patri-
　　　mony.　　20
Lat. See how Arruntius sits, and Lepidus!
Trio. Let hem alone; they will be marked
　　anon.
[1] Sen. I'll do with others.
[2] Sen.　　　　So will I.
[3] Sen.　　　　　　And I.
　　Men grow not in the state but as they
　　are planted
　　Warm in his favors.
Cot.　　　　　Noble Sejanus!
Hat. Honored Sejanus!
Lat.　　　Worthy and great Sejanus!
Arr. [*Aside.*] Gods! How the sponges
　　open and take in
　　And shut again! Look, look! Is not he
　　blessed
　　That gets a seat in eye-reach of him?
　　More
　　That comes in ear- or tongue-reach? O,
　　but most　　30

Can claw his subtile elbow, or with a
    buzz
Flyblow his ears?
PRÆT[OR].   Proclaim the senate's peace,
And give last summons by the edict.
PRÆ.   Silence!
In name of Cæsar and the senate! Si-
    lence!
"Memmius Regulus, and Fulcinius Trio,
consuls, these present kalends of June, with
the first light, shall hold a senate in the
Temple of Apollo Palatine; all that are
fathers, and are registered fathers,[1] that
have right of ent'ring the senate, we [40
warn or command you be frequently pres-
ent; take knowledge the business is the
commonwealth's.   Whosoever is absent,
his fine or mulct will be taken, his excuse
will not be taken."
TRIO. Note who are absent, and record
    their names.
REG. Fathers conscript, may what I am
    to utter
Turn good and happy for the common-
    wealth!
And thou, Apollo, in whose holy house
We here are met, inspire us all with
    truth,   50
And liberty of censure to our thought!
The majesty of great Tiberius Cæsar
Propounds to this grave senate the
    bestowing
Upon the man he loves, honored Sejanus,
The tribunitial dignity and power.
Here are his letters, signéd with his
    signet.
What pleaseth now the fathers to be
    done?
SEN. Read, read hem, open, publicly read
    hem.
COT. Cæsar hath honored his own great-
    ness much
In thinking of this act.
TRIO.   It was a thought 60
Happy, and worthy Cæsar.
LAT.   And the lord
As worthy it, on whom it is directed!
HAT. Most worthy!
SAN.   Rome did never boast the virtue
That could give envy bounds, but his;
    Sejanus—
[1] SEN. Honored and noble!
[2] SEN.   Good and great Sejanus!

    [1] *I.e.*, conscript fathers

ARR. [*Aside.*] O, most tame slavery, and
    fierce flattery!
PRÆ.   Silence!   *The epistle is read.*
"Tiberius Cæsar to the senate, greeting.
If you, conscript fathers, with your children, be in health, it is abundantly well;
we with our friends here are so. The [70
care of the commonwealth, howsoever we
are removed in person, cannot be absent
to our thought, although oftentimes, even
to princes most present, the truth of their
own affairs is hid; than which nothing
falls out more miserable to a state, or
makes the art of governing more difficult.
But, since it hath been our easeful happiness to enjoy both the aids and industry
of so vigilant a senate, we profess to [80
have been the more indulgent to our
pleasures, not as being careless of our office,
but rather secure of the necessity. Neither
do these common rumors of many and infamous libels published against our retirement, at all afflict us, being born more
out of men's ignorance than their malice,
and will, neglected, find their own grave
quickly; whereas, too sensibly acknowledged, it would make their obloquy [90
ours.   Nor do we desire their authors,
though found, be censured, since in a free
state, as ours, all men ought to enjoy their
minds and tongues free."
(ARR. The lapwing, the lapwing!)
"Yet in things which shall worthily and
more near concern the majesty of a prince,
we shall fear to be so unnaturally cruel
to our own fame, as to neglect them. True
it is, conscript fathers, that we have [100
raised Sejanus from obscure and almost
unknown gentry"—
(SEN. How, how!)
"to the highest and most conspicuous
point of greatness, and, we hope, deserv-
ingly; yet not without danger, it being a
most bold hazard in that sov'reign who,
by his particular love to one, dares adventure the hatred of all his other subjects."
(ARR. This touches; the blood turns.)
"But we affy [2] in your loves and un- [111
derstandings, and do no way suspect the
merit of our Sejanus to make our favors
offensive to any."
(SEN. O, good, good!)
"Though we could have wished his zeal

    [2] Trust.

had run a calmer course against Agrippina
and our nephews, howsoever the openness
of their actions declared them delinquents,
and that he would have remembered   [120
no innocence is so safe but it rejoiceth
to stand in the sight of mercy—the use
of which in us he hath so quite taken away
toward them, by his loyal fury, as now our
clemency would be thought but wearied
cruelty, if we should offer to exercise it."
(ARR.   I thank him; there I looked for 't.
    A good fox!)
"Some there be that would interpret this
his public severity to be particular ambition, and that, under a pretext of   [130
service to us, he doth but remove his own
lets, alleging the strengths he hath made to
himself, by the prætorian soldiers, by his
faction in court and senate, by the offices
he holds himself, and confers on others,
his popularity and dependents, his urging
and almost driving us to this our unwilling
retirement, and, lastly, his aspiring to be
our son-in-law."
(SEN. This 's strange!   140
ARR. I shall anon believe your vultures,
    Marcus.)
"Your wisdoms, conscript fathers, are
able to examine and censure these suggestions. But were they left to our absolving
voice, we durst pronounce them, as we
think them, most malicious."
(SEN. O, he has restored all; list!)
"Yet are they offered to be averred, and
on the lives of the informers. What we
should say, or rather what we should   [150
not say, lords of the senate, if this be
true, our gods and goddesses confound
us if we know! Only we must think,
we have placed our benefits ill, and conclude that, in our choice, either we were
wanting to the gods, or the gods to us."
    The Senators shift their places.
(ARR. The place grows hot; they shift.)
"We have not been covetous, honorable
fathers, to change; neither is it now any
new lust that alters our affection,   [160
or old loathing, but those needful jealousies
of state, that warn wiser princes hourly
to provide their safety, and do teach them
how learned a thing it is to beware of the
humblest enemy—much more of those
great ones whom their own employed
favors have made fit for their fears."

([1] SEN. Away!
[2] SEN.   Sit farder.
COT.   Let's remove—
ARR. Gods! How the leaves drop off,
    this little wind!)
"We therefore desire that the offices   [170
he holds be first seized by the senate, and
himself suspended from all exercise of
place or power—"
(SEN. How!
SAN. [*Pushing through.*] By your leave!
ARR. Come, porcpisce.[1]—Where's Hate-
    rius?
    His gout keeps him most miserably
    constant!—
    Your dancing shows a tempest.)
SEJ.   Read no more!
REG. Lords of the senate, hold your
    seats; read on.
SEJ. These letters, they are forged.
REG.   A guard! Sit still.   180

        Laco enters with the Guards.

ARR. There's change!
REG.   Bid silence, and read forward.
    PRÆ. Silence!—"and himself suspended
from all exercise of place or power but
till due and mature trial be made of his
innocency, which yet we can faintly apprehend the necessity to doubt. If, conscript fathers, to your more searching wisdoms there shall appear farther cause
—or of farder proceeding, either to seizure
of lands, goods, or more—it is not our   [190
power that shall limit your authority, or
our favor that must corrupt your justice;
either were dishonorable in you, and
both uncharitable to ourself. We would
willingly be present with your counsels in
this business; but the danger of so potent
a faction, if it should prove so, forbids
our attempting it, except one of the consuls
would be entreated for our safety, to undertake the guard of us home; then we   [200
should most readily adventure. In the
meantime, it shall not be fit for us to importune so judicious a senate, who know
how much they hurt the innocent that
spare the guilty, and how grateful a
sacrifice to the gods is the life of an ingrateful person. We reflect not in this on Sejanus (notwithstanding, if you keep an

_____
[1] Porpoise.

eye upon him—and there is Latiaris, a
senator, and Pinnarius Natta, two   [210
of his most trusted ministers, and so professed, whom we desire not to have apprehended) but as the necessity of the cause
exacts it."
REG. A guard on Latiaris!
ARR.   O, the spy,
    The reverend spy is caught! Who pities
        him?
    Reward, sir, for your service.   Now
        you ha' done
    Your property,[1] you see what use is
        made?
        [Exeunt Latiaris and Natta, guarded.]
    Hang up the instrument.
SEJ.   Give leave.
LAC.   Stand, stand!
    He comes upon his death, that doth
        advance   220
    An inch toward my point.
SEJ.   Have we no friends here?
ARR. Hush't!   Where now are all the
    hails and acclamations?

                [Enter] Macro.[2]

[MAC.] Hail to the consuls, and this noble
    senate!
SEJ. [Aside.] Is Macro here? O, thou art
    lost, Sejanus!
MAC. Sit still and unaffrighted, reverend
    fathers;
    Macro, by Cæsar's grace the new-made
        provost,
    And now possessed of the prætorian
        bands,
    An honor late belonged to that proud
        man,
    Bids you be safe, and, to your constant
        doom [3]   229
    Of his deservings, offers you the surety
    Of all the soldiers, tribunes, and cen-
        turions
    Received in our command.
REG.   Sejanus, Sejanus,
    Stand forth, Sejanus!
SEJ.   Am I called?
MAC.   Ay, thou,
    Thou insolent monster, art bid stand.
SEJ.   Why, Macro,

[1] Performed your office.
[2] The word Senate is repeated here.
[3] Firm judgment.

It hath been otherwise between you
    and I;
This court, that knows us both, hath
    seen a difference,
And can, if it be pleased to speak, con-
    firm
Whose insolence is most.
MAC.   Come down, Typhœus!
    If mine be most, lo, thus I make it more;
    Kick up thy heels in air, tear off thy
        robe,   240
    Play with thy beard and nostrils. Thus
        'tis fit
    (And no man take compassion of thy
        state)
    To use th' ingrateful viper, tread his
        brains
    Into the earth.
REG.   Forbear!
MAC.   If I could lose
    All my humanity now, 'twere well to
        torture
    So meriting a traitor.—Wherefore, fa-
        thers,
    Sit you amazed and silent, and not
        censure
    This wretch, who, in the hour he first
        rebelled
    Gainst Cæsar's bounty, did condemn
        himself?
    Phlegra, the field where all the sons of
        earth   250
    Mustered against the gods, did ne'er
        acknowledge
    So proud and huge a monster.
REG.   Take him hence;
    And all the gods guard Cæsar!
TRIO.   Take him hence.
HAT. Hence.
COT.   To the dungeon with him.
SAN.   He deserves it.
SEN. Crown all our doors with bays.
SAN.   And let an ox,
    With gilded horns and garlands, straight
        be led
    Unto the Capitol.
HAT.   And sacrificed
    To Jove, for Cæsar's safety.
TRIO.   All our gods
    Be present still to Cæsar!
COT.   Phœbus.
SAN.   Mars.
HAT. Diana.
SAN.   Pallas.

SEN.   Juno, Mercury,   260
All guard him!
MAC.   Forth, thou prodigy of men.
               [*Exit Sejanus, guarded.*]
COT. Let all the traitor's titles be de-
   faced.
TRIO. His images and statues be pulled
   down.
HAT. His chariot-wheels be broken.
ARR.   And the legs
Of the poor horses, that deserved naught,
Let them be broken too!
LEP.   O violent change,
And whirl of men's affections!
ARR.   Like as both
Their bulks and souls were bound on
   Fortune's wheel,
And must act only with her motion.
   [*Exeunt All but*] Lepidus, Arruntius.
[LEP.] Who would depend upon the popu-
   lar air,   270
Or voice of men, that have today
   beheld
(That which, if all the gods had fore-
   declared,
Would not have been believed) Sejanus'
   fall?
He that this morn rose proudly as the
   sun,
And, breaking through a mist of clients'
   breath,
Came on as gazed at and admired as
   he
When superstitious Moors salute his
   light!
That had our servile nobles waiting
   him
As common grooms, and hanging on
   his look   279
No less than human life on destiny!
That had men's knees as frequent as the
   gods,
And sacrifices more than Rome had
   altars!
And this man fall! Fall? Ay, without
   a look
That durst appear his friend, or lend
   so much
Of vain relief, to his changed state, as
   pity!
ARR. They that before, like gnats, played
   in his beams,
And thronged to circumscribe him, now
   not seen,

Nor deign to hold a common seat with
   him!
Others, that waited him unto the
   senate,   289
Now inhumanely ravish him to prison,
Whom but this morn they followed as
   their lord;
Guard through the streets, bound like
   a fugitive;
Instead of wreaths give fetters, strokes
   for stoops,
Blind shame for honors, and black taunts
   for titles!
Who would trust slippery Chance?
LEP.   They that would make
Themselves her spoil, and foolishly
   forget,
When she doth flatter, that she comes
   to prey.
Fortune, thou hadst no deity, if men
Had wisdom; we have placéd thee so
   high
By fond belief in thy felicity.   300
SEN. (*Shout within.*) The gods guard Cæ-
   sar! All the gods guard Cæsar!

        [*Enter*] Macro, Regulus, Senators.

[MAC.] Now, great Sejanus, you that awed
   the state,
And sought to bring the nobles to your
   whip;
That would be Cæsar's tutor, and dis-
   pose
Of dignities and offices; that had
The public head still bare to your de-
   signs,
And made the general voice to echo
   yours;
That looked for salutations twelve
   score off,
And would have pyramids, yea, temples,
   reared
To your huge greatness—now you lie
   as flat   310
As was your pride advanced!
REG.   Thanks to the gods!
SEN. And praise to Macro, that hath
   savéd Rome!
Liberty, liberty, liberty! Lead on,
And praise to Macro, that hath savéd
   Rome!
[*Exeunt All but*] Arruntius, Lepidus. [*Enter*]
                   Terentius.

[ARR.] I prophesy, out of this senate's
　　flattery,
That this new fellow, Macro, will be-
　　come
A greater prodigy in Rome than he
That now is fall'n.
TER.　　　　¡O you whose minds are good,
And have not forced all mankind from
　　your breasts,
That yet have so much stock of virtue
　　left　　　　　　　　　　　　　　320
To pity guilty states, when they are
　　wretched,
Lend your soft ears to hear, and eyes to
　　weep,
Deeds done by men beyond the acts of
　　Furies.
The eager multitude (who never yet
Knew why to love or hate, but only
　　pleased
T' express their rage of power) no sooner
　　heard
The murmur of Sejanus in decline,
But with that speed and heat of appe-
　　tite,
With which they greedily devour the
　　way
To some great sports or a new thea-
　　ter,　　　　　　　　　　　　　　330
They filled the Capitol and Pompey's
　　Cirque [1]
Where, like so many mastives [2] biting
　　stones,
As if his statues now were sensive [3]
　　grown
Of their wild fury, first, they tear them
　　down,
Then, fast'ning ropes, drag them along
　　the streets,
Crying in scorn, "This, this was that
　　rich head
Was crowned with girlands [4] and with
　　odors, this
That was in Rome so reverencéd! Now
The fornace and the bellows shall to
　　work,
The great Sejanus crack, and piece by
　　piece　　　　　　　　　　　　　　340
Drop in the founder's pit."
LEP.　　　　　　　　　O popular rage!
TER. The whilst the senate at the Temple
　　of Concord

Make haste to meet again, and throng-
　　ing cry,
"Let us condemn him, tread him down
　　in water,
While he doth lie upon the bank. Away!"
Where some, more tardy, cry unto their
　　bearers,
"He will be censured ere we come; run,
　　knaves,"
And use that furious diligence, for fear
Their bondmen should inform against
　　their slackness,
And bring their quaking flesh unto the
　　hook.　　　　　　　　　　　　　350
The rout, they follow with confuséd
　　voice,
Crying they are glad; say they could
　　ne'er abide him;
Inquire what man he was, what kind
　　of face,
What beard he had, what nose, what
　　lips; protest
They ever did presage h' would come to
　　this,
They never thought him wise, nor val-
　　iant, ask
After his garments, when he dies; what
　　death.
And not a beast of all the herd demands
What was his crime, or who were his
　　accusers,　　　　　　　　　　　359
Under what proof or testimony he fell.
There came, says one, a huge long-
　　worded letter
From Capreæ against him. Did there
　　so?
O, they are satisfied; no more.
LEP.　　　　　　　　　　　　　Alas!
They follow Fortune, and hate men
　　condemned,
Guilty or not.
ARR.　　　　　But had Sejanus thrived
In his design, and prosperously oppressed
The old Tiberius, then, in that same
　　minute,
These very rascals, that now rage like
　　Furies,
Would have proclaimed Sejanus emperor.
LEP. But what hath followed?
TER.　　　　　Sentence by the senate,
To lose his head, which was no sooner
　　off　　　　　　　　　　　　　　371
But that and th' unfortunate trunk
　　were seized

---

[1] Circus, stadium.　　　　[3] Sensitive.
[2] Mastiffs.　　　　　　　　[4] Garlands.

By the rude multitude, who, not content
With what the forward justice of the
　　state
Officiously had done, with violent rage
Have rent it limb from limb. A thousand
　　heads,
A thousand hands, ten thousand tongues
　　and voices,
Employed at once in several acts of
　　malice!
Old men not staid with age, virgins with
　　shame,
Late wives with loss of husbands, moth-
　　ers of children,　　　　　　　　380
Losing all grief in joy of his sad fall,
Run quite transported with their cruelty!
These mounting at his head, these at
　　his face,
These digging out his eyes, those with
　　his brain
Sprinkling themselves, their houses, and
　　their friends;
Others are met, have ravished thence
　　an arm,
And deal small pieces of the flesh for
　　favors;
These with a thigh, this hath cut off
　　his hands,
And this his feet; these fingers, and
　　these toes;
That hath his liver, he his heart; there
　　wants　　　　　　　　　　　　390
Nothing but room for wrath, and place
　　for hatred!
What cannot oft be done, is now o'er-
　　done.
The whole, and all of what was great
　　Sejanus,
And, next to Cæsar, did possess the world,
Now torn and scattered, as he needs
　　no grave;
Each little dust covers a little part.
So lies he nowhere, and yet often buried!

[Enter] Nuntius.[1]

[Arr.] More of Sejanus?
Nun.　　　　　Yes.
Lep.　　　　　　　　What can be added?
　　We know him dead.
Nun.　　　　　Then there begin your pity.
　　There is enough behind to melt ev'n
　　Rome　　　　　　　　　　　　400

[1] The names *Arruntius, Lepidus,* and *Terentius*
are repeated here.

And Cæsar into tears; since never
　　slave
Could yet so highly offend, but tyranny,
In torturing him, would make him worth
　　lamenting.
A son and daughter to the dead Se-
　　janus
(Of whom there is not now so much
　　remaining
As would give fast'ning to the hang-
　　man's hook)
Have they drawn forth for farder sac-
　　rifice;
Whose tenderness of knowledge, unripe
　　years,
And childish silly [2] innocence was such
As scarce would lend them feeling of
　　their danger;　　　　　　　　410
The girl so simple, as she often asked
Where they would lead her, for what
　　cause they dragged her,
Cried she would do no more, that she
　　could take
Warning with beating.　And, because
　　our laws
Admit no virgin immature to die,
The wittily and strangely cruel Macro
Delivered her to be deflowered and
　　spoiled
By the rude lust of the licentious hang-
　　man,
Then to be strangled with her harmless
　　brother.
Lep.　O, act most worthy hell and lasting
　　night　　　　　　　　　　　　420
To hide it from the world!
Nun.　　　　　　　　Their bodies thrown
Into the Gemonies (I know not how,
Or by what accident returned), the
　　mother,
Th' expulséd Apicata, finds them there,
Whom when she saw lie spread on the
　　degrees,[3]
After a world of fury on herself,
Tearing her hair, defacing of her face,
Beating her breasts and womb, kneeling
　　amazed,
Crying to heaven, then to them, at
　　last
Her drownéd voice gat up above her
　　woes,　　　　　　　　　　　　430
And with such black and bitter execra-
　　tions

[2] Simple.　　　　　　　　[3] Steps.

As might affright the gods, and force
the sun
Run backward to the east, nay, make the
old
Deforméd chaos rise again, t' o'erwhelm
Them, us, and all the world, she fills
the air,
Upbraids the heavens with their partial
dooms,[1]
Defies their tyrannous powers, and de-
mands
What she and those poor innocents have
transgressed,
That they must suffer such a share in
vengeance,
Whilst Livia, Lygdus, and Eudemus
live,   440
Who, as she says, and firmly vows to
prove it
To Cæsar and the senate, poisoned
Drusus?
LEP. Confederates with her husband?
NUN.   Ay.
LEP.   Strange act!
ARR. And strangely opened. What says
now my monster,
The multitude? They reel now, do they
not?
NUN. Their gall is gone, and now they
gin to weep
The mischief they have done.
ARR.   I thank hem, rogues.
NUN. Part are so stupid, or so flexible,
As they believe him innocent; all
grieve;

[1] Unfair judgments.

And some whose hands yet reek with
his warm blood,   450
And gripe the part which they did tear
of him,
Wish him collected and created new.
LEP. How Fortune plies her sports, when
she begins
To practice hem! Pursues, continues,
adds,
Confounds with varying her impassioned
moods!
ARR. Dost thou hope, Fortune, to redeem
thy crimes,
To make amends for thy ill-placéd
favors
With these strange punishments? For-
bear, you things
That stand upon the pinnacles of state,
To boast your slippery height; when you
do fall,   460
You pash [2] yourselves in pieces, ne'er to
rise;
And he that lends you pity is not wise.
TER. Let this example move th' insolent
man
Not to grow proud and careless of the
gods.
It is an odious wisdom to blaspheme,
Much more to slighten or deny their
powers;
For whom the morning saw so great
and high,
Thus low and little, fore the even doth
lie.   [Exeunt.]

[2] Dash.

THE END.

This tragedy was first acted in the year 1603 by the King's Majesty's Servants. The principal tragedians were:

Ric. Burbadge	*Will. Shakespeare*
Aug. Philips	*Joh. Hemings*
Will. Sly	*Hen. Condell*
Joh. Lowin	*Alex. Cooke*

With the allowance of the Master of Revels.

VOLPONE, OR THE FOX[1]

BY

BEN JONSON

To the most noble and most equal sisters, the two famous universities, for their love and acceptance shown to his poem in the presentation, Ben Jonson, the grateful acknowledger, dedicates both it and himself.

Never, most equal sisters, had any man a wit so presently [2] excellent as that it could raise itself, but there must come both matter, occasion, commenders, and favorers to it. If this be true, and that [10 the fortune of all writers doth daily prove it, it behoves the careful to provide well toward these accidents, and, having acquired them, to preserve that part of reputation most tenderly wherein the benefit of a friend is also defended. Hence it is that I now render myself grateful and am studious to justify the bounty of your act, to which, though your mere authority were satisfying, yet, it being an [20 age wherein poetry and the professors [3] of it hear so ill [4] on all sides, there will a reason be looked for in the subject. It is certain, nor can it with any forehead be opposed, that the too much license of poetasters in this time hath much deformed their mistress, that every day their manifold and manifest ignorance doth stick unnatural reproaches upon her. But for their petulancy it were an act of the [30 greatest injustice either to let the learned suffer, or so divine a skill, which indeed should not be attempted with unclean hands, to fall under the least contempt. For, if men will impartially and not asquint look toward the offices and function of a poet, they will easily conclude to themselves the impossibility of any man's being the good poet without first being a good man. He that is said [40

to be able to inform young men to all good disciplines, inflame grown men to all great virtues, keep old men in their best and supreme state or, as they decline to childhood, recover them to their first strength; that comes forth the interpreter and arbiter of nature, a teacher of things divine no less than human, a master in manners, and can alone, or with a few, effect the business of mankind— [50 this, I take him, is no subject for pride and ignorance to exercise their railing rhetoric upon. But it will here be hastily answered that the writers of these days are other things; that not only their manners but their natures are inverted, and nothing remaining with them of the dignity of poet but the abused name, which every scribe usurps; that now, especially in dramatic or, as they term it, stage [60 poetry, nothing but ribaldry, profanation, blasphemy, all license of offense to God and man is practiced. I dare not deny a great part of this, and am sorry I dare not, because in some men's abortive features (and would they had never boasted the light) it is overtrue; but that all are embarked in this bold adventure for hell is a most uncharitable thought and, uttered, a more malicious slander. For my par- [70 ticular [5] I can, and from a most clear conscience, affirm that I have ever trembled to think toward the least profaneness, have loathed the use of such foul and unwashed bawdry as is now made the food of the scene; [6] and, howsoever I cannot escape from some the imputation of sharpness but that they will say I have taken a pride or lust to be bitter, and not my youngest infant but hath come [80 into the world with all his teeth, I would ask of these supercilious politics [7] what

---

[1] The title continues: "A Comedy, Acted in the Year 1605, by the K[ing's] Majesty's Servants."   [3] Practitioners.

[2] Actually.   [4] Are so ill spoken of.

[5] In my own case.   [7] Politicians, intriguers.

[6] Stage.

nation, society, or general order or state I have provoked?—what public person?—whether I have not in all these preserved their dignity, as mine own person, safe? My works are read, allowed [1] (I speak of those that are entirely mine); look into them. What broad reproofs have I used? Where have I been particular, where [90 personal, except to a mimic, cheater, bawd, or buffoon—creatures for their insolencies worthy to be taxed? Yet to which of these so pointingly as he might not either ingenuously have confessed or wisely dissembled his disease? But it is not rumor can make men guilty, much less entitle me to other men's crimes. I know that nothing can be so innocently writ or carried but may be made obnoxious to con- [100 struction;[2] marry, whilst I bear mine innocence about me I fear it not. Application [3] is now grown a trade with many; and there are that profess to have a key for the deciphering of everything. But let wise and noble persons take heed how they be too credulous or give leave to these invading interpreters to be overfamiliar with their fames, who cunningly and often utter their own virulent malice under [110 other men's simplest meanings. As for those that will (by faults which charity hath raked [4] up or common honesty concealed) make themselves a name with the multitude, or, to draw their rude and beastly claps, care not whose living faces they intrench with their petulant styles, may they do it without a rival, for me! I choose rather to live graved [5] in obscurity than share with them in so prepos- [120 terous a fame. Nor can I blame the wishes of those severe and wiser patriots, who, providing [6] the hurts these licentious spirits may do in a state, desire rather to see fools and devils and those antique relics of barbarism retrieved, with all other ridiculous and exploded follies, than behold the wounds of private men, of princes and nations, for, as Horace makes Trebatius speak among these, 130

Sibi quisque timet, quanquam est intactus, et odit.[7]

And men may justly impute such rages, if continued, to the writer as his sports. The increase of which lust in liberty, together with the present trade of the stage in all their misc'line [8] interludes, what learned or liberal soul doth not already abhor, where nothing but the filth of the time is uttered, and that with such impropriety of phrase, such [140 plenty of solecisms, such dearth of sense, so bold prolepses, so racked metaphors, with brothelry able to violate the ear of a pagan, and blasphemy to turn the blood of a Christian to water? I cannot but be serious in a cause of this nature, wherein my fame and the reputations of divers honest and learned are the question, when a name so full of authority, antiquity, and all great mark is through [150 their insolence become the lowest scorn of the age, and those men subject to the petulancy of every vernaculous [9] orator, that were wont to be the care of kings and happiest monarchs. This is it that hath not only rapt [10] me to present indignation, but made me studious heretofore, and, by all my actions, to stand off from them, which may most appear in this my latest work, which you, most [160 learned arbitresses, have seen, judged, and to my crown approved, wherein I have labored for their instruction and amendment, to reduce not only the ancient forms but manners of the scene, the easiness, the propriety, the innocence, and, last, the doctrine, which is the principal end of poesy, to inform men in the best reason of living. And, though my catastrophe may, in the strict rigor of comic law, [170 meet with censure, as turning back to my promise, I desire the learned and charitable critic to have so much faith in me to think it was done of industry, for with what ease I could have varied it nearer his scale (but that I fear to boast my own faculty) I could here insert. But my special aim being to put the snaffle in their mouths that cry out, "We never

---

[1] *I.e.*, passed by the censor.
[2] Through interpretation.
[3] Reading of cloaked allusions.
[4] Covered.
[5] Buried.
[6] Foreseeing.

[7] " Everybody fears for himself and is vexed, although he is untouched " (*Sermones*, II, i, 23).
[8] Miscelline, miscellaneous.
[9] Scurrilous.   [10] Transported.

punish vice in our interludes," etc., [180 I took the more liberty, though not without some lines of example, drawn even in the ancients themselves, the goings out [1] of whose comedies are not always joyful, but ofttimes the bawds, the servants, the rivals, yea, and the masters are mulcted —and fitly, it being the office of a comic poet to imitate justice and instruct to life as well as purity of language, or stir up gentle affections,[2] to which I shall [190 take the occasion elsewhere to speak.

For the present, most reverenced sisters, as I have cared to be thankful for your affections past, and here made the understanding acquainted with some ground of your favors, let me not despair their continuance to the maturing of some worthier fruits, wherein, if my muses be true to me, I shall raise the despised head of poetry again, and, stripping her out [200 of those rotten and base rags wherewith the times have adulterated her form, restore her to her primitive habit, feature, and majesty, and render her worthy to be embraced and kissed of all the great and master spirits of our world. As for the vile and slothful, who never affected an act worthy of celebration, or are so inward [3] with their own vicious natures as they worthily fear her and think it [210 a high point of policy to keep her in contempt with their declamatory and windy invectives, she shall out of just rage incite her servants (who are "genus irritabile" [4]) to spout ink in their faces, that shall eat farder [5] than their marrow, into their fames; and not Cinnamus the barber,[6] with his art, shall be able to take out the brands; but they shall live and be read till the wretches die, as things worst deserving [220 of themselves in chief and then of all mankind.

[From my house in the Blackfriars, this 11th day of February, 1607.] [7]

THE PERSONS OF THE PLAY

VOLPONE [the Fox], a magnifico.
MOSCA [the Gadfly], his parasite.
VOLTORE [the Vulture], an advocate.
CORBACCIO [the Crow], an old gentleman.
CORVINO [the Raven], a merchant.
AVOCATORI, four magistrates.
NOTARIO, the register.
NANO, a dwarf.
CASTRONE, an eunuch.
GREGE [or MOB].

POLITIC WOULD-BE, a knight.
PEREGRINE, a gent[leman] traveler.
BONARIO, a young gentleman.

FINE MADAME WOULD-BE, the knight's wife.
CELIA, the merchant's wife.

COMMANDADORI, officers [of justice].
MERCATORI, three merchants.
ANDROGYNO, a hermaphrodite.
SERVITORE, a servant; WOMEN [SERVANTS].

THE SCENE: Venice.

[TIME: Contemporary.]

THE ARGUMENT

V olpone, childless, rich, feigns sick, despairs,
O ffers his state to hopes of several heirs,
L ies languishing; his parasite receives
P resents of all, assures, deludes, then weaves
O ther cross plots, which ope themselves, are told.
N ew tricks for safety are sought; they thrive, when, bold,
E ach tempts th' other again, and all are sold.

[1] Conclusions.   [2] Feelings.

PROLOGUE

Now, luck yet send us, and a little wit
    Will serve to make our play hit;
According to the palates of the season,
    Here is rime, not empty of reason.
This we were bid to credit from our poet,
    Whose true scope, if you would know it,
In all his poems still hath been this measure:
    To mix profit with your pleasure;

[3] Familiar.
[4] "Genus irritabile vatum" (Horace, Epistles, II, 2, 102): "The excitable race of poets."
[5] Farther.
[6] The barber was also a surgeon.
[7] From 1607 edn.

And not as some, whose throats their envy
    failing, 9
Cry hoarsely, "All he writes is railing,"
And, when his plays come forth, think
    they can flout them,
With saying he was a year about them.
To these there needs no lie, but this his
    creature,[1]
Which was two months since no feature;
And, though he dares give them five lives
    to mend it,
'Tis known five weeks fully penned it,
From his own hand, without a coadjutor,
    Novice, journeyman, or tutor.
Yet thus much I can give you as a token
Of his play's worth: no eggs are broken,
Nor quaking custards [2] with fierce teeth
    affrighted, 21
Wherewith your rout are so delighted;
Nor hales he in a gull, old ends reciting,
To stop gaps in his loose writing;
With such a deal of monstrous and forced
    action,
As might make Bet'lem a faction; [3]
Nor made he his play for jests stol'n from
    each table,
But makes jests to fit his fable;
And so presents quick [4] comedy refined
    As best critics have designed. 30
The laws of time, place, persons he observ-
    eth;
From no needful rule he swerveth.
All gall and copp'ras from his ink he drain-
    eth;
Only a little salt remaineth,
Wherewith he'll rub your cheeks till, red
    with laughter,
They shall look fresh a week after.

Act I. Scene i.

[A room in Volpone's house.][5]

Volpone, Mosca.

VOLP. Good morning to the day; and next
    my gold!
Open the shrine that I may see my saint.

[1] Creation, *i.e.*, the play.
[2] An allusion to the tricks sometimes played
with immense custards at the lord mayors' and
other official feasts, and apparently later transferred to the theater (Gifford).
[3] Make Bedlam, the madhouse, more confused.
[4] Living, lively.
[5] The scene remains the same throughout the
act, and the action is continuous.

[*Mosca opens the curtain, revealing Vol-
    pone's treasure.*]

Hail, the world's soul and mine! More
    glad than is
The teeming earth to see the longed-for
    sun
Peep through the horns of the celestial
    Ram,
Am I, to view thy splendor darkening
    his,
That, lying here amongst my other
    hoards,
Show'st like a flame by night, or like
    the day
Strook [6] out of chaos, when all darkness
    fled
Unto the center.[7] O, thou son of Sol, 10
But brighter than thy father, let me
    kiss
With adoration thee and every relic
Of sacred treasure in this blessed room.
Well did wise poets, by thy glorious
    name,
Title that age which they would have
    the best,
Thou being the best of things, and far
    transcending
All style of joy in children, parents,
    friends,
Or any other waking dream on earth.
Thy looks when they to Venus did as-
    cribe,
They should have given her twenty
    thousand Cupids; 20
Such are thy beauties and our loves!
    Dear saint,
Riches, the dumb god, that giv'st all
    men tongues,
That canst do naught, and yet mak'st
    men do all things,
The price of souls, even hell, with thee
    to boot,
Is made worth heaven! Thou art virtue,
    fame,
Honor, and all things else. Who can
    get thee,
He shall be noble, valiant, honest, wise—
Mos. And what he will, sir. Riches are
    in fortune
A greater good than wisdom is in na-
    ture.
VOLP. True, my beloved Mosca. Yet I
    glory 30

[6] Struck.   [7] *I.e.*, of the earth.

More in the cunning purchase[1] of my
    wealth
Than in the glad possession, since I gain
No common way: I use no trade, no
    venter;[2]
I wound no earth with plowshares; I
    fat no beasts
To feed the shambles, have no mills
    for iron,
Oil, corn, or men to grind hem[3] into
    poulder;[4]
I blow no subtle glass, expose no ships
To threat'nings of the furrow-facéd sea;
I turn no moneys in the public bank,
Nor usure[5] private.

Mos.   No, sir, nor devour   40
Soft prodigals. You shall ha' some will
    swallow
A melting heir as glibly as your Dutch
Will pills of butter, and ne'er purge for 't;
Tear forth the fathers of poor families
Out of their beds, and coffin them alive
In some kind, clasping prison, where
    their bones
May be forthcoming when the flesh is
    rotten.
But your sweet nature doth abhor these
    courses;
You loathe the widow's or the orphan's
    tears
Should wash your pavements, or their
    piteous cries   50
Ring in your roofs, and beat the air for
    vengeance.

Volp. Right, Mosca; I do loathe it.

Mos.   And besides, sir,
You are not like a thresher that doth
    stand
With a huge flail, watching a heap of corn,
And, hungry, dares not taste the small-
    est grain,
But feeds on mallows and such bitter
    herbs,
Nor like the merchant, who hath filled
    his vaults
With Romagnia and rich Candian wines,
Yet drinks the lees of Lombard's vinegar.
You will not lie in straw, whilst moths
    and worms   60
Feed on your sumptuous hangings and
    soft beds;

You know the use of riches, and dare
    give now
From that bright heap, to me, your
    poor observer,[6]
Or to your dwarf, or your hermaphrodite,
Your eunuch, or what other household
    trifle
Your pleasure allows maint'nance—

Volp.   Hold thee, Mosca;
Take of my hand; thou strik'st on truth
    in all,
And they are envious term thee parasite.
Call forth my dwarf, my eunuch, and
    my fool,
And let hem make me sport. [Exit
    Mosca.] What should I do   70
But cocker up[7] my genius, and live free
To all delights my fortune calls me to?
I have no wife, no parent, child, ally,
To give my substance to; but whom I
    make
Must be my heir; and this makes men
    observe[8] me.
This draws new clients daily to my
    house,
Women and men of every sex and age,
That bring me presents, send me plate,
    coin, jewels,
With hope that when I die (which they
    expect
Each greedy minute) it shall then re-
    turn   80
Tenfold upon them, whilst some, cov-
    etous
Above the rest, seek to engross[9] me
    whole,
And counterwork the one unto the other,
Contend in gifts, as they would seem in
    love—
All which I suffer, playing with their
    hopes,
And am content to coin hem into profit,
And look upon their kindness, and take
    more,
And look on that, still bearing them in
    hand,[10]
Letting the cherry knock against their
    lips,
And draw it by their mouths, and back
    again.—   90
How now!

---

[1] Gain by underhand methods.   [4] Powder.
[2] Venture.   [5] Usury.
[3] Them.

[6] Dutiful attendant.   [8] Take notice of.
[7] Indulge.   [9] Absorb.
[10] Deceiving them.

Act I. Scene ii.

Nano, Androgyno, Castrone, Volpone, Mosca.

[Nan.] Now, room for fresh gamesters,
　　who do will you to know
They do bring you neither play nor
　　university show,
And therefore do entreat you that what-
　　soever they rehearse
May not fare a whit the worse for the
　　false pace of the verse.[1]
If you wonder at this, you will wonder
　　more ere we pass,
For know, here [*Points to Androgyno.*]
　　is enclosed the soul of Pythagoras,
That juggler divine, as hereafter shall
　　follow—
Which soul, fast and loose, sir, came
　　first from Apollo,
And was breathed into Æthalides, Mer-
　　curius his son,
Where it had the gift to remember all
　　that ever was done.　　　　　　　10
From thence it fled forth, and made
　　quick transmigration
To goldilocked Euphorbus, who was
　　killed in good fashion
At the siege of old Troy, by the cuck-
　　old of Sparta.
Hermotimus was next (I find it in my
　　charta [2]),
To whom it did pass, where no sooner
　　it was missing
But with one Pyrrhus of Delos it learned
　　to go a-fishing;
And thence did it enter the sophist of
　　Greece.
From Pythagore, she went into a beauti-
　　ful piece,
Hight [3] Aspasia, the meretrix; [4] and the
　　next toss of her
Was again of [5] a whore she became a
　　philosopher,　　　　　　　　　20
Crates the Cynic, as itself doth relate it.
Since, kings, knights, and beggars,
　　knaves, lords, and fools gat it,
Besides ox and ass, camel, mule, goat,
　　and brock,[6]

In all which it hath spoke, as in the cob-
　　bler's cock.
But I come not here to discourse of that
　　matter,
Or his "one," "two," or "three," or his
　　great oath, "by quater," [7]
His musics, his trigon,[8] his golden thigh,[9]
Or his telling how elements shift; but I
Would ask how of late thou hast suffered
　　translation,
And shifted thy coat in these days of
　　reformation.　　　　　　　　　30
And. Like one of the reformed, a fool, as
　　you see,
Counting all old doctrine heresy.
Nan. But not on thine own forbid meats [10]
　　hast thou ventered?
And. On fish, when first a Carthusian I
　　entered.
Nan. Why, then thy dogmatical silence
　　hath left thee?
And. Of that an obstreperous lawyer be-
　　reft me.
Nan. O wonderful change, when Sir
　　Lawyer forsook thee!
For Pythagore's sake, what body then
　　took thee?
And. A good dull moil [11]
Nan.　　　　　And how! By that means
　　Thou wert brought to allow of the eat-
　　ing of beans?　　　　　　　　40
And. Yes.
Nan.　　　But from the moil into whom
　　didst thou pass?
And. Into a very strange beast, by some
　　writers called an ass;
By others, a precise, pure, illuminate
　　brother [12]
Of those devour flesh, and sometimes
　　one another,
And will drop you forth a libel or a
　　sanctified lie
Betwixt every spoonful of a Nativity pie.
Nan. Now quit thee, for heaven, of that
　　profane nation,
And gently report thy next transmigra-
　　tion.
And. To the same that I am.

---

[1] The verse of this interlude or debate based
on Lucian's dialogue of a cobbler and a cock is
in the old-fashioned tumbling meter. In the
original the sixty-two lines of the passage are
printed in italics.　　　　　　[4] Hetaira.
[2] Paper.　　　　　　　　　　[5] From being.
[3] Called.　　　　　　　　　　[6] Badger.

[7] By four.
[8] Triangular harp.
[9] According to legend, Pythagoras actually
showed his golden thigh to Abaris, priest of the
Hyperboreans, and also exhibited it once at the
Olympic games.　　　　　　[11] Mule.
[10] Forbidden foods.　　　　[12] *I.e.*, Puritan.

NAN.   A creature of delight?
And, what is more than a fool, an her-
  maphrodite?   50
Now, pray thee, sweet soul, in all thy
  variation,
Which body wouldst thou choose to
  take up thy station?
AND. Troth, this I am in; even here would
  I tarry.
NAN. Cause [1] here the delight of each sex
  thou canst vary?
AND. Alas, those pleasures be stale and
  forsaken;
  No, 'tis your fool wherewith I am so
  taken,
The only one creature that I can call
  blessed,
For all other forms I have proved most
  distressed.
NAN. Spoke true, as thou wert in Pythag-
  oras still.
This learned opinion we celebrate will, 60
Fellow eunuch, as behooves us, with all
  our wit and art,
To dignify that whereof ourselves are
  so great and special a part.—

VOLP. Now, very, very pretty! Mosca,
  this
Was thy invention?
MOS.   If it please my patron;
  Not else.
VOLP.   It doth, good Mosca.
MOS.   Then it was, sir.

SONG

Fools, they are the only nation
Worth men's envy or admiration,
Free from care or sorrow-taking,
Selves and others merry making;
All they speak or do is sterling.   70
Your fool he is your great man's dearling [2]
And your ladies' sport and pleasure;
Tongue and bable [3] are his treasure.
E'en his face begetteth laughter,
And he speaks truth free from slaughter; [4]
He's the grace of every feast,
And sometimes the chiefest guest,
Hath his trencher and his stool,
When wit waits upon the fool.
  O, who would not be   80
  He, he, he?

One knocks without.
VOLP. Who's that? Away! Look, Mosca.
MOS.   Fool, begone!—
[*Exeunt Nano, Castrone, and Androgyno.*]
'Tis Signior Voltore, the advocate;
I know him by his knock.
VOLP.   Fetch me my gown,
My furs, and nightcaps. Say my couch
  is changing,
And let him entertain himself awhile
Without i' th' gallery.—[*Exit Mosca.*]
  Now, now, my clients
Begin their visitation! Vulture, kite,
Raven, and gorcrow,[5] all my birds of
  prey,
That think me turning carcass, now they
  come.   90
I am not for hem yet.—

[*Enter Mosca, with the gown, etc.*]
                   How now! The news?
MOS. A piece of plate, sir.
VOLP.   Of what bigness?
MOS.   Huge,
Massy, and antique, with your name
  inscribed
And arms engraven.
VOLP.   Good! And not a fox
Stretched on the earth, with fine delusive
  sleights
Mocking a gaping crow? Ha, Mosca?
MOS.   Sharp, sir.
VOLP. Give me my furs. [*Puts on his dress-
  ing gown.*] Why dost thou laugh so,
  man?
MOS. I cannot choose, sir, when I appre-
  hend
What thoughts he has without now, as he
  walks:
That this might be the last gift he should
  give;   100
That this would fetch you; if you died
  today,
And gave him all, what he should be
  tomorrow;
What large return would come of all
  his venters;
How he should worshiped be and reverenced,
Ride with his furs and footcloths,[6]
  waited on
By herds of fools and clients, have clear
  way

---

[1] Because.   [3] Babble.
[2] Darling.   [4] *I.e.*, with safety.
[5] Carrion crow.   [6] A caparison of a horse.

Made for his moil, as lettered as him-
    self,
Be called the great and learned advocate,
And then concludes there's naught im-
    possible.
VOLP. Yes, to be learned, Mosca.
Mos.   O, no. Rich 110
    Implies it. Hood an ass with reverend
    purple,
So you can hide his two ambitious [1] ears,
And he shall pass for a cathedral doctor.[2]
VOLP. My caps, my caps, good Mosca.
    Fetch him in.
Mos. Stay, sir; your ointment for your
    eyes.
VOLP.   That's true;
    Despatch, despatch! I long to have pos-
    session
Of my new present.
Mos.   That, and thousands more,
    I hope to see you lord of.
VOLP.   Thanks, kind Mosca.
Mos. And that, when I am lost in blended
    dust,
    And hundred such as I am, in succes-
    sion—   120
VOLP. Nay, that were too much, Mosca.
Mos.   You shall live
    Still to delude these harpies.
VOLP.   Loving Mosca,
'Tis well! My pillow now, and let him
    enter.—   [Exit Mosca.]
    Now, my feigned cough, my phthisic,
    and my gout,
    My apoplexy, palsy, and catarrhs,
    Help, with your forcéd functions, this
    my posture,
    Wherein this three year I have milked
    their hopes.
    He comes; I hear him—Uh! uh! uh! uh!
    O—

Act I. Scene iii.

Mosca, Voltore, Volpone.

[Mos. (*To Voltore.*)] You still are what you
    were, sir. Only you,
Of all the rest, are he commands his love,
And you do wisely to preserve it thus,
With early visitation and kind notes
Of your good meaning to him, which I
    know

[1] Moving, flapping.
[2] One who holds a university chair.

Cannot but come most grateful.—Pa-
    tron! Sir!
Here's Signior Voltore is come—
VOLP.   What say you?
Mos. Sir, Signior Voltore is come this
    morning
To visit you.
VOLP.   I thank him.
Mos.   And hath brought
    A piece of antique plate, bought of S[t].
    Mark,[3]   10
With which he here presents you.
VOLP.   He is welcome.
    Pray him to come more often.
Mos.   Yes.
VOLT.   What says he?
Mos. He thanks you, and desires you see
    him often.
VOLP. Mosca!
Mos.   My patron?
VOLP.   Bring him near. Where is he?
    I long to feel his hand.
Mos.   The plate is here, sir.
VOLT. How fare you, sir?
VOLP.   I thank you, Signior Voltore.
    Where is the plate? Mine eyes are bad.
VOLT. [*Giving the plate to him.*]   I'm sorry
    To see you still thus weak.
Mos. [*Aside.*]   That he is not weaker.
VOLP. You are too munificent.
VOLT.   No, sir; would to heaven
    I could as well give health to you as
    that plate!   20
VOLP. You give, sir, what you can; I
    thank you. Your love
    Hath taste in this, and shall not be un-
    answered.
    I pray you see me often.
VOLT.   Yes, I shall, sir.
VOLP. Be not far from me.
Mos.   Do you observe that, sir?
VOLP. Hearken unto me still; it will con-
    cern you.
Mos. You are a happy man, sir; know
    your good.
VOLP. I cannot now last long—
[4] (Mos.   You are his heir, sir.
VOLT. Am I?)
VOLP.   I feel me going. Uh! uh! uh! uh!
    I am sailing to my port. Uh! uh! uh! uh!

[3] *I.e.*, at a shop in St. Mark's Place.
[4] Jonson frequently uses parentheses to indicate asides and other passages incidental to
the main action.

And I am glad I am so near my haven.   30

Mos. Alas, kind gentleman!   Well, we
must all go—

Volt. But, Mosca—

Mos.   Age will conquer.

Volt.   Pray thee, hear me.
Am I inscribed his heir for certain?

Mos.   Are you?
I do beseech you, sir, you will vouchsafe
To write me i' your family. All my hopes
Depend upon your worship. I am lost
Except the rising sun do shine on me.

Volt. It shall both shine and warm thee,
Mosca.

Mos.   Sir,
I am a man that hath not done your
love
All the worst offices; here I wear your
keys,   40
See all your coffers and your caskets
locked,
Keep the poor inventory of your jewels,
Your plate, and moneys, am your stew-
ard, sir,
Husband your goods here.

Volt.   But am I sole heir?

Mos. Without a partner, sir—confirmed
this morning.
The wax is warm yet, and the ink scarce
dry
Upon the parchment.

Volt.   Happy, happy me!
By what good chance, sweet Mosca?

Mos.   Your desert, sir;
I know no second cause.

Volt.   Thy modesty
Is loath to know it; well, we shall requite
it.   50

Mos. He ever liked your course, sir; that
first took him.
I oft have heard him say how he admired
Men of your large profession, that could
speak
To every cause, and things mere con-
traries,
Till they were hoarse again, yet all be
law;
That with most quick agility could turn,
And re-turn, make knots and undo them,
Give forkéd counsel, take provoking gold
On either hand, and put it up—these
men,
He knew, would thrive with their hu-
mility.   60

And, for his part, he thought he should
be blessed
To have his heir of such a suffering spirit,
So wise, so grave, of so perplexed a
tongue,
And loud withal, that would not wag,
nor scarce
Lie still, without a fee, when every word
Your worship but lets fall is a cecchine![1]—
          Another knocks.
Who's that? One knocks; I would not
have you seen, sir.
And yet—pretend you came and went
in haste;
I'll fashion an excuse. And, gentle sir,
When you do come to swim in golden
lard,   70
Up to the arms in honey, that your chin
Is borne up stiff with fatness of the flood,
Think on your vassal; but remember me.
I ha' not been your worst of clients.

Volt.   Mosca!—

Mos. When will you have your inventory
brought, sir?
Or see a copy of the will? (Anon!)
I'll bring hem to you, sir. Away, begone;
Put business i' your face. [*Exit Voltore.*]

Volp.   Excellent Mosca!
Come hither; let me kiss thee.

Mos.   Keep you still, sir.
Here is Corbaccio.

Volp.   Set the plate away.   80
The vulture's gone, and the old raven's
come.

Act I. Scene iv.

Mosca, Corbaccio,[2] Volpone.

[Mos.] Betake you to your silence and
your sleep.—
     [*Puts the plate among the treasures.*]
Stand there and multiply.—Now we
shall see
A wretch who is indeed more impotent
Than this can feign to be, yet hopes to
hop
Over his grave.

         [*Enter Corbaccio.*]
         Signior Corbaccio!
Yo' are very welcome, sir.

Corb.   How does your patron?

Mos. Troth, as he did, sir; no amends.

---

[1] Sequin, a gold coin.   [2] Enters later.

CORB.   What? Mends he?
Mos. No, sir; he is rather worse.
CORB.   That's well. Where is he?
Mos. Upon his couch, sir, newly fall'n
    asleep.
CORB. Does he sleep well?
Mos.   No wink, sir, all this night, 10
    Nor yesterday; but slumbers.
CORB.   Good! He should take
    Some counsel of physicians. I have
        brought him
    An opiate here from mine own doctor—
Mos. He will not hear of drugs.
CORB.   Why? I myself
    Stood by while 'twas made, saw all th'
        ingredients,
    And know it cannot but most gently
        work.
    My life for his, 'tis but to make him
        sleep.
VOLP. [Aside.] Ay, his last sleep, if he
    would take it.
Mos.   Sir,
    He has no faith in physic.
CORB.   Say you, say you?
Mos. He has no faith in physic. He does
        think   20
    Most of your doctors are the greater
        danger,
    And worse disease, t' escape. I often
        have
    Heard him protest that your physician
    Should never be his heir.
CORB.   Not I his heir?
Mos. Not your physician, sir.
CORB.   O, no, no, no,
    I do not mean it.
Mos.   No, sir, nor their fees
    He cannot brook; he says they flay a
        man
    Before they kill him.
CORB.   Right, I do conceive you.
Mos. And then they do it by experiment,
    For which the law not only doth absolve
        hem,   30
    But gives them great reward; and he is
        loath
    To hire his death so.
CORB.   It is true, they kill
    With as much license as a judge.
Mos.   Nay, more,
    For he but kills, sir, where the law con-
        demns,
    And these can kill him too.

CORB.   Ay, or me,
    Or any man. How does his apoplex?[1]
    Is that strong on him still?
Mos.   Most violent.
    His speech is broken, and his eyes are
        set,
    His face drawn longer than 'twas wont—
CORB.   How? How?
    Stronger than he was wont?
Mos.   No, sir; his face 40
    Drawn longer than 'twas wont.
CORB.   O, good!
Mos.   His mouth
    Is ever gaping, and his eyelids hang.
CORB.   Good.
Mos. A freezing numbness stiffens all his
        joints,
    And makes the color of his flesh like lead.
CORB.   'Tis good.
Mos. His pulse beats slow and dull.
CORB.   Good symptoms still.
Mos. And from his brain—
CORB.   Ha? How? Not from his brain?
Mos. Yes, sir, and from his brain—
(CORB.   I conceive you; good.)
Mos. Flows a cold sweat, with a continual
        rheum,[2]
    Forth the resolvéd[3] corners of his eyes.
CORB. Is 't possible? Yet I am better, ha!
    How does he with the swimming of his
        head?   51
Mos. O, sir, 'tis past the scotomy;[4] he
        now
    Hath lost his feeling, and hath left[5] to
        snort;
    You hardly can perceive him, that he
        breathes.
CORB. Excellent, excellent! Sure I shall
        outlast him.
    This makes me young again, a score of
        years.
Mos. I was a-coming for you, sir.
CORB.   Has he made his will?
    What has he given me?
Mos.   No, sir.
CORB.   Nothing? Ha?
Mos. He has not made his will, sir.
CORB.   O, O, O! 59
    What then did Voltore, the lawyer, here?
Mos. He smelt a carcass, sir, when he
        but heard

---

[1] Apoplexy.   [2] Discharge.   [3] Loosened.
[4] Dizziness, with dimness of sight.
[5] Ceased.

My master was about his testament;
As I did urge him to it for your good—
CORB. He came unto him, did he?　I
　thought so.
MOS. Yes, and presented him this piece
　of plate.
CORB. To be his heir?
MOS.　　　　　　　I do not know, sir.
CORB.　　　　　　　　　　True;
　I know it too.
MOS. [*Aside.*]　By your own scale, sir.
CORB.　　　　　　　　　　Well,
　I shall prevent him yet. See, Mosca,
　look!
Here I have brought a bag of bright
　cecchines
Will quite weigh down his plate.
MOS.　　　　　Yea, marry, sir.　70
　This is true physic, this your sacred
　medicine;
No talk of opiates to this great elixir!
CORB. 'Tis *aurum palpabile*, if not *pota-
　bile*.[1]
MOS. It shall be ministered to him in his
　bowl?
CORB. Ay, do, do, do.
MOS.　　　　　Most blessed cordial!
　This will recover him.
CORB.　　　　　　Yes, do, do, do.
MOS. I think it were not best, sir.
CORB.　　　　What?
MOS.　　　　　　　To recover him.
CORB. O, no, no, no; by no means.
MOS.　　　　　　　Why, sir, this
　Will work some strange effect, if he but
　feel it.
CORB. 'Tis true; therefore forbear. I'll
　take my venter;　　　　　　80
Give me 't again.
MOS.　　　　At no hand;[2] pardon me.
　You shall not do yourself that wrong,
　sir. I
Will so advise you, you shall have it all.
CORB. How?
MOS.　　　　All, sir; 'tis your right, your
　own; no man
Can claim a part. 'Tis yours without a
　rival,
Decreed by destiny.
CORB.　　　　How, how, good Mosca?
MOS. I'll tell you, sir. This fit he shall
　recover—

CORB. I do conceive you.
MOS.　　　　And, on first advantage
　Of his gained sense, will I reimportune
　him
Unto the making of his testament,　90
And show him this.
CORB.　　　　Good, good.
MOS.　　　　　　　'Tis better yet,
　If you will hear, sir.
CORB.　　　　Yes, with all my heart.
MOS. Now would I counsel you, make
　home with speed;
There, frame a will, whereto you shall
　inscribe
My master your sole heir.
CORB.　　　　　And disinherit
　My son?
MOS.　O, sir, the better, for that color[3]
　Shall make it much more taking.
CORB.　　　　　O, but[4] color?
MOS. This will, sir, you shall send it unto
　me.
　Now, when I come to enforce, as I will
　do,
Your cares, your watchings, and your
　many prayers,　　　　　　100
Your more than many gifts, your this
　day's present,
And, last, produce your will, where
　without thought
Or least regard unto your proper issue,
A son so brave and highly meriting,
The stream of your diverted love hath
　thrown you
Upon my master, and made him your
　heir,
He cannot be so stupid or stone dead
But out of conscience and mere grati-
　tude—
CORB. He must pronounce me his?
MOS.　　　　　　'Tis true.
CORB.　　　　　　　　This plot
　Did I think on before.
MOS.　　　　　I do believe it.　110
CORB. Do you not believe it?
MOS.　　　　Yes, sir.
CORB.　　　　　　Mine own project.
MOS. Which when he hath done, sir—
CORB.　　　　　Published me his heir?
MOS. And you so certain to survive him—
CORB.　　　　　　　　Ay.
MOS. Being so lusty a man—
CORB.　　　　　　'Tis true.

---

[1] Palpable gold, if not potable.—"Potable
gold" was a medicine.　　　[2] By no means.
[3] Pretense.　　　　　　　[4] Merely.

Mos.   Yes, sir—

Corb. I thought on that too. See, how
  he should be

The very organ to express my thoughts!

Mos. You have not only done yourself a
  good—

Corb. But multiplied it on my son?

Mos.   'Tis right, sir.

Corb. Still, my invention.

Mos.   'Las, sir! Heaven knows
  It hath been all my study, all my care 120
  (I e'en grow gray withal) how to work
  things—

Corb. I do conceive, sweet Mosca.

Mos.   You are he
  For whom I labor here.

Corb.   Ay, do, do, do.
  I'll straight about it.

Mos. [Aside.]   Rook go with you,[1] raven!

Corb. I know thee honest.

Mos. [Aside.]   You do lie, sir!

Corb.   And—

Mos. [Aside.] Your knowledge is no better
  than your ears, sir.

Corb. I do not doubt to be a father to
  thee.

Mos. [Aside.] Nor I to gull my brother
  of his blessing.

Corb. I may ha' my youth restored to
  me; why not?

Mos. [Aside.] Your worship is a precious
  ass!

Corb.   What say'st thou?   130

Mos. I do desire your worship to make
  haste, sir.

Corb. 'Tis done, 'tis done; I go.   [Exit.]

Volp. [Springing from his bed.]   O, I
  shall burst!
  Let out my sides, let out my sides—

Mos.   Contain
  Your flux of laughter, sir. You know
  this hope
  Is such a bait it covers any hook.

Volp. O, but thy working, and thy placing it!
  I cannot hold; good rascal, let me kiss
  thee.
  I never knew thee in so rare a humor.

Mos. Alas, sir, I but do as I am taught—
  Follow your grave instructions, give
  hem words,   140
  Pour oil into their ears, and send them
  hence.

[1] May you be rooked.

Volp. 'Tis true, 'tis true. What a rare
  punishment
  Is avarice to itself!

Mos.   Ay, with our help, sir.

Volp. So many cares, so many maladies,
  So many fears attending on old age,
  Yea, death so often called on, as no wish
  Can be more frequent with hem, their
  limbs faint,
  Their senses dull, their seeing, hearing,
  going,
  All dead before them, yea, their very
  teeth,
  Their instruments of eating, failing
  them—   150
  Yet this is reckoned life! Nay, here was
  one,
  Is now gone home, that wishes to live
  longer—
  Feels not his gout nor palsy, feigns him-
  self
  Younger by scores of years, flatters his
  age
  With confident belying it, hopes he may
  With charms like Æson have his youth
  restored,
  And with these thoughts so battens, as
  if fate
  Would be as easily cheated on as he,
  And all turns air! Who's that there,
  now? A third?   Another knocks.

Mos. Close, to your couch again; I hear
  his voice.   160
  It is Corvino, our spruce merchant.

Volp. [Lying on his bed.]   Dead!

Mos. Another bout, sir, with your eyes.—
  Who's there?

Act I. Scene v.

Mosca, Corvino, Volpone.

[Mos.] Signior Corvino!   Come most
  wished for! O,
  How happy were you, if you knew it,
  now!

Corv. Why? What? Wherein?

Mos.   The tardy hour is come, sir.

Corv. He is not dead?

Mos.   Not dead, sir, but as good;
  He knows no man.

Corv.   How shall I do then?

Mos.   Why, sir?

Corv. I have brought him here a pearl.

Mos.   Perhaps he has

So much remembrance left as to know
   you, sir;
He still [1] calls on you; nothing but your
   name
Is in his mouth. Is your pearl orient,[2]
   sir?
Corv. Venice was never owner of the
   like.   10
Volp. Signior Corvino!
Mos.   Hark!
Volp.   Signior Corvino!
Mos. He calls you; step and give it him.—
   H' is here, sir,
And he has brought you a rich pearl.
Corv.   How do you, sir?—
   Tell him it doubles the twelve caract.[3]
Mos.   Sir,
   He cannot understand; his hearing's
      gone;
And yet it comforts him to see you—
Corv.   Say
   I have a diamant [4] for him, too.
Mos.   Best show 't, sir;
   Put it into his hand—'tis only there
   He apprehends. He has his feeling yet.
   See how he grasps it!
Corv.   'Las, good gentleman! 20
   How pitiful the sight is!
Mos.   Tut, forget, sir.
   The weeping of an heir should still be
      laughter
   Under a visor.[5]
Corv.   Why, am I his heir?
Mos. Sir, I am sworn; I may not show
   the will
   Till he be dead. But here has been Cor-
      baccio,
   Here has been Voltore, here were others
      too;
   I cannot number hem, they were so
      many,
   All gaping here for legacies; but I,
   Taking the vantage of his naming you,
   "Signior Corvino, Signior Corvino,"
      took   30
   Paper and pen and ink and there I
      asked him
   Whom he would have his heir. "Cor-
      vino." Who
   Should be executor? "Corvino." And

To any question he was silent to,
I still interpreted the nods he made,
Through weakness, for consent, and
   sent home th' others,
Nothing bequeathed them, but to cry
   and curse.
Corv. O, my dear Mosca! (*They embrace.*)
   Does he not perceive us?
Mos. No more than a blind harper. He
   knows no man,
   No face of friend, nor name of any serv-
      ant,   40
   Who 'twas that fed him last, or gave
      him drink—
   Not those he hath begotten or brought up
   Can he remember.
Corv.   Has he children?
Mos.   Bastards,
   Some dozen or more, that he begot on
      beggars,
   Gypsies and Jews and blackmoors,
      when he was drunk.
   Knew you not that, sir? 'Tis the com-
      mon fable.
   The dwarf, the fool, the eunuch are all
      his;
   H' is the true father of his family,
   In all save me; but he has given hem
      nothing.
Corv. That's well, that's well! Art sure
   he does not hear us?   50
Mos. Sure, sir? Why, look you, credit
   your own sense.—[*Shouts at Volpone.*]
   The pox approach, and add to your
      diseases,
   If it would send you hence the sooner, sir.
   For your incontinence, it hath deserved
      it
   Throughly [6] and throughly, and the
      plague to boot!—
   (You may come near, sir.) Would you
      would once close
   Those filthy eyes of yours, that flow
      with slime
   Like two frog-pits; [7] and those same
      hanging cheeks,
   Covered with hide instead of skin—
      (Nay, help, sir!)
   That look like frozen dishclouts set on
      end!   60
Corv. Or like an old smoked wall, on
   which the rain
   Ran down in streaks!

[1] Continually.   [3] Carat.
[2] Lustrous.   [4] Diamond.
[5] *I.e.*, an heir's sorrow is actually disguised
happiness.

[6] Thoroughly.   [7] Frog's eyes (?).

Mos.   Excellent, sir! Speak out.
You may be louder yet. A culvering [1]
Dischargéd in his ear would hardly bore
it.

Corv. His nose is like a common sewer,
still running.

Mos. 'Tis good! And what his mouth?

Corv.   A very draught.

Mos. O, stop it up—

Corv.   By no means.

Mos.   Pray you, let me.
Faith, I could stifle him rarely with a
pillow
As well as any woman that should keep [2]
him.

Corv. Do as you will; but I'll be gone.

Mos.   Be so;   70
It is your presence makes him last so
long.

Corv. I pray you use no violence.

Mos.   No, sir? Why?
Why should you be thus scrupulous,
pray you, sir?

Corv. Nay, at your discretion.

Mos.   Well, good sir, begone.

Corv. I will not trouble him now to take [3]
my pearl?

Mos. Pooh! Nor your diamant? What
a needless care
Is this afflicts you? Is not all here yours?
Am not I here, whom you have made?
Your creature
That owe my being to you?

Corv.   Grateful Mosca!
Thou art my friend, my fellow, my companion,   80
My partner, and shalt share in all my
fortunes.

Mos. Excepting one.

Corv.   What's that?

Mos.   Your gallant wife,
sir.—   [Exit Corvino precipitately.]
Now is he gone. We had no other means
To shoot him hence but this.

Volp.   My divine Mosca!
Thou hast today outgone thyself.—
(Another knocks.)   Who's there?
I will be troubled with no more. Pre-
pare
Me music, dances, banquets, all delights;
The Turk is not more sensual in his
pleasures

Than will Volpone. [Exit Mosca.] Let
me see. A pearl?
A diamant? Plate? Cecchines? Good
morning's purchase.   90
Why, this is better than rob churches,
yet;
Or fat by eating once a month a man—

[Enter Mosca.]

Who is 't?

Mos.   The beauteous Lady Would-be,
sir,
Wife to the English knight, Sir Politic
Would-be
(This is the style, sir, is directed me),
Hath sent to know how you have slept
tonight,
And if you would be visited.

Volp.   Not now.
Some three hours hence—

Mos.   I told the squire [4] so much.

Volp. When I am high with mirth and
wine, then, then!
Fore heaven, I wonder at the desperate
valure [5]   100
Of the bold English, that they dare
let loose
Their wives to all encounters!

Mos.   Sir, this knight
Had not his name for nothing; he is
politic,
And knows, howe'er his wife affect
strange airs,
She hath not yet the face to be dishonest.[6]
But, had she Signior Corvino's wife's
face—

Volp. Has she so rare a face?

Mos.   O, sir, the wonder,
The blazing star of Italy! A wench
O' the first year, a beauty ripe as har-
vest!
Whose skin is whiter than a swan all
over,   110
Than silver, snow, or lilies! A soft lip
Would tempt you to eternity of kissing!
And flesh that melteth in the touch to
blood!
Bright as your gold, and lovely as your
gold!

Volp. Why had not I known this before?

Mos.   Alas, sir,
Myself but yesterday discovered it.

---

[1] Culverin, a small cannon.
[2] Care for.   [3] Take away (from Volpone).

[4] Messenger.   [5] Valor.   [6] Unchaste.

VOLP. How might I see her?

MOS.　　　　　　　　O, not possible;
She's kept as warily as is your gold;
Never does come abroad, never takes
　air
But at a windore.[1] All her looks are
　sweet,　　　　　　　　　　　120
As the first grapes or cherries, and are
　watched
As near as they are.

VOLP.　　　　　　　I must see her—

MOS.　　　　　　　　　　　　Sir,
There is a guard of ten spies thick upon
　her,
All his whole household, each of which
　is set
Upon his fellow, and have all their
　charge,
When he goes out, when he comes in,
　examined.

VOLP. I will go see her, though but at her
　windore.

MOS. In some disguise then.

VOLP.　　　　　　That is true; I must
Maintain mine own shape still the same.
We'll think.　　　　　　　[Exeunt.]

ACT II. SCENE i.

[Before Corvino's house on St. Mark's
　　　　　　　　　　　Place.]

Politic Would-be, Peregrine.

[POL.] Sir, to a wise man all the world's his
　soil:
It is not Italy nor France nor Europe
That must bound me, if my fates call me
　forth.
Yet I protest it is no salt [2] desire
Of seeing countries, shifting a religion,
Nor any disaffection to the state
Where I was bred, and unto which I owe
My dearest plots,[3] hath brought me out,
　much less
That idle, antique, stale, gray-headed
　project
Of knowing men's minds and manners,
　with Ulysses,　　　　　　　10
But a peculiar humor of my wife's,
Laid for this height [4] of Venice, to ob-
　serve,

To quote, [5] to learn the language, and so
　forth—
I hope you travel, sir, with license? [6]

PER.　　　　　　　　　　　　　Yes.

POL. I dare the safelier converse. How
　long, sir,
Since you left England?

PER.　　　　　　　　Seven weeks.

POL.　　　　　　　　　　　So lately!
You ha' not been with my lord ambassa-
　dor?

PER. Not yet, sir.

POL.　　　　Pray you, what news, sir, vents
　our climate? [7]
I heard last night a most strange thing
　reported
By some of my lord's followers, and I
　long　　　　　　　　　　　20
To hear how 'twill be seconded.[8]

PER.　　　　　　　　What was 't, sir?

POL. Marry, sir, of a raven that should
　build
In a ship royal of the king's.[9]

PER. [Aside.]　　　　　　This fellow,
Does he gull me, trow? [10] Or is gulled?—
　Your name, sir?

POL. My name is Politic Would-be.

PER. [Aside.]　　　O, that speaks him.—
　A knight, sir?

POL.　　　　A poor knight, sir.

PER.　　　　　　　　　Your lady
Lies here in Venice, for intelligence
Of tires [11] and fashions and behavior
Among the courtesans? The fine Lady
　Would-be?

POL. Yes, sir; the spider and the bee oft-
　times　　　　　　　　　　　30
Suck from one flower.

PER.　　　　　　　　Good Sir Politic,
I cry you mercy; I have heard much of
　you.
'Tis true, sir, of your raven.

POL.　　　　　　　On your knowledge?

PER. Yes, and your lion's whelping in the
　Tower.

[1] Window.
[2] Wanton.
[3] Plans.
[4] Latitude.
[5] Make notes.
[6] Required of men of rank by the English
government.
[7] *I.e.*, does our country give forth?
[8] Followed up.
[9] Probably a reference to an actual event of
the day, like the following allusions to the lion's
whelping, the Woolwich whale, etc.
[10] Do you suppose?
[11] Attires.

Pol. Another whelp!

Per. 　　　　　　　　　Another, sir.

Pol. 　　　　　　　　　Now, heaven!
What prodigies be these?　The fires at
　Berwick!
And the new star!　These things concur-
　ring, strange,
And full of omen!　Saw you those
　meteors?

Per. I did, sir.

Pol. 　　Fearful!　Pray you, sir, confirm me.
Were there three porcpisces [1] seen above
　the bridge, 　　　　　　　　　　40
As they give out?

Per. 　　　　　　Six, and a sturgeon, sir.

Pol. I am astonished.

Per. 　　　　　　　Nay, sir, be not so;
I'll tell you a greater prodigy than these.

Pol. What should these things portend!

Per. 　　　　　　　　The very day
(Let me be sure) that I put forth from
　London,
There was a whale discovered in the
　river,
As high as Woolwich, that had waited
　there,
Few know how many months, for the
　subversion
Of the Stode fleet.

Pol. 　　　　　Is 't possible?　Believe it,
'Twas either sent from Spain, or the
　archduke's— 　　　　　　　　　50
Spinola's whale, upon my life, my credit!
Will they not leave these projects?
　Worthy sir,
Some other news.

Per. 　　　Faith, Stone the fool is dead,
And they do lack a tavern fool extremely.

Pol. Is Mas' Stone dead?

Per. 　　　H' is dead, sir; why, I hope
You thought him not immortal?—
　[Aside.] O, this knight,
Were he well-known, would be a precious
　thing
To fit our English stage; he that should
　write
But such a fellow, should be thought to
　feign
Extremely, if not maliciously.

Pol. 　　　　　　　Stone dead! 60

Per. Dead.　Lord!　How deeply, sir, you
　apprehend it!
He was no kinsman to you?

[1] Porpoises.

Pol. 　　　　　　　That I know of.
Well, that same fellow was an unknown
　fool.

Per. And yet you knew him, it seems?

Pol. 　　　　　　　　I did so.　Sir,
I knew him one of the most dangerous
　heads
Living within the state, and so I held
　him.

Per. Indeed, sir?

Pol. 　　　　While he lived, in action,
He has received weekly intelligence,
Upon my knowledge, out of the Low
　Countries, 　　　　　　　　　　69
For all parts of the world, in cabbages,
And those dispensed again to ambas-
　sadors,
In oranges, muskmelons, apricots,
Limons,[2] pome-citrons,[3] and suchlike—
　sometimes
In Colchester oysters, and your Selsey
　cockles.

Per. You make me wonder.

Pol. 　　　　　Sir, upon my knowledge.
Nay, I've observed him, at your public
　ordinary,
Take his advertisement [4] from a traveler,
A concealed statesman, in a trencher of
　meat,
And instantly, before the meal was done,
Convey an answer in a toothpick.

Per. 　　　　　　　　Strange! 80
How could this be, sir?

Pol. 　　　　　Why, the meat was cut
So like his character, and so laid as he
Must easily read the cipher.

Per. 　　　　　　　　I have heard
He could not read, sir.

Pol. 　　　　　　So 'twas given out,
In polity, by those that did employ him;
But he could read, and had your lan-
　guages,
And to 't as sound a noddle—

Per. 　　　　　　　I have heard, sir,
That your babions [5] were spies, and that
　they were
A kind of subtle nation near to China.

Pol. Ay, ay, your Mamuluchi.[6]　Faith
　they had 　　　　　　　　　　90
Their hand in a French plot or two; but
　they

[2] Lemons.　　　　　　　[4] Information.
[3] Citrons.　　　　　　　[5] Baboons.
[6] Mamelukes, a kind of Islamite soldier.

Were so extremely given to women as
They made discovery of all; yet I
Had my advices here, on Wednesday
　last,
From one of their own coat, they were
　returned,
Made their relations,[1] as the fashion is,
And now stand fair for fresh employ-
　ment.

PER. [*Aside.*]　　　　Heart!
This Sir Pol will be ignorant of noth-
　ing.—
It seems, sir, you know all.

POL.　　　　　　　Not all, sir; but
I have some general notions.　I do
　love　　　　　　　　　　　　　100
To note and to observe.　Though I live
　out,
Free from the active torrent, yet I'ld
　mark
The currents and the passages of things
For mine own private use, and know the
　ebbs
And flows of state.

PER.　　　　　Believe it, sir, I hold
Myself in no small tie [2] unto my fortunes
For casting me thus luckily upon you,
Whose knowledge, if your bounty equal it,
May do me great assistance in instruction
For my behavior and my bearing,
　which　　　　　　　　　　　110
Is yet so rude and raw—

POL.　　　　Why? Came you forth
Empty of rules for travel?

PER.　　　　　　　Faith, I had
Some common ones, from out that vulgar
　grammar,
Which he that cried Italian to me taught
　me.

POL. Why, this it is that spoils all our
　brave bloods,
Trusting our hopeful gentry unto ped-
　ants,
Fellows of outside, and mere bark. You
　seem
To be a gentleman of ingenuous race—
I not profess it, but my fate hath been
To be where I have been consulted
　with,　　　　　　　　　　　120
In this high kind, touching some great
　men's sons,
Persons of blood and honor.

PER.　　　　　Who be these, sir?

ACT II. SCENE ii.

[*The same.*]

Mosca [*with Assistants carrying material for
　a platform*], *Politic, Peregrine, Volpone,
　　　　　　　　　Nano, Grege.*[3]

[Mos.] Under that windore, there 't must
　be.　The same.

POL. Fellows, to mount a bank.[4]　Did your
　instructor
In the dear tongues [5] never discourse to
　you
Of the Italian mountebanks?

PER.　　　　　　　Yes, sir.

POL.　　　　　　　　Why,
Here shall you see one.

PER.　　　　　They are quacksalvers,
Fellows that live by venting [6] oils and
　drugs.

POL. Was that the character he gave you
　of them?

PER. As I remember.

POL.　　　　　Pity his ignorance.
They are the only knowing men of
　Europe!
Great general scholars, excellent physi-
　cians,　　　　　　　　　　　10
Most admired statesmen, professed fa-
　vorites
And cabinet counselors to the greatest
　princes—
The only languaged men of all the world!

PER. And, I have heard, they are most
　lewd [7] impostors,
Made all of terms and shreds, no less be-
　liers
Of great men's favors than their own vile
　med'cines,
Which they will utter [8] upon monstrous
　oaths,
Selling that drug for twopence ere they
　part,
Which they have valued at twelve crowns
　before.

POL. Sir, calumnies are answered best with
　silence.　　　　　　　　　　20
Yourself shall judge.—Who is it mounts,
　my friends?

Mos. Scoto of Mantua,[9] sir.

―――――――――――
[1] Reports.　　　　　　　[2] Obligation.

[3] Last three enter later.　　　　[6] Vending.
[4] Bench, platform.　　　　　[7] Ignorant.
[5] Modern languages.　　　　[8] Vend.
[9] An actual Italian juggler who was then in
England.

POL.   Is 't he? Nay, then
I'll proudly promise, sir, you shall behold
Another man than has been fant'sied [1]
to you.
I wonder yet that he should mount his
bank
Here in this nook, that has been wont t'
appear
In face of the Piazza!—Here he comes.

[*Enter Volpone, disguised as a mountebank,
followed by Nano, also disguised, and
Grege.*]

VOLP. Mount, zany. [2]
GRE. Follow, follow, follow, follow, follow!
POL. See how the people follow him! H' is
a man   30
May write ten thousand crowns in bank
here. Note,
            [*Volpone mounts the platform.*]
Mark but his gesture; I do use to observe
The state he keeps in getting up.
PER.   'Tis worth it, sir.
VOLP. Most noble gentlemen and my
worthy patrons! It may seem strange that
I, your Scoto Mantuano, who was ever
wont to fix my bank in face of the public
Piazza, near the shelter of the Portico to the
Procuratia, should now, after eight months'
absence from this illustrous city of [40
Venice, humbly retire myself into an obscure nook of the Piazza.
POL. [*Aside.*] Did not I now object the
same?
PER. [*Aside.*]   Peace, sir.
VOLP. Let me tell you I am not, as your
Lombard proverb saith, cold on my feet, or
content to part with my commodities at a
cheaper rate than I accustomed—look not
for it; nor that the calumnious reports of
that impudent detractor and shame to
our profession (Alessandro Buttone, I [50
mean), who gave out, in public, I was condemned *a' sforzato* [3] to the galleys for
poisoning the Cardinal Bembo's—cook,
hath at all attached, [4] much less dejected
me. No, no, worthy gentlemen! To tell you
true, I cannot endure to see the rabble of
these ground *ciarlitani*, [5] that spread their
cloaks on the pavement as if they meant to
do feats of activity, and then come in

lamely with their moldy tales out of [60
Boccaccio, like stale Tabarine, [6] the fabu-
list, [7] some of them discoursing their travels,
and of their tedious captivity in the Turks'
galleys, when indeed, were the truth known,
they were the Christians' galleys, where
very temperately they eat bread and drunk
water as a wholesome penance, enjoined
them by their confessors, for base pilferies.
POL. [*Aside.*] Note but his bearing, and
contempt of these.
VOLP. These turdy-facey-nasty- [70
patey-lousy-fartical rogues, with one poor
groatsworth of unprepared antimony,
finely wrapped up in several *scartoccios*, [8] are
able, very well, to kill their twenty a week,
and play; yet these meager, starved spirits,
who have half stopped the organs of their
minds with earthy oppilations, [9] want not
their favorers among your shriveled, salad-
eating artisans, who are overjoyed that they
may have their half-pe'rth of physic; [80
though it purge hem into another world, 't
makes no matter.
POL. [*Aside.*] Excellent! Ha' you heard
better language, sir?
VOLP. Well, let hem go. And, gentlemen, honorable gentlemen, know that for
this time our bank, being thus removed
from the clamors of the *canaglia*, [10] shall
be the scene of pleasure and delight, for
I have nothing to sell, little or nothing to
sell.   90
POL. [*Aside.*] I told you, sir, his end.
PER. [*Aside.*]   You did so, sir.
VOLP. I protest I and my six servants
are not able to make of this precious liquor
so fast as it is fetched away from my lodging by gentlemen of your city, strangers of
the *terrafirma*, [11] worshipful merchants, ay,
and senators too, who ever since my arrival
have detained me to their uses by their
splendidous liberalities—and worthily. For
what avails your rich man to have his [100
magazines stuffed with *moscadelli*, [12] or of the
purest grape, when his physicians prescribe
him, on pain of death, to drink nothing but
water cocted [13] with anis seeds? O health,
health! The blessing of the rich! The riches

[6] Tabarin, a popular French mountebank.
[7] A professional teller of tales.
[8] Twists of paper.   [11] Mainland.
[9] Obstructions.   [12] Muscatel.
[10] Canaille, mob.   [13] Boiled.

[1] Represented.   [4] Attacked.
[2] A subordinate buffoon.   [5] Trivial charlatans.
[3] To hard labor.

of the poor! Who can buy thee at too dear
a rate, since there is no enjoying this world
without thee? Be not then so sparing of
your purses, honorable gentlemen, as to
abridge the natural course of life—   [110
PER. [*Aside.*] You see his end?
POL. [*Aside.*]   Ay, is 't not good?
VOLP. For, when a humid flux, or
catarrh, by the mutability of air, falls from
your head into an arm or shoulder, or any
other part, take you a ducat, or your
cecchine of gold, and apply to the place
affected; see what good effect it can work.
No, no, 'tis this blessed *unguento*,[1] this rare
extraction, that hath only power to disperse all malignant humors[2] that   [120
proceed either of hot, cold, moist, or windy
causes—
PER. [*Aside.*] I would he had put in dry
too.
POL. [*Aside.*]   Pray you, observe.
VOLP. To fortify the most indigest[3] and
crude stomach, ay, were it of one that,
through extreme weakness, vomited blood,
applying only a warm napkin to the place,
after the unction and fricace;[4] for the
vertigine[5] in the head, putting but a drop
into your nostrils, likewise behind the   [130
ears, a most sovereign and approved remedy, the *mal caduco*,[6] cramps, convulsions,
paralyses, epilepsies, *tremorcordia*,[7] retired[8] nerves, ill vapors of the spleen, stop-
pings of the liver, the stone, the strangury,
hernia ventosa, iliaca passio;[9] stops a
dysenteria immediately; easeth the torsion
of the small guts; and cures *melancholia
hypocondriaca*, being taken and applied
according to my printed receipt.   [140
(*Pointing to his bill and his glass.*) For this
is the physician, this the medicine; this
counsels, this cures; this gives the direction,
this works the effect; and, in sum, both together may be termed an abstract of the
theoric and practic in the Æsculapian art.[10]
'Twill cost you eight crowns. And, Zan
Fritada, pray thee, sing a verse extempore
in honor of it.   149
POL. [*Aside.*] How do you like him, sir?
PER. [*Aside.*]   Most strangely, I!

POL. [*Aside.*] Is not his language rare?
PER. [*Aside.*]   But[11] alchemy,
I never heard the like—or Broughton's[12]
books.

SONG

Had old Hippocrates or Galen,
That to their books put med'cines all in,
But known this secret, they had never
(Of which they will be guilty ever)
Been murderers of so much paper,
Or wasted many a hurtless taper;
No Indian drug had e'er been famed,
Tabacco,[13] sassafras not named;   160
Ne[14] yet of guacum[15] one small stick, sir,
Nor Raymond Lully's[16] great elixir;
Ne had been known the Danish Gonswart,[17]
Or Paracelsus, with his long sword.[18]

PER. [*Aside.*] All this, yet, will not do;
eight crowns is high.
VOLP. No more.—Gentlemen, if I had
but time to discourse to you the miraculous
effects of this my oil, surnamed Oglio del
Scoto, with the countless catalogue of those
I have cured of th' aforesaid and   [170
many more diseases, the patents and privi-
leges of all the princes and commonwealths
of Christendom, or but the depositions of
those that appeared on my part before the
signiory of the Sanita and most learned
College of Physicians, where I was authorized, upon notice taken of the admirable
virtues of my medicaments, and mine own
excellency in matter of rare and unknown
secrets, not only to disperse them   [180
publicly in this famous city, but in all the
territories that happily joy under the
government of the most pious and magnificent states of Italy! But may some
other gallant fellow say, "O, there be
divers that make profession to have as good
and as experimented receipts as yours."
Indeed, very many have assayed, like apes,
in imitation of that which is really and
essentially in me, to make of this oil,   [190
bestowed great cost in furnaces, stills,
alembics, continual fires, and preparation

[11] Except for.
[12] Hugh Broughton was a fanatical commentator on the Old Testament.
[13] Tobacco.   [15] Guaiacum, a kind of resin.
[14] Nor.   [16] Fourteenth century alchemist.
[17] Johan Gansfort, or Wessel, a fifteenth century scholar.
[18] In the hollow handle of which his familiar
spirit was supposed to reside.

[1] Ointment.   [6] Epilepsy.
[2] Fluids.   [7] Palpitating heart.
[3] Disordered.   [8] Overtired.
[4] Salve.   [9] Varieties of colic.
[5] Vertigo.
[10] The theory and practice of medicine.

of the ingredients (as indeed there goes to it six hundred several simples, besides some quantity of human fat, for the conglutination, which we buy of the anatomists), but, when these practitioners come to the last decoction, blow, blow, puff, puff, and all flies *in fumo*.[1] Ha, ha, ha! Poor wretches! I rather pity their folly and in- [200 discretion than their loss of time and money, for those may be recovered by industry, but to be a fool born is a disease incurable. For myself I always from my youth have endeavored to get the rarest secrets, and book them, either in exchange or for money; I spared nor cost nor labor, where anything was worthy to be learned. And, gentlemen, honorable gentlemen, I will undertake, by virtue of chymi- [210 cal[2] art, out of the honorable hat that covers your head, to extract the four elements; that is to say, the fire, air, water, and earth, and return you your felt without burn or stain. For, whilst others have been at the balloo,[3] I have been at my book, and am now past the craggy paths of study, and come to the flowery plains of honor and reputation.

Pol. [*Aside.*] I do assure you, sir, that is his aim. 220

Volp. But to our price—

Per. [*Aside.*]　And that withal, Sir Pol.

Volp. You all know, honorable gentlemen, I never valued this *ampulla*, or vial, at less than eight crowns; but for this time I am content to be deprived of it for six; six crowns is the price, and less in courtesy I know you cannot offer me. Take it or leave it; howsoever, both it and I am at your service. I ask you not as the value of the thing, for then I should de- [230 mand of you a thousand crowns; so the Cardinals Montalto, Fernese, the great Duke of Tuscany, my gossip,[4] with divers other princes, have given me; but I despise money. Only to show my affection to you, honorable gentlemen, and your illustrous state here, I have neglected the messages of these princes, mine own offices, framed my journey hither, only to present you with the fruits of my travels.—Tune [240 your voices once more to the touch of your

instruments, and give the honorable assembly some delightful recreation.

Per. What monstrous and most painful circumstance
Is here, to get some three or four gazettes,[5]
Some threepence i' th' whole, for that 'twill come to.

Song

You that would last long, list to my song;
Make no more coil,[6] but buy of this oil.
Would you be ever fair and young?
Stout of teeth, and strong of tongue?　250
Tart of palate? Quick of ear?
Sharp of sight? Of nostril clear?
Moist of hand? And light of foot?
Or, I will come nearer to 't,
Would you live free from all diseases?
Do the act your mistress pleases?
Yet fright all aches[7] from your bones?
Here's a med'cine for the nones.[8]

Volp. Well, I am in a humor at this time to make a present of the small [260 quantity my coffer contains—to the rich in courtesy, and to the poor for God's sake. Wherefore now mark: I asked you six crowns; and six crowns at other times you have paid me; you shall not give me six crowns, nor five, nor four, nor three, nor two, nor one; nor half a ducat; no, nor a muccinigo.[9] Six—pence it will cost you, or six hundred pound—expect no lower price, for, by the banner of my front, I will [270 not bate a bagatine[10]—that I will have, only, a pledge of your loves, to carry something from amongst you, to show I am not contemned by you. Therefore, now, toss your handkerchiefs cheerfully, cheerfully; and be advertised that the first heroic spirit that deigns to grace me with a handkerchief, I will give it a little remembrance of something beside, shall please it better than if I had presented it with a [280 double pistolet.[11]

Per. [*Aside.*]　Will you be that heroic spark, Sir Pol?

Celia, at the windo', throws down her handkerchief.

O, see! The windore has prevented[12] you.

---

[1] In smoke.　　　　　[2] Chemical.
[3] Probably a misprint for *balloon*, a game of ball.　　　　　　[4] Intimate friend.
[5] Small Italian coins.　　[7] Pronounced *aitches*.
[6] Fuss.　　　　　　　[8] Occasion.
[9] Moccinigo, an Italian coin.
[10] An Italian coin.
[11] A Spanish gold coin.　　[12] Anticipated

VOLP. Lady, I kiss your bounty; and for this timely grace you have done your poor Scoto of Mantua I will return you, over and above my oil, a secret of that high and inestimable nature shall make you forever enamored on that minute wherein your eye first descended on so mean, [290 yet not altogether to be despised, an object. Here is a poulder concealed in this paper, of which, if I should speak to the worth, nine thousand volumes were but as one page, that page as a line, that line as a word, so short is this pilgrimage of man (which some call life) to the expressing of it. Would I reflect on the price? Why, the whole world were but as an empire, that empire as a province, that province as [300 a bank, that bank as a private purse to the purchase of it. I will only tell you it is the poulder that made Venus a goddess (given her by Apollo), that kept her perpetually young, cleared her wrinkles, firmed her gums, filled her skin, colored her hair; from her derived [1] to Helen, and at the sack of Troy unfortunately lost; till now, in this our age, it was as happily recovered, by a studious antiquary, out of some ruins [310 of Asia, who sent a moiety of it to the court of France (but much sophisticated[2]), wherewith the ladies there now color their hair. The rest, at this present, remains with me, extracted to a quintessence, so that, wherever it but touches, in youth it perpetually preserves, in age restores, the complexion; seats your teeth, did they dance like virginal jacks,[3] firm as a wall; makes them white as ivory, that were black as— [320

ACT II. SCENE iii.

[The same.]

Corvino, Politic, Peregrine.

[CORV.] Spite o' the devil, and my shame! Come down here;
Come down! No house but mine to make your scene?
Signior Flaminio,[4] will you down, sir? Down?

[1] Transmitted.
[2] Adulterated.
[3] Attachments to the keys of a virginal.
[4] This name. like the following ones, is associated with the Italian *commedia dell' arte* of the day.

What, is my wife your Franciscina, sir?
No windores on the whole Piazza here
To make your properties but mine? But mine?
He beats away the Mountebank, etc.[5]
Heart! Ere tomorrow I shall be new christened,
And called the Pantalone di Besogniosi [6]
About the town.
PER.   What should this mean, Sir Pol?
POL. Some trick of state, believe it; I will home.   10
PER. It may be some design on you.
POL.   I know not.
I'll stand upon my guard.
PER.   It is your best, sir.
POL. This three weeks, all my advices, all my letters,
They have been intercepted.
PER.   Indeed, sir?
Best have a care.
POL.   Nay, so I will.
PER.   This knight,
I may not lose him, for my mirth, till night.   [*Exeunt.*]

ACT II. SCENE iv.

[A room in Volpone's house.]

Volpone, Mosca.

VOLP. O, I am wounded!
MOS.   Where, sir?
VOLP.   Not without;
Those blows were nothing—I could bear them ever.
But angry Cupid, bolting from her eyes,
Hath shot himself into me like a flame,
Where now he flings about his burning heat,
As in a fornace [7] an ambitious fire,
Whose vent is stopped. The fight is all within me.
I cannot live except thou help me, Mosca;
My liver melts, and I, without the hope
Of some soft air from her refreshing breath,   10
Am but a heap of cinders.
MOS.   'Las, good sir,

[5] This stage direction appears as a marginal note opposite the first line of the scene.
[6] Fool of Beggars.
[7] Furnace.

Would you had never seen her!

VOLP.   Nay, would thou
Hadst never told me of her!

MOS.   Sir, 'tis true;
I do confess I was unfortunate,
And you unhappy; but I'm bound in
    conscience,
No less than duty, to effect my best
To your release of torment, and I will,
    sir.

VOLP. Dear Mosca, shall I hope?

MOS.   Sir, more than dear,
I will not bid you to despair of aught
Within a human compass.

VOLP.   O, there spoke 20
My better angel. Mosca, take my
    keys,
Gold, plate, and jewels—all 's at thy de-
    votion;
Employ them how thou wilt. Nay, coin
    me too,
So thou in this but crown my longings,
    Mosca.

MOS. Use but your patience.

VOLP.   So I have.

MOS.   I doubt not
To bring success to your desires.

VOLP.   Nay, then,
I not repent me of my late disguise.

MOS. If you can horn [1] him, sir, you need
    not.

VOLP.   True.
Besides, I never meant him for my heir.
Is not the color o' my beard and eye-
    brows   30
To make me known?

MOS.   No jot.

VOLP.   I did it well.

MOS. So well, would I could follow you
    in mine
With half the happiness! And yet I
    would
Escape your epilogue. [2]

VOLP.   But were they gulled
With a belief that I was Scoto?

MOS.   Sir,
Scoto himself could hardly have dis-
    tinguished!
I have not time to flatter you now; we'll
    part,
And, as I prosper, so applaud my art.
                          [Exeunt.]

[1] Cuckold.
[2] I.e., a similar beating from Corvino.

ACT II. SCENE V.

[A room in Corvino's house.]

Corvino, Celia, Servatore. [3]

[CORV.] Death of mine honor, with the
    city's fool?
A juggling,   tooth-drawing,   prating
    mountebank?
And at a public windore? Where, whilst
    he,
With his strained action and his dole of
    faces, [4]
To his drug-lecture draws your itching
    ears,
A crew of old, unmarried, noted lechers
Stood leering up like satyrs; and you
    smile
Most graciously, and fan your favors
    forth,
To give your hot spectators satisfaction!
What, was your mountebank their call?
    Their whistle?   10
Or were you enamored on his copper
    rings,
His saffron jewel, with the toadstone [5]
    in 't,
Or his embroidered suit, with the cope
    stitch,
Made of a hearse cloth? Or his old tilt [6]
    feather?
Or his starched beard? Well, you shall
    have him, yes!
He shall come home, and minister unto
    you
The fricace for the mother. [7] Or, let me
    see,
I think you had rather mount; would
    you not mount?
Why, if you'll mount, you may; yes,
    truly, you may!
And so you may be seen, down to th'
    foot.   20
Get you a cittern, Lady Vanity,
And be a dealer with the virtuous man;
Make one. I'll but protest myself a cuck-
    old,
And save your dowry. I'm a Dutch-
    man, I!
For, if you thought me an Italian,

[3] Enters later.   [4] Grimaces.
[5] A fossil or semi-precious stone, popularly
supposed to have come from the head of a toad.
[6] Tilted.   [7] Hysteria.

You would be damned ere you did this,
  you whore!
Thou'ldst tremble to imagine that the
  murder
Of father, mother, brother, all thy race,
Should follow as the subject of my jus-
  tice.
CEL. Good sir, have patience.
CORV. [*Drawing his dagger*.]   What
  couldst thou propose [1]   30
Less to thyself than, in this heat of wrath
And stung with my dishonor, I should
  strike
This steel unto thee, with as many stabs
As thou wert gazed upon with goatish
  eyes?
CEL. Alas, sir, be appeased! I could not
  think
My being at the windore should more now
Move your impatience than at other
  times.
CORV. No? Not to seek and entertain a
  parley
With a known knave, before a multi-
  tude?
You were an actor with your handker-
  chief,   40
Which he most sweetly kissed in the re-
  ceipt,
And might, no doubt, return it with a
  letter,
And point the place where you might
  meet; your sister's,
Your mother's, or your aunt's might
  serve the turn.
CEL. Why, dear sir, when do I make these
  excuses,
Or ever stir abroad but to the church?
And that so seldom—
CORV.   Well, it shall be less;
And thy restraint before was liberty
To what I now decree; and therefore
  mark me.
First, I will have this bawdy light
  dammed up,   50
And, till 't be done, some two or three
  yards off
I'll chalk a line, o'er which if thou but
  chance
To set thy desp'rate foot, more hell,
  more horror,
More wild, remorseless rage shall seize
  on thee

Than on a conjuror that had heedless
  left
His circle's safety ere his devil was laid.
Then here's a lock which I will hang upon
  thee,
And, now I think on 't, I will keep thee
  backwards; [2]
Thy lodging shall be backwards; thy
  walks backwards;
Thy prospect, all be backwards; and no
  pleasure   60
That thou shalt know but backwards.
  Nay, since you force
My honest nature, know it is your own,
Being too open, makes me use you thus.
Since you will not contain your subtle
  nostrils
In a sweet room, but they must snuff
  the air
Of rank and sweaty passengers—(*Knock
  within.*) One knocks.
Away, and be not seen, pain of thy life;
Not look toward the windore; if thou
  dost—
Nay, stay, hear this—let me not pros-
  per, whore,
But I will make thee an anatomy, [3]   70
Dissect thee mine own self, and read a
  lecture
Upon thee to the city, and in public.
Away!—   [*Exit Celia.*

          Enter Servitore.]

          Who's there?
SER.   'Tis Signior Mosca, sir.

          ACT II. SCENE vi.

          [*The same.*]

          Corvino, Mosca.

[CORV.] Let him come in. His master's
  dead; there's yet
Some good to help the bad.—My Mosca,
  welcome!
I guess your news.
MOS.   I fear you cannot, sir.
CORV. Is 't not his death?
MOS.   Rather the contrary.
CORV. Not his recovery?
MOS.   Yes, sir.
CORV.   I am cursed,

----

[1] Expect.

[2] In the rear of the house.   [3] Cadaver.

I am bewitched, my crosses meet to
vex me.
How? How? How? How?

Mos.　　　　　Why, sir, with Scoto's oil;
Corbaccio and Voltore brought of it,
Whilst I was busy in an inner room—

Corv. Death!　　That damned mounte-
bank! But for the law　　　　　10
Now, I could kill the rascal. 'T cannot be
His oil should have that virtue. Ha'
not I
Known him a common rogue, come fid-
dling in
To th' *osteria*,[1] with a tumbling whore,
And, when he has done all his forced
tricks, been glad
Of a poor spoonful of dead wine, with
flies in 't?
It cannot be. All his ingredients
Are a sheep's gall, a roasted bitch's
marrow,
Some few sod [2] earwigs, pounded cater-
pillars,
A little capon's grease, and fasting
spittle—　　　　　20
I know hem to a dram.

Mos.　　　　　I know not, sir;
But some on 't, there, they poured into
his ears,
Some in his nostrils, and recovered him,
Applying but the fricace.

Corv.　　　　　Pox o' that fricace!

Mos. And since, to seem the more officious
And flatt'ring of his health, there they
have had,
At extreme fees, the College of Physicians
Consulting on him, how they might
restore him,
Where one would have a cataplasm [3]
of spices,
Another a flayed ape clapped to his
breast,　　　　　30
A third would ha' it a dog, a fourth an
oil,
With wild cats' skins. At last, they all
resolved
That to preserve him was no other means
But some young woman must be straight
sought out,
Lusty, and full of juice, to sleep by him;
And to this service most unhappily,
And most unwillingly, am I now em-
ployed,

Which here I thought to preacquaint
you with,
For your advice, since it concerns you
most,
Because I would not do that thing might
cross　　　　　40
Your ends, on whom I have my whole
dependence, sir.
Yet, if I do it not, they may delate [4]
My slackness to my patron, work me
out
Of his opinion, and there all your hopes,
Venters, or whatsoever are all frustrate!
I do but tell you, sir. Besides, they are
all
Now striving who shall first present him;
therefore,
I could entreat you, briefly conclude
somewhat;
Prevent hem if you can.

Corv.　　　　　Death to my hopes!
This is my villainous fortune! Best to
hire　　　　　50
Some common courtesan.

Mos.　　　　　Ay, I thought on that, sir;
But they are all so subtle, full of art—
And age again doting and flexible,
So as—I cannot tell—we may, per-
chance,
Light on a quean may cheat us all.

Corv.　　　　　'Tis true.

Mos. No, no. It must be one that has no
tricks, sir,
Some simple thing, a creature made [5]
unto it—
Some wench you may command. Ha'
you no kinswoman?
Godso [6]—think, think, think, think,
think, think, think, sir.
One o' the doctors offered there his
daughter.　　　　　60

Corv. How!

Mos.　　　　Yes, Signior Lupo, the physician.

Corv. His daughter?

Mos.　　　　And a virgin, sir. Why, alas,
He knows the state of 's body, what it is—
That naught can warm his blood, sir,
but a fever,
Nor any incantation raise his spirit.
A long forgetfulness hath seized that
part.

---

[1] Hostelry.　　[2] Sodden, boiled.　　[3] Poultice.

[4] Blame, denounce.
[5] Prepared beforehand.
[6] Gadso, catso, a term of impatience.

Besides, sir, who shall know it? Some
  one or two—
Corv. I pray thee give me leave. [*Walks
  aside.*] If any man
But I had had this luck—the thing in
  'tself,
I know, is nothing.—Wherefore should
  not I   70
As well command my blood and my af-
  fections
As this dull doctor? In the point of
  honor,
The cases are all one of wife and daugh-
  ter.
Mos. [*Aside.*] I hear him coming.[1]
Corv.   She shall do 't; 'tis done.
'Slight! If this doctor, who is not en-
  gaged,
Unless 't be for his counsel, which is
  nothing,
Offer his daughter, what should I, that
  am
So deeply in? I will prevent him. Wretch!
Covetous wretch!—Mosca, I have de-
  termined.
Mos. How, sir?
Corv. We 'll make all sure. The party
  you wot [2] of   80
Shall be mine own wife, Mosca.
Mos.   Sir, the thing,
But that I would not seem to counsel
  you,
I should have motioned [3] to you at the
  first;
And, make your count,[4] you have cut
  all their throats.[5]
Why, 'tis directly taking a possession!
And in his next fit we may let him go.
'Tis but to pull the pillow from his
  head,
And he is thratled.[6] 'T had been done
  before
But for your scrupulous doubts.
Corv.   Ay, a plague on 't,
My conscience fools my wit! Well, I'll
  be brief,   90
And so be thou, lest they should be be-
  fore us.
Go home, prepare him, tell him with
  what zeal
And willingness I do it; swear it was

On the first hearing, as thou mayst do
  truly,
Mine own free motion.
Mos.   Sir, I warrant you,
I'll so possess him with it that the rest
Of his starved clients shall be banished
  all,
And only you received. But come not,
  sir,
Until I send, for I have something else
To ripen for your good—you must not
  know 't.   100
Corv. But do not you forget to send now.
Mos.   Fear not. [*Exit.*]

Act II. Scene vii.

[*The same.*]

Corvino, Celia.

Corv. Where are you, wife? My Celia!
  Wife!

[*Enter Celia.*]

                    What, blubbering?
Come, dry those tears. I think thou
  thought'st me in earnest?
Ha! By this light, I talked so but to
  try thee.
Methinks the lightness of the occasion
Should ha' confirmed thee. Come, I am
  not jealous.
Cel. No?
Corv.   Faith, I am not, I, nor never was;
It is a poor, unprofitable humor.
Do not I know, if women have a will,
They'll do gainst all the watches o' the
  world,
And that the fiercest spies are tamed
  with gold?   10
Tut, I am confident in thee; thou shalt
  see 't.
And see I'll give thee cause, too, to
  believe it.
Come, kiss me. Go, and make thee ready
  straight,
In all thy best attire, thy choicest jewels;
Put hem all on, and with hem thy best
  looks;
We are invited to a solemn feast,
At old Volpone's, where it shall appear
How far I am free from jealousy or fear.
                                        [*Exeunt.*]

---

[1] *I.e.*, into my trap.   [4] Count on it.
[2] Know.   [5] Worsted them all.
[3] Suggested.   [6] Throttled.

ACT III. SCENE i.

[A street.]

Mosca.

[Mos.] I fear I shall begin to grow in love
    With my dear self and my most pros-
       p'rous parts,
They do so spring and burgeon; I can feel
A whimsy i' my blood. I know not how,
Success hath made me wanton. I could
    skip
Out of my skin now, like a subtle snake,
I am so limber. O! Your parasite
Is a most precious thing, dropped from
    above,
Not bred 'mongst clods and clotpolls [1]
    here on earth.
I muse the mystery [2] was not made a
    science,   10
It is so liberally professed! Almost
All the wise world is little else, in nature,
But parasites or sub-parasites. And yet
I mean not those that have your bare
    town-art,
To know who's fit to feed hem, have no
    house,
No family, no care, and therefore mold
Tales for men's ears to bait that sense,
    or get
Kitchen invention and some stale re-
    ceipts
To please the belly and the groin, nor
    those,
With their court-dog tricks, that can
    fawn and fleer,   20
Make their revenue out of legs and
    faces,[3]
Echo my lord, and lick [4] away a moth—
But your fine, elegant rascal, that can
    rise
And stoop, almost together, like an ar-
    row,
Shoot through the air as nimbly as a
    star,
Turn short as doth a swallow, and be
    here,
And there, and here, and yonder, all
    at once,
Present to any humor, all occasion,
And change a visor [5] swifter than a
    thought!

[1] Clodpolls, blockheads.   [4] Flick.
[2] I wonder that the profession.
[3] Bows and smiles.   [5] Facial expression.

This is the creature had the art born
    with him,   30
Toils not to learn it, but doth practice it
Out of most excellent nature, and such
    sparks
Are the true parasites, others but their
    zanies.

ACT III. SCENE ii.

[The same.]

Mosca, Bonario.

[Mos. (Aside.)] Who's this? Bonario, old
    Corbaccio's son?
The person I was bound to seek.—Fair
    sir,
You are happ'ly met.
Bon.   That cannot be by thee.
Mos. Why, sir?
Bon.   Nay, pray thee, know thy way,
    and leave me;
I would be loath to interchange discourse
With such a mate [6] as thou art.
Mos.   Courteous sir,
Scorn not my poverty.
Bon.   Not I, by heaven;
But thou shalt give me leave to hate thy
    baseness.
Mos. Baseness?
Bon.   Ay; answer me, is not thy sloth
Sufficient argument? Thy flattery?   10
Thy means of feeding?
Mos.   Heaven be good to me!
These imputations are too common, sir,
And easily stuck on virtue when she's
    poor.
You are unequal [7] to me, and howe'er
Your sentence may be righteous, yet you
    are not,
That, ere you know me, thus proceed in
    censure.
St. Mark bear witness gainst you, 'tis
    inhuman.   [Weeps.]
Bon. [Aside.] What! Does he weep? The
    sign is soft and good!
I do repent me that I was so harsh.
Mos. 'Tis true that, swayed by strong
    necessity,   20
I am enforced to eat my careful bread
With too much obsequy; [8] 'tis true, be-
    side,
That I am fain to spin mine own poor
    raiment

[6] Fellow.   [7] Unfair.   [8] Obsequiousness.

Out of my mere observance,[1] being not
　born
To a free fortune; but that I have done
Base offices, in rending friends asunder,
Dividing families, betraying counsels,
Whispering false lies, or mining men
　with praises,
Trained [2] their credulity with perjuries,
Corrupted chastity, or am in love　　30
With mine own tender ease, but would
　not rather
Prove the most rugged and laborious
　course,
That might redeem my present estima-
　tion,
Let me here perish, in all hope of good-
　ness.
Bon. [Aside.] This cannot be a personated
　passion.—
I was to blame, so to mistake thy nature;
Pray thee, forgive me, and speak out thy
　business.
Mos. Sir, it concerns you; and, though I
　may seem
At first to make a main offense in man-
　ners,
And in my gratitude unto my master,　40
Yet for the pure love which I bear all
　right,
And hatred of the wrong, I must reveal
　it.
This very hour your father is in purpose
To disinherit you—
Bon.　　　　　How!
Mos.　　　　　And thrust you forth
As a mere stranger to his blood; 'tis true,
　sir.
The work no way engageth me but as
I claim an interest in the general state
Of goodness and true virtue, which I hear
T' abound in you, and for which mere
　respect,
Without a second aim, sir, I have done
　it.　　　　　　　　　　　　　　50
Bon. This tale hath lost thee much of the
　late trust
Thou hadst with me; it is impossible.
I know not how to lend it any thought
My father should be so unnatural.
Mos. It is a confidence that well becomes
Your piety; [3] and formed, no doubt, it is
From your own simple innocence, which
　makes

Your wrong more monstrous and ab-
　horred. But, sir,
I now will tell you more. This very
　minute
It is or will be doing; and, if you　　60
Shall be but pleased to go with me, I'll
　bring you,
I dare not say where you shall see, but
　where
Your ear shall be a witness of the deed,
Hear yourself written bastard, and pro-
　fessed
The common issue of the earth.
Bon.　　　　　　　　I'm mazed!
Mos. Sir, if I do it not, draw your just
　sword,
And score your vengeance on my front
　and face;
Mark me your villain. You have too
　much wrong,
And I do suffer for you, sir. My heart　69
Weeps blood in anguish—
Bon.　　　Lead; I follow thee. [Exeunt.]

Act III. Scene iii.

[A room in Volpone's house.] [4]

Volpone, Nano, Androgyno, Castrone.

[Volp.] [5] Mosca stays long, methinks.—
　Bring forth your sports,
And help to make the wretched time
　more sweet.
Nan. Dwarf, fool, and eunuch, well met
　here we be.
A question it were now, whether [6] of us
　three,
Being all the known delicates of a rich
　man,
In pleasing him, claim the precedency
　can?
Cas. I claim for myself.
And.　　　　　And so doth the fool.
Nan. 'Tis foolish indeed; let me set you
　both to school.
First, for your dwarf, he's little and
　witty,　　　　　　　　　　9
And everything, as it is little, is pretty;
Else why do men say to a creature of my
　shape,

---

[1] Service.　　　[2] Enticed. led on.　　　[3] Filial love.

[4] The scene remains the same to the end of the
act.
[5] The following short debate through line 20
is printed in italics in the original.
[6] Which.

So soon as they see him, "It's a pretty
    little ape"?
And why a pretty ape but for pleasing
    imitation
Of greater men's action in a ridiculous
    fashion?
Beside, this feat [1] body of mine doth not
    crave
Half the meat, drink, and cloth one of
    your bulks will have.
Admit your fool's face be the mother of
    laughter,
Yet, for his brain, it must always come
    after;
And, though that do feed him, it's a
    pitiful case,
His body is beholding [2] to such a bad
    face.   *One knocks.* 20
VOLP. Who's there? My couch! Away!
    Look, Nano, see!
        [*Exeunt Androgyno and Castrone.*]
Give me my caps first—go, inquire. [*Exit
    Nano.*] Now, Cupid
Send it be Mosca, and with fair return!
NAN. [*Within.*] It is the beauteous Mad-
    am—
VOLP.   Would-be—is it?
NAN. The same.
VOLP. Now torment on me! Squire her in,
For she will enter, or dwell here forever.
Nay, quickly. [*Lies down on his couch.*]
    That my fit were past! I fear
A second hell too, that my loathing this
Will quite expel my appetite to the other.
Would she were taking now her tedious
    leave.   30
Lord, how it threats me what I am to
    suffer!

Act III. Scene iv.

*Lady [Politic Would-be], Volpone, Nano,
    Women 2.[3]*

[LADY.] I thank you, good sir. Pray you
    signify
Unto your patron I am here.—This band
Shows not my neck enough.—(I trouble
    you, sir;
Let me request you bid one of my women
Come hither to me.) In good faith, I am
    dressed
Most favorably today! It is no matter;
'Tis well enough.

[1] Delicate, dainty.   [2] Beholden.
[3] The waiting-women enter later.

[*Enter 1 Waiting-woman.*]
        Look, see these petulant things,
How they have done this!
VOLP. [*Aside.*]   I do feel the fever
Ent'ring in at mine ears. O, for a
    charm   9
To fright it hence!
LADY.   Come nearer. Is this curl
In his right place, or this? Why is this
    higher
Than all the rest? You ha' not washed
    your eyes yet?
Or do they not stand even i' your head?
Where's your fellow? Call her.
                [*Exit 1 Woman.*]
NAN. [*Aside.*]   Now St. Mark
Deliver us! Anon she'll beat her women
Because her nose is red.

[*Enter 1 and 2 Women.*]

LADY.   I pray you view
This tire,[4] forsooth. Are all things apt,
    or no?
[1] WOM. One hair a little here sticks out,
    forsooth.
LADY. Does 't so, forsooth? And where was
    your dear sight
When it did so, forsooth? What now!
    Bird-eyed?[5]   20
And you, too? Pray you, both approach
    and mend it.
Now, by that light, I muse yo' are not
    ashamed!
I, that have preached these things so oft
    unto you,
Read you the principles, argued all the
    grounds,
Disputed every fitness, every grace,
Called you to counsel of so frequent
    dressings—
(NAN. More carefully than of your fame
    or honor.)
LADY. Made you acquainted what an
    ample dowry
The knowledge of these things would be
    unto you,
Able alone to get you noble husbands 30
At your return—and you thus to neglect
    it!
Besides, you seeing what a curious [6]
    nation

[4] Headress.   [6] Fastidious.
[5] Sharp-eyed.

Th' Italians are, what will they say of
    me?
"The English lady cannot dress herself."
Here's a fine imputation to our country!
Well, go your ways, and stay i' the next
    room.
This fucus [1] was too coarse too; it's no
    matter.—
Good sir, you 'll give hem entertainment?
    [Exeunt Nano and Waiting-women.]
Volp. [Aside.] The storm comes toward
    me.
Lady.   How does my Volp[one]?
Volp. Troubled with noise, I cannot sleep;
    I dreamt   40
That a strange fury entered now my
    house,
And with the dreadful tempest of her
    breath
Did cleave my roof asunder.
Lady.   Believe me, and I
Had the most fearful dream, could I
    remember 't—
Volp. [Aside.] Out on my fate! I ha'
    given her the occasion
How to torment me; she will tell me hers.
Lady. Methought the golden mediocrity,[2]
Polite and delicate—
Volp.   O, if you do love me,
No more! I sweat and suffer at the
    mention   49
Of any dream; feel how I tremble yet.
Lady. Alas, good soul! The passion of the
    heart.
Seed pearl were good now, boiled with
    syrup of apples,
Tincture of gold, and coral, citron pills,[3]
Your elecampane [4] root, myrobalans [5]—
Volp. Ay me, I have ta'en a grasshopper
    by the wing!
Lady. Burnt silk and amber. You have
    muscadel
Good i' the house—
Volp.   You will not drink, and part?
Lady. No, fear not that. I doubt we shall
    not get
Some English saffron (half a dram would
    serve),
Your sixteen cloves, a little musk, dried
    mints,   60
Bugloss, and barley meal—

Volp. [Aside.]   She's in again!
Before, I feigned diseases; now I have
    one.
Lady. And these applied with a right
    scarlet cloth—
Volp. [Aside.] Another flood of words! A
    very torrent!
Lady. Shall I, sir, make you a poultice?
Volp.   No, no, no!
I am very well; you need prescribe no
    more.
Lady. I have a little studied physic; but
    now
I am all for music, save, i' the forenoons,
An hour or two for painting. I would
    have
A lady, indeed, t' have all—letters and
    arts,   70
Be able to discourse, to write, to paint,
But principal, as Plato holds, your music
(And so does wise Pythagoras, I take it)
Is your true rapture, when there is con-
    cent [6]
In face, in voice, and clothes, and is,
    indeed,
Our sex's chiefest ornament.
Volp.   The poet
As old in time as Plato, and as knowing,
Says that your highest female grace is
    silence.
Lady. Which of your poets? Petrarch?
    Or Tasso? Or Dante?
Guarini? Ariosto? Aretine?   80
Cieco di Hadria? I have read them all.
Volp. [Aside.] Is everything a cause to
    my destruction?
Lady. I think I ha' two or three of hem
    about me.
Volp. [Aside.] The sun, the sea will sooner
    both stand still
Than her eternal tongue! Nothing can
    scape it.
Lady. Here's Pastor Fido—
Volp. [Aside.]   Profess obstinate silence;
That's now my safest.
Lady.   All our English writers,
I mean such as are happy in th' Italian,
Will deign to steal out of this author,
    mainly,
Almost as much as from Montagnié.   90
He has so modern and facile a vein,
Fitting the time, and catching the court
    ear!

[1] Cosmetic.   [3] Peels.
[2] Golden mean.   [4] A herb used as a tonic.
[5] A dried fruit, once used as a medicine.

[6] Harmony, agreement.

Your Petrarch is more passionate, yet
  he,
In days of sonneting, trusted hem with
  much;
Dante is hard, and few can understand
  him.
But for a desperate wit there's Aretine;
Only his pictures are a little obscene—
You mark me not?
VOLP.   Alas, my mind's perturbed.
LADY. Why, in such cases, we must cure
  ourselves,
  Make use of our philosophy—
VOLP.   Oi me!   100
LADY. And, as we find our passions do
  rebel,
  Encounter hem with reason, or divert
  hem
By giving scope unto some other humor
Of lesser danger, as, in politic bodies,
There's nothing more doth overwhelm
  the judgment
And cloud the understanding than too
  much
Settling and fixing, and, as 'twere, sub-
  siding
Upon one object. For the incorporating
Of these same outward things into that
  part
Which we call mental, leaves some cer-
  tain fæces   110
That stop the organs, and, as Plato says,
Assassinates our knowledge.
VOLP. [Aside.]   Now, the spirit
  Of patience help me!
LADY.   Come, in faith, I must
  Visit you more a-days, and make you
  well.
  Laugh and be lusty.
VOLP. [Aside.]   My good angel save me!
LADY. There was but one sole man in all
  the world
With whom I e'er could sympathize, and
  he
Would lie you, often, three, four hours
  together
To hear me speak, and be sometime so
  rapt
As he would answer me quite from the
  purpose,   120
Like you; and you are like him, just. I'll
  discourse,
And 't be but only, sir, to bring you
  asleep,

How we did spend our time and loves
  together
For some six years.
VOLP.   O, O, O, O, O, O!
LADY. For we were *cœtanei*,[1] and brought
  up—
VOLP. [*Aside*.] Some power, some fate,
  some fortune rescue me!

ACT III. SCENE V.

Mosca, Lady, Volpone.

[MOS.] God save you, madam!
LADY.   Good sir.
VOLP.   Mosca, welcome,
  Welcome to my redemption!
MOS.   Why, sir?
VOLP. [*Aside*.]   O,
  Rid me of this my torture, quickly,
  there—
My madam with the everlasting voice.
The bells, in time of pestilence, ne'er
  made
Like noise, or were in that perpetual
  motion!
The Cockpit[2] comes not near it. All
  my house,
But now, steamed like a bath with her
  thick breath;
A lawyer could not have been heard, nor
  scarce
Another woman, such a hail of words   10
She has let fall. For hell's sake, rid her
  hence.
MOS. [*Aside*.] Has she presented?
VOLP. [*Aside*.]   O, I do not care;
  I'll take her absence upon any price,
  With any loss.
MOS.   Madam—
LADY.   I ha' brought your patron
  A toy, a cap here, of mine own work.
MOS.   'Tis well.
  I had forgot to tell you I saw your knight
  Where you'ld little think it.
LADY.   Where?
MOS.   Marry,
  Where yet, if you make haste, you may
  apprehend him,
Rowing upon the water in a gondole,
With the most cunning courtesan of
  Venice.   20
LADY. Is 't true?

---

[1] Of the same age.
[2] Where cockfighting and other noisy entertainments were held.

Mos.   Pursue hem, and believe your eyes;
Leave me to make your gift.—
                        [Exit Lady.]
                I knew 'twould take,
For, lightly,[1] they that use themselves
   most license
Are still most jealous.
Volp.   Mosca, hearty thanks
For thy quick fiction and delivery of
   me.
Now to my hopes, what say'st thou?

              [Enter Lady.]
Lady.   But do you hear, sir?
Volp. *[Aside.]* Again! I fear a paroxysm.
Lady.   Which way
Rowed they together?
Mos.   Toward the Rialto.
Lady. I pray you lend me your dwarf.
Mos.   I pray you take him.—*[Exit Lady.]*
Your hopes, sir, are like happy blossoms,
   fair,   30
And promise timely fruit, if you will
   stay
But the maturing; keep you at your
   couch.
Corbaccio will arrive straight with the
   will;
When he is gone, I'll tell you more.
                         [Exit.]
Volp.   My blood,
My spirits are returned; I am alive,
And, like your wanton gamester at
   primero,[2]
Whose thought had whispered to him,
   "Not go less,"
Methinks I lie, and draw [3]—*[Draws the
   curtains across his bed.]* for an en-
   counter.[3]

Act III. Scene vi.

Mosca, Bonario.

[Mos.] Sir, here concealed you may hear
   all. *[Shows Bonario the hiding place.]*
But, pray you,
Have patience, sir. *(One knocks.)* The
   same's your father knocks;
I am compelled to leave you.   *[Exit.]*
Bon.   Do so.—Yet
Cannot my thought imagine this a truth.
                 [Hides himself.]

---

[1] Generally.   [2] A card game.
[3] Terms in primero, used punningly.

Act III. Scene vii.

Mosca, Corvino, Celia, Bonario, Volpone.

[Mos.] Death on me! You are come too
   soon. What meant you?
Did not I say I would send?
Corv.   Yes, but I feared
You might forget it, and then they pre-
   vent us.
Mos. Prevent?—*[Aside.]*   Did e'er man
   haste so for his horns?
A courtier would not ply it so for a
   place.—
Well, now there's no helping it, stay
   here;
I'll presently return.   *[Exit.]*
Corv.   Where are you, Celia?
You know not wherefore I have brought
   you hither?
Cel. Not well, except you told me.
Corv.   Now I will:
   Hark hither.   *[They step aside.*

       Enter Mosca.]

Mos. *(To Bonario.)*   Sir, your father
   hath sent word   10
It will be half an hour ere he come;
And therefore, if you please to walk the
   while
Into that gallery—at the upper end,
There are some books to entertain the
   time;
And I'll take care no man shall come
   unto you, sir.
Bon. Yes, I will stay there.—*[Aside.]* I
   do doubt this fellow.   *[Exit.]*
Mos. There! He is far enough; he can
   hear nothing.
And, for his father, I can keep him off.
          [Draws Volpone's curtains.]
Corv. Nay, now, there is no starting back,
   and therefore
Resolve upon it. I have so decreed.   20
It must be done. Nor would I move 't
   afore,
Because I would avoid all shifts and
   tricks
That might deny me.
Cel.   Sir, let me beseech you,
Affect not these strange trials; if you
   doubt
My chastity, why, lock me up forever;
Make me the heir of darkness. Let me
   live

Where I may please your fears, if not
  your trust.

Corv. Believe it, I have no such humor, I.
  All that I speak I mean; yet I am not
    mad—
  Not horn-mad,[1] see you? Go to, show
    yourself   30
  Obedient, and a wife.

Cel.   O heaven!

Corv.   I say it,
  Do so.

Cel.   Was this the train?[2]

Corv.   I have told you reasons:
  What the physicians have set down,
    how much
  It may concern me, what my engage-
    ments are,
  My means, and the necessity of those
    means
  For my recovery; wherefore, if you be
  Loyal and mine, be won; respect my
    venture.

Cel. Before your honor?

Corv.   Honor? Tut, a breath!
  There's no such thing in nature—a mere
    term   39
  Invented to awe fools. What is my gold
  The worse for touching, clothes for be-
    ing looked on?
  Why, this 's no more. An old decrepit
    wretch
  That has no sense, no sinew; takes his
    meat
  With others' fingers; only knows to gape
  When you do scald his gums; a voice, a
    shadow;
  And what can this man hurt you?

Cel. [Aside.]   Lord! What spirit
  Is this hath entered him?

Corv.   And, for your fame,
  That's such a jig.[3] As if I would go tell it,
  Cry it on the Piazza! Who shall know it
  But he that cannot speak it, and this
    fellow,   50
  Whose lips are i' my pocket? Save
    yourself
  (If you'll proclaim 't, you may), I know
    no other
  Should come to know it.

Cel.   Are heaven and saints then
    nothing?
  Will they be blind or stupid?

[1] Raving mad, with a reference to cuckoldry.
[2] Trick.   [3] Trifle.

Corv.   How!

Cel.   Good sir,
  Be jealous still, emulate them, and think
  What hate they burn with toward every
    sin.

Corv. I grant you; if I thought it were a
    sin,
  I would not urge you. Should I offer
    this
  To some young Frenchman, or hot
    Tuscan blood
  That had read Aretine, conned all his
    prints,   60
  Knew every quirk within lust's laby-
    rinth,
  And were professed critic in lechery,
  And I would look upon him and applaud
    him,
  This were a sin; but here, 'tis contrary,
  A pious work, mere charity for physic,
  And honest polity to assure mine own.

Cel. O heaven! Canst thou suffer such
  a change?

Volp. [Aside.] Thou art mine honor,
  Mosca, and my pride,
  My joy, my tickling, my delight! Go
  bring hem.

Mos. Please you draw near, sir.

Corv.   Come on! What? 70
  You will not be rebellious? By that
    light—

Mos. Sir, Signior Corvino, here, is come
  to see you.

Volp. O!

Mos.   And, hearing of the consultation
    had
  So lately for your health, is come to
    offer,
  Or rather, sir, to prostitute—

Corv.   Thanks, sweet Mosca.

Mos. Freely, unasked, or unentreated—

Corv.   Well.

Mos. As the true, fervent instance of his
    love,
  His own most fair and proper wife, the
    beauty
  Only of price in Venice—

Corv.   'Tis well urged.

Mos. To be your comfortress, and to pre-
    serve you.   80

Volp. Alas, I am past already! Pray you,
  thank him
  For his good care and promptness; but
    for that,

'Tis a vain labor e'en to fight gainst
heaven—
Applying fire to a stone—uh, uh, uh,
uh!—
Making a dead leaf grow again. I take
His wishes gently, though; and you may
tell him
What I have done for him. Marry, my
state is hopeless.
Will him to pray for me, and t' use his
fortune
With reverence when he comes to 't.
Mos.   Do you hear, sir?
Go to him with your wife.
Corv.   Heart of my father! 90
Wilt thou persist thus? Come, I pray
thee, come.
Thou seest 'tis nothing, Celia. By this
hand,
I shall grow violent. Come, do 't, I say.
Cel. Sir, kill me rather; I will take down
poison,
Eat burning coals, do anything—
Corv.   Be damned!
Heart, I will drag thee hence home by
the hair;
Cry thee a strumpet through the streets;
rip up
Thy mouth unto thine ears; and slit
thy nose,
Like a raw rochet![1] Do not tempt me;
come.
Yield, I am loath—Death! I will buy
some slave   100
Whom I will kill, and bind thee to him
alive,
And at my windore hang you forth,
devising
Some monstrous crime, which I, in cap-
ital letters,
Will eat into thy flesh with aqua fortis
And burning corsives[2] on this stubborn
breast.
Now, by the blood thou hast incensed,
I'll do 't!
Cel. Sir, what you please, you may; I
am your martyr.
Corv. Be not thus obstinate; I ha' not
deserved it.
Think who it is entreats you. Pray thee,
sweet—
Good faith, thou shalt have jewels,
gowns, attires,   110

What thou wilt think and ask. Do but
go kiss him.
Or touch him but. For my sake. At my
suit—
This once. No? Not? I shall remember
this.
Will you disgrace me thus? Do you
thirst my undoing?
Mos. Nay, gentle lady, be advised.
Corv.   No, no.
She has watched her time. God's pre-
cious, this is scurvy,
'Tis very scurvy; and you are—
Mos.   Nay, good sir.
Corv. An arrant locust—by heaven, a
locust!—
Whore, crocodile, that hast thy tears
prepared,
Expecting how thou'lt bid hem flow—
Mos.   Nay, pray you, sir! 120
She will consider.
Cel.   Would my life would serve
To satisfy.
Corv.   'Sdeath! If she would but
speak to him,
And save my reputation, 'twere some-
what;
But spitefully to affect my utter ruin—
Mos. Ay, now you have put your fortune
in her hands.
Why, i' faith, it is her modesty; I must
quit [3] her.
If you were absent, she would be more
coming;
I know it, and dare undertake for her.
What woman can before her husband?
Pray you,
Let us depart and leave her here.
Corv.   Sweet Celia, 130
Thou mayst redeem all yet; I'll say no
more.
If not, esteem yourself as lost. Nay,
stay there.
                  [Exeunt Corvino and Mosca.]
Cel. O God and his good angels! Whither,
whither
Is shame fled human breasts, that with
such ease
Men dare put off your honors and their
own?
Is that, which ever was a cause of life,[4]
Now placed beneath the basest circum-
stance,

[1] A fish.   [2] Corrosives.

[3] Acquit, excuse.   [4] I.e., wedlock.

And modesty an exile made for money?

VOLP. (*He leaps off from his couch.*) Ay,
in Corvino, and such earth-fed minds,
That never tasted the true heaven of
love.   140
Assure thee, Celia, he that would sell
thee
Only for hope of gain, and that uncertain,
He would have sold his part of Paradise
For ready money, had he met a cope-
man.[1]
Why art thou mazed to see me thus re-
vived?
Rather applaud thy beauty's miracle;
'Tis thy great work, that hath, not now
alone,
But sundry times, raised me in several
shapes,
And but this morning, like a mounte-
bank,   149
To see thee at thy windore. Ay, before
I would have left my practice,[2] for thy
love,
In varying figures I would have con-
tended
With the blue Proteus or the hornéd
flood.[3]
Now art thou welcome.

CEL.   Sir!

VOLP.   Nay, fly me not,
Nor let thy false imagination
That I was bedrid make thee think I
am so;
Thou shalt not find it. I am now as
fresh,
As hot, as high, and in as jovial plight
As when, in that so celebrated scene
At recitation of our comedy   160
For entertainment of the great Valois,[4]
I acted young Antinous, and attracted
The eyes and ears of all the ladies pres-
ent
To admire each graceful gesture, note,
and footing.

SONG

Come, my Celia, let us prove,
While we can, the sports of love.
Time will not be ours forever;
He, at length, our good will sever.

Spend not then his gifts in vain.
Suns that set may rise again;   170
But, if once we lose this light,
'Tis with us perpetual night.
Why should we defer our joys?
Fame and rumor are but toys.
Cannot we delude the eyes
Of a few poor household spies,
Or his easier ears beguile,
Thus removéd by our wile?
'Tis no sin love's fruits to steal,
But the sweet thefts to reveal.   180
To be taken, to be seen,
These have crimes accounted been.

CEL. Some serene[5] blast me, or dire lightning strike
This my offending face!

VOLP.   Why droops my Celia?
Thou hast in place of a base husband
found
A worthy lover; use thy fortune well,
With secrecy and pleasure. See, behold,
What thou art queen of—not in expec-
tation,
As I feed others, but possessed and
crowned.
See here a rope of pearl, and each more
orient   190
Than that the brave Egyptian queen
caroused;[6]
Dissolve and drink hem. See, a car-
buncle,
May put out both the eyes of our St.
Mark;
A diamant, would have bought Lollia
Paulina,[7]
When she came in like starlight, hid
with jewels
That were the spoils of provinces. Take
these,
And wear and lose hem; yet remains
an earring
To purchase them again, and this whole
state.
A gem but worth a private patrimony
Is nothing; we will eat such at a meal. 200
The heads of parrots, tongues of night-
ingales,
The brains of peacocks and of estriches[8]
Shall be our food, and, could we get the
phœnix,

---

[1] Chapman, dealer.   [2] Plotting.
[3] A reference to the story of Acheloüs, god of
the Grecian river.
[4] Henry VI was entertained at Venice in 1574.

[5] The damp evening air.
[6] *I.e.*, Cleopatra drank.
[7] Mistress of Emperor Claudius.
[8] Ostriches.

Though nature lost her kind, she were
  our dish.
CEL. Good sir, these things might move a
  mind affected
With such delights; but I, whose inno-
  cence
Is all I can think wealthy, or worth th'
  enjoying,
And which, once lost, I have naught to
  lose beyond it,
Cannot be taken with these sensual
  baits.   209
If you have conscience—
VOLP.   'Tis the beggar's virtue;
If thou hast wisdom, hear me, Celia.
Thy baths shall be the juice of July-
  flowers,[1]
Spirit of roses and of violets,
The milk of unicorns, and panthers'
  breath [2]
Gathered in bags and mixed with Cre-
  tan wines.
Our drink shall be preparéd gold and
  amber,
Which we will take until my roof whirl
  round
With the vertigo, and my dwarf shall
  dance,
My eunuch sing, my fool make up the
  antic,[3]
Whilst we, in changéd shapes, act Ovid's
  tales,   220
Thou, like Europa now, and I like Jove,
Then I like Mars, and thou like Erycine;
So of the rest, till we have quite run
  through
And wearied all the fables of the gods.
Then will I have thee in more modern
  forms,
Attired like some sprightly dame of
  France,
Brave Tuscan lady, or proud Spanish
  beauty,
Sometimes unto the Persian sophy's
  wife,
Or the grand signior's mistress, and,
  for change,
To one of our most artful courtesans, 230
Or some quick Negro, or cold Russian;

And I will meet thee in as many shapes,
Where we may so transfuse our wan-
  d'ring souls
Out at our lips, and score up sums of
  pleasures,

    That the curious shall not know
    How to tell [4] them as they flow,
    And the envious, when they find
    What their number is, be pined.[5]

CEL. If you have ears that will be pierced,
  or eyes
That can be opened, a heart may be
  touched,   240
Or any part that yet sounds man about
  you,
If you have touch of holy saints or
  heaven,
Do me the grace to let me scape. If not,
Be bountiful and kill me. You do know
I am a creature, hither ill betrayed,
By one whose shame I would forget it
  were;
If you will deign me neither of these
  graces,
Yet feed your wrath, sir, rather than
  your lust
(It is a vice comes nearer manliness),
And punish that unhappy crime of
  nature,   250
Which you miscall my beauty. Flay my
  face,
Or poison it with ointments, for seducing
Your blood to this rebellion. Rub these
  hands
With what may cause an eating leprosy,
E'en to my bones and marrow—anything
That may disfavor me, save in my honor.
And I will kneel to you, pray for you,
  pay down
A thousand hourly vows, sir, for your
  health,
Report and think you virtuous—
VOLP.   Think me cold,
Frozen, and impotent, and so report
  me?   260
That I had Nestor's hernia, thou wouldst
  think.
I do degenerate, and abuse my nation,
To play with opportunity thus long;
I should have done the act, and then
  have parleyed.
Yield, or I'll force thee.   [Seizes her.]

---

[1] Gillyflowers.
[2] It was a common belief that panthers had
fragrant breaths. Panther was also the name
of a sweet-smelling drug.
[3] Pageant.
[4] Count.   [5] Pained.

CEL. 　　　　　O! Just God!
VOLP. 　　　　　　　　In vain—
BON. (*He leaps out from where Mosca had
　　placed him.*) Forbear, foul ravisher!
　　Libidinous swine!
Free the forced lady, or thou di'st, im-
　　postor.
But that I am loath to snatch thy pun-
　　ishment
Out of the hand of justice, thou shouldst
　　yet
Be made the timely sacrifice of ven-
　　geance 　　　　　　　　　　　　　270
Before this altar and this dross, thy
　　idol.—
Lady, let's quit the place; it is the den
Of villainy. Fear naught; you have a
　　guard.
And he ere long shall meet his just re-
　　ward. 　　[*Exeunt Bonario and Celia.*]
VOLP. Fall on me, roof, and bury me in
　　ruin!
Become my grave, that wert my shelter!
　　O!
I am unmasked, unspirited, undone,
Betrayed to beggary, to infamy—

ACT III. SCENE viii.

Mosca, Volpone.

[MOS.] Where shall I run, most wretched
　　shame of men,
To beat out my unlucky brains?
VOLP. 　　　　　　　　Here, here.
What! Dost thou bleed?
MOS. 　　　　O, that his well-driv'n sword
Had been so courteous to have cleft me
　　down
Unto the navel, ere I lived to see
My life, my hopes, my spirits, my pa-
　　tron, all
Thus desperately engagéd by my error!
VOLP. Woe on thy fortune!
MOS. 　　　　　　And my follies, sir.
VOLP. Th' hast made me miserable.
MOS. 　　　　　　　And myself, sir.
Who would have thought he would have
　　hearkened so? 　　　　　　　　　10
VOLP. What shall we do?
MOS. 　　　　I know not; if my heart
Could expiate the mischance, I'ld pluck
　　it out.
Will you be pleased to hang me, or cut
　　my throat?

And I'll requite you, sir. Let's die like
　　Romans,[1]
Since we have lived like Grecians.[2]
　　　　　　　　They knock without.
VOLP. 　　　　Hark! Who's there?
I hear some footing; officers, the *saffi*,[3]
Come to apprehend us! I do feel the
　　brand
Hissing already at my forehead; now
Mine ears are boring.
MOS. 　　　　To your couch, sir; you
Make that place good, however. [*Vol-
　　pone lies down.*] Guilty men 　　20
Suspect what they deserve still.—Si-
　　gnior Corbaccio!

ACT III. SCENE ix.

Corbaccio, Mosca, Voltore,[4] *Volpone.*

[CORB.] Why, how now, Mosca?
MOS. 　　　　　O, undone, amazed, sir.
Your son, I know not by what accident,
Acquainted with your purpose to my
　　patron,
Touching your will and making him your
　　heir,
Entered our house with violence, his
　　sword drawn,
Sought for you, called you wretch, un-
　　natural,
Vowed he would kill you.
CORB. 　　　　　　　　Me?
MOS. 　　　　　　　Yes, and my patron.
CORB. This act shall disinherit him indeed;
Here is the will.
MOS. 　　　　　'Tis well, sir.
CORB. 　　　　　　　　Right and well.
Be you as careful now for me.

[*Enter Voltore behind.*]

MOS. 　　　　　　My life, sir, 　　10
Is not more tendered;[5] I am only yours.
CORB. How does he? Will he die shortly,
　　think'st thou?
MOS. 　　　　　I fear
He'll outlast May.
CORB. 　　　　Today?
MOS. 　　　　　No, last out May, sir.
CORB. Couldst thou not gi' him a dram?
MOS. 　　　　O, by no means, sir.
CORB. Nay, I'll not bid you.

---

[1] *I.e.*, commit suicide. 　　[4] Enters later.
[2] Greeks, roisterers. 　　　　[5] Attended to.
[3] Police.

Volt. [*Coming forward.*] This is a
knave, I see.

Mos. [*Aside.*] How! Signior Voltore! Did
he hear me?

Volt. Parasite!

Mos. Who's that?—O, sir, most timely
welcome—

Volt. Scarce
To the discovery of your tricks, I fear.
You are his, "only"? And mine also,
are you not?

Mos. Who? I, sir!

Volt. You, sir. What devise is this 20
About a will?

Mos. A plot for you, sir.

Volt. Come,
Put not your foists [1] upon me; I shall
scent hem.

Mos. Did you not hear it?

Volt. Yes, I hear Corbaccio
Hath made your patron there his heir.

Mos. 'Tis true,
By my device, drawn to it by my plot,
With hope—

Volt. Your patron should reciprocate?
And you have promised?

Mos. For your good I did, sir.
Nay, more, I told his son, brought, hid
him here,
Where he might hear his father pass the
deed,
Being persuaded to it by this thought,
sir, 30
That the unnaturalness, first, of the act,
And then his father's oft disclaiming in
him
(Which I did mean t' help on), would
sure enrage him
To do some violence upon his parent,
On which the law should take sufficient
hold,
And you be stated in a double hope.
Truth be my comfort and my conscience,
My only aim was to dig you a fortune
Out of these two old rotten sepulchers—

Volt. I cry thee mercy, Mosca.

Mos. Worth your patience 40
And your great merit, sir. And see the
change!

Volt. Why, what success?

Mos. Most hapless! You must help, sir.
Whilst we expected th' old raven, in
comes

[1] Tricks.

Corvino's wife, sent hither by her
husband—

Volt. What, with a present?

Mos. No, sir, on visitation
(I'll tell you how anon), and, staying long,
The youth he grows impatient, rushes
forth,
Seizeth the lady, wounds me, makes her
swear
(Or he would murder her, that was his
vow)
T' affirm my patron to have done her
rape— 50
Which how unlike it is, you see!—and
hence,
With that pretext he's gone, t' accuse his
father,
Defame my patron, defeat you—

Volt. Where's her husband?
Let him be sent for straight.

Mos. Sir, I'll go fetch him.

Volt. Bring him to the Scrutineo.[2]

Mos. Sir, I will.

Volt. This must be stopped.

Mos. O, you do nobly, sir.
Alas, 'twas labored all, sir, for your good;
Nor was there want of counsel in the
plot;
But Fortune can at any time o'erthrow
The projects of a hundred learned clerks,
sir. 60

Corb. [*Cupping his ear.*] What's that?

Volt. Wilt please you, sir, to go along?
[*Exit with Corbaccio.*]

Mos. Patron, go in, and pray for our success.

Volp. [*Rising.*] Need makes devotion;
heaven your labor bless! [*Exeunt.*]

Act IV. Scene i.

[*A street.*]

Politic, Peregrine.

[Pol.] I told you, sir, it was a plot; you see
What observation is! You mentioned me
For some instructions; I will tell you, sir
(Since we are met here in this height of
Venice),
Some few particulars I have set down,
Only for this meridian,[3] fit to be known
Of your crude [4] traveler; and they are
these.

[2] Senate House.   [4] Inexperienced.
[3] Special locality.

I will not touch, sir, at your phrase, or
　　clothes,
For they are old.

PER.　　　　　　Sir, I have better.

POL.　　　　　　　　　　　　Pardon;
　I meant, as they are themes.

PER.　　　　　　　O, sir, proceed.　　10
　I'll slander you no more of wit, good sir.

POL. First, for your garb, [1] it must be
　　grave and serious,
　Very reserved and locked; not tell a secret
　On any terms, not to your father; scarce
　A fable, but with caution; make sure
　　choice
　Both of your company and discourse;
　　beware
　You never speak [2] a truth—

PER.　　　　　　How!

POL.　　　　　　　　Not to strangers,
　For those be they you must converse [3]
　　with most;
　Others I would not know, sir, but at
　　distance,
　So as I still might be a saver in hem; [4]　20
　You shall have tricks else passed upon
　　you hourly.
　And then, for your religion, profess none,
　But wonder at the diversity of all;
　And, for your part, protest, were there
　　no other
　But simply the laws o' th' land, you
　　could content you.
　Nic. Machiavel and Monsieur Bodine [5]
　　both
　Were of this mind. Then must you learn
　　the use
　And handling of your silver fork at meals,
　The metal of your glass (these are main
　　matters
　With your Italian), and to know the
　　hour　　　30
　When you must eat your melons and
　　your figs.

PER. Is that a point of state too?

POL.　　　　　　　　Here it is.
　For your Venetian, if he see a man
　Preposterous in the least, he has him
　　straight;

He has; he strips him. I'll acquaint you,
　　sir.
I now have lived here 'tis some fourteen
　　months.
Within the first week of my landing here
All took me for a citizen of Venice,
I knew the forms so well.

PER. [Aside.]　　　　　And nothing else.

POL. I had read Contarene, [6] took me a
　　house,　　　40
　Dealt with my Jews to furnish it with
　　movables—
　Well, if I could but find one man, one
　　man
　To mine own heart, whom I durst trust,
　　I would—

PER. What, what, sir?

POL.　　　Make him rich, make him a
　　fortune.
He should not think again.　I would
　　command it.

PER. As how?

POL.　　With certain projects that I have,
　Which I may not discover.

PER. [Aside.]　　　　　If I had
　But one to wager with, I would lay odds
　　now
　He tells me instantly.

POL.　　　　　　　One is, and that
　I care not greatly who knows, to serve
　　the state　　　50
　Of Venice with red herrings for three
　　years,
　And at a certain rate from Rotterdam,
　Where I have correspondence.　There's
　　a letter,
　Sent me from one o' th' states, and to
　　that purpose.
　He cannot write his name, but that's his
　　mark.

PER. He is a chaundler? [7]

POL.　　　　　No, a cheesemonger.
　There are some other too with whom I
　　treat
　About the same negotiation;
　And I will undertake it.　For 'tis thus
　(I'll do 't with ease; I have cast [8] it all):
　　your hoy [9]　　　60
　Carries but three men in her, and a boy;

---

[1] Demeanor.

[2] Original reads *spake*.

[3] Associate.

[4] *I.e.*, so that I might not lose any money
through them.

[5] Jean Bodin, a sixteenth century French political philosopher.

[6] Cardinal Gasparo Contraini, author of a
work on Venice.

[7] Chandler, dealer in provisions.

[8] Calculated.

[9] A small coasting vessel.

And she shall make me three returns a
  year;
So, if there come but one of three, I save;
If two, I can defalk.[1] But this is, now,
If my main project fail.
PER.   Then you have others?
POL. I should be loath to draw the subtle
  air
Of such a place without my thousand
  aims.
I'll not dissemble, sir; where'er I come,
I love to be considerative; and, 'tis true,
I have at my free hours thought upon   70
Some certain goods unto the state of
  Venice,
Which I do call my cautions, and, sir,
  which
I mean, in hope of pension, to propound
To the Great Council, then unto the
  Forty,
So to the Ten. My means are made al-
  ready—
PER. By whom?
POL.   Sir, one that, though his place
  b' obscure,
Yet he can sway, and they will hear him.
  H'is
A *commandadore*.
PER.   What! A common sergeant?
POL. Sir, such as they are, put it in their
  mouths,
What they should say, sometimes; as
  well as greater.   80
I think I have my notes to show you—
PER.   Good sir.
POL. But you shall swear unto me, on your
  gentry,
Not to anticipate—
PER.   I, sir?
POL.   Nor reveal
A circumstance—My paper is not with
  me.
PER. O, but you can remember, sir.
POL.   My first is
Concerning tinder boxes. You must
  know
No family is here without its box.
Now, sir, it being so portable a thing,
Put case that you or I were ill affected
Unto the state, sir; with it in our pockets,
Might not I go into the Arsenal,   91
Or you come out again, and none the
  wiser?

PER. Except yourself, sir.
POL.   Go to, then. I therefore
Advertise to the state how fit it were
That none but such as were known
  patriots,
Sound lovers of their country, should be
  suffered
T' enjoy them in their houses, and even
  those
Sealed at some office, and at such a
  bigness
As might not lurk in pockets.
PER.   Admirable!
POL. My next is, how t' inquire, and be re-
  solved   100
By present demonstration, whether a
  ship,
Newly arrived from Soria [2] or from
Any suspected part of all the Levant,
Be guilty of the plague; and, where they
  use
To lie out forty, fifty days sometimes,
About the Lazaretto, for their trial,
I'll save that charge and loss unto the
  merchant,
And in an hour clear the doubt.
PER.   Indeed, sir?
POL. Or—I will lose my labor.
PER.   My faith, that's much.
POL. Nay, sir, conceive [3] me. 'Twill cost
  me, in onions,   110
Some thirty livres—
PER.   Which is one pound sterling.
POL. Beside my waterworks; for this I do,
  sir:
First, I bring in your ship twixt two brick
  walls
(But those the state shall venter); on the
  one
I strain me a fair tarpauling, and in that
I stick my onions, cut in halves; the
  other
Is full of loopholes, out at which I thrust
The noses of my bellows; and those
  bellows
I keep, with waterworks, in perpetual
  motion,   119
Which is the easi'st matter of a hundred.
Now, sir, your onion, which doth nat-
  urally
Attract th' infection, and your bellows
  blowing
The air upon him, will show instantly,

---

[1] Cut off, reduce.   [2] Syria.   [3] Understand.

By his changed color, if there be con-
tagion,
Or else remain as fair as at the first.
Now 'tis known, 'tis nothing.
PER.　　　　　　　　　You are right, sir.
POL. I would I had my note.
PER.　　　　　　　　　Faith, so would I;
But you ha' done well for once, sir.
POL.　　　　　　　　　Were I false,
Or would be made so, I could show you
reasons
How I could sell this state now to the
Turk,　　　　　　　　　　　　　130
Spite of their galleys or their—
　　　　　　　　　[Examines his notes.]
PER.　　　　　　　　　Pray you, Sir Pol.
POL. I have hem not about me.
PER. [Aside.]　　　　　That I feared.—
They are there, sir?
POL.　　　　　　No, this is my diary,
Wherein I note my actions of the day.
PER. Pray you, let's see, sir. What is here?
Notandum,[1]　　　　　　　[Reads.]
"A rat had gnawn my spur leathers;
notwithstanding,
I put on new, and did go forth; but first
I threw three beans over the threshold.
Item,
I went and bought two toothpicks,
whereof one
I burst immediately, in a discourse　140
With a Dutch merchant, 'bout ragion'
del stato.[2]
From him I went and paid a moccinigo
For piecing my silk stockings; by the way
I cheapened[3] sprats; and at St. Mark's I
urined."
Faith, these are politic notes!
POL.　　　　　　　　Sir, I do slip
No action of my life, thus but I quote it.
PER. Believe me, it is wise!
POL.　　　　　Nay, sir, read forth.

ACT IV. SCENE ii.

[The same.]

[Enter, at a distance,] Lady, Nano, Women,
　　　　　　　　　　　Politic, Peregrine.

[LADY.] Where should this loose knight be,
trow? Sure, h' is housed.
NAN. Why, then he's fast.

LADY.　　　Ay, he plays both[4] with me.
I pray you stay. This heat will do more
harm
To my complexion than his heart is
worth.
(I do not care to hinder, but to take
him.) [Rubs her cheeks.]
How it comes off!
[1] WOM.　　　My master's yonder.
LADY.　　　　　　　　　　Where?
[2] WOM. With a young gentleman.
LADY.　　　　　　　That same's the party—
In man's apparel! Pray you, sir, jog my
knight;
I will be tender to his reputation,
However he demerit.
POL. [Spying his Wife at a distance.]　My
lady!
PER.　　　Where?　　　　　　　　　10
POL. 'Tis she indeed, sir; you shall know
her. She is,
Were she not mine, a lady of that merit,
For fashion and behavior; and for beauty
I durst compare—
PER.　　　It seems you are not jealous,
That dare commend her.
POL.　　　　　Nay, and for discourse—
PER. Being your wife, she cannot miss
that.
POL. [Approaching his Wife.]　　Madam,
Here is a gentleman; pray you, use him
fairly;
He seems a youth, but he is—
LADY.　　　　　　　　　None?
POL.　　　　　　　　　　Yes, one
Has put his face as soon into the
world—
LADY. You mean, as early? But today?
POL.　　　　　　　　　How's this?　20
LADY. Why, in this habit, sir; you appre-
hend me.
Well, Master Would-be, this doth not
become you;
I had thought the odor, sir, of your good
name
Had been more precious to you; that you
would not
Have done this dire massacre on your
honor.
One of your gravity and rank besides!
But knights, I see, care little for the oath
They make to ladies—chiefly their own
ladies.

---

[1] Let it be noted; take notice.
[2] Politics.　　　　　　　[3] Bargained for.
[4] I.e., both fast and loose.

Pol. Now, by my spurs, the symbol of my
　knighthood—
(Per. Lord, how his brain is humbled for
　an oath!)　　　　　　　　　　　　　30
Pol. I reach [1] you not.
Lady.　　　　　Right, sir, your polity
May bear it through thus.—[To Pere-
　grine.] Sir, a word with you.
I would be loath to contest publicly
With any gentlewoman, or to seem
Froward or violent, as the courtier says;
It comes too near rusticity in a lady,
Which I would shun by all means. And
　however
I may deserve from Master Would-be,
　yet
T' have one fair gentlewoman thus be
　made
Th' unkind instrument to wrong an-
　other,　　　　　　　　　　　　　40
And one she knows not, ay, and to
　persever,[2]
In my poor judgment, is not warranted
From being a solecism in [3] our sex,
If not in manners.
Per.　　　　　How is this!
Pol.　　　　　　　　　Sweet madam,
Come nearer to your aim.
Lady.　　　　　　　Marry, and will, sir.
Since you provoke me with your im-
　pudence
And laughter of your light land-siren
　here,
Your Sporus, your hermaphrodite—
Per.　　　　　　　　What's here?
Poetic fury and historic storms! [4]
Pol. The gentleman, believe it, is of
　worth　　　　　　　　　　　　　50
And of our nation.
Lady.　　　Ay, your Whitefriars [5] nation.
Come, I blush for you, Master Would-be,
　I,
And am ashamed you should ha' no more
　forehead [6]
Than thus to be the patron, or St.
　George,
To a lewd harlot, a base fricatrice,[7]
A female devil, in a male outside.
Pol.　　　　　　　　　　　Nay,

And you be such a one, I must bid adieu
To your delights. The case appears too
　liquid.[8]　　　　　　　　　　　[Exit.]
Lady. Ay, you may carry 't clear, with
　your state face!　　　　　　　　59
But, for your carnival concupiscence,[9]
Who here is fled for liberty of con-
　science,
From furious persecution of the marshal,
Her will I disc'ple.[10]
Per.　　　　　This is fine, i' faith!
And do you use this often? Is this part
Of your wit's exercise gainst you have
　occasion?
Madam—
Lady.　　　　　Go to, sir.
Per.　　　　　　Do you hear me, lady?
Why, if your knight have set you to beg
　shirts,
Or to invite me home, you might have
　done it
A nearer way by far.
Lady.　　　　　　This cannot work you
Out of my snare.
Per.　　　Why, am I in it, then?　70
Indeed, your husband told me you were
　fair,
And so you are, only your nose inclines,
That side that's next the sun, to the
　queenapple.[11]
Lady. This cannot be endured by any
　patience.

ACT IV. SCENE iii.

[The same.]

Mosca, Lady, Peregrine [, Nano, Women].

[Mos.] What's the matter, madam?
Lady.　　　　　　　　　If the senate
Right not my quest in this, I will protest
　hem
To all the world no aristocracy.
Mos. What is the injury, lady?
Lady.　　　　　Why, the callet [12]
You told me of, here I have ta'en dis-
　guised.
Mos. Who? This? What means your
　ladyship? The creature

---

[1] Comprehend.　　　　　[3] Crime against.
[2] Persevere.　　　　　　[4] Dramatic stormings.
[5] Disreputable district in London where evil-
doers were not followed by the law.
[6] Modesty.　　　　　　　[7] Prostitute.

[8] Clear.
[9] The object of your carnal desire.
[10] Disciple, discipline.
[11] A particularly red apple.
[12] Wench.

I mentioned to you is apprehended now
Before the senate; you shall see her—
LADY.　　　　　　　　　　　　　　Where?
MOS. I'll bring you to her. This young gentleman,
I saw him land this morning at the
　　port.　　　　　　　　　　　　　　　10
LADY. Is 't possible! How has my judgment wandered!
Sir, I must, blushing, say to you I have
　　erred
And plead your pardon.
PER.　　　　　　What, more changes yet?
LADY. I hope yo' ha' not the malice to remember
A gentlewoman's passion. If you stay
In Venice here, please you to use me,
　　sir—
MOS. Will you go, madam?
LADY.　　Pray you, sir, use me; in faith,
The more you see me, the more I shall conceive
You have forgot our quarrel.
　　　　　　　　　　[Exeunt All but Peregrine.]
PER.　　　　　　　　　　　This is rare!
Sir Politic Would-be? No, Sir Politic
　　Bawd,　　　　　　　　　　　　　20
To bring me thus acquainted with his
　　wife!
Well, wise Sir Pol, since you have practiced thus
Upon my freshmanship, I'll try your
　　salthead,[1]
What proof it is against a counterplot.
　　　　　　　　　　　　　　　　[Exit.]

ACT IV. SCENE iv.

[The Senate.]

Voltore, Corbaccio, Corvino, Mosca.

[VOLT.] Well, now you know the carriage
　　of the business,
Your constancy is all that is required
Unto the safety of it.
MOS.　　　　　　　　　　　Is the lie
Safely conveyed[2] amongst us? Is that
　　sure?
Knows every man his burden?[3]
CORV.　　　　　　　Yes.
MOS.　　　　　　　　　Then shrink not.
CORV. But knows the advocate the truth?
MOS.　　　　　　　　　　　　O, sir,

By no means; I devised a formal tale
That salved your reputation. But be
　　valiant, sir.
CORV. I fear no one but him, that this his
　　pleading
Should make him stand for a co-heir—
MOS.　　　　　　　Co-halter!　10
Hang him; we will but use his tongue,
　　his noise,
As we do Croaker's[4] here.
CORV.　　　　　　Ay, what shall he do?
MOS. When we ha' done, you mean?
CORV.　　　　　　　Yes.
MOS.　　　　　　　　　Why, we'll think—
Sell him for mummia![5] He's half dust
　　already.—
　　(To Voltore.) Do not you smile to see
　　this buffalo,[6]
How he doth sport it with his head?—
　　[Aside.] I should,
If all were well and past.—(To Corbaccio.)
Sir, only you
Are he that shall enjoy the crop of all,
And these not know for whom they toil.
CORB.　　　　　　　　　　Ay, peace.
MOS. (To Corvino.) But you shall eat it.—
　　[Aside.] Much!—(Then to Voltore
　　again.) Worshipful sir,　20
Mercury sit upon your thund'ring tongue,
Or the French Hercules,[7] and make your
　　language
As conquering as his club, to beat along,
As with a tempest, flat, our adversaries;
But much more yours, sir.
VOLT.　　　　Here they come; ha' done.
MOS. I have another witness, if you need,
　　sir,
I can produce.
VOLT.　　　　　　Who is it?
MOS.　　　　　　　　　Sir, I have her.

ACT IV. SCENE v.

[The same.]

Avocatori 4, Bonario, Celia, Voltore, Corbaccio, Corvino, Mosca, Notario, Commandadori.

[AVOC. 1.] The like of this the senate
　　never heard of.

---

[4] Corbaccio's.
[5] Mummy, a medicine.
[6] A horned animal; i.e., a cuckold.
[7] I.e., Ognius, regarded as the symbol of eloquence. See Lucian.

[1] Salthood, lechery.
[2] Arranged.　　　[3] Refrain of a song; part.

Avoc. 2. 'Twill come most strange to them when we report it.

Avoc. 4. The gentlewoman has been ever held

Of unreprovéd name.

Avoc. 3.   So the young man.

Avoc. 4. The more unnatural part, that of his father.

Avoc. 2. More of the husband.

Avoc. 1.   I not know to give

His act a name, it is so monstrous!

Avoc. 4. But the impostor, he is a thing created

T' exceed example!

Avoc. [1.]   And all aftertimes! 9

Avoc. 2. I never heard a true voluptuary Described but him.

Avoc. 3.   Appear yet those were cited?

Not. All but the old magnifico, Volpone.

Avoc. 1. Why is not he here ?

Mos.   Please your fatherhoods,

Here is his advocate. Himself's so weak,

So feeble—

Avoc. 4.   What are you?

Bon.   His parasite,

His knave, his pander. I beseech the court

He may be forced to come, that your grave eyes

May bear strong witness of his strange impostures.

Volt. Upon my faith and credit with your virtues,

He is not able to endure the air.   20

Avoc. 2. Bring him, however.

Avoc. 3.   We will see him.

Avoc. 4.   Fetch him.

Volt. Your fatherhoods' fit pleasures be obeyed;   [Exeunt Commandadori.]

But sure, the sight will rather move your pities

Than indignation. May it please the court,

In the meantime, he may be heard in me.

I know this place most void of prejudice,

And therefore crave it, since we have no reason

To fear our truth should hurt our cause.

Avoc. 3.   Speak free.

Volt. Then know, most honored fathers, I must now   29

Discover to your strangely abuséd ears,

The most prodigious and most frontless [1] piece

Of solid impudence and treachery

That ever vicious nature yet brought forth

To shame the state of Venice. This lewd woman,

That wants no artificial looks or tears

To help the visor she has now put on,

Hath long been known a close [2] adulteress

To that lascivious youth there; not suspected,

I say, but known, and taken in the act

With him, and by this man, the easy husband,   40

Pardoned, whose timeless [3] bounty makes him now

Stand here, the most unhappy, innocent person

That ever man's own goodness made accused.

For these not knowing how to owe [4] a gift

Of that dear grace, but with their shame, being placed

So above all powers of their gratitude,

Began to hate the benefit, and, in place

Of thanks, devise t'extirp [5] the memory

Of such an act, wherein I pray your fatherhoods

To observe the malice, yea, the rage of creatures   50

Discovered in their evils, and what heart

Such take, even from their crimes. But that anon

Will more appear. This gentleman, the father,

Hearing of this foul fact,[6] with many others,

Which daily strook at his too tender ears,

And, grieved in nothing more than that he could not

Preserve himself a parent (his son's ills

Growing to that strange flood), at last decreed

To disinherit him.

Avoc. 1.   These be strange turns!

---

[1] Shameless.   [4] Own.

[2] Secret.   [5] Extirpate.

[3] Untimely.   [6] Deed.

Avoc. 2. The young man's fame was ever
  fair and honest.   60
Volt. So much more full of danger is his
  vice,
  That can beguile so, under shade of
  virtue.
  But, as I said, my honored sires, his
  father
  Having this settled purpose, by what
  means
  To him betrayed we know not, and this
  day
  Appointed for the deed, that parricide—
  I cannot style him better—by confeder-
  acy
  Preparing this his paramour to be there,
  Entered Volpone's house (who was the
  man,
  Your fatherhoods must understand,
  designed   70
  For the inheritance), there sought his
  father—
  But with what purpose sought he him,
  my lords?
  I tremble to pronounce it, that a son
  Unto a father, and to such a father,
  Should have so foul, felonious intent!
  It was to murder him—when, being pre-
  vented
  By his more happy absence, what then
  did he?
  Not check his wicked thoughts; no, now
  new deeds!
  (Mischief doth ever end where it begins.)
  An act of horror, fathers! He dragged
  forth   80
  The aged gentleman that had there
  lyen [1] bedrid
  Three years and more, out of his inno-
  cent couch,
  Naked upon the floor; there left him;
  wounded
  His servant in the face; and with this
  strumpet,
  The stale to his forged practice,[2] who
  was glad
  To be so active (I shall here desire
  Your fatherhoods to note but my col-
  lections [3]
  As most remarkable), thought at once
  to stop

[1] Lain.
[2] Decoy to his invented plot.
[3] Inferences, conclusions.

His father's ends, discredit his free choice
In the old gentleman, redeem them-
  selves   90
By laying infamy upon this man,
To whom, with blushing, they should
  owe their lives.
Avoc. 1. What proofs have you of this?
Bon.   Most honored fathers,
  I humbly crave there be no credit given
  To this man's mercenary tongue.
Avoc. 2.   Forbear.
Bon. His soul moves in his fee.
Avoc. 3.   O, sir!
Bon.   This fellow
  For six sols [4] more would plead against
  his Maker.
Avoc. 1. You do forget yourself.
Volt.   Nay, nay, grave fathers,
  Let him have scope. Can any man im-
  agine
  That he will spare his accuser, that
  would not   100
  Have spared his parent?
Avoc. 1.   Well, produce your proofs.
Cel. I would I could forget I were a
  creature.
Volt. Signior Corbaccio!
                    [Corbaccio advances.]
Avoc. 4.   What is he?
Volt.   The father.
Avoc. 2. Has he had an oath?
Not.   Yes.
Corb.   What must I do now?
Not. Your testimony's craved.
Corb.   Speak to the knave?
  I'll ha' my mouth first stopped with
  earth; my heart
  Abhors his knowledge. I disclaim in [5]
  him.
Avoc. 1. But for what cause?
Corb.   The mere portent of nature!
  He is an utter stranger to my loins.
Bon. Have they made [6] you to this?
Corb.   I will not hear thee,
  Monster of men, swine, goat, wolf, par-
  ricide!   111
  Speak not, thou viper.
Bon.   Sir, I will sit down,
  And rather wish my innocence should
  suffer
  Than I resist the authority of a father.
Volt. Signior Corvino!
                     [Corvino advances.]
[4] Small coins.   [5] Disown.   [6] Worked, wrought.

Avoc. 2.   This is strange.
Avoc. 1.   Who's this?
Not. The husband.
Avoc. 4.   Is he sworn?
Not.   He is.
Avoc. 3.   Speak then.
Corv. This woman, please your father-
   hoods, is a whore,
   Of most hot exercise, more than a par-
   trich,[1]
   Upon record—
Avoc. 1.   No more.
Corv.   Neighs like a jennet.
Not. Preserve the honor of the court.
Corv.   I shall, 120
   And modesty of your most reverend
   ears.
   And yet I hope that I may say these
   eyes
   Have seen her glued unto that piece of
   cedar,
   That fine, well-timbered gallant, and
   that here   [Points to Celia's face.]
   The letters may be read, thorough [2] the
   horn,[3]
   That make the story perfect.
Mos.   Excellent, sir!
Corv. [Aside to Mosca.] There is no shame
   in this now, is there?
Mos. [Aside.]   None.
Corv. Or, if I said I hoped that she were
   onward
   To her damnation, if there be a hell
   Greater than whore and woman, a good
   Catholic   130
   May make the doubt.
Avoc. 3.   His grief hath made him
   frantic.
Avoc. 1. Remove him hence. *She swoons.*
Avoc. 2.   Look to the woman!
Corv.   Rare!
   Prettily feigned again!
Avoc. 4.   Stand from about her!
Avoc. 1. Give her the air.
Avoc. 3. [To Mosca.]   What can you say?
Mos.   My wound,
   May 't please your wisdoms, speaks for
   me, received
   In aid of my good patron, when he
   missed

His sought-for father, when that well-
   taught dame
Had her cue given her to cry out a rape.
Bon. O most laid [4] impudence! Fathers—
Avoc. 3.   Sir, be silent.
   You had your hearing free; so must they
   theirs.   140
Avoc. 2. I do begin to doubt th' imposture
   here.
Avoc. 4. This woman has too many
   moods.
Volt.   Grave fathers,
   She is a creature of a most professed
   And prostituted lewdness.
Corv.   Most impetuous,
   Unsatisfied—grave fathers!
Volt.   May her feignings
   Not take your wisdoms; but this day
   she baited
   A stranger, a grave knight, with her
   loose eyes
   And more lascivious kisses. This man
   saw hem
   Together on the water in a gondola.
Mos. Here is the lady herself that saw
   hem too,   150
   Without, who then had in the open
   streets
   Pursued them but for saving her knight's
   honor.
Avoc. 1. Produce that lady.
Avoc. 2.   Let her come. [Exit Mosca.]
Avoc. 4.   These things,
   They strike with wonder.
Avoc. 3.   I am turned a stone.

Act IV. Scene vi.

[The same.]

Mosca, Lady, Avocatori, etc.

[Mos.] Be resolute, madam.
Lady.   Ay, this same is she.
   Out, thou chameleon harlot! Now thine
   eyes
   Vie tears with the hyena. Dar'st thou
   look
   Upon my wrongèd face? I cry your
   pardons.
   I fear I have forgettingly transgressed
   Against the dignity of the court—
Avoc. 2.   No, madam.
Lady. And been exorbitant—

---

[1] Partridge.   [2] Through.
[3] The child's A B C card, or hornbook, had a thin covering of horn. The inevitable allusion to cuckoldry is also present.

[4] Carefully plotted.

Avoc. 2. You have not, lady.

Avoc. 4. These proofs are strong.

Lady. Surely, I had no purpose
To scandalize your honors or my sex's.

Avoc. 3. We do believe it.

Lady. Surely you may believe it.　10

Avoc. 2. Madam, we do.

Lady. Indeed you may; my breeding
Is not so coarse—

Avoc. 4. We know it.

Lady. To offend
With pertinacy[1]—

Avoc. 3. Lady—

Lady. Such a presence!
No, surely.

Avoc. 1. We well think it.

Lady. You may think it.

Avoc. 1. Let her o'ercome.—What witnesses have you,
To make good your report?

Bon. Our consciences.

Cel. And heaven, that never fails the
innocent.

Avoc. 4. These are no testimonies.

Bon. Not in your courts,
Where multitude and clamor overcomes.

Avoc. 1. Nay, then you do wax insolent.

Volpone is brought in, as impotent. [*Lady
Would-be kisses him.*]

Volt. Here, here,　20
The testimony comes that will convince
And put to utter dumbness their bold
tongues!
See here, grave fathers, here's the rav-
isher,
The rider on men's wives, the great im-
postor,
The grand voluptuary! Do you not think
These limbs should affect venery? Or
these eyes
Covet a concubine? Pray you, mark
these hands.
Are they not fit to stroke a lady's breasts?
Perhaps he doth dissemble?

Bon. So he does.

Volt. Would you ha' him tortured?

Bon. I would have him proved.　30

Volt. Best try him then with goads, or
burning irons;
Put him to the strappado.[2] I have heard

The rack hath cured the gout; faith,
give it him,
And help him of a malady. Be courteous.
I'll undertake, before these honored
fathers,
He shall have yet as many left diseases
As she has known adulterers, or thou
strumpets.
O, my most equal[3] hearers, if these deeds,
Acts of this bold and most exorbitant
strain,　39
May pass with suffrance, what one citizen
But owes the forfeit of his life, yea, fame,
To him that dares traduce him? Which
of you
Are safe, my honored fathers? I would
ask,
With leave of your grave fatherhoods, if
their plot
Have any face or color like to truth?
Or if, unto the dullest nostril here,
It smell not rank, and most abhorréd
slander?
I crave your care of this good gentleman,
Whose life is much endangered by their
fable;
And, as for them, I will conclude with
this,　50
That vicious persons, when they are
hot and fleshed
In impious acts, their constancy abounds.
Damned deeds are done with greatest
confidence.

Avoc. 1. Take hem to custody, and sever
them.

Avoc. 2. 'Tis pity two such prodigies
should live.

Avoc. 1. Let the old gentleman be returned with care.

[*Exeunt Commandadori with Volpone.*]
I am sorry our credulity wronged him.

Avoc. 4. These are two creatures!

Avoc. 3. I have an earthquake in me.

Avoc. 2. Their shame, even in their
cradles, fled their faces.

Avoc. 4. [*To Voltore.*] You have done a
worthy service to the state, sir,　60
In their discovery.

Avoc. 1. You shall hear, ere night,
What punishment the court decrees
upon hem.

[*Exeunt Avocatori, Notario, and Commandadori with Bonario and Celia.*]

---

[1] Pertinacity.　　　[2] A kind of torture.　　　[3] Impartial.

VOLT. We thank your fatherhoods. How like you it?

MOS. Rare!

I'ld ha' your tongue, sir, tipped with gold for this;

I'ld ha' you be the heir to the whole city;

The earth I'ld have want men ere you want living.

They are bound to erect your statue in St. Mark's.

Signior Corvino, I would have you go And show yourself, that you have conquered.

CORV. Yes.

MOS. It was much better that you should profess 70

Yourself a cuckold thus than that the other

Should have been proved.

CORV. Nay, I considered that;

Now it is her fault.

MOS. Then it had been yours.

CORV. True. I do doubt this advocate still.

MOS. I' faith,

You need not; I dare ease you of that care.

CORV. I trust thee, Mosca.

MOS. As your own soul, sir.
         [Exit Corvino.]

CORB. Mosca!

MOS. Now for your business, sir.

CORB. How! Ha' you business?

MOS. Yes, yours, sir.

CORB. O, none else?

MOS. None else, not I.

CORB. Be careful then.

MOS. Rest you with both your eyes, sir.

CORB. Despatch it.

MOS. Instantly.

CORB. And look that all, 80 Whatever, be put in, jewels, plate, moneys,

Household stuff, bedding, cortines.[1]

MOS. Cortine rings, sir; Only the advocate's fee must be deducted.

CORB. I'll pay him now; you'll be too prodigal.

MOS. Sir, I must tender it.

CORB. Two cecchines is well?

MOS. No, six, sir.

CORB. 'Tis too much.

MOS. He talked a great while; You must consider that, sir.

CORB. Well, there's three—

MOS. I'll give it him.

CORB. Do so, and there's for thee. [Exit.]

MOS. [Aside.] Bountiful bones! What horrid, strange offense

Did he commit gainst nature, in his youth, 90

Worthy this age?—You see, sir, how I work

Unto your ends; take you no notice.

VOLT. No; I'll leave you.

MOS. All is yours, the devil and all, Good advocate!—[Exit Voltore.] Madam, I'll bring you home.

LADY. No, I'll go see your patron.

MOS. That you shall not; I'll tell you why. My purpose is to urge My patron to reform his will, and for The zeal you have shown today, whereas before

You were but third or fourth, you shall be now

Put in the first, which would appear as begged 100

If you were present. Therefore—

LADY. You shall sway me. [Exeunt.]

ACT V. SCENE i.

[A room in Volpone's house.]

Volpone.

[VOLP.] Well, I am here, and all this brunt is past.

I ne'er was in dislike with my disguise

Till this fled moment; here 'twas good, in private;

But in your public—cave [2] whilst I breathe.

Fore God, my left leg gan [3] to have the cramp,

And I apprehended straight some power had strook me

With a dead palsy. Well, I must be merry,

And shake it off. A many of these fears

Would put me into some villainous disease,

Should they come thick upon me; I'll prevent hem. 10

---

[1] Curtains. [2] Beware. [3] Began.

Give me a bowl of lusty wine to fright
This humor from my heart. (*He drinks.*)
   Hum, hum, hum!
'Tis almost gone already; I shall con-
   quer.
Any device now of rare, ingenious knav-
   ery,
That would possess me with a violent
   laughter,
Would make me up again. (*Drinks
   again.*) So, so, so, so!
This heat is life; 'tis blood by this time.—
   Mosca!

ACT V. SCENE ii.

[*The same.*]

Mosca, Volpone, Nano, Castrone.[1]

[Mos.] How now, sir? Does the day look
   clear again?
Are we recovered, and wrought out of
   error,
Into our way, to see our path before us?
Is our trade free once more?
VOLP.   Exquisite Mosca!
Mos. Was it not carried learnedly?
VOLP.   And stoutly.
Good wits are greatest in extremities.
Mos. It were a folly beyond thought to
   trust
Any grand act unto a cowardly spirit.
You are not taken with it enough, me-
   thinks?
VOLP. O, more than if I had enjoyed the
   wench;   10
The pleasure of all womankind's not like
   it.
Mos. Why, now you speak, sir. We must
   here be fixed;
Here we must rest. This is our master-
   piece;
We cannot think to go beyond this.
VOLP.   True,
Thou hast played thy prize, my precious
   Mosca.
Mos.   Nay, sir,
To gull the court—
VOLP.   And quite divert the torrent
Upon the innocent.
Mos.   Yes, and to make
So rare a music out of discords—
VOLP.   Right.

---

[1] Last two enter later.

That yet to me 's the strangest (how th'
   hast borne it!),
That these, being so divided mongst
   themselves,   20
Should not scent somewhat or [2] in me or
   thee,
Or doubt their own side.
Mos.   True, they will not see 't.
Too much light blinds hem, I think.
   Each of hem
Is so possessed and stuffed with his own
   hopes
That anything unto the contrary,
Never so true, or never so apparent,
Never so palpable, they will resist it—
VOLP. Like a temptation of the devil.
Mos.   Right, sir.
Merchants may talk of trade, and your
   great signiors
Of land that yields well; but, if Italy 30
Have any glebe [3] more fruitful than these
   fellows,
I am deceived. Did not your advocate
   rare?
VOLP. O—"My most honored fathers, my
   grave fathers,
Under correction of your fatherhoods,
What face of truth is here? If these
   strange deeds
May pass, most honored fathers"—I had
   much ado
To forbear laughing.
Mos.   'T seemed to me you sweat, sir.
VOLP. In troth, I did a little.
Mos.   But confess, sir,
Were you not daunted?
VOLP.   In good faith, I was
A little in a mist, but not dejected;   40
Never but still myself.
Mos.   I think it, sir.
Now, so truth help me, I must needs
   say this, sir,
And out of conscience for your advocate,
He has taken pains, in faith, sir, and
   deserved,
In my poor judgment, I speak it under
   favor,
Not to contrary you, sir, very richly—
Well—to be cozened.
VOLP.   Troth, and I think so too,
By that I heard him in the latter end.
Mos. O, but before, sir. Had you heard
   him first

---

[2] Either.   [3] Cultivated ground.

Draw it to certain heads, then ag-
    gravate,[1]   50
Then use his vehement figures—I looked
    still
When he would shift a shirt; and doing
    this
Out of pure love, no hope of gain—
VOLP.   'Tis right.
I cannot answer him, Mosca, as I would,
Not yet; but for thy sake, at thy en-
    treaty,
I will begin even now—to vex hem all,
This very instant.
MOS.   Good sir.
VOLP.   Call the dwarf
And eunuch forth.
MOS.   Castrone, Nano!

        [*Enter Castrone and Nano.*]

NANO.   Here.
VOLP. Shall we have a jig[2] now?
MOS.   What you please, sir.
VOLP.   Go,
Straight give out about the streets, you
    two,   60
That I am dead. Do it with constancy,
Sadly,[3] do you hear? Impute it to the
    grief
Of this late slander.
        [*Exeunt Castrone and Nano.*]
MOS.   What do you mean, sir?
VOLP.   O,
I shall have instantly my vulture, crow,
Raven, come flying hither, on the news,
To peck for carrion, my she-wolf, and all,
Greedy, and full of expectation—
MOS. And then to have it ravished from
    their mouths?
VOLP. 'Tis true. I will ha' thee put on a
    gown,
And take upon thee, as thou wert mine
    heir;   70
Show hem a will. Open that chest, and
    reach
Forth one of those that has the blanks;
    I'll straight
Put in thy name.
MOS.   It will be rare, sir.
        [*Gives him a paper.*]
VOLP.   Ay,
When they e'en gape, and find themselves
    deluded—

MOS. Yes.
VOLP.   And thou use them scurvily!
    Despatch;
    Get on thy gown.
MOS. [*Putting on a gown.*]   But what,
    sir, if they ask
    After the body?
VOLP.   Say it was corrupted.
MOS. I'll say it stunk, sir, and was fain t'
    have it
    Coffined up instantly, and sent away.
VOLP. Anything; what thou wilt. Hold,
    here's my will.   80
    Get thee a cap, a count-book, pen and
    ink,
    Papers afore thee; sit as thou wert taking
    An inventory of parcels. I'll get up
    Behind the cortine, on a stool, and
    harken;
    Sometime peep over; see how they do
    look,
    With what degrees their blood doth leave
    their faces.
    O, 'twill afford me a rare meal of laugh-
    ter!
MOS. [*Following Volpone's directions.*] Your
    advocate will turn stark dull upon it.
VOLP. It will take off his oratory's edge.
MOS. But your clarissimo,[4] old round-
    back, he   90
Will crump you like a hog louse, with
    the touch.
VOLP. And what Corvino?
MOS.   O, sir, look for him
    Tomorrow morning with a rope and a
    dagger
    To visit all the streets; he must run mad.
    My lady, too, that came into the court
    To bear false witness for your wor-
    ship—
VOLP.   Yes,
And kissed me fore the fathers, when my
    face
    Flowed all with oils—
MOS.   And sweat, sir. Why, your gold
    Is such another med'cine, it dries up
    All those offensive savors; it trans-
    forms   100
    The most deforméd, and restores hem
    lovely,
    As 'twere the strange poetical girdle.[5]
    Jove

---

[1] Make his accusations.
[2] Entertainment, jest.   [3] Seriously.
[4] Grandee.
[5] Jonson's marginal note reads: "Cestus."

Could not invent t' himself a shroud more
   subtile
To pass Acrisius'[1] guards. It is the thing
Makes all the world her grace, her youth,
   her beauty.
VOLP. I think she loves me.
MOS.   Who? The lady, sir?
   She's jealous of you.
VOLP.   Dost thou say so?
                 [*Knocking within.*]
MOS.   Hark!
   There's some already.
VOLP.   Look.
MOS.   It is the vulture;
   He has the quickest scent.
VOLP.   I'll to my place;
   Thou to thy posture.
           [*Goes behind the curtain.*]
MOS.   I am set.
VOLP.   But, Mosca, 110
   Play the artificer now; torture hem
   rarely.

ACT V. SCENE iii.

[*The same.*]

Voltore, Mosca, Corbaccio,[2] *Corvino,*[2] *Lady,*[2]
                           Volpone.

[VOLT.] How now, my Mosca?
MOS. [*Writing.*]   "Turkey carpets,
   nine—"
VOLT. Taking an inventory? That is well.
MOS. "Two suits of bedding, tissue—"
VOLT.   Where's the will?
   Let me read that the while.

[*Enter Servants with Corbaccio in a chair.*]

CORB.   So, set me down,
   And get you home. [*Exeunt Servants.*]
VOLT.   Is he come now to trouble us?
MOS. "Of cloth of gold, two more—"
CORB.   Is it done, Mosca?
MOS. "Of several vellets,[3] eight—"
VOLT.   I like his care.
CORB. Dost thou not hear?

[*Enter Corvino.*]

CORV.   Ha! Is the hour come, Mosca?
   Volpone peeps from behind a traverse.
VOLP. [*Aside.*] Ay, now they muster.

---

[1] Danaë's father's.
[2] Enters later.   [3] Velvets.

CORV.   What does the advocate here,
   Or this Corbaccio?
CORB.   What do these here?

[*Enter Lady Would-be.*]

LADY.   Mosca! 10
   Is his thread spun?
MOS.   "Eight chests of linen—"
VOLP. [*Aside.*]   O,
   My fine Dame Would-be, too!
CORB.   Mosca, the will,
   That I may show it these, and rid hem
     hence.
MOS. "Six chests of diaper,[4] four of dam-
   ask."—There! [*Gives them the will.*]
CORB. Is that the will?
MOS.   "Down beds, and bolsters—"
VOLP. [*Aside.*]   Rare!
   Be busy still. Now they begin to flut-
   ter;
   They never think of me. Look, see, see,
   see!
   How their swift eyes run over the long
   deed,
   Unto the name, and to the legacies, 19
   What is bequeathed them there—
MOS.   "Ten suits of hangings—"
VOLP. [*Aside.*] Ay, i' their garters, Mosca.
   Now their hopes
   Are at the gasp.
VOLT.   Mosca the heir!
CORB.   What's that?
VOLP. [*Aside.*] My advocate is dumb.
   Look to my merchant;
   He has heard of some strange storm—
   a ship is lost;
   He faints. My lady will swoon. Old
   glazen-eyes,
   He hath not reached his despair yet.
CORB.   All these
   Are out of hope; I am, sure, the man.
                [*Takes the will.*]
CORV.   But, Mosca—
MOS. "Two cabinets—"
CORV.   Is this in earnest?
MOS.   "One
   Of ebony—"
CORV.   Or do you but delude me?
MOS. "The other, mother of pearl."—I'm
   very busy.   30
   Good faith, it is a fortune thrown upon
   me—

---

[4] Fine linen.

"Item, one salt [1] of agate"—not my seeking.

LADY. Do you hear, sir?

MOS.　　　　　"A perfumed box"—pray you, forbear;
　You see I am troubled—"made of an onyx—"

LADY.　　　　　How!

MOS. Tomorrow or next day, I shall be at leisure
　To talk with you all.

CORV.　　　　Is this my large hope's issue?

LADY. Sir, I must have a fairer answer.

MOS.　　　　　　　　　　Madam!
　Marry, and shall. Pray you, fairly quit my house.
　Nay, raise no tempest with your looks; but, hark you,　　　　39
　Remember what your ladyship offered me
　To put you in an heir; go to, think on 't,
　And what you said e'en your best madams did
　For maintenance; and why not you? Enough.
　Go home, and use the poor Sir Pol, your knight, well,
　For fear I tell some riddles. Go, be melancholic.　　[Exit Lady Would-be.]

VOLP. [Aside.] O, my fine devil!

CORV.　　　　Mosca, pray you a word.

MOS. Lord! Will not you take your despatch hence yet?
　Methinks, of all, you should have been th' example.
　Why should you stay here? With what thought, what promise?
　Hear you! Do not you know I know you an ass?　　　　50
　And that you would most fain have been a wittol [2]
　If fortune would have let you? That you are
　A declared cuckold, on good terms? This pearl,
　You'll say, was yours? Right. This diamant?
　I'll not deny 't, but thank you. Much here else?
　It may be so. Why, think that these good works
　May help to hide your [3] bad. I'll not betray you;

Although you be but extraordinary,
And have it only in title, it sufficeth.
Go home; be melancholy too, or mad.　60
　　　　　　　[Exit Corvino.]

VOLP. [Aside.] Rare Mosca! How his villainy becomes him!

VOLT. Certain he doth delude all these for me.

CORB. Mosca the heir?

VOLP. [Aside.]　　　O, his four eyes have found it.

CORB. I am cozened, cheated, by a parasite-slave;
Harlot,[4] t' hast gulled me.

MOS.　　　Yes, sir. Stop your mouth,
Or I shall draw the only tooth is left.
Are not you he, that filthy, covetous wretch,
With the three legs,[5] that here, in hope of prey,
Have, any time this three year, snuffed about
With your most grov'ling nose, and would have hired　70
Me to the pois'ning of my patron, sir?
Are not you he that have today in court
Professed the disinheriting of your son?
Perjured yourself? Go home, and die, and stink;
If you but croak a syllable, all comes out.
Away, and call your porters! Go, go, stink!　　　[Exit Corbaccio.]

VOLP. [Aside.] Excellent varlet!

VOLT.　　　Now, my faithful Mosca,
I find thy constancy—

MOS.　　　　　Sir?

VOLT.　　　　　　　Sincere.

MOS. [Writing.]　　　　"A table
Of porphyry"—I marl [6] you'll be thus troublesome.

VOLT. Nay, leave off now; they are gone.

MOS.　　　Why, who are you?　80
What? Who did send for you? O, cry you mercy,
Reverend sir! Good faith, I am grieved for you,
That any chance of mine should thus defeat
Your (I must needs say) most deserving travails;
But I protest, sir, it was cast upon me,
And I could almost wish to be without it,

---

[1] Saltcellar.
[2] A passive cuckold.　　[3] Original reads you.
[4] Knave.
[5] In reference to his cane.　　[6] Marvel.

But that the will o' th' dead must be
　observed.
Marry, my joy is that you need it not;
You have a gift, sir (thank your educa-
　tion),
Will never let you want, while there are
　men　　　　　　　　　　　　　　　90
And malice to breed causes.[1]　Would I
　had
But half the like, for all my fortune, sir!
If I have any suits (as I do hope,
Things being so easy and direct, I shall
　not),
I will make bold with your obstreperous
　aid,
Conceive me—for your fee, sir. In mean-
　time,
You that have so much law, I know ha'
　the conscience
Not to be covetous of what is mine.
Good sir, I thank you for my plate;
　'twill help
To set up a young man.　Good faith, you
　look　　　　　　　　　　　　　　100
As you were costive; best go home and
　purge, sir.　　　　　　　[Exit Voltore.]
VOLP. [Coming from behind the curtain.]
　Bid him eat lettuce well.[2]　My witty
　mischief,
Let me embrace thee.　O, that I could
　now
Transform thee to a Venus!—Mosca, go,
Straight take my habit of clarissimo,
And walk the streets.　Be seen; torment
　hem more.
We must pursue as well as plot.　Who
　would
Have lost this feast?
Mos.　　　　　I doubt it will lose them.
VOLP. O, my recovery shall recover all.
That I could now but think on some dis-
　guise　　　　　　　　　　　　　110
To meet hem in, and ask hem questions!
How I would vex hem still at every turn!
Mos. Sir, I can fit you.
VOLP.　　　　　　　　Canst thou?
Mos.　　　　　　　　　　Yes, I know
One o' the commandadori,[3] sir, so like
　you;
Him will I straight make drunk, and
　bring you his habit.

[1] Lawsuits.
[2] I.e., as a soporific.
[3] Original has commandatori.

VOLP. A rare disguise, and answering thy
　brain!
O, I will be a sharp disease unto hem.
Mos. Sir, you must look for curses—
VOLP.　　　　　　　　　Till they burst;
The fox fares ever best when he is curst.
　　　　　　　　　　　　　[Exeunt.]

ACT V. SCENE iv.

[A room in Politic's house.]

Peregrine, [disguised,] Mercatori 3, Woman,
　　　　　　　　　　　　　　　Politic.[4]

[PER.] Am I enough disguised?
MER. 1.　　　　　　　　I warrant you.
PER. All my ambition is to fright him
　only.
MER. 2. If you could ship him away,
　'twere excellent.
MER. 3. To Zant or to Aleppo!
PER.　　　　　　　Yes, and ha' his
Adventures put i' th' Book of Voyages,[5]
And his gulled story registered for truth.
Well, gentlemen, when I am in a while,
And that you think us warm in our dis-
　course,
Know your approaches.
MER. 1.　　　　　Trust it to our care.
　　　　　　　　　　　[Exeunt Mercatori.

Enter Woman.]

PER. Save you, fair lady!　Is Sir Pol
　within?　　　　　　　　　　　　10
WOM. I do not know, sir.
PER.　　　　　　　Pray you, say unto him
Here is a merchant, upon earnest busi-
　ness,
Desires to speak with him.
WOM.　　　　　　I will see, sir. [Exit.]
PER.　　　　　　　　　　Pray you.
I see the family is all female here.

[Enter Woman.]

WOM. He says, sir, he has weighty affairs
　of state
That now require him whole; some other
　time
You may possess him.
PER.　　　　　　　Pray you, say again,
If those require him whole, these will
　exact[6] him,

[4] Last two enter later.
[5] By Hakluyt.　　　　　　[6] Finish off.

Whereof I bring him tidings.— [*Exit
Woman.*] What might be
His grave affair of state now? How to
make   2G
Bolognian sausages here in Venice, spar-
ing
One o' th' ingredients!

[Enter Woman.]

Wom.   Sir, he says he knows
By your word "tidings" that you are
no statesman,
And therefore wills you stay.
Per.   Sweet, pray you, return [1] him:
I have not read so many proclamations,
And studied them for words as he has
done,
But—here he deigns to come.
                                         [Exit Woman.

Enter Sir Politic.]

Pol.   Sir, I must crave
Your courteous pardon. There hath
chanced today
Unkind disaster twixt my lady and me;
And I was penning my apology   30
To give her satisfaction, as you came
now.
Per. Sir, I am grieved I bring you worse
disaster.
The gentleman you met at th' port to-
day,
That told you he was newly arrived—
Pol.   Ay, was
A fugitive punk? [2]
Per.   No, sir, a spy set on you;
And he has made relation to the senate
That you professed to him to have a
plot
To sell the state of Venice to the Turk.
Pol. O me!
Per.   For which warrants are signed by
this time,
To apprehend you, and to search your
study   40
For papers—
Pol.   Alas, sir, I have none but notes
Drawn out of playbooks—
Per.   All the better, sir.
Pol. And some essays. What shall I do?
Per.   Sir, best
Convey yourself into a sugar chest,

[1] Answer.   [2] Prostitute.

Or, if you could lie round, a frail [3] were
rare,
And I could send you aboard.
Pol.   Sir, I but talked so
For discourse' sake merely.
                          They knock without.
Per.   Hark! They are there.
Pol. I am a wretch, a wretch!
Per.   What will you do, sir?
Ha' you ne'er a curran-butt [4] to leap
into?
They'll put you to the rack; you must
be sudden.   50
Pol. Sir, I have an engine [5]—
Mer. 3. [*Within.*]   Sir Politic Would-be?
Mer. 2. [*Within.*]   Where is he?
Pol.   That I have
thought upon before time.
Per. What is it?
Pol.   (I shall ne'er endure the torture.)
Marry, it is, sir, of a tortoise shell,
Fitted for these extremities; pray you,
sir, help me. [*Brings out his contrivance.*]
Here I have a place, sir, to put back my
legs
(Please you to lay it on, sir), with this cap
And my black gloves. I'll lie, sir, like
a tortoise,
Till they are gone.
Per.   And call you this an engine?
Pol. Mine own device.—Good sir, bid my
wife's women   60
To burn my papers.   [*Exit Peregrine.*]

They rush in.

Mer. 1.   Where's he hid?
Mer. 3.   We must
And will sure find him.
Mer. 2.   Which is his study?

[Enter Peregrine.]

Mer. 1.   What
Are you, sir?
Per.   I am a merchant that came here
To look upon this tortoise.
Mer. 3.   How?
Mer. 1.   St. Mark!
What beast is this?
Per.   It is a fish.
Mer. 2.   Come out here!

[3] A basket made of rushes.
[4] Wine cask.
[5] Contrivance.

PER. Nay, you may strike him, sir, and
　　tread upon him;
He'll bear a cart.
MER. 1.　　　　　What, to run over him?
PER.　　　　　　　　　　　　　　　Yes.
MER. 3. Let's jump upon him.
MER. 2.　　　　　　Can he not go?
PER.　　　　　　　　　　He creeps, sir.
MER. 1. [*Drawing a weapon.*] Let's see him
　creep.
PER.　　No, good sir, you will hurt him.
MER. 2. Heart, I'll see him creep, or prick
　　his guts.　　　　　　　　　　　　70
MER. 3. Come out here!
PER.　　　Pray you, sir.—(Creep a little!)
MER. 1.　　　　　　　　　　　　Forth.
MER. 2. Yet furder.
PER.　　　　　　　　Good sir!—(Creep!)
MER. 2.　　　　　　We'll see his legs.
They pull off the shell and discover him.
MER. 3. Godso, he has garters!
MER. 1.　　　　　　　　Ay, and gloves!
MER. 2.　　　　　　　　　　　Is this
Your fearful tortoise?
PER. [*Discovering himself.*]　　　Now, Sir
　Pol, we're even;
For your next project I shall be pre-
　pared.
I am sorry for the funeral of your notes,
　sir.
MER. 1. 'Twere a rare motion [1] to be seen
　in Fleet Street.
MER. 2. Ay, i' the term.
MER. 1.　　　　　Or Smithfield, in the fair.
MER. 3. Methinks 'tis but a melancholic
　sight.
PER. Farewell, most politic tortoise!
　　[*Exeunt Peregrine and Merchants.*

Enter Woman.]

POL.　　　　　　　Where's my lady?　80
Knows she of this?
WOM.　　　　　I know not, sir.
POL.　　　　　　　　　　　Inquire.—
O, I shall be the fable of all feasts,
The freight of the *gazetti*,[2] ship boys'
　tale,
And, which is worst, even talk for ordi-
　naries.
WOM. My lady's come most melancholic
　home,

---

[1] Puppet show.
[2] The theme of the newspapers.

And says, sir, she will straight to sea
　for physic.
POL. And I, to shun this place and clime
　forever,
Creeping with house on back, and think
　it well
To shrink my poor head in my politic
　shell.　　　　　　　　　　　[*Exeunt.*]

ACT V. SCENE v.

[*A room in Volpone's house.*]

*Volpone, Mosca, the first in the habit of a
commandadore, the other of a clarissimo.*

[VOLP.] Am I then like him?
MOS.　　　　　O, sir, you are he;
No man can sever you.
VOLP.　　　　　　　Good.
MOS.　　　　　　　　But what am I?
VOLP. Fore heaven, a brave clarissimo;
　thou becom'st it!
Pity thou wert not born one.
MOS. [*Aside.*]　　　　　　If I hold
My made one, 'twill be well.
VOLP.　　　　　　I'll go and see
What news first at the court.　[*Exit.*]
MOS.　　　　　　　Do so. My fox
Is out on his hole, and, ere he shall re-
　enter,
I'll make him languish in his borrowed
　case,[3]
Except he come to composition[4] with
　me.—
Androgyno, Castrone, Nano!

[*Enter Androgyno, Castrone, and Nano.*]

ALL.　　　　　　　　　　　Here!　10
MOS. Go, recreate yourselves abroad; go,
　sport.—　　　　　　　　　　[*Exeunt.*]
So, now I have the keys, and am pos-
　sessed.
Since he will needs be dead afore his
　time,
I'll bury him, or gain by him. I am his
　heir,
And so will keep me till he share at
　least.
To cozen him of all were but a cheat
Well placed; no man would construe it
　a sin.
Let his sport pay for 't. This is called
　the Fox Trap.　　　　　　　[*Exit.*]

---

[3] Disguise.　　　[4] Agreement, terms.

Act V. Scene vi.

[*A street.*]

Corbaccio, Corvino, Volpone.[1]

[CORB.] They say the court is set.

CORV.   We must maintain
Our first tale good, for both our reputations.

CORB. Why, mine's no tale; my son would
there have killed me.

CORV. That's true; I had forgot. Mine is,
I am sure.
But for your will, sir—

CORB.   Ay, I'll come upon him
For that hereafter, now his patron's dead.

[*Enter Volpone.*]

VOLP. Signior Corvino! And Corbaccio!
Sir,
Much joy unto you.

CORV.   Of what?

VOLP.   The sudden good
Dropped down upon you—

CORB.   Where?

VOLP.   (And none knows how.)
From old Volpone, sir.

CORB.   Out, arrant knave! 10

VOLP. Let not your too much wealth, sir,
make you furious.

CORB. Away, thou varlet!

VOLP.   Why, sir?

CORB.   Dost thou mock me?

VOLP. You mock the world, sir. Did you
not change wills?

CORB. Out, harlot!

VOLP.   O! Belike you are the man,
Signior Corvino? Faith, you carry it
well;
You grow not mad withal. I love your
spirit.
You are not overleavened with your
fortune.
You should ha' some would swell now,
like a wine fat,[2]
With such an autumn.—Did he gi' you
all, sir?

CORV. Avoid, you rascal!

VOLP.   Troth, your wife has shown 20
Herself a very woman; but you are
well.
You need not care; you have a good
estate

To bear it out, sir, better by this
chance—
Except Corbaccio have a share?

CORB.   Hence, varlet!

VOLP. You will not be a'known,[3] sir; why,
'tis wise.
Thus do all gamesters, at all games, dissemble;
No man will seem to win.—[*Exeunt Corvino and Corbaccio.*] Here comes my
vulture,
Heaving his beak up i' the air, and snuffing.

Act V. Scene vii.

[*The same.*]

Voltore, Volpone.

[VOLT.] Outstripped thus by a parasite?
A slave?
Would run on errands? And make legs[4]
for crumbs?
Well, what I'll do—

VOLP.   The court stays for your[5]
worship.
I e'en rejoice, sir, at your worship's
happiness,
And that it fell into so learned hands,
That understand the fingering.

VOLT.   What do you mean?

VOLP. I mean to be a suitor to your worship,
For the small tenement out of reparations[6]—
That at the end of your long row of
houses,
By the Piscaria. It was, in Volpone's
time,   10
Your predecessor, ere he grew diseased,
A handsome, pretty, customed[7] bawdy-house
As any was in Venice, none dispraised,
But fell with him; his body and that
house
Decayed together.

VOLT.   Come, sir, leave your prating.

VOLP. Why, if your worship give me but
your hand
That I may ha' the refusal, I have done.
'Tis a mere toy to you, sir—candle-rents.[8]

---

[1] Enters later.   [2] Vat.

[3] Acknown, recognized.   [6] Out of repair.
[4] Bows.   [7] Well patronized.
[5] Original reads *you.*   [8] Pin money.

As your learned worship knows—

VOLT. What do I know?

VOLP. Marry, no end of your wealth, sir;
　　God decrease it! 20

VOLT. Mistaking knave! What, mock'st
　　thou my misfortune?

VOLP. His blessing on your heart, sir;
　　would 'twere more!— [Exit Voltore.]
　　Now to my first again, at the next corner.
　　　　　　　　　　　　　　　　[Exit.]

ACT V. SCENE viii.

[The Senate.]

*Corbaccio, Corvino, (Mosca passant,)[1]
Volpone.*

[CORB.] See, in our habit![2] See the impu-
　　dent varlet!

CORV. That I could shoot mine eyes at
　　him, like gunstones![3]

[Enter Volpone.]

VOLP. But is this true, sir, of the parasite?

CORB. Again, t' afflict us? Monster!

VOLP. In good faith, sir,
　　I am heartily grieved a beard of your
　　grave length
　　Should be so overreached. I never
　　brooked[4]
　　That parasite's hair; methought his nose
　　should cozen;
　　There still was somewhat in his look
　　did promise
　　The bane of a clarissimo.

CORB. Knave—

VOLP. [To Corvino.] Methinks 9
　　Yet you, that are so traded i' the world,
　　A witty merchant, the fine bird, Corvino,
　　That have such moral emblems[5] on
　　your name,
　　Should not have sung your[6] shame,
　　and dropped your cheese
　　To let the fox laugh at your emptiness.

CORV. Sirrah, you think the privilege of
　　the place
　　And your red, saucy cap, that seems to
　　me

---

[1] *I.e.*, passing over the stage.
[2] *I.e.*, of a clarissimo.
[3] Cannon balls.
[4] Could endure.
[5] Allegorical pictures with mottoes.
[6] Original reads *you*.

Nailed to your jolthead[7] with those
　　two cecchines,[8]
Can warrant your abuses. Come you
　　hither;
You shall perceive, sir, I dare beat you.
　　Approach!

VOLP. No haste, sir; I do know your valure
　　well, 20
　　Since you durst publish what you are,
　　sir.

CORV. Tarry;
　　I'ld speak with you.

VOLP. Sir, sir, another time—

CORV. Nay, now.

VOLP. O God, sir! I were a wise man,
　　Would stand the fury of a distracted
　　cuckold. *Mosca walks by hem.*

CORB. What, come again?

VOLP. [Aside.] Upon hem, Mosca;
　　save me.

CORB. The air's infected where he
　　breathes.

CORV. Let's fly him.
　　　　　[Exeunt Corvino and Corbaccio.]

VOLP. Excellent basilisk! Turn upon the
　　vulture.

ACT V. SCENE ix.

[The same.]

Voltore, Mosca, Volpone.

[VOLT.] Well, flesh fly, it is summer with
　　you now;
　　Your winter will come on.

MOS. Good advocate,
　　Pray thee not rail, nor threaten out of
　　place thus;
　　Thou'lt make a solecism, as madam
　　says.
　　Get you a biggin[9] more; your brain
　　breaks loose. [Exit.]

VOLT. Well, sir.

VOLP. Would you ha' me beat the inso-
　　lent slave?
　　Throw dirt upon his first good clothes?

VOLT. This same
　　Is doubtless some familiar.[10]

VOLP. Sir, the court,
　　In troth, stays for you. I am mad, a
　　mule
　　That never read Justinian should get
　　up 10

---

[7] Blockhead.
[8] *I.e.*, gold buttons.
[9] Lawyer's coif.
[10] Familiar spirit.

And ride an advocate. Had you no quirk
To avoid gullage, sir, by such a creature?
I hope you do but jest; he has not done 't.
This 's but confederacy to blind the rest.
You are the heir?

Volt.   A strange, officious,
Troublesome knave! Thou dost torment me.

Volp.   I know—
It cannot be, sir, that you should be cozened.
'Tis not within the wit of man to do it;
You are so wise, so prudent; and 'tis fit
That wealth and wisdom still should go together.   [*Exeunt.*] 20

Act V. Scene x.

[*The same.*]

Avocatori 4, Notario, Commandadore, Bonario, Celia, Corbaccio, Corvino, Voltore, Volpone.

[Avoc. 1.] Are all the parties here?

Not.   All but the advocate.

Avoc. 2. And here he comes.

[*Enter Voltore and Volpone.*]

Avoc. [1.]   Then bring hem forth to sentence.

Volt. O, my most honored fathers, let your mercy
Once win upon your justice, to forgive—
I am distracted—

(Volp.   What will he do now?)

Volt.[1]   O,
I know not which t' address myself to first,
Whether your fatherhoods or these innocents—

(Corv. Will he betray himself?)

Volt.   Whom equally
I have abused, out of most covetous ends—

(Corv. The man is mad!)

Corb.   What's that?

Corv.   He is possessed.) 10

Volt. For which, now strook in conscience, here I prostrate
Myself at your offended feet for pardon.

Avoc. 1, 2. Arise.

[1] Original reads *Volp.*

Cel.   O heaven, how just thou art!

Volp. [*Aside.*]   I am caught
I' mine own noose—

Corv. [*To Corbaccio.*]   Be constant,
sir; naught now
Can help but impudence.

Avoc. 1.   Speak forward.

Com.   Silence!

Volt. It is not passion in me, reverend fathers,
But only conscience, conscience, my good sires,
That makes me now tell truth. That parasite,
That knave, hath been the instrument of all.

Avoc. [1.] Where is that knave? Fetch him.

Volp.   I go.   [*Exit.*]

Corv.   Grave fathers, 20
This man's distracted; he confessed it now;
For, hoping to be old Volpone's heir,
Who now is dead—

Avoc. 3.   How?

Avoc. 2.   Is Volpone dead?

Corv. Dead since, grave fathers—

Bon.   O sure vengeance!

Avoc. 1.   Stay!
Then he was no deceiver?

Volt.   O, no, none;
The parasite, grave fathers.

Corv.   He does speak
Out of mere envy, cause the servant's made
The thing he gaped for. Please your fatherhoods,
This is the truth, though I'll not justify
The other, but he may be somedeal[2] faulty. 30

Volt. Ay, to your hopes as well as mine, Corvino;
But I'll use modesty.[3] Pleaseth your wisdoms
To view these certain notes, and but confer[4] them;
As I hope favor, they shall speak clear truth.

Corv. The devil has entered him!

Bon.   Or bides in you.

Avoc. 4. We have done ill, by a public officer
To send for him, if he be heir.

[2] Somewhat.   [3] Moderation.   [4] Compare.

Avoc. 2.   For whom?
Avoc. 4. Him that they call the parasite.
Avoc. 3.   'Tis true;
He is a man of great estate, now left.
Avoc. 4. Go you, and learn his name, and
    say the court   40
Entreats his presence here, but to the
    clearing
Of some few doubts.   [*Exit Notario.*]
Avoc. 2.   This same's a labyrinth!
Avoc. 1. Stand you unto your first report?
Corv.   My state,
My life, my fame—
(Bon.   Where is 't?)
Corv.   Are at the stake.
Avoc. 1. Is yours so too?
Corb.   The advocate's a knave,
And has a forkéd tongue—
Avoc. 2.   Speak to the point.[1]
Corb. So is the parasite too.
Avoc. 1.   This is confusion.
Volt. I do beseech your fatherhoods,
    read but those— [*Gives them papers.*]
Corv. And credit nothing the false spirit
    hath writ.
It cannot be but he is possessed, grave
    fathers. [*Exeunt.*]   50

Act V. Scene xi.

[*A street.*]

Volpone, Nano, Androgyno, Castrone.[2]

[Volp.] To make a snare for mine own
    neck, and run
My head into it willfully, with laughter,
When I had newly scaped, was free and
    clear!
Out of mere wantonness! O, the dull
    devil
Was in this brain of mine when I de-
    vised it,
And Mosca gave it second; he must now
Help to sear up this vein, or we bleed
    dead.—

[*Enter Nano, Androgyno, and Castrone.*]

How now! Who let you loose? Whither
    go you now?
What, to buy gingerbread, or to drown
    kittlings?[3]

[1] This speech is printed in parenthesis in the original.
[2] Last three enter later.   [3] Kittens.

Nan. Sir, Master Mosca called us out of
    doors,   10
And bid us all go play, and took the keys.
And. Yes.
Volp.   Did Master Mosca take the keys?
    Why, so!
I am farder in. These are my fine con-
    ceits!
I must be merry, with a mischief to me!
What a vile wretch was I, that could
    not bear
My fortune soberly? I must ha' my
    crotchets
And my conundrums! Well, go you,
    and seek him;
His meaning may be truer than my fear.
Bid him, he straight come to me to the
    court;
Thither will I, and, if 't be possible, 20
Unscrew my advocate, upon new hopes.
When I provoked him, then I lost my-
    self.   [*Exeunt.*]

Act V. Scene xii.

[*The Senate.*]

Avocatori, etc.

[Avoc. 1.] These things can ne'er be
    reconciled. He here
         [*Points to the papers.*]
Professeth that the gentleman was
    wronged,
And that the gentlewoman was brought
    thither,
Forced by her husband, and there left.
Volt.   Most true.
Cel. How ready is heaven to those that
    pray!
Avoc. 1.   But that
Volpone would have ravished her, he
    holds
Utterly false, knowing his impotence.
Corv. Grave fathers, he is possessed;
    again, I say,
Possessed; nay, if there be possession
And obsession, he has both.
Avoc. 3.   Here comes our officer. 10

[*Enter Volpone.*]

Volp. The parasite will straight be here,
    grave fathers.
Avoc. 4. You might invent some other
    name, Sir Varlet.
Avoc. 3. Did not the notary meet him?

VOLP.   Not that I know.
Avoc. 4. His coming will clear all.
Avoc. 2.   Yet it is misty.
VOLT. May 't please your fatherhoods—
        Volpone whispers the Advocate.
VOLP.   Sir, the parasite
    Willed me to tell you that his master
        lives;
    That you are still the man; your hopes
        the same;
    And this was only a jest—
VOLT.   How?
VOLP.   Sir, to try
    If you were firm, and how you stood
        affected.
VOLT. Art sure he lives?
VOLP.   Do I live, sir?
VOLT.   O me! 20
    I was too violent.
VOLP.   Sir, you may redeem it.
    They said you were possessed; fall
        down, and seem so.
    I'll help to make it good.—(*Voltore falls.*)
    God bless the man!—
    (Stop your wind hard, and swell.) See,
        see, see, see!
    He vomits crooked pins! His eyes are
        set,
    Like a dead hare's hung in a poulter's
        shop!
    His mouth's running away! Do you
        see, signior?
    Now 'tis in his belly.
(CORV.   Ay, the devil!)
VOLP. Now in his throat.
(CORV.   Ay, I perceive it plain.)
VOLP. 'Twill out, 'twill out! Stand clear.
    See where it flies,   30
    In shape of a blue toad, with a bat's
        wings!
    Do not you see it, sir?
CORB.   What? I think I do.
CORV. 'Tis too manifest.
VOLP.   Look! He comes t' himself!
VOLT. Where am I?
VOLP.   Take good heart; the worst
    is past, sir.
    You're dispossessed.
Avoc. 1.   What accident is
    this?
Avoc. [2.] Sudden and full of wonder!
Avoc. 3.   If he were
    Possessed, as it appears, all this is
        nothing.

CORV. He has been often subject to
    these fits.
Avoc. 1. Show him that writing.—Do
    you know it, sir?
VOLP. [*Whispering to Voltore.*] Deny it,
    sir; forswear it; know it not.   40
VOLT. Yes, I do know it well; it is my hand
    But all that it contains is false.
BON.   O, practice! [1]
Avoc. 2. What maze is this!
Avoc. 1.   Is he not guilty then
    Whom you there name the parasite?
VOLT.   Grave fathers,
    No more than his good patron, old
        Volpone.
Avoc. 4. Why, he is dead.
VOLT.   O, no, my honored fathers,
    He lives—
Avoc. 1.   How! Lives?
VOLT.   Lives.
Avoc. 2.   This is subtler yet!
Avoc. 3. You said he was dead.
VOLT.   Never.
Avoc. 3.   You said so.
CORV.   I heard so.
Avoc. 4. Here comes the gentleman; make
    him way.

                [Enter Mosca.]

Avoc. 3.   A stool!
Avoc. 4. [*Aside.*] A proper man; and,
    were Volpone dead,   50
    A fit match for my daughter.
Avoc. 3.   Give him way.
VOLP. [*Aside to Mosca.*] Mosca, I was
    a'most lost; the advocate
    Had betrayed all; but now it is recov-
        ered.
    All's o' the hinge again.—Say I am
        living.
Mos. What busy knave is this!—Most
    reverend fathers,
    I sooner had attended your grave pleas-
        ures,
    But that my order for the funeral
    Of my dear patron did require me—
(VOLP.   Mosca!)
Mos. Whom I intend to bury like a
    gentleman.
VOLP. [*Aside.*] Ay, quick,[2] and cozen me
    of all.
Avoc. 2.   Still stranger!   60
    More intricate!

[1] Deceit.   [2] Alive.

Avoc. 1.　　　　And come about again!

Avoc. 4. [*Aside*.] It is a match; my
　daughter is bestowed.

(Mos. Will you gi' me half?

Volp.　　　　First I'll be hanged.

Mos.　　　　　I know
　Your voice is good; cry not so loud.)

Avoc. 1.　　　　Demand
　The advocate.—Sir, did you not affirm
　Volpone was alive?

Volp.　　　　Yes, and he is;
　This gent'man told me so.—(Thou
　shalt have half.)

Mos. Whose drunkard is this same?
　Speak, some that know him;
　I never saw his face.—(I cannot now
　Afford it you so cheap.

Volp.　　No?)

Avoc. 1.　　What say you?　70

Volt. The officer told me.

Volp.　　　　I did, grave fathers,
　And will maintain he lives, with mine
　own life,
　And that this creature [*Points to Mosca*.]
　　told me.—(I was born
　With all good stars my enemies.)

Mos.　　　　Most grave fathers,
　If such an insolence as this must pass
　Upon me, I am silent; 'twas not this
　For which you sent, I hope.

Avoc. 2.　　　　Take him away.

(Volp. Mosca!)

Avoc. 3.　　Let him be whipped.

(Volp.　　Wilt thou betray me?
　Cozen me?)

Avoc. 3.　　And taught to bear him-
　　self
　Toward a person of his rank

Avoc. 4.　　　　Away!　80
　　　　[*Commendadore seizes Volpone*.]

Mos. I humbly thank your fatherhoods.

Volp.　　　　Soft, soft!—
　[*Aside*.] Whipped?
　And lose all that I have? If I con-
　　fess,
　It cannot be much more.

Avoc. 4.　　　Sir, are you mar-
　　ried?

Volp. They'll be allied anon; I must
　be resolute.
　The fox shall here uncase.
　　　　　He puts off his disguise.

(Mos.　　　Patron!)

Volp.　　　　Nay, now

My ruins shall not come alone; your
　match
I'll hinder sure. My substance shall
　not glue you,
Nor screw you, into a family.

(Mos.　　　　Why, patron!)

Volp. I am Volpone, and this is my
　knave;　　　[*Points to Mosca*.]
This [*To Voltore*.] his own knave; this
　[*To Corbaccio*.] avarice's fool;　90
This [*To Corvino*.] a chimera of wittol,
　fool, and knave;
And, reverend fathers, since we all
　can hope
Naught but a sentence, let's not now
　despair it.
You hear me brief.

Corv.　May it please your fatherhoods—

Com.　　　　Silence!

Avoc. 1. The knot is now undone by
　miracle.

Avoc. 2. Nothing can be more clear.

Avoc. 3.　　　Or can more prove
　These innocent.

Avoc. 1.　　Give hem their liberty.
　　　　[*Bonario and Celia are released*.]

Bon. Heaven could not long let such
　gross crimes be hid.

Avoc. 1. If this be held the highway to
　get riches,
May I be poor!

Avoc. 3.　　This 's not the gain, but tor-
　　ment.　　　　　　100

Avoc. 1. These possess wealth, as sick
　men possess fevers,
　Which trulier may be said to possess
　them.

Avoc. 2. Disrobe that parasite.

Corv. ⎫
Mos. ⎭　　　Most honored fathers—

Avoc. 1. Can you plead aught to stay the
　course of justice?
If you can, speak.

Corv. ⎫
Volt. ⎭　　We beg favor.

Cel.　　　　And mercy.

Avoc. 1. You hurt your innocence, suing
　for the guilty.
Stand forth; and first the parasite.
　You appear
T' have been the chiefest minister, if
　not plotter,
In all these lewd impostures, and now,
　lastly,

Have with your impudence abused [1]
the court,   110
And habit of a gentleman of Venice,
Being a fellow of no birth or blood—
For which our sentence is, first, thou be
whipped,
Then live perpetual prisoner in our
galleys.
VOLP. I thank you for him.
MOS.   Bane to thy wolvish nature!
AVOC. 1. Deliver him to the saffi.— [*Mosca
is led away.*] Thou, Volpone,
By blood and rank a gentleman, canst
not fall
Under like censure; but our judgment
on thee
Is that thy substance all be straight
confiscate
To the hospital of the Incurabili; 120
And, since the most was gotten by
imposture,
By feigning lame, gout, palsy, and
such diseases,
Thou art to lie in prison, cramped with
irons,
Till thou beest sick and lame indeed.
Remove him!
      [*Volpone is removed from the bar.*]
VOLP. This is called mortifying of a
fox.
AVOC. 1. Thou, Voltore, to take away the
scandal
Thou hast giv'n all worthy men of thy
profession,
Art banished from their fellowship and
our state.—
Corbaccio!—Bring him near.—We here
possess   129
Thy son of all thy state,[2] and confine
thee
To the monastery of San Spirito,
Where, since thou knew'st not how to
live well here,
Thou shalt be learned to die well.
CORB.   Ha! What said he?
COM. You shall know anon, sir.
AVOC. [1.]   Thou, Corvino, shalt

[1] Imposed on.   [2] Estate.   [3] Pillory.

Be straight embarked from thine own
house, and rowed
Round about Venice, through the Grand
Canal,
Wearing a cap, with fair, long ass's ears,
Instead of horns, and so to mount, a
paper
Pinned on thy breast, to the *berlino!*[3]
CORV.   Yes,
And have mine eyes beat out with stink-
ing fish,   140
Bruised fruit, and rotten eggs—'tis well.
I am glad
I shall not see my shame yet.
AVOC. 1.   And, to expiate
Thy wrongs done to thy wife, thou art
to send her
Home to her father, with her dowry
trebled.
And these are all your judgments—
(ALL.   Honored fathers—)
AVOC. 1. Which may not be revoked.
Now you begin,
When crimes are done and past, and
to be punished,
To think what your crimes are. Away
with them!
Let all that see these vices thus re-
warded,
Take heart, and love to study hem.
Mischiefs feed   150
Like beasts, till they be fat, and then
they bleed.   [*Exeunt.*]

Volpone [*comes forward*].

The seasoning of a play is the applause.
Now, though the fox be punished by
the laws,
He yet doth hope there is no suff'ring due
For any fact which he hath done gainst
you.
If there be, censure him; here he doubt-
ful stands.
If not, fare jovially, and clap your
hands.   [*Exit.*]

THE END.

This comedy was first acted in the year 1605 by the King's Majesty's Servants.
The principal comedians were:

Ric. Burbadge	*Will. Sly*	*Joh. Lowin*
Hen. Condell	*Joh. Hemings*	*Alex. Cooke*

With the allowance of the Master of Revels.

THE ALCHEMIST[1]

BY

BEN JONSON

THE PERSONS OF THE PLAY

SUBTLE, *the alchemist.*
FACE, *the housekeeper.*
DOLL COMMON, *their colleague.*
DAPPER, *a [lawyer's] clerk.*

DRUGGER, *a tabacco-man.*[14]
LOVEWIT, *master of the house.*
EPICURE MAMMON, *a knight.*
[PERTINAX] SURLY, *a gamester.*
TRIBULATION [WHOLESOME], *a pastor of Amsterdam.*
ANANIAS, *a deacon there.*
KASTRIL, *the angry boy.*
DA[ME] PLIANT, *his sister, a widow.*
NEIGHBORS.
OFFICERS.
MUTES.

[1] The title continues: "A Comedy, Acted in the Year 1610 by the King's Majesty's Servants." After the title-page appears a dedication to Mary, Lady Wroth.
[2] This address appears in the 1612 edn. only.
[3] *I.e.*, a person who accepts other peoples' judgments on faith.
[4] The Hoe copy reads *dances and antics.*
[5] Practitioners.
[6] Natural endowments.
[7] The Hoe copy reads *many.*
[8] Surpassing deficiency.
[9] Robustiously.
[10] An incomplete fall in wrestling.
[11] Copious supply, abundance of wit.
[12] Publish.
[13] Selection and moderation. [14] Tobacconist.

THE SCENE: [*A house in the Blackfriars district,*] *London.*

[TIME: *A single day in the autumn of 1610.*]

THE ARGUMENT [1]

T he sickness [2] hot, a master quit, for fear,
H is house in town and left one servant
  there.
E ase him corrupted, and gave means to
  know
A cheater and his punk,[3] who, now brought
  low,
L eaving their narrow practice, were be-
  come
C oz'ners at large, and, only wanting some
H ouse to set up, with him they here con-
  tract
E ach for a share, and all begin to act.
M uch company they draw and much
  abuse,[4]   9
I n casting figures,[5] telling fortunes, news,
S elling of flies,[6] flat bawdry, with the
  stone,[7]
T ill it and they and all in fume are gone.

PROLOGUE

Fortune, that favors fools, these two short
  hours
  We wish away, both for your sakes and
  ours,
Judging spectators; and desire in place,
  To th' author justice, to ourselves but
  grace.
Our scene is London, cause we would make
  known
  No country's mirth is better than our
  own;
No clime breeds better matter for your
  whore,
  Bawd, squire, impostor, many persons
  more,
Whose manners, now called humors, feed
  the stage,
  And which have still [8] been subject for
  the rage   10
Or spleen of comic writers. Though, this
  pen
  Did never aim to grieve, but better, men,
Howe'er the age he lives in doth endure

The vices that she breeds, above their
  cure.
But, when the wholesome remedies are
  sweet
  And in their working gain and profit
  meet,
He hopes to find no spirit so much diseased
  But will with such fair correctives be
  pleased;
For here he doth not fear who can apply.
  If there be any that will sit so nigh   20
Unto the stream, to look what it doth run,
  They shall find things they'ld think or
  wish were done;
They are so natural follies, but so shown,
  As even the doers may see, and yet not
  own.

ACT I. SCENE i.

[*A room in Lovewit's house.*] [9]

Face, Subtle, Doll Common.

[FACE.] Believe 't, I will.
SUB.   Thy worst. I fart at thee!
DOLL. Ha' you your wits? Why, gentle-
  men! For love—
FACE. Sirrah, I'll strip you—
SUB.   What to do? Lick figs [10]
  Out at my—
FACE.   Rogue, rogue, out of all your
  sleights! [11]
DOLL. Nay, look ye! Sovereign, general,
  are you madmen?
SUB. O, let the wild sheep loose. I'll gum
  your silks
  With good strong water,[12] an [13] you come.
DOLL.   Will you have
  The neighbors hear you? Will you betray
  all?
  Hark! I hear somebody.
FACE.   Sirrah—
SUB.   I shall mar
  All that the tailor has made, if you
  approach.   10

---

[1] Summary of the plot.
[2] The plague.
[3] Mistress.
[4] Deceive.
[5] Horoscopes.
[6] Familiar spirits.
[7] Philosophers' stone.
[8] Always.
[9] The scene and the action are continuous throughout the act.
[10] For this vulgar allusion, *cf.* Rabelais, bk. IV, ch. 45.
[11] Cease your tricks!
[12] *I.e.*, some chemical preparation which he carries in his hand.   [13] If.

FACE. You most notorious whelp, you in-
　　solent slave,
　Dare you do this?
SUB.　　　　Yes, faith; yes, faith.
FACE.　　　　　　　　Why, who
　Am I, my mungril? [1] Who am I?
SUB.　　　　　　　I'll tell you,
　Since you know not yourself.
FACE.　　　　　Speak lower, rogue.
SUB. Yes. You were once (time's not long
　　past) the good,
　Honest, plain, livery-three-pound-thrum [2]
　　that kept
　Your master's worship's house here in the
　　Friars [3]
　For the vacations [4]—
FACE.　　　　　Will you be so loud?
SUB. Since, by my means, translated sub-
　　urb-captain.[5]
FACE. By your means, Doctor Dog?
SUB.　　　Within man's memory,　20
　All this I speak of.
FACE.　　　Why, I pray you, have I
　Been countenanced by you, or you by
　　me?
　Do but collect,[6] sir, where I met you
　　first.
SUB. I do not hear well.
FACE.　　　　Not of this, I think it.
　But I shall put you in mind, sir—at Pie
　　Corner,
　Taking your meal of steam in from cooks'
　　stalls,
　Where, like the father of hunger, you did
　　walk
　Piteously costive, with your pinched
　　horn-nose
　And your complexion of the Roman
　　wash,[7]
　Stuck full of black and melancholic
　　worms,　　　　　　　　　30
　Like poulder corns [8] shot at th' artillery
　　yard.
SUB. I wish you could advance your voice
　　a little.

FACE. When you went pinned up in the
　　several rags
　Yo' had raked and picked from dunghills
　　before day,
　Your feet in moldy slippers for your
　　kibes,[9]
　A felt of rug,[10] and a thin-threaden cloak
　That scarce would cover your no-
　　buttocks—
SUB.　　　　　　So, sir!
FACE. When all your *alchemy* and your
　　algebra,
　Your *minerals*, *vegetals*, and *animals*,[11]
　Your conjuring, coz'ning, and your dozen
　　of trades　　　　　　　40
　Could not relieve your corpse with so
　　much linen
　Would make you tinder but to see a
　　fire,[12]
　I ga' you count'nance, credit for your
　　coals,
　Your stills, your glasses, your *materials*,
　Built you a fornace,[13] drew you cus-
　　tomers,
　Advanced all your black arts, lent you,
　　beside,
　A house to practice in—
SUB.　　　　Your master's house?
FACE. Where you have studied the more
　　thriving skill
　Of bawdry since.
SUB.　　　Yes, in your master's house.
　You and the rats here kept possession.
　Make it not strange.[14] I know yo' were
　　one could keep　　　　　51
　The butt'ry-hatch still locked and save
　　the chippings,[15]
　Sell the dole-beer [16] to aqua-vitæ-men,[17]
　The which, together with your Christ-
　　mas vails [18]
　At post-and-pair,[19] your letting out of
　　counters,[20]
　Made you a pretty stock, some twenty
　　marks,

[1] Mongrel.
[2] An inferior servant wearing a livery made out
of weaver's warp.
[3] The Blackfriars, a district in London.
[4] *I.e.*, between the terms of court.
[5] Pander, since the stews were generally located in the suburbs.
[6] Recollect.
[7] *I.e.*, swarthy (?).
[8] Powder corns, grains of powder.

[9] Chilblains.　　　　[10] A hat of coarse cloth.
[11] Throughout the play Jonson italicizes terms
associated with alchemy. The present editors
have not glossed these except where intelligibility demands.
[12] *I.e.*, as would make you sufficient tinder to
provide a fire.　　　　　　[13] Furnace.
[14] Do not counterfeit ignorance.
[15] Scraps of bread.
[16] Beer intended to be given to the poor.
[17] Liquor-dealers.　　　[19] A game of cards.
[18] Tips.　　　　　　[20] *I.e.*, to the gamesters.

And gave you credit to converse with
  cobwebs
Here since your mistress' death hath
  broke up house.
FACE. You might talk softlier, rascal.
SUB.   No, you scarab,
I'll thunder you in pieces. I will teach
  you   60
How to beware to tempt a Fury again
That carries tempest in his hand and
  voice.
FACE. The place has made you valiant.
SUB.   No, your clothes.
Thou vermin, have I ta'en thee out of
  dung,
So poor, so wretched, when no living
  thing
Would keep thee company but a spider
  or worse?
Raised thee from brooms, and dust, and
  wat'ring-pots,
Sublimed thee, and *exalted* thee, and
  fixed thee
I' the *third region*, called our *state of
  grace?*
Wrought thee to *spirit*, to *quintessence*,
  with pains   70
Would twice have won me the *philos-
  ophers' work?*
Put thee in words and fashion? Made
  thee fit
For more than ordinary fellowships?
Giv'n thee thy oaths, thy quarreling
  dimensions?
Thy rules to cheat at horse race, cockpit,
  cards,
Dice, or whatever gallant tincture [1] else?
Made thee a second in mine own great
  art?
And have I this for thank? Do you
  rebel?
Do you fly out i' the *projection?* [2]
Would you be gone now?
DOLL.   Gentlemen, what mean you? 80
  Will you mar all?
SUB.   Slave, thou hadst had no name—
DOLL. Will you undo yourselves with
  civil war?
SUB. Never been known, past *equi cliba-
  num*,
The heat of horse dung, under ground,
  in cellars,

[1] Inclination to gallantry.
[2] On the completion of the experiment.

Or an alehouse darker than deaf John's—
  been lost
To all mankind but laundresses and
  tapsters,
Had not I been.
DOLL.   Do you know who hears you,
  sovereign?
FACE. Sirrah—
DOLL.   Nay, general, I thought you
  were civil.
FACE. I shall turn desperate, if you grow
  thus loud.
SUB. And hang thyself, I care not.
FACE.   Hang thee, collier, 90
And all thy pots and pans! In picture
  I will,
Since thou hast moved me—
[3] (DOLL.   O, this'll o'erthrow all.)
FACE. Write thee up bawd in Paul's,[4] have
  all thy tricks
Of coz'ning with a hollow coal, dust,
  scrapings,
Searching for things lost, with a sieve and
  shears,
Erecting *figures* in your rows of *houses*,
And taking in of shadows with a glass,[5]
Told [6] in red letters, and a face cut for
  thee
Worse than Gamaliel Ratsey's.[7]
DOLL.   Are you sound?
Ha' you your senses, masters?
FACE.   I will have 100
A book, but barely reckoning thy im-
  postures,
Shall prove a true *philosophers' stone* to
  printers.
SUB. Away, you trencher-rascal!
FACE.   Out, you dog leech!
The vomit of all prisons—
DOLL.   Will you be
Your own destructions, gentlemen?
FACE.   Still spewed out
For lying too heavy o' the basket.[8]
SUB.   Cheater!
FACE. Bawd!

[3] Jonson frequently encloses in parenthesis
passages that are aside or are incidental to the
main action.
[4] St. Paul's Cathedral, a common meeting
place for all London.
[5] A method of divination.
[6] Written.
[7] A highwayman hanged in 1605.
[8] Taking more than his share of the prisoners'
food.

SUB.   Cowherd!
FACE.   Conjurer!
SUB.   Cutpurse!
FACE.   Witch!
DOLL.   O me!
  We are ruined, lost! Ha' you no more
    regard
  To your reputations? Where's your
    judgment? 'Slight,[1]
  Have yet some care of me, o' your
    republic—   110
FACE. Away, this brach![2] I'll bring thee,
    rogue, within
  The statute of sorcery, tricesimo tertio
  Of Harry the Eight,[3] ay, and perhaps
    thy neck
  Within a noose, for laund'ring[4] gold and
    barbing[5] it.
DOLL. You'll bring your head within a
    coxcomb,[6] will you?

She catcheth out Face his sword, and breaks
                          Subtle's glass.

  And you, sir, with your *menstrue!*[7]
    Gather it up.
  'Sdeath, you abominable pair of stink-
    ards,
  Leave off your barking, and grow one
    again,
  Or, by the light that shines, I'll cut your
    throats.
  I'll not be made a prey unto the mar-
    shal[8]   120
  For ne'er a snarling dogbolt[9] o' you both.
  Ha' you together cozened all this while
  And all the world, and shall it now be
    said
  Yo' have made most courteous shift to
    cozen yourselves?—
  [*To Face.*] You will accuse him? You
    will bring him in
  Within the statute? Who shall take your
    word—
  A whoreson, upstart, apocryphal cap-
    tain,
  Whom not a Puritan in Blackfriars will
    trust

---

[1] By God's light, a mild oath. *Cf.* also *Od's
precious, 'Slid*, etc.   [2] Bitch.
[3] In the thirty-third year of Henry the
Eighth, *i.e.*, 1541.
[4] "Sweating," *i.e.*, washing in acid.
[5] Clipping.   [7] Solvent.
[6] Fool's cap.   [8] Prison warden.
[9] Useless arrow; hence, a worthless thing.

  So much as for a feather?—[*To Subtle.*]
    And you too
  Will give the cause, forsooth? You will
    insult,[10]   130
  And claim a primacy in the divisions?
  You must be chief, as if you only had
  The poulder to project[11] with, and the
    work
  Were not begun out of equality?
  The venter[12] tripartite? All things in
    common?
  Without priority? 'Sdeath, you per-
    petual curs,
  Fall to your couples again, and cozen
    kindly
  And heartily and lovingly, as you should,
  And lose not the beginning of a term,[13]
  Or, by this hand, I shall grow factious
    too   140
  And take my part and quit you.
FACE.   'Tis his fault;
  He ever murmurs, and objects his pains,
  And says the weight of all lies upon
    him.
SUB. Why, so it does.
DOLL.   How does it? Do not we
  Sustain our parts?
SUB.   Yes, but they are not equal.
DOLL. Why, if your part exceed today, I
    hope
  Ours may tomorrow match it.
SUB.   Ay, they *may*.
DOLL. "May," murmuring mastiff? Ay,
    and do. Death on me!
  Help me to thrattle[14] him.
                          [*Strives to choke him.*]
SUB.   Dorothy! Mistress Dorothy!
  Od's precious, I'll do anything. What
    do you mean?   150
DOLL. Because o' your *fermentation* and
    cibation?
SUB. Not I, by heaven—
DOLL. Your *Sol* and *Luna*—[*To Face.*]
    Help me!
SUB. Would I were hanged then! I'll
    conform myself.
DOLL. Will you, sir? Do so then, and
    quickly. Swear.
SUB. What should I swear?

---

[10] Behave insolently.
[11] Apply the elixir to the metal to be transmuted.   [12] Venture.
[13] A term of court, when London was crowded
with visitors.   [14] Throttle.

DOLL.   To leave your faction, sir,
And labor kindly in the commune [1] work.
SUB. Let me not breathe if I meant aught
 beside.
I only used those speeches as a spur
To him.
DOLL. I hope we need no spurs, sir.
 Do we?
FACE. 'Slid, prove today who shall shark [2]
 best.
SUB.   Agreed.   160
DOLL. Yes, and work close and friendly.
SUB.   'Slight, the knot
 Shall grow the stronger for this breach,
 with me.   [*They shake hands.*]
DOLL. Why, so, my good baboons! Shall
 we go make
A sort [3] of sober, scurvy, precise neigh-
 bors,[4]
That scarce have smiled twice sin' the
 king came in,[5]
A feast of laughter at our follies? Rascals,
Would run themselves from breath to see
 me ride,[6]
Or you t' have but a hole to thrust your
 heads in,
For which you should pay ear-rent.[7] No,
 agree.
And may Don Provost [8] ride a-feasting [9]
 long   170
In his old velvet jerkin and stained
 scarfs,
My noble sovereign and worthy general,
Ere we contribute a new crewel [10] garter
To his most worsted worship.
SUB.   Royal Doll!
 Spoken like Claridiana,[11] and thyself.
FACE. For which at supper thou shalt sit
 in triumph,
And not be styled Doll Common, but
 Doll Proper,
Doll Singular. The longest cut at
 night
Shall draw thee for his Doll Particular.
    [*A bell rings.*]

SUB. Who's that? One rings. To the
 window, Doll. Pray heaven 180
The master do not trouble us this
 quarter.
FACE. O, fear not him. While there dies
 one a week
O' the plague, he's safe from thinking
 toward London.
Beside, he's busy at his hopyards now;
I had a letter from him. If he do,
He'll send such word for airing o' the
 house
As you shall have sufficient time to quit
 it.
Though we break up a fortnight, 'tis no
 matter.
SUB. Who is it, Doll?
DOLL. A fine young quodling.[12]
FACE.   O,
My lawyer's clerk I lighted on last
 night   190
In Holborn at the Dagger. He would
 have
(I told you of him) a familiar,[13]
To rifle [14] with at horses and win cups.
DOLL. O, let him in.
SUB.   Stay. Who shall do 't?
FACE.   Get you
Your robes on; I will meet him, as [15]
 going out.
DOLL. And what shall I do?
FACE. Not be seen; away!—[*Exit Doll*]
Seem you very reserved.
SUB.   Enough. [*Exit.*]
FACE. [*Shouting to Subtle.*] God be
 w' you, sir.
I pray you let him know that I was here.
His name is Dapper.—[*Pretends to leave.*]
 I would gladly have stayed, but—

ACT I. SCENE ii.

Dapper, Face, Subtle.

[DAP.] Captain, I am here.
FACE. Who's that?—He's come, I think,
 doctor.—
Good faith, sir, I was going away.
DAP.   In truth,
I am very sorry, captain.
FACE.   But I thought
Sure I should meet you.

---

[1] Common.
[2] Swindle, cozen.
[3] Crowd.
[7] *I.e.*, lose your ears in the pillory.
[8] *I.e.* the hangman, part of whose perquisites was the clothes of the criminal.
[9] Thriving.
[10] A worsted yarn, with a pun on *cruel.*
[11] Heroine of the romance, *The Mirror of Knighthood.*

[4] *I.e.*, the Puritans.
[5] In 1603.
[6] *I.e.*, carted as a bawd.

[12] Codling, a green apple; here an immature young man. [14] Raffle, hold a lottery
[13] Familiar spirit. [15] As if.

DAP.　　　　　　　Ay, I am very glad.
I had a scurvy writ or two to make,
And I had lent my watch last night to
　one
That dines today at the shrief's,[1] and
　so was robbed
Of my pass-time.

[*Enter Subtle in his robes.*]

　　　　　　　　Is this the cunning [2] man?
FACE. This is his worship.
DAP.　　　　　　　Is he a doctor?
FACE.　　　　　　　　　　Yes.
DAP. And ha' you broke [3] with him, cap-
　tain?
FACE.　　　　Ay.
DAP.　　　　　　　And how?　10
FACE. Faith, he does make the matter,
　sir, so dainty [4]
I know not what to say.
DAP.　　　　　　Not so, good captain.
FACE. Would I were fairly rid on 't, be-
　lieve me.
DAP. Nay, now you grieve me, sir. Why
　should you wish so?
I dare assure you, I'll not be ungrate-
　ful.
FACE. I cannot think you will, sir. But
　the law
Is such a thing—and then he says Read's
　matter
Falling so lately [5]—
DAP.　　　　　　Read? He was an ass,
And dealt, sir, with a fool.
FACE.　　　　　It was a clerk, sir.
DAP. A clerk?
FACE.　　Nay, hear me, sir. You know the
　law　　　　　　　　　　　　　　　20
Better, I think—
DAP.　　　I should, sir, and the danger.
You know I showed the statute to
　you?
FACE.　　　　　　　　You did so.
DAP. And will I tell then? By this hand
　of flesh,
Would it might never write good court-
　hand [6] more,

---

[1] Sheriff's.
[2] Learned, especially in magic.
[3] Broached the question.
[4] *I.e.*, he has so many scruples.
[5] Dr. Simon Read had been recently convicted
as a magician.
[6] Handwriting of the law courts.

If I discover.[7] What do you think of me,
That I am a chiaus? [8]
FACE.　　　　What's that?
DAP.　　　　　　　The Turk was here.
As one would say, do you think I am a
　Turk?
FACE. I'll tell the doctor so.
DAP.　　　　　Do, good sweet captain.
FACE. Come, noble doctor, pray thee, let's
　prevail;
This is the gentleman, and he is no
　chiaus.　　　　　　　　　　　　　30
SUB. Captain, I have returned you all my
　answer.
I would do much, sir, for your love—
　but this
I neither may, nor can.
FACE.　　　　　　Tut, do not say so.
You deal now with a noble fellow, doctor,
One that will thank you richly; and
　h' is no chiaus.
Let that, sir, move you.
SUB.　　　　　　Pray you, forbear.
FACE.　　　　　　　　　He has
Four angels [9] here.
SUB.　　You do me wrong, good sir.
FACE. Doctor, wherein? To tempt you
　with these spirits?
SUB. To tempt my ar̀ and love, sir, to my
　peril.
Fore [10] heav'n, I scarce can think you
　are my friend,　　　　　　　　40
That so would draw me to apparent
　danger.
FACE. I draw you? A horse draw you,
　and a halter,
You and your flies together—
DAP.　　　　　　Nay, good captain.
FACE. That know no difference of men.
SUB.　　　　　　Good words, sir.
FACE. Good deeds, sir, Doctor Dogs'-
　meat. 'Slight, I bring you
No cheating Clim o' the Cloughs or
　Claribels,[11]
That look as big as five-and-fifty and
　flush,[12]
And spit out secrets like hot custard—
DAP.　　　　　　　　Captain!

---

[7] Reveal.
[8] Chouse, a Turkish messenger, like the one
who had recently cheated some London merchants.
[9] Gold coins.　　　　　[10] Before.
[11] Heroes of romantic tales.
[12] The highest hand at primero, a card game.

FACE. Nor any melancholic underscribe,
Shall tell the vicar; but a special gentle,[1]
That is the heir to forty marks a year, 51
Consorts with the small poets of the time,
Is the sole hope of his old grandmother;
That knows the law and writes you six fair hands,
Is a fine clerk and has his ciph'ring perfect,
Will take his oath o' the Greek Xenophon,
If need be, in his pocket, and can court
His mistress out of Ovid.
DAP. Nay, dear captain—
FACE. Did you not tell me so?
DAP. Yes; but I'ld ha' you
Use Master Doctor with some more respect. 60
FACE. Hang him, proud stag, with his broad velvet head!
But for your sake I'ld choke ere I would change
An article of breath with such a puckfist![2]
Come, let's be gone.
SUB. Pray you, le' me speak with you.
DAP. His worship calls you, captain.
FACE. I am sorry
I e'er embarked myself in such a business.
DAP. Nay, good sir; he did call you.
FACE. Will he take then?
SUB. First, hear me—
FACE. Not a syllable, 'less you take.
SUB. Pray ye, sir—
FACE. Upon no terms but an *assumpsit*.[3]
SUB. Your humor must be law.
He takes the money.
FACE. Why now, sir, talk 70
Now I dare hear you with mine honor. Speak.
So may this gentleman too.
SUB. [*Pretending to whisper to Face.*] Why, sir—
FACE. No whisp'ring.
SUB. Fore heav'n, you do not apprehend the loss
You do yourself in this.
FACE. Wherein? For what?

<hr />

[1] Gentleman.
[2] Puffball, a worthless person.
[3] Legal term for a contract involving an initial payment.

SUB. Marry, to be so importunate for one
That, when he has it, will undo you all;
He'll win up all the money i' the town.
FACE. How!
SUB. Yes, and blow up gamester after gamester,
As they do crackers in a puppet play.
If I do give him a familiar, 80
Give you him all you play for; never set[4] him,
For he will have it.
FACE. Y' are mistaken, doctor.
Why, he does ask one but for cups and horses,
A rifling fly—none o' your great familiars.
DAP. Yes, captain, I would have it for all games.
SUB. I told you so.
FACE. [*Drawing Dapper aside.*] 'Slight, that's a new business!
I understood you, a tame bird,[5] to fly
Twice in a term or so, on Friday nights
When you had left the office, for a nag
Of forty or fifty shillings.
DAP. Ay, 'tis true, sir; 90
But I do think now I shall leave the law,
And therefore—
FACE. Why, this changes quite the case.
Do you think that I dare move him?
DAP. If you please, sir;
All's one to him, I see.
FACE. What? For that money?
I cannot with my conscience, nor should you
Make the request, methinks.
DAP. No, sir, I mean
To add consideration.
FACE. Why, then, sir,
I'll try.—[*To Subtle.*] Say that it were for all games, doctor?
SUB. I say then not a mouth shall eat for[6] him
At any ordinary but o' the score;[7] 100
That is a gaming mouth, conceive me.
FACE. Indeed!
SUB. He'll draw you all the treasure of the realm,
If it be set him.
FACE. Speak you this from art?
SUB. Ay, sir, and reason too, the ground of art.

<hr />

[4] Stake against.
[5] A familiar spirit.
[6] On account of.
[7] On credit.

H' is o' the only best complexion
The Queen of Fairy loves.
FACE.   What! Is he?
SUB.   Peace!
He'll overhear you. Sir, should she but
    see him—
FACE. What?
SUB.   Do not you tell him.
FACE.   Will he win at cards too?
SUB. The spirits of dead Holland, living
    Isaac,[1]
You'ld swear, were in him—such a
    vigorous luck   110
As cannot be resisted. 'Slight, he'll put
Six o' your gallants to a cloak,[2] indeed.
FACE. A strange success, that some man
    shall be born to!
SUB. He hears you, man—
DAP.   Sir, I'll not be ingrateful.
FACE. Faith, I have a confidence in his
    good nature.
You hear, he says he will not be ingrate-
    ful.
SUB. Why, as you please; my venture
    follows yours.
FACE. Troth, do it, doctor; think him
    trusty, and make him.
He may make us both happy in an
    hour—
Win some five thousand pound, and send
    us two on 't.   120
DAP. Believe it, and I will, sir.
FACE.   And you shall, sir.
You have heard all?
                    Face takes him aside.
DAP.   No, what was 't? Nothing, I, sir.
FACE. Nothing?
DAP.   A little, sir.
FACE.   Well, a rare star
Reigned at your birth.
DAP.   At mine, sir? No!
FACE.   The doctor
Swears that you are—
SUB.   Nay, captain, yo'll tell all now.
FACE. Allied to the Queen of Fairy.
DAP.   Who? That I am?
Believe it, no such matter.
FACE.   Yes, and that
Yo' were born with a caul o' your head.[3]

DAP.   Who says so?
FACE.   Come,
You know it well enough, though you
    dissemble it.
DAP. I' fac,[4] I do not; you are mistaken.
FACE.   How!   130
Swear by your fac, and in a thing so
    known
Unto the doctor? How shall we, sir,
    trust you
I' the other matter? Can we ever think,
When you have won five or six thousand
    pound,
You'll send us shares in 't, by this rate?
DAP.   By Jove, sir,
I'll win ten thousand pound, and send
    you half.
I' fac 's no oath.
SUB.   No, no, he did but jest.
FACE. Go to. Go thank the doctor. He's
    your friend,
To take it so.
DAP.   I thank his worship.
FACE.   So?
Another angel.
DAP.   Must I?
FACE.   Must you? 'Slight,   140
What else is thanks? Will you be triv-
    ial?—[*Dapper gives Subtle money.*]
Doctor,
When must he come for his familiar?
DAP. Shall I not ha' it with me?
SUB.   O, good sir,
There must a world of ceremonies pass;
You must be bathed and fumigated
    first;
Besides, the Queen of Fairy does not
    rise
Till it be noon.
FACE.   Not if she danced tonight.[5]
SUB. And she must bless it.
FACE.   Did you never see
Her royal grace yet?
DAP.   Whom?
FACE.   Your aunt of Fairy?
SUB. Not since she kissed him in the cra-
    dle, captain;   150
I can resolve[6] you that.
FACE.   Well, see her grace,
Whate'er it cost you, for a thing that I
    know.
It will be somewhat hard to compass;
    but,

---

[1] Whalley suggests these are the names of
well-known gamblers of the period.
[2] *I.e.*, strip them to a single cloak for all.
[3] An old superstition connected with good
luck.
[4] In faith.   [5] Last night.   [6] Tell.

However, see her. You are made, be-
    lieve it,
If you can see her. Her grace is a lone
    woman,
And very rich; and, if she take a fancy,
She will do strange things. See her, at
    any hand.[1]
'Slid, she may hap to leave you all she
    has!
It is the doctor's fear.
DAP.   How will 't be done, then?
FACE. Let me alone; take you no thought.
    Do you   160
But say to me, "Captain, I'll see her
    grace."
DAP. Captain, I'll see her grace.
FACE.   Enough. *One knocks without.*
SUB.   Who's there?
    Anon.—(Conduct him forth by the back
    way.)
    Sir, against one a-clock prepare your-
    self;
    Till when, you must be fasting; only
    take
    Three drops of vinegar in at your nose,
    Two at your mouth, and one at either
    ear;
    Then bath[2] your fingers' ends and wash
    your eyes,
    To sharpen your five senses, and cry
    "hum"
    Thrice, and then "buzz" as often; and
    then come.   [*Exit.*]   170
FACE. Can you remember this?
DAP.   I warrant you.
FACE. Well then, away. 'Tis but your be-
    stowing
    Some twenty nobles 'mong her grace's
    servants,
    And put on a clean shirt. You do not
    know
    What grace her grace may do you in
    clean linen.   [*Exeunt.*]

ACT I. SCENE iii.

Subtle, Drugger, Face.[3]

[SUB. (*Within.*)] Come in! (Good wives,
    I pray you forbear me now;
    Troth, I can do you no good till after-
    noon.)

[*Enter Subtle and Drugger.*]

SUB. What is your name, say you? Abel
    Drugger?
DRUG.   Yes, sir.
SUB. A seller of tabacco?
DRUG.   Yes, sir.
SUB.   Umh!
    Free of the Grocers?[4]
DRUG.   Ay, and[5] 't please you.
SUB.   Well.
    Your business, Abel?
DRUG.   This, and 't please your worship:
    I am a young beginner, and am building
    Of a new shop, and 't like your worship,
    just
    At corner of a street.   (Here's the plot[6]
    on 't.)
    And I would know by art, sir, of your
    worship,   10
    Which way I should make my door, by
    necromancy,
    And where my shelves, and which should
    be for boxes,
    And which for pots. I would be glad to
    thrive, sir.
    And I was wished[7] to your worship by
    a gentleman,
    One Captain Face, that says you know
    men's planets,
    And their good angels, and their bad.
SUB.   I do,
    If I do see hem.[8]—

[*Enter Face.*]

FACE.   What! My honest Abel?
    Thou art well met here.
DRUG.   Troth, sir, I was speaking,
    Just as your worship came here, of your
    worship.
    I pray you speak for me to Master
    Doctor.   20
FACE. He shall do anything. Doctor, do
    you hear?
    This is my friend, Abel, an honest
    fellow;
    He lets me have good tabacco, and he
    does not
    Sophisticate[9] it with sack lees or oil,
    Nor washes it in muscadel and grains,[10]

---

[1] Rate.   [3] All actually enter later.
[2] Bathe.

[4] *I.e.,* a member of the Grocers' Guild.
[5] If it.   [7] Recommended.
[6] Plat, diagram.   [8] Them.
[9] Adulterate.
[10] Grains of paradise, a spice.

Nor buries it in gravel under ground,
Wrapped up in greasy leather or pissed
　clouts,
But keeps it in fine lily pots,[1] that,
　opened,
Smell like conserve of roses, or French
　beans.　　　　　　　　　　　　　　29
He has his maple block,[2] his silver tongs,
Winchester pipes, and fire of juniper [3]—
A neat, spruce, honest fellow, and no
　goldsmith.[4]

SUB. H' is a fortunate fellow; that I am
　sure on.
FACE. Already, sir, ha' you found it?
　Lo thee,[5] Abel!
SUB. And in right way toward riches.
FACE.　　　　　　　　　　　Sir!
SUB.　　　　　　　　　　This summer
He will be of the clothing [6] of his com-
　pany,
And next spring called to the scarlet;[7]
　spend what he can—
FACE. What, and so little beard?
SUB.　　　　　Sir, you must think
He may have a receipt to make hair
　come.
But he'll be wise, preserve his youth,
　and fine [8] for 't;　　　　　　　40
His fortune looks for him another way.
FACE. 'Slid, doctor, how canst thou know
　this so soon?
I am amused [9] at that.
SUB.　　　　　By a rule, captain,
In metoposcopy,[10] which I do work by—
A certain star i' the forehead, which
　you see not.
Your chestnut- or your olive-colored
　face
Does never fail, and your long ear doth
　promise.
I knew 't by certain spots too in his
　teeth
And on the nail of his mercurial finger.
FACE. Which finger's that?
SUB.　　　　His little finger. Look.　50
Yo' were born upon a Wednesday?
DRUG.　　　　　Yes, indeed, sir.

SUB. The thumb, in chiromanty [11] we give
　Venus,
The forefinger to Jove, the midst to
　Saturn,
The ring to Sol, the least to Mercury,
Who was the lord, sir, of his horoscope,
His house of life being Libra, which for-
　showed
He should be a merchant, and should
　trade with balance.
FACE. Why, this is strange! Is 't not,
　honest Nab?
SUB. There is a ship now coming from
　Ormus,
That shall yield him such a commodity 60
Of drugs—[Points to the plan.] This
　is the west, and this the south?
DRUG. Yes, sir.
SUB.　　　And those are your two sides?
DRUG.　　　　　　　　　　Ay, sir.
SUB. Make me your door then, south;
　your broad side, west;
And on the east side of your shop, aloft,
Write Mathlai, Tarmiel, and Baraborat;
Upon the north part, Rael, Velel, Thiel.
They are the names of those Mercurial
　spirits
That do fright flies from boxes.
DRUG.　　　　　　　　　　Yes, sir.
SUB.　　　　　　　　　　　And
Beneath your threshold bury me a load-
　stone
To draw in gallants that wear spurs;
　the rest,　　　　　　　　　70
They'll seem [12] to follow.
FACE.　　　　That's a secret, Nab!
SUB. And on your stall a puppet, with a
　vise [13]
And a court-fucus,[14] to call city dames;
You shall deal much with minerals.
DRUG.　　　　　　Sir, I have,
At home, already—
SUB.　　　Ay, I know you have ars'nic,
Vitriol, sal tartar, argaile,[15] alkali,
Cinoper.[16] I know all.—This fellow, cap-
　tain,
Will come, in time, to be a great distiller,
And give a say [17]—I will not say directly,
But very fair—at the philosophers'
　stone.　　　　　　　　　　80

[1] Ornamental jars.
[2] For shredding tobacco.
[3] At which customers could light their pipes.
[4] Usurer.　　　　　　[7] Become alderman.
[5] Behold thyself.　　[8] Pay a fine.
[6] Wear the livery.　　[9] Amazed.
[10] Divination by observing the forehead.
Original reads *metaposcopy*.
[11] Chiromancy.　　　[13] Screw, clamp.
[12] Be seen.　　　　[14] A cosmetic used at court.
[15] Argol, tartar deposited by wine.
[16] Cinnabar.　　　　[17] An assay, attempt.

FACE. Why, how now, Abel! Is this true?
DRUG. [*Drawing Face aside.*]   Good captain,
  What must I give?
FACE.   Nay, I'll not counsel thee.
  Thou hear'st what wealth (he says, spend what thou canst)
  Thou 'rt like to come to.
DRUG.   I would gi' him a crown.
FACE. A crown? And toward such a fortune? Heart,
  Thou shalt rather gi' him thy shop. No gold about thee?
DRUG. Yes, I have a portague [1] I ha' kept this half year.
FACE. Out on thee, Nab! 'Slight, there was such an offer.
  Shalt keep 't no longer. I'll gi' it him for thee?—Doctor,
  Nab prays your worship to drink this, and swears   90
  He will appear more grateful, as your skill
  Does raise him in the world.
DRUG.   I would entreat
  Another favor of his worship.
FACE.   What is 't, Nab?
DRUG. But to look over, sir, my almanac,
  And cross out my ill-days, that I may neither
  Bargain, nor trust upon them.
FACE.   That he shall, Nab.
  Leave it; it shall be done gainst afternoon.
SUB. And a direction for his shelves.
FACE.   Now, Nab,
  Art thou well pleased, Nab?
DRUG.   Thank, sir, both your worships.
FACE.   Away! [*Exit Drugger.*]
  Why, now, you smoky persecutor of nature!   100
  Now do you see that something's to be done
  Beside your beech-coal and your corsive [2] waters,
  Your crosslets, [3] crucibles, and cucurbites? [4]
  You must have stuff brought home to you, to work on?
  And yet you think I am at no expense
  In searching out these veins, then following hem,

Then trying hem out. Fore God, my intelligence
  Costs me more money than my share oft comes to
  In these rare works.
SUB.   You are pleasant, sir.—How now?

ACT I. SCENE iv.

Face, Doll, Subtle.

[SUB.] What says my dainty Dolkin?
DOLL.   Yonder fishwife
  Will not away. And there's your giantess,
  The bawd of Lambeth.
SUB.   Heart, I cannot speak with hem.
DOLL. Not afore night, I have told hem in a voice
  Thorough the trunk, [5] like one of your familiars.
  But I have spied Sir Epicure Mammon.
SUB.   Where?
DOLL. Coming along, at far end of the lane,
  Slow of his feet, but earnest of his tongue
  To one that's with him.
SUB.   Face, go you and shift. [6]—
                    [*Exit Face.*]
  Doll, you must presently [7] make ready too.   10
DOLL. Why, what's the matter?
SUB.   O, I did look for him
  With the sun's rising. Marvel, he could sleep!
  This is the day I am to perfect for him
  The *magisterium*, our *great work*, the *stone*,
  And yield it, made, into his hands—of which
  He has this month talked as he were possessed. [8]
  And now he's dealing pieces on 't away.
  Methinks I see him ent'ring ordinaries,
  Dispensing for the pox, and plaguy houses, [9]
  Reaching [10] his dose, walking Moorfields for lepers,   20
  And off'ring citizens' wives pomander bracelets [11]

[1] A gold coin.
[2] Corrosive.
[3] Vessels.
[4] Retorts.
[5] Through the speaking tube.
[6] Change your clothes.   [7] At once.
[8] *I.e.*, as if he owned it.
[9] House˵ infested with the plague.
[10] Offering.
[11] As a protection against disease.

As his preservative, made of the *elixir;*
Searching the spital [1] to make old bawds
  young,
And the highways for beggars to make
  rich.
I see no end of his labors. He will make
Nature ashamed of her long sleep,
  when art,
Who's but a stepdame, shall do more
  than she
In her best love to mankind ever could.
If his dream last, he'll turn the age to
  gold.   [*Exeunt.*]

ACT II. SCENE i.

[*The same.*] [2]

Mammon, Surly.

[MAM.] Come on, sir. Now you set your
  foot on shore
In *Novo Orbe;* [3] here's the rich Peru,
And there within, sir, are the golden
  mines,
Great Salomon's [4] Ophir! He was
  sailing to 't
Three years, but we have reached it in
  ten months.
This is the day wherein to all my
  friends
I will pronounce the happy word, "Be
  rich;
This day you shall be *spectatissimi.*" [5]
You shall no more deal with the hollow [6]
  die
Or the frail card; no more be at charge
  of keeping   10
The livery-punk [7] for the young heir
  that must
Seal at all hours in his shirt; no more,
If he deny, ha' him beaten to 't, as he is
That brings him the commodity. No
  more
Shall thirst of satin, or the covetous
  hunger
Of velvet entrails [8] for [9] a rude-spun cloak,

To be displayed at Madam Augusta's, [10]
  make
The sons of **sword** and hazard fall
  before
The golden calf, and on their knees,
  whole nights,
Commit idolatry with wine and trump-
  ets,   20
Or go a-feasting after drum and en-
  sign.
No more of this. You shall start up
  young viceroys,
And have your punks and punkettees, [11]
  my Surly.
And unto thee I speak it first, "Be
  rich."
Where is my Subtle there? Within, ho!
[FACE.] (*Within.*)   Sir,
  He'll come to you by-and-by.
MAM.   That's his firedrake, [12]
  His lungs, [13] his Zephyrus, he that puffs
  his coals
Till he firk [14] nature up in her own cen-
  ter.
You are not faithful, [15] sir. This night
  I'll change
All that is metal in my [16] house to
  gold,   30
And early in the morning will I send
To all the plumbers and the pewter-
  ers,
And buy their tin and lead up, and to
  Lothbury
For all the copper.
SUR.   What, and turn that too?
MAM. Yes, and I'll purchase Devonshire
  and Cornwall,
And make them perfect Indies! You
  admire [17] now?
SUR. No, faith.
MAM.   But, when you see th' effects
  of the great med'cine,
Of which one part projected on a hun
  dred
Of Mercury, or Venus, or the Moon   3,
Shall turn it to as many of the Sun [18]
Nay, to a thousand, so *ad infinitum*—
You will believe me.

SUR. Yes, when I see 't, I will.
But, if my eyes do cozen me so, and I
Giving hem no occasion, sure I'll have
A whore shall piss hem out next day.
MAM. Ha! Why?
Do you think I fable with you? I assure you,
He that has once the *Flower of the Sun*,
The perfect *ruby*, which we call *elixir*,
Not only can do that, but by its virtue
Can confer honor, love, respect, long life;   50
Give safety, valure, [1] yea, and victory
To whom he will. In eight-and-twenty days
I'll make an old man of fourscore a child.
SUR. No doubt; he's that already.
MAM. Nay, I mean,
Restore his years, renew him, like an eagle,
To the fifth age, [2] make him get sons and daughters,
Young giants (as our philosophers have done,
The ancient patriarchs afore the flood),
But, taking once a week on a knife's point
The quantity of a grain of mustard of it,   60
Become stout Marses and beget young Cupids.
SUR. The decayed vestals of Pickt-hatch [3] would thank you,
That keep the fire alive there.
MAM. 'Tis the secret
Of nature naturized gainst all infections,
Cures all diseases coming of all causes,
A month's grief in a day, a year's in twelve,
And, of what age soever, in a month,
Past all the doses of your drugging doctors.
I'll undertake, withal, to fright the plague
Out o' the kingdom in three months.
SUR. And I'll   70

Be bound, the players shall sing your praises then,
Without their poets. [4]
MAM. Sir, I'll do 't. Meantime,
I'll give away so much unto my man,
Shall serve th' whole city with preservative
Weekly, each house his dose, and at the rate—
SUR. As he that built the Waterwork does with water?
MAM. You are incredulous.
SUR. Faith, I have a humor;
I would not willingly be gulled. Your *stone*
Cannot transmute me.
MAM. Pertinax Surly,
Will you believe antiquity? Records? 80
I'll show you a book where Moses and his sister
And Salomon have written of the art;
Ay, and a treatise penned by Adam—
SUR. How!
MAM. O' the *philosophers' stone*, and in High Dutch.
SUR. Did Adam write, sir, in High Dutch?
MAM. He did,
Which proves it was the primitive tongue.
SUR. What paper?
MAM. On cedar board.
SUR. O, that, indeed, they say,
Will last gainst worms.
MAM. 'Tis like your Irish wood
Gainst cobwebs. I have a piece of Jason's fleece too,
Which was no other than a book of alchemy,   90
Writ in large sheepskin, a good fat ramvellam. [5]
Such was Pythagoras' thigh, [6] Pandora's tub,
And all that fable of Medea's charms.
The manner of our work: the bulls, our fornace,
Still breathing fire; our *argent-vive*, [7] the dragon;
The dragon's teeth, *mercury sublimate*,
That keeps the whiteness, hardness, and the biting;

---

[1] Valor.
[2] *I.e.*, of the seven ages of man.
[3] A low district in London.

[4] Plays were not given when the plague was raging.   [7] Quicksilver.
[5] Vellum made of ram skin.
[6] *Cf.* note on *Volpone*, I, ii, 27.

And they are gathered into Jason's
  helm,
Th' *alembic*, and then sowed in Mars his
  field,
And thence sublimed so often, till they
  are fixed.   100
Both this, th' Hesperian garden, Cad-
  mus' story,
Jove's shower, the boon of Midas, Argus' eyes,
Boccace his Demogorgon, thousands
  more,
All abstract riddles of our *stone.*—How
  now?

Act II. Scene ii.

Mammon, Face, Surly.

[Mam.] Do we succeed? Is our day come?
  And holds it?
Face. The evening will set red upon you,
  sir;
You have color for it, crimson; the red
  ferment
Has done his office; three hours hence
  prepare you
To see projection.
Mam.   Pertinax, my Surly,
Again I say to thee, aloud, "Be rich."
This day thou shalt have ingots, and
  tomorrow
Give lords th' affront.—Is it, my
  Zephyrus, right?
Blushes the bolt's-head? [1]
Face.   Like a wench with child, sir,
That were but now discovered to her
  master.   10
Mam. Excellent witty Lungs!—My only
  care is
Where to get stuff enough now to pro-
  ject on;
This town will not half serve me.
Face.   No, sir? Buy
The covering off o' churches.
Mam.   That's true.
Face.   Yes.
Let hem stand bare, as do their audi-
  tory,[2]
Or cap hem new with shingles.
Mam.   No, good thatch;
Thatch will lie light upo' the rafters,
  Lungs.

Lungs, I will manumit thee from the
  fornace;
I will restore thee thy complexion,
  Puff,
Lost in the embers, and repair this
  brain,   20
Hurt wi' the fume o' the metals.
Face.   I have blown, sir,
Hard for your worship, thrown by many
  a coal,
When 'twas not beech, weighed those
  I put in, just,[3]
To keep your heat still even. These
  bleared eyes
Have waked to read your several colors,
  sir,
Of the *pale citron,* the *green lion,* the
  crow,
The *peacock's tail,* the *plumed swan.*
Mam.   And lastly
Thou hast descried the *flower,* the
  sanguis agni? [4]
Face. Yes, sir.
Mam.   Where's master?
Face.   At 's prayers, sir, he;
Good man, he's doing his devotions   30
For the success.
Mam.   Lungs, I will set a period
To all thy labors; thou shalt be the
  master
Of my seraglia.[5]
Face.   Good, sir.
Mam.   But do you hear?
I'll geld you, Lungs.
Face.   Yes, sir.
Mam.   For I do mean
To have a list of wives and concubines
Equal with Salomon, who had the *stone*
Alike with me; and I will make me a
  back
With the *elixir,* that shall be as tough
As Hercules, to encounter fifty a night.—
Thou'rt sure thou saw'st it *blood?*
Face.   Both *blood and spirit,* sir.   40
Mam. I will have all my beds blown up,
  not stuffed;
Down is too hard. And then, mine
  oval room
Filled with such pictures as Tiberius
  took
From Elephantis, and dull Aretine
But coldly imitated. Then, my glasses

---

[1] Flask.   [2] Auditors, congregation.

[3] Exactly.   [5] Seraglio.
[4] Blood of the Lamb.

Cut in more subtle angles to disperse
And multiply the figures, as I walk
Naked between my *succubæ*.[1] My mists
I'll have of perfume, vapored 'bout the
    room,
To lose ourselves in, and my baths like
    pits   50
To fall into, from whence we will come
    forth,
And roll us dry in gossamer and roses.—
Is it arrived at *ruby?*—Where I spy
A wealthy citizen or rich lawyer
Have a sublimed pure wife, unto that
    fellow
I'll send a thousand pound to be my
    cuckold.
FACE. And I shall carry it?
MAM.   No. I'll ha' no bawds
But fathers and mothers. They will
    do it best,
Best of all others. And my flatterers
Shall be the pure and gravest of
    divines   60
That I can get for money; my mere
    fools
Eloquent burgesses; and then my poets
The same that writ so subtly of the
    fart,
Whom I will entertain still for that
    subject.
The few that would give out themselves
    to be
Court- and town-stallions, and, each-
    where, belie
Ladies who are known most innocent,
    for them,
Those will I beg to make me eunuchs of;
And they shall fan me with ten es-
    trich [2] tails
Apiece, made in a plume to gather
    wind.   70
We will be brave, Puff, now we ha' the
    med'cine.
My meat shall all come in, in Indian
    shells,
Dishes of agate set in gold, and studded
With emeralds, sapphires, hyacinths,[3]
    and rubies.
The tongues of carps, dormice, and
    camels' heels,
Boiled i' the spirit of *Sol*, and dissolved
    pearl

(Apicius' diet gainst the epilepsy)—
And I will eat these broths with spoons
    of amber,
Headed with diamant [4] and carbuncle.
My footboy shall eat pheasants, calvered
    salmons,[5]   80
Knots,[6] godwits,[7] lampreys; I myself
    will have
The beards of barbels [8] served instead of
    salads;
Oiled mushrooms; and the swelling
    unctuous paps
Of a fat pregnant sow, newly cut off,
Dressed with an exquisite and poignant
    sauce,
For which I'll say unto my cook,
    "There's gold;
Go forth, and be a knight."
FACE.   Sir, I'll go look
A little how it heightens.
MAM.   Do.—[*Exit Face.*] My shirts
I'll have of taffeta-sarsnet,[9] soft and
    light
As cobwebs; and for all my other rai-
    ment,   90
It shall be such as might provoke the
    Persian,
Were he to teach the world riot anew.
My gloves of fishes' and birds' skins,
    perfumed
With gums of Paradise, and Eastern
    air—
SUR. And do you think to have the *stone*
    with this?
MAM. No, I do think t' have all this with
    the *stone.*
SUR. Why, I have heard he must be
    homo frugi,
A pious, holy, and religious man,
One free from mortal sin, a very virgin.
MAM. That makes it, sir; he is so. But
    I buy it;   100
My venter brings it me. He, honest
    wretch,
A notable, superstitious, good soul,
Has worn his knees bare, and his slip-
    pers bald,
With prayer and fasting for it. And,
    sir, let him

[1] Paramours.   [3] An ancient precious stone.
[2] Ostrich.

[4] Diamond.
[5] Specially prepared salmon, perhaps pickled
[6] Robin-snipes, a kind of sandpiper.
[7] Wading birds of the snipe family.
[8] A fresh-water fish.
[9] Fine silk.

Do it alone, for me, still. Here he comes.
Not a profane word afore him; 'tis
　poison.—

ACT II. SCENE iii.

Mammon, Subtle, Surly, Face.[1]

[MAM.] Good morrow, father.

SUB.　　　　　　Gentle son, good morrow,
And to your friend there. What is he
　is with you?

MAM. An heretic that I did bring along
In hope, sir, to convert him.

SUB.　　　　　　Son, I doubt[2]
Yo' are covetous, that thus you meet
　your time
I' the just point, prevent your day[3] at
　morning.
This argues something worthy of a fear
Of importune and carnal appetite.
Take heed you do not cause the blessing
　leave you,
With your ungoverned haste. I should
　be sorry　　　　　　　　　　　10
To see my labors, now e'en at perfection,
Got by long watching and large patience,
Not prosper where my love and zeal
　hath placed hem—
Which[4] (heaven I call to witness, with
　yourself,
To whom I have poured my thoughts),
　in all my ends,
Have looked no way but unto public
　good,
To pious uses and dear charity,
Now[5] grown a prodigy with men;
　wherein
If you, my son, should now prevaricate,
And to your own particular lusts em-
　ploy　　　　　　　　　　　　20
So great and catholic a bliss, be sure
A curse will follow, yea, and overtake
Your subtle and most secret ways.

MAM.　　　　　　I know, sir;
You shall not need to fear me; I but
　come
To ha' you confute this gentleman.

SUR.　　　　　　　　Who is,
Indeed, sir, somewhat costive of belief
Toward your *stone*—would not be gulled.

SUB.　　　　　　　　　　Well, son,
All that I can convince him in is this:
The work is done; bright *Sol* is in his
　robe.
We have a *med'cine of the triple soul*,　30
The *glorified spirit*. Thanks be to heaven,
And make us worthy of it!—Ulen
　Spiegel![6]

FACE. [*Within.*] Anon, sir.

SUB.　　　　　　Look well to the register,
And let your heat still lessen by degrees
To the *aludels*.[7]

FACE. [*Within.*] Yes, sir.

SUB.　　　　　　　Did you look
O' the *bolt's-head* yet?

FACE. [*Within.*] Which? On *D*, sir?

SUB.　　　　　　　　　Ay.
What's the complexion?

FACE. [*Within.*] Whitish.

SUB.　　　　　　Infuse vinegar,　40
To draw his *volatile substance* and his
　tincture;
And let the water in *glass E* be feltered,[8]
And put into the *gripe's egg*. Lute[9]
　him well,
And leave him closed *in balneo*.[10]

FACE. [*Within.*]　　　　　I will, sir.

SUR. What a brave language here is!
　Next to canting.[11]

SUB. I have another work you never saw,
　son,
That three days since passed the *philos-
　ophers' wheel*,
In the lent[12] heat of *Athanor*,[13] and 's
　become
Sulphur o' nature.

MAM.　　　　　　But 'tis for me?

SUB.　　　　　　What need you?
You have enough, in that is perfect.

MAM.　　　　　　O, but—　50

SUB. Why, this is covetise![14]

MAM.　　　　　No, I assure you,
I shall employ it all in pious uses,
Founding of colleges and grammar
　schools,
Marrying young virgins, building hos-
　pitals,
And now and then a church.

[6] Owl Glass, the hero of a popular German
jest book.

[7] Alchemical vessels.　　[12] Mild.
[8] Filtered.　　　　　　　[13] Furnace.
[9] Seal.　　　　　　　　　[14] Covetousness.
[10] In a pan of warm water.
[11] Cant, rogues' jargon.

[1] Enters later.　　　　　　[2] Fear.
[3] Come before your time.
[4] *I.e.*, I who.
[5] From 1640 edn. Original has *no*.

[*Enter Face.*]

SUB. How now?

FACE. Sir, please you,
Shall I not change the felter?

SUB. Marry, yes;
And bring me the complexion of *glass B.*
[*Exit Face.*]

MAM. Ha' you another?

SUB. Yes, son; were I assured
Your piety were firm, we would not
want
The means to glorify it. But I hope the
best. 60
I mean to tinct *C* in *sand-heat* tomorrow,
And give him *imbibition.*

MAM. Of white oil?

SUB. No, sir, of red. *F* is come over the
helm too,
I thank my Maker, in *S[t]. Mary's
bath,*
And shows *lac virginis.*[1] Blessed be
heaven!
I sent you of his *fæces* there *calcined;*
Out of that *calx* I ha' won the *salt of
mercury.*

MAM. By pouring on your *rectified water?*

SUB. Yes, and *reverberating* in *Athanor.*—

[*Enter Face.*]

How now? What color says it?

FACE. The ground black, sir. 70

MAM. That's your *crow's head?*

SUR. [*Aside.*] Your coxcomb's, is 't
not?

SUB. No, 'tis not perfect. Would it were
the *crow!*
That work wants something.

SUR. [*Aside.*] O, I looked for this;
The hay[2] is a-pitching.

SUB. Are you sure you loosed hem
I' their own *menstrue?*

FACE. Yes, sir, and then married hem,
And put hem in a *bolt's-head* nipped to
digestion,
According as you bade me, when I set
The *liquor of Mars* to *circulation*
In the same heat.

SUB. The process then was right.

FACE. Yes, by the token, sir, the *retort*
brake, 80

[1] Milk of the Virgin.
[2] Net for catching rabbits.

And what was saved was put into the
pelican,
And signed with *Hermes' seal.*[3]

SUB. I think 'twas so.
We should have a new *amalgama.*

SUR. [*Aside.*] O, this ferret
Is rank as any polecat.

SUB. But I care not;
Let him e'en die; we have enough be-
side,
In *embryon. H* has his *white shirt* on?

FACE. Yes, sir,
He's ripe for *inceration;* he stands warm
In his *ash-fire.* I would not you should
let
Any die now, if I might counsel, sir,
For luck's sake to the rest. It is not
good. 90

MAM. He says right.

SUR. [*Aside.*] Ay, are you bolted?[4]

FACE. Nay, I know 't, sir;
I have seen th' ill fortune. What is
some three ounces
Of fresh *materials?*

MAM. Is 't no more?

FACE. No more, sir,
Of gold, t' *amalgam* with some six of
mercury.

MAM. Away, here's money. What will
serve?

FACE. Ask him, sir.

MAM. How much?

SUB. Give him nine pound;
you may gi' him ten.

SUR. [*Aside.*] Yes, twenty, and be cozened,
do.

MAM. There 'tis. [*Gives Face the money.*]

SUB. This needs not, but that you will
have it so,
To see conclusions of all. For two
Of our inferior works are at *fixation;* 100
A third is in *ascension.* Go your ways.
Ha' you set the *oil of Luna* in *kemia?*

FACE. Yes, sir.

SUB. And the *philosophers' vinegar?*

FACE. Ay. [*Exit.*]

SUR. [*Aside.*] We shall have a salad!

MAM. When do you make *projection?*

SUB. Son, be not hasty. I *exalt* our
med'cine
By hanging him *in balneo vaporoso,*
And giving him solution; then *congeal*
him,

[3] *I.e.,* hermetically sealed. [4] Dislodged.

And then *dissolve* him; then again *congeal* him;
For look, how oft I iterate the work,
So many times I add unto his virtue.   110
As, if at first one ounce convert a hundred,
After his second loose, he'll turn a thousand;
His third solution, ten; his fourth, a hundred;
After his fifth, a thousand thousand ounces
Of any imperfect metal, into pure
Silver or gold, in all examinations,
As good as any of the natural mine.
Get you your stuff here against afternoon,
Your brass, your pewter, and your andirons.
MAM. Not those of iron?
SUB.   Yes, you may bring them too; 120
We'll change all metals.
SUR. [*Aside.*]   I believe you in that.
MAM. Then I may send my spits?
SUB.   Yes, and your racks.
SUR. And dripping pans, and pothangers, and hooks?
Shall he not?
SUB.   If he please.
SUR.   To be an ass.
SUB. How, sir!
MAM.   This gent'man you must bear withal.
I told you he had no faith.
SUR.   And little hope, sir;
But much less charity, should I gull myself.
SUB. Why, what have you observed, sir, in our art
Seems so impossible?
SUR.   But your whole work; no more.
That you should hatch gold in a fornace, sir,   130
As they do eggs in Egypt!
SUB.   Sir, do you
Believe that eggs are hatched so?
SUR.   If I should?
SUB. Why, I think that the greater miracle.
No egg but differs from a chicken more
Than metals in themselves.
SUR.   That cannot be.

The egg's ordained by nature to that end,
And is a chicken *in potentia.*[1]
SUB. The same we say of lead and other metals,
Which would be gold if they had time.
MAM.   And that
Our art doth furder.[2]
SUB.   Ay, for 't were absurd 140
To think that nature in the earth bred gold
Perfect i' the instant; something went before.
There must be *remote matter.*
SUR.   Ay, what is that?
SUB. Marry, we say—
MAM.   Ay, now it heats. Stand, father;
Pound him to dust.
SUB.   It is, of the one part,
A humid exhalation, which we call
Materia liquida, or the *unctuous water;*
On th' other part, a certain crass and viscous
Portion of earth; both which, concorporate,
Do make the *elementary matter* of gold,   150
Which is not yet *propria materia,*
But commune to all metals and all stones;
For, where it is forsaken of that moisture,
And hath more dryness, it becomes a stone;
Where it retains more of the humid fatness,
It turns to *sulphur* or to *quicksilver,*
Who are the parents of all other metals.
Nor can this *remote matter* suddenly
Progress so from extreme unto extreme
As to grow gold, and leap o'er all the means.[3]   160
Nature doth first beget th' imperfect; then
Proceeds she to the perfect. Of that airy
And oily water, *mercury* is engendered;
Sulphur o' the fat and earthy part; the one,
Which is the last, supplying the place of male,
The other of the female, in all metals.
Some do believe hermaphrodeity,

[1] Potentially.
[2] Further.
[3] Intermediate stages.

That both do act and suffer. But these
two
Make the rest ductile, malleable, extensive.
And even in gold they are; for we do
find   170
Seeds of them by our fire, and gold in
them,
And can produce the *species* of each
metal
More perfect thence than nature doth in
earth.
Beside, who doth not see in daily practice
Art can beget bees, hornets, beetles,
wasps
Out of the carcasses and dung of creatures—
Yea, scorpions of an herb, being rightly
placed?
And these are living creatures, far more
perfect
And excellent than metals.

MAM.   Well said, father!
Nay, if he take you in hand, sir, with
an argument,   180
He'll bray [1] you in a mortar.

SUR.   Pray you, sir, stay.
Rather than I'll be brayed, sir, I'll be-
lieve
That alchemy is a pretty kind of game,
Somewhat like tricks o' the cards, to
cheat a man
With charming.

SUB.   Sir?

SUR.   What else are all your terms,
Whereon no one o' your writers grees
with other?
Of your *elixir*, your *lac virginis*,
Your *stone*, your *med'cine*, and your
chrysosperm,
Your *sal*, your *sulphur*, and your *mer-
cury*,
Your *oil of height*, your *tree of life*, your
blood,   190
Your *marchesite*, your *tutie*, your
magnesia,
Your *toad*, your *crow*, your *dragon*, and
your *panther*,
Your *sun*, your *moon*, your *firmament*,
your *adrop*,
Your *lato*, *azoch*, *zernich*, *chibrit*, *heau-
tarit*,

[1] Pulverize.

And then your *red man* and your
white woman,
With all your broths, your *menstrues*, and
materials
Of piss and eggshells, women's terms,
man's blood,
Hair o' the head, burnt clouts, chalk,
merds,[2] and clay,
Poulder of bones, scalings of iron, glass,
And worlds of other strange *ingredi-
ents*   200
Would burst a man to name?

SUB.   And all these, named,
Intending but one thing, which **art our**
writers
Used to obscure their art.

MAM.   Sir, so I told him—
Because [3] the simple idiot should not
learn it,
And make it vulgar.

SUB.   Was not all the knowledge
Of the Egyptians writ in mystic sym-
bols?
Speak not the Scriptures oft in parables?
Are not the choicest fables of the poets,
That were the fountains and first springs
of wisdom,
Wrapped in perplexéd allegories?

MAM.   I urged that,   210
And cleared to him that Sisyphus was
damned
To roll the ceaseless stone, only because
He would have made ours common.—
(Doll is seen.) Who is this?

SUB. God's precious!—What do you mean?
Go in, good lady,
Let me entreat you.—[*Exit Doll*.]
Where's this varlet?

[*Enter Face*.]

FACE.   Sir?

SUB. You very knave! Do you use me
thus?

FACE.   Wherein, sir?

SUB. Go in and see, you traitor. Go!
                       [*Exit Face*.]

MAM.   Who is it, sir?

SUB. Nothing, sir; nothing.

MAM.   What's the matter, good sir?
I have not seen you thus distempered.
Who is 't?

[2] Fæces.
[3] In order that.

Sub. All arts have still had, sir, their
    adversaries;   220
But ours the most ignorant.—

Face returns.

                            What now?
Face. 'Twas not my fault, sir; she would
    speak with you.
Sub. Would she, sir? Follow me. [*Exit.*]
Mam.   Stay, Lungs!
Face.   I dare not, sir.
Mam. How! Pray thee, stay.
Face.   She's mad, sir, and
    sent hither—
Mam. Stay, man; what is she?
Face.   A lord's sister, sir.—
    (He'll be mad too.
Mam.   I warrant thee.[1]) Why sent
    hither?
Face. Sir, to be cured.
Sub. [*Within.*]   Why, rascal!
Face.   Lo you!—Here, sir!
                            He goes out.
Mam. Fore God, a Bradamante,[2] a brave
    piece.
Sur. Heart, this is a bawdyhouse! I'll be
    burnt else.
Mam. O, by this light, no. Do not wrong
    him. H' is   230
Too scrupulous that way; it is his vice.
No, h' is a rare physician (do him right),
An excellent Paracelsian, and has done
Strange cures with mineral physic. He
    deals all
With spirits, he; he will not hear a word
Of Galen or his tedious recipes.—

Face again.

                    How now, Lungs?
Face. Softly, sir; speak softly. I meant
    To ha' told your worship all. This[3]
    must not hear.
Mam. No, he will not be gulled; let him
    alone.
Face. Y' are very right, sir; she is a most
    rare scholar,   240
And is gone mad with studying Brough-
    ton's[4] works.
If you but name a word touching the
    Hebrew,

[1] *I.e.*, I guarantee to protect you against
Subtle.
[2] Heroine in Ariosto's *Orlando Furioso.*
[3] *I.e.*, Surly.   [4] A rabbinical scholar.

She falls into her fit, and will discourse
So learnedly of genealogies
As you would run mad, too, to hear her,
    sir.
Mam. How might one do t' have confer-
    ence with her, Lungs?
Face. O, divers have run mad upon the
    conference.
I do not know, sir. I am sent in haste
To fetch a vial.
Sur.   Be not gulled, Sir Mammon.
Mam. Wherein? Pray ye, be patient.
Sur.   Yes, as you are, 250
And trust confederate knaves and bawds
    and whores.
Mam. You are too foul, believe it.—
    Come here, Ulen.
One word.
Face.   I dare not, in good faith.
Mam.   Stay, knave.
Face. H' is extreme angry that you saw
    her, sir.
Mam. Drink that. [*Gives him money.*]
    What is she when she's out of her
    fit?
Face. O, the most affablest creature, sir!
    So merry!
So pleasant! She'll mount you up, like
    quicksilver,
Over the helm, and *circulate* like *oil;*
A very *vegetal;* discourse of state,   259
Of mathematics, bawdry, anything—
Mam. Is she no way accessible? No means,
No trick to give a man a taste of her—
    wit—
Or so?—Ulen!
Face.   I'll come to you again, sir. [*Exit.*]
Mam. Surly, I did not think one o' your
    breeding
Would traduce personages of worth.
Sur.   Sir Epicure,
Your friend to use, yet still loath to be
    gulled.
I do not like your philosophical bawds.
Their *stone* is lechery enough to pay
    for,
Without this bait.
Mam.   Heart, you abuse yourself.
I know the lady, and her friends, and
    means,   270
The original of this disaster. Her brother
Has told me all.
Sur.   And yet you ne'er saw her
Till now?

Mam.   O, yes, but I forgot. I have,
  believe it,
One o' the treacherous'st memories, I
  do think,
Of all mankind.
Sur.   What call you her brother?
Mam.   My lord—
He wi' not have his name known, now
  I think on 't.
Sur. A very treacherous memory!
Mam.   O' my faith—
Sur. Tut, if you ha' it not about you,
  pass it
Till we meet next.
Mam.   Nay, by this hand, 'tis true.
He's one I honor, and my noble friend;
And I respect his house.
Sur.   Heart! Can it be 281
That a grave sir, a rich, that has no
  need,
A wise sir, too, at other times, should
  thus
With his own oaths and arguments make
  hard means
To gull himself?   And this be your
  elixir,
Your *lapis mineralis*, and your *lunary*,
Give me your honest trick yet at primero
Or gleek,[1] and take your *lutum sapi-
  entis*,
Your *menstruum simplex!*   I'll have
  gold before you,   289
And with less danger of the *quicksilver*,
Or the hot *sulphur*.

          [*Enter Face.*]

Face. (*To Surly.*)   Here's one from
  Captain Face, sir,
Desires you meet him i' the Temple
  Church
Some half hour hence, and upon earnest
  business.—
(*He whispers Mammon.*) Sir, if you
  please to quit us now, and come
Again within two hours, you shall have
My master busy examining o' the works;
And I will steal you in unto the party,
That you may see her converse.—Sir,
  shall I say
You'll meet the captain's worship?
Sur.   Sir, I will.—
[*Aside.*] But by attorney, and to a
  second purpose.   300

Now I am sure it is a bawdyhouse;
I'll swear it, were the marshal here to
  thank me.
The naming this commander doth con-
  firm it.
Don Face! Why, h' is the most auten-
  tic [2] dealer
I' these commodities, the superintend-
  ent
To all the quainter [3] traffickers in town!
He is their visitor, and does ap-
  point
Who lies with whom, and at what hour,
  what price,
Which gown, and in what smock, what
  fall,[4] what tire.[5]
Him will I prove, by a third person, to
  find   310
The subtleties of this dark labyrinth,
Which if I do discover, dear Sir Mam-
  mon,
You'll give your poor friend leave,
  though no *philosopher*,
To laugh; for you that are, 't is thought,
  shall weep.
Face. Sir, he does pray you'll not forget.
Sur.   I will not, sir.
Sir Epicure, I shall leave you.   [*Exit.*]
Mam.   I follow you straight.
Face. But do so, good sir, to avoid sus-
  picion.
This gent'man has a parlous head.
Mam.   But wilt thou, Ulen,
Be constant to thy promise?
Face.   As my life, sir.
Mam. And wilt thou insinuate what I am,
  and praise me,   320
And say I am a noble fellow?
Face.   O, what else, sir?
And that you'll make her royal with the
  stone,
An empress, and yourself King of Ban-
  tam.
Mam. Wilt thou do this?
Face.   Will I, sir?
Mam.   Lungs, my Lungs,
  I love thee!
Face.   Send your stuff, sir, that my
  master
May busy himself about projection.
Mam. Th' hast witched me, rogue.   Take,
  go.   [*Gives him money.*]

----

[1] Card games.

[2] Authentic.   [4] Collar, ruff.
[3] More crafty.   [5] Headdress.

FACE.   Your jack [1] and all, sir.

MAM. Thou art a villain! I will send my jack,

And the weights too. Slave, I could bite thine ear.

Away, thou dost not care for me.

FACE.   Not I, sir?   330

MAM. Come, I was born to make thee, my good weasel,

Set thee on a bench, and ha' thee twirl a chain

With the best lord's vermin of hem all.

FACE.   Away, sir.

MAM. A count, nay, a count palatine—

FACE.   Good sir, go.

MAM. Shall not advance thee better; no, nor faster.   [*Exit.*]

Act II. Scene iv.

Subtle, Face, Doll.

[SUB.] Has he bit? Has he bit?

FACE.   And swallowed too, my Subtle.

I ha' given him line, and now he plays, i' faith.

SUB. And shall we twitch him?

FACE.   Thorough both the gills.

A wench is a rare bait, with which a man

No sooner 's taken, but he straight firks [2] mad.

SUB. Doll, my Lord What's-hum's sister, you must now

Bear yourself ſtatelich.[3]

DOLL.   O, let me alone,

I'll not forget my race, I warrant you.

I'll keep my distance, laugh and talk aloud,

Have all the tricks of a proud, scurvy lady,   10

And be as rude as her woman.

FACE.   Well said, sanguine! [4]

SUB. But will he send his andirons?

FACE.   His jack too,

And 's iron shoeing-horn; I ha' spoke to him. Well,

I must not lose my wary gamester yonder.

SUB. O, Monsieur Caution, that will not be gulled?

FACE. Ay, if I can strike a fine hook into him now!

The Temple Church, there I have cast mine angle.

Well, pray for me. I'll about it.

           (*One knocks.*)

SUB.   What, more gudgeons!

Doll, scout, scout!—[*Doll goes to the window.*] Stay, Face, you must go to the door.

Pray God it be my Anabaptist.—Who is 't, Doll?   20

DOLL. I know him not. He looks like a gold-end man.[5]

SUB. God's so! [6] 'Tis he, he said he would send—what call you him?—

The sanctified elder, that should deal

For Mammon's jack and andirons. Let him in.

Stay, help me off first with my gown.— [*Exit Face with the gown.*] Away,

Madam, to your withdrawing chamber.— [*Exit Doll.*] Now,

In a new tune, new gesture, but old language.—

This fellow is sent from one negotiates with me

About the *stone* too, for the holy Brethren

Of Amsterdam, the exiled Saints, that hope   30

To raise their discipline [7] by it. I must use him

In some strange fashion now, to make him admire me.

Act II. Scene v.

Subtle, Face, Ananias.

[SUB.] Where is my drudge?

FACE. [*Entering.*]   Sir!

SUB.   Take away the *recipient*,

And rectify your *menstrue* from the *phlegma*.

Then pour it o' the *Sol* in the *cucurbite*,

And let hem macerate together.

FACE.   Yes, sir.

And save the ground?

SUB.   No; *terra damnata*

Must not have entrance in the *work*.—

Who are you?

ANA. A faithful Brother,[8] if it please you.

---

[1] A turnspit moved by weights.
[2] Runs.   [3] Stately.   [4] Red face.
[5] One who buys odds and ends of gold.
[6] A mild oath.
[7] Form of church government.
[8] *I.e.*, a Puritan.

Sub. What's that?
A Lullianist? A Ripley? [1] *Filius artis?* [2]
Can you *sublime* and *dulcify? Calcine?*
Know you the *sapor pontic? Sapor*
stiptic? 10
Or what is *homogene* or *heterogene?*
Ana. I understand no heathen language,
truly.
Sub. Heathen, you Knipperdolling? [3] Is
ars sacra,
Or *chrysopœia,* or *spagyrica,*
Or the *pamphysic* or *panarchic* knowledge
A heathen language?
Ana. Heathen Greek, I take it.
Sub. How? Heathen Greek?
Ana. All's heathen but the Hebrew.
Sub. Sirrah, my varlet, stand you forth
and speak to him
Like a *philosopher;* answer i' the lan-
guage.
Name the vexations and the martyriza-
tions 20
Of metals in the *work.*
Face. Sir, *putrefaction,*
Solution, ablution, sublimation,
Cohobation, calcination, ceration, and
Fixation.
Sub. This is heathen Greek to you
now?—
And when comes *vivification?*
Face. After *mortification.*
Sub. What's *cohobation?*
Face. 'Tis the pouring on
Your *aqua regis,* and then drawing him
off,
To the *trine circle* of the *seven spheres.*
Sub. What's the proper passion of metals?
Face. *Malleation.*
Sub. What's your *ultimum supplicium*
auri?
Face. *Antimonium.* 30
Sub. This 's heathen Greek to you?—And
what's your *mercury?*
Face. A very *fugitive,* he will be gone, sir.
Sub. How know you him?
Face. By his *viscosity,*
His *oleosity,* and his *suscitability.*
Sub. How do you *sublime* him?
Face. With the *calce of eggshells,*
White *marble, talc.*

[1] Followers of Lully and Ripley, two earlier
alchemists.
[2] Son of the art?
[3] An Anabaptist leader.

Sub. Your *magisterium* now,
What's that?
Face. Shifting, sir, your *elements,*
Dry into cold, cold into moist, moist in-
To hot, hot into dry.
Sub. This is heathen Greek to you
still?—
Your *lapis philosophicus?*
Face. 'Tis a *stone,* 40
And not a *stone;* a *spirit,* a *soul,* and a
body;
Which if you do *dissolve,* it is *dissolved;*
If you *coagulate,* it is *coagulated;*
If you make it to *fly,* it *flieth.*
Sub. Enough.—[*Exit Face.*]
This 's heathen Greek to you? What are
you, sir?
Ana. Please you, a servant of the exiled
Brethren,
That deal with widows' and with or-
phans' goods,
And make a just account unto the
Saints—
A deacon.
Sub. O, you are sent from Master
Wholesome,
Your teacher?
Ana. From Tribulation Wholesome, 50
Our very zealous pastor.
Sub. Good! I have
Some orphans' goods to come here.
Ana. Of what kind, sir?
Sub. Pewter and brass, andirons and
kitchenware,
Metals that we must use our *med'cine*
on,
Wherein the Brethren may have a penn'-
orth
For ready money.
Ana. Were the orphans' parents
Sincere professors?
Sub. Why do you ask?
Ana. Because
We then are to deal justly, and give, in
truth,
Their utmost value.
Sub. 'Slid, you'ld cozen else,
And if their parents were not of the
faithful? 60
I will not trust you, now I think on 't,
Till I ha' talked with your pastor. Ha'
you brought money
To buy more coals?
Ana. No, surely.

Sub.   No? How so?

Ana. The Brethren bid me say unto you, sir,
Surely they will not venter any more
Till they may see *projection*.

Sub.   How!

Ana.   Yo' have had
For the *instruments*, as bricks and lome,[1] and glasses,
Already thirty pound, and for *materials*,
They say, some ninety more; and they have heard since
That one at Heidelberg made it of an egg   70
And a small paper of pin dust.[2]

Sub.   What's your name?

Ana. My name is Ananias.

Sub.   Out, the varlet
That cozened the apostles! Hence, away!
Flee, mischief! Had your holy consistory
No name to send me of another sound
Than wicked Ananias? Send your elders
Hither, to make atonement for you, quickly,
And gi' me satisfaction; or out goes
The fire, and down th' *alembics*, and the *fornace*,
Piger Henricus, or what not.   Thou wretch!   80
Both *sericon* and *bufo* shall be lost,
Tell hem. All hope of rooting out the bishops
Or th' antichristian hierarchy shall perish,
If they stay threescore minutes; the *aqueity*,
Terreity, and *sulphureity*
Shall run together again, and all be annulled,
Thou wicked Ananias!—[*Exit Ananias.*]
This will fetch hem,
And make hem haste towards their gulling more.
A man must deal like a rough nurse, and fright   89
Those that are froward, to an appetite.

Act II. Scene vi.

Face [in his uniform], Subtle, Drugger.

[Face.] H' is busy with his spirits, but we'll upon him.

[1] A vessel.
[2] Dust from the manufacture of pins.

Sub. How now!   What mates,[3] what Bayards[4] ha' we here?

Face. I told you he would be furious.—
Sir, here's Nab
Has brought yo' another piece of gold to look on
(We must appease him. Give it me.) and prays you
You would devise—(What is it, Nab?)

Drug.   A sign, sir.

Face. Ay, a good lucky one, a thriving sign, doctor.

Sub. I was devising now.

Face. [*Aside to Subtle.*]   'Slight, do not say so;
He will repent he ga' you any more.—
What say you to his constellation, doctor, The Balance?

Sub.   No, that way is stale and common.   11
A townsman born in Taurus gives the Bull,
Or the bull's head; in Aries, the Ram—
A poor device! No, I will have his name
Formed in some mystic character, whose *radii*,
Striking the senses of the passers-by,
Shall, by a virtual influence,[5] breed affections[6]
That may result upon the party owns it,
As thus—

Face. Nab!

Sub.   He first shall have *a bell*— that's *Abel*;
And by it standing one whose name is *Dee*,[7]   20
In a *rug*[8] gown; there's *D*, and *rug*— that's *Drug*;
And right anenst[9] him a dog snarling "*er*"—
There's Drugger, Abel Drugger. That's his sign.
And here's now mystery and hieroglyphic!

Face. Abel, thou art made.

[3] Wretches.
[4] Blind fools—named from a legendary blind horse of Charlemagne.
[5] *I.e.*, an influence deriving from the virtue or power of the symbol.
[6] Inclinations.
[7] Referring to the mathematician and astrologer, Dr. John Dee, popularly regarded as a magician, who had recently died.
[8] Coarse cloth.
[9] Beside.

DRUG. [*Bowing.*]   Sir, I do thank his
  worship.
FACE. Six o' thy legs [1] more will not do it,
  Nab.—
  He has brought you a pipe of tabacco,
  doctor.
DRUG.   Yes, sir.
  I have another thing I would impart—
FACE. Out with it, Nab.
DRUG.   Sir, there is lodged hard by me
  A rich young widow—
FACE.   Good! A *bona roba?* [2]   31
DRUG. But nineteen at the most.
FACE.   Very good, Abel.
DRUG. Marry, sh' is not in fashion yet· she
  wears
  A hood, but 't stands acop. [3]
FACE.   No matter, Abel.
DRUG. And I do now and then give her a
  fucus—
FACE. What! Dost thou deal, Nab?
SUB.   I did tell you, captain.
DRUG. And physic too sometime, sir, for
  which she trusts me
  With all her mind. She's come up here
  of purpose
  To learn the fashion.
FACE.   Good! (His match too!)
  On, Nab.
DRUG. And she does strangely long to
  know her fortune.   40
FACE. God's lid, Nab, send her to the
  doctor, hither.
DRUG. Yes, I have spoke to her of his
  worship already;
  But she's afraid it will be blown abroad,
  And hurt her marriage.
FACE.   Hurt it? 'Tis the way
  To heal it, if 'twere hurt—to make it
  more
  Followed and sought. Nab, thou shalt
  tell her this.
  She'll be more known, more talked of;
  and your widows
  Are ne'er of any price till they be famous;
  Their honor is their multitude of suitors.
  Send her; it may be thy good fortune.
  What?   50
  Thou dost not know?
DRUG.   No, sir, she'll never marry
  Under a knight; her brother has made
  a vow.

FACE. What, and dost thou despair, my
  little Nab,
  Knowing what the doctor has set down
  for thee,
  And seeing so many o' the city dubbed?
  One glass o' thy water, with a madam I
  know,
  Will have it done, Nab. What's her
  brother? A knight?
DRUG. No, sir, a gentleman newly warm
  in his land, sir,
  Scarce cold in his one-and-twenty, that
  does govern
  His sister here, and is a man himself   60
  Of some three thousand a year, and is
  come up
  To learn to quarrel, and to live by his
  wits,
  And will go down again, and die i' the
  country.
FACE. How! To quarrel?
DRUG.   Yes, sir, to carry quarrels
  As gallants do, and manage hem by line. [4]
FACE. 'Slid, Nab, the doctor is the only
  man
  In Christendom for him. He has made
  a table,
  With mathematical demonstrations,
  Touching the art of quarrels. He will
  give him
  An instrument to quarrel by. Go, bring
  hem both,   76
  Him and his sister. And, for thee, with
  her
  The doctor haply may persuade. [5] Go to!
  Shalt give his worship a new damask suit
  Upon the premises.
SUB.   O, good captain!
FACE.   He shall;
  He is the honestest fellow, doctor. Stay
  not,
  No offers; bring the damask and the
  parties.
DRUG. I'll try my power, sir.
FACE.   And thy will too, Nab.
SUB. 'Tis good tabacco, this! What is 't an
  ounce?
FACE. He'll send you a pound, doctor.
SUB.   O, no.
FACE.   He will do 't.
  It is the goodest soul!—Abel, about it.
  (Thou shalt know more anon. Away, be-
  gone.)—   [*Exit Abel.*]   81

---

[1] Bows.   [2] Fine wench.
[3] On the top of her head, not tilted.
[4] Rule.   [5] Plead.

A miserable rogue, and lives with cheese,
And has the worms. That was the cause,
  indeed,
Why he came now; he dealt with me in
  private,
To get a med'cine for hem.
Sub.   And shall, sir. This works.
Face. A wife, a wife for one on us, my dear
  Subtle!
We'll e'en draw lots, and he that fails
  shall have
The more in goods, the other has in tail.
Sub. Rather the less, for she may be so
  light
She may want grains.[1]
Face.   Ay; or be such a burden 90
A man would scarce endure her for the
  whole.
Sub. Faith, best let's see her first, and
  then determine.
Face. Content, but Doll must ha' no
  breath on 't.
Sub.   Mum!
Away, you, to your Surly yonder; catch
  him.
Face. Pray God I ha' not stayed too long.
Sub.   I fear it. [Exeunt.]

Act III. Scene i.

[*The street before Lovewit's house.*]

Tribulation, Ananias.

[Tri.] These chastisements are common
  to the Saints,
And such rebukes we of the separation [2]
Must bear with willing shoulders as the
  trials
Sent forth to tempt our frailties.
Ana.   In pure zeal,
I do not like the man; he is a heathen,
And speaks the language of Canaan,
  truly.
Tri. I think him a profane person indeed.
Ana.   He bears
The visible mark of the beast in his
  forehead.
And, for his *stone*, it is a work of darkness,
And with *philosophy* blinds the eyes of
  man.   10
Tri. Good brother, we must bend unto all
  means
That may give furtherance to the holy
  cause.

[1] Groins, with a pun on the measure of weight.
[2] Dissenting sect.

Ana. Which his cannot. The sanctified
  cause
Should have a sanctified course.
Tri.   Not always necessary.
The children of perdition are ofttimes
Made instruments even of the greatest
  works.
Beside, we should give somewhat to [3]
  man's nature,
The place he lives in, still about the fire
And fume of metals, that intoxicate
The brain of man and make him prone
  to passion.   20
Where have you greater atheists than
  your cooks?
Or more profane or choleric than your
  glassmen?
More antichristian than your bell-
  founders?
What makes the devil so devilish, I
  would ask you,
Sathan, our common enemy, but his
  being
Perpetually about the fire, and boiling
Brimstone and arsenic? We must give,
  I say,
Unto the motives and the stirrers-up
Of humors in the blood. It may be so.
Whenas [4] the *work* is done, the *stone* is
  made,   30
This heat of his may turn into a zeal,
And stand up for the beauteous discipline
Against the menstruous cloth and rag of
  Rome.
We must await his calling and the com-
  ing
Of the good spirit. You did fault t' up-
  braid him
With the Brethren's blessing of Heidel-
  berg, weighing
What need we have to hasten on the work
For the restoring of the silenced Saints,[5]
Which ne'er will be but by the *philos-
  ophers' stone*.   39
And so a learned elder, one of Scotland,
Assured me, *aurum potabile* [6] being
The only med'cine for the civil magistrate
T' incline him to a feeling of the cause,
And must be daily used in the disease.

[3] Make allowance for.
[4] When.
[5] Non-conformist clergy not permitted to
preach.
[6] Drinkable gold, an elixir; here a bribe.

Ana. I have not edified [1] more, truly, by man,
Not since the beautiful light first shone on me;
And I am sad my zeal hath so offended.
Tri. Let us call on him then.
Ana.　　　　　　　The motion's good,
And of the spirit. I will knock first.—
　[*Knocks*.] Peace be within!
　　　　　　[*Exeunt into the house*.] [2]

ACT III. SCENE ii.

[*A room in Lovewit's house*.] [3]

Subtle, Tribulation, Ananias.

[Sub.] O, are you come? 'Twas time. Your threescore minutes
Were at the last thread, you see; and down had gone
Furnus acediæ, turris circulatorius;
Lembec, [4] *bolt's-head, retort,* and *pelican*
Had all been cinders. Wicked Ananias!
Art thou returned? Nay, then it goes down yet.
Tri. Sir, be appeased; he is come to humble
Himself in spirit, and to ask your patience,
If too much zeal hath carried him aside
From the due path.
Sub.　　　　Why, this doth qualify! [5]　10
Tri. The Brethren had no purpose, verily,
To give you the least grievance, but are ready
To lend their willing hands to any project
The spirit and you direct.
Sub.　　　　　This qualifies more!
Tri. And, for the orphans' goods, let them be valued,
Or what is needful else to the holy work,
It shall be numbered; here, by me, the Saints
Throw down their purse before you.
Sub.　　　　　This qualifies most!
Why, thus it should be, now you understand.
Have I discoursed so unto you of our stone,　20

And of the good that it shall bring your cause?
Showed you (beside the main [6] of hiring forces
Abroad, drawing the Hollanders, your friends,
From th' Indies to serve you with all their fleet)
That even the med'cinal use shall make you a faction
And party in the realm? As, put the case
That some great man in state, he have the gout,
Why, you but send three drops of your *elixir*,
You help him straight; there you have made a friend.
Another has the palsy or the dropsy;　30
He takes of your incombustible stuff,
He's young again; there you have made a friend.
A lady that is past the feat of body,
Though not of mind, and hath her face decayed
Beyond all cure of paintings, you restore
With the *oil of talc;* there you have made a friend—
And all her friends. A lord that is a leper,
A knight that has the boneache, or a squire
That hath both these, you make hem smooth and sound
With a bare *fricace* [7] of your *med'cine;* still　40
You increase your friends.
Tri.　　　　Ay, 'tis very pregnant.
Sub. And then the turning of this lawyer's pewter
To plate at Christmas—
Ana.　　　　Christ-tide, I pray you.
Sub. Yet, [8] Ananias!
Ana.　　　　I have done.
Sub.　　　　　Or changing
His parcel [9] gilt to massy gold. You cannot
But raise you friends. Withal, to be of power
To pay an army in the field, to buy

---

[1] Been edified.
[2] They perhaps simply pass from the outer to the inner stage by the drawing of the traverse.
[3] The scene and action are continuous through the remainder of the act.　　　　[5] Mollify.
[4] Alembic.

[6] Important matter.
[7] Rubbing.
[8] An exclamation of impatience.
[9] Partly.

The King of France out of his realms,
  or Spain
Out of his Indies—what can you not do
Against lords spiritual or temporal 50
That shall oppone [1] you?

TRI.   Verily, 'tis true.
  We may be temporal lords ourselves, I
    take it.

SUB. You may be anything, and leave off
    to make
  Long-winded exercises, or suck up
  Your "ha!" and "hum!" in a tune. I
    not deny,
  But such as are not gracéd in a state,
  May, for their ends, be adverse in re-
    ligion,
  And get a tune to call the flock together,
  For, to say sooth, a tune does much with
    women
  And other phlegmatic people; it is your
    bell.   60

ANA. Bells are profane; a tune may be
    religious.

SUB. No warning with you? Then fare-
    well my patience.
  'Slight, it shall down; I will not be thus
    tortured.

TRI. I pray you, sir.

SUB.   All shall perish. I have spoke it.

TRI. Let me find grace, sir, in your eyes;
    the man,
  He stands corrected. Neither did his
    zeal,
  But as yourself, allow a tune somewhere,
  Which now, being toward [2] the *stone*,
    we shall not need.

SUB. No, nor your holy vizard,[3] to win
    widows
  To give you legacies; or make zealous
    wives   70
  To rob their husbands for the common
    cause;
  Nor take the start of bonds broke but
    one day,[4]
  And say they were forfeited by provi-
    dence.
  Nor shall you need o'er night to eat huge
    meals,
  To celebrate your next day's fast the
    better,

The whilst the Brethren and the Sisters,
    humbled,
  Abate the stiffness of the flesh. Nor cast
  Before your hungry hearers scrupulous
    bones,[5]
  As whether a Christian may hawk or
    hunt,   79
  Or whether matrons of the holy assembly
  May lay their hair out, or wear doublets,
  Or have that idol, starch, about their
    linen.

ANA. It is indeed an idol.

TRI.   Mind him not, sir.
  I do command thee, spirit (of zeal, but
    trouble),
  To peace within him! Pray you, sir, go
    on.

SUB. Nor shall you need to libel gainst
    the prelates,
  And shorten so your ears [6] against the
    hearing
  Of the next wiredrawn grace; nor of
    necessity
  Rail against plays, to please the alder-
    man
  Whose daily custard you devour; nor
    lie   90
  With zealous rage till you are hoarse.
    Not one
  Of these so singular arts! Nor call your-
    selves
  By names of Tribulation, Persecution,
  Restraint, Long-patience, and suchlike,
    affected
  By the whole family or wood [7] of you,
  Only for glory, and to catch the ear
  Of the disciple.

TRI.   Truly, sir, they are
  Ways that the godly Brethren have in-
    vented
  For propagation of the glorious cause,
  As very notable means, and whereby
    also   100
  Themselves grow soon and profitably
    famous.

SUB. O, but the *stone*, all's idle to it! Noth-
    ing!
  The art of angels, nature's miracle,
  The *divine secret* that doth fly in clouds
  From east to west, and whose tradition
  Is not from men, but *spirits*.

[1] Oppose.
[2] Near to owning.
[3] Mask, sanctimonious expression.
[4] *I.e.*, foreclose obligations just expired.
[5] Dry bones of discussion on small points.
[6] Lose your ears in a pillory.
[7] Crowd.

ANA.   I hate traditions;
   I do not trust them——
TRI.   Peace!
ANA.   They are popish all.
   I will not peace. I will not——
TRI.   Ananias!
ANA. Please the profane, to grieve the
   godly; I may not.   109
SUB. Well, Ananias, thou shalt overcome.
TRI. It is an ignorant zeal that haunts
   him, sir—
   But truly else a very faithful Brother,
   A botcher,[1] and a man by revelation
   That hath a competent knowledge of
   the truth.
SUB. Has he a competent sum there i'
   the bag
   To buy the goods within? I am made
   guardian,
   And must, for charity and conscience'
   sake,
   Now see the most be made for my poor
   orphan,
   Though I desire the Brethren, too, good
   gainers.
   There they are within. When you have
   viewed and bought hem,   120
   And ta'en the inventory of what they
   are,
   They are ready for *projection;* there's no
   more
   To do. Cast on the *med'cine,* so much
   silver
   As there is tin there, so much gold as
   brass,
   I'll gi' it you in by weight.
TRI.   But how long time,
   Sir, must the Saints expect [2] yet?
SUB.   Let me see,
   How's the moon now? Eight, nine, ten
   days hence,
   He will be *silver potate;* then three days
   Before he *citronize;* some fifteen days,
   The *magisterium* will be perfected.   130
ANA. About the second day of the third
   week
   In the ninth month?
SUB.   Yes, my good Ananias.
TRI. What will the orphans' goods arise
   to, think you?
SUB. Some hundred marks, as much as
   filled three cars,[3]

Unladed now; you'll make six millions
   of hem.
   But I must ha' more coals laid in.
TRI.   How!
SUB.   Another load,
   And then we ha' finished. We must
   now increase
   Our fire to *ignis ardens;* we are past
   Fimus equinus, balnei, cineris,
   And all those lenter heats. If the holy
   purse   140
   Should with this draught fall low, and
   that the Saints
   Do need a present sum, I have [a] [4] trick
   To melt the pewter you shall buy now
   instantly,
   And with a *tincture* make you as good
   Dutch dollars
   As any are in Holland.
TRI.   Can you so?
SUB. Ay, and shall bide the third exami-
   nation.
ANA. It will be joyful tidings to the
   Brethren.
SUB. But you must carry it secret.
TRI.   Ay; but stay—
   This act of coining, is it lawful?
ANA.   Lawful?
   We know [5] no magistrate; or, if we did,
   This's foreign coin.
SUB.   It is no coining, sir.   151
   It is but casting.
TRI.   Ha! You distinguish well.
   Casting of money may be lawful.
ANA.   'Tis, sir.
TRI. Truly, I take it so.
SUB.   There is no scruple,
   Sir, to be made of it; believe Ananias;
   This case of conscience he is studied in.
TRI. I'll make a question of it to the Breth-
   ren.
ANA. The Brethren shall approve it law-
   ful, doubt not.
   Where shall 't be done?
SUB.   For that we'll talk anon.
                   Knock without.
   There's some to speak with me. Go in,
   I pray you,   160
   And view the parcels. That's the in-
   ventory.
   I'll come to you straight.—[*Exeunt Trib-
   ulation and Ananias.*] Who is it?—
   Face, appear!

[1] Tailor, a cant term for Puritan.
[2] Wait.   [3] Carts.
[4] From 1640 edn.   [5] Acknowledge.

Act III. Scene iii.

Subtle, Face, Doll.[1]

[Sub.] How now? Good prize?

Face.   Good pox! Yond' costive cheater Never came on.

Sub.   How then?

Face.   I ha' walked the round Till now, and no such thing.

Sub.   And ha' you quit him?

Face. Quit him? And hell would quit him too, he were happy.

'Slight! Would you have me stalk like a mill jade,

All day, for one that will not yield us grains?

I know him of old.

Sub.   O, but to ha' gulled him Had been a maistry.[2]

Face.   Let him go, black boy!

And turn thee, that some fresh news may possess thee.

A noble count, a don of Spain (my dear   10

Delicious compeer, and my party-[3] bawd),

Who is come hither private for his conscience

And brought munition with him, six great slops,[4]

Bigger than three Dutch hoys,[5] beside round trunks,[6]

Furnished with pistolets[7] and pieces of eight,[7]

Will straight be here, my rogue, to have thy bath

(That is the color[8]) and to make his batt'ry

Upon our Doll, our castle, our Cinque Port,[9]

Our Dover pier, our what thou wilt. Where is she?

She must prepare perfumes, delicate linen,   20

The bath in chief, a banquet, and her wit,

For she must milk his epididymis—

Where is the doxy?

Sub.   I'll send her to thee,

And but despatch my brace of little John Leydens[10]

And come again myself.

Face.   Are they within then?

Sub. Numb'ring the sum.

Face. How much?

Sub.   A hundred marks, boy. [*Exit.*]

Face. Why, this 's a lucky day. Ten pounds of Mammon!

Three o' my clerk! A portague o' my grocer!

This o' the Brethren! Beside reversions

And states to come i' the widow and my count!   30

My share today will not be bought for forty—

[*Enter Doll.*]

Doll.   What?

Face. Pounds, dainty Dorothy! Art thou so near?

Doll. Yes. Say, lord general, how fares our camp?

Face. As with the few that had entrenched themselves

Safe, by their discipline, against a world, Doll,

And laughed within those trenches, and grew fat

With thinking on the booties, Doll, brought in

Daily by their small parties. This dear hour

A doughty don is taken with my Doll;

And thou mayst make his ransom what thou wilt,   40

My dowsabel;[11] he shall be brought here, fettered

With thy fair looks, before he sees thee, and thrown

In a down bed as dark as any dungeon,

Where thou shalt keep him waking with thy drum—

Thy drum, my Doll, thy drum—till he be tame

As the poor blackbirds were i' the great frost,[12]

Or bees are with a basin, and so hive him

---

[1] Enters later.   [5] Ships.
[2] Mastery, achievement.   [6] Trunk hose.
[3] Partner.   [7] Gold coins.
[4] Loose breeches.   [8] Pretext.
[9] One of five strategic Channel towns.

[10] Puritans, so called from their leader, John Bockholdt, or John of Leyden.
[11] Sweetheart.   [12] Of 1608.

I' the swan-skin coverlid and cambric
sheets,
Till he work honey and wax, my little
God's-gift.[1]
DOLL. What is he, general?
FACE.   An adalantado,[2]   50
A grandee, girl. Was not my Dapper
here yet?
DOLL. No.
FACE.   Nor my Drugger?
DOLL.   Neither.
FACE.   A pox on hem,
They are so long a-furnishing! Such
stinkards
Would not be seen upon these festival
days.—

[Enter Subtle.]

How now! Ha' you done?
SUB.   Done. They are gone; the sum
Is here in bank, my Face. I would we
knew
Another chapman[3] now would buy hem
outright.
FACE. 'Slid, Nab shall do 't against he ha'
the widow,
To furnish household.
SUB.   Excellent, well thought on.
Pray God he come.
FACE.   I pray he keep away   60
Till our new business be o'erpast.
SUB.   But, Face,
How cam'st thou by this secret don?
[FACE.][4]   A spirit
Brought me th' intelligence in a paper
here,
As I was conjuring yonder in my circle
For Surly; I ha' my flies abroad. Your
bath
Is famous, Subtle, by my means. Sweet
Doll,
You must go tune your virginal, no los-
ing
O' the least time. And—do you hear?—
good action!
Firk like a flounder; kiss like a scallop,
close;
And tickle him with thy mother-tongue.
His great   70

Verdugoship[5] has not a jot of lan-
guage[6]—
So much the easier to be cozened, my
Dolly.
He will come here in a hired coach, ob-
scure,
And our own coachman, whom I have
sent, as guide,
No creature else. *(One knocks.)* Who's
that?   *[Exit Doll.]*
SUB.   It i' not he?
FACE. O, no, not yet this hour.

[Enter Doll.]

SUB.   Who is 't?
DOLL.   Dapper,
Your clerk.
FACE.   God's will then, Queen of Fairy,
On with your tire[7]—*[Exit Doll.]* and, doc-
tor, with your robes.
Let's despatch him for God's sake.
SUB.   'Twill be long.
FACE. I warrant you, take but the cues
I give you,   80
It shall be brief enough. *[Goes to the
window.]* 'Slight, here are more!
Abel and, I think, the angry boy, the
heir
That fain would quarrel.
SUB.   And the widow?
FACE.   No,
Not that I see. Away!—*[Exit Subtle.]*
O, sir, you are welcome.

ACT III. SCENE iv.

Face, Dapper, Drugger, Kastril.[8]

[FACE.] The doctor is within, a-moving for
you.
(I have had the most ado to win him to
it')
He swears you'll be the dearling o' the
dice;
He never heard her highness dote till
now, he says.
Your aunt has giv'n you the most
gracious words
That can be thought on.
DAP.   Shall I see her grace?
FACE. See her, and kiss her too.—

---

[1] Alluding to the etymological meaning of
Dorothea.
[2] Adelantado, a Spanish governor.
[3] Dealer.   [4] From 1612 edn.

[5] Hangmanship; a word coined from the
Spanish.
[6] *I.e.*, he cannot speak English.
[7] Attire.   [8] The last two enter later.

[Enter Drugger and Kastril.]

                     What, honest Nab!
Hast brought the damask?

NAB.   No, sir; here's tabacco.

FACE. 'Tis well done, Nab. Thou'lt bring
   the damask too?

DRUG. Yes. Here's the gentleman, captain, Master Kastril,   10
I have brought to see the doctor.

FACE.   Where's the widow?

DRUG. Sir, as he likes, his sister, he says,
   shall come.

FACE. O, is it so? Good time. Is your
   name Kastril, sir?

KAS. Ay, and the best o' the Kastrils—
   I'ld be sorry else—
By fifteen hundred a year. Where is this
   doctor?
My mad tabacco-boy here tells me of
   one
That can do things. Has he any skill?

FACE.   Wherein, sir?

KAS. To carry a business, manage a
   quarrel fairly,
Upon fit terms.

FACE   It seems, sir, yo' are but young
   About the town, that can make that a
   question.   20

KAS. Sir, not so young but I have heard
   some speech
Of the angry boys,[1] and seen hem take
   tabacco,
And in his shop; and I can take it too.
And I would fain be one of hem, and go
   down
And practice i' the country.

FACE.   Sir, for the duello,
The doctor, I assure you, shall inform
   you
To the least shadow of a hair, and show
   you
An instrument he has of his own making,
Wherewith, no sooner shall you make
   report
Of any quarrel, but he will take the
   height on 't   30
Most instantly, and tell in what degree
Of safety it lies in, or mortality,
And how it may be borne, whether in a
   right line
Or a half circle, or may else be cast
Into an angle blunt, if not acute—

All this he will demonstrate; and then,
   rules
To give and take the lie by.

KAS.   How? To take it?

FACE. Yes, in oblique [2] he'll show you, or
   in circle; [2]
But ne'er in diameter.[3] The whole
   town
Study his theorems, and dispute them
   ordinarily   40
At the eating academies.

KAS.   But does he teach
Living by the wits too?

FACE.   Anything whatever.
You cannot think that subtlety but he
   reads it.
He made me a captain. I was a stark
   pimp,
Just o' your standing, fore I met with
   him;
It i' not two months since. I'll tell you
   his method:
First, he will enter you at some ordinary.

KAS. No, I'll not come there. You shall
   pardon me.

FACE.   For why, sir?

KAS. There's gaming there, and tricks.

FACE.   Why, would you be
   A gallant, and not game?

KAS.   Ay, 'twill spend a man.   50

FACE. Spend you? It will repair you when
   you are spent.
How do they live by their wits there,
   that have vented
Six times your fortunes?

KAS.   What, three thousand a year!

FACE. Ay, forty thousand.

KAS.   Are there such?

FACE.   Ay, sir,
And gallants yet. Here's a young gentleman
Is born to nothing—*[Indicates Dapper.]*
   forty marks a year,
Which I count nothing. H' is to be
   initiated,
And have a fly o' the doctor. He will win
   you
By unresistible luck, within this fortnight,
Enough to buy a barony. They will set
   him   60

[1] Roisterers.

[2] *I.e.*, the lie circumstantial.
[3] *I.e.*, the lie direct.

Upmost, at the groom porter's,[1] all the
　　Christmas,
And, for the whole year through at every
　　place
Where there is play, present him with the
　　chair,
The best attendance, the best drink,
　　sometimes
Two glasses of Canary—and pay noth-
　　ing—
The purest linen and the sharpest knife,
The partrich [2] next his trencher, and
　　somewhere
The dainty bed, in private, with the
　　dainty.
You shall ha' your ordinaries bid for
　　him,
As playhouses for a poet, and the mas-
　　ter　　　　　　　　　　　　　　　　70
Pray him aloud to name what dish he
　　affects,
Which must be buttered shrimps; and
　　those that drink
To no mouth else will drink to his, as
　　being
The goodly president mouth of all the
　　board.
KAS. Do you not gull one?
FACE.　　　'Od's my life! Do you think it?
You shall have a cast [3] commander (can
　　but get
In credit with a glover or a spurrier
For some two pair of either's ware afore-
　　hand)
Will, by most swift posts, dealing with
　　him,
Arrive at competent means to keep
　　himself,　　　　　　　　　　　　80
His punk, and naked boy in excellent
　　fashion,
And be admired for 't.
KAS.　　　　　Will the doctor teach this?
FACE. He will do more, sir: when your
　　land is gone
(As men of spirit hate to keep earth
　　long),
In a vacation,[4] when small money is
　　stirring,
And ordinaries suspended till the term,

He'll show a perspective [5] where on one
　　side
You shall behold the faces and the per-
　　sons
Of all sufficient young heirs in town,　89
Whose bonds are current for commodity;
On th' other side, the merchants' forms,
　　and others
That, without help of any second broker,
Who would expect a share, will trust such
　　parcels;
In the third square, the very street and
　　sign
Where the commodity dwells, and does
　　but wait
To be delivered, be it pepper, soap,
Hops, or tabacco, oatmeal, woad,[6] or
　　cheeses—
All which you may so handle, to enjoy
To your own use, and never stand
　　obliged.
KAS. I' faith, is he such a fellow?
FACE.　　　Why, Nab here knows him.　100
And then for making matches for rich
　　widows,
Young gentlewomen, heirs, the for-
　　tunat'st man!
He's sent to, far and near, all over
　　England,
To have his counsel and to know their
　　fortunes.
KAS. God's will, my suster [7] shall see him.
FACE.　　　　　　　I'll tell you, sir,
What he did tell me of Nab. It's a
　　strange thing!
(By the way, you must eat no cheese,
　　Nab; it breeds melancholy,
And that same melancholy breeds worms
　　—but pass it.)
He told me, honest Nab here was ne'er
　　at tavern　　　　　　　　　　109
But once in 's life.
DRUG.　　Truth, and no more I was not.
FACE. And then he was so sick—
DRUG.　　　Could he tell you that too?
FACE. How should I know it?
DRUG.　In troth, we had been a-shooting,
And had a piece of fat ram-mutton to
　　supper,
That lay so heavy o' my stomach—

---

[1] An officer of the court who superintended
gaming.
[2] Partridge.
[3] Cassed, cashiered, dismissed.
[4] Of the law courts.

[5] A picture the appearance of which changes
according to the angle of vision.
[6] A plant which produced blue dye.
[7] Provincial form for *sister*.

FACE.   And he has no head
  To bear any wine; for what with the
    noise o' the fiddlers
  And care of his shop, for he dares keep
    no servants—
DRUG. My head did so ache—
FACE.   As he was fain to be brought
  home,
  The doctor told me. And then a good
    old woman—
DRUG. Yes, faith, she dwells in Seacoal
  Lane—did cure me
  With sodden [1] ale and pellitory o' the
    wall [2]—   120
  Cost me but twopence. I had another
    sickness
  Was worse than that.
FACE.   Ay, that was with the grief
  Thou took'st for being cessed [3] at eigh-
    teenpence
  For the waterwork.
DRUG.   In truth, and it was like
  T' have cost me almost my life.
FACE.   Thy hair went off?
DRUG. Yes, sir; 'twas done for spite.
FACE.   Nay, so says the doctor.
KAS. Pray thee, tabacco-boy, go fetch my
  suster;
  I'll see this learned boy before I go;
  And so shall she.
FACE.   Sir, he is busy now;
  But, if you have a sister to fetch
    hither,   130
  Perhaps your own pains may command
    her sooner,
  And he by that time will be free.
KAS.   I go. [Exit.]
FACE. Drugger, she's thine. The damask!
  —[Exit Abel.] (Subtle and I
  Must wrastle for her.) Come on, Master
    Dapper;
  You see how I turn clients here
    away,
  To give your cause despatch; ha' you
    performed
  The ceremonies were enjoined you?
DAP.   Yes, o' the vinegar
  And the clean shirt.
FACE.   'Tis well. That shirt may do you
  More worship than you think. Your
    aunt's afire,

[1] Heated.
[2] Wall-pellitory, a herb.
[3] Assessed.

But that she will not show it, t' have a
  sight on you.   140
Ha' you provided for her grace's serv-
  ants?
DAP. Yes, here are sixscore Edward shil-
  lings—
FACE.   Good!
DAP. And an old Harry's sovereign—
FACE.   Very good!
DAP. And three James shillings, and an
  Elizabeth groat—
  Just twenty nobles.
FACE.   O, you are too just.
  I would you had had the other noble in
    Marys.
DAP. I have some Philip and Marys.
FACE.   Ay, those same
  Are best of all. Where are they? Hark,
  the doctor.

ACT III. SCENE V.

*Subtle, Face, Dapper, Doll.[4] Subtle disguised
              like a Priest of Fairy.*

[SUB.] Is yet her grace's cousin come?
FACE.   He is come.
SUB. And is he fasting?
FACE.   Yes.
SUB.   And hath cried "hum"?
FACE. Thrice, you must answer.
DAP.   Thrice.
SUB.   And as oft "buzz"?
FACE. If you have, say.
DAP.   I have.
SUB.   Then, to her coz,
  Hoping that he hath vinegared his senses,
  As he was bid, the Fairy Queen dispenses,
  By me, this robe, the petticoat of For-
    tune,
  Which that he straight put on, she doth
    importune.
  And though to Fortune near be her
    petticoat,
  Yet nearer is her smock, the queen doth
    note;   10
  And therefore even of that a piece she
    hath sent,
  Which, being a child, to wrap him in was
    rent,
  And prays him for a scarf he now will
    wear it
  (With as much love as then her grace
    did tear it)

[4] Enters later.

About his eyes (*They blind him with a rag.*) to show he is fortunate.

And, trusting unto her to make his state,
He'll throw away all worldly pelf about him;
Which that he will perform, she doth not doubt him.

FACE. She need not doubt him, sir. Alas, he has nothing
But what he will part withal as willingly, 20
Upon her grace's word (throw away your purse),
As she would ask it. (Handkerchiefs and all!)
She cannot bid that thing but he'll obey.
(If you have a ring about you, cast it off,
Or a silver seal at your wrist; her grace will send

He throws away, as they bid him.

Her fairies here to search you; therefore deal
Directly [1] with her highness. If they find
That you conceal a mite, you are undone.)

DAP. Truly, there's all.

FACE. All what?

DAP. My money; truly.

FACE. Keep nothing that is transitory about you. 30
(Bid Doll play music.)

Doll enters with a cittern. They pinch him.

Look, the elves are come
To pinch you, if you tell not truth. Advise you.

DAP. O! I have a paper with a spur ryal [2] in 't.

FACE. *Ti, ti.*
They knew 't, they say.

SUB. *Ti, ti, ti, ti.* He has more yet.

FACE. *Ti, ti-ti-ti.* I' the tother [3] pocket?

SUB. *Titi, titi, titi, titi.*
They must pinch him or he will never confess, they say.

[They pinch him again.]

DAP. O, O!

FACE. Nay, pray you, hold. He is her grace's nephew.—
Ti, ti, ti? What care you? Good faith, you shall care.—

Deal plainly, sir, and shame the fairies.
Show 39
You are an innocent.

DAP. By this good light, I ha' nothing.

SUB. *Titi, tititota.* He does equivocate, she says—
Ti, ti do ti, ti ti do, ti da—and swears by the light when he is blinded.

DAP. By this good dark, I ha' nothing but a half crown
Of gold about my wrist, that my love gave me;
And a leaden heart I wore sin' she forsook me.

FACE. I thought 'twas something. And would you incur
Your aunt's displeasure for these trifles? Come,
I had rather you had thrown away twenty half crowns. [*Removes the coin.*]
You may wear your leaden heart still.—
How now?

SUB. [*Aside.*] What news, Doll?

DOLL. [*Aside.*] Yonder's your knight, Sir Mammon. 50

FACE. [*Aside.*] God's lid, we never thought of him till now!
Where is he?

DOLL. [*Aside.*] Here hard by. H' is at the door.

SUB. [*Aside.*] And you are not ready now?
Doll, get his suit.— [*Exit Doll.*]
He must not be sent back.

FACE. [*Aside.*] O, by no means.
What shall we do with this same puffin here,
Now he's o' the spit?

SUB. [*Aside.*] Why, lay him back awhile
With some device.—

[Enter Doll with Face's clothes.]

Ti, titi, tititi. Would her grace speak with me?
I come.—Help, Doll!

FACE. (*He speaks through the keyhole, the Other knocking.*) Who's there?
Sir Epicure,
My master's i' the way. Please you to walk
Three or four turns but till his back be turned, 60
And I am for you.—Quickly, Doll!

---

[1] Honestly.
[2] Spur royal, a gold coin.
[3] Other.

Sub.   Her grace
Commends her kindly to you, Master
    Dapper.
Dap. I long to see her grace.
Sub.   She now is set
At dinner in her bed, and she has sent you
From her own private trencher a dead
    mouse
And a piece of gingerbread, to be merry
    withal
And stay your stomach, lest you faint
    with fasting;
Yet if you could hold out till she saw
    you, she says,
It would be better for you.
Face.   Sir, he shall
Hold out, and 'twere this two hours, for
    her highness;   70
I can assure you that. We will not lose
All we ha' done.—
Sub.   He must not see nor speak
To anybody till then.
Face.   For that we'll put, sir,
A stay in 'is mouth.
Sub.   Of what?
Face.   Of gingerbread.
Make you it fit. He that hath pleased
    her grace
Thus far, shall not now crinkle ¹ for a
    little.—
Gape, sir, and let him fit you.
                              [*They gag him.*]
Sub. [*Aside.*]   Where shall we now
Bestow him?
Doll. [*Aside.*]   I' the privy.
Sub.   Come along, sir;
I must now show you Fortune's privy
    lodgings.
Face. Are they perfumed, and his bath
    ready?
Sub.   All.   80
Only the fumigation's somewhat strong.
Face. [*Through the keyhole.*] Sir Epicure,
I am yours, sir, by-and-by.²
    [*Exeunt Subtle and Doll with Dapper.*]

Act IV. Scene i.

[*The same.*]

*Face, Mammon, Doll.*³

[Face.] O, sir, yo' are come i' the only
    finest time!
Mam. Where's master?

¹ Turn aside.   ² Immediately.   ³ Enters later.

Face. Now preparing for *projection*, sir.
Your stuff will b' all changed shortly.
Mam.   Into gold?
Face. To gold and silver, sir.
Mam.   Silver I care not for.
Face. Yes, sir, a little to give beggars.
Mam.   Where's the lady?
Face. At hand here. I ha' told her such
    brave things o' you,
Touching your bounty and your noble
    spirit—
Mam.   Hast thou?
Face. As she is almost in her fit to see
    you.
But, good sir, no divinity i' your confer-
    ence,
For fear of putting her in rage.⁴
Mam.   I warrant thee. 10
Face. Six men will not hold her down.
    And then,
If the old man should hear or see you—
Mam.   Fear not.
Face. The very house, sir, would run
    mad. You know it,
How scrupulous he is and violent
Gainst the least act of sin. Physic or
    mathematics,
Poetry, state,⁵ or bawdry, as I told you,
She will endure, and never startle; but
No word of controversy.
Mam.   I am schooled, good Ulen.
Face. And you must praise her house,˙
    remember that,
And her nobility.⁶
Mam.   Let me alone; 20
No herald, no, nor antiquary, Lungs,
Shall do it better. Go.
Face. [*Aside.*]   Why, this is yet
A kind of modern⁷ happiness,⁸ to have
Doll Common for a great lady. [*Exit.*]
Mam.   Now, Epicure.
Heighten thyself; talk to her all in gold;
Rain her as many showers as Jove did
    drops
Unto his Danaë; show the god a miser,
Compared with Mammon. What! The
    stone will do 't.
She shall feel gold, taste gold, hear gold,
    sleep gold;

⁴ Insanity.
⁵ Matters of state; politics.
⁶ Family.
⁷ With a pun on the meaning *common.*
⁸ Fitness, appropriateness.

Nay, we will *concumbere* [1] gold. I will be
puissant 30
And mighty in my talk to her.—

[Enter Face with Doll.]

Here she comes.
FACE. [*Aside.*] To him, Doll; suckle him.—
This is the noble knight
I told your ladyship—
MAM. Madam, with your pardon,
I kiss your vesture.
DOLL. Sir, I were uncivil
If I would suffer that; my lip to you,
sir.
MAM. I hope my lord your brother be in
health, lady.
DOLL. My lord my brother is, though I
no lady, sir.
(FACE. Well said, my Guinea bird. [2])
MAM. Right noble madam—
(FACE. O, we shall have most fierce idola-
try.)
MAM. 'Tis your prerogative.
DOLL. Rather your courtesy. 40
MAM. Were there naught else t' enlarge
your virtues to me,
These answers speak your breeding and
your blood.
DOLL. Blood we boast none, sir; a poor
baron's daughter.
MAM. "Poor"!—and gat you? Profane
not. Had your father
Slept all the happy remnant of his life
After that act, lyen [3] but there still, and
panted,
H' had done enough to make himself,
his issue,
And his posterity noble.
DOLL. Sir, although
We may be said to want the gilt and
trappings,
The dress of honor, yet we strive to
keep 50
The seeds and the materials.
MAM. I do see
The old ingredient, virtue, was not lost,
Nor the drug, money, used to make your
compound.
There is a strange nobility i' your eye,
This lip, that chin! Methinks you do
resemble
One o' the Austriac [4] princes.

FACE. [*Aside.*] Very like!
Her father was an Irish costermonger. [5]
MAM. The house of Valois, just, had
such a nose,
And such a forehead yet the Medici
Of Florence boast.
DOLL. Troth, and I have been likened 60
To all these princes.
FACE. [*Aside.*] I'll be sworn, I heard it.
MAM. I know not how! It is not any one,
But e'en the very choice of all their
features.
FACE. [*Aside.*] I'll in, and laugh. [*Exit.*]
MAM. A certain touch, or air,
That sparkles a divinity beyond
An earthly beauty!
DOLL. O, you play the courtier.
MAM. Good lady, gi' me leave—
DOLL. In faith, I may not,
To mock me, sir.
MAM. To burn i' this sweet flame;
The phœnix never knew a nobler death.
DOLL. Nay, now you court the courtier,
and destroy 70
What you would build. This art, sir,
i' your words,
Calls your whole faith in question.
MAM. By my soul—
DOLL. Nay, oaths are made o' the same
air, sir.
MAM. Nature
Never bestowed upon mortality
A more unblamed, [6] a more harmonious
feature;
She played the stepdame in all faces else.
Sweet madam, le' me be particular—
DOLL. Particular, [7] sir? I pray you, know
your distance.
MAM. In no ill sense, sweet lady, but to
ask
How your fair graces pass the hours.
I see 80
Yo' are lodged here i' the house of a rare
man,
An excellent artist—but what's that
to you?
DOLL. Yes, sir; I study here the mathe-
matics,
And distillation.
MAM. O, I cry your pardon.
H' is a divine instructor, can extract
The souls of all things by his art, call all

---

[1] Lie with.   [3] Lain.
[2] Prostitute.   [4] Austrian.
[5] Apple seller.   [7] Personal.
[6] Unblemished.

The virtues and the miracles of the sun
Into a temperate fornace, teach dull na-
ture
What her own forces are—a man the
emp'ror
Has courted above Kelly,[1] sent his
medals   90
And chains t' invite him.

DOLL.   Ay, and for his physic, sir—

MAM. Above the art of Esculapius,
That drew the envy of the Thunderer!
I know all this, and more.

DOLL.   Troth, I am taken, sir,
Whole with these studies that contemplate nature.

MAM. It is a noble humor; but this form
Was not intended to so dark a use.
Had you been crooked, foul, of some
coarse mold,
A cloister had done well; but such a
feature,
That might stand up the glory of a
kingdom,   100
To live recluse is a mere solecism,
Though in a nunnery. It must not be.
I muse [2] my lord your brother will per-
mit it!
You should spend half my land first,
were I he.
Does not this diamant better on my
finger
Than i' the quarry?

DOLL.   Yes.

MAM.   Why, you are like it.
You were created, lady, for the light.
Here, you shall wear it; take it, the first
pledge
Of what I speak, to bind you to believe
me.

DOLL. In chains of adamant?

MAM.   Yes, the strongest bands. 110
And take a secret too—here, by your
side,
Doth stand this hour the happiest man
in Europe.

DOLL. You are contented, sir?

MAM.   Nay, in true being,
The envy of princes and the fear of
states.

DOLL. Say you so, Sir Epicure?

MAM.   Yes, and thou shalt prove it,
Daughter of honor. I have cast mine
eye

Upon thy form, and I will rear this
beauty
Above all styles.

DOLL.   You mean no treason, sir?

MAM. No, I will take away that jealousy.[3]
I am the lord of the *philosophers' stone,*
And thou the lady.

DOLL.   How, sir! Ha' you that? 121

MAM. I am the master of the *maistry.*
This day the good old wretch here o'
the house
Has made it for us; now he's at *projec-
tion.*
Think therefore thy first wish now; let
me hear it,
And it shall rain into thy lap—no shower,
But floods of gold, whole cataracts, a
deluge,
To get a nation on thee.

DOLL.   You are pleased, sir,
To work on the ambition of our sex.

MAM. I am pleased the glory of her sex
should know   130
This nook here of the Friars is no climate
For her to live obscurely in, to learn
Physic and surgery for the constable's
wife
Of some odd hundred [4] in Essex; but
come forth,
And taste the air of palaces; eat, drink
The toils of emp'rics,[5] and their boasted
practice—
Tincture of pearl and coral, gold and
amber;
Be seen at feasts and triumphs; [6] have
it asked
What miracle she is; set all the eyes
Of court afire, like a burning glass,   140
And work hem into cinders, when the
jewels
Of twenty states adorn thee, and the
light
Strikes out the stars that,[7] when thy
name is mentioned,
Queens may look pale, and, we but show-
ing our love,
Nero's Poppæa may be lost in story!
Thus will we have it.

DOLL.   I could well consent, sir.
But in a monarchy how will this be?

[3] Suspicion.
[4] A division of a county.
[5] The results of the toil of experimenters.
[6] Festivities.   [7] So that.

[1] The partner of Dee.   [2] Am astonished.

The prince will soon take notice, and
  both seize
You and your *stone*, it being a wealth
  unfit
For any private subject.
MAM.   If he knew it.   150
DOLL. Yourself do boast it, sir.
MAM.   To thee, my life.
DOLL. O, but beware, sir! You may come
  to end
The remnant of your days in a loathed
  prison
By speaking of it.
MAM.   'Tis no idle fear.
We'll therefore go with all, my girl, and
  live
In a free state, where we will eat our
  mullets,
Soused in high-country wines, sup pheas-
  ants' eggs,
And have our cockles boiled in silver
  shells,
Our shrimps to swim again, as when
  they lived,
In a rare butter made of dolphins'
  milk,   160
Whose cream does look like opals, and
  with these
Delicate meats set ourselves high for
  pleasure,
And take us down again, and then renew
Our youth and strength with drinking
  the *elixir*,
And so enjoy a perpetuity
Of life and lust! And thou shalt ha'
  thy wardrobe
Richer than Nature's, still to change
  thyself,
And vary oft'ner, for thy pride, than
  she,
Or Art, her wise and almost equal serv-
  ant.

[Enter Face.]

FACE. Sir, you are too loud. I hear you
  every word   170
Into the laboratory. Some fitter place;
The garden, or great chamber above.—
  [Aside.] How like you her?
MAM. *[Aside.]* Excellent, Lungs. There's
  for thee.   *[Gives him money.]*
FACE. *[Aside.]*   But do you hear?
Good sir, beware, no mention of the
  rabbins.

MAM. *[Aside.]* We think not on hem.
FACE.   O, it is well, sir.—*[Exeunt
  Mammon and Doll.]* Subtle!

ACT IV. SCENE ii.

[The same.]

Face, Subtle, Kastril, Dame Pliant.[1]

[FACE.] Dost thou not laugh?
SUB.   Yes. Are they gone?
FACE.   All's clear.
SUB. The widow is come.
FACE.   And your quarreling disciple?
SUB. Ay.
FACE.   I must to my captainship again
  then.
SUB. Stay, bring hem in first.
FACE.   So I meant. What is she?
  A bonnibel?[2]
SUB.   I know not.
FACE.   We'll draw lots.
  You'll stand to that?
SUB.   What else?
FACE.   O, for a suit,
  To fall now like a cortine[3]— flap!
SUB.   To th' door, man.
FACE. You'll ha' the first kiss, cause[4] I
  am not ready.   *[Exit.]*
SUB. Yes, and perhaps hit you through
  both the nostrils.[5]
FACE. *[Within.]* Who would you speak
  with?
KAS. *[Within.]*   Where's the captain?
FACE. *[Within.]*   Gone, sir,   10
  About some business.
KAS. *[Within.]*   Gone?
FACE. *[Within.]*   He'll return straight.
  But Master Doctor, his lieutenant, is
  here.

[Enter Kastril and Dame Pliant.]

SUB. Come near, my worshipful boy, my
  terræ fili,
That is, my boy of land; make thy approaches.
Welcome. I know thy lusts and thy desires,
And I will serve and satisfy hem. Begin;

---

[1] Last two enter later.   [3] Curtain.
[2] Fair lass.   [4] Because
[5] "Put your nose out of joint."

Charge me from thence, or thence, or in this line.

Here is my center; ground thy quarrel.

KAS.　　　　　　　　　　　　You lie!

SUB. How, child of wrath and anger! The loud lie?

For what, my sudden boy?

KAS.　　　　Nay, that look you to;　20
I am aforehand.

SUB.　　　　O, this 's no true grammar,
And as ill logic! You must render causes,[1]
　child,
Your first and second intentions, know
　your canons
And your divisions, moods, degrees, and
　differences,
Your predicaments, substance, and ac-
　cident,
Series extern and intern, with their
　causes,
Efficient, material, formal, final,
And ha' your elements perfect.

KAS.　　　　　　　　What is this?
The angry[2] tongue he talks in?

SUB.　　　　　　　That false precept
Of being aforehand has deceived a
　number,　　　　　　　　　　　30
And made hem enter quarrels often-
　times
Before they were aware, and afterward
Against their wills.

KAS.　　　How must I do then, sir?

SUB. I cry this lady mercy; she should
　first
Have been saluted. I do call you lady,
Because you are to be one ere 't be long,
　　　　　　　　　　　He kisses her.
My soft and buxom widow.

KAS.　　　　　　　　Is she, i' faith?

SUB. Yes, or my art is an egregious liar.

KAS. How know you?

SUB.　　　　By inspection on her forehead,
And subtlety of her lip, which must be
　tasted　　　　　　　　　　　40
Often to make a judgment. (He kisses
　her again.)—[Aside.] 'Slight, she melts
Like a myrobalan![3]— Here is yet a line
In rivo frontis[4] tells me he is no knight.

PLI. What is he then, sir?

SUB.　　　　　　Let me see your hand.

O, your linea Fortunæ[5] makes it plain,
And stella[6] here in monte Veneris,[7]
But, most of all, junctura annularis.[8]
He is a soldier, or a man of art, lady,
But shall have some great honor shortly.

PLI.　　　　　　　　　　　Brother,
He's a rare man, believe me!

[Enter Face, in his uniform.]

KAS.　　　　　　Hold your peace!　50
Here comes the tother rare man.—Save
　you, captain.

FACE. Good Master Kastril! Is this your
　sister?

KAS.　　Ay, sir.
Please you to kuss[9] her, and be proud
　to know her?

FACE. I shall be proud to know you, lady.
　　　　　　　　　　　[Kisses her.]

PLI.　　　　　　　　　Brother,
He calls me lady, too.

KAS.　　　　　Ay, peace. I heard it.

FACE. [Taking Subtle aside.] The count is
　come.

SUB.　　　Where is he?

FACE.　　　　　　　　At the door.

SUB. Why, you must entertain him.

FACE.　　　　　　　　What'll you do
With these the while?

SUB.　　Why, have hem up, and show hem
Some fustian book, or the dark glass.[10]

FACE.　　　　　　　Fore God,
She is a delicate dabchick![11] I must have
　her.　　　　　　　　　　[Exit.]　60

SUB. [Aside.] Must you?　Ay, if your
　fortune will, you must.—
Come, sir, the captain will come to us
　presently.
I'll ha' you to my chamber of demon-
　strations,
Where I'll show you both the grammar
　and logic
And rhetoric of quarreling; my whole
　method
Drawn out in tables; and my instrument
That hath the several scale upon 't
　shall make you
Able to quarrel at a straw's breadth by
　moonlight

[1] The following terms are from scholastic logic.
[2] Quarrel-provoking.
[3] A kind of dried plum.
[4] The vein of the forehead.
[5] Line of Fortune.
[6] The star.
[7] Mount of Venus.
[8] The ring joint.
[9] Kiss.
[10] Polished black stone into which astrologers gazed.
[11] Water hen.

And, lady, I'll have you look in a glass,
Some half an hour, but to clear your
　eyesight　　　　　　　　　　　70
Against you see[1] your fortune, which
　is greater
Than I may judge upon the sudden,
　trust me.　　　　　　　　[*Exeunt.*]

ACT IV. SCENE iii.

[*The same.*]

Face, Subtle, Surly.[2]

[FACE.] Where are you, doctor?
SUB. [*Within.*]　　　　I'll come to you
　presently.
FACE. I will ha' this same widow, now I
　ha' seen her,
On any composition.[3]

[*Enter Subtle.*]

SUB.　　　　　　　What do you say?
FACE. Ha' you disposed of them?
SUB.　　　　　　　I ha' sent hem up.
FACE. Subtle, in troth, I needs must have
　this widow.
SUB. Is that the matter?
FACE.　　　　　　Nay, but hear me.
SUB.　　　　　　　　　Go to!
If you rebel once, Doll shall know it
　all;
Therefore be quiet, and obey your
　chance.
FACE. Nay, thou art so violent now. Do
　but conceive:
Thou art old, and canst not serve—
SUB.　　　　　　Who cannot? I?　10
'Slight, I will serve her with thee, for a—
FACE.　　　　　　　　　Nay,
But understand; I'll gi' you composi-
　tion.
SUB. I will not treat with thee. What!
　Sell my fortune?
'Tis better than my birthright. Do not
　murmur.
Win her, and carry her. If you grumble,
　Doll
Knows it directly.
FACE.　　　　Well, sir, I am silent.
Will you go help to fetch in Don in state?

[1] In preparation for seeing.
[2] Last two enter later.
[3] Terms.

SUB. I follow you, sir.—[*Exit Face.*] We
　must keep Face in awe,
Or he will overlook[4] us like a tyran.[5]

[*Enter Face with*] *Surly like a Spaniard.*

Brain of a tailor! Who comes here?
　Don John!　　　　　　　　　20
SUR. *Senores, beso las manos á vuestras
　mercedes.*[6]
SUB. Would you had stooped a little, and
　kissed our *anos.*
FACE. Peace, Subtle!
SUB.　　Stab me; I shall never hold, man.
He looks in that deep ruff like a head in
　a platter,
Served in by a short cloak upon two
　trestles.[7]
FACE. Or what do you say to a collar of
　brawn,[8] cut down
Beneath the souse,[9] and wriggled[10]
　with a knife?
SUB. 'Slud,[11] he does look too fat to be a
　Spaniard.
FACE. Perhaps some Fleming or some
　Hollander got him
In d'Alva's time—Count Egmont's bas-
　tard.
SUB.　　Don,　　　　　　　　30
Your scurvy, yellow, Madrid face is
　welcome.
SUR. *Gratia.*[12]
SUB.　　He speaks out of a fortification.
Pray God he ha' no squibs in those deep
　sets.[13]
SUR. *Por dios, senores, muy linda casa!*[14]
SUB. What says he?
FACE.　　Praises the house, I think;
I know no more but's action.
SUB.　　　　　　　Yes, the *casa,*
My precious Diego, will prove fair
　enough
To cozen you in. Do you mark? You
　shall
Be cozened, Diego.

[4] Look down upon, despise.
[5] Tyrant.
[6] Gentlemen, I kiss your worships' hands.
[7] Stilts.
[8] Roll of boar's flesh.
[9] Ear.
[10] Cut into wrinkles, like a ruff.
[11] God's Lord, a mild oath.
[12] Thanks.
[13] Plaits of the ruff.
[14] By Jove, sirs, a very fine house!

FACE.   Cozened, do you see,
My worthy Donzel,[1] cozened.
SUR.   *Entiendo.*[2] 40
SUB. Do you intend it? So do we, dear
Don.
Have you brought pistolets or porta-
gues,[3]
My solemn Don?—(*He [, i.e., Face,] feels
his pockets.*) Dost thou feel any?
FACE.   Full.
SUB. You shall be emptied, Don, pumped
and drawn
Dry, as they say.
FACE.   Milked, in troth, sweet Don.
SUB. See all the monsters [4]—the great
lion of all, Don.
SUR. *Con licencia, se puede ver á esta se-
nora?* [5]
SUB. What talks he now?
FACE.   O' the *senora.*
SUB.   O, Don,
That is the lioness, which you shall see
Also, my Don.
FACE.   'Slid, Subtle, how shall we do? 50
SUB. For what?
FACE.   Why, Doll's employed, you know.
SUB.   That's true.
Fore heav'n, I know not. He must stay,
that's all.
FACE. Stay? That he must not, by no
means.
SUB.   No? Why?
FACE. Unless you'll mar all. 'Slight, he'll
suspect it;
And then he will not pay, not half so
well.
This is a traveled punk-master, and
does know
All the delays—a notable hot rascal,
And looks already rampant.
SUB.   'Sdeath, and Mammon
Must not be troubled.
FACE.   Mammon, in no case!
SUB. What shall we do then?
FACE.   Think; you must be sudden. 60
SUR. *Entiendo que la senora es tan hermosa,
que codicio tan
Á verla como la bien aventuranza de mi
vida.*[6]

FACE. *Mi vida?* 'Slid, Subtle, he puts me
in mind o' the widow.
What dost thou say to draw her to 't—
ha!—
And tell her it is her fortune? All our
venter
Now lies upon 't. It is but one man
more,
Which on 's chance [7] to have her; and
beside,
There is no maidenhead to be feared
or lost.
What dost thou think on 't, Subtle?
SUB.   Who, I? Why—
FACE. The credit of our house too is en-
gaged.   70
SUB. You made me an offer for my share
erewhile.
What wilt thou gi' me, i' faith?
FACE.   O, by that light,
I'll not buy now. You know your doom [8]
to me.
E'en take your lot; obey your chance,
sir; win her,
And wear her—out for me.
SUB.   'Slight, I'll not work her then.
FACE. It is the common cause; therefore
bethink you.
Doll else must know it, as you said.
SUB.   I care not.
SUR. *Senores, porque se tarda tanta?* [9]
SUB. Faith, I am not fit; I am old.
FACE.   That's now no reason, sir.
SUR. *Puede ser de hazer burla de mi
amor?* [10]   80
FACE. You hear the Don too? By this air
I call,
And loose the hinges—Doll!
SUB.   A plague of hell—
FACE. Will you then do?
SUB.   Yo' are a terrible rogue!
I'll think of this. Will you, sir, call the
widow?
FACE. Yes, and I'll take her too with all
her faults,
Now I do think on 't better.
SUB.   With all my heart, sir.
Am I discharged o' the lot?
FACE.   As you please.
SUB.   Hands. [*They shake hands.*]

---

[1] Little Don.   [3] Gold coins.
[2] I understand.   [4] *I.e.*, see the sights.
[5] By your leave, may I see this lady?
[6] I understand that the lady is so beautiful
that I desire to see her as much as the good
fortune of my life.

[7] Whichever of us should chance.
[8] Decision.
[9] Sirs, why so much delay?
[10] Can it be you are making a jest of my love?

FACE. Remember now, that upon any change
You never claim her.

SUB.   Much good joy and health to you, sir.
Marry a whore? Fate, let me wed a witch first.   90

SUR. *Por estas honradas barbas* [1]—

SUB.   He swears by his beard.
Despatch, and call the brother too.
                                        [*Exit Face.*]

SUR. *Tengo duda, senores, que no me hagan alguna traycion.* [2]

SUB. How, *issue on?* Yes, *præsto, senor.* [3]
Please you
Enthratha the *chambratha*, worthy Don,
Where, if it please the Fates, in your *bathada,*
You shall be soaked, and stroked, and tubbed, and rubbed,
And scrubbed, and fubbed, [4] dear Don, before you go.
You shall, in faith, my scurvy babion [5] Don,
Be curried, clawed, and flawed, [6] and tawed, [7] indeed.   100
I will the heartlier go about it now,
And make the widow a punk so much the sooner,
To be revenged on this impetuous Face;
The quickly doing of it is the grace.
                                        [*Exeunt.*]

ACT IV. SCENE iv.

[*Another room in the same.*]

Face, Kastril, Da[me] Pliant, Subtle, Surly. [8]

[FACE.] Come, lady. I knew the doctor would not leave
Till he had found the very nick of her fortune.

KAS. To be a countess, say you?

[FACE.] [9]   A Spanish countess, sir.

PLI. Why, is that better than an English countess?

FACE. Better? 'Slight, make you that a question, lady?

---

[1] By these honored hairs—
[2] I fear, sirs, that you are playing me some trick.
[3] Quickly, sir.   [5] Baboon.
[4] Cheated.   [6] Flayed.
[7] Soaked in preparation for tanning.
[8] Last two enter later.
[9] From 1612 edn.

KAS. Nay, she is a fool, captain; you must pardon her.

FACE. Ask from your courtier to your Inns of Court man,
To your mere milaner; [10] they will tell you all
Your Spanish jennet is the best horse; your Spanish
Stoop is the best garb; [11] your Spanish beard   10
Is the best cut; your Spanish ruffs are the best
Wear; your Spanish pavin the best dance;
Your Spanish titillation in a glove
The best perfume; and for your Spanish pike,
And Spanish blade, let your poor captain speak.—
Here comes the doctor.

[*Enter Subtle with a paper.*]

SUB.   My most honored lady,
For so I am now to style you, having found,
By this my scheme, [12] you are to undergo
An honorable fortune very shortly,
What will you say now, if some—

FACE.   I ha' told her all, sir,   20
And her right worshipful brother here, that she shall be
A countess; do not delay hem, sir. A Spanish countess!

SUB. Still, my scarce-worshipful captain, you can keep
No secret! Well, since he has told you, madam,
Do you forgive him, and I do.

KAS.   She shall do that, sir.
I'll look to 't; 'tis my charge.

SUB.   Well then, naught rests
But that she fit her love now to her fortune.

PLI. Truly, I shall never brook a Spaniard.

SUB.   No?

PLI. Never sin' eighty-eight [13] could I abide hem,
And that was some three year afore I was born, in truth.   30

---

[10] Milliner, dealer in fancy articles.
[11] Bearing.
[12] Horoscope.
[13] 1588, the date of the destruction of the Armada.

SUB. Come, you must love him, or be miserable;
Choose which you will.
FACE.   By this good rush, persuade her,
She will cry [1] strawberries else within this twelvemonth.
SUB. Nay, shads and mack'rel, which is worse.
FACE.   Indeed, sir?
KAS. God's lid, you shall love him, or I'll kick you.
PLI.   Why,
I'll do as you will ha' me, brother.
KAS.   Do,
Or by this hand I'll maul you.
FACE.   Nay, good sir,
Be not so fierce.
SUB.   No, my enragéd child;
She will be ruled. What, when she comes to taste
The pleasures of a countess! To be courted—   40
FACE. And kissed and ruffled!
SUB.   Ay, behind the hangings.
FACE. And then come forth in pomp!
SUB.   And know her state!
FACE. Of keeping all th' idolators o' the chamber
Barer to her than at their prayers!
SUB.   Is served
Upon the knee!
FACE.   And has her pages, huishers, [2]
Footmen, and coaches—
SUB.   Her six mares—
FACE.   Nay, eight!
SUB. To hurry her through London to th' Exchange, [3]
Bet'lem, [4] the China-houses [5]—
FACE.   Yes, and have
The citizens gape at her, and praise her tires,
And my lord's goose-turd bands, [6] that rides with her!   50
KAS. Most brave! [7] By this hand, you are not my suster
If you refuse.
PLI.   I will not refuse, brother.

[1] Hawk on the street.
[2] Ushers.
[3] Where shops were located.
[4] Bethlehem Hospital, where people visited the insane for amusement.
[5] Where ware from China was shown.
[6] Green-colored collars.
[7] Fine.

[Enter Surly.]

SUR. Que es esto, senores, que non se venga? Esta tardanza me mata! [8]
FACE.   It is the count come;
The doctor knew he would be here, by his art.
SUB. En gallanta madama, Don, gallantissima!
SUR. Por todos los dioses, la mas acabada Hermosura, que he visto en mi vida! [9]
FACE. Is 't not a gallant language that they speak?
KAS. An admirable language! Is 't not French?   60
FACE. No, Spanish, sir.
KAS.   It goes like law French,
And that, they say, is the court-liest language.
FACE.   List, sir.
SUR. El sol ha perdido su lumbre, con el Resplandor que træ esta dama! Valgame dios! [10]
FACE. He admires your sister.
KAS.   Must not she make court'sy?
SUB. 'Od's will, she must go to him, man, and kiss him!
It is the Spanish fashion for the women
To make first court.
FACE.   'Tis true he tells you, sir;
His art knows all.
SUR.   Porque no se acude? [11]
KAS. He speaks to her, I think?
FACE.   That he does, sir.   70
SUR. Por el amor de dios, que es esto que se tarda? [12]
KAS. Nay, see; she will not understand him!—Gull!
Noddy!
PLI.   What say you, brother?
KAS.   Ass, my suster,
Go kuss him, as the cunning man would ha' you;
I'll thrust a pin i' your buttocks else.
FACE.   O, no, sir.

[8] What's the matter, sirs, that nobody comes? This delay is killing me.
[9] By all the gods, the most finished beauty that I have seen in my life.
[10] The sun has lost his light in comparison with the splendor which this lady brings! God bless me!
[11] Why don't you draw near?
[12] For the love of God, why this delay?

Sur. *Senora mia, mi persona muy indigna*
   esta
Á llegar á tanta hermosura.[1] [*Kisses her.*]
Face. Does he not use her bravely?
Kas.   Bravely, i' faith!
Face. Nay, he will use her better.
Kas.   Do you think so?
Sur. *Senora, si sera servida, entremos.*[2]   80
                    [*Exit with Dame Pliant.*]
Kas. Where does he carry her?
Face.   Into the garden, sir.
   Take you no thought; I must interpret
   for her.
Sub. [*Aside to Face.*] Give Doll the word.—
                    [*Exit Face*].
   Come, my fierce child, advance;
   We'll to our quarreling lesson again.
Kas.   Agreed.
   I love a Spanish boy with all my heart.
Sub. Nay, and by this means, sir, you shall
   be brother
To a great count.
Kas.   Ay, I knew that at first.
   This match will advance the house of
   the Kastrils.
Sub. Pray God your sister prove but
   pliant!
Kas.   Why,
   Her name is so, by her other husband.
Sub.   How!   90
Kas. The Widow Pliant. Knew you not
   that?
Sub.   No, faith, sir;
   Yet, by erection of her figure,[3] I guessed it.
   Come, let's go practice.
Kas.   Yes, but do you think, doctor,
   I e'er shall quarrel well?
Sub.   I warrant you. [*Exeunt.*]

Act IV. Scene v.

[*Another room in the same.*]

Doll, Mammon, Face, Subtle.[4]

[Doll.] (*In her fit of talking.*) For after
   Alexander's death [5]—
Mam.   Good lady—

---

[1] Madam, my person is entirely unworthy to
come near to such beauty.

[2] Madam, if you will, let us go in.

[3] Casting of her horoscope, with an obvious
double meaning.

[4] Last two to enter later.

[5] The following speeches by Doll are inco-
herent extracts from Hugh Broughton's *Concent
of Scripture.*

Doll. That Perdiccas and Antigonus were
   slain,
   The two that stood, Seleuc' and Ptol-
   omy—
Mam. Madam—
Doll.   Made up the two legs, and the
   fourth beast,
   That was Gog-north and Egypt-south,
   which after
   Was called Gog-iron-leg and South-iron-
   leg—
Mam.   Lady—
Doll. And then Gog-horned.   So was
   Egypt, too.
   Then Egypt-clay-leg, and Gog-clay-leg—
Mam.   Sweet madam —
Doll. And last Gog-dust, and Egypt-dust,
   which fall
   In the last link of the fourth chain. And
   these   10
   Be stars in story, which none see, or look
   at—
Mam. What shall I do?
Doll.   For, as he says, except
   We call the rabbins and the heathen
   Greeks—
Mam. Dear lady—
Doll.   To come from Salem, and from
   Athens,
   And teach the people of Great Britain—

[*Enter Face, in his livery.*]

Face.   What's the matter, sir?
Doll. To speak the tongue of Eber and
   Javan [6]—
Mam.   O,
   Sh' is in her fit.
Doll.   We shall know nothing—
Face.   Death, sir,
   We are undone!
Doll.   Where then a learned linguist
   Shall see the ancient used communion
   Of vowels and consonants—
Face.   My master will hear!   20
Doll. A wisdom which Pythagoras held
   most high—
Mam. Sweet honorable lady!
Doll.   To comprise
   All sounds of voices, in few marks of
   letters—
Face. Nay, you must never hope to lay
   her now.   *They* [*all*] *speak together.*

---

[6] *I.e.,* of the Hebrews and the Greeks.

DOLL. And so we may arrive by Talmud skill [1]
And profane Greek to raise the building up
Of Helen's house against the Ismaelite,
King of Thogarma, and his habergeons
Brimstony, blue, and fiery; and the force
Of King Abaddon, and the beast of Cittim, 30
Which Rabbi David Kimchi, Onkelos,
And Aben Ezra do interpret Rome.
FACE. How did you put her into 't?
MAM. Alas, I talked
Of a fift [2] monarchy I would erect
With the *philosophers' stone*, by chance, and she
Falls on the other four straight.
FACE. Out of Broughton!
I told you so. 'Slid, stop her mouth.
MAM. Is 't best?
FACE. She'll never leave else. If the old man hear her,
We are but fæces, ashes.
SUB. [*Within.*] What's to do there?
FACE. O, we are lost! Now she hears him, she is quiet. 40
MAM. Where shall I hide me?
SUB. How! What sight is here?
Upon Subtle's entry they disperse.
Close [3] deeds of darkness, and that shun the light!
Bring him again. Who is he? What, my son!
O, I have lived too long.
MAM. Nay, good, dear father,
There was no unchaste purpose.
SUB. Not? And flee me
When I come in?
MAM. That was my error.
SUB. Error?
Guilt, guilt, my son; give it the right name. No marvel
If I found check in our *great work* within,
When such affairs as these were managing!
MAM. Why, have you so?
SUB. It has stood still this half hour,
And all the rest of our *less works* gone back. 51
Where is the instrument of wickedness,
My lewd, false drudge?

MAM. Nay, good sir, blame not him;
Believe me, 'twas against his will or knowledge.
I saw her by chance.
SUB. Will you commit more sin,
T' excuse a varlet?
MAM. By my hope, 'tis true, sir.
SUB. Nay, then I wonder less, if you, for whom
The blessing was prepared, would so tempt heaven,
And lose your fortunes.
MAM. Why, sir?
SUB. This 'll retard
The *work* a month at least.
MAM. Why, if it do, 60
What remedy? But think it not, good father.
Our purposes were honest. [4]
SUB. As they were,
So the reward will prove. (*A great crack and noise within.*)—How now! Ay me!
God and all saints be good to us.—

[Enter Face.]
What's that?
FACE. O, sir, we are defeated! All the works
Are flown *in fumo;* every glass is burst;
Fornace and all rent down, as if a bolt
Of thunder had been driven through the house.
Retorts, receivers, pelicans, boltheads,
All strook [5] in shivers!
Subtle falls down as in a swoon.
Help, good sir! Alas, 70
Coldness and death invades him. Nay, Sir Mammon,
Do the fair offices of a man! You stand,
As you were readier to depart than he.—
One knocks.
Who's there?—My lord her brother is come.
MAM. Ha, Lungs?
FACE. His coach is at the door. Avoid his sight,
For he's as furious as his sister is mad.
MAM. Alas!
FACE. My brain is quite undone with the fume, sir;
I ne'er must hope to be mine own man again.

---

[1] In the original this speech and the following dialogue including Face's final speech are printed in parallel columns.
[2] Fifth. [3] Secret. [4] Chaste. [5] Struck.

MAM. Is all lost, Lungs? Will nothing be
  preserved
  Of all our cost?
FACE.   Faith, very little, sir; 80
  A peck of coals or so, which is cold
  comfort, sir.
MAM. O, my voluptuous mind! I am justly
  punished.
FACE. And so am I, sir.
MAM.   Cast from all my hopes—
FACE. Nay, certainties, sir.
MAM.   By mine own base affections.
              Subtle seems come to himself.
SUB. O, the cursed fruits of vice and lust!
MAM.   Good father,
  It was my sin. Forgive it.
SUB.   Hangs my roof
  Over us still, and will not fall, O justice,
  Upon us for this wicked man?
FACE.   Nay, look, sir;
  You grieve him now with staying in his
  sight.
  Good sir, the nobleman will come too,
  and take you,   90
  And that may breed a tragedy.
MAM.   I'll go.
FACE. Ay, and repent at home, sir. It may
  be
  For some good penance you may ha' it
  yet;
  A hundred pound to the box at Bet'lem—
MAM.   Yes.
FACE. For the restoring such as—ha' their
  wits.
MAM.   I'll do 't.
FACE. I'll send one to you to receive it.
MAM.   Do.
  Is no *projection* left?
FACE.   All flown, or stinks, sir.
MAM. Will naught be saved that's good
  for *med'cine*, think'st thou?
FACE. I cannot tell, sir. There will be per-
  haps
  Something about the scraping of the
  shards   100
  Will cure the itch—[*Aside.*] though not
  your itch of mind, sir.—
  It shall be saved for you, and sent home.
  Good sir,
  This way, for fear the lord should meet
  you.   [*Exit Mammon.*]
SUB.   Face!
FACE. Ay.
SUB.   Is he gone?

FACE.   Yes, and as heavily
  As all the gold he hoped for were in his
  blood.
  Let us be light though.
SUB.   Ay, as balls, and bound
  And hit our heads against the roof for
  joy;
  There's so much of our care now cast
  away.
FACE. Now to our Don.
SUB.   Yes, your young widow by this
  time
  Is made a countess, Face; sh' has been in
  travail   110
  Of a young heir for you.
FACE.   Good, sir.
SUB.   Off with your case,[1]
  And greet her kindly, as a bridegroom
  should,
  After these common hazards.
FACE.   Very well, sir.
  Will you go fetch Don Diego off the
  while?
SUB. And fetch him over too, if you'll be
  pleased, sir.
  Would Doll were in her place, to pick his
  pockets now!
FACE. Why, you can do it as well, if you
  would set to 't.
  I pray you, prove your virtue.[2]
SUB.   For your sake, sir.   [*Exeunt.*]

ACT IV. SCENE vi.

[*Another room in the same.*]

Surly, Da[me] Pliant, Subtle, Face.[3]

[SUR.] Lady, you see into what hands you
  are fall'n,
  'Mongst what a nest of villains, and how
  near
  Your honor was t' have catched a certain
  clap,
  Through your credulity, had I but been
  So punctually forward, as place, time,
  And other circumstance would ha' made
  a man;
  For yo' are a handsome woman—would
  yo' were wise too!
  I am a gentleman come here disguised,
  Only to find the knaveries of this citadel·

---

[1] *I.e.*, his present costume.
[2] Power.
[3] Last two enter later.

And where I might have wronged your
    honor, and have not,   10
I claim some interest in your love. You
    are,
They say, a widow, rich; and I'm a
    bachelor,
Worth naught; your fortunes may make
    me a man,
As mine ha' preserved you a woman.
    Think upon it,
And whether I have deserved you or no.
PLI.   I will, sir.
SUR. And for these household-rogues, let
    me alone
To treat with them.

[Enter Subtle.]

SUB.   How doth my noble Diego,
And my dear madam countess? Hath the
    count   18
Been courteous, lady, liberal and open?
Donzel, methinks you look melancholic
After your *coitum*,[1] and scurvy! Truly,
I do not like the dullness of your eye;
It hath a heavy cast—'tis upsee Dutch,[2]
And says you are a lumpish whoremaster.
Be lighter; I will make your pockets so.
         He falls to picking of them.
SUR. [*Disclosing himself.*] Will you, Don
    bawd and pickpurse? [*Beats him.*]
    How now? Reel you?
Stand up, sir; you shall find, since I am
    so heavy,
I'll gi' you equal weight.
SUB.   Help! Murder!
SUR.   No, sir,
There's no such thing intended. A good
    cart [3]
And a clean whip shall ease you of that
    fear.   30
I am the Spanish Don that should be
    cozened,
Do you see? Cozened? Where's your
    Captain Face,
That parcel [4] broker, and whole bawd,
    all rascal?

[Enter Face in his uniform.]

FACE. How, Surly!
SUR.   O, make your approach,
    good captain.

---

[1] Coition.   [2] In the Dutch fashion.
[3] Bawds were "carted" through the city as a
punishment.   [4] Partial. part.

I have found from whence your copper
    rings and spoons
Come now, wherewith you cheat abroad
    in taverns.
'Twas here you learned t' anoint your
    boot with brimstone,
Then rub men's gold on 't for a kind of
    touch,
And say, 'twas naught, when you had
    changed the color,
That you might ha't for nothing? And
    this doctor,   40
Your sooty, smoky-bearded compeer,
    he
Will close you so much gold, in a *bolt's-
    head*,
And, on a turn, convey i' the stead an-
    other
With *sublimed mercury*, that shall burst
    i' the heat,
And fly out all *in fumo!* Then weeps
    Mammon;
Then swoons his worship. [*Exit Face.*]
    Or he is the Faustus,
That casteth figures and can conjure,
    cures
Plague, piles, and pox, by the ephemer-
    ides,[5]
And holds intelligence with all the bawds
And midwives of three shires, while you
    send in   50
(Captain!—What! Is he gone?) damsels
    with child,
Wives that are barren, or the waiting-
    maid
With the green sickness? [*Seizes Subtle
    as he attempts to escape.*] Nay, sir,
    you must tarry,
Though he be scaped, and answer by the
    ears,[6] sir.

ACT IV. SCENE vii.

[The same.]

*Face, Kastril, Surly, Subtle, Drugger,[7]
    Ananias,[7] Da[me] Pliant, Doll.[7]*

[FACE. (*To Kastril.*)] Why, now's the
    time, if ever you will quarrel
Well, as they say, and be a true-born
    child.
The doctor and your sister both are
    abused.

---

[5] Astrological almanacs.   [7] Enters later.
[6] Referring to punishment in the pillory.

Kas. Where is he? Which is he? He is a
slave,
Whate'er he is, and the son of a whore.—
Are you
The man, sir, I would know?
Sur.　　　　　　　I should be loath,
sir,
To confess so much.
Kas.　　　　　　Then you lie i' your throat.
Sur.　　　　　　　　　　　How!
Face. [*To Kastril.*] A very arrant rogue,
sir, and a cheater,
Employed here by another con-
jurer
That does not love the doctor, and would
cross him　　　　　　　　　　　10
If he knew how.
Sur.　　　　　Sir, you are abused.
Kas.　　　　　　　　　You lie—
And 'tis no matter.
Face.　　　　　Well said, sir! He is
The impudent'st rascal—
Sur.　　You are indeed. Will you hear me,
sir?
Face. By no means. Bid him be gone.
Kas.　　　　　　Begone, sir, quickly!
Sur. This 's strange!—Lady, do you in-
form your brother.
　　　　[*Dame Pliant whispers to Kastril.*]
Face. There is not such a foist ¹ in all the
town.
The doctor had him ² presently,³ and
finds yet
The Spanish count will come here.—
[*Aside.*] Bear up, Subtle.
Sub. Yes, sir, he must appear within this
hour.
Face. And yet this rogue would come in
a disguise,　　　　　　　　　20
By the temptation of another spirit,
To trouble our art, though he could
not hurt it!
Kas.　　　　Ay,
I know.—[*To Pliant.*] Away, you talk
like a foolish mauther.⁴
Sur. Sir, all is truth she says.
Face.　　　　　　Do not believe
him, sir.
He is the lying'st swabber! Come your
ways, sir.
Sur. You are valiant out of company!
Kas.　　　　　Yes, how then, sir?

¹ Rogue.　　　　　　³ In actual presence.
² *I.e.*, the count(?).　　⁴ Wench.

[*Enter Drugger with a piece of cloth.*]

Face. Nay, here's an honest fellow too
that knows him
And all his tricks. (Make good what I
say, Abel.
This cheater would ha' cozened thee
o' the widow.)
He owes this honest Drugger here
seven pound　　　　　　　30
He has had ⁵ on him in twopenny'orths
of tabacco.
Drug. Yes, sir. And h' has damned him-
self ⁶ three terms to pay me.
Face. And what does he owe for lotium? ⁷
Drug.　　　　　Thirty shillings, sir;
And for six syringes.
Sur.　　　　　　Hydra of villainy!
Face. [*To Kastril.*] Nay, sir, you must
quarrel him out o' the house.
Kas.　　　　　　　　I will.—
Sir, if you get not out o' doors, you lie;
And you are a pimp.
Sur.　　　　　Why, this is madness, sir,
Not valure in you; I must laugh at this.
Kas. It is my humor; you are a pimp and
a trig,⁸
And an Amadis de Gaul, or a Don
Quixote.　　　　　　　　40
Drug. Or a Knight o' the Curious Cox-
comb, do you see?

　　　　　[*Enter Ananias.*]

Ana. Peace to the household!
Kas.　　　　I'll keep peace for no man.
Ana. Casting of dollars is concluded
lawful.
Kas. Is he the constable?
Sub.　　　　　Peace, Ananias.
Face.　　　　　　No, sir.
Kas. Then you are an otter, and a shad,
a whit,
A very tim.⁹
Sur.　　　　　You'll hear me, sir?
Kas.　　　　　　I will not.
Ana. What is the motive?
Sub.　　　　Zeal in the young gentleman
Against his Spanish slops—
Ana.　　　　　They are profane,
Lewd, superstitious, and idolatrous
breeches.

⁵ Charged.　　　　　⁷ Lotion.
⁶ *I.e.*, sworn.　　　⁸ Coxcomb.
⁹ A term of abuse which has baffled the
editors.

Sur. New rascals!

Kas.　　　　　　　Will you be gone, sir?

Ana.　　　　　　　　　　　Avoid, Sathan! 50
Thou art not of the light! That ruff of
　pride
About thy neck betrays thee, and is
　the same
With that which the unclean birds, in
　seventy-seven,[1]
Were seen to prank it with on divers
　coasts.
Thou look'st like antichrist, in that lewd
　hat.

Sur. I must give way.

Kas.　　　　　　　　Begone, sir.

Sur.　　　　　　　　　　But I'll take
A course with you—

Ana.　　　　Depart, proud Spanish fiend!

Sur. Captain and doctor—

Ana.　　　　　　　Child of perdition!

Kas.　　　　　　　Hence, sir!—[*Exit Surly.*]
Did I not quarrel bravely?

Face.　　　　　　　　Yes, indeed, sir.

Kas. Nay, and I give my mind to 't, I
　shall do 't.　　　　　　　　　　　60

Face. O, you must follow, sir, and
　threaten him tame.
He'll turn again else.

Kas.　　　　　I'll re-turn him then. [*Exit.*]

Face. Drugger, this rogue prevented[2] us
　for thee;
We had determined that thou shouldst
　ha' come
In a Spanish suit, and ha' carried her so;
　and he,
A brokerly slave, goes, puts it on him-
　self.
Hast brought the damask?

Drug.　　　Yes, sir.

Face.　　　　　　Thou must borrow
A Spanish suit. Hast thou no credit
　with the players?

Drug. Yes, sir; did you never see me play
　the Fool?

Face. I know not, Nab.—[*Aside.*] Thou
　shalt, if I can help it.—　　　　　70
Hieronimo's[3] old cloak, ruff, and hat
　will serve;
I'll tell thee more when thou bring'st
　hem.　　　　　　　　[*Exit Drugger.*]

Ana. (*Subtle hath whispered with him this
　while.*)　　　　　　　Sir, I know
The Spaniard hates the Brethren, and
　hath spies
Upon their actions; and that this was
　one
I make no scruple.—But the holy Synod
Have been in prayer and meditation
　for it;
And 'tis revealed no less to them than me
That casting of money is most lawful.

Sub.　　　　　　　　　　　True.
But here I cannot do it; if the house
Should chance to be suspected, all
　would out,　　　　　　　　　　80
And we be locked up in the Tower for-
　ever,
To make gold there for th' state, never
　come out;
And then are you defeated.

Ana.　　　　　　　　　I will tell
This to the elders and the weaker
　Brethren,
That the whole company of the sepa-
　ration
May join in humble prayer again.

(Sub.　　　　　　　　And fasting.)

Ana. Yea, for some fitter place. The peace
　of mind
Rest with these walls!

Sub.　　　　　Thanks, courteous Ananias.
　　　　　　　　　　　[*Exit Ananias.*]

Face. What did he come for?

Sub.　　　　　　About casting dollars,
Presently out of hand. And so I told
　him　　　　　　　　　　　　90
A Spanish minister came here to spy
Against the faithful—

Face.　　　　　I conceive. Come, Subtle,
Thou art so down upon the least disaster!
How wouldst thou ha' done, if I had not
　helped thee out?

Sub. I thank thee, Face, for the angry
　boy, i' faith.

Face. Who would ha' looked[4] it should
　ha' been that rascal
Surly? He had dyed his beard and all.
　Well, sir,
Here's damask come to make you a suit.

Sub.　　　　　　　　Where's Drugger?

Face. He is gone to borrow me a Spanish
　habit;
I'll be the count now.

Sub.　　　　But where's the widow? 100
Face. Within, with my lord's sister;
　Madam Doll
Is entertaining her.
Sub.　　　　　　By your favor, Face,
Now she is honest, I will stand again.
Face. You will not offer it?
Sub.　　　　Why?
Face.　　　　　　Stand to your word,
Or—here comes Doll. She knows—
Sub.　　　　Yo' are tyrannous still.
Face. Strict for my right.—

[Enter Doll.]

　　　　How now, Doll? Hast told her
The Spanish count will come?
Doll.　　　　Yes; but another is come
You little looked for!
Face.　　　　Who's that?
Doll.　　　　Your master;
The master of the house.
Sub.　　　　How, Doll!
Face.　　　　　　She lies.
This is some trick. Come, leave your
　quiblins,[1] Dorothy.　　　　　110
Doll. Look out and see.
　　　　[Face goes to the window.]
Sub.　　　　Art thou in earnest?
Doll.　　　　'Slight,
Forty o' the neighbors are about him,
　talking.
Face. 'Tis he, by this good day.
Doll.　　　　'Twill prove ill day
For some on us.
Face.　　　　We are undone, and taken.
Doll. Lost, I am afraid.
Sub.　　　You said he would not come,
While there died one a week within the
　liberties.[2]
Face. No; 'twas within the walls.
Sub.　　　Was 't so? Cry you mercy.
I thought the liberties. What shall we
　do now, Face?
Face. Be silent; not a word, if he call or
　knock.
I'll into mine old shape again, and meet
　him,　　　　　120
Of Jeremy, the butler. I' the meantime,
Do you two pack up all the goods and
　purchase[3]

[1] Quibbles, equivocations.
[2] Slum district just outside the walls of the city.
[3] Plunder, booty.

That we can carry i' the two trunks
　I'll keep him
Off for today, if I cannot longer; and
　then
At night I'll ship you both away to
　Ratcliff,
Where we'll meet tomorrow, and there
　we'll share.
Let Mammon's brass and pewter keep
　the cellar;
We'll have another time for that. But,
　Doll,
Pray thee, go heat a little water quickly;
Subtle must shave me. All my captain's
　beard　　　　　130
Must off, to make me appear smooth
　Jeremy.
You'll do 't?
Sub.　　　　Yes, I'll shave you as well as
　I can.
Face. And not cut my throat, but trim
　me?
Sub.　　　　You shall see, sir.　　*[Exeunt.]*

Act V. Scene i.

[The street before Lovewit's house.]
Lovewit, Neighbors.

[Love.] Has there been such resort, say
　you?
Nei. 1.　　　　Daily, sir.
Nei. 2. And nightly, too.
Nei. 3.　　　　Ay, some as brave as lords.
Nei. 4. Ladies and gentlewomen.
Nei. 5.　　　　　　Citizens' wives.
Nei. 1. And knights.
Nei. 6.　　　　In coaches.
Nei. 2.　　　　　　Yes, and oyster women.
Nei. 1. Beside other gallants.
Nei. 3.　　　　Sailors' wives.
Nei. 4.　　　　　　Tabacco men.
Nei. 5. Another Pimlico![4]
Love.　　　What should my knave advance
To draw this company? He hung out
　no banners
Of a strange calf with five legs to be seen,
Or a huge lobster with six claws?
Nei. 6.　　　　　　No, sir.
Nei. 3. We had gone in then, sir.
Love.　　　　He has no gift 10
Of teaching i' the nose[5] that e'er I
　knew of.

[4] A popular summer resort.
[5] *I.e.*, like a Puritan.

You saw no bills set up that promised cure
Of agues or the toothache?
NEI. 2.   No such thing, sir!
LOVE. Nor heard a drum strook for babions or puppets?
NEI. 5. Neither, sir.
LOVE.   What device should he bring forth now?
I love a teeming wit as I love my nour-ishment.
Pray God he ha' not kept such open house
That he hath sold my hangings and my bedding!
I left him nothing else. If he have eat hem,
A plague o' the moth, say I! Sure he has got   20
Some bawdy pictures to call all this ging: [1]
The Friar and the Nun; or the new motion [2]
Of the knight's courser covering the parson's mare;
The boy of six year old with the great thing.
Or 't may be he has the fleas that run at tilt
Upon a table, or some dog to dance?
When saw you him?
NEI. 1.   Who, sir, Jeremy?
NEI. 2.   Jeremy butler?
We saw him not this month.
LOVE.   How!
NEI. 4.   Not these five weeks, sir.
NEI. [6.] [3] These six weeks, at the least.
LOVE.   Yo' amaze me, neighbors!
NEI. 5. Sure, if your worship know not where he is,   30
He's slipped away.
NEI. 6.   Pray God he be not made away.
                              He knocks.
LOVE. Ha! It's no time to question, then.
NEI. 6.   About
Some three weeks since I heard a dole-ful cry,
As I sat up a-mending my wife's stock-ings.
LOVE. This 's strange that none will answer! Didst thou hear
A cry, say'st thou?

NEI. 6.   Yes, sir, like unto a man
That had been strangled an hour, and could not speak.
NEI. 2. I heard it, too, just this day three weeks, at two a-clock
Next morning.
LOVE.   These be miracles, or you make hem so!
A man an hour strangled, and could not speak,   40
And both you heard him cry?
NEI. 3.   Yes, downward, [4] sir.
LOVE. Thou art a wise fellow. Give me thy hand, I pray thee.
What trade art thou on?
NEI. 3.   A smith and 't please your worship.
LOVE. A smith? Then lend me thy help to get this door open.
NEI. 3. That I will presently, sir; but fetch my tools—   [*Exit.*]
NEI. 1. Sir, best to knock again afore you break it.

ACT V. SCENE ii.

[*The same.*]

Lovewit, Face, Neighbors.

[LOVE. (*Knocking again.*)] I will.

[*Enter Face dressed as a butler.*]

FACE.   What mean you, sir?
NEI. 1, 2, 4.   O, here's Jeremy!
FACE. Good sir, come from the door.
LOVE.   Why, what's the matter?
FACE. Yet farder; [5] you are too near yet.
LOVE.   I' the name of wonder,
What means the fellow?
FACE.   The house, sir, has been visited.
LOVE. What, with the plague? Stand thou then farder.
FACE.   No, sir,
I had it not.
LOVE.   Who had it then? I left
None else but thee i' the house.
FACE.   Yes, sir, my fellow,
The cat that kept [6] the butt'ry, had it on her
A week before I spied it; but I got her

---

[1] Gang.
[2] Puppet show.
[3] From 1640 edn.
[4] Hathaway suggests that this is a slang term of negation.
[5] Farther.
[6] Guarded.

Conveyed away i' the night. And so I
  shut   10
The house up for a month—
LOVE.   How!
FACE.   Purposing then, sir,
  T' have burnt rose-vinegar, treacle, and
    tar,
  And ha' made it sweet, that you should
    ne'er ha' known it,
  Because I knew the news would but
    afflict you, sir.
LOVE. Breathe less, and farder off! Why,
  this is stranger!
  The neighbors tell me all here that the
    doors
  Have still been open—
FACE.   How, sir!
LOVE.   Gallants, men and women,
  And of all sorts, tag-rag, been seen to
    flock here
  In threaves [1] these ten weeks, as to a
    second Hogsden,
  In days of Pimlico and Eye-bright. [2]
FACE.   Sir, 20
  Their wisdoms will not say so.
LOVE.   Today they speak
  Of coaches and gallants; one in a French
    hood
  Went in, they tell me; and another
    was seen
  In a velvet gown at the windore; [3]
    divers more
  Pass in and out.
FACE.   They did pass through the doors
    then,
  Or walls, I assure their eyesights and
    their spectacles;
  For here, sir, are the keys, and here
    have been,
  In this my pocket, now above twenty
    days!
  And for before, I kept the fort alone
    there.
  But that 'tis yet not deep i' the after-
    noon,   30
  I should believe my neighbors had seen
    double
  Through the black pot, and made these
    apparitions!
  For, on my faith to your worship, for
    these three weeks
  And upwards, the door has not been
    opened.

[1] Droves.   [2] A tavern.   [3] Window.

LOVE.   Strange!
NEI. 1. Good faith, I think I saw a coach.
NEI. 2.   And I too,
  I'ld ha' been sworn.
LOVE.   Do you but think it now?
  And but one coach?
NEI. 4.   We cannot tell, sir; Jeremy
  Is a very honest fellow.
FACE.   Did you see me at all?
NEI. 1. No; that we are sure on.
NEI. 2.   I'll be sworn o' that.
LOVE. Fine rogues to have your testi-
  monies built on!   40

[*Enter Third Neighbor, with his tools.*]

NEI. 3. Is Jeremy come?
NEI. 1.   O, yes; you may leave your
    tools;
  We were deceived, he says.
NEI. 2.   He has had the keys,
  And the door has been shut these three
    weeks.
NEI. 3.   Like enough!
LOVE. Peace, and get hence, you change-
  lings.

[*Enter Surly and Mammon.*]

FACE. [*Aside.*]   Surly come!
  And Mammon made acquainted! They'll
    tell all.
  How shall I beat them off? What shall
    I do?
  Nothing's more wretched than a guilty
    conscience.

ACT V. SCENE iii.

[*The same.*]

Surly, Mammon, Lovewit, Face, Neigh-
* bors, Kastril, Ananias, Tribulation,*
* Dapper, Subtle.* [4]

[SUR.] No, sir, he was a great physician.
  This,
  It was no bawdyhouse, but a mere
    chancel!
  You knew the lord and his sister.
MAM.   Nay, good Surly—
SUR. The happy word, "Be rich"—
MAM.   Play not the tyran—
SUR. Should be today pronounced to all
  your friends.

[4] The last five enter later.

And where be your andirons now, and
　your brass pots,
That should ha' been golden flagons
　and great wedges?
MAM. Let me but breathe. What, they
　ha' shut their doors,
Methinks!　　*Mammon and Surly knock.*
SUR.　　Ay, now 'tis holiday with them.
MAM.　　　　　　　　Rogues,
Cozeners, impostors, bawds!
FACE.　　　　　What mean you, sir?　10
MAM. To enter if we can.
FACE.　　　　　Another man's house?
Here is the owner, sir; turn you to
　him,
And speak your business.
MAM.　　　　　Are you, sir, the owner?
LOVE. Yes, sir.
MAM.　　　And are those knaves within,
　your cheaters?
LOVE. What knaves? What cheaters?
MAM.　　　　Subtle and his Lungs.
FACE. The gentleman is distracted, sir!
　No lungs
Nor lights ha' been seen here these
　three weeks, sir,
Within these doors, upon my word.
SUR.　　　　　　　Your word,
Groom arrogant?
FACE.　　Yes, sir, I am the housekeeper,
And know the keys ha' not been out o'
　my hands.　　　　　　　20
SUR. This 's a new Face?
FACE.　　　　You do mistake the
　house, sir.
What sign was 't at?
SUR.　　　　You rascal! This is one
O' the confederacy. Come, let's get
　officers,
And force the door.
LOVE.　　　Pray you, stay, gentle-
　men.
SUR. No, sir, we'll come with warrant.
MAM.　　　　　Ay, and then
We shall ha' your doors open.
　　　[Exeunt Mammon and Surly.]
LOVE.　　　　What means this?
FACE. I cannot tell, sir.
NEI. 1.　　These are two o' the gallants
That we do think we saw.
FACE.　　　　Two o' the fools?
You talk as idly as they. Good faith,
　sir,
I think the moon has crazed 'em all.

[Enter Kastril.]

(O me,　　　　　　　　　　30
The angry boy come too? He'll make a
　noise,
And ne'er away till he have betrayed us
　all.)　　　　　*Kastril knocks.*
KAS. What, rogues, bawds, slaves, you'll
　open the door anon!
Punk, cockatrice,[1] my suster! By this
　light,
I'll fetch the marshal to you. You are
　a whore
To keep your castle—
FACE.　　Who would you speak with, sir?
KAS. The bawdy doctor, and the cozen-
　ing captain,
And Puss, my suster.
LOVE.　　　　This is something, sure.
FACE. Upon my trust, the doors were
　never open, sir.
KAS. I have heard all their tricks told me
　twice over　　　　　　　40
By the fat knight and the lean gentle-
　man.
LOVE. Here comes another.

[Enter Ananias and Tribulation.]

FACE. *[Aside.]*　　　　Ananias too?
And his pastor?
TRI.　　The doors are shut against us.
　　　They beat, too, at the door.
ANA. Come forth, you seed of sulphur,
　sons of fire!
Your stench, it is broke forth; abomina-
　tion
Is in the house.
KAS.　　　Ay, my suster's there.
ANA.　　　　　　The place,
It is become a cage of unclean birds.
KAS. Yes, I will fetch the scavenger and
　the constable.
TRI. You shall do well.
ANA.　　　We'll join to weed them out.
KAS. You will not come then, punk de-
　vice,[2] my suster!　　　　50
ANA. Call her not sister; she is a harlot
　verily.
KAS. I'll raise the street.
LOVE.　　　Good gentlemen, a word.
ANA. Sathan avoid, and hinder not our
　zeal!

[1] Here, a prostitute.
[2] Perfect harlot, possibly with a pun on *point-
device.*

[*Exeunt Ananias, Tribulation, and Kastril.*]

Love. The world's turned Bet'lem.

Face.   These are all broke loose
Out of S[t]. Kather'ne's, where they use
  to keep
The better sort of madfolks.

Nei. 1.   All these persons
We saw go in and out here.

Nei. 2.   Yes, indeed, sir.

Nei. 3. These were the parties.

Face.   Peace, you drunkards! Sir,
I wonder at it. Please you to give me
  leave
To touch the door; I'll try an the lock
  be changed.   60

Love. It mazes me!

Face. [*Going to the door.*]   Good faith, sir,
  I believe
There's no such thing. 'Tis all *deceptio
  visus.*[1]—

[*Aside.*] Would I could get him away.
                Dapper cries out within.

Dap.   Master Captain! Master Doctor!

Love. Who's that?

Face.   (Our clerk within, that I
  forgot!)—I know not, sir.

Dap. For God's sake, when will her grace
  be at leisure?

Face.   Ha!
Illusions, some spirit o' the air!—(His
  gag is melted,
And now he sets out the throat.[2])

Dap.   I am almost stifled—

(Face. Would you were altogether.)

Love.   'Tis i' the house.
  Ha! List!

Face.   Believe it, sir, i' the air.

Love.   Peace, you—

Dap. Mine aunt's grace does not use me
  well.

Sub. [*Within.*]   You fool,   70
Peace; you'll mar all.

Face. [*Through the keyhole, but is overheard
  by Lovewit.*]   Or you will else,
  you rogue.

Love. O, is it so? Then you converse
  with spirits!—
Come, sir. No more o' your tricks, good
  Jeremy.
The truth, the shortest way.

[1] Optical illusion.
[2] "Lets off his mouth."

Face.   Dismiss this rabble, sir.—
[*Aside.*] What shall I do? I am catched.

Love.   Good neighbors,
I thank you all. You may depart.—
[*Exeunt Neighbors.*] Come, sir.—
You know that I am an indulgent
  master;
And therefore conceal nothing. What's
  your med'cine,
To draw so many several sorts of wild
  fowl?

Face. Sir, you were wont to affect mirth
  and wit—   80
But here's no place to talk on 't i' the
  street.
Give me but leave to make the best of
  my fortune,
And only pardon me th' abuse of your
  house;
It's all I beg. I'll help you to a widow,
In recompense, that you shall gi' me
  thanks for,
Will make you seven years younger,
  and a rich one.
'Tis but your putting on a Spanish cloak.
I have her within. You need not fear
  the house;
It was not visited.

Love.   But by me, who came
Sooner than you expected.

Face.   It is true, sir.   90
Pray you, forgive me.

Love.   Well; let's see your widow.
                                [*Exeunt.*]

Act V. Scene iv.

[*A room in Lovewit's house.*]

Subtle, Dapper [blindfolded], Face, Doll.[3]

[Sub.] How! Ha' you eaten your gag?

Dap.   Yes, faith, it crumbled
Away i' my mouth.

Sub.   You ha' spoiled all then.

Dap.   No!
I hope my aunt of Fairy will forgive me.

Sub. Your aunt's a gracious lady; but in
  troth
You were to blame.

Dap.   The fume did overcome me,
And I did do 't to stay my stomach.
  Pray you
So satisfy her grace.

[3] Last two enter later.

[Enter Face in his uniform.]

                    Here comes the captain.
FACE. How now! Is his mouth down?
SUB.   Ay, he has spoken!
FACE. (A pox, I heard him, and you too.)
    He's undone then.—
    (I have been fain to say the house is
        haunted   10
With spirits, to keep churl back.
SUB.   And hast thou done it?
FACE. Sure, for this night.
SUB.   Why, then triumph and sing
Of Face so famous, the precious king
Of present wits.
FACE.   Did you not hear the coil [1]
About the door?
SUB.   Yes, and I dwindled with it.)
FACE. Show him his aunt, and let him be
    despatched;
I'll send her to you.   *[Exit.]*
SUB.   Well, sir, your aunt her
    grace
Will give you audience presently, on
    my suit,
And the captain's word that you did
    not eat your gag
In any contempt of her highness.
        [Removes the blindfold from his eyes.]
DAP.   Not I, in troth, sir.   20

[Enter] Doll like the Queen of Fairy.

SUB. Here she is come. Down o' your
    knees and wriggle;
She has a stately presence.
                    [Dapper kneels.]
    Good! Yet nearer,
And bid, "God save you!"
DAP.   Madam!
SUB.   And your aunt.
DAP. And my most gracious aunt, God
    save your grace.
DOLL. Nephew, we thought to have been
    angry with you;
But that sweet face of yours hath
    turned the tide,
And made it flow with joy, that ebbed
    of love.
Arise, and touch our velvet gown.
SUB.   The skirts,
And kiss hem. So!
DOLL.   Let me now stroke that head.

Much, nephew, shalt thou win; much shalt
    thou spend.   30
Much shalt thou give away; much shalt
    thou lend.
SUB. (Ay, much, indeed.)—Why do you
    not thank her grace?
DAP. I cannot speak for joy.
SUB.   See, the kind wretch!
Your grace's kinsman right.
DOLL.   Give me the bird.—
Here is your fly in a purse, about your
    neck, cousin;
Wear it, and feed it about this day
    sev'night,
On your right wrist—
SUB.   Open a vein with a pin
And let it suck but once a week; till then,
You must not look on 't.
DOLL.   No. And, kinsman,
Bear yourself worthy of the blood you
    come on.   40
SUB. Her grace would ha' you eat no
    more Woolsack [2] pies
Nor Dagger [2] frume'ty.[3]
DOLL.   Nor break his fast
In Heaven [2] and Hell.[2]
SUB.   She's with you everywhere!
Nor play with costermongers, at mum-
    chance,[4] traytrip,[4]
God-make-you-rich [4] (whenas your aunt
    has done it); but keep
The gallant'st company and the best
    games—
DAP.   Yes, sir.
SUB. Gleek [4] and primero; [4] and what you
    get, be true to us.
DAP. By this hand, I will.
SUB.   You may bring 's a thousand pound
Before tomorrow night, if but three
    thousand
Be stirring, an you will.
DAP.   I swear I will then.   50
SUB. Your fly will learn you all games.
FACE. *[Within.]*   Ha' you done there?
SUB. Your grace will command him no
    more duties?
DOLL.   No;
But come and see me often. I may
    chance
To leave him three or four hundred
    chests of treasure,

[1] Disturbance.

[2] Name of a tavern.
[3] Frumenty, wheat boiled in milk, etc.
[4] A game of chance.

And some twelve thousand acres of fairy land,
If he game well and comely with good gamesters.

Sub. There's a kind aunt! Kiss her departing part.—
But you must sell your forty mark a year now.

Dap. Ay, sir, I mean.

Sub. Or gi't away; pox on 't!

Dap. I'll gi't mine aunt. I'll go and fetch the writings. 60

Sub. 'Tis well; away. [*Exit Dapper.*

Enter Face.]

Face. Where's Subtle?

Sub. Here. What news?

Face. Drugger is at the door; go take his suit,
And bid him fetch a parson presently.
Say he shall marry the widow. Thou shalt spend
A hundred pound by the service!—
[*Exit Subtle.*
Now, Queen Doll,
Ha' you packed up all?

Doll. Yes.

Face. And how do you like The Lady Pliant?

Doll. A good, dull innocent.

[*Enter Subtle.*]

Sub. Here's your Hieronimo's cloak and hat.

Face. Give me hem.

Sub. And the ruff too?

Face. Yes; I'll come to you presently.
[*Exit.*

Sub. Now he is gone about his project, Doll, 70
I told you of, for the widow.

Doll. 'Tis direct Against our articles.

Sub. Well, we'll fit him, wench.
Hast thou gulled her of her jewels or her bracelets?

Doll. No; but I will do 't.

Sub. Soon at night, my Dolly,
When we are shipped, and all our goods aboard,
Eastward for Ratcliff, we will turn our course

To Brainford, westward, if thou say'st the word,
And take our leaves of this o'erweening rascal,
This peremptory Face.

Doll. Content; I am weary of him.

Sub. Thou hast cause, when the slave will run a-wiving, Doll, 80
Against the instrument that was drawn between us.

Doll. I'll pluck his bird as bare as I can.

Sub. Yes, tell her
She must by any means address some present
To th' cunning man, make him amends for wronging
His art with her suspicion, send a ring,
Or chain of pearl; she will be tortured else
Extremely in her sleep, say, and ha' strange things
Come to her. Wilt thou?

Doll. Yes.

Sub. My fine flittermouse,[1]
My bird o' the night! We'll tickle it at the Pigeons,[2]
When we have all, and may unlock the trunks, *They kiss.* 90
And say this 's mine and thine, and thine and mine—

[*Enter Face.*]

Face. What now! A-billing?

Sub. Yes, a little exalted
In the good passage of our stock-affairs.

Face. Drugger has brought his parson; take him in, Subtle,
And send Nab back again to wash his face.

Sub. I will—and shave himself?

Face. If you can get him.
[*Exit Subtle.*

Doll. You are hot upon it, Face, whate'er it is!

Face. A trick that Doll shall spend ten pound a month by.

[*Enter Subtle.*]

Is he gone?

Sub. The chaplain waits you i' the hall, sir. 99

[1] Bat.
[2] An inn at Brainford, or Brentford.

FACE. I'll go bestow him.　　　　　[*Exit.*]
DOLL.　　He'll now marry her instantly.
SUB. He cannot yet; he is not ready.
　Dear Doll,
　Cozen her of all thou canst. To deceive
　him
　Is no deceit, but justice, that would
　break
　Such an inextricable tie as ours was.
DOLL. Let me alone to fit him.

　　　　　　[*Enter Face.*]

FACE.　　　　　Come, my venturers;
　You ha' packed up all? Where be the
　trunks? Bring forth.
SUB. Here.
FACE.　　　Let 's see hem. Where's the
　money?
SUB.　　　　Here,
　In this.
FACE.　　Mammon's ten pound; eight
　score before;
　The Brethren's money this; Drugger's
　and Dapper's.　　　　　　　　109
　What paper's that?
DOLL.　　The jewel of the waiting-maid's,
　That stole it from her lady, to know
　certain—
FACE. If she should have precedence of
　her mistress?
DOLL.　　　　Yes.
FACE. What box is that?
SUB.　　　The fishwife's rings, I think,
　And th' alewife's single money.[1] Is 't
　not, Doll?
DOLL. Yes; and the whistle that the sail-
　or's wife
　Brought you, to know and her husband
　were with Ward.[2]
FACE. We'll wet it tomorrow; and our
　silver beakers
　And tavern cups. Where be the French
　petticoats
　And girdles and hangers?[3]
SUB.　　　　Here, i' the trunk,
　And the bolts of lawn.
FACE.　　Is Drugger's damask there,　120
　And the tabacco?
SUB.　　　Yes.
FACE.　　　　Give me the keys.
DOLL. Why you the keys?

[1] Small change.
[2] A notorious pirate.
[3] Loops from which swords were hung.

SUB.　　　　No matter, Doll; because
　We shall not open hem before he comes.
FACE. 'Tis true, you shall not open them,
　indeed;
　Nor have hem forth. Do you see? Not
　forth, Doll.
DOLL.　　　　　No!
FACE. No, my smock-rampant. The right
　is, my master
　Knows all, has pardoned me, and he
　will keep hem.
　Doctor, 'tis true—you look [4]—for [5] all
　your figures;
　I sent for him, indeed. Wherefore, good
　partners,
　Both he and she, be satisfied, for here　130
　Determines [6] the indenture tripartite
　Twixt Subtle, Doll, and Face. All I
　can do
　Is to help you over the wall, o' the back
　side,
　Or lend you a sheet to save your velvet
　gown, Doll.
　Here will be officers presently; bethink
　you
　Of some course suddenly to scape the
　dock,
　For thither you'll come else. (*Some
　knock.*) Hark you, thunder!
SUB. You are a precious fiend!
OFFICERS. [*Without.*]　　Open the door!
FACE. Doll, I am sorry for thee, i' faith;
　but hear'st thou?
　It shall go hard but I will place thee
　somewhere;　　　　　　　　　　140
　Thou shalt ha' my letter to Mistress
　Amo—
DOLL.　　　　Hang you—
FACE. Or Madam Cæsarean.
DOLL.　　　　Pox upon you, rogue!
　Would I had but time to beat thee!
FACE.　　　　　Subtle,
　Let 's know where you set up next; I'll
　send you
　A customer now and then, for old ac-
　quaintance.
　What new course ha' you?
SUB.　　　　Rogue, I'll hang myself,
　That I may walk a greater devil than
　thou,
　And haunt thee i' the flockbed [7] and the
　buttery.　　　　　　　　　[*Exeunt.*]

[4] Stare.　　[5] In spite of.　　[6] Terminates.
[7] A bed stuffed with pieces of wool or cloth.

ACT V. SCENE v.

[*Another room in the same.*]

Lovewit [*in Spanish costume, Parson*], *Officers, Mammon, Surly, Face, Kastril, Ananias, Tribulation, Drugger, Da[me] Pliant.*[1]

[LOVE.] What do you mean, my masters?
MAM. [*Without.*] 　　　　Open your door,
　Cheaters, bawds, conjurers.
OFF. [*Without.*] 　　Or we'll break it open.
LOVE. What warrant have you?
OFF. [*Without.*] 　　Warrant enough, sir,
　doubt not,
　If you'll not open it.
LOVE. 　　　　Is there an officer there?
OFF. [*Without.*] Yes, two or three for[2]
　failing.
LOVE. 　　　Have but patience,
　And I will open it straight.

[*Enter Face, as butler.*]

FACE. 　　　　　Sir, ha' you done?
　Is it a marriage? Perfect?
LOVE. 　　　　　Yes, my brain.
FACE. Off with your ruff and cloak then;
　be yourself, sir.
　　　　　[*Lovewit takes off his disguise.*]
SUR. [*Without.*] Down with the door!
KAS. [*Without.*] 'Slight, ding[3] it open.
LOVE. [*Opening the door.*] 　　Hold,
　Hold, gentlemen, what means this vio-
　lence? 　　　　　　　　10

[*Enter Mammon, Surly, Kastril, Ananias, Tribulation, and Officers.*]

MAM. Where is this collier?
SUR. 　　　　And my Captain Face?
MAM. These day-owls.
SUR. 　That are birding[4] in men's purses.
MAM. Madam Suppository.
KAS. 　　　　　Doxy, my sister.
ANA. 　　　　　Locusts
　Of the foul pit.
TRI. 　　Profane as Bel and the Dragon.
ANA. Worse than the grasshoppers, or the
　lice of Egypt.

LOVE. Good gentlemen, hear me. Are you
　officers,
　And cannot stay this violence?
OFF. [1.] 　　　　　Keep the peace.
LOVE. Gentlemen, what is the matter?
　Whom do you seek?
MAM. The chymical[5] cozener.
SUR. 　　　　And the captain pander.
KAS. The nun my suster.
MAM. 　　　　Madam Rabbi.
ANA. 　　　　　Scorpions 20
　And caterpillars.
LOVE. 　　Fewer at once, I pray you.
OFF. [1.] One after another, gentlemen, I
　charge you,
　By virtue of my staff—
ANA. 　　　　They are the vessels
　Of pride, lust, and the cart.
LOVE. 　　　Good zeal, lie still
　A little while.
TRI. 　　　Peace, Deacon Ananias.
LOVE. The house is mine here, and the
　doors are open; 　　　　　　（
　If there be any such persons as you seek
　for,
　Use your authority; search on, o' God's
　name.
　I am but newly come to town, and, find-
　ing
　This tumult 'bout my door, to tell you
　true, 　　　　　　　　30
　It somewhat mazed me, till my man here,
　fearing
　My more displeasure, told me he had
　done
　Somewhat an insolent part, let out my
　house
　(Belike presuming on my known aversion
　From any air o' the town while there was
　sickness)
　To a doctor and a captain, who, what
　they are
　Or where they be, he knows not.

They enter.[6]

MAM. 　　　　Are they gone?
LOVE. You may go in and search, sir.—
　　[*Exit Mammon.*] Here I find
　The empty walls worse than I left hem,
　smoked,

---

[1] All except Lovewit and the Parson are without or enter later.
[2] For fear of. 　　[3] Break. 　　[4] Thieving.

[5] Chemical.
[6] *I.e.*, the Officers, Tribulation, and Ananias
start their search.

A few cracked pots, and glasses, and a
    fornace; 40
The ceiling filled with poesies of the
    candle,
And "Madam with a dildo" [1] writ o' the
    walls.
Only one gentlewoman I met here,
That is within, that said she was a
    widow—

Kas. Ay, that's my suster; I'll go thump
    her. Where is she? [*Exit.*]

Love. And should ha' married a Spanish
    count, but he,
When he came to 't, neglected her so
    grossly
That I, a widower, am gone through with
    her.

Sur. How! Have I lost her then?

Love. Were you the Don, sir?
Good faith, now she does blame yo'
    extremely, and says 50
You swore and told her you had ta'en the
    pains
To dye your beard, and umber o'er your
    face,
Borrowed a suit and ruff, all for her
    love—
And then did nothing. What an over-
    sight
And want of putting forward, sir, was
    this!
Well fare an old hargubuzier [2] yet,
Could prime his poulder, and give fire,
    and hit,
All in a twinkling!

Mammon comes forth.

Mam. The whole nest are fled!

Love. What sort of birds were they?

Mam. A kind of choughs,
Or thievish daws, sir, that have picked
    my purse 60
Of eight score and ten pounds within
    these five weeks,
Beside my first materials, and my goods
That lie i' the cellar, which I am glad
    they ha' left,
I may have home yet.

Love. Think you so, sir?

Mam. Ay.

Love. By order of law, sir, but not other-
    wise.

Mam. Not mine own stuff?

Love. Sir, I can take no knowledge
That they are yours, but by public
    means.
If you can bring certificate that you were
    gulled of hem,
Or any formal writ out of a court
That you did cozen yourself, I will not
    hold them. 70

Mam. I'll rather lose hem.

Love. That you shall not, sir,
By me, in troth; upon these terms, they
    are yours.
What, should they ha' been, sir, turned
    into gold, all?

Mam. No.
I cannot tell. It may be they should.
    What then?

Love. What a great loss in hope have you
    sustained!

Mam. Not I; the commonwealth has.

Face. Ay, he would ha' built
The city new, and made a ditch about it
Of silver, should have run with cream
    from Hogsden,
That every Sunday in Moorfields the
    younkers [3]
And tits [4] and tomboys should have fed
    on, gratis. 80

Mam. I will go mount a turnip-cart, and
    preach
The end o' the world within these two
    months.—Surly,
What! In a dream?

Sur. Must I needs cheat myself
With that same foolish vice of honesty?
Come, let us go and hearken [5] out the
    rogues.
That Face I'll mark for mine, if e'er I
    meet him.

Face. If I can hear of him, sir, I'll bring
    you word
Unto your lodging; for, in troth, they
    were strangers
To me. I thought hem honest as myself,
    sir.

They come forth.

Tri. 'Tis well, the Saints shall not lose all
    yet. Go 90
And get some carts—

Love. For what, my zealous friends?

---

[1] Fragment of a ballad.
[2] Harquebusier, musketeer.
[3] Youths.
[4] Wenches.
[5] Inquire, search.

ANA. To bear away the portion of the righteous

Out of this den of thieves.

LOVE.   What is that portion?

ANA. The goods sometimes the orphans', that the Brethren

Bought with their silver pence.

LOVE.   What, those i' the cellar

The knight Sir Mammon claims?

ANA.   I do defy

The wicked Mammon; so do all the Brethren,

Thou profane man! I ask thee with what conscience

Thou canst advance that idol against us,

That have the seal? [1] Were not the shillings numbered   100

That made the pounds? Were not the pounds told out

Upon the second day of the fourth week

In the eighth month, upon the table dormant, [2]

The year of the last patience of the Saints,

Six hundred and ten?

LOVE.   Mine earnest, vehement botcher,

And deacon also, I cannot dispute with you;

But, if you get you not away the sooner,

I shall confute you with a cudgel.

ANA.   Sir!

TRI. Be patient, Ananias.

ANA.   I am strong,

And will stand up, well girt, against an host   110

That threaten Gad in exile.

LOVE.   I shall send you

To Amsterdam, to your cellar.

ANA.   I will pray there,

Against thy house. May dogs defile thy walls,

And wasps and hornets breed beneath thy roof,

This seat of falsehood, and this cave of coz'nage!

          [*Exeunt Ananias and Tribulation.*]

Drugger enters, and he beats him away.

LOVE. Another too?

DRUG.   Not I, sir; I am no Brother.

LOVE. Away, you Harry Nicholas! [3] Do you talk?   [*Exit Drugger.*]

---

[1] *I.e.*, of the chosen of God.

[2] Fixed, stationary.   [3] A notorious fanatic.

FACE. No, this was Abel Drugger.—(*To the Parson.*) Good sir, go,

And satisfy him; tell him all is done.

He stayed too long a-washing of his face.   120

The doctor, he shall hear of him at Westchester,

And of the captain, tell him, at Yarmouth, or

Some good port-town else, lying for a wind.—   [*Exit Parson.*]

If you [can] [4] get off the angry child now, sir—

[*Enter Kastril and Dame Pliant.*]

KAS. (*To his sister.*) Come on, you ewe; you have matched most sweetly, ha' you not?

Did not I say I would never ha' you tupped

But by a dubbed boy, [5] to make you a lady-tom?

'Slight, you are a mammet! [6] O, I could touse you now.

Death, mun [7] you marry, with a pox!

LOVE.   You lie, boy;

As sound as you; and I'm aforehand with you.

KAS. [*To Pliant.*]   Anon!   130

LOVE. Come, will you quarrel? I will feeze [8] you, sirrah;

Why do you not buckle to your tools?

KAS.   God's light,

This is a fine old boy as e'er I saw!

LOVE. What, do you change your copy [9] now? Proceed;

Here stands my dove. Stoop [10] at her if you dare.

KAS. 'Slight, I must love him! I cannot choose, i' faith,

And I should be hanged for 't! Suster, I protest

I honor thee for this match.

LOVE.   O, do you so, sir?

KAS. Yes, and thou canst take tabacco and drink, old boy,

I'll give her five hundred pound more to her marriage   140

Than her own state.

---

[4] From 1612 edn.   [7] Must.

[5] *I.e.*, a knight.   [8] Flog.

[6] Puppet.   [9] Theme, " tune."

[10] Swoop (a term of falconry). The name Kastril meant a hawk.

LOVE.   Fill a pipeful, Jeremy.

FACE. Yes; but go in and take it, sir.

LOVE.   We will.
I will be ruled by thee in anything,
Jeremy.

KAS. 'Slight, thou art not hidebound; thou
art a jovy [1] boy!
Come, let 's in, I pray thee, and take our
whiffs.

LOVE. Whiff in with your sister, brother
boy.—[*Exeunt Kastril and Dame
Pliant.*]
                     That master
That had received such happiness by a
servant,
In such a widow, and with so much
wealth,
Were very ungrateful if he would not
be
A little indulgent to that servant's
wit,   150
And help his fortune, though with some
small strain
Of his own candor.[2]—[*To the audience.*]
Therefore, gentlemen

And kind spectators, if I have outstripped
An old man's gravity or strict canon,
think
What a young wife and a good brain may
do—
Stretch age's truth sometimes, and crack
it too.—
Speak for thyself, knave.

FACE.   So I will, sir.—Gentlemen,
My part a little fell in this last scene,
Yet 'twas decorum.[3] And though I am
clean
Got off from Subtle, Surly, Mammon,
Doll,   160
Hot Ananias, Dapper, Drugger, all
With whom I traded, yet I put myself
On you, that are my country; [4] and this
pelf
Which I have got, if you do quit [5] me,
rests
To feast you often and invite new guests.
                        [*Exeunt.*]

THE END.

[1] Jovial.   [2] Integrity.   [3] Dramatic propriety.   [4] Jury.   [5] Acquit.

This comedy was first acted in the year 1610 by the King's Majesty's Servants. The
principal comedians were:

Ric. Burbadge	*Joh. Hemings*
Joh. Lowin	*Will. Ostler*
Hen. Condell	*Joh. Underwood*
Alex. Cooke	*Nic. Tooly*
Rob. Armin	*Will. Eglestone*

With the allowance of the Master of Revels.

THE HUE AND CRY AFTER CUPID[1]

BY

BEN JONSON

[*DRAMATIS PERSONÆ*

CUPID.
VULCAN.
HYMEN.
VENUS.

PYRACMON ⎫
BRONTES ⎬ *Cyclopes.*
STEROPES ⎭
GRACES 1, 2, and 3.

SCENE: *Imaginary.*

TIME: *Contemporary.*]

The worthy custom of honoring worthy marriages with these noble solemnities hath of late years advanced itself frequently with us, to the reputation no less of our court than nobles, expressing besides (through the difficulties of expense and travel, with the cheerfulness of undertaking) a most real affection in the personators, to those for whose sake they would sustain these persons. It behoves then us, that are trusted with a part of their honor in these celebrations, to do nothing in them beneath the dignity of either. With this proposed part of judgment, I adventure to give that abroad, which in my first conception I intended honorably fit; and, though it hath labored since, under censure, I, that know truth to be always of one stature and so like a rule as [2] *who bends it the least way must needs do an injury to the right, cannot but smile at their tyrannous ignorance, that will offer to slight me (in these things being an artificer) and give themselves a peremptory license to judge, who have never touched so much as to the bark or utter* [3] *shell of any knowl-*edge. *But their daring dwell with them. They have found a place to pour out their follies, and I a seat to sleep out the passage.*

The scene to this masque was a high, steep, red cliff, advancing itself into the clouds, figuring the place from whence (as I have been, not fabulously, informed) the honorable family of the Radcliffes first took their name, a clivo rubro,[4] *and is to be written with that orthography, as I have observed out of M[aster] Camden in his mention of the Earls of Sussex. This cliff was also a note of height, greatness, and antiquity, before which, on the two sides, were erected two pilasters, charged with spoils and trophies of Love and his mother, consecrate to marriage; amongst which were old and young persons figured, bound with roses, the wedding garments, rocks and spindles, hearts transfixed with arrows, others flaming, virgins' girdles, girlonds,[5] and worlds of suchlike, all wrought round and bold; and overhead two personages, Triumph and Victory, in flying postures, and twice so big as the life, in place of the arch, and holding a girlond of myrtle for the key— all which, with the pillars, seemed to be of burnished gold, and embossed out of the metal. Beyond the cliff was seen nothing but clouds, thick and obscure, till on the sudden, with a solemn music, a bright sky breaking forth, there were discovered first two doves,*

[1] This title was assigned to the masque by Gifford. The title in the 1616 folio reads: "The Description of the Masque, with the Nuptial Songs, at the Lord Viscount Haddington's Marriage at Court on the Shrove Tuesday at Night. 1608." On this occasion the bride was Lady Elizabeth Ratcliffe, or Radcliffe, daughter of Robert Earl of Sussex.

[2] That.   [3] Outer.   [4] From a red cliff.   [5] Garlands.

*then two swans,[1] with silver gears,[2] drawing
forth a triumphant chariot, in which Venus
sat, crowned with her star, and beneath her
the three Graces, or* Charites, *Aglaia,
Thalia, Euphrosyne, all attired according
to their antique figures. These from their
chariot alighted on the top of the cliff, and,
descending by certain abrupt and winding
passages, Venus having left her star only
flaming in her seat, came to the earth, the
Graces throwing girlonds all the way, and
began to speak.*

VENUS. It is no common cause, ye will
    conceive,
  My lovely Graces, makes your goddess
    leave
  Her state in heaven, tonight to visit
    earth.
  Love late is fled away, my eldest birth,
  Cupid, whom I did joy to call my son;
  And, whom long absent, Venus is un-
    done.
  Spy, if you can, his footsteps on this
    green,
  For here, as I am told, he late hath
    been,
  With divers of his brethren,[3] lending
    light
  From their best flames to gild a glorious
    night,   10
  Which I not grudge at, being done for
    her
  Whose honors to mine own I still prefer.
  But he not yet returning, I am in fear
  Some gentle Grace or innocent Beauty
    here
  Be taken with him, or he hath surprised
  A second Psyche, and lives here dis-
    guised.
  Find ye no tract [4] of his strayed feet?
1 GRACE.   Not I.
2 GRACE. Nor I.
3 GRACE.   Nor I.

[1] Jonson's note runs: "Both doves and swans
were sacred to this goddess, and as well with the
one as the other; her chariot is induced by
Ovid, L. x and xi, *Metamor.*" The editors of the
present text omit most of Jonson's notes on this
masque and a small amount of similar material
incorporated in the stage directions.
[2] Trappings.
[3] "Alluding to the Loves in the Queen's
Masque before" (Jonson's note referring to his
Masque of Beauty).
[4] Track, trace.

VENUS.   Stay, nymphs,
  we then will try
  A nearer way. Look [5] all these ladies'
    eyes,
  And see if there he not concealéd lies, 20
  Or in their bosoms twixt their swelling
    breasts
  (The wag affects to make himself such
    nests).
  Perchance he hath got some simple
    heart to hide
  His subtle shape in. I will have him
    cried,[6]
  And all his virtues told, that, when
    they know
  What sprite he is, she soon may let
    him go,
  That guards him now, and think her-
    self right blessed
  To be so timely rid of such a guest.
  Begin, soft Graces, and proclaim reward
  To her that brings him in. Speak to
    be heard.   30
1 GRACE. Beauties, have ye seen this toy,
  Calléd Love, a little boy,
  Almost naked, wanton, blind,
  Cruel now, and then as kind?
  If he be amongst ye, say.
  He is Venus' runaway.
2 GRACE. She that will but now discover
  Where the wingéd wag doth hover,
  Shall tonight receive a kiss,
  How or where herself would wish;   40
  But who brings him to his mother,
  Shall have that kiss, and another.
3 GRACE. H' hath of marks about him
    plenty;
  You shall know him among twenty.
  All his body is a fire,
  And his breath a flame entire,
  That being shot, like lightning, in,
  Wounds the heart, but not the skin.
1 GRACE. At his sight, the sun hath turned;
  Neptune in the waters burned;   50
  Hell hath felt a greater heat;
  Jove himself forsook his seat.
  From the center [7] to the sky
  Are his trophies rearéd high.
2 GRACE. Wings he hath, which though
    ye clip,
  He will leap from lip to lip,

[5] Look at, examine.
[6] Proclaimed by the public crier.
[7] Center of the world.

Over liver, lights, and heart,
But not stay in any part;
And, if chance his arrow misses,
He will shoot himself in kisses.   60
3 GRACE. He doth bear a golden bow,
And a quiver, hanging low,
Full of arrows that outbrave
Dian's shafts, where, if he have
Any head more sharp than other,
With that first he strikes his mother.
1 GRACE. Still the fairest are his fuel.
When his days are to be cruel,
Lovers' hearts are all his food,
And his baths their warmest blood.   70
Naught but wounds his hand doth
season,
And he hates none like to Reason.
2 GRACE. Trust him not; his words, though
sweet,
Seldom with his heart do meet.
All his practice is deceit,
Every gift it is a bait,
Not a kiss but poison bears,
And most treason in his tears.
3 GRACE. Idle minutes are his reign;
Then the straggler makes his gain   80
By presenting maids with toys,
And would have ye think hem joys;
'Tis the ambition of the elf
To have all childish as himself.
1 GRACE. If by these ye please to know
him,
Beauties, be not nice,[1] but show him.
2 GRACE. Though ye had a will to hide
him,
Now, we hope, ye'll not abide him—
3 GRACE. Since ye hear his falser play,
And that he is Venus' runaway.   90

*At this, from behind the trophies, Cupid
discovered himself and came forth
armed, attended with twelve Boys, most
anticly attired, that represented the
Sports and pretty Lightnesses that accompany Love, under the titles of* Joci
and Risus, *and are said to wait on*
Venus, *as she is Prefect of Marriage.*

CUPID. Come, my little jocund Sports,
Come away; the time now sorts [2]
With your pastime. This same night
Is Cupid's day. Advance your light.
With your revel fill the room,
That our triumphs be not dumb.

[1] Scrupulous.   [2] Agrees.

*Wherewith they fell into a subtle, capricious
dance, to as odd a music, each of them
bearing two torches, and nodding with
their antic faces, with other variety of
ridiculous gesture, which gave much
occasion of mirth and delight to the
spectators.   The dance ended, Cupid
went forward.*

CUPID. Well done, antics! Now my bow
And my quiver bear to show
That these Beauties here may know
By what arms this feat was done,   100
That hath so much honor won
Unto Venus and her son.

*At which his Mother apprehended him and,
circling him in with the Graces, began
to demand.*

VENUS. What feat, what honor is it that
you boast,
My little straggler? I had given you
lost,
With all your games here.
CUPID.   Mother?
VENUS.   Yes, sir, she.
What might your glorious cause of
triumph be?
Ha' you shot Minerva or the Thespian
dames?
Heat [3] aged Ops again with youthful
flames?
Or have you made the colder Moon to
visit
Once more a sheepcote? Say, what con-
quest is it   110
Can make you hope such a renown to
win?
Is there a second Hercules brought to
spin?
Or, for some new disguise, leaves Jove
his thunder?
CUPID. Nor that, nor those, and yet no
less a wonder—
Which to tell, I may not stay.
And there slips from her.

*Here Hymen, the God of Marriage, entered,
and was so induced here as you have
him described in my* Hymenæi.

Hymen's presence bids away;
'Tis already at his night;

[3] Heated.

He can give you farther light.
You, my Sports, may here abide
Till I call to light the bride.   120
HYMEN. Venus, is this a time to quit your
    car?
To stoop to earth, to leave alone your
    star,
Without your influence, and, on such a
    night,
Which should be crowned with your
    most cheering sight,
As [1] you were ignorant of what were
    done
By Cupid's hand, your all-triumphing
    son?
Look on this state, [2] and, if you yet
    not know
What crown there shines, whose scepter
    here doth grow,
Think on thy loved Æneas; and what
    name
Maro, the golden trumpet [3] of his
    fame,   130
Gave him, read thou in this: a prince
    that draws
By example more than others do by
    laws,
That is so just to his great act and
    thought,
To do, not what kings may, but what
    kings ought;
Who, out of piety, unto peace is vowed,
To spare his subjects, yet to quell the
    proud,
And dares esteem it the first fortitude
To have his passions, foes at home, sub-
    dued;
That was reserved, until the Parcæ spun
Their whitest wool and then his thread
    begun,   140
Which thread, when treason would
    have burst, [4] a soul
(Today renowned and added to my roll)
Opposed; and, by that act, to his name
    did bring
The honor to be saver of his king—
This king, whose worth, if gods for vir-
    tue love,
Should Venus with the same affections
    move

[1] As if.   [2] Canopied throne.   [3] Trumpeter.
[4] Jonson's note runs: "In that monstrous
conspiracy of E[arl] Gowry." Haddington aided
the future James I to put down the conspiracy
in 1600.

As her Æneas, and no less endear
Her love to his safety than when she
    did cheer,
After a tempest, long-afflicted Troy,
Upon the Lybian shore, and brought
    them joy.   150
VENUS. I love, and know his virtues,
    and do boast
Mine own renown when I renown him
    most.
My Cupid's absence I forgive and praise,
That me to such a present grace could
    raise.
His champion shall hereafter be my care.
But speak his bride, and what her vir-
    tues are.
HYMEN. She is a noble virgin, styled the
    Maid
Of the Red Cliff, and hath her dowry
    weighed
No less in virtue, blood, and form than
    gold;
Thence, where my pillar's reared (you
    may behold)   160
Filled with Love's trophies, doth she
    take her name.
Those pillars did uxorious Vulcan frame
Against [5] this day; and underneath that
    hill
He and his Cyclopes are forging still
Some strange and curious piece t' adorn
    the night,
And give these gracéd nuptials greater
    light.

*Here Vulcan presented himself, as over-
    hearing Hymen, attired in a cassock
    girt to him, with bare arms, his hair
    and beard rough, his hat of blue and
    ending in a cone, in his hand a ham-
    mer and tongs, as coming from the forge.*

VULCAN. Which I have done—the best of
    all my life—
And have my end, if it but please my
    wife,
And she commend it, to the labored
    worth.
Cleave, solid rock, and bring the wonder
    forth!   170

*At which, with a loud and full music,
    the cliff parted in the midst and dis-*

[5] In preparation for.

covered an illustrious [1] *concave, filled with an ample and glistering light, in which an artificial sphere was made of silver, eighteen foot in the diameter, that turned perpetually; the* coluri [2] *were heightened with gold; so were the arctic and antarctic circles, the tropics, the equinoctial, the meridian and horizon; only the zodiac was of pure gold, in which the Masquers, under the characters of the twelve signs, were placed, answering them in number, whose offices, with the whole frame, as it turned, Vulcan went forward to describe.*

VULCAN. It is a sphere I have formed round and even,
In due proportion to the sphere of heaven,
With all his [3] lines and circles that compose
The perfect'st form, and aptly do disclose
The heaven of marriage (which I title it),
Within whose zodiac I have made to sit,
In order of the signs, twelve sacred powers
That are presiding at all nuptial hours:
1. The first, in Aries' place, respecteth pride
    Of youth and beauty, graces in the bride.   180
2. In Taurus, he loves strength and manliness,
    The virtues which the bridegroom should profess.
3. In Gemini, that noble power is shown,
    That twins their hearts, and doth of two make one.
4. In Cancer, he that bids the wife give way
    With backward yielding to her husband's sway.
5. In Leo, he that doth instill the heat
    Into the man, which from the following seat
6. Is tempered so as he that looks from thence
    Sees yet they keep a Virgin innocence.   190

7. In Libra's room, rules he that doth supply
    All happy beds with sweet equality.
8. The Scorpion's place he fills, that makes the jars,
    And stings in wedlock little strifes and wars,
9. Which he in th' Archer's throne doth soon remove
    By making with his shafts new wounds of love.
10. And those the follower with more heat inspires,
    As in the Goat the sun renews his fires.
11. In wet Aquarius' stead, reigns he that showers
    Fertility upon the genial bowers.   200
12. Last, in the Fishes' place, sits he doth say,
    "In married joys all should be dumb as they."
And this hath Vulcan for his Venus done,
To grace the chaster triumph of her son.
VENUS. And for this gift will I to heaven return,
And vow forever that my lamp shall burn
With pure and chastest fire, or never shine
But when it mixeth with thy sphere and mine.

Here Venus returned to her chariot with the Graces, while Vulcan, calling out the Priests of Hymen, who were the musicians, was interrupted by Pyracmon (one of the Cyclopes), . . . Brontes, and Steropes. . . .

VULCAN. Sing then, ye priests.
PYRACMON.   Stay, Vulcan, shall not these   209
Come forth and dance?
VULCAN.   Yes, my Pyracmon, please
The eyes of these spectators with our art.
PYRACMON. Come here, then, Brontes; bear a Cyclop's part,
And Steropes; both with your sledges stand,
And strike a time unto them as they land,

---

[1] Brilliantly lighted.
[2] The great circles of the celestial sphere intersecting at the poles.   [3] Its.

And, as they forwards come, still guide
    their paces
In musical and sweet proportioned
    graces,
While I upon the work and frame at-
    tend,
And Hymen's priests forth, at their
    seasons, send
To chaunt their hymns, and make this
    square admire
Our great artificer, the god of fire.   220

*Here the Musicians, attired in yellow,
with wreaths of marjoram, and veils like
Hymen's priests, sung the first staff of the
following epithalamion, which, because it
was sung in pieces between the dances,
showed to be so many several songs, but
was made to be read an entire poem. After
the song, they came forth (descending in
an oblique motion) from the zodiac, and
danced their first dance; then, music inter-
posed (but varied with voices, only keeping
the same chorus), they danced their second
dance. So after, their third and fourth
dances, which were all full of elegancy and
curious device. The two latter were made
by M[aster] Tho. Giles,[1] the two first by
M[aster] Hie. Herne,[2] who, in the persons
of the two Cyclopes, beat a time to them with
their hammers. The tunes were M[aster]
Alphonso Ferrabosco's.[3] The device and act
of the scene M[aster] Inigo Jones [4] his, with
addition of the trophies. For the invention
of the whole and the verses, Assertor qui
dicat esse meos, imponet plagiario pu-
dorem.[5]
The attire of the Masquers throughout
was most graceful and noble, partaking of
the best both ancient and later figure; the
colors carnation and silver, enriched both
with embroidery [6] and lace; the dressing of
their heads, feathers and jewels; and so*

*excellently ordered to the rest of the habit
as all would suffer under any description
after the show. Their performance of all, so
magnificent and illustrous that nothing can
add to the seal of it but the subscription of
their names:* [7]

The Duke of Lennox	*Lord Hay*
Earl of Arundel	*Lord Sankre*
Earl of Pembroke	*Sir Ro. Riche*
Earl of Montgomery	*Sir Jo. Kennethie*
Lord D'Aubigny	*[Master of Mar]*[8]
Lord of Walden	*Mr. Ersskins*

EPITHALAMION

Up, youths and virgins, up, and praise
The god whose nights outshine his days—
Hymen, whose hallowed rites
Could never boast of brighter lights;
Whose bands pass liberty.
Two of your troop, that with the morn were
    free,
Are now waged to his war.
And what they are,
If you'll perfection see,
Yourselves must be.   10
Shine, Hesperus, shine forth, thou wishéd
    star!

What joy or honors can compare
With holy nuptials, when they are
Made out of equal parts
Of years, of states, of hands, of hearts,
When, in the happy choice,
The spouse and spouséd have the fore-
    most voice?
Such, glad of Hymen's war,
Live what they are,
And long perfection see;   20
And such ours be.
Shine, Hesperus, shine forth, thou wishéd
    star!

The solemn state of this one night
Were fit to last an age's light;

---

[1] Formerly Master of the Children of Paul's
and later instructor in music to the princes
royal.
   [2] Hierome Herne, a minor musician and
dancing master.
   [3] A well-known Italian dancing master.
   [4] The most famous architect of the day and
inventor of scenery and costumes for court
masques. He was on constantly shifting terms
of enmity and friendship with Jonson.
   [5] The declarer who calls them mine will bring
shame upon the plagiarist.
   [6] Embroidery.

[7] Gifford in his 1816 edn. of Jonson, VII, 94,
quotes a letter from Rowland White to the Earl
of Shrewsbury: "The great masque intended for
my L. Haddington's marriage is now *the only
thing thought upon* at court, by 5 English: L.
Arundel, L. Pemb., L. Montgomery, L. Theoph.
Howard, and Sir Robt. Rich; and by 7 Scots:
D. Lennox, D'Aubigny, Hay, Mr. of Mar, young
Erskine, Sankier, and Kennedy. It will cost
them about 300 *l.* a man."
   [8] Supplied from White's letter **above.**

But there are rites behind
Have less of state, but more of kind: [1]
Love's wealthy crop of kisses,
And fruitful harvest of his mother's blisses.
Sound then to Hymen's war—
That what these are,   30
Who will perfection see,
May haste to be.
Shine, Hesperus, shine forth, thou wishéd
    star!

Love's commonwealth consists of toys;
His council are those antic boys,
Games, Laughter, Sports, Delights,
That triumph with him on these nights,
To whom we must give way,
For now their reign begins, and lasts till
    day.
They sweeten Hymen's war,   40
And, in that jar,
Make all that married be,
Perfection see.
Shine, Hesperus, shine forth, thou wishéd
    star!

Why stays the bridegroom to invade
Her that would be a matron made?
Good night, whilst yet we may
Good night, to you a virgin, say;
Tomorrow rise the same   49
Your mother is, and use a nobler name.
Speed well in Hymen's war

  ᵕ Nature.

That what you are,
By your perfection we
And all may see.
Shine, Hesperus, shine forth, thou wishéd
    star!

Tonight is Venus' vigil kept.
This night no bridegroom ever slept;
And, if the fair bride do,
The married say, 'tis his fault, too.
Wake then, and let your lights   60
Wake too; for they'll tell nothing of your
    nights
But that in Hymen's war
You perfect are.
And such perfection we
Do pray should be.
Shine, Hesperus, shine forth, thou wishéd
    star!

That, ere the rosy-fingered morn
Behold nine moons, there may be born
A babe, t' uphold the fame   69
Of Radcliffe's blood and Ramsey's [2] name,
That may, in his great seed,
Wear the long honors of his father's deed.
Such fruits of Hymen's war
Most perfect are;
And all perfection we
Wish you should see.
Shine, Hesperus, shine forth, thou wishéd
    star!

  [2] The family name of Viscount Haddington.

THE SAD SHEPHERD
OR
A TALE OF ROBIN HOOD

BY

BEN JONSON

THE PERSONS OF THE PLAY

ROBIN HOOD, *the chief woodman,*[1] *master of the feast.*
MARIAN, *his lady, the mistress.*

THEIR FAMILY [2]

FRIAR TUCK, *the chaplain and steward.*
LITTLE JOHN, *bow bearer.*[3]
SCARLET } *two brothers, huntsmen.*
SCATHLOCK }
GEORGE A GREENE, *huisher* [4] *of the bower.*[5]
MUCH, *Robin Hood's bailiff or acater.*[6]

THE GUESTS INVITED

CLARION, *the rich*
LIONEL, *the courteous*
ALKEN, *the sage* } *shepherds.*
EGLAMOUR, *the sad*
KAROLIN, *the kind*

MELLIFLEUR, *the sweet*
AMIE, *the gentle* } *shepherdesses.*
EARINE, *the beautiful*

THE TROUBLES UNEXPECTED

MAUDLIN, *the envious, the Witch of Papple-wick.*
DOUCE, *the proud, her daughter.*
LOREL, *the rude, a swine'ard,* [7] *the witch's son.*
PUCK-HAIRY, *or Robin Goodfellow, their hine.*[8]

THE RECONCILER

REUBEN, *a devout hermit.*

The scene is Sherwood, consisting of a landtshape [9] *of forest, hills, valleys, cottages, a castle, a river, pastures, herds, flocks, all full of country simplicity. Robin Hood's bower; his well; the witch's dimble;* [10] *the swine'ard's oak; the hermit's cell.*

[TIME: *Late Middle Ages.*]

PROLOGUE [11]

He that hath feasted you these forty years,
And fitted fables for your finer ears,
Although at first he scarce could hit the bore,[12]

Yet you, with patience heark'ning more and more,
At length have grown up to him, and made known
The working of his pen is now your own.
He prays you would vouchsafe, for your own sake,
To hear him this once more, but sit awake.
And, though he now present you with such wool
As from mere [13] English flocks his muse can pull,   10
He hopes when it is made up into cloth,

---

[1] Huntsman.   [2] Followers.
[3] An under officer charged with the prevention of trespassing.
[4] Usher, doorkeeper.   [5] Rustic cottage.
[6] Caterer, purchaser of provisions.
[7] Swineherd.   [9] Landscape.
[8] Hind, servant.   [10] Dingle, narrow valley.
[11] In the original the prologue follows the argument of the first act.
[12] *I.e.*, suit the caliber of your intelligence.

[13] Pure.

Not the most curious head here will be
　　loath
To wear a hood of it, it being a fleece
To match or [1] those of Sicily or Greece.
His scene is Sherwood, and his play a tale
Of Robin Hood's inviting from the Vale
Of Be'voir [2] all the shepherds to a feast,
Where by the casual absence of one guest
The mirth is troubled much, and in one
　　man　　　　　　　　　　　　　　　　　19
As much of sadness shown as passion can—
The sad young shepherd, whom we here
　　present,

*The Sad Shepherd passeth silently over the
　　　　　　　　　　　　　　　　　stage.*

Like his woes' figure, dark and discontent
For his lost love, who in the Trent is said
To have miscarried. 'Las! What knows the
　　head
Of a calm river whom the feet have
　　drowned?
Hear what his sorrows are, and, if they
　　wound
Your gentle breasts, so that the end crown
　　all,
Which in the scope of one day's chance
　　may fall,
Old Trent will send you more such tales
　　as these,
And shall grow young again as one doth
　　please.　　　　　　　　　　　　　　　30

*Here the Prologue, thinking to end, returns
　　upon a new purpose and speaks on.*

But here's an heresy of late let fall,
That mirth by no means fits a pastoral.
Such say so, who can make none, he pre-
　　sumes;
Else there's no scene more properly as-
　　sumes
The sock. [3] For whence can sport in kind [4]
　　arise
But from the rural routs and families?
Safe on this ground then, we not fear today
To tempt your laughter by our rustic play;
Wherein if we distaste, [5] or be cried down,
We think we therefore shall not leave the
　　town,　　　　　　　　　　　　　　　40

[1] Either.
[2] Belvoir, the seat of the Earls of Rutland.
[3] Shoe worn by actors of classical comedy.
[4] In nature, naturally.　　[5] Disgust, displease.

Nor that the forewits, [6] that would draw
　　the rest
Unto their liking, always like the best.
The wise and knowing critic will not say,
This worst, or better is, before he weigh
Where [7] every piece be perfect in the kind, [8]
And then, though in themselves he differ-
　　ence find,
Yet, if the place require it where they stood,
The equal fitting makes them equal good.
You shall have love and hate and jealousy,
As well as mirth and rage and melancholy,
Or whatsoever else may either move　　51
Or stir affections, [9] and your likings prove.
But that no style for pastoral should go
Current but what is stamped with "Ah"
　　and "O,"
Who judgeth so, may singularly err,
As if all poesy had one character
In which what were not written, were not
　　right,
Or that the man who made such one poor
　　flight
In his whole life, had with his wingéd skill
Advanced him upmost on the muses' hill, 60
When he like poet yet remains, as those
Are painters who can only make a rose.
From such your wits redeem you, or your
　　chance,
Lest to a greater height you do advance
Of folly, to contemn those that are known
Artificers, and trust such as are none.

The Argument of the First Act

Robin Hood, having invited all the
shepherds and shepherdesses of the Vale
of Be'voir to a feast in the Forest of Sherwood, and, trusting to his mistress, Maid
Marian, with her woodmen, to kill him
venison against [10] the day, having left the
like charge with Friar Tuck, his chaplain
and steward, to command the rest of his
merry men to see the bower made ready
and all things in order for the enter-　[10
tainment, meeting with his guests at their
entrance into the wood, welcomes and
conducts them to his bower, where, by
the way, he receives the relation of the
Sad Shepherd, Eglamour, who is fallen
into a deep melancholy for the loss of his
beloved Earine, reported to have been
drowned in passing over the Trent some

[6] Critics.　　　　[7] Whether.　　　　[8] Type.
[9] Emotions.　　　　[10] In preparation for.

few days before. They endeavor in what they can to comfort him, but, his dis- [20 ease having taken so strong root, all is in vain, and they are forced to leave him. In the meantime Marian is come from hunting with the huntsmen, where the lovers interchangeably express their loves. Robin Hood inquires if she hunted the deer at force [1] and what sport he made, how long he stood, and what head [2] he bore; all which is briefly answered with a relation of breaking him up,[3] and the [30 raven and her bone, the suspect [4] had of that raven to be Maudlin, the Witch of Papplewick, whom one of the huntsmen met i' the morning at the rousing of the deer, and is confirmed by her, being then in Robin Hood's kitchen, i' the chimney corner broiling the same bit which was thrown to the raven at the quarry [5] or fall of the deer. Marian, being gone in to show the deer to some of the shepherdesses, [40 returns instantly to the scene discontented, sends away the venison she had killed to her they call the Witch, quarrels with her love, Robin Hood, abuseth him and his guests, the shepherds, and so departs, leaving them all in wonder and perplexity.

Act I. Scene i.

[Robin Hood's bower.] [6]

Eglamour.

EG. Here she was wont to go, and here, and here—
Just where those daisies, pinks, and violets grow!
The world may find the spring by following her,
For other print her airy steps ne'er left.
Her treading would not bend a blade of grass,
Or shake the downy blowball [7] from his stalk!
But like the soft west wind she shot along,

---

[1] Ran the deer down with dogs instead of slaying it with weapons.
[2] Horns.   [4] Suspicion.
[3] *I.e.*, cutting up the deer.   [5] Cutting up.
[6] The scene remains the same throughout the act.
[7] Dandelion's head gone to seed.

And, where she went, the flowers took thickest root,
As she had sowed hem [8] with her odorous foot.

Act I. Scene ii.

[To him,] Marian, Tuck, John, Woodmen, etc.

MAR. Know you, or can you guess, my merry men,
What 'tis that keeps your master Robin Hood
So long both from his Marian and the wood?
TUCK. Forsooth, madam, he will be here by noon,
And prays it of your bounty, as a boon,
That you by then have killed him venison some
To feast his jolly friends, who hither come
In threaves [9] to frolic with him and make cheer.
Here's Little John hath harbored [10] you a deer,
I see by his tackling.[11]
JOHN.   And a hart of ten,[12]   10
I trow he be, madam, or blame your men,
For by his slot,[13] his entries,[14] and his port,[15]
His frayings,[16] fewmets [17] he doth promise sport
And standing fore [18] the dogs; he bears a head
Large and well-beamed, with all rights summed [19] and spread.
MAR. Let's rouse him quickly, and lay on the hounds.
JOHN. Scathlock is ready with them on the grounds;
So is his brother Scarlet. Now they 'ave found
His lair, they have him sure within the pound.[20]

---

[8] Them.   [11] Equipment.
[9] Numbers.   [12] *I.e.*, ten-pronged horns.
[10] Tracked down.   [13] Track.
[14] Openings made in the thickets by the deer.
[15] Weight indicated by the depth of his footprints.
[16] Velvet rubbed from his antlers.
[17] Dung of a deer.   [18] Before.
[19] With all tines completed.
[20] *I.e.*, in a hopeless position.

Mar. Away then! When my Robin bids
    a feast,   20
'Twere sin in Marian to defraud a guest.
[*Exeunt Marian and John with the Wood-*
                             men.]

Act I. Scene iii.

Tuck, George a Greene, Much, Eglamour.[1]

Tuck. And I, the chaplain, here am left
    to be
Steward today, and charge you all in fee[2]
To don your liveries, see the bower
    dressed,
And fit the fine devices for the feast.
You, George, must care to make the
    baldric[3] trim,
And garland that must crown or her or
    him
Whose flock this year hath brought the
    earliest lamb.
George. Good Father Tuck, at your com-
    mands I am
To cut the table out o' the greensward,
Or any other service for my lord,   10
To carve the guests large seats and these
    laid in
With turf as soft and smooth as the
    mole's skin,
And hang the bulléd[4] nosegays 'bove
    their heads . . . .[5]
The piper's bank whereon to sit and
    play,
And a fair dial to mete out the day.
Our master's feast shall want no just
    delights;
His entertainments must have all the
    rites.
Much. Ay, and all choice that plenty
    can send in—
Bread, wine, acates,[6] fowl, feather, fish,
    or fin,
For which my father's nets have swept
    the Trent.   20

Eglamour falls in with them.

Eg. And ha' you found her?
Much.   Whom?
Eg.   My drownéd love,
Earine! The sweet Earine!

The bright and beautiful Earine!
Have you not heard of my Earine?
Just by your father's mills (I think I am
    right—
Are not you Much the Miller's son?)—
Much.   I am.
Eg. And baily[7] to brave Robin Hood?
Much.   The same.
Eg. Close by your father's mills, Earine,
Earine was drowned! O my Earine!
    (Old Maudlin tells me so, and Douce, her
        daughter.)   30
Ha' you swept the river, say you, and
    not found her?
Much. For fowl and fish we have.
Eg.   O, not for her?
You are goodly friends, right charita-
    ble men!
Nay, keep your way and leave me; make
    your toys,
Your tales, your poesies, that you talked
    of—all
Your entertainments. You not injure me.
Only if I may enjoy my cypress wreath,
And you will let me weep, 'tis all I ask,
Till I be turned to water as was she!
And, troth, what less suit can you grant
    a man?   40
Tuck. His fantasy[8] is hurt; let us now
    leave him;
The wound is yet too fresh to admit
    searching.   [*Exit.*]
Eg. Searching? Where should I search,
    or on what track?
Can my slow drop of tears or this dark
    shade
About my brows enough describe her
    loss?
Earine! O, my Earine's loss!
No, no, no, no; this heart will break first.
George. How will this sad disaster strike
    the ears
Of bounteous Robin Hood, our gentle
    master!   [*Exit.*]
Much. How will it mar his mirth, abate
    his feast,   50
And strike a horror into every guest!
                          [*Exit.*]
Eg. If I could knit whole clouds about
    my brows,
And weep like Swithin[9] or those wat'ry
    signs,

---

[1] Enters later   [3] Belt.
[2] Fealty.   [4] Swollen, budding.
[5] The rime and sense indicate that at least one
line has here dropped out.   [6] Cates, dainties.

[7] Bailiff.   [8] Imagination.
[9] Patron saint of rainy weather.

The Kids [1] that rise then, and drown all
  the flocks
Of those rich shepherds dwelling in this
  vale,
Those careless shepherds that did let
  her drown,
Then I did something; or could make old
  Trent
Drunk with my sorrow, to start out in
  breaches
To drown their herds, their cattle, and
  their corn,
Break down their mills, their dams, o'er-
  turn their weirs,   60
And see their houses and whole liveli-
  hood
Wrought into water with her, all were
  good—
I'ld kiss the torrent and those whirls of
  Trent
That sucked her in, my sweet Earine!
When they have cast their body [2] on
  the shore,
And it comes up as tainted as them-
  selves,
All pale and bloodless, I will love it still,
For all that they can do, and make hem
  mad
To see how I will hug it in mine arms,
And hang upon the looks, dwell on her
  eyes,   70
Feed round about her lips, and eat her
  kisses,
Suck of her drownèd flesh!—and where's
  their malice? [3]
Not all their envious sousing can change
  that.
But I will study some revenge past this!
I pray you, give me leave, for I will study,
Though all the bells, pipes, tabors, tim-
  burines [4] ring,
That you can plant about me; I will study.

Act I. Scene iv.

To him, Robin Hood, Clarion, Mellifleur,
Lionel, Amie, Alken, Tuck, Servants,
*   with music of all sorts.*

Rob. Welcome, bright Clarion and sweet
  Mellifleur,
The courteous Lionel, fair Amie, all

My friends and neighbors, to the jolly
  bower
Of Robin Hood and to the greenwood
  walks!
Now that the shearing of your sheep is
  done,
And the washed flocks are lighted [5] of
  their wool,
The smoother ewes are ready to receive
The mounting rams again; and both do
  feed,
As either promised, to increase your
  breed
At eaning [6] time, and bring you lusty
  twins.   10
Why should or you or we so much forget
The season in ourselves as not to make
Use of our youth and spirits to awake
The nimble hornpipe [7] and the timbu-
  rine,
And mix our songs and dances in the
  wood,
And each of us cut down a triumph
  bough?
Such were the rites the youthful June
  allow.
Cla. They were, gay Robin; but the sourer
  sort
Of shepherds [8] now disclaim in [9] all such
  sport,
And say our flocks the while are poorly
  fed,   20
When with such vanities the swains are
  led.
Tuck. Would they, wise Clarion, were
  not hurried more
With covetise [10] and rage, when to their
  store
They add the poor man's eanling, [11] and
  dare sell
Both fleece and carcass, not gi'ing him
  the fell,
When to one goat they reach that prickly
  weed,
Which maketh all the rest forbear to
  feed,
Or strew tods' [12] hairs, or with their tails
  do sweep
The dewy grass, to doff the simpler
  sheep,

[1] A group of stars supposed to influence hurricanes.
[2] *I.e.*, the body held by the waters.
[3] Power to harm.   [4] Tambourines.
[5] Lightened.   [7] A musical instrument.
[6] Yeaning, lambing.
[8] Satirical allusion to the Puritans.
[9] Declaim against.   [11] Yeanling, lamb.
[10] Covetousness.   [12] Foxes'.

Or dig deep pits their neighbor's neat [1]
to vex, 30
To drown the calves and crack the heif-
ers' necks,
Or with pretense of chasing thence the
brock [2]
Send in a cur to worry the whole flock!
Lio. O friar, those are faults that are not
seen;
Ours open and of worst example been. [3]
They call ours pagan pastimes, that in-
fect
Our blood with ease, our youth with all
neglect,
Our tongues with wantonness, our
thoughts with lust;
And what they censure [4] ill, all others
must.
Rob. I do not know what their sharp sight
may see 40
Of late, but I should think it still might
be,
As 'twas, a happy age, when on the
plains
The woodmen met the damsels, and the
swains,
The neat'ards, [5] plowmen, and the pipers
loud,
And each did dance, some to the kit or
crowd, [6]
Some to the bagpipe; some the tabret [7]
moved,
And all did either love or were beloved.
Lio. The dextrous shepherd then would
try his sling,
Then dart his hook at daisies, then
would sing,
Sometimes would wrastle.
Cla. Ay, and with a lass, 50
And give her a new garment on the
grass [8]
After a course [9] at barleybreak or base. [10]
Lio. And all these deeds were seen with-
out offense,
Or the least hazard o' their innocence.
Rob. Those charitable times had no mis-
trust;
Shepherds knew how to love and not
to lust.

Cla. Each minute that we lose thus, I
confess,
Deserves a censure on us, more or less,
But that a sadder chance hath given
allay [11]
Both to the mirth and music of this
day. 60
Our fairest shepherdess we had of late,
Here upon Trent, is drowned, for whom
her mate,
Young Eglamour, a swain, who best
could tread
Our country dances, and our games did
lead,
Lives like the melancholy turtle, [12]
drowned
Deeper in woe than she in water, crowned
With yew and cypress, and will scarce
admit
The physic of our presence to his fit.
Lio. Sometimes he sits, and thinks all
day, then walks,
Then thinks again, and sighs, weeps,
laughs, and talks, 70
And twixt his pleasing frenzy [13] and sad
grief
Is so distracted as [14] no sought relief
By all our studies can procure his peace.
Cla. The passion finds in him that [15] large
increase
As we doubt hourly we shall lose him too.
Rob. You should not cross him then,
whate'er you do,
For fant'sy stopped will soon take fire
and burn
Into an anger, or to a frenzy turn.
Cla. Nay, so we are advised by Alken
here,
A good sage shepherd, who, although he
wear 80
An old worn hat and cloak, can tell us
more
Than all the forward fry that boast their
lore.
Lio. See, yonder comes the brother of
the maid,
Young Karolin! How curious and
afraid
He is at once, willing to find him out,
And loath to offend him.
Alk. Sure he's here about.

[1] Cattle.
[2] Badger.
[3] Are.
[4] Judge.
[5] Neatherds.
[6] Two varieties of fiddle.
[7] Taboret, a small drum.
[8] Stain her dress green.
[9] Round.
[10] Varieties of boys' games.
[11] Abatement, check.
[12] Turtledove.
[13] Happy delirium.
[14] That.
[15] Such.

Act I. Scene v.

Robin Hood, Clarion, Mellifleur, Lionel, Amie, Alken, Karolin; Eglamour, sitting upon a bank by.

Cla. See where he sits.
Eg.   It will be rare, rare, rare!
An exquisite revenge! But peace, no
    words—
Not for the fairest fleece of all the flock!
If it be known afore, 'tis all worth noth-
    ing.
I'll carve it on the trees and in the turf,
On every greensworth [1] and in every path,
Just to the margin of the cruel Trent.
There will I knock the story in the
    ground,
In smooth great pebble and moss fill it
    round,
Till the whole country read how she
    was drowned,   10
And with the plenty of salt tears there
    shed
Quite alter the complexion of the spring.
Or I will get some old, old grandam
    thither,
Whose rigid foot, but dipped into the
    water,
Shall strike that sharp and sudden cold
    throughout
As it shall lose all virtue; and those
    nymphs,
Those treacherous nymphs, pulled in
    Earine,
Shall stand curled up like images of ice,
And never thaw. Mark, never! A sharp
    justice!
Or, stay, a better! When the year's at
    hottest,   20
And that the Dog Star foams, and the
    streams boils
And curls and works and swells ready
    to sparkle,
To fling a fellow with a fever in,
To set it all on fire till it burn
Blue as Scamander fore the walls of Troy
When Vulcan leaped into him to con-
    sume him!
Rob. A deep-hurt fant'sy!
                    [*They approach him.*]
Eg.   Do you not approve it?
Rob. Yes, gentle Eglamour, we all ap-
    prove,

[1] Greensward.

And come to gratulate your just revenge,
Which, since it is so perfect, we now
    hope   30
You'll leave all care thereof and mix
    with us
In all the proffered solace of the spring.
Eg. A spring, now she is dead! Of what?
    Of thorns?
Briars and brambles? Thistles? Burs
    and docks?
Cold hemlock? Yew? The mandrake
    or the box?
These may grow still; but what can
    spring beside?
Did not the whole earth sicken when she
    died?
As if there since did fall one drop of dew
But what was wept for her, or any stalk
Did bear a flower, or any branch a
    bloom,   40
After her wreath was made! In faith, in
    faith,
You do not fair to put these things upon
    me,
Which can in no sort be. Earine,
Who had her very being and her name
With the first knots [2] or buddings of
    the spring,
Born with the primrose and the violet,
Or earliest roses blown, when Cupid
    smiled,
And Venus led the Graces out to dance,
And all the flowers and sweets in na-
    ture's lap
Leaped out, and made their solemn con-
    juration   50
To last but while she lived! Do not I
    know
How the vale withered the same day, how
    Dove,
Dean, Eye, and Erwash, Idel, Snite,
    and Soare
Each broke his urn, [3] and twenty waters
    more
That swelled proud Trent shrunk them-
    selves dry? That, since,
No sun or moon or other cheerful star
Looked out of heaven, but all the cope [4]
    was dark,
As it were hung so for her exequies!
And not a voice or sound to ring her
    knell

[2] Swellings.
[3] Flow(?).   [4] Vault of the sky.

But of that dismal pair, the scritching
owl [1] 60
And buzzing hornet! Hark, hark, hark,
the foul
Bird! How she flutters with her wicker [2]
wings!
Peace! You shall hear her scritch.

CLA. Good Karolin, sing.
Help to divert this fant'sy.

KAR. All I can.

The Song, which while Karolin sings, Egla-
mour reads.

Though I am young and cannot tell
Either what Death or Love is well,
Yet I have heard they both bear darts,
And both do aim at human hearts.
And then again I have been told,
Love wounds with heat,[3] as Death with
cold, 70
So that I fear they do but bring
Extremes to touch, and mean one thing.

As in a ruin we it call
One thing to be blown up or fall,
Or to our end like way may have
By a flash of lightning or a wave,
So Love's inflaméd shaft or brand
May kill as soon as Death's cold hand,
Except Love's fires the virtue have
To fright the frost out of the grave. 80

EG. Do you think so? Are you in that
good heresy,
I mean opinion? If you be, say nothing.
I'll study it as a new philosophy,
But by myself alone. Now you shall
leave me.
Some of these nymphs here will reward
you—this,
This pretty maid, although but with a
kiss. *He forces Amie to kiss him.*[4]
Lived my Earine, you should have
twenty;
For every line here, one I would allow
hem
From mine own store, the treasure I
had in her.
Now I am as poor as you.

KAR. And I a wretch! 90

CLA. Yet keep an eye upon him, Karolin.
Eglamour goes out and Karolin follows him.

[1] Screech owl.   [4] *I.e.*, Karolin, the singer.
[2] Pliant(?), ominous(?).
[3] Original reads *heart.*

MEL. Alas, that ever such a generous spirit
As Eglamour's should sink by such a loss!

CLA. The truest lovers are least fortunate:
Look 't [5] all their lives and legends, what
they call
The lovers' scriptures, Heliodore's or
Tatii,
Longi, Eustathii, Prodomi,[6] you'll find it!
What think you, father?

ALK. I have known some few,
And read of more, wh' have had their
dose, and deep,
Of these sharp bittersweets.

LIO. But what is this 100
To jolly Robin, who the story [7] is
Of all beatitude in love?

CLA. And told
Here every day with wonder on the
wold.[8]

LIO. And with Fame's voice.

ALK. Save that some folk delight
To blend all good of others with some
spite.

CLA. He and his Marian are the sum and
talk
Of all that breathe here in the greenwood walk.

MEL. Or Be'voir Vale.

LIO. The turtles of the wood.

CLA. The billing pair.

ALK. And so are understood
For simple loves, and sampled [9] lives
beside. 110

MEL. Faith, so much virtue should not
be envied.

ALK. Better be so than pitied, Mellifleur,
For gainst all envy virtue is a cure,
But wretched pity ever calls on scorns.—
[*Horns within.*]
The deer's brought home; I hear it by
their horns.

ACT I. SCENE vi.

To Robin, etc., Marian, John, Scarlet,
Scathlock.[10]

ROB. My Marian, and my mistress!

MAR. My loved Robin!

MEL. The moon's at full; the happy pair
are met.

[5] Original reads *looks.*
[6] Authors of late Greek romances, the last four
names being Latin genitives.
[7] Example.   [9] Exemplary.
[8] Original reads *world.*   [10] Enters later.

Mar. How hath this morning paid me for
  my rising—
First, with my sports, but most with
  meeting you.
I did not half so well reward my hounds
As she hath me today, although I gave
  them
All the sweet morsels called tongue, ears,
  and dowcets! [1]

Rob. What, and the inchpin? [2]

Mar. Yes.

Rob. Your sports then pleased you?

Mar. You are a wanton.

Rob. *One,* I do confess,
I *want*ed till you came; but now I have
  you   10
I'll grow to your embraces, till two souls,
Distilléd into kisses through our lips,
Do make one spirit of love. [*Kisses her.*]

Mar. O Robin, Robin!

Rob. Breathe, breathe awhile. What says
  my gentle Marian?

Mar. Could you so long be absent?

Rob. What, a week?
Was that so long?

Mar. How long are lovers' weeks,
Do you think, Robin, when they are
  asunder?
Are they not pris'ners' years?

Rob. To some they seem so,
But, being met again, they are schoolboys' hours—

Mar. That have got leave to play, and
  so we use them.   20

Rob. Had you good sport i' your chase
  today?

John. O, prime!

Mar. A lusty stag.

Rob. And hunted ye at force?

Mar. In a full cry.

John. And never hunted change! [3]

Rob. You had stanch hounds then?

Mar. Old and sure; I love
No young rash dogs, no more than changing friends.

Rob. What relays set you?

John. None at all; we laid not
In one fresh dog.

Rob. He stood not long then?

Scar. Yes,
Five hours and more. A great, large deer!

Rob. What head?

John. Forkéd! A hart of ten.

Mar. He is good venison,
According to the season i' the blood,   30
I'll promise all your friends for whom he
  fell.

John. But at his fall there happed a
  chance.

Mar. Worth mark.

Rob. Ay, what was that, sweet Marian?
  He kisses her.

Mar. You'll not hear?

Rob. I love these interruptions in a story;
  He kisses her again.
They make it sweeter.

Mar. You do know as soon
As the assay [4] is taken.
  He kisses her again.

Rob. On, my Marian.
I did but take the assay.

Mar. You stop one's mouth,
And yet you bid hem speak!—When the
  arbor's [5] made—

Rob. Pulled down, and paunch turned
  out—

Mar. He that undoes him [6]
Doth cleave the brisket bone, upon the
  spoon   40
Of which a little gristle grows; you call
  it—

Rob. The raven's bone. [7]

Mar. Now o'erhead sat a raven
On a sere bough—a grown, great bird,
  and hoarse,
Who, all the while the deer was breaking
  up,
So croaked and cried for 't as all the
  huntsmen,
Especially old Scathlock, thought it omi-
  nous,
Swore it was mother Maudlin, whom he
  met
At the day-dawn just as he roused the deer
Out of his lair; but we made shift to run
  him
Off his four legs, and sunk him ere we
  left.   50

[*Enter Scathlock.*]

Is the deer come?

Scath. He lies within o' the dresser. [8]

Mar. Will you go see him, Mellifleur?

---

[1] Doucets.
[2] Sweetbread. [3] Followed a cross scent.
[4] Test of quality. [6] Cuts him up.
[5] Disemboweling is.
[7] Because it was given to the ravens.
[8] Block on which meat is dressed.

Mel. I attend you.
Mar. Come, Amie, you'll go with us?
Amie. I am not well.
Lio. She's sick o' the young shepherd that
bekissed her.
Mar. Friend, cheer your friends up; we
will eat him merrily.
[*Exeunt Marian, Mellifleur, and Amie.*]
Alk. Saw you the raven, friend?
Scath. Ay, quha suld let me? [1]
I suld be afraid o' you, sir, suld I?
Clar. Huntsman,
A dram more of civility would not hurt
you.
Rob. Nay, you must give [2] them all their
rudenesses;
They are not else themselves without
their language. 60
Alk. And what do you think of her?
Scath. As of a witch.
They call her a wise woman, but I think
her
An arrant witch.
Clar. And wherefore think you so?
Scath. Because I saw her since, broiling
the bone
Was cast her at the quarry.
Alk. Where saw you her?
Scath. I' the chimley nuik,[3] within; she's
there now.
Rob. Marian!

Act I. Scene vii.

To them, Marian.

[Rob.] Your hunt holds in [4] his tale still,
and tells more.
Mar. My hunt? What tale?
Rob. How! Cloudy, Marian!
What look is this?
Mar. A fit one, sir, for you.
Hand off, rude ranger!—(*To Scathlock.*)
Sirrah, get you in,
And bear the venison hence. It is too
good
For these coarse, rustic mouths that
cannot open,
Or spend a thank for 't. A starved mut-
ton's carcass
Would better fit their palates. See it
carried

To mother Maudlin's, whom you call
the witch, sir.
Tell her I sent it to make merry with. 10
She'll turn [5] us thanks at least! Why
stand'st thou, groom?
Rob. I wonder he can move, that he's not
fixed,
If that his feeling be the same with
mine!
I dare not trust the faith of mine own
senses;
I fear [6] mine eyes and ears. This is not
Marian!
Nor am I Robin Hood! I pray you ask
her,
Ask her, good shepherds, ask her all for
me—
Or rather ask yourselves—if she be she,
Or I be I.
Mar. Yes, and you are the spy,
And the spied spy that watch upon my
walks 20
To inform what deer I kill or give away!
Where! When! To whom! But spy your
worst, good spy.
I will dispose of this where least you like!
Fall to your cheesecakes, curds, and
clawted [7] cream,
Your fools,[8] your flauns,[9] and of ale a
stream
To wash it from your livers. Strain ewes'
milk
Into your cider sillabubs, and be drunk
To [10] him whose fleece hath brought the
earliest lamb
This year, and wears the baudric [11] at your
board,
Where you may all go whistle, and
record 30
This i' your dance, and foot it lustily.
She leaves them.
Rob. I pray you, friends, do you hear and
see as I do?
Did the same accents strike your ears,
and objects
Your eyes, as mine?
Alk. We taste the same reproaches.
Lio. Have seen the changes.
Rob. Are we not all changed,
Transforméd from ourselves?

---

[1] Who should stop me? [3] Chimney nook.
[2] Grant, allow. [4] Huntsman holds to.

[5] Return. [9] Pancakes.
[6] Doubt. [10] In honor of.
[7] Clouted, clotted. [11] Baldric.
[8] Custards.

Lio.   I do not know.
   The best is silence.
Alk.   And to await the issue.
Rob. The dead or lazy wait for 't! I will
    find it.   [*Exeunt.*]

The Argument of the Second Act

The Witch Maudlin, having taken the
shape of Marian to abuse Robin Hood and
perplex his guests, cometh forth with her
daughter, Douce, reporting in what confusion she hath left them, defrauded them
of their venison, made them suspicious each
of the other, but most of all Robin Hood so
jealous of his Marian as she hopes no effect
of love would ever reconcile them, glorying
so far in the extent of her mischief as [10
she confesseth to have surprised Earine,
stripped her of her garments to make her
daughter appear fine at this feast in them,
and to have shut the maiden up in a tree
as her son's prize, if he could win her, or his
prey, if he would force her. Her son, a rude,
bragging swine'ard, comes to the tree to
woo her (his mother and sister stepping
aside to overhear him) and first boasts his
wealth to her and his possessions— [20
which move not. Then he presents her
gifts such as himself is taken with, but she
utterly shows a scorn and loathing both of
him and them. His mother is angry, rates
him, instructs him what to do the next time,
and persuades her daughter to show herself
about the bower, tells how she shall know
her mother, when she is transformed, by
her broidered belt. Meanwhile the young
shepherdess Amie, being kissed by [30
Karolin, Earine's brother, before, falls in
love, but knows not what love is, but de-
scribes her disease so innocently that
Marian pities her. When Robin Hood and
the rest of his guests, invited, enter to
Marian, upbraiding her with sending away
their venison to mother Maudlin by Scathlock, which she denies, Scathlock affirms
it, but, seeing his mistress weep and to
forswear it, begins to doubt his own [40
understanding rather than affront her
farder,[1] which makes Robin Hood and
the rest to examine themselves better. But
Maudlin, entering like herself, the witch,
comes to thank her for her bounty, at

[1] Farther.

which Marian is more angry, and more
denies the deed. Scathlock enters, tells he
has brought it again, and delivered it to the
cook. The witch is inwardly vexed the
venison is so recovered from her by [50
the rude huntsman, and murmurs and
curses, bewitches the cook, mocks poor
Amie and the rest, discovereth her ill nature, and is a mean of reconciling them all.
For the Sage Shepherd suspecteth her mischief, if she be not prevented,[2] and so
persuadeth to seize on her. Whereupon
Robin Hood despatcheth out his woodmen
to hunt and take her, which ends the act.

Act II. Scene i.

[*The witch's dimble, with the swineherd's
oak at one side.*]

Maudlin, Douce [*dressed in Earine's clothes*].

Maud. Have I not left 'em in a brave
     confusion,
   Amazed their expectation, got their veni-
     son,
   Troubled their mirth and meeting, made
     them doubtful
   And jealous of each other, all distracted,
   And, i' the close, uncertain of themselves?
   This can your mother do, my dainty
     Douce:
   Take any shape upon her, and delude
   The senses best acquainted with their
     owners!
   The jolly Robin, who hath bid this feast,
   And made this solemn invitation,   10
   I ha' possesséd so with syke [3] dislikes
   Of his own Marian that, albee [4] he know
     her
   As doth the vaulting [5] hart his venting [6]
     hind,
   He ne'er fra hence sall nase [7] her i' the
     wind,
   To his first liking.
Douce.   Did you so distaste him?
Maud. As far as her proud scorning him
     could bate,
   Or blunt the edge of any lover's temper.
Douce. But were ye like her, mother?
Maud.   So like, Douce,
   As, had she seen me her sel', her sel' had
     doubted   19

[2] Anticipated.
[3] Sic, such.
[4] Albeit, although.
[5] Vaulting.
[6] Scenting, smelling.
[7] From hence shall nose (smell).

Whether had been the liker of the twa!
This can your mother do, I tell you,
　daughter!
I ha' but dight [1] ye yet i' the outdress [2]
And parel [3] of Earine; but this raiment,
These very weeds, sall make ye as, but
　coming
In view or ken of Eglamour, your form
Shall show too slippery [4] to be looked
　upon,
And all the forests swear you to be she!
They shall rin [5] after ye, and wage the
　odds,
Upo' their own deceivéd sights, ye are
　her,
Whilst she, poor lass, is stocked up [6] in a
　tree—　　　　　　　　　　　　30
Your brother Lorel's prize! For so my
　largess
Hath lotted her to be your brother's mis-
　tress,
Gif [7] she can be reclaimed [8]—gif not, his
　prey!
And here he comes new claithéd, [9] like a
　prince
Of swine'ards. Syke he seems, dight i'
　the spoils
Of those he feeds—a mighty lord of
　swine!
He is comand [10] now to woo. Let's step
　aside,
And hear his lovecraft. See, he opes the
　door,
And takes her by the hand, and helps her
　forth.
This is true courtship, and becomes his
　ray. [11]　　　　　　　　　　　　40

Act II. Scene ii.

[The same.]

Lorel, Earine, Maudlin, Douce.

Lor. Ye kind to others, but ye coy to me,
　Deft mistress, whiter than the cheese new
　　pressed,
　Smoother than cream, and softer than
　　the curds,

Why start ye from me ere ye hear me tell
My wooing errand and what rents I
　have?
Large herds and pastures! Swine and
　ky [12] mine own!
And though my nase be camused, [13] my
　lips thick,
And my chin bristled, Pan, great Pan,
　was such,
Who was the chief of herdsmen, and our
　sire!　　　　　　　　　　　　9
I am na [14] fay, na incubus, na changelin',
But a good man that lives o' my awn
　gear. [15]
This house, these grounds, this stock is
　all mine awn.
Ear. How better 'twere to me, this were
　not known!
Maud. [Aside.] She likes it not; but it is
　boasted well.
Lor. An hundred udders for the pail I
　have,
　That gi' me milk and curds, that make
　　me cheese
　To cloy the markets! Twenty swarm of
　　bees,
　Whilk [16] all the summer hum about the
　　hive,
　And bring me wax and honey in bilive. [17]
　An aged oak, the king of all the field, 20
　With a broad beech there grows afore my
　　dur, [18]
　That mickle mast [19] unto the farm doth
　　yield.
　A chestnut, whilk hath larded mony [20] a
　　swine,
　Whose skins I wear to fend [21] me fra the
　　cold;
　A poplar green, and with a carvéd seat,
　Under whose shade I solace in the heat,
　And thence can see gang [22] out and in my
　　neat.
　Twa trilland [23] brooks each from his
　　spring doth meet
　And make a river to refresh my feet,
　In which each morning, ere the sun doth
　　rise,　　　　　　　　　　　　30
　I look myself, and clear my pleasant eyes,
　Before I pipe, for therein I have skill

[1] Dressed.
[2] Outer dress.
[3] Apparel.
[4] Uncertain.
[5] Run.
[6] Imprisoned.
[7] If.
[8] Tamed, as a hawk.
[9] Clothed.
[10] Coming. In many later words in this play
the northern ending -and is used for participles
in -ing.
[11] Array, dress.
[12] Kine.
[13] Flat.
[14] No.
[15] Own property.
[16] Which.
[17] Belive, quickly.
[18] Before my door.
[19] Much food (nuts).
[20] Fattened many.
[21] Defend, protect.
[22] Go.
[23] Trickling.

'Bove other swine'ards. Bid me, and I will
Straight play to you, and make you melody.

EAR. By no means. Ah, to me all minstrelsy
Is irksome, as are you.

LOR.   Why scorn you me?
Because I am a herdsman, and feed swine! *He draws out other presents.*
I am a lord of other gear. This fine,
Smooth bauson's [1] cub, the young grice of a gray,[2]   39
Twa tiny urshins,[3] and this ferret gay.

EAR. Out on hem! What are these?

LOR.   I give hem ye
As presents, Mrs.[4]—

EAR.   O, the fiend and thee!
Gar [5] take them hence; they fewmand [6] all the claithes,
And prick my coats.[7] Hence with hem, limmer lown,[8]
Thy vermin and thyself; thyself art one!
Ay, lock me up—all's well when thou art gone.
     [*Lorel shuts her in the tree again.*]

ACT II. SCENE iii.

[*The same.*]

Lorel, Maudlin, Douce.

LOR. Did you hear this? She wished me at the fiend
With all my presents!

MAUD.   A too lucky end
She wishend [9] thee, foul limmer, dritty [10] lown!
Gude [11] faith, it dules [12] me that I am thy mother.
And see, thy sister scorns thee for her brother.
Thou woo thy love, thy mistress, with twa hedgehogs,
A stinkand brock, a polecat? Out, thou howlet! [13]
Thou shouldst ha' given her a madge-owl,[14] and then

Tho' hadst made a present o' thyself, owlspiegle! [15]

DOUCE. Why, mother, I have heard ye bid to give,   10
And often as the cause calls.

MAUD.   I know well,
It is a witty [16] part sometimes to give;
But what? To wham? [17] No monsters, nor to maidens.
He suld present them with mare [18] pleasand things,
Things natural, and what all women covet
To see: the common parent of us all,
Which maids will twire [19] at tween their fingers thus;
With which [20] his sire gat him, he s' [21] get another,
And so beget posterity upon her.
This he should do! False gelden,[22] gang thy gait,   20
And do thy turns betimes; or I s' gar take
Thy new breikes [23] fra thee, and thy duiblet [24] too.
The talleur [25] and the souter [26] sall undo
All they ha' made, except thou manlier woo!   *Lorel goes out.*

DOUCE. Gud mother, gif you chide him, he'll do wairs.[27]

MAUD. Hang him! I geif [28] him to the devil's erse.[29]
But ye, my Douce, I charge ye, show yoursel'
To all the shepherds baudly.[30] Gang amang hem,
Be mickel i' their eye, frequent and fugeand,[31]
And, gif they ask ye of Earine,   30
Or of these claithes, say that I ga' hem ye,
And say no more. I ha' that wark [32] in hand,

---

[1] Badger's.
[2] Cub of a badger.
[3] Hedgehogs.
[4] *I.e.*, mistress.
[5] Cause to.
[6] Soil—a form perhaps invented by Jonson.
[7] Make holes in my petticoats.
[8] Rascally loon.
[9] Wished.
[10] Dirty.
[11] Good.
[12] Grieves.
[13] Owl.
[14] Barn owl.
[15] Mirror of an owl, a term of contempt derived from *Eulenspiegel*, the hero of certain medieval German jest books.
[16] Clever.
[17] Whom.
[18] More.
[19] Peer.
[20] That which.
[21] Shall. Put later in the original the first person of this form reads '*is*.
[22] Gelding.
[23] Breeks, breeches.
[24] Doublet.
[25] Tailor.
[26] Cobbler.
[27] Worse.
[28] Give.
[29] Arse.
[30] Joyously.
[31] Figent, lively.
[32] Work.

That web upo' the luime,[1] shall gar hem think

By then, they feelin' their own frights and fears,

I s' pu'[2] the world or nature 'bout their ears.

But hear ye, Douce, bycause[3] ye may meet me

In mony shapes today, where'er you spy

This brodered[4] belt with characters, 'tis I.

A Gypsan[5] lady, and a right beldame,

Wrought it by moonshine for me, and starlight, 40

Upo' your grannam's[6] grave, that very night

We earthed her in the shades, when our dame Hecate

Made it her gang-night[7] over the kirk-yard,

With all the barkand parish-tikes set at her,

While I sat whirland of my brazen spindle.

At every twisted thrid[8] my rock[9] let fly

Unto the sewster,[10] who did sit me nigh,

Under the town turnpike, which ran each spell

She stitchèd in the work, and knit it well.

See ye take tent[11] to this, and ken your mother. [*Exeunt.*] 50

Act II. Scene iv.

[*Before Robin Hood's bower.*]

Marian, Mellifleur, Amie.

MAR. How do you, sweet Amie? Yet?

MEL. She cannot tell;

If she could sleep, she says, she should do well.

She feels a hurt, but where, she cannot show

Any least sign that she is hurt or no.

Her pain's not doubtful to her, but the seat

Of her pain is. Her thoughts, too, work and beat,

Oppressed with cares, but why she cannot say.

All matter of her care is quite away.

MAR. Hath any vermin[12] broke into your fold?

Or any rot seized on your flock, or cold? 10

Or hath your feighting[13] ram burst his hard horn,

Or any ewe her fleece or bag hath torn,

My gentle Amie?

AMIE. Marian, none of these.

MAR. Ha' you been stung by wasps or angry bees,

Or rased[14] with some rude bramble or rough brier?

AMIE. No, Marian, my disease is somewhat nigher.

I weep, and boil away myself in tears;

And then my panting heart would dry those fears.

I burn, though all the forest lend a shade,

And freeze, though the whole wood one fire were made.

MAR. Alas! 20

AMIE. I often have been torn with thorn and brier,

Both in the leg and foot, and somewhat higher,

Yet gave not then such fearful shrieks as these. Ah!

I often have been stung too with curst[15] bees,

Yet not remember that I then did quit

Either my company or mirth for it. Ah!

And therefore what it is that I feel now,

And know no cause of it, nor where, nor how

It entered in me, nor least print can see,

I feel, afflicts me more than brier or bee. O! 30

How often when the sun, heaven's brightest birth,

Hath with his burning fervor cleft the earth,

Under a spreading elm or oak hard by

A cool, clear fountain could I sleeping lie,

Safe from the heat! But now no shady tree

Nor purling brook can my refreshing be.

---

[1] Loom.	[4] Embroidered.	
[2] Pull.	[5] Egyptian, gipsy.	
[3] Because.	[6] Grandam's, grandmother's.	
[7] Night when spirits walk.		
[8] Thread.	[10] Sempstress.	
[9] Spindle.	[11] Attention.	

[12] Obnoxious animal.	[14] Scratched
[13] Fighting.	[15] Angry.

Oft when the meadows were grown rough
  with frost,
The rivers ice-bound, and their currents
  lost,
My thick, warm fleece I wore was my
  defense;
Or large, good fires I made drave [1]
  winter thence.   40
But now my whole flock's fells, nor this
  thick grove,
Enflamed to ashes, can my cold remove.
It is a cold and heat that doth outgo
All sense of winter's and of summer's
  so.

ACT II. SCENE V.

[*The same.*]

[*To them,*] *Robin Hood, Clarion, Lionel,*
                            Alken.

ROB. O, are you here, my mistress?
MAR.   Ay, my love!
She, seeing him, runs to embrace him. He
                     puts her back.
Where should I be but in my Robin's
  arms,
The sphere which I delight in so to
  move?
ROB. What, "the rude ranger" and "spied
  spy"? Hand off!
You are "for no such rustics."
MAR.   What means this?
Thrice worthy Clarion, or wise Alken,
  know ye?
ROB. 'Las, no, not they! "A poor, starved
  mutton's carcass
Would better fit their palates than your
  venison."
MAR. What riddle is this? Unfold your-
  self, dear Robin.
ROB. You ha' not sent your venison hence
  by Scathlock   10
To mother Maudlin?
MAR.   I to mother Maudlin!
Will Scathlock say so?
ROB.   Nay, we will all swear so.
For all did hear it when you gave the
  charge so,
Both Clarion, Alken, Lionel, myself.
MAR. Good honest shepherds, masters of
  your flocks,
Simple and virtuous men, no others'
  hirelings,

[1] Drove.

Be not you made to speak against your
  conscience
That which may soil the truth. I send
  the venison
Away? By Scathlock, and to mother
  Maudlin?
I came to show it here to Mellifleur, 20
I do confess; but Amie's falling ill
Did put us off it. Since, we employed
  ourselves
In comforting of her.

Scathlock enters.

                   O, here he is!—
Did I, sir, bid you bear away the venison
To mother Maudlin?
SCATH.   Ay, gude faith, madam,
Did you, and I ha' done it.
MAR.   What ha' you done?
SCATH. Obeyed your hests,[2] madam, done
  your commands.
MAR. Done my commands, dull groom?
  Fetch it again,
Or kennel with the hounds.—Are these
  the arts,
Robin, you rede [3] your rude ones o'
  the wood   30
To countenance your quarrels and mis-
  takings?
Or are the sports to entertain your
  friends
Those forméd jealousies? [4] Ask of
  Mellifleur
If I were ever from her here, or Amie,
Since I came in with them, or saw this
  Scathlock
Since I related to you his tale o' the
  raven.
SCATH. Ay, say you so? *Scathlock goes out.*
MEL.   She never left my side
Since I came in here, nor I hers.
CLA.   This 's strange!
Our best of senses were deceived, our
  eyes, then!
LIO. And ears too.
MAR. What you have concluded on, 40
Make good, I pray you.
AMIE.   O my heart, my heart!
MAR. My heart it is, is wounded, pretty
  Amie.
Report not you your griefs; I'll tell
  for all.

[2] Behests.   [4] *I.e.,* suspicions of those kinds.
[3] Counsel.

MEL. Somebody is to blame there is a fault.
MAR. Try if you can take rest. A little
  slumber
Will much refresh you, Amie.

                              [*Amie sleeps.*]
ALK.   What's her grief?
MAR. She does not know, and therein she
  is happy.

ACT II. SCENE vi.

[*The same.*]

*To them, John, Maudlin, and Scathlock
                                    after.*

JOHN. Here's mother Maudlin come to
  give you thanks,
  Madam, for some late gift she hath re-
    ceived—
  Which she's not worthy of, she says,
    but crakes [1]
  And wonders of it, hops about the house,
  Transported with the joy.
MAUD.   Send me a stag,
                      (*She danceth.*)
  A whole stag, madam, and so fat a deer!
  So fairly hunted, and at such a time too,
  When all your friends were here!
ROB.   Do you mark this, Clarion?
  Her own acknowledgment?
MAUD.   'Twas such a bounty
  And honor done to your poor beads-
    woman,   10
  I know not how to owe [2] it but to thank
    you;
  And that I come to do. I shall go round
  And giddy with the toy [3] of the good
    turn.

	Look out, look out,	
	Gay folk about,	
She	And see me spin	
turns	The ring I am in	
round	Of mirth and glee,	
	With thanks for fee	
	The heart puts on,	20
	For th' venison	
	My lady sent,	
	Which shall be spent	
	In draughts of wine,	
	To fume up fine	
	Into the brain,	
till	And down again	
she	Fall in a swoun,[4]	
falls.	Upo' the groun'.	29

---

[1] Cracks, chatters.   [3] Surprising thought.
[2] Own, acknowledge.   [4] Swoon.

ROB. Look to her; she is mad.
MAUD. [*Rising.*]   My son hath sent you
  A pot of strawberries gathered i' the
    wood
  (His hogs would else have rooted up or
    trod);
  With a choice dish of wildings [5] here to
    scald
  And mingle with your cream.
MAR.   Thank you, good Maudlin,
  And thank your son. Go, bear hem in to
    Much,
  Th' acater; let him thank her. Surely,
    mother,
  Your were mistaken, or my woodmen
    more,
  Or most myself, to send you all our
    store
  Of venison, hunted for ourselves this
    day.
  You will not take it, mother, I dare
    say,   40
  If we'ld entreat you, when you know
    our guests;
  Red deer is head still of the forest feasts.
MAUD. But I knaw [6] ye, a right free-
    hearted lady,
  Can spare it out of superfluity.
  I have departit [7] it 'mong my poor neigh-
    bors,
  To speak your largess.
MAR.   I not gave it, mother;
  You have done wrong then. I know how
    to place
  My gifts, and where; and when to find
    my seasons
  To give, not throw away my courtesies.
MAUD. Count you this thrown away?
MAR.   What's ravished from me 50
  I count it worse, as stolen; I lose my
    thanks.
  But leave this quest. They fit not you
    nor me,
  Maudlin, contentions of this quality.—

Scathlock enters.

                              How now?
SCATH. Your stag's returned upon my
    shoulders;
  He has found his way into the kitchen
    again
  With his two legs, if now your cook can
    dress him.

---

[5] Crab apples.   [6] Know.   [7] Divided.

'Slid,[1] I thought the swine'ard would ha'
   beat me,
He looks so big,[2] the sturdy karl,[3]
   lewd[4] Lorel!

MAR. There, Scathlock, for thy pains;
   thou hast deserved it.
               Marian gives him gold.

MAUD. Do you give a thing, and take a
   thing, madam?   60

MAR. No, Maudlin, "you had imparted
   to your neighbors;"
As much good do 't them! I ha' done
   no wrong.

THE FIRST CHARM

MAUD.
   The spit stand still, no broaches turn
   Before the fire, but let it burn
   Both sides and haunches till the whole
   Converted be into one coal!

CLA. What devil's paternoster mumbles
   she?

ALK. Stay, you will hear more of her
   witchery.

MAUD.
   The swilland[5] dropsy enter in
   The lazy cuke[6] and swell his skin;   70
   And the old mortmal[7] on his shin
   Now prick and itch withouten blin.[8]

CLA. Speak out, hag, we may hear your
   devil's matins.

MAUD.
   The pain we call S[t]. Anton's fire,
   The gout, or what we can desire,
   To cramp a cuke in every limb,
   Before they dine yet, seize on him.

ALK. A foul, ill spirit hath possessèd
   her.

AMIE. [*From her sleep.*] O Karol, Karol,
   call him back again!

LIO. Her thoughts do work upon her in
   her slumber,   80
And may express some part of her
   disease.

ROB. Observe and mark, but trouble not
   her ease.

---

[1] By God's lid, a mild oath.
[2] Menacing.
[3] Churl, fellow.
[4] Rude.
[5] Swelling.
[6] Cuckold(?).
[7] Mormal, ulcer.
[8] Without stopping.

AMIE. O, O!

MAR.   How is 't, Amie?

MEL.   Wherefore start you?

AMIE. [*Awakening.*] O Karol! He is fair
   and sweet.

MAUD.   What then?
Are there not flowers as sweet and fair
   as men?
The lily is fair, and rose is sweet.

AMIE.   Ay, so!
Let all the roses and the lilies go.
Karol is only fair to me.

MAR.   And why?

AMIE. Alas, for Karol, Marian, I could
   die!
Karol, he singeth sweetly too.

MAUD.   What then? 90
Are there not birds sing sweeter far than
   men?

AMIE. I grant the linnet, lark, and bull-
   finch sing,
But best the dear, good angel[9] of the
   spring,
The nightingale.

MAUD.   Then why, then why, alone,
Should his notes please you?

AMIE.   I not long agone[10]
Took a delight with wanton kids to
   play,
And sport with little lambs a summer's
   day,
And view their frisks. Methought it
   was a sight
Of joy to see my two brave rams to
   fight!   99
Now Karol only all delight doth move;
All that is Karol, Karol I approve!
This very morning but,[11] I did bestow
(It was a little gainst my will, I know)
A single kiss upon the seely[12] swain,
And now I wish that very kiss again.
His lip is softer, sweeter than the rose;
His mouth and tongue with dropping
   honey flows;
The relish of it was a pleasing thing.

MAUD. Yet, like the bees, it had a little
   sting.

AMIE. And sunk, and sticks yet in my
   marrow deep;   110
And what doth hurt me I now wish to
   keep.

MAR. Alas, how innocent her story is!

---

[9] Messenger.
[10] Ago.
[11] Just this morning.
[12] Simple.

AMIE. I do remember, Marian, I have
    oft
With pleasure kissed my lambs and
    puppies soft;
And once a dainty, fine roe-fawn I
    had,
Of whose outskipping bounds I was as
    glad
As of my health, and him I oft would
    kiss;
Yet had his no such sting or pain as
    this.
They never pricked or hurt my heart;
    and, for
They were so blunt and dull, I wish no
    more.   120
But this, that hurts and pricks, doth
    please; this sweet
Mingled with sour I wish again to
    meet;
And that delay, methinks, most tedious
    is
That keeps or hinders me of Karol's
    kiss.
MAR. We'll send for him, sweet Amie, to
    come to you.
MAUD. But I will keep him off, if charms
    will do it.   *She goes murmuring out.*
CLA. Do you mark the murmuring hag,
    how she doth mutter?
ROB. I like her not; and less her manners
    now.
ALK. She is a shrewd, deforméd piece, I
    vow.
LIO. As crooked as her body.
ROB.   I believe   130
    She can take any shape, as Scathlock
    says.
ALK. She may deceive the sense, but
    really
    She cannot change herself.
ROB.   Would I could see her
    Once more in Marian's form, for I am
        certain
    Now it was she abused us, as I think
    My Marian, and my love, now in-
        nocent—
    Which faith I seal unto her with this
        kiss,
    And call you all to witness of my pen-
        ance.   [*Kisses Marian.*]
ALK. It was believed before, but now
    confirmed,
    That we have seen the monster.   140

ACT II. SCENE vii.

[*The same.*]

To them, Tuck, John, Much, Scarlet.

TUCK.   Hear you how
    Poor Tom, the cook, is taken! [1] All his
        joints
    Do crack, as if his limbs were tied with
        points; [2]
    His whole frame slackens; and a kind of
        rack
    Runs down along the spondils [3] of his
        back;
    A gout or cramp now seizeth on his
        head,
    Then falls into his feet; his knees are
        lead;
    And he can stir his either hand no
        more
    Than a dead stump, to his office, as
        before.
ALK. He is bewitched.
CLA.   This is an argument   10
    Both of her malice and her power, we
        see.
ALK. She must by some device restrainéd
        be,
    Or she'll go far in mischief.
ROB.   Advise how,
    Sage Shepherd, we shall put it straight
        in practice.
ALK. Send forth your woodmen then
    into the walks,
    Or let 'em prick [4] her footing hence; a
        witch
    Is sure a creature of melancholy,
    And will be found or sitting in her
        fourm, [5]
    Or else at relief, [6] like a hare.
CLA.   You speak,
    Alken, as if you knew the sport of witch-
        hunting,   20
    Or starting of a hag.

*Enter George to the Huntsmen, who by
    themselves continue the scene, the Rest
                                going off.*

ROB.   Go, sirs, about it.
    Take George here with you; he can help
        to find her.

[1] Bewitched.   [4] Track.
[2] Laces.   [5] Form, bed of a hare.
[3] Vertebræ.   [6] Feeding.

Leave Tuck and Much behind to dress
the dinner
I' the cook's stead.

MUCH.　　　We'll care to get that done.

ROB. Come, Marian, let's withdraw into
the bower.

ACT II. SCENE viii.

[*The same.*]

John, Scarlet, Scathlock, George, Alken.[1]

JOHN. Rare sport, I swear, this hunting
of the witch
Will make us.

SCAR.　　　Let's advise upon 't like
huntsmen.

GEORGE. And [2] we can spy her once, she
is our own.

SCATH. First, think which way she four-
meth,[3] on what wind—
Or north or south.

GEORGE.　　For, as the shepherd said,
A witch is a kind of hare.

SCATH.　　And marks the weather,
As the hare does.

JOHN.　Where shall we hope to find her?
　　　　　　　　Alken returns.

ALK. I have asked leave to assist you,
jolly huntsmen,
If an old shepherd may be heard among
you,
Not jeered or laughed at.

JOHN.　　　Father, you will see　10
Robin Hood's household know more
courtesy.

SCATH. Who scorns at eld,[4] peels off his
own young hairs.

ALK. Ye say right well.　Know ye the
Witch's Dell?

SCATH. No more than I do know the walks
of hell.

ALK. Within a gloomy dimble she doth
dwell
Down in a pit, o'ergrown with brakes
and briers,
Close by the ruins of a shaken abbey,
Torn with an earthquake down unto the
ground,
'Mongst graves and grots, near an old
charnel house,
Where you shall find her sitting in her
fourm　　　　　　　　　　　　　20

As fearful and melancholic as that
She is about, with caterpillars' kells [5]
And knotty cobwebs, rounded in with
spells.
Thence she steals forth to relief, in the
fogs
And rotten mists, upon the fens and
bogs,
Down to the drownéd lands of Lincoln-
shire,
To make ewes cast their lambs, swine
eat their farrow,
The housewife's tun not work,[6] nor the
milk churn!
Writhe children's wrists, and suck their
breath in sleep,
Get vials of their blood!　And, where
the sea　　　　　　　　　　　　30
Casts up his slimy owze,[7] search for a
weed
To open locks with, and to rivet charms,
Planted about her in the wicked feat [8]
Of all her mischiefs, which are mani-
fold.

JOHN. I wonder such a story could be
told
Of her dire deeds.

GEORGE.　　　I thought a witch's banks [9]
Had enclosed nothing but the merry
pranks
Of some old woman.

SCAR.　　　　Yes, her malice more.

SCATH. As it would quickly appear had
we the store
Of his collects.[10]

GEORGE.　　Ay, this gude, learned man　40
Can speak her right.

SCAR.　He knows her shifts and haunts.

ALK. And all her wiles and turns;　the
venomed plants
Wherewith she kills; where the sad mandrake grows,
Whose groans are deathful; the dead-
numbing nightshade,
The stupefying hemlock, adder's tongue,
And martagan;[11] the shrieks of luckless[12]
owls
We hear, and croaking night crows in
the air;

[1] Enters later.　　　　　[3] Crouches.
[2] If.　　　　　　　　　　[4] Age.

[5] Cauls, cocoons.　　　[7] Ooze.
[6] Ferment.　　　　　　[8] Performance.
[9] *I.e.*, the banks of the dimble.
[10] Collections of information.
[11] Martagon, a kind of lily.
[12] Ominous of ill luck.

Green-bellied snakes; blue firedrakes [1]
  in the sky,
And giddy flittermice [2] with leather wings;
The scaly beetles, with their haber-
  geons,   50
That make a humming murmur as they fly!
There in the stocks [3] of trees white fays
  do dwell,
And span-long elves that dance about
  a pool,
With each a little changeling in their
  arms!
The airy spirits play with falling stars,
And mount the sphere of fire to kiss the
  moon,
While she sits reading by the glowworm's
  light
Or rotten wood, o'er which the worm
  hath crept,
The baneful schedule of her nocent [4]
  charms,
And binding characters through which
  she wounds   60
Her puppets, [5] the sigilla [6] of her witch-
  craft.
All this I know, and I will find her for you,
And show you her sitting in her fourm.
  I'll lay
My hand upon her, make her throw her
  scut
Along her back, when she doth start be-
  fore us.
But you must give her law; [7] and you
  shall see her
Make twenty leaps and doubles, cross
  the paths,
And then squat down beside us.
JOHN.   Crafty crone!
I long to be at the sport, and to report it.
SCAR. We'll make this hunting of the witch
  as famous   70
As any other blast of venery. [8]
SCATH. Hang her, foul hag! She'll be a
  stinking chase.
I had rather ha' the hunting of her heir.
GEORGE. If we could come to see her, cry
  "so haw" [9] once.
ALK. That I do promise, or I am no good
  hag-finder.   [*Exeunt.*]

---

[1] Firedragons.   [5] *I.e.*, images in wax or cloth.
[2] Bats.   [6] Signatures.
[3] Trunks.   [7] A fair start.
[4] Hurtful.   [8] Famous story of hunting.
[9] A huntsman's cry of discovery.

THE ARGUMENT OF THE THIRD ACT

Puck-Hairy discovers himself in the
forest, and discourseth his offices, with
their necessities, briefly; after which,
Douce, entering in the habit of Earine, is
pursued by Karol, who, mistaking her at
first to be his sister, questions her how she
came by those garments. She answers, by
her mother's gift. The Sad Shepherd coming in the while, she runs away affrighted,
and leaves Karol suddenly; Eglamour, [10
thinking it to be Earine's ghost he saw, falls
into a melancholic expression of his fant'sy
to Karol, and questions him sadly about
that point, which moves compassion in
Karol of his mistake still. When Clarion
and Lionel enter to call Karol to Amie,
Karol reports to them Eglamour's passion with much regret. Clarion resolves
to seek him, Karol to return with Lionel.
By the way, Douce and her mother, [20
in the shape of Marian, meet them, and
would divert them, affirming Amie to be
recovered, which Lionel wondered at to
be so soon. Robin Hood enters; they tell
him the relation of the witch, thinking
her to be Marian; Robin, suspecting her
to be Maudlin, lays hold of her girdle
suddenly, but, she striving to get free,
they both run out, and he returns with
the belt broken. She, following in her [30
own shape, demanding it, but at a distance, as fearing to be seized upon again,
and seeing she cannot recover it, falls into
a rage and cursing, resolving to trust to
her old arts, which she calls her daughter
to assist her. The shepherds, content with
this discovery, go home triumphing, make
the relation to Marian. Amie is gladded [10]
with the sight of Karol, etc. In the meantime, enters Lorel, with purpose to [40
ravish Earine, and, calling her forth to
that lewd end, he, by the hearing of Clarion's footing, [11] is stayed and forced to commit her hastily to the tree again, where
Clarion, coming by and hearing a voice
singing, draws near unto it; but Eglamour,
hearing it also and knowing it to be Earine's, falls into a superstitious commendation of it, as being an angel's, and in the
air; when Clarion espies a hand put [50
forth from the tree, and makes towards it,

---

[10] Gladdened.   [11] Footsteps.

leaving Eglamour to his wild fant'sy, who quitteth the place; and, Clarion beginning to court the hand and make love to it, there ariseth a mist suddenly, which darkening all the place, Clarion loseth himself and the tree where Earine is enclosed, lamenting his misfortune, with the unknown nymph's misery. The air clearing, enters the witch with her son and [60 daughter, tells them how she had caused that late darkness, to free Lorel from surprisal, and his prey from being rescued from him, bids him look to her, and lock her up more carefully, and follow her to assist a work she hath in hand of recovering her lost girdle, which she laments the loss of, with cursings, execrations, wishing confusion to their feast and meeting; sends her son and daughter to gather [70 certain simples for her purpose, and bring them to her dell. This Puck, hearing, prevents, and shows her error still. The huntsmen, having found her footing, follow the tract,[1] and prick after her. She gets to her dell, and takes her form.[2] Enter [the huntsmen]. Alken has spied her sitting with her spindle, threads, and images. They are eager to seize her presently,[3] but Alken persuades them to let her begin [80 her charms, which they do. Her son and daughter come to her; the huntsmen are affrighted as they see her work go forward; and, overhasty to apprehend her, she escapeth them all by the help and delusions of Puck.

Act III. Scene i.

[*The forest.*][4]

Puck-Hairy.

[Puck.] The fiend hath much to do that keeps a school,
  Or is the father of a family,
  Or governs but a country academy.
  His labors must be great, as are his cares,
  To watch all turns, and cast [5] how to prevent hem.
This dame of mine here, Maud, grows high in evil,
  And thinks she does all, when 'tis I, her devil,

---

[1] Track.
[2] *I.e.* her human figure.   [3] Immediately.
[4] The scene remains the same through the act.
[5] Plan.

That both delude her and must yet protect her.
She's confident in mischief, and presumes
The changing of her shape will still [6] secure her;   10
But that may fail, and divers hazards meet
Of other consequence, which I must look to—
Not let her be surprised on the first catch.
I must go dance about the forest now,
And firk [7] it like a goblin till I find her.
Then will my service come worth acceptation,
When not expected of her; when the help
Meets the necessity, and both do kiss,
'Tis called the timing of a duty, this.
                    [*Exit.*]

Act III. Scene ii.

Karol, Douce [in the dress of Earine]. *To*
them, Eglamour.

Kar. Sure, you are very like her! I conceived
  You had been she, seeing you run afore me,
  For such a suit she made her gainst this feast,
  In all resemblance, or the very same;
  I saw her in it. Had she lived t' enjoy it,
  She had been there an acceptable guest
  To Marian and the gentle Robin Hood,
  Who are the crown and girlond [8] of the wood.
Douce. I cannot tell; my mother gave it me,
  And bade me wear it.
Kar.   Who, the wise, good woman, 10
  Old Maud of Papplewick?
Douce.   Yes.—[*Aside.*] This sullen man,
  I cannot like him.—I must take my leave.

Eglamour enters and Douce goes out.

Eg. What said she to you?
Kar.   Who?
Eg.   Earine.
  I saw her talking with you, or her ghost,

---

[6] Always.   [7] Frisk.   [8] Garland.

For she indeed is drowned in old Trent's
  bottom.
Did she not tell who would ha' pulled her
  in,
And had her maidenhead upon the place,
The river's brim, the margin of the
  flood?
No ground is holy enough (you know my
  meaning);
Lust is committed in kings' palaces,   20
And yet their majesty's not violated!
No words!
KAR.   How sad and wild his thoughts
  are! Gone?
  Eglamour goes out, but comes in again.
EG. But she, as chaste as was her name,
  Earine,
Died undeflowered; and now her sweet
  soul hovers
Here in the air above us, and doth haste
To get up to the moon and Mercury,
And whisper Venus in her orb; then
  spring
Up to old Saturn, and come down by
  Mars,
Consulting Jupiter, and seat herself
Just in the midst with Phœbus, temp'ring
  all   30
The jarring spheres, and giving to the
  world
Again his first and tuneful planeting.[1]
O, what an age will here be of new con-
  cords!
Delightful harmony, to rock old sages,
Twice infants, in the cradle o' specula-
  tion,
And throw a silence upon all the crea-
  tures!
  *He goes out again but returns as soon as
                                  before.*
KAR. A cogitation of the highest rapture!
EG. The loudest seas and most enragéd
  winds
Shall lose their clangor; tempest shall
  grow hoarse,
Loud thunder dumb, and every spece [2] of
  storm,   40
Laid in the lap of list'ning nature, hushed
To hear the changéd chime of this eighth
  sphere.
Take tent, and hearken for it; lose it not.
                   Eglamour departs.

[1] An allusion to the music of the spheres.
[2] Species.

Act III. Scene iii.

Clarion, Lionel, Karol.

CLA. O, here is Karol! Was not that the
  Sad
Shepherd slipped from him?
LIO.   Yes, I guess it was.—
Who was that left you, Karol?
KAR.   The lost [3] man,
Whom we shall never see himself again,
Or ours, I fear; he starts away from hand
  so,
And all the touches or soft stroke of rea-
  son
Ye can apply! No colt is so unbroken,
Or hawk yet half so haggard or un-
  manned! [4]
He takes all toys that his wild fant'sy
  proffers,
And flies away with them. He now con-
  ceives   10
That my lost sister, his Earine,
Is lately turned a sphere amid the seven,
And reads a music lecture to the planets!
And with this thought he's run to call
  hem hearers.
CLA. Alas, this is a strained but innocent
  fant'sy!
I'll follow him, and find him if I can.
Meantime, go you with Lionel, sweet
  Karol;
He will acquaint you with an accident,[5]
Which much desires your presence on the
  place.   [*Exit.*]

Act III. Scene iv.

Karol, Lionel.

KAR. What is it, Lionel, wherein I may
  serve you?
Why do you so survey and circumscribe
  me,
As if you stuck one eye into my breast,
And with the other took my whole dimen-
  sions?
LIO. I wish you had a window i' your
  bosom,
Or i' your back, I might look thorough
  you,
And see your in-parts, Karol, liver, heart;
For there the seat of Love is, whence the
  boy,

[3] Original reads *last*.
[4] Untamed or unmastered.   [5] Happening.

The wingéd archer, hath shot home a
    shaft
Into my sister's breast, the innocent
    Amie,   10
Who now cries out, upon her bed, on
    Karol,
Sweet-singing Karol, the delicious Karol,
That kissed her like a Cupid! In your
    eyes,
She says, his stand is, and between your
    lips
He runs forth his divisions [1] to her ears,
But will not bide there, 'less yourself do
    bring him.
Go with me, Karol, and bestow a visit
In charity upon the afflicted maid,
Who pineth with the languor of your
    love.

To them, Maud and Douce, but Maud ap-
pearing like Marian.

MAR.[2] Whither intend you? Amie is re-
    covered,   20
Feels no such grief as she complained of
    lately.
This maiden hath been with her from her
    mother
Maudlin, the cunning woman, who hath
    sent her
Herbs for her head, and simples of that
    nature
Have wrought upon her a miraculous
    cure,
Settled her brain to all our wish and
    wonder.
LIO. So instantly? You know I now but
    left her,
Possessed with such a fit almost to a
    frenzy;
Yourself, too, feared her,[3] Marian, and
    did urge
My haste to seek out Karol and to bring
    him.   30
MAR. I did so. But the skill of that wise
    woman,
And her great charity of doing good,
Hath by the ready hand of this deft
    lass,
Her daughter, wrought effects beyond
    belief,

And to astonishment; we can but thank,
And praise, and be amazed, while we tell
    it.   *They go out.*
LIO. 'Tis strange that any art should so
    help nature
In her extremes.
KAR.   Then it appears most real,
When th' other is deficient.

Enter Robin Hood.

ROB.   Wherefore stay you
    Discoursing here, and haste not with
        your succors   40
To poor afflicted Amie, that so needs
    them?
LIO. She is recovered well, your Marian
    told us
But now here. See, she is returned t' af-
    firm it!

Enter Maudl[in] like Marian. Maudl[in],
espying Robin Hood, would run out,
but he stays her by the girdle, and runs
in with her.

ROB. My Marian?
MAR.   Robin Hood! Is he here?
ROB.   Stay;
What was 't you ha' told my friend?
He returns with the girdle broken and she in
*   her own shape.*
MAUD.   Help, murder, help!
You will not rob me, outlaw? Thief,
    restore
My belt that ye have broken!
ROB.   Yes, come near.
MAUD. Not i' your gripe.
ROB.   Was this the charméd circle,[4]
The copy [5] that so cozened and deceived
    us?
I'll carry hence the trophy of your
    spoils.   50
My men shall hunt you too upon the
    start,[6]
And course [7] you soundly.
MAUD.   I shall make hem sport,
And send some home without their legs
    or arms.
I'll teach hem to climb stiles, leap ditches,
    ponds,
And lie i' the waters, if they follow me.

---

[1] Melodies.
[2] While Maudlin is still undiscovered she is
referred to as Marian.   [3] For her.

[4] Spell.
[5] Disguise, assumed shape.
[6] Without a fair start.   [7] Pursue.

Rob. Out, murmuring hag!

[*Exeunt All but Maudlin.*]

Maud.　　　　　I must use all my powers,
Lay all my wits to piecing of this loss.
Things run unluckily.　　Where's my
Puck-Hairy?

Act III. Scene v.

Maud, Puck.

[Maud.] Hath he forsook me?

Puck.　　　　　At your beck, madam.

Maud. O Puck, my goblin! I have lost
my belt;
The strong thief, Robin Outlaw, forced
it from me.

Puck. They are other clouds and blacker
threat you, dame;
You must be wary, and pull in your
sails,
And yield unto the weather of the tempest.
You think your power's infinite as your
malice,
And would do all your anger prompts you
to;
But you must wait occasions, and obey
them.

Sail in an eggshell, make a straw your
mast,　　　　　　　　　　　　　　10
A cobweb all your cloth,[1] and pass unseen,
Till you have scaped the rocks that are
about you.

Maud. What rocks about me?

Puck.　　　　　　　I do love, madam,
To show you all your dangers, when you
are past hem!
Come, follow me; I'll once more be your
pilot,
And you shall thank me.　　　[*Exit.*]

Maud.　　　　　Lucky, my loved goblin!

Lorel meets her.

Where are you gaang [2] now?

Lor.　　　　　　　Unto my tree,
To see my maistress.

Maud.　　　　　Gang thy gait, and try
Thy turns with better luck, or hang
thysel'.

The End.[3]

[1] Sail.　　　　　　　　　　[2] Going(?).

[3] The play, of course, is actually unfinished,
but F. G. Waldron published a completion of it
in 1783, reprinted by W. W. Greg in his edition
of the play (Bang's *Materialen*, 1905).

FRANCIS BEAUMONT AND
JOHN FLETCHER

When the first collected folio of Beaumont and Fletcher, containing a masque and some thirty-four plays, none of the latter having previously been printed, was published in 1647, long after the deaths of its authors, no attempt was made to discriminate between the parts of the famous collaborators; nor did the 1679 folio, in spite of its eighteen additional plays, suggest that a separation was desirable or feasible. But recent investigation has tended more and more strongly toward such a distinction, until, for instance, C. M. Gayley in his *Beaumont the Dramatist* is sure of only six plays as the joint product of Swinburne's Castor and Pollux of the English drama—although E. H. C. Oliphant in his *The Plays of Beaumont and Fletcher* prefers eight and allows the two men three more with the assistance of Massinger. Moreover, contrary to the older impression growing out of the longer dramatic career and larger output of Fletcher, virtually all modern critics insist that Beaumont was the greater dramatist. But the disentangling of the web has not ended here, since the hands of Massinger and Field, not to mention those of William Rowley, Shirley, Shakespeare, and others have been identified in a considerable part of the work which for many years masqueraded under the label of "Beaumont and Fletcher." The whole situation provides a striking commentary on the conditions of Elizabethan dramatic publication and authorship.

Both Beaumont and Fletcher brought a new respectability to the Stuart drama, for both came from excellent families and were able to picture the life of the upper classes, especially in comedies of manners and "fashion," with ease and authenticity. Fletcher's father eventually became Bishop of London, and his uncle, Giles Fletcher, himself an author, was the parent of the two Spenserian poets, Phineas and Giles the Younger. Beaumont (born about 1584) was the youngest son of a prominent judge, and his brother John early became recognized as a poet. Fletcher entered Cambridge about 1591, when he was some twelve years of age, and perhaps intended to take orders like his father, but the latter's loss of Elizabeth's favor soon afterward may account for the lack of any record of the boy's graduation; Beaumont went to Oxford in 1597, but by 1600 had transferred himself to the Inner Temple, though not necessarily because of any particular ambition to follow his father's profession of the law. The date at which the two men began to write, and even the date of their first collaboration, cannot be exactly established, but Beaumont published his first poetry about 1602, and seems soon to have become a friend of Jonson and a member of his circle—Dryden, in fact, preserving the story that Jonson had such a regard for the other's judgment that he submitted all his plays to him for criticism, especially as regarded plot. Probably both of the future collaborators had independently written a play or two apiece before their intimacy began, sometime between 1604 and 1606; but they rapidly became such friends that a tradition runs to the effect that they shared rooms on the Bankside and owned all things in common. Since almost no one holds to a date much earlier than 1606 for their first significant collaboration, and since Beaumont's marriage in 1613 and his non-professional attitude toward the drama led to an almost complete cessation of activity in literary creation after that date, the partnership was not actually very long in duration. After the year 1616 had seen the deaths of both Beaumont and his twenty-year senior, Shakespeare, Fletcher continued to write so prolifically and successfully, both alone and in his favorite collaboration, as to become the leading English dramatist, easily overshadowing Jonson in popularity. Fletcher died of the plague in 1625.

The Knight of the Burning Pestle is generally considered to have been written about 1607–8, although Oliphant, on the evidence of the printer's epistle, etc., prefers 1610. Some critics also believe it to have been written entirely by Beaumont, at least in its initial composition, but Oliphant, saying that none of Beaumont's unaided work is extant, agrees with earlier critics in attributing a small portion of it to Fletcher. According to the frank admission of the publisher in the prefatory epistle to the anonymous first quarto edition in 1613, the play was composed in little more than a week, and, upon being produced at the Blackfriars by the Children of the Queen's Revels, was promptly rejected by its audience, which obviously must have been restless under its satire as well as bored by its form. For, in addition to poking fun at the taste and manners of the London tradesman, the play is a burlesque not only of such popular romantic dramas as *Mucedorus* and Heywood's *The Four Prentices of London* but also of such fictional romances, in both verse and prose, as Rafe's own favorite *Palmerin of England*. The question of Beaumont's debt to *Don Quixote* has likewise produced much controversy, since no English translation of Cervantes' work has definitely been shown to have been printed before 1612, although the manuscript was apparently circulated before this date; moreover, though Fletcher used much Spanish material in later plays, Beaumont never did, and there is no evidence to show that either could read Spanish. French or English translations were usually available in some form or other. Scholarly opinion today inclines toward the rejection of the Spanish influence on the play and toward the stressing of the English motives, conventions, and tendencies of the time. The present text is based on the 1613 quarto as reprinted by R. M. Alden in the Belles-Lettres Series (New York, 1912), but these readings have been checked by reference to those given by H. S. Murch in his critical edition for the Yale Series in English in 1908, and by A. R. Waller in the Cambridge edition of the plays of Beaumont and Fletcher.

No serious question has ever been raised as to Fletcher's complete authorship of *The Faithful Shepherdess*, since the first quarto (undated, but probably issued about 1609–10, a year or two after the production by the Children of the Queen's Revels) bears his name, as do the four other editions preceding the second folio, in which there was no distinction of authors. This pastoral drama, or rather pastoral "tragi-comedy," which Fletcher carefully defines in his preface, is in the Italian tradition of Guarini's *Il Pastor Fido*, itself modeled after Tasso's *Aminta;* but these authors, as well as Spenser, merely furnished some general suggestions and a few incidental details without in any way detracting from Fletcher's originality. The plot, largely because of the several pairings of lovers necessitated by the author's desire to illustrate all the gradations of love from the most sensual to the most chaste, is rather complicated, but the poetry is fresh and graceful. Though the play was not a stage success, it has retained the enthusiasm of readers, and its influence is shown in Milton's *Comus*, both in theme and in versification. The present text follows the first quarto as given by Greg in the third volume of the Variorum edition, but, since different copies of the quarto vary, in rare cases Waller's readings in the Cambridge edition have been adopted.

Philaster, or Love Lies a-Bleeding, produced about 1609 and first printed in an imperfect quarto in 1620, was the earliest play of its authors, either singly or together, to achieve a popular success; it was the first important play to spring from their collaboration; and it was their first play to be acted by Shakespeare's company. It belongs to the type of romantic drama or tragi-comedy which was then coming into vogue, with its rapidity of action, its spectacular scenes, its contrast of love and lust, its mingling of humor and seriousness, its sentimentalities, its glittering but shallow characters drawn from the nobility, and its poetical passages. In spite of Thorndike's opinion, expressed in 1901, that these tragi-comedies of Beaumont and Fletcher influenced Shakespeare in *Cymbeline* and *The Winter's Tale*, the general view today is that the influence was in the opposite direction. *Philaster*, although held by Oliphant to be mostly by Beaumont, has given scholars an excellent opportunity to apply their tests of authorship to its various parts. These tests, after eliminating the negligible external evidence, depend upon the following internal elements: versification, especially Fletcher's free approximation of conversational prose effects by the use of weak (*i.e.*, double, triple, or even quadruple) endings for his lines, with a general avoidance of rime (*The Faithful Shepherdess* is an obvious exception), and a favoring of the end-stop; diction and recurring rhetorical devices, such as repetition of words, constructions, and ideas; and mental attitude, shown in the use of certain types of material, such as Fletcher's greater fondness for questionable moral situations and furtive innuendo, and Beaumont's more truly philosophical and speculative outlook. No source for *Philaster* has been discovered, though resemblances to parts of Sidney's *Arcadia* and Montemayor's *Diana* have been noted. The basis of the present text is the 1622 quarto ("second impression, corrected and amended") as reproduced by A. H. Thorndike in the Belles-Lettres Series (New York, 1906), but these readings have been checked with those of the same quarto as given in the Variorum edition by P. A. Daniel and in the Cambridge by Waller.

The Maid's Tragedy was apparently produced about 1611, and was printed anonymously in 1619. A revised edition was brought out in 1622, and another in 1630, containing the authors' names. Both the record of publications and the stage history of the play attest its extreme popularity, for it went through many editions, and leading actors appeared in it, or adaptations of it, on into the nineteenth century. Although Beaumont, famed for his plotting ability, is usually given credit for the major part of the tragedy, there are still some rather unnatural and unplausible aspects of both plot and motivation, but these are almost overlooked in the intensity and interest of the action. The tragedy of blood, lust, and revenge reaches one of its highest points in this play. No source for the plot is known, but the character and some of the acts of Aspatia are not unlike those of Sidney's deserted Parthenia. The present text follows Thorndike's reprint of the 1622 quarto in the Belles-Lettres Series (New York, 1906), checked by the readings of the same quarto given in the Variorum edition by Daniel and in the Cambridge by Waller.

THE KNIGHT OF THE BURNING PESTLE[1]

[BY

FRANCIS BEAUMONT AND JOHN FLETCHER][2]

To His Many Ways Endeared Friend,
Master Robert Keysar[3]

Sir:

This unfortunate child, who in eight days, as lately I have learned, was begot and born, soon after was by his parents (perhaps because he was so unlike his brethren) exposed to the wide world, who, for want of judgment or not understanding the privy mark of irony about it (which showed it was no offspring of any vulgar brain), utterly rejected it, so that for want of acceptance it was even [10 ready to give up the ghost and was in danger to have been smothered in perpetual oblivion, if you out of your direct antipathy to ingratitude had not been moved both to relieve and cherish it, wherein I must needs commend both your judgment, understanding, and singular love to good wits. You afterwards sent it to me, yet being an infant and somewhat ragged. I have fostered it privately [20 in my bosom these two years, and now to show my love return it to you, clad in good, lasting clothes which scarce memory will wear out, and able to speak for itself, and withal, as it telleth me, desirous to try his fortune in the world, where, if yet it be welcome, father, foster-father, nurse, and child—all have their desired end. If it be slighted or traduced, it hopes his father will beget him a younger [30 brother who shall revenge his quarrel and challenge the world either of fond[4]

and merely literal interpretation or illiterate misprision.[5] Perhaps it will be thought to be of the race of *Don Quixote.* We both may confidently swear it is his elder above a year, and therefore may by virtue of his birthright challenge the wall of[6] him. I doubt not but they will meet in their adventures, and I hope [40 the breaking of one staff will make them friends; and perhaps they will combine themselves and travel through the world to seek their adventures. So I commit him to his good fortune, and myself to your love.

Your assured friend,
W. B.[7]

[To the Readers of This Comedy[8]

Gentlemen:

The world is so nice[9] in these our times that for apparel there is no fashion; for music (which is a rare art, though now slighted), no instrument; for diet, none but the French kickshews[10] that are delicate; and, for plays, no invention but that which now runneth an invective way, touching some particular person, or else it is contemned before it is thoroughly understood. This is all that I have to say: [10 that the author had no intent to wrong anyone in this comedy, but, as a merry passage, here and there interlaced it with delight, which he hopes will please all, and be hurtful to none.

---

[1] The title at the head of the text is *The Famous History of the Knight of the Burning Pestle.*
[2] The names of the authors do not appear until the second quarto (1635).
[3] Concerning Keysar nothing is known.
[4] Foolish.

[5] Misapprehension.
[6] *I.e.,* take precedence of.
[7] Walter Burre, the publisher.
[8] The address "To the Readers," the prologue, and the dramatis personæ are all from the 1635 edn.
[9] Fastidious.
[10] Kickshaws.

PROLOGUE [1]

Where the bee can suck no honey, she leaves her sting behind; and, where the bear cannot find origanum [2] to heal his grief, he blasteth all other leaves with his breath. We fear it is like to fare so with us—that, seeing you cannot draw from our labors sweet content, you leave behind you a sour mislike, and with open reproach blame our good meanings, because you cannot reap the wonted mirth. Our intent was at this time to move [11 inward delight, not outward lightness, and to breed (if it might be) soft smiling, not loud laughing, knowing it to the wise to be a great pleasure to hear counsel mixed with wit, as to the foolish to have sport mingled with rudeness. They were banished the theater of Athens, and from Rome hissed, that brought parasites on the stage with apish actions, or fools [20 with uncivil habits, or courtesans with immodest words. We have endeavored to be as far from unseemly speeches to make your ears glow as we hope you will be free from unkind reports or mistaking the author's intention (who never aimed at any one particular in this play) to make our cheeks blush. And thus I leave it, and thee to thine own censure, to like or dislike.—*Vale.*[3]   30

THE SPEAKERS' NAMES

THE PROLOGUE.
Then A CITIZEN.
THE CITIZEN'S WIFE, *and* RAFE,[4] *her man, sitting below amidst the spectators.*
[VENTUREWELL,] *a rich merchant.*
JASPER, *his apprentice.*
MASTER HUMPHREY, *a friend to the merchant.*
LUCE, *merchant's daughter.*
MISTRESS MERRYTHOUGHT, *Jasper's mother.*
MICHAEL, *a second son of Mistress Merrythought.*
OLD MASTER MERRYTHOUGHT.

[TIM,] *a squire.*
[GEORGE,] *a dwarf.*
A TAPSTER.
A BOY *that danceth and singeth.*
AN HOST.
A BARBER.
[THREE CAPTIVE] KNIGHTS.[5]
[CAPTIVE WOMAN.]
A CAPTAIN.
A SERGEANT.
SOLDIERS.
[BOYS.
POMPIONA, *daughter of the King of Moldavia.*

SCENE: *London, Moldavia, etc.*

TIME: *Indefinite.*

INDUCTION

Several Gentlemen sitting on stools on the stage; the Citizen, his Wife, and Rafe standing below among the audience.]

Enter Prologue.

[PRO.] From all that's near the court, from all that's great,
Within the compass of the city [6] walls,
We now have brought our scene—

Enter Citizen [, *climbing onto the stage*].

CIT. Hold your peace, Goodman [7] Boy!
PRO. What do you mean, sir?
CIT. That you have no good meaning. This seven years there hath been plays at this house,[8] I have observed it, you have still girds [9] at citizens; and now you call your play *The London Merchant.* Down with your title,[10] boy! Down with [11 your title!
PRO. Are you a member of the noble city?
CIT. I am.

---

[1] This prologue is an almost exact reproduction of "The Prologue at the Blackfriars" prefixed to Lyly's *Sappho and Phao.*
[2] Marjoram.
[3] Farewell.
[4] Colloquial for *Ralph.*
[5] Early edns. read *Two Knights.*
[6] The business district of London, as opposed to Westminster, the court.
[7] Master.
[8] Probably Whitefriars, a private theater.
[9] Sneers.
[10] A sign hung or set on the stage to announce the name of the play.

Pro. And a freeman? [1]

Cit. Yea, and a grocer.

Pro. So, grocer, then, by your sweet favor, we intend no abuse to the city.

Cit. [2] No, sir! Yes, sir! If you were [20 not resolved to play the Jacks,[3] what need you study for new subjects, purposely to abuse your betters? Why could not you be contented, as well as others, with the legend of Whittington, or the life and death of Sir Thomas Gresham, with the building of the Royal Exchange, or the story of Queen Eleanor, with the rearing of London Bridge upon woolsacks? [4]   29

Pro. You seem to be an understanding man. What would you have us do, sir?

Cit. Why, present something notably in honor of the commons of the city.

Pro. Why, what do you say to the life and death of fat Drake, or the repairing of Fleet privies?

Cit. I do not like that; but I will have a citizen, and he shall be of my own trade.

Pro. O, you should have told us your mind a month since; our play is ready [40 to begin now.

Cit. 'Tis all one for that; I will have a grocer, and he shall do admirable [5] things.

Pro. What will you have him do?

Cit. Marry, I will have him—

Wife. (Below.[6]) Husband, husband!

Rafe. (Below.[7]) Peace, mistress!

Wife. Hold thy peace, Rafe; I know what I do, I warrant tee.[8] —Husband, [50 husband!

Cit. What sayst thou, cunny? [9]

Wife. Let him kill a lion with a pestle, husband! Let him kill a lion with a pestle!

Cit. So he shall.—I'll have him kill a lion with a pestle.

Wife. Husband!   Shall I come up, husband?

Cit. Ay, cunny.—Rafe, help your mistress this way.—Pray, gentlemen, [60

make her a little room.—I pray you, sir, lend me your hand to help up my wife. I thank you, sir.—So.

[Wife is pulled onto the stage.]

Wife. By your leave, gentlemen all; I'm something troublesome. I'm a stranger here; I was ne'er at one of these plays, as they say, before; but I should have seen [10] Jane Shore once; and my husband hath promised me, any time this twelvemonth, to carry me to the Bold Beauchamps, [70 but in truth he did not. I pray you, bear with me.

Cit. Boy, let my wife and I have a couple stools and then begin; and let the grocer do rare things. [Stools are brought.]

Pro. But, sir, we have never a boy [11] to play him; everyone hath a part already.

Wife. Husband, husband, for God's sake, let Rafe play him! Beshrew me, if I do not think he will go beyond them all. [80

Cit. Well remembered, wife.—Come up, Rafe.—I'll tell you, gentlemen; let them but lend him a suit of reparel [12] and necessaries, and, by Gad, if any of them all blow wind in the tail on him,[13] I'll be hanged.

[Rafe leaps onto the stage.]

Wife. I pray you, youth, let him have a suit of reparel!—I'll be sworn, gentlemen, my husband tells you true. He will act you sometimes at our house that [90 all the neighbors cry out on him; he will fetch you up a couraging part so in the garret that we are all as feared, I warrant you, that we quake again. We'll fear [14] our children with him; if they be never so unruly, do but cry, "Rafe comes, Rafe comes!" to them, and they'll be as quiet as lambs.—Hold up thy head, Rafe; show the gentlemen what thou canst do. Speak a huffing [15] part; I warrant you, [100 the gentlemen will accept of it.

Cit. Do, Rafe, do.

Rafe. "By heaven, methinks, it were an easy leap

---

[1] In this case, a member of one of the great tradesmen's guilds.

[2] The original prints the remainder of this scene in extremely irregular verse.

[3] Act like low fellows.

[4] Allusions to actual plays of the period.

[5] Wonderful.

[6] Marginal note in the original reads *Wife below.*

[7] Marginal note in the original reads *Rafe below.*

[8] Thee.

[9] Cony, pet.

[10] Was to have seen.

[11] The play was first performed by the Children of Her Majesty's Revels.

[12] Apparel.

[13] A vulgar expression for *find fault with him.*

[14] Frighten.

[15] Blustering.

To pluck bright honor from the pale-
faced moon,
Or dive into the bottom of the sea,
Where never fathom line touched any
ground,
And pluck up drownéd honor from the
lake of hell." [1]

CIT. How say you, gentlemen, is it not
as I told you?

WIFE. Nay, gentlemen, he hath [110
played before, my husband says, *Mucedorus*, before the wardens of our Company.

CIT. Ay, and he should have played
Jeronimo [2] with a shoemaker for a wager.

PRO. He shall have a suit of apparel,
if he will go in.

CIT. In, Rafe, in, Rafe, and set out the
grocery [3] in their kind, [4] if thou lov'st me.
[*Exit Rafe.*]

WIFE. I warrant, our Rafe will look
finely when he's dressed.   120

PRO. But what will you have it called?

CIT. *The Grocer's Honor.*

PRO. Methinks *The Knight of the Burning Pestle* were better.

WIFE. I'll be sworn, husband, that's
as good a name as can be.

CIT. Let it be so.—Begin, begin; my
wife and I will sit down.

PRO. I pray you, do.   129

CIT. What stately music have you?
You have shawms? [5]

PRO. Shawns? No.

CIT. No? I'm a thief if my mind did
not give [6] me so. Rafe plays a stately part,
and he must needs have shawns. I'll be
at the charge of them myself rather than
we'll be without them.

PRO. So you are like to be.

CIT. Why, and so I will be; there's
two shillings. [*Gives money.*] Let's [140
have the waits [7] of Southwark; they are
as rare fellows as any are in England;
and that will fetch them all o'er the water
with a vengeance, as if they were mad.

PRO. You shall have them. Will you
sit down then?

CIT. Ay.—Come, wife.

WIFE. Sit you merry all, gentlemen;

I'm bold to sit amongst you for my ease.
[*Citizen and Wife sit down.*]

PRO. From all that's near the court,
from all that's great,   150
Within the compass of the city walls,
We now have brought our scene. Fly
far from hence
All private taxes, [8] immodest phrases,
Whatever may but show like vicious!
For wicked mirth never true pleasure
brings,
But honest minds are pleased with hon-
est things.—
Thus much for that we do; but for
Rafe's part you must answer for yourself.

CIT. Take you no care for Rafe; he'll
discharge himself, I warrant you.   160
[*Exit Prologue.*]

WIFE. I' faith, gentlemen, I'll give my
word for Rafe.

ACTUS PRIMI SCENA PRIMA. [9]

[*A room in Venturewell's house.*]

*Enter Merchant [Venturewell] and Jasper,
his prentice.*

MERCH. Sirrah, I'll make you know you
are my prentice,
And whom my charitable love redeemed
Even from the fall of fortune; gave
thee heat
And growth, to be what now thou art;
new-cast [10] thee,
Adding the trust of all I have at home,
In foreign staples, [11] or upon the sea,
To thy direction; tied the good opinions
Both of myself and friends to thy en-
deavors.
So fair were thy beginnings. But with
these,
As I remember, you had never charge 10
To love your master's daughter, and
even then
When I had found a wealthy husband
for her.
I take it, sir, you had not. But, however,
I'll break the neck of that commission,
And make you know you are but a
merchant's factor.

JASP. Sir, I do liberally confess I am yours,
Bound both by love and duty to your
service,

---

[1] A slightly inaccurate quotation from Shakespeare's *I Henry IV*, I, iii.
[2] The conventional allusion to *The Spanish
Tragedy*.   [5] Wind instruments.
[3] Grocers.   [6] Misgive.
[4] In their proper livery.   [7] Musicians.
[8] Criticisms of individuals.   [10] Remade.
[9] Scene one of act one.   [11] Markets.

In which my labor hath been all my
profit;
I have not lost in bargain, nor delighted
To wear your honest gains upon my
back;   20
Nor have I given a pension to my blood,[1]
Or lavishly in play consumed your stock;
These, and the miseries that do attend
them,
I dare with innocence proclaim are
strangers
To all my temperate actions. For your
daughter,
If there be any love to my deservings
Borne by her virtuous self, I cannot
stop it;
Nor am I able to refrain[2] her wishes.
She's private to herself and best of
knowledge[3]
Whom she'll make so happy as to sigh
for;   30
Besides, I cannot think you mean to
match her
Unto a fellow of so lame a presence,
One that hath little left of nature in
him.
MERCH. 'Tis very well, sir; I can tell
your wisdom
How all this shall be cured.
JASP.   Your care becomes you.
MERCH. And thus it must be, sir: I here
discharge you
My house and service; take your liberty;
And, when I want a son, I'll send for
you.   *Exit.*
JASP. These be the fair rewards of them
that love!   39
O, you that live in freedom, never prove
The travail of a mind led by desire!

Enter Luce.

LUCE. Why, how now, friend?   Struck
with my father's thunder?
JASP. Struck, and struck dead, unless the
remedy
Be full of speed and virtue; I am now,
What I expected long, no more your
father's.
LUCE. But mine.
JASP.   But yours, and only yours, I am;

That's all I have to keep me from the
statute.[4]
You dare be constant still?
LUCE.   O, fear me not!
In this I dare be better than a woman.
Nor shall his anger nor his offers move me,
Were they both equal to a prince's
power.   51
JASP. You know my rival?
LUCE.   Yes, and love him dearly,
Even as I love an ague or foul weather.
I prithee, Jasper, fear him not.
JASP.   O, no!
I do not mean to do him so much kind-
ness.
But to our own desires: you know the plot
We both agreed on?
LUCE.   Yes, and will perform
My part exactly.
JASP.   I desire no more.
Farewell, and keep my heart; 'tis yours.
LUCE.   I take it;
He must do miracles makes me forsake
it.   *Exeunt.* 60

CIT. Fie upon 'em, little infidels! What
a matter's here now? Well, I'll be hanged
for a halfpenny, if there be not some
abomination knavery in this play. Well,
let 'em look to 't; Rafe must come, and if
there be any tricks a-brewing—
WIFE. Let 'em brew, and bake too,
husband, a[5] God's name; Rafe will find
all out, I warrant you, and[6] they were
older than they are.—   70

[Enter Boy.]

I pray, my pretty youth, is Rafe ready?
BOY. He will be presently.
WIFE. Now, I pray you, make my commendations unto him, and withal carry
him this stick of licoras.[7] Tell him his
mistress sent it him, and bid him bite a
piece; 'twill open his pipes the better, say.
                                [Exit Boy.]

[SCENA SECUNDA.

The same.]

Enter Merchant and Master Humphrey.

MERCH. Come, sir, she's yours; upon my
faith, she's yours.

---

[1] A license to my passion.
[2] Restrain.
[3] *I.e.*, she is secret and knows best.

[4] Against masterless men.   [6] If.
[5] In.   [7] Licorice.

You have my hand. For other idle lets [1]
Between your hopes and her, thus with
    a wind
They are scattered and no more. My
    wanton prentice,
That like a bladder blew himself with
    love,
I have let out, and sent him to discover
New masters yet unknown.
HUM.   I thank you, sir;
    Indeed, I thank you, sir; and, ere I stir,
    It shall be known, however you do deem,
    I am of gentle blood and gentle seem.   10
MERCH. O, sir, I know it certain.
HUM.   Sir, my friend,
    Although, as writers say, all things have
        end,
    And that we call a pudding hath his two,
    O, let it not seem strange, I pray, to you,
    If in this bloody simile I put
    My love, more endless than frail things
        or gut!

WIFE. Husband, I prithee, sweet lamb,
tell me one thing, but tell me truly.—
Stay, youths, I beseech you, till I question
my husband.   20
    CIT. What is it, mouse?
    WIFE. Sirrah, didst thou ever see a
prettier child? How it behaves itself, I
warrant ye, and speaks and looks and
perts [2] up the head!—I pray you, brother,
with your favor, were you never none of
M[aster] Monkester's [3] scholars?
    CIT. Chicken, I prithee heartily, con-
tain thyself; the childer [4] are pretty childer;
but, when Rafe comes, lamb—   30
    WIFE. Ay, when Rafe comes, conny!—
Well, my youth, you may proceed.

MERCH. Well, sir, you know my love, and
    rest, I hope,
    Assured of my consent; get but my
        daughter's,
    And wed her when you please. You must
        be bold,
    And clap in close unto her; come, I know
    You have language good enough to win
        a wench.

[1] Obstacles.
[2] Cocks.
[3] Richard Mulcaster, until 1608 Headmaster
of St. Paul's School, encouraged the acting of
plays among his pupils.
[4] Children.

WIFE. A whoreson [5] tyrant! H'as been
an old stringer [6] in 's days, I warrant him.

HUM. I take your gentle offer, and withal
    Yield love again for love reciprocal.   [41
MERCH. What, Luce! Within there!

Enter Luce.

LUCE.   Called you, sir?
MERCH.   I did.
    Give entertainment to this gentleman,
    And see you be not froward.—To her,
        sir;
    My presence will but be an eyesore to
        you.   *Exit.*
HUM. Fair Mistress Luce, how do you do?
    Are you well?
    Give me your hand, and then I pray
        you tell
    How doth your little sister and your
        brother,
    And whether you love me or any other.
LUCE. Sir, these are quickly answered.
HUM.   So they are,   50
    Where women are not cruel. But how
        far
    Is it now distant from this place we are
        in,
    Unto that blessed place, your father's
        warren?
LUCE. What makes you think of that, sir?
HUM.   Even that face;
    For, stealing rabbits whilom [7] in that
        place,
    God Cupid, or the keeper, I know not
        whether, [8]
    Unto my cost and charges brought you
        thither,
    And there began—
LUCE.   Your game, sir.
HUM.   Let no game,
    Or anything that tendeth to the same,
    Be evermore remembered, thou fair
        killer,   60
    For whom I sat me down, and brake my
        tiller. [9]

WIFE. There's a kind gentleman, I
warrant you; when will you do as much for
me, George?

[5] Rascally.   [8] Which.
[6] Libertine.   [9] Crossbow.
[7] Formerly.

LUCE. Beshrew me, sir, I am sorry for
  your losses,
  But, as the proverb says, I cannot cry.
  I would you had not seen me!
HUM.   So would I,
  Unless you had more maw [1] to do me
  good.
LUCE. Why, cannot this strange passion
  be withstood?   69
  Send for a constable, and raise the town.
HUM. O, no! My valiant love will batter
  down
  Millions of constables, and put to flight
  Even that great watch of Midsummer
  Day at night. [2]
LUCE. Beshrew me, sir, 'twere good I
  yielded then;
  Weak women cannot hope, where val-
  iant men
  Have no resistance.
HUM.   Yield, then; I am full
  Of pity, though I say it, and can pull
  Out of my pocket thus a pair of gloves.
  Look, Lucy, look; the dog's tooth nor
  the dove's
  Are not so white as these; and sweet
  they be,   80
  And whipped [3] about with silk, as you
  may see.
  If you desire the price, shoot [4] from your
  eye
  A beam to this place, and you shall espy
  "F S," [5] which is to say, my sweetest
  honey,
  They cost me three and twopence, or
  no money.
LUCE. Well, sir, I take them kindly, and
  I thank you.
  What would you more?
HUM.   Nothing.
LUCE.   Why, then, farewell.
HUM. Nor so, nor so; for, lady, I must
  tell,
  Before we part, for what we met to-
  gether.
  God grant me time and patience and
  fair weather!   90
LUCE. Speak, and declare your mind in
  terms so brief.

HUM. I shall. Then, first and foremost,
  for relief
  I call to you, I, if that you can afford it;
  I care not at what price, for, on my word,
  it
  Shall be repaid again, although it cost me
  More than I'll speak of now, for love
  hath tossed me
  In furious blanket like a tennis ball,
  And now I rise aloft, and now I fall.
LUCE. Alas, good gentleman, alas the
  day!
HUM. I thank you heart[i]ly; and, as I
  say,   100
  Thus do I still continue without rest,
  I' th' morning like a man, at night a
  beast,
  Roaring and bellowing mine own dis-
  quiet,
  That much I fear forsaking of my diet
  Will bring me presently to that quan-
  dary
  I shall bid all adieu.
LUCE.   Now, by S[t]. Mary,
  That were great pity!
HUM.   So it were, beshrew me;
  Then, ease me, lusty [6] Luce, and pity
  show me.
LUCE. Why, sir, you know my will is
  nothing worth
  Without my father's grant; get his
  consent,   110
  And then you may with assurance try me.
HUM. The worshipful your sire will not
  deny me;
  For I have asked him, and he hath
  replied,
  "Sweet Master Humphrey, Luce shall
  be thy bride."
LUCE. Sweet Master Humphrey, then
  I am content.
HUM. And so am I, in truth.
LUCE.   Yet take me with you; [7]
  There is another clause must be annexed,
  And this it is (I swore, and will perform
  it):
  No man shall ever joy [8] me as his wife
  But he that stole me hence. If you dare
  venter, [9]   120
  I am yours (you need not fear; my
  father loves you);
  If not, farewell forever!

[1] Appetite, desire.
[2] The annual military muster of the guilds.
[3] Embroidered.
[4] From 1711 edn. Original reads *sute*.
[5] Evidently the trade-mark or price mark.

[6] Jolly.
[7] Understand me fully.

[8] Enjoy.
[9] Venture.

Hum.   Stay, nymph, stay.
I have a double gelding, colored bay,
Sprung by his father from Barbarian [1]
    kind;
Another for myself, though somewhat
    blind,
Yet true as trusty tree.
Luce.   I am satisfied;
And so I give my hand. Our course
    must lie
Through Waltham Forest, where I have
    a friend
Will entertain us. So, farewell, Sir Hum-
    phrey,
And think upon your business.
                                    Exit Luce.
Hum.   Though I die, 130
I am resolved to venter life and limb
For one so young, so fair, so kind, so
    trim.   *Exit Humphrey.*

Wife. By my faith and troth, George,
and as I am virtuous, it is e'en the kindest
young man that ever trod on shoe leather.
—Well, go thy ways; if thou hast her not,
'tis not thy fault, faith.

Cit. I prithee, mouse, be patient; a [2]
shall have her, or I'll make some [of] [3] 'em
smoke [4] for 't.   140

Wife. That's my good lamb, George.—
Fie, this stinking tobacco kills men! [5]
Would there were none in England!—Now,
I pray, gentlemen, what good does this
stinking tobacco do you? Nothing, I war-
rant. You make chimneys a [6] your faces!—
O, husband, husband, now, now! There's
Rafe, there's Rafe.

[Scena Tertia.]

*Enter Rafe, like a grocer in 's shop with
    two Prentices, [Tim and George,] read-
    ing Palmerin of England.*

Cit. Peace, fool! Let Rafe alone.—
Hark you, Rafe; do not strain yourself
too much at the first.—Peace!—Begin,
Rafe.

Rafe. [*Reading.*] [7] "Then Palmerin and
Trineus, snatching their launces from

their dwarfs, and clasping their helmets,
galloped amain after the giant; and Palmerin, having gotten a sight of him, came
posting amain, saying, 'Stay, traitor- [10
ous thief! For thou mayst not so carry
away her that is worth the greatest lord
in the world;' and with these words gave
him a blow on the shoulder that he
stroke [8] him besides [9] his elephant. And
Trineus, coming to the knight that had
Agricola behind him, set him soon besides
his horse, with his neck broken in the
fall, so that the princess, getting out of
the throng, between joy and grief, [20
said, 'All happy knight, the mirror of all
such as follow arms, now may I be well
assured of the love thou bearest me.' "—
I wonder why the kings do not raise an
army of fourteen or fifteen hundred thousand men, as big as the army that the
Prince of Portigo brought against Rosicleer, and destroy these giants; they do
much hurt to wandering damsels that
go in quest of their knights.   30

Wife. Faith, husband, and Rafe says
true; for they say the King of Portugal
cannot sit at his meat but the giants and
the ettins [10] will come and snatch it from
him.

Cit. Hold thy tongue!—On, Rafe!

Rafe. And certainly those knights are
much to be commended, who, neglecting
their possessions, wander with a squire
and a dwarf through the deserts to [40
relieve poor ladies.

Wife. Ay, by faith, are they, Rafe;
let 'em say what they will, they are indeed. Our knights neglect their possessions well enough, but they do not the rest.

Rafe. There are no such courteous
and fair well-spoken knights in this age;
they will call one "the son of a whore"
that Palmerin of England would have
called "fair sir"; and one that Rosi- [50
cleer would have called "right beauteous
damsel" they will call "damned bitch."

Wife. I'll be sworn will they, Rafe;
they have called me so an hundred times
about a scurvy pipe of tobacco.

---

[1] *I.e.*, Barbary.
[2] He.
[3] From 1635 edn.
[4] Suffer.
[5] Me(?).
[6] Of.
[7] The following passage is actually a con-
densed quotation from Munday's translation
of *Palmerin de Oliva*

[8] Struck.
[9] Off.
[10] Another word for *giants*.

RAFE. But what brave spirit could be content to sit in his shop, with a flappet [1] of wood and a blue apron before him, selling mithridatum and dragon's-water [2] to visited [3] houses, that might pursue [60 feats of arms, and, through his noble achievements, procure such a famous history to be written of his heroic prowess?

CIT. Well said, Rafe; some more of those words, Rafe!
WIFE. They go finely, by my troth.

RAFE. Why should not I then pursue this course, both for the credit of myself and our company? For, amongst all the worthy books of achievements, I do [70 not call to mind that I yet read of a grocer-errant. I will be the said knight.—Have you heard of any that hath wandered unfurnished of his squire and dwarf? My elder prentice Tim shall be my trusty squire, and little George my dwarf. Hence, my blue aporn! [4]   Yet, in remembrance of my former trade, upon my shield shall be portrayed a burning pestle, and I will be called the Knight o' th' Burning Pestle.

WIFE. Nay, I dare swear thou wilt [81 not forget thy old trade; thou wert ever meek.

RAFE. Tim!
TIM. Anon.
RAFE. My beloved squire, and George my dwarf, I charge you that from henceforth you never call me by any other name but "the right courteous and valiant Knight of the Burning Pestle," and [90 that you never call any female by the name of a woman or wench, but "fair lady," if she have her desires; if not, "distressed damsel;" that you call all forests and heaths "deserts," and all horses "palfreys."

WIFE. This is very fine, faith.—Do the gentlemen like Rafe, think you, husband?
CIT. Ay, I warrant thee; the players would give all the shoes in their shop [100 for him.

RAFE. My beloved squire Tim, stand out. Admit this were a desert, and over it a knight-errant pricking, [5] and I should bid you inquire of his intents, what would you say?
TIM. Sir, my master sent me to know whither you are riding?
RAFE. No, thus: "Fair sir, the right courteous and valiant Knight of the [110 Burning Pestle commanded me to inquire upon what adventure you are bound, whether to relieve some distressed damsels, or otherwise."

CIT. Whoresome [6] blockhead, cannot remember!
WIFE. I' faith, and Rafe told him on 't before; all the gentlemen heard him.—Did he not, gentlemen? Did not Rafe tell him on 't?

GEORGE. Right courteous and valiant Knight of the Burning Pestle, here is a distressed damsel to have a halfpennyworth of pepper.

WIFE. That's a good boy! See, the little boy can hit it; by my troth, it's a fine child.

RAFE. Relieve her, with all courteous language. Now shut up shop; no more my prentice, but my trusty squire [130 and dwarf. I must bespeak my shield and arming [7] pestle. [Exeunt Tim and George.]

CIT. Go thy ways, Rafe! As I'm a true man, thou art the best on 'em all.
WIFE. Rafe, Rafe!
RAFE. What say you, mistress?
WIFE. I prithee, come again quickly, sweet Rafe.
RAFE. By-and-by. [8]   Exit Rafe.

[SCENA QUARTA.

A room in Merrythought's house.]

Enter Jasper and his mother, Mistress Merrythought.

MIST. MER. Give thee my blessing? No, I'll ne'er give thee my blessing; I'll

---

[1] Ledge, i.e., of the counter.
[2] Medicines used against the plague.
[3] I.e., by the plague.   [4] Apron.

see thee hanged first; it shall ne'er be said I gave thee my blessing. Th' art thy father's own son, of the right blood of the Merrythoughts. I may curse the time that e'er I knew thy father; he hath spent all his own and mine too; and, when I tell him of it, he laughs, and dances, and sings, and cries, "A merry heart lives [10 long-a." And thou art a wastethrift, and art run away from thy master that loved thee well, and art come to me; and I have laid up a little for my younger son Michael, and thou think'st to bezzle [1] that, but thou shalt never be able to do it.—Come hither, Michael! Come, Michael.

Enter Michael.

Down on thy knees; thou shalt have my blessing.   19

MICH. [Kneeling.] I pray you, mother, pray to God to bless me.

MIST. MER. God bless thee! [Michael rises.] But Jasper shall never have my blessing; he shall be hanged first; shall he not, Michael? How say'st thou?

MICH. Yes, forsooth, mother, and grace of God.

MIST. MER. That's a good boy!

WIFE. Ay, faith, it's a fine-spoken child.

JASP. Mother, though you forget a parent's love,   30
I must preserve the duty of a child.
I ran not from my master, nor return
To have your stock maintain my idleness.

WIFE. Ungracious child, I warrant him; hark, how he chops logic [2] with his mother!—Thou hadst best tell her she lies; do tell her she lies.

CIT. If he were my son, I would hang him up by the heels, and flay him, and salt him, whoreson haltersack. [3]   40

JASP. My coming only is to beg your love,
Which I must ever, though I never gain it;
And, howsoever you esteem of me,

[1] Embezzle, squander.
[2] Argues.   [3] Gallows bird.

There is no drop of blood hid in these veins
But, I remember well, belongs to you
That brought me forth, and would be glad for you
To rip them all again, and let it out.

MIST. MER. Ay, faith, I had sorrow enough for thee, God knows; but I'll hamper thee well enough. Get thee [50 in, thou vagabond, get thee in, and learn of thy brother Michael.

[Exeunt Jasper and Michael.]

OLD MER. ([Singing] within.)

Nose, nose, jolly red nose,
And who gave thee this jolly red nose?

MIST. MER. Hark, my husband! He's singing and hoiting, [4] and I'm fain to cark and care, and all little enough.—Husband! Charles! Charles Merrythought!

Enter Old Merrythought.

OLD MER. [Singing.]

Nutmegs and ginger, cinnamon and cloves—
And they gave me this jolly red nose.   60

MIST. MER. If you would consider your state, you would have little list [5] to sing, iwis. [6]

OLD MER. It should never be considered, while it were an estate, if I thought it would spoil my singing.

MIST MER. But how wilt thou do, Charles? Thou art an old man, and thou canst not work, and thou hast not forty shillings left, and thou eatest good [70 meat, and drinkest good drink, and laughest.

OLD MER. And will do.

MIST. MER. But how wilt thou come by it, Charles?

OLD MER. How? Why, how have I done hitherto this forty years? I never came into my dining room but at eleven and six a-clock I found excellent meat and drink a th' table; my clothes were [80 never worn out but next morning a tailor brought me a new suit; and without question it will be so ever; use makes perfectness. If all should fail, it is but a little

[4] Making merry.   [5] Desire.   [6] Certainly.

straining myself extraordinary and laugh myself to death.

WIFE. It's a foolish old man this, is not he, George?

CIT. Yes, cunny.

WIFE. Give me a penny i' th' purse [90 while I live, George.

CIT. Ay, by Lady, cunny; hold thee there.[1]

MIST. MER. Well, Charles, you promised to provide for Jasper, and I have laid up for Michael. I pray you, pay Jasper his portion. He's come home, and he shall not consume Michael's stock; he says his master turned him away, but, I promise you truly, I think he ran away.   100

WIFE. No, indeed, Mistress Merrythought; though he be a notable gallows,[2] yet I'll assure you his master did turn him away, even in this place. 'Twas, i' faith, within this half hour, about his daughter; my husband was by.

CIT. Hang him, rogue! He served him well enough. Love his master's daughter! By my troth, cunny, if there were a thousand boys, thou wouldst spoil them [110 all with taking their parts. Let his mother alone with him.

WIFE. Ay, George; but yet truth is truth.

OLD MER. Where is Jasper? He's welcome, however. Call him in; he shall have his portion. Is he merry?

Enter Jasper and Michael.

MIST. MER. Ay, foul chive[3] him, he is too merry!—Jasper! Michael!

OLD MER. Welcome, Jasper! Though [120 thou runn'st away, welcome! God bless thee! 'Tis thy mother's mind thou shouldst receive thy portion. Thou hast been abroad, and I hope hast learned experience enough to govern it; thou art of sufficient years. Hold thy hand—one, two, three, four, five, six, seven, eight, nine, there's ten shillings for thee. [*Gives money.*] Thrust thyself into the world with that,

and take some settled course. If [130 fortune cross thee, thou hast a retiring place. Come home to me; I have twenty shillings left. Be a good husband,[4] that is, wear ordinary clothes, eat the best meat, and drink the best drink; be merry, and give to the poor; and, believe me, thou hast no end of thy goods.

JASP. Long may you live free from all thought of ill,
And long have cause to be thus merry still!
But, father—   140

OLD MER. No more words, Jasper; get thee gone. Thou hast my blessing; thy father's spirit upon thee! Farewell, Jasper!
[*Sings.*]

But yet, or ere you part (O, cruel!),
Kiss me, kiss me, sweeting, mine own dear jewel!

So, now begone; no words.   *Exit Jasper.*

MIST. MER. So, Michael, now get thee gone too.

MICH. Yes, forsooth, mother; but I'll have my father's blessing first.   150

MIST. MER. No, Michael; 'tis no[5] matter for his blessing. Thou hast my blessing; begone. I'll fetch my money and jewels, and follow thee; I'll stay no longer with him, I warrant thee.—[*Exit Michael.*] Truly, Charles, I'll be gone too.

OLD MER. What, you will not?

MIST. MER. Yes, indeed will I.

OLD MER. [*Singing.*]

Heigh-ho, farewell, Nan!   159
I'll never trust wench more again, if I can.

MIST. MER. You shall not think, when all your own is gone, to spend that I have been scraping up for Michael.

OLD MER. Farewell, good wife; I expect it not. All I have to do in this world is to be merry, which I shall, if the ground be not taken from me; and, if it be, [*Sings.*]

When earth and seas from me are reft,
The skies aloft for me are left.   169
Exeunt.

Boy danceth. Music.

FINIS ACTUS PRIMI.

Stand by your belief.
[2] Gallows bird.   [3] Ill befall.

[4] Be economical.
[5] From 1635 edn. Original has *now.*

WIFE. I'll be sworn he's a merry old gentleman for all that. Hark, hark, husband, hark! Fiddles, fiddles! Now surely they go finely. They say 'tis present death for these fiddlers to tune their rebecks before the great Turk's grace, is 't not, George? But look, look! Here's a youth dances!—Now, good youth, do a turn a th' toe.—Sweetheart, i' faith, I'll have Rafe come and do some of his gambols.— He'll ride the wild mare,[1] gentle- [180 men, 'twould do your hearts good to see him.—I thank you, kind youth; pray, bid Rafe come.

CIT. Peace, cunny!—Sirrah, you scurvy boy, bid the players send Rafe; or, by God's——,[2] and they do not, I'll tear some of their periwigs beside their heads; this is all riffraff.   [Exit Boy.]

ACTUS SECUNDI SCENA PRIMA.

[A room in Venturewell's house.]

Enter Merchant and Humphrey.

MERCH. And how, faith, how goes it now, son Humphrey?

HUM. Right worshipful, and my beloved friend
And father dear, this matter's at an end.

MERCH. 'Tis well; it should be so. I'm glad the girl
Is found so tractable.

HUM.   Nay, she must whirl
From hence (and you must wink, for so, I say,
The story[3] tells) tomorrow before day.

WIFE. George, dost thou think in thy conscience now 'twill be a match? Tell me but what thou think'st, sweet [10 rogue. Thou seest the poor gentleman, dear heart, how it labors and throbs, I warrant you, to be at rest! I'll go move the father for 't.

CIT. No, no; I prithee, sit still, honeysuckle; thou'lt spoil all. If he deny him, I'll bring half a dozen good fellows myself, and in the shutting of an evening knock 't up, and there's an end.

WIFE. I'll buss thee for that, i' [20 faith, boy. Well, George, well, you have

[1] Play at seesaw.
[2] To be filled in by the actor.
[3] I.e., the plan of eloping.

been a wag in your days, I warrant you; but God forgive you, and I do with all my heart.

MERCH. How was it, son? You told me that tomorrow
Before daybreak you must convey her hence.

HUM. I must, I must; and thus it is agreed:
Your daughter rides upon a brown-bay steed,
I on a sorrel, which I bought of Brian,   29
The honest host of the red roaring Lion,
In Waltham situate. Then, if you may,
Consent in seemly sort, lest, by delay,
The Fatal Sisters come, and do the office,
And then you'll sing another song.

MERCH.   Alas,
Why should you be thus full of grief to me,
That do as willing as yourself agree
To anything, so it be good and fair?
Then, steal her when you will, if such a pleasure
Content you both; I'll sleep and never see it,
To make your joys more full. But tell me why   40
You may not here perform your marriage?

WIFE. God's blessing a thy soul, old man! I' faith, thou art loath to part true hearts. I see a has her, George; and I'm as glad on 't!—Well, go thy ways, Humphrey; for a fair-spoken man, I believe thou hast not thy fellow within the walls of London; and I should say the suburbs too, I should not lie.—Why dost not rejoice with me, George?   50

CIT. If I could but see Rafe again, I were as merry as mine host, i' faith.

HUM. The cause you seem to ask, I thus declare—
Help me, O Muses nine! Your daughter sware
A foolish oath, and more it was the pity;
Yet none but myself within this city
Shall dare to say so, but a bold defiance
Shall meet him, were he of the noble science;[4]

[4] I.e., a fencer.

And yet she sware, and yet why did
she swear?
Truly, I cannot tell, unless it were   60
For her own ease, for, sure, sometimes
an oath,
Being sworn thereafter, is like cordial
broth;
And thus it was she swore, never to
marry
But such a one whose mighty arm could
carry
(As meaning me, for I am such a one)
Her bodily away, through stick and
stone,
Till both of us arrive, at her request,
Some ten miles off, in the wild Wal-
tham Forest.
MERCH. If this be all, you shall not need
to fear
Any denial in your love. Proceed;   70
I'll neither follow, nor repent the deed.
HUM. Good night, twenty good nights,
and twenty more,
And twenty more good nights—that
makes threescore!   *Exeunt.*

[SCENA SECUNDA.

Waltham Forest.]

*Enter Mistress Merrythought and her son
Michael.*

MIST. MER. Come, Michael; art thou
not weary, boy?
MICH. No, forsooth, mother, not I.
MIST. MER. Where be we now, child?
MICH. Indeed, forsooth, mother, I cannot tell, unless we be at Mile End. Is not
all the world Mile End, mother?
MIST. MER. No, Michael, not all the
world, boy; but I can assure thee, Michael,
Mile End is a goodly matter. There [10
has been a pitchfield,[1] my child, between
the naughty Spaniels and the Englishmen; and the Spaniels ran away, Michael,
and the Englishmen followed. My neighbor Coxstone was there, boy, and killed
them all with a birding piece.
MICH. Mother, forsooth—
MIST. MER. What says my white[2] boy?
MICH. Shall not my father go with us
too?   20

MIST. MER. No, Michael, let thy father
go snick up;[3] he shall never come between
a pair of sheets with me again while he
lives. Let him stay at home, and sing for
his supper, boy. Come, child, sit down,
and I'll show my boy fine knacks, indeed.
[*They sit down; and she opens a casket.*]
Look here, Michael; here's a ring, and
here's a brooch, and here's a bracelet, and
here's two rings more, and here's money
and gold by th' eye,[4] my boy.   30
MICH. Shall I have all this, mother?
MIST. MER. Ay, Michael, thou shalt
have all, Michael.

CIT. How lik'st thou this, wench?
WIFE. I cannot tell; I would have Rafe,
George; I'll see no more else, indeed-law;[5]
and, I pray you, let the youths understand so much by word of mouth; for, I
tell you truly, I'm afraid a my boy. Come,
come, George, let's be merry and [40
wise; the child's a fatherless child; and
say they should put him into a strait pair
of gaskins,[6] 'twere worse than knotgrass;[7]
he would never grow after it.

Enter Rafe, Squire, and Dwarf.

CIT. Here's Rafe, here's Rafe!
WIFE. How do you do, Rafe? You are
welcome, Rafe, as I may say. It's a good
boy; hold up thy head, and be not afraid.
We are thy friends, Rafe; the gentlemen
will praise thee, Rafe, if thou play'st [50
thy part with audacity. Begin, Rafe, a
God's name!

RAFE. My trusty squire, unlace my
helm; give me my hat. Where are we, or
what desert may this be?
DWARF. Mirror of knighthood, this
is, as I take it, the perilous Waltham
Down, in whose bottom stands the enchanted valley.
MIST. MER. O, Michael, we are be- [60
trayed, we are betrayed! Here be giants!
Fly, boy! Fly, boy, fly!
Exeunt Mother and Michael [, *leaving the
casket*].

[3] Go hang.
[4] In unlimited quantity.
[5] An exclamation of annoyance.
[6] Tight breeches.
[7] A concoction of this was supposed to retard
growth.

[1] Perhaps an allusion to a sham battle fought
on this drill ground by the trained bands.
[2] Dear.

RAFE. Lace on my helm again. What
    noise is this?
  A gentle lady, flying the embrace
  Of some uncourteous knight! I will re-
    lieve her.
  Go, squire, and say the knight that
    wears this pestle
  In honor of all ladies swears revenge
  Upon that recreant coward that pur-
    sues her.
  Go, comfort her, and that same gentle
    squire
  That bears her company.
SQUIRE.   I go, brave knight. [*Exit.*] 70
RAFE. My trusty dwarf and friend, reach
    me my shield,
  And hold it while I swear. First, by my
    knighthood;
  Then by the soul of Amadis de Gaul,
  My famous ancestor; then by my sword
  The beauteous Brionella girt about me;
  By this bright burning pestle, of mine
    honor
  The living trophy; and by all respect
  Due to distressèd damsels, here I vow
  Never to end the quest of this fair
    lady
  And that forsaken squire till by my
    valor   80
  I gain their liberty!
DWARF.   Heaven bless the knight
  That thus relieves poor errant gentle-
    women!   *Exit* [*with Rafe*].

WIFE. Ay, marry, Rafe, this has some
savor in 't; I would see the proudest of
them all offer to carry his books after him.
But, George, I will not have him go away
so soon; I shall be sick if he go away, that
I shall. Call Rafe again, George, call Rafe
again; I prithee, sweetheart, let him come
fight before me, and let's ha' some [90
drums and some trumpets, and let him kill
all that comes near him, and thou lov'st
me, George!
  CIT. Peace a little, bird; he shall kill
them all, and they were twenty more on
'em than there are.

Enter Jasper.

JASP. Now, Fortune, if thou beest not
    only ill,
  Show me thy better face, and bring
    about

Thy desperate wheel, that I may climb
    at length,   99
And stand. This is our place of meeting,
If love have any constancy. O age
Where only wealthy men are counted
    happy!
How shall I please thee, how deserve
    thy smiles,
When I am only rich in misery?
My father's blessing and this little coin
Is my inheritance—a strong revenue!
From earth thou art, and to the earth I
    give thee.   [*Throws away the money.*]
There grow and multiply, whilst fresher
    air
Breeds me a fresher fortune.—(*Spies the
    casket.*) How! Illusion?
What, hath the devil coined himself
    before me?   110
'Tis metal good; it rings well. I am wak-
    ing,
And taking too, I hope. Now, God's dear
    blessing
Upon his heart that left it here! 'Tis
    mine;
These pearls, I take it, were not left
    for swine.   *Exit* [*with the casket*].

WIFE. I do not like that this unthrifty
youth should embezzle away the money;
the poor gentlewoman his mother will
have a heavy heart for it, God knows.
  CIT. And reason good, sweetheart. 119
  WIFE. But let him go; I'll tell Rafe a
tale in 's ear shall fetch him again with a
wanion,[1] I warrant him, if he be above
ground; and besides, George, here are a
number of sufficient gentlemen can witness, and myself, and yourself, and the
musicians, if we be called in question.
But here comes Rafe, George; thou shalt
hear him speak as [2] he were an emperal.[3]

[SCENA TERTIA.

Another part of the forest.]

Enter Rafe and Dwarf.

RAFE. Comes not Sir Squire again?
DWARF.   Right courteous knight,
  Your squire doth come, and with him
    comes the lady,

---

[1] Vengeance.
[2] From 1635 edn.; original reads *an*.
[3] Imperial, *i.e.*, emperor.

Enter Mistress Merr[ythought] and Michael and Squire.

For and [1] the Squire of Damsels, as I take it.

RAFE. Madam, if any service or devoir
Of a poor errant knight may right your wrongs,
Command it; I am prest [2] to give you succor,
For to that holy end I bear my armor.

MIST. MER. Alas, sir, I am a poor gentlewoman, and I have lost my money in this forest!   10

RAFE. Desert, you would say, lady; and not lost
Whilst I have sword and lance. Dry up your tears,
Which ill befits the beauty of that face,
And tell the story, if I may request it,
Of your disastrous fortune.

MIST. MER. Out, alas! I left a thousand pound, a thousand pound, e'en all the money I had laid up for this youth, upon the sight of your mastership—you looked so grim, and, as I may say it,   [20 saving your presence, more like a giant than a mortal man.

RAFE. I am as you are, lady; so are they
All mortal. But why weeps this gentle squire?

MIST. MER. Has he not cause to weep, do you think, when he hath lost his inheritance?

RAFE. Young hope of valor, weep not;
I am here
That will confound thy foe, and pay it dear   29
Upon his coward head that dares deny
Distresséd squires and ladies equity.
I have but one horse, on which shall ride
This lady fair behind me, and, before,
This courteous squire. Fortune will give us more
Upon our next adventure. Fairly speed
Beside us, squire and dwarf, to do us need!   *Exeunt.*

CIT. Did not I tell you, Nell, what your man would do? By the faith of my body, wench, for clean action and good delivery they may all cast their caps   [40 at him.[3]

WIFE. And so they may, i' faith, for, I dare speak it boldly, the twelve companies of London cannot match him, timber for timber.[4] Well, George, and he be not inveigled by some of these paltry players, I ha' much marvel. But, George, we ha' done our parts, if the boy have any grace to be thankful.

CIT. Yes, I warrant thee, duckling.   50

[SCENA QUARTA.

Another part of the forest.]

Enter Humphrey and Luce.

HUM. Good Mistress Luce, however I in fault am
For your lame horse, you're welcome unto Waltham;
But which way now to go, or what to say,
I know not truly, till it be broad day.

LUCE. O, fear not, Master Humphrey; I am guide
For this place good enough.

HUM.   Then up and ride;
Or, if it please you, walk, for your repose;
Or sit, or, if you will, go pluck a rose [5]—
Either of which shall be indifferent
To your good friend and Humphrey, whose consent   10
Is so entangled ever to your will
As the poor harmless horse is to the mill.

LUCE. Faith, and you say the word, we'll e'en sit down,
And take a nap.

HUM.   'Tis better in the town,
Where we may nap together, for, believe me,
To sleep without a snatch would mickle grieve me.

LUCE. You're merry, Master Humphrey.

HUM.   So I am,
And have been ever merry from my dam.

LUCE. Your nurse had the less labor.

HUM.   Faith, it may be,
Unless it were by chance I did beray [6] me.   20

Enter Jasper.

JASP. Luce! Dear friend Luce!

LUCE.   Here, Jasper.

---

[1] And also.
[2] Ready.   [3] Take off their hats to him.

[4] Man for man.
[5] A vulgar euphemism.   [6] Befoul.

JASP.   You are mine.

HUM. If it be so, my friend, you use me
    fine.
    What do you think I am?

JASP.   An arrant noddy.

HUM. A word of obloquy! Now, by God's
    body,
    I'll tell thy master, for I know thee well.

JASP. Nay, and you be so forward for to
    tell,
    Take that, and that! [*Beats him.*] And
    tell him, sir, I gave it,
    And say I paid you well.

HUM.   O, sir, I have it,
    And do confess the payment! Pray, be
    quiet.

JASP. Go, get you to your nightcap
    and the diet   30
    To cure your beaten bones.

LUCE.   Alas, poor Humphrey!
    Get thee some wholesome broth, with
    sage and comfrey,[1]
    A little oil of roses and a feather
    To noint [2] thy back withal.

HUM.   When I came hether,[3]
    Would I had gone to Paris with John
    Dory![4]

LUCE. Farewell, my pretty nump; [5] I am
    very sorry
    I cannot bear thee company.

HUM.   Farewell!
    The devil's dam was ne'er so banged in
    hell.   *Exeunt. Manet* [6] *Humphrey.*

WIFE. This young Jasper will prove me
anotherthings,[7] a my conscience, and   [40
he may be suffered. George, dost not see,
George, how a swaggers, and flies at the
very heads a folks, as he were a dragon?
Well, if I do not do his lesson [8] for wronging the poor gentleman, I am no true
woman. His friends that brought him
up might have been better occupied, iwis,
than ha' taught him these fegaries; [9] he's
e'en in the high way to the gallows, God
bless him!   50

CIT. You're too bitter, cunny; the
young man may do well enough for all
this.

---

[1] A herb used to cure wounds.   [3] Hither.
[2] Anoint.   [4] The subject of a popular song.
[5] Blockhead; or, perhaps, a nickname for
Humphrey.
[6] Remains.   [8] Teach him.
[7] Otherwise.   [9] Vagaries, pranks.

WIFE. Come hither, Master Humphrey;
has he hurt you? Now, beshrew his fingers
for 't! Here, sweetheart, here's some green
ginger for thee. Now, beshrew my heart,
but a has peppernel [10] in 's head as big as
a pullet's egg! Alas, sweet lamb, how thy
temples beat! Take the peace on him,[11]   [60
sweetheart, take the peace on him.

Enter a Boy.

CIT. No, no; you talk like a foolish
woman. I'll ha' Rafe fight with him, and
swinge him up well-favoredly.—Sirrah
Boy, come hither. Let Rafe come in and
fight with Jasper.

WIFE. Ay, and beat him well; he's an
unhappy [12] boy.

BOY. Sir, you must pardon us; the plot
of our play lies contrary, and 'twill   [70
hazard the spoiling of our play.

CIT. Plot me no plots! I'll ha' Rafe
come out; I ll make your house too hot
for you else.

BOY. Why, sir, he shall; but, if anything fall out of order, the gentlemen must
pardon us.

CIT. Go your ways, Goodman Boy!—
[*Exit Boy.*] I'll hold [13] him a penny he shall
have his bellyful of fighting now. Ho,   [80
here comes Rafe! No more! [14]

*Enter Rafe, Mistress Merry[thought], Mi-
chael, Squire, and Dwarf.*

RAFE. What knight is that, squire? Ask
    him if he keep
    The passage, bound by love of lady fair,
    Or else but prickant.[15]

HUM.   Sir, I am no knight,
    But a poor gentleman, that this same
    night
    Had stolen from me, on yonder green,
    My lovely wife, and suffered (to be seen
    Yet extant on my shoulders) such a
    greeting
    That whilst I live I shall think of that
    meeting.

WIFE. Ay, Rafe, he beat him un-   [90
mercifully, Rafe; and thou spar'st him,
Rafe, I would thou wert hanged.

CIT. No more, wife, no more.

---

[10] A lump.
[11] Have him bound to keep the peace.
[12] Mischievous.   [14] *I.e.*, Silence!
[13] Wager.   [15] Pricking, traveling.

RAFE. Where is the caitiff wretch hath
done this deed?
Lady, your pardon, that I may proceed
Upon the quest of this injurious knight.—
And thou, fair squire, repute me not
the worse
In leaving the great venture of the purse
And the rich casket, till some better
leisure.

Enter Jasper and Luce.

HUM. Here comes the broker [1] hath pur-
loined my treasure.   100
RAFE. Go, squire, and tell him I am here,
An errant knight-at-arms, to crave de-
livery
Of that fair lady to her own knight's
arms.
If he deny, bid him take choice of
ground,
And so defy him.
SQUIRE.   From the knight that bears
The golden pestle, I defy thee, knight,
Unless thou make fair restitution
Of that bright lady.
JASP.   Tell the knight that sent thee
He is an ass; and I will keep the wench,
And knock his headpiece.
RAFE.   Knight, thou art but dead,   110
If thou recall not thy uncourteous terms.

WIFE. Break 's pate, Rafe; break 's pate,
Rafe, soundly!

JASP. Come, knight; I am ready for you.
Now your pestle
(*Snatches away his pestle.*)
Shall try what temper, sir, your mor-
tar 's of.
"With that he stood upright in his
stirrups,
And gave the Knight of the Calfskin
such a knock   [*Knocks Rafe down.*]
That he forsook his horse and down he
fell;
And then he leaped upon him, and,
plucking off his helmet—"
HUM. Nay, and my noble knight be down
so soon,   120
Though I can scarcely go,[2] I needs must
run.   *Exeunt* [3] *Humphrey and Rafe.*

[1] With a pun on the meaning of *pander.*
[2] Walk.
[3] Original reads *Exit.*

WIFE. Run, Rafe; run, Rafe! Run for
thy life, boy! Jasper comes, Jasper comes!

JASP. Come, Luce, we must have other
arms for you;
Humphrey and golden pestle, both
adieu!   *Exeunt.*

WIFE. Sure the devil (God bless us!)
is in this springald![4] Why, George, didst
ever see such a firedrake?[5] I am afraid my
boy's miscarried;[6] if he be, though he were
Master Merrythought's son a thou-   [130
sand times, if there be any law in England,
I'll make some of them smart for 't.
CIT. No, no; I have found out the matter, sweetheart. Jasper is enchanted; as
sure as we are here, he is enchanted. He
could no more have stood in Rafe's hands
than I can stand in my lord mayor's. I'll
have a ring to discover all enchantments,
and Rafe shall beat him yet. Be no more
vexed, for it shall be so.   140

[SCENA QUINTA.

Before the Bell Inn at Waltham.]

*Enter Rafe, Squire, Dwarf, Mistress Merry-
thought, and Michael.*

WIFE. O, husband, here's Rafe again!—
Stay, Rafe, let me speak with thee. How
dost thou, Rafe? Art thou not shrowdly [7]
hurt?—The foul great lungis [8] laid un-
mercifully on thee; there's some sugar
candy for thee. Proceed; thou shalt have
another bout with him.
CIT. If Rafe had him at the fencing
school, if he did not make a puppy of him,
and drive him up and down the school,   [10
he should ne'er come in my shop more.

MIST. MER. Truly, Master Knight of
the Burning Pestle, I am weary.
MICH. Indeed-law, mother, and I am
very hungry.
RAFE. Take comfort, gentle dame, and
you, fair squire;
For in this desert there must needs be
placed
Many strong castles held by courteous
knights;

[4] Young man.
[5] Fiery dragon.
[6] Ruined.
[7] Shrewdly, severely.
[8] Lout.

And, till I bring you safe to one of those,
I swear by this my order ne'er to leave
   you.   20

WIFE. Well said, Rafe!—George, Rafe
was ever comfortable,[1] was he not?
  CIT. Yes, duck.
  WIFE. I shall ne'er forget him. When
we had lost our child (you know it was
strayed almost, alone, to Puddle Wharf,
and the criers were abroad for it, and there
it had drowned itself but for a sculler),
Rafe was the most comfortablest to me.
"Peace, mistress," says he, "let it go; [30
I'll get you another as good." Did he not,
George, did he not say so?
  CIT. Yes, indeed did he, mouse.

  DWARF. I would we had a mess of
pottage and a pot of drink, squire, and
were going to bed!
  SQUIRE. Why, we are at Waltham
town's end, and that's the Bell Inn.
  DWARF. Take courage, valiant knight,
    damsel, and squire!
I have discovered, not a stonecast off, 40
An ancient castle, held by the old knight
Of the most holy Order of the Bell,
Who gives to all knights-errant enter-
    tain.[2]
There plenty is of food, and all pre-
    pared
By the white hands of his own lady
    dear.
He hath three squires that welcome
    all his guests:
The first, high[t][3] Chamberlino, who
    will see
Our beds prepared, and bring us snowy
    sheets,
Where never footman stretched his
    buttered hams;[4]
The second, hight Ta[p]stero, who will
    see   50
Our pots full filléd, and no froth therein;
The third, a gentle squire, Ostlero hight,
Who will our palfreys slick with wisps
    of straw,
And in the maunger[5] put them oats
    enough,

And never grease their teeth with candle
  snuff.[6]

  WIFE. That same dwarf's a pretty
boy, but the squire's a groutnole.[7]

  RAFE. Knock at the gates, my squire,
    with stately lance.   [Squire knocks.]

Enter Tapster.

  TAP. Who's there?—You're welcome,
gentlemen. Will you see a room?   60
  DWARF. Right courteous and valiant
Knight of the Burning Pestle, this is the
Squire Tapstero.
  RAFE. Fair Squire Tapstero, I a wander-
    ing knight,
Hight of the Burning Pestle, in the
    quest
Of this fair lady's casket and wrought
    purse,
Losing myself in this vast wilderness,
Am to this castle well by fortune
    brought,
Where, hearing of the goodly entertain
Your knight of holy Order of the Bell 70
Gives to all damsels and all errant
    knights,
I thought to knock, and now am bold
    to enter.
  TAP. An 't please you see a chamber,
you are very welcome.   *Exeunt.*

  WIFE. George, I would have something
done, and I cannot tell what it is.
  CIT. What is it, Nell?
  WIFE. Why, George, shall Rafe beat
nobody again? Prithee, sweetheart, let
him.   80
  CIT. So he shall, Nell; and, if I join with
him, we'll knock them all.

[SCENA SEXTA.

A room in Venturewell's house.]

Enter Humphrey and Merchant.

  WIFE. O, George, here's Master Humphrey again now, that lost Mistress Luce,
and Mistress Lucy's father. Master Hum-

---

[1] Comforting.   [3] Called.
[2] Entertainment.
[4] The calves of running footmen were greased
to prevent cramps.   [5] Manger.

[6] An ostler's trick to keep horses from eating
their feed.
[7] Blockhead.

phrey will do somebody's errant,[1] I'll warrant him.

HUM. Father, it's true in arms I ne'er shall clasp her,
For she is stol'n away by your man Jasper.

WIFE. I thought he would tell him.

MERCH. Unhappy that I am, to lose my child!   9
Now I begin to think on Jasper's words,
Who oft hath urged to me thy fool-ishness.
Why didst thou let her go? Thou lov'st her not,
That wouldst bring home thy life, and not bring her.

HUM. Father, forgive me.   Shall I tell you true?
Look on my shoulders; they are black and blue.
Whilst to and fro fair Luce and I were winding,
He came and basted me with a hedge binding.

MERCH. Get men and horses straight; we will be there
Within this hour.   You know the place again?

HUM. I know the place where he my loins did swaddle;   20
I'll get six horses, and to each a saddle.

MERCH. Meantime I'll go talk with Jasper's father.   *Exeunt.*

WIFE. George, what wilt thou lay with me now, that Master Humphrey has not Mistress Luce yet? Speak, George, what wilt thou lay with me?

CIT. No, Nell; I warrant thee Jasper is at Puckeridge with her by this.

WIFE. Nay, George, you must consider Mistress Lucy's feet are tender; and [30 besides 'tis dark; and, I promise you truly, I do not see how he should get out of Waltham Forest with her yet.

CIT. Nay, cunny, what wilt thou lay with me that Rafe has her not yet?

WIFE. I will not lay against Rafe, honey, because I have not spoken with him. But look, George; peace! Here comes the merry old gentleman again.

[1] Errand, expedition.

[SCENA SEPTIMA.

A room in Merrythought's house.]

Enter Old Merrythought.

OLD. MER. [*Singing.*]

When it was grown to dark midnight,
   And all were fast asleep,
In came Margaret's grimely [2] ghost,
   And stood at William's feet.

I have money, and meat and drink be-forehand, till tomorrow at noon; why should I be sad? Methinks I have half a dozen jovial spirits within me!   [*Sings.*]

I am three merry men, and three merry men!

To what end should any man be sad [10 in this world? Give me a man that, when he goes to hanging, cries, "Troll [3] the black bowl to me!"—and a woman that will sing a catch in her travail! I have seen a man come by my door with a seri-ous face, in a black cloak, without a hat-band, carrying his head as if he looked for pins in the street; I have looked out of my window half a year after, and have spied that man's head upon London Bridge.[4] [20 'Tis vile.   Never trust a tailor that does not sing at his work; his mind is of nothing but filching.

WIFE. Mark this, George; 'tis worth noting: Godfrey my tailor, you know, never sings, and he had fourteen yards to make this gown; and, I'll be sworn, Mistress Pennistone the draper's wife had one made with twelve.   29

OLD MER. [*Singing.*]

'Tis mirth that fills the veins with blood,
More than wine, or sleep, or food.
Let each man keep his heart at ease;
No man dies of that disease.
He that would his body keep
From diseases, must not weep;
But whoever laughs and sings,
Never he his body brings
Into fevers, gouts, or rheums,

[2] Grim-looking.   [3] Pass.
[4] The heads of traitors and heretics were here displayed upon poles.

Or ling'ringly his lungs consumes,
Or meets with achës in the bone,   40
Or catarrhs or griping stone,
But contented lives for aye.
The more he laughs, the more he may.

WIFE. Look, George; how say'st thou
by this, George? Is 't not a fine old man?—
Now, God's blessing a thy sweet lips!—
When wilt thou be so merry, George?
Faith, thou art the frowning'st little thing,
when thou art angry, in a country.

Enter Merchant.

CIT. Peace, cony; thou shalt see [50
him taken down too, I warrant thee. Here's
Luce's father come now.

OLD MER. [*Singing.*]

As you came from Walsingham,
    From that holy land,
There met you not with my true love
    By the way as you came?

MERCH. O, Master Merrythought, my
    daughter's gone!
This mirth becomes you not; my daugh-
    ter's gone!
OLD. MER. [*Singing.*]

Why, an if she be, what care I?
Or let her come, or go, or tarry.   60

MERCH. Mock not my misery; it is your
    son
(Whom I have made my own, when all
    forsook him)
Has stol'n my only joy, my child, away.
OLD. MER. [*Singing.*]

He set her on a milk-white steed,
    And himself upon a gray;
He never turned his face again,
    But he bore her quite away.

MERCH. Unworthy of the kindness I have
    shown
To thee and thine! Too late I well per-
    ceive
Thou art consenting to my daughter's
    loss.   70
OLD MER. Your daughter! What a
stir 's here wi' your daughter? Let her go,
think no more on her, but sing loud. If

both my sons were on the gallows, I would
sing,

Down, down, down—they fall
Down, and arise they never shall.

MERCH. O, might I behold her once again,
    And she once more embrace her aged
    sire!
OLD MER. Fie, how scurvily this goes! [80
"And she once more embrace her aged
sire"? You'll make a dog on her, will
ye? She cares much for her aged sire, I
warrant you.   [*Sings.*]

She cares not for her daddy,
    Nor she cares not for her mammy,
For she is, she is, she is, she is
    My Lord of Lowgave's lassy.

MERCH. For this thy scorn I will pursue
That son of thine to death.   90
OLD MER. Do; and when you ha' killed
him,   [*Sings.*]

Give him flowers enow, palmer, give him
    flowers enow;
Give him red and white, and blue, green,
    and yellow.

MERCH. I'll fetch my daughter—
OLD MER. I'll hear no more a your
daughter; it spoils my mirth.
MERCH. I say, I'll fetch my daughter.
OLD MER. [*Singing.*]

Was never man for lady's sake—
    Down, down—   100
Tormented as I, poor Sir Guy—
    De derry down—
For Lucy's sake, that lady bright—
    Down, down—
As ever men beheld with eye—
    De derry down.

MERCH. I'll be revenged, by heaven!
                                   Exeunt.
                Music.

FINIS ACTUS SECUNDI.

WIFE. How dost thou like this, George?
CIT. Why, this is well, cony; but, if
Rafe were hot once, thou shouldst see
more.   111
WIFE. The fiddlers go again, husband.

CIT. Ay, Nell; but this is scurvy music. I gave the whoreson gallows money, and I think he has not got me the waits of Southwark. If I hear 'em [1] not anan,[2] I'll twinge him by the ears.—You musicians, play "Baloo"![3]

WIFE. No, good George, let's ha' "Lachrymæ"!   120

CIT. Why, this is it, cony.

WIFE. It's all the better, George. Now, sweet lamb, what story is that painted upon the cloth? The Confutation[4] of St. Paul?

CIT. No, lamb; that's [5] Rafe and Lucrece.

WIFE. Rafe and Lucrece? Which Rafe? Our Rafe?   129

CIT. No, mouse; that was a Tartarian.[6]

WIFE. A Tartarian? Well, I would the fiddlers had done, that we might see our Rafe again!

ACTUS TERTIUS. SCENA PRIMA.

[*Waltham Forest.*]

Enter Jasper and Luce.

JASP. Come, my dear dear; though we have lost our way,
We have not lost ourselves. Are you not weary
With this night's wand'ring, broken from your rest,
And frighted with the terror that attends
The darkness of this [7] wild unpeopled place?

LUCE. No, my best friend; I cannot either fear,
Or entertain a weary thought, whilst you
(The end of all my full desires) stand by me.
Let them that lose their hopes, and live to languish   9
Amongst the number of forsaken lovers,
Tell the long, weary steps, and number time,

Start at a shadow, and shrink up their blood,
Whilst I, possessed with all content and quiet,
Thus take my pretty love, and thus embrace him.   [*Embraces him.*]

JASP. You have caught me, Luce, so fast that, whilst I live,
I shall become your faithful prisoner,
And wear these chains forever. Come, sit down,
And rest your body, too-too delicate
For these disturbances. [*They sit down.*]
So, will you sleep?
Come, do not be more able [8] than you are;   20
I know you are not skillful in these watches,
For women are no soliders. Be not nice,[9]
But take it;[10] sleep, I say.

LUCE.   I cannot sleep;
Indeed, I cannot, friend.

JASP.   Why, then we'll sing,
And try how that will work upon our senses.

LUCE. I'll sing, or say, or anything but sleep.

JASP. Come, little mermaid, rob me of my heart
With that enchanting voice.

LUCE.   You mock me, Jasper.

SONG

JASP. Tell me, dearest, what is love?
LUCE. 'Tis a lightning from above;   30
  'Tis an arrow; 'tis a fire;
  'Tis a boy they call Desire;
      'Tis a smile
      Doth beguile
JASP. The poor hearts of men that prove.

  Tell me more, are women true?
LUCE. Some love change, and so do you.
JASP. Are they fair and never kind?
LUCE. Yes, when men turn with the wind.
JASP.   Are they froward?   40
LUCE.   Ever toward,[11]
  Those that love, to love anew.

JASP. Dissemble it no more; I see the god
Of heavy sleep lay on his heavy mace
Upon your eyelids.
LUCE.   I am very heavy. [*Sleeps.*]

---

[1] Original reads *him.*
[2] Anon, at once.
[3] A ballad tune.
[4] Her blunder for *Conversion.*
[5] From 1635 edn. Original reads *that.*
[6] His blunder for *Tarquin. Tartarian* was also a cant term for *thief.*
[7] From 1635 edn. Original has *these.*

[8] Capable of endurance.   [10] Acquiesce, agree.
[9] Foolish.   [11] Apt.

JASP. Sleep, sleep; and quiet rest crown
  thy sweet thoughts!
Keep from her fair blood distempers,
  startings,
Horrors, and fearful shapes! Let all her
  dreams
Be joys and chaste delights, embraces,
  wishes,
And such new pleasures as the ravished
  soul   50
Gives to the senses!—So; my charms
  have took.—
Keep her, you powers divine, whilst I
  contemplate
Upon the wealth and beauty of her mind!
She is only fair and constant, only kind,
And only to thee, Jasper. O, my joys!
Whither will you transport me? Let
  not fullness
Of my poor buried hopes come up to-
  gether
And overcharge my spirits! I am weak.
Some say (however ill) the sea and
  women
Are governed by the moon; both ebb
  and flow,   60
Both full of changes; yet to them that
  know,
And truly judge, these but opinions are,
And heresies, to bring on pleasing war
Between our tempers, that without
  these were
Both void of after-love and present
  fear,
Which are the best of Cupid. O, thou
  child
Bred from despair, I dare not enter-
  tain thee,
Having a love without the faults of
  women,
And greater in her perfect goods than
  men—
Which to make good, and please my-
  self the stronger,   70
Though certainly I am certain of her
  love,
I'll try her, that the world and memory
May sing to aftertimes her constancy.—
                      [*Draws his sword.*]
Luce! Luce! Awake!
LUCE.   Why do you fright me, friend,
With those distempered looks? What
  makes [1] your sword

[1] Does.

Drawn in your hand? Who hath of-
  fended you?
I prithee, Jasper, sleep; thou art wild
  with watching.
JASP. Come, make your way to heaven,
  and bid the world,
With all the villainies that stick upon it,
Farewell; you're for another life.
LUCE.   O, Jasper,   80
How have my tender years committed
  evil,
Especially against the man I love,
Thus to be cropped untimely?
JASP.   Foolish girl,
Canst thou imagine I could love his
  daughter
That flung me from my fortune into
  nothing?
Dischargéd me his service, shut the
  doors
Upon my poverty, and scorned my
  prayers,
Sending me, like a boat without a mast,
To sink or swim? Come; by this hand
  you die.
I must have life and blood to satisfy   90
Your father's wrongs.

WIFE. Away, George, away! Raise
the watch at Ludgate, and bring a mittimus from the justice for this desperate
villain!—Now, I charge you, gentlemen,
see the king's peace kept!—O, my heart,
what a varlet's this to offer manslaughter
upon the harmless gentlewoman!
CIT. I warrant thee, sweetheart, we'll
have him hampered.   100

LUCE. O, Jasper, be not cruel!
If thou wilt kill me, smile, and do it
  quickly,
And let not many deaths appear before
  me.
I am a woman, made of fear and love,
A weak, weak woman; kill not with
  thy eyes;
They shoot me through and through.
  Strike, I am ready;
And, dying, still I love thee.

Enter Merchant, Humphrey, and his Men.
MERCH.   Whereabouts?
JASP. [*Aside.*] No more of this; now to
  myself again.

Hum. There, there he stands, with sword, like martial knight,
Drawn in his hand; therefore beware the fight, 110
You that be wise, for, were I good Sir Bevis,
I would not stay his coming, by your leaves.

Merch. Sirrah, restore my daughter!

Jasp. Sirrah, no.

Merch. Upon him, then!

[*They set upon Jasper and take Luce from him.*]

Wife. So; down with him, down with him, down with him! Cut him i' th' leg, boys, cut him i' th' leg!

Merch. Come your ways, minion; I'll provide a cage
For you, you're grown so tame.—Horse her away. 119

Hum. Truly, I'm glad your forces have the day. *Exeunt. Manet Jasper.*

Jasp. They are gone, and I am hurt; my love is lost,
Never to get again. O, me unhappy!
Bleed, bleed and die! I cannot. O, my folly,
Thou hast betrayed me! Hope, where art thou fled?
Tell me, if thou beest anywhere remaining.
Shall I but see my love again? O, no!
She will not deign to look upon her butcher,
Nor is it fit she should; yet I must venter.
O, Chance, or Fortune, or whate'er thou art
That men adore for powerful, hear my cry, 130
And let me loving live, or losing die! *Exit.*

Wife. Is a gone, George?

Cit. Ay, cony.

Wife. Marry, and let him go, sweetheart. By the faith a my body, a has put me into such a fright that I tremble (as they say) as 'twere an aspine leaf. Look a my little finger, George, how it shakes. Now, i' truth, every member of my body is the worse for 't. 140

Cit. Come, hug in mine arms, sweet mouse; he shall not fright thee any more. Alas, mine own dear heart, how it quivers!

[Scena Secunda.

Before the Bell Inn at Waltham.]

Enter Mistress Merrythought, Rafe, Michael, Squire, Dwarf, Host, and a Tapster.

Wife. O, Rafe! How dost thou, Rafe? How hast thou slept tonight? [1] Has the knight used thee well?

Cit. Peace, Nell; let Rafe alone.

Tap. Master, the reckoning is not paid.

Rafe. Right courteous knight, who, for the order's sake
Which thou hast ta'en, hang'st out the holy Bell,
As I this flaming pestle bear about,
We render thanks to your puissant self,
Your beauteous lady, and your gentle squires 10
For thus refreshing of our wearied limbs,
Stiffened with hard achievements in wild desert.

Tap. Sir, there is twelve shillings to pay.

Rafe. Thou merry Squire Tapstero, thanks to thee
For comforting our souls with double jug;
And, if advent'rous fortune prick thee forth,
Thou jovial squire, to follow feats of arms,
Take heed thou tender [2] every lady's cause,
Every true knight, and every damsel fair;
But spill the blood of treacherous Saracens, 20
And false enchanters that with magic spells
Have done to death full many a noble knight.

Host. Thou valiant Knight of the Burning Pestle, give ear to me. There is twelve shillings to pay, and, as I am a true knight, I will not bate a penny.

Wife. George, I pray thee, tell me, must Rafe pay twelve shillings now?

[1] Last night. [2] Treat with care.

CIT. No, Nell, no; nothing but the old knight is merry with Rafe.   30

WIFE. O, is 't nothing else? Rafe will be as merry as he.

RAFE. Sir Knight, this mirth of yours becomes you well;
But, to requite this liberal courtesy,
If any of your squires will follow arms,
He shall receive from my heroic hand
A knighthood, by the virtue of this pestle.
HOST. Fair knight, I thank you for your noble offer;
Therefore, gentle knight,
Twelve shillings you must pay, or I must cap [1] you.   40

WIFE. Look, George! Did not I tell thee as much? The Knight of the Bell is in earnest. Rafe shall not be beholding [2] to him; give him his money, George, and let him go snick up.
CIT. Cap Rafe? No.—Hold your hand, Sir Knight of the Bell; there's your money. [Gives money.] Have you anything to say to Rafe now? Cap Rafe?
WIFE. I would you should know it, [50 Rafe has friends that will not suffer him to be capped for ten times so much, and ten times to the end of that.—Now take thy course, Rafe.

MIST. MER. Come, Michael; thou and I will go home to thy father. He hath enough left to keep us a day or two, and we'll set fellows abroad to cry [3] our purse and our casket. Shall we, Michael?
MICH. Ay, I pray, mother; in truth [60 my feet are full of chilblains with traveling.

WIFE. Faith, and those chilblains are a foul trouble. Mistress Merrythought, when your youth comes home, let him rub all the soles of his feet, and the heels, and his ankles, with a mouse skin; or, if none of your people can catch a mouse, when he goes to bed, let him roll his feet in the warm embers, and, I warrant you, he [70 shall be well; and you may make him put his fingers between his toes, and smell to

them; it's very sovereign for his head, if he be costive.

MIST. MER. Master Knight of the Burning Pestle, my son Michael and I bid you farewell. I thank your worship heartily for your kindness.
RAFE. Farewell, fair lady, and your tender squire.
If, pricking through these deserts, I do hear   80
Of any traitorous knight, who through his guile
Hath light [4] upon your casket and your purse,
I will despoil him of them, and restore them.
MIST. MER. I thank your worship.
    Exit with Michael.
RAFE. Dwarf, bear my shield; squire, elevate my lance.
And now farewell, you Knight of holy Bell.

CIT. Ay, ay, Rafe, all is paid.

RAFE. But yet, before I go, speak, worthy knight,
If aught you do of sad [5] adventures know,
Where errant knight [6] may through his prowess win   90
Eternal fame, and free some gentle souls
From endless bonds of steel and ling'ring pain.
HOST. Sirrah, go to Nick the barber, and bid him prepare himself, as I told you before, quickly.
TAP. I am gone, sir.   *Exit Tapster.*
HOST. Sir Knight, this wilderness affordeth none
But the great venter, where full many a knight
Hath tried his prowess, and come off with shame,
And where I would not have you lose your life   100
Against no man, but furious fiend of hell.
RAFE. Speak on, Sir Knight; tell what he is and where,
For here I vow, upon my blazing badge,

---

[1] Arrest.   [2] Beholden.
[3] *I.e.*, have public criers announce the loss of.
[4] Lit.
[5] Important.   [6] Original reads *Knights.*

Never to blaze a day in quietness,
But bread and water will I only eat,
And the green herb and rock shall be
　my couch,
Till I have quelled [1] that man, or beast,
　or fiend
That works such damage to all errant
　knights.

HOST. Not far from hence, near to a
　craggy cliff,　109
At the north end of this distressèd town,
There doth stand a lowly house,
Ruggedly builded, and in it a cave
In which an ugly giant now doth wone,[2]
Yclepéd [3] Barbaroso; in his hand
He shakes a naked lance of purest steel,
With sleeves turned up; and him be-
　fore he wears
A motley garment, to preserve his
　clothes
From blood of those knights which he
　massacres,
And ladies gent;[4] without his door doth
　hang
A copper basin on a prickant [5] spear,[6] 120
At which no sooner gentle knights can
　knock
But the shrill sound fierce Barbaroso
　hears,
And, rushing forth, brings in the errant
　knight
And sets him down in an enchanted
　chair;
Then with an engine,[7] which he hath
　prepared
With forty teeth, he claws his courtly
　crown,
Next makes him wink,[8] and underneath
　his chin
He plants a brazen piece of mighty
　bord,[9]
And knocks his bullets [10] round about
　his cheeks,
Whilst with his fingers and an instru-
　ment　130

With which he snaps his hair off he
　doth fill
The wretch's ears with a most hideous
　noise.
Thus every knight adventurer he doth
　trim,
And now no creature dares encounter
　him.

RAFE. In God's name, I will fight him.
　Kind sir,
Go but before me to this dismal cave,
Where this huge giant Barbaroso dwells,
And, by that virtue that [11] brave Rosi-
　cleer
That damnéd brood of ugly giants slew,
And Palmerin Frannarco overthrew, 140
I doubt not but to curb this traitor
　foul,
And to the devil send his guilty soul.

HOST. Brave-sprighted [12] knight, thus far
　I will perform
This your request: I'll bring you within
　sight
Of this most loathsome place, inhabited
By a more loathsome man, but dare
　not stay,
For his main force soops [13] all he sees
　away.

RAFE. Saint George, set on before!
　March, squire and page!　*Exeunt.*

WIFE. George, dost think Rafe will
confound the giant?　150

CIT. I hold my cap to a farthing he
does. Why, Nell, I saw him wrastle with
the great Dutchman, and hurl him.

WIFE. Faith, and that Dutchman was
a goodly man, if all things were answerable to his bigness. And yet they say there
was a Scotchman higher than he, and that
they two and a knight met, and saw one
another for nothing. But of all the sights
that ever were in London, since I was [160
married, methinks the little child that was
so fair grown about the members was the
prettiest; that and the hermaphrodite.

CIT. Nay, by your leave, Nell, Ninivy [14]
was better.

WIFE. Ninivy! O, that was the story
of Jone and the wall,[15] was it not, George?

CIT. Yes, lamb.

[1] Killed.
[2] Dwell.
[3] Called.
[4] Gentle, noble.
[5] With point upward.
[6] The basin and spear advertised the barber-
surgeon.　[7] Instrument, *i.e.*, comb.
[8] *I.e.*, close his eyes to anoint them with perfume.
[9] Circumference. The barber's basin, which
was held up by the customer, had a semicircular
opening to fit around his neck.
[10] Balls of soap.

[11] By which.　[12] Brave-spirited.　[13] Sweeps.
[14] A popular puppet show about Ninevah.
[15] *I.e.*, Jonah and the whale.

[SCENA TERTIA.

Before Merrythought's house.]

Enter Mistress Merrythought.

WIFE. Look, George, here comes Mistress Merrythought again! And I would have Rafe come and fight with the giant; I tell you true, I long to see 't.

CIT. Good Mistress Merrythought, begone, I pray you, for my sake; I pray you, forbear a little; you shall have audience presently. I have a little business.

WIFE. Mistress Merrythought, if it please you to refrain your passion a [10 little, till Rafe have despatched the giant out of the way, we shall think ourselves much bound to you. I thank you, good Mistress Merrythought.

Exit Mist[ress] Merrythou[ght].

Enter a Boy.

CIT. Boy, come hither. Send away Rafe and this whoreson giant quickly.

BOY. In good faith, sir, we cannot; you'll utterly spoil our play, and make it to be hissed; and it cost money; you will not suffer us to go on with our plot.— [20 I pray, gentlemen, rule him.

CIT. Let him come now and despatch this, and I'll trouble you no more.

BOY. Will you give me your hand of that?

WIFE. Give him thy hand, George, do; and I'll kiss him. I warrant thee, the youth means plainly.[1]

BOY. I'll send him to you presently.

WIFE. [*Kissing him.*] I thank you, [30 little youth.—(*Exit Boy.*) Faith, the child hath a sweet breath, George; but I think it be troubled with the worms. *Carduus Benedictus* [2] and mare's milk were the only thing in the world for 't.—O, Rafe's here, George!—God send thee good luck, Rafe!

[SCENA QUARTA.

Before a barber's shop.]

Enter Rafe, Host, Squire, and Dwarf.

HOST. Puissant knight, yonder his mansion is.
Lo, where the spear and copper basin are!

[1] Sincerely.
[2] The Blessed Thistle, regarded as a panacea.

Behold that string, on which hangs many a tooth,
Drawn from the gentle jaw of wand'ring knights!
I dare not stay to sound; [3] he will appear. *Exit Host.*

RAFE. O, faint not, heart! Susan, my lady dear,
The cobbler's maid in Milk Street, for whose sake
I take these arms, O, let the thought of thee
Carry thy knight through all adventerous deeds;
And, in the honor of thy beauteous self, 10
May I destroy this monster Barbaroso!—
Knock, squire, upon the basin till it break
With the shrill strokes, or till the giant speak. [*Squire knocks upon the basin.*]

Enter Barber.

WIFE. O, George, the giant, the giant!—Now, Rafe, for thy life!

BARBER. What fond unknowing wight is this that dares
So rudely knock at Barbaroso's cell,
Where no man comes but leaves his fleece behind?

RAFE. I, traitorous caitiff, who am sent by fate
To punish all the sad enormities 20
Thou hast committed against ladies gent
And errant knights. Traitor to God and men,
Prepare thyself! This is the dismal hour
Appointed for thee to give strict account
Of all thy beastly, treacherous villainies.

BARBER. Foolhardy knight, full soon thou shalt aby [4]
This fond reproach; thy body will I bang; *He takes down his pole.*
And, lo, upon that string thy teeth shall hang!
Prepare thyself, for dead soon shalt thou be.

RAFE. Saint George for me! *They fight.*

BARBER. Gargantua for me! 30

[3] Blow horn.   [4] Pay for.

WIFE. To him, Rafe, to him! Hold up the giant; set out thy leg before, Rafe!

CIT. Falsify[1] a blow, Rafe, falsify a blow! The giant lies open on the left side.

WIFE. Bear 't off, bear 't off still! There, boy!—O, Rafe's almost down, Rafe's almost down!

RAFE. Susan, inspire me! Now have up again.

WIFE. Up, up, up, up, up! So, Rafe! Down with him, down with him, Rafe!

CIT. Fetch him o'er the hip, boy! 41
[Rafe knocks the Barber down.]

WIFE. There, boy! Kill, kill, kill, kill, kill, Rafe!

CIT. No, Rafe; get all out of him first.

RAFE. Presumptuous man, see to what desperate end
Thy treachery hath brought thee! The just gods,
Who never prosper those that do despise them,
For all the villainies which thou hast done
To knights and ladies, now have paid thee home
By my stiff arm, a knight adventurous. 50
But say, vile wretch, before I send thy soul
To sad Avernus, whither it must go,
What captives hold'st thou in thy sable cave?

BARBER. Go in, and free them all; thou hast the day.

RAFE. Go, squire and dwarf, search in this dreadful cave,
And free the wretched prisoners from their bonds.
Exeunt[2] *Squire and Dwarf.*

BARBER. I crave for mercy, as thou art a knight,
And scorn'st to spill the blood of those that beg.

RAFE. Thou showed'st no mercy, nor shalt thou have any;
Prepare thyself, for thou shalt surely die. 60

Enter Squire, leading One winking, with a basin under his chin.

SQUIRE. Behold, brave knight, here is one prisoner,
Whom this wild man hath uséd as you see.

WIFE. This is the first wise word I heard the squire speak.

RAFE. Speak what thou art, and how thou hast been used,
That I may give [him][3] condign punishment.

1 KNI. I am a knight that took my journey post
Northward from London; and in courteous wise
This giant trained me to his loathsome den 69
Under pretense of killing of the itch;
And all my body with a powder strewed,
That smarts and stings, and cut away my beard,
And my curled locks wherein were ribands tied,
And with a water washed my tender eyes
(Whilst up and down about me still he skipped),
Whose virtue is that, till my eyes be wiped
With a dry cloth, for this my foul disgrace
I shall not dare to look a dog i' th' face.

WIFE. Alas, poor knight!—Relieve him, Rafe; relieve poor knights, whilst you live.

RAFE. My trusty squire, convey him to the town, 81
Where he may find relief.—Adieu, fair knight. *Exit* [1] *Knight.*

Enter Dwarf, leading One with a patch o'er his nose.

DWARF. Puissant knight, of the Burning Pestle hight,
See here another wretch, whom this foul beast

---

[1] Counterfeit.
[2] Original reads *Exit.*

[3] From 1635 edn. Original reads *That that I may give.*

Hath scorched [1] and scored in this inhuman wise.

RAFE. Speak me thy name, and eke thy place of birth,
And what hath been thy usage in this cave.

2 KNI. I am a knight, Sir Pockhole is my name,
And by my birth I am a Londoner,
Free by my copy,[2] but my ancestors   90
Were Frenchmen [3] all; and, riding hard this way
Upon a trotting horse, my bones did ache,
And I, faint knight, to ease my weary limbs,
Light at this cave, when straight this furious fiend
With sharpest instrument of purest steel
Did cut the gristle of my nose away,
And in the place this velvet plaster stands.
Relieve me, gentle knight, out of his hands!

WIFE. Good Rafe, relieve Sir Pockhole, and send him away, for in truth his breath stinks.   101

RAFE. Convey him straight after the other knight.—
Sir Pockhole, fare you well.

2 KNI.   Kind sir, good night. *Exit.*
                     Cries within.

MAN. Deliver us!
WOMAN. Deliver us!

WIFE. Hark, George, what a woeful cry there is! I think some woman lies-in there.

MAN. Deliver us!
WOMAN. Deliver us!   110

RAFE. What ghastly noise is this? Speak, Barbaroso,
Or, by this blazing steel, thy head goes off!

BARBER. Prisoners of mine, whom I in diet keep.
Send lower down into the cave,

[1] Scotched, cut.
[2] Certificate of citizenship.
[3] In allusion to the "French disease," a common name for the pox or syphilis.

And in a tub that's heated smoking hot
There may they find them, and deliver them.

RAFE. Run, squire and dwarf; deliver them with speed.
            Exeunt Squire and Dwarf.

WIFE. But will not Rafe kill this giant? Surely I am afeard, if he let him go, he will do as much hurt as ever he did.   120

CIT. Not so, mouse, neither, if he could convert him.

WIFE. Ay, George, if he could convert him; but a giant is not so soon converted as one of us ordinary people. There's a pretty tale of a witch that had the devil's mark about her (God bless us!), that had a giant to her son, that was called Lob-lie-by-the-fire; didst never hear it, George?

Enter Squire, leading a Man, with a glass of lotion in his hand, and the Dwarf, leading a Woman, with diet bread [4] and drink.

CIT. Peace, Nell, here comes the prisoners.

DWARF. Here be these pinéd wretches, manful knight,   131
That for these six weeks have not seen a wight.

RAFE. Deliver what you are, and how you came
To this sad cave, and what your usage was.

MAN. I am an errant knight that followed arms
With spear and shield; and in my tender years
I stricken was with Cupid's fiery shaft,
And fell in love with this my lady dear,
And stole her from her friends in Turnbull Street,[5]
And bore her up and down from town to town,   140
Where we did eat and drink, and music hear,
Till at the length at this unhappy town
We did arrive, and, coming to this cave,
This beast us caught and put us in a tub,
Where we this two months sweat, and should have done

[4] Special bread prepared for invalids.
[5] A disreputable district.

Another month, if you had not relieved
us.

WOMAN. This bread and water hath our
diet been,
Together with a rib cut from a neck
Of burnéd mutton; hard hath been our
fare.   149
Release us from this ugly giant's snare!

MAN. This hath been all the food we have
received;
But only twice a day, for novelty,
He gave a spoonful of this hearty broth   *Pulls out a syringe.*
To each of us, through this same slender
quill.

RAFE. From this infernal monster you
shall go,
That useth knights and gentle ladies
so!—
Convey them hence.
                             Exeunt Man and Woman.

CIT. Cony, I can tell thee, the gentlemen like Rafe.

WIFE. Ay, George, I see it well [160
enough.—Gentlemen, I thank you all
heartily for gracing my man Rafe; and,
I promise you, you shall see him oft'ner.

BARBER. Mercy, great knight! I do recant my ill,
And henceforth never gentle blood will
spill.

RAFE. I give thee mercy; but yet shalt
thou swear
Upon my burning pestle, to perform
Thy promise uttered.

BARBER. I swear and kiss.
                             [*Kisses the pestle.*]

RAFE.   Depart then, and amend.—
                             [*Exit Barber.*]
Come, squire and dwarf; the sun grows
towards his set,   170
And we have many more adventures
yet.   *Exeunt.*

CIT. Now Rafe is in this humor I know
he would ha' beaten all the boys in the
house, if they had been set on him.

WIFE. Ay, George, but it is well as it
is. I warrant you, the gentlemen do consider what it is to overthrow a giant. But
look, George; here comes Mistress Merrythought and her son Michael.—Now you

are welcome, Mistress Merrythought;   [180
now Rafe has done, you may go on.

[SCENA QUINTA.

Before Merrythought's house.]

Enter Mistress Merrythought and Michael.

MIST. MER. Mick, my boy—

MICH. Ay, forsooth, mother.

MIST. MER. Be merry, Mick; we are
at home now, where, I warrant you, you
shall find the house flung out at the windows. [*Music within.*] Hark! Hey, dogs,
hey! This is the old world,[1] i' faith, with
my husband. If I get in among 'em, I'll
play 'em such a lesson that they shall
have little list to come scraping hither   [10
again.—Why, Master Merrythought! Husband! Charles Merrythought!

OLD MER. (*Within.*)

If you will sing, and dance, and laugh,
And hollo, and laugh again,
And then cry, "There, boys, there!" why,
then,
One, two, three, and four,
We shall be merry within this hour.

MIST. MER. Why, Charles, do you not
know your own natural wife? I say, open
the door, and turn me out those mangy   [20
companions; 'tis more than time that they
were fellow and fellowlike with you. You
are a gentleman, Charles, and an old man,
and father of two children; and I myself
(though I say it) by my mother's side
niece to a worshipful gentleman and a
conductor;[2] ha[3] has been three times
in his majesty's service at Chester, and
is now the fourth time, God bless him and
his charge, upon his journey.   30

OLD MER. [*Singing.*]

Go from my window, love, go;
Go from my window, my dear!
The wind and the rain will drive you back
again;
You cannot be lodgéd here.

Hark you, Mistress Merrythought, you
that walk upon adventures, and forsake
your husband, because he sings with never

---

[1] Way.
[2] Military leader.   [3] He.

a penny in his purse, what shall I think
myself the worse? Faith, no; I'll be merry.

You come not here; here's none but   [40
lads of mettle, lives of a hundred years
and upwards; care never drunk their
bloods, nor want made 'em warble, "Heigh-
ho, my heart is heavy."

Mist. Mer. Why, Mr.[1] Merrythought,
what am I that you should laugh
me to scorn thus abruptly? Am I not
your fellow-feeler, as we may say, in all
our miseries? Your comforter in health
and sickness? Have I not brought you   [50
children? Are they not like you, Charles?
Look upon thine own image, hard-hearted
man! And yet for all this—

Old Mer. (*Within.*)

> Begone, begone, my juggy,[2] my puggy, [3]
> Begone, my love, my dear!
> The weather is warm, 'twill do thee no
>   harm;
> Thou canst not be lodgéd here.—

Be merry, boys! Some light music, and
more wine!

Wife. He's not in earnest, I hope,   [60
George, is he?

Cit. What if he be, sweetheart?

Wife. Marry, if he be, George, I'll make
bold to tell him he's an ingrant [4] old man
to use his bedfellow so scurvily.

Cit. What! How does he use her,
honey?

Wife. Marry, come up, Sir Saucebox!
I think you'll take his part, will you not?
Lord, how hot you are grown! You   [70
are a fine man, an you had a fine dog; [5] it becomes you sweetly!

Cit. Nay, prithee, Nell, chide not, for,
as I am an honest man and a true Christian grocer, I do not like his doings.

Wife. I cry you mercy, then, George!
You know we are all frail and full of
infirmities.—D'e hear, Mr. Merrythought? May I crave a word with you?

Old Mer. (*Within.*)   Strike up   [80
lively, lads!

[1] Master.
[2] Diminutive of Joan.
[3] Term of endearment.
[4] Wife's confusion of *ignorant* and *ingrate*.
[5] A mark of gentility.

Wife. I had not thought, in truth,
Mr. Merrythought, that a man of your
age and discretion (as I may say), being
a gentleman, and therefore known by your
gentle conditions,[6] could have used so
little respect to the weakness of his wife,
for your wife is your own flesh, the staff
of your age, your yokefellow, with whose
help you draw through the mire of   [90
this transitory world; nay, she's your own
rib! And again—

Old Mer. [*Singing.*]

> I come not hither for thee to teach;
> I have no pulpit for thee to preach;
> I would thou hadst kissed me under the
>   breech,
>   As thou art a lady gay.

Wife. Marry, with a vengeance! I
am heartily sorry for the poor gentlewoman, but, if I were thy wife, i' faith,
graybeard, i' faith—   100

Cit. I prithee, sweet honeysuckle, be
content.

Wife. Give me such words, that am
a gentlewoman born! Hang him, hoary
rascal! Get me some drink, George; I am
almost molten with fretting. Now, beshrew his knave's heart for it!

[*Exit Citizen.*]

Old Mer. Play me a light lavalto.[7]
Come, be frolic. Fill the good fellows
wine.   110

Mist. Mer. Why, Mr. Merrythought,
are you disposed to make me wait here?
You'll open, I hope; I'll fetch them that
shall open else.

Old Mer. Good woman, if you will
sing, I'll give you something; if not—

Song

> You are no love for me, Margret;
>   I am no love for you.—

Come aloft,[8] boys, aloft!

Mist. Mer. Now a churl's fart in   [120
your teeth, sir!—Come, Mick, we'll not
trouble him; a shall not ding us i' th' teeth

[6] Qualities.   [8] Be merry.
[7] Lavolta, a lively dance.

with his bread and his broth, that he shall not. Come, boy; I'll provide for thee, I warrant thee. We'll go to Master Venterwell's, the merchant; I'll get his letter to mine host of the Bell in Waltham; there I'll place thee with the tapster. Will not that do well for thee, Mick? And let me alone for that old cuckoldly knave [130 your father; I'll use him in his kind,[1] I warrant ye.   [Exeunt.

Enter Citizen with beer.]

WIFE. Come, George, where's the beer?
CIT. Here, love.
WIFE. This old fornicating fellow will not out of my mind yet.—Gentlemen, I'll begin to you all; and I desire more of your acquaintance with all my heart.—[Drinks.] Fill the gentlemen some beer, George.

FINIS ACTUS TERTII.

Music.

ACTUS QUARTUS. SCENA PRIMA.

[A street.]
Boy danceth.

WIFE. Look, George, the little boy 's come again; methinks he looks something like the Prince of Orange in his long stocking, if he had a little harness[2] about his neck. George, I will have him dance "Fading."—"Fading" is a fine jig, I'll assure you, gentlemen.—Begin, brother.—Now a capers, sweetheart!—Now a turn a th' toe, and then tumble! Cannot you tumble, youth?   10
BOY. No, indeed, forsooth.
WIFE. Nor eat fire?
BOY. Neither.
WIFE. Why, then, I thank you heartily; there's twopence to buy you points[3] withal.   [Exit Boy.]

Enter Jasper and Boy.

JASP. There, boy, deliver this. [Gives a letter.] But do it well.
Hast thou provided me four lusty fellows, Able to carry me? And art thou perfect In all thy business?

[1] According to his own nature.
[2] Armor.
[3] Laces for fastening clothes.

BOY.   Sir, you need not fear;   19
I have my lesson here, and cannot miss it.
The men are ready for you and what else Pertains to this employment.
JASP.   There, my boy. [Gives money.] Take it, but buy no land.
BOY.   Faith, sir, 'twere rare To see so young a purchaser. I fly, And on my wings carry your destiny.   Exit.
JASP. Go and be happy!—Now, my latest hope,
Forsake me not, but fling thy anchor out,
And let it hold! Stand fixed, thou rolling stone,   28
Till I enjoy my dearest! Hear me, all You powers, that rule in men, celestial!   Exit.

WIFE. Go thy ways; thou art as crooked a sprig as ever grew in London. I warrant him, he'll come to some naughty end or other, for his looks say no less. Besides, his father (you know, George) is none of the best; you heard him take me up like a flirt-gill,[4] and sing bawdy songs upon me; but, i' faith, if I live, George—
CIT. Let me alone, sweetheart; I have a trick in my head shall lodge him in the [40 Arches[5] for one year, and make him sing *peccavi*[6] ere I leave him; and yet he shall never know who hurt him neither.
WIFE. Do, my good George, do!
CIT. What shall we have Rafe do now, boy?
BOY. You shall have what you will, sir.
CIT. Why, so, sir, go and fetch me him then, and let the Sophy of Persia come and christen him a child.[7]   50
BOY. Believe me, sir, that will not do so well; 'tis stale; it has been had before at the Red Bull.[8]
WIFE. George, let Rafe travel over great hills, and let him be very weary, and come to the King of Cracovia's house, covered with velvet; and there let the king's daughter stand in her window, all in beaten gold, combing her golden locks

[4] Loose woman.   [5] A prison.   [6] I have sinned.
[7] *I. e.*, a member of his nation. (The passage alludes to *The Travels of the Three English Brothers*, a play by Day, Rowley, and Wilkins.)
[8] A rival theater.

with a comb of ivory; and let her spy [60
Rafe, and fall in love with him, and come
down to him, and carry him into her
father's house; and then let Rafe talk
with her.

CIT. Well said, Nell; it shall be so.—
Boy, let's ha't done quickly.

BOY. Sir, if you will imagine all this
to be done already, you shall hear them
talk together; but we cannot present a
house covered with black velvet, and [70
a lady in beaten gold.

CIT. Sir Boy, let's ha't as you can, then.

BOY. Besides, it will show ill-favoredly
to have a grocer's prentice to court a
king's daughter.

CIT. Will it so, sir? You are well read
in histories! [1] I pray you, what was Sir
Dagonet? Was not he prentice to a grocer
in London? Read the play of *The Four
Prentices of London*,[2] where they toss [80
their pikes so. I pray you, fetch him in, sir,
fetch him in.

BOY. It shall be done.—[*To audience.*]
It is not our fault, gentlemen. *Exit.*

WIFE. Now we shall see fine doings, I
warrant tee, George. O, here they come;
how prettily the King of Cracovia's
daughter is dressed!

[SCENA SECUNDA.

A hall in the palace of the King of Moldavia.]

Enter Rafe and the Lady, Squire, and Dwarf.

CIT. Ay, Nell, it is the fashion of that
country, I warrant tee.

LADY. Welcome, Sir Knight, unto my
    father's court,
King of Moldavia, unto me, Pompiona,
His daughter dear! But, sure, you do
    not like
Your entertainment, that will stay with
    us
No longer but a night.

RAFE.   Damsel right fair,
I am on many sad adventures bound,
That call me forth into the wilderness;
Besides, my horse's back is something
    galled,   10
Which will enforce me ride a sober pace.
But many thanks, fair lady, be to you

For using errant knight with courtesy!

LADY. But say, brave knight, what is your
    name and birth?

RAFE. My name is Rafe; I am an
    Englishman,
As true as steel, a hearty Englishman,
And prentice to a grocer in the Strond [3]
By deed indent,[4] of which I have one
    part;
But, Fortune calling me to follow arms,
On me this holy order I did take   20
Of Burning Pestle, which in all men's
    eyes
I bear, confounding ladies' enemies.

LADY. Oft have I heard of your brave
    countrymen,
And fertile soil, and store of wholesome
    food;
My father oft will tell me of a drink
In England found, and nippitato [5] called,
Which driveth all the sorrow from your
    hearts.

RAFE. Lady, 'tis true; you need not lay
    your lips
To better nippitato than there is.

LADY. And of a wild fowl he will often
    speak,   30
Which   poudered [6]-beef-and-mustard
    calléd is;
For there have been great wars twixt us
    and you.
But truly, Rafe, it was not long [7] of me.
Tell me then, Rafe, could you contented
    be
To wear lady's favor in your shield?

RAFE. I am a knight of religious order,
And will not wear a favor of a lady's
That trusts in Antichrist and false
    traditions.

CIT. Well said, Rafe! Convert her, if
thou canst.   40

RAFE. Besides, I have a lady of my own
In merry England, for whose virtuous
    sake
I took these arms; and Susan is her name,
A cobbler's maid in Milk Street, whom I
    vow
Ne'er to forsake whilst life and pestle last.

LADY. Happy that cobbling dame, whoe'er
    she be,

[1] Fiction.   [2] By Thomas Heywood.

[3] Strand.   [6] Salted.
[4] Indenture.   [7] Because.
[5] Strong liquor.

That for her own, dear Rafe, hath gotten thee!
Unhappy I, that ne'er shall see the day
To see thee more, that bear'st my heart
away!

RAFE. Lady, farewell; I needs must take
my leave.   50
LADY. Hard-hearted Rafe, that ladies dost
deceive!

CIT. Hark thee, Rafe; there's money
for thee. [*Gives money.*] Give something
in the King of Cracovia's house; be not
beholding to him.

RAFE. Lady, before I go, I must remember
Your father's officers, who, truth to tell,
Have been about me very diligent.
Hold up thy snowy hand, thou princely
maid!
There's twelvepence for your father's
chamberlain;   60
And another shilling for his cook,
For, by my troth, the goose was roasted
well;
And twelvepence for your father's
horse keeper,
For nointing my horse' back, and for
his butter [1]
There is another shilling; to the maid
That washed my boothose [2] there's an
English groat,
And twopence to the boy that wiped my
boots;
And last, fair lady, there is for yourself
Threepence to buy you pins at Bumbo
Fair.
LADY. Full many thanks; and I will keep
them safe   70
Till all the heads be off, for thy sake,
Rafe.
RAFE. Advance, my squire and dwarf! I
cannot stay.
LADY. Thou kill'st my heart in parting
thus away.   *Exeunt.*

WIFE. I commend Rafe yet, that he
will not stoop to a Cracovian; there's
properer [3] women in London than any are
there, iwis. But here comes Master Humphrey and his love again now, George.
CIT. Ay, cony; peace.

[SCENA TERTIA.

A room in Venturewell's house.]

*Enter Merchant, Humphrey, Luce, and a
Boy.*

MERCH. Go, get you up; [4] I will not be
entreated;
And, gossip [5] mine, I'll keep you sure
hereafter
From gadding out again with boys and
unthrifts.[6]
Come, they are women's tears; I know
your fashion.—
Go, sirrah, lock her in, and keep the key
Safe as you love your life.—
                Exeunt [7] *Luce and Boy.*
                Now, my son Humphrey,
You may both rest assuréd of my love
In this, and reap your own desire.
HUM. I see this love you speak of, through
your daughter,
Although the hole be little, and here-
after   10
Will yield the like in all I may or can,
Fitting a Christian and a gentleman.
MERCH. I do believe you, my good son,
and thank you,
For 'twere an impudence to think you
flattered.
HUM. It were, indeed; but shall I tell you
why?
I have been beaten twice about the
lie.
MERCH. Well, son, no more of compliment.
My daughter
Is yours again; appoint the time and
take her.
We'll have no stealing for it; I myself
And some few of our friends will see
you married.   20
HUM. I would you would, i' faith, for, be
it known,
I ever was afraid to lie alone.
MERCH. Some three days hence, then.
HUM.   Three days! Let me see;
'Tis somewhat of the most; [8] yet I
agree,
Because I mean against [9] the appointed
day
To visit all my friends in new array.

[1] Used to rub the horse's back.
[2] Leggings.   [3] Handsomer.

[4] Upstairs.   [7] Original reads *Exit.*
[5] Relative.   [8] Rather long.
[6] Prodigals.   [9] In preparation for

Enter Servant.

SER. Sir, there's a gentlewoman without would speak with your worship.

MERCH. What is she?

SER. Sir, I asked her not.   30

MERCH. Bid her come in. [*Exit Servant.*]

Enter Mistress Merrythought and Michael.

MIST. MER. Peace be to your worship! I come as a poor suitor to you, sir, in the behalf of this child.

MERCH. Are you not wife to Merrythought?

MIST. MER. Yes, truly. Would I had ne'er seen his eyes! Ha has undone me and himself and his children; and there he lives at home, and sings and hoits [40 and revels among his drunken companions! But, I warrant you, where to get a penny to put bread in his mouth he knows not; and therefore, if it like your worship, I would entreat your letter to the honest host of the Bell in Waltham that I may place my child under the protection of his tapster, in some settled course of life.

MERCH. I'm glad the heavens have heard my prayers. Thy husband,
When I was ripe in sorrows, laughed at me;   50
Thy son, like an unthankful wretch, I having
Redeemed him from his fall, and made him mine,
To show his love again first stole my daughter,
Then wronged this gentleman, and, last of all,
Gave me that grief had almost brought me down
Unto my grave, had not a stronger hand
Relieved my sorrows. Go, and weep as I did,
And be unpitied, for I here profess
An everlasting hate to all thy name.

MIST. MER. Will you so, sir? How [60 say you by that? —Come, Mick; let him keep his wind to cool his porridge. We'll go to thy nurse's, Mick; she knits silk stockings, boy; and we'll knit too, boy, and be beholding to none of them all.

Exeunt Michael and Mother.

Enter a Boy with a letter.

BOY. Sir, I take it you are the master of this house.

MERCH. How then, boy?

BOY. Then to yourself, sir, comes this letter.   70

MERCH. From whom, my pretty boy?

BOY. From him that was your servant; but no more
Shall that name ever be, for he is dead.
Grief of your purchased [1] anger broke his heart.
I saw him die, and from his hand received
This paper, with a charge to bring it hither.
Read it, and satisfy yourself in all.

LETTER

MERCH. "Sir, that I have wronged your love I must confess, in which I have purchased to myself, besides mine [80 own undoing, the ill opinion of my friends. Let not your anger, good sir, outlive me, but suffer me to rest in peace with your forgiveness. Let my body (if a dying man may so much prevail with you) be brought to your daughter, that she may truly know my hot flames are now buried, and withal receive a testimony of the zeal I bore her virtue. Farewell forever, and be ever happy!   JASPER."

God's hand is great in this. I do forgive him;   91
Yet I am glad he's quiet, where I hope
He will not bite again.—Boy, bring the body,
And let him have his will, if that be all.

BOY. 'Tis here without, sir.

MERCH.   So, sir; if you please,
You may conduct it in; I do not fear it.

HUM. I'll be your usher, boy, for, though I say it,
He owed me something once, and well did pay it.   *Exeunt.*

Enter Luce, alone.

LUCE. If there be any punishment inflicted
Upon the miserable more than yet I feel,   100

[1] Acquired.

Let it together seize me, and at once
Press down my soul! I cannot bear the
pain
Of these delaying tortures.—Thou that
art
The end of all, and the sweet rest of all,
Come, come, O Death! Bring me to
thy peace,
And blot out all the memory I nourish
Both of my father and my cruel friend!—
O, wretched maid, still living to be
wretched,
To be a say [1] to Fortune in her changes,
And grow to number times and woes
together,   110
How happy had I been, if, being born,
My grave had been my cradle!

Enter Servant.

SER.   By your leave,
Young mistress, here's a boy hath
brought a coffin.
What a would say, I know not; but your
father
Charged me to give you notice. Here
they come.   [*Exit.*]

Enter Two bearing a coffin, Jasper in it.

LUCE. For me I hope 'tis come, and 'tis
most welcome.
BOY. Fair mistress, let me not add greater
grief
To that great store you have already.
Jasper
(That whilst he lived was yours, now dead
And here enclosed) commanded me to
bring   120
His body hither, and to crave a tear
From those fair eyes (though he deserved
not pity)
To deck his funeral, for so he bid me
Tell her for whom he died.
LUCE.   He shall have many.—
Good friends, depart a little, whilst I
take
My leave of this dead man that once I
loved. *Exeunt Coffin Carrier and Boy.*
Hold yet a little, life, and then I give thee
To thy first heavenly being. O, my
friend!
Hast thou deceived me thus, and got
before me?

<hr/>

[1] Subject for experiment.

I shall not long be after. But, believe
me,   130
Thou wert too cruel, Jasper, gainst
thyself,
In punishing the fault I could have pardoned,
With so untimely death. Thou didst
not wrong me,
But ever wert most kind, most true,
most loving,
And I the most unkind, most false, most
cruel!
Didst thou but ask a tear? I'll give thee
all,
Even all my eyes can pour down, all my
sighs,
And all myself. Before thou goest from
me
There are but sparing rites; but, if thy
soul   139
Be yet about this place, and can behold
And see what I prepare to deck thee
with,
It shall go up, borne on the wings of
peace,
And satisfied. First will I sing thy dirge,
Then kiss thy pale lips, and then die
myself,
And fill one coffin and one grave to-
gether.

SONG

Come, you whose loves are dead,
   And, whiles I sing,
   Weep and wring
Every hand, and every head
Bind with cypress and sad yew;   150
Ribands black and candles blue
For him that was of men most true!

Come with heavy mourning,[2]
   And on his grave
   Let him have
Sacrifice of sighs and groaning;
Let him have fair flowers enow,
White and purple, green and yellow,
For him that was of men most true!

Thou sable cloth, sad cover of my joys,
I lift thee up, and thus I meet with
death.   161
[*Removes the cloth, and Jasper rises out of
the coffin.*]
JASP. And thus you meet the living!
LUCE.   Save me, heaven!

<hr/>

[2] Moaning(?).

JASP. Nay, do not fly me, fair; I am no
  spirit.
  Look better on me; do you know me yet?
LUCE. O, thou dear shadow of my friend!
JASP.   Dear substance,
  I swear I am no shadow. Feel my hand;
  It is the same it was. I am your Jasper,
  Your Jasper that's yet living, and yet
    loving.
  Pardon my rash attempt, my foolish
    proof   169
  I put in practice of your constancy,
  For sooner should my sword have drunk
    my blood,
  And set my soul at liberty than drawn
  The least drop from that body, for
    which boldness
  Doom me to anything; if death, I take it,
  And willingly.
LUCE.   This death I'll give you for it.
                          [Kisses him.]
  So, now I am satisfied you are no spirit,
  But my own truest, truest, truest friend.
  Why do you come thus to me?
JASP.   First, to see you;
  Then to convey you hence.
LUCE.   It cannot be;
  For I am locked up here, and watched
    at all hours,   180
  That 'tis impossible for me to scape.
JASP. Nothing more possible.   Within
    this coffin
  Do you convey yourself. Let me alone;
  I have the wits of twenty men about me;
  Only I crave the shelter of your closet [1]
  A little, and then fear me [2] not. Creep
    in,
  That they may presently convey you
    hence.
  Fear nothing, dearest love; I'll be your
    second.
[Luce places herself in the coffin and Jasper
            puts the cloth over her.]
  Lie close. So; all goes well yet.—Boy!

[Enter Coffin Carrier and Boy.]

BOY.   At hand, sir.
JASP. Convey away the coffin, and be wary.
BOY. 'Tis done already.
[Exeunt Coffin Carrier and Boy with the
                                 coffin.]
JASP.   Now must I go conjure. 191
                                  Exit.

[1] Private room.   [2] I.e., for me.

Enter Merchant.

MERCH. Boy, boy!

[Enter Boy.]

BOY. Your servant, sir.
MERCH. Do me this kindness, boy.
Hold, here's a crown. Before thou bury
the body of this fellow, carry it to his
old merry father, and salute him from me,
and bid him sing; he hath cause.
BOY. I will, sir.   190
MERCH. And then bring me word what
tune he is in, and have another crown; but
do it truly. I have fitted him a bargain now
will vex him.
BOY. God bless your worship's health,
sir!
MERCH. Farewell, boy.   Exeunt.

[SCENA QUARTA.

Before Merrythought's house.]

Enter Master Merrythought.

WIFE. Ah, old Merrythought, art thou
there again? Let's hear some of thy songs.
OLD MER. [Singing.]

  Who can sing a merrier note
  Than he that cannot change a groat?

Not a denier [3] left, and yet my heart leaps!
I do wonder yet, as old as I am, that any
man will follow a trade, or serve, that may
sing and laugh, and walk the streets. My
wife and both my sons are I know not
where; I have nothing left, nor know I   [10
how to come by meat to supper; yet am
I merry still, for I know I shall find it upon
the table at six a-clock; therefore, hang
thought!   [Sings.]

  I would not be a serving-man
    To carry the cloak bag still,
  Nor would I be a falconer
    The greedy hawks to fill;
  But I would be in a good house,
    And have a good master too;   20
  But I would eat and drink of the best,
    And no work would I do.

This is it that keeps life and soul together—
mirth; this is the philosophers' stone that
they write so much on, that keeps a man
ever young.

[3] Penny.

Enter a Boy.

Boy. Sir, they say they know all your money is gone, and they will trust you for no more drink.

Old Mer. Will they not? Let [30 am [1] choose! The best is, I have mirth at home, and need not send abroad for that. Let them keep their drink to themselves. [*Sings.*]

For Jillian of Berry, she dwells on a hill,
And she hath good beer and ale to sell,
And of good fellows she thinks no ill;
   And thither will we go now, now, now,
     now,
   And thither will we go now.

And, when you have made a little stay,
You need not ask what is to pay,   40
But kiss your hostess, and go your way;
   And thither, etc.

Enter another Boy.

2 Boy. Sir, I can get no bread for supper.

Old Mer. Hang bread and supper! Let's preserve our mirth, and we shall never feel hunger, I'll warrant you. Let's have a catch. Boy, follow me; come, sing this catch.

Ho, ho, nobody at home!   50
Meat, nor drink, nor money ha' we none.
   Fill the pot, Eedy,
   Never more need I.

Old Mer. So, boys, enough. Follow me. Let's change our place, and we shall laugh afresh.   *Exeunt.*

Wife. Let him go, George; a shall not have any countenance from us, nor a good word from any i' th' company, if I may strike stroke in 't.[2]   60

Cit. No more a sha' not, love. But, Nell, I will have Rafe do a very notable matter now, to the eternal honor and glory of all grocers.—Sirrah! You there, boy! Can none of you hear?

[Enter Boy.]

Boy. Sir, your pleasure?

Cit. Let Rafe come out on May Day in the morning, and speak upon a conduit, with all his scarfs about him, and his feathers, and his rings, and his knacks.   70

[1] 'Em.   [2] *I.e.*, have anything to do with it.

Boy. Why, sir, you do not think of our plot; what will become of that, then?

Cit. Why, sir, I care not what become on 't. I'll have him come out, or I'll fetch him out myself; I'll have something done in honor of the city. Besides, he hath been long enough upon adventures. Bring him out quickly; or, if I come in amongst you—

Boy. Well, sir, he shall come out, but if our play miscarry, sir, you are like [80 to pay for 't.   *Exit Boy.*

Cit. Bring him away then!

Wife. This will be brave, i' faith! George, shall not he dance the morris too, for the credit of the Strand?

Cit. No, sweetheart, it will be too much for the boy. O, there he is, Nell! He's reasonable well in reparel; but he has not rings enough.

Enter Rafe [dressed as the Lord of the May].

Rafe. London, to thee I do present the
   merry month of May;   90
Let each true subject be content to
   hear me what I say.
For from the top of conduit head, as
   plainly may appear,
I will both tell my name to you, and
   wherefore I came here.
My name is Rafe, by due descent though
   not ignoble I,
Yet far inferior to the flock of gracious
   grocery;[3]
And by the common counsel of my fellows in the Strand,
With gilded staff and crosséd scarf, the
   May Lord here I stand.
Rejoice, O English hearts, rejoice! Rejoice, O lovers dear!
Rejoice, O city, town, and country!
   Rejoice, eke every shire!
For now the fragrant flowers do spring
   and sprout in seemly sort,   100
The little birds do sit and sing, the
   lambs do make fine sport;
And now the birchen tree doth bud,
   that makes the schoolboy cry;
The morris rings, while hobbyhorse doth
   foot it featously;[4]
The lords and ladies now abroad, for
   their disport and play,

[3] A parody of part of the Ghost's opening speech in *The Spanish Tragedy.*
[4] Neatly, expertly.

Do kiss sometimes upon the grass, and
   sometimes in the hay;
Now butter with a leaf of sage is good
   to purge the blood;
Fly Venus and phlebotomy, for they
   are neither good;
Now little fish on tender stone begin
   to cast their bellies,[1]
And sluggish snails, that erst were mute,[2]
   do creep out of their shellës;
The rumbling rivers now do warm, for
   little boys to paddle;   110
The sturdy steed now goes to grass,
   and up they hang his saddle;
The heavy hart, the bellowing buck,
   the rascal,[3] and the pricket [4]
Are now among the yeoman's peas,
   and leave the fearful thicket.
And be like them, O you, I say, of this
   same noble town,
And lift aloft your velvet heads, and,
   slipping off your gown,
With bells on legs, and napkins [5] clean
   unto your shoulders tied,
With scarfs and garters as you please,
   and "Hey for our town!" cried,
March out, and show your willing minds,
   by twenty and by twenty,
To Hogsdon or to Newington, where ale
   and cakes are plenty;
And let it ne'er be said for shame that
   we, the youths of London,   120
Lay thrumming of [6] our caps at home,
   and left our custom undone.
Up, then, I say, both young and old,
   both man and maid a-maying,
With drums and guns that bounce [7]
   aloud, and merry tabor playing!
Which to prolong, God save our king,
   and send his country peace,
And root out treason from the land!
And so, my friends, I cease. [*Exit*.]

     Finis Actus Quarti.

    Actus Quintus. Scena Prima.

[*A room in Venturewell's house.*]

    Enter Merchant, solus.[8]

Merch. I will have no great store of
company at the wedding—a couple of neighbors and their wives; and we will have a
capon in stewed broth, with marrow, and
a good piece of beef stuck with rosemary.

    Enter Jasper, his face mealed.[9]

Jasp. Forbear thy pains, fond man! It
   is too late.
Merch. Heaven bless me! Jasper?
Jasp.   Ay, I am his ghost,
Whom thou hast injured for his con-
   stant love,
Fond worldly wretch, who dost not
   understand
In death that true hearts cannot parted
   be!   10
First, know thy daughter is quite borne
   away
On wings of angels, through the liquid
   air,
To far out of thy reach, and never more
Shalt thou behold her face; but she
   and I
Will in another world enjoy our loves,
Where neither father's anger, poverty,
Nor any cross that troubles earthly
   men
Shall make us sever our united hearts.
And never shalt thou sit or be alone
In any place, but I will visit thee   20
With ghastly looks, and put into thy
   mind
The great offenses which thou didst to
   me.
When thou art at thy table with thy
   friends,
Merry in heart, and filled with swelling
   wine,
I'll come in midst of all thy pride and
   mirth,
Invisible to all men but thyself,
And whisper such a sad tale in thine
   ear
Shall make thee let the cup fall from
   thy hand,
And stand as mute and pale as Death
   itself.
Merch. Forgive me, Jasper! O, what
   might I do,   30
Tell me, to satisfy thy troubled ghost?
Jasp. There is no means; too late thou
   think'st of this.
Merch. But tell me what were best for
   me to do?

[1] Spawn.
[2] Mewed (?).
[3] A lean young deer.
[4] A yearling buck.
[5] Handkerchiefs.
[6] Setting tufts on.
[7] Boom, bang.
[8] Alone.
[9] Whitened with flour.

JASP. Repent thy deed, and satisfy my
   father,
And beat fond Humphrey out of thy
   doors.   *Exit Jasper.*

Enter Humphrey.

WIFE. Look, George; his very ghost
would have folks beaten.

HUM. Father, my bride is gone, fair Mis-
   tress Luce;
My soul's the fount of vengeance, mis-
   chief's sluice.
MERCH. Hence, fool, out of my sight;
   with thy fond passion   40
Thou hast undone me.   *[Beats him.]*
HUM.   Hold, my father dear,
For Luce thy daughter's sake, that had
   no peer!
MERCH. Thy father, fool? There's some
   blows more; begone.—   *[Beats him.]*
Jasper, I hope thy ghost be well appeased
To see thy will performed. Now will
   I go
To satisfy thy father for thy wrongs.
                    Exit.
HUM. What shall I do? I have been beaten
   twice,
And Mistress Luce is gone. Help me,
   device!
Since my true love is gone, I never more,
Whilst I do live, upon the sky will pore,
But in the dark will wear out my shoe
   soles   51
In passion in Saint Faith's Church under
   Paul's.[1]   *Exit.*

WIFE. George, call Rafe hither; if you
love me, call Rafe hither. I have the
bravest [2] thing for him to do, George;
prithee, call him quickly.
CIT. Rafe! Why, Rafe, boy!

Enter Rafe.

RAFE. Here, sir.
CIT. Come hither, Rafe; come to thy
mistress, boy.   60
WIFE. Rafe, I would have thee call
all the youths together in battle ray,[3] with
drums, and guns, and flags, and march
to Mile End in pompous fashion, and

there exhort your soldiers to be merry and
wise, and to keep their beards from burning, Rafe; and then skirmish, and let your
flags fly, and cry, "Kill, kill, kill!" My
husband shall lend you his jerkin, Rafe,
and there's a scarf; for the rest, the [70
house shall furnish you, and we'll pay
for 't. Do it bravely, Rafe; and think before whom you perform, and what person
you represent.
RAFE. I warrant you, mistress; if I do
it not for the honor of the city and the
credit of my master, let me never hope for
freedom! [4]
WIFE. 'Tis well spoken, i' faith. Go
thy ways; thou art a spark indeed.   80
CIT. Rafe, Rafe, double your files
bravely, Rafe!
RAFE. I warrant you, sir.   *Exit Rafe.*
CIT. Let him look narrowly to his service; [5] I shall take him else. I was there myself a pikeman once, in the hottest of the
day, wench, had my feather shot sheer
away, the fringe of my pike burnt off with
powder, my pate broken with a scouring
stick,[6] and yet, I thank God, I am here.   90
               Drum within.
WIFE. Hark, George, the drums!
CIT. Ran, tan, tan, tan; ran, tan! O,
wench, an thou hadst but seen little Ned
of Algate, Drum [7] Ned, how he made it
roar again, and laid on like a tyrant, and
then stroke softly till the ward [8] came up,
and then thundered again, and together
we go! "Sa, sa, sa, bounce!" quoth the
guns; "Courage, my hearts!" quoth the
captains; "Saint George!" quoth the [100
pikemen; and withal, here they lay, and
there they lay. And yet for all this I am
here, wench.
WIFE. Be thankful for it, George, for
indeed 'tis wonderful.

[SCENA SECUNDA.

A street in London.]

*Enter Rafe and his Company with drums
               and colors.*

RAFE. March fair, my hearts! Lieutenant, beat the rear up.—Ancient,[9] let
your colors fly; but have a great care of

---

[1] Near St. Paul's Cathedral.
[2] Finest.   [3] Array.

[4] *I.e.,* full membership in his company.
[5] Equipment.
[6] Ramrod.   [8] Guard.
[7] Drummer.   [9] Standard bearer.

the butchers' hooks at Whitechapel; they have been the death of many a fair ancient.[1]—Open your files that I may take a view both of your persons and munition.—Sergeant, call a muster.

SERG. A stand![2]—William Hammerton, pewterer? 10

HAM. Here, captain.

RAFE. A corselet and a Spanish pike; 'tis well. Can you shake it with a terror?

HAM. I hope so, captain.

RAFE. Charge upon me. [*He charges on Rafe.*] 'Tis with the weakest; put more strength, William Hammerton, more strength. As you were, again!—Proceed, sergeant. 19

SERG. George Greengoose, poulterer?

GREEN. Here.

RAFE. Let me see your piece, Neighbor Greengoose. When was she shot in?

GREEN. And 't[3] like you, Master Captain, I made a shot even now, partly to scour her, and partly for audacity.

RAFE. It should seem so certainly, for her breath is yet inflamed; besides, there is a main[4] fault in the touchhole—it runs and stinketh; and I tell you, moreover, [30 and believe it, ten such touchholes would breed the pox in the army. Get you a feather,[5] neighbor, get you a feather, sweet oil, and paper, and your piece may do well enough yet. Where's your powder?

GREEN. Here.

RAFE. What, in a paper? As I am a soldier and a gentleman, it craves a martial court! You ought to die for 't. Where's your horn? Answer me to that. 40

GREEN. An 't like you, sir, I was oblivious.

RAFE. It likes me not you should be so; 'tis a shame for you, and a scandal to all our neighbors, being a man of worth and estimation, to leave your horn behind you; I am afraid 'twill breed example. But let me tell you no more on 't.—Stand, till I view you all. What's become o' th' nose of your flask? 50

1 SOLD. Indeed-law, captain, 'twas blown away with powder.

RAFE. Put on a new one at the city's charge.—Where's the stone of this piece?

2 SOLD. The drummer took it out to light tobacco.

RAFE. 'Tis a fault, my friend; put it in again.—You want a nose, and you a stone.—Sergeant, take a note on 't, for I mean to stop it in the pay.—Remove, [60 and march! [*They march.*] Soft and fair, gentlemen, soft and fair! Double your files! As you were! Faces about! Now, you with the sodden face, keep in there! Look to your match, sirrah; it will be in your fellow's flask anon! So; make a crescent now! Advance your pikes! Stand and give ear!—Gentlemen, countrymen, friends, and my fellow soldiers, I have brought you this day from the shops [70 of security and the counters of content to measure out in these furious fields honor by the ell and prowess by the pound. Let it not, O, let it not, I say, be told hereafter, the noble issue of this city fainted; but bear yourselves in this fair action like men, valiant men, and free men! Fear not the face of the enemy, nor the noise of the guns, for, believe me, brethren, the rude rumbling of a brewer's car is far [80 more terrible, of which you have a daily experience; neither let the stink of powder offend you, since a more valiant stink is nightly with you. To a resolved mind his home is everywhere. I speak not this to take away the hope of your return, for you shall see (I do not doubt it), and that very shortly, your loving wives again and your sweet children, whose care doth bear you company in baskets.[6] Remember, [90 then, whose cause you have in hand, and, like a sort[7] of true-born scavengers, scour me this famous realm of enemies. I have no more to say but this: stand to your tacklings,[8] lads, and show to the world you can as well brandish a sword as shake an apron. Saint George, and on, my hearts!

OMNES. St. George, St. George! *Exeunt.*

WIFE. 'Twas well done, Rafe! I'll [100 send thee a cold capon afield and a bottle

---

1 Flag.
2 Halt!
3 If it. Emended by Dyce. Original reads *And*.
4 Serious.
5 A sharp blade placed in the musket rest.
6 Lunch baskets(?).
7 Company.   8 Tackle, equipment.

of March beer, and, it may be, come myself to see thee.

CIT. Nell, the boy has deceived me much; I did not think it had been in him. He has performed such a matter, wench, that, if I live, next year I'll have him captain of the galley foist [1] or I'll want my will.

[SCENA TERTIA.

A room in Merrythought's house.]

Enter Old Merrythought.

OLD MER. Yet, I thank God, I break not a wrinkle more than I had, not a stoop, boys! Care, live with cats; I defy thee! My heart is as sound as an oak; and, though I want drink to wet my whistle, I can sing.
[*Sings.*]

Come no more there, boys, come no more there,
For we shall never whilst we live come any more there.

Enter a Boy [and a Coffin Carrier] with a coffin.

BOY. God save you, sir!
OLD MER. It's a brave boy. Canst thou sing?　　　　　　　　　　10
BOY. Yes, sir, I can sing; but 'tis not so necessary at this time.
OLD MER. [*Singing.*]

Sing we, and chant it,
Whilst love doth grant it.

BOY. Sir, sir, if you knew what I have brought you, you would have little list to sing.
OLD MER. [*Singing.*]

O, the Mimon round,
Full long, long I have thee sought,
And now I have thee found,　　　　20
And what hast thou here brought?

BOY. A coffin, sir, and your dead son Jasper in it.　　　[*Exit with Coffin Carrier.*]
OLD MER. Dead? Why, farewell he!
[*Sings.*]

Thou wast a bonny boy, and I did love thee.

Enter Jasper.

JASP. Then, I pray you, sir, do so still.

[1] Barge used in the Lord Mayors' pageants.

OLD MER. Jasper's ghost?　　　[*Sings.*]

Thou art welcome from Stygian lake so soon;
Declare to me what wondrous things in Pluto's court are done.

JASP. By my troth, sir, I ne'er came [30 there; 'tis too hot for me, sir.
OLD MER. A merry ghost, a very merry ghost!　　　[*Sings.*]

And where is your true love? O, where is yours?

JASP. Marry, look you, sir!
Heaves up the coffin [, and Luce steps forth].
OLD MER. Ah, ha! Art thou good at that, i' faith?　　　[*Sings.*]

With hey, trixy, terlery-whiskin,
The world it runs on wheels;
When the young man's ——,　　　40
Up goes the maiden's heels.

Mistress Merrythought and Michael within.

MIST. MER. What, Mr. Merrythought, will you not let 's in? What do you think shall become of us?
OLD MER. [*Singing.*]

What voice is that, that calleth at our door?

MIST. MER. You know me well enough; I am sure I have not been such a stranger to you.
OLD MER. [*Singing.*]

And some they whistled, and some they sung,
"Hey, down, down!"　　　50
And some did loudly say,
Ever as the Lord Barnet's horn blew,
"Away, Musgrave, away!"

MIST. MER. You will not have us starve here, will you, Mr. Merrythought?
JASP. Nay, good sir, be persuaded; she is my mother. If her offenses have been great against you, let your own love remember she is yours, and so forgive her.
LUCE. Good Mr. Merrythought, let [60 me entreat you; I will not be denied.
MIST. MER. Why, Mr. Merrythought, will you be a vext [2] thing still?
OLD MER. Woman, I take you to my

[2] Ill-tempered.

love again; but you shall sing before you enter; therefore despatch your song and so come in.

Mist. Mer. Well, you must have your will, when all's done.—Mick, what song canst thou sing, boy?   70

Mich. I can sing none, forsooth, but "A lady's daughter of Paris properly."

{ Mist. Mer.
{ [Mich.]

Song

It was a lady's daughter, etc.

[Merrythought opens the door and Mistress Merrythought and Michael enter.]

Old Mer. Come, you're welcome home again.   *[Sings.]*

> If such danger be in playing,
>   And jest must to earnest turn,
> You shall go no more a-maying—

Merch. (*Within.*) Are you within, sir, Master Merrythought?   80

Jasp. It is my master's voice! Good sir, go hold him in talk, whilst we convey ourselves into some inward room.
    [Exit with Luce.]

Old Mer. What are you? Are you merry? You must be very merry, if you enter.

Merch. I am, sir.

Old Mer. Sing, then.

Merch. Nay, good sir, open to me.

Old Mer. Sing, I say, or, by the merry heart, you come not in!   91

Merch. Well, sir, I'll sing.   *[Sings.]*

Fortune, my foe, etc.

[Merrythought opens the door and Venture-well enters.]

Old Mer. You are welcome, sir; you are welcome. You see your entertainment; pray you, be merry.

Merch. O, Mr. Merrythought, I'm come to ask you
    Forgiveness for the wrongs I offered you
And your most virtuous son! They're infinite;
Yet my contrition shall be more than they.   100

I do confess my hardness broke his heart,
For which just heaven hath given me punishment
More than my age can carry. His wand'ring spirit,
Not yet at rest, pursues me everywhere,
Crying, "I'll haunt thee for thy cruelty."
My daughter, she is gone, I know not how,
Taken invisible, and whether living
Or in grave, 'tis yet uncertain to me.
O, Master Merrythought, these are the weights
Will sink me to my grave! Forgive me, sir.   110

Old Mer. Why, sir, I do forgive you; and be merry.
And, if the wag in 's lifetime played the knave,
Can you forgive him too?

Merch.   With all my heart, sir.

Old Mer. Speak it again, and heartly.

Merch.   I do, sir.

Now, by my soul, I do.

Old Mer. *[Singing.]*

> With that came out his paramour;
> She was as white as the lily flower.
>   Hey, troll, trolly, lolly!

Enter Luce and Jasper.

> With that came out her own dear knight;
> He was as true as ever did fight, etc.   120

Sir, if you will forgive him, clap their hands together; there's no more to be said [1] i' th' matter.

Merch. I do, I do.

Cit. I do not like this! Peace, boys! Hear me, one of you! Everybody's part is come to an end but Rafe's, and he's left out.

Boy. 'Tis long of yourself, sir; we have nothing to do with his part.   130

Cit. Rafe, come away!—Make on him, as you have done of the rest, boys; come.

Wife. Now, good husband, let him come out and die.

Cit. He shall, Nell.—Rafe, come away quickly, and die, boy!

Boy. 'Twill be very unfit he should die

---

[1] From 1635 edn. Original reads *sad*.

sir, upon no occasion—and in a comedy too.   139

CIT. Take you no care of that, Sir Boy; is not his part at an end, think you, when he's dead?—Come away, Rafe!

Enter Rafe, with a forked arrow through his head.

RAFE.[1] When I was mortal, this my costive corpse
Did lap up figs and raisins in the Strand,
Where, sitting, I espied a lovely dame,
Whose master wrought with lingel [2] and with awl,
And underground he vampied [3] many a boot.
Straight did her love prick forth me, tender sprig,
To follow feats of arms in warlike wise
Through Waltham Desert, where I did perform   150
Many achievements, and did lay on ground
Huge Barbaroso, that insulting giant,
And all his captives soon set at liberty.
Then honor pricked me from my native soil
Into Moldavia, where I gained the love
Of Pompiona, his beloved daughter,
But yet proved constant to the black-thumbed maid,
Susan, and scornéd Pompiona's love;
Yet liberal I was, and gave her pins,
And money for her father's officers.   160
I then returnéd home, and thrust myself
In action, and by all men chosen was
Lord of the May, where I did flourish it,
With scarfs and rings, and posy in my hand.
After this action I preferréd was,
And chosen city captain at Mile End,
With hat and feather, and with leading staff,
And trained my men, and brought them all off clear,
Save one man that berayed him with the noise.

But all these things I Rafe did undertake   170
Only for my beloved Susan's sake.
Then coming home, and sitting in my shop
With apron blue, Death came into my stall
To cheapen [4] *aqua vitæ;* but ere I
Could take the bottle down and fill a taste,
Death caught a pound of pepper in his hand,
And sprinkled all my face and body o'er,
And in an instant vanishéd away.

CIT. 'Tis a pretty fiction, i' faith.

RAFE. Then took I up my bow and shaft in hand,   180
And walked into Moorfields to cool myself;
But there grim cruel Death met me again,
And shot this forkéd arrow through my head.
And now I faint. Therefore be warned by me,
My fellows every one, of forkéd heads!
Farewell, all you good boys in merry London!
Ne'er shall we more upon Shrove Tuesday meet,
And pluck down houses of iniquity.[5]—
My pain increaseth—I shall never more
Hold open, whilst another pumps both legs,   190
Nor daub a satin gown with rotten eggs;
Set up a stake,[6] O, never more I shall!
I die! Fly, fly, my soul, to Grocers' Hall!
O, O, O, etc.

WIFE. Well said, Rafe! Do your obeisance to the gentlemen, and go your ways.
Well said, Rafe!   *Exit Rafe.*

OLD MER. Methinks all we, thus kindly and unexpectedly reconciled, should not depart without a song.   200

---

[1] Many parts of the following passage are a parody of the opening speech of Andrea's Ghost in *The Spanish Tragedy.*
[2] Waxed thread.
[3] Patched.

[4] Bargain for.
[5] An annual custom of the London apprentices.
[6] To which cocks were tied for targets to be thrown at.

MERCH. A good motion.

OLD MER. Strike up, then!

SONG

Better music ne'er was known
Than a choir of hearts in one.
Let each other that hath been
Troubled with the gall or spleen
Learn of us to keep his brow
Smooth and plain, as ours are now.
Sing, though before the hour of dying;
He shall rise, and then be crying,   210
"Hey, ho, 'tis naught but mirth
That keeps the body from the earth!"

Exeunt omnes.

EPILOGUS

CIT. Come, Nell, shall we go? The
play's done.

WIFE. Nay, by my faith, George, I
have more manners than so; I'll speak to
these gentlemen first.—I thank you all,
gentlemen, for your patience and countenance to Rafe, a poor fatherless child;
and, if I might see you at my house,   [220
it should go hard but I would have a pottle [1] of wine and a pipe of tabacco for you,
for, truly, I hope you do like the youth,
but I would be glad to know the truth. I
refer it to your own discretions, whether
you will applaud him or no, for I will wink,
and whilst [2] you shall do what you will.
I thank you with all my heart. God give
you good night!—Come, George.

[*Exeunt.*]

FINIS.

[1] Bottle.   [2] In the meantime.

THE FAITHFUL SHEPHERDESS

BY

JOHN FLETCHER [1]

[DRAMATIS PERSONÆ

PERIGOT.	SATYR.
THENOT.	SHEPHERDS.
DAPHNIS.	
ALEXIS.	CLORIN.
SULLEN SHEPHERD.	AMORET.
OLD SHEPHERD.	AMARILLIS.
PRIEST OF PAN.	CLOE.
GOD OF THE RIVER.	SHEPHERDESSES.

SCENE: *Thessaly.*

TIME: *Mythical.*]

TO THE READER

If you be not reasonably assured of your knowledge in this kind of poem, lay down the book, or read this, which I would wish had been the prologue. It is a pastoral tragi-comedy, which the people, seeing when it was played, having ever had a singular gift in defining, concluded to be a play of country hired shepherds in gray cloaks, with curtailed dogs in strings, some- [10 times laughing together, and some- times killing one another; and, missing Whitsun ales, cream, wassail, and mor- ris dances, began to be angry. In their error I would not have you fall, lest you incur their censure.[2] Understand, there- fore, a pastoral to be a representation of shepherds and shepherdesses with their actions and passions, which must be such as may agree with their natures, at least not exceeding former fictions and vul- [20 gar traditions; they are not to be adorned with any art but such improper [3] ones as nature is said to bestow, as singing and poetry, or such as experience may teach them, as the virtues of herbs and foun- tains, the ordinary course of the sun, moon, and stars, and suchlike. But you are ever to remember shepherds to be such as all the ancient poets, and modern of under- standing, have received them; that [30 is, the owners of flocks, and not hirelings. A tragi-comedy is not so called in respect of mirth and killing, but in respect it wants deaths, which is enough to make it no tragedy, yet brings some near it, which is enough to make it no comedy, which must be a representation of familiar people, with such kind of trouble as no life be ques- tioned,[4] so that a god is as lawful in this as in a tragedy, and mean people as in a [40 comedy. Thus much I hope will serve to justify my poem, and make you understand it; to teach you more for nothing, I do not know that I am in conscience bound.

JOHN FLETCHER.

---

[1] Commendatory verses by Nathan Field, Francis Beaumont, Ben Jonson, and George Chapman, and dedicatory verses to Sir Walter Aston, Sir William Skipwith, and Sir Robert Townshend follow here.

[2] *I.e.*, the criticism which they received.

[3] *I.e.*, common to all men.
[4] *I.e.*, be put in danger.

Actus Primi Scena Prima.[1]

[*A glade in a wood.*][2]

Enter Clorin, a shepherdess, having buried
her love in an arbor.

[Clorin.] Hail, holy earth, whose cold
    arms do embrace
The truest man that ever fed his flocks
By the fat plains of fruitful Thessaly!
Thus I salute thy grave; thus do I pay
My early vows and tribute of mine eyes
To thy still-lovéd ashes; thus I free
Myself from all ensuing heats and fires
Of love; all sports, delights, and games
That shepherds hold full dear, thus put
    I off.
Now no more shall these smooth brows
    be girt   10
With youthful coronals, and lead the
    dance;
No more the company of fresh fair
    maids
And wanton shepherds be to me de-
    lightful,
Nor the shrill, pleasing sound of merry
    pipes
Under some shady dell, when the cool
    wind
Plays on the leaves—all be far away,
Since thou art far away, by whose dear
    side
How often have I sat crowned with fresh
    flowers
For summer's queen, whilst every shep-
    herd's boy
Puts on his lusty green, with gaudy
    hook [3]   20
And hanging scrip of finest cordevan.[4]
But thou art gone, and these are gone
    with thee,
And all are dead but thy dear memory.
That shall outlive thee, and shall ever
    spring,
Whilst there are pipes, or jolly shep-
    herds sing.
And here will I, in honor of thy love,

Dwell by thy grave, forgetting all those
    joys
That former times made precious to
    mine eyes,
Only rememb'ring what my youth did
    gain
In the dark, hidden, virtuous [5] use of
    herbs.   30
That will I practice, and as freely give
All my endeavors, as I gained them free.
Of all green wounds I know the remedies
In men or cattle, be they stung with
    snakes,
Or charmed with powerful words of
    wicked art,
Or be they lovesick, or, through too
    much heat
Grown wild or lunatic, their eyes or ears
Thickened with misty film of dulling
    rheum;
These I can cure, such secret virtue lies
In herbs appliéd by a virgin's hand. 40
My meat shall be what these wild woods
    afford,
Berries and chestnuts, plantains, on
    whose cheeks
The sun sits smiling, and the lofty fruit
Pulled from the fair head of the
    straight-grown pine.
On these I'll feed with free content, and
    rest,
When night shall blind the world, by
    thy side blessed.

Enter a Satyr [with a basket of fruit].

Sat. Through [6] yon same bending plain,
That flings his arms down to the main,
And through these thick woods have I
    run,
Whose bottom never kissed the sun 50
Since the lusty spring began;
All to please my master Pan,
Have I trotted without rest
To get him fruit, for at a feast
He entertains this coming night
His paramour, the Syrinx bright.—
But, behold, a fairer sight!
             He stands amazed.
By that heavenly form of thine,
Brightest fair, thou art divine,
Sprong [7] from great immortal race 60

---

[1] The first scene of the first act.
[2] The setting, which apparently remains unchanged throughout the play, consists of
Clorin's bower (or cottage) in the inner stage,
a wood on one side of the main stage, and a hill
with a well on the other.
[3] Crook.
[4] Cordovan leather.

[5] Efficacious.   [7] Sprung.
[6] Perhaps pronounced *thorough*.

Of the gods; for in thy face
Shines more awful majesty
Than dull weak mortality
Dare with misty eyes behold,
And live. Therefore on this mold
Lowly do I bend my knee
In worship of thy deity.
Deign it, goddess, from my hand
To receive whate'er this land
From her fertile womb doth send   70
Of her choice fruits, and but lend
Belief to that the satyr tells:
Fairer by the famous wells
To this present day ne'er grew,
Never better nor more true.
Here be grapes, whose lusty blood
Is the learned poets' good,
Sweeter yet did never crown
The head of Bacchus; nuts more brown
Than the squirrel's teeth that crack
them.   80
Deign, O fairest fair, to take them!
For these black-eyed Dryope
Hath oftentimes commanded me
With my claspéd knee to climb—
See how well the lusty time
Hath decked their rising cheeks in
red,
Such as on your lips is spread!
Here be berries for a queen—
Some be red, some be green;
These are of that luscious meat   90
The great god Pan himself doth eat;
All these, and what the woods can yield,
The hanging mountain, or the field,
I freely offer, and ere long
Will bring you more, more sweet and
strong,
Till when, humbly leave I take,
Lest the great Pan do awake,
That sleeping lies in a deep glade
Under a broad beech's shade.
I must go, I must run   100
Swifter than the fiery sun.   *Exit.*
CLO. And all my fears go with thee!
What greatness, or what private hidden
power,
Is there in me, to draw submission
From this rude man and beast? Sure
I am mortal,
The daughter of a shepherd; he was
mortal,
And she that bore me mortal; prick my
hand,

And it will bleed; a fever shakes me, and
The selfsame wind that makes the young
lambs shrink
Makes me acold; my fear says I am
mortal.   110
Yet I have heard (my mother told it
me,
And now I do believe it), if I keep
My virgin-flower uncropped, pure, chaste,
and fair,
No goblin, wood god, fairy, elf, or fiend,
Satyr, or other power that haunts these
groves
Shall hurt my body, or by vain illusion
Draw me to wander after idle fires,
Or voices calling me in dead of night
To make me follow, and so toll me on
Through mires and standing pools. 120
Else why should this rough thing, who
never knew
Manners nor smooth humanity, whose
heats [1]
Are rougher than himself and more mis-
shapen,
Thus mildly kneel to me? Sure there is
a power
In that great name of virgin that binds
fast
All rude, uncivil bloods, all appetites
That break their confines. Then, strong
chastity,
Be thou my strongest guard, for here
I'll dwell
In opposition against fate and hell!
                                   [*Exit.*]

*Enter an Old Shepherd, with four couple of
Shepherds and Shepherdesses [, among
whom are Perigot and Amoret].* [2]

OLD SHEP. Now we have done this holy
festival   130
In honor of our great god, and his rites
Performed, prepare yourselves for chaste
And uncorrupted fires, that, as the priest
With powerful hand shall sprinkle on
your brows
His pure and holy water, ye may be
From all hot flames of lust and loose
thoughts free.
Kneel, shepherds, kneel; here comes the
priest of Pan.   [*They kneel.*]

[1] Passions.
[2] Added by Dyce.

Enter Priest.

PRIEST. [*Sprinkling them with water.*] Shep-
  herds, thus I purge away
Whatsoever this great day
Or the past hours gave not good   140
To corrupt your maiden blood.
From the high rebellious heat
Of the grapes, and strength of meat,
From the wanton quick desires
They do kindle by their fires
I do wash you with this water.
Be you pure and fair hereafter.
From your livers [1] and your veins
Thus I take away the stains;
All your thoughts be smooth and fair; 150
Be ye fresh and free as air.
Never more let lustful heat
Through your purgéd conduits [2] beat,
Or a plighted troth be broken,
Or a wanton verse be spoken
In a shepherdess's ear.
Go your ways; ye are all clear.
    They rise and sing in praise of Pan.

THE SONG

Sing his praises that doth keep
  Our flocks from harm,
Pan, the father of our sheep;   160
  And arm in arm
Tread we softly in a round,
Whilst the hollow neighboring ground
Fills the music with her sound.

Pan, O great god Pan, to thee
  Thus do we sing,
Thou that keep'st us chaste and free
  As the young spring!
Ever be thy honor spoke,
From that place the Morn is broke 170
To that place Day doth unyoke!

Exeunt omnes but Perigot and Amoret.
PERI. Stay, gentle Amoret, thou fair-
  browed maid;
Thy shepherd prays thee stay, that holds
  thee dear,
Equal with his soul's good.
AMO.   Speak; I give
Thee freedom, shepherd, and [3] thy
  tongue be still [4]
The same it ever was, as free from ill
As he whose conversation never knew
The court or city; be thou ever true!

---

[1] The supposed seat of desire.   [3] If.
[2] Veins.   [4] Always.

PERI. When I fall off from my affection,
  Or mingle my clean thoughts with foul
  desires,   180
First, let our great god cease to keep
  my flocks,
That, being left alone without a guard,
The wolf, or winter's rage, summer's
  great heat
And want of water, rots, or what to us
Of ill is yet unknown, fall speedily,
And in their general ruin let me go!
AMO. I pray thee, gentle shepherd, wish
  not so.
I do believe thee; 'tis as hard for me
To think thee false, and harder, than
  for thee
To hold me foul.
PERI.   O, you are fairer far 190
Than the chaste blushing morn, or that
  fair star
That guides the wand'ring seaman
  through the deep,
Straighter than the straightest pine
  upon the steep
Head of an aged mountain, and more
  white
Than the new milk we strip before day-
  light
From the full-freighted bags of our fair
  flocks;
Your hair more beauteous than those
  hanging locks
Of young Apollo!
AMO.   Shepherd, be not lost;
Y' are sailed too far already from the
  coast
Of our discourse.
PERI.   Did you not tell me once 200
I should not love alone, I should not
  lose
Those many passions, vows, and holy
  oaths
I've sent to heaven? Did you not give
  your hand,
Even that fair hand, in hostage? Do
  not, then,
Give back again those sweets to other
  men
You yourself vowed were mine.
AMO. Shepherd, so far as maiden's mod-
  esty
May give assurance, I am once more
  thine;
Once more I give my hand. Be ever free

From that great foe to faith, foul jeal-
   ousy!   210
PERI. I take it as my best good, and de-
   sire,
For stronger confirmation of our love,
To meet this happy night in that fair
   grove
Where all true shepherds have rewarded
   been
For their long service. Say, sweet, shall
   it hold?
AMO. Dear friend, you must not blame
   me if I make
A doubt of what the silent night may do,
Coupled with this day's heat, to move
   your blood.
Maids must be fearful. Sure you have
   not been
Washed white enough, for yet I see a
   stain   220
Stick in your liver; go and purge again.
PERI. O, do not wrong my honest, simple
   truth!
Myself and my affections are as pure
As those chaste flames that burn be-
   fore the shrine
Of the great Dian; only my intent
To draw you thither was to plight our
   troths,
With interchange of mutual chaste em-
   braces
And ceremonious tying of our souls.
For to that holy wood is consecrate
A virtuous well, about whose flowery
   banks   230
The nimble-footed fairies dance their
   rounds
By the pale moonshine, dipping often-
   times
Their stolen children, so to make them
   free
From dying flesh and dull mortality.
By this fair fount hath many a shep-
   herd sworn,
And given away his freedom, many a
   troth
Been plight, which neither envy nor old
   time
Could ever break, with many a chaste
   kiss given
In hope of coming happiness. By this
Fresh fountain many a blushing maid 240
Hath crowned the head of her long-
   lovéd shepherd

With gaudy flowers, whilst he happy sung
Lays of his love and dear captivity.
There grows all herbs fit to cool looser
   flames
Our sensual parts provoke, chiding our
   bloods,
And quenching by their power those
   hidden sparks
That else would break out, and provoke
   our sense
To open fires; so virtuous is that place.
Then, gentle shepherdess, believe, and
   grant.
In troth, it fits not with that face to
   scant   250
Your faithful shepherd of those chaste
   desires
He ever aimed at, and—
AMO. Thou hast prevailed; farewell. This
   coming night
Shall crown thy chaste hopes with long-
   wished delight.
PERI. Our great god Pan reward thee for
   that good
Thou hast given thy poor shepherd!
   Fairest bud
Of maiden virtues, when I leave to be
The true admirer of thy chastity,
Let me deserve the hot polluted name
Of a wild woodman, or affect some dame
Whose often prostitution hath begot 261
More foul diseases than ever yet the hot
Sun bred through his burnings, whilst
   the Dog [1]
Pursues the raging Lion,[1] throwing fog
And deadly vapor from his angry breath,
Filling the lower world with plague and
   death!   *Ex*[*it*] *Am*[*oret*].

Enter [*Amarillis,*] *another shepherdess that*
                is in love with Perigot.

AMAR. Shepherd, may I desire to be be-
   lieved,
What I shall blushing tell?
PERI.   Fair maid, you may.
AMAR. Then, softly thus: I love thee, Peri-
   got,
And would be gladder to be loved
   again   270
Than the cold earth is in his frozen arms
To clip [2] the wanton spring. Nay, do
   not start,

---

[1] Sign of the zodiac.   [2] Embrace.

Nor wonder that I woo thee, thou that
 art
The prime of our young grooms, even
 the top
Of all our lusty shepherds. What dull
 eye,
That never was acquainted with desire,
Hath seen thee wrastle, run, or cast
 the stone
With nimble strength and fair delivery,
And hath not sparkled fire, and speedily
Sent secret heat to all the neighboring
 veins?   280
Who ever heard thee sing, that brought
 again
That freedom back was lent unto thy
 voice?
Then, do not blame me, shepherd, if I
 be
One to be numbered in this company,
Since none that ever saw thee yet were
 free.
PERI. Fair shepherdess, much pity I can
 lend
To your complaints; but sure I shall
 not love.
All that is mine, myself and my best
 hopes,
Are given already. Do not love him,
 then,
That cannot love again; on other men 290
Bestow those heats, more free, that may
 return
You fire for fire, and in one flame equal
 burn.
AMAR. Shall I rewarded be so slenderly
For my affection, most unkind of men?
If I were old, or had agreed with art
To give another nature to my cheeks,
Or were I common mistress to the love
Of every swain, or could I with such
 ease
Call back my love as many a wanton
 doth,
Thou mightst refuse me, shepherd; but
 to thee   300
I am only fixed and set. Let it not be
A sport, thou gentle shepherd, to abuse
The love of silly [1] maid.
PERI.   Fair soul, you use
These words to little end; for, know, I
 may
Better call back that time was yesterday,
 Weak.

Or stay the coming night, than bring
 my love
Home to myself again, or recreant
 prove.
I will no longer hold you with delays.
This present night I have appointed
 been
To meet that chaste fair that enjoys my
 soul,   310
In yonder grove, there to make up our
 loves.
Be not deceived no longer; choose again.
These neighboring plains have many a
 comely swain,
Fresher and freer [2] far than I e'er was;
Bestow that love on them, and let me
 pass.
Farewell; be happy in a better choice!
                                 Exit.
AMAR. Cruel, thou hast struck me deader
 with thy voice
Than if the angry heavens with their
 quick flames
Had shot me through. I must not leave
 to love;
I cannot; no, I must enjoy thee, boy, 320
Though the great dangers twixt my
 hopes and that
Be infinite. There is a shepherd dwells
Down by the moor, whose life hath ever
 shown
More sullen discontent than Saturn's
 brow
When he sits frowning on the births of
 men—
One that doth wear himself away in
 loneness,
And never joys, unless it be in breaking
The holy plighted troths of mutual souls;
One that lusts after every several beauty,
But never yet was known to love or
 like,   330
Were the face fairer or more full of truth
Than Phœbe in her fullness, or the youth
Of smooth Lyæus, whose nigh-starvéd
 flocks
Are always scabby, and infect all sheep
They feed withal, whose lambs are ever
 last,
And die before their weaning, and whose
 dog
Looks, like his master, lean and full of
 scurf,

[2] More liberal.

Not caring for the pipe or whistle. This
　man may,
If he be well wrought, do a deed of won-
　der,　　　　　　　　　　　　　　　339
Forcing me passage to my long desires.
And here he comes, as fitly to my pur-
　pose
As my quick thoughts could wish for.

Enter Sullen [Shepherd].

SULL. Fresh beauty, let me not be thought
　uncivil,
　Thus to be partner of your loneness;
　　'twas
My love (that ever-working passion)
　drew
Me to this place to seek some remedy
For my sick soul. Be not unkind and
　fair,
For such the mighty Cupid in his doom
Hath sworn to be avenged on. Then
　give room
To my consuming fires that so I may　350
Enjoy my long desires, and so allay
Those flames that else would burn my
　life away.
AMAR. Shepherd, were I but sure thy
　heart were sound
　As thy words seem to be, means might
　　be found
To cure thee of thy long pains; for to me
That heavy, youth-consuming misery
The lovesick soul endures never was
　pleasing.
I could be well content with the quick
　easing
Of thee and thy hot fires, might it
　procure
Thy faith and farther service to be
　sure.　　　　　　　　　　　　　360
[SULL.] [1] Name but that work, danger, or
　what can
Be compassed by the wit or art of man,
And, if I fail in my performance, may
I never more kneel to the rising day!
AMAR. Then thus I try thee, shepherd.
　This same night
That now comes stealing on, a gentle pair
Have promised equal love, and do
　appoint
To make yon wood the place where
　hands and hearts

[1] From 1634 edn.

Are to be tied forever. Break their
　meeting
And their strong faith, and I am ever
　thine.　　　　　　　　　　　　370
SULL. Tell me their names, and, if I do
　not move,
By my great power, the center of their
　love
From his fixed being, let me never more
Warm me by those fair eyes I thus adore.
AMAR. Come; as we go, I'll tell thee what
　they are,
And give thee fit directions for thy work.
　　　　　　　　　　　　　　Exeunt.

Enter Cloe.

CLOE. How have I wronged the times or
　men, that thus
After this holy feast I pass unknown
And unsaluted? 'Twas not wont to be
Thus frozen with the younger com-
　pany　　　　　　　　　　　　380
Of jolly shepherds; 'twas not then held
　good
For lusty grooms [2] to mix their quicker
　blood
With that dull humor, most unfit to be
The friend of man, cold and dull chastity.
Sure I am held not fair, or am too old,
Or else not free enough, or from my
　fold
Drive not a flock sufficient great to
　gain
The greedy eyes of wealth-alluring
　swain.
Yet, if I may believe what others say,
My face has foil [3] enough; nor can they
　lay　　　　　　　　　　　　390
Justly too strict a coyness to my charge;
My flocks are many, and the downs as
　large
They feed upon. Then, let it ever be
Their coldness, not my virgin-modesty,
Makes me complain.

Enter Thenot.

THE.　　　　　　　Was ever man but I
Thus truly taken with uncertainty? [4]
Where shall that man be found that
　loves a mind

[2] Merry fellows.
[3] Beauty.
[4] Bewitched with "the desire of things in-
compatible" (Greg).

Made up in constancy, and dares not find
His love rewarded? Here, let all men know,
A wretch that lives to love his mistress so.   400
CLOE. Shepherd, I pray thee stay. Where hast thou been?
Or whither go'st thou? Here be woods as green
As any; air as fresh and sweet
As where smooth Zephyrus plays on the fleet
Face of the curléd streams, with flowers as many
As the young spring gives, and as choice as any;
Here be all new delights, cool streams and wells,
Arbors o'ergrown with woodbines, caves, and dells.
Choose where thou wilt, whilst I sit by and sing,
Or gather rushes, to make many a ring   410
For thy long fingers; tell thee tales of love—
How the pale Phoebe, hunting in a grove,
First saw the boy Endymion, from whose eyes
She took eternal fire that never dies,
How she conveyed him softly in a sleep,
His temples bound with poppy, to the steep
Head of old Latmus, where she stoops each night,
Gilding the mountain with her brother's light,
To kiss her sweetest.
THE.   Far from me are these
Hot flashes, bred from wanton heat and ease;   420
I have forgot what love and loving meant;
Rimes, songs, and merry rounds,[1] that oft are sent
To the soft ear of maid, are strange to me.
Only I live t' admire a chastity
That neither pleasing age,[2] smooth tongue, or gold
Could ever break upon, so sure a mold

Is that her mind was cast in. 'Tis to her
I only am reserved; she is my form I stir
By, breathe, and move; 'tis she, and only she,   429
Can make me happy, or give misery.
CLOE. Good shepherd, may a stranger crave to know
To whom this dear observance [3] you do owe?
THE. You may, and by her virtue learn to square
And level out your life; for to be fair,
And nothing virtuous, only fits the eye
Of gaudy youth and swelling vanity.
Then, know, she's called the Virgin of the Grove,
She that hath long since buried her chaste love,
And now lives by his grave, for whose dear soul
She hath vowed herself into the holy roll   440
Of strict virginity. 'Tis her I so admire,
Not any looser blood or new desire.
                                        [Exit.]
CLOE. Farewell, poor swain! Thou art not for my bend; [4]
I must have quicker souls, whose words may tend
To some free action. Give me him dare love
At first encounter, and as soon dare prove!

THE SONG

Come, shepherds, come!
Come away without delay,
Whilst the gentle time doth stay.
  Green woods are dumb,   450
And will never tell to any
Those dear kisses and those many
Sweet embraces that are given—
Dainty pleasures that would even
Raise in coldest age a fire,
And give virgin-blood desire.
  Then, if ever,
  Now or never,
  Come and have it;
  Think not I   460
  Dare deny,
  If you crave it.

[1] Roundelays.   [2] Youth.   [3] Homage.   [4] Bent, purpose.

Enter Daphnis.

[CLOE. (*Aside.*)] Here comes another.
 Better be my speed,
Thou god of blood! But certain, if I
 read
Not false, this is that modest shepherd,
 he
That only dare salute, but ne'er could
 be
Brought to kiss any, hold discourse, or
 sing,
Whisper, or boldly ask that wishéd thing
We all are born for—one that makes
 loving faces,
And could be well content to covet
 graces,   470
Were they not got by boldness. In
 this thing
My hopes are frozen; and, but fate doth
 bring
Him hither, I would sooner choose
A man made out of snow, and freer use
An eunuch to my ends. But since he
 is here,
Thus I attempt him.—Thou, of men
 most dear,
Welcome to her that only for thy sake
Hath been content to live! Here, boldly
 take
My hand in pledge, this hand that
 never yet
Was given away to any, and but sit 480
Down on this rushy bank whilst I go
 pull
Fresh blossoms from the boughs, or
 quickly cull
The choicest delicates from yonder
 mead,
To make thee chains or chaplets, or
 to spread
Under our fainting bodies, when delight
Shall lock up all our senses. How the
 sight
Of those smooth rising cheeks renew
 the story
Of young Adonis, when in pride and glory
He lay infolded twixt the beating arms
Of willing Venus! Methinks stronger
 charms   490
Dwell in those speaking eyes, and on
 that brow
More sweetness than the painters can
 allow

To their best pieces. Not Narcissus, he
That wept himself away in memory
Of his own beauty, nor Silvanus' boy,
Nor the twice-ravished maid, for whom
 old Troy
Fell by the hand of Pyrrhus, may to
 thee
Be otherwise compared than some dead
 tree
To a young fruitful olive.
DAPH.   I can love, 499
But I am loath to say so, lest I prove
Too soon unhappy.
CLOE.   Happy, thou wouldst say.
My dearest Daphnis, blush not. If the
 day
To thee and thy soft heats be enemy,
Then take the coming night. Fair
 youth, 'tis free
To all the world. Shepherd, I'll meet
 thee, then,
When darkness hath shut up the eyes of
 men,
In yonder grove. Speak, shall our
 meeting hold?
Indeed ye are too bashful; be more bold,
And tell me ay.
DAPH.   I am content to say so,
And would be glad to meet, might I
 but pray so   510
Much from your fairness, that you
 would be true.
CLOE. Shepherd, thou hast thy wish.
DAPH.   Fresh maid, adieu.
Yet one word more. Since you have
 drawn me on
To come this night, fear not to meet
 alone
That man that will not offer to be ill,
Though your bright self would ask it,
 for his fill
Of this world's goodness. Do not fear
 him, then,
But keep your pointed [1] time. Let
 other men
Set up their bloods to sale; mine shall
 be ever
Fair as the soul it carries, and un-
 chaste never.   *Exit.* 520
CLOE. Yet am I poorer than I was before.
Is it not strange, among so many a score
Of lusty bloods, I should pick out these
 things

---

[1] Appointed.

Whose veins, like a dull river far from
    springs,
Is still the same, slow, heavy, and unfit
For stream or motion, though the strong
    winds hit
With their continual power upon his
    sides?
O, happy be your names that have been
    brides,
And tasted those rare sweets for which
    I pine!
And far more heavy be thy grief and
    tine,[1]   530
Thou lazy swain, that mayst relieve
    my needs,
Than his upon whose liver always feeds
A hungry vulture!

Enter Alexis.

ALEX.   Can such beauty be
Safe in his [2] own guard, and not draw
    the eye
Of him that passeth on, to greedy gaze
Or covetous desire, whilst in a maze
The better part contemplates, giving
    rein
And wishéd freedom to the laboring
    vein? [3]
Fairest and whitest, may I crave to
    know
The cause of your retirement, why ye
    go   540
Thus all alone? Methinks the downs are
    sweeter,
And the young company of swains more
    meeter,
Than these forsaken and untrodden
    places.
Give not yourself to loneness, and those
    graces
Hide from the eyes of men, that were
    intended
To live amongst us swains.
CLOE.   Thou art befriended,
Shepherd; in all my life I have not seen
A man in whom greater contents hath
    been
Than thou thyself art. I could tell thee
    more,
Were there but any hope left to re-
    store   550
My freedom lost. O, lend me all thy red,

Thou shamefast [4] Morning, when from
    Tithon's bed
Thou risest ever maiden!
ALEX.   If for me,
Thou sweetest of all sweets, these flashes
    be,
Speak, and be satisfied. O, guide her
    tongue,
My better angel; force my name among
Her modest thoughts, that the first
    word may be—
CLOE. Alexis, when the sun shall kiss the
    sea,
Taking his rest by the white Thetis'
    side,
Meet me in the holy wood, where I'll
    abide   560
Thy coming, shepherd.
ALEX.   If I stay behind,
An everlasting dullness, and the wind,
That as he passeth by shuts up the
    stream
Of Rhine or Volga, whilst the sun's
    hot beam
Beats back again, seize me, and let me
    turn
To coldness more than ice! O, how I
    burn
And rise in youth and fire! I dare not
    stay.
CLOE. My name shall be your word.
ALEX.   Fly, fly, thou day! *Exit.*
CLOE. My grief is great, if both these
    boys should fail;
He that will use all winds must shift
    his sail.   *Exit.* 570

ACTUS SECUNDUS. SCENA PRIMA.

[The same.]

Enter an Old Shepherd, with a bell ringing,
    and the Priest of Pan following.

PRIEST. Shepherds all, and maidens fair,
Fold your flocks up, for the air
Gins [5] to thicken, and the sun
Already his great course hath run.
See the dewdrops, how they kiss
Every little flower that is,
Hanging on their velvet heads,
Like a rope of crystal beads.
See the heavy clouds low [6] falling,

---

[1] Teen, sorrow.   [2] Its.   [3] *I.e.*, pulsing blood.

[4] Modest.
[5] Begins.
[6] From 1656 edn. Original reads *lowde.*

And bright Hesperus down calling   10
The dead Night from underground,
At whose rising mists unsound,[1]
Damps and vapors fly apace,
Hovering o'er the wanton face
Of these pastures, where they come,
Striking dead both bud and bloom.
Therefore, from such danger lock
Every one his lovéd flock;
And let your dogs lie loose without,
Lest the wolf come as a scout   20
From the mountain, and, ere day,
Bear a lamb or kid away;
Or the crafty thievish fox
Break upon your simple flocks.
To secure yourselves from these,
Be not too secure in ease.
Let one eye his watches keep,
Whilst the tother[2] eye doth sleep;
So you shall good shepherds prove,
And forever hold the love   30
Of our great god. Sweetest slumbers
And soft silence fall in numbers
On your eyelids! So, farewell.
Thus I end my evening's knell.   *Exeunt.*

Enter Clorin, the shepherdess, sorting of
herbs, and telling the natures of them.

CLO. Now let me know what my best
    art hath done,
Helped by the great power of the vir-
    tuous moon
In her full light. O, you sons of earth,
You only brood, unto whose happy birth
Virtue was given, holding more of nature
Than man, her first-born and most
    perfect creature,   40
Let me adore you! You, that only can
Help or kill nature, drawing out that
    span
Of life and breath even to the end of
    time;
You, that these hands did crop long
    before prime
Of day, give me your names, and, next,
    your hidden power.
This is the clote,[3] bearing a yellow
    flower;
And this, black horehound. Both are
    very good

[1] Unwholesome.
[2] That other.
[3] The name is applied to both the burdock and
the yellow water lily.

For sheep or shepherd bitten by a wood[4]
Dog's venomed tooth. These rhamnus[5]
    branches are,
Which, stuck in entries or about the
    bar   50
That holds the door fast, kill all enchant-
    ments, charms
(Were they Medea's verses) that do
    harms
To men or cattle. These for frenzy be
A speedy and a sovereign remedy—
The bitter wormwood, sage, and mari-
    gold—
Such sympathy with man's good they do
    hold.
This tormentil, whose virtue is to part
All deadly killing poison from the heart.
And here, narcissus root, for swellings
    best;
Yellow lysimachus,[6] to give sweet rest   60
To the faint shepherd, killing, where it
    comes,
All busy gnats and every fly that hums.
For leprosy, darnel and celandine,
With calamint, whose virtues do refine
The blood of man, making it free and
    fair
As the first hour it breathed, or the best
    air.
Here, other two; but your rebellious use
Is not for me, whose goodness is abuse.
Therefore, foul standergrass,[7] from me
    and mine
I banish thee, with lustful turpentine—   70
You that entice the veins and stir the
    heat
To civil mutiny, scaling the seat
Our reason moves in, and deluding it
With dreams and wanton fancies till
    the fit
Of burning lust be quenched, by ap-
    petite
Robbing the soul of blessedness and
    light.
And thou, light varvin[8] too, thou must
    go after,
Provoking easy souls to mirth and
    laughter;
No more shall I dip thee in water now,

[4] Mad.
[5] A thorny shrub. Dyce's emendation for
Ramuus.
[6] Loosestrife.
[7] A variety of orchid.
[8] Vervain.

And sprinkle every post and every
bough   80
With thy well-pleasing juice, to make
the grooms
Swell with high mirth, as with joy all
the rooms.

Enter Thenot.[1]

THE. This is the cabin where the best of
all
Her sex that ever breathed, or ever
shall
Give heat or happiness to the shep-
herd's side,
Doth only to her worthy self abide.
Thou blessed star, I thank thee for thy
light,
Thou by whose power the darkness of
sad night
Is banished from the earth, in whose
dull place
Thy chaster beams play on the heavy
face   90
Of all the world, making the blue sea
smile
To see how cunningly thou dost be-
guile
Thy brother of his brightness, giving
day
Again from chaos; whiter than that way
That leads to Jove's high court, and
chaster far
Than chastity itself, yon blessed star
That nightly shines; thou, all the con-
stancy
That in all women was or e'er shall be,
From whose fair eyeballs flies that holy
fire
That poets[2] style the mother of de-
sire,   100
Infusing into every gentle breast
A soul of greater price, and far more
blessed
Than that quick power which gives a
difference
Twixt man and creatures of a lower
sense!
CLO. Shepherd, how cam'st thou hither
to this place?
No way is trodden; all the verdant grass

The spring shot up stands yet unbruiséd
here
Of any foot; only the dappled deer,
Far from the fearéd sound of crooked
horn,
Dwells in this fastness.
THE.   Chaster than the morn, 110
I have not wandered, or by strong
illusion
Into this virtuous place have made in-
trusion;
But hither am I come (believe me, fair)
To seek you out, of whose great good
the air
Is full, and strongly labors, whilst the
sound
Breaks against heaven, and drives into
a stound[3]
The amazéd shepherd, that such virtue
can
Be resident in lesser than a man.
CLO. If any art I have, or hidden skill,
May cure thee of disease or festered
ill   120
Whose grief or greenness to another's
eye
May seem unpossible of remedy,
I dare yet undertake it.
THE.   'Tis no pain
I suffer through disease, no beating vein
Conveys infection dangerous to the heart,
No part impostumed, to be cured by art,
This body holds, and yet a feller[4] grief
Than ever skillful hand did give relief,
Dwells on my soul, and may be healed
by you,
Fair, beauteous virgin.
CLO.   Then, shepherd, let me sue 130
To know thy grief; that man yet never
knew
The way to health that durst not show
his sore.
THE. Then, fairest, know, I love you.
CLO.   Swain, no more!
Thou hast abused the strictness of this
place,
And offered sacrilegious foul disgrace
To the sweet rest of these interréd
bones,
For fear of whose ascending, fly at
once,

---

[1] From 1629 edn. Original reads *Shepherd.*
The following speech heads also read *Shep.* in
the original.
[2] From 1629 edn. Original reads *ports.*

[3] Astonishment. From 1634 edn. Original has
stround.
[4] Crueler.

Thou and thy idle passions, that the
  sight
Of death and speedy vengeance may
  not fright
Thy very soul with horror.
[THE.] [1]   Let me not, 140
Thou all perfection, merit such a blot
For my true, zealous faith.
CLO.   Dar'st thou abide
To see this holy earth at once divide,
And give her body up? For sure it will,
If thou pursu'st with wanton flames
  to fill
This hallowed place; therefore repent
  and go,
Whilst I with praye[r]s appease his
  ghost below,
That else would tell thee what it were
  to be
A rival in that virtuous love that he
Embraces yet.
THE.   'Tis not the white or red 150
Inhabits in your cheek that thus can
  wed
My mind to adoration; nor your eye,
Though it be full and fair; your fore-
  head high
And smooth as Pelops' shoulder; not
  the smile
Lies watching in those dimples to be-
  guile
The easy soul; your hands and fingers
  long,
With veins enameled richly, nor your
  tongue,
Though it spoke sweeter than Arion's
  harp;
Your hair woven into many a curious
  warp,
Able in endless error to infold [2] 160
The wand'ring soul; not the true, per-
  fect mold
Of all your body, which as pure doth
  show
In maiden whiteness as the Alpsian
  snow—
All these, were but your constancy
  away,
Would please me less than a black,
  stormy day
The wretched seaman toiling through
  the deep.

But, whilst this honored strictness you
  dare keep,
Though all the plagues that e'er be-
  gotten were
In the great womb of air were settled
  here,
In opposition, I would, like the tree, 170
Shake off those drops of weakness, and
  be free
Even in the arm of danger.
CLO.   Wouldst thou have
Me raise again, fond [3] man, from silent
  grave
Those sparks that long ago were buried
  here
With my dead friend's cold ashes?
THE.   Dearest dear,
I dare not ask it, nor you must not
  grant;
Stand strongly to your vow, and do
  not faint.
Remember how he loved ye, and be
  still
The same opinion speaks ye. Let not
  will,
And that great god of women, ap-
  petite,   180
Set up your blood again; do not invite
Desire and fancy from their long exile,
To seat them once more in a pleasing
  smile.
Be, like a rock, made firmly up gainst
  all
The power of angry heaven or the
  strong fall
Of Neptune's battery. If ye yield, I
  die
To all affection; 'tis that loyalty
Ye tie unto this grave I so admire.
And yet there's something else I would
  desire,   189
If you would hear me, but withal deny.
O, Pan, what an uncertain destiny
Hangs over all my hopes! I will retire,
For, if I longer stay, this double fire
Will lick my life up.
CLO.   Do; and let time wear out
What art and nature cannot bring about.
THE. Farewell, thou soul of virtue, and be
  blessed
Forever, whilst I wretched rest
Thus to myself! Yet grant me leave to
  dwell

[1] From 1629 edn.
[2] From 1634 edn. Original has *unfold*.
[3] Foolish.

In kenning [1] of this arbor; yon same dell,
O'ertopped with mourning cypress and
　sad yew,　　　　　　　　　　　200
Shall be my cabin, where I'll early rue,
Before the sun hath kissed this dew
　away,
The hard uncertain chance which faith
　doth lay
Upon this head.
CLO.　　　　The gods give quick release
And happy cure unto thy hard disease! [2]
　　　　　　　　　　　　　　Exeunt.

Enter Sullen Shepherd.

SULL. I do not love this wench that I
　should meet,
For never did my unconstant eye yet
　greet
That beauty, were it sweeter or more fair
Than the new blossoms when the morn-
　ing air
Blows gently on them, or the breaking
　light　　　　　　　　　　　210
When many maiden blushes to our
　sight
Shoot from his early face—were all
　these set
In some neat form before me, 'twould
　not get
The least love from me. Some desire it
　might,
And present burning. All to me in sight
Are equal; be they fair or black or
　brown,
Virgin or careless wanton, I can crown
My appetite with any; swear as oft,
And weep, as any; melt my words as
　soft　　　　　　　　　　　219
Into a maiden's ears, and tell how long
My heart has been her servant, and
　how strong
My passions are; call her unkind and
　cruel;
Offer her all I have to gain the jewel
Maidens so highly praise; then loathe,
　and fly.
This do I hold a blessed destiny.

Enter Amarillis.

AMAR. Hail, shepherd! Pan bless both
　thy flock and thee
For being mindful of thy word to me!

SULL. Welcome, fair shepherdess! Thy
　loving swain
Gives thee the selfsame wishes back
　again,
Who till this present hour ne'er knew
　that eye　　　　　　　　　　230
Could make me cross mine arms, or
　daily die
With fresh consumings. Boldly tell
　me, then,
How shall we part their faithful loves,
　and when?
Shall I belie him to her? Shall I swear
His faith is false and he loves every-
　where?
I'll say he mocked her the other day to
　you,
Which will by your confirming show as
　true,
For she [3] is of so pure an honesty,
To think, because she [3] will not, none
　will lie.
Or else to him I'll slander Amoret,　240
And say she but seems chaste. I'll
　swear she met
Me mongst the shady sycamores last
　night,
And loosely offered up her flame and
　sprite
Into my bosom, made a wanton bed
Of leaves and many flowers, where she
　spread
Her willing body to be pressed by me.
There have I carved her name on many
　a tree,
Together with mine own. To make this
　show
More full of seeming—Hobinal, you
　know,
Son to the aged shepherd of the glen,　250
Him I have sorted out of many men,
To say he found us at our private sport,
And roused us fore our time by his re-
　sort.
This to confirm, I've promised to the
　boy
Many a pretty knack and many a toy,
As gren [4] to catch him birds, with bow
　and bolt
To shoot at nimble squirrels in the holt,
A pair of painted buskins, and a lamb
Soft as his own locks or the down of
　swan.

[1] View.　　[2] Dis-ease, discomfort.　[3] Early edns. read *he.*　[4] Snare.

This I have done to win ye, which doth
   give   260
Me double pleasure. Discord makes me
   live.
AMAR. Loved swain, I thank ye. These
   tricks might prevail
With other rustic shepherds, but will
   fail
Even once to stir, much more to over-
   throw,
His fixéd love from judgment, who doth
   know
Your nature, my end, and his chosen's
   merit.
Therefore some stronger way must force
   his spirit,
Which I have found: give second, and
   my love
Is everlasting thine.
SULL.   Try me, and prove.
AMAR. These happy pair of lovers meet
   straightway,   270
Soon as they fold their flocks up with
   the day,
In the thick grove bordering upon yon
   hill,
In whose hard side nature hath carved a
   well,
And, but that matchless spring which
   poets know,
Was ne'er the like to this. By it doth
   grow
About the sides all herbs which witches
   use,
All simples good for medicine or abuse,
All sweets that crown the happy nup-
   tial day
With all their colors. There the month
   of May   279
Is ever dwelling; all is young and green:
There's not a grass on which was ever
   seen
The falling autumn or cold winter's hand,
So full of heat and virtue is the land
About this fountain, which doth slowly
   break,
Below yon mountain's foot, into a creek
That waters all the valley, giving fish
Of many sorts to fill the shepherd's
   dish.
This holy well, my grandam that is
   dead,
Right wise in charms, hath often to me
   said,

Hath power to change the form of any
   creature,   290
Being thrice dipped over the head, into
   what feature
Or shape 'twould please the letter-down
   to crave,
Who must pronounce this charm too,
   which she gave   [Shows a scroll.]
Me on her deathbed, told me what, and
   how,
I should apply unto the patients' brow
That would be changed, casting them
   thrice asleep,
Before I trusted them into this deep.
All this she showed me, and did charge
   me prove
This secret of her art, if crossed in
   love.
I'll this attempt now, shepherd.   I
   have here   300
All her prescriptions, and I will not
   fear
To be myself dipped. Come, my temples
   bind
With these sad herbs, and, when I sleep
   you find,
As you do speak your charm, thrice
   down me let,
And bid the water raise me Amoret;
Which being done, leave me to my af-
   fair,
And, ere the day shall quite itself out-
   wear,
I will return unto my shepherd's arm.
Dip me again, and then repeat this
   charm,
And pluck me up myself, whom freely
   take,   310
And the hott'st fire of thine affection
   slake.
SULL. And, if I fit thee not, then fit not
   me.
I long the truth of this well's power to
   see.   Exeunt.[1]

Enter Daphnis.

DAPH. Here will I stay, for this the covert is
Where I appointed Cloe. Do not miss,
Thou bright-eyed virgin; come, O, come,
   my fair!

[1] In the first quarto only here follows: "ACTUS
SECUNDUS. SCENA QUARTA"—the only attempt in
the play to divide acts into shorter scenes.

Be not abused [1] with fear, or let cold care
Of honor stay thee from thy shepherd's arm,
Who would as hard be won to offer harm
To thy chaste thoughts, as whiteness from the day,　　　320
Or yon great round [2] to move another way.
My language shall be honest, full of truth;
My flame, as smooth and spotless as my youth.
I will not entertain that wand'ring thought,
Whose easy current may at length be brought
To a loose vastness.

ALEX. (Within.)　　　　Cloe!

DAPH.　　　　　　　　'Tis her voice,
And I must answer.—Cloe!—O, the choice
Of dear embraces, chaste and holy strains
Our hands shall give! I charge you, all my veins,
Through which the blood and spirit take their way,　　　330
Lock up your disobedient heats, and stay
Those mutinous desires that else would grow
To strong rebellion; do not wilder show
Than blushing modesty may entertain.

ALEX. (Within.) Cloe!

DAPH.　　　　There sounds that blessed name again,
And I will meet it. Let me not mistake.

Enter Alexis.

This is some shepherd. Sure, I am awake.
What may this riddle mean? I will retire,
To give myself more knowledge.
　　　　　　　　　　　　[Retires.]

ALEX.　　　　　　　　O, my fire,
How thou consum'st me!—Cloe, answer me!　　　340
Alexis, strong Alexis, high and free,
Calls upon Cloe. See, mine arms are full
Of entertainment, ready for to pull
That golden fruit which too-too long hath hung

[1] Cheated.　　　　　[2] I.e., the moon.

Tempting the greedy eye. Thou stayest too long;
I am impatient of these mad delays;
I must not leave unsought those many ways
That lead into this center, till I find
Quench for my burning lust. I come, unkind!　　　　*Exit Alexis.*

DAPH. [Coming forward.] Can my imagination work me so much ill　　　350
That I may credit this for truth and still
Believe mine eyes? Or shall I firmly hold
Her yet untainted, and these sights but bold
Illusion? Sure, such fancies oft have been
Sent to abuse true love, and yet are seen
Daring to blind the virtuous thought [3] with error.
But be they far from me with their fond terror!
I am resolved my Cloe yet is true.

CLOE. (Within.) Cloe!

[DAPH.]　　　　　　　Hark! Cloe! Sure, this voice is new,
Whose shrillness, like the sounding of a bell,　　　360
Tells me it is a woman.—Cloe, tell
Thy blessed name again.

CLOE. (Within.)　　　　　　Here!

[DAPH.] O, what a grief is this, to be so near
And not encounter!

Enter Cloe.

CLOE.　　　　　　Shepherd, we are met;
Draw close into the covert, lest the wet,
Which falls like lazy mists upon the ground,
Soak through your startups. [4]

DAPH.　　　　　Fairest, are you found?
How have we wandered, that the better part
Of this good night is perished? O, my heart!
How have I longed to meet ye, how to kiss　　　370
Those lily hands, how to receive the bliss
That charming tongue gives to the happy ear

[3] From 1634 edn. Original reads *though*.
[4] Rustic shoes.

Of him that drinks your language! But
  I fear
I am too much unmannered, far too
  rude,
And almost grown lascivious, to intrude
These hot behaviors, where regard of
  fame,
Honor, and modesty, a virtuous name,
And such discourse as one fair sister
  may
Without offense unto the brother say,
Should rather have been tendered. But,
  believe,   380
Here dwells a better temper. Do not
  grieve,
Then, ever-kindest, that my first salute
Seasons so much of fancy.[1] I am mute
Henceforth to all discourses but shall be
Suiting to your sweet thoughts and
  modesty.
Indeed, I will not ask a kiss of you,
No, not to wring your fingers, nor to sue
To those blessed pair of fixéd stars for
  smiles.
All a young lover's cunning, all his
  wiles,   389
And pretty wanton dyings shall to me
Be strangers; only to your chastity
I am devoted ever.
CLOE.   Honest swain,
  First let me thank you, then return
    again
As much of my love.—[Aside.] No,
  thou art too cold,
Unhappy boy, not tempered to my
  mold;
Thy blood falls heavy downward. 'Tis
  not fear
To offend in boldness wins; they never
  wear
Deservéd favors that deny to take
When they are offered freely. Do I
  wake,
To see a man of his youth, years, and
  feature,   400
And such a one as we call goodly crea-
  ture,
Thus backward? What a world of
  precious art
Were merely [2] lost, to make him do his
  part!
But I will shake him off, that dares not
  hold.

Let men that hope to be beloved be
  bold.—
Daphnis, I do desire, since we are met
So happily, our lives and fortunes set
Upon one stake, to give assurance now,
By interchange of hands and holy vow,
Never to break again. Walk you that
  way,   410
Whilst I in zealous meditation stray
A little this way. When we both have
  ended
These rites and duties, by the woods be-
  friended
And secrecy of night, retire and find
An aged oak, whose hollowness may bind
Us both within his body. Thither go.
It stands within yon bottom.
DAPH.   Be it so. *Ex[it] Daph[nis]*.
CLOE. And I will meet there never more
  with thee,
Thou idle shamefastness!
ALEX. [*Within.*]   Cloe!
CLOE.   'Tis he
That dare, I hope, be bolder.
ALEX. [*Within.*]   Cloe!
CLOE.   Now, 420
Great Pan, for Syrinx' sake, bid speed
  our plow!   *Exit Cloe.*

ACTUS TERTIUS. SCENA PRIMA.

[*The same.*]

*Enter the Sullen Shepherd, with Amarillis
          in a sleep.*

SULL. From thy forehead thus I take
These herbs, and charge thee not awake
Till in yonder holy well
Thrice, with powerful magic spell
Filled with many a baleful word,
Thou hast been dipped. Thus, with my
  cord
Of blasted hemp, by moonlight twined,
I do thy sleepy body bind.
I turn thy head into the east,
And thy feet into the west,   10
Thy left arm to the south put forth,
And thy right unto the north.
I take thy body from the ground,
In this deep and deadly sound,[3]
And into this holy spring
I let thee slide down by my string.—
        [*Lowers her into the well.*]
Take this maid, thou holy pit,

[1] Amorousness.   [2] Wholly.   [3] Swound, swoon.

To thy bottom; nearer yet.
In thy water pure and sweet,
By thy leave I dip her feet.   20
Thus I let her lower yet,
That her ankles may be wet.
Yet down lower, let her knee
In thy waters washéd be.
There stop. Fly away,
Everything that loves the day!
Truth, that hath but one face,
Thus I charm thee from this place.
Snakes that cast your coats for new,
Chameleons that alter hue,   30
Hares that yearly sexes change,
Proteus alt'ring oft and strange,
Hecate with shapés three,
Let this maiden changéd be,
With this holy water wet,
To the shape of Amoret!
Cynthia, work thou with my charm!—
Thus I draw thee, free from harm,
[*Draws her from the well, in the shape of
                                   Amoret.*]
Up out of this blessed lake.
Rise both like her and awake!   40
                              She awaketh.
AMAR. Speak, shepherd, am I Amoret to
    sight?
  Or hast thou missed in any magic
    rite,
  For want of which any defect in me
  May make our practices discovered be?
SULL. By yonder moon, but that I here
    do stand,
  Whose breath hath thus re-formed thee,
    and whose hand
  Let thee down dry, and plucked thee up
    thus wet,
  I should myself take thee for Amoret!
  Thou art in clothes, in feature, voice,
    and hue
  So like that sense cannot distinguish
    you.   50
AMAR. Then this deceit, which cannot
    crosséd be,
  At once[1] shall lose her him, and gain
    thee me.
  Hither she needs must come, by promise
    made;
  And, sure, his nature never was so bad,
  To bid a virgin meet him in the wood
  When night and fear are up, but under-
    stood

[1] Simultaneously.

'Twas his part to come first. Being come,
    I'll say
  My constant love made me come first
    and stay;
  Then will I lead him further to the
    grove.
  But stay you here, and, if his own true
    love   60
  Shall seek him here, set her in some wrong
    path,
  Which say her lover lately trodden hath.
  I'll not be far from hence. If need there
    be,
  Here is another charm [*Gives a scroll.*],
    whose power will free
  The dazzled sense, read by the moon-
    beams clear,
  And in my own true shape make me
    appear.

                  Enter Perigot.

SULL. Stand close; here's Perigot, whose
    constant heart
  Longs to behold her in whose shape thou
    art.   [*Retires with Amarillis.*]
PERI. This is the place.—Fair Amoret!—
    The hour
  Is yet scarce come. Here every sylvan
    power   70
  Delights to be about yon sacred well,
  Which they have blessed with many a
    powerful spell;
  For never traveler in dead of night,
  Nor strayéd beasts have fall'n in; but,
    when sight
  Hath failed them, then their right way
    they have found
  By help of them, so holy is the ground.
  But I will farther seek, lest Amoret
  Should be first come, and so stray long
    unmet.—
  My Amoret, Amoret!   *Exit.*[2]
AMAR.   Perigot!
PERI. [*Within.*] My love!
AMAR.   I come, my love!   *Exit.*
SULL.   Now she hath got   80
  Her own desires, and I shall gainer be
  Of my long-looked-for hopes as well as
    she.
  How bright the moon shines here, as if
    she strove
  To show her glory in this little grove

[2] Original reads *Ex. Amarillis. Perigot.*

Enter Amoret.

To some new-lovéd shepherd!—[*Aside*.]
   Yonder is
Another Amoret. Where differs this
From that? But that she Perigot hath
   met,
I should have ta'en this for the counter-
   feit.
Herbs, woods, and springs, the power
   that in you lies,
If mortal men could know your prop-
   erties!   90
AMO. Methinks it is not night; I have no
   fear,
Walking this wood, of lion or of bear,
Whose names at other times have made
   me quake,
When any shepherdess in her tale spake
Of some of them that underneath a wood
Have torn true lovers that together
   stood.
Methinks there are no goblins, and men's
   talk,
That in these woods the nimble fairies
   walk,
Are fables—such a strong heart I have
   got
Because I come to meet with Peri-
   got.—   100
My Perigot! Who's that? My Perigot?
SULL. Fair maid!
AMO.   Aye me, thou art not Perigot?
SULL. But I can tell ye news of Perigot.
An hour together under yonder tree
He sat with wreathéd arms, and called
   on thee
And said, "Why, Amoret, stayest thou
   so long?"
Then starting up, down yonder path he
   flung,
Lest thou hadst missed thy way. Were
   it daylight,
He could not yet have borne him out of
   sight.
AMO. Thanks, gentle shepherd; and be-
   shrew [1] my stay,   110
That made me fearful I had lost my way.
As fast as my weak legs (that cannot be
Weary with seeking him) will carry me,
I'll follow; and, for this thy care of me,
Pray Pan thy love may ever follow thee!
                           Exit.

Curse.

SULL. How bright she was, how lovely
   did she show!
Was it not pity to deceive her so?
She plucked her garments up, and tripped
   away,
And with a virgin innocence did pray
For me that perjured [2] her. Whilst
   she was here   120
Methought the beams of light that did
   appear
Were shot from her; methought the
   moon gave none
But what it had from her. She was
   alone
With me; if then her presence did so
   move,
Why did not I essay to win her love?
She would (not sure) [3] have yielded
   unto me.
Women love only opportunity,
And not the man; or, if she had denied,
Alone, I might have forced her to have
   tried
Who had been stronger. O, vain fool,
   to let   130
Such blessed occasion pass! I'll follow yet.
My blood is up; I cannot now forbear.

Enter Alex[is] and Cloe.

I come, sweet Amoret!—[*Aside*.] Soft,
   who is here?
A pair of lovers? He shall yield her me;
Now lust is up, alike all women be.
                           [*Retires*.]
ALEX. Where shall we rest? But for the
   love of me,
Cloe, I know, ere this would weary be.
CLOE. Alexis, let us rest here, if the place
Be private, and out of the common
   trace [4]   139
Of every shepherd; for, I understood,
This night a number are about the
   wood.
Then let us choose some place, where,
   out of sight,
We freely may enjoy our stol'n delight.
ALEX. Then boldly here, where we shall
   ne'er be found.
No shepherd's way lies here; 'tis hallowed
   ground.
No maid seeks here her strayéd cow
   or sheep.

---

[2] Swore falsely to.   [4] Track, path.
[3] *I.e.*, perhaps (?)

Fairies and fauns and satyrs do it keep.
Then, carelessly rest here, and clip and
    kiss,
And let no fear make us our pleasures
    miss.
CLOE. Then, lie by me; the sooner we
    begin,   150
The longer ere the day descry our sin.
                            [*They lie down.*]
SULL. [*Coming forward.*] Forbear to touch
    my love; or, by yon flame,
The greatest power that shepherds
    dare to name,
Here where thou sit'st, under this holy
    tree,
Her to dishonor, thou shalt buried be!
ALEX. If Pan himself should come out
    of the lawns,[1]
With all his troops of satyrs and of
    fauns,
And bid me leave, I swear by her two
    eyes
(A greater oath than thine), I would not
    rise!
SULL. Then, from the cold earth never
    thou shalt move,   160
But lose at one stroke both thy life and
    love.   [*Wounds him.*]
CLOE. Hold, gentle shepherd!
SULL.   Fairest shepherdess,
Come you with me; I do not love ye
    less
Than that fond man that would have
    kept you there
From me of more desert.
ALEX.   O, yet forbear
To take her from me! Give me leave to
    die
By her!

*The Satyr enters; he [2] runs one way and
                              she another.*

SAT.   Now, whilst the moon doth rule
    the sky,
And the stars, whose feeble light
Gives a pale shadow to the night,
Are up, great Pan commanded me   170
To walk this grove about, whilst he,
In a corner of the wood,
Where never mortal foot hath stood,
Keeps dancing, music, and a feast,
To entertain a lovely guest;
Where he gives her many a rose—

[1] Glades.   [2] *I.e.*, Sullen Shepherd.

Sweeter than the breath that blows
The leaves—grapes, berries of the best.
I never saw so great a feast.   179
But to my charge. Here must I stay,
To see what mortals lose their way,
And by a false fire, seeming bright,
Train them in and leave them right.
Then must I watch if any be
Forcing of a chastity.
If I find it, then in haste
Give my wreathéd horn a blast,
And the fairies all will run,
Wildly dancing by the moon,
And will pinch him to the bone   190
Till his lustful thoughts be gone.
ALEX. O, death!
SAT. Back again about this ground;
Sure, I hear a mortal sound.—
I bind thee by this powerful spell,
By the waters of this well,
By the glimmering moonbeams bright,
Speak again, thou mortal wight!
ALEX. O!
SAT.[3] Here the foolish mortal lies,   200
Sleeping on the ground.—Arise!—
The poor wight is almost dead;
On the ground his wounds have bled,
And his clothes fouled with his blood.
To my goddess in the wood
Will I lead him, whose hands pure
Will help this mortal wight to cure.
                     [*Exit, supporting Alexis.*]

            Enter Cloe again.

CLOE. Since I beheld yon [4] shaggy man,
    my breast
Doth pant; each bush, methinks, should
    hide a beast.
Yet my desire keeps still above my
    fear.   210
I would fain meet some shepherd, knew I
    where,
For from one cause of fear I am most
    free:
It is impossible to ravish me,
I am so willing. Here upon this ground
I left my love, all bloody with his wound;
Yet, till that fearful shape made me
    be gone,
Though he were hurt, I furnished was
    of one;

[3] Original here repeats *Speak again, thou
mortal wight.*
[4] From 1634 edn. Original has *you.*

But now both lost.—Alexis, speak or
  move,
If thou hast any life; thou art yet my
  love!—
He's dead, or else is with his little
  might   220
Crept from the bank for fear of that ill
  sprite.—
Then, where art thou that struck'st my
  love? O, stay!
Bring me thyself in change, and then
  I'll say
Thou hast some justice. I will make
  thee trim
With flowers and garlands that were
  meant for him;
I'll clip thee round with both mine arms,
  as fast
As I did mean he should have been em-
  braced.
But thou art fled.—What hope is left
  for me?
I'll run to Daphnis in the hollow tree,
Who I did mean to mock; though hope
  be small   230
To make him bold, rather than none at
  all,
I'll try him; his heart, and my behavior
  too,
Perhaps may teach him what he ought
  to do.   *Exit.*

Enter the Sullen Shepherd.

SULL. This was the place. 'Twas but my
  feeble sight,
Mixed with the horror of my deed, and
  night,
That shaped these fears, and made me
  run away,
And lose my beauteous, hardly-gotten
  prey.—
Speak, gentle shepherdess! I am alone,
And tender love for love.—But she is gone
From me, that, having struck her lover
  dead,   240
For silly fear left her alone and fled.
And see, the wounded body is removed
By her of whom it was so well beloved.

*Enter Perigot, and Amarillis in the shape of
                                  Amoret.*

But all these fancies must be quite
  forgot.

I must lie close; here comes young Peri-
  got,
With subtle Amarillis in the shape
Of Amoret. Pray, love, he may not
  scape!   *[Retires.]*
AMAR. Beloved Perigot, show me some
  place
Where I may rest my limbs weak with
  the chase
Of thee, an hour before thou cam'st
  at least.   250
PERI. Beshrew my tardy steps! Here
  shalt thou rest
Upon this holy bank. No deadly snake
Upon this turf herself in folds doth make;
Here is no poison for the toad to feed.
Here boldly spread thy hands—no
  venomed weed
Dares blister them; no slimy snail dare
  creep
Over thy face when thou art fast asleep;
Here never durst the babbling cuckoo
  spit; [1]
No slough [2] of falling star did ever hit
Upon this bank. Let this thy cabin be;
This other, set with violets, for me.   261
                              [They lie down.]
AMAR. Thou dost not love me, Perigot.
PERI.   Fair maid,
You only love to hear it often said;
You do not doubt.
AMAR.   Believe me, but I do.
PERI. What, shall we now begin again to
  woo?
'Tis the best way to make your lover
  last,
To play with him when you have caught
  him fast.
AMAR. By Pan I swear, beloved Perigot,
And by yon moon, I think thou lov'st
  me not.
PERI. By Pan I swear—and, if I falsely
  swear,   270
Let him not guard my flocks. Let
  foxes tear
My earliest lambs, and wolves, whilst
  I do sleep,
Fall on the rest—a rot among my sheep.
I love thee better than the careful ewe
The new-yeaned lamb that is of her own
  hue.

[1] An allusion to cuckoo-spit, a frothy secre-
tion exuded by the larvæ of certain insects.
[2] Shell.

I dote upon thee more than that young
   lamb
Doth on the bag that feeds him from
   his dam!
Were there a sort [1] of wolves got in
   my fold,
And one ran after thee, both young and
   old
Should be devoured, and it should be
   my strife   280
To save thee whom I love above my
   life.

AMAR. How should I trust thee, when I
   see thee choose
Another bed, and dost my side refuse?

PERI. 'Twas only that the chaste thoughts
   might be shown
'Twixt thee and me, although we were
   alone.

AMAR. Come, Perigot will show his power,
   that he
Can make his Amoret, though she
   weary be,
Rise nimbly from her couch and come
   to his.
Here, take thy Amoret; embrace and
   kiss.   [Comes to him.]

PERI. What means my love?

AMAR.   To do as lovers should, 290
That are to be enjoyed, not to be wooed.
There's ne'er a shepherdess in all the
   plain
Can kiss thee with more art; there's
   none can feign
More wanton tricks.

PERI.   Forbear, dear soul, to try
Whether my heart be pure; I'll rather
   die
Than nourish one thought to dishonor
   thee.

AMAR. Still think'st thou such a thing
   as chastity
Is amongst women? Perigot, there's
   none
That with her love is in a wood alone,
And would come home a maid; be not
   abused   300
With thy fond first belief; let time be
   used.   [Perigot rises.]
Why dost thou rise?

PERI.   My true heart thou hast slain!

AMAR. Faith, Perigot, I'll pluck thee
   down again.

[1] Pack.

PERI. Let go, thou serpent, that into
   my breast
Hast with thy cunning dived!—Art not
   in jest?

AMAR. Sweet love, lie down.

PERI.   Since this I live to see,
Some bitter north wind blast my flocks
   and me!

AMAR. You swore you loved, yet will not
   do my will.

PERI. O, be as thou wert once, I'll love
   thee still!

AMAR. I am as still I was, and all my
   kind,   310
Though other shows we have, poor
   men to blind.

PERI. Then, here I end all love; and,
   lest my vain
Belief should ever draw me in again,
Before thy face, that hast my youth
   misled,
I end my life! My blood be on thy
   head!   [Offers to kill himself.]

AMAR. [Rising.] O, hold thy hands, thy
   Amoret doth cry!

PERI. Thou counsel'st well; first, Amoret
   shall die,
That is the cause of my eternal smart!
        He runs after her.

AMAR. O, hold!

PERI.   This steel shall pierce thy lustful
   heart!   [Exeunt.]

*The Sullen Shepherd steps out and uncharms
        her.*

SULL. Up and down, everywhere,   320
I strew the herbs to purge the air.
Let your odor drive hence
All mists that dazzle sense.
Herbs and springs, whose hidden might
Alters shapes, and mocks the sight,
Thus I charge ye to undo
All before I brought ye to!
Let her fly, let her scape;
Give again her own shape!   [Retires.]

*Enter Amarillis [in her own shape] [2] [, fol-
        lowed by Perigot].*

AMAR. Forbear, thou gentle swain! Thou
   dost mistake;   330
She whom thou follow'dst fled into the
   brake,

[2] From 1629 edn.

And, as I crossed thy way, I met thy
　　wrath,
The only fear of which near slain me hath.
PERI. Pardon, fair shepherdess; my rage
　　and night
Were both upon me, and beguiled my
　　sight.
But far be it from me to spill the blood
Of harmless maids that wander in the
　　wood!　　　　　　　*Ex[it Amarillis].*

Enter Amoret.

AMO. Many a weary step, in yonder path,
Poor hopeless Amoret twice trodden
　　hath,　　　　　　　　　　　　339
To seek her Perigot, yet cannot hear
His voice.—My Perigot! She loves thee
　　dear
That calls.
PERI.　　　　　　See yonder where she is!
　　How fair
She shows, and yet her breath infests
　　the air!
AMO. My Perigot!
PERI.　　　　　　　　Here.
AMO.　　　　　　　　　Happy!
PERI.　　　　　　　　　Hapless! First
　　It lights on thee; the next blow is the
　　worst.　　　　　　　　　*[Wounds her.]*
AMO. Stay, Perigot! My love, thou art un-
　　just.　　　　　　　　　　　*[Falls.]*
PERI. Death is the best reward that's
　　due to lust.　　　　　*Exit Perigot.*
SULL. *[Aside.]* Now shall their love be
　　crossed, for, being struck,
　　I'll throw her in the fount, lest being
　　took
By some night-traveler, whose honest
　　care　　　　　　　　　　　　350
May help to cure her—
　　　　　　　　　　　[Comes forward.]
　　　　　　Shepherdess, prepare
Yourself to die!
AMO.　　　　　　No mercy I do crave.
Thou canst not give a worse blow than
　　I have.
Tell him that gave me this, who loved
　　him too,
He struck my soul, and not my body
　　through;
Tell him, when I am dead, my soul
　　shall be
At peace, if he but think he injured
　　me.

SULL. In this fount be thy grave. Thou
　　wert not meant
Sure for a woman, thou art so innocent.—
　　　　　　He flings her into the well.
She cannot scape, for, underneath the
　　ground,　　　　　　　　　　360
In a long hollow the clear spring is bound,
Till on yon side, where the morn's sun
　　doth look,
The struggling water breaks out in a
　　brook.　　　　　　　　　　*Exit.*

*The God of the River riseth with Amoret in
　　　　　　　　his arms.*

GOD. What powerful charms my streams
　　do bring
Back again unto their spring,
With such force that I their god,
Three times striking with my rod,
Could not keep them in their ranks?
My fishes shoot into the banks;
There's not one that stays and feeds;　370
All have hid them in the weeds.
Here's a mortal almost dead,
Fall'n into my riverhead,
Hallowed so with many a spell,
That till now none ever fell.
'Tis a female young and clear,
Cast in by some ravisher.
See, upon her breast a wound,
On which there is no plaster bound.
Yet, she's warm; her pulses beat;　　380
'Tis a sign of life and heat.—
If thou be'st a virgin pure,
I can give a present cure.
Take a drop into thy wound,
From my watery lock[s], [1] more round
Than orient pearl, and far more pure
Than unchaste flesh may endure.—
See, she pants, and from her flesh
The warm blood gusheth out afresh.
She is an unpolluted maid;　　　　390
I must have this bleeding stayed.
From my banks I pluck this flower
With holy hand, whose virtuous power
Is at once to heal and draw.
The blood returns. I never saw
A fairer mortal. Now doth break
Her deadly slumber.—Virgin, speak.
AMO. Who hath restored my sense, given
　　me new breath,
And brought me back out of the arms of
　　death?

[1] From 1629 edn.

God. I have healed thy wounds.
Amo.   Ay me!   400
God. Fear not him that succored thee.
  I am this fountain's god; below,
  My waters to a river grow,
  And twixt two banks with osiers set,
  That only prosper in the wet,
  Through the meadows do they glide,
  Wheeling still on every side,
  Sometimes winding round about,
  To find the evenest channel out.
  And, if thou wilt go with me,   410
  Leaving mortal company,
  In the cool streams shalt thou lie,
  Free from harm as well as I.
  I will give thee for thy food
  No fish that useth [1] in the mud,
  But trout and pike, that love to swim
  Where the gravel from the brim
  Through the pure streams may be seen;
  Orient pearl fit for a queen
  Will I give, thy love to win,   420
  And a shell to keep them in;
  Not a fish in all my brook
  That shall disobey thy look,
  But, when thou wilt, come sliding by,
  And from thy white hand take a fly;
  And, to make thee understand
  How I can my waves command,
  They shall bubble, whilst I sing,
  Sweeter than the silver string.

THE SONG

  Do not fear to put thy feet   430
  Naked in the river sweet;
  Think not leech or newt or toad
  Will bite thy foot when thou hast trod;
  Nor let the water rising high,
  As thou wad'st in, make thee cry
  And sob; but ever live with me,
  And not a wave shall trouble thee.

Amo. Immortal power, that rul'st this
  holy flood,
I know myself unworthy to be wooed
By thee, a god, for ere this, but for
  thee,   440
I should have shown my weak mortality.
Besides, by holy oath betwixt us twain,
I am betrothed unto a shepherd swain,
Whose comely face, I know, the gods
  above
May make me leave to see, but not to
  love.

[1] Lives.

God. May he prove to thee as true!
  Fairest virgin, now adieu.
  I must make my waters fly,
  Lest they leave their channels dry,   449
  And beasts that come unto the spring
  Miss their morning's watering,
  Which I would not; for of late
  All the neighbor people sate
  On my banks, and from the fold
  Two white lambs of three weeks old
  Offered to my deity;
  For which this year they shall be free
  From raging floods that, as they pass,
  Leave their gravel in the grass;
  Nor shall their meads be overflown   460
  When their grass is newly mown.
Amo. For thy kindness to me shown,
  Never from thy banks be blown
  Any tree, with windy force,
  Cross [2] thy streams, to stop thy course;
  May no beast that comes to drink,
  With his horns cast down thy brink;
  May none that for thy fish do look,
  Cut thy banks to dam thy brook;
  Barefoot may no neighbor wade   470
  In thy cool streams, wife nor maid,
  When the spawns on stones do lie,
  To wash their hemp, and spoil the fry!
God. Thanks, virgin. I must down again.
  Thy wound will put thee to no pain.
  Wonder not so soon 'tis gone;
  A holy hand was laid upon.   Exit.
Amo. And I, unhappy born to be,
  Must follow him that flies from me.
                                    [Exit.]

[ACTUS QUARTUS. SCENA PRIMA.[3]

The same.]

Enter Perigot.

Peri. She is untrue, unconstant, and
    unkind.
  She's gone, she's gone! Blow high, thou
    northwest wind,
  And raise the sea to mountains; let the
    trees
  That dare oppose thy raging fury loese [4]
  Their firm foundation, creep into the
    earth,

[2] Across.
[3] From 1629 edn. The act division in the
original is indicated merely by Finis actus
terti[u]s.
[4] Lose.

And shake the world as at the monstrous birth
Of some new prodigy, whilst I constant stand,
Holding this trusty boar spear in my hand,
And falling thus upon it.

Enter to Perigot,[1] *Amarillis running.*

AMAR. Stay thy dead-doing hand! Thou art too hot   10
Against thyself. Believe me, comely swain,
If that thou diest, not all the showers of rain
The heavy clouds send down can wash away
That foul unmanly guilt the world will lay
Upon thee. Yet thy love untainted stands.
Believe me, she is constant; not the sands
Can be so hardly numbered as she won.
I do not trifle, shepherd; by the moon
And all those lesser lights our eyes do view,
All that I told thee, Perigot, is true. 20
Then be a free man; put away despair
And will to die; smooth gently up that fair,
Dejected forehead; be as when those eyes
Took the first heat.
PERI.   Alas, he double dies
That would believe, but cannot! 'Tis not well
Ye keep me thus from dying, here to dwell
With many worse companions. But, O, death!
I am not yet enamored of this[2] breath
So much but I dare leave it; 'tis not pain
In forcing of a wound, nor after-gain 30
Of many days, can hold me from my will.
'Tis not myself, but Amoret, bids kill.
AMAR. Stay but a little, little—but one hour—
And, if I do not show thee, through the power
Of herbs and words I have, as dark as night,

[1] Original reads *Perigot to enter.*
[2] From 1634 edn. Original reads *his.*

Myself turned to thy Amoret, in sight,
Her very figure, and the robe she wears,
With tawny buskins, and the hook she bears
Of thine own carving, where your names are set,
Wrought underneath with many a curious fret, 40
The primrose-chaplet, tawdry-lace,[3] and ring,
Thou gav'st her for her singing, with each thing
Else that she wears about her, let me feel
The first fell stroke of that revenging steel!
PERI. I am contented, if there be a hope,
To give it entertainment for the scope
Of one poor hour. Go; you shall find me next
Under yon shady beech, even thus perplexed,
And thus believing.
AMAR.   Bind, before I go,
Thy soul by Pan unto me, not to do 50
Harm or outrageous wrong upon thy life
Till my return.
PERI.   By Pan, and by the strife
He had with Phœbus for the mastery,
When golden Midas judged their minstrelsy,
I will not!   *Exeunt.*

Enter Satyr with Alexis, hurt.

SAT. Softly gliding as I go,
With this burthen full of woe,
Through still silence of the night
Guided by the glowworm's light,
Hither am I come at last. 60
Many a thicket have I passed;
Not a twig that durst deny me,
Not a bush that durst descry[4] me
To the little bird that sleeps
On the tender spray; nor creeps
That hardy worm with pointed tail,
But if[5] I be under sail,
Flying faster than the wind,
Leaving all the clouds behind,
But doth hide her tender head 70
In some hollow tree, or bed

[3] Lace bought at the fair of St. Audrey at Ely.
[4] Reveal.   [5] Unless.

Of seeded nettles; not a hare
Can be started from his fare
By my footing; nor a wish
Is more sudden, nor a fish
Can be found with greater ease
Cut the vast unbounded seas,
Leaving neither print nor sound,
Than I, when nimbly on the ground
I measure many a league an hour.   80
But, behold, the happy bower
That must ease me of my charge,
And by holy hand enlarge [1]
The soul of this sad man that yet
Lies fast bound in deadly fit.
Heaven and great Pan succor it!—
Hail, thou beauty of the bower,
Whiter than the paramour
Of my master! Let me crave   89
Thy virtuous help, to keep from grave
This poor mortal that here lies,
Waiting when the Destinies
Will undo his thread of life.
View the wound, by cruel knife
Trenched into him.

[Enter Clorin.]

CLO. What art thou call'st me from my
        holy rites,
And with the feared name of death
        affrights
My tender ears? Speak me thy name
        and will.
SAT. I am the satyr that did fill
Your lap with early fruit, and will,   100
When I hap to gather more,
Bring ye better and more store.
Yet I come not empty now:
See, a blossom from the bough;
But beshrew his heart that pulled it,
And his perfect sight that culled it
From the other springing blooms!
For a sweeter youth the grooms
Cannot show me, nor the downs,
Nor the many neighboring towns.   110
Low in yonder glade I found him;
Softly in mine arms I bound him;
Hither have I brought him sleeping
In a trance, his wounds fresh weeping,
In remembrance such youth may
Spring and perish in a day.
CLO. Satyr, they wrong thee that do
        term thee rude;

[1] Free.

Though thou be'st outward-rough and
        tawny-hued,
Thy manners are as gentle and as fair
As his who brags himself born only
        heir   120
To all humanity.—Let me see thy wound.
This herb will stay the current, being
        bound
Fast to the orifice, and this restrain
Ulcers and swellings, and such inward
        pain
As the cold air hath forced into the sore;
This to draw out such putrefying gore
As inward falls.
SAT.   Heaven grant it may do good!
CLO. Fairly wipe away the blood.
Hold him gently, till I fling
Water of a virtuous spring   130
On his temples; turn him twice
To the moonbeams; pinch him thrice,
That the laboring soul may draw
From his great eclipse.
SAT.   I saw
His eyelids moving.
CLO.   Give him breath;
All the danger of cold death
Now is vanished! With this plaster
And this unction do I master
All the festered ill that may
Give him grief another day.   140
SAT. See, he gathers up his sprite,
And begins to hunt for light;
Now a [2] gaps and breathes again.
How the blood runs to the vein
That erst was empty!
ALEX.   O my heart!
My dearest, dearest Cloe! O, the smart
Runs through my side! I feel some
        pointed thing
Pass through my bowels, sharper than
        the sting
Of scorpion.—
Pan, preserve me!—What are you?   150
Do not hurt me; I am true
To my Cloe, though she fly,
And leave me to this destiny.
There she stands, and will not lend
Her smooth white hand to help her
        friend.
But I am much mistaken, for that face
Bears more austerity and modest grace,
More reproving and more awe,
Than these eyes yet ever saw

[2] He.

In my Cloe. O, my pain   160
Eagerly renews again!
Give me your help for his sake you love
   best.
CLO. Shepherd, thou canst not possible
   take rest,
Till thou hast laid aside all heats, desires,
Provoking thoughts that stir up lusty
   fires,
Commerce with wanton eyes, strong
   blood, and will
To execute. These must be purged until
The vein grow whiter; then repent, and
   pray
Great Pan to keep you from the like
   decay,
And I shall undertake your cure with
   ease;   170
Till when, this virtuous plaster [1] will
   displease [2]
Your tender sides. Give me your hand,
   and rise!
Help him a little, satyr, for his thighs
Yet are feeble.
ALEX. [Rising.]   Sure, I have lost much
   blood.
SAT. 'Tis no matter; 'twas not good.
Mortal, you must leave your wooing;
Though there be a joy in doing,
Yet it brings much grief behind it.
They best feel it that do find it.
CLO. Come, bring him in; I will attend his
   sore.—   180
When you are well, take heed you lust
   no more.   [They retire.]
SAT. Shepherd, see what comes of kissing;
By my head, 'twere better missing.—
Brightest, if there be remaining
Any service, without feigning
I will do it. Were I set
To catch the nimble wind, or get
Shadows gliding on the green,
Or to steal from the great queen
Of fairies all her beauty,   190
I would do it, so much duty
Do I owe those precious eyes.
CLO. I thank thee, honest satyr. If the
   cries
Of any other that be hurt or ill
Draw thee unto them, prithee, do thy
   will
To bring them hether.

[1] From 1629 edn. Original reads *Playsters*.
[2] Discomfort.

SAT. I will; and, when the weather
Serves to angle in the brook,
I will bring a silver hook,
With a line of finest silk,   200
And a rod as white as milk,
To deceive the little fish.
So I take my leave, and wish
On this bower may ever dwell
Spring and summer!
CLO.   Friend, farewell.
     Exit [*with Alexis and Satyr*].

   Enter Amoret, seeking her Love.

AMO. This place is ominous; for here I lost
My love and almost life, and since have
   crossed
All these woods over; never a nook or
   dell,
Where any little bird or beast doth dwell,
But I have sought it; never a bending
   brow   210
Of any hill, or glade the wind sings
   through,
Nor a green bank or shade where shep-
   herds use
To sit and riddle, sweetly pipe, or
   choose
Their valentines, but I have missed [3] to
   find
My love in. Perigot! O, too unkind,
Why hast thou fled me? Whither art
   thou gone?
How have I wronged thee? Was my
   love alone
To thee worthy this scorned recompense?
   'Tis well;
I am content to feel it. But I tell
Thee, shepherd, and these lusty woods
   shall hear,   220
Forsaken Amoret is yet as clear
Of any stranger fire as heaven is
From foul corruption, or the deep abyss
From light and happiness; and thou
   mayst know
All this for truth, and how that fatal
   blow
Thou gav'st me, never from desert of
   mine
Fell on my life, but from suspect [4] of
   thine,
Or fury more than madness. There-
   fore here,

[3] Failed.   [4] Suspicion.

Since I have lost my life, my love, my
 dear,
Upon this cursèd place, and on this
 green   230
That first divorced us, shortly shall be
 seen
A sight of so great pity that each eye
Shall daily spend his spring in memory
Of my untimely fall.

Enter Amarillis.

AMAR. [*Aside.*]   I am not blind,
 Nor is it through the working of my
  mind
That this shows Amoret. Forsake me, all
That dwell upon the soul, but what
 men call
Wonder, or, more than wonder, miracle!
For, sure, so strange as this, the oracle
Never gave answer of; it passeth dreams,
Or madmen's fancy, when the many
 streams   241
Of new imagination rise and fall.
'Tis but an hour since these ears heard
 her call
For pity to young Perigot, whilst he,
Directed by his fury, bloodily
Lanched [1] up her breast, which bloodless
 fell and cold;
And, if belief may credit what was told,
After all this, the melancholy swain
Took her into his arms, being almost
 slain,
And to the bottom of the holy well 250
Flung her, forever with the waves to
 dwell.
'Tis she, the very same, 'tis Amoret,
And living yet! The great powers will
 not let
Their virtuous love be crossed.—Maid,
 wipe away
Those heavy drops of sorrow, and allay
The storm that yet goes high, which,
 not depressed,
Breaks heart and life and all before it
 rest.
Thy Perigot—
AMO.   Where, which is Perigot?
AMAR. Sits there below, lamenting much,
 God wot,
Thee and thy fortune. Go and comfort
 him: 260

[1] Lanced.

And thou shalt find him underneath a
 brim
Of sailing [2] pines that edge yon mountain in.
AMO. I go, I run. Heaven grant me I may
 win
His soul again!   [*Exit Amoret.*] [3]

Enter Sullen.

SULL.   Stay, Amarillis, stay!
 You are too fleet; 'tis two hours yet to
  day.
I have performed my promise; let us sit
And warm our bloods together, till the
 fit
Come lively on us.
AMAR.   Friend, you are too keen;
 The morning riseth, and we shall be seen.
 Forbear a little.
SULL.   I can stay no longer. 270
AMAR. Hold, shepherd, hold! Learn not
 to be a wronger
Of your word. Was not your promise
 laid,
To break their loves first?
SULL.   I have done it, maid.
AMAR. No; they are yet unbroken, met
 again,
And are as hard to part yet as the stain
Is from the finest lawn.
SULL.   I say they are
 Now at this present parted, and so far
 That they shall never meet.
AMAR.   Swain, 'tis not so;
 For do but to yon hanging mountain go,
 And there believe your eyes.
SULL.   You do but hold 280
 Off with delays and trifles.—Farewell,
  cold
And frozen bashfulness, unfit for men!—
Thus I salute thee, virgin!
     [*Attempts to seize her.*]
AMAR.   And thus, then,
 I bid you follow; catch me if you can!
         Exit.
SULL. And, if I stay behind, I am no
 man! [*Exit, running after her.*]

Enter Perigot.

PERI. Night, do not steal away; I woo
 thee yet
To hold a hard hand o'er the rusty bit

[2] "*I.e.*, of which masts are made" (Greg).
[3] From 1629 edn.

That guides thy lazy team.   Go back
    again,
Boötes, thou that driv'st thy frozen
    wain
Round as a ring, and bring a second
    night   290
To hide my sorrows from the coming
    light;
Let not the eyes of men stare on my
    face
And read my falling; give me some black
    place,
Where never sunbeam shot his whole-
    some light,
That I may sit and pour out my sad
    sprite
Like running water, never to be known
After the forcéd fall and sound is gone.

Enter Amoret, looking of [1] *Perigot.*

AMO.   This is the bottom.[2]—Speak, if
    thou be here,
My Perigot! Thy Amoret, thy dear,
Calls on thy lovéd name.
PERI.   What [art] [3] thou dare   300
Tread these forbidden paths, where
    death and care
Dwell on the face of darkness?
AMO.   'Tis thy friend,
Thy Amoret, come hither to give end
To these consumings.   Look up, gentle
    boy;
I have forgot those pains and dear
    annoy
I suffered for thy sake, and am content
To be thy love again.   Why hast thou
    rent
Those curléd locks where I have often
    hung
Ribands and damask-roses, and have
    flung
Waters distilled, to make thee fresh
    and gay,   310
Sweeter than nosegays on a bridal day?
Why dost thou cross thine arms, and
    hang thy face
Down to thy bosom, letting fall apace
From those two little heavens, upon the
    ground,
Showers of more price, more orient, and
    more round
Than those that hang upon the moon's
    pale brow?

¹ For.   ² Dale.   ³ From 1629 edn.

Cease these complainings, shepherd; I
    am now
The same I ever was, as kind and free,
And can forgive before you ask of me;
Indeed, I can and will.
PERI.   So spoke my fair! 320
O, you great working powers of earth
    and air,
Water and forming fire, why have you
    lent
Your hidden virtues of so ill intent?
Even such a face, so fair, so bright of
    hue,
Had Amoret; such words, so smooth
    and new,
Came flowing from her tongue; such
    was her eye,
And such the pointed sparkle that did
    fly
Forth like a bleeding shaft.   All is the
    same,
The robe and buskins, painted hook,
    and frame
Of all her body.   O me, Amoret!   330
AMO. Shepherd, what means this riddle?
    Who hath set
So strong a difference twixt myself and
    me
That I am grown another? Look, and see
The ring thou gav'st me, and about my
    wrist
That curious bracelet thou thyself didst
    twist
From those fair tresses.   Know'st thou
    Amoret?
Hath not some newer love forced thee
    forget
Thy ancient faith?
PERI.   Still nearer to my love!
These be the very words she oft did
    prove
Upon my temper; so she still would
    take   340
Wonder into her face, and silent make
Signs with her head and hand, as who
    would say,
"Shepherd, remember this another day."
AMO. Am I not Amoret?   Where was I
    lost?
Can there be heaven and time and men,
    [and] [4] most
Of these unconstant?   Faith, where
    art thou fled?

⁴ From 1629 edn.

Are all the vows and protestations
  dead,
The hands held up, the wishes and the
  heart?
Is there not one remaining, not a part
Of all these to be found? Why, then, I
  see   350
Men never knew that virtue, constancy.
PERI. Men ever were most blessed, till
  cross fate
Brought love and women forth, unfor-
  tunate
To all that ever tasted of their smiles;
Whose actions are all double, full of
  wiles,
Like to the subtle hare, that fore the
  hounds
Makes many turnings, leaps, and many
  rounds,
This way and that way, to deceive the
  scent
Of her pursuers.
AMO.   'Tis but to prevent
Their speedy coming on, that seek her
  fall;   360
The hands of cruel men, more bestial,
And of a nature more refusing good
Than beasts themselves, or fishes of the
  flood.
[PERI.] ¹ Thou art all these, and more than
  nature meant
When she created all: frowns, joys,
  content;
Extreme fire for an hour, and presently
Colder than sleepy poison, or the sea
Upon whose face sits a continual frost;
Your actions ever driven to the most,
Then down again as low, that none can
  find   370
The rise or falling of a woman's mind.
AMO. Can there be any age or days or time
Or tongues of men guilty so great a crime
As wronging simple maid? O, Perigot,
Thou that wast yesterday without a
  blot,
Thou that wast every good and every-
  thing
That men call blessed, thou that wast the
  spring
From whence our looser grooms drew all
  their best,
Thou that wast always just and al-
  ways blessed

¹ From 1629 edn.

In faith and promise, thou that hadst
  the name   380
Of virtuous given thee, and made good
  the same
Ev'n from thy cradle, thou that wast
  that all
That men delighted in! O, what a fall
Is this, to have been so, and now to be
The only best in wrong and infamy!
And I to live to know this! And by me,
That loved thee dearer than mine eyes, or
  that
Which we esteem our honor, virgin
  state!
Dearer than swallows love the early
  morn,
Or dogs of chase the sound of merry
  horn;   390
Dearer than thou canst love thy new
  love, if thou hast
Another, and far dearer than the last;
Dearer than thou canst love thyself,
  though all
The self-love were within thee that did
  fall
With that coy swain that now is made
  a flower,
For whose dear sake Echo weeps many a
  shower!
And am I thus rewarded for my flame?
Loved worthily to get a wanton's name?
Come, thou forsaken willow, wind my
  head,
And noise it to the world, my love is
  dead!   400
I am forsaken, I am cast away,
And left for every lazy groom to say
I was unconstant, light, and sooner lost
Than the quick clouds we see, or the
  chill frost
When the hot sun beats on it! Tell me
  yet,
Canst thou not love again thy Amoret?
PERI. Thou art not worthy of that blessed
  name;
I must not know thee. Fling thy wanton
  flame
Upon some lighter blood that may be
  hot   409
With words and feignéd passions; Perigot
Was ever yet unstained, and shall not
  now
Stoop to the meltings of a borrowed
  brow.

Amo. Then hear me, heaven, to whom
  I call for right,
And you, fair twinkling stars, that crown
  the night;
And hear me, woods, and silence of this
  place,
And ye, sad hours, that move a sullen
  pace;
Hear me, ye shadows, that delight to
  dwell
In horrid darkness, and ye powers of
  hell,
Whilst I breathe out my last! I am that
  maid,   419
That yet-untainted Amoret, that played
The careless prodigal, and gave away
My soul to this young man that now
  dares say
I am a stranger, not the same, more
  wild;
And thus with much belief I was be-
  guiled.
I am that maid that have delayed,
  denied,
And almost scorned the loves of all
  that tried
To win me but this swain, and yet
  confess
I have been wooed by many with no
  less
Soul of affection, and have often had
Rings, belts, and cracknels sent me from
  the lad   430
That feeds his flocks down westward;
  lambs and doves
By young Alexis; Daphnis sent me
  gloves—
All which I gave to thee.   Nor these
  nor they
That sent them did I smile on, or e'er
  lay
Up to my after-memory.   But why
Do I resolve to grieve, and not to die?
Happy had been the stroke thou gav'st,
  if home,
By this time had I found a quiet room,
Where every slave is free, and every
  breast,
That living bred new care, now lies at
  rest;   440
And thither will poor Amoret.
Peri.   Thou must.
Was ever any man so loath to trust
His eyes as I? Or was there ever yet

Any so like as this to Amoret?
For whose dear sake I promise, if there
  be
A living soul within thee, thus to free
Thy body from it.   *He hurts her again.*
Amo. [*Falling.*]   So, this work hath end.
Farewell, and live; be constant to thy
  friend
That loves thee next.

Enter Satyr; Perigot runs off.

Sat. See, the day begins to break,   450
And the light shoots [1] like a streak
Of subtle fire; the wind blows cold,
Whilst the morning doth unfold;
Now the birds begin to rouse,
And the squirrel from the boughs
Leaps to get him nuts and fruit.
The early lark, that erst was mute,
Carols to the rising day
Many a note and many a lay;
Therefore here I end my watch,   460
Lest the wand'ring swain should catch
Harm, or lose himself.
Amo.   Ah me!
Sat. Speak again, whate'er thou be.
I am ready; speak, I say!
By the dawning of the day,
By the power of night and Pan,
I enforce thee, speak again!
Amo. O, I am most unhappy!
Sat. Yet more blood!
Sure, these wanton swains are wood.   470
Can there be a hand or heart
Dare commit so vild [2] a part
As this murder? By the moon,
That hid herself when this was done,
Never was a sweeter face;
I will bear her to the place
Where my goddess keeps, [3] and crave
Her to give her life or grave.   *Exeunt.*

Enter Clorin.

Clo. Here whilst one patient takes his
  rest secure,   479
I steal abroad to do another cure.—
Pardon, thou buried body of my love,
That from thy side I dare so soon re-
  move;
I will not prove unconstant, nor will leave
Thee for an hour alone. When I deceive

[1] From 1634 edn. Original reads *shutts.*
[2] Vile.   [3] Dwells.

My first-made vow, the wildest of the
   wood
Tear me, and o'er thy grave let out my
   blood!
I go by wit to cure a lover's pain,
Which no herb can; being done, I'll
   come again.   *Exit.*

Enter Thenot.

THE. Poor shepherd, in this shade forever lie
And, seeing thy fair Clorin's cabin,
   die!   [*Lies down.*]   490
O, hapless love, which being answered,
   ends!
And, as a little infant cries and bends
His tender brows, when, rolling of his
   eye,
He hath espied something that glisters
   nigh,
Which he would have, yet, give it him,
   away
He throws it straight, and cries afresh
   to play
With something else—such my affection,
   set
On that which I should loathe, if I could
   get.

Enter Clorin.

CLO. [*Aside.*] See, where he lies! Did
   ever man but he
Love any woman for her constancy   500
To her dead lover, which she needs
   must end
Before she can allow him for her friend,
And he himself must needs the cause
   destroy
For which he loves, before he can en-
   joy?
Poor shepherd, heaven grant I at once
   may free
Thee from thy pain, and keep my loy-
   alty!—
Shepherd, look up.
THE.   Thy brightness doth amaze;
So Phœbus may at noon bid mortals
   gaze.
Thy glorious constancy appears so bright,
I dare not meet the beams with my
   weak sight.   510
CLO. Why dost thou pine away thyself
   for me?

THE. Why dost thou keep such spotless
   constancy?
CLO. Thou holy shepherd, see what for
   thy sake
Clorin, thy Clorin, now dare undertake.
                   He starts up.
THE. Stay there, thou constant Clorin!
   If there be
Yet any part of woman left in thee,
To make thee light, think yet before
   thou speak.
CLO. See, what a holy vow for thee I
   break—
I, that already have my fame far spread
For being constant to my lover dead.
THE. Think yet, dear Clorin, of your love,
   how true,   521
If you had died, he would have been to
   you.
CLO. Yet, all I'll lose for thee—
THE.   Think but how blessed
A constant woman is above the rest!
CLO. And offer up myself, here on this
   ground,
To be disposed by thee.
THE.   Why dost thou wound
His heart with malice against women
   more,
That hated all the sex but thee before?
How much more pleasant had it been to
   me
To die than [to] [1] behold this change in
   thee!   530
Yet, yet return; let not the woman sway.
CLO. Insult not on [2] her now, nor use de-
   lay,
Who for thy sake hath ventured all her
   fame.
THE. Thou hast not ventured, but bought
   certain shame.
Your sex's curse, foul falsehood, must
   and shall,
I see, once in your lives light on you all.
I hate thee now. Yet turn!
CLO.   Be just to me;
Shall I at once lose both my fame and
   thee?
THE. Thou hadst no fame; that which
   thou didst like good
Was but thy appetite that swayed thy
   blood   540
For that time to the best, for as a blast

---

[1] From 1634 edn.
[2] Do not behave insolently toward.

That through a house comes, usually
    doth cast
Things out of order, yet by chance may
    come
And blow some one thing to his proper
    room,
So did thy appetite, and not thy zeal,
Sway thee by chance to do some one
    thing well.
Yet turn!
CLO.   Thou dost but try me, if I would
Forsake thy dear embraces for my old
Love's, though he were alive; but do not
    fear.
THE. I do contemn thee now, and dare
    come near,   550
And gaze upon thee; for methinks that
    grace,
Austerity, which sate upon that face,
Is gone, and thou like others.   False
    maid, see,
This is the gain of foul inconstancy!
                                                Exit.
CLO. 'Tis done.—Great Pan, I give thee
    thanks for it!—
What art could not have healed is cured
    by wit.

                Enter Thenot again.

THE. Will ye be constant yet?   Will ye
    remove
Into the cabin to your buried love?
CLO. No, let me die, but by thy side re-
    main.
THE. There's none shall know that thou
    didst ever stain   560
Thy worthy strictness, but shalt honored
    be,
And I will lie again under this tree,
And pine and die for thee with more
    delight
Than I have sorrow now to know thee
    light.
CLO. Let me have thee, and I'll be where
    thou wilt.
THE. Thou art of women's race, and full
    of guilt.
Farewell all hope of that sex!   Whilst I
    thought
There was one good, I feared to find
    one naught;
But, since their minds I all alike espy,
Henceforth I'll choose, as others, by
    mine eye.   [*Exit.*]   570

CLO. Blessed be ye powers that gave such
    quick redress,
And for my labors sent so good success!
I rather choose, though I a woman be,
He should speak ill of all than die for
    me.   [*Exit.*] [1]

            ACTUS QUINTUS. SCENA PRIMA.

                  [*The same.*]

          Enter Priest and Old Shepherd.

PRIEST. Shepherds, rise, and shake off
    sleep!
See, the blushing morn doth peep
Through the windows, whilst the sun
To the mountain tops is run,
Gilding all the vales below
With his rising flames, which grow
Greater by his climbing still.
Up, ye lazy grooms, and fill
Bag and bottle for the field!   9
Clasp your cloaks fast, lest they yield
To the bitter northeast wind.
Call the maidens up, and find
Who lay longest, that she may
Go without a friend all day;
Then reward your dogs, and pray
Pan to keep you from decay.
So unfold, and then away!—
What, not a shepherd stirring?   Sure,
    the grooms
Have found their beds too easy, or the
    rooms
Filled with such new delight and heat
    that they   20
Have both forgot their hungry sheep and
    day.
Knock, that they may remember what
    a shame
Sloth and neglect lays on a shepherd's
    name.
OLD SHEP. It is to little purpose.   Not a
    swain
This night hath known his lodging here,
    or lain
Within these cotes.   The woods, or
    some near town
That is a neighbor to the bordering down,
Hath drawn them thither 'bout some
    lusty sport,
Or spicéd wassail bowl, to which resort
All the young men and maids of many
    a cote,   30

[1] Original edn. here adds *Finis actus quartus.*

Whilst the trim minstrel strikes his
merry note.
PRIEST. God pardon sin!—Show me the
way that leads
To any of their haunts.
OLD SHEP.   This to the meads,
And that down to the woods.
PRIEST.   Then, this for me.
Come, shepherd, let me crave your
company.   *Exeunt.*

Enter Clorin in her cabin, Alexis with her.[1]

CLO. Now your thoughts are almost pure,
And your wound begins to cure.
Strive to banish all that's vain,
Lest it should break out again.
ALEX. Eternal thanks to thee, thou holy
maid!   40
I find my former wand'ring thoughts
well stayed
Through thy wise precepts; and my
outward pain
By thy choice herbs is almost gone again.
Thy sex's vice and virtue are revealed
At once; for what one hurt another
healed.
CLO. May thy grief more appease!
Relapses are the worst disease.
Take heed how you in thought offend;
So mind and body both will mend.

Enter Satyr with Amoret.

AMO. Be'st thou the wildest creature of
the wood,   50
That bear'st me thus away, drowned in
my blood,
And dying, know I cannot injured be;
I am a maid; let that name fight for me.
SAT. Fairest virgin, do not fear
Me, that doth thy body bear,
Not to hurt, but healed to be;
Men are ruder far than we.—
See, fair goddess, in the wood
They have let out yet more blood.
Some savage man hath struck her
breast,   60
So soft and white, that no wild beast
Durst 'a' touched, asleep or wake—
So sweet that adder, newt, or snake
Would have lain, from arm to arm,
On her bosom to be warm

All a night, and, being hot,
Gone away and stung her not.
Quickly clap herbs to her breast.
A man, sure, is a kind of beast.   69
CLO. With spotless hand on spotless breast
I put these herbs, to give thee rest,
Which, till it heal thee, there will bide,
If both be pure; if not, off slide.—
See, it falls off from the wound!
Shepherdess, thou art not sound,
Full of lust.
SAT.   Who would have thought it?
So fair a face!
CLO.   Why, that hath brought it.
AMO. For aught I know or think, these
words my last,
Yet Pan so help me as my thoughts are
chaste!
CLO. And so may Pan bless this my
cure,   80
As all my thoughts are just and pure!
Some uncleanness nigh doth lurk,
That will not let my medicines work.—
Satyr, search if thou canst find it.
SAT. Here away methinks I wind [2] it.
Stronger yet!—O, here they be;
Here, here, in a hollow tree
Two fond mortals have I found.
CLO. Bring them out; they are unsound.

Enter Cloe and Daphnis.

SAT. By the fingers thus I wring ye;   90
To my goddess thus I bring ye;
Strife is vain; come gently in.—
I scented them; they're full of sin.
CLO. Hold, satyr; take this glass,
Sprinkle over all the place,
Purge the air from lustful breath,
To save this shepherdess from death,
And stand you still whilst I do dress
Her wound, for fear the pain increase.
SAT. From this glass I throw a drop   100
Of crystal water on the top
Of every grass, on flowers a pair.—
Send a fume, and keep the air
Pure and wholesome, sweet and blessed,
Till this virgin's wound be dressed.
CLO. Satyr, help to bring her in.
SAT. By Pan, I think she hath no sin,
        [*Carries Amoret into the bower.*]
She is so light.—Lie on these leaves.
Sleep, that mortal sense deceives,

---

[1] Early edns. here erroneously add *and Ama-*
rillis.

[2] *I.e.,* catch wind of.

Crown thine eyes and ease thy pain; 110
Mayst thou soon be well again!

CLO. Satyr, bring the shepherd near;
Try him, if his mind be clear.

SAT. Shepherd, come.

DAPH.	My thoughts are pure.

SAT. The better trial to endure.

CLO. In this flame his finger thrust,
Which will burn him if he lust;
But if not, away will turn,
As loath unspotted flesh to burn.

[*Satyr holds Daphnis' finger to the flame.*]
See, it gives back; let him go.	120

SAT.[1] Farewell, mortal; keep thee so.—
	[*Exit Daphnis.*]
Stay, fair nymph; fly not so fast;
We must try if you be chaste.—
Here's a hand that quakes for fear;
Sure, she will not prove so clear.

CLO. Hold her finger to the flame;
That will yield her praise or shame.

SAT. To her doom she dares not stand,
	[*Holds Cloe's finger to the flame.*]
But plucks away her tender hand,
And the taper darting sends	130
His hot beams at her fingers' ends.—
O, thou art foul within, and hast
A mind, if nothing else, unchaste!

ALEX. Is not that Cloe? 'Tis my love,
'tis she!
Cloe, fair Cloe!

CLOE.	My Alexis!

ALEX.	He.

CLOE. Let me embrace thee.

CLO.	Take her hence,
Lest her sight disturb his sense.

ALEX. Take not her; take my life first!

CLO. See, his wound again is burst!
Keep her near, here in the wood,	140
Till I have stopped these streams of
blood.	[*Exeunt Cloe and Satyr.*]
Soon again he ease shall find,
If I can but still his mind.
This curtain thus I do display,
To keep the piercing air away.
	[*Draws the traverse across the bower.*]

Enter Old Shepherd and Priest.

PRIEST. Sure, they are lost forever; 'tis
in vain
To find them out with trouble and
much pain

[1] In the original, this speech head has dropped
so that it precedes the next line.

That have a ripe desire and forward will
To fly the company of all but ill.
What shall be counseled now? Shall
we retire,	150
Or constant follow still that first desire
We had to find them?

OLD SHEP.	Stay a little while,
For, if the morning's mist do not beguile
My sight with shadows, sure I see a
swain;
One of this jolly troop's come back
again.

Enter Thenot.

PRIEST. Dost thou not blush, young
shepherd, to be known
Thus without care leaving thy flocks
alone,
And following what desire and present
blood
Shapes out before thy burning sense
for good,
Having forgot what tongue hereafter
may	160
Tell to the world thy falling off, and say
Thou art regardless both of good and
shame,
Spurning at virtue and a virtuous name?
And like a glorious,[2] desperate man that
buys
A poison of much price, by which he
dies,
Dost thou lay out for lust, whose only
gain
Is foul disease, with present age and
pain,
And then a grave? These be the fruits
that grow
In such hot veins, that only beat to know
Where they may take most ease, and
grow ambitious	170
Through their own wanton fire and
pride delicious.

THE. Right holy sir, I have not known this
night
What the smooth face of mirth was, or
the sight
Of any looseness; music, joy, and ease
Have been to me as bitter drugs to
please
A stomach lost with weakness, not a
game

[2] Boastful.

That I am skilled at throughly; nor a dame,
Went her tongue smoother than the feet of time,
Her beauty ever-living like the rime
Our blessed Tityrus [1] did sing of yore;
No, were she more enticing that the store   181
Of fruitful summer, when the loaden tree
Bids the faint traveler be bold and free;
'Twere but to me like thunder gainst the bay,
Whose lightning may inclose, but never stay
Upon his charméd branches; such am I
Against the catching flames of woman's eye.

PRIEST. Then, wherefore hast thou wandered?

THE.   'Twas a vow
That drew me out last night, which I have now
Strictly performed, and homewards go to give   190
Fresh pasture to my sheep, that they may live.

PRIEST. 'Tis good to hear ye, shepherd, if the heart
In this well-sounding music bear his part.
Where have you left the rest?

[THE.] [2]   I have not seen,
Since yesternight we met upon this green
To fold our flocks up, any of that train;
Yet have I walked these woods round, and have lain
All this long night under an aged tree;
Yet neither wand'ring shepherd did I see,   199
Or shepherdess; or drew into mine ear
The sound of living thing, unless it were
The nightingale, among the thick-leaved spring,
That sits alone in sorrow, and doth sing
Whole nights away in mourning; or the owl,
Or our great enemy,[3] that still doth howl
Against the moon's cold beams.

[1] Either Virgil or Chaucer.   [3] I.e., the wolf.
[2] From 1629 edn.

PRIEST.   Go, and beware
Of after-falling.

THE.   Father, 'tis my care.
   Exit Thenot.

Enter Daphnis.

OLD SHEP. Here comes another straggler. Sure I see
A shame in this young shepherd.— Daphnis?

DAPH.   He.

PRIEST. Where hast left the rest, that should have been   210
Long before this grazing upon the green
Their yet-imprisoned flocks?

DAPH.   Thou holy man,
Give me a little breathing, till I can
Be able to unfold what I have seen—
Such horror, that the like hath never been
Known to the ear of shepherd. O, my heart
Labors a double motion to impart
So heavy tidings! You all know the bower
Where the chaste Clorin lives, by whose great power
Sick men and cattle have been often cured.   220
There lovely Amoret, that was assured [4]
To lusty Perigot, bleeds out her life,
Forced by some iron hand and fatal knife;
And, by her, young Alexis.

Enter Amarillis, running from her Sullen Shepherd.

AMAR.   If there be
Ever a neighbor brook or hollow tree,
Receive my body, close me up from lust
That follows at my heels! Be ever just,
Thou god of shepherds, Pan, for her dear sake
That loves the rivers' brinks, and still doth shake
In cold remembrance of thy quick pursuit.   230
Let me be made a reed, and, ever mute,
Nod to the waters' fall, whilst every blast
Sings through my slender leaves that I was chaste!

[4] Affianced.

PRIEST. This is a night of wonder.—
  Amarill,
Be comforted; the holy gods are still
Revengers of these wrongs.
AMAR.   Thou blessed man,
Honored upon these plains, and loved
  of Pan,
Hear me, and save from endless infamy
My yet unblasted flower, virginity!
By all the garlands that have crowned
  that head,   240
By thy chaste office, and the marriage
  bed
That still is blessed by thee, by all the
  rites
Due to our god, and by those virgin
  lights
That burn before his altar, let me not
Fall from my former state, to gain the
  blot
That never shall be purged! I am not
  now
That wanton Amarillis; here I vow
To heaven and thee, grave father, if I
  may
Scape this unhappy night, to know the
  day
A virgin, never after to endure   250
The tongues or company of men un-
  pure!
I hear him come; save me!
PRIEST.   Retire awhile
Behind this bush, till we have known
  that vile
Abuser of young maidens. [*They retire.*]

Enter Sullen.

SULL.   Stay thy pace,
Most lovéd Amarillis; let the chase
Grow calm and milder; fly me not so
  fast;
I fear the pointed brambles have unlaced
Thy golden buskins. Turn again, and see
Thy shepherd follow, that is strong and
  free,   259
Able to give thee all content and ease.
I am not bashful, virgin; I can please
At first encounter, hug thee in mine
  arm,
And give thee many kisses, soft and warm
As those the sun prints on the [1] smiling
  cheek

<hr>

[1] From 1634 edn. Original has *thy.*

Of plums or mellow peaches; I am sleek
And smooth as Neptune when stern
  Æolus
Locks up his surly winds, and nimbly
  thus
Can show my active youth. Why dost
  thou fly?
Remember, Amarillis, it was I   269
That killed Alexis for thy sake, and set
An everlasting hate twixt Amoret
And her beloved Perigot; 'twas I
That drowned her in the well, where she
  must lie
Till time shall leave to be. Then, turn
  again,
Turn with thy open arms, and clip the
  swain
That hath performed all this; turn, turn,
  I say;
I must not be deluded.
PRIEST. [*Coming forward.*]   Monster,
  stay!
Thou that art like a canker to the state
Thou liv'st and breath'st in, eating with
  debate [2]
Through every honest bosom, forcing
  still   280
The veins of any men may serve thy
  will;
Thou that hast offered with a sinful hand
To seize upon this virgin that doth stand
Yet trembling here!
SULL.   Good holiness, declare
What had the danger been, if being bare
I had embraced her; tell me, by your
  art,
What coming wonders would that sight
  impart?
PRIEST. Lust and branded soul.
SULL.   Yet, tell me more;
Hath not our mother Nature, for her
  store
And great increase, said it is good and
  just,   290
And willed that every living creature
  must
Beget his like?
PRIEST.   Ye are better read than I,
I must confess, in blood and lechery.—
Now to the bower, and bring this beast
  along,
Where he may suffer penance for his
  wrong.   [*Exeunt.*]

[2] Discord.

Enter Perigot, with his hand bloody.

PERI. Here will I wash it in the morning's
dew,
Which she on every little grass doth
strew
In silver drops against the sun's appear.[1]
'Tis holy water, and will make me
clear.—
My hand will not be cleansed.—My
wrongéd love,   300
If thy chaste spirit in the air yet move,
Look mildly down on him that yet doth
stand
All full of guilt, thy blood upon his hand.
And, though I struck thee undeservedly,
Let my revenge on her that injured thee
Make less a fault which I intended not,
And let these dewdrops wash away my
spot!—
It will not cleanse. O, to what sacred
flood
Shall I resort to wash away this blood?
Amidst these trees the holy Clorin
dwells   310
In a low cabin of cut boughs, and heals
All wounds; to her I will myself ad-
dress,
And my rash faults repentantly confess;
Perhaps she'll find a means, by art or
prayer,
To make my hand, with chaste blood
stainéd, fair.
That done, not far hence, underneath
some tree
I'll have a little cabin built, since she
Whom I adored is dead; there will I give
Myself to strickness,[2] and, like Clorin,
live.   *Exit.*

*The curtain is drawn; Clorin appears sitting
in the cabin, Amoret sitting on the one
side of her, Alexis and Cloe on the other,
the Satyr standing by.*

CLO. Shepherd, once more your blood is
stayed;   320
Take example by this maid,
Who is healed ere you be pure,
So hard it is lewd lust to cure.
Take heed, then, how you turn your eye
On these other lustfully.—
And, shepherdess, take heed lest you
Move his willing eye thereto;

Let no wring nor pinch nor smile
Of yours his weaker sense beguile.—
Is your love yet true and chaste,   330
And forever so to last?
ALEX. I have forgot all vain desires,
All looser thoughts, ill-tempered fires.
True love I find a pleasant fume,
Whose moderate heat can ne'er con-
sume.
CLOE. And I a new fire feel in me,
Whose chaste flame[3] is not quenched to
be.
CLO. Join your hands with modest touch,
And forever keep you such.

Enter Perigot.

PERI. [*Aside.*] Yon is her cabin; thus far
off I'll stand,   340
And call her forth; for my unhallowed
hand
I dare not bring so near yon sacred
place.—
Clorin, come forth, and do a timely
grace
To a poor swain.
CLO.   What art thou that dost call?
Clorin is ready to do good to all.
Come near.
PERI.   I dare not.
CLO.   Satyr, see
Who it is that calls on me.
SAT. There, at hand,[4] some swain doth
stand,
Stretching out a bloody hand.
PERI. Come, Clorin, bring thy holy waters
clear,   350
To wash my hand.
CLO.   What wonders have been here
Tonight! Stretch forth thy hand, young
swain;
Wash and rub it, whilst I rain
Holy water.
PERI.   Still you pour,
But my hand will never scour.
CLO. Satyr, bring him to the bower.
We will try the sovereign power
Of other waters.
SAT.   Mortal, sure,
'Tis the blood of maiden pure
That stains thee so.

[1] Appearance.   [2] Strictness.

[3] From 1656 edn. Original reads *base end.*
[4] From 1634 edn. Original reads *there's a*
hand.

*The Satyr leadeth him to the bower, where
he spieth Amoret, and kneeleth down;
she knoweth him.*

PERI.   Whate'er thou be, 360
Beest thou her sprite, or some divinity
That in her shape thinks good to walk
this grove,
Pardon poor Perigot!
AMO.   I am thy love,
Thy Amoret, forevermore thy love;
Strike [1] once more on my naked breast,
I'll prove
As constant still. O, canst thou love me
yet,
How soon could I my former griefs forget!
PERI. So overgreat with joy that you live,
now
I am, that no desire of knowing how
Doth seize me. Hast thou still power to
forgive?   370
AMO. Whilst thou hast power to love, or I
to live.
More welcome now than hadst thou
never gone
Astray from me!
PERI.   And, when thou lov'st alone,
And not I, death or some ling'ring pain
That's worse, light on me!
CLO.   Now your stain
Perhaps will cleanse thee [2] once again.
See, the blood that erst did stay,
With the water drops away.
All the powers again are pleased,
And with this new knot are appeased. 380
Join your hands, and rise together;
Pan be blessed that brought you hither!

Enter Priest and Old Shepherd.

Go back again, whate'er thou art; unless
Smooth maiden thoughts possess thee,
do not press
This hallowed ground.—Go, satyr, take
his hand,
And give him present trial.
SAT.   Mortal, stand,
Till by fire I have made known
Whether thou be such a one
That mayst freely tread this place.
Hold thy hand up.—[*Holds the Priest's
hand to the flame.*] Never was   390
More untainted flesh than this.—
Fairest, he is full of bliss.

[1] From 1634 edn. Original reads *stick*.
[2] *I.e.*, be cleansed for thee.

CLO. Then boldly speak; why dost thou
seek this place?
PRIEST. First, honored virgin, to behold
thy face,
Where all good dwells that is; next, for
to try
The truth of late report was given to
me—
Those shepherds that have met with
foul mischance
Through much neglect and more ill
governance,
Whether the wounds they have may yet
endure
The open air, or stay a longer cure; 400
And lastly, what the doom may be shall
light
Upon those guilty wretches, through
whose spite
All this confusion fell; [3] for to this place,
Thou holy maiden, have I brought the
race
Of these offenders, who have freely told
Both why and by what means they gave
this bold
Attempt upon their lives.
CLO.   Fume all the ground,
And sprinkle holy water, for unsound
And foul infection gins to fill the air;
It gathers yet more strongly; [take a
pair] [4]   410
Of censers filled with frankincense and
myrrh,
Together with cold camphire; [5] quickly
stir
Thee, gentle satyr, for the place begins
To sweat and labor with the abhorréd
sins
Of those offenders. Let them not come
nigh,
For full of itching flame and leprosy
Their very souls are, that the ground
goes back,
And shrinks to feel the sullen weight of
black
And so unheard-of venom.—Hie thee
fast,
Thou holy man, and banish from the
chaste   420
These manlike monsters; let them never
more

[3] From 1629 edn. Original reads *full*.
[4] From 1629 edn.
[5] Camphor, supposedly an antaphrodisiac.

Be known upon these downs, but, long
　before
The next sun's rising, put them from
　the sight
And memory of every honest wight.
Be quick in expedition, lest the sores
Of these weak patients break into new
　gores.　　　　　　　　*Ex[it] Priest.*
PERI. My dear, dear Amoret, how happy
　are
Those blessed pairs, in whom a little jar
Hath bred an everlasting love, too
　strong　　　　　　　　　　429
For time or steel or envy to do wrong!
How do you feel your hurts? Alas, poor
　heart,
How much I was abused! Give me the
　smart,
For it is justly mine.
AMO.　　　　　　　I do believe.
It is enough, dear friend; leave off to
　grieve,
And let us once more, in despite of ill,
Give hands and hearts again.
PERI.　　　　　　　With better will
Than e'er I went to find in hottest day
Cool crystal of the fountain, to allay
My eager thirst. May this band never
　break!
Hear us, O heaven!
AMO.　　　Be constant.
PERI.　　　　　　Else Pan wreak　440
With double vengeance my disloyalty!
Let me not dare to know the company
Of men, or any more behold those eyes!
AMO. Thus, shepherd, with a kiss all envy [1]
　dies.

Enter Priest.

PRIEST. Bright maid, I have performed
　your will. The swain
In whom such heat and black rebellions
　reign
Hath undergone your sentence [and dis-
　grace]; [2]
Only the maid I have reserved,[3] whose
　face
Shows much amendment; many a tear
　doth fall
In sorrow of her fault. Great fair,
　recall　　　　　　　　　　450
Your heavy doom, in hope of better
　days,

[1] Ill will.　[2] From 1629 edn.　[3] Preserved.

Which I dare promise; once again up-
　raise
Her heavy spirit, that near drownéd
　lies
In self-consuming care that never dies.
CLO. I am content to pardon; call her in.—
The air grows cool again, and doth be-
　gin
To purge itself. How bright the day
　doth show
After this stormy cloud!—Go, satyr, go,
And with this taper boldly try her hand.
If she be pure and good, and firmly
　stand　　　　　　　　　　460
To be so still, we have performed a work
Worthy the gods themselves.
　　　　　　Satyr brings Amarillis in.
SAT. Come forward, maiden; do not lurk,
Nor hide your face with grief and shame.
Now or never get a name
That may raise thee, and recure [4]
All thy life that was impure.
Hold your hand unto the flame.
If thou beest a perfect dame,
Or hast truly vowed to mend,　　470
This pale fire will be thy friend.—
　　　[*Holds her hand to the flame.*]
See, the taper hurts her not!
Go thy ways; let never spot
Henceforth seize upon thy blood.
Thank the gods, and still be good.
CLO. Young shepherdess, now ye are
　brought again
To virgin state, be so, and so remain
To thy last day, unless the faithful love
Of some good shepherd force thee to
　remove;
Then labor to be true to him, and
　live　　　　　　　　　　480
As such a one that ever strives to give
A blessed memory to aftertime;
Be famous for your good, not for your
　crime.—
Now, holy man, I offer up again
These patients, full of health and free
　from pain.
Keep them from after-ills; be ever near
Unto their actions; teach them how to
　clear
The tedious way they pass through from
　suspect;
Keep them from wrong in others, or neg-
　lect

[4] Recover, cure.

Of duty in themselves; correct the blood   490
With thrifty bits[1] and labor; let the flood
Or the next neighboring spring give remedy
To greedy thirst and travail, not the tree
That hangs with wanton clusters; let not wine,
Unless in sacrifice or rites divine,
Be ever known of shepherds; have a care,
Thou man of holy life! Now do not spare
Their faults through much remissness, nor forget
To cherish him whose many pains and sweat
Hath giv'n increase and added to the downs.   500
Sort all your shepherds from the lazy clowns
That feed their heifers in the budded brooms.
Teach the young maidens strictness, that the grooms
May ever fear to tempt their blowing youth.
Banish all compliment, but single truth,
From every tongue and every shepherd's heart;
Let them use persuading, but no art.
Thus, holy priest, I wish to thee and these
All the best goods and comforts that may please.
ALL. And all those blessings heaven did ever give,   510
We pray upon this bower may ever live.
PRIEST. Kneel, every shepherd, whilst with powerful hand
I bless your after-labors, and the land
You feed your flocks upon. Great Pan defend you
From misfortune, and amend you;
Keep you from those dangers still
That are followed by your will;
Give ye means to know at length
All your riches, all your strength,
Cannot keep your foot from falling   520
To lewd lust, that still is calling
At your cottage, till his power
Bring again that golden hour
Of peace and rest to every soul;

[1] Scanty fare.

May his care of you control
All diseases, sores, or pain
That in aftertime may reign
Either in your flocks or you;
Give ye all affections new,
New desires, and tempers new,   530
That ye may be ever true!
Now rise, and go; and, as ye pass away,
Sing to the God of Sheep that happy lay
That honest Dorus[2] taught ye—Dorus, he
That was the soul and god of melody.
They all sing [and strew flowers on the ground].

THE SONG

All ye woods and trees and bowers,
All ye virtues and ye powers
That inhabit in the lakes,
In the pleasant springs or brakes,
Move your feet   540
    To our sound,
Whilst we greet
    All this ground
With his honor and his name
That defends our flocks from blame.[3]

He is great, and he is just;
He is ever good, and must
Thus be honored. Daffadillies,
Roses, pinks, and lovéd lilies,
Let us fling,   550
Whilst we sing,
Ever holy,
Ever holy,
Ever honored, ever young!
Thus great Pan is ever sung!

Exeunt [all except Clorin and Satyr].

SAT. Thou divinest, fairest, brightest,
Thou most powerful maid and whitest,
Thou most virtuous and most blessed,
Eyes of stars, and golden-tresséd
Like Apollo, tell me, sweetest,   560
What new service now is meetest
For the satyr? Shall I stray
In the middle air, and stay
The sailing rack, or nimbly take
Hold by the moon, and gently make
Suit to the pale queen of the night
For a beam to give thee light?
Shall I dive into the sea,
And bring thee coral, making way
Through the rising waves that fall   570

[2] Probably a reference to Spenser and *The Shepherd's Calendar.*
[3] Harm.

In snowy fleeces? Dearest, shall
I catch thee wanton fauns, or flies
Whose woven wings the summer dyes
Of many colors, get thee fruit,
Or steal from heaven old Orpheus' lute?
All these I'll venter [1] for, and more,
To do her service all these woods adore.

CLO. No other service, satyr, but thy
    watch
About these thicks,[2] lest harmless people
    catch
Mischief or sad mischance.   580

SAT. Holy virgin, I will dance
Round about these woods as quick
As the breaking light, and prick [3]
Down the lawns and down the vales
Faster than the windmill-sails.
So I take my leave, and pray
All the comforts of the day,
Such as Phœbus' heat doth send
On the earth, may still befriend
Thee and this arbor!

CLO.   And to thee   590
All thy master's love be free!   *Exeunt.*

[1] Venture.   [2] Thickets.   [3] Spur, speed.

FINIS. THE PASTORAL OF THE FAITHFUL SHEPHERDESS.

PHILASTER,
OR
LOVE LIES A-BLEEDING [1]

BY
FRANCIS BEAUMONT AND JOHN FLETCHER

[The scene being in Sicily.
The persons represented in the play are these, viz.:

THE KING.
PHILASTER, *heir to the crown.*
PHARAMOND, *Prince of Spain.*
DION, *a lord.*
CLEREMONT } *noble gentlemen,*
THRASILINE } *his associates.*
ARETHUSA, *the king's daughter.*
GALATEA, *a wise, modest lady attending the*
princess.
MEGRA, *a lascivious lady.*

AN OLD WANTON LADY, *or crone.*
ANOTHER LADY *attending the princess.*
EUPHRASIA, *daughter of Dion, but disguised*
like a page and called Bellario.
AN OLD CAPTAIN.
FIVE CITIZENS.
A COUNTRY FELLOW.
TWO WOODMEN.
THE KING'S GUARD AND TRAIN.]* [2]

[TIME: Indefinite.]

ACTUS I. SCENA i.

[The presence chamber in the palace.]

Enter Dion, Cleremont, and Thrasiline. [3]

CLE. Here's nor lords nor ladies.

DI. Credit me, gentlemen, I wonder at
it. They received strict charge from the
king to attend here; besides, it was boldly
published that no officer should forbid
any gentleman that desired to attend and
hear.

CLE. Can you guess the cause?

DI. Sir, it is plain—about the Spanish
prince that's come to marry our king- [10
dom's heir and be our sovereign.

THRA. Many that will seem to know
much say she looks not on him like a maid
in love.

DI. Faith, sir, the multitude, that seldom know anything but their own opinions,
speak that they would have; but the prince,
before his own approach, received so many
confident messages from the state that I
think she's resolved to be ruled.   20

CLE. Sir, it is thought with her he shall
enjoy both these kingdoms of Sicily and
Calabria.

DI. Sir, it is without controversy so
meant. But 'twill be a troublesome labor
for him to enjoy both these kingdoms with
safety, the right heir to one of them living,
and living so virtuously—especially, the
people admiring the bravery of his mind
and lamenting his injuries.   30

CLE. Who? Philaster?

DI. Yes; whose father, we all know, was
by our late King of Calabria unrighteously
deposed from his fruitful Sicily. Myself
drew some blood in those wars, which I
would give my hand to be washed from.

CLE. Sir, my ignorance in state policy
will not let me know why, Philaster being

[1] The title-page continues: "As It Hath Been
Divers Times Acted at the Globe and Blackfriars by His Majesty's Servants."
[2] From 1630 edn.
[3] So all other quartos. 1622 edn. reads
Trasiline.

heir to one of these kingdoms, the king should suffer him to walk abroad with [40 such free liberty.

DI. Sir, it seems your nature is more constant than to inquire after state news. But the king, of late, made a hazard of both the kingdoms, of Sicily and his own, with offering but to imprison Philaster, at which the city was in arms, not to be charmed down by any state order or proclamation, till they saw Philaster ride through the streets pleased and without a guard, [50 at which they threw their hats and their arms from them, some to make bonfires, some to drink, all for his deliverance— which wise men say is the cause the king labors to bring in the power of a foreign nation to awe his own with.

Enter Galatea, Megra, and a Lady.[1]

THRA. See, the ladies! What's the first?

DI. A wise and modest gentlewoman that attends the princess.

CLE. The second? 60

DI. She is one that may stand still discreetly enough and ill-favoredly dance her measure, simper when she is courted by her friend, and slight her husband.

CLE. The last?

DI. Faith, I think she is one whom the state keeps for the agents of our confederate princes; she'll cog[2] and lie with a whole army, before the league shall break. Her name is common through the kingdom, [70 and the trophies of her dishonor advanced beyond Hercules' Pillars. She loves to try the several constitutions of men's bodies, and, indeed, has destroyed the worth of her own body by making experiment upon it for the good of the commonwealth.

CLE. She's a profitable member.

LA. Peace, if you love me! You shall see these gentlemen stand their ground and not court us. 80

GAL. What if they should?

MEG. What if they should!

LA. [*To Galatea.*] Nay, let her alone.— What if they should? Why, if they should,

---

[1] The order of the last two characters has been transposed and the speech heads *La.* and *Meg.* reversed by all other modern editors in the dialogue preceding the entrance of the King. But the *Lady* is probably the "old wanton lady, or crone."

[2] Cheat.

I say they were never abroad. What foreigner would do so? It writes them directly untraveled.

GAL. Why, what if they be?

MEG. What if they be!

LA. [*To Galatea.*] Good madam, let [90 her go on.—What if they be? Why, if they be, I will justify, they cannot maintain discourse with a judicious lady, nor make a leg[3] nor say, "Excuse me."

GAL. Ha, ha, ha!

LA. Do you laugh, madam?

DI. Your desires upon you, ladies!

LA. Then you must sit beside us.

DI. I shall sit near you then, lady.

LA. Near me, perhaps; but there's a lady endures no stranger; and to me [101 you appear a very strange fellow.

MEG. Methinks he's not so strange; he would[4] quickly to be acquainted.

THRA. Peace, the king!

Enter King, Pharamond, Arethusa, and Train.

KING. To give a stronger testimony of love
Than sickly promises (which commonly
In princes find both birth and burial
In one breath), we have drawn you, worthy sir,
To make your fair endearments to our daughter, 110
And worthy services known to our subjects,
Now loved and wondered at; next, our intent
To plant you deeply our immediate heir
Both to our blood and kingdoms. For this lady
(The best part of your life, as you confirm me,
And I believe), though her few years and sex
Yet teach her nothing but her fears and blushes,
Desires without desire, discourse and knowledge
Only of what herself is to herself,
Make her feel moderate health; and, when she sleeps, 120
In making no ill day, knows no ill dreams.
Think not, dear sir, these undivided parts

---

[3] Bow.   [4] Wishes.

That must mold up a virgin, are put on
To show her so, as borrowed ornaments
To talk of her perfect love to you, or add
An artificial shadow to her nature.
No, sir; I boldly dare proclaim her yet
No woman. But woo her still, and think
   her modesty
A sweeter mistress than the offered lan-
   guage
Of any dame, were she a queen, whose
   eye   130
Speaks common loves and comforts to
   her servants.[1]
Last, noble son (for so I now must call
   you),
What I have done thus public is not only
To add comfort in particular
To you or me, but all, and to confirm
The nobles and the gentry of these king-
   doms
By oath to your succession, which shall
   be
Within this month at most.
THRA. [*Aside.*] This will be hardly done.
CLE. [*Aside.*] It must be ill done, if it be
   done.   140
DI. [*Aside.*] When 'tis at best, 'twill be but
   half done, whilst [2]
So brave a gentleman is wronged and
   flung off.
THRA. [*Aside.*] I fear.
CLE. [*Aside.*] Who does not?
DI. [*Aside.*] I fear not for myself, and
   yet I fear too.
Well, we shall see, we shall see. No more.
PHA. Kissing your white hand, mistress, I
   take leave
To thank your royal father, and thus far
To be my own free trumpet. Under-
   stand,
Great king, and these your subjects, mine
   that must be   150
(For so deserving you have spoke me,
   sir,
And so deserving I dare speak myself),
To what a person, of what eminence,
Ripe expectation, of what faculties,
Manners, and virtues, you would wed
   your kingdoms;
You in me have your wishes. O, this
   country!

By more than all the gods, I hold it
   happy—
Happy in their dear memories that have
   been
Kings great and good; happy in yours
   that is;   159
And from you (as a chronicle to keep
Your noble name from eating age) do I
Open [3] myself most happy. Gentle-
   men,
Believe me in a word, a prince's word,
There shall be nothing to make up a
   kingdom
Mighty and flourishing, defensèd, feared,
Equal to be commanded and obeyed,
But through the travails of my life I'll
   find it,
And tie it to this country. By all the
   gods,
My reign shall be so easy to the subject
That every man shall be his prince him-
   self,   170
And his own law—yet I his prince and
   law.
And, dearest lady, to your dearest self
(Dear in the choice of him whose name
   and luster
Must make you more and mightier) let
   me say
You are the blessed'st living, for, sweet
   princess,
You shall enjoy a man of men to be
Your servant; you shall make him yours,
   for whom
Great queens must die,
THRA. [*Aside.*] [4] Miraculous!
CLE. [*Aside.*] This speech calls him   [180
Spaniard, being nothing but a large inven-
tory of his own commendations.

Ent[er] Philaster.

DI. [*Aside.*] I wonder what's his price,
for certainly he'll sell himself, he has so
praised his shape.—But here comes one
more worthy those large speeches than the
large speaker of them. Let me be swallowed
quick, if I can find, in all the anatomy of
yon man's virtues, one sinew sound enough
to promise for him he shall be con-   [190
stable. By this sun, he'll ne'er make king

---

[1] Lovers.
[2] Here and in a few other passages the line
division has been regularized.
[3] Reveal, declare.
[4] In several speeches, such as the following, although prose is used, it may be scanned as
rough iambics.

unless it be of trifles, in my poor judgment.

PHI. [*Kneeling.*] Right noble sir, as low as
  my obedience,
And with a heart as loyal as my knee,
I beg your favor.

KING.   Rise; you have it, sir.
                [*Philaster rises.*]

DI. Mark but the king, how pale he looks!
  He fears!
O, this same whoreson [1] conscience, how
  it jades us!

KING. Speak your intent, sir.

PHI.   Shall I speak um freely?
Be still my royal sovereign.

KING.   As a subject,   200
We give you freedom.

DI. [*Aside.*]   Now it heats.

PHI.   Then thus I turn
My language to you, prince—you, foreign
  man!
Ne'er stare nor put on wonder, for you
  must
Endure me, and you shall. This earth
  you tread upon
(A dowry, as you hope, with this fair
  princess),
By my dead father (O, I had a father,
Whose memory I bow to!) was not left [2]
To your inheritance, and I up and living—
Having myself about me and my sword,
The souls of all my name and memories,
These arms and some few friends beside
  the gods—   211
To part so calmly with it, and sit still
And say, "I might have been." I tell
  thee, Pharamond,
When thou art king, look I be dead and
  rotten,
And my name ashes, as I; for, hear me,
  Pharamond,
This very ground thou goest on, this fat
  earth
My father's friends made fertile with
  their faiths,
Before that day of shame shall gape and
  swallow
Thee and thy nation, like a hungry grave,
Into her hidden bowels. Prince, it shall.
By the just gods, it shall!

----

[1] Rascally.
[*] The order of this and the preceding line is
  reversed in the original.

PHA.   He's mad; beyond cure, mad.   221

DI. [*Aside.*] Here's a fellow has some fire
  in 's veins;
The outlandish [3] prince looks like a tooth-
  drawer.

PHA. Sir Prince of Poppingjays,[4] I'll make
  it well appear
To you I am not mad.

KING.   You displease us;
You are too bold.

PHI.   No, sir, I am too tame,
Too much a turtle,[5] a thing born without
  passion,
A faint shadow that every drunken cloud
Sails over, and makes nothing.

KING.   I do not fancy this.
Call our physicians; sure, he's somewhat
  tainted.[6]   230

THRA. [*Aside.*] I do not think 'twill prove
  so.

DI. [*Aside.*] H'as given him a general
purge already, for all the right he has;
and now he means to let him blood. Be
constant, gentlemen; by heaven, I'll run
his hazard,[7] although I run my name out
of the kingdom!

CLE. [*Aside.*] Peace, we are all one soul.

PHA. What you have seen in me to stir
  offense   239
I cannot find, unless it be this lady,
Offered into mine arms with the succes-
  sion,
Which I must keep (though it hath
  pleased your fury
To mutiny within you) without disput-
  ing
Your genealogies, or taking knowledge
Whose branch you are. The king will
  leave it me,
And I dare make it mine. You have your
  answer.

PHI. If thou wert sole inheritor to him
That made the world his,[8] and couldst
  see no sun
Shine upon anything but thine; were
  Pharamond
As truly valiant as I feel him cold,   250
And ringed amongst the choicest of his
  friends
(Such as would blush to talk such serious
  follies,

----

[3] Foreign.   [6] Mentally unbalanced.
[4] Popinjays.   [7] *I.e.*, I'll run a risk for him.
[5] Turtledove.   [8] *I.e.*, Alexander the Great.

Or back such belied [1] commendations),
And from this presence, spite of [all] [2]
these bugs, [3]
You should hear further from me.

KING. Sir, you wrong the prince;
I gave you not this freedom to brave our
best friends.
You deserve our frown. Go to; be better
tempered.

PHI. It must be, sir, when I am nobler
used.

GAL. [*Aside.*] Ladies,   260
This would have been a pattern of suc-
cession,
Had he ne'er met this mischief. By my
life,
He is the worthiest the true name of
man
This day within my knowledge.

MEG. [*Aside.*] I cannot tell what you may
call your knowledge;
But the other is the man set in my eye.
O, 'tis a prince of wax! [4]

GAL. [*Aside.*]   A dog it is. [5]

KING. Philaster, tell me
The injuries you aim at in your riddles.

PHI. If you had my eyes, sir, and sufferance, [6]   270
My griefs upon you, and my broken
fortunes,
My wants great, and now-nothing hopes
and fears,
My wrongs would make ill riddles to be
laughed at.
Dare you be still my king, and right me
[not]? [7]

KING. Give me your wrongs in private.

PHI.   Take them,
And ease me of a load would bow strong
Atlas.   *They whisper.*

CLE. [*Aside.*] He dares not stand the
shock.

DI. [*Aside.*] I cannot blame him; there's
danger in 't. Every man in this age [280
has not a soul of crystal for all men to read
their actions through; men's hearts and faces
are so far asunder that they hold no intelligence. Do but view yon stranger well, and
you shall see a fever through all his bravery, [8]

and feel him shake like a true tenant. [9] If he
give not back his crown again upon the report of an elder gun, [10] I have no augury.

KING. Go to;
Be more yourself, as you respect our
favor;   290
You'll stir us else. Sir, I must have you
know
That y' are and shall be, at our pleasure,
what fashion we
Will put upon you. Smooth your brow,
or by the gods—

PHI. I am dead, sir; y' are my fate. It was
not I
Said I was wronged. I carry all about
me
My weak stars lead me to, all my weak
fortunes.
Who dares in all this presence speak (that
is
But man [11] of flesh, and may be mortal),
tell me
I do not most entirely love this prince,
And honor his full virtues!

KING.   Sure, he's possessed! 300

PHI. Yes, with my father's spirit. It's
here, O king,
A dangerous spirit! Now he tells me,
king,
I was a king's heir, bids me be a king,
And whispers to me these are all my
subjects.
'Tis strange he will not let me sleep, but
dives
Into my fancy, and there gives me shapes
That kneel and do me service, cry me
king.
But I'll suppress him; he's a factious
spirit,
And will undo me.—[*To Pharamond.*]
Noble sir, your hand;
I am your servant.

KING.   Away! I do not like this. 310
I'll make you tamer, or I'll dispossess you
Both of life and spirit. For this time
I pardon your wild speech, without so
much
As your imprisonment.

*Exeunt K[ing], Pha[ramond], Are[thusa, and
Train].*

---

[1] Lying.   [3] Bugbears.
[2] Supplied from other quartos.
[4] *I.e.*, perfect like a wax model.
[5] "A dog of wax" was a cant phrase indicating contempt.
[6] Suffering.   [7] From 1628 edn.   [8] Insolence.

[9] *I.e.*, "one who has only temporary possession" (Dyce).
[10] Popgun.
[11] From 1620 edn. Original reads *men.*

Di. I thank you, sir; you dare not for the people.

Gal. Ladies, what think you now of this brave fellow?

Meg. A pretty talking fellow, hot at hand. But eye yon stranger; is he not a fine complete gentleman? O, these strangers, I do affect[1] them strangely! [320 They do the rarest home-things, and please the fullest! As I live, I could love all the nation over and over for his sake.

Gal. Gods comfort your poor head-piece, lady! 'Tis a weak one, and had need of a nightcap.　　　　*Exeunt*[2] *Ladies.*

Di. [*Aside.*] See, how his fancy labors! Has he not spoke
Home and bravely? What a dangerous train
Did he give fire to! How he shook the king,
Made his soul melt within him, and his blood　　　　　　　　　　　　　330
Run into whey! It stood upon his brow
Like a cold, winter dew.

Phi.　　　　　　　　Gentlemen,
You have no suit to me? I am no minion.
You stand, methinks, like men that would be courtiers,
If you[3] could well be flattered at a price
Not to undo your children. Y' are all honest.
Go, get you home again, and make your country
A virtuous court, to which your great ones may,
In their diseaséd age, retire and live recluse.

Cle. How do you, worthy sir?

Phi.　　　　　　　Well, very well;　340
And so well that, if the king please, I find
I may live many years.

Di.　　　　　　　The king must please,
Whilst we know what you are and who you are,
Your wrongs and injuries. Shrink not, worthy sir,
But add your father to you, in whose name
We'll waken all the gods, and conjure up
The rods of vengeance, the abuséd people,
Who, like to raging torrents, shall swell high,

And so begirt the dens of these male dragons
That, through the strongest safety, they shall beg　　　　　　　　　　350
For mercy at your sword's point.

Phi.　　　　　　　Friends, no more;
Our ears may be corrupted. 'Tis an age
We dare not trust our wills to. Do you love me?

Thra. Do we love heaven and honor?

Phi. My Lord Dion, you had
A virtuous gentlewoman called you father;
Is she yet alive?

Di.　　　　　　Most honored sir, she is,
And, for the penance but of an idle dream,
Has undertook a tedious pilgrimage.

Enter a Lady.

Phi. Is it to me, or any of these gentlemen, you come?　　　　　　360

La. To you, brave lord; the princess would entreat
Your present company.

Phi. The princess send for me! Y' are mistaken.

La. If you be called Philaster, 'tis to you.

Phi. Kiss her fair hand, and say I will attend her.　　　　　[*Exit Lady.*]

Di. Do you know what you do?

Phi. Yes; go to see a woman.

Cle. But do you weigh the danger you are in?

Phi. Danger in a sweet face?
By Jupiter, I must not fear a woman!　370

Thra. But are you sure it was the princess sent?
It may be some foul train[4] to catch your life.

Phi. I do not think it, gentlemen; she's noble.
Her eye may shoot me dead, or those true red
And white friends in her face may steal my soul out;
There's all the danger in 't. But, be what may,
Her single[5] name hath armed me.
　　　　　　　　　Exit Phil[aster].

Di.　　　　　　　Go on.
And be as truly happy as thou'rt fearless!—

---

[1] Admire.　　　　　　[3] Mason suggests *I.*
[2] Original reads *Exit.*
[4] Trick, plot.　　　　　[5] Mere.

Come, gentlemen, let's make our friends
  acquainted,
Lest the king prove false.   380
          Exeunt [1] *Gentlemen.*

[SCENA ii.

Arethusa's chambers in the palace.]

Enter Arethusa and a Lady.

ARE. Comes he not?
LA.   Madam?
ARE.   Will Philaster come?
LA. Dear madam, you were wont
  To credit me at first.
ARE.   But didst thou tell me so?
  I am forgetful, and my woman's strength
  Is so o'ercharged with dangers like to
    grow
  About my marriage that these under-
    things
  Dare not abide in such a troubled sea.
  How looked he when he told thee he
    would come?
LA. Why, well.   10
ARE. And not a little fearful?
LA. Fear, madam? Sure, he knows not
  what it is.
ARE. You all are of his faction; the whole
    court
  Is bold in praise of him, whilst I
  May live neglected, and do noble things,
  As fools in strife throw gold into the sea,
  Drowned in the doing. But I know he
    fears.
LA. Fear, madam! Methought, his looks
  hid more
  Of love than fear.
ARE.   Of love? To whom? To you?
  Did you deliver those plain words I sent,
  With such a winning gesture and quick
    look   21
  That you have caught him?
LA.   Madam, I mean to you.
ARE. Of love to me! Alas, thy ignorance
  Lets thee not see the crosses of our births!
  Nature, that loves not to be questionéd
  Why she did this or that, but has her
    ends,
  And knows she does well, never gave the
    world
  Two things so opposite, so contrary,
  As he and I am. If a bowl of blood

[1] Original reads *Exit.*

Drawn from this arm of mine would poi-
  son thee,   30
  A draught of his would cure thee. Of
    love to me!
LA. Madam, I think I hear him.
ARE.   Bring him in.—[*Exit Lady.*]
  You gods, that would not have your
    dooms withstood,
  Whose holy wisdoms at this time it is
  To make the passions of a feeble maid
  The way unto your justice, I obey.

Enter Phil[aster with Lady].

LA. Here is my Lord Philaster.
ARE.   O, it is well.
  Withdraw yourself.   [*Exit Lady.*]
PHI.   Madam, your messenger
  Made me believe you wished to speak
    with me.
ARE. 'Tis true, Philaster; but the words
    are such   40
  I have to say and do so ill beseem
  The mouth of woman that I wish them
    said,
  And yet am loath to speak them. Have
    you known
  That I have aught detracted from your
    worth?
  Have I in person wronged you, or have
    set
  My baser instruments to throw disgrace
  Upon your virtues?
PHI.   Never, madam, you.
ARE. Why, then, should you, in such a
    public place,
  Injure a princess, and a scandal lay 49
  Upon my fortunes, famed to be so great,
  Calling a great part of my dowry in ques-
    tion?
PHI. Madam, this truth which I shall
  speak will be
  Foolish; but, for your fair and virtuous
    self.
  I could afford myself to have no right
  To anything you wished.
ARE.   Philaster, know
  I must enjoy these kingdoms.
PHI.   Madam, both?
ARE. Both, or I die; by heaven, I die, Phil-
    aster,
  If I not calmly may enjoy them both.
PHI. I would do much to save that noble
  life,
  Yet would be loath to have posterity 60

Find in our stories that Philaster gave
His right unto a scepter and a crown
To save a lady's longing.

ARE.   Nay, then, hear:
I must and will have them, and more—

PHI.   What more?

ARE. Or lose that little life the gods pre-
    pared
To trouble this poor piece of earth withal.

PHI. Madam, what more?

ARE.   Turn then away thy face.

PHI. No.

ARE. Do.

PHI. I can endure it. Turn away my
    face?   70
I never yet saw enemy that looked
So dreadfully but that I thought myself
As great a basilisk [1] as he, or spake
So horrible but that I thought my tongue
Bore thunder underneath, as much as his,
Nor beast that I could turn from.   Shall
    I then
Begin to fear sweet sounds? A lady's
    voice,
Whom I do love? Say you would have
    my life.
Why, I will give it you, for it is of me
A thing so loathed, and unto you that
    ask   80
Of so poor use, that I shall make no price.
If you entreat, I will unmovedly hear.

ARE. Yet, for my sake, a little bend thy
    looks.

PHI. I do.

ARE.   Then know I must have them
    and thee.

PHI. And me?

ARE.   Thy love—without which all
    the land
Discovered yet will serve me for no use
But to be buried in.

PHI.   Is 't possible?

ARE. With it, it were too little to bestow
On thee. Now, though thy breath do
    strike me dead
(Which, know, it may), I have unripped
    my breast.   90

PHI. Madam, you are too full of noble
    thoughts
To lay a train for this contemnéd life,
Which you may have for asking. To sus-
    pect

[1] A fabulous creature whose breath and look
were fatal.

Were base, where I deserve no ill. Love
    you!
By all my hopes, I do, above my life!
But how this passion should proceed
    from you
So violently, would amaze a man
That would be jealous. [2]

ARE. Another soul into my body shot
Could not have filled me with more
    strength and spirit   100
Than this thy breath. But spend not
    hasty time
In seeking how I came thus. 'Tis the gods,
The gods, that make me so; and, sure,
    our love
Will be the nobler and the better blessed,
In that the secret justice of the gods
Is mingled with it. Let us leave, and kiss,
Lest some unwelcome guest should fall
    betwixt us,
And we should part without it.

PHI.   'Twill be ill
I should abide here long.

ARE.   'Tis true; and worse
You should come often. How shall we
    devise   110
To hold intelligence, [3] that our true loves,
On any new occasion, may agree
What path is best to tread?

PHI.   I have a boy,
Sent by the gods, I hope, to this intent,
Not yet seen in the court. Hunting the
    buck,
I found him sitting by a fountain's side,
Of which he borrowed some to quench his
    thirst,
And paid the nymph again as much in
    tears.
A garland lay him by, made by himself
Of many several flowers bred in the bay, [4]
Stuck in that mystic order that the rare-
    ness   121
Delighted me; but ever when he turned
His tender eyes upon um, he would weep,
As if he meant to make um grow again.
Seeing such pretty, helpless innocence
Dwell in his face, I asked him all his
    story.
He told me that his parents gentle died,
Leaving him to the mercy of the fields,

[2] Suspicious.
[3] Communication.
[4] "An indentation, recess in a range of hills,
etc." (*N.E.D.*)

Which gave him roots; and of the crystal
  springs,
Which did not stop their courses; and the
  sun,   130
Which still, he thanked him, yielded him
  his light.
Then took he up his garland, and did
  show
What every flower, as country people
  hold,
Did signify, and how all, ordered thus,
Expressed his grief, and, to my thoughts,
  did read
The prettiest lecture of his country art
That could be wished, so that methought
  I could
Have studied it. I gladly entertained
Him, who was glad to follow, and have
  got
The trustiest, loving'st, and the gentlest
  boy   140
That ever master kept. Him will I send
To wait on you, and bear our hidden love.
ARE. 'Tis well; no more.

Enter Lady.

LA. Madam, the prince is come to do
  his service.
ARE. What will you do, Philaster, with
  yourself?
PHI. Why, that which all the gods have
  appointed out for me.
ARE. Dear, hide thyself!—
  Bring in the prince.   [*Exit Lady.*]
PHI.   Hide me from Pharamond!
When thunder speaks, which is the voice
  of God,
Though I do reverence, yet I hide me
  not;   150
And shall a stranger prince have leave to
  brag
Unto a foreign nation that he made
Philaster hide himself?
ARE.   He cannot know it.
PHI. Though it should sleep forever to the
  world,
It is a simple sin to hide myself,
Which will forever on my conscience lie.
ARE. Then, good Philaster, give him scope
  and way
In what he says, for he is apt to speak
What you are loath to hear. For my
  sake, do.
PHI. I will.   160

Enter Pharamond [with Lady].

PHA. My princely mistress, as true lovers
  ought,   [*Exit Lady.*]
I come to kiss these fair hands, and to
  show,
In outward ceremonies, the dear love
Writ in my heart.
PHI. If I shall have an answer no directlier,
  I am gone.
PHA.   To what would he have answer?
ARE. To his claim unto the kingdom.
PHA. Sirrah, I forbare [1] you before the
  king—
PHI. Good sir, do so still; I would not talk
  with you.
PHA. But now the time is fitter. Do but
  offer   170
To make mention of right to any king-
  dom,
Though it be scarce habitable—
PHI.   Good sir, let me go.
PHA. And, by the gods—
PHI.   Peace, Pharamond! If thou—
ARE. Leave us, Philaster.
PHI. I have done.
PHA. You are gone! By heaven, I'll fetch
  you back.
PHI. You shall not need.
PHA.   What now?
PHI.   Know, Pharamond,
I loathe to brawl with such a blast as
  thou,
Who art naught but a valiant voice, but,
  if
Thou shalt provoke me further, men shall
  say   180
Thou wert—and not lament it.
PHA.   Do you slight
My greatness so, and in the chamber of
  the princess?
PHI. It is a place to which I must confess
I owe a reverence; but, were 't the
  church,
Ay, at the altar, there's no place so safe,
Where thou dar'st injure me, but I dare
  kill thee.
And for your greatness, know, sir, I can
  grasp
You and your greatness thus, thus into
  nothing.
Give not a word, not a word back! Fare-
  well.   *Exit.*

[1] Forbore.

PHA. 'Tis an odd fellow, madam; we must
    stop   190
His mouth with some office when we are
    married.
ARE. You were best make him your con-
    troller.
PHA. I think he would discharge it well.
    But, madam,
I hope our hearts are knit; but yet so slow
The ceremonies of state are that 'twill be
    long
Before our hands be so. If then you
    please,
Being agreed in heart, let us not wait
For dreaming form, but take a little
    stolen
Delights, and so prevent [1] our joys to
    come.
ARE. If you dare speak such thoughts, 200
    I must withdraw in honor.
                  Exit Are[thusa].
PHA. The constitution of my body will
never hold out till the wedding; I must seek
elsewhere.   *Exit Ph[aramond].*

ACTUS II. SCENA i.

[*A hall in the palace.*]

Enter Philaster and Bellario.

PHI. And thou shalt find her honorable,
    boy,
Full of regard unto thy tender youth,
For thine own modesty, and, for my sake,
Apter to give than thou wilt be to ask,
Ay, or deserve.
BEL.   Sir, you did take me up
When I was nothing, and only yet am
    something
By being yours. You trusted me un-
    known,
And that which you were apt to conster [2]
A simple innocence in me, perhaps
Might have been craft, the cunning of a
    boy   10
Hardened in lies and theft, yet ventured
    you
To part my miseries and me, for which
I never can expect to serve a lady
That bears more honor in her breast than
    you.
PHI. But, boy, it will prefer [3] thee. Thou
    art young,

[1] Anticipate.
[2] Construe, interpret.
[3] Advance.

And bearest a childish, overflowing love
To them that clap thy cheeks and speak
    thee fair yet;
But, when thy judgment comes to rule
    those passions,
Thou wilt remember best those careful
    friends
That placed thee in the noblest way of
    life.   20
She is a princess I prefer thee to.
BEL. In that small time that I have seen
    the world,
I never knew a man hasty to part
With a servant he thought trusty. I
    remember
My father would prefer the boys he kept
To greater men than he, but did it not
Till they were grown too saucy for him-
    self.
PHI. Why, gentle boy, I find no fault at all
In thy behavior.
BEL.   Sir, if I have made 29
A fault of ignorance, instruct my youth;
I shall be willing, if not apt, to learn.
Age and experience will adorn my mind
With larger knowledge; and, if I have
    done
A willful fault, think me not past all hope
For once. What master holds so strict a
    hand
Over his boy that he will part with him
Without one warning? Let me be cor-
    rected
To break my stubbornness, if it be so,
Rather than turn me off; and I shall
    mend.
PHI. Thy love doth plead so prettily to
    stay   40
That, trust me, I could weep to part
    with thee.
Alas, I do not turn thee off! Thou
    knowest
It is my business that doth call thee hence;
And, when thou art with her, thou
    dwellest with me.
Think so, and 'tis so; and, when time is
    full,
That thou hast well discharged this
    heavy trust,
Laid on so weak a one, I will again
With joy receive thee. As I live, I will!
Nay, weep not, gentle boy. 'Tis more
    than time
Thou didst attend the princess.

BEL.   I am gone. 50
But, since I am to part with you, my
    lord,
And none knows whether I shall live to
    do
More service for you, take this little
    prayer:
Heaven bless your loves, your fights, all
    your designs!
May sick men, if they have your wish, be
    well,
And heaven hate those you curse, though
    I be one!   *Exit.*
PHI. The love of boys unto their lords is
    strange.
I have read wonders of it; yet this boy
For my sake (if a man may judge by
    looks
And speech) would outdo story. I may
    see   60
A day to pay him for his loyalty.
                        Exit Phi[laster].

Enter Pharamond.

PHA. Why should these ladies stay so
long? They must come this way. I know
the queen employs um not, for the reverend
mother[1] sent me word they would all be
for the garden. If they should all prove
honest[2] now, I were in a fair taking.[3] I
was never so long without sport in my life,
and, in my conscience, 'tis not my fault.
O, for our country ladies![4]—Here's one [70
bolted; I'll hound at her.—[Madam!][5]

Enter Galatea.

GAL. Your grace!
PHA. Shall I not be a trouble?
GAL. Not to me, sir.
PHA. Nay, nay, you are too quick. By
this sweet hand—
GAL. You'll be forsworn, sir; 'tis but
an old glove. If you will talk at distance,
I am for you; but, good prince, be not
bawdy, nor do not brag; these two I [80
bar; and then, I think, I shall have
sense enough to answer all the weighty
apothegms your royal blood shall manage.

---

[1] *I.e.,* the lady in charge of the maids of honor.
[2] Chaste.
[3] Dilemma.
[4] *I.e.,* ladies of our country (Spain).
[5] From 1620 edn.

PHA. Dear lady, can you love?
GAL. "Dear," prince? How dear? I
ne'er cost you a coach yet, nor put you to
the dear repentance of a banquet. Here's
no scarlet, sir, to blush the sin out it was
given for. This wire[6] mine own hair [90
covers; and this face has been so far from
being dear to any that it ne'er cost penny
painting; and, for the rest of my poor
wardrobe, such as you see, it leaves no
hand[7] behind it to make the jealous mercer's
wife curse our good doings.
PHA. You mistake me, lady.
GAL. Lord, I do so; would you or I
could help it!
PHA. Do ladies of this country use [100
to give no more respect to men of my
full being?
GAL. Full being! I understand you not,
unless your grace means growing to fatness;
and then your only remedy (upon my
knowledge, prince) is, in a morning, a cup
of neat white wine brewed with carduus,[8]
then fast till supper—about eight you may
eat; use exercise, and keep a sparrow
hawk; you can shoot in a tiller;[9] but, [110
of all, your grace must fly phlebotomy,
fresh pork, conger, and clarified whey; they
are all dullers of the vital spirits.
PHA. Lady, you talk of nothing all this
while.
GAL. 'Tis very true, sir; I talk of you.
PHA. [*Aside.*] This is a crafty wench; I
like her wit well; 'twill be rare to stir up a
leaden appetite. She's a Danaë, and must
be courted in a shower of gold.— [120
[*Shows her money.*] Madam, look here; all
these, and more than—
GAL. What have you there, my lord?
Gold? Now, as I live, 'tis fair gold! You
would have silver for it, to play with the
pages. You could not have taken me in a
worse time; but, if you have present use,
my lord, I'll send my man with silver and
keep your gold for you.
PHA. Lady, lady!   130
GAL. She's coming, sir, behind, will take
white money.[10]—[*Aside.*] Yet for all this
I'll match ye. [*Takes gold.*]
        Exit GAL[ATEA] *behind the hangings.*

---

[6] Used as a frame for the headdress.
[7] Record of indebtedness.
[8] A panacea made from a kind of thistle.
[9] With a crossbow.   [10] *I.e.,* silver.

PHA. If there be but two such more in this kingdom, and near the court, we may even hang up our harps. Ten such camphire [1] constitutions as this will call the golden age again in question, and teach the old way for every ill-faced husband to get his own children; and what a mis- [140 chief that will breed, let all consider!—

Enter Megra.

Here's another; if she be of the same last, the devil shall pluck her on.—Many fair mornings, lady!

MEG. As many mornings bring as many days,
Fair, sweet, and hopeful to your grace!

PHA. [*Aside.*] She gives good words yet; sure this wench is free.—
If your more serious business do not call you,
Let me hold quarter [2] with you; we'll talk
An hour out quickly.

MEG. What would your grace talk of?

PHA. Of some such pretty subject as yourself. 151
I'll go no further than your eye, or lip;
There's theme enough for one man for an age.

MEG. Sir, they stand right, and my lips are yet even,
Smooth, young enough, ripe enough, and red enough,
Or my glass wrongs me.

PHA. O, they are two twinned cherries dyed in blushes,
Which those fair suns above with their bright beams
Reflect upon and ripen. Sweetest beauty,
Bow down those branches, that the longing taste 160
Of the faint looker-on may meet those blessings,
And taste and live. [*They kiss.*][3]

MEG. [*Aside.*] O, delicate, sweet prince!
She that hath snow enough about her heart
To take the wanton spring of ten such lines off,
May be a nun without probation.—Sir,

[1] Camphor was formerly considered to possess the property of coldness.
[2] Friendly intercourse.
[3] From 1620 edn.

You have in such neat poetry gathered a kiss
That, if I had but five lines of that number,
Such pretty, begging blanks,[4] I should commend
Your forehead or your cheeks, and kiss you too.

PHA. Do it in prose; you cannot miss it, madam. 170

MEG. I shall, I shall.

PHA. By my life, but you shall not;
I'll prompt you first. [*Kisses her.*] Can you do it now?

MEG. Methinks 'tis easy, now I ha' done 't before;
But yet I should stick at it. [*Kisses him.*]

PHA. Stick till tomorrow;
I'll ne'er part you, sweetest. But we lose time.
Can you love me?

MEG. Love you, my lord? How would you have me love you?

PHA. I'll teach you in a short sentence, cause I will not load your memory. This is all: love me, and lie with me. 180

MEG. Was it "lie with you" that you said? 'Tis impossible.

PHA. Not to a willing mind, that will endeavor. If I do not teach you to do it as easily in one night as you'll go to bed, I'll lose my royal blood for 't.

MEG. Why, prince, you have a lady of your own that yet wants teaching.

PHA. I'll sooner teach a mare the old measures [5] than teach her anything [190 belonging to the function. She's afraid to lie with herself if she have but any masculine imaginations about her. I know, when we are married, I must ravish her.

MEG. By mine honor, that's a foul fault, indeed; but time and your good help will wear it out, sir.

PHA. And for any other I see, excepting your dear self, dearest lady, I had rather be Sir Tim the schoolmaster, and [200 leap a dairymaid, madam.

MEG. Has your grace seen the court star, Galatea?

PHA. Out upon her! She's as cold of her favor as an apoplex;[6] she sailed by but now.

MEG. And how do you hold her wit, sir?

[4] Blank verses.   [5] Stately dances.
[6] Apoplexy.

PHA. I hold her wit? The strength of all the guard cannot hold it, if they were tied to it; she would blow um out of the king-dom. They talk of Jupiter; he's but [210 a squib-cracker to her. Look well about you, and you may find a tongue-bolt.[1] But speak, sweet lady, shall I be freely welcome?

MEG. Whither?

PHA. To your bed. If you mistrust my faith, you do me the unnoblest wrong.

MEG. I dare not, prince, I dare not.

PHA. Make your own conditions, my purse shall seal um, and what you [220 dare imagine you can want, I'll furnish you withal. Give two hours to your thoughts every morning about it. Come, I know you are bashful. Speak in my ear; will you be mine? Keep this. [*Gives a ring.*] And, with it, me. Soon I will visit you.

MEG. My lord, my chamber's most unsafe; but, when 'tis night, I'll find some means to slip into your lodging; till [230 when—

PHA. Till when, this and my heart go with thee!   *Exeunt.*

Enter Galatea from behind the hangings.

GAL. O, thou pernicious petticoat prince, are these your virtues? Well, if I do not lay a train to blow your sport up, I am no woman; and, Lady Towsabel,[2] I'll fit you for 't.   *Exit Gal[atea].*

[SCENA ii.

Arethusa's chambers in the palace.]

Enter Arethusa and a Lady.

ARE. Where's the boy?

LA. Within, madam.

ARE. Gave you him gold to buy him clothes?

LA. I did.

ARE. And has he done 't?

LA. Yes, madam.

ARE. 'Tis a pretty, sad-talking[3] boy, is it not? Asked you his name?

LA. No, madam.   10

Enter Galatea.

ARE. O, you are welcome. What good news?

GAL. As good as anyone can tell your grace, That says she has done that you would have wished.

ARE. Hast thou discovered?

GAL. I have strained a point of modesty for you.

ARE. I prithee, how?

GAL. In listening after bawdry. I see, let a lady live never so modestly, she shall be sure to find a lawful time to hearken after bawdry. Your prince, brave Phara- [20 mond, was so hot on 't!

ARE. With whom?

GAL. Why, with the lady I suspected. I can tell the time and place.

ARE. O, when, and where?

GAL. Tonight, his lodging.

ARE. Run thyself into the presence;[4] min-gle there again With other ladies; leave the rest to me.— [*Exit Galatea.*]
If destiny (to whom we dare not say, Why thou didst this) have not decreed it so,   30
In lasting leaves (whose smallest charac-ters Were never altered), yet this match shall break.—
Where's the boy?

LA. Here, madam.

Enter Bellario.

ARE. Sir, you are sad to change your serv-ice, is 't not so?

BEL. Madam, I have not changed; I wait on you, To do him service.

ARE.   Thou disclaim'st[5] in me. Tell me thy name.

BEL. Bellario.

ARE. Thou canst sing and play?   40

BEL. If grief will give me leave, madam, I can.

ARE. Alas, what kind of grief can thy years know? Hadst thou a curst[6] master when thou went'st to school? Thou art not capable of other grief; Thy brows and cheeks are smooth as wa-ters be

---

[1] With an allusion to Jupiter's thunderbolt.
[2] A contemptuous form of Dowsabell, a sweetheart.
[3] Serious-talking.
[4] Presence chamber.   [6] Ill-tempered.
[5] Renouncest all share.

When no breath troubles them.   Believe
me, boy,
Care seeks out wrinkled brows and hol-
low eyes,
And builds himself caves, to abide in
them.
Come, sir, tell me truly, doth your lord
love me?
BEL. Love, madam? I know not what
it is.   50
ARE. Canst thou know grief, and never
yet knew'st love?
Thou art deceived, boy.   Does he speak
of me
As if he wished me well?
BEL.   If it be love
To forget all respect of his own friends
With thinking of your face; if it be love
To sit cross-armed and think away the
day,
Mingled with starts, crying your name as
loud
And hastily as men i' the streets do fire;
If it be love to weep himself away
When he but hears of any lady dead   60
Or killed, because it might have been
your chance;
If, when he goes to rest (which will not
be),
Twixt every prayer he says, to name you
once,
As others drop a bead, be to be in love,
Then, madam, I dare swear he loves you.
ARE. O, y' are a cunning boy, and taught
to lie
For your lord's credit! But thou knowest
a lie
That bears this sound is welcomer to me
Than any truth that says he loves me
not.
Lead the way, boy.—[To Lady.] Do you
attend me too.—   70
'Tis thy lord's business hastes me thus.
Away!   Exeunt.

[SCENA iii.

Before Pharamond's lodging in the palace
yard.]

Enter Dion, Cleremont, Thrasiline, Megra,
Galatea.

DI. Come, ladies, shall we talk a round?
As men

Do walk a mile, women should talk an
hour
After supper; 'tis their exercise.
GAL. 'Tis late.
MEG. 'Tis all
My eyes will do to lead me to my
bed.
GAL. I fear they are so heavy they'll
scarce find
The way to your own lodging with um
tonight.

Enter Pharamond.

THRA. The prince!
PHA. Not abed, ladies? Y' are good sit-
ters-up.   10
What think you of a pleasant dream, to
last
Till morning?
MEG. I should choose, my lord, a pleasing
wake before it.

Enter Arethusa and Bellario.

ARE. 'Tis well, my lord; y' are courting
of these ladies.—
Is 't not late, gentlemen?
CLE. Yes, madam.
ARE. Wait you there.   *Exit Arethusa.*
MEG. [Aside.] She's jealous, as I live.—
Look you, my lord,
The princess has a Hylas, an Adonis.
PHA. His form is angel-like.   20
MEG. Why, this is he must, when you are
wed,
Sit by your pillow, like young Apollo,
with
His hand and voice binding your
thoughts in sleep;
The princess does provide him for you
and for herself.
PHA. I find no music in these boys.
MEG.   Nor I.
They can do little, and that small they
do,
They have not wit to hide.
DI.   Serves he the princess?
THRA. Yes.
DI.   'Tis a sweet boy; how brave [1] she
keeps him!
PHA. Ladies all, good rest; I mean to kill a
buck

[1] Richly dressed.

Tomorrow morning ere y'ave done your
dreams.   30

Meg. All happiness attend your grace!—
[*Exit Pharamond.*]   Gentlemen, good
rest.—

Come, shall we to bed?

Gal.   Yes.—All, good night.
Exit Gal[atea with] Meg[ra].

Di. May your dreams be true to you!—
What shall we do, gallants?   'Tis late.
The king
Is up still; see, he comes, a guard
along
With him.

Enter King, Arethusa, and Guard.

King.   Look your intelligence be true.

Are. Upon my life, it is; and I do hope
Your highness will not tie me to a
man
That in the heat of wooing throws me
off,
And takes another.   40

Di. What should this mean?

King. If it be true,
That lady had been better have em-
braced
Cureless diseases.   Get you to your rest.
Ex[eunt] Are[thusa], Bell[ario].
You shall be righted.—Gentlemen, draw
near;
We shall employ you.   Is young Phara-
mond
Come to his lodging?

Di.   I saw him enter there.

King. Haste, some of you, and cunningly
discover
If Megra be in her lodging. [*Exit Dion.*]

Cle. Sir,   50
She parted hence but now, with other
ladies.

King. If she be there, we shall not need to
make
A vain discovery of our suspicion.—
[*Aside.*] You gods, I see that who un-
righteously
Holds wealth or state from others shall
be cursed
In that which meaner men are blessed
withal;
Ages to come shall know no male of
him
Left to inherit, and his name shall be

Blotted from earth; if he have any child
It shall be crossly matched; the gods
themselves   60
Shall sow wild strife betwixt her lord and
her.
Yet, if it be your wills, forgive the sin
I have committed; let it not fall
Upon this understanding child of mine!
She has not broke your laws.   But how
can I
Look to be heard of gods that must be
just,
Praying upon the ground I hold by
wrong?

Enter Dion.

Di. Sir, I have asked, and her women
swear she is within; but they, I think, are
bawds.   I told um I must speak with   [70
her; they laughed, and said their lady lay
speechless.   I said my business was important; they said their lady was about it.
I grew hot, and cried my business was a
matter that concerned life and death; they
answered, so was sleeping, at which their
lady was.   I urged again, she had scarce
time to be so since last I saw her.   They
smiled again, and seemed to instruct me
that sleeping was nothing but lying   [80
down and winking.[1]   Answers more direct
I could not get; in short, sir, I think she is
not there.

King. 'Tis then no time to dally.—You o'
th' guard,
Wait at the back door of the prince's
lodging,
And see that none pass thence, upon your
lives.—   [*Exeunt Guards.*]
Knock, gentlemen; knock loud; louder
yet.   [*They knock.*]
What, has their pleasure taken off their
hearing?—
I'll break your meditations.—Knock
again!—
Not yet?   I do not think he sleeps, having
this   90
Larum [2] by him.—Once more.—Phara-
mond!   Prince!

Pharamond above.

Pha. What saucy groom knocks at this
dead of night?

_____
[1] Closing the eyes.   [2] Alarum.

Where be our waiters? [1] By my vexéd
    soul,
He meets his death that meets me, for
    this boldness.
KING. Prince, you wrong your thoughts;
    we are your friends.
    Come down.
PHA.   The king?
KING.   The same, sir. Come down;
    We have cause of present counsel with
    you.
PHA. If your grace please
    To use me, I'll attend you to your
    chamber.

Pha[ramond] below.

KING. No, 'tis too late, prince; I'll make
    bold with yours.   100
PHA. I have some private reasons to my-
    self
    Makes me unmannerly, and say you
    cannot.—
    Nay, press not forward, gentlemen; he
    must come
    Through my life that comes here.
KING. Sir, be resolved [2] I must and will
    come.—Enter!
PHA. I will not be dishonored.
    He that enters, enters upon his
    death.
    Sir, 'tis a sign you make no stranger of
    me,
    To bring these renegadoes to my cham-
    ber
    At these unseasoned hours.
KING.   Why do you 110
    Chafe yourself so? You are not wronged
    nor shall be;
    Only I'll search your lodging, for some
    cause
    To ourself known.—Enter, I say.
PHA.   I say, no.

Meg[ra] above.

MEG. Let um enter, prince, let um en-
    ter;
    I am up and ready.[3] I know their
    business;
    'Tis the poor breaking of a lady's
    honor
    They hunt so hotly after; let um enjoy
    it.—

[1] Attendants.   [2] Convinced.   [3] Dressed.

You have your business, gentlemen. I
    lay here.
O, my lord the king, this is not noble in
    you
To make public the weakness of a
    woman!   120
KING. Come down.
MEG. I dare, my lord. Your whootings [4]
    and your clamors,
    Your private whispers and your broad
    fleerings,
    Can no more vex my soul than this base
    carriage.[5]
    But I have vengeance yet in store for
    some
    Shall, in the most contempt you can
    have of me,
    Be joy and nourishment.
KING.   Will you come down?
MEG. Yes, to laugh at your worst; but I
    shall wring you,
    If my skill fail me not.   *[Exit above.]*
KING. Sir, I must dearly chide you for
    this looseness;   130
    You have wronged a worthy lady; but
    no more.—
    Conduct him to my lodging and to bed.
    [Exeunt Pharamond and Attendants.]
CLE. Get him another wench, and you
bring him to bed indeed.
DI. 'Tis strange a man cannot ride a
    stag [6]
    Or two, to breathe himself, without a
    warrant.
    If this gear [7] hold, that lodgings be
    searched thus,
    Pray God we may lie with our own wives
    in safety,
    That they be not by some trick of state
    mistaken!

Enter [Attendants] with Megra.

KING. Now, lady of honor, where's your
    honor now?   140
    No man can fit your palate but the
    prince.
    Thou most ill-shrouded rottenness, thou
    piece
    Made by a painter and a pothe-
    cary,

[4] Hootings.   [6] A romping girl.
[5] Behavior.   [7] Matter.

Thou troubled sea of lust, thou wilderness
Inhabited by wild thoughts, thou swoln
  cloud
Of infection, thou ripe mine of all dis-
  eases,
Thou all-sin, all-hell, and, last, all-devils,
  tell me,
Had you none to pull on with your
  courtesies
But he that must be mine, and wrong my
  daughter?
By all the gods, all these, and all the
  pages,   150
And all the court shall hoot thee through
  the court,
Fling rotten oranges, make ribald
  rimes,
And sear thy name with candles upon
  walls!
Do you laugh, Lady Venus?
MEG. Faith, sir, you must pardon me;
I cannot choose but laugh to see you
  merry.
If you do this, O king, nay, if you dare
  do it,
By all those gods you swore by, and as
  many
More of my own, I will have fellows, and
  such
Fellows in it as shall make noble
  mirth!   160
The princess, your dear daughter, shall
  stand by me
On walls, and sung in ballads, any-
  thing.
Urge me no more; I know her and her
  haunts,
Her lays,[1] leaps, and outlays, and will
  discover all,
Nay, will dishonor her. I know the
  boy
She keeps, a handsome boy, about
  eighteen,
Know what she does with him, where,
  and when.
Come, sir, you put me to a woman's madness,
The glory of a fury; and, if I do
  not   169
Do it to the height—
KING.   What boy is this she raves
  at?

[1] Hiding places.

MEG. Alas, good-minded prince, you know
  not these things?
I am loath to reveal um. Keep this
  fault
As you would keep your health from the
  hot air
Of the corrupted people, or, by heaven,
I will not fall alone. What I have
  known
Shall be as public as a print; all
  tongues
Shall speak it as they do the language
  they
Are born in, as free and commonly; I'll
  set it,
Like a prodigious star,[2] for all to gaze
  at,
And so high and glowing that other king-
  doms far and foreign   180
Shall read it there, nay, travel with it,
  till they find
No tongue to make it more, nor no more
  people;
And then behold the fall of your fair
  princess!
KING. Has she a boy?
CLE. So please your grace, I have seen a
  boy wait
On her, a fair boy.
KING.   Go, get you to your quarter,
For this time I'll study to forget you.
MEG. Do you study to forget me, and I'll
  study
To forget you.
          Ex[eunt] K[ing], Meg[ra], Guard.
CLE. Why, here's a male spirit fit   [190
for Hercules. If ever there be Nine Worthies of women, this wench shall ride astride
and be their captain.
DI. Sure, she has a garrison of devils in
her tongue, she uttered such balls of wildfire. She has so nettled[3] the king that all
the doctors in the country will scarce cure
him. That boy was a strange-found-out antidote to cure her infection; that boy, that
princess' boy; that brave, chaste, vir- [200
tuous lady's boy! And a fair boy, a well-
spoken boy, all these considered, can make
nothing else—but there I leave you, gentlemen.
THRA. Nay, we'll go wander with you.
                              Exeunt.

[2] Portentous comet.
[3] From 1620 edn. Original reads metled.

ACTUS III. SCENA i.

[*The court of the palace.*]

Enter Cle[remont], Di[on], Thra[siline].

CLE. Nay, doubtless, 'tis true.

DI. Ay; and 'tis the gods
That raised this punishment to scourge
  the king
With his own issue. Is it not a shame
For us that should write noble [1] in the
  land,
For us that should be freemen, to behold
A man that is the bravery of his age,
Philaster, pressed down from his royal
  right
By this regardless [2] king, and only look
And see the scepter ready to be cast   10
Into the hands of that lascivious lady
That lives in lust with a smooth boy, now
  to be
Married to yon strange prince, who, but
  that people
Please to let him be a prince, is born a
  slave
In that which should be his most noble
  part,
His mind?

THRA.   That man that would not stir
  with you
To aid Philaster, let the gods forget
That such a creature walks upon the
  earth!

CLE. Philaster is too backward in 't himself.   19
The gentry do await it, and the people
Against their nature are all bent for
  him,
And like a field of standing corn, that's
  moved
With a stiff gale, their heads bow all one
  way.

DI. The only cause that draws Philaster
  back
From this attempt is the fair princess'
  love,
Which he admires, and we can now confute.

THRA. Perhaps he'll not believe it.

DI. Why, gentlemen, 'tis without question
  so.

CLE. Ay, 'tis past speech she lives dis-
  honestly.

But how shall we, if he be curious,[3]
  work   30
Upon his faith?

THRA. We all are satisfied within ourselves.

DI. Since it is true, and tends to his own
  good,
I'll make this new report to be my knowledge;
I'll say I know it; nay, I'll swear I saw it.

CLE. It will be best.

THRA.   'Twill move him.

Enter Philas[ter].

DI.   Here he comes.
Good morrow to your honor; we have
  spent
Some time in seeking you.

PHI.   My worthy friends,
You that can keep your memories to
  know
Your friend in miseries, and cannot
  frown   40
On men disgraced for virtue, a good day
Attend you all! What service may I do
Worthy your acceptation?

DI.   My good lord,
We come to urge that virtue, which we
  know
Lives in your breast, forth. Rise, and
  make a head; [4]
The nobles and the people are all dulled
With this usurping king, and not a man
That ever heard the word, or knew such a
  thing
As virtue, but will second your attempts.

PHI. How honorable is this love in you   50
To me that have deserved none! Know,
  my friends
(You that were born to shame your poor
  Philaster
With too much courtesy), I could afford
To melt myself in thanks; but my designs
Are not yet ripe. Suffice it that ere long
I shall employ your loves; but yet the
  time
Is short of what I would.

DI. The time is fuller, sir, than you expect;
That which hereafter will not, perhaps,
  be reached
By violence, may now be caught. As for
  the king,   60

---

[1] *I.e.*, rank as nobles.   [2] Neglectful.   [3] Scrupulous, skeptical.   [4] Raise an army.

You know the people have long hated
  him;
But now the princess, whom they
  loved—
PHI. Why, what of her?
DI.   Is loathed as much as he.
PHI. By what strange means?
DI.   She's known a whore.
PHI.   Thou liest!
DI. My lord—
PHI. Thou liest,
      Offers to draw and is held.
And thou shalt feel it! I had thought
  thy mind
Had been of honor. Thus to rob a lady
Of her good name is an infectious sin
Not to be pardoned.   Be it false as
  hell,   70
'Twill never be redeemed, if it be sown
Amongst the people, fruitful to increase
All evil they shall hear. Let me alone
That I may cut off falsehood whilst it
  springs!
Set hills on hills betwixt me and the man
That utters this, and I will scale them all,
And from the utmost top fall on his neck,
Like thunder from a cloud.
DI.   This is most strange;
Sure, he does love her.
PHI.   I do love fair truth. 79
She is my mistress, and who injures her
Draws vengeance from me. Sirs, let go
  my arms.
THRA. Nay, good my lord, be patient.
CLE. Sir, remember this is your honored
  friend
That comes to do his service, and will
  show you
Why he uttered this.
PHI.   I ask your pardon, sir;
My zeal to truth made me unmannerly.
Should I have heard dishonor spoke of
  you,
Behind your back, untruly, I had been
As much distempered and enraged as
  now.
DI. But this, my lord, is truth.
PHI.   O, say not so! 90
Good sir, forbear to say so. 'Tis then
  truth
That womankind is false. Urge it no
  more;
It is impossible. Why should you think
The princess light?

DI.   Why, she was taken at it.
PHI. 'Tis false! By heaven, 'tis false! It
  cannot be!
Can it? Speak, gentlemen; for God's
  love, speak!
Is 't possible? Can women all be damned?
DI. Why, no, my lord.
PHI.   Why, then, it cannot be.
DI. And she was taken with her boy.
PHI.   What boy?
DI. A page, a boy that serves her.
PHI.   O, good gods! 100
A little boy?
DI.   Ay; know you him, my lord?
PHI. [*Aside.*] Hell and sin know him!—
Sir, you are deceived;
I'll reason it a little coldly with you.
If she were lustful, would she take a
  boy,
That knows not yet desire? She would
  have one
Should meet her thoughts and know the
  sin he acts,
Which is the great delight of wickedness.
You are abused,[1] and so is she, and I.
DI. How you, my lord?
PHI.   Why, all the world's abused
In an unjust report.
DI.   O, noble sir, your virtues 110
Cannot look into the subtle thoughts of
  woman!
In short, my lord, I took them, I myself.
PHI. Now, all the devils, thou didst! Fly
  from my rage!
Would thou hadst ta'en devils engend'-
  ring plagues,
When thou didst take them! Hide thee
  from mine eyes!
Would thou hadst ta'en thunder on thy
  breast
When thou didst take them, or been
  strucken dumb
Forever, that this foul deed might have
  slept
In silence!
THRA. [*Aside.*]   Have you known him
  so ill-tempered?
CLE. [*Aside.*] Never before.
PHI.   The winds that are let loose 120
From the four several corners of the
  earth,
And spread themselves all over sea and
  land,

[1] Deceived.

Kiss not a chaste one. What friend bears a sword
To run me through?

Di.   Why, my lord, are you
So moved at this?

Phi.   When any fall from virtue,
I am distracted; I have an interest in 't.

Di. But, good my lord, recall yourself, and think
What's best to be done.

Phi.   I thank you; I will do it.
Please you to leave me; I'll consider of it.
Tomorrow I will find your lodging forth,   130
And give you answer.

Di.   All the gods direct you
The readiest way!

Thra. [Aside.]   He was extreme impatient.

Cle. [Aside.] It was his virtue and his noble mind.

Exit Di[on, with] Cle[remont], Thra[siline].

Phi. I had forgot to ask him where he took them;
I'll follow him. O, that I had a sea
Within my breast to quench the fire I feel!
More circumstances will but fan this fire.
It more afflicts me now, to know by whom
This deed is done, than simply that 'tis done,   139
And he that tells me this is honorable,
As far from lies as she is far from truth.
O, that like beasts we could not grieve ourselves
With that we see not! Bulls and rams will fight
To keep their females, standing in their sight;
But take um from them, and you take at once
Their spleens away, and they will fall again
Unto their pastures, growing fresh and fat,
And taste the waters of the springs as sweet
As 'twas before, finding no start in sleep.
But miserable man—

Enter Bellario.

[Aside.]   See, see, you gods,   150
He walks still; and the face you let him wear

When he was innocent is still the same,
Not blasted! Is this justice? Do you mean
To entrap mortality, that you allow
Treason so smooth a brow? I cannot now
Think he is guilty.

Bel.   Health to you, my lord!
The princess doth commend her love, her life,
And this, unto you.   [*Gives a letter.*]

Phi.   O, Bellario,
Now I perceive she loves me; she does show it
In loving thee, my boy; she has made thee brave.   160

Bel. My lord, she has attired me past my wish,
Past my desert, more fit for her attendant,
Though far unfit for me who do attend.

Phi. Thou art grown courtly, boy.—
[*Aside.*] O, let all women
That love black deeds, learn to dissemble here,
Here, by this paper! She does write to me
As if her heart were mines of adamant
To all the world besides; but, unto me,
A maiden snow that melted with my looks.—
Tell me, my boy, how doth the princess use thee?   170
For I shall guess her love to me by that.

Bel. Scarce like her servant, but as if I were
Something allied to her, or had preserved
Her life three times by my fidelity;
As mothers fond do use their only sons,
As I'd use one that's left unto my trust,
For whom my life should pay if he met harm,
So she does use me.

Phi.   Why, this is wondrous well.
But what kind language does she feed thee with?

Bel. Why, she does tell me she will trust my youth   180
With all her loving secrets, and does call me
Her pretty servant; bids me weep no more
For leaving you; she'll see my services
Regarded; and such words of that soft strain

That I am nearer weeping when she ends
Than ere she spake.

Phi.   This is much better still.

Bel. Are you not ill, my lord?

Phi.   Ill? No, Bellario.

Bel. Methinks your words
Fall not from off your tongue so evenly,
Nor is there in your looks that quietness
That I was wont to see.

Phi.   Thou art deceived, boy. 191
And she strokes thy head?

Bel. Yes.

Phi. And she does clap thy cheeks?

Bel.   She does, my lord.

Phi. And she does kiss thee, boy? Ha!

Bel.   How, my lord?

Phi. She kisses thee?

Bel.   Never, my lord, by heaven.

Phi. That's strange; I know she does.

Bel.   No, by my life.

Phi. Why, then she does not love me.
Come, she does.
I bade her do it; I charged her, by all
charms
Of love between us, by the hope of
peace   200
We should enjoy, to yield thee all de-
lights
Naked as to her bed; I took her oath
Thou shouldst enjoy her. Tell me, gentle
boy,
Is she not parallelless? Is not her breath
Sweet as Arabian winds when fruits are
ripe?
Are not her breasts two liquid ivory
balls?
Is she not all a lasting mine of joy?

Bel. Ay, now I see why my disturbéd
thoughts
Were so perplexed. When first I went to
her,   209
My heart held augury. You are abused;
Some villain has abused you. I do
see
Whereto you tend. Fall rocks upon his
head
That put this to you! 'Tis some subtile
train
To bring that noble frame of yours to
naught.

Phi. Thou think'st I will be angry with
thee. Come,
Thou shalt know all my drift. I hate her
more

Than I love happiness, and placed thee
there
To pry with narrow eyes into her deeds.
Hast thou discovered? Is she fall'n to
lust,
As I would wish her? Speak some comfort to me.   220

Bel. My lord, you did mistake the boy
you sent.
Had she the lust of sparrows or of goats,
Had she a sin that way, hid from the
world,
Beyond the name of lust, I would not aid
Her base desires; but what I came to
know
As servant to her, I would not reveal
To make my life last ages.

Phi. [Aside.]   O, my heart!
This is a salve worse than the main
disease.—
Tell me thy thoughts, for I will know the
least
That dwells within thee, or will rip thy
heart   230
To know it. I will see thy thoughts as
plain
As I do now thy face.

Bel.   Why, so you do.
She is (for aught I know), by all the
gods,
As chaste as ice! But, were she foul as
hell,
And I did know it thus, the breath of
kings,
The points of swords, tortures, nor bulls
of brass [1]
Should draw it from me.

Phi.   Then 'tis no time
To dally with thee; I will take thy life,
For I do hate thee. I could curse thee
now'

Bel. If you do hate, you could not curse
me worse;   240
The gods have not a punishment in store
Greater for me than is your hate.

Phi.   Fie, fie,
So young and so dissembling! Tell me
when
And where thou didst enjoy her, or let
plagues
Fall on me, if I destroy thee not!
                   [Draws his sword.]

[1] An instrument of torture causing death by
roasting.

BEL. By heaven, I never did; and, when I
 lie
 To save my life, may I live long and
  loathed!
 Hew me asunder, and, whilst I can think,
 I'll love those pieces you have cut away
 Better than those that grow, and kiss
  those limbs   250
 Because you made um so.
PHI.   Fear'st thou not death?
 Can boys contemn that?
BEL.   O, what boy is he
 Can be content to live to be a man,
 That sees the best of men thus passion-
  ate,
 Thus without reason?
PHI.   O, but thou dost not know
 What 'tis to die.
BEL.   Yes, I do know, my lord.
 'Tis less than to be born, a lasting sleep,
 A quiet resting from all jealousy,
 A thing we all pursue. I know, besides,
 It is but giving over of a game   260
 That must be lost.
PHI.   But there are pains, false boy,
 For perjured souls. Think but on those,
  and then
 Thy heart will melt, and thou wilt utter
  all.
BEL. May they fall all upon me whilst I
 live,
 If I be perjured, or have ever thought
 Of that you charge me with! If I be false,
 Send me to suffer in those punishments
 You speak of; kill me!
PHI.   O, what should I do?
 Why, who can but believe him? He
  does swear
 So earnestly that, if it were not true,   270
 The gods would not endure him. Rise,
  Bellario;
 Thy protestations are so deep, and thou
 Dost look so truly when thou utter'st
  them
 That, though I know um false as were
  my hopes,
 I cannot urge thee further. But thou wert
 To blame to injure me, for I must love
 Thy honest looks, and take no revenge
  upon
 Thy tender youth. A love from me to
  thee
 Is firm, whate'er thou doest; it troubles
 me

That I have called the blood out of thy
 cheeks,   280
That did so well become thee. But, good
 boy,
Let me not see thee more; something is
 done
That will distract me, that will make me
 mad,
If I behold thee. If thou tender'st [1] me,
Let me not see thee.
BEL.   I will fly as far
 As there is morning, ere I give distaste
 To that most honored mind. But,
  through these tears
 Shed at my hopeless parting, I can see
 A world of treason practiced upon you,
 And her, and me. Farewell forevermore!
 If you shall hear that sorrow struck me
  dead,   291
 And after find me loyal, let there be
 A tear shed from you in my memory,
 And I shall rest at peace.
          Exit Bell[ario].
PHI.   Blessing be with thee,
 Whatever thou deserv'st! O, where
  shall I
 Go bathe this body? Nature too unkind,
 That made no medicine for a troubled
  mind!   *Ex[it] Phi[laster].*

[SCENA ii.

Arethusa's chambers in the palace.]

Enter Arethusa.

ARE. I marvel my boy comes not back
  again;
 But that I know my love will question
  him
 Over and over—how I slept, waked,
  talked,
 How I remembered him when his dear
  name
 Was last spoke, and how, when I sighed,
  wept, sung,
 And ten thousand such—I should be
  angry at his stay.

Enter King.

KING. What, at your meditations? Who
 attends you?
ARE. None but my single self. I need no
  guard;
 I do no wrong, nor fear none.

[1] Regardest.

King. Tell me, have you not a boy?
Are.   Yes, sir.   10
King. What kind of boy?
Are.   A page, a waiting-boy.
King. A handsome boy?
Are.   I think he be not ugly;
Well qualified and dutiful I know him;
I took him not for beauty.
King. He speaks and sings and plays?
Are.   Yes, sir.
King. About eighteen?
Are.   I never asked his age.
King. Is he full of service?
Are. By your pardon, why do you ask?
King. Put him away.
Are.   Sir?
King.   Put him away, I say.
H'as done you that good service shames
    me to speak of.   20
Are. Good sir, let me understand you.
King.   If you fear me,
Show it in duty; put away that boy.
Are. Let me have reason for it, sir, and
    then
Your will is my command.
King. Do not you blush to ask it? Cast
    him off,
Or I shall do the same to you. Y' are one
Shame with me, and so near unto my-
    self
That, by my life, I dare not tell myself
What you, myself, have done.
Are. What I have done, my lord?   30
King. 'Tis a new language, that all love
    to learn;
The common people speak it well al-
    ready;
They need no grammar. Understand
    me well;
There be foul whispers stirring. Cast
    him off,
And suddenly. Do it! Farewell.
                                    Exit King.
Are. Where may a maiden live securely
    free,
Keeping her honor fair? Not with the
    living.
They feed upon opinions, errors, dreams,
And make um truths; they draw a
    nourishment   39
Out of defamings, grow upon disgraces,
And, when they see a virtue fortified
Strongly above the battery of their
    tongues,

O, how they cast [1] to sink it, and, de-
    feated
(Soul-sick with poison), strike the mon-
    uments
Where noble names lie sleeping, till
    they sweat,
And the cold marble melt.

Enter Philaster.

Phi. Peace to your fairest thoughts, dear-
    est mistress!
Are. O, my dearest servant, I have a war
    within me!
Phi. He must be more than man that
    makes these crystals
Run into rivers. Sweetest fair, the
    cause?   50
And, as I am your slave, tied to your
    goodness,
Your creature, made again from what
    I was
And newly-spirited, I'll right your honor.
Are. O, my best love, that boy!
Phi.   What boy?
Are. The pretty boy you gave me—
Phi.   What of him?
Are. Must be no more mine.
Phi. Why?
Are.   They are jealous of him.
Phi. Jealous! Who?
Are.   The king.
Phi. [*Aside.*]   O, my misfortune!
Then 'tis no idle jealousy.—Let him go.
Are. O, cruel!
Are you hard-hearted too? Who shall
    now tell you   60
How much I loved you? Who shall
    swear it to you,
And weep the tears I send? Who shall
    now bring you
Letters, rings, bracelets? Lose his health
    in service?
Wake tedious nights in stories of your
    praise?
Who shall sing your crying elegies,
And strike a sad soul into senseless
    pictures,
And make them mourn? Who shall
    take up his lute,
And touch it till he crown a silent sleep
Upon my eyelids, making me dream,
    and cry,
"O, my dear, dear Philaster!"

[1] Plan.

PHI. [*Aside.*] O, my heart! 70
Would he had broken thee, that made
  thee know
This lady was not loyal!—Mistress,
Forget the boy; I'll get thee a far better.
ARE. O, never, never such a boy again
As my Bellario!
PHI. 'Tis but your fond affection.
ARE. With thee, my boy, farewell forever
All secrecy in servants! Farewell, faith,
And all desire to do well for itself!
Let all that shall succeed thee for thy
  wrongs
Sell and betray chaste love! 80
PHI. And all this passion for a boy?
ARE. He was your boy, and you put him
  to me,
And the loss of such must have a mourn-
  ing for.
PHI. O, thou forgetful woman!
ARE. How, my lord?
PHI. False Arethusa!
Hast thou a medicine to restore my wits,
When I have lost um? If not, leave to
  talk
And do thus.
ARE. Do what, sir? Would you sleep?
PHI. Forever, Arethusa. O, you gods,
Give me a worthy patience! Have I
  stood, 90
Naked, alone, the shock of many for-
  tunes?
Have I seen mischiefs numberless and
  mighty
Grow like a sea upon me? Have I taken
Danger as stern as death into my
  bosom,
And laughed upon it, made it but a
  mirth,
And flung it by? Do I live now like him,
Under this tyrant king, that languish-
  ing
Hears his sad bell and sees his mourners?
  Do I
Bear all this bravely, and must sink
  at length
Under a woman's falsehood? O, that
  boy, 100
That cursed boy! None but a villain
  boy
To ease your lust?
ARE. Nay, then, I am betrayed.
I feel the plot cast for my overthrow.
O, I am wretched!

PHI. Now you may take that little right
  I have
To this poor kingdom. Give it to your
  joy,
For I have no joy in it. Some far place,
Where never womankind durst set her
  foot
For [1] bursting with her poisons, must
  I seek,
And live to curse you. 110
There dig a cave, and preach to birds
  and beasts
What woman is, and help to save them
  from you:
How heaven is in your eyes, but in
  your hearts
More hell than hell has; how your
  tongues, like scorpions,
Both heal and poison; how your thoughts
  are woven
With thousand changes in one subtle
  web,
And worn so by you; how that foolish
  man,
That reads the story of a woman's face
And dies believing it, is lost forever;
How all the good you have is but a
  shadow, 120
I' th' morning with you, and at night
  behind you,
Past and forgotten; how your vows are
  frosts,
Fast for a night, and with the next sun
  gone;
How you are, being taken all together,
A mere confusion, and so dead a chaos
That love cannot distinguish. These
  sad texts,
Till my last hour, I am bound to utter
  of you.
So, farewell all my woe, all my delight!
  Exit Phi[laster].
ARE. Be merciful, ye gods, and strike me
  dead!
What way have I deserved this? Make
  my breast 130
Transparent as pure crystal, that the
  world,
Jealous of me, may see the foulest
  thought
My heart holds. Where shall a woman
  turn her eyes
To find out constancy?

[1] For fear of.

Enter Bell[ario].

                 Save me, how black
And guiltily, methinks, that boy looks
   now!—
O, thou dissembler, that, before thou
   spak'st,
Wert in thy cradle false, sent to make
   lies
And betray innocents! Thy lord and
   thou
May glory in the ashes of a maid
Fooled by her passion; but the con-
   quest is   140
Nothing so great as wicked. Fly away!
Let my command force thee to that
   which shame
Would do without it. If thou under-
   stood'st
The loathéd office thou hast undergone,
Why, thou wouldst hide thee under heaps
   of hills,
Lest men should dig and find thee.
Bᴇʟ.   O, what god,
   Angry with men, hath sent this strange
     disease
Into the noblest minds? Madam, this
   grief
You add unto me is no more than drops
To seas, for which they are not seen to
   swell.   150
My lord hath struck his anger through
   my heart,
And let out all the hope of future joys.
You need not bid me fly; I came to part,
To take my latest leave. Farewell for-
   ever!
I durst not run away in honesty
From such a lady, like a boy that stole
Or made some grievous fault. The power
   of gods
Assist you in your sufferings! Hasty
   time
Reveal the truth to your abuséd lord
And mine, that he may know your worth,
   whilst I   160
Go seek out some forgotten place to
   die!   *Exit Bell[ario].*
Aʀᴇ. Peace guide thee! Th'ast over-
   thrown me once;
Yet, if I had another Troy to lose,
Thou, or another villain with thy looks,
Might talk me out of it, and send me
   naked,

My hair disheveled, through the fiery
   streets.

Enter a Lady.

Lᴀ. Madam, the king would hunt, and
   calls for you
With earnestness.
Aʀᴇ.   I am in tune to hunt!
Diana, if thou canst rage with a maid
As with a man,[1] let me discover thee   170
Bathing, and turn me to a fearful hind,
That I may die pursued by cruel hounds,
And have my story written in my
   wounds!   *Exeunt.*

Aᴄᴛᴜs IV. Sᴄᴇɴᴀ i.

[Outside the palace.]

*Enter King, Pharamond, Arethusa, Gala-
   tea, Megra, Dion, Cleremont, Thrasiline, and Attendants.*

Kɪɴɢ. What, are the hounds before and
   all the woodmen?
Our horses ready and our bows bent?
Dɪ.   All, sir.
Kɪɴɢ. [*To Pharamond.*] Y' are cloudy,
   sir. Come, we have forgotten
Your venial trespass; let not that sit
   heavy
Upon your spirit; here's none dare utter it.
Dɪ. [*Aside.*] He looks like an old surfeited stallion after his leaping, dull as a
dormouse. See how he sinks! The wench
has shot him between wind and water,
and, I hope, sprung a leak.   10
Tʜʀᴀ. [*Aside.*] He needs no teaching;
he strikes sure enough. His greatest fault
is, he hunts too much in the purlieus;
would he would leave off poaching!
Dɪ. [*Aside.*] And, for his horn, h'as left
it at the lodge where he lay late. O, he's
a precious limehound![2] Turn him loose
upon the pursue[3] of a lady, and, if he lose
her, hang him up i' th' slip.[4] When my
fox bitch, Beauty, grows proud,[5] I'll   [20
borrow him.
Kɪɴɢ. Is your boy turned away?

[1] *I.e.,* Actaeon.
[2] A hunting dog led by a lime, or leash.
[3] Pursuit.
[4] Noose by which hounds are held.
[5] Sexually excited.

ARE. You did command, sir, and I obeyed you.

KING. 'Tis well done. Hark ye further. [*All except Cleremont, Dion, and Thrasiline retire. The King and Arethusa talk apart.*]

CLE. Is 't possible this fellow should repent? Methinks that were not noble in him; and yet he looks like a mortified member, as if he had a sick man's salve [1] in 's mouth. If a worse man had done [30 this fault now, some physical justice [2] or other would presently (without the help of an almanac [3]) have opened the obstructions of his liver, and let him blood with a dog whip.

DI. See, see how modestly yon lady looks, as if she came from churching with her neighbors! Why, what a devil can a man see in her face but that she's honest?

THRA. Faith, no great matter to [40 speak of—a foolish twinkling with the eye, that spoils her coat; [4] but he must be a cunning herald that finds it.

DI. See how they muster [5] one another! O, there's a rank regiment where the devil carries the colors, and his dam drum major! Now the world and the flesh come behind with the carriage. [6]

CLE. Sure this lady has a good turn done her against her will; before, she [50 was common talk; now none dare say cantharides [7] can stir her. Her face looks like a warrant, willing and commanding all tongues, as they will answer it, to be tied up and bolted when this lady means to let herself loose. As I live, she has got her a goodly protection and a gracious, and may use her body discreetly for her health' sake, once a week, excepting Lent and dog days. O, if they were to be [60 got for money, what a large sum would come out of the city for these licenses!

KING. To horse, to horse! We lose the morning, gentlemen. *Exeunt.*

---

[1] An allusion to such religious pamphlets as Thomas Becon's *The Sick Man's Salve* (1561) and William Perkins' *Salve for a Sick Man* (1595).

[2] *I.e.*, a justice acting as a physician.

[3] Almanacs gave directions for bloodletting.

[4] "The allusion is to mullets, or stars, introduced into coats of arms to distinguish the younger branches of a family, which of course denote inferiority" (Mason).

[5] Set off.　　　[6] Baggage.　　　[7] A provocative.

[SCENA ii.

A forest.]

Enter two Woodmen.

1 WOOD. What, have you lodged [8] the deer?

2 WOOD. Yes, they are ready for the bow.

1 WOOD. Who shoots?

2 WOOD. The princess.

1 WOOD. No, she'll hunt.

2 WOOD. She'll take a stand, I say.

1 WOOD. Who else?

2 WOOD. Why, the young stranger [10 prince.

1 WOOD. He shall shoot in a stone-bow [9] for me. [10] I never loved his beyond-sea-ship since he forsook the say, for paying ten shillings. [11] Hew as there at the fall of a deer, and would needs (out of his mightiness) give ten groats for the dowcets; [12] marry, the steward would have the velvethead, [13] into the bargain, to turf [14] his hat withal. I think he should love venery; [20 he is an old Sir Tristram; [15] for, if you be remembered, he forsook the stag once to strike a rascal milking [16] in a meadow, and her he killed in the eye. Who shoots else?

2 WOOD. The Lady Galatea.

1 WOOD. That's a good wench, and [17] she would not chide us for tumbling of her women in the brakes. She's liberal, and, by the gods, they say she's honest, and whether that be a fault, I have nothing [30 to do. There's all?

2 WOOD. No, one more—Megra.

1 WOOD. That's a firker, [18] i' faith, boy. There's a wench will ride her haunches as hard after a kennel of hounds as a hunting saddle, and, when she comes home, get um clapped, [19] and all is well again. I have known her lose herself three times in one afternoon (if the woods have been answerable [20]), and it has been work enough [40 for one man to find her, and he has sweat

---

[8] Entrapped.

[9] With a crossbow for shooting stones.

[10] For all I care.

[11] Refused the assay, or slitting of the deer, to avoid paying the customary keeper's fee.

[12] Doucets.

[13] The down-covered horns of a young deer.

[14] Re-cover.　　　　　[17] If.　　[18] A lively one.

[15] An expert huntsman.　　　　[19] Rubbed.

[16] A lean doe feeding.　　　[20] Suitable.

for it. She rides well and she pays well.
Hark! Let's go.   *Exeunt.*

Enter Philaster.

PHI. O, that I had been nourished in these
        woods
   With milk of goats and acorns, and not
        known
   The right of crowns nor the dissembling
        trains
   Of women's looks, but digged myself a
        cave
   Where I, my fire, my cattle, and my
        bed
   Might have been shut together in one
        shed,
   And then had taken me some mountain
        girl,   50
   Beaten with winds, chaste as the hard-
        ened rocks
   Whereon she dwells, that might have
        strewed my bed
   With leaves and reeds, and with the skins
        of beasts,
   Our neighbors, and have borne at her big
        breasts
   My large, coarse issue! This had been a
        life
   Free from vexation.

Enter Bellario.

BEL. [*To himself.*]   O, wicked men!
   An innocent may walk safe among
        beasts;
   Nothing assaults me here. See, my
        grieved lord
   Sits as his soul were searching out a way
   To leave his body!—Pardon me, that
        must   60
   Break thy last commandment, for I
        must speak.
   You that are grieved can pity; hear,
        my lord!
PHI. Is there a creature yet so miserable
   That I can pity?
BEL.   O, my noble lord,
   View my strange fortune, and bestow
        on me,
   According to your bounty (if my service
   Can merit nothing), so much as may
        serve
   To keep that little piece I hold of life
   From cold and hunger!

PHI.   Is it thou? Begone!
   Go, sell those misbeseeming clothes thou
        wear'st,   70
   And feed thyself with them.
BEL. Alas, my lord, I can get nothing for
        them!
   The silly country people think 'tis trea-
        son
   To touch such gay things.
PHI.   Now, by the gods, this is
   Unkindly done, to vex me with thy
        sight.
   Th' art fall'n again to thy dissembling
        trade.
   How shouldst thou think to cozen me
        again?
   Remains there yet a plague untried for
        me?
   Even so thou wep[t]'st, and look[ed]'st,
        and spok'st when first   79
   I took thee up. Curse on the time! If thy
   Commanding tears can work on any
        other,
   Use thy art; I'll not betray it. Which
        way
   Wilt thou take, that I may shun thee,
   For thine eyes are poison to mine, and I
   Am loath to grow in rage? This way, or
        that way?
BEL. Any will serve; but I will choose to
        have
   That path in chase that leads unto my
        grave.
   Exit Phi[laster, with] Bel[lario], severally.

Enter Dion and the Woodmen.

DI. This is the strangest sudden chance!
   —You, woodmen!
1 WOOD. My lord Dion?
DI. Saw you a lady come this way   [90
on a sable horse studded with stars of
white?
2 WOOD. Was she not young and tall?
DI. Yes. Rode she to the wood or to the
        plain?
2 WOOD. Faith, my lord, we saw none.
                        Exeunt [1] *Woodmen.*
DI. Pox of your questions then!—

Enter Cleremont.

                   What, is she found?
CLE. Nor will be, I think.
[1] Original reads *Exit.*

Di. Let him seek his daughter himself. She cannot stray about a little necessary natural business, but the whole court [100 must be in arms. When she has done, we shall have peace.

Cle. There's already a thousand fatherless tales amongst us. Some say her horse ran away with her; some, a wolf pursued her; others, 'twas a plot to kill her, and that armed men were seen in the wood; but questionless she rode away willingly.

Enter King and Thrasiline.

King. Where is she?

Cle. Sir, I cannot tell.

King. How's that? Answer me so again!

Cle. Sir, shall I lie? 110

King. Yes, lie and damn, rather than tell me that.

I say again, where is she? Mutter not!—Sir, speak you; where is she?

Di. Sir, I do not know.

King. Speak that again so boldly, and, by heaven,

It is thy last!—You, fellows, answer me; Where is she? Mark me, all; I am your king.

I wish to see my daughter; show her me.

I do command you all, as you are subjects,

To show her me! What! Am I not your king?

If ay, then am I not to be obeyed? 120

Di. Yes, if you command things possible and honest.

King. Things possible and honest! Hear me, thou,

Thou traitor, that dar'st confine thy king to things

Possible and honest! Show her me,

Or, let me perish, if I cover not

All Sicily with blood!

Di. Faith, I cannot,

Unless you tell me where she is.

King. You have betrayed me; y' have let me lose

The jewel of my life. Go, bring her me, 129

And set her here before me. 'Tis the king

Will have it so, whose breath can still the winds,

Uncloud the sun, charm down the swelling sea,

And stop the floods of heaven. Speak, can it not?

Di. No.

King. No? Cannot the breath of kings do this?

Di. No; nor smell sweet itself, if once the lungs

Be but corrupted.

King. Is it so? Take heed!

Di. Sir, take you heed how you dare the powers

That must be just.

King. Alas! What are we kings?

Why do you gods place us above the rest,

To be served, flattered, and adored, till we 140

Believe we hold within our hands your thunder?

And, when we come to try the power we have,

There's not a leaf shakes at our threat'-nings.

I have sinned, 'tis true, and here stand to be punished;

Yet would not thus be punished. Let me choose

My way, and lay it on!

Di. [*Aside.*] He articles [1] with the gods. Would somebody would draw bonds for the performance of covenants betwixt them! 150

Enter Pha[ramond], Galatea, and Megra.

King. What, is she found?

Pha. No; we have ta'en her horse;

He galloped empty by. There's some treason.

You, Galatea, rode with her into the wood.

Why left you her?

Gal. She did command me.

King. Command! You should not.

Gal. 'Twould ill become my fortunes and my birth

To disobey the daughter of my king.

King. Y' are all cunning to obey us for our hurt;

But I will have her.

Pha. If I have her not, 160

By this hand, there shall be no more Sicily.

---

[1] Bargains.

Dɪ. [*Aside.*]   What, will he carry it to
 Spain in 's pocket?

Pʜᴀ. I will not leave one man alive but
 the king,
 A cook, and a tailor.

Dɪ. [*Aside.*] Yes; you may do well to
spare your lady-bedfellow; and her you may
keep for a spawner.

Kɪɴɢ. [*Aside.*] I see the injuries I have
 done must be revenged.

Dɪ. Sir, this is not the way to find her
 out.

Kɪɴɢ. Run all; disperse yourselves. The
 man that finds her,   170
 Or (if she be killed) the traitor, I'll make
 him great.

Dɪ. I know some would give five thousand
 pounds to find her.

Pʜᴀ. Come, let us seek.

Kɪɴɢ. Each man a several way; here I myself.

Dɪ. Come, gentlemen, we here.

Cʟᴇ. Lady, you must go search too.

Mᴇɢ. I had rather be searched myself.

                     Exeunt [1] *omnes.*

[Sᴄᴇɴᴀ iii.

Another part of the forest.]

Enter Arethusa.

Aʀᴇ. Where am I now?   Feet, find me out
 a way,
 Without the counsel of my troubled head.
 I'll follow you boldly about these woods,
 O'er mountains, through brambles, pits,
 and floods.
 Heaven, I hope, will ease me.   I am sick.
                     [*She sits down.*] [2]

Enter Bellario.

Bᴇʟ. [*Aside.*] Yonder's my lady.   God
 knows I want nothing,
 Because I do not wish to live; yet I
 Will try her charity.—O, hear, you that
 have plenty!
 From that flowing store drop some on
 dry ground.—See,   9
 The lively red is gone to guard her heart!
 I fear she faints.—Madam, look up!—
 She breathes not.—
 Open once more those rosy twins, and
 send

[1] Original reads *Exit.*   [2] From 1620 edn.

Unto my lord your latest farewell!—O,
 she stirs.—
 How is it, madam?   Speak comfort.

Aʀᴇ. 'Tis not gently done,
 To put me in a miserable life,
 And hold me there.   I prithee, let me
 go.
 I shall do best without thee; I am well.

Enter Philaster.

Pʜɪ. [*Aside.*] I am to blame to be so
 much in rage.
 I'll tell her coolly when and where I
 heard   20
 This killing truth.   I will be temperate
 In speaking, and as just in hearing.—
 O, monstrous!   Tempt me not, you gods!
 Good gods,
 Tempt not a frail man!   What's he that
 has a heart
 But he must ease it here!

Bᴇʟ. My lord, help, help!   The princess!

Aʀᴇ. I am well; forbear.

Pʜɪ. [*Aside.*] Let me love lightning; let me
 be embraced
 And kissed by scorpions, or adore the
 eyes   29
 Of basilisks, rather than trust the tongues
 Of hell-bred woman!   Some good god
 look down,
 And shrink these veins up!   Stick me
 here a stone,
 Lasting to ages in the memory
 Of this damned act!—Hear me, you
 wicked ones!
 You have put hills of fire into this
 breast,
 Not to be quenched with tears, for which
 may guilt
 Sit on your bosoms!   At your meals and
 beds
 Despair await you!   What, before my
 face?
 Poison of asps between your lips!   Dis-
 eases
 Be your best issues!   Nature make a
 curse,   40
 And throw it on you!

Aʀᴇ.   Dear Philaster, leave
 To be enraged, and hear me.

Pʜɪ.   I have done;
 Forgive my passion.   Not the calméd
 sea,
 When Aeolus locks up his windy brood,

Is less disturbed than I. I'll make you
  know 't.
Dear Arethusa, do but take this sword,
            [*Offers his drawn sword.*] [1]
And search how temperate a heart I
  have;
Then you and this your boy may live and
  reign
In lust without control.—Wilt thou,
  Bellario?
I prithee, kill me; thou art poor, and
  mayst   50
Nourish ambitious thoughts; when I am
  dead,
This way were freer. Am I raging now?
If I were mad, I should desire to live.
Sirs,[2] feel my pulse, whether you have
  known
A man in a more equal tune to die.
BEL. Alas, my lord, your pulse keeps mad-
  man's time!
So does your tongue.
PHI.   You will not kill me, then?
ARE. Kill you?
BEL.   Not for the world.
PHI.   I blame not thee,
Bellario; thou has done but that which
  gods
Would have transformed themselves to
  do. Begone;   60
Leave me without reply. This is the
  last
Of all our meeting.—(*Exit Bell*[*ario*].)
Kill me with this sword.
Be wise, or worse will follow; we are two
Earth cannot bear at once. Resolve to
  do,
Or suffer.
ARE. If my fortune be so good to let me
  fall
Upon [3] thy hand, I shall have peace in
  death.
Yet tell me this: will there be no slan-
  ders,
No jealousy in the other world, no ill
  there?
PHI. No.   70
ARE. Show me then the way.
PHI. Then guide my feeble hand,
  You that have power to do it, for I must
Perform a piece of justice!—If your
  youth

[1] From 1620 edn.   [3] At.
[2] Formerly applied to both sexes.

Have any way offended heaven, let
  prayers
Short and effectual reconcile you to it.
ARE. I am prepared.

        Enter a Country Fellow.

COUN. [*Aside.*] I'll see the king, if he be
in the forest; I have hunted him these two
hours. If I should come home and not [80
see him, my sisters would laugh at me. I
can see nothing but people better horsed
than myself, that outride me; I can hear
nothing but shouting. These kings had
need of good brains; this whooping is able
to put a mean man out of his wits.—
There's a courtier with his sword drawn;
by this hand, upon a woman, I think!
PHI. Are you at peace?
ARE.   With heaven and earth. 89
PHI. May they divide thy soul and body!
                 [*Wounds her.*]
COUN. Hold, dastard! Strike a woman!
Th' art a craven. I warrant thee, thou
wouldst be loath to play half a dozen venies
at wasters [4] with a good fellow for a
broken head.
PHI. Leave us, good friend.
ARE. What ill-bred man art thou, to in-
  trude thyself
Upon our private sports, our recreations?
COUN. God 'uds [5] me, I understand you
not; but I know the rogue has hurt you.
PHI. Pursue thy own affairs. It will be ill
  To multiply blood upon my head, which
    thou   102
Wilt force me to.
COUN. I know not your rhetoric; but I
can lay it on, if you touch the woman.
                They fight.
PHI. Slave, take what thou deservest!
ARE.   Heavens guard my lord!
COUN. O, do you breathe?
PHI. I hear the tread of people. I am hurt.
  The gods take part against me. Could
    this boor
Have held me thus else? I must shift
    for life,   110
Though I do loathe it. I would find a
    course
To lose it rather by my will than force.
               Exit Philaster.
COUN. I cannot follow the rogue. I
pray thee, wench, come and kiss me now.

[4] Bouts at cudgels.   [5] God judge.

*Enter Phara[mond], Dion, Cle[remont], Thra-
si[line], and Woodmen.*

PHA. What art thou?

COUN. Almost killed I am for a foolish
woman; a knave has hurt her.

PHA. The princess, gentlemen! —Where's
the wound, madam? Is it dangerous?

ARE. He has not hurt me. 120

COUN. By God, she lies; h'as hurt her in
the breast; look else.

PHA. O sacred spring of innocent blood!

DI. 'Tis above wonder! Who should
dare this?

ARE. I felt it not.

PHA. Speak, villain, who has hurt the
princess?

COUN. Is it the princess?

DI. Ay. 130

COUN. Then I have seen something yet.

PHA. But who has hurt her?

COUN. I told you, a rogue; I ne'er saw
him before, I.

PHA. Madam, who did it?

ARE. Some dishonest wretch;
Alas, I know him not, and do forgive him!

COUN. He's hurt too; he cannot go far;
I made my father's old fox [1] fly about his
ears.

PHA. How will you have me kill [140
him?

ARE. Not at all; 'tis some distracted fellow.

PHA. By this hand, I'll leave ne'er a
piece of him bigger than a nut, and bring
him all to you in my hat.

ARE. Nay, good sir,
If you do take him, bring him quick [2] to
me,
And I will study for a punishment
Great as his fault. 149

PHA. I will.

ARE. But swear.

PHA. By all my love, I will.—
Woodmen, conduct the princess to the
king,
And bear that wounded fellow to dressing.—
Come, gentlemen, we'll follow the chase
close.

*Exeunt [3] Are[thusa], Pha[ramond], Di[on],
Cle[remont], Thra[siline], and 1 Woodman.*

---

[1] Broad sword.   [3] Original reads *Exit.*
[2] Alive.

COUN. I pray you, friend, let me see the
king.

2 WOOD. That you shall, and receive
thanks.

COUN. If I get clear with this, I'll go to
see no more gay sights.   *Exeunt.* [4]

[SCENA iv.

Another part of the forest.]

Enter Bellario.

BEL. A heaviness near death sits on my
brow,
And I must sleep. Bear me, thou gentle
bank,
Forever, if thou wilt. You sweet ones
all,   [*Lies down.*]
Let me unworthy press you; I could wish
I rather were a corse strewed o'er with
you
Than quick above you. Dullness shuts
mine eyes,
And I am giddy. O, that I could take
So sound a sleep that I might never
wake!   [*Sleeps.*]

Enter Philaster.

PHI. I have done ill; my conscience calls
me false
To strike at her that would not strike at
me.   10
When I did fight, methought I heard her
pray
The gods to guard me. She may be
abused,
And I a loathéd villain; if she be,
She will conceal who hurt her. He has
wounds
And cannot follow; neither knows he me.
Who's this? Bellario sleeping? If thou
beest
Guilty, there is no justice that thy
sleep   *Cry within.*
Should be so sound, and mine, whom
thou hast wronged,
So broken. Hark! I am pursued. You
gods,
I'll take this offered means of my
escape.   20
They have no mark to know me but my
wounds,

---

[4] In original, stage direction appears at end of
preceding speech.

If she be true; if false, let mischief light
On all the world at once! Sword, print
    my wounds
Upon this sleeping boy! I ha' none, I
    think,
Are mortal, nor would I lay greater on
    thee.   *Wounds him.*
Bel. O, death, I hope, is come!   Blessed
    be that hand!
It meant me well. Again, for pity's sake!
Phi. I have caught myself;
                        Phi[laster] falls.
The loss of blood hath stayed my flight.
    Here, here
Is he that stroke [1] thee. Take thy full
    revenge;   30
Use me, as I did mean thee, worse than
    death;
I'll teach thee to revenge. This luckless
    hand
Wounded the princess; tell my followers [2]
Thou didst receive these hurts in staying
    me,
And I will second thee. Get a reward.
Bel. Fly, fly, my lord, and save yourself!
Phi.   How's this?
Wouldst thou I should be safe?
Bel.   Else were it vain
For me to live. These little wounds I
    have
Ha' not bled much. Reach me that noble
    hand;
I'll help to cover you.
Phi.   Art thou true to me?   40
Bel. Or let me perish loathed! Come,
    my good lord,
Creep in among those bushes. Who does
    know
But that the gods may save your much-
    loved breath?
Phi. Then I shall die for grief, if not for
    this,
That I have wounded thee. What wilt
    thou do?
Bel. Shift for myself well. Peace! I hear
    um come. [*Philaster conceals himself.*]
[Voices.] (*Within.*) Follow, follow, follow!
    That way they went.
Bel. With my own wounds I'll bloody
    my own sword.
I need not counterfeit to fall; heaven
    knows
That I can stand no longer. [*Falls.*]   50

[1] Struck.   [2] Pursuers.

Enter Pharamond, Dion, Cleremont, Thrasi-
                                    line.

Pha. To this place we have tracked him
    by his blood.
Cle. Yonder, my lord, creeps one away.
Di. Stay, sir! What are you?
Bel. A wretched creature, wounded in
    these woods
By beasts. Relieve me, if your names
    be men,
Or I shall perish.
Di.   This is he, my lord,
Upon my soul, that hurt her. 'Tis the
    boy,
That wicked boy that served her.
Pha.   O, thou damned
In thy creation! What cause couldst
    thou shape
To hurt the princess?
Bel.   Then I am betrayed.   60
Di. Betrayed!   No, apprehended.
Bel.   I confess
(Urge it no more) that, big with evil
    thoughts,
I set upon her, and did make my aim
Her death. For charity, let fall at once
The punishment you mean, and do not
    load
This weary flesh with tortures.
Pha.   I will know
Who hired thee to this deed.
Bel.   Mine own revenge.
Pha. Revenge! For what?
Bel.   It pleased her to receive
Me as her page and, when my fortunes
    ebbed,
That men strid [3] o'er them careless, she
    did shower   70
Her welcome graces on me, and did swell
My fortunes till they overflowed their
    banks,
Threat'ning the men that crossed um,
    when, as swift
As storms arise at sea, she turned her
    eyes
To burning suns upon me, and did dry
The streams she had bestowed, leaving
    me worse
And more contemned than other little
    brooks,
Because I had been great. In short, I
    knew

[3] Strode.

I could not live, and therefore did desire
To die revenged.

PHA.   If tortures can be found 80
Long as thy natural life, resolve to feel
The utmost rigor.

                Philaster creeps out of a bush.

CLE.   Help to lead him hence.

PHI. Turn back, you ravishers of inno-
cence!
Know ye the price of that you bear away
So rudely?

PHA.   Who's that?

DI.   'Tis the Lord Philaster.

PHI. 'Tis not the treasure of all kings in
one,
The wealth of Tagus, nor the rocks of
pearl
That pave the court of Neptune, can
weigh down
That virtue. It was I that hurt the prin-
cess.
Place me, some god, upon a pyramis [1] 90
Higher than hills of earth, and lend a
voice
Loud as your thunder to me, that from
thence
I may discourse to all the underworld
The worth that dwells in him!

PHA.   How's this?

BEL.   My lord, some man
Weary of life, that would be glad to die.

PHI. Leave these untimely courtesies,
Bellario.

BEL. Alas, he's mad! Come, will you lead
me on?

PHI. By all the oaths that men ought
most to keep,
And gods do punish most when men do
break,
He touched her not.—Take heed, Bel-
lario,   100
How thou dost drown the virtues thou
hast shown
With perjury.—By all that's good, 'twas
I!
You know she stood betwixt me and my
right.

PHA. Thy own tongue be thy judge!

CLE.   It was Philaster.

DI. Is 't not a brave boy?
Well, sirs, I fear me we were all deceived.

PHI. Have I no friend here?

DI.   Yes.

PHI.   Then show it. Some
Good body lend a hand to draw us
nearer.
Would you have tears shed for you when
you die?
Then lay me gently on his neck, that
there   110
I may weep floods and breathe forth my
spirit.
'Tis not the wealth of Plutus, nor the
gold   [*Embraces Bellario.*]
Locked in the heart of earth, can buy
away
This armful from me; this had been a
ransom
To have redeemed the great Augustus
Cæsar,
Had he been taken. You hard-hearted
men,
More stony than these mountains, can
you see
Such clear, pure blood drop, and not
cut your flesh
To stop his life, to bind whose bitter
wounds
Queens ought to tear their hair, and
with their tears   120
Bathe um?—Forgive me, thou that art
the wealth
Of poor Philaster!

Enter King, Arethusa, and a Guard.

KING.   Is the villain ta'en?

PHA. Sir, here be two confess the deed;
but say [2]
It was Philaster—

PHI.   Question it no more;
It was.

KING.   The fellow that did fight with him
Will tell us that.

ARE.   Ay me! I know he will.

KING. Did not you know him?

ARE.   Sir, if it was he,
He was disguised.

PHI.   I was so.—O, my stars,
That I should live still!

KING.   Thou ambitious fool,
Thou that hast laid a train for thy own
life!—   130
Now [3] I do mean to do, I'll leave to
talk.
Bear him to prison.

---

[1] Pyramid.

[2] Suppose.   [3] Now that.

ARE. Sir, they did plot together to take hence
This harmless life; should it pass unrevenged,
I should to earth go weeping. Grant me, then,
By all the love a father bears his child,
Their custodies, and that I may appoint
Their tortures and their deaths.

DI. Death? Soft; our law will not reach that for this fault.

KING. 'Tis granted; take um to you with a guard.— 140
Come, princely Pharamond, this business past,
We may with more security go on
To your intended match.

CLE. [*Aside.*] I pray that this action lose not Philaster the hearts of the people.

DI. [*Aside.*] Fear it not; their overwise heads will think it but a trick.

Exeunt omnes.[1]

ACTUS V. SCENA i.

[*Outside the palace.*]

Enter Dion, Cleremont, Thrasiline.

THRA. Has the king sent for him to death?

DI. Yes; but the king must know 'tis not in his power to war with heaven.

CLE. We linger time; the king sent for Philaster and the headsman an hour ago.

THRA. Are all his wounds well?

DI. All. They were but scratches, but the loss of blood made him faint.

CLE. We dally, gentlemen. 10

THRA. Away!

DI. We'll scuffle hard before he perish.

Exeunt.

[SCENA ii.

A room in a prison.]

Enter Philaster, Arethusa, Bellario.

ARE. Nay, faith, Philaster, grieve not; we are well.

BEL. Nay, good my lord, forbear; we're wondrous well.

PHI. O, Arethusa, O, Bellario,
Leave to be kind!

I shall be shut[2] from heaven, as now from earth,
If you continue so. I am a man
False to a pair of the most trusty ones
That ever earth bore; can it bear us all?
Forgive, and leave me. But the king hath sent
To call me to my death. O, show it me, 10
And then forget me! And for thee, my boy,
I shall deliver words will mollify
The hearts of beasts to spare thy innocence.

BEL. Alas, my lord, my life is not a thing
Worthy your noble thoughts! 'Tis not a life;
'Tis but a piece of childhood thrown away.
Should I outlive you, I should then outlive
Virtue and honor; and, when that day comes,
If ever I shall close these eyes but once,
May I live spotted for my perjury, 20
And waste my[3] limbs to nothing!

ARE. And I (the woeful'st maid that ever was,
Forced with my hands to bring my lord to death)
Do by the honor of a virgin swear
To tell no hours beyond it![4]

PHI. Make me not hated so.

ARE. Come from this prison all joyful to our deaths!

PHI. People will tear me, when they find you true
To such a wretch as I; I shall die loathed.
Enjoy your kingdoms peaceably, whilst I 29
Forever sleep forgotten with my faults.
Every just servant, every maid in love,
Will have a piece of me, if you be true.

ARE. My dear lord, say not so.

BEL. A piece of you?
He was not born of women that can cut
It and look on.

PHI. Take me in tears betwixt you, for my heart
Will break with shame and sorrow.

[1] In the original *Finis actus quarti* is inserted here.

[2] From 1620 edn. Original reads *shot*.

[3] From 1630 edn. Original reads *by*.

[4] *I.e.*, to die.

ARE.   Why, 'tis well.
BEL. Lament no more.
PHI.   What would you have done
  If you had wronged me basely, and had
    found
  Your [1] life no price compared to mine?[1]
  For love, sirs,   40
  Deal with me truly.
BEL.   'Twas mistaken, sir.
PHI. Why, if it were?
BEL.   Then, sir, we would have asked
  Your pardon.
PHI.   And have hope to enjoy it?
ARE. Enjoy it? Ay.
PHI.   Would you indeed? Be plain.
BEL. We would, my lord.
PHI.   Forgive me, then.
ARE.   So, so.
BEL. 'Tis as it should be now.
PHI.   Lead to my death. *Exeunt.*

[SCENA iii.

A state room in the palace.]

Enter King, Dion, Cleremont, Thrasiline.

KING. Gentlemen, who saw the prince?
CLE. So please you, sir, he's gone to see
    the city
  And the new platform, with some gentle-
    men
  Attending on him.
KING.   Is the princess ready
  To bring her prisoner out?
THRA.   She waits your grace.
KING. Tell her we stay.
              [*Exit Thrasiline.*] [2]
DI. [*Aside.*]   King, you may be de-
    ceived yet.
  The head you aim at cost more setting
    on
  Than to be lost so lightly. If it must off,
  Like a wild overflow, that soops [3] be-
    fore him
  A golden stack, and with it shakes down
    bridges,   10
  Cracks the strong hearts of pines, whose
    cable-roots
  Held out a thousand storms, a thousand
    thunders,
  And, so made mightier, takes whole
    villages

Upon his back, and in that heat of pride
Charges strong towns, towers, castles,
    palaces,
And lays them desolate, so shall thy
    head,
Thy noble head, bury the lives of thou-
    sands,
That must bleed with thee like a sacri-
    fice,
In thy red ruins.

*Enter Philaster, Arethusa, Bellario in a
    robe and garland [, and Thrasiline].*

KING.   How now? What masque is this?
BEL. Right royal sir, I should   20
  Sing you an epithalamion of these lovers,
  But having lost my best airs with my
    fortunes,
  And wanting a celestial harp to strike
  This blessed union on, thus in glad story
  I give you all. These two fair cedar
    branches,
  The noblest of the mountain where they
    grew,
  Straightest and tallest, under whose
    still shades
  The worthier beasts have made their
    lairs, and slept
  Free from [the fervor of] [4] the Sirian
    star
  And the fell thunderstroke, free from
    the clouds   30
  When they were big with humor,[5] and
    delivered
  In thousand spouts their issues to the
    earth
  (O, there was none but silent quiet
    there),
  Till never-pleaséd Fortune shot up
    shrubs,
  Base underbrambles, to divorce these
    branches;
  And for a while they did so, and did reign
  Over the mountain, and choke up his
    beauty
  With brakes, rude thorns, and thistles,
    till the sun
  Scorched them even to the roots and
    dried them there.   39
  And now a gentle gale hath blown again,
  That made these branches meet and
    twine together,
  Never to be divided. The god that sings

---

[1] Mason's emendation for *my . . . yours* of
all early edns.
[2] From 1620 edn.   [3] Sweeps.
[4] From 1620 edn.   [5] Moisture.

His holy numbers [1] over marriage beds
Hath knit their noble hearts; and here
  they stand,
Your children, mighty king; and I have
  done.

KING. How, how?

ARE.   Sir, if you love it in plain truth
(For now there is no masquing in 't),
  this gentleman,
The prisoner that you gave me, is be-
  come
My keeper, and through all the bitter
  throes
Your jealousies and his ill fate have
  wrought him,   50
Thus nobly hath he struggled, and at
  length
Arrived here my dear husband.

KING.   Your dear husband!—
Call in the Captain of the Citadel—
There you shall keep your wedding.
  I'll provide
A masque shall make your Hymen turn
  his saffron
Into a sullen coat, and sing sad requiems
To your departing souls.
Blood shall put out your torches; and,
  instead
Of gaudy flowers about your wanton
  necks,
An ax shall hang, like a prodigious
  meteor,   60
Ready to crop your loves' sweets. Hear,
  you gods!
From this time do I shake all title off
Of father to this woman, this base
  woman;
And what there is of vengeance in a
  lion
Chased among dogs or robbed of his
  dear young,
The same, enforced more terrible, more
  mighty,
Expect from me!

ARE. Sir, by that little life I have left to
  swear by,
There's nothing that can stir me from
  myself.
What I have done, I have done without
  repentance,   70
For death can be no bugbear unto me,
So long as Pharamond is not my headsman.

[1] Verses.

DI. [Aside.] Sweet peace upon thy soul,
  thou worthy maid,
Whene'er thou diest! For this time I'll
  excuse thee,
Or be thy prologue. [2]

PHI.   Sir, let me speak next,
And let my dying words be better with
  you
Than my dull, living actions. If you aim
At the dear life of this sweet innocent,
Y' are a tyrant and a savage monster.
Your memory shall be as foul behind
  you,   80
As you are living; all your better deeds
Shall be in water writ, but this in marble;
No chronicle shall speak you, though
  your own,
But for the shame of men. No monu-
  ment,
Though high and big as Pelion, shall be
  able
To cover this base murther, make it
  rich
With brass, with purest gold, and shin-
  ing jasper,
Like the pyramidës; lay on epitaphs
Such as make great men gods; my little
  marble,
That only clothes my ashes, not my
  faults,   90
Shall far outshine it. And for after-
  issues [3]
Think not so madly of the heavenly
  wisdoms
That they will give you more for your
  mad rage
To cut off, unless it be some snake, or
  something
Like yourself, that in his birth shall
  strangle you.
Remember my father, king! There was
  a fault,
But I forgive it. Let that sin persuade
  you
To love this lady; if you have a soul,
Think, save her, and be savéd. For my-
  self,   99
I have so long expected [4] this glad hour,
So languished under you, and daily
  withered,
That, by the gods, it is a joy to die;
I find a recreation in 't.

[2] I.e., precede thee in death.   [4] Awaited.
[3] Future offspring.

Enter a Messenger.

MESS. Where's the king?

KING.　　　Here.

MESS.　　　　Get you to your strength,
And rescue the Prince Pharamond from
　　danger.
He's taken prisoner by the citizens,
Fearing [1] the Lord Philaster.

DI. [*Aside.*]　　　O, brave followers!
Mutiny, my fine, dear countrymen,
　　mutiny!
Now, my brave, valiant foremen, show
　　your weapons
In honor of your mistresses!　　110

Enter another Messenger.

[2] MESS. Arm, arm, arm, arm!

KING. A thousand devils take um!

DI. [*Aside.*] A thousand blessings on um!

[2] MESS. Arm, O king! The city is in
　　mutiny,
Led by an old gray ruffian, who comes
　　on
In rescue of the Lord Philaster.

KING. Away to the citadel!—

Exit with Are[thusa], Phi[laster], Bellario.
　　　　　　　I'll see them safe,
And then cope with these burghers. Let
　　the guard
And all the gentlemen give strong at-
　　tendance.

Exit King; manent [2] Dion, Cleremont,
　　　　　　　　　　Thrasiline.

CLE. The city up! This was above our
　　wishes.　　120

DI. Ay, and the marriage too. By my
life, this noble lady has deceived us all.
A plague upon myself, a thousand plagues,
for having such unworthy thoughts of her
dear honor! O, I could beat myself! Or
do you beat me, and I'll beat you, for we
had all one thought.

CLE. No, no, 'twill but lose time.

DI. You say true. Are your swords
sharp?—Well, my dear countrymen [130
What-ye-lacks,[3] if you continue, and fall
not back upon the first broken shin, I'll
have ye chronicled and chronicled, and
cut and chronicled, and all-to [4] bepraised
and sung in sonnets, and bathed [5] in new,

brave ballads, that all tongues shall troll
you *in sæcula sæculorum,*[6] my kind can-
carriers.

THRA. What if a toy [7] take um i' th'
heels now, and they run all away, [140
and cry, "The devil take the hindmost"?

DI. Then the same devil take the foremost too, and souse him for his breakfast!
If they all prove cowards, my curses fly
among them, and be speeding! May they
have murrains [8] reign to keep the gentlemen at home unbound in easy frieze!
May the moths branch [9] their velvets, and
their silks only be worn before sore [150
eyes! May their false lights undo um, and
discover presses,[10] holes, stains, and old-
ness in their stuffs, and make them shop-
rid! May they keep whores and horses,
and break,[11] and live mewed up with necks
of beef and turnips! May they have many
children, and none like the father! May
they know no language but that gibberish they prattle to their parcels,[12] unless
it be the goatish [13] Latin they write in [160
their bonds—and may they write that false,
and lose their debts!

Enter the King.

KING. Now the vengeance of all the
gods confound them! How they swarm
together! What a hum they raise!—Devils
choke your wild throats!—If a man had
need to use their valors, he must pay a
brokage for it, and then bring um on, and
they will fight like sheep. 'Tis Philaster,
none but Philaster, must allay this [170
heat. They will not hear me speak, but
fling dirt at me and call me tyrant. O, run,
dear friend, and bring the Lord Philaster!
Speak him fair; call him prince; do him
all the courtesy you can; commend me to
him. O, my wits, my wits!

Exit Cleremont.

DI. [*Aside.*]　　O, my brave countrymen!
As I live, I will not buy a pin out of your
walls [14] for this. Nay, you shall cozen me,
and I'll thank you, and send you [180
brawn and bacon, and soil [15] you every long

---

[1] Fearing for.
[2] Remain.
[3] Shopkeepers, who used this cry.
[4] Completely.
[5] Heath suggests *bawled.*

[6] Forever and ever.
[7] Trifle, whim.
[8] Plagues.
[9] Eat patterns on.
[10] Creases.
[11] "Go broke."
[12] Conveyances.
[13] Foul.
[14] Outside of your shops.
[15] Fatten.

vacation a brace of foremen,[1] that at Michaelmas shall come up fat and kicking.

KING. What they will do with this poor prince, the gods know, and I fear.

DI. [*Aside.*] Why, sir, they'll flay him, and make church buckets[2] on 's skin, to quench rebellion; then clap a rivet in 's sconce, and hang him up for [a][3] sign.

Enter Cleremont with Philaster.

KING. O, worthy sir, forgive me! Do not make   190
Your miseries and my faults meet together,
To bring a greater danger. Be yourself,
Still sound amongst diseases. I have wronged you;
And, though I find it last, and beaten to it,
Let first your goodness know it. Calm the people,
And be what you were born to. Take your love,
And with her my repentance, all my wishes,
And all my prayers. By the gods, my heart speaks this;
And, if the least fall from me not performed,
May I be strook with thunder!
PHI.   Mighty sir, 200
I will not do your greatness so much wrong,
As not to make your word truth. Free the princess
And the poor boy, and let me stand the shock
Of this mad sea-breach, which I'll either turn,
Or perish with it.
KING.   Let your own word free them.
PHI. Then thus I take my leave, kissing your hand,
And hanging on your royal word. Be kingly,
And be not moved, sir. I shall bring your peace
Or never bring myself back.
KING. All the gods go with thee.
                                        Exeunt omnes.

[1] Geese.
[2] Leather buckets kept in the church in case of fire.   [3] From 1620 edn.

[SCENA iv.

A street.]

Enter an old Captain and Citizens with Pharamond.

CAP. Come, my brave myrmidons, let's fall on. Let your[4] caps swarm, my boys, and your nimble tongues forget your mother-gibberish of "what do you lack?" And set your mouths up,[5] children, till your palates fall frighted half a fathom past the cure of bay salt and gross pepper, and then cry, "Philaster, brave Philaster!" Let Philaster be deeper in request, my dingdongs,[6] my pairs of dear indentures, [10 kings of clubs,[7] than your cold water chamblets[8] or your paintings spitted with copper.[9] Let not your hasty[10] silks, or your branched cloth of bodkin, [11] or your tissues, dearly beloved of spiced cake and custards, your Robin Hoods, Scarlets, and Johns, tie your affections in darkness to your shops. No, dainty duckers, [12] up with your three-piled spirits, your wrought valors; [13] and let your uncut cholers [14] make the king [20 feel the measure of your mightiness. Philaster! Cry, my rose-nobles,[15] cry!

ALL. Philaster! Philaster!

CAP. How do you like this, my lord prince? These are mad boys, I tell you; these are things that will not strike their topsails to a foist,[16] and let a man of war, an argosy, hull and cry "cockles." [17]

PHA. Why, you rude slave, do you know what you do?

CAP. My pretty prince of puppets, we do know,   30
And give your greatness warning that you talk
No more such bug's [18] words, or that soldered crown

[4] From 1620 edn. Original reads *our*.
[5] 1620 edn. has *ope*.
[6] Hearties.
[7] *I.e.*, apprentices, who were bound by indentures and preferred the club as a weapon.
[8] Camlets, a kind of watered cloth.
[9] Painted cloths interwoven with copper.
[10] Shoddy.
[11] Embroidered cloth of gold and silk.
[12] *I.e.*, those who bow before their customers.
[13] With a pun on *velours*.
[14] With a pun on *collars*.
[15] Name of a coin.
[16] A small pleasure boat.
[17] Lie idle and be meanly engaged.
[18] Bugbear's; *i.e.*, swaggering.

Shall be scratched with a musket. Dear
　　Prince Pippin,
Down with your noble blood, or, as I
　　live,
I'll have you coddled.—Let him loose,
　　my spirits;
Make us a round ring with your bills, my
　　Hectors,
And let me see what this trim man
　　dares do.
Now, sir, have at you! Here I lie,
And with this swashing [1] blow (do you
　　see, sweet prince?)
I could hulk [2] your grace, and hang you
　　up cross-legged,　　　　　　　　40
Like a hare at a poulter's, [3] and do this
　　with this wiper. [4]

PHA. You will not see me murdered,
　　wicked villains?

1 CIT. Yes, indeed, will we, sir; we have
　　not seen one for a great while.

CAP. He would have weapons, would he?
Give him a broadside, my brave boys,
with your pikes; branch me his skin in
flowers like a satin, and between every
flower a mortal cut.—Your royalty shall
ravel!—Jag him, gentlemen; I'll have him
cut to the kell, [5] then down the seams. [50
O, for a whip to make him galloon-laces! [6]
I'll have a coachwhip.

PHA. O, spare me, gentlemen!

CAP. Hold, hold; the man begins to fear
and know himself. He shall for this time
only be seeled up, [7] with a feather through
his nose, that he may only see heaven, and
think whither he's going. Nay, my beyond-
sea sir, we will proclaim you. You would
be king! Thou tender heir apparent　　[60
to a church ale, [8] thou slight prince of
single sarcenet, [9] thou royal ringtail, [10] fit to
fly at nothing but poor men's poultry, and
have every boy beat thee from that too
with his bread and butter!

PHA. Gods keep me from these hell-
hounds!

1 CIT. Shall 's geld him, captain?

CAP. No, you shall spare his dowcets, my
　　dear donsels; [11]
As you respect the ladies, let them
　　flourish.　　　　　　　　　　　70
The curses of a longing woman kills
As speedy as a plague, boys.

1 CIT. I'll have a leg, that's certain.

2 CIT. I'll have an arm.

3 CIT. I'll have his nose, and at mine
own charge build a college and clap 't upon
the gate. [12]

4 CIT. I'll have his little gut to string a
kit [13] with; for certainly a royal gut will
sound like silver.　　　　　　　　80

PHA. Would they were in thy belly, and
I past my pain once!

5 CIT. Good captain, let me have his
liver to feed ferrets.

CAP. Who will have parcels else? Speak.

PHA. Good gods, consider me! I shall
be tortured.

1 CIT. Captain, I'll give you the trimming of your two-hand sword, and let me
have his skin to make false scabbards.　90

2 CIT. He had no horns, sir, had he?

CAP. No, sir, he's a pollard. [14] What
wouldst thou do with horns?

2 CIT. O, if he had had, I would have
made rare hafts and whistles of um; but
his shin bones, if they be sound, shall
serve me.

Enter Philaster.

ALL. Long live Philaster, the brave
　　Prince Philaster!

PHI. I thank you, gentlemen. But why are
　　these
Rude weapons brought abroad, to teach
　　your hands　　　　　　　　　　100
Uncivil trades?

CAP.　　　　　　My royal Rosicleer,
We are thy myrmidons, thy guard, thy
　　roarers;
And, when thy noble body is in durance,
Thus do we clap our musty murrions [15]
　　on,
And trace [16] the streets in terror. Is it
　　peace,
Thou Mars of men? Is the king sociable,
And bids thee live? Art thou above thy
　　foemen,

---

[1] Slashing.
[2] Disembowel.
[3] Poulterer's.
[4] Ramrod.
[5] Caul.
[6] Tape used for trimming or binding.
[7] As a hawk's eyelids were temporarily sewed
together.
[8] *I.e.*, a bastard child conceived at a church
festivity.
[9] Thin silk.
[10] A sort of kite.
[11] Young dons, young fellows.
[12] In allusion to Brasenose College, Oxford.
[13] Cittern.
[14] Unhorned animal.
[15] Helmets.
[16] Walk.

And free as Phœbus? Speak. If not,
this stand [1]
Of royal blood shall be abroach, atilt,
And run even to the lees of honor.　110
PHI. Hold, and be satisfied. I am myself,
Free as my thoughts are; by the gods,
I am!
CAP. Art thou the dainty darling of the
king?
Art thou the Hylas to our Hercules?
Do the lords bow, and the regarded
scarlets [2]
Kiss their gummed golls,[3] and cry, "We
are your servants"?
Is the court navigable and the presence
stuck
With flags of friendship? If not, we are
thy castle,
And this man sleeps.
PHI. I am what I do desire to be, your
friend;　120
I am what I was born to be, your prince.
PHA. Sir, there is some humanity in you;
You have a noble soul. Forget my name,
And know my misery; set me safe
aboard
From these wild cannibals, and, as I
live,
I'll quit this land forever. There is
nothing—
Perpetual prisonment, cold, hunger,
sickness
Of all sorts, of all dangers, and al-
together
The worst company of the worst men,
madness, age,　129
To be as many creatures as a woman,
And do as all they do, nay, to despair—
But I would rather make it a new na-
ture,
And live with all these, than endure one
hour
Amongst these wild dogs.
PHI. I do pity you.—Friends, discharge
your fears;
Deliver me the prince. I'll warrant you
I shall be old enough to find my safety.
3 CIT. Good sir, take heed he does not
hurt you;
He's a fierce man, I can tell you, sir.
CAP. Prince, by your leave, I'll have a
surcingle,[4]　140

And make [5] you like a hawk. (*He strives.*)[6]
PHI. Away, away, there is no danger in
him!
Alas, he had rather sleep to shake his
fit off!
Look you, friends, how gently he leads!
Upon my word,
He's tame enough; he need[s] no further
watching.
Good my friends, go to your houses,
And by me have your pardons and my
love;
And know there shall be nothing in my
power
You may deserve, but you shall have
your wishes.
To give you more thanks were to flatter
you.　150
Continue still your love; and for an
earnest
Drink this.　　　　　[*Gives money.*]
ALL. Long mayst thou live, brave prince,
brave prince, brave prince!
　　　Exeunt [7] *Phi[laster] and Pharamond.*
CAP. Go thy ways, thou art the king of
courtesy!—
Fall off again, my sweet youths. Come,
And every man trace to his house again,
And hang his pewter up; then to the
tavern,
And bring your wives in muffs. We will
have music;
And the red grape shall make us dance
and rise, boys.　　　　　*Exeunt.*

[SCENA v.

An apartment in the palace.]

*Enter King, Arethusa, Galatea, Megra,
Cleremont, Dion, Thrasiline, Bellario, and
　　　　　　　　　　　　Attendants.*

KING. Is it appeased?
DI. Sir, all is quiet as this dead of night,
As peaceable as sleep. My Lord Philaster
Brings on the prince himself.
KING.　　　　　　　Kind gentlemen,
I will not break the least word I have
given
In promise to him. I have heaped a
world
Of grief upon his head, which yet I hope
To wash away.

---

[1] Cask, *i.e.*, Pharamond.　[3] Perfumed hands.
[2] Courtiers clad in scarlet.　[4] Band.
[5] Train.　　　　　[7] Original reads *Exit.*
[6] *I.e.*, Pharamond tries to get away.

Enter Philaster and Pharamond.

CLE.   My lord is come.

KING.   My son!
Blessed be the time that I have leave to
    call
Such virtue mine!   Now thou art in
    mine arms,   10
Methinks I have a salve unto my breast
For all the stings that dwell there.
    Streams of grief
That I have wrought thee, and as much
    of joy
That I repent it, issue from mine eyes;
Let them appease thee.   Take thy right.
    Take her
(She is thy right too), and forget to urge
My vexéd soul with that I did before.

PHI.   Sir, it is blotted from my memory,
Past and forgotten.—For you, Prince of
    Spain,
Whom I have thus redeemed, you have
    full leave   20
To make an honorable voyage home.
And, if you would go furnished to your
    realm
With fair provision, I do see a lady,
Methinks, would gladly bear you com-
    pany.
How like you this piece?

MEG.   Sir, he likes it well,
For he hath tried it, and hath found it
    worth
His princely liking.   We were ta'en
    abed;
I know your meaning.   I am not the first
That nature taught to seek a fellow
    forth.
Can shame remain perpetually in me,   30
And not in others?   Or have princes
    salves
To cure ill names, that meaner people
    want?

PHI.   What mean you?

MEG.   You must get another ship,
To bear the princess and her boy to-
    gether.

DI.   How now!

MEG.   Others took me, and I took her and
    him
At that all women may be ta'en some-
    time.
Ship us all four, my lord; we can endure
Weather and wind alike.

KING.   Clear thou thyself, or know not me
    for father.   40

ARE.   This earth, how false it is!   What
    means is left for me
To clear myself?   It lies in your belief.
My lords, believe me; and let all things
    else
Struggle together to dishonor me.

BEL.   O, stop your ears, great king, that I
    may speak
As freedom would!   Then I will call this
    lady
As base as are her actions.   Hear me, sir;
Believe your heated blood when it
    rebels
Against your reason, sooner than this
    lady.

MEG.   By this good light, he bears it
    handsomely.   50

PHI.   This lady?   I will sooner trust the
    wind
With feathers, or the troubled sea with
    pearl,
Than her with anything.   Believe her
    not.
Why, think you, if I did believe her
    words,
I would outlive 'em?   Honor cannot take
Revenge on you.   Then what were to be
    known
But death?

KING.   Forget her, sir, since all is knit
Between us.   But I must request of you
One favor, and will sadly be denied.

PHI.   Command, whate'er it be.

KING.   Swear to be true   60
To what you promise.

PHI.   By the powers above,
Let it not be the death of her or him,
And it is granted!

KING.   Bear away that boy
To torture; I will have her cleared or
    buried.

PHI.   O, let me call my word back, worthy
    sir!
Ask something else; bury my life and
    right
In one poor grave; but do not take away
My life and fame at once.

KING.   Away with him!   It stands irrevo-
    cable.

PHI.   Turn all your eyes on me.   Here
    stands a man,   70
The falsest and the basest of this world.

Set swords against this breast, some
  honest man,
For I have lived till I am pitiéd!
My former deeds were hateful; but this
  last
Is pitiful, for I unwillingly
Have given the dear preserver of my
  life
Unto his torture. Is it in the power
Of flesh and blood to carry this, and live?
  Offers to kill himself.
ARE. Dear sir, be patient yet! O, stay
  that hand!
KING. Sirs, strip that boy.
DI.   Come, sir; your tender flesh 80
Will try [1] your constancy.
BEL.   O, kill me, gentlemen!
DI. No.—Help, sirs!
BEL.   Will you torture me?
KING.   Haste there.
Why stay you?
BEL.   Then I shall not break my vow,
You know, just gods, though I discover
  all.
KING. How's that? Will he confess?
DI.   Sir, so he says.
KING. Speak then.
BEL.   Great king, if you command
This lord to talk with me alone, my
  tongue
Urged by my heart, shall utter all the
  thoughts
My youth hath known; and stranger
  things than these
You hear not often.
KING.   Walk aside with him. 90
  [*Dion and Bellario walk apart.*]
DI. Why speak'st thou not?
BEL.   Know you this face, my lord?
DI. No.
BEL. Have you not seen it, nor the like?
DI. Yes, I have seen the like, but readily
I know not where.
BEL.   I have been often told
In court of one Euphrasia, a lady,
And daughter to you, betwixt whom
  and me
They that would flatter my bad face
  would swear
There was such strange resemblance
  that we two
Could not be known asunder, dressed
  alike.

[1] From 1620 edn. Original reads *tire.*

DI. By heaven, and so there is!
BEL.   For her fair sake, 100
Who now doth spend the springtime of
  her life
In holy pilgrimage, move to the king
That I may scape this torture.
DI.   But thou speak'st
As like Euphrasia as thou dost look.
How came it to thy knowledge that she
  lives
In pilgrimage?
BEL.   I know it not, my lord;
But I have heard it, and do scarce
  believe it.
DI. O, my shame! Is 't possible? Draw
  near
That I may gaze upon thee. Art thou
  she,
Or else her murderer? [2] Where wert
  thou born? 110
BEL. In Syracusa.
DI.   What's thy name?
BEL.   Euphrasia.
DI. O, 'tis just, 'tis she!
Now I do know thee. O, that thou hadst
  died,
And I had never seen thee nor my
  shame!
How shall I own thee? Shall this tongue
  of mine
E'er call thee daughter more?
BEL. Would I had died indeed! I wish it
  too;
And so [I] [3] must have done by vow, ere
  published
What I have told, but that there was no
  means
To hide it longer. Yet I joy in this, 120
The princess is all clear.
KING.   What, have you done?
DI. All 's discovered.
PHI.   Why then hold you me?
All is discovered! Pray you, let me go.
  He offers to stab himself.
KING. Stay him!
ARE.   What is discovered?
DI.   Why, my shame.
It is a woman; let her speak the rest.
PHI. How? That again!
DI. It is a woman.

[2] Some barbarous peoples believed that the
murderer assumed the shape of the person he
murdered.
[3] From 1620 edn.

PHI. Blessed be you powers that favor
  innocence!
KING. Lay hold upon that lady.
                [*Megra is seized.*]
PHI. It is a woman, sir!—Hark, gentle-
  men,   130
  It is a woman!—Arethusa, take
  My soul into thy breast, that would be
    gone
  With joy. It is a woman! Thou art fair,
  And virtuous still to ages, in despite
  Of malice.
KING. Speak you, where lies his shame?
BEL.   I am his daughter.
PHI. The gods are just.
DI. I dare accuse none; but, before you
  two,
  The virtue of our age, I bend my knee
  For mercy.   [*Kneels.*]
PHI. [*Raising him.*]   Take it freely, for
  I know,   140
  Though what thou didst were undis-
    creetly done,
  'Twas meant well.
ARE. And, for me,
  I have a power to pardon sins, as oft
  As any man has power to wrong me.
CLE. Noble and worthy!
PHI.   But, Bellario
  (For I must call thee still so), tell me
    why
  Thou didst conceal thy sex. It was a
    fault,
  A fault, Bellario, though thy other deeds
  Of truth outweighed it.   All these
    jealousies   150
  Had flown to nothing if thou hadst dis-
    covered
  What now we know.
BEL.   My father oft would speak
  Your worth and virtue; and, as I did
    grow
  More and more apprehensive,[1] I did
    thirst
  To see the man so raised. But yet all
    this
  Was but a maiden longing, to be lost
  As soon as found, till, sitting in my
    window,
  Printing my thoughts in lawn,[2] I saw a
    god,
  I thought (but it was you), enter our
    gates.

[1] Quick to understand.   [2] *I.e.*, embroidering.

  My blood flew out and back again, as
    fast   160
  As I had puffed it forth and sucked
    it in
  Like breath. Then was I called away in
    haste
  To entertain you. Never was a man,
  Heaved from a sheepcote to a scepter,
    raised
  So high in thoughts as I. You left a kiss
  Upon these lips then, which I mean to
    keep
  From you forever. I did hear you talk,
  Far above singing. After you were gone,
  I grew acquainted with my heart, and
    searched   169
  What stirred it so. Alas, I found it love,
  Yet far from lust, for, could I but have
    lived
  In presence of you, I had had my end.
  For this I did delude my noble father
  With a feigned pilgrimage, and dressed
    myself
  In habit of a boy; and, for I knew
  My birth no match for you, I was past
    hope
  Of having you; and, understanding well
  That when I made discovery of my sex
  I could not stay with you, I made a vow,
  By all the most religious things a maid
  Could call together, never to be known,
  Whilst there was hope to hide me from
    men's eyes,   182
  For other than I seemed, that I might
    ever
  Abide with you. Then sat I by the fount,
  Where first you took me up.
KING.   Search out a match
  Within our kingdom, where and when
    thou wilt,
  And I will pay thy dowry; and thyself
  Wilt well deserve him.
BEL.   Never, sir, will I
  Marry; it is a thing within my vow.
  But, if I may have leave to serve the
    princess,   190
  To see the virtues of her lord and her,
  I shall have hope to live.
ARE.   I, Philaster,
  Cannot be jealous, though you had a lady
  Dressed like a page to serve you; nor
    will I
  Suspect her living here.—Come, live
    with me;

Live free as I do. She that loves my
lord,
Cursed be the wife that hates her!

PHI. I grieve such virtue should be laid in
earth
Without an heir.—Hear me, my royal
father.
Wrong not the freedom of our souls so
much, 200
To think to take revenge of that base
woman;
Her malice cannot hurt us. Set her free
As she was born, saving from shame and
sin.

KING. Set her at liberty.—But leave the
court;
This is no place for such.—You, Pharamond,
Shall have free passage, and a conduct
home
Worthy so great a prince. When you
come there,

Remember 'twas your faults that lost
you her,
And not my purposed will.

PHA. I do confess,
Renownéd sir. 210

KING. Last, join your hands in one. En-
joy, Philaster,
This kingdom, which is yours, and,
after me,
Whatever I call mine. My blessing on
you!
All happy hours be at your marriage
joys,
That you may grow yourselves over all
lands,
And live [1] to see your plenteous branches
spring
Wherever there is sun! Let princes learn
By this to rule the passions of their blood;
For what heaven wills can never be
withstood. *Exeunt omnes.*

[1] From 1620 edn. Original reads *like*.

FINIS.

THE MAID'S TRAGEDY[1]

[BY

FRANCIS BEAUMONT AND JOHN FLETCHER][2]

SPEAKERS

KING.
LYSIPPUS, *brother to the king.*
AMINTOR [, *a noble gentleman*].[3]
EVADNE, *wife to Amintor.*
MELANTIUS } *brothers to Evadne.*
DIPHILUS
ASPATIA, *troth-plight wife to Amintor.*
CALIANAX, *an old humorous* [4] *lord, and father to Aspatia.*
CLEON } *gentlemen.*
STRATO
DIAGORAS, *a servant.*

[LORDS, GENTLEMEN, SERVANTS, *etc.*]
ANTIPHILA } *waiting gentlewomen to Aspatia.*
OLYMPIAS
DULA, *a lady* [, *attendant on Evadne*].
[LADIES.]

NIGHT
CYNTHIA
NEPTUNE
ÆOLUS } *masquers.*
[SEA GODS]
[WINDS]

[SCENE: *Rhodes.*

TIME: *Indefinite.*]

ACTUS I. SCEN[A] i.

[*An apartment in the palace.*]

Enter Cleon, Strato, Lysippus, Diphilus.

CLE. The rest are making ready, sir.

LYS.[5] So let them; there's time enough.

DIPH. You are the brother to the king, my lord; we'll take your word.

LYS. Strato, thou hast some skill in poetry; what think'st [thou][6] of the[7] masque? Will it be well?

STRA. As well as masques can be.

LYS. As masques can be?

STRA. Yes; they must commend [10 their king, and speak in praise of the assembly, bless the bride and bridegroom in person of some god; they're tied to rules of flattery.

CLE. See, good my lord, who is returned!

Enter Melantius.

LYS. Noble Melantius, the land by me welcomes thy virtues home to Rhodes—thou that with blood abroad buyest our peace! The breath of kings is like the breath of gods; my brother wished [20 thee here, and thou art here. He will be too kind, and weary thee with often welcomes; but the time doth give thee a welcome above his or all the world's.

MEL. My lord, my thanks; but these scratched limbs of mine have spoke my love and truth unto my friends more than my tongue e'er could. My mind's the same it [8

Ever was to you. Where I find worth,
I love the keeper till he let it go, 31
And then I follow it.

DIPH. Hail, worthy brother!
He that rejoices not at your return
In safety is mine enemy forever.

MEL. I thank thee, Diphilus. But thou art faulty:

[1] The title continues: "As It Hath Been Divers Times Acted at the Blackfriars by the King's Majesty's Servants."

[2] The authors' names do not appear until the third quarto (1630).

[3] From 1630 edn.   [4] Temperamental.

[5] From 1619 edn. Original reads *Stra.*

[6] From 1619 edn.

[7] Suggested by Seward. Early edns. read *a.*

[8] Although the preceding passage is printed as prose in all the early edns., it may be scanned in rough iambics.

1233

I sent for thee to exercise thine arms
With me at Patria; thou cam'st not,
  Diphilus;
'Twas ill.
DIPH.   My noble brother, my excuse
Is my king's strict command, which
  you, my lord,
Can witness with me.
LYS.   'Tis true, Melantius; 40
He might not come till the solemnity
Of this great match were past.
DIPH.   Have you heard of it?
MEL. Yes, I have given cause to those
  that
Envy my deeds abroad to call me game-
  some.
I have no other business here at Rhodes.
LYS. We have a masque tonight, and you
  must tread
A soldier's measure.
MEL. These soft and silken wars are not
  for me;
The music must be shrill and all con-
  fused
That stirs my blood; and then I dance
  with arms.   50
But is Amintor wed?
DIPH. This day.
MEL. All joys upon him, for he is my
  friend.
Wonder not that I call a man so young
  my friend.
His worth is great; valiant he is and
  temperate,
And one that never thinks his life his
  own,
If his friend need it. When he was a
  boy,
As oft as I returned (as, without boast,
I brought home conquest), he would
  gaze upon me
And view me round to find in what one
  limb   60
The virtue lay to do these things he
  heard;
Then would he wish to see my sword,
  and feel
The quickness of the edge, and in his
  hand
Weigh it. He oft would make me smile
  at this.
His youth did promise much, and his
  ripe years
Will see it all performed.—

Enter Aspatia, passing by.

                Hail, maid and wife!
Thou fair Aspatia, may the holy knot
That thou hast tied today last till the
  hand
Of age undo 't! Mayst thou bring a
  race   69
Unto Amintor that may fill the world
Successively with soldiers!
ASP.   My hard fortunes
Deserve not scorn, for I was never
  proud
When they were good.   *Exit Aspatia.*
MEL.   How's this?
LYS.   You are mistaken,[1]
For she is not married.
MEL.   You said Amintor was.
DIPH. 'Tis true; but—
MEL.   Pardon me; I did receive
Letters at Patria from my Amintor,
That he should marry her.
DIPH.   And so it stood
In all opinion long; but your arrival
Made me imagine you had heard the
  change.
MEL. Who hath he taken then?
LYS.   A lady, sir, 80
That bears the light about her, and
  strikes dead
With flashes of her eye—the fair Evadne,
Your virtuous sister.
MEL.   Peace of heart betwixt them!
But this is strange.
LYS.   The king, my brother, did it
To honor you; and these solemnities
Are at his charge.
MEL. 'Tis royal, like himself. But I am
  sad
My speech bears so unfortunate a sound
To beautiful Aspatia. There is rage
Hid in her father's breast. Calianax 90
Bent long against me, and he should
  not think,
If I could call it back, that I would take
So base revenges as to scorn the state
Of his neglected daughter. Holds he still
His greatness with the king?
LYS.   Yes. But this lady
Walks discontented, with her wat'ry eyes
Bent on the earth. The unfrequented
  woods

---

[1] Here and in a few other passages the line
division has been regularized.

Are her delight; and, when she sees a
    bank
Stuck full of flowers, she with a sigh will
    tell   99
Her servants what a pretty place it were
To bury lovers in, and make her maids
Pluck 'em, and strow her over like a
    corse.
She carries with her an infectious grief
That strikes all her beholders; she will
    sing
The mournful'st things that ever ear
    hath heard,
And sigh, and sing again; and, when the
    rest
Of our young ladies, in their wanton [1]
    blood,
Tell mirthful tales in course,[2] that fill
    the room
With laughter, she will with so sad a
    look   109
Bring forth a story of the silent death
Of some forsaken virgin, which her grief
Will put in such a phrase that, ere she
    end,
She'll send them weeping one by one
    away.
MEL. She has a brother under my com-
    mand,
Like her—a face as womanish as hers,
But with a spirit that hath much out-
    grown
The number of his years.

Enter Amintor.

CLE.   My lord the bridegroom!
MEL. I might run fiercely, not more hast-
    ily,
Upon my foe. I love thee well, Amintor,
My mouth is much too narrow for my
    heart;   120
I joy to look upon those eyes of thine.
Thou art my friend, but my disordered
    speech
Cuts off my love.
AMIN.   Thou art Melantius;
All love is spoke in that. A sacrifice,
To thank the gods Melantius is returned
In safety! Victory sits on his sword,
As she was wont. May she build there
    and dwell,
And may thy armor be, as it hath been,

Only thy valor and thine innocence!
What endless treasures would our ene-
    mies give   130
That I might hold thee still thus!
MEL.   I am poor
In words; but credit me, young man,
    thy mother
Could no more but weep for joy to see
    thee
After long absence. All the wounds I
    have
Fetched not so much away, nor all the
    cries
Of widowéd mothers. But this is peace,
And that was war.
AMIN.   Pardon, thou holy god
Of marriage bed, and frown not I am
    forced,
In answer of such noble tears as those,
To weep upon my wedding day!   140
MEL. I fear thou art grown too fickle,
    for I hear
A lady mourns for thee, men say, to
    death,
Forsaken of thee, on what terms[3] I
    know not.
AMIN. She had my promise; but the king
    forbade it,
And made me make this worthy change,
    thy sister,
Accompanied with graces about her,
With whom I long to lose my lusty
    youth
And grow old in her arms.
MEL.   Be prosperous!

Enter Messenger.

MESS.[4] My lord, the masquers rage for
    you.
LYS. We are gone. Cleon, Strato, Diphi-
    lus!   150
AMIN. We'll all attend you.—
    [Exeunt All but Amintor and Melantius.]
                    We shall trouble you
With our solemnities.
MEL.   Not so, Amintor;
But, if you laugh at my rude carriage
In peace, I'll do as much for you in war,
When you come thither. Yet I have a
    mistress
To bring to your delights; rough though
    I am,

[1] Lively.   [2] Turn.
[3] Under what circumstances.
[4] Original reads *Serv.*

I have a mistress, and she has a heart,
She says; but, trust me, it is stone, no
　better.
There is no place that I can challenge.
But you stand still, and here my way
　lies.　　　*Exit [with Amintor].*　160

[SCENA ii.

A hall in the palace, with Spectators in a
　　　　　　　　　　　　balcony.]

Enter Calianax with Diagoras.

CAL. Diagoras, look to the doors better,
for shame! You let in all the world, and
anon the king will rail at me. Why, very
well said.[1] By Jove, the king will have the
show i' th' court!

DIAG. Why do you swear so, my lord?
You know he'll have it here.

CAL. By this light, if he be wise, he
will not.

DIAG. And, if he will not be wise, [10
you are forsworn.

CAL. One may swear[2] his heart out
with swearing, and get thanks on no side.
I'll be gone, look to 't who will.

DIAG. My lord, I shall never keep
them out. Pray, stay; your looks will
terrify them.

CAL. My looks terrify them, you cox-
combly ass, you! I'll be judge[d] by all
the company whether thou hast not a [20
worse face than I.

DIAG. I mean, because they know you
and your office.

CAL. Office! I would I could put it
off! I am sure I sweat quite through my
office. I might have made room at my
daughter's wedding—they ha' near killed
her among them; and now I must do service for him that hath forsaken her. Serve[3]
that will!　　　*Exit Calianax.*　30

DIAG. He's so humorous since his daughter was forsaken! (*Knock within.*) Hark,
hark! There, there! So, so! Codes, codes![4]
What now?

MEL. (*Within.*) Open the door!

DIAG. Who's there?

MEL. Melantius.

DIAG. I hope your lordship brings no
troop with you, for, if you do, I must
return them.　　　*[Opens the door.]*　40

Enter Melantius and a Lady.

MEL. None but this lady, sir.

DIAG. The ladies are all placed above,
save those that come in the king's troop;
the best of Rhodes sit there, and there's
room.

MEL. I thank you, sir.—When I have
seen you placed, madam, I must attend
the king; but, the masque done, I'll wait
on you again.

　　　[Exit Melantius, Lady, other door.][5]

DIAG. Stand back there!—Room for [50
my Lord Melantius!—Pray, bear back
—this is no place for such youths and
their trulls—let the doors shut again.—
Ay!—Do your heads itch? I'll scratch
them for you. [*Shuts door.*] So, now
thrust and hang.—[*Knocking within.*]
Again! Who is 't now?—I cannot blame
my Lord Calianax for going away. Would
he were here! He would run raging among
them, and break a dozen wiser heads [60
than his own in the twinkling of an eye.
—What's the news now?

[VOICE.] (*Within.*) I pray you, can
you help me to the speech of the master
cook?

DIAG. If I open the door, I'll cook some
of your calves' heads. Peace, rogues!—
[*Knocking within.*] Again! Who is 't?

MEL. (*Within.*) Melantius.

Enter Calianax to Melantius.

CAL. Let him not in.　　　70
DIAG. O, my lord, a[6] must.—

[*Opens door. Enter Melantius.*]

Make room there for my lord.—Is your
lady placed?
MEL. Yes, sir.
　I thank you.—My Lord Calianax, well
　　met.
　Your causeless hate to me I hope is
　　buried.
CAL. Yes, I do service for your sister here,
　That brings my own poor child to time-
　　less[7] death.
　She loves your friend Amintor, such
　　another
　False-hearted lord as you.

---

[1] Done.　　　　　[3] Let him serve.
[2] Folio reads *wear.*　[4] Corruption of *God's* (?).

[5] From 1619 edn. Thus, Diagoras is guarding
two doors, one to the gallery, and one to the
outside.　　　　　[6] He.　　[7] Untimely.

MEL.   You do me wrong, 80
A most unmanly one, and I am slow
In taking vengeance; but be well advised.
CAL. It may be so.—Who placed the lady
there
So near the presence of the king?
MEL.   I did.
CAL. My lord, she must not sit there.
MEL.   Why?
CAL. The place is kept for women of more
worth.
MEL. More worth than she?   It mis-
becomes your age
And place to be thus womanish. Forbear!
What you have spoke, I am content to
think
The palsy shook your tongue to.
CAL.   Why, 'tis well, 90
If I stand here to place men's wenches.
MEL.   I
Shall forget this place, thy age, my
safety,
And, through all, cut that poor sickly
week
Thou hast to live away from thee.
CAL. Nay, I know you can fight for your
whore.
MEL. Bate [1] the king, and, be he flesh and
blood,
A lies that says it!   Thy mother at
fifteen
Was black and sinful to her.
DIAG.   Good my lord—
MEL. Some god pluck threescore years
from that fond [2] man,
That I may kill him and not stain mine
honor!   100
It is the curse of soldiers that in peace
They shall be braved by such ignoble
men
As, if the land were troubled, would
with tears
And knees beg succor from 'em. Would
that blood,
That sea of blood, that I have lost in
fight,
Were running in thy veins, that it might
make thee
Apt to say less, or able to maintain,
Shouldst thou say more! This Rhodes,
I see, is naught
But a place privileged to do men wrong.
CAL. Ay, you may say your pleasure.

Enter Amintor.

AMIN.   What vild [3] injury 110
Has stirred my worthy friend, who is
as slow
To fight with words as he is quick of
hand?
MEL. That heap of age, which I should
reverence
If it were temperate—but testy years
Are most contemptible.
AMIN.   Good sir, forbear.
CAL. There is just such another as your-
self.
AMIN. He will wrong you, or me, or any
man,
And talk as if he had no life to
lose,
Since this our match. The king is coming
in;
I would not for more wealth than I
enjoy   120
He should perceive you raging. He did
hear
You were at difference now, which has-
tened him.   *Hautboys play within.*
CAL. Make room there!

*Enter King, Evadne, Aspatia, Lords, and
Ladies.*

KING. Melantius, thou art welcome, and
my love
Is with thee still; but this is not a
place
To brabble [4] in.—Calianax, join hands.
CAL. He shall not have mine hand.
KING.   This is no time
To force you to 't. I do love you
both.
Calianax, you look well to your office;
And you, Melantius, are welcome
home.—   130
Begin the masque.
MEL. Sister, I joy to see you and your
choice;
You looked with my eyes when you
took that man.
Be happy in him!   *Recorders [play].*
EVAD.   O, my dearest brother,
Your presence is more joyful than this
day
Can be unto me.

[1] Except.   [2] Foolish.   [3] Vile.   [4] Quarrel.

The Masque

Night rises in mists.

NIGHT. Our reign is come, for in the raging
sea
The sun is drowned, and with him fell
the Day.
Bright Cynthia, hear my voice! I am
the Night,
For whom thou bear'st about thy bor-
rowed light.   140
Appear! No longer thy pale visage
shroud,
But strike thy silver horns quite through
a cloud,
And send a beam upon my swarthy
face,
By which I may discover all the place
And persons, and how many longing
eyes
Are come to wait on our solemnities.

Enter Cynthia.

How dull and black am I! I could not
find
This beauty [1] without thee, I am so
blind;
Methinks they show like to those east-
ern streaks
That warn us hence before the morning
breaks.   150
Back, my pale servant, for these eyes
know how
To shoot far more and quicker rays
than thou.
CYNTH. Great queen, they be a troop for
whom alone
One of my clearest moons I have put on—
A troop that looks as if thyself and I
Had plucked our reins in and our whips
laid by,
To gaze upon these mortals that appear
Brighter than we.
NIGHT.   Then let us keep 'em here,
And never more our chariots drive
away,
But hold our places and outshine the
Day.   160
CYNTH. Great queen of shadows, you are
pleased to speak
Of more than may be done. We may not
break

[1] Referring to the ladies of the court.

The gods' decrees, but, when our time
is come,
Must drive away, and give the Day our
room.
Yet, whilst our reign lasts, let us stretch
our power
To give our servants one contented
hour,
With such unwonted solemn grace and
state
As may forever after force them hate
Our brother's glorious beams, and wish
the Night
Crowned with a thousand stars and our
cold light,   170
For almost all the world their service
bend
To Phœbus, and in vain my light I
lend,
Gazed on unto my setting from my rise
Almost of none but of unquiet eyes.
NIGHT. Then shine at full, fair queen,
and by thy power
Produce a birth—to crown this happy
hour—
Of nymphs and shepherds; let their
songs discover,
Easy and sweet, who is a happy lover;
Or, if thou woot, [2] then call thine own
Endymion   179
From the sweet flow'ry bed he lies upon,
On Latmus' top, thy pale beams drawn
away,
And of this long night let him make
this day.
CYNTH. Thou dream'st, dark queen; that
fair boy was not mine,
Nor went I down to kiss him. Ease and
wine
Have bred these bold tales. Poets,
when they rage,
Turn gods to men, and make an hour
an age.
But I will give a greater state and
glory,
And raise to time a noble memory
Of what these lovers are.—Rise, rise, I
say,
Thou power of deeps, thy surges laid
away,   190
Neptune, great king of waters, and by
me
Be proud to be commanded!

[2] Wilt.

Neptune rises.

NEP.   Cynthia, see
Thy word hath fetched me hither; let
    me know
Why I ascend.
CYNTH.   Doth this majestic show
Give thee no knowledge yet?
NEP.   Yes, now I see
Something intended, Cynthia, worthy
    thee.
Go on; I'll be a helper.
CYNTH.   Hie thee, then,
And charge the Wind fly from his rocky
    den;
Let loose thy subjects; only Boreas,   199
Too foul for our intentions as he was,
Still keep him fast chained. We must
    have none here
But vernal blasts and gentle winds
    appear,
Such as blow flowers, and through the
    glad boughs sing
Many soft welcomes to the lusty spring.
These are our music. Next, thy wat'ry
    race
Bring on in couples (we are pleased to
    grace
This noble night), each in their richest
    things
Your own deeps or the broken vessel
    brings.
Be prodigal, and I shall be as kind   209
And shine at full upon you.
NEP.   O, the wind-
Commanding Æolus!

Enter Æolus out of a rock.

ÆOL.   Great Neptune!
NEP.   He.
ÆOL. What is thy will?
NEP.   We do command thee free
Favonius and thy milder winds, to wait
Upon our Cynthia; but tie Boreas
    strait.
He's too rebellious.
ÆOL.   I shall do it. [*Exit.*]
NEP.   Do.
[ÆOL. (*Within.*)] Great master of the flood
    and all below,
Thy full command has taken.—O, the
    Main!
Neptune!
NEP.   Here.

[*Enter Æolus with Favonius and other
                                    Winds.*]
ÆOL.   Boreas has broke his chain,
And, struggling with the rest, has got
    away.
NEP. Let him alone; I'll take him up at
    sea.   220
He will not long be thence. Go once
    again,
And call out of the bottoms of the main
Blue Proteus and the rest; charge them
    put on
Their greatest pearls, and the most
    sparkling stone
The beaten rock breeds, till this night
    is done
By me a solemn honor to the Moon.
Fly, like a full sail.
ÆOL.   I am gone. [*Exit.*]
CYNTH.   Dark Night,
Strike a full silence, do a thorough
    right
To this great chorus, that our music
    may
Touch high as heaven, and make the
    east break day   230
At midnight.   *Music.*

[FIRST] SONG

[*During the song enter Proteus and other Sea
                                    Deities.*]
Cynthia, to thy power and thee
    We obey.
Joy to this great company!
    And no day
Come to steal this night away,
    Till the rites of love are ended,
And the lusty bridegroom say,
    "Welcome, light, of all befriended!"

Pace out, you wat'ry powers below;   240
    Let your feet,
Like the galleys when they row,
    Even beat.
Let your unknown measures, set
    To the still winds, tell to all
That gods are come, immortal, great,
    To honor this great nuptial.
                            The measure.

SECOND SONG

Hold back thy hours, dark Night, till we
    have done;
    The Day will come too soon.

Young maids will curse thee, if thou
　　steal'st away,　　　　　　　　　250
And leav'st their blushes open to the day.
　　Stay, stay, and hide
　　The blushes of the bride.

Stay, gentle Night, and with thy darkness
　　cover
　　The kisses of her lover.
Stay, and confound her tears and her shrill
　　cryings,
Her weak denials, vows, and often-dyings.
　　Stay, and hide all.
　　But help not, though she call.

NEP. Great queen of us and heaven, hear
　　what I bring　　　　　　　　　260
To make this hour a full one.
　　　　　　　　　Another measure.[1]
CYNTH.　　　　　　　Speak, sea's king.
NEP. Thy tunes my Amphitrite joys to
　　have,
When they will dance upon the rising
　　wave,
And court me as the sails. My Tritons,
　　play
Music to lead a storm! I'll lead the way.
　　　　　　　　　　　　　Measure.

[THIRD] SONG

To bed, to bed! Come, Hymen, lead the
　　bride,
And lay her by her husband's side.
　　Bring in the virgins every one,
　　That grieve to lie alone,
That they may kiss while they may say, "A
　　maid;"　　　　　　　　　　　270
Tomorrow 'twill be other [2] kissed and said.
　　Hesperus, be long a-shining,
　　Whilst these lovers are a-twining.

ÆOL. [*Within.*] Ho, Neptune!
NEP.　　　　　　　　Æolus!

[*Enter Æolus.*]

ÆOL.　　　　　　　The sea goes high;
Boreas hath raised a storm. Go and
　　apply
Thy trident; else, I prophesy, ere day
Many a tall ship will be cast away.
Descend with all the gods and all their
　　power,
To strike a calm.

CYNTH. A thanks to everyone and to
　　gratulate　　　　　　　　　280
So great a service, done at my desire,
Ye shall have many floods, fuller and
　　higher
Than you have wished for; no ebb shall
　　dare
To let the Day see where your dwelling[s]
　　are.
Now back unto your government in
　　haste,
Lest your proud charge should swell
　　above the waste,
And win upon the island.
NEP.　　　　　　　　We obey.
Neptune descends and the Sea Gods. [Exeunt
　　Favonius and other Winds.]
CYNTH. Hold up thy head, dead Night;
　　see'st thou not Day?
The east begins to lighten. I must down,
And give my brother place.
NIGHT.　　　　　　　O, I could frown
To see the Day, the Day that flings his
　　light　　　　　　　　　　291
Upon my kingdoms and contemns old
　　Night!
Let him go on and flame! I hope to see
Another wildfire in his axletree,
And all fall drenched. But I forget.—
　　Speak, queen.
The Day grows on; I must no more be
　　seen.
CYNTH. Heave up thy drowsy head again
　　and see
A greater light, a greater majesty,
Between our set [3] and us! Whip up thy
　　team.
The Day breaks here, and yon same
　　flashing stream [4]　　　　　300
Shot from the south. Say, which way
　　wilt thou go?
NIGHT. I'll vanish into mists.
CYNTH.　　　　　　I into Day. *Exeunt.*

FINIS MASQUE

KING. Take lights there!—Ladies, get the
　　bride to bed.—
We will not see you laid. Good night,
　　Amintor.
We'll ease you of that tedious cere-
　　mony.

---

[1] Fleay's emendation for *if not her measure.*
[2] Otherwise.

[3] Seward's emendation for *sect.*
[4] The "effulgence of the court" (Thorndike).

Were it my case, I should think time
  run slow.
If thou beest noble, youth, get me a boy
That may defend my kingdoms from my
  foes.
AMIN. All happiness to you!
KING.   Good night, Melantius.
                        Exeunt.

ACTUS II. [SCENA i.

Anteroom to Evadne's bedchamber.]

Enter Evadne, Aspatia, Dula, and other
*   Ladies.*

DUL. Madam, shall we undress you for
  this fight?
The wars are nak'd that you must make
  tonight.
EVAD. You are very merry, Dula.
DUL.   I should be
Far merrier, madam, if it were with me
As it is with you.
[EVAD.   How's that?
DUL.   That I might go
To bed with him wi' th' credit that you
  do.][1]
EVAD. Why, how now, wench?
DUL.   Come, ladies, will you help?
EVAD. I am soon undone.
DUL.   And as soon done;
Good store of clothes will trouble you at
  both.
EVAD. Art thou drunk, Dula?
DUL.   Why, here's none but we. 10
EVAD. Thou think'st belike[2] there is no
  modesty
When we are alone.
DUL.   Ay, by my troth,
You hit my thoughts aright.
EVAD. You prick me, lady.
DUL.   'Tis against my will.
Anon you must endure more and lie still;
You're best to practice.
EVAD.   Sure, this wench is mad.
DUL. No, faith, this is a trick that I have
  had
Since I was fourteen.
EVAD.   'Tis high time to leave it.
DUL. Nay, now I'll keep it till the trick
  leave me.   19
A dozen wanton words put in your head
Will make you livelier in your husband's
  bed.

EVAD. Nay, faith, then take it.[3]
DUL.   Take it, madam! Where?
We all, I hope, will take it that are here.
EVAD. Nay, then I'll give you o'er.
DUL.   So will I make
The ablest man in Rhodes, or his heart,
  ache.
EVAD. Wilt take my place tonight?
DUL.   I'll hold your cards
Against any two I know.
EVAD.   What wilt thou do?
DUL. Madam, we'll do 't, and make 'em
  leave play too.
EVAD. Aspatia, take her part.
DUL.   I will refuse it.
She will pluck down a side;[4] she does not
  use it.   30
EVAD. Do, I prithee.[5]
DUL.   You will find the play
Quickly, because your head lies well
  that way.
EVAD. I thank thee, Dula. Would thou
  couldst instill
Some of thy mirth into Aspatia!
Nothing but sad thoughts in her breast
  do dwell;
Methinks, a mean betwixt you would
  do well.
DUL. She is in love; hang me, if I were so,
But I could run[6] my country. I love too
To do those things that people in love
  do.
ASP. It were a timeless smile should prove
  my cheek.[7]   40
It were a fitter hour for me to laugh,
When at the altar the religious priest
Were pacifying the offended powers
With sacrifice than now. This should
  have been
My night; and all your hands have been
  employed
In giving me a spotless offering
To young Amintor's bed, as we are now
For you. Pardon, Evadne. Would my
  worth
Were great as yours, or that the king,
  or he,
Or both, thought so! Perhaps he found
  me worthless,   50
But till he did so, in these ears of mine,

---

[1] From 1619 edn.   [2] Perhaps.

[3] *I.e.*, the trick.
[4] Cause the loss of the game.
[5] From 1619 edn. Original reads *Why, do.*
[6] Ride at a hot pace.   [7] Audacity.

These credulous ears, he poured the
　　sweetest words
That art or love could frame. If he were
　　false,
Pardon it, heaven! And, if I did want
Virtue, you safely may forgive that too,
For I have lost none that I had from you.
Evad. Nay, leave this sad talk, madam.
Asp. 　　　　　　　Would I could!
Then I should leave the cause.
Evad. See, if you have not spoiled all
　　Dula's mirth!
Asp. Thou think'st thy heart hard; but,
　　if thou beest caught, 　　　　60
Remember me; thou shalt perceive a
　　fire
Shot suddenly into thee.
Dul. 　　　　　That's not so good;
Let 'em shoot anything but fire, I fear
'em not.
Asp. Well, wench, thou mayst be taken.
Evad. Ladies, good night; I'll do the rest
　　myself.
Dul. Nay, let your lord do some.
Asp. [*Singing.*]

　　Lay a garland on my hearse
　　　Of the dismal yew—

Evad. That's one of your sad songs,
　　madam.
Asp. Believe me, 'tis a very pretty one. 70
Evad. How is it, madam?

　　　　　Song

Asp. Lay a garland on my hearse
　　　Of the dismal yew;
　　　Maidens, willow branches bear;
　　　Say I diéd true.

　　My love was false, but I was firm
　　　From my hour of birth.
　　Upon my buried body lay
　　　Lightly gentle earth!

Evad. Fie on 't, madam! The words　[80
are so strange, they are able to make one
dream of hobgoblins.—"I could never
have the power"—sing that, Dula.
Dul. [*Singing.*]

　　I could never have the power
　　To love one above an hour,
　　But my heart would prompt mine eye
　　On some other man to fly.

Venus, fix mine eyës fast,
Or, if not, give me all that I shall see at
　　last! 　　　　　　　　　　89
Evad. So, leave me now.
Dul. 　　　　Nay, we must see you laid.
Asp. Madam, good night. May all the
　　marriage joys
That longing maids imagine in their
　　beds
Prove so unto you! May no discontent
Grow twixt your love and you! But, if
　　there do,
Inquire of me, and I will guide your
　　moan,
Teach you an artificial [1] way to grieve,
To keep your sorrow waking. Love your
　　lord
No worse than I; but, if you love so
　　well,
Alas, you may displease him! So did I.
This is the last time you shall look on
　　me.— 　　　　　　　　　100
Ladies, farewell. As soon as I am dead,
Come all and watch one night about
　　my hearse;
Bring each a mournful story and a tear,
To offer at it when I go to earth;
With flattering ivy clasp my coffin
　　round;
Write on my brow my fortune; let my
　　bier
Be borne by virgins that shall sing by
　　course
The truth of maids and perjuries of
　　men.
Evad. Alas, I pity thee. 　*Exit Evadne.*
Omnes. 　　　　　Madam, good night.
1 Lady. Come, we'll let in the bride-
　　groom.
Dul. 　　　Where's my lord? 　　110
1 Lady. Here, take this light.

　　　Enter Amintor.

Dul. 　　　You'll find her in the dark.
1 Lady. Your lady's scarce abed yet;
　　you must help her.
Asp. Go, and be happy in your lady's
　　love.
May all the wrongs that you have done
　　to me
Be utterly forgotten in my death!
I'll trouble you no more; yet I will take

[1] Artful.

A parting kiss, and will not be denied.
[*Kisses Amintor.*]
You'll come, my lord, and see the virgins weep
When I am laid in earth, though you yourself
Can know no pity. Thus I wind myself   120
Into this willow garland, and am prouder
That I was once your love, though now refused,
Than to have had another true to me.
So with [my][1] prayers I leave you, and must try
Some yet unpracticed way to grieve and die.   *Exit Aspatia.*

DUL. Come, ladies, will you go?
OMNES.   Good night, my lord.
AMIN. Much happiness unto you all!
                    Exeunt [Dula and] Ladies.
I did that lady wrong. Methinks, I feel
Her grief shoot suddenly through all my veins;
Mine eyes run. This is strange at such a time.   130
It was the king first moved me to 't; but he
Has not my will in keeping. Why do I
Perplex myself thus? Something whispers me,
"Go not to bed." My guilt is not so great
As mine own conscience, too sensible,[2]
Would make me think; I only brake a promise,
And 'twas the king that forced me. Timorous flesh,
Why shak'st thou so? Away, my idle fears!

Enter Evadne.

Yonder she is, the luster of whose eye
Can blot away the sad remembrance   140
Of all these things.—O, my Evadne, spare
That tender body; let it not take cold!
The vapors of the night will not fall here.
To bed, my love; Hymen will punish us
For being slack performers of his rites.
Cam'st thou to call me?
EVAD.   No.

AMIN.   Come, come, my love,
And let us lose ourselves to one another.
Why art thou up so long?
EVAD.   I am not well.
AMIN. To bed then; let me wind thee in these arms
Till I have banished sickness.
EVAD.   Good my lord,   150
I cannot sleep.
AMIN.   Evadne, we'll watch;
I mean no sleeping.
EVAD.   I'll not go to bed.
AMIN. I prithee, do.
EVAD.   I will not for the world.
AMIN. Why, my dear love?
EVAD.   Why? I have sworn I will not.
AMIN. Sworn!
EVAD.   Ay.
AMIN.   How? Sworn, Evadne?
EVAD. Yes, sworn, Amintor—and will swear again,
If you will wish to hear me.
AMIN. To whom have you sworn this?
EVAD. If I should name him, the matter were not great.
AMIN. Come, this is but the coyness of a bride.   160
EVAD. The coyness of a bride?
AMIN.   How prettily
That frown becomes thee!
EVAD.   Do you like it so?
AMIN. Thou canst not dress thy face in such a look
But I shall like it.
EVAD.   What look likes[3] you best?
AMIN. Why do you ask?
EVAD. That I may show you one less pleasing to you.
AMIN. How's that?
EVAD. That I may show you one less pleasing to you.
AMIN. I prithee, put thy jests in milder looks;
It shows as thou wert angry.
EVAD.   So perhaps   170
I am indeed.
AMIN.   Why, who has done thee wrong?
Name me the man, and by thyself I swear,
Thy yet unconquered self, I will revenge thee!
EVAD. Now I shall try thy truth. If thou dost love me,

---

[1] From 1630 edn.   [2] Sensitive.   [3] Pleases.

Thou weigh'st not anything compared
　with me.
Life, honor, joys eternal, all delights
This world can yield, or hopeful people
　feign,
Or in the life to come, are light as air
To a true lover when his lady frowns,
And bids him, "Do this." Wilt thou
　kill this man?　　　　　　　　　180
Swear, my Amintor, and I'll kiss the sin
Off from thy lips.

AMIN.　　　　I wo' not swear, sweet love,
Till I do know the cause.

EVAD.　　　　　I would thou wouldst.
Why, it is thou that wrong'st me. I
　hate thee.
Thou shouldst have killed thyself.

AMIN. If I should know that, I should
　quickly kill
The man you hated.

EVAD.　　　　Know it, then, and do 't.

AMIN. O, no! What look soe'er thou
　shalt put on
To try my faith, I shall not think thee
　false;
I cannot find one blemish in thy face, 190
Where falsehood should abide. Leave,
　and to bed.
If you have sworn to any of the virgins
That were your old companions, to
　preserve
Your maidenhead a night, it may be done
Without this means.

EVAD.　　　　A maidenhead, Amintor,
At my years?

AMIN.　　　Sure she raves. This cannot be
Thy natural temper. Shall I call thy
　maids?
Either thy healthful sleep hath left
　thee long,
Or else some fever rages in thy blood.

EVAD. Neither, Amintor. Think you I
　am mad,　　　　　　　　　　　200
Because I speak the truth?

AMIN.　　　　　　[Is this the truth?] [1]
Will you not lie with me tonight?

EVAD.　　　　　　　　　Tonight?
You talk as if [you thought] [1] I would
　hereafter.

AMIN. Hereafter? Yes, I do.

EVAD.　　　　　　You are deceived.
Put off amazement, and with patience
　mark

[1] From 1619 edn.

What I shall utter, for the oracle
Knows nothing truer. 'Tis not for a
　night
Or two that I forbear thy bed, but ever.

AMIN. I dream. Awake, Amintor!

EVAD.　　　　　You hear right; 209
I sooner will find out the beds of snakes,
And with my youthful blood warm their
　cold flesh,
Letting them curl themselves about
　my limbs,
Than sleep one night with thee. This is
　not feigned,
Nor sounds it like the coyness of a bride.

AMIN. Is flesh so earthly to endure all
　this?
Are these the joys of marriage? Hymen,
　keep
This story, that will make succeeding
　youth
Neglect thy ceremonies, from all ears;
Let it not rise up for thy shame and
　mine
To after ages; we will scorn thy laws, 220
If thou no better bless them. Touch the
　heart
Of her that thou hast sent me, or the
　world
Shall know; there's not an altar that
　will smoke
In praise of thee; we will adopt us sons;
Then virtue shall inherit, and not blood.
If we do lust, we'll take the next we
　meet,
Serving ourselves as other creatures do,
And never take note of the female more,
Nor of her issue.—I do rage in vain;
She can but jest.—O, pardon me, my
　love!　　　　　　　　　　　230
So dear the thoughts are that I hold of
　thee,
That I must break forth. Satisfy my
　fear;
It is a pain, beyond the hand of death,
To be in doubt. Confirm it with an oath,
If this be true.

EVAD.　　　　　　Do you invent the form;
Let there be in it all the binding words
Devils and conjurers can put together,
And I will take it. I have sworn be-
　fore,
And here by all things holy do again,
Never to be acquainted with thy bed!
Is your doubt over now?　　　　241

AMIN. I know too much; would I had
doubted still!
Was ever such a marriage night as this!
You powers above, if you did ever mean
Man should be used thus, you have
thought a way
How he may bear himself, and save
his honor.
Instruct me in it, for to my dull eyes
There is no mean, no moderate course
to run;
I must live scorned, or be a murderer.
Is there a third? Why is this night so
calm?   250
Why does not heaven speak in thunder
to us,
And drown her voice?
EVAD.   This rage will do no good.
AMIN. Evadne, hear me. Thou has ta'en
an oath,
But such a rash one that to keep it
were
Worse than to swear it. Call it back to
thee;
Such vows as those never ascend to
the heaven;
A tear or two will wash it quite away.
Have mercy on my youth, my hopeful
youth,
If thou be pitiful, for, without boast,
This land was proud of me. What lady
was there   260
That men called fair and virtuous in
this isle,
That would have shunned my love? It
is in thee
To make me hold this worth. O, we
vain men,
That trust all our reputation
To rest upon the weak and yielding
hand
Of feeble woman! But thou art not
stone;
Thy flesh is soft, and in thine eyes doth
dwell
The spirit of love; thy heart cannot be
hard.
Come, lead me from the bottom of de-
spair
To all the joys thou hast, I know thou
wilt,   270
And make me careful lest the sudden
change
O'ercome my spirits.

EVAD.   When I call back this oath,
The pains of hell environ me!
AMIN. I sleep, and am too temperate.
Come to bed!
Or by those hairs, which, if thou hast
a soul
Like to thy locks, were threads for kings
to wear
About their arms——
EVAD.   Why, so perhaps they are.
AMIN. I'll drag thee to my bed, and make
thy tongue
Undo this wicked oath, or on thy flesh
I'll print a thousand wounds to let out
life!   280
EVAD. I fear thee not; do what thou
dar'st to me!
Every ill-sounding word or threat'ning
look
Thou show'st to me will be revenged at
full.
AMIN. It will not, sure, Evadne.
EVAD. Do not you hazard that.
AMIN.   Ha' ye your champions?
EVAD. Alas, Amintor, think'st thou I
forbear
To sleep with thee because I have put
on
A maiden's strictness?   Look upon
these cheeks,
And thou shalt find the hot and rising
blood   289
Unapt for such a vow. No; in this heart
There dwells as much desire and as
much will
To put that wished act in practice as
ever yet
Was known to woman; and they have
been shown
Both. But it was the folly of thy youth
To think this beauty, to what land[1]
soe'er
It shall be called, shall stoop to any
second.
I do enjoy the best, and in that height
Have sworn to stand or die. You guess
the man.
AMIN. No; let me know the man that
wrongs me so,
That I may cut his body into motes, 300
And scatter it before the northern wind.
EVAD. You dare not strike him.

---

[1] Bullen suggests *hand*, to fit the figure of
falconry in the passage.

AMIN.   Do not wrong me so.
Yes, if his body were a poisonous plant
That it were death to touch, I have a soul
Will throw me on him.

EVAD.   Why, 'tis the king.

AMIN.   The king!

EVAD. What will you do now?

AMIN.   'Tis not the king!

EVAD. What did he make this match for, dull Amintor?

AMIN. O, thou hast named a word that wipes away
All thoughts revengeful! In that sacred name,
"The king," there lies a terror. What frail man   310
Dares lift his hand against it? Let the gods
Speak to him when they please; till when, let us
Suffer and wait.

EVAD. Why should you fill yourself so full of heat,
And haste so to my bed? I am no virgin.

AMIN. What devil put it in thy fancy, then,
To marry me?

EVAD.   Alas, I must have one
To father children, and to bear the name
Of husband to me, that my sin may be
More honorable!

AMIN. What a strange thing am I!   320

EVAD. A miserable one; one that myself
Am sorry for.

AMIN.   Why, show it then in this:
If thou hast pity, though thy love be none,
Kill me; and all true lovers, that shall live
In after ages crossed in their desires,
Shall bless thy memory, and call thee good,
Because such mercy in thy heart was found,
To rid a ling'ring wretch.

EVAD.   I must have one
To fill thy room again, if thou wert dead;
Else, by this night, I would! I pity thee.   330

AMIN. These strange and sudden injuries have fall'n
So thick upon me that I lose all sense

Of what they are. Methinks, I am not wronged;
Nor is it aught, if from the censuring world
I can but hide it. Reputation,
Thou art a word, no more!—But thou hast shown
An impudence so high that to the world
I fear thou wilt betray or shame thyself.

EVAD. To cover shame, I took thee; never fear
That I would blaze [1] myself.

AMIN.   Nor let the king   340
Know I conceive he wrongs me; then mine honor
Will thrust me into action; that my flesh
Could bear with patience. And it is some ease
To me in these extremes that I know this
Before I touched thee; else, had all the sins
Of mankind stood betwixt me and the king,
I had gone through 'em to his heart and thine.
I have lost one desire; 'tis not his crown
Shall buy me to thy bed, now I resolve [2]
He has dishonored thee. Give me thy hand.   350
Be careful of thy credit, and sin close; [3]
'Tis all I wish. Upon thy chamber floor
I'll rest tonight, that morning visitors
May think we did as married people use.
And, prithee, smile upon me when they come,
And seem to toy, as if thou hadst been pleased
With what we did.

EVAD.   Fear not; I will do this.

AMIN. Come, let us practice; and, as wantonly
As ever loving bride and bridegroom met,
Let's laugh and enter here.

EVAD.   I am content.   360

AMIN. Down all the swellings of my troubled heart!
When we walk thus entwined, let all eyes see
If ever lovers better did agree.

Exit [with Evadne].

[1] Proclaim.   [2] Am convinced.   [3] Privately.

[SCENA ii.

A room in the house of Calianax.]

Enter Aspatia, Antiphila, and Olympias.

ASP. Away, you are not sad! Force it no
        further.
    Good gods, how well you look! Such a
        full color
    Young bashful brides put on; sure, you
        are new married!
ANT. Yes, madam, to your grief.
ASP.   Alas, poor wenches!
    Go learn to love first; learn to lose your-
        selves;
    Learn to be flattered, and believe and
        bless
    The double tongue that did it; make a
        faith
    Out of the miracles of ancient lovers,
    Such as speak truth and died in 't; and,
        like me,
    Believe all faithful, and be miserable.   10
    Did you ne'er love yet, wenches? Speak,
        Olympias; [1]
    Thou hast an easy temper, fit for stamp.
OLYM. Never.
ASP.   Nor you, Antiphila?
ANT.   Nor I.
ASP. Then, my good girls, be more than
        women, wise;
    At least be more than I was; and be sure
    You credit anything the light gives life
        to,
    Before a man. Rather believe the sea
    Weeps for the ruined merchant, when he
        roars;
    Rather, the wind courts but the preg-
        nant sails,
    When the strong cordage cracks; rather,
        the sun   20
    Comes but to kiss the fruit in wealthy
        autumn,
    When all falls blasted. If you needs
        must love
    (Forced by ill fate), take to your maiden
        bosoms
    Two dead-cold aspics, and of them make
        lovers.
    They cannot flatter nor forswear; one
        kiss
    Makes a long peace for all. But man—

[1] This line follows l. 8 in original. Emended
by Theobald.

O, that beast man! Come, let's be sad,
    my girls;
That down-cast of thine eye, Olympias,
Shows a fine sorrow.—Mark, Antiphila;
Just such another was the nymph
    Oenone's,   30
When Paris brought home Helen.—
    Now, a tear;
And then thou art a piece expressing
    fully
The Carthage queen, when from a cold
    sea rock,
Full with her sorrow, she tied fast her
    eyes
To the fair Trojan ships, and, having
    lost them,
Just as thine does, down stole a tear.—
    Antiphila,
What would this wench do, if she were
    Aspatia?
Here she would stand, till some more
    pitying god
Turned her to marble!— 'Tis enough,
    my wench!
Show me the piece of needlework you
    wrought.   40
ANT. Of Ariadne, madam?
ASP. [*Examining the needlework.*]   Yes,
    that piece.—
    This should be Theseus; h'as a cozening
        face.—
    You meant him for a man?
ANT.   He was so, madam.
ASP. Why, then, 'tis well enough.—Never
        look back;
    You have a full wind and a false heart,
        Theseus.—
    Does not the story say his keel was
        split,
    Or his masts spent, or some kind rock
        or other
    Met with his vessel?
ANT.   Not as I remember.
ASP. It should ha' been so. Could the
        gods know this,
    And not, of all their number, raise a
        storm?   50
    But they are all as ill. This false smile
    Was well expressed; just such another
        caught me.—
    [*To Theseus.*] You shall not go so.—
    Antiphila, in this place work a quick-
        sand,
    And over it a shallow, smiling water,

And his ship plowing it, and then a
　Fear.
Do that Fear to the life, wench.

ANT.　　　　　　　'Twill wrong the story.

ASP. 'Twill make the story, wronged by
　wanton poets,
　Live long and be believed. But where's
　the lady?

ANT. There, madam.　　　　　　60

ASP. Fie, you have missed it here, Anti-
　phila;
　You are much mistaken, wench.
　These colors are not dull and pale
　enough
　To show a soul so full of misery
　As this sad lady's was. Do it by me,
　Do it again by me, the lost Aspatia;
　And you shall find all true but the wild
　island.
　I stand upon the sea-breach now, and
　think
　Mine arms thus, and mine hair blown
　with the wind,
　Wild as that desert; and let all about
　me　　　　　　　　　　　　　70
　Tell that I am forsaken. Do my face
　(If thou hadst ever feeling of a sor-
　row)
　Thus, thus, Antiphila: strive to make
　me look
　Like Sorrow's monument; and the trees
　about me,
　Let them be dry and leafless; let the
　rocks
　Groan with continual surges; and, be-
　hind me,
　Make all a desolation. Look, look,
　wenches,
　A miserable life [1] of this poor picture!

OLYM. Dear madam!

ASP.　　　I have done. Sit down; and let us
　Upon that point fix all our eyes, that
　point there.　　　　　　　　80
　Make a dull silence, till you feel a sudden
　sadness
　Give us new souls.

Enter Calianax.

CAL. The king may do this, and he may
　not do it.
　My child is wronged, disgraced.—Well,
　how now, huswives? [2]

───────────────
[1] Living representation.　　　　[2] Hussies.

What, at your ease? Is this a time to
　sit still?
Up, you young lazy whores, up, or I'll
　swenge [3] you!

OLYM. Nay, good my lord—

CAL. You'll lie down shortly. Get you in,
　and work!
　What, are you grown so resty [4] you want
　heats?
　We shall have some of the court boys do
　that office.　　　　　　　90

ANT. My lord, we do no more than we
　are charged.
　It is the lady's pleasure we be thus
　In grief; she is forsaken.

CAL.　　　　　　　There's a rogue too,
　A young dissembling slave!—Well, get
　you in.—
　I'll have a bout with that boy. 'Tis high
　time
　Now to be valiant; I confess my youth
　Was never prone that way. What, made
　an ass?
　A court stale? [5] Well, I will be valiant,
　And beat some dozen of these whelps; I
　will!
　And there's another of 'em, a trim,
　cheating soldier;　　　　　　100
　I'll maul that rascal; has outbraved me
　twice;
　But now, I thank the gods, I am val-
　iant.—
　Go, get you in.—I'll take a course with
　all.　　　　　　　*Exeunt om[nes].*

ACTUS III. [SCENA i.

Anteroom to Evadne's bedchamber.]

Enter Cleon, Strato, and Diphilus.

CLE. Your sister is not up yet.

DIPH. O, brides must take their morning's rest; the night is troublesome.

STRA. But not tedious.

DIPH. What odds, he has not my
sister's maidenhead tonight?

STRA. No; it's odds against any bridegroom living, he ne'er gets it while he
lives.

DIPH. Y' are merry with my sister; [10
you'll please to allow me the same freedom
with your mother.

───────────────
[3] Swinge, beat.　　　　[5] Laughingstock.
[4] Restive, sluggish.

Stra. She's at your service.

Diph. Then she's merry enough of herself; she needs no tickling.—Knock at the door.

Stra. We shall interrupt them.

Diph. No matter; they have the year before them.—[*Strato knocks.*] Good morrow, sister. Spare yourself today; the [20 night will come again.

Enter Amintor.

Amin. Who's there? My brother! I'm no readier yet. Your sister is but now up.

Diph. You look as you had lost your eyes tonight; I think you ha' not slept.

Amin. I' faith, I have not.

Diph.   You have done better, then.

Amin. We ventured for a boy; when he is twelve,
A shall command against the foes of Rhodes.
Shall we be merry?   29

Stra. You cannot; you want sleep.

Amin.   'Tis true.—(*Aside.*) But she,
As if she had drunk Lethe, or had made
Even with heaven, did fetch so still a sleep,
So sweet and sound——

Diph.   What's that?

Amin.   Your sister frets
This morning, and does turn her eyes upon me,
As people on their headsman. She does chafe,
And kiss, and chafe again, and clap my cheeks.
She's in another world.

Diph. Then I had lost; I was about to lay
You had not got her maidenhead tonight.[1]

Amin. [*Aside.*] Ha! He does not mock me?
—Y'ad lost indeed;   40
I do not use to bungle.

Cle.   You do deserve her.

Amin. (*Aside.*) I laid my lips to hers, and that wild breath,
That was so rude and rough to me last night,
Was sweet as April. I'll be guilty too,
If these be the effects.

---

[1] Last night.

Enter Melantius.

Mel. Good day, Amintor, for to me the name
Of brother is too distant; we are friends,
And that is nearer.

Amin.   Dear Melantius!
Let me behold thee. Is it possible?

Mel. What sudden gaze is this?

Amin.   'Tis wondrous strange! 50

Mel. Why does thine eye desire so strict a view
Of that it knows so well? There's nothing here
That is not thine.

Amin.   I wonder much, Melantius,
To see those noble looks that make me think
How virtuous thou art; and, on the sudden,
'Tis strange to me thou shouldst have worth and honor,
Or not be base, and false, and treacherous,
And every ill. But——

Mel.   Stay, stay, my friend;
I fear this sound will not become our loves.
No more embrace me.

Amin.   O, mistake me not! 60
I know thee to be full of all those deeds
That we frail men call good; but by the course
Of nature thou shouldst be as quickly changed
As are the winds, dissembling as the sea,
That now wears brows as smooth as virgins' be,
Tempting the merchant to invade his face,
And in an hour calls his billows up,
And shoots 'em at the sun, destroying all
A carries on him.—(*Aside.*) O, how near am I
To utter my sick thoughts!   70

Mel. But why, my friend, should I be so by nature?

Amin. I have wed thy sister, who hath virtuous thoughts
Enough for one whole family; and it is strange
That you should feel no want.

Mel. Believe me, this is compliment too cunning for me.

DIPH. What should I be then by the course of nature,
They having both robbed me of so much virtue?
STRA. O, call the bride, my Lord Amintor, that we may see her blush, and turn her eyes down. It is the prettiest sport!
AMIN. Evadne!
EVAD. (*Within.*) My lord?
AMIN. Come forth, my love; 81
Your brothers do attend to wish you joy.
EVAD. I am not ready yet.
AMIN. Enough, enough.
EVAD. They'll mock me.
AMIN. Faith, thou shalt come in.

Enter Evadne.

MEL. Good morrow, sister. He that understands
Whom you have wed, need not to wish you joy.
You have enough; take heed you be not proud.
DIPH. O, sister, what have you done?
EVAD. I done! Why, what have I done?
STRA. My Lord Amintor swears you are no maid now. 90
EVAD. Push!
STRA. I' faith, he does.
EVAD. I knew I should be mocked.
DIPH. With a truth.
EVAD. If 'twere to do again, In faith I would not marry.
AMIN. (*Aside.*) Nor I, by heaven!
DIPH. Sister, Dula swears she heard you cry two rooms off.
EVAD. Fie, how you talk!
DIPH. Let's see you walk.
EVAD. By my troth, y' are spoiled.
MEL. Amintor!
AMIN. Ha!
MEL. Thou art sad.
AMIN. Who, I? I thank you for that.
Shall Diphilus, thou, and I sing a catch? 100
MEL. How!
AMIN. Prithee, let's.
MEL. Nay, that's too much the other way.
AMIN. I am so lightened with my happiness!—
How dost thou, love? Kiss me.
EVAD. I cannot love you; you tell tales of me.
AMIN. Nothing but what becomes us.—
Gentlemen,

Would you had all such wives, and all the world,
That I might be no wonder! Y' are all sad.
What, do you envy me? I walk, methinks, 109
On water, and ne'er sink, I am so light.
MEL. 'Tis well you are so.
AMIN. Well! How can I be other,
When she looks thus?—Is there no music there?
Let's dance.
MEL. Why, this is strange, Amintor!
AMIN. I do not know myself; yet I could wish
My joy were less.
DIPH. I'll marry too, if it will make one thus.
EVAD. (*Aside.*) Amintor, hark.
AMIN. [*Aside.*] What says my love?—I must obey.
EVAD. [*Aside.*] You do it scurvily; 'twill be perceived. 119
CLE. My lord, the king is here.

Enter King and Lysip[pus].

AMIN. Where?
STRA. And his brother.
KING. Good morrow, all!—
Amintor, joy on joy fall thick upon thee!—
And, madam, you are altered since I saw you;
I must salute you; you are now another's.
How liked you your night's rest?
EVAD. Ill, sir.
AMIN. Indeed,
She took but little.
LYS. You'll let her take more,
And thank her too, shortly.
KING. Amintor, wert thou truly honest [1] till Thou wert married?
AMIN. Yes, sir.
KING. Tell me, then, how shows The sport unto thee?
AMIN. Why, well.
KING. What did you do? 130
AMIN. No more, nor less, than other couples use;
You know what 'tis; it has but a coarse name.

[1] Chaste.

KING. But, prithee, I should think, by her
  black eye,
And her red cheek, she should be quick
  and stirring
In this same business; ha?
AMIN.   I cannot tell;
I ne'er tried other, sir, but I perceive
She is as quick [1] as you deliveréd.
KING. Well, you'll trust me then, Amintor,
  to choose
A wife for you again?
AMIN.   No, never, sir.
KING. Why, like you this so ill?
AMIN.   So well I like her.   140
For this I bow my knee in thanks to
  you,
And unto heaven will pay my grateful
  tribute
Hourly, and do hope we shall draw out
A long contented life together here,
And die both, full of gray hairs, in one
  day,
For which the thanks is yours. But, if
  the powers
That rule us please to call her first
  away,
Without pride spoke, this world holds
  not a wife
Worthy to take her room.
KING. [Aside.]   I do not like this.—
All forbear the room but you, Amin-
  tor,   150
And your lady.
[Exeunt All but the King, Amintor, and
                          Evadne.]
              I have some speech with you,
That may concern your after living well.
AMIN. [Aside.] A will not tell me that he
  lies with her?
If he do, something heavenly stay my
  heart,
For I shall be apt to thrust this arm of
  mine
To acts unlawful!
KING.   You will suffer me
To talk with her, Amintor, and not have
A jealous pang?
AMIN.   Sir, I dare trust my wife
With whom she dares to talk, and not be
  jealous.   [Retires.]
KING. How do you like Amintor?
EVAD.   As I did, sir.   160
KING. How's that?

¹ *I.e.*, quickened with child.

EVAD. As one that, to fulfill your will and
  pleasure,
I have given leave to call me wife and
  love.
KING. I see there is no lasting faith in sin;
They that break word with heaven will
  break again
With all the world, and so dost thou
  with me.
EVAD. How, sir?
KING.   This subtle woman's ignorance
Will not excuse you; thou hast taken
  oaths,
So great that, methought, they did mis-
  become
A woman's mouth, that thou wouldst
  ne'er enjoy   170
A man but me.
EVAD.   I never did swear so;
You do me wrong.
KING.   Day and night have heard it.
EVAD. I swore indeed that I would never
  love
A man of lower place; but, if your for-
  tune
Should throw you from this height, I
  bade you trust
I would forsake you, and would bend to
  him
That won your throne. I love with my
  ambition,
Not with my eyes. But, if I ever yet
Touched any other, leprosy light here
Upon my face, which for your royalty
I would not stain!   181
KING. Why, thou dissemblest, and it is
  in me
To punish thee.
EVAD.   Why, it is in me, then,
Not to love you, which will more afflict
Your body than your punishment can
  mine.
KING. But thou hast let Amintor lie with
  thee.
EVAD. I ha' not.
KING.   Impudence! He says himself so.
EVAD. A lies.
KING.   A does not.
EVAD.   By this light, he does,
Strangely and basely, and I'll prove it
  so!
I did not only shun him for a night,   190
But told him I would never close with
  him.

KING. Speak lower; 'tis false.

EVAD. I am no man
To answer with a blow; or, if I were,
You are the king. But urge [me][1] not;
'tis most true.

KING. Do not I know the uncontrolléd
thoughts
That youth brings with him, when his
blood is high
With expectation and desire of that
He long hath waited for? Is not his
spirit,
Though he be temperate, of a valiant
strain
As this our age hath known? What could
he do, 200
If such a sudden speech had met his
blood,
But ruin thee forever, if he had not killed
thee?
He could not bear it thus; he is as we,
Or any other wronged man.

EVAD. It is dissembling.

KING. Take him! Farewell; henceforth
I am thy foe,
And what disgraces I can blot thee with
look for.

EVAD. Stay, sir!—Amintor!—You shall
hear.—Amintor!

AMIN. [Coming forward.] What, my love?

EVAD. Amintor, thou hast an ingenious[2]
look,
And shouldst be virtuous; it amazeth
me 210
That thou canst make such base, malicious lies!

AMIN. What, my dear wife?

EVAD. Dear wife! I do despise thee.
Why, nothing can be baser than to sow
Dissension amongst lovers.

AMIN. Lovers! Who?

EVAD. The king and me—

AMIN. O, God!

EVAD. Who should live long, and love
without distaste,
Were it not for such pickthanks[3] as
thyself.
Did you lie with me? Swear now, and be
punished
In hell for this!

AMIN. The faithless sin I made
To fair Aspatia is not yet revenged; 220
It follows me.—I will not lose a word

To this wild[4] woman; but to you, my
king,
The anguish of my soul thrusts out this
truth:
Y' are a tyrant!—and not so much to
wrong
An honest man thus, as to take a pride
In talking with him of it.

EVAD. Now, sir, see
How loud this fellow lied!

AMIN. You that can know to wrong, should
know how men
Must right themselves—what punishment is due
From me to him that shall abuse my
bed. 230
It is not death; nor can that satisfy,
Unless I send your lives[5] through all
the land,
To show how nobly I have freed myself.

KING. Draw not thy sword; thou knowest
I cannot fear
A subject's hand. But thou shalt feel
the weight
Of this, if thou dost rage.

AMIN. The weight of that!
If you have any worth, for heaven's
sake, think
I fear not swords; for, as you are mere
man,
I dare as easily kill you for this deed 239
As you dare think to do it. But there is
Divinity about you that strikes dead
My rising passions; as you are my king,
I fall before you, and present my sword
To cut mine own flesh, if it be your will.
Alas, I am nothing but a multitude
Of walking[6] griefs! Yet, should I mur-
der you,
I might before the world take the ex-
cuse
Of madness; for, compare[7] my injuries,
And they will well appear too sad a
weight 249
For reason to endure. But fall I[8] first
Amongst my sorrows, ere my treacher-
ous hand
Touch holy things! But why (I know
not what

---

[1] From 1630 edn. [2] Ingenuous. [3] Talebearers.

[4] Dyce suggests *vild*, i.e., vile.
[5] Life histories.
[6] So all edns. except original, which reads
waking.
[7] Examine. [8] *I.e.*, may I fall.

I have to say), why did you choose out me
To make thus wretched?   There were thousands, fools
Easy to work on, and of state [1] enough,
Within the island.
EVAD.   I would not have a fool;
It were no credit for me.
AMIN.   Worse and worse!
Thou, that dar'st talk unto thy husband thus,
Profess thyself a whore, and, more than so,
Resolve to be so still!—It is my fate   260
To bear and bow beneath a thousand griefs,
To keep that little credit with the world!—
But there were wise ones too; you might have ta'en
Another.
KING.   No; for I believe thee honest,
As thou wert valiant.
AMIN.   All the happiness [2]
Bestowed upon me turns into disgrace.
Gods, take your honesty again, for I
Am loaden with it!—Good my lord the king,
Be private in it.
KING.   Thou mayst live, Amintor,
Free as thy king, if thou wilt wink at this,   270
And be a means that we may meet in secret.
AMIN. A bawd! Hold, hold, my breast! A bitter curse
Seize me, if I forget not all respects
That are religious, on another word [3]
Sounded like that, and through a sea of sins
Will wade to my revenge, though I should call
Pains here and after life upon my soul!
KING. Well, I am resolute [4] you lay not with her;
And so I leave you.   Exit King.
EVAD.   You must needs be prating;
And see what follows!
AMIN.   Prithee, vex me not.   280
Leave me; I am afraid some sudden start
Will pull a murther on me.

[1] Estate, position.
[2] Good fortune.
[3] I.e., a repetition of bawd (?).
[4] Convinced.

EVAD.   I am gone;
I love my life well.   Exit Evadne.
AMIN.   I hate mine as much.
This 'tis to break a troth! I should be glad,
If all this tide of grief would make me mad.   Exit.

[SCENA ii.

A room in the palace.]

Enter Melantius.

MEL. I'll know the cause of all Amintor's griefs,
Or friendship shall be idle.[5]

Enter Calianax.

CAL.   O, Melantius,
My daughter will die!
MEL.   Trust me, I am sorry;
Would thou hadst ta'en her room!
CAL.   Thou art a slave,
A cutthroat slave, a bloody, treacherous slave!
MEL. Take heed, old man; thou wilt be heard to rave,
And lose thine offices.
CAL.   I am valiant grown
At all these years, and thou art but a slave!
MEL. Leave! Some company will come, and I respect
Thy years, not thee, so much that I could wish   10
To laugh at thee alone.
CAL.   I'll spoil your mirth.
I mean to fight with thee. There lie, my cloak!
This was my father's sword, and he durst fight.
Are you prepared?
MEL.   Why wilt thou dote thyself
Out of thy life? Hence, get thee to bed,
Have careful looking-to, and eat warm things,
And trouble not me; my head is full of thoughts
More weighty than thy life or death can be.
CAL. You have a name in war, where you stand safe
Amongst a multitude; but I will try   20

[5] Vain.

What you dare do unto a weak old man
In single fight. You'll give ground, I fear.
Come, draw!

MEL. I will not draw, unless thou pull'st
    thy death
Upon thee with a stroke. There's no
    one blow
That thou canst give hath strength
    enough to kill me.
Tempt me not so far, then; the power
    of earth
Shall not redeem thee.

CAL. [*Aside.*]   I must let him alone;
He's stout and able; and, to say the
    truth,
However I may set a face and talk, 30
I am not valiant. When I was a youth,
I kept my credit with a testy trick
I had amongst cowards, but durst never
    fight.

MEL. I will not promise to preserve your
    life,
If you do stay.

CAL. [*Aside.*]   I would give half my land
That I durst fight with that proud man
    a little.
If I had men to hold him, I would beat
    him
Till he ask me mercy.

MEL.   Sir, will you be gone?

CAL. [*Aside.*] I dare not stay; but I will
go home, and beat my servants all [40
over for this.   *Exit Calianax.*

MEL. This old fellow haunts me.
But the distracted carriage of mine
    Amintor
Takes deeply on me.[1] I will find the
    cause;
I fear his conscience cries he wronged
    Aspatia.

Enter Amintor.

AMIN. [*Aside.*] Men's eyes are not so
    subtle to perceive
My inward misery; I bear my grief
Hid from the world. How art thou
    wretched then?
For aught I know, all husbands are
    like me;
And every one I talk with of his wife 50
Is but a well dissembler of his woes,
As I am. Would I knew it! For the
    rareness

[1] Affects me deeply.

Afflicts me now.

MEL. Amintor, we have not enjoyed
our friendship of late, for we were wont
to charge [2] our souls in talk.

AMIN. Melantius, I can tell thee a
good jest of Strato and a lady the last day.

MEL. How was 't?

AMIN. Why, such an odd one!   60

MEL. I have longed to speak with you,
not of an idle jest, that's forced, but of
matter you are bound to utter to me.

AMIN. What is that, my friend?

MEL. I have observed your words fall
    from your tongue
Wildly, and all your carriage
Like one that strove to show his merry
    mood,
When he were ill disposed. You were
    not wont
To put such scorn into your speech, or
    wear
Upon your face ridiculous jollity. 70
Some sadness sits here, which your
    cunning would
Cover o'er with smiles, and 'twill not
    be.
What is it?

AMIN.   A sadness here! What cause
Can fate provide for me to make me so?
Am I not loved through all this isle?
    The king
Rains greatness on me. Have I not
    received
A lady to my bed, that in her eye
Keeps mounting fire, and on her tender
    cheeks
Inevitable [3] color, in her heart   79
A prison for all virtue? Are not you,
Which is above all joys, my constant
    friend?
What sadness can I have? No; I am
    light,
And feel the courses of my blood more
    warm
And stirring than they were. Faith,
    marry too,
And you will feel so unexpressed [4] a joy
In chaste embraces that you will indeed
Appear another.

MEL.   You may shape, Amintor,
Causes to cozen the whole world withal,
And yourself too; but 'tis not like a
    friend

[2] Weigh down.   [3] Irresistible.   [4] Inexpressible.

To hide your soul from me. 'Tis not
your nature   90
To be thus idle. I have seen you stand
As you were blasted midst of all your
    mirth,
Call thrice aloud, and then start, feign-
    ing joy
So coldly!—World, what do I here? A
    friend
Is nothing. Heaven, I would ha' told
    that man
My secret sins! I'll search [1] an unknown
    land,
And there plant friendship; all is with-
    ered here.
Come with a compliment! I would have
    fought,
Or told my friend a lied, ere soothed [2]
    him so.—
Out of my bosom!   100
AMIN. But there is nothing.
MEL.   Worse and worse! Farewell!
    From this time have acquaintance, but
    no friend.
AMIN. Melantius, stay; you shall know
    what that is.
MEL. See how you played with friendship!
    Be advised
How you give cause unto yourself to say
You ha' lost a friend.
AMIN.   Forgive what I ha' done,
For I am so o'ergone with injuries
Unheard of, that I lose consideration
Of what I ought to do. O, O!
MEL.   Do not weep.
What is 't? May I once but know the
    man   110
Hath turned my friend thus!
AMIN.   I had spoke at first
But that—
MEL.   But what?
AMIN.   I held it most unfit
For you to know. Faith, do not know
    it yet.
MEL. Thou seest my love, that will keep
    company
With thee in tears; hide nothing, then,
    from me,
For, when I know the cause of thy dis-
    temper,
With mine old armor I'll adorn myself,
My resolution, and cut through thy
    foes,

[1] *I.e.*, search for.   [2] Flattered.

Unto thy quiet, till I place thy heart
As peaceable as spotless innocence.   120
What is it?
AMIN.   Why, 'tis this—it is too big
To get out—let my tears make way
    awhile.
MEL. Punish me strangely, heaven, if he
    escape
Of life or fame, that brought this youth
    to this!
AMIN. Your sister—
MEL.   Well said.
AMIN.   You'll wish 't unknown,
When you have heard it.
MEL.   No.
AMIN.   —is much to blame,
And to the king has given her honor
    up,
And lives in whoredom with him.
MEL.   How's this?
Thou art run mad with injury indeed;
Thou couldst not utter this else. Speak
    again,   130
For I forgive it freely; tell thy griefs.
AMIN. She's wanton; I am loath to say
    "a whore,"
Though it be true.
MEL. Speak yet again, before mine anger
    grow
Up beyond throwing down. What are
    thy griefs?
AMIN. By all our friendship, these.
MEL.   What, am I tame?
After mine actions, shall the name of
    friend
Blot all our family, and strike the brand
Of whore upon my sister, unrevenged?
My shaking flesh, be thou a witness for
    me,   140
With what unwillingness I go to scourge
This railer, whom my folly hath called
    friend?
I will not take thee basely; thy sword
                    [*Draws his sword.*]
Hangs near thy hand; draw it, that I
    may whip
Thy rashness to repentance. Draw thy
    sword!
AMIN. Not on thee, did thine anger go as
    high
As the wild surges. Thou shouldst do
    me ease
Here and eternally, if thy noble hand
Would cut me from my sorrows.

MEL. This is base
And fearful.[1] They that use to utter lies 150
Provide not blows but words to qualify [2]
The men they wronged. Thou hast a guilty cause.

AMIN. Thou pleasest me; for so much more like this
Will raise my anger up above my griefs
(Which is a passion easier to be borne)
And I shall then be happy.

MEL. Take, then, more
To raise thine anger: 'tis mere cowardice
Makes thee not draw; and I will leave thee dead,
However. But, if thou art so much pressed
With guilt and fear as not to dare to fight, 160
I'll make thy memory loathed, and fix a scandal
Upon thy name forever.

AMIN. [Drawing his sword.] Then I draw,
As justly as our magistrates their swords
To cut offenders off. I knew before
'Twould grate your ears; but it was base in you
To urge a weighty secret from your friend,
And then rage at it. I shall be at ease,
If I be killed; and, if you fall by me,
I shall not long outlive you.

MEL. Stay awhile.— 169
The name of friend is more than family,
Or all the world besides; I was a fool.
Thou searching human nature, that didst wake
To do me wrong, thou art inquisitive,
And thrusts me upon questions that will take
My sleep away! Would I had died, ere known
This sad dishonor!—Pardon me, my friend! [Sheathes his sword.]
If thou wilt strike, here is a faithful heart;
Pierce it, for I will never heave my hand
To thine. Behold the power thou hast in me!

I do believe my sister is a whore, 180
A leprous one. Put up thy sword, young man.

AMIN. How should I bear it, then, she being so?
I fear, my friend, that you will lose me shortly; [Sheathes his sword.]
And I shall do a foul act on myself,
Through these disgraces.

MEL. Better half the land
Were buried quick [3] together. No, Amintor;
Thou shalt have ease. O, this adulterous king
That drew her to 't! Where got he the spirit
To wrong me so?

AMIN. What is it, then, to me,
If it be wrong to you?

MEL. Why, not so much. 190
The credit of our house is thrown away.
But from his iron den I'll waken Death,
And hurl him on this king. My honesty
Shall steel my sword; and on my horrid point
I'll wear my cause, that shall amaze the eyes
Of this proud man, and be too glittering
For him to look on.

AMIN. I have quite undone my fame.

MEL. Dry up thy watery eyes, 199
And cast a manly look upon my face,
For nothing is so wild as I, thy friend,
Till I have freed thee. Still this swelling breast.
I go thus from thee, and will never cease
My vengeance till I find my heart at peace.

AMIN. It must not be so. Stay. Mine eyes would tell
How loath I am to this; but, love and tears,
Leave me awhile, for I have hazarded
All that this world calls happy!—Thou hast wrought
A secret from me, under name of friend,
Which art could ne'er have found, nor torture wrung 210
From out my bosom. Give it me again,
For I will find it, wheresoe'er it lies,
Hid in the mortal'st part. Invent a way
To give it back.

___

[1] Cowardly.   [2] Mollify.   [3] Alive.

MEL.   Why would you have it back?
  I will to death pursue him with revenge.
AMIN. Therefore I call it back from thee,
  for I know
  Thy blood so high that thou wilt stir
  in this,
  And shame me to posterity. Take to
  thy weapon!   [*Draws his sword.*]
MEL. Hear thy friend, that bears more
  years than thou.
AMIN. I will not hear. But draw, or I—
MEL.   Amintor! 220
AMIN. Draw, then; for I am full as reso-
  lute
  As fame and honor can enforce me be.
  I cannot linger. Draw!
MEL. [*Drawing his sword.*]   I do. But is
  not
  My share of credit equal with thine,
  If I do stir?
AMIN.   No; for it will be called
  Honor in thee to spill thy sister's blood,
  If she her birth abuse; and on the king
  A brave revenge; but on me, that have
  walked
  With patience in it, it will fix the name
  Of fearful cuckold. O, that word! Be
  quick.   230
MEL. Then, join with me.
AMIN.   I dare not do a sin,
  Or else I would. Be speedy.
MEL. Then, dare not fight with me, for
  that's a sin.—
  [*Aside.*] His grief distracts him.—Call
  thy thoughts again,
  And to thyself pronounce the name of
  friend,
  And see what that will work. I will not
  fight.
AMIN. You must.
MEL. [*Sheathing his sword.*]   I will be
  killed first. Though my passions
  Offered the like to you, 'tis not this earth
  Shall buy my reason to it. Think awhile,
  For you are (I must weep when I speak
  that)   240
  Almost besides yourself.
AMIN. [*Sheathing his sword.*]   O, my soft
  temper!
  So many sweet words from thy sister's
  mouth
  I am afraid would make me take her to
  Embrace, and pardon her. I am mad
  indeed,

And know not what I do. Yet have a
  care
  Of me in what thou doest.
MEL.   Why, thinks my friend
  I will forget his honor, or, to save
  The bravery of our house, will lose his
  fame,
  And fear to touch the throne of majesty?
AMIN. A curse will follow that; but rather
  live   250
  And suffer with me.
MEL.   I will do what worth
  Shall bid me, and no more.
AMIN.   Faith, I am sick,
  And desperately I hope; yet, leaning
  thus,
  I feel a kind of ease.
MEL.   Come, take again
  Your mirth about you.
AMIN.   I shall never do 't.
MEL. I warrant you. Look up; we'll
  walk together.
  Put thine arm here; all shall be well
  again.
AMIN. Thy love (O, wretched!), ay, thy
  love, Melantius.
  Why, I have nothing else.
MEL.   Be merry, then. *Exeunt.*

Enter Melantius again.

MEL. This worthy young man may do
  violence   260
  Upon himself; but I have cherished
  him
  To my best power, and sent him smiling from me,
  To counterfeit again. Sword, hold thine
  edge;
  My heart will never fail me.—

Enter Diphilus.[1]

                    Diphilus!
  Thou com'st as [2] sent.
DIPH.   Yonder has been such laughing.
MEL. Betwixt whom?
DIPH.   Why, our sister and the king.
  I thought their spleens would break;
  they laughed us all
  Out of the room.
MEL. They must weep, Diphilus.
DIPH.   Must they?

---

[1] In original, direction appears a line later.
[2] As if.

MEL. 　　　　　　　They must.
Thou art my brother; and, if I did be-
　lieve 　　　　　　　　　　270
Thou hadst a base thought, I would rip
　it out,
Lie where it durst.
DIPH. 　　　You should not; I would first
Mangle myself and find it.
MEL. 　　　　　　　That was spoke
According to our strain. Come, join
　thy hands to mine,
And swear a firmness to what project I
Shall lay before thee.
DIPH. 　　　　You do wrong us both.
People hereafter shall not say there
　passed
A bond, more than our loves, to tie our
　lives
And deaths together. 　　　　　279
MEL. It is as nobly said as I would wish.
Anon [1] I'll tell you wonders: we are
　wronged.
DIPH. But I will tell you now, we'll right
　ourselves.
MEL. Stay not; prepare the armor in my
　house;
And what friends you can draw unto
　our side,
Not knowing of the cause, make ready
　too.
Haste, Diph[ilus]; the time requires it,
　haste!— 　　　　　　Exit Diphilus.
I hope my cause is just; I know my blood
Tells me it is; and I will credit it.
To take revenge, and lose myself withal,
Were idle, and to scape impossible 　290
Without I had the fort, which (misery!)
Remaining in the hands of my old en-
　emy,
Calianax—but I must have it. See

Enter Calianax.

Where he comes shaking by me!—Good
　my lord,
Forget your spleen to me. I never
　wronged you,
But would have peace with every man.
CAL. 　　　　　　　　　'Tis well.
If I durst fight, your tongue would lie
　at quiet.
MEL. Y' are touchy without all cause.
CAL. 　　　　　　　Do, mock me.

[1] At once.

MEL. By mine honor, I speak truth.
CAL. 　　　　Honor? Where is 't?
MEL. See, what starts you make 　300
Into your hatred, to my love
And freedom to you. I come with resolu-
　tion
To obtain a suit of you.
CAL. 　　　　　　A suit of me!
'Tis very like it should be granted, sir.
MEL. Nay, go not hence.
'Tis this: you have the keeping of the
　fort,
And I would wish you, by the love you
　ought
To bear unto me, to deliver it
Into my hands.
CAL. 　　　I am in hope thou art mad,
To talk to me thus.
MEL. 　　　　But there is a reason 　310
To move you to it: I would kill the king
That wronged you and your daughter.
CAL. 　　　　　　　Out, traitor!
MEL. Nay, but stay; I cannot scape, the
　deed once done,
Without I have this fort.
CAL. 　　　And should I help thee?
Now thy treacherous mind betrays it-
　self.
MEL. Come, delay me not.
Give me a sudden answer, or already
Thy last is spoke! Refuse not offered
　love 　　　　　　　　　318
When it comes clad in secrets.
CAL. [*Aside.*] 　　　　　If I say
I will not, he will kill me; I do see 't
Writ in his looks; and should I say I will,
He'll run and tell the king.—I do not
　shun
Your friendship, dear Melantius; but
　this cause
Is weighty. Give me but an hour to
　think.
MEL. Take it.—[*Aside.*] I know this goes
　unto the king;
But I am armed. 　　　　*Exit Melantius.*
CAL. 　　　　Methinks I feel myself
But twenty now again. This fighting
　fool 　　　　　　　　　327
Wants policy; I shall revenge my girl,
And make her red [2] again. I pray my legs
Will last that pace that I will carry them;
I shall want breath before I find the
　king. 　　　　　　　　　*Exit.*

[2] *I.e.*, healthy.

Actus IV. [Scena i.

Evadne's apartment.]

Enter Melantius, Evadne, and Ladies.[1]

MEL. Save you!

EVAD.   Save you, sweet brother.

MEL. In my blunt eye, methinks, you look [2] Evadne.

EVAD. Come, you would make me blush.

MEL.   I would, Evadne; I shall displease my ends else.

EVAD.   You shall, if you Commend [3] me; I am bashful. Come, sir, how do I look?

MEL.   I would not have your women hear me Break into commendations of you; 'tis not Seemly.

EVAD. [*To Ladies.*]   Go wait me in the gallery.— Now speak.

MEL.   I'll lock the door first.
                                Exeunt Ladies.

EVAD.   Why?

MEL. I will not have your gilded things, that dance   10 In visitation with their Milan skins,[4] Choke up my business.

EVAD.   You are strangely disposed, sir.

MEL. Good madam, not to make you merry.

EVAD. No; if you praise me, 'twill make me sad.

MEL. Such a sad commendations I have for you.

EVAD. Brother, The court hath made you witty, and learn to riddle.

MEL. I praise the court for 't; has it learned you nothing?

EVAD. Me?

MEL.   Ay, Evadne; thou art young and handsome, A lady of a sweet complexion,   20 And such a flowing carriage that it cannot Choose but inflame a kingdom.

EVAD.   Gentle brother!

MEL. 'Tis yet in thy repentance, foolish woman, To make me gentle.

EVAD.   How is this?

MEL.   'Tis base; And I could blush, at these years, through all My honored scars, to come to such a parley.

EVAD. I understand you not.

MEL.   You dare not, fool! They that commit thy faults fly the remembrance.

EVAD. My faults, sir! I would have you know I care not If they were written here, here in my forehead.   30

MEL. Thy body is too little for the story, The lusts of which would fill another woman,[5] Though she had twins within her.

EVAD.   This is saucy. Look you intrude no more! There's your way.

MEL. Thou art my way, and I will tread upon thee Till I find truth out.

EVAD.   What truth is that you look for?

MEL. Thy long-lost honor. Would the gods had set me Rather to grapple with the plague, or stand [6] One of their loudest bolts! Come, tell me quickly,   39 Do it without enforcement, and take heed You swell me not above my temper.

EVAD.   How, sir? Where got you this report?

MEL.   Where there was people, In every place.

EVAD.   They and the seconds of it Are base people. Believe them not; they lied.

MEL. Do not play with mine anger; do not, wretch!   [*Seizes her.*] I come to know that desperate fool that drew thee From thy fair life. Be wise, and lay him open.

EVAD. Unhand me, and learn manners! Such another Forgetfulness forfeits your life.

---

[1] Original has *a Lady*.   [4] Gloves.
[2] *I.e.*, look like.
[3] Theobald's emendation for *Command*.

[5] The account of whose lusts would cover the body of another woman.   [6] Withstand.

MEL. Quench me this mighty humor, and
    then tell me   50
Whose whore you are; for you are one,
    I know it.
Let all mine honors perish but I'll find
    him,
Though he lie locked up in thy blood!
    Be sudden;
There is no facing it;[1] and be not flattered.
The burnt air, when the Dog reigns, is
    not fouler
Than thy contagious name, till thy re-
    pentance
(If the gods grant thee any) purge thy
    sickness.
EVAD. Begone! You are my brother;
    that's your safety.
MEL. I'll be a wolf first. 'Tis, to be thy
    brother,
An infamy below the sin of coward. 60
I am as far from being part of thee
As thou art from thy virtue. Seek a
    kindred
Mongst sensual beasts, and make a goat
    thy brother;
A goat is cooler. Will you tell me yet?
EVAD. If you stay here and rail thus, I
    shall tell you
I'll ha' you whipped! Get you to your
    command,
And there preach to your sentinels, and
    tell them
What a brave man you are. I shall laugh
    at you.
MEL. Y' are grown a glorious[2] whore!
    Where be your fighters?
What mortal fool durst raise thee to
    this daring,   70
And I alive! By my just sword, h'ad safer
Bestride a billow when the angry North
Plows up the sea, or made heaven's fire
    his food!
Work me no higher. Will you discover
    yet?
EVAD. The fellow's mad. Sleep, and speak
    sense.
MEL. Force my swoln heart no further;
    I would save thee.
Your great maintainers are not here—
    they dare not.
Would they were all, and armed! I
    would speak loud;

Here's one should thunder to 'em! Will
    you tell me?
Thou hast no hope to scape. He that
    dares most,   80
And damns away his soul to do thee serv-
    ice,
Will sooner snatch meat from a hungry
    lion
Than come to rescue thee. Thou hast
    death about thee—
Has undone thine honor, poisoned thy
    virtue,
And, of a lovely rose, left thee a canker.[3]
EVAD. Let me consider.
MEL.   Do, whose child thou wert,
Whose honor thou hast murdered, whose
    grave opened,
And so pulled on[4] the gods that in their
    justice
They must restore him flesh again and
    life,
And raise his dry bones to revenge this
    scandal.   90
EVAD. The gods are not of my mind; they
    had better
Let 'em lie sweet still in the earth; they'll
    stink here.
MEL. Do you raise mirth out of my easi-
    ness?
Forsake me, then, all weaknesses of
    nature
That make men women! [Draws his
    sword.] Speak, you whore, speak truth,
Or, by the dear soul of thy sleeping
    father,
This sword shall be thy lover! Tell,
    or I'll kill thee;
And, when thou hast told all, thou wilt
    deserve it.
EVAD. You will not murther me?   99
MEL. No; 'tis a justice, and a noble one,
To put the light out of such base of-
    fenders.
EVAD. Help!
MEL. By thy foul self, no human help
    shall help thee,
If thou criest! When I have killed thee,
    as I
Have vowed to do, if thou confess not,
    naked
As thou hast left thine honor will I
    leave thee,

---

[1] I.e., there is nothing to be gained by main-
taining a false appearance.   [2] Boasting.

[3] Dog-rose; also a disease of plants.
[4] Provoked.

That on thy branded flesh the world
  may read
Thy black shame and my justice. Wilt
  thou bend yet?
EVAD. Yes.
MEL. Up, and begin your story.   110
EVAD. O, I am miserable!
MEL. 'Tis true, thou art. Speak truth
  still.
EVAD. I have offended; noble sir, forgive
  me!
MEL. With what secure [1] slave?
EVAD.   Do not ask me, sir;
  Mine own remembrance is a misery
  Too mighty for me.
MEL.   Do not fall back again;
  My sword's unsheathéd yet.
EVAD.   What shall I do?
MEL. Be true, and make your fault less.
EVAD.   I dare not tell.
MEL. Tell, or I'll be this day a-killing thee.
EVAD. Will you forgive me, then?   120
MEL. Stay; I must ask mine honor first.
  I have too much foolish nature in me.
  Speak.
EVAD. Is there none else here?
MEL. None but a fearful conscience;
  that's too many.
  Who is 't?
EVAD.   O, hear me gently! It was
  the king.
MEL. No more! My worthy father's and
  my services
  Are liberally rewarded! King, I thank
  thee!
  For all my dangers and my wounds thou
  hast paid me
  In my own metal: these are soldiers'
  thanks!—
  How long have you lived thus, Evadne?
EVAD.   Too long. 130
MEL. Too late you find it. Can you be
  sorry?
EVAD. Would I were half as blameless!
MEL. Evadne, thou wilt to thy trade
  again.
EVAD. First to my grave.
MEL.   Would gods thou
  hadst been so blessed!
  Dost thou not hate this king now?
  Prithee, hate him.
  Couldst thou not curse him? I com-
  mand thee, curse him;

[1] Overconfident.

Curse till the gods hear, and deliver
  him
To thy just wishes. Yet I fear, Evadne,
You had rather play your game out.
EVAD.   No; I feel
Too many sad confusions here, to let
  in   140
Any loose flame hereafter.
MEL. Dost thou not feel, amongst all
  those, one brave anger
That breaks out nobly, and directs
  thine arm
To kill this base king?
EVAD.   All the gods forbid it!
MEL. No, all the gods require it;
  They are dishonored in him.
EVAD.   'Tis too fearful.
MEL. Y' are valiant in his bed, and bold
  enough
To be a stale whore, and have your
  madam's name
Discourse for grooms and pages, and
  hereafter,
When his cool majesty hath laid you
  by,   150
To be at pension with some needy sir
For meat and coarser clothes; thus far
  you know
No fear. Come, you shall kill him.
EVAD.   Good sir!
MEL. An 'twere to kiss him dead, thou'dst
  smother him.
Be wise, and kill him. Canst thou live,
  and know
What noble minds shall make thee,
  see thyself
Found out with every finger, made the
  shame
Of all successions, and in this great
  ruin
Thy brother and thy noble husband
  broken?
Thou shalt not live thus. Kneel, and
  swear to help me,   160
When I shall call thee to it; or, by
  all
Holy in heaven and earth, thou shalt
  not live
To breathe a full hour longer; not a
  thought!
Come, 'tis a righteous oath. Give me
  thy hand[s],
And, both to heaven held up, swear, by
  that wealth

This lustful thief stole from thee, when
　　I say it,
To let his foul soul out.

EVAD.　　　　　　　　Here I swear it;
And, all you spirits of abuséd ladies,
Help me in this performance!

MEL. Enough.　This must be known to
　　none　　　　　　　　　　　　　　170
But you and I, Evadne—not to your
　　lord,
Though he be wise and noble, and a
　　fellow
Dares step as far into a worthy action
As the most daring, ay, as far as justice.
Ask me not why.　Farewell!
　　　　　　　　　　　　Exit Mel[antius].

EVAD. Would I could say so to my black
　　disgrace!
O, where have I been all this time?
　　How friended,
That I should lose myself thus desper-
　　ately,
And none for pity show me how I
　　wandered?　　　　　　　　　　　179
There is not in the compass of the light
A more unhappy creature; sure, I am
　　monstrous,
For I have done those follies, those mad
　　mischiefs,
Would dare [1] a woman.　O, my loaden
　　soul,
Be not so cruel to me; choke not up
The way to my repentance!—

Enter Amintor.

　　　　　　　　　　　　　　O, my lord!

AMIN. How now?

EVAD.　　My much abuséd lord! [*Kneels.*]

AMIN.　　　　　　　　This cannot be!

EVAD. I do not kneel to live; I dare not
　　hope it.
The wrongs I did are greater.　Look
　　upon me,
Though I appear with all my faults.

AMIN.　　　　　　　　Stand up!　　189
This is no new way to beget more sorrow!
Heaven knows I have too many.　Do
　　not mock me;
Though I am tame, and bred up with
　　my wrongs,
Which are my foster-brothers, I may
　　leap,

[1] Frighten.

Like a hand-wolf,[2] into my natural
　　wildness,
And do an outrage.　Prithee, do not
　　mock me.

EVAD. My whole life is so leprous, it
　　infects
All my repentance.　I would buy your
　　pardon,
Though at the highest set,[3] even with
　　my life,
That slight contrition—that's [4] no sacri-
　　fice
For what I have committed.

AMIN.　　　　　　　Sure, I dazzle;　200
There cannot be a faith in that foul
　　woman,
That knows no god more mighty than
　　her mischiefs.
Thou dost still worse, still number on
　　thy faults,
To press my poor heart thus.　Can I
　　believe
There's any seed of virtue in that woman
Left to shoot up, that dares go on in
　　sin
Known, and so known as thine is? O,
　　Evadne!
Would there were any safety [5] in thy
　　sex
That I might put a thousand sorrows
　　off,
And credit thy repentance! But I must
　　not.　　　　　　　　　　　　210
Thou hast brought me to that dull
　　calamity,
To that strange misbelief of all the world
And all things that are in it, that I
　　fear
I shall fall like a tree, and find my grave,
Only rememb'ring that I grieve.

EVAD.　　　　　　　　　My lord,
Give me your griefs.　You are an inno-
　　cent,
A soul as white as heaven.　Let not my
　　sins
Perish [6] your noble youth.　I do not fall
　　here
To shadow by dissembling with my
　　tears　　　　　　　　　　　　219
(As all say women can) or to make less

[2] Hand-raised, tamed wolf.
[3] Stake.
[4] From 1630 edn.　Original reads *that.*
[5] Trustworthiness.　　　　　　[6] Destroy.

What my hot will hath done, which
    heaven and you
Knows to be tougher than the hand of
    time
Can cut from man's remembrance. No,
    I do not.
I do appear the same, the same Evadne,
Dressed in the shames I lived in, the
    same monster.
But these are names of honor to what
    I am;
I do present myself the foulest creature,
Most poisonous, dangerous, and de-
    spised of men,
Lerna e'er bred or Nilus. I am hell,
Till you, my dear lord, shoot your light
    into me,   230
The beams of your forgiveness; I am
    soul-sick,
And wither with the fear of one con-
    demned,
Till I have got your pardon.
AMIN.   Rise, Evadne!
Those heavenly powers that put this
    good into thee
Grant a continuance of it! I forgive thee.
Make thyself worthy of it, and take
    heed,
Take heed, Evadne, this be serious.
Mock not the powers above, that can
    and dare
Give thee a great example of their jus-
    tice
To all ensuing eyes, if thou play'st   240
With thy repentance, the best sacrifice.
EVAD. I have done nothing good to win
    belief,
My life hath been so faithless. All the
    creatures,
Made for heaven's honors, have their
    ends, and good ones,
All but the cozening crocodiles, false
    women.
They reign here like those plagues, those
    killing sores,
Men pray against; and, when they die,
    like tales
Ill told and unbelieved, they pass away,
And go to dust forgotten. But, my
    lord,
Those short days I shall number to my
    rest   250
(As many must not see me), shall—
    though too late.

Though in my evening—yet perceive
    a will
(Since I can do no good, because a
    woman)
Reach constantly at something that is
    near it.
I will redeem one minute of my age,
Or, like another Niobe, I'll weep
Till I am water.
AMIN.   I am now dissolved.
My frozen soul melts. May each sin
    thou hast,
Find a new mercy! Rise; I am at
    peace.
Hadst thou been thus, thus excellently
    good   260
Before that devil-king tempted thy
    frailty,
Sure thou hadst made a star. Give me
    thy hand;
From this time I will know thee; and,
    as far
As honor gives me leave, be thy Amintor.
When we meet next, I will salute thee
    fairly,
And pray the gods to give thee happy
    days.
My charity shall go along with thee,
Though my embraces must be far from
    thee.
I should ha' killed thee, but this sweet
    repentance
Locks up my vengeance, for which thus
    I kiss thee—   270
The last kiss we must take—and would
    to heaven
The holy priest that gave our hands to-
    gether
Had given us equal virtues! Go,
    Evadne;
The gods thus part our bodies. Have a
    care
My honor falls no farther. I am well,
    then.
EVAD. All the dear joys here, and above
    hereafter,
Crown thy fair soul! Thus I take leave,
    my lord;
And never shall you see the foul
    Evadne
Till she have tried all honored means
    that may
Set her in rest and wash her stains
    away.   *Exeunt.*   280

[SCENA ii.

A hall in the palace.]

Banquet. Enter King, Calianax. Hautboys play within.

KING. I cannot tell how I should credit this
From you, that are his enemy.

CAL. I am sure
He said it to me; and I'll justify it
What way he dares oppose—but with my sword.

KING. But did he break,[1] without all circumstance,[2]
To you, his foe, that he would have the fort
To kill me, and then scape?

CAL. If he deny it,
I'll make him blush.

KING. It sounds incredibly.

CAL. Ay, so does everything I say of late.

KING. Not so, Calianax.

CAL. Yes, I should sit 10
Mute, whilst a rogue with strong arms
cuts your throat.

KING. Well, I will try him; and, if this be true,
I'll pawn my life I'll find it; if 't be false,
And that you clothe your hate in such a lie,
You shall hereafter dote in your own house,
Not in the court.

CAL. Why, if it be a lie,
Mine ears are false, for I'll be sworn I heard it.
Old men are good for nothing; you were best
Put me to death for hearing, and free him
For meaning it. You would 'a' trusted me 20
Once, but the time is altered.

KING. And will still,
Where I may do with justice to the world.
You have no witness.

CAL. Yes, myself.

KING. No more,
I mean, there were that heard it.

CAL. How? No more?
Would you have more? Why, am not I enough
To hang a thousand rogues?

KING. But so you may
Hang honest men too, if you please.

CAL. I may!
'Tis like I will do so; there are a hundred
Will swear it for a need too, if I say it.

KING. Such witnesses we need not.

CAL. And 'tis hard 30
If my word cannot hang a boisterous knave.

KING. Enough.—Where's Strato?

STRA. Sir?

Enter Strat[o].

KING. Why, where's all the company?
Call Amintor in;

EVADNE. Where's my brother, and Melantius?
Bid him come too; and Diphilus. Call all
That are without there.—(*Exit Strat[o].*)
If he should desire
The combat of you, 'tis not in the power
Of all our laws to hinder it, unless
We mean to quit 'em.

CAL. Why, if you do think 40
'Tis fit an old man and a councilor
To fight for what he says, then you may grant it.

Enter Amint[or], Evad[ne], Melant[ius], Diph[ilus], Lysip[pus], Cle[on], Stra[to], Diag[oras].

KING. Come, sirs!—Amintor, thou art yet a bridegroom,
And I will use thee so; thou shalt sit down.—
Evadne, sit; and you, Amintor, too;
This banquet is for you, sir.—Who has brought
A merry tale about him, to raise laughter
Amongst our wine? Why, Strato, where art thou?
Thou wilt chop out with them[3] unseasonably,
When I desire 'em not. 50

STRA. 'Tis my ill luck, sir, so to spend them, then.

KING. Reach me a bowl of wine.—Melantius, thou
Art sad.

MEL.[4] I should be, sir, the merriest here,

---

[1] Impart.　　[2] Without any ceremony.
[3] *I.e.,* blurt out tales.
[4] From 1619 edn. Original reads *Amint.*

But I ha' ne'er a story of mine own
Worth telling at this time.
KING.　　　　　　Give me the wine.—
Melantius, I am now considering
How easy 'twere for any man we trust
To poison one of us in such a bowl.
MEL. I think it were not hard, sir, for a
knave.
CAL. [*Aside.*] Such as you are.　　60
KING. I' faith, 'twere easy. It becomes
us well
To get plain-dealing men about our-
selves,
Such as you all are here.—Amintor, to
thee,
And to thy fair Evadne.　　[*Drinks.*]
MEL. (*Aside.*)　　　Have you thought
Of this, Calianax?
CAL. [*Aside.*]　　　Yes, marry, have I.
MEL. [*Aside.*] And what's your resolu-
tion?
CAL. [*Aside.*]　　　Ye shall have it—
[*To himself.*] Soundly, I warrant you.
KING. Reach to Amintor, Strato.
AMIN.　　　　　　Here, my love.
　　[*Drinks and hands the cup to Evadne.*]
This wine will do thee wrong, for it will
set
Blushes upon thy cheeks; and, till thou
dost　　　　　　　　　　　70
A fault, 'twere pity.
KING.　　　　Yet I wonder much
Of [1] the strange desperation of these
men
That dare attempt such acts here in our
state.
He could not scape that did it.
MEL.　　　　　Were he known,
Unpossible.
KING. It would be known, Melantius.
MEL. It ought to be. If he got then away,
He must wear all our lives upon his
sword.
He need not fly the island; he must
leave
No one alive.
KING.　　No; I should think no man
Could kill me, and scape clear, but that
old man.　　　　　　　　　80
CAL. But I! Heaven bless me! I! Should
I, my liege?
KING. I do not think thou wouldst; but
yet thou mightst,

¹ At.

For thou hast in thy hands the means
to scape,
By keeping of the fort.—He has, Melan-
tius,
And he has kept it well.
MEL.　　　　　From cobwebs, sir,
'Tis clean swept; I can find no other
art
In keeping of it now.　'Twas ne'er be-
sieged
Since he commanded.
CAL.　　　　　I shall be sure
Of your good word; but I have kept it
safe
From such as you.
MEL.　　Keep your ill temper in.　90
I speak no malice; had my brother kept
it,
I should ha' said as much.
KING.　　　　You are not merry.
Brother, drink wine. Sit you all still!—
　　(*Aside.*) Calianax,
I cannot trust thus. I have thrown out
words
That would have fetched warm blood
upon the cheeks
Of guilty men, and he is never moved;
He knows no such thing.
CAL.　　　　Impudence may scape,
When feeble virtue is accused.
KING.　　　　　　A must,
If he were guilty, feel an alteration
At this our whisper, whilst we point
at him.　　　　　　　　　100
You see he does not.
CAL.　　Let him hang himself.
What care I what he does? This he did
say.
KING. Melan[tius], you can easily con-
ceive
What I have meant, for men that are
in fault
Can subtly apprehend when others aim
At what they do amiss; but I forgive
Freely before this man. Heaven do so
too!
I will not touch thee, so much as with
shame
Of telling it. Let it be so no more.
CAL. Why, this is very fine!
MEL.　　　　I cannot tell　110
What 'tis you mean; but I am apt
enough
Rudely to thrust into ignorant fault.

But let me know it. Happily [1] 'tis naught
But misconstruction; and, where I am clear,
I will not take forgiveness of the gods,
Much less of you.

KING. Nay, if you stand so stiff,
I shall call back my mercy.

MEL. I want smoothness
To thank a man for pardoning of a crime
I never knew.

KING. Not to instruct your knowledge, but to show you 120
My ears are everywhere; you meant to kill me,
And get the fort to scape.

MEL. Pardon me, sir;
My bluntness will be pardoned. You preserve
A race of idle people here about you,
Eaters and talkers, to defame the worth
Of those that do things worthy. The man that uttered this
Had perished without food, be 't who it will,
But for this arm, that fenced him from the foe;
And, if I thought you gave a faith to this,
The plainness of my nature would speak more. 130
Give me a pardon (for you ought to do 't)
To kill him that spake this.

CAL. [Aside.] Ay, that will be
The end of all; then I am fairly paid
For all my care and service.

MEL. That old man,
Who calls me enemy, and of whom I
(Though I will never match my hate so low)
Have no good thought, would yet, I think, excuse me,
And swear he thought me wronged in this.

CAL. Who, I?
Thou shameless fellow, didst thou not speak to me
Of it thyself?

MEL. O, then it came from him! 140

CAL. From me! Who should it come from but from me?

MEL. Nay, I believe your malice is enough;

[1] Haply.

But I ha' lost my anger.—Sir, I hope
You are well satisfied.

KING. Lysip[pus], cheer
Amintor and his lady.—There's no sound
Comes from you; I will come and do 't myself.

AMIN. [Aside.] You have done already, sir, for me, I thank you.

KING. Melantius, I do credit this from him,
How slight soe'er you make 't.

MEL. 'Tis strange you should.

CAL. 'Tis strange a should believe an old man's word 150
That never lied in 's life!

MEL. I talk not to thee.—
Shall the wild words of this distempered man,
Frantic with age and sorrow, make a breach
Betwixt your majesty and me? 'Twas wrong
To hearken to him; but to credit him,
As much at least as I have power to bear—
But pardon me—whilst I speak only truth,
I may commend myself—I have bestowed
My careless blood with you, and should be loath
To think an action that would make me lose 160
That and my thanks too. When I was a boy,
I thrust myself into my country's cause,
And did a deed that plucked five years from time,
And styled me man then. And for you, my king,
Your subjects all have fed by virtue of
My arm. This sword of mine hath plowed the ground,
And reaped the fruit in peace;
And you yourself have lived at home in ease.
So terrible I grew that, without swords,
My name hath fetched you conquest;
and my heart 170
And limbs are still the same; my will as great
To do you service. Let me not be paid
With such a strange distrust.

KING.   Melant[ius],
I held it great injustice to believe
Thine enemy, and did not; if I did,
I do not; let that satisfy.—What, struck
With sadness,[1] all? More wine!
CAL.   A few fine words
Have overthrown my truth. Ah, thou'rt
a villain!
MEL. (*Aside.*) Why, thou wert better
let me have the fort.
Dotard, I will disgrace thee thus for-
ever.   180
There shall no credit lie upon thy words.
Think better, and deliver it.
CAL.   My liege,
He's at me now again to do it.—Speak!
Deny it, if thou canst.—Examine him
Whilst he is hot, for, if he cool again,
He will forswear it.
KING.   This is lunacy,
I hope, Melantius.
MEL.   He hath lost himself
Much, since his daughter missed the
happiness
My sister gained; and, though he call
me foe,
I pity him.
CAL.   A pity! A pox upon you! 190
MEL. Mark his disordered words; and
at the masque
Diagoras knows he raged and railed
at me,
And called a lady "whore," so innocent
She understood him not. But it be-
comes
Both you and me too to forgive dis-
traction.[2]
Pardon him, as I do.
CAL.   I'll not speak for thee,
For all thy cunning.—If you will be
safe,
Chop off his head, for there was never
known
So impudent a rascal.
KING.   Some that love him
Get him to bed. Why, pity should not
let   200
Age make itself contemptible; we must
be
All old. Have him away.
MEL. [*Aside.*]   Calianax,
The king believes you Come, you shall
go home,

And rest; you ha' done well. You'll
give it up,
When I have used you thus a month,
I hope.
CAL. Now, now, 'tis plain, sir; he does
move me still.
He says he knows I'll give him up the
fort,
When he has used me thus a month. I
am mad,
Am I not, still?
OMNES. Ha, ha, ha!   210
CAL. I shall be mad indeed, if you do
thus.
Why should you trust a sturdy fellow
there
(That has no virtue in him; all's in his
sword)
Before me? Do but take his weapons
from him,
And he's an ass; and I am a very fool,
Both with him and without him, as you
use me.
OMNES. Ha, ha, ha!
KING. 'Tis well, Cal[ianax]; but, if you
use
This once again, I shall entreat some
other
To see your offices be well discharged.—
Be merry, gentlemen.—It grows some-
what late.—   221
Amintor, thou wouldst be abed again.
AMIN. Yes, sir.
KING.   And you, Evadne.—Let me take
Thee in my arms, Melantius, and be-
lieve
Thou art, as thou deservest to be, my
friend
Still and forever.—Good Cal[ianax],
Sleep soundly; it will bring thee to
thyself.
Exeunt omnes.   Manent [3] *Mel[antius] and
Cal[ianax].*
CAL. Sleep soundly! I sleep soundly now,
I hope;
I could not be thus else.—How dar'st
thou stay
Alone with me, knowing how thou hast
used me?   230
MEL. You cannot blast me with your
tongue, and that's
The strongest part you have about you.
CAL.   ]

---

[1] Seriousness.   [2] Madness.   [3] Remain.

Do look for some great punishment for
　　this,
For I begin to forget all my hate,
And take 't unkindly that mine enemy
　Should use me so extraordinarily scur-
　　vily.
MEL. I shall melt too, if you begin to take
Unkindnesses; I never meant you hurt.
CAL. Thou'lt anger me again.　Thou
　　wretched rogue,
　"Meant me no hurt"!　Disgrace me with
　　the king!　　　　　　　　　　240
　Lose all my offices!　This is no hurt,
　Is it?　I prithee, what dost thou call
　　hurt?
MEL. To poison men, because they love
　　me not;
　To call the credit of men's wives in ques-
　　tion;
　To murder children betwixt me and
　　land—
　This I call hurt.
CAL.　　　All this thou think'st is sport;
　For mine is worse.　But use thy will
　　with me;
　For betwixt grief and anger I could cry.
MEL. Be wise, then, and be safe; thou
　　mayst revenge—
CAL. Ay, o' th' king!　I would revenge of
　　thee.　　　　　　　　　　　　250
MEL. That you must plot yourself.
CAL.　　　　　　　I'm a fine plotter.
MEL. The short is, I will hold thee with
　　the king
　In this perplexity, till peevishness
　And thy disgrace have laid thee in thy
　　grave.
　But, if thou wilt deliver up the fort,
　I'll take thy trembling body in my arms,
　And bear thee over dangers.　Thou
　　shalt hold
　Thy wonted state.
CAL.　　　　　If I should tell the king,
　Canst thou deny 't again?
MEL.　　　　　　　Try, and believe.
CAL. Nay, then, thou canst bring any-
　　thing about.　　　　　　　　260
　Thou shalt have the fort.
MEL. Why, well.
　Here let our hate be buried; and this
　　hand
　Shall right us both.　Give me thy aged
　　breast
　To compass.

CAL.　　　Nay, I do not love thee yet;
　I cannot well endure to look on thee;
　And, if I thought it were a courtesy,
　Thou shouldst not have it.　But I am
　　disgraced;
　My offices are to be ta'en away;
　And, if I did but hold this fort a day,
　I do believe the king would take it from
　　me,　　　　　　　　　　　271
　And give it thee, things are so strangely
　　carried.
　Ne'er thank me for 't; but yet the king
　　shall know
　There was some such thing in 't I told
　　him of,
　And that I was an honest man.
MEL.　　　　　　　　　He'll buy
　That knowledge very dearly.—

Enter Diphilus.

　　　　　　　　　　　Diph[ilus],
　What news with thee?
DIPH.　　　　　This were a night indeed
　To do it in; the king hath sent for her.
MEL. She shall perform it then.—Go,
　　Diph[ilus],
　And take from this good man, my
　　worthy friend,　　　　　　　280
　The fort; he'll give it thee.
DIPH.　　　　　　Ha' you got that?
CAL. Art thou of the same breed?　Canst
　　thou deny
　This to the king too?
DIPH.　　　　　　With a confidence
　As great as his.
CAL. Faith, like enough.
MEL. Away, and use him kindly.
CAL.　　　　　　　Touch not me;
　I hate the whole strain.　If thou follow
　　me
　A great way off, I'll give thee up the
　　fort—
　And hang yourselves!
MEL.　　　Begone.
DIPH.　　　　　He's finely wrought.[1]
　　Exeunt Cal[ianax], Diph[ilus].
MEL. This is a night, spite of astrono-
　　mers,[2]　　　　　　　　290
　To do the deed in.　I will wash the stain
　That rests upon our house off with his
　　blood.

[1] Wrought up, excited.
[2] Astrologers.

Enter Amintor.

AMIN. Melantius, now assist me. If thou
   beest
That which thou say'st, assist me. I
   have lost
All my distempers, and have found a
   rage
So pleasing! Help me.
MEL. [*Aside.*]   Who can see him thus,
   And not swear vengeance?—What's
   the matter, friend?
AMIN. Out with thy sword; and, hand in
   hand with me,
Rush to the chamber of this hated king,
And sink him with the weight of all his
   sins   300
To hell forever.
MEL.   'Twere a rash attempt,
Not to be done with safety. Let your
   reason
Plot your revenge, and not your passion.
AMIN. If thou refusest me in these ex-
   tremes,
Thou art no friend. He sent for her to
   me;
By heaven, to me, myself! And, I must
   tell ye,
I love her as a stranger; there is worth
In that vild woman, worthy things,
   Melantius;
And she repents. I'll do 't myself alone,
Though I be slain. Farewell.
MEL. [*Aside.*]   He'll overthrow   310
My whole design with madness.—
   Amintor,
Think what thou doest. I dare as much
   as valor,
But 'tis the king, the king, the king,
   Amintor,
With whom thou fightest!—(*Aside.*) I
   know he's honest,[1]
And this will work with him.
AMIN.   I cannot tell
What thou hast said; but thou hast
   charmed my sword
Out of my hand, and left me shaking
   here,
Defenseless.
MEL.   I will take it up for thee.
AMIN. What a wild beast is uncollected[2]
   man!

[1] Loyal.
[2] Not self-controlled.

The thing that we call honor bears us all
Headlong unto sin, and yet itself is
   nothing.   321
MEL. Alas, how variable are thy thoughts!
AMIN. Just like my fortunes. I was run
   to [3] that
I purposed to have chid thee for. Some
   plot
I did distrust thou hadst against the
   king,
By that old fellow's carriage. But take
   heed;
There's not the least limb growing to
   a king
But carries thunder in 't.
MEL.   I have none
Against him.
AMIN.   Why, come, then; and still
   remember
We may not think revenge.
MEL.   I will remember. *Exeunt.*   330

ACTUS V. [SCENA i.

An anteroom opening upon the king's bed-
chamber curtained off on the inner
stage.]

Enter Evadne and a Gentleman [of the bed-
chamber].

EVAD. Sir, is the king abed?
GENT.   Madam, an hour ago.
EVAD. Give me the key, then, and let
   none be near;
'Tis the king's pleasure.
GENT. I understand you, madam; would
   'twere mine!
I must not wish good rest unto your
   ladyship.
EVAD. You talk, you talk.
GENT. 'Tis all I dare do, madam; but
   the king
Will wake, and then—
EVAD. Saving your imagination, pray,
   good night, sir.
GENT. A good night be it, then, and a
   long one, madam.   10
I am gone.   *Exit.*
EVAD. The night grows horrible, and all
   about me
Like my black purpose. O, the con-
   science   *King abed.*
Of a lost virgin, whither wilt thou pull
   me?

[3] *I.e.*, just on the point of doing.

To what things dismal as the depth of
hell
Wilt thou provoke me? Let no woman
dare
From this hour be disloyal, if her heart
be flesh,
If she have blood, and can fear. 'Tis a
daring
Above that desperate fool's that left
his peace,
And went to sea to fight; 'tis so many
sins,   20
An age cannot prevent [1] 'em, and so
great
The gods want mercy for. Yet I must
through 'em.
I have begun a slaughter on my honor,
And I must end it there.—A sleeps.
Good heavens!
Why give you peace to this untemperate
beast,
That hath so long transgressed you?
I must kill him,
And I will do 't bravely; the mere joy
Tells me, I merit in it. Yet I must not
Thus tamely do it as he sleeps—that
were
To rock him to another world. My
vengeance   30
Shall take him waking, and then lay be-
fore him
The number of his wrongs and punish-
ments.
I'll shape his sins like Furies, till I
waken
His evil angel, his sick conscience,
And then I'll strike him dead.—King,
by your leave!—
            Ties his arms to the bed.
I dare not trust your strength; your
grace and I
Must grapple upon even terms no more.
So, if he rail me not from my resolu-
tion,
I shall be strong enough.—My lord the
king!
My lord!—A sleeps, as if he meant to
wake   40
No more.—My lord!—Is he not dead
already?—
Sir! My lord!
KING. Who's that?
EVAD. O, you sleep soundly, sir!

[1] Recount (?). 1619 edn. has *repent.*

KING.   My dear Evadne,
I have been dreaming of thee; come to
bed.
EVAD. I am come at length, sir; but how
welcome?
KING. What pretty new device is this,
Evadne?
What, do you tie me to you? By my love,
This is a quaint one. Come, my dear,
and kiss me.
I'll be thy Mars; to bed, my Queen of
Love.   50
Let us be caught together, that the
gods
May see and envy our embraces.
EVAD.   Stay, sir, stay;
You are too hot, and I have brought
you physic
To temper your high veins.
KING. Prithee, to bed then; let me take
it warm.
There thou shalt know the state of my
body better.
EVAD. I know you have a surfeited, foul
body,
And you must bleed. [*Draws a knife.*]
KING. Bleed!
EVAD. Ay, you shall bleed. Lie still; and,
if the devil,   60
Your lust, will give you leave, repent.
This steel
Comes to redeem the honor that you
stole,
King, my fair name, which nothing but
thy death
Can answer to the world.
KING.   How's this, Evadne?
EVAD. I am not she; nor bear I in this
breast
So much cold spirit to be called a woman.
I am a tiger; I am anything
That knows not pity. Stir not! If thou
dost,
I'll take thee unprepared, thy fears
upon thee,
That make thy sins look double, and
so send thee   70
(By my revenge, I will!) to look [2] those
torments
Prepared for such black souls.
KING. Thou dost not mean this; 'tis im-
possible.
Thou art too sweet and gentle.

[2] Behold.

EVAD.   No, I am not;
I am as foul as thou art, and can number
As many such hells here. I was once
    fair;
Once I was lovely, not a blowing rose
More chastely sweet, till thou, thou,
    thou, foul canker
(Stir not!), didst poison me. I was a
    world of virtue,
Till your cursed court and you (hell
    bless you for 't!)   80
With your temptations on temptations
Made me give up mine honor, for which,
    king,
I am come to kill thee.
KING.   No!
EVAD.   I am.
KING.   Thou art not!
I prithee, speak not these things. Thou
    art gentle,
And wert not meant thus rugged.
EVAD.   Peace, and hear me.
Stir nothing but your tongue, and that
    for mercy
To those above us, by whose lights I vow,
Those blessed fires [1] that shot to see
    our sin,
If thy hot soul had substance with thy
    blood,
I would kill that too; which, being past
    my steel,   90
My tongue shall reach.   Thou art a
    shameless villain,
A thing out of the overcharge of nature,
Sent like a thick cloud to disperse a
    plague
Upon weak, catching [2] women—such
    a tyrant
That for his lust would sell away his
    subjects,
Ay, all his heaven hereafter!
KING.   Hear, Evadne,
Thou soul of sweetness, hear! I am thy
    king.
EVAD. Thou art my shame!   Lie still;
    there's none about you,
Within your cries; all promises of safety
Are but deluding dreams. Thus, thus,
    thou foul man,   100
Thus I begin my vengeance! *Stabs him.*
KING.   Hold, Evadne!
I do command thee hold.
EVAD.   I do not mean, sir,

To part so fairly with you; we must
    change
More of these love tricks yet.
KING.   What bloody villain
Provoked thee to this murther?
EVAD.   Thou, thou monster!
KING. O!
EVAD. Thou kept'st me brave [3] at court,
    and whored me, king;
Then married me to a young, noble
    gentleman,
And whored me still.
KING.   Evadne, pity me!
EVAD. Hell take me, then!   This for my
    lord, Amintor!   110
This for my noble brother!   And this
    stroke
For the most wronged of women!
                        Kills him.
KING.   O, I die!
EVAD. Die all our faults together!   I for-
    give thee.   *Exit.* [4]

Enter Two of the bedchamber.

1. Come, now she's gone, let's enter;
the king expects it, and will be angry.
2. 'Tis a fine wench; we'll have a snap
at her one of these nights, as she goes from
him.
1. Content. How quickly he had done
with her! I see kings can do no more   [120
that way than other mortal people.
2. How fast [5] he is! I cannot hear him
    breathe.
1. Either the tapers give a feeble light,
Or he looks very pale.
2.   And so he does.
Pray heaven he be well; let's look.—
    Alas!
He's stiff, wounded, and dead!   Treason,
    treason!
1. Run forth and call! *Exit [2] Gent[leman].*
2. Treason, treason!
1.   This will be laid on us.
Who can believe a woman could do this?

Enter Cleon and Lysippus.

CLE. How now!   Where's the traitor?
1. Fled, fled away; but there her woeful
    act   131
Lies still.

---

[1] Shooting stars.   [2] Easily infected.
[3] Well-dressed.   [5] Fast asleep.
[4] Original reads *Exeunt.*

CLE. Her act! A woman!

LYS.　　　　　　　　　Where's the body?

1.　　　　　　　　　　　　　　There.

LYS. Farewell, thou worthy man! There
were two bonds
That tied our loves, a brother and a
king,
The least of which might fetch a flood
of tears;
But such the misery of greatness is,
They have no time to mourn. Then,
pardon me!
Sirs, which way went she?

Enter Strato.

STRA.　　　　　　　　　Never follow her,
For she, alas, was but the instrument.
News is now brought in that Melantius
Has got the fort, and stands upon the
wall,　　　　　　　　　　　　142
And with a loud voice calls those few
that pass
At this dead time of night, delivering
The innocence of this act.

LYS.　　　　　　　　　　Gentlemen,
I am your king.

STRA.　　　　　We do acknowledge it.

LYS. I would I were not! Follow, all;
for this
Must have a sudden stop.　　*Exeunt.*

[SCENA ii.

Before the fort.]

*Enter Melant[ius], Diph[ilus], Cal[ianax] on
the walls.*

MEL. If the dull people can believe I am
armed
(Be constant, Diph[ilus]), now we have
time
Either to bring our banished honors
home,
Or create new ones in our ends.

DIPH.　　　　　　　　　I fear not;
My spirit lies not that way.—Courage,
Calianax!

CAL. Would I had any! You should
quickly know it.

MEL. Speak to the people; thou art eloquent.

CAL. 'Tis a fine eloquence to come to the
gallows.
You were born to be my end; the devil
take you!

Now must I hang for company? 'Tis
strange　　　　　　　　　　　10
I should be old, and neither wise nor
valiant.

*Enter Lysip[pus], Diag[oras], Cleon, Strat[o],
Guard.*

LYS. See where he stands, as boldly confident
As if he had his full command about
him.

STRA. He looks as if he had the better
cause, sir;
Under your gracious pardon, let me
speak it!
Though he be mighty-spirited, and for-
ward
To all great things, to all things of that
danger
Worse men shake at the telling of, yet
certainly
I do believe him noble, and this action
Rather pulled on than sought. His
mind was ever　　　　　　　20
As worthy as his hand.

LYS.　　　　　　　'Tis my fear, too.
Heaven forgive all!—Summon him,
Lord Cleon.

CLE. Ho, from the walls there!

MEL.　　　　Worthy Cleon, welcome.
We could 'a' wished you here, lord;
you are honest.

CAL. (*Aside.*) Well, thou art as flattering a knave, though
I dare not tell thee so—

LYS.　　　　　　　　Melantius!

MEL.　　　　　　　　　　　Sir?

LYS. I am sorry that we meet thus; our
old love
Never required such distance. Pray
heaven,
You have not left yourself, and sought
this safety
More out of fear than honor! You have
lost　　　　　　　　　　　30
A noble master, which your faith, Melantius,
Some think might have preserved; yet
you know best.

CAL. [*Aside.*] When time was,[1] I was mad;
some that dares fight
I hope will pay this rascal.

[1] Once upon a time.

MEL. Royal young man, those tears look
  lovely on thee;
  Had they been shed for a deserving one,
  They had been lasting monuments. Thy
    brother,
  Whilst he was good, I called him king,
    and served him
  With that strong faith, that most un-
    wearied valor,
  Pulled people from the farthest sun to
    seek him,   40
  And buy his friendship. I was then his
    soldier.
  But, since his hot pride drew him to
    disgrace me,
  And brand my noble actions with his
    lust
  (That never-cured dishonor of my sister,
  Base stain of whore, and, which is worse,
    the joy
  To make it still so), like myself, thus I
  Have flung him off with my allegiance,
  And stand here, mine own justice, to
    revenge
  What I have suffered in him, and this
    old man
  Wronged almost to lunacy.
CAL.   Who, I? 50
  You would draw me in. I have had no
    wrong;
  I do disclaim ye all.
MEL.   The short is this:
  'Tis no ambition to lift up myself
  Urgeth me thus; I do desire again
  To be a subject, so I may be free.
  If not, I know my strength, and will
    unbuild
  This goodly town. Be speedy, and be
    wise,
  In a reply.
STRA.   Be sudden, sir, to tie
  All up again. What's done is past re-
    call,
  And past you to revenge; and there are
    thousands   60
  That wait for such a troubled hour as
    this.
  Throw him the blank.
LYS.   Melantius, write in that
  Thy choice; my seal is at it.
        [Throws a paper to Melantius.]
MEL. It was our honors drew us to this act,
  Not gain; and we will only work our
    pardons.

CAL. Put my name in too.
DIPH.   You disclaimed us all
  But now, Calianax.
CAL.   That's all one.
  I'll not be hanged hereafter by a trick;
  I'll have it in.
MEL.   You shall, you shall.—
  Come to the back gate, and we'll call
    you king,   70
  And give you up the fort.
LYS.   Away, away! *Exeunt omnes.*

[SCENA iii.

An anteroom to Amintor's apartment.]

*Enter Aspatia in man's apparel [and with
  her face disguised with counterfeit scars].*

ASP. This is my fatal hour. Heaven
    may forgive
  My rash attempt, that causelessly hath
    laid
  Griefs on me that will never let me rest,
  And put a woman's heart into my
    breast.
  It is more honor for you that I die,
  For she that can endure the misery
  That I have on me, and be patient
    too,
  May live and laugh at all that you can
    do.—
        Enter Servant.
  God save you, sir!
SER.   And you, sir! What's your
    business?
ASP. With you, sir, now; to do me the
    fair office   10
  To help me to your lord.
SER.   What, would you serve him?
ASP. I'll do him any service; but, to haste,
  For my affairs are earnest, I desire
  To speak with him.
SER. Sir, because you are in such haste,
    I would
  Be loath to delay you longer. You can
    not.
ASP. It shall become you, though, to tell
    your lord.
SER. Sir, he will speak with nobody.
ASP.   This is most strange.
  Art thou gold-proof? There's for thee;
    help me to him.   [*Gives money.*]
SER. Pray be not angry, sir; I'll do my
    best.   *Exit.* 20

Asp. How stubbornly this fellow an-
swered me!
There is a vild, dishonest trick in man,
More than in women. All the men I
meet
Appear thus to me, are harsh and rude,
And have a subtilty in everything,
Which love could never know; but we
fond women
Harbor the easiest and the smoothest
thoughts,
And think all shall go so. It is unjust
That men and women should be matched
together.

Enter Amintor and his Man.

Amin. Where is he?
Ser.　　　　There, my lord.
Amin.　　　　What would you, sir? 30
Asp. Please it your lordship to command
your man
Out of the room, I shall deliver things
Worthy your hearing.
Amin.　　　　Leave us. [*Exit Servant.*]
Asp. (*Aside.*)　　　　O, that that shape
Should bury falsehood in it!
Amin.　　　　Now your will, sir.
Asp. When you know me, my lord, you
needs must guess
My business; and I am not hard to
know;
For, till the chance of war marked this
smooth face
With these few blemishes, people would
call me
My sister's picture, and her mine. In
short,　　　　39
I am the brother to the wronged Aspatia.
Amin. The wronged Aspatia! Would thou
wert so too
Unto the wronged Amintor! Let me
kiss
That hand of thine, in honor that I
bear
Unto the wronged Aspatia. Here I
stand
That did it. Would he could not! Gentle
youth,
Leave me, for there is something in thy
looks
That calls my sins in a most hideous
form
Into my mind; and I have grief enough
Without thy help.

Asp.　　　　I would I could with credit!
Since I was twelve years old, I had not
seen　　　　50
My sister till this hour I now arrived;
She sent for me to see her marriage—
A woeful one! But they that are above
Have ends in everything. She used few
words,
But yet enough to make me understand
The baseness of the injuries you did her.
That little training I have had is war;
I may behave myself rudely in peace;
I would not, though. I shall not need
to tell you
I am but young, and would be loath to
lose　　　　60
Honor, that is not easily gained again.
Fairly I mean to deal; the age is strict
For [1] single combats; and we shall be
stopped,
If it be published. If you like your
sword,
Use it; if mine appear a better to you,
Change; for the ground is this, and this
the time,
To end our difference. [*Draws.*]
Amin.　　　　Charitable youth,
If thou beest such, think not I will main-
tain
So strange a wrong; and, for thy sister's
sake,
Know that I could not think that des-
perate thing　　　　70
I durst not do; yet, to enjoy this world,
I would not see her, for, beholding thee,
I am I know not what. If I have aught
That may content thee, take it, and be-
gone,
For death is not so terrible as thou;
Thine eyes shoot guilt into me.
Asp.　　　　Thus, she swore
Thou wouldst behave thyself, and give
me words
That would fetch tears into my eyes;
and so
Thou dost indeed. But yet she bade me
watch
Lest I were cozened; and be sure to
fight　　　　80
Ere I returned.
Amin.　　　　That must not be with me.
For her I'll die directly; but against her
Will never hazard it.

──────
[1] Against.

Asp.   You must be urged.
I do not deal uncivilly with those
That dare to fight; but such a one as you
Must be used thus.   *She strikes him.*
Amin.   I prithee, youth, take heed.
Thy sister is a thing to me so much
Above mine honor that I can endure
All this—Good gods! A blow I can en-
   dure!
But stay not, lest thou draw a timeless
   death   90
Upon thyself.
Asp.   Thou art some prating fellow,
One that hath studied out a trick to
   talk,
And move soft-hearted people; to be
   kicked—   *She kicks him.*
Thus to be kicked!—(*Aside.*) Why
   should he be so slow
In giving me my death?
Amin.   A man can bear
No more, and keep his flesh. Forgive
   me, then!
I would endure yet, if I could. Now
   show   [*Draws.*]
The spirit thou pretendest, and under-
   stand
Thou hast no hour to live.
      They fight [; Aspatia is wounded].
                 What dost thou mean?
Thou canst not fight. The blows thou
   mak'st at me   100
Are quite besides;[1] and those I offer
   at thee,
Thou spread'st thine arms, and tak'st
   upon thy breast,
Alas, defenseless!
Asp.   I have got enough,
And my desire. There is no place so fit
For me to die as here.   [*Falls.*]

*Enter Evadne, her hands bloody, with a
                                   knife.*

Evad. Amintor, I am loaden with events,
That fly to make thee happy; I have
   joys
That in a moment can call back thy
   wrongs,
And settle thee in thy free state again.
It is Evadne still that follows thee,   110
But not her mischiefs.
Amin. Thou canst not fool me to believe
   again;

[1] To one side.

But thou hast looks and things so full
   of news
That I am stayed.
Evad. Noble Amintor, put off thy amaze,
Let thine eyes loose, and speak. Am I
   not fair?
Looks not Evadne beauteous with these
   rites now?
Were those hours half so lovely in thine
   eyes
When our hands met before the holy
   man?
I was too foul within to look fair then; 120
Since I knew ill, I was not free till now.
Amin. There is presage of some impor-
   tant thing
About thee, which it seems thy tongue
   hath lost.
Thy hands are bloody, and thou hast
   a knife.
Evad. In this consists thy happiness and
   mine.
Joy to Amintor, for the king is dead!
Amin. Those have most power to hurt us
   that we love;
We lay our sleeping lives within their
   arms.
Why, thou hast raised up mischief to
   his height,
And found one to outname[2] thy other
   faults;   130
Thou hast no intermission of thy sins,
But all thy life is a continued ill.
Black is thy color now, disease thy na-
   ture.
"Joy to Amintor!" Thou hast touched
   a life,
The very name of which had power to
   chain
Up all my rage, and calm my wildest
   wrongs.
Evad. 'Tis done; and, since I could not
   find a way
To meet thy love so clear as through
   his life,
I cannot now repent it.
Amin. Couldst thou procure the gods to
   speak to me,   140
To bid me love this woman and forgive,
I think I should fall out with them. Be-
   hold,
Here lies a youth whose wounds bleed
   in my breast,

[2] Surpass.

Sent by a violent fate to fetch his death
From my slow hand! And, to augment
  my woe,
You now are present, stained with a
  king's blood
Violently shed. This keeps night here,
And throws an unknown wilderness [1]
  about me.

ASP. O, O, O!

AMIN. No more; pursue me not.

EVAD.   Forgive me then, 150
And take me to thy bed; we may not
  part.   [Kneels.]

AMIN. Forbear, be wise, and let my rage
go this way.

EVAD. 'Tis you that I would stay, not it.

AMIN.   Take heed;
It will return with me.

EVAD.   If it must be,
I shall not fear to meet it. Take me
  home.

AMIN. Thou monster of cruelty, forbear!

EVAD. For heaven's sake, look more calm!
  Thine eyes are sharper
Than thou canst make thy sword.

AMIN.   Away, away!
Thy knees are more to me than violence.
I am worse than sick to see knees fol-
  low me   160
For that I must not grant. For God's
  sake, stand.

EVAD. Receive me, then.

AMIN.   I dare not stay thy language.
In midst of all my anger and my grief,
Thou dost awake something that trou-
  bles me,
And says I loved thee once. I dare not
  stay;
There is no end of woman's reasoning.
                       Leaves her.

EVAD. [Rising.] Amintor, thou shalt love
  me now again.
Go; I am calm. Farewell, and peace
  forever!
Evadne, whom thou hat'st, will die
  for thee.   Kills herself. 169

AMIN. I have a little human nature yet,
That's left for thee, that bids me stay
  thy hand.   Returns.

EVAD. Thy hand was welcome, but it
  came too late.
O, I am lost! The heavy sleep makes
  haste.   She dies.

[1] Wildness.

ASP. O, O, O!

AMIN. This earth of mine doth tremble,
  and I feel
A stark affrighted motion in my blood.
My soul grows weary of her house, and I
All over am a trouble to myself.
There is some hidden power in these
  dead things   179
That calls my flesh into 'em; I am cold.
Be resolute and bear 'em company.
There's something yet, which I am loath
  to leave.
There's man enough in me to meet the
  fears
That death can bring; and yet would it
  were done!
I can find nothing in the whole dis-
  course
Of death I durst not meet the boldest
  way;
Yet still, betwixt the reason and the act,
The wrong I to Aspatia did stands up;
I have not such another fault to answer.
Though she may justly arm herself
  with scorn   190
And hate of me, my soul will part less
  troubled,
When I have paid to her in tears my
  sorrow.
I will not leave this act unsatisfied,
If all that's left in me can answer it.

ASP. Was it a dream? There stands Amintor still,
Or I dream still.

AMIN. How dost thou? Speak; receive
  my love and help.
Thy blood climbs up to his old place
  again;
There's hope of thy recovery.

ASP. Did you not name Aspatia?

AMIN.   I did. 200

ASP. And talked of tears and sorrow unto
  her?

AMIN. 'Tis true; and, till these happy
  signs in thee
Stayéd my course, 'twas thither I was
  going.

ASP. Thou art there already, and these
  wounds are hers.
Those threats I brought with me sought
  not revenge,
But came to fetch this blessing from thy
  hand.
I am Aspatia yet.

AMIN. Dare my soul ever look abroad again?

ASP. I shall sure live, Amintor; I am well.
A kind of healthful joy wanders within me.　210

AMIN. The world wants lines to excuse thy loss;
Come, let me bear thee to some place of help.

ASP. Amintor, thou must stay; I must rest here;
My strength begins to disobey my will.
How dost thou, my blessed soul? I would fain live
Now, if I could. Wouldst thou have loved me, then?

AMIN. Alas,
All that I am 's not worth a hair from thee!

ASP. Give me thy hand; mine hands grope up and down,
And cannot find thee; I am wondrous sick.　220
Have I thy hand, Amintor?

AMIN. Thou greatest blessing of the world, thou hast.

ASP. I do believe thee better than my sense.
O, I must go! Farewell! *Dies.*

AMIN. She sounds.[1]—Aspatia!—Help! For God's sake, water,
Such as may chain life ever to this frame!—
Aspatia, speak!—What, no help? Yet I fool![2]
I'll chafe her temples. Yet there nothing stirs.
Some hidden power tell her Amintor calls,
And let her answer me!—Aspatia, speak!—　230
I have heard, if there be any life, but bow
The body thus, and it will show itself.
O, she is gone! I will not leave her yet.
Since out of justice we must challenge nothing,
I'll call it mercy, if you'll pity me,
You heavenly powers, and lend for some few years
The blessed soul to this fair seat again!
No comfort comes; the gods deny me too.

---

[1] Swounds, swoons.　　　[2] Act foolishly.

I'll bow the body once again.—Aspatia!—
The soul is fled forever, and I wrong　240
Myself, so long to lose her company.
Must I talk now? Here's to be with thee, love! *Kills himself.*

Enter Servant.

SER. This is a great grace to my lord, to have the new king come to him. I must tell him he is entering.—O, God!—Help, help!

Enter Lysip[pus], Melant[ius], Cal[ianax],
Cleon, Diph[ilus], Strato.

LYS. Where's Amintor?

STRA. O, there, there!

LYS. How strange is this!

CAL. What should we do here?

MEL. These deaths are such acquainted things with me　250
That yet my heart dissolves not. May I stand
Stiff here forever! Eyes, call up your tears!
This is Amintor. Heart, he was my friend.
Melt! Now it flows.—Amintor, give a word
To call me to thee.

AMIN. O!

MEL. Melantius calls his friend Amintor. O!
Thy arms are kinder to me than thy tongue!
Speak, speak!

AMIN. What?　260

MEL. That little word was worth all the sounds
That ever I shall hear again.

DIPH. O, brother,
Here lies your sister slain! You lose yourself
In sorrow there.

MEL. Why, Diphilus, it is
A thing to laugh at, in respect of this.
Here was my sister, father, brother, son—
All that I had.—Speak once again; what youth
Lies slain there by thee?

AMIN. 'Tis Aspatia.

My last is said. Let me give up my soul
Into thy bosom.   [*Dies.*]   270
CAL. What's that? What's that? Aspatia!
MEL.   I never did
  Repent the greatness of my heart till
    now;
  It will not burst at need.
    CAL. My daughter dead here too! And
you have all fine new tricks to grieve; but
I ne'er knew any but direct crying.
MEL. I am a prattler; but no more.
            [*Offers to stab himself.*]
DIPH.   Hold, brother!
LYS. Stop him.
DIPH. Fie, how unmanly was this offer
  in you!
  Does this become our strain?   280
    CAL. I know not what the matter
is, but I am grown very kind, and am
friends with you. You have given me that
among you will kill me quickly; but I'll
go home, and live as long as I can. [*Exit.*]

MEL. His spirit is but poor that can be
  kept
  From death for want of weapons.
  Is not my hands a weapon sharp enough
  To stop my breath? Or, if you tie down
    those,
  I vow, Amintor, I will never eat,   290
  Or drink, or sleep, or have to do with
    that
  That may preserve life! This I swear
    to keep.
LYS. Look to him, though, and bear those
  bodies in.
  May this a fair example be to me
  To rule with temper;[1] for, on lustful
    kings,
  Unlooked-for, sudden deaths from God
    are sent,
  But cursed is he that is their instrument.
                  [*Exeunt.*]
            FINIS.

[1] Temperance, self-restraint.

THOMAS MIDDLETON AND WILLIAM ROWLEY

No partnership in the composition of Elizabethan plays was conducted with more success than that of Thomas Middleton and William Rowley, for their joint efforts resulted in better work than either dramatist produced independently. Thomas Middleton was christened son of William Middleton and Anne Snow at St. Lawrence in the Old Jewry on April 18, 1580. As a lad in his teens he published *The Wisdom of Solomon Paraphrased* (1597) and *Micro-Cynicon, Six Snarling Satires* (1599), but meanwhile, in April, 1598, had matriculated at Queen's College, Oxford. There is no record of his connection with the theater until May 22, 1602, when Henslowe records in his Diary a payment made to him together with Munday, Drayton, and Webster "in earnest of a book called *Cæsar's Fall.*" From this time almost to his death numerous references to his dramatic activity show that he sometimes wrote alone but more often with other well-known dramatists, notably Dekker and Rowley. Two satirical tales, *The Black Book* and *Father Hubbard's Tale*, published in 1604, reveal his early interest in the seamy side of London life, which he was to turn to good account in his comedies of manners written between 1604 and 1611. Among these may be mentioned *A Trick to Catch the Old One; A Mad World, My Masters;* and *Michaelmas Term*—all dealing with the duping of an unsuspecting victim by London sharpers; *Your Five Gallants*, which reveals the wiles of five different types of swindlers and ruffians; and that laughter-provoking farce, *A Chaste Maid in Cheapside*. Middleton's one unaided tragedy, *Women, Beware Women*, written about 1612, was followed in 1613 by his first masque, *The Triumphs of Truth;* and until his death he was in demand as a writer of this type of entertainment. The temporary amalgamation of the companies of Princess Elizabeth and Prince Charles in 1614 or 1615 brought Middleton and Rowley together, and their period of collaboration began shortly thereafter. Little is known of William Rowley's life. He was born about 1585, or perhaps earlier, and died in February, 1626. He was writing for the stage as early as 1607, and he not only achieved something of a reputation as an actor, but collaborated with a number of the best dramatists of the time. The best results of his collaboration with Middleton are *A Fair Quarrel, The Changeling*, and *The Spanish Gipsy*. From 1620 until his death Middleton held the office of city chronologer. He was buried in the Newington Butts Parish Church on July 4, 1627.

Middleton possesses no unusual poetic gifts, and his style is often uneven. His strength lies rather in his constructive skill, and in his fine dramatic sense, which enables him to give rapidity of movement and effectiveness to his scenes, and to make very real his pictures of low life in London. These features are well illustrated by *A Trick to Catch the Old One*, which was composed between 1604 and 1606, entered in the Stationers' Register October 7, 1607, and issued in two quartos dated 1608, and again in 1616. The plot, ingeniously contrived save for the lack of moral justice in the *dénouement*, is presumably of Middleton's own invention, and the materials of the play are drawn from the dramatist's experience in London life. The present text is based on photostats of the copy of the 1608 quarto, with readings from photostats of the 1616 quarto—both in the possession of the Huntington Library—with permission of the authorities of the library.

The Changeling, the best of Middleton and Rowley's joint efforts, although written between 1622 and the date of its performance at Whitehall on January 4, 1624, was not published until 1653. The story of Beatrice Joanna and Deflores is drawn from John Reynolds' *The Triumphs of God's Revenge against the Crying and Execrable Sin of Murther*, entered in the Stationers' Register June 7, 1621, and published later the same year; and one episode in the story is derived from Leonard Digges' translation of the Spanish novel

1279

of Cespedes, *Gerardo, the Unfortunate Spaniard* (1622). For the sub-plot, which gives the play its name, no source is known. According to Miss Pauline G. Wiggin (*An Inquiry into the Authorship of the Middleton-Rowley Plays*, Boston, 1897), "the first and last scenes, as well as the underplot," of the play are by Rowley. The play has been accorded high praise as a psychological tragedy and as one of the most successful plays written in collaboration in the whole range of Elizabethan drama. The present text is based on photostats of the copy of the 1653 quarto in the Harvard College Library, and reference has been made to the editions by Dyce and Bullen.

A TRICK TO CATCH THE OLD ONE

BY

T[HOMAS] M[IDDLETON]

[*DRAMATIS PERSONÆ*

THEODORUS WITGOOD.	SIR LANCELOT.
PECUNIUS LUCRE, *his uncle.*	HOST.
WALKADINE HOARD.	GEORGE, *Lucre's servant.*
ONESIPHORUS HOARD, *his brother.*	ARTHUR, *Hoard's servant.*

LIMBER ⎫
KIX ⎪
LAMPREY ⎬ *friends of Hoard.*
SPICHCOCK ⎭

CREDITORS, GENTLEMEN, DRAWER, BOY
   SCRIVENER, SERVANTS, *etc.*

HARRY DAMPIT ⎫ *usurers.*
GULF ⎭

COURTESAN.
MISTRESS LUCRE.

SAM FREEDOM, *son of Mistress Lucre.*
MONEYLOVE.

JOYCE, *Hoard's niece.*
LADY FOXTONE.
AUDREY, *Dampit's servant.*

SCENE: *Leicestershire and London.*

TIME: *Contemporary.*

ACTUS I. SCENA i.

A street in a town in Leicestershire.]

Enter Witgood, a gentleman, solus.

WIT. All's gone! Still thou'rt a gentleman—that's all; but a poor one—that's nothing. What milk brings thy meadows forth now? Where are thy goodly uplands and thy downlands? All sunk into that little pit, lechery. Why should a gallant pay but two shillings for his ordinary that nourishes him, and twenty times two for his brothel that consumes him? But where's Longacre?[2] In my uncle's conscience, [10 which is three years' voyage about. He that sets out upon his conscience ne'er finds the way home again; he is either swallowed in the quicksands of law quillets,[3] or splits upon the piles of a præmunire. Yet these old fox-brained and ox-browed uncles have still defenses for their avarice, and apologies for their practices, and will thus greet our follies:

> He that doth his youth expose   20
>   To brothel, drink, and danger,
> Let him that is his nearest kin
>   Cheat him before a stranger—

and that's his uncle; 'tis a principle in usury. I dare not visit the city; there I should be too soon visited by that horrible plague, my debts, and by that means I lose a virgin's love, her portion, and her virtues. Well, how should a man live now that has no living—hum? Why, are there not [30 a million of men in the world that only sojourn upon their brain, and make their wits their mercers; and am I but one amongst that million, and cannot thrive upon 't? Any trick, out of the compass of law, now would come happily to me.

Enter Courtesan.

COUR. My love!

WIT. My loathing! Hast thou been the secret consumption of my purse, and now

com'st to undo my last means, my [40
wits? Wilt leave no virtue in me, and yet
thou ne'er the better?

    Hence, courtesan, round-webbed taran-
      tula,[1]
    That dryest the roses in the cheeks of
      youth!

Cour. I have been true unto your
pleasure; and all your lands thrice racked [2]
was never worth the jewel which I prodigally gave you, my virginity.

    Lands mortgaged may return, and more
      esteemed,
    But honesty,[3] once pawned, is ne'er re-
      deemed.   50

Wit. Forgive; I do thee wrong
    To make thee sin, and then to chide thee
      for 't.

Cour. I know I am your loathing now.
    Farewell.

Wit. Stay, best invention,[4] stay!

Cour. I that have been the secret consumption of your purse, shall I stay now to
undo your last means, your wits? Hence,
courtesan, away!

Wit. I prithee, make me not mad at my
own weapon. Stay (a thing few [60
women can do, I know that, and therefore
they had need wear stays); be not contrary.
Dost love me? Fate has so cast [5] it that all
my means I must derive from thee.

Cour. From me? Be happy then;
    What lies within the power of my per-
      formance
    Shall be commanded of thee.

Wit.   Spoke like
    An honest drab, i' faith! It may prove
      something.
    What trick is not an embryon at first,
    Until a perfect shape come over it?   70

Cour. Come, I must help you. Where-
    abouts left you?
    I'll proceed.
    Though you beget, 'tis I must help to
      breed.
    Speak, what is 't? I'd fain conceive it.

Wit. So, so, so. Thou shalt presently
take the name and form upon thee of a rich

country widow, four hundred a year valiant [6] in woods, in bullocks, in barns, and
in rye stacks. We'll to London, and to my
covetous uncle.   80

Cour. I begin to applaud thee; our
states being both desperate, they are soon
resolute. But how for horses?

Wit. Mass, that's true; the jest will be
of some continuance. Let me see; horses
now, a bots [7] on 'em! Stay, I have acquaintance with a mad host, never yet
bawd to thee. I have rinsed the whoreson's
gums in mull-sack [8] many a time and often.
Put but a good tale into his ear now, [90
so it come off cleanly, and there's horse
and man for us, I dare warrant thee.

Cour. Arm your wits then speedily;
    There shall want nothing in me, either in
behavior, discourse, or fashion,
    That shall discredit your intended pur-
      pose.
    I will so artfully disguise my wants,
    And set so good a courage on my state,
    That I will be believed.

Wit. Why, then, all's furnished. [100
I shall go nigh to catch that old fox, mine
uncle, though he make but some amends
for my undoing. Yet there's some comfort
in 't: he cannot otherwise choose (though
it be but in hope to cozen me again) but
supply any hasty want that I bring to town
with me. The device well and cunningly
carried, the name of a rich widow and four
hundred a year in good earth will so conjure up a kind of usurer's love in him [110
to me that he will not only desire my
presence—which at first shall scarce be
granted him; I'll keep off a [9] purpose—but
I shall find him so officious to deserve, so
ready to supply! I know the state of an old
man's affection so well: if his nephew be
poor indeed, why, he lets God alone with
him; but, if he be once rich, then he'll be
the first man that helps him.

Cour. 'Tis right the world; [10] for, [120
in these days, an old man's love to his
kindred is like his kindness to his wife—
'tis always done before he comes at it.

Wit. I owe thee for that jest. Begone!
Here's all my wealth; prepare thyself.
Away! I'll to mine host with all possible

---

[1] Here and in a few other passages the original
prose has been changed into verse. Later, some
line divisions have also been regularized.
[2] Rented at excessively high rates.
[3] Chastity.
[4] Referring to her as the instrument for his
plan described below.   [5] Planned.

[6] Worth.   [9] On.
[7] Plague.   [10] Exactly the way of the world.
[8] Spiced and heated wine.

haste, and, with the best art and most profitable form, pour the sweet circumstance into his ear, which shall have the gift to turn all the wax to honey.—[*Exit* [130 *Courtesan.*] How now? O, the right worshipful seniors of our country!

[*Enter Onesiphorus Hoard, Limber, and Kix.*] [1]

O. Hoa. Who's that?

Lim. O, the common rioter; take no note of him.

Wit. [*Aside.*] You will not see me now; the comfort is,
Ere it be long you will scarce see yourselves.　　　　　[*Exit.*]

O. Hoa. I wonder how he breathes; h'as consumed all
Upon that courtesan.

Lim.　　　　　We have heard so much.

O. Hoa. You have heard all truth.　His uncle and my brother　　　140
Have been these three years mortal adversaries.
Two old, tough spirits, they seldom meet but fight,
Or quarrel when 'tis calmest.　I think their anger
Be the very fire that keeps their age alive.

Lim. What was the quarrel, sir?

O. Hoa. Faith, about a purchase,[2] fetching over a young heir.　Master Hoard, my brother, having wasted much time in beating the bargain, what did me old Lucre, but, as his conscience moved him, knowing　[150 the poor gentleman, stepped in between 'em and cozened him himself.

Lim. And was this all, sir?

O. Hoa. This was e'en it, sir; yet for all this I know no reason but the match might go forward betwixt his wife's son and my niece.　What though there be a dissension between the two old men?　I see no reason it should put a difference between the two younger; 'tis as natural for old folks　[160 to fall out as for young to fall in.　A scholar comes a-wooing to my niece; well, he's wise, but he's poor.　Her son comes a-wooing to my niece; well, he's a fool, but he's rich.

---

[1] These characters, represented in the speech heads of the original by the numbers 1, 2, and 3 only, were first identified by Dyce. The following speech heads have been altered accordingly.　　　　[2] Booty.

Lim. Ay, marry, sir?

O. Hoa. Pray now, is not a rich fool better than a poor philosopher?

Lim. One would think so, i' faith.

O. Hoa. She now remains at London with my brother, her second uncle, [170 to learn fashions, practice music; the voice between her lips, and the viol between her legs, she'll be fit for a consort [3] very speedily. A thousand good pound is her portion; if she marry, we'll ride up and be merry.

Kix. A match, if it be a match.　*Exeunt.*

[Scena ii.

Another street in the same town.]

Enter at one door, Witgood; at the other, Host.

Wit. Mine host!

Host. Young Master Witgood.

Wit. I have been laying [4] all the town for thee.

Host. Why, what's the news, bully Hadland?

Wit. What geldings are in the house, of thine own?　Answer me to that first.

Host. Why, man, why?

Wit. Mark me what I say.　I'll [10 tell thee such a tale in thine ear that thou shalt trust me spite of thy teeth, furnish me with some money willy-nilly, and ride up with me thyself *contra voluntatem et professionem.*[5]

Host. How?　Let me see this trick, and I'll say thou hast more art than a conjuror.

Wit. Dost thou joy in my advancement?　　　　　　20

Host. Do I love sack and ginger?

Wit. Comes my prosperity desiredly to thee?

Host. Come forfeitures to a usurer, fees to an officer, punks to an host, and pigs to a parson desiredly?　Why, then, la!

Wit. Will the report of a widow of four hundred a year, boy, make thee leap and sing and dance, and come to thy place again?　　　　　　30

Host. Wilt thou command me now? I am thy spirit; conjure me into any shape.

Wit. I ha' brought her from her friends, turned back the horses by a sleight; not

---

[3] With the double meaning, *concert* and *husband.*　　　[4] Searching.

[5] Contrary to your wish and profession.

so much as one amongst her six men, goodly, large, yeomanly fellows, will she trust with this her purpose—by this light, all unmanned,[1] regardless of her state, neglectful of vainglorious ceremony, all for my love. O, 'tis a fine little vol- [40 uble tongue, mine host, that wins a widow!

HOST. No, 'tis a tongue with a great T, my boy, that wins a widow.

WIT. Now, sir, the case stands thus. Good mine host, if thou lov'st my happiness, assist me.

HOST. Command all my beasts i' th' house.

WIT. Nay, that's not all neither. Prithee, take truce with thy joy, and listen to me. Thou know'st I have a wealthy [50 uncle i' th' city, somewhat the wealthier by my follies. The report of this fortune, well and cunningly carried, might be a means to draw some goodness from the usuring rascal, for I have put her in hope already of some estate that I have either in land or money. Now, if I be found true in neither, what may I expect but a sudden breach of our love, utter dissolution of the match, and confusion [60 of my fortunes forever?

HOST. Wilt thou but trust the managing of thy business with me?

WIT. With thee? Why, will I desire to thrive in my purpose? Will I hug four hundred a year, I that know the misery of nothing? Will that man wish a rich widow, that has ne'er a hole to put his head in? With thee, mine host? Why, believe it, sooner with thee than with a [70 covey of counselors.

HOST. Thank you for your good report, i' faith, sir; and, if I stand you not in stead, why, then, let an host come off *hic et hæc hostis*,[2] a deadly enemy to dice, drink, and venery. Come, where's this widow?

WIT. Hard at Park End.

HOST. I'll be her serving-man for once.

WIT. Why, there we let off together, keep full time; my thoughts were strik- [80 ing then just the same number.

HOST. I knew 't. Shall we then see our merry days again?

WIT. Our merry nights—[*Aside.*] which ne'er shall be more seen.   *Exeunt.*

---

[1] Without attendants.
[2] A pun on the meaning *host* and *enemy* is intended.

[SCENA iii.

A street in London.]

Enter at several doors old Lucre and old Hoard, Gentlemen [, i.e., Lamprey, Spichcock, Freedom, and Moneylove,] coming between them to pacify 'em.

LAMP. Nay, good Master Lucre, and you, Master Hoard, anger is the wind which you're both too much troubled withal.

HOARD. Shall my adversary thus daily affront me, ripping up the old wound of our malice, which three summers could not close up, into which wound the very sight of him drops scalding lead instead of balsamum?   10

LUC. Why, Hoard, Hoard, Hoard, Hoard, Hoard! May I not pass in the state of quietness to mine own house? Answer me to that, before witness, and why? I'll refer the cause to honest, even-minded gentlemen, or require the mere indifferences[3] of the law to decide this matter. I got the purchase, true. Was 't not any man's case? Yes. Will a wise man stand as a bawd, whilst another wipes [20 his nose[4] of the bargain? No; I answer no in that case.

LAMP. Nay, sweet Master Lucre.

HOARD. Was it the part of a friend? No, rather of a Jew. Mark what I say— when I had beaten the bush to the last bird, or, as I may term it, the price to a pound, then, like a cunning usurer, to come in the evening of the bargain and glean all my hopes in a minute, to en- [30 ter, as it were, at the back door of the purchase? For thou ne'er cam'st the right way by it.

LUC. Hast thou the conscience to tell me so without any impeachment to thyself?

HOARD. Thou that canst defeat thy own nephew, Lucre, lap his lands into bonds, and take the extremity of thy kindred's forfeitures, because he's a [40 rioter, a wastethrift, a brothel-master, and so forth—what may a stranger expect from thee but *vulnera dilacerata*,[5] as the poet says, dilacerate dealing?

---

[3] Impartialities.   [5] Lacerated wounds.
[4] *I.e.,* cheats him.

LUC. Upbraidest thou me with nephew? Is all imputation laid upon me? What acquaintance have I with his follies? If he riot, 'tis he must want it; if he surfeit, 'tis he must feel it; if he drab it, 'tis he must lie by 't. What's this to me?   50

HOARD. What's all to thee? Nothing, nothing; such is the gulf of thy desire and the wolf of thy conscience. But be assured, old Pecunius Lucre, if ever fortune so bless me that I may be at leisure to vex thee, or any means so favor me that I may have opportunity to mad thee, I will pursue it with that flame of hate, spirit of malice, unrepressed wrath, that I will blast thy comforts.   60

LUC. Ha, ha, ha!

LAMP. Nay, Master Hoard, you're a wise gentleman—

HOARD. I will so cross thee—

LUC. And I thee.

HOARD. So without mercy fret thee—

LUC. So monstrously oppose thee—

HOARD. Dost scoff at my just anger? O, that I had as much power as usury has over thee!   70

LUC. Then thou wouldst have as much power as the devil has over thee.

HOARD. Toad!

LUC. Aspic!

HOARD. Serpent!

LUC. Viper!

SPI. Nay, gentlemen, then we must divide you perforce.

LAMP. When the fire grows too unreasonable hot, there's no better way [80 than to take off the wood.

Exeunt. Mane[n]t [1] *Sam [Freedom] and Moneylove.*

SAM. A word, good signior.

MON. How now, what's the news?

SAM. 'Tis given me to understand that you are a rival of mine in the love of Mistress Joyce, Master Hoard's niece. Say me ay, say me no?

MON. Yes, 'tis so.

SAM. Then look to yourself. You cannot live long; I'm practicing every [90 morning. A month hence I'll challenge you.

MON. Give me your hand upon 't; there's my pledge I'll meet you.

             Strikes him. Exit.

---

[1] Remain.

SAM. O, O! What reason had you for that, sir, to strike before the month? You knew I was not ready for you, and that made you so crank.[2] I am not such a coward to strike again, I warrant you. My ear has the law of her side, for it burns [100 horribly. I will teach him to strike a naked face, the longest day of his life. 'Slid,[3] it shall cost me some money, but I'll bring this box into the chancery.   *Exit.*

[SCENA iv.

Another street in London.]

Enter Witgood and the Host.

HOST. Fear you nothing, sir; I have lodged her in a house of credit, I warrant you.

WIT. Hast thou the writings?

HOST. Firm, sir.

WIT. Prithee, stay, and behold two the most prodigious rascals that ever slipped into the shape of men—Dampit, sirrah, and young Gulf, his fellow caterpillar.   10

HOST. Dampit? Sure, I have heard of that Dampit.

WIT. Heard of him? Why, man, he that has lost both his ears may hear of him—a famous, infamous trampler of time:[4] his own phrase. Note him well. That Dampit, sirrah, he in the uneven beard and the serge cloak, is the most notorious, usuring, blasphemous, atheistical, brothel-vomiting rascal that we [2? have in these latter times now extant, whose first beginning was the stealing of a masty [5] dog from a farmer's house.

HOST. He looked as if he would obey the commandment well, when he began first with stealing.

WIT. True. The next town he came at, he set the dogs together by th' ears.

HOST. A sign he should follow the law, by my faith.   30

WIT. So it followed, indeed; and, being destitute of all fortunes, staked his masty against a noble,[6] and by great fortune his dog had the day. How he made it up ten shillings, I know not, but his own boast is that he came to town with but

---

[2] Lively.   [3] God's eyelid, a mild oath.
[4] Lawyer.   [5] Mastiff.   [6] Gold coin.

ten shillings in his purse, and now is credibly worth ten thousand pound.

HOST. How the devil came he by it?

[Enter Dampit and Gulf.]

WIT. [*Aside.*] How the devil came [40 he not by it? If you put in the devil once, riches come with a vengeance. H'as been a trampler of the law, sir; and the devil has a care of his footmen. The rogue has spied me now; he nibbled me finely once, too.—A pox search you!—[*Turns to Dampit.*] O, Master Dampit!—[*Aside.*] The very loins of thee!—Cry you mercy,[1] Master Gulf; you walk so low I promise you I saw you not, sir.   50

GULF. He that walks low walks safe, the poets tell us.

WIT. [*Aside.*] And nigher hell by a foot and a half than the rest of his fellows.— But, my old Harry!

DAMP. My sweet Theodorus!

WIT. 'Twas a merry world when thou cam'st to town with ten shillings in thy purse.

DAMP. And now worth ten thou- [60 sand pound, my boy. Report it. Harry Dampit, a trampler of time, say, he would be up in a morning, and be here with his serge gown, dashed up to the hams in a cause, have his feet stink about Westminster Hall and come home again, see the galleons, the galleasses. the great armadoes[2] of the law; then there be hoys and petty vessels, oars[3] and scullers of the time. There be picklocks of the [70 time too. Then would I be here; I would trample up and down like a mule. Now to the judges: "May it please your reverend-honorable fatherhoods!" Then to my counselor: "May it please your worshipful patience!" Then to the examiner's office: "May it please your mastership's gentleness!" Then to one of the clerks: "May it please your worshipful lousiness!"—for I find him scrubbing in [80 his codpiece. Then to the hall again, then to the chamber again—

WIT. And when to the cellar again?

DAMP. E'en when thou wilt again. Tramplers of time, motions[4] of Fleet

Street, and visions of Holborn! Here I have fees of one, there I have fees of another; my clients come about me, the fooliaminy[5] and coxcombry of the country. I still trashed[6] and trotted for [90 other men's causes. Thus was poor Harry Dampit made rich by others' laziness, who though they would not follow their own suits, I made 'em follow me with their purses.

WIT. Didst thou so, old Harry?

DAMP. Ay, and I soused 'em with bills of charges, i' faith; twenty pound a year have I brought in for boat hire, and I ne'er stepped into boat in my life.   100

WIT. Tramplers of time!

DAMP. Ay, tramplers of time, rascals of time, bull-beggars![7]

WIT. Ah, thou'rt a mad old Harry!— Kind Master Gulf, I am bold to renew my acquaintance.

GULF. I embrace it, sir.   *Exeunt.*

MUSIC.

Incipit[8]

ACT[US] II. [SCENA i.

A room in Lucre's house.]

Enter Lucre.

LUC. My adversary evermore twits me with my nephew, forsooth, my nephew. Why may not a virtuous uncle have a dissolute nephew? What though he be a brotheler, a wastethrift, a common surfeiter, and, to conclude, a beggar? Must sin in him call up shame in me? Since we have no part in their follies, why should we have part in their infamies? For my strict hand toward his mortgage, that I deny not; [10 I confess I had an uncle's pen'worth. Let me see, half in half; true. I saw neither hope of his reclaiming nor comfort in his being, and was it not then better bestowed upon his uncle than upon one of his aunts? —I need not say bawd, for everyone knows what "aunt" stands for in the last translation.[9]—

[1] I beg your pardon.
[2] Armadas, large warships.
[3] Rowboats.
[4] Puppet shows.
[5] One of Dampit's coinages.
[6] Tramped.
[7] Hobgoblins.
[8] Begins.
[9] Tralation, metaphor.

[*Enter Servant.*]

Now, sir?

SER.[1] There's a country serving- [20 man, sir, attends to speak with your worship.

LUC. I'm at best leisure now; send him in to me. [*Exit Servant.*]

Enter Host like a serving-man.

HOST. Bless your venerable worship.

LUC. Welcome, good fellow.

HOST. [*Aside.*] He calls me thief[2] at first sight, yet he little thinks I am an host.

LUC. What's thy business with me?

HOST. Faith, sir, I am sent from [30 my mistress to any sufficient gentleman indeed, to ask advice upon a doubtful point. 'Tis indifferent, sir, to whom I come, for I know none, nor did my mistress direct me to any particular man, for she's as mere[3] a stranger here as myself; only I found your worship within, and 'tis a thing I ever loved, sir, to be despatched as soon as I can.

LUC. [*Aside.*] A good, blunt honesty; I like him well.—What is thy mistress? [40

HOST. Faith, a country gentlewoman, and a widow, sir. Yesterday was the first flight of us; but now she intends to stay till a little term[4] business be ended.

LUC. Her name, I prithee?

HOST. It runs there in the writings, sir, among her lands: Widow Medler.

LUC. Medler? Mass, have I ne'er heard of that widow?

HOST. Yes, I warrant you, have [50 you, sir; not the rich widow in Staffordshire?

LUC. Cud's[5] me, there 'tis indeed; thou hast put me into memory. There's a widow indeed; ah, that I were a bachelor again!

HOST. No doubt your worship might do much then; but she's fairly promised to a bachelor already.

LUC. Ah, what is he, I prithee?

HOST. A country gentleman too, [60 one whom your worship knows not, I'm sure; h'as spent some few follies in his youth, but marriage, by my faith, begins to call him home. My mistress loves him,

sir, and love covers faults, you know: one Master Witgood, if ever you have heard of the gentleman.

LUC. Ha! Witgood, say'st thou?

HOST. That's his name indeed, sir my mistress is like to bring him to a goodly [70 seat yonder—four hundred a year, by my faith.

LUC. But, I pray, take me with you.[6]

HOST. Ay, sir.

LUC. What countryman might this young Witgood be?

HOST. A Leicestershire gentleman, sir.

LUC. [*Aside.*] My nephew, by th' Mass, my nephew! I'll fetch out more of this, i' faith. A simple country fellow! I'll [80 work 't out of him.—And is that gentleman, say'st thou, presently[7] to marry her?

HOST. Faith, he brought her up to town, sir; h'as the best card in all the bunch for 't, her heart; and I know my mistress will be married ere she go down.[8] Nay, I'll swear that, for she's none of those widows that will go down first, and be married after; she hates that, I can tell you, sir.

LUC. By my faith, sir, she is like to [90 have a proper gentleman and a comely; I'll give her that gift.

HOST. Why, does your worship know him, sir?

LUC. I know him? Does not all the world know him? Can a man of such exquisite qualities be hid under a bushel?

HOST. Then your worship may save me a labor, for I had charge given me to inquire after him. 100

LUC. Inquire of him? If I might counsel thee, thou shouldst ne'er trouble thyself further; inquire of him no more but of me; I'll fit thee. I grant he has been youthful, but is he not now reclaimed? Mark you that, sir. Has not your mistress, think you, been wanton in her youth? If men be wags, are there not women wagtails?

HOST. No doubt, sir.

LUC. Does not he return wisest [110 that comes home whipped with his own follies?

HOST. Why, very true, sir.

LUC. The worst report you can hear of him, I can tell you, is that he has been a kind gentleman, a liberal, and a worthy.

---

[1] Original reads *Scr. 2.*
[2] *Good fellow* was a cant phrase for *thief.*
[3] Absolute.   [5] God's.
[4] Pertaining to court sessions.
[6] Tell me your meaning.
[7] Immediately.   [8] *I.e.,* to the country.

Who but lusty Witgood, thrice-noble Witgood!

HOST. Since your worship has so much knowledge in him, can you resolve [120 me, sir, what his living might be? My duty binds me, sir, to have a care of my mistress' estate; she has been ever a good mistress to me, though I say it. Many wealthy suitors has she nonsuited for his sake; yet, though her love be so fixed, a man cannot tell whether his non-performance may help to remove it, sir; he makes us believe he has lands and living.

LUC. Who, young Master Wit- [130 good? Why, believe it, he has as goodly a fine living out yonder—what do you call the place?

HOST. Nay, I know not, i' faith.

LUC. Hum—see, like a beast, if I have not forgot the name—pooh! And out yonder again, goodly grown woods and fair meadows—pax [1] on 't, I can ne'er hit of that place neither. He? Why, he's Witgood of Witgood Hall. He an un- [140 known thing?

HOST. Is he so, sir? To see how rumor will alter! Trust me, sir, we heard once he had no lands, but all lay mortgaged to an uncle he has in town here.

LUC. Push! [2] 'Tis a tale, 'tis a tale.

HOST. I can assure you, sir, 'twas credibly reported to my mistress.

LUC. Why, do you think, i' faith, he was ever so simple to mortgage his lands [150 to his uncle, or his uncle so unnatural to take the extremity of such a mortgage?

HOST. That was my saying still, sir.

LUC. Pooh, ne'er think it.

HOST. Yet that report goes current.

LUC. Nay, then you urge me. Cannot I tell that best that am his uncle?

HOST. How, sir? What have I done!

LUC. Why, how now! In a sown,[3] man?

HOST. Is your worship his uncle, [160 sir?

LUC. Can that be any harm to you, sir?

HOST. I do beseech you, sir, do me the favor to conceal it. What a beast was I to utter so much! Pray, sir, do me the kindness to keep it in; I shall have my coat pulled o'er my ears, an 't [4] should be known; for the truth is, an 't please your worship, to prevent much rumor and many suitors,

[1] Pox.   [2] Pish!   [3] Swoon.   [4] If it.

they intend to be married very sud- [170 denly and privately.

LUC. And dost thou think it stands with my judgment to do them injury? Must I needs say the knowledge of this marriage comes from thee? Am I a fool at fifty-four? Do I lack subtilty now, that have got all my wealth by it? There's a leash of angels [5] for thee. Come, let me woo thee; speak, where lie they?

HOST. So I might have no anger, [180 sir—

LUC. Passion of me, not a jot. Prithee, come.

HOST. I would not have it known it came by my means.

LUC. Why, am I a man of wisdom?

HOST. I dare trust your worship, sir; but I'm a stranger to your house; and to avoid all intelligencers, I desire your worship's ear.   190

LUC. [Aside.] This fellow's worth a matter of trust.—Come, sir. [Host whispers to him.] Why, now, thou'rt an honest lad.— [Aside.] Ah, Sirrah Nephew!

HOST. Please you, sir, now I have begun with your worship, when shall I attend for your advice upon that doubtful point? I must come warily now.

LUC. Tut, fear thou nothing; tomorrow's evening shall resolve the doubt.   200

HOST. The time shall cause my attendance.   *Exit.*

LUC. Fare thee well.—There's more true honesty in such a country serving-man than in a hundred of our cloak companions; [6] I may well call 'em companions, for, since blue coats [7] have been turned into cloaks, we can scarce know the man from the master.—George!

[*Enter George.*]

GEO. Anon, sir?   210

LUC. List hither. [*Whispers.*] Keep the place secret. Commend me to my nephew; I know no cause, tell him, but he might see his uncle.

GEO. I will, sir.

LUC. And, do you hear, sir, take heed you use him with respect and duty.

GEO. [*Aside.*] Here's a strange alteration! One day he must be turned out like

[5] Three gold coins.
[6] Servants, knaves.   [7] Servants' livery.

a beggar, and now he must be called [220 in like a knight.   *Exit.*

Luc. Ah, sirrah, that rich widow! Four hundred a year! Beside, I hear she lays claim to a title of a hundred more. This falls unhappily that he should bear a grudge to me now, being likely to prove so rich. What is 't, trow, that he makes me a stranger for? Hum—I hope he has not so much wit to apprehend that I cozened him. He deceives me then? Good heaven, [230 who would have thought it would ever have come to this pass! Yet he's a proper gentleman, i' faith, give him his due— marry, that's his mortgage; but that I ne'er mean to give him. I'll make him rich enough in words, if that be good, and, if it come to a piece of money, I will not greatly stick for 't. There may be hope some of the widow's lands, too, may one day fall upon me, if things be carried wisely.—[240

[Enter George.]

Now, sir, where is he?

Geo. He desires your worship to hold him excused; he has such weighty business it commands him wholly from all men.

Luc. Were those my nephew's words?

Geo. Yes, indeed, sir.

Luc. [*Aside.*] When men grow rich, they grow proud too, I perceive that. He would not have sent me such an answer once within this twelvemonth. See [250 what 'tis when a man comes to his lands!— Return to him again, sir; tell him his uncle desires his company for an hour. I'll trouble him but an hour, say; 'tis for his own good, tell him. And, do you hear, sir, put "worship" upon him. Go to, do as I bid you; he's like to be a gentleman of worship very shortly.

Geo. [*Aside.*] This is good sport, i' faith.   *Exit.*   260

Luc. Troth, he uses his uncle discourteously now. Can he tell what I may do for him? Goodness may come from me in a minute, that comes not in seven year again. He knows my humor; I am not so usually good. 'Tis no small thing that draws kindness from me; he may know that and [1] he will. The chief cause that invites me to do him most good is the

sudden astonishing of old Hoard, [270 my adversary. How pale his malice will look at my nephew's advancement! With what a dejected spirit he will behold his fortunes, whom but last day he proclaimed rioter, penurious makeshift, despised brothel-master! Ha, ha! 'Twill do me more secret joy than my last purchase, more precious comfort than all these widow's revenues.—Now, sir—

Enter Witgood [, shown in by George].

Geo. With much entreaty he's at [280 length come, sir.   [*Exit.*]

Luc. O, nephew, let me salute you, sir! You're welcome, nephew.

Wit. Uncle, I thank you.

Luc. Y'ave a fault, nephew; you're a stranger here.   Well, heaven give you joy!

Wit. Of what, sir?

Luc. Hah, we can hear!
You might have known your uncle's
    house, i' faith,   290
You and your widow. Go to, you were
    to blame,
If I may tell you so without offense.

Wit. How could you hear of that, sir?

Luc.   O, pardon me!
It was your will to have kept it from me,
    I perceive now.

Wit. Not for any defect of love, I protest, uncle.

Luc. O, 'twas unkindness,[2] nephew! Fie, fie, fie!

Wit. I am sorry you take it in that sense, sir.   300

Luc. Pooh, you cannot color it, i' faith, nephew.

Wit. Will you but hear what I can say in my just excuse, sir?

Luc. Yes, faith, will I, and welcome.

Wit. You that know my danger i' th' city, sir, so well, how great my debts are, and how extreme my creditors, could not out of your pure judgment, sir, have wished us hither.   310

Luc. Mass, a firm reason indeed.

Wit. Else, my uncle's house, why, 't 'ad been the only make-match—

Luc. Nay, and thy credit.

Wit. My credit?   Nay, my counte-

[1] If.

[2] Perhaps *unnaturalness*, forgetfulness of the relationship due a relative.

nance. Push, nay, I know, uncle, you would have wrought it so by your wit you would have made her believe in time the whole house had been mine.   319

Luc. Ay, and most of the goods too—

Wit. La, you there! Well, let 'em all prate what they will, there's nothing like the bringing of a widow to one's uncle's house.

Luc. Nay, let nephews be ruled as they list, they shall find their uncle's house the most natural place when all's done.

Wit. There they may be bold.

Luc. Life, they may do anything there, man, and fear neither beadle nor som-   [330 ner.[1] An uncle's house! A very Cole Harbor.[2] Sirrah, I'll touch thee near now. Hast thou so much interest in thy widow that by a token thou couldst presently send for her?

Wit. Troth, I think I can, uncle.

Luc. Go to, let me see that.

Wit. Pray, command one of your men hither, uncle.

Luc. George!   340

[Enter George.]

Geo. Here, sir.

Luc. Attend my nephew.—[*Witgood whispers to George, who goes out.—Aside.*] I love a' life[3] to prattle with a rich widow; 'tis pretty, methinks, when our tongues go together—and then to promise much and perform little. I love that sport a' life, i' faith; yet I am in the mood now to do my nephew some good, if he take me handsomely.—What, have you despatched?   350

Wit. I ha' sent, sir.

Luc. Yet I must condemn you of unkindness, nephew.

Wit. Heaven forbid, uncle!

Luc. Yes, faith, must I. Say your debts be many, your creditors importunate, yet the kindness of a thing is all, nephew. You might have sent me close[4] word on 't without the least danger or prejudice to your fortunes.   360

Wit. Troth, I confess it, uncle; I was to blame there; but, indeed, my intent was to have clapped it up suddenly, and

so have broke forth like a joy to my friends, and a wonder to the world. Beside, there's a trifle of a forty pound matter toward the setting of me forth; my friends should ne'er have known on 't; I meant to make shift for that myself.

Luc. How, nephew? Let me not   [370 hear such a word again, I beseech you. Shall I be beholding[5] to you?

Wit. To me? Alas, what do you mean, uncle?

Luc. I charge you, upon my love, you trouble nobody but myself.

Wit. Y'ave no reason for that, uncle.

Luc. Troth, I'll ne'er be friends with you while you live, and you do.

Wit. Nay, and you say so, uncle,   [380 here's my hand; I will not do 't—

Luc. Why, well said! There's some hope in thee when thou wilt be ruled. I'll make it up fifty, faith, because I see thee so reclaimed. Peace; here comes my wife with Sam, her tother[6] husband's son.

[Enter Mistress Lucre and Sam Freedom.]

Wit. Good aunt—

Sam. Cousin Witgood! I rejoice in my salute; you're most welcome to this noble city, governed with the sword in the   [390 scabbard.

Wit. [*Aside.*] And the wit in the pommel.[7]—Good Master Sam Freedom, I return the salute.

Luc. By the Mass, she's coming, wife; let me see now how thou wilt entertain her.

Wife. I hope I am not to learn, sir, to entertain a widow; 'tis not so long ago since I was one myself.

[Enter Courtesan.]

Wit. Uncle—   400

Luc. She's come indeed.

Wit. My uncle was desirous to see you, widow, and I presumed to invite you.

Cour. The presumption was nothing, Master Witgood. Is this your uncle, sir?

Luc. Marry am I, sweet widow; and his good uncle he shall find me; ay, by this smack that I give thee [*Kisses her.*], thou'rt welcome.—Wife, bid the widow welcome the same way again.   410

---

[1] Summoner.
[2] Cold Harbor, where debtors found sanctuary.
[3] As life, dearly.   [4] Secret.

[5] Beholden.   [6] Other.
[7] The amount of wit in the knob on the hilt of a sword; *i.e.*, no wit at all.

SAM. [*Aside*.] I am a gentleman now too by my father's occupation, and I see no reason but I may kiss a widow by my father's copy;[1] truly, I think the charter[2] is not against it. Surely these are the words, "The son, once a gentleman, may revel it, though his father were a dauber"[3] —'tis about the fifteen page. I'll to her. [*Attempts to kiss the Courtesan, who rebuffs him.*]

LUC. Y' are not very busy now; a word with thee, sweet widow— 420

SAM. [*Aside*.] Coad's nigs![4] I was never so disgraced since the hour my mother whipped me.

LUC. Beside, I have no child of mine own to care for; she's my second wife, old, past bearing. Clap sure to him, widow; he's like to be my heir, I can tell you.

COUR. Is he so, sir?

LUC. He knows it already, and the knave's proud on 't; jolly rich widows [430 have been offered him here i' th' city, great merchants' wives; and do you think he will once look upon 'em? Forsooth, he'll none. You are beholding to him i' th' country, then, ere we could be; nay, I'll hold a wager, widow, if he were once known to be in town, he would be presently sought after; nay, and happy were they that could catch him first.

COUR. I think so. 440

LUC. O, there would be such running to and fro, widow! He should not pass the streets for 'em; he'd be took up in one great house or other presently. Fah! They know he has it, and must have it. You see this house here, widow; this house and all comes to him, goodly rooms, ready furnished, ceiled with plaster of Paris, and all hung about with cloth of arras.—Nephew!

WIT. Sir. 450

LUC. Show the widow your house; carry her into all the rooms, and bid her welcome.—You shall see, widow.—[*Aside to Witgood.*] Nephew, strike all sure above and thou beest a good boy—ah!

WIT. Alas, sir, I know not how she would take it!

LUC. The right way, I warrant t'ee. A pox, art an ass? Would I were in thy stead! Get you up; I am ashamed of you.— [460

[*Exeunt Witgood and Courtesan.*] So, let 'em agree as they will now. Many a match has been struck up in my house a[5] this fashion. Let 'em try all manner of ways, still there's nothing like an uncle's house to strike the stroke in. I'll hold my wife in talk a little. —Now, 'Ginny, your son there goes a-wooing to a poor gentlewoman but of a thousand portion. See my nephew, a lad of less hope, strikes at four hundred [470 a year in good rubbish.[6]

WIFE. Well, we must do as we may, sir.

LUC. I'll have his money ready told[7] for him again[8] he come down. Let me see, too. By th' Mass, I must present the widow with some jewel, a good piece a[9] plate, or such a device; 'twill hearten her on well. I have a very fair standing cup; and a good high standing cup will please a widow above all other pieces. *Exit.* 480

WIFE. Do you mock us with your nephew?—I have a plot in my head, son— i' faith, husband, to cross you.

SAM. Is it a tragedy plot, or a comedy plot, good mother?

WIFE. 'Tis a plot shall vex him. I charge you, of my blessing, son Sam, that you presently withdraw the action of your love from Master Hoard's niece.

SAM. How, mother! 490

WIFE. Nay, I have a plot in my head, i' faith. Here, take this chain of gold and this fair diamond. Dog me the widow home to her lodging, and at thy best opportunity fasten 'em both upon her. Nay, I have a reach;[10] I can tell you thou art known what thou art, son, among the right worshipful, all the twelve companies.[11]

SAM. Truly, I thank 'em for it.

WIFE. He? He's a scab to thee— [500 and so certify her thou hast two hundred a year of thyself, besides thy good parts—a proper person and a lovely. If I were a widow, I could find in my heart to have thee myself, son; ay, from 'em all.

SAM. Thank you for your good will, mother; but, indeed, I had rather have a stranger. And, if I woo her not in that violent fashion, that I will make her be glad to take these gifts ere I leave [510

---

¹ Example. ² *I.e.*, of a trade guild.
³ Plasterer. ⁴ God's nigs, a meaningless oath.
⁵ In. ⁹ Of.
⁶ Money. ¹⁰ Scheme.
⁷ Counted. ¹¹ *I.e.*, of the trade guilds.
⁸ Against, by the time that.

her, let me never be called the heir of your
body.

WIFE. Nay, I know there's enough in
you, son, if you once come to put it forth.

SAM. I'll quickly make a bolt or a shaft
on 't.[1]   *Exeunt.*

[SCENA ii.

A street in London.]

Enter Hoard and Moneylove.

MON. Faith, Master Hoard, I have bestowed many months in the suit of your
niece, such was the dear love I ever bore to
her virtues; but, since she hath so extremely
denied me, I am to lay out for my fortunes
elsewhere.

HOARD. Heaven forbid but you should,
sir! I ever told you my niece stood otherwise affected.[2]

MON. I must confess you did, sir; [10
yet, in regard of my great loss of time, and
the zeal with which I sought your niece,
shall I desire one favor of your worship.

HOARD. In regard of those two, 'tis hard
but you shall, sir.

MON. I shall rest grateful. 'Tis not full
three hours, sir, since the happy rumor of a
rich country widow came to my hearing.

HOARD. How? A rich country widow?

MON. Four hundred a year landed.   20

HOARD. Yea?

MON. Most firm, sir; and I have learnt
her lodging. Here my suit begins, sir; if I
might but entreat your worship to be a
countenance for me, and speak a good word
(for your words will pass), I nothing doubt
but I might set fair for the widow; nor shall
your labor, sir, end altogether in thanks;
two hundred angels—

HOARD. So, so. What suitors has [30
she?

MON. There lies the comfort, sir; the
report of her is yet but a whisper, and only
solicited by young riotous Witgood, nephew
to your mortal adversary.

HOARD. Ha! Art certain he's her suitor?

MON. Most certain, sir; and his uncle
very industrious to beguile the widow, and
make up the match.

HOARD. So? Very good.   40

MON. Now, sir, you know this young

[1] A proverb meaning *to succeed or fail.*
[2] Was in love with another.

Witgood is a spendthrift, dissolute fellow.

HOARD. A very rascal.

MON. A midnight surfeiter.

HOARD. The spume of a brothel house.

MON. True, sir; which, being well told
in your worship's phrase, may both heave
him out of her mind, and drive a fair way
for me to the widow's affections.

HOARD. Attend me about five.   50

MON. With my best care, sir.   *Exit.*

HOARD. Fool, thou hast left thy treasure
with a thief,

To trust a widower with a suit in love!
Happy revenge, I hug thee! I have not
only the means laid before me, extremely to
cross my adversary, and confound the last
hopes of his nephew, but thereby to enrich
my state, augment my revenues, and build
mine own fortunes greater. Ha, ha!

I'll mar your phrase, o'erturn your
flatteries,   60

Undo your windings, policies, and plots,
Fall like a secret and despatchful plague
On your securéd comforts. Why, I am
able

To buy three of Lucre, thrice outbid him,
Let my outmonies [3] be reckonéd and all.

Enter three Creditors.

1 [CRED.] I am glad of this news.

2 [CRED.] So are we, by my faith.

3 [CRED.] Young Witgood will be a gallant again now.

HOARD. [*Aside.*] Peace!   70

1 [CRED.] I promise you, Master Cockpit, she's a mighty rich widow.

2 [CRED.] Why, have you ever heard of
her?

1 [CRED.] Who? Widow Medler? She
lies open to much rumor.

3 [CRED.] Four hundred a year, they
say, in very good land.

1 [CRED.] Nay, take 't of my word, if
you believe that, you believe the least. [80

2 [CRED.] And to see how close he keeps
it!

1 [CRED.] O, sir, there's policy in that
to prevent better suitors.

3 [CRED.] He owes me a hundred pound,
and I protest I ne'er looked for a penny.

1 [CRED.] He little dreams of our coming; he'll wonder to see his creditors upon
him.   *Exeunt* [*Creditors*].

[3] Money put out in loans.

HOARD. Good! His creditors! I'll follow.
This makes for me.   90
All know the widow's wealth; and 'tis
well known
I can estate her fairly, ay, and will.
In this one chance shines a twice happy
fate;
I both deject my foe and raise my state.
Exit.

MUSIC.

Incipit.
ACT[US] III. [SCENA i.

Witgood's room.]

Witgood with his Creditors.

WIT. Why, alas, my creditors, could you
find no other time to undo me but now?
Rather your malice appears in this than the
justness of the debt.
1 [CRED.] Master Witgood, I have forborne my money long.
WIT. I pray, speak low, sir. What do
you mean?
2 [CRED.] We hear you are to be married
suddenly to a rich country widow.   10
WIT. What can be kept so close but you
creditors hear on 't! Well, 'tis a lamentable
state that our chiefest afflictors should first
hear of our fortunes. Why, this is no good
course, i' faith, sirs. If ever you have hope
to be satisfied, why do you seek to confound
the means that should work it? There's
neither piety, no, nor policy in that. Shine
favorably now, why, I may rise and spread
again to your great comforts.   20
1 [CRED.] He says true, i' faith.
WIT. Remove me now, and I consume forever.
2 [CRED.] Sweet gentleman!
WIT. How can it thrive which from the sun
you sever?
3 [CRED.] It cannot, indeed.
WIT. O, then, show patience! I shall have
enough
To satisfy you all.
1 [CRED.]   Ay, if we could
Be content, a shame take us!
WIT.   For, look you,
I am but newly sure [1] yet to the widow,
And what a rend might this discredit
make!   30

¹ Engaged.

Within these three days will I bind you
lands
For your securities.
1 [CRED.]   No, good Master Witgood.
Would 'twere as much as we dare trust
you with!
WIT. I know you have been kind; however, now,
Either by wrong report or false incitement
Your gentleness is injured. In such
A state as this a man cannot want
foes.
If on the sudden he begin to rise,
No man that lives can count his enemies.
You had some intelligence, I warrant
ye,   40
From an ill-willer.
2 [CRED.] Faith, we heard you brought
up a rich widow, sir, and were suddenly to
marry her.
WIT. Ay, why, there it was; I knew 'twas
so; but, since you are so well resolved [2] of
my faith toward you, let me be so much
favored of you, I beseech you all—
ALL. O, it shall not need, i' faith,
sir!—   50
WIT. As to lie still awhile, and bury my
debts in silence, till I be fully possessed of
the widow; for the truth is—I may tell you
as my friends—
ALL. O—O—O!—
WIT. I am to raise a little money in the
city, toward the setting forth of myself, for
my own credit and your comfort. Now, if
my former debts should be divulged, all
hope of my proceedings were quite [60
extinguished.
1 [CRED.] Do you hear, sir? I may deserve your custom hereafter. Pray, let my
money be accepted before a stranger's.
Here's forty pound I received as I came to
you. If that may stand you in any stead,
make use on 't. [*Offers money, which Witgood at first refuses.*] Nay, pray, sir; 'tis at
your service.
WIT. You do so ravish me with kindness
that   70
I'm constrained to play the maid, and
take it.
1 [CRED. (*Aside to Witgood.*)] Let none
of them see it, I beseech you.
WIT. [*Taking money. (Aside.)*] Fah!

² Satisfied.

1 [CRED. (*Aside.*)] I hope I shall be first in
your remembrance
After the marriage rites.
WIT. [*Aside.*]   Believe it firmly.
1 [CRED.] So.—What, do you walk, sirs?
2 [CRED.] I go.—[*Aside to Witgood.*]
Take no care, sir, for money to furnish you;
within this hour I'll send you suffi-   [80
cient.—Come, Master Cockpit, we both
stay for you.
3 [CRED.] I ha' lost a ring, i' faith; I'll
follow you presently.—[*Exeunt 1 and 2
Creditors.*] But you shall find it, sir. I
know your youth and expenses have dis-
furnished you of all jewels. There's a ruby
of twenty pound price, sir; bestow it upon
your widow. [*Offers a ring, which Witgood
at first refuses.*] What, man! 'Twill   [90
call up her blood to you; beside, if I might
so much work with you, I would not have
you beholding to those bloodsuckers for
any money.
WIT. [*Taking ring.*] Not I, believe it.
3 [CRED.] They're a brace of cutthroats.
WIT. I know 'em.
3 [CRED.] Send a note of all your wants
to my shop, and I'll supply you instantly.
WIT. Say you so? Why, here's my   [100
hand then; no man living shall do 't but
thyself.
3 [CRED.] Shall I carry it away from 'em
both, then?
WIT. I' faith, shalt thou.
3 [CRED.] Troth, then, I thank you, sir.
WIT. Welcome, good Master Cockpit.
—(*Exit [3 Creditor].*) Ha, ha, ha! Why, is
not this better now than lying abed? I perceive there's nothing conjures up wit   [110
sooner than poverty, and nothing lays it
down sooner than wealth and lechery! This
has some savor yet. O, that I had the
mortgage from mine uncle as sure in possession as these trifles! I would forswear
brothel at noonday, and muscadine and
eggs [1] at midnight.

Enter Courtesan.

COUR. Master Witgood, where are you?
WIT. Holla!
COUR. Rich news!   120
WIT. Would 'twere all in plate!
COUR. There's some in chains and jew-
els. I am so haunted with suitors, Master

[1] A concoction used as an aphrodisiac.

Witgood, I know not which to despatch
first.
WIT. You have the better term,[2] by my
faith.
COUR. Among the number one Master
Hoard, an ancient gentleman.
WIT. Upon my life, my uncle's   [130
adversary.
COUR. It may well hold so, for he rails on
you,
Speaks shamefully of him.
WIT.   As I could wish it.
COUR. I first denied him, but so cunningly
It rather promised him assuréd hopes
Than any loss of labor.
WIT.   Excellent!
COUR. I expect him every hour with gen-
tlemen,
With whom he labors to make good his
words,
To approve [3] you riotous, your state con-
sumed,
Your uncle—   140
WIT. Wench, make up thy own fortunes
now; do thyself a good turn once in thy
days. He's rich in money, movables, and
lands. Marry him. He's an old, doting
fool, and that's worth all. Marry him.
'Twould be a great comfort to me to see
thee do well, i' faith. Marry him. 'Twould
ease my conscience well to see thee well
bestowed; I have a care of thee, i' faith.
COUR. Thanks, sweet Master Wit-   [150
good.
WIT. I reach at farder happiness. First, I
am sure it can be no harm to thee, and there
may happen goodness to me by it. Prosecute it well; let's send up for our [4] wits, now
we require their best and most pregnant
assistance.
COUR. Step in; I think I hear 'em.
    Exit [with Witgood].

*Enter Hoard and Gentlemen with the Host
[as] serving-man.*

HOARD. Art thou the widow's man? By
my faith, sh'as a company of proper [5]   [160
men then.
HOST. I am the worst of six, sir; good
enough for bluecoats.

[2] The time for lawsuits, at which many dissolute people came to London.
[3] Prove.   [5] Handsome.
[4] From 1616 edn. Original reads *out*.

HOARD. Hark hither. I hear say thou art in most credit with her.

HOST. Not so, sir.

HOARD. Come, come, thou'rt modest. There's a brace of royals; [1] prithee, help me to th' speech of her. [*Gives him money.*]

HOST. I'll do what I may, sir, al- [170 ways saving myself harmless.

HOARD. Go to, do 't, I say; thou shalt hear better from me.

HOST. [*Aside.*] Is not this a better place than five mark a year standing wages? Say a man had but three such clients in a day, methinks he might make a poor living on 't. Beside, I was never brought up with so little honesty to refuse any man's money; never. What gulls there are a this side the [180 world! Now know I the widow's mind, none but my young master comes in her clutches. Ha, ha, ha! *Exit.*

HOARD. Now, my dear gentlemen, stand firmly to me;

You know his follies and my worth.

1 [GENT.] We do, sir.

2 [GENT.] But, Master Hoard, are you sure he is not i' th' house now?

HOARD. Upon my honesty, I chose this time

A purpose, fit; the spendthrift is abroad. Assist me; here she comes.—

[Enter Courtesan.]

Now, my sweet widow. 190
COUR. Y' are welcome, Master Hoard.

HOARD. Despatch, sweet gentlemen, despatch.—

I am come, widow, to prove those my words

Neither of envy sprung nor of false tongues,

But such as their [2] deserts and actions

Do merit and bring forth, all which these gentlemen,

Well known and better reputed, will confess.

COUR. I cannot tell

How my affections may dispose of me;

But surely, if they find him so desert-less, 200

They'll have that reason to withdraw themselves;

And therefore, gentlemen, I do entreat you,

As you are fair in reputation

And in appearing form, so shine in truth.

I am a widow, and, alas, you know,

Soon overthrown! 'Tis a very small thing

That we withstand, our weakness is so great.

Be partial unto neither, but deliver,

Without affection, [3] your opinion.

HOARD. And that will drive it home. 210
COUR. Nay, I beseech your silence, Master Hoard;

You are a party.

HOARD. Widow, not a word.

1 [GENT.] The better first to work you to belief,

Know neither of us owe him flattery,

Nor tother [4] malice, but unbribéd censure [5]—

So help us our best fortunes!

COUR. It suffices.

1 [GENT.] That Witgood is a riotous, un-done man,

Imperfect both in fame and in estate,

His debts wealthier than he, and executions

In wait for his due body, we'll maintain 220

With our best credit and our dearest blood.

COUR. Nor land nor living, say you? Pray, take heed

You do not wrong the gentleman.

1 [GENT.] What we speak

Our lives and means are ready to make good.

COUR. Alas, how soon are we poor souls beguiled!

2 [GENT.] And for his uncle—

HOARD. Let that come to me.

His uncle, a severe extortioner;

A tyrant at a forfeiture; greedy of others' Miseries; one that would undo his brother, 229

Nay, swallow up his father, if he can,

Within the fadoms [6] of his conscience.

1 [GENT.] Nay, believe it, widow,

You had not only matched yourself to wants,

But in an evil and unnatural stock.

HOARD. [*Aside to Gentlemen.*] Follow hard, gentlemen, follow hard.

COUR. Is my love so deceived? Before you all
I do renounce him; on my knees I vow
He ne'er shall marry me.

WIT. [*Looking in. (Aside.)*] Heaven knows he never meant it!

HOARD. [*Aside to Gentlemen.*] There take her at the bound.   240

1 [GENT.] Then, with a new and pure affection,
Behold yon gentleman, grave, kind, and rich,
A match worthy yourself; esteeming him,
You do regard your state.

HOARD. [*Aside to Gentlemen.*] I'll make her a jointure, say.

1 [GENT.] He can join land to land, and will possess you
Of what you can desire.

2 [GENT.]   Come, widow, come.

COUR. The world is so deceitful!

1 [GENT.]   There, 'tis deceitful
Where flattery, want, and imperfection lies;
But none of these in him. Push!

COUR.   Pray, sir—   250

1 [GENT.] Come, you widows are ever most backward when you should do yourselves most good; but, were it to marry a chin not worth a hair now, then you would be forward enough. Come, clap hands! A match!

HOARD. With all my heart, widow.—
Thanks, gentlemen.
I will deserve [1] your labor and thy love.

COUR. Alas, you love not widows but for wealth!
I promise you I ha' nothing, sir.

HOARD.   Well said, widow,   260
Well said; thy love is all I seek, before
These gentlemen.

COUR.   Now I must hope the best.

HOARD. My joys are such they want to be expressed.

COUR. But, Master Hoard, one thing I must remember you of, before these gentlemen, your friends: how shall I suddenly avoid the loathed soliciting of that perjured Witgood, and his tedious, dissembling uncle, who this very day hath appointed a meeting for the same [270

purpose too, where, had not truth come forth, I had been undone, utterly undone?

HOARD. What think you of that, gentlemen?

1 [GENT.] 'Twas well devised.

HOARD. Hark thee, widow. Train [2] out young Witgood single; hasten him thither with thee, somewhat before the hour, where, at the place appointed, these gentlemen and myself will wait the oppor- [280 tunity, when, by some slight removing him from thee, we'll suddenly enter and surprise thee, carry thee away by boat to Cole Harbor, have a priest ready, and there clap it up instantly. How lik'st it, widow?

COUR. In that it pleaseth you, it likes me well.

HOARD. I'll kiss thee for those words.
Come, gentlemen;
Still must I live a suitor to your favors,
Still to your aid beholding.

1 [GENT.]   We're engaged, sir;
'Tis for our credits now to see 't well ended.   290

HOARD. 'Tis for your honors, gentlemen; nay, look to 't.
Not only in joy, but I in wealth excel.
No more sweet widow, but, sweet wife, farewell.

COUR. Farewell, sir.
        Exeunt [*Hoard and Gentlemen*].

Enter Witgood.

WIT. O, for more scope! I could laugh eternally!
Give you joy, Mistress Hoard. I promise your fortune was good, forsooth. Y'ave fell upon wealth enough, and there's young gentlemen enow can help you to the rest. Now it requires our wits. Carry thy- [300 self but heedfully now, and we are both—

[*Enter Host.*]

HOST. Master Witgood, your uncle.

Enter Lucre.

WIT. [*Aside.*] Cud's me! Remove thyself awhile; I'll serve for him.
        [*Exeunt Courtesan and Host.*]

LUC. Nephew, good morrow, nephew.

WIT. The same to you, kind uncle.

[1] Reward.

[2] Lure.

Luc. How fares the widow? Does the
  meeting hold?
Wit. O, no question of that, sir.
Luc. I'll strike the stroke, then, for thee;
  no more days.[1]   309
Wit. The sooner the better, uncle. O,
she's mightily followed!
Luc. And yet so little rumored!
Wit. Mightily! Here comes one old
gentleman, and he'll make her a jointure of
three hundred a year, forsooth; another
wealthy suitor will estate his son in his lifetime, and make him weigh down the widow;
here a merchant's son will possess her with
no less than three goodly lordships[2] at once,
which were all pawns to his father.   320
Luc. Peace, nephew, let me hear no
more of 'em; it mads me. Thou shalt prevent[3] 'em all. No words to the widow of
my coming hither. Let me see—'tis now
upon nine. Before twelve, nephew, we will
have the bargain struck, we will, faith, boy.
Wit. O, my precious uncle!
                              Exit [with Lucre].

[Scena ii.

A room in Hoard's house.]
Hoard and his Niece.

Hoard. Niece, sweet niece, prithee,
have a care to my house; I leave all to thy
discretion. Be content to dream awhile.
I'll have a husband for thee shortly; put
that care upon me, wench, for in choosing
wives and husbands I am only fortunate;
I have that gift given me.   *Exit.*
Niece. But 'tis not likely you should
  choose for me,
  Since nephew to your chiefest enemy   9
  Is he whom I affect. But, O, forgetful!
  Why dost thou flatter thy affections so,
  With name of him that for a widow's bed
  Neglects thy purer love? Can it be so,
  Or does report dissemble?—

        [Enter George.]
                              How now, sir?
Geo. A letter, with which came a private
  charge.
Niece. Therein I thank your care.—
                              [Exit George.]
  I know this hand—(*Reads.*)
"Dearer than sight,

¹ Delays.   ² Manors.   ³ Anticipate.

What the world reports of me, yet believe
not; rumor will alter shortly. Be thou constant; I am still the same that I was in [20
love, and I hope to be the same in fortunes.
          Theodorus Witgood."
I am resolved. No more shall fear or
  doubt
Raise their pale powers to keep affection
  out.   *Exit.*

[Scena iii.

A room in a tavern.]
*Enter, with a Drawer, Hoard and two Gentle-
                              men.*

Dra. You're very welcome, gentle-
men.—Dick, show those gentlemen the
Pomegranate[4] there.
Hoard. Hist!
Dra. Up those stairs, gentlemen.
Hoard. Pist,[5] drawer!
Dra. Anon, sir.
Hoard. Prithee, ask at the bar if a
gentlewoman came not in lately.
Dra. William, at the bar, did you [10
see any gentlewoman come in lately? Speak
you ay, speak you no?
[William.] (*Within.*) No, none came in
yet but Mistress Florence.
Dra. He says none came in yet, sir, but
one Mistress Florence.
Hoard. What is that Florence?   A
widow?
Dra. Yes, a Dutch widow.
Hoard. How?   20
Dra. That's an English drab, sir—give
your worship good morrow.   [*Exit.*]
Hoard. A merry knave, i' faith! I shall
remember a Dutch widow the longest day
of my life.
1 [Gent.] Did not I use most art to win
the widow?
2 [Gent.] You shall pardon me for that,
sir; Master Hoard knows I took her at best
vantage.   30
Hoard. What's that, sweet gentlemen,
what's that?
2 [Gent.] He will needs bear me down,
that his art only wrought with the widow
most.
Hoard. O, you did both well, gentlemen, you did both well, I thank you.
1 [Gent.] I was the first that moved her.

⁴ The name of one of the rooms.   ⁵ Hist!

HOARD.　　　　　　　You were, i' faith.

2 [GENT.] But it was I that took her at
　the bound.

HOARD. Ay, that was you. Faith, gentle-
　men, 'tis right.　　　　　　　　　　40

1 [GENT.] I boasted least, but 'twas I
　joined their hands.

HOARD. By th' Mass, I think he did. You
　did all well,
　Gentlemen, you did all well. Contend
　no more.

1 [GENT.] Come, yon room's fittest.

HOARD.　　　　　　True, 'tis next the door.
　　　　　　　　　　　Exit [with Gentlemen].

*Enter [Drawer,] Witg[ood], Court[esan], and
　　　　　　　　　　　　　　　　　Host.*

DRA. You're very welcome. Please you
to walk upstairs; cloth's laid, sir.

COUR. Upstairs? Troth, I am weary,
Master Witgood.

WIT. Rest yourself here awhile, widow;
we'll have a cup of muscadine in this　[50
little room.

DRA. A cup of muscadine? You shall
have the best, sir.

WIT. But do you hear, sirrah?

DRA. Do you call? Anon, sir.

WIT. What is there provided for dinner?

DRA. I cannot readily tell you, sir. If
you please, you may go into the kitchen
and see yourself, sir; many gentlemen of
worship do use to do it, I assure you,　[60
sir.　　　　　　　　　　　　　　　*[Exit.]*

HOST. A pretty, familiar, priggin [2] rascal; he has his part without book.

WIT. Against you are ready to drink to
me, widow, I'll be present to pledge you.

COUR. Nay, I commend your care; 'tis
done well of you.—*[Exit Witgood.]* 'Las,[3]
what have I forgot!

HOST. What, mistress?

COUR. I slipped my wedding ring off　[70
when I washed, and left it at my lodging.
Prithee, run; I shall be sad without it.—
[Exit Host.] So, he's gone.—Boy!

[Enter Boy.]

BOY. Anon, forsooth.

COUR. Come hither, sirrah.　　Learn

[1] Original reads *3*, but see III, i, 251–6.
[2] Prigging; usually *thieving*, here *smart*.
[3] Emended by Bullen. Early edns. read *asse*,
but apparently a letter has dropped out.

secretly if one Master Hoard, an ancient
gentleman, be about house.

BOY. I heard such a one named.

COUR. Commend me to him.

Enter Hoard with Gentlemen.

HOARD.　　　　　I'll do thy commendations!

COUR. O, you come well. Away, to boat,
　begone!　　　　　　　　　　　　80

HOARD. Thus wise men are revenged, give
　two for one.　　　　　　　　*Exeunt.*

Enter Witgood and Vintner.

WIT. I must request
You, sir, to show extraordinary care.
My uncle comes with gentlemen, his
　friends,
And 'tis upon a making.[4]

VIN.　　　　　　　　　　Is it so?
I'll give a special charge, good Master
　Witgood.
May I be bold to see her?

WIT.　　　　　　　　　Who? The widow?
With all my heart, i' faith; I'll bring you
　to her.

VIN. If she be a Staffordshire gentlewoman, 'tis much if I know her not.　　90

WIT. How now? Boy! Drawer!

VIN. Hie!

[Enter Boy.]

BOY. Do you call, sir?

WIT. Went the gentlewoman up that
was here?

BOY. Up, sir? She went out, sir.

WIT. Out, sir?

BOY. Out, sir. One Master Hoard, with
a guard of gentlemen, carried her out at
back door, a pretty while since, sir.　　100

WIT. Hoard? Death and darkness!
Hoard?

Enter Hoard.

HOST. The devil of ring I can find.

WIT. How now? What news? Where's
the widow?

HOST. My mistress? Is she not here, sir?

WIT. More madness yet!

HOST.　　　　　She sent me for a ring.

WIT. A plot, a plot!—To boat! She's stole
　away.

HOST. What?　　　　　　　　　　109

[4] Mating.

Enter Lucre with Gentlemen.

Wit. Follow! Inquire! Old Hoard, my
uncle's adversary—   [*Exit Host.*]
Luc. Nephew, what's that?
Wit.   Thrice-miserable wretch!
Luc. Why, what's the matter?
Vin.   The widow's borne away, sir.
Luc. Ha, passion of me!—A heavy wel-
come, gentlemen.
1 [Gent.] The widow gone?
Luc. Who durst attempt it?
Wit. Who but old Hoard, my uncle's
adversary?
Luc. How?
Wit. With his confederates.
Luc. Hoard, my deadly enemy?—Gentle-
men, stand to me;   120
I will not bear it; 'tis in hate of me;
That villain seeks my shame, nay,
thirsts [1] my blood.
He owes me mortal malice.
I'll spend my wealth on this despiteful
plot,
Ere he shall cross me and my nephew
thus.
Wit. So maliciously!

Enter Host.

Luc. How now, you treacherous rascal?
Host. That's none of my name, sir.
Wit. Poor soul, he knew not on 't!
Luc. I'm sorry. I see then 'twas a mere
plot.   130
Host. I traced 'em nearly—
Luc.   Well?
Host.   And hear for certain
They have took Cole Harbor.
Luc.   The devil's sanctuary!
They shall not rest, I'll pluck her from
his arms—
Kind and dear gentlemen,
If ever I had seat within your breasts—
1 [Gent.] No more, good sir; it is a wrong
to us
To see you injured in a cause so just.
We'll spend our lives but we will right
our friends.
Luc. Honest and kind! Come, we have
delayed too long.   139
Nephew, take comfort; a just cause is
strong.   *Exeunt* [*All but Witgood*].

[1] Early edns read *thrifts.*

Wit. That's all my comfort, uncle. Ha,
ha, ha!
Now may events fall luckily and well;
He that ne'er strives, says wit, shall ne'er
excel.   *Exit.*

[Scena iv.

A room in Dampit's house.]

Enter Dampit, the usurer, drunk.

Damp. When did I say my prayers?
In *anno* '88, when the great armado was
coming; and in *anno* '99, when the great
thunder and lightning was, I prayed heartily then, i' faith, to overthrow Poovies'
new buildings; I kneeled by my great iron
chest, I remember.

[*Enter Audrey.*]

Aud. Master Dampit, one may hear
you before they see you. You keep sweet
hours, Master Dampit; we were all   [10
abed three hours ago.
Damp. Audrey?
Aud. O, y' are a fine gentleman!
Damp. So I am, i' faith, and a fine
scholar. Do you use to go to bed so early,
Audrey?
Aud. Call you this early, Master Dam-
pit?
Damp. Why, is 't not one of clock i' th'
morning? Is not that early enough? [20
Fetch me a glass of fresh beer.
Aud. Here, I have warmed your night-
cap for you, Master Dampit.
Damp. Draw it on then. I am very weak,
truly. I have not eaten so much as the
bulk of an egg these three days.
Aud. You have drunk the more, Master
Dampit.
Damp. What's that?
Aud. You mought,[2] and you would,   [30
Master Dampit.
Damp. I answer you, I cannot. Hold
your prating; you prate too much, and
understand too little. Are you answered?
Give me a glass of beer.
Aud. May I ask you how you do, Mas-
ter Dampit?
Damp. How do I? I' faith, naught.
Aud. I ne'er knew you do otherwise.
Damp. I eat not one pennort [3] of   [40

[2] Might.   [3] Pennyworth.

bread these two years. Give me a glass of fresh beer. I am not sick, nor I am not well.

AUD. Take this warm napkin about your neck, sir, whilst I help to make you unready.[1]

DAMP. How now, Audrey-prater, with your scurvy devices, what say you now?

AUD. What say I, Master Dampit? I say nothing but that you are very weak. [50

DAMP. Faith, thou hast more cunny-catching[2] devices than all London.

AUD. Why, Master Dampit, I never deceived you in all my life.

DAMP. Why was that? Because I never did trust thee.

AUD. I care not what you say, Master Dampit.

DAMP. Hold thy prating. I answer thee, thou art a beggar, a quean, and a bawd. [60 Are you answered?

AUD. Fie, Master Dampit! A gentleman, and have such words!

DAMP. Why, thou base drudge of infortunity, thou kitchen-stuff drab of beggary, roguery, and coxcombry, thou cavernesed[3] quean of foolery, knavery, and bawdreaminy, I'll tell thee what, I will not give a louse for thy fortunes.

AUD. No, Master Dampit? And [70 there's a gentleman comes a-wooing to me, and he doubts[4] nothing but that you will get me from him.

DAMP. I? If I would either have thee or lie with thee for two thousand pound, would I might be damned! Why, thou base, impudent quean of foolery, flattery, and coxcombry, are you answered?

AUD. Come, will you rise and go to bed, sir? 80

DAMP. Rise, and go to bed too, Audrey? How does Mistress Proserpine?

AUD. Fooh!

DAMP. She's as fine a philosopher of a stinkard's wife as any within the liberties.[5] Fah, fah, Audrey!

AUD. How now, Master Dampit?

DAMP. Fie upon 't, what a choice of stinks here is! What hast thou done, Au-

drey? Fie upon 't, here's a choice of [90 stinks indeed! Give me a glass of fresh beer, and then I will to bed.

AUD. It waits for you above, sir.

DAMP. Foh! I think they burn horns in Barnard's Inn. If ever I smelt such an abominable stink, usury forsake me. [Exit.

AUD. They be the stinking nails of his trampling feet, and he talks of burning horns. Exit.

Incipit
ACT[US] IV. [SCENA i.]

Enter at Cole Harbor, Hoard, the Widow, [Lamprey, Spichcock,] and Gentlemen, he married now.

1 [GENT.] Join hearts, join hands,
  In wedlock's bands,
  Never to part
  Till death cleave your heart.
  [*To Hoard.*] You shall forsake all other women;
  [*To Courtesan.*] You lords, knights, gentlemen, and yeomen.
  What my tongue slips
  Make up with your lips.

HOARD. Give you joy, Mistress Hoard; let the kiss come about.—[*One knocks.*]
  Who knocks? Convey my little pig-eater[6] out. 10

LUC. [*Within.*] Hoard!

HOARD. Upon my life, my adversary, gentlemen!

LUC. [*Within.*] Hoard, open the door, or we will force it ope.
  Give us the widow.

HOARD. Gentlemen, keep 'em out.

LAMP. He comes upon his death that enters here.

LUC. [*Within.*] My friends, assist me!

HOARD. He has assistants, gentlemen.

LAMP. Tut, nor him nor them we in this action fear.

LUC. [*Within.*] Shall I, in peace, speak one word with the widow?

COUR. Husband and gentlemen, hear me but a word.

HOARD. Freely, sweet wife.

COUR. Let him in peaceably; 20
  You know we're sure from any act of his.

HOARD. Most true.

---

[1] Undress you. [2] Cheating.
[3] Another of Dampit's coinages, of doubtful meaning. [4] Fears.
[5] The slum district just outside the walls of the city.
[6] Term of endearment.

Cour. [1] You may stand by and smile at
　his old weakness.
　Let me alone to answer him.

Hoard. 　　　　　　　　　Content;
　'Twill be good mirth, i' faith. How
　think you, gentlemen?

Lamp. Good gullery!

Hoard. 　Upon calm conditions let him in.

Luc. [*Within.*] All spite and malice!

Lamp. 　　　　　　Hear me, Master Lucre.
　So you will vow a peaceful entrance
　With those your friends, and only exer-
　cise
　Calm conference with the widow, with-
　out fury,　　　　　　　　　　　　30
　The passage shall receive you.

Enter Lucre [, Gentlemen, and Host].

Luc. 　　　　　　　　　I do vow it.

Lamp. Then enter and talk freely. Here
　she stands.

Luc. O, Master Hoard, your spite has
　watched [2] the hour!
　You're excellent at vengeance, Master
　Hoard.

Hoard. Ha, ha, ha!

Luc. 　　　　I am the fool you laugh at.
　You are wise, sir, and know the seasons
　well.—
　Come hither, widow. Why is it thus?
　O, you have done me infinite disgrace,
　And your own credit no small injury!
　Suffer mine enemy so despitefully　40
　To bear you from my nephew? O, I
　had rather
　Half my substance had been forfeit and
　begged by some
　Starved rascal!

Cour. 　　　　　Why, what would you
　wish me do, sir?
　I must not overthrow my state for love.
　We have too many presidents [3] for that;
　From thousands of our wealthy undone
　widows
　One may derive some wit. I do confess
　I loved your nephew, nay, I did affect
　him
　Against the mind and liking of my
　friends, [4]
　Believed his promises, lay here in hope　50
　Of flattered living and the boast of lands.

[1] Early edns. read *Luc.*　　　[3] Precedents.
[2] Awaited.
[4] From 1616 edn. Original reads *friend.*

Coming to touch his wealth and state
　indeed,
　It appears dross; I find him not the
　man,
　Imperfect, mean, scarce furnished of
　his needs—
　In words, fair lordships; in performance,
　hovels.
　Can any woman love the thing that is
　not?

Luc. Broke you for this?

Cour. 　　　　Was it not cause too much?
　Send to inquire his state; most part of
　it
　Lay two years mortgaged in his uncle's
　hands.

Luc. Why, say it did; you might have
　known my mind.　　　　　　　　60
　I could have soon restored it.

Cour. Ay, had I but seen any such thing
　performed,
　Why, 'twould have tied my affection,
　and contained
　Me in my first desires. Do you think,
　i' faith,
　That I could twine such a dry oak as
　this,
　Had promise in your nephew took ef-
　fect?

Luc. Why, and there's no time past; and
　rather than
　My adversary should thus thwart my
　hopes,
　I would—

Cour. Tut, y'ave been ever full of golden
　speech.　　　　　　　　　　　　70
　If words were lands, your nephew would
　be rich.

Luc. Widow, believe it, I vow by my
　best bliss,
　Before these gentlemen, I will give in
　The mortgage to my nephew instantly,
　Before I sleep or eat.

1 [Gent.] [5] 　　　　　We'll pawn our
　credits,
　Widow, what he speaks shall be per-
　formed
　In fullness.

Luc. 　　　　Nay, more. I will estate him
　In farther blessings; he shall be my
　heir;
　I have no son;
　I'll bind myself to that condition.　80

[5] Of Lucre's party.

Cour. When I shall hear this done, I
   shall soon yield
   To reasonable terms.
Luc.   In the mean season,
   Will you protest, before these gentle-
   men,
   To keep yourself as you are now at this
   present?
Cour. I do protest, before these gentle-
   men,
   I will be as clear then as I am now.
Luc. I do believe you. Here's your own
   honest servant;
   I'll take him along with me.
Cour.   Ay, with all my heart.
Luc. He shall see all performed, and
   bring you word.
Cour. That's all I wait for.   90
Hoard. What, have you finished, Master
   Lucre? Ha, ha, ha, ha!
Luc. So laugh, Hoard, laugh at your
   poor enemy, do;
   The wind may turn; you may be laughed
   at too.
   Yes, marry, may you, sir.—Ha, ha, ha!
        Exeunt [*Lucre, Gentlemen, and Host*].
Hoard. Ha, ha, ha! If every man that
   swells in malice
   Could be revenged as happily as I,
   He would choose hate, and forswear
   amity.—
   What did he say, wife, prithee?
Cour. Faith, spoke to ease his mind.
Hoard. O—O—O!
Cour.   You know now, little to
   any purpose.   100
Hoard. True, true, true!
Cour.   He would do mountains now.
Hoard. Ay, ay, ay, ay.
Lamp.   Y'ave struck him dead, Master
   Hoard.
Spi. And his nephew desperate.
Hoard.   I know 't, sirs, I.
   Never did man so crush his enemy.
                       Exeunt.

[Scena ii.

A room in Lucre's house.]

Enter Lucre with Gentlemen, [*and Host,*]
           meeting Sam Freedom.

Luc. My son-in-law, Sam Freedom,
   where's my nephew?
Sam. O, man in lamentation, father!

Luc.   How!
Sam. He thumps his breast like a gal-
lant dicer that has lost his doublet, and
stands in 's shirt to do penance.
Luc. Alas, poor gentleman!
Sam. I warrant you may hear him sigh
in a still evening to your house at High-
gate.
   Luc. I prithee, send him in.   10
Sam. Were it to do a greater matter,
I will not stick with you, sir, in regard you
married my mother.   [*Exit.*]
Luc. Sweet gentlemen, cheer him up;
I will but fetch the mortgage and return
to you instantly.   *Exit.*
1 [Gent.] We'll do our best, sir.—See
   where he comes,
   E'en joyless and regardless of all form.

[Enter Witgood.]

2 [Gent.] Why, how now, Master Witgood? Fie! You a firm scholar, and [20
an understanding gentleman, and give
your best parts to passion?
   1 [Gent.] Come, fie!
Wit. O, gentlemen—
1 [Gent.] Sorrow of me, what a sigh was
   there, sir!
   Nine such widows are not worth it.
Wit. To be borne from me by that lecher,
   Hoard!
1 [Gent.] That vengeance is your uncle's,
   being done
   More in despite to him than wrong to
   you.
   But we bring comfort now.
Wit.   I beseech you, gentlemen— 30
2 [Gent.] Cheer thyself, man; there's
   hope of her, i' faith.
Wit. Too gladsome to be true.

Enter Lucre.

Luc.   Nephew, what cheer?
   Alas, poor gentleman, how art thou
   changed!
   Call thy fresh blood into thy cheeks
   again.
   She comes.
Wit.   Nothing afflicts me so much,
   But that it is your adversary, uncle,
   And merely plotted in despite of you.
Luc. Ay, that's it mads me, spites me!
I'll spend my wealth ere he shall carry her

so, because I know 'tis only to spite me. [40
Ay, this is it. Here, nephew. [*Gives a
paper.*] Before these kind gentlemen, I
deliver in your mortgage my promise to
the widow. See, 'tis done. Be wise; you're
once more master of your own. The widow
shall perceive now you are not altogether
such a beggar as the world reputes you;
you can make shift to bring her to three
hundred a year, sir.

1 [GENT.] Berlady,[1] and that's no toy,
    sir.

LUC.   A word, nephew.   50

1 [GENT. (*To Host.*)] Now you may certify
    the widow.

LUC. You must conceive it aright, nephew,
    now;
    To do you good I am content to do this.

WIT. I know it, sir.

LUC. But your own conscience can tell I
    had it
    Dearly enough of you.

WIT.   Ay, that's most certain.

LUC. Much money laid out, beside many
    a journey
    To fetch the rent; I hope you'll think
    on 't, nephew.

WIT. I were worse than a beast else, i'
    faith.

LUC. Although to blind the widow and
    the world,   60
    I out of policy do 't, yet there's a con-
    science, nephew.

WIT. Heaven forbid else!

LUC.   When you are full possessed,
    'Tis nothing to return it.

WIT. Alas, a thing quickly done, uncle!

LUC. Well said! You know I give it you
    but in trust.

WIT. Pray, let me understand you rightly,
    uncle:
    You give it me but in trust?

LUC. No.

WIT. That is, you trust me with it?

LUC. True, true.   70

WIT. [*Aside.*] But, if ever I trust you with
    it again,
    Would I might be trussed up for my
    labor!

LUC. You can all witness, gentlemen,
    and you, Sir Yeoman?

HOST. My life for yours, sir, now, I
know my mistress's mind too well toward

your nephew; let things be in preparation,
and I'll train her hither in most excellent
fashion.   *Exit.*   79

LUC. A good old boy!—Wife! 'Ginny!

Enter Wife.

WIFE. What's the news, sir?

LUC. The wedding day's at hand.
Prithee, sweet wife, express thy house-
wifery. Thou'rt a fine cook, I know 't;
thy first husband married thee out of an
alderman's kitchen; go to, he raised thee
for raising of paste. What! Here's none
but friends; most of our beginnings must
be winked at.—Gentlemen, I invite you
all to my nephew's wedding against [90
Thursday morning.

1 [GENT.] With all our hearts, and we
shall joy to see your enemy so mocked.

LUC. He laughed at me, gentlemen;
ha, ha, ha!   *Exeunt* [*All but Witgood*].

WIT. He has no conscience, faith,
would laugh at them. They laugh at one
another.
Who then can be so cruel? Troth,
    not I;
I rather pity now than aught envy.   100
I do conceive such joy in mine own
happiness I have no leisure yet to laugh
at their follies.—
[*To the mortgage.*] Thou soul of my es-
    tate, I kiss thee!
I miss life's comfort when I miss thee.
O, never will we part again,
Until I leave the sight of men!
We'll ne'er trust conscience of our kin,
Since cozenage brings that title in. [*Exit.*]

[SCENA iii.

A street in London.]

Enter three Creditors.

1 [CRED.] I'll wait these seven hours but
I'll see him caught.

2 [CRED.] Faith, so will I.

3 [CRED.] Hang him, prodigal! He's
stripped of the widow.

1 [CRED.] A my troth, she's the wiser; she
has made the happier choice. And I wonder
of what stuff those widows' hearts are made
of, that will marry unfledged boys before
comely thrum-chinned [2] gentlemen.   10

Enter a Boy.

Boy. News, news, news!

1 [CRED.] What, boy?

Boy. The rioter is caught.

1 [CRED.] So, so, so, so! It warms me at the heart; I love a' life to see dogs upon men. O, here he comes.

Enter Witgood, with Serjeants.

WIT. My last joy was so great it took away the sense of all future afflictions. What a day is here o'ercast! How soon a black tempest rises!   20

1 [CRED.] O, we may speak with you now, sir! What's become of your rich widow? I think you may cast your cap at [1] the widow, may you not, sir?

2 [CRED.] He a rich widow? Who, a prodigal, a daily rioter, and a nightly vomiter? He a widow of account? He a hole i' th' Counter! [2]

WIT. You do well, my masters, to tyrannize over misery, to afflict the afflicted; [30 'tis a custom you have here amongst you. I would wish you never leave it, and I hope you'll do as I bid you.

1 [CRED.] Come, come, sir, what say you extempore now to your bill of a hundred pound? A sweet debt for froating [3] your doublets.

2 [CRED.] Here's mine of forty.

3 [CRED.] Here's mine of fifty.   39

WIT. Pray, sirs—you'll give me breath?

1 [CRED.] No, sir, we'll keep you out of breath still; then we shall be sure you will not run away from us.

WIT. Will you but hear me speak?

2 [CRED.] You shall pardon us for that, sir. We know you have too fair a tongue of your own. You overcame us too lately, a shame take you! We are like to lose all that for want of witnesses. We dealt in policy then; always when we strive to be [50 most politic we prove most coxcombs—*non plus ultra.*[4] I perceive by us we're not ordained to thrive by wisdom, and therefore we must be content to be tradesmen.

WIT. Give me but reasonable time, and I protest I'll make you ample satisfaction.

---

[1] Give up.
[2] London prison for debtors.
[3] Rubbing, probably with perfume.
[4] *I.e.,* go no further.

1 [CRED.] Do you talk of reasonable time to us?

WIT. 'Tis true, beasts know no reasonable time.   60

2 [CRED.] We must have either money or carcass.

WIT. Alas, what good will my carcass do you?

3 [CRED.] O, 'tis a secret delight we have amongst us! We that are used to keep birds in cages have the heart to keep men in prison, I warrant you.

WIT. [*Aside.*] I perceive I must crave a little more aid from my wits. Do but [70 make shift for me this once, and I'll forswear ever to trouble you in the like fashion hereafter; I'll have better employment for you, and I live.—You'll give me leave, my masters, to make trial of my friends, and raise all means I can?

1 [CRED.] That's our desires, sir.

Enter Host.

HOST. Master Witgood.

WIT. O, art thou come?

HOST. May I speak one word with [80 you in private, sir?

WIT. No, by my faith, canst thou; I am in hell here, and the devils will not let me come to thee.

CIT.[5] Do you call us devils? You shall find us Puritans.—Bear him away; let 'em talk as they go. We'll not stand to hear 'em.—Ah, sir, am I a devil? I shall think the better of myself as long as I live. A devil, i' faith!   *Exeunt.*   90

[SCENA iv.

A room in Hoard's house.]

Enter Hoard.

HOARD. What a sweet blessing hast thou, Master Hoard, above a multitude! Wilt thou never be thankful? How dost thou think to be blessed another time? Or dost thou count this the full measure of thy happiness? By my troth, I think thou dost. Not only a wife large in possessions, but spacious in content; she's rich, she's young, she's fair, she's wise.[6] When I wake, I think of her lands—that revives me; [10

---

[5] Probably meaning *citizens, i.e., creditors.*
[6] From 1616 edn. Original reads *wife.*

when I go to bed, I dream of her beauty—
and that's enough for me. She's worth four
hundred a year in her very smock, if a man
knew how to use it. But the journey will
be all, in troth, into the country, to ride to
her lands in state and order following—my
brother and other worshipful gentlemen,
whose companies I ha' sent down for
already, to ride along with us in their goodly
decorum beards, their broad velvet [20
chashocks,[1] and chains of gold twice or
thrice double, against which time I'll entertain some ten men of mine own into liveries, all of occupations or qualities; I will
not keep an idle man about me, the sight
of which will so vex my adversary Lucre—
for we'll pass by his door a purpose, make
a little stand for [the][2] nonce, and have our
horses curvet before the window—certainly
he will never endure it, but run up [30
and hang himself presently.—

[Enter Servant.]

How now, sirrah, what news? Any that
offer their service to me yet?

SER. Yes, sir, there are some i' th' hall
that wait for your worship's liking, and
desire to be entertained.

HOARD. Are they of occupation?

SER. They are men fit for your worship,
sir.   39

HOARD. Say'st so? Send 'em all in.—
[Exit Servant.] To see ten men ride after
me in watchet[3] liveries, with orange-
tawny capes—'twill cut his comb, i' faith.

Enter All[4] [, i.e., Tailor, Barber, Perfumer,
Falconer, and Huntsman].

How now? Of what occupation are you,
sir?

TAIL. A tailor, an 't please your worship

HOARD. A tailor? O, very good. You
shall serve to make all the liveries.—What
are you, sir?

BAR. A barber, sir.   50

HOARD. A barber? Very needful. You
shall shave all the house, and, if need
require, stand for a reaper i' th' summer
time.—You, sir?

PER. A perfumer.

HOARD. I smelt you before. Perfumers,
of all men, had need carry themselves
uprightly; for if they were once knaves
they would be smelt out quickly.—To you,
sir?   60

FAL. A falc'ner, an 't please your worship.

HOARD. Sa ho, sa ho, sa ho![5]—And
you, sir?

HUNT. A huntsman, sir.

HOARD. There, boy, there, boy, there,
boy![6] I am not so old but I have pleasant
days to come. I promise you, my masters,
I take such a good liking to you that I entertain you all. I put you already [70
into my countenance, and you shall be
shortly in my livery. But especially you
two, my jolly falc'ner and my bonny huntsman, we shall have most need of you at my
wife's manor-houses i' th' country. There's
goodly parks and champion[7] grounds for
you; we shall have all our sports within ourselves; all the gentlemen a th' country shall
be beholding to us and our pastimes.

FAL. And we'll make your[8] worship [80
admire, sir.

HOARD. Say'st thou so? Do but make
me admire, and thou shall want for nothing.—My tailor.

TAIL. Anon, sir.

HOARD. Go presently in hand with the
liveries.

TAIL. I will, sir.

HOARD. My barber.

BAR. Here, sir.   90

HOARD. Make 'em all trim fellows,
louse 'em well—especially my huntsman—
and cut all their beards of the Polonian[9]
fashion.—My perfumer.

PER. Under your nose, sir.

HOARD. Cast a better savor upon the
knaves, to take away the scent of my
tailor's feet, and my barber's lotium
water.[10]

PER. It shall be carefully per- [100
formed, sir.

HOARD. But you, my falc'ner and
huntsman, the welcom'st men alive, i'
faith!

---

[1] Cassocks.   [2] Added by Dyce.   [3] Pale blue.
[4] This direction appears at the end of the speech
in the original.

[5] A hawking cry.   [7] Champaign.
[6] A hunting cry.
[8] From 1616 edn. Original reads *you*.
[9] Polish.
[10] A preparation of urine used as a cosmetic.

HUNT. And we'll show you that, sir, shall deserve your worship's favor.

HOARD. I prithee, show me that.—Go, you knaves all, and wash your lungs i' th' buttery, go.—[*Exeunt Tailor, Barber, etc.*] By th' Mass, and well remembered! [110 I'll ask my wife that question.—Wife, Mistress Jane Hoard!

Enter Courtesan, altered in apparel.

COUR. Sir, would you with me?

HOARD. I would but know, sweet wife, which might stand best to thy liking, to have the wedding dinner kept here or i' th' country?

COUR. Hum! Faith, sir, 'twould like me better here; here you were married, here let all rites be ended.   120

HOARD. Could a marquesse [1] give a better answer? Hoard, bear thy head aloft; thou'st a wife will advance it.—

[*Enter Host with a letter.*]

What haste comes here now? Yea, a letter? Some dreg of my adversary's malice. Come hither; what's the news?

HOST. A thing that concerns my mistress, sir.   [*Gives letter to Courtesan.*]

HOARD. Why, then it concerns me, knave.   130

HOST. Ay, and you, knave, too (cry your worship mercy). You are both like to come into trouble, I promise you, sir; a precontract.[2]

HOARD. How? A precontract, say'st thou?

HOST. I fear they have too much proof on 't, sir. Old Lucre, he runs mad up and down, and will to law as fast as he can; young Witgood laid hold on [140 by his creditors, he exclaims upon you a tother side, says you have wrought his undoing by the injurious detaining of his contract.

HOARD. Body a me!

HOST. He will have utmost satisfaction; The law shall give him recompense, he says.

COUR. [*Aside.*] Alas, his creditors so

[1] Marchioness.

[2] "A pre-contract of marriage could not be set aside without the mutual consent of the parties" (Bullen).

merciless! My state being yet uncertain, I deem it not unconscionable to fur- [150 der him.

HOST. True, sir.

HOARD. Wife, what says that letter? Let me construe it.

COUR. Cursed be my rash and unadviséd words!

[*Tears and stamps upon the letter.*]

I'll set my foot upon my tongue, And tread my inconsiderate grant to dust.

HOARD. Wife—

HOST. [*Aside.*] A pretty shift, i' faith! I commend a woman when she can [160 make away a letter from her husband handsomely, and this was cleanly done, by my troth.

COUR. I did, sir; Some foolish words I must confess did pass, Which now litigiously he fastens on me.

HOARD. Of what force? Let me examine 'em.

COUR. Too strong, I fear; would I were well freed of him!   170

HOARD. Shall I compound?

COUR. No, sir, I'd have it done some nobler way Of your side; I'd have you come off with honor; Let baseness keep with them. Why, have you not The means, sir? The occasion's offered you.

HOARD. Where, how, dear wife?

COUR. He is now caught by his creditors; the slave's needy; his debts petty. He'll rather bind himself to all inconveniences than rot in prison; by this only [180 means you may get a release from him. 'Tis not yet come to his uncle's hearing. Send speedily for the creditors. By this time he's desperate; he'll set his hand to anything. Take order for his debts, or discharge 'em quite. A pax on him, let's be rid of a rascal!

HOARD. Excellent! Thou dost astonish me.—Go, run, make haste; Bring both the creditors and Witgood hither.   190

HOST. [*Aside.*] This will be some revenge yet.   [*Exit.*]

HOARD. In the mean space I'll have a release drawn.—
Within there!

[*Enter Servant.*]

SER. [1] Sir?

HOARD. Sirrah, come, take directions; go to my scrivener.

COUR. [*Aside.*] I'm yet like those whose riches lie in dreams;
If I be waked, they're false. Such is my fate,
Who ventures deeper than the desperate state.
Though I have sinned, yet could I become new,　　　　　199
For, where I once vow, I am ever true.

HOARD. Away, despatch! On my displeasure, quickly.—[*Exit Servant.*] Happy occasion! Pray heaven he be in the right vein now to set his hand to 't, that nothing alter him; grant that all his follies may meet in him at once, to besot him enough! I pray for him, i' faith, and here he comes.

[*Enter Witgood and Creditors.*]

WIT. What would you with me now, my uncle's spiteful adversary?　　　　　210

HOARD. Nay, I am friends.

WIT. Ay, when your mischief's spent.

HOARD. I heard you were arrested.

WIT. Well, what then?
You will pay none of my debts, I am sure.

HOARD. A wise man cannot tell;
There may be those conditions 'greed upon
May move me to do much.

WIT. Ay, when?—'Tis thou,
Perjuréd woman! (O, no name is vild [2]
Enough to match thy treachery!) That art
The cause of my confusion.

COUR. Out, you Penurious slave!

HOARD. Nay, wife, you are too forward;　　　　　220
Let him alone; give losers leave to talk.

WIT. Shall I remember thee of another promise
Far stronger than the first?

COUR. I'd fain know that.

WIT. 'Twould call shame to thy cheeks.

COUR. Shame!

WIT. Hark in your ear.—
[*Draws Courtesan aside.*]
Will he come off, think'st thou, and pay my debts roundly?

COUR. Doubt nothing; there's a release a-drawing and all, to which you must set your hand.

WIT. Excellent!　　　　　230

COUR. But methinks, i' faith, you might have made some shift to discharge this yourself, having in the mortgage, and never have burdened my conscience with it.

WIT. A my troth, I could not, for my creditors' cruelties extend to the present.

COUR. No more.—[*Aloud.*] Why, do your worst for that. I defy you.

WIT. Y' are impudent. I'll call up witnesses.

COUR. Call up thy wits, for thou hast been devoted　　　　　240
To follies a long time.

HOARD. Wife, y' are too bitter.—
Master Witgood, and you, my masters, you shall hear a mild speech come from me now, and this it is: 't 'as been my fortune, gentlemen, to have an extraordinary blessing poured upon me alate, and here she stands; I have wedded her, and bedded her, and yet she is little the worse. Some foolish words she hath passed to you in the country, and some peevish [3] debts you owe [250 here in the city. Set the hare's head to the goose-giblet [4]—release you her of her words, and I'll release you of your debts, sir.

WIT. Would you so? I thank you for that, sir; I cannot blame you, i' faith.

HOARD. Why, are not debts better than words, sir?

WIT. Are not words promises, and are not promises debts, sir?

HOARD. [*Aside.*] He plays at [260 backracket with me. [5]

1 [CRED.] Come hither, Master Witgood, come hither; be ruled by fools once.
[*Creditors take Witgood aside.*]

2 [CRED.] We are citizens, and know what belong to 't.

1 [CRED.] Take hold of his offer. Pax

---

[1] Original reads *1.*　　　　　[2] Vile.

[3] Small.
[4] *I.e.,* let equivalents balance each other.
[5] *I.e.,* he hits the ball back at me.

on her, let her go. If your debts were once discharged, I would help you to a widow myself worth ten of her.

3 [CRED.] Mass, partner, and now [270 you remember me on 't, there's Master Mulgrave's sister newly fallen a widow.

1 [CRED.] Cud's me, as pat as can be! There's a widow left for you, ten thousand in money, beside plate, jewels, *et cetera*. I warrant it a match; we can do all in all with her. Prithee, despatch; we'll carry thee to her presently.

WIT. My uncle will ne'er endure me when he shall hear I set my hand to a [280 release.

2 [CRED.] Hark, I'll tell thee a trick for that. I have spent five hundred pound in suits in my time; I should be wise. Thou'rt now a prisoner; make a release; take 't of my word, whatsoever a man makes as long as he is in durance, 'tis nothing in law, not thus much.

WIT. Say you so, sir? 289

3 [CRED.] I have paid for 't; I know 't.

WIT. Proceed then; I consent.

3 [CRED.] Why, well said.

HOARD. How now, my masters, what have you done with him?

1 [CRED.] With much ado, sir, we have got him to consent.

HOARD. Ah—a—a! And what came his debts to now?

1 [CRED.] Some eightscore odd pounds, sir. 300

HOARD. Naw, naw, naw, naw, naw! Tell me the second time; give me a lighter sum. They are but desperate debts, you know, ne'er called in but upon such an accident. A poor, needy knave, he would starve and rot in prison. Come, come, you shall have ten shillings in the pound, and the sum down roundly.

1 [CRED.] You must make it a mark, sir.

HOARD. Go to then; tell your money [310 in the meantime; you shall find little less there.—[*Gives money.*] Come, Master Witgood, you are so unwilling to do yourself good now!—

[*Enter Scrivener.*]

Welcome, honest scrivener.—Now you shall hear the release read.

SCRI. [*Reading.*] "Be it known to all men, by these presents, that I, Theodorus

Witgood, gentleman, sole nephew to Pecunius Lucre, having unjustly made [320 title and claim to one Jane Medler, late widow of Anthony Medler, and now wife to Walkadine Hoard, in consideration of a competent sum of money to discharge my debts, do forever hereafter disclaim any title, right, estate, or interest in or to the said widow, late in the occupation of the said Anthony Medler, and now in the occupation of Walkadine Hoard; as also neither to lay claim by virtue of any former [330 contract, grant, promise, or demise, to any of her manor[s], manor houses, parks, groves, meadow grounds, arable lands, barns, stacks, stables, dove holes, and cunny borrows,[1] together with all her cattle, money, plate, jewels, borders, chains, bracelets, furnitures, hangings, movables or immovables. In witness whereof, I, the said Theodorus Witgood, have interchangeably set to my hand and seal before [340 these presents, the day and date above written."

WIT. What a precious fortune hast thou slipped here, like a beast as thou art!

HOARD. Come, unwilling heart, come.

WIT. Well, Master Hoard, give me the pen; I see
'Tis vain to quarrel with our destiny.   [*Signs.*]

HOARD. O, as vain a thing as can be! You cannot commit a greater absurdity, sir. So, so; give me that hand now; before [350 all these presents, I am friends forever with thee.

WIT. Troth, and it were pity of my heart now, if I should bear you any grudge, i' faith.

HOARD. Content. I'll send for thy uncle against the wedding dinner; we will be friends once again.

WIT. I hope to bring it to pass myself, sir.

HOARD. How now? Is 't right, my [360 masters?

1 [CRED.] 'Tis something wanting, sir; yet it shall be sufficient.

HOARD. Why, well said; a good conscience makes a fine show nowadays. Come, my masters, you shall all taste of my wine ere you depart.

ALL. We follow you, sir.

[*Exeunt Hoard and Scrivener.*]

---

[1] Rabbit burrows.

WIT. [*Aside.*] I'll try these fellows now.
—A word, sir. What, will you carry [370
me to that widow now?

1 [CRED.] Why, do you think we were
in earnest, i' faith? Carry you to a rich
widow? We should get much credit by that.
A noted rioter! A contemptible prodigal!
'Twas a trick we have amongst us to get
in our money. Fare you well, sir.
Exeunt [Creditors].

WIT. Farewell, and be hanged, you short
pig-haired, ram-headed rascals! He that
believes in you shall ne'er be saved, [380
I warrant him. By this new league I shall
have some access unto my love.
She [, i.e., Niece,] is above.

NIECE. Master Witgood!

WIT. My life!

NIECE. Meet me presently; that note
directs you. [*Drops him a paper.*] I would
not be suspected. Our happiness attends
us. Farewell!

WIT. A word's enough.   *Exeunt.* [1]

[SCENA v.]

Dampit the usurer in his bed, Audrey spinning by. [Boy.]

SONG [*by Audrey*]

Let the usurer cram him, in interest that
    excel,
There's pits enow to damn him, before he
    comes to hell;
In Holborn some, in Fleet Street some,
Where'er he come there's some, there's
    some.

DAMP. *Trahe, trahito,* draw the curtain;
give me a sip of sack more.

Enter Gentlemen [, i.e., Lamprey and Spichcock].

LAMP. Look you; did not I tell you he
lay like the devil in chains, when he was
bound for a thousand year?

SPI. But I think the devil had no [10
steel bedstaffs; [2] he goes beyond him for that.

LAMP. Nay, do but mark the conceit [3] of
his drinking; one must wipe his mouth for
him with a muckinder, [4] do you see, sir?

SPI. Is this the sick trampler? Why, he
is only bedrid with drinking.

LAMP. True, sir. He spies us.

DAMP. What, Sir Tristram? You come
and see a weak man here, a very weak
man—   20

LAMP. If you be weak in body, you
should be strong in prayer, sir.

DAMP. O, I have prayed too much,
poor man!

LAMP. There's a taste of his soul for
you!

SPI. Fah, loathsome!

LAMP. I come to borrow a hundred
pound of you, sir.

DAMP. Alas, you come at an ill [30
time! I cannot spare it, i' faith; I ha' but
two thousand i' th' house.

AUD. Ha, ha, ha!

DAMP. Out, you gernative [5] quean, the
mullipoop [6] of villainy, the spinner of
concupiscenty!

Enter other Gentleman [, i.e., Sir Lancelot].

LAN. Yea, gentlemen, are you here before us? How is he now?

LAMP. Faith, the same man still. The
tavern bitch has bit him i' the head. [7]   40

LAN. We shall have the better sport
with him. Peace!—And how cheers Master Dampit now?

DAMP. O, my bosom, Sir Lancelot, how
cheer I? Thy presence is restorative.

LAN. But I hear a great complaint of
you, Master Dampit, among gallants.

DAMP. I am glad of that, i' faith.
Prithee, what?

LAN. They say you are waxed proud [50
alate, and, if a friend visit you in the afternoon, you'll scarce know him.

DAMP. Fie, fie! Proud? I cannot remember any such thing. Sure, I was
drunk then.

LAN. Think you so, sir?

DAMP. There 'twas, i' faith; nothing
but the pride of the sack; and so certify
'em.—Fetch sack, sirrah.

BOY. A vengeance sack you once!   60
    [*Exit Boy, who returns with sack.*]

AUD. Why, Master Dampit, if you hold
on as you begin, and lie a little longer, you

---

[1] In original, stage direction appears after preceding line.
[2] For preparing a feather bed.
[3] Fancy, singularity.   [4] Handkerchief.
[5] Grinning, peevish.
[6] Another unintelligible coinage by Dampit.
[7] *I.e.,* he is drunk.

need not take care how to dispose your wealth; you'll make the vintner your heir.

DAMP. Out, you babliaminy, you unfeathered, cremitoried quean, you cullisance of scabiosity!

AUD. Good words, Master Dampit, to speak before a maid and a virgin! 69

DAMP. Hang thy virginity upon the pole of carnality!

AUD. Sweet terms! My mistress shall know 'em.

LAMP. Note but the misery of this usuring slave. Here he lies, like a noisome dunghill, full of the poison of his drunken blasphemies; and they to whom he bequeaths all grudge him the very meat that feeds him, the very pillow that eases him. Here may a usurer behold his [80 end. What profits it to be a slave in this world, and a devil i' th' next?

DAMP. Sir Lancelot, let me buss thee, Sir Lancelot; thou art the only friend that I honor and respect.

LAN. I thank you for that, Master Dampit.

DAMP. Farewell, my bosom Sir Lancelot.

LAN. Gentlemen, and you love me, [90 let me step behind you, and one of you fall a-talking of me to him.

LAMP. Content.—Master Dampit—

DAMP. So, sir.

LAMP. Here came Sir Lancelot to see you e'en now.

DAMP. Hang him, rascal!

LAMP. Who, Sir Lancelot?

DAMP. Pythagorical rascal!

LAMP. Pythagorical? 100

DAMP. Ay, he changes his cloak when he meets a serjeant.

LAN. What a rogue's this!

LAMP. I wonder you can rail at him, sir; he comes in love to see you.

DAMP. A louse for his love! His father was a comb maker; I have no need of his crawling love. He comes to have longer day, the superlative rascal!

LAN. 'Sfoot,[1] I can no longer en- [110 dure the rogue!—Master Dampit, I come to take my leave once again, sir.

DAMP. Who? My dear and kind Sir Lancelot, the only gentleman of England? Let me hug thee; farewell, and a thousand.

[1] God's foot, a mild oath.

LAMP. Composed of wrongs and slavish flatteries!

LAN. Nay, gentlemen, he shall show you more tricks yet; I'll give you another taste of him. 120

LAMP. Is 't possible?

LAN. His memory is upon departing.

DAMP. Another cup of sack!

LAN. Mass, then 'twill be quite gone! Before he drink that, tell him there's a country client come up, and here attends for his learned advice.

LAMP. Enough.

DAMP. One cup more, and then let the bell toll. I hope I shall be weak [130 enough by that time.

LAMP. Master Dampit—

DAMP. Is the sack spouting?

LAMP. 'Tis coming forward, sir. Here's a countryman, a client of yours, waits for your deep and profound advice, sir.

DAMP. A coxcombry? Where is he? Let him approach. Set me up a peg higher.

LAMP. [To Sir Lancelot.] You must draw near, sir. 140

DAMP. Now, good man fooliaminy, what say you to me now?

LAN. Please your good worship, I am a poor man, sir—

DAMP. What make [2] you in my chamber then?

LAN. I would entreat your worship's device in a just and honest cause, sir.

DAMP. I meddle with no such matters; I refer 'em to Master No-man's office. [150

LAN. I had but one house left me in all the world, sir, which was my father's, my grandfather's, my great-grandfather's, and now a villain has unjustly wrung me out, and took possession on 't.

DAMP. Has he such feats? Thy best course is to bring thy *ejectione firmæ;* [3] and in seven year thou mayst shove him out by the law.

LAN. Alas, an 't please your wor- [160 ship, I have small friends and less money!

DAMP. Hoyday! This gear will fadge [4] well. Hast no money? Why, then, my advice is, thou must set fire a th' house, and so get him out.

LAMP. That will break strife, indeed.

LAN. I thank your worship for your hot counsel, sir.—Altering but my voice a little,

[2] Do.   [3] Writ of ejection.   [4] Work.

you see he knew me not. You may observe by this that a drunkard's mem- [170 ory holds longer in the voice than in the person. But, gentlemen, shall I show you a sight? Behold the little divedapper [1] of damnation, Gulf the usurer, for his time worse than tother.

Enter Hoard with Gulf.

LAMP. What's he comes with him?

LAN. Why, Hoard, that married lately the Widow Medler.

LAMP. O, I cry you mercy, sir.

HOARD. Now, gentlemen visitants, [180 how does Master Dampit?

LAN. Faith, here he lies, e'en drawing in, sir, good canary as fast as he can, sir; a very weak creature, truly, he is almost past memory.

HOARD. Fie, Master Dampit! You lie lazing abed here, and I come to invite you to my wedding dinner. Up, up, up!   189

DAMP. Who's this? Master Hoard? Who hast thou married, in the name of foolery?

HOARD. A rich widow.

DAMP. A Dutch widow?

HOARD. A rich widow; one Widow Medler.

DAMP. Medler? She keeps open house.

HOARD. She did, I can tell you, in her tother husband's days—open house for all comers; horse and man was welcome, [200 and room enough for 'em all.

DAMP. There's too much for thee, then; thou mayst let out some to thy neighbors.

GULF. What, hung alive in chains? O spectacle! Bedstaffs of steel? *"O monstrum horrendum, informe, ingens, cui lumen ademptum!"* [2] O Dampit, Dampit, here's a just judgment shown upon usury, extortion, and trampling villainy!   210

LAN. [*Aside.*] This exc'llent thief rails upon the thief!

GULF. Is this the end of cutthroat usury, brothel, and blasphemy? Now mayst thou see what race a usurer runs.

DAMP. Why, thou rogue of universal-

ity, do not I know thee? Thy sound is like the cuckoo, the Welsh ambassador; [3] thou cowardly slave, that offers to fight with a sick man when his weapon's [220 down! Rail upon me in my naked bed? Why, thou great Lucifer's little vicar, I am not so weak but I know a knave at first sight. Thou inconscionable rascal, thou that goest upon Middlesex juries, and will make haste to give up thy verdit [4] because thou wilt not lose thy dinner, are you answered?

GULF. An 't were not for shame— [229

Draws his dagger.

DAMP. Thou wouldst be hanged then.

LAMP. Nay, you must exercise patience, Master Gulf, always in a sick man's chamber.

LAN. He'll quarrel with none, I warrant you, but those that are bedrid.

DAMP. Let him come, gentlemen; I am armed. Reach my close-stool [5] hither.

LAN. Here will be a sweet fray anon. I'll leave you, gentlemen.

LAMP. Nay, we'll along with [240 you.—Master Gulf—

GULF. Hang him, usuring rascal!

LAN. Push, set your strength to his, your wit to his!

AUD. Pray, gentlemen, depart; his hour's come upon him.—Sleep in my bosom, sleep.

LAN. Nay, we have enough of him, i' faith; keep him for the house.

Now make your best.   250

For thrice his wealth I would not have his breast.

GULF. A little thing would make me beat him now he's asleep.

LAN. Mass, then 'twill be a pitiful day when he wakes. I would be loath to see that day come.

GULF. You overrule me, gentlemen, i' faith.   *Exeunt.*

ACTUS V. [SCENA i.]

A room in Lucre's house.]

Enter Lucre and Witgood.

WIT. Nay, uncle, let me prevail with you so much. I' faith, go, now he has invited you.

---

[1] Didapper, dabchick.
[2] "O horrible monster, misshapen, huge, from whom sight is taken away!" (Virgil's *Æneid*, iii, 658).

[3] Nares conjectures that the cuckoo was so named because it migrated from the west.
[4] Verdict.   [5] Chamber pot.

Luc. I shall have great joy there when he has borne away the widow!

Wit. Why, la, I thought where I should find you presently. Uncle, a my troth, 'tis nothing so.

Luc. What's nothing so, sir? Is not he married to the widow? 10

Wit. No, by my troth, is he not, uncle.

Luc. How?

Wit. Will you have the truth on 't? He is married to a whore, i' faith.

Luc. I should laugh at that.

Wit. Uncle, let me perish in your favor if you find it not so, and that 'tis I that have married the honest woman.

Luc. Ha! I'd walk ten mile afoot to see that, i' faith. 20

Wit. And see 't you shall, or I'll ne'er see you again.

Luc. A quean, i' faith? Ha, ha, ha!
Exeunt.

[SCENA ii.

A room in Hoard's house.]

Enter Hoard, tasting wine, the Host following in a livery cloak.

Hoard. Pup, pup, pup, pup! I like not this wine. Is there never a better tierce ¹ in the house?

Host. Yes, sir, there are as good tierce in the house as any are in England.

Hoard. Desire your mistress, you knave, to taste 'em all over; she has better skill.

Host. [*Aside.*] Has she so? The better for her, and the worse for you. *Exit.*

Hoard. Arthur! 10

[*Enter Arthur.*]

Is the cupboard of plate set out?

Art. All's in order, sir. [*Exit.*]

Hoard. I am in love with my liveries every time I think on 'em; they make a gallant show, by my troth.—Niece!

[*Enter Niece.*]

Niece. Do you call, sir?

Hoard. Prithee, show a little diligence, and overlook the knaves a little; they'll filch and steal today, and send whole pasties home to their wives; and thou beest [20 a good niece, do not see me purloined.

¹ A small cask.

Niece. Fear it not, sir.—[*Aside.*] I have cause; though the feast be prepared for you, yet it serves fit for my wedding dinner too.
[*Exit.*]

Enter two Gentlemen [*, i.e., Lamprey and Spichcock*].

Hoard. Master Lamprey and Master Spichcock, two the most welcome gentlemen alive! Your fathers and mine were all free a th' fishmongers.²

Lamp. They were indeed, sir. You see bold guests, sir, soon entreated. 30

Hoard. And that's best, sir.—

[*Enter Servant.*]

How now, sirrah?

Ser. There's a coach come to th' door, sir. [*Exit.*]

Hoard. My Lady Foxtone, a my life!— Mistress Jane Hoard! Wife!—Mass, 'tis her ladyship indeed!—

[*Enter Lady Foxtone.*]

Madam, you are welcome to an unfurnished house, dearth of cheer, scarcity of attendance. 40

Lad. You are pleased to make the worst, sir.

Hoard. Wife!

[*Enter Courtesan.*]

Lad. Is this your bride?

Hoard. Yes, madam.—Salute my Lady Foxtone.

Cour. Please you, madam, awhile to taste the air in the garden?

Lad. 'Twill please us well.
Exeunt [*Lady and Courtesan*].

Hoard. Who would not wed? The most delicious life! 50
No joys are like the comforts of a wife.

Lamp. So we bachelors think, that are not troubled with them.

[*Enter Servant.*]

Ser. Your worship's brother with another ancient gentleman are newly alighted, sir. [*Exit.*]

Hoard. Master Onesiphorus Hoard? Why, now our company begins to come in.—

² Members of the Company of Fishmongers.

[Enter Onesiphorus Hoard, Limber, and Kix.]

My dear and kind brother, welcome, i' faith.

O. Hoa.[1] You see we are men at an   [60 hour, brother.

Hoard. Ay, I'll say that for you, brother; you keep as good an hour to come to a feast as any gentleman in the shire.— What, old Master Limber and Master Kix! Do we meet, i' faith, jolly gentlemen?

Lim. We hope you lack guess,[2] sir?

Hoard. O, welcome, welcome! We lack still such guess as your worships.

O. Hoa. Ah, Sirrah Brother, have   [70 you catched up Widow Medler?

Hoard. From 'em all, brother; and I may tell you I had mighty enemies, those that stuck sore; old Lucre is a sore fox, I can tell you, brother.

O. Hoa. Where is she? I'll go seek her out; I long to have a smack at her lips.

Hoard. And most wishfully,[3] brother, see where she comes.

[Enter Courtesan and Lady.]

Give her a smack[4] now we may hear   [80 it all the house over.

Cour. *[Aside.]* O heaven, I am betrayed! *(Both [, i.e., Courtesan and Onesiphorus Hoard,] turn back.)* I know that face.

Hoard. Ha, ha, ha! Why, how now? Are you both ashamed?—Come, gentlemen, we'll look another way

O. Hoa. Nay, brother, hark you. Come, y' are disposed to be merry.   90

Hoard. Why do we meet else, man?

O. Hoa. That's another matter. I was ne'er so fraid in my life but that you had been in earnest.

Hoard. How mean you, brother?

O. Hoa. You said she was your wife?

Hoard. Did I so? By my troth, and so she is.

O. Hoa. By your troth, brother?   99

Hoard. What reason have I to dissemble with my friends, brother? If marriage can make her mine, she is mine. Why—

O. Hoa. Troth, I am not well of a sudden. I must crave pardon, brother; I came to see you, but I cannot stay dinner, i' faith.

Hoard. I hope you will not serve me so, brother?

Lim. By your leave, Master Hoard—

Hoard. What now? What now?   [110 Pray, gentlemen, you were wont to show yourselves wise men.

Lim. But you have shown your folly too much here.

Hoard. How?

Kix. Fie, fie! A man of your repute and name!

You'll feast your friends, but cloy 'em first with shame.

Hoard. This grows too deep; pray, let us reach the sense.

Lim. In your old age dote on a courtesan!

Hoard. Ha!

Kix. Marry a strumpet!   120

Hoard. Gentlemen!

O. Hoa. And Witgood's quean!

Hoard. O! Nor lands nor living?

O. Hoa. Living!

Hoard. *[To Courtesan.]*   Speak!

Cour.   Alas, you know, at first, sir, I told you I had nothing!

Hoard. Out, out! I am cheated; infinitely cozened!

Lim. Nay, Master Hoard—

Enter Witgood, [Niece,] and Lucre.

Hoard. A Dutch widow! A Dutch widow! A Dutch widow!

Luc. Why, nephew, shall I trace thee still a liar?

Wilt make me mad? Is not yon thing the widow?   130

Wit. Why, la, you are so hard a belief, uncle!

By my troth, she's a whore.

Luc.   Then thou'rt a knave.

Wit. *Negatur argumentum,*[5] uncle.

Luc. *Probo tibi,*[6] nephew.   He that knows a woman to be a quean must needs be a knave; thou say'st thou know'st her to be one; *ergo,* if she be a quean, thou'rt a knave.

Wit. *Negatur sequela majoris,*[7] uncle. He that knows a woman to be a   [140 quean must needs be a knave; I deny that.

---

[1] Through the rest of this scene in the original this speech head reads *Ony.* or *On.*

[2] Guests.   [4] Early edns. read *smerck.*

[3] Exactly on your wish.

[5] Proof is denied.   [6] I'll prove it to you.

[7] The conclusion of your major premise is denied.

HOARD. Lucre and Witgood, y' are both villains; get you out of my house!

LUC. Why, didst not invite me to thy wedding dinner?

WIT. And are not you and I sworn perpetual friends before witness, sir, and were both drunk upon 't?

HOARD. Daintily abused! Y'ave put a junt [1] upon me! 149

LUC. Ha, ha, ha!

HOARD.   A common strumpet!

WIT.   Nay, now
You wrong her, sir; if I were she, I'd have
The law on you for that; I durst depose for her
She ne'er had common use nor common thought.

COUR. Despise me, publish me, I am your wife.
What shame can I have now but you'll have part?
If in disgrace you share, I sought not you;
You pursuéd me, nay, forc[é]d me.
Had I friends would follow it,
Less than your action has been proved a rape.

O. HOA. Brother! 160

COUR. Nor did I ever boast of lands unto you,
Money, or goods; I took a plainer course,
And told you true, I'd nothing.
If error were committed, 'twas by you;
Thank your own folly. Nor has my sin been
So odious, but worse has been forgiven;
Nor am I so deformed, but I may challenge
The utmost power of any old man's love.
She that tastes not sin before, twenty to one but she'll taste it after. Most of you [170 old men are content to marry young virgins, and take that which follows; where, marrying one of us, you both save a sinner and are quit from a cuckold forever.
"And more, in brief, let this your best thoughts win,
She that knows sin, knows best how to hate sin." [2]

HOARD. Cursed be all malice! Black are the fruits of spite,

And poison first their owners. O, my friends,
I must embrace shame, to be rid of shame!
Concealed disgrace prevents a public name. 180
Ah, Witgood! Ah, Theodorus!

WIT. Alas, sir, I was pricked in conscience to see her well bestowed, and where could I bestow her better than upon your pitiful worship? Excepting but myself, I dare swear she's a virgin; and now, by marrying your niece, I have banished myself forever from her. She's mine aunt now, by my faith, and there's no meddling with mine aunt, you know—a sin [190 against my nuncle. [3]

COUR. [Kneeling.] Lo, gentlemen, before you all
In true reclaiméd form I fall.
Henceforth forever I defy [4]
The glances of a sinful eye,
Waving of fans (which some suppose
Tricks of fancy [5]), treading of toes,
Wringing of fingers, biting the lip,
The wanton gait, th' alluring trip, 199
All secret friends and private meetings,
Close-borne letters and bawds' greetings,
Feigning excuse to women's labors
When we are sent for to th' next neighbor's,
Taking false physic, and ne'er start
To be let blood, though sign be at heart,[6]
Removing chambers, shifting beds,
To welcome friends in husbands' steads,
Them to enjoy, and you to marry,
They first served, while you must tarry,
They to spend, and you to gather, 210
They to get, and you to father—
These and thousand thousand more,
New reclaimed, I now abhor.

LUC. [To Witgood.] Ah, here's a lesson, rioter, for you!

WIT. I must confess my follies; I'll down too.   [Kneels.]
And here forever I disclaim
The cause of youth's undoing, game,
Chiefly dice, those true outlanders,
That shake out beggars, thieves, and panders,
Soul-wasting surfeits, sinful riots, 220

---

[1] Fraud.
[2] Quotation marks were often used to call attention to sententious passages.

[3] Uncle.   [4] Renounce.   [5] Love.
[6] According to the almanacs a propitious time for bloodletting.

Queans' evils, doctors' diets,
Pothecaries' drugs, surgeons' glisters,
Stabbing of arms [1] for a common mis-
    tress,
Riband favors, ribald speeches,
Dear perfumed jackets, penniless
    breeches,
Dutch flapdragons,[2] healths in urine,

[1] To drink off one's blood mixed with wine.
[2] Tidbits swallowed from burning brandy.

Drabs that keep a man too sure in—
I do defy you all.
Lend me each honest hand, for here I rise
A reclaimed man, loathing the general
    vice.   230
HOARD. So, so, all friends! The wedding
    dinner cools.
Who seem most crafty prove ofttimes
    most fools.   [*Exeunt.*]
             FINIS.

THE CHANGELING[1]

BY

IHOMAS MIDDLETON AND WILLIAM ROWLEY

DRAMATIS PERSONÆ

VERMANDERO, [governor of the castle of Alicant and] father to Beatrice.
TOMASO DE PIRACQUO, a noble lord.
ALONZO DE PIRACQUO, his brother, suitor to Beatrice.
ALSEMERO, a nobleman, afterwards married to Beatrice.
JASPERINO, his friend.
ALIBIUS, a jealous doctor.
LOLLIO, his man.
PEDRO, friend to Antonio.

ANTONIO, the changeling.
FRANCISCUS, the counterfeit madman.
DEFLORES, servant to Vermandero.
MADMEN.
SERVANTS.

BEATRICE [JOANNA], daughter to Vermandero.
DIAPHANTA, her waiting-woman.
ISABELLA, wife to Alibius.

THE SCENE: Alligant.[2]

[TIME: Contemporary.]

ACTUS PRIMUS. [SCENA PRIMA.

Outside a temple.]

Enter Alsemero.

[ALS.] 'Twas in the temple where I first
    beheld her,
And now again the same. What omen yet
Follows of that? None but imaginary.
Why should my hopes or fate be timor-
    ous?
The place is holy; so is my intent.
I love her beauties to the holy purpose;
And that, methinks, admits comparison
With man's first creation, the place
    blessed,
And is his right home back, if he achieve
    it.
The church hath first begun our inter-
    view,   10
And that's the place must join us into
    one;
So there's beginning and perfection too.

Enter Jasperino.

JAS. O sir, are you here? Come, the wind's
    fair with you;
Y' are like to have a swift and pleasant
    passage.
ALS. Sure, y' are deceived, friend; 'tis con-
    trary,
In my best judgment.
JAS.   What, for Malta?
If you could buy a gale amongst the
    witches,
They could not serve you such a lucky
    pennyworth   18
As comes a[3] God's name.
ALS.   Even now I observed
The temple's vane to turn full in my face;
I know 'tis against me.
JAS.   Against you?
Then you know not where you are.
ALS.   Not well, indeed.
JAS. Are you not well, sir?
ALS.   Yes, Jasperino,
Unless there be some hidden malady
Within me that I understand not.

---

[1] The title continues: "As It Was Acted with Great Applause at the Private House in Drury Lane, and Salisbury Court."   [2] Alicant.

[3] In.

Jas.   And that
I begin to doubt,[1] sir. I never knew
Your inclinations to travels at a pause
With any cause to hinder it, till now.
Ashore you were wont to call your serv-
    ants up,
And help to trap[2] your horses for the
    speed;   30
At sea I have seen you weigh the anchor
    with 'em,
Hoist sails for fear to lose the foremost
    breath,
Be in continual prayers for fair winds—
And have you changed your orisons?[3]
Als.   No, friend;
I keep the same church, same devotion.
Jas. Lover I'm sure y' are none; the stoic
    was[4]
Found in you long ago; your mother nor
Best friends, who have set snares of
    beauty, ay,
And choice ones too, could never trap
    you that way.
What might be the cause?
Als.   Lord, how violent   40
Thou art! I was but meditating of
Somewhat I heard within the temple.
Jas.   Is this
Violence? 'Tis but idleness compared
With your haste yesterday.
Als.   I'm all this while
A-going, man.

Enter Servants.

Jas. Backwards, I think, sir. Look,
your servants.
1 Ser. The seamen call. Shall we board
your trunks?
Als. No, not today.   50
Jas. 'Tis the critical day, it seems, and
the sign in Aquarius.[5]
2 Ser. We must not to sea today; this
smoke will bring forth fire.
Als. Keep all on shore; I do not know the
    end,
Which needs I must do, of an affair in
    hand
Ere I can go to sea.

---

[1] Fear.   [2] Prepare.   [3] Prayers.
[4] In the original line ends with *stoic.* Other
instances of faulty line division later in the play
have been altered silently, and a few passages of
very rough verse have been printed as prose.
[5] *I.e.,* favorable for sailing.

1 Ser.   Well, your pleasure.
2 Ser. Let him e'en take his leisure too;
we are safer on land.
                                Exeunt Serv[ants].

Enter Beatrice Joanna,[6] Diaphanta, and
    Servants. [Alsemero kisses Beatrice.]

Jas. [*Aside.*] How now! The laws   [60
of the Medes are changed sure. Salute a
woman! He kisses too! Wonderful! Where
learnt he this? And does it perfectly too.
In my conscience,[7] he ne'er rehearsed it
before. Nay, go on; this will be stranger
and better news at Valencia than if he had
ransomed half Greece from the Turk.
Bea. You are a scholar, sir?
Als.   A weak one, lady.
Bea. Which of the sciences is this love you
    speak of?
Als. From your tongue I take it to be
    music.   70
Bea. You are skillful in 't; can sing at first
    sight.
Als. And I have showed you all my skill
    at once;
I want more words to express me further,
And must be forced to repetition.
I love you dearly.
Bea.   Be better advised, sir.
Our eyes are sentinels unto our judg-
    ments,
And should give certain judgment what
    they see;
But they are rash sometimes, and tell us
    wonders
Of common things, which, when our
    judgments find,
They can then check the eyes, and call
    them blind.   80
Als. But I am further, lady; yesterday
Was mine eyes' employment, and hither
    now
They brought my judgment, where are
    both agreed.
Both houses then consenting, 'tis agreed;
Only there wants the confirmation
By the hand royal. That's your part, lady.
Bea. O, there's one above me, sir.—
    [*Aside.*] For five days past
To be recalled! Sure mine eyes were
    mistaken;

---

[6] In the original *Joanna* appears after *Servants.*
[7] To my knowledge.

This was the man was meant me. That
  he should come
So near his time, and miss it!   90
  JAS. We might have come by the carriers from Valencia, I see, and saved all our
sea-provision; we are at farthest sure. Methinks I should do something too; I meant
to be a venturer in this voyage. Yonder's
another vessel; I'll board her. If she be
lawful prize, down goes her topsail.

                    [*Goes to Diaphanta.*]

         Enter Deflores.

DEF. Lady, your father—
BEA.   Is in health, I hope.
DEF. Your eye shall instantly instruct you,
  lady;
  He's coming hitherward.
BEA.   What needed then 100
Your duteous preface? I had rather
He had come unexpected; you must stall [1]
A good presence with unnecessary blab-
  bing;
And how welcome for your part you are,
I'm sure you know.
DEF. [*Aside.*]   Will 't never mend,
  this scorn,
One side nor other? Must I be enjoined
To follow still [2] whilst she flies from me?
  Well,
Fates, do your worst, I'll please myself
  with sight
Of her at all opportunities,
If but to spite her anger. I know she had
Rather see me dead than living; and yet
She knows no cause for 't but a peevish
  will.   112
ALS. You seemed displeaséd, lady, on the
  sudden.
BEA. Your pardon, sir; 'tis my infirmity.
Nor can I other reason render you
Than his or hers, of [3] some particular thing
They must abandon as a deadly poison,
Which to a thousand other tastes were
  wholesome;
Such to mine eyes is that same fellow
  there,
The same that report speaks of the
  basilisk. [4]   120

[1] Forestall, anticipate.   [2] Always.
[3] Emended by Dyce. Original reads *or*.
[4] A fabulous creature whose look was supposed
to be fatal.

ALS. This is a frequent frailty in our nature;
There's scarce a man amongst a thousand
  found
But hath his imperfection: one distastes
The scent of roses, which to infinites [5]
Most pleasing is and odoriferous;
One, oil, the enemy of poison;
Another, wine, the cheerer of the heart
And lively refresher of the countenance.
Indeed, this fault, if so it be, is general;
There's scarce a thing but is both loved
  and loathed.   130
Myself, I must confess, have the same
  frailty.
BEA. And what may be your poison, sir?
  I am bold with you.
ALS. And what might be your desire, per-
  haps—a cherry?
BEA. I am no enemy to any creature
My memory has, but yon gentleman.
ALS. He does ill to tempt your sight, if he
  knew it.
BEA. He cannot be ignorant of that, sir.
I have not spared to tell him so; and I
  want
To help myself, since he's a gentleman
In good respect [6] with my father, and
  follows him.   140
ALS. He's out of his place then now.
               [*They walk aside.*]
JAS. I am a mad wag, wench.
DIA. So methinks; but, for your comfort,
I can tell you we have a doctor in the city
that undertakes the cure of such.
JAS. Tush, I know what physic is best
for the state of mine own body.
DIA. 'Tis scarce a well-governed state, I
believe.
JAS. I could show thee such a [150
thing with an ingredian [7] that we two would
compound together, and, if it did not tame
the maddest blood i' th' town for two hours
after, I'll ne'er profess physic again.
DIA. A little poppy, sir, were good to
cause you sleep.
JAS. Poppy? I'll give thee a pop i' th'
lips for that first, and begin there. Poppy
is one simple indeed, and cuckoo [8] (what-
you-call 't) another. I'll discover no [160
more now; another time I'll show thee all.
                   [*Exit.*]

[5] Many people.   [6] Repute.
[7] Ingredience, mixture.
[8] The cuckoo-flower, with an obvious pun.

Enter Vermandero and Servants.

BEA. My father, sir.

VER. O Joanna, I came to meet thee. Your devotion's ended?

BEA. For this time, sir.—
[*Aside.*] I shall change my saint, I fear me; I find
A giddy turning in me.—Sir, this while
I am beholding to this gentleman,
Who left his own way to keep me company,
And in discourse I find him much desirous
To see your castle. He hath deserved it, sir,
If ye please to grant it.

VER. With all my heart, sir. 170
Yet there's an article between; I must know
Your country. We use not to give survey
Of our chief strengths to strangers; our citadels
Are placed conspicuous to outward view,
On promonts' tops, but within our secrets.

ALS. A Valencian, sir.

VER. A Valencian?
That's native, sir. Of what name, I beseech you?

ALS. Alsemero, sir.

VER. Alsemero? Not the son
Of John de Alsemero?

ALS. The same, sir.

VER. My best love bids you welcome.

BEA. He was wont 180
To call me so, and then he speaks a most
Unfeignéd truth.

VER. O sir, I knew your father;
We two were in acquaintance long ago,
Before our chins were worth iulan down,[1]
And so continued till the stamp of time
Had coined us into silver. Well, he's gone;
A good soldier went with him.

ALS. You went together in that, sir.

VER. No, by Saint Jacques, I came behind him;
Yet I have done somewhat too. An unhappy day 190
Swallowed him at last at Gibraltar,
In fight with those rebellious Hollanders.
Was it not so?

ALS. Whose death I had revenged,
Or followed him in fate, had not the late league [2]
Prevented me.

VER. Ay, ay, 'twas time to breathe.—
O Joanna, I should ha' told thee news;
I saw Piracquo lately.

BEA. [*Aside.*] That's ill news.

VER. He's hot preparing for this day of triumph;
Thou must be a bride within this sevennight.

ALS. [*Aside.*] Ha! 200

BEA. Nay, good sir, be not so violent; with speed
I cannot render satisfaction
Unto the dear companion of my soul,
Virginity, whom I thus long have lived with,
And part with it so rude and suddenly.
Can such friends divide, never to meet again,
Without a solemn farewell?

VER. Tush, tush! There's a toy.[3]

ALS. [*Aside.*] I must now part, and never meet again
With any joy on earth.—Sir, your pardon;
My affairs call on me.

VER. How, sir? By no means. 210
Not changed so soon, I hope? You must see my castle
And her best entertainment ere we part;
I shall think myself unkindly used else.
Come, come, let's on; I had good hope your stay
Had been awhile with us in Alligant.
I might have bid you to my daughter's wedding.

ALS. [*Aside.*] He means to feast me, and poisons me beforehand.—
I should be dearly glad to be there, sir,
Did my occasions suit as I could wish.

BEA. I shall be sorry if you be not there
When it is done, sir; but not so suddenly. 221

VER. I tell you, sir, the gentleman's complete,
A courtier and a gallant, enriched
With many fair and noble ornaments.
I would not change him for a son-in-law
For any he in Spain, the proudest he,
And we have great ones, that you know.

---

[1] The first growth of the beard.

[2] An armistice signed in 1609.   [3] Trifle.

ALS.   He's much
  Bound to you, sir.
VER.   He shall be bound to me
  As fast as this tie can hold him; I'll want
  My will else.
BEA. [*Aside.*]   I shall want mine, if you
  do it.   230
VER. But come. By the way I'll tell you
  more of him.
ALS. [*Aside.*] How shall I dare to venture
  in his castle,
  When he discharges murderers[1] at the
    gate?
  But I must on, for back I cannot go.
BEA. [*Aside.*] Not this serpent[2] gone yet?
                          [*Drops her glove.*]
VER.   Look, girl, thy glove's fall'n.
  Stay, stay. Deflores, help a little.
[*Exeunt Vermandero, Alsemero, and Serv-
                                    ants.*]
DEF. [*Offering her her glove.*]   Here, lady.
BEA. Mischief on your officious forward-
    ness!
  Who bade you stoop? They touch my
    hand no more.
  There! For tother's[3] sake I part with
    this.   [*Throws down the other glove.*]
  Take um, and draw thine own skin off
    with um!   240
Exeunt [*Beatrice, Diaphanta, and Attend-
                                    ants*].
DEF. Here's a favor come with a mischief!
    Now I know
  She had rather wear my pelt tanned in a
    pair
  Of dancing pumps than I should thrust
    my fingers
  Into her sockets here. I know she hates me,
  Yet cannot choose but love her.
  No matter! If but to vex her, I'll haunt
    her still;
  Though I get nothing else, I'll have my
    will.   *Exit.*

              [SCENA SECUNDA.

  A room in the house of Alibius.]

        Enter Alibius and Lollio.

ALIB. Lollio, I must trust thee with a
    secret,
  But thou must keep it.
LOL. I was ever close to a secret, sir.

ALIB. The diligence that I have found in
    thee,
  The care and industry already past,
  Assures me of thy good continuance.
  Lollio, I have a wife.
LOL. Fie, sir, 'tis too late to keep her
secret; she's known to be married all the
town and country over.   10
ALIB. Thou goest too fast, my Lollio.
    That knowledge
  I allow no man can be barred it;
  But there is a knowledge which is
    nearer,
  Deeper, and sweeter, Lollio.
LOL. Well, sir, let us handle that be-
tween you and I.
ALIB. 'Tis that I go about, man. Lollio,
  My wife is young.
LOL. So much the worse to be kept
secret, sir.   20
ALIB. Why, now thou meet'st the sub-
    stance of the point;
  I am old, Lollio.
LOL. No, sir, 'tis I am old Lollio.
ALIB. Yet why may not this concord and
    sympathize?
  Old trees and young plants often grow
    together,
  Well enough agreeing.
LOL. Ay, sir, but the old trees raise
themselves higher and broader than the
young plants.
ALIB. Shrewd application! There's the
    fear, man;   30
  I would wear my ring on my own finger;
  Whilst it is borrowed, it is none of
    mine,
  But his that useth it.
LOL. You must keep it on still then; if
it but lie by, one or other will be thrusting
into 't.
ALIB. Thou conceiv'st me, Lollio. Here
    thy watchful eye
  Must have employment. I cannot al-
    ways be at home.
LOL. I dare swear you cannot.
ALIB. I must look out.   40
LOL. I know 't, you must look out; 'tis
every man's case.
ALIB. Here, I do say, must thy employ-
    ment be—
  To watch her treadings, and in my ab-
    sence
  Supply my place.

Lol. I'll do my best, sir; yet surely I cannot see who you should have cause to be jealous of.

Alib. Thy reason for that, Lollio? 'Tis a comfortable question.　50

Lol. We have but two sorts of people in the house, and both under the whip—that's fools and madmen; the one has not wit enough to be knaves, and the other not knavery enough to be fools.

Alib. Ay, those are all my patients, Lollio.
I do profess the cure of either sort.
My trade, my living 'tis; I thrive
　by it.
But here's the care that mixes with my
　thrift:
The daily visitants, that come to see　60
My brainsick patients, I would not
　have
To see my wife. Gallants I do ob-
　serve
Of quick, enticing eyes, rich in habits,
Of stature and proportion very comely.
These are most shrewd temptations,
　Lollio.

Lol. They may be easily answered, sir.
If they come to see the fools and madmen, you and I may serve the turn, and let my mistress alone. She's of neither sort.

Alib. 'Tis a good ward;[1] indeed, come they
　to see　70
Our madmen or our fools, let um see no
　more
Than what they come for. By that con-
　sequent
They must not see her; I'm sure she's no
　fool.

Lol. And I'm sure she's no madman.

Alib. Hold that buckler fast. Lollio, my
　trust
Is on thee, and I account it firm and
　strong.
What hour is 't, Lollio?

Lol.　　　　　　Towards belly hour, sir.

Alib. Dinner time? Thou mean'st twelve
　a-clock?

Lol. Yes, sir, for every part has his hour:
we wake at six and look about us—　[80
that's eye hour; at seven we should pray—
that's knee hour; at eight walk—that's leg
hour; at nine gather flowers and pluck
a rose[2]—that's nose hour; at ten we

drink—that's mouth hour; at eleven lay about us for victuals—that's hand hour; at twelve go to dinner—that's belly hour.

Alib. Profoundly, Lollio! It will be long
Ere all thy scholars learn this lesson, and
I did look to have a new one entered—
　stay,　90
I think my expectation is come home.

Enter Pedro, and Antonio like an idiot.

Ped. Save you, sir. My business speaks
　itself;
This sight takes off the labor of my
　tongue.

Alib. Ay, ay, sir, 'tis plain enough you
　mean him for my patient.

Ped. And, if your pains prove but commodious, to give but some little strength to
his sick and weak part of nature in him,
these are [*Gives him money.*] but patterns to
show you of the whole pieces that will follow to you, beside the charge of diet, washing, and other necessaries, fully defrayed.

Alib. Believe it, sir, there shall no care be
　wanting.　102

Lol. Sir, an officer in this place may deserve something. The trouble will pass through my hands.

Ped. 'Tis fit something should come to your hands then, sir. [*Gives him money.*]

Lol. Yes, sir, 'tis I must keep him sweet,[3] and read to him. What is his name?

Ped. His name is Antonio; marry, we use but half to him, only Tony.　111

Lol. Tony, Tony, 'tis enough, and a very good name for a fool.—What's your name, Tony?

Ant. He, he, he! Well, I thank you, cousin. He, he, he!

Lol. Good boy, hold up your head.—He can laugh; I perceive by that he is no beast.

Ped. Well, sir,
If you can raise him but to any height,
Any degree of wit, might he attain,　121
As I might say, to creep but on all four
Towards the chair of wit, or walk on
　crutches,
'Twould add an honor to your worthy
　pains,
And a great family might pray for you,
To which he should be heir, had he dis-
　cretion

---

[1] Guard, defense.　　[2] *I.e.*, relieve ourselves.　　[3] Clean.

To claim and guide his own. Assure
you, sir,
He is a gentleman.

LOL. Nay, there's nobody doubted that.
At first sight I knew him for a gentleman;
he looks no other yet.   131

PED. Let him have good attendance and
sweet lodging.

LOL. As good as my mistress lies in, sir;
and, as you allow us time and means, we
can raise him to the higher degree of discretion.

PED. Nay, there shall no cost want, sir.

LOL. He will hardly be stretched up to
the wit of a magnifico.

PED. O, no, that's not to be expected;
far shorter will be enough.   141

LOL. I'll warrant you [I'll] [1] make him
fit to bear office in five weeks; I'll undertake to wind him up to the wit of constable.

PED. If it be lower than that, it might
serve turn.

LOL. No, fie; to level him with a head-
borough, [2] beadle, or watchman were but
little better than he is. Constable I'll [150
able him; [3] if he do come to be a justice
afterwards, let him thank the keeper. Or
I'll go further with you. Say I do bring
him up to my own pitch; say I make him
as wise as myself.

PED. Why, there I would have it.

LOL. Well, go to; either I'll be as errant
a fool as he, or he shall be as wise as I, and
then I think 'twill serve his turn.   159

PED. Nay, I do like thy wit passing well.

LOL. Yes, you may; yet if I had not
been a fool, I had had more wit than I
have too. Remember what state [4] you
find me in.

PED. I will, and so leave you. Your
best cares, I beseech you.   Ex[it] Ped[ro].

ALIB. Take you none with you; leave
um all with us.

ANT. O, my cousin's gone! Cousin,
cousin, O!   170

LOL. Peace, peace, Tony! You must
not cry, child; you must be whipped if you
do. Your cousin is here still; I am your
cousin, Tony.

ANT. He, he! Then I'll not cry, if thou
beest my cousin. He, he, he!

LOL. I were best try his wit a little, that
I may know what form [5] to place him in.

ALIB. Ay, do, Lollio, do.

LOL. I must ask him easy ques-   [180
tions at first.—Tony, how many true [6] fingers has a tailor on his right hand?

ANT. As many as on his left, cousin.

LOL. Good. And how many on both?

ANT. Two less than a deuce, cousin.

LOL. Very well answered. I come to
you again, cousin Tony. How many fools
goes to [7] a wise man?

ANT. Forty in a day sometimes, cousin.

LOL. Forty in a day? How prove [190
you that?

ANT. All that fall out amongst themselves, and go to a lawyer to be made friends.

LOL. A parlous fool! He must sit in the
fourth form at least, I perceive that.—I
come again, Tony. How many knaves
make an honest man?

ANT. I know not that, cousin.

LOL. No, the question is too hard for
you. I'll tell you, cousin. There's [200
three knaves may make an honest man—a
serjeant, a jailor, and a beadle; the serjeant
catches him, the jailor holds him, and the
beadle lashes him; and, if he be not honest
then, the hangman must cure him.

ANT. Ha, ha, ha! That's fine sport,
cousin.

ALIB. This was too deep a question for
the fool, Lollio.

LOL. Yes, this might have served [210
yourself, though I say 't.—Once more and
you shall go play, Tony.

ANT. Ay, play at pushpin, cousin. Ha, he!

LOL. So thou shalt. Say how many
fools are here.

ANT. Two, cousin; thou and I.

LOL. Nay, y' are too forward there,
Tony. Mark my question! How many
fools and knaves are here: a fool before a
knave, a fool behind a knave, between [220
every two fools a knave—how many fools,
how many knaves?

ANT. I never learnt so far, cousin.

ALIB. Thou putt'st too hard questions
to him, Lollio.

LOL. I'll make him understand it easily.
—Cousin, stand there.

ANT. Ay, cousin.

[1] Supplied by Dyce.   [2] Constable.
[3] I.e., qualify him for.   [4] Position.
[5] Class.   [6] Honest.   [7] Make.

Lol. Master, stand you next the fool.

Alib. Well, Lollio.   230

Lol. Here's my place. Mark now, Tony, there a fool before a knave.

Ant. That's I, cousin.

Lol. Here's a fool behind a knave—that's I; and between us two fools there is a knave—that's my master; 'tis but we three, that's all.

Ant. We three, we three, cousin.

                              Madmen within.

1 [Mad.] (*Within.*) Put's head i' th' pillory; the bread's too little.   240

2 [Mad.] (*Within.*) Fly, fly, and he catches the swallow.

3 [Mad.] (*Within.*) Give her more onion, or the devil put the rope about her crag.[1]

Lol. You may hear what time of day it is; the chimes of Bedlam goes.

Alib. Peace, peace, or the wire [2] comes!

3 [Mad.] (*Within.*) Cat whore, cat [249 whore! Her parmasant, her parmasant! [3]

Alib. Peace, I say!—Their hour's come; they must be fed, Lollio.

Lol. There's no hope of recovery of that Welsh madman; was undone by a mouse that spoiled him a parmasant; lost his wits for 't.

Alib. Go to your charge, Lollio; I'll to mine.

Lol. Go you to your madmen's ward; let me alone with your fools.   260

Alib. And remember my last charge, Lollio.   *Exit.*

Lol. Of which your patients do you think I am? Come, Tony, you must amongst your schoolfellows now. There's pretty scholars amongst um, I can tell you; there's some of 'em at *stultus, stulta, stultum.*[4]

Ant. I would see the madmen, cousin, if they would not bite me.   270

Lol. No, they shall not bite thee, Tony.

Ant. They bite when they are at dinner, do they not, coz?

Lol. They bite at dinner, indeed, Tony. Well, I hope to get credit by thee; I like thee the best of all the scholars that ever I brought up, and thou shalt prove a wise man, or I'll prove a fool myself.   *Exeunt.*

---

[1] Neck.   [2] Whip.   [3] Parmesan cheese.
[4] The beginning of the Latin declension of *stupid.*

Actus Secundus. [Scena Prima.

A room in the castle.]

Enter Beatrice and Jasperino severally.

Bea. O, sir, I'm ready now for that fair service
Which makes the name of friend sit glorious on you!
Good angels and this conduct be your guide!   [*Gives a paper.*]
Fitness of time and place is there set down, sir.

Jas. The joy I shall return rewards my service.   *Exit.*

Bea. How wise is Alsemero in his friend!
It is a sign he makes his choice with judgment.
Then I appear in nothing more approved
Than making choice of him, for, 'tis a principle,
He that can choose   10
That bosom well who of his thoughts partakes,
Proves most discreet in every choice he makes.
Methinks I love now with the eyes of judgment,
And see the way to merit, clearly see it.
A true deserver like a diamond sparkles;
In darkness you may see him—that's in absence,
Which is the greatest darkness falls on love;
Yet is he best discerned then
With intellectual eyesight.   What's Piracquo
My father spends his breath for? And his blessing   20
Is only mine as I regard his name,
Else it goes from me, and turns head against me,
Transformed into a curse. Some speedy way
Must be remembered. He's so forward too,
So urgent that way, scarce allows me breath
To speak to my new comforts.

Enter Deflores.

Def. [*Aside.*]   Yonder's she;
Whatever ails me, now alate especially!
I can as well be hanged as refrain seeing her.

Some twenty times a day, nay, not so
    little,
Do I force errands, frame ways and ex-
    cuses,   30
To come into her sight; and I have small
    reason for 't,
And less encouragement, for she baits
    me still
Every time worse than other; does pro-
    fess herself
The cruelest enemy to my face in town;
At no hand can abide the sight of me,
As if danger or ill luck hung in my
    looks.
I must confess my face is bad enough,
But I know far worse has better fortune,
And not endured alone, but doted on;
And yet such pick-haired [1] faces, chins
    like witches',   40
Here and there five hairs, whispering
    in a corner
As if they grew in fear one of another,
Wrinkles like troughs, where swine-
    deformity swills
The tears of perjury, that lie there like
    wash
Fallen from the slimy and dishonest
    eye—
Yet such a one plucks sweets without
    restraint,
And has the grace of beauty to his sweet.
Though my hard fate has thrust me out
    to servitude,
I tumbled into th' world a gentleman.
She turns her blessed eye upon me now,
And I'll endure all storms before I part
    with 't.   51
BEA. [Aside.] Again?
This ominous ill-faced fellow more dis-
    turbs me
Than all my other passions.
DEF. [Aside.]   Now 't begins again;
I'll stand this storm of hail, though the
    stones pelt me.
BEA. Thy business? What's thy busi-
    ness?
DEF. [Aside.]   Soft and fair!
I cannot part so soon now.
BEA. [Aside.]   The villain's fixed.—
Thou standing toad-pool—
DEF. [Aside.]   The shower falls
    amain now.

BEA. Who sent thee? What's thy errand?
    Leave my sight!
DEF. My lord your father charged me
    to deliver   60
A message to you.
BEA.   What, another since?
Do 't, and be hanged then; let me be rid
    of thee.
DEF. True service merits mercy.
BEA.   What's thy message?
DEF. Let beauty settle but in patience,
    You shall hear all.
BEA.   A dallying, trifling torment!
DEF. Signior Alonzo de Piracquo, lady,
    Sole brother to Tomaso de Piracquo—
BEA. Slave, when wilt make an end?
DEF.   Too soon I shall.
BEA. What all this while of him?
DEF.   The said Alonzo,
With the foresaid Tomaso—
BEA.   Yet again? 70
DEF. Is new alighted.
BEA.   Vengeance strike the news!
Thou thing most loathed, what cause
    was there in this
To bring thee to my sight?
DEF.   My lord your father
Charged me to seek you out.
BEA.   Is there no other
To send his errand by?
DEF.   It seems 'tis my luck
To be i' th' way still.
BEA.   Get thee from me!
DEF.   So.—
[Aside.] Why, am not I an ass to devise
    ways
Thus to be railed at? I must see her still!
I shall have a mad qualm within this
    hour again,
I know 't; and, like a common Garden
    bull,[2]   80
I do but take breath to be lugged [3] again.
What this may bode I know not; I'll
    despair the less,
Because there's daily presidents [4] of
    bad faces
Beloved beyond all reason. These foul
    chops
May come into favor one day mongst
    his fellows.
Wrangling has proved the mistress of
    good pastime.

---

[1] Thin-bearded.

[2] Bulls were baited at Paris Garden.
[3] Pulled, baited.   [4] Precedents.

As children cry themselves asleep, I
   ha' seen
Women have chid themselves abed to
   men.   *Exit Def[lores].*
Bea. I never see this fellow but I think
   Of some harm towards me; danger's
   in my mind still;   90
I scarce leave trembling of an hour after.
The next good mood I find my father in,
I'll get him quite discarded. O, I was
Lost in this small disturbance, and forgot
Affliction's fiercer torrent that now
   comes
To bear down all my comforts!

Enter Vermandero, Alonzo, Tomaso.

Ver.   Y' are both welcome,
But an especial one belongs to you, sir,
To whose most noble name our love
   presents
The addition[1] of a son, our son Alonzo.
Alon. The treasury of honor cannot bring
   forth   100
A title I should more rejoice in, sir.
Ver. You have improved it well.—Daugh-
   ter, prepare;
The day will steal upon thee suddenly.
Bea. [*Aside.*] Howe'er, I will be sure to
   keep the night,[2]
If it should come so near me.
      [*Beatrice takes Vermandero aside.*]
Tom.   Alonzo!
Alon.   Brother?
Tom. In troth, I see small welcome in her
   eye.
Alon. Fie, you are too severe a censurer[3]
Of love in all points. There's no bring-
   ing on[4] you.
If lovers should mark everything a
   fault,   109
Affection would be like an ill-set book,
Whose faults might prove as big as half
   the volume.
Bea. That's all I do entreat.
Ver.   It is but reasonable;
I'll see what my son says to 't.—Son
   Alonzo,
Here's a motion made but to reprieve
A maidenhead three days longer; the
   request
Is not far out of reason, for indeed
The former time is pinching.

Alon.   Though my joys
Be set back so much time as I could
   wish
They had been forward, yet, since she
   desires it,
The time is set as pleasing as before. 120
I find no gladness wanting.
Ver.   May I ever
Meet it in that point still! Y' are nobly
   welcome, sirs.
     Exeunt Ver[mandero] and Bea[trice].
Tom. So; did you mark the dullness of
   her parting now?
Alon. What dullness? Thou art so ex-
   ceptious[5] still!
Tom. Why, let it go then; I am but a fool
To mark your harms so heedfully.
Alon.   Where's the oversight?
Tom. Come, your faith's cozened in her,
   strongly cozened.
Unsettle your affection with all speed
Wisdom can bring it to; your peace is
   ruined else.
Think what a torment 'tis to marry
   one   130
Whose heart is leaped into another's
   bosom.
If ever pleasure she receive from thee,
It comes not in thy name, or of thy gift.
She lies but with another in thine arms,
He the half-father unto all thy children
In the conception; if he get 'em not,
She helps to get 'em for him in his[6]
   passions, and how dangerous
And shameful her restraint may go in
   time to,
It is not to be thought on without suf-
   ferings.
Alon. You speak as if she loved some
   other, then.   140
Tom. Do you apprehend so slowly?
Alon.   Nay, and that
Be your fear only, I am safe enough.
Preserve your friendship and your coun-
   sel, brother,
For times of more distress; I should de-
   part
An enemy, a dangerous, deadly one,
To any but thyself, that should but think
She knew the meaning of inconstancy,
Much less the use and practice; yet
   w' are friends.

---

[1] Title. [2] *I.e.*, watch. [3] Judge. [4] Persuading.

[5] Captions.   [6] *I.e.*, the husband's.

Pray, let no more be urged; I can endure
Much, till I meet an injury to her;   150
Then I am not myself.   Farewell, sweet
   brother;
How much w' are bound to heaven to
   depart lovingly.   *Exit.*
Tom. Why, here is love's tame madness;
   thus a man
Quickly steals into his vexation.   *Exit.*

[Scena Secunda.

Another room in the castle.]

Enter Diaphanta and Alsemero.

Dia. The place is my charge; you have
   kept your hour,
And the reward of a just meeting bless
   you!
I hear my lady coming.   Complete
   gentleman,
I dare not be too busy with my praises;
Th' are dangerous things to deal with.
                        Exit.
Als.   This goes well;
These women are the ladies' cabinets,
Things of most precious trust are lock[ed]
   into 'em.

Enter Beatrice.

Bea. I have within mine eye all my de-
   sires.
Requests that holy prayers ascend
   heaven for,
And brings 'em down to furnish our
   defects,   10
Come not more sweet to our necessities
Than thou unto my wishes.
Als.   W' are so like
In our expressions, lady, that, unless I
   borrow
The same words, I shall never find their
   equals.
Bea. How happy were this meeting, this
   embrace,
If it were free from envy!   This poor
   kiss
It has an enemy, a hateful one,
That wishes poison to 't.   How well were
   I now,
If there were none such name known
   as Piracquo,
Nor no such tie as the command of
   parents!   20

I should be but too much blessed.
Als.   One good service
Would strike off both your fears, and
   I'll go near it too,
Since you are so distressed.   Remove
   the cause,
The command ceases; so there's two
   fears blown out
With one and the same blast.
Bea.   Pray, let me find [1] you, sir.
What might that service be, so strangely
   happy?
Als. The honorablest piece 'bout man,
   valor.
I'll send a challenge to Piracquo in-
   stantly.
Bea. How?   Call you that extinguishing
   of fear,
When 'tis the only way to keep it flam-
   ing?   30
Are not you ventured in the action,
That's all my joys and comforts?
Pray, no more, sir.
Say you prevailed; you're danger's and
   not mine then.
The law would claim you from me, or
   obscurity
Be made the grave to bury you alive.
I'm glad these thoughts come forth;
   O, keep not one
Of this condition, sir!   Here was a course
Found to bring sorrow on her way to
   death;
The tears would ne'er 'a' dried, till dust
   had choked 'em.
Blood guiltiness becomes a fouler vis-
   age.—   40
[*Aside.*] And now I think on one; I was
   to blame—
I ha' marred so good a market with my
   scorn.
'T had been done questionless.   The
   ugliest creature
Creation framed for some use!   Yet to
   see
I could not mark so much where it should
   be!
Als. Lady—
Bea. [*Aside.*]   Why, men of art make
   much of poison,
Keep one to expel another.   Where was
   my art?
Als. Lady, you hear not me.
   [1] Understand.

Bea.　　　　　　　I do especially, sir.
The present times are not so sure of our
　side
As those hereafter may be; we must
　use 'em then　　　　　　　　　　50
As thrifty folks their wealth, sparingly
　now,
Till the time opens.
Als.　　　　　You teach wisdom, lady.
Bea. Within there, Diaphanta!

Enter Diaphanta.

Dia.　　　　　　Do you call, madam?
Bea. Perfect your service, and conduct
　this gentleman
The private way you brought him.
Dia.　　　　　　　I shall, madam.
Als. My love's as firm as love e'er built
　upon.
　　Ex[eunt] Dia[phanta] and Als[emero].

Enter Deflores.

Def. [*Aside.*] I've watched this meeting,
　and do wonder much
What shall become of tother. I'm sure
　both
Cannot be served unless she transgress;
　happily [1]　　　　　　　　　　59
Then I'll put in for one; for, if a woman
Fly from one point, from him she makes
　a husband,
She spreads and mounts then like arith-
　metic
(One, ten, a hundred, a thousand, ten
　thousand),
Proves in time sutler to an army royal.
Now do I look to be most richly railed at;
Yet I must see her.
Bea. [*Aside.*]　　Why, put case [2] I loathed
　him
As much as youth and beauty hates a
　sepulcher,
Must I needs show it? Cannot I keep
　that secret,
And serve my turn upon him? See, he's
　here.—
Deflores!
Def. [*Aside.*]　　Ha, I shall run mad with
　joy!　　　　　　　　　　　　70
She called me fairly by my name, De-
　flores,
And neither rogue nor rascal.

Bea.　　　　　　　What ha' you done
To your face alate? Y'ave met with
　some good physician;
Y'ave pruned [3] yourself, methinks. You
　were not wont
To look so amorously.[4]
Def.　　　　　　　Not I.—[*Aside.*] 'Tis
The same physnomy,[5] to a hair and
　pimple,
Which she called scurvy scarce an hour
　ago.
How is this?
Bea.　　　　Come hither; nearer, man.
Def. [*Aside.*] I'm up to the chin in heaven!
Bea.　　　　　　　Turn, let me see.
Vaugh, 'tis but the heat of the liver, I
　perceive 't;　　　　　　　　　80
I thought it had been worse.
Def. [*Aside.*]　　　Her fingers touched me!
She smells all amber.[6]
Bea. I'll make a water for you shall cleanse
　this
Within a fortnight.
Def.　　　With your own hands, lady?
Bea. Yes, mine own, sir; in a work of
　cure
I'll trust no other.
Def. [*Aside.*]　　'Tis half an act of pleasure
To hear her talk thus to me.
Bea.　　　　　　　When w' are used
To a hard face, 'tis not so unpleasing;
It mends still in opinion, hourly mends;
I see it by experience.
Def. [*Aside.*]　　　　I was blessed　90
To light upon this minute; I'll make
　use on 't.
Bea. Hardness becomes the visage of a
　man well;
It argues service, resolution, manhood,
If cause were of employment.
Def.　　　　　　　'Twould be soon seen
If e'er your ladyship had cause to use
　it;
I would but wish the honor of a service
So happy as that mounts to.
Bea.　　　　　　　We shall try you.—
O, my Deflores!
Def. [*Aside.*] How's that? She calls me
　hers
Already! "My Deflores!"—You were
　about
To sigh out somewhat, madam?

[3] Preened.　　　　[4] Like one to be loved.
[5] Physiognomy.　　　　　　[6] Ambergris.

---

[1] Haply, perhaps.　　　　[2] *I.e.*, suppose.

BEA.   No, was I? 100
I forgot—O!—

DEF.   There 'tis again, the very
fellow on 't.

BEA. You are too quick, sir.

DEF. There's no excuse for 't now; I
heard it twice, madam;
That sigh would fain have utterance.
Take pity on 't,
And lend it a free word. 'Las, how it
labors
For liberty! I hear the murmur yet
Beat at your bosom.

BEA.   Would creation—

DEF. Ay, well said, that's it.

BEA.   Had formed me man!

DEF. Nay, that's not it.

BEA.   O, 'tis the soul of freedom!
I should not then be forced to marry
one   110
I hate beyond all depths; I should have
power
Then to oppose my loathings, nay, re-
move 'em
Forever from my sight.

DEF. [Aside.]   O blessed occasion!—
Without change to your sex you have
your wishes;
Claim so much man in me.

BEA.   In thee, Deflores?
There's small cause for that.

DEF.   Put it not from me;
It's a service that I kneel for to you.
                    [Kneels.]

BEA. You are too violent to mean faithfully.
There's horror in my service, blood and
danger;
Can those be things to sue for?

DEF.   If you knew 120
How sweet it were to me to be employed
In any act of yours, you would say
then
I failed, and used not reverence enough
When I receive the charge on 't.

BEA. [Aside.]   This is much,
Methinks; belike his wants are greedy;
and,
To such, gold tastes like angel's food.
Rise!

DEF. I'll have the work first.

BEA. [Aside.]   Possible his need
Is strong upon him.—There's to encourage thee;   [Gives money.]

As thou art forward, and thy service
dangerous,
Thy reward shall be precious.

DEF.   That I have thought on; 130
I have assured myself of that beforehand,
And know it will be precious; the thought
ravishes!

BEA. Then take him to thy fury!

DEF.   I thirst for him.

BEA. Alonzo de Piracquo.

DEF. [Rising.]   His end's upon him;
He shall be seen no more.

BEA.   How lovely now
Dost thou appear to me! Never was
man
Dearlier rewarded.

DEF.   I do think of that.

BEA. Be wondrous careful in the execution.

DEF. Why, are not both our lives upon
the cast?

BEA. Then I throw all my fears upon thy
service.   140

DEF. They ne'er shall rise to hurt you.

BEA.   When the deed's done,
I'll furnish thee with all things for thy
flight;
Thou mayst live bravely in another
country.

DEF. Ay, ay;
We'll talk of that hereafter.

BEA. [Aside.]   I shall rid myself
Of two inveterate loathings at one
time,
Piracquo, and his dog-face.   Exit.

DEF.   O my blood!
Methinks I feel her in mine arms already,
Her wanton fingers combing out this
beard,
And, being pleased, praising this bad
face.   150
Hunger and pleasure, they'll commend
sometimes
Slovenly dishes, and feed heartily on
'em—
Nay, which is stranger, refuse daintier
for 'em.
Some women are odd feeders.—I'm too
loud.
Here comes the man goes supperless
to bed,
Yet shall not rise tomorrow to his din-
ner.

Enter Alonzo.

ALON. Deflores.

DEF.   My kind, honorable lord?

ALON. I am glad I ha' met with thee.

DEF.   Sir?

ALON.   Thou canst show me
The full strength of the castle?

DEF.   That I can, sir.

ALON. I much desire it.

DEF.   And if the ways and straits 160
Of some of the passages be not too tedious for you,
I will assure you, worth your time and
   sight, my lord.

ALON. Puh, that shall be no hindrance.

DEF.   I'm your servant, then.
'Tis now near dinner time; gainst [1]
   your lordship's rising
I'll have the keys about me.

ALON.   Thanks, kind Deflores.

DEF. [*Aside.*] He's safely thrust upon me
   beyond hopes.   *Exeunt.*

ACTUS TERTIUS. [SCENA PRIMA.

The top of a narrow stairway in the castle.]

Enter Alonzo and Deflores. (*In the act
time* [2] *Deflores hides a naked rapier.*)

DEF. Yes, here are all the keys. I was
   afraid, my lord,
I'd wanted for the postern [3] —this
   is it.
I've all, I've all, my lord. This for the
   sconce.[4]

ALON. 'Tis a most spacious and impregnable fort.

DEF. You'll tell me more, my lord. This
   descent
Is somewhat narrow; we shall never
   pass
Well with our weapons. They'll but
   trouble us.

ALON. Thou say[e]st true.

DEF.   Pray, let me help your lordship.

ALON. 'Tis done. Thanks, kind Deflores.

DEF.   Here are hooks, my lord,
To hang such things on purpose.   10
           [*Hangs up the two swords.*]

ALON. Lead; I'll follow thee.

Ex[eunt] at one door and enter at the other.

[1] In anticipation of.
[2] *I.e.,* between the acts.
[3] Lacked the postern key.
[4] Isolated fortification.

A landing place on the stairway.]

DEF. All this is nothing; you shall see
   anon
A place you little dream on.

ALON.   I am glad
I have this leisure; all your master's house
Imagine I ha' taken a gondola.

DEF. All but myself, sir—[*Aside.*] which
   makes up my safety.—
My lord, I'll place you at a casement here
Will show you the full strength of all the
   castle.
Look, spend your eye awhile upon that
   object.

ALON. Here's rich variety, Deflores.

DEF.   Yes, sir.

ALON. Goodly munition.

DEF.   Ay, there's ordnance, sir—   10
No bastard metal, will ring you a peal
   like bells
At great men's funerals. Keep your eye
   straight, my lord.
Take special notice of that sconce before
   you;
There you may dwell awhile.
     [*Takes the rapier which he has hidden.*]

ALON.   I am upon 't.

DEF. And so am I.   [*Stabs him.*]

ALON.   Deflores! O Deflores!
Whose malice hast thou put on?

DEF.   Do you question
A work of secrecy? I must silence you.
             [*Stabs him.*]

ALON. O, O, O!

DEF.   I must silence you.—[*Stabs him.*]
So here's an undertaking well accom-
   plished.
This vault serves to good use now. Ha,
   what's that   20
Threw sparkles in my eye? O, 'tis a
   diamond
He wears upon his finger. It was well
   found;
This will approve [5] the work. What, so
   fast on?
Not part in death? I'll take a speedy
   course then.
Finger and all shall off. [*Cuts off the
   finger.*] So, now I'll clear
The passages from all suspect [6] or fear.
                Exit with body.

[5] Bear witness to.   [6] Suspicion.

[SCENA TERTIA.

A room in the house of Alibius.]

Enter Isabella and Lollio.

ISA. Why, sirrah! Whence have you commission
To fetter the doors against me? If you
Keep me in a cage, pray, whistle to me;
Let me be doing something.

LOL. You shall be doing, if it please you;
I'll whistle to you, if you'll pipe after.

ISA. Is it your master's pleasure, or your own,
To keep me in this pinfold?

LOL. 'Tis for my master's pleasure,
lest, being taken in another man's [10
corn, you might be pounded in another
place.

ISA. 'Tis very well, and he'll prove very
wise.

LOL. He says you have company enough
in the house, if you please to be sociable, of
all sorts of people.

ISA. Of all sorts? Why, here's none but
fools and madmen.

LOL. Very well. And where will [20
you find any other, if you should go abroad?
There's my master and I to boot, too.

ISA. Of either sort one, a madman and
a fool.

LOL. I would ev'n participate of both
then if I were as you. I know y' are half
mad already; be half foolish too.

ISA. Y' are a brave, saucy rascal! Come
on, sir;
Afford me then the pleasure of your
bedlam.
You were commending once today to
me   30
Your last-come lunatic—what a proper [1]
Body there was without brains to guide it,
And what a pitiful delight appeared
In that defect, as if your wisdom had
found
A mirth in madness. Pray, sir, let me
partake,
If there be such a pleasure.

LOL. If I do not show you the hand-
somest, discreetest madman, one that I
may call the understanding madman,
then say I am a fool.   40

ISA. Well, a match,[2] I will say so.

LOL. When you have a taste of the
madman, you shall, if you please, see
Fool's College, o' th' side. I seldom lock
there; 'tis but shooting a bolt or two, and
you are amongst 'em. (*Ex[it]. Enter presently.*[3])—Come on, sir; let me see how
handsomely you'll behave yourself now.

Enter Loll[io], Franciscus.

FRAN. How sweetly she looks! O, but
there's a wrinkle in her brow as deep as [50
philosophy. Anacreon, drink to my mistress' health; I'll pledge it. Stay, stay,
there's a spider in the cup! No, 'tis but a
grapestone. Swallow it; fear nothing,
poet; so, so, lift higher.

ISA. Alack, alack, 'tis too full of pity
To be laughed at! How fell he mad?
Canst thou tell?

LOL. For love, mistress. He was a
pretty poet, too, and that set him forwards
first. The Muses then forsook him; [60
he ran mad for a chambermaid, yet she
was but a dwarf neither.

FRAN. Hail, bright Titania!
Why stand'st thou idle on these flow'ry
banks?
Oberon is dancing with his Dryads;
I'll gather daisies, primrose, violets,
And bind them in a verse of poesy.

LOL. [*Showing him a whip.*] Not too
near! You see your danger.   69

FRAN. O, hold thy hand, great Diomede!
Thou feed'st thy horses well; they shall
obey thee.
Get up! Bucephalus kneels.   [*Kneels.*]

LOL. You see how I awe my flock; a
shepherd has not his dog at more obedience.

ISA. His conscience is unquiet; sure that
was
The cause of this. A proper gentleman!

FRAN. Come hither, Aesculapius; hide the
poison.

LOL. [*Hiding the whip.*] Well, 'tis hid. [79

FRAN. Didst thou never hear of one
Tiresias, a famous poet?

LOL. Yes, that kept tame wild geese.

FRAN. That's he, I am the man.

LOL. No?

FRAN. Yes; but make no words on 't. I
was a man seven years ago.

---

[1] Handsome.   [2] It is agreed.   [3] *I.e.*, after the following off-stage speech.

Lol. A stripling, I think, you might.
Fran. Now I'm a woman, all feminine.
Lol. I would I might see that!
Fran. Juno struck me blind.   90
Lol. I'll ne'er believe that; for a woman,
they say, has an eye more than a man.
Fran. I say she struck me blind.
Lol. And Luna made you mad; you
have two trades to beg with.
Fran. Luna is now big-bellied, and
    there's room
For both of us to ride with Hecate.
I'll drag thee up into her silver sphere,
And there we'll kick the Dog—and beat
    the bush—
That barks against the witches of the
    night.   100
The swift *lycanthropi* [1] that walks the
    round,
We'll tear their wolvish skins, and save
    the sheep.   [*Snatches at Lollio.*]
Lol. Is 't come to this? Nay, then, my
poison comes forth again.   [*Shows the
whip.*] Mad slave, indeed, abuse your
keeper!
Isa. I prithee, hence with him, now he
    grows dangerous.
                          [*Let Franciscus*] *sing.*

Fran.   Sweet love, pity me;
    Give me leave to lie with thee.

Lol. No, I'll see you wiser first. To
your own kennel!   111
Fran. No noise; she sleeps. Draw all the
    curtains round;
Let no soft sound molest the pretty soul
But love, and love creeps in at a mouse-
    hole.
Lol. I would you would get into your
hole! (*Exit Fra[nciscus].*)—Now, mistress, I
will bring you another sort; you shall be
fooled another while.—Tony, come hither,
Tony! Look who's yonder, Tony.

Enter Antonio.

Ant. Cousin, is it not my aunt? [2]   120
Lol. Yes, 'tis one of um, Tony.
Ant. He, he! How do you, uncle?
Lol. Fear him not, mistress; 'tis a
gentle nidget; [3] you may play with him—
as safely with him as with his bauble.

Isa. How long hast thou been a fool?
Ant. Ever since I came hither, cousin.
Isa. Cousin? I'm none of thy cousins,
fool.   129
Lol. O, mistress, fools have always so
much wit as to claim their kindred.
Madman. (*Within.*) Bounce, bounce!
He falls, he falls!
Isa. Hark you, your scholars in the up-
per room are out of order.
Lol. Must I come amongst you there?—
Keep you the fool, mistress; I'll go up and
play left-handed Orlando amongst the
madmen.   *Exit.*
Isa. Well, sir.   140
Ant. [*Revealing himself.*] 'Tis opportune-
    ful now, sweet lady! Nay,
Cast no amazing [4] eye upon this change.
Isa. Ha!
Ant. This shape of folly shrouds your
    dearest love,
The truest servant to your powerful
    beauties,
Whose magic had this force thus to
    transform me.
Isa. You are a fine fool indeed!
Ant.   O, 'tis not strange!
Love has an intellect that runs through
    all
The scrutinous sciences, and, like
A cunning poet, catches a quantity 150
Of every knowledge, yet brings all
    home
Into one mystery, into one secret.
That he proceeds in.
Isa.   Y' are a parlous fool.
Ant. No danger in me; I bring naught but
    love
And his soft-wounding shafts to strike
    you with.
Try but one arrow; if it hurt you,
I'll stand you twenty back in recom-
    pense.   [*Kisses her.*]
Isa. A forward fool too!
Ant.   This was Love's teaching.
A thousand ways he [5] fashioned out my
    way,
And this I found the safest and the
    nearest,   160
To tread the galaxia to my star.
Isa. Profound withal! Certain, you
    dreamed of this;
Love never taught it waking.

---

[1] Lycanthropes, werewolves.
[2] Slang term for *procuress.*   [3] Idiot.
[4] Wondering.   [5] Original reads *she.*

ANT.   Take no acquaintance
Of these outward follies. There's within
A gentleman that loves you.
ISA.   When I see him,
I'll speak with him; so, in the meantime,
      keep
Your habit; it becomes you well enough.
As you are a gentleman, I'll not discover
      you.
That's all the favor that you must
      expect.
When you are weary, you may leave the
      school,   170
For all this while you have but played the
      fool.

Enter Lollio.

ANT. And must again.—He, he! I thank
      you, cousin;
I'll be your valentine tomorrow morning.
LOL. How do you like the fool, mistress?
ISA. Passing well, sir.
LOL. Is he not witty, pretty well, for a
fool?
ISA. If he hold on as he begins, he is
like to come to something.   179
LOL. Ay, thank a good tutor. You may
put him to 't; he begins to answer pretty
hard questions.—Tony, how many is five
times six?
ANT. Five times six is six times five.
LOL. What arithmetician could have
answered better? How many is one hun-
dred and seven?
ANT. One hundred and seven is seven
hundred and one, cousin.
LOL. This is no wit to speak on!—Will
you be rid of the fool now?   191
ISA. By no means; let him stay a little.
MADMAN. (*Within.*) Catch there, catch
the last couple in hell! [1]
LOL. Again must I come amongst you?
Would my master were come home! I am
not able to govern both these wards to-
gether.   *Exit.*
ANT. Why should a minute of love's hour
      be lost?   199
ISA. Fie, out again! I had rather you kept
Your other posture; you become not
      your tongue
When you speak from [2] your clothes.

ANT.   How can he freeze
Lives near so sweet a warmth? Shall I
      alone
Walk through the orchard of the Hes-
      perides,
And, cowardly, not dare to pull an apple?

Enter Lol[lio] above.

This with the red cheeks I must venter [3]
      for.   [*Attempts to kiss her.*]
ISA. Take heed; there's giants keep 'em.
LOL. [*Aside.*] How now, fool, are you
good at that? Have you read Lipsius? [4]
He's past *Ars Amandi*; [5] I believe I   [210
must put harder questions to him, I per-
ceive that.
ISA. You are bold without fear too.
ANT.   What should I fear,
Having all joys about me? Do you smile,
And love shall play the wanton on your
      lip,
Meet and retire, retire and meet again;
Look you but cheerfully, and in your eyes
I shall behold mine own deformity,
And dress myself up fairer. I know this
      shape
Becomes me not, but in those bright
      mirrors   220
I shall array me handsomely.
LOL.   Cuckoo, cuckoo! *Exit.*
[*Cries of*] *Madmen above, some as birds,
                         others as beasts.*
ANT. What are these?
ISA.   Of fear enough to part us;
Yet are they but our schools of lunatics,
That act their fantasies in any shapes,
Suiting their present thoughts: if sad,
      they cry;
If mirth be their conceit, they laugh
      again;
Sometimes they imitate the beasts and
      birds,
Singing or howling, braying, barking—all
As their wild fancies prompt um.

Enter Lollio.

ANT.   These are no fears.
ISA. But here's a large one, my man.
ANT. Ha, he! That's fine sport, indeed,
cousin.   232

---

[1] In the game of barleybreak the last couple
left in the center were said to be in hell.

[2] Out of keeping with.

[3] Venture.

[4] A humanist writer, with an obvious pun.

[5] Reference to Ovid's *Art of Love.*

Lol. I would my master were come home! 'Tis too much for one shepherd to govern two of these flocks; nor can I believe that one churchman can instruct two benefices at once. There will be some incurable mad of the one side, and very fools on the other.—Come, Tony.

Ant. Prithee, cousin, let me stay here still. 241

Lol. No, you must to your book now; you have played sufficiently.

Isa. Your fool has grown wondrous witty.

Lol. Well, I'll say nothing; but I do not think but he will put you down one of these days. *Exeunt Lol[lio] and Ant[onio].*

Isa. Here the restrainéd current might
  make breach,
Spite of the watchful bankers.[1] Would a
  woman stray, 250
She need not gad abroad to seek her sin;
It would be brought home one ways or
  other.
The needle's point will to the fixéd north;
Such drawing artics [2] womens' beauties
  are.

Enter Lollio.

Lol. How dost thou, sweet rogue?

Isa. How now?

Lol. Come, there are degrees; one fool may be better than another.

Isa. What's the matter?

Lol. Nay, if thou giv'st thy mind to fool's flesh, have at thee! 261

Isa. You bold slave, you!

Lol. I could follow now as t'other fool did.
"What should I fear,
Having all joys about me? Do you but
  smile,
And love shall play the wanton on your
  lip,
Meet and retire, retire and meet again;
Look you but cheerfully, and in your
  eyes
I shall behold my own deformity, 270
And dress myself up fairer. I know this
  shape
Becomes me not—"
And so as it follows. But is not this the
more foolish way? Come, sweet rogue;

kiss me, my little Lacedaemonian. Let me feel how thy pulses beat. Thou hast a thing about thee would do a man pleasure; I'll lay my hand on 't.

Isa. Sirrah, no more! I see you have dis-
  covered
This love's knight errant, who hath made
  adventure 280
For purchase of my love. Be silent,
  mute,
Mute as a statue, or his injunction
For me enjoying, shall be to cut thy
  throat;
I'll do it, though for no other purpose;
  and
Be sure he'll not refuse it.

Lol.   My share, that's all;
I'll have my fool's part with you.

Isa.   No more! Your master.

Enter Alibius.

Alib. Sweet, how dost thou?

Isa.   Your bounden servant, sir.

Alib. Fie, fie, sweetheart, no more of that.

Isa. You were best lock me up.

Alib. In my arms and bosom, my sweet
  Isabella, 290
I'll lock thee up most nearly.—Lollio,
We have employment, we have task in
  hand.
At noble Vermandero's, our castle cap-
  tain,
There is a nuptial to be solemnized—
Beatrice Joanna, his fair daughter,
  bride—
For which the gentleman hath bespoke
  our pains,
A mixture of our madmen and our
  fools,
To finish, as it were, and make the fag [3]
Of all the revels, the third night from the
  first;
Only an unexpected passage over,[4] 300
To make a frightful pleasure, that is all,
But not the all I aim at. Could we so act
  it,
To teach it in a wild, distracted measure,
Though out of form and figure, breaking
  time's head,
It were no matter—'twould be healed
  again

---

[1] Dike builders. [2] *I.e.*, points of attraction.

[3] End.
[4] *I.e.*, of fools and madmen across the stage.

In one age or other, if not in this.
This, this, Lollio, there's a good reward
   begun,
And will beget a bounty, be it known.

Lol. This is easy, sir, I'll warrant you.
You have about you fools and madmen
that can dance very well; and, 'tis no [311
wonder, your best dancers are not the wisest men; the reason is, with often jumping
they jolt their brains down into their feet,
that their wits lie more in their heels than
in their heads.

Alib. Honest Lollio, thou giv'st me a good
   reason,
And a comfort in it.

Isa.   Y'ave a fine trade on 't.
Madmen and fools are a staple com-
   modity.

Alib. O wife, we must eat, wear clothes,
   and live.   320
Just at the lawyer's haven we arrive—
By madmen and by fools we both do
   thrive.   *Exeunt.*

[Scena Quarta.

A room in the castle.]

*Enter Vermandero, Alsemero, Jasperino, and
                                    Beatrice.*

Ver. Valencia speaks so nobly of you, sir,
I wish I had a daughter now for you.

Als. The fellow of this creature were a
   partner
For a king's love.

Ver.   I had her fellow once, sir,
But heaven has married her to joys
   eternal;
'Twere sin to wish her in this vale again.
Come, sir, your friend and you shall see
   the pleasures
Which my health chiefly joys in.

Als. I hear the beauty of this seat largely.[1]

Ver. It falls much short of that.
                       Exeunt. Manet [2] *Beatrice.*

Bea.   So, here's one step   10
Into my father's favor; time will fix him.
I have got him now the liberty of the
   house.
So wisdom, by degrees, works out her
   freedom,
And if that eye be darkened that offends
   me—

---
[1] Widely   [2] Remains.

I wait but that eclipse—this gentleman
Shall soon shine glorious in my father's
   liking,
Through the refulgent virtue of my love.

Enter Deflores.

Def. [*Aside.*] My thoughts are at a banquet; for the deed,
I feel no weight in 't; 'tis but light and
   cheap
For the sweet recompense that I set
   down for 't.   20

Bea. Deflores!

Def.   Lady!

Bea.   Thy looks promise cheerfully.

Def. All things are answerable, time, circumstance,
Your wishes, and my service.

Bea.   Is it done, then?

Def. Piracquo is no more.

Bea. My joys start at mine eyes; our
   sweet'st delights
Are evermore born weeping.

Def.   I've a token for you.

Bea. For me?

Def. But it was sent somewhat unwillingly;
I could not get the ring without the finger.   [*Shows the finger and ring.*]

Bea. Bless me, what hast thou done?

Def.   Why, is that more   30
Than killing the whole man? I cut his
   heartstrings;
A greedy hand thrust in a dish at court
In a mistake hath had as much as this.

Bea. 'Tis the first token my father made
   me send him.

Def. And I made him send it back again
For his last token. I was loath to leave it,
And I'm sure dead men have no use of
   jewels;
He was as loath to part with 't, for it stuck
As if the flesh and it were both one sub-
   stance.

Bea. At the stag's fall, the keeper has his
   fees.   40
'Tis soon applied; all dead men's fees are
   yours, sir.
I pray, bury the finger, but the stone
You may make use on shortly; the true
   value,
Take 't of my truth, is near three hundred
   ducats.

DEF. 'Twill hardly buy a capcase [1] for
  one's conscience though,
To keep it from the worm, as fine as 'tis.
Well, being my fees, I'll take it;
Great men have taught me that, or else
  my merit
Would scorn the way on 't.

BEA.   It might justly, sir.
Why, thou mistak'st, Deflores; 'tis not
  given   50
In state [2] of recompense.

DEF.   No, I hope so, lady;
  You should soon witness my contempt
  to 't then.

BEA. Prithee—thou look'st as if thou wert
  offended.

DEF. That were strange, lady; 'tis not
  possible
My service should draw such a cause
  from you.
Offended? Could you think so? That
  were much
For one of my performance, and so warm
Yet in my service.

BEA. 'Twere misery in me to give you
  cause, sir.

DEF. I know so much, it were so—
  misery   60
In her most sharp condition.

BEA.   'Tis resolved then;
Look you, sir, here's three thousand
  golden florins;
I have not meanly thought upon thy
  merit.

DEF. What! Salary? Now you move me.

BEA.   How, Deflores?

DEF. Do you place me in the rank of ver-
  minous fellows,
To destroy things for wages? Offer
  gold?
The lifeblood of man? Is anything
Valued too precious for my recompense?

BEA. I understand thee not.

DEF.   I could ha' hired   69
A journeyman in murder at this rate—
And mine own conscience might have
  [slept at ease] [3] —
And have had the work brought home.

BEA. [Aside.]   I'm in a labyrinth.
What will content him? I would fain be
  rid of him.
I'll double the sum, sir.

[1] Bandbox.   [2] Place.
[3] Added by editor of 1816 edn.

DEF.   You take a course
To double my vexation; that's the good
  you do.

BEA. [Aside]. Bless me, I am now in worse
  plight than I was;
I know not what will please him.—For
  my fear's sake,
I prithee, make away with all speed
  possible;
And, if thou beest so modest not to name
The sum that will content thee, paper
  blushes not.   80
Send thy demand in writing; it shall
  follow thee.
But, prithee, take thy flight.

DEF.   You must fly too, then.

BEA. I?

DEF. I'll not stir a foot else.

BEA.   What's your meaning?

DEF. Why, are not you as guilty? In, I'm
  sure,
As deep as I? And we should stick to-
  gether.
Come, your fears counsel you but ill;
  my absence
Would draw suspect upon you instantly;
There were no rescue for you.

BEA. [Aside.]   He speaks home!

DEF. Nor is it fit we two, engaged so
  jointly,
Should part and live asunder.

BEA.   How now, sir?   90
This shows not well.

DEF. What makes your lip so strange?
This must not be betwixt us.

BEA.   The man talks wildly!

DEF. Come, kiss me with a zeal now.

BEA. [Aside.] Heaven, I doubt [4] him!

DEF. I will not stand so long to beg 'em
  shortly.

BEA. Take heed, Deflores, of forgetfulness;
'Twill soon betray us.

DEF.   Take you heed first.
Faith, y' are grown much forgetful; y' are
  to blame in 't.

BEA. [Aside.] He's bold, and I am blamed
  for 't.

DEF.   I have eased
You of your trouble; think on 't. I'm in
  pain,   100
And must be eased of [5] you; 'tis a charity.
Justice invites your blood to understand
  me.

[4] Fear.   [5] By.

BEA. I dare not.

DEF.   Quickly!

BEA.   O, I never shall!
Speak it yet further off, that I may lose
What has been spoken, and no sound
    remain on 't.
I would not hear so much offense again
For such another deed.

DEF.   Soft, lady, soft!
The last is not yet paid for. O, this act
Has put me into spirit; I was as greedy
    on 't
As the parched earth of moisture, when
    the clouds weep.   110
Did you not mark, I wrought myself
    into 't,
Nay, sued and kneeled for 't? Why was
    all that pains took?
You see I have thrown contempt upon
    your gold;
Not that I want it,[1] for I do piteously.
In order I will come unto 't, and make
    use on 't,
But 'twas not held so precious to begin
    with,
For I place wealth after the heels of
    pleasure;
And, were not I resolved in my belief
That thy virginity were perfect in thee,
I should but take my recompense with
    grudging,   120
As if I had but half my hopes I agreed
    for.

BEA. Why, 'tis impossible thou canst be so
    wicked,
Or shelter such a cunning cruelty,
To make his death the murderer of my
    honor!
Thy language is so bold and vicious
I cannot see which way I can forgive it
With any modesty.

DEF.   Push![2] You forget yourself.
A woman dipped in blood, and talk of
    modesty!

BEA. O misery of sin! Would I'd been
    bound
Perpetually unto my living hate   130
In that Piracquo than to hear these
    words!
Think but upon the distance that crea-
    tion
Set twixt thy blood and mine, and keep
    thee there.

DEF. Look but into your conscience; **read**
    me there.
'Tis a true book; you'll find me **there**
    your equal.
Push! Fly not to your birth, but settle
    you
In what the act has made you; y' are no
    more now.
You must forget your parentage[3] to me;
Y' are the deed's creature. By that name
You lost your first condition, and I
    challenge you,   140
As peace and innocency has turned you
    out,
And made you one with me.

BEA.   With thee, foul villain?

DEF. Yes, my fair murd'ress. Do you urge
    me,
Though thou writ'st "maid," thou whore
    in thy affection?
'Twas changed from thy first love, and
    that's a kind
Of whoredom in thy heart; and he's
    changed now
To bring thy second on, thy Alsemero,
Whom, by all sweets that ever darkness
    tasted,
If I enjoy thee not, thou ne'er enjoy'st!
I'll blast the hopes and joys of mar-
    riage;   150
I'll confess all. My life I rate at nothing.

BEA. Deflores!

DEF.   I shall rest from all lovers' plagues
    then;
I live in pain now; that shooting eye
Will burn my heart to cinders.

BEA.   O, sir, hear me!

DEF. She that in life and love refuses me,
In death and shame my partner she shall
    be.

BEA. [*Kneeling.*] Stay, hear me once for
    all. I make thee master
Of all the wealth I have in gold and
    jewels;
Let me go poor unto my bed with honor,
And I am rich in all things!

DEF.   Let this silence thee: 160
The wealth of all Valencia shall not
    buy
My pleasure from me.
Can you weep Fate from its determined
    purpose?
So soon may [you][4] weep me.

---

[1] *I.e.*, want it not.   [2] Pish!

[3] Relationship.   [4] Added by Dyce.

BEA. Vengeance begins.
Murder, I see, is followed by more sins.
Was my creation in the womb so cursted
It must engender with a viper first?

DEF. [*Raising her.*] Come, rise and shroud
your blushes in my bosom;
Silence is one of pleasure's best receipts.
Thy peace is wrought forever in this
yielding. 170
'Las! How the turtle pants! Thou'lt
love anon
What thou so fear'st and faint'st to
venture on. *Exeunt.*

ACTUS QUARTUS.

[DUMB SHOW]

*Enter Gentlemen, Vermandero meeting them
with action of wonderment at the flight of
Piracquo. Enter Alsemero with Jasperino and Gallants; Vermandero points to
him, the Gentlemen seeming to applaud
the choice. Alsemero, Jasperino, and
Gentlemen; Beatrice the bride following
in great state, accompanied with Diaphanta, Isabella, and other Gentlewomen;
Deflores after All, smiling at the accident.[1] Alonzo's ghost appears to Deflores
in the midst of his smile, startles him,
showing him the hand whose finger he had
cut off. They pass over in great solemnity.*

[SCENA PRIMA.

Alsemero's chamber in the castle.]

Enter Beatrice.

BEA. This fellow has undone me endlessly;
Never was bride so fearfully distressed.
The more I think upon th' ensuing night,
And whom I am to cope with in em-
braces,
One both ennobléd[2] in blood and mind,
So clear in understanding—that's my
plague now—
Before whose judgment will my fault
appear
Like malefactors' crimes before tri-
bunals.
There is no hiding on 't, the more I dive
Into my own distress. How a wise
man 10

Stands for [3] a great calamity! There's
no venturing
Into his bed, what course soe'er I light
upon,
Without my shame, which may grow up
to danger.
He cannot but in justice strangle me
As I lie by him, as a cheater use me.
'Tis a precious craft to play with a false
die
Before a cunning gamester. Here's his
closet,
The key left in 't, and he abroad i' th'
park!
Sure 'twas forgot; I'll be so bold as look
in 't. [*Passes to the inner stage.*]
Bless me! A right physician's closet 'tis,
Set round with vials, every one her mark
too. 21
Sure he does practice physic for his own
use,
Which may be safely called your great
man's wisdom.
What manuscript lies here? *The Book of
Experiment,*
Called Secrets in Nature. So 'tis; 'tis so.
[*Reads.*] "How to know whether a woman
be with child or no."
I hope I am not yet; if he should try
though!
Let me see. [*Reads.*] "Folio forty-five"—
here 'tis,
The leaf tucked down upon 't, the place
suspicious. 29
[*Reads.*] "If you would know whether a
woman be with child or not, give her two
spoonfuls of the white water in glass C——"
Where's that glass C? O yonder, I see 't
now—
[*Reads.*] "and, if she be with child, she
sleeps full twelve hours after; if not, not."
None of that water comes into my belly;
I'll know you from a hundred. I could
break you now,
Or turn you into milk, and so beguile
The master of the mystery; but I'll look
to you.
Ha! That which is next is ten times
worse: 40
[*Reads.*] "How to know whether a
woman be a maid or not."
If that should be applied, what would
become of me?

---

[1] Event. [2] Original repeats *both* here. [3] Exposed to.

Belike he has a strong faith of my purity,
That never yet made proof; but this he calls

[*Reads.*] "A merry sleight, but true experiment; the author Antonius Mizaldus.
Give the party you suspect the quantity of
a spoonful of the water in the glass M,
which, upon her that is a maid, makes [50
three several effects: 'twill make her in-
continently [1] gape, then fall into a sudden
sneezing, last into a violent laughing; else,
dull, heavy, and lumpish."
Where had I been?
I fear it; yet 'tis seven hours to bedtime.

Enter Diaphanta.

DIA.   Cud's,[2] madam, are you here?
BEA.   [*Aside.*]   Seeing that wench now,
A trick comes in my mind; 'tis a nice piece
Gold cannot purchase.—I come hither, wench,
To look [3] my lord.
DIA.   Would I had such a cause 60
To look him too!—Why, he's i' th' park, madam.
BEA.   There let him be.
DIA.   Ay, madam, let him compass
Whole parks and forests, as great rangers do;
At roosting-time a little lodge can hold 'em.
Earth-conquering   Alexander,   that
thought the world
Too narrow for him, in the end had but his pit-hole.
BEA.   I fear thou art not modest, Diaphanta.
DIA.   Your thoughts are so unwilling to be known, madam.
'Tis ever the bride's fashion, towards bedtime,
To set light by her joys, as if she owed [4]
'em not.   70
BEA.   Her joys? Her fears thou wouldst say.
DIA.   Fear of what?
BEA.   Art thou a maid, and talk'st so to a maid?
You leave a blushing business behind;
Beshrew your heart for 't!
DIA.   Do you mean good sooth, madam?
BEA.   Well, if I'd thought upon the fear at first,
Man should have been unknown.

DIA.   Is 't possible?
BEA.   I will give a thousand ducats to that woman
Would try what my fear were, and tell me true
Tomorrow, when she gets from 't; as she likes,
I might perhaps be drawn to 't.
DIA.   Are you in earnest? 80
BEA.   Do you get the woman, then chal-
lenge me,
And see if I'll fly from 't; but, I must tell you
This by the way, she must be a true maid.
Else there's no trial; my fears are not hers else.
DIA.   Nay, she that I would put into your hands, madam,
Shall be a maid.
BEA.   You know I should be shamed else,
Because she lies for me.
DIA.   'Tis a strange humor!
But are you serious still? Would you resign
Your first night's pleasure, and give money too?
BEA.   As willingly as live.—[*Aside.*] Alas, the gold   90
Is but a by-bet to wedge in the honor!
DIA.   I do not know how the world goes abroad
For faith or honesty; there's both re-
quired in this.
Madam, what say you to me, and stray no further?
I've a good mind, in troth, to earn your money.
BEA.   Y' are too quick, I fear, to be a maid.
DIA.   How? Not a maid? Nay, then you urge me, madam;
Your honorable self is not a truer,
With all your fears upon you—
BEA.   [*Aside.*]   Bad enough then.
DIA.   Than I with all my lightsome joys about me.   100
BEA.   I'm glad to hear 't. Then you dare put your honesty [5]
Upon an easy trial.
DIA.   Easy? Anything.
BEA.   I'll come to you straight.
[*Goes to the closet.*]

---

[1] Immediately.   [2] God's, part of a mild oath.
[3] Look for.   [4] Owned.

[5] Chastity.

Dia.   She will not search me, will she,
Like the forewoman of a female jury?
Bea. Glass M. Ay, this is it. Look, Diaphanta;
You take no worse than I do.   [*Drinks.*]
Dia.   And, in so doing,
I will not question what 'tis, but take it.
                                        [*Drinks.*]
Bea. [*Aside.*] Now if the experiment be
true, 'twill praise itself,
And give me noble ease. Begins already.
                              [*Diaphanta gapes.*]
There's the first symptom; and what
haste it makes   110
To fall into the second, there by this
time!   [*Diaphanta sneezes.*]
Most admirable secret! On the contrary,
It stirs not me a whit, which most concerns it.
Dia. Ha, ha, ha!
Bea. [*Aside.*]   Just in all things, and in
order
As if 'twere circumscribed; one accident [1]
Gives way unto another.
Dia. Ha, ha, ha!
Bea. How now, wench?
Dia.   Ha, ha, ha! I'm so, so light
At heart—ha, ha, ha!—so pleasurable!
But one swig more, sweet madam.
Bea.   Ay, tomorrow,   120
We shall have time to sit by 't.
Dia.   Now I'm sad again.
Bea. [*Aside.*] It lays [2] itself so gently
too!—Come, wench.
Most honest Diaphanta I dare call thee
now.
Dia. Pray, tell me, madam, what trick call
you this?
Bea. I'll tell thee all hereafter; we must
study
The carriage of this business.
Dia.   I shall carry 't well,
Because I love the burthen.
Bea.   About midnight
You must not fail to steal forth gently,
That I may use the place.
Dia.   O, fear not, madam,
I shall be cool by that time. The bride's
place,   130
And with a thousand ducats! I'm for a
justice now.
I bring a portion with me; I scorn small
fools.   *Exeunt.*

[1] Effect, symptom.   [2] Allays.

[Scena Secunda.

Another room in the castle.]

Enter Vermandero and Servant.

Ver. I tell thee, knave, mine honor is in
question,
A thing till now free from suspicion,
Nor ever was there cause. Who of my
gentlemen
Are absent? Tell me, and truly, how
many, and who?
Ser. Antonio, sir, and Franciscus.
Ver. When did they leave the castle?
Ser. Some ten days since, sir, the one
intending to
Briamata, th' other for Valencia.
Ver. The time accuses um. A charge of
murder
Is brought within my castle gate, Piracquo's murder.   10
I dare not answer faithfully their absence.
A strict command of apprehension
Shall pursue um suddenly, and either
wipe
The stain off clear, or openly discover it.
Provide me wingéd warrants for the
purpose.   *Exit Servant.*
See, I am set on again.

Enter Tomaso.

Tom. I claim a brother of you.
Ver.   Y' are too hot;
Seek him not here.
Tom.   Yes, 'mongst your dearest bloods,
If my peace find no fairer satisfaction.
This is the place must yield account for
him,   20
For here I left him; and the hasty tie
Of this snatched marriage gives strong
testimony
Of his most certain ruin.
Ver.   Certain falsehood!
This is the place indeed. His breach of
faith
Has too much marred both my abuséd
love,
The honorable love I reserved for him,
And mocked my daughter's joy. The
prepared morning
Blushed at his infidelity; he left
Contempt and scorn to throw upon those
friends

Whose belief hurt 'em. O, 'twas most
   ignoble   30
To take his flight so unexpectedly,
And throw such public wrongs on those
   that loved him!
Tom. Then this is all your answer?
Ver.   'Tis too fair
For one of his alliance; and I warn you
That this place no more see you.   *Exit.*

Enter Deflores.

Tom.   The best is
There is more ground to meet a man's
   revenge on.—
Honest Deflores?
Def.   That's my name indeed.
Saw you the bride? Good, sweet sir,
   which way took she?
Tom. I have blessed mine eyes from seeing
   such a false one.
Def. [*Aside.*] I'd fain get off; this man's
   not for my company.   40
I smell his brother's blood when I come
   near him.
Tom. Come hither, kind and true one; I
   remember
My brother loved thee well.
Def.   O, purely, dear sir!—
[*Aside.*] Methinks I am now again a-
   killing on him,
He brings it so fresh to me.
Tom.   Thou canst guess, sirrah—
One honest friend has an instinct of
   jealousy—
At some foul, guilty person.
Def. 'Las, sir, I am so charitable I think
   none
Worse than myself! You did not see the
   bride then?
Tom. I prithee, name her not. Is she not
   wicked?   50
Def. No, no; a pretty, easy, round-
   packed sinner,
As your most ladies are, else you might
   think
I flattered her; but, sir, at no hand wicked,
Till th' are so old their chins and noses [1]
   meet,
And they salute witches. I'm called, I
   think, sir.—
[*Aside.*] His company ev'n o'erlays my
   conscience.   *Exit.*

Tom. That Deflores has a wondrous honest
   heart!
He'll bring it out in time, I'm assured on 't.
O, here's the glorious master of the day's
   joy!
'T [2] will not be long till he and I do
   reckon.—Sir!   60

Enter Alsemero.

Als. You are most welcome.
Tom.   You may call that word back;
I do not think I am, nor wish to be.
Als. 'Tis strange you found the way to
   this house, then.
Tom. Would I'd ne'er known the cause!
   I'm none of those, sir,
That come to give you joy, and swill
   your wine.
'Tis a more precious liquor that must lay
The fiery thirst I bring.
Als.   Your words and you
Appear to me great strangers.
Tom.   Time and our swords
May make us more acquainted. This the
   business:
I should have a brother in your place; 70
How treachery and malice have disposed
   of him,
I'm bound to inquire of him which holds
   his right,
Which never could come fairly.
Als.   You must look
To answer for that word, sir.
Tom.   Fear you not,
I'll have it ready drawn at our next meet-
   ing.
Keep your day solemn. [3] Farewell, I dis-
   turb it not;
I'll bear the smart with patience for a
   time.   *Exit.*
Als. 'Tis somewhat ominous this; a quar-
   rel entered
Upon this day. My innocence relieves me;

Enter Jasperino.

I should be wondrous sad else.—Jas-
   perino,   80
I have news to tell thee, strange news.
Jasp.   I ha' some too,
I think as strange as yours. Would I
   might keep

---

[1] Emended by Dyce. Original reads *sins and vices.*

[2] Emended by Dyce. Original reads *I.*
[3] *I.e.*, celebrate your wedding day.

Mine, so my faith and friendship might
   be kept in 't!
Faith, sir, dispense a little with my zeal,
   And let it cool in this.

ALS.   This puts me on,
   And blames thee for thy slowness.

JAS.   All may prove nothing,
   Only a friendly fear that leaped from me,
   sir.

ALS. No question, it may prove nothing;
   let's partake it though.

JAS. 'Twas Diaphanta's chance—for to
   that wench
   I pretend [1] honest love, and she deserves
   it—   90
   To leave me in a back part of the house,
   A place we chose for private conference.
   She was no sooner gone but instantly
   I heard your bride's voice in the next
      room to me,
   And, lending more attention, found
      Deflores
   Louder than she.

ALS.   Deflores?   Thou art out now.

JAS. You'll tell me more anon.

ALS.   Still I'll prevent [2] thee.
The very sight of him is poison to her.

JAS. That made me stagger too; but Diaphanta
   At her return confirmed it.

ALS.   Diaphanta! 100

JAS. Then fell we both to listen, and words
   passed
   Like those that challenge interest in a
      woman.

ALS. Peace! Quench thy zeal; 'tis dangerous to thy bosom.

JAS. Then truth is full of peril.

ALS.   Such truths are.
   O, were she the sole glory of the earth,
   Had eyes that could shoot fire into king's
      breasts,
   And touched,[3] she sleeps not here! Yet I
      have time,
   Though night be near, to be resolved [4]
      hereof.
   And, prithee, do not weigh me by my
      passions.

JAS. I never weighed friend so.

ALS.   Done charitably! 110
   That key will lead thee to a pretty secret,
                      [*Gives key.*]
   By a Chaldean taught me, and I've

[1] Profess. [2] Anticipate. [3] Tainted. [4] Satisfied.

My study upon some. Bring from my
   closet
A glass inscribed there with the letter M,
   And question not my purpose.

JAS.   It shall be done, sir. *Exit.*

ALS. How can this hang together? Not an
   hour since
Her woman came pleading her lady's fears,
Delivered her for the most timorous virgin
That ever shrunk at man's name, and
   so modest
She charged her weep out her request to
   me   120
That she might come obscurely to my
   bosom.

Enter Beatrice.

BEA. [*Aside.*] All things go well; my woman's preparing yonder
For her sweet voyage, which grieves me
   to lose.
Necessity compels it. I lose all, else.

ALS. [*Aside.*] Push! Modesty's shrine is
   set in yonder forehead.
I cannot be too sure though.—My Joanna!

BEA. Sir, I was bold to weep a message
   to you;
Pardon my modest fears.

ALS. [*Aside.*]   The dove's not meeker;
   She's abused, questionless.—O, are you
   come, sir?

Enter Jasperino [with vial].

BEA. [*Aside.*] The glass, upon my life! I
   see the letter.   130

JAS. [*Giving vial.*] Sir, this is M.

ALS.   'T's it.

BEA. [*Aside.*]   I am suspected.

ALS. How fitly our bride comes to partake
   with us!

BEA. What is 't, my lord?

ALS.   No hurt.

BEA.   Sir, pardon me;
   I seldom taste of any composition.

ALS. But this, upon my warrant, you shall
   venture on.

BEA. I fear 'twill make me ill.

ALS.   Heaven forbid that.

BEA. [*Aside.*] I'm put now to my cunning;
   th' effects I know,
If I can now but feign 'em handsomely.
                           [*Drinks.*]

ALS. It has that secret virtue, it ne'er
missed, sir,
Upon a virgin.

JAS.   Treble-qualitied?   140

[*Beatrice gapes and sneezes.*]

ALS. By all that's virtuous it takes there—
proceeds!

JAS. This is the strangest trick to know a
maid by.

BEA. Ha, ha, ha!
You have given me joy of heart to drink,
my lord.

ALS. No, thou hast given me such joy of
heart
That never can be blasted.

BEA.   What's the matter, sir?

ALS. [*Aside.*] See now 'tis settled in a
melancholy.
Keep both the time and method.—My
Joanna,
Chaste as the breath of heaven, or
morning's womb,
That brings the day forth! Thus my love
encloses thee.   *Exeunt.*   150

[SCENA TERTIA.

A room in the house of Alibius.]

Enter Isabella [with a letter,] and Lollio.

ISA. O heaven! Is this the waning[1] moon?
Does love turn fool, run mad, and all at
once?
Sirrah, here's a madman, akin to the fool
too,
A lunatic lover.

LOL. No, no, not he I brought the letter
from.

ISA. [*Giving him the letter.*] Compare his inside with his out, and tell me.

LOL. The out's mad, I'm sure of that; I
had a taste on 't. [*Reads letter.*] "To the
bright Andromeda, chief chambermaid to
the Knight of the Sun, at the sign of   [10
Scorpio, in the middle region, sent by the
bellows-mender of Aeolus. Pay the post."
This is stark madness!

ISA. Now mark the inside. [*Takes the
letter and reads.*] "Sweet lady, having now
cast off this counterfeit cover of a madman,
I appear to your best judgment a true and
faithful lover of your beauty."

LOL. He is mad still.

ISA. "If any fault you find, chide   [20
those perfections in you which have made
me imperfect; 'tis the same sun that causeth
to grow and enforceth to wither—"

LOL. O rogue!

ISA. "Shapes and transshapes, destroys
and builds again. I come in winter to you,
dismantled of my proper ornaments; by
the sweet splendor of your cheerful smiles I
spring and live a lover."

LOL. Mad rascal still!   30

ISA. "Tread him not under foot, that
shall appear an honor to your bounties. I
remain—mad till I speak with you, from
whom I expect my cure, from
Yours all, or one beside himself,
FRANCISCUS."

LOL. You are like to have a fine time
on 't. My master and I may give over our
professions; I do not think but you can cure
fools and madmen faster than we, with
little pains too.   40

ISA. Very likely.

LOL. One thing I must tell you,[2] mistress: you perceive that I am privy to your
skill;[3] if I find you minister once, and set up
the trade, I put in for my thirds. I shall be
mad or fool else.

ISA. The first place is thine, believe it,
Lollio,
If I do fall.

LOL.   I fall upon you.

ISA.   So.

LOL. Well, I stand to my venture.

ISA. But thy counsel now. How   [50
shall I deal with 'em?

LOL. Why,[4] do you mean to deal with um?

ISA. Nay, the fair understanding[5]—how to
use um.

LOL. Abuse[6] um! That's the way to
mad the fool, and make a fool of the madman, and then you use um kindly.[7]

ISA. 'Tis easy; I'll practice. Do thou observe it.
The key of thy wardrobe.

LOL. [*Giving key.*] There. Fit yourself
for um, and I'll fit um both for you.   [60

ISA. Take thou no further notice than the
outside.   *Exit.*

LOL. Not an inch; I'll put you to the inside.

---

[1] Emended by editor of 1816. Original has
waiting.

[2] Original reads *your.*   [3] Profession.
[4] Emended by Dyce.   Original reads *We.*
[5] *I.e.*, the proper meaning of my words.
[6] Deceive.   [7] According to their nature.

Enter Alibius.

ALIB. Lollio, art there? Will all be perfect, think'st thou?

Tomorrow night, as if to close up the Solemnity, Vermandero expects us.

LOL. I mistrust the madmen most. The fools will do well enough; I have taken pains with them.

ALIB. Tush! They cannot miss. The more absurdity,

The more commends it, so [1] no rough behaviors   70

Affright the ladies. They're nice [2] things, thou know'st.

LOL. You need not fear, sir; so long as we are there with our commanding peesles [3] they'll be as tame as the ladies themselves.

ALIB. I will see them once more rehearse before they go.

LOL. I was about it, sir. Look you to the madmen's morris, and let me alone with the other. There is one or two that I mistrust their fooling. I'll instruct them, and [80 then they shall rehearse the whole measure.

ALIB. Do so; I'll see the music prepared. But, Lollio,

By the way, how does my wife brook her restraint?

Does she not grudge at it?

LOL. So, so. She takes some pleasure in the house; she would abroad else. You must allow her a little more length; she's kept too short.

ALIB. She shall along to Vermandero's with us—   89

That will serve her for a month's liberty.

LOL. What's that on your face, sir?

ALIB. Where, Lollio? I see nothing.

LOL. Cry you mercy, [4] sir, 'tis your nose; it showed like the trunk of a young elephant. [5]

ALIB. Away, rascal! I'll prepare the music, Lollio.   *Ex[it] Ali[bius].*

LOL. Do, sir, and I'll dance the whilst.— Tony, where art thou, Tony?

Enter Antonio.

ANT. Here, cousin. Where art thou?

LOL. Come, Tony, the footmanship [100 I taught you.

[1] Provided that.   [2] Fastidious.
[3] Pizzles, whips.   [4] I beg your pardon.
[5] A variation on the jest about the cuckold's horns.

ANT. I had rather ride, cousin.

LOL. Ay, a whip take you! But I'll keep you out. Vault in. Look you, Tony! Fa, la, la, la, la.   [*Dances.*]

ANT. [*Dancing.*] Fa, la, la, la, la.

LOL. There, an honor. [6]

ANT. Is this an honor, coz?

LOL. Yes, and it please your worship. 109

ANT. Does honor bend in the hams, coz?

LOL. Marry, does it, as low as worship, squireship, nay, yeomandry itself sometimes, from whence it first stiffened. There rise, a caper.

ANT. Caper after an honor, coz?

LOL. Very proper, for honor is but a caper, rise[s] as fast and high, has a knee or two, and falls to th' ground again. You can remember your figure, [7] Tony?   *Exit.*

ANT. Yes, cousin; when I see thy figure, I can remember mine.   121

Enter Isabella [, dressed as a madwoman].

ISA. Hey, how she treads the air! Shough, shough, tother way! He burns his wings else. Here's wax enough below, Icarus, more than will be canceled these eighteen moons. He's down, he's down! What a terrible fall he had!

Stand up, thou son of Cretan Daedalus, And let us tread the lower labyrinth; I'll bring thee to the clue.   130

ANT. Prithee, coz, let me alone.

ISA.   Art thou not drowned? About thy head I saw a heap of clouds Wrapped like a Turkish turbant; on thy back

A crook'd chameleon-colored rainbow hung

Like a tiara down unto thy hams.

Let me suck out those billows in thy belly;

Hark, how they roar and rumble in the streets!

Bless thee from the pirates!

ANT. Pox upon you, let me alone!

ISA. Why shouldst thou mount so high as Mercury,   140

Unless thou hadst reversion of his place? Stay in the moon with me, Endymion, And we will rule these wild, rebellious waves,

That would have drowned my love.

[6] Obeisance.   [7] Dance.

ANT. I'll kick thee, if again thou touch me,
Thou wild unshapen antic; I am no fool,
You bedlam!

ISA. But you are, as sure as I am, mad.
[*Reveals herself.*]
Have I put on this habit of a frantic,
With love as full of fury, to beguile   150
The nimble eye of watchful jealousy,
And am I thus rewarded?

ANT.   Ha! Dearest beauty!

ISA. No, I have no beauty now,
Nor never had but what was in my gar-
ments.
You a quick-sighted lover! Come not
near me.
Keep your caparisons; y' are aptly clad.
I came a feigner, to return stark mad.
                              Exit.

ANT. Stay, or I shall change condition,
And become as you are.   159

Enter Lollio.[1]

LOL. Why, Tony, whither now? Why, fool—

ANT. Whose fool, usher of idiots? You coxcomb!
I have fooled too much.

LOL. You were best be mad another while
then.

ANT. So I am, stark mad; I have cause
enough.
And I could throw the full effects on thee,
And beat thee like a fury.

LOL. Do not, do not; I shall not forbear
the gentleman under the fool, if you do.
Alas! I saw through your foxskin before
now! Come, I can give you comfort. [170
My mistress loves you; and there is as
arrant a madman i' th' house as you are a
fool, your rival, whom she loves not. If
after the masque we can rid her of him,
you earn her love, she says, and the fool
shall ride her.

ANT. May I believe thee?

LOL. Yes, or you may choose whether you
will or no.

ANT. She's eased of him; I have a good
quarrel on 't.

LOL. Well, keep your old station yet, and
be quiet.   180

ANT. Tell her *I* will deserve her love.

LOL. And you are like to have your desire.
                        [*Exit Antonio.*]

---

[1] This stage direction appears before Antonio's speech in the original.

Enter Franciscus.

FRAN. [*Singing.*] "Down, down, down, a-
down a-down—" and then with a
horse trick [2]
To kick Latona's forehead, and break
her bowstring.

LOL. [*Aside.*] This is tother counterfeit;
I'll put him out of his humor.—[*Reads Franciscus' letter.*] "Sweet lady, having now
cast this counterfeit cover of a madman,
I appear to your best judgment a   [189
true and faithful lover of your beauty."
This is pretty well for a madman.

FRAN. Ha! What's that?

LOL. "Chide those perfections in you
which [have] made me imperfect."

FRAN. I am discovered to the fool.

LOL. I hope to discover the fool in you
ere I have done with you. "Yours all, or one
beside himself, FRANCISCUS." This madman will mend sure.

FRAN. What do you read, sirrah?   200

LOL. Your destiny, sir. You'll be hanged
for this trick, and another that I know.

FRAN. Art thou of counsel with thy
mistress?

LOL. Next her apron strings.

FRAN. Give me thy hand.

LOL. Stay, let me put yours in my pocket
first. [*Puts the letter away.*] Your hand
is true,[3] is it not? It will not pick? I   [209
partly fear it, because I think it does lie.

FRAN. Not in a syllable.

LOL. So if you love my mistress so well
as you have handled the matter here, you
are like to be cured of your madness.

FRAN. And none but she can cure it.

LOL. Well, I'll give you over then, and
she shall cast your water [4] next.

FRAN. Take for thy pains past.   218
                        [*Gives money.*]

LOL. I shall deserve more, sir, I hope.
My mistress loves you, but must have
some proof of your love to her.

FRAN. There I meet my wishes.

LOL. That will not serve; you must
meet her enemy and yours.

FRAN. He's dead already.

LOL. Will you tell me that, and I parted
but now with him?

FRAN. Show me the man.   228

---

[2] Caper.   [3] Honest.
[4] *I.e.*, diagnose your disease.

LOL. Ay, that's a right course now. See him before you kill him, in any case; and yet it needs not go so far neither. 'Tis but a fool that haunts the house and my mistress in the shape of an idiot; bang but his fool's coat well-favoredly, and 'tis well.

FRAN. Soundly, soundly!

LOL. Only reserve him till the masque be past; and, if you find him not now in the dance yourself, I'll show you. In, in! My master!   [*Dances.*] [239

FRAN. He handles him like a feather. Hey!   [*Exit.*]

Enter Alibius.

ALIB. Well said.[1] In a readiness, Lollio?

LOL. Yes, sir.

ALIB. Away then, and guide them in, Lollio.
Entreat your mistress to see this sight.
Hark, is there not one incurable fool
That might be begged?[2] I have friends.

LOL. I have him for you, one that shall deserve it too.

ALIB. Good boy, Lollio!
          The Madmen and Fools dance.
'Tis perfect. Well, fit but once these strains,   250
We shall have coin and credit for our pains.   *Exeunt.*

ACTUS QUINTUS. [SCENA PRIMA.

A corridor in the castle.]

Enter Beatrice. A clock strikes one.

BEA. One struck, and yet she lies by 't!
O, my fears!
This strumpet serves her own ends, 'tis apparent now,
Devours the pleasure with a greedy appetite,
And never minds my honor or my peace,
Makes havoc of my right. But she pays dearly for 't;
No trusting of her life with such a secret
That cannot rule her blood to keep her promise.
Beside, I have some suspicion of her faith to me,
Because I was suspected of my lord,   9

And it must come from her. (*Strike two.*)[3]
Hark! By my horrors,
Another clock strikes two!

Enter Deflores.

DEF.   Pist! Where are you?

BEA. Deflores!

DEF. Ay. Is she not come from him yet?

BEA. As I am a living soul, not!

DEF.   Sure the devil
Hath sowed his itch within her. Who'd trust a waiting-woman?

BEA. I must trust somebody.

DEF.   Push! They're termagants,
Especially when they fall upon their masters
And have their ladies' first fruits. Th' are mad whelps;
You cannot stave 'em off from game royal. Then
You are so harsh[4] and hardy, ask no counsel;
And I could have helped you to a apothecary's daughter   20
Would have fall'n off before eleven, and thank you too.

BEA. O me, not yet! This whore forgets herself.

DEF. The rascal fares so well. Look, y' are undone;
The day-star, by this hand! See Phosphorus[5] plain yonder.

BEA. Advise me now to fall upon some ruin;
There is no counsel safe else.

DEF.   Peace! I ha 't now,
For we must force a rising; there's no remedy.

BEA. How? Take heed of that.

DEF. Tush! Be you quiet, or else give over all.   29

BEA. Prithee, I ha' done then.

DEF.   This is my reach:[6] I'll set
Some part afire of Diaphanta's chamber.

BEA. How? Fire, sir? That may endanger the whole house.

DEF. You talk of danger when your fame's on fire.

BEA. That's true; do what thou wilt now.

---

[1] Well done.
[2] Be appointed the fool's guardian to control and enjoy his estate.

[3] This stage direction in the original appears at the end of the speech.   [4] Rough, rude.
[5] Original reads *Bosphorus*.   [6] Trick.

DEF.   Push! I aim
At a most rich success strikes all dead
    sure.
The chimney being afire, and some light
    parcels
Of the least danger in her chamber only,
If Diaphanta should be met by chance
    then
Far from her lodging, which is now sus-
    picious,
It would be thought her fears and af-
    frights then   40
Drove her to seek for succor; if not seen
Or met at all, as that's the likeliest,
For her own shame she'll hasten towards
    her lodging.
I will be ready with a piece high-charged,
As 'twere to cleanse the chimney,
    there [1] 'tis proper now;
But she shall be the mark.
BEA.   I'm forced to love thee now,
Cause thou provid'st so carefully for
    my honor.
DEF. 'Slid, it concerns the safety of us
    both,
Our pleasure and continuance.
BEA.   One word now,
Prithee; how for the servants?
DEF.   I'll despatch them,   50
Some one way, some another in the
    hurry,
For buckets, hooks, ladders. Fear not you,
The deed shall find its time; and I've
    thought since
Upon a safe conveyance for the body
    too.
How this fire purifies wit! Watch you
    your minute.
BEA. Fear keeps my soul upon 't; I can-
    not stray from 't.

Enter Alonzo's Ghost.

DEF. Ha! What art thou that tak'st
    away the light
'Twixt that star and me? I dread thee
    not.—
'Twas but a mist of conscience; all's
    clear again.   [*Exit.*]
BEA. Who's that, Deflores? Bless me, it
    slides by!   [*Exit Ghost.*]   60
Some ill thing haunts the house; 't has
    left behind it

---

[1] Where.

A shivering sweat upon me; I'm afraid
    now.
This night hath been so tedious! O,
    this strumpet!
Had she a thousand lives, he should
    not leave her
Till he had destroyed the last.   List!
    O, my terrors!   *Struck three a-clock.*
Three struck by St. Sebastian's!
WITHIN.   Fire, fire, fire!
BEA. Already!   How rare is that man's
    speed!
How heartily he serves me!   His face
    loathes [2] one;
But, look upon his care, who would not
    love him?
The East is not more beauteous than
    his service.   70
WITHIN. Fire, fire, fire!

*Enter Deflores; Servants pass over.   Ring
    a bell.*

DEF. Away, despatch!   Hooks, buckets,
    ladders!   That's well said.
The fire bell rings; the chimney works.
    My charge!
The piece is ready.   *Exit.*

Enter Diaphanta.

BEA.   Here's a man worth loving!—
O, y' are a jewel!
DIA.   Pardon frailty, madam;
In troth, I was so well, I ev'n forgot myself.
BEA. Y' have made trim work!
DIA. What?
BEA.   Hie quickly to your chamber;
Your reward follows you.
DIA.   I never made
So sweet a bargain.   *Exit.*

Enter Alsemero.

ALS.   O, my dear Joanna!   80
Alas, art thou risen too?   I was coming,
My absolute treasure!
BEA.   When I missed you,
I could not choose but follow.
ALS.   Th'art all sweetness.
The fire is not so dangerous.
BEA.   Think you so, sir?
ALS. I prithee, tremble not; believe me,
    'tis not.

---

[2] Repels.

Enter Vermandero, Jasperino.

VER. O, bless my house and me!
ALS.   My lord your father.

Enter Deflores with a piece.

VER. Knave, whither goes that piece?
DEF.   To scour the chimney. *Exit.*
VER. O, well said, well said!
    That fellow's good on all occasions.   89
BEA. A wondrous necessary man, my lord.
VER. He hath a ready wit; he's worth 'em
    all, sir.
    Dog [1] at a house of fire; I ha' seen him
    singed ere now.— *The piece goes off.*
    Ha, there he goes!
BEA.   'Tis done!
ALS.   Come, sweet, to bed now;
    Alas, thou wilt get cold.
BEA.   Alas, the fear keeps that out!
    My heart will find no quiet till I hear
    How Diaphanta, my poor woman, fares;
    It is her chamber, sir, her lodging cham-
    ber.
VER. How should the fire come there?
BEA. As good a soul as ever lady coun-
    tenanced,   99
    But in her chamber negligent and heavy.
    She scaped a mine twice.
VER.   Twice?
BEA.   Strangely twice, sir.
VER. Those sleepy sluts are dangerous in
    a house,
    And they be ne'er so good.

Enter Deflores.

DEF.   O poor virginity,
    Thou hast paid dearly for 't!
VER.   Bless us, what's that?
DEF. A thing you all knew once—Dia-
    phanta's burnt.
BEA. My woman! O, my woman!
DEF.   Now the flames
    Are greedy of her; burnt, burnt, burnt
    to death, sir!
BEA. O, my presaging soul!
ALS.   Not a tear more!
    I charge you by the last embrace I gave
    you   109
    In bed before this raised us.
BEA.   Now you tie me;
    Were it my sister, now she gets no more.

[1] An adept.

Enter Servant.

VER. How now?
SER.   All danger's past; you may now
    take
    Your rests, my lords; the fire is throughly
    quenched.
    Ah, poor gentlewoman, how soon was
    she stifled!
BEA. Deflores, what is left of her inter,
    And we as mourners all will follow her.
    I will entreat that honor to my servant
    Ev'n of my lord himself.
ALS.   Command it, sweetness.
BEA. Which of you spied the fire first?
DEF.   'Twas I, madam.
BEA. And took such pains in 't too? A
    double goodness!   120
    'Twere well he were rewarded.
VER.   He shall be.—
    Deflores, call upon me.
ALS.   And upon me, sir.
             Exeunt [All but Deflores].
DEF. Rewarded?   Precious!   Here's a
    trick beyond me.
    I see in all bouts, both of sport and wit,
    Always a woman strives for the last
    hit.   *Exit.*

[SCENA SECUNDA.

A room in the castle].

Enter Tomaso.

TOM. I cannot taste the benefits of life
    With the same relish I was wont to do.
    Man I grow weary of, and hold his
    fellowship
    A treacherous, bloody friendship, and,
    because
    I am ignorant in whom my wrath should
    settle,
    I must think all men villains, and the
    next
    I meet, whoe'er he be, the murderer
    Of my most worthy brother.   Ha!
    What's he?

Enter Deflores, passes over the stage.

O, the fellow that some call honest
    Deflores—   9
But methinks honesty was hard bestead
To come there for a lodging; as if a
    queen

Should make her palace of a pesthouse.
I find a contrariety in nature
Betwixt that face and me.   The least
  occasion
Would give me game upon him; yet he's
  so foul
One would scarce touch [him] [1] with a
  sword he loved
And made account of—so most deadly
  venomous,
He would go near to poison any weapon
That should draw blood on him.   One
  must resolve
Never to use that sword again in fight   20
In way of honest manhood that strikes
  him.
Some river must devour 't; 'twere not fit
That any man should find it.   What,
  again?

Enter Deflores.

He walks a [2] purpose by, sure, to choke
  me up,
To infect my blood.
DEF.   My worthy, noble lord!
TOM. Dost offer to come near and breathe
  upon me?   [*Strikes him.*]
DEF. A blow!   [*Draws.*]
TOM.   Yea, are you so prepared?
I'll rather like a soldier die by th' sword
Than like a politician by thy poison.
                                [*Draws.*]
DEF. Hold, my lord, as you are honorable!
TOM. All slaves that kill by poison are
  still cowards.   31
DEF. [*Aside.*] I cannot strike; I see his
  brother's wounds
Fresh-bleeding in his eye, as in a crys-
  tal.—
I will not question this; I know y' are
  noble.
I take my injury with thanks given, sir,
Like a wise lawyer, and as a favor
Will wear it for the worthy hand that
  gave it.—
[*Aside.*] Why this from him that yester-
  day appeared
So strangely loving to me?
O, but instinct is of a subtler strain!   40
Guilt must not walk so near his lodge
  again;
He came near me now.   *Exit.*

<hr/>

[1] Added by Dyce.   [2] On.

TOM. All league with mankind I renounce
  forever,
Till I find this murderer; not so much
As common courtesy but I'll lock up;
For, in the state of ignorance I live in,
A brother may salute his brother's
  murderer,
And wish good speed to th' villain in a
  greeting.

Enter Verman[dero], Ali[bius], and Isabella.

VER. Noble Piracquo!
TOM.   Pray, keep on your way, sir;
I've nothing to say to you.
VER.   Comforts bless you, sir.   50
TOM. I have forsworn compliment, in troth
  I have, sir;
As you are merely man, I have not left
A good wish for you, nor any here.
VER. Unless you be so far in love with
  grief,
You will not part from 't upon any
  terms.
We bring that news will make a welcome
  for us.
TOM. What news can that be?
VER.   Throw no scornful smile
Upon the zeal I bring you; 'tis worth
  more, sir.
Two of the chiefest men I kept about me
I hide not from the law or your just
  vengeance.   60
TOM. Ha!
VER. To give your peace more ample
  satisfaction,
Thank these discoverers.
TOM.   If you bring that calm,
Name but the manner I shall ask for-
  giveness in
For that contemptuous smile upon you;
I'll perfect it with reverence that belongs
Unto a sacred altar.   [*Kneels.*]
VER. [*Raising him.*]   Good sir, rise.
Why, now you overdo as much a this
  hand
As you fell short a tother.—Speak,
  Alibius.
ALIB. 'Twas my wife's fortune, as she is
  most lucky   70
At a discovery, to find out lately
Within our hospital of fools and madmen
Two counterfeits slipped into these
  disguises,

Their names Franciscus and Antonio.

VER. Both mine, sir, and I ask no favor
for 'em.

ALIB. Now that which draws suspicion
to their habits,
The time of their disguisings, agrees
justly
With the day of the murder.

TOM. O blessed revelation!

VER. Nay, more, nay, more, sir—I'll not
spare mine own
In way of justice—they both feigned
a journey   80
To Briamata, and so wrought out their
leaves;
My love was so abused in 't.

TOM.   Time's too precious
To run in waste now; you have brought
a peace
The riches of five kingdoms could not
purchase.
Be my most happy conduct. I thirst for
'em.
Like subtile lightning will I wind about
'em,
And melt their marrow in 'em. *Exeunt.*

[SCENA TERTIA.

Alsemero's apartment in the castle.]

Enter Alsemero and Jasperino.

JAS. Your confidence, I'm sure, is now of
proof;
The prospect from the garden has
showed
Enough for deep suspicion.

ALS.   The black mask
That so continually was worn upon 't
Condemns the face for ugly ere 't be seen,
Her despite to him, and so seeming
bottomless.

JAS. Touch it home then; 'tis not a shallow
probe
Can search this ulcer soundly; I fear
you'll find it
Full of corruption. 'Tis fit I leave you.
She meets you opportunely from that
walk;   10
She took the back door at his parting
with her.   *Ex[it] Jas[perino].*

ALS. Did my fate wait for this unhappy
stroke
At my first sight of woman?—She's here.

Enter Beatrice.

BEA. Alsemero!

ALS.   How do you?

BEA.   How do I?
Alas, how do you? You look not well.

ALS. You read me well enough; I am not
well.

BEA. Not well, sir? Is 't in my power to
better you?

ALS. Yes.

BEA. Nay, then y' are cured again.   19

ALS. Pray, resolve [1] me one question, lady.

BEA. If I can.

ALS. None can so sure: are you honest?

BEA. Ha, ha, ha! That's a broad question,
my lord.

ALS. But that's not a modest answer, my
lady.
Do you laugh? My doubts are strong
upon me.

BEA. 'Tis innocence that smiles, and no
rough brow
Can take away the dimple in her cheek.
Say I should strain a tear to fill the vault,
Which would you give the better faith to?

ALS. 'Twere but hypocrisy of a sadder
color,   30
But the same stuff; neither your smiles
nor tears
Shall move or flatter me from my belief:
You are a whore!

BEA.   What a horrid sound it hath!
It blasts a beauty to deformity;
Upon what face soever that breath falls,
It strikes it ugly. O, you have ruined
What you can ne'er repair again.

ALS. I'll all demolish, and seek out truth
within you,
If there be any left. Let your sweet
tongue
Prevent your heart's rifling; there I'll
ransack   40
And tear out my suspicion.

BEA.   You may, sir;
'Tis an easy passage; yet, if you please,
Show me the ground whereon you lost
your love.
My spotless virtue may but tread on that
Before I perish.

ALS.   Unanswerable.
A ground you cannot stand on. You fall
down

[1] Answer.

Beneath all grace and goodness when
you set
Your ticklish heel on 't. There was a visor
O'er that cunning face, and that became
you;   49
Now Impudence in triumph rides upon 't.
How comes this tender reconcilement else
'Twixt you and your despite, your ran-
corous loathing,
Deflores? He that your eye was sore at
sight of,
He's now become your arm's supporter,
your
Lip's saint!
BEA.   Is there the cause?
ALS.   Worse, your lust's devil,
Your adultery!
BEA.   Would any but yourself say that,
'Twould turn him to a villain!
ALS.   'Twas witnessed
By the counsel of your bosom, Dia-
phanta.
BEA. Is your witness dead then?
ALS.   'Tis to be feared
It was the wages of her knowledge; poor
soul,   60
She lived not long after the discovery.
BEA. Then hear a story of not much less
horror
Than this your false suspicion is beguiled
with;
To your bed's scandal I stand up inno-
cence,
Which even the guilt of one black other
deed
Will stand for proof of; your love has
made me
A cruel murd'ress.
ALS.   Ha!
BEA.   A bloody one.
I have kissed poison for 't, stroked a
serpent,
That thing of hate, worthy in my esteem
Of no better employment; and him,
most worthy   70
To be so employed I caused to murder
That innocent Piracquo, having no
Better means than that worst to assure
Yourself to me.
ALS.   O, the place itself e'er since
Has crying been for vengeance, the
temple,
Where blood and beauty first unlaw-
fully

Fired their devotion and quenched the
right one!
'Twas in my fears at first; 'twill have it
now.
O, thou art all deformed!
BEA.   Forget not, sir,
It for your sake was done. Shall greater
dangers   80
Make the less welcome?
ALS.   O, thou shouldst have gone
A thousand leagues about to have
avoided
This dangerous bridge of blood! Here
we are lost.
BEA. Remember, I am true unto your bed.
ALS. The bed itself's a charnel, the sheets
shrouds
For murdered carcasses. It must ask pause
What I must do in this; meantime you
shall   87
Be my prisoner only. Enter my closet.
                                        Exit Beatrice.
I'll be your keeper yet. O, in what part
Of this sad story shall I first begin?—Ha!
This same fellow has put me in.[1]—
Deflores!

Enter Deflores.

DEF. Noble Alsemero!
ALS.   I can tell you
News, sir; my wife has her commended
to you.
DEF. That's news indeed, my lord; I
think she would
Commend me to the gallows if she could,
She ever loved me so well. I thank her.
ALS. What's this blood upon your band,[2]
Deflores?
DEF. Blood? No, sure; 'twas washed since.
ALS.   Since when, man?
DEF. Since tother day I got a knock
In a sword-and-dagger school; I think
'tis out.   100
ALS. Yes, 'tis almost out, but 'tis per-
ceived though.
I had forgot my message. This it is—
What price goes murder?
DEF.   How, sir?
ALS.   I ask you, sir.
My wife's behindhand with [3] you, she
tells me,

---

[1] Given me the cue.   [2] Collar.
[3] In arrears of payment to.

For a brave, bloody blow you gave for
  her sake
Upon Piracquo.
DEF.   Upon? 'Twas quite through
  him sure.
Has she confessed it?
ALS.   As sure as death to both of you;
And much more than that.
DEF.   It could not be much more.
'Twas but one thing, and that—she is a
  whore.
ALS. I could not choose but follow. O cun-
  ning devils!   110
How should blind men know you from
  fair-faced saints?
BEA. (*Within.*) He lies! The villain does
  belie me!
DEF. Let me go to her, sir.
ALS.   Nay, you shall to her.—
  Peace, crying crocodile, your sounds are
  heard.
  Take your prey to you; get you into her,
  sir.   *Exit Def[lores]*.
I'll be your pander now; rehearse again
Your scene of lust, that you may be
  perfect
When you shall come to act it to the
  black audience,
Where howls and gnashings shall be
  music to you.   119
Clip [1] your adult'ress freely; 'tis the pilot
Will guide you to the *mare mortuum*,[2]
Where you shall sink to fadoms [3] bottom-
less.

*Enter Vermandero, Alibius, Isabella, To-
  maso, Franciscus, and Antonio.*

VER. O Alsemero! I have a wonder for
  you.
ALS. No, sir, 'tis I, I have a wonder for
  you.
VER. I have suspicion near as proof itself
For Piracquo's murder.
ALS.   Sir, I have proof
Beyond suspicion for Piracquo's murder.
VER. Beseech you, hear me; these two
  have been disguised
E'er since the deed was done.
ALS.   I have two other
That were more close disguised than
  your two could be   130
E'er since the deed was done.

---

[1] Embrace.   [2] Dead sea.   [3] Fathoms.

VER. You'll hear me—these mine own
  servants—
ALS. Hear me—those nearer than your
  servants
That shall acquit them, and prove them
  guiltless.
FRAN. That may be done with easy truth,
  sir.
TOM. How is my cause bandied through
  your delays!
'Tis urgent in blood and calls for haste.
Give me a brother alive or dead—
Alive, a wife with him; if dead, for
  both   139
A recompense for murder and adultery.
BEA. (*Within.*) O, O, O!
ALS.   Hark! 'Tis coming to you.
DEF. (*Within.*) Nay, I'll along for com-
  pany.
BEA. (*Within.*)   O, O!
VER. What horrid sounds are these?
ALS. Come forth, you twins of mischief!

*Enter Deflores, bringing in Beatrice
  [wounded].*

DEF. Here we are. If you have any more
To say to us, speak quickly. I shall not
Give you the hearing else; I am so stout
  yet,
And so, I think, that broken rib of man-
  kind.
VER. An host of enemies entered my
  citadel
Could not amaze like this! Joanna!
  Beatrice Joanna!   150
BEA. O, come not near me, sir; I shall
  defile you!
I am that of your blood [4] was taken
  from you
For your better health; look no more
  upon 't,
But cast it to the ground regardlessly.
Let the common sewer [5] take it from
  distinction.
Beneath the stars, upon yon meteor
                    [*Points to Deflores.*]
Ever hung [6] my fate 'mongst things cor-
  ruptible;
I ne'er could pluck it from him; my
  loathing

---

[4] That part of your blood which.
[5] Original reads *shewer*.
[6] Emended by Dyce. Original has *hang*.

Was prophet to the rest, but ne'er
  believed.
Mine honor fell with him, and now my
  life.—   160
Alsemero, I am a stranger to your bed;
Your bed was cozened on the nuptial
  night—
For which your false bride died.
ALS.   Diaphanta!
DEF. Yes, and the while I coupled with
  your mate
At barleybreak; now we are left in hell.
VER. We are all there; it circumscribes
  [us] [1] here.
DEF. I loved this woman in spite of her
  heart;
  Her love I earned out of Piracquo's
  murder.
TOM. Ha! My brother's murtherer?
DEF.   Yes, and her honor's prize 169
  Was my reward. I thank life for nothing
  But that pleasure; it was so sweet to me
  That I have drunk up all, left none
  behind
  For any man to pledge me.
VER.   Horrid villain!
  Keep life in him for further tortures.
DEF.   No!
  I can prevent you; here's my penknife
  still.
  It is but one thread more [Stabs him-
  self.]—and now 'tis cut.—
  Make haste, Joanna, by that token to
  thee,   177
  Canst not forget, so lately put in mind;
  I would not go to leave thee far behind.
                                    Dies.
BEA. Forgive me, Alsemero, all forgive!
  'Tis time to die when 'tis a shame to live.
                                    Dies.
VER. O, my name is entered now in that
  record
  Where till this fatal hour 'twas never
  read.
ALS. Let it be blotted out; let your heart
  lose it,
  And it can never look you in the face,
  Nor tell a tale behind the back of life
  To your dishonor. Justice hath so right
  The guilty hit that innocence is quit
  By proclamation, and may joy again.—
  Sir, you are sensible of what truth hath
  done;   190

'Tis the best comfort that your grief can
  find.
TOM. Sir, I am satisfied; my injuries
  Lie dead before me. I can exact no more,
  Unless my soul were loose, and could
  o'ertake
  Those black fugitives that are fled from
  thence,
  To take a second vengeance; but there
  are wraths
  Deeper than mine, 'tis to be feared, about
  'em.
ALS. What an opacous body had that
  moon
  That last changed on us! Here's beauty
  changed
  To ugly whoredom; here servant-obe-
  dience   200
  To a master-sin, imperious murder;
  I, a supposed husband, changed embraces
  With wantonness—but that was paid
  before.
  Your change is come too, from an igno-
  rant wrath
  To knowing friendship.—Are there any
  more on's?
ANT. Yes, sir, I was changed too from a
little ass as I was to a great fool as I am; and
had like to ha' been changed to the gallows,
but that you know my innocence [2] always
excuses me.   210
FRAN. I was changed from a little wit to
  be stark mad,
  Almost for the same purpose.
ISA. [To Alibius.]   Your change is still
  Behind, but deserve best your transformation.
  You are a jealous coxcomb, keep schools
  of folly,
  And teach your scholars how to break
  your own head.
ALIB. I see all apparent, wife, and will
  change now
  Into a better husband, and never keep
  Scholars that shall be wiser than myself.
ALS. [To Vermandero.] Sir, you have yet
  a son's duty living.
  Please you, accept it. Let that your
  sorrow,   220
  As it goes from your eye, go from your
  heart.
  Man and his sorrow at the grave must
  part.

[1] Added by Dyce.

[2] Idiocy.

EPILOGUE

ALS. All we can do to comfort one an-
other,
To stay a brother's sorrow for a brother,
To dry a child from the kind father's
eyes,
Is to no purpose—it rather multiplies.

Your only smiles have power to cause
relive
The dead again, or in their rooms to give
Brother a new brother, father a child;
If these appear, all griefs are reconciled.

Exeunt omnes.

FINIS.

PHILIP MASSINGER

Although Philip Massinger will never be estimated above the second rank of Elizabethan playwrights, he is becoming more and more admired by modern readers and critics because of his qualities of simplicity, saneness, and dramatic (rather than lyrical) effectiveness. He belongs to the third and last generation of Elizabethan writers for the stage, since he was born in 1584, established his contacts with the theater just as Shakespeare was beginning to bring his work to an end and as Beaumont and Fletcher were producing their most famous plays, and died in 1640, just before the closing of the theaters by the Puritans. Massinger's birth into a family of education, his early patronage by the Pembrokes, and his partial education at Oxford, all started his career under favorable auspices. When he left college for London without a degree, probably about 1606, he seems to have gradually won for himself the confidence of such men as Field, Tourneur, Dekker, and Fletcher, with all of whom he eventually collaborated. His work with Fletcher from 1613 to 1623 for the King's Men has given his own friends and contemporaries, such as Sir Aston Cockayne, as well as many later scholars, plenty of opportunities to claim for him large portions of plays generally attributed to the more famous member of the intimate partnership which succeeded that of Beaumont and Fletcher on the retirement and death of the former. With the exception of the two years from 1623 to 1625, when for some unknown reason Massinger transferred his talents to the Queen's Men, his characters were created for the King's Men during the remaining years of his life. But, although he wrote many plays, both alone and in collaboration with other dramatists, he was never prosperous, and is known to have borrowed money at least once from old Philip Henslowe.

The two plays here printed from Massinger's individual pen, *A New Way to Pay Old Debts* and *The Maid of Honor*, represent his work at its best and most characteristic, for his two fortes were comedy and tragi-comedy; tragedy he is known to have practiced rarely, in such plays as *The Duke of Milan* and *The Fatal Dowry*, although Bishop Warburton's unfortunate cook is reputed to have consumed the manuscripts of several of Massinger's unprinted plays in his culinary operations. *A New Way to Pay Old Debts*, which was printed in 1633 and perhaps acted about 1625 or 1626, is not only one of the few Elizabethan plays which could be successfully produced for a modern audience almost without alteration, but, because of its being founded directly on Middleton's *A Trick to Catch the Old One*, it also affords an extremely interesting comparison between the spirits of the two men as well as between those of their generations. For in this comedy, as well as in his tragi-comedy, *The Maid of Honor* (printed in 1632 and probably acted less than a decade before), Massinger reveals himself as close to the cleanest and most high-minded of the playwrights of his age, though unluckily the same statement cannot be made about all of his writings, some of which are gratuitously coarse. Not only morality but also religion often bear leading parts in his works, although there is no necessity for accusing him of turning Roman Catholic because he presents adherents of this church in a particularly heroic light in some of his plays. His women are especially attractive, and in fact offer more variety and interest than his men, who, like his plots, tend to lack originality. The story of *The Maid of Honor*, for instance, derives from Boccaccio's "Camiola and Rolande" through the intermediary of Painter's *Palace of Pleasure*.

The present text of *The Maid of Honor* is based on the careful critical edition (London, 1927) prepared by Eva A. W. Bryne for the Bryn Mawr series of dissertations editing Massinger's plays; her readings are drawn from a collation of nine copies of the first, and only early, quarto, all of which vary slightly among themselves, corrections having apparently been made by the printer as the pages were going through the press. Her text, however, has been checked with that of the 1632 quarto in the Newberry Library. The text of *A New Way to Pay Old Debts* is based on a copy of the 1633 edition in the Newberry Library at Chicago, compared with A. H. Cruikshank's edition (Oxford, 1926) and Brander Matthews' in volume three of Gayley's *Representative English Comedies.*

A NEW WAY TO PAY OLD DEBTS[1]

BY

PHILIP MASSINGER

DRAMATIS PERSONÆ

LOVELL, *an English lord.*
SIR GILES OVERREACH, *a cruel extortioner.*
[FRANK] WELLBORN, *a prodigal.*
[TOM] ALLWORTH, *a young gentleman, page*
  to Lord Lovell.
GREEDY, *a hungry justice of peace.*
MARALL, *a term driver;* [2] *a creature of Sir*
  Giles Overreach.
ORDER [, *a steward*] ⎫
AMBLE [, *an usher*] ⎪ *servants to the Lady*
FURNACE [, *a cook*] ⎬ *Allworth.*
WATCHALL [, *a porter*] ⎭

WILLDO, *a parson.*
TAPWELL, *an alehouse keeper.*
THREE CREDITORS [, SERVANTS, *etc.*]

THE LADY ALLWORTH, *a rich widow.*
MARGARET, *Overreach his daughter.*
WAITING-WOMAN.
CHAMBERMAID.
FROTH, *Tapwell's wife.*

[SCENE: *The country near Nottingham.*

TIME: *Contemporary.*]

ACTUS PRIMUS. SCENA PRIMA.

[*Before Tapwell's house.*]

Wellborn, Tapwell, Froth.

WELL. No booze? Nor no tobacco?
TAP.   Not a suck, sir,
  Nor the remainder of a single can
  Left by a drunken porter, all night
  palled [3] too.
FROTH. Not the dropping of the tap for
  your morning's draught, sir.
  'Tis verity, I assure you.
WELL.   Verity, you brach! [4]
  The devil turned precisian? [5] Rogue,
  what am I?

TAP. Troth, durst I trust you with a look-
  ing-glass
  To let you see your trim shape, you
  would quit [6] me
  And take the name yourself.
WELL.   How, dog?
TAP.   Even so, sir.
  And I must tell you, if you but ad-
  vance   10
  Your Plimworth cloak [7] you shall be soon
  instructed
  There dwells, and within call, if it please
  your worship,
  A potent monarch called the constable,
  That does command a citadel called the
  stocks,
  Whose guards are certain files of rusty
  billmen [8]
  Such as with great dexterity will hale
  Your tattered, lousy—
WELL.   Rascal! Slave!
FROTH.   No rage, sir.

---

[1] The title continues: "A Comedy. As It
Hath Been Often Acted at the Phœnix in Drury
Lane by the Queen's Majesty's Servants." On
the following pages appear the dedication to
the Earl of Carnarvon and two commendatory
poems by Sir Henry Moody and Sir Thomas
Jay.
[2] One who moves from court to court during
sessions.
[3] Paled, become flat.
[4] Bitch.   [5] Puritan.

[6] Acquit.
[7] Plymouth cloak; *i.e.*, a cudgel.
[8] Watchmen armed with pikes.

TAP. At his own peril. Do not put yourself
   In too much heat, there being no water
     near
   To quench your thirst; and sure, for
     other liquor,   20
   As mighty ale or beer, they are things, I
     take it,
   You must no more remember—not in a
     dream, sir.
WELL. Why, thou unthankful villain,
     dar'st thou talk thus?
   Is not thy house, and all thou hast, my
     gift?
TAP. I find it not in chalk; and Timothy
     Tapwell
   Does keep no other register.
WELL.   Am not I he
   Whose riots fed and clothed thee? Wert
     thou not
   Born on my father's land, and proud to
     be
   A drudge in his house?
TAP.   What I was, sir, it skills [1] not;
   What you are, is apparent. Now, for a
     farewell,   30
   Since you talk of father, in my hope it
     will torment you,
   I'll briefly tell your story. Your dead
     father,
   My quondam master, was a man of wor-
     ship,
   Old Sir John Wellborn, justice of peace
     and quorum, [2]
   And stood fair to be *custos rotulorum;* [3]
   Bare the whole sway of the shire, kept a
     great house,
   Relieved the poor, and so forth; but, he
     dying,
   And the twelve hundred a year coming
     to you,
   Late Master Francis, but now forlorn
     Wellborn—
WELL. Slave, stop, or I shall lose my-
     self!
FROTH.   Very hardly;   40
   You cannot out of your way.
TAP.   But to my story.
   You were then a lord of acres, the prime
     gallant,
   And I your underbutler. Note the change
     now.

[1] Matters.
[2] One of the most eminent justices.
[3] Custodian of the records.

You had a merry time of 't—hawks and
     hounds,
With choice of running horses; mistresses
Of all sorts and all sizes, yet so hot
As their embraces made your lordships [4]
     melt,
Which your uncle, Sir Giles Overreach,
     observing,
Resolving not to lose a drop of 'em
On foolish mortgages, statutes, and
     bonds,   50
For a while supplied your looseness, and
     then left you.
WELL. Some curate hath penned this in-
     vective, mongrel,
   And you have studied it.
TAP.   I have not done yet.
   Your land gone, and your credit not
     worth a token, [5]
   You grew the common borrower; no man
     scaped
   Your paper pellets, [6] from the gentle-
     man
   To the beggars on highways, that sold
     you switches
   In your gallantry.
WELL.   I shall switch your brains out!
TAP. Where poor Tim Tapwell, with a
     little stock,
   Some forty pounds or so, bought a small
     cottage,   60
   Humbled myself to marriage with my
     Froth here,
   Gave entertainment—
WELL.   Yes, to whores and canters, [7]
     Clubbers by night.
TAP.   True, but they brought in profit,
   And had a gift to pay for what they
     called for,
   And stuck [8] not like your mastership.
     The poor income
   I gleaned from them hath made me in my
     parish
   Thought worthy to be scavenger, and in
     time
   May rise to be overseer of the poor,
   Which if I do, on your petition, Wellborn,
   I may allow you thirteenpence a quarter,
   And you shall thank my worship.

[4] Estates.
[5] A counter used as a substitute for money.
[6] *I.e.,* I.O.U's.
[7] Users of thieves' cant.
[8] *I. e.,* delayed payment.

WELL.   Thus, you dogbolt,[1] 71
And thus—   *Beats and kicks him.*
TAP. [*To Froth.*]   Cry out for help!
WELL.   Stir, and thou diest.
Your potent prince, the constable, shall
    not save you.
Hear me, ungrateful hellhound! Did
    not I
Make purses for you? Then you licked
    my boots,
And thcught your holy day [2] cloak too
    coarse to clean 'em.
'Twas I that, when I heard thee swear if
    ever
Thou couldst arrive at forty pounds thou
    wouldst
Live like an emperor, 'twas I that
    gave it
In ready gold. Deny this, wretch!
TAP.   I must, sir, 80
For, from the tavern to the taphouse, all,
On forfeiture of their licenses, stand
    bound
Never to remember who their best guests
    were,
If they grew poor like you.
WELL.   They are well rewarded
That beggar themselves to make such
    cuckolds rich.
Thou viper, thankless viper! Impudent
    bawd!
But, since you are grown forgetful, I will
    help
Your memory, and tread thee into mor-
    tar,
Not leave one bone unbroken.
                     [*Beats him again.*]
TAP.   O!
FROTH.   Ask mercy.

Enter Allworth.

WELL. 'Twill not be granted.
ALL.   Hold—for my sake, hold! 90
Deny me, Frank? They are not worth
    your anger.
WELL. For once thou hast redeemed them
    from this scepter. [*Shows*] *his cudgel.*
But let 'em vanish, creeping on their
    knees,
And, if they grumble, I revoke my par-
    don.

[1] A worthless arrow, *i.e.*, a contemptible
fellow.   [2] Holiday.

FROTH. This comes of your prating, hus-
    band; you presumed
On your ambling wit, and must use your
    glib tongue,
Though you are beaten lame for 't.
TAP.   Patience, Froth;
There's law to cure our bruises.
            They go off on their hands and knees.
WELL.   Sent to your mother?
ALL. My lady, Frank, my patroness, my
    all!
She's such a mourner for my father's
    death,   100
And, in her love to him, so favors me
That I cannot pay too much observance
    to her.
There are few such stepdames.
WELL.   'Tis a noble widow,
And keeps her reputation pure and clear
From the least taint of infamy; her life,
With the splendor of her actions, leaves
    no tongue
To envy or detraction. Prithee, tell me,
Has she no suitors?
ALL.   Even the best of the shire, Frank,
My lord excepted, such as sue and send,
And send and sue again, but to no pur-
    pose.   110
Their frequent visits have not gained her
    presence.
Yet she's so far from sullenness and
    pride
That I dare undertake you shall meet
    from her
A liberal entertainment. I can give you
A catalogue of her suitors' names.
WELL.   Forbear it,
While I give you good counsel. I am
    bound to it;
Thy father was my friend, and that
    affection
I bore to him, in right descends to
    thee.
Thou art a handsome and a hopeful
    youth,
Nor will I have the least affront stick on
    thee,   120
If I with any danger can prevent it.
ALL. I thank your noble care; but, pray
    you, in what
Do I run the hazard?
WELL.   Art thou not in love?
Put it not off with wonder.
ALL.   In love, at my years?

WELL. You think you walk in clouds, but are trans[pa]rent.
I have heard all, and the choice that you have made,
And with my finger can point out the north star
By which the loadstone of your folly's guided.
And, to confirm this true, what think you of 129
Fair Margaret, the only child and heir
Of cormorant Overreach? Does it blush and start,
To hear her only named? Blush at your want
Of wit and reason.
ALL. You are too bitter, sir.
WELL. Wounds of this nature are not to be cured
With balms, but corrosives. I must be plain:
Art thou scarce manumised [1] from the porter's lodge [2]
And yet sworn servant to the pantofle, [3]
And dar'st thou dream of marriage? I fear
'Twill be concluded for impossible
That there is now, nor e'er shall be hereafter, 140
A handsome page or player's boy of fourteen
But either loves a wench, or drabs love him—
Court-waiters [4] not exempted.
ALL. This is madness.
Howe'er you have discovered my intents,
You know my aims are lawful; and, if ever
The queen of flowers, the glory of the spring,
The sweetest comfort to our smell, the rose,
Sprang from an envious brier, I may infer
There's such disparity in their conditions
Between the goddess of my soul, the daughter, 150
And the base churl of her father.

[1] Manumitted, freed.
[2] Where servants were punished.
[3] Slipper; i.e., he is still a page.
[4] Pages at court.

WELL. Grant this true,
As I believe it, canst thou ever hope
To enjoy a quiet bed with her whose father
Ruined thy state?
ALL. And yours too.
WELL. I confess it.
True, I must tell you as a friend, and freely,
That, where impossibilities are apparent,
'Tis indiscretion to nourish hopes.
Canst thou imagine (let not self-love blind thee)
That Sir Giles Overreach, that, to make her great
In swelling titles, without touch of conscience 160
Will cut his neighbor's throat, and I hope his own too,
Will e'er consent to make her thine?
Give o'er,
And think of some course suitable to thy rank,
And prosper in it.
ALL. You have well advised me.
But in the meantime you that are so studious
Of my affairs wholly neglect your own.
Remember yourself, and in what plight you are.
WELL. No matter, no matter.
ALL. Yes, 'tis much material. [5]
You know my fortune and my means; yet something
I can spare from myself to help your wants.
WELL. How's this? 170
ALL. Nay, be not angry; there's eight pieces
To put you in better fashion.
WELL. Money from thee?
From a boy? A stipendary? [6] One that lives
At the devotion of a stepmother
And the uncertain favor of a lord?
I'll eat my arms first. Howsoe'er blind Fortune
Hath spent the utmost of her malice on me—
Though I am vomited out of an alehouse,
And, thus accoutered, know not where to eat,

[5] Very important.
[6] Stipendiary.

Or drink, or sleep, but underneath this
　canopy [1]—　　　　　　　　　　180
Although I thank thee, I despise thy
　offer,
And, as I in my madness broke my state
Without th' assistance of another's brain,
In my right wits I'll piece it; at the worst,
Die thus and be forgotten.

ALL.　　　　　A strange humor!　*Exeunt.*

ACTUS PRIMI SCENA SECUNDA.[2]

[*A room in Lady Allworth's house.*]

Order, Amble, Furnace, Watchall.

ORD. Set all things right, or, as my name is
　Order,
And by this staff of office that commands
　you,
This chain and double ruff, symbols of
　power,
Whoever misses in his function,
For one whole week makes forfeiture of
　his breakfast
And privilege in the wine cellar.

AMB.　　　　　　　　　You are merry,
　Good Master Steward.

FURN.　　　　　　　Let him; I'll be angry.

AMB. Why, fellow Furnace, 'tis not twelve
　a-clock yet,
Nor dinner taking up; then, 'tis allowed,
Cooks by their places may be choleric.

FURN. You think you have spoke wisely,
　Goodman Amble,　　　　　　　　11
My lady's go-before! [3]

ORD.　　　　　　Nay, nay, no wrangling.

FURN. Twit me with the authority of the
　kitchen?
At all hours and all places, I'll be angry;
And, thus provoked, when I am at my
　prayers,
I will be angry.

AMB.　　　　　There was no hurt meant.

FURN. I am friends with thee; and yet I
　will be angry.

ORD. With whom?

FURN.　　　　No matter whom—yet, now I
　think on 't,
I am angry with my lady.

WATCH.　　　　　　Heaven forbid, man!

ORD. What cause has she given thee?

FURN.　　　　　　　Cause enough, Master
　Steward.　　　　　　　　　　　20
I was entertained [4] by her to please her
　palate,
And, till she forswore eating, I performed
　it.
Now, since our master, noble Allworth,
　died,
Though I crack my brains to find out
　tempting sauces,
And raise fortifications in the pastry
Such as might serve for models in the
　Low Countries,
Which, if they had been practiced at
　Breda,
Spinola might have thrown his cap at it, [5]
　and ne'er took it—

AMB. But you had wanted matter there to
　work on.

FURN. Matter?　　With six eggs and a
　strike [6] of rye meal　　　　　　30
I had kept the town till doomsday, per-
　haps longer.

ORD. But what's this to your pet against
　my lady?

FURN. What's this? Marry, this: when I
　am three parts roasted
And the fourth part parboiled to prepare
　her viands,
She keeps her chamber, dines with a
　panada [7]
Or water gruel my sweat never thought
　on.

ORD. But your art is seen in the dining
　room.

FURN.　　　　By whom?
By such as pretend love to her, but come
To feed upon her. Yet, of all the harpies
That do devour her, I am out of charity
With none so much as the thin-gutted
　squire　　　　　　　　　　　　41
That's stolen into commission.

ORD.　　　　　　　　　Justice Greedy?

FURN. The same, the same. Meat's cast
　away upon him;
It never thrives. He holds this para-
　dox:
Who eats not well, can ne'er do justice
　well.

---

[4] Employed.
[5] Given it up as a bad job.
[6] A measure varying from one-half to four
bushels.
[7] A boiled bread pudding.

---

[1] *I.e.*, the sky.
[2] The second scene of the first act.
[3] *I.e.*, usher.

His stomach's as insatiate as the grave,
Or strumpets' ravenous appetites.
WATCH. One knocks.

Allworth knocks, and enters.

ORD. Our late young master!
AMB. Welcome, sir.
FURN. Your hand.
If you have a stomach, a cold bakemeat's
ready.
ORD. His father's picture in little.
FURN. We are all your servants. 50
AMB. In you he lives.
ALL. At once, my thanks to
all;
This is yet some comfort. Is my lady
stirring?

*Enter the Lady Allworth, Waiting-Woman,
Chambermaid.*

ORD. Her presence answer for us.
LADY. Sort those silks well.
I'll take the air alone.
Exeunt Waiting-Woman and Chambermaid.
FURN. You air and air;
But will you never taste but spoonmeat [1]
more?
To what use serve I?
LADY. Prithee, be not angry;
I shall, ere long. I' the meantime, there
is gold
To buy thee aprons and a summer
suit.
FURN. I am appeased, and Furnace now
grows cook.
LADY. And, as I gave directions, if this
morning 60
I am visited by any, entertain 'em
As heretofore; but say, in my excuse,
I am indisposed.
ORD. I shall, madam.
LADY. Do, and leave me.—
Nay, stay you, Allworth.
Exeunt Order, Amble, Furnace, Watchall.
ALL. I shall gladly grow here,
To wait on your commands.
LADY. So soon turned courtier!
ALL. Style not that courtship, madam,
which is duty
Purchased on your part.
LADY. Well, you shall o'ercome;
I'll not contend in words. How is it with
Your noble master?

[1] Liquid diet.

ALL. Ever like himself,
No scruple lessened in the full weight of
honor. 70
He did command me, pardon my pre-
sumption,
As his unworthy deputy to kiss
Your ladyship's fair hands.
LADY. I am honored in
His favor to me. Does he hold his pur-
pose
For the Low Countries?
ALL. Constantly, good madam;
But he will in person first present his
service.
LADY. And how approve you of his course?
You are yet,
Like virgin parchment, capable of any
Inscription, vicious or honorable.
I will not force your will, but leave you
free 80
To your own election.
ALL. Any form you please
I will put on; but, might I make my
choice,
With humble emulation I would follow
The path my lord marks to me.
LADY. 'Tis well answered,
And I commend your spirit. You had a
father—
Blessed be his memory!—that some few
hours
Before the will of heaven took him from
me,
Who did commend you, by the dearest
ties
Of perfect love between us, to my charge;
And therefore what I speak you are
bound to hear 90
With such respect as if he lived in me.
He was my husband, and, howe'er you
are not
Son of my womb, you may be of my love,
Provided you deserve it.
ALL. I have found you,
Most honored madam, the best mother to
me,
And, with my utmost strengths of care
and service,
Will labor that you never may repent
Your bounties showered upon me.
LADY. I much hope it.
These were your father's words: "If e'er
my son 99
Follow the war, tell him it is a school

Where all the principles tending to
   honor
Are taught, if truly followed. But for
   such
As repair thither as a place in which
They do presume they may with license
   practice
Their lusts and riots, they shall never
   merit
The noble name of soldiers. To dare
   boldly
In a fair cause, and for the country's
   safety
To run upon the cannon's mouth un-
   daunted;
To obey their leaders, and shun muti-
   nies;   109
To bear with patience the winter's
   cold
And summer's scorching heat, and not to
   faint,
When plenty of provision fails, with
   hunger—
Are the essential parts make up a sol-
   dier,
Not swearing, dice, or drinking."
ALL.   There's no syllable
You speak but is to me an oracle,
Which but to doubt were impious.
LADY.   To conclude:
Beware ill company, for often men
Are like to those with whom they do con-
   verse;
And from one man I warned you, and
   that's Wellborn,
Not cause he's poor—that rather claims
   your pity—   120
But that he's in his manners so de-
   bauched,
And hath to vicious courses sold him-
   self.
'Tis true, your father loved him while he
   was
Worthy the loving; but, if he had lived
To have seen him as he is, he had cast
   him off,
As you must do.
ALL.   I shall obey in all things.
LADY. You follow me to my chamber; you
   shall have gold
To furnish you like my son, and still
   supplied
As I hear from you.
ALL.   I am still your creature. *Exeunt.*

ACTUS PRIMI SCENA TERTIA.

[*A hall in the same.*]

Overreach, Greedy, Order, Amble, Furnace,
                              Watchall, Marall.

GREEDY. Not to be seen?
OVER.   Still cloistered up? Her rea-
   son,
I hope, assures her, though she make
   herself
Close prisoner ever for her husband's
   loss,
'Twill not recover him.
ORD.   Sir, it is her will,
Which we that are her servants ought
   to serve it
And not dispute. Howe'er, you are
   nobly welcome;
And, if you please to stay, that you may
   think so,
There came not six days since from
   Hull a pipe
Of rich Canary, which shall spend itself
For my lady's honor.
GREEDY.   Is it of the right race?   10
ORD. Yes, Master Greedy.
AMB. [*Aside.*]   How his mouth runs
   o'er!
FURN. [*Aside.*] I'll make it run, and run.—
   Save your good worship!
GREEDY. Honest Master Cook, thy hand
   again! How I love thee!
Are the good dishes still in being? Speak,
   boy.
FURN. If you have a mind to feed, there
   is a chine
Of beef, well seasoned.
GREEDY.   Good!
FURN.   A pheasant, larded.
GREEDY. That I might now give thanks
   for 't!
FURN.   Other kuckshaws.[1]
Besides, there came last night from the
   forest of Sherwood
The fattest stag I ever cooked.
GREEDY.   A stag, man?
FURN. A stag, sir—part of it prepared for
   dinner,   20
And baked in puff paste.
GREEDY.   Puff paste too, Sir Giles!
A ponderous chine of beef! A pheasant
   larded!

[1] Kickshaws.

And red deer too, Sir Giles, and baked
　in puff paste!
All business set aside, let us give thanks
　here.
FURN. How the lean skeleton's raped! [1]
OVER. 　　　　　　You know we cannot.
MAR. Your worships are to sit on a com-
　mission,
　And, if you fail to come, you lose the
　cause.
GREEDY. Cause me no causes. I'll prove
　't, for such a dinner
We may put off a commission: you shall
　find it
Henrici decimo quarto [2] —
OVER. 　　　　　　Fie, Master Greedy! 30
　Will you lose me a thousand pounds
　for a dinner?
No more, for shame! We must forget
　the belly
When we think of profit.
GREEDY. 　　　Well, you shall o'errule me.
　I could ev'n cry now.—Do you hear,
　Master Cook?
Send but a corner of that immortal
　pasty,
And I in thankfulness will by your boy
Send you—a brace of threepences.
FURN. 　　　　　Will you be so prodigal?

Enter Wellborn.

OVER. Remember me to your lady.—
　Who have we here?
WELL. You know me.
OVER. 　　　　I did once, but now I will not;
　Thou art no blood of mine. Avaunt,
　thou beggar! 　　　　　　　　　　40
If ever thou presume to own me more,
I'll have thee caged and whipped.
GREEDY. 　　　　　I'll grant the warrant.
　Think of Pie Corner, Furnace!
　　　Exeunt Overreach, Greedy, Marall.
WATCH. 　　　　　　Will you out, sir?
I wonder how you durst creep in.
ORD. 　　　　　　　　This is rudeness
　And saucy impudence.
AMB. 　　　　　　　Cannot you stay
　To be served, among your fellows, from
　the basket, [3]
But you must press into the hall?

[1] Rapt, transported.
[2] In a law enacted in the fourteenth year of
Henry's reign.
[3] Of scraps.

FURN. 　　　　　　　Prithee, vanish
Into some outhouse, though it be the
　pigsty;
My scullion shall come to thee.

Enter Allworth.

WELL. 　　　　　　　　This is rare.
O, here's Tom Allworth.—Tom!
ALL. 　　　　　We must be strangers; 50
　Nor would I have you seen here for a
　million. 　　　　　　　*Exit Allworth.*
WELL. Better and better. He contemns
　me too!

Enter [Waiting-] Woman and Chambermaid.

WOMAN. Foh, what a smell's here! What
　thing's this?
CHAM. 　　　　　A creature
　Made out of the privy; let us hence,
　for love's sake,
　Or I shall sown. [4]
WOMAN. 　　I begin to feel faint already.
*Exeunt [Waiting-] Woman and Chamber-
　　　　　　　　　　　　　　maid.*
WATCH. Will you know your way?
AMB. 　　　　　Or shall we teach it you
　By the head and shoulders?
WELL. 　　　　　　No; I will not stir.
　Do you mark, I will not. Let me see
　the wretch
　That dares attempt to force me. Why,
　you slaves, 　　　　　　　　　　59
Created only to make legs [5] and cringe,
To carry in a dish and shift a trencher,
That have not souls only to hope a
　blessing
Beyond blackjacks [6] or flagons—you that
　were born
Only to consume meat and drink, and
　batten
Upon reversions!—Who advances? Who
Shows me the way?
ORD. 　　　　　　　My lady!

*Enter Lady, [Waiting-] Woman, Chamber-
　　　　　　　　　　　　　　maid.*

CHAM. 　　　　　Here's the monster.
WOMAN. Sweet madam, keep your glove
　to your nose.

[4] Sound, swoon. 　　　　[6] Leather jugs.
[5] Bows.

CHAM.　　　　　　Or let me
Fetch some perfumes may be predomi-
nant;
You wrong yourself else.
WELL.　　　　Madam, my designs
Bear me to you.
LADY. To me?
WELL.　　And, though I have met with 70
But ragged entertainment from your
grooms here,
I hope from you to receive that noble
usage
As may become the true friend of your
husband,
And then I shall forget these.
LADY.　　　　　　I am amazed
To see and hear this rudeness. Dar'st
thou think,
Though sworn, that it can ever find belief
That I, who to the best men of this
country
Denied my presence since my husband's
death,
Can fall so low as to change words with
thee?　　　　　　　79
Thou son of infamy, forbear my house,
And know and keep the distance that's
between us,
Or, though it be against my gentler
temper,
I shall take order you no more shall be
An eyesore to me.
WELL.　　　　Scorn me not, good lady;
But, as in form you are angelical,
Imitate the heavenly natures and vouch-
safe
At the least awhile to hear me. You will
grant
The blood that runs in this arm is as
noble
As that which fills your veins; those
costly jewels,
And those rich clothes you wear, your
men's observance　　　　　90
And women's flattery are in you no
virtues,
Nor these rags, with my poverty, in
me vices.
You have a fair fame, and, I know, de-
serve it;
Yet, lady, I must say, in nothing more
Than in the pious sorrow you have
shown
For your late noble husband.

ORD. [Aside.]　　　　How she starts!
FURN. [Aside.] And hardly can keep finger
from the eye
To hear him named.
LADY.　　　Have you aught else to say?
WELL. That husband, madam, was once
in his fortune
Almost as low as I; want, debts, and
quarrels　　　　　　　100
Lay heavy on him. Let it not be thought
A boast in me, though I say I relieved
him.
'Twas I that gave him fashion; mine
the sword
That did on all occasions second his;
I brought him on and off with honor,
lady;
And, when in all men's judgments he
was sunk
And in his own hopes not to be bunged
up,
I stepped unto him, took him by the
hand,
And set him upright.
FURN. [Aside.]　　Are not we base rogues,
That could forget this?
WELL.　　I confess, you made him 110
Master of your estate; nor could your
friends,
Though he brought no wealth with him,
blame you for 't,
For he had a shape, and to that shape
a mind,
Made up of all parts either great or
noble—
So winning a behavior not to be
Resisted, madam.
LADY.　　　　　'Tis most true, he had.
WELL. For his sake, then, in that I was
his friend,
Do not contemn me.
LADY.　　　For what's past, excuse me;
I will redeem it.—Order, give the gentle-
man
A hundred pounds.
WELL.　　No, madam, on no terms. 120
I will nor beg nor borrow sixpence of
you,
But be supplied elsewhere, or want
thus ever.
Only one suit I make, which you deny
not
To strangers; and 'tis this.
　　　　　　　　　Whispers to her.

LADY.   Fie! Nothing else?

WELL. Nothing, unless you please to charge your servants

To throw away a little respect upon me.

LADY. What you demand is yours.

WELL.   I thank you, lady.

Now what can be wrought out of such a suit

Is yet in supposition. I have said all;

When you please, you may retire.—[*Exit Lady.*] Nay, all's forgotten;   130

And for a lucky omen to my project

Shake hands and end all quarrels in the cellar.

ORD. Agreed, agreed.

FURN.   Still merry Master Wellborn!

Exeunt.

ACTUS SECUNDI SCENA PRIMA.

[*A room in Overreach's house.*]

Overreach, Marall.

OVER. He's gone, I warrant thee; this commission crushed him.

MAR. Your worship have the way on 't,[1] and ne'er miss

To squeeze these unthrifts[2] into air; and yet

The chapfallen justice did his part, returning

For your advantage the certificate,

Against his conscience and his knowledge too

(With your good favor), to the utter ruin

Of the poor farmer.

OVER.   'Twas for these good ends

I made him a justice; he that bribes his belly

Is certain to command his soul.

MAR.   I wonder, 10

Still with your license, why your worship, having

The power to put this thin-gut in commission,

You are not in 't yourself?

OVER.   Thou art a fool.

In being out of office I am out of danger;

Where,[3] if I were a justice, besides the trouble,

I might or[4] out of willfulness or error

Run myself finely into a *præmunire*,[5]

And so become a prey to the informer.

No, I'll have none of 't. 'Tis enough I keep

Greedy at my devotion;[6] so he serve   20

My purposes, let him hang or damn, I care not.

Friendship is but a word.

MAR.   You are all wisdom.

OVER. I would be worldly wise; for the other wisdom,

That does prescribe as a well-governed life,

And to do right to others as ourselves,

I value not an atom.

MAR.   What course take you,

With your good patience, to hedge in the manor

Of your neighbor, Master Frugal, as 'tis said

He will nor sell nor borrow nor exchange?

And his land, lying in the midst of your many lordships,   30

Is a foul blemish.

OVER.   I have thought on 't, Marall,

And it shall take. I must have all men sellers,

And I the only purchaser.

MAR.   'Tis most fit, sir.

OVER. I'll therefore buy some cottage near his manor,

Which done, I'll make my men break ope his fences,

Ride o'er his standing corn, and in the night

Set fire on his barns, or break his cattle's legs.

These trespasses draw on suits and suits, expenses,

Which I can spare, but will soon beggar him.

When I have harried him thus two or three year,   40

Though he sue *in forma pauperis*,[7] in spite

Of all his thrift and care he'll grow behindhand.

MAR. The best I ever heard! I could adore you.

OVER. Then, with the favor of my man of law,

---

[1] Emended by Gifford. Original reads *out.*

[2] Spendthrifts.

[3] Whereas.   [4] Either.

[5] A legal writ; here a scrape or predicament.

[6] *I. e.*, interests.

[7] In the status of a pauper.

I will pretend some title. Want will
force him
To put it to arbitrament; then, if he sell
For half the value, he shall have ready
money,
And I possess his land.
MAR.   'Tis above wonder!
Wellborn was apt[1] to sell, and needed
not
These fine arts, sir, to hook him in.
OVER.   Well thought on. 50
This varlet, Marall, lives too long to
upbraid me
With my close cheat[2] put upon him.
Will nor cold
Nor hunger kill him?
MAR.   I know not what to think on 't.
I have used all means, and the last
night I caused
His host, the tapster, to turn him out
of doors,
And have been since with all your
friends and tenants
And on the forfeit of your favor charged
them,[3]
Though a crust of moldy bread would
keep him from starving,
Yet they should not relieve him. This
is done, sir.
OVER. That was something, Marall; but
thou must go further,   60
And suddenly, Marall.
MAR.   Where and when you please, sir.
OVER. I would have thee seek him out
and, if thou canst,
Persuade him that 'tis better steal than
beg;
Then, if I prove he has but robbed a
henroost,
Not all the world shall save him from
the gallows.
Do anything to work him to despair,
And 'tis thy masterpiece.
MAR.   I will do my best, sir.
OVER. I am now on my main work with
the Lord Lovell,
The gallant-minded, popular Lord Lov-
ell,
The minion of the people's love. I
hear   70
He's come into the country, and my
aims are

To insinuate myself into his knowledge,
And then invite him to my house.
MAR.   I have you;
This points at my young mistress.
OVER.   She must part with
That humble title, and write "honor-
able,"
"Right honorable," Marall, my "right
honorable" daughter,
If all I have, or e'er shall get, will
do it.
I will have her well attended; there are
ladies
Of errant knights decayed and brought
so low
That for cast[4] clothes and meat will
gladly serve her.   80
And 'tis my glory, though I come from
the city,
To have their issue whom I have un-
done,
To kneel to mine as bondslaves.
MAR.   'Tis fit state, sir.
OVER. And therefore I'll not have a cham-
bermaid
That ties her shoes, or any meaner
office,
But such whose fathers were right wor-
shipful.
'Tis a rich man's pride, there having
ever been
More than a feud, a strange antipathy,
Between us and true gentry.

                Enter Wellborn.

MAR.   See who's here, sir.
OVER. Hence, monster! Prodigy!
WELL.   Sir, your wife's nephew; 90
She and my father tumbled in one belly.
OVER. Avoid my sight! Thy breath's
infectious, rogue!
I shun thee as a leprosy or the plague.—
Come hither, Marall.—[*Aside.*] This is
the time to work him.
MAR. I warrant you, sir.
                        Exit Over[*reach*].
WELL.   By this light, I think he's mad.
MAR. Mad? Had you took compassion
on yourself,
You long since had been mad.
WELL.   You have took a course,
Between you and my venerable uncle,
To make me so.

MAR.   The more pale-spirited you,
That would not be instructed. I swear
    deeply—   100
WELL. By what?
MAR.   By my religion.
WELL. [*Aside.*]   Thy religion!
The devil's creed!—But what would
    you have done?
MAR. Had there been but one tree in all
    the shire,
Nor any hope to compass a penny
    halter,
Before, like you, I had outlived my
    fortunes,
A withe had served my turn to hang
    myself.
I am zealous in your cause; pray you,
    hang yourself,
And presently,[1] as you love your credit.
WELL.   I thank you.
MAR. Will you stay till you die in a ditch,
    or lice devour you?
Or, if you dare not do the feat your-
    self,   110
But that you'll put the state to charge
    and trouble,
Is there no purse to be cut, house to be
    broken,
Or market women with eggs, that you
    may murther,
And so despatch the business?
WELL.   Here's variety,
I must confess; but I'll accept of
    none
Of all your gentle offers, I assure you.
MAR. Why, have you hope ever to eat
    again,
Or drink, or be the master of three
    farthings?
If you like not hanging, drown your-
    self! Take some course
For your reputation.
WELL.   'Twill not do, dear tempter,   120
With all the rhetoric the fiend hath
    taught you.
I am as far as thou art from despair;
Nay, I have confidence, which is more
    than hope,
To live, and suddenly, better than ever.
MAR. Ha, ha! These castles you build
    in the air
Will not persuade me or to give or lend
A token to you.

[1] At once.

WELL.   I'll be more kind to thee.
Come, thou shalt dine with me.
MAR.   With you?
WELL.   Nay, more, dine gratis.
MAR. Under what hedge, I pray you?
    Or at whose cost?
Are they padders[2] or Abram-men[3]
    that are your consorts?   130
WELL. Thou art incredulous; but thou
    shalt dine
Not alone at her house, but with a
    gallant lady—
With me and with a lady.
MAR.   Lady? What lady?
With the Lady of the Lake,[4] or Queen
    of Fairies?
For I know it must be an enchanted
    dinner.
WELL. With the Lady Allworth, knave.
MAR.   Nay, now there's hope
Thy brain is cracked.
WELL.   Mark there, with what respect
I am entertained.
MAR.   With choice, no doubt, of dog
    whips.
Why, dost thou ever hope to pass her
    porter?
WELL. 'Tis not far off; go with me. Trust
    thine own eyes.   140
MAR. Troth, in my hope, or my assurance
    rather,
To see thee curvet and mount like a dog
    in a blanket,
If ever thou presume to pass her thresh-
    old,
I will endure thy company.
WELL.   Come along then. *Exeunt.*

ACTUS SECUNDI SCENA SECUNDA.

[*A room in Lady Allworth's house.*]

*Allworth, Waiting-Woman, Chambermaid,
    Order, Amble, Furnace, Watchall.*

WOMAN. Could you not command your
    leisure one hour longer?
CHAM. Or half an hour?
ALL.   I have told you what my haste is.
Besides, being now another's, not mine
    own,
Howe'er I much desire to enjoy you
    longer,

[2] Footpads.
[3] Beggars who feigned insanity.
[4] In the *Morte d'Arthur.*

My duty suffers, if, to please myself,
I should neglect my lord.

WOMAN.   Pray you, do me the favor
To put these few quince cakes into your
    pocket;
They are of mine own preserving.

CHAM.   And this marmulade;[1]
'Tis comfortable for your stomach.

WOMAN.   And, at parting,
Excuse me if I beg a farewell from you. 10

CHAM. You are still before me. I move the
    same suit, sir.
          [*Allworth*] *kisses 'em severally.*

FURN. How greedy these chamberers are
    of a beardless chin!
I think the tits [2] will ravish him.

ALL.   My service
To both.

WOMAN.   Ours waits on you.

CHAM.   And shall do ever.

ORD. You are my lady's charge; be there-
    fore careful
That you sustain your parts.

WOMAN.   We can bear, I warrant you.

Exeunt [*Waiting-*] *Woman and Chambermaid.*

FURN. Here, drink it off. The ingredients
    are cordial,
And this the true elixir; it hath boiled
Since midnight for you. 'Tis the quin-
    tessence
Of five cocks of the game, ten dozen of
    sparrows,   20
Knuckles of veal, potato roots and mar-
    row,
Currall [3] and ambergris. Were you two
    years elder,
And I had a wife or gamesome mistress,
I durst trust you with neither. You need
    not bait [4]
After this, I warrant you, though your
    journey's long;
You may ride on the strength of this till
    tomorrow morning.

ALL. Your courtesies overwhelm me. I
    much grieve
To part from such true friends, and yet
    find comfort—   28
My attendance on my honorable lord,
Whose resolution holds to visit my lady,
Will speedily bring me back.

Knocking at the gate; Marall and Wellborn
          within. [*Exit Watchall.*]

MAR.   Dar'st thou venture further?

WELL. Yes, yes, and knock again.

ORD.   'Tis he; disperse!

AMB. Perform it bravely.

FURN.   I know my cue; ne'er doubt me.

They go off several ways [*, Allworth re-*
                      maining.

Enter Watchall with Wellborn and Marall.]

WATCH. Beast that I was, to make you
    stay! Most welcome;
You were long since expected.

WELL.   Say so much
To my friend, I pray you.

WATCH. For your sake, I will, sir.

MAR. [*Aside.*] For his sake!

WELL. [*Aside.*]   Mum; this is nothing.

MAR.   More than ever
I would have believed, though I had
    found it in my primer.[5]

ALL. When I have given you reasons for
    my late harshness,
You'll pardon and excuse me, for, be-
    lieve me,   40
Though now I part abruptly, in my
    service
I will deserve it.

MAR. [*Aside.*]   Service! With a ven-
    geance!

WELL. I am satisfied. Farewell, Tom.

ALL.   All joy stay with you!
                 Exit Allw[*orth*].

Enter Amble.

AMB. You are happily encountered; I yet
    never
Presented one so welcome as I know
You will be to my lady.

MAR. [*Aside.*]   This is some vision,
Or, sure, these men are mad, to worship
    a dunghill;
It cannot be a truth.

WELL.   Be still a pagan,
An unbelieving infidel; be so, miscreant,
And meditate on blankets and on dog
    whips!   50

Enter Furnace.

FURN. I am glad you are come; until I
    know your pleasure
I knew not how to serve up my lady's
    dinner.

---

[1] Marmalade.   [3] Coral.
[2] Chits.   [4] Eat.

[5] "The original primers were books of prayers
for children" (Cruikshank).

MAR. [*Aside.*] His pleasure! Is it possible?

WELL.   What's thy will?

FURN. Marry, sir, I have some grouse, and turkey chicken,

Some rails and quails, and my lady willed me ask you

What kind of sauces best affect your palate

That I may use my utmost skill to please it.

MAR. [*Aside.*] The devil's entered this cook. Sauce for his palate,

That, on my knowledge, for almost this twelvemonth

Durst wish but cheese parings, and brown bread on Sundays.   60

WELL. That way I like 'em best.

FURN.   It shall be done, sir.

Exit Furnace.

WELL. What think you of "the hedge we shall dine under"?

Shall we feed gratis?

MAR. [*Aside.*]   I know not what to think.

Pray you, make me not mad.

Enter Order.

ORD.   This place becomes you not;

Pray you, walk, sir, to the dining room.

WELL.   I am well here,

Till her ladyship quits her chamber.

MAR. [*Aside.*]   Well here, say you?

'Tis a rare change! But yesterday you thought

Yourself well in a barn, wrapped up in peas-straw.

Enter [Waiting-] Woman and Chambermaid.

WOMAN. O, sir, you are wished for.

CHAM.   My lady dreamt, sir, of you.

WOMAN. And the first command she gave, after she rose,   70

Was, her devotions done, to give her notice

When you approached here.

CHAM.   Which is done, on my virtue.

MAR. [*Aside.*] I shall be converted; I begin to grow

Into a new belief, which saints nor angels

Could have won me to have faith in.

WOMAN.   Sir, my lady!

Enter Lady [Allworth].

LADY. I come to meet you, and languished till I saw you.

This first kiss is for form; I allow a second

To such a friend.   [*Kisses Wellborn.*]

MAR. [*Aside.*]   To such a friend!

Heaven bless me!

WELL. I am wholly yours; yet, madam, if you please

To grace this gentleman with a salute—   80

MAR. [*Aside.*] Salute me at his bidding!

WELL.   I shall receive it

As a most high favor.

LADY.   Sir, you may command me.

[*Advances to kiss Marall, who draws back.*]

WELL. Run backward from a lady? And such a lady?

MAR. To kiss her foot is to poor me a favor

I am unworthy of—

                    Offers to kiss her foot.

LADY.   Nay, pray you, rise,

And, since you are so humble, I'll exalt you.

You shall dine with me today at mine own table.

MAR. Your ladyship's table? I am not good enough

To sit at your steward's board.

LADY.   You are too modest;

I will not be denied.

Enter Furnace.

FURN.   Will you still be babbling   90

Till your meat freeze on the table? The old trick still;

My art ne'er thought on!

LADY.   Your arm, Master Wellborn.—

[*To Marall.*] Nay, keep us company.

MAR.   I was never so graced.

Exeunt Wellborn, Lady [Allworth], Amble, Marall, [Waiting-] Woman [, and Chambermaid].

ORD. So we have played our parts, and are come off well;

But, if I know the mystery, why my lady

Consented to it, or why Master Wellborn

Desired it, may I perish!

Furn.   Would I had
  The roasting of his heart that cheated
    him,
  And forces the poor gentleman to these
    shifts!
  By fire (for cooks are Persians, and
    swear by it),   100
  Of all the griping and extorting tyrants
  I ever heard or read of, I ne'er met
  A match to Sir Giles Overreach.
Watch.   What will you take
  To tell him so, fellow Furnace?
Furn.   Just as much
  As my throat is worth, for that would be
    the price on 't.
  To have a usurer that starves himself
  And wears a cloak of one-and-twenty
    years
  On a suit of fourteen groats, bought of
    the hangman,
  To grow rich, and then purchase,[1] is too
    common;
  But this Sir Giles feeds high, keeps many
    servants,   110
  Who must at his command do any out-
    rage.
  Rich in his habit, vast in his expenses,
  Yet he to admiration[2] still increases
  In wealth and lordships.
Ord.   He frights men out of their estates,
  And breaks through all law nets, made
    to curb ill men,
  As they were cobwebs. No man dares
    reprove him.
  Such a spirit to dare and power to do
    were never
  Lodged so unluckily.

Enter Amble.

Amb.   Ha, ha! I shall burst.
Ord. Contain thyself, man.
Furn.   Or make us partakers
  Of your sudden mirth.
Amb.   Ha, ha! My lady has got   120
  Such a guest at her table—this term
    driver, Marall,
  This snip of an attorney!
Furn.   What of him, man?
Amb. The knave thinks still he's at the
    cook's shop in Ram Alley,[3]

Where the clerks[4] divide, and the elder
    is to choose;[5]
  And feeds so slovenly!
Furn.   Is this all?
Amb.   My lady
  Drank to him for fashion' sake, or to
    please Master Wellborn.
  As I live, he rises, and takes up a dish
  In which there were some remnants of a
    boiled capon,
  And pledges her in white broth!
Furn.   Nay, 'tis like   129
  The rest of his tribe.
Amb.   And, when I brought him wine,
  He leaves his stool and after a leg or two
  Most humbly thanks my worship.
Ord.   Rose already!
Amb. I shall be chid.

Enter Lady [Allworth], Wellborn, Marall.

Furn. [*Aside.*]   My lady frowns.
Lady.   You wait well!
  Let me have no more of this; I observed
    your jeering.
  Sirrah, I'll have you know, whom I
    think worthy
  To sit at my table, be he ne'er so mean,
  When I am present, is not your com-
    panion.[6]
Ord. [*Aside.*] Nay, she'll preserve what's
    due to her.
Furn. [*Aside.*]   This refreshing
  Follows your flux of laughter.
Lady. [*To Wellborn.*]   You are master
  Of your own will. I know so much of
    manners   140
  As not to inquire your purposes; in a
    word,
  To me you are ever welcome, as to a
    house
  That is your own.
Well. [*Aside to Marall.*]   Mark that.
Mar. [*Aside.*]   With reverence, sir,
  And it like[7] your worship.
Well.   Trouble yourself no farther,
  Dear madam; my heart's full of zeal and
    service,
  However in my language I am sparing.—
  Come, Master Marall.
Mar.   I attend your worship.
                Exeunt Wellb[orn], Mar[all].

---

[1] Acquire real estate by any other means than
inheritance.
[2] In a wonderful fashion.
[3] A street in London famous for its restaurants.

[4] Lawyers.
[5] Have first choice of his portion.
[6] *I.e.*, kind.   [7] If it please.

LADY. I see in your looks you are sorry,
   and you know me
An easy mistress. Be merry; I have for-
   got all.—
Order and Furnace, come with me; I
   must give you   150
Further directions.
ORD.   What you please.
FURN.   We are ready. [*Exeunt.*]

ACTUS SECUNDI SCENA TERTIA.

[*The country near Lady Allworth's house.*]

Wellborn, Marall.

WELL. I think I am in a good way.
MAR.   Good sir, the best way,
The certain best way.
WELL.   There are casualties
That men are subject to.
MAR.   You are above 'em;
And, as you are already worshipful,
I hope ere long you will increase in wor-
   ship,
And be right worshipful.
WELL.   Prithee, do not flout me.
What I shall be, I shall be. Is 't for your
   ease
You keep your hat off?
MAR.   Ease, and it like your worship?
I hope Jack Marall shall not live so long,
To prove himself such an unmannerly
   beast,   10
Though it hail hazelnuts, as to be covered
When your worship's present.
WELL. (*Aside.*)   Is not this a true rogue
That, out of mere hope of a future
   coz'nage,[1]
Can turn thus suddenly?   'Tis rank
   already.
MAR. I know your worship's wise, and
   needs no counsel;
Yet, if in my desire to do you service
I humbly offer my advice (but still
Under correction), I hope I shall not
Incur your high displeasure.
WELL.   No; speak freely.
MAR. Then, in my judgment, sir, my
   simple judgment   20
(Still with your worship's favor), I could
   wish you
A better habit, for this cannot be
But much distasteful to the noble lady

[1] With a pun on *cousinage*, intimacy.

(I say no more) that loves you, for, this
   morning
To me (and I am but a swine to her),
Before th' assurance of her wealth
   perfumed you,
You savored not of amber.[2]
WELL.   I do now then?
[*Marall*] *kisses the end of his* [*Wellborn's*]
           cudgel.
MAR. This your batoon [3] hath got a touch
   of it.
Yet, if you please, for change I have
   twenty pounds here
Which out of my true love I presently 30
Lay down at your worship's feet; 'twill
   serve to buy you
A riding suit.
WELL.   But where's the horse?
MAR.   My gelding
Is at your service; nay, you shall ride me
Before your worship shall be put to the
   trouble
To walk afoot. Alas, when you are lord
Of this lady's manor, as I know you will
   be,
You may with the lease of glebe land,
   called Knave's Acre,
A place I would manure,[4] requite your
   vassal.
WELL. I thank thy love, but must make no
   use of it.
What's twenty pounds?
MAR.   'Tis all that I can make, sir. 40
WELL. Dost thou think, though I want
   clothes, I could not have 'em
For one word to my lady?
MAR.   As I know not that!
WELL. Come, I'll tell thee a secret, and so
   leave thee.
I'll not give her the advantage, though
   she be
A gallant-minded lady, after we are
   married
(There being no woman but is sometimes
   froward),
To hit me in the teeth, and say she was
   forced
To buy my wedding clothes, and took
   me on
With a plain riding suit and an ambling
   nag.

[2] Ambergris.
[3] Baton, stick.
[4] Maneuver, operate, possess.

No, I'll be furnished something like
  myself,   50
And so farewell. For thy suit touching
  Knave's Acre,
When it is mine, 'tis thine.
MAR.   I thank your worship.—
                              Exit Wellb[orn].
How [I] ¹ was cozened in the calcula-
  tion
Of this man's fortune! My master
  cozened too,
Whose pupil I am in the art of undoing
  men,
For that is our profession! Well, well,
  Master Wellborn,
You are of a sweet nature and fit again
  to be cheated,
Which, if the Fates please, when you are
  possessed
Of the land and lady, you, sans question,
  shall be.
I'll presently think of the means.
                          Walk by, musing. ²

                Enter Overreach.

OVER. [*To a Servant within.*]   Sirrah,
  take my horse.   60
I'll walk to get me an appetite; 'tis but a
  mile,
And exercise will keep me from being
  pursy.
Ha! Marall! Is he conjuring? Perhaps
The knave has wrought the prodigal to
  do
Some outrage on himself, and now he
  feels
Compunction in his conscience for 't.
  No matter,
So it be done.—Marall!
MAR.   Sir.
OVER.   How succeed we
In our plot on Wellborn?
MAR.   Never better, sir.
OVER. Has he hanged or drowned himself?
MAR.   No, sir, he lives—
Lives once more to be made a prey to
  you,   70
A greater prey than ever.
OVER.   Art thou in thy wits?
If thou art, reveal this miracle, and
  briefly.

¹ Added by Cruickshank.
² Matthews' reading; original reads *masing.*

MAR. A lady, sir, is fall'n in love with him.
OVER. With him? What lady?
MAR.   The rich Lady Allworth.
OVER. Thou dolt! How dar'st thou speak
  this?
MAR.   I speak truth;
And I do so but once a year, unless
It be to you, sir. We dined with her
  ladyship,
I thank his worship.
OVER.   His worship!
MAR.   As I live, sir,
I dined with him at the great lady's
  table,
Simple as I stand here, and saw when she
  kissed him,   80
And would at his request have kissed
  me too;
But I was not so audacious as some
  youths are,
And dare do anything, be it ne'er so
  absurd,
And sad after performance.
OVER.   Why, thou rascal,
To tell me these impossibilities!
Dine at her table? And kiss him? Or
  thee?
Impudent varlet, have not I myself,
To whom great countesses' doors have
  oft flew open,
Ten times attempted, since her hus-
  band's death,
In vain to see her, though I came—a
  suitor?   90
And yet your good solicitorship and
  rogue Wellborn
Were brought into her presence, feasted
  with her!
But that I know thee a dog that cannot
  blush,
This most incredible lie would call up
  one
On thy buttermilk cheeks.
MAR.   Shall I not trust my eyes, sir,
Or taste? I feel her good cheer in my
  belly.
OVER. You shall feel me, if you give not
  over, sirrah.
Recover your brains again, and be no
  more gulled
With a beggar's plot, assisted by the
  aids
Of serving-men and chambermaids, for
  beyond these   100

Thou never saw'st a woman, or I'll quit [1]
you
From my employments.

MAR.   Will you credit this yet?
On my confidence of their marriage, I
offered Wellborn—
(*Aside.*) I would give a crown now I
durst say "his worship"—
My nag and twenty pounds.

OVER.   Did you so, idiot? [2]
Strikes him down.
Was this the way to work him to despair,
Or rather to cross me?

MAR.   Will your worship kill me?

OVER. No, no; but drive the lying spirit
out of you.

MAR. He's gone.

OVER.   I have done then. Now,
forgetting
Your late imaginary feast and lady,   110
Know my Lord Lovell dines with me
tomorrow.
Be careful naught be wanting to receive
him;
And bid my daughter's women trim her
up;
Though they paint her, so she catch the
lord I'll thank 'em.
There's a piece for my late blows.
[*Gives money.*]

MAR. (*Aside.*)   I must yet suffer.
But there may be a time—

OVER.   Do you grumble?

MAR.   No, sir. [*Exeunt.*]

ACTUS TERTII SCENA PRIMA.

[*The country near Overreach's house.*]

Lovell, Allworth, Servants.

LOV. Walk the horses down the hill. Something in private
I must impart to Allworth. *Exeunt servi.* [3]

ALL.   O, my lord,
What sacrifice of reverence, duty, watch-
ing,
Although I could put off the use of sleep,
And ever wait on your commands [to]
serve 'em,
What dangers, though ne'er so horrid
shapes,

[1] Release, discharge.
[2] Emended by Coxeter. Original reads *I doe.*
Cf. V, i, 215.
[3] Servants.

Nay, death itself, though I should run
to meet it,
Can I, and with a thankful willingness,
suffer!
But still the retribution will fall short
Of your bounties showered upon me.

LOV.   Loving youth,   10
Till what I purpose be put into act,
Do not o'erprize it. Since you have
trusted me
With your soul's nearest, nay, her
dearest secret,
Rest confident 'tis in a cabinet locked
Treachery shall never open. I have
found you
(For so much to your face I must profess,
Howe'er you guard [4] your modesty with a
blush for 't)
More zealous in your love and service
to me
Than I have been in my rewards.

ALL.   Still great ones,
Above my merit.

LOV.   Such your gratitude calls 'em;   20
Nor am I of that harsh and rugged tem-
per
As some great men are taxed with, who
imagine
They part from the respect due to their
honors
If they use not all such as follow 'em,
Without distinction of their births, like
slaves.
I am not so conditioned; I can make
A fitting difference between my footboy
And a gentleman by want compelled to
serve me.

ALL. 'Tis thankfully acknowledged. You
have been   29
More like a father to me than a master.
Pray you, pardon the comparison.

LOV.   I allow it;
And, to give you assurance I am pleased
in 't,
My carriage and demeanor to your mis-
tress,
Fair Margaret, shall truly witness for me
I can command my passions.

ALL.   'Tis a conquest
Few lords can boast of when they are
tempted.—O!

LOV. Why do you sigh?   Can you be
doubtful of me?

[4] Adorn.

By that fair name I in the wars have
    purchased
And all my actions hitherto untainted,
I will not be more true to mine own
    honor   40
Than to my Allworth!
ALL.   As you are the brave Lord Lovell,
    Your bare word only given is an assur-
    ance
Of more validity and weight to me
Than all the oaths bound up with im-
    precations,
Which, when they would deceive, most
    courtiers practice;
Yet, being a man (for, sure, to style you
    more
Would relish of gross flattery), I am
    forced
Against my confidence of your worth and
    virtues
To doubt, nay, more, to fear.
Lov.   So young, and jealous?
ALL. Were you to encounter with a single
    foe,   50
The victory were certain; but to stand
The charge of two such potent enemies,
At once assaulting you, as wealth and
    beauty,
And those too seconded with power, is
    odds
Too great for Hercules.
Lov.   Speak your doubts and fears,
    Since you will nourish 'em, in plainer
    language
That I may understand 'em.
ALL.   What's your will,
    Though I lend arms against myself
    (provided
They may advantage [1] you), must be
    obeyed.
My much-loved lord, were Margaret
    only fair,   60
The cannon of her more than earthly
    form,
Though mounted high, commanding all
    beneath it,
And rammed with bullets of her sparkling
    eyes,
Of all the bulwarks that defend your
    senses
Could batter none [2] but that which
    guards your sight.

But, when the well-tuned accents of her
    tongue
Make music to you, and with numerous [3]
    sounds
Assault your hearing (such as if Ulysses
Now lived again, howe'er he stood the
    Sirens,
Could not resist), the combat must grow
    doubtful   70
Between your reason and rebellious
    passions.
Add this too: when you feel her touch,
    and breath
Like a soft western wind when it glides
    o'er
Arabia, creating gums and spices,
And, in the van, the nectar of her lips,
Which you must taste, bring the battalia [4]
    on,
Well armed, and strongly lined [5] with her
    discourse
And knowing manners, to give enter-
    tainment—
Hippolytus himself would leave Diana
To follow such a Venus.
Lov.   Love hath made you 80
    Poetical, Allworth.
ALL.   Grant all these beat off
    (Which, if it be in man to do, you'll do it),
Mammon, in Sir Giles Overreach, steps
    in
With heaps of ill-got gold, and so much
    land,
To make her more remarkable, as would
    tire
A falcon's wings in one day to fly over.
O my good lord! These powerful aids,
    which would
Make a misshapen negro beautiful
(Yet are but ornaments to give her
    luster,   89
That in herself is all perfection), must
Prevail for her. I here release your
    trust;
'Tis happiness enough for me to serve
    you
And sometimes with chaste eyes to look
    upon her.
Lov. Why, shall I swear?
ALL.   O, by no means, my lord;
    And wrong not so your judgment to the
    world

---

[1] Help.
[2] Emended by Gifford. Original reads *more*.

[3] Rhythmical.
[4] Army.   [5] Strengthened. Original reads *liv'd*.

As from your fond indulgence to a boy,
Your page, your servant, to refuse a
   blessing
Divers great men are rivals for.

Lov.   Suspend
Your judgment till the trial. How far is it
To Overreach' house?

ALL.   At the most, some half hour's
   riding;   100
You'll soon be there.

Lov.   And you the sooner freed
From your jealous fears.

ALL.   O, that I durst but hope it!
                          Exeunt.

ACTUS TERTII SCENA SECUNDA.

[*A room in Overreach's house.*]

Overreach, Greedy, Marall.

OVER. Spare for no cost; let my dressers
   crack with the weight
Of curious viands.

GREEDY.   *Store indeed's no sore,*[1] sir.

OVER. That proverb fits your stomach,
   Master Greedy.
And let no plate be seen but what's pure
   gold,
Or such whose workmanship exceeds the
   matter
That it is made of; let my choicest linen
Perfume the room, and, when we wash,
   the water,
With precious powders mixed, so please
   my lord
That he may with envy wish to bathe so
   ever.

MAR. 'Twill be very chargeable.[2]

OVER.   Avaunt, you drudge!   10
Now all my labored ends are at the
   stake,
Is 't a time to think of thrift? Call in my
   daughter.—   [*Exit Marall.*]
And, Master Justice, since you love
   choice dishes,
And plenty of 'em—

GREEDY.   As I do, indeed, sir,
Almost as much as to give thanks for 'em.

OVER. I do confer that providence, with
   my power
Of absolute command to have abundance,
To your best care.

GREEDY.   I'll punctually discharge it
And give the best directions. Now am I
In mine own conceit[3] a monarch—at
   the least,   20
Archpresident of the boiled, the roast,
   the baked,
For which I will eat often and give
   thanks
When my belly's braced up like a drum—
   and that's pure justice.

OVER. I[t] must be so. Should the foolish
   girl prove modest,   *Exit Greedy.*
She may spoil all. She had it not from
   me,
But from her mother; I was ever forward,
As she must be, and therefore I'll prepare her.

[*Enter*] *Margaret.*

Alone—and let your women wait without.

MARG. Your pleasure, sir?

OVER.   Ha, this is a neat dressing!
These orient pearls and diamonds well
   placed too!   30
The gown affects[4] me not; it should have
   been
Embroidered o'er and o'er with flowers
   of gold;
But these rich jewels and quaint fashion
   help it.
And how below, since oft the wanton
   eye,
The face observed, descends unto the
   foot,
Which, being well proportioned, as
   yours is,
Invites as much as perfect white and red,
Though without art? How like you
   your new woman,
The Lady Downfall'n?

MARG.   Well, for a companion;
Not as a servant.

OVER.   Is she humble, Meg, 40
And careful too, her ladyship forgotten?

MARG. I pity her fortune.

OVER.   Pity her? Trample on her!
I took her up in an old tamine[5] gown
(Even starved for want of twopenny
   chops) to serve thee;
And, if I understand she but repines
To do thee any duty, though ne'er so
   servile,

---

[1] Harm. Sententious sayings are frequently
indicated by italics.   [2] Costly.

[3] Thought, opinion.
[4] Pleases.   [5] Thin woolen stuff.

I'll pack her to her knight, where I have
  lodged him,
Into the Counter [1] and there let 'em
  howl together.
MARG. You know your own ways; but, for
  me, I blush
When I command her that was once
  attended   50
With persons not inferior to myself
In birth.
OVER.   In birth? Why, art thou not
  my daughter,
The blessed child of my industry and
  wealth?
Why, foolish girl, was 't not to make thee
  great
That I have ran, and still pursue, those
  ways
That hale down curses on me, which I
  mind not?
Part with these humble thoughts, and
  apt [2] thyself
To the noble state I labor to advance
  thee,
Or, by my hopes to see thee honorable,
I will adopt a stranger to my heir,   60
And throw thee from my care. Do not
  provoke me.
MARG. I will not, sir; mold me which way
  you please.

Enter Greedy.

OVER. How! Interrupted?
GREEDY.   'Tis matter of importance.
The cook, sir, is self-willed, and will not
  learn
From my experience. There's a fawn
  brought in, sir,
And, for my life, I cannot make him
  roast it
With a Norfolk dumpling in the belly of
  it;
And, sir, we wise men know, without the
  dumpling
'Tis not worth threepence.
OVER.   Would it were whole in thy belly,
To stuff it out! Cook it any way; prithee,
  leave me.   70
GREEDY. Without order for the dumpling?
OVER.   Let it be dumpled
Which way thou wilt, or tell him I will
  scald him
In his own caldron.

GREEDY.   I had lost my stomach
Had I lost my Mistress Dumpling I'll
  give thanks for.
OVER. But to our business, Meg. You
  have heard who dines here?
                             Exit Greedy.
MARG. I have, sir.
OVER.   'Tis an honorable man;
A lord, Meg, and commands a regiment
Of soldiers, and, what's rare, is one
  himself,
A bold and understanding one; and to be
A lord and a good leader, in one volume,
Is granted unto few but such as rise [3]
  up   81
The kingdom's glory.

Enter Greedy.

GREEDY.   I'll resign my office,
If I be not better obeyed.
OVER.   'Slight, art thou frantic?
GREEDY. Frantic?   'Twould make me
  a frantic [4] and stark mad,
Were I not a justice of peace and coram [5]
  too,
Which this rebellious cook cares not a
  straw for.
There are a dozen of woodcocks—
OVER.   Make thyself
Thirteen, the baker's dozen.
GREEDY.   I am contented,
So they may be dressed to my mind. He
  has found out
A new device for sauce, and will not dish
  'em   90
With toasts and butter. My father was a
  tailor,
And my name, though a justice, Greedy
  Woodcock;
And, ere I'll see my linage [6] so abused,
I'll give up my commission.
OVER. [*To Cook within.*] Cook! Rogue,
  obey him!
I have given the word; pray you, now
  remove yourself
To a collar of brawn,[7] and trouble me no
  farther.
GREEDY. I will, and meditate what to eat
  at dinner.   *Exit Greedy.*

[1] One of the London prisons.   [2] Fit.
[3] Raise.
[4] *I.e.*, an insane person.
[5] Obsolete corruption of *quorum.*
[6] Lineage.   [7] Neck of a boar.

OVER. And, as I said, Meg, when this gull
　　disturbed us,
This honorable lord, this colonel,[1]
I would have thy husband.
MARG. 　　　There's too much disparity　100
Between his quality and mine to hope it.
OVER. I more than hope 't, and doubt not
　　to effect it.
Be thou no enemy to thyself; my wealth
Shall weigh his titles down, and make
　　you equals.
Now for the means to assure him thine,
　　observe me:
Remember he's a courtier and a soldier,
And not to be trifled with; and, therefore,
　　when
He comes to woo you, see you do not
　　coy it.[2]
This mincing modesty hath spoiled many
　　a match　　　　　　　　　109
By a first refusal, in vain after hoped
　　for.
MARG. You'll have me, sir, preserve the
　　distance that
Confines a virgin?
OVER. 　　　　　Virgin me no virgins!
I must have you lose that name, or you
　　lose me.
I will have you private—start not—I
　　say, private.
If thou art my true daughter, not a
　　bastard,
Thou wilt venture alone with one man,
　　though he came
Like Jupiter to Semele, and come off,
　　too;
And therefore, when he kisses you, kiss
　　close.
MARG. I have heard this is the strumpet's
　　fashion, sir,
Which I must never learn.
OVER. 　　　　Learn anything,　120
And from any creature that may make
　　thee great—
From the devil himself.
MARG. [Aside.] 　　This is but devilish
　　doctrine!
OVER. Or, if his blood grow hot, suppose
　　he offer
Beyond this, do not you stay till it
　　cool,
But meet his ardor; if a couch be near,
Sit down on 't, and invite him.

[1] Trisyllabic here.　　[2] Behave coyly.

MARG. 　　　　　　In your house,
Your own house, sir? For heaven's sake,
　　what are you then?
Or what shall I be, sir?
OVER. 　　　　　Stand not cn form;
Words are no substances.
MARG. 　　　　Though you could dispense
With your own honor, cast aside re-
　　ligion,　　　　　　　130
The hopes of heaven or fear of hell,
　　excuse me.
In worldly policy this is not the way
To make me his wife; his whore, I grant
　　it may do.
My maiden honor so soon yielded up,
Nay, prostituted, cannot but assure him
I, that am light to him, will not hold
　　weight
When he is tempted by others; so, in
　　judgment,
When to his lust I have given up my
　　honor,
He must and will forsake me.
OVER. 　　　　　How? Forsake thee?
Do I wear a sword for fashion? Or is this
　　arm　　　　　　　　140
Shrunk up or withered? Does there live a
　　man
Of that large list I have encountered
　　with
Can truly say I e'er gave inch of
　　ground
Not purchased with his blood that did
　　oppose me?
Forsake thee when the thing is done?
　　He dares not.
Give me but proof he has enjoyed thy
　　person,
Though all his captains, echoes to his
　　will,
Stood armed by his side to justify the
　　wrong,
And he himself in the head of his bold
　　troop,　　　　　　　149
Spite of his lordship and his colonel-
　　ship,
Or the judge's favor, I will make him
　　render
A bloody and a strict accompt,[3] and
　　force him,
By marrying thee, to cure thy wounded
　　honor!
I have said it.

[3] Account.

Enter Marall.

MAR.   Sir, the man of honor's come,
Newly alighted.
OVER.   In, without reply.
And do as I command, or thou art lost.
                              Exit Marg[aret].
Is the loud music I gave order for
Ready to receive him?
MAR.   'Tis, sir.
OVER.   Let 'em sound
A princely welcome.—[*Exit Marall.*]
Roughness, awhile leave me,
For fawning now, a stranger to my
    nature,   160
Must make way for me.

*Loud music.   Enter Lovell, Greed[y], All-
              w[orth], Mar[all].*

LOV.   Sir, you meet your trouble.
OVER. What you are pleased to style so is
    an honor
Above my worth and fortunes.
ALL. [*Aside.*]   Strange, so humble.
OVER. A justice of peace, my lord.
                    Presents Greedy to him.
LOV.   Your hand, good sir.
GREEDY. [*Aside.*] This is a lord, and some
    think this a favor;
But I had rather have my hand in my
    dumpling.
OVER. Room for my lord.
LOV.   I miss, sir, your fair daughter
To crown my welcome.
OVER.   May it please my lord
To taste a glass of Greek wine first, and
    suddenly
She shall attend my lord.
LOV.   You'll be obeyed, sir.   170
          Exeunt omnes præter [1] *Over[reach].*
OVER. 'Tis to my wish. As soon as come,
    ask for her!—
Why, Meg! Meg Overreach!—

[*Enter Margaret.*]

                    How! Tears in your eyes!
Ha! Dry 'em quickly, or I'll dig 'em
    out.
Is this a time to whimper? Meet that
    greatness
That flies into thy bosom; think what 'tis
For me to say, "My honorable daugh-
    ter,"

[1] All except.

And thou, when I stand bare, to say,
    "Put on,"[2]
Or, "Father, you forget yourself." No
    more.
But be instructed, or expect—He
    comes.—

Enter Lovell, Greedy, Allworth, Marall.
                              They salute.
A black-browed girl, my lord.
LOV. [*Kissing her.*]   As I live,
a rare one.   180
ALL. [*Aside.*] He's took already. I am
    lost.
OVER. [*Aside.*]   That kiss
Came twanging off; I like it.—Quit the
    room.—   *The Rest off.*
A little bashful, my good lord, but you,
I hope, will teach her boldness.
LOV.   I am happy
In such a scholar, but—
OVER.   I am past learning,
And therefore leave you to yourselves.—
    (*To his Daughter.*) Remember!
                              Exit Overreach.
LOV. You see, fair lady, your father is
    solicitous
To have you change the barren name of
    virgin
Into a hopeful wife.
MARG.   His [3] haste, my lord,
Holds no power o'er my will.
LOV.   But o'er your duty.   190
MARG. Which, forced too much, may
    break.
LOV.   Bend rather, sweetest.
Think of your years.
MARG.   Too few to match with yours—
And choicest fruits, too soon plucked,
    rot and wither.
LOV. Do you think I am old?
MARG.   I am sure I am too young.
LOV. I can advance you.
MARG.   To a hill of sorrow,
Where every hour I may expect to fall,
But never hope firm footing. You are
    noble,
I of a low descent, however rich;
And tissues [4] matched with scarlet [5]
    suit but ill.

[2] *I.e.*, put on your hat.
[3] Emended by Gifford. Original reads *he.*
[4] Silk clothes.
[5] A scarlet gown, worn as a mark of dignity.

O, my good lord, I could say more, but
  that   200
I dare not trust these walls.

Lov.   Pray you, trust my ear then.

Enter Over[reach behind], list'ning.

OVER. Close at it! Whispering! This is
  excellent!
And, by their postures, a consent on
  both parts.

Enter Greed[y behind].

GREEDY. Sir Giles, Sir Giles!

OVER.   The great fiend stop
  that clapper!

GREEDY. It must ring out, sir, when my
  belly rings noon.
The baked-meats are run out, the roast
  turned powder.

OVER. I shall powder you.

GREEDY.   Beat me to dust, I care not;
In such a cause as this, I'll die a martyr.

OVER. Marry, and shall, you barathrum
  of the shambles! [1]   *Strikes him.*

GREEDY. How! Strike a justice of peace?
'Tis petty treason,   210
Edwardi quinto. [2] But that you are my
  friend,
I could commit you without bail or
  mainprize. [3]

OVER. Leave your bawling, sir, or I shall
  commit you
Where you shall not dine today. Disturb my lord
When he is in discourse?

GREEDY.   Is 't a time to talk
When we should be munching?

Lov.   Ha! I heard some noise.

OVER. Mum, villain; vanish! Shall we
  break a bargain
Almost made up?   *Thrust Greedy off.*

Lov.   Lady, I understand you,
And rest most happy in your choice,
  believe it;
I'll be a careful pilot to direct   220
Your yet uncertain bark to a port of
  safety.

MARG. So shall your honor save two lives,
  and bind us
Your slaves forever.

[1] Gulf of the butcher shops; glutton.
[2] According to a law enacted in the fifth year
of Edward's reign.
[3] An undertaking of suretyship.

Lov.   I am in the act rewarded,
Since it is good; howe'er, you must put
  on
An amorous carriage towards me to
  delude
Your subtle father.

MARG.   I am prone to that.

Lov. Now break we off our conference.—
Sir Giles!
Where is Sir Giles?

Enter Overreach and the Rest.

OVER.   My noble lord! And how
Does your lordship find her?

Lov.   Apt, Sir Giles, and coming;
And I like her the better.

OVER.   So do I too.   230

Lov. Yet, should we take forts at the first
  assault,
'Twere poor in the defendant; I must
  confirm her
With a love letter or two, which I must
  have
Delivered by my page, and you give way
  to 't.

OVER. With all my soul—a towardly gen-
  tleman!—
Your hand, good Master Allworth.
  Know my house
Is ever open to you.

ALL. (*Aside.*)   'Twas shut till now.

OVER. Well done, well done, my honorable
  daughter!
Th' art so already. Know this gentle
  youth,
And cherish him, my honorable daugh-
  ter.   240

MARG. I shall, with my best care.
             Noise within, as of a coach.

OVER.   A coach!

GREEDY.   More stops
Before we go to dinner! O my guts!

Enter Lady [Allworth] and Wellborn.

LADY.   If I find welcome,
You share in it; if not, I'll back again,
Now I know your ends, for I come armed
  for all
Can be objected.

Lov.   How! The Lady Allworth!

OVER. And thus attended!

*Lovell salutes the Lady; the Lady salutes
                Margaret.*

MAR.   No, I am a dolt!
The spirit of lies had entered me!
OVER.   Peace, patch! [1]
'Tis more than wonder! An astonish-
ment
That does possess me wholly!
LOV.   Noble lady,
This is a favor, to prevent [2] my visit, 250
The service of my life can never equal.
LADY. My lord, I laid wait for you, and
much hoped
You would have made my poor house
your first inn;
And therefore, doubting that you might
forget me
Or too long dwell here, having such
ample cause
In this unequaled beauty for your stay,
And fearing to trust any but myself
With the relation of my service to
you,
I borrowed so much from my long re-
straint
And took the air in person to invite
you.   260
LOV. Your bounties are so great they rob
me, madam,
Of words to give you thanks.
LADY.   Good Sir Giles Overreach!—
                              Salutes him.
How doest thou, Marall? Liked you my
meat so ill
You'll dine no more with me?
GREEDY.   I will, when you please,
And it like your ladyship.
LADY.   When you please, Master
Greedy;
If meat can do it, you shall be satisfied.—
And now, my lord, pray take into your
knowledge
This gentleman; howe'er his outside's
coarse,   *Presents Wellborn.*
His inward linings are as fine and fair
As any man's. Wonder not I speak at
large. [3]   270
And howsoe'er his humor carries him
To be thus accoutered, or what taint
soever
For his wild life hath stuck upon his
fame, [4]
He may ere long with boldness rank
himself

With some that have contemned him.—
Sir Giles Overreach,
If I am welcome, bid him so.
OVER.   My nephew!
He has been too long a stranger. Faith,
you have;
Pray, let it be mended.
                    Lovell conferring with Wellborn.
MAR.   Why, sir, what do you mean?
This is "rogue Wellborn, monster,
prodigy,
That should hang or drown himself;"
no man of worship,   280
Much less your nephew.
OVER.   Well, sirrah, we shall reckon
For this hereafter.
MAR. [*Aside.*]   I'll not lose my jeer,
Though I be beaten dead for 't.
WELL.   Let my silence plead
In my excuse, my lord, till better leisure
Offer itself to hear a full relation
Of my poor fortunes.
LOV.   I would hear, and help 'em.
OVER. Your dinner waits you.
LOV.   Pray you, lead; we follow.
LADY. Nay, you are my guest.—Come,
dear Master Wellborn.
                    Exeunt. Manet [5] Greedy.
GREEDY. "Dear Master Wellborn!" so
she said. Heaven! Heaven!
If my belly would give me leave, I could
ruminate   290
All day on this. I have granted twenty
warrants
To have him committed, from all prisons
in the shire,
To Nottingham jail. And now "Dear
Master Wellborn"!
And "My good nephew"!—but I play
the fool
To stand here prating, and forget my
dinner.—

                    Enter Marall.

Are they set, Marall?
MAR. Long since. Pray you, a word, sir.
GREEDY. No wording now.
MAR.   In troth, I must. My master,
Knowing you are his good friend, makes
bold with you
And does entreat you, more guests being
come in   299
Than he expected, especially his nephew,

---

[1] Fool.   [3] Freely.
[2] Anticipate.   [4] Reputation.
[5] Remains.

The table being full too, you would
    excuse him
And sup with him on the cold meat.
GREEDY.   How! No dinner
    After all my care?
MAR.   'Tis but a penance for
A meal; besides, you broke your fast.
GREEDY.   That was
But a bit to stay my stomach. A man
    in commission
Give place to a tatterdemalion!
MAR.   No bug [1] words, sir;
    Should his worship hear you—
GREEDY.   Lose my dumpling too,
And buttered toasts, and woodcocks?
MAR.   Come, have patience.
If you will dispense a little with your
    worship,
And sit with the waiting-women, you
    have dumpling,   310
Woodcock, and buttered toasts too.
GREEDY.   This revives me;
I will gorge there sufficiently.
MAR.   This is the way, sir. *Exeunt.*

ACTUS TERTII SCENA TERTIA.

[*The same.*]

Overreach, as from dinner.

OVER. She's caught! O women! She
    neglects my lord,
    And all her compliments applied to
        Wellborn!
    The garments of her widowhood laid
        by,
    She now appears as glorious as the
        spring.
    Her eyes fixed on him, in the wine she
        drinks,
    He being her pledge, she sends him
        burning kisses,
    And sits on thorns till she be private
        with him.
    She leaves my meat to feed upon his
        looks,
    And, if in our discourse he be but named,
    From her a deep sigh follows. But why
        grieve I   10
    At this? It makes for me; if she prove
        his,
    All that is hers is mine, as I will work
        him.

[1] Pompous, conceited.

Enter Marall.

MAR. Sir, the whole board is troubled at
    your rising.
OVER. No matter, I'll excuse it. Prithee,
    Marall,
    Watch an occasion to invite my nephew
    To speak with me in private.
MAR.   Who? "The rogue
    The lady scorned to look on"?
OVER.   You are a wag.

Enter Lady [Allworth] and Wellborn.

MAR. See, sir, she's come, and cannot
    be without him.
LADY. With your favor, sir, after a plen-
    teous dinner,   19
    I shall make bold to walk a turn or two
    In your rare garden.
OVER.   There's an arbor too,
    If your ladyship please to use it.
LADY.   Come, Master Wellborn.
    Exeunt Lady [Allworth] and Wellborn.
OVER. Grosser and grosser! Now I be-
    lieve the poet
    Feigned not, but was historical, when
        he wrote
    Pasiphaë was enamored of a bull.
    This lady's lust's more monstrous.—
        My good lord,

Enter Lord Lovell, Margaret, and the Rest.

    Excuse my manners.
LOV.   There needs none, Sir Giles—
    I may ere long say father, when it
        pleases
    My dearest mistress to give warrant
        to it.
OVER. She shall seal to it, my lord, and
    make me happy.   30

Enter Wellb[orn] and the Lad[y].

MARG. My lady is returned.
LADY.   Provide my coach;
    I'll instantly away. My thanks, Sir
        Giles,
    For my entertainment.
OVER.   'Tis your nobleness
    To think it such.
LADY.   I must do you a further wrong
    In taking away your honorable guest.
LOV. I wait on you, madam; farewell,
    good Sir Giles.

LADY. Good Mistress Margaret!—Nay,
  come, Master Wellborn,
  I must not leave you behind; in sooth,
  I must not.
OVER. Rob me not, madam, of all joys
  at once;
  Let my nephew stay behind. He shall
  have my coach,   40
  And, after some small conference be-
  tween us,
  Soon overtake your ladyship.
LADY.   Stay not long, sir.
LOV. This parting kiss! [*Kisses Margaret.*]
  You shall every day hear from me
  By my faithful page.
ALL.   'Tis a service I am proud of.
Exeunt Lovell, Lady [Allworth], Allworth,
                    Margaret, Marall.
OVER. Daughter, to your chamber.—
  You may wonder, nephew,
  After so long an enmity between us,
  I should desire your friendship.
WELL.   So I do, sir;
  'Tis strange to me.
OVER.   But I'll make it no wonder;
  And, what is more, unfold my nature
  to you.
  We worldly men, when we see friends
  and kinsmen   50
  Past hopes sunk in their fortunes, lend
  no hand
  To lift 'em up, but rather set our feet
  Upon their heads to press 'em to the
  bottom,
  As, I must yield, with you I practiced
  it.
  But, now I see you in a way to rise,
  I can and will assist you. This rich lady
  (And I am glad of 't) is enamored of
  you;
  'Tis too apparent, nephew.
WELL.   No such thing—
  Compassion rather, sir.
OVER.   Well, in a word,
  Because your stay is short, I'll have
  you seen   60
  No more in this base shape; nor shall
  she say
  She married you like a beggar, or in
  debt.
WELL. (*Aside.*) He'll run into the noose
  and save my labor.
OVER. You have a trunk of rich clothes
  not far hence

In pawn; I will redeem 'em. And, that
  no clamor
May taint your credit for your petty
  debts,
You shall have a thousand pounds to
  cut 'em off,
And go a free man to the wealthy
  lady.
WELL. This done, sir, out of love, and no
  ends else—
OVER. As it is, nephew.
WELL.   Binds me still your servant. 70
OVER. No compliments; you are stayed
  for. Ere y'ave supped,
  You shall hear from me.—My coach,
  knaves, for my nephew!—
  Tomorrow I will visit you.
WELL.   Here's an uncle
  In a man's extremes! [1] How much they
  do belie you,
  That say you are hard-hearted!
OVER.   My deeds, nephew,
  Shall speak my love; what men report
  I weigh not.   *Exeunt.*

FINIS ACTUS TERTII.

ACTUS QUARTI SCENA PRIMA.

[*A room in Lady Allworth's house.*]

Lovell, Allworth.

LOV. 'Tis well; give me my cloak; I now
  discharge you
  From further service. Mind your own
  affairs;
  I hope they will prove successful.
ALL.   What is blessed
  With your good wish, my lord, cannot
  but prosper.
  Let aftertimes report, and to your
  honor,
  How much I stand engaged, [2] for I want
  language
  To speak my debt. Yet, if a tear or two
  Of joy for your much goodness can
  supply
  My tongue's defects, I could—
LOV.   Nay, do not melt;
  This ceremonial thanks to me 's super-
  fluous.   10
OVER. (*Within.*) Is my lord stirring?
LOV. 'Tis he! O, here's your letter. Let
  him in.

[1] Extremities.   [2] Indebted.

Enter Over[reach], Greed[y], Mar[all].

OVER. A good day to my lord!

LOV.   You are an early riser,
Sir Giles.

OVER.   And reason, to attend your
lordship.

LOV. And you too, Master Greedy, up
so soon?

GREEDY. In troth, my lord, after the sun
is up,
I cannot sleep, for I have a foolish stom-
ach
That croaks for breakfast. With your
lordship's favor,
I have a serious question to demand   19
Of my worthy friend Sir Giles.

LOV.   Pray you, use your pleasure.

GREEDY. How far, Sir Giles, and, pray
you, answer me
Upon your credit, hold you it to be
From your manor house to this of my
Lady Allsworth's?

OVER. Why, some four mile.

GREEDY.   How! Four mile? Good Sir
Giles,
Upon your reputation think better,
For, if you do abate but one half-quarter
Of five, you do yourself the greatest
wrong
That can be in the world; for four miles'
riding
Could not have raised so huge an appe-
tite   29
As I feel gnawing on me.

MAR.   Whether you ride
Or go afoot, you are that way still pro-
vided,
And it please your worship.

OVER.   How now, sirrah? Prating
Before my lord! No difference? Go to
my nephew,
See all his debts discharged, and help
his worship
To fit on his rich suit.

MAR. [*Aside.*]   I may fit you too.
Tossed like a dog still!   *Exit Marall.*

LOV.   I have writ this morning
A few lines to my mistress, your fair
daughter.

OVER. 'Twill fire her, for she's wholly
yours already.—
Sweet Master Allworth, take my ring.
'Twill carry you

To her presence, I dare warrant you;
and there plead   40
For my good lord, if you shall find occasion.
That done, pray ride to Nottingham;
get a license,
Still by this token. I'll have it despatched,
And suddenly, my lord, that I may
say
My "honorable," nay, "right honorable"
daughter.

GREEDY. Take my advice, young gentleman; get your breakfast.
'Tis unwholesome to ride fasting. I'll
eat with you
And eat to purpose.

OVER.   Some Fury's in that gut!
Hungry again! Did you not devour this
morning
A shield of brawn,[1] and a barrel of Colchester oysters?   50

GREEDY. Why, that was, sir, only to
scour my stomach,
A kind of a preparative. Come, gentleman,
I will not have you feed like the hangman of Vlushing [2]
Alone, while I am here.

LOV.   Haste your return.

ALL. I will not fail, my lord.

GREEDY.   Nor I, to line
My Christmas coffer.[3]
                    Exeunt Greedy and Allworth.

OVER.   To my wish, we are private.
I come not to make offer with my daugh-
ter
A certain portion—that were poor and
trivial.
In one word, I pronounce all that is
mine,   59
In lands or leases, ready coin or goods,
With her, my lord, comes to you; nor
shall you have
One motive to induce you to believe
I live too long, since every year I'll
add
Something unto the heap, which shall
be yours too.

LOV. You are a right kind father.

---

[1] "The thick skin on the flanks of a boar: a
piece of this was filled up with meat and cooked
till soft" (Cruikshank).
[2] Flushing.   [3] *I.e.*, his stomach.

OVER.   You shall have reason
To think me such. How do you like
    this seat?
It is well wooded, and well watered, the
    acres
Fertile and rich. Would it not serve
    for change,
To entertain your friends in a summer
    progress?[1]   69
What thinks my noble lord?
LOV.   'Tis a wholesome air,
And well-built pile; and she that's mis-
    tress of it
Worthy the large revenue.
OVER.   She the mistress?
It may be so for a time, but, let my lord
Say only that he likes it, and would
    have it,
I say, ere long 'tis his.
LOV.   Impossible.
OVER. You do conclude too fast, not know-
    ing me,
Nor the engines[2] that I work by. 'Tis
    not alone
The Lady Allworth's lands, for those
    once Wellborn's
(As by her dotage on him I know they will
    be)
Shall soon be mine; but point out any
    man's   80
In all the shire, and say they lie con-
    venient
And useful for your lordship, and once
    more
I say aloud, they are yours.
LOV.   I dare not own
What's by unjust and cruel means ex-
    torted;
My fame and credit are more dear to
    me
Than so to expose 'em to be censured by
The public voice.
OVER.   You run, my lord, no hazard.
Your reputation shall stand as fair
In all good men's opinions as now;
Nor can my actions, though condemned
    for ill,   90
Cast any foul aspersion upon yours,
For, though I do contemn report my-
    self
As a mere sound, I still will be so tender
Of what concerns you, in all points of
    honor,

That the immaculate whiteness of your
    fame
Nor your unquestioned integrity
Shall e'er be sullied with one taint or
    spot
That may take from your innocence and
    candor.[3]
All my ambition is to have my daugh-
    ter
Right honorable, which my lord can
    make her.   100
And, might I live to dance upon my
    knee
A young Lord Lovell, borne by her unto
    you,
I write *nil ultra*[4] to my proudest hopes.
As for possessions and annual rents,
Equivalent to maintain you in the port[5]
Your noble birth and present state re-
    quires,
I do remove that burthen from your
    shoulders
And take it on mine own, for, though
    I ruin
The country to supply your riotous
    waste,
The scourge of prodigals, want, shall
    never find you.   110
LOV. Are you not frighted with the im-
    precations
And curses of whole families, made
    wretched
By your sinister practices?
OVER.   Yes, as rocks are,
When foamy billows split themselves
    against
Their flinty ribs, or as the moon is moved
When wolves, with hunger pined, howl
    at her brightness.
I am of a solid temper and like these
Steer on a constant course. With mine
    own sword,
If called into the field, I can make that
    right
Which fearful enemies murmured at as
    wrong.   120
Now, for these other piddling com-
    plaints
Breathed out in bitterness, as when they
    call me
Extortioner, tyrant, cormorant, or in-
    truder

[1] Journey.   [2] Devices.
[3] Immaculateness.
[4] Nothing beyond.   [5] Style of living.

On my poor neighbor's right, or grand
incloser
Of what was common, to my private
use,
Nay, when my ears [1] are pierced with
widows' cries,
And undone orphants [2] wash with tears
my threshold,
I only think what 'tis to have my daugh-
ter
Right honorable; and 'tis a powerful
charm   129
Makes me insensible of remorse or pity
Or the least sting of conscience.

Lov.   I admire [3]
The toughness of your nature.

Over.   'Tis for you,
My lord, and for my daughter, I am
marble;
Nay, more, if you will have my char-
acter
In little, I enjoy more true delight
In my arrival to my wealth these dark
And crooked ways than you shall e'er
take pleasure
In spending what my industry hath
compassed.
My haste commands me hence. In one
word, therefore,   139
Is it a match?

Lov.   I hope that is past doubt now.

Over. Then rest secure; not the hate of
all mankind here,
Nor fear of what can fall on me hereafter
Shall make me study aught but your
advancement
One story higher. An earl, if gold can
do it!
Dispute not my religion nor my faith.
Though I am borne thus headlong by
my will,
You may make choice of what belief
you please;
To me they are equal. So, my lord,
good morrow.   Exit.

Lov. He's gone—I wonder how the earth
can bear
Such a portent! I, that have lived a
soldier,   150
And stood the enemy's violent charge
undaunted,

To hear this blasphemous beast am
bathed all over
In a cold sweat. Yet, like a mountain,
he,
Confirmed in atheistical [4] assertions,
Is no more shaken than Olympus is
When angry Boreas loads his double
head
With sudden drifts of snow.

Enter Amble, Lady [Allworth], [Waiting-]
Woman.

Lady.   Save you, my lord!
Disturb I not your privacy?

Lov.   No, good madam;
For your own sake I am glad you came
no sooner,
Since this bold, bad man, Sir Giles
Overreach,   160
Made such a plain discovery [5] of himself,
And read this morning such a devilish
matins
That I should think it a sin next to his
But to repeat it.

Lady.   I ne'er pressed, my lord,
On others' privacies; yet, against my
will,
Walking, for health' sake, in the gallery
Adjoining to your lodgings, I was made
(So vehement and loud he was) partaker
Of his tempting offers.

Lov.   Please you to command
Your servants hence, and I shall gladly
hear   170
Your wiser counsel.

Lady.   'Tis, my lord, a woman's,
But true and hearty.—[To Amble.] Wait
in the next room,
But be within call; yet not so near to
force me
To whisper my intents.

Amb.   We are taught better
By you, good madam.

Woman.   And well know our distance.

Lady. Do so, and talk not; 'twill become
your breeding.—
     Exeunt Amble and [Waiting-] *Woman.*
Now, my good lord, if I may use my
freedom,
As to an honored friend—

Lov.   You lessen else
Your favor to me.

---

[1] Original read *cares.*
[2] Orphans.   [3] Wonder at.
[4] Godless.   [5] Revelation.

LADY.   I dare then say thus: 179
As you are noble (howe'er common men
Make sordid wealth the object and sole
    end
Of their industrious aims), 'twill not
    agree
With those of eminent blood, who are
    engaged
More to prefer [1] their honors than to
    increase
The state left to 'em by their ances-
    tors,
To study large additions to their for-
    tunes
And quite neglect their births—though
    I must grant
Riches, well got, to be a useful servant,
But a bad master.
LOV.   Madam, 'tis confessed. 189
But what infer you from it?
LADY.   This, my lord:
That as all wrongs, though thrust into
    one scale,
Slide of themselves off when right fills
    the other
And cannot bide the trial, so all wealth,
I mean if ill-acquired, cemented to
    honor
By virtuous ways achieved and bravely
    purchased,
Is but as rubbage [2] poured into a river
(Howe'er intended to make good the
    bank),
Rendering the water, that was pure be-
    fore,
Polluted and unwholesome. I allow
The heir of Sir Giles Overreach,
    Margaret,   200
A maid well qualified and the richest
    match
Our north part can make boast of; yet
    she cannot,
With all that she brings with her, fill [3]
    their mouths,
That never will forget who was her
    father,
Or that my husband Allworth's lands
    and Wellborn's
(How wrung from both needs now no
    repetition)
Were real motive that more worked
    your lordship

To join your families than her form and
    virtues.
You may conceive the rest.
LOV.   I do, sweet madam,
And long since have considered it. I
    know,   210
The sum of all that makes a just man
    happy
Consists in the well choosing of his wife;
And there, well to discharge it, does
    require
Equality of years, of birth, of fortune,
For beauty, being poor and not cried
    up
By birth or wealth, can truly mix with
    neither.
And wealth, where there's such differ-
    ence in years
And fair descent, must make the yoke
    uneasy.
But I come nearer.
LADY.   Pray you, do, my lord.
LOV. Were Overreach' states thrice cen-
    tupled, his daughter   220
Millions of degrees much fairer than
    she is,
Howe'er I might urge presidents [4] to
    excuse me,
I would not so adulterate my blood
By marrying Margaret, and so leave my
    issue
Made up of several pieces, one part
    scarlet
And the other London blue. [5] In my own
    tomb
I will inter my name first.
LADY. (Aside.)   I am glad to hear this.—
Why then, my lord, pretend you mar-
    riage to her?
Dissimulation but ties false knots
On that straight line by which you
    hitherto   230
Have measured all your actions.
LOV.   I make answer,
And aptly, with a question. Wherefore
    have you
That, since your husband's death, have
    lived a strict
And chaste nun's life, on the sudden
    given yourself
To visits and entertainments? Think
    you, madam,

[1] Promote.
[2] Rubbish.   [3] I.e., stop.

[4] Precedents.
[5] Cloth symbolical of the servant class.

'Tis not grown public conference? Or
  the favors
Which you too prodigally have thrown
  on Wellborn,
Being too reserved before, incur not
  censure?
LADY. I am innocent here; and, on my
  life, I swear   239
My ends are good.
LOV.   On my soul, so are mine
To Margaret; but leave both to the
  event. [1]
And, since this friendly privacy does serve
But as an offered means unto ourselves
To search each other farther, you having
  shown
Your care of me, I my respect to you,
Deny me not, but still in chaste words,
  madam,
An afternoon's discourse.
LADY.   So I shall hear you. [Exeunt.]

ACTUS QUARTI SCENA SECUNDA.

[Before Tapwell's house.]

Tapwell, Froth.

TAP. Undone, undone! This was your
  counsel, Froth.
FROTH. Mine! I defy thee. Did not Mas-
  ter Marall
(He has marred all, I am sure) strictly
  command us,
On pain of Sir Giles Overreach' dis-
  pleasure,
To turn the gentleman out of doors?
TAP.   'Tis true;
But now he's his uncle's darling, and has
  got
Master Justice Greedy, since he filled
  his belly,
At his commandment, to do anything.
  Woe, woe to us!
FROTH.   He may prove merciful. 9
TAP. Troth, we do not deserve it at his
  hands.
Though he knew all the passages [2] of our
  house,
As the receiving of stolen goods, and
  bawdry,
When he was rogue Wellborn no man
  would believe him,
And then his information could not hurt
  us;

But now he is "right worshipful" again,
Who dares but doubt [3] his testimony?
  Methinks,
I see thee, Froth, already in a cart,
For a close [4] bawd, thine eyes ev'n pelted
  out
With dirt and rotten eggs, and my hand
  hissing   19
If I scape the halter, with the letter R [5]
Printed upon it.
FROTH.   Would that were the worst!
That were but nine days' wonder. As
  for credit,
We have none to lose, but we shall lose
  the money
He owes us, and his custom—there's the
  hell on 't.
TAP. He has summoned all his creditors
  by the drum,
And they swarm about him like so many
  soldiers
On the pay day, and has found out such
  a new way
To pay his old debts as 'tis very likely
He shall be chronicled for it!
FROTH.   He deserves it
More than ten pageants. But are you
  sure his worship   30
Comes this way, to my lady's?
  A cry within: "Brave Master Wellborn!"
TAP.   Yes. I hear him.
FROTH. Be ready with your petition and
  present it
To his good grace.

Enter Wellb[orn] in a rich habit, [Marall,]
  Greed[y], Ord[er], Furn[ace], three Creditors; Tapw[ell], kneeling, delivers his
                              bill of debt.

WELL.   How's this? Petitioned, too?
But note what miracles the payment of
A little trash, and a rich suit of clothes,
Can work upon these rascals! I shall be,
I think, Prince Wellborn.
MAR.   When your worship's married,
You may be—I know what I hope to
  see you.
WELL. Then look thou for advancement.
MAR.   To be known
Your worship's bailiff is the mark I shoot
  at.   40

[1] Outcome.　　　　[2] Occurrences.

[3] Fear.
[4] Secret.　　　　[5] Standing for "Rogue."

WELL. And thou shalt hit it.

MAR.   Pray you, sir, despatch

These needy followers, and for my admittance,[1]

Provided you'll defend me from Sir Giles,

This interim, Tapwell and Froth flattering
                and bribing Justice Greedy.

Whose service I am weary of, I'll say
something

You shall give thanks for.

WELL.   Fear me not [2] Sir Giles.

GREEDY. Who? Tapwell? I remember
thy wife brought me

Last New Year's tide a couple of fat
turkeys.

TAP. And shall do every Christmas, let
your worship

But stand my friend now.

GREEDY.   How? With Master Wellborn?

I can do anything with him on such
terms.—   50

[*To Wellborn.*] See you this honest couple? They are good souls

As ever drew out faucet. Have they
not

A pair of honest faces?

WELL.   I o'erheard you,

And the bribe he promised. You are
cozened in 'em,

For of all the scum that grew rich by my
riots

This, for a most unthankful knave, and
this,

For a base bawd and whore, have worst
deserved me,[3]

And therefore speak not for 'em. By
your place

You are rather to do me justice. Lend me
your ear.—

[*Aside.*] Forget his turkeys, and call in
his license,   60

And at the next fair I'll give you a yoke
of oxen

Worth all his poultry.

GREEDY.   I am changed on the sudden

In my opinion!—Come near; nearer,
rascal.

And, now I view him better, did you e'er
see

One look so like an archknave? His very
countenance,

Should an understanding judge but look
upon him,

Would hang him, though he were innocent.

TAP. ⎫   Worshipful sir!
FROTH. ⎭

GREEDY. No, though the great Turk came,
instead of turkeys,

To beg any favor, I am inexorable.

Thou hast an ill name; besides thy musty
ale,   70

That hath destroyed many of the king's
liege people,

Thou never hadst in thy house, to stay
men's stomachs,

A piece of Suffolk cheese or gammon of
bacon,

Or any esculent, as the learned call it,

For their emolument, but sheer drink
only,

For which gross fault I here do damn thy
license,

Forbidding thee ever to tap or draw;

For instantly I will in mine own person

Command the constable to pull down
thy sign,

And do it before I eat.

FROTH.   No mercy?

GREEDY.   Vanish! 80

If I show any, may my promised oxen
gore me!

TAP. Unthankful knaves are ever so rewarded.

              Exeunt Greedy, Tapwell, Froth.

WELL. Speak, what are you?

1 CRED.   A decayed vintner, sir,

That might have thrived, but that your
worship broke me

With trusting you with muscadine and
eggs,

And five-pound suppers, with your after-
drinkings,

When you lodged upon the Bankside.

WELL.   [I] [4] remember.

1 CRED. I have not been hasty, nor e'er
laid to arrest you;

And therefore, sir—

WELL.   Thou art an honest fellow. 89

I'll set thee up again; see his bill paid.—
What are you?

2 CRED.   A tailor once, but now
mere botcher.[5]

I gave you credit for a suit of clothes,

Which was all my stock, but, you failing
   in payment,
I was removed from the shopboard,[1] and
   confined
Under a stall.[2]

WELL.   See him paid—and botch
   no more.

2 CRED. I ask no interest, sir.

WELL.   Such tailors need not;
If their bills are paid in one-and-twenty
   year,
They are seldom losers.—[To 3 Creditor.]
   O, I know thy face;
Thou wert my surgeon. You must tell
   no tales;
Those days are done. I will pay you in
   private.   100

ORD. A royal gentleman!

FURN.   Royal as an emperor!
He'll prove a brave master; my good
   lady knew
To choose a man.

WELL.   See all men else discharged;
And, since *old debts are cleared by a new
   way,*
A little bounty will not misbecome me.
There's something, honest cook, for thy
   good breakfasts.—
[To Order.] And this, for your respect.
   Take 't; 'tis good gold,
And I able to spare it.

ORD.   You are too munificent.

FURN. He was ever so.

WELL.   Pray you, on before.

3 CRED.   Heaven bless you!

MAR. At four a-clock the rest know where
   to meet me.   110
   Exeunt Ord[er], Furn[ace], Credit[ors].

WELL. Now, Master Marall, what's the
   weighty secret
You promised to impart?

MAR.   Sir, time nor place
Allow me to relate each circumstance.
This only, in a word: I know Sir Giles
Will come upon you for security
For his thousand pounds, which you
   must not consent to.
As he grows in heat, as I am sure he
   will,
Be you but rough, and say he's in your
   debt
Ten times the sum, upon sale of your
   land.

I had a hand in 't (I speak it to my
   shame)   120
When you were defeated [3] of it.

WELL.   That's forgiven.

MAR. I shall deserve 't then. Urge him to
   produce
The deed in which you passed it over to
   him,
Which I know he'll have about him, to
   deliver
To the Lord Lovell with many other
   writings
And present monies. I'll instruct you
   further,
As I wait on your worship. If I play not
   my price [4]
To your full content and your uncle's
   much vexation,
Hang up Jack Marall.

WELL.   I rely upon thee. *Exeunt.*

ACTUS QUARTI SCENA ULTIMA.[5]

[*A room in Overreach's house.*]

Allworth, Margaret.

ALL. Whether to yield the first praise to
   my lord's
Unequaled temperance or your constant
   sweetness
That I yet live, my weak hands fastened
   on
Hope's anchor, spite of all storms of
   despair,
I yet rest doubtful.

MARG.   Give it to Lord Lovell,
For what in him was bounty, in me's
   duty.
I make but payment of a debt to which
My vows, in that high office[6] registered,
Are faithful witnesses.

ALL.   'Tis true, my dearest;
Yet, when I call to mind how many fair
   ones   10
Make willful shipwrack of their faiths,
   and oaths
To God and man, to fill the arms of greatness,
And you rise up [no] [7] less than a glorious
   star,

---

[1] A tailor's workbench.   [2] Bench.
[3] Defrauded.
[4] Prize (in a game); *i.e.*, part.
[5] The last scene of the fourth act.
[6] *I.e.*, heaven.   [7] Added by Dodsley.

To the amazement of the world, that hold
out
Against the stern authority of a father,
And spurn at honor when it comes to
court you,
I am so tender of your good that, faintly,[1]
With your wrong I can wish myself that
right
You yet are pleased to do me.
MARG.   Yet and ever.
To me what's title, when content is want-
ing?   20
Or wealth, raked up together with much
care
And to be kept with more, when the
heart pines
In being dispossessed of what it longs for
Beyond the Indian [2] mines?   Or the
smooth brow
Of a pleased sire, that slaves me to his
will,
And, so his ravenous humor may be
feasted
By my obedience, and he see me great,
Leaves to my soul nor faculties nor power
To make her own election?
ALL.   But the dangers
That follow the repulse—
MARG.   To me they are nothing. 30
Let Allworth love, I cannot be unhappy.
Suppose the worst, that in his rage he
kill me.
A tear or two, by you dropped on my
hearse
In sorrow for my fate, will call back life
So far as but to say that I die yours;
I then shall rest in peace. Or should he
prove
So cruel, as one death would not suffice
His thirst of vengeance, but with ling'ring
torments
In mind and body I must waste to air,
In poverty joined with banishment, so
you share   40
In my afflictions, which I dare not wish
you,
So high I prize you, I could undergo 'em
With such a patience as should look
down
With scorn on his worst malice.
ALL.   Heaven avert
Such trials of your true affection to me!
Nor will it unto you, that are all mercy,

Show so much rigor. But, since we must
run
Such desperate hazards, let us do our best
To steer between 'em.
MARG.   Your lord's ours, and sure;
And, though but a young actor, second
me   50
In doing to the life what he has plotted,

Enter Overreach [behind].

The end may yet prove happy. Now, my
Allworth—   [*Sees her father.*]
ALL. [*Aside.*] To your letter, and put on a
seeming anger.
MARG. I'll pay my lord all debts due to his
title;
And when, with terms not taking from
his honor,
He does solicit me, I shall gladly hear
him.
But in this peremptory, nay, command-
ing way,
To appoint a meeting and, without my
knowledge,
A priest to tie the knot can ne'er be
undone
Till death unloose it, is a confidence [3] 60
In his lordship will deceive him.
ALL.   I hope better,
Good lady.
MARG.   Hope, sir, what you please.
For me
I must take a safe and secure course; I
have
A father, and without his full consent,
Though all lords of the land kneeled for
my favor,
I can grant nothing.
OVER. [*Coming forward.*]   I like this obe-
dience.—
But whatsoever my lord writes must and
shall be
Accepted and embraced. Sweet Master
Allworth,
You show yourself a true and faithful
servant
To your good lord; he has a jewel of
you.   70
How? Frowning, Meg? Are these looks
to receive
A messenger from my lord? What's this?
Give me it.

MARG. A piece of arrogant paper, like th'
inscriptions. *Overreach read[s] the letter.*
OVER. "Fair mistress, from your servant
learn, all joys
That we can hope for, if deferred, prove
toys;
Therefore this instant, and in private,
meet
A husband, that will gladly at your
feet
Lay down his honors, tend'ring them to
you
With all content, the church being paid
her due."—   79
Is this the arrogant piece of paper? Fool,
Will you still be one? In the name of
madness what
Could his good honor write more to
content you?
Is there aught else to be wished, after
these two,
That are already offered: marriage first,
And lawful pleasure after? What would
you more?
MARG. Why, sir, I would be married like
your daughter,
Not hurried away i' th' night I know not
whither,
Without all ceremony—no friends invited
To honor the solemnity.
ALL.   An 't please your honor,
For so before tomorrow I must style
you,   90
My lord desire[s] this privacy, in respect
His honorable kinsmen are far off,
And his desires to have it done brook
not
So long delay as to expect[1] their com-
ing;
And yet he stands resolved, with all due
pomp,
As running at the ring, plays, masques,
and tilting,
To have his marriage at court celebrated,
When he has brought your honor up to
London.
OVER. He tells you true; 'tis the fashion,
on my knowledge.
Yet the good lord, to please your peevish-
ness,   100
Must put it off, forsooth, and lose a night,
In which perhaps he might get two boys
on thee.

[1] Wait for,

Tempt me no farther; if you do, this
goad[2]   [*Points to his sword.*]
Shall prick you to him.
MARG.   I could be contented,
Were you but by to do a father's part
And give me in the church.
OVER.   So my lord have you,
What do I care who gives you? Since
my lord
Does purpose to be private, I'll not cross
him.
I know not, Master Allworth, how my
lord
May be provided, and therefore there's a
purse   110
Of gold—'twill serve this night's expense;
tomorrow
I'll furnish him with any sums. In the
meantime,
Use my ring to my chaplain; he is
beneficed
At my manor of Gotam,[3] and called
Parson Willdo.
'Tis no matter for a license; I'll bear him
out in 't.
MARG. With your favor, sir, what warrant
is your ring?
He may suppose I got that twenty ways,
Without your knowledge; and then to be
refused
Were such a stain upon me! If you
pleased, sir,
Your presence would do better.
OVER.   Still perverse? 120
I say again, I will not cross my lord;
Yet I'll prevent you too.—Paper and
ink there!
ALL. I can furnish you.
OVER.   I thank you; I can write then.
                              Writes on his book.
ALL. You may, if you please, put out the
name of my lord,
In respect he comes disguised, and only
write,
"Marry her to this gentleman."
OVER.   Well advised.—(*Margaret kneels.*)
'Tis done; away!—My blessing, girl?
Thou hast it.
Nay, no reply; begone.—Good Master
Allworth,
This shall be the best night's work you
ever made.

[2] Emended by Gifford. Original reads *good.*
[3] Gotham.

ALL. I hope so, sir.　　　　　130

Exeunt Allworth and Margaret.

OVER. Farewell!—Now all's cocksure.
Methinks I hear already knights and
　ladies
Say, "Sir Giles Overreach, how is it with
Your honorable daughter?　Has her
　honor
Slept well tonight?" or, "Will her honor
　please
To accept this monkey?　Dog?　Or
　paraquit?" [1]
(This is state in ladies) "Or my eldest son
To be her page, and wait upon her
　trencher?"
My ends, my ends are compassed! Then
　for Wellborn
And the lands. Were he once married to
　the widow,　　　　　140
I have him here. I can scarce contain
　myself,
I am so full of joy, nay, joy all over. *Exit.*

THE END OF THE FOURTH ACT

ACTUS QUINTI SCENA PRIMA. [2]

[*A room in Lady Allworth's house.*]

Lovell, Lady [Allworth], Amble.

LADY. By this you know how strong the
　motives were
That did, my lord, induce me to dispense
A little with my gravity to advance,
In personating some few favors to him,
The plots and projects of the downtrod
　Wellborn.
Nor shall I e'er repent, although I suffer
In some few men's opinions for 't, the
　action,
For he that ventured all for my dear
　husband
Might justly claim an obligation from
　me
To pay him such a courtesy, which
　had I　　　　　10
Coyly or overcuriously [3] denied,
It might have argued me of little love
To the deceased.
LOV.　　　　What you intended, madam,
For the poor gentleman hath found good
　success,
For, as I understand, his debts are paid,

And he once more furnished for fair em-
　ployment.
But all the arts that I have used to raise
The fortunes of your joy and mine, young
　Allworth,
Stand yet in supposition, though I hope
　well,
For the young lovers are in wit more
　pregnant　　　　　20
Than their years can promise; and for
　their desires,
On my knowledge, they are equal.
LADY.　　　　　　—As my wishes
Are with yours, my lord. Yet give me
　leave to fear
The building, though well grounded. To
　deceive
Sir Giles, that's both a lion and a fox
In his proceedings, were a work beyond
The strongest undertakers—not the trial
Of two weak innocents.
LOV.　　　　　Despair not, madam.
*Hard things are compassed oft by easy
　means;*
And judgment, being a gift derived from
　heaven,　　　　　30
Though sometimes lodged i' th' hearts of
　worldly men,
That ne'er consider from whom they re-
　ceive it,
Forsakes such as abuse the giver of it—
Which is the reason that the politic
And cunning statesman, that believes he
　fathoms
The counsels of all kingdoms on the
　earth,
Is by simplicity oft overreach[ed]. [4]
LADY. May he be so! Yet in his name to
　express it
Is a good omen.
LOV.　　　　May it to myself　　　39
Prove so, good lady, in my suit to you!
What think you of the motion? [5]
LADY.　　　　　　　Troth, my lord,
My own unworthiness may answer for
　me,
For had you, when that I was in my
　prime
(My virgin flower uncropped), presented
　me
With this great favor, looking on my
　lowness
Not in a glass of self-love, but of truth.

[1] Parakeet.
[2] Original reads *Quinta.*　　　[3] Overcarefully.
[4] Added by Coxeter.　　　　　[5] Proposal.

I could not but have thought it as a
  blessing
Far, far beyond my merit.
Lov.   You are too modest,
And undervalue that which is above
My title, or whatever I call mine.   50
I grant, were I a Spaniard, to marry
A widow might disparage me; but, being
A true-born Englishman, I cannot find
How it can taint my honor. Nay, what's
  more,
That which you think a blemish is to me
The fairest luster. You already, madam,
Have given sure proofs how dearly you
  can cherish
A husband that deserves you, which con-
  firms me
That, if I am not wanting in my care
To do you service, you'll be still the
  same   60
That you were to your Allworth. In a
  word,
Our years, our states, our births are not
  unequal,
You being descended nobly, and allied
  so;
If then you may be won to make me
  happy,
But join your lips to mine, and that shall
  be
A solemn contract.
Lady.   I were blind to my own good
Should I refuse it. [*Kisses him.*] Yet, my
  lord, receive me
As such a one, the study of whose whole
  life
Shall know no other object but to please
  you.
Lov. If I return not with all tender-
  ness   70
Equal respect to you, may I die wretched!
Lady. There needs no protestation, my
  lord,
To her that cannot doubt.—

Enter Wellborn [handsomely appareled].[1]

                    You are welcome, sir.
Now you look like yourself.
Well.   And will continue
Such in my free acknowledgment that I
  am

---

[1] In the original the stage direction follows
Lady Allworth's speech.

Your creature, madam, and will never
  hold
My life mine own, when you please to
  command it.
Lov. It is a thankfulness that well be-
  comes you.
You could not make choice of a better
  shape
To dress your mind in.
Lady.   For me, I am happy   80
That my endeavors prospered. Saw you
  of late
Sir Giles, your uncle?
Well.   I heard of him, madam,
By his minister, Marall; he's grown into
  strange passions
About his daughter. This last night he
  looked for
Your lordship at his house, but, missing
  you,
And she not yet appearing, his wisehead[2]
Is much perplexed and troubled.
Lov.   It may be,
Sweetheart, my project took.

*Enter Over[reach], with distracted looks, driv-
ing in Marall before him [with a box].*

Lady.   I strongly hope.
Over. Ha! Find her, booby, thou huge
  lump of nothing;
I'll bore thine eyes out else.
Well. [*Aside.*]   May it please
  your lordship,   90
For some ends of mine own but to with-
  draw
A little out of sight, though not of hearing,
You may perhaps have sport.
Lov.   You shall direct me. *Steps aside.*
Over. I shall *sol fa*[3] you, rogue!
Mar.   Sir, for what cause
Do you use me thus?
Over.   Cause, slave? Why, I am angry,
And thou a subject only fit for beating,
And so to cool my choler. Look to the
  writing;
Let but the seal be broke upon the box
That has slept in my cabinet these three
  years,
I'll rack thy soul for 't.
Mar. (*Aside.*)   I may yet cry quit-
  tance,   100
Though now I suffer, and dare not resist.

---

[2] *I.e.*, his "wisehood," "wisdomship."
[3] Play a tune on, beat.

Over. Lady, by your leave, did you see my daughter, lady?

And the lord her husband? Are they in your house?

If they are, discover, that I may bid 'em joy;

And, as an entrance to her place of honor,

See your ladyship on her left hand, and make curtseys

When she nods on you, which you must receive

As a special favor.

Lady.　　　　　When I know, Sir Giles,

Her state requires such ceremony, I shall pay it;　　　　　109

But in the meantime, as I am myself,

I give you to understand I neither know

Nor care where her honor is.

Over.　　　　　When you once see her

Supported and led by the lord her husband,

You'll be taught better.—Nephew!

Well.　　　　　Sir.

Over.　　　　　No more?

Well. 'Tis all I owe you.

Over.　　　　　Have your redeemed rags

Made you thus insolent?

Well. (*In scorn.*)　　　　　Insolent to you?

Why, what are you, sir, unless in your years,

At the best, more than myself?

Over. [*Aside.*]　　　　　His fortune swells him.

'Tis rank [1] he's married.

Lady.　　　　　This is excellent!

Over. Sir, in calm language, though I seldom use it,　　　　　120

I am familiar with the cause that makes you

Bear up thus bravely. There's a certain buzz

Of a stol'n marriage—do you hear?—of a stol'n marriage,

In which, 'tis said, there's somebody hath been cozened.

I name no parties.

Well.　　　　　Well, sir, and what follows?

Over. Marry, this, since you are peremptory: remember,

Upon mere hope of your great match, I lent you

A thousand pounds. Put me in good security,

And suddenly, by [2] mortgage or by statute,

Of some of your new possessions, or I'll have you　　　　　130

Dragged in your lavender [3] robes to the jail. You know me,

And therefore do not trifle.

Well.　　　　　Can you be

So cruel to your nephew, now he's in

The way to rise? Was this the courtesy

You did me "in pure love, and no ends else"?

Over. End me no ends! Engage the whole estate,

And force your spouse to sign it, you shall have

Three or four thousand more, to roar and swagger

And revel in bawdy taverns.

Well.　　　　　And beg after—　139

Mean you not so?

Over.　　　　　My thoughts are mine, and free.

Shall I have security?

Well.　　　　　No, indeed, you shall not,

Nor bond, nor bill, nor bare acknowledgment;

Your great looks fright not me.

Over.　　　　　But my deeds shall.

Outbraved?

　　　　　They both draw. The Servants enter.

Lady.　　　　　Help, murther! Murther!

Well.　　　　　Let him come on,

With all his wrongs and injuries about him,

Armed with his cutthroat practices to guard him;

The right that I bring with me will defend me,

And punish his extortion.

Over.　　　　　That I had thee

But single in the field!

Lady.　　　　　You may; but make not

My house your quarreling scene.

Over.　　　　　Were 't in a church, 150

By heaven and hell, I'll do 't!

Mar. [*Aside to Wellborn.*]　　　　　Now put him to

The showing of the deed.

Well.　　　　　This rage is vain, sir.

For fighting, fear not, you shall have your hands full

Upon the least incitement; and whereas

[1] Gross, plain.

[2] Emended by Coxeter. Original reads *my*.

[3] *I.e.,* pawned.

You charge me with a debt of a thousand
　pounds,
If there be law (howe'er you have no
　conscience),
Either restore my land or I'll recover
A debt that's truly due to me from you,
In value ten times more than what you
　challenge.[1]

OVER. I in thy debt! O impudence! Did
　I not purchase　　　　　　　　160
　The land left by thy father, that rich
　　land
　That had continuéd in Wellborn's name
　Twenty descents, which, like a riotous
　　fool,
　Thou didst make sale of? Is not here
　　inclosed
　The deed that does confirm it mine?

MAR. [Aside.]　　　　　　　　Now, now!

WELL. I do acknowledge none; I ne'er
　passed o'er
　Any such land. I grant for a year or two
　You had it in trust, which if you do
　　discharge,
　Surrend'ring the possession, you shall
　　ease
　Yourself and me of chargeable suits in
　　law,　　　　　　　　　　　170
　Which, if you prove not honest, as I
　　doubt it,
　Must of necessity follow.

LADY.　　　　　　　In my judgment
　He does advise you well.

OVER.　　　　　Good! Good! Conspire
　With your new husband, lady; second
　　him
　In his dishonest practices; but, when
　This manor is extended [2] to my use,
　You'll speak in an humbler key, and sue
　　for favor.

LADY. Never; do not hope it.

WELL.　　　　　Let despair first seize me.

OVER. Yet, to shut up thy mouth, and
　make thee give
　Thyself the lie, the loud lie, I draw
　　out　　　　　　　　　　　180
　The precious evidence; if thou canst for-
　　swear
　Thy hand and seal, and make a forfeit of
　Opens the box [and shows the document].
　Thy ears to the pillory—see, here's that
　will make
　My interest clear.—Ha!

LADY.　　　　A fair skin of parchment.

WELL. Indented, I confess, and labels
　too;
　But neither wax nor words. How! Thun-
　　derstrook? [3]
　Not a syllable to insult with? My wise
　　uncle,
　Is this your precious evidence? Is this
　　that makes
　Your interest clear?

OVER.　　　I am o'erwhelmed with wonder!
　What prodigy is this? What subtle
　　devil　　　　　　　　　　190
　Hath razed out the inscription, the wax
　Turned into dust? The rest of my deeds
　　whole
　As when they were delivered, and this
　　only
　Made nothing! Do you deal with
　　witches, rascal?
　There is a statute for you, which will
　　bring
　Your neck in a hempen circle; yes, there
　　is.
　And now 'tis better thought, for, cheater,
　　know
　This juggling shall not save you.

WELL.　　　　　　　To save thee
　Would beggar the stock of mercy.

OVER.　　　　　　　　Marall!

MAR.　　　　　　　　　　Sir.

OVER. (Flattering him.) Though the wit-
　nesses are dead, your testimony—　200
　Help with an oath or two; and for thy
　　master,
　Thy liberal master, my good honest
　　servant,
　I know you will swear anything to dash
　This cunning sleight. Besides, I know
　　thou art
　A public notary, and such stand in law
　For a dozen witnesses. The deed, being
　　drawn too
　By thee, my careful Marall, and deliv-
　　ered
　When thou wert present, will make good
　　my title.
　Wilt thou not swear this?

MAR.　　　　　I? No, I assure you.
　I have a conscience not seared up like
　　yours;　　　　　　　　　210
　I know no deeds.

OVER.　　　　　Wilt thou betray me?

---

[1] Claim.　　　　　　[2] Seized for debt.

[3] Thunderstruck.

MAR.   Keep him
From using of his hands, I'll use my
  tongue
To his no little torment.
OVER.   Mine own varlet
Rebel against me?
MAR.   Yes, and uncase [1] you too.
The "idiot," the "patch," the "slave,"
  the "booby,"
The property fit only to be beaten
For your morning exercise, your "foot-
  ball," or
"Th' unprofitable lump of flesh," your
  "drudge,"
Can now anatomize [2] you, and lay open
All your black plots, and level with the
  earth   220
Your hill of pride, and, with these
  gabions [3] guarded,
Unload my great artillery and shake,
Nay, pulverize the walls you think de-
  fend you.
LADY. How he foams at the mouth with
  rage!
WELL.   To him again.
OVER. O, that I had thee in my gripe; I
  would tear thee
Joint after joint!
MAR.   I know you are a tearer,
But I'll have first your fangs pared off,
  and then
Come nearer to you, when I have dis-
  covered,[4]
And made it good before the judge, what
  ways   229
And devilish practices you used to cozen
With an army of whole families, who yet
  live,
And, but [5] enrolled for soldiers, were able
To take in [6] Dunkirk.
WELL.   All will come out.
LADY.   The better.
OVER. But that I will live, rogue, to torture
  thee,
And make thee wish, and kneel in vain,
  to die,
These swords that keep thee from me
  should fix here,
Although they made my body but one
  wound,

But I would reach thee.
LOV. (*Aside.*)   Heaven's hand is in this;
One bandog [7] worry the other!
OVER.   I play the fool,
And make my anger but ridiculous; 240
There will be a time and place, there will
  be, cowards,
When you shall feel what I dare do.
WELL.   I think so.
You dare do any ill, yet want true valor
To be honest and repent.
OVER.   They are words I know not,
Nor e'er will learn. Patience, the beg-
  gar's virtue,

Enter Greedy and Parson Willdo.

Shall find no harbor here.—After these
  storms
At length a calm appears. Welcome,
  most welcome!
There's comfort in thy looks. Is the deed
  done?
Is my daughter married? Say but so, my
  chaplain,   249
And I am tame.
WILLDO.   Married? Yes, I assure you.
OVER. Then vanish, all sad thoughts!
  There's more gold for thee.
My doubts and fears are in the titles
  drowned
Of my "right honorable," my "right
  honorable" daughter.
GREEDY. Here will I be feasting! At least
  for a month
I am provided. Empty guts, croak no
  more.
You shall be stuffed like bagpipes, not
  with wind,
But bearing [8] dishes.
OVER.   Instantly be here?
                    Whisp'ring to Willdo.
To my wish! To my wish! Now you that
  plot against me,
And hoped to trip my heels up, that
  contemned me,   *Loud music.*
Think on 't and tremble.—They come!
  I hear the music.   260
A lane there for my lord!
WELL.   This sudden heat
May yet be cooled, sir.
OVER.   Make way there for my lord!

---

[1] Flay.   [2] Dissect.
[3] Cylinders filled with earth and used for
fortification.   [5] If only.
[4] Revealed.   [6] Capture.
[7] A ferocious dog kept chained.
[8] Substantial.

Enter Allworth and Margaret.

MARG. Sir, first your pardon, then your
     blessing, with
     Your full allowance of the choice I have
     made,
     As ever you could make use of your
     reason.   *Kneeling.*
     Grow not in passion, since you may as
     well
     Call back the day that's past, as untie
     the knot
     Which is too strongly fastened. Not to
     dwell
     Too long on words, this's my husband.
OVER.   How!
ALL. So I assure you; all the rites of mar-
     riage,   270
     With every circumstance, are past. Alas,
     sir,
     Although I am no lord, but a lord's
     page,
     Your daughter and my loved wife mourns
     not for it;
     And, for "right honorable" son-in-law,
     you may say,
     Your "dutiful" daughter.
OVER.   Devil! Are they married?
WILLDO. Do a father's part, and say,
     "Heaven give 'em joy!"
OVER. Confusion and ruin! Speak, and
     speak quickly,
     Or thou art dead.
WILLDO.   They are married.
OVER.   Thou hadst better
     Have made a contract with the king of
     fiends
     Than these. My brain turns!
WILLDO.   Why this rage to me? 280
     Is not this your letter, sir, and these the
     words?
     "Marry her to this gentleman."
OVER.   It cannot—
     Nor will I e'er believe it—'sdeath, I will
     not!—
     That I, that in all passages I touched
     At worldly profit have not left a print
     Where I have trod for the most curious
     search
     To trace my footsteps, should be gulled
     by children,
     Baffled and fooled, and all my hopes and
     labors
     Defeated and made void.

WELL.   As it appears,
     You are so, my grave uncle.
OVER.   Village nurses 290
     Revenge their wrongs with curses; I'll
     not waste
     A syllable, but thus I take the life
     Which, wretched, I gave to thee.
                 Offers to kill Margaret.
LOV. [*Rushing forward.*]   Hold, for
     your own sake!
     Though charity to your daughter hath
     quite left you,
     Will you do an act, though in your hopes
     lost here,
     Can leave no hope for peace or rest here-
     after?
     Consider; at the best you are but a man,
     And cannot so create your aims but that
     They may be crossed.
OVER.   Lord, thus I spit at thee 299
     And at thy counsel, and again desire thee,
     And as thou art a soldier, if thy valor
     Dares show itself where multitude and
     example
     Lead not the way, let's quit the house,
     and change
     Six words in private.
LOV.   I am ready.
LADY.   Stay, sir.
     Contest with one distracted?
WELL.   You'll grow like him,
     Should you answer his vain challenge.
OVER.   Are you pale? [1]
     Borrow his help; though Hercules call it
     odds,
     I'll stand against both, as I am hemmed
     in thus.
     Since, like Libyan lion in the toil,
     My fury cannot reach the coward hun-
     ters,   310
     And only spends itself, I'll quit the place.
     Alone I can do nothing; but I have
     servants
     And friends to second me; and, if I make
     not
     This house a heap of ashes (by my
     wrongs,
     What I have spoke I will make good!)
     or leave [2]
     One throat uncut—if it be possible,
     Hell add to my afflictions!
                     Exit Overreach.

[1] Afraid.
[2] Emended by Gifford. Original reads *leav'd.*

MAR.   Is 't not brave sport?

GREEDY. Brave sport? I am sure it has
ta'en away my stomach;
I do not like the sauce.

ALL.   Nay, weep not, dearest,
Though it express your pity; what's
decreed   320
Above, we cannot alter.

LADY.   His threats move me
No scruple, madam.

MAR.   Was it not a rare trick,
And it please your worship, to make the
deed nothing?
I can do twenty neater, if you please
To purchase and grow rich, for I will be
Such a solicitor and steward for you
As never worshipful had.

WELL.   I do believe thee.
But first discover the quaint [1] means you
used
To raze out the conveyance?

MAR.   They are mysteries
Not to be spoke in public: certain min-
erals   330
Incorporated in the ink and wax.
Besides, he gave me nothing, but still
fed me
With hopes and blows; and that was the
inducement
To this conumbrum.[2] If it please your
worship
To call to memory, this mad beast once
caused me
To urge you or to drown or hang your-
self;
I'll do the like to him, if you command
me.

WELL. You are a rascal! He that dares be
false
To a master, though unjust, will ne'er be
true   339
To any other. Look not for reward
Or favor from me; I will shun thy sight
As I would do a basilisk's. Thank my
pity
If thou keep thy ears; howe'er, I will take
order
Your practice shall be silenced.

GREEDY.   I'll commit him,
If you'll have me, sir.

WELL.   That were to little purpose;
His conscience be his prison. Not a word,
But instantly begone!

[1] Ingenious.   [2] Conundrum.

ORD.   Take this kick with you.

AMB. And this.

FURN.   If that I had my cleaver here,
I would divide your knave's head.

MAR.   This is the haven   349
False servants still arrive at.

Exit Mar[all].

Enter Over[reach].

LADY.   Come again!

LOV. Fear not, I am your guard.

WELL.   His looks are ghastly.

WILLDO. Some little time I have spent,
under your favors,
In physical [3] studies, and, if my judgment err not,
He's mad beyond recovery. But observe
him,
And look to yourselves.

OVER.   Why, is not the whole world
Included in myself? To what use then
Are friends and servants? Say there were
a squadron
Of pikes, lined through with shot, [4] when
I am mounted
Upon my injuries, shall I fear to charge
'em?
No; I'll through the battalia, and, that
routed,   360

Flourishing his sword sheathed.[5]

I'll fall to execution. Ha! I am feeble;
Some undone widow sits upon mine arm,
And takes away the use of 't; and my
sword,
Glued to my scabbard with wronged
orphans' tears,
Will not be drawn. Ha! What are these?
Sure, hangmen
That come to bind my hands, and then
to drag me
Before the judgment seat. Now they are
new shapes,
And do appear like Furies, with steel
whips
To scourge my ulcerous soul. Shall I
then fall
Ingloriously, and yield? No; spite of
Fate,   370
I will be forced to hell like to myself.

[3] Medical.
[4] Interspersed with musketeers.
[5] Emended by Gifford. Original reads *unsheathed.*

Though you were legions of accursèd
  spirits,
Thus would I fly among you.
                [*Runs forward and falls.*]
WELL.[1]   There's no help;
Disarm him first, then bind him.
GREEDY.   Take a *mittimus*,[2]
And carry him to Bedlam.
LOV.   How he foams!
WELL. And bites the earth!
WILLDO.   Carry him to some dark room;
  There try what art can do for his recov-
  ery.
MARG. O my dear father!
                They force Overreach off.
ALL.   You must be patient, mistress.
LOV. Here is a president to teach wicked
  men
  That when they leave religion, and turn
    atheists,   380
  Their own abilities leave 'em. Pray you,
    take comfort;
  I will endeavor you shall be his guardians
  In his distractions. And for your land,
    Master Wellborn,
  Be it good or ill in law, I'll be an umpire
  Between you and this, th' undoubted
    heir
  Of Sir Giles Overreach. For me, here's
    the anchor
  That I must fix on.
ALL.   What you shall determine,
  My lord, I will allow of.[3]

[1] This speech head is placed before the preceding line in the original.
[2] A writ of committal.
[3] Agree to.

WELL.   'Tis the language
  That I speak too; but there is something
    else
  Beside the repossession of my land   390
  And payment of my debts, that I must
    practice.
  I had a reputation, but 'twas lost
  In my loose course, and, till I redeem it
  Some noble way, I am but half made up.
  It is a time of action; if your lordship
  Will please to confer a company upon me
  In your command, I doubt not in my
    service
  To my king and country but I shall do
    something
  That may make me right again.
LOV.   Your suit is granted
  And you loved for the motion.
WELL. [*To the audience.*]   Nothing
  wants then   400
  But your allowance—

THE EPILOGUE

But your allowance, and in that our all
Is comprehended, it being known nor we
Nor he that wrote the comedy can be
  free
Without your manumission, which if you
Grant willingly, as a fair favor due
To the poet's and our labors (as you may,
For we despair not, gentlemen, of the
  play),
We jointly shall profess your grace hath
  might   409
To teach us action, and him how to write.
                [*Exeunt.*]

FINIS.

THE MAID OF HONOR [1]

BY

PHILIP MASSINGER

THE ACTORS' NAMES

ROBERTO, *King of Sicily.*
FERDINAND, *Duke of Urbin.*
BERTOLDO, *the king's natural brother, a Knight of Malta.*
GONZAGA, *a Knight of Malta, general to the Duchess of Siena.*
ASTUTIO, *a counselor of state.*
FULGENTIO, *the minion of Roberto.*
ADORNI, *a follower of Camiola's father.*
AMBASSADOR *from the Duke of Urbin.*
SIGNIOR SYLLI, *a foolish self-lover.*
ANTHONIO } *two rich heirs, city bred.*
GASPARO }
PIERIO, *a colonel to Gonzaga.*
RODERIGO } *captains to Gonzaga.*
JACOMO }

DRUSO } *captains to Duke Ferdinand.*
LIVIO }
PAULO, *a priest, Camiola's confessor.*
[BISHOP.]
[PAGE.]
SCOUT.
SOLDIERS.
SERVANTS.
JAILOR.
DWARF.
MUTES.

AURELIA, *Duchess of Siena.*
CAMIOLA, *the Maid of Honor.*
CLARINDA, *her woman.* [2]

[SCENE: *Sicily and the Sienese.*

TIME: *Fourteenth century.*]

ACT I. SCENE i.

[*The council chamber in the palace at Palermo.*]

Astutio, Adorni.

ADOR. Good day to your lordship.
AST.   Thanks, Adorni.
ADOR. May I presume to ask if the ambassador
  Employed by Ferdinand, the Duke of Urbin,
  Hath audience this morning?

Enter Fulgent[io].

AST.   'Tis uncertain;
  For, though a counselor of state, I am not
  Of the cabinet council. But there's one,
    if he please,
  That may resolve [3] you.
ADOR.   I will move [4] him.—Sir! [5]
FUL. If you have a suit, show water; [6] I am
    blind else.
ADOR. A suit, yet of a nature not to prove
  The quarry [7] that you hawk for. If your
    words   10

[3] Satisfy, inform.   [4] Appeal to.
[5] As frequently the original reads *Sr.*, a form which may sometimes be an abbreviation for *Signior.*
[6] Give me an eye wash (*i.e.*, a bribe) to clear my sight.
[7] "A hunting phrase, meaning to try out a special prey on the hawk which is being trained to capture that particular kind of game"(Bryne).

Are not like Indian wares, and every
　　scruple
To be weighed and rated, one poor syl-
　　lable
Vouchsafed in answer of a fair demand
Cannot deserve a fee.
FUL. 　　　　　　It seems you are ignorant.
I neither speak nor hold my peace for
　　nothing—
And yet for once I care not if I answer
One single question gratis.
ADOR. 　　　　　　I much thank you.
Hath the ambassador audience, sir, to-
　　day?
FUL. Yes.
ADOR. 　　　At what hour?
FUL. 　　　　　　I promised not so much.
A syllable you begged; my charity gave
　　it. 　　　　　　　　　　　　　20
Move me no further. 　　*Exit Fulgentio.*
AST. 　　　　　　This you wonder at?
With me, 'tis usual.
ADOR. 　　　　Pray you, sir, what is he?
AST. A gentleman, yet no lord. He hath
　　some drops
Of the king's blood running in his veins,
　　derived
Some ten degrees off. His revenue lies
In a narrow compass, the king's ear, and
　　yields him
Every hour a fruitful harvest. Men may
　　talk
Of three crops in a year in the Fortunate
　　Islands,
Or profit made by wool; but, while there
　　are suitors,
His sheep shearing, nay, shaving to the
　　quick, 　　　　　　　　　　30
Is in every quarter of the moon, and
　　constant.
In the time of trussing a point,[1] he can
　　undo
Or make a man. His play or recrea-
　　tion
Is to raise this up, or pull down that, and,
　　though
He never yet took orders, makes more
　　bishops
In Sicily than the pope himself.

*Enter Bertoldo, Gasparo, Anthonio, a
　　　　　　　　　　Servant.*

ADOR. 　　　　　　　　Most strange!

[1] Tying the laces of the hose.

AST. The presence fills. He in the Malta
　　habit
Is the natural brother of the king—a by-
　　blow.[2]
ADOR. I understand you.
GASP. 　　　　　　Morrow to my uncle.
ANT. And my late guardian.—But at
　　length I have 　　　　　　　40
The reins in my own hands.
AST. 　　　　　　Pray you, use 'em well,
Or you'll too late repent it.
BERT. 　　　　　　With this jewel,
Presented to Camiola, prepare
This night a visit for me.—(*Exit Servant.*)
I shall have
Your company, gallants, I perceive, if
　　that
The king will hear of war.
ANT. 　　　　　　Sir, I have horses
Of the best breed in Naples, fitter far
To break a rank than crack a lance,[3] and
　　are
In their career of such incredible swift-
　　ness
They outstrip swallows.
BERT. 　　　And such may be useful 50
To run away with, should we be defeated.
You are well provided, signior.
ANT. 　　　　　　Sir, excuse me.
All of their race by instinct know a
　　coward
And scorn the burthen. They come on
　　like lightning,
Foundered in a retreat.
BERT. 　　　　　By no means back 'em,
Unless you know your courage sym-
　　pathize
With the daring of your horse.
ANT. 　　　　My lord, this is bitter.
GASP. I will raise me a company of foot,
And, when at push of pike I am to enter
A breach, to show my valor I have
　　bought me 　　　　　　　60
An armor cannon-proof.
BERT. 　　　You will not leap then
O'er an outwork in your shirt?
GASP. 　　　　　　I do not like
Activity that way.
BERT. 　　　　You had rather stand
A mark to try their muskets on?
GASP. 　　　　　　If I do
No good, I'll do no hurt.
BERT. 　　　　'Tis in you, signior,

[2] Illegitimate child. [3] *I.e.*, in a tournament.

A Christian resolution, and becomes you!
But I will not discourage you.
ANT.   You are, sir,
A Knight of Malta, and, as I have heard,
Have served against the Turk.
BERT.   'Tis true.
ANT.   Pray you, show us
The difference between the city valor   70
And service in the field.
BERT.   'Tis somewhat more
Than roaring [1] in a tavern or a brothel,
Or to steal a constable from a sleeping
  watch,
Then burn their halberds, or, safe
  guarded by
Your tenants' sons, to carry away a
  Maypole
From a neighbor village. You will not
  find there
Your masters of dependencies [2] to take up
A drunken brawl or to get you the names
Of valiant chevaliers, fellows that will be,
For a cloak with thrice-dyed velvet, and
  a cast [3] suit,   80
Kicked down the stairs. A knave with
  half a britch [4] there
And no shirt (being a thing superfluous
And worn out of his memory), if you bear
  not
Yourselves both in and upright, [5] with a
  provant [6] sword
Will slash your scarlets and your plush a
  new way,
Or, with the hilts, thunder about your
  ears
Such music as will make your worships
  dance
To the doleful tune of "Lachryma." [7]
GASP.   I must tell you
In private, as you are my princely friend,
I do not like such fiddlers.
BERT.   No? They are useful   90
For your imitation. I remember you
When you came first to the court and
  talked of nothing

---

[1] Roistering.
[2] Bravoes who managed duels between inexperienced contestants.
[3] Cast-off.
[4] Breech, a pair of breeches.
[5] I.e., erectly, like a soldier.
[6] Provided by the quartermaster; i.e., of
inferior quality.
[7] Generally "Lachrymæ," a popular song by
Dowland.

But your rents and your entradas, [8] ever
  chiming
The golden bells in your pockets; you be-
  lieved
The taking of the wall [9] as a tribute due
  to
Your gaudy clothes, and could not walk
  at midnight
Without a causeless quarrel, as if men
Of coarser outsides were in duty bound
To suffer your affronts; but, when you
  had been
Cudgeled well twice or thrice, and from
  the doctrine [10]   100
Made profitable uses, you concluded
The sovereign means to teach irregular [11]
  heirs
Civility, with conformity of manners,
Were two or three sound beatings.
ANT.   I confess
They did much good upon me.
GASP.   And on me [12] —
The principles that they read were sound.
BERT.   You'll find
The like instructions in the camp.
AST.   The king!

A flourish. Enter Roberto, Fulgentio, Am-
                      bassador, Attendants.

ROB. [*Ascending the throne.*] We sit pre-
  pared to hear.
AMB.   Your majesty
Hath been long since familiar, I doubt
  not,
With the desperate fortunes of my lord;
  and pity   110
Of the much that your confederate hath
  suffered,
You being his last refuge, may persuade
  you
Not alone to compassionate, but to lend
Your royal aids to stay him in his fall
To certain ruin. He too late is conscious
That his ambition to encroach upon
His neighbor's territories with the danger
  of
His liberty, nay, his life, hath brought in
  question

---

[8] Income.
[9] In passing a person, walking nearest the wall,
where the street was cleanest.
[10] Lesson.   [11] Unruly.
[12] Here and in a few other passages the line
division has been regularized.

His own inheritance; but youth and heat
Of blood, in your interpretation, may
Both plead and mediate for him. I must
　grant it　　　　　　　　　　　　121
An error in him, being denied the favors
Of the fair Princess of Siena (though
He sought her in a noble way) t' endeavor
To force affection by surprisal of
Her principal seat, Siena.

Rob.　　　　　　　　Which now proves
　The seat of his captivity, not triumph.
Heaven is still just.

Amb.　　　　　　　And yet that justice is
　To be with mercy tempered, which
　　heaven's deputies
Stand bound to minister. The injured
　duchess,　　　　　　　　　　　130
By reason taught, as nature, could not,
　with
The reparation of her wrongs, but aim at
A brave revenge; and my lord feels too
　late
That innocence will find friends. The
　great Gonzaga,
The honor of his Order (I must praise
Virtue, though in an enemy), he whose
　fights
And conquests hold one number, rallying
　up
Her scattered troops, before we could get
　time
To victual or to man the conquered city,
Sat down before it, and, presuming
　that　　　　　　　　　　　　140
'Tis not to be relieved, admits no parley,
Our flags of truce hung out in vain; nor
　will he
Lend an ear to composition,[1] but exacts,
With the rendering up the town, the
　goods and lives
Of all within the walls and of all sexes
To be at his discretion.

Rob.　　　　　　　　Since injustice
　In your duke meets this correction, can
　you press us,
With any seeming argument of reason,
In foolish pity to decline[2] his dangers,
To draw 'em on ourself? Shall we not
　be　　　　　　　　　　　　150
Warned by his harms? The league pro-
　claimed between us
Bound neither of us farther than to aid
Each other, if by foreign force invaded;

_____
[1] Making of terms.　　　　[2] Turn aside.

And so far in my honor I was tied.
But, since without our counsel or allow-
　ance
He hath took arms, with his good leave
　he must
Excuse us if we steer not on a rock
We see and may avoid. Let other mon-
　archs
Contend to be made glorious by proud
　war
And with the blood of their poor subjects
　purchase　　　　　　　　　　160
Increase of empire and augment their
　cares
In keeping that which was by wrongs
　extorted,
Gilding unjust invasions with the trim
Of glorious conquests; we, that would be
　known
The father of our people, in our study
And vigilance for their safety must not
　change
Their plowshares into swords, or force
　them from
The secure shade of their own vines to be
Scorched with the flames of war, or for
　our sport
Expose their lives to ruin.

Amb.　　　　　　　Will you then　170
　In his extremity forsake your friend?

Rob. No; but preserve ourself.

Bert.　　　　　　　Cannot the beams
　Of honor thaw your icy fears?

Rob.　　　　　　　　Who's that?

Bert. A kind of brother, sir, howe'er your
　subject;
Your father's son, and one who blushes
　that
You are not heir to his brave spirit and
　vigor,
As to his kingdom.

Rob.　　　　　　　How's this?

Bert.　　　　　　　Sir, to be
　His living chronicle and to speak his
　　praise
Cannot deserve your anger.

Rob.　　　　　　　Where's your warrant
　For this presumption?

Bert.　　　　Here, sir, in my heart.　180
　Let sycophants, that feed upon your
　　favors,
Style coldness in you caution, and prefer
Your ease before your honor, and con-
　clude

To eat and sleep supinely is the end
Of human blessings. I must tell you, sir,
Virtue, if not in action, is a vice,
And, when we move not forward, we go
  backward.
Nor is this peace, the nurse of drones and
  cowards,
Our health, but a disease.
GASP.   Well urged, my lord.
ANT. Perfit [1] what is so well begun.
AMB.   And bind   190
My lord your servant.
ROB.   Hair-brained fool! What reason
Canst thou infer [2] to make this good?
BERT.   A thousand,
Not to be contradicted. But consider
Where your command lies. 'Tis not, sir,
  in France,
Spain, Germany, Portugal, but in Sicily,
An island, sir. Here are no mines of gold
Or silver to enrich you; no worm spins
Silk in her womb to make distinction
Between you and a peasant in your
  habits;
No fish lives near our shores, whose blood
  can dye   200
Scarlet or purple; all that we possess,
With beasts we have in common. Nature
  did
Design us to be warriors, and to break
  through
Our ring, the sea, by which we are en-
  vironed;
And we by force must fetch in what is
  wanting
Or precious to us. Add to this, we are
A populous nation, and increase so fast
That, if we by our providence are not
  sent
Abroad in colonies, or fall by the sword,
Not Sicily, though now it were more
  fruitful   210
Than when 'twas styled the "granary of
  great Rome,"
Can yield our numerous fry bread. We
  must starve,
Or eat up one another.
ADOR.   The king hears
With much attention.
AST.   And seems moved with what
Bertoldo hath delivered.
BERT.   May you live long, sir,
The king of peace, so you deny not us

[1] Perfect.   [2] Bring forward.

The glory of the war; let not our nerves
Shrink up with sloth, nor for want of em-
  ployment
Make younger brothers thieves.   'Tis
  their swords, sir,
Must sow and reap their harvest.   If
  examples   220
May move you more than arguments,
  look on England,
The empress of the European isles,
And unto whom alone ours yields prece-
  dence.
When did she flourish so as when she was
The mistress of the ocean? Her navies,
Putting a girdle round about the world
When the Iberian [3] quaked, her worthies
  named; [4]
And the fair flower-de-luce [5] grew pale,
  set by
The red rose and the white! Let not our
  armor
Hung up, or our unrigged armada, make
  us   230
Ridiculous to the late poor snakes our
  neighbors,
Warmed in our bosoms, and to whom
  again
We may be terrible, while we spend our
  hours
Without variety, confined to drink,
Dice, cards, or whores. Rouse us, sir,
  from the sleep
Of idleness, and redeem our mortgaged
  honors.
Your birth, and justly, claims my father's
  kingdom;
But his heroic mind descends to me.
I will confirm so much.
ADOR.   In his looks he seems
To break ope Janus' temple.
AST.   How these younglings   240
  Take fire from him!
ADOR.   It works an alteration
Upon the king.
ANT.   I can forbear no longer.
War, war, my sovereign!
FUL.   The king appears
Resolved, and does prepare to speak.
ROB.   Think not
Our counsel's built upon so weak a base

[3] Spaniard, in reference to the Spanish Armada.
[4] *I.e.*, England's navy made her great men.
[5] *I.e.*, France.

As to be overturned or shaken with
Tempestuous winds of words. As I, my
　　lord,
Before resolved you, I will not engage
My person in this quarrel, neither press
My subjects to maintain it; yet, to
　　show　　　　　　　　　　　　　　250
My rule is gentle and that I have feeling
Of your master's sufferings, since these
　　gallants, weary
Of the happiness of peace, desire to taste
The bitter sweets of war, we do con-
　　sent
That, as adventure[r]s and volunteers,
No way compelled by us, they may make
　　trial
Of their boasted valors.
BERT.　　　　　　　　We desire no more.
ROB. 'Tis well; and, but my grant in this,
　　expect not
Assistance from me.　Govern as you
　　please
The province you make choice of, for I
　　vow,　　　　　　　　　　　　　　260
By all things sacred, if that thou mis-
　　carry
In this rash undertaking, I will hear it
No otherwise than as a sad disaster
Fallen on a stranger, nor will I esteem
That man my subject who in thy ex-
　　tremes
In purse or person aids thee.　Take your
　　fortune.
You know me; I have said it.　So, my
　　lord,
You have my absolute answer.
AMB.　　　　　　　　　　My prince pays
In me his duty.
ROB.　　　　　　Follow me, Fulgentio,
And you, Astutio.
Exeunt Roberto, Fulgentio, Astutio, Attend-
　　　　　　　　　　　　　　ants.
GASP.　　　　What a frown he threw　270
At his departure on you!
BERT.　　　　　　　　　Let him keep
His smiles for his state catamite;[1] I care
　　not.
ANT. Shall we aboard tonight?
AMB.　　　　　　　Your speed, my lord,
Doubles the benefit.
BERT.　　　　　　　I have a business
Requires despatch; some two hours hence
　　I'll meet you.　　　　　　　*Exeunt.*
[1] Male prostitute.

[*A room in Camiola's house at Palermo.*]

Signior Sylli, walking fantastically before,
　　　　followed by Camiola and Clarinda.

CAM. Nay, signior, this is too much cere-
　　mony
In my own house.
SYL.　　　　　　　What's gracious abroad
Must be in private practiced.
CLAR.　　　　　　For your mirth' sake
Let him alone; he has been all this morn-
　　ing
In practice with a peruged[2] gentleman
　　usher,
To teach him his true amble and his
　　postures
Sylli walking by and practicing his postures.
When he walks before a lady.
SYL.　　　　　　You may, madam,
Perhaps, believe that I in this use art
To make you dote upon me by exposing
My more than most rare features to
　　your view.　　　　　　　　　　　10
But I, as I have ever done, deal simply,
A mark of sweet simplicity ever noted
I' the family of the Syllis.　Therefore,
　　lady,
Look not with too much contemplation
　　on me;
If you do, you are i' the suds.[3]
CAM.　　　　　　　You are no barber?
SYL. Fie, no! Not I.　But my good parts
　　have drawn
More loving hearts out of fair ladies'
　　bellies
Than the whole trade have done teeth.[4]
CAM.　　　　　　　　　Is 't possible?
SYL. Yes, and they live too, marry, much
　　condoling[5]
The scorn of their Narcissus, as they
　　call me,　　　　　　　　　　　20
Because I love myself—
CAM.　　　　　　　Without a rival.
What philters or love powders do you
　　use
To force affection?　I see nothing in
Your person but I dare look on, yet
　　keep
My own poor heart still.

[2] Peruked, bewigged.
[3] *I.e.,* in a pickle.
[4] The barber was also surgeon and dentist.
[5] Lamenting.

Syl.　　　　You are warned—be armed;
And do not lose the hope of such a hus-
band
In being too soon enamored.
Clar.　　　　　　Hold in your head,
Or you must have a martingale.
Syl.　　　　　　I have sworn
Never to take a wife but such a
one
(O, may your ladyship prove so strong!)
as can　　　　　　　　　　　　30
Hold out a month against me.
Cam.　　　　　　Never fear it;
Though your best taking part, your
wealth, were trebled,
I would not woo you. But, since in your
pity
You please to give me caution, tell me
what
Temptations I must fly from.
Syl.　　　　　　The first is
That you never hear me sing, for I am
a Syri.[1]
If you observe, when I warble, the dogs
howl
As ravished with my ditties, and you
will
Run mad to hear me.
Cam.　　　　I will stop my ears,
And keep my little wits.
Syl.　　　　Next, when I dance, 40
And come aloft thus [Capers.], cast not
a sheep's eye
Upon the quivering of my calf.
Cam.　　　　　　Proceed, sir.
Syl. But on no terms (for 'tis a main
point) dream not
Of the strength of my back, though it
will bear a burthen
With any porter.
Cam.　　　　I mean not to ride you.
Syl. [2] Nor I your little ladyship, till you
have
Performed the covenants. Be not taken
with
My pretty spider-fingers, nor my
eyes
That twinkle [3] on both sides.
Cam. [Aside.]　　Was there ever such
A piece of motley [4] heard of!—(One

knocks.)　Who's that? — You may
spare
The catalogue of my dangers.
　　　　　　　　　　Exit Clarinda.
Syl.　　　　No, good madam; 51
I have not told you half.
Cam.　　　　Enough, good signior;
If I eat more of such sweetmeats, I shall
surfeit.—

Enter Clarinda.

Who is 't?
Clar.　　　The brother of the king.
Syl.　　　　　Nay, start not.
The brother of the king! Is he no more?
Were it the king himself, I'll give him
leave
To speak his mind to you, for I am not
jealous;
And, to assure your ladyship of so much,
I'll usher him in—[Aside.] and, that
done, hide myself.　　Exit Syl[li].
Cam. Camiola, if ever, now be constant. 60
This is indeed a suitor whose sweet
presence,
Courtship,[5] and loving language would
have staggered
The chaste Penelope; and, to increase
The wonder, did not modesty forbid it,
I should ask that from him he sues to
me for.
And yet my reason, like a tyran,[6] tells
me
I must nor give nor take it.

Enter Sylli and Bertoldo.

Syl.　　　　　I must tell you
You lose your labor. 'Tis enough to
prove it,
Signior Sylli came before you; and you
know
First come, first served; yet you shall
have my countenance　　　　70
To parley with her, and I'll take special
care
That none shall interrupt you.
Bert.　　　　You are courteous.
Syl. Come, wench, wilt thou hear wis-
dom?
Clar.　　Yes, from you, sir.
　　　　Steps aside [with Sylli].

---

[1] A double pun on *Siren* and *Sirius*, the Dog
Star (Bryne).
[2] Original has *Cam.*
[3] Wink.　　　　　　　　　[4] *I.e.*, fool.
[5] Courtliness.　　　　　　　[6] Tyrant.

BERT. (*Kisseth her.*) If forcing this sweet favor from your lips,
Fair madam, argue me of too much boldness,
When you are pleased to understand I take
A parting kiss, if not excuse, at least
'Twill qualify, the offense.

CAM. A parting kiss, sir?
What nation, envious of the happiness
Which Sicily enjoys in your sweet presence, 80
Can buy you from her, or what climate yield
Pleasures transcending those which you enjoy here,
Being both beloved and honored, the North Star
And guider of all hearts, and, to sum up
Your full accompt [1] of happiness in a word,
The brother of the king?

BERT. Do you alone
And with an unexampled cruelty
Enforce my absence and deprive me of
Those blessings which you with a polished phrase
Seem to insinuate that I do possess, 90
And yet tax me as being guilty of
My willful exile? What are titles to me,
Or popular suffrage, or my nearness to
The king in blood, or fruitful Sicily,
Though it confessed no sovereign but myself,
When you, that are the essence of my being,
The anchor of my hopes, the real substance
Of my felicity, in your disdain
Turn all to fading and deceiving shadows?

CAM. You tax me without cause.

BERT. You must confess it. 100
But, answer love with love, and seal the contract
In the uniting of our souls, how gladly
(Though now I were in action, and assured,
Following my fortune, that plumed Victory
Would make her glorious stand upon my tent)
Would I put off my armor in my heat

[1] Account.

Of conquest and like Anthony pursue
My Cleopatra! Will you yet look on me
With an eye of favor?

CAM. Truth bear witness for me
That in the judgment of my soul you are 110
A man so absolute and circular [2]
In all those wished-for rarities that may take
A virgin captive that, though at this instant
All sceptered monarchs of our western world
Were rivals with you, and Camiola worthy
Of such a competition, you alone
Should wear the garland.

BERT. If so, what diverts
Your favor from me?

CAM. No mulct [3] in yourself,
Or in your person, mind, or fortune.

BERT. What then?

CAM. The consciousness of mine own wants. Alas, sir, 120
We are not parallels, but, like lines divided,
Can ne'er meet in one center. Your birth, sir,
Without addition, were an ample dowry
For one of fairer fortunes, and this shape,
Were you ignoble, far above all value;
To this, so clear a mind, so furnished with
Harmonious faculties molded from heaven,
That, though you were Thersites in your features,
Of no descent, and Irus in your fortunes,
Ulysses-like, you would force all eyes and ears 130
To love, but seen, and, when heard, wonder at
Your matchless story. But all these bound up
Together in one volume! Give me leave
With admiration to look upon 'em,
But not presume in my own flattering hopes
I may or can enjoy 'em.

BERT. How you ruin
What you would seem to build up! I know no

[2] Perfect, complete. [3] Defect.

Disparity between us; you are an heir
Sprung from a noble family, fair, rich,
young,
And every way my equal.
CAM.   Sir, excuse me;   140
One ærie with proportion ne'er dis-
closes [1]
The eagle and the wren. Tissue [2] and
frieze
In the same garment, monstrous! But
suppose
That what's in you excessive were di-
minished,
And my desert supplied; the strongest
bar,
Religion, stops our entrance. You are, sir,
A Knight of Malta, by your Order
bound
To a single life; you cannot marry me,
And I assure myself you are too noble
To seek me, though my frailty should
consent,   150
In a base path.
BERT.   A dispensation, lady,
Will easily absolve me.
CAM.   O, take heed, sir!
When what is vowed to heaven is dis-
pensed with,
To serve our ends on earth, a curse must
follow,
And not a blessing.
BERT.   Is there no hope left me?
CAM. Nor to myself, but is a neighbor to
Impossibility.   True love should walk
On equal feet; in us it does not, sir.
But rest assured, excepting this, I shall
be
Devoted to your service.
BERT.   And this is your   160
Determinate sentence?
CAM.   Not to be revoked.
BERT. Farewell then, fairest cruel! All
thoughts in me
Of women perish. Let the glorious light
Of noble war extinguish Love's dim
taper,
That only lends me light to see my folly.
Honor, be thou my ever-living mistress,
And fond affection, as thy bondslave,
serve thee!   Exit Ber[toldo].
CAM. How soon my sun is set, he being
absent,

---

[1] One nest of natural dimensions never hatches.
[2] Rich cloth.

Never to rise again!   What a fierce
battle
Is fought between my passions!—Me-
thinks   170
We should have kissed at parting.
SYL. [Aside.]   I perceive
He has his answer; now must I step in
To comfort her.—[Comes forward.] You
have found, I hope, sweet lady,
Some difference between a youth of my
pitch [3]
And this bugbear [4] Bertoldo. Men are
men;
The king's brother is no more.   Good
parts will do it,
When titles fail. Despair not; I may be
In time entreated.
CAM.   Be so now—to leave me.—
Lights for my chamber. O my heart!
               Exeunt Camiola and Clarinda.
SYL.   She now,
I know, is going to bed to ruminate
Which way to glut herself upon my
person.   181
But for my oath' sake I will keep her
hungry,
And, to grow full myself, I'll straight—
to supper.   Exit.

THE END OF THE FIRST ACT.

ACT II. SCENE i.

[The council chamber in the palace at Palermo.]

Roberto, Fulgentio, Astutio.

ROB. Embarked tonight, do you say?
FUL.   I saw him aboard, sir.
ROB. And without taking of his leave?
AST.   'Twas strange!
ROB. Are we grown so contemptible?
FUL.   'Tis far
From me, sir, to add fuel to your anger,
That, in your ill opinion of him, burns
Too hot already; else I should affirm
It was a gross neglect.
ROB.   A willful scorn
Of duty and allegiance; you give it
Too fair a name. But we shall think on 't.
Can you

---

[3] The height to which falcons were trained to
fly.
[4] Hobgoblin.

Guess what the numbers were that fol-
　lowed him　　　　　　　　　　10
In his desperate action?

FUL.[1]　　　　More than you think, sir.
All ill-affected spirits in Palermo,
Or [2] to your government or person, with
The turbulent swordmen, such whose
　poverty forced 'em
To wish a change, are gone along with
　him—
Creatures devoted to his undertakings,
In right or wrong—and to express their
　zeal
And readiness to serve him, ere they
　went,
Profanely took the sacrament on their
　knees
To live and die with him.

ROB.　　　　　O most impious!　20
Their loyalty to us forgot?

FUL.　　　　　　　　I fear so.

AST. Unthankful as they are!

FUL.　　　　Yet this deserves not
One troubled thought in you, sir; with
　your pardon,
I hold that their remove from hence
　makes more
For your security than danger.

ROB.　　　　　　　　True;
And, as I'll fashion it, they shall feel it
　too.
Astutio, you shall presently be des-
　patched
With letters, writ and signed with our
　own hand,
To the Duchess of Siena, in excuse
Of these forces sent against her. If you
　spare　　　　　　　　　　30
An oath to give it credit, that we never
Consented to it, swearing for the king,
Though false, it is no perjury.

AST.　　　　　　　I know it.
They are not fit to be state agents, sir,
That without scruple of their conscience
　cannot
Be prodigal in such trifles.

FUL.　　　　　Right, Astutio.

ROB. You must, beside, from us take some
　instructions
To be imparted, as you judge 'em use-
　ful,
To the general, Gonzaga. Instantly
Prepare you for your journey.

AST.　　　　　　With the wings　40
Of loyalty and duty.　　Exit Astutio.

FUL.　　　　　　　I am bold
To put your majesty in mind—

ROB.　　　　　　Of my promise
And aids to further you in your amorous
　project
To the fair and rich Camiola. There's
　my ring;
Whatever you shall say that I entreat,
Or can command by power, I will make
　good.

FUL. Ever your majesty's creature.

ROB.　　　　　　Venus prove
Propitious to you!　　Exit Robert[o].

FUL.　　　　All sorts to [3] my wishes.
Bertoldo was my hindrance; he removed,
I now will court her in the conquerous [4]
　style:　　　　　　　　　　50
"Come, see, and overcome." [5]—Boy!

Enter Page.

PAGE.　　　　　Sir, your pleasure?

FUL. Haste to Camiola; bid her prepare
An entertainment suitable to a fortune
She could not hope for. Tell her I vouch-
　safe
To honor her with a visit.

PAGE.　　　　　'Tis a favor
Will make her proud.

FUL.　I know it.

PAGE.　　　I am gone, sir. Exit Page.

FUL. Entreaties fit not me; a man in
　grace
May challenge awe and privilege by
　his place.　　　　Exit Fulgentio.

ACT II. SCENE ii.

[*A room in Camiola's house.*]

Sylli, Adorni, Clarinda.

ADOR. So melancholy, say you?

CLAR.　　　　　Never given
To such retirement.

ADOR.　　　Can you guess the cause?

CLAR. If it hath not its birth and being
　from
The brave Bertoldo's absence, I confess
It is past my apprehension.

SYL.　　　　　You are wide,[6]

─────────

[1] Original reads *Roberto*.　　　[2] Either.
[3] Consorts with, fits.　　　[4] Conquering.
[5] Cæsar's famous phrase.
[6] Wide of the mark.

The whole field wide. I, in my under-
standing,
Pity your ignorance; yet, if you will
Swear to conceal it, I will let you know
Where her shoe wrings her.
CLAR.   I vow, signior,
By my virginity.
SYL.   A perilous oath   10
In a waiting-woman of fifteen, and is,
indeed,
A kind of nothing.
ADOR.   I'll take one of something,
If you please to minister it.
SYL.   Nay, you shall not swear.
I had rather take your word, for, should
you vow,
"Damn me, I'll do this!"—you are sure
to break.
ADOR. I thank you, signior; but resolve
us.
SYL.   Know, then,
Here walks the cause: she dares not
look upon me;
My beauties are so terrible and enchant-
ing
She cannot endure my sight.
ADOR.   There I believe you.
SYL. But the time will come, be com-
forted, when I will   20
Put off this visor of unkindness to her,
And show an amorous and yielding
face.
And, until then, though Hercules him-
self
Desire to see her, he had better eat
His club than pass her threshold, for
I'll be
Her Cerberus to guard her.
ADOR.   A good dog!

Enter Page.

CLAR. Worth twenty porters.
PAGE.   Keep you open house here?
No groom to attend a gentleman? O,
I spy one.
SYL. He means not me, I am sure.
PAGE.   You, Sirrah Sheepshead,
With a face cut on a catstick,[1] do you
hear?   30
You, yeoman fewterer,[2] conduct me to

---

[1] Stick used in the game of cat, here referring
to a pair of thin legs.
[2] A menial attendant of dogs.

The lady of the mansion, or my poniard
Shall disembogue thy soul.
SYL.   O, terrible! "Disembogue"!
I talk of Hercules, and here is one
Bound up in *decimo sexto*.[3]
PAGE.   Answer, wretch!
SYL. Pray you, little gentleman, be not
so furious.
The lady keeps her chamber.
PAGE.   And we present?
Sent in an embassy to her? But here is
Her gentlewoman. Sirrah, hold my
cloak,
While I take a leap at her lips. Do it,
and neatly,   40
Or, having first tripped up thy heels,
I'll make
Thy back my footstool.
              Page kisses Clar[inda].
SYL.   Tamburlaine in little!
Am I turned Turk? What an office am
I put to!
CLAR. My lady, gentle youth, is indis-
posed.
PAGE. Though she were dead and buried,
only tell her
The great man in the court, the brave
Fulgentio,
Descends to visit her, and it will raise
her
Out of the grave for joy.

Enter Fulgen[tio].

SYL.   Here comes another!
The devil, I fear, in his holiday clothes.
PAGE.   So soon!
My part is at an end then.—Cover my
shoulders;   50
When I grow great, thou shalt serve
me.
FUL. [*To Sylli.*]   Are you, sirrah,
An implement of the house?
SYL.   Sure, he will make
A joins-stool[4] of me!
FUL. [*To Adorni.*]   Or, if you belong
To the lady of the place, command her
hither.
ADOR. I do not wear her livery, yet ac-
knowledge
A duty to her, and as little bound
To serve your peremptory will as she
is

---

[3] A very small book; hence a diminutive person.
[4] Joint stool.

To obey your summons. 'Twill become
you, sir,
To wait her leisure; then, her pleasure
known,
You may present your duty.
FUL. 　　　　　　Duty? Slave, 60
I'll teach you manners.
ADOR. 　　　I am past learning. Make not
A tumult in the house.
FUL. 　　　　　Shall I be braved thus?
　　　　　　　　　　　　They draw.
SYL. O, I am dead! And now I soun. [1]
　　　　　　　　　　　Falls on his face.
CLAR. 　　　　　　　　Help! Murther!
PAGE. Recover, sirrah; the lady's here.

Enter Cam[iola].

SYL. 　　　　　　　　　Nay, then
I am alive again, and I'll be valiant.
　　　　　　　　　　　　　[*Rises.*]
CAM. What insolence is this? 　Adorni,
hold,
Hold, I command you!
FUL. 　　　Saucy groom!
CAM. 　　　　　　　　Not so, sir;
However in his life he had dependence
Upon my father, he is a gentleman
As well born as yourself. Put on your
hat. 　　　　　　　　　　　　70
FUL. In my presence, without leave?
SYL. 　　　　　　He has mine, madam.
CAM. And I must tell you, sir, and in
plain language,
Howe'er your glittering outside prom-
ise gentry,[2]
The rudeness of your carriage and be-
havior
Speaks you a coarser thing.
SYL. 　　　　　She means a clown, sir—
I am her interpreter for want of a bet-
ter.
CAM. I am a queen in mine own house,
nor must you
Expect an empire here.
SYL. 　　　　Sure, I must love her
Before the day, the pretty soul's so
valiant.
CAM. What are you, and what would you
with me?
FUL. 　　　　　　Proud one, 　　80
When you know what I am, and what
I came for,

[1] Sound, swoon. 　[2] Gentility, good breeding.

And may on your submission proceed
to,[3]
You in your reason must repent the
coarseness
Of my entertainment.
CAM. 　　Why, fine man? What are you?
FUL. A kinsman of the king's.
CAM. 　　　　　I cry you mercy,[4]
For his sake, not your own. But grant
you are so,
'Tis not impossible but a king may
have
A fool to his kinsman—no way mean-
ing you, sir.
FUL. You have heard of Fulgen[tio]?
CAM. 　　　　　　Long since, sir—
A suit-broker in court. He has the
worst 　　　　　　　　　　　90
Report among good men I ever heard
of,
For bribery and extortion. 　In their
prayers
Widows and orphans curse him for a
canker
And caterpillar in the state. I hope,
sir,
You are not the man, much less em-
ployed by him
As a smock-agent [5] to me.
FUL. 　　　　　　　I reply not
As you deserve, being assured you know
me—
Pretending ignorance of my person
only
To give me a taste of your wit. 'Tis
well and courtly;
I like a sharp wit well.
SYL. 　　　　I cannot endure it, 100
Nor any of the Syllis.
FUL. 　　　　　More I know too.
This harsh induction [6] must serve as a
foil
To the well-tuned observance [7] and re-
spect
You will hereafter pay me, being made
Familiar with my credit with the king,
And that (contain your joy) I deign
to love you.
CAM. Love me? I am not raped [8] with it.

[3] So all editors except Bryne who reads *so,*
stating "the *s* in *so* not clear." However, the
Newberry copy plainly reads *fo.*
[4] I beg forgiveness.
[5] Pander. 　　　　　[7] Deference.
[6] Introduction. 　　[8] Rapt, transported.

FUL.   Hear 't again:
I love you honestly. Now you admire [1]
me.
CAM. I do indeed, it being a word so sel-
dom
Heard from a courtier's mouth.   But,
pray you, deal plainly,   110
Since you find me simple. What might
be the motives
Inducing you to leave the freedom of
A bachelor's life, on your soft neck to
wear
The stubborn yoke of marriage? And,
of all
The beauties in Palermo, to choose me,
Poor me? That is the main point you
must treat of.
FUL. Why, I will tell you. Of a little
thing
You are a pretty peat,[2] indifferently [3]
fair too,
And, like a new-rigged ship, both tight
and yare,[4]
Well trussed to bear. Virgins of giant
size   120
Are sluggards at the sport, but for my
pleasure
Give me a neat, well-timbered gamester
like you;
Such need no spurs—the quickness of
your eye
Assures an active spirit.
CAM.   You are pleasant, sir;
Yet I presume that there was one thing
in me,
Unmentioned yet, that took you more
than all
Those parts you have remembered.
FUL.   What?
CAM.   My wealth, sir.
FUL. You are i' the right; without that,
beauty is
A flower worn in the morning, at night
trod on.
But, beauty, youth, and fortune meet-
ing in you,   130
I will vouchsafe to marry you.
CAM.   You speak well;
And in return excuse me, sir, if I
Deliver reasons why upon no terms
I'll marry you. I fable not.

SYL. [Aside.]   I am glad
To hear this; I began to have an ague.
FUL. Come, your wise reasons.
CAM. Such as they are, pray you, take
them:
First, I am doubtful whether you are
a man,
Since, for your shape, trimmed up in a
lady's dressing,
You might pass for a woman; now I
love   140
To deal on certainties. And, for the
fairness
Of your complexion, which you think
will take me,
The color, I must tell you, in a man
Is weak and faint, and never will hold
out
If put to labor—give me the lovely
brown,
A thick-curled hair of the same dye,
broad shoulders,
A brawny arm full of veins, a leg with-
out
An artificial calf. I suspect yours—
But let that pass.
SYL. [Aside.]   She means me all this
while,
For I have every one of those good
parts.   150
O Sylli! Fortunate Sylli!
CAM.   You are moved, sir.
FUL. Fie! No; go on.
CAM.   Then, as you are a courtier,
A graced one too, I fear you have been
too forward.
And so much for your person.   Rich
you are,
Devilish rich, as 'tis reported, and sure
have
The aids of Satan's little fiends to get it;
And what is got upon his back must be
Spent, you know where—the proverb's
stale. One word more,
And I have done.
FUL.   I'll ease you of the trouble, 159
Coy and disdainful!
CAM.   Save me, or else he'll beat me!
FUL. No, your own folly shall; and, since
you put me
To my last charm, look upon this and
tremble.   *Shows the king's ring.*
CAM. At the sight of a fair ring? The
king's, I take it.

I have seen him wear the like. If he
    hath sent it
As a favor to me—
Ful.   Yes, 'tis very likely,
His dying mother's gift, prized at [1] his
    crown!
By this he does command you to be
    mine;
By his gift you are so. You may yet
    redeem all.
Cam. You are in a wrong account still.
    Though the king may
Dispose of my life and goods, my mind's
    mine own,   170
And shall be never yours. The king—
    heaven bless him!—
Is good and gracious, and,being in himself
Abstemious from base and goatish loose-
    ness,
Will not compel, against their wills,
    chaste maidens
To dance in his minions' circles. I be-
    lieve,
Forgetting it when he washed his hands,
    you stole it
With an intent to awe me. But you are
    cozened;
I am still myself, and will be.
Ful.   A proud haggard,[2]
And not to be reclaimed! Which of
    your grooms,
Your coachman, fool, or footman, min-
    isters   180
Night-physic to you?
Cam.   You are foul-mouthed.
Ful.   Much fairer
Than thy black soul; and so I will pro-
    claim thee.
Cam. Were I a man, thou durst not speak
    this.
Ful.   Heaven
So prosper me, as I resolve to do it
To all men, and in every place. Scorned
    by
A tit of tenpence! [3]
         Exeunt [4] Fulgentio and his Page.
Syl.   Now I begin to be valiant.
Nay, I will draw my sword. O, for a
    brother! [5]

---

[1] *I.e.*, at the value of. [2] Wild female hawk.
[3] A girl not worth tenpence.
[4] Original reads *Exit.*
[5] *I.e.*, a sworn brother. Some copies of the
original read *butcher*, *i.e.*, bravo.

Do a friend's part; pray you, carry him
    the length of 't.
I give him three years and a day to
    match my Toledo,
And then we'll fight like dragons.
Ador.   Pray, have patience.   190
Cam. I may live to have vengeance. My
    Bertoldo
Would not have heard this.
Ador.   Madam—
Cam.   Pray you, spare
Your language.—[*To Sylli.*] Prithee, fool
    and make me merry.
Syl. That is my office ever.
Ador.   I must do,
Not talk; this glorious gallant shall hear
    from me.   *Exeunt.*

Act II. Scene iii.

[Before the walls of Siena.]

*The chambers [6] discharged; a flourish as
to an assault. Gonzaga, Pierio, Roderigo, Jacomo, Soldiers.*

Gonz. Is the breach made assaultable?
Pier.   Yes, and the moat
Filled up; the cannoneer hath done his
    parts.
We may enter six abreast.
Rod.   There's not a man
Dares show himself upon the wall.
Jac.   Defeat not
The soldiers' hoped-for spoil.
Pier.   If you, sir,
Delay the assault, and the city be given
    up
To your discretion, you in honor cannot
Use the extremity of war—but, in
Compassion to 'em, you to us prove
    cruel.
Jac. And an enemy to yourself.
Rod.   A hindrance to   10
The brave revenge you have vowed.
Gonz.   Temper your heat
And lose not by too sudden rashness
    that
Which, be but patient, will be offered
    to you.
Security [7] ushers ruin; proud contempt
Of an enemy three parts vanquished
    with desire

---

[6] Small cannon used for theatrical purposes.
[7] Want of caution.

And greediness of spoil, have often
      wrested
A certain victory from the conqueror's
      gripe.
Discretion is the tutor of the war,
Valor the pupil; and, when we command
With lenity, and your direction's fol-
      lowed   20
With cheerfulness, a prosperous end
      must crown
Our works well undertaken.
Rod.   Ours are finished—
Pier. If we make use of fortune.
Gonz.   Her false smiles
Deprive you of your judgments. The
      condition
Of our affairs exacts a double care,
And, like bifronted Janus, we must look
Backward as forward. Though a flat-
      tering calm
Bids us urge on, a sudden tempest raised,
Not feared, much less expected, in our
      rear
May foully fall upon us, and distract [1]
      us   30
To our confusion.—

Enter Scout.

                        Our scout! What brings
Thy ghastly looks and sudden speed?
Scout.   Th' assurance
Of a new enemy.
Gonz.   This I foresaw and feared.
What are they, know'st thou?
Scout.   They are by their colors
Sicilians, bravely mounted, and the
      brightness
Of their rich armors doubly gilded with
Reflection of the sun.
Gonz.   From Sicily?
The king in league! No war proclaimed!
      'Tis foul;
But this must be prevented, not dis-
      puted.
Ha, how is this? Your estridge [2] plumes,
      that but   40
E'en now like quills of porcupines seemed
      to threaten
The stars, drop at the rumor of a shower,
And like to captive colors sweep the
      earth!
Bear up; but, in great dangers, greater
      minds

Are never proud. Shall a few loose
      troops, untrained
But in a customary ostentation,
Presented as a sacrifice to your valors,
Cause a dejection in you?
Pier.   No dejection.
Rod. However startled, where you lead
      we'll follow.
Gonz. 'Tis bravely said. We will not
      stay their charge,   50
But meet 'em man to man, and horse
      to horse.
Pierio, in our absence hold our place,
And with our footmen [3] and those sickly
      troops
Prevent a sally. I in mine own person,
With part of the cavallerie,[4] will bid
These hunters welcome to a bloody
      breakfast.—
But I lose time.
Pier.   I'll to my charge. *Exit Pierio.*
Gonz.   And we
To ours. I'll bring you on.
Jac.   If we come off,
It is not amiss; if not, my state is set-
      tled.   *Exeunt. Alarm.*

Act II. Scene iv.

[*The citadel of Siena.*]

Ferdinand, Druso, Livio, above.[5]

Fer. No aids from Sicily? Hath hope
      forsook us,
And that vain comfort to affliction, pity,
By our vowed friend denied us? We
      can nor live
Nor die with honor. Like beasts in a
      toil,
We wait the leisure of the bloody hunter,
Who is not so far reconciled unto us,
As in one death to give a period
To our calamities; but in delaying
The fate we cannot fly from, starved
      with wants,   9
We die this night to live again tomorrow
And suffer greater torments.
Dru.   There is not
Three days' provision for every soldier,
At an ounce of bread a day, left in the
      city.
Liv. To die the beggar's death, with
      hunger made

---

[1] Draw apart, scatter.   [2] Ostrich.
[3] Foot soldiers.
[4] Cavalry.   [5] *I.e.,* on the walls.

Anatomies [1] while we live, cannot but crack
Our heartstrings with vexation.

FER.   Would they would break,
Break altogether! How willingly, like Cato,
Could I tear out my bowels rather than
Look on the conqueror's insulting face,
But that religion and the horrid dream
To be suffered in the other world denies it!   21

Enter Soldier.

What news with thee?

SOLD.   From the turret of the fort,
By the rising clouds of dust, through which, like lightning,
The splendor of bright arms sometimes brake through,
I did descry some forces making towards us;
And from the camp, as emulous of their glory,
The general (for I know him by his horse),
And bravely seconded, encountered 'em.
Their greetings were too rough for friends, their swords
And not their tongues exchanging courtesies.   30
By this the main battalias are joined,
And, if you please to be spectators of
The horrid issue, I will bring you where
As in a theater you may see their fates
In purple gore presented.

FER.   Heaven, if yet
Thou art appeased for my wrong done to Aurelia,
Take pity of my miseries!—Lead the way, friend.   [*Exeunt.*]

ACT II. SCENE v.

[*A plain near the walls.*]

*A long charge; after, a flourish for victory.
Gonzaga; Jacomo; Roderigo, wounded.
Bertoldo, Gasparo, Anthonio prisoners.
            [Officers and Soldiers.]*

GONZ. We have 'em yet, though they cost us dear. This was
Charged home, and bravely followed.
(*To Jacomo and Roderigo.*) Be to yourselves

[1] Skeletons.

True mirrors to each other's worth; and, looking
With noble emulation on his [2] wounds,
The glorious livery of triumphant war,
Imagine these with equal grace appear
Upon yourself. [3] The bloody sweat you have suffered
In this laborious, nay, toilsome harvest,
Yields a rich crop of conquest; and the spoil,
Most precious balsam to a soldier's hurts,   10
Will ease and cure 'em. Let me look upon
The prisoners' faces.—(*To Gasparo and Anthon[io].*) O, how much transformed
From what they were! O Mars! Were these toys fashioned
To undergo the burthen of thy service?
The weight of their defensive armor bruised
Their weak, effeminate limbs, and would have forced 'em
In a hot day without a blow to yield.

ANT. This insultation [4] shows not manly in you.

GONZ. To men I had forborne it; you are women,
Or, at the best, loose carpet knights. [5]
What fury   20
Seduced you to exchange your ease in court
For labor in the field? Perhaps you thought
To charge through dust and blood an arméd foe
Was but like graceful running at the ring [6]
For a wanton mistress' glove, and the encounter
A soft impression on her lips. But you
Are gaudy butterflies, and I wrong myself
In parling [7] with you.

GASP.   Væ victis! [8] Now we prove it.

ROD. But here's one fashioned in another mold,

[2] *I.e.*, Roderigo's.   [3] *I.e.*, Jacomo.
[4] Scornful exultation.
[5] Knights who have been created in court, not on the battlefield.
[6] One of the favorite sports at a tournament.
[7] Parleying, speaking.
[8] Woe to the vanquished!

And made of tougher metal.

GONZ.   True; I owe him   30
For this wound bravely given.

BERT.   O, that mountains
Were heaped upon me that I might ex-
pire,
A wretch no more remembered!

GONZ.   Look up, sir.
To be o'ercome deserves no shame. If
you
Had fallen ingloriously, or could accuse
Your want of courage in resistance,
'twere
To be lamented; but, since you per-
formed
As much as could be hoped for from a
man,
Fortune his enemy, you wrong your-
self
In this direction.[1] I am honored in   40
My victory o'er you; but to have these
My prisoners is, in my true judgment,
rather
Captivity than a triumph. You shall
find
Fair quarter from me, and your many
wounds,
Which I hope are not mortal, with such
care
Looked to and cured, as if your nearest
friend
Attended on you.

BERT.   When you know me better,
You will make void this promise. Can
you call me
Into your memory?

GONZ.   The brave Bertoldo!
A brother of our order! By Saint John,
Our holy patron, I am more amazed,   51
Nay, thunderstrook [2] with thy apostasy
And precipice [3] from the most solemn
vows
Made unto heaven, when this, the
glorious badge
Of our Redeemer, was conferred upon
thee
By the great master, than if I had seen
A reprobate Jew, an atheist, Turk, or
Tartar
Baptized in our religion!

BERT.   This I looked for,
And am resolved to suffer.

GONZ.   Fellow soldiers,
Behold this man, and, taught by his
example,   60
Know that 'tis safer far to play with
lightning
Than trifle in things sacred.   In my
rage   *Weeps.*
I shed these at the funeral of his virtue,
Faith, and religion.   Why, I will tell
you
He was a gentleman so trained up and
fashioned
For noble uses, and his youth did prom-
ise
Such certainties, more than hopes, of
great achievements,
As—if the Christian world had stood
opposed
Against the Ottoman race to try the
fortune
Of one encounter—this Bertoldo had
been,   70
For his knowledge to direct, and match-
less courage
To execute, without a rival by
The votes of good men chosen general,
As the prime soldier and most deserv-
ing
Of all that wear the cross, which now
in justice
I thus tear from him.

BERT.   Let me die with it
Upon my breast.

GONZ.   No; by this thou wert sworn
On all occasions as a knight to guard
Weak ladies from oppression, and never
To draw thy sword against 'em, where-
as thou,   80
In hope of gain or glory, when a prin-
cess,
And such a princess as Aurelia is,
Was dispossessed by violence of what
was
Her true inheritance, against thine oath
Hast to thy uttermost labored to up-
hold
Her falling enemy. But thou shalt pay
A heavy forfeiture, and learn too late
Valor employed in an ill quarrel turns
To cowardice, and Virtue then puts on
Foul Vice's visor.   This is that which
cancels   90
All friendship's bands between us.—
Bear 'em off;

I will hear no reply. And let the ransom
Of these, for they are yours, be highly
　rated.
In this I do but right, and let it be
Styled justice and not willful cruelty.
　　　　　　　　　　　　　　Exeunt.

The End of the Second Act.

Act III. Scene i.

[Before the walls of Siena.]

Gonzaga, Astutio, Roderigo, Jacomo.

Gonz. What I have done, sir, by the law
　of arms
I can and will make good.
Ast. 　　　　　I have no commission
　To expostulate[1] the act. These letters
　speak
　The king my master's love to you, and
　his
　Vowed service to the duchess, on whose
　person
　I am to give attendance.
Gonz. 　　　　　　At this instant
　She's at Pienza. You may spare the
　trouble
Of riding thither; I have advertised her
Of our success, and on what humble
　terms　　　　　　　　　　　　　9
Siena stands. Though presently[2] I can
Possess it, I defer it, that she may
Enter her own, and, as she please, dispose
　of
The prisoners and the spoil.
Ast. 　　　　　　　I thank you, sir.
I' the meantime, if I may have your
　license,
I have a nephew, and one once my ward,
For whose liberties and ransoms I would
　gladly
Make composition.
Gonz. 　　　　　They are, as I take it,
　Called Gasparo and Anthonio.
Ast. 　　　　　　　The same, sir.
Gonz. For them, you must treat with
　these [*Indicating Roderigo and Jacomo*];
　but, for Bertoldo,
He is mine own. If the king will ransom
　him,　　　　　　　　　　　　　20
He pays down fifty thousand crowns;
　if not,
He lives and dies my slave.

Ast. 　　　　　　　Pray you, a word.—
[*Aside to Gonzaga.*] The king will rather
　thank you to detain him
Than give one crown to free him.
Gonz. [*Aside.*] 　　　At his pleasure.—
I'll send the prisoners under guard; my
　business
Calls me another way. 　*Exit Gonzaga.*
Ast. 　　　　　My service waits you.—
Now, gentlemen, do not deal like mer-
　chants with me,
But noble captains; you know, in great
　minds,
Posse et nolle nobile.[3]
Rod. 　　　　　　　Pray you, speak
Our language.
Jac. 　I find not in my commission　30
　An officer's bound to speak or under-
　stand
More than his mother tongue.
Rod. 　　　　　　If he speaks that
After midnight, 'tis remarkable.
Ast. 　　　　　　In plain terms, then,
Anthonio is your prisoner; Gasparo,
　yours.
Jac. You are i' the right.
Ast. 　　　　At what sum do you rate
　Their several ransoms?
Rod. 　　　　　I must make my market
As the commodity cost me.
Ast. 　　　　　　As it cost you?
You did not buy your captainship?
　Your desert,
I hope, advanced you.
Rod. 　　　　　　How? It well appears
You are no soldier. Desert in these
　days?　　　　　　　　　　　　40
Desert may make a sergeant to a colo-
　nel,
And it may hinder him from rising
　higher;
But, if it ever get a company,
A company, pray you, mark me, with-
　out money
Or private service done for the general's
　mistress,
With a commendatory epistle from
　her,
I will turn lanceprisado.[4]
Jac. 　　　　　　Pray you, observe, sir:
I served two prenticeships, just fourteen
　year,

1 Discuss, examine. 　　　 2 Immediately.

3 It is noble to have the power and to refuse.
4 Lance-corporal.

Trailing the puissant pike, and half so
  long
Had the right-hand file; and I fought
  well, 'twas said, too.   50
But I might have served, and fought,
  and served till doomsday,
And never have carried a flag but for the
  legacy
A buxom widow of threescore bequeathed
  me;
And that too, my back knows, I labor[ed]
  hard for,
But was better paid.
Ast.   You are merry with yourselves.
  But this is from the purpose.
Rod.   To the point then.
  Prisoners are not ta'en every day; and,
    when
We have 'em, we must make the best
  use of 'em.
Our pay is little to the part we should
  bear,
And that so long a-coming that 'tis
  spent   60
Before we have it, and hardly wipes off
  scores
At the tavern and the ordinary.
Jac.   You may add, too,
  Our sport took up [1] on trust.
Rod.   Peace, thou smock vermin!
  Discover commanders' secrets!—In a
    word, sir,
We have required,[2] and find our prison-
  ers rich.
Two thousand crowns apiece our com-
  panies cost us,
And so much each of us will have, and
  that
In present pay.
Jac.   It is too little; yet,
  Since you have said the word, I am con-
    tent,
But will not go a gazet [3] less.
Ast.   Since you are not   70
  To be brought lower, there is no evad-
    ing;
I'll be your paymaster.
Rod.   We desire no better.
Ast. But not a word of what's agreed be-
  tween us,
Till I have schooled my gallants.
Jac.   I am dumb, sir.

[1] Obtained.
[2] Inquired, investigated.   [3] A small coin.

Enter a Guard; Bertoldo, Anthonio, Gasparo,
in irons.

Bert. And where removed now? Hath the
  tyrant found out
Worse usage for us?
Ant.   Worse it cannot be.
  My grewhound [4] has fresh straw and
    scraps in his kennel;
But we have neither.
Gasp.   Did I ever think
  To wear such garters [5] on silk stockings,
    or
That my too curious [6] appetite, that
    turned   80
At the sight of godwits, [7] pheasant,
    partridge, quails,
Larks, woodcocks, calvered [8] salmon, as
    coarse diet,
Would leap at a moldy crust?
Ant.   And go without it,
  So oft as I do? O, how have I jeered
The city entertainment! A huge shoulder
Of glorious, fat ram-mutton, seconded
With a pair of tame cats [9] or conies, [10] a
    crab [11] tart,
With a worthy loin of veal, and valiant
    capon,
Mortified [12] to grow tender—these I
    scorned,
From their plentiful horn of abundance,
    though invited.   90
But now I could carry my own stool to a
    tripe,
And call their chitterlings charity, and
    bless the founder.
Bert. O, that I were no farther sensible
  Of my miseries than you are! You, like
    beasts,
Feel only stings of hunger, and complain
    not
But when you are empty; but your
    narrow souls,
If you have any, cannot comprehend
How insupportable the torments are
Which a free and noble soul, made cap-
    tive, suffers.
Most miserable men! And what am I,
    then,   100

[4] Greyhound.   [9] Hares.
[5] *I.e.*, shackles.   [10] Rabbits.
[6] Finical.   [11] Crab apple.
[7] Snipes.   [12] Castrated.
[8] Perhaps pickled.

That envy you? Fetters, though made of
　　gold,
Express base thralldom; and all delicates
Prepared by Median cooks for epicures,
When not our own, are bitter; quilts
　　filled high
With gossamer and roses cannot yield
The body soft repose, the mind kept
　　waking
With anguish and affliction.

Ast. 　　　　　　My good lord—

Bert. This is no time nor place for
　　flattery, sir.
　　Pray you, style me as I am, a wretch for-
　　saken
　　Of the world, as myself.

Ast. 　　　　　　I would it were 110
　　In me to help you.

Bert. 　　Ay, if that you want power, sir,
　　Lip-comfort cannot cure me. Pray you,
　　leave me
　　To mine own private thoughts. *Walks by.*[1]

Ast. 　　　　　　My valiant nephew!
　　And my more than warlike ward! I am
　　glad to see you
　　After your glorious conquests. Are these
　　chains
　　Rewards [2] for your good service? If they
　　are,
　　You should wear 'em on your necks,
　　since they are massy,
　　Like aldermen [3] of the war.

Ant. 　　　　　　You jeer us too!

Gasp. Good uncle, name not, as you are a
　　man of honor,
　　That fatal word of war; the very sound [4]
　　of 't 　　　　　　　　　　　　120
　　Is more dreadful than a cannon.

Ant. 　　　　　　But redeem us
　　From this captivity, and I'll vow here-
　　after
　　Never to wear a sword, or cut my
　　meat
　　With a knife that has an edge or point;
　　I'll starve first.

Gasp. I will cry "broom" or "cat's
　　meat" [5] in Palermo,
　　Turn porter, carry burthens—anything
　　Rather than live a soldier.

Ast. 　　　　　　This should have
　　Been thought upon before. At what
　　price, think you,
　　Your two wise heads are rated?

Ant. 　　　　　　A calf's head is
　　More worth than mine; I am sure it had
　　more brains in't, 　　　　　　　130
　　Or I had never come here.

Rod. 　　　　　　And I will eat it
　　With bacon, if I have not speedy ran-
　　som.

Ant. And a little garlic too, for your own
　　sake, sir;
　　'Twill boil in your stomach else.

Gasp. 　　　　　　Beware of mine,
　　Or the horns [6] may choke you; I am
　　married, sir.

Ant. You shall have my row of houses
　　near the palace.

Gasp. And my villa; all—

Ant. 　　　　　　All that we have.[7]

Ast. Well, have more wit hereafter; for
　　this time,
　　You are ransomed.

Jac. 　　　　　　Off with their irons.

Rod. 　　　　　　Do, do.
　　If you are ours again, you know your
　　price. 　　　　　　　　　　　140

Ant. Pray you, despatch [8] us. I shall ne'er
　　believe
　　I am a free man, till I set my foot
　　In Sicily again, and drink Palermo,
　　And in Palermo too.

Ast. 　　　　　　The wind sits fair;
　　You shall aboard tonight. With the
　　rising sun
　　You may touch upon the coast. But
　　take your leaves
　　Of the late general first.

Gasp. 　　　　　　I will be brief.

Ant. And I. My lord, heaven keep you!

Gasp. 　　　　　　Yours, to use
　　In the way of peace; but as your soldiers,
　　never.

Ant. A pox of [9] war! No more of war.

Exeunt Roderig[o], Jaco[mo], Anthonio,
　　　　　　　　　　　　Gasparo.

Bert. 　　　　　　Have you 150
　　Authority to loose their bonds, yet leave

---

[1] Stage direction follows next line in original.
[2] Original reads *rewardee*.
[3] London aldermen still wear heavy gold
chains.
[4] The Newberry copy reads *summon*.
[5] Common cries of public vendors.

[6] The time-worn allusion to the sign of
cuckoldry.
[7] In the original here follows the unnecessary
stage direction, *To Astutio.*
[8] Hasten. 　　　　　　[9] A plague on.

The brother of your king, whose worth
  disdains
Comparison with such as these, in irons?
If ransom may redeem them, I have
  lands,
A patrimony of mine own, assigned me
By my deceaséd sire, to satisfy
Whate'er can be demanded for my
  freedom.
Ast. I wish you had, sir; but the king,
  . who yields
No reason for his will, in his displeasure
Hath seized on all you had; nor will
  Gonzaga,   160
Whose prisoner now you are, accept of
  less
Than fifty thousand crowns.
Bert.   I find it now
That misery ne'er comes alone. But,
  grant
The king is yet inexorable, time
May work him to a feeling of my suffer-
  ings.
I have friends that swore their lives and
  fortunes were
At my devotion—and among the rest
Yourself, my lord, when, forfeited to the
  law
For a foul murther, and in cold blood
  done,
I made your life my gift, and reconciled
  you   170
To this incenséd king and got your par-
  don.
Beware ingratitude. I know you are rich,
And may pay down the sum.
Ast.   I might, my lord;
But pardon me.
Bert.   And will Astutio prove then
(To please a passionate man—the king's
  no more)
False to his maker and his reason,
  which
Commands more than I ask? O summer
  friendship,
Whose flattering leaves, that shadowed
  us in our
Prosperity, with the least gust drop off
In th' autumn of adversity! How   180
  like
A prison is to a grave! When dead, we
  are
With solemn pomp brought thither, and
  our heirs.

Masking their joy in false, dissembled
  tears,
Weep o'er the hearse; but earth no
  sooner covers
The earth brought thither, but they turn
  away
With inward smiles, the dead no more
  remembered.
So, entered in a prison—
Ast.   My occasions
Command me hence, my lord.
Bert.   Pray you, leave me, do;
And tell the cruel king that I will wear
These fetters till my flesh and they are
  one   190
Incorporated substance. In myself,
As in a glass, I'll look on human frailty,
And curse the height of royal blood,
  since I,
In being born near to Jove, am near his
  thunder.
Cedars once shaken with a storm, their
  own   Exit Astutio.
Weight grubs their roots out.—Lead me
  where you please;
I am his, not fortune's, martyr, and will
  die
The great example of his cruelty.
                              Exit cum suis.[1]

Act III. Scene ii.

[A grove near the palace near Palermo.]

Adorni.

Ador. He undergoes my challenge and
  contemns it,
And threatens me with the late edict
  made
Gainst duelists—the [2] altar cowards fly to.
But I, that am engaged, and nourish in
  me
A higher aim than fair Camiola dreams
  of,
Must not sit down thus. In the court I
  dare not
Attempt him; and in public he's so
  guarded
With a herd of parasites, clients, fools,
  and suitors
That a musket cannot reach him. My
  designs

---

[1] With his attendants.
[2] Suggested by Davies. Original reads *then.*

Admit of no delay. This is her birth-
day,   10
Which, with a fit and due solemnity,
Camiola celebrates; and on it all such
As love or serve her usually present
A tributary duty. I'll have something
To give, if my intelligence prove true,
Shall find acceptance. I am told, near
this grove
Fulgentio every morning makes his
markets [1]
With his petitioners; I may present him
With a sharp petition!—Ha, 'tis he!
My fate
Be ever blessed for 't!   [*Retires.*]

Enter [2] Fulgen[tio and Page].

FUL.   Command such as wait me 20
Not to presume, at the least for half an
hour,
To press on my retirements.
PAGE.   I will say, sir,
You are at your prayers.
FUL.   That will not find belief;
Courtiers have something else to do.
Begone, sir.—   [*Exit Page.*]
Challenged! 'Tis well! And by a groom!
Still better!
Was this shape made to fight? I have a
tongue yet,
Howe'er no sword, to kill him; and what
way
This morning I'll resolve of.
                          Exit Fulgentio.
ADOR.   I shall cross
Your resolution, or suffer for you.
                          Exit Adorni.

ACT III. SCENE iii.

[*A room in Camiola's house.*]

*Camiola, divers Servants with presents,
Sylli, Clarinda.*

SYL. What are all these?
CLAR.   Servants with several presents,
And rich ones too.
1 SERV.   With her best wishes, madam,
Of many such days to you, the Lady
Petula
Presents you with this fan.
2 SERV.   This diamond
From your aunt Honoria.

[1] Dealings.   [2] Original reads *Exit.*

3 SERV.   This piece of plate
From your uncle, old Vincentio, with
your arms
Graven upon it.
CAM.   Good friends they are too—
Munificent in their love and favor to
me.—
[*To Clarinda.*] Out of my cabinet return
such jewels   9
As this directs you.—[*Gives Servants
money.*] For your pains; and yours;
Nor must you be forgotten. Honor
me
With the drinking of a health.
1 SERV.   Gold, on my life!
2 SERV. She scorns to give base silver.
3 SERV.   Would she had been
Born every month in the year!
1 SERV.   Month? Every day.
2 SERV. Show such another maid.
3 [SERV.]   All happiness wait you!
SYLLI. I'll see your will done.
          Exeunt Sylli, Clarinda, Servants.

Enter Adorni, wounded.

CAM.   How, Adorni wounded?
ADOR. A scratch got in your service, else
not worth
Your observation. I bring not, madam,
In honor of your birthday, antique plate
Or pearl for which the savage Indian
dives   20
Into the bottom of the sea, nor diamonds
Hewn from steep rocks with danger.
Such as give
To those that have what they themselves
want, aim at
A glad return with profit. Yet despise
not
My offering at the altar of your favor,
Nor let the lowness of the giver lessen
The height of what's presented, since it is
A precious jewel, almost forfeited,
And dimmed with clouds of infamy,
redeemed
And in its natural splendor, with addi-
tion,   30
Restored to the true owner.
CAM.   How is this?
ADOR. Not to hold you in suspense, I
bring you, madam,
Your wounded reputation cured, the
sting

Of virulent malice, festering your fair
name,
Plucked out and trod on. That proud
man, that was
Denied the honor of your bed, yet durst
With his untrue reports strumpet your
fame,
Compelled by me, hath given himself the
lie,
And in his own blood wrote it. [*Gives her
a paper.*] You may read
"Fulgentio" subscribed.

CAM.　　　　　　　I am amazed! 40

ADOR. It does deserve it, madam. Com-
mon service
Is fit for hinds, and the reward propor-
tioned
To their conditions. Therefore, look not
on me
As a follower of your father's fortunes, or
One that subsists on yours. You frown!
My service
Merits not this aspect.

CAM.　　　　　Which of my favors,
I might say bounties, hath begot and
nourished
This more than rude presumption?
Since you had
An itch to try your desperate valor,
wherefore
Went you not to the war? Couldst thou
suppose　　　　　　　　　　　50
My innocence could ever fall so low
As to have need of thy rash sword to
guard it
Against malicious slander? O, how much
Those ladies are deceived and cheated
when
The clearness and integrity of their
actions
Do not defend themselves, and stand
secure
On their own bases! Such as in a color [1]
Of seeming service give protection to 'em,
Betray their own strengths. Malice
scorned puts out　　　　　　　59
Itself, but argued gives a kind of credit
To a false accusation. In this, this your
Most memorable service, you believed
You did me right; but you have wronged
me more
In your defense of my undoubted honor
Than false Fulgentio could.

[1] Pretense.

ADOR.　　　　　I am sorry what was
So well intended is so ill received;
Yet, under your correction, you wished

Ente[r] Clarinda.

Bertoldo had been present.

CAM.　　　　　　　True, I did.
But he and you, sir, are not parallels,
Nor must you think yourself so.

ADOR.　　　　　　I am what 70
You'll please to have me.

CAM.　　　　If Bertoldo had
Punished Fulgentio's insolence, it had
shown
His love to her whom in his judgment he
Vouchsafed to make his wife—a height,
I hope,
Which you dare not aspire to. The same
actions
Suit not all men alike. But I perceive
Repentance in your looks. For this time,
leave me;
I may forgive, perhaps forget, your
folly.
Conceal yourself till this storm be blown
over.
You will be sought for, yet, for my
estate [2]　　　　　　　　　　80
Can hinder it, shall not suffer in my
service.　　　*Gives him her hand to kiss.*

ADOR. [*Aside.*] This is something yet,
though I missed the mark I shot at.
　　　　　　　　　　　Exit Adorni.

CAM. This gentleman is of a noble temper,
And I too harsh, perhaps, in my reproof.
Was I not, Clarinda?

CLAR.　　　I am not to censure [3]
Your actions, madam; but there are a
thousand
Ladies, and of good fame, in such a cause
Would be proud of such a servant.

CAM.　　　　　　　　It may be.

Enter a Servant.

Let me offend in this kind.—Why,
uncalled for?

SERV. The signiors, madam, Gasparo and
Anthonio,　　　　　　　　90
Selected friends of the renowned Ber-
toldo,
Put ashore this morning.

CAM.　　　　　　Without him?

[2] Rank, position.　　　　　　[3] Judge.

SERV. I think so.

CAM.   Never think more then.

SERV.   They have been at court,
Kissed the king's hand, and, their first
     duties done
To him, appear ambitious [1] to tender
To you their second service.

CAM.   Wait 'em hither. *Exit* [2] *Servant.*
Fear, do not rack me! Reason, now if
     ever,
Haste with thy aids and tell me such a
     wonder
As my Bertoldo is, with such care
     fashioned,
Must not, nay, cannot, in heaven's
     providence   100

Enter Anthonio, Gasparo, Serv[ant].

So soon miscarry!—Pray you, forbear;
     ere you
Take the privilege, as strangers, to
     salute me—
Excuse my manners—make me first
     understand
How it is with Bertoldo.

GASP. [3]   The relation
Will not, I fear, deserve your thanks.

ANT.   I wish
Some other should inform you.

CAM.   Is he dead?
You see, though with some fear, I dare
     inquire it.

GASP. Dead! Would that were the worst;
     a debt were paid then
Kings in their birth owe nature.

CAM.   Is there aught
More terrible than death?

ANT.   Yes, to a spirit   110
Like his: cruel imprisonment, and that
Without the hope of freedom.

CAM.   You abuse me.
The royal king cannot, in love to virtue,
Though all springs of affection were dried
     up,
But pay his ransom.

GASP.   When you know what 'tis,
You will think otherwise. No less will do
     it
Than fifty thousand crowns.

CAM.   A pretty sum,
The price weighed with the purchase!
     Fifty thousand?
To the king 'tis nothing. He that can
     spare more
To his minion for a masque cannot but
     ransom   120
Such a brother at a million. You wrong
The king's magnificence.

ANT.   In your opinion;
But 'tis most certain. He does not alone
In himself refuse to pay it, but forbids
All other men.

CAM.   Are you sure of this?

GASP.   You may read
The edict to that purpose, published by
     him;
That will resolve you.

CAM.   Possible! Pray you, stand off.
If I do not mutter treason to myself,
My heart will break. Yet I will not curse
     him;
He is my king. The news you have de-
     livered   130
Makes me weary of your company; we'll
     salute
When we meet next. I'll bring you to the
     door.
Nay, pray you, no more compliments.

GASP.   One thing more,
And that's substantial: let your Adorni
Look to himself.

ANT.   The king is much incensed
Against him for Fulgentio.

CAM.   As I am,
For your slowness to depart.

BOTH.   Farewell, sweet lady.
          Exeunt Gaspa[ro], Antho[nio].

CAM. O more than impious times, when
     not alone
Subordinate ministers of justice are
Corrupted and seduced, but kings them-
     selves,   140
The greater wheels by which the lesser
     move,
Are broken or disjointed! Could it be,
     else,
A king, to soothe his politic ends, should
     so far
Forsake his honor as at once to break
Th' adamant chains of nature and
     religion
To bind up atheism [4] as a defense

---

[1] Emended by Gifford. Original reads *ambitions.*

[2] Original reads *Exeunt.*

[3] Original reads *Ber.*

[4] Godlessness, dishonor.

To his dark counsels? Will it ever be
That to deserve too much is dangerous,
And virtue, when too eminent, a crime?
Must she serve fortune still, or, when
   stripped of   150
Her gay and glorious favors, lose the
   beauties
Of her own natural shape? O my Ber-
   toldo,
Thou only sun in honor's sphere, how
   soon
Art thou eclipsed and darkened—not the
   nearness
Of blood prevailing on the king, nor
   all
The benefits to the general good dis-
   pensed,
Gaining a retribution! But that
To owe a courtesy to a simple virgin
Would take from the deserving, I find in
   me
Some sparks of fire, which, fanned with
   honor's breath,   160
Might rise into a flame and in men
   darken
Their usurped splendor. Ha! My aim is
   high,
And, for the honor of my sex, to fall so
Can never prove inglorious. 'Tis re-
   solved.—
Call in Adorni.
CLAR.   I am happy in
Such employment, madam.
                  Exit Clarin[da].
CAM.   He's a man,
I know, that at a reverend distance
   loves me;
And such are ever faithful. What a sea
Of melting ice I walk on! What strange
   censures
Am I to undergo! But good intents   170
Deride all future rumors.

    Enter [1] *Clarin[da] and Adorn[i].*

ADOR.   I obey
Your summons, madam.
CAM.   Leave the place, Clarinda;
One woman, in a secret of such weight,
Wise men may think too much.—
                  [*Exit Clarinda.*]
                 Nearer, Adorni.
I warrant it with a smile.

[1] Original reads *Exit*.

ADOR.   I cannot ask
Safer protection. What's your will?
CAM.   To doubt
Your ready desire to serve me, or prepare
   you
With the repetition of former merits,
Would, in my diffidence, wrong you. But
   I will,
And without circumstance, in the trust
   that I   180
Impose upon you, free you from sus-
   picion.
ADOR. I foster none of you.
CAM.   I know you do not.
You are, Adorni, by the love you owe
   me—
ADOR. The surest conjuration.
CAM.   Take me with you [2]—
Love born of duty. But advance no
   further.
You are, sir, as I said, to do me service,
To undertake a task in which your faith,
Judgment, discretion—in a word, your
   all
That's good—must be engaged; nor
   must you study,   189
In the execution, but what may make
For the ends I aim at.
ADOR.   They admit no rivals.
CAM. You answer well. You have heard
   of Bertoldo's
Captivity, and the king's neglect, the
   greatness
Of his ransom—fifty thousand crowns,
   Adorni,
Two parts of my estate?
ADOR. [*Aside.*]   To what tends this?
CAM. Yet I so love the gentleman, for to
   you
I will confess my weaknesses, that I
   purpose
Now, when he is forsaken by the king
And his own hopes, to ransom him, and
   receive him
Into my bosom as my lawful hus-
   band—   200
      Adorni starts and seems troubled.
Why change you color?
ADOR.   'Tis in wonder of
Your virtue, madam.
CAM.   You must therefore to
Siena for me, and pay to Gonzaga
This ransom for his liberty; you shall

[2] *I.e.*, don't go too fast.

Have bills of exchange along with you.
Let him swear
A solemn contract to me; for you must
be
My principal witness, if he should—but
why
Do I entertain these jealousies? [1] You
will do this?

ADOR. Faithfully, madam—(*Aside.*) but
not live long after.

CAM. One thing I had forgot: besides his
freedom   210
He may want accommodations; furnish
him
According to his birth. And from Cami-
ola
Deliver this kiss, printed on your lips,
                                    Kisses him.
Sealed on his hand. You shall not see my
blushes.
I'll instantly despatch you.
                                    Exit Camiola.

ADOR.   I am half
Hanged out of the way already.—Was
there ever
Poor lover so employed against himself
To make way for his rival? I must do it.
Nay, more, I will. If loyalty can find
Recompense beyond hope or imagina-
tion,   220
Let it fall on me in the other world
As a reward, for in this I dare not hope
it.   *Exit.*

THE END OF THE THIRD ACT.

ACT IV. SCENE i.

[*Before the walls of Siena.*]

Gonzaga, Pierio, Roderigo, Jacomo.

GONZ. You have seized upon the citadel,
and disarmed
All that could make resistance?

PIER.   Hunger had
Done that before we came, nor was the
soldier
Compelled to seek for prey; the famished
wretches,
In hope of mercy, as a sacrifice offered
All that was worth the taking.

GONZ.   You proclaimed,
On pain of death, no violence should be
offered
To any woman?

[1] Suspicions.

ROD.   But it needed not,
For famine had so humbled 'em, and took
off
The care of their sex's honor that there
was not   10
So coy a beauty in the town but would
For half a moldy biscuit sell herself
To a poor bezonian,[2] and without shriek-
ing.

GONZ. Where is the duke of Urbin?

JAC.   Under guard,
As you directed.

GONZ.   See the soldiers set
In rank and file, and, as the duchess
passes,
Bid 'em vail [3] their ensigns; and charge
'em on their lives
Not to cry "whores"!

JAC.   The devil cannot fright 'em
From their military license. Though
they know
They are her subjects, and will part with
being   20
To do her service, yet, since she is a
woman,
They will touch at her britch [4] with their
tongues; and that is all
That they can hope for.

A shout, and a general cry within, "*Whores,*
                                    whores!"

GONZ.   O, the devil! They are at it!
Hell stop their bawling throats. Again!
Make up,
And cudgel them into jelly.

ROD.   To no purpose;
Though their mothers [5] were there, they
would have the same name for 'em.
                                    Exeunt.

ACT IV. SCENE ii.

[*Another part of the camp.*]

Roderigo, Jacomo, Pierio, Gonzaga, Aurelia,
under a canopy. Astutio presents her
with letters. Loud music. She reads the
                                    letters.

GONZ. I do beseech your highness not to
ascribe
To the want of discipline the barbarous
rudeness
Of the soldier in his profanation of
Your sacred name and virtues.

[2] Recruit, beggar.   [3] Lower.   [4] Breech.
[5] Emended by Gifford. Original reads *mouthes*

Aur.   No, lord general;
I've heard my father say oft 'twas a custom
Usual in the camp, nor are they to be punished
For words, that have in fact [1] deserved so well.
Let the one excuse the other.
All.   Excellent, princess!
Aur. But, for [2] these aids from Sicily sent against us
To blast our spring of conquest in the bud,   10
I cannot find, my lord ambassador,
How we should entertain 't but as a wrong,
With purpose to detain us from our own,
Howe'er the king endeavors in his letters
To mitigate the affront.
Ast.   Your grace hereafter
May hear from me such strong assurances
Of his unlimited desires to serve you
As will, I hope, drown in forgetfulness
The memory of what's past.
Aur.   We shall take time
To search the depth of 't further, and proceed   20
As our council shall direct us.
Gonz.   We present you
With the keys of the city; all lets [3] are removed.
Your way is smooth and easy; at your feet
Your proudest enemy falls.
Aur.   We thank your valors.
A victory without blood is twice achieved,
And the disposure of it, to us tendered,
The greatest honor. Worthy captains, thanks!
My love extends itself to all.
Gonz.   Make way there!

A Guard made. Aurelia passes thorough 'em.
Loud music. Exeunt.

Act IV. Scene iii.

[*A room in the prison at Siena.*]

Bertoldo, with a small book, in fetters.
                    Jailor. [4]

Bert. 'Tis here determined (great examples, armed
With arguments, produced to make it good)
That neither tyrants nor the wrested laws,
The people's frantic rage, sad exile, want,
Nor that which I endure, captivity,
Can do a wise man any injury.
Thus Seneca, when he wrote it, thought.
But then
Felicity courted him. His wealth exceeding
A private man's, happy in the embraces
Of his chaste wife Paulina, his house full
Of children, clients, servants, flattering friends,   11
Soothing his lip-positions, [5] and created
Prince of the senate, by the general voice,
As his pupils' new [6] suffrage [7] —then no doubt
He held and did believe this. But no sooner
The prince's frowns and jealousies had thrown him
Out of security's lap, and a centurion
Had offered him what choice of death he pleased,
But told him die he must, when straight the armor
Of his so boasted fortitude fell off,   20
             Throws away the book.
Complaining of his frailty. Can it then
Be censured womanish weakness in me, if,
Thus clogged with irons, and the period
To close up all calamities [8] denied me,
Which was presented Seneca, I wish
I ne'er had being, at least never knew
What happiness was, or argue with heaven's justice,
Tearing my locks, and in defiance throwing
Dust in the air, or, falling on the ground, thus
With my nails and teeth to dig a grave, or rend   30
The bowels of the earth, my stepmother,
And not a natural parent, or thus practice

---

[1] Deed, achievement.
[2] As for.
[3] Hindrances.
[4] Probably on guard on the outer stage.
[5] Utterances.
[6] Emended by Bryne. Original reads *pupil news.*
[7] Choice by vote.   [8] *I.e.,* death.

To die, and, as I were insensible,
Believe I had no motion? *Lies on his face.*

Enter Gonzaga, Adorn[i], Jailor.

GONZ.   There he is.
I'll not inquire by whom his ransom's
    paid—
I am satisfied that I have it—nor allege
One reason to excuse his cruel usage,
As you may interpret it. Let it suffice
It was my will to have it so. He is yours
    now;
Dispose of him as you please.
                                Exit Gonzaga.
ADOR.   Howe'er I hate him, 40
As one preferred before me, being a man
He does deserve my pity. Sir, he sleeps.
Or is he dead? Would he were a saint in
    heaven
('Tis all the hurt I wish him), but was not
Born to such happiness. (*Kneels by him.*)
—No, he breathes—come near,
And, if 't be possible without his feeling,
Take off his irons. (*His irons taken off.*)
So; now leave us private. *Exit Jailor.*
He does begin to stir; and, as trans-
    ported
With a joyful dream, how he stares and
    feels his legs,
As yet uncertain whether it can be   50
True or fantastical!
BERT. [*Rising.*]   Ministers of mercy,
Mock not calamity. Ha, 'tis no vision!
Or, if it be, the happiest that ever
Appeared to sinful flesh! Who's here?
    His face
Speaks him Adorni—but some glorious
    angel,
Concealing its divinity in his shape,
Hath done this miracle, it being not an
    act
For wolvish man. Resolve me, if thou
    look'st for
Bent knees in adoration?
ADOR.   O, forbear, sir!
I am Adorni, and the instrument   60
Of your deliverance; but the benefit
You owe another.
BERT.   If he has a name,
As soon as spoken, 'tis writ on my heart
I am his bondman.
ADOR.   To the shame of men,
This great act is a woman's.

BERT.   The whole sex
For her sake must be deified. How I
    wander
In my imagination, yet cannot
Guess who this phœnix should be!
ADOR.   'Tis Camiola.
BERT. Pray you, speak 't again; there's
    music in her name.
Once more, I pray you, sir.
ADOR.   Camiola, 70
The Maid of Honor.
BERT.   Cursed atheist [1] that I was,
Only to doubt it could be any other,
Since she alone, in the abstract of her-
    self,
That small but ravishing substance, com-
    prehends
Whatever is, [2] or can be wished, in the
Idea [3] of a woman! O, what service
Or sacrifice of duty can I pay her,
If not to live and die her charity's slave,
Which is resolved already!
ADOR.   She expects not 79
Such a dominion o'er you. Yet, ere I
Deliver her demands, give me your hand.
On this, as she enjoined me, with my
    lips
I print her love and service, by me sent
    you.
BERT. I am o'erwhelmed with wonder!
ADOR.   You must now,
Which is the sum of all that she desires,
By a solemn contract bind yourself,
    when she
Requires it, as a debt due for your free-
    dom,
To marry her.
BERT.   This does engage me further.
A payment! An increase of obligation.
To marry her!—'Twas my *nil ultra* [4]
    ever—   90
The end of my ambition! O, that now
The holy man, she present, were pre-
    pared
To join our hands, but with that speed
    my heart
Wishes mine eyes might see her!
ADOR.   You must swear this.
BERT. Swear it? Collect all oaths and im-
    precations,
Whose least breach is damnation, and
    those

---

[1] Skeptic.
[2] Original read *it.*
[3] Ideal pattern.
[4] Nothing beyond.

Ministered to me in a form more dread-
　　ful;
Set heaven and hell before me, I will take
　　'em.
False to Camiola? Never.—Shall I now
Begin my vows to you?
ADOR.　　　　　　I am no churchman;　100
Such a one must file it on record. You
　　are free;
And, that you may appear like to your-
　　self,
For so she wished, there's [1] gold, with
　　which you may
Redeem your trunks and servants, and
　　whatever
Of late you lost. I have found out the
　　captain
Whose spoil they were; his name is Ro-
　　derigo.
BERT. I know him.
ADOR.　　　　　　I have done my parts.
BERT.　　　　　　So much, sir,
As I am ever yours for 't. Now, me-
　　thinks,
I walk in air! Divine Camiola—
But words cannot express thee. I'll build
　　to thee　　　　　　110
An altar in my soul, on which I'll offer
A still-increasing sacrifice of duty.
　　　　　　　　　　Exit Ber[toldo].
ADOR. What will become of me now is
　　apparent.
Whether a poniard or a halter be
The nearest way to hell (for I must
　　thither
After I have killed myself) is somewhat
　　doubtful.
This Roman resolution of self-murther
Will not hold water at the high tribunal
When it comes to be argued; my good
　　genius　　　　　　119
Prompts me to this consideration. He
That kills himself to avoid misery fears
　　it,
And, at the best, shows but a bastard
　　valor.
This life's a fort committed to my trust,
Which I must not yield up till it be
　　forced.
Nor will I. He's not valiant that dares
　　die,
But he that boldly bears calamity. *Exit.*

[1] Emended by Bryne. Different copies of the
quarto read *thee's* or *hee's.*

ACT IV. SCENE iv.

[The council chamber in the palace at Siena.]

*A flourish. Pierio, Roderigo, Jacomo, Gon-
　　zaga, Aurelia, Ferdinand, Astutio,
　　　　　　　　　　　Attendants.*

AUR. A seat here for the duke! It is our
　　glory
To overcome with courtesies, not rigor.
The lordly Roman, who held it the
　　height
Of human happiness to have kings and
　　queens
To wait by his triumphant chariot
　　wheels,
In his insulting pride, deprived himself
Of drawing near the nature of the gods,
Best known for such, in being merciful.
Yet give me leave, but still with gentle
　　language
And with the freedom of a friend, to
　　tell you　　　　　　10
To seek by force what courtship could
　　not win
Was harsh [2] and never taught in Love's
　　mild school.
Wise poets feign that Venus' coach is
　　drawn
By doves and sparrows, not by bears and
　　tigers.
I spare the application.
FER.　　　　　　In my fortune,
Heaven's justice hath confirmed it; yet,
　　great lady,
Since my offense grew from excess of love,
And [3] not to be resisted, having paid too
With the loss of liberty the forfeiture
Of my presumption, in your clemency　20
It may find pardon.
AUR.　　　　　　You shall have just cause
To say it hath. The charge of the long
　　siege
Defrayed, and the loss my subjects have
　　sustained
Made good, since so far I must deal with
　　caution,
You have your liberty.
FER.　　　　　　I could not hope for
Gentler conditions.
AUR.　　　　　　My Lord Gonzaga,

[2] Emended by Gifford. Original reads *not
harsh.*
[3] *I.e.,* and a love, etc.

Since my coming to Siena, I have heard much
  Of your prisoner, brave Bertoldo.
Gonz.   Such an one,
  Madam, I had.
Ast.   And have still, sir, I hope.
Gonz. Your hopes deceive you. He is ran-
  somed, madam.   30
Ast. By whom, I pray you, sir?
Gonz.   You had best inquire
  Of your intelligencer. I am no informer.
Ast. [Aside.] I like not this.
Aur.   He is, as 'tis reported,
  A goodly gentleman, and of noble parts—
  A brother of your order.
Gonz.   He was, madam,
  Till he against his oath wronged you, a
    princess,
  Which his religion bound him from.
Aur.   Great minds
  For trial of their valors oft maintain
  Quarrels that are unjust, yet without
    malice;
  And such a fair construction I make of
    him.   40
  I would see that brave enemy.
Gonz.   My duty
  Commands me to seek for him.
Aur.   Pray you, do,
  And bring him to our presence.
                              Exit Gonzaga.
Ast. [Aside.]   I must blast
  His entertainment.—May it please your
    excellency,
  He is a man debauched, and, for his riots,
  Cast off by the king my master; and that,
    I hope, is
  A crime sufficient.
Fer.   To you, his subjects,
  That like as your king likes.

Enter Gonzaga, Bertoldo, richly habited;
                              Adorni.

Aur.   But not to us;
  We must weigh with our own scale.—
    [Aside.] This is he, sure.
  How soon mine eye had found him!
    What a port   50
  He bears! How well his bravery [1] be-
    comes him!
  A prisoner, nay, a princely suitor, rather!
  But I am too sudden.
  ¹ Fine clothes.

Gonz.   Madam, 'twas his suit,
  Unsent for, to present his service to you
  Ere his departure.
Aur. [Aside.]   With what majesty
  He bears himself!
Ast.   The devil, I think, supplies him.
  Ransomed, and thus rich too!
          Bertoldo,² kneeling, kisses her hand.
Aur.   You ill deserve
  The favor of our hand—(We are not well;
  Give us more air.)
                              She descends suddenly.
Gonz.   What sudden qualm is this?
Aur.—That lifted yours against me.
Bert. [Kissing her hand.]   Thus
  once more   60
  I sue for pardon.
Aur. (Aside.)   Sure his lips are poisoned
  And through these veins force passage to
    my heart,
  Which is already seized upon.
Bert.   I wait, madam,
  To know what your commands are; my
    designs
  Exact me in another place.
Aur.   Before
  You have our license to depart? If man-
    ners,
  Civility of manners, cannot teach you
  T' attend our leisure, I must tell you, sir,
  That you are still our prisoner—[To
    Gonzaga.] nor had you
  Commission to free him.
Gonz.   How's this, madam? 70
Aur. You were my substitute and wanted
    power
  Without my warrant to dispose of him,
  I will pay back his ransom ten times over
  Rather than quit my interest.
Bert.   This is
  Against the law of arms.
Aur. (Aside.)   But not of love.—
  Why, hath your entertainment, sir, been
    such,
  In your restraint, that with the wings of
    fear
  You would fly from it?
Bert.   I know no man, madam,
  Enamored of his fetters, or delighting
  In cold or hunger, or that would in
    reason   80
  Prefer straw in a dungeon before
  A down bed in a palace.
  ² Original reads Ferdinand.

AUR.   How!—[To Gonzaga.] Come
    nearer.
Was his usage such?
GONZ.   Yes; and it had been worse
    Had I foreseen this.
AUR.   O thou misshaped monster!
    In thee it is confirmed that such as
        have
    No share in nature's bounties know no
        pity
    To such as have 'em. Look on him with
        my eyes,
    And answer, then, whether this were a
        man
    Whose cheeks of lovely fullness should
        be made   89
    A prey to meager famine? Or these eyes,
    Whose every glance store Cupid's emp-
        tied quiver,
    To be dimmed with tedious watching?
        Or these lips,
    These ruddy lips, of whose fresh color
        cherries
    And roses were but copies, should grow
        pale
    For want of nectar? Or these legs, that
        bear
    A burthen of more worth than is sup-
        ported
    By Atlas' wearied shoulders, should be
        cramped
    With the weight of iron? O, I could
        dwell ever
    On this description!
BERT.   Is this in derision
    Or pity of me?
AUR.   In your charity   100
    Believe me innocent. Now you are my
        prisoner,
    You shall have fairer quarter. You will
        shame
    The place where you have been, should
        you now leave it
    Before you are recovered. I'll conduct
        you
    To more convenient lodgings, and it shall
        be
    My care to cherish you. Repine who
        dare;
    It is our will. You'll follow me?
BERT.   To the center,
    Such a Sybilla guiding me.
    Exeunt Aurelia, Bertoldo [, and Attendants].
GONZ.   Who speaks first?

FER. We stand as we had seen Medusa's
    head.   *All amazed.*
PIER. I know not what to think, I am so
    amazed.   110
ROD. Amazed! I am thunderstrook.
JAC.   We are enchanted,
    And this is some illusion.
ADOR. [*Aside.*]   Heaven forbid!
    In dark despair it shows a beam of hope.
    Contain thy joy, Adorni.
AST.   Such a princess,
    And of so long-experienced reservedness,
    Break forth, and on the sudden, into
        flashes
    Of more than doubted [1] looseness!

                [*Enter Aurelia and Bertoldo.*]

GONZ. [*Aside.*]   They come again,
    Smiling, as I live, his arm circling her
        waist!
    I shall run mad. Some fury hath pos-
        sessed her.
    If I speak, I may be blasted. Ha! I'll
        mumble   120
    A prayer or two, and cross myself, and
        then,
    Though the devil fart fire, have at him.
AUR.   Let not, sir,
    The violence of my passions nourish in
        you
    An ill opinion; or, grant my carriage
    Out of the road and garb of private
        women,
    'Tis still done with decorum. As I am
    A princess, what I do is above censure,
    And to be imitated.
BERT.   Gracious madam,   128
    Vouchsafe a little pause, for I am so rapt
    Beyond myself that, till I have collected
    My scattered faculties, I cannot tender
    My resolution.
AUR.   Consider of it.
    I will not be long from you.
                   Bertoldo walking by, musing.
GONZ. [*Aside.*]   Pray I cannot!
    This curséd object strangles my devotion.
    I must speak, or I burst.—Pray you, fair
        lady,
    If you can, in courtesy direct me to
    The chaste Aurelia.
AUR.   Are you blind? Who are we?
GONZ. Another kind of thing. Her blood
    was governed

[1] Suspected.

By her discretion, and not ruled her
　reason.
The reverence and majesty of Juno　140
Shined in her looks, and, coming to the
　camp,
Appeared a second Pallas. I can see
No such divinities in you. If I
Without offense may speak my thoughts,
　you are,
As it were, a wanton Helen.

AUR.　　　　　　　　　Good! Ere long
You shall know me better.

GONZ.　　　　　Why, if you are Aurelia,
How shall I dispose of the soldier?

AST.　　　　　　　　May it please you
To hasten my despatch?

AUR.　　　　　　　　Prefer your suits
Unto Bertoldo; we will give him hearing,
And you'll find him your best advocate.
　　　　　　　　　　　　Exit Aurelia.

AST.　　　　　　　This is rare!　150
GONZ. What are we come to?

ROD.　　　　　　Grown up in a moment
A favorite!

FERD.　　　He does take state already.

BERT. [*Aside.*] No, no, it cannot be. Yet
　but [1] Camiola
There is no step between me and a crown.
Then my ingratitude—a sin in which
All sins are comprehended! Aid me,
　virtue,
Or I am lost.

GONZ.　　　May it please your excel-
　lence—
Second me, sir.

BERT. [*Aside.*]　　Then my so horrid
　oaths,
And hell-deep imprecations made against
　it!

AST. The king, your brother, will thank
　you for th' advancement　160
Of his affairs.

BERT. [*Aside.*]　And yet who can hold
　out
Against such batteries as her power and
　greatness
Raise up against my weak defenses!

GONZ.　　　　　　　　　　　　Sir,

Enter Aurelia.

Do you dream, waking?—'Slight,[2] she's
　here again!

[1] Except for.
[2] By God's light, a mild oath.

BERT. Walks she on woolen feet!

AUR.　　　　　　You dwell too long
In your deliberation, and come
With a cripple's pace to that which you
　should fly to.

BERT. It is confessed. Yet why should I,
　to win
From you that hazard all to my poor
　nothing,
By false play send you off a loser from
　me?　170
I am already too-too much engaged
To the king my brother's anger; and who
　knows
But that his doubts and politic fears,
　should you
Make me his equal, may draw war
　upon
Your territories? Were that breach made
　up,
I should with joy embrace what now I
　fear
To touch but with due reverence.

AUR.　　　　　　　　That hinderance
Is easily removed. I owe the king
For a royal visit, which I straight will
　pay him;
And, having first reconciled you to his
　favor,　180
A dispensation shall meet with us.

BERT. I am wholly yours.

AUR.　　　　　On this book seal it.

GONZ. [*Aside.*] What, hand and lip too!
　Then the bargain's sure.—
You have no employment for me?

AUR.　　　　　　　　Yes, Gonzaga;
Provide a royal ship.

GONZ.　　　　　A ship? Saint John,
Whither are we bound now?

AUR.　　　　　You shall know hereafter.
My lord, your pardon for my too much
　trenching
Upon your patience.

ADOR. (*Whispers to Bertoldo.*)　Camiola!

AUR. How do you?

BERT.　　　Indisposed; but I attend you.
　　　　　　　　Exeunt [All but Adorni].

ADOR. The heavy curse that waits on per-
　jury　190
And foul ingratitude pursue thee ever!
Yet why from me this? In this breach of
　faith
My loyalty finds reward! What poisons
　him

Proves mithridate [1] to me. I have per-
　formed
All she commanded, punctually, and now
In the clear mirror of my truth she may
Behold his falsehood. O, that I had
　wings
To bear me to Palermo! This, once
　known,
Must change her love into a just disdain,
And work her to compassion of my
　pain.　　　　　　　　*Exit.* 200

Act IV. Scene v.

[*A room in Camiola's house.*]

Sylli, Camiola, Clarinda, at several doors.

Syl. Undone! Undone! Poor I, that
　whilom [2] was
　The top and ridge of my house, am on
　　the sudden
　Turned to the pitifullest animal
　Of the lignage [3] of the Syllis!
Cam.　　　　　　What's the matter?
Syl. The king—break, girdle, break!
Cam.　　　　　Why, what of him?
Syl. Hearing how far you doted on my
　person,
　Growing envious of my happiness, and
　　knowing
　His brother nor his favorite, Fulgentio,
　Could get a sheep's eye from you, I being
　　present,
　Is come himself a suitor, with the awl　10
　Of his authority to bore my nose,
　And take you from me—O, O, O!
Cam.　　　　　　　Do not roar so.
　The king?
Syl.　　The king! Yet loving Sylli is not
　So sorry for his own as your misfortune;
　If the king should carry you, or you bear
　　him,
　What a loser should you be! He can but
　　make you
　A queen, and what a simple thing is that
　To the being my lawful spouse. The
　　world can never
　Afford you such a husband.
Cam.　　　　　　　I believe you.
　But how are you sure the king is so
　　inclined?　　　　　　　　　　　　20
　Did not you dream this?

Syl.　　　　　With these eyes I saw him
　Dismiss his train and lighting from his
　　coach,
　Whispering Fulgentio in the ear.
Cam.　　　　　　　　　　If so,
　I guess the business.
Syl.　　　　　　It can be no other
　But to give me the bob,[4] that being a
　　matter
　Of main importance. Yonder they are; I
　　dare not
　Be seen, I am so desperate. If you forsake
　　me,

Enter [5] *Rob*[*erto*], *Ful*[*gentio*].

　Send me word that I may provide a
　　willow garland
　To wear when I drown myself. O Sylli,
　　O Sylli!　　　　　　*Exit, crying.*
Ful. It will be worth your pains, sir, to
　　observe　　　　　　　　　　　30
　The constancy and bravery of her spirit.
　Though great men tremble at your
　　frowns, I dare
　Hazard my head your majesty, set off [6]
　With terror, cannot fright her.
Rob.　　　　　　May she answer
　My expectation!
Ful.　　　　　　There she is.
Cam.　　　　　　My knees thus
　Bent to the earth, while my vows are
　　sent upward
　For the safety of my sovereign, pay the
　　duty
　Due for so great an honor, in this favor
　Done to your humblest handmaid.
Rob.　　　　　You mistake me;　39
　I come not, lady, that you may report
　The king, to do you honor, made your
　　house
　(He being there) his court, but to correct
　Your stubborn disobedience. A pardon
　For that, could you obtain it, were well
　　purchased
　With this humility.
Cam.　　　　　　A pardon, sir?
　Till I am conscious of an offense,
　I will not wrong my innocence to beg one.
　What is my crime, sir?
Rob.　　　　　Look on him I favor,
　By you scorned and neglected.
Cam.　　　　　　Is that all, sir?

Rob. No, minion, though that were too
    much. How can you   50
    Answer the setting on your desperate
    bravo
    To murther him?
Cam.   With your leave, I must not
    kneel, sir,
    While I reply to this, but thus rise up
    In my defense and tell you as a man
    (Since, when you are unjust, the deity
    Which you may challenge as a king parts
    from you)
    'Twas never read in Holy Writ, or moral,
    That subjects on their loyalty were
    obliged
    To love their sovereign's vices. Your
    grace, sir,
    To such an undeserver is no virtue.   60
Ful. What think you now, sir?
Cam.   Say you should love wine,
    You being the king, and, cause [1] I am
    your subject,
    Must I be ever drunk? Tyrants, not
    kings,
    By violence from humble vassals force
    The liberty of their souls. I could not
    love him;
    And to compel affection, as I take it,
    Is not found in your prerogative.
Rob. (*Aside.*)   Excellent virgin!
    How I admire her confidence!
Cam.   He complains
    Of wrong done him; but be no more a
    king
    Unless you do me right. Burn your
    decrees,   70
    And of your laws and statutes make a
    fire
    To thaw the frozen numbness of delin-
    quents,
    If he escape unpunished. Do your edicts
    Call it death in any man that breaks into
    Another's house to rob him, though of
    trifles?
    And shall Fulgentio, your Fulgentio, live,
    Who hath committed more than sacri-
    lege
    In the pollution of my clear fame
    By his malicious slanders?
Rob.   Have you done this?
    Answer truly, on your life.
Ful.   In the heat of blood   80
    Some such thing I reported.

[1] Because.

Rob.   Out of my sight!
    For I vow, if by true penitence thou win
    not
    This injured virgin to sue out thy pardon,
    Thy grave is digged already.
Ful. [*Aside.*]   By my own folly
    I have made a fair hand of 't.
           Exit Fulgentio.
Rob.   You shall know, lady,
    While I wear a crown, justice shall use
    her sword
    To cut offenders off, though nearest to us.
Cam. Ay, now you show whose deputy
    you are.
    If now I bath [2] your feet with tears, it
    cannot
    Be censured superstition.
Rob.   You must rise;   90
    Rise in our favor and protection ever.
           Kisses her.
Cam. Happy are subjects, when the prince
    is still
    Guided by justice, not his passionate
    will.   *Exeunt.*

THE END OF THE FOURTH ACT.

ACT V. SCENE i.

[*The same.*]

Camiola, Sylli.

Cam. You see how tender I am of the quiet
    And peace of your affection, and what
    great ones
    I put off in your favor.
Syl.   You do wisely,
    Exceeding wisely; and, when I have said
    I thank you for 't, be happy.
Cam.   And good reason,
    In having such a blessing.
Syl.   When you have it;
    But the bait is not yet ready. Stay the
    time,
    While I triumph by myself. King, by
    your leave,
    I have wiped your royal nose [3] without a
    napkin.[4]
    You may cry, "Willow, willow!" [5] for
    your brother;   10
    I'll only say, "Go by!" [6] for my fine
    favorite,

[2] Bathe.   [4] Handkerchief.
[3] *I.e.*, cheated you.   [5] A cry of sorrow.
[6] Wait a little. The well-known catch phrase
from *The Spanish Tragedy.*

He may graze where he please; his lips
  may water
Like a puppy's o'er a fermenty [1] pot,
  while Sylli
Out of his two-leaved cherry-stone dish,[2]
  drinks nectar!
I cannot hold out any longer; heaven forgive me!
'Tis not the first oath I have broke; I
  must take
A little for a preparative.
        Offers to kiss and embrace her.

CAM.   By no means.
If you forswear yourself, we shall not
  prosper.
I'll rather lose my longing.

SYL.   Pretty soul!
How careful it is of me! Let me buss
  yet   20
Thy little dainty foot for 't. That, I'm
  sure, is
Out of my oath.

CAM.   Why, if thou canst dis-
  pense with 't
So far, I'll not be scrupulous; such a favor
My amorous shoemaker steals.

SYL.   O most rare leather!
               Kisses her shoe often.
I do begin at the lowest, but in time
I may grow higher.

CAM.   Fie, you dwell too long there!
Rise, prithee, rise.

        Enter Clarinda, hastily.

SYL.   O, I am up already.
CAM. How I abuse my hours!—What news
  with thee now?
CLAR. Off with that gown; 'tis mine, mine
  by your promise.
Signior Adorni is returned! Now upon
  entrance! [3]   30
Off with it, oft with it, madam!

CAM.   Be not so hasty.
When I go to bed, 'tis thine.

SYL.   You have my grant,[4] too.
But, do you hear, lady, though I give
  way to this,
You must hereafter ask my leave be-
  fore
You part with things of moment.

---

[1] Frumenty, hulled wheat boiled in milk.
[2] *I.e.*, Camiola's lips.
[3] Now ready to enter.   [4] Consent.

CAM.   Very good;
When I'm yours, I will be governed.

SYL.   Sweet obedience!

          Enter Adorni.

CAM. You are well returned.
ADOR.   I wish that the success
Of my service had deserved it.

CAM.   Lives Bertoldo?
ADOR. Yes, and returned with safety.

CAM.   'Tis not then
In the power of fate to add to or take
  from   40
My perfit happiness; and yet he should
Have made me his first visit.

ADOR.   So I think too;
But he—

SYL.   Durst not appear, I being present;
That's his excuse, I warrant you.

CAM.   Speak, where is he?
With whom? Who hath deserved more
  from him, or
Can be of equal merit? I in this
Do not except the king.

ADOR.   He's at the palace
With the Duchess of Siena. One coach
  brought 'em hither,
Without a third. He's very gracious with
  her;
You may conceive the rest.

CAM.   My jealous fears   50
Make me to apprehend.

ADOR.   Pray you, dismiss
Signior Wisdom, and I'll make relation
  to you
Of the particulars.

CAM.   Servant,[5] I would have you
To haste unto the court.

SYL.   I will outrun
A footman for your pleasure.

CAM.   There observe
The duchess' train and entertainment.

SYL.   Fear not;
I will discover all that is of weight,
To the liveries of her pages and her foot-
  men.
This is fit employment for me.
                  Exit Sylli.

CAM.   Gracious with
The duchess! Sure, you said so?

ADOR.   I will use   60
All possible brevity to inform you,
  madam,

---

[5] This word also meant *lover*.

Of what was trusted to me, and discharged
With faith and loyal duty.

CAM. I believe it.
You ransomed him, and supplied his
wants—imagine
That is already spoken. And what vows
Of service he made to me is apparent;
His joy of me, and wonder too, per-
spicuous.
Does not your story end so?

ADOR. Would the end
Had answered [1] the beginning! In a
word, 69
Ingratitude and perjury at the height
Cannot express him.

CAM. Take heed.

ADOR. Truth is armed,
And can defend itself. It must out,
madam.
I saw (the presence [2] full) the amorous
duchess
Kiss and embrace him; on his part ac-
cepted
With equal ardor; and their willing hands
No sooner joined, but a remove [3] was
published,
And put in execution.

CAM. The proofs are
Too pregnant. O Bertoldo!

ADOR. He's not worth
Your sorrow, madam.

CAM. Tell me, when you saw this,
Did not you grieve, as I do now to hear
it? 80

ADOR. His precipice from goodness raising
mine,
And serving as a foil to set my faith off,
I had little reason.

CAM. In this you confess
The devilish malice of your disposition.
As you were a man, you stood bound to
lament it,
And not, in flattery of your false hopes,
To glory in it. When good men pursue
The path marked out by virtue, the
blessed saints
With joy look on it, and seraphic angels
Clap their celestial wings in heavenly
plaudits 90
To see [4] a scene of grace so well presented,

[1] Corresponded to. [2] Presence chamber.
[3] Removal, withdrawal from the room.
[4] Gifford's reading. Original reads be.

The fiends and men made up of envy
mourning,
Whereas now, on the contrary, as far
As their divinity can partake of passion,
With me they weep, beholding a fair
temple,
Built in Bertoldo's loyalty, turned to
ashes
By the flames of his inconstancy, the
damned
Rejoicing in the object.—'Tis not well
In you, Adorni.

ADOR. [Aside.] What a temper dwells
In this rare virgin!—Can you pity him
That hath shown none to you?

CAM. I must not be 101
Cruel by his example. You, perhaps,
Expect now I should seek recovery
Of what I have lost, by tears, and with
bent knees
Beg his compassion. No; my towering
virtue,
From the assurance of my merit, scorns
To stoop so low. I'll take a nobler
course
And, confident in the justice of my cause,
The king his brother and new mistress,
judges,
Ravish him from her arms. You have
the contract 110
In which he swore to marry me?

ADOR. 'Tis here, madam.

CAM. He shall be then against his will
my husband;
And, when I have him, I'll so use him!
Doubt not
But that, your honesty being unques-
tioned,
This writing, with your testimony, clears
all.

ADOR. [Aside.] And buries me in the dark
mists of error.

CAM. I'll presently to court; pray you, give
order
For my caroche.[5]

ADOR. [Aside.] A cart for me were
fitter,
To hurry me to the gallows.
Exit Ador[ni].

CAM. O false men!
Inconstant! Perjured! My good angel
help me 120
In these my extremities!

[5] Carriage.

Enter Sylli.

SYL.　　If you ever will see brave sight,
Lose it not now.　Bertoldo and the
　　duchess
Are presently to be married.　There's
　　such pomp
And preparation.
CAM.　　　　　If I marry, 'tis
This day or never.
SYL.　　　　　Why, with all my heart;
Though I break this, I'll keep the next
　　oath I make,
And then it is quit.
CAM.　　　Follow me to my cabinet.[1]
You know my confessor, Father Paulo?
SYL.　　　　　　Yes.　Shall he
Do the feat for us?
CAM.　　　　　I will give in writing
Directions to him, and attire myself　130
Like a virgin bride; and something I will
　　do
That shall deserve men's praise—and
　　wonder too.
SYL.　And I, to make all know I am not
　　shallow,
Will have my points of cochineal and
　　yellow.　　　　　　*Exeunt.*

ACT V. SCENE ii.

[*The presence chamber in the palace at
Palermo.*]

*Loud music.　Astutio, Gonzaga, Roderigo,
Jacomo, Pierio, Roberto, Bertoldo, Aurelia, [Ferdinand,] Bishop, with Attendants.*

ROB.　Had our division been greater,
　　madam,
Your clemency, the wrong being done to
　　you,
In pardon of it, like the rod of concord,
Must make a perfect union.—Once more
With a brotherly affection we receive you
Into our favor.　Let it be your study
Hereafter to deserve this blessing, far
Beyond your merit.
BERT.　　　　As the princess' grace
To me is without limit, my endeavors
With all obsequiousness to serve her
　　pleasures　　　　　　　　　　10
Shall know no bounds; nor will I, being
　　made

[1] Private room.

Her husband, e'er forget the duty that
I owe her as a servant.
AUR.　　　　　I expect not
But fair equality, since I well know,
If that superiority be due,
'Tis not to me.　When you are made my
　　consort,
All the prerogatives of my high birth
　　canceled,
I'll practice the obedience of a wife,
And freely pay it.　Queens themselves,
　　if they
Make choice of their inferiors, only aim-
　　ing　　　　　　　　　　　　20
To feed their sensual appetites, and to
　　reign
Over their husbands, in some kind com-
　　mit
Authorized whoredom; nor will I be
　　guilty
In my intent of such a crime.
GONZ.　　　　　This done,
As it is promised, madam, may well
　　stand for
A president [2] to great women; but, when
　　once
The griping hunger of desire is cloyed,
And the poor fool advanced, brought on
　　his knees,
Most of your eagle breed, I'll not say all,
Ever excepting you, challenge [3] again　30
What in hot blood they parted from.
AUR.　　　　　　You are ever
An enemy of our sex; but you, I hope,
　　sir,
Have better thoughts.
BERT.　　　　　I dare not entertain
An ill one of your goodness.
ROB.　　　　　To my power
I will enable [4] him, to prevent all danger
Envy can raise against your choice.　One
　　word more
Touching the articles.

Enter Fulgen[tio], Cam[iola], Syl[li], Ador[ni].

FUL.　　　　　In you alone
Lie all my hopes; you can or kill or save
　　me.
But pity in you will become you better
(Though I confess in justice 'tis denied
　　me)　　　　　　　　　　　40
Than too much rigor.

[2] Precedent.
[3] Lay claim to, demand.　　　[4] Elevate.

Cam.   I will make your peace
As far as it lies in me, but must first
Labor to right myself.

Aur. [*To Roberto.*]   Or add or alter
What you think fit. In him I have my all;
Heaven make me thankful for him!

Rob.   On to the temple.

Cam. Stay, royal sir; and, as you are a king,
Erect one here, in doing justice to
An injured maid.

Aur.   How's this?

Bert. [*Aside.*]   O, I am blasted!

Rob. I have given some proof, sweet lady,
of my promptness
To do you right; you need not, therefore,
doubt me.   50
And rest assured that, this great work
despatched,
You shall have audience and satisfaction
To all you can demand.

Cam.   To do me justice
Exacts your present care, and can admit
Of no delay. If, ere my cause be heard,
In favor of your brother you go on, sir,
Your scepter cannot right me. He's the man,
The guilty man, whom I accuse; and you
Stand bound in duty, as you are supreme,
To be impartial. Since you are a judge,
As a delinquent look on him, and not   61
As on a brother. Justice painted blind
Infers her ministers are obliged to hear
The cause, and, truth the judge, deter-
mine of it,
And, not swayed or by favor or affection,
By a false gloss or wrested comment, alter
The true intent and letter of the law.

Rob. Nor will I, madam.

Aur. [*To Bertoldo.*]   You seem troubled, sir.

Gonz. His color changes, too.

Cam.   The alteration
Grows from his guilt. The goodness of
my cause   70
Begets such confidence in me that I bring
No hired tongue to plead for me, that
with gay,
Rhetorical flourishes may palliate
That which, stripped naked, will appear
deformed.
I stand here mine own advocate; and my
truth,
Delivered in the plainest language, will

Make good itself; nor will I, if the king
Give suffrage to it, but admit of you,
My greatest enemy, and this stranger
prince,
To sit assistants with him.

Aur.   I ne'er wronged you.   80

Cam. In your knowledge of the injury, I
believe it;
Nor will you, in your justice, when you
are
Acquainted with my interest in this man
Which I lay claim to.

Rob.   Let us take our seats.
What is your title to him?

Cam. [*Giving a paper to the King.*]   By
this contract,
Sealed solemnly before a reverend man,
I challenge him for my husband.

Syl. [*Aside.*]   Ha! Was I
Sent for the friar for this? O Sylli!
Sylli!—
Some cordial, or I faint.

Rob.   This writing is
Authentical.

Aur.   But, done in heat of blood,   90
Charmed by her flatteries as no doubt he
was,
To be dispensed with.

Fer.   Add this, if you please:
The distance and disparity between
Their births and fortunes.

Cam.   What can Innocence hope for,
When such as sit her judges are cor-
rupted!
Disparity of birth or fortune, urge you?
Or Siren charms? Or, at his best, in me
Wants [1] to deserve him? Call some few
days back
And, as he was, consider him, and you
Must grant him my inferior. Imagine
You saw him now in fetters, with his
honor,   101
His liberty lost, with her black wings
Despair
Circling his miseries, and this [2] Gonzaga
Trampling on his afflictions; the great
sum
Proposed for his redemption; the king
Forbidding payment of it; this near kins-
man, [3]

[1] Deficiencies.

[2] Emended by all editors. Original has *his*.

[3] The reading of the Princeton copy. Other
copies examined by Bryne read *kinsmen*.

With his protesting followers and friends,
Falling off from him; by the whole world
    forsaken;
Dead to all hope, and buried in the grave
Of his calamities; and then weigh duly
What she deserved, whose merits now
    are doubted,   111
That as his better angel in her bounties
Appeared unto him, his great ransom
    paid,
His wants, and with a prodigal hand,
    supplied—
Whether then, being my manumised [1]
    slave,
He owed not himself to me?
AUR.   Is this true?
ROB. In his silence 'tis acknowledged.
GONZ.   If you want
A witness to this purpose, I'll depose it.
CAM. If I have dwelt too long on my
    deservings
To this unthankful man, pray you,
    pardon me;   120
The cause required it. And, though now
    I add
A little in my painting to the life
His barbarous ingratitude, to deter
Others from imitation, let it meet with
A fair interpretation. This serpent,
Frozen to numbness, was no sooner
    warmed
In the bosom of my pity and compassion,
But in return he ruined his preserver,
The prints the irons had made in his
    flesh   129
Still ulcerous; but all that I had done,
My benefits, in sand or water writ-
    ten,
As they had never been, no more re-
    membered!
And on what ground but his ambitious
    hopes
To gain this duchess' favor?
AUR.   Yes; the object—
Look on it better, lady—may excuse
The charge of [2] his affection.
CAM.   The object!
In what? Forgive me, modesty, if I say
You look upon your form in the false
    glass
Of flattery and self-love, and that de-
    ceives you.

That you were a duchess, as I take it, was
    not   140
Charactered on your face; and, that not
    seen,
For other feature,[3] make all these that are
Experienced in women judges of 'em,
And, if they are not parasites, they must
    grant,[4]
For beauty without art, though you
    storm at it,
I may take the right-hand file.
GONZ.   Well said, i' faith!
I see fair women on no terms will yield
Priority in beauty.
CAM.   Down, proud heart!
Why do I rise up in defense of that
Which, in my cherishing of it, hath un-
    done me?   150
No, madam, I recant—you are all
    beauty,
Goodness, and virtue, and poor I not
    worthy
As a foil to set you off. Enjoy your con-
    quest,
But do not tyrannize. Yet, as I am,
In my lowness, from your height you may
    look on me
And in your suffrage to me make him know
That, though to all men else I did appear
The shame and scorn of women, he
    stands bound
To hold me as her masterpiece.
ROB. [To Bertoldo.]   By my life,
You have shown yourself of such an
    abject temper,   160
So poor and low-conditioned, as I grieve
    for
Your nearness to me.
FER.   I am changed in my
Opinion of you, lady, and profess
The virtues of your mind an ample fortune
For an absolute monarch.
GONZ. [To Bertoldo.]   Since you
    are resolved
To damn yourself, in your forsaking of
Your noble order for a woman, do it
For this. You may search through the
    world, and meet not
With such another phœnix.
AUR.   On the sudden
I feel all fires of love quenched in the
    water   170

[1] Manumitted, freed.
[2] Accusation against.

[3] I.e., as far as other features are concerned.
[4] Supply that.

Of compassion.—Make your peace; you have
My free consent; for here I do disclaim
All interest in you, and, to further your
Desires, fair maid, composed of worth and honor,
The dispensation procured by me,
Freeing Bertoldo from his vow, makes way
To your embraces.

BERT.　　　　　　　　O, how have I strayed,
And willfully, out of the noble tract [1]
Marked me by virtue! Till now, I was never
Truly a prisoner. To excuse my late　180
Captivity, I might allege the malice
Of fortune, you, that conquered me, confessing
Courage in my defense was no way wanting.
But now I have surrendered up my strengths
Into the power of vice, and on my forehead
Branded with mine own hand in capital letters,
DISLOYAL and INGRATEFUL. Though barred from
Human society, and hissed into
Some desert ne'er yet haunted with the curses　189
Of men and women, sitting as a judge
Upon my guilty self, I must confess
It justly falls upon me, and one tear,
Shed in compassion of my sufferings, more
Than I can hope for.

CAM.　　　　　　　　This compunction
For the wrong that you have done me, though you should
Fix here, and your true sorrow move no further,
Will, in respect I loved once, make these eyes
Two springs of sorrow for you.

BERT.　　　　　　　　In your pity
My cruelty shows more monstrous; yet I am not,
Though most ingrateful, grown to such a height　200
Of impudence as in my wishes only
To ask your pardon. If, as now I fall
Prostrate before your feet, you will vouchsafe

[1] Track, course.

To act your own revenge, treading upon me
As a viper eating through the bowels of
Your benefits, to whom with liberty
I owe my being, 'twill take from the burthen
That now is insupportable.

CAM.　　　　　　　　Pray you, rise.
As I wish peace and quiet to my soul,
I do forgive you heartily. Yet, excuse me,　210
Though I deny myself a blessing that,
By the favor of the duchess, seconded
With your submission, is offered to me,
Let not the reason I allege for 't grieve you:
You have been false once. I have done. And if,
When I am married, as this day I will be,
As a perfit sign of your atonement [2] with me,
You wish me joy, I will receive it for
Full satisfaction of all obligations
In which you stand bound to me.

BERT.　　　　　　　　I will do it,　220
And, what's more, in despite of sorrow, live
To see myself undone, beyond all hope
To be made up again.

SYL. [Aside.]　　　　　　　My blood begins
To come to my heart again.

CAM.　　　　　　　　Pray you, Signior Syl,
Call in the holy friar. He's prepared
For finishing the work.

SYL.　　　　　　　　I knew I was
The man. Heaven make me thankful!

ROB.　　　　　　　　Who is this?

AST. His father was the banker of Palermo,
And this the heir of his great wealth; his wisdom
Was not hereditary.

SYL.　　Though you know me not,　230
Your majesty owes me a round sum; I have
A seal or two to witness. Yet, if you please
To wear my colors and dance at my wedding,
I'll never sue you.

ROB.　　　　　　　　And I'll grant your suit.

SYL. Gracious madonna, noble general,
Brave captains, and my quondam rivals, wear 'em,

[2] Reconciliation.

Since I am confident you dare not harbor
A thought but that way current.[1] *Exit.*

AUR.   For my part
I cannot guess the issue.

Enter Syl[li] with [Father Paulo].

SYL.   Do your duty;
And with all speed you can you may despatch us.   240

PAUL. Thus, as a principal ornament to
  the church,
I seize her.

ALL.   How!

ROB.   So young, and so religious!

PAUL. She has forsook the world.

SYL.   And Sylli too!
I shall run mad.

ROB.   Hence with the fool!—
  (*Syl[li] thrust off.*) Proceed, sir.

PAUL. Look on this Maid of Honor, now
Truly honored in her vow
She pays to heaven. Vain delight
By day or pleasure of the night
She no more thinks of. This fair hair
(Favors for great kings to wear)   250
Muw [2] now be shorn; her rich array
Changed into a homely gray.
The dainties with which she was fed
And her proud flesh pamperéd
Must not be tasted; from the spring,
For wine, cold water we will bring,
And with fasting mortify
The feasts of sensuality.
Her jewels, beads; and she must look
Not in a glass, but holy book,   260
To teach her the ne'er-erring way
To immortality. O, may
She, as she purposes to be
A child new-born to piety,
Persever [3] in it, and good men,
With saints and angels, say, Amen!

CAM. This is the marriage, this the port to
  which
My vows must steer me! Fill my spread-
  ing sails
With the pure wind of your devotions
  for me
That I may touch the secure haven,
  where   270
Eternal happiness keeps her residence,
Temptations to frailty never entering!
I am dead to the world, and thus dispose

Of what I leave behind me; and, dividing
My state into three parts, I thus be-
  queath it:
The first to the fair nunnery, to which
I dedicate the last and better part
Of my frail life; a second portion
To pious uses; and the third to thee,   279
Adorni, for thy true and faithful service.
And, ere I take my last [4] farewell, with
  hope
To find a grant, my suit to you is that
You would for my sake pardon this
  young man,
And to his merits love him, and no
  further.

ROB. I thus confirm it.
                  Gives his hand to Fulgen[tio].

CAM. (*To Bertoldo.*) And, as e'er you hope,
Like me, to be made happy, I conjure
  you
To reassume your order, and, in fighting
Bravely against the enemies of our faith,
Redeem your mortgaged honor.

GONZ.[5]   I restore this.
                  [Gives him] the white cross.
Once more brothers in arms.

BERT.   I'll live and die so.   290

CAM. To you my pious wishes! And, to
  end
All differences, great sir, I beseech you
To be an arbitrator, and compound
The quarrel long continuing between
The duke and duchess.

ROB.   I'll take it into
My special care.

CAM.   I am then at rest. Now, father,
Conduct me where you please.
                  Exeunt Paulo and Camiola.

ROB.   She well deserves
Her name, the Maid of Honor! May
  she stand
To all posterity a fair example   299
For noble maids to imitate, since to live
In wealth and pleasure is common, but to
  part with
Such poisoned baits is rare, there being
  nothing
Upon this stage of life to be commended,
Though well begun, till it be fully ended.
                                        Exeunt.

THE END.

[1] Tending in that direction.
[2] May.   [3] Persevere.

[4] Emended by all editors. Original reads
mytake lust.   [5] Original reads *Rob.*

JOHN FORD

Because of his disdain of the orthodox moral code of his time and his sympathetic treatment of forbidden love, John Ford is often regarded as the most modern of Elizabethan and Stuart dramatists. He was baptized at Ilsington in Devonshire, April 17, 1586, was probably the John Ford who entered Exeter College, Oxford, in March, 1601, and was certainly the John Ford who was admitted to the Middle Temple in November, 1602. He first appeared in print with *Fame's Memorial* (1606), a long elegy on the death of the Earl of Devonshire, and he published other occasional pieces before he finally committed himself to a dramatic career. His first venture in dramatic work may well have been in the writing or revising of *A Bad Beginning Makes a Good Ending*, which was acted by the King's Men at court in 1612/13, and which was one of the four unprinted plays of Ford that were destroyed by Warburton's cook. His career as a playwright definitely begins, however, in 1621, when he joined with Thomas Dekker and William Rowley in the composition of *The Witch of Edmonton*. He collaborated with Dekker in several other plays and with Webster in at least one. After about 1624, however, he seems to have worked alone, and his reputation rests chiefly upon his three unaided tragedies of forbidden love, *'Tis Pity She's a Whore*, *The Broken Heart*, and *Love's Sacrifice*. He was still writing for the stage in May, 1638, but the date of his death is unknown.

On April 19, 1621, Elizabeth Sawyer, who was later to assume the title rôle in *The Witch of Edmonton*, was executed for witchcraft. On April 27, Henry Goodcole's *Wonderful Discovery of E. Sawyer, a Witch* was entered in the Stationers' Register, and was published later the same year. From this work the authors drew materials for *The Witch of Edmonton*, which was acted December 29, 1621, at Whitehall by the Prince's Servants. Studies of the proportionate shares of the three collaborators in the play have not led to agreement beyond a few general conclusions (see M. L. Hunt's *Thomas Dekker*, F. E. Pierce in *Anglia*, XXXVI, and H. Dugdale Sykes in *N. & Q.*, December 18, 1926). Rowley's share in the play seems to be indeterminable, but is probably slight, being confined chiefly to those scenes in which Cuddy Banks appears. To Dekker may be assigned the witch scenes, the greater share in the character of Susan, and a considerable part in the prose passages. According to Sykes and others, Ford is responsible for the greater part of the play—its main structure; the characters of Sir Arthur Clarington, Frank Thorney, and Winnifride; and some part in the character of Susan and in the prose passages, especially those dealing with Old Carter and his household. The present text is based upon photostats of the quarto of 1658 in the Harvard College Library; some use has been made of the Gifford-Dyce edition of Ford's works.

The Broken Heart, printed in 1633, was probably written not long before its entry in the Stationers' Register, March 28 of that year. No literary source for the play has been discovered, but, in view of ll. 15–16 of the prologue and the arguments of Stuart Pratt Sherman (*PMLA*, 1909, and the introduction to his edition in the Belles-Lettres Series), it appears to have been based upon the experiences of Sir Philip Sidney, Penelope Devereux, and Lord Rich, the triangle celebrated in Sidney's *Astrophel and Stella*. "In *The Broken Heart*," Sherman says, "Ford throws down the gauntlet to orthodox morality by placing a thoroughly pure woman in a genuine moral dilemma. . . . By establishing the tragic conflict of Penthea in her own spirit, he makes of her a distinctly modern type of heroine." The present text is based upon Henry De Vocht's reprint of the 1633 quarto in the Royal Library of The Hague; reference has been made to the Gifford-Dyce edition of Ford's works.

In *The Chronicle History of Perkin Warbeck*, entered in the Stationers' Register February 24, 1634, and published the same year, Ford turned aside from his interest in romantic love to produce a type of play which, as he seems to suggest in his prologue, had been neglected for a generation. He derived the materials for the play from Bacon's *History of the Reign of Henry the Seventh* (1622) and Thomas Gainsford's *True and Wonderful History of Perkin Warbeck* (1618), and apparently chose the Shakespearean chronicle play as his model. His plot, however, is simpler than Shakespeare's, and the play as a whole, though rapid in movement, lacks intensity and variety. Nevertheless, it fills a gap among Shakespeare's chronicle plays, and it has often received high praise as a play not unworthy to rank among the few plays of the kind that deserve distant comparison with those of the master dramatist. The present text is based upon Henry De Vocht's reprint of the 1634 quarto, and reference has been made to the Gifford-Dyce edition of Ford's works and to the edition by Mildred C. Struble.

THE WITCH OF EDMONTON[1]

BY

WILLIAM ROWLEY, THOMAS DEKKER, AND JOHN FORD

ACTORS' NAMES

SIR ARTHUR CLARINGTON.
OLD THORNEY, *a gentleman.*
OLD CARTER, *a rich yeoman.*
OLD BANKS, *a countryman.*
W. MAGO[2] } *two countrymen.*
W. HAMLUC[2] }
THREE OTHER COUNTRYMEN.
WARBECK } *suitors to Carter's daughters.*
SOMERTON }
FRANK, *Thorney's son.*
YOUNG CUDDY BANKS, *the clown.*
FOUR MORRIS DANCERS.[3]
OLD RATCLIFFE.
SAWGUT, *an old fiddler.*
POLDAVIS, *a barber's boy.*[4]

JUSTICE.
CONSTABLE.
OFFICERS.
SERVING-MEN.
DOG, *a familiar.*[5]
A SPIRIT.

WOMEN

MOTHER SAWYER, *the witch.*
ANN, *Ratcliffe's wife.*
SUSAN } *Carter's daughters.*
KATHERINE }
WINNIFRIDE, *Sir Arthur's maid.*
[JANE, *Carter's maid.*

SCENE: *Edmonton and its vicinity; London.*

TIME: *Early seventeenth century.*]

The whole argument is this distich.

Forced marriage, murder; murder, blood
requires.
Reproach, revenge; revenge, hell's help
desires.

PROLOGUE

The town of Edmonton hath lent the stage
A devil[6] and a witch, both in an age.
To make comparisons it were uncivil
Between so even a pair, a witch and devil;
But, as the year doth with his plenty bring
As well a latter as a former spring,
So has this witch enjoyed the first, and
reason
Presumes she may partake the other season.
In acts deserving name, the proverb says,
"Once good, and ever." Why not so in
plays?   10
Why not in this, since, gentlemen, we
flatter
No expectation? Here is mirth and matter.
                                    MR. BIRD.[7]

ACT[US] I. SCEN[A] i.

[*A room in Sir Arthur's House at Edmonton.*]

*Enter Frank Thorney; Winnifride, with
child.*[8]

FRANK. Come, wench. Why, here's a
business soon despatched.
Thy heart I know is now at ease; thou
need'st not

[1] The title continues: "A Known True Story,
Composed into a Tragi-Comedy by Divers Well-
Esteemed Poets, William Rowley, Thomas
Dekker, John Ford, etc. Acted by the Prince's
Servants, Often at the Cockpit in Drury Lane,
Once at Court, with Singular Applause."
[2] Probably the names of actual actors.
W. Mago, however, is not referred to by name
in the play itself.
[3] Who appear first as the above-mentioned
countrymen.
[4] Merely referred to in the play.
[5] *I.e.,* a familiar spirit.
[6] An allusion to *The Merry Devil of Edmonton,*
printed anonymously in 1608.
[7] Master Theophilus Bird.   [8] *I.e.,* pregnant.

1445

Fear what the tattling gossips in their
   cups
Can speak against thy fame. Thy child
   shall know
Who to call dad now.

WIN.   You have discharged [1]
The true part of an honest man; I cannot
Request a fuller satisfaction
Than you have freely granted. Yet
   methinks
'Tis an hard case, being lawful man and
   wife,
We should not live together.

FRANK.   Had I failed   10
In promise of my truth to thee, we must
Have then been ever sundered; now the
   longest
Of our forbearing either's company
Is only but to gain a little time
For our continuing thrift, that so here-
   after
The heir that shall be born may not have
   cause
To curse his hour of birth, which made
   him feel
The misery of beggary and want—
Two devils that are occasions to enforce
A shameful end. My plots aim but to
   keep   20
My father's love.

WIN.   And that will be as difficult
To be preserved, when he shall under-
   stand
How you are married, as it will be now,
Should you confess it to him.

FRANK.   Fathers are
Won by degrees, not bluntly, as our
   masters
Or wrongéd friends are; and besides I'll use
Such dutiful and ready means that ere
He can have notice of what's past, th'
   inheritance
To which I am born heir shall be assured.
That done, why, let him know it; if he
   like it not,   30
Yet he shall have no power in him left
To cross the thriving of it.

WIN.   You who had
The conquest of my maiden love may
   easily

[1] Here and in a few later passages the line
division has been regularized. Some passages
printed in the original as prose have been divided into verse.

Conquer the fears of my distrust. And
   whither
Must I be hurried?

FRANK.   Prithee, do not use
A word so much unsuitable to the con-
   stant
Affections of thy husband. Thou shalt
   live
Near Waltham Abbey with thy uncle
   Selman.
I have acquainted him with all at large.[2]
He'll use thee kindly; thou shalt want
   no pleasures   40
Nor any other fit supplies whatever
Thou canst in heart desire.

WIN.   All these are nothing
Without your company.

FRANK.   Which thou shalt have
Once every month at least.

WIN.   Once every month!
Is this to have an husband?

FRANK.   Perhaps oft'ner;
That's as occasion serves.

WIN.   Ay, ay; in case
No other beauty tempt your eye, whom
   you
Like better, I may chance to be re-
   membered,
And see you now and then. Faith, I did
   hope
You'ld not have used me so; 'tis but
   my fortune.   50
And yet, if not for my sake, have some
   pity
Upon the child I go with, that's your own.
And, less you'll be a cruel-hearted father,
You cannot but remember that.
Heaven knows how—

FRANK.   To quit which fear at once,
As by the ceremony late performed
I plighted thee a faith as free from
   challenge
As any double thought, once more, in
   hearing
Of heaven and thee, I vow that never
   henceforth
Disgrace, reproof, lawless affections,
   threats,   60
Or what can be suggested gainst our
   marriage,
Shall cause me falsify that bridal oath
That binds me thine. And, Winnifride,
   whenever

[2] At length, fully.

The wanton heat of youth, by subtle
baits
Of beauty, or what woman's art can
practice,[1]
Draw me from only loving thee, let
heaven
Inflict upon my life some fearful ruin!
I hope thou dost believe me.

WIN.　　　　　　　　Swear no more;
I am confirmed, and will resolve to do
What you think most behooveful for us.

FRANK.　　　　　　　Thus, then:　70
Make thyself ready; at the furthest house
Upon the green without the town your
uncle
Expects you. For a little time, farewell!

WIN.　　　　　　　　　　Sweet,
We shall meet again as soon as thou
canst possibly?

FRANK. We shall. One kiss!—Away!

　　　　　　　　　[Exit Winnifride.]

Ent[er] Sir Art[hur] Clarington.

SIR ART.　　　　Frank Thorney!

FRANK.　　　　　　　　Here, sir.

SIR ART. Alone? Then must I tell thee in
plain terms
Thou hast wronged thy master's house
basely and lewdly.

FRANK. Your house, sir?

SIR ART.　　　Yes, sir. If the nimble devil
That wantoned in your blood rebelled
against　　　　　　　　　　　79
All rules of honest duty, you might, sir,
Have found out some more fitting place
than here
To have built a stews in. All the country
whispers
How shamefully thou hast undone a
maid,
Approved for modest life, for civil car-
riage,
Till thy prevailing perjuries enticed her
To forfeit shame. Will you be honest yet,
Make her amends and marry her?

FRANK.　　　　　　　　So, sir,
I might bring both myself and her to
beggary;
And that would be a shame worse than
the other.

SIR ART. You should have thought on this
before, and then　　　　　　　90

Your reason would have overswayed the
passion
Of your unruly lust. But, that you may
Be left without excuse, to salve the
infamy
Of my disgracéd house, and cause[2] you
are
A gentleman, and both of you my serv-
ants,
I'll make the maid a portion.

FRANK.　　　　　So you promised me
Before, in case I married her. I know
Sir Arthur Clarington deserves the credit
Report hath lent him, and presume you
are
A debtor to your promise. But upon　100
What certainty shall I resolve? Excuse me
For being somewhat rude.

SIR ART.　　　　　　　'Tis but reason.
Well, Frank, what think'st thou of two
hundred pounds
And a continual friend?

FRANK.　　　Though my poor fortunes
Might happily[3] prefer me to a choice
Of a far greater portion, yet, to right
A wrongéd maid and to preserve your
favor,
I am content to accept your proffer.

SIR ART.　　　　　　　　Art thou?

FRANK. Sir, we shall every day have need
to employ
The use of what you please to give.

SIR ART.　　　　　　Thou shalt have 't.　110

FRANK. Then I claim your promise. We
are man and wife.

SIR ART. Already?

FRANK.　　　　　And more than so; I have
promised her
Free entertainment in her uncle's house
Near Waltham Abbey, where she may
securely
Sojourn, till time and my endeavors work
My father's love and liking.

SIR ART.　　　　　　　Honest Frank!

FRANK. I hope, sir, you will think I cannot keep her
Without a daily charge.

SIR ART.　　　　　　As for the money,
'Tis all thine own! And, though I can-
not make thee
A present payment, yet thou shalt be
sure　　　　　　　　　　120
I will not fail thee.

---

[1] Scheme.

[2] Because.　　　　　　[3] Haply, perhaps.

FRANK. But our occasions—

SIR ART. Nay, nay,
Talk not of your occasions. Trust my bounty;
It shall not sleep. Hast married her, i' faith, Frank?
'Tis well, 'tis passing well! Then, Winnifride,
Once more thou art an honest [1] woman. Frank,
Thou hast a jewel. Love her; she'll deserve it.
And when to Waltham?

FRANK. She is making ready;
Her uncle stays for her.

SIR ART. Most provident speed.
Frank, I will be [thy] [2] friend, and such a friend!
Thou'lt bring her thither?

FRANK. Sir, I cannot; newly 130
My father sent me word I should come to him.

SIR ART. Marry, and do; I know thou hast a wit
To handle him.

FRANK. I have a suit t' ye.

SIR ART. What is 't?
Anything, Frank; command it.

FRANK. That you'll please
By letters to assure my father that
I am not married.

SIR ART. How!

FRANK. Someone or other
Hath certainly informed him that I purposed
To marry Winnifride, on which he threatened
To disinherit me. To prevent it,
Lowly I crave your letters, which he, seeing, 140
Will credit; and I hope, ere I return,
On such conditions as I'll frame, his lands
Shall be assured.

SIR ART. But what is there [3] to quit [4]
My knowledge of the marriage?

FRANK. Why, you were not
A witness to it.

SIR ART. I conceive; and then—
His land confirmed, thou wilt acquaint him throughly
With all that's past.

FRANK. I mean no less.

SIR ART. Provided
I never was made privy to it.

FRANK. Alas, sir,
Am I a talker?

SIR ART. Draw thyself the letter;
I'll put my hand to it. I commend thy policy; 150
Th' art witty, witty Frank; nay, nay, 'tis fit.
Despatch it.

FRANK. I shall write effectually. *Exit.*

SIR ART. Go thy way, cuckoo. Have I caught the young man?
One trouble, then, is freed. He that will feast
At other's cost must be a bold-faced guest.

Enter Win[nifride] in a riding suit.

WIN. I have heard the news; all now is safe;
The worst is past.

SIR ART. Thy lip, wench! [*Kisses her.*]
I must bid
Farewell, for fashion's sake; but I will visit thee
Suddenly, girl. This was cleanly carried;
Ha! Was 't not, Win?

WIN. Then were my happiness, 160
That I in heart repent I did not bring him
The dower of a virginity. Sir, forgive me;
I have been much to blame. Had not my lewdness [5]
Given way to your immoderate waste of virtue,
You had not with such eagerness pursued
The error of your goodness.

SIR ART. Dear, dear Win,
I hug this art of thine; it shows how cleanly
Thou canst beguile, in case occasion serve
To practice; it becomes thee. Now we share
Free scope enough, without control or fear, 170
To interchange our pleasures; we will surfeit
In our embraces, wench. Come, tell me, when
Wilt thou appoint a meeting?

---

[1] Chaste.　　[2] Added in Gifford-Dyce edn.
[3] Emended by Gifford. Original reads *that.*
[4] *I.e.,* rid myself of.

[5] Suggested by Dyce. Original reads *laundress.*

Win. What to do?

Sir Art. Good, good, to con the lesson of our loves,
Our secret game.

Win. O, blush to speak it further!
As y' are a noble gentleman, forget
A sin so monstrous; 'tis not gently done
To open a curéd wound. I know you speak
For trial; troth, you need not.

Sir Art. I for trial?
Not I, by this good sunshine!

Win. Can you name 180
That syllable of good, and yet not tremble
To think to what a foul and black in-tent
You use it for an oath? Let me resolve [1] you:
If you appear in any visitation
That brings not with it pity for the wrongs
Done to abuséd Thorney, my kind hus-band;
If you infect mine ear with any breath
That is not throughly perfumed with sighs
For former deeds of lust, may I be cursed 189
Even in my prayers, when I vouchsafe
To see or hear you! I will change my life
From a loose whore to a repentant wife.

Sir Art. Wilt thou turn monster now?
Art not ashamed
After so many months to be honest at last?
Away, away! Fie on 't!

Win. My resolution
Is built upon a rock. This very day
Young Thorney vowed, with oaths not to be doubted,
That never any change of love should cancel
The bonds in which we are to either bound
Of lasting truth—and shall I, then, for my part 200
Unfile the sacred oath set on record
In heaven's book? Sir Arthur, do not study
To add to your lascivious lust the sin
Of sacrilege, for, if you but endeavor

By any unchaste word to tempt my constancy,
You strive as much as in you lies to ruin
A temple hallowed to the purity
Of holy marriage. I have said enough;
You may believe me.

Sir Art. Get you to your nunnery;
There freeze in your old cloister! This is fine! 210

Win. Good angels guide me! Sir, you'll give me leave
To weep and pray for your conversion?

Sir Art. Yes.
Away to Waltham! Pox on your honesty!
Had you no other trick to fool me? Well,
You may want money yet.

Win. None that I'll send for
To you, for hire of a damnation.
When I am gone, think on my just com-plaint.
I was your devil; O, be you my saint!
Exit Win[nifride].

Sir Art. Go, go thy ways, as changeable a baggage
As ever cozened knight. I'm glad I'm rid of her. 220
Honest? Marry, hang her! Thorney is my debtor;
I thought to have paid him too; but fools have fortune. *Exit S[ir] A[rthur].*

Scen[a] ii.

[*A room in Carter's house at Edmonton.*]

Enter Old Thorney and Old Carter.

O. Thor. You offer, Mr. Carter, like a gentleman; I cannot find fault with it, 'tis so fair.

O. Cart. No gentleman I, Mr. Thorney. Spare the mastership; call me by my name, John Carter. "Master" is a title my father, nor his before him, were acquainted with— honest Hertfordshire yeomen. Such an one am I; my word and my deed shall be proved one at all times. I mean to give you [10 no security for the marriage money.

O. Thor. How? No security? Although it need not so long as you live, yet who is he has surety of his life one hour? "Men," the proverb says, "are mortal;" else, for my part, I distrust you not, were the sum double.

O. Cart. Double, treble, more or less,

---
[1] Inform.

I tell you, Mr. Thorney, I'll give no security. Bonds and bills are but terriers to [20 catch fools, and keep lazy knaves busy; my security shall be present payment. And we here about Edmonton hold present payment as sure as an alderman's bond in London, Mr. Thorney.

O. Thor. I cry you mercy,[1] sir; I understood you not.

O. Cart. I like young Frank well; so does my Susan too. The girl has a fancy to him, which makes me ready in my [30 purse. There be other suitors within, that make much noise to little purpose. If Frank love Sue, Sue shall have none but Frank. 'Tis a mannerly girl, Mr. Thorney, though but an homely man's daughter. There have worse faces looked out of black bags, man.

O. Thor. You speak your mind freely and honestly. I marvel my son comes not; I am sure he will be here some time [40 today.

O. Cart. Today or tomorrow, when he comes he shall be welcome to bread, beer, and beef, yeoman's fare; we have no kickshaws: full dishes, whole bellyfulls. Should I diet three days at one of the slender city suppers, you might send me to Barber-Surgeons' Hall [2] the fourth day, to hang up for an anatomy.[3] Here come they that—How now, girls? Every day [50 playday with you?

Enter Warbeck with Susan, Somerton with Katherine.

Valentine's day too, all by couples? Thus will young folks do when we are laid in our graves, Mr. Thorney; here's all the care they take. And how do you find the wenches, gentlemen? Have they any mind to a loose gown and a strait shoe? Win 'em and wear 'em. They shall choose for themselves by my consent.

Warb. You speak like a kind father.—
[*The young people stand aside in pairs.*]
Sue, thou hearest   60
The liberty that's granted thee; what sayest thou?
Wilt thou be mine?

[1] I beg your pardon.
[2] Many barbers performed duties now given to surgeons.
[3] Skeleton.

Sus.   Your what, sir? I dare swear
Never your wife.
Warb.   Canst thou be so unkind,
Considering how dearly I affect [4] thee,
Nay, dote on thy perfections?
Sus.   You are studied,
Too scholarlike in words; I understand not.
I am too coarse for such a gallant's love
As you are.
Warb.   By the honor of gentility—
Sus. Good sir, no swearing; yea and nay
with us   69
Prevails above all oaths you can invent.
Warb. By this white hand of thine—
Sus.   Take a false oath?
Fie, fie! Flatter the wise; fools not regard it—
And one of these am I.
Warb.   Dost thou despise me?
O. Cart. Let 'em talk on, Mr. Thorney;
I know Sue's mind. The fly may buzz about the candle; he shall but singe his wings when all's done. Frank, Frank is he has her heart.
Som. But shall I live in hope, Kate?   79
Kat. Better so than be a desperate man.
Som. Perhaps thou think'st it is thy portion
I level at. Wert thou as poor in fortunes
As thou art rich in goodness, I would rather
Be suitor for the dower of thy virtues
Than twice thy father's whole estate;
and, prithee,
Be thou resolved [5] so.
Kat.   Mr. Somerton,
It is an easy labor to deceive
A maid that will believe men's subtile promises;
Yet I conceive of you as worthily
As I presume you do deserve.
Som.   Which is   90
As worthily in loving thee sincerely
As thou art worthy to be so beloved.
Kat. I shall find time to try you.
Som.   Do, Kate, do;
And, when I fail, may all my joys forsake me!
O. Cart. Warbeck and Sue are at it still. I laugh to myself, Mr. Thorney, to see how earnestly he beats the bush, while the bird is flown into another's bosom. A very un-

[4] Love.   [5] Convinced.

thrift, Mr. Thorney; one of the country roaring lads. We have such as well as the [100 city, and as arrant rakehells as they are, though not so nimble at their prizes of wit. Sue knows the rascal to an hair's breadth, and will fit him accordingly.

O. THOR. What is the other gentleman?

O. CART. One Somerton—the honester man of the two by five pounds in every stone weight; a civil fellow. He has a fine, convenient estate of land in West Ham, by Essex. M[aster] Ranges, that dwells [110 by Enfield, sent him hither. He likes Kate well; I may tell you I think she likes him as well. If they agree, I'll not hinder the match for my part. But that Warbeck is such another—I use him kindly for Mr. Somerton's sake, for he came hither first as a companion of his. Honest men, Mr. Thorney, may fall into knaves' company now and then.

WARB. Three hundred a year jointure, Sue.

SUS. Where lies it? 120 By sea or by land? I think by sea.

WARB. Do I look like a captain?

SUS. Not a whit, sir. Should all that use the seas be reckoned captains, There's not a ship should have a scullion in her To keep her clean.

WARB. Do you scorn me, Mrs.[1] Susan? Am I a subject to be jeered at?

SUS. Neither Am I a property for you to use As stale [2] to your fond, [3] wanton, loose discourse. Pray, sir, be civil.

WARB. Wilt be angry, wasp?

O. CART. God-a-mercy, Sue! She'll [130 firk [4] him, on my life, if he fumble with her.

Enter Frank.

Mr. Francis Thorney, you are welcome indeed; your father expected your coming. How does the right worshipful knight, Sir Arthur Clarington, your master?

FRANK. In health this morning.—Sir, my duty.

O. THOR. Now You come as I could wish.

WARB. [Aside.] Frank Thorney, ha!

SUS. You must excuse me.

FRANK. Virtuous Mrs. Susan! Kind Mrs. Katherine! (Salutes [5] them.)— Gentlemen, to both 139 Good time o' th' day.

SOM. The like to you.

WARB. [Aside to Somerton.] 'Tis he. A word, friend. On my life, this is the man Stands fair in crossing Susan's love to me.

SOM. [Aside to Warbeck.] I think no less; be wise, and take no notice on 't. He that can win her, best deserves her.

WARB. [Aside to Somerton.] Marry A serving-man? Mew!

SOM. [Aside to Warbeck.] Prithee, friend, no more.

O. CART. Gentlemen all, there's within a slight dinner ready, if you please to taste of it. Mr. Thorney, Mr. Francis, Mr. Somerton!—Why, girls! What, huswives! Will you spend all your fore- [150 noon in tittle-tattles? Away! It's well, i' faith.—Will you go in, gentlemen?

O. THOR. We'll follow presently; my son and I Have a few words of business.

O. CART. At your pleasure. Ex[eunt] the Rest.

O. THOR. I think you guess the reason, Frank, for which I sent for you.

FRANK. Yes, sir.

O. THOR. I need not tell you With what a labyrinth of dangers daily The best part of my whole estate's encumbered; Nor have I any clew to wind it out 159 But what occasion proffers me, wherein If you should falter, I shall have the shame, And you the loss. On these two points rely Our happiness or ruin. If you marry With wealthy Carter's daughter, there's a portion Will free my land, all which I will instate,[6] Upon the marriage, to you; otherwise I must be of necessity enforced To make a present sale of all; and yet, For aught I know, live in as poor distress,

---

[1] Mistress. [2] Dupe. [3] Foolish. [4] Chastise. [5] Kisses. [6] Assign.

Or worse, than now I do. You hear the
   sum? 170
I told you thus before. Have you con-
   sidered on 't?
FRANK. I have, sir; and however I could
   wish
To enjoy the benefit of single freedom—
For that I find no disposition in me
To undergo the burthen of that care
That marriage brings with it—yet, to
   secure
And settle the continuance of your credit,
I humbly yield to be directed by you
In all commands.
O. THOR.   You have already used
Such thriving protestations to the maid
That she is wholly yours. And—speak
   the truth— 181
You love her, do you not?
FRANK.   'Twere pity, sir,
I should deceive her.
O. THOR.   Better y' had been unborn.
But is your love so steady that you
   mean—
Nay, more, desire—to make her your
   wife?
FRANK.   Else, sir,
It were a wrong not to be righted.
O. THOR.   True,
It were. And you will marry her?
FRANK.   Heaven prosper it,
I do intend it.
O. THOR.   O, thou art a villain!
A devil like a man! Wherein have I 189
Offended all the powers so much, to be
Father to such a graceless, godless son?
FRANK. To me, sir, this? O, my cleft heart!
O. THOR.   To thee,
Son of my curse. Speak truth and blush,
   thou monster!
Hast thou not married Winnifride, a maid
Was fellow servant with thee?
FRANK. [Aside.]   Some swift spirit
Has blown this news abroad; I must out-
   face it.
O. THOR. D' you study for excuse? Why,
   all the country
Is full on 't.
FRANK.   With your license, 'tis not
   charitable,
I am sure it is not fatherly, so much
To be o'erswayed with credulous con-
   ceit [1] 200

[1] Thought, belief.

Of mere [2] impossibilities; but fathers
Are privileged to think and talk at
   pleasure.
O. THOR. Why, canst thou yet deny thou
   hast no wife?
FRANK. What do you take me for? An
   atheist?
One that nor hopes the blessedness of
   life
Hereafter, neither fears the vengeance
   due
To such as make the marriage bed an
   inn,
Which travelers day and night,
After a toilsome lodging, leave at pleas-
   ure?
Am I become so insensible of losing 210
The glory of creation's work, my soul?
O, I have lived too long!
O. THOR.   Thou hast, dissembler.
Darest thou persever [3] yet, and pull
   down wrath
As hot as flames of hell to strike thee
   quick
Into the grave of horror? I believe thee
   not;
Get from my sight!
FRANK.   Sir, though mine
   innocence
Needs not a stronger witness than the
   clearness
Of an unperished conscience, yet for that
I was informed how mainly you had been
Possessed of this untruth, to quit all
   scruple, 220
Please you peruse this letter; 'tis to you.
O. THOR. From whom?
FRANK.   Sir Arthur Clar-
   ington, my master.
O. THOR. [After reading.] Well, sir.
FRANK. [Aside.]   On every side
I am distracted,
Am waded deeper into mischief
Than virtue can avoid. But on I must.
Fate leads me; I will follow.—There you
   read
What may confirm you.
O. THOR.   Yes, and wonder
   at it.
Forgive me, Frank; credulity abused me.
My tears express my joy, and I am
   sorry
I injured innocence.

[2] Absolute.   [3] Persevere

FRANK.   Alas, I knew 230
Your rage and grief proceeded from your
    love
To me; so I conceived it.
O. THOR.   My good son,
I'll bear with many faults in thee here-
    after;
Bear thou with mine.
FRANK.   The peace is soon
    concluded.

Enter Old Carter [and Susan].

O. CART. Why, Mr. Thorney, d' ye mean
to talk out your dinner? The company
attends your coming. What must it be,
Mr. Frank, or son Frank? I am plain Dun-
stable.[1]
O. THOR. Son, brother, if your daughter
    like to have it so.   240
FRANK. I dare be confident she's not al-
    tered
From what I left her at our parting last.
Are you, fair maid?
SUS.   You took too sure
    possession
Of an engagéd heart.
FRANK.   Which now I challenge.
O. CART. Marry, and much good may
it do thee, son. Take her to thee. Get me a
brace of boys at a burthen, Frank; the nurs-
ing shall not stand thee in a penny-worth
of milk. Reach her home and spare not!
When's the day?   250
O. THOR. Tomorrow, if you please. To use
    ceremony
Of charge and custom were to little
    purpose;
Their loves are married fast enough
    already.
O. CART. A good motion. We'll e'en have
an household dinner, and let the fiddlers go
scrape. Let the bride and bridegroom dance
at night together; no matter for the guests.
Tomorrow, Sue, tomorrow.—Shall 's to
dinner now?
O. THOR. We are on all sides pleased, I
    hope.   260
SUS. Pray heaven I may deserve the bless-
    ing sent me.
Now my heart is settled.
FRANK.   So is mine.
O. CART. Your marriage money shall be

received before your wedding shoes can
be pulled on. Blessing on you both!
FRANK. [*Aside.*] No man can hide his
    shame from heaven that views him;
In vain he flees whose destiny pursues
    him.   *Exeunt omnes.*

ACT[US] II. SCEN[A] i.

[*A field near Edmonton.*]

Enter Elizabeth Sawyer gathering sticks.

SAWY. And why on me? Why should the
    envious world
Throw all their scandalous malice upon
    me?
Cause I am poor, deformed, and igno-
    rant,
And like a bow buckled and bent to-
    gether
By some more strong in mischiefs than
    myself,
Must I for that be made a common
    sink
For all the filth and rubbish of men's
    tongues
To fall and run into? Some call me
    witch,
And, being ignorant of myself, they go
About to teach me how to be one, urg-
    ing   10
That my bad tongue—by their bad
    usage made so—
Forspeaks[2] their cattle, doth bewitch
    their corn,
Themselves, their servants, and their
    babes at nurse.
This they enforce upon me, and in part

Enter O[ld] Banks.

Make me to credit it. And here comes
    one
Of my chief adversaries.
O. BANK. Out, out upon thee, witch!
SAWY.   Dost call me witch?
O. BANK. I do, witch, I do; and worse
I would, knew I a name more hateful.
What makest[3] thou upon my ground? [20
SAWY. Gather a few rotten sticks to
warm me.
O. BANK. Down with them when I bid
thee, quickly; I'll make thy bones rattle in
thy skin else.

---

[1] Proverbial for outspoken and honest.   [2] Bewitches.   [3] Doest.

Sawy. You won't, churl, cutthroat,
miser! There they be. [*Throws them down.*]
Would they stuck cross thy throat, thy
bowels, thy maw, thy midriff!

O. Bank. Say'st thou me so? Hag, [30
out of my ground! [*Beats her.*]

Sawy. Dost strike me, slave, curmudgeon? Now, thy bones aches, thy joints
cramps, and convulsions stretch and crack
thy sinews!

O. Bank. Cursing, thou hag! Take
that and that! [*Beats her and*] *exit.*

Sawy. Strike, do, and withered may
　　that hand and arm
Whose blows have lamed me drop from
　　the rotten trunk.
Abuse me! Beat me! Call me hag and
　　witch! 40
What is the name, where and by what
　　art learned,
What spells, what charms, or invoca-
　　tions,
May the thing called Familiar be pur-
　　chased?

Enter Young Banks and three or four more
[Countrymen].

Y. Bank. A new head for the tabor,
and silver tipping for the pipe; remember
that, and forget not five leash of new bells.

1 [Count.] Double bells! Crooked Lane [1]
ye shall have 'em straight in. Crooked
Lane! Double bells all, if it be possible.

Y. Bank. Double bells? Double [50
coxcombs! Trebles, buy me trebles, all
trebles, for our purpose is to be in the
altitudes.

2 [Count.] All trebles? Not a mean? [2]

Y. Bank. Not one. The morris is so
cast we'll have neither mean nor bass in
our company, fellow Rowland.

3 [Count.] What? Nor a counter? [3]

Y. Bank. By no means, no hunting
counter; [4] leave that to Enfield [5] Chase [60
men. All trebles, all in the altitudes. Now
for the disposing of parts in the morris,
little or no labor will serve.

2 [Count.] If you that be minded to
follow your leader know me—an ancient

---

[1] A shopping district in London.
[2] Tenor.　　　　　　　[3] Countertenor.
[4] Following the trail in the wrong direction.
[5] The original spelling, *Envile*, indicates the
pronunciation.

honor belonging to our house—for a fore-
horse [i' th'] [6] team and fore-gallant [7] in a
morris, my father's stable is not unfurnished.

3 [Count.] So much for the fore- [70
horse; but how for a good hobbyhorse? [8]

Y. Bank. For a hobbyhorse? Let me
see an almanac. Midsummer moon, let
me see ye. "When the moon's in the full,
then's wit in the wane." No more. Use
your best skill; your morris will suffer an
eclipse.

1 [Count.] An eclipse?

Y. Bank. A strange one.

2 [Count.] Strange? 80

Y. Bank. Yes, and most sudden. Remember the fore-gallant, and forget the
hobbyhorse! The whole body of your
morris will be darkened.—There be of
us—but 'tis no matter. Forget the hobbyhorse!

1 [Count.] Cuddy Banks, have you
forgot since he paced it from Enfield
Chase to Edmonton? Cuddy, honest
Cuddy, cast thy stuff. 90

Y. Bank. Suffer may ye all! It shall
be known, I can take mine ease as well
as another man. Seek your hobbyhorse
where you can get him.

1 [Count.] Cuddy, honest Cuddy, we
confess, and are sorry for our neglect.

2 [Count.] The old horse shall have a
new bridle.

3 [Count.] The caparisons new painted.

4 [Count.] The tail repaired. The [100
snaffle and the bosses new saffroned o'er. [9]

1 [Count.] Kind—

2 [Count.] Honest—

3 [Count.] Loving, ingenious—

4 [Count.] Affable Cuddy.

Y. Bank. To show I am not flint, but
affable, as you say, very well stuffed, a
kind of warm dough or puffpaste, I relent, I connive, most affable Jack. Let
the hobbyhorse provide a strong back, [110
he shall not want a belly when I am in
'em—but [*Sees Sawyer.*]—'uds me, [10] Mother
Sawyer!

---

[6] Added in Gifford-Dyce edn.
[7] Leader of the dancers.
[8] A performer in a morris.
[9] The original gives this sentence to the first
countryman.
[10] God's me; a mild oath.

1 [COUNT.] The old witch of Edmonton! If our mirth be not crossed—

2 [COUNT.] Bless us, Cuddy, and let her curse her tother [1] eye out.—What dost now?

Y. BANK. "Ungirt, unblessed," says the proverb; but my girdle shall [120 serve [2] a riding knot; [3] and a fig for all the witches in Christendom!—What wouldst thou?

1 [COUNT.] The devil cannot abide to be crossed.

2 [COUNT.] And scorns to come at any man's whistle.

3 [COUNT.] Away—

4 [COUNT.] With the witch!

OMN[ES]. Away with the witch [130 of Edmonton! *Ex[eunt] in strange posture.*

SAWY. Still vexed? Still tortured? That curmudgeon Banks
Is ground of all my scandal; I am shunned
And hated like a sickness, made a scorn
To all degrees and sexes. I have heard old beldams
Talk of familiars in the shape of mice,
Rats, ferrets, weasels, and I wot not what,
That have appeared, and sucked, some say, their blood;
But by what means they came acquainted with them
I'm now ignorant. Would some power, good or bad, 140
Instruct me which way I might be revenged
Upon this churl, I'd go out of myself,
And give this fury leave to dwell within
This ruined cottage ready to fall with age,
Abjure all goodness, be at hate with prayer,
And study curses, imprecations,
Blasphemous speeches, oaths, detested oaths,
Or anything that's ill, so I might work
Revenge upon this miser, this black cur,
That barks and bites, and sucks the very blood 150
Of me and of my credit. 'Tis all one

To be a witch as to be counted one.
Vengeance, shame, ruin light upon that canker!

Enter Dog.

DOG. Ho! Have I found thee cursing? Now thou art
Mine own.

SAWY.   Thine? What art thou?

DOG.   He thou hast so often
Importuned to appear to thee, the devil.

SAWY. Bless me! The devil?

DOG. Come, do not fear; I love thee much too well
To hurt or fright thee; if I seem terrible,
It is to such as hate me. I have found 160
Thy love unfeigned, have seen and pitiéd
Thy open wrongs, and come, out of my love,
To give thee just revenge against thy foes.

SAWY. May I believe thee?

DOG.   To confirm 't, command me
Do any mischief unto man or beast,
And I'll effect it, on condition
That, uncompelled, thou make a deed of gift
Of soul and body to me.

SAWY.   Out, alas!
My soul and body?

DOG.   And that instantly,
And seal it with thy blood. If thou deniest, 170
I'll tear thy body in a thousand pieces.

SAWY. I know not where to seek relief. But shall I,
After such covenants sealed, see full revenge
On all that wrong me?

DOG.   Ha, ha! Silly woman!
The devil is no liar to such as he loves.
Didst ever know or hear the devil a liar
To such as he affects?

SAWY. Then [4] I am thine; at least so much of me
As I can call mine own.

DOG.   Equivocations?
Art mine or no? Speak, or I'll tear—

SAWY.   All thine. 180

DOG. Seal 't with thy blood.
Sucks her arm. Thunder and lightning.
See! Now I dare call thee mine!

---

[1] Other.   [2] *I.e.*, serve as.
[3] Running knot, slip knot, used for hanging. Original reads *knit.*
[4] Emended by Dyce. Original reads *when.*

For proof, command me; instantly I'll
 run
To any mischief; goodness can I none.
SAWY. And I desire as little. There's an
 old churl,
One Banks—
DOG.   That wronged thee: he lamed
 thee, called thee witch.
SAWY. The same; first upon him I'ld be
 revenged.
DOG. Thou shalt; do but name how.
SAWY.   Go, touch his life.
DOG. I cannot.
SAWY. Hast thou not vowed? Go, kill
 the slave!
DOG.   I wonnot.
SAWY. I'll cancel, then, my gift.
DOG.   Ha, ha!
SAWY.   Dost laugh?   190
 Why wilt not kill him?
DOG.   Fool, because I cannot.
 Though we have power, know it is cir-
 cumscribed
 And tied in limits. Though he be cursed
 to thee,
 Yet of himself he is loving to the world,
 And charitable to the poor. Now men
 That, as he, love goodness, though in
 smallest measure,
 Live without compass of our reach. His
 cattle
 And corn I'll kill and mildew; but his
 life—
 Until I take him, as I late found thee,
 Cursing and swearing—I have no power
 to touch.   200
SAWY. Work on his corn and cattle, then.
DOG.   I shall.
 The witch of Edmonton shall see his
 fall,
 If she at least put credit in my power,
 And in mine only, make orisons to me,
 And none but me.
SAWY.   Say how and in what manner.
DOG. I'll tell thee. When thou wishest
 ill,
 Corn, man, or beast wouldst spoil or
 kill,
 Turn thy back against the sun,
 And mumble this short orison:
 "If thou to death or shame pursue
 'em,   210
 Sanctibicetur nomen tuum." [1]

[1] Hallowed be thy name.

SAWY. "If thou to death or shame pur-
 sue 'em,
 Sanctibicetur nomen tuum."
DOG. Perfect! Farewell. Our first-made
 promises
 We'll put in execution against Banks.
        Exit.
SAWY. Contaminetur nomen tuum.[2] I'm
 an expert scholar,
 Speak Latin, or I know not well what
 language,
 As well as the best of 'em. But who
 comes here?

    Enter Y[oung] Ba[nks].

 The son of my worst foe. "To death pur-
 sue 'em,
 Ei sanctibicetur nomen tuum."   220
Y. BANK. [Aside.] What's that she mum-
bles? The devil's paternoster? Would
it were else!—Mother Sawyer, good mor-
row.
SAWY. Ill morrow to thee, and all the
 world that flout
 A poor old woman! "To death pursue
 'em,
 And sanctibicetur nomen tuum."
Y. BANK. Nay, good Gammer Sawyer,
 whate'er it pleases
 My father to call you, I know you are—
SAWY.   A witch.
Y. BANK. A witch? Would you were else,
 i' faith!
SAWY.   Your father   230
 Knows I am by this.[3]
Y. BANK.   I would he did.
SAWY. And so in time may you.
 Y. BANK. I would I might else! But,
witch or no witch, you are a motherly
woman, and, though my father be a kind
of God-bless-us, as they say, I have an
earnest suit to you; and, if you'll be so
kind to ka me one good turn, I'll be so
courteous as to kob you another.[4]
SAWY. What's that? To spurn, beat me,
 and call me witch,   240
 As your kind father doth?
 Y. BANK. My father? I am ashamed
to own him. If he has hurt the head of thy
credit, there's money to buy thee a plaster.
[Gives money.] And a small courtesy I
would require at thy hands.

[2] Cursed be thy name. [3] I.e., by this time.
[4] Serve me, and I'll serve you.

Sawy. You seem a good young man, and—
  [*Aside.*] I must dissemble,
The better to accomplish my revenge.—
But—for this silver, what wouldst have
  me do?
Bewitch thee?   250
Y. Bank. No, by no means; I am be-
witched already. I would have thee so
good as to unwitch me, or witch another
with me for company.
Sawy. I understand thee not; be plain,
  my son.
Y. Bank. As a pikestaff, mother. You
know Kate Carter?
Sawy. The wealthy yeoman's daughter?
  What of her?
Y. Bank. That same party has be-
witched me.   260
Sawy. Bewitched thee?
Y. Bank. Bewitched me, *hisce auribus.*[1]
I saw a little devil fly out of her eye like
a burbolt,[2] which sticks at this hour up
to the feathers in my heart. Now, my request is, to send one of thy what-d'ye-
call-'ems either to pluck that out, or stick
another as fast in hers. Do, and here's
my hand; I am thine for three lives.
Sawy. [*Aside.*] We shall have sport.—
  Thou art in love with her?   270
Y. Bank. Up to the very hilts, mother.
Sawy. And thou'ldst have me make her
  love thee too?
Y. Bank. [*Aside.*] I think she'll prove
a witch in earnest.—Yes, I could find in
my heart to strike her three-quarters deep
in love with me too.
Sawy. But dost thou think that I can
  do 't, and I alone?
Y. Bank. Truly, Mother Witch, I do
verily believe so; and, when I see it done,
I shall be half persuaded so too.   280
Sawy. It's enough. What art can do be
  sure of.
Turn to the west, and, whatsoe'er thou
  hearest
Or seest, stand silent, and be not afraid.

*She stamps. Enter the Dog. He fawns and
                                leaps upon her.*

Y. Bank. Afraid, Mother Witch?—
[*Aside.*] Turn my face to the west? I

said I should always have a backfriend[3]
of her; and now it's out. And[4] her little
devil should be hungry, come sneaking be-
hind me, like a cowardly catchpole,[5] and
clap his talents[6] on my haunches!— [290
'Tis woundy[7] cold, sure.—[*Aside.*] I dud-
der[8] and shake like an aspen leaf, every
joint of me.
Sawy. "To scandal and disgrace pursue
  'em,
Et sanctibicetur nomen tuum." Exit Dog.
How now, my son, how is 't?
Y. Bank. Scarce in a clean life, Mother
Witch. But did your goblin and you spout
Latin together?
Sawy. A kind of charm I work by. Didst
  thou hear me?   300
Y. Bank. I heard I know not the devil
what mumble in a scurvy bass tone, like
a drum that had taken cold in the head
the last muster. Very comfortable words;
what were they? And who taught them
you?
Sawy. A great learned man.
Y. Bank. Learned man? Learned devil,
it was as soon! But what? What comfortable news about the party?   310
Sawy. Who? Kate Carter? I'll tell
thee. Thou know'st the stile at the west
end of thy father's peasfield. Be there
tomorrow night after sunset, and the first
live thing thou seest be sure to follow, and
that shall bring thee to thy love.
Y. Bank. In the peasfield? Has she
a mind to codlings[9] already? The first
living thing I meet, you say, shall bring
me to her?   320
Sawy. To a sight of her, I mean. She
will seem wantonly coy, and flee thee;
but follow her close and boldly. Do but
embrace her in thy arms once, and she is
thine own.
Y. Bank. At the stile at the west end
of my father's peasland, the first live thing
I see, follow and embrace her, and she
shall be thine. Nay, and I come to embracing once, she shall be mine; I'll [330
go near to make at eaglet[10] else. *Exit.*

[3] This word meant both *supporter* and *secret
enemy.*
[4] If.
[5] Sheriff's officer.
[6] Talons.
[7] Extremely.
[8] Dodder, shiver.
[9] Green peas, with a pun on *cuddlings.*
[10] Probably a term from some game of the
period.

[1] By these ears.
[2] Blunt-headed arrow.

SAWY. A ball well bandied! Now the set's half won.

The father's wrong I'll wreak upon the son.   *Exit.*

SCEN[A] ii.

[*Old Carter's house.*]

Enter Carter, Warbeck, Somerton.

[O.] CART. How now, gentlemen! Cloudy? I know, Mr. Warbeck, you are in a fog about my daughter's marriage.

WARB. And can you blame me, sir?

[O.] CART. Nor you me justly. Wedding and hanging are tied up both in a proverb; and destiny is the juggler that unties the knot. My hope is you are reserved to a richer fortune than my poor daughter.

WARB. However, your promise—   10

[O.] CART. Is a kind of debt, I confess it.

WARB. Which honest men should pay.

[O.] CART. Yet some gentlemen break in that point now and then, by your leave, sir.

SOM. I confess thou hast had a little wrong in the wench; but patience is the only salve to cure it. Since Thorney has won the wench, he has most reason to wear her.   20

WARB. Love in this kind admits no reason to wear her.

[O.] CART. Then Love's a fool, and what wise man will take exception?

SOM. Come, frolic Ned, were every man master of his own fortune, Fate might pick straws, and Destiny go a-woolgathering.

WARB. You hold yours in a string, though. 'Tis well; but, if there be any   [30 equity, look thou to meet the like usage ere long.

SOM. In my love to her sister Katherine? Indeed, they are a pair of arrows drawn out of one quiver, and should fly at an even length, if she do run after her sister.

WARB. Look for the same mercy at my hands as I have received at thine.

SOM. She'll keep a surer compass; I have too strong a confidence to mistrust her.   40

WARB. And that confidence is a wind that has blown many a married man ashore at Cuckold's Haven, I can tell you; I wish yours more prosperous though.

[O.] CART. Whate'er you wish, I'll master my promise to him.

WARB. Yes, as you did to me.

[O.] CART. No more of that, if you love me. But for the more assurance, the next offered occasion shall consummate the   [50 marriage; and that once sealed—

Enter Young Thorney and Susan [*, and stand aside*].

SOM. Leave the manage of the rest to my care. But see, the bridegroom and bride comes—the new pair of Sheffield knives, fitted both to one sheath.

WARB. The sheath might have been better fitted, if somebody had their due. But—

[O.] CART. No harsh language, if thou lovest me. Frank Thorney has done—   [60

WARB. No more than I, or thou, or any man, things so standing, would have attempted.

SOM. Good morrow, Mr. Bridegroom.

WARB. Come, give thee joy. Mayst thou live long and happy in thy fair choice!

Y. THOR. I thank ye, gentlemen. Kind Mr. Warbeck, I find you loving.

WARB. Thorney, that creature (much good do thee with her!)—

Virtue and beauty hold fair mixture in her;   70

She's rich, no doubt, in both. Yet were she fairer,

Thou art right worthy of her. Love her, Thorney.

'Tis nobleness in thee; in her but duty.

The match is fair and equal; the success I leave to censure.[1] Farewell, Mrs. Bride!

Till now elected, thy old scorn deride.
                                                Exit.

SOM. Good Mr. Thorney—

[O.] CART. Nay, you shall not part till you see the barrels run atilt, gentlemen.
                            Exit [*with Somerton*].

SUS. Why change you your face,   [80 sweetheart?

Y. THOR. Who, I? For nothing.

SUS. Dear, say not so; a spirit of your constancy cannot endure this change for nothing. I have observed strange variations in you.

Y. THOR. In me?

_____
[1] Judgment.

Sus. In you, sir. Awake, you seem to
dream, and in your sleep you utter sudden
and distracted accents, like one at en- [90
mity with peace. Dear loving husband, if I
  May dare to challenge any interest in
    you,
  Give me the reason fully; you may trust
  My breast as safely as your own.
Y. Thor.   With what?
  You half amaze me; prithee—
Sus.   Come, you shall not,
  Indeed you shall not, shut me from
    partaking
  The least dislike that grieves you; I am
    all yours.
Y. Thor. And I all thine.
Sus.   You are not, if you keep
  The least grief from me. But I find the
    cause;
  It grew from me.
Y. Thor.   From you?
Sus.   From some distaste 100
  In me or my behavior; you are not kind
  In the concealment. 'Las, sir, I am
    young,
  Silly, and plain; more, strange to those
    contents
  A wife should offer. Say but in what I
    fail,
  I'll study satisfaction.
Y. Thor.   Come, in nothing.
Sus. I know I do; knew I as well in
    what,
  You should not long be sullen. Prithee,
    love,
  If I have been immodest or too bold,
  Speak 't in a frown; if peevishly too nice,
  Show 't in a smile. Thy liking is the
    glass
  By which I'll habit my behavior.   111
Y. Thor. Wherefore dost weep now?
Sus.   You, sweet, have the power
  To make me passionate as an April day—
  Now smile, then weep; now pale, then
    crimson red.
  You are the powerful moon of my blood's
    sea,
  To make it ebb or flow into my face,
  As your looks change.
Y. Thor.   Change thy conceit,[1] I prithee.
  Thou art all perfection: Diana herself
  Swells in thy thoughts and moderates
    thy beauty.   119

[1] Figure of speech.

Within thy left eye amorous Cupid sits,
Feathering love shafts, whose golden
  heads he dipped
In thy chaste breast; in the other lies
Blushing Adonis scarfed in modesties;
And, still as wanton Cupid blows love
  fires,
Adonis quenches out unchaste desires;
And from these two I briefly do imply
A perfect emblem of thy modesty.
Then, prithee, dear, maintain no more
  dispute,
For, where thou speak'st, it's fit all
  tongues be mute.
Sus. Come, come, those golden strings of
  flattery   130
Shall not tie up my speech, sir; I must
  know
The ground of your disturbance.
Y. Thor.   Then look here,
  For here, here is the fen in which this
  hydra
Of discontent grows rank.
Sus.   Heaven shield it! Where?
Y. Thor. In mine own bosom; here the
  cause has root.
  The poisoned leeches twist about my
    heart,
  And will, I hope, confound me.
Sus.   You speak riddles.
Y. Thor. Take 't plainly, then. 'Twas
  told me by a woman
Known and approved in palmistry,
I should have two wives.
Sus.   Two wives? Sir, I take it 140
Exceeding likely; but let not conceit
Hurt you. You are afraid to bury me?
Y. Thor. No, no, my Winnifride.
Sus. How say you? Winnifride? You
  forget me.
Y. Thor. No, I forget myself, Susan.
Sus.   In what?
Y. Thor. Talking of wives, I pretend
  Winnifride,
  A maid that at my mother's waited on
    me
  Before thyself.
Sus.   I hope, sir, she may live
  To take my place. But why should all
    this move you?
Y. Thor. [Aside.] The poor girl! She
  has 't before thee,   150
  And that's the fiend torments me.
Sus.   Yet why should this

Raise mutiny within you? Such presages
Prove often false. Or say it should be
   true?
Y. Thor. That I should have another wife?
Sus.   Yes, many;
If they be good, the better.
Y. Thor.   Never any
Equal to thee in goodness.
Sus. Sir, I could wish I were much better
   for you,
Yet, if I knew your fate
Ordained you for another, I could wish—
So well I love you and your hopeful
   pleasure—   160
Me in my grave, and my poor virtues
   added
To my successor.
Y. Thor.   Prithee, prithee, talk not
Of death or graves; thou art so rare a
   goodness
As Death would rather put itself to
   death
Than murther thee. But we, as all
   things else,
Are mutable and changing.
Sus.   Yet you still move
In your first sphere of discontent. Sweet,
   chase
Those clouds of sorrow, and shine clearly
   on me.
Y. Thor. At my return I will.
Sus.   Return? Ah me!
Will you, then, leave me?
Y. Thor.   For a time I must.   170
But how? As birds their young, or
   loving bees
Their hives, to fetch home richer dain-
   ties.
Sus.   Leave me?
Now has my fear met its effect. You
   shall not;
Cost it my life, you shall not.
Y. Thor.   Why? Your reason?
Sus. Like to the lapwing have you all
   this while
With your false love deluded me, pre-
   tending
Counterfeit senses for your discontent;
And now at last it is by chance stole
   from you.
Y. Thor. What? What by chance?
Sus.   Your preappointed meeting
Of single combat with young Warbeck.
Y. Thor.   Ha!   180

Sus. Even so. Dissemble not; 'tis too
   apparent.
Then in his look I read it. Deny it not;
I see 't apparent. Cost it my undoing,
And unto that my life, I will not leave
   you.
Y. Thor. Not until when?
Sus.   Till he and you be friends.
Was this your cunning? And then flam
   me off
With an old witch, two wives, and
   Winnifride?
Y 'are not so kind, indeed, as I imagined.
Y. Thor. [Aside.] And you more fond [1]
   by far than I expected.   189
It is a virtue that attends thy kind.—
But of our business within. And, by
   this kiss,
I'll anger thee no more; troth, chuck,
   I will not.
Sus. You shall have no just cause.
Y. Thor.   Dear Sue, I shall not.
                       Exeunt.

Act[us] III. Scen[a] i.

[*The village green in Edmonton.*]

Enter Cuddy Banks and Morris Dancers.

1 [Dan.] Nay, Cuddy, prithee, do not
leave us now; if we part all this night, we
shall not meet before day.

2 [2] [Dan.] I prithee, Banks, let's keep
together now.

Clow. [3] If you were wise, a word would
serve; but, as you are, I must be forced to
tell you again, I have a little private business, an hour's work. It may prove but an
half hour's, as luck may serve: and [10
then I take horse, and along with you.
Have we e'er a witch in the morris?

1 [Dan.] No, no; no woman's part but
Maid Marian and the hobbyhorse.

Clow. I'll have a witch; I love a witch.

1 [Dan.] Faith, witches themselves are
so common nowadays that the counterfeit
will not be regarded. They say we have
three or four in Edmonton besides Mother
Sawyer.   20

2 [Dan.] I would she would dance her
part with us.

---

[1] With a pun on the meaning *foolish.*

[2] Original reads *1.*

[3] *I.e., Clown,* previously *Young Banks.*

3 [Dan.] So would not I, for, if she comes, the devil and all comes along with her.

Clow. Well, I'll have a witch; I have loved a witch ever since I played at cherry pit.[1] Leave me, and get my horse dressed. Give him oats; but water him not till I come. Whither do we foot it first?   30

2 [Dan.] To Sir Arthur Clarington's first; then whither thou wilt.

Clow. Well, I am content. But we must up to Carter's, the rich yeoman; I must be seen on hobbyhorse there.

1 [Dan.] O, I smell him now! I'll lay my ears Banks is in love, and that's the reason he would walk melancholy by himself.

Clow. Ha! Who was that said I   [40 was in love?

1 [Dan.] Not I.

2 [Dan.] Nor I.

Clow. Go to, no more of that. When I understand what you speak, I know what you say; believe that.

1 [Dan.] Well, 'twas I; I'll not deny it. I meant no hurt in 't. I have seen you walk up to Carter's of Chessum. Banks, were not you there last Shrovetide?   50

Clow. Yes, I was ten days together there the last Shrovetide.

2 [Dan.] How could that be, when there are but seven days in the week?

Clow. Prithee, peace! I reckon *stila nova* [2] as a traveler; thou understandest as a freshwater farmer that never sawest a week beyond sea. Ask any soldier that ever received his pay but in the Low Countries, and he'll tell thee there are eight days   [60 in the week there hard by. How dost thou think they rise in High Germany, Italy, and those remoter places?

3 [Dan.] Ay, but simply there are but seven days in the week yet.

Clow. No, simply as thou understandest. Prithee, look but in the lover's almanac. When he has been but three days absent, "O," says he, "I have not seen my love these seven years." There's a long   [70 cut! When he comes to her again and embraces her, "O," says he, "now methinks I am in heaven." And that's a pretty step! He that can get up to heaven in ten days

need not repent his journey; you may ride a hundred days in a caroche,[3] and be further off than when you set forth. But, I pray you, good morris mates, now leave me. I will be with you by midnight.

1 [Dan.] Well, since he will be   [80 alone, we'll back again and trouble him no more.

Omn[es]. But remember, Banks.

Clow. The hobbyhorse shall be remembered. But hark you; get Poldavis, the barber's boy, for the witch, because he can show his art better than another.—
                         Exeunt [All but Clown].
Well, now to my walk. I am near the place where I should meet—I know not what. Say I meet a thief, I must follow him,   [90 if to the gallows; say I meet a horse, or hare, or hound, still I must follow. Some slow-paced beast, I hope. Yet love is full of lightness in the heaviest lovers. Ha! My guide is come.

[Enter the Dog.]

A water dog! I am thy first man, sculler; I go with thee; ply no other but myself. Away with the boat! Land me but at Katherine's Dock, my sweet Katherine's Dock, and I'll be a fare to thee.   [100 That way? Nay, which way thou wilt; thou know'st the way better than I. Fine, gentle cur it is, and well brought up, I warrant him. We go a-ducking, spaniel; thou shalt fetch me the ducks, pretty, kind rascal.

Enter Spirit in shape of Katherine, vizarded,
                              and takes it [4] off.

Spir. [*Aside.*] Thus throw I off mine own essential horror,
  And take the shape of a sweet, lovely maid
  Whom this fool dotes on. We can meet his folly,   109
  But from his virtues must be runaways.
  We'll sport with him; but, when we reckoning call,
  We know where to receive; th' witch pays for all.   *Dog barks.*

Clow. Ay? Is that the watchword? She's come. Well, if ever we be married,

it shall be at Barking Church, in memory
of thee. Now come behind, kind cur.

> And have I met thee, sweet Kate?
> I will teach thee to walk so late.

O, see, we meet in meter. [*The Spirit moves
away.*] What! Dost thou trip from [120
me? O, that I were upon my hobbyhorse; I
would mount after thee so nimble! "Stay,
nymph; stay, nymph," singed Apollo.

> "Tarry and kiss me. Sweet nymph, stay!
> Tarry and kiss me, sweet."

We will to Chessum Street, and then to the
house stands in the highway.—Nay, by
your leave, I must embrace you.
　　　　　　　　Ex[eunt] Spir[it] and Banks.
[*Within.*] O, help, help! I am drowned,
I am drowned!　　　　　*Enter wet.* [130
　Dog. Ha, ha, ha, ha!
　Clow. This was an ill night to go a-wooing in. I find it now in Pond's almanac.
Thinking to land at Katherine's Dock, I
was almost at Gravesend. I'll never go to a
wench in the dog days again; yet 'tis cool
enough.—Had you never a paw in this dog-
trick? A mangie [1] take that black hide of
yours! I'll throw you in at Limehouse in
some tanner's pit or other.　　　　　　140
　Dog. Ha, ha, ha, ha!
　Clow. How now! Who's that laughs
at me? Hist to him!—(*Dog barks.*) Peace,
peace! Thou didst but thy kind [2] neither;
'twas my own fault.
　Dog. Take heed how thou trustest the
devil another time.
　Clow. How now! Who's that speaks?
I hope you have not your reading tongue
about you.　　　　　　　　　　　150
　Dog. Yes, I can speak.
　Clow. The devil you can! You have
read Æsop's fables, then; I have played one
of your parts then—the dog that catched
at the shadow in the water. Pray you, let
me catechize you a little. What might one
call your name, dog?
　Dog. My dame calls me Tom.
　Clow. 'Tis well, and she may call me
Ass; so there's an whole one betwixt [160
us, Tom-Ass. She said I should follow you,
indeed. Well, Tom, give me thy fist; we

are friends. You shall be mine ingle. [3] I love
you, but, I pray you, let's have no more of
these ducking devices.
　Dog. Not, if you love me. Dogs love
where they are beloved; cherish me, and
I'll do anything for thee.
　Clow. Well, you shall have jowls and
livers; I have butchers to my friends [170
that shall bestow 'em. And I will keep
crusts and bones for you, if you'll be a kind
dog, Tom.
　Dog. Anything; I'll help thee to thy
love.
　Clow. Wilt thou? That promise shall
cost me a brown loaf, though I steal it out
of my father's cupboard. You'll eat stolen
goods, Tom, will you not?
　Dog. O, best of all; the sweetest [180
bits those.
　Clow. You shall not starve, ningle [4]
Tom; believe that. If you love fish, I'll
help you to maids [5] and soles; I'm acquainted with a fishmonger.
　Dog. Maids and soles? O, sweet bits!
Banqueting stuff those.
　Clow. One thing I would request you,
ningle, as you have played the knavish
cur with me a little, that you would [190
mingle amongst our morris dancers in the
morning. You can dance?
　Dog. Yes, yes, anything; I'll be there,
but unseen to any but thyself. Get thee
gone before; fear not my presence. I have
work tonight; I serve more masters, more
dames, than one.
　Clow. He can serve Mammon and the
devil too.
　Dog. It shall concern thee and thy love's
　purchase.　　　　　　　　　　　200
> There's a gallant rival loves the maid,
> And likely is to have her. Mark what a
> 　mischief,
> Before the morris ends, shall light on
> 　him!

　Clow. O, sweet ningle, thy neuf [6] once
again; friends must part for a time. Farewell, with this remembrance; shalt have
bread too when we meet again. If ever there
were an honest devil, 'twill be the devil
of Edmonton, I see. Farewell, Tom; I
prithee, dog me as soon as thou canst. [210
　　　　　　　　　　　　Ex[it] Banks.

---

[1] Mange.　　[2] *I.e.,* according to thy nature.

[3] Crony.　　　　　　[5] Female skates.
[4] *I.e.,* mine ingle.　　[6] Fist.

Dog. I'll not miss thee, and be merry
with thee.
Those that are joys denied must take
delight
In sins and mischiefs; 'tis the devil's
right. *Ex[it] Dog.*

[Scena ii.

The neighborhood of Edmonton.]

Enter Young Thorney, Winnifride as a boy.

Frank. Prithee, no more! Those tears
give nourishment
To weeds and briers in me, which shortly
will
O'ergrow and top my head; my shame
will sit
And cover all that can be seen of me.
Win. I have not shown this cheek in
company.
Pardon me now. Thus singled with
yourself,
It calls a thousand sorrows round about,
Some going before, and some on either
side,
But infinite behind, all chained together.
Your second adulterous marriage leads;
That's the sad eclipse—th' effects must
follow, 11
As plagues of shame, spite, scorn, and
obloquy.
Y. Thor. Why, hast thou not left one
hour's patience
To add to all the rest? One hour bears us
Beyond the reach of all these enemies.
Are we not now set forward in the flight,
Provided with the dowry of my sin
To keep us in some other nation?
While we together are, we are at home
In any place.
Win. 'Tis foul, ill-gotten coin, 20
Far worse than usury or extortion.
Y. Thor. Let my father, then, make the
restitution,
Who forced me take the bribe. It is his
gift
And patrimony to me; so I receive it.
He would not bless, nor look a father on
me,
Until I satisfied his angry will.
When I was sold, I sold myself again—
Some knaves have done 't in lands, and I
in body—

For money, and I have the hire. But,
sweet, no more; 29
'Tis hazard of discovery, our discourse;
And then prevention takes off all our
hopes.
For only but to take her leave of me
My wife is coming.
Win. Who coming? Your wife?
Y. Thor. No, no; thou art here. The
woman—I knew
Not how to call her now; but after this
day
She shall be quite forgot and have no
name
In my remembrance. See, see! She's
come.

Enter Susan.

Go lead
The horses to the hill's top; there I'll
meet thee.
Sus. Nay, with your favor let him stay a
little;
I would part with him too, because he
is 40
Your sole companion; and I'll begin with
him,
Reserving you the last.
Y. Thor. Ay, with all my heart.
Sus. You may hear, if it please you, sir.
Y. Thor. No, 'tis not fit.
Some rudiments, I conceive, they must
be,
To overlook my slippery footings. And
so—
Sus. No, indeed, sir.
Y. Thor. Tush, I know it must be so,
And 'tis necessary. On! But be brief.
[*Walks forward.*]
Win. What charge soe'er you lay upon
me, mistress,
I shall support it faithfully—being hon-
est—
To my best strength.
Sus. Believe 't shall be no other. 50
I know you were commended to my hus-
band
By a noble knight.
Win. O, gods! O, mine eyes!
Sus. How now! What ail'st thou, lad?
Win. Something hit mine eye—it makes it
water still—
Even as you said "commended to my
husband."

Some dor [1] I think it was. I was, for-
sooth,
Commended to him by Sir Arthur Clar-
ington.
Sus. Whose servant once my Thorney was
himself.
That title, methinks, should make you
almost fellows,
Or at the least much more than a ser-
vant;　　　　　　　　　　　　　　60
And I am sure he will respect you so.
Your love to him, then, needs no spur
from me,
And what for my sake you will ever do,
'Tis fit it should be bought with some-
thing more
Than fair entreats. Look, here's a jewel
for thee,
A pretty, wanton label for thine ear;
And I would have it hang there, still to
whisper
These words to thee, "Thou hast my
jewel with thee."
It is but earnest of a larger bounty,
When thou return'st with praises of thy
service,　　　　　　　　　　　　70
Which I am confident thou wilt deserve.
Why, thou art many now besides thyself:
Thou mayst be servant, friend, and wife
to him;
A good wife is, then, all. A friend can
play
The wife and servant's part, and shift
enough;
No less the servant can the friend and
wife.
'Tis all but sweet society, good counsel,
Interchanged loves, yes, and counsel-
keeping.
Y. Thor. Not done yet?
Sus. Even now, sir.　　　　　　　　80
Win. Mistress, believe my vow; your
severe eye,
Were it present to command, your boun-
teous hand,
Were it then by to buy or bribe my
service,
Shall not make me more dear or near
unto him
Than I shall voluntary. I'll be all your
charge,
Servant, friend, wife to him.
Sus.　　　　　　　　　　　Wilt thou?

[1] Beetle.

Now blessings go with thee for 't! Cour-
tesies
Shall meet thee coming home.
Win.　　　　　　　Pray you, say plainly,
Mistress, are you jealous of him? If you
be,
I'll look to him that way too.
Sus.　　　　　　　Say'st thou so?　90
I would thou hadst a woman's bosom
now;
We have weak thoughts within us. Alas,
There's nothing so strong in us as sus-
picion;
But I dare not, nay, I will not think
So hardly of my Thorney.
Win.　　　　　　Believe it, mistress,
I'll be no pander to him; and, if I find
Any loose, lubric [2] scapes in him, I'll
watch him,
And at my return protest I'll show you
all.
He shall hardly offend without my
knowledge.　　　　　　　　　99
Sus. Thine own diligence is that I press,
And not the curious eye over his faults.
Farewell. If I should never see thee more,
Take it forever.
Y. Thor. (Gives his sword.) Prithee, take
that along with thee, and haste thee
To the hill's top; I'll be there instantly.
Ex[it] Win[nifride].
Sus. No haste, I prithee; slowly as thou
canst.
Pray, let him obey me now; 'tis happily
His last service to me. My power is
e'en
A-going out of sight.
Y. Thor.　　　　　Why would you delay?
We have no other business now but to
part.　　　　　　　　　　　110
Sus. And will not that, sweetheart, ask a
long time?
Methinks it is the hardest piece of work
That e'er I took in hand.
Y. Thor.　　　　　Fie, fie! Why, look,
I'll make it plain and easy to you—
farewell!　　　　　　　　Kisses.
Sus. Ah, 'las, I am not half perfect in it
yet;
I must have it read over an hundred
times.
Pray you, take some pains; I confess my
dullness.

[2] Lubricous, lascivious.

Y. Thor. [*Aside.*] What a thorn this rose
grows on! Parting were sweet;
But what a trouble 'twill be to obtain
it!—
Come, again and again, farewell!—
(*Kisses.*) Yet wilt return?   120
All questions of my journey, my stay,
employment,
And revisitation, fully I have answered
all.
There's nothing now behind but—
nothing.
Sus.   And
That "nothing" is more hard than any-
thing,
Than all the everythings. This request—
Y. Thor.   What is it?
Sus. That I may bring you through one
pasture more
Up to yon knot of trees; amongst those
shadows
I'll vanish from you—they shall teach
me how.
Y. Thor. Why, 'tis granted; come, walk,
then.
Sus.   Nay, not too fast.
They say slow things have best perfec-
tion;   130
The gentle shower wets to fertility,
The churlish storm may mischief with
his bounty;
The baser beasts take strength even from
the womb,
But the lord lion's whelp is feeble long.
                          Exeunt.

[Scena iii.

A field with a small grove.]

Enter Dog.[1]

Dog. Now for an early mischief and a
sudden!
The mind's about it now; one touch from
me
Soon sets the body forward.

Enter Young Thorney, Susan.

Y. Thor. Your request is out; yet will you
leave me?
Sus. What? So churlishly? You'll make
me stay forever
Rather than part with such a sound from
you.

---

[1] The Dog is, of course, invisible to all but the
audience.

Y. Thor. Why, you almost anger me,
Pray you, begone.
You have no company, and 'tis very
early;
Some hurt may betide you homewards.
Sus.   Tush! I fear none;
To leave you is the greatest hurt I can
suffer.   10
Besides, I expect your father and mine
own
To meet me back, or overtake me with
you.
They began to stir when I came after you.
I know they'll not be long.
Y. Thor. [*Aside.*] So! I shall have more
trouble. (*Dog rubs him.*) Thank you
for that.
Then I'll ease all at once. 'Tis done
now—
What I ne'er thought on.—You shall not
go back.
Sus. Why, shall I go along with thee?
Sweet music!
Y. Thor. No, to a better place.
Sus.   Any place I;
I'm there at home where thou pleasest to
have me.   20
Y. Thor. At home? I'll leave you in your
last lodging;
I must kill you.
Sus.   O, fine! You'ld fright me from
you.
Y. Thor. You see I had no purpose; I'm
unarmed;
'Tis this minute's decree, and it must be.
Look, this will serve your turn.
                     [*Draws a knife.*]
Sus.   I'll not turn from it,
If you be ear[ne]st, sir; yet you may tell
me
Wherefore you'll kill me.
Y. Thor.   Because you are a whore.
Sus. There's one deep wound already. A
whore!
'Twas ever further from me than the
thought
Of this black hour. A whore?
Y. Thor.   Yes, I'll prove it,   30
And you shall confess it. You are my
whore—
No wife of mine; the word admits no
second.
I was before wedded to another, have her
still.

I do not lay the sin unto your charge;
'Tis all mine own. Your marriage was
my theft,
For I espoused your dowry, and I have
it.
I did not purpose to have added mur-
ther;
The devil did not prompt me. Till this
minute
You might have safe returned; now you
cannot.
You have dogged your own death.
                              Stabs her.
Sus.   And I deserve it;   40
I'm glad my fate was so intelligent.[1]
'Twas some good spirit's motion. Die?
O, 'twas time!
How many years might I have slept in
sin,
Sin of my most hatred, too, adultery?
Y. Thor. Nay, sure, 'twas likely that the
most was past,
For I meant never to return to you
After this parting.
Sus.   Why, then, I thank you more.
You have done lovingly, leaving yourself,
That you would thus bestow me on
another.
Thou art my husband, Death, and I em-
brace thee   50
With all the love I have. Forget the stain
Of my unwitting sin; and then I come
A crystal virgin to thee. My soul's purity
Shall with bold wings ascend the doors
of Mercy,
For Innocence is ever her companion.
Y. Thor. Not yet mortal? I would not
linger you,
Or leave you a tongue to blab.
                        [*Stabs her again.*]
Sus. Now heaven reward you ne'er the
worse for me!
I did not think that Death had been so
sweet,
Nor I so apt to love him. I could ne'er
die better,   60
Had I stayed forty years for preparation,
For I'm in charity with all the world.
Let me for once be thine example,
heaven;
Do to this man as I him free forgive,
And may he better die and better live.
                              Moritur.[2]

---

[1] Communicative.   [2] She dies.

Y. Thor. 'Tis done; and I am in! Once
past our height,
We scorn the deep'st abyss. This follows
now,
To hele [3] her wounds by dressing of the
weapon.
Arms, thighs, hands, any place; we must
not fail   *Wounds himself.*
Light scratches, giving such deep ones.
The best I can   70
To bind myself to this tree. Now's the
storm,
Which if blown o'er, many fair days may
follow.   *Dog ties him.*
So, so, I'm fast; I did not think I could
Have done so well behind me. How
prosperous
And effectual mischief sometimes is!
Help! Help!
Murther, murther, murther!

Enter Carter and Old Thorney.

[O.] Cart. Ha! Whom tolls the bell for?
Y. Thor.   O, O!
O. Thor.   Ah me!
The cause appears too soon. My child,
my son!
[O.] Cart. Susan, girl, child! Not speak
to thy father? Ha!
Y. Thor. O, lend me some assistance to
o'ertake   80
This hapless woman.
O. Thor.   Let's o'ertake the murtherers.
Speak whilst thou canst; anon may be too
late.
I fear thou hast death's mark upon thee
too.
Y. Thor. I know them both; yet such an
oath is passed
As pulls damnation up if it be broke.
I dare not name 'em. Think what forced
men do.
O. Thor. Keep oath with murtherers?
That were a conscience
To hold the devil in.
Y. Thor.   Nay, sir, I can describe 'em,
Shall show them as familiar as their
names.   89
The taller of the two at this time wears
His satin doublet white, but crimson-
lined,
Hose of black satin, cloak of scarlet—

---

[3] *I.e.*, conceal the source of.

O. Thor.　　　　　　　　　Warbeck,
　Warbeck, Warbeck!—Do you list to this,
　　sir?
[O.] Cart. Yes, yes, I listen you; here's
　nothing to be heard.
Y. Thor. Th' other's cloak branched [1] vel-
　vet, black, velvet-lined his suit.
O. Thor. I have 'em already. Somerton,
　Somerton!
　Binal [2] revenge all this. Come, sir, the
　　first work
　Is to pursue the murtherers, when we
　　have
　Removed these mangled bodies hence.
[O.] Cart. Sir, take that carcass there,
　and give me this.　　　　　　　　100
　I'll not own her now; she's none of mine.
　Bob me off with a dumb show? No, I'll
　　have life.
　This is my son too, and, while there's life
　　in him,
　'Tis half mine; take you half that silence
　　for 't.—
　When I speak, I look to be spoken to.
　Forgetful slut!
O. Thor.　　　　Alas, what grief may do
　　now!—
　Look, sir, I'll take this load of sorrow
　　with me.
[O.] Cart. Ay, do, and I'll have this.—[Exit
　Old Thorney, carrying Susan.] How do
　you, sir?
Y. Thor. O, very ill, sir.
[O.] Cart. Yes, I think so; but 'tis well
　you can speak yet.　　　　　　　110
　There's no music but in sound; sound it
　　must be.
　I have not wept these twenty years be-
　　fore,
　And that I guess was ere that girl was
　　born;
　Yet now methinks, if I but knew the way,
　My heart's so full I could weep night and
　　day.　　　　　　　　　　　Exeunt.

[Scena iv.
Before Sir Arthur Clarington's house.]
*Enter Sir Arthur Clarington, Warbeck,
　　　　　　　　　　　　　　Somerton.*

Sir Art. Come, gentlemen, we must all
　help to grace
　The nimble-footed youth of Edmonton,

[1] Embroidered with a figured pattern.
[2] Twofold.

That are so kind
To call us up today with an high morris.
Warb. I could wish it for the best it
were the worst now. Absurdity's in my
opinion ever the best dancer in a morris.
Som. I could rather sleep than see 'em.
Sir Art. Not well, sir?
Som. Faith, not ever thus leaden; [10
yet I know no cause for 't.
Warb. Now am I beyond mine own
condition highly disposed to mirth.
Sir Art. Well, you may have yet a morris
　to help both:
To strike you in a dump, and make him
　merry.

Enter Fiddler and Morris, all but Banks.

Fiddl. Come, will you set yourselves
in morris ray? [3] The fore-bell, second bell,
tenor, and great bell; Maid Marian for the
same bell. But where's the weathercock
now? The hobbyhorse?　　　　　　20
1 [Dan.] Is not Banks come yet? What
a spite 'tis!
Sir Art. When set you forward, gentlemen?
1 [Dan.] We stay but for the hobbyhorse, sir; all our footmen are ready.
Som. 'Tis marvel your horse should be
behind your foot.
2 [Dan.] Yes, sir, he goes further about;
we can come in at the wicket, but the [30
broad gate must be opened for him.

Enter Banks, Hobbyhorse, and Dog.

Sir Art. O, we stayed for you, sir.
Clow. Only my horse wanted a shoe,
sir; but we shall make you amends ere we
part.
Sir Art. Ay? Well said. Make 'em drink
　ere they begin.

Ent[er] Serv[ants] with beer.

Clow. A bowl, I prithee, and a little for
my horse; he'll mount the better. Nay,
give me. I must drink to him; he'll not
pledge else.—[Drinks.] Here, hobby. [40
(*Holds him the bowl.*) I pray you. No? Not
drink?—You see, gentlemen, we can but
bring our horse to the water; he may
choose whether he'll drink or no.

[3] Array.

Som. A good moral made plain by history.

1 [Dan.] Strike up, Father Sawgut, strike up.

Fiddl. E'en when you will, children. Now in the name of the best foot for- [50 ward!—[*The fiddle makes no sound.*] How now! Not a word in thy guts? I think, children, my instrument has caught cold on the sudden.

Clow. [*Aside.*] My ningle's knavery; black Tom's doing.

Omn[es]. Why, what mean you, Father Sawgut?

Clow. Why, what would you have him do? You hear his fiddle is speechless.   60

Fiddl. I'll lay mine ear to my instrument that my poor fiddle is bewitched. I played "The Flowers in May" e'en now, as sweet as a violet; now 'twill not go against the hair. You see I can make no more music than a beetle of a cow turd.

Clow. Let me see, Father Sawgut. [*Takes the fiddle.*] Say once you had a brave hobbyhorse that you were beholding [1] to. I'll play and dance too.—Ningle, [70 away with it.

Dog plays the morris, which ended, enter a Constable and Officers.

Omn[es]. Ay, marry, sir!

Con. Away with jollity! 'Tis too sad an hour.—

Sir Arthur Clarington, your own assistance,

In the king's name, I charge, for apprehension

Of these two murderers, Warbeck and Somerton.

Sir Art. Ha! Flat murtherers?

Som. Ha, ha, ha! This has awakened my melancholy.

Warb. And struck my mirth down [80 flat.—Murtherers?

Con. The accusation is flat against you, gentlemen.—

Sir, you may be satisfied with this.— [*Shows warrant.*]

I hope you'll quietly obey my power; 'Twill make your cause the fairer.

Ambo.[2] O, with all our hearts, sir.

[1] Beholden.
[2] *I.e.*, both Somerton and Warbeck.

Clow. There's my rival taken up for hangman's meat. Tom told me he was about a piece of villainy.—Mates and morris men, you see here's no longer [90 piping, no longer dancing; this news of murder has slain the morris. You that go the footway, fare ye well; I am for a gallop. —Come, ningle.

Exe[unt Banks and Dog].

Fiddl. (*Strikes his fiddle.*) Ay? Nay, and my fiddle be come to himself again, I care not. I think the devil has been abroad amongst us today; I'll keep thee out of thy fit now, if I can.

Exe[unt Fiddler and Morris].

Sir Art. These things are full of horror, full of pity.   100

But, if this time be constant to the proof, The guilt of both these gentlemen I dare take

Upon mine own danger; yet, howsoever, sir,

Your power must be obeyed.

Warb.   O, most willingly, sir.

'Tis a most sweet affliction; I could not meet

A joy in the best shape with better will. Come, fear not, sir; nor judge nor evidence

Can bind him o'er who's freed by conscience.

Som. Mine stands so upright to the middle zone   109

It takes no shadow to 't; it goes alone.

Exeunt.

Act[us] IV. Scen[a] i.

[*The village green in Edmonton.*]

Enter Old Banks and two or three Countrymen.

O. Bank. My horse this morning runs most piteously of the glanders, whose nose yesternight was as clean as any man's here now coming from the barber's; and this, I'll take my death upon 't, is long [3] of this jadish witch, Mother Sawyer.

1 [Count.] I took my wife and a servingman in our town of Edmonton, thrashing in my barn together such corn as country wenches carry to market, and, examin- [10 ing my polecat [4] why she did so, she swore

[3] Because.
[4] Harlot.

in her conscience she was bewitched. And what witch have we about us but Mother Sawyer?

2 [COUNT.] Rid the town of her, else all our wives will do nothing else but dance about other country Maypoles.

3 [COUNT.] Our cattle fall, our wives fall, our daughters fall, and maidservants fall; and we ourselves shall not be able to [20 stand, if this beast be suffered to graze amongst us.

Enter W. Hamluc with thatch and a link.[1]

HAML. Burn the witch, the witch, the witch, the witch!

OMN[ES]. What hast got there?

HAML. A handful of thatch plucked off a hovel of hers; and they say, when 'tis burning, if she be a witch, she'll come running in.

O. BANK. Fire it, fire it! I'll stand [30 between thee and home for any danger.

As that burns enter the Witch.

SAWY. Diseases, plagues, the curse of an old woman follow and fall upon you!

OMN[ES]. Are you come, you old trot?

O. BANK. You hot whore, must we fetch you with fire in your tail?

1 [COUNT.] This thatch is as good as a jury to prove she is a witch.

OMN[ES]. Out, witch! Beat her, kick her, set fire on her! 40

SAWY. Shall I be murthered by a bed of serpents? Help, help!

Enter Sir Arthur Clarington and a Justice.

OMN[ES]. Hang her, beat her, kill her!

JUST. How now? Forbear this violence!

SAWY. A crew of villains, a knot of bloody hangmen, set to torment me, I know not why.

JUST. Alas, neighbor Banks, are you a ringleader in mischief? Fie, to abuse an aged woman! 50

O. BANK. Woman? A she-hellcat, a witch! To prove her one, we no sooner set fire on the thatch of her house, but in she came running as if the devil had sent her in a barrel of gunpowder, which trick as surely proves her a witch as the pox in a snuffling nose is a sign a man is a whoremaster.

¹ Torch.

JUST. Come, come. Firing her thatch? Ridiculous!

Take heed, sirs, what you do; unless your proofs

Come better armed, instead of turning her   60

Into a witch, you'll prove yourselves stark fools.

OMN[ES]. Fools?

JUST. Arrant fools.

O. BANK. Pray, Mr. Justice What-do-you-call-'em, hear me but in one thing: this grumbling devil owes me I know no good will ever since I fell out with her.

SAWY. And breakedst my back with beating me.

O. BANK. I'll break it worse. 70

SAWY. Wilt thou?

JUST. You must not threaten her; 'tis against law. Go on.

O. BANK. So, sir, ever since, having a dun cow tied up in my backside,[2] let me go thither, or but cast mine eye at her, and, if I should be hanged, I cannot choose, though it be ten times in an hour, but run to the cow, and, taking up her tail, kiss—saving your worship's reverence—my cow [80 behind, that the whole town of Edmonton has been ready to bepiss themselves with laughing me to scorn.

JUST. And this is long of her?

O. BANK. Who the devil else? For is any man such an ass to be such a baby, if he were not bewitched?

SIR ART. Nay, if she be a witch, and the harms she does end in such sports, she may scape burning. 90

JUST. Go, go! Pray, vex her not; she is a subject,

And you must not be judges of the law

To strike her as you please.

OMN[ES]. No, no, we'll find cudgel enough to strike her.

O. BANK. Ay; no lips to kiss but my cow's—!

Exeunt [Old Banks and Countrymen].

SAWY. Rots and foul maladies eat up thee and thine!

JUST. Here's none now, Mother Sawyer, but this gentleman,

Myself, and you. Let us to some mild questions;   100

Have you mild answers. Tell us honestly

³ Back yard.

And with a free confession—we'll do
  our best
  To wean you from it—are you a witch,
    or no?

Sawy. I am none!

Just.   Be not so furious.

Sawy.   I am none!
  None but base curs so bark at me. I'm
  none.
  Or would I were! If every poor old
  woman
  Be trod on thus by slaves, reviled,
    kicked, beaten,
  As I am daily, she to be revenged
  Had need turn witch.

Sir Art.   And you to be revenged
  Have sold your soul to th' devil.

Sawy.   Keep thine own from him.

Just. You are too saucy and too bitter.

Sawy.   Saucy? 111
  By what commission can he send my soul
  On the devil's errand more than I can
  his?
  Is he a landlord of my soul, to thrust it,
  When he list, out of door?

Just.   Know whom you speak to.

Sawy. A man; perhaps no man. Men in
  gay clothes,
  Whose backs are laden with titles and
    honors,
  Are within far more crooked than I am,
  And, if I be a witch, more witchlike.

Sir Art. Y' are a base hellhound.— 120
  And now, sir, let me tell you, far and near
  She's bruited for a woman that maintains
  A spirit that sucks her.

Sawy.   I defy thee.

Sir Art.   Go, go.
  I can, if need be, bring an hundred voices,
  E'en here in Edmonton, that shall loud
    proclaim
  Thee for a secret and pernicious witch.

Sawy. Ha, ha!

Just.   Do you laugh? Why laugh you?

Sawy.   At my name,
  The brave name this knight gives me—
  witch.

Just. Is the name of witch so pleasing to
  thine ear?

Sir Art. Pray, sir, give way, and let her
  tongue gallop on.   130

Sawy. A witch! Who is not?
  Hold not that universal name in scorn,
  then.

What are your painted things in princes'
  courts,
Upon whose eyelids lust sits, blowing
  fires
To burn men's souls in sensual hot desires,
Upon whose naked paps a lecher's
  thought
Acts sin in fouler shapes than can be
  wrought?

Just. But those work not as you do.

Sawy.   No, but far worse.
  These by enchantments can whole lord-
  ships [1] change
  To trunks of rich attire, turn plows and
  teams   140
  To Flanders mares and coaches, and huge
  trains
  Of servitors to a French butterfly.
  Have you not city witches who can turn
  Their husbands' wares, whole standing
  shops of wares,
  To sumptuous tables, gardens of stol'n
  sin,
  In one year wasting what scarce twenty
  win?
  Are not these witches?

Just.   Yes, yes; but the law
  Casts not an eye on these.

Sawy.   Why then on me,
  Or any lean old beldam? Reverence once
  Had wont to wait on age; now an old
  woman,   150
  Ill-favored grown with years, if she be
  poor,
  Must be called bawd or witch. Such so
  abused
  Are the coarse witches; tother are the
  fine,
  Spun for the devil's own wearing.

Sir Art.   And so is thine.

Sawy. She on whose tongue a whirlwind
  sits to blow
  A man out of himself, from his soft
  pillow
  To lean his head on rocks and fighting
  waves,
  Is not that scold a witch? The man of
  law
  Whose honeyed hopes the credulous
  client draws—
  As bees by tinkling basins—to swarm to
  him   160

[1] Estates.

From his own hive to work the wax in
his—
He is no witch, not he!
SIR ART.   But these men-witches
Are not in trading with hell's merchan-
dise,
Like such as you are, that for a word, a
look,
Denial of a coal of fire, kill men,
Children, and cattle.
SAWY.   Tell them, sir, that do so.
Am I accused for such an one?
SIR ART.   Yes; 'twill be sworn.
SAWY.   Dare any swear I ever tempted
maiden
With golden hooks flung at her chastity
To come and lose her honor; and, being
lost,   170
To pay not a denier [1] for 't? Some slaves
have done it.
Men-witches can, without the fangs of
law
Drawing once one drop of blood, put
counterfeit pieces
Away for true gold.
SIR ART.   By one thing she speaks
I know now she's a witch, and dare no
longer
Hold conference with the fury.
JUST.   Let's, then, away.—
Old woman, mend thy life; get home and
pray. *Exeunt [Sir Arthur and Justice].*
SAWY.   For his confusion!—

Enter Dog.

My dear Tom-boy, welcome!
I'm torn in pieces by a pack of curs
Clapped all upon me, and for want of
thee.   180
Comfort me; thou shalt have the teat
anon.
DOG.   Bow, wow! I'll have it now.
SAWY.   I am dried up
With cursing and with madness, and
have yet
No blood to moisten these sweet lips of
thine.
Stand on thy hind legs up—kiss me, my
Tommy,
And rub away some wrinkles on my
brow
By making my old ribs to shrug for joy

[1] Penny.

Of thy fine tricks. What has thou done?
Let's tickle.
Hast thou struck the horse lame as I bid
thee?
DOG.   Yes;
And nipped the sucking child.
SAWY.   Ho, ho, my dainty,   190
My little pearl! No lady loves her hound,
Monkey, or parrakeet, as I do thee.
DOG.   The maid has been churning butter
nine hours, but it shall not come.
SAWY.   Let 'em eat cheese and choke.
DOG.   I had rare sport
Among the clowns i' th' morris.
SAWY.   I could dance
Out of my skin to hear thee. But, my
curl-pate,
That jade, that foul-tongued whore, Nan
Ratcliffe,
Who, for a little soap licked by my sow,
Struck and almost had lamed it, did not
I charge thee   200
To pinch that quean to th' heart?
DOG.   Bow, wow, wow! Look
here else.

Enter Ann Ratcliffe mad.

RATC.   See, see, see! The man i' th'
moon has built a new windmill; and what
running there's from all quarters of the
city to learn the art of grinding!
SAWY.   Ho, ho, ho! I thank thee, my
sweet mongrel.
RATC.   Hoyda! A pox of the devil's false
hopper! All the golden meal runs into the
rich knaves' purses, and the poor [210
have nothing but bran. Hey derry down!—
Are not you Mother Sawyer?
SAWY.   No, I am a lawyer.
RATC.   Art thou? I prithee, let me
scratch thy face, for thy pen has flayed off
a great many men's skins. You'll have
brave doings in the vacation, for knaves
and fools are at variance in every village.
I'll sue Mother Sawyer, and her own sow
shall give in evidence against her.   220
SAWY.   *[To Dog.]* Touch her.
RATC.   O, my ribs are made of a paned
hose,[2] and they break! There's a Lan-
cashire hornpipe in my throat; hark, how
it tickles it, with doodle, doodle, doodle,
doodle! Welcome, serjeants! Welcome,

[2] Hose made by sewing strips together.

devil!—Hands, hands! Hold hands, and
dance around, around, around.   [*Dances.*]

*Enter Old Banks, his son the Clown, Old
Ratcliffe, Country Fellows.*

O. RATC. She's here; alas, my poor wife
is here!   230

O. BANK. Catch her fast, and have her
into some close chamber, do, for she's, as
many wives are, stark mad.

CLOW. The witch! Mother Sawyer, the
witch, the devil!

O. RATC. O, my dear wife! Help, sirs!
                    Car[*ry*] *her* [1] *off.* [2]

O. BANK. You see your work, Mother
Bumby.[3]

SAWY. My work? Should she and all
you here run mad, is the work mine?   [240

CLOW. No, on my conscience, she would
not hurt a devil of two years old.—

Enter Old Ratcliffe and the Rest.

How now? What's become of her?

O. RATC. Nothing; she's become nothing
but the miserable trunk of a wretched
woman. We were in her hands as reeds in a
mighty tempest. Spite of our strengths,
away she brake; and nothing in her mouth
being heard but "the devil, the witch, the
witch, the devil!" she beat out her   [250
own brains, and so died.

CLOW. It's any man's case, be he never
so wise, to die when his brains go a-woolgathering.

O. BANK. Masters, be ruled by me; let's
all to a justice.—Hag, thou hast done this,
and thou shalt answer it.

SAWY. Banks, I defy thee.

O. BANK. Get a warrant first to examine
her; then ship her to Newgate. Here's   [260
enough, if all her other villainies were
pardoned, to burn her for a witch.—
You have a spirit, they say, comes to you in
the likeness of a dog; we shall see your cur
at one time or other. If we do, unless it be
the devil himself, he shall go howling to
the goal [4] in one chain, and thou in another.

SAWY. Be hanged thou in a third, and
do thy worst!

CLOW. How, father? You send the   [270

[1] *I.e.*, Ann Ratcliffe.
[2] This stage direction follows the preceding
line in the original.
[3] A reference to Lyly's *Mother Bombie.*
[4] Gaol, jail.

poor dumb thing howling to th' goal? He
that makes him howl makes me roar.

O. BANK. Why, foolish boy, dost thou
know him?

CLOW. No matter if I do or not. He's
bailable, I am sure, by law. But, if the dog's
word will not be taken, mine shall.

O. BANK. Thou bail for a dog?

CLOW. Yes, or a bitch either, being my
friend. I'll lie by the heels myself   [280
before puppison [5] shall; his dog days are
not come yet, I hope.

O. BANK. What manner of dog is it?
Didst ever see him?

CLOW. See him? Yes, and given him a
bone to gnaw twenty times. The dog is
no court foisting [6] hound that fills his belly
full by base wagging his tail; neither is it
a citizen's water spaniel, enticing his master
to go a-ducking twice or thrice a week,   [290
whilst his wife makes ducks and drakes
at home. This is no Paris Garden bandog [7] neither, that keeps a bow-wow-
wowing to have butchers bring their curs
thither; and, when all comes to all, they
run away like sheep. Neither is this the
Black Dog of Newgate.[8]

O. BANK. No, Goodman Son-fool, but
the dog of hellgate.

CLOW. I say, Goodman Father-   [300
fool, it's a lie.

OMN[ES]. He's bewitched.

CLOW. A gross lie, as big as myself. The
devil in St. Dunstan's will as soon drink
with this poor cur as with any Temple Bar
laundress that washes and wrings lawyers.

DOG. Bow, wow, wow, wow!

OMN[ES]. O, the dog's here, the dog's
here.   309

O. BANK. It was the voice of a dog.

CLOW. The voice of a dog? If that
voice were a dog's, what voice had my
mother? So am I a dog. Bow, wow, wow!
It was I that barked so, father, to make
coxcombs of these clowns.

O. BANK. However, we'll be coxcombed
no longer. Away, therefore, to th' justice
for a warrant; and then, Gammer Gurton,
have at your needle of witchcraft!

[5] Probably equivalent to *his puppyship.*
[6] Cheating; also stinking.
[7] Fierce dog used for bear baiting.
[8] A probable allusion to a lost play of a similar
title.

SAWY. And prick thine own eyes out. Go,
　peevish fools!　　　　　　　　　　320
Exe[unt Old Banks, Ratcliffe, and Coun-
　　　　　　　　　　　　　trymen].

CLOW. Ningle, you had liked to have
spoiled all with your bow-ings. I was glad
to put 'em off with one of my dogtricks
on a sudden; I am bewitched, little Cost-
me-naught, to love thee.—A pox!—That
morris makes me spit in thy mouth. I
dare not stay.　Farewell, ningle; you
whoreson [1] dog's nose!—Farewell, witch!
　　　　　　　　　　　　　　　Exit.

DOG. Bow, wow, wow, wow!

SAWY. Mind him not; he's not　[330
worth thy worrying.　Run at a fairer
game, that foul-mouthed knight, scurvy Sir
Arthur.　Fly at him, my Tommy, and pluck
out 's throat.

DOG. No, there['s] a dog already biting 's
conscience.

SAWY. That's a sure bloodhound.　Come,
　let's home and play;
Our black work ended, we'll make holi-
　day.　　　　　　　　　　*Exeunt.*

SCEN[A] ii.

[A bedroom in Carter's house.]

*Enter Katherine. A bed thrust forth; on it
　　　　　　　Frank in a slumber.*

KAT. Brother, brother!　So sound asleep?
　That's well.

FRANK. [*Waking.*] No, not I, sister; he
　that's wounded here
As I am—all my other hurts are bitings
Of a poor flea—but he that here once
　bleeds
Is maimed incurably.

KAT.　　　　My good sweet brother—
For now my sister must grow up in you—
Though her loss strikes you through,
　and that I feel
The blow as deep, I pray thee, be not
　cruel
To kill me too, by seeing you cast away
In your own helpless sorrow.　Good love,
　sit up;　　　　　　　　　　10
And, if you can give physic to yourself,
I shall be well.

FRANK.　　　　I'll do my best.

KAT.　　　　　　　I thank you.
What do you look about for?

---
[1] Rascally.

FRANK.　　　　Nothing, nothing;
But I was thinking, sister—

KAT.　　　　　Dear heart, what?

FRANK. Who but a fool would thus be
　bound to a bed,
Having this room to walk in?

KAT.　　　　Why do you talk so?
Would you were fast asleep!

FRANK.　　　No, no; I'm not idle.[2]
But here's my meaning: being robbed as
　I am,
Why should my soul, which married was
　to hers,
Live in divorce, and not fly after her?　20
Why should not I walk hand in hand
　with Death,
To find my love out?

KAT.　　　　That were well indeed,
Your time being come; when Death is
　sent to call you,
No doubt you shall meet her.

FRANK.　　　　Why should not I
Go without calling?

KAT.　　　Yes, brother, so you might,
Were there no place to go when y' are
　gone
But only this.

FRANK.　　Troth, sister, thou say'st true,
For, when a man has been an hundred
　years
Hard traveling o'er the tottering bridge
　of age,　　　　　　　　　　29
He's not the thousand part upon his way.
All life is but a wand'ring to find home;
When we are gone, we are there.　Happy
　were man,
Could here his voyage end; he should
　not, then,
Answer how well or ill he steered his soul
By heaven's or by hell's compass; how
　he put in—
Losing blessed goodness' shore—at such
　a sin;
Nor how life's dear provision he has
　spent;
Nor how far he in 's navigation went
Beyond commission.　This were a fine
　reign,
To do ill and not hear of it again;　40
Yet then were man more wretched than
　a beast;
For, sister, our dead pay [3] is sure the
　best.

---
[2] Light-headed.　　　　[3] Retribution.

KAT. 'Tis so, the best or worst; and I wish heaven
To pay—and so I know it will—that traitor,
That devil Somerton, who stood in mine eye
Once as an angel, home to his deservings.
What villain but himself, once loving me,
With Warbeck's soul would pawn his own to hell
To be revenged on my poor sister?

FRANK.   Slaves!
A pair of merciless slaves! Speak no more of them.   50

KAT. I think this talking hurts you.

FRANK. Does me no good, I'm sure;
I pay for 't everywhere.

KAT.   I have done, then.
Eat, if you cannot sleep; you have these two days
Not tasted any food.—[Calls.] Jane, is it ready?

FRANK. What's ready? What's ready?

KAT. I have made ready a roasted chicken for you.

[Enter Jane with chicken.]

Sweet, wilt thou eat?

FRANK. A pretty stomach on a sudden, yes.
There's one in the house can play upon a lute.   60
Good girl, let's hear him too.

KAT.   You shall, dear brother.
[Exit Jane.]
Would I were a musician; you should hear   Lute plays.
How I would feast your ear! Stay, mend your pillow,
And raise you higher.

FRANK.   I am up too high,
Am I not, sister, now?

KAT.   No, no; 'tis well.
Fall to, fall to.—A knife! Here's never a knife.
Brother, I'll look out yours.
[Picks up his coat.]

Enter Dog, shrugging as it were for joy, and
                                        dances.

FRANK.   Sister, O sister,
I am ill upon a sudden, and can eat nothing.

KAT. In very deed you shall. The want of food
Makes you so faint. Ha! [Sees the bloody knife.] Here's none in your pocket;   70
I'll go fetch a knife.   Exit.

FRANK.   Will you? 'Tis well;
All's well.

She gone, he searches first one, then the other,
    pocket. Knife found. Dog runs off.
    He lies on one side. The Spirit of
    Susan, his second wife, comes to the
    bed's side. He stares at it, and, turning
    to the other side, it's there too. In the
    meantime, Winnifride as a page comes
    in, stands at his bed's feet sadly. He,
    frighted, sits upright. The Spirit van-
                                        ishes.

FRANK.   What art thou?

WIN.   A lost creature.

FRANK. So am I too.—Win? Ah, my she-page!

WIN. For your sake I put on
A shape that's false; yet do I wear a heart
True to you as your own.

FRANK.   Would mine and thine
Were fellows in one house! Kneel by me here.
On this side now? How dar'st thou come to mock me
On both sides of my bed?

WIN.   When?

FRANK.   But just now.
Outface me, stare upon me with strange postures,   80
Turn my soul wild by a face in which were drawn
A thousand ghosts leaped newly from their graves
To pluck me into a winding sheet!

WIN.   Believe it,
I came no nearer to you than yon place
At your bed's feet, and of the house had leave,
Calling myself your horse boy, in to come
And visit my sick master.

FRANK.   Then 'twas my fancy—
Some windmill in my brains for want of sleep.

WIN. Would I might never sleep, so you could rest!

But you have plucked a thunder on your
head,   90
Whose noise cannot cease suddenly.
  Why should you
Dance at the wedding of a second
  wife,
When scarce the music which you heard
  at mine
Had ta'en a farewell of you? O, this was
  ill!
And they who thus can give both hands
  away
In th' end shall want their best limbs.
FRANK.   Winnifride—
  The chamber door fast?
WIN.   Yes.
FRANK.   Sit thee, then, down,
  And, when th'ast heard me speak, melt
  into tears.
Yet I, to save those eyes of thine from
  weeping,
Being to write a story of us two,   100
Instead of ink dipped my sad pen in
  blood.
When of thee I took leave, I went abroad
Only for pillage, as a freebooter,
What gold soe'er I got to make it
  thine.
To please a father, I have heaven dis-
  pleased;
Striving to cast two wedding rings in
  one,
Through my bad workmanship I now
  have none.
I have lost her and thee.
WIN.   I know she's dead;
  But you have me still.
FRANK.   Nay, her this hand
  Murdered; and so I lose thee too.
WIN.   O me!   110
FRANK. Be quiet, for thou my evidence
  art,
Jury, and judge. Sit quiet, and I'll tell all.

As they whisper, enter at one end o' th' stage
Old Carter and Katherine, Dog at th'
other, pawing softly at Frank.

KAT. I have run madding up and down to
  find you,
  Being laden with the heaviest news that
  ever
  Poor daughter carried.
[O.] CART.   Why? Is the boy dead?

KAT.   Dead, sir!
  O father, we are cozened. You are told
  The murtherer sings in prison, and he
  laughs here.
This villain killed my sister. See else,
  see,
A bloody knife in 's pocket!
[O.] CART.   Bless me, patience!
FRANK. [*Seeing them.*] The knife, the knife,
  the knife!   120
KAT. What knife?   *Exit Dog.*
FRANK.   To cut my chicken up,
  my chicken!—
Be you my carver, father.
[O.] CART.   That I will.
KAT. [*Aside.*] How the devil steels our
  brows after doing ill!
FRANK. My stomach and my sight are
  taken from me;
All is not well within me.
[O.] CART. I believe thee, boy—I that
have seen so many moons clap their horns
on other men's foreheads to strike them
sick, yet mine to scape and be well; I that
never cast away a fee upon urinals,   [130
but am as sound as an honest man's conscience when he's dying, I should cry out
as thou dost, "All is not well within me,"
felt I but the bag of thy imposthumes.
Ah, poor villain! Ah, my wounded rascal!
All my grief is, I have now small hope of
thee.
FRANK. Do the surgeons say my wounds
are dangerous then?
[O.] CART. Yes, yes, and there's no   [140
way with thee but one.
FRANK. Would he were here to open
them!
[O.] CART. I'll go to fetch him; I'll make
an holiday to see thee as I wish.
                    Exit to fetch Officers.
FRANK. A wondrous kind old man!
WIN. [*Aside to Frank.*] Your sin's the
blacker so to abuse his goodness.—Master,
how do you?
FRANK. Pretty well now, boy; I   [150
have such odd qualms come cross my
stomach. I'll fall to; boy, cut me.
WIN. [*Aside.*] You have cut me, I'm
sure.—A leg or wing, sir?
FRANK. No, no, no! A wing?—[*Aside.*]
Would I had wings but to soar up yon
tower! But here's a clog that hinders me.—
What's that?

Father with her in a coffin.

[O.] CART. That? What? O, now I see
her; 'tis a young wench, my daughter, [160
sirrah, sick to the death; and, hearing thee to
be an excellent rascal for letting blood, she
looks out at a casement, and cries, "Help,
help! Stay that man! Him I must have or
none."

FRANK. For pity's sake, remove her! See,
she stares
With one broad open eye still in my face!

[O.] CART. Thou puttest both hers out,
like a villain as thou art; yet, see, she
is willing to lend thee one again to [170
find out the murtherer, and that's thyself.

FRANK. Old man, thou liest!

[O.] CART. So shalt thou—
i' th' goal.
Run for officers!

KAT. O, thou merciless slave!
She was—though yet above ground—in
her grave
To me; but thou hast torn it up
again.
Mine eyes, too much drowned, now
must feel more rain.

[O.] CART. Fetch officers.

Exit Katherine.

FRANK. For whom?

[O.] CART. For thee, sirrah, sirrah!
Some knives have foolish posies [1] upon [180
them, but thine has a villainous one.
[*Takes knife from Frank's pocket.*] Look!
O, it is enameled with the heart blood of
thy hated wife, my beloved daughter!
What say'st thou to this evidence? Is 't
not sharp? Does 't not strike home? Thou
canst not answer honestly and without
a trembling heart to this one point, this
terrible, bloody point.

WIN. I beseech you, sir, strike [190
him no more; you see he's dead already.

[O.] CART. O, sir, you held his horses;
you are as arrant a rogue as he. Up go
you too.

FRANK. As y' are a man, throw not upon
that woman
Your loads of tyranny, for she's innocent.

[O.] CART. How? How? A woman?
Is 't grown to a fashion for women in all
countries to wear the breeches?

WIN. I am not as my disguise [200

[1] Inscriptions.

speaks me, sir, his page, but his first, only
wife, his lawful wife.

[O.] CART. How? How? More fire i'
th' bedstraw!

WIN. The wrongs which singly fell on
your daughter
On me are multiplied; she lost a life,
But I an husband and myself must lose
If you call him to a bar for what he has
done.

[O.] CART. He has done it, then?

WIN. Yes, 'tis confessed to me.

FRANK. Dost thou betray me? 210

WIN. O, pardon me, dear heart! I am
mad to lose thee,
And know not what I speak; but, if thou
didst,
I must arraign this father for two sins,
Adultery and murther.

Enter Katherine.

KAT. Sir, they are come.

[O.] CART. Arraign me for what thou
wilt, all Middlesex knows me better for an
honest man than the middle of a market
place knows thee for an honest woman.—
Rise, sirrah, and don your tacklings; rig
yourself for the gallows, or I'll carry [220
thee thither on my back. Your trull shall to
th' goal go with you. There be as fine
Newgate birds as she, that can draw him in.
Pox on 's wounds!

FRANK. I have served thee, and my wages
now are paid;
Yet my worst punishment shall, I hope,
be stayed. *Exeunt.*

ACT[US] V. SCEN[A] i.

[*Mother Sawyer's hut.*]

Enter Mother Sawyer alone.

SAWY. Still wronged by every slave, and
not a dog
Bark in his dame's defense? I am called
witch,
Yet am myself bewitched from doing
harm.
Have I given up myself to thy black
lust
Thus to be scorned? Not see me in
three days?
I'm lost without my Tomalin. Prithee,
come;

Revenge to me is sweeter far than life.
Thou art my raven, on whose coal-
black wings
Revenge comes flying to me. O, my
best love!
I am on fire, even in the midst of ice,   10
Raking my blood up, till my shrunk
knees feel
Thy curled head leaning on them. Come,
then, my darling;
If in the air thou hover'st, fall upon me
In some dark cloud; and, as I oft have
seen
Dragons and serpents in the elements,
Appear thou now so to me. Art thou i'
th' sea?
Muster up all the monsters from the
deep,
And be the ugliest of them, so that my
bulch [1]
Show but his swarth cheek to me, let
earth cleave
And break from hell, I care not! Could
I run   20
Like a swift powder mine beneath the
world,
Up would I blow it, all to find out thee,
Though I lay ruined in it. Not yet
come!
I must, then, fall to my old prayer:
Sanctibicetur nomen tuum.
Not yet come! Worrying of wolves,
biting of mad dogs, the manges, and the—

Enter Dog [, now white].

Dog. How now! Whom art thou cursing?
Sawy. Thee! Ha! No, 'tis my black cur
I am cursing
For not attending on me.
Dog.   I am that cur.   30
Sawy. Thou liest. Hence! Come not
nigh me.
Dog.   Baw, waw!
Sawy. Why dost thou thus appear to me
in white,
As if thou wert the ghost of my dear
love?
Dog. I am dogged—list not to tell
thee; yet, to torment thee, my whiteness
puts thee in mind of thy winding sheet.[2]
Sawy. Am I near death?

[1] Bull calf, a term of endearment.
[2] Original reads *sweet.*

Dog. Yes, if the dog of hell be near
thee; when the devil comes to thee as a
lamb, have at thy throat!   40
Sawy. Off, cur!
Dog. He has the back of a sheep, but
the belly of an otter; devours by sea and
land. Why am I in white? Didst thou not
pray to me?
Sawy. Yes, thou dissembling hellhound! Why now in white more than at
other times?
Dog. Be blasted with the news! Whiteness is day's footboy, a forerunner [50
to light, which shows thy old riveled [3]
face. Villains are stripped naked; the
witch must be beaten out of her cockpit.
Sawy. Must she? She shall not; thou
art a lying spirit.
Why to mine eyes art thou a flag of
truce?
I am at peace with none; 'tis the black
color,
Or none, which I fight under. I do not like
Thy puritan paleness; glowing furnaces
Are far more hot than they which flame
outright.
If thou my old dog art, go and bite
such   60
As I shall set thee on.
Dog. I will not.
Sawy. I'll sell myself to twenty thou-
sand fiends
To have thee torn in pieces, then.
Dog. Thou canst not; thou art so ripe
to fall into hell, that no more of my kennel
will so much as bark at him that hangs
thee.
Sawy. I shall run mad.
Dog. Do so; thy time is come to [70
curse, and rave, and die. The glass of thy
sins is full, and it must run out at gallows.
Sawy. It cannot, ugly cur. I'll confess
nothing;
And, not confessing, who dare come
and swear
I have bewitched them? I'll not confess
one mouthful.
Dog. Choose, and be hanged or burned.
Sawy. Spite of the devil and thee, I'll
muzzle up
My tongue from telling tales.
Dog. Spite of thee and the devil, thou'lt
be condemned.

[3] Shriveled.

Sawy. Yes, when?

Dog.   And, ere the executioner 80
   Catch thee full in 's claws, thou'lt con-
     fess all.

Sawy. Out, dog!

Dog.   Out, witch! Thy trial is at hand.
   Our prey being had, the devil does
     laughing stand. *The Dog stands aloof.*

Enter Old Banks, Ratcliffe, and Countrymen.

   O. Bank. She's here; attach her.—
Witch, you must go with us.

                     [They seize her.]

Sawy. Whither? To hell?

   O. Bank. No, no, no, old crone; your
mittimus shall be made thither, but your
own jailors shall receive you.—Away with
her!   90

Sawy. My Tommy! My sweet Tom-boy!
   O, thou dog!
   Dost thou now fly to thy kennel and for-
     sake me?
   Plagues and consumptions—
                 Exeunt [All but Dog].

Dog. Ha, ha, ha, ha!
   Let not the world witches or devils
     condemn;
   They follow us, and then we follow them.

[Enter] Young Banks to the Dog.

Clow. I would fain meet with mine
ingle once more. He has had a claw
amongst um. My rival that loved my
wench is like to be hanged like an [100
innocent.[1] A kind cur where he takes,
but, where he takes not, a dogged rascal. I
know the villain loves me. No!—(*[Dog]
barks.*) Art thou there? *[Sees Dog.]*—That's
Tom's voice, but 'tis not he; this is a dog
of another hair, this. Bark, and not speak
to me? Not Tom, then; there's as much
difference betwixt Tom and this as betwixt
white and black.

Dog. Hast thou forgot me?   110

Clow. That's Tom again.—Prithee,
ningle, speak. Is thy name Tom?

Dog. Whilst I served my old Dame
Sawyer, 'twas; I'm gone from her now.

Clow.[2] Gone? Away with the witch,
then, too! She'll never thrive if thou
leav'st her; she knows no more how to
kill a cow, or a horse, or a sow, without
thee, than she does to kill a goose.

[1] Fool, idiot.   [2] Original reads *Dog.*

Dog. No, she has done killing now, [120
but must be killed for what she has done;
she's shortly to be hanged.

Clow. Is she? In my conscience, if
she be, 'tis thou hast brought her to the
gallows, Tom.

Dog. Right. I served her to that purpose; 'twas part of my wages.

Clow. This was no honest servant's
part, by your leave, Tom. This remember,
I pray you, between you and I; I [130
entertained you ever as a dog, not as a
devil.

Dog. True; and so I used thee doggedly,
    not devilishly;
I have deluded thee for sport to laugh
    at.
The wench thou seek'st after thou never
    spakest with,
But a spirit in her form, habit, and
    likeness.
Ha, ha!

Clow. I do not, then, wonder at the
change of your garments, if you can enter
into shapes of women too.   140

Dog. Any shape, to blind such silly
eyes as thine; but chiefly those coarse
creatures, dog, or cat, hare, ferret, frog,
toad.

Clow. Louse or flea?

Dog. Any poor vermin.

Clow. It seems you devils have poor,
thin souls, that you can bestow yourselves
in such small bodies. But, pray you, Tom,
one question at parting—I think I [150
shall never see you more—where do you
borrow those bodies that are none of your
own? The garment-shape you may hire
at broker's.

Dog. Why wouldst thou know that?
Fool, it avails thee not.

Clow. Only for my mind's sake, Tom,
and to tell some of my friends.

Dog. I'll thus much tell thee: thou never
    art so distant   152
From an evil spirit but that thy oaths,
Curses, and blasphemies pull him to
    thine elbow.
Thou never tell'st a lie but that a devil
Is within hearing it; thy evil purposes
Are ever haunted; but, when they come
    to act—
As thy tongue slandering, bearing false
    witness,

Thy hand stabbing, stealing, cozening,
    cheating—
He's then within thee. Thou play'st;
    he bets upon thy part.
Although thou lose, yet he will gain by
    thee.

CLOW. Ay? Then he comes in the shape
    of a rook.

DOG. The old cadaver of some self-
    strangled wretch   170
We sometimes borrow, and appear
    human;
The carcass of some disease-slain strum-
    pet
We varnish fresh, and wear as her first
    beauty.
Didst never hear? If not, it has been
    done.
An hot, luxurious lecher in his twines,
When he has thought to clip his dal-
    liance,
There has provided been for his em-
    brace
A fine, hot, flaming devil in her place.

CLOW. Yes, I am partly a witness to
this, but I never could embrace her. [180
I thank thee for that, Tom. Well, again I
thank thee, Tom, for all this counsel;
without a fee too! There's few lawyers of
thy mind now. Certainly, Tom, I begin to
pity thee.

DOG. Pity me? For what?

CLOW. Were it not possible for thee to
become an honest dog yet? 'Tis a base
life that you lead, Tom, to serve witches,
to kill innocent children, to kill [190
harmless cattle, to stroy corn and fruit,
etc. 'Twere better yet to be a butcher and
kill for yourself.

DOG. Why, these are all my delights,
my pleasures, fool.

CLOW. Or, Tom, if you could give your
mind to ducking—I know you can swim,
fetch, and carry—some shopkeeper in
London would take great delight in you,
and be a tender master over you. Or [200
if you have a mind to the game either at
bull or bear, I think I could prefer you
to Moll Cutpurse.

DOG. Ha, ha! I should kill all the game
—bulls, bears, dogs, and all; not a cub to
be left.

CLOW. You could do, Tom; but you
must play fair; you should be staved off

else. Or, if your stomach did better like to
serve in some nobleman's, knight's, [210
or gentleman's kitchen, if you could brook
the wheel and turn the spit (your labor
could not be much) when they have roast
meat (that's but once or twice in the week
at most), here you might lick your own
toes very well. Or, if you could translate
yourself into a lady's arming puppy, there
you might lick sweet lips, and do many
pretty offices. But to creep under an old
witch's coats, and suck like a great [220
puppy! Fie upon 't! I have heard beastly
things of you, Tom.

DOG. Ha, ha!
The worse thou heard'st of me, the bet-
    ter 'tis.
Shall I serve thee, fool, at the selfsame
    rate?

CLOW. No, I'll see thee hanged; thou
shalt be damned first! I know thy qualities
too well; I'll give no suck to such whelps.
Therefore henceforth I defy thee. Out,
and avaunt!   230

DOG. Nor will I serve for such a silly
    soul.
I am for greatness now, corrupted great-
    ness;
There I'll shug [1] in, and get a noble
    countenance;
Serve some Briarean footcloth-strider, [2]
That has an hundred hands to catch at
    bribes,
But not a finger's nail of charity.
Such, like the dragon's tail, shall pull
    down hundreds
To drop and sink with him. I'll stretch
    myself,
And draw this bulk small as a silver
    wire,   239
Enter at the least pore tobacco fume
Can make a breach for. Hence, silly
    fool!
I scorn to prey on such an atom soul.

CLOW. Come out, come out, you cur!
I will beat thee out of the bounds of
Edmonton, and tomorrow we go in procession, and after thou shalt never come
in again. If thou goest to London, I'll
make thee go about by Tyburn, stealing
in by Thieving Lane. If thou canst rub
thy shoulder against a lawyer's gown, [250

[1] Crawl, sneak.
[2] A rider on a horse trapped for state occasions.

as thou passest by Westminster Hall, do;
if not, to the stairs amongst the bandogs;
take water, and the devil go with thee!
Exeunt Y[oung] Banks, Dog barking.

[SCENA ii.

Near Tyburn.]

*Enter Justice, Sir Arthur, [Somerton,]
Warbeck, Carter, Kate.*

JUST. Sir Arthur, though the bench
hath mildly censured your errors, yet you
have indeed been the instrument that
wrought all their misfortunes; I would
wish you paid down your fine speedily and
willingly.

SIR ART. I'll need no urging to it.

[O.] CART. If you should, 'twere a
shame to you, for, if I should speak my
conscience, you are worthier to be   [10
hanged of the two, all things considered;
and now make what you can of it. But I
am glad these gentlemen are freed.

WARB. We knew our innocence.

SOM.   And therefore feared it not.

KAT. But I am glad that I have you safe.
                              Noise within.

JUST. How now! What noise is that?

[O.] CART. Young Frank is going the
wrong way. Alas, poor youth! Now I
begin to pity him.   [*Exeunt.*]

[SCENA iii.

Another place near Tyburn.]

*Enter Y[oung] Thorney and Halberts. Enter,
as to see the execution, O[ld] Carter,
O[ld] Thorney, Katherine, Winnifride
weeping.*

O. THOR. Here let our sorrows wait him; to
    press nearer
The place of his sad death, some appre-
    hensions
May tempt our grief too much, at height
    already.—
Daughter, be comforted.

WIN.   Comfort and I
Are too far separated to be joined,
But in eternity. I share too much
Of him that's going thither.

[O.] CART. Poor woman, 'twas not thy
    fault; I grieve to see
Thee weep for him that hath my pity too.

WIN. My fault was lust; my punishment
    was shame.   10
Yet I am happy that my soul is free
Both from consent, foreknowledge, and
    intent
Of any murther but of mine own honor,
Restored again by a fair satisfaction,
And since not to be wounded.

O. THOR.   Daughter, grieve not
For what necessity forceth; rather
    resolve
To conquer it with patience.—Alas,
    she faints!

WIN. My griefs are strong upon me; my
    weakness scarce
Can bear them.

[VOICES.] (*within.*) Away with her! Hang
    her, witch!

*Enter Sawyer to execution; Officers with
Halberts; Country People.*

[O.] CART. The witch, that instru-   [20
ment of mischief! Did not she witch the
devil into my son-in-law, when he killed
my poor daughter?—Do you hear, Mother
Sawyer?

SAWY. What would you have? Cannot a
    poor old woman
Have your leave to die without vexa-
    tion?

[O.] CART. Did not you bewitch Frank
to kill his wife? He could never have
done 't without the devil.

SAWY. Who doubts it? But is every devil
    mine?   30
Would I had one now whom I might
    command
To tear you all in pieces! Tom would
    have done 't
Before he left me.

[O.] CART. Thou didst bewitch Ann
Ratcliffe to kill herself.

SAWY. Churl, thou liest; I never did her
    hurt.
Would you were all as near your ends as
    I am,
That gave evidence against me for it!

[1] COUNT. I'll be sworn, Mr. Carter, she
bewitched Gammer Washbowl's sow to cast
her pigs a day before she would have   [40
farried.[1] Yet they were sent up to London
and sold for as good Westminster dog pigs [2]

———
[1] Farrowed.   [2] Male pigs.

at Bartholomew Fair as ever great-bellied
alewife longed for.

SAWY. These dogs will mad me; I was
well resolved
  To die in my repentance. Though 'tis
true
  I would live longer if I might, yet since
  I cannot, pray, torment me not; my
conscience
  Is settled as it shall be. All take heed
  How they believe the devil; at last he'll
  cheat you. 50
[O.] CART. Th'adst best confess all truly.
SAWY. Yet again?
  Have I scarce breath enough to say my
prayers,
  And would you force me to spend that
in bawling?
  Bear witness, I repent all former evil;
  There is no damnéd conjuror like the
devil.
OMN[ES]. Away with her, away!
                    [*She is led away.*]

Enter Frank to execution, Officers, Justice,
    Sir Arthur, Warbeck, Somerton.

O. THOR. Here's the sad object which I
yet must meet
  With hope of comfort, if a repentant end
  Make him more happy than misfortune
would
  Suffer him here to be.
FRANK. Good sirs, turn from me. 60
  You will revive affliction almost killed
  With my continual sorrow.
O. THOR. O, Frank, Frank!
  Would I had sunk in mine own wants,
or died
  But one bare minute ere thy fault was
acted!
FRANK. To look upon your sorrows
executes me
  Before my execution.
WIN. Let me pray you, sir—
FRANK. Thou much-wronged woman, I
must sigh for thee,
  As he that's only loath to leave the
world
  For that he leaves thee in it unprovided,
  Unfriended; and for me to beg a pity
  From any man to thee when I am gone
  Is more than I can hope; nor, to say
truth, 72

Have I deserved it. But there is a pay-
ment
  Belongs to goodness from the great
exchequer
  Above; it will not fail thee, Winnifride.
  Be that thy comfort.
O. THOR. Let it be thine too,
Untimely-lost young man.
FRANK. He is not lost
  Who bears his peace within him. Had I
spun
  My web of life out at full length, and
dreamed
  Away my many years in lusts, in sur-
feits, 80
  Murthers of reputations, gallant sins
  Commended or approved, then, though
I had
  Died easily, as great and rich men do,
  Upon my own bed, not compelled by
justice,
  You might have mourned for me indeed;
my miseries
  Had been as everlasting as remediless.
  But now the law hath not arraigned,
condemned
  With greater rigor my unhappy fact [1]
  Than I myself have every little sin
  My memory can reckon from my child-
hood. 90
  A court hath been kept here, where I
am found
  Guilty; the difference is, my impartial
judge
  Is much more gracious than my faults
  Are monstrous to be named; yet they
are monstrous.
O. THOR. Here's comfort in this penitence.
WIN. It speaks
  How truly you are reconciled, and
quickens
  My dying comfort, that was near expiring
  With my last breath. Now this re-
pentance makes thee
  As white as innocence; and my first sin
with thee,
  Since which I knew none like it, by my
sorrow 100
  Is clearly canceled. Might our souls
together
  Climb to the height of their eternity,
  And there enjoy what earth denied us,
happiness!

[1] Deed.

But, since I must survive, and be the
monument
Of thy loved memory, I will preserve it
With a religious care, and pay thy
ashes
A widow's duty, calling that end best
Which, though it stain the name, makes
the soul blessed.
FRANK. Give me thy hand, poor woman;
do not weep.
Farewell! Thou dost forgive me?
WIN.   'Tis my part   110
To use that language.
FRANK.   O, that my example
Might teach the world hereafter what a
curse
Hangs on their heads who rather choose
to marry
A goodly portion than a dower of vir-
tues!—
Are you there, gentlemen? There is not
one
Amongst you whom I have not
wronged.—[To Carter.] You most—
[I] [1] robbed you of a daughter; but
she is
In heaven, and I must suffer for it
willingly.
[O.] CART. Ay, ay, she's in heaven, and I
am glad to see thee so well prepared   [120
to follow her. I forgive thee with all my
heart; if thou hadst not had ill counsel, thou
wouldst not have done as thou didst—the
more shame for them.
SOM. Spare your excuse to me; I do con-
ceive
What you would speak. I would you
could as easily
Make satisfaction to the law as to my
wrongs.
I am sorry for you.
WARB.   And so am I,
And heartily forgive you.
KAT.   I will pray for you
For her sake, who I am sure did love
you dearly.   130
SIR ART. Let us part friendly too; I am
ashamed
Of my part in thy wrongs.
FRANK.   You are all merciful,
And send me to my grave in peace. Sir
Arthur,

Heavens send you a new heart!—[To Old
Thorney.] Lastly, to you, sir;
And, though I have deserved not to be
called
Your son, yet give me leave upon my
knees
To beg a blessing.   [Kneels.]
O. THOR.   Take it; let me wet
Thy cheeks with the last tears my griefs
have left me.
O, Frank, Frank, Frank!
FRANK.   Let me beseech you, gentle-
men,
To comfort my old father, keep him with
ye;   140
Love this distresséd widow, and, as
often
As you remember what a graceless
man
I was, remember likewise that these are
Both free, both worthy of a better
fate
Than such a son or husband as I have
been.
All help me with your prayers.—On,
on; 'tis just
That law should purge the guilt of blood
and lust.   Exit [with Officers].
[O.] CART. Go thy ways. I did not think
to have shed one tear for thee, but thou
hast made me water my plants spite   [150
of my heart.—M[aster] Thorney, cheer up,
man; whilst I can stand by you, you shall
not want help to keep you from falling.
We have lost our children, both on 's,[2] the
wrong way, but we cannot help it; better
or worse, 'tis now as 'tis.
O. THOR. I thank you, sir; you are more
kind than I
Have cause to hope or look for.
[O.] CART. Mr. Somerton, is Kate yours
or no?   160
SOM. We are agreed.
KAT. And, but my faith is passed, I
should fear to be married, husbands are so
cruelly unkind. Excuse me that I am thus
troubled.
SOM. Thou shalt have no cause.
JUST.[3] Take comfort, Mistress Winnifride.
   —Sir Arthur,

---

[1] The spreading of the type in the original
shows that this word has obviously fallen out.

[2] Of us.
[3] The content of the following speech indicates that it should be assigned to the Justice
rather than to Old Carter, as in the original.

For his abuse to you and to your husband,
Is by the bench enjoined to pay you
down   169
A thousand marks.
SIR ART.   Which I will soon discharge.
WIN. Sir, 'tis too great a sum to be employed
Upon my funeral.
     [O.] CART. Come, come! If luck had
served, Sir Arthur, and every man had his
due, somebody might have tottered ere
this, without paying fines, like it as you
list.—Come to me, Winnifride; shalt be welcome.—Make much of her, Kate, I charge
you. I do not think but she's a good wench,
and hath had wrong as well as we. [180
So let's every man home to Edmonton with
heavy hearts, yet as merry as we can, though
not as we would.

JUST. Join, friends, in sorrow; make of
all the best.
Harms past may be lamented, not
redressed.   *Exeunt.*

EPILOGUE

Win[nifride].

I am a widow still, and must not sort [1]
A second choice without a good report,
Which though some widows find, and
few deserve,
Yet I dare not presume, but will not
swerve
From modest hopes. All noble tongues
are free;   190
The gentle may speak one kind word for
me.
                               PHEN.[2]

              FINIS.

[1] Select.   [2] This author is unidentified.

THE BROKEN HEART[1]

BY

JOHN FORD[2]

THE SCENE: *Sparta.*

[THE TIME: *About the eighth century, B.C.*]

THE SPEAKERS' NAMES FITTED TO THEIR QUALITIES

AMYCLAS, *common*[3] *to the kings of Laconia.*
ITHOCLES, *Honor of Loveliness: a favorite.*
ORGILUS, *Angry: son to Crotolon.*
BASSANES, *Vexation: a jealous nobleman.*
ARMOSTES, *an Appeaser: a councilor of state.*
CROTOLON, *Noise: another councilor.*
PROPHILUS, *Dear: friend to Ithocles.*
NEARCHUS, *Young Prince: Prince of Argos.*
TECNICUS, *Artist: a philosopher.*
HEMOPHIL, *Glutton* ⎫ *two courtiers.*
GRONEAS, *Tavern Haunter* ⎭
AMELUS, *Trusty: friend to Nearchus.*
PHULAS, *Watchful: servant to Bassanes.*

CALANTHA, *Flower of Beauty: the king's daughter.*
PENTHEA, *Complaint: sister to Ithocles [and wife to Bassanes].*
EUPHRANEA, *Joy: a maid of honor [and daughter to Crotolon].*
CHRISTALLA, *Crystal* ⎫ *maids of honor.*
PHILEMA, *a Kiss* ⎭
GRAUSIS,[4] *Old Beldam: overseer of Penthea.*

PERSONS INCLUDED

THRASUS, *Fierceness: Father of Ithocles.*
APLOTES, *Simplicity: Orgilus so disguised.*
[COURTIERS, OFFICERS, ATTENDANTS, ETC.]

THE PROLOGUE

Our scene is Sparta. He whose best of art
Hath drawn this piece calls it *The Broken Heart.*
The title lends no expectation here
Of apish laughter, or of some lame jeer
At place or persons; no pretended clause[5]
Of jests, fit for a brothel, courts applause
From vulgar admiration; such low songs,
Tuned to unchaste ears, suit not modest tongues.
The Virgin Sisters then deserved fresh bays
When Innocence and Sweetness crowned their lays;   10
Then vices gasped for breath, whose whole commerce
Was whipped to exile by unblushing verse.
This law we keep in our presentment now,
Not to take freedom more than we allow;[6]
What may be here thought a fiction, when Time's youth
Wanted some riper years, was known a truth,
In which, if words have clothed the subject right,
You may partake a pity with delight.

---

[1] The title continues: "A Tragedy. Acted by the King's Majesty's Servants at the Private House in the Blackfriars. *Fide Honor.*"
[2] The author's name does not appear on the title-page, but is affixed to the adulatory dedication (here omitted) to William, Lord Craven, Baron of Hampsted Marshall. The Latin motto is also an anagram of Ford's name, used elsewhere instead of his signature.
[3] *I.e.*, a name common.
[4] Throughout the text of the original, almost invariably misprinted *Gransis.*
[5] Conclusion, *i.e.*, by substituting different words for those expected or implied.
[6] Sanction.

ACTUS PRIMUS. SCENA PRIMA.

[*A room in Crotolon's house.*]

Enter Crotolon and Orgilus.

CROT. Dally not further; I will know the reason
That speeds thee to this journey.
ORG.   Reason? Good sir,
I can yield many.
CROT.   Give me one, a good one;
Such I expect, and ere we part must have.
Athens? Pray, why to Athens? You intend not
To kick against the world, turn cynic, stoic,
Or read the logic lecture, or become
An Areopagite,[1] and judge in causes
Touching the commonwealth? For, as I take it,
The budding of your chin cannot prognosticate   10
So grave an honor.
ORG.   All this I acknowledge.
CROT. You do! Then, son, if books and love of knowledge
Inflame you to this travel, here in Sparta
You may as freely study.
ORG.   'Tis not that, sir.
CROT. Not that, sir! As a father, I command thee
To acquaint me with the truth.
ORG.   Thus I obey 'e.
After so many quarrels as dissension,
Fury, and rage had broached in blood, and sometimes
With death to such confederates as sided
With now-dead Thrasus and yourself, my lord,   20
Our present king, Amyclas, reconciled
Your eager swords and sealed a gentle peace.
Friends you professed yourselves, which to confirm,
A resolution for a lasting league
Betwixt your families was entertained,
By joining in a Hymenean bond
Me and the fair Penthea, only daughter
To Thrasus.
CROT.   What of this?
ORG.   Much, much, dear sir.   28
A freedom of converse, an interchange
Of holy and chaste love, so fixed our souls

In a firm growth of [2] union, that no time
Can eat into the pledge; we had enjoyed
The sweets our vows expected, had not cruelty
Prevented all those triumphs [3] we prepared for,
By Thrasus his untimely death.
CROT.   Most certain.
ORG. From this time sprouted up that poisonous stalk
Of aconite, whose ripened fruit hath ravished
All health, all comfort of a happy life,
For Ithocles, her brother, proud of youth,
And prouder in his power, nourished closely   40
The memory of former discontents,
To glory in revenge. By cunning partly,
Partly by threats, a [4] woos at once and forces
His virtuous sister to admit a marriage
With Bassanes, a nobleman, in honor
And riches, I confess, beyond my fortunes.
CROT. All this is no sound reason to importune
My leave for thy departure.
ORG.   Now it follows.
Beauteous Penthea, wedded to this torture   49
By an insulting brother, being secretly
Compelled to yield her virgin freedom up
To him who never can usurp her heart,
Before contracted mine, is now so yoked
To a most barbarous thralldom, misery,
Affliction, that he savors not humanity,
Whose sorrow melts not into more than pity
In hearing but her name.
CROT.   As how, pray?
ORG.   Bassanes,
The man that calls her wife, considers truly
What heaven of perfections he is lord of
By thinking fair Penthea his; this thought   60
Begets a kind of monster-love, which love
Is nurse unto a fear so strong and servile
As brands all dotage with a jealousy.
All eyes who gaze upon that shrine of beauty,

[1] A member of the highest Athenian court of justice.

[2] Some copies of the original insert *holy* here.
[3] Celebrations.   [4] He.

He doth resolve,[1] do homage to the miracle;
Someone, he is assured, may now or then,
If opportunity but sort,[2] prevail.
So much, out of a self-unworthiness,
His fears transport him—not that he
  finds cause   69
In her obedience, but his own distrust.
CROT. You spin out your discourse.
ORG.   My griefs are violent;
For, knowing how the maid was heretofore
Courted by me, his jealousies grow wild
That I should steal again into her favors,
And undermine her virtues, which the
  gods
Know I nor dare nor dream of. Hence,
  from hence
I undertake a voluntary exile—
First, by my absence to take off the cares
Of jealous Bassanes; but chiefly, sir,
To free Penthea from a hell on earth; 80
Lastly, to lose the memory of some-
  thing
Her presence makes to live in me afresh.
CROT. Enough, my Orgilus, enough. To
  Athens
I give a full consent.—Alas, good lady!—
We shall hear from thee often?
ORG.   Often.
CROT.   See,
Thy sister comes to give a farewell.

Enter Euphranea.

EUPH.   Brother!
ORG. Euphranea, thus upon thy cheeks I
  print
A brother's kiss, more careful of thine
  honor,
Thy health, and thy well-doing than my
  life.   89
Before we part, in presence of our father,
I must prefer a suit to 'e.
EUPH.   You may style it,
My brother, a command.
ORG.   That you will promise
To pass never to any man, however [3]
Worthy, your faith, till, with our
  father's leave,
I give a free consent.

[1] Conclude.
[2] Occur.
[3] Here and in a few other passages the line
division has been regularized.

CROT.   An easy motion! [4]
I'll promise for her, Orgilus.
ORG.   Your pardon.
Euphranea's oath must yield me satis-
  faction.
EUPH. By Vesta's sacred fires I swear.
CROT.   And I
By great Apollo's beams join in the vow,
Not without thy allowance to bestow her
On any living.
ORG.   Dear Euphranea,   101
Mistake me not; far, far 'tis from my
  thought,
As far from any wish of mine, to hinder
Preferment to an honorable bed
Or fitting fortune. Thou art young and
  handsome,
And 'twere injustice—more, a tyranny—
Not to advance thy merit. Trust me,
  sister,
It shall be my first care to see thee
  matched
As may become thy choice and our con-
  tents.
I have your oath.
EUPH.   You have. But mean
  you, brother,   110
To leave us, as you say?
CROT.   Ay, ay, Euphranea;
He has just grounds direct him. I will
  prove
A father and a brother to thee.
EUPH.   Heaven
Does look into the secrets of all hearts.
Gods, you have mercy with 'e, else—
CROT.   Doubt nothing
Thy brother will return in safety to us.
ORG. Souls sunk in sorrows never are with-
  out 'em;
They change fresh airs, but bear their
  griefs about 'em.   *Exeunt omnes.*

SCENE ii.

[*A room in the palace.*]

*Flourish. Enter Amyclas the king, Armostes,
    Prophilus, and Attendants.*

AMY. The Spartan gods are gracious; our
  humility
Shall bend before their altars, and perfume
Their temples with abundant sacrifice.

[4] Proposal.

See, lords, Amyclas, your old king, is
    ent'ring
Into his youth again! I shall shake off
This silver badge of age, and change this
    snow
For hairs as gay as are Apollo's locks;
Our heart leaps in new vigor.
ARM.   May old time
Run back to double your long life, great
    sir!
AMY. It will, it must, Armostes; thy bold
    nephew,   10
Death-braving Ithocles, brings to our
    gates
Triumphs and peace upon his conquering
    sword.
Laconia is a monarchy at length,
Hath in this latter war trod under
    foot
Messene's pride; Messene bows her neck
To Lacedemon's royalty. O, 'twas
A glorious victory, and doth deserve
More than a chronicle—a temple, lords,
A temple to the name of Ithocles!—
Where didst thou leave him, Prophilus?
PRO.   At Pephon, 20
Most gracious sovereign; twenty of the
    noblest
Of the Messenians there attend your
    pleasure
For such conditions as you shall propose
In settling peace and liberty of life.
AMY. When comes your friend, the gen-
    eral?
PRO.   He promised
To follow with all speed convenient.

*Enter Crotolon, Calantha, Christalla, Philema
    [with a garland], and Euphranea.*

AMY. Our daughter!—Dear Calantha, the
    happy news,
The conquest of Messene, hath already
Enriched thy knowledge.
CAL.   With the circumstance
And manner of the fight, related faith-
    fully   30
By Prophilus himself.—But, pray, sir,
    tell me
How doth the youthful general demean
His actions in these fortunes?
PRO.   Excellent princess,
Your own fair eyes may soon report a
    truth

Unto your judgment, with what modera-
    tion,
Calmness of nature, measure, bounds,
    and limits
Of thankfulness and joy, a doth digest
Such amplitude of his success as would
In others, molded of a spirit less clear,
Advance 'em to comparison with heaven.
But Ithocles—
CAL.   Your friend—
PRO.   He is so, madam, 41
In which the period [1] of my fate consists;
He, in this firmament of honor, stands
Like a star fixed, not moved with any
    thunder
Of popular applause or sudden lightning
Of self-opinion; he hath served his coun-
    try,
And thinks 'twas but his duty.
CROT.   You describe
A miracle of man.
AMY.   Such, Crotolon,
On forfeit of a king's word, thou wilt find
    him.—
Hark, warning of his coming! All attend
    him.   *Flourish.* 50

*Enter Ithocles, Hemophil, and Groneas, the
    rest of the Lords ushering him in.*

AMY. Return into these arms, thy home,
    thy sanctuary,
Delight of Sparta, treasure of my bosom,
Mine own, own Ithocles!
ITH.   Your humblest subject.
ARM. Proud of the blood I claim an in-
    terest in,
As brother to thy mother, I embrace
    thee,
Right noble nephew.
ITH.   Sir, your love's too partial.
CROT. Our country speaks by me, who by
    thy valor,
Wisdom, and service shares in this great
    action,
Returning thee, in part [2] of thy due merits,
A general welcome.
ITH.   You exceed in bounty. 60
CAL. Christalla, Philema, the chaplet.—
    [*Takes the chaplet from them.*] Ith-
    ocles,
Upon the wings of Fame the singular
And chosen fortune of an high attempt

---

[1] Summation.   [2] On behalf.

Is borne so past the view of common
    sight
That I myself with mine own hands have
    wrought,
To crown thy temples, this provincial
    garland.[1]
Accept, wear, and enjoy it as our gift
Deserved, not purchased.

ITH.   Y' are a royal maid.
AMY. She is in all our daughter.
ITH.   Let me blush,
    Acknowledging how poorly I have
       served,   70
What nothings I have done, compared
    with th' honors
Heaped on the issue of a willing mind;
In that lay mine ability, that only.
For who is he so sluggish from his birth,
So little worthy of a name or country,
That owes not out of gratitude for life
A debt of service, in what kind soever
Safety or counsel of the commonwealth
Requires, for payment?
CAL.   A speaks truth.
ITH.   Whom heaven
    Is pleased to style victorious, there, to
       such,   80
Applause runs madding, like the drunken
    priests
In Bacchus' sacrifices, without reason,
Voicing the leader-on a demigod,
Whenas, indeed, each common soldier's
    blood
Drops down as current coin in that hard
    purchase
As his whose much more delicate condi-
    tion
Hath sucked the milk of ease. Judgment
    commands,
But resolution executes. I use not,
Before this royal presence, these fit
    slights
As in contempt of such as can direct; 90
My speech hath other end—not to at-
    tribute
All praise to one man's fortune, which is
    strength'd
By many hands. For instance, here is
    Prophilus,
A gentleman—I cannot flatter truth—
Of much desert; and, though in other
    rank,

[1] *I.e.*, one "conferred on those who . . . had
added a *Province* to the empire" (Gifford).

Both Hemophil and Groneas were not
    missing
To wish their country's peace; for, in a
    word,
All there did strive their best, and 'twas
    our duty.
AMY. Courtiers turn soldiers?—We vouch-
    safe our hand.
    [*Hemophil and Groneas kiss his hand.*]
    Observe [2] your great example.
HEM.   With all diligence. 100
GRO. Obsequiously and hourly.
AMY.   Some repose
    After these toils are needful. We must
    think on
Conditions for the conquered; they ex-
    pect [3] 'em.
On!—Come, my Ithocles.
EUPH.   Sir, with your favor,
    I need not a supporter.
PRO.   Fate instructs me.
Exeunt. Manent [4] *Hemophil, Groneas, Chris-*
    talla, et Philema. Hemophil stays
    Christalla; Groneas, Philema.
CHRIS. With me?
PHIL.   Indeed, I dare not stay.
HEM.   Sweet lady,
    Soldiers are blunt—your lip.
CHRIS.   Fie, this is rudeness;
    You went not hence such creatures.
GRO.   Spirit of valor
    Is of a mounting nature.
PHIL.   It appears so.— 109
    Pray, in earnest, how many men apiece
    Have you two been the death of?
GRO.   Faith, not many;
    We were composed of mercy.
HEM.   For our daring,
    You heard the general's approbation
    Before the king.
CHRIS.   You "wished your country's
    peace;"
That showed your charity. Where are
    your spoils,
Such as the soldier fights for?
PHIL.   They are coming.
CHRIS. By the next carrier, are they not?
GRO.   Sweet Philema,
    When I was in the thickest of mine
      enemies,
Slashing off one man's head, another's
    nose,
Another's arms and legs—

[2] Do homage to.   [3] Await.   [4] Remain.

PHIL. And all together [1] — 120

GRO. Then would I with a sigh remember thee,
And cry, "Dear Philema, 'tis for thy sake
I do these deeds of wonder!"—Dost not love me
With all thy heart now?

PHIL. Now as heretofore.
I have not put my love to use; [2] the principal
Will hardly yield an interest.

GRO. By Mars,
I'll marry thee!

PHIL. By Vulcan, y' are forsworn,
Except my mind do alter strangely.

GRO. One word.

CHRIS. You lie beyond all modesty. Forbear me! 129

HEM. I'll make thee mistress of a city; 'tis
Mine own by conquest.

CHRIS. By petition; sue for 't
In forma pauperis. [3] City? Kennel! [4] Gallants,
Off with your feathers; [5] put on aprons, gallants.
Learn to reel, thrum, [6] or trim a lady's dog,
And be good, quiet souls of peace, hobgoblins!

HEM. Christalla!

CHRIS. Practice to drill hogs, in hope
To share in the acorns. Soldiers? Corncutters,
But not so valiant; they ofttimes draw blood,
Which you durst never do. When you have practiced 139
More wit or more civility, we'll rank 'e
I' th' list of men; till then, brave things-at-arms,
Dare not to speak to us—most potent Groneas!—

PHIL. And Hemophil the hardy!—at your services.

GRO. They scorn us as they did before we went.

HEM. Hang 'em! Let us scorn them, and be revenged.
Exeunt Chri[stalla] et Philema.

[1] Gifford-Dyce reading. Original reads *altogether.*
[2] *I.e.,* lent it out for profit.
[3] In the status of a pauper. [4] Gutter!
[5] Gifford-Dyce reading. Original reads *fathers.*
[6] Provide with fringe.

GRO. Shall we?

HEM. We will; and, when we slight them thus,
Instead of following them, they'll follow us;
It is a woman's nature.

GRO. 'Tis a scurvy one. *Exeunt omnes.*

SCENE iii.

[The palace gardens adjoining a grove.]

Enter Tecnicus, a philosopher, and Orgilus disguised like a scholar of his.

TEC. Tempt not the stars, young man; thou canst not play
With the severity of fate. This change
Of habit and disguise in outward view
Hides not the secrets of thy soul within thee
From their quick-piercing eyes, which dive at all times
Down to thy thoughts; in thy aspect I note
A consequence of danger.

ORG. Give me leave,
Grave Tecnicus, without foredooming destiny,
Under thy roof to ease my silent griefs,
By applying to my hidden wounds the balm 10
Of thy oraculous lectures. If my fortune
Run such a crooked byway as to wrest
My steps to ruin, yet thy learned precepts
Shall call me back and set my footings straight.
I will not court the world.

TEC. Ah, Orgilus,
Neglects in young men of delights and life
Run often to extremities; they care not
For harms to others who contemn their own.

ORG. But I, most learned artist, am not so much
At odds with nature that I grutch [7] the thrift 20
Of any true deserver; nor doth malice [8]
Of present hopes so check them with despair
As that I yield to thought of more affliction

[7] Grudge. [8] Misfortune.

Than what is incident to frailty; where-
fore
Impute not this retiréd course of living
Some little time to any other cause
Than what I justly render—the infor-
mation
Of an unsettled mind; as the effect
Must clearly witness.

Tec.   Spirit of truth inspire thee!
On these conditions I conceal thy
change,   30
And willingly admit thee for an audi-
tor.—
I'll to my study.

Org.   I to contemplations
In these delightful walks.—
                              [*Exit Tecnicus.*]
                    Thus metamorphized [1]
I may without suspicion hearken after
Penthea's usage and Euphranea's faith.
Love, thou art full of mystery!   The
deities
Themselves are not secure [2] in search-
ing out
The secrets of those flames, which,
hidden, waste
A breast made tributary to the laws
Of beauty; physic yet hath never
found   40
A remedy to cure a lover's wound.—
Ha! Who are those that cross yon
private walk
Into the shadowing grove in amorous
foldings?

Prophilus passeth over, supporting Euphra-
nea, and whispering.

My sister—O, my sister? 'Tis Euphra-
nea
With Prophilus!   Supported too!   I
would
It were an apparition!   Prophilus
Is Ithocles his friend.   It strangely
puzzles me.
Again?   Help me, my book; this scholar's
habit
Must stand my privilege; [3] my mind is
busy,
Mine eyes and ears are open.
                    Walk by, reading.

[1] Metamorphosed.
[2] Certain.
[3] *I.e.,* must become my right to walk here.

Enter again Prophilus and Euphranea.

Pro.   Do not waste   50
The span of this stol'n time, lent by the
gods
For precious use, in niceness. [4]   Bright
Euphranea,
Should I repeat old vows, or study new,
For purchase of belief to my desires—

Org. [*Aside.*] Desires?

Pro.   My service, my integrity—

Org. [*Aside.*] That's better.

Pro.   I should but repeat a lesson
Oft conned without a prompter but
thine eyes.
My love is honorable.

Org. [*Aside.*]   So was mine
To my Penthea—chastely honorable.

Pro. Nor wants there more addition to
my wish   60
Of happiness than having thee a wife—
Already sure of Ithocles, a friend
Firm and unalterable.

Org. [*Aside.*]   But a brother
More cruel than the grave.

Euph.   What can you look for,
In answer to your noble protestations,
From an unskillful maid, but language
suited
To a divided mind?

Org. [*Aside.*]   Hold out, Euphranea!

Euph. Know, Prophilus, I never under-
valued,
From the first time you mentioned
worthy love,
Your merit, means, or person; it had
been   70
A fault of judgment in me, and a dull-
ness
In my affections, not to weigh and thank
My better stars that offered me the
grace
Of so much blissfulness.   For, to speak
truth,
The law of my desires kept equal pace
With yours, nor have I left that resolu-
tion;
But only, in a word, whatever choice
Lives nearest in my heart must first
procure
Consent both from my father and my
brother,
Ere he can own me his.

[4] Coyness.

ORG. [*Aside.*]   She is forsworn else. 80
PRO. Leave me that task.
EUPH.   My brother, ere he parted
To Athens, had my oath.
ORG. [*Aside.*]   Yes, yes, a had, sure.
PRO. I doubt not, with the means the
    court supplies,
But to prevail at pleasure.
ORG. [*Aside.*]   Very likely!
PRO. Meantime, best, dearest, I may
    build my hopes
On the foundation of thy constant
    suff'rance
In any opposition.
EUPH.   Death shall sooner
Divorce life and the joys I have in living
Than my chaste vows from truth.
PRO.   On thy fair hand
I seal the like.
ORG. [*Aside.*]   There is no faith in
    woman.   90
Passion, O, be contained! My very
    heartstrings
Are on the tenters.[1]
EUPH.   Sir, we are overheard.
Cupid protect us! 'Twas a stirring, sir,
Of someone near.
PRO.   Your fears are needless, lady;
None have access into these private
    pleasures
Except some near in court, or bosom
    student
From Tecnicus his oratory,[2] granted
By special favor lately from the king
Unto the grave philosopher.
EUPH.   Methinks
I hear one talking to himself—I see
    him.   100
PRO. 'Tis a poor scholar, as I told you,
    lady.
ORG. [*Aside.*] I am discovered.—[*As if
    studying aloud.*] Say it: is it possible,
With a smooth tongue, a leering counte-
    nance,
Flattery, or force of reason—I come t'e,[3]
    sir—
To turn or to appease the raging sea?
Answer to that.—Your art? What art
    to catch
And hold fast in a net the sun's small
    atoms?

No, no; they'll out, they'll out; ye may
    as easily
Outrun a cloud driven by a northern
    blast
As fiddle-faddle so! Peace, or speak
    sense.   110
EUPH. Call you this thing a scholar? 'Las,
    he's lunatic.
PRO. Observe him, sweet; 'tis but his rec-
    reation.
ORG. But will you hear a little! You are
    so tetchy.
You keep no rule in argument. Philoso-
    phy
Works not upon impossibilities,
But natural conclusions.—Mew!—Ab-
    surd!
The metaphysics are but speculations
Of the celestial bodies, or such accidents
As, not mixed perfectly, in the air en-
    gendered
Appear to us unnatural; that's all.   120
Prove it; yet, with a reverence to your
    gravity,
I'll balk illiterate sauciness, submitting
My sole opinion to the touch of writers.
PRO. Now let us fall in with him.
          [*They come forward.*]
ORG.   Ha, ha, ha!
These apish boys, when they but taste
    the grammates [4]
And principles of theory, imagine
They can oppose their teachers. Con-
    fidence
Leads many into errors.
PRO.   By your leave, sir.
EUPH. Are you a scholar, friend?
ORG.   I am, gay creature,
With pardon of your deities, a mush-
    room   130
On whom the dew of heaven drops now
    and then;
The sun shines on me too, I thank his
    beams!
Sometime I feel their warmth; and eat
    and sleep.
PRO. Does Tecnicus read [5] to thee?
ORG.   Yes, forsooth.
He is my master surely; yonder door
Opens upon his study.
PRO.   Happy creatures!
Such people toil not, sweet, in heats of
    state,

---

[1] Tenterhooks.
[2] Lecture hall.
[3] He addresses an imaginary opponent.

[4] Rudiments.   [5] Lecture.

Nor sink in thaws of greatness; their affections

Keep order with the limits of their modesty;[1]

Their love is love of virtue.—What's thy name?   140

Org. Aplotes, sumptuous master, a poor wretch.

Euph. Dost thou want anything?

Org.   Books, Venus, books.

Pro. Lady, a new conceit[2] comes in my thought,

And most available for both our comforts.

Euph. My lord—

Pro.   Whiles I endeavor to deserve Your father's blessing to our loves, this scholar

May daily at some certain hours attend[3]

What notice I can write of my success,

Here in this grove, and give it to your hands;

The like from you to me. So can we never,   150

Barred of our mutual speech, want sure intelligence,

And thus our hearts may talk when our tongues cannot.

Euph. Occasion is most favorable; use it.

Pro. Aplotes, wilt thou wait us twice a day,

At nine i' the morning and at four at night,

Here in this bower, to convey such letters As each shall send to other? Do it willingly,

Safely, and secretly, and I will furnish Thy study, or what else thou canst desire.

Org. Jove, make me thankful, thankful, I beseech thee,   160

Propitious Jove! I will prove sure and trusty.

You will not fail me books?

Pro.   Nor aught besides Thy heart can wish. This lady's name's Euphranea,

Mine Prophilus.

Org.   I have a pretty memory;

It must prove my best friend. I will not miss

One minute of the hours appointed.

Pro.   Write

The books thou wouldst have bought thee in a note,

Or take thyself some money.

Org.   No, no money;

Money to scholars is a spirit invisible;

We dare not finger it. Or[4] books or nothing.   170

Pro. Books of what sort thou wilt. Do not forget

Our names.

Org.   I warrant 'e, I warrant 'e.

Pro. Smile, Hymen, on the growth of our desires;

We'll feed thy torches with eternal fires!

     Exeunt. Manet Org[ilus].

Org. Put out thy torches, Hymen, or their light

Shall meet a darkness of eternal night!

Inspire me, Mercury, with swift deceits.

Ingenious Fate has leapt into mine arms,

Beyond the compass of my brain. Mortality

Creeps on the dung of earth, and cannot reach   180

The riddles which are purposed by the gods.

Great arts best write themselves in their own stories;

They die too basely who outlive their glories.   *Exit.*

Actus Secundus. Scena Prima.

[*A room in Bassanes' house.*]

Enter Bassanes and Phulas.

Bass. I'll have that window next the street dammed up;

It gives too full a prospect to temptation,

And courts a gazer's glances. There's a lust

Committed by the eye, that sweats and travails,

Plots, wakes, contrives, till the deformed bear whelp,

Adultery, be licked into the act,

The very act. That light shall be dammed up;

D'e hear, sir?

Phu.   I do hear, my lord; a mason Shall be provided suddenly.[5]

---

[1] Moderation.   [2] Idea.   [3] Await.   [4] Either.   [5] At once.

BASS. Some rogue, 9
Some rogue of your confederacy, factor [1]
For slaves and strumpets, to convey
close [2] packets
From this spruce springal [3] and the
tother [4] youngster,
That gaudy earwrig,[5] or my lord your
patron,
Whose pensioner you are! I'll tear thy
throat out,
Son of a cat, ill-looking hound's head,
rip up
Thy ulcerous maw, if I but scent a paper,
A scroll but half as big as what can
cover
A wart upon thy nose, a spot, a pimple,
Directed to my lady; it may prove
A mystical preparative to lewdness.   20
PHU. Care shall be had. I will turn every
thread
About me to an eye.—[Aside.] Here's a
sweet life!
BASS. The city housewives, cunning in the
traffic
Of chamber merchandise, set all at
price
By wholesale; yet they wipe their
mouths and simper,
Cull, [6] kiss, and cry "sweetheart," and
stroke the head
Which they have branched; [7] and all is
well again!
Dull clods of dirt, who dare not feel the
rubs [8]
Stuck on the foreheads.
PHU.   'Tis a villainous world;
One cannot hold his own in 't.
BASS.   Dames at court,   30
Who flaunt in riots, run another bias; [9]
Their pleasure heaves the patient ass that
suffers
Up on the stilts of office, titles, in-
comes;
Promotion justifies the shame, and sues
for 't.
Poor Honor, thou art stabbed, and
bleed'st to death
By such unlawful hire! The country
mistress

Is yet more wary, and in blushes hides
Whatever trespass draws her troth to
guilt.
But all are false. On this truth I am
bold:
No woman but can fall, and doth, or
would.—   40
Now for the newest news about the
city;
What blab the voices, sirrah?
PHU.   O, my lord,
The rarest, quaintest, strangest, tickling
news
That ever—
BASS.   Heyday! Up and ride me, rascal!
What is 't?
PHU.   Forsooth, they say, the king has
mewed [10]
All his gray beard, instead of which is
budded
Another of a pure carnation color,
Speckled with green and russet.
BASS.   Ignorant block!
PHU. Yes, truly; and 'tis talked about the
streets
That, since Lord Ithocles came home,
the lions   50
Never left roaring, at which noise the
bears
Have danced their very hearts out.
BASS.   Dance out thine too.
PHU. Besides, Lord Orgilus is fled to
Athens
Upon a fiery dragon, and 'tis thought
A never can return.
BASS.   Grant it, Apollo!
PHU. Moreover, please your lordship,
'tis reported
For certain that whoever is found jealous
Without apparent proof that 's wife is
wanton
Shall be divorced; but this is but she-
news—
I had it from a midwife. I have more
yet.   60
BASS. Antic, no more! Idiots and stupid
fools
Grate my calamities. Why to be fair
Should yield presumption of a faulty
soul? [11]
Look to the doors.

---

[1] Agent.   [3] Youth.
[2] Secret.   [4] That other.
[5] Earwig.
[6] Coll, "neck," embrace.
[7] A conventional allusion to cuckoldry.
[8] Knobs, horns.   [9] Direction.

[10] Moulted.
[11] *I.e.*, why should beauty arouse suspicion of a
faulty soul?

PHU. [*Aside.*]   The horn of plenty crest
  him!   *Exit Phul[as].*
BASS. Swarms of confusion huddle in my
  thoughts
In rare distemper.—Beauty? O, it is
An unmatched blessing or a horrid curse.

Enter Penthea and Grausis, an old lady.

[*Aside.*] She comes, she comes! So shoots
  the morning forth,
  Spangled with pearls of transparent
  dew.
The way to poverty is to be rich,   70
As I in her am wealthy; but for her,
In all contents a bankrupt.—Loved
  Penthea!
How fares my heart's best joy?
GRAU.   In sooth, not well.
She is so oversad.
BASS.   Leave chattering, magpie.—
Thy brother is returned, sweet, safe and
  honored
With a triumphant victory; thou shalt
  visit him.
We will to court, where, if it be thy
  pleasure,
Thou shalt appear in such a ravishing
  luster
Of jewels above value that the dames
Who brave it there, in rage to be out-
  shined,   80
Shall hide them in their closets, and un-
  seen
Fret in their tears, whiles every won-
  d'ring eye
Shall crave none other brightness but thy
  presence.
Choose thine own recreations; be a
  queen
Of what delights thou fanciest best, what
  company,
What place, what times; do anything, do
  all things
Youth can command, so thou wilt chase
  these clouds
From the pure firmament of thy fair
  looks.
GRAU. Now 'tis well said, my lord.—What,
  lady! Laugh;
Be merry! Time is precious.
BASS. [*Aside.*]   Furies whip thee! 90
PEN. Alas, my lord, this language to your
  handmaid

Sounds as would music to the deaf; I need
No braveries [1] nor cost of art to draw
The whiteness of my name into offense;
Let such, if any such there are, who covet
A curiosity of admiration,
By laying out their plenty to full view,
Appear in gaudy outsides; my attires
Shall suit the inward fashion of my
  mind,
From which, if your opinion, nobly
  placed,   100
Change not the livery your words be-
  stow,
My fortunes with my hopes are at the
  highest.
BASS. This house, methinks, stands some-
  what too much inward; [2]
It is too melancholy. We'll remove
Nearer the court. Or what thinks my
  Penthea
Of the delightful island we command?
Rule me as thou canst wish.
PEN.   I am no mistress.
Whither you please, I must attend; all
  ways
Are alike pleasant to me.
GRAU.   Island? Prison!
A prison is as gaysome; we'll no is-
  lands.   110
Marry, out upon 'em! Whom shall we
  see there?
Seagulls, and porpoises, and water rats,
And crabs, and mews, and dogfish—
  goodly gear
For a young lady's dealing—or an old
  one's!
On no terms islands; I'll be stewed first.
BASS. [*Aside.*]   Grausis,
You are a juggling bawd.—This sadness,
  sweetest,
Becomes not youthful blood.—[*Aside.*]
  I'll have you pounded. [3] —
For my sake put on a more cheerful
  mirth;
Thou'lt mar thy cheeks, and make me old
  in griefs.—
[*Aside.*] Damnable bitch fox!
GRAU.   I am thick of hearing 120
Still, [4] when the wind blows southerly.—
  What think 'e,
If your fresh lady breed young bones, my
  lord?

[1] Fineries.   [3] Impounded.
[2] Secret, secluded.   [4] Always.

Would not a chopping boy d'e good at
  heart?
But, as you said—
Bass. [*Aside.*]   I'll spit thee on a stake,
Or chop thee into collops!
Grau.   Pray, speak louder.
Sure, sure the wind blows south still.
Pen.   Thou prat'st madly.
Bass. 'Tis very hot; I sweat extremely.—
Now?

Enter Phulas.

Phu. A herd of lords, sir.
Bass.   Ha?
Phu.   A flock of ladies.
Bass. Where?
Phu.   Shoalds [1] of horses.
Bass.   Peasant, how?
Phu.   Caroches [2]
In drifts; th' one enter, th' other stand
  without, sir.   130
And now I vanish.   *Exit Phulas.*

*Enter Prophilus, Hemophil, Groneas, Chris-
talla, and Philema.*

Pro.   Noble Bassanes!
Bass. Most welcome, Prophilus; ladies,
  gentlemen,
To all my heart is open; you all honor
  me—
[*Aside.*] A tympany [3] swells in my head al-
  ready—
Honor me bountifully.—[*Aside.*] How
  they flutter,
Wagtails and jays together!
Pro.   From your brother
By virtue of your love to him, I require
Your instant presence, fairest.
Pen.   He is well, sir?
Pro. The gods preserve him ever! Yet,
  dear beauty,
I find some alteration in him lately, 140
Since his return to Sparta.—My good
  lord,
I pray, use no delay.
Bass.   We had not needed
An invitation, if his sister's health
Had not fallen into question.—Haste,
  Penthea,
Slack not a minute.—Lead the way, good
  Prophilus;
I'll follow step by step.

  [1] Shoals.   [2] Coaches.   [3] Distension.

Pro.   Your arm, fair madam.
Exeunt omnes sed [4] *Bass[anes] et Grau[sis].*
Bass. One word with your old bawdship:
  th' hadst been better
Railed at the sins thou worshipp'st than
  have thwarted
My will. I'll use thee cursedly.
Grau.   You dote; 149
You are beside yourself. A politician
In jealousy? No, y' are too gross, too
  vulgar.
Pish, teach not me my trade; I know my
  cue.
My crossing you sinks me into her trust,
By which I shall know all; my trade's a
  sure one.
Bass. Forgive me, Grausis; 'twas consid-
  eration
I relished [5] not; but have a care now.
Grau.   Fear not,
I am no new-come-to 't.
Bass.   Thy life's upon it,
And so is mine. My agonies are infinite.
        Exeunt omnes.

Scene ii.

[*Ithocles' apartment in the palace.*]

Enter Ithocles, alone.

Ith. Ambition? 'Tis of vipers' breed; it
  gnaws
A passage through the womb that gave
  it motion.
Ambition, like a seeléd [6] dove, mounts
  upward,
Higher and higher still, to perch on
  clouds,
But tumbles headlong down with heavier
  ruin.
So squibs and crackers fly into the air;
Then, only breaking with a noise, they
  vanish
In stench and smoke. Morality,[7] applied
To timely practice, keeps the soul in
  tune,
At whose sweet music all our actions
  dance.   10
But this is form of books and school-
  tradition; [8]
It physics not the sickness of a mind

  [4] But.   [7] Moralization.
  [5] Understood.   [8] *I.e.,* pedantry.
  [6] With eyelids sewed together.

Broken with griefs. Strong fevers are not eased
With counsel, but with best receipts and means—
Means, speedy means and certain; that's the cure.

Enter Armostes and Crotolon.

ARM. You stick, Lord Crotolon, upon a point
Too nice and too unnecessary; Prophilus
Is every way desertful. I am confident
Your wisdom is too ripe to need instruction
From your son's tutelage.
CROT.   Yet not so ripe, 20
My Lord Armostes, that it dares to dote
Upon the painted [1] meat of smooth persuasion,
Which tempts me to a breach of faith.
ITH.   Not yet
Resolved, my lord? Why, if your son's consent
Be so available, [2] we'll write to Athens
For his repair [3] to Sparta. The king's hand
Will join with our desires; he has been moved to 't.
ARM. Yes, and the king himself importuned Crotolon
For a despatch.
CROT.   Kings may command; their wills
Are laws not to be questioned.
ITH.   By this marriage 30
You knit an union so devout, so hearty,
Between your loves to me and mine to yours,
As if mine own blood had an interest in it;
For Prophilus is mine, and I am his.
CROT. My lord, my lord!—
ITH.   What, good sir? Speak your thought.
CROT. Had this sincerity been real once,
My Orgilus had not been now unwived,
Nor your lost sister buried in a bridebed.
Your uncle here, Armostes, knows this truth,
For, had your father Thrasus lived—but peace 40
Dwell in his grave! I have done.
ARM.   Y' are bold and bitter.

ITH. [*Aside.*] A presses home the injury; it smarts.—
No reprehensions, uncle; I deserve 'em.
Yet, gentle sir, consider what the heat
Of an unsteady youth, a giddy brain,
Green indiscretion, flattery of greatness,
Rawness of judgment, willfulness in folly,
Thoughts vagrant as the wind and as uncertain,
Might lead a boy in years to; 'twas a fault,
A capital fault, for then I could not dive 50
Into the secrets of commanding love,
Since when, experience, by the extremities [4] (in others),
Hath forced me to collect. [5] And, trust me, Crotolon,
I will redeem those wrongs with any service
Your satisfaction can require for current.
ARM. Thy acknowledgment is satisfaction.
What would you more?
CROT.   I'm conquered; if Euphranea
Herself admit the motion, let it be so;
I doubt not my son's liking.
ITH.   Use my fortunes,
Life, power, sword, and heart—all are your own. 60

Enter Bassanes, Prophilus, Calantha, Penthea, Euphranea, Christalla, Philema, and Grausis.

ARM. The princess, with your sister.
CAL.   I present 'e
A stranger here in court, my lord, for, did not
Desire of seeing you draw her abroad,
We had not been made happy in her company.
ITH. You are a gracious princess.—Sister, wedlock
Holds too severe a passion in your nature,
Which can engross all duty to your husband,
Without attendance on so dear a mistress.—
[*To Bassanes.*] 'Tis not my brother's pleasure, I presume,
T' immure her in a chamber.

---

[1] Counterfeit.   [2] Serviceable.   [3] Return.   [4] Extremes.   [5] Understand.

BASS.   'Tis her will; 70
She governs her own hours. Noble
  Ithocles,
We thank the gods for your success and
  welfare.
Our lady has of late been indisposed,
Else we had waited on you with the first.

ITH. How does Penthea now?

PEN.   You best know, brother,
From whom my health and comforts
  are derived.

BASS. [*Aside.*] I like the answer well; 'tis
  sad [1] and modest.
There may be tricks yet, tricks.—Have
  an eye, Grausis!

CAL. Now, Crotolon, the suit we joined in
  must not
Fall by too long demur.[2]

CROT.   'Tis granted, princess, 80
For my part.

ARM.   With condition that his son
Favor the contract.

CAL.   Such delay is easy.—
The joys of marriage make thee, Pro-
  philus,
A proud deserver of Euphranea's love,
And her of thy desert!

PRO.   Most sweetly gracious!

BASS. The joys of marriage are the heaven
  on earth,
Life's paradise, great princess, the soul's
  quiet,
Sinews of concord, earthly immortality,
Eternity of pleasures—no restoratives
Like to a constant woman!—[*Aside.*]
  But where is she?   90
'Twould puzzle all the gods but to create
Such a new monster.—I can speak by
  proof,
For I rest in Elysium; 'tis my happiness.

CROT. Euphranea, how are you resolved—
  speak freely—
In your affections to this gentleman?

EUPH. Nor more nor less than as his love
  assures me,
Which—if your liking with my brother's
  warrants—
I cannot but approve in all points
  worthy.

CROT. So, so!—[*To Prophilus.*] I know
  your answer.

ITH.   'T had been pity   99
To sunder hearts so equally concented.[3]

[1] Serious.   [2] Delay.   [3] Harmonized.

Enter Hemophil.

HEM. The king, Lord Ithocles, commands
  your presence—
And, fairest princess, yours.

CAL.   We will attend him.

Enter Groneas.

GRO. Where are the lords? All must unto
  the king
Without delay; the Prince of Argos—

CAL.   Well, sir?

GRO. Is coming to the court, sweet lady.

CAL.   How!
The Prince of Argos?

GRO.   'Twas my fortune, madam,
T' enjoy the honor of these happy tidings.

ITH. Penthea!—

PEN.   Brother?

ITH.   Let me an hour hence
Meet you alone within the palace grove;
I have some secret with you.—Prithee,
  friend,   110
Conduct her thither, and have special
  care
The walks be cleared of any to disturb us.

PRO. I shall.

BASS. [*Aside.*]   How's that?

ITH.   Alone, pray be alone.—
I am your creature, princess.—On, my
  lords!   *Exeunt [All but] Bassanes.*

BASS. Alone, alone? What means that
  word "alone"?
Why might not I be there?—Hum!—
He's her brother.
Brothers and sisters are but flesh and
  blood,
And this same whoreson [4] court ease is
  temptation
To a rebellion in the veins; besides,
His fine friend Prophilus must be her
  guardian.   120
Why may not he despatch a business
  nimbly
Before the other come?—Or—pand'ring,
  pand'ring
For one another—be 't to sister, mother,
Wife, cousin, anything—'mongst youths
  of mettle
Is in request; it is so—stubborn fate!
But, if I be a cuckold, and can know it,
I will be fell,[5] and fell.

[4] Rascally.   [5] Ruthless.

Enter Groneas.

Gro.　　　　　My lord, y' are called for.

Bass. Most heartily I thank ye. Where's
　　my wife, pray?

Gro. Retired amongst the ladies.

Bass.　　　　　　　Still I thank 'e.
　　There's an old waiter [1] with her; saw you
　　her too?　　　　　　　　　　　　130

Gro. She sits i' th' presence lobby fast
　　asleep, sir.

Bass. Asleep? Sleep, sir?

Gro.　　　　　Is your lordship troubled?
　　You will not to the king?

Bass.　　　　　　Your humblest vassal.

Gro. Your servant, my good lord.

Bass.　　　I wait your footsteps.
　　　　　　　　　　　　　Exeunt.

Scene the Third.

[*The palace gardens adjoining a grove.*]

[*Enter*] *Prophilus, Penthea.*

Pro. In this walk, lady, will your brother
　　find you;
　　And, with your favor, give me leave a
　　little
　　To work a preparation. In his fashion
　　I have observed of late some kind of
　　slackness
　　To such alacrity as nature [once] [2]
　　And custom took delight in, sadness
　　grows
　　Upon his recreations, which he hoards
　　In such a willing [3] silence that to question
　　The grounds will argue [little][2] skill in
　　friendship,
　　And less good manners.

Pen.　　　　Sir, I'm not inquisitive　10
　　Of secrecies without an invitation.

Pro. With pardon, lady, not a syllable
　　Of mine implies so rude a sense; the
　　drift—

Enter Orgilus [, *disguised as before*].

[*To Orgilus.*] Do thy best
　　To make this lady merry for an hour.
　　　　　　　　　　　　　Exit.

Org. Your will shall be a law, sir.

Pen.　　　　　Prithee, leave me;

---

[1] Attendant, watcher.
[2] Supplied by Gifford-Dyce.
[3] Resolute.

　　I have some private thoughts I would
　　account with;
　　Use thou thine own.

Org.　　Speak on, fair nymph; our souls
　　Can dance as well to music of the spheres
　　As any's who have feasted with the
　　gods.　　　　　　　　　　　　20

Pen. Your school terms [4] are too trouble-
　　some.

Org.　　　　What heaven
　　Refines mortality from dross of earth
　　But such as uncompounded [5] beauty
　　hallows
　　With glorified perfection?

Pen.　　　　　　Set thy wits
　　In a less wild proportion.

Org.　　　　　　　Time can never
　　On the white table of unguilty faith
　　Write counterfeit dishonor; turn those
　　eyes,
　　The arrows of pure love, upon that fire,
　　Which once rose to a flame, perfumed
　　with vows
　　As sweetly scented as the incense smok-
　　ing　　　　　　　　　　　　30
　　The holiest artars, virgin tears (like
　　On Vesta's odors), sprinkled dews to
　　feed 'em [6]
　　And to increase their fervor.

Pen.　　　　　　　Be not frantic!

Org. All pleasures are but mere imagina-
　　tion,
　　Feeding the hungry appetite with steam
　　And sight of banquet, whilst the body
　　pines,
　　Not relishing the real taste of food;
　　Such is the leanness of a heart divided
　　From intercourse of troth-contracted
　　loves;
　　No horror should deface that precious
　　figure　　　　　　　　　　　40
　　Sealed with the lively stamp of equal
　　souls.

Pen. Away! Some Fury hath bewitched
　　thy tongue.
　　The breath of ignorance, that flies from
　　thence,
　　Ripens a knowledge in me of afflictions

---

[4] *I.e.*, rhetorical language.
[5] Unadorned, simple.
[6] This incoherency may be intentional, but
Gifford emends as follows:
　　"On Vesta's altars . . .
　　. . . the holiest odors, virgins' tears,
　　. . . sprinkled, like dews, to feed them."

Above all suff'rance.—Thing of talk, begone!
Begone, without reply!

ORG.   Be just, Penthea,
In thy commands; when thou send'st forth a doom
Of banishment, know first on whom it lights.
Thus I take off the shroud, in which my cares
Are folded up from view of common eyes.   [*Discloses himself.*] 50
What is thy sentence next?

PEN.   Rash man! Thou layest
A blemish on mine honor, with the hazard
Of thy too desperate life; yet I profess,
By all the laws of ceremonious wedlock,
I have not given admittance to one thought
Of female change since cruelty enforced
Divorce betwixt my body and my heart.
Why would you fall from goodness thus?

ORG.   O, rather
Examine me, how I could live to say
I have been much, much wronged. 'Tis for thy sake   60
I put on this imposture; dear Penthea,
If thy soft bosom be not turned to marble,
Thou't [1] pity our calamities; my interest
Confirms me thou art mine still.

PEN.   Lend your hand;
With both of mine I clasp it thus, thus kiss it,
Thus kneel before ye.

ORG.   You instruct my duty.

PEN. We may stand up.—Have you aught else to urge
Of new demand? As for the old, forget it;
'Tis buried in an everlasting silence,
And shall be, shall be ever. What more would ye?   70

ORG. I would possess my wife; the equity
Of very reason bids me.

PEN.   Is that all?

ORG. Why, 'tis the all of me, myself.

PEN.   Remove
Your steps some distance from me.—At this space
A few words I dare change; but first put on
Your borrowed shape.

[1] Thou wilt.

ORG.   You are obeyed; 'tis done.
     [*He resumes his disguise.*]

PEN. How, Orgilus, by promise I was thine
The heavens do witness; they can witness too
A rape done on my truth; [2] how I do love thee   79
Yet, Orgilus, and yet, must best appear
In tendering [3] thy freedom, for I find
The constant preservation of thy merit,
By thy not daring to attempt my fame
With injury of any loose conceit,
Which might give deeper wounds to discontents.
Continue this fair race; [4] then, though I cannot
Add to thy comfort, yet I shall more often
Remember from what fortune I am fallen,
And pity mine own ruin.—Live, live happy,
Happy in thy next choice, that thou mayst people   90
This barren age with virtues in thy issue!
And O, when thou art married, think on me
With mercy, not contempt! I hope thy wife,
Hearing my story, will not scorn my fall.—
Now let us part.

ORG.   Part! Yet advise thee better:
Penthea is the wife to Orgilus,
And ever shall be.

PEN.   Never shall nor will.

ORG. How!

PEN.   Hear me; in a word I'll tell thee why.
The virgin dowry which my birth bestowed   99
Is ravished by another; my true love
Abhors to think that Orgilus deserved
No better favors than a second bed.

ORG. I must not take this reason.

PEN.   To confirm it
Should I outlive my bondage, let me meet
Another worse than this and less desired,
If, of all men alive, thou shouldst but touch
My lip or hand again?

[2] Troth.   [4] Course.
[3] Having a care of.

ORG.　　　　　　　　　　　Penthea, now
I tell 'e, you grow wanton in my suffer-
　ance;
Come, sweet, th' art mine.
PEN.　　　　　　Uncivil sir, forbear, 109
Or I can turn affection into vengeance!
Your reputation, if you value any,
Lies bleeding at my feet.　Unworthy
　man,
If ever henceforth thou appear in lan-
　guage,
Message, or letter to betray my frailty,
I'll call thy former protestations lust,
And curse my stars for forfeit of my
　judgment.
Go thou, fit only for disguise and
　walks,[1]
To hide thy shame.　This once I spare
　thy life.
I laugh at mine own confidence; my
　sorrows
By thee are made inferior to my for-
　tunes.　　　　　　　　　　　　120
If ever thou didst harbor worthy love,
Dare not to answer.　My good genius
　guide me
That I may never see thee more!—Go
　from me!
ORG. I'll tear my veil of politic French [2]
　off,
And stand up like a man resolved to
　do;
Action, not words, shall show [3] me.—O
　Penthea!　　　　　　*Exit Orgilus.*
PEN. A sighed my name, sure, as he
　parted from me;
I fear I was too rough.　Alas, poor
　gentleman,
A looked not like the ruins of his
　youth,　　　　　　　　　　　129
But like the ruins of those ruins. Honor,
How much we fight with weakness to
　preserve thee!　　　　*[Walks aside.]*

Enter Bassanes and Grausis.

BASS. Fie on thee!　Damn thee, rotten
　maggot, damn thee!
Sleep? Sleep at court? And now? Aches,[4]
　convulsions,

Imposthumes, rhemes,[5] gouts, palsies
　clog thy bones
A dozen years more yet!
GRAU.　　　　　Now y' are in hu-
　mors.
BASS. She's by herself; there's hope of
　that.　She's sad too;
She's in strong contemplation; yes, and
　fixed.
The signs are wholesome.
GRAU.　　　　Very wholesome, truly.
BASS. Hold your chops,[6] nightmare!—
　Lady, come; your brother
Is carried to his closet;[7] you must
　thither.　　　　　　　　　　140
PEN. Not well, my lord?
BASS.　　　　A sudden fit; 'twill off!
Some surfeit or disorder.—How dost,
　dearest?
PEN. Your news is none o' the best.

Enter Prophilus.

PRO.　　　　　　　The chief of men,
The excellentest Ithocles, desires
Your presence, madam.
BASS.　　　　　We are hasting to him.
PEN. In vain we labor in this course of
　life
To piece our journey out at length, or
　crave
Respite of breath; our home is in the
　grave.
BASS. Perfect philosophy!
[PEN.][8]　　　　　Then let us care
To live so, that our reckonings may fall
　even　　　　　　　　　　　　150
When w' are to make account.
PRO.　　　　　　　　He cannot fear
Who builds on noble grounds; sickness
　or pain
Is the deserver's exercise;[9] and such
Your virtuous brother to the world is
　known.
Speak comfort to him, lady; be all
　gentle.
Stars fall but in the grossness of our
　sight;
A good man dying, th' earth doth lose a
　light.　　　　　　　　*Exeunt omnes.*

[1] *I.e.*, for secret meeting.
[2] A characteristic Elizabethan anachronism.
[3] Reveal.
[4] Pronounced *aitches*.

[5] Remes, rheums.　　[6] Jaws.　　[7] Chamber.
[8] Emended by Gifford-Dyce.　Original assigns
this speech to Bassanes.
[9] Discipline.

Actus Tertius. Scena Prima.

[*The study of Tecnicus.*]

Enter Tecnicus, and Orgilus in his own shape.

Tec. Be well advised; let not a resolution
Of giddy rashness choke the breath of
reason.

Org. It shall not, most sage master.

Tec.   I am jealous,[1]
For, if the borrowed shape so late put on
Inferred a consequence, we must con-
clude
Some violent design of sudden nature
Hath shook that shadow off, to fly upon
A new-hatched execution.[2] Orgilus,
Take heed thou hast not, under our
integrity,
Shrouded unlawful plots; our mortal
eyes   10
Pierce not the secrets of your hearts;
the gods
Are only privy to them.

Org.   Learned Tecnicus,
Such doubts are causeless; and, to clear
the truth
From misconceit,[3] the present state com-
mands me.
The Prince of Argos comes himself in
person
In quest of great Calantha for his bride,
Our kingdom's heir; besides, mine only
sister,
Euphranea, is disposed to Prophilus;
Lastly, the king is sending letters for me
To Athens, for my quick repair to
court.   20
Please to accept these reasons.

Tec.   Just ones, Orgilus,
Not to be contradicted; yet beware
Of an unsure foundation; no fair colors[4]
Can fortify a building faintly jointed.
I have observed a growth in thy aspect
Of dangerous extent, sudden, and—
look to 't—
I might add, certain—

Org.   My aspect? Could art
Run through mine inmost thoughts, it
should not sift
An inclination there more than what
suited
With justice of mine honor.

Tec.   I believe it.   30
But know then, Orgilus, what honor is.
Honor consists not in a bare opinion
By doing any act that feeds content,
Brave in appearance, cause we think it
brave;
Such honor comes by accident, not
nature,
Proceeding from the vices of our passion,
Which makes our reason drunk. But real
honor
Is the reward of virtue, and acquired
By justice or by valor which for bases
Hath justice to uphold it. He then
fails   40
In honor, who for lucer [or][5] revenge
Commits thefts, murthers, treasons, and
adulteries,
With suchlike, by intrenching on just
laws,
Whose sovereignty is best preserved by
justice.
Thus, as you see how honor must be
grounded
On knowledge, not opinion—for opinion
Relies on probability and accident,
But knowledge on necessity and truth—
I leave thee to the fit consideration
Of what becomes the grace of real
honor,   50
Wishing success to all thy virtuous mean-
ings.

Org. The gods increase thy wisdom, reverend oracle,
And in thy precepts make me ever
thrifty!   *Exit Org[ilus].*

Tec. I thank thy wish.—Much mystery
of fate
Lies hid in that man's fortunes; curiosity
May lead his actions into rare attempts.
But let the gods be moderators still;
No human power can prevent their
will.—

Enter Armostes [with a casket].

From whence come 'e?

Arm.   From King Amyclas—pardon
My interruption of your studies. Here,
In this sealed box, he sends a treasure
dear   61
To him as his crown. A prays your grav-
ity

---

[1] Suspicious.   [2] Achievement, enterprise.
[3] Misconception.   [4] Reasons, excuses.

[5] Emended by Gifford. Original has *of.*

You would examine, ponder, sift, and
bolt
The pith and circumstance of every tittle
The scroll within contains.

TEC.   What is 't, Armostes?

ARM. It is the health of Sparta, the king's
life,
Sinews and safety of the common-
wealth—
The sum of what the oracle delivered
When last he visited the prophetic
temple
At Delphos. What his reasons are, for
which,   70
After so long a silence, he requires
Your counsel now, grave man, his
majesty
Will soon himself acquaint you with.

TEC. [*Taking the casket.*] Apollo
Inspire my intellect!—The Prince of
Argos
Is entertained?

ARM.   He is, and has demanded
Our princess for his wife, which I con-
ceive
One special cause the king importunes
you
For resolution[1] of the oracle.

TEC. My duty to the king, good peace to
Sparta,
And fair day to Armostes!

ARM. Like to Tecnicus! *Exeunt.* 80

[SCENE ii.

Ithocles' apartment in the palace.]

Soft music.

A SONG

Can you paint a thought, or number
Every fancy in a slumber?
Can you count soft minutes roving
From a dial's point by moving?
Can you grasp a sigh, or, lastly,
Rob a virgin's honor chastely?
 No, O, no! Yet you may
Sooner do both that and this,
This and that, and never miss,
 Than by any praise display   10
Beauty's beauty—such a glory,
As beyond all fate, all story,
 All arms, all arts,
  All loves, all hearts,
 Greater than those or they,
Do, shall, and must obey.

[1] Interpretation.

*During which time enters Prophilus, Bas-
sanes, Penthea, Grausis, passing over
the stage; Bassanes and Grausis enter
again softly, stealing to several stands,*[2]
and listen.

BASS. All silent, calm, secure.—Grausis,
no creaking?
No noise? Dost hear nothing?

GRAU.   Not a mouse,
Or whisper of the wind.

BASS.   The floor is matted;
The bedposts sure are steel or marble.—
Soldiers   20
Should not affect, methinks, strains so
effeminate;
Sounds of such delicacy are but fawn-
ings
Upon the sloth of luxury;[3] they heighten
Cinders of covert lust up to a flame.

GRAU. What do you mean, my lord?
Speak low; that gabbling
Of yours will but undo us.

BASS.   Chamber combats
Are felt, not heard.

PRO. [*Within.*] A wakes.

BASS.   What's that?

ITH. [*Within.*] Who's there?
Sister?—All quit the room else.

BASS.   'Tis consented!

Enter Prophilus.

PRO. Lord Bassanes, your brother would
be private;
We must forbear; his sleep hath newly
left him.   30
Please 'e withdraw.

BASS.   By any means; 'tis fit.

PRO. Pray, gentlewoman, walk too.

GRAU. Yes, I will, sir. *Exeunt omnes.*

Ithocles discovered[4] *in a chair, and Penthea.*

ITH. Sit nearer, sister, to me; nearer yet.
We had one father, in one womb took
life,
Were brought up twins together, yet
have lived
At distance, like two strangers. I could
wish
That the first pillow whereon I was
cradled
Had proved to me a grave.

[2] Different positions.   [3] Lust.
[4] By the drawing of the curtain from the inner
stage.

PEN. You had been happy;
Then had you never known that sin of life
Which blots all following glories with
a vengeance, 40
For forfeiting the last will of the dead,
From whom you had your being.
ITH. Sad Penthea,
Thou canst not be too cruel; my rash spleen
Hath with a violent hand plucked from thy bosom
A lover-blessed heart, to grind it into dust
For which mine's now a-breaking.
PEN. Not yet, heaven,
I do beseech thee! First let some wild fires
Scorch, not consume it! May the heat be cherished
With desires infinite, but hopes impossible!
ITH. Wronged soul, thy prayers are heard.
PEN. Here, lo, I breathe, 50
A miserable creature, led to ruin
By an unnatural brother!
ITH. I consume
In languishing affections [1] for that trespass,
Yet cannot die.
PEN. The handmaid to the wages
Of country toil drinks the untroubled [2] streams
With leaping kids and with the bleating lambs,
And so allays her thirst secure,[3] whiles I
Quench my hot sighs with fleetings [4] of my tears.
ITH. The laborer doth eat his coarsest bread,
Earned with his sweat, and lies him down to sleep, 60
Whiles [5] every bit I touch turns in digestion
To gall as bitter as Penthea's curse.
Put me to any penance for my tyranny,
And I will call thee merciful.
PEN. Pray, kill me;
Rid me from living with a jealous husband.

[1] Emotions.
[2] The last two words are misplaced at the head of the line in the original.
[3] Unmolested.
[4] Flowings, streams.
[5] Gifford-Dyce reading. Original reads *Which*.

Then we will join in friendship, be again
Brother and sister.—Kill me, pray; nay, will 'e?
ITH. How does thy lord esteem thee?
PEN. Such an one
As only you have made me: a faith-breaker,
A spotted whore. Forgive me. I am one 70
In art,[6] not in desires, the gods must witness.
ITH. Thou dost belie thy friend.
PEN. I do not, Ithocles;
For she that's wife to Orgilus, and lives
In known adultery with Bassanes,
Is at the best a whore. Wilt kill me now?
The ashes of our parents will assume
Some dreadful figure, and appear to charge
Thy bloody guilt, that hast betrayed their name 78
To infamy in this reproachful match.
ITH. After my victories abroad, at home
I meet despair; ingratitude of nature
Hath made my actions monstrous. Thou shalt stand
A deity, my sister, and be worshipped
For thy resolvéd martyrdom; wronged maids
And married wives shall to thy hallowed shrine
Offer their orisons, and sacrifice
Pure turtles,[7] crowned with myrtle, if thy pity
Unto a yielding brother's pressure lend
One finger but to ease it.
PEN. O, no more!
ITH. Death waits to waft me to the Stygian banks, 90
And free me from this chaos of my bondage;
And, till thou wilt forgive, I must endure.
PEN. Who is the saint you serve?
ITH. Friendship, or [nearness] [8]
Of birth to any but my sister, durst not
Have moved that question; as a secret, sister,
I dare not murmur to myself—
PEN. Let me,
By your new protestations I conjure 'e,
Partake her name.

[6] Act, practice (?).   [8] Supplied by Gifford.
[7] Turtledoves.

ITH.   Her name?—'Tis—'tis—
I dare not.
PEN. All your respects [1] are forged.
ITH.   They are not.—Peace!
Calantha is—the princess—the king's
daughter—   100
Sole heir of Sparta.—Me most miser-
able,
Do I now love thee? For my injuries,
Revenge thyself with bravery, and gos-
sip
My treasons to the king's ears; do.
Calantha
Knows it not yet, nor Prophilus, my
nearest.
PEN. Suppose you were contracted to her,
would it not
Split even your very soul to see her
father
Snatch her out of your arms against
her will,
And force her on the Prince of Argos?
ITH.   Trouble not
The fountains of mine eyes with thine
own story;   110
I sweat in blood for 't.
PEN.   We are reconciled.
Alas, sir, being children, but two
branches
Of one stock, 'tis not fit we should divide.
Have comfort; you may find it.
ITH.   Yes, in thee;
Only in thee, Penthea mine.
PEN.   If sorrows
Have not too much dulled my infected
brain,
I'll cheer invention for an active strain. [2]
ITH. Mad man! Why have I wronged a
maid so excellent?

Enter Bassanes with a poniard; Prophilus,
Groneas, Hemophil, and Grausis.

BASS. I can forbear no longer; more, I
will not.
Keep off your hands, or fall upon my
point.   120
Patience is tired, for, like a slow-paced
ass,
Ye ride my easy nature, and proclaim
My sloth to vengeance a reproach and
property. [3]

[1] Supply *for me.*
[2] *I.e.,* I will try to contrive some plan.
[3] Characteristic condition.

ITH. The meaning of this rudeness?
PRO.   He's distracted.
PEN. O, my grieved lord!—
GRAU.   Sweet lady, come not near
him;
He holds his perilous weapon in his
hand
To prick a cares not whom nor where—
see, see, see!
BASS. My birth is noble.   Though the
popular blast
Of vanity, as giddy as thy youth,
Hath reared thy name up to bestride
a cloud,   130
Or progress in the chariot of the sun,
I am no clod of trade, to lackey pride,
Nor, like your slave of expectation, [4]
wait [5]
The bawdy hinges of your doors, or
whistle
For mystical conveyance to your bed
sports.
GRO. Fine humors!   They become him.
HEM.   How a stares,
Struts, puffs, and sweats!   Most ad-
mirable [6] lunacy!
ITH. But that I may conceive the spirit
of wine
Has took possession of your soberer
custom,
I'd say you were unmannerly.
PEN.   Dear brother!— 140
BASS. Unmannerly!—Mew,   kitling! [7]—
Smooth Formality
Is usher to the rankness of the blood,
But Impudence bears up the train.   In-
deed, sir,
Your fiery mettle, or your springal [8]
blaze
Of huge renown, is no sufficient royalty [9]
To print upon my forehead the scorn,
"cuckold."
ITH. His jealousy has robbed him of his
wits;
A talks a knows not what.
BASS.   Yes, and a knows
To whom a talks—to one that franks [10]
his lust
In swine-security of bestial incest.   150
ITH. Ha, devil!

[4] Attendance.
[5] Attend.
[6] Wonderful.
[7] Kitten.
[8] Youthful.
[9] Right.
[10] Fattens.

BASS. 　I will hallo [1] 't, though I blush more
To name the filthiness than thou to act it.
ITH. Monster!
PRO. 　Sir, by our friendship—
PEN. 　By our bloods—
Will you quite both undo us, brother?
GRAU. 　Out on him!
These are his megrims, firks,[2] and melancholies.
HEM. Well said, old touchhole!
GRO. 　Kick him out at doors!
PEN. With favor, let me speak.—My lord, what slackness
In my obedience hath deserved this rage?
Except humility and silent duty
Have drawn on your unquiet, my simplicity 　　160
Ne'er studied your vexation.
BASS. 　Light of beauty,
Deal not ungently with a desperate wound!
No breach of reason dares make war with her
Whose looks are sovereignty, whose breath is balm.
O, that I could preserve thee in fruition
As in devotion!
PEN. 　Sir, may every evil
Locked in Pandora's box shower, in your presence,
On my unhappy head, if, since you made me
A partner in your bed, I have been faulty
In one unseemly thought against your honor! 　　170
ITH. Purge not his griefs, Penthea.
BASS. 　Yes, say on,
Excellent creature!—[To Ithocles.] Good, be not a hinderance
To peace and praise of virtue.—O, my senses
Are charmed with sounds celestial!— On, dear, on;
I never gave you one ill word; say, did I?
Indeed, I did not.
PEN. 　Nor, by Juno's forehead,
Was I e'er guilty of a wanton error.
BASS. A goddess! Let me kneel.

[1] Proclaim. 　　　　　　　[2] Freaks.

GRAU. 　Alas, kind animal!
ITH. No; but for penance—
BASS. 　Noble sir, what is it?
With gladness I embrace it; yet, pray, let not 　　180
My rashness teach you to be too unmerciful.
ITH. When you shall show good proof that manly wisdom,
Not overswayed by passion or opinion,
Knows how to lead judgment, then this lady,
Your wife, my sister, shall return in safety
Home, to be guided by you; but, till first
I can out of clear evidence approve it,
She shall be my care.
BASS. 　Rip my bosom up,
I'll stand the execution with a constancy;
This torture is unsufferable.
ITH. 　Well, sir, 　　190
I dare not trust her to your fury.
BASS. 　But
Penthea says not so.
PEN. 　She needs no tongue
To plead excuse who never purposed wrong.
HEM. [To Grausis.] Virgin of reverence and antiquity,
Stay you behind.
GRO. [To Grausis.] 　The court wants not your diligence.
　　Exeunt omnes sed Bass[anes] et Graus[is].
GRAU. What will you do, my lord? My lady's gone;
I am denied to follow.
BASS. 　I may see her,
Or speak to her once more?
GRAU. 　And feel her too, man;
Be of good cheer, she's your own flesh and bone.
BASS. Diseases desperate must find cures alike. 　　200
She swore she has been true.
GRAU. 　True, on my modesty.
BASS. Let him want truth who credits not her vows!
Much wrong I did her, but her brother infinite;
Rumor will voice me the contempt of manhood,

Should I run on thus. Some way I must
   try
To outdo art, and cry [1] a jealousy.
Exeunt omnes.

[SCENE iii.

A room in the palace.]

Flourish. Enter Amyclas, Nearchus, leading Calantha, Armostes, Crotolon, Euphranea, Christalla, Philema, and Amelus.

AMY. Cousin of Argos, what the heavens
   have pleased
In their unchanging counsels to conclude
For both our kingdoms' weal, we must
   submit to;
Nor can we be unthankful to their
   bounties,
Who, when we were even creeping to
   our graves,
Sent us a daughter, in whose birth our
   hope
Continues of succession. As you are
In title next, being grandchild to our
   aunt,
So we in heart desire you may sit nearest
Calantha's love, since we have ever
   vowed   10
Not to enforce affection by our will,
But by her own choice to confirm it
   gladly.
NEAR. You speak the nature of a right
   just father.
I come not hither roughly to demand
My cousin's thralldom, but to free
   mine own.
Report of great Calantha's beauty,
   virtue,
Sweetness, and singular perfections,
   courted
All ears to credit what I find was published
By constant truth, from which, if any
   service
Of my desert can purchase fair construction,   20
This lady must command it.
CAL.   Princely sir,
So well you know how to profess observance [2]

That you instruct your hearers to become
Practitioners in duty, of which number
I'll study to be chief.
NEAR.   Chief, glorious virgin,
In my devotions, as in all men's wonder.
AMY. Excellent cousin, we deny no liberty;
Use thine own opportunities.—Armostes,
We must consult with the philosophers;
The business is of weight.
ARM.   Sir, at your pleasure.   30
AMY. You told me, Crotolon, your son's
   returned
From Athens? Wherefore comes a not
   to court
As we commanded?
CROT.   He shall soon attend
Your royal will, great sir.
AMY.   The marriage
Between young Prophilus and Euphranea
Tastes of too much delay.
CROT.   My lord—
AMY.   Some pleasures
At celebration of it would give life
To th' entertainment of the prince our
   kinsman;
Our court wears gravity more than we
   relish.
ARM. Yet the heavens smile on all your
   high attempts   40
Without a cloud.
CROT.   So may the gods protect us.
CAL. A prince a subject?
NEAR.   Yes, to beauty's scepter;
As all hearts kneel, so mine.
CAL.   You are too courtly.

To them, Ithocles, Orgilus, Prophilus.

ITH. Your safe return to Sparta is most
   welcome;
I joy to meet you here, and, as occasion
Shall grant us privacy, will yield you
   reasons
Why I should covet to deserve the title
Of your respected friend; for, without
   compliment,
Believe it, Orgilus, 'tis my ambition.
ORG. Your lordship may command me
   your poor servant.   50
ITH. [*Aside.*] So amorously close? So
   soon? My heart!

---

[1] Decry, disprove.   [2] Courtship.

Pro. What sudden change is next?

Ith. 　　　　　　　　　Life to the king,
To whom I here present this noble gentleman,
New come from Athens. Royal sir, vouchsafe
Your gracious hand in favor of his merit.

Crot. [*Aside.*] My son preferred by Ithocles!

Amy. 　　　　Our bounties
Shall open to thee, Orgilus; for instance—
Hark in thine ear—if, out of those inventions
Which flow in Athens, thou hast there engrossed [1]
Some rarity of wit, to grace the nuptials　　　　　　　　　　　　60
Of thy fair sister, and renown our court
In th' eyes of this young prince, we shall be debtor
To thy conceit; think on 't.

Org. 　　　　Your highness honors me.

Near. My tongue and heart are twins.

Cal. 　　　　　　A noble birth,
Becoming such a father.—Worthy Orgilus,
You are a guest most wished for.

Org. 　　　　　　May my duty
Still rise in your opinion, sacred princess!

Ith. Euphranea's brother, sir; a gentleman
Well worthy of your knowledge.

Near. 　　　　We embrace him,
Proud of so dear acquaintance.

Amy. 　　　　　All prepare　70
For revels and disport; the joys of Hymen,
Like Phœbus in his luster, puts to flight
All mists of dullness. Crown the hours with gladness.
No sounds but music, no discourse but mirth!

Cal. Thine arm, I prithee, Ithocles.—
Nay, good
My lord, keep on your way; I am provided.

Near. I dare not disobey.

Ith. 　　　Most heavenly lady! 　*Exeunt.*

[1] Acquired, learned.

A room in Crotolon's house.]

Enter Crotolon, Orgilus.

Crot. The king hath spoke his mind.

Org. 　　　　　　His will he hath;
But, were it lawful to hold plea against
The power of greatness, not the reason, haply
Such undershrubs as subjects sometimes might
Borrow of nature justice, to inform
That license [2] sovereignty holds without check
Over a meek obedience.

Crot. 　　　　How resolve you
Touching your sister's marriage? Prophilus
Is a deserving and a hopeful youth. 　9

Org. I envy not his merit, but applaud it;
Could wish [3] him thrift [4] in all his best desires,
And with a willingness inleague our blood
With his, for purchase of full growth in friendship.
He never touched on any wrong that maliced [5]
The honor of our house nor stirred our peace;
Yet, with your favor, let me not forget
Under whose wing he gathers warmth and comfort,
Whose creature he is bound, made, and must live so.

Crot. Son, son, I find in thee a harsh condition; [6]
No courtesy can win it; 'tis too rancorous. 　　　　　　　　　20

Org. Good sir, be not severe in your construction.
I am no stranger to such easy calms
As sit in tender bosoms. Lordly Ithocles
Hath graced my entertainment in abundance,
Too humbly hath descended from that height
Of arrogance and spleen which wrought the rape
On grieved Penthea's purity; his scorn
Of my untoward fortunes is reclaimed

[2] To control that authority.
[3] Suggested by Gifford-Dyce. Original reads *with.*
[4] Success.
[5] Sought to injure.
[6] Disposition.

Unto a courtship, almost to a fawning.
I'll kiss his foot, since you will have it
  so.   30
CROT. Since I will have it so? Friend, I
  will have it so,
Without our ruin by your politic plots,
Or wolf of hatred snarling in your breast.
You have a spirit, sir, have ye? A fa-
  miliar
That posts i' th' air for your intelligence?
Some such hobgoblin hurried you from
  Athens,
For yet you come unsent for.
ORG.   If unwelcome,
I might have found a grave there.
CROT.   Sure, your business
Was soon despatched, or your mind al-
  tered quickly.
ORG. 'Twas care, sir, of my health cut
  short my journey;   40
For there a general infection
Threatens a desolation.
CROT.   And I fear
Thou hast brought back a worse infection
  with thee—
Infection of thy mind, which, as thou
  say'st,
Threatens the desolation of our family.
ORG. Forbid it, our dear genius![1] I will
  rather
Be made a sacrifice on Thrasus' monu-
  ment,
Or kneel to Ithocles, his son, in dust,
Than woo a father's curse. My sister's
  marriage
With Prophilus is from my heart con-
  firmed.   50
May I live hated, may I die despised,
If I omit to further it in all
That can concern me!
CROT.   I have been too rough.
My duty to my king made me so earnest.
Excuse it, Orgilus.
ORG.   Dear sir!—

Enter to them, Prophilus, Euphranea, Itho-
*   cles, Groneas, Hemophil.*

CROT.   Here comes
Euphranea with Prophilus and Ithocles.
ORG. Most honored! Ever famous!
ITH.   Your true friend;
On earth not any truer.—With smooth[2]
  eyes

[1] Tutelary spirit.   [2] Kindly.

Look on this worthy couple; your consent
Can only make them one.
ORG.   They have it.—Sister, 60
Thou pawn'dst to me an oath, of which
  engagement
I never will release thee, if thou aim'st
At any other choice than this.
EUPH.   Dear brother
At him, or none.
CROT.   To which my blessing's added.
ORG. Which, till a greater ceremony per-
  fect—
Euphranea, lend thy hand. Here, take
  her, Prophilus;
Live long a happy man and wife; and
  further,
That these in presence may conclude an
  omen,
Thus for a bridal song I close my wishes:

Comforts lasting; loves increasing,   70
Like soft hours never ceasing;
Plenty's pleasure; peace complying,
Without jars, or tongues envying;
Hearts by holy union wedded
More than theirs by custom bedded;
Fruitful issues; life so gracéd,
Not by age to be defacéd,
Budding, as the year ensu'th,
Every spring another youth—
All what thought can add beside   80
Crown this bridegroom and this bride!

PRO. You have sealed joy close to my
  soul.—Euphranea,
Now I may call thee mine.
ITH.   I but exchange
One good friend for another.
ORG.   If these gallants
Will please to grace a poor invention
By joining with me in some slight device,
I'll venture on a strain my younger days
Have studied for delight.
HEM.   With thankful willingness
I offer my attendance.
GRO.   No endeavor
Of mine shall fail to show itself.
ITH.   We will 90
All join to wait on thy directions, Orgilus.
ORG. O, my good lord, your favors flow
  towards
A too unworthy worm—but as you
  please;
I am what you will shape me.
ITH.   A fast friend.

CROT. I thank thee, son, for this acknowl-
edgment;
It is a sight of gladness.
ORG. But my duty. *Exeunt omnes.*

[SCENE v.

Calantha's apartment in the palace.]

*Enter Calantha, Penthea, Christalla, Phi-
lema.*

CAL. Whoe'er would speak with us, deny
his entrance;
Be careful of our charge.
CHRIS. We shall, madam.
CAL. Except the king himself, give none
admittance;
Not any.
PHIL. Madam, it shall be our care.

Exeunt [All but] Calantha, Penthea.

CAL. Being alone, Penthea, you have
granted
The opportunity you sought, and might
At all times have commanded.
PEN. 'Tis a benefit
Which I shall owe your goodness even in
death for.
My glass [1] of life, sweet princess, hath few
minutes
Remaining to run down; the sands are
spent,   10
For by an inward messenger I feel
The summons of departure short and
certain.
CAL. You feed too much your melancholy.
PEN. Glories
Of human greatness are but pleasing
dreams
And shadows soon decaying; on the stage
Of my mortality my youth hath acted
Some scenes of vanity, drawn out at
length
By varied pleasures, sweetened in the
mixture,
But tragical in issue; beauty, pomp,
With every sensuality our giddiness   20
Doth frame an idol, are unconstant
friends,
When any troubled passion makes as-
sault
On the unguarded castle of the mind.
CAL. Contemn not your condition for the
proof
[1] Hourglass.

Of bare opinion only.[2] To what end
Reach all these moral texts?
PEN. To place before 'e
A perfect mirror, wherein you may see
How weary I am of a ling'ring life,
Who count the best a misery.
CAL. Indeed
You have no little cause; yet none so
great   30
As to distrust a remedy.
PEN. That remedy
Must be a winding sheet, a fold of lead,
And some untrod-on corner in the
earth.—
Not to detain your expectation, princess,
I have an humble suit.
CAL. Speak; I enjoy it.
PEN. Vouchsafe, then, to be my executrix,
And take that trouble on 'e to dispose
Such legacies as I bequeath, impartially.
I have not much to give—the pains are
easy;
Heaven will reward your piety, and
thank it   40
When I am dead. For sure I must not
live;
I hope I cannot.
CAL. Now, beshrew thy sadness;
Thou turn'st me too much woman.
[*Weeps.*]
PEN. [*Aside.*] Her fair eyes
Melt into passion. Then I have assurance
Encouraging my boldness.—In this paper
My will was charactered, which you, with
pardon,
Shall now know from mine own mouth.
CAL. Talk on, prithee;
It is a pretty earnest.[3]
PEN. I have left me
But three poor jewels to bequeath. The
first is
My youth, for, though I am much old in
griefs,   50
In years I am a child.
CAL. To whom that?
PEN. To virgin wives, such as abuse not
wedlock
By freedom of desires, but covet chiefly
The pledges of chaste beds for ties of love,
Rather than ranging of their blood; and
next

[2] On account of your experience from mere
public opinion.
[3] A small advance payment, a foretaste.

To married maids, such as prefer the
number
Of honorable issue in their virtues
Before the flattery of delights by mar-
riage.
May those be ever young!

CAL.   A second jewel
You mean to part with?

PEN.   'Tis my fame, I trust   60
By scandal yet untouched; this I be-
queath
To Memory, and Time's old daughter,
Truth.
If ever my unhappy name find mention
When I am fall'n to dust, may it deserve
Beseeming charity without dishonor!

CAL. How handsomely thou play'st with
harmless sport
Of mere imagination! Speak the last.
I strangely like thy will.

PEN.   This jewel, madam,
Is dearly precious to me; you must use
The best of your discretion to employ   70
This gift as I intend it.

CAL.   Do not doubt me.

PEN. 'Tis long agone since first I lost my
heart;
Long I have lived without it, else for cer-
tain
I should have given that too; but instead
Of it, to great Calantha, Sparta's heir,
By service bound and by affection vowed,
I do bequeath, in holiest rites of love,
Mine only brother, Ithocles.

CAL.   What said'st thou?

PEN. Impute not, heaven-blessed lady, to
ambition   79
A faith as humbly perfect as the prayers
Of a devoted suppliant can endow it.
Look on him, princess, with an eye of
pity.
How like the ghost of what he late ap-
peared
A moves before you!

CAL.   Shall I answer here,
Or lend my ear too grossly?

PEN.   First his heart
Shall fall in cinders, scorched by your
disdain,
Ere he will dare, poor man, to ope an eye
On these divine looks, but with low-bent
thoughts
Accusing such presumption, as, for
words,

A dares not utter any but of service.   90
Yet this lost creature loves 'e. Be a
princess
In sweetness as in blood; give him his
doom,
Or raise him up to comfort.

CAL.   What new change
Appears in my behavior, that thou dar'st
Tempt my displeasure?

PEN.   I must leave the world
To revel [in] [1] Elysium, and 'tis just
To wish my brother some advantage
here;
Yet, by my best hopes, Ithocles is ig-
norant
Of this pursuit. But, if you please to kill
him,
Lend him one angry look or one harsh
word,   100
And you shall soon conclude how strong
a power
Your absolute authority holds over
His life and end.

CAL.   You have forgot, Penthea,
How still I have a father.

PEN.   But remember
I am a sister, though to me this brother
Hath been, you know, unkind, O, most
unkind!

CAL. Christalla, Philema, where are 'e?—
Lady,
Your check [2] lies in my silence.

Enter Christalla and Philema.

BOTH.   Madam, here.

CAL. I think 'e sleep, 'e drones! Wait on
Penthea
Unto her lodging.—[*Aside.*] Ithocles?
Wronged lady!   110

PEN. My reckonings are made even;
death or fate
Can now nor strike too soon, nor force
too late.   *Exeunt.*

ACTUS QUARTUS. SCENA PRIMA.

[*Ithocles' apartment in the palace.*]

Enter Ithocles and Armostes.

ITH. Forbear your inquisition; curiosity
Is of too subtle and too searching nature,
In fears of love too quick, too slow of
credit.

[1] Supplied by Gifford-Dyce.   [2] Censure.

I am not what you doubt [1] me.

ARM.   Nephew, be, then,
As I would wish.—[*Aside.*]   All is not
right.—Good heaven
Confirm your resolutions for depend-
    ence
On worthy ends, which may advance
    your quiet!
ITH.   I did the noble Orgilus much injury,
But grieved Penthea more; I now repent
    it.
Now, uncle, now; this "now" is now too
    late.   10
So provident [2] is folly in sad issue
That after-wit, like bankrupts' debts,
    stand tallied [3]
Without all possibilities of payment.
Sure, he's an honest, very honest gentle-
    man;
A man of single [4] meaning.
ARM.   I believe it;
Yet, nephew, 'tis the tongue informs our
    ears;
Our eyes can never pierce into the
    thoughts,
For they are lodged too inward. But I
    question
No truth in Orgilus.—The princess, sir.
ITH.   The princess? Ha!
ARM.   With her the Prince of Argos.   20

Enter Nearchus, leading Calantha; Amelus,
                    Christalla, Philema.

NEAR.   Great fair one, grace my hopes
    with any instance
Of livery,[5] from the allowance of your
    favor;
This little spark—
        [*Tries to take a ring from her finger.*]
CAL.   A toy!
NEAR.   Love feasts on toys,
For Cupid is a child.   Vouchsafe this
    bounty;
It cannot be [de][6]nied.
CAL.   You shall not value,
Sweet cousin, at a price, what I count
    cheap,
So cheap that let him take it who dares
    stoop for 't,
And give it at next meeting to a mistress;

1 Suspect.   3 Reckoned up.
2 Productive.   4 Sincere.
5 Badge of service.
6 Supplied by Gifford-Dyce.

She'll thank him for 't, perhaps.
                    Casts it to Ithocles.
AME.   The ring, sir, is   29
The princess's; I could have took it up.
ITH.   Learn manners, prithee.—To the
    blessed owner,
Upon my knees—
NEAR.   Y' are saucy.
CAL.   This is pretty!
I am, belike, "a mistress." Wondrous
    pretty!
Let the man keep his fortune, since he
    found it;
He's worthy on 't.—On, cousin!
ITH.   [*To Amelus.*]   Follow, spaniel:
I'll force 'e to a fawning else.
AME.   You dare not.
        Exeunt. Manent Itho[cles] et Armost[es].
ARM.   My lord, you were too forward.
ITH.   Look 'e, uncle,
Some such there are whose liberal con-
    tents
Swarm without care in every sort of
    plenty,
Who after full repasts can lay them
    down   40
To sleep; and they sleep, uncle—in which
    silence
Their very dreams present 'em choice of
    pleasures,
Pleasures—observe me, uncle—of rare
    object;
Here heaps of gold, there increments of
    honors,
Now change of garments, then the votes
    of people,
Anon varieties of beauties, courting,
In flatteries of the night, exchange of
    dalliance.
Yet these are still but dreams. Give me
    felicity
Of which my senses waking are par--
    takers,
A real, visible, material happiness;   50
And then, too, when I stagger in ex-
    pectance
Of the least comfort that can cherish
    life—
I saw it, sir, I saw it, for it came
From her own hand.
ARM.   The princess threw it t'e.
ITH.   True; and she said—well I remember
    what.
Her cousin prince would beg it.

ARM.   Yes, and parted
 In anger at your taking on 't.
ITH.   Penthea,
 O, thou hast pleaded with a powerful
  language!
 I want a fee to gratify thy merit;
 But I will do——
ARM.   What is 't you say?
ITH.   In anger, 60
 In anger let him part, for could his
  breath,
 Like whirlwinds, toss such servile slaves
  as lick
 The dust his footsteps print into a vapor,
 It durst not stir a hair of mine, it should
  not;
 I'd rend it up by th' roots first. To be
  anything
 Calantha smiles on is to be a blessing
 More sacred than a petty prince of Argos
 Can wish to equal, or in worth or title.
ARM. Contain yourself, my lord. Ixion,
  aiming 69
 To embrace Juno, bosomed but a cloud,
 And begat Centaurs; 'tis an useful
  moral.
 Ambition hatched in clouds of mere opin-
  ion
 Proves but in birth a prodigy.
ITH.   I thank 'e;
 Yet, with your license, I should seem un-
  charitable
 To gentler fate, if, relishing the dainties
 Of a soul's settled peace, I were so feeble
 Not to digest it.
ARM.   He deserves small trust
 Who is not privy counselor to himself.

Enter Nearchus, Orgilus, and Amelus.

NEAR. Brave me?
ORG.   Your excellence mistakes
  his temper,
 For Ithocles in fashion of his mind 80
 Is beautiful, soft, gentle, the clear mirror
 Of absolute perfection.
AME.   Was 't your modesty
 Termed any of the prince his servants
  "spaniel"?
 Your nurse, sure, taught you other lan-
  guage.
ITH.   Language!
NEAR. A gallant man-at-arms is here, a
  doctor

In feats of chivalry, blunt and rough-
  spoken,
Vouchsafing not the fustian of civility,
Which [less] [1] rash spirits style good man-
  ners!
ITH. Manners!
ORG. No more, illustrious sir; 'tis match-
  less Ithocles.
NEAR. You might have understood who I
  am.
ITH.   Yes,   90
 I did; else—but the presence [2] calmed
  th' affront—
 Y' are cousin to the princess.
NEAR.   To the king, too;
 A certain instrument that lent support-
  ance
 To your colossic greatness—to that king
  too,
 You might have added.
ITH.   There is more divinity
 In beauty than in majesty.
ARM.   O, fie, fie!
NEAR. This odd youth's pride turns heretic
  in loyalty.
 Sirrah, low mushrooms never rival ce-
  dars! *Exeunt Nearchus et Amelus.*
ITH. Come back!—What pitiful dull thing
  am I
 So to be tamely scolded at! Come
  back!—   100
 Let him come back, and echo once
  again
 That scornful sound of "mushroom"!
  Painted colts—
 Like heralds' coats gilt o'er with crowns
  and scepters—
 May bait a muzzled lion.
ARM.   Cousin, cousin,
 Thy tongue is not thy friend.
ORG.   In point of honor
 Discretion knows no bounds. Amelus
  told me
 'Twas all about a little ring.
ITH.   A ring
 The princess threw away, and I took up.
 Admit she threw 't to me, what arm of
  brass
 Can snatch it hence? No; could a grind
  the hoop   110
 To powder, a might sooner reach my
  heart

[1] Supplied by Gifford.
[2] *I.e.*, of the princess.

Than steal and wear one dust [1] on 't.
  Orgilus,
I am extremely wronged.

ORG.   A lady's favor
  Is not to be so slighted.

ITH.   Slighted!

ARM.   Quiet
  These vain, unruly passions, which will
    render ye
  Into a madness.

ORG.   Griefs will have their vent.

Enter Tecnicus [with a scroll].

ARM. Welcome; thou com'st in season, rev-
    erend man,
  To pour the balsam of a suppling [2] pa-
    tience
  Into the festering wound of ill-spent fury.

ORG. [*Aside.*] What makes he here?

TEC.   The hurts are yet but [3] mortal,
  Which shortly will prove deadly. To
    the king,   121
  Armostes, see in safety thou deliver
  This sealed-up counsel; bid him with a
    constancy
  Peruse the secrets of the gods.—O
    Sparta,
  O Lacedemon! Double-named, but one
  In fate! When kingdoms reel—mark
    well my saw—
  Their heads must needs be giddy. Tell
    the king
  That henceforth he no more must inquire
    after
  My aged head; Apollo wills it so.
  I am for Delphos.

ARM.   Not without some conference
  With our great master.

TEC.   Never more to see him; 131
  A greater prince commands me.—Itho-
    cles,
  When youth is ripe, and age from time
    doth part,
  The lifeless trunk shall wed the broken
    heart.

ITH. What's this, if understood?

TEC.   List, Orgilus;
  Remember what I told thee long before;
  These tears shall be my witness.

[1] One particle.
[2] Healing. Suggested by Gifford-Dyce; original
reads *supplying*.
[3] Gifford-Dyce suggests *not* but retains original.

ARM.   'Las, good man!

TEC. *Let craft with courtesy awhile confer;*
  Revenge proves its own executioner.

ORG. Dark sentences are for Apollo's
    priests;   140
  I am not Œdipus.

TEC.   My hour is come.
  Cheer up the king; farewell to all.—O
    Sparta,
  O Lacedemon!   *Exit Tecn[icus].*

ARM.   If prophetic fire
  Have warmed this old man's bosom, we
    might construe
  His words to fatal sense.

ITH.   Leave to the
    powers
  Above us the effects of their decrees;
  My burthen lies within me. Servile
    fears
  Prevent no great effects.—Divine Ca-
    lantha!

ARM. The gods be still propitious!
               Exeunt. Manet Org[ilus].

ORG.   Something oddly
  The bookman prated, yet a talked it
    weeping: 150
  "*Let craft with courtesy awhile confer;*
  Revenge proves its own executioner."
  Con it again.—For what? It shall not
    puzzle me;
  'Tis dotage of a withered brain.—Pen-
    thea
  Forbade me not her presence; I may see
    her,
  And gaze my fill. Why, see her, then, I
    may,
  When, if I faint to speak—I must be
    silent.   *Exit Org[ilus].*

[SCENE ii.

A room in Bassanes' house.]

Enter Bassanes, Grausis, and Phulas.

BASS. Pray, use your recreations; all the
    service
  I will expect is quietness amongst 'e;
  Take liberty at home, abroad, at all
    times,
  And in your charities appease the gods,
  Whom I, with my distractions, have
    offended.

GRAU. Fair blessings on thy heart!

PHU. [*Aside.*]   Here's a rare change!

My lord, to cure the itch, is surely
  gelded;
The cuckold in conceit [1] hath cast his
  horns.
BASS. Betake 'e to your several occasions;
  And, wherein I have heretofore been
    faulty,   10
  Let your constructions mildly pass it
    over.
  Henceforth I'll study reformation; more
  I have not for employment.
GRAU.   O sweet man!
  Thou art the very "Honeycomb of
    Honesty."
PHU. The "Garland of Goodwill." [2]—Old
  lady, hold up
  Thy reverend snout, and trot behind me
    softly,
  As it becomes a moil [3] of ancient carriage.
        Exeunt. Manet Bass[anes].
BASS. Beasts, only capable of sense, enjoy
  The benefit of food and ease with thank-
    fulness;
  Such silly creatures, with a grudging,
    kick not   20
  Against the portion nature hath be-
    stowed;
  But men, endowed with reason and the
    use
  Of reason, to distinguish from the chaff
  Of abject scarcity the quintessence,
  Soul, and elixir of the earth's abundance,
  The treasures of the sea, the air, nay,
    heaven,
  Repining at these glories of creation,
  Are verier beasts than beasts; and of
    those beasts
  The worst am I—I, who was made a
    monarch
  Of what a heart could wish for—a chaste
    wife—   30
  Endeavored what in me lay to pull down
  That temple built for adoration only,
  And level 't in the dust of causeless
    scandal.
  But, to redeem a sacrilege so impious,
  Humility shall pour, before the deities
  I have incensed, a largeness [4] of more pa-
    tience
  Than their displeaséd altars can require.

[1] Imagination.
[2] A popular miscellany of the time.
[3] Mule.
[4] Bounty, liberality.

No tempests of commotion shall disquiet
The calms of my composure.

Enter Orgilus.

ORG.   I have found thee,
  Thou patron of more horrors than the
    bulk   40
  Of manhood, hooped about with ribs of
    iron,
  Can cram within thy breast. Penthea,
    Bassanes,
  Cursed by thy jealousies—more, by thy
    dotage—
  Is left a prey to words. [5]
BASS.   Exercise
  Your trials for addition to my penance;
  I am resolved.
ORG.   Play not with misery
  Past cure; some angry minister of fate
    hath
  Deposed the empress of her soul, her
    reason,
  From its most proper throne; but, what's
    the miracle
  More new, I, I have seen it, and yet
    live!   50
BASS. You may delude my senses, not my
    judgment;
  'Tis anchored into a firm resolution;
  Dalliance of mirth or wit can ne'er unfix
    it.
  Practice [6] yet further.
ORG.   May thy death of love to her
  Damn all thy comforts to a lasting fast
  From every joy of life! Thou barren
    rock,
  By thee we have been split in ken [7] of
    harbor.

*Enter Ithocles, Penthea, her hair about her
  ears, [Armostes,] Philema, Christalla.*

ITH. Sister, look up; your Ithocles, your
    brother,
  Speaks t'e; why do you weep? Dear,
    turn not from me.—
  Here is a killing sight; lo, Bassanes,   60
  A lamentable object!
ORG.   Man, dost see 't?
  Sports are more gamesome; am I yet in
    merriment?
  Why dost not laugh?

[5] *I.e.*, scandal.   [6] Carry on.   [7] Sight.

BASS. Divine and best of ladies,
Please to forget my outrage; mercy ever
Cannot but lodge under a roof [1] so ex-
cellent.
I have cast off that cruelty of frenzy
Which once appeared impostors, and then
juggled
To cheat my sleeps of rest.
ORG. Was I in earnest?
PEN. Sure, if we were all Sirens, we should
sing pitifully.
And 'twere a comely music, when in
parts 70
One sung another's knell. The turtle
sighs
When he hath lost his mate; and yet
some say
A must be dead first. 'Tis a fine deceit
To pass away in a dream; indeed, I've
slept
With mine eyes open a great while. No
falsehood
Equals a broken faith; there's not a hair
Sticks on my head but, like a leaden
plummet,
It sinks me to the grave. I must creep
thither;
The journey is not long.
ITH. But thou, Penthea,
Hast many years, I hope, to number
yet, 80
Ere thou canst travel that way.
BASS. Let the sun [2] first
Be wrapped up in an everlasting dark-
ness,
Before the light of nature, chiefly formed
For the whole world's delight, feel an
eclipse
So universal!
ORG. Wisdom, look 'e, begins
To rave!—Art thou mad too, antiquity?
PEN. Since I was first a wife, I might have
been
Mother to many pretty, prattling babes;
They would have smiled when I smiled,
and for certain
I should have cried when they cried.—
Truly, brother, 90
My father would have picked me out a
husband,

And then my little ones had been no
bastards;
But 'tis too late for me to marry now—
I am past childbearing; 'tis not my fault.
BASS. Fall on me, if there be a burning
Ætna,
And bury me in flames! Sweats hot as
sulphur
Boil through my pores! Affliction hath
in store
No torture like to this.
ORG. Behold a patience!
Lay by thy whining, gray dissimulation;
Do something worth a chronicle. Show
justice 100
Upon the author of this mischief; dig out
The jealousies that hatched this thrall-
dom first
With thine own poniard. Every antic
rapture
Can roar as thine does.
ITH. Orgilus, forbear.
BASS. Disturb him not; it is a talking
motion [3]
Provided for my torment. What a fool
am I
To bawdy passion! Ere I'll speak a word,
I will look on and burst.
PEN. [To Orgilus.] I loved you once.
ORG. Thou didst, wronged creature, in de-
spite of malice;
For it I love thee ever.
PEN. Spare your hand; 110
Believe me, I'll not hurt it.
ORG. Pain my heart too.
[PEN.] [4] Complain not though I wring it
hard. I'll kiss it;
O, 'tis a fine soft palm!—Hark, in thine
ear;
Like whom do I look, prithee?—Nay, no
whispering.
Goodness! We had been happy; too
much happiness
Will make folk proud, they say—but that
is he— Points at Ithocles.
And yet he paid for 't home. Alas, his
heart
Is crept into the cabinet of the princess;
We shall have points [5] and bride laces.
Remember,

---

[1] Emended by Gifford-Dyce; original reads
roof.
[2] Emended by Gifford-Dyce; original reads
swan.

[3] Puppet.
[4] This speech is assigned to Orgilus in the
original.
[5] Tagged laces.

When we last gathered roses in the gar-
    den, 120
I found my wits, but truly you lost yours.
That's he, and still 'tis he.
ITH.   Poor soul, how idly [1]
    Her fancies guide her tongue!
BASS. [Aside.]   Keep in, vexation,
    And break not into clamor.
ORG. [Aside.]   She has tutored me;
    Some powerful inspiration checks my
      laziness.[2]—
    Now let me kiss your hand, grieved
      beauty.
PEN.   Kiss it.—
    Alack, alack, his lips be wondrous cold.
    Dear soul, h'as lost his color; have 'e
      seen
    A straying heart? All crannies! Every
      drop
    Of blood is turn[é]d to an amethyst, 130
    Which married bachelors hang in their
      ears.
ORG. Peace usher her into Elysium!—
    If this be madness, madness is an oracle.
                  Exit Org[ilus].
ITH. Christalla, Philema, when slept my
    sister,
    Her ravings are so wild?
CHRIS.   Sir, not these ten days.
PHIL. We watch by her continually; be-
    sides,
    We cannot any way pray her to eat.
BASS. O, misery of miseries!
PEN.   Take comfort;
    You may live well, and die a good old
    man.
    By yea and nay, an oath not to be
      broken, 140
    If you had joined our hands once in the
      temple—
    'Twas since my father died, for had he
      lived
    He would have done 't—I must have
      called you father.
    O, my wracked honor, ruined by those
      tyrants,
    A cruel brother and a desperate dotage!
    There is no peace left for a ravished
      wife
    Widowed by lawless marriage; to all
      memory
    Penthea's, poor Penthea's, name is
      strumpeted.

But, since her blood was seasoned by
    the forfeit
Of noble shame with mixtures of pollu-
    tion, 150
Her blood—'tis just—be henceforth
    never heightened
With taste of sustenance! Starve; let
    that fullness
Whose plurisy [3] hath fevered faith and
    modesty—
Forgive me; O, I faint!
    [*Falls into the arms of her Attendants.*]
ARM.   Be not so willful,
    Sweet niece, to work thine own destruc-
    tion.
ITH.   Nature
    Will call her daughter monster!—What!
    Not eat?
    Refuse the only ordinary means
    Which are ordained for life? Be not, my
    sister,
    A murth'ress to thyself.—Hear'st thou
    this, Bassanes?
BASS. Foh! I am busy, for I have not
    thoughts 160
    Enow to think; all shall be well anon.
    'Tis tumbling in my head; there is a
    mastery
    In art to fatten and keep smooth the
    outside;
    Yes, and to comfort up the vital spirits
    Without the help of food, fumes or per-
    fumes,
    Perfumes or fumes. Let her alone; I'll
    search out
    The trick on 't.
PEN.   Lead me gently; heavens reward
    ye.
    Griefs are sure friends; they leave with-
    out control
    Nor cure nor comforts for a leprous soul.
    Exeunt the Maids supporting Penthea.
BASS. I grant 'e, and will put in practice
    instantly 170
    What you shall still admire.[4] 'Tis won-
    derful;
    'Tis super-singular, not to be matched;
    Yet, when I've done 't, I've done 't.—Ye
    shall all thank me.   *Exit Bassanes.*
ARM. The sight is full of terror.
ITH.   On my soul
    Lies such an infinite clog of massy dull-
    ness

---

[1] Madly.   [2] Procrastination.   [3] Superabundance.   [4] Wonder at.

As that I have not sense enough to feel
  it.—
See, uncle, th' augury [1] thing returns
  again;
Shall 's welcome him with thunder? We
  are haunted,
And must use exorcism to conjure down
This spirit of malevolence.
ARM.   Mildly, nephew. 180

Enter Nearchus and Amelus.

NEAR. I come not, sir, to chide your late
  disorder,
  Admitting that th' inurement to a rough-
  ness
  In soldiers of your years and fortunes,
  chiefly,
  So lately prosperous, hath not yet shook
  off
  The custom of the war in hours of leisure;
  Nor shall you need excuse, since y' are to
  render
  Account to that fair excellence, the
  princess,
  Who in her private gallery expects it
  From your own mouth alone. I am a
  messenger
  But to her pleasure.
ITH.   Excellent Nearchus, 190
  Be prince still of my services, and con-
  quer
  Without the combat of dispute; I hon-
  or 'e.
NEAR. The king is on a sudden indisposed;
  Physicians are called for. 'Twere fit,
  Armostes,
  You should be near him.
ARM.   Sir, I kiss your hands.
  Exeunt. Manent Nearchus et Amelus.
NEAR. Amelus, I perceive Calantha's
  bosom
  Is warmed with other fires than such as
  can
  Take strength from any fuel of the love
  I might address to her. Young Ithocles,
  Or ever I mistake, is lord ascendant 200
  Of her devotions—one, to speak him
  truly,
  In every disposition nobly fashioned.
AME. But can your highness brook to be
  so rivaled,
  Considering th' inequality of the persons?

[1] Foreboding.

NEAR. I can, Amelus, for affections in-
  jured
By tyranny or rigor of compulsion,
Like tempest-threatened trees unfirmly
  rooted,
Ne'er spring to timely growth. Observe,
  for instance,
Life-spent Penthea and unhappy Orgilus.
AME. How does your grace determine?
NEAR.   To be jealous 210
In public of what privately I'll further;
And, though they shall not know, yet
  they shall find it.   *Exeunt omnes.*

[SCENE iii.

An apartment in the palace.]

*Enter Hemophil and Groneas leading Amy-
  clas, and placing him in a chair; followed
  by Armostes [with a box], Crotolon, and
                                    Prophilus.*

AMY. Our daughter is not near?
ARM.   She is retired, sir,
  Into her gallery.
AMY.   Where's the prince our cousin?
PRO. New walked into the grove, my lord.
AMY.   All leave us
  Except Armostes, and you, Crotolon;
  We would be private.
PRO.   Health unto your majesty!
  Exeunt Prophilus, Hemophil, et Groneas.
AMY. What! Tecnicus is gone?
ARM.   He is to Delphos,
  And to your royal hands presents this
  box.
AMY. Unseal it, good Armostes; therein
  lies
  The secrets of the oracle. Out with it.
        [*Armostes removes the scroll.*]
  Apollo live our patron! Read, Ar-
  mostes.   10
ARM. "*The plot in which the vine takes root
  Begins to dry from head to foot;
  The stock soon withering, want of sap
  Doth cause to quail* [2] *the budding grape;
  But from the neighboring elm a dew
  Shall drop, and feed the plot anew.*"
AMY.   That is the oracle. What exposi-
  tion
  Makes the philosopher?
ARM.   This brief one only.
  "*The plot is Sparta; the dried vine the king;*

[2] Die.

The quailing grape his daughter; but the
thing   20
Of most importance, not to be revealed,
Is a near prince, the elm—the rest con-
cealed.

                     TECNICUS."

AMY. Enough; although the opening [1] of
     this riddle
Be but itself a riddle, yet we construe
How near our laboring age draws to a
     rest.
But must Calantha quail too? That
     young grape
Untimely budded! I could mourn for her;
Her tenderness hath yet deserved no rigor
So to be crossed by fate.

ARM.   You misapply, sir. 29
With favor let me speak it—what Apollo
Hath clouded in hid sense. I here con-
     jecture
Her marriage with some neighb'ring
     prince, the dew
Of which befriending elm shall ever
     strengthen
Your subjects with a sovereignty of
     power.

CROT. Besides, most gracious lord, the
     pith of oracles
Is to be then digested when th' events
Expound their truth, not brought as soon
     to light
As uttered. Truth is child of Time; and
     herein
I find no scruple, rather cause of comfort,
With unity of kingdoms.

AMY.   May it prove so, 40
For weal of this dear nation!—Where is
     Ithocles?—
Armostes, Crotolon, when this withered
     vine
Of my frail carcass, on the funeral pile
Is fired into its ashes, let that young man
Be hedged about still with your cares and
     loves.
Much owe I to his worth, much to his
     service.—
Let such as wait come in now.

ARM.   All attend here!

Enter Ithocles, Calantha, Prophilus, Orgilus,
*   Euphranea, Hemophil, and Groneas.*

CAL. Dear sir! King! Father!
ITH.   O my royal master!

[1] *I.e.*, interpretation.

AMY. Cleave not my heart, sweet twins of
     my life's solace,
With your forejudging fears; there is no
     physic   50
So cunningly restorative to cherish
The fall of age, or call back youth and
     vigor,
As your consents in duty. I will shake off
This languishing disease of time, to
     quicken
Fresh pleasures in these drooping hours
     of sadness.
Is fair Euphranea married yet to Pro-
     philus?

CROT. This morning, gracious lord.
ORG.   This very morning,
Which, with your highness' leave, you
     may observe too.
Our sister looks, methinks, mirthful and
     sprightly,
As if her chaster fancy could already 60
Expound the riddle of her gain in losing
A trifle maids know only that they know
     not.
Pish! Prithee, blush not; 'tis but honest
     change
Of fashion in the garment, loose for
     strait,
And so the modest maid is made a wife.
Shrewd business—is 't not, sister?

EUPH.   You are pleasant.
AMY. We thank thee, Orgilus; this mirth
     becomes thee.
But wherefore sits the court in such a
     silence?
A wedding without revels is not seemly.

CAL. Your late indisposition, sir, forbade
     it.   70
AMY. Be it thy charge, Calantha, to set
     forward
The bridal sports, to which I will be
     present;
If not, at least consenting.—Mine own
     Ithocles,
I have done little for thee yet.

ITH.   Y' have built me
To the full height I stand in.

CAL. [*Aside.*]   Now or never!—
May I propose a suit?
AMY.   Demand, and have it.
CAL. Pray, sir, give me this young man,
     and no further
Account him yours than he deserves in
     all things

To be thought worthy mine; I will
esteem him
According to his merit.

AMY.   Still th' art my daughter, 80
Still grow'st upon my heart.—[*To
Ithocles.*] Give me thine hand.—
Calantha, take thine own. In noble
actions
Thou'lt find him firm and absolute.—I
would not
Have parted with thee, Ithocles, to any
But to a mistress who is all what I am.

ITH. A change, great king, most wished
for, cause the same!

CAL. [*Aside to Ithocles.*] Th' art mine. Have
I now kept my word?

ITH. [*Aside to Calantha.*]   Divinely.

ORG. Rich fortunes guard, the[1] favor of a
princess
Rock thee, brave man, in ever-crownéd
plenty!
Y' are minion of the time; be thankful for
it.—   90
[*Aside.*] Ho! Here's a swinge[2] in destiny.
Apparent,
The youth is up on tiptoe, yet may stum-
ble.

AMY. On to your recreations.—Now convey me
Unto my bedchamber. None on his forehead
Wear a distempered look.

OMNES.   The gods preserve 'e!

CAL. [*Aside to Ithocles.*] Sweet, be not
from my sight.

ITH. [*Aside to Calantha.*]   My whole
felicity!

*Exeunt, carrying out of the King; Orgilus
                              stays Ithocles.*

ORG. Shall I be bold, my lord?

ITH.   Thou canst not, Orgilus.
Call me thine own, for Prophilus must
henceforth
Be all thy sister's. Friendship, though it
cease not   99
In marriage, yet is oft at less command
Than when a single freedom can dispose
it.

ORG. Most right, my most good lord, my
most great lord,
My gracious, princely lord, I might add,
royal.

ITH. Royal! A subject royal?

ORG.   Why not, pray, sir?
The sovereignty of kingdoms in their
nonage
Stooped to desert, not birth; there's as
much merit
In clearness of affection[3] as in puddle
Of generation.[4] You have conquered love
Even in the loveliest; if I greatly err
not,
The son of Venus hath bequeathed his
quiver   110
To Ithocles his manage,[5] by whose
arrows
Calantha's breast is opened.

ITH.   Can 't be possible?

ORG. I was myself a piece of suitor once,
And forward in preferment too—so for-
ward
That, speaking truth, I may without
offense, sir,
Presume to whisper that my hopes and
—hark 'e—
My certainty of marriage stood assured
With as firm footing—by your leave—as
any's
Now at this very instant—but—

ITH.   'Tis granted;
And, for a league of privacy between
us,   120
Read o'er my bosom and partake a
secret:
The princess is contracted mine.

ORG.   Still, why not?
I now applaud her wisdom; when your
kingdom
Stands seated in your will, secure and
settled,
I dare pronounce you will be a just mon-
arch;
Greece must admire and tremble.

ITH.   Then the sweetness
Of so imparadised a comfort, Orgilus!
It is to banquet with the gods.

ORG.   The glory
Of numerous children, potency of nobles,
Bent knees, hearts paved to tread on!

ITH.   With a friendship 130
So dear, so fast as thine.

ORG.   I am unfitting
For office; but for service—

---

[1] Emended by Gifford-Dyce; original reads *to*.
[2] Sway.
[3] Nobility of mental tendencies.
[4] Birth.
[5] To Ithocles' management.

ITH. We'll distinguish
Our fortunes merely in the title; partners
In all respects else but the bed.
ORG. The bed?
Forfend it, Jove's own jealousy, till
lastly
We slip down in the common earth to-
gether,
And there our beds are equal, save some
monument
To show this was the king, and this the
subject.—
List, what sad sounds are these?—Ex-
tremely sad ones!
ITH. Sure, from Penthea's lodgings.
ORG. Hark! A voice too. 140

Soft, sad music.

A SONG

O, no more, no more, too late
    Sighs are spent; the burning tapers
Of a life as chaste as fate,
    Pure as are unwritten papers,
Are burnt out. No heat, no light
Now remains; 'tis ever night.

Love is dead; let lovers' eyes,
    Locked in endless dreams,
    Th' extremes of all extremes,
Ope no more, for now Love dies, 150
    Now Love dies, implying
Love's martyrs must be ever, ever dying.

ITH. O, my misgiving heart!
ORG. A horrid stillness
Succeeds this deathful air; let's know the
reason.
Tread softly; there is mystery in mourn-
ing. *Exeunt.*

[SCENE iv.

Penthea's apartment in the palace.]

*Enter Christalla and Philema, bringing in
    Penthea in a chair, veiled; two other
    Servants placing two chairs, one on the
    one side, and the other with an engine[1]
    on the other. The Maids sit down at her
    feet, mourning. The Servants go out;
        meet them Ithocles and Orgilus.*

SERV. [*Aside to Orgilus.*] 'Tis done; that on
    her right hand.

[1] Mechanical contrivance.

ORG. Good; begone!
    [*Exeunt Servants.*]
ITH. Soft peace enrich this room!
ORG. How fares the lady?
PHIL. Dead!
CHRIS. Dead!
PHIL. Starved!
CHRIS. Starved!
ITH. Me miserable!
ORG. Tell us
How parted she from life.
PHIL. She called for music,
And begged some gentle voice to tune a
farewell
To life and griefs. Christalla touched the
lute;
I wept the funeral song.
CHRIS. Which scarce was ended
But her last breath sealed up these hollow
sounds,
"O, cruel Ithocles and injured Orgilus!"
So down she drew her veil, so died.
ITH. So died! 10
ORG. Up! You are messengers of death; go
from us;
Here's woe enough to court without a
prompter!
Away; and—hark ye—till you see us
next,
No syllable that she is dead.—Away;
    Exeunt Phil[ema] et Chri[stalla].
Keep a smooth brow.—My lord—
ITH. Mine only sister!
Another is not left me.
ORG. Take that chair;
I'll seat me here in this. Between us sits
The object of our sorrows; some few
tears
We'll part among us; I perhaps can mix
One lamentable story to prepare 'em.—
There, there; sit there, my lord.
ITH. Yes, as you please. 21
*Ithocles sits down, and is catched in the
    engine.*
What means this treachery?
ORG. Caught! You are caught,
Young master; 'tis thy throne of corona-
tion,
Thou fool of greatness! See, I take this
veil off;
Survey a beauty withered by the flames
Of an insulting Phaëton, her brother.
ITH. Thou mean'st to kill me basely.
ORG. I foreknew

The last act of her life, and trained [1] thee
hither
To sacrifice a tyrant to a turtle.
You dreamt of kingdoms, did 'e? How to
bosom   30
The delicacies of a youngling princess,
How with this nod to grace that subtle
courtier,
How with that frown to make this noble
tremble,
And so forth, whiles Penthea's groans and
tortures,
Her agonies, her miseries, afflictions
Ne'er touched upon your thought? As
for my injuries,
Alas, they were beneath your royal
pity;
But yet they lived, thou proud man, to
confound thee.
Behold thy fate, this steel!
                                   [*Draws a dagger.*]

ITH.   Strike home! A courage
As keen as thy revenge shall give it wel-
come.   40
But, prithee, faint not; if the wound
close up,
Tent [2] it with double force, and search it
deeply.
Thou look'st that I should whine and beg
compassion,
As loath to leave the vainness of my
glories.
A statelier resolution arms my confidence,
To cozen thee of honor; neither could I
With equal trial of unequal fortune
By hazard of a duel; 'twere a bravery
Too mighty for a slave intending mur-
ther.
On to the execution, and inherit   50
A conflict with thy horrors!

ORG.   By Apollo,
Thou talk'st a goodly language! For
requital
I will report thee to thy mistress richly.
And take this peace along: some few
short minutes
Determined,[3] my resolves shall quickly
follow
Thy wrathful ghost; then, if we tug for
mastery,
Penthea's sacred eyes shall lend new
courage.

Give me thy hand; be healthful in thy
parting
From lost mortality! Thus, thus I free it!
                                   Kills him.
ITH. Yet, yet, I scorn to shrink.
ORG.   Keep up thy spirit.   60
I will be gentle even in blood; to linger [4]
Pain, which I strive to cure, were to be
cruel.   [*Stabs him again.*]
ITH. Nimble in vengeance, I forgive thee.
Follow
Safety, with best success.   O, may it
prosper!—
Penthea, by thy side thy brother
bleeds—
The earnest of his wrongs to thy forced
faith.
Thoughts of ambition, or delicious ban-
quet,
With beauty, youth, and love, together
perish
In my last breath, which on the sacred
altar
Of a long-looked-for peace—now—moves
—to heaven.   *Moritur.*[5] 70
ORG. Farewell, fair spring of manhood.
Henceforth welcome
Best expectation of a noble suff'rance.
I'll lock the bodies safe, till what must
follow
Shall be approved.—Sweet twins, shine
stars forever!—
In vain they build their hopes whose life
is shame;
No monument lasts but a happy name.
                                   Exit Orgilus.

ACTUS QUINTUS.   SCENA PRIMA.

[*A room in Bassanes' house.*]

Enter Bassanes, alone.

BASS. Athens!—To Athens I have sent,
the nursery
Of Greece for learning and the fount of
knowledge,
For here in Sparta there's not left
amongst us
One wise man to direct; we're all turned
madcaps.
'Tis said Apollo is the god of herbs;
Then certainly he knows the virtue of
'em.

---

[1] Lured.   [3] Brought to a termination.
[2] Probe.

[4] Prolong.   [5] He dies.

To Delphos I have sent too. If there
  can be
A help for nature, we are sure yet.

Enter Orgilus.

ORG.   Honor
  Attend thy counsels ever!
BASS.   I beseech thee
  With all my heart, let me go from thee
    quietly;   10
  I will not aught to do with thee of all
    men.
  The doubles [1] of a hare—or, in a morning,
  Salutes from a splay-footed witch—to
    drop
  Three drops of blood at th' nose just
    and no more—
  Croaking of ravens, or the screech of
    owls—
  Are not so boding mischief as thy cross-
    ing
  My private meditations. Shun me,
    prithee;
  And, if I cannot love thee heartily,
  I'll love thee as well as I can.
ORG.   Noble Bassanes,
  Mistake me not.
BASS.   Phew!   Then we shall be
    troubled.   20
  Thou wert ordained my plague—heaven
    make me thankful,
  And give me patience too, heaven, I
    beseech thee.
ORG. Accept a league of amity, for hence-
    forth
  I vow by my best genius, in a syllable,
  Never to speak vexation. I will study
  Service and friendship, with a zealous
    sorrow
  For my past incivility towards 'e.
BASS. Heyday, good words, good words! I
    must believe 'em,
  And be a coxcomb for my labor.
ORG.   Use not
  So hard a language; your misdoubt is
    causeless.   30
  For instance, if you promise to put on
  A constancy of patience, such a patience
  As chronicle or history ne'er mentioned,
  As follows not example, but shall stand
  A wonder and a theme for imitation,

The first, the index pointing to a second,
  I will acquaint 'e with an unmatched
    secret,
  Whose knowledge to your griefs shall
    set a period.
BASS. Thou canst not, Orgilus; 'tis in the
    power   39
  Of the gods only; yet, for satisfaction,
  Because I note an earnest in thine
    utterance,
  Unforced and naturally free, be resolute [2]
  The virgin bays shall not withstand the
    lightning
  With a more careless [3] danger than my
    constancy
  The full of thy relation. Could it move
  Distraction in a senseless marble statue,
  It should find me a rock. I do expect
    now
  Some truth of unheard moment.
ORG.   To your patience
  You must add privacy, as strong in
    silence
  As mysteries locked up in Jove's own
    bosom.   50
BASS. A skull hid in the earth a treble age
  Shall sooner prate.
ORG.   Lastly, to such direction
  As the severity of a glorious action
  Deserves to lead your wisdom and your
    judgment,
  You ought to yield obedience.
BASS.   With assurance
  Of will and thankfulness.
ORG.   With manly courage
  Please then to follow me.
BASS.   Where'er, I fear not.
                   Exeunt omnes.

SCENE ii.

[*A room of state in the palace.*]

*Loud music. Enter Groneas and Hemophil,
  leading Euphranea; Christalla and
  Philema, leading Prophilus; Nearchus
  supporting Calantha; Crotolon and
  Amelus. Cease loud music; All make a
                       stand.*

CAL. We miss our servant Ithocles and
  Orgilus;
  On whom attend they?
CROT.   My son, gracious princess,

---

[1] Doublings. Reading of Gifford-Dyce; original
reads *doublers.*

[2] Certain.   [3] *I.e.*, heedlessness of.

Whispered some new device, to which
these revels
Should be but usher, wherein 1 con-
ceive
Lord Ithocles and he himself are actors.
CAL. A fair excuse for absence. As for
Bassanes,
Delights   to   him   are   troublesome.
Armostes
Is with the king?
CROT.   He is.
CAL.   On to the dance!—
Dear cousin, hand you the bride; the
bridegroom must be
Intrusted to my courtship.   Be not
jealous,   10
Euphranea; I shall scarcely prove a
temptress.—
Fall to our dance.   *Music.*

Nearchus dance with Euphranea, Prophilus
with Calantha, Christalla with Hem-
ophil, Philema with Groneas.   Dance
the first change,[1] during which enter
Armostes.

ARM. (*In Calantha's ear.*)   The king
your father's dead.
CAL. To the other change.
ARM.   Is 't possible?   *Dance again.*

Enter Bassanes.

BASS. [*In Calantha's ear.*]   O, madam!
Penthea, poor Penthea's starved.
CAL.   Beshrew thee!—
Lead to the next.
BASS.   Amazement dulls my senses.
                              Dance again.

Enter Orgilus.

ORG. [*In Calantha's ear.*] Brave Ithocles
is murthered, murthered cruelly.
CAL. How dull this music sounds! Strike
up more sprightly;
Our footings are not active like our heart,
Which treads the nimbler measure.
ORG.   I am thunderstrook.
                 Last change. Cease music.
CAL. So! Let us breathe awhile.—Hath
not this motion   20
Raised fresher color on your cheeks?

NEAR.   Sweet princess,
A perfect purity of blood enamels
The beauty of your white.
CAL.   We all look cheerfully;
And, cousin, 'tis, methinks, a rare pre-
sumption
In any who prefers our lawful pleasures
Before their own sour censure, to in-
terrupt
The custom of this ceremony bluntly.
NEAR. None dares, lady.
CAL. Yes, yes; some hollow voice delivered
to me
How that the king was dead.
ARM.   The king is dead. 30
That fatal news was mine; for in mine
arms
He breathed his last, and with his crown
bequeathed 'e
Your mother's wedding ring, which here
I tender.
CROT. Most strange!
CAL.   Peace crown his ashes! We are
queen, then.
NEAR. Long live Calantha! Sparta's sov-
ereign queen!
OMNES. Long live the queen!
CAL.   What whispered Bassanes?
BASS. That my Penthea, miserable soul,
Was starved to death.
CAL.   She's happy; she hath finished
A long and painful progress.—A third
murmur
Pierced mine unwilling ears.
ORG.   That Ithocles 40
Was murthered—rather butchered—had
not bravery
Of an undaunted spirit, conquering ter-
ror,
Proclaimed his last act triumph over
ruin.
ARM. How? Murthered!
CAL.   By whose hand?
ORG.   By mine; this weapon
Was instrument to my revenge.   The
reasons
Are just, and known; quit him of these,
and then
Never lived gentleman of greater merit,
Hope, or abiliment[2] to steer a kingdom.
CROT. Fie, Orgilus!
EUPH.   Fie, brother!
CAL.   You have done it?

BASS. How it was done let him report,
the forfeit　　　　　　　　　50
Of whose allegiance to our laws doth
covet
Rigor of justice; but that done it is,
Mine eyes have been an evidence of
credit
Too sure to be convinced.[1] Armostes,
rent [2] not
Thine arteries with hearing the bare
circumstances
Of these calamities. Thou 'st lost a
nephew,
A niece, and I a wife. Continue man
still;
Make me the pattern of digesting [3]
evils,
Who can outlive my mighty ones, not
shrinking　　　　　　　　　59
At such a pressure as would sink a soul
Into what 's most of death, the worst of
horrors.
But I have sealed a covenant with sad-
ness,
And entered into bonds without condi-
tion,
To stand these tempests calmly. Mark
me, nobles,
I do not shed a tear, not for Penthea!
Excellent misery!
CAL.　　　　　　　We begin our reign
With a first act of justice: thy confession,
Unhappy Orgilus, dooms thee a sen-
tence;
But yet thy father's or thy sister's
presence
Shall be excused.—Give, Crotolon, a
blessing　　　　　　　　　70
To thy lost son; Euphranea, take a
farewell;
And both be gone.
CROT. [To Orgilus.]　　　Confirm thee,
noble sorrow,
In worthy resolution!
EUPH.　　　　　　Could my tears speak,
My griefs were slight.
ORG.　　　All goodness dwell amongst ye!
Enjoy my sister, Prophilus; my ven-
geance
Aimed never at thy prejudice.
CAL.　　　　　　　　　Now withdraw.
Exeunt Crotolon, Prophilus, et Euphranea.

[1] Confuted.　　　[3] Stomaching, enduring.
[2] Rend.

Bloody relater of thy stains in blood,
For that thou hast reported him, whose
fortunes
And life by thee are both at once
snatched from him,
With honorable mention, make thy
choice　　　　　　　　　80
Of what death likes thee best; there's
all our bounty.—
But, to excuse delays, let me, dear
cousin,
Entreat you and these lords see execution
Instant before 'e part.
NEAR.　　　　　　Your will commands us.
ORG. One suit, just queen, my last:
vouchsafe your clemency
That by no common hand I be divided
From this my humble frailty.
CAL.　　　　　　　　To their wisdoms
Who are to be spectators of thine end
I make the reference. Those that are
dead
Are dead; had they not now died, of
necessity　　　　　　　　　90
They must have paid the debt they owed
to nature
One time or other.—Use despatch, my
lords;
We'll suddenly prepare our coronation.
Exeunt Calantha, Philema, Christalla.
ARM. 'Tis strange these tragedies should
never touch on
Her female pity.
BASS.　　　　She has a masculine spirit;
And wherefore should I pule, and, like
a girl,
Put finger in the eye? Let's be all
toughness,
Without distinction betwixt sex and sex.
NEAR. Now, Orgilus, thy choice?
ORG.　　　　　　　　To bleed to death.
ARM. The executioner?
ORG.　　　　　　Myself, no surgeon;　100
I am well skilled in letting blood. Bind
fast
This arm, that so the pipes may from
their conduits
Convey a full stream; here's a skillful
instrument.　　　[Shows his dagger.]
Only I am a beggar to some charity
To speed me in this execution
By lending th' other prick to th' tother
arm,
When this is bubbling life out.

Bass.   I am for 'e;
It most concerns my art, my care, my
    credit.—
Quick, fillet both his [1] arms.
Org.   Gramercy, friendship!
Such courtesies are real which flow
    cheerfully   110
Without an expec[ta]tion of requital.
Reach me a staff in this hand.
                    [*They give him a staff.*]
                            If a proneness
Or custom in my nature from my
    cradle
Had been inclined to fierce and eager
    bloodshed,
A coward guilt, hid in a coward quaking,
Would have betrayed fame to ignoble
    flight
And vagabond pursuit of dreadful safety;
But look upon my steadiness, and scorn
    not
The sickness of my fortune, which,
    since Bassanes
Was husband to Penthea, had lain
    bedrid.   120
We trifle time in words. Thus I show
    cunning
In opening of a vein too full, too lively.
                            [*Opens the vein.*]
Arm. Desperate courage!
Org.   Honorable infamy!
Hem. I tremble at the sight.
Gro.   Would I were loose!
Bass. It sparkles like a lusty wine new
    broached;
The vessel must be sound from which it
    issues.
Grasp hard this other stick; I'll be as
    nimble—
But, prithee, look not pale. Have at
    'e! Stretch out
Thine arm with vigor and unshook
    virtue.   [*Opens the other vein.*]
Good! O, I envy not a rival, fitted   130
To conquer in extremities. This pastime
Appears majestical; some high-tuned
    poem
Hereafter shall deliver to posterity
The writer's glory and his subject's
    triumph.
How is 't, man? Droop not yet.
Org.   I feel no palsies.

On a pair-royal [2] do I wait in death:
My sovereign, as his liegeman; on my
    mistress,
As a devoted servant; and on Ithocles,
As if no brave, yet no unworthy enemy.
Nor did I use an engine to entrap   140
His life out of a slavish fear to combat
Youth, strength, or cunning,[3] but for
    that I durst not
Engage [4] the goodness of a cause on for-
    tune,
By which his name might have outfaced
    my vengeance.
O Tecnicus, inspired with Phœbus' fire!
I call to mind thy augury; 'twas per-
    fect:
"*Revenge proves its own executioner.*"
When feeble man is bending to his
    mother,
The dust a was first framed on, thus he
    totters.
Bass. Life's fountain is dried up.
Org.   So falls the standards 150
Of my prerogative in being a creature!
A mist hangs o'er mine eyes; the sun's
    bright splendor
Is clouded in an everlasting shadow.
Welcome, thou ice, that sitt'st about my
    heart;
No heat can ever thaw thee.   *Dies.*
Near.   Speech hath left him.
Bass. A has shook hands with time; his
    funeral urn
Shall be my charge. Remove the blood-
    less body.
The coronation must require attendance;
That past, my few days can be but one
    mourning.   *Exeunt.*

[Scene iii.

A temple.]

*An altar covered with white; two lights of
    virgin wax, during which music of
    recorders. Enter Four bearing Ithocles
    on a hearse, or in a chair, in a rich
    robe, and a crown on his head; place
    him on one side of the altar. After
    him enter Calantha in a white robe
    and crowned; Euphranea, Philema,
    Christalla, in white; Nearchus, Armostes
    Crotolon, Prophilus, Amelus, Bassanes*

Hemophil, and Groneas.   Calantha
goes and kneels before the altar; the
Rest stand off, the women kneeling be-
hind.   Cease recorders during her de-
votions.   Soft music.   Calantha and the
Rest rise, doing obeisance to the altar.

CAL. Our orisons are heard; the gods are
    merciful.—
  Now tell me, you whose loyalties pays
    tribute
  To us your lawful sovereign, how un-
    skillful
  Your duties or obedience is to render
  Subjection to the scepter of a virgin,
  Who have been ever fortunate in princes
  Of masculine and stirring composi-
    tion.
  A woman has enough to govern wisely
  Her own demeanors, passions, and di-
    visions.[1]
  A nation warlike and inured to prac-
    tice   10
  Of policy and labor cannot brook
  A feminate authority; we therefore
  Command your counsel how you may
    advise us
  In choosing of a husband whose abili-
    ties
  Can better guide this kingdom.
NEAR.   Royal lady,
  Your law is in your will.
ARM.   We have seen tokens
  Of constancy too lately to mistrust it.
CROT. Yet, if your highness settle on a
    choice
  By your own judgment both allowed and
    liked of,
  Sparta may grow in power, and pro-
    ceed   20
  To an increasing height.
CAL.   Hold you the same
    mind?
BASS. Alas, great mistress, reason is so
    clouded
  With the thick darkness of my infinite
    woes
  That I forecast nor dangers, hopes, or
    safety.
  Give me some corner of the world to wear
    out
  The remnant of the minutes I must
    number,

[1] Uncertainties.

  Where I may hear no sounds but sad
    complaints
  Of virgins who have lost contracted
    partners;
  Of husbands howling that their wives
    were ravished
  By some untimely fate; of friends
    divided   30
  By churlish opposition; or of fathers
  Weeping upon their children's slaugh-
    tered carcasses;
  Or daughters groaning o'er their fathers'
    hearses;
  And I can dwell there, and with these
    keep consort [2]
  As musical as theirs.   What can you
    look for
  From an old, foolish, peevish, doting man
  But craziness of age?
CAL. Cousin of Argos!
NEAR.   Madam?
CAL.   Were I presently
  To choose you for my lord, I'll open
    freely
  What articles I would propose to treat
    on   40
  Before our marriage.
NEAR.   Name them, virtuous lady.
CAL. I would presume you would retain
    the royalty
  Of Sparta in her own bounds; then in
    Argos
  Armostes might be viceroy; in Messene
  Might Crotolon bear sway; and Bas-
    sanes—
BASS. I, queen? Alas, what I?
CAL.   Be Sparta's mar-
    shal.
  The multitudes of high employments
    could not
  But set a peace to private griefs. These
    gentlemen,
  Groneas and Hemophil, with worthy
    pensions,
  Should wait upon your person in your
    chamber.   50
  I would bestow Christalla on Amelus;
  She'll prove a constant wife.   And
    Philema
  Should into Vesta's temple.
BASS.   This is a testament!
  It sounds not like conditions on a
    marriage.

[2] Harmony.

NEAR. All this should be performed.

CAL. Lastly, for Prophilus,
He should be, cousin, solemnly invested
In all those honors, titles, and prefer-
ments
Which his dear friend and my neglected
husband
Too short a time enjoyed.

PRO. I am unworthy
To live in your remembrance.

EUPH. Excellent lady! 60

NEAR. Madam, what means that word,
"neglected husband"?

CAL. Forgive me.—Now I turn to thee,
thou shadow
Of my contracted lord! Bear witness
all,
I put my mother's [1] wedding ring upon
His finger; 'twas my father's last be-
quest.

[*Places a ring on the finger of Ithocles.*]
Thus I new-marry him whose wife I
am;
Death shall not separate us. O my
lords,
I but deceived your eyes with antic
gesture,
When one news straight came huddling
on another
Of death, and death, and death! Still
I danced forward; 70
But it strook home, and here, and in an
instant.
Be [2] such mere women, who with shrieks
and outcries
Can vow a present end to all their sor-
rows,
Yet live to vow new pleasures, and out-
live them.
They are the silent griefs which cut the
heartstrings;
Let me die smiling.

NEAR. 'Tis a truth too ominous.

CAL. One kiss on these cold lips, my last!—
[*Kisses Ithocles.*] Crack, crack!—
Argos now's Sparta's king.—Command
the voices
Which wait at th' altar now to sing the
song
I fitted for my end.

NEAR. Sirs, the song! 80

---

[1] Original reads *mother*, perhaps a survival of
an old genitive.
[2] *I.e.*, there be.

A SONG

ALL. Glories, pleasures, pomps, delights,
and ease
Can but please
[Th']³ outward senses when the mind
Is ⁴ untroubled or by peace refined.

1 [VOICE.] Crowns may flourish and decay;
Beauties shine, but fade away.

2 [VOICE.] Youth may revel, yet it must
Lie down in a bed of dust.

3 [VOICE.] Earthly honors flow and waste;
Time alone doth change and
last. 90

ALL. Sorrows mingled with contents pre-
pare
Rest for care;
Love only reigns in death, though art
Can find no comfort for a broken
heart.

[*Calantha dies.*]

ARM. Look to the queen!

BASS. Her heart is broke, indeed.
O, royal maid, would thou hadst missed
this part;
Yet 'twas a brave one. I must weep
to see
Her smile in death.

ARM. Wise Tecnicus! Thus said he:
"*When youth is ripe, and age from time
doth part,
The lifeless trunk shall wed the broken
heart.*" 100
'Tis here fulfilled.

NEAR. I am your king.

OMNES. Long live
Nearchus, King of Sparta!

NEAR. Her last will
Shall never be digressed from; wait in
order
Upon these faithful lovers, as becomes
us.—
The counsels of the gods are never known
Till men can call th' effects of them
their own. [*Exeunt.*]

FINIS.

THE EPILOGUE

WHERE noble judgments and clear eyes
are fixed
To grace endeavor, there sits Truth,
not mixed

---

[3] A space here indicates that something has
dropped out.
[4] Original reads *Is not.*

With ignorance; those censures [1] may command
Belief which talk not till they understand.
Let some say, "This was flat;" some, "Here the scene
Fell from its height;" another, that the mean
Was "ill observed" in such a growing passion
As it transcended either state or fashion.

[1] Opinions.

Some few may cry, "'Twas pretty well," or so,
"But—" and there shrug in silence; yet we know   10
Our writer's aim was in the whole addressed
Well to deserve of *all*, but please the *best*,
Which granted, by th' allowance of this strain,
The *Broken Heart* may be pieced up again.

FINIS.

THE CHRONICLE HISTORY OF
PERKIN WARBECK [1]

[BY
JOHN FORD]

THE SCENE: *The continent of Great Britain.*

[THE TIME: *1499 and the years preceding.*]

THE PERSONS PRESENTED

HENRY THE SEVENTH.
[LORD] DAWBNEY.[2]
SIR WILLIAM STANLEY.
[EARL OF] OXFORD.
[EARL OF] SURREY.
[Fox,] *Bishop of Durham.*
URSWICK, *chaplain to King Henry.*
SIR ROBERT CLIFFORD.
LAMBERT SIMNEL.
HIALAS,[3] *a Spanish agent.*
CONSTABLE, OFFICERS, [POST,][4] SERVING-
　MEN *and* SOLDIERS.

JAMES THE FOURTH, *King of Scotland.*
EARL OF HUNTLEY.

EARL OF CRAWFORD.
LORD DALIELL.
MARCHMOUNT, *a herald.*

PERKIN WARBECK.
[STEPHEN] FRION, *his secretary.*
[JOHN A WATER,] *Mayor of Cork.*
HERON, *a mercer.*
SKETON, *a tailor.*
ASTLEY, *a scrivener.*

WOMEN

LADY KATHERINE GORDON, *wife to Perkin.*
COUNTESS OF CRAWFORD.
JANE DOUGLAS, *Lady Kath[erine's] maid*

PROLOGUE

Studies have of this nature been of late
So out of fashion, so unfollowed, that
It is become more justice [6] to revive
The antic [7] follies of the times than strive
To countenance wise industry. No want
Of art doth render wit or [8] lame or scant
Or slothful in the purchase of fresh bays,
But want of truth in them who give the
　praise
To their self-love, presuming to outdo
The writer, or—for need—the actors too. 10
But such this author's silence best befits,
Who bids them be in love with their own
　wits.
From him to clearer judgments we can
　say
He shows a history couched in a play—
A history of noble mention, known
Famous and true; most noble, cause [9] our
　own;
Not forged from Italy, from France, from
　Spain,
But chronicled at home; as rich in strain
Of brave attempts as ever fertile rage [10]
In action could beget to grace the stage. 20

[1] The title continues· "A Strange Truth. Acted (Sometimes) by the Queen's Majesty's Servants at the Phœnix in Drury Lane. *Fide Honor.*" The Latin motto is an anagram of Ford's name used elsewhere instead of his signature.
[2] *I.e.*, Giles, Baron Daubeney.
[3] *I.e.*, Don Pedro Ayala.　　[4] Messenger.
[5] Here follow the dedicatory epistle to William Cavendish, Earl of Newcastle, signed by John Ford, and five commendatory poems.
[6] Judiciousness, wisdom.
[7] Antique, ancient.　　　　[8] Either.
[9] Because.　　　[10] Poetic inspiration.

We cannot limit scenes, for the whole land
Itself appeared too narrow to withstand
Competitors for kingdoms; nor is here
Unnecessary mirth forced, to endear
A multitude. On these two rests the fate
Of worthy expectation—truth and state.

ACTUS PRIMUS. SCENA PRIMA.

[*The presence chamber at Westminster.*]

Enter King Henry, Durham, Oxford, Sur-
rey, Sir William Stanley, Lord Cham-
berlain, Lord Dawbney; the King
supported to his throne by Stanley and
Durham. A Guard.

KING. Still [1] to be haunted, still to be
    pursued,
    Still to be frighted with false appari-
      tions
    Of pageant majesty and new-coined
      greatness,
    As if we were a mockery king in state,
    Only ordained to lavish sweat and blood
    In scorn and laughter to the ghosts of
      York, [2]
    Is all below our merits; yet, my lords,
    My friends and counselors, yet we sit
      fast
    In our own royal birthright. The rent
      face
    And bleeding wounds of England's
      slaughtered people   10
    Have been by us as by the best physi-
      cian
    At last both throughly cured and set in
      safety;
    And yet for all this glorious work of
      peace
    Ourself is scarce secure.
DUR.   The rage of malice
    Conjures fresh spirits with the spells of
      York.
    For ninety years ten English kings and
      princes,
    Threescore great dukes and earls, a
      thousand lords
    And valiant knights, two hundred fifty
      thousand
    Of English subjects have in civil wars
    Been sacrificed to an uncivil thirst   20

Of discord and ambition. This hot
    vengeance
Of the just powers above to utter ruin
And desolation had reigned on, but that
Mercy did gently sheathe the sword
    of justice
In lending to this blood-shrunk common-
    wealth
A new soul, new birth, in your sacred
    person.
DAW. Edward the Fourth, after a doubt-
    ful fortune,
    Yielded to nature, leaving to his sons,
    Edward and Richard, the inheritance
    Of a most bloody purchase. [3]   These
      young princes,   30
    Richard the tyrant, [4] their unnatural
      uncle,
    Forced to a violent grave, so just is
      heaven.
    Him hath your majesty by your own
      arm,
    Divinely strengthened, pulled from his
      boar's sty [5]
    And struck the black usurper to a car-
      cass.
    Nor doth the house of York decay in
      honors,
    Though Lancaster doth repossess his
      right,
    For Edward's daughter is King Henry's
      queen,
    A blessed union, and a lasting blessing
    For this poor panting island, if some
      shreds,   40
    Some useless remnant of the house of
      York,
    Grudge not at this content.
OX.   Margaret of Burgundy
    Blows fresh coals of division.
SUR.   Painted fires,
    Without or heat to [6] scorch or light to
      cherish.
DAW. York's headless trunk, her father;
    Edward's fate,
    Her brother king; the smothering of her
      nephews
    By tyrant Gloucester, [7] brother to her
      nature;

---

[1] Always.
[2] *I.e.*, Simnel and Warbeck, pretenders to the
throne, who were supported by the Yorkist
faction.

[3] Acquisition.   [4] *I.e.*, Richard III.
[5] A reference to the arms of Richard III.
[6] Emended by Gifford-Dyce. Original reads *to*
heat or.
[7] *I.e.*, Richard III.

Nor Gloucester's own confusion (all
   decrees
Sacred in heaven) can move this woman-
   monster,
But that she still from the unbottomed
   mine   50
Of devilish policies doth vent the ore
Of troubles and sedition.
Ox.   In her age—
   Great sir, observe the wonder—she
     grows fruitful,
Who in her strength of youth was always
   barren,
Nor are her births as other mothers'
   are,
At nine or ten months' end—she has been
   with child
Eight or seven years at least; whose
   twins [1] being born—
A prodigy in nature—even the youngest
Is fifteen years of age at his first entrance
As soon as known i' th' world, tall strip-
   lings, strong   60
And able to give battle unto kings,
   Idols of Yorkish malice.
Daw.[2]   And but idols!
A steely hammer crushes 'em to pieces.
King. Lambert, the eldest, lords, is in
   our service,
Preferred by an officious care of duty
From the scullery to a falc'ner—strange
   example!—
Which shows the difference between
   noble natures
And the baseborn. But for the upstart
   duke,
The new revived York, Edward's sec-
   ond son,
Murdered long since i' th' Tower, he
   lives again   70
And vows to be your king.
Stan.   The throne is filled, sir.
King. True, Stanley; and the lawful heir
   sits on it.
A guard of angels and the holy prayers
Of loyal subjects are a sure defense
Against all force and counsel of intru-
   sion.
But now, my lords, put case [3] some of
   our nobles,

Our great ones, should give counte-
   nance and courage
To trim Duke Perkin. You will all con-
   fess
Our bounties have unthriftily been
   scattered
Amongst unthankful men.
Daw.   Unthankful beasts, 80
Dogs, villains, traitors!
King.   Dawbney, let the guilty
Keep silence; I accuse none, though I
   know
Foreign attempts against a state and
   kingdom
Are seldom without some great friends
   at home.
Stan. Sir, if no other abler reasons else
Of duty or allegiance could divert
A headstrong resolution, yet the dangers
So lately passed by men of blood and
   fortunes
In Lambert Simnel's party must com-
   mand
More than a fear, a terror, to conspir-
   acy.   90
The highborn Lincoln, son to De la
   Pole,
The Earl of Kildare, [the][4] Lord Ger-
   aldine,
Francis, Lord Lovell, and the German
   baron
Bold Martin Swart, with Broughton
   and the rest—
Most spectacles of ruin, some of mercy—
Are presidents [5] sufficient to forewarn
The present times, or any that live in
   them,
What folly, nay, what madness, 'twere
   to lift
A finger up in all defense but yours,
Which can be but impostorous in a
   title.   100
King. Stanley, we know thou lov'st us,
   and thy heart
Is figured on thy tongue; nor think we
   less
Of any's here.—How closely we have
   hunted
This cub, since he unlodged, from hole
   to hole,
Your knowledge is our chronicle. First
   Ireland,
The common stage of novelty, presented

---

[1] These youths were not actually her sons, but
were impostors put forward by her.
[2] Gifford-Dyce's emendation for Ox.
[3] Suppose.
[4] Supplied by Gifford-Dyce.   [5] Precedents.

This gewgaw to oppose us; there the Geraldines
And Butlers once again stood in support
Of this colossic statue.   Charles of France   109
Thence called him into his protection,
Dissembled him the lawful heir of England;
Yet this was all but French dissimulation,
Aiming at peace with us, which being granted
On honorable terms on our part, suddenly
This smoke of straw was packed from France again
T' infect some grosser air. And now we learn—
Mauger the malice of the bastard Nevill,
Sir Taylor, and a hundred English rebels—
They're all retired to Flanders, to the dam
That nursed this eager whelp, Margaret of Burgundy.   120
But we will hunt him there too; we will hunt him,
Hunt him to death, even in the beldam's closet,
Though the archduke were his buckler.
SUR. She has styled him "the fair white rose of England."
DAW. Jolly gentleman, more fit to be a swabber
To the Flemish after a drunken surfeit.

Enter Urswick.

UR. Gracious sovereign, please you peruse this paper.   [The King reads.]
DUR. The king's countenance gathers a sprightly blood.
DAW. Good news, believe it.
KING.   Urswick, thine ear.
    Th'ast lodged [1] him?
UR.   Strongly safe, sir.   130
KING. Enough. Is Barley come too?
UR.   No, my lord.
KING. No matter—phew, he's but a running weed,
    At pleasure to be plucked up by the roots!

[1] Thou hast entrapped.

But more of this anon.—I have bethought me.
My lords, for reasons which you shall partake,
It is our pleasure to remove our court
From Westminster to th' Tower. We will lodge
This very night there; give, Lord Chamberlain,
A present order for it.
STAN. [Aside.]   The Tower!—I shall, sir.
KING. Come, my true, best, fast friends.
    These clouds will vanish;   140
The sun will shine at full; the heavens are clearing.   Exeunt. Flourish.

[SCENA SECUNDA.

A room in Huntley's house at Edinburgh.]

Enter Huntley and Daliell.

HUNT. You trifle time, sir.
DAL.   O, my noble lord,
    You conster [2] my griefs to so hard a sense
    That where the text is argument [3] of pity,
    Matter of earnest love, your gloss corrupts it
With too much ill-placed mirth.
HUNT.   Much mirth, Lord Daliell?
    Not so, I vow. Observe me, sprightly gallant.
I know thou art a noble lad, a handsome,
Descended from an honorable ancestry,
Forward and active, dost resolve to wrestle
And ruffle in the world by noble actions   10
For a brave mention to posterity.
I scorn not thy affection to my daughter,
Not I, by good St. Andrew; but this bugbear,
This whoresome [4] tale of honor—honor, Daliell!—
So hourly chats and tattles in mine ear
The piece of royalty that is stitched up
In my Kate's blood [5] that 'tis as dangerous
For thee, young lord, to perch so near an eaglet
As foolish for my gravity to admit it.
I have spoke all at once.

[2] Construe, interpret.
[3] Evidence.   [4] Whoreson, rascally.
[5] Huntley had married Annabella, daughter of James I of Scotland.

Dal.　　　　　　　Sir, with this truth　20
You mix such wormwood that you leave
　no hope
For my disordered palate e'er to relish
A wholesome taste again. Alas, I know,
　sir,
What an unequal distance lies between
Great Huntley's daughter's birth and
　Daliell's fortunes.
She's the king's kinswoman, placed near
　the crown,
A princess of the blood, and I a subject.
Hunt. Right; but a noble subject—put in
　that too.
Dal. I could add more, and in the rightest
　line　　　　　　　　　　　　　29
Derive my pedigree from Adam Mure,
A Scottish knight, whose daughter was
　the mother
To him who first begot the race of
　Jameses
That sway the scepter to this very day.
But kindreds are not ours when once the
　date
Of many years have swallowed up the
　memory
Of their originals; so pasture fields
Neighboring too near the ocean are
　sooped [1] up
And known no more; for, stood I in my
　first
And native [2] greatness, if my princely
　mistress
Voutsafed [3] me not her servant,[4] 'twere
　as good　　　　　　　　　　40
I were reduced to clownery,[5] to nothing,
As to a throne of wonder.
Hunt. [*Aside.*]　Now, by Saint Andrew,
A spark of mettle! [6] A [7] has a brave fire
　in him.
I would a had my daughter, so I knew 't
　not.
But must not be so, must not.—Well,
　young lord,
This will not do yet. If the girl be head-
　strong
And will not hearken to good counsel,
　steal her
And run away with her; dance galliards,[8]
　do,

And frisk about the world to learn the
　languages.
'Twill be a thriving trade; you may set up
　by 't.　　　　　　　　　　50
Dal. With pardon, noble Gordon, this dis-
　dain
Suits not your daughter's virtue or my
　constancy.
Hunt. You are angry.—[*Aside.*] Would a
　would beat me; I deserve it.—
Daliell, thy hand; w' are friends. Follow
　thy courtship.
Take thine own time and speak; if thou
　prevail'st
With passion more than I can with my
　counsel,
She's thine. Nay, she is thine; 'tis a fair
　match,
Free and allowed. I'll only use my
　tongue,
Without a father's power; use thou thine.
Self do, self have. No more words; win
　and wear her.　　　　　　　60
Dal. You bless me; I am now too poor
　in thanks
To pay the debt I owe you.
Hunt.　　　　　　Nay, th' art poor [9]
Enough.—[*Aside.*] I love his spirit in-
　finitely.—
Look ye, she comes. To her now, to her,
　to her!

Enter Katherine and Jane.

Kath. The king commands your presence,
　sir.
Hunt.　The gallant—
This—this—this lord—this servant,
　Kate, of yours—
Desires to be your master.
Kath.　　　　　　I acknowledge him
A worthy friend of mine.
Dal.　　　　　Your humblest creature.
Hunt. [*Aside.*] So, so, the game's afoot!
　I'm in cold hunting;
The hare and hounds are parties.[10]
Dal.　　　　　　Princely lady,　70
How most unworthy I am to employ
My services in honor of your virtues,
How hopeless my desires are to enjoy

---

[1] Supped.
[2] Inherited.
[3] Vouchsafed.
[4] Suitor.
[5] Base birth.
[6] A high-spirited young man.
[7] He.
[8] Lively dances.
[9] Here, as in many other passages throughout the play, lines which have obviously been wrongly divided by the printer have been silently regularized.
[10] Confederates.

Your fair opinion, and much more your
    love,
Are only matter of despair, unless
Your goodness give large warrant to my
    boldness,
My feeble-winged ambition.
HUNT. [*Aside.*]   This is scurvy.[1]
KATH. My lord, I interrupt you not.
HUNT. [*Aside.*]   Indeed!
Now, on my life, she'll court him.—Nay,
    nay, on, sir.
DAL. Oft have I tuned the lesson of my
    sorrows   80
To sweeten discord and enrich your pity;
But all in vain. Here had my comforts
    sunk,
And never risen again to tell a story
Of the despairing lover, had not now,
Even now, the earl your father—
HUNT. [*Aside.*]   A means me, sure.
DAL. After some fit disputes of your con-
    dition,
Your highness and my lowness, given a
    license
Which did not more embolden than en-
    courage
My faulting [2] tongue.
HUNT.   How, how? How's that?
    Embolden?
Encourage? I encourage ye? D'e [3] hear,
    sir?   90
A subtle trick, a quaint one! Will you
    hear, man?
What did I say to you? Come, come, to
    th' point.
KATE. It shall not need, my lord.
HUNT.   Then hear me, Kate.—
Keep you on that hand of her, I on
    this.—
Thou stand'st between a father and a
    suitor,
Both striving for an interest in thy heart.
He courts thee for affection, I for duty;
He as a servant pleads; but, by the
    privilege
Of nature though I might command, my
    care   99
Shall only counsel what it shall not force.
Thou canst but make one choice; the
    ties of marriage
Are tenures not at will, but during life.
Consider whose thou art, and who—a
    princess,

A princess of the royal blood of Scotland,
In the full spring of youth and fresh in
    beauty.
The king that sits upon the throne is
    young,
And yet unmarried, forward in attempts
On any least occasion to endanger
His person; wherefore, Kate, as I am
    confident
Thou dar'st not wrong thy birth and
    education   110
By yielding to a common servile rage
Of female wantonness, so I am confident
Thou wilt proportion all thy thoughts to
    side [4]
Thy equals, if not equal thy superiors.
My Lord of Daliell, young in years, is
    old
In honors, but nor eminent in titles
Or in estate that may support or add to
The expectation of thy fortunes. Settle
Thy will and reason by a strength of
    judgment,
For, in a word, I give thee freedom; take
    it.   120
If equal fates have not ordained to pitch
Thy hopes above my height, let not thy
    passion
Lead thee to shrink mine honor in ob-
    livion.
Thou art thine own; I have done.
DAL.   O, y' are all oracle,
The living stock and root of truth and
    wisdom!
KATH. My worthiest lord and father, the
    indulgence
Of your sweet composition [5] thus com-
    mands
The lowest of obedience. You have
    granted
A liberty so large that I want skill   129
To choose without direction of example,
From which I daily learn by how much
    more
You take off from the roughness of a
    father,
By so much more I am engaged to tender
The duty of a daughter. For respects
Of birth, degrees of title, and advance-
    ment,
I nor admire nor slight them; all my
    studies
Shall ever aim at this perfection only—

_____
[1] Wretched.   [2] Failing.   [3] Do ye.   [4] Match.   [5] Nature.

To live and die so, that you may not
　　blush
In any course of mine to own me yours.
HUNT. Kate, Kate, thou grow'st upon my
　　heart like peace,　　　　　　140
　　Creating every other hour a jubilee.
KATE. To you, my Lord of Daliell, I ad-
　　dress
Some few remaining words. The general
　　fame,
That speaks your merit even in vulgar
　　tongues,
Proclaims it clear; but in the best, a
　　president.[1]
HUNT. Good wench, good girl, i' faith!
KATH.　　　　　　For my part, trust me,
　　I value mine own worth at higher rate
Cause you are pleased to prize it. If the
　　stream
Of your protested service—as you term
　　it—
Run in a constancy more than a compli-
　　ment,　　　　　　150
It shall be my delight that worthy love
Leads you to worthy actions, and these
　　guide ye
Richly to wed an honorable name.[2]
So every virtuous praise in after ages
Shall be your heir, and I in your brave
　　mention
Be chronicled the mother of that issue,
That glorious issue.
HUNT.　　　　O, that I were young again!
　　She'd make me court proud danger, and
　　suck spirit
From reputation.
KATH.　　　　To the present motion[3]
Here's all that I dare answer: when a
　　ripeness　　　　　　160
Of more experience, and some use of
　　time,
Resolves to treat the freedom of my
　　youth
Upon exchange of troths, I shall desire
No surer credit of a match with virtue
Than such as lives in you. Meantime my
　　hopes are
Preserved secure in having you a friend.
DAL. You are a blessed lady, and instruct
　　Ambition not to soar a farther flight
Than in the perfumed air of your soft
　　voice.—

My noble Lord of Huntley, you have
　　lent　　　　　　170
A full extent of bounty to this parley,
And for it shall command your humblest
　　servant.
HUNT. Enough. We are still friends, and
　　will continue
A hearty love.—O, Kate, thou art mine
　　own!—
No more. My Lord of Crawford!

Enter Crawford.

CRAW.　　　　　　　　From the king
I come, my Lord of Huntley, who in
　　council
Requires your present aid.
HUNT.　　　　　　Some weighty business!
CRAW. A secretary from a Duke of York,
　　The second son to the late English
　　Edward,
Concealed I know not where these four-
　　teen years,　　　　　　180
Craves audience from our master; and
　　'tis said
The duke himself is following to the
　　court.
HUNT. Duke upon duke! 'Tis well, 'tis
　　well; here's bustling
For majesty. My lord, I will along with
　　ye.
CRAW. My service, noble lady!
KATH.　　　　　　Please ye walk, sir?
DAL. [*Aside.*] "Times have their changes;
　　sorrow makes men wise;
The sun itself must set as well as rise."[4]
Then, why not I?—Fair madam, I wait
　　on ye.　　　　　　*Exeunt omnes.*

[SCENA TERTIA.

A room in the Tower of London.]

*Enter Durham, Sir Robert Clifford, and
　　　　　　　　Urswick. Lights.*

DUR. You find, Sir Robert Clifford, how
　　securely
King Henry, our great master, doth com-
　　mit
His person to your loyalty; you taste
His bounty and his mercy even in this,
That at a time of night so late, a place
So private as his closet, he is pleased

---

[1] Model, pattern.
[2] Reputation, career.　　　　　　[3] Proposal.

[4] Quotation marks were often used to call attention to sententious passages.

To admit you to his favor. Do not falter
In your discovery; [1] but, as you covet
A liberal grace and pardon for your
    follies,
So labor to deserve it by laying open   10
All plots, all persons that contrive against
    it.
URS. Remember not the witchcraft or the
    magic,
The charms and incantations, which the
    sorceress
Of Burgundy hath cast upon your rea-
    son.
Sir Robert, be your own friend now; dis-
    charge
Your conscience freely. All of such as
    love you
Stand sureties for your honesty and
    truth.
Take heed you do not dally with the
    king;
He is wise as he is gentle.
CLIF.   I am miserable,
If Henry be not merciful.
URS.   The king comes.   20

Enter King Henry.

KING. Clifford!
CLIF. [*Kneeling.*]   Let my weak knees
    rot on the earth,
If I appear as leap'rous [2] in my treach-
    eries
Before your royal eyes, as to mine own
I seem a monster by my breach of truth.
KING. Clifford, stand up; for instance [3] of
    thy safety,
I offer thee my hand.
CLIF.   A sovereign balm
For my bruised soul, I kiss it with a
    greediness.   [*Rises.*]
Sir, you are a just master, but I—
KING.   Tell me,
Is every circumstance thou hast set down
With thine own hand within this paper
    true?   30
Is it a sure intelligence of all
The progress of our enemies' intents
Without corruption?
CLIF.   True, as I wish heaven,
Or my infected honor white again.
KING. We know all, Clifford, fully, since
    this meteor,

This airy apparition, first discradled [4]
From Tournay into Portugal, and thence
Advanced his fiery blaze for adoration
To th' superstitious Irish; since the
    beard   39
Of this wild comet, conjured into France,
Sparkled in antic flames in Charles his
    court,
But shrunk again from thence, and, hid
    in darkness,
Stole out of [5] Flanders, flourishing the
    rags
Of painted power on the shore of Kent.
Whence he was beaten back with shame
    and scorn,
Contempt, and slaughter of some naked
    outlaws.
But tell me what new course now shapes
    Duke Perkin?
CLIF. For Ireland, mighty Henry; so in-
    structed
By Stephen Frion, sometimes [6] secretary
In the French tongue unto your sacred
    excellence,   50
But Perkin's tutor now.
KING.   A subtle villain,
That Frion, Frion. You, my Lord of Dur-
    ham,
Knew well the man.
DUR.   French both in heart and actions.
KING. Some Irish heads work in this mine
    of treason;
Speak [7] 'em.
CLIF.   Not any of the best; your fortune
Hath dulled their spleens. Never had
    counterfeit
Such a confuséd rabble of lost bank-
    routs [8]
For counselors: first Heron, a broken
    mercer;
Then John a Water, sometimes Major [9] of
    Cork;
Sketon, a tailor; and a scrivener   60
Called Astley. And whate'er these list [10]
    to treat of,
Perkin must hearken to; but Frion, cun-
    ning
Above these dull capacities, still prompts
    him

---

[1] Disclosure.   [2] Leprous.   [3] Proof.

[4] Left its cradle, emerged.
[5] Suggested by Struble. Original reads *into*.
[6] Sometime, formerly.
[7] Reveal.   [9] Mayor.
[8] Bankrupts.   [10] Please.

To fly to Scotland to young James the
　Fourth,
And sue for aid to him. This is the latest
Of all their resolutions.

KING.　　　　　　　　　Still more Frion!
Pestilent adder, he will hiss out poison
As dang'rous as infectious. We must
　match 'em.
Clifford, thou hast spoke home; we give
　thee life.
But, Clifford, there are people of our
　own　　　　　　　　　　　　　　　70
Remain behind untold; who are they,
　Clifford?
Name those, and we are friends, and will
　to rest.
'Tis thy last task.

CLIF.　　　　　　O, sir, here I must break
A most unlawful oath to keep a just one.

KING. Well, well, be brief, be brief.

CLIF.　　　　　　　　　The first in rank
Shall be John Ratcliffe, Lord Fitzwater,
　then
Sir Simon Mountford and Sir Thomas
　Thwaites,
With William Dawbney, Cressoner, Ast-
　wood,
Worsley the Dean of Paul's, two other
　friars,　　　　　　　　　　　　79
And Robert Ratcliffe.

KING.　　　　Churchmen are turned devils.
These are the principal?

CLIFF.　　　　　　　One more remains
Unnamed, whom I could willingly forget.

KING. Ha, Clifford! One more?

CLIF.　　　　Great sir, do not hear him;
For, when Sir William Stanley, your lord
　chamberlain,
Shall come into the list, as he is chief,
I shall lose credit with ye; yet this lord
Last named is first against you.

KING.　　　　　　　　Urswick, the light!
View well my face, sirs; is there blood
　left in it?

DUR. You alter strangely, sir.

KING.　　　　　　Alter, Lord Bishop?
Why, Clifford stabbed me, or I dreamed
　a stabbed me.—　　　　　　　　90
Sirrah, it is a custom with the guilty
To think they set their own stains off by
　laying
Aspersions on some nobler than them-
　selves.
Lies wait on treasons, as I find it here.

Thy life again is forfeit; I recall
My word of mercy, for I know thou
　dar'st
Repeat the name no more.

CLIF.　　　　　I dare, and once more,
Upon my knowledge, name Sir William
　Stanley
Both in his counsel and his purse the
　chief　　　　　　　　　　　　　99
Assistant to the feign[é]d Duke of York.

DUR. Most strange!

URS.　　　　　　　Most wicked!

KING.　　　　　　　　Yet again, once more.

CLIF. Sir William Stanley is your secret
　enemy,
And, if time fit, will openly profess it.

KING. Sir William Stanley! Who? Sir
　William Stanley?
My chamberlain, my counselor, the love,
The pleasure of my court, my bosom
　friend,
The charge and the controlment of my
　person,
The keys and secrets of my treasury,
The all of all I am! I am unhappy.　109
Misery of confidence—let me turn traitor
To mine own person, yield my scepter up
To Edward's sister and her bastard duke!

DUR. You lose your constant temper.

KING.　　　　　　　Sir William Stanley!
O, do not blame me; he, 'twas only he,
Who, having rescued me in Bosworth
　Field
From Richard's bloody sword, snatched
　from his head
The kingly crown, and placed it first on
　mine.
He never failed me. What have I de-
　served
To lose this good man's heart, or he his
　own?

URS. The night doth waste. This passion
　ill becomes ye;　　　　　　　　120
Provide against your danger.

KING.　　　　　　　　Let it be so.
Urswick, command straight Stanley to
　his chamber;
'Tis well we are i' th' Tower; set a guard
　on him.
Clifford, to bed; you must lodge here to-
　night.
We'll talk with you tomorrow. My sad
　soul
Divines strange troubles.

DAW. [*Within.*]   Ho! The king, the king!
    I must have entrance.
KING.   Dawbney's voice! Admit him.
    What new combustions huddle next, to
      keep
    Our eyes from rest?—The news?

Enter Dawbney.

DAW.   Ten thousand Cornish,
    Grudging to pay your subsidies, have
      gathered   130
    A head.[1] Led by a blacksmith and a
      lawyer,
    They make for London, and to them is
      joined
    Lord Audley. As they march, their num-
      ber daily
    Increases; they are—
KING.   Rascals!—Talk no more;
    Such are not worthy of my thoughts to-
      night.
    And, if I cannot sleep, I'll wake.—To bed.
    When counsels fail, and there's in man no
      trust,
    Even then an arm from heaven fights for
      the just.   *Exeunt.*

FINIS ACTUS PRIMI.

ACTUS SECUNDUS. SCENA PRIMA.

[*The presence chamber in the palace at*
Edinburgh.]

Enter above, Countess of Crawford, Kath-
erine, Jane, with other Ladies.

COUN. Come, ladies, here's a solemn prep-
    aration
    For entertainment of this English prince;
    The king intends grace more than
      ordinary.
    'Twere pity now if a should prove a
      counterfeit.
KATH. Bless the young man, our nation
      would be laughed at
    For honest [2] souls through Christendom.
      My father
    Hath a weak stomach to the business,
      madam,
    But that the king must not be crossed.
COUN.   A brings
    A goodly troop, they say, of gallants with
      him,

     [1] Armed force.   [2] Trusting, simple.

    But very modest people, for they strive
      not   10
    To fame [3] their names too much; their
      godfathers
    May be beholding [4] to them, but their
      fathers
    Scarce owe them thanks. They are
      disguiséd princes,
    Brought up, it seems, to honest trades.
      No matter,
    They will break forth in season.
JANE.   Or break out; [5]
    For most of 'em are broken, by report.—
    The king!
KATH.   Let us observe 'em and be silent.
                    Flourish.

Enter [below] King James, Huntley, Craw-
ford, and Daliell [, with other Noblemen].

K. JA. The right of kings, my lords, ex-
    tends not only
    To the safe conservation of their own,
    But also to the aid of such allies   20
    As change of time and state hath often-
      times
    Hurled down from careful crowns to
      undergo
    An exercise of sufferance in both for-
      tunes.
    So English Richard, surnamed Cœur-de-
      Lion,
    So Robert Bruce, our royal ancestor,
    Forced by the trial of the wrongs they
      felt,
    Both sought and found supplies from
      foreign kings
    To repossess their own. Then grudge
      not,[6] lords,
    A much distresséd prince. King Charles
      of France
    And Maximilian of Bohemia both   30
    Have ratified his credit by their letters.
    Shall we then be distrustful? No, com-
      passion
    Is one rich jewel that shines in our
      crown,
    And we will have it shine there.
HUNT.   Do your will, sir.
K. JA. The young duke is at hand. Daliell,
    from us
    First greet him, and conduct him on;
      then Crawford

     [3] Boast.   [5] *I.e.,* rebel.
     [4] Beholden.   [6] Do not begrudge aid to.

Shall meet him next; and Huntley, last
  of all,
Present him to our arms. Sound sprightly
  music,
Whilst majesty encounters majesty.
                              Hautboys.

*Daliell goes out, brings in Perkin at the
door, where Crawford entertains him,
and from Crawford, Huntley salutes him
and presents him to the King. They
embrace; Perkin in state retires some
few paces back, during which ceremony
the noblemen slightly salute Frion,
Heron, a mercer, Sketon, a tailor,
Astley, a scrivener, with John a Water,*[1]
*all Perkin's followers. Salutations
                        ended, cease music.*

WAR. Most high, most mighty king! That
  now there stands   40
Before your eyes, in presence of your
  peers,
A subject of the rarest kind of pity
That hath in any age touched noble
  hearts,
The vulgar [2] story of a prince's ruin
Hath made it too apparent. Europe
  knows,
And all the western world, what per-
  secution
Hath raged in malice against us, sole
  heir
To the great throne of old Plantagenets.
How from our nursery we have been
  hurried
Unto the sanctuary, from the sanctu-
  ary   50
Forced to the prison, from the prison
  haled
By cruel hands to the tormentor's fury
Is registered already in the volume
Of all men's tongues, whose true rela-
  tion draws
Compassion, melted into weeping eyes
And bleeding souls. But our misfortunes
  since
Have ranged a larger progress through
  strange lands,
Protected in our innocence by heaven.
Edward the Fift, our brother, in his
  tragedy
Quenched their hot thirst of blood,
  whose hire to murther   60

Paid them their wages of despair and
  horror.
The softness of my childhood smiled
  upon
The roughness of their task, and robbed
  them farther
Of hearts to dare, or hands to execute.
Great king, they spared my life, the
  butchers spared it,
Returned the tyrant, my unnatural
  uncle,
A truth [3] of my despatch. I was con-
  veyed
With secrecy and speed to Tournay,
  fostered
By obscure means, taught to unlearn
  myself.   69
But, as I grew in years, I grew in sense
Of fear and of disdain—fear of the
  tyrant
Whose power swayed the throne then,
  when disdain
Of living so unknown, in such a servile
And abject lowness, prompted me to
  thoughts
Of recollecting who I was. I shook off
My bondage, and made haste to let my
  aunt
Of Burgundy acknowledge me her kins-
  man,
Heir to the crown of England, snatched
  by Henry
From Richard's head—a thing scarce
  known i' th' world.
K. JA. My lord, it stands not with your
  counsel now   80
To fly upon invectives. If you can
Make this apparent what you have
  discoursed
In every circumstance, we will not
  study
An answer, but are ready in your cause.
WAR. You are a wise and just king, by the
  powers
Above reserved beyond all other aids
To plant me in mine own inheritance,
To marry these two kingdoms in a love
Never to be divorced while time is
  time.
As for the manner, first of my escape, 90
Of my conveyance next, of my life since,
The means and persons who were instru-
  ments,

---

[1] Original reads *Watring*.   [2] Common.   [3] Pledge.

Great sir, 'tis fit I overpass in silence,
Reserving the relation to the secrecy
Of your own princely ear, since it concerns
Some great ones living yet, and others dead,
Whose issue might be questioned. For your bounty,
Royal magnificence to him that seeks it,
We vow hereafter to demean ourself
As if we were your own and natural brother,   100
Omitting no occasion in our person
To express a gratitude beyond example.
K. JA. He must be more than subject who can utter
The language of a king, and such is thine.
Take this for answer: be whate'er thou art,
Thou never shalt repent that thou hast put
Thy cause and person into my protection.
Cousin of York, thus once more we embrace thee.
Welcome to James of Scotland! For thy safety,
Know such as love thee not shall never wrong thee.   110
Come, we will taste awhile our court delights,
Dream hence afflictions past, and then proceed
To high attempts of honor. On, lead on!
Both thou and thine are ours, and we will guard ye.
Lead on! *Exeunt. Manent* [1] *Ladies above.*
COUN.   I have not seen a gentleman
Of a more brave aspect or goodlier carriage;
His fortunes move not him.—Madam, y' are passionate. [2]
KATH. Beshrew me, [3] but his words have touched me home,
As if his cause concerned me. I should pity him   119
If a should prove another than he seems.

Enter Crawford.

CRAW. Ladies, the king commands your presence instantly
For entertainment of the duke.

KATH.   The duke
Must then be entertained, the king obeyed;
It is our duty.
COUN.   We will all wait on him.
                                    Exeunt.

[SCENA SECUNDA.

A room in the Tower of London.]

Flourish.   Enter King Henry [and his Train]; Oxford, Durham, Surrey.

KING. Have ye condemned my chamberlain?
DUR.   His treasons
Condemned him, sir, which were as clear and manifest
As foul and dangerous. Besides, the guilt
Of his conspiracy pressed him so nearly [4]
That it drew from him free confession
Without an importunity.
KING.   O, lord bishop,
This argued shame and sorrow for his folly,
And must not stand in evidence against
Our mercy and the softness of our nature.
The rigor and extremity of law   10
Is sometimes too-too bitter, but we carry
A chancery [5] of pity in our bosom.
I hope we may reprieve him from the sentence
Of death; I hope we may.
DUR.   You may, you may,
And so persuade your subjects that the title
Of York is better, nay, more just and lawful,
Than yours of Lancaster! So Stanley holds—
Which if it be not treason in the highest,
Then we are traitors all, perjured and false,
Who have took oath to Henry and the justice   20
Of Henry's title: Oxford, Surrey, Dawbney,
With all your other peers of state and church,

[4] Closely.
[5] A chancellorship, whose holder could lighten sentences.

[1] Remain.
[2] Compassionate, moved.
[3] A mild oath.

Forsworn, and Stanley true alone to
heaven
And England's lawful heir!

Ox.   By Vere's old honors,
I'll cut his throat dares speak it.

Sur.   'Tis a quarrel
To engage a soul in.

King.   What a coil [1] is here
To keep my gratitude sincere and per-
fect!
Stanley was once my friend, and came
in time
To save my life; yet, to say truth, my
lords,
The man stayed long enough t' endan-
ger it.   30
But I could see no more into his heart
Than what his outward actions did
present,
And for 'em have rewarded 'em so fully
As that there wanted nothing in our
gift
To gratify his merit, as I thought,
Unless I should divide my crown with
him,
And give him half—though now I well
perceive
'Twould scarce have served his turn
without the whole.
But I am charitable, lords; let justice
Proceed in execution, whiles I mourn   40
The loss of one whom I esteemed a
friend.

Dur. Sir, he is coming this way.

King.   If a speak to me,
I could deny him nothing; to prevent it,
I must withdraw. Pray, lords, commend
my favors
To his last peace, which I with him will
pray for.
That done, it doth concern us to consult
Of other following troubles.
          Exeunt [King Henry with his Train].

Ox.   I am glad
He's gone. Upon my life, he would have
pardoned
The traitor, had a seen him.

Sur.   'Tis a king
Composed of gentleness.

Dur.   Rare and unheard of!   50
But every man is nearest to [2] himself;
And that the king observes. 'Tis fit a
should.

[1] Tumult.   [2] Closest to most concerned for.

Enter Stanley, Executioner, Urswick, and
Dawbney.

Stan. May I not speak with Clifford ere
I shake
This piece of frailty off?

Daw.   You shall; he's sent for.

Stan. I must not see the king?

Dur.   From him, Sir William,
These lords and I am sent; he bade us
say
That he commends his mercy to your
thoughts,
Wishing the laws of England could
remit
The forfeit of your life as willingly
As he would in the sweetness of his
nature   60
Forget your trespass. But howe'er your
body
Fall into dust, he vows, the king him-
self
Doth vow to keep a requiem for your
soul,
As for a friend close treasured in his
bosom.

Ox. Without remembrance of your errors
past,
I come to take my leave, and wish you
heaven.

Sur. And I. Good angels guard ye!

Stan.   O, the king,
Next to my soul, shall be the nearest
subject
Of my last prayers. My grave Lord of
Durham,
My Lords of Oxford, Surrey, Dawbney,
all,   70
Accept from a poor dying man a fare-
well.
I was as you are, once—great, and stood
hopeful
Of many flourishing years; but fate and
time
Have wheeled about to turn me into
nothing.

Enter Clifford.

Daw. Sir Robert Clifford comes—the
man, Sir William,
You so desire to speak with.

Dur.   Mark their meeting.

Clif. Sir William Stanley, I am glad your
conscience

Before your end hath emptied every
　　burthen
Which charged it, as that [1] you can
　　clearly witness
How far I have proceeded in a duty　80
That both concerned my truth and the
　　state's safety.
STAN. Mercy, how dear is life to such as
　　hug it!
Come hither; by this token think on me!
Makes a cross on Clifford's face with his
　　　　　　　　　　　　　finger.
CLIF. This token? What? I am abused!
STAN.　　　　　　　　　　You are not.
　I wet upon your cheeks a holy sign,
　The cross, the Christian's badge, the
　　　traitor's infamy.
　Wear, Clifford, to thy grave this painted
　　　emblem;
　Water shall never wash it off; all eyes
　That gaze upon thy face shall read there
　　　written　89
　A state-informer's character, more ugly
　Stamped on a noble name than on a
　　　base.
　The heavens forgive thee! Pray, my
　　　lords, no change [2]
　Of words; this man and I have used too
　　　many.
CLIF. Shall I be disgraced
　Without reply?
DUR.　　　　　Give losers leave to talk;
　His loss is irrecoverable.
STAN.　　　　　　　　　Once more,
　To all a long farewell! The best of great-
　　　ness
　Preserve the king! My next suit is, my
　　　lords,
　To be remembered to my noble brother,
　Derby, my much-grieved brother. O,
　　　persuade him　100
　That I shall stand no blemish to his
　　　house
　In chronicles writ in another age.
　My heart doth bleed for him and for his
　　　sighs.
　Tell him, he must not think the style [3]
　　　of Derby,
　Nor being husband to King Henry's
　　　mother,
　The league with peers, the smiles of for-
　　　tune, can
　Secure his peace above the state of man.

I take my leave, to travel to my dust.
　"Subjects deserve their deaths whose
　　　kings are just."—
　[*To Urswick.*] Come, confessor.—[*To
　　　Executioner.*] On with thy ax, friend,
　　　on!　110
Exeunt [Urswick, Stanley, and Executioner].
CLIF. Was I called hither by a traitor's
　　breath
　To be upbraided? Lords, the king shall
　　know it.

Enter King Henry with a white staff. [4]

KING. The king doth know it, sir; the
　　king hath heard
　What he or you could say. We have
　　given credit
　To every point of Clifford's information,
　The only evidence gainst Stanley's
　　head.
　A dies for 't; are you pleased?
CLIF.　　　　　　　I pleased, my lord!
KING. No echoes. For your service we
　　dismiss
　Your more attendance on the court.
　　Take ease,
　And live at home; but, as you love your
　　life,　120
　Stir not from London without leave
　　from us.
　We'll think on your reward. Away!
CLIF.　　　　　　I go, sir. *Exit Clifford.*
KING. Die all our griefs with Stanley!
　　Take this staff
　Of office, Dawbney; henceforth be our
　　chamberlain.
DAW. I am your humblest servant.
KING.　　　　　　　　We are followed
　By enemies at home, that will not cease
　To seek their own confusion. 'Tis most
　　true
　The Cornish under Audley are marched
　　on
　As far as Winchester. But let them
　　come;
　Our forces are in readiness; we'll catch
　　'em　130
　In their own toils.
DAW.　　　　Your army, being mustered,
　Consists in all, of horse and foot, at least
　In number six-and-twenty thousand—
　　men

---

[1] So that.　　　[2] Exchange.　　　[3] Title.

[4] Emblematic of the Lord Chamberlain's office.

Daring and able, resolute to fight,
And loyal in their truths.
KING.　　　　　We know it, Dawbney.
For them we order thus: Oxford in chief,
Assisted by bold Essex and the Earl
Of Suffolk, shall lead on the first battalia.[1] —
Be that your charge.
Ox.　　　　I humbly thank your majesty.
KING. The next division we assign to
Dawbney.　　　　　　　　　　　140
These must be men of action, for on those
The fortune of our fortunes must rely.
The last and main ourself commands in person,
As ready to restore the fight at all times
As to consummate an assuréd victory.
DAW. The king is still oraculous.[2]
KING.　　　　　　　　But, Surrey,
We have employment of more toil for thee,
For our intelligence comes swiftly to us
That James of Scotland late hath entertained
Perkin the counterfeit with more than common　　　　　　　　　　150
Grace and respect, nay, courts him with rare favors.
The Scot is young and forward; we must look for
A sudden storm to England from the north,
Which to withstand, Durham shall post to Norham
To fortify the castle and secure
The frontiers against an invasion there.
Surrey shall follow soon, with such an army
As may relieve the bishop and encounter
On all occasions the death-daring Scots.
You know your charges all; 'tis now a time　　　　　　　　　　160
To execute, not talk. Heaven is our guard still.
War must breed peace; such is the fate of kings.　　　　　　　*Exeunt.*

[1] Division.　　　　　[2] Oracular, wise.

[SCENA TERTIA.

A room in the palace at Edinburgh.]

Enter Crawford and Daliell.

CRAW. 'Tis more than strange; my reason cannot answer
Such argument of fine imposture, couched
In witchcraft of persuasion, that it fashions
Impossibilities, as if appearance
Could cozen truth itself. This dukeling mushroom
Hath doubtless charmed the king.
DAL.　　　　　　　A courts the ladies
As if his strength of language chained attention
By power of prerogative.
CRAW.　　　　　　　It madded
My very soul to hear our master's motion.　　　　　　　　　　9
What surety both of amity and honor
Must of necessity ensue upon
A match betwixt some noble of our nation
And this brave prince, forsooth!
DAL.　　　　　　'Twill prove too fatal;
Wise Huntley fears the threat'ning. Bless the lady
From such a ruin.
CRAW.　　　　　How the council privy
Of this young Phaëton do screw their faces
Into a gravity their trades, good people,
Were never guilty of! The meanest of 'em
Dreams of at least an office in the state.
DAL. Sure, not the hangman's; 'tis bespoke already　　　　　　　　　　20
For service to their rogueships.—Silence!

Enter King James and Huntley.

K. JA.　　　　　　　　Do not
Argue against our will; we have descended
Somewhat—as we may term it—too familiarly
From justice of our birthright to examine
The force of your allegiance—sir, we have—
But find it short of duty.
HUNT.　　　　　　　Break my heart,
Do, do, king! Have my services, my loyalty—

Heaven knows untainted ever—drawn
  upon me
Contempt now in mine age, when I but
  wanted [1]   29
A minute of a peace not to be troubled,
My last, my long one? Let me be a
  dotard,
A bedlam,[2] a poor sot,[3] or what you
  please
To have me, so you will not stain your
  blood,
Your own blood, royal sir, though mixed
  with mine,
By marriage of this girl to a straggler!
Take, take my head, sir; whilst my
  tongue can wag,
It cannot name him other.

K. JA.   Kings are counterfeits
In your repute, grave oracle, not pres-
  ently [4]
Set on their thrones with scepters in their
  fists.
But use your own detraction; [5] 'tis our
  pleasure   40
To give our cousin York for wife our
  kinswoman,
The Lady Katherine. Instinct of sover-
  eignty
Designs the honor, though her peevish
  father
Usurps our resolution.[6]

HUNT.   O, 'tis well,
Exceeding well. I never was ambitious
Of using congees to my daughter-queen—
A queen? Perhaps a quean! Forgive me,
  Daliell,
Thou honorable gentleman. None here
Dare speak one word of comfort?

DAL.   Cruel misery!
CRAW. The lady, gracious prince, maybe
  hath settled   50
Affection on some former choice.

DAL.   Enforcement
Would prove but tyranny.

HUNT.   I thank 'e heartily.
Let any yeoman of our nation challenge
An interest in the girl, then the king
May add a jointure of ascent in titles,
Worthy a free consent; now a pulls down
What old desert hath builded.

---

[1] Lacked.   [3] Fool.
[2] Lunatic.   [4] I.e., if not actually.
[5] I.e., speak to your own injury.
[6] Power of decision.

K. JA.   Cease persuasions.
I violate no pawns of faiths, intrude
  not
On private loves. That I have played
  the orator
For kingly York to virtuous Kate, her
  grant   60
Can justify, referring her contents
To our provision.[7] The Welsh Harry [8]
  henceforth
Shall therefore know, and tremble to
  acknowledge,
That not the painted idol of his policy
Shall fright the lawful owner from a
  kingdom.
We are resolved.

HUNT.   Some of thy subjects' hearts,
King James, will bleed for this.

K. JA.   Then shall their bloods
Be nobly spent. No more disputes; he is
  not
Our friend who contradicts us.

HUNT.   Farewell, daughter!
My care by one is lessened: thank the
  king for 't.[9]   70
I and my griefs will dance now.—Look,
  lords, look;
Here's hand in hand already!

K. JA.   Peace, old frenzy!—

*Enter Warbeck, leading Katherine, com-
  plimenting; Countess of Crawford, Jane,
  Frion, Major of Cork, Astley, Heron,
              and Sketon.*

How like a king a looks! Lords, but observe
The confidence of his aspect. Dross
  cannot
Cleave to so pure a metal. Royal
  youth!
Plantagenet undoubted!

HUNT. [*Aside.*]   Ho, brave lady!
But no Plantagenet, by'r Lady, yet,
By red rose or by white.

WAR.   An union this way
Settles possession in a monarchy
Established rightly, as is my inherit-
  ance.   80
Acknowledge me but sovereign of this
  kingdom,

---

[7] Oversight.
[8] Henry VII's grandfather was a **Welshman**.
[9] Original has *Enter* in the margin.

Your heart, fair princess, and the hand
  of providence
Shall crown you queen of me and my
  best fortunes.
KATH. Where my obedience is, my lord, a
  duty,
Love owes true service.
WAR.   Shall I—
K. JA.   Cousin, yes,
Enjoy her; from my hand accept your
  bride;   [He joins their hands.]
And may they live at enmity with com-
  fort
Who grieve at such an equal pledge of
  troths!
Y' are the prince's wife now.
KATH.   By your gift, sir.
WAR. Thus I take seizure of mine own.
KATH.   I miss yet 90
A father's blessing. Let me find it.
  [Kneels.] Humbly
Upon my knees I seek it.
HUNT.   I am Huntley,
Old Alexander Gordon, a plain subject,
Nor more nor less; and, lady, if you
  wish for
A blessing, you must bend your knees to
  heaven,
For heaven did give me you. Alas, alas,
What would you have me say? May all
  the happiness
My prayers ever sued to fall upon
  you
Preserve you in your virtues!—Prithee,
  Daliell,
Come with me, for I feel thy griefs as
  full   100
As mine. Let's steal away and cry
  together.
DAL. My hopes are in their ruins.
            Exeunt Huntley and Daliell.
K. JA.   Good, kind Huntley
Is overjoyed. A fit solemnity
Shall perfit [1] these delights.—Crawford,
  attend
Our order for the preparation.
Exeunt. Manent Frion, Major, Astley,
          Heron, et Sketon.
FRI. Now, worthy gentlemen, have I not
  followed
My undertakings with success? Here's
  entrance
Into a certainty above a hope.

[1] Perfect.

HER. Hopes are but hopes; I was ever
confident, when I traded but in rem- [110
nants, that my stars had reserved me to
the title of a viscount at least. Honor is
honor, though cut out of any stuffs.

SKE. My brother Heron hath right
wisely delivered his opinion; for he that
threads his needle with the sharp eyes of
industry shall in time go through-stitch [2]
with the new suit of preferment.

AST. Spoken to the purpose, my fine-
witted brother Sketon; for as no in- [120
denture but has its counterpawn,[3] no
noverint [4] but his [5] condition or defeasance;
so no right but may have claim, no claim
but may have possession, any act of parliament to the contrary notwithstanding.

FRI. You are all read in mysteries of state,
  And quick of apprehension, deep in judg-
    ment,
Active in resolution; and 'tis pity
Such counsel should lie buried in obscurity.
But why, in such a time and cause of
  triumph, 130
Stands the judicious Major of Cork so
  silent?
Believe it, sir, as English Richard prospers,
You must not miss employment of high
  nature.
MAJ. If men may be credited in their
mortality, which I dare not peremptorily
aver but they may or not be, presumptions
by this marriage are then, in sooth, of
fruitful expectation. Or else I must not
justify other men's belief more than other
should rely on mine.   140
FRI. Pith of experience! Those that have
  borne office
Weigh every word before it can drop
  from them.
But, noble counselors, since now the
  present
Requires in point of honor—pray, mistake not—
Some service to our lord, 'tis fit the Scots
Should not engross all glory to themselves
At this so grand and eminent solemnity.

[2] Finish thoroughly.
[3] Indentures were torn in two, each person
keeping half.
[4] Writ, deed, bond.   [5] Its.

Ske. The Scots? The motion is defied.
I had rather, for my part, without trial of
my country, suffer persecution under   [150
the pressing iron of reproach, or let my skin
be punched [1] full of oilet-holes [2] with the
bodkin of derision.

Ast. I will sooner lose both my ears on
the pillory of forgery.

Her. Let me first live a bankrout, and
die in the lousy Hole [3] of hunger, without
compounding for sixpence in the pound.

Maj. If men fail not in their expecta-
tions, there may be spirits also that   [160
disgest [4] no rude affronts, Master Secretary Frion, or I am cozened—which is
possible, I grant.

Fri. Resolved like men of knowledge! At
this feast then,
In honor of the bride, the Scots, I
    know,
Will in some show, some masque, or
    some device
Prefer their duties. Now it were un-
    comely
That we be found less forward for our
    prince
Than they are for their lady; and by how
    much   169
We outshine them in persons of account,
By so much more will our endeavors
    meet with
A livelier applause. Great emperors
Have for their recreations undertook
Such kind of pastimes; as for the con-
    ceit, [5]
Refer it to my study. The performance
You all shall share a thanks in. 'Twill
    be grateful.

Her. The motion is allowed. I have
stole to a dancing school when I was a
prentice.

Ast. There have been Irish hub-   [180
bubs, [6] when I have made one too.

Ske. For fashioning of shapes and cutting a cross caper, [7] turn me off to my trade
again.

Maj. Surely there is, if I be not deceived, a kind of gravity in merriment, as
there is, or perhaps ought to be, respect of

persons in the quality of carriage, which is,
as it is construed, either so or so.
                              [Demonstrates.]
Fri. Still you come home to me; upon
    occasion   190
I find you relish courtship [8] with discre-
    tion,
And such are fit for statesmen of your
    merits.
Pray 'e wait [9] the prince, and in his ear
    acquaint him
With this design. I'll follow and di-
    rect 'e.   Exeunt; mane[t] Frion.
O, the toil
Of humoring this abject scum of man-
    kind,
Muddy-brained peasants! Princes feel
    a misery
Beyond impartial sufferance, whose ex-
    tremes
Must yield to such abettors. Yet [10] our
    tide
Runs smoothly without adverse winds.
    Run on!   200
Flow to a full sea! Time alone debates
Quarrels forewritten in the book of fates.
                              Exit.

ACTUS TERTIUS. SCENA PRIMA.

[The presence chamber at Westminster.]

Enter King Henry, his gorget [11] on, his sword,
    plume of feathers, leading staff; [12] and
                              Urswick.

King. How runs the time of day?
Urs.   Past ten, my lord.
King. A bloody hour will it prove to some,
Whose disobedience, like the sons o' th'
    Earth, [13]
Throw a defiance gainst the face of
    heaven.
Oxford, with Essex and stout De la Pole,
Have quieted the Londoners, I hope,
And set them safe from fear.
Urs.   They are all silent.
King. From their own battlements they
    may behold
Saint George's Fields o'erspread with
    arméd men,

---

[1] Suggested by Gifford-Dyce. Original reads
pincht.   [2] Eyelet-holes.
[3] One of the worst cells in the Counter Prison.
[4] Digest.   [6] Celebrations.
[5] Idea.   [7] A movement in dancing.

[8] Court behavior.   [9] Await.   [10] Thus far.
[11] A piece of armor for the throat.
[12] A baton borne by a commanding officer.
[13] I.e., the Titans.

Amongst whom our own royal standard
  threatens   10
Confusion to opposers. We must learn
To practice war again in time of peace,
Or lay our crown before our subjects'
  feet—
Ha, Urswick, must we not?

URS.   The powers who seated
King Henry on his lawful throne will ever
Rise up in his defense.

KING.   Rage shall not fright
The bosom of our confidence. In Kent
Our Cornish rebels, cozened of their
  hopes,
Met brave resistance by that country's [1]
  earl,
George Abergeny,[2] Cobham, Poynings,
  Guilford,   20
And other loyal hearts; now, if Black-
  heath
Must be reserved the fatal tomb to
  swallow
Such stiff-necked abjects as with weary
  marches
Have traveled from their homes, their
  wives and children,
To pay, instead of subsidies, their lives,
We may continue sovereign. Yet, Urs-
  wick,
We'll not abate one penny what in parlia-
  ment
Hath freely been contributed; we must
  not.
Money gives soul to action. Our competi-
  tor,
The Flemish counterfeit, with James of
  Scotland,   30
Will prove what courage need and want
  can nourish,
Without the food of fit supplies. But,
  Urswick,
I have a charm in secret that shall loose
The witchcraft wherewith young King
  James is bound,
And free it at my pleasure without blood-
  shed.

URS. Your majesty's a wise king, sent from
  heaven,
Protector of the just.

KING.   Let dinner cheerfully
Be served in; this day of the week is
  ours,
Our day of providence; for Saturday

Yet never failed in all my undertak-
  ings   40
To yield me rest at night. (*A flourish.*)
  What means this warning?
Good fate, speak peace to Henry!

Enter Dawbney, Oxford, and Attendants.

DAW.   Live the king,
Triumphant in the ruin of his enemies!

OX. The head of strong rebellion is cut off,
The body hewed in pieces.

KING.   Dawbney, Oxford,
Minions to noblest fortunes, how yet
  stands
The comfort of your wishes?

DAW.   Briefly thus:
The Cornish under Audley, disappointed
Of flattered expectation, from the Kent-
  ish
(Your majesty's right trusty liegemen)
  flew,   50
Feathered by rage and heartened by
  presumption,
To take the field even at your palace
  gates,
And face you in your chamber royal.
  Arrogance
Improved their ignorance, for they, sup-
  posing,
Misled by rumor, that the day of battle
Should fall on Monday, rather braved
  your forces
Than doubted [3] any onset; yet this morn-
  ing,
When in the dawning I by your direc-
  tion
Strove to get Dartford Strand bridge,
  there I found
Such a resistance as might show what
  strength   60
Could make. Here arrows hailed in
  showers upon us
A full yard long at least, but we pre-
  vailed.
My Lord of Oxford, with his fellow peers
Environing the hill, fell fiercely on them
On the one side, I on the other, till, great
  sir
(Pardon the oversight), eager of doing
Some memorable act, I was engaged
Almost a prisoner, but was freed as soon
As sensible of danger. Now the fight

[1] County's.   [2] Abergavenny.   [3] Feared.

Began in heat, which, quenched in the blood of   70
Two thousand rebels, and as many more
Reserved to try your mercy, have returned
A victory with safety.

KING.   Have we lost
An equal number with them?

Ox.   In the total
Scarcely four hundred. Audley, Flammock, Joseph,
The ringleaders of this commotion,
Railed [1] in ropes, fit ornaments for traitors,
Wait your determinations.

KING.   We must pay
Our thanks where they are only due. O, lords,   79
Here is no victory, nor shall our people
Conceive that we can triumph in their falls.
Alas, poor souls! Let such as are escaped
Steal to the country back without pursuit.
There's not a drop of blood spilt but hath drawn
As much of mine. Their swords could have wrought wonders
On their king's part, who faintly were unsheathed
Against their prince, but wounded their own breasts.
Lords, we are debtors to your care; our payment
Shall be both sure and fitting your deserts.

DAW. Sir, will you please to see those rebels, heads   90
Of this wild monster-multitude?

KING.   Dear friend,
My faithful Dawbney, no. On them our justice
Must frown in terror; I will not vouchsafe
An eye of pity to them. Let false Audley
Be drawn upon an hurdle from the Newgate
To Tower Hill in his own coat of arms,
Painted on paper, with the arms reversed,
Defaced, and torn; there let him lose his head.
The lawyer and the blacksmith shall be hanged,

Quartered, their quarters into Cornwall sent   100
Examples to the rest, whom we are pleased
To pardon and dismiss from further quest.[2]
My Lord of Oxford, see it done.

Ox.   I shall, sir.

KING. Urswick!

URS.   My lord?

KING.   To Dinham, our high treasurer,
Say we command commissions be new granted
For the collection of our subsidies
Through all the west, and that speedily.
Lords, we acknowledge our engagements due
For your most constant services.

DAW.   Your soldiers 109
Have manfully and faithfully acquitted
Their several duties.

KING.   For it we will throw
A largess free amongst them, which shall hearten
And cherish up [3] their loyalties. More yet
Remains of like employment; not a man
Can be dismissed till enemies abroad,
More dangerous than these at home, have felt
The puissance of our arms. O happy kings
Whose thrones are raiséd in their subjects' hearts!   *Exeunt omnes.*

[SCENA SECUNDA.

A room in the palace at Edinburgh.]

Enter Huntley and Daliell.

HUNT. Now, sir, a modest [4] word with you, sad gentleman.
Is not this fine, I trow,[5] to see the gambolds,[6]
To hear the jigs,[7] observe the frisks, b' enchanted
With the rare discord of bells, pipes, and tabors,
Hotchpotch of Scotch and Irish twingle-twangles,

[1] Tied in a row.

[2] Inquest, inquiry.   [4] Quiet.
[3] Cheer, encourage.
[5] Here merely an expression of contempt.
[6] Gambols.   [7] Lively songs or ballads.

Like to so many quiristers [1] of Bedlam
Trolling a catch! [2] The feasts, the manly
    stomachs,
The healths in usquebaugh [3] and bonny-
    clabber, [4]
The ale in dishes never fetched from
    China,
The hundred thousand knacks [5] not to
    be spoken of—   10
And all this for King Oberon and Queen
    Mab—
Should put a soul int'e. Look 'e, good
    man,
How youthful I am grown. But, by
    your leave,
This new queen-bride must henceforth
    be no more
My daughter; no, bur [6] Lady, 'tis unfit.
And yet you see how I do bear this
    change,
Methinks courageously, then shake off
    care
In such a time of jollity.
DAL.   Alas, sir,
How can you cast a mist upon your
    griefs,
Which, howsoe'er you shadow, but pre-
    sent   20
To any judging eye the perfect sub-
    stance,
Of which mine are but counterfeits?
HUNT.   Foh, Daliell!
Thou interrupts the part I bear in
    music
To this rare bridal feast. Let us be
    merry,
Whilst flattering calms secure us against
    storms.
Tempests, when they begin to roar, put
    out
The light of peace, and cloud the sun's
    bright eye
In darkness of despair; yet we are safe.
DAL. I wish you could as easily forget
The justice of your sorrows as my
    hopes   30
Can yield to destiny.
HUNT.   Pish! Then I see
Thou dost not know the flexible condi-
    tion

Of my apt nature. I can laugh, laugh
    heartily,
When the gout cramps my joints; let
    but the stone
Stop in my bladder, I am straight a-
    singing;
The quartan-fever, shrinking every limb,
Sets me a-capering straight. Do but
    betray me,
And bind me a friend ever. What! I
    trust
The losing of a daughter, though I
    doted
On every hair that grew to trim her
    head,   40
Admits not any pain like one of these.
Come, th' art deceived in me. Give me
    a blow,
A sound blow on the face, I'll thank thee
    for 't.
I love my wrongs. Still th' art deceived
    in me.
DAL. Deceived? O, noble Huntley, my
    few years
Have learnt experience of too ripe an
    age
To forfeit fit credulity. Forgive
My rudeness; I am bold.
HUNT.   Forgive me first
A madness of ambition; by example
Teach me humility, for patience scorns
Lectures, which schoolmen use to read
    to boys   51
Uncapable of injuries. Though old,
I could grow tough in fury, and disclaim
Allegiance to my king, could fall at odds
With all my fellow peers that durst not
    stand
Defendants gainst the rape done on
    mine honor.
But kings are earthly gods; there is no
    meddling
With their anointed bodies; for their
    actions
They only are accountable to heaven.
Yet in the puzzle of my troubled brain
One antidote's reserved against the
    poison   61
Of my distractions; 'tis in thee t' apply
    it.
DAL. Name it; O, name it quickly, sir!
HUNT.   A pardon
For my most foolish slighting thy de-
    serts;

---

[1] Choristers.   [3] Whiskey.
[2] Singing a round song.
[4] Coagulated sour milk.   [6] By our.
[5] Knickknacks, trifles.

I have culled out this time to beg it.
Prithee,
Be gentle. Had I been so, thou hadst
owned
A happy bride, but now a castaway,
And never child of mine more.

DAL.   Say not so, sir;
It is not fault in her.

HUNT.   The world would prate
How she was handsome; young I know
     she was,   70
Tender and sweet in her obedience—
But lost now. What a bankrupt am I
     made
Of [1] a full stock of blessings! Must I
     hope
A mercy from thy heart?

DAL.   A love, a service,
A friendship to posterity.[2]

HUNT.   Good angels
Reward thy charity! I have no more
But prayers left me now.

DAL.   I'll lend you mirth, sir,
If you will be in consort.[3]

HUNT.   Thank ye truly.
I must; yes, yes, I must. Here's yet
     some ease,
A partner in affliction; look not angry. 80

DAL. Good, noble sir!   [Flourish.]

HUNT.   O, hark! We may be quiet;
The king and all the others come, a
     meeting
Of gaudy sights. This day's the last of
     revels;
Tomorrow sounds of war; then new ex-
     change.
Fiddles must turn to swords. Unhappy
     marriage!

*Flourish. Enter King James; Warbeck
leading Katherine; Crawford, Countess,
and Jane [, with other Ladies]. Huntley
and Daliell fall among them.*

K. JA. Cousin of York, you and your
     princely bride
Have liberally enjoyed such soft de-
lights
As a new-married couple could forethink;
Nor has our bounty shortened [4] expecta-
tion.
But after all those pleasures of repose, 90

Or amorous safety, we must rouse the
     ease
Of dalliance with achievements of more
     glory
Than sloth and sleep can furnish. Yet,
     for farewell,
Gladly we entertain a truce with time
To grace the joint endeavors of our
     servants.

WAR. My royal cousin, in your princely
     favor
The extent of bounty hath been so un-
     limited
As only an acknowledgment in words
Would breed suspicion in [5] our state
     and quality.
When we shall, in the fullness of our
     fate,   100
Whose minister, necessity, will perfit,[6]
Sit on our own throne; then our arms,
     laid open
To gratitude, in sacred memory
Of these large benefits, shall twine them
     close,
Even to our thoughts and heart, without
     distinction.
Then James and Richard, being in effect
One person, shall unite and rule one
     people,
Divisible in titles only.

K. JA.   Seat ye.
Are the presenters ready?

CRAW.   All are entering.

HUNT. Dainty sport toward, Daliell! Sit;
     come, sit,   110
Sit and be quiet. Here are kingly bug's
     words! [7]

*Enter at one door four Scotch Antics,[8] ac-
cordingly habited; enter at another
four Wild Irish in trowses,[9] long-
haired and accordingly habited. Music.
The Masquers dance.*

K. JA. To all a general thanks!

WAR.   In the next room
Take your own shapes again; you shall
     receive
Particular acknowledgment.
                  [Exeunt Masquers.]

---

[1] From.
[2] *i.e.*, remembered by posterity.
[3] Harmony.   [4] Come short of.
[5] As to.
[6] *I.e.*, bring our destiny to perfection.
[7] Words of a bug, or bogey; swaggering
language.
[8] Burlesque performers.   [9] Close-fitting trousers.

K. JA.   Enough
Of merriments.—Crawford, how far's
    our army
Upon the march?
CRAW.   At Hedonhall, great king;
Twelve thousand, well prepared.
K. JA.   Crawford, tonight
Post thither. We in person with the
    prince
By four a-clock tomorrow after dinner
Will be w'e.[1] Speed away!
CRAW.   I fly, my lord. [*Exit.*] 120
K. JA. Our business grows to head now.
    Where's your secretary,
That he attends 'e not to serve?
WAR.   With Marchmount,
    Your herald.
K. JA.   Good! The proclamation's
    ready;
By that it will appear how the English
    stand
Affected to your title. Huntley, com-
    fort
Your daughter in her husband's ab-
    sence; fight
With prayers at home for us, who for
    your honors
Must toil in fight abroad.
HUNT.   Prayers are the weapons
Which men so near their graves as I
    do use.
I've little else to do.
K. JA.   To rest, young beauties! 130
We must be early stirring; quickly part.
"A kingdom's rescue craves both speed
    and art."
Cousins, good night.   *Flourish.*
WAR.   Rest to our cousin king.
KATH. Your blessing, sir.
HUNT. Fair blessings on your highness!
    Sure, you need 'em.
Exeunt omnes; manent Warb[eck, Jane,]
    et Katherine.
WAR. Jane, set the lights down, and from
    us return
To those in the next room this little
    purse;
Say we'll deserve [2] their loves.
JANE.   It shall be done, sir. [*Exit.*]
WAR. Now, dearest, ere sweet sleep shall
    seal those eyes,
Love's precious tapers, give me leave to
    use   140

A parting ceremony, for tomorrow
It would be sacrilege to intrude upon
The temple of thy peace. Swift as the
    morning
Must I break from the down of thy em-
    braces,
To put on steel, and trace the paths
    which lead
Through various hazards to a careful [3]
    throne.
KATH. My lord, I would fain go w'e;
    there's small fortune
In staying here behind.
WAR.   The churlish brow
Of war, fair dearest, is a sight of horror
For ladies' entertainment. If thou
    hear'st   150
A truth of my sad ending by the hand
Of some unnatural subject, thou withal
Shalt hear how I died worthy of my
    right,
By falling like a king; and in the close,
Which my last breath shall sound, thy
    name, thou fairest,
Shall sing a requiem to my soul, unwill-
    ing
Only of greater glory, cause [4] divided
From such a heaven on earth as life
    with thee.
But these are chimes for funerals. My
    business
Attends on fortune of a sprightlier
    triumph,   160
For love and majesty are reconciled,
And vow to crown thee empress of the
    west.
KATH. You have a noble language, sir;
    your right
In me is without question, and how-
    ever
Events of time may shorten my deserts
In others' pity, yet it shall not stagger
Or constancy or duty in a wife.
You must be king of me; and my poor
    heart
Is all I can call mine.
WAR.   But we will live,
Live, beauteous virtue, by the lively
    test   170
Of our own blood to let the "counter-
    feit"
Be known the world's contempt.
KATH.   Pray, do not use

---

[1] With ye.   [2] Reward.   [3] Full of care.   [4] Because.

That word; it carries fate in 't. The first
suit
I ever made, I trust your love will grant.

WAR. Without denial, dearest.

KATH. That hereafter,
If you return with safety, no adventure
May sever us in tasting any fortune.
I ne'er can stay behind again.

WAR. Y' are lady
Of your desires, and shall command
your will;
Yet 'tis too hard a promise.

KATH. What our destinies 180
Have ruled out in their books we must
not search,
But kneel to.

WAR. Then to fear when hope is
fruitless,
Were to be desperately miserable,
Which poverty our greatness dares not
dream of,
And much more scorns to stoop to.
Some few minutes
Remain yet; let's be thrifty in our hopes.
Exeunt.

[SCENA TERTIA.

*The presence chamber in the palace at
Westminster.*]

Enter King Henry, Hialas, and Urswick.

KING. Your name is Pedro Hialas, a
Spaniard?

HIAL. Sir, a Castilian born.

KING. King Ferdinand,
With wise Queen Isabel, his royal con-
sort,
Write 'e[1] a man of worthy trust and
candor.
Princes are dear to heaven who meet
with subjects
Sincere in their employments; such I
find
Your commendation, sir. Let me de-
liver
How joyful I repute the amity
With your most fortunate master, who
almost
Comes near a miracle in his success 10
Against the Moors, who had devoured
his country
Entire now to his scepter. We for our
part

[1] Report ye.

Will imitate his providence,[2] in hope
Of partage[3] in the use on 't. We
repute
The privacy of his advisement to us
By you, intended an ambassador
To Scotland for a peace between our
kingdoms,
A policy of love which well becomes
His wisdom and our care.

HIAL. Your majesty
Doth understand him rightly.

KING. Else 20
Your knowledge can instruct me;
wherein, sir,
To fall on ceremony would seem use-
less,
Which shall not need, for I will be as
studious
Of your concealment in our conference
As any council shall advise.

HIAL. Then, sir,
My chief request is that, on notice
given,
At my despatch in Scotland you will
send
Some learned man of power and ex-
perience
To join entreaty with me.

KING. I shall do it,
Being that way well provided by[4] a
servant 30
Which may attend 'e ever.

HIAL. If King James
By any indirection should perceive
My coming near your court, I doubt
the issue
Of my employment.

KING. Be not your own herald;
I learn sometimes without a teacher.

HIAL. Good days
Guard all your princely thoughts!

KING. Urswick, no further
Than the next open gallery attend him.
A hearty love go with you!

HIAL. Your vowed beadsman.[5]
Ex[eunt] Ursw[ick] and Hialas.

KING. King Ferdinand is not so much a
fox
But that a cunning huntsman may in
time 40
Fall on the scent. In honorable actions
Safe imitation best deserves a praise.—

[2] Foresight.
[3] Share.
[4] With.
[5] Devoted servant.

Enter Urswick.

What, the Castilian's passed away?

Urs.　　　　　　　　　　　He is,
And undiscovered.　The two hundred marks
Your majesty conveyed,[1] a gently pursed
With a right modest gravity.

King.　　　　　　　　　What was 't
A muttered in the earnest [2] of his wisdom?
A spoke not to be heard.　'Twas about—

Urs.　　　　　　　　　　Warbeck:
How if King Henry were but sure of subjects,
Such a wild runagate might soon be caged,　　　　　　　　　　　　50
No great ado withstanding.

King.　　　　　Nay, nay; something
About my son Prince Arthur's match.

Urs.　　　　　　　　Right, right, sir.
A hummed it out, how that King Ferdinand
Swore that the marriage twixt the Lady Katherine,
His daughter, and the Prince of Wales, your son,
Should never be consummated as long
As any Earl of Warwick lived in England,
Except by new creation.

King.　　　　　　　I remember
'Twas so, indeed.　The king his master swore it?

Urs. Directly, as he said.

King.　　　　　　An Earl of Warwick! 60
Provide a messenger for letters instantly
To Bishop Fox.　Our news from Scotland creeps,
It comes so slow.　We must have airy spirits;
Our time requires depatch.—[*Aside.*]
The Earl of Warwick!
Let him be son to Clarence, younger brother
To Edward!　Edward's daughter is, I think,
Mother to our Prince Arthur.—Get a messenger.　　　　　　*Exeunt.*

---

[1] Sent.　　　　　　　　[2] Soberness.

[SCENA QUARTA.

Before the castle of Norham.]

*Enter King James, Warbeck, Crawford,
Daliell, Heron, Astley, Major, Sketon,
　　　　　　　　　　and Soldiers.*

K. Ja. We trifle time against these castle walls;
The English prelate will not yield.
Once more
Give him a summons.　　　　*Parley.*

*Enter above, Durham, armed, a truncheon
　　　　in his hand, and Soldiers.*

War.　　　　　See, the jolly clerk [3]
Appears, trimmed [4] like a ruffian!

K. Ja.　　　　　　　　Bishop, yet
Set ope the ports, and to your lawful sovereign,
Richard of York, surrender up this castle,
And he will take thee to his grace; else Tweed
Shall overflow his banks with English blood,
And wash the sand that cements those hard stones,
From their foundation.

Dur.　　　Warlike King of Scotland, 10
Vouchsafe a few words from a man enforced
To lay his book aside and clap on arms
Unsuitable to my age or my profession.
Courageous prince, consider on what grounds
You rend the face of peace, and break a league
With a confederate king that courts your amity.
For whom too?　For a vagabond, a straggler,
Not noted in the world by birth or name,
An obscure peasant, by the rage of hell
Loosed from his chains to set great kings at strife.　　　　　　　　　20
What nobleman, what common man of note,
What ordinary subject hath come in,
Since first you footed on our territories,
To only feign a welcome?　Children laugh at
Your proclamations, and the wiser pity

---

[3] Ecclesiastic.　　　　　　[4] Armed.

So great a potentate's abuse by one
Who juggles merely with the fawns [1]
and youth
Of an instructed compliment.   Such
spoils,
Such slaughters as the rapine of your
soldiers
Already have committed, is enough   30
To show your zeal in a conceited jus-
tice.[2]
Yet, great king, wake not yet my mas-
ter's vengeance,
But shake that viper off which gnaws
your entrails.
I and my fellow subjects are resolved,
If you persist, to stand your utmost fury
Till our last blood drop from us.

WAR.   O, sir, lend
Me ear to this seducer of my honor!—
What shall I call thee, thou gray-bearded
scandal,
That kick'st against the sovereignty to
which
Thou owest allegiance?—Treason is
boldfaced   40
And eloquent in mischief.   Sacred king,
Be deaf to his known malice.

DUR.   Rather yield
Unto those holy motions which inspire
The sacred heart of an anointed body.
It is the surest policy in princes
To govern well their own than [3] seek en-
croachment
Upon another's right.

CRAW. [Aside.]   The king is serious,
Deep in his meditation[s]. [4]

DAL. [Aside.]   Lift them up
To heaven, his better genius!

WAR.   Can you study
While such a devil raves?   O, sir!

K. JA.   Well, bishop,   50
You'll not be drawn to mercy?

DUR.   Conster me
In like case by a subject of your own.
My resolution's fixed.   King James, be
counseled.
A greater fate waits on thee.

                    Exit Durham cum suis.[5]

K. JA.   Forage through
The country; spare no prey of life or
goods.

WAR. O, sir, then give me leave to yield
to nature;
I am most miserable.   Had I been
Born what this clergyman would by
defame [6]
Baffle belief with, I had never sought
The truth of mine inheritance with rapes
Of women or of infants murthered,
virgins   61
Deflowered, old men butchered, dwell-
ings fired,
My land depopulated, and my people
Afflicted with a kingdom's devastation.
Show more remorse,[7] great king, or I
shall never
Endure to see such havoc with dry eyes.
Spare, spare my dear, dear England!

K. JA.   You fool [8] your piety,
Ridiculously careful of an interest
Another man possesseth.   Where's your
faction?
Shrewdly the bishop guessed of your
adherents,   70
When not a petty burgess of some town,
No, not a villager, hath yet appeared
In your assistance.   That should make
'e whine,
And not your country's sufferance,[9]
as you term it.

DAL. [Aside.] The king is angry.

CRAW. [Aside.]   And the
passionate duke
Effeminately dolent.[10]

WAR.   The experience
In former trials, sir, both of mine own
Or other princes cast out of their thrones,
Have so acquainted me how misery
Is destitute of friends or of relief   80
That I can easily submit to taste
Lowest reproof without contempt or
words.

                    Enter Frion.

K. JA. An humble-minded man!—Now,
what intelligence
Speaks Master Secretary Frion?

FRI.   Henry
Of England hath in open field o'erthrown
The armies who opposed him in the
right
Of this young prince.

---

[1] Fawnings.   [2] Imagined act of justice.
[3] Rather than. [4] Added by Gifford-Dyce.
[5] With his men.

[6] Defamation.   [9] Suffering.
[7] Pity.   [10] Doleful.
[8] Make foolish.

K. Ja.   His subsidies,[1] you mean.
More, if you have it?
Fri.   Howard, Earl of Surrey,
Backed by twelve earls and barons of
the north,
An hundred knights and gentlemen of
name,   90
And twenty thousand soldiers, is at
hand
To raise your siege. Brooke, with a
goodly navy,
Is admiral at sea; and Dawbney follows
With an unbroken army for a second.
War. 'Tis false! They come to side with
us.
K. Ja.   Retreat!
We shall not find them stones and walls
to cope with.
Yet, Duke of York, for such thou sayest
thou art,
I'll try thy fortune to the height. To
Surrey,
By Marchmount, I will send a brave
defiance
For single combat. Once [2] a king will
venter [3]   100
His person to an earl, with condition
Of spilling lesser blood.[4] Surrey is bold,
And James resolved.[5]
War.   O, rather, gracious sir,
Create me [6] to this glory, since my cause
Doth interest [7] this fair quarrel; valued
least,
I am his equal.
K. Ja.   I will be the man.—
March softly off. "Where victory can
reap
A harvest crowned with triumph, toil is
cheap."   Exeunt omnes.

ACTUS QUARTUS. SCENA PRIMA.

[*The English camp near Ayton, on the
border.*]

*Enter Surrey, Durham, Soldiers, with drums
and colors.*

Sur. Are all our braving enemies shrunk
back,
Hid in the fogs of their distempered [8]
climate,

---

[1] Auxiliaries.   [2] For once.   [3] Venture.
[4] With the intention of spilling less blood.
[5] Resolute.   [7] Is concerned in.
[6] *I.e.*, advance me.   [8] Intemperate.

Not daring to behold our colors wave
In spite of this infected air? Can they
Look on the strength of Cundrestine
defaced,
The glory of Hedonhall devasted,[9] that
Of Edington cast down, the pile of
Fulden
O'erthrown, and this the strongest of
their forts,
Old Ayton Castle, yielded and demol-
ished,
And yet not peep abroad? The Scots
are bold,   10
Hardy in battle; but it seems the cause
They undertake, considered, appears
Unjointed in the frame on 't.
Dur.   Noble Surrey,
Our royal master's wisdom is at all times
His fortune's harbinger, for when he
draws
His sword to threaten war, his provi-
dence
Settles on peace, the crowning of an
empire.   *Trumpet.*
Sur. Rank all in order; 'tis a herald's
sound,
Some message from King James. Keep a
fixed station.

*Enter Marchmount and another Herald in
their coats.*

March. From Scotland's awful majesty
we come   20
Unto the English general.
Sur.   To me?
Say on.
March.   Thus then: the waste and
prodigal
Effusion of so much guiltless blood
As in two potent armies of necessity
Must glut the earth's dry womb, his
sweet compassion
Hath studied to prevent, for which to
thee,
Great Earl of Surrey, in a single fight
He offers his own royal person, fairly
Proposing these conditions only, that,
If victory conclude our master's right, 30
The earl shall deliver for his ransom
The town of Berwick to him, with the
fishgarths; [10]
If Surrey shall prevail, the king will pay

---

[9] Devastated.   [10] Weirs.

A thousand pounds down present for his freedom,
And silence further arms. So speaks King James.
Sur. So speaks King James! So like a king a speaks.
Heralds, the English general returns
A sensible devotion from his heart,
His very soul, to this unfellowed [1] grace.
For let the king know, gentle heralds, truly, 40
How his descent from his great throne to honor
A stranger subject with so high a title
As his compeer in arms, hath conquered more
Than any sword could do, for which— my loyalty
Respected—I will serve his virtues ever
In all humility. But Berwick, say,
Is none of mine to part with. "In affairs
Of princes, subjects cannot traffic rights
Inherent to the crown." My life is mine;
That I dare freely hazard; and—with pardon 50
To some unbribed vainglory—if his majesty
Shall taste a change of fate, his liberty
Shall meet no articles.[2] If I fall, falling
So bravely, I refer me to his pleasure
Without condition; and for this dear favor,
Say, if not countermanded, I will cease
Hostility, unless provoked.
March.   This answer
We shall relate unpartially.
Dur.   With favor,
Pray have a little patience.—[Aside to Surrey.] Sir, you find
By these gay flourishes how wearied travail 60
Inclines to willing rest; here's but a prologue,
However confidently uttered, meant
For some ensuing acts of peace. Consider
The time of year, unseasonableness of weather,
Charge, barrenness of profit; and occasion
Presents itself for honorable treaty,
Which we may make good use of. I will back,

[1] Unique.
[2] I.e., no conditions shall be imposed.

As sent from you in point of noble gratitude,
Unto King James, with these his heralds. You
Shall shortly hear from me, my lord, for order 70
Of breathing or proceeding; and King Henry,
Doubt not, will thank the service.
Sur. [Aside to Durham.]   To your wisdom,
Lord Bishop, I refer it.
Dur. [Aside to Surrey.]   Be it so, then.
Sur. Heralds, accept this chain and these few crowns.
March. Our duty, noble general.
Dur.   In part
Of retribution [3] for such princely love,
My lord the general is pleased to show
The king your master his sincerest zeal,
By further treaty, by no common man.
I will myself return with you.
Sur.   Y' oblige 80
My faithfullest affections t'e, Lord Bishop.
March. All happiness attend your lordship!
Sur.   Come, friends
And fellow soldiers! We, I doubt, shall meet
No enemies but woods and hills to fight with.
Then 'twere as good to feed and sleep at home.
We may be free from danger, not secure.
                          Exeunt omnes.

[SCENA SECUNDA.

The Scottish camp.]

Enter Warbeck and Frion.

War. Frion, O Frion, all my hopes of glory
Are at a stand! The Scottish king grows dull,
Frosty, and wayward, since this Spanish agent
Hath mixed discourses with him. They are private;
I am not called to council now. Confusion
On all his crafty shrugs! I feel the fabric
Of my designs are tottering.

[3] In partial payment.

Fri.   Henry's policies
Stir with too many engines.[1]
War.   Let his mines,
Shaped in the bowels of the earth, blow
    up
Works raised for my defense, yet can
    they never   10
Toss into air the freedom of my birth,
Or disavow my blood Plantagenet's.
I am my father's son still. But, O, Frion,
When I bring into count with my dis-
    asters
My wife's compartnership,[2] my Kate's,
    my life's,
Then, then my frailty feels an earth-
    quake. Mischief
Damn Henry's plots! I will be England's
    king,
Or let my aunt of Burgundy report
My fall in the attempt deserved[3] our
    ancestors!
Fri. You grow too wild in passion. If you
    will   20
Appear a prince indeed, confine your
    will
To moderation.
War.   What a saucy rudeness
Prompts this distrust! If? If I will
    appear?
Appear a prince? Death throttle such
    deceits
Even in their birth of utterance! Curséd
    cozenage
Of trust! Ye make me mad. 'Twere
    best, it seems,
That I should turn impostor to myself,
Be mine own counterfeit, belie the truth
Of my dear mother's womb, the sacred
    bed
Of a prince murthered and a living
    baffled.   30
Fri. Nay, if you have no ears to hear, I
    have
No breath to spend in vain.
War.   Sir, sir, take heed!
Gold and the promise of promotion
    rarely
Fail in temptation.
Fri.   Why to me this?
War.   Nothing.
Speak what you will; we are not sunk so
    low

But your advice may piece again the
    heart
Which many cares have broken. You
    were wont
In all extremities to talk of comfort;
Have ye none left now? I'll not interrupt
    ye.
Good, bear with my distractions. If
    King James   40
Deny us dwelling here, next whither
    must I?
I prithee, be not angry.
Fri.   Sir, I told ye
Of letters come from Ireland—how the
    Cornish
Stomach their last defeat, and humbly
    sue
That with such forces as you could par-
    take[4]
You would in person land in Cornwall,
    where
Thousands will entertain your title
    gladly.
War. Let me embrace thee, hug thee.
    Th'ast revived
My comforts; if my cousin king will fail,
Our cause will never.—Welcome, my tried
    friends!   50

Enter Major, Heron, Astley, Sketon.

You keep your brains awake in our
    defense.
Frion, advise with them of these affairs,
In which be wondrous secret; I will listen
What else concerns us here. Be quick
    and wary.   *Ex[it] Warbeck.*
Ast. Ah, sweet young prince!—Secre-
tary, my fellow counselors and I have consulted, and jump[5] all in one opinion
directly: that, if this Scotch garboils[6] do
not fadge[7] to our minds, we will pell-mell
run amongst the Cornish choughs[8] [60
presently and in a trice.
Ske. 'Tis but going to sea and, leaping
ashore, cut ten or twelve thousand unnecessary throats, fire seven or eight
towns, take half a dozen cities, get into the
market place, crown him Richard the
Fourth, and the business is finished.
Maj. I grant ye, quoth I, so far forth
as men may do, no more than men may

---

[1] Contrivances.   [3] Was worthy of.
[2] Copartnership.

[4] Bring together.   [6] Tumults.   [8] Crows.
[5] Agree.   [7] Succeed.

do. For it is good to consider when [70
consideration may be to the purpose;
otherwise—still you shall pardon me—
little said is soon amended.

FRI. Then you conclude the Cornish
action surest?

HER. We do so, and doubt not but to
thrive abundantly. Ho, my masters, had
we known of the commotion when we set
sail out of Ireland, the land had been ours
ere this time.   80

SKE. Pish, pish! 'Tis but forbearing
being an earl or a duke a month or two
longer. I say, and say it again, if the work
go not on apace, let me never see new
fashion more. I warrant ye, I warrant ye;
we will have it so, and so it shall be.

AST. This is but a cold, phlegmatic
country, not stirring enough for men of
spirit. Give me the heart of England for
my money!   90

SKE. A man may batten there in a week
only, with hot loaves and butter, and a
lusty cup of muscadine [1] and sugar at
breakfast, though he make never a meal
all the month after.

MAJ. Surely, when I bore office, I found
by experience that to be much troublesome was to be much wise and busy. I
have observed how filching and bragging has
been the best service in these last [100
wars, and therefore conclude peremptorily
on the design in England. If things and
things may fall out, as who can tell what
or how—but the end will show it.

FRI. Resolved like men of judgment.
    Here to linger [2]
More time is but to lose it. Cheer the
    prince
And haste him on to this; on this de-
    pends
Fame in success, or glory in our ends.
                        Exeunt omnes.

[SCENA TERTIA.

Another part of the same.]

*Enter King James, Durham, and Hialas on
                        either side.*

HIAL. France, Spain, and Germany com-
    bine a league
Of amity with England. Nothing wants

For settling peace through Christen-
    dom but love
Between the British monarchs, James
    and Henry.

DUR. The English merchants, sir, have
    been received
With general procession into Antwerp;
The emperor confirms the combination.

HIAL. The King of Spain resolves a
    marriage
For Katherine his daughter with Prince
    Arthur.

DUR. France courts this holy contract.

HIAL.   What can hinder 10
A quietness in England—

DUR.   But your suffrage
To such a silly creature, mighty sir,
As is but in effect an apparition,
A shadow, a mere trifle?

HIAL.   To this union
The good of both the church and com-
    monwealth
Invite 'e—

DUR.   To this unity, a mystery
Of providence points out a greater
    blessing
For both these nations than our human
    reason
Can search into. King Henry hath a
    daughter,
The Princess Margaret; I need not
    urge   20
What honor, what felicity can follow
On such affinity twixt two Christian
    kings
Inleagued by ties of blood. But sure I
    am,
If you, sir, ratify the peace proposed,
I dare both motion [3] and effect this mar-
    riage
For weal of both the kingdoms.

K. JA.   Dar'st thou, Lord Bishop?

DUR. Put it to trial, royal James, by
    sending
Some noble personage to the English
    court
By way of embassy.

HIAL.   Part of the business
Shall suit my mediation.

K. JA.   Well; what heaven 30
Hath pointed out to be, must be. You
    two
Are ministers, I hope, of blessed fate.

---

[1] A sweet wine.   [2] Delay.   [3] Move, propose.

But herein only I will stand acquitted—
No blood of innocents shall buy my
  peace.
For Warbeck, as you nick [1] him, came to
  me
Commended by the states of Christen-
  dom,
A prince, though in distress. His fair
  demeanor,
Lovely behavior, unappalléd spirit,
Spoke him not base in blood, however
  clouded.
The brute beasts have both rocks and
  caves to fly to,   40
And men the altars of the church; to
  us
He came for refuge. "Kings come near
  in nature
Unto the gods in being touched with
  pity."
Yet, noble friends, his mixture with our
  blood,
Even with our own, shall no way inter-
  rupt
A general peace. Only I will dismiss
  him
From my protection, throughout my
  dominions
In safety, but not ever to return.
HIAL. You are a just king.
DUR.   Wise, and herein happy.
K. JA. Nor will we dally in affairs of
  weight.   50
Huntley, lord bishop, shall with you to
  England
Ambassador from us. We will throw
  down
Our weapons. Peace on all sides now.
  Repair
Unto our council; we will soon be with
  you.
HIAL. Delay shall question no despatch;
  heaven crown it.
          Exeunt Durham and Hialas.
K. JA. A league with Ferdinand? A mar-
  riage
With English Margaret? A free re-
  lease
From restitution for the late affronts?
Cessation from hostility? And all
For Warbeck, not delivered, but dis-
  missed.   60
We could not wish it better.—Daliell!

[1] Nickname.

                    Enter Daliell.
DAL.   Here, sir.
K. JA. Are Huntley and his daughter sent
  for?
DAL.   Sent for
And come, my lord.
K. JA.   Say to the English prince
We want his company.
DAL.   He is at hand, sir.

Enter Warbeck, Katherine, Jane, Frion,
*   Heron, Sketon, Major, Astley.*

K. JA. Cousin, our bounty, favors, gentle-
  ness,
Our benefits, the hazard of our person,
Our people's lives, our land hath evi-
  denced
How much we have engaged on your
  behalf.
How trivial and how dangerous our
  hopes
Appear, how fruitless our attempts in
  war,   70
How windy, rather smoky, your assur-
  ance
Of party [2] shows, we might in vain
  repeat!
But now obedience to the mother church,
A father's care upon his country's weal,
The dignity of state, directs our wis-
  dom
To seal an oath of peace through Chris-
  tendom,
To which we are sworn already. 'Tis
  you
Must only seek new fortunes in the
  world,
And find an harbor elsewhere. As I
  promised   79
On your arrival, you have met no usage
Deserves repentance in your being here;
But yet I must live master of mine own.
However, what is necessary for you
At your departure, I am well content
You be accommodated with, provided
Delay prove not my enemy.
WAR.   It shall not,
Most glorious prince. The fame of my
  designs
Soars higher than report of ease and
  sloth
Can aim at. I acknowledge all your
  favors

[2] Support.

Boundless and singular, am only
wretched   90
In words as well as means to thank the
grace
That flowed so liberally. Two empires
firmly
You're lord of—Scotland and Duke
Richard's heart.
My claim to mine inheritance shall
sooner
Fail than my life to serve you, best of
kings.
And, witness Edward's blood in me, I am
More loath to part with such a great
example
Of virtue than all other mere respects.
But, sir, my last suit is, you will not
force
From me what you have given—this
chaste lady,   100
Resolved on all extremes.[1]
KATH.   I am your wife;
No human power can or shall divorce
My faith from duty.
WAR.   Such another treasure
The earth is bankrout of.
K. JA.   I gave her, cousin,
And must avow the gift, will add withal
A furniture [2] becoming her high birth
And unsuspected [3] constancy, provide
For your attendance. We will part good
friends.   *Exeunt* [4] *King and Daliell.*
WAR. The Tudor hath been cunning in
his plots.   109
His Fox of Durham would not fail at last.
But what! Our cause and courage are
our own.
Be men, my friends, and let our cousin
king
See how we follow fate as willingly
As malice follows us. Y' are all resolved
For the west parts of England?
OMNES.   Cornwall, Cornwall!
FRI. The inhabitants expect you daily.
WAR.   Cheerfully
Draw all our ships out of the harbor,
friends;
Our time of stay doth seem too long.
We must
Prevent [5] intelligence. About it sud-
denly!

OMNES. A prince, a prince, a prince!   120
                    Exeunt Counselors.
WAR. Dearest, admit not into thy pure
thoughts
The least of scruples, which may charge
their softness
With burden of distrust. Should I prove
wanting
To noblest courage now, here were the
trial.
But I am perfect, sweet; I fear no change
More than thy being partner in my
sufferance.
KATH. My fortunes, sir, have armed me
to encounter
What chance soe'er they meet with.—
Jane, 'tis fit
Thou stay behind, for whither wilt thou
wander?
JANE. Never till death will I forsake my
mistress,   130
Nor then, in wishing to die with 'e
gladly.
KATH. Alas, good soul!
FRI.   Sir, to your aunt of Burgundy
I will relate your present undertakings.
From her expect on all occasions wel-
come.
You cannot find me idle in your services.
WAR. Go, Frion, go! Wise men know how
to soothe
Adversity, not serve it. Thou hast
waited
Too long on expectation. "Never yet
Was any nation read of so besotted
In reason as to adore the setting sun."
Fly to the archduke's court; say to the
duchess   141
Her nephew, with fair Katherine his
wife,
Are on their expectation to begin
The raising of an empire. If they fail,
Yet the report will never. Farewell,
Frion.—   *Exit Frion.*
This man, Kate, has been true, though
now of late
I fear too much familiar with the Fox.

                    Enter Huntley and Daliell.

HUNT. I come to take my leave. You need
not doubt
My interest in this sometime child of
mine.

---

[1] Extremities.
[2] Portion.
[3] Not distrusted.
[4] Original reads *Exit.*
[5] Forestall.

She's all yours now, good sir. O, poor
    lost creature,   150
Heaven guard thee with much patience!
    If thou canst
Forget thy title to old Huntley's family,
As much of peace will settle in thy mind
As thou canst wish to taste but in thy
    grave.
Accept my tears yet, prithee; they are
    tokens
Of charity as true as of affection.

KATH. This is the cruel'st farewell!

HUNT.   Love, young gentleman,
    This model of my griefs. She calls you
    husband.
Then be not jealous of a parting kiss:
It is a father's, not a lover's offering. 160
Take it, my last.—[*Kisses her.*] I am too
    much a child.
Exchange of passion is to little use;
So [1] I should grow too foolish. Goodness
    guide thee!   *Exit Hunt[ley].*

KATH. Most miserable daughter!—Have
    you aught
To add, sir, to our sorrows?

DAL.   I resolve,
    Fair lady, with your leave, to wait on all
    Your fortunes in my person, if your lord
    Vouchsafe me entertainment.

WAR. We will be bosom friends, most
    noble Daliell,
For I accept this tender of your love 170
Beyond ability of thanks to speak it.
Clear thy drowned eyes, my fairest;
    time and industry
Will show us better days, or end the
    worst.   *Exeunt omnes.*

[SCENA QUARTA.

The presence chamber at Westminster.]

Enter Oxford and Dawbney.

OX. No news from Scotland yet, my lord?

DAW.   Not any
    But what King Henry knows himself. I
        thought
    Our armies should have marched that
        way; his mind,
    It seems, is altered.

OX.   Victory attends
    His standard everywhere.

DAW.   Wise princes, Oxford,
    Fight not alone with forces. Providence

[1] Thus.

Directs and tutors strength; else ele-
    phants
And barbéd [2] horses might as well prevail
As the most subtile stratagems of war.

OX. The Scottish king showed more than
    common bravery   10
In proffer of a combat hand to hand
With Surrey.

DAW.   And but showed it. North-
    ern bloods
Are gallant, being fired, but the cold
    climate,
Without good store of fuel, quickly
    freezeth
The glowing flames.

OX.   Surrey, upon my life,
    Would not have shrunk an hair's
        breadth.

DAW.   May a forfeit
    The honor of an English name and
        nature,
    Who would not have embraced it with a
        greediness
    As violent as hunger runs to food!   19
    'Twas an addition [3] any worthy spirit
    Would covet, next to immortality,
    Above all joys of life. We all missed
        shares
    In that great opportunity.

Enter King Henry and Urswick, whispering.

OX.   The king!
    See, a comes smiling.

DAW.   O, the game runs smooth
    On his side, then, believe it. Cards, well
        shuffled
    And dealt with cunning, bring some
        gamester thrift,
    But others must rise losers.

KING.   The train [4] takes?

URS. Most prosperously.

KING.   I knew it should not miss.
    He fondly [5] angles who will hurl his bait
    Into the water cause the fish at first   30
    Plays round about the line and dares not
        bite.
Lords, we may reign your king yet.
    Dawbney, Oxford,
Urswick, must Perkin wear the crown?

DAW.   A slave!

OX. A vagabond!

[2] Barded, armored.   [4] Plot.
[3] Honor.   [5] Foolishly.

URS.   A glowworm!

KING.   Now, if Frion,
His practiced politician, wear a brain
Of proof, King Perkin will in progress ride
Through all his large dominions. Let us
  meet him,
And tender homage. Ha, sirs? Liegemen
  ought
To pay their fealty.

DAW.   Would the rascal were,   39
With all his rabble, within twenty miles
Of London.

KING.   Farther off is near enough
To lodge him in his home. I'll wager odds
Surrey and all his men are either idle
Or hasting back. They have not work, I
  doubt,
To keep them busy.

DAW.   'Tis a strange conceit, sir.

KING. Such voluntary favors as our people
In duty aid us with, we never scattered
On cobweb parasites, or lavished out
In riot or a needless hospitality.
No undeserving favorite doth boast   50
His issues [1] from our treasury; our charge
Flows through all Europe, proving us but
  steward
Of every contribution which provides
Against the creeping canker of disturb-
  ance.
Is it not rare, then, in this toil of state
Wherein we are embarked, with breach
  of sleep,
Cares, and the noise of trouble, that our
  mercy
Returns nor thanks nor comfort? Still
  the west
Murmur and threaten innovation,[2]
Whisper our government tyrannical,   60
Deny us what is ours, nay, spurn their
  lives,
Of which they are but owners by our gift.
It must not be.

Ox.   It must not, should not.

Enter a Post. [3]

KING.   So then—
To whom?

POST.   This packet to your sacred
  majesty.

KING. Sirrah, attend without. [*Exit Post.*]

Ox. News from the north, upon my life.

DAW.   Wise Henry
Divines aforehand of events; with him
Attempts and execution are one act.

KING. Urswick, thine ear: Frion is caught;
  the man
Of cunning is outreached. We must be
  safe.   70
Should reverend Morton, our archbishop,
  move
To a translation higher yet,[4] I tell thee
My Durham owns a brain deserves that
  see.[5]
He's nimble in his industry, and mount-
  ing.[6]
Thou hear'st me?

URS.   And conceive your highness fitly.

KING. Dawbney and Oxford, since our
  army stands
Entire, it were a weakness to admit
The rust of laziness to eat amongst them.
Set forward toward Salisbury; the plains
Are most commodious for their exer-
  cise.   80
Ourself will take a muster of them there,
And or disband them with reward or else
Dispose as best concerns us.

DAW.   Salisbury?
Sir, all is peace at Salisbury.

KING.   Dear friend,
The charge must be our own; we would a
  little
Partake the pleasure with our subjects'
  ease.—
Shall I entreat your loves?

Ox.   Command our lives.

KING. Y' are men know how to do, not to
  forethink.
My bishop is a jewel tried and perfect;
A jewel, lords. The post who brought
  these letters   90
Must speed another to the Mayor of
  Exeter.
Urswick, dismiss him not.

URS.   He waits your pleasure.

KING. Perkin a king? A king?

URS.   My gracious lord.

KING. Thoughts busied in the sphere of
  royalty
Fix not on creeping worms, without their
  stings

---

[1] Monetary grants.   [2] Revolution.
[3] This stage direction follows the King's speech
in the original.

[4] *I.e.*, die.   [6] Ambitious.
[5] *I.e.*, of Canterbury.

Mere excrements of earth. The use of time
Is thriving safety and a wise prevention
Of ills expected. W' are resolved for Salisbury.   *Exe[unt] omnes.*

[SCENA QUINTA.

The coast of Cornwall.]

A general shout within. Enter Warbeck, Daliell, Katherine, and Jane.

WAR. After so many storms as wind and seas
Have threatened to our weather-beaten ships,
At last, sweet fairest, we are safe arrived
On our dear mother earth, ingrateful only
To heaven and us in yielding sustenance
To sly usurpers of our throne and right.
These general acclamations are an omen
Of happy process [1] to their welcome lord.
They flock in troops, and from all parts with wings   9
Of duty fly to lay their hearts before us.
Unequaled pattern of a matchless wife,
How fares my dearest yet?
KATH.   Confirmed in health,
By which I may the better undergo
The roughest face of change; but I shall learn
Patience to hope, since silence courts affliction
For comforts, to this truly noble gentleman,
Rare unexampled pattern of a friend,
And my beloved Jane, the willing follower
Of all misfortunes.
DAL.   Lady, I return   19
But barren crops of early protestations,
Frost-bitten in the spring of fruitless hopes.
JANE. I wait but as the shadow to the body;
For, madam, without you, let me be nothing.
WAR. None talk of sadness; we are on the way
Which leads to victory. Keep cowards' thoughts
With desperate sullenness. The lion faints not,

Locked in a grate,[2] but loose disdains all force
Which bars his prey—and we are lion-hearted—
Or else no king of beasts. (*Another shout [within].*) Hark, how they shout,
Triumphant in our cause! Bold confidence   30
Marches on bravely, cannot quake at danger.

Enter Sketon.

SKE. Save King Richard the Fourth! Save thee, king of hearts! The Cornish blades are men of mettle, have proclaimed, through Bodnam and the whole county, my sweet prince monarch of England. Four thousand tall yeomen, with bow and sword, already vow to live and die at the foot of King Richard.

Enter Astley.

AST. The mayor, our fellow coun- [40
selor, is servant for an emperor. Exeter is appointed for the rendezvous, and nothing wants to victory but courage and resolution. *Sigillatum et datum decimo Septembris, anno regni regis primo, et cætera; confirmatum est.*[3] All's cocksure.[4]
WAR. To Exeter! To Exeter, march on!
Commend us to our people. We in person
Will lend them double spirits; tell them so.
SKE. AND AST.   King Richard!   King Richard!   50
WAR. A thousand blessings guard our lawful arms!
A thousand horrors pierce our enemies' souls!
Pale fear unedge their weapons' sharpest points
And, when they draw their arrows to the head,
Numbness shall strike their sinews! Such advantage
Hath majesty in its pursuit of justice
That on the proppers-up of Truth's old throne
It both enlightens counsel and gives heart

[1] Progress.

[2] Cage.
[3] Sealed and dated on the tenth of September, in the first year of the king's reign, etc. Confirmed.   [4] Perfectly safe.

To execution, whiles [1] the throats of traitors
Lie bare before our mercy. O, divinity   60
Of royal birth! How it strikes dumb the tongues
Whose prodigality of breath is bribed
By trains to greatness! Princes are but men
Distinguished in the fineness of their frailty,
Yet not so gross in beauty of the mind,
For there's a fire more sacred purifies
The dross of mixture. Herein stand the odds:
"Subjects are men on earth; kings, men and gods."   *Exeunt omnes.*

ACTUS QUINTUS. SCENA PRIMA.

[*St. Michael's Mount, Cornwall.*]

Enter Katherine and Jane in riding suits,
with one Servant.

KATH. It is decreed; and we must yield to fate,
Whose angry justice, though it threaten ruin,
Contempt, and poverty, is all but trial
Of a weak woman's constancy in suffering.
Here, in a stranger's and an enemy's land,
Forsaken and unfurnished of all hopes
But such as wait on misery, I range
To meet affliction wheresoe'er I tread.
My train and pomp of servants is reduced
To one kind gentlewoman and this groom.   10
Sweet Jane, now whither must we?
JANE.   To your ships,
Dear lady, and turn home.
KATH.   Home! I have none.
Fly thou to Scotland; thou hast friends will weep
For joy to bid thee welcome. But, O, Jane,
My Jane, my friends are desperate of comfort,
As I must be of them. The common charity,
Good people's alms and prayers of the gentle,

Is the revenue must support my state.
As for my native country, since it once
Saw me a princess in the height of greatness   20
My birth allowed me, here I make a vow
Scotland shall never see me, being fallen
Or lessened in my fortunes. Never, Jane,
Never to Scotland more will I return.
Could I be England's queen—a glory, Jane,
I never fawned on—yet the king who gave me
Hath sent me with my husband from his presence,
Delivered us suspected to his [2] nation,
Rendered us spectacles to time and pity.
And is it fit I should return to such   30
As only listen after our descent
From happiness enjoyed, to misery
Expected, though uncertain? Never, never!
Alas, why dost thou weep, and that poor creature
Wipe his wet cheeks too? Let me feel alone
Extremities, who know [3] to give them harbor.
Nor thou nor he has cause. You may live safely.
JANE. There is no safety whiles your dangers, madam,
Are every way apparent.
SERV.   Pardon, lady
I cannot choose but show my honest heart—   40
You were ever my good lady.
KATH.   O, dear souls,
Your shares in grief are too-too much!

Enter Daliell.

DAL.   I bring,
Fair princess, news of further sadness yet
Than your sweet youth hath been acquainted with.
KATH. Not more, my lord, than I can welcome. Speak it;
The worst, the worst I look for.
DAL.   All the Cornish
At Exeter were by the citizens
Repulsed, encountered by the Earl of Devonshire
And other worthy gentlemen of the country.

---

[1] While   [2] Perkin's.   [3] Know how.

Your husband marched to Taunton, and
   was there   50
Affronted [1] by King Henry's chamber-
   lain,
The king himself in person with his army
Advancing nearer to renew the fight
On all occasions. But the night before
The battles [2] were to join, your husband
   privately,
Accompanied with some few horse, de-
   parted
From out the camp, and posted none
   knows whither.
KATH. Fled without battle given?
DAL.   Fled, but followed
By Dawbney, all his parties [3] left to taste
King Henry's mercy—for to that they
   yielded—   60
Victorious without bloodshed.
KATH.   O, my sorrows!
If both our lives had proved the sacrifice
To Henry's tyranny, we had fallen like
   princes,
And robbed him of the glory of his pride.
DAL. Impute it not to faintness or to
   weakness
Of noble courage, lady, but foresight;
For by some secret friend he had in-
   telligence
Of being bought and sold by his base fol-
   lowers.
Worse yet remains untold.
KATH.   No, no, it cannot.
DAL. I fear y' are betrayed: the Earl of
   Oxford   70
Runs hot in your pursuit.
KATH.   A shall not need;
We'll run as hot in resolution gladly
To make the earl our jailor.
JANE.   Madam, madam,
   They come, they come!

Enter Oxford with Followers.

DAL.   Keep back! Or he who dares
Rudely to violate the law of honor
Runs on my sword.
KATH.   Most noble sir, forbear.
What reason draws you hither, gentle-
   men?
Whom seek 'e?
Ox.   All stand off!—With favor, lady,
From Henry, England's king, I would
   present

[1] Confronted.   [2] Armies.   [3] Allies.

Unto the beauteous princess, Katherine
   Gordon,   80
The tender of a gracious entertainment.
KATH. We are that princess, whom your
   master king
Pursues with reaching arms to draw into
His power. Let him use his tyranny;
We shall not be his subjects.
Ox.   My commission
Extends no further, excellentest lady,
Than to a service; 'tis King Henry's
   pleasure
That you, and all that have relation t'e,
Be guarded as becomes your birth and
   greatness,
For, rest assured, sweet princess, that
   not aught   90
Of what you do call yours shall find dis-
   turbance,
Or any welcome other than what suits
Your high condition.
KATH.   By what title, sir,
May I acknowledge you?
Ox.   Your servant, lady,
Descended from the line of Oxford's earls,
Inherits what his ancestors before him
Were owners of.
KATH.   Your king is herein royal,
That by a peer so ancient in desert
As well as blood commands us to his
   presence.
Ox. Invites 'e, princess, not commands.
KATH.   Pray, use 100
Your own phrase as you list. To your
   protection
Both I and mine submit.
Ox.   There's in your number
A nobleman whom fame hath bravely
   spoken.
To him the king my master bade me
   say
How willingly he courts his friendship;
   far
From an enforcement, more than what in
   terms
Of courtesy so great a prince may hope
   for.
DAL. My name is Daliell.
Ox.   'Tis a name hath won
Both thanks and wonder from report, my
   lord.
The court of England emulates your
   merit,   110
And covets to embrace 'e.

DAL.   I must wait on
The princess in her fortunes.
Ox.   Will you please,
Great lady, to set forward?
KATH.   Being driven
By fate, it were in vain to strive with
    heaven.   *Exeunt omnes.*

[SCENA SECUNDA.

Salisbury.]

*Enter King Henry, Surrey, Urswick, and a
                    guard of Soldiers.*

KING. The counterfeit, King Perkin, is
    escaped—
Escape, so let him; he is hedged too fast
Within the circuit of our English pale
To steal out of our ports, or leap the walls
Which guard our land.   The seas are
    rough and wider
Than his weak arms can tug with.—Sur-
    rey, henceforth
Your king may reign in quiet; turmoils
    past,
Like some unquiet dream, have rather
    busied
Our fancy than affrighted rest of state.
But, Surrey, why, in articling a peace   10
With James of Scotland, was not restitu-
    tion
Of losses which our subjects did sustain
By the Scotch inroads questioned?
SUR.   Both demanded
And urged, my lord, to which the king
    replied,
In modest merriment, but smiling ear-
    nest,
How that our master Henry was much
    abler
To bear the detriments than he repay
    them.
KING. The young man, I believe, spake
    honest truth;
A studies to be wise betimes.[1]—Has, Urs-
    wick,
Sir Rice ap Thomas and Lord Brooke our
    steward   20
Returned the Western gentlemen full
    thanks
From us for their tried loyalties?
URS.[2]   They have—

[1] Early.
[2] Suggested by Weber.   Original has *Sur.*

Which, as if health and life had reigned
    amongst 'em,
With open hearts they joyfully received.
KING. Young Buckingham is a fair-
    natured prince,
Lovely in hopes, and worthy of his
    father.
Attended by an hundred knights and
    squires
Of special name, he tendered humble
    service,
Which we must ne'er forget; and Devon-
    shire's wounds,
Though slight, shall find sound cure in
    our respect.[3]   30

*Enter Dawbney with [a Guard, conducting]
    Warbeck, Heron, John a Water, Astley,
                                Sketon.*

DAW. Life to the king, and safety fix his
    throne!
I here present you, royal sir, a shadow
Of majesty, but in effect a substance
Of pity—a young man, in nothing grown
To ripeness but th' ambition of your
    mercy,
Perkin, the Christian world's strange
    wonder.
KING.   Dawbney,
We observe no wonder.   I behold, 'tis
    true,
An ornament of nature, fine and polished,
A handsome youth indeed, but not ad-
    mire [4] him.
How came he to thy hands?
DAW.   From sanctuary   40
At Bewley, near Southampton, regis-
    tered,
With these few followers, for persons
    privileged.
KING. I must not thank you, sir; you were
    to blame
To infringe the liberty of houses sacred.
Dare we be irreligious?
DAW.   Gracious lord,
They voluntarily resigned themselves
Without compulsion.
KING.   So? 'Twas very well;
'Twas very, very well.—Turn now thine
    eyes,
Young man, upon thyself and thy past
    actions.

[3] In respect to us, at our hands.
[4] Wonder at.

What revels in combustion through our
  kingdom   50
A frenzy of aspiring youth hath danced,
Till, wanting breath, thy feet of pride
  have slipped
To break thy neck!
WAR.   But not my heart; my heart
Will mount till every drop of blood be
  frozen
By death's perpetual winter. If the sun
Of majesty be darkened, let the sun
Of life be hid from me in an eclipse
Lasting and universal. Sir, remember
There was a shooting in of light when
  Richmond,
Not aiming at a crown, retired, and
  gladly,   60
For comfort to the Duke of Britain's [1]
  court.
Richard, who swayed the scepter, was re-
  puted
A tyrant then; yet then a dawning glim-
  mered
To some few wandering remnants, prom-
  ising day
When first they ventured on a frightful
  shore
At Milford Haven—
DAW.   Whither speeds his boldness?
Check his rude tongue, great sir.
KING.   O, let him range.
The player's on the stage still; 'tis his part;
A does but act.—What followed?
WAR.   Bosworth Field,
Where, at an instant, to the world's
  amazement,   70
A morn to Richmond and a night to
  Richard
Appeared at once. The tale is soon
  applied:
Fate, which crowned these attempts
  when least assured,
Might have befriended others like re-
  solved.
KING. A pretty gallant! Thus your aunt
  of Burgundy,
Your   duchess-aunt,   informed   her
  nephew; so
The lesson, prompted and well conned,
  was molded
Into familiar dialogue, oft rehearsed,
Till, learnt by heart, 'tis now received for
  truth.

WAR. Truth, in her pure simplicity, wants
  art   80
To put a feignéd blush on. Scorn wears
  only
Such fashion as commends to gazers' eyes
Sad ulcerated novelty, far beneath
The sphere of majesty. In such a court
Wisdom and gravity are proper robes,
By which the sovereign is best distin-
  guished
From zanies [2] to his greatness.
KING.   Sirrah, shift
Your antic [3] pageantry, and now appear
In your own nature, or you'll taste the
  danger
Of fooling out of season.
WAR.   I expect 90
No less than what severity calls justice,
And politicians safety. Let such beg
As feed on alms, but, if there can be
  mercy
In a protested enemy, then may it
Descend to these poor creatures, whose
  engagements,
To th' bettering of their fortunes, have
  incurred
A loss of all. To them if any charity
Flow from some noble orator, in death
I owe the fee of thankfulness.
KING.   So brave!
What a bold knave is this!—Which of
  these rebels   100
Has been the Mayor of Cork?
DAW.   This wise formality.
Kneel to the king, 'e rascals!
KING.   Canst thou hope
A pardon where thy guilt is so apparent?
MAYOR. Under your good favors, as men
are men, they may err; for I confess, re-
spectively, in taking great parts, the one
side prevailing, the other side must go
down. Herein the point is clear, if the
proverb hold, that hanging goes by destiny,
that it is to little purpose to say this [110
thing or that shall be thus or thus; for, as
the Fates will have it, so it must be; and
who can help it?
DAW. O, blockhead! Thou a privy-coun-
  selor?
Beg life, and cry aloud, "Heaven save
  King Henry!"
MAYOR. Every man knows what is best,
as it happens; for my own part, I believe it

---

[1] Bretagne's.

[2] Clownish imitators.   [3] Fantastic, fanciful.

is true, if I be not deceived, that kings must
be kings and subjects subjects; but which
is which, you shall pardon me for that. [120
Whether we speak or hold our peace, all are
mortal; no man knows his end.

KING. We trifle time with follies.

OMNES.   Mercy, mercy!

KING. Urswick, command the dukeling
     and these fellows
     To Digby, the lieftenant [1] of the Tower;
     With safety let them be conveyed to
        London.
     It is our pleasure no uncivil outrage,
     Taunts, or abuse be suffered to their
        persons;
     They shall meet fairer law than they de-
        serve.
     Time may restore their wits, whom vain
        ambition   130
     Hath many years distracted.

WAR.   Noble thoughts
     Meet freedom in captivity. The Tower?
     Our childhood's dreadful nursery!

KING.   No more.

URS. Come, come, you shall have leisure
     to bethink 'e.

Exit Ursw[ick] with Perkin and his [Follow-
                             ers].

KING. Was ever so much impudence in
     forgery?
     The custom, sure, of being styled a king
     Hath fastened in his thought that he is
        such;
     But we shall teach the lad another lan-
        guage.
     'Tis good we have him fast.

DAW.   The hangman's physic
     Will purge this saucy humor.

KING.   Very likely;   140
     Yet we could temper mercy with ex-
        tremity,
     Being not too far provoked.

Enter Oxford, Katherine in her richest attire,
       [Daliell,] Jane, and Attendants.

OX.   Great sir, be pleased,
     With your accustomed grace to enter-
        tain
     The Princess Katherine Gordon.

KING.   Oxford, herein
     We must beshrew [2] thy knowledge of our
        nature.

   [1] Lieutenant.   [2] Deprecate.

A lady of her birth and virtues could not
Have found us so unfurnished of good
    manners
As not, on notice given, to have met her
Half way in point of love.—Excuse, fair
    cousin,
The oversight. O, fie! You may not
    kneel;   150
'Tis most unfitting. First, vouchsafe this
    welcome,
A welcome to your own, for you shall
    find us
But guardian to your fortune and your
    honors.

KATH. My fortunes and mine honors are
    weak champions,
As both are now befriended, sir. How-
    ever,
Both bow before your clemency.

KING.   Our arms
Shall circle them from malice.—A sweet
    lady!
Beauty incomparable!—Here lives maj-
    esty
At league with love.

KATH.   O, sir, I have a husband.

KING. We'll prove your father, husband,
    friend, and servant.   160
Prove what you wish to grant us.—
    Lords, be careful
A patent presently be drawn for issuing
A thousand pounds from our exchequer
    yearly
During our cousin's life.—Our queen
    shall be
Your chief companion, our own court
    your home,
Our subjects all your servants.

KATH.   But my husband?

KING. [*To Daliell.*] By all descriptions,
    you are noble Daliell,
Whose generous truth hath famed a rare
    observance.
We thank 'e; 'tis a goodness gives addi-
    tion
To every title boasted from your an-
    cestry,   170
In all most worthy.

DAL.   Worthier than your praises,
Right princely sir, I need not glory in.

KING. Embrace him, lords.—[*To Kath-*
    erine.] Whoever calls you mistress
Is lifted in our charge. A goodlier beauty
Mine eyes yet ne'er encountered.

KATH.   Cruel misery
Of fate! What rests [1] to hope for?
KING.   Forward, lords,
To London.—Fair, ere long I shall pre-
sent 'e
With a glad object, peace, and Huntley's
blessing.   *Exeunt omnes.*

[SCENA TERTIA.

The Tower Hill, London.]

*Enter Constable and Officers; Warbeck,
Urswick, and Lambert Simnel like a
falconer [, followed by a Mob]. A pair
of stocks.*

CONST. Make room there! Keep off,
I require 'e; and none come within twelve
foot of his majesty's new stocks, upon
pain of displeasure.—Bring forward the
malefactors.—Friend, you must to this
gear [2]—no remedy.—Open the hole, and
in with his legs, just in the middle hole;
there, that hole.—[*Warbeck is put in the
stocks.*] Keep off, or I'll commit you all.
Shall not a man in authority be [10
obeyed?—So, so, there; 'tis as it should be.
Put on the padlock, and give me the key.—
Off, I say, keep off!
URS. Yet, Warbeck, clear thy conscience.
 Thou hast tasted
King Henry's mercy liberally; the law
Has forfeited thy life; an equal [3] jury
Have doomed thee to the gallows; twice,
 most wickedly,
Most desperately, hast thou escaped
 the Tower,
Inveigling to thy party with thy witch-
 craft
Young Edward, Earl of Warwick, son
 to Clarence,   20
Whose head must pay the price of that
 attempt.
Poor gentleman, unhappy in his fate,
And ruined by thy cunning! So a mon-
 grel
May pluck the true stag down. Yet,
 yet confess
Thy parentage; for yet the king has
 mercy.
LAM. You would be Dick the Fourth;
 very likely!
Your pedigree is published; you are
 known

For Osbeck's son of Tournay, a loose
 runagate,
A landloper; [4] your father was a Jew,
Turned Christian merely to repair his
 miseries.   30
Where's now your kingship?
WAR.   Baited to my death?
Intolerable cruelty! I laugh at
The Duke of Richmond's practice on
 my fortunes.
"Possession of a crown ne'er wanted
 heralds."
LAM. You will not know who I am?
URS.   Lambert Simnel,
Your predecessor in a dangerous uproar,
But, on submission, not alone received
To grace, but by the king vouchsafed
 his service.
LAM. I would be Earl of Warwick, toiled
 and ruffled
Against my master, leaped to catch the
 moon,   40
Vaunted my name Plantagenet, as you
 do;
An earl, forsooth, whenas in truth I
 was,
As you are, a mere rascal! Yet his maj-
 esty,
A prince composed of sweetness—heaven
 protect him!—
Forgave me all my villainies, reprived [5]
The sentence of a shameful end, ad-
 mitted
My surety [6] of obedience to his service;
And I am now his falconer, live plen-
 teously,
Eat from the king's purse, and enjoy
 the sweetness
Of liberty and favor, sleep securely. 50
And is not this, now, better than to
 buffet
The hangman's clutches, or to brave
 the cordage
Of a tough halter which will break your
 neck?
So, then, the gallant totters!—Prithee,
 Perkin,
Let my example lead thee; be no longer
A counterfeit. Confess and hope for
 pardon.
WAR. For pardon? Hold, my heart-
 strings, whiles contempt

---

[1] Remains. [2] Business. [3] Impartial.

[4] Vagabond.   [6] Accepted my oath.
[5] Reprieved.

Of injuries, in scorn, may bid defiance
To this base man's foul language!—
    Thou poor vermin,
How dar'st thou creep so near me? Thou
    an earl?   60
Why, thou enjoy'st as much of happi-
    ness
As all the swinge [1] of slight ambition
    flew at.
A dunghill was thy cradle. So a puddle,
By virtue of the sunbeams, breathes
    a vapor
To infect the purer air, which drops
    again
Into the muddy womb that first ex-
    haled it.
Bread and a slavish ease, with some as-
    surance
From the base beadle's whip, crowned
    all thy hopes.
But, sirrah, ran there in thy veins one
    drop   69
Of such a royal blood as flows in mine,
Thou wouldst not change condition to
    be second
In England's state, without the crown
    itself.
Coarse creatures are incapable of ex-
    cellence.
But let the world, as all to whom I am
This day a spectacle, to time deliver,[2]
And by tradition fix [3] posterity,
Without another chronicle than truth,
How constantly my resolution suffered
A martyrdom of majesty.
LAM.   He's past
Recovery; a Bedlam cannot cure him.   80
URS. Away, inform the king of his be-
    havior.
LAM. Perkin, beware the rope! The
    hangman's coming.
URS. If yet thou hast no pity of thy
    body,
Pity thy soul!   *Exit Simnel.*

Enter Katherine, Jane, Daliell, and Ox-
                                        ford.

JANE.   Dear lady!
Ox.   Whither will 'e,
Without respect of shame?
KATH.   Forbear me,[4] sir,

And trouble not the current of my
    duty.—
O, my loved lord! Can any scorn be
    yours
In which I have no interest?—Some
    kind hand
Lend me assistance that I may partake
Th' infliction of this penance.—My
    life's dearest,   90
Forgive me. I have stayed too long from
    tendering
Attendance on reproach; yet bid me
    welcome.
WAR. Great miracle of constancy! My
    miseries
Were never bankrout of their confi-
    dence
In worst afflictions, till this. Now I feel
    them.
Report and thy deserts, thou best of
    creatures,
Might to eternity have stood a pattern
For every virtuous wife without this
    conquest.
Thou hast outdone belief; yet may
    their ruin
In after-marriages be never pitied,   100
To whom thy story shall appear a fable!
Why wouldst thou prove so much un-
    kind to greatness
To glorify thy vows by such a servitude?
I cannot weep; but trust me, dear, my
    heart
Is liberal of passion.—Harry Richmond,
A woman's faith hath robbed thy fame
    of triumph!
Ox. Sirrah, leave off your juggling, and
    tie up
The devil that ranges in your tongue.
URS.   Thus witches,
Possessed, even [to] [5] their deaths de-
    luded, say
They have been wolves and dogs, and
    sailed in eggshells   110
Over the sea, and rid on fiery dragons,
Passed in the air more than a thousand
    miles
All in a night. The enemy of mankind
Is powerful, but false; and falsehood
    confident.
Ox. Remember, lady, who you are; come
    from
That impudent impostor.

---

[1] Sway.   [3] Assure.
[2] Proclaim.   [4] Let me alone.
                               [5] Supplied by Gifford-Dyce.

KATH.   You abuse us,
For, when the holy churchman joined
    our hands,
Our vows were real then; the ceremony
Was not in apparition,[1] but in act.—
Be what these people term thee, I am
    certain   120
Thou art my husband; no divorce in
    heaven
Has been sued out between us; 'tis in-
    justice
For any earthly power to divide us.
Or we will live or let us die together.
There is a cruel mercy.
WAR.   Spite of tyranny
We reign in our affections, blessed
    woman!
Read in my destiny the wrack of honor;
Point out, in my contempt of death, to
    memory
Some miserable happiness, since herein,
Even when I fell, I stood enthroned a
    monarch   130
Of one chaste wife's troth, pure and
    uncorrupted.
Fair angel of perfection, immortality
Shall raise thy name up to an adora-
    tion,
Court every rich opinion of true merit,
And saint it in the calendar of Virtue,
When I am turned into the selfsame
    dust
Of which I was first formed.
Ox.   The Lord Ambassador
Huntley, your father, madam, should
    a look on
Your strange subjection in a gaze so
    public,
Would blush on your behalf, and wish
    his country   140
Unleft for entertainment to such sorrow.
KATH. Why art thou angry, Oxford? I
    must be
More peremptory in my duty. Sir,
Impute it not unto immodesty
That I presume to press you to[2] a
    legacy
Before we part forever.
WAR.   Let it be, then,
My heart, the rich remains of all my
    fortunes.
KATH. Confirm it with a kiss, pray.
WAR. [*Kissing her.*]   O, with that

I wish to breathe my last! Upon thy
    lips,
Those equal twins of comeliness, I
    seal   150
The testament of honorable vows.
Whoever be that man that shall un-
    kiss
This sacred print next, may he prove
    more thrifty
In this world's just applause, not more
    desertful!
KATH. By this sweet pledge of both our
    souls, I swear
To die a faithful widow to thy bed,
Not to be forced or won. O, never,
    never!

Enter Surrey, Dawbney, Huntley, and
Crawford.

DAW. Free   the   condemnéd   person;
    quickly free him!
What has a yet confessed?
    [*Warbeck is released from the stocks.*]
URS.   Nothing to purpose;
But still a will be king.
SUR.   Prepare your journey   160
To a new kingdom, then.—Unhappy
    madam,
Willfully foolish!—See, my lord am-
    bassador,
Your lady daughter will not leave the
    counterfeit
In this disgrace of fate.
HUNT.   I never pointed[3]
Thy marriage, girl; but yet, being mar-
    ried,
Enjoy thy duty to a husband freely.
The griefs are mine. I glory in thy con-
    stancy,
And must not say I wished that I had
    missed
Some partage in these trials of a patience.
KATH. You will forgive me, noble sir?
HUNT.   Yes, yes;   170
In every duty of a wife and daughter
I dare not disavow thee. To your hus-
    band—
For such you are, sir—I impart a fare-
    well
Of manly pity. What your life has
    passed through,
The dangers of your end will make ap-
    parent.

[1] Appearance.   [2] For.   [3] Appointed.

And I can add, for comfort to your suf-
ferance,
No cordial but the wonder of your
frailty,
Which keeps so firm a station. We are
parted.
WAR. We are. A crown of peace renew
thy age,
Most   honorable   Huntley.—Worthy
Crawford,   180
We may embrace; I never thought thee
injury.
CRAW. Nor was I ever guilty of neglect
Which might procure such thought. I
take my leave, sir.
WAR. To you, Lord Daliell—what? Ac-
cept a sigh;
'Tis hearty and in earnest.
DAL.   I want utterance.
My silence is my farewell.
KATH.   O, O!
JANE.   Sweet madam,
What do you mean?—[To Daliell.] My
lord, your hand.
DAL.   Dear lady,
Be pleased that I may wait[1] 'e to your
lodging.
            Exeunt Daliell, Katherine, Jane.

Enter Sheriff and Officers, Sketon, Astley,
Heron, and Mayor, with halters about
their necks.

OX. Look 'e; behold your followers, ap-
pointed
To wait on 'e in death!
WAR.   Why, peers of England, 190
We'll lead 'em on courageously. I read
A triumph over tyranny upon
Their several foreheads. Faint not in
the moment
Of victory! Our ends, and Warwick's
head,
Innocent Warwick's head—for we are
prologue
But to his tragedy—conclude the wonder
Of Henry's fears; and then the glorious
race
Of fourteen kings, Plantagenets, de-
termines[2]
In this last issue male. Heaven be obeyed!
Impoverish time of its amazement,
friends,   200

[1] Attend.   [2] Terminates.

And we will prove as trusty in our pay-
ments
As prodigal to nature in our debts.
Death? Pish! 'Tis but a sound; a name
of air;
A minute's storm, or not so much. To
tumble
From bed to bed, be massacred alive
By some physicians for a month or two,
In hope of freedom from a fever's tor-
ments,
Might stagger manhood. Here the pain
is past
Ere sensibly 'tis felt. Be men of spirit!
Spurn coward passion! So illustrious
mention   210
Shall blaze our names, and style us
kings o'er death.
DAW. Away, impostor beyond president!
No chronicle records his fellow.
            Ex[eunt] all Officers and Prisoners.
HUNT.   I have
Not thoughts left; 'tis sufficient in such
cases
Just laws ought to proceed.

Enter King Henry, Durham, and Hialas.

KING.   We are resolved.
Your business, noble lords, shall find
success
Such as your king importunes.
HUNT.   You are gracious.
KING. Perkin, we are informed, is armed
to die;
In that we'll honor him. Our lords shall
follow
To see the execution; and from hence 220
We gather this fit use: that "public
states,
As our particular bodies, taste most
good
In health when purgéd of corrupted
blood."   Exeunt omnes.
            FINIS.

EPILOGUE

Here has appeared, though in a several[3]
fashion,
The threats of majesty, the strength of
passion,
Hopes of an empire, change of fortunes—
all

[3] Separate.

What can to theaters of greatness fall,
Proving their weak foundations. Who
  will please,
Amongst such several sights, to censure [1]
  these
No births abortive, nor a bastard brood

  [1] Judge.

(Shame to a parentage or fosterhood),
May warrant,[2] by their loves, all just
  excuses,[3]   9
And often find a welcome to the Muses.

FINIS.

  [2] Authorize, sanction.   [3] Deserved defenses (?)

JAMES SHIRLEY

Shirley has been called "the last of the Elizabethans" partly because he was actually the last of the dramatists of his age to be born (in 1596, in London) and the last to die (in 1666, from exposure in the Great Fire), but even more because his work bears an extremely close and interesting relationship to that of his fellows while at the same time, especially in comedy, it anticipates much of the material and characters of the Restoration, if not its spirit. After attending the Merchant Tailors' School, Oxford, and Cambridge as an Anglican, he was converted to Roman Catholicism and abandoned what might have been a career in the church for school-teaching at St. Albans Grammar School, in Hertfordshire. In 1624, however, he gave up his head-mastership, and took up his residence at Gray's Inn, London, although there is no evidence that he ever actually became a lawyer. But in the following year his first play, *Love Tricks*, was licensed, and he continued to write voluminously for the stage, first for the Queen's Men and later for the King's. Not one of the least significant phases of his life was his four-year sojourn in Ireland, where the production of several of his plays in his friend John Ogilby's new Dublin theater marks one of the earliest signs of dramatic activity in that country. During the first days of the Civil War Shirley attended his patron, the Duke of Newcastle, on some of the Royalist campaigns, but after the defeat at Marston Moor he returned to his former profession of school-teaching, the closing of the theaters in 1642 precluding his earning a living in the manner he would have preferred. Nevertheless, he continued to write for the reading public, and saw that his plays as well as his poems and some pot-boiling works were put into print. He also edited the first collected edition of Beaumont and Fletcher, and according to tradition essayed to write for the stage once more after the Restoration, but if so none of his attempts struck the popular taste sufficiently to be known today as his.

It was both an advantage and a handicap to Shirley to have had before him the examples of his great predecessors; in fact, the playwright was so steeped in his study of these men that scarcely one of his scenes but has its parallels which have gone before. At the same time, however, so great was Shirley's ingenuity and dramatic sense that out of this material he was able to construct plays of considerable effectiveness and even originality—plays which in general read with naturalness and ease even though they fall sadly short in the usual Elizabethan poetry. He can claim to have written successfully in four different fields: masques, such as the lavishly produced *The Triumph of Peace* (1634); comedies of manners, such as *Hyde Park* (1632) and *The Lady of Pleasure* (1635), all dealing with the lower levels of fashionable society in the time of Charles I; tragi-comedies, such as *The Young Admiral* (1633) and *The Politician* (1639); and pure tragedies, the best of which are clearly *The Traitor* (1631) and *The Cardinal* (1641), decadent as these are in their excessive ingenuity, their reminiscences of other plays, their horrors, and their use of the old motives of lust, madness, and revenge.

The basis of the present text of *The Lady of Pleasure* is the copy of the first quarto (1637) in the Newberry Library at Chicago; that of *The Cardinal* the Library of Congress copy, dated 1652, in the 1653 collection, entitled *Six New Plays*. In both cases reference has sometimes been made to the not overreliable six-volume edition of *The Dramatic Works and Poems of James Shirley* (1833) by Alexander Dyce, which used many notes left by William Gifford.

THE LADY OF PLEASURE[1]

BY

JAMES SHIRLEY

PERSONS OF THE COMEDY

LORD.
SIR THOMAS BORNWELL.
SIR WILLIAM SCENTLOVE.
MR.[2] ALEX[ANDER] KICKSHAW.
MR. JOHN LITTLEWORTH.
MR. HAIRCUT [, a barber].
MR. FREDERICK [, Lady Bornwell's nephew].
STEWARD to the Lady Aretina.
STEWARD to the Lady Celestina.

SECRETARY [to Lord].
SERVANTS, etc.

ARETINA, Sir Thomas Bornwell's lady.
CELESTINA, a young widow.
ISABELLA [NOVICE] ⎱ [Kinswomen of Ce-
MARIANA [NOVICE] ⎰ lestina].
MADAM DECOY [, a procuress].
[GENTLEWOMAN.]

SCENE: The Strand.

[TIME: Contemporary.][3]

THE FIRST ACT. [SCENE i.

A room in Bornwell's house.]

Enter Aretina and her Steward.

STEW. Be patient, madam; you may have
your pleasure.
ARE. 'Tis that I came to town for. I
would not
Endure again the country conversation,[4]
To be the lady of six shires! The men,
So near the primitive making they re-
tain
A sense of nothing but the earth, their
brains
And barren heads standing as much in
want
Of plowing as their ground! To hear
a fellow
Make himself merry and his horse, with
whistling
"Sellinger's Round"![5] To observe with
what solemnity 10

They keep their wakes,[6] and throw for
pewter candlesticks!
How they become the morris,[7] with
whose bells
They ring all in to Whitsun ales,[8] and
sweat
Through twenty scarfs and napkins,
till the hobbyhorse
Tire, and the Maid Marian, dissolved
to a jelly,
Be kept for spoon meat![9]
STEW. These, with your pardon, are no
argument
To make the country life appear so
hateful,
At least to your particular,[10] who en-
joyed
A blessing in that calm, would you be
pleased 20
To think so, and the pleasure of a kingdom.
While your own will commanded what
should move
Delights, your husband's love and power
joined

<hr>

[1] The title continues: "A Comedy, As It Was
Acted by Her Majesty's Servants at the Private
House in Drury Lane."
[2] *I.e.*, Master
[3] Here follows a brief dedication to Richard,
Lord Lovelace of Hurley.
[4] Association.
[5] An old-fashioned country dance tune.
[6] Annual parish festivals.
[7] A dance in which the hobbyhorse and Maid
Marian were characters.
[8] Parish festivals held at Whitsuntide.
[9] Liquid food eaten with a spoon.
[10] In your case.

To give your life more harmony. You lived there
Secure and innocent, beloved of all,
Praised for your hospitality, and prayed for;
You might be envied, but malice knew
Not where you dwelt. I would not prophesy,
But leave to your own apprehension
What may succeed your change.
ARE. You do imagine, 30
No doubt, you have talked wisely, and confuted
London past all defense. Your master should
Do well to send you back into the country,
With title of superintendent-baily.[1]
STEW. How, madam!
ARE. Even so, sir.
STEW. I am a gentleman,
Though now your servant.[2]
ARE. A country gentleman,
By your affection to converse with stubble.
His tenants will advance your wit, and plump it so
With beef and bag pudding!
STEW. You may say your pleasure;
It becomes not me dispute.
ARE. Complain to the 40
Lord of the soil, your master.
STEW. Y' are a woman
Of an ungoverned passion, and I pity you.

Enter Sir Thomas Bornwell.

BORN. How now![3] What's the matter?
STEW. Nothing, sir. [*Exit.*]
BORN. Angry, sweetheart?
ARE. I am angry with myself,
To be so miserably restrained in things
Wherein it doth concern your love and honor
To see me satisfied.
BORN. In what, Aretina?
Dost thou accuse me? Have I not obeyed

All thy desires? Against mine own opinion
Quitted the country, and removed the hope 50
Of our return, by sale of that fair lordship[4]
We lived in? Changed a calm and retire[d] life
For this wild town, composed of noise and charge?[5]
ARE. What charge more than is necessary for
A lady of my birth and education?
BORN. I am not ignorant how much nobility
Flows in your blood—your kinsmen great and powerful
I' th' state; but with this lose not your memory
Of being my wife. I shall be studious,
Madam, to give the dignity of your birth 60
All the best ornaments which become my fortune,
But would not flatter it to ruin both,
And be the fable of the town, to teach
Other men loss of wit by mine, employed
To serve your vast expenses.
ARE. Am I then
Brought in the balance? So, sir!
BORN. Though you weigh
Me in a partial[6] scale, my heart is honest,
And must take liberty to think you have
Obeyed no modest counsel, to effect,[7]
Nay, study, ways of pride and costly ceremony: 70
Your change of gaudy furniture, and pictures
Of this Italian master, and that Dutchman's;
Your mighty looking-glasses, like artillery,
Brought home[8] on engines; the superfluous plate,
Antique and novel; vanities of tires;[9]
Fourscore-pound suppers for my lord, your kinsman,
Banquets for tother[10] lady aunt, and cousins,

[1] Bailiff.
[2] Here and in several other passages the line division has been somewhat regularized, although much of the original meter is rather rough.
[3] Gifford-Dyce's reading. Original reads *how.*
[4] Estate
[5] Expense.
[6] Prejudiced.
[7] Affect, desire.
[8] Gifford-Dyce's reading. Original reads *whom.*
[9] Headdresses.
[10] The other.

And perfumes that exceed all; train of
servants
To stifle us at home and show abroad
More motley than the French or the
Venetian,   80
About your coach, whose rude postil-
lion
Must pester [1] every narrow lane, till
passengers [2]
And tradesmen curse your choking up
their stalls,
And common cries pursue your lady-
ship,
For hind'ring o' their market.

ARE.   Have you done, sir?
BORN. I could accuse the gaiety of your
wardrobe
And prodigal embroideries,[3] under which
Rich satins, plushes, cloth of silver,
dare
Not show their own complexions; your
jewels,
Able to burn out the spectators' eyes,   90
And show like bonefires [4] on you by the
tapers.
Something might here be spared, with
safety [5] of
Your birth and honor, since the truest
wealth
Shines from the soul, and draws up
just admirers.
I could urge something more.

ARE.   Pray do; I like
Your homily of thrift.
BORN.   I could wish, madam,
You would not game so much.
ARE.   A gamester too?
BORN. But are not come to that acquaint-
ance [6] yet
Should teach you skill enough to raise
your profit.
You look not through the subtilty of
cards   100
And mysteries of dice, nor can you save
Charge with the box,[7] buy petticoats
and pearls,
And keep your family by the precious
income.

Nor do I wish you should. My poorest
servant
Shall not upbraid my tables nor his hire,
Purchased beneath my honor.   You
make play
Not a pastime but a tyranny, and vex
Yourself and my estate by 't.

ARE.   Good! Proceed.
BORN. Another game you have, which
consumes more
Your fame than purse—your revels in
the night,   110
Your meetings called the "Ball," [8] to
which appear,
As to the Court of Pleasure, all your
gallants
And ladies, thither bound by a subpœna
Of Venus, and small Cupid's high dis-
pleasure;
'Tis but the Family of Love [9] translated
Into more costly sin! There was a play
on 't,
And, had the poet not been bribed to
a modest
Expression of your antic gambols in 't,
Some darks [10] had been discovered, and
the deeds too.
In time he may repent, and make some
blush   120
To see the second part danced on the
stage.
My thoughts acquit you for dishonor-
ing me
By any foul act; but the virtuous know
'Tis not enough to clear ourselves, but
the
Suspicions of our shame.

ARE.   Have you concluded
Your lecture?
BORN.   I ha' done; and, howsoever
My language may appear to you, it
carries
No other than my fair and just intent
To your delights, without curb to their
modest [11]
And noble freedom.

ARE.   I'll not be so tedious   130
In my reply, but, without art or ele-
gance,

---

[1] Obstruct.   [3] Embroideries.
[2] Passer-by   [4] Bonfires.
[5] Gifford-Dyce's reading. Original reads *which
safely.*
[6] Emended by Gifford-Dyce. Original reads
repentance.
[7] Dice box.

[8] The newly invented subscription dance,
upon which Shirley wrote a play.
[9] A religious sect, object of scandalous charges;
also the title of a play by Middleton.
[10] Secrets.   [11] Moderate.

Assure you I keep still my first opinion;
And, though you veil your avaricious
meaning
With handsome names of modesty and
thrift,
I find you would intrench and wound
the liberty
I was born with. Were my desires un-
privileged
By example, while my judgment thought
'em fit,
You ought not to oppose; but, when
the practice
And tract [1] of every honorable lady   139
Authorize me, I take it great injustice
To have my pleasures circumscribed
and taught me.
A narrow-minded husband is a thief
To his own fame, and his preferment
too;
He shuts his parts and fortunes from
the world,
While, from the popular vote and knowl-
edge, men
Rise to employment in the state.
BORN.   I have
No great ambition to buy preferment
At so dear rate.
ARE.   Nor I to sell my honor
By living poor and sparingly. I was not
Bred in that ebb of fortune, and my
fate   150
Shall not compel me to 't.
BORN.   I know not,
Madam; but you pursue these ways—
ARE.   What ways?
BORN. In the strict sense of honesty, I
dare
Make oath they are innocent.
ARE.   Do not divert,
By busy troubling of your brain, those
thoughts
That should preserve 'em.
BORN.   How was that?
ARE.   'Tis English.
BORN. But carries some unkind sense.

Enter Madam Decoy.

DEC. Good morrow, my sweet madam.
ARE.   Decoy, welcome!
This visit is a favor.
DEC.   Alas, sweet madam,
I cannot stay. I came but to present 160

[1] Course of action

My service to your ladyship; I could
not
Pass by your door but I must take the
boldness
To tender my respects.
ARE.   You oblige me, madam;
But I must not dispense so with your
absence.
DEC. Alas, the coach, madam, stays for
me at the door.
ARE. Thou sha't command mine; prithee,
sweet Decoy—
DEC. I would wait on you, madam, but
I have many
Visits to make this morning; I beseech—
ARE. So you will promise to dine with
me.
DEC.   I shall
Present a guest.
ARE.   Why, then good morrow,
madam.   170
DEC. A happy day shine on your ladyship!
                                Exit.

Enter Steward.

ARE. What's your news, sir?
STEW.   Madam, two gentlemen.
ARE. What gentlemen? Have they no
names?
STEW.   They are
The gentleman with his own head of
hair,
Whom you commended for his horse-
ship
In Hyde Park, and becoming the saddle,
The tother day.
ARE.   What circumstance is this
To know him by?
STEW.   His name's at my tongue's end—
He liked the fashion of your pearl chain,
madam,
And borrowed it for his jeweler to
take   180
A copy by it.
BORN. [*Aside.*]   What cheating gallant's
this?
STEW. That never walks without a lady's
busk, [2]
And plays with fans—Mr. Alexander
Kickshaw—
I thought I should remember him.
ARE.   What's the other?
STEW. What an unlucky memory I have!

[2] Corset.

The gallant that still [1] danceth in the
street,
And wears a gross of ribbon in his hat;
That carries oringado [2] in his pocket,
And sugarplums to sweeten his dis-
course;   189
That studies compliment, defies all wit
On black,[3] and censures plays that are
not bawdy—
Mr. John Littleworth.
ARE.   They are welcome; but
Pray, entertain them a small time, lest I
Be unprovided.
BORN.   Did they ask for me?
STEW. No, sir.
BORN.   It matters not; they must be
welcome.
ARE. Fie! How's this hair disordered?
Here's a curl
Straddle[s] [4] most impiously. I must to
my closet.   *Exit.*
BORN. Wait on 'em; my lady will return
again.—   [*Exit Steward.*]
I have to such a height fulfilled her
humor,
All application's [5] dangerous. These
gallants   200
Must be received, or she will fall into
A tempest, and the house be shook with
names
Of all her kindred. 'Tis a servitude
I may in time shake off.

*Enter Alexander [Kickshaw] and Little-
worth.*

AL. }
LIT. }   Save you, Sir Thomas!
BORN. Save you, gentlemen!
AL.   I kiss your hand.
BORN. What day [6] is it abroad?
LIT. The morning rises from your lady's
eye;
If she look clear, we take the happy
omen
Of a fair day.
BORN.   She'll instantly appear,
To the discredit of your compliment; 210
But you express your wit thus.
AL.   And you, modesty,
Not to affect [7] the praises of your own.

[1] Always.   [2] Candied orange peel.
[3] In black, in print.
[4] Supplied by Gifford-Dyce.
[5] *I.e.*, all pleading to be reasonable is.
[6] Weather.   [7] Appear to be pleased with.

BORN. Leaving this subject, what game's
now on foot?
What exercise carries the general vote? [8]
O' th' town now, nothing moves with-
out your knowledge.
AL. The cocking [9] now has all the noise;
I'll have
A hundred pieces of one battle. O,
These birds of Mars!
LIT.   Venus is Mars his bird too.
AL. Why, and the pretty doves are
Venus's,
To show that kisses draw the chariot. 220
LIT. I am for that skirmish.
BORN.   When shall we have
More booths and bagpipes upon Ban-
stead Downs?
No mighty race is expected?—But my
lady
Returns!

Enter Aretina.

ARE.   Fair morning to you, gentlemen!
You went not late to bed by your early
visit.
You do me honor.
AL.   It becomes our service.
ARE. What news abroad? You hold pre-
cious intelligence.
LIT. All tongues are so much busy with
your praise
They have not time to frame other dis-
course.
Will please you, madam, taste a sugar-
plum?   230
BORN. What does the goldsmith think
the pearl is worth
You borrowed of my lady?
AL.   'Tis a rich one.
BORN. She has many other toys, whose
fashion you
Will like extremely. You have no in-
tention
To buy any of her jewels?
AL.   Understand me—
BORN. You had rather sell, perhaps. But,
leaving this,
I hope you'll dine with us.
AL.   I came a-purpose.
ARE. And where were you last night?
AL.   I, madam? Where
I slept not; it had been sin, where so
much

[8] Approval.   [9] Cockfighting.

Delight and beauty was to keep me wak-
　ing.　240
There is a lady, madam, will be worth
Your free society; my conversation
Ne'er knew so elegant and brave [1] a
　soul,
With most incomparable flesh and blood,
So spirited, so courtly, speaks the lan-
　guages,
Sings, dances, plays o' th' lute to ad-
　miration,
Is fair and paints not, games too, keeps
　a table,
And talks most witty satire, has a wit
Of a clean [2] Mercury—
LIT.　　　　　　Is she married?
AL.　　　　　　　　No.　249
ARE.　A virgin?
AL.　　Neither.
LIT.　　　　What! A widow? Something
Of this wide commendation might have
　been
Excused.　This such a prodigy?
AL.　　　　　　　　　　　Repent,
Before I name her.　She did never see
Yet full sixteen, an age, in the opinion
Of wise men, not contemptible.　She
　has
Mourned out her year, too, for the
　honest knight
That had compassion of her youth, and
　died
So timely.　Such a widow is not com-
　mon;
And now she shines more fresh and
　tempting
Than any natural virgin.
ARE.　　　　　What's her name?　260
AL.　She was christened Celestina; by her
　husband,
The Lady Bellamour.　This ring was
　hers.
BORN.　You borrowed it to copy out the
　posy. [3]
AL.　Are they not pretty rubies?　'Twas
　a grace
She was pleased to show me, that I
　might have one
Made of the same fashion, for I love
All pretty forms.
ARE.　　　　　　And is she glorious?
AL.　She is full of jewels, madam; but I am

Most taken with the bravery [4] of her
　mind,
Although her garments have all grace
　and ornament.　270
ARE.　You have been high in praises.
AL.　　　　　　　　I come short;
No flattery can reach her.
BORN.　[Aside.]　　　　Now my lady
Is troubled, as she feared to be eclipsed;
This news will cost me somewhat.
ARE.　　　　　　　　You deserve
Her favor, for this noble character.
AL.　And I possess it, by my star's benevo-
　lence.
ARE.　You must bring us acquainted.
BORN.　　　　　　　I pray, do, sir;
I long to see her too.—Madam, I have
Thought upon 't, and corrected my
　opinion.
Pursue what ways of pleasure your
　desires　280
Incline you to, not only with my state,
But with my person; I will follow
　you.
I see the folly of my thrift, and will
Repent in sack and prodigality,
To your own heart's content.
ARE.　　　　　　But do not mock.
BORN.　Take me to your embraces, gen-
　tlemen,
And tutor me.
LIT.　　　　And will you kiss the ladies?
BORN.　And sing and dance.　I long to see
　this beauty.
I would fain lose a hundred pounds at
　dice now.
Thou sha't have another gown and petti-
　coat　290
Tomorrow.　Will you sell my running
　horses?
We have no Greek wine in the house, I
　think;
Pray, send one of our footmen to the
　merchant,
And throw the hogsheads of March-
　beer [5] into
The kennel, [6] to make room for sacks and
　claret.
What think you to be drunk yet before
　dinner?
We will have constant music, and main-
　tain

[1] Fine.　　　　　[3] Inscription in a ring.
[2] Veritable.

[4] Finery, excellence.　　[6] Channel, gutter.
[5] Bock beer.

Them and their fiddles in fantastic
    liveries;
I'll tune my voice to catches. I must
    have
My dining room enlarged, to invite am-
    bassadors.   300
We'll feast the parish in the fields, and
    teach
The military men new discipline,
Who shall charge all their new artillery
With oranges and lemons,[1] boy, to play
All dinner upon our capons.
AL.   He's exalted!
BORN. I will do anything to please my
    lady—
Let that suffice—and kiss o' th' same
    condition.
I am converted; do not you dispute,
But patiently allow the miracle.

Enter Servant.

ARE. I am glad to hear you, sir, in so good
    tune.   310
SER. Madam, the painter.
ARE.   I am to sit this morning.
BORN. Do, while I give new directions to
    my steward.
AL. With your favor, we'll wait on you;
    sitting's but
A melancholy exercise without
Some company to discourse.
ARE.   It does conclude
A lady's morning work. We rise, make
    fine,
Sit for our picture, and 'tis time to dine.
LIT. Praying's forgot.
AL.   'Tis out of fashion. *Exeunt.*

[SCENE ii.

A room in Celestina's house.]
Enter Celestina and her Steward.

CEL. Fie, what an air this room has!
STEW.   'Tis perfumed.
CEL. With some cheap stuff. Is it your
    wisdom's thrift
To infect my nostrils thus? Or is 't to
    favor
The gout in your worship's hand, you are
    afraid
To exercise your pen in your account
    book?

[1] Lemons.

Or do you doubt my credit to discharge
    Your bills?
STEW. Madam, I hope you have not
    found
My duty, with the guilt of sloth or
    jealousy,
Unapt to your command.
CEL.   You can extenuate
Your faults with language, sir; but I
    expect   10
To be obeyed. What hangings have we
    here?
STEW. They are arras, madam.
CEL.   Impudence! I know 't.
I will have fresher and more rich, not
    wrought
With faces that may scandalize a Chris-
    tian,
With Jewish stories stuffed with corn and
    camels.
You had best wrap all my chambers in
    wild Irish,
And make a nursery of monsters here,
To fright the ladies comes to visit me.
STEW. Madam, I hope—
CEL.   I say I will have other, 19
Good Master Steward, of a finer loom—
Some silk and silver, if your worship
    please
To let me be at so much cost. I'll have
Stories to fit the seasons of the year,
And change as often as I please.
STEW.   You shall, madam.
CEL. I am bound to your consent, for-
    sooth! And is
My coach brought home?
STEW.   This morning I expect it.
CEL. The inside, as I gave direction,
    Of crimson plush?
STEW.   Of crimson camel plush.
CEL. Ten thousand moths consume 't!
    Shall I ride through
The streets in penance, wrapped up
    round in haircloth?   30
Sell 't to an alderman; 'twill serve his
    wife
To go a-feasting to their country house,
Or fetch a merchant's nurse child, and
    come home
Laden with fruit and cheesecakes. I
    despise it!
STEW. The nails adorn it, madam, set in
    method
And pretty forms.

CEL. But single gilt, I warrant.

STEW. No, madam.

CEL. Another solecism! O, fie!
This fellow will bring me to a consump-
tion
With fretting at his ignorance. Some
lady
Had rather never pray than go to church
in 't. 40
The nails not double gilt? To market
wo't? [1]
'Twill hackney out to Mile End, or con-
vey
Your city tumblers [2] to be drunk with
cream
And prunes at Islington.

STEW. Good madam, hear me.

CEL. I'll rather be beholding [3] to my aunt,
The countess, for her mourning coach
than be
Disparaged so. Shall any juggling trades-
man
Be at charge to shoe his running horse
with gold,
And shall my coach nails be but single
gilt?
How dare these knaves abuse me so?

STEW. Vouchsafe 50
To hear me speak.

CEL. Is my sedan yet finished,
And liveries for my men-mules,[4] accord-
ing
As I gave charge?

STEW. Yes, madam, it is finished,
But without tilting-plumes [5] at the four
corners;
The scarlet's pure, but not embroideréd.

CEL. What mischief were it to your con-
science
Were my coach lined with tissue,[6] and
my harness
Covered with needlework? If my sedan
Had all the story of the prodigal
Embroderéd with pearl?

STEW. Alas, good madam, 60
I know 'tis your own cost; I am but your
steward,
And would discharge my duty the best
way.
You have been pleased to hear me; 'tis
not for

My profit that I manage your estate
And save expense, but for your honor,
madam.

CEL. How, sir, my honor?

STEW. Though you hear it not,
Men's tongues are liberal in your char-
acter,
Since you began to live thus high. I know
Your fame [7] is precious to you.

CEL. I were best
Make you my governor, audacious var-
let! 70
How dare you interpose your doting
counsel?
Mind your affairs with more obedience,
Or I shall ease you of an office, sir.
Must I be limited to please your honor,
Or, for the vulgar breath, confine my
pleasures?
I will pursue 'em in what shapes I fancy,
Here and abroad; my entertainments
shall
Be oft'ner and more rich. Who shall con-
trol me?
I live i' th' Strand, whither few ladies
come
To live, and purchase more than fame. I
will 80
Be hospitable then, and spare no cost
That may engage all generous report
To trumpet forth my bounty and my
bravery,
Till the court envy, and remove. I'll have
My house the academy of wits, who shall
Exalt [their genius] [8] with rich sack and
sturgeon,
Write panegyrics of my feasts, and
praise
The method of my witty superfluities.
The horses shall be taught, with frequent
waiting 89
Upon my gates, to stop in their career
Toward Charing Cross, spite of the
coachman's fury;
And not a tilter [9] but shall strike his
plume
When he sails by my window; my bal-
cony
Shall be the courtier's idol, and more
gazed at
Than all the pageantry at Temple Bar
By country clients.

---

[1] With it.
[2] Prostitutes.
[3] Beholden.
[4] Chairmen.
[5] Plumes for a canopy.
[6] Fine silk cloth.
[7] Reputation.　[8] Supplied by Gifford-Dyce.
[9] One riding to the tilting grounds.

STEW.   Sure, my lady's mad.
CEL. [*Striking him.*] Take that for your ill
  manners.
STEW.   Thank you, madam.
  I would there were less quicksilver in
  your fingers.   *Exit.*
CEL. There's more than simple honesty in
  a servant
  Required to his full duty; none should
  dare   100
  But with a look, much less a saucy lan-
  guage,
  Check at their mistress' pleasure. I'm
  resolved
  To pay for some delight; my estate will
  bear it;
  I'll rein it shorter when I please.

Enter Steward.

STEW.   A gentleman
  Desires to speak with your ladyship.
CEL.   His name?
STEW. He says you know him not; he
  seems to be
  Of quality.
CEL.   Admit him.—[*Exit Steward.*]

Enter Haircut.[1]

                    Sir, with me?
HAIR. Madam, I know not how you may
  receive
  This boldness from me; but my fair in-
  tents,   109
  Known, will incline you to be charitable.
CEL. No doubt, sir.
HAIR.   He must live obscurely, madam,
  That hath not heard what virtues you
  possess;
  And I, a poor admirer of your fame,
  Am come to kiss your hand.
CEL.   That all your business?
HAIR. Though it were worth much travel,
  I have more
  In my ambition.
CEL.   Speak it freely, sir.
HAIR. You are a widow.
CEL.   So.
HAIR.   And I a bachelor.
CEL. You come a-wooing, sir, and would
  perhaps
  Show me a way to reconcile these two.

---

[1] In the original this stage direction appears
at the end of Celestina's speech.

HAIR. And bless my stars for such a happi-
  ness.   120
CEL. I like you, sir, the better, that you do
  not
  Wander about, but shoot home to the
  meaning;
  'Tis a confidence will make a man
  Know sooner what to trust to; but I
  never
  Saw you before, and I believe you come
  not
  With hope to find me desperate upon
  marriage.
  If maids, out of their ignorance of what
  Men are, refuse these offers, widows may,
  Out of their knowledge, be allowed some
  coyness.
  And yet I know not how much happi-
  ness   130
  A peremptory answer may deprive me of;
  You may be some young lord, and,
  though I see not
  Your footmen and your groom, they may
  not be
  Far off, in conference with your horse.
  Please you
  To instruct me with your title, against
  which
  I would not willingly offend.
HAIR.   I am
  A gentleman; my name is Haircut,
  madam.
CEL. Sweet Mr. Haircut, are you a court-
  ier?
HAIR. Yes.
CEL.   I did think so, by your confidence.
  Not to detain you, sir, with circum-
  stance,[2]   140
  I was not so unhappy in my husband
  But that 'tis possible I may be a wife
  Again; but I must tell you he that wins
  My affection shall deserve me.
HAIR.   I will hope,
  If you can love, I sha' not present,
  madam,
  An object to displease you in my person;
  And, when time and your patience shall
  possess you
  With further knowledge of me, and the
  truth
  Of my devotion, you will not repent
  The offer of my service.
CEL.   You say well.   150

---

[2] Detailed narration.

How long do you imagine you can love,
sir?
Is it a quotidian,[1] or will it hold
But every other day?
HAIR. You are pleasant,[2] madam.
CEL. Does 't take you with a burning at
the first,
Or with a cold fit? For you gentle-
men
Have both your summer and your winter
service.
HAIR. I am ignorant what you mean; but
I shall never
Be cold in my affection to such beauty.
CEL. And 'twill be somewhat long ere I be
warm in 't.
HAIR. If you vouchsafe me so much honor,
madam,   160
That I may wait on you sometimes, I sha'
not
Despair to see a change.
CEL.   But now I know
Your mind, you shall not need to tell it
when
You come again; I shall remember it.
HAIR. You make me fortunate.

Enter Steward.

STEW.   Madam, your kinswomen,
The Lady Novice and her sister, are
New lighted from their coach.
CEL.   I did expect 'em;
They partly are my pupils. I'll attend
'em.   [*Exit Steward.*]
HAIR. Madam, I have been too great a
trespasser   169
Upon your patience; I'll take my leave.
You have affairs, and I have some em-
ployment
Calls me to court; I shall present again
A servant[3] to you.   *Exit Ha[ircut].*
CEL.   Sir, you may present,
But not give fire, I hope.—Now to the
ladies.
This recreation's past; the next must
be
To read to them some court philosophy.
                                        Exit.[4]

[1] Something of daily occurrence.
[2] Facetious.
[3] *I.e.*, present myself as a servant, with a pun
on the meaning *lover*.
[4] Original reads *Exeunt.*

THE SECOND ACT. [SCENE i.

A room in Bornwell's house.]

Enter Sir Thomas Bornwell.

[BORN.] 'Tis a strange humor I have under-
taken,
To dance, and play, and spend as fast as
she does;
But I am resolved. It may do good upon
her,
And fright her into thrift. Nay, I'll en-
deavor
To make her jealous too; if this do not
Allay her gamboling, she's past a woman,
And only a miracle must tame her.

Enter Steward.

STEW. 'Tis Mr. Frederick, my lady's
nephew.
BORN.   What of him?
STEW. Is come from the university.
BORN.   By whose directions?
STEW. It seems, my lady's.
BORN.   Let me speak with him   10
Before he see his aunt.—[*Exit Steward.*]
I do not like it.—

Enter [Steward, with] Mr. Frederick.

Mr. Frederick, welcome! I expected not
So soon your presence. What's the hasty
cause?
FRED. These letters from my tutor will ac-
quaint you. [*Gives Bornwell letters.*]
STEW. Welcome home, sweet Mr. Fred-
erick!
FRED.   Where's my aunt?
STEW. She's busy about her painting in
her closet;[5]
The outlandish[6] man of art is copying
out
Her countenance.
FRED.   She is sitting for her picture?
STEW. Yes, sir; and when 'tis drawn she
will be hanged
Next the French cardinal in the dining
room.   20
But, when she hears you're come, she
will dismiss
The Belgic gentleman, to entertain
Your worship.
FRED.   Change of air has made you
witty.   [*Exit Steward.*]

[5] Chamber   [6] Foreign.

BORN. Your tutor gives you a handsome
    character,
    Frederick, and is sorry your aunt's
      pleasure
    Commands you from your studies; but I
      hope
    You have no quarrel to the liberal arts.
    Learning is an addition [1] beyond
    Nobility of birth. Honor of blood,
    Without the ornament of knowledge,
      is   30
    A glorious [2] ignorance.
FRED. I never knew more sweet and happy
    hours
    Than I employed upon my books. I
      heard
    A part of my philosophy, and was so
    Delighted with the harmony of nature
    I could have wasted my whole life
      upon 't.
BORN. [*Aside.*] 'Tis pity a rash indulgence
    should corrupt
    So fair a genius! She's here; I'll observe.

Enter Aretina, Alexander, Littleworth, Stew-
                             ard.

FRED. My most loved aunt!
ARE.   Support me; I shall faint.
LIT. What ails your ladyship?
ARE.   Is that Frederick,   40
    In black?
AL.   Yes, madam; but the doublet's
    satin.
ARE. The boy's undone!
FRED.   Madam, you appear troubled.
ARE. Have I not cause? Was not I trusted
    with
    Thy education, boy, and have they sent
    thee
    Home like a very scholar?
AL.   'Twas ill done,
    Howe'er they used him in the university,
    To send him to his friends thus.
FRED.   Why, sir, black
    (For 'tis the color that offends your eye-
    sight)
    Is not, within my reading, any blemish;
    Sables are no disgrace in heraldry.   50
AL. 'Tis coming from the college thus that
    makes it
    Dishonorable. While you ware [3] it for

[1] Title, ornament.
[2] Vainglorious.   [3] Wore.

    Your father, it was commendable; or,
    were
    Your aunt dead, you might mourn, and
    justify.
ARE. What luck [4] I did not send him into
    France!
    They would have given him generous
    education,
    Taught him another garb, to wear his
    lock
    And shape as gaudy as the summer, how
    To dance, and wag his feather *à la mode*,
    To compliment and cringe,[5] to talk not
    modestly,   60
    Like, "ay, forsooth," and "no, forsooth,"
    to blush,
    And look so like a chaplain! There he
    might
    Have learned a brazen confidence, and
    observed
    So well the custom of the country that
    He might by this time have invented
    fashions
    For us, and been a benefit to the king-
    dom,
    Preserved our tailors in their wits, and
    saved
    The charge of sending into foreign courts
    For pride and antic fashions. Observe
    In what a posture he does hold his hat
    now!   70
FRED. Madam, with your pardon, you
    have practiced
    Another dialect than was taught me
    when
    I was commended to your care and breed-
    ing.
    I understand not this. Latin or Greek
    Are more familiar to my apprehension;
    Logic was not so hard in my first lectures
    As your strange language.
ARE.   Some strong waters—O!
LIT. [*Offering a box.*] Comfits will be as
    comfortable to your stomach, madam.
ARE. I fear he's spoiled forever! He did
    name
    Logic, and may, for aught I know, be
    gone   80
    So far to understand it. I did always
    Suspect they would corrupt him in the
    college.—
    Will your Greek saws and sentences dis-
    charge

[4] *I.e.*, bad luck.   [5] Bow.

The mercer? Or is Latin a fit language
To court a mistress in?—Mr. Alexander,
If you have any charity, let me
Commend him to your breeding. I sus-
   pect
I must employ my doctor first, to purge
The university that lies in 's head;
It alters his complexion.[1]

AL.   If you dare   90
Trust me to serve him—

ARE.   Mr. Littleworth,
Be you joined in commission.

LIT.   I will teach him
Postures and rudiments.

ARE.   I have no patience
To see him in this shape; it turns my
   stomach.
When he has cast his academic skin,
He shall be yours. I am bound in con-
   science
To see him bred; his own state shall
   maintain
The charge, while he's my ward.—Come
   hither, sir.

FRED. What does my aunt mean to do
   with me?

STEW. To make you a fine gentleman, and
   translate you   100
Out of your learned language, sir, into
The present Goth and Vandal, which is
   French.

BORN. [Aside.] Into what mischief will
   this humor ebb?
She will undo the boy; I see him ruined.
My patience is not manly, but I must
Use stratagem to reduce her—open ways
Give me no hope.   Exit.

STEW.   You shall be obeyed, madam.
Exeunt [All but Frederick and Steward].

FRED. Mr. Steward, are you sure we do
   not dream?
Was 't not my aunt you talked to?

STEW.   One that loves you
Dear as her life. These clothes do not be-
   come you;   110
You must have better, sir—

FRED.   These are not old.

STEW. More suitable to the town and time;
   we keep
No Lent here, nor is 't my lady's pleasure
   you
Should fast from anything you have a
   mind to—

[1] Disposition.

Unless it be your learning, which she
   would have you
Forget with all convenient speed that
   may be,
For the credit of your noble family.
The case is altered since we lived i' th'
   country;
We do not invite the poor o' th' parish
To dinner, keep a table for the tenants;
Our kitchen does not smell of beef; the
   cellar   121
Defies the price of malt and hops; the
   footmen
And coachdrivers may be drunk like
   gentlemen
With wine, nor will three fiddlers upon
   holidays,
With aid of bagpipes, that called in the
   country
To dance and plow the hall up with their
   hobnails
Now make my lady merry. We do feed
Like princes, and feast nothing but
   princes;
And are these robes fit to be seen amongst
   'em?

FRED. My lady keeps a court then! Is Sir
   Thomas   130
Affected with this state and cost?

STEW.   He was not,
But is converted; and I hope you wo' not
Persist in heresy, but take a course
Of riot, to content your friends; you shall
Want nothing, if you can be proud, and
   spend it
For my lady's honor. Here are a hun-
   dred
Pieces will serve you till you have new
   clothes;
I will present you with a nag of mine,
Poor tender of my service—please you
   accept.
My lady's smile more than rewards me
   for it.   140
I must provide fit servants to attend you,
Monsieurs, for horse and foot.

FRED.   I shall submit,
If this be my aunt's pleasure, and be
   ruled;
My eyes are opened with this purse already,
And sack will help to inspire me. I must
   spend it?

STEW. What else, sir?

FRED.   I'll begin with you. To encourage
You to have still a special care of me,
There is five pieces—not for your nag.
STEW. No, sir; I hope it is not.
FRED.   Buy a beaver [1]
For thy own block; I shall be ruled. Who does   150
Command the wine cellar?
STEW.   Who command but you, sir?
FRED. I'll try to drink a health or two, my aunt's,
Or anybody's; and, if that foundation
Stagger me not too much, I will commence
In all the arts of London.
STEW.   If you find, sir,
The operation of the wine exalt
Your blood to the desire of any female
Delight, I know your aunt wo' not deny
Any of her chambermaids to practice on;
She loves you but too well.
FRED.   I know not how   160
I may be for that exercise.—Farewell, Aristotle!
Prithee, commend me to the library
At Westminster; my bones I bequeath thither,
And to the learned worms that mean to visit 'em.
I will compose myself; I begin to think
I have lost time indeed.—Come, to the wine cellar.   *Exit [with Steward].*

[SCENE ii.

A room in Celestina's house.]

Enter Celestina, Mariana, Isabella.

MAR. But shall we not, madam, expose ourselves
To censure for this freedom?
CEL.   Let them answer
That dare mistake us. Shall we be so much
Cowards, to be frighted from our pleasure,
Because men have malicious tongues, and show
What miserable souls they have? No, cousin,
We hold our life and fortunes upon no
Man's charity; if they dare show so little

Discretion to traduce our fames, we will
Be guilty of so much wit to laugh at 'em.
ISA. 'Tis a becoming fortitude.
CEL.   My stars   11
Are yet kind to me; for, in a happy minute
Be 't spoke, I'm not in love, and men shall never
Make my heart lean with sighing, nor with tears
Draw on my eyes the infamy of spectacles.
'Tis the chief principle to keep your heart
Under your own obedience; jest, but love not.
I say my prayers, yet can wear good clothes,
And only satisfy my tailor for 'em.
I wo' not lose my privilege.   20
MAR. And yet they say your entertainments are—
Give me your pardon, madam—to proclaim
Yourself a widow, and to get a husband.
CEL. As if a lady of my years, some beauty,
Left by her husband rich, that had mourned for him
A twelvemonth too, could live so obscure i' th' town
That gallants would not know her, and invite
Themselves, without her chargeable [2] proclamations!
Then we are worse than citizens.[3] No widow
Left wealthy can be throughly warm in mourning,   30
But some one noble blood or lusty kindred
Claps in with his gilt coach and Flandrian trotters,
And hurries her away to be a countess.
Courtiers have spies, and great ones with large [4] titles,
Cold in their own estates, would warm themselves
At a rich city bonefire.
ISA.   Most true, madam.

---

[1] Beaver hat.
[2] Expensive.
[3] Dwellers in the city, *i.e.*, middle-class persons.
[4] Gifford-Dyce's reading. Original reads *charge.*

CEL. No matter for corruption of the
blood—
Some undone courtier made her husband
rich,
And this new lord receives it back again.
Admit it were my policy, and that   40
My entertainments pointed to acquaint
me
With many suitors, that I might be safe
And make the best election, could you
blame me?
MAR. Madam, 'tis wisdom.
CEL.   But I should be
In my thoughts miserable, to be fond [1]
Of leaving the sweet freedom I possess,
And court myself into new marriage
fetters.
I now observe men's several wits and
windings,
And can laugh at their follies.
MAR.   You have given
A most ingenious satisfaction.   50
CEL. One thing I'll tell you more, and this
I give you
Worthy your imitation, from my prac-
tice:
You see me merry, full of song and danc-
ing,
Pleasant in language, apt to all delights
That crown a public meeting; but you
cannot
Accuse me of being prodigal of my favors
To any of my guests. I do not summon,
By any wink, a gentleman to follow me
To my withdrawing chamber; I hear all
Their pleas in court, nor can they boast
abroad   60
(And do me justice [2]) after a salute
They have much conversation with my
lip.
I hold the kissing of my hand a courtesy,
And he that loves me must, upon the
strength
Of that, expect [3] till I renew his favor.
Some ladies are so expensive in their
graces
To those that honor 'em, and so prodigal,
That in a little time they have nothing
but
The naked sin left to reward their serv-
ants,

Whereas a thrift in our rewards will
keep   70
Men long in their devotion, and preserve
Ourselves in stock, to encourage those
that honor us.
ISA. This is an art worthy a lady's practice.
CEL. It takes not from the freedom of our
mirth,
But seems to advance it, when we can
possess
Our pleasures with security of our honor;
And, that preserved, I welcome all the
joys
My fancy can let in. In this I have given
The copy of my mind, nor do I blush
You understand it.

Enter Celestina's Gentlewoman.

ISA.   You have honored us.   80
GEN. Madam, Sir William Scentlove's
come to wait on you.
CEL. There's one would be a client.—Make
excuse
For a few minutes. [*Exit Gentlewoman.*]
MAR.   One that comes a-wooing?
CEL. Such a thing he would seem, but in
his guiltiness
Of little land, his expectation is not
So valiant as it might be. He wears [rich] [4]
clothes,
And feeds with noblemen; to some, I
hear,
No better than a wanton emissary
Or scout for Venus' wild fowl, which
made tame,
He thinks no shame to stand court
sentinel,   90
In hope of the reversion.
MAR.   I have heard
That some of them are often my lord's
tasters;
The first fruits they condition for and will
Exact as fees, for the promotion.
CEL. Let them agree; there's no account
shall lie
For me among their traffic.

Enter Gentlewo[man].

GEN.   Mr. Haircut, madam,
Is new come in, to tender you his service.
CEL. Let him discourse a little with Sir
William.   *Exit [Gentlewoman].*

---

[1] Foolishly desirous.
[2] Gifford-Dyce's reading.   Original reads
justific.   [3] Wait.
[4] Supplied by Gifford-Dyce.

Mar. What is this gentleman, Mr. Hair-
　cut, madam?
　I note him very gallant, and much
　　courted　　　　　　　　　　　　　　100
By gentlemen of quality.
Cel.　　　　　　　　　　I know not,
　More than a trim, gay man; he has some
　　great office,
　Sure, by his confident behavior.
　He would be entertained under the title
　Of servant to me, and I must confess
　He is the sweetest of all men that visit
　　me.
Isa. How mean you, madam?
Cel.　　　　　　　　He is full of powder;
　He will save much in perfume for my
　　chamber,
　Were he but constant here.—Give 'em
　　access.

Enter Sir Will[iam] Scentlove, Mr. Haircut.

Scent. Madam, the humblest of your
　　servants is　　　　　　　　　　　110
　Exalted to a happiness, if you smile
　Upon my visit.
Hair.　　　　　　I must beg your charity
　Upon my rudeness, madam; I shall
　　give
　That day up lost to any happiness,
　When I forget to tender you my serv-
　　ice.
Cel. You practice courtship, gentlemen.
Scent.　　　　　　　　　But cannot
　Find where with more desert to exercise
　　it.—
　What lady's this, I pray?
Cel.　　　　　　　　　A kinswoman
　Of mine, Sir William.
Scent.　　　　　I am more her servant.
　　　　　　　　　[*Takes Mariana aside.*]
Cel. You came from court, now, I pre-
　sume.
Hair.　　　　　'Tis, madam,　　　　　120
　The sphere I move in, and my destiny
　Was kind to place me there, where I
　　enjoy
　All blessings that a mortal can possess,
　That lives not in your presence; and I
　　should
　Fix my ambition, when you would vouch-
　　safe
　Me so much honor to accept from me
　An humble entertainment there.

Cel.　　　　　　　　　　　　But by
　What name shall I be known? In what
　　degree
　Shall I be of kinred [1] to you?
Hair.　　　　　　How mean you, madam?
Cel. Perhaps you'll call me sister—I shall
　take it　　　　　　　　　　　　　130
　A special preferment; or it may be
　I may pass under title of your mistress,
　If I seem rich and fair enough to engage
　Your confidence to own me.
Hair.　　　　　　　I would hope—
Cel. But 'tis not come to that yet; you
　will, sir,
　Excuse my mirth.
Hair.　　　　　Sweet madam!
Cel.　　　　　　　　　　Shall I take
　Boldness to ask what place you hold in
　　court?
　'Tis an uncivil curiosity,
　But you'll have mercy to a woman's
　　question.
Hair. My present condition, madam, car-
　ries　　　　　　　　　　　　　　140
　Honor and profit, though not to be named
　With that employment I expect i' th'
　　state,
　Which shall discharge the first maturity
　Upon your knowledge; until then, I beg
　You allow a modest silence.
Cel.　　　　　　　I am charmed, sir;
　And, if you scape ambassador, you can-
　　not
　Reach a preferment wherein I'm against
　　you.
　But where's Sir William Scentlove?
Hair.　　　　　　　　　Give him leave
　To follow his nose, madam; while he
　　hunts
　In view, he'll soon be at a fault.[2]
Cel.　　　　　　　You know him?　　150
Hair. Know Scentlove? Not a page but
　can decipher him;
　The waiting-women know him to a
　　scruple.
　He's called the blister-maker of the town.
Cel. What's that?
Hair.[3]　　　　　　The laundry ladies can
　resolve [4] you,

---

[1] Kindred.
[2] *I.e.*, while now he can see the quarry, he'll
soon lose the scent.
[3] Emended by Gifford-Dyce. Original reads
Isa.　　　　　　　　　　[4] Inform.

And you may guess—an arrant epicure
As this day lives, born to a pretty wit,
A knight, but no gentleman. I must
Be plain to you; your ladyship may have
Use of this knowledge, but conceal the
    author.

SCENT. I kiss your fairest hand.

MAR.   You make a difference;   160
Pray reconcile 'em to an equal whiteness.

SCENT. You wound my meaning, lady.

CEL.   Nay, Sir William
Has the art of compliment.

SCENT.   Madam, you honor me
'Bove my desert of language.

CEL.   Will you please
To enrich me with your knowledge of
    that gentleman?

SCENT. Do you not know him, madam?

CEL.   What is he?

SCENT. A camphire[1] ball. You shall know
    more hereafter;
He shall tell you himself, and save my
    character.
Till then—you see he's proud.

CEL.   One thing, gentlemen,
I observe in your behavior, which is
    rare   170
In two that court one mistress: you pre-
    serve
A noble friendship.   There's no gum
    within
Your hearts; you cannot fret,[2] or show an
    envy
Of one another's hope. Some would not
    govern
Their passions with that temper!

SCENT.   The whole world
Sha' not divorce our friendship.—Mr.
    Haircut!
Would I had lives to serve him! He is
    lost
To goodness does not honor him.

HAIR.   My knight!

CEL. [Aside.] This is right playing at
    court shuttlecock.

Enter Gentlew[oman].

GEN. Madam, there is a gentleman de-
    sires   180
To speak wi'e, one Sir Thomas Born-
    well.

---
[1] Camphor.
[2] Gum was used to stiffen velvet, which
thereafter fretted easily.

CEL.   Bornwell?

GEN. He says he is a stranger to your lady-
    ship.

SCENT. I know him.

HAIR.   Your neighbor, madam.

SCENT.   Husband to
The lady that so revels in the Strand.

HAIR. He has good parts, they say, but
    cannot help
His lady's bias.

CEL.   They have both much fame
I' th' town, for several merits. Pray, ad-
    mit him.   [*Exit Gentlewoman.*]

HAIR. [*Aside.*] What comes he for?

Enter Sir Thomas.

BORN. Your pardon, noble lady, that I
    have
Presumed, a stranger to your knowl-
    edge—   [*Kisses Celestina.*]

CEL.   Sir,   190
Your worth was here before you, and
    your person
Cannot be here ingrateful.

BORN.   'Tis the bounty
Of your sweet disposition, madam.—[*To
    Isabella.*] Make me
Your servant, lady, by her fair example,
To favor me.—[*Offers to kiss Isabella, who
    turns her cheek. Aside.*] I never knew
    one turn
Her cheek to a gentleman that came to
    kiss her,
But sh'ad a stinking breath.—Your serv-
    ant, gentlemen.
Will Scentlove, how is 't?

CEL.   I am sorry, coz,
To accuse you; we in nothing more be-
    tray   199
Ourselves to censure of ridiculous pride
Than answering a fair salute too rudely.
O, it shows ill upon a gentlewoman
Not to return the modest lip, if she
Would have the world believe her breath
    is not
Offensive.

BORN.   Madam, I have business
With you.   [*The Rest step aside.*]

SCENT.   His looks are pleasant.

CEL.   With me, sir?

BORN. I hear you have an ex'llent wit,
    madam;
I see you're fair.

CEL. The first is but report;
And do not trust your eyesight for the last,
Cause I presume y' are mortal, and may err. 210
HAIR. He is very gamesome.
BORN. Y'ave an ex'llent voice
(They say you catched it from a dying swan),
Which, joined to the sweet harmony of your lute,
You ravish all mankind.
CEL. Ravish mankind?
BORN. With their consent.
CEL. It were the stranger rape;
But there's the less indictment lies against it,
And there is hope your little honesties [1]
Cannot be much the worse, for men do rather
Believe they had a maidenhead than put
Themselves to th' rack of memory how long 220
'Tis since they left the burden of their innocence.
BORN. Why, you are bitter, madam!
CEL. So is physic;
I do not know your constitution.
BORN. You shall, if please you, madam.
CEL. Y' are too hasty;
I must examine what certificate
You have first, to prefer you.
BORN. Fine! Certificate?
CEL. Under your lady's hand and seal.
BORN. Go to.
I see you are a wag.
CEL. But take heed how
You trust to 't.
BORN. I can love you in my wedlock
As well as that young gallant o' th' first hair 230
Or the knight bachelor, and can return
As amorous delight to thy soft bosom.
CEL. Your person and your language are both strangers.
BORN. But may be more familiar; I have those
That dare make affidavit for my body.
CEL. D'e mean your surgeon?
BORN. My surgeon, madam?
I know not how you value my abilities,
But I dare undertake as much, to express
My service to your ladyship, and with

[1] Chastities.

As fierce ambition fly to your commands
As the most valiant of these lay siege to you. 241
CEL. You dare not, sir.
BORN. How, madam?
CEL. I will justify 't.
You dare not marry me; and I imagine
Some here, should I consent, would fetch a priest
Out of the fire.
BORN. I have a wife indeed.
CEL. And there's a statute not repealed, I take it.
BORN. Y' are in the right; I must confess y'ave hit
And bled me in a master vein.
CEL. You think
I took you on the advantage; use your best
Skill at defense, I'll come up to your valor, 250
And show another work you dare not do:
You dare not, sir, be virtuous.
BORN. I dare,
By this fair hand I dare, and ask a pardon
If my rude words offend thy innocence,
Which, in a form so beautiful, would shine
To force a blush in them suspected it,
And from the rest draw wonder.
HAIR. I like not
Their secret parley; shall I interrupt 'em?
ISA. By no means, sir.
SCENT. Sir Thomas was not wont
To show so much a courtier.
MAR. He cannot 260
Be prejudicial to you. Suspect not
Your own deserts so much; he's married.
BORN. I have other business, madam.
You keep music;
I came to try how you can dance.
CEL. You did?—[Aside.] I'll try his humor
out of breath.—
Although I boast no cunning, sir, in revels,
If you desire to show your art that way,
I can wait on you.
BORN. You much honor me;
Nay, all must join to make a harmony.
They dance.
BORN. I have nothing now, madam, but to beseech, 270
After a pardon for my boldness, you

Would give occasion to pay my gratitude.
I have a house will be much honor[é]d,
If you vouchsafe your presence, and a wife
Desires to present herself your servant.
I came with the ambition to invite you;
Deny me not. Your person you shall trust
On fair security.

CEL.   Sir, although I use not
This freedom with a stranger, you shall have
No cause to hold me obstinate.

BORN.   You grace me.   280
Sir William Scentlove—

HAIR.   I must take my leave.
You will excuse me, madam; court at-
    tendances—

CEL. By any means.

BORN.   Ladies, you will vouchsafe
Your company?

ISA. }
MAR. }   We wait upon you, sir.

                            Exeunt.

THE THIRD ACT. [SCENE i.

A dressing room.]

Enter Lord, unready; [1] *Haircut preparing
    his periwig; table and looking-glass.*

LORD. What hour is 't?

HAIR.   'Bout three a-clock, my lord.

LORD.[2] 'Tis time to rise.

HAIR.   Your lordship went but late
To bed last night.

LORD.   'Twas early in the morning.

Enter Secre[tary].

SEC. [*Calling back.*] Expect awhile.—My
    lord is busy?

LORD. What's the matter?

SEC.   Here is a lady
Desires access to you upon some affairs
She says may specially concern your
    lordship.

LORD. A lady? What her name?

SEC.   Madam Decoy.

LORD. Decoy? Prithee, admit her.—

Enter Decoy.

                    Have you business, madam,   9
With me?

DEC.   And such, I hope, as will not be
Offensive to your lordship.

---

[1] Partly dressed.   [2] Original reads *Bor.*

LORD.   I pray, speak it.

DEC. I would desire your lordship's ear
    more private.

LORD. [*To Secretary and Haircut.*] Wait i'
    th' next chamber till I call.—(*Exeunt
    [Haircut and Secretary].*) Now, madam.

DEC. Although I am a stranger to your
    lordship,
I would not lose a fair occasion offered
To show how much I honor and would
    serve you.

LORD. Please you to give me the par-
    ticular,
That I may know the extent of my en-
    gagement.
I am ignorant by what desert you should
Be encouraged to have care of me.

DEC.   My lord,   20
I will take boldness to be plain; beside
Your other excellent parts, you have
    much fame
For your sweet inclination to our sex.

LORD. How d'e mean, madam?

DEC.   I' that way your lordship
Hath honorably practiced upon some
Not to be named, your noble constancy
To a mistress hath deserved our general
    vote,
And I, a part of womankind, have
    thought
How to express my duty.

LORD.   In what, madam?

DEC. Be not so strange, my lord.   I
    know the beauty   30
And pleasures of your eyes—that hand-
    some creature
With whose fair life all your delight took
    leave,
And to whose memory you have paid
    too much
Sad tribute.

LORD.   What's all this?

DEC.   This: if your lo[rd]s[hip]
Accept my service, in pure zeal to cure
Your melancholy, I could point where
    you might
Repair your loss.

LORD.   Your ladyship, I conceive,
Doth traffic in flesh merchandise.

DEC.   To men
Of honor, like yourself. I am well known
To some in court, and come not with am-
    bition   40
Now to supplant your officer.

LORD.   What is
The lady of pleasure you prefer?
DEC.   A lady
Of birth and fortune, one upon whose
  virtue
I may presume, the Lady Aretina.
LORD. Wife to Sir Thomas Bornwell?
DEC.   The same, sir.
LORD. Have you prepared her?
DEC. Not for your lordship, till I have
  found your pulse.
I am acquainted with her disposition;
She has a very appliable [1] nature.
LORD. And, madam, when expect you to
  be whipped   50
For doing these fine favors?
DEC.   How, my lord?
Your lordship does but jest, I hope; you
  make
A difference between a lady that
Does honorable offices, and one
They call a bawd. Your lordship was not
  wont
To have such coarse opinion of our prac-
  tice.
LORD. The Lady Aretina is my kins-
  woman.
DEC. What if she be, my lord? The nearer
  blood,
The dearer sympathy.
LORD.   I'll have thee carted.[2]
DEC. Your lordship wo' not so much stain
  your honor   60
And education to use a woman
Of my quality—
LORD.   'Tis possible you may
Be sent off with an honorable convoy
Of halberdiers.
DEC.   O, my good lord!
LORD. Your ladyship [3] shall be no protec-
  tion,
If thou but stay'st three minutes.
DEC.   I am gone.—
When next you find rebellion in your
  blood,
May all within ten mile o' th' court turn
  honest! [4]   *Exit.*
LORD. I do not find that proneness, since
  the fair
Bella Maria died; my blood is cold,   70

Nor is there beauty enough surviving
To heighten me to wantonness.—Who
  waits?

Enter Haircut.

And what said my lady?
HAIR. The silent language of her face, my
  lord,
Was not so pleasant as it showed upon
Her entrance.
LORD.   Would any man that meets
This lady take her for a bawd?
HAIR.   She does
The trade an honor, credit to the pro-
  fession.
We may in time see baldness, quarter
  noses,
And rotten legs to take the wall of [5]
  footcloths.[6]   80
LORD. I ha' thought better.—[*To Secretary
  within.*] Call the lady back.
I wo' not lose this opportunity.
Bid her not fear. The favor is not com-
  mon,
And I'll reward it.—I do wonder much
Will Scentlove was not here today.
HAIR. I heard him say this morning he
  would wait
Upon your lordship.—She is returned,
  sir.

Enter Secre[tary] and Decoy.

SEC. Madam, be confident; my lord's not
  angry.
LORD. You return welcome, madam; you
  are better
Read in your art, I hope, than to be
  frighted   90
With any shape of anger, when you bring
Such news to gentlemen. Madam, you
  shall
Soon understand how I accept the office.
DEC. You are the first lord, since I studied
  carriage,[7]
That showed such infidelity and fury
Upon so kind a message. Every gentle-
  man
Will show some breeding, but if one right
  honorable
Should not have noble blood—

---

[1] Pliable, compliant.
[2] Bawds were punished by being whipped
through the streets at the tail of a cart.
[3] Station as a lady.   [4] Chaste

[5] Take precedence over.
[6] The caparison of a horse.
[7] Acting as a go-between.

LORD.   You shall return
My compliment in a letter to my Lady
Aretina.   Favor me with a little pa-
tience.—   100
Show her that chamber.
DEC.   I'll attend your lordship.
[*Exeunt Decoy and Haircut.   Secretary pre-
pares to write.*]
LORD. Write—"Madam, where your honor
is in danger,
My love must not be silent."—

Enter Scentlove and Kickshaw.

                      Scentlove and Kickshaw!
KICK. Your lordship's busy.
LORD. Writing a letter.—Nay, it sha' not
bar
Any discourse.
SEC.   "—silent."
LORD. "Though I be no physician, I may
Prevent a fever in your blood."—And
where
Have you spent the morning's conversa-
tion?
SCENT. Where you would have given the
best Barbary   110
In your stable to have met on honorable
terms.
LORD. What new beauty? You acquaint
yourselves
With none but wonders.
SCENT.   'Tis too low—a miracle.
LORD. 'Twill require a strong faith.
SEC.   "—your blood."
LORD. "If you be innocent, preserve your
fame, lest this Decoy,
Madam, betray it, to your repent-
ance."—
By what name is she known?
SCENT.   Ask Alexander;
He knows her.
AL.   Whom?
SCENT.   The Lady Celestina.
LORD. He has a vast knowledge of ladies.
'Las, poor Alexander!
When dost thou mean thy body shall lie
fallow?   120
AL. When there is mercy in a petticoat.
I must turn pilgrim for some breath.
LORD.   I think
'Twere cooler travel, if you examine it,
Upon the hoof through Spain.
SCENT.   Through Ethiopia.

LORD. Nay, less laborious to serve a pren-
ticeship
In Peru, and dig gold out of the mine,
Where all the year is dog days.
SEC.   "— to repentance."
LORD. "In brief, this lady, could you fall
from virtue,
Within my knowledge, will not blush to
be a bawd."
SCENT. But, hang 't, 'tis honorable journey-
work;   130
Thou art famous by 't, and thy name's
up.
AL.   So, sir!
Let me ask you a question, my dear
knight:
Which is less servile, to bring up the
pheasant
And wait, or sit at table uncontrolled
And carve to my own appetite?
SCENT.   No more;
Th' art witty, as I am.
SEC.   "— a bawd."
SCENT.   How's that?
AL. O, you are famous by 't, and your
name's up, sir.
LORD. "Be wise, and reward my caution
with
Timely care of yourself, so I shall not
repent
To be known your loving kinsman and
servant"—   140
Gentlemen, the Lady Celestina,
Is she so rare a thing?
AL.   If you'll have my
Opinion, my lord, I never saw
So sweet, so fair, so rich a piece of nature.
LORD. I'll show thee a fairer presently, to
shame
Thy eyes and judgment; look o' that.—
[*Shows him a picture.*] So, I'll sub-
scribe. [*Signs his name.*]
Seal it; I'll excuse your pen for the direc-
tion.
AL. Bella Maria's picture! She was hand-
some.
SCENT. But not to be compared—
LORD. Your patience, gentlemen; I'll re-
turn instantly.   *Exit.* 150
AL. Whither is my lord gone?
SEC. To a lady i' th' next chamber.
SCENT.   What is she?
SEC. You shall pardon me; I am his secre-
tary.

SCENT. I was wont to be of his counsel. A
　new officer,
And I not know 't? I am resolved to
　batter
All other with the praise of Celestina.
I must retain him.

Enter Lord.

LORD. 　　　　　Has not that object—
Convinced your erring judgments?
AL. 　　　　　What, this picture?
LORD. Were but your thoughts as capable
　as mine 　　　　　159
Of your idea, you would wish no thought
That were not active in her praise, above
All worth and memory of her sex.
SCENT. 　　　　　She was fair,
I must confess; but, had your lordship
　looked
With eyes more narrow and some less
　affection
Upon her face—
AL. 　　　　　I do not love the copies
Of any dead; they make me dream of
　goblins.
Give me a living mistress, with but half
The beauty of Celestina. Come, my lord,
'Tis pity that a lord of so much flesh
Should waste upon a ghost, when they
　are living 　　　　　170
Can give you a more honorable consump-
　tion.
SCENT. Why, do you mean, my lord, to
　live an infidel?
Do, and see what will come on 't; observe
　still
And dote upon your vigils; build a cham-
　ber
Within a rock, a tomb among the worms,
Not far off, where you may in proof
　apocryphal
Court 'em not devour the pretty pile
Of flesh your mistress carried to the
　grave.
There are no women in the world; all eyes
And tongue and lips are buried in her
　coffin! 　　　　　180
LORD. Why, do you think yourselves com-
　petent judges
Of beauty, gentlemen?
BOTH. 　　　　　What should hinder us?
AL. I have seen and tried as many as an-
　other
With a mortal back.

LORD. 　　　　　Your eyes are bribed,
And your hearts chained to some desires;
　you cannot
Enjoy the freedom of a sense.
AL. 　　　　　Your lordship
Has a clear eyesight, and can judge and
　penetrate.
LORD. I can, and give a perfect censure[1] of
Each line and point; distinguish beauty
　from
A thousand forms, which your corrupted
　optics 　　　　　190
Would pass for natural.
SCENT. 　　　　　I desire no other
Judge should determine[2] us, and, if your
　lordship
Dare venture but your eyes upon this
　lady,
I'll stand their justice, and be confident
You shall give Celestina victory
And triumph o'er all beauties past and
　living.
AL. I dare, my lord, venture a suit of
　clothes
You will be o'ercome.
LORD. 　You do not know my fortitude.
SCENT. Nor frailty; you dare not trust
　yourself to see her.
LORD. Think you so, gentlemen? I dare
　see this creature 　　　　　200
To make you know your errors, and the
　difference
Of her whose memory is my saint. Not
　trust
My senses? I dare see and speak with
　her.
Which holds the best acquaintance to
　prepare
My visit to her?
SCENT. 　　　　　I will do 't, my lord.
AL. She is a lady free in entertainments.
LORD. I would give this advantage to your
　cause.
Bid her[3] appear in all the ornaments
Did ever wait on beauty, all the riches
Pride can put on, and teach her face more
　charm 　　　　　210
Than ever poet dressed up Venus in;
Bid her be all the Graces and the Queen
Of Love in one, I'll see her, Scentlove,
　and

---

[1] Judgment. 　　　　　[2] Decide for.
[3] Emended by Gifford-Dyce. Original reads
him.

Bring off my heart, armed but [with a] [1]
　single thought
Of one that is dead, without a wound,
　and, when
I have made your folly prisoner, I'll
　laugh at you.
SCENT. She shall expect you; trust to me
　for knowledge.
LORD. I'm for the present somewhere else
　engaged;
　Let me hear from you. 　　　　[*Exit.*]
SCENT. 　　　　So! I am glad he's yet
So near conversion.
AL. 　　　　I am for Aretina. 　220
SCENT. No mention of my lord.
AL. 　　　　Prepare his lady;
'Tis time he were reduced [2] to the old
　sport.
One lord like him more would undo the
　court. 　　　　*Exit* [*with Scentlove*].

[SCENE ii.

A room in Bornwell's house.]

Enter Aretina with a letter; Decoy.

DEC. He is the ornament of your blood,
　madam;
I am much bound to his lordship.
ARE. 　　　　He gives you
A noble character.
DEC. 　　　　'Tis his goodness, madam.
ARE. [*Aside.*] I wanted such an engine.[3]
　My lord has
Done me a courtesy to disclose her na-
　ture;
I now know one to trust, and will employ
　her.—
Touching my lord, for reasons which I
　shall
Offer to your ladyship hereafter, I
Desire you would be silent; but, to
　show
How much I dare be confident in your
　secrecy, 　　　　　　10
I pour my bosom forth. I love a gentle-
　man,
On whom there wo' not need [4] much con-
　juration
To meet.—Your ear. 　　[*Whispers to her.*]
DEC. 　　　　I apprehend you, and I shall
Be happy to be serviceable. I am sorry

　[1] Supplied by Gifford-Dyce.
　[2] Brought back. 　　　　[3] Device.
　[4] Gifford-Dyce's reading. Original reads *meet*.

Your ladyship did not know me before
　now.
I have done offices, and not a few
Of the nobility but have done feats
Within my house, which is convenient
For situation and artful chambers
And pretty pictures to provoke the
　fancy. 　　　　　　20

Enter Littleworth.

LIT. Madam, all pleasures languish in your
　absence.
ARE. Your pardon a few minutes, sir.—
　[*Walks aside with Decoy.*] You must
Contrive it thus.
LIT. 　　　　I attend, and shall account it
Honor to wait on your return.
ARE. 　　　　He must not
Have the least knowledge of my name or
　person.
DEC. I have practiced that already for
　some great ones,
And dare again, to satisfy you, madam;
I have a thousand ways to do sweet
　offices.
LIT. [*To himself.*] If this Lady Aretina
　should be honest, 　　　　　29
I ha' lost time. She's free as air; I must
Have closer conference, and, if I have art,
Make her affect me in revenge.
DEC. 　　　　This evening?
Leave me to manage things.
ARE. 　　　　You will oblige me.
DEC. You shall commend my art, and
　thank me after. 　　　　*Ex*[*it*].
ARE. I hope the revels are maintained
　within.
LIT. By Sir Thomas and his mistress.
ARE. 　　　　How? His mistress?
LIT. The Lady Celestina; I ne'er saw
Eyes shoot more amorous interchange.
ARE. 　　　　Is 't so?
LIT. He wears her favor with o'er-pride[5]—
ARE. 　　　　Her favor?
LIT. A feather that he ravished from her
　fan— 　　　　　　40
And is so full of courtship, which she
　smiles on.
ARE. 'Tis well.
LIT. 　　And praises her beyond all poetry.
ARE. I'm glad he has so much wit.
LIT. [*Aside.*] 　　　　Not jealous!

　[5] Immense pride.

ARE. [*Aside.*] This secures me. What
   would make other ladies pale
With jealousy, gives but a license to my
   wand'rings.
Let him now tax me, if he dare; and
   yet
Her beauty's worth my envy, and I wish
Revenge upon it, not because he loves,
But that it shines above my own.

Enter Alex[ander].

AL.   Dear madam!
ARE. [*Aside.*] I have it.—You two gentle-
   men profess   50
Much service to me; if I have a way
To employ your wit and secrecy—
BOTH.   You'll honor us.
ARE. You gave a high and worthy char-
   acter
Of Celestina.
AL.   I remember, madam.
ARE. Do either of you love her?
AL.   Not I, madam.
LIT. I would not, if I might.
ARE.   She's now my guest
And, by a trick, invited by my husband
To disgrace me. You, gentlemen, are
   held
Wits of the town, the consuls that do
   govern
The senate here, whose jeers are all
   authentic.   60
The taverns and the ordinaries are
Made academies, where you come, and
   all
Your sins and surfeits made the time's
   example.
Your very nods can quell a theater;
No speech or poem good without your
   seal;
You can protect scurrility, and publish;
By your authority believed, no rapture
Ought to have honest meaning.
AL.   Leave our characters.
LIT. And name the employment.
ARE.   You must exercise
The strength of both your wits upon this
   lady,   70
And talk her into humbleness or anger,
Both which are equal, to my thought. If
   you
Dare undertake this slight thing for my
   sake,

My favor shall reward it; but be faith-
   ful,
And seem to let all spring from your own
   freedom.
AL. This all? We can defame her. If you
   please,
My friend shall call her whore, or any-
   thing,
And never be endangered to a duel.
ARE. How's that?
AL. He can endure a cudgeling, and no
   man   80
Will fight after so fair a satisfaction.
But leave us to our art, and do not limit
   us.
ARE. They are here; begin not till I whis-
   per you.

*Enter Sir Thomas, Celestina, Mariana, Isa-
   bella.*

ARE.[1] *Je vous prie, madame, d'excuser
l'importunité de mes affaires, qui m'ont fait
offenser, par mon absence, une dame de
laquelle j'ai reçu tant d'obligation.*
   CEL. *Pardonnez-moi, madame; vous me
faites trop d'honneur.*   89
   ARE. *C'est bien de la douceur de votre na-
turel, que vous tenez cette langage. Mais
j'espère que mon mari n'a pas manqué de
vous entretenir en mon absence.*
   CEL. *En vérité, monsieur nous a fort
obligé.*
   ARE. *Il eût trop failli, s'il n'eût taché de
tout son pouvoir à vous rendre toutes sortes de
services.*
   CEL. *C'est de sa bonté qu'il nous a tant
favorisé.*   100
   ARE. *De la vôtre plutôt, madame, que
vous fait donner d'interprétation si bénigne
à ses efforts.*
   CEL. *Je vois bien que la victoire sera tou-
jours à madame, et de langage et de la
courtesie.*
   ARE. *Vraiment, madame, que jamais per-
sonne a plus désiré l'honneur de votre
compagnie que moi.*
   CEL. *Laissons-en, je vous supplie,* [110
*des compliments, et permettez à votre servante
de vous baiser les mains.*

[1] The French as well as some of the English
which follows has been printed as prose, although in the original an unsuccessful attempt
at line division has been made.

ARE. *Vous m'obligez trop.*[1]

BORN. I have no more patience; let's be merry again
In our own language. Madam, our mirth cools.—

Enter Frederick [, intoxicated, and Steward].

Our nephew!

ARE. Passion of my brain!

FRED. Save you, gentlemen! Save you, ladies!

ARE. I am undone! 120

FRED. I must salute, no matter at which end I begin. [*Kisses Celestina.*]

ARE. There's a compliment!

CEL. Is this your nephew, madam?

ARE. *Je vous prie, madame, d'excuser les habits et le rude comportement de mon cousin. Il est tout fraîchement venu de l'université, où on l'a tout gâté.*

CEL. *Excusez-moi, madame; il est bien accompli.*[2] 130

FRED. This language should be French by the motions of your heads and the mirth of your faces.

[1] ARE. I beg you, madam, to pardon the importunity of my affairs, which have made me offend, by my absence, a lady from whom I have received so much obligation.
CEL. Pardon me, madam; you do me too much honor.
ARE. It is indeed from the kindness of your good nature that you use such language. But I hope that my husband has not failed to entertain you in my absence.
CEL. In truth, your husband has been very kind.
ARE. He would have been too remiss if he hadn't tried with all his might to render you all kinds of services.
CEL. It is out of his good nature that he has been so good to us.
ARE. It is your good nature rather that makes you give such a gracious interpretation to his efforts.
CEL. I see indeed that the victory will always be madam's both in language and in courtesy.
ARE. Truly, madam, no one ever more desired the honor of your company than I.
CEL. Leave compliments, I pray you, and permit your servant to kiss your hand.
ARE. You are too kind.
[2] ARE. I beg you, madam, to excuse the dress and the rude behavior of my kinsman. He has but lately come from the university, where they completely corrupted him.
CEL. Excuse me, madam; he is indeed accomplished.

ARE. I am dishonored.

FRED. 'Tis one of the finest tongues for ladies to show their teeth in. If you'll Latin, I am for you, or Greek it; my tailor has not put me into French yet. *Mille basia, basia mille.*[3] 139

CEL. *Je ne vous entends pas, monsieur*— I understand you not, sir.

FRED. Why, so?
You and I then shall be in charity,
For, though we should be abusive, we ha' the benefit
Not to understand one another. Where's my aunt?
I did hear music somewhere, and my brains,
Tuned with a bottle of your capering claret,
Made haste to show their dancing.

LIT. [*Offering sweetmeats to Celestina.*]
　　　　　　　　Please you, madam,
They are very comfortable.[4]

STEW. 　　　　　　　Alas, madam,
How would you have me help it? I did use 150
All means I could, after he heard the music,
To make him drunk, in hope so to contain him;
But the wine made him lighter, and his head
Flew hither, ere I missed his heels.

AL. Nay, he spoke Latin to the lady.

ARE. O, most unpardonable! Get him off
Quickly, and discreetly; or, if I live—

STEW. 'Tis not in my power; he swears I am
An absurd, sober fellow, and, if you keep
A servant in his house to cross his humor, 160
When the rich sword and belt comes home, he'll kill him.

ARE. What shall I do? Try your skill, Master Littleworth.

LIT. He has ne'er a sword.—Sweet Mr. Frederick—

BORN. 'Tis pity, madam, such a scion should
Be lost. But you are clouded.

CEL. 　　　　　　　Not I, sir;
I never found myself more clear at heart.

[3] A thousand kisses, kisses a thousand.
[4] Comforting.

Born. I could play with a feather; your
　fan, lady.—
　Gentlemen, Aretina, ta, ra, ra, ra! Come,
　madam.
Fred. Why, my good tutor in election?
　You might have been a scholar.
Lit.　　　　　　　　But I thank　170
　My friends they brought me up a little
　better.
　Give me the town wits, that deliver jests
　Clean from the bow, that whistle in the
　air,
　And cleave the pin at twelvescore! La-
　dies do
　But laugh at a gentleman that has any
　learning;
　'Tis sin enough to have your clothes sus-
　pected.
　Leave us, and I will find a time to instruct
　you.
　Come, here are sugarplums. 'Tis a good
　Frederick.
Fred. Why, is not this my aunt's house in
　the Strand?
　The noble rendezvous? Who laughs at
　me?　　　　　　　　　　　　　　180
　Go, I will root here if I list,[1] and talk
　Of rhetoric, logic, Latin, Greek, or any-
　thing,
　And understand 'em too. Who says the
　contrary?
　Yet, in a fair way, I contemn all
　learning,
　And will be as ignorant as he, or he,
　Or any taffeta, satin, scarlet, plush,
　Tissue, or cloth-a-bodkin [2] gentleman,
　Whose manners are most gloriously in-
　fected.—
　Did you laugh at me, lady?
Cel.　　　　　　　　　Not I, sir;
　But, if I did show mirth upon your
　question,　　　　　　　　　　　190
　I hope you would not beat me, little
　gentleman.
Fred. How, "little gentleman"? You
　dare not say
　These words to my new clothes and
　fighting sword.
Are. Nephew Frederick!
Fred.　　　　　　"Little gentleman"!
　This an affront both to my blood and
　person!

[1] Please.
[2] Baudekin was a rich gold and silk cloth.

I am a gentleman of as tall [3] a birth
As any boast nobility; though my clothes
Smell o' the lamp, my coat [4] is honorable,
Right honorable, full of or and argent.—
A "little gentleman"!
Born.　　　　Coz, you must be patient;
My lady meant you no dishonor, and
You must remember she's a woman.　202
Fred. Is she a woman? That's another
　matter.—
D'e hear? My uncle tells me what you
　are.
Cel. So, sir.
Fred.　　You called me "little gentle-
　man."
Cel. I did, sir.
Fred. A little pink [5] has made a lusty ship
　Strike her topsail. The Crow [6] may beard
　the Elephant; [6]
A whelp [7] may tame the Tiger,[6] spite of
　all
False decks [8] and murderers; [9] and a
　"little gentleman"　　　　　　　210
Be hard enough to grapple with your
　ladyship,
Top and topgallant.—Will you go drink,
　uncle,
Tother enchanted bottle? You and I
Will tipple, and talk philosophy.
Born.　　　　　　Come, nephew.—
You will excuse a minute's absence,
　madam.—
Wait you on us.
Stew.　　　　　My duty, sir.
Ex[eunt] All but [Aretina and] Cel[estina] and
　　　　　　Alex[ander] and Little[worth].
Are.　　　　　　　Now, gentlemen.
Al. Madam, I had rather you accuse my
　language
For speaking truth than virtue suffer in
My further silence; and it is my wonder
That you, whose noble carriage hath de-
　served　　　　　　　　　　　220
All honor and opinion, should now
Be guilty of ill manners.
Cel.　　　　　　What was that
You told me, sir?
Lit.　　　Do you not blush, madam,
To ask that question?

[3] High.　　　　　　　　[4] Coat of arms.
[5] A small coasting vessel.
[6] Probably the name of a ship of war.
[7] A small ship.
[8] Barricades raised against boarders.
[9] Cannon discharging grapeshot.

CEL.　　　　　　　　You amaze rather
My cheek to paleness. What mean you
by this?
I am not troubled with the hiccup, gen-
tlemen,
[1] You should bestow this fright upon me.[2]
LIT.　　　　　　　　　　　Then
Pride and ill memory go together.
CEL.　　　　　　　　　　How, sir?
AL. The gentleman on whom you exercise
Your thin wit was a nephew to the lady
Whose guest you are, and, though her
modesty　　　　　　　　231
Look calm on the abuse of one so near
Her blood, the affront was impious.
LIT.　　　　　　I am ashamed on 't.
You an ingenious lady, and well man-
nered?
I'll teach a bear as much civility.
CEL. You may be master of the college,
sir,
For aught I know.
LIT.　　　　　What college?
CEL.[3]　　　　　　　Of the bears.
Have you a plot upon me? D'e possess
Your wits, or know me, gentlemen?

Enter Bornwell [behind].

BORN.　　　　　　　　　How's this?
AL. [*Aside.*] Know you? Yes, we do know
you to an atom.　　　　　　240
LIT. Madam, we know what stuff your
soul is made on.
CEL. But do not bark so like a mastive,[4]
pray.—
[*Aside.*] Sure they are mad.—Let your
brains stand awhile
And settle, gentlemen. You know not
me.
What am I?
LIT.　　　Th' art a puppet, a thing made
Of clothes and painting, and not half so
handsome
As that which played Susanna in the fair.
CEL. I heard you visited those canvas
tragedies,
One of their constant audience, and so
taken

With Susan that you wished yourself a
rival　　　　　　　　　250
With the two wicked elders.
AL.　　　　　　　　You think this
Is wit now. Come, you are—
CEL.　　　　　What, I beseech you?
Your character will be full of salt and
satire,
No doubt. What am I?
AL.　　　　　Why, you are a woman—
CEL. And that's at least a bow [5] wide of
your knowledge.
AL. Would be thought handsome, and
might pass i' th' country
Upon a market day, but miserably
Forfeit to pride and fashions, that if
heaven
Were a new gown, you'd not stay in 't a
fortnight.
CEL. It must be miserably out of fashion
then.　　　　　　　　260
Have I no sin but pride?
AL.　　　　　　　Hast any virtue,
Or but a good face, to excuse that want?
CEL. You praised it yesterday.
AL.　　　　　　That made you proud.
CEL. More pride?
AL.　　　You need not to close up the
praise;
I have seen a better countenance in a
sybil.
CEL. When you wore spectacles of sack,[6]
mistook
The painted cloth,[7] and kissed it for your
mistress.
AL. Let me ask you a question: how much
Have you consumed in expectation
That I would love you?
CEL.　　　　Why, I think as much　270
As you have paid away in honest debts
This seven year. 'Tis a pretty impu-
dence,
But cannot make me angry.
LIT.　　　　　　　　Is there any
Man that will cast away his limbs upon
her?
AL. You do not sing so well as I im-
agined,
Nor dance; you reel in your coranto,[8]
and pinch

[1] Supply *so that.*
[2] A reference to the belief that fright cured
the hiccups.
[3] In the original this speech head appears at
the beginning of the next line.
[4] Mastiff.

[5] Bowshot.
[6] *I.e.,* had drunk too much sack.
[7] Cheap wall hangings.
[8] A lively dance.

Your petticoat too hard; y'ave no good
　ear
To th' music, and incline too much one
　shoulder,
As you were dancing on the rope, and
　falling.　　　　　　　　　　　　279
You speak abominable French, and make
A curtsy like a dairymaid.—[Aside.] Not
　mad?
LIT. [Aside.] Do we not sting her hand-
　somely?
BORN. [Aside.]　　　　　　A conspiracy!
AL. Your state is not so much as 'tis re-
　ported.
When you confer [1] notes, all your hus-
　band's debts
And your own reconciled—but that's
　not it
Will so much spoil your marriage.
CEL.　　　　　　　　　　As what, sir?
Let me know all my faults.
AL.　　　　　　　Some men do whisper
You are not overhonest.
CEL.　　　　　　　All this shall not
Move me to more than laughter, and
　some pity,
Because you have the shapes of gentle-
　men,　　　　　　　　　　　　290
And, though you have been insolent
　upon me,
I will engage no friend to kick or cudgel
　you,
To spoil your living and your limbs to-
　gether.
I leave that to diseases that offend you,
And spare my curse, poor silken vermin,
　and
Hereafter shall distinguish men from
　monkeys.
BORN. [Coming forward.] Brave soul!—
You brace of horseleeches!—I have
　heard
Their barbarous language, madam; y' are
　too merciful.
They shall be silent to your tongue; pray,
　punish 'em.
CEL. They are things not worth my char-
　acter,[2] nor mention　　　　　　300
Of any clean breath, so lost in honesty
They cannot satisfy for wrongs enough,
Though they should steal out of the
　world at Tyburn.[3]

LIT. We are hanged already.
CEL. Yet I will talk a little to the pil-
　chards.[4] —
You two, that have not twixt you both
　the hundred
Part of a soul, coarse woolen-witted
　fellows,
Without a nap, with bodies made for
　burdens,
You, that are only stuffings for apparel,
As you were made but engines [5] for your
　tailors　　　　　　　　　　　　310
To frame their clothes upon, and get
　them custom,
Until men see you move, yet then you
　dare not,
Out of your guilt of being the ignobler
　beast,
But give a horse the wall, whom you excel
Only in dancing of the brawls,[6] because
The horse was not taught the French
　way! Your two faces,
One fat, like Christmas, tother lean, like
　Candlemas
And prologue to a Lent, both bound to-
　gether,
Would figure Janus, and do many cures
On agues and the green disease [7] by
　frighting;　　　　　　　　　　320
But neither can, with all the characters
And conjuring circles, charm a woman,
　though
Sh'ad fourscore years upon her and but
　one
Tooth in her head, to love or think well
　of you;
And I were miserable to be at cost
To court such a complexion [8] as your
　malice
Did impudently insinuate. But I waste
　time,
And stain my breath in talking to such
　tadpoles.
Go home and wash your tongues in bar-
　ley water,
Drink [9] clean tobacco, be not hot i' th'
　mouth,　　　　　　　　　　　　330
And you may scape the beadle; so I leave
　you

[1] Compare.　　　　　　[2] Characterizing.
[3] Place of execution.

[4] A term of contempt, perhaps *sardines*.
[5] *I.e.*, manikins.
[6] A French dance like a cotillion.
[7] Greensickness, chlorosis (?).
[8] Disposition.　　　　　　[9] **Smoke.**

To shame, and your own garters![1] —
Sir, I must
Entreat you, for my honor, do not pen-
ance 'em—
They are not worth your anger. How I
shall
Acquit your lady's silence!
Born.   Madam, I
Am sorry to suspect, and dare revenge—
Cel. No cause of mine.
Born. It must become me to attend you
home.
Cel. You are noble.—Farewell, mush-
rooms!   [*Exit with Bornwell.*]
Are.   Is she gone?
Lit. I think we peppered her.
Al.   I am glad 'tis over;   340
But I repent no service for you,
madam.—

Enter Servant, with a letter [*and a jewel*].
To me? From whence?—A jewel! A
good preface.
Be happy the conclusion.
Are.   Some love letter. *He[2] smiles*
upon 't.
Lit. He has a hundred mistresses. You
may
Be charitable, madam; I ha' none.
He surfeits, and I fall away i' th' kidneys.
Al. I'll meet.—   [*Exit Servant.*
Aside.] 'Tis some great lady, question-
less, that has
Taken notice, and would satisfy her
appetite.
Are. Now, Mr. Alexander, you look bright
o' the sudden;   350
Another spirit's in your eye.
Al.   Not mine, madam;
Only a summons to meet a friend.
Are. What friend?
Al.[3]   By this jewel, I know her not.
Are. 'Tis a she-friend. I'll follow, gentle-
men;
We may have a game at sant[4] before
you go.
Al. I shall attend you, madam.
Lit.   'Tis our duty.
              [*Exit with Alexander.*]
Are. I blush while I converse with my
own thoughts.

[1] *I.e.*, for hanging themselves.
[2] *I.e.*, Alexander.   [3] Original reads *Lit.*
[4] Cent, a game at cards.

Some strange fate governs me, but I must
on;
The ways are cast already, and we thrive
When our sin fears no eye nor perspective.[5]   *Exit.*   360

THE FOURTH ACT. [SCENE i.

A room in Decoy's house.]

Enter two Men leading Alexander, blinded,[6]
and go off suddenly.

Al. I am not hurt; my patience to obey
'em,
Not without fear to ha' my throat cut
else,
Did me a courtesy. Whither ha' they
brought me?   [*Pulls off bandage.*]
'Tis devilish dark; the bottom of a well
At midnight, with but two stars on the
top,
Were broad day to this darkness. I but
think
How like a whirlwind these rogues caught
me up,
And smotheréd[7] my eyesight. Let me
see.
These may be spirits, and, for aught I
know,
Have brought me hither over twenty
steeples.   10
Pray heaven they were not bailiffs (that's
more worth
My fear) and this a prison! All my debts
Reek in my nostril, and my bones begin
To ache with fear to be made dice; and
yet
This is too calm and quiet for a prison.
What if the riddle prove I am rob'ed?
And yet
I did not feel 'em search me. [*Music
within.*] How now? Music?

Enter Decoy, like an old woman, with a light.
And a light? What beldam's this? I
cannot pray.—
What art?
Dec.   A friend. Fear not, young
man; I am
No spirit.
Al.   Off!
Dec.   Despise me not for age,   20
Or this coarse outside, which I wear not
out

[5] Telescope.   [6] Blindfolded.   [7] Smothered.

Of poverty. Thy eyes be witness, 'tis
No cave or beggar's cell th' art brought to; let
That gold speak here's no want, which thou mayst spend,
And find a spring to tire even prodigality,
If thou beest wise. [*Gives him a purse.*]

AL.　　　　　　　　The devil was a coiner
From the beginning; yet the gold looks current.

DEC. Th' art still in wonder. Know, I am mistress of
This house, and of a fortune that shall serve
And feed thee with delights. 'Twas I sent for thee;　　　30
The jewel and the letter came from me.
It was my art thus to contrive our meeting,
Because I would not trust thee with my fame,
Until I found thee worth a woman's honor.

AL. [*Aside.*] Honor and fame? The devil means to have
A care on 's credit. Though she sent for me,
I hope she has another customer
To do the trick withal; I would not turn
Familiar [1] to a witch.

DEC.　　　　　　What say'st? Canst thou
Dwell in my arms tonight? Shall we change kisses,　　　40
And entertain the silent hours with pleasure,
Such as old Time shall be delighted with,
And blame the too swift motion of his wings,
While we embrace?

AL. [*Aside.*]　　　　Embrace? She has had no teeth
This twenty years, and the next violent cough
Brings up her tongue; it cannot possibly
Be sound at root. I do not think but one
Strong sneeze upon her, and well meant, would make
Her quarters fall away; one kick would blow
Her up like gunpowder, and loose all her limbs.　　　50
She is so cold an incubus would not heat her;

Her phlegm would quench a furnace, and her breath
Would damp a musket bullet.

DEC.　　　　　　　　Have you, sir,
Considered?

AL.　　　　What?

DEC.　　　　　　My proposition.
Canst love?

AL.　　I could have done. Whom do you mean?
I know you are pleased but to make sport.

DEC.　　　Thou art not
So dull of soul as thou appear'st.

AL. [*Aside.*]　　　　　　This is
But some device; my grannam has some trick in 't.—
Yes, I can love.

DEC.　　　　But canst thou affect [2] me?

AL. Although to reverence so grave a matron　　　60
Were an ambitious word in me, yet since
You give me boldness, I do love you.

DEC.　　　　　　　　Then
Thou art my own.

AL. [*Aside.*]　　Has she no cloven foot?

DEC. And I am thine, and all that I command
Thy servants; from this minute thou art happy,
And fate in thee will crown all my desires.
I grieved a proper [3] man should be compelled
To bring his body to the common market.
My wealth shall make thee glorious; and, the more
To encourage thee, howe'er this form may fright　　　70
Thy youthful eyes, yet thou wo't find, by light
Of thy own sense, for other light is banished
My chamber, when our arms tie lovers' knots,
And kisses seal the welcome of our lips,
I shall not there affright thee, nor seem old,
With riveled [4] veins; my skin is smooth and soft
As ermines, with a spirit to meet thine,

1 Familiar spirit.　　　2 Fancy, love.　　3 Handsome.　　4 Shriveled.

Active and equal to the Queen of Love's
When she did court Adonis.

AL. [*Aside.*] This doth more
Confirm she is a devil, and I am 80
Within his own dominions. I must on,
Or else be torn a-pieces. I have heard
These succubae must not be crossed.

DEC. We trifle
Too precious time away; I'll show you a
prospect
Of the next chamber, and then out the
candle.

AL. Have you no sack i' th' house? I
would go armed
Upon this breach.

DEC. It sha' not need.

AL. One word,
Mother—have not you been a cat in
your days?

DEC. I am glad you are so merry, sir. You
observe
That bed? [*Opens a door.*]

AL. A very brave one.

DEC. When you are 90
Disrobed, you can come thither in the
dark.
You sha' not stay for me. Come, as you
wish
For happiness. *Exit.*

AL. I am preferred, if I
Be modest and obey. She cannot have
The heart to do me harm, and [1] she were
Hecate
Herself. I will have a strong faith, and
think
I march upon a mistress, the less evil.
If I scape fire now, I defy the devil. *Exit.*

[SCENE ii.

A room in Bornwell's house.]

Enter Fred[erick], Little[worth], Steward.

FRED. And how d'e like me now?

STEW. Most excellent.

FRED. Your opinion, Mr. Littlewor[th].

LIT. Your French tailor
Has made you a perfect gentleman; I
may
Converse now with you, and preserve my
credit.
D'e find no alteration in your body
With these new clothes?

[1] If.

FRED. My body altered? No.

LIT. You are not yet in fashion then. That
must
Have a new motion, garb, and posture
too,
Or all your pride is cast away; it is not
The cut of your apparel makes a gallant,
But the geometrical wearing of your
clothes. 11

STEW. Mr. Littleworth tells you right; you
wear your hat
Too like a citizen.

LIT. 'Tis like a midwife.
Place it with best advantage of your hair.
Is half your feather molted? This does
make
No show; it should spread over, like a
canopy.
Your hot-reined monsieur wears it for a
shade
And cooler to his back. Your doublet
must
Be more unbuttoned hereabouts; you'll
not
Be a sloven else. A foul shirt is no blem-
ish; 20
You must be confident, and outface clean
linen.
Your doublet and your breeches must be
allowed
No private meeting here; your cloak's
too long.
It reaches to your buttock, and doth
smell
Too much of Spanish gravity; the
fashion
Is to wear nothing but a cape; a coat
May be allowed a covering for one elbow,
And some, to avoid the trouble, choose
to walk
In *quirpo*,[2] thus.

STEW. [*Aside.*] Your coat and
cloak's a-brushing
In Long Lane, Lumbard.[3]

FRED. But what if it rain? 30

LIT. Your belt about your shoulder is suffi-
cient
To keep off any storm; beside, a reed
But waved discreetly has so many pores
It sucks up all the rain that falls about
one.

[2] *Cuérpo* (Span.); *i.e.*, in your shirt.
[3] The Lombard district was famous for pawn-
shops.

With this defense, when other men have
  been
Wet to the skin through all their cloaks,
  I have
Defied a tempest, and walked by the
  taverns
Dry as a bone.
STEW. [*Aside.*]   Because he had no
  money
To call for wine.
FRED.   Why, you do walk enchanted.
  Have you such pretty charms in town?
  But stay.   40
Who must I have to attend me?
LIT.   Is not that
  Yet thought upon?
STEW.   I have laid out [1] for servants.
LIT. They are everywhere.
STEW.   I cannot yet be furnished
  With such as I would put into his
  hands.
FRED. Of what condition must they be,
  and how
  Many in number, sir?
LIT.   Beside your fencing,
  Your singing, dancing, riding, and
    French master,
  Two may serve domestic, to be constant
    waiters
  Upon a gentleman: a fool, a pimp.
STEW. For these two officers I have in-
  quired,   50
  And I am promised a convenient
    whiskin.[2]
  I could save charges, and employ the pie-
    wench,
  That carries her intelligence in white-
    pots; [3]
  Or 'tis but taking order with the woman
  That holds the ballads—she could fit him
    with
  A concubine to any tune; but I
  Have a design to place a fellow with
    him
  That has read all Sir Pandarus' works, a
    Trojan [4]
  That lies concealed, and is acquainted
    with
  Both city and suburban fripperies,[5] 60
  Can fetch 'em with a spell at midnight to
    him,

And warrant which are for his turn; can,
  for
A need, supply the surgeon too.
FRED.   I like
  Thy providence; [6] such a one deserves a
    livery twice a year.
STEW. It sha' not need; a cast [7] suit of your
  worship's
  Will serve; he'll find a cloak to cover it,
  Out of his share with those he brings to
    bed to you.
FRED. But must I call this fellow pimp?
LIT.   It is
  Not necessary—or [8] Jack or Harry,
  Or what he's known abroad by, will
    sound better,   70
  That men may think he is a Christian.
FRED. But hear you, Mr. Littleworth: is
  there not
  A method and degrees of title in
  Men of this art?
LIT.   According to the honor
  Of men that do employ 'em. An emperor
  May give this office to a duke; a king
  May have his viceroy to negotiate for
    him;
  A duke may use a lord; the lord a knight;
  A knight may trust a gentleman; and,
    when   79
  They are abroad and merry, gentlemen
  May pimp to one another.
FRED.   Good, good fellowship!
  But for the fool now, that should wait on
    me,
  And break me jests?
LIT.   A fool is necessary.
STEW. By any [9] means.
FRED.   But which of these two servants
  Must now take place? [10]
LIT.   That question, Mr. Frederick,
  The school of heraldry should conclude
    upon;
  But, if my judgment may be heard, the
    fool
  Is your first man; and it is known a
    point
  Of state to have a fool.
STEW.   But, sir, the other
  Is held the finer servant; his employ-
    ments   90
  Are full of trust, his person clean and
    nimble,

[1] Been on the lookout.
[2] Go-between.   [4] Sly rascal.
[3] Milkpuddings.   [5] Suburban prostitutes.

[6] Foresight.   [8] Either.
[7] Discarded.   [9] All.   [10] Precedence.

And none so soon can leap into prefer-
ment,
Where fools are poor.
LIT.   Not all; there's story for 't:
Princes have been no wiser than they
should be.
Would any nobleman, that were no fool,
Spend all in hope of the philosophers'
stone,
To buy new lordships in another coun-
try?
Would knights build colleges, or gentle-
men
Of good estates challenge the field, and
fight,
Because a whore wo' not be honest?
Come,   100
Fools are a family over all the world;
We do affect one naturally; indeed
The fool is lieger [1] with us.
STEW.   Then the pimp
Is extraordinary.
FRED.   Do not you fall out
About their places.—Here's my noble
aunt!

Enter Aretina.

LIT. How do you like your nephew, madam,
now?
ARE. Well!—Turn about, Frederick.—
Very well!
FRED.[2] Am I not now a proper gentleman?
The virtue of rich clothes! Now could I
take
The wall of Julius Cæsar, affront   110
Great Pompey's upper lip, and defy the
senate.
Nay, I can be as proud as your own heart,
madam;
You may take that for your comfort. I
put on
That virtue with my clothes, and I doubt
not
But in a little time I shall be impudent
As any page, or player's boy. I am
Beholding to this gentleman's good disci-
pline;
But I shall do him credit in my practice.
Your steward has some pretty notions,
too,
In moral mischief.

ARE.   Your desert in this   120
Exceeds all other service, and shall bind
me
Both to acknowledge and reward.
LIT.   Sweet madam,
Think me but worth your favor; I would
creep
Upon my knees to honor you, and, for
every
Minute you lend to my reward, I'll pay
A year of serviceable tribute.
ARE.   You
Can compliment.
LIT. [*Aside.*]   Thus still she puts me off;
Unless I speak the downright word, she'll
never
Understand me. A man would think that
creeping
Upon one's knees were English to a
lady.   130

Enter Alex[ander].

AL. How is 't, Jack?—Pleasures attend
you, madam!
How does my plant of honor?
ARE.   Who is this?
AL. 'Tis Alexander.
ARE.   Rich and glorious!
LIT. 'Tis Alexander the Great.
AL.   And my Bucephalus
Waits at the door.
ARE.   Your case is altered, sir.
AL. I cannot help these things. The Fates
will have it.
'Tis not my land does this.
LIT.   But thou hast a plow
That brings it in.
ARE.   Now he looks brave and lovely.
FRED. Welcome, my gallant Macedonian.
AL. Madam, you gave your nephew for my
pupil.   140
I read [3] but in a tavern; if you'll honor us,
The Bear at the bridge foot shall enter-
tain you.
A drawer [4] is my Ganymede; he shall
skink [5]
Brisk nectar to us. We will only have
A dozen partridge in a dish; as many
pheasants,
Quails, cocks, and godwits [6] shall come
marching up

---

[1] Ledger, resident, as an ordinary ambassador.
[2] Original reads *Are*.

[3] Lecture, teach.
[4] Waiter.

[5] Draw.
[6] Snipe.

Like the trained-band;[1] a fort of sturgeon
Shall give most bold defiance to an army,
And triumph o'er the table.

ARE.　　　　　　　　　Sir, it will
But dull the appetite to hear more, and
　mine　　　　　　　　　　　　　150
Must be excused. Another time I may
Be your guest.

AL.　　　　　'Tis grown in fashion
　now with ladies.
When you please, I'll attend you. Little-
　worth!—
Come, Frederick.

FRED.　　　We'll have music; I love noise.
We will outroar the Thames, and shake
　the bridge, boy. Ex[it with Alexander].

LIT. Madam, I kiss your hand; would you
　would think
Of your poor servant. Flesh and blood is
　frail,
And troublesome to carry without help.

ARE. A coach will easily convey it, or
You may take water at Strand Bridge.

LIT.　　　　　　　　　But I　160
Have taken fire.

ARE.　　　　The Thames will cool—

LIT. But never quench my heart; your
　charity
Can only do that.

ARE.　　　　　　I will keep it cold
Of purpose.

LIT.　　　Now you bless me, and I dare
Be drunk in expectation.　　　　[Exit.]

ARE.　　　　　　　I am confident
He knows me not, and I were worse than
　mad
To be my own betrayer.—Here's my
　husband.

Enter Born[well].

BORN. Why, how now, Aretina? What!
　Alone?
The mystery of this solitude? My house
Turn desert o' the sudden? All the game-
　sters　　　　　　　　　　　　170
Blown up? Why is the music put to
　silence?
Or ha' their instruments caught a cold,
　since we
Gave 'em the last heat? I must know thy
　ground
Of melancholy.

[1] London militia.

ARE.　　　　　You are merry, as
You came from kissing Celestina.

BORN.　　　　　　　　　　　　　I
Feel her yet warm upon my lip; she is
Most excellent company. I did not think
There was that sweetness in her sex. I
　must
Acknowledge 'twas thy cure to disen-
　chant me　　　　　　　　　　　179
From a dull husband to an active lover.
With such a lady I could spend more
　years
Than since my birth my glass hath run
　soft minutes,
And yet be young. Her presence has a
　spell
To keep off age; she has an eye would
　strike
Fire through an adamant.

ARE.　　　　　　I have heard as much
Bestowed upon a dull-faced chamber-
　maid,
Whom love and wit would thus com-
　mend. True beauty
Is mocked when we compare thus, itself
　being
Above what can be fetched to make it
　lovely,
Or could our thoughts reach something
　to declare　　　　　　　　　　190
The glories of a face, or body's elegance
(That touches but our sense), when
　beauty spreads
Over the soul, and calls up understanding
To look what [2] thence is offered, and ad-
　mire!
In both I must acknowledge Celestina
Most excellently fair, fair above all
The beauties I ha' seen, and one most
　worthy
Man's love and wonder.

BORN.　　　　　Do you speak, Aretina,
This with a pure sense to commend? Or
　is 't
The mockery of my praise?

ARE.　　　　　Although it shame　200
Myself, I must be just, and give her all
The excellency of women; and, were I
A man—

BORN.　　　What then?

ARE.　　　　　I know not with what loss
I should attempt her love. She is a piece
So angelically moving, I should think

[2] Gifford-Dyce's reading. Original reads *when*,

Frailty excused to dote upon her form,
And almost virtue to be wicked with her.
                                        Exit.
Born. What should this mean? This is no
        jealousy,
Or she believes I counterfeit. I feel
Something within me, like a heat, to
        give   210
Her cause, would Celestina but consent.
What a frail thing is man! It is not worth
Our glory to be chaste, while we deny
Mirth and converse with women. He is
        good
That dares the tempter, yet corrects his
        blood.   *Exit.*

[Scene iii.

A room in Celestina's house.

Enter] *Celestina, Mariana, Isabella.*

Cel. I have told you all my knowledge;
        since he is pleased
    To invite himself, he shall be entertained,
    And you shall be my witnesses.
Mar.   Who comes with him?
Cel. Sir William Scentlove, that prepared
        me for
    The honorable encounter. I expect
    His lordship every minute.

Enter Scentlove.

Scent.   My lord is come.

Enter Lord, Haircut.

Cel. He has honored me.
Scent.   My lord, your periwig is awry!
Lord. You, sir—
*While Haircut is busy about his hair, Scent-
                love goes to Celestina.*
Scent. You may guess at the gentleman
        that's with him.   9
    It is his barber, madam, d'e observe,
    And your ladyship wants a shaver.
Hair.   She is here, sir.
    I am betrayed.—Scentlove, your plot. I
        may
    Have opportunity to be revenged. *Exit.*
Scent. She in the midst.
Lord.   She's fair, I must confess;
    But does she keep this distance out of
        state?
Cel. Though I am poor in language to
        express

How much your lordship honors me, my
        heart
Is rich and proud in such a guest. I shall
Be out of love with every air abroad,
And, for his grace done my unworthy
        house,   20
Be a fond prisoner, become anchorite,
And spend my hours in prayer, to reward
The blessing and the bounty of this
        presence.
Lord. Though you could turn each place
        you move in, to
A temple, rather than a wall should hide
So rich a beauty from the world, it were
Less want to lose our piety and your
        prayer.
A throne were fitter to present you to
Our wonder, whence your eyes, more
        worth than all
They look on, should chain every heart
        a prisoner.   30
Scent. [*Aside.*] 'Twas pretty well come
        off.
Lord.   By your example
    I shall know how to compliment; in this,
    You more confirm my welcome.
Cel.   I shall love
    My lips the better, if their silent lan-
        guage
    Persuade your lordship but to think so
        truly.
Lord. You make me smile, madam.
Cel.   I hope you came not
    With fear that any sadness here should
        shake
    One blossom from your eye. I should be
        miserable
    To present any object should displease
        you.
Lord. You do not, madam.
Cel.   As I should account   40
    It no less sorrow, if your lordship should
    Lay too severe a censure on my free-
        dom.
    I wo' not court a prince against his jus-
        tice,
    Nor bribe him with a smile to think me
        honest.
    Pardon, my lord, this boldness and the
        mirth
    That may flow from me. I believe my
        father
    Thought of no winding sheet when he
        begot me.

LORD. [*Aside.*] She has a merry soul.—It will become
Me ask your pardon, madam, for my rude
Approach, so much a stranger to your knowledge.   50
CEL. Not, my lord, so much stranger to my knowledge;
Though I have but seen your person afar off,
I am acquainted with your character,
Which I have heard so often I can speak it.
LORD. You shall do me an honor.
CEL.   If your lordship will Be patient.
LORD.   And glad to hear my faults.
CEL. That, as your conscience can agree upon 'em.
However, if your lordship give me privilege,
I'll tell you what's the opinion of the world.
LORD. You cannot please me better.
CEL.   Y' are a lord   60
Born with as much nobility as would,
Divided, serve to make ten noblemen
Without a herald, but with so much spirit
And height of soul as well might furnish twenty.
You are learned, a thing not compatible now
With native honor, and are master of
A language that doth chain all ears,[1] and charm
All hearts, where you persuade; a wit so flowing,
And prudence to correct it, that all men
Believe they only meet in you, which, with   70
A spacious memory, make up the full wonders.
To these, you have known valor, and upon
A noble cause know how to use a sword
To honor's best advantage, though you wear none.
You are as bountiful as the showers that fall
Into the Spring's green bosom, as you were
Created lord of Fortune, not her steward;

[1] Gifford-Dyce reading. Original reads *years*.

So constant to tne cause in which you make
Yourself an advocate, you dare all dangers;
And men had rather you should be their friend   80
Than justice or the bench bound up together.
LORD. But did you hear all this?
CEL.   And more, my lord.
LORD. Pray, let me have it, madam.
CEL. To all these virtues there is added one
(Your lordship will remember, when I name it,
I speak but what I gather from the voice
Of others)—it is grown to a full fame [2]
That you have loved a woman.
LORD.   But one, madam?
CEL. Yes, many. Give me leave to smile, my lord;
I shall not need to interpret in what sense.   90
But you have showed yourself right honorable,
And, for your love to ladies, have deserved,
If their vote might prevail, a marble statue.
I make no comment on the people's text.
My lord, I should be sorry to offend.
LORD. You cannot, madam; these are things we owe
To nature for.
CEL.   And honest men will pay Their debts.
LORD.   If they be able, or compound.
CEL. She had a hard heart would be unmerciful,   99
And not give day [3] to men so promising;
But you owed women nothing.
LORD.   Yes, I am Still in their debt, and I must owe them love;
It was part of my character.
CEL.   With your lordship's Pardon, I only said you had a fame
For loving women; but of late men say
You have, against the imperial laws of love,
Restrained the active flowings of your blood,

[2] Report.
[3] "Good day," *i.e.*, notice, attention.

And with a mistress buried all that is
Hoped for in love's succession, as all
beauty
Had died with her, and left the world be-
nighted! 110
In this you more dishonor all our sex
Than you did grace a part, when every-
where
Love tempts your eye to admire a glori-
ous harvest,
And everywhere as full-blown ears sub-
mit
Their golden heads, the laden trees bow
down
Their willing fruit, and court your
amorous tasting.
LORD. I see men would dissect me to a
fiber.
But do you believe this?
CEL. It is my wonder,
I must confess, a man of nobler earth
Than goes to vulgar composition 120
(Born and bred high, so unconfined, so
rich
In fortunes, and so read in all that
sum
Up human knowledge, to feed gloriously,
And live at court, the only sphere where-
in
True beauty moves, nature's most
wealthy garden,
Where every blossom is more worth than
all
The Hesperian fruit by jealous dragon
watched,
Where all delights do circle appetite,
And pleasures multiply by being tasted)
Should be so lost with thought of one,
turn ashes. 130
There's nothing left, my lord, that can
excuse you,
Unless you plead what I am ashamed to
prompt
Your wisdom to.
LORD. What's that?
CEL. That you have played
The surgeon with yourself.
LORD. And am made eunuch?
CEL. It were much pity.
LORD. Trouble not yourself;
I could convince your fears with demon-
stration
That I am man enough, but knew not
where,

Until this meeting, beauty dwelt. The
court
You talked of must be where the Queen
of Love is,
Which moves but with your person; in
your eye 140
Her glory shines, and only at that flame
Her wanton boy doth light his quick'ning
torch.
CEL. Nay, now you compliment; I would
it did,
My lord, for your own sake.
LORD. You would be kind,
And love me then?
CEL. My lord, I should be loving
Where I found worth to invite it, and
should cherish
A constant man.
LORD. Then you should me, madam.
CEL. But is the ice about your heart fallen
off?
Can you return to do what love com-
mands?— 149
Cupid, thou shalt have instant sacrifice,
And I dare be the priest.
LORD. Your hand, your lip.
[*Kisses her.*]
Now I am proof gainst all temptation.
CEL. Your meaning, my good lord?
LORD. I, that have strength
Against thy voice and beauty, after
this
May dare the charms of womankind.—
Thou art,
Bella Maria, unprofanéd yet;
This magic has no power upon my
blood.—
Farewell, madam! If you durst be the
example
Of chaste as well as fair, thou wert a
brave one.
CEL. I hope your lordship means not this
for earnest; 160
Be pleased to grace a banquet.
LORD. Pardon, madam.—
Will Scentlove, follow; I must laugh at
you.
CEL. My lord, I must beseech you stay,
for honor
For her whose memory you love best.
LORD. Your pleasure.
CEL. And, by that virtue you have now
professed,
I charge you to believe me too; I can

Now glory that you have been worth my
trial,
Which, I beseech you, pardon. Had not
you
So valiantly recovered in this conflict,
You had been my triumph, without hope
of more   170
Than my just scorn upon your wanton
flame;
Nor will I think these noble thoughts
grew first
From melancholy for some female loss,
As the fantastic world believes, but from
Truth and your love of innocence, which
shine
So bright in the two royal luminaries
At court,[1] you cannot lose your way to
chastity.
Proceed, and speak of me as honor guides
you.   *Exit Lord.*
I am almost tired.—Come, ladies, we'll
beguile
Dull time, and take the air another while.
                                   Exeunt.

The Fifth Act. [Scene i.

A room in Bornwell's house.]

Enter Aretina and Servant [with a purse].

Are. But hath Sir Thomas lost five hun-
dred pounds
Already?
Ser.   And five hundred more he bor-
rowed.
The dice are notable devourers, madam;
They make no more of pieces than of
pebbles,
But thrust their heaps together to en-
gender.
"Two hundred more!" the caster[2] cries
this[3] gentleman.
"I am w'e. I ha' that to nothing, sir."
The caster
Again: " 'Tis covered!"—and the table
too,
With sums that frighted me. Here one
sneaks out,   9
And with a martyr's patience smiles upon
His money's executioner, the dice,
Commands a pipe of good tobacco, and
I' th' smoke on 't vanishes. Another
makes

The bones vault o'er his head, swears
that ill-throwing
Has put his shoulder out of joint, calls for
A bonesetter, that looks to th' box, to bid
His master send him some more hundred
pounds,
Which lost, he takes tobacco, and is
quiet.
Here a strong arm throws in and in, with
which
He brusheth all the table,[4] pays the
rooks[5]   20
That went their smelts[6] apiece upon his
hand,
Yet swears he has not drawn a stake this
seven year.
But I was bid make haste; my master
may
Lose this five hundred pounds ere I come
thither.   *Exit.*
Are. If we both waste so fast, we shall
soon find
Our state is not immortal. Something in
His other ways appear not well already.

Enter Sir Thomas [with Servants].

Born. Ye tortoises, why make you no
more haste?
Go pay to th' master of the house that
money,
And tell the noble gamesters I have an-
other   30
Superfluous thousand pound; at night I'll
visit 'em.
D'e hear?
Ser.   Yes, and please you.
Born.   Do 't, ye drudges.—
                               [*Exeunt Servants.*]
Ta, ra, ra!—Aretina!
Are.   You have a pleasant humor, sir.
Born. What, should a gentleman be sad?
Are.   You have lost—
Born. A transitory sum; as good that
way
As another.
Are.   Do you not vex within for 't?
Born. I had rather lose a thousand more
than one
Sad thought come near my heart for 't.
Vex for trash?
Although it go from other men like drops

---

[1] Charles I and Queen Henrietta Maria.
[2] Thrower of dice.   [3] *I.e.*, to this.

[4] Wins all the stakes.
[5] Gulls, fools.   [6] Bet their half-guineas.

Of their life blood, we lose with the
alacrity   40
We drink a cup of sack, or kiss a mistress.
No money is considerable with a game-
ster;
They have souls more spacious than
kings. Did two
Gamesters divide the empire of the world,
They'd make one throw for 't all, and he
that lost
Be no more melancholy than to have
played for
A morning's draught. Vex a rich soul for
dirt,
The quiet of whose every thought is
worth
A province!
ARE.   But, when dice have consumed
all,
Your patience will not pawn for as much
more.   50
BORN. Hang pawning! Sell outright, and
the fear's over.
ARE. Say you so? I'll have another coach
tomorrow
If there be rich above ground.
BORN.   I forgot
To bid the fellow ask my jeweler
Whether the chain of diamonds be made
up;
I will present it to my Lady Bellamour,
Fair Celestina.
ARE.   This gown I have worn
Six days already; it looks dull. I'll give it
My waiting-woman, and have one of
cloth
Of gold embrodered; shoes and pant-
ables [1]   60
Will show well of the same.
BORN.   I have invited
A covey of ladies, and as many gentlemen
Tomorrow, to the Italian ordinary;
I shall have rarities and regalias [2]
To pay for, madam; music, wanton
songs,
And tunes of silken petticoats to dance
to.
ARE. And tomorrow have I invited half
the court
To dine here. What misfortune 'tis your
company
And ours should be divided! After dinner
I entertain 'em with a play.

[1] Slippers.   [2] Regalos, delicacies.

BORN.   By that time 70
Your play inclines to the epilogue, shall
we
Quit our Italian host, and whirl in
coaches
To the Dutch magazine of sauce,[3] the
Stillyard, [4]
Where deal,[5] and backrag,[6] and what
strange wine else
They dare but give a name to in the
reckoning,
Shall flow into our room, and drown
Westphalias,[7]
Tongues, and anchovies, like some little
town
Endangered by a sluice, through whose
fierce ebb
We wade, and wash ourselves into a boat,
And bid our coachmen drive their
leather tenements   80
By land, while we sail home with a fresh
tide
To some new rendezvous.
ARE.   If you have not
Pointed [8] the place, pray, bring your
ladies hither;
I mean to have a ball tomorrow night,
And a rich banquet for 'em, where we'll
dance
Till morning rise and blush to interrupt
us.
BORN. Have you no ladies i' th' next room
to advance
A present mirth? What a dull house you
govern!
Farewell! A wife's no company.—Are-
tina,
I've summed up my estate, and find we
may have   90
A month good yet.
ARE.   What mean you?
BORN.   And I'd rather
Be lord one month of pleasures, to the
height
And rapture of our senses, than be years
Consuming what we have in foolish tem-
perance,
Live in the dark, and no fame wait upon
us!

[3] Storehouse of sauce, tavern.
[4] The Steelyard, in the former German trading
district of the same name.
[5] An unidentified kind of German wine.
[6] Baccarach, a Rhenish wine.
[7] Westphalian hams.   [8] Appointed.

I will live so posterity shall stand
At gaze when I am mentioned.

ARE.   A month good!
And what shall be done then?

BORN.   I'll over sea,
And trail a pike. With watching, march-
  ing, lying
In trenches, with enduring cold and
  hunger,   100
And, taking here and there a musket shot,
I can earn every week four shillings,
  madam;
And, if the bullets favor me to snatch
Any superfluous limb, when I return
With good friends, I despair not to be
  enrolled
Poor Knight of Windsor.[1] For your
  course, madam,
No doubt you may do well; your friends
  are great;
Or, if your poverty and their pride can-
  not
Agree, you need not trouble much in-
  vention
To find a trade to live by; there are cus-
  tomers.   110
Farewell; be frolic, madam! If I live,
I will feast all my senses, and not fall
Less than a Phaëton from my throne of
  pleasure,
Though my estate flame like the world
  about me.

ARE. 'Tis very pretty!—

Enter Decoy.

Madam Decoy!   *Exit* [*Bornwell*].

DEC.   What! Melancholy
After so sweet a night's work? Have
  not I
Showed myself mistress of my art?

ARE.   A lady.

DEC. That title makes the credit of the
  act
A story higher. Y'ave not seen him yet?
I wonder what he'll say.

ARE.   He's here.

Enter Alexander and Frederick.

AL.   Bear up,   120
My little myrmidon; does not Jack
  Littleworth
Follow?

[1] A pensioned knight who had quarters in
Windsor Castle.

FRED.   Follow? He fell into the Thames
At landing.

AL.   The devil shall dive for him,
Ere I endanger my silk stockings for
  him.
Let the watermen alone; they have drags
  and engines.
When he has drunk his julep, I shall
  laugh
To see him come in pickled the next tide.

FRED. He'll never sink, he has such a cork
  brain.

AL. Let him be hanged or drowned, all's
  one to me;   129
Yet he deserves to die by water, cannot [2]
Bear his wine credibly.

FRED.   Is not this my aunt?

AL. And another handsome lady; I must
  know her.   [*Takes Decoy aside.*]

FRED. [*Aside.*] My blood is rampant too;
  I must court somebody—
As good my aunt as any other body.

ARE. Where have you been, cousin?

FRED.   At the bridge
At the Bear's foot, where our first health
  began
To the fair Aretina, whose sweet com-
  pany
Was wished by all. We could not get a
  lay,
A tumbler, a device, a *bona roba* [3]
For any money; drawers were grown
  dull.   140
We wanted our true firks [4] and our
  vagaries.—
When were you in drink, aunt?

ARE.   How?

FRED.   Do not ladies
Play the good fellows too? There's no
  true mirth
Without 'em. I have now such tickling
  fancies!
That doctor of the chair of wit has read
A precious lecture, how I should behave
Myself to ladies; as now, for example—

ARE. Would you practice upon me?

FRED.   I first salute you. [*Kisses her.*]
You have a soft hand, madam; are you so
All over?

ARE. Nephew!

FRED.   Nay, you should but smile.   150
                   [*Kisses her again.*]

[2] *I.e.*, who cannot.
[3] Four synonyms for *courtesan*.   [4] Tricks.

And then again I kiss you, and thus draw
Off your white glove, and start, to see
    your hand
More excellently white. I grace my own
Lip with this touch, and, turning gently
    thus,
Prepare you for my skill in palmistry,
Which, out of curiosity, no lady
But easily applies [1] to. The first line
I look [2] with most ambition to find out,
Is Venus' girdle, a fair semicircle,
Enclosing both the mount of Sol and
    Saturn;   160
If that appear, she's for my turn—a lady
Whom nature has prepared for the ca-
    reer;
And, Cupid at my elbow, I put forward.
You have this very line, aunt.
ARE.   The boy's frantic!
FRED. You have a couch or pallet; I can
    shut
The chamber door. Enrich a stranger,
    when
Your nephew's coming into play!
ARE.   No more.
FRED. Are you so coy to your own flesh
    and blood?
AL. [Coming forward.] Here, take your
    playfellow; I talk of sport,
And she would have me marry her.   170
FRED. Here's Littleworth.—

        Enter Littleworth, wet.

Why, how now, tutor?
LIT.   I ha' been fishing.
FRED. And what ha' you caught?
LIT.   My belly full of water.
AL. Ha, ha! Where's thy rapier?
LIT.   My rapier is drowned,
And I am little better. I was up by th'
    heels,
And out came a tun of water, beside
    wine.
AL. 'T has made thee sober.
LIT.   Would you have me drunk
With water?
ARE.   I hope your fire is quenched by
    this time.
FRED. It is not now, as when your worship
    "walked   179
By all the taverns, Jack, dry as a bone."

AL. You had store of fish under water,
    Jack.
LIT. It has made a poor John [3] of me.
FRED. I do not think but if we cast an
    angle
Into his belly, we might find some pil-
    chards.
LIT. And boiled, by this time.—Dear
    madam, a bed.
AL. Carry but the water spaniel to a grass
    plot,
Where he may roll himself; let him but
    shake
His ears twice in the sun, and you may
    grind him
Into a posset.
FRED.   Come, thou shalt to my bed,
Poor pickerel.
DEC.   Alas, sweet gentleman!   190
LIT. I have ill luck and I should smell by
    this time;
I am but new ta'en, I am sure.—Sweet
    gentlewoman!
DEC. Your servant.
LIT.   Pray, do not pluck off my skin;
It is so wet, unless you have good eyes,
You'll hardly know it from a shirt.
DEC.   Fear nothing.
    Exeunt [All but Aretina and Alexander]. [4]
ARE. [Aside.] He has sack enough, and I
    may find his humor.
AL. And how is 't with your ladyship? You
    look
Without a sunshine in your face.
ARE.   You are glorious
In mind and habit.
AL.   Ends of gold and silver!
ARE. Your other clothes were not so rich.
    Who was   200
Your tailor, sir?
AL.   They were made for me long since;
They have known but two bright days
    upon my back.
I had a humor, madam, to lay things by;
They will serve two days more. I think
    I ha' gold enough
To go to th' mercer. I'll now allow myself
A suit a week, as this, with necessary
Dependences, beaver, silk stockings, gar-
    ters,
And roses,[5] in their due conformity;

[1] Yields.
[2] Emended by Gifford-Dyce. Original reads
look.

[3] A poor John was a small dried fish.
[4] This stage direction follows the next line in the
original.   [5] Rosettes.

Boots are forbid a clean leg but to ride
  in.   209
My linen every morning comes in new;
The old goes to great bellies.
ARE.   You are charitable.
AL. I may dine w'e sometime, or at the
  court,
To meet good company, not for the table.
My clerk o' th' kitchen's here, a witty
  epicure,
A spirit, that, to please me with what's
  rare,
Can fly a hundred mile a day to market,
And make me Lord of Fish and Fowl. I
  shall
Forget there is a butcher; and to make
My footman nimble he shall feed on
  nothing
But wings of wild fowl.
ARE.   These ways are costly. 220
AL. Therefore I'll have it so; I ha' sprung
  a mine.
ARE. You make me wonder, sir, to see
  this change
Of fortune; your revenue was not late
So plentiful.
AL.   Hang dirty land and lordships!
I wo' not change one lodging I ha' got
For the Chamber of London.
ARE.   Strange, of such a sudden
To rise to this estate! No fortunate hand
At dice could lift you up so, for 'tis since
Last night; yesterday you were no such
  monarch.
AL. There be more games than dice.
ARE.   It cannot be   230
A mistress, though your person is worth
  love;
None possibly are rich enough to feed
As you have cast the method of your
  riots.
A princess, after all her jewels, must
Be forced to sell her provinces.
AL. [Showing a jewel.]   Now you talk
Of jewels, what do you think of this?
ARE.   A rich one.
AL. You'll honor me to wear 't. This
  other toy
I had from you. This chain I borrowed
  of you;
A friend had it in keeping. [Gives her the
  jewelry.] If your ladyship
Want any sum, you know your friend,
  and Alexander.   240

ARE. Dare you trust my security?
AL.   There's gold;
I shall have more tomorrow.
ARE.   You astonish me.
Who can supply these?
AL.   A dear friend I have.
She promised we should meet again i' th'
  morning.
ARE. Not that I wish to know
More of your happiness than I have a
  ready
Heart to congratulate, be pleased to lay
My wonder.
AL.   'Tis a secret—
ARE.   Which I'll die
Ere I'll betray.
AL.   You have always wished me well;
But you shall swear not to reveal the
  party.   250
ARE. I'll lose the benefit of my tongue.
AL.   Nor be
Afraid at what I say. What think you
  first
Of an old witch, a strange, ill-favored
  hag,
That, for my company last night, has
  wrought
This cure upon my fortune? I do sweat
To think upon her name.
ARE.   How, sir, a witch?
AL. I would not fright your ladyship too
  much
At first, but witches are akin to spirits.
The truth is—nay, if you look pale al-
  ready,   259
I ha' done.
ARE.   Sir, I beseech you.
AL.   If you have
But courage then to know the truth, I'll
  tell you
In one word: my chief friend is—the
  devil!
ARE. What devil? How I tremble!
AL.   Have a heart;
'Twas a she-devil too, a most insatiate,
Abominable devil, with a tail
Thus long.
ARE.   Goodness defend me! Did you see
  her?
AL. No, 'twas i' th' dark; but she appeared
  first to me
I' th' likeness of a beldam,[1] and was
  brought,

---

[1] Original reads *bedlam*.

I know not how nor whither, by two
   goblins, 269
More hooded than a hawk.

ARE.   But would you venter [1]
   Upon a devil?

AL.   Ay, for means.

ARE. [Aside.]   How black
   An impudence is this!—But are you sure
   It was the devil you enjoyed?

AL.   Say nothing;
   I did the best to please her; but, as
   sure
   As you live, 'twas a hell-cat.

ARE.   D'e not quake?

AL. I found myself in the very room [2] i' th'
   morning,
   Where two of her familiars had left me.

Enter Servant.

SER. My lord is come to visit you.

AL.   No words,
   As you respect my safety. I ha' told
   tales
   Out of the devil's school; if it be
   known, 280
   I lose a friend. 'Tis now about the
   time
   I promised her to meet again; at my
   Return I'll tell you wonders. Not a
   word!   *Exit.*

ARE. [*Looking in a mirror.*] 'Tis a false
   glass; sure I am more deformed.
What have I done? My soul is miserable.

Enter Lord.

LORD. I sent you a letter, madam.

ARE.   You expressed
   Your noble care of me, my lord.

Enter Bornwell, Celestina.

BORN.   Your lordship
   Does me an honor.

LORD.   Madam, I am glad
   To see you here; I meant to have kissed
   your hand 289
   Ere my return to court.

CEL.   Sir Thomas has
   Prevailed to bring me, to his trouble,
   hither.

LORD. You do him grace.

[1] Venture.
[2] Emended by Gifford-Dyce. Original reads
the very same in.

BORN.   Why, what's the matter,
   madam?
   Your eyes are tuning "Lachrimæ." [3]

ARE.   As you
   Do hope for heaven, withdraw, and give
   me but
   The patience of ten minutes.

BORN.   Wonderful!
   I wo' not hear you above that proportion.
   She talks of heaven.—Come, where must
   we to counsel?

ARE. You shall conclude [4] me when you
   please.   [*Exit.*]

BORN.   I follow.

LORD. [*Aside.*] What alteration is this? I,
   that so late 299
   Stood the temptation of her eye and voice,
   Boasted a heart 'bove all licentious flame,
   At second view turn renegade, and think
   I was too superstitious, and full
   Of phlegm, not to reward her amorous
   courtship
   With manly freedom.

CEL.   I obey you, sir.

BORN. I'll wait upon your lordship presently.   [*Exit.*]

LORD. [*Aside.*] She could not want a cun-
   ning to seem honest
   When I neglected her. I am resolved.—
   You still look pleasant, madam.

CEL.   I have cause,
   My lord, the rather for your presence,
   which 310
   Hath power to charm all trouble in my
   thoughts.

LORD. I must translate that compliment,
   and owe
   All that is cheerful in myself to these
   All-quick'ning smiles; and, rather than
   such bright
   Eyes should repent their influence upon
   me,
   I would release the aspects, and quit the
   bounty
   Of all the other stars. Did you not think
   me
   A strange and melancholy gentleman
   To use you so unkindly?

CEL.   Me, my lord?

LORD. I hope you made no loud complaint;
   I would not 320
   Be tried by a jury of ladies.

[3] *I.e.*, beginning to weep. "Lachrimæ" was a
melancholy song.   [4] Stop.

CEL.   For what, my lord?

LORD. I did not meet that noble entertainment
You were late pleased to show me.

CEL.   I observed
No such defect in your lordship, but a brave
And noble fortitude.

LORD.   A noble folly;
I bring repentance for 't. I know you have,
Madam, a gentle faith, and wo' not ruin
What you have built to honor you.

CEL.   What's that?

LORD. If you can love, I'll tell your ladyship.   329

CEL. I have a stubborn soul else.

LORD.   You are all
Composed of harmony.

CEL.   What love d'e mean?

LORD. That which doth perfect both. Madam, you have heard
I can be constant, and, if you consent
To grace it so, there is a spacious dwelling
Prepared within my heart for such a mistress.

CEL. Your mistress, my good lord?

LORD.   Why, my good lady,
Your sex doth hold it no dishonor
To become mistress to a noble servant
In the now court Platonic way. Consider
Who 'tis that pleads to you; my birth and present   340
Value can be no stain to your embrace.
But these are shadows when my love appears,
Which shall in his first miracle return
Me in my bloom of youth, and thee a virgin,
When I, within some new Elysium,
Of purpose made and meant for us, shall be
In everything Adonis but in his
Contempt of love, and court thee from a Daphne
Hid in the cold rind of a bashful tree,
With such warm language and delight, till thou   350
Leap from that bays into the Queen of Love,
And pay my conquest with composing garlands
Of thy own myrtle for me.

CEL.   What's all this?

LORD. Consent to be my mistress, Celestina,
And we will have it springtime all the year,
Upon whose invitations, when we walk,
The winds shall play soft descant [1] to our feet,
And breathe rich odors to re-pure the air;
Green bowers on every side shall tempt our stay,
And violets stoop to have us tread upon 'em.   360
The red rose shall grow pale, being near thy cheek,
And the white blush, o'ercome with such a forehead.
Here laid, and measuring with ourselves some bank,
A thousand birds shall from the woods repair,
And place themselves so cunningly behind
The leaves of every tree that, while they pay
Us [2] tribute of their songs, thou sha't imagine
The very trees bear music, and sweet voices
Do grow in every arbor. Here can we
Embrace and kiss, tell tales, and kiss again,   370
And none but heaven our rival.

CEL.   When we are
Weary of these, what if we shift our paradise,
And through a grove of tall and even pine
Descend into a valley, that shall shame
All the delights of Tempe, upon whose
Green plush the Graces shall be called to dance
To please us, and maintain their fairy revels
To the harmonious murmurs of a stream
That gently falls upon a rock of pearl.
Here doth the nymph, forsaken Echo, dwell,   380
To whom we'll tell the story of our love,
Till at our surfeit and her want of joy
We break her heart with envy. Not far off,
A grove shall call us to a wanton river
To see a dying swan give up the ghost,

[1] Melody.

[2] Gifford-Dyce's reading. Original reads *As.*

The fishes shooting up their tears in bub-
bles
That they must lose the genius of their
waves—
And such love linsey-woolsey, to no pur-
pose!
LORD. You chide me handsomely; pray,
tell me how　　　　　　389
You like this language.
CEL.　　　　Good my lord, forbear.
LORD. You need not fly out of this circle,
madam;
These widows so are full of circumstance!
I'll undertake, in this time I ha' courted
Your ladyship for the toy, to ha' broken
ten,
Nay, twenty colts—virgins, I mean—and
taught 'em
The amble, or what pace I most affected.
CEL. Y' are not my lord again—the lord I
thought you;
And I must tell you now you do forget
Yourself and me.
LORD.　　　You'll not be angry, madam?
CEL. Nor rude (though gay men have a
privilege)　　　　　　400
It shall appear. There is a man, my lord,
Within my acquaintance, rich in worldly
fortunes,
But cannot boast any descent of blood,
Would buy a coat of arms.
LORD.　　　　He may, and legs
Booted and spurred, to ride into the
country.
CEL. But these will want antiquity, my
lord,
The seal of honor. What's a coat cut out
But yesterday, to make a man a gentle-
man?　　　　　　408
Your family, as old as the first virtue
That merited an escutcheon, doth owe [1]
A glorious coat of arms; if you will sell now
All that your name doth challenge in that
ensign,
I'll help you to a chapman [2] that shall pay,
And pour down wealth enough for 't.
LORD.　　　　Sell my arms?
I cannot, madam.
CEL.　　　Give but your consent,
You know not how the state may be in-
clined
To dispensation; we may prevail
Upon the Herald's office afterward.

[1] Own.　　　　　　　　[2] Merchant.

LORD. I'll sooner give these arms to th'
hangman's ax,
My head, my heart, to twenty execu-
tions,　　　　　　420
Than sell one atom from my name.
CEL.　　　　　　Change that,
And answer him would buy my honor
from me—
Honor, that is not worn upon a flag
Or pennon that without the owner's dan-
gers
An enemy may ravish and bear from
me,
But that which grows and withers with
my soul,
Beside the body's stain. Think, think,
my lord,
To what you would unworthily betray
me,
If you would not, for price of gold or
pleasure
(If that be more your idol) lose the
glory　　　　　　430
And painted honor of your house. I ha'
done.
LORD. Enough to rectify a satyr's blood.
Obscure my blushes here.

Enter Scentlove and Haircut [behind].

HAIR.　　　Or this or fight with me.
It shall be no exception that I wait
Upon my lord. I am a gentleman;
You may be less and be a knight. The
office
I do my lord is honest, sir. How many
Such you have been guilty of, heaven
knows.
SCENT. 'Tis no fear of your sword, but that
I would not
Break the good laws established against
duels.　　　　　　440
HAIR. Off with your periwig, and stand
bare.　　　[*Scentlove removes his wig.*]
LORD.　　　From this
Minute I'll be a servant to thy goodness.
A mistress in the wanton sense is com-
mon;
I'll honor you with chaste thoughts, and
call you so.
CEL. I'll study to be worth your fair opin-
ion.
LORD. Scentlove, your head was used to a
covering
Beside a hat; when went the hair away?

SCENT. I laid a wager, my lord, with Hair-
cut,
Who thinks I shall catch cold, that I'll
stand bare 449
This half hour.
HAIR. Pardon my ambition,
Madam. I told you truth; I am a gen-
tleman,
And cannot fear that name is drowned in
my
Relation to my lord.
CEL. I dare not think so.
HAIR. From henceforth call my service
duty, madam.
That pig's head, that betrayed me to
your mirth,
Is doing penance for 't.
SCENT. Why may not I,
My lord, begin a fashion of no hair?
CEL. Do you sweat, Sir William?
SCENT. Not with store of nightcaps.

Enter Aretina, Bornwell.

ARE. Heaven has dissolved the clouds that
hung upon
My eyes, and, if you can with mercy
meet 460
A penitent, I throw my own will off,
And now in all things obey yours. My
nephew
Send back again to th' college, and my-
self
To what place you'll confine me.
BORN. Dearer now
Than ever to my bosom, thou sha't
please
Me best to live at thy own choice. I did
But fright thee with a noise of my
expenses;
The sums are safe, and we have wealth
enough, 468
If yet we use it nobly. My lord—madam,
Pray, honor [us] [1] tonight.
ARE. I beg your presence
And pardon.
BORN. I know not how my Aretina
May be disposed tomorrow for the coun-
try.
CEL. You must not go before you both
have done
Me honor to accept an entertainment
Where I have power; on those terms I'm
your guest.

[1] Supplied by Gifford-Dyce.

BORN. You grace us, madam.
ARE. [*Aside.*] Already
I feel a cure upon my soul, and promise
My after-life to virtue. Pardon, heaven,
My shame, yet hid from the world's eye.

Enter Decoy. [2]

DEC. Sweet madam! 480
ARE. Not for the world be seen here! We
are lost.
I'll visit you at home.—[*Aside.*] But not
to practice
What she expects; my counsel may recover her. [*Exit Decoy.*]

Enter Alexander.

AL. Where's madam?—Pray, lend me a
little money;
My spirit has deceived me. Proserpine
Has broke her word.
ARE. Do you expect to find
The devil true to you?
AL. Not too loud!
ARE. I'll voice it
Louder, to all the world, your horrid sin,
Unless you promise me religiously
To purge your foul blood by repentance,
sir. 490
AL. Then I'm undone.
ARE. Not while I have power
To encourage you to virtue. I'll endeavor
To find you out some nobler way at court
To thrive in.
AL. Do 't, and I'll forsake the devil
And bring my flesh to obedience. You
shall steer me.—
My lord, your servant.
LORD. You are brave again.
AL. Madam, your pardon.
BORN. Your offense requires
Humility.
AL. Low as my heart.—Sir Thomas,
I'll sup with you, a part of satisfaction.
BORN. Our pleasures cool. Music! And,
when our ladies 500
Are tired with active motion, to give
Them rest, in some new rapture to ad-
vance
Full mirth, our souls shall leap into a
dance. *Exeunt.*

FINIS.

[2] This stage direction follows the next line in the
original.

THE CARDINAL[1]

BY

JAMES SHIRLEY

PERSONS

KING OF NAVARRE.
CARDINAL.
COLUMBO, *the cardinal's nephew.*
[COUNT D']ALVAREZ.
HERNANDO, *a colonel.*
ALPHONSO [, *a captain*].
LORDS.
[ANTONIO,] *secretary to the duchess.*
COLONELS.
ANTONELLI, *the cardinal's servant.*

SURGEON.
GUARD.
ATTENDANTS, *etc.*

DUCHESS ROSAURA.
VALERIA } *ladies.*
CELINDA }
PLACENTIA, *a lady that waits upon the duchess.*

SCENE: *Navarre.*

[TIME: *Contemporary.*]

[1] The title continues: "A Tragedy As It Was Acted at the Private House in Blackfriars." The unimportant dedication, "To My Worthily Honored Friend, G. B., Esq.," is omitted.
[2] The prologue appears before the cast in the original.
[3] Because we hang out no placard, "The Cardinal" recalls Richelieu in France.
[4] Alluding to the cardinal himself.
[5] Here follows a complimentary poem by Hall

PROLOGUE[2]

The Cardinal! Cause[3] we express no scene,
We do believe most of you gentlemen
Are at this hour in France,[3] and busy there,
Though you vouchsafe to lend your bodies
   here;
But keep your fancy active, till you know,
By th' progress of our play, 'tis nothing so.
A poet's art is to lead on your thought
Through subtle paths and workings of a
   plot,
And, where your expectation does not
   thrive,   9
If things fall better, yet you may forgive.
I will say nothing positive; you may
Think what you please; we call it but a
   "play."
Whether the comic Muse, or ladies' love,
Romance, or direful tragedy it prove,
The bill determines not; and, would you be
Persuaded, I would have 't a comedy,

For all the purple in the name and state
Of him that owns it;[4] but 'tis left to fate.
Yet I will tell you, ere you see it played,
What the author—and he blushed too, when
   he said,   20
Comparing with his own (for 't had been
   pride,
He thought, to build his wit a pyramide
Upon another's wounded fame), this play
Might rival with his best, and dared to
   say—
Troth, I am out. He said no more. You,
   then,
When 'tis done, may say your pleasures,
   gentlemen.[5]

ACT I. [SCENE i.

A room in the king's palace.]

Enter two Lords at one door; Secretary at the
*   other.*

1 Lo. Who is that?
2 Lo.   The duchess' secretary.
1 Lo. Signior!
SEC.   Your lordship's servant.
1 Lo. How does her grace since she left
   her mourning

For the young Duke Mendoza, whose
timeless [1] death
At sea left her a virgin and a widow?

2 Lo. She's now inclining to a second
bride.[2] —
When is the day of mighty marriage
To our great cardinal's nephew, Don
Columbo?

Sec. When they agree. They wo' not steal
to church.
I guess the ceremonies will be loud and
public. 10
Your lordships will excuse me. *Exit.*

1 Lo. When they agree? Alas, poor lady,
she
Dotes not upon Columbo when she
thinks
Of the young Count d'Alvarez, divorced
from her
By the king's power.

2 Lo. And counsel of the cardinal to advance
His nephew to the duchess' bed. 'Tis
not well.

1 Lo. Take heed; the cardinal holds intelligence [3]
With every bird i' th' air.

2 Lo. Death on his purple pride!
He governs all, and yet Columbo is 20
A gallant gentleman.

1 Lo. The darling of the war, whom vic-
tory
Hath often courted; a man of daring
And most exalted spirit. Pride in him
Dwells like an ornament, where so much
honor
Secures his praise.

2 Lo. This is no argument
He should usurp and wear Alvarez' title
To the fair duchess; men of coarser
blood
Would not so tamely give this treasure
up.

1 Lo. Although Columbo's name is great
in war, 30
Whose glorious art and practice is above
The greatness of Alvarez, yet he can-
not
Want soul, in whom alone survives the
virtue
Of many noble ancestors, being the last
Of his great family.

2 Lo. 'Tis not safe, you'll say.
To wrastle with the king.[4]

1 Lo. More danger if the cardinal be dis-
pleased,
Who sits at helm of state. Count d'Al-
varez
Is wiser to obey the stream than, by
Insisting on his privilege to her love, 40
Put both their fates upon a storm.

2 Lo. If wisdom, not inborn fear, make
him compose,[5]
I like it. How does the duchess bear
herself?

1 Lo. She moves by the rapture [6] of an-
other wheel [7]
That must be obeyed, like some sad
passenger,
That looks upon the coast his wishes fly
to,
But is transported by an adverse wind,
Sometimes a churlish pilot.

2 Lo. She has a sweet and noble nature.

1 Lo. That 49
Commends Alvarez; Hymen cannot tie
A knot of two more equal hearts and
blood.

Enter Alphonso.

2 Lo. Alphonso!

Alph. My good lord.

1 Lo. What great affair
Hath brought you from the confines?

Alph. Such as will
Be worth your counsels, when the king
hath read
My letters from the governor. The
Aragonians,
Violating their confederate oath and
league,
Are now in arms; they have not yet
marched towards us,
But 'tis not safe to expect,[8] if we may
timely
Prevent invasion.

2 Lo. Dare they be so insolent?

1 Lo. This storm I did foresee. 60

2 Lo. What have they but the sweetness of
the king
To make a crime?

---

[1] Untimely.
[2] Bridegroom. [3] Communication.

[4] Here and in several other passages the line
division has been regularized.
[5] Agree. [7] *I.e.*, steering wheel.
[6] Energy, force. [8] Wait.

1 Lo.   But how appears the cardinal
    At this news?
ALPH.   Not pale, although
    He knows they have no cause to think
        him innocent,
    As by whose counsel they were once sur-
        prised.
1 Lo. There is more
    Than all our present art can fathom in
    This story, and I fear I may conclude
    This flame has breath at home to cherish
        it.
    There's treason in some hearts, whose
        faces are   70
    Smooth to the state.
ALPH.   My lords, I take my leave.
2 Lo. Your friends, good captain. *Exeunt.*

[SCENE ii.

A room in the duchess' palace.]

Enter Duchess, Valeria, Celinda.

VAL. Sweet madam, be less thoughtful;
        this obedience
    To passion will destroy the noblest
        frame
    Of beauty that this kingdom ever
        boasted.
CEL. This sadness might become your
        other habit
    And ceremonies black for him that died.
    The times of sorrow are expired; and all
    The joys that wait upon the court, your
        birth,
    And a new Hymen, that is coming to-
        wards you,
    Invite a change.
DUCH.   Ladies, I thank you both.
    I pray, excuse a little melancholy   10
    That is behind; my year of mourning
        hath not
    So cleared my account with sorrow but
        there may
    Some dark thoughts stay, with sad re-
        flections,
    Upon my heart for him I lost. Even this
    New dress and smiling garment, meant
        to show
    A peace concluded twixt my grief and
        me,
    Is but a sad remembrance. But I resolve
    To entertain more pleasing thoughts;
        and, if

You wish me heartily to smile, you
        must
    Not mention grief, not in advice to
        leave it.   20
    Such counsels open but afresh the
        wounds
    Ye would close up, and keep alive the
        cause,
    Whose bleeding you would cure. Let's
        talk of something
    That may delight. You two are read in
        all
    The histories of our court. Tell me,
        Valeria,
    Who has thy vote for the most handsome
        man?—
    [*Aside.*] Thus I must counterfeit a peace,
        when all
    Within me is at mutiny.
VAL.   I have examined
    All that are candidates for the praise of
        ladies,
    But find—may I speak boldly to your
        grace?   30
    And will you not return it in your mirth
    To make me blush?
DUCH.   No, no; speak freely.
VAL. I wo' not rack your patience,
        madam; but
    Were I a princess, I should think Count
        d'Alvarez
    Had sweetness to deserve[1] me from the
        world.
DUCH. [*Aside.*] Alvarez! She's a spy upon
        my heart.
VAL. He's young and active, and composed
        most sweetly.
DUCH. I have seen a face more tempting.
VAL.   It had then
    Too much of woman in 't. His eyes speak
        movingly,
    Which may excuse his voice, and lead
        away   40
    All female pride his captive; his hair,
        black,
    Which, naturally falling into curls—
DUCH. Prithee, no more; thou art in love
        with him.—
    The man in your esteem, Celinda, now?
CEL. Alvarez is, I must confess, a gentle-
        man
    Of handsome composition; but with
    His mind, the greater excellence, I think

[1] Be worthy of.

Another may delight a lady more,
If man be well considered. That's
  Columbo,
Now, madam, voted to be yours.
DUCH. [*Aside.*]   My torment! 50
VAL. [*Aside.*] She affects [1] him not.
CEL. He has person, and a bravery beyond
  All men that I observe.
VAL.   He is a soldier,
  A rough-hewn man, and may show well
    at distance.
  His talk will fright a lady; War and
    grim-
  Faced Honor are his mistresses; he raves
  To hear a lute; Love meant him not his
    priest.—
  Again your pardon, madam. We may
    talk,
  But you have art to choose, and crown
    affection. [*Celinda and Valeria retire.*]
DUCH. What is it to be born above these
    ladies,   60
  And want their freedom! They are not
    constrained,
  Nor slaved by their own greatness, or
    the king's,
  But let their free hearts look abroad and
    choose
  By their own eyes to love. I must repair
  My poor afflicted bosom, and assume
  The privilege I was born with, which now
    prompts me
  To tell the king he hath no power nor art
  To steer a lover's soul.—

Enter Secretary.

      What says Count d'Alvarez?
SEC. Madam, he'll attend you.
DUCH. Wait you, as I directed. When he
    comes,   70
  Acquaint me privately.
SEC.   Madam, I have news;
  'Tis now arrived the court we shall have
    wars.
DUCH. [*Aside.*] I find an army here of
    killing thoughts.
SEC. The king has chosen Don Columbo
    general,
  Who is immediately to take his leave.
DUCH. [*Aside.*] What flood is let into my
    heart!—How far
  Is he to go?
  [1] Likes.

SEC.   To Aragon.
DUCH.   That's well
  At first. He should not want a pilgrimage
  To the unknown world, if my thoughts
    might convey him.   79
SEC. 'Tis not impossible he may go thither.
DUCH. How?
SEC. To the unknown other world. He
    goes to fight;
  That's in his way. Such stories are in
    nature.
DUCH. Conceal this news.
SEC.   He wo' not be long absent;
  The affair will make him swift to kiss
    your grace's hand.   [*Exit.*]
DUCH. He cannot fly
  With too much wing to take his leave.—
    [*To the Ladies.*] I must
  Be admitted to your conference. Ye have
  Enlarged my spirits; they shall droop no
    more.
CEL. We are happy if we may advance
    one thought   90
  To your grace's pleasure.
VAL. Your eye before was in eclipse; these
    smiles
  Become you, madam.
DUCH. [*Aside.*] I have not skill to contain
    myself.

Enter Placentia.

PLA. The cardinal's nephew, madam, Don
    Columbo.
DUCH. Already? Attend him.
             Ex[it] Plac[entia].
VAL.   Shall we take our leave?
DUCH. He shall not know, Celinda, [2] how
    you praised him.
CEL. [3] If he did, madam, I should have the
    confidence
  To tell him my free thoughts.

Enter Columbo.

DUCH. My lord, while I'm in study to
    requite   100
  The favor you ha' done me, you increase
  My debt to such a sum, still by a new
    honoring
  Your servant, I despair of my own free-
    dom.

[2] Original reads *Valeria*, but *cf.* ll. 45ff. The
reversing of the two names here and later in the
scene was first suggested by Gifford.
  [3] Original reads *Val.*

Col. Madam, he kisseth your white hand,
　　that must
　Not surfeit in this happiness—and, la-
　　dies,
　I take your smiles for my encouragement!
　I have not long to practice these court
　　tactics.　　　　　　　　[*Kisses them.*]
Cel. [*Aside.*] He has been taught to kiss.
Duch.　　　　　　There's something, sir,
　Upon your brow I did not read before.
Col. Does the character please you,
　　madam?
Duch.　　　　More,　　　　　　　　110
　Because it speaks you cheerful.
Col.　　　　　　　　'Tis for such
　Access of honor as must make Columbo
　Worth all your love; the king is pleased
　　to think
　Me fit to lead his army.
Duch.　　　　　　　How, an army?
Col. We must not use the priest, till I
　　bring home
　Another triumph that now stays for me
　To reap it in the purple field of glory.
Duch. But do you mean to leave me, and
　　expose
　Yourself to the devouring war?　　No
　　enemy
　Should divide us; the king is not so
　　cruel.　　　　　　　　　　　　120
Col. The king is honorable; and this grace
　More answers my ambition than his gift
　Of thee and all thy beauty, which I can
　Love, as becomes thy soldier, and fight
　　　　　　　　　　　　　She weeps.
　To come again, a conqueror of thee.
　Then I must chide this fondness.[1]

　　　　　Enter Secretary.

Sec. Madam, the king and my Lord Car-
　　dinal.　　　　　　　　　　[*Exit.*]

　Enter King, Cardinal, and Lords.

King. Madam, I come to call a servant[2]
　　from you,
　And strengthen his excuse; the public
　　cause
　Will plead for your consent.　At his
　　return　　　　　　　　　　130
　Your marriage shall receive triumphant
　　ceremonies;
　Till then you must dispense.
　　　　[*He walks aside with the Duchess.*]

[1] Foolishness.　　　　　　　[2] Lover.

Car. [*Walking aside with Columbo.*]　　She
　　appears sad
　To part with him.—I like it fairly,
　　nephew.
Cel.[3] Is not the general a gallant man?
　What lady would deny him a small
　　courtesy?
Val. Thou hast converted me, and I begin
　To wish it were no sin.
Cel. Leave that to narrow consciences.
Val.　　　　　　　You are pleasant.
Cel. But he would please one better.　Do
　　such men
　Lie with their pages?
Val.　　Wouldst thou make a shift?　140
Cel. He is going to a bloody business;
　'Tis pity he should die without some heir.
　That lady were hard-hearted now that
　　would
　Not help posterity, for the mere good
　O' th' king and commonwealth.
Val. Thou art wild; we may be observed.
Duch. Your will must guide me; happiness
　　and conquest
　Be ever waiting on his sword!
Col.　　　　　　　　　　Farewell.
Ex[eunt] K[ing], Col[umbo], Card[inal], and
　　　　　　　　　　　　　　Lo[rds].
Duch. Pray, give leave to examine a few
　　thoughts;　　　　　　　　　149
　Expect me in the garden.
Ladies.　　We attend. *Ex[eunt] Ladies.*
Duch. This is above all expectation
　　happy.
　Forgive me, Virtue, that I have dis-
　　sembled,
　And witness with me I have not a
　　thought
　To tempt or to betray him, but secure
　The promise I first made to love and
　　honor.

　　　　　Enter Secretary.

Sec. The Count d'Alvarez, madam.
Duch.　　　　　　　Admit him,
　And let none interrupt us.—[*Exit Secre-
　　tary.*] How shall I
　Behave[4] my looks?　The guilt of my neg-
　　lect,
　Which had no seal from hence, will call
　　up blood

[3] The original reverses the names of *Cel.* and
Val. throughout this dialogue.
[4] Control.

To write upon my cheeks the shame and
   story   160
In some red letter.

Enter d'Alvarez.

D'ALV.   Madam, I present
   One that was glad to obey your grace,
     and come
To know what your commands are.
DUCH.   Where I once
   Did promise love, a love that had the
     power
And office of a priest to chain my heart
To yours, it were injustice to command.
D'ALV. But I can look upon you, madam,
   as
   Becomes a servant; with as much humil-
     ity,
   In tenderness of[1] your honor and great
     fortune,
   Give up, when you call back your bounty,
     all that   170
   Was mine, as I had pride to think them
     favors.
DUCH. Hath love taught thee no more
   assurance in
   Our mutual vows thou canst suspect it
     possible
I should revoke a promise made to
   heaven
And thee so soon? This must arise from
   some
Distrust of thy own faith.
D'ALV.   Your grace's pardon;
   To speak with freedom, I am not so old
In cunning to betray, nor young in time,
Not to see when and where I am at loss,
And how to bear my fortune and my
     wounds,   180
   Which, if I look for health, must still
     bleed inward,
A hard and desperate condition.
I am not ignorant your birth and great-
     ness
   Have placed you to grow up with the
     king's grace
And jealousy, which to remove, his
   power
Hath chosen a fit object for your beauty
To shine upon, Columbo, his great favor-
   ite.
I am a man on whom but late the king

[1] Regard for.

Has pleased to cast a beam, which was
   not meant   189
To make me proud, but wisely to direct
And light me to my safety. O, dear
   madam,
I will not call more witness of my love
(If you will let me still give it that name)
Than this, that I dare make myself a
   loser,
And to your will give all my blessings up.
Preserve your greatness, and forget a
   trifle
That shall at best, when you have drawn
   me up,
But hang about you like a cloud, and dim
The glories you are born to.
DUCH.   Misery
   Of birth and state! That I could shift
     into   200
A meaner blood, or find some art to purge
That part which makes my veins un-
     equal! Yet
Those nice distinctions have no place in
   us;
There's but a shadow difference, a title.
Thy stock partakes as much of noble sap
As that which feeds the root of kings; and
   he
That writes a lord hath all the essence of
   Nobility.
D'ALV.   'Tis not a name that makes
   Our separation; the king's displeasure
Hangs a portent to fright us, and the
     matter   210
That feeds this exhalation[2] is the car-
   dinal's
Plot to advance his nephew; then Co-
   lumbo,
A man made up for some prodigious act,
Is fit to be considered. In all three
There is no character you fix upon
But has a form of ruin to us both.
DUCH. Then you do look on these with
   fear?
D'ALV.   With eyes
   That should think tears a duty, to lament
Your least unkind fate; but my youth
     dares boldly
Meet all the tyranny o' th' stars, whose
     black   220
Malevolence but shoot my single tragedy.
You are above the value of many worlds
Peopled with such as I am.

[2] Meteor.

DUCH.   What if Columbo,
  Engaged to war, in his hot thirst of
    honor
  Find out the way to death?
D'ALV.   'Tis possible.
DUCH. Or say (no matter by what art or
    motive)
  He gives his title up, and leave me to
  My own election?
D'ALV.   If I then be happy
  To have a name within your thought,
    there can
  Be nothing left to crown me with new
    blessing.   230
  But I dream thus of heaven, and wake
    to find
  My amorous soul a mockery. When the
    priest
  Shall tie you to another, and the joys
  Of marriage leave no thought at leisure to
  Look back upon Alvarez, that must
    wither
  For loss of you, yet then I cannot lose
  So much of what I was once in your
    favor,
  But in a sigh pray still you may live
    happy.   *Exit.*
DUCH. My heart is in a mist; some good
    star smile
  Upon my resolution, and direct   240
  Two lovers in their chaste embrace to
    meet!
  Columbo's bed contains my winding
    sheet.   *Exit.*

ACT II. [SCENE i.

*Columbo's tent outside the walls of a frontier
city.*]

*Enter General Columbo, Hernando, two Colo-
nels, Alphonso, two Captains, and other
Officers, as at a council of war.*

COL. I see no face in all this council that
  Hath one pale fear upon 't, though we
    arrived not
  So timely to secure the town, which gives
  Our enemy such triumph.
1 COL.   'Twas betrayed.
ALPH. The wealth of that one city
  Will make the enemy glorious.[1]
1 COL.   They dare
  Not plunder it.
   [1] Boastful.

ALPH.   They give fair quarter yet;
  They only seal up men's estates, and
    keep
  Possession for the city's use; they take up
  No wares without security, and he   10
  Whose single credit will not pass puts in
  Two lean comrades, upon whose bonds
    'tis not
  Religion to deny 'em.
COL.   To repair this
  With honor, gentlemen?
HER.   My opinion is
  To expect awhile.
COL.   Your reason?
HER.   Till their own
  Surfeit betray 'em, for their soldier[s],
  Bred up with coarse and common bread,
    will show
  Such appetites on the rich cates they find,
  They will spare our swords a victory,
    when their own
  Riot and luxury destroys 'em.
1 COL.   That   20
  Will show our patience too like a fear.
  With favor of his excellence, I think
  The spoil of cities takes not off the cour-
    age,
  But doubles it on soldiers; besides,
  While we have tameness to expect, the
    noise
  Of their success and plenty will increase
  Their army.
HER.   'Tis considerable; we do not
  Exceed in foot or horse, our muster not
  'Bove sixteen thousand both, and the
    infantry
  Raw, and not disciplined to act.
ALPH.   Their hearts,   30
  But with a brave thought of their coun-
    try's honor,
  Will teach 'em how to fight, had they not
    seen
  A sword. But we decline [2] our own too
    much;
  The men are forward in their arms, and
    take
  The use with avarice of fame.
         They rise, and talk privately.
COL.   Colonel,
  I do suspect you are a coward.
HER.   Sir!
COL. Or else a traitor; take your choice.
  No more.
   [2] Undervalue.

I called you to a council, sir, of war;
Yet keep your place.
HER.   I have worn other names.
COL. Deserve 'em. Such   40
Another were enough to unsoul an army.
Ignobly talk of patience, till they drink
And reel to death? We came to fight, and
    force 'em
To mend their pace; thou hast no honor
    in thee,
Not enough noble blood to make a blush
For thy tame eloquence.
HER.   My lord, I know
My duty to a general; yet there are
Some that have known me here. Sir, I
    desire
To quit my regiment.
COL.   You shall have license.—
Ink and paper!   50

    Enter with paper and standish.[1]

1 COL. The general's displeased.
2 COL.   How is 't, Hernando?
HER. The general has found out em-
    ployment for me;
He is writing letters back.
ALPH. }
1]CAP. }   To his mistress?
HER. Pray, do not trouble me; yet, prithee,
    speak,
And flatter not thy friend. Dost think I
    dare
Not draw my sword, and use it, when
    cause
With honor calls to action?
ALPH. }
[1]COL. } With the most valiant man alive.
HER. You'll do me some displeasure in
    your loves.
Pray, to your places.   60
COL. So; bear those letters to the king;
It speaks my resolution, before
Another sun decline, to charge the
    enemy.
HER. [*Aside.*] A pretty court way
Of dismissing an officer.—I obey; success
Attend your counsels!   *Exit.*
COL. If here be any dare not look on dan-
    ger,
And meet it like a man, with scorn of
    death,
I beg his absence; and a coward's fear
Consume him to a ghost!

[1] A stand for writing.

1 COL.   None such here. 70
COL. Or, if in all your regiments you find
One man that does not ask to bleed with
    honor,
Give him a double pay to leave the army;
There's service to be done will call the
    spirits
And aid of men.
1 COL.   You give us all new flame.
COL. I am confirmed, and you must lose no
    time;
The soldier that was took last night, to
    me
Discovered[2] their whole strength, and
    that we have
A party in the town, the river that   79
Opens the city to the west unguarded.
We must this night use art and resolu-
    tions.
We cannot fall ingloriously.
1 CAP. That voice is every man's.

    Enter Soldier and Secretary with a letter.

COL. What now?
SOL. Letters.
COL. Whence?
SOL. From the duchess.
COL. They are welcome.—[*Takes the let-
    ter.*]
Meet at my tent again this evening;
Yet stay, some wine.—The duchess'
    health!   90
See it go round.   [*Opens the letter.*]
SEC.   It wo' not please his excellence.
1 COL. The duchess' health!   [*Drinks.*]
2 CAP. To me! More wine.
SEC. The clouds are gathering, and his eyes
    shoot fire;
Observe what thunder follows.
2 CAP. The general has but ill news. I
    suspect
The duchess sick, or else the king.
1 CAP.   May be
The cardinal.
2 CAP.   His soul has long been looked
    for.
COL. [*Aside.*] She dares not be so insolent.
    It is
The duchess' hand. How am I shrunk in
    fame   100
To be thus played withal! She writes,
    and counsels,

[2] Revealed.

Under my hand, to send her back a free
Resign of all my interest to her person,
Promise, or love; that there's no other
   way,
With safety of my honor, to revisit her.
The woman is possessed with some bold
   devil,
And wants an exorcism; or I am grown
A cheap, dull, phlegmatic fool, a post
   that's carved
I' th' common street, and holding out my
   forehead
To every scurril wit to pin disgrace   110
And libels on 't.—Did you bring this to
   me, sir?
My thanks shall warm your heart.
                 Draws a pistol.

Sec.   Hold, hold, my lord!
   I know not what provokes this tempest,
     but
   Her grace ne'er showed more freedom
    from a storm
   When I received this paper. If you have
   A will to do an execution,
   Your looks, without that engine, sir, may
    serve.
   I did not like the employment.
Col.   Ha! Had she
   No symptom, in her eye or face, of anger,
   When she gave this in charge?
Sec.   Serene as I   120
   Have seen the morning rise upon the
    spring;
   No trouble in her breath, but such a wind
   As came to kiss and fan the smiling
    flowers.
Col. No poetry.
Sec.   By all the truth in prose,
   By honesty and your own honor, sir,
   I never saw her look more calm and gentle.
Col. I am too passionate; you must for-
   give me.
   I have found it out; the duchess loves me
    dearly.
   She expressed a trouble in her when I
    took   129
   My leave, and chid me with a sullen eye.
   'Tis a device to hasten my return;
   Love has a thousand arts. I'll answer it
   Beyond her expectation, and put
   Her soul to a noble test.—Your patience,
    gentlemen;
   The king's health will deserve a sacrifice
   of wine.   [*Sits at the table and writes.*]

Sec. [*Aside.*] I am glad to see this change,
   and thank my wit
   For my redemption.
1 Col. Sir, the soldier's curse on him loves
   not our master!
2 Col. And they curse loud enough to be
   heard.
2 Cap. Their curse has the nature of gunpowder.   140
Sec. They do not pray with half the noise.
1 Col. Our general is not well mixed;
   He has too great a portion of fire.
2 Col. His mistress cool him (her complexion [1]
   Carries some phlegm) when they two
   meet in bed!
2 Cap. A third may follow.
1 Cap.   'Tis much pity
   The young duke lived not to take the
   virgin off.
1 Col. 'Twas the king's act to match two
   rabbit-suckers.[2]
2 Col. A common trick of state;   150
   The little great man marries, travels then
   Till both grow up, and dies when he
   should do
   The feat. These things are still unlucky
   On the male side.
Col. This to the duchess' fair hand.
              [*Gives Secretary a letter.*]
Sec.   She will think
   Time hath no wing, till I return.   [*Exit.*]
Col.   Gentlemen,
   Now each man to his quarter, and en-
   courage
   The soldier. I shall take a pride to know
   Your diligence, when I visit all your
   Several commands.
Omnes.   We shall expect.
2 Col.   And move   160
   By your directions.
Col.   Y' are all noble.   *Exeunt.*

[Scene ii.

A room in the duchess' palace.]

Enter Cardinal, Duchess, Placentia.

Car. I shall perform a visit daily, madam,
   In th' absence of my nephew, and be
   happy
   If you accept my care.
Duch.   You have honored me

[1] Temperament.   [2] Sucking rabbits, children

And, if your entertainment have not been
Worthy your grace's person, 'tis because
Nothing can reach it in my power; but,
    where
There is no want of zeal, other defect
Is only a fault to exercise your mercy.
CAR. You are bounteous in all. I take my
    leave,
My fair niece, shortly, when Columbo
    has   10
Purchased more honors to prefer [1] his
    name
And value to your noble thoughts; mean-
    time,
Be confident you have a friend, whose
    office
And favor with the king shall be effectual
To serve your grace.
DUCH.   Your own good deeds reward
    you,
Till mine rise equal to deserve their bene-
    fit.—   *Exit Cardinal.*
Leave me awhile.—   *Exit Placen[tia].*
Do not I walk upon the teeth of serpents,
And, as I had a charm against their poi-
    son,
Play with their stings? The cardinal is
    subtle,   20
Whom 'tis not wisdom to incense, till I
Hear to what destiny Columbo leaves
    me.
May be the greatness of his soul will
    scorn
To own what comes with murmur, if he
    can
Interpret me so happily.—Art come?

Enter Secretary with a letter.

SEC. His excellence salutes your grace.
DUCH.   Thou hast
A melancholy brow. How did he take my
    letter?
SEC. As he would take a blow; with so
    much sense
Of anger his whole soul boiled in his face,
And such prodigious flame in both his
    eyes   30
As they'd been th' only seat of fire, and at
Each look a salamander leaping forth,
Not able to endure the furnace.
DUCH.   Ha! Thou dost
Describe him with some horror.

[1] Advance.

SEC.   Soon as he
Had read again, and understood your
    meaning,
His rage had shot me with a pistol, had
    not
I used some soft and penitential language
To charm the bullet.
DUCH.   Wait at some more distance.—
My soul doth bath itself in a cold dew.
Imagine I am opening of a tomb.   40
                        [*Opens the letter.*]
Thus I throw off the marble, to discover
What antic posture death presents in this
Pale monument to fright me. (*Reads.*)
    Ha!
My heart, that called my blood and
    spirits to
Defend it from the invasion of my fears,
Must keep a guard about it still, lest this
Strange and too mighty joy crush it to
    nothing.—
Antonio.
SEC.   Madam.
DUCH.   Bid my steward give thee
Two thousand ducats. Art sure I am
    awake?   49
SEC. I shall be able to resolve [2] you, madam,
When he has paid the money.
DUCH. Columbo now is noble.
                        Exit Duch[ess].
SEC.   This is better
Than I expected—if my lady be
Not mad, and live to justify her bounty.
                                        Exit.

[SCENE iii.

A room in the king's palace.]

Enter King, Alvarez, Hernando, Lords.

KING. The war is left to him, but we must
    have
You reconciled, if that be all your dif-
    ference.
His rage flows like a torrent, when he
    meets
With opposition. Leave to wrastle with
    him,
And his hot blood retreats into a calm,
And then he chides his passion. You shall
    back
With letters from us.
HER.   Your commands are not
To be disputed.

[2] Inform.

King.　　　　　Alvarez. [*Takes him aside.*]

1 Lo.　　　　　　　　　　Lose not
Yourself by cool submission; he will find
His error, and the want of such a soldier.

2 Lo. Have you seen the cardinal?

Her.　　　　　　　　　　Not yet. 11

1 Lo. He wants no plot—

Her.　　　　　　　The king I must obey;
But let the purple gownman place his
　　engines[1]
I' th' dark, that wounds me.

2 Lo.　　　　　　　　　Be assured
Of what we can to friend you; and the
　　king
Cannot forget your service.

Her.　　　　　　　　　I am sorry
For that poor gentleman.

D'Alv.　　　　　　I must confess, sir,
The duchess has been pleased to think
　　me worthy
Her favors, and in that degree of honor
That has obliged my life to make the
　　best　　　　　　　　　　　　20
Return of service, which is not, with bold
Affiance in her love, to interpose
Against her happiness and your election.
I love so much her honor I have quitted
All my desires, yet would not shrink to
　　bleed
Out my warm stock of life, so the last
　　drop
Might benefit her wishes.

King.　　　　　　　　I shall find
A compensation for this act, Alvarez;
It hath much pleased us.

Enter Duchess with a letter; Gentleman Usher.

Duch.　　　　　　Sir, you are the king,
And in that sacred title it were sin　　30
To doubt a justice. A'l that does concern
My essence in this world, and a great part
Of the other bliss, lives in your breath.

King. What intends the duchess?

Duch. That will instruct you, sir.—[*Gives
him the letter.*] Columbo has,
Upon some better choice or discontent,
Set my poor soul at freedom.

King.　　　　'Tis his character.[2]　*Reads.*[3]
"Madam, I easily discharge all my pretensions to your love and person; I leave you to
your own choice; and, in what you have　[40

---

[1] Plots.　　　　　　　　[2] Handwriting.
[3] The letter is divided into lines of verse in the
original.

obliged yourself to me, resume a power to
cancel, if you please.
　　　　　　　　　　　Columbo."

This is strange!

Duch.　　　　Now do an act to make
Your chronicle beloved and read forever.

King. Express yourself.

Duch.　　　　Since by divine infusion,
For 'tis no art could force the general to
This change, second this justice, and
　　bestow
The heart you would have given from
　　me, by
Your strict commands to love Columbo,
　　where　　　　　　　　　　　　50
'Twas meant by heaven; and let your
　　breath return
Whom you divorced, Alvarez, mine.

Lords.　　　　　　　　　　This is
But justice, sir.

King.　　　　It was decreed above;
And, since Columbo has released his
　　interest,
Which we had wrought him, not without
　　some force
Upon your will, I give you your own
　　wishes.
Receive your own Alvarez. When you
　　please
To celebrate your nuptial, I invite
Myself your guest.

Duch.　　　　Eternal blessings crown you!

Omnes. And every joy your marriage! 60

Exit King, who meets the Cardinal; they confer.

D'Alv. I know not whether I shall wonder
　　most
Or joy to meet this happiness.

Duch.　　　　　　　Now the king
Hath planted us, methinks we grow
　　already,
And twist our loving souls, above the
　　wrath
Of thunder to divide us.

D'Alv.　　　　　　Ha! The cardinal
Has met the king! I do not like this con-
　　ference;
He looks with anger this way. I expect
A tempest.

Duch.　　　Take no notice of his presence;
Leave me to meet, and answer it. If the
　　king
Be firm in 's royal word, I fear no light-
　　ning.　　　　　　　　　　　　70
Expect me in the garden.

D'ALV.　　　　　　　　　　　　I obey,
But fear a shipwreck on the coast. *Exit.*
CAR.　　　　　　　　　　　　Madam.
DUCH. My lord.
CAR. The king speaks of a letter that has
　　brought
　A riddle in 't.
DUCH.　　　　　'Tis easy to interpret.
CAR. From my nephew? May I deserve
　　the favor?
　　　　　　　　[Duchess hands him the letter.]
DUCH. [*Aside.*] He looks as though his
　　eyes would fire the paper.
　They are a pair of burning glasses, and
　His envious blood doth give 'em flame.
CAR. [*Aside.*] What lethargy could thus
　　unspirit him?　　　　　　　　　　　80
　I am all wonder.—Do not believe,
　　madam,
　But that Columbo's love is yet more
　　sacred
　To honor and yourself than thus to for-
　　feit
　What I have heard him call the glorious
　　wreath
　To all his merits, given him by the king,
　From whom he took you with more pride
　　than ever
　He came from victory. His kisses hang
　Yet panting on your lips; and he but now
　Exchanged religious farewell to return,
　But with more triumph, to be yours.
DUCH.　　　　　　　　　　　My lord,
　You do believe your nephew's hand was
　　not　　　　　　　　　　　　　　91
　Surprised or strained[1] to this?
CAR. Strange arts and windings in the
　　world! Most dark
　And subtle progresses! Who brought this
　　letter?
DUCH. I inquired not his name; I thought
　　it not
　Considerable[2] to take such narrow
　　knowledge.
CAR. Desert and honor urged it here, nor
　　can
　I blame you to be angry; yet his person
　Obliged you should have given a nobler
　　pause
　Before you made your faith and change
　　so violent　　　　　　　　　　　100
　From his known worth into the arms of
　　one,

However fashioned to your amorous
　wish,
　Not equal to his cheapest fame,[3] with all
　The gloss of blood and merit.
DUCH.　　　　　　　This comparison,
　My good lord cardinal, I cannot think
　Flows from an even justice; it betrays
　You partial where your blood runs.
CAR.　　　　　　　　　I fear, madam,
　Your own takes too much license, and
　　will soon
　Fall to the censure of unruly tongues.
　Because Alvarez has a softer cheek,　110
　Can like a woman trim his wanton hair,
　Spend half a day with looking in the
　　glass
　To find a posture to present himself,
　And bring more effeminacy than man
　Or honor to your bed, must he supplant
　　him?
　Take heed, the common murmur, when
　　it catches
　The scent of a lost fame—
DUCH.　　　　　My fame, Lord Cardinal?
　It stands upon an innocence as clear
　As the devotions you pay to heaven.
　I shall not urge, my lord, your soft in-
　　dulgence　　　　　　　　　　　120
　At my next shrift.
CAR.　　　　　You are a fine court lady!
DUCH. And you should be a reverend
　　churchman.
CAR.　　　　　One
　That, if you have not thrown off mod-
　　esty,
　Would counsel you to leave Alvarez.
DUCH.　　　　　　　　　　　Cause
　You dare do worse than marriage, must
　　not I
　Be admitted what the church and law
　　allows me?
CAR. Insolent! Then you dare marry him?
DUCH.　　　　　　　　　　　Dare?
　Let your contracted flame and malice,
　　with
　Columbo's rage, higher than that, meet
　　us
　When we approach the holy place,
　　clasped hand　　　　　　　　　　130
　In hand we'll break through all your
　　force, and fix
　Our sacred vows together there.
CAR.　　　　　　　　　　　I knew

---

[1] Compelled.　　　[2] Weighty, important.

[3] Reputation.

When, with as chaste a brow, you
  promised fair
To another. You are no dissembling
  lady!
Duch. Would all your actions had no
  falser lights
About 'em!
Car. Ha!
Duch. The people would not talk and
  curse so loud.
Car. I'll have you chid into a blush for
  this.
Duch. Begin at home, great man; there's
  cause enough.   140
  You turn the wrong end of the perspec-
    tive [1]
  Upon your crimes, to drive them to a
    far
  And lesser sight; but let your eyes look
    right,
  What giants would your pride and surfeit
    seem!
  How gross your avarice, eating up whole
    families!
  How vast are your corruptions and abuse
  Of the king's ear, at which you hang a
    pendant,
  Not to adorn, but ulcerate, while the
    honest
  Nobility, like pictures in the arras,
  Serve only for court ornament. If they
    speak,   150
  'Tis when you set their tongues, which
    you wind up
  Like clocks, to strike at the just[2] hour
    you please.
  Leave, leave, my lord, these usurpa-
    tions,
  And be what you were meant, a man to
    cure,
  Not let in, agues to religion.
  Look on the church's wounds.
Car.   You dare presume,
  In your rude spleen to me, to abuse the
    church?
Duch. Alas, you give false aim, my lord;
  'tis your
  Ambition and scarlet sins that rob   159
  Her altar of the glory and leave wounds
  Upon her brow, which fetches grief and
    paleness
  Into her cheeks, making her troubled
    bosom

Pant with her groans, and shroud her
  holy blushes
Within your reverend purples.
Car.   Will you now take breath?
Duch. In hope, my lord, you will behold
  yourself
  In a true glass, and see those injust acts
  That so deform you, and by timely cure
  Prevent a shame, before the short-haired
    men [3]
  Do crowd and call for justice. I take
    leave.   *Exit.*
Car. This woman has a spirit that may
  rise   170
  To tame the devil's. There's no dealing
    with
  Her angry tongue; 'tis action and revenge
  Must calm her fury. Were Columbo
    here,
  I could resolve; but letters shall be sent
  To th' army, which may wake him into
    sense
  Of his rash folly, or direct his spirit
  Some way to snatch his honor from this
    flame.
  All great men know, "The soul of life is
    fame."   *Exit.*

Act III. [Scene i.]

An apartment in the king's palace.]

Enter Valeria, Celinda.

Val. I did not think, Celinda, when I
  praised
  Alvarez to the duchess, that things thus
  Would come about. What does your
    ladyship
  Think of Columbo now? It staggers all
  The court he should forsake his mis-
    tress; I
  Am lost with wonder yet.
Cel.   'Tis very strange,
  Without a spell; but there's a fate in love.
  I like him ne'er the worse.

Enter two Lords.

1 Lo. Nothing but marriages and triumph
  now!
Val. What new access of joy makes you,
  my lord,   10
So pleasant?
1 Lo.   There's a packet come to court

---

[1] Telescope.   [2] Exact.   [3] Perhaps an allusion to the Puritans.

Makes the king merry; we are all con-
cerned in 't.
Columbo hath given the enemy a great
And glorious defeat, and is already
Preparing to march home.
CEL. He thrived the better for my prayers.
2 Lo.   You have been
His great admirer, madam.
1 Lo.   The king longs
To see him.
VAL.   This news exalts the cardinal.

Enter Cardinal.

1 Lo. [*Aside.*]   He's here.
He appears with discontent; the mar-
riage   19
With Count d'Alvarez hath a bitter taste,
And not worn off his palate. But let us
leave him.
LADIES. [*Aside.*] We'll to the duchess.
                   Exeunt. Manet [1] *Car[dinal].*
CAR. He has not won so much upon the
Aragon
As he has lost at home; and his neglect
Of what my studies had contrived to add
More luster to our family by the access
Of the great duchess' fortune, cools his
triumph,
And makes me wild.

Enter Hernando.

HER.   My good Lord Cardinal!
CAR. You made complaint to th' king
about your general.
HER. Not a complaint, my lord; I did but
satisfy   30
Some questions o' the king's.
CAR.   You see he thrives
Without your personal valor or advice,
Most grave and learned in the wars.
HER.   My lord,
I envy not his fortune.
CAR.   'Tis above
Your malice, and your noise not worth
his anger;
'Tis barking gainst the moon.
HER.   More temper would
Become that habit.
CAR. The military thing would show some
spleen.
I'll blow an army of such wasps about
The world. Go look [2] your sting you left
i' th' camp, sir.   40

[1] Remains.   [2] Look for.

Enter King and Lords.

HER. The king!—This may be one day
counted [3] for.   *Exit.*
KING. All things conspire, my lord, to
make you fortunate.
Your nephew's glory—
CAR.   'Twas your cause and justice
Made him victorious; had he been so
valiant
At home, he had had another conquest
to
Invite, and bid her welcome to new wars.
KING. You must be reconciled to provi-
dence, my lord.
I heard you had a controversy with
The duchess; I will have you friends.
CAR. I am not angry.
KING.   For my sake, then,   50
You shall be pleased, and with me grace
the marriage.
A churchman must show charity, and
shine
With first example: she's a woman.
CAR. You shall prescribe in all things, sir.
You cannot
Accuse my love, if I still wish my
nephew
Had been so happy, to be constant to
Your own and my election; yet my brain
Cannot reach how this comes about; I
know
My nephew loved her with a near affec-
tion.

Enter Hernando.

KING. He'll give you fair account at his
return.—   60
Colonel, your letters may be spared; the
general
Has finished, and is coming home. [*Exit.*]
HER. I am glad on 't, sir.—My good Lord
Cardinal,
'Tis not impossible but some man pro-
voked
May have a precious mind to cut your
throat.
CAR. You shall command me, noble col-
onel; [4]
I know you wo' not fail to be at th'
wedding.
HER. 'Tis not Columbo that is married,
sir.

[3] Accounted.   [4] Trisyllabic.

CAR. Go teach the postures of the pike and
    musket;   69
Then drill your myrmidons into a ditch,
Where starve,[1] and stink in pickle.—You
    shall find
Me reasonable. You see the king expects
    me.
IER. So does the devil.
Some desperate hand may help you on
    your journey.   *Exeunt.*

[SCENE ii.

A room in the duchess' palace.]

Enter Secretary and Servants.

SEC. Here, this; ay, this will fit your
part: you shall wear the slashes, because
you are a soldier. Here's for the blue [2]
mute.

1 [SERV.] This doublet will never fit me;
pox on 't![3] Are these breeches good
enough for a prince too? Pedro plays but a
lord, and he has two laces more in a seam.

SEC. You must consider Pedro is a foolish lord; he may wear what lace he [10
please.

2 [SERV.] Does my beard fit my clothes
well, gentlemen?

SEC. Pox o' your beard!

3 [SERV.] That will fright away the hair.

1 [SERV.] This fellow plays but a mute,
and he is so troublesome, and talks.

3 [SERV.] Mr.[4] Secretary might have let
Jaques play the soldier; he has a black
patch already.   20

2 [SERV.] By your favor, Mr. Secretary,
I was asked who writ this play for us.

SEC. For us? Why, art thou any more
than a blue mute?

2 [SERV.] And, by my troth, I said I
thought it was all your own.

SEC. Away, you coxcomb!

4 [SERV.] Dost think he has no more wit
than to write a comedy? My lady's chaplain made the play, though he is con- [30
tent, for the honor and trouble of the business, to be seen in 't.

Enter Fifth Servant.

5 [SERV.] Did anybody see my head,
gentlemen? 'Twas here but now. I shall
have never a head to play my part in.

SEC. Is thy head gone? 'Tis well thy
part was not in 't. Look, look about; has
not Jaques it?

4 [SERV.] I his head? 'T wo' not come
on upon my shoulders.   40

SEC. Make haste, gentlemen; I'll see
whether the king has supped. Look every
man to his wardrope [5] and his part.
                Exit [with Fifth Servant].

2 [SERV.] Is he gone? In my mind, a
masque had been fitter for a marriage.

4 [SERV.] Why, mute? There was no
time for 't, and the scenes are troublesome.

2 [SERV.] Half a score deal tacked together in the clouds.[6] What's that? A
throne, to come down and dance; all [50
the properties have been paid forty times
over, and are in the court stock, but the
secretary must have a play to show his wit.

4 [SERV.] Did not I tell thee 'twas the
chaplain's? Hold your tongue, mute.

1 [SERV.] Under the rose, and would
this cloth of silver doublet might never
come off again, if there be any more plot
than you see in the back of my hand.

2 [SERV.] You talk of a plot! I'll [60
not give this for the best poet's plot in the
world, and if it be not well carried.

4 [SERV.] Well said, mute.

3 [SERV.] Ha, ha! Pedro, since he put on
his doublet, has repeated but three lines,
and he has broke five buttons.

2 [SERV.] I know not; but, by this false
beard, and here's hair enough to hang a
reasonable honest man, I do not remember,
to say, a strong line indeed in the [70
whole comedy but when the chambermaid
kisses the captain.

3 [SERV.] Excellent, mute!

Enter another Servant.

5 [SERV.] They have almost supped, and
I cannot find my head yet.

4 [SERV.] Play in thine own.

5 [SERV.] Thank you for that! So I may
have it made a property! If I have not a
head found me, let Mr. Secretary play my
part himself without it.   80

Enter Secretary.

SEC. Are you all ready, my masters?
The king is coming through the gallery.

---

[1] Die.
[2] Color worn by servants.
[3] A plague on it!
[4] *I.e.*, Master.
[5] Wardrobe.
[6] Ten planks nailed together under the roof of
the stage.

Are the women dressed?

1 [SERV.] Rogero wants a head.

SEC. Here, with a pox to you, take mine! You a player? You a puppy dog! Is the music ready?

Enter Gentleman Usher.

GENT. Gentlemen, it is my lady's pleasure that you expect till she call for you. There are a company of cavaliers in [90 gallant equipage, newly alighted, have offered to present their revels in honor of this Hymen; and 'tis her grace's command that you be silent till their entertainment be over.

1 [SERV.] Gentlemen?

2 [SERV.] Affronted?

5 [SERV.] Mr. Secretary, there's your head again; a man's a man. Have I broken my sleep to study fifteen lines for an [100 ambassador, and after that a constable, and is it come to this?

SEC. Patience, gentlemen, be not so hot; 'tis but deferred, and the play may do well enough cold.

4 [SERV.] If it be not presented, the chaplain will have the greatest loss; he loses his wits. *Hautboys.*

SEC. This music speaks the king upon entrance. Retire, retire, and grumble [110 not. *Exeunt [All but Secretary].*

Enter King, Cardinal, Alvarez, Duchess, Celinda, Valeria, Placentia, Lords, Hernando. They being set, enter Columbo and five more, in rich habits, vizarded; between every two a Torchbearer. They dance, and after beckon to Alvarez, as desirous to speak with him.

D'ALV. With me!
They embrace and whisper.

KING. Do you know the masquers, madam?

DUCH. Not I, sir.

CAR. There's one—but that my nephew is abroad,
And has more soul than thus to jig upon
Their hymeneal night, I should suspect
'Twere he.
The Masquers lead in Alvarez.

DUCH. Where's my Lord Alvarez?
Recorders.

KING. Call in the bridegroom.

Enter Columbo. Four Masquers bring in Alvarez dead, in one of their habits, and, having laid him down, exeunt [the four Masquers].

DUCH. What mystery is this?

CAR. We want the bridegroom still.

KING. Where is Alvarez? 119
Columbo points to the body; they unvizard it, and find Alvar[ez] bleeding.

DUCH. O, 'tis my lord! He's murdered!

KING. Who durst commit this horrid act?

COL. [*Removing his mask.*] I, sir.

KING. Columbo? Ha!

COL. Yes; Columbo, that dares stay
To justify that act.

HER. Most barbarous!

DUCH. O, my dearest lord!

KING. Our guard seize on them all. This sight doth shake
All that is man within me.—Poor Alvarez,
Is this thy wedding day?

Enter Guard.

DUCH. If you do think there is a heaven, or pains
To punish such black crimes i' th' other world,
Let me have swift and such exemplar[1] justice 130
As shall become this great assassinate.
You will take off our faith else, and, if here
Such innocence must bleed, and you look on,
Poor men, that call you gods on earth. will doubt
To obey your laws, nay, practice to be devils,
As fearing, if such monstrous sins go on,
The saints will not be safe in heaven.

KING. You shall,
You shall have justice.

CAR. [*Aside.*] Now to come off[2] were brave.[3]

Enter Servant.

SERV. The masquers, sir, are fled; their horse, prepared 139
At gate, expected to receive 'em, where

[1] Exemplary.
[2] Escape, get clear. [3] Fine.

They quickly mounted. Coming so like
   friends,
None could suspect their haste, which is
   secured
By advantage of the night.

Col. I answer for 'em all; 'tis stake
   enough
For many lives. But, if that poniard
Had voice, it would convince they were
   but all
Spectators of my act. And now, if you
Will give your judgments leave, though
   at the first
Face of this object your cool bloods were
   frighted,   149
I can excuse this deed, and call it justice,
An act your honors and your office, sir,
Is bound to build a law upon for others
To imitate. I have but took his life,
And punished her with mercy, who had
   both
Conspired to kill the soul of all my fame.
Read there—and read an injury as deep
In my dishonor as the devil knew
A woman had capacity or malice
To execute. Read there how you were
   cozened, sir,
    [*Gives the King the duchess' letter.*]
Your power affronted, and my faith; her
   smiles,   160
A juggling witchcraft to betray, and
   make
My love her horse to stalk withal, and
   catch
Her curléd minion.

Car.   Is it possible
The duchess could dissemble so, and for-
   feit
Her modesty with you, and to us all?
Yet I must pity her. My nephew has
Been too severe, though this affront
   would call
A dying man from prayers, and turn him
   tiger,
There being nothing dearer than our
   fame,
Which, if a common man, whose blood
   has no   170
Ingredient of honor, labor to
Preserve, a soldier (by his nearest tie
To glory) is, above all others, bound
To vindicate. And yet it might have
   been less bloody.

Her. [*Aside.*] Charitable devil!

King. (*Reads.*) "I pray, my lord, release under your hand what you dare challenge in my love or person, as a just forfeit
to myself. This act will speak you honorable to my thoughts, and, when you   [180
have conquered thus yourself, you may
proceed to many victories, and after, with
safety of your fame, visit again
          The lost Rosaura."
To this your answer was a free resign?

Col. Flattered with great opinion of her
   faith,
And my desert of her (with thought that
   she,
Who seemed to weep and chide my easy
   will
To part with her, could not be guilty of
A treason or apostasy so soon,   190
But rather meant this a device to make
Me expedite the affairs of war), I sent
That paper, which her wickedness, not
   justice,
Applied [1] (what I meant trial) her di-
   vorce.
I loved her so, I dare call heaven to wit-
   ness,
I knew not whether [2] I loved most, while
   she
With him whose crimson penitence I pro-
   voked [3]
Conspired my everlasting infamy.
Examine but the circumstance.

Car.   'Tis clear.
This match was made at home, before
   she sent   200
That cunning writ, in hope to take him
   off,
As knowing his impatient soul would
   scorn
To own a blessing came on crutches to
   him.
It was not well to raise his expectation
(Had you, sir, no affront?) to ruin him
With so much scandal and contempt.

King.   We have
Too plentiful a circumstance to accuse
You, madam, as the cause of your own
   sorrows,
But not without an accessary more
Than young Alvarez.

Car.   Any other instrument? 210

King. Yes; I am guilty, with herself, and
   Don

---

[1] Considered as.   [2] Which.   [3] Caused.

Columbo, though our acts looked several
　ways,
That thought a lover might so soon be
　ransomed,
And did exceed the office of a king
To exercise dominion over hearts
That owe to the prerogative of heaven
Their choice or separation; you must,
　therefore,
When you do kneel for justice and re-
　venge,
Madam, consider me a lateral agent
In poor Alvarez' tragedy.　　　　220
1 Lo. It was your love to Don Columbo,
　sir.
Her. [Aside.] So, so! The king is charmed.
　Do you observe
How, to acquit Columbo, he would draw
Himself into the plot. Heaven, is this
　justice?
Car. Your judgment is divine in this.
King.　　　　　　　　　　And yet
Columbo cannot be secure, and we
Just in his pardon, that durst make so
　great
And insolent a breach of law and duty.
2 Lo. [Aside.] Ha! Will he turn again?
King.　　　　　　　And should we leave
This guilt of blood to heaven, which cries,
　and strikes　　　　　　　　230
With loud appeals the palace of eternity?
Yet here is more to charge Columbo
　than
Alvarez' blood, and bids me punish it,
Or be no king.
Her. [Aside.]　　　　　'Tis come about,
　my lords.
King. And, if I should forgive
His timeless death, I cannot the offense,
That with such boldness struck at me.
　Has my
Indulgence to your merits, which are
　great,
Made me so cheap your rage could meet
　no time
Nor place for your revenge but where
　my eyes　　　　　　　　　240
Must be affrighted, and affronted with
The bloody execution? This contempt
Of majesty transcends my power to par-
　don,
And you shall feel my anger, sir.
Her. Thou shalt have one short prayer
　more for that.

Col. Have I, i' th' progress of my life,
No actions to plead me up deserving
Against this ceremony?
Car.　　　　　　　　Contain yourself.
Col. I must be dumb then. Where is
　honor
And gratitude of kings, when they for-
　get　　　　　　　　　　250
Whose hand secured their greatness?
　Take my head off;
Examine then which of your silken lords,
As I have done, will throw himself on
　dangers;
Like to a floating island move in blood;
And, where your great defense calls him
　to stand
A bulwark, upon his bold breast to
　take
In death, that you may live. But soldiers
　are
Your valiant fools, whom, when your
　own securities
Are bleeding, you can cherish, but, when
　once
Your state and nerves are knit, not think-
　ing when　　　　　　　　260
To use their surgery again, you cast
Them off, and let them hang in dusty
　armories,
Or make it death to ask for pay.
King.　　　　　　　　　　No more.
We thought to have put your victory
　and merits
In balance with Alvarez' death, which,
　while
Our mercy was to judge, had been your
　safety;
But the affront to us, made greater by
This boldness to upbraid our royal
　bounty,
Shall tame, or make you nothing.
[2] Lo. [Aside.]　　　　　　Excellent!
Her. [Aside.] The cardinal is not pleased.
Car.　　　　　　　Humble yourself　270
To th' king.
Col.　　　And beg my life? Let cowards
　do 't
That dare not die; I'll rather have no
　head
Than owe it to his charity.
King.　　　　To th' Castle with him!—
　　　　[The Guard take Columbo away.]
Madam, I leave you to your grief, and
　what

The king can recompense to your tears,
 or honor
Of your dead lord, expect.
Duch. This shows like justice. *Exeunt.*

Act IV. [Scene i.

A room in the king's palace.]

Enter two Lords, Hernando.

1 Lo. This is the age of wonders.
2 Lo.   Wondrous mischiefs!
Her. Among those guards, which some
 call tutelar angels,
 Whose office is to govern provinces,
 Is there not one will undertake Navarre?
 Hath heaven forsook us quite?
1 [Lo.]   Columbo at large!
2 [Lo.] And graced now more than ever.
1 [Lo.]   He was not pardoned;
 That word was prejudicial to his fame.
Her. But, as the murder done had been a
 dream
 Vanished to memory, he's courted as
 Preserver of his country. With what
  chains   10
 Of magic does this cardinal hold the
  king?
2 [Lo.] What will you say, my lord, if they
 enchant
 The duchess now and by some impudent
 art
 Advance a marriage to Columbo yet?
Her. Say! I'll say no woman can be
 saved; nor is 't
 Fit, indeed, any should pretend to
 heaven
 After one such impiety in their sex.
 And yet my faith has been so staggered,
 since
 The king restored Columbo, I'll be now
 Of no religion.
1 [Lo.]   'Tis not possible 20
 She can forgive the murder; I observed
 Her tears.
Her.   Why, so did I, my lord;
 And, if they be not honest, 'tis to be
 Half damned to look upon a woman
 weeping.
 When do you think the cardinal said his
 prayers?
2 [Lo.] I know not.
Her.   Heaven forgive my want of
 charity,

But, if I were to kill him, he should
 have
No time to pray; his life could be no
 sacrifice,
Unless his soul went too.
1 [Lo.]   That were too much.
Her. When you mean to despatch him,
 you may give   30
Time for confession. They have injured
 me
After another rate.
2 [Lo]. You are too passionate, cousin.

Enter Columbo, Colonels, Alphonso, Court-
iers. They pass over the stage.

Her. How the gay men do flutter to con-
 gratulate
His goal [1] delivery! There's one honest
 man.
What pity 'tis a gallant fellow should
Depend on knaves for his preferment!
1 [Lo.] Except this cruelty upon Alvarez,
Columbo has no mighty stain upon him;
But for his uncle—
Her.   If I had a son 40
Of twelve years old that would not fight
 with him,
And stake his soul against his cardinal's
 cap,
I would disinherit him. Time has took a
 lease
But for three lives, I hope; a fourth may
 see
Honesty walk without a crutch.
2 [Lo.]   This is
But air and wildness.
Her.   I'll see the duchess.
1 [Lo.][2] You may do well to comfort her;
We must attend the king.
Her.   Your pleasures.
        Exit Her[nando].

Enter King and Cardinal.

1 [Lo. *Aside.*] A man of a brave soul.
2 [Lo. *Aside.*]   The less his safety.
The king and cardinal in consult! 50
King. Commend us to the duchess, and
 employ
What language you think fit and powerful

---

[1] Gaol, jail.
[2] In the original this speech head introduces
the following line.

To reconcile her to some peace.—My
　　lords.

CAR. Sir, I possess all for your sacred uses.
　　　　　　　　　　　　Exeunt severally.

[SCENE ii.

A room in the duchess' palace.]

Enter Secretary and Celinda.

SEC. Madam, you are the welcom'st lady
　　living.
CEL. To whom, Mr. Secretary?
SEC. 　　　　　　　If you have mercy
　　To pardon so much boldness, I durst say,
　　To me—I am a gentleman.
CEL. 　　　　　　　And handsome.
SEC. But my lady has much wanted you.
CEL. Why, Mr. Secretary?
SEC. You are the prettiest—
CEL. So!
SEC. The wittiest—
CEL. So! 　　　　　　　　　　　　　10
SEC. The merriest lady i' th' court.
CEL. And I was wished to make the duch-
　　ess pleasant?
SEC. She never had so deep a cause of sor-
　　row;
　　Her chamber's but a coffin of a larger
　　Volume, wherein she walks so like a
　　ghost,
　　'Twould make you pale to see her.
CEL. 　　　　　　　　　　Tell her grace
　　I attend here.
SEC. 　　　　　I shall most willingly.—
　　[*Aside.*] A spirited lady! Would I had
　　her in my closet!
　　She is excellent company among the
　　lords.
　　Sure she has an admirable treble.—
　　Madam. 　　　　　　　　*Exit.* 20
CEL. I do suspect this fellow would be nib-
　　bling,
　　Like some whose narrow fortunes will not
　　rise
　　To wear things when the invention's rare
　　and new,
　　But, treading on the heel of pride, they
　　hunt
　　The fashion when 'tis crippled, like fell
　　tyrants.
　　I hope I am not old yet. I had the honor
　　To be saluted by our cardinal's nephew
　　This morning. There's a man!

Enter Secretary.

SEC. 　　　　　　　　　I have prevailed.
　　Sweet madam, use what eloquence you
　　can
　　Upon her, and, if ever I be useful 　　30
　　To your ladyship's service, your least
　　breath commands me. 　　　　　[*Exit.*]

Enter Duchess.

DUCH. Madam, I come to ask you but one
　　question:
　　If you were in my state, my state of grief,
　　I mean an exile from all happiness
　　Of this world, and almost of heaven (for
　　my
　　Affliction is finding out despair),
　　What would you think of Don Columbo?
CEL. 　　　　　　　　　　　　Madam?
DUCH. Whose bloody hand wrought all
　　this misery.
　　Would you not weep as I do, and wish
　　rather 　　　　　　　　　　　　39
　　An everlasting spring of tears to drown
　　Your sight than let your eyes be cursed
　　to see
　　The murderer again, and glorious?
　　So careless of his sin that he is made
　　Fit for new parricide, even while his soul
　　Is purpled o'er, and reeks with innocent
　　blood?
　　But do not, do not answer me; I know
　　You have so great a spirit (which I want,
　　The horror of his fact [1] surprising all
　　My faculties), you would not let him live.
　　But I, poor I, must suffer more. There's
　　not 　　　　　　　　　　　　　50
　　One little star in heaven will look on me,
　　Unless to choose me out the mark, on
　　whom
　　It may shoot down some angry influence.

Enter Placentia.

PLA. Madam, here's Don Columbo says
　　he must
　　Speak with your grace.
DUCH. 　　But he must not, I charge you.—
　　　　　　　　　　　　[*Exit Placentia.*]
　　None else wait?—Is this well done,
　　To triumph in his tyranny? Speak,
　　madam,
　　Speak but your conscience.

[1] Deed.

Enter Columbo and Secretary.

SEC.　　　　　　Sir, you must not see her.

COL. Not see her? Were she cabled up
　above
The search of bullet or of fire, were
　she　　　　　　　　　　　　　　60
Within her grave, and that the toughest
　mine
That ever nature teemed and groaned
　withal,
I would force some way to see her.—[*Exit
　Secretary.*] Do not fear
I come to court you, madam; y' are not
　worth
The humblest of my kinder thoughts. I
　come
To show the man you have provoked,
　and lost,
And tell you what remains of my re-
　venge.
Live, but never presume again to marry;
I'll kill the next at th' altar, and quench
　all
The smiling tapers with his blood. If,
　after,　　　　　　　　　　　　70
You dare provoke the priest and heaven
　so much
To take another, in thy bed I'll cut him
　from
Thy warm embrace, and throw his heart
　to ravens.

CEL. This will appear an unexampled
　cruelty.

COL. Your pardon, madam. Rage and my
　revenge,
Not perfect, took away my eyes. You are
A noble lady—this not worth your eye-
　beam—
One of so slight a making and so thin
An autumn leaf is of too great a value
To play, which shall be soonest lost i' th'
　air.　　　　　　　　　　　　80
Be pleased to own me by some name in
　your
Assurance; I despise to be received
There. Let her witness that I call you
　mistress;
Honor me to make these pearls your
　carcanet.　　　　[*Gives her a necklace.*]

CEL. My lord, you are too humble in your
　thoughts.

COL. [*Aside.*] There's no vexation too
　great to punish her.　　　　*Exit.*

Enter Secretary.

SEC. Now, madam?

CEL. Away, you saucy fellow!—Madam, I
Must be excused, if I do think more hon-
　orably
Than you have cause, of this great lord.

DUCH.　　　　　　Why, is not　90
All womankind concerned to hate what's
　impious?

CEL. For my part—

DUCH.　　　　Antonio, is this a woman?

SEC. I know not whether she be man or
　woman;
I should be nimble to find out the experi-
　ment.
She looked with less state when Columbo
　came.

DUCH. Let me entreat your absence.—
　[*Aside.*] I am cozened in her.—
I took you for a modest, honest [1] lady.

CEL. Madam, I scorn any accuser; and,
Deducting the great title of a duchess,
I shall not need one grain of your dear
　honor　　　　　　　　　　　100
To me make full weight. If your grace be
　jealous,
I can remove.　　　　　　　　*Exit.*

SEC.　　　　　She is gone.

DUCH.　　　　　　Prithee, remove
My fears of her return.—(*Ex*[*it*] *Sec-
　*[*retary*].) She is not worth
Considering; my anger's mounted higher.
He need not put in caution for my next
Marriage. Alvarez, I must come to thee,
Thy virgin, wife, and widow; but not till
I ha' paid those tragic duties to thy
　hearse
Become [2] my piety and love. But how?
Who shall instruct a way?

Enter Placentia.

PLA.　　　　　　Madam, Don　110
Hernando much desires to speak with
　you.

DUCH. Will not thy own discretion think I
　am
Unfit for visit?

PLA.　　　　Please your grace, he brings
Something he says imports your ear, and
　love
Of the dead Lord Alvarez.

DUCH.　　　　　Then admit him.

1 Chaste.　　　　　2 *I.e.*, which become.

Enter Hernando.

HER. I would speak, madam, to yourself.

DUCH.   Your absence. [*Exit Placentia.*]

HER. I know not how your grace will censure so
Much boldness, when you know the
affairs I come for.

DUCH. My servant has prepared me to
receive it,
If it concern my dead lord.

HER.   Can you name 120
So much of your Alvarez in a breath,
Without one word of your revenge? O,
madam,
I come to chide you, and repent my great
Opinion of your virtue, that can walk,
And spend so many hours in naked soli-
tude,
As if you thought that no arrears were due
To his death, when you had paid his
funeral charges,
Made your eyes red, and wept a handker-
cher.
I come to tell you that I saw him bleed;
I, that can challenge nothing in his
name   130
And honor, saw his murdered body warm
And panting with the labor of his spirits,
Till my amazed soul shrunk and hid
itself,
While barbarous Columbo, grinning,
stood
And mocked the weeping wounds. It is
too much
That you should keep your heart alive so
long
After this spectacle, and not revenge it.

DUCH. You do not know the business of
my heart,
That censure me so rashly; yet I thank
you.   139
And, if you be Alvarez' friend, dare tell
Your confidence that I despise my life,
But know not how to use it in a service
To speak me his revenger. This will need
No other proof than that to you, who
may
Be sent with cunning to betray me, I
Have made this bold confession. I so
much
Desire to sacrifice to that hovering ghost
Columbo's life that I am not ambitious
To keep my own two minutes after it.

HER. If you will call me coward, which is
equal   150
To think I am a traitor, I forgive it
For this brave resolution, which time
And all the destinies must aid. I beg
That I may kiss your hand for this, and
may
The soul of angry honor guide it.

DUCH.   Whither?

HER. To Don Columbo's heart.

DUCH. It is too weak, I fear, alone.

HER. Alone? Are you in earnest? Why,
will it not   158
Be a dishonor to your justice, madam,
Another arm should interpose? But that
It were a saucy act to mingle with you,
I durst, nay, I am bound in the revenge
Of him that's dead (since the whole world
has interest
In every good man's loss) to offer it.
Dare you command me, madam?

DUCH.   Not command;
But I should more than honor such a
truth
In man, that durst, against so mighty
odds,
Appear Alvarez' friend and mine. The
cardinal—

HER. Is for the second course. Columbo
must
Be first cut up; his ghost must lead the
dance.   170
Let him die first.

DUCH. But how?

HER. How? With a sword; and, if I under-
take it,
I wo' not lose so much of my own honor
To kill him basely.

DUCH.   How shall I reward
This infinite service? 'Tis not modesty
While now my husband groans beneath
his tomb,
And calls me to his marble bed, to prom-
ise
What this great act might well deserve,
myself,   179
If you survive the victor; but, if thus
Alvarez' ashes be appeased, it must
Deserve an honorable memory;
And, though Columbo (as he had all
power,
And grasped the fates) has vowed to kill
the man
That shall succeed Alvarez—

Her.　　　　　　　　　　Tyranny!
Duch. Yet, if ever
　I entertain a thought of love hereafter,
　Hernando from the world shall challenge
　　it,
　Till when, my prayers and fortune shall
　　wait on you.
Her. This is too mighty recompense.
Duch.　　　　　　　'Tis all just. 190
Her. If I outlive Columbo, I must not
　Expect security at home.
Duch.　　　　　　　　Thou canst
　Not fly where all my fortunes and my
　　love
　Shall not attend to guard thee.
Her.　　　　　　　　　If I die—
Duch. Thy memory
　Shall have a shrine, the next within my
　　heart,
　To my Alvarez.
Her.　　　　　　Once again your hand.
　Your cause is so religious you need not
　Strengthen it with your prayers; trust it
　　to me.

Enter Placentia and Cardinal.

Pla. Madam, the cardinal.
Duch.　　　　　　Will you appear? 200
Her. And [1] he had all the horror of the
　devil
　In 's face, I would not balk him.
　　He stares upon the Cardinal in his exit.
Car. [*Aside.*] What makes [2] Hernando
　here? I do not like
　They should consult; I'll take no note.—
　　The king
　Fairly salutes your grace, by whose com-
　　mand
　I am to tell you, though his will and
　　actions,
　Illimited, stoop not to satisfy
　The vulgar inquisition, he is
　Yet willing to retain a just opinion
　With those that are placed near him;
　　and, although　　　　　　　210
　You look with nature's eye upon your-
　　self,
　Which needs no perspective to reach, nor
　　art
　Of any optic [3] to make greater what
　Your narrow sense applies [4] an injury

(Ourselves still nearest to ourselves),
　but there's
　Another eye that looks abroad, and walks
　In search of reason and the weight of
　　things,
　With which, if you look on him, you will
　　find
　His pardon to Columbo cannot be　219
　So much against his justice as your erring
　Faith would persuade your anger.
Duch.　　　　　　　Good my lord,
　Your phrase has too much landshape,[5]
　　and I cannot
　Distinguish at this distance; you present
　The figure perfect, but indeed my eyes
　May pray your lordship find excuse, for
　　tears
　Have almost made them blind.
Car.　　　　　Fair, peace restore 'em!
　To bring the object nearer, the king says
　He could not be severe to Don Columbo
　Without injustice to his other merits,
　Which call more loud for their reward
　　and honor　　　　　　　　230
　Than you for your revenge; the kingdom
　　made
　Happy by those, you only, by the last,
　Unfortunate; nor was it rational
　(I speak the king's own language) he
　　should die
　For taking one man's breath, without
　　whose valor
　None now had been alive without dis-
　　honor.
Duch. In my poor understanding, 'tis the
　　crown
　Of virtue to proceed in its own tract,[6]
　Not deviate from honor. If you acquit
　A man of murder, cause he has done
　　brave　　　　　　　　　　240
　Things in the war, you will bring down
　　his valor
　To a crime, nay, to a bawd, if it secure
　A rape, and but teach those that deserve
　　well
　To sin with greater license. But dispute
　Is now too late, my lord; 'tis done; and
　　you,
　By the good king, in tender [7] of my sor-
　　rows,
　Sent to persuade me 'tis unreasonable
　That justice should repair me.

---

[1] If.　　　　　　　[3] Magnifying glass.
[2] Does.　　　　　　[4] Interprets as.

[5] Landscape.
[6] Track.　　　　　　[7] Consideratï

Car.   You mistake,
For, if Columbo's death could make
  Alvarez   249
Live, the king had given him up to law,
Your bleeding sacrifice, but, when his
  life
Was but another treasure thrown away
To obey a clamorous statute, it was wis-
  dom
To himself, and common safety, to take
  off
This killing edge of law, and keep
  Columbo
To recompense the crime by noble acts
And sorrow, that in time might draw
  your pity.
Duch. This is a greater tyranny than that
Columbo exercised; he killed my lord,
And you have not the charity to let 260
Me think it worth a punishment.
Car.   To that,
In my own name, I answer: I condemn
And urge the bloody guilt against my
  nephew;
'Twas violent and cruel, a black deed,
A deed whose memory doth make me
  shudder,
An act that did betray a tyrannous
  nature,
Which he took up in war, the school of
  vengeance,
And, though the king's compassion spare
  him here,
Unless his heart
Weep itself out in penitent tears here-
  after—   270
Duch. This sounds
As you were now a good man.
Car.   Does your grace
Think I have conscience to allow the
  murder?
Although, when it was done, I did obey
The stream of nature, as he was my kins-
  man,
To plead he might not pay his forfeit life,
Could I do less for one so near my blood?
Consider, madam, and be charitable;
Let not this wild injustice make me
  lose   279
The character I bear, and reverend habit.
To make you full acquainted with my
  innocence,
I challenge here my soul and heaven to
  witness.

If I had any thought or knowledge with
My nephew's plot, or person, when he
  came
Under the smooth pretense of friend to
  violate
Your hospitable laws, and do that act
Whose frequent mention draws this tear,
  a whirlwind
Snatch me to endless flames!
Duch.   I must believe,
And ask your grace's pardon. I confess
I ha' not loved you since Alvarez' death,
Though we were reconciled.
Car.   I do not blame 291
Your jealousy,[1] nor any zeal you had
To prosecute revenge against me, ma-
  dam,
As I then stood suspected, nor can yet
Implore your mercy to Columbo. All
I have to say is, to retain my first
Opinion and credit with your grace,
Which you may think I urge not out of
  fear
Or ends[2] upon you (since, I thank the
  king,   299
I stand firm on the base of royal favor),
But for your own sake, and to show I
  have
Compassion of your sufferings.
Duch.   You have cleared
A doubt, my lord, and by this fair remon-
  strance
Given my sorrow so much truce, to think
That we may meet again and yet be
  friends.
But be not angry, if I still remember
By whom Alvarez died, and weep, and
  wake
Another justice with my prayers.
Car.   All thoughts
That may advance a better peace dwell
  with you!   Exit.
Duch. How would this cozening statesman
  bribe my faith   310
With flatteries to think him innocent!
No; if his nephew die, this cardinal must
  not
Be long-lived. All the prayers of a
  wronged widow
Make firm Hernando's sword, and my
  own hand
Shall have some glory in the next re-
  venge.

[1] Mistrust.   [2] Designs.

I will pretend my brain with grief dis-
　tracted;
It may gain easy credit, and, beside
The taking off examination
For great Columbo's death, it makes
　what act　　　　　　　　　　　319
I do, in that believed want of my reason,
Appear no crime, but my defense. Look
　down,
Soul of my lord, from thy eternal shade,
And unto all thy blessed companions
　boast
Thy duchess busy to revenge thy ghost!
　　　　　　　　　　　　　　Exit.

[SCENE iii.

A lonely spot outside the city.]

*Enter Columbo, Hernando, Alphonso, Colo-
　nel.*

COL. Hernando, now I love thee, and do
　half
　Repent the affront my passion threw
　upon thee.
HER. You wo' not be too prodigal o' your
　penitence.
COL. This makes good thy nobility of
　birth;
　Thou mayst be worth my anger and my
　sword,
　If thou dost execute as daringly
　As thou provok'st a quarrel. I did think
　Thy soul a starve'ing, or asleep.
HER.　　　　　　　　You'll find it
　Active enough to keep your spirit wak-
　ing,
　Which, to exasperate, for yet I think　10
　It is not high enough to meet my rage—
　D'e smile?
COL.　　This noise is worth it.—Gentle-
　men,
　I'm sorry this great soldier has engaged
　Your travail; all his business is to talk.
HER. A little of your lordship's patience.
　You shall have other sport, and swords
　that will
　Be as nimble 'bout your heart as you can
　wish.
　'Tis pity more than our two single lives
　Should be at stake.
COLONEL.　　Make that no scruple, sir.
HER. To him then that survives, if fate
　allow　　　　　　　　　　　　20

That difference, I speak, that he may tell
The world I came not hither on slight
　anger,
But to revenge my honor, stained and
　trampled on
By this proud man. When general, he
　commanded
My absence from the field.
COL.　　　　　　I do remember,
　And I'll give your soul now a discharge.
HER.　　　　　　　　　I come
　To meet it, if your courage be so fortu-
　nate.
　But there is more than my own injury
　You must account for, sir, if my sword
　prosper,
　Whose point and every edge is made more
　keen　　　　　　　　　　　　30
　With young Alvarez' blood, in which I
　had
　A noble interest. Does not that sin be-
　numb
　Thy arteries, and turn the guilty flowings
　To trembling jelly in thy veins? Canst
　hear
　Me name that murder, and thy spirits
　not
　Struck into air, as thou wert shot by
　some
　Engine from heaven?
COL.　　You are the duchess' champion!
　Thou hast given me a quarrel now. I
　grieve
　It is determined all must fight, and I
　Shall lose much honor in his fall.
HER.　　　　　　　That duchess　40
　(Whom but to mention with thy breath
　is sacrilege),
　An orphan of thy making, and con-
　demned
　By thee to eternal solitude, I come
　To vindicate; and, while I am killing
　thee,
　By virtue of her prayers sent up for
　justice,
　At the same time in heaven I am par-
　doned for 't.
COL. I cannot hear the bravo.
HER.　　　　　　　Two words more,
　And take your chance. Before you all I
　must
　Pronounce that noble lady without
　knowledge　　　　　　　　　　49
　Or thought of what I undertake for her.

Poor soul, she's now at her devotions,
Busy with heaven, and wearing out the
  earth
With her stiff knees, and bribing her
  good angel
With treasures of her eyes, to tell her
  lord
How much she longs to see him. My
  attempt
Needs no commission from her. Were I
A stranger in Navarre, the inborn right
Of every gentleman to Alvarez' loss
Is reason to engage their swords and
  lives   59
Against the common enemy of virtue.
Col. Now have you finished? I have an
  instrument
Shall cure this noise, and fly up to thy
  tongue
To murder all thy words.
Her.   One little knot
Of phlegm, that clogs my stomach, and
  I ha' done:
You have an uncle, called a cardinal.
Would he were lurking now about thy
  heart,
That the same wounds might reach you
  both, and send
Your reeling souls together! Now have
  at you!
Alph. We must not, sir, be idle.
      They fight; Columbo's Second slain.
Her. What think you now of praying?
Col.   Time enough. 70
        He kills Hernando's Second.
Commend me to my friend; the scales
  are even.
I would be merciful, and give you time
Now to consider of the other world;
You'll find your soul benighted pres-
  ently.
Her. I'll find my way i' th' dark.
They fight, and close; Columbo gets both the
    swords, and Hernando takes up the Sec-
              ond's weapon.
Col.   A stumble's dangerous.
Now ask thy life. Ha!
Her.   I despise to wear it,
A gift from any but the first bestower.
Col. I scorn a base advantage. Ha!
Columbo throws away one of the swords.
    They fight; Hernando wounds Columbo.
Her.   I am now
Out of your debt.

Col.   Th'ast done 't and I forgive thee.
Give me thy hand. When shall we meet
  again?   80
Her. Never, I hope.
Col. I feel life ebb apace, yet I'll look
  upwards,
And show my face to heaven.   [*Dies.*]
Her.   The matter's done;
I must not stay to bury him.   *Exit.*

ACT V. [Scene i.

A garden.]

Enter two Lords.

1 Lo. Columbo's death doth much afflict
  the king.
2 Lo. I thought the cardinal would have
  lost his wits
At first, for 's nephew; it drowns all the
  talk
Of the other that were slain.
1 [Lo.]   We are friends.
I do suspect Hernando had some interest,
And knew how their wounds came.
2 [Lo.]   His flight confirms it,
For whom the cardinal has spread his
  nets.
1 [Lo.] He is not so weak to trust himself
  at home
To his enemy's gripe.
2 [Lo.]   All strikes not me so much
As that the duchess, most oppresséd
  lady,   10
Should be distracted, and before Columbo
Was slain.
1 [Lo.]   But that the cardinal should be
  made
Her guardian is to me above that wonder.
2 [Lo.] So it pleased the king; and she,
  with that small stock
Of reason left her, is so kind and smooth
Upon him.
1 [Lo.]   She's turned a child again. A
  madness,
That would ha' made her brain and blood
  boil high,
In which distemper she might ha'
  wrought something—
2 [Lo.] Had been to purpose.
1 [Lo.] The cardinal is cunning, and, how-
    e'er   20

His brow does smile, he does suspect
   Hernando
Took fire from her, and waits a time to
   punish it.
2 [Lo.] But what a subject of disgrace and
   mirth
Hath poor Celinda made herself by pride,
In her belief Columbo was her servant! [1]
Her head hath stooped much since he
   died, and she
Almost ridiculous at court.

Enter Cardinal, Antonelli, Servant.

1 [Lo.]   The cardinal
Is come into the garden, now—
CAR.   Walk off.—[*Exeunt Lords.*]
   It troubles me the duchess by her loss
   Of brain is now beneath my great re-
     venge.   30
   She is not capable to feel my anger,
   Which, like to unregarded thunder spent
   In woods, and lightning aimed at sense-
     less trees,
   Must idly fall, and hurt her not, not to
   That sense her guilt deserves. A fatal
     stroke,
   Without the knowledge for what crime,
     to fright her
   When she takes leave, and make her tug
     with death,
   Until her soul sweat, is a pigeon's tor-
     ment,
   And she is sent a babe to the other world.
   Columbo's death will not be satisfied, 40
   And I but wound her with a two-edged
     feather.
   I must do more. I have all opportunity
   (She by the king now made my charge),
     but she's
   So much a turtle [2] I shall lose by killing
     her,
   Perhaps do her a pleasure and prefer-
     ment;
   That must not be.

Enter Celinda with a parchment.

ANT. [*Stopping her.*] Is not this she that
   would be thought to have been
Columbo's mistress? Madam, his grace
   is private,
And would not be disturbed; you may
   displease him.

[1] Admirer.   [2] Turtledove.

CEL. What will your worship wager that
   he shall   50
   Be pleased again before we part?
ANT. I'll lay this diamond, madam, gainst
   a kiss,
And trust yourself to keep the stakes.
CEL.   'Tis done.
     [*Approaches the Cardinal.*]
ANT. [*Aside.*] I have long had an appe-
   tite to this lady;
But the lords keep her up so high—this
   toy
May bring her on.
CAR. This interruption tastes not of good
   manners.
CEL. But where necessity, my lord, com-
   pels,
   The boldness may meet pardon, and,
     when you
   Have found my purpose, I may less ap-
     pear   60
   Unmannerly.
CAR.   To th' business.
CEL.   It did please
   Your nephew, sir, before his death, to
     credit me
   With so much honorable favor, I
   Am come to tender to his near'st of blood,
   Yourself, what does remain a debt to him.
   Not to delay your grace with circum-
     stance,
   That deed, if you accept, makes you my
     heir
   Of no contemptible estate.   *He reads.*
     —[*Aside.*] This way
   Is only left to tie up scurrile tongues
   And saucy men, that since Columbo's
     death   70
   Venture to libel on my pride and folly;
   His greatness and this gift, which I enjoy
   Still for my life (beyond which term a
     kingdom's
   Nothing), will curb the giddy spleens of
     men
   That live on impudent rime, and railing at
   Each wandering fame [3] they catch.
CAR.   Madam, this bounty
   Will bind my gratitude, and care to serve
     you.
CEL. I am your grace's servant.
CAR.   Antonelli! *Whisper.*
   And, when this noble lady visits me,
   Let her not wait.   80

[3] Rumor.

Cᴇʟ. [*Aside.*] What think you, my officious sir? His grace
Is pleased, you may conjecture. I may keep
Your gem; the kiss was never yours.
Aɴᴛ. [*Aside.*] Sweet madam—
Cᴇʟ. [*Aside.*] Talk if you dare; you know I must not wait.
And so, farewell for this time. [*Exit.*]
Cᴀʀ. 'Tis in my brain already, and it forms
Apace—good, excellent revenge, and pleasant!
She's now within my talons; 'tis too cheap
A satisfaction for Columbo's death, 89
Only to kill her by soft charm or force.
I'll rifle first her darling chastity;
'Twill be after time enough to poison her,
And she to th' world be thought her own destroyer.
As I will frame the circumstance, this night
All may be finished; for the colonel,
Her agent in my nephew's death (whom I
Disturbed at counsel with her), I may reach him
Hereafter, and be master of his fate.
We starve our conscience when we thrive in state. *Exeunt.*

[Sᴄᴇɴᴇ ii.

A room in the duchess' palace.]

Enter Secretary and Placentia.

Sᴇᴄ. Placentia, we two are only left
Of my lady's servants; let us be true
To her and one another, and be sure,
When we are at prayers, to curse the cardinal.
Pʟᴀ. I pity my sweet lady.
Sᴇᴄ. I pity her too, but am a little angry;
She might have found another time to lose
Her wits.
Pʟᴀ. That I were a man!
Sᴇᴄ. What wouldst thou do, Placentia?
Pʟᴀ. I would revenge my lady.
Sᴇᴄ. 'Tis better being a woman; thou mayst do 10
Things that may prosper better, and the fruit
Be thy own another day.

Pʟᴀ. Your wit still loves
To play the wanton.
Sᴇᴄ. 'Tis a sad time, Placentia;
Some pleasure would do well. The truth is, I
Am weary of my life, and I would have
One fit of mirth before I leave the world.
Pʟᴀ. Do not you blush to talk thus wildly?
Sᴇᴄ. 'Tis good manners
To be a little mad after my lady. 19
But I ha' done. Who is with her now?
Pʟᴀ. Madam Valeria.
Sᴇᴄ. Not Celinda? There's a lady for my humor!
A pretty book of flesh and blood, and well
Bound up, in a fair letter too. Would I
Had her with all the errata!
Pʟᴀ. She has not
An honorable fame.
Sᴇᴄ. Her fame? That's nothing;
A little stain; her wealth will fetch again
The color, and bring honor into her cheeks
As fresh. If she were mine, and I had her
Exchequer, I know the way to make her honest— 30
Honest to th' touch, the test, and the last trial.
Pʟᴀ. How, prithee?
Sᴇᴄ. Why, first I would marry her—that's a verb material;
Then I would print her with an *index
Expurgatorius*, a table drawn
Of her court heresies; and, when she's read
Cum privilegio,[1] who dares call her whore?
Pʟᴀ. I'll leave you, if you talk thus.
Sᴇᴄ. I ha' done.
Placentia, thou mayst be better company
After another progress; and now, tell me, 40
Didst ever hear of such a patient madness
As my lady is possessed with? She has raved
But twice; and she would fright the cardinal,
Or at a supper if she did but poison him,
It were a frenzy I could bear withal.
She calls him her dear governor—
_____
[1] With license.

Enter Hernando disguised, having a letter.

PLA.   Who is this?

HER. Her secretary!—Sir,
  Here is a letter, if it may have so
  Much happiness to kiss her grace's hand.

SEC. From whom?

HER.   That's not in your commis-
    sion, sir,   50
  To ask, or mine to satisfy; she will
    want
  No understanding when she reads.

SEC.   Alas!
  Under your favor, sir, you are mistaken;
  Her grace did never more want under-
    standing.

HER. How?

SEC. Have you not heard? Her skull is
    broken, sir,
  And many pieces taken out; she's mad.

HER. The sad fame of her distraction
  Has too much truth, it seems.

PLA.   If please you, sir,
  To expect awhile, I will present the
    letter.   60

HER. Pray, do.—   *Exit Placen[tia].*
  How long has she been thus distempered,
    sir?

SEC. Before the cardinal came to govern
    here,
  Who, for that reason, by the king was
    made
  Her guardian. We are now at his devo-
    tion.[1]

HER. A lamb given up to a tiger! May
    diseases
  Soon eat him through his heart!

SEC.   Your pardon, sir.
  I love that voice; I know it too a little.
  Are not you—be not angry, noble sir;
  I can with ease be ignorant again,   70
  And think you are another man; but, if
  You be that valiant gentleman they
    call—

HER. Whom? What?

SEC. That killed—I would not name him,
    if I thought
  You were not pleased to be that very
    gentleman.

HER. Am I betrayed?

SEC. The devil sha' not
  Betray you here. Kill me, and I will take
  My death you are the noble colonel.

[1] Power of disposal.

We are all bound to you for the general's
    death,   80
  Valiant Hernando! When my lady knows
  You are here, I hope 'twill fetch her
    wits again.
  But do not talk too loud; we are not all
  Honest[2] i' th' house; some are the car-
    dinal's creatures.

HER. Thou wert faithful to thy lady. I
    am glad
  'Tis night. But tell me how the church-
    man uses
  The duchess.

Enter Antonelli.

SEC. He carries angels in his tongue and
    face, but I
  Suspect his heart. This is one of his
    spawns.—
  Signior Antonelli.

ANT.   Honest Antonio! 90

SEC. And how, and how—a friend of mine
  —where is
  The cardinal's grace?

HER. [*Aside.*]   That will be never an-
    swered.

ANT. He means to sup here with the duch-
    ess.

SEC.   Will he?

ANT. We'll have the charming bottles at
    my chamber.
  Bring that gentleman; we'll be mighty
    merry.

HER. [*Aside.*] I may disturb your jollity.

ANT.   Farewell, sweet—[*Exit.*]

SEC. Dear Antonelli!—[*Aside.*] A round
    pox confound you!
  This is court rhetoric at the back stairs.

Enter Placentia.

PLA. Do you know this gentleman?

SEC.   Not I.

PLA. My lady presently dismissed Va-
    leria,   100
  And bade me bring him to her bed-
    chamber.

SEC. The gentleman has an honest face.

PLA.   Her words
  Fell from her with some evenness and
    joy.—
  Her grace desires your presence.

[2] Loyal.

HER.   I'll attend her.
            Exit [with Placentia].
SEC. I would this soldier had the cardinal
   Upon a promontory. With what a spring
   The churchman would leap down! It
      were a spectacle
   Most rare to see him topple from the
      precipice,
   And souse in the salt water with a noise
   To stun the fishes; and, if he fell into   110
   A net, what wonder would the simple
      sea gulls
   Have, to draw up the o'ergrown lobster,[1]
   So ready boiled! He shall have my good
      wishes.
   This colonel's coming may be lucky; I
   Will be sure none shall interrupt 'em.

Enter Celinda.

CEL.   Is
   Her grace at opportunity?
SEC.   No, sweet madam;
   She is asleep, her gentlewoman says.
CEL. My business is but visit. I'll expect.
SEC. That must not be, although I like
   your company.   119
CEL. You are grown rich, Mr. Secretary.
SEC. I, madam? Alas!
CEL. I hear you are upon another pur-
   chase.
SEC. I upon a purchase?
CEL.   If you want any sum—
SEC. If I could purchase your sweet favor,
   madam?
CEL. You shall command me, and my
   fortune, sir.
SEC. [*Aside.*] How's this?
CEL.   I have observed you, sir, a staid
   And prudent gentleman—and I shall
      want—
SEC. Not me?
CEL. (*Aside.*) A father for some infant.
   He has credit
   I' th' world. I am not the first cast
      lady   130
   Has married a secretary.
SEC. Shall I wait upon you?
CEL.   Whither?
SEC.   Any whither.
CEL. I may chance lead you then—
SEC. I shall be honored to obey. My blood
   Is up, and in this humor I'm for any-
      thing.

[1] An allusion to the color of the cardinal's robes.

CEL. Well, sir, I'll try your manhood.
SEC.   'Tis my happiness;
   You cannot please me better.
CEL. [*Aside.*]   This was struck
   I' th' opportunity.
SEC.   I am made forever.
                       [*Exeunt.*]

[SCENE iii.

Another room in the same.]

Enter Hernando and Duchess.

HER. Dear madam, do not weep.
DUCH.   Y' are very welcome.
   I ha' done; I wo' not shed a tear more
   Till I meet Alvarez; then I'll weep for
      joy.
   He was a fine young gentleman, and sung
      sweetly;
   And you had heard him but the night
      before
   We were married, you would ha' sworn
      he had been
   A swan, and sung his own sad epitaph.
   But we'll talk o' the cardinal.
HER.   Would his death
   Might ransom your fair sense! He should
      not live
   To triumph in the loss. Beshrow[2] my
      manhood,   10
   But I begin to melt.
DUCH.   I pray, sir, tell me,
   For I can understand, although they say
   I have lost my wits; but they are safe
      enough,
   And I shall have 'em when the cardinal
      dies,
   Who had a letter from his nephew, too,
   Since he was slain.
HER.   From whence?
DUCH. I know not where he is. But in
      some bower
   Within a garden he is making chaplets,
   And means to send me one; but I'll not
      take it;
   I have flowers enough, I thank him,
      while I live.   20
HER. But do you love your governor?
DUCH. Yes, but I'll never marry him; I am
      promised
   Already.
HER.   To whom, madam?

[2] Beshrew, curse.

Duch.   Do not you
Blush when you ask me that? Must not
   you be
My husband? I know why, but that's a
   secret.
Indeed, if you believe me, I do love
No man alive so well as you. The cardi-
   nal
Shall never know 't; he'll kill us both; and
   yet
He says he loves me dearly, and has
   promised   29
To make me well again. But I'm afraid
One time or other he will give me poison.
Her. Prevent him, madam, and take
   nothing from him.
Duch. Why, do you think 'twill hurt me?
Her.   It will kill you.
Duch. I shall but die, and meet my dear-
   loved lord,
Whom, when I have kissed, I'll come
   again and work
A bracelet of my hair for you to carry
   him,
When you are going to heaven; the
   poesy [1] shall
Be my own name, in little tears, that I
Will weep next winter, which, congealed
   i' th' frost,
Will show like seed pearl. You'll deliver
   it?   40
I know he'll love and wear it for my sake.
Her. She is quite lost.
Duch.   I pray, give me, sir, your
   pardon.
I know I talk not wisely; but, if you
   had
The burthen of my sorrow, you would
   miss
Sometimes your better reason. Now I'm
   well.
What will you do when the cardinal
   comes?
He must not see you for the world.
Her.   He sha' not;
I'll take my leave before he come.
Duch.   Nay, stay;
I shall have no friend left me when you
   go.
He will but sup; he sha' not stay to lie
   wi' me.   50
I have the picture of my lord abed;
Three are too much this weather.

[1] Posy, inscription.

Enter Placentia.

Pla.   Madam, the cardinal.
Her. He shall sup with the devil.
Duch.   I dare not stay;
The red cock [2] will be angry. I'll come
   again. *Exeunt [Duchess and Placentia].*
Her. This sorrow is no fable. Now I find
My curiosity is sadly satisfied.—
Ha! If the duchess in her straggled wits
Let fall words to betray me to the car-
   dinal,
The panther will not leap more fierce to
   meet
His prey, when a long want of food hath
   parched   60
His starvéd maw, than he to print his
   rage,
And tear my heartstrings. Everything
   is fatal;
And yet she talked sometimes with chain
   of sense,
And said she loved me. Ha! They come
   not yet.
I have a sword about me, and I left
My own security to visit death.
Yet I may pause a little, and consider
Which way does lead me to 't most hon-
   orably.
Does not the chamber that I walk in
   tremble?   69
What will become of her, and me, and all
The world in one small hour? I do not
   think
Ever to see the day again; the wings
Of night spread o'er me like a sable
   hearsecloth;
The stars are all close mourners too; but I
Must not alone to the cold, silent grave,
I must not.—If thou canst, Alvarez, open
That ebon curtain, and behold the man,
When the world's justice fails, shall right
   thy ashes,
And feed their thirst with blood! Thy
   duchess is   79
Almost a ghost already, and doth wear
Her body like a useless upper garment,
The trim and fashion of it lost.—Ha!

Enter Placentia.

Pla. You need not doubt me, sir. My lady
   prays
You would not think it long; she in my
   ear

[2] *I.e.*, the cardinal.

Commanded me to tell you that, when last
She drank, she had happy wishes to your health.

HER. And did the cardinal pledge it?

PLA.   He was not
Invited to 't, nor must he know you are here.

HER. What do they talk of, prithee?

PLA. His grace is very pleasant   90
              A lute is heard.
And kind to her; but her returns [1] are after
The sad condition of her sense, sometimes Unjointed.

HER.   They have music.

PLA.   A lute only.
His grace prepared, they say, the best of Italy,
That waits upon my lord.

HER.   He thinks the duchess
Is stung with a tarantula.

PLA.   Your pardon;
My duty is expected.   *Exit.*

HER.   Gentle lady!—
A voice too?

         SONG (*within*)

STRE. Come, my Daphne, come away;
    We do waste the crystal day.   100
    'Tis Strephon calls.

DA.   What says my love?

STRE. Come, follow to the myrtle grove,
    Where Venus shall prepare
    New chaplets for thy hair.

DA.   Were I shut up within a tree,
    I'd rend my bark to follow thee.

STRE. My shepherdess, make haste;
    The minutes slide too fast.

DA.   In those cooler shades will I,
    Blind as Cupid, kiss thine eye.   110

STRE. In thy bosom then I'll stay;
    In such warm snow who would not lose his way?

CHOR. We'll laugh, and leave the world behind,
    And gods themselves that see,
    Shall envy thee and me,
    But never find
    Such joys, when they embrace a deity.

[HER.] If at this distance I distinguish, 'tis not
Church music; and the air's wanton, and no anthem

---

[1] Replies.

Sung to 't, but some strange ode of love and kisses.   120
What should this mean?—Ha, he is coming hither.
I am betrayed; he marches in her hand.
I'll trust a little more; mute as the arras,
My sword and I here.
      [*With drawn sword*] *he observes.*

Enter Cardinal, Duchess, Antonelli, and
                   Attendants.

CAR. Wait you in the first chamber, and let none
Presume to interrupt us.—
           Ex[eunt] *Serv*[ants].
       [*Aside.*] She is pleasant;
Now for some art to poison all her innocence.

DUCH. [*Aside.*] I do not like the cardinal's humor; he
Little suspects what guest is in my chamber.   129

CAR. Now, madam, you are safe.
              [*Embraces her.*]

DUCH.   How means your lordship?

CAR. Safe in my arms, sweet duchess.

DUCH.   Do not hurt me.

CAR. Not for the treasures of the world! You are
My pretty charge. Had I as many lives
As I have careful thoughts to do you service,
I should think all a happy forfeit to
Delight your grace one minute; 'tis a heaven
To see you smile.

DUCH.   What kindness call you this?

CAR. It cannot want a name while you preserve
So plentiful a sweetness; it is love.

DUCH. Of me? How shall I know 't, my lord?   140

CAR. By this, and this, swift messengers to whisper
Our hearts to one another.   *Kisses.*

DUCH. Pray, do you come a-wooing?

CAR.   Yes, sweet madam;
You cannot be so cruel to deny me.

DUCH. What, my lord?

CAR.   Another kiss.

DUCH.   Can you
Dispense with this, my lord?—(*Aside.*)
    Alas, I fear
Hernando is asleep, or vanished from me.

CAR. [*Aside.*] I have mocked my blood
    into a flame; and what
My angry soul had formed for my re-
    venge   149
Is now the object of my amorous sense.
I have took a strong enchantment from
    her lips,
And fear I shall forgive Columbo's death,
If she consent to my embrace.—Come,
    madam.
DUCH. Whither, my lord?
CAR.   But to your bed or couch,
Where, if you will be kind, and but
    allow
Yourself a knowledge, Love, whose shape
    and raptures
Wise poets have but glorified in dreams,
Shall make your chamber his eternal
    palace,
And with such active and essential
    streams
Of new delights glide o'er your bosom,
    you   160
Shall wonder to what unknown world you
    are
By some blessed change translated. Why
    d'e pause,
And look so wild? Will you deny your
    governor?
DUCH. How came you by that cloven foot?
CAR.   Your fancy
Would turn a traitor to your happiness.
I am your friend; you must be kind.
DUCH.   Unhand me,
Or I'll cry out a rape.
CAR.   You wo' not, sure?
DUCH. I have been cozened with Her-
    nando's shadow;
Here's none but heaven to hear me.—
    Help! A rape!
CAR. Are you so good at understanding?
    Then,   170
I must use other argument.
    He forces her. [*Hernando rushes forth.*]
HER. Go to, cardinal!
        Strikes him. Ex[it] Duch[ess].
CAR. Hernando? Murder! Treason!
    Help!
HER. An army sha' not rescue thee. Your
    blood
Is much inflamed; I have brought a
    lancet wi' me
Shall open your hot veins, and cool your
    fever.

To vex thy parting soul, it was the same
Engine that pierced [1] Columbo's heart.
CAR.   Help! Murder!
    [*Hernando stabs him.*]

Enter Antonelli and Servants.

ANT. Some ring the bell; 'twill raise the
    court.   179
My lord is murdered! 'Tis Hernando!
            The bell rings.
HER. I'll make you all some sport.—[*Stabs
    himself.*] So; now we are even.
Where is the duchess? I would take my
    leave
Of her, and then bequeath my curse
    among you.   *Her[nando] falls.*

*Enter King, Duchess, Valeria, Lords,
                         Guard.*

KING. How come these bloody objects?
HER. With a trick my sword found out. I
    hope he's paid.
1 Lo. [*Aside.*] I hope so too.—A surgeon
    for my Lord Cardinal!
KING. Hernando?
DUCH. Justice! O, justice, sir, against a
    ravisher!
HER. Sir, I ha' done you service.
KING.   A bloody service.
HER. 'Tis pure scarlet.   190

Enter Surgeon.

CAR. [*Aside.*] After such care to perfect
    my revenge,
Thus banded [2] out o' th' world by a
    woman's plot!
HER. I have preserved the duchess from a
    rape.
Good night to me and all the world
    forever.   *Dies.*
KING. So impious!
DUCH.   'Tis most true; Alvarez' blood
Is now revenged; I find my brain return,
And every straggling sense repairing
    home.
CAR. I have deserved you should turn from
    me, sir.
My life hath been prodigiously wicked;
My blood is now the kingdom's balm.
    O, sir,   200

[1] Emended by Gifford-Dyce. Original reads
pinc'd.
[2] Bandied.

I have abused your ear, your trust, your
     people,
And my own sacred office; my conscience
Feels now the sting. O, show your char-
     ity,
And with your pardon, like a cool, soft
     - gale,
Fan my poor sweating soul, that wanders
     through
Unhabitable climes and parchéd deserts.
But I am lost, if the great world forgive
     me,
Unless I find your mercy for a crime
You know not, madam, yet, against your
     life,
I must confess, more than my black in-
     tents   210
Upon your honor; y' are already poi-
     soned.
KING. By whom?
CAR.   By me,
In the revenge I owed Columbo's loss.
With your last meat was mixed a poison
     that
By subtle and by sure degrees must let
In death.
KING.   Look to the duchess, our physi-
     cians!
CAR. Stay! I will deserve her mercy,
     though I cannot
Call back the deed. In proof of my re-
     pentance,   219
If the last breath of a now dying man
May gain your charity and belief, re-
     ceive
This ivory box; in it an antidote
'Bove that they boast the great magis-
     tral [1] medicine.
That powder, mixed with wine, by a most
     rare
And quick access to the heart, will for-
     tify it
Against the rage of the most nimble
     poison.
I am not worthy to present her with it.
O, take it, and preserve her innocent life.
1 Lo. Strange, he should have a good thing
     in such readiness.
CAR. 'Tis that, which in my jealousy and
     state,   230
Trusting to false predictions of my
     birth,
That I should die by poison, I preserved

[1] Sovereign, effectual.

For my own safety. Wonder not I made
That my companion was to be my refuge.

Enter Servant with a bowl of wine.   .

1 Lo. Here's some touch of grace.
CAR. In greater proof of my pure thoughts,
     I take
This first, and with my dying breath
     confirm
My penitence; it may benefit her life,
But not my wounds. [*He drinks.*] O,
     hasten to preserve her;
And, though I merit not her pardon, let
     not   240
Her fair soul be divorced.
            [*The Duchess drinks.*]
KING. This is some charity; may it pros-
     per, madam!
VAL. How does your grace?
DUCH. And must I owe my life to him
     whose death
Was my ambition? Take this free ac-
     knowledgment;
I had intent this night with my own hand
To be Alvarez' justicer.
KING.   You were mad,
And thought past apprehension of re-
     venge.
DUCH. That shape I did usurp, great sir, to
     give
My art more freedom and defense; but,
     when   250
Hernando came to visit me, I thought
I might defer my execution,
Which his owe [2] rage supplied without
     my guilt,
And, when his lust grew high, met with
     his blood.
1 Lo. The cardinal smiles.
CAR.   Now my revenge has met
With you, my nimble duchess! I have
     took
A shape [3] to give my act more freedom
     too,
And now I am sure she's poisoned with
     that dose
I gave her last.
KING.   Th' art not so horrid?
DUCH. Ha, some cordial!
CAR.   Alas, no preservative   260
Hath wings to overtake it. Were her
     heart

[2] Own.   [3] Disguise, trick.

Locked in a quarry, it would search and kill

Before the aids can reach it. I am sure
You sha' not now laugh at me.

KING. How came you by that poison?

CAR. 　　　　　I prepared it,
Resolving, when I had enjoyed her, which
The colonel prevented, by some art
To make her take it, and by death con-
clude
My last revenge. You have the fatal
story.

KING. This is so great a wickedness it
will　　　　　　　　　　　　　　270
Exceed belief.

CAR. 　　　　　I knew I could not live.

SURG. Your wounds, sir, were not desperate.

CAR. 　　Not mortal?
Ha, were they not mortal?

SURG. 　　　　If I have skill in surgery.

CAR. Then I have caught myself in my
own engine.

2 LO. It was your fate, you said, to die by
poison.

CAR. That was my own prediction to
abuse
Your faith. No human art can now re-
sist it;
I feel it knocking at the seat of life;
It must come in. I have wracked all my
own
To try your charities. Now it would be
rare　　　　　　　　　　　　　280
If you but waft me with a little prayer;
My wings that flag may catch the wind,
but 'tis
In vain; the mist is risen, and there's
none
To steer my wand'ring bark. 　　Dies.

1 LO. 　　　　　He's dead.

KING. 　　　　　With him
Die all deceivéd trust.

2 LO. This was a strange impiety.

KING. 　　　　　When men
Of gifts and sacred function once decline
From virtue, their ill deeds transcend
example.

DUCH. The minute's come that I must
take my leave, too.
Your hand, great sir; and, though you
be a king,　　　　　　　　　290

We may exchange forgiveness. Heaven
forgive,
And all the world! I come, I come,
Alvarez! 　　　　　　　　　　Dies.

KING. Dispose their bodies for becoming
funeral.
How much are kings abused by those
they take
To royal grace, whom, when they cherish
most
By nice indulgence, they do often arm
Against themselves, from whence this
maxim springs:
None have more need of perspectives than
kings. 　　　　　　　　　　Exeunt.

EPILOGUE

[VOICE.] (*Within.*) Mr. Pollard! Where's
Mr. Pollard, for the epilogue?
　　He is thrust upon the stage, and falls.

EPI. [*Rising.*] I am coming to you, gentle-
men; the poet
Has helped me thus far on my way, but
I'll
Be even with him: the play is a tragedy,
The first that ever he composed for us,
Wherein he thinks he has done prettily,

Enter Servant.

And I am sensible.[1]—I prithee, look.
Is nothing out of joint? Has he broke
nothing?

SERV. No, sir, I hope.

EPI. Yes, he has broke his epilogue all to
pieces. 　　　　　　　　　　10
Canst thou put it together again?

SERV. 　　　　　　　Not I, sir.

EPI. Nor I. Prithee, begone!—[*Exit Serv-*
ant.] Hum!—Mr. Poet,
I have a teeming mind to be revenged.—
[*To audience.*] You may assist, and not
be seen in 't now,
If you please, gentlemen, for I do know
He listens to the issue of his cause;
But blister not your hands in his ap-
plause,
Your private smile, your nod, or hum,
to tell
My fellows that you like the business
well. 　　　　　　　　　　19
And, when without a clap you go away,

[1] Satisfied.

I'll drink a small beer health to his
   second day,
And break his heart, or make him swear
   and rage
He'll write no more for the unhappy
   stage.

But that's too much; so we should lose.
   Faith, shew it,
And, if you like his play, 't 's as well he
   knew it.

FINIS.